OXFORD PAPERBACK REFERENCE

A Dictionary of
Architec

Professor James Stevens Curl is a leading British architectural historian. His many stimulating studies include *The English Heritage Book of Victorian Churches, Egyptomania: The Egyptian Revival as a Recurring Theme in the History of Taste, A Celebration of Death, Classical Architecture*, and *The Art and Architecture of Freemasonry* (which won the Sir Banister Fletcher Award for Best Book of the Year on Architecture in 1992). From 1970 to 1973 he was Architectural Editor of the *Survey of London*, and was Architectural Adviser to the Scottish Committee for European Architectural Heritage Year 1975.

John Sambrook spent nearly twenty years with the Greater London Council producing measured drawings for the *Survey of London*. Today, he combines a career as a freelance illustrator with his principal occupation as a manufacturer of metal fanlight-windows.

Oxford Paperback Reference

Abbreviations
ABC of Music
Accounting
Archaeology*
Architecture*
Art and Artists
Art Terms*
Astronomy
Bible
Biology
British Women Writers
Buddhism*
Business
Card Games
Chemistry
Christian Church
Classical Literature
Classical Mythology*
Colour Medical
Colour Science
Computing
Dance*
Dates
Earth Sciences
Ecology
Economics
Engineering*
English Etymology
English Folklore*
English Grammar
English Language
English Literature
English Place-Names
Euphemisms
Film*
Finance and Banking
First Names
Food and Nutrition
Fowler's Modern English Usage
Geography
Handbook of the World*
Humorous Quotations
Irish Literature*
Jewish Religion
Kings and Queens*
King's English
Law
Linguistics
Literary Quotations
Literary Terms
London Place Names*
Mathematics
Medical
Medicines*
Modern Design*
Modern Quotations
Modern Slang
Music
Nursing
Opera
Paperback Encyclopedia
Philosophy
Physics
Plant-Lore
Plant Sciences
Political Biography
Political Quotations
Politics
Popes
Proverbs
Psychology*
Quotations
Sailing Terms
Saints
Science
Shakespeare
Ships and the Sea
Sociology
Statistics*
Superstitions
Synonyms and Antonyms
Theatre
Twentieth-Century Art
Twentieth-Century Poetry
Twentieth-Century World History
Weather Facts
Who's Who in Opera
Who's Who in the Twentieth Century
Word Games
World History*
World Mythology
World Religions*
Writers' Dictionary
Zoology

* forthcoming

A Dictionary of Architecture

JAMES STEVENS CURL

With line-drawings by

the Author and John Sambrook

OXFORD
UNIVERSITY PRESS

OXFORD
UNIVERSITY PRESS
Great Clarendon Street, OX2 6DP
Oxford University Press is a department of the University of Oxford and furthers the University's aim of excellence in research, scholarship, and education by publishing worldwide in
Oxford New York
Athens Auckland Bangkok Bogotá Buenos Aires Calcutta Cape Town Chennai Dar es Salaam Delhi Florence Hong Kong Istanbul Karachi Kuala Lumpur Madrid Melbourne Mexico City Mumbai Nairobi Paris São Paulo Singapore Taipei Tokyo Toronto Warsaw
and associated companies in Berlin Ibadan

First published 1999

First issued as an Oxford University Press paperback 2000

British Library Cataloguing in Publication Data
Data available

Library of Congress Cataloging in Publication Data
Data available
ISBN 0-19-280017-5

10 9 8 7 6 5 4 3 2 1

Typeset by Best-set Typesetter Ltd., Hong Kong
Printed in Great Britain
by Cox & Wyman Ltd,
Reading, Berkshire

In Memoriam

Stephen Ernest Dykes Bower
18 April 1903–11 November 1994

and

James Edmund Kennedy Esdaile
21 September 1910–18 January 1994

Preface

This book is intended to help the subject of architecture to become more accessible to the general public, but it is also hoped that students and even professionals will turn to it for helpful information. It does not have pretensions to completeness, for that is not attainable in a Concise Dictionary, but it does provide a wide range of entries, including biographies of architects and others who have made contributions to architecture; architectural terms; architectural styles; building types; and certain regional and national movements. There are no essays on the architecture of individual countries, for such entries are more suited to an encyclopedia than to a dictionary. While the scope of the book has been restricted to the British Isles, Europe, the United States of America, Canada, Australia, and Latin America, aspects of the subject associated with the Indian Subcontinent, the Near and Far East, and former Colonial architecture are included when deemed necessary. In particular, those influences on exoticism (Buddhism, China, India, Islam, and Japan) in Western architecture are mentioned, although no attempt has been made to include the vast terminology of Chinese and Japanese architecture that would itself fill volumes. The inclusion of some architects from Japan and elsewhere needs explanation: those who are listed have made an acknowledged contribution to the increasingly international nature of architecture, and their work has been perceived as influential. Illustrations are provided where appropriate, for pictures can do so much more than words to clarify meaning.

I have been guided throughout the preparation of the book by Mr Angus Phillips, Senior Commissioning Editor, Trade Books, of Oxford University Press. His patience and good humour were unfailing throughout the project. My collaborator, Mr John Sambrook, worked with me to help to make this Dictionary useful, and provided drawings to that end: I am grateful to him and to his family for hospitality when discussing the work. I am also indebted to Mr Ashley Barker, Professor Charles MacCallum, Professor Newton Watson, and Professor Michael Welbank for support. Financial assistance towards the costs of research and preparation was given by a Royal Institute of British Architects Research Award made in 1993 which continued until the end of 1996: I therefore express my gratitude to the RIBA Historical Research Trust for helping to fund the project. I received further help in the form of a Small Personal Research Grant from The British Academy, to which body I acknowledge my indebtedness, and I was also fortunate enough to obtain grants from The Worshipful Company of Tylers and Bricklayers and from The Worshipful Company of Chartered Architects: to both those Livery Companies of the City of London and to The British Academy I extend my warmest thanks. Mr Mark Le Fanu and Mr Gareth Shannon of the Society of Authors courteously and gallantly assisted in many ways, as did Miss Ingrid Curl, Mr Ronald Dudley, Lady Freeman, Fru Lisbeth Ehlers, Dr Timothy Mowl, Mr John Simpson, and Dr David Watkin. Dictionaries cannot be prepared without sustained and time-consuming work, and this book has been no exception, involving having time off from my duties at De Montfort University. I am grateful to my colleagues (especially Professors David Chiddick, Brian Field, George Henderson, and Vincent Shacklock, and Dr Judith Roberts) for their forbearance.

Edmund Burke (1729–97), in his influential work *On the Sublime and Beautiful* (1757), observed that he had no 'great opinion of a definition, the celebrated remedy for the cure of . . . uncertainty and confusion', whereas Erasmus (*c*.1469–1536), in his *Adagia* (1500), went further, stating that 'every definition is dangerous'. In spite of these reservations, I have attempted to define architectural terms, bearing in mind the view of Dr Samuel Johnson (1709–84) that 'dictionaries are like watches; the worst is better than none, and the best cannot be expected to go quite true'. My primary source for these has been my own experience and study of architecture over more than four decades. As a young student, faced with a bewildering and daunting array of unfamiliar words necessary to describe architecture, I began to haunt dusty second-hand and antiquarian bookshops, and acquired certain volumes, including John Parker's very useful *A Glossary of Terms used in Grecian, Roman, Italian, and Gothic Architecture* in the 1850 edition, Thomas Rickman's *Attempt to Discriminate the Styles of Architecture in England from the Conquest to the Reformation* in the 1848 edition, and Matthew Holbeche Bloxam's *Principles of Gothic Ecclesiastical Architecture* in the 1882 edition, that helped to form a familiarity with architectural terminology. Other sources consulted during the compilation of this Dictionary were *An Encyclopaedia of Architecture, Historical, Theoretical, and Practical*, by Joseph Gwilt (originally published in 1842), and revised in 1903 by Papworth, *An Architectural and Engineering Dictionary, Containing Correct Nomenclature and Derivation of the Terms Employed by Architects, Builders, and Workmen*, by Peter Nicholson (1835), *A Treatise on the Decorative Part of Civil Architecture*, by Sir William Chambers (in the Gwilt edition of 1825), *A Dictionary of Architecture and Building, Biographical, Historical, and Descriptive*, by Russell Sturgis (1901–2), that wonderful mine of information, *The Dictionary of Architecture*, edited by Wyatt Angelicus van Sandau Papworth, and issued by The Architectural Publication Society (1852–92), and a very useful booklet dealing with aspects of timber-framed construction, the *Practical Handbook in Archaeology No 5, Recording Timber-Framed Buildings: An Illustrated Glossary*, by N. W. Alcock, M. W. Barley, P. W. Dixon, and R. A. Meeson, published by the Council for British Archaeology (York, 1996). Two exhaustive American productions dealing with terms deserve citation for the thoroughness of scholarship and fullness of coverage: *Dictionary of Architecture and Construction*, published by McGraw-Hill (1975), and *Illustrated Dictionary of Historic Architecture*, published by Dover (1983), both edited by Cyril M. Harris, contain an enormous amount of information (the *Illustrated Dictionary* is especially useful as it contains 2,100 illustrations drawn from many historical sources as well as many originals). William Bell Dinsmoor's *The Architecture of Greece* (1950) and D. S. Robertson's *Handbook of Greek and Roman Architecture* (1945) are useful sources for terms from Classical Antiquity. A. L. Osborne's *Dictionary of English Domestic Architecture* (1954) is also worth consulting, not least for its illustrations. Glen L. Pride's *Glossary of Scottish Building* (1975), revised and expanded as *Dictionary of Scottish Building* (1996), is essential for terms used in the North. No lexicographer, in Dr Johnson's immortal phrase, 'a harmless drudge', can afford not to consult *The Oxford English Dictionary*: I have used the

1933 edition, edited by James A. H. Murray, Henry Bradley, W. A. Craigie, and C. T. Onions. Other standard foreign-language Dictionaries have been used, including P. G. W. Glare's *Oxford Latin Dictionary* (1985) and Cassell's various Dictionaries of European languages. The *Oxford Companion* volumes dealing with *Art* and the *Decorative Arts*, edited by Harold Osborne (1970 and 1975 respectively), have also been consulted, as has *The Oxford Dictionary of Art*, edited by Ian Chilvers and Harold Osborne, with Dennis Farr as Consultant Editor (1988). In a Concise Dictionary it is not possible to include expansive accounts, especially of ornament, so readers are referred to the splendid *Dictionary of Ornament* by Philippa Lewis and Gillian Darley (1986), which contains highly informative and scholarly entries graced with over 1,300 illustrations. It also includes useful biographies of those who influenced the development, use, or invention of ornament. Again including biographies and information about designers is *The Penguin Dictionary of Design and Designers* by Simon Jervis (1984). C20 art-historical terms and movements have mushroomed, and it is difficult to determine what permanence, if any, can be assessed. I have included those movements and terms that appear to have had some significance, however short, but my entries dealing with them are necessarily brief (though reams have been published). Fuller accounts of the second half of the century may be consulted in John A. Walker's *Glossary of Art, Architecture, and Design since 1945*, published by the Library Association and G. K. Hall (1992), a thorough and scholarly tome with comprehensive bibliographies for those who wish to pursue things further.

Terms are one thing, biographies another. I have had to make judgements concerning who is to be included on grounds of importance, contributions, quality, and so on. Many personalities (however unattractive) have entries because, by common consent, they are reckoned to be or to have been of significance. Others are included because of publications, perhaps a very small but important output in terms of buildings, and others for reasons of quality, influence, or other matters. A biography's presence does not mean approval or disapproval by the compiler: it is there because in my judgement it has to be. Some may find fault with inclusions or omissions, length or otherwise of entries, and, in some instances, failure to join in choruses of uncritical admiration. No compiler can hope to please everyone, but this Dictionary is an attempt to provide as informative a book as is possible within the parameters given. Anybody familiar with historical research will know that a work of this kind is only a staging-post on an endless journey. Errors are inevitable, and the indulgence of those who find them is humbly asked. Indeed, to have mistakes pointed out can only assist the compiler.

Certain source-books have provided the foundations for the biographical entries. The *Dictionary of National Biography* (from 1917), the various comparable dictionaries of other countries (e.g. *Dictionary of American Architects*, the Danish Weilbach *Kunstnerleksikon*, and the German *Allgemeines Künstler-Lexikon*), and other standard sources have been used. The Papworth-Architectural Publications Society *Dictionary of Architecture* (1852–92) and Sturgis *Dictionary of Architecture and Building* (1901–2) contain many entries on architects, but many of these have been superseded by later scholarship and should be treated with caution. For architects in the British Isles Sir Howard Colvin's definitive *A Biographical Dictionary of British Architects 1600–1840* (1995), John Harvey's *English Mediaeval*

Architects: A Biographical Dictionary down to 1550 (1987), Peter Eden's *Dictionary of Land Surveyors and Local Cartographers of Great Britain and Ireland, 1550–1850* (1979), Rolf Loeber's *A Biographical Dictionary of Architects in Ireland 1600–1720* (1981), A. Stuart Gray's *Edwardian Architecture: A Biographical Dictionary* (1985), Felstead, Franklin, and Pinfield's *Directory of British Architects 1834–1900* (1993), Pevsner's *Buildings of England, Scotland, Wales, and Ireland* (from 1951), and the many monographs listed in the Recommendations for Further Reading at the end of this book are essential, and I have drawn on them (with acknowledgement) where appropriate.

Apart from the scholarly books devoted to single individual architects (and they grow in number each year), much information has been extracted from more general books. For example, French architects of C18 and C19 are discussed in useful works such as Allan Braham's *The Architecture of the French Enlightenment* (1980) and Robin Middleton and David Watkin's *Neoclassical and 19th-Century Architecture* (1987), while an enormous amount of information on German architects is enshrined in David Watkin and Tilman Mellinghoff's *German Architecture and the Classical Ideal 1740–1840* (1987). Many articles in the *Macmillan Encylopaedia of Architects*, edited by Adolf K. Placzek (1982), are almost short monographs with substantial bibliographies far more comprehensive than can be hoped for in a Concise Dictionary, so I have referred readers to this work, as Placzek (1982), where I consider the article in question provides information (especially references) impossible to include in the present book. Other publications, such as *Contemporary Architects*, edited by Muriel Emanuel (1980, 1994) and Ann Lee Morgan and Colin Naylor (1987), and *International Dictionary of Architects and Architecture*, edited by Randall J. van Vynckt (1993), contain lists of buildings, bibliographies, and other published matter (including some illustrations) that are more expansive than possible in my own Dictionary. In many instances entries are based on personal knowledge, or on information kindly provided by individuals. In all cases, sources for biographies are given at the end of each entry, although citations also contain recommendations for further reading intended to guide, rather than indicate the origins of material.

Some words are necessary concerning the arrangement of the *Dictionary*. When an entry incorporates a term defined in its own right, this is indicated by an asterisk before the term at its first mention (e.g. *spandrel in the entry for **apron**). However, a rigorous adherence to this system would involve too many asterisks in an entry and thus make it difficult to read. The commonest terms (e.g. **door**, **pavement**, **tower**, and **wall**) are only cross-referenced where it is considered helpful for the reader to turn to those specific entries. Italics have been used to draw attention to alternative names or otherwise employed for clarity. In the instances where a term has more than one meaning, each has been prefaced by a number in **bold** type (**1. 2. 3.**, etc.), with the most usual meaning given first, and the least usual given last: in some cases, however, the numbering will have no particular significance, as where two or more meanings carry equal weight. At the end of many entries there are references by author and date to the Bibliography (Further Reading) which, while extensive, is not comprehensive: some of these references are given to guide those wishing to delve further, while others refer to sources, or to material connected with the entry in some other way. As far as names are concerned, surnames including 'de', 'du', 'Le', 'van', 'von', etc., are given under the main name: de Soissons is placed under S, Le Corbusier under C, van de Velde under V, and von Klenze under K.

The compiler of a Dictionary such as this incurs many obligations, not least to his sources, the numbers of which are only outlined in the Bibliography at the end of the book. However, he is also indebted to fellow-scholars (who have helped with suggestions, information, and in other ways), to archivists, to librarians, and to many other people. I have made use of several libraries, including The Bodleian Library of the University of Oxford, The British Library, The RIBA British Architectural Library, Cambridge University Library, the Library of The Queen's University of Belfast, and the Library of De Montfort University, Leicester. I owe a considerable debt to the staffs of all those great collections, but especially to Mrs Ann Perry and Mrs Mary Weston, of the last-named institution, who successfully tracked down elusive information for me. Miss Claudia Merrick, Mr Paul Nash, Miss Jane Oldfield, Mr Richard Reed, and Mr Trevor Todd, all of the RIBA, have been most helpful and diligent in obtaining material. Mr Victor Belcher, Sir Howard Colvin, Frau Eva Eissmann, Mr John Fisher, Mr John Greenacombe, Mr Paul Grinke, Miss Hermione Hobhouse, Mr Ralph Hyde, Mr Joseph Kilner, Dr Karin Kryger, Mr Julian Litten, Professor Stanisław Mossakowski, Mr Richard Sidwell, Dr Gavin Stamp, the late Sir John Summerson, Professor Peter Swallow, Mr Henry Vivian-Neal, Professor David Walker, and Richard Weston have my thanks for their individual acts of kindness and other help. Mrs Margaret Reed, of Starword, prepared the typescripts and disks, and has my thanks for this arduous task. My wife, Professor Dorota Iwaniec, and my friends have had to put up with my monkish devotion to the book, and have my gratitude for their patience.

Finally, the *Dictionary* is dedicated to the memory of Stephen Dykes Bower and Edmund Esdaile, who corresponded with me for more than a quarter of a century, and who loved architecture, words, and the English language. I remember the many happy hours spent in their company with a mixture of pleasure in their recollection and sadness that they cannot be repeated.

J.S.C.

Burley-on-the-Hill, Rutland, and Holywood, Co. Down
1993–9

Note on Illustrations

All the illustrations have been drawn by the Author except for those marked JJS which have been prepared by John Sambrook. Plans of buildings are not drawn to the same scale: they are provided to show arrangements, geometries, and other architectural aspects.

Contents

Aalto, Hugo Alvar Henrik (1898–1976). Finnish architect, among the most important C20 designers, he started his career as a *Neoclassicist in Jyväskylä (1923–7), but, influenced by *CIAM and by **Aino Marsio** (1894–1949)—his wife and partner from 1925—became involved in *International *Modernism after his office moved to Turku. The Standard Apartment Block, Turku (1927–9), incorporated prefabricated *concrete units, while the *Turun Sanomat* Building (1928–30) was the first of his designs to incorporate Le *Corbusier's *'Five Points of a New Architecture'. One of the most significant of his early buildings was the Viipuri Library (1927, 1930–5), with its undulating ceiling, which established his credentials as an architect of international stature with his own distinctive idiosyncrasies. In the Turku years Aalto's reputation grew, not least because of his furniture designs in which bent plywood played a considerable part: his three-legged stacking-stool (1938) is ubiquitous. Timber also enjoyed a growing role in his architecture, as in his country's Pavilion at the Paris Exposition Universelle (1937) and the Villa Mairea at Noormarkku (1937–9). His more personal style, in which curved walls, mono-pitched roofs, and brick-and-timber construction were prominent, evolved after the 1939–45 war: perhaps the most memorable designs are the Baker House Halls of Residence at Massachusetts Institute of Technology (MIT), Cambridge, Mass., with its serpentine walls and projecting staircases (1946–9); the Town Hall at Säynätsalo, with its brickwork and monopitched roofs (1949–52); and the Finlandia Conference Centre and Concert Hall, Helsinki (1962–75). His interest in all aspects of design extended to many artefacts: his celebrated vases, for example, are still given as wedding-presents in Finland today. In 1952 Aalto married **Elisse Mäkiniemi** (d. 1994). who worked on many later projects, taking over the practice after his death.

Fleig (1963–78); Porphyrios (1982); Quantrill (1995); Schildt (1984–91); Weston (1995)

Aaron's rod. **1.** Ornament in the form of a staff with budding leaves. **2.** Ornamented rod with a serpent twined around it, not to be confused with the *caduceus.

abaciscus. **1.** Small *abacus or *abaculus. **2.** Square border enclosing part or the entire pattern of a *mosaic. **3.** *Tessera or *abaculus* in a mosaic. **4.** Small tile.

abaculus. *Abaciscus in the sense of a small *abacus or a *mosaic *tessera.

abacus (*pl.* **abaci**). **1.** Flat-topped plate, also called *tailloir*, the upper member of a *capital of a column on which the *architrave rests. The *Greek *Doric abacus is the simplest, consisting of a square unmoulded block, called *plinthus*, but abaci vary according to the *Order used. **2.** Flat slab supported on a *podium or legs, used as a sideboard or for the display of plate, etc., in Antiquity. **3.** *Panel on an *Antique wall.

Abadie, Paul (1783–1868). French architect. In 1805 he joined *Percier's office in Paris, and in 1818 became Architect to the City of Angoulême and the Département de Charente. He designed the Palais de Justice (1825), *Hôtel of the Prefecture (1828), the School, and the Grain Market, all in Angoulême. His son, also **Paul Abadie** (1812–84), became Diocesan Architect to Angoulême, Périgueux, and La Rochelle in 1848, and in 1861 Inspector-General of Diocesan Buildings. He designed the Hôtel de Ville at Angoulême, but is best known for his somewhat drastic over-restorations of the Cathedral Church of St-Pierre (1854–82) at Angoulême and the Byzantino-*Romanesque Church of St-Front at Périgueux (1852–1901), both of which owe more to conjecture than archaeology. He used the same style for his Church of Sacré-Cœur, Montmartre, Paris (1874–1919). In 1874 he succeeded *Viollet-le-Duc as Architect of Notre Dame in Paris.

Hautecœur (1943–57)

abamurus. *Buttress or reinforcing wall.

abated. Stone surface cut away or lowered, leaving a sculpted ornament or design in low relief (e.g. on the *metope of a *Greek *Doric temple).

abat-jour. **1.** Anything that serves to throw daylight downward, or in a given direction, such as a sloped or bevelled *cill, or splayed *jambs. **2.** Skylight, set in a sloping aperture.

abaton. **1.** Inaccessible place. **2.** Building in Rhodes containing trophies created by Artemisia (*fl.* C4 BC), and closed to all but a select few.

abat-son. **1.** Anything to reflect sound downwards or outwards, such as a *louvre. **2.** Series of sloping louvres in a *belfry.

abat-vent. *Louvre in an external wall, such as is found in the *belfry-*stage of a *steeple, permitting the admission of light and air, but acting as a baffle to the elements, while allowing the emission of sound.

abat-voix. *Tester, or *canopy to reflect sound behind and on top of a *pulpit, common in late-C17 churches, e.g. those of *Wren in the City of London.

abbey. *See* monastery.

Abel, John (*c.*1578–1675). English architect and master-carpenter. He designed and built several elaborate *timber-framed structures in the English and Welsh Border Counties, including the Market Halls at Brecon, Wales (1624—demolished), Kington, Herefordshire (1654—demolished 1820), and Leominster, Herefordshire (1633—dismantled 1861 and reconstructed as a house named Grange Court). He also built the stone Grammar School at Kington (1625), and was probably responsible for the rumbustious *Carolean timber screen at Abbey Dore Church, Herefordshire (1633).

Colvin (1995)

Abercrombie, Sir (Leslie) Patrick (1879–1957). Influential British architect and town-planner. He worked at the University of Liverpool (1907–9) under (Sir) C. H. *Reilly and S. D. *Adshead, edited the *Town Planning Review*, and produced a series of reports on the growth and condition of several European cities. After Adshead was appointed to the Chair of Town Planning at University College London, Abercrombie became Professor of Civic Design at Liverpool in 1915, a post he held until 1935, when he succeeded Adshead in London. During those twenty years Abercrombie produced a multitude of studies and reports on many areas in England and Wales, and, during his Presidency of the Town Planning Institute, published *The Preservation of Rural England* (1926) which led to the formation of the Council for the Preservation of Rural England (CPRE). He championed the idea of a Green Belt around London, and contributed to the Royal Commission on the Distribution of the Industrial Population, the report of which (*Barlow Report*) appeared in 1940. Abercrombie, in association with J. H. Forshaw, was appointed to prepare a plan for post-war rebuilding in the County of London, and was also given the task of planning the whole area around the County. The results were the *County of London Plan* (1943) and the *Greater London Plan* (1944) which provided the basic skeleton of post-war development policies, including the *New Towns programme, from 1946. Abercrombie became an internationally acclaimed figure in town and regional planning: many of his former students became established in positions of authority.

Abercrombie (1926, 1933, 1959); *DNB* (1971); Stephenson and Pool (1944)

Abramovitz, Max (1908–). Chicago-born architect, educated in the USA and at the École des *Beaux-Arts in Paris. He worked with Wallace K. *Harrison and Jacques-André *Fouilhoux, and was Harrison's partner 1945–76 (*see* Harrison).

Abramovitz (1963)

abrevoir. **1.** Joint between stones in masonry. **2.** Elaborate water-tank.

Absolute architecture. The antithesis of *Functionalism, it was proposed as a purposeless architecture by Walter Pichler and Hans *Hollein in the 1960s, the opposite of objectivity (*Sachlichkeit*). Its forms were to be created by imagination rather than by consideration of need. It was also used by Bruce *Goff to describe his investigations of structure and the enclosure of space.

Conrads (1970); Long (1977, 1988)

Abstract Representation. Synthesis of *Late-*Modernism and *Post-Modernism in which analogies, associations, ornament, and symbolism were subtly suggested rather than clearly quoted.

Jencks (1983)

abstraction. Omission or severe simplification of details in drawings of a building or landscape, leaving essentials of massing, form, and solids, so that the basis of a design can be explained.

abuse. 1. Violation of established uses in Classical architecture. **2.** Corruption of form. Abuses according to *Palladio included *brackets, *consoles, or *modillions supporting (or seeming to support) a major structural load, e.g. a column; broken or open-topped *pediments; exaggerated overhangs of *cornices; and *rusticated or banded columns (*see* band). *Perrault and others identified further abuses: *pilasters and columns physically joined, especially at the corner of a building; *coupled columns (which Perrault himself employed at the east front of the Louvre in Paris); distortion of *metopes by making them wider and rectangular instead of square in abnormally large *intercolumniations; omission of the bottom part of the *Ionic *abacus; *Giant *Orders instead of an *assemblage of *Orders; an inverted *cavetto moulding joining the *plinth under a column-base to the cornice of a *pedestal; *architrave-cornices (as in *Hellenistic *Ionic); and *entablatures broken or interrupted immediately above a column. However, through use many abuses have become acceptable aspects of *Classicism.

Gwilt (1903); Papworth (1852)

abutment. 1. Any solid structure, such as a *pier, which receives the thrust of an *arch or *vault. **2.** Point at which a roof-structure rests on a wall.

abutment-piece. *Cill or *sole-plate (*see* sole-piece).

acanthus. Conventionalized representation of the leaf of the *Acanthus spinosus* plant, found on the lower parts of *Corinthian and *Composite *capitals, and also used for enrichment of various elements in Classical architecture. *Vitruvius tells of how a basket, placed over the grave of a maiden of Corinth, and protected by a tile, became festooned in acanthus-stalks and leaves, and was copied by *Callimachus in stylized form, thus creating the Corinthian capital.

Typical stylized form of acanthus-leaf.

Acanthus-leaves arranged in typical Classical style above an astragal moulding.

acanthus

accessory. Element in a composition not essential (unlike an *accompaniment) to the use or character of the building, but which enhances the general effect.

accolade. Two *ogee curves meeting above or within an arch, and rising to a *finial, usually associated with late-*Gothic work, e.g. over a *doorway or in a *screen.

accompaniment. 1. Ornament further enriching another ornament. **2.** Building or ornament closely connected with, or essential to, the completeness of the design, such as the *wings of a *Palladian *villa. *See* accessory.

accouplement. Pair of *coupled columns or *pilasters.

accumulation. Collection of features derived from different periods used to suggest a chronological sequence of building even though construction may have taken place at the one time. *See* additive.

Achaemenian, Achaemenid. Period in Persian architecture from the time of Cyrus the Great (d. 529 BC) until the death of Darius (330 BC). Its most elaborate buildings include the vast palace complex at Persepolis (518–*c*.460 BC) which included large relief decorations, while the *apadana (or Hall of the

Hundred Columns) had elaborate *capitals with vertical *volutes and animal-heads. *Reliefs of green, yellow, and blue glazed bricks were employed at the palaces of Susa, and the rock-cut tombs at Naksh-i-Rustam employ similar capitals to those at Persepolis, with door-surrounds derived from Egyptian precedents.

Cruickshank (1996); Lloyd and Müller (1986)

Achievement of Arms. Collected armorial ensigns consisting of *shield of arms, crest, helm, mantling,* and *motto,* with *supporters* and *heraldic badge* as appropriate. It is corrupted as *hatchment,* and this term denotes an *Achievement of Arms* painted on a diamond-shaped frame hung on a house following a death (and thereafter displayed in a church).

Norroy and Ulster King of Arms

achromatic. Architecture without colour, or only with white and black, or white and gold, commonly found in early examples of the *Greek Revival.

acorn. *Finial or other *termination representing the fruit or seed of the oak-tree, often used instead of an *urn or *pine-cone.

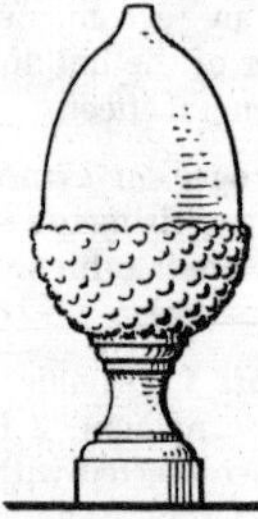

acorn. Acorn-shaped cast-iron finial (*c.*1820), Mecklenburgh Square, London. (*JJS*)

acrolithus, acrolith. *Antique or *Neoclassical statue with hands, feet, and face of marble, the rest being of wood concealed by drapery.

acropodium. **1.** *Pedestal, usually elaborate and high, supporting a statue. **2.** *Terminal pedestal resting on representations of feet.

acropolis. Elevated part of the city, or the citadel, in Ancient Greece, especially the Athenian acropolis (from *acro-*, meaning highest or topmost, and *polis*, meaning city).

Dinsmoor (1950)

acrostolium. Part of the prow of an *Antique warship, often circular, spiral, or shaped to resemble an animal: representations can be found on e.g. the *columna rostrata.

acroter, acroterion, acroterium (*pl.* **acroteria**). **1.** *Plinth or *fastigium*, one placed over the *apex and one over each end of a *Classical *pediment, left unadorned but often carrying a statue or other ornament. Those on each side are *acroteria angularia*. **2.** Ornament or statue with no plinth in those positions, or ornament forming one object with its plinth at the apex and ends of a pediment. **3.** *Ridge of a Classical temple. **4.** *Horn or *ear of an altar, *stele, or *sarcophagus.

Dinsmoor (1950)

acroter. Ornamental *acroter, acroterion,* or *acroterium*, one of two *acroteria angularia* from the Temple of Aphaia, Aegina (beginning of C5 BC). (*JJS*)

Action architecture. **1.** Architecture evolved from sketches without precise working-drawings and using materials ready to hand. **2.** Creation of form through constant repetition and evolution of one concept. An example of Action architecture is Boston City Hall, Mass. (1964–9), by Kallmann, McKinnell, & Knowles.

Collins (1965); Jencks (1973*a*); Kallmann (1959)

Adam, James (1732–94). Distinguished Scots architect, he was the third son of William *Adam. He toured Italy (1760–3), accompanied by George *Richardson, before joining the family firm in London. While in Italy he met *Clérisseau, and the two men travelled to Rome. Adam visited Naples and *Paestum, but his plans to see Sicily and Greece did not work out. His studies of *Pompeian decorations and *grotesques became important for his work as an interior designer, as *The Works in Architecture of Robert and James Adam* (1773–1822) proves. Although, by the time he returned to England, his brother Robert *Adam had established the vocabulary of the 'Adam style', James must share in the credit for the many distinguished buildings under their joint authorship. In his own right he was responsible for the *Ionic gateway at Cullen House, Banff (1767), Hertford Shire and Town Hall (1767–9), the *façades of Portland Place, London (1776), and several buildings in Glasgow. In 1769 James succeeded his brother as Architect of the King's Works.

Adam (1975); Bolton (1922); Colvin (1995); King (1991); Rykwert and Rykwert (1985)

Adam, John (1721–92). Scots architect. The eldest son of William *Adam, he became Master-Mason to the Board of Ordnance on the death of his father in 1748. He took his brother **Robert** into partnership, and over the next decade they completed the impressive military structures at Fort George and elsewhere in the Scottish Highlands that William had begun in the aftermath of the Jacobite Rising of 1745–6. A competent designer who drew on the vocabulary of *Palladianism, John was nevertheless the business-manager of the partnership, which survived until 1758 when Robert set up his own practice in London. Works identifiable as by John and Robert were illustrated in *Vitruvius Scoticus*, published by John's son **William** (1751–1839) in 1811. His buildings include the completion of Hopetoun House, West Lothian (1750–6), the Adam family *mausoleum in Greyfriars Churchyard, Edinburgh (1753), the Court House and other structures at Inveraray, Argyll (1755–61), and Moffat House, Moffat, Dumfries (1761). By the 1770s John had retired from practice, but was closely involved in the business affairs of his brothers **James** and Robert. When the Adelphi speculation, Strand, London, got into severe difficulties in 1772 John was forced to mortgage the family seat at Blair Adam to stave off bankruptcy.

Colvin (1995); Fleming (1962); King (1991)

Adam, Robert (1728–92). One of the most celebrated of British architects, decorators, and interior designers in the later part of C18. The second surviving son of William *Adam, he matriculated at Edinburgh University, and knew the leading figures of the Scottish Enlightenment. On the death of William, he entered into partnership with his brother **John**, and by 1754 had enough capital to set out on the *Grand Tour. In Italy he employed *Clérisseau (who joined him in his travels, instructed the young Scot in draughtsmanship, and influenced him to appreciate the possibilities of *Neoclassicism), studied Classical Antiquities, and met *Piranesi (who incorporated a monument to Adam in his *Antichità Romane* (1756), and later dedicated his *Campo Marzio* (1762) to 'Roberto Adam'). In 1755 Adam and Clérisseau visited Naples and *Herculaneum to see the excavations, and in 1757 proceeded to Spalato, where they surveyed the huge Roman Palace: their labours were published as *Ruins of the Palace of Emperor Diocletian at Spalatro in Dalmatia* (1764), illustrated with magnificent engravings.

Adam settled in London in 1758, was joined by his brothers **James** and **William** (1738–1822), and set out to establish himself as the leading architect in Great Britain. From that time Robert was the dominant director of the family firm, assisted by James and William, while **John** helped out with capital. His fellow-Scots the Duke of Argyll and the Earl of Bute supported him, and in 1761 he obtained one of the two posts of Architect of the King's Works. He began to change domestic architecture (dominated then by *Burlingtonian *Palladianism) by providing a fresh vocabulary of *Classicism with elements drawn from a range of sources from Antiquity to the *Cinquecento. He advertised himself as an authority on *Antique Roman architecture, and in 1773 the first sumptuous volume of the *Works in Architecture of Robert and James Adam* appeared, in which the brothers staked their claim to have 'brought about . . . a kind of revolution' in English architecture. At Kedleston Hall, Derbyshire, for example, the Adam Brothers took over and completed the house after Matthew *Brettingham and James *Paine had started the central *block and the *quadrants: the Adams were responsible for the noble, domed *Pantheon-like *saloon and the *triumphal arch applied to the south front, while the Palladian marble hall was a reworking of Paine's version of *Palladio's reconstruction of *Vitruvius' *Egyptian hall. Indeed, it was in interior design that the Adam Brothers had their greatest influence: essentially, they eschewed a violent change of established canons, but they succeeded in evolving a Neoclassical style that avoided Greek severity or old-fashioned

Palladianism by expanding the available ranges of decorative elements and by inventing a sumptuous and elegant array of details drawn from various sources. Their ceilings were often enriched with painted panels by talented Italian artists, while Joseph Rose sen. (*c*.1723–80) and jun. (1745–99) realized their designs for plasterwork. The firm employed several draughtsmen to facilitate its enormous practice: among them were George *Richardson, Joseph *Bonomi, and Antonio Zucchi. The Adams juxtaposed room-plans of various shapes and forms that had their origins in Antique interiors from Spalato and from the Roman *thermae. Such variations of form and the judicious use of *apses, *niches, and *colonnaded *screens created spatial complexities that were a welcome contrast to the older Palladian arrangements.

At Syon House, Isleworth, Middlesex, the remodelled interiors (1762–9) demonstrate the exploitation of varied geometrical forms, although the projected central Pantheon-like *rotunda was not executed, but the anteroom (which was built) displays an eclectic Neoclassical *polychrome treatment incorporating detached Greek *Ionic columns (with *capitals based on those of the Athenian Erechtheion) supporting an elegant *entablature, over which are gilded statues. To whet the client's appetite for Antique authenticity, the blue-grey marble column-shafts are Roman, rescued from the bed of the River Tiber. Other fine Adam interiors include Osterley Park, Middlesex (1763–80), Newby Hall, Yorkshire (*c*.1770–*c*.1780), Derby House (later 26), Grosvenor Square, London (1773–4—demolished 1861), and the beautiful Library at Kenwood House, Hampstead (1767–9). As far as ingenious planning is concerned, the most intricate examples are at two London houses: 20 St James's Square and 20 Portman Square, although the decorative details are thin and shallow compared with earlier works.

Perhaps because of a frustrated desire to 'raise a great public building . . . in the monumental manner', the brothers in 1768 began their scheme to erect 24 first-rate houses between the north bank of the Thames and The Strand, the whole set on a mighty *podium of vaulted areas intended as warehouses. Called The Adelphi, the speculation was ruined by a national credit crisis, and the brothers were forced to stave off bankruptcy by disposing of the property in a lottery. Later, James Adam designed the unified *façade of Portland Place incorporating *stucco details for the central elements of each block on either side. Other unified *terrace-house designs include Charlotte Square, Edinburgh (1791–1807), and the south and east sides of Fitzroy Square, London (1790–4)—the latter with elegant attenuated Grecian detail.

In the last years of his life Robert Adam obtained a number of commissions for large buildings, including the Register House, Edinburgh (1774–92), Edinburgh University (1789–93), and the large *Picturesque houses in the *Castle style (that is, with elements derived from medieval castle architecture, but with Classical interiors), including Culzean Castle, Ayrshire (1777–92), and Seton Castle, East Lothian (1790–1). Adam also designed distinguished *mausolea, among which may be cited the rectangular Templetown mausoleum, capped with an *urn and two ash-chests, at Castle Upton, Co. Antrim (1789), and the circular *Doric drum of the Hume monument at Calton Old Burying Ground, Edinburgh (1778).

The Adam firm was wound up in 1794, although William Adam produced unsuccessful designs for the completion of Edinburgh University in 1815. William went bankrupt in 1801, and between 1818 and 1821 sold all his brothers' possessions. While the *Works* . . . provided a definitive vocabulary of what became known as the 'Adam style', details designed by Robert and his brothers were pirated even during their lifetimes, and there was an Adam Revival dating from 1862 which still goes on, though often as a travesty.

Adam (1975); Bolton (1922); Colvin (1995); Fleming (1962); King (1991); Placzek (1982—a very full account by Prof. Stillman); Rowan (1985); Rykwert and Rykwert (1985); Stillman (1966, 1988)

Adam, Robert (1948–). English architect. An important figure in the *New Classicism, he combines scholarship with a willingness to embrace modern materials, functions, and technological developments. No dry respecter of canonical buildings, he has argued that *Classicism, as the common architectural language of the Western world, is accessible and capable of continuous development. Among his works are West Walk House, The Close, Salisbury, Wiltshire (1983), Aamdahl (UK) Headquarters, Dogmersfield Park, Odiham, Hampshire (1985), the Director's House, Accademia Britannica, Rome (1992), and a project to extend the Ashmolean Museum, Oxford (1995). Among his many publications is *Classical Architecture: A Complete Handbook* (1990).

Emanuel (1994); Powers (1987)

Adam, William (1689–1748). As a Presbyterian Whig, Adam was acceptable both to the aristocracy and to the protagonists of the Scottish Enlightenment in post-1715 Scotland, and quickly established himself as the leading architect in that country. An entrepreneur with many interests, he invested in property in Edinburgh, and purchased a country estate at Blair Crambeth in Kinross, renamed Blair Adam. In 1728 Adam became Clerk and Storekeeper of the Works in Scotland, and from 1730 Mason to the Board of Ordnance in North Britain, which brought him many lucrative building-contracts for *forts and other structures after 1745.

As an architect he took his architectural elements from a wide series of precedents, creating an eclectic mix that was lively and often startlingly original. While he imbibed much from *Gibbs and *Vanbrugh, it also appears he knew something of Continental *Baroque architecture from a visit to The Netherlands. Adam endeavoured to publicize his own designs and those of other Scots architects in a book, but the volume languished until 1811 when it was published as *Vitruvius Scoticus*, consisting of plates without an explanatory text.

Adam was the founder of the famous Adam dynasty, including **Robert** and **James**. His most important buildings include Hopetoun House, West Lothian (1723–48), Haddo House, Aberdeenshire (1732–5), the erection of Inveraray Castle, Argyll, to designs by Roger *Morris (1745–8), Mavisbank House, Loanhead, Midlothian (1723–7), and Floors Castle, Roxburghshire (1721–6).

Adam (1980); Colvin (1995); Fleming (1962); Gifford (1989)

Adams, Henry Percy (1865–1930). English architect, who took over Stephen Salter's practice, which in 1913 became Adams, Holden, & Pearson (*see* Holden, Charles Henry).

Gray (1985)

Adams, Maurice Bingham (1849–1933). English architect, best remembered for his part in the making of Bedford Park, Chiswick, the artists' colony founded in 1875, where he designed several of the houses (illustrated in *Artists' Homes* (1883)), supervised the erection of Norman *Shaw's Church of St Michael and All Angels, and designed the north aisle and parish-hall (1887). He was also responsible for the exquisite Chapel of All Souls, added to St Michael's in 1909. He designed several public libraries for John Passmore Edwards (1823–1911), the philanthropist. His work is generally in a free *Arts-and-Crafts style. He was the author of *Modern Cottage Architecture* (1904).

Adams (1883, 1904); Gray (1985); Greeves (1975)

additive. A method of *agglutinative* or *serial* design involving asymmetrical plans and elevations, where the interior spaces and volumes are suggested by, and even dictate, the exterior treatment of projections, roofs, and other features. Derived from the theories of A. W. N. *Pugin, additive design can also include *accumulation (suggesting a sequence of building additions of different styles and periods). *See* articulation and concatenation.

addorsed. Opposite of *affronted. Set back-to-back, such as two identical figures facing in opposite directions.

Adelcrantz, Carl Fredrik (1716–96). Swedish architect, son of the architect **Göran Josuae Adelcrantz** (1668–1739), he was a pupil of Carl Gustav Tessin (*see* Tessin, Nicodemus the Younger). Appointed Supervisor of Court Buildings in Stockholm (1741), he remodelled the riding-master's quarters at Ulriksdal as a theatre in the *Rococo style (1753). Drawing on *Chambers's *Designs for Chinese Buildings* (1757), he created the charming *Chinoiserie *pavilion at Drottningholm (1763–9), and designed two more theatres (Drottningholm (1764–6) and the Royal Opera in Stockholm (1777–82)). In 1768–74 he built the Adolf-Fredrik Church in Stockholm, much influenced by French *Classicism, and remodelled other Stockholm buildings in a Neoclassical style.

Fogelmarck (1957)

Adhocism. Design, essentially a *collage*, where every part of a building, or each element of a building-complex, is designed with scant regard to the whole, and often involves disparate parts taken from catalogues.

Jencks (1968, 1972)

Adler, Dankmar (1844–1900). *See* Sullivan, Louis Henry.

adobe. Sun-dried unburned clay or earth building-brick or -block (*clay-bat*) made with straw, found in Cambridgeshire (England), Spain, and Latin America. Compare *cob, *pisé de terre, and *tabia.

Adshead, Stanley Davenport (1868–1946). Cheshire-born English architect, he moved to London in 1890 and worked with William *Flockhart for whom he superintended the building of Rosehaugh, Avoch, Ross and Cromarty, a vast mansion of great magnificence. In 1898 he set up his own practice; his most successful work (in partnership with Stanley C. Ramsay) is undoubtedly the delightful Neo-*Regency Duchy of Cornwall Estate, Kennington, South London (1913), modelled on modest early C19 stock-brick London housing. In 1912 he was appointed to the Leverhulme Chair of Civic Design at the University of Liverpool, and, in 1914, to the Chair of Town Planning at the University of London.

DNB (1959); Gray (1985)

Advocacy planning. Term coined by the American planner Paul Davidoff in 1965, meaning architectural design and planning for powerless, inarticulate inner-city groups, notably when resisting destructive schemes by planning authorities, government agencies, or similar bodies. Among its early practitioners were ARCH (Architects' Renewal Committee in Harlem), a group formed by the architect C. Richard Hatch in 1964.

Davidoff (1965); Lopen (1965)

adyton, adytum. Innermost unlit chamber of a Greek temple whence oracles were delivered. *See* secos.

aedes, aedis. Small *Antique dedicated (not consecrated) *shrine or building, often circular on plan, either *monopteral or a *rotunda with *peristyle.

aedicule, aedicula (*pl.* **aedicules, aediculae**). **1.** *Shrine or *sacellum within a temple *cella, either a large *niche or a *pedestal supporting two or more columns carrying an *entablature and *pediment thus forming a frame or *canopied housing for a cult-statue. **2.** Architectural frame around a *doorway, niche, or window-aperture consisting of two columns or *pilasters over which is an entablature with pediment, like a miniature *distyle* building: such an opening is said to be *aediculated*.

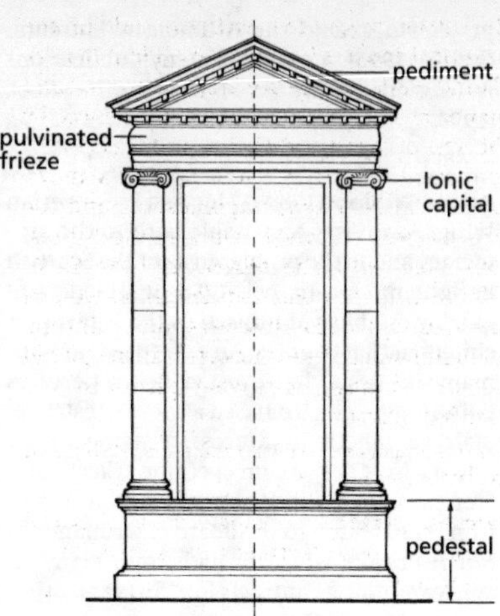

aedicule. The Order is Roman Ionic, with a pulvinated frieze and triangular pediment.

aegicrane, aegicranium (*pl.* **aegicranes, aegicrania**). Classical ornament of sculpted ram's or goat's head or skull. *Not* aegricane. *See* bucranium.

Aelric (*fl.* *c.*1124–53). Northumbrian mason, probably of Saxon origin. He was perhaps the designer of the Abbey Church at Dunfermline, Scotland (*c.*1125–50).

Harvey (1987)

Aeolic. *Primitive type of *Ionic *capital with *volutes seeming to grow from the *shaft, and a *palmette between the volutes.

Aeolic capital (*JJS*)

Aesthetic Movement. British and American artistic reaction against much of overblown Victorian design which enjoyed a vogue from the 1860s, associated with the cult of the Beautiful and Art for Art's Sake. Plain materials and surfaces were preferred to profuse and inappropriate ornament. It was influenced by the arts of Japan and China, and was closely connected with the *Arts-and-Crafts movement, *Art Nouveau, *Japonaiserie, and the *Queen Anne Revival. The architect most connected with the Movement was E. W. *Godwin, but its main manifestations were in late-Victorian decorative arts and painting, often influenced by exotic orientalism, giving it a rich, strange, somewhat perfumed and decadent flavour.

Aslin (1969); Burke *et al.* (1986); Lambourne (1996); Lewis and Darley (1986)

aetoma, aetos. 1. *Ridge of a Classical temple. **2.** Apex *acroterium. **3.** *Pediment *tympanum.

Affleck, Raymond Tait (1922–89). Canadian architect, whose interests in multi-purpose spaces are best expressed in the Place Bonaventure, Montreal (1964–8), by Affleck Desbarats Dimakopoulos Lebensold Sise: it is a vast complex with internal circulation routes and spaces, but its architectural style is a somewhat forbidding example of *Brutalism.

Kalman (1994)

affronted. Opposite of *addorsed. Identical figures or animals facing each other, for example, with busts on each side of an opening, as in the tower of Alexander 'Greek' *Thomson's St Vincent Street Church, Glasgow (1857–9).

agger. 1. Mound or *rampart formed by the earth and stones excavated from a ditch. **2.** *Piers carrying the domed structures of a *Byzantine church. **3.** Roman road-foundation.

agglutinative. *See* additive.

agora. Public open space in a Greek city, surrounded by fine architecture. *See* forum.

Agostino di Duccio (1418–81). Florentine sculptor and architect, he worked (*c.*1450–7) on *Alberti's *Tempio Malatestiano* at Rimini, where he created refined and original *personifications of the Liberal Arts. He designed the early *Renaissance *façade of the Oratorio di San Bernardino at Perugia (1457–61), on which both coloured marble and *terracotta are used to great effect. He was also responsible for the decorations on the monumental Porta San Pietro in the same city (1473–81).

Heydenreich and Lotz (1974); Pope-Hennessy (1958)

agrafe, agraffe. *Keystone decorated with relief sculpture.

Agrest and Gandelsonas. American architects, founded by Argentine-born Diana Agrest (1944–) and Mario Gandelsonas (1938–). They have written on the 'analytical decomposition' of architecture, and, with their house on Sag Pond, Sagaponack, Long Island, NY (1990–4), have demonstrated the architectural possibilities of this with a cluster of disparate elements, using timber cladding, and suggesting tradition that is half-forgotten.

Jodidio (1996)

Agricultural Order. Type of *Corinthian *capital with *volutes replaced by representations of animal-heads, *acanthus-leaves replaced by those of mangel-wurzel and turnip, and other allusions to agriculture.

aguilla. *Obelisk, *spire, or similar object.

Ahrends, Burton, & Koralek. British architectural practice founded in 1961 by Peter Ahrends, Richard Burton, and Paul Koralek (all 1933–) after they won first prize in the competition to design the Berkeley Library for Trinity College, Dublin (1960, built 1961–7). Other works include St Andrew's College, Booterstown, Dublin (1968–72); Trinity College Arts Faculty Building, Dublin (1968–79); extensions to Keble College, Oxford (1972–80); Templeton College, Oxford (1969–96); Portsmouth Polytechnic Library (1975–90); the John Lewis Store, Kingston upon Thames, Surrey (1979–90); and the J. Sainsbury Supermarket, Canterbury, Kent (1982–4—with a roof suspended on cables from steel uprights). They were also responsible for eleven stations and two bridges for the Docklands Light Railway, London (1987–93). The firm received unwelcome publicity when its prize-winning (1982–6) proposal for the extension to the National Gallery in London was described by the Prince of Wales as a 'carbuncle', and the design was not realized. However, Hooke Park College, Dorset (1983–90), Burton House, London (1988), and the British Embassy in Moscow (1996–9), among many other projects, demonstrate the resilience of ABK.

Information from ABK (1997); Emanuel (1994)

Aichel, Jan Blažej Santini (1667–1723). *See* Santini-Aichel, Jan Blažej.

Aida, Takefumi (1937–). *See* Architext.

Aigner, Chrystian Piotr (1756–1841). One of the leading architects and theorists of Polish *Neoclassicism, he was responsible for embellishing the Garden of Allusions at Puławy with its circular temple of the Sybil (1798–1801), *Gothic house, and remarkable *rotunda-church with *portico based on the Roman *Pantheon (1800–3). He also designed the Namiestnikowski Palace (1818–19), and the Pantheon-like Church of St Alexander (1818–25), both in Warsaw.

Lorentz and Rottermund (1984)

aileron. Half-*gable or half-*pediment concealing a *lean-to roof, *aisle-roof, or similar.

Aillaud, Émile (1902–88). French architect. He attempted to counter the rigid effects of using prefabricated *concrete panel-construction by arranging the masses of building on curving snake-like plans, as at Les Courtillières, Pantin (1955–60).

Dhuys (1983)

aisle. 1. Part of a church on either side of the *nave or *choir, divided from the latter by means of *arcades, *colonnades, or *piers supporting the *clearstorey. Aisles are commonly of less height than the nave, and the normal *basilican form consists of a clearstoreyed nave with a *lean-to aisle on each side, sometimes doubled so that there are two aisles on each side, but in England there are countless medieval churches with only one aisle. *Transepts (called *cross-aisles*) may also have aisles to the liturgical east or west, but often have only an eastern aisle to accommodate *chapels. In German *hall-churches (*Hallenkirchen*) the aisles and nave are the same height, so there are no clearstoreys, but the aisle-windows are long and tall. **2.** Compartment of a *timber-framed barn, hall, or house, defined by a row of *posts separating it from the main body of the building. **3.** Walk or passage in a theatre, church, or hall giving access to rows of seats. **4.** Covered and enclosed burial-ground attached to a church. **5.** Flanking wing of a building.

Aitchison, George, jun. (1825–1910). British architect, the son of **George Aitchison** (1792–1861), architect, by whom he was trained, and whose partner he became in 1859. An expert in interior design, his finest work is the house he designed for Frederic, Baron Leighton of Stretton (1830–96), at Holland Park Road, Kensington, which includes the Arab Hall (added 1877–9, built to display the collection of glazed tiles Leighton had acquired during his visits to the East) and the artist's studio. Aitchison enjoyed a considerable reputation, being Professor of Architecture at the Royal Academy (1887–1905) and President of the Royal Institute of British Architects (1896–9). He opposed too slavish a following of historical styles: his furniture designs were published in *Gewerbehalle* and in *The Cabinet Maker and Art Furnisher* (1884), and he brought out a new edition of James Ward's *The Principles of Ornament* in 1892.

DNB (1920); Jervis (1984); Richardson (1980)

ajaraca. Spanish ornament on brick walls formed of patterns a half-brick in depth.

ajimez, aximez. Window-aperture in *Moorish architecture with *colonnettes or *mullions dividing it into arch-headed *lights.

ajour, à jour, ajouré. Pierced *panel of some material, e.g. marble, to allow the admission of air and light.

ala (*pl.* alae). **1.** Rectangular room on each side of the main *cella of an *Etruscan temple, each with its own door, approached from a deep *portico. **2.** Small room or *alcove on each side of a *vestibule or *atrium in a Roman house. **3.** Space between the *naos and flanking *colonnade of a Greek temple.

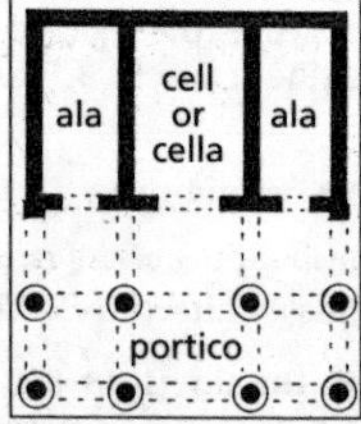

ala. Plan of Etruscan temple derived from descriptions in Vitruvius. (*JJS after Author*)

alabaster. Massive, fine-grained partly translucent type of gypsum (calcium sulphate), coloured white, yellow, red, and brown, called *bastard alabaster*, often employed for church fittings and monuments. *Oriental* or *calcareous alabaster* is a translucent calcium carbonate, yellowish-white in colour, broken with milky veins. Thin slabs of oriental alabaster were often used in window-*lights (especially in Italy), and the *sarcophagus of Pharaoh Seti I, now in Sir John *Soane's Museum, London, is made of this material.

Alan of Walsingham (*fl.* C14). *See* Walsingham, Alan of.

Álava, Juan de (*c*.1480–1537). Spanish master-mason involved in the building of the Catedral Nueva at Salamanca (1512) and Seville Cathedral (1513). Later, he worked with members of the *Colonia family at Plasencia Cathedral (notably around the *crossing), and from 1521 he built the *cloisters of Santiago de Compostela Cathedral, in the *Plateresque style, which are among the largest and most beautiful in Spain. From 1524 he was engaged in building the Church of San Esteban at Salamanca (completed 1610), and was in charge of the works at Salamanca Cathedral from 1526. His work spans a late flowering of *Gothic to early *Renaissance styles.

Kubler and Soria (1959)

Alavoine, Jean-Antoine (1778–1834). French architect. He rebuilt the central *spire of Rouen Cathedral after it burned down in 1822, and designed the Colonne de Juillet, Place de la Bastille, Paris, modified and completed by L.-J. *Duc. He was a pioneer in the use of cast iron as a building material, as in his restorations of the Cathedrals of Sées (1817–23) and Rouen (from 1823).

Chirol (1920)

albanega. *Spandrel between a *Moorish horseshoe *arch and a rectangular *frame (*alfiz*) around it.

Alberic (*fl.* 1249–53). English mason. He was overseer of the building of the east *cloister at Westminster Abbey (1249–53), and was also engaged on the construction of the *chapter-house there. He probably worked under Henry de *Reyns.

Harvey (1987)

Albert, Prince Francis (Albert) Augustus Charles Emmanuel, Duke of Saxony and Prince of Saxe-Coburg and Gotha (1819–61). Born at Schloss Rosenau, near Coburg, Prince Albert married the young Queen Victoria in 1840, and was created Prince Consort in 1857. In 1841 he chaired the Royal Commission to oversee the decorations of the new Palace of Westminster that were to act as a catalyst to improve the quality of British art, design, and manufactures. The Prince joined the Society of Arts and became its President in 1843; in this capacity he encouraged the application of science and art to industrial purposes. Around this time two important figures, (Sir) Henry Cole (1808–82) and Professor Ludwig Grüner (1801–82), became closely involved with the Prince. The latter acted as art-adviser, encouraging a taste for *Renaissance *polychromy, *grotesques, and the *Rundbogenstil that were to be so influential in the buildings at South Kensington. The former became Chairman of the Society of Arts, and promoted model designs commissioned from artists which coined the term 'art manufactures': he was an energetic organizer, becoming Prince Albert's chief lieutenant for the remarkable Great Exhibition of 1851 in *Paxton's Crystal Palace, of which the Prince was an enthusiastic promoter.

Albert was also President of the Society for Improving the Condition of the Labouring Classes, and helped to encourage the building of exemplary dwellings: the Society erected four 'Model Houses for Families' as part of the 1851 Exhibition, designed by Henry *Roberts and paid for by the Prince. Later, Albert proposed using the profits of the Great Exhibition to found an establishment where science and art could be applied to industry of all nations. This was the beginning of South Kensington, a complex of museums, scientific institutions, and places of learning, known as Albertopolis, which had at its nucleus the Schools of Design. The Victoria & Albert Museum, a national museum of fine and applied art, is probably the Prince's most lasting memorial.

As an influence on architecture the Prince was significant. Not only was polychromy favoured from the late 1840s, but many of Grüner's other Italianizing enthusiasms took root. Albert himself was involved in a number of design projects, including the *Italianate Osborne House, Isle of Wight (with the London builder Thomas *Cubitt from 1845), the Royal Dairy at the Model Farms at Windsor, alterations at Buckingham Palace, and Balmoral Castle (an essay in the *Scottish Baronial style executed by William Smith (1817–91) of Aberdeen). However, Prince

Albert's importance in the history of design lies in the immense improvements that became apparent from the time of the 1862 London Exhibition, which he encouraged, but did not live to see realized.

Ames (1967); Curl (1983); *DNB* (1917); Hobhouse (1983); Rhodes James (1983); Scheele (1977)

Alberti, Leon Battista (1404–72). *Uomo universale* of the Italian early *Renaissance, and architect of genius (though never involved in the actual building of his designs), he was the first architectural theorist of the Renaissance, and established the moral and intellectual essence of architecture, placing it in realms more exalted than those inhabited by the master-craftsman of the medieval period (although there had been exceptions then).

Born in Genoa, educated at Padua and Bologna, he visited Florence in 1428 where he became acquainted with leading intellectuals: in his *De Pictura* (the Italian version of 1436 is dedicated to *Brunelleschi) he provided the first written description of the principles of *perspective. His admiration for the achievements of Brunelleschi and his appreciation of the importance of architecture in the revitalization of the spirit of Antiquity led him to a study of theoretical and archaeological bases, and therefore to Rome, where he became closely involved in the Papal Court from 1431. In *Descriptio urbis Romanae* (1443), a key work of Roman topography, his understanding of Antiquity and of Renaissance principles of *proportion is displayed. He became an intimate of Tommaso Parentucelli, who became Pope Nicholas V (1447–55), and Alberti became consultant to the Papacy on architectural and restoration projects. In 1452 he presented his *De re aedificatoria* (On the Art of Building) to the Pope: the book (published complete in 1486), intended to be a modern equivalent of *Vitruvius's great work, encapsulated concerns with the *Orders and proportion, extolled *Antique architecture, gave practical advice, and explained the principles of Roman civic design and how they had contemporary significance. The book was translated into English by *Leoni and first published in 1726–9 as *The Architecture of L. B. Alberti*, with subsequent editions of 1739 and 1753–5: a new edition, edited by Joseph Rykwert, was published in 1966.

Alberti prepared plans (from 1450) for the transformation of the medieval church of San Francesco in Rimini into a *mortuary-chapel-cum-*mausoleum for Sigismondo Malatesta (1417–68), Lord of Rimini. He encased the *Gothic structure in Classical *ashlar fabric, with an unfinished front (the first Renaissance example of a Classical west front on a *basilican church), the lower part of which is based on a Roman *triumphal arch (symbolizing Christian triumph over death). The *Tempio Malatestiano* (as it became known) was a deeply serious building, evoking the power and severity of Ancient Roman architecture.

C15 perception of the *Romanesque Church of San Miniato al Monte, Florence, as Antique probably inspired Alberti in his designs for the west front of the Gothic Church of Santa Maria Novella in that city (1456–70), executed in a skin of coloured marble applied to the brick structure behind. This celebrated front is an attempted solution to the problem of providing a Classical *façade for the traditional basilican shape of a *clearstoreyed *nave with *lean-to *aisles: the Orders framing the central doorway (itself based on that of the Roman *Pantheon) and the *blind *arcading merge the triumphal-arch theme with the treatment of the façade of San Miniato. Above, the crowning *pediment is carried on an *entablature and four *pilasters, suggesting a *temple-front, and large *scrolls hide the roofs of the aisles. There are clear geometrical relationships between the various parts of the façade and the whole, and these complex interconnections are the first use of *harmonic proportions in the Renaissance period. This design was carried out for Giovanni Rucellai, for whom Alberti also prepared a scheme for the façade of the new *palazzo (erected under the direction of Bernardo di Matteo Gambarelli, called *Rossellino, *c.*1460). The Palazzo Rucellai was the first domestic Renaissance building in which each storey was defined by an Order (but owes something to Brunelleschi's Palazzo di Parte Guelfa).

Alberti again entered the service of the Papacy under Pope Pius II (1458–64), for whom the architect may have played a part in the rebuilding of Pienza, and was probably involved in the design of the Benediction Loggia at the Vatican. He was very likely responsible for the barrel-vaulted mortuary-chapel (Cappella Rucellai) at the Church of San Pancrazio, Florence, of 1460–7, and certainly designed the exquisite marble shrine (*c.*1467) of the Holy Sepulchre (articulated with pilasters) for that *chapel. Also dating from the

1460s is Alberti's Church of San Sebastiano, Mantua, built on a Greek-cross plan, and with an entrance temple-front originally intended to have six pilasters carrying a broken entablature and pediment: the arch linking the two parts of the pediment and the elimination of two of the pilasters suggests the triumphal arch of Tiberius at Orange (late C1 BC) and also a certain freedom of expression, but the real model is probably Diocletian's Palace at Spalato (*c.* AD 300) and the Antique façades of the tombs of Annia Regilla (near the *Via Appia*) and of the Cercenii (south of Rome—a point emphasized by the similarity of the plan of San Sebastiano to that tomb). Another precedent for the plan can be found in the Greek Library at Hadrian's *Villa at Tivoli.

In 1464, on the death of Pius II, Alberti devoted himself to the service of the Gonzaga family of Mantua. In 1470 he was involved in the construction of the *rotunda of the Florentine Church of Santissima Annunziata, which is derived from Santa Maria degli Angeli in Florence (1434), in turn derived from

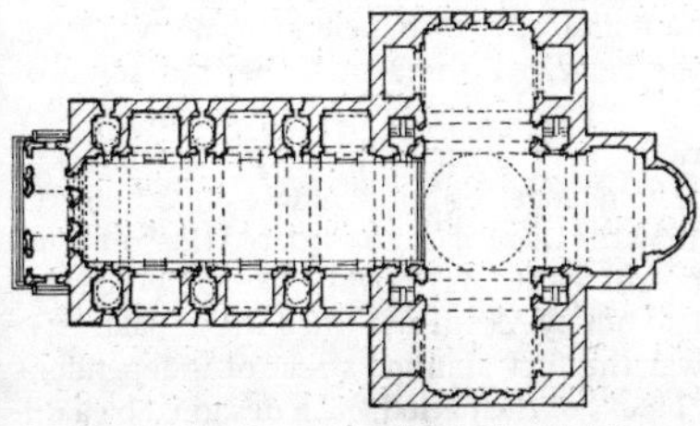

Plan of Sant'Andrea, Mantua, showing massive internal buttresses (wall-piers) subdividing the aisles into chapels.

the so-called temple of 'Minerva Medica' in Rome (*c.* AD 250), although *Michelozzo di Bartolommeo was involved earlier. For the Gonzagas, he designed his great Church of Sant'Andrea in Mantua (commenced 1470), where the influence of Roman exemplars is clear. The nave is roofed with a gigantic coffered barrel-*vault (the largest and heaviest to be erected since Antiquity): to carry this, Alberti drew on the structural principles of Roman *thermae, and formed massive *abutments at right angles to the axis of the nave, between which he created large barrel-vaulted and smaller domed chapels in what would have been the 'aisles' of a normal basilican arrangement. Furthermore, the elevation of the nave arcades consists of three interlocked triumphal arches, and the west front combines an Antique temple-front with a triumphal arch that echoes the arches of the interior as well as the great barrel-vault within. The grand interior with chapels instead of aisles is the precedent for most Italian and Counter-Reformation churches of C16.

Alberti (1988); Borsi (1989); Heydenreich and Lotz (1974); Rykwert (1966); Wittkower (1988)

Albini, Franco (1905–77). Influential Italian architect, born near Como, Albini rose to eminence in the 1930s. His first important building was the Pavilion for the Istituto Nazionale della Assicurazione at the Milan Congress (1935). He established a reputation as a designer of exhibitions and displays, and had considerable success with his Fabio Filzi communal housing project in Milan (designed with Renato Camus and Giancarlo Palanti, 1936), which won the silver medal at the Paris International Exhibition (1937). After the 1939–45 war his renovation of the Palazzo Bianco Museum (1950–61) and the Tesoro di San Lorenzo (1952), both in Genoa, brought him new fame. His remarkably sophisticated Department Store, *La Rinascente*, Piazza Fiume, Rome (with Franca Helg), of 1957–62, suggested elements (e.g. the crowning *cornice) of a *Renaissance *palazzo, although the construction was a matt-black steel frame with reddish infill panels.

From 1945–6, with Giancarlo Palanti, he was editor of the influential Italian architectural journal *Casabella*, and for a long period was a member of *CIAM. His work was various and eclectic, and reflected the independence of Italian designs from the tyrannies of *Modernist orthodoxy.

Albini (1981); Lampugnani (1988); Leet (1990); Moschini (1979*a*)

alcázar. Castle or fortified *palace in Spain.

alcove. 1. Large *niche. **2.** Recess or part of a chamber defined by an *estrade, partition, or *balustrade, for a bed. **3.** Arched recess or niche in the wall of any building or room. **4.** Covered retreat, bower, summer-house, or recess in a wall or hedge in a garden or pleasure-ground provided with seats.

Aldrich, Henry (1648–1710). Canon and Dean of Christ Church, Oxford, Aldrich was a polymath, virtuoso, and architect, one of the forerunners of *Palladianism, architect of several Oxford buildings, and author of a *Vitruvian-

Palladian book on architecture, *Elementa Architecturae Civilis* (not published until 1789). He designed Peckwater *Quadrangle at Christ Church (1707–14), built by William *Townesend (which anticipates *Wood's Queen Square, Bath, by two decades, and is the first Palladian *palace-fronted composition in England), probably designed the Fellows' Building (1706–12) at Corpus Christi College (which shows certain affinities with Peckwater Quad), and may have been the architect of All Saints' Church (1701–10), although the *steeple was a compromise between Aldrich's original design and an alternative by Nicholas *Hawksmoor.

Aldrich (1789); Colvin (1995); *DNB* (1917); Hiscock (1960)

Aleijadinho, António Francisco Lisboa, *known as* **O** (1738–1814). The leading practitioner of *Baroque and *Rococo in Brazil, he was born the illegitimate son of the Portuguese architect **Manuel Francisco Lisboa** near Ouro Prêto, Brazil. The 'little cripple' (as O Aleijadinho means) suffered from a disease (possibly syphilis or leprosy) that gradually cost him his toes, fingers, sight, and skin. In spite of these disadvantages he succeeded in transforming traditional types of Lusitanian church-architecture by means of the most rich and imaginative applied sculptural decoration, much of it carved by himself in the soft soapstone found in abundance in the interior captaincy of Minas Gerais, where gold and diamonds were mined. The capital, Ouro Prêto, acquired numerous *chapels, altars, doorways, and *façades by Aleijadinho, and his masterpieces are recognized as the Churches of São Francisco de Assis (1766–94), Ouro Prêto (with twin cylindrical towers set on either side of a curved front in which is set a sumptuous carved *door-case, while the interior of the Church is remarkably unified, undulating, and elegant), and Bom Jesus de Matosinhos in Congonhas de Campo near Ouro Prêto (with 12 carved figures guarding the entrance to the Church, while the rest of the ensemble is a synthesis of dramatic, powerful, and richly plastic elements, evolved over a long period from 1777 to 1805).

Bazin (1963); Brétas (1951); Kubler and Soria (1959); Norberg-Schulz (1986*a*)

Alen, William van (1882–1954). Born in Brooklyn, New York, he studied at the École des *Beaux-Arts in Paris before setting up his practice in New York. The firm became known for its very tall commercial buildings in which the Classical allusims to *base, *shaft, and *capital were abandoned. Van Alen's most celebrated work is the Chrysler Building, New York (1928–30), a monument not only to Walter P. Chrysler, but also to corporate advertising. The *Art Deco upper part of this *skyscraper incorporates eagle-head and radiator-cap *gargoyles as well as a series of semicircular forms recalling hub-caps.

Bletter and Robinson (1975); National Institute for Architectural Education (1964); Placzek (1982)

Aleotti, Giovanni Battista (1546–1636). *See* Scamozzi, Vincenzo.

Alessi, Galeazzo (1512–72). Born in Perugia and trained in Rome (where he was influenced by *Michelangelo), he became the leading mid-C16 architect in Genoa and Milan. His first important building was Santa Maria di Carignano, Genoa (1549–72): it is a Greek *cross on plan within a square, with a projecting *apse and a dome surrounded by four smaller domes, clearly based on *Bramante's scheme for San Pietro in Rome. His domestic architecture, especially the Villa Cambiaso of 1548, has elements derived from the Palazzo Farnese in Rome, but some of the exterior elevational treatment is very rich, with open-topped *pediments and *Michelangeloesque window-surrounds. In 1550 the Doge of Genoa ordered the construction of the Strada Nuova (1558–70), which was laid out by Alessi, and lined with *palaces: it was the first planned street of independent *blocks of the period, each designed by a different architect, but with an overall control of certain architectural features, heights, and scale to ensure a degree of harmony. These palaces became internationally known after the publication of Peter Paul Rubens's (1577–1640) *Palazzi di Genova* (1622–52). Alessi's enormous Palazzo Marino (1557) in Milan was richly treated on its elevations, and its *cortile was an outstanding example of *Mannerist decoration. His Churches of Santi Paolo e Barnaba (1561) and Santa Maria presso San Celso (1568), both in Milan, deserve note, the former for the distinct divisions between *nave, *presbytery, and *choir, and the latter for its size and decorations, completed by Martino *Bassi after Alessi's death.

Alessi (1974); Brown (1980); Heydenreich and Lotz (1974)

alette. 1. *Ala or wing of a building. **2.** *Jamb or *piedroit. **3.** In Classical architecture the visible parts of a *pier flanking *engaged columns or *pilasters, and usually forming the *abutment of arches. **4.** Semi-visible rear pilaster among several columnar elements.

Alexander, Christopher (1936–). Viennese-born English architect and theorist, he founded the Center for Environmental Structures (CES) in 1967 at the University of California in Berkeley. He experimented with the application of scientific principles to planning theory, evolving complex mathematical formulae to attempt to reproduce conditions by which primitive cultures create forms in harmony with their environments. A supporter of self-build housing, he was involved in the evolution of user-designed apartment-buildings at St-Quentin-en-Yvelines, near Paris (1974), and elsewhere. His publications include *Notes on the Synthesis of Form* (1964), *A Pattern Language* (1977), and *The Timeless Way of Building* (1979).

Curtis (1996); Emanuel (1994)

Alexander the Mason III (*fl.* *c*.1235–57). English? master-mason in charge of the works at Lincoln Cathedral *c*.1240. He was probably responsible for the building of the *nave, *chapter-house, and the *Galilee, together with the upper parts of the west front and the rebuilding of the lower stage of the *crossing-tower. He was an important and innovative designer, and had a profound influence on English *Gothic, notably with his polygonal chapter-house and *vault, the *screen-front at the west, and the lierne vaults in the nave. The last led to the evolution of patterned vaulting in Europe. Among other innovations were the trellis-patterns on the west front and central tower. He also may have designed the lower stages of the towers of the Churches of St Wulfram, Grantham, Lincolnshire, and St Mary Magdalene, Newark, Nottinghamshire. He may have been the same Alexander (*fl.* *c*.1224–40) who was master-mason at Worcester Cathedral, which also had a polygonal chapter-house, and was possibly involved in works at Le Mans Cathedral, France.

Harvey (1987)

alexandrian work. *See* opus alexandrinum.

Alfieri, Benedetto Innocente (1699–1767). Piedmontese Roman-born lawyer-turned-architect, he succeeded *Juvarra as architect in Turin in 1739, completing the latter's Palazzo Reale and Teatro Regio. His own Parish Church at Carignano (1757–64) has an elliptical plan, a spectacularly enriched interior, and a contrasting plain *façade. His design for the west front of the Cathedral of St-Pierre at Geneva (1752–6) is an advanced *Neoclassical style. He published *Il nuovo teatro regio di Torino* in 1740.

Bellini (1978); Cancro (1992); Pommer (1967)

alfiz. *See* albanega.

Algardi, Alessandro (1595–1654). A native of Bologna who settled in Rome, he designed the Villa Doria-Pamphili (1640s), situated in beautiful gardens outside the Porta San Pancrazio, and the *Baroque façade of the Church of Sant'Ignazio (1649). He was also a successful sculptor.

Montagu (1985)

Algarotti, Francesco (1712–64). Influential figure of the Enlightenment, from Venice, he became artistic adviser to King Frederick II of Prussia (reigned 1740–86), and was largely responsible for introducing *Palladianism to Potsdam and Berlin. His writings on architecture (much influenced by *Lodoli, from whom he gleaned a considerable part of his ideas) were of considerable importance in the development of architectural theory, and include *Il Newtonianismo per le Dame ovvero Dialoghi sopra la Luce e i Colori* (Newtonianism . . . or Dialogue on Light and Colours—actually a treatise on optics—1737) and *Opere del Conte Algarotti* (Works of Count Algarotti—1791–4).

Journal of Architectural Historians, 4/2 (1944), 23–9; Kaufmann (1955); Rykwert (1980)

Alhambra. **1.** One of the most exquisite, elaborate, and richly ornamented of all *Moorish palaces in Spain (mostly 1338–90), it consists of a series of joined pavilions, with two great courts set at right angles to each other. Channels of water, linking pools with fountains, add to the overall effect of a Paradise on earth. **2.** Garden-building in an exotic Moresque style, such as *Chambers's 'Alhambra' at Kew Gardens (1758), named after the celebrated buildings at Granada.

Blair and Bloom (1994)

alicatado. Wall-finish of uniformly shaped coloured glazed *tiles (*azulejos) commonly found in Spain and Latin America.

aliform. **1.** Wing-shaped. **2.** Building with additions resembling wings.

Allason, Thomas (1790–1852). English architect. After visiting Greece (from 1814), he published *Picturesque Views of the Antiquities of Pola in Istria* (1817), and claimed he was the first to spot *entasis on the *shafts of Greek columns, although C. R. *Cockerell and *Haller von Hallerstein, whom Allason had met while in Athens, had also observed this. His main work was the Alliance Fire Office, Bartholomew Lane, London (1841—demolished), and he planned and carried out designs for houses on the Ladbroke Estate, Kensington, in a severe, *stripped Classical style from 1823: his own house in Linden Gardens (demolished) was illustrated in *Loudon's *Encyclopaedia of Cottage, Farm, and Villa Architecture* (1846), and he designed a studio for the artist William Mulready (1786–1863) at Linden Grove, Bayswater (1827). He also oversaw the development of the Pitt Estate, Kensington (from 1844), and was involved in the d'Este Estate, Ramsgate, Kent.

Colvin (1995); Papworth (1852); Sheppard (1973)

allée. Straight gravel or grass garden-walk, defined by trees or hedges, and usually terminated by an *eye-catcher.

allège. Thinner part of a wall, e.g. between a window-cill and the floor.

allering. 1. *Aloring*, *battlement, or parapet-wall. **2.** Gutter, *gallery, passage, or walkway behind a parapet on top of a building. **3.** *Alura, or *clearstorey gallery as at Ely Cathedral. **4.** Uppermost part of a wall on which the roof-structure rests. **5.** Walkway in a *cloister.

alley. 1. *Allée, or long straight garden-walk, usually with trees on each side. **2.** Walk in a garden bordered with trees, shrubs, or bushes, or in a maze. **3.** Long, narrow area for open-air games. **4.** *Aisle. **5.** Pedestrian passage between houses or walls. **6.** Passage between rows of seats, as in a church.

Allio, Domenico dell' (d. 1563). Italian architect of the three-storeyed arcaded courtyard at the *Landhaus* (Seat of Regional Government), Graz (1557–65), one of the earliest and best examples of an assured Italian *Renaissance style in Austria.

Sitwell and Schneiders (1959)

Allio, Donato Felice d' (*c*.1680–1770). Descended from a family of Italians who settled in Austria, he was the architect of the *Salesianerinnen-Kloster* (Salesian Monastery), Vienna (1717–30), an assured *Baroque ensemble with a two-storey church-façade of the *scroll type and a plan consisting of an ellipse on the long axis. His greatest, but unfinished, work is the Abbey of Klosterneuburg (begun 1730).

Bourke (1962)

Alliprandi, Giovanni Battista (1665–*c*.1720). Architect of the Garden Palace of Liblice (1699–1706) and the Palais Lobkowicz, Prague (1702–5), who explored powerful curved bow-centrepieces, and contributed to the extraordinary richness of *Baroque buildings in Bohemia.

Neumann, J. (1970); Norberg-Schulz (1986*a*); Sheppard (1973)

Allom, Thomas (1804–72). London-born architect, articled to Francis *Goodwin (1784–1835), Allom's skills gained him employment as a topographical artist: he was a frequent exhibitor at the Royal Academy, and often produced drawings for his fellow-architects. His designs include St Peter's Church, Kensington Park Road, London (1855–7), and some spectacular ranges of *stucco-faced houses in Kensington Park Gardens (1850s).

DNB (1917); Felstead, Franklin, and Pinfield (1993); Sheppard (1973)

almena. Upright solid part of a *battlement shaped like a trapezium with serrated sides, characteristic of *Moorish architecture.

crenel or embrasure
cop or merlon

almena (*JJS*)

almery. *Aumbry.

almond. Term for the 'egg' in *egg-and-dart mouldings, distinguished by a *fillet around the 'egg'.

almonry. 1. Place where alms were distributed. **2.** Residence of an almoner. **3.** Building in a *monastery where food for the poor was received, often associated with the almoner's rooms.

Almqvist, Osvald (1884–1950). Swedish architect. With Sigurd *Lewerentz and others, he founded an independent architectural school, and studied the tradition of *vernacular architecture as part of the search for a national style, but became a pioneer of non-*Historicist architecture with such designs as the industrial village, Berglagsbyn, Domnarfvet, Dalecarlia (1916–20), and the hydro-electric power-stations of Forshuvudfors (1917–21), Hammarfors (1925–8) and Krångfors (1925–8).

Linn (1967)

almshouse. 1. Establishment founded and endowed by private charity for the reception, housing, and support of the aged poor. Almshouses often consisted of groups of dwellings, sometimes with a *chapel and dining-hall. Many English almshouses were erected following the dissolution of the monasteries: some are very simple *terraces of houses, but others, e.g. the Beauchamp Almshouses at Newland, Worcestershire (complete with church), of 1862–4, have architectural pretensions. **2.** House where the alms of a *monastery were distributed and the hospitality dispensed.

Bailey (1988); Godfrey (1955)

altana. *Loggia, covered roof-terrace or *belvedere, common in medieval Venice and *Renaissance Rome.

altar. Block, *pedestal, stand, or table on which to place or sacrifice offerings to a deity. Jewish altars had *horn-like ornaments at each corner, and this type of decoration also occurred in Classical Antiquity, with simplified horns or *ears, also known as *acroteria. Classical altar-tops have similarities to *cinerarium- and *sarcophagus-lids, and influenced the design of Neoclassical gate-piers, tops of *door-cases, and the like.

Christian altars, consecrated for celebration of the Eucharist, are elevated tables with a plane top, usually of stone, although the Reformation insisted on replacing them with wooden *Communion- or Holy-tables. In a church the high altar is the chief altar and is sited at the east end of the *chancel. The *sides (*horns*) of altars are termed *Epistle (south) and *Gospel (north).

altar-facing. Detachable finish or cover for the front part of an altar, facing the *nave, often of fabric woven into intricate designs of great beauty, also called *altar-frontal* or *antependium*.

altar of credence. *Credence-table, or table of *prothesis.

altar of repose. *Niche or side-altar where the Host is placed from Maundy Thursday until Good Friday. *See* Easter Sepulchre.

altar-piece. Painting or sculpture set up above and behind an altar.

altar-rail. Rail dividing the rest of the *chancel from the *sacrarium*, at which Communicants kneel during the Eucharist.

altar-screen. Separates the *presbytery or *sacrarium* from the *ambulatory to the east, also called *altar-wall*.

altar-slab, altar-stone. Slab of stone forming the top of an altar, also called *mensa*.

altar-stair, altar-steps. Steps up to the elevated area where an altar is placed.

altar-table. Timber 'Holy Table', used instead of stone altars in post-Reformation churches.

altar-tomb. Monumental *tomb-chest, also called a *high tomb*, resembling an altar, but never used as such, sometimes supporting recumbent *effigies or with memorial brasses on top, and occasionally embellished with *weepers in *niches around its sides. Altar-tombs are sometimes protected by ornate canopies.

alto-rilievo. Carved work projecting by at least half its thickness from the background on which it is sculpted.

alura, alure, ailure. Gangway, *gallery, garden-walk, passage, walkway, or *allering behind *battlements. A *clearstorey gallery, as at Ely Cathedral, the passages in a *cloister, or other covered passage, *ambulatory, or walkway.

Álvares, Baltasar (*fl.* 1570–1620). Portuguese architect, responsible for the Jesuit Church at Oporto (*c.*1590–1610), with its busy *Mannerist twin-towered *façade. His uncle, **Afonso** (*fl.* 1551–75), designed work in the *Cinquecento style at Leira Cathedral (from 1551).

Kubler and Soria (1959)

Álvarez, Mario Roberto (1913–). Leading Argentinian architect who, in his role as Architect to the Ministry of Public Works in that city, became an important promoter of the *Modern Movement, developing prefabrication techniques, engineering, and town-planning. His buildings include the San Martin Sanatorium, Buenos Aires (1937), and the IBM Argentina Headquarters (1978–84).

Emanuel (1994); Trabucco (1965)

Amadeo, Homodeo, Homodeus, *or* **Omodeo, Giovanni Antonio** (1447–1522). Important architect, engineer, and sculptor, he was born in Pavia, where he worked on the *Certosa in the 1460s, designing (with Ambrogio Fossano) the *Renaissance *screen-façade (1480s, but built over the next 150 years) which conceals the *basilican form of *clearstoreyed *nave and *aisles. He imbibed the early *Renaissance style when working as a sculptor on the Portinari *Chapel in the Church of Sant'Eustorgio, Milan, and subsequently (1470–3) designed the Colleoni Chapel at Santa Maria Maggiore, Bergamo, which resembles the former. His designs demonstrate the mixing of the Classical principles favoured by Tuscan architects with the love of decoration found in Northern Italy. He collaborated with *Bramante in the latter's works in Milan, and was involved in the design (1490s) of the *Gothic domical *vault and lantern at Milan Cathedral (*c.*1500) with Francesco di *Giorgio and Giovanni Giacomo Dolcebuono.

Heydenreich and Lotz (1974)

ambitus. 1. Consecrated area surrounding a grave or tomb, or the burial-ground attached to a church. **2.** Space in a *loculus in a *catacomb or *hypogeum surrounding the body or coffin, or around a funerary *urn or *cinerarium in a *columbarium or other tomb.

ambo, ambon (*pl.* **ambones**). *Gradus, lectorium, lectricium*, or *lectern or *pulpit, properly a singing-desk, approached by steps, particularly associated with *Early Christian churches, where there were often two ambones, one on the north (for the reading or chanting of the *Gospel) and one on the south (for the *Epistle) side of the *choir or *presbytery: in San Clemente in Rome the ambones balance each other on each side, and are attached to the *cancelli, or low *screen-walls defining the choir within the main volume of the *nave. Later ambones were connected to constructions separating the *sanctuary from the *nave.

ambry. *Aumbry.

ambulacrum. 1. *Atrium, *court, or *parvis, sometimes with a fountain in the centre, surrounded by *arcades or *colonnades, and often planted with trees, in front of a *basilica. **2.** Any walk or avenue with formally arranged tree-planting.

ambulatio (*pl.* **ambulationes**). **1.** Promenade, or *xystum open to the sky. **2.** Covered promenade, or *xystus, defined by fragrant formal planting or by a *colonnade, or both. **3.** *Ambulatory, volume, or walkway bounded by the colonnade of a temple *peristyle and the wall of the *cella.

ambulatory. 1. Any place in which to process, walk, or promenade, whether partially or totally covered or uncovered, such as an *ambulatio or a *cloister. **2.** *Aisle linking the *chancel-aisles behind the high-altar in a large church: it can be canted, semicircular, or straight on plan, with *chapels to the east and the *sanctuary to the west.

ambulatory church. 1. Church arranged with an *ambulatory between the *sanctuary and chapels to the east, i.e. with an *aisle linking the *chancel-aisles behind the high altar. **2.** *Early Christian or *Byzantine church with a domed area bounded on at least three sides by aisles and *galleries, so forming a cross on plan, also known as a *cross-domed church*.

American bond. *See* brick.

American Directory. *See* Directoire.

American Order. *Capital resembling that of the *Corinthian *Order with the *acanthus leaves replaced by *corn-cobs, corn-ears, and tobacco-leaves, invented by *Latrobe for the United States Capitol in Washington, DC.

Ammanati *or* **Ammannati, Bartolomeo** (1511–92). Born near Florence, Ammannati was a gifted *Mannerist sculptor, but he also designed buildings, including the elegant Ponte Santa Trinità in Florence (1567–70), rebuilt after its destruction in 1944. He was involved in the design of the Villa Giulia in Rome (1551–5) with *Vignola and *Vasari, and later extended the Palazzo Pitti, Florence (1558–70), for which he designed the heavily *rusticated garden-front and *cortile, where the influence of the Mint in Venice by *Sansovino (with whom Ammannati had worked earlier) is clear. He supervised the construction (and may have played a part in the design) of *Michelangelo's entrance *vestibule and staircase to the Library of San Lorenzo, Florence (1524–50s).

He was also responsible for the Tempietto della Vittoria near Arezzo (1572), and probably built most of the Palazzo Provinciale, Lucca (1577–8), in which the centrepiece is composed of a *Serlian *loggia derived from that employed by Vasari at the Uffizi in Florence.

Fossi (1967); Heydenreich and Lotz (1974)

Ammann, Othmar (1879–1965). Swiss-born engineer, who settled in the United States in 1904, and over 35 years designed bridges in the New York area. In 1925 he joined the Port of New York Authority for which he designed the Bayonne Bridge (opened in 1931) as a graceful *parabolic two-hinged steel-arch structure, which made his name. In the same year his George Washington Bridge was opened, with twice the span of any then existing suspension-bridge, and steel-framed towers suggesting vestigial *Classicism. His elegant Bronx-Whitestone Suspension Bridge was the first to use shallow plate-*girders as stiffeners instead of the more usual deep *trusses. In 1946 he formed a partnership with Charles Whitney, establishing one of the leading engineering firms in the world. His majestic Verrazano-Narrows Bridge, New York (completed 1964), was even longer than his earlier structures.

Billington (1983); Stüssi (1974)

Ammonite Order. Type of *capital similar to the *Ionic Order, used on early C19 domestic architecture in Kent and Sussex, with *volutes resembling the whorled chambered fossilized shells, called *snake-stones*, of a genus of cephalopods. The fossils were once supposed to be coiled petrified snakes, and were so called from their resemblance to the *Cornu Ammonis*, or involuted horn of Jupiter Ammon. The Ammonite Order was employed by the architect-developer Amon *Wilds (*c*.1762–1833), who may have derived his version from designs by *Piranesi, and who probably used it as an identification with his own name.

Colvin (1995)

Amoretto (*pl.* **Amoretti, Amorettoes**). *See* Amorino.

Amorino (*pl.* **Amorini**). Winged male baby, or young child, often chubby and knowing, also called Amoretto, Little Love, *Cherub, or *Cupid, as distinct from a *putto, which is without wings.

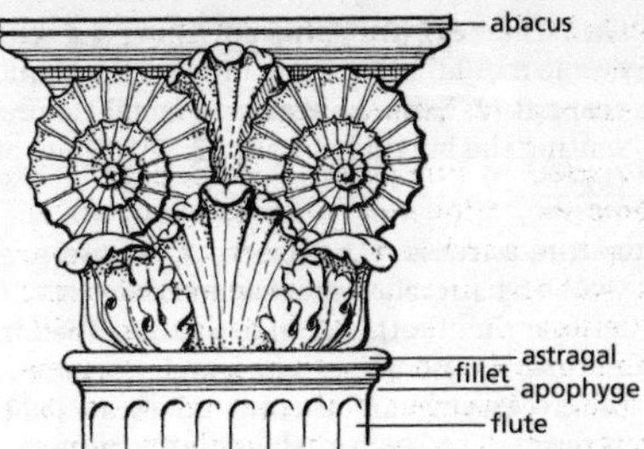

Ammonite capital. Typical example as used by Amon and Amon Henry Wilds in the 1820s. (*JJS*)

amphi-. Prefix, meaning on both sides, or the same at front and rear. For example:

amphi-antis: a Classical temple with an *in antis* (*see* anta) *portico at each end;

amphi-prostyle: *apteral temple without flanking *colonnades, but with a *prostyle portico at each end of the *cella.

amphitheatre. **1.** Roman building-type resembling two *theatres joined together to form an *arena, elliptical on plan (viz. the Colosseum in Rome). **2.** Bowl-like garden feature, planted or not, sometimes used for open-air performances, with tiers.

Amsterdam School. Group of Netherlands architects influenced by *Berlage and Frank Lloyd *Wright, including van der *Mey, *Kramer, and de *Klerk, who built sculptured and *Picturesque brick structures much influenced by *Expressionism and by Dutch *vernacular traditions from *c*.1912 to *c*.1936. The antithesis of the buildings of the De *Stijl group, their work was publicized in the *Modernist magazine *Wendingen* (1918–36), edited by *Wijdeveld.

Nederlandse Architectuur, 1910–1930: Amsterdamse School (Amsterdam: Stedelijk Museum, 1975)

Analogical architecture. Aldo *Rossi's term to describe his own architecture in Italy in the 1970s, in which he saw analogies with historical buildings, *vernacular architecture, engineering, and simple forms.

Ferlenga (1987)

anathyrosis. Smooth *dressing of the margin of *ashlar stone or of the *drums comprising the *shaft of a Classical column to ensure an accurate *masonry joint.

anchor. **1.** Misnomer for the arrow-head, dart, or tongue-like ornament alternating with the *egg-like form enriching e.g. the *ovolo moulding or the *echinus of the *Ionic *capital. **2.** Exposed head of a metal tie preventing the bulging of walls. **3.** *Attribute of Hope.

ancon, anconis (*pl.* ancones). **1.** *Console resembling a scrolled bracket, narrower at the bottom than at the top (i.e. wedge-shaped in elevation), also acting as an arch *keystone, often carrying an ornamental element. **2.** *Console, *crossette, shouldering-piece, or *truss supporting each end of the *cornice over the *antepagmenta of apertures in Classical architecture, and properly wedge-shaped or tapering, although the term is loosely given to parallel-sided *consoles*, *parotides*, or *prothyrides*. **3.** *Quoin or two adjacent sides of a rectangle. **4.** Cramp employed in masonry to join two stones. **5.** Projection left on a column-shaft *drum to enable it to be lifted by ropes.

Anderson, John MacVicar (1835–1915). Glasgow-born Scots architect, articled to his uncle, William *Burn, whose partner he became: he continued to practise after Burn's death in 1870. As well as carrying out additions to various London clubs, he was responsible for the handsome Classical *façade of Coutts's Bank in the centre of the *Nash terrace at The Strand, London (demolished), and the British Linen Bank (now Bank of Scotland), Threadneedle Street (both 1903).

Gray (1985)

Anderson, Sir Robert Rowand (1834–1921). One of the most gifted architects Scotland has produced, he started work in Sir George Gilbert *Scott's office. Among his buildings are All Saints' Church, Edinburgh (1864–78), the Catholic Apostolic Church, Edinburgh (1871–94), the Medical School (1874–86) and McEwan Hall (1884–90), Edinburgh University, the Central Station Hotel in Glasgow (1878–84), and Govan Parish Church (1884–8): the last is one of the finest works of the *Gothic Revival in Scotland. He designed the well-mannered wings and terrace at Pollok House, Glasgow (1890s), and the Pearce Institute, Govan (1903–5). A meticulous conservationist, his sensitive work at e.g. Iona Abbey (1874–6), Paisley Abbey (1898–1907), and Sweetheart Abbey, near Dumfries (1911–14), may be cited. Among his many important designs, Mount Stuart, Rothesay, Bute (from 1878), and the National Portrait Gallery and Museum of Antiquities, Edinburgh (1884–9), are of considerable interest. His Revivalism was scrupulous and scholarly: his Central Station Hotel draws on Scandinavian C17 precedents to great effect, while elsewhere his work is clearly influenced by the architecture of his native Scotland. He published works on the medieval architecture of France and Italy (1870–5), and, with others, edited a volume dealing with Scottish architecture from C12 to C17.

DNB (1993); Paterson (1921)

Ando, Tadao (1941–). Internationally recognized largely self-educated Japanese architect. After travelling in Africa, Europe, and the USA he founded Tadao Ando Architect & Associates in Osaka in 1969. Drawing on traditional materials and *vernacular styles, he also used modern techniques of construction, and produced the concept of 'defensive architecture' which turned away from the street and looked inwards A leader of *Critical Regionalism, he was responsible for the Wall-House at Sumiyoshi, Osaka (1979—which exploits his interest in an architecture stripped to elemental minimals), the Rokko housing, Kobe (1983–93), the Church on the Water, Tomamu, Hokkaido (1988), the Naoshima Museum and Hotel, Kagawa (1990–5), the cylindrical Meditation Space, UNESCO Headquarters, Paris (1994–5), and the Suntory Museum, Osaka (1994). The Naoshima complex shows how Ando employs rigorous geometries and concrete, yet responds with great sensitivity to the site.

Ando (1989); Curtis (1996); Dal Co (1996); Frampton (1991); Jodidio (1997*a*); Pare (1997)

Andrea di Cione (*fl.* 1343–68). *See* Orcagna, Andrea.

Andrews, John (1933–). Australian-born architect, who made his name with Scarborough College, University of Toronto (1962–9): the latter is a *megastructure, employing the raw materials and chunky forms of New *Brutalism with a large internal street. He also designed the Student Housing Complex, Guelph University (1965–8) and the CN Tower (1975), both in Ontario, during his time in Canada. His Gund Hall Graduate School of Design at Harvard University (1968) was hailed by Philip *Johnson as one of the six 'greatest buildings' of C20, although its huge studio-space and large areas of glass created some problems. Later buildings in Australia include the American Express Tower, Sydney (1976), in which a service-tower forms one of the corners of the triangular plan, while solar glare is controlled by a light tubular structure supporting the anti-sun glass. He designed several large buildings for universities, including the Chemical Engineering Building of the University of Queensland (1976), and the School of Australian Environmental Studies (1978), at Griffith University, near Brisbane. His Merlin Hotel, Perth (1984), has a cruciform plan with huge atria and courts. His Intelsat Building, Washington, DC (1988), attracted considerable praise.

Drew (1972); Emanuel (1994)

Androuet. *See* Cerceau.

angel light. Small, roughly triangular *light between subordinate arched window-*tracery, especially in English *Perpendicular work.

angle-buttress. *See* buttress.

angle-capital. *Capital at the corner of a *colonnade or *portico. In the *Ionic *Order the front and side of a normal capital differ, so to obtain *volutes on both sides of the corner the volutes at the external angle are splayed outwards at 45° (or 135° to the planes of the front and side elevations). An angle-capital is not the same as an *angular capital.

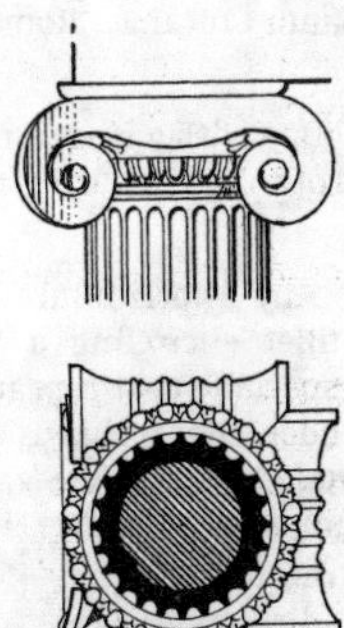

angle- *or* **corner-capital** (*JJS*)

angle-leaf. One of four carved claws, griffes, leaves, or *spurs projecting from the lower *torus of a *pier-base in medieval architecture covering one of the corners of the square *plinth below.

angle-modillion. *Modillion set diagonally at the external corner of a *Classical *cornice, properly regarded as an *abuse, although occasionally occurring in Roman Antiquity.

angle-post. Vertical *post at the corner of a *timber-framed structure: if rising through one storey only, as in jettied construction, it is a *storey-post*.

angle-roll. *Bowtell, or plain rounded moulding.

angle-round. *Battlemented parapet on continuous *corbelling set over a curved corner of a tower or wall, especially in C17 Scottish architecture.

angle-shaft. **1.** Decorative *colonnette at an external corner of a building. **2.** Colonnette in the *jamb of a *Romanesque door- or window-aperture.

angle-stone. *Quoin.

angle-tie. **1.** *Angle-brace*, *dragon-tie*, or *horizontal brace* linking the wall-plates at the corner of a hipped roof; or supporting one end of a *dragon-beam (the other set on the mitring of the wall-plates). **2.** Any timber acting as a *tie between two other timbers to stop them spreading.

anglo-chinois. French term for a type of irregular informal landscape-garden supposedly evolved from Chinese prototypes and embellished with buildings in the Chinese Taste popularized by *Chambers. *See* Chinoiserie, Sharawadgi.

Anglo-Saxon architecture. English architecture from the end of C6 to the Norman Conquest (1066), also called *Saxon* architecture. Much Anglo-Saxon building was of timber, but from *c.*672 the more significant structures were of masonry, usually *rag or *rubble. Later, freestone *dressings, including *quoins set alternately horizontally and on end (known as *long-and-short work), raised *lesenes (as at Earl's Barton Church, Northamptonshire), horizontal *string-courses, *blind arcades on vertical strips, paired semicircular headed openings separated by *baluster-like *colonnettes in towers, triangular-topped openings, and roughly carved outsized elements framing doorways, were common motifs. The raised lesenes, strings, and long-and-short work suggest that the rubble panels thus created were originally intended to be *rendered with plaster or some kind of *stucco. Occasionally, rubble was laid in a *herring-bone pattern. Window-openings were usually small. Churches consisted of a *nave (often with a storey over (e.g. Deerhurst, Gloucestershire)) and a *chancel divided from the nave by an *arch (e.g. Wittering, Soke of Peterborough) or by three arches (e.g. Bradwell-juxta-Mare, Essex). Northern chancels were usually square-ended, but in the South were sometimes *apsidal. All Saints Church, Brixworth, Northamptonshire, has nave-arcades partly made of recycled Roman bricks and tiles: this suggests a *basilica, but it appears the 'aisles' were subdivided by walls to form chambers, called *porticus*, although there seems to have been an *apse at one end and a two-storeyed porch at the other, with chambers on each side. Thus Brixworth is one of the grandest surviving examples of Anglo-Saxon architecture, although certain structures, such as the New *Minster at Winchester, Hampshire (begun 903–destroyed), seem to have been more ambitious, owing much to *Carolingian precedent.

Cruickshank (1996); Stoll (1967)

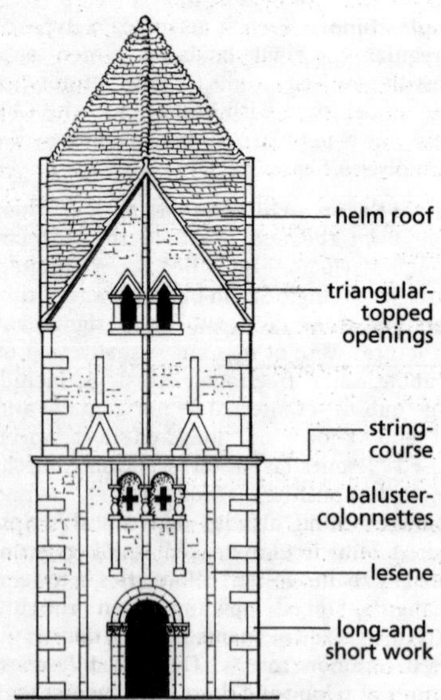

Anglo-Saxon architecture. Church-tower incorporating typical Anglo-Saxon motifs. (*JJS*)

angular capital. Type of *Ionic 'diagonal' *capital, with four identical faces and therefore eight *volutes, supposedly an *abuse invented by *Scamozzi, and known as the *Modern* or *Scamozzian* Ionic *Order. Thus, if it is used, no special *angle-capital is needed at the return angle of a *portico. However, it can be seen as having *Antique origins, for it is found at the top part of all Roman *Composite capitals, and indeed existed independently as the 'diagonal' Ionic capital, fashionable in *Pompeii, and conspicuous on the portico of the temple of Saturn, Rome (*c.* AD 320).

angular *or* **Scamozzi capital** (*JJS*)

annular. Ring-shaped. An annular *vault springs from two concentric walls circular on plan, as in Santa Costanza, Rome (*c.* AD 325 and later).

annulated. Fitted with a ring or rings, as in a *Gothic band of a shaft, securing a thin *shaft to a *pier.

annulet. 1. Any horizontal *shaft-ring, *band, or *fillet encircling a *colonnette or column, especially that repeated three to five times under the *echinus of a Greek *Doric *capital. **2.** *List, *listella*, or vertical fillet between column-*flutes in Classical architecture.

Anreith, Anton (1754–1822). German-born architect, sculptor, and woodcarver, who settled in the Cape Colony, South Africa (1776), bringing South-German *Rococo to the region. He built the less successful *Neoclassical façade of the Lutheran Church, Cape Town.

Bosdari (1954); Meintjes (1951)

anse de panier. *See* arch.

anta (*pl.* **antae**). **1.** Square or rectangular *pier formed by the thickening of the end of a wall, e.g. in Greek temples, where the side-walls or *pteromata* terminate. Where *porticoes were formed by carrying the side-walls out beyond the front wall of the *naos and placing columns in a line between the antae, the columns, portico, and temple are described as *in antis*. Greek antae can have *capitals and *bases differing from those of the *Order proper, unlike Roman *pilasters, which are usually identical to the columns save for having rectangular plans. Furthermore, antae have either very slight or no *entasis, and therefore have parallel sides. **2.** Another term for an *antepagmentum.

ante-chamber. Room leading to an apartment beyond, often used as a waiting-room.

ante-chapel. Part of a *chapel situated at its west end, similar to *transepts, serving as a volume leading to the chapel proper. Examples include Magdalen and Merton College Chapels, Oxford.

ante-choir. Fore-choir, or area corresponding to the thickness of the *pulpitum or *choir-screen, as at Southwell *Minster, Nottinghamshire (*c*.1320–40).

ante-church. Ante-nave, fore-church, or *narthex at the west end of a church, with *aisles and *nave, sometimes a few *bays long. A good example is the five-aisled *Galilee at Durham Cathedral (*c*.1170–80).

ante-court. First *court of a great house, preceding the *cour d'honneur, giving access to the service-wings.

antefix, antefixum (*pl.* **antefixes, antefixa**). **1.** Decorative termination of the covering-tiles over the joints of the roof-tiles placed on the *eaves-tiles or on top of the *cyma of the *cornice, and sometimes on the *ridge-crest of a Greek temple. It was frequently embellished with the *anthemion motif. **2.** Ornament on the *frieze of early Classical temples, or over *pediment *acroteria, often of *terracotta. Antefixum (*not* antefixa) was also applied to lions'-heads on the *cymatium of temples, but this appears to be an error.

Antelami, *or* **Antelmi, Benedetto degli** (*fl.* 1177–1233). Italian sculptor and architect, responsible for the towering octagonal *Romanesque *Baptistry at Parma (1196–1216, but not completed until 1270): the exterior treatment has four tiers of open *colonnaded *galleries. Also attributed to him are the Cathedral at Fidenza (late C12 and early C13), and the Church of Sant'Andrea at Vercelli (1219–26) in which the transition from *Romanesque to *Gothic is clearly expressed.

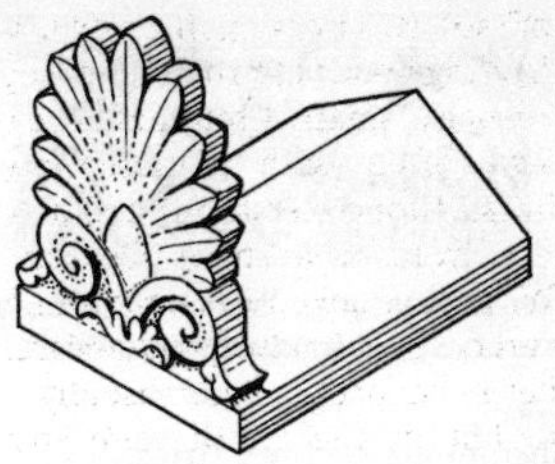
antefix (*JJS*)

Forster (1961)

ante-mural(e). Defensive breastworks, outworks, or walls before a city-wall, castle, or fortress, such as a *barbican.

ante-nave. *See* ante-church.

antepagment, antepagmentum (*pl.* **antepagments, antepagmenta**). **1.** Face of a *jamb of an aperture, or a moulded *architrave. Its top horizontal part, *supercilium* or *antepagmentum superius* is really a moulding over the *lintel, and has a *section identical to that of the vertical parts of the architrave: it is often expressed as a lintel by means of a *crossette whereby it projects slightly beyond the tops of the antepagmenta, and the mouldings return at the ends, forming ears, elbows, lugs, or shoulders. **2.** *Anta or *pilaster.

antependium. *See* altar-facing.

anteris, anteridos (*pl.* **anterides**). **1.** *Buttress, counter-fort, erisma, sperone, or spur supporting or strengthening a wall. **2.** Type of *anta or *pilaster, called *sperone*, more like a *lesene than in Classical architecture.

anthemion (*pl.* **anthemia**). **1.** Decorative group of leafy forms resembling a radiating cluster of flowers on the same plant, and called by some a honeysuckle: it occurs in Classical architecture above *acroteria, on *antefixa, on *cornices, on the *hypotrachelium of some varieties of the Greek *Ionic *Order, and elsewhere, often used alternately with the *palmette or lotus in horizontal

anthemion and palmette. Anthemion alternating with palmette on a frieze, with scrolls and other ornament.

embellishments such as *friezes, and sometimes instead of the *fleuron on the *Corinthian *capital. **2.** William *Wilkins, in *Prolusiones Architectonicae* (1837), thought it referred to the *Ionic *volute, but this seems to be discounted.

Anthemios of Tralles (*fl.* first half of C6). Greek mathematician and theorist, celebrated for the Church of Hagia Sophia, Constantinople (532–7). He was commissioned by Emperor Justinian (527–65) to design this huge structure, largely because of his reputation as an engineer. The building employed four massive *buttresses and two hemi-domes to contain the outward thrust of the low saucer-dome on *pendentives. In this master-work of *Byzantine architecture, Anthemios was assisted by *Isidorus of Miletus.

Huxley (1959); Krautheimer (1986); Mainstone (1988); Mango (1972, 1986)

Anthon, George David (1714–81). Danish architect. He was appointed Professor of Architecture at the Old Academy, Copenhagen (1748), and Royal Building-Inspector (1751), becoming Master-Builder to the Royal Court in 1760. He carried out the brickwork for *Eigtved's Frederik's Hospital, and directed building works at Christian's Church after Eigtved's death, although he himself was responsible for the design and creation of the *spire (1769). In 1756 he prepared designs for Frederik's Church, which were not realized, and which were developments of proposals by Eigtved and *Jardin. Other works included the Castle of Bregentved, essentially after Eigtved's designs (1754), restoration at Kronborg Castle (1761), and building at Fredensborg (1762). In 1759 he published *Anvisning til Civil-Bygningskunsten* (Directions for Civic Architecture), which went into further editions in 1772 and 1818.

Sturgis *et al.* (1901–2); Weilbach (1947–)

antic. 1. *Grotesque ornamental representation of human, animal, and floral forms bizarrely mingled. **2.** Deliberately monstrous, fantastic, and caricatured ornamental representations of fauna and flora used in decorations. **3.** *Caryatid(e) or other humanoid representation, but incongruously formed and inappropriately positioned. **4.** Distorted, leering mask, suggesting the irrational, wild nature, and the realm of unreason.

anticlastic. Of a double-curved surface, of which the two curvatures (transverse to each other) lie in opposite directions, convex in length and concave in breadth, or vice versa. This condition can be seen in e.g. a *hyperbolic *paraboloid roof. *See* synclastic.

anticum. 1. Latin equivalent of *pronaos, the space between the front of the *cella and the *colonnade of a *portico. **2.** Gate or a front door, or a variety of porch in front of a main door. **3.** *Temple-front. **4.** *Anta, but its use for this is erroneous.

Antique. Pertaining to Graeco-Roman Antiquity, or the Classical civilizations of the Graeco-Roman world.

antis, in. *See* anta.

Antistates (*fl.* C6 BC). One of the architects (the others were Antimachides, Kallaeschros, and Porinos) engaged by Peisistratos (560–527 BC) to build the temple of Jupiter Olympius, Athens, mentioned by *Vitruvius.

Dinsmoor (1950); Lawrence (1983)

Antoine, Jacques-Denis (1733–1801). French architect, active in the *Louis Seize period, appointed in 1766 to build the severely *Neoclassical Hôtel des Monnaies (the Mint), Quai de Conti, Paris (1768–75), reckoned by *Quatremère de Quincy to be one of the finest French public buildings. He completed the *Barrières des Fermiers Généraux* (toll-gates), Paris, after *Ledoux was dismissed in 1787. His town-houses for the aristocracy, including the rigorously plain Hôtel Brochet de Saint-Prest, now École des Ponts-et-Chaussées (*c.*1768–74), and the Hôtel de Jaucourt, Rue de Varennes (1770), as well as his country residences, among which may be mentioned the Château de Herces in Berchères-sur-Vesgre, near Houdan (1770–2), are in a strict Neoclassical style. As architect to the Révérends Pères de la Charité, he built hospitals, including the Hôpital de la Charité, Paris (*c.*1760s), believed to be the first building with a *portico of baseless Greek *Doric columns to be erected in the French capital.

Braham (1980); Hautecœur (1952); Middleton and Watkin (1987); Placzek (1982)

Antolini, Giovanni Antonio (1756–1841). Italian *Neoclassical architect, who came from Faenza, and who settled in Milan in 1800 after a long stay in Rome. He was much influenced by French Neoclassicists, as his monumental scheme for the Foro Buonaparte, Milan (1801), shows, but his realized projects are few.

Antolini (1806); Meeks (1966); Mezzanotte (1966); Middleton and Watkin (1987)

Antonelli, Alessandro (1798–1888). Professor of Architecture at Turin (1836–57). Addicted to the *temple-front, he employed it in several buildings, including the Sanctuary at Boca (from 1830), the Parish Church at Oleggio (1853–8), and the Cathedral at Novara (from 1854). He is regarded as one of the last great masters of *Neoclassicism in Italy, and is famed for the Mole Antonelliana (a former synagogue), Turin (1863–84), one of the tallest masonry structures ever erected: rising in a series of stages defined by *Orders, it was crowned by a *pagoda-like spire. He also added the very tall *cupola and *lantern over the *crossing of the Church of San Gaudenzio, Novara (from 1841), and remodelled the Duomo, also at Novara (1854–69), essentially a *basilica, but using columns extensively, both inside and out.

Brino (1972); Meeks (1966); Rosso (1989)

Antonine column. Monumental *Tuscan-*Doric column in Rome supposedly commemorating Emperor Antoninus Pius (AD 138–61). Set on a large *pedestal, its *shaft is embellished with sculptured reliefs arranged in a spiral band, and contains a circular staircase similar to the *Trajanic column (AD 112–13). It actually commemorates Emperor Marcus Aurelius Antoninus (AD 161–80), hence the confusion.

Antonio di Vicenzo (*c*.1350–1401/2). *See* Vicenzo.

apadana, apadhana. Square porticoed, free-standing *hypostyle hall such as that in Persepolis built by Darius I (*c.* C6–C5 BC). *See* Achaemenian, Achaemenid.

apex. Top of a cone, *gable, *obelisk, *pediment, or *pyramid. The *saddle-stone is the topmost stone at the apex of a gable or pediment.

Apolline. Type of decoration drawing on the *attributes of the Greek sun-god Apollo, first found in Classical Antiquity and revived during the *Renaissance and *Baroque periods, especially during the reign of *Louis Quatorze (1643–1715). Common motifs were the head of Apollo surrounded by sun-rays (the *sunburst), the chariot, the lyre, and the sun.

Apollodorus of Damascus (*fl.* AD 98–123). Damascus-born, he became architect to Emperor Trajan (98–117), and is credited with most of the Imperial buildings of the latter's reign, including the *thermae and forum of Trajan, the enormous Ulpian *basilica, Trajan's column, and the nearby market complex. He seems to have given the Roman thermae their definitive form, was an important influence on the Roman Imperial style, and brought a sound knowledge of advanced constructional techniques to bear on his various projects (not least of which was the huge bridge over the fast-flowing Danube, at Drobeta, constructed in *c*.104). It would be tempting to connect Apollodorus with the building of the *Pantheon and the *Villa Adriana* at Tivoli, in the reign of Hadrian (117–38), but the evidence is lacking. He was the author of several technical treatises, now lost, and enjoyed a considerable reputation in his lifetime.

MacDonald (1965–86); Ward-Perkins (1981, 1986)

apophyge, apophysis, apothesis. 1. Outward curve, called *congé or scape, connecting the *shaft of a Classical column to the *fillets over the *base and under the *astragal beneath the *capital. **2.** *Hypotrachelium of the *Tuscan capital or the slightly concave *trachelium beneath the *echinus of certain archaic Greek *Doric capitals.

applied. 1. Moulding or any other feature planted on to a surface (*appliqué*). **2.** *Engaged, as a column.

apron. 1. Panel below a window-cill, often carved and enriched. **2.** In an apron- or *curtain-wall, a *spandrel or infill-panel between a window-cill above and a window-head below, as in a tall building. **3.** Ornamental work below the *cornice or *eaves of a *verandah, i.e. *valance.

apse, apsis (*pl.* **apses, apsides**). Recess, generally semicircular on plan, and *vaulted, projecting from an external wall, the interior forming a large, deep volume. It is often a feature terminating the *nave of a *basilica, containing the high altar. Apses forming *chapels were built on the eastern sides of *transepts of larger churches (e.g. Lincoln Cathedral), and some, termed *apse-chapels*, were arranged round a semicircular apse-aisle or *ambulatory as in the complex *chevet form of larger French churches. Some apses are canted rather than curved on plan.

apsidiole. *Apse-chapel, or a small apsidal chapel projecting from a larger apse.

apteral. 1. Adjective describing a Classical temple with a *portico at one or both ends, with no flanking *colonnades. **2.** Said of a church without *aisles, and especially of a liturgical west front with a gabled roof and no lean-to aisle-walls sloping to meet the *nave.

aqueduct. Structure for artificially conveying a constant supply of water, consisting of a channel (usually covered to prevent evaporation and/or pollution) supported on *piers over valleys, roads, etc., and cut through hills. Numerous *Antique remains of aqueducts survive, the most impressive being the huge arcaded structure over the Roman Campagna, and that over the River Gard in France. Some C19 aqueducts carrying canals, such as *Telford's Pont-y-Cysyllte (1795–1805), consist of cast-iron structures carried on massive piers.

Ward-Perkins (1981)

ara (*pl.* **arae**). Roman altar. It could be a large, public, commemorative structure, like the sumptuous *Ara Pacis* (erected by Emperor Augustus to mark the establishment of Imperial power and the coming of peace in 13 BC), or a small altar in a private house by which the protection of the deities was invoked.

arabesque. Decorative *scroll-work and other ornament loosely derived from branches, leaves, tendrils, and vegetation, sometimes called *Moresque* ornament, arranged in imaginatively intertwined symmetrical geometrical patterns. Usually defined as free from human or animal figures, it is quite distinct from *grotesque ornament.

Ward-Jackson (1967*a*)

arabesque. Panel of arabesque ornament.

Arabian. Vague term suggesting *Moorish, Moresque, or other architecture of Islamic origin.

araeostyle. *See* intercolumniation.

ARAU. (Atelier de Recherche et d'Action Urbaine). Belgian architectural pressure group formed in 1968 by Maurice Culot to study problems posed by drastic urban redevelopment (especially arguing for conservation and restoration). It became known through the journal *Archives d'Architecture Moderne* from 1975.

Walker (1992)

arbalestina, arbalesteria. *See* balistaria.

Arbeitsrat für Kunst. Group of German architects established in 1918 by Bruno *Taut, which included Otto *Bartning, Walter *Gropius, Erich *Mendelsohn, and Max *Taut, with several artists. Taut wanted the group to wield political influence similar to the Soldiers' and Workers' Councils, but this failed, and Gropius took over the leadership in 1919. When the latter took up his post at the *Bauhaus in Weimar, the programme there reflected the ideals of the *Arbeitsrat* (Work Council for Art), which called for the establishment of a community of architects and artists who would work towards the fusion of the arts under the wing of architec-

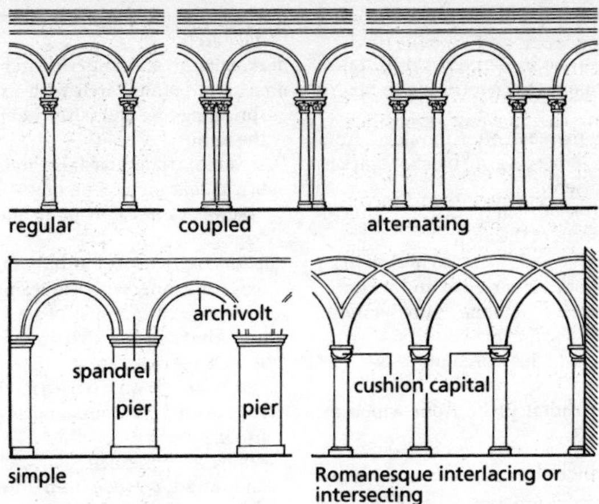

arcade. Regular, coupled, alternating (resembling a series of partly overlapping serlianas), simple, and Romanesque interlacing arcades, the last producing pointed arches. (*JJS*)

ture, the symbolic *Bauprojekt*. The group exhibited and published widely, but disbanded in 1921 through lack of funds.

Boyd Whyte (1982)

arbour. Garden-building constructed of timber, lattice-work, and wicker-work, intended to be covered with climbing plants.

arcade. 1. Series of arches on the same plane, supported by *colonnettes, columns, *piers, or *pilasters. Varieties of arcade include:

alternating: with arches springing from the ends of two-column *colonnades, resembling a series of overlapping *serlianas;

blind: arcade *engaged with or attached to a wall, also called *surface-* or *wall-arcade*;

coupled: carried on *coupled columns;

interlacing or *intersecting*: overlapping arcades, e.g. *Romanesque overlapping arcades, producing a series of pointed arches, as in Southwell *Minster, Nottinghamshire (C12);

nave: series of arches on *piers separating the *nave from the *aisle and supporting the *clearstorey in a church;

regular: any series of repetitive arches, also called a *simple* arcade;

screen: arcade standing on its own as a feature, or used as a *screen;

simple: see *regular* above;

surface: see *blind* above;

wall: see *blind* above.

2. Row of vertical *arcade-posts* carrying the *arcade-plate*, and set between the nave or central area and aisles of a *timber-framed aisled building. **3.** Top-lit roofed passage with shops on either side, known as a *shopping-arcade*, equivalent to the *galerie*, *galleria*, or *passage* on the Continent.

Alcock, Barley, Dixon, and Meeson (1996); Geist (1983); MacKeith (1986)

arch. Construction, known as an *arch-ring*, made of truncated wedge-shaped *blocks (arch-stones or *voussoirs) that by mutual pressure stay in place, set out in a curved form to span an opening and carry a superimposed load, as an alternative to a *lintel: such construction is termed *arcuated, as opposed to *trabeated. Terms associated with an arch include:

abutment: solid structure from which an arch springs, and which resists the outward *thrust* (all arches will collapse unless adequately supported);

archivolt: concentric ring of mouldings round an arch, like an *architrave bent around the top of the arch;

chord: horizontal distance between *abutments* taken from the *springing-line* on one side to that of the other, also called the *span*;

crown: highest point of the *intrados*, also called *vertex*;

extrados: upper curve of each *voussoir* or outer extremity of the *archivolt*;

flank: see *haunch* below;

haunch: curved part on the top of the section between the *crown*, the portion of the arch it-

self, and the extremity of the *span*, also called *flank*;
height: *rise* of an arch, or vertical distance between the *chord* to the *crown* or highest point of the *intrados*;
impost: projecting member, often moulded, from which an arch *springs*, e.g. a *block, *bracket, *corbel, or *dosseret;
intrados: lower curve of each *voussoir*, i.e. coinciding with the *soffit of the arch;
keystone: central large wedge-shaped *voussoir* in an arch, often elaborately carved as an *ancon;
section of the cavity: vertical plane figure bounded by the *span* and the *intrados*;
springing: point at which an arch unites with its support;
springing-line: horizontal plane from which an arch begins to rise.

Types of arches include:

acute arch: see *lancet*-arch;
anse de panier: *three-centred* arch resembling a basket-handle, also known as a *basket-handled* arch, usually formed by a segment of a circle connected to two other segments with smaller radii, but sometimes constructed using five or seven centres to give a similar shape;
back arch: see *rear* arch;
basket arch: see *anse de panier*;
bell arch: arch supported on two *corbels with curved faces above the reveals, so that the resulting compound curve of the opening resembles a bell;
Caernarfon arch: see *Welsh* arch;
camber arch: *flat* arch with a slight upward curve to the intrados, or a very low *segmental* arch;
canted arch: similar to a *corbel* arch, but with straight haunches set at an angle of 45° from the vertical;
catenary arch: formed like an inverted *catenary, similar to a *parabolic* arch, but less sharp and more elegant;
compound arch: *Order* or *recessed* arch consisting of several concentric arches with vertical supports, successively placed within and behind each other, each smaller than that in front, as in a *Romanesque doorway;
contrasted arch: as *ogee* arch;
corbel arch: *false* or *pseudo*-arch formed by means of horizontal blocks corbelled out from each side of the opening to be bridged until the latter is closed;
cusped arch: see *foil* arch;
depressed arch: see *anse-de-panier*, *four-centred*, and *three-centred* arch;
diaphragm arch: *transverse* arch across a nave supporting a gable between sections of a timber roof to prevent the spread of fire;
diminished arch: *segmental* arch, less than a *semicircular* arch;
discharging arch: see *relieving* arch;
drop arch: pointed arch with its centres on the springing-line and with the *span* longer than the radius;
Dutch arch: triangular false arch constructed of bricks laid on a slope of 45° starting from a *skew-back at each *jamb and meeting at an *apex;
elliptical arch: formed as half an ellipse with its axis coinciding with the springing-line;
equilateral arch: pointed *two-centred* arch of two arcs, the radii of which are equal to the span;
false arch: see *corbel* arch;
flat arch: *straight* arch with a level or slightly *cambered* soffit, the voussoirs seeming to form a lintel;
Florentine arch: semicircular arch with extrados and intrados struck from different centres, so that the voussoirs increase in length towards the top;
foil arch: *cusped* or *foliated* arch associated with *Gothic, *Moorish, and *Islamic styles. Foil arches can have *trefoils*, *cinquefoils*, or *multifoils* within a pointed arch, can have a series of small arcs cut in the intrados, as in the *Moorish multifoil* or *scalloped* arch, or can themselves be in the form of *foils, such as the *pointed trefoil* or *round trefoil* arch;
foliated arch: see *foil* arch;
four-centred arch: *depressed* arch, the characteristic form of late-*Perpendicular openings, with upper central arcs with centres below the springing-line, flanked by two arcs with centres on the springing-line;
French arch: *Dutch* arch;
gauged arch: *flat* arch, with a slightly *cambered *soffit, formed of voussoirs made of precisely cut stones, or, more usually, finely rubbed bricks (known as *rubbers*), with very fine lime-putty joints;
horseshoe arch: usually associated with Islamic styles, such arches are *horseshoe* (semicircular on straight piers narrowing towards the base below the springing-line), *pointed horseshoe* (pointed with arcs continuing to narrow the opening below the springing-line), and *round horseshoe* (semicircular with arcs continuing to narrow the opening below the springing-line);
interlacing arches: *intersecting* semicircular *Romanesque arches in a *blind *arcade, overlapping and forming pointed arches;
inverted arch: built upside-down, used in foundations;
Italian pointed arch: with intrados and extrados struck from different centres, and voussoirs increasing in size towards the apex. Similar to a *Florentine* arch, but pointed;

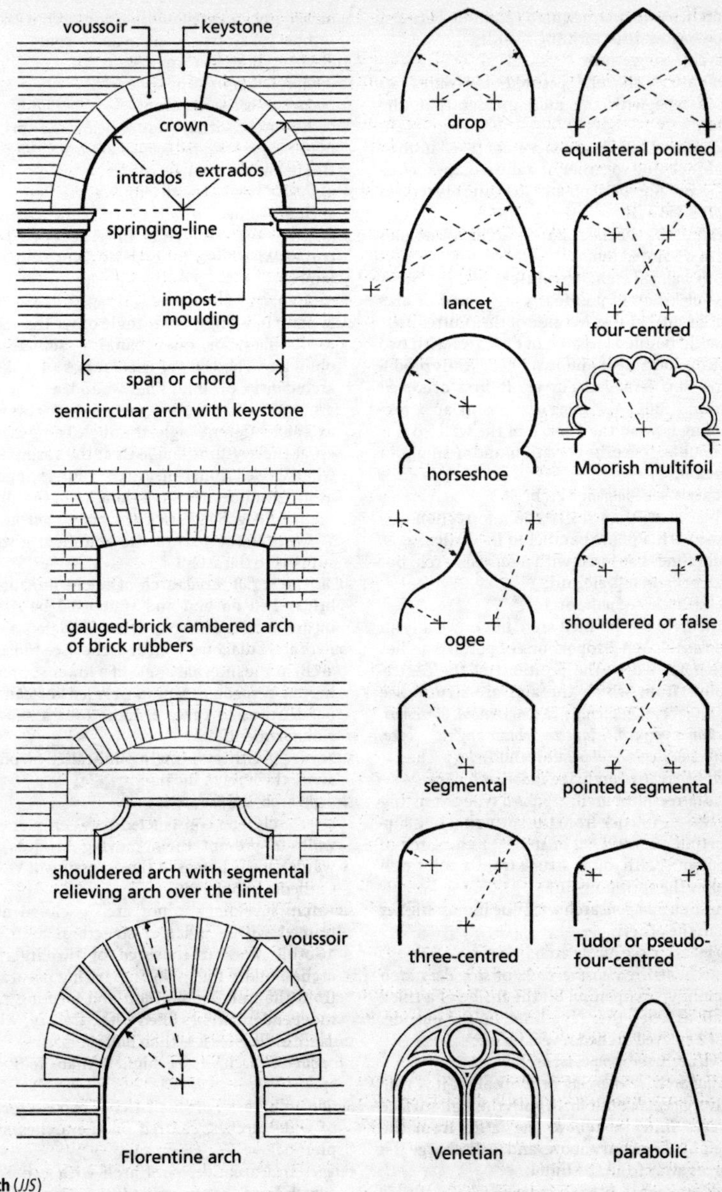
voussoir
keystone
crown
intrados
extrados
springing-line
impost
moulding
span or chord
semicircular arch with keystone
gauged-brick cambered arch
of brick rubbers
shouldered arch with segmental
relieving arch over the lintel
voussoir
Florentine arch
drop
equilateral pointed
lancet
four-centred
horseshoe
Moorish multifoil
ogee
shouldered or false
segmental
pointed segmental
three-centred
Tudor or pseudo-
four-centred
Venetian
parabolic

arch (*JJS*)

jack arch: *segmental* brick arch spanning between iron beams, thus forming a vault;
keel arch: see *ogee* arch;
lancet arch: sharply pointed *two-centred* or *acute* type with the radii greater than the span;
mitre arch: *triangular pseudo*-arch of two flat stone slabs leaning together at a mitred apex, common in *Anglo-Saxon architecture; also called a *pediment* arch;
Moorish arch: *horseshoe*-shaped arch, sometimes with a pointed top;
Moorish multifoil arch: see *foil* arch;
obtuse-angled arch: pointed type formed of arcs with centres on either side of the centre-line;
ogee arch: pointed *keel*-arch of four arcs with two centres outside it and two inside, thus producing two S-shaped curves. It first occurred around 1300. A *nodding ogee* has its apex projecting beyond the *naked of the wall, so it is a double *ogee in elevation and a single in section;
Order arch: see *compound* arch;
parabolic arch: shaped like the intersection of a cone with a plane parallel to its vertical axis, sometimes confused with a *catenary* arch, but sharper and less elegant;
pediment arch: see *mitre* arch;
pointed arch: any pointed arch, but especially an *equilateral* arch. Proportions of pointed arches are governed by the positions of the centre-points from which the arcs are struck. See *acute*, *drop*, *equilateral*, *foil*, *four-centred*, *horseshoe*, *Italian pointed*, *lancet*, *obtuse-angled*, *ogee*, *Saracenic*, *segmental pointed*, and *Tudor* arches;
pseudo-four-centred arch: see *Tudor* arch;
pseudo-three-centred arch: *depressed* type consisting of two arcs struck from the springing-line supporting a central *flat* or *straight pseudo*-arch of voussoirs with joints struck from a point well below the springing-line;
raking arch: *rampant* arch with one impost higher than the other;
rampant arch: see *raking* arch;
rear arch: *arrière voussure*, *back*, or *secondary* arch spanning an opening on the inside of a thick wall, as when there is a lintel on the outside, but a splayed arched reveal inside;
recessed arch: see *compound* arch;
relieving arch: *discharging* or *safety* arch, it is usually *segmental*, built flush with the wall-surface over a lintel to relieve the latter from the weight of masonry above, and to discharge the forces away from the lintel;
round horseshoe arch: see *horseshoe* arch;
round trefoil arch: see *foil* arch;
rowlock arch: has small voussoirs laid in a series of concentric rings;
safety arch: see *relieving* arch;
Saracenic arch: pointed *stilted*, *striped* arch with alternate voussoirs of contrasting colours;
scalloped arch: see *foil* arch;
scheme arch: *segmental* or *skene* arch;
secondary arch: see *rear* arch;
segmental arch: with its centre below the springing-line. A *segmental pointed* arch has *two* centres below the springing-line;
semicircular arch: with its centre on the springing-line;
shouldered arch: flat arch or lintel supported on corbels with *quadrants above rising from the jambs;
skene arch: see *scheme* arch;
skew arch: has jambs at an angle other than 90° to its face, or one spanning something obliquely. The beds of the courses of a skew arch consist of spiral lines wound, as it were, around a cylinder, every part of which cuts the axis at a different angle, the angle being greatest at the keystone and least at the springing; when viewed from beneath the courses appear as straight lines. *Skew* is a slope, as in the abutment of a gauged-brick *flat* or *straight* arch. *Skewback* is the part of the abutment giving support to the arch;
soldier arch: *flat pseudo*-arch of uncut ungauged bricks laid on end and supported by some means such as an L-shaped metal angle;
squinch arch: diagonal arch or arches (see *trumpet*-arch) in the internal angle of a tower supporting an octagonal *spire, or used instead of pendentives to carry a dome over a square compartment;
stilted arch: with its springing-line raised on piers above the level of the impost;
straight arch: see *flat* arch;
strainer arch: one constructed between piers or walls to prevent them moving inwards towards each other, as at the *crossing of Wells Cathedral, Somerset;
sub-arch: subsidiary minor arch enclosed and framed within a larger structural arch. In *Gothic work it consisted of two inferior arches, under the main arch, rising naturally from the middle *mullion and forming two independent arches filled with *tracery;
surbased arch: rises less than half its span;
surmounted arch: rises higher than half its span;
Syrian arch: series of small arches above a series of wider arches, centred on the arches and piers below;
three-centred arch: *depressed* arch with two arcs struck from the springing-line with a central arc struck from below it. A *depressed three-centred* arch has the central arc struck from a point very much lower than the springing-line;

transverse arch: divides a compartment of a vault from another, spanning from wall to wall or from wall to pier, forming a *bay;

trefoil arch: see *foil* arch;

triangular arch: see *mitre* arch;

triumphal arch: monumental arched free-standing structure, invented by the Romans, and a significant precedent for later *façade treatments in which columnar and *trabeated elements were mixed with *arcuated forms. Many Roman examples survive, including that of Septimius Severus (AD 203), with two smaller arches flanking a wider central arch with a richly coffered vault. The form was revived during the *Renaissance period, and there are many fine Neoclassical examples, including the Carrousel arch, Paris, by *Percier and *Fontaine (1806–7);

trumpet-arch: *squinch*-like part of a cone, i.e. with the arches getting wider and higher towards the extremities;

Tudor arch: *pseudo-four-centred* late-*Perpendicular arch, similar to the *four-centred* type, but with shanks starting as quarter-circles (with centres on the springing-line) continuing as straight lines to the apex. It is very *depressed*, and often expressed as a single lintel;

two-centred arch: *acute* or *lancet* arch;

Venetian arch: semicircular arch framing two semicircular-headed *lights separated by a colonnette above which is a *roundel in the space between the tops of the smaller arches and the main intrados;

and

Welsh arch: *Caernarfon* arch, comprising a wide keystone resting on two corbels shaped to fit the keystone.

Gwilt (1903); Papworth (1852); Parker (1850); Sturgis *et al.* (1901–2)

archaeology. Systematic scientific study of remains and monuments of earlier periods. Revivals of architectural styles usually have an archaeological phase in which accurate recording of extant buildings and details informs architectural design, as in the *Greek Revival.

arch-band. Raised band or strip (*arc-doubleau*) below the *soffit of an arch or *vault.

arch-bar. Metal rectangular bar under a *flat-* or *soldier*-arch supporting the *voussoirs.

arch-beam. Curved beam or a *collar-brace*.

arch-brace. Curved brace in timber-framed construction found in pairs which together form an arched shape.

arch-brick. Wedge-shaped brick (called *compass-brick*, *feather-edged brick*, or *voussoir*) for constructing an arch or a wall curved on plan.

arch-buttant. *As* arch-buttress.

arch-buttress. Flying *buttress, arched butment, or *arc-boutant*.

Archer, John Lee (1791–1852). Irish-born architect, who was John *Rennie's draughtsman from 1812 until he set up his own architectural and engineering practice in 1818. In 1826 he was appointed Civil Engineer to the Government of Van Diemen's Land, for which he designed several distinguished Classical buildings, including the Custom House (later Parliament House) and the Churches of St George (1837–8) and St John (1834–5), all in Hobart.

Colvin (1995); Robertson (1970); Smith (1962)

Archer, Thomas (*c*.1668–1743). English architect, who made the *Grand Tour and absorbed the lessons provided by the works of *Bernini and *Borromini. His reputation rests upon a handful of fine and accomplished *Baroque buildings, including the north front of, and cascade house at, Chatsworth, Derbyshire (1704–5), the garden-pavilion at Wrest Park, Bedfordshire (1709–11), and three churches (St Philip, Birmingham (now the Cathedral of 1710–15), St Paul, Deptford (1713–30), and St John, Smith Square, Westminster (1713–28)). The last-named building (damaged in the 1939–45 war), has four Baroque towers worthy of Borromini, and open-topped *pediments framing *aedicules. St Paul's, Deptford, is his finest surviving church, with a centralized space, powerfully modelled wall-surfaces and *entablatures, and an elegant tower.

Colvin (1995); Downes (1966); Summerson (1993); Whiffen (1950*a*)

arch-façade. Screen-wall into which are set deep, plain arches, as at the west front of Lincoln Cathedral.

Archigram. Group of designers formed by Peter *Cook and others in 1960, influenced by Cedric *Price (especially his Fun Palace of 1961), and disbanded in 1975. Archigram provided the precedents for the so-called *High Tech style, and promoted its architectural ideas through seductive futuristic graphics by means of exhibitions and the magazine *Archigram*: buildings designed by the group resembled machines or machine-parts, and structures exhibited their services and structural elements picked out in strong colours. The group's vision of disposable, flexible, easily extended constructions was influential, although very few of its projects were realized (the capsule at Expo 70 in Osaka, Japan, was one). Richard *Rogers's architecture derives from Archigram ideas, while Price's notions of expendability influenced Japanese *Metabolism. Unrealized but influential projects include the Fulham Study (1963), Instant City (1968), and the Inflatable Suit-Home (1968).

Archigram (1961–70); *Architectural Design*, 35/11 (Nov. 1965), 534–5; Cook (1991); Klotz (1986); Lampugnani (1982)

architect. Person capable of preparing the *plans, *elevations, and *sections of the design of a sophisticated building with an aesthetic content and to supervise its construction in accordance with the drawings and specifications. *Soane described an architect's business as that of making 'designs and estimates', directing 'the works', and valuing 'the different parts': he declared the architect as the 'intermediate agent between the employer, whose honour and interest he is to study, and the mechanic, whose rights he is to defend'. Soane emphasized the architect's position as implying great trust, being 'responsible for the mistakes, negligences, and ignorance of those he employs'. *Ruskin suggested that one who is neither a sculptor nor painter could not be an architect, but only a builder, and Frank Lloyd *Wright stated that an architect cannot bury his mistakes, unlike a physician.

Colvin (1995); Papworth (1852); Sturgis *et al.* (1901–2)

architectonic. 1. Pertaining to architecture or to the arrangement of knowledge. **2.** Suggesting in e.g. music or sculpture the qualities of architecture. **3.** In the plural, the science of architecture or the systematic ordering of knowledge.

Architects' Co-Partnership. Firm of English architects, founded in 1939 and restructured in 1945. It fostered team-work and often used industrialized components in its buildings. Its most celebrated building is the Rubber Factory at Bryn Mawr (1946–9), with which Ove *Arup was associated. It also built several schools, study-bedrooms on hexagonal plans at St John's College, Oxford (1960), and St Paul's Cathedral Choir School, London (1967).

Emanuel (1994)

architecture. *Ruskin, in his *Seven Lamps* (1849), stated that architecture was the 'art which so disposes and adorns the edifices raised by man . . . that the sight of them' contributes 'to his mental health, power, and pleasure', which proposes aesthetic, beneficial, and spiritual aspects rather than a utilitarian or *Functionalist agenda. He also opined, in the same book, that 'architecture' should be confined to 'that art which, . . . admitting . . . the necessities and common uses' of a building 'impresses on its form certain characters venerable or beautiful, but otherwise unnecessary'. He went on to note that 'no one would call the laws architectural which determine the height of a breastwork or the position of a bastion. But if to the stone facing of that bastion be added an unnecessary feature, as a cable moulding, *that* is Architecture. It would be similarly unreasonable to call battlements or machicolations architectural features, so long as they consist only of an advanced gallery supported on projecting masses, with open intervals beneath for offence. But if these projecting masses be carved beneath into rounded courses, which are useless, and if the headings of the intervals be arched and trefoiled, which is useless, *that* is Architecture.' Such a simplistic and prolix definition is revealing of Ruskin's attitudes, which, to a large extent, became the general view of the subject for the next eighty years or so.

Architecture is concerned with the creation of order out of chaos, a respect for organization, the manipulation of geometry, and the creation of a work in which aesthetics plays a far greater role than anything likely to be found in a humdrum building. Sir Henry Wotton's (1568–1639) statement that 'well building hath three conditions: Commodity, Firmness, and Delight' seems to have originated from *Vitruvius, who insisted that architecture derives from order, arrangement, eurythmy (or harmony of proportion), symmetry, propriety, and economy. *Wren spoke of 'Beauty, Firmness, and Convenience' in architecture. These definitions suggest that there is much in the built fabric that falls into the category of non-architecture. Architecture might be described as the art and science of designing a building having qualities of beauty, geometry, emotional and spiritual power, intellectual content and complexity, soundness of construction, convenient planning, many virtues of different kinds, durable and pleasing materials, agreeable colouring and decorations, serenity and dynamism, good proportions and acceptable scale, and many mnemonic associations drawing on a great range of precedents. Doubtless there are many more aspects that some would consider essential other than those suggested above. Philip *Johnson, in the *New York Times* (1964), went so far as to claim that 'architecture is the art of how to waste space'.

Gwilt (1903); Nicholson (1835); Papworth (1852); Ruskin, *The Seven Lamps of Architecture*, ch. I (first edn. 1849)

Architecture Machine. Title of book by Nicholas Negroponte in which artificial intelligence in architectural design was proposed, involving the employment of computers to such an extent that they would eventually function like colleagues.

Negroponte (1970)

architecture parlante. Architecture expressive of its purpose, a term first used in print by L. *Vaudoyer in respect of the French C18 Neoclassicists, notably *Ledoux.

Bergdoll (1994*a*)

Architecture Studio. French architectural practice founded in Paris in 1973. It was responsible for the Institut du Monde Arabe, Paris (1981–7—with Jean *Nouvel, Soria, and Lezènes), the French Embassy, Muscat, Oman (1987–9), the Lycée du Futur, Jaunay-Clan, France (1986–7), the Lycée Jules Verne, Cergy-Le-Haut, France (1991–3), and the European Parliament Buildings, Strasbourg, France (1994–7).

Jodidio (1996*a*)

Architext. Group of Japanese architects (including Takefumi Aida (1937–), Takamitsu *Azuma, Mayumi Miyawaki, Makoto Suzuki, and Minoru Takeyama (1934–)) founded in 1971. Opposed to the incipient totalitarianism of *Modernism (and especially *Metabolism), the group (based on the journal of the same name) promoted contradiction, discontinuity, individualism, and pluralism.

Architext (1976); *Japan Architect*, 51/232 (1976), 19–80

architrave. **1.** Essentially a formalized beam or *lintel, it is the lowest of the three main parts of an *entablature, itself often divided into *fasciae. **2.** *Antepagmentum consisting of plain or elaborate mouldings framing a doorway, *niche, panel, window-aperture, or other opening, properly with the same *section and number of *fasciae as on an entablature architrave. If the vertical mouldings of the architrave turn outwards horizontally as though at the ends of a lintel, then turn vertically, then run horizontally again across the top of the opening, they comprise an *eared*, or *lugged*, architrave; and if the vertical mouldings turn outwards horizontally, again as though at the ends of a lintel, then turn vertically, then run horizontally for a distance equal to the short vertical run, then drop vertically, then run horizontally along the top, they comprise a *shouldered* architrave, and the projecting shoulders are called *crossettes. Architraves often stop against an *architrave-*, *plinth-*, or *skirting-*block against which a *plinth or *skirting also stops. An architrave narrower at the top than at the bottom, i.e. with *battered sides, is called a *Vitruvian opening*.

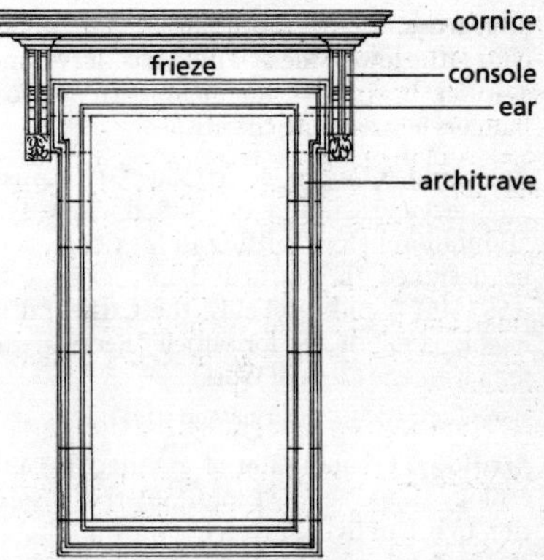

architrave. Classical window-surround with consoles, cornice, and eared architrave.

architrave cornice. *Entablature (usually of the *Ionic *Order) with no *frieze.

archivolt. **1.** Collection of *fasciae and other mouldings in a concentric ring forming an ornamental curved *band around a Classical arch terminating on a *platband at the springing: it is really an *architrave bent around the head of an arch. **2.** Erroneous term for the intrados or *soffit of an arch or vault.

Archizoom. (Studio Archizoom Associati). Group of Florentine architects, founded in 1966, devoted to anti-*Functionalism, and employing elements from popular 'culture' and even from *Kitsch. It was associated with *Supersensualism, anti-design, and so-called 'banal' design, and was promoted in *Casabella*, *Domus*, and *Architectural Design*.

Branzi (1984); Walker (1992)

arch Order. 1. Engaged columns, bases, *pedestals, and *entablature attached to an *arcuated structure as in a *triumphal arch*, or a series of superimposed Orders and arches as in the Roman Colosseum. **2.** Successive planes of diminishing concentric arches with *colonnettes, as in a *compound* arch or a *Romanesque doorway.

arch-rib. Vault-rib across a *nave or *aisle at right angles to the main axis.

arch-ring. Load-bearing curved part of an arched structure made of *voussoirs.

arch-stone. *Voussoir or keystone.

arch-truss. *Truss with an arched upper chord (the lower side of which is concave) and a lower horizontal member, with vertical hangers between the chords.

Arciniega, Claudio de (*c*.1520–93). Spanish architect and sculptor. He worked with Gil de *Hontañon before settling in Mexico, where he designed the Cathedral in Mexico City (1563–1667) and, probably, the Cathedral of Puebla (1557–1649), for which *Becerra was for a time the Clerk of Works.

Marco Dorta (1951); Kubler and Soria (1959)

Arcology. Combination of architecture and ecology supported by Paolo *Soleri as a solution to urban living involving the building of *megastructures able to contain up to three million people. Arcosanti, a future self-sufficient community powered by solar energy in the desert of Arizona, was commenced in the 1970s and has been under construction ever since.

Soleri (1969); Wall (1971)

arcosolium (*pl.* **arcosolia**). *Loculus with an arched or vaulted top in a Roman *catacomb, *hypogeum, or other type of tomb, usually big enough to contain a *sarcophagus.

arcuated. Structure erected using *arches, rather than columns and *lintels (*columnar and *trabeated structure).

arcus. 1. Roman arch. **2.** Entrance to a *basilica, or a porch or gateway to a church. **3.** Area in front of a basilica. **4.** Apse.

arcus choralis. 1. *Screen between the *choir and *nave in a *basilica, often of lattice-work. **2.** Arch between choir and nave in the same position, also called *arcus ecclesiae* or *arcus presbyterii*.

arcus toralis. As *arcus choralis* **1**.

arcus triumphalis. 1. *Triumphal *arch. **2.** Arch between the *nave and sanctuary in a *basilica.

arena. 1. Central area of an *amphitheatre surrounded by seats for spectators where public competitions, displays, or games take place. **2.** Building for public performances, contests, or displays, usually in the open. **3.** *Theatre without a *proscenium, loosely called 'theatre-in-the-round'. **4.** Part of a theatre used by the performers. **5.** The main body of a church.

Arens, Johann August (1757–1806). Hamburg-born architect, he studied with *Harsdorff and de *Wailly. Through Goethe he was called to Weimar to rebuild the *Schloss* (Castle—1789–92), but his most remarkable building there is the so-called Roman House in the Park, with its primitivist *Doric columns at the lower level supporting a temple-like structure (1790–2). Much of his output is in Hamburg, where, with C. F. *Hansen, he practised a refined and mature *Neoclassicism of which he was one of the most distinguished exponents of his time in Northern Germany.

Grundmann (1957); Watkin and Mellinghoff (1987); Wietek (1972)

Ariss, John (*c*.1725–99). English-born architect, who settled in Maryland *c*.1751, and who seems to have been the first, or one of the first, professional architects to work in the American Colonies. Steeped in English *Palladianism and in the architectural language of James *Gibbs, he was probably responsible for some of the more imposing Virginian houses, such as Mount Airey, Richmond County.

Pierson and Jordy (1970–86); Waterman (1945); Whiffen and Koeper (1983)

ark. 1. Receptacle for storing the scrolls in a synagogue. *See* echal. **2.** Type of cupboard or press for hanging priests' vestments in a church.

Arnolfo di Cambio (*c.*1245–*c.*1302). Master-mason and sculptor, perhaps born in Colle Val d'Elsa, Tuscany, but also referred to in the early C16 as a German, he assisted Nicola *Pisano of Siena in the 1260s, before going to Rome in 1277, where he designed a number of sepulchral monuments. His most important surviving tomb is that of Cardinal de Braye (d. 1282) in the Church of San Domenico at Orvieto. He evolved a type of tomb designed to be set against a wall, with a *gabled *canopy carried on *colonnettes protecting an *effigy on a *sarcophagus, which established the precedent for a century or so. He was probably familiar with French *Gothic architecture, and was master-mason for the new Cathedral in Florence (begun 1294–6), responsible for the *nave and *aisles, and for an earlier version of the present east end, possibly influenced by Rhineland precedents (especially Cologne Cathedral). His other Florentine designs (according to *Vasari) include the great Church of Santa Croce (begun 1294–5) and the Palazzo Vecchio (1299–1323).

Romanini (1980); Vasari (1568); White (1987)

aronade. *Battlement with an arc placed on the centre of an otherwise straight top of each cop or merlon, not extending the full width of each cop.

Aronco, Raimondo d' (1857–1932). Important Italian architect responsible for the graceful buildings at the International Exposition of Decorative Arts held at Turin (1902), where *Art Nouveau (called in Italy *Stile Liberty*), was vigorously in evidence. The central rotunda at Turin was an ebullient design, much ornamented, with low symmetrical wings. D'Aronco's buildings marked a climax of the style, even though his particular architectural language was greatly influenced by the *Sezession in its Austrian manifestation. The d'Aronco mausoleum at Udine (1898) demonstrated other aspects of his eclecticism, with its *battered walls, Egyptianizing heads, and influences from *Wagner and *Viollet-le-Duc.

Meeks (1966); Tschudi-Madsen (1967)

Arquitectonica. American architectural firm founded in 1977 by Peru-born Bernardo Fort-Brescia (1951–), his wife, the US-born Laurinda Hope-Spear (1950–), and Hervin A. Romney (who left the partnership in 1984). Their works include Spear House, Miami (1976–8); the Atlantis Condominium, Miami (1980–2); the Mulder House (1983–5) and the Banco de Crédito (1983–8), both in Lima, Peru; the North Dade Justice Center, Miami (1984–7); the Banque de Luxembourg Headquarters, Luxembourg (1994); the Center for Innovative Technology, Herndon, Va. (1985–8); and Miami International Airport (1997). Their US Embassy, Lima, Peru (1993–5), is clad in coloured panels which, with the allusions to irregular cyclopean masonry, suggest pre-Columbian precedents, although their work is in the mainstream of new Modernist architecture.

Emanuel (1994); Jodidio (1993, 1996, 1997)

Arras, Matthias of (d. 1352). French architect of the *Gothic Cathedral of St Vitus in Prague, Bohemia, commenced 1344, and influenced by the Cathedral in Narbonne. Matthias was also responsible for the restoration of Prague Castle (from 1333).

Sturgis *et al.* (1901–2)

arris. Sharp crease-like edge formed where two surfaces join, such as the corner of a brick or between the *flutes of a Greek *Doric column.

arrow-head. Pointed element in *egg-and-dart ornament.

arrow-loop. *Balistraria or loophole.

Arruda, Diogo (*fl.* 1508–31). Leading Portuguese architect working within the *Manueline style, responsible for the remarkable *nave and *chapter-house of the Church of the Order of Christ at Tomar (1510–14): it has a mass of extraordinary and exuberant decoration, including net-like *vaults over the two-storey space, and external ornament combining Royal coats-of-arms, emblems, musical instruments, ropes, sails, and marine flora and fauna. Arruda's brother, **Francisco** (*fl.* 1510–47), was responsible for the strange and exotic tower at the Jeronymite Monastery at Belém (1515–20).

Kubler and Soria (1959)

Art Deco. Fashionable style of European and American design and interior decoration (also known as the *Style Moderne*) that superseded *Art Nouveau in the period immediately before and after the 1914–18 war. In the 1920s and 1930s it evolved further, and took its name from the Exposition Interational des Arts-Décoratifs et Industriels Modernes in Paris in 1924–5: the official publication of the Exposition, *Encyclopédie des arts décoratifs et industriels modernes au XXième siècle*, in 12 volumes with many illustrations, disseminated the elements of a style derived from the more severe geometrical patterns evolved as a reaction to *Art Nouveau. Archaeological aspects also influenced the style: the discovery of Pharaoh Tutankhamun's tomb in 1922 led to a new enthusiasm for Ancient Egyptian motifs and themes such as strong colouring, pyramidal compositions, and stepped forms. However, the canted arch, *chevron, stepped corbelled arch, and stepped *gable (themselves pyramidal compositions) owed more to what C18 designers imagined was Egyptian, derived from publications such as *Piranesi's *Diverse maniere d'adornare i cammini* (Different Ways of Decorating Fireplaces—1769) and from exotic *Egyptian Revival stage-sets. Investigations of *Aztec and other *Meso-American architecture with its stepped forms were also influential. Late Art Deco designs were often concerned with aerodynamics, speed, and *streamlining to emphasize the style's Modernist pretensions. Robert *Mallet-Stevens was the most important of the French architects working with Art Deco elements, but the style also flourished in the USA, where William van *Alen's Chrysler Building, New York (1928–30), is perhaps its most celebrated architectural example. Simplified and vulgarized elements of Art Deco entered *Post-Modern designs from the 1960s.

Bletter and Robinson (1975); Brunhammer (1984); Curl (1994); Escritt (1997); Hillier (1985)

articulation. Architectural composition in which elements and parts of the building are expressed logically, distinctly, and consistently, with clear joints.

Artinatural. Style lying between the formal and informal, defined by Batty *Langley in his *Practical Geometry* (1726) and *New Principles of Gardening* (1728) as 'regular irregularity': in landscape-gardens this signified a symmetrical geometry overlaid by asymmetrical elements such as serpentine paths.

Symes (1993)

Artisan Mannerism. English architecture created by masons (rather than architects) in the period *c.*1615–*c.*1675, and based on *Mannerist *pattern-books. Such craftsmen

Art Deco. Typical Art Deco door and door-surround with stepped top, chevrons, and other typical detail of the style. (*JJS*)

were not trained in the theory and vocabulary of the Classical language of architecture, so their creations often have a curious scale, are strangely proportioned, and frequently display an ignorance of how Classical elements are put together which some commentators have found refreshing and others distressing.

Mowl and Earnshaw (1995); Summerson (1993); Wüsten (1951)

Art Nouveau. Style of architecture and the decorative arts that flourished in Europe and the USA from *c.*1888 to *c.*1914, featuring asymmetrical compositions; attenuated blooms, foliage, roots, and stems with sinuous flowing lines, as though floating in water; the dream-maiden (female figure with long wavy tendril-like hair known as *femme-fleur); stylized *rose-bowls; intertwining plant-forms; and indeterminate *whiplash curved tendrils. It evolved from some late-*Gothic Revival patterns, and owed something, perhaps, to *Auricular and *Rococo ornament. Proto-typical Art Nouveau *capitals at Blackfriars Railway Bridge (1862–4) and Holborn Viaduct (1863–9), both in London, demonstrate that the essence of the style was in place in the early 1860s, while the illustrations in *Viollet-le-Duc's hugely influential *Entretiens sur l'Architecture* (Lectures in Architecture—1872) spread images of free-flowing curved forms throughout Europe and America. Certain artists associated with the *Arts-and-Crafts movement, notably Arthur H. *Mackmurdo,

William *Morris, and C. F. A. *Voysey produced celebrated designs that fall firmly within the style. Named after the Paris shop (*Maison de l'Art Nouveau*) of the art-dealer Siegfried Bing (1838–1905—which stocked artefacts that were not reproductions of styles of earlier periods, but were modern and often oriental, and had interiors designed by Henry van de *Velde (1896)), the style was associated first with the *Aesthetic Movement, and then with modernity (in France it was also known as the *Style Moderne*, in Spain as *Modernismo, *Estilo Modernista, or *Modernisme (Catalan), in The Netherlands as *Nieuwe Kunst* (New Art), in Germany, Austria-Hungary, and Scandinavia as *Jugendstil* (Youth style), and in Italy as *Stile *Floreale* or *Stile Liberty* (from Liberty's shop in London which stocked Art Nouveau objects), so its new, youthful, and modern associations were emphasized by its various names). In architecture the style reached its heights of virtuosity with the buildings of d'*Aronco in Milan, *Gaudí in Barcelona, *Guimard in Paris, *Horta in Brussels, and *Shekhtel' in Moscow. Drawings by Aubrey Beardsley (1872–98), furniture by Louis Majorelle (1859–1926), designs by Margaret Macdonald (1865–1933) and her husband C. R. *Mackintosh, graphic work by Alphonse Mucha (1860–1939), glassware by Louis Comfort Tiffany (1848–1913), and architectural designs by Émile André (1871–1933), *Basile, *Hankar, *Hoffmann, *Jourdain, Jules Lavirotte (1864–1924), *Olbrich, and Louis *Sullivan, all display characteristic Art Nouveau elements. Journals such as *L'Art Décoratif* (Decorative Art), *Die Jugend* (Youth), *Kunst und Kunsthandwerk* (Art and Craft), *Pan*, and *The Studio* disseminated the style, which was also promoted in German-speaking countries by various *Sezession groups (in Austria-Hungary the preferred term was *Sezessionstil* rather than *Jugendstil*).

Loyer (1986, 1991); Nicoletti (1978); Pevsner and Richards (1973); Russell (1979); Tschudi-Madsen (1967)

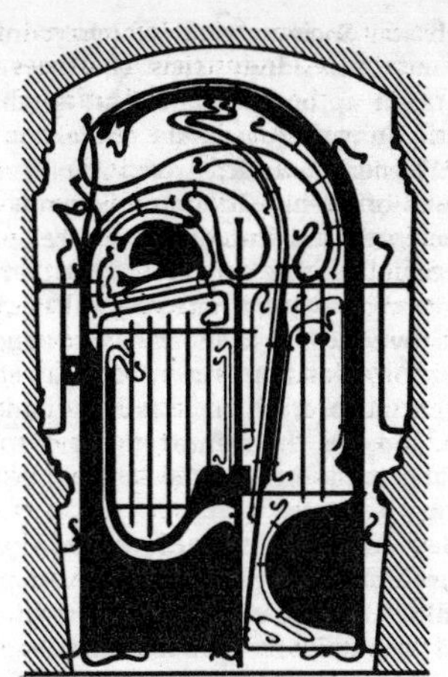

Art Nouveau. Metal gate to the Castel Béranger, Paris (1894–5), by Hector Guimard. Note the free, flowing forms and asymmetry. (*JJS*)

Arts-and-Crafts. Widely influential late-C19 English movement that attempted to re-establish the skills of craftsmanship threatened by mass-production and industrialization. While the medieval craft-guilds were revered as ideals, the movement had its origins in the ideas of Jean-Jacques Rousseau (1712–78), who proposed that manual skills should be acquired by everybody, no matter from what social class, but owed its immediate impetus to the polemical publications and widespread influence of *Pugin and *Ruskin. The latter founded the Guild of St George in 1871 to promote the transition from theory to practice, but the most important personality associated with the Arts-and-Crafts movement was William *Morris, who sought to revive medieval standards and methods of making artefacts while holding truth to materials, constructional methods, and function to be the essence of design. Learning the problems and solutions of providing designs for objects in his own living-accommodation, Morris set up a company in 1861 capable of undertaking any species of decoration, from pictures to a consideration of the smallest work in which artistic beauty could be incorporated. Morris, Marshall, Faulkner, & Co, with which Ford Madox Brown (1821–93), Dante Gabriel Rossetti (1828–82), Edward Burne-Jones (1833–98), and Philip *Webb were closely associated, embraced medieval craftsmanship as the ideal, opposed mass-production, and encouraged design and decoration intricately allied to the properties of materials and the logical methods of construction, drawing on traditional and *vernacular precedents. The movement gave rise to the Century Guild (founded by *Mackmurdo in 1882), the *Art-Workers' Guild (1884), the Guild of Handicraft (founded by *Ashbee in 1888), and the Arts-and-Crafts

Exhibition Society (1888) which promoted Arts-and-Crafts ideals. Soon the movement was taken up on the Continent, notably in Austria-Hungary (where the *Sezession and the *Wiener Werkstätte were two of its most obvious offspring), Belgium, Germany, The Netherlands, and Scandinavia (where it is still influential at the end of C20). Other key figures were Walter Crane (1845–1915), W. K. *Lethaby (who had an enormous influence on education, was appointed Principal of the Central School of Arts and Crafts in London in 1896, and was the mentor of the *Barnsley brothers and Ernest *Gimson), and E. S. *Prior.

The chief legacy of the movement to architecture was the appreciation of *vernacular buildings leading to elements derived from them being widely used in the *Domestic Revival (which grew out of the *Gothic Revival and aspects of the *Picturesque). Important developments in housing such as at Bedford Park, Chiswick (from the 1870s), Bournville, near Birmingham, Warwickshire (from the 1890s), Letchworth, Hertfordshire (from 1903), and Port Sunlight, Cheshire (from the 1880s), all employed themes drawn from vernacular architecture and set the agenda for domestic architecture in Britain until 1939. So admired was English domestic architecture that a major study of it by Hermann *Muthesius was published in *Das Englische Haus* (The English House—1904/5), and regular articles also appeared in architectural journals as well as in the influential art journal *The Studio* (which strongly supported the Arts-and-Crafts movement as a whole). Two American disciples of Morris, Elbert Hubbard (1856–1915) and Gustav Stickley (1857–1942), helped to promote the movement in the USA.

Finally, the movement was in the vanguard of recording, studying, and preserving old buildings, and argued for the careful *conservation of ancient fabric rather than wholesale or drastic 'restorations'. Morris himself founded the Society for the Protection of Ancient Buildings (SPAB) which has been an influential agent ever since.

Davey (1980, 1995); Hawkes (1986); Kaplan (1987); Kornwolf (1972); Lewis and Darley (1986); Richardson (1983); Stansky (1996); Winter (1997)

Art-Workers' Guild. Founded in 1884 as a forum for discussion for architects, craftsmen, and designers, it promoted *Arts-and-Crafts ideals, and still continues at the end of C20. Its Masters have included *Sedding, *Morris, and several distinguished architects.

Stansky (1996)

Arup, Sir Ove Nyquist (1895–1988). Born to Danish parents in Newcastle upon Tyne, Arup founded the engineering and consultancy firm of Arup & Arup in 1938. He worked with *Tecton in London on such projects as Highpoint (1936–8), the Penguin Pool at London Zoo (1939), and Finsbury Health Centre (1938–9), and was among the first in England to design load-bearing *concrete walls using slip-form shuttering (moulds for concrete that can be moved and reused as work progresses). In 1949 he founded Ove Arup & Partners, and in 1963, with Philip *Dowson, Ronald Hobbs, and others, he formed Arup Associates, a multi-professional firm notable for its elegant approach to design problems. From the beginning of his career Arup was a Modernist, and was a founding-member of *MARS. He worked with the *Smithsons on the School at Hunstanton, Norfolk (1949, and 1952–4), with *Utzon on the Sydney Opera House (1956–74), and with *Piano and *Rogers on the Centre Pompidou in Paris (1971–7), but his own command of elegance in structure and design can best be seen in his Kingsgate footbridge over the River Wear at Durham (1963). The firm has also been responsible for the development at Finsbury Avenue, London (1984), the latter part of the huge Broadgate development, Liverpool Street. Arup was involved (1977–80) as a consultant to Rogers for the Lloyd's Headquarters Building, City of London.

Brawne (1983); Dunster (1997); Emanuel (1994)

Asam Brothers (**Cosmas Damian** (1686–1739) *and* **Egid Quirin** (1692–1750)). Although C. D. Asam was primarily a painter of *frescoes, and his brother a sculptor, together they designed and made some of the foremost examples of *Baroque architecture in Bavaria. They were supported by the Abbot of Tegernsee who sent them on a study-visit to Rome after the death of their father **Georg Asam** (1649–1711). On their return to Bavaria they were employed as decorators of several churches, especially after C. D. Asam demonstrated his mastery of theatrical effects and dramatic perspectives in the ceiling-frescoes of the *Dreifaltigkeitskirche* (Church of the Holy Trinity) in Munich (1715). In 1714 he started

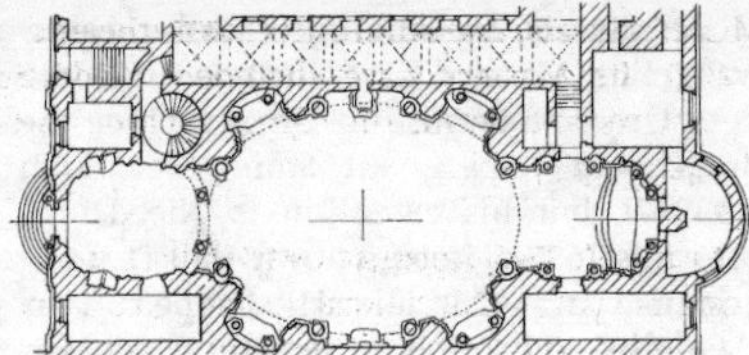

Plan of the Benedictine Abbey Church of Weltenburg showing elliptical nave and, behind the high-altar, the apse from which light floods.

work on the Benedictine Abbey of Weltenburg, where Roman influences are plainly demonstrated, for the *nave of the church is an ellipse on plan, light-sources are difficult to discern, and the rich colouring and gilding are reminiscent of *Bernini's Sant'Andrea at Quirinale. However, Bernini placed the high-altar on the shorter axis of the ellipse, whereas at Weltenburg Asam set the high-altar on the longer axis. E. Q. Asam also contributed to the works at Weltenburg from 1721, and the collaboration created a stunning work, the climax of which is the stage-like *aedicule of *Solomonic columns within which an equestrian St George, bathed in yellow light that pours from above and behind, slays a fearsome dragon. A sculptured figure of C. D. Asam leans elegantly over the gallery high above the elliptical nave, smiling down at visitors as if in welcome.

The brothers decorated many churches, including the *Pfarrkirche* (Parish Church) St Jakobi, Innsbruck (1722–3), but it was in the few they designed and built that they demonstrated their mastery of spatial illusion, lighting effects, and other melodramatic aspects of design they had learned in Rome. Weltenburg is sensational, but so is the Augustinian Priory Church at Rohr (1717–25), where the Virgin rises from her coffin, carried up to Heaven by angels within an *aedicule, the broken *pediment of which features in its centre clouds, *putti, and a *sunburst of glory. At the tiny Church of St Johann Nepomuk (often known as the *Asamkirche*), Munich (1733–40), lighting, drama, theatrical effects, and intensity of expression reached new heights, while the delicate and fanciful *Ursulinenkirche* (Church of the Ursulines), Straubing (1736–41), built on a quatrefoil plan, also employs dramatic lighting sources from on high, and makes more overt the visual expression of earthly and heavenly realms. The Asams were masters of drama and illusion, rarely failing to delight the eye and move the emotions.

Bourke (1962); Hitchcock (1968*a*); Powell (1959); Rupprecht and Mülbe (1987)

Ashbee, Charles Robert (1863–1942). English *Arts-and-Crafts designer, celebrated for his metalwork, but also an architect, with some sixty buildings, most of them houses, to his credit. He was influenced by *Morris, *Ruskin, and idealistic Socialism, worked for a time with *Bodley, and in 1888 founded the School and Guild of Handicraft, which exhibited at the 1889 and later Arts-and-Crafts exhibitions. This co-operative group of craftsmen worked for a while in the East End of London. In 1893–4 Ashbee designed a house (destroyed 1968) for his mother at 37 Cheyne Walk, London, the interiors of which were decorated by the Guild, and this was followed by other houses (notably 72–3 (destroyed) and 38–9 Cheyne Walk) in the *Queen Anne Revival style (1897–1903). The Guild designed furniture for Baillie *Scott's house for the reigning Grand Duke of Hesse at Darmstadt in 1898, exhibited at the Vienna *Sezession in 1900, moved to Chipping Campden in Gloucestershire in 1901, but failed in 1905. Ashbee was in the forefront of *conservation, and carried out many restorations, new buildings, and extensions in Chipping Campden, all of which were carefully considered in order to respect the character of the place. His sensitivity was well tested when he adapted a ruined chapel of *c.*1100 as a dwelling-house at Broad Campden (*c.*1906–7). He was one of the first British architects to realize the importance of Frank Lloyd *Wright, and he was in the vanguard of endeavour to bring order and care to the planning of towns and cities. Mindful of the huge losses of historic buildings through redevelopment, he began a process of surveying London buildings that led to the important *Survey of London* volumes. He published *A Book of Cottages and Little Houses* (1906).

Crawford (1985); *DNB* (1959); Service (1975, 1977)

ash-chest. *See* cinerarium.

ashlar. 1. Class of *masonry consisting of blocks of accurately dressed, cut, squared, and finished stone (the Roman *opus quadratum), faced and with clean sharp *arrises, forming perfect courses, laid in mortar. It is contrasted with *rubble. Thin slabs of similar masonry, used as a facing to a brick wall or as paving slabs, were also termed *ashlar*, although *bastard ashlar* is preferred. Finished work featuring the *faces of each stone projecting beyond the line of the joints is *rustication, or rusticated ashlar, and can be of several types. **2.** Large clay-based block larger than a brick, such as *faïence or *terracotta (US).

ashlar-piece. *See* roof.

ashlering. *See* roof.

Asiatic base. *Base of the *Ionic *Order, unlike the *Attic base, consisting of a lower *fluted and *reeded cylinder with a reeded *torus above it.

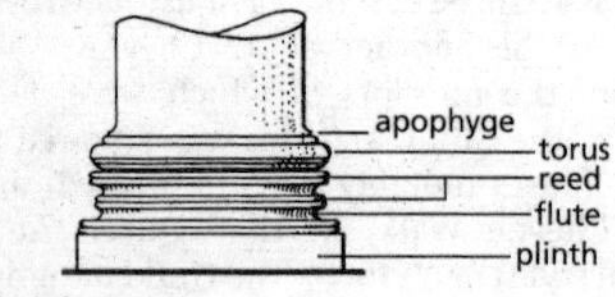

Asiatic base (*JJS*)

Aslin, Charles Herbert (1893–1959). Pioneer of C20 prefabricated design, who, as County Architect for Hertfordshire 1945–58, used the potential of light industry to produce prefabricated standardized components for the County school-building programme.

Emanuel (1980)

Asplund, Erik Gunnar (1885–1940). One of the most prominent of Swedish architects of the first half of C20. His first works show the influence of *National Romanticism (the villas Selander (1913) and Ruth (1914)), but after a period in Germany he adopted *Neoclassicism. His mastery of Neoclassical themes was demonstrated in Stockholm at the Skandia Cinema (with its *Pompeian interior colouring (1922–3)), in the Public Library (with its great *drum exposing the shape of the reading-room rising up from the simple, blocky mass of the rest of the building (1920–8)), and in the Swedish Pavilion for the 1924–5 Exposition in Paris. For the Woodland Cemetery, part of Stockholm South Cemetery, he and *Lewerentz prepared designs in which Neoclassicism and Romanticism were subtly mingled. The austere funerary Chapel, for example, combined vernacular and Classical themes, and was set in a wooded landscape of moving serenity. With his designs for the Stockholm Exhibition (1930), Asplund demonstrated that he had become a Modernist, and his handling of steel and glass was greatly admired for its elegance and lightness. Other Modernist buildings include the Bredenberg Department Store, Stockholm (1933–7), but his extension to Nicodemus *Tessin's 1672 Göteborg Town Hall (1934–7, designed in 1925) mixed *stripped *Neoclassicism and a modern structural grid. His Woodland Crematorium, Stockholm South Cemetery (1935–40), has a beautifully crafted *portico contrasting with the solemn, cave-like main *chapel behind, demonstrating his incorporation of aspects of historical architecture with contemporary design, and his ability to anchor his buildings within a landscape that is partly natural and partly contrived.

Ahlberg (1943); Asplund (1985, 1988); Asplund *et al.* (1931); Caldenby and Hultin (1986); Holmdahl *et al.* (1981); Maré (1955); Nagy (1974); Wrede (1980)

Asprucci, Antonio (1723–1808). Important *Neoclassical architect working in Rome. His best-known works are the sumptuous interiors of the Villa Borghese, Rome (from 1782), and the enlivening of the Borghese Gardens with arches, pavilions, pools, ruins, and temples, including the *Ionic Temple of Aesculapius (1787) and the Chiesetta di Piazza di Siena (*c.*1787), with its *portico of unfluted Greek *Doric columns. Antonio was the first Italian architect to revive the Greek Doric style. He used several Egyptianizing motifs in his Neoclassical designs. His son, **Mario Asprucci** (1764–1804), also worked on the Villa Borghese Gardens in the 1780s and 1790s (the plan of which was by the Scots landscape-painter Jacob More (*c.*1740–93)), and was responsible for the original designs for Ickworth House, Suffolk (*c.*1795), executed, with some modifications, by Francis *Sandys from 1796.

Lavagnino (1961); Meeks (1966)

Assche, Simon van (*fl.* C15). Flemish architect of the *Gothic Cloth Hall at Ghent (Gent), Belgium (1426–41).

Baedeker, *Belgium* (1931)

assemblage of Orders. Arrangement of *Orders on a Classical *façade of several *storeys, set one above the other and defining the storeys, with the vertical axes of the columns coinciding and lining up: this is called *supercolumniation* or an arrangement of *superimposed* Orders. The hierarchy places *Tuscan at the lowest storey, then *Doric, *Ionic, *Corinthian, and finally *Composite.

While the *Antique precedent for such superimposition or assemblage was the Colosseum in Rome, its external wall having Doric, Ionic, and Corinthian Orders associated with an *arcuated structure, the topmost Order was again Corinthian, but it was an Order of *pilasters. *Serlio was the first to codify the *five* Orders in his *L'Architettura* (1584), which had appeared in six parts from between 1537 and 1551, with illustrations augmenting the information in 1575, and so the five Orders set above each other (in the hierarchy described above) was essentially a *Renaissance invention, and was widely disseminated.

asses' ears. Type of *ear or *horn.

Assyrian architecture. When the Assyrians of Northern Mesopotamia became dominant in the region towards the end of the second millennium BC they took over principles of design established by their *Sumerian predecessors. They used brilliant colouring in their architecture (usually by means of coloured glazed bricks), and sculptured decorations in relief as well as free-standing objects. The great Palace of Sargon at Khorsabad (C8 BC) incorporated many repeated motifs such as arches, winged lions and bulls with humanoid heads, gigantic *reedings, and two-stepped crenellations, although columns were little used: it stood on a vast brick *plinth, and was reached by ramps and stairs. Assyrian temple-platforms resembled flat-topped stepped *pyramids, with the 'steps' formed of a continuous ramp that led around the square plan to reach the summit. Vaulting and even domed construction were apparently known to the Assyrians.

Cruickshank (1996); Lloyd and Müller (1986)

astragal, astragulus. **1.** *Baguette, *bead, chaplet, small convex moulding, or *roundel, especially the ring of semicircular section at the top of the *shaft of most Classical columns (except Greek *Doric), defining the bottom of the *capital, or a similar type of moulding further defining *architrave *fasciae, often ornamented, usually with *bead-and-reel. **2.** In Scotland, glazing-bars in a window-frame, dividing the *lights into panes.

astragulum Lesbium. *Astragal embellished, usually with *bead-and-reel.

astreated. Decorated with stars.

astylar. Classical exterior or interior with no columns or *pilasters.

Atelier 5. Group of Swiss architects established at Berne in 1955 by Erwin Fritz (d. 1992), Samuel Gerber (retired 1969), Rolf Hesterberg (1927–), Hans Hostettler (1925– , retired 1990), and Alfredo Pini (1932–). The firm is best known for its many housing developments in Switzerland, the most celebrated of which is the unified Halen complex of housing at Herrenschwanden, near Berne (1955–61), influenced by Le *Corbusier's unrealized project for housing at La Sainte-Baume (1948), but also incorporating a grid-plan similar to that of the old town of Berne. Atelier 5's later work includes extensions to the Court House, Berne (1976–81), Students' Housing, University of Stuttgart, Vaihingen, Germany (1966–72), the Flamatt 3 Housing Development (1988), and Housing at Ried, Niederwangen (1990).

Blaser (1982); Emanuel (1994)

Athens Charter. In 1933, the fourth *CIAM congress investigated thirty-three major cities, and evolved principles based on Le *Corbusier's notions of the distribution and ordering of the functions of the city, including rigid zoning, housing in high-rise blocks, and wholesale destruction of existing urban fabric. Le Corbusier published the dogma of Modernist urban planning in his *La Charte d'Athènes* in 1943 (published as *The Athens Charter* in 1973), in which such functions were treated concisely, simplistically, and crudely. Great damage was inflicted on countless towns and cities through the widespread acceptance of the ideas enshrined in the Charter.

Jeanneret-Gris (1973)

Atkinson, Robert Frank (1871–1923). Articled to John Francis *Doyle (1840–1913) of Liverpool, Atkinson opened his own office in London, and in 1912 designed the Midland Adelphi Hotel in Liverpool (completed in modified form by Stanley Hamp). In 1907 he collaborated with the Chicago architect Daniel H. *Burnham on the design of the steel-framed Selfridges Store in Oxford Street, London, although the architect of the façade was Francis S. *Swales, who placed a *Giant *Order of *Ionic columns (based on Philibert de l'*Orme's Tuileries Palace in Paris), with panels of metal and glass between them, on the ground-floor base. This building set the style for grand Classical stores and offices in Great Britain until 1939.

Gray (1985)

atlantes. *See* atlas.

atlas, atlantis (*pl.* **atlantes, atlantides**). Sculptured well-developed male figure, rather than a column, used as a support for an *entablature, or other architectural element, e.g. *balcony. In form, the figure seems to sustain a great burden, and the arms and shoulders are used to hold up the superstructure, unlike a canephora, *caryatid, or *telamon, which supports the entablature on its head. Some sources state that atlantes (or *gigantes*) were Greek equivalents of Roman telamones, and that they were also called *Persians*, but male standing figures dressed in oriental fashion, telamones (often with Egyptianizing attributes), canephorae, and caryatides are always straight and unbowed, and are wholly unlike atlantes, which often occur in *Baroque architecture, especially in Central Europe. The Greek temple of Zeus Olympius, Agraces (or Agrigentum), had atlantes standing on screen-walls between the *engaged *Doric columns to help to support the entablature with heads *and arms* (*c.*480 BC).

Curl (1992); Dinsmoor (1950)

atrium (*pl.* **atria**). **1.** Small *court or principal room in a Roman house, called *cavaedium* or *cavum aedium*, usually surrounded by a roofed area, supported on columns, disposed with the *compluvium* or roofless opening in the centre. Rainwater was channelled into an *impluvium*, *cistern, pool, or tank set under the opening in the floor. Types of domestic atrium include:

atrium Corinthium: with more than four columns (i.e. a *peristyle) supporting the edge of the *compluvium*;
atrium displuvatium: with the roof sloping away from the *compluvium*, the rain being carried away by means of gutters and pipes;
atrium testudinatum: with no *compluvium*, but crowned with an arched *vault (*testudo*);
atrium tetrastylum: with four columns, one at each corner supporting the *compluvium*;
atrium Tuscanicum: insignificant and *astylar with the roof carried on two beams with two short beams or trimmers.

2. Open court surrounded by a roofed *arcaded or *colonnaded walk, laid out before the west end of an *Early Christian, *Byzantine or medieval church, sometimes planted with trees, and often with a fountain in the centre. An interesting survival is the atrium of Sant'Ambrogio, Milan (*c.*1140). In this sense, the atrium was the forerunner of the *cloister. **3.** Top-lit volume surrounded by several storeys within a building.

Robertson (1945)

attached. *See* engaged.

Attic base. Commonest type of *base of a Classical column (used with all *Orders except Greek *Doric and (properly) *Tuscan) consisting of (usually) a *plinth over which is a large convex *torus ring, a *fillet, then a convex *scotia, then another fillet above which is a torus smaller than the lower ring, then a fillet, then the *apophyge and the *shaft.

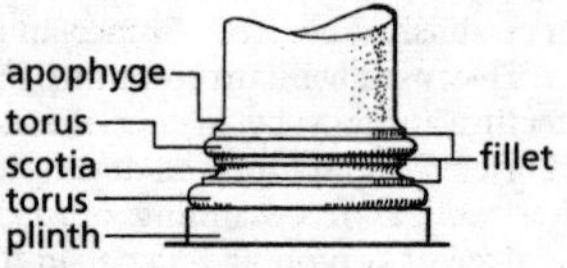

Attic base (*JJS*)

Attic door-case. *Battered or *Vitruvian opening, its dimension at the threshold wider than at the top, the whole framed by an *architrave, often with *fasciae.

Vitruvius Pollio IV. vi. 1, 2, 6

Attic Order. Subordinate *Order, perhaps of *pilasters, adorning the front of an *Attic storey over the main *entablature, and lining up with the Orders used below.

Attic storey. In Classical architecture, a storey erected over the main *entablature, often with an *Attic *Order relating to the Orders below, but sometimes treated very plainly, as in the Attic storey of a *triumphal arch, or the Attic of the *Choragic Monument of Thrasyllus, Athens (added 279 BC).

Atticurges, Atticurgic. Seems to refer to anything 'in the Athenian style', and might allude to an *Attic base or an *Attic door-case.

attribute. Object expressing the authority or character of a personage (mythical or otherwise) or a deity, used to suggest the use of a building. A lyre represents Apollo, a dove Venus, a grid-iron St Lawrence, a flaying-knife St Bartholomew, and a trident Neptune.

Thus lyres are found on concert-halls and tridents on buildings associated with marine affairs.

Atwood, Charles Bowler (1849–95). Massachusetts-born and -educated architect, who worked for *Ware and van Brunt from 1866 before opening his own office in 1872, later joining Daniel H. *Burnham of Chicago in 1891. His work in the 1880s showed an ever-developing fluency in the use of Classical motifs, and it was this facility that helped to get him the position of chief designer for the World's Columbian Exposition, Chicago, 1893. The accuracy and power of his Classical architecture was best seen at the Terminal Railroad Station at the Exposition, based on Roman *thermae, which influenced the design of many railway-stations in the United States thereafter. His Fine Arts Building (later Museum of Science and Industry) of 1893 was a noble essay in the Graeco-Roman *Neoclassical style. It was Atwood who helped to apply a logical and scholarly architectural language to tall buildings, including the Reliance (1894–5) and the Fisher (1895–6) Buildings, two of the most important works of the Chicago School: towers clad in glass and *terracotta, they represent a significant step in the evolution of the metal-framed *skyscraper, the outside skin of which was visibly non-structural.

Jenkins (1895); Woltersdorf (1924)

Atwood, William (*fl.* 1490–1557). English freemason. He was master-mason at Wells Cathedral, Somerset, from 1490, and rebuilt the south *cloister there (completed 1508).

Harvey (1987)

auditory. 1. Ancient name for the *nave of a church, where the Gospel could be heard. **2.** From C17, churches of the Reformed religion adopted a wide, almost square, plan so that the *lectern and *pulpit were more clearly visible and the Word could be heard, and such buildings were essentially religious auditoria, called *auditory churches*.

Landale-Drummond (1934)

aumbry. Recess in a church wall in which sacred vessels are kept, usually near an altar, also called *almery*, *ambry*, and *aumery*.

aureole. Halo or Glory surrounding the figure of Christ, the Virgin, or a Saint. If almond-shaped, it is formed of two interlocking segmental arcs, the whole figure called a *mandala or a *vesica piscis. A circular halo surrounding a head only is called a *nimbus*.

Auricular. Style of C16 and C17 ornament made with curved, smooth, undulating forms with flowing lines and ripple-like elements reminiscent of the human ear. Called the *Cartilaginous*, *Dutch Grotesque*, *Lobate*, or *Oleaginous* style, it was found in *antic, *grotesque, and *Mannerist ornament, and probably influenced *Rococo and *Art Nouveau detail.

Austin, Henry (1804–91). Connecticut-born architect, who trained in the office of *Town & *Davis, and mastered several historical styles. His works at New Haven, Connecticut, include the Yale Library (now Dwight Chapel, of 1842–5), based on King's College *Chapel, Cambridge, and the gateway at Grove Street Cemetery (1848–9) that incorporates a *battered *pylon-form and *papyrus-bud *capitals of the *Egyptian Revival. For the Railway Station (1848–9) he employed *Italianate, *Chinoiserie, and *Indian styles, while his City Hall (1861–2) is *High *Victorian *Gothic Revival. He exploited exotic styles in a number of villas, one of the best of which was the Moses Yale Beach House, Wallingford, Conn. (1850), in which Indian and Italian motifs promiscuously mingled. In his last years in practice he designed several timber houses using the *Stick style (e.g. the W. J. Clark House, Stony Creek, Branford, Connecticut (1879–80)).

Brown, E. M. (1976); Carrott (1978); Placzek (1982)

Austin, Hubert James (1841–1915). *See* Paley, Edward Graham (1823–95).

avant-corps. Porch, *pavilion, or other structure projecting from the *corps de logis, or advanced before it.

Averlino, Antonio (*c.*1400–69). *See* Filarete.

axial. Describes a layout disposed symmetrically about an *axis, such as a *basilican church.

axis. 1. Straight line laid down as a guide on either side of which elements of the plan are symmetrically or systematically disposed. In a sphere it would run through the centre. *See* axial. **2.** Thickness of the thinnest portion of the *Ionic *volute cushion, i.e. the *fillet. **3.** Hanging-*stile of a door.

axonometric projection. Geometrical drawing of a work of architecture. Its plan is produced to *scale, but moved round at an angle of 60° and 30° to the normal *axis (or set at 45°, whichever is convenient or creates the best impression). The vertical lines are then also projected from the plan to scale, thus the only parts distorted and not to scale are any curves and diagonals. This is useful to give an idea of the three-dimensional form of a building, more or less to scale, and can be exploded to show the interior, etc.

Fraser Reekie (1946)

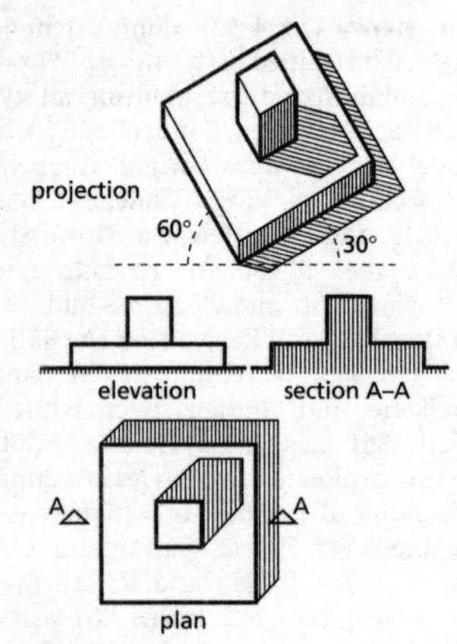

axonometric projection

Aylmer, John (*c*.1471–1548). English master-mason. A partner of John *Vertue, he contracted in 1506 to build the *vault of St George's *Chapel, Windsor, Berkshire, including flying *buttresses, cresting, etc. He also built the Savoy Hospital, London (1512–19), and carried out various works at the Tower of London.

Harvey (1987)

Aymonino, Carlo (1926–). Rome-born architect. He edited the architectural journal *Casabella-Continuità* (1959–64), but he is perhaps best known for his many writings on typologies, cities, and urbanism. He designed the Monte Amiata housing development, Gallaratese, Milan (built 1967–73), in collaboration with several other architects (including Aldo *Rossi): blocks of apartments (mostly seven storeys high) were arranged geometrically around a vast space. Aymonino was involved in several city-centre planning schemes, including those at Bologna and Turin (both 1962), Reggio Emilia (with Constantino Dardi, 1971), and Florence (with Aldo Rossi, 1978).

Aymonino (1971, 1975, 1975*a*); Conforti (1980); Emanuel (1994)

Azéma, Léon (1888–1978). French architect. With Louis-Hippolyte Boileau (1878–1948) and Jacques Carlu (1890–1976) he designed the Palais de Chaillot, Paris (completed 1937), in a monumental stripped Classical style. Among other works the forbidding Ossuary at Douaumont (1923–7), by Azéma and others, containing the bones of unidentifiable dead at Verdun in the 1914–18 war, and his solo design for the Church of St-Antoine de Padoue, Paris (1933–6), may be cited.

Curl (1993); Placzek (1982)

Aztec architecture. A people who settled on the island of Texcoco *c*.1325, the Aztecs soon came to dominate Meso-America in what is now Mexico. The previously dominant people, the Toltecs, built storeyed *pyramids adorned with fearsome sculpture, and the Aztecs seem to have adopted their architecture, adding the double pyramid to the repertoire of building types. Their capital, Tenochtitlán (now Mexico City), and the city of Cholula were adorned with pyramids and temples. The surviving pyramid at Tenayuca (*c*.1450–1500) has a steep stair on one side, and rows of sculptured serpent-heads on the base on the three other sides. An early C16 pyramid at El Tepozteco and the rock-cut structures at Malinalco of the same period represent the chief architectural remains. Aztec architecture inspired the *Art Deco style.

Cruickshank (1996); Gendrop and Heyden (1986); Kubler (1984)

azulejo. Glazed earthenware lustrous *tile, brightly coloured and ornamented with geometrical and floral patterns, found in *alicatado work in the Iberian Peninsula and Latin America. The term is also applied to Dutch or Delft glazed tiles in which the predominant colour is blue.

Azuma, Takamitsu (1933–). Japanese architect, who worked in Junzo *Sakakura's office before becoming a founder-member of *Architext in 1971. He evolved a concept of 'oppositional harmonies' in architecture by deliberately placing disparate elements together and even emphasizing them in order to create tension. His own house in Tokyo

(1967) is a tall *concrete tower set among traditionally built single-storey houses. Other works include the Satsuki Kindergarten in Osaka (1969–73), many individual private houses, and the K Flat housing development, Mejiro, Tokyo (with **Rie Azuma**, his daughter) (1991–2).

Bognar (1985, 1990–2); Emanuel (1994)

Babb, George Fletcher (1836–1915). American architect. He designed several buildings in New Jersey before forming a partnership with Walter Cook (1846–1916) in New York in 1877: Babb & Cook designed the cast-iron office-building, 55 Broadway, New York (1881—demolished). They were joined by Daniel W. Willard in 1884: as Babb, Cook, & Willard, the firm's most celebrated design was the De Vinne Press Building, Lafayette Street, New York (1885–6), but it was responsible for many other architectural works, mostly in New York.

Schull (1980); Scully (1971)

Babcock, Charles (1829–1913). American architect. He worked with *Upjohn (1853–8), was one of the founding-members of the American Institute of Architects, and later designed a number of buildings for Cornell University, Ithaca, NY, including the *Gothic house for the University's President (1871) and Franklin Hall (1881).

Wodehouse (1976)

Babylonian architecture. Mesopotamian architecture *c.*4000–1250 BC. Early inhabitants of the region were the Sumerians, who, as early as the fourth millennium, had evolved a sophisticated architecture using brick, and who set the architectural agenda, virtually until *Hellenistic times. They built arches with *voussoirs and *vaults, and used cedar-wood in great quantities. In important buildings, walls were decorated with coloured *terracotta cones placed in geometrical patterns, while other characteristic elements were walls with slightly projecting decorative *buttresses, vertical channelling, and stepped or triangular *battlements. Staged towers, known as *ziggurats, and resembling a pile of diminishing square platforms, each stage smaller than that below, were associated with temples: an impressive example was the enormous ziggurat at Ur (C22 BC), with huge staircases giving access to the sanctuary on top. The main characteristics of Babylonian architecture were absorbed by the *Assyrians near the end of the second millennium BC.

Cruickshank (1996); Lloyd and Müller (1986)

Bacchic ornament. Associated with Bacchus, Roman deity of wine and fertility, among whose *attributes are asses, grapevines, laurels, panthers, rams, serpents, and tigers, it was found in Antiquity, and from *Renaissance times was used when associations with sensual pleasure were desired. It was regarded as the opposite of *Apolline decoration, and was widely used in *Neoclassical design.

Lewis and Darley (1986)

Bachelier, Nicolas (d. 1556). French architect, born in Arras, he was a protagonist of *Renaissance design. He designed the Hôtel de Bagis, Toulouse (1538–46), and the *châteaux at Pibrac (*c.*1540), Castelnau d'Estrèfons (1546), and Lasserre-les-Montastruc (1555–6).

Blunt (1982); Graillot (1914); Hautecœur (1943–57)

bacino (*pl.* **bacini**). Coloured glazed earthenware plates and roundels set into the exterior walls of Italian *Romanesque buildings, mostly churches.

back. 1. *Principal rafter in a roof. **2.** Top or visible part of e.g. a slate. **3.** Rear part of something, or its hidden side.

Backsteingotik. Simplified medieval *Gothic architecture constructed of brick, as in the town-halls of Lübeck or Toruń, or in the vast brick churches of Northern Germany and Poland.

Backström, Sven Mauritz (1903–92). Swedish architect. Entered into partnership with Leif Axel Reinius (1907–   ), designing some of the most influential buildings of the 1940s, when Sweden's relative isolation encouraged the evolution of an indigenous style using natural materials, traditional roof-forms, and much timber. The firm invented the Y-shaped housing block with the three arms joined to a central circulation-core, as at Gröndal, Stockholm (1943–5), and planned the suburb of Vällingby (1956–7), among many other projects.

Emanuel (1980)

Bacon, Edmund Norwood (1910–). Born in Philadelphia, USA, he contributed to architecture and town-planning, especially in his native city, and was the author of numerous works on planning.

Bacon (1974)

Bacon, Henry (1866–1924). Illinois-born American architect, much influenced by his elder brother, **Francis Henry Bacon** (1856–1940), architect, who had been involved in archaeological expeditions in Asia Minor in the 1880s. In 1889 Henry Bacon himself travelled in Greece and Asia Minor, before returning to the prestigious firm of *McKim, Mead, & White, where he contributed to the designs of Rhode Island State House (1891–1903), the World's Columbian Exposition and the Brooklyn Museum (both 1893), and the J. P. Morgan Library (1902–6). In 1897 he set up his own practice, producing buildings of scholarly refinement and exquisite detail, including a large number of monuments and *mausolea. His expertise in this field led to the commission to design the Lincoln Memorial in Washington, DC (1911–22), which terminates the axis of the Mall at the Potomac River: it is one of the finest examples of Neoclassical *Greek Revival architecture in the world.

Hitchcock (1977); Kidney (1974); Scully (1988)

Badger, Daniel D. (1806–84). American designer who established in New York one of the USA's largest iron-foundries, and manufactured cast-iron kits-of-parts for entire buildings at his Architectural Iron Works, including the Haughwout Store, Broadway, New York (1856).

Gayle and Gillon (1974); Handlin (1985)

Badovici, Jean (1893–1956). Romanian architect and critic, who edited *L'Architecture Vivante* (1923–5), the de luxe Paris journal that promoted Modern architecture and design. He built two houses for himself, at Vézelay (1924) and near the Pont de Sèvres, Paris (1934), and collaborated with Eileen *Gray on 'E-1027', the *Maison en Bord de Mer*, a house at Roquebrune-Cap-Martin in the South of France (1926–9) which is a classic Modern building of the period (it filled a whole issue of *L'Architecture Vivante*). Badovici was a friend of Le *Corbusier (who painted murals in the Roquebrune-Cap-Martin house in 1929), and was one of the most influential writers of the *Modern Movement.

Badovici (1923, 1925, 1926–30, 1931, 1937); Badovici (ed.) (1975); Badovici and Gray (1929)

baffle-entry. *See* entry.

bagnet, bagnette. *See* baguet.

bague. *See* baguet.

baguet, baguette, *also* **bagnet, bagnette. 1.** Small convex moulding with a semicircular *section, similar to a *bead or an *astragal, called a *chaplet* when ornamented. **2.** Frame ornamented with a bead-moulding.

Bähr, Georg (1666–1738). One of the most gifted architects of the *Baroque in Germany, he was born in Fürstenwalde, Saxony, and trained as a carpenter, becoming *Ratszimmermeister* (Master Carpenter) to the City of Dresden in 1705. He was responsible for the *Pfarrkirche* (Parish Church) at Loschwitz, near Dresden (1705–8), which was a variation of the *Baroque ellipse on plan (being a distorted octagon), the *Dreifaltigkeitskirche* (Church of the Holy Trinity) at Schmiedeberg, south of Dresden (1713–16), and the *Dorfkirche* (Village Church) at Forchheim, near Chemnitz (1719–26), both of which are Greek crosses on plan. His reputation rests on his greatest work, the *Frauenkirche* (Church of Our Lady), Dresden (1722–43), the finest centrally planned Protestant church ever conceived. On the strength of that one building (one of the most grievous losses of the bombing of Dresden in 1944–5—under reconstruction from 1996), Bähr must be considered a master of the Baroque style, fully in control of complex geometries and structure, who gave Dresden a great domed church that rose majestically by the banks of the Elbe. The plan was, in essence, circular, but set inside a square, with the *chancel within part of an ellipse, and with staircases, capped with elegant turrets, placed diagonally in relation to the square four corners. Eight massive *piers supported the very high stone-vaulted dome with its huge lantern, and, between those piers, three tiers of *galleries were fitted, the fronts of the lowest tier being glazed, and known as *Bettstübchen* (Little Bedrooms), *Hoflogen* (Court Boxes), or *Ranglogen* (Gallery Boxes). The altar was given prominence by being raised on a platform, while the organ-pipes rose up behind it, increasing the theatrical effects of a stunning interior. This building, capable of containing a congregation of almost 4,000, was the epitome of the Protestant *auditory church.

Hempel (1965); Landale-Drummond (1934); Popp (1924); Sponsel (1893)

bailey. 1. External wall or defences surrounding a *keep or *motte of a medieval castle. **2.** Area between the circuits of walls or defences of a castle, also called a *ward*, or any court within the walls, hence *outer bailey* or *inner bailey*.

Baillargé (*or* Baillairgé) Family. Dynasty of French-Canadian architects active in Quebec for two centuries. **Jean** (1726–1805) and **François** (1759–1830) were responsible for the first phases of the reconstruction of the Cathedral of Notre-Dame, Quebec (1768–1818), while **Thomas** (1791–1859) designed the severe front (1843). Thomas, as Diocesan Architect of Quebec, was also responsible for the elegant interior of the Church of St-François-de-Sales, Île d'Orléans (1835–44), and made alterations to the *façade of the Church of Ste-Famille, Île d'Orléans (begun 1743), including the central *clocher at the gable-peak of 1843. Among his other churches are Sainte-Croix de Lotbinière (1835) and Saint-François-Xavier (1835–49) at Saint-François-du-Lac, Sainte-Geneviève at Pierrefonds (1837–44), and Saint-Joseph at Lauzon (1830–2).

Charles-Philippe-Ferdinand (1826–1906), architect, civil engineer, and surveyor, was influenced by the publications of Minard *Lafever, as demonstrated in his designs for the *Greek Revival Music Hall, Quebec (1851–3). He designed many buildings, including the Church of Saint-Romuald, Quebec (1854–6), and the New Quebec Prison (1860–3). He had a fine architectural library and published many articles.

Baillairgé (1899, 1900, 1979); Cameron (1989); Kalman (1994); Noppen, Paulette, and Tremblay (1979)

Baillie Scott, Mackay Hugh (1865–1945). *See* Scott.

Bailly, Antoine-Nicolas-Louis (1810–92). French architect, a pupil of *Debret and *Duban, he specialized in the French *Renaissance Revival. He was appointed by *Haussmann to design the Tribunal de Commerce, Paris (1858–64), based on the Town Hall in Brescia, and containing a sumptuous vaulted staircase of considerable grandeur. His *Mairie* of the fourth *arrondissement* (1862–7) is probably his best work, owing much to C17 French precedent.

Hautecœur (1957); Middleton and Watkin (1987)

Baird, John (1798–1859). Scots architect, whose Glasgow practice was second only in importance to that of David *Hamilton. He rarely strayed from a sedate *Classicism in his work, although there were forays into *Jacobethan (Cairnhill House, Airdrie, 1841) and *Tudor Revival (Urie House, Fetteresso, Kincardineshire, 1855). He is remembered today primarily for his experiments with iron construction, including the cast-iron hammer-beam roof of the Argyle Arcade, Glasgow (1827–8), and the cast-iron fronted Gardner's Warehouse, 36 Jamaica Street, Glasgow (1855–6). Baird was assisted by James Thomson (1835–1905), who became his partner, and Alexander 'Greek' *Thomson worked in the office 1836–49.

Colvin (1995); Gomme and Walker (1987)

Bakema, Jakob Berend (1914–81). Groningen-born Dutch architect, who worked under van *Eesteren and for the municipality of Rotterdam before setting up a partnership with J. H. van den Broek (1898–1978) in 1948. In 1947 Bakema had joined *CIAM, and in 1963 *Team X (10), while in 1959–64 he was joint Editor of *Forum* (which promoted the cause of *Structuralism). Both partners favoured the ideals of *Modernism and of De *Stijl, attacking the conservative craft-orientated beliefs of the Delft School. Their Lijnbaan Centre in Rotterdam (1949–54) was a precedent for many shopping 'malls', while their Civic Centre at Marl in Germany of 1958–62 (four tower-blocks linked by lower slab-blocks) is representative of a type that became widely influential over the following decades. The partnership's Town Hall at Terneuzen (1968) and the Psychiatric Hospital in Middelharnis (1973–4) both have aspects reminiscent of *Constructivism. The firm had a great influence on developments in Britain and

Germany, but Bakema's assertion that architecture is the three-dimensional expression of human behaviour savours of the cliché, while his campaigns to jettison craft traditions and any historical references arguably have done damage.

Gubitosi and Izzo (1976); Joedicke (1963*a*, 1976)

Baker, Sir Herbert (1862–1946). Kent-born architect who worked for Ernest *George and Harold *Peto (1882–7) before opening his own office and then emigrating to Cape Colony, South Africa. He quickly became a protégé of Cecil John Rhodes (1853–1902) and Lord Milner (1854–1925), under whose aegis he began to create a distinctive architecture for British South Africa, drawing together English *vernacular elements, aspects of the *Arts-and-Crafts movement, Dutch *Colonial architecture, *Baroque architecture of the *Wren Revival, and much else. He adapted his eclectic style for later buildings in Rhodesia, Kenya, India, and England. For Rhodes he built the house known as Groote Schuur, Rondebosch (1893–8), in which Dutch-Colonial elements were well to the fore, followed by Government Buildings in Bloemfontein, and the masterly Union Buildings, Pretoria (1909–13), with twin *cupolas derived from Wren's work at Greenwich. Baker was then appointed joint architect (with *Lutyens) for the design of the Imperial Capital of New Delhi, and designed (from 1913) the north and south Secretariat Blocks as well as the circular Legislative Building. At New Delhi he introduced Indian architectural features such as *chattris, and successfully combined Western and Eastern elements. Baker set up an office in London in 1912, and in 1917 he was appointed Principal Architect to the Imperial War Graves Commission, in which capacity he encouraged design of the highest calibre. Thereafter, he was responsible for some of the most grandiose developments in London, including the enormous Bank of England works (1921–39) which destroyed *Soane's building (apart from the *screen-wall), India House (1925), and South Africa House (1930–5) in Trafalgar Square. These buildings cannot really be described as wholly successful, for Baker seems to have been happier using *Classicism with a strong dose of *Arts-and-Crafts influence: in this respect his beautifully articulated war-memorial cloister at Winchester College, Hampshire (1922–5), demonstrates a sensitivity not so apparent in his grander buildings.

Baker (1934, 1944); Gray (1985); Greig (1970); Irving (1981); Stamp (1977)

balanced sash. Window-frame with two vertically sliding *sashes hung on chains or cords draped over pulleys in the boxed frame and fixed at the other end to weights which balance the sashes and facilitate easy and smooth movement.

balanced winder. *Dancing step* or *winder* of a curving section or turn of a *stair, with the narrowest parts of the wedge-shaped treads the same size as the treads of a straight flight in the same stair.

Balat, Alphonse-Hubert-François (1818–95). Belgian architect, consultant to King Leopold II (1865–1909) from 1851, he was much influenced by the theories of *Viollet-le-Duc in his search for a rational approach to design and for ever-increasing simplicity, and drew on the immense vocabulary of *Classicism while also experimenting with contemporary advances in engineering and constructional techniques, which influenced his pupil *Horta and other exponents of *Art Nouveau in Belgium. His best-known works are the Palais des Beaux-Arts (1870s), various galleries, conservatories, and pavilions at the Royal Palace of Laeken (1882–5), and the Grand Stair, State Rooms, and main elevations of the Royal Palace (1885–90), all in Brussels.

Placzek (1982); Tschudi-Madsen (1967)

balcon. 1. Curved row of *theatre-seats projecting beyond a stack of *boxes above the pit. **2.** Boxes situated on the proscenium of a theatre.

balcone. Large important group of windows forming an architectural feature.

balconet, balconette. 1. False *balcony, or railing at the outer plane of a window-opening reaching to the floor, and having, when the window is open, the appearance of a balcony. Common in France, Spain, and Italy. **2.** Ornamental railing on a window-*cill to prevent flower-pots from falling, called *vignette.

balcony. 1. Platform or open *gallery built out from the *naked of a wall, supported on *brackets, *consoles, *corbels, or columns, or *cantilevered. Normally constructed in front of windows or other apertures, it is unroofed, with a balustrade, parapet, or railing around the platform, is capable of bearing the weight of one or more persons, and is usually slightly below the floor-level within the building. **2.** Projecting gallery with seats in an *auditorium at a higher level than the stalls.

baldachin, baldachino, baldacchino, baldaquin. Permanent *canopy, especially over an altar, throne, or tomb, usually supported on columns. *Compare* **ciborium**.

Baldessari, Luciano (1896–1982). Rovereto-born Italian architect, who, with Luigi *Figini and Gino Pollini, designed the Rationalist De Angeli Building in Milan (1929–32). With Gio *Ponti he built the Cima Chocolate Factory in Milan (1932–3). He worked on many exhibition-buildings, notably pavilions for the Milan Trade Fair (1933, 1951, 1952, 1953, and 1954). Baldessari was an exponent of *Rationalism, who retreated from *Functionalism early in his career. He built an apartment-block in the Hansa Quarter, Berlin (1957–8), and the Fratelli Fontana Technical Institute, Rovereto (1961–73).

Lampugnani (1988); Veronesi (1957)

bale. Type of tomb found in the Cotswolds in England, essentially an *altar-tomb supporting a stone half-cylinder resembling a woollen bale.

balection. *See* bolection.

balistraria *or* **ballistraria** (*pl.* **balistrariae**). **1.** Arbalestina, arbalisteria, arrow-loop, loophole, or similar aperture, frequently cruciform, in a medieval wall through which bowmen (*arbalesters*) fired arrows or bolts. **2.** Store-room for *arbalests* (crossbows) or similar weapons.

balistraria

balk, baulk. 1. Any large piece of squared timber. **2.** *Lintel or summer-beam. **3.** Upper roof-*tie, or *balk-tie*, between rafters. **4.** Earthen ridge dividing areas of land.

ball-flower. Characteristic ornament of the *Second Pointed style of *Gothic (C14), resembling a small ball, just visible, enclosed within a broken ball with a trefoil or quatrefoil opening, normally placed at regular intervals in a continuous hollow moulding.

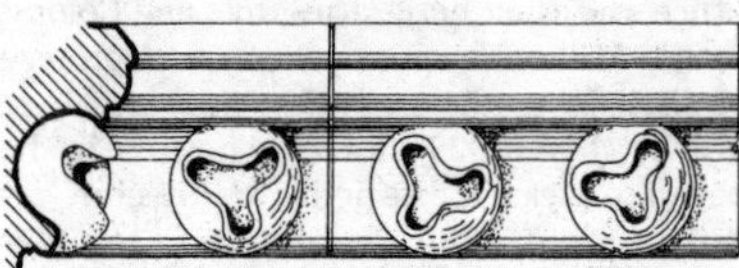

ball-flower. From a string-course, Church of St Nicholas, Kiddington, Oxfordshire. (*After Parker*)

balloon. 1. Large ball, *balloon*, globe, or sphere placed above a column or *pier as a termination. **2.** Globe under a cross on a church *spire or *dome. **3.** System of *timber-framed construction common in Scandinavia and the USA in which the corner *posts and *studs are continuous in one piece from *cill or *sole-plate to roof-plate, the intermediate floor-joists being secured to them without mortises and tenons.

Ballu, Théodore (1817–85). Parisian architect, renowned for the early *Renaissance-style La Trinité Church (1861–7) near the Gare St-Lazare in Paris. Ballu completed *Gau's Ste-Clotilde (1846–57), the first *Gothic Revival church in Paris; restored the Tour St-Jacques de la Boucherie (1854–8); and designed the *Flamboyant Revival free-standing tower, and restored the rest of the fabric of St-Germain l'Auxerrois, with its *lantern-top, beside *Hittorff's Mairie du Ier (1858–63). He also built the Hôtel de Ville, Paris (1874–82).

Ballu (1868); Delaborde (1887); Hautecœur (1957); Sédille (1886)

Baltard, Louis-Pierre (1764–1846). French architect, academic, and theorist. He became Professor at the École Polytechnique, Paris, in 1796, and later helped to prepare many of the plates for the Napoleonic *Description de l'Égypte*, the major source-book of the *Egyptian Revival. He designed the Palais de Justice in Lyons, with its *façade composed of a long line of twenty-four huge *Corinthian columns (1835–41) and the Salle des Pas

Perdus consisting of a series of low-domed spaces: the design is typical of the type of official architecture promoted by *Quatremère de Quincy, and based on Roman Antiquity. He was also responsible for the prison of the Quartier Perrache (1830), the artillery arsenal (1840–6), and other important buildings in Lyons. He published several books, including *Recueil des Monuments Antiques* (1801).

Baltard (1818, 1875); Egbert (1980); Hautecœur (1952–5); Kaufmann (1955); Middleton and Watkin (1987); Sturgis *et al.* (1901–2)

Baltard, Victor (1805–74). French architect and academic, the son of L.-P. *Baltard. As City Architect of Paris, he redecorated and rebuilt many Parisian churches, but his chief works were the iron-and-glass Halles Centrales, Paris (1852–9—demolished)—with Félix-Emmanuel Callet (1792–1854)—and the remarkable Church of St-Augustin (1860–71)—with cast-iron columns inside and a French *Renaissance exterior. He also added the Chapelle des Catéchismes (1853) to *Chalgrin's great Church of St-Philippe-du-Roule (1768–84). He published *Villa Médicis à Rome* (1847) and, with Callet, *Monographie des halles centrales de Paris* (1863 and 1873).

Baltard and Callet (1863); Benevolo (1971); Deconchy (1875); Garnier (1874); Middleton and Watkin (1987)

balteus. **1.** Strap-like element around the *baluster-side, *cushion, coussinet, or *volute of the *Ionic *capital: it refers both to the central strap visible at the side of the capital and to those seeming to join the volutes at the ends of the cushion visible on the fronts of the volutes as well. **2.** *Praecentio*, wide step, or landing occurring at every eighth seat in an *Antique *theatre or *amphitheatre, affording a passage for spectators so that those seated would not be disturbed.

baluster. Upright support in a *balustrade: it may be a square, circular, turned, or ornamented bar or rod, very small in thickness (as in a stair balustrade); it can be a miniature column; or it can be the bellied, bulbed type of *colonnette (*columella*), with base, shaft, and capital, circular, polygonal, or square on plan, with elaborate profiles, in some cases given distinctive features depending on which *Order is used elsewhere. The thickest part of a baluster is called the *belly*, and the thin part the *sleeve*. *Banister* is sometimes used instead of *baluster*, while *banisters* signifies a balustrade.

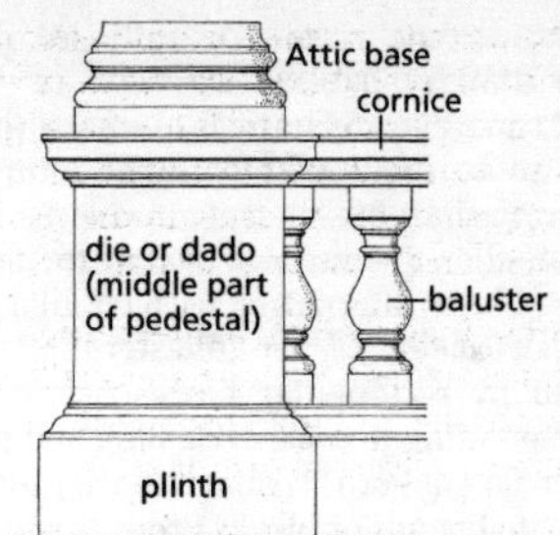

baluster. Balustrade terminating in a pedestal supporting a column.

baluster-shaft. Short, thick *colonnette with pronounced *entasis between openings (usually in towers) in *Anglo-Saxon architecture: it is also the *baluster-column* in Italian *campanili.

baluster-side. Form like a rolled-up mattress, like a *baluster laid on its side, also known as a *bolster, *cushion, *pulvin, or pulvinus, joining the *volutes of an *Ionic *capital.

balustrade. **1.** Row of *balusters supporting a hand-rail of a stair. **2.** Series of balusters between *pedestals, *plinths, and *copings or *cornices, forming a type of parapet.

balustrade Order. Order of *balustrade columns, actually miniature versions from the Classical *Orders.

balustrata. A *chancel-*screen.

balustrum. Altar-rail, *cancelli, or *chancel-*screen. The last is more usually termed *balustrata, while *balustrum* usually refers to the low *balustrade or wall defining a *choir, as in San Clemente, Rome.

band. **1.** Flat raised horizontal strip on a *façade, occasionally ornamented, sometimes coinciding with *cills or floor-levels, also called a *band-course*, *band-moulding*, *belt-course*, or *string-course*. The term can therefore be applied to the *fasciae on an *architrave, and sometimes (though rarely) to a *fillet, *list, or *taenia. In Classical *Orders *dentils and *modillions project from such bands called *dentil-* or *modillion-bands*. **2.** Plain *block interrupting an architectural element, such as a column. In this sense, *banded* is used to describe the condition. Examples are *banded architrave* (one with projecting blocks placed at regular intervals between which the architrave is visible, as in a *Gibbs surround);

banded, *blocked*, *ringed*, or *rusticated column* (with shaft interrupted by plain or *rusticated square or cylindrical blocks, although some authorities prefer to use *banded* to mean a column-shaft made up of alternating larger and smaller drums, and *blocked* to indicate square blocks alternating with circular shaft-drums); *banded pilaster* (pilaster-shaft interrupted by rectangular blocks at intervals, corresponding to *banded columns*); and *banded rustication* (smooth *ashlar alternating with rusticated bands or blocks projecting beyond the *naked of the wall). **3.** *Bond*, in Scots, hence *inband* (header) and *outband* (stretcher or *quoin with long side on face and short on reveals).

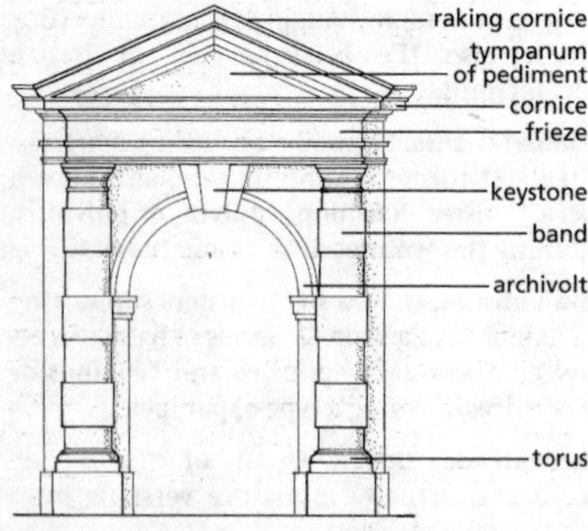

band. Gateway with banded Tuscan columns.

banded. *See* band.

banded impost. When the *section of a medieval *pier is identical to that of the arch above, the horizontal mouldings, etc., at the springing of the arch, form a *banded impost*.

bandelet. 1. Small flat plain moulding, greater than a *fillet and smaller than a *band or *fascia, such as the taenia of the *Doric *Order. **2.** *Annulet. **3.** *Band of a shaft.

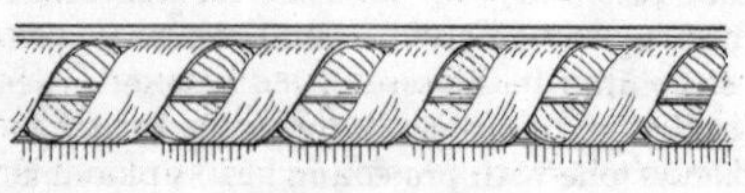

banderol. Also called *ribbon-moulding.*

banderol, banderole, bannerol. 1. Sculptured *band, often inscribed, especially resembling a ribbon or continuous spiral *scroll. **2.** Enriched string-course.

band of a shaft. *Annulets, *bandelets, bandlets, or *shaft-rings around *colonnettes and slender *shafts in *Gothic architecture, at the junctions of *monolithic lengths, often tying the shafts to the *pier behind, as in a *cluster arrangement.

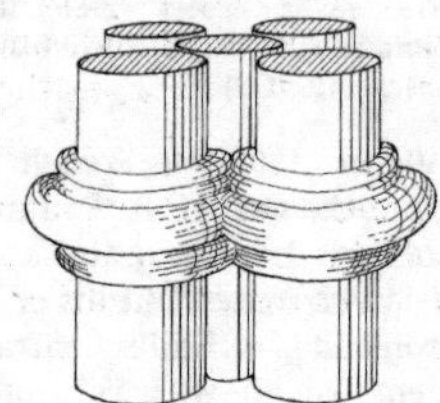

band of a shaft

band-work. Type of *arabesque, also occurring in *Rococo C-scroll frames and in *parterre gardens.

Banfi, Gianluigi (1910–45). *See* BBPR.

Banham, Peter Reyner (1922–88). British architectural critic, historian, and polemicist. He was a promoter and chronicler of New *Brutalism and the *Machine Aesthetic in *Architectural Review* and elsewhere, and he quickly became recognized as an influential observer of contemporary architecture and design. His *Theory and Design in the First Machine Age* (1960) was a reassessment of the history of the *Modern Movement: it was followed by *The New Brutalism* (1966), *The Architecture of the Well-Tempered Environment* (1969—in which he described architecture determined by its mechanical services), *Los Angeles: The Architecture of Four Ecologies* (1971), *Age of the Masters* (1975), and *Megastructure* (1976). He left the Bartlett School of Architecture, University College London (where he had a Personal Chair), in 1976 to take up academic posts in the USA, after which he published *Scenes in America Deserta* (1982) and enthusiastic interpretations of American life and urban developments. He was a prolific writer contributing to *New Society* and many other journals, and was vitriolic about the retreat from the Modern Movement known as *Neo-Liberty in Italy, which he described as 'infantile regression'. Believing that the design of a machine, such as a refrigerator, could be subjected to the same processes of research and analysis as any building, or painting, he combined meticulous attention to source-material (learned from his mentor *Pevsner) with his ability to look at problems from new positions.

Architectural Design, 30/9 (1960), 375–6; *Architectural Review*, 125/747 (April 1959), 231–5, and 126/754 (Dec. 1959), 341–4; Banham (1960, 1966, 1971, 1975, 1976); *DNB* (1996)

banister. *See* baluster.

banner. Ornament in the form of a pole with flag, found on metal railings, and, with a counter-balance, used as a weather-vane or *banneret*.

banquet, banquette. **1.** Narrow footpath beside an *aqueduct or road. **2.** Raised standing-place or platform behind a rampart. **3.** Window-seat.

baptistery, baptistry, baptisterium. Building or part of a church containing the *font used for the Sacrament of Baptism, modelled on the cold bath, or *baptisterium*, of a Roman *frigidarium* in a *therma, often consisting of a sunken circular pool in a circular building. Baptisteries such as those in Parma and Pisa were detached buildings, one polygonal and the other circular, and the form was recalled in some apsidal baptisteries physically joined to churches.

bar. **1.** Single piece of wood or metal, of any shape in *section, placed horizontally, like the rail of a gate, to form an obstruction, or *latch-bar* dropped into a mortise behind a door or shutter to fasten it shut. **2.** Horizontal timber *ledge* fixed to the back of a *barred* or ledged door to which the door-finish and hinges are fixed. **3.** Gateway or gatehouse (such as the Micklegate, York), a barrier, or a toll-gate (toll-bar) on a highway. **4.** Enclosure or barrier in a court of justice marking off the precinct of a judge's seat, at which prisoners are stationed for arraignment, trial, and sentence, or a particular court of law, or a barrier separating the seats of the benchers or readers from the rest of a hall, to which students were 'called' from the body of the hall (hence barristers 'called to the bar'). **5.** Barrier or counter over which drink (or food) is served in an inn, hotel, etc., or the room in which it is installed. **6.** Pieces of timber forming the horizontal and vertical glazed divisions of a *sash in a window, called *bar of a sash*, *glazing-*, *sash-*, or *window-bar*. The upright at the junction of two planes of a canted *bay-window is called the *angle-bar*. **7.** Flowing patterns in *Gothic *tracery, all the stonework having moulded *sections the same as the *mullions from which they rise, is *bar-tracery*, because the patterns are similar to those capable of being formed using wrought-iron bars.

Barabino, Carlo Francesco (1768–1835). Italian *Neoclassical architect, who became City Architect of Genoa in 1818. His Teatro Carlo Felice, Genoa (1825–32), is an important early example of the Greek *Doric Revival in Italy. He designed several *temple-fronts (Church of the Rosary (1824), Church of San Siro (1820–1), and Santissima Annunziata (1830–43), all in Genoa), and was responsible for the Cimitero di Staglieno, Genoa, projected before 1825, with its competent *Pantheon-like *chapel (with Greek Doric *portico), erected under the direction of Giovanni Antonio Resasco (1799–1872) in 1844–61. The cemetery is one of the most brilliantly sited in Europe, and its conception was entirely Barabino's.

Curl (1993); Meeks (1966); Mezzanotte (1966); de Negri (1977)

barbacan, barbican. **1.** Double fortified tower erected over a gate or a bridge, often very strong and high, and serving as a watch-tower. **2.** Advanced outwork or structure flanking the approach to a fortified gateway. **3.** *Balistraria, in the sense of a loophole.

Barbet, Jean (1591–*c*.1650). French architect who worked for Cardinal Richelieu (1585–1642). His *Livre d'Architecture d'Autels et de Cheminées* (1632) illustrated altar- and chimney-pieces, many of them in an elaborate *Mannerist style. Inigo *Jones was influenced by Barbet's designs, some of which reappeared in Robert Pricke's *The Architects Store-House* (1672).

Jervis (1984); Lewis and Darley (1986)

Barbon, Nicholas (*c*.1638–98). Born in London, he not only became one of the most important developers there after the Great Fire (1666), but instituted fire insurance. He built houses at Red Lion Fields, near Gray's Inn, and in the 1690s carried out improvements at Chancery Lane and Lincoln's Inn. It is unclear whether or not he was his own architect, but his housing developments were of great significance, and set the pattern for London *terrace-housing for years to come. He was involved in the rebuilding of the Temple after it was destroyed by fire in 1678/9, with which Roger *North was concerned in an architectural capacity, but Barbon's designs for the *cloisters in Pump Court, Middle Temple (1679), were rejected in favour of a 'model' prepared by *Wren.

Barbon (1976); Colvin (1995); *DNB* (1917); Summerson (1988)

Barelli, Agostino (1627–79). Bologna-born Italian architect, who designed the Theatine Church of San Bartolomeo there (1653), but whose main importance is that he introduced the Italian *Baroque style to Bavaria, notably with his designs for the *Theatinerkirche* (Church of the Theatines) of St Kajetan, Munich (1663–90), modelled on Sant'Andrea della Valle in Rome, the mother-church of the Theatines. The Munich church was completed by Enrico *Zuccalli. Barelli was also responsible for the central block with the high roof at Schloss Nymphenburg, Munich (from 1663), altered by *Effner and Cuvilliés.

Bourke (1962); Lieb (1988); Powell (1959)

barge. **1.** Coping on a *gable, so a barge-stone is one of the stones forming the raked top of a gable. **2.** Projecting ledge or drip at the base of a chimney following the line of the pitched roof, also called a *water-table.

barge-board. Also called *berge-*, *gable-*, *parge-*, or *verge-board*, an inclined board (often decorated) above a *gable under the *barge-course and covering the *barge-couples or used instead of the last.

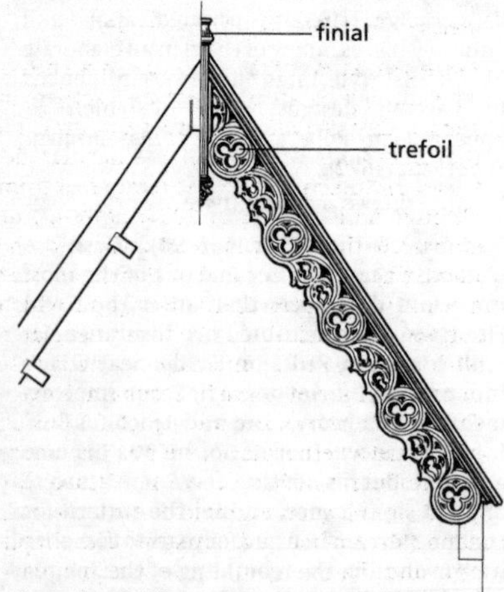

barge-board *(After A. W. N. Pugin)*

barge-couple. Rafters under the *barge-course serving as grounds for the *barge-boards and to which the *soffits are fixed, or simply supporting the roof over the *gable if there are no barge-boards.

barge-course. **1.** Part of a tiled roof projecting beyond the *barge-boards, or, if the latter are omitted, projecting over the *gable and sealed with mortar or parging, called a *parged *verge. **2.** *Coping on a gable roof of tumbled brickwork.

barley-sugar. Column or *colonnette twisted like a corkscrew, or a *spiral column.

Barlow, William Henry (1812–1902). Woolwich-born English civil-engineer, who, as consulting engineer to the Midland Railway, was responsible (with R. M. *Ordish) for the design of the iron-and-glass terminus-shed at St Pancras, London (1864–8), an immense pointed vault that was widely copied. He was an advocate of the use of steel in structures, published papers on a wide variety of engineering and scientific subjects, and advised on the reconstruction of the Tay Bridge (1882–7) after the disaster of 1879.

DNB (1917)

barn. Building to store agricultural produce, especially grain, to protect it from the weather. Barns of the Middle Ages often had architectural pretensions. Examples include the C13 barn at Great Coxwell, Berkshire, and the (probably) C12 barley-barn at Cressing Temple, Essex, both with timber *nave-and-*aisle interiors.

Barnes, Edward Larrabee (1915–). Chicago-born architect who studied under *Gropius and *Breuer at Harvard, later opening an office in New York. He employed bold geometries, evoking forms used by Le *Corbusier, but, influenced by *vernacular architecture, his designs often respond with sensitivity to their surroundings. Indeed, Barnes was one of the first architects of the *Modernist tendency to become a proponent of *contextual design. His Walker Art Center in Minneapolis, Minn. (1971–4), employs the simplest of forms, and in 1988 Barnes designed an urban sculpture-garden to enhance it. His museum interiors are treated as simply as possible, but the exteriors are given a civic presence, as at the Dallas Museum of Art (1983–4). Later work of his office became more *Historicist, as with the Allen Library at the University of Washington in Seattle (1991), with *Neo-Gothic *gables and *finials, and the Judicial Office Building, Washington, DC, which had Neoclassical and *Beaux-Arts influences.

Diamonstein (1980, 1985); Emanuel (1994); van Vynckt (1993)

Barnet, James J. (1827–1904). Scots-born Australian architect. He was Colonial Architect for New South Wales (1862–90), and produced numerous competent buildings, including the Venice-inspired General Post Office, Sydney (1865–74); the Lands Department, Sydney (1876–90), a *palazzo-like *Renaissance Revival building; the Court House and Government Buildings, Bathurst (1878–80), a charming symmetrical composition featuring *verandahs; and the arcaded Court House, Goulburn (1887). He also designed the *Gothic railway-station associated with Rookwood Cemetery, Sydney (1868), for funerals by train.

Cruickshank (1996); Curl (1993)

Barnsley, Ernest Arthur (1863–1926). Birmingham-born English architect, who was articled to *Sedding, later entering into partnership with Ernest *Gimson. He designed a number of buildings in the *Arts-and-Crafts *vernacular manner (some with his brother, S. H. *Barnsley, including The Leasowes, Sapperton, Gloucestershire). His largest building was Rodmarton Manor, near Cirencester (1912–26), completed by Norman Jewson and held by some to be the last great country-house built in England.

Gray (1985)

Barnsley, Sidney Howard (1865–1926). Birmingham-born English architect, educated at the Royal Academy Schools, articled to R. Norman *Shaw, he travelled in Greece with Robert Schultz *Weir, with whom he collaborated on *Byzantine Architecture in Greece* (1901). His finest work is the Church of St Sophia, Lower Kingswood, Surrey (1891), in a free *Byzantine style, which includes several *Antique fragments. Barnsley joined his brother and *Gimson when they moved to the Cotswolds, and settled at Sapperton where Sidney designed his own cottage. He also designed a number of buildings in an *Arts-and-Crafts *vernacular style.

Gray (1985)

Baronial. *See* Scottish Baronial.

Baroque. Style of C17 and C18 European architecture derived from late-*Renaissance *Mannerism and evolving into *Rococo before *Neoclassicism eclipsed it. Theatrical and exuberant, it employed convex and concave flowing curves in *plan, *elevation, and *section, optical illusions, interpenetrating ellipses in plans that were often extensions of the centralized type, complicated geometries and relationships between volumes of different shapes and sizes, emphatic overstatement, daring colour, exaggerated modelling, and much architectural and symbolic rhetoric. Associated with the Counter-Reformation, the style reached maturity with the C17 works of *Bernini and *Borromini: it achieved heights of inventiveness and beauty in Central Europe, especially Austria, Bavaria, and Bohemia (e.g. the churches of the *Asams and the *Dientzenhofers); the epitome of exotic over-ornamentation in the Iberian peninsula and Latin America; and a chasteness where a strong *Classicism was never far away in France. In England, however, where the Counter-Reformation had little direct architectural impact, the curved, swaying, swelling forms were generally eschewed in favour of emphasized modelling of wall-surfaces, as in the work of *Hawksmoor. There was a European Baroque Revival that was evident in the years immediately before and after 1900. In landscape-design, the Baroque style was associated especially with the huge formal gardens of France, notably at Versailles.

Norberg-Schulz (1986, 1986*a*); Pevsner (1960)

Barragán, Luis (1902–87). Mexican architect who trained as an engineer and settled in Mexico City in 1936. His early work drew on the precedents of Mexican *vernacular domestic architecture, and also on themes from *Islamic architecture. In 1936, however, he embraced the *International style and the ideas of Le *Corbusier, and in 1940 he evolved a personal architectural language in which simple geometrical forms were associated with water, planting, and the imaginative use of colour. His own house in Tacubaya, Mexico City (1947), shows his mixing of Corbusian motifs with vernacular elements. The house and stud-farm at San Cristobal, Mexico City (1967–8), is a good example of his late work, almost dream-like in its imagery. The simplicity and bareness of some designs have inspired *Minimalism.

Ambasz (1976); Arets and van der Bergh (1990); Emanuel (1994); Irizarry (1983); Rispa (1996)

Barre, Eloy de la (1764–1833). French architect. A pupil of J.-D. *Antoine and *Chalgrin, he succeeded A.-T. *Brongniart as architect of the Paris Bourse, and indeed completed that important Neoclassical building. He played a significant part in architectural developments in Paris from about 1810.

Sturgis *et al.* (1901–2)

Barré, Jean-Benoît-Vincent (*c.*1732–1824). French architect. The best of his town-houses (e.g. Hôtel Grimod de la Reynière, Champs-Élysées, Paris (1769)), are known to us only through drawings, but his ingeniously planned Château Montgeoffroy (1771–6), Anjou, survives. He designed some of the *fabriques in the celebrated Parc de Méréville, and built the Château du Marais, Remarde, south of Paris. He designed the Place Royale, Brussels, Belgium, realized by Barnabé Guimard in the 1770s.

Saur (1993)

Barre, William Joseph (1830–67). Irish architect from Newry, Co. Down. He assisted Thomas *Duff until the latter's death, and set up on his own in 1850. He designed several important buildings in Belfast, including the *Italianate Ulster Hall (1859–62—one of the largest music-halls in the British Isles when built), the *Second Pointed Duncairn Presbyterian Church (1860–2), the *polychrome round-arched Moat, Old Holywood Road (1863–4), the High-Victorian Clanwilliam (later Danefort) House (1864), the polychrome Lombardic-Romanesque Methodist Church, University Road (1864–5), the Venetian *palazzo of Bryson House, Bedford Street (1865–7), the *Gothic Revival Albert Memorial clock-tower (1865–9), and the opulent round-arched former Bank at Castle Junction (1864–9), encrusted with lavishly carved detail. His buildings were florid and eclectic, with robust ornament.

Brett (1967); Larmour (1987)

barrel. Describes a form (*barrel-vault*) like a half-cylinder or extruded semicircular arch with a smooth underside. A *barrel-ceiling* is like the underside of a true barrel-vault.

barrow. *Tumulus, or large mound of stones and earth over a burial.

Barry, Sir Charles (1795–1860). London-born English architect and fine draughtsman. In Rome and Florence he studied *Renaissance architecture, and these investigations were to be of great importance in the development of his work. He set up his practice in London, and designed several competent *Gothic Revival churches including St Peter's, Brighton (1824–8), and Holy Trinity, Cloudesley Square, Islington (1826–8), before turning his attention to public buildings, where he would demonstrate his mastery of *Classicism. The Royal Institution of Fine Arts (now the City Art Gallery), Manchester (1824–35), in a Grecian style, was followed by the Travellers' Club, Pall Mall, London (1830–2), a refined essay in the *Quattrocento style, which was to mark the beginning of the *Italianate Renaissance Revival. The Reform Club, next door to the Travellers', followed in 1838–41, a vast *Cinquecento *palazzo, which has a fine glass-roofed *cortile of the greatest sumptuousness, and signals Barry's transition from the use of low relief to robust high relief, culminating in his Bridgewater House, Green Park, London (1846–51). At this time, he tended to experiment with Northern Renaissance architecture, the most outstanding examples being the *Jacobethan Highclere Castle, Hampshire (1842–*c.*1850), and Free Cinquecento Halifax Town Hall (1859–62), the latter completed by his son, E. M. *Barry.

Barry's most celebrated building is the Palace of Westminster and Houses of Parliament (1835–60), the ingenious and complex plan of which is essentially Classical. Barry would have preferred an Italianate design, but was obliged to use the Gothic or *Elizabethan styles by the rules of the commissioning authorities. Indeed, the façade to the river is symmetrical, in a late-*Georgian manner, and could easily have been clothed in Classical garb. The importance of this vast building, however, lies in its *Gothic Revival *Picturesque composition and exquisite *Perpendicular detail inside and out (mostly designed by A. W. N. *Pugin). The choice of Gothic for such a prestigious building gave considerable impetus to the Gothic Revival, while the work earned Barry his Knighthood in 1852.

Barry's rich clients enabled him to produce buildings that were not only exceedingly grand, but opulently detailed, and some of his work tended to over-lavishness after 1840. His was a significant figure in garden-history: he placed sumptuous flower-gardens around the mansions he designed, thus replacing the subtle Georgian concept of the house set within a Picturesque landscape.

Barry (1867); Colvin (1995); Colvin (ed.) (1973); *DNB* (1917); Hitchcock (1954, 1977); Port (1976); Whiffen (1950)

Barry, Edward Middleton (1830–80). Son of **Charles**, Barry worked in the office of T. H. *Wyatt before joining his father's office where he helped prepare drawings for the Palace of Westminster and Houses of Parliament. He was a competent architect, responsible for some opulent Victorian buildings, including the Royal Opera House, Covent Garden (1857–8), the Floral Hall, Covent Garden (1857–8), and Charing Cross Station Hotel, London (1864). He completed the Palace of Westminster and was largely responsible for the eclectic Halifax Town Hall (1859–62). He completed *Basevi's Fitzwilliam Museum, Cambridge (1870–5).

DNB (1917); Dixon and Muthesius (1985); Port (1976); Summerson (1970)

Barthélèmy, Jacques-Eugène (1799–1882). French architect, whose Notre-Dame de Bon-Sécours, near Rouen (1840–7), is one of the most important early examples of C13 *Gothic Revival in France. As Diocesan Architect of Rouen, he carried out numerous restorations, including work at St-Maclou, Rouen.

Saur (1993)

bartisan, bartizan. *Battlemented unroofed *turret or *parapet, circular or square, projecting on *corbels or *machicolations from an angle at the top of a tower or wall. *See* tourelle.

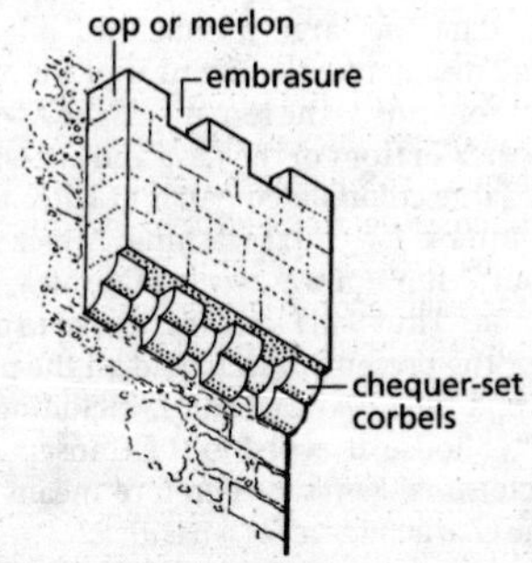

bartisan with plain crenellation (*JJS*)

Bartning, Otto (1883–1959). Karlsruhe-born German architect and Lutheran theologian, who began his career as an *Expressionist, and later directed the *Hochschule für Handwerk und Baukunst* (High School for Craft and Architecture) in Weimar (1926–30) which took over the functions of the *Bauhaus after it moved. In his role as Director, Bartning attempted to revive the *Arts-and-Crafts traditions that had been undermined by the *Gropius régime there. A traditionalist and a Christian, he is best known as a designer of Protestant churches, nearly all centrally planned. His Pressa Church, or *Stahlkirche* (Steel Church), Cologne (1928), was designed with a steel frame and glazed walls using a hyperbola on plan set on a low square base, whereas the Church of the Resurrection, or *Rundkirche* (Round Church), Essen (1930), was circular on plan. Both owe much to C18 prototypes, at least in their overall arrangement, although the architecture was stark and simple. After the 1939–45 war Bartning was closely involved in the programme to provide prefabricated timber churches for the German Evangelical Relief Organization.

Bartning (1959); Mayer (1958); Pollak (1926); Siemon (1958)

base. **1.** Anything on which an object rests, the term is given primarily to the foot or lowest member of a *colonnette, column, or *pier on which the shaft or mass of construction sits. The base of a column is therefore that part between the bottom of the shaft and the pavement, *pedestal, or *plinth. Bases differ according to the *Order used, although the *Attic base is commonly used on all Orders except the Greek *Doric (which has no base) and the *Tuscan (except in impure Tuscan Orders). Greek *Ionic *Asiatic bases are embellished with horizontal *reeds and other mouldings. Typical bases of the *Ionic, *Corinthian, and *Composite Orders are also referred to by the term *spira*. Bases of *pilasters are usually identical to those of the columns used in the same *portico or building, and may continue with the same profile when used as a continuous skirting or wall-base, but the bases of *antae may differ (though not usually). Medieval bases have far greater variety: pier bases, for example, are invariably set on a circular, polygonal, or square plinth, and have many mouldings. **2.** Lowest, thickest part of a wall, such as a *plinth or a *skirting, or the lowest visible element of a building, like a platform, plinth, or *podium called the *basement.

basement. **1.** Lower part of the walls of a building, especially if distinguished by an architectural treatment, such as *rustication or *battering, as in Palladian compositions. **2.** Storey behind the wall described above, above the ground or wholly or partly underneath it, supporting the principal storey.

Basevi, George (1794–1845). London-born architect, related to the Jewish families of Disraeli and *Ricardo, one of several pupils of *Soane. After a tour of Greece and Italy in 1816, he returned to London well able to provide an eclectic architecture in growing demand at that time. From 1820, when he established his practice, he designed several London squares and terraces, including Belgrave Square (1825–40), Alexander Square (1827–30), Thurloe Square (*c.*1839–45), and, from 1833, Pelham Crescent, Pelham Place, Egerton Crescent, and Walton Place for the trustees of the Smith's Charity Estate. In these developments he reinterpreted the late-C18 domestic architecture of London, giving it a new freshness without slavish archaeological or antiquarian bias. Like many of his contemporaries, Basevi was capable of designing in many styles, including *Gothic, and was responsible for the *Tudor Revival Dr Fryer's *Almshouses and Truesdale's Hospital in Stamford, Lincolnshire, of 1832, both agreeable essays in that style. His best-known work is the Fitzwilliam Museum, Cambridge (1836–45), completed by C. R. *Cockerell and E. M. *Barry, which eloquently demonstrates the change from Regency to Victorian taste: a new opulence, far removed from the chilly *Greek Revival that had been *de rigueur* for public buildings in the two decades since 1815, was evident in a noble synthesis of Graeco-Roman and *Renaissance themes. The monumental *portico with its flanking *colonnades terminating in end-pavilions was derived from *Antique precedent at Brescia, and further *gravitas* was given by the *Attic-storey rising above the *pediment. In collaboration with Sydney *Smirke he designed the Conservative Club in St James's Street (1843–4). Had he not fallen to his premature death while inspecting the west tower of Ely Cathedral, Cambridgeshire, he could well have been the greatest Classical architect of his generation.

Bolton (1925); Colvin (1995); Papworth (1852)

Basile, Ernesto (1857–1932). Palermo-born architect who designed many buildings in Rome and Sicily, including those for the Palermo Exhibition (1891–2). One of the chief protagonists of the *Stile Liberty, the Italian version of *Art Nouveau, he displayed his work at the Turin Exhibition (1902), the Venice Biennale (1903), and in *The Studio* (1904). His elegantly linear Art Nouveau architecture is perhaps best represented by the Villino Florio (1899–1902), the Hotel Villa Igiea (1899–1901), and the Utveggio House (1901) in Palermo. He also designed the Villino Basile and the Villino Fassini (1903), both in Palermo. One of his most impressive buildings was his extension to *Bernini's Montecitorio Palace, Rome (1902–27), in a sumptuous *Renaissance style. After the 1914–18 war his architecture became more Classical, as at the Istituto Provinciale Antitubercolare (1920–5) and the Albergo Diorno (1925), both in Palermo, with which he demonstrated his opposition to the growing influence of *Functionalism.

Borsi (1966); Caronia Roberti (1935); Meeks (1966); Nicoletti (1978); Pirrone (1971); Zevi (1973)

basilica (*pl.* **basilicas** *or* **basilicae**). Roman building-type with a *clearstoreyed *nave, two or more lower lean-to *aisles on each side of the nave, and an *apse at the end of the nave, originally for public functions, but later adapted for Christian worship, and the precedent for medieval church design. Early basilicas include that of Trajan in Rome (*c.* AD 113), and the very important Constantinian basilica of San Pietro, Rome (begun *c.*333), the model for Christian churches for nearly two millennia. The latter building had two aisles on each side of the nave and a lateral *transept between the apse and the nave to accommodate the large numbers of pilgrims wishing to venerate the shrine over the *martyrium containing the remains of the Apostle; a *narthex in front of the nave and aisles; and a very large colonnaded *atrium with a central fountain for ritual washing. Attached to the south transept were two *mausolea, both *rotundas. Thus San Pietro (destroyed to make way for the present church) had all the prototypes of a medieval cathedral, including the *chapter-house attached to the transept, and the *cloisters. *Basilican* therefore means having the characteristics of a basilica.

Krautheimer (1986); Ward-Perkins (1981)

basin. **1.** Bowl for the water in a fountain, or an artificial pool fed by *cascades or fountains. **2.** Large ornamental pond.

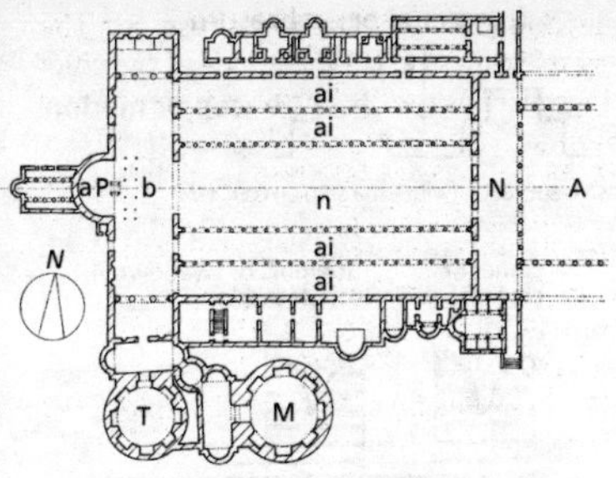

Plan showing the basilican arrangement that was to be the model for later medieval churches (although the orientation differs from the usual one of altar at the east end). It consists of a nave (n) flanked by two aisles (ai) on each side, a transeptal arrangement in which stood the high-altar on a bema (b) over the Shrine of St Peter (P), an apse (a), a narthex (N) or entrance-porch, and an atrium (A). Attached to the church were the circular mausolea of Honorius (later the tomb of St Petronilla (T)) and another (later Santa Maria della Febbre (M)).

Hypothetical section through clearstoreyed nave and lean-to double aisles looking towards the high altar and Solomonic columns seen through the great arch.

basilica. Constantinian basilica of San Pietro, Rome (begun *c.*333)

basket. 1. *Bell of the *capital of the *Corinthian *Order. **2.** *Byzantine and *Romanesque capital carved with interwoven strips resembling a basket-weave. **3.** *Corbeil, or ornament resembling a basket filled with fruit and flowers, often with *festoons. **4.** Type of *arch, as in *basket-handled* arch.

basket-weave. Any pattern resembling interweaving rushes, etc. *See also* brick.

bas-relief. *See* relief.

Bassae Order. Greek *Ionic Order with a *capital similar to an *angular capital, that is with *volutes on all sides, but with a high curved join between the volutes set under an *abacus. Developed by C. R. *Cockerell from his studies of the temple of Apollo Epicurius at Bassae.

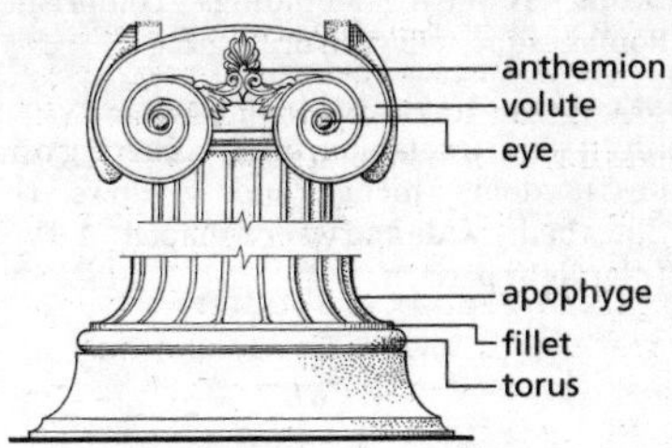

Bassae Order (*JJS*)

Bassi, Martino (1542–91). Milanese architect. He succeeded *Alessi at Santa Maria presso San Celso, and from 1573 worked on the rebuilding of the *Early Christian *rotunda of San Lorenzo, Milan. He also worked on Milan Cathedral from 1587, and at the Sacro Monte, Varallo, from 1578.

Bassi (1572); Heydenreich and Lotz (1974); Wittkower (1974)

Bastard Brothers (**John** (1688–1770) *and* **William** (*c.*1689–1766)). English architect-builders who worked in Dorset, and rebuilt Blandford Forum in a *vernacular *Baroque style from 1731 after that town had been destroyed by fire. They employed the *capital with *volutes turned inwards (*see* Borromini capital) which had been used by *Archer, derived from *Borromini, as well as exploiting *Rococo motifs. Among their more important buildings are the Town Hall (1734), the Church (1735–9), and two Inns (1734–5).

Colvin (1995); Summerson (1993)

bastel, bastle. Fortified farmhouse, with accommodation for livestock on the *vaulted ground-floor, usually found in the Border counties of Scotland and England, and dating from mid-C16 to mid-C17.

bastion. 1. Defensive projection, usually canted on plan and with *battered sides, at an angle of a fortress from which the ground in front of *ramparts may be viewed and raked with fire. **2.** In gardens, a vantage-point in a corner, or a raised projection, like an arrow-head bastion.

bastle. *See* bastel.

bath-house. C18 feature in gardens, often erected over a spring, and containing changing-rooms and fireplaces as well as a bath.

bâtons rompus. Mouldings comprising *Romanesque *chevron or *zig-zag.

bat's-wing. 1. Fluted half-*patera, resembling a semicircular fan, often occurring over late-C18 doors, niches, and windows, the *flutes being wide and wedge-shaped. **2.** Type of *fanlight pattern.

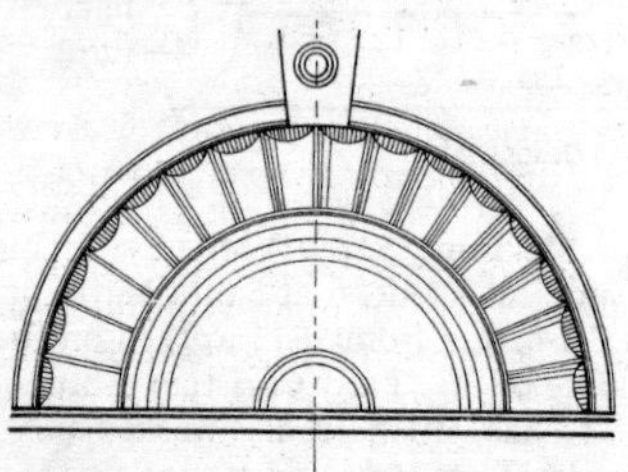

bat's-wing. Stucco example from Suffolk Place, London, 1820s, by John Nash.

batter. Slope, or inclination from the perpendicular, as in a *Vitruvian opening or on a retaining-wall or battered Egyptian *pylon-tower.

battery. Raised strip in a garden overlooking a view, and resembling a *bastion or gun-batteries. Sometimes a garden-battery will be embellished with real cannon.

battlement. *Parapet with higher and lower alternate parts. The indentations between the higher parts are the *carnels*, *crenels*, *embrasures*, *loops*, or *wheelers*, and the uprights between the indentations are the *cops*, *kneelers*, or *merlons*: a *crenellated* or *embattled* wall is therefore one with battlements, on *Perpendicular churches often ornamented with quatrefoils. Miniature decorative battlements occur in a number of places in architecture including the *transoms of *tracery and the *capitals of *piers in the *Perpendicular style of *Gothic: even *Tudor *chimney-pots have them. An *almena is a merlon with sloping, notched sides. A *Guelphic* or *swallowtail* battlement, common in medieval Italian architecture, has V-shaped notches in the tops of the merlon, giving a horn-like effect.

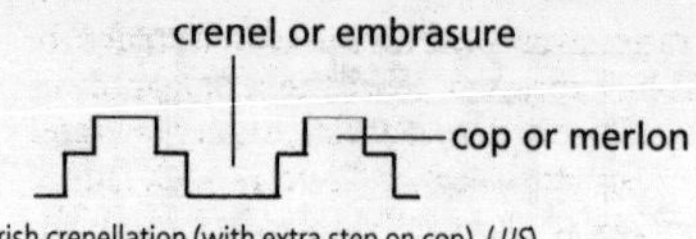

Irish crenellation (with extra step on cop). (*JJS*)

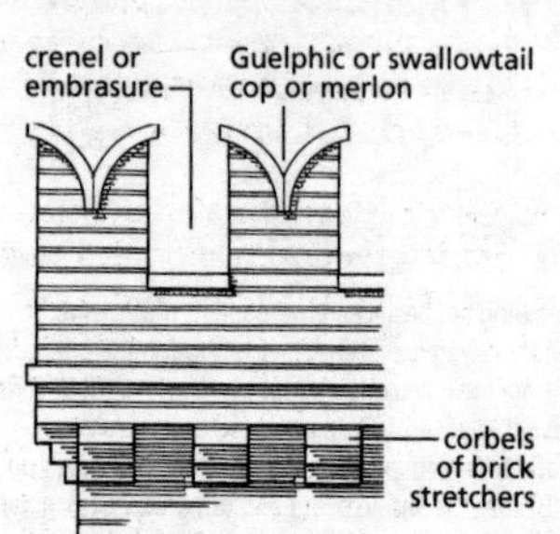

Guelphic or swallowtail crenellation on stretcher corbels, C19 warehouse in Bristol, Somerset. (*JJS*)

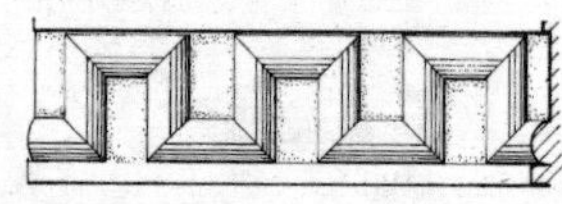

Romanesque embattled moulding, Lincoln Cathedral (mid-C12). (*After Parker*)

battlement

Baud, Benjamim (*c*.1807–75). English architect. He was *Wyatville's assistant during the remodelling of Windsor Castle, Berkshire (1826–40). In 1838 he won the competition to design the West of London and Westminster Cemetery, Brompton, London, which contained so many buildings for *catacomb 'burial' that it never had any possibility of recouping the capital expended upon it. After disastrous litigation with the Cemetery Company, Baud carried on a minor architectural practice and produced many drawings and paintings. He designed the eccentric *mausoleum in Lowther churchyard, Westmorland (1857), for William, 2nd Earl of Lonsdale (1787–1872). With Michael *Gandy he published *Architectural Illustrations of Windsor Castle* (1842) containing a text by John *Britton.

Colvin (1995); Curl (1993); Sheppard (1983)

Baudot, Joseph-Eugène-Anatole de (1834–1915). French architect. A pupil of *Labrouste and *Viollet-le-Duc, he is remembered primarily for the Church of St-Jean de Montmartre, Paris (1894–1902), in which Baudot used *reinforced *concrete and brick reinforced with steel rods. This building was influenced by Viollet-le-Duc's *Entretiens* (1863–72), and demonstrates Baudot's search for a rational architecture in which structure would be expressed. Even then, St-Jean owes much to medieval *Gothic prototypes, and indeed Baudot's earlier Church of St-Lubin, Rambouillet (1865–9), was Gothic in spirit, but with iron *piers. As a pioneer of reinforced-concrete construction, however, Baudot is of considerable importance.

Baudot (1905, 1916); Collins (1959); Hitchcock (1977)

Bauhaus. German school of design (literally Building House), the ideals of which dominated C20 architecture after the 1914–18 war. Contrary to belief, it had no Department of Architecture until 1927. In 1919 the *Grossherzogliche Sächsische Kunstgewerbeschule* (Grand-Ducal Saxon School of Arts and Crafts) and the *Grossherzogliche Sächsische Hochschule für Bildende Kunst* (Grand-Ducal Saxon High School for Fine Art), two important art-schools founded in 1906 by Wilhelm Ernst, the Grand Duke of Saxe-Weimar (1901–18), to promote the ideals of the *Arts-and-Crafts movement, were merged to become the *Staatliches Bauhaus Weimar* (State Building House, Weimar). Walter *Gropius had been proposed by Henry van de *Velde to succeed him as Director in 1915, but Gropius was serving in the army, and was unable to take up the post until 1919. Under his leadership the School moved away from its original ideals, although Gropius claimed his innovatory policies were derived from the ideas promoted by the *Deutscher Werkbund.

The Bauhaus became a centre for *Modernist theorizing, especially from 1922, when Theo van Doesburg (1883–1931) was there, propagating *Constructivist and De *Stijl ideas. Thereafter, self-dramatization was the *forte* of the institution, for although the Bauhaus claimed to be inspired by the notions of unifying art and technology, it did nothing of the sort, and its protagonists accelerated the sundering of 'design' from craftsmanship. As a State-subsidized but overtly Left-wing institution, it was perceived as a threat to local private craft-workshops, and in 1925 opposition grew so intense it was disbanded, and its functions taken over by the *Hochschule für Handwerk und Baukunst* (High School for Handicrafts and Architecture), directed by Otto *Bartning, who was more sympathetic to Arts-and-Crafts ideals.

After Weimar had proved hostile, the industrial town of Dessau became host to the Bauhaus, and a new building, designed by Gropius, was erected there (1925–6), which became a paradigm of the *International Modern style: the complex included three wings, a large glass-fronted workshop-*block, and residences for the 'Masters', or professors, at the institution. The Bauhaus became the State School of Art of Anhalt, and a new department of architecture was established under the direction of Hannes *Meyer. He was to succeed Gropius as Director of the Bauhaus in 1928, and promoted the Collectivist and Socialist flavour of the institution, encouraging inexpensive designs affordable by the working classes. Meyer's insistence (backed by Ludwig *Hilbersheimer, who taught architecture) that building was not an aesthetic process, and that everything depended on the marriage between function and economy, led to dissent. Eventually the Bürgermeister (Mayor) of Dessau was obliged to remove Meyer from his post in 1930. Meyer's successor was *Mies van der Rohe, who demanded rigorous standards of quality as well as a ferocious work-ethic concentrated on building and development: this régime alienated the Leftists, and the ructions which followed led to the closure of the Bauhaus, partly as a consequence of the increasing influence of the National Socialist German Workers' Party (Nazis). Under Mies van der Rohe it moved to Berlin-Steglitz in 1932, but finally closed in 1933.

Later, emigration of Bauhaus members led to the spread of its anti-crafts and anti-*Historicist ideals throughout the world: in the USA its message was promoted at Harvard by Gropius and *Breuer, at Chicago by László Moholy-Nagy (1895–1946), and at the Armour Institute, Chicago (now Institute of Technology), by Mies van der Rohe and others. The Bauhaus was promoted as an ideal by Sigfried *Giedion and by (Sir) Nikolaus *Pevsner who saw it as the Modernist educational academy *par excellence*. The Ulm *Hochschule für Gestaltung* (Ulm High School for Construction), founded in 1950, was the German successor of the Bauhaus.

Bayer (1938); Curtis (1996); Gropius (1965); Jervis (1984); Naylor (1985); Wingler (1969)

baulk-tie. *See* roof.

Baurscheit, Jan Pieter van (1699–1768). Architect of German descent, he was one of the most talented designers working in the *Rococo style in The Netherlands. Originally influenced by *Marot, who introduced the

Style *Louis Quatorze to The Hague, he evolved his own architectural language in which Flemish and South-German decorative devices were mingled. His works include the Town Hall, Vlissingen (1730), the Hotel de Fraula, Antwerp (1737), the Town Hall, Lier (1740–4), and the Hotel den Grooten Robijn, Antwerp (*c.*1749).

Musgrove (1987)

Bautista, Francisco (1594–1679). Spanish Jesuit priest and architect. He was responsible for the Churches of San Salvador del Mundo and San Isidro el Real, Madrid (1626–51), based on the Church of *Il Gesù* in Rome, and precedents for many later churches in Spain and Latin America of the *Gesù* type.

Kubler and Soria (1959)

Bawa, Geoffrey (1919–). London-educated Sri Lankan architect, who made his name by mixing modern techniques with Sri Lankan *vernacular architecture. His best-known buildings are the Triton Hotel, Ahungalla (1982), new Parliament Building, Sri Jayawardenepura, Kotte (1982), and the University of Ruhunu, Matara (1980–6).

Curtis (1996); Emanuel (1994); Khan (1995); Taylor (1986)

bawn. Walled enclosure protected by circular, polygonal, or square *flankers (low towers) at the corners, and associated with a fortified house, especially in C17 Ulster.

bay. 1. Regular structural subdivision of a building, such as a church: in the latter case the building is divided along its long axis by bays defined by the *buttresses, *piers, and *vaults, with windows inserted into the *curtain-wall of each bay. In Classical buildings bays may be marked by *Orders, vaults, roof-*trusses, or beams, but it is erroneous to describe, say, an C18 Georgian domestic *façade in terms of bays, as the number of windows may not relate to structure: five *windows* wide would be more correct. **2.** Part of a framed building between the main supporting timbers. The term describes units, such as a two-bay hall, or a *half-bay* used as a *cross-entry. **3.** Free or light-space in a *sash-window. *See also* bay-window.

Bayer, Herbert (1900–85). Born at Haag, near Salzburg, he studied architecture before joining the *Bauhaus in Weimar in 1921. In 1925 he became head of the typographic workshops at Dessau, and designed the journal *Bauhaus*. He promoted a single-alphabet sans-serif typography, and designed the celebrated typeface *Universal* (1925–8). He established his own firm in Berlin in 1928, working with *Gropius, *Breuer, and others at the Paris *Deutscher Werkbund Exhibition of 1930. He emigrated to the USA in 1938, helping with the Museum of Modern Art's Bauhaus exhibition of that year. He became a design consultant in Aspen, Colo., in 1946.

Bayer (1938); Jervis (1984); Neumann, E. (1970)

bay-leaf. Classical decoration based on the bay-leaf, often in *garlands, and usually applied to a *torus moulding or a *pulvinated *frieze.

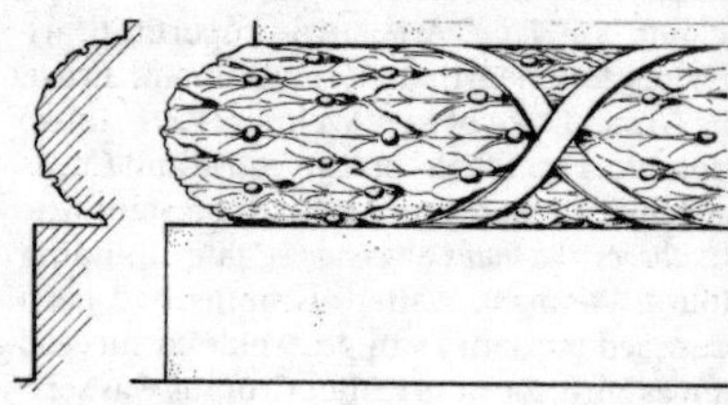

bay-leaf garland

bay-window. Projection from a house-front, circular, rectangular, segmental, or canted on plan, largely filled with windows. A segmental bay is defined as a *bow, common in the *Regency period. A bay-window on an upper floor only is an *oriel.

Bazhenov, Vasily Ivanovich (1737–99). Born in Kaluga, he was one of the greatest Russian architects, whose contribution to *Neoclassicism is of great importance. In 1767 he was appointed architect in charge of the reconstruction of the Kremlin in Moscow, his team including M. F. *Kazakov (whose Senate Building of 1776 is an outstanding memorial to the whole scheme). Bazhenov produced a design for a *Gothic palace (with much *polychrome lace-like detail) at Tsaritsyno, and appears to have been responsible for a series of eclectic garden *fabriques. A convinced Freemason, his severe Neoclassicism has parallels with the work of other known Freemason-architects throughout Europe. His best surviving buildings are the Dolgov and Yushkov Houses, the bell-tower of the Skorbyashchenskaya Church, and the Pashkov Palace of 1784–6, all in Moscow. His last great building was the moated St Michael or Engineer's fortress at St Petersburg, with its golden *flèche and detached *pavilions.

Hamilton (1983); Middleton and Watkin (1987)

Bazzani, Cesare (1873–1939). Italian architect who worked in Rome and created the Museo d'Arte Moderne there for the Exhibition of 1911. His style was eclectic *Historicist in approach, and his buildings include the Biblioteca Nazionale, Florence (1907–35), and the Ministero dell' Educazione Nazionale, Rome (1913–28).

Borsi (1966); Meeks (1966)

BBPR. Architectural Partnership founded in Milan in 1932 by Gianluigi Banfi (1910–45), Lodovico Barbiano di Belgiojoso (1909–), Enrico Peressutti (1908–76), and Ernesto Nathan *Rogers. Like many Italian Modernists, BBPR backed Fascism, hoping it would continue to favour progressive architecture, and many early works are associated with the Fascist regime. The firm's Heliotherapy Clinic, Legnano (1937–8—now demolished), was an intelligent and sensitive design, while the restoration of the *cloisters of the monastery of San Simpliciano, Milan (1940)—which included offices for the firm—was an eloquent testimony to a sympathy for historic buildings that ran counter to orthodox *Modernism. As Fascist Italy became tightly bound to the Nazi Axis, any 'progressive' tendencies vanished in Italy, although BBPR managed to erect the Central Post Office Complex in the EUR Quarter of Rome (1940), the only building there not to succumb to the *stripped *Classicism of *Piacentini: such bravado led to BBPR's falling from favour. After the 1939–45 war BBPR's search for a severe geometry that could yet express emotion led to the memorial erected in the Cimitero Monumentale, Milan (1946), to the victims of the concentration camps (Banfi himself had perished at Mauthausen). In 1954–6 the conversion of the Sforza Castle into a museum again demonstrated great sensitivity to older fabric, but the Torre Velasca, Milan (1954–8), with its projecting upper storeys, the whole reminiscent of a medieval tower, demonstrated a rejection of the rigid dogmas of *International Modernism, bringing the wrath of American and British critics down on BBPR for the allusive qualities of the building. Subsequently, the possibilities of exposed steelwork and glass were elegantly exploited on a curved frontage to great effect at the Chase Manhattan Bank, Milan (1969).

Belgiojoso (1979); Morgan and Naylor (1987); Placzek (1982)

bead. 1. Convex moulding, often of semicircular *section, also called *astragal, *baguet(te), half-round, or *roundel. If ornamented, it is a *chaplet*. A *bead-moulding* is a bead that does not project, also called a *reed if several occur together in parallel lines. *Beading* is enrichment consisting of a row of small balls resembling a string of beads, called *beadwork*, or *pearling*, common in *Romanesque work, and revived in C18. **2.** A prayer (referring to beads on a string as mnemonics for prayers), so a *bead-* or *bede-house* was a type of *almshouse, the inmates of which were required to pray in an adjacent *chapel or church for the founder's soul.

bead-and-reel. *Astragal carved in semblance of a continuous row of bead-like and spool- or reel-like elements, arranged usually with one bead then two reels, then a bead, in series.

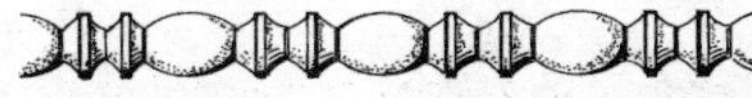

bead-and-reel

beak-head. *Romanesque carving in the form of a series of animal-, bird- (*bird's-head*), or humanoid-heads with long pointed beaks (or tongues) curving around a lower *roll-moulding, as in a church doorway. Heads with stumpier cone-like beaks are *cats'-heads*.

Romanesque *beak-head* ornament, Church of St Ebbe, Oxford. A variant is the *cat's head*

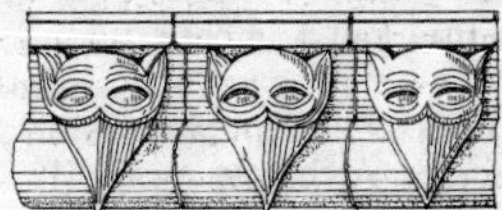

Romanesque *cat's-head* ornament, Church of Sts Peter and Paul, Tickencote, Rutland. (*After Parker*)

beak-head

beak-moulding. Pendent *fillet on the edge of a *larmier, with a channel or curved groove behind, as on a *Doric *anta *capital.

beam. Horizontal structural element supported at each end by some means, such as walls, columns, *piers, etc. A beam employed as a *lintel supports a weight. Beams are further defined by adjectives, as in *tie-beam. *See* truss.

Beaudouin, Eugène-Elie (1898–1983). Paris-born French architect who specialized in low-cost housing, notably at Cité de la Muette at Drancy (from 1934), in which industrialized components were used. Among his other works the Maison du Peuple, Clichy (1937–9—with *Prouvé), and extensions to the Palais des Nations, Geneva, Switzerland (1967–73—with *Nervi and others), should be cited. His work produced hard and uncompromising environments.

Emanuel (1994)

Beauregard, Guyot de (d. 1551). French architect responsible for the *Renaissance *façade of the Hôtel de Savoie, Mechelen, Belgium (1517–26). *See* Kelderman.

Baedeker, *Belgium* (1931)

Beautiful. One of three C18 aesthetic categories, with the *Picturesque and the *Sublime. Edmund *Burke, in his *A Philosophical Enquiry into the Origin of our Ideas of the Sublime and Beautiful* (1756), perhaps the most influential C18 English work on aesthetics, especially in the 1757 expanded edition, did not accept that architectural Beauty was connected with proportions of an idealized human body, denied that there was any 'inner sense' of Beauty, and argued against the notion of mathematical means of measuring it. Beauty was a property which causes love, and consisted of relative smallness, smoothness, absence of angularity, and brightness of colour. Sir Uvedale *Price and Richard Payne *Knight held that the Beautiful had a smooth, undulating appearance, with no harshness, surprises, or broken lines, a concept which they applied to landscapes. Archibald Alison (1757–1839) believed that architectural Beauty of proportion was dependent upon an association of fitness of form, shape, size, and scale for the function. Apprehension of the Beautiful should be accompanied by pleasure, which Alison defined as the 'emotion of Taste'. *See* Kant.

Burke (1757); Osborne (1970)

Beaux-Arts. Florid Classical style evolved in the *École Nationale Supérieure des Beaux-Arts*, the main official art-school in France, founded in 1795, when it became a separate institution from the old *Académie Royale*. The School was very influential, and ofter started young architects in their careers with the award of the Prix de Rome (from 1723), intended to perpetuate the academic traditions of training. The Beaux-Arts style, as it came to be known, evolved in the second half of C19, especially in Paris, where most of the important architects trained, including several (e.g. *Hunt, *McKim, and *Richardson) from the USA. Examples of the Beaux-Arts architectural style include *Garnier's *Opéra*, Paris (1861–75), *Polaert's *Palais de Justice*, Brussels (1866–83), and *Girault's *Petit Palais*, Paris (1897–1900). Scholarly, self-confident, grand, and lush, the style was perfectly attuned to the mood of Europe and America in the two decades before 1914.

Chilvers, Osborne, and Farr (1988); Drexler (1977); Egbert (1980); Middleton (1982)

Beazley, Samuel (1786–1851). English architect, playwright, novelist, and wit. He was the leading designer of theatres of his time. Among his works were the Royal Lyceum, London (1816, rebuilt 1831–4, reconstructed 1902, leaving the *portico), the Theatre Royal, Birmingham (1820—demolished 1956), the County Library and Reading Rooms, Leamington Spa, Warwickshire (1820–1), Drury Lane Theatre, London (1822, with *Ionic *colonnade added in 1831), and many other theatres in Belgium, Latin America, and India. He designed the new town at Ashford, Kent, for the employees of the North Kent Railway (1851), as well as the Lord Warden Hotel, Dover (1848–53). He was responsible for several country-houses, commercial buildings, and much else, and published on many subjects.

Colvin (1995); Harbron (1936)

Becerra, Francisco (*c*.1545–1605). Spanish-born architect. He settled in Mexico in 1573, where he worked on the Cathedral of Puebla, probably to designs by Claudio de *Arciniega. He was mostly responsible for the design of the Cathedrals of Cuzco (1582–1654) and Lima (1582–1662), both in Peru and built from 1598. Becerra adopted the somewhat severe style of mid-C16 Spain, although the *façade of Cuzco Cathedral was an ornate and rather clumsy *Baroque.

Kubler and Soria (1959); Marco Dorta (1951)

bed. Prepared horizontal surface with a layer of mortar on which bricks, stones, *tiles, etc., lie; also the under-surface in contact with the mortar-layer. The *bed-joint* is therefore where those surfaces meet, and the term is also applied to the joints between the *voussoirs of an arch. In Classical architecture the *bed-moulding* is part of the *entablature, lying between the *corona and the *frieze, or any moulding over which any horizontal moulding projects.

Bedford, Francis Octavius (1784–1858). English architect. With J. P. *Gandy and William *Wilkins he was engaged by the Society of *Dilettanti to accompany Sir William *Gell on a tour of Greece and Asia Minor to collect material. Their researches led to the publication (1817) of *The Unedited Antiquities of Attica* and (1840) the third volume of *The Antiquities of Ionia*. Much later (1912) the fifth part of *The Antiquities of Ionia*, containing work by Bedford, Gandy, and Gell, was published, edited by *Lethaby.

As an architect he produced some of the finest essays in the *Greek Revival style, including the Churches of St John, Waterloo Road, lambeth (1823–4), St George, Camberwell (1822–4—gutted), Holy Trinity, Southwark (1823–4—now the Henry Wood Hall, as converted by *Arup Associates), and St Luke, West Norwood (1823–5—altered by *Street (1870–9)), all in London. His pre-ecclesiological *Gothic Revival churches are thin and spindly.

Colvin (1995); Crook (1972*a*); Pevsner (1983): *Buildings of England, London 2: South*

beehive. Structure built of coursed *rubble on a circular plan, each successive course slightly *corbelled over the course below and slightly less in diameter so that, as each course is completed, a roughly conical or beehive-shaped *thole or tholos is formed, actually covered with a corbelled or fake dome. The finest example from Antiquity is the *Mycenaean 'Treasury of Atreus' (C13 BC). Inhabited beehive-houses in Southern Italy are called *trulli*, the prehistoric Sardinian versions of which are called *nuraghi*.

Beer Family. Celebrated family working mostly in South Germany and Switzerland, which created some of the finest *Baroque churches in the German-speaking lands. Although there was a **Georg Beer** (d. 1600) working in Stuttgart in C16, the Beers came from the Bregenzerwald, and, with the *Moosbruggers and the *Thumbs, were important protagonists of the *Vorarlberg School. The first member of the family to come to eminence in C17 was **Michael Beer** (d. 1666), who worked at the Abbey Church of St Lorenz, Kempten (1652–66), which on plan is a mixture of the longitudinal and centralized type, with a domed octagon set between *chancel and *nave. His son, **Franz** (1660–1726), one of the most talented of the family, earned his apprenticeship at the prototypical Vorarlberg Abbey Church at Obermarchtal (1686–92), a *Wandpfeiler (wall-pier) building with slightly projecting transeptal bay, three-bay nave, and three-bay *choir, designed by Michael Thumb. Franz Beer's next building (much under the Thumb influence) was the former Benedictine Abbey Church at Irsee (1699–1704), another *Wandpfeiler* building with transeptal *chapels, apsidal *choir, and twin-towered *façade: inside is the charming *pulpit in the form of a ship, complete with sail and *putti climbing the rope-ladders. Another *Wandpfeiler* building was his *Heiligenkreuzkirche* (Holy Cross Church), Donauwörth (1717–22), completed by Josef *Schmutzer. Beer's most brilliant work can be found in Switzerland, starting with the former Benedictine Abbey Church at Rheinau, near Schaffhausen (1704–11), again of the *Wandpfeiler* type with twin-towered façade. Inside, *galleries are set back from the *piers, so that *bays and verticality are emphasized. Beer's masterpiece is the former Cistercian Abbey Church of St Urban, near Langenthal (1711–36), with double *pilasters on the wall-piers, and, like Rheinau, set-back galleries. Beer was involved in the designs of the great Benedictine Abbey Church of Weingarten, north of Lake Constance (1714–24), not far from which, near Ravensburg, he designed the Premonstratensian Church at Weissenau (1717–24). **Johann Michael Beer** (1696–1780) was responsible for the handsome twin-towered façade (and probably the choir) of the former Benedictine Abbey Church (now

Cathedral) at St Gallen in Switzerland (1760s), together with his nephew **Johann Ferdinand Beer** (1731–89).

Bourke (1962); Lieb and Dieth (1976); Oechslin (1973)

Behne, Adolf (1885–1948). German architect, theorist, and critic. He was associated with the avant-garde before and after the 1914–18 war, and was involved in the *Deutscher Werkbund, *Arbeitsrat für Kunst, and *Gläserne Kette, all of which he promoted in *Die Wiederkehr der Kunst* (The Return to Art—1919). He used the term *Reklamerarchitektur* (Advertising Architecture) to describe the works of *Mendelsohn and others. In 1920 he published *Ruf zum Bauen* (A Call to Build), and in 1923–5 his best-known book, *Der moderne Zweckbau* (The Modern Functional Building), which promoted *Functionalism and the *Modern Movement. In his *Entartete Kunst* (Degenerate Art) he described art and architecture banned by the Nazis, and continued to publish many articles and polemics until his death.

Behne (1919, 1920, 1926, 1988); Saur (1994)

Behnisch, Günter (1922–). German architect, born near Dresden, Saxony. The most celebrated work of his Stuttgart firm Behnisch & Partners is the Olympiapark, Munich (1967–72), designed for the 1972 Olympic Games. The spectacular tent-roof covering the stadium, sports-hall, and swimming-pool was designed with Frei *Otto. The firm also built many schools, using prefabricated components, including the Hohenstaufen-Gymnasium, Göppingen (1956–9), the Secondary School, Lorch (1973), and the Study Centre for the Lutheran Church in Stuttgart-Birkach (1977–80). More recently the Technical School, Bruchsal (1983), Catholic University Library, Eichstätt (1987), German Postal Museum, Frankfurt-am-Main (1990), Central Bank of Bavaria, Schwabing, Munich (1992), and office-buildings in Nuremberg and Salzburg have enhanced the firm's reputation, while the Federal Parliament Building in Bonn (1992) has consolidated it.

Emanuel (1994); Lampugnani (1988); Meyhöfer (1995)

Behrendt, Walter Curt (1884–1945). German-born American architect and architectural writer. He worked with the Ministry for Housing and Town Planning (1919–26) and in the Ministry of Finance (1927–33), in which positions he promoted the *Modern Movement in public building projects in Prussia and throughout the Weimar Republic. Like others of the avant-garde, he had been involved in the *Deutscher Werkbund, and later joined Der *Ring. He left Germany in 1934 and settled in the USA, where he taught at Buffalo, NY (1937–41), Dartmouth College, Hanover (1941–5), and elsewhere. He became a disciple of Frank Lloyd *Wright. His writings include *Städtebau und Wohnungswesen in den Vereinigten Staaten* (Town Planning and Housing in the United States—1926), *Der Sieg des neuen Baustils* (The Victory of the New Architectural Style—1927), *Modern Building: Its Nature, Problems, and Forms* (1937), and *Roots of Contemporary American Architecture* (1972).

Behrendt (1920, 1937); Saur (1994)

Behrens, Peter (1868–1940). Hamburg-born artist, who became an architect under the influence of the teachings of William *Morris. A founder-member of the Munich *Sezession in 1893, his early graphic work was heavily influenced by *Art Nouveau. From 1898 he became interested in the problems of designing mass-produced artefacts. In 1899 he was invited to Darmstadt by Ernst Ludwig II, reigning Grand Duke of Hesse (1892–1918), where he designed his own house for the artists' colony of *Mathildenhöhe*: incorporating a severe geometry with *Gothic *ogee *gable and dormer-windows, it was designed as a whole, inside and out, drawing on the ideas of van de *Velde and *Mackintosh. From 1907 his work became more *Neoclassical: the crematorium at Delstern, near Hagen, in Westphalia (1906–7), is a good example. He became a founder of the *Deutscher Werkbund and was appointed architect to the first electrical company in Berlin, the AEG, for which he designed the turbine-hall (1908–10), factories, offices, shops, workers' housing, and all manner of artefacts until 1914.

His Berlin office gained an international reputation for progressive design, and in *c.*1910 Le *Corbusier, W. *Gropius, and *Mies van der Rohe all worked there. There was much that was Neoclassical in his AEG work, and the influence of *Schinkel was strong in his Haus Schröder, Hagen-Eppenhausen, Westphalia (1908), and Haus Wiegand, Berlin (1911–13). The Imperial German Embassy in St Petersburg (1911–12), a powerful essay in *stripped Classicism, influenced many architects, including the Scandinavian Neoclassicists of the 1920s and 1930s. In

1920–4 he built the offices of the I. G. Farben (now Höchst) Dyeworks in Frankfurt-am-Main, an *Expressionist essay with touches of proto-*Art Deco.

From 1922 Behrens was Director of the School of Architecture in the Vienna Academy of Arts, a post he held until 1936, when he became Head of the Department of Architecture of the Prussian Academy of Arts, Berlin. He designed one house in England: 'New Ways', 508 Wellingborough Road, Northampton (1923–5), for Wenman Joseph Bassett-Lowke (1877–1953), which incorporated an earlier room from 78 Derngate designed by *Mackintosh in 1907.

Behrens (1901); Buddensieg and Rogge (1984); Weber (1966); Windsor (1981)

Bélanger, François-Joseph (1744–1818). Paris-born architect, the most important landscape-architect and the most refined of the *Neoclassicists working in the France of *Louis Seize. Appointed *Dessinateur des Menus-Plaisirs du Roi* in 1767, he met Charles-Joseph, Prince de Ligne (1735–1814), in 1769, for whom he designed *fabriques for the celebrated gardens at Belœi, Belgium. In 1770–1 he designed the lovely *pavillon à l'antique* for the Comte de Lauraguais's Hôtel de Brancas in Paris. For Charles-Philippe, Comte d'Artois (1757–1836—later King Charles X—to whom he had become *premier architecte*), his design for the exquisite *Parva sed Apta* (small but fitting) Neoclassical Pavillon de Bagatelle in the Bois de Boulogne, Paris, was erected in 64 days in 1777 to win a bet with Queen Marie-Antoinette. The main bedroom was designed as a tent, and the whole building set in the most celebrated 'English' garden of the period (1778–80), with many *Gothick, *Chinoiserie, and other *fabriques*, designed by Bélanger and created by the Scots landscape-gardener Thomas Blaikie (1750–1838). At Neuilly, the Folie Saint-James (*c.*1780) was placed in a large jardin *anglo-chinois in which were many famous *fabriques*, including *kiosks, *grottoes, Chinese pavilions, and a massive artificial rock (the *Grand Rocher*, known as the Eighth Wonder of the World) containing a bathroom, reservoir, grotto, and art gallery. He designed the extraordinary gardens and *fabriques* at Méréville, near Étampes, for the Court Banker, Jean-Joseph, Marquis de Laborde (1724–94), held to be superior to anything by William *Kent, from 1784, and was succeeded there by Hubert *Robert, who dishonestly claimed the designs were his alone. Bélanger's dome of the Halle au Blé in Paris (1808–13), probably the first such iron-and-glass structure in the world, replaced the timber-and-glass dome by Legrand and Molinos (1782).

Braham (1980); Deming (1984); Middleton and Watkin (1987); Mosser and Teyssot (1991)

Belcher, John (1841–1913). One of the most distinguished late-Victorian and Edwardian British architects, he joined his father, **John** (*c.*1816–90), in practice in London in 1865, remaining until 1875. He made his name with the Genoese-inspired *Mannerist *Baroque Hall of the Incorporated Chartered Accountants, Great Swan Alley, City of London (1888–93), designed in association with Arthur Beresford *Pite. The building was adorned with a lively frieze carved by (Sir) William Hamo Thorneycroft (1850–1925), while Henry Bates designed the *terms and *corbels. The ideals of revived *Classicism and the *Arts-and-Crafts movement were fused in the building, as they were in Belcher's own career, for he was not only responsive to the spirit of the Italian *Renaissance (and especially the Genoese *palazzi*), but he was a founder-member of the *Art Workers' Guild. In 1898–1902 his office produced Colchester Town Hall with a fine *campanile and vigorous main *façade, enlivened by a *Giant *Order carrying broken *pediments. From 1897 John James *Joass joined Belcher, becoming his partner in 1905, and the firm evolved an assured and robust Baroque, culminating in the massive *Wrenaissance Ashton Memorial, Lancaster (1904–9). He published *Essentials in Architecture* (1893), and with Mervyn E. *Macartney, a collection of photographs and drawings of *Later Renaissance Architecture in England* (1901), which had a considerable effect on contemporary architecture. Belcher and Joass designed the Franco-British White City Exhibition in 1908, displaying their mastery of opulent late-Baroque to great effect.

DNB (1927); Gray (1985); Service (1975, 1977)

belection. *See* bolection.

Belfast. *See* truss.

belfry. **1.** Bell-tower, generally attached to a church or other building, and sometimes standing separate. **2.** *Stage of a tower in which bells are hung and from which the sound is emitted, called the *belfry-stage*, identified by its (usually) *louvred openings. **3.** Framing on which bells are supported.

Belgiojoso, Lodovico Barbiano di (1909–). *See* BBPR.

bell. 1. Ancient Egyptian bell-like *capital. **2.** *Basket, corbeille, or vase-like solid part of a *Corinthian and *Composite capital from which leaves, scrolls, etc., spring. **3.** Bell-shaped *First Pointed *Gothic capital **4.** One of many small bell-shaped forms (*campanulae*) suspended from the *eaves of *pagodas, etc., in *Chinoiserie buildings. **5.** *Gutta of the *Doric *Order.

bell-arch. Arch springing from curved-ended *corbels, creating a bell-shaped aperture.

bell-cage. Structure supporting bells in a *belfry.

bell-canopy. Roof of some kind to protect a bell or bells, often with a *gable.

bell-capital. *See* bell.

bell-cast. 1. Sprocketed *eaves with *sprockets or cocking-pieces fixed to the top of the common rafters above the eaves so that the roof above the eaves has a flatter pitch. **2.** Projecting finish, or *bell-cast piece*, at the bottom of *harling, *render, or *roughcast finish on a wall, resembling the base of a bell, forming a drip.

bell-cote *or* **bell-gable.** Small *gable, usually set over the west wall of a church or over the east wall of the *nave immediately above the *chancel-arch, containing a bell or bells suspended within arched openings. Over the chancel-arch a bell-cote is called a Sancte-cote, as it carries the *Sanctus* bell.

Bell, Edward Ingress (1837–1914). *See* Webb, Sir Aston (1849–1930).

bell-flower. *See* husk.

Bell, Henry (1647–1711). Born in King's Lynn, Norfolk, Bell, English gentleman-architect, appears to have been partly responsible for the replanning and rebuilding of Northampton after the fire of 1675, and to have designed All Saints' Church there (1677–80) as well as some of the *façades of houses in the Market Place. Bell's other works are all in King's Lynn: they include the charming Customs House (1683), built as an Exchange; the Market Cross (1707–10)—demolished; two altar-pieces; probably the Duke's Head Inn (*c*.1684); and various houses. He was also responsible for North Runcton Church, Norfolk (1703–13), and may have designed other buildings in Huntingdonshire, Norfolk, and Suffolk. He wrote an essay on painting, published posthumously in 1728.

Colvin (1995)

Bell, John (*fl.* 1478–88). English master-mason. He worked on the upper *stages of the *crossing-tower at Durham Cathedral (1483–90). He may be the same Bell who worked at York *Minster in 1472, at King's College *Chapel, Cambridge, in the 1480s, and at Great St Mary's Church, Cambridge, until 1503.

Harvey (1987)

Bellot, Dom Paul (1876–1944). French architect and Benedictine monk, a disciple of *Choisy and *Viollet-le-Duc, trained (1894–1901) at the École des *Beaux-Arts, Paris. He designed many buildings in Belgium, England, France, The Netherlands, and Portugal. He was responsible for the Benedictine Monastery of St-Paul-de-Wisques, Oosterhout, Brabant, The Netherlands (1906–20), which greatly impressed *Berlage. Quarr Abbey, Isle of Wight (1907–14), his outstanding architectural achievement, is a master-work of *Expressionism in brick, with a church of 1911–12 that is wholly original, having a short, low *nave, a long *choir, and a stunning eastern tower with brick arches inspired, perhaps, by the *Moorish architecture of Spain. It astonished *Pevsner, no less. Bellot established a studio at Oosterhout, and later (from 1928) at St Paul's Abbey, Wisques, near Saint-Omer, France, and explored the architectural possibilities of load-bearing brick parabolic arches and corbelling, arguing that such investigations were more in the spirit of medieval architecture than was possible in a strictly archaeologically based *Gothic Revival. Among his finest buildings are the glowing *polychrome Church of Notre-Dame-des-Trévois, Troyes (1931–4), the Convent Church of Ste-Bathilde, Vanves (1933–6), both in France, and the lovely Church at Bloemendaal (1923–4), in The Netherlands.

He visited Montreal, Canada, in 1934, to give a series of lectures (published in 1939) in which he stressed that the modern architect should emulate, not imitate, the lessons of the Middle Ages, and also in which he roundly denounced Le *Corbusier as an 'architecte bolchéviste militant': these lectures promoted the building of several churches in what became known as the 'Dom Bellot style', featuring parabolic arches, polychrome brickwork, and powerful geometries. Bellot's disciple Adrian Dufresne (1904–82) designed the Church of Ste-Thérèse-de-Lisieux, Beauport, near Quebec City (1936), in that style, partly influenced by Bellot's own Church at Noordhoek, The Netherlands (1921–2). Bellot himself, with Félix Racicot (1903–73) and another architect-monk, Dom Claude-Marie Côté, designed (1935) spectacular additions to the Abbaye de St-Benoît-du-Lac, begun in 1939, a dramatically composed work, with brick *cloisters again featuring parabolic arches. At the Oratoire St-Joseph, Montreal, he worked with Lucien Parent (1893–1956) on the completion of the building, his principal contribution being the great polygonal concrete dome and the canted arches of the interior.

Bellot (1948); Culot and Meade (1996); Kalman (1994); *Perspectives on Architecture*, 27 (Feb.–Mar. 1997), 54–7; Willis (1997)

bell-roof. Roof with an exterior profile resembling a bell-like form.

bell-tower. High tower, attached to or detached from a building such as a church, with a *belfry-stage containing bells, and called *campanile in Italian.

Belluschi, Pietro (1899–1994). Italian-born architect and engineer, he settled in the USA in the 1920s, and joined the Portland, Oreg., office of the architect Albert Ernest Doyle (1877–1928) in 1925, which he reorganized under his own name in 1943. In the 1930s Belluschi established his architectural reputation with several commercial, domestic, and religious buildings, among which the Art Museum (1931–8), Finley Mortuary (1936–7), Sutor House (1937–8), and Church of St Thomas More (1939–41), all in Portland, should be mentioned. With his US National Bank of Oregon, Salem (1940–1), he showed an inclination to *International Modernism, a tendency reinforced with his Equitable Life Assurance Building, Portland (1944–8), one of the first examples of an aluminium-and-glass *curtain-wall enclosing a *concrete-framed tower, a building-type that became very common thereafter. From 1951 he was appointed Dean of the School of Architecture and Planning at Massachusetts Institute of Technology (MIT), and his practice was absorbed by *Skidmore, Owings, & Merrill (SOM). Fond of the phrase 'eliminate, refine, and integrate', he had built up a huge and successful commercial practice, and collaborated with others while involved at MIT, notably with Eduardo Catalano (1917–) and Holge Westermann for the Juilliard School of Music and Alice Tully Hall at the Lincoln Center, New York (1955–70), with a travertine marble *façade masking the buildings behind it. On relinquishing his position at MIT in 1965 he again established an architectural practice in Portland, often working with other architects. Among the later works are numerous churches, the San Francisco Symphony Hall, California (with SOM—1980), and the Baltimore Symphony Hall, Maryland (with Jung, Brannen, Associates—1982).

Gubitosi and Izzo (1974); Heyer (1978); Stubblebine (1953)

belt-course. *See* band.

Beltrami, Luca (1854–1933). *See* Sommaruga, Giuseppe (1867–1917).

belvedere. Any raised structure or tower erected over the roof of a dwelling-house or on a vantage-point in a landscape from which pleasant scenery may be viewed. Such a building in a garden might be in the form of a Classical temple, and is also termed a *gazebo, mirador, or *summer-house.

bema. **1.** Platform, rostrum, or raised floor in the *apse of a *basilica. **2.** *Chancel, *sanctuary, or raised part of a church containing the altar. **3.** Raised part of the *nave, enclosed by a balustrade, *cancelli, or *screen, allotted to the clergy. **4.** Elevated *pulpit in *synagogues for readings.

bench. *Pew. A *bench-end* is therefore the terminal timber facing of a church-pew, frequently decorated with *poppy-heads, *blind tracery, and the like. A *bench-table* or *bench-table stone* is a low projecting course of *masonry, its lowest part chamfered, forming a seat against medieval walls in e.g. *cloisters.

Benedetto da Maiano (1442–97). *See* Maiano.

Benedictine. Monastic Order based on the rules of St Benedict (480–543), who established the great Abbey at Monte Cassino from which the arts of agriculture, architecture, and writing were disseminated. In C9 the Rule was regularized, and the Order confined its activities to Western Europe. An exemplary

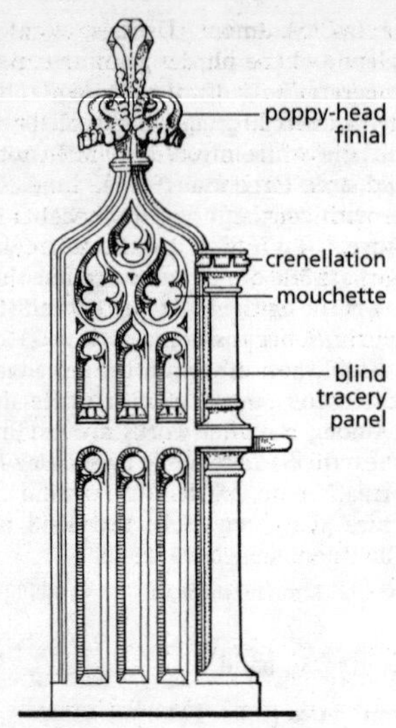

bench-end. Medieval example with blind tracery panels and poppy-head finial. (*JJS*)

plan for the Benedictine Monastery of St Gall in Switzerland survives, and demonstrates the sophistication of the architecture as early as *c*.820: the plan of the church itself is similar to that used for several later churches.

Eschapasse (1963); Evans (1972)

Bengal cottage. Mid-C19 European garden building with *cob (or similar) walls, *bamboo doors and window-frames, and a reed-covered roof.

Benjamin, Asher (1771–1845). Massachusetts-born American architect who published *The Country Builder's Assistant* (1797) and *The American Builder's Companion* (1806), among other works, the sources of the design of countless buildings in New England. Five other titles followed, and Benjamin's books went into many editions: they were clear, practical, and well-illustrated volumes containing examples of various architectural styles from late-*Georgian to *Greek Revival. Benjamin thought highly of the *Federal-style architecture of Charles *Bulfinch. He practised as an architect in Boston from 1803, and several of his buildings may still be seen there, including the African Meeting House (1805), West Church (1806), and Charles Street Meeting House (1807). He was responsible for the reticent and handsome 54–5 and 70–5 Beacon Street. Benjamin was the architect for many buildings in Massachusetts, Vermont, Connecticut, Rhode Island, and New Hampshire, while his *Practical House Carpenter* (1830) was the most popular architectural book in C19 USA, and the source for an enormous range of buildings and street-furniture. He also published *Elements of Architecture* (1843), which includes technological information, including notes on the uses of cast iron. Most of his writings have been reprinted.

Benjamin (1838, 1854, 1972, 1972*a* 1976, 1976*a–c*); Embury (1917)

Benoît-Lévy, Georges (1880–1971). French theorist, founder of the Association Française des Cités-Jardins (1903), based on Ebenezer *Howard's ideas in England for *Garden Cities. It achieved a few pleasant garden suburbs, but little more. Benoit-Lévy was a prolific writer, however, and his thought was widely disseminated.

Benoît-Lévy (1911, 1932)

Benš, Adolf (1894–1982). Czech architect. He designed numerous buildings in the crisp up-to-date *International Modern style, including the Electric Administration Building, Holešovice District, Prague (1926–35—with Josef Kříž), a villa at Troja, Prague (1928), and his own house in the Baba District, Prague (1937). His best-known work was Prague Airport (1931–5). He was Professor of Architecture at the School of Industrial Arts in Prague from 1945 to 1970.

Leśnikowski (1996); Šlapeta (1978); Vondrová *et al.* (1978)

Benson, William (1682–1754). English architect. He designed Wilbury House, Wiltshire (1710), the first example of the Revival of the style of Inigo *Jones's domestic architecture in C18 England, derived in this case from John *Webb's Amesbury House, Wiltshire (1661). Wilbury was illustrated in volume 1 of *Vitruvius Britannicus* (1715—plates 51–2). Interested in hydraulics, Benson provided a system of piped water-supply for Shaftesbury, Dorset (1715), and designed water-works for the gardens of Herrenhausen, near Hanover, for King George I (1714–27). He curried such favour that he was appointed to the Surveyorship of the Works in 1718, having had the octogenarian *Wren dismissed. In the fifteen months he held the post he managed to remove any subordinate with talent, although he appointed Colen *Campbell as his

Deputy. Benson and Campbell seem to have planned to have the Houses of Parliament demolished (by claiming the House of Lords was structurally unsound) in order to further their plans to design a huge new Palladian building, but their views were challenged and they were dismissed in 1719, but not before new State Rooms at Kensington Palace (1718–20) were commenced, probably to Campbell's designs. *Hawksmoor claimed that Benson got more in one year for 'confusing the King's Works' than Wren obtained in forty years of 'honest endeavours'. Benson seems to have been involved in the building of Campbell's Stourhead, Wiltshire, and contributed to the building of the new *chancel of the Parish Church at Quarley, Hampshire (1723).

Colvin (1995); *DNB* (1917)

Bentley, John Francis (1839–1902). Doncaster-born English architect. He joined the London office of Henry *Clutton, working on the Jesuit Church in Farm Street and on Clutton's delightful little church of St Francis of Assisi, Notting Dale, London, where he designed the high-altar, *baptistery, and much else. In 1862 he converted to Roman Catholicism and set up his own practice, obtaining much work from his Church, including the Holy Rood, Watford, Hertfordshire (1883–90), a firmly English mix of *Second and Third Pointed Gothic, with an exquisite high-altar, *reredos, Rood-loft, and Rood. His greatest building is Westminster Cathedral (1894–1903), an Italo-*Byzantine building with a red-and-white striped exterior influenced by Norman *Shaw's New Scotland Yard. An eclectic tour-de-force, other precedents were San Marco, Venice, San Vitale in Ravenna, the *Romanesque *Duomo* in Pisa, the *Domkirche* (Cathedral Church) in Speier, Sant'Ambrogio in Milan, the *Certosa in Pavia, and Hagia Sophia in Constantinople (Istanbul). Romanesque and Byzantine elements fuse, but the plan is not unlike *Vignola's church of *Il Gesù* in Rome: the series of saucer-domes (constructed of *concrete) recall those of St-Front, Périgueux.

DNB (1920); de L'Hôpital (1919); Scott-Moncrieff (1924)

berceau. **1.** *Arbour of trellises covered with plants. **2.** Trees trained in *espalier fashion, with branches arched to form an *arbour.

Berg, Max (1870–1947). Stettin- (now Szczecin-) born German architect, who became City Architect of Breslau (now Wrocław), where he designed the gigantic *Jahrhunderthalle* (Century Hall—1910–13), one of the first buildings in which the *arcuated possibilities of *reinforced *concrete were exploited on a large scale in the huge ribbed dome with rings of *clearstorey-lights rising up above. It was intended as the centrepiece of a huge park laid out to commemorate the centenary of the defeat of Napoleon at the Battle of Leipzig, hence the name of the hall. It was one of the most adventurous and advanced structures to be built before 1914. He also designed many buildings in and around Breslau to cope with the increase in population when the creation of the Polish Corridor drove many Germans into Silesia after 1918, but retired and settled in Berlin in 1925.

Biegański (1972); Konwiarz (1926)

Berlage, Hendrik Petrus (1856–1934). Amsterdam-born architect, one of the most influential figures in The Netherlands, who was himself influenced by the work of *Sullivan and *Wright. He entered into partnership with the engineer Theodorus Sanders in 1884, and opened his own office in 1889. His early work was essentially in the *Renaissance Revival style, and in the 1890s he produced several *Art Nouveau graphic designs, culminating in the Villa Henny, The Hague (1898), a full-blown Art Nouveau work of architecture with furnishings much influenced by the design philosophies of *Morris and *Pugin. Berlage's most celebrated building is the Amsterdam Stock Exchange (1897–1903), which revealed his respect for the expressive power of constructional arched brickwork. The robust detailing and his love of brickwork and clear expressive functions (such as the *kneelers from which the segmental arches in the hall spring, and the junctions between load-bearing structure and metal *trusses) made him a precursor of the *Amsterdam School, while his writings earned him the respect of the young, aspiring members of the avant-garde. Berlage, like *Behrens, designed furniture, graphics, and all manner of artefacts: he was also an important town-planner. Although he was a delegate to *CIAM in 1928, he never actually joined, and claims for him as a proto-Modernist are much exaggerated. In fact, when *Rietveld asked him to join a group (that included Le *Corbusier, *Lurçat, Hannes *Meyer, and other Modernists) to have a photograph taken at the 1929 CIAM conference, Berlage refused, saying that everything he had built up was being destroyed by the very same collection of people.

Berlage (1996); Polano (1988); Reinink (1975); Singelenberg (1972); Singelenberg and Bock (1975)

berm. **1.** Horizontal surface lying between a moat and the slope of a *rampart in military architecture. **2.** Area between a ditch and a bank. **3.** Continuously sloping bank of earth against a wall, as in a fortified city-wall.

Bernard de Soissons (*fl.* C13). *See* Soissons.

Bernini, Giovanni Lorenzo (1598–1680). Sculptor, architect, painter, and poet, who made an outstanding contribution to the evolution of *Baroque. Born in Naples, his family settled in Rome (*c.*1605), where he spent the rest of his life. By the age of 20 he was famous, and from the election of Pope Urban VIII (1623–44) his rise was meteoric. In 1624 he began work on his gigantic *baldacchino in San Pietro, Rome, a tour-de-force with four *barley-sugar columns that alluded to the columns taken from the Herodian Temple in Jerusalem and set up over the tomb of the Apostle in the Constantinian *basilica that preceded the later church. Those columns, and the extravagance and grandeur of the object, made clear the continuity of the Church from the Old Testament, and celebrated the Church Triumphant of the Counter-Reformation.

Bernini was a master of the theatrical, as his sensational Cornaro Chapel in the Church of Santa Maria della Vittoria, Rome (1645–52), demonstrates. In the Ecstasy of St Teresa, a smiling angel thrusts its spear into the bosom of the swooning Saint, carried aloft in clouds, illuminated by gilded-rod *sunbursts and concealed lighting, and placed within an *aedicule above the altar. The whole vision is viewed by members of the Cornaro family, as though in theatre-boxes: it is a stunning, unforgettable, and magical creation. He also used theatrical techniques of false perspective, concealed lighting, and optical devices at the Scala Regia, Vatican Palace (1663–6), to emphasize the illusion of great length and size.

He designed the Four Rivers Fountain (1648–51) in the Piazza Navona, Rome (a powerful *base for the *Antique *obelisk recovered from excavations), and the elephant carrying another Antique obelisk on its back

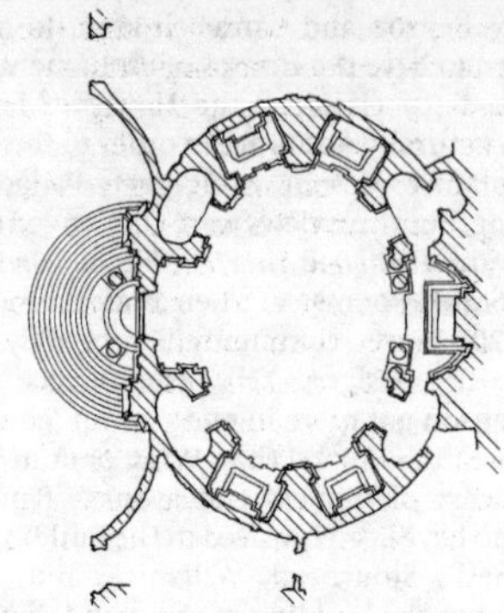

Plan of Sant'Andrea al Quirinale, Rome, showing elliptical nave surrounded by chapels with high-altar on the short axis opposite the entrance.

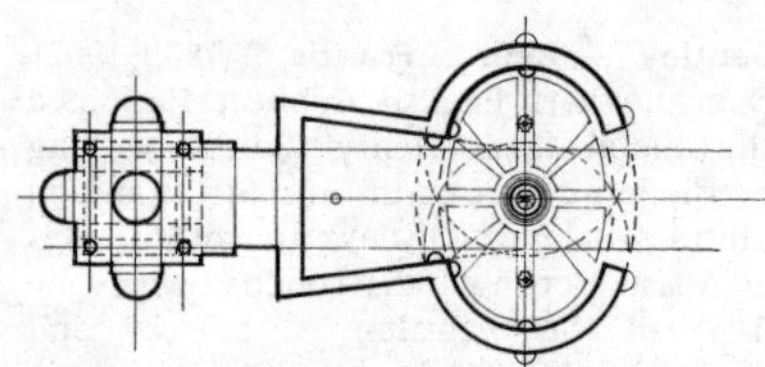

Diagrammatic plan of the Basilica and Piazza of San Pietro, Rome, showing Bernini's elliptical urban space and the converging colonnades in front of the church.

Bernini

outside the Church of Santa Maria sopra Minerva. His designs for the Papal tombs in St Peter's (Urban VIII, 1627–47, and Alexander VII, 1671–8) employed an essentially pyramidal composition where the figures were set against a fat obelisk-form. These were the precedents for countless such pyramidal funerary monuments set up in churches throughout Europe thereafter (there are many examples in England).

As an architect, Bernini was also outstanding. His finest church is Sant'Andrea al Quirinale (1658–70), an ellipse with the high-altar set on the short axis, and a series of *chapels off the centralized volume. A triumphant, vigorous, richly coloured space, it was widely influential in Roman Catholic countries during the Baroque period, notably in Central Europe. Also elliptical was his Piazza di San Pietro, with the Ancient Egyptian obelisk (re-erected by Domenico *Fontana in 1586) at its centre, on the main axis of the *basilica: the great *colonnades of the severe *Tuscan *Order around the wider parts of the ellipse become straight colonnades as they approach *Maderno's façade, but they are not parallel, being closer together as they branch off from the ellipse. These points, and the fact that the ground rises up to the steps before the façade, employ theatrical techniques to make the approach to the church seem longer and more impressive, while creating the illusion that Maderno's somewhat weak front is taller. There is a symbolic aspect too, for the great curved arms of the colonnade reach out to embrace the faithful to the bosom of Mother Church.

In secular architecture he was equally influential. His Palazzo Chigi (later Odescalchi) of 1664–6, which has a centrepiece of eight *Giant *pilasters with rusticated wings on either side, provided the precedent for many European princely palaces. At the same time he produced proposals for the east side of the Louvre in Paris: although never realized, it was an important model for other architects.

Borsi (1984); Brauer and Wittkower (1970); Fagiolo dell'Arco and Carandini (1977–8); Lavin (1980); Lavin *et al.* (1981); Varriano (1986); Wittkower (1981, 1982)

Bertotti-Scamozzi, Ottavio (1719–90). Doyen of the *Palladian Revival in Italy, he edited Palladio's work, producing the important *Le fabbriche e i disegni di Andrea Palladio raccolti e illustrati* (The Buildings and Designs of Andrea Palladio collected and illustrated—1776–83) and *Le terme dei Romani, disegnate da A. Palladio* (The Baths of Rome, Drawn by A. Palladio—1785), publications which have tended to obscure his own architectural significance. He was well-connected, and knew such figures as *Algarotti and *Quarenghi, while he seems to have been sought-after as a cicerone by those *cognoscenti* on the *Grand Tour, and produced a guide-book to the architectural sights of Vicenza in 1761. His own buildings in and around Vicenza, unsurprisingly, are strongly influenced by Palladianism: his Casa Muzzi, Riello (1770), is clearly based on the Villino Cerato di Montecchio Precalcino (1540s), while the Palazzo Franceschini a San Marco, Vicenza (1770), though essentially Palladian in compostion, betrays certain tentative aspects of *Neoclassicism. In the last decade of his life his work became more severe and bare (e.g. Palazzo Braghetta sul Corso (1780) and Teatro Eretenio (1781–4)).

Bertotti-Scamozzi (1776–83, 1797); Kamm-Kyburz (1983); Olivato (1975)

Berty, Thomas (*c.*1485–1555). English master-mason. He was engaged on the buildings of the Priory of St Mary Overie, Southwark, including the top *stage of what is now the tower of Southwark Cathedral. In the 1530s he worked on the *vaults of the *presbytery *aisles of Winchester Cathedral. Berty was in charge of the Royal building-works at Calshot Castle and Cowes Castle, Isle of Wight, and in the 1540s he built Hurst Castle. He seems to have been a key figure in the transformation of *Perpendicular *Gothic into *Tudor *Renaissance, as can be seen in Winchester Cathedral, where the *chantry-chapels of Bishops Fox and Gardiner show the change in the 1520s and 1530s.

Harvey (1987)

Bestelmeyer, German (1874–1942). German traditionalist architect, best known as one of the founders of Der *Block, and as a critic of *Modernism. He designed several new buildings and remodelled existing ones at the University of Munich (1906–22), and was responsible for the German Pavilion at the International Art Exhibition, Rome (1911). His Germanic Museum (now the Busch-Reisinger Museum of Central and North European Art, Harvard University, Cambridge, Mass. (1914–17)) is well known. In 1916 he won the competition to design a House of Friendship, Istanbul, Turkey, and during the inter-war period designed several large projects, including the *Luftwaffe* District Headquarters Building, Munich (1933–9), all in a simplified Neoclassical style.

Lane (1985); Rittich (1938); Thiersch (1961)

béton. *Concrete. *Béton brut* is raw concrete, exposed after the *formwork is struck, and sometimes showing impressions (board-marked concrete) of the timber boards of which the formwork is constructed.

Bettino, Antonio (*fl.* 1650–80). Italian architect who designed the Church of San Filippo Neri, Chieri (1664–73), and Santi Maurizio e Lazzaro, Turin (1679–1704), generally agreed to be his greatest work. He was also responsible for San Filippo Neri, Turin (begun 1675), but *Guarini took this over.

Pommer (1967); Tamburini (1968)

Betto, Jean (1647–1722). The Betto family provided architects who practised in and around

Nancy, Lorraine, in C17 and C18. Jean is the most celebrated, remembered for the interior design of the Cathedral (1699–1736), but his son, **Jacques**, and grandson, also **Jacques** (1714–), carried out designs for various churches in Nancy.

Bauchal (1887); Hautecœur (1950)

Beverley, Robert of (*fl.* 1253–85). English master-mason. He worked on the *choir and *transept of Beverley *Minster, Yorkshire (completed *c.*1260), and from 1253 was engaged on work at Westminster Abbey and Palace. In 1260 he became King's Master-Mason and Chief Mason of Westminster Abbey. In 1271 he became Surveyor of the Royal Works at the Tower of London, the castles of Windsor, Rochester, and Hadleigh, and the manors of Guildford, Kempton, and Havering. He designed the Byward and Middle towers of the Tower of London, complete with their beautiful internal *vaults. These works and his contributions at Westminster Abbey (including the first four *bays of the *nave) have assured him a secure place in the history of English architecture. He was no mean sculptor, either, and was responsible for the image of King Henry III (1276) from which the famous *effigy was copied.

Harvey (1987)

Beyaert, Henri (1823–94). Belgian architect who, like his contemporary Alphonse *Balat, made an eclectic contribution to the development of *fin-de-siècle* architecture in Brussels, notably in his harmonious blending of white stone, blue stone, and brick. He was particularly interested in the use of iron in architecture, and influenced his assistants, Paul *Hankar and Victor *Horta. His best-known classical work is the Banque Nationale, Brussels (1860–5), but he later experimented with *Gothic and *Renaissance Revivals.

Beyaert (1880–92); Kennes, Vanderperren, and Victoire (1978); Martiny (1980); Puttemans (1976)

Bianchi, Pietro (1787–1849). Italian Neo-classical architect from the Ticino area. A pupil of Luigi *Cagnola, he was responsible for the Church of San Francesco di Paola, Naples (1817–31), with its high, windowless drum and *Pantheon-like dome, and serenely beautiful interior. Much influenced by French precedent, the curved *colonnades on either side of the *portico were based on *Bernini's Piazza di San Pietro in Rome. They were designed by Leopoldo Laperuta and Antonio de Simone from 1808 for an earlier scheme proposed under the French occupation.

Meeks (1966); Middleton and Watkin (1987)

Bianco *or* **Bianchi, Bartolommeo** (*c.*1590–1657). Como-born architect who worked in the *Baroque style in Genoa. His Jesuit College, now the University (1630–6), built on a dramatically sloping site, has a staircase rising from the vaulted entrance-vestibule to the *arcaded *cortile at the far end of which is a splendid symmetrical double stair rising the full height of the building. The chief influence on Bianco was Galeazzo *Alessi, who also constructed *palazzi* on sloping sites.

Watkin (1986); Wittkower (1982)

Bibiena. *See* Galli da Bibiena.

Bicknell, Julian (1945–). English architect. His works include alterations to the stables (1977), re-creation of the garden-hall (1980), and the design of the new library (1982) at Castle Howard, Yorkshire. Henbury *Rotonda, a house near Macclesfield, Cheshire, is a convincing essay in C20 *Palladianism (1983–7) based on the Villa Capra, Vicenza, and on *Campbell's Mereworth Castle, Kent. His work draws on the *Arts-and-Crafts, Classical, and vernacular traditions, involving close collaboration with craftsmen.

Personal information; Powers (1987)

Bidlake, William Henry (1861–1938). Son of the Wolverhampton church-architect **George Bidlake** (1829–92). In 1887 he set up in practice with John Cotton (1844–) in Birmingham, from where he developed a large practice. He designed several fine late *Arts-and-Crafts houses, one of which (his own), 'Woodgate', 37 Hartopp Road, Sutton Coldfield, was published by *Muthesius in *Das Englische Haus* (The English House).

Gray (1985)

Biedermeier. Central-European style of architecture, decorative arts, painting, and interior design from *c.*1815 to *c.*1860, especially in Berlin, Vienna, and Munich. The name derives from the fictional (1854) character, Wieland Gottlieb Biedermaier, a comfortable, middle-class figure of fun, *Bieder* meaning virtuous, and Maier being a common German surname, like Jones. The style was robustly comfortable, decently proportioned, essentially *Neoclassical, with *Empire and *Regency touches.

Chilvers, Osborne, and Farr (1988); Gentil (1990)

Biegański, Piotr (1905–). Polish architect who contributed to the restoration of Warsaw's Old Town (1947–54), and helped, with Jan *Zachwatowicz, to evolve Polish theories of *conservation. He prepared prizewinning designs for the competition to design the new opera-house in Leipzig, Germany, in 1952, but the building erected (1956–60) under the direction of the German architect Kunz Nierade owed little to his work. He was a prolific author, writing on many aspects of historic buildings.

Biegański (1972); Puget (1994); Warsaw Polytechnic (1967)

biforate window. Type of medieval window, common in Italy, with a *colonnette subdividing it into two arched *lights, also called a *Venetian arch or *bifore*.

biforis, biforus (*pl.* **bifora**). **1.** *Antique two-leaved door or window according to *Vitruvius. **2.** Building or room with two doors or other openings.

Bigelow, Jacob (1786–1879). Rumford Professor of Medicine at Harvard University, responsible for the design of Mount Auburn Cemetery, Cambridge, Mass., with its *Egyptian Revival gateway and lodges (1825–42).

Carrott (1978)

Bigio, Nanni di Baccio (d. 1568). Florentine architect who settled in Rome in the 1540s. He designed the Porta del Pòpolo (1561–4), unquestionably his best work, and was appointed Architect to the Papal Palace for life in 1567, in which capacity he supervised construction of the Castel Sant'Angelo, various fortifications, and the church of San Martin degli Svizzeri.

Ackerman (1986); Wittkower and Jaffé (1972)

bilection. *See* bolection.

Bill, Max (1908–94). Swiss architect who trained at the Dessau *Bauhaus (1927–9) and designed many timber houses in the 1940s, but who also revived the Bauhaus programme at the *Hochschule für Gestaltung* (High School for Construction) in Ulm in Germany, for which he designed a new building (1953–5). He designed several exhibition buildings, including the Swiss Pavilions at the World's Fair, New York (1938), the Milan *Triennale* (1951), and the Venice *Biennale* (1952), the Ulm City Pavilion, Baden-Württemberg Exhibition, Stuttgart (1955), and the *Bilden und Gestalten* (Form and Construction) section, Swiss National Exhibition, Lausanne (1964). He was a prolific writer, and published much on aspects of *Modernism.

Bill (1945, 1952, 1955, 1969); Hüttinger (1977); Staber (1964)

billet. One of a series of short chamfered, cylindrical, prismatic, rectangular, segmental, or square projecting members in, or forming, a decorative continuous moulding, its axis parallel to the direction of the series, with sometimes two or more rows of this ornament placed one above the other, with the billets of one row alternating with those of the other. It is characteristic of *Romanesque architecture. Cylindrical billets resemble short lengths of dowel.

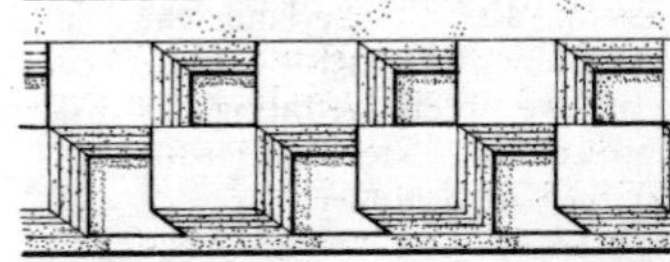

alternating cubical billets, Church of St Augustine, Canterbury, Kent

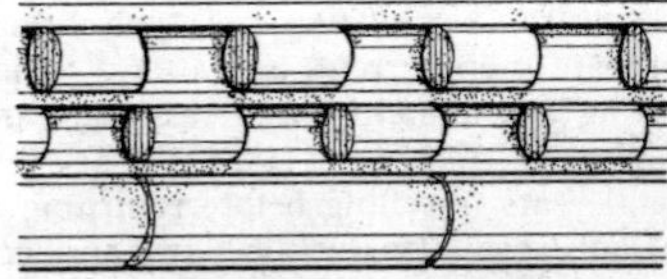

cylindrical billets, Binham Priory, Norfolk

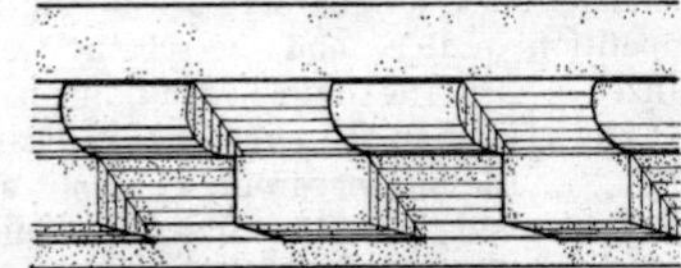

half-cylindrical and prismatic billets, Church of St Mary de Castro, Leicester

billet (*After Parker*)

Billing, Hermann (1867–1946). German architect, celebrated as a designer of houses and fine interiors in the early years of C20, often in a zestful *Jugendstil manner. He evolved a massive simplified *Rundbogenstil shortly afterwards. His buildings include the *Rathaus*, Kiel (1903–11), the powerful *Kunsthalle*, Mannheim (1906–7), and the new University buildings, Freiburg-im-Breisgau (1907–11).

In the 1920s he turned to a simplified *Neoclassicism.

Billing (1904); Martin (1930)

Billings, Robert William (1813–74). English architect, better known for his fine illustrations and draughtsmanship, as in *History and Description of St Paul's Cathedral* (1837), *Churches of London* (1839), and *Durham Cathedral* (1843). His most celebrated work was *Baronial and Ecclesiastical Antiquities of Scotland* (1845–52), an important book for Scots antiquarianism, and a major source-book of the *Scottish Baronial style. He also published several works on *Gothic architecture. He had an extensive practice, specializing in restoration. He designed Castle Wemyss, Renfrewshire, various works at Dalziell Castle, Motherwell, Lanarkshire (1859), the Church of St John, Crosby-on-Eden, Cumberland (1854), and a fine monument in Carlisle Cemetery consisting of two interpenetrating *obelisks in memory of Peter *Nicholson (1856).

Billings (1845–52); *DNB* (1917)

Bindesbøll, Michael Gottlieb Birkner (1800–56). Danish Neoclassical architect. In Paris during the 1820s he was influenced by the new theories of Classical *polychromy that were then current, and after a period working as an architectural assistant and studying in Copenhagen (1824–33), he spent several years travelling before returning to the Danish capital to work on his masterpiece, the museum in Copenhagen to hold Bertel Thorvaldsen's (1770–1844) sculptures (1839–47). Bindesbøll's designs were selected in a competition in 1839, and the scheme was finalized in 1840. The completed building has five Graeco-Egyptian *battered or *Vitruvian openings on the entrance-front, set *in antis*, as it were, between *antae and under an *Ionic *entablature from which the *frieze has been elided. This *portico seems to have been derived from a synthesis of *Schinkel's first project for the *Neue Wache* Guard House, *Unter den Linden* (1816), mixed with his *Lustgarten* Museum-front, both in Berlin. The same battered motifs are repeated (to a smaller scale) on two storeys around the windows of the side-walls. The *stucco exterior is painted ochre, with architectural elements picked out in blue, green, and white, and the vaulted interiors painted red, green, and ochre are admirable settings for the white marble sculptures. The airy central courtyard (in which Thorvaldsen's body was buried) has its surrounding walls painted with images of trees: these murals create an extraordinary and memorable backdrop to the sculptor's grave. On three sides of the building is a painted frieze, set just above the *plinth, that depicts the transportation of the exhibits from Rome to Copenhagen. The Museum made an important contribution to the C19 debate about polychromy in Classical architecture. Bindesbøll also designed a lunatic-asylum near Aarhus, a charming complex of very simple brick buildings set in a specially created landscape intended to benefit the patients by its beauty and serenity (1850–1); another mental hospital at Oringa, Zeeland (1854–7); the Town Halls of Thisted (1851–3), Flensburg (1852), Stege (1853–4), and Naestved (1855–6); and the Medical Association housing-block, Copenhagen (1853–5), all of which were accomplished works. His son, **Thorvald** (1846–1908), was also an architect, and became the most prolific of designers in the *Art Nouveau style: he also designed the Carlsberg Lager-Beer label.

Bramsen (1959); Bruun and Fenger (1892); Millech (1960); Wanscher (1903)

Biotecture. Architecture influenced by biology, such as in the work of *Soleri. *See* Arcology.

Jencks (1971)

bird's-beak. Moulding, the *section of which consists of an *ovolo at the top under which is an *ogee or hollow, forming a sharp point at the junction of the two: the section resembles a bird's beak. Common in *Renaissance work.

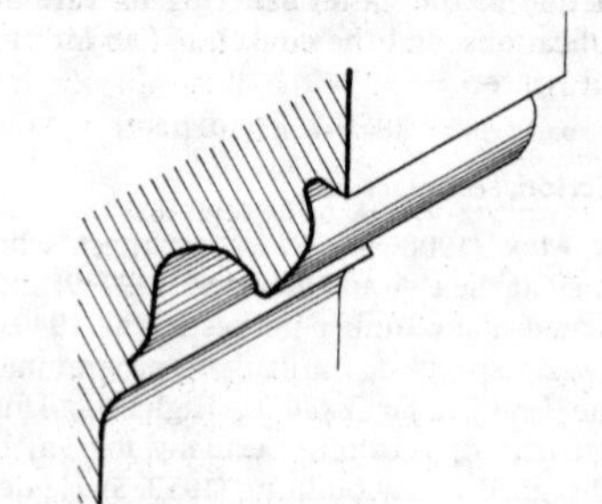

bird's-beak

bird's-head. *See* beak-head.

bird's-mouth. Triangular right-angled notch formed in the end of a timber (e.g. *rafter) to enable it to be securely fixed to a rectangular timber (e.g. a *wall-plate).

Birkerts, Gunnar (1925–). Latvian-born American architect, who settled in the USA in 1949, where his architecture, much influenced by the work of Eero *Saarinen, has been admired. His Museum of Glass, Corning, NY (1976), exploits curved glazed forms. Other works include the Law Library, Duke University, NC (1989), and the Kemper Museum of Contemporary Art, Kansas, Mo. (1991).

Emanuel (1994)

Blackburn, William (1750–90). English architect, he made his name as a designer of prisons following the Penitentiary Act (1779), and was a pioneer of radial design. His work included the County Gaols at Oxford (*c.*1785–1805), Ipswich, Suffolk (1786–90), Gloucester (1788–91), Monmouth (1788–90), and Dorchester, Dorset (1789–95). He was also responsible for the Houses of Correction at Northleach, Gloucestershire (1787–91), and Horsley, Gloucestershire (1787–91), among others.

DNB (1917); Colvin (1995)

Blacket, Edmund Thomas (1817–83). English-born architect, he emigrated to Australia in 1842, completed the Anglican Cathedral in Sydney (from 1845), and designed several churches in the *Gothic Revival style as Diocesan Architect, including St Mark's, Darling Point, Sydney (1847–75). He designed the University of Sydney (1854–60), an essay in *Tudor *Gothic, with a great hall based on Westminster Hall in London. He was also responsible for the Cathedral Church of St George, Perth, Western Australia. In later years he was assisted by his son, **Cyril** (*fl.* 1874–80).

Cruickshank (1996); Herman (1954, 1963)

blade. 1. *Back or principal *rafter. **2.** Main element of a *cruck *truss.

blank. *Blind, meaning with no openings. *Blank door* or *window* is a sealed recess with the appearance of a door or window placed to create symmetry in a *façade. A *blank, blind,* or *dead* wall has no apertures.

blind. 1. As *blank. Anything *engaged or attached to a wall, with no openings or glazing, used decoratively, such as an *arcade or *tracery, is described as *blind*, as in a *blind arcade* or *blind tracery*. **2.** Device for partially or wholly preventing light from passing through an opening, such as a piece of flexible material attached at the top to a roller on which it is unwound or wound, or a *screen with fixed or moveable slats (*Venetian blind*).

blind storey. 1. Wall-façade at the top of a building, essentially a raised *parapet, without rooms behind it, and unroofed, for architectural effect or to conceal e.g. a roof. **2.** *Tribune of a church.

blocage. Mass of *rubble-stones of various sizes mixed with mortar, often used inside the *dressed faces of *Romanesque walls and *piers. It was not always stable, and led to many structural failures.

block. 1. Piece of stone, *terracotta, etc., prepared for building and bigger than a brick. **2.** Rectangular plain element at the bottom of a door-*architrave, also stopping the *skirt or *plinth in Classical architecture. **3.** Row or mass of buildings connected together, as in a *terrace, set against a street on the front and bounded by other streets, often of mixed use. **4.** Most significant building in an architectural composition, e.g. a *corps de logis with wings. **5.** One of a series of projecting blocks on *architraves, columns, or *pilasters as in a *Gibbs surround: in such cases the architrave, column, or pilaster is said to be *banded* or *blocked*. *See* band. **6.** Small triangular piece of timber in the angle between two other timbers, e.g. at the top of two *cruck *blades.

block-capital. *Cushion *capital.

block-cornice. Italian *Renaissance *entablature with a series of plain undecorated *modillions treated as *corbels supporting a normal *cornice, often with the *bed-mouldings suppressed, or converted into a simplified *architrave.

Block, Der. Group of Berlin-based traditionalist architects formed in 1928 to resist the *Modernist *Ring group. Its origins lay in acrimony that arose when Paul *Bonatz prepared a plan at the behest of the *Deutscher Werkbund for the *Weissenhofsiedlung in Stuttgart, in which houses with pitched roofs were proposed. Disputes followed, and *Mies van der Rohe's Modernist solution was accepted. Bonatz and his colleague Paul Schmitthenner (1884–1972) withdrew from the scheme in protest, and, with other architects, including *Bestelmeyer and Paul

*Schultze-Naumburg, formed an association which proposed to promote an architecture suited to the tastes and needs of ordinary people, and on regional and national conditions, rather than imposed upon an unwilling populace by a Leftist élite. It later became associated with German Nationalism.

Tafuri and Dal Co (1986)

block-house. Structure, frequently of timber, often for defensive purposes, constructed of logs.

blocking-course. 1. *Masonry or brickwork laid on a *cornice to hold the latter down, as large projecting cornices are effectively *cantilevers, and need weights or forces to anchor them and prevent them from falling. **2.** Course of stone or brick forming a projecting *band without mouldings at the base of a building, i.e. an unmoulded *plinth. **3.** Plain band or *string-course.

blocking-out. *Boasting in *masonry, or preparation for a finish on a wall by means of timber grounds or battens.

block-plan. Drawing of buildings and layouts in simplified, undetailed form.

Blom, Holger (1906–96). Swedish architect who, as Director of Parks in Stockholm, instituted a comprehensive plan for landscaping the city (1937–72). His ideas have been widely adopted since the 1939–45 war.

Emanuel (1994)

Blom, Piet (1934–). Amsterdam-born architect who became one of the most important protagonists of Dutch *Structuralism. He is best known for the 'Kasbah' housing at Hengelo (1965–73) and 't Speelhuis centre and housing at Helmond (1975–8).

Emanuel (1994)

Blomfield, Sir Arthur William (1829–99). English architect. After the obligatory Continental tour, he established a successful practice in London, carrying out numerous commissions for churches, private houses, schools, and other buildings. His best-known works are the skilful rebuilding of the *nave and south *transept of St Mary Overie (now Southwark Cathedral), in the *Gothic style (1890–7), and the *Italianate *basilica of St Barnabas, Jericho, Oxford, with a fine *Gothic *campanile.

DNB (1917)

Blomfield, Charles James (1862–1932). Eldest son of Sir Arthur *Blomfield, he was articled to his father, and became Architect to the Dean and Chapter of Southwark Cathedral. He carried out sensitive restorations at St Cross, Winchester, and St Mary Redcliffe, Bristol. His new buildings include additions at Eton College, Buckinghamshire, and at Wellington College, Berkshire (1906), where he built the new dining-hall in a free *Renaissance style.

Gray (1985)

Blomfield, Sir Reginald Theodore (1856–1942). Cousin of C. J. *Blomfield, he entered the office of his uncle, Sir Arthur *Blomfield, in 1881. Two years later he set up his own London practice, began writing and drawing for publication, and was involved in the founding of the *Art-Workers' Guild. He designed 51 and 53 Frognal, Hampstead, the Talbot Building at Lady Margaret Hall, Oxford (1910–15), the former United Universities Club of 1906 (known as his *Champs-Élysées* style) at the corner of Suffolk Street and Pall Mall East, and the Regent Street Quadrant and part of Piccadilly Circus of 1910–23. Other works were war cemeteries and the Menin Gate, Ypres, Belgium (1926). His writings include *The Formal Garden in England* (1892); *A History of Renaissance Architecture in England, 1500–1800* (1897), a source-book for the *Wrenaissance and *Georgian Revival; *A History of French Architecture, 1494–1661* and *1661–1774* (1911 and 1921); and *Memoirs of an Architect* (1932). He published a scathing and witty attack on the fashionable *International *Modernism then being promoted by *The Architectural Review*: it was called, appropriately, *Modernismus* (1934). He also wrote elegantly on *Vauban (1938) and Norman *Shaw (1940).

Blomfield (1892, 1897, 1932, 1934, 1938, 1940, 1974); *DNB* (1959); Fellows (1985); Gray (1985)

Blomstedt, Aulis (1906–79). Finnish architect and theoretician, whose architecture has been influential. His apartment-blocks and *terrace-houses at Tapiola, Espoo (1962–5), are boldly conceived, with strong, rhythmic patterns.

Pallasmaa (1980); Salokorpi (1970); Tempel (1968)

Blond, Jean-Baptiste-Alexandre Le (1679–1719). French architect. He trained in Paris, where he built the *Hôtel de Clermont, Rue de Varennes (1708–14). His elegant architecture is perhaps best appreciated from the Reynault

House, Châtillon-sur-Bagneux (*c.*1709–14). In 1716 or 1717 he was engaged by Peter the Great to superintend the works at St Petersburg, Russia, where he introduced the *Rococo style at the palace of Peterhof (later doubled in length by *Rastrelli). A fine draughtsman, he prepared illustrations for Félibien's history of Saint-Denis (1706) and d'Aviler's *Cours* in the 1710 edition, which he also edited.

Gallet (1972, 1972*a*); Hautecœur (1950); Kimball (1980); Mariette (1927–9)

Blondel, Jacques-François (1705–74). Rouen-born French architect, who was an important teacher, theorist, and writer. He revered French architecture, and especially the work of *Gabriel, *Mansart, and *Perrault. His independent School of Architecture, opened in Paris in 1743, included among its students *Boullée, *Chambers, *Ledoux, and de *Wailly. He was appointed Professor at the Académie Royale d'Architecture in 1762, and his lectures and theories were set out in his *Cours d'architecture* (1771–7), completed by Pierre Patte. His many books included *De la Distribution des Maisons de Plaisance et de la Décoration des Édifices en Général* (1737–8), the monumental four-volume encylopedia of French buildings, *L'Architecture Françoise . . .* (1752–6), and *Discours sur la Manière d'étudier l'Architecture* (1747), with a later edition of 1754. Among his surviving works are part of the Place des Armes, Metz (1760s), and a *screen in Strasbourg Cathedral (*c.*1767).

Blondel and Patte (1771–7); Braham (1980); Eriksen (1974); Gallet (1972*a*); Hautecœur (1950); Herrmann (1962); Kaufmann (1955); Rykwert (1980)

Blondel, Nicolas-François (1617–86). French military engineer and mathematician, who became the first Director of the Royal Academy of Architecture and *Ingénieur du Roi*. His *Cours d'Architecture* (1675, 1683, and 1698) was an important architectural textbook in which the *Orders were given prominence, and the principles of *Classicism and a rational approach to architecture were promoted and explained. He did not design many buildings but was responsible for the huge monumental Parisian *Portes*, those of St-Antoine, St-Bernard, and St-Denis, all 1671.

Blondel (1698); Blunt (1982); Hautecœur (1948); Herrmann (1973); Teyssèdre (1967)

Blore, Edward (1787–1879). English architect, he contributed to the final designs of Sir Walter Scott's Abbotsford, provided all the architectural drawings for *The Provincial Antiquities and Picturesque Scenery of Scotland*, and published his *The Monumental Remains of Noble and Eminent Persons* (1824). Soon he established himself as a reliable architect, designing the Mall front (destroyed) and other works at Buckingham Palace (1832), becoming Surveyor to Westminster Abbey (1827–49), and carrying out works at Hampton Court and Windsor Castle. He built up an enormous practice, designing country-houses in his favoured *Tudor and *Elizabethan styles (Crom Castle, Co. Fermanagh, Ireland (1838–41), is a good example), and building and restoring churches.

Colvin (1995); *DNB* (1917)

Blouet, Guillaume-Abel (1795–1853). Architect and theorist of mid-C19 France. He worked with *Gilbert in Rome and later in Paris, where he was appointed architect to the Arc de Triomphe de l'Étoile in 1831 (with Gilbert as his deputy): he added the *Attic storey to *Chalgrin's arch. Blouet travelled to Greece in 1828 and prepared studies of the *Doric temple at Aegina (published in 1838), which showed the building brilliantly coloured, with strong blue and red predominating. With Gilbert and *Hittorff, Blouet was an important protagonist of the use of colour in Greek architecture. His reputation as a scholar of *Antique architecture was further enhanced by his *Restauration des thermes d'Antonin Caracalla à Rome* (Restoration of the Baths of Caracalla in Rome—1828).

Blouet determined to use architecture to further social and moral aims, and his ideas were developed from those of François-Marie-Charles Fourier (1772–1837) and Claude-Henri de Rouvroy, Comte de Saint-Simon (1760–1825). In 1836 he toured America to look at prisons, and on his return designed a number of formal corrective institutions, including the penal-farm colony at Mettray, near Tours (designed 1839). He became an authority on the design of prisons. His utilitarian aims were promoted through his teaching, and in 1846 he succeeded L.-P. *Baltard as Professor of the Theory of Architecture at the École des Beaux-Arts, a post he held until his death. In 1847 he commenced work on the *Supplément à la traité théorique et pratique de l'art de bâtir de Jean Rondelet*, essentially a catalogue of early C19 achievements in engineering.

Hautecœur (1943–57); Middleton and Watkin (1987)

Blow, Detmar Jellings (1867–1939). London-born *Arts-and-Crafts architect who travelled to Italy with *Ruskin in 1889, and then worked for Philip *Webb on East Knoyle Church, Wiltshire. A member of the *Art-Workers' Guild from 1892, he laid the stonework for two cottages by *Gimson in Leicestershire, and then acted as clerk of works for *Lethaby at Brockhampton Church, Herefordshire. He designed a cottage for the Cheap Cottages Exhibition at Letchworth (1905), and from 1906 (when he was joined in partnership by the *Beaux-Arts architect Fernand Billerey) worked on numerous town- and country-houses, notably on the Duke of Westminster's estates. He designed Government House, Salisbury (now Harare), Rhodesia (now Zimbabwe), carried out sensitive repairs and alterations to many churches, and designed Happisburgh Manor, Norfolk (a flint-and-brick house on a *butterfly plan with a thatched roof). He was one of the most gifted architects of his generation.

Gray (1985); Miller (1989)

Blum, Hans (*fl.* 1550). German compiler of an influential and much-published work on the *Orders based on *Serlio, *Quinque Columnarum exacta descriptio atque deliniatio cum symmetrica earum distributione* (1550), later published in London as *The Book of Five Collumnes of Architecture . . . Gathered . . . by H. Bloome out of Antiquities*, of which the 1608 edition was probably the finest. Some German editions also contained designs by Blum.

Blum (1550); Harris (1990)

board. Thin, long slab of timber no more than 5 cm thick.

board-marked concrete. *See* béton.

boast. 1. To cut material, especially stone, to the general form, leaving it for later carving into, say, a *capital. Such a form, awaiting fine *dressing, is called *boasted* or *bossage*. **2.** To dress stone with a boaster or drove (a broad chisel): *boasted* or *droved* dressings have regular marks like ribands or small chequers; irregular rough dressings are *random-tooled* or *random-droved*.

Boberg, Ferdinand (1860–1946). Swedish architect. His early designs were influenced by the theories of *Viollet-le-Duc as well as by the works of H. H. *Richardson and *Sullivan, but his most important achievements were several large civic buildings, including the Central Post Office, Stockholm (1898–1904). He designed many exhibitions, including the Baltic Exposition Building, Malmö (1914), and a great number of private houses, notably the Villa Bergsgarden (1905–6). His mature designs were rich in decoration and materials, with simple, bold massing in the Swedish *Neoclassical tradition, but with exotic, even oriental allusions in his interpretation of *Art Nouveau. His reputation has been largely eclipsed by the works of *Asplund, *Lewerentz, *Östberg, and *Tengbom, but he was one of the major architectural figures in Scandinavia from 1884 until 1915. From the time he closed his office in 1915 he recorded much of Sweden's historical architecture in a series of portfolios supported by subscription.

Ahlberg (1925); Eaton (1972); Walton (1994)

Böblinger Family. South-German master-masons among whom **Hans** (1412–82) and his son **Matthäus** (d. 1505) were the most important. Hans worked under *Ensinger on the *Frauenkirche* (Church of Our Lady) in Esslingen on the Neckar. Matthäus, who seems to have been apprenticed at Cologne, joined his father at Esslingen, later becoming master-mason of Ulm *Minster (*c.*1480), where he succeeded Ensinger and designed the upper stages of the spectacular western tower. However, the beautiful octagon and perforated masonry *spire were not completed until the 1890s by August Beyer, according to Böblinger's drawings, forming the tallest such ensemble in Europe.

Baum (1956); Bucher (1979)

Bodley, George Frederick (1827–1907). Hull-born English architect, one of the most successful and sensitive of the *Gothic Revival. A student of George Gilbert *Scott in the 1840s, his first churches include St Michael and All Angels, Brighton (1859–61), an essay in C13 *polychromy of the *'muscular' type; All Saints', Jesus Lane, Cambridge (1862–9), which marks Bodley's rejection of Continental influences in favour of English *Second Pointed; and St John the Baptist, Tue Brook, Liverpool (1868–71), representing a glowing and refined English C14 Second Pointed revival of the utmost delicacy, with glorious colour all over the walls, roof, and furnishings (beautifully restored by S. E. *Dykes Bower). From 1869 to 1897 Bodley was in partnership with Thomas *Garner, designing several churches, including the exquisite and scholarly Holy Angels, Hoar Cross, Staffordshire (1872–1900); St Augustine's, Pendlebury, Manchester (1870–4), with the internal *buttress arrangement of Albi Cathedral translated into English Second Pointed (the *buttresses being pierced to form *aisle-passages); and St Mary the Virgin, Clumber Park, Nottinghamshire (1886–9), a cruciform church with a central tower and spire, the ensemble being in Bodley's most elegant flowing Second Pointed style. Bodley designed most of Clumber on his own, as he did with St Mary's, Eccleston, Cheshire (1894–9), again nominally C14 in style, with stone rib-vaulting throughout. His Holy Trinity, Prince Consort Road, Kensington, London (1902), is light and airy, quite unlike his earlier work. His last great church was the Cathedral of Sts Peter and Paul, Washington, DC (1906–76, finally completed in 1990).

Clarke (1969); *DNB* (1920); Dixon and Muthesius (1985); Eastlake (1970)

Bodley, Sir Josias (*c.*1550–1617). Exeter-born military engineer, brother of the founder of the Bodleian Library in Oxford. He saw service in Ireland from 1598 in the war against Hugh, The O'Neill, Second 'Great' Earl of Tyrone (*c.*1540–1616), which only came to an end in 1603. He remained in Ireland, having been appointed by the Privy Council as Superintendent of Castles. In 1609 he was entrusted with the survey for the Plantation of Ulster, and in 1612 became Director-General of the Fortifications and Buildings in Ireland. He built a range of fortifications, but his largest works were the *ramparts and fortifications of the City of London's new town of Coleraine in the specially created County of Londonderry (largely colonized by the City and its Livery Companies).

Curl (1986); Loeber (1981)

Bodt, Jean de (1670–1745). Huguenot military engineer and architect who left France after 1685, trained in The Netherlands, arrived in England in 1688, served in King William III's army in Ireland (1690–1) and in Flanders (1692–5), and worked for a while in England, producing grand *Baroque designs for Whitehall and Greenwich Palaces (1698), neither of which was realized. He eventually moved to Berlin in 1699 (where he was known as **Johann von Bodt** or **von Bott**). He completed (*c.*1706) the *Baroque *Zeughaus* (Arsenal) on *Unter den Linden* (begun by *Nering, with sculptures by *Schlüter), built the great Fortuna Gate of the *Stadtschloss* (Town Palace), Potsdam (1701), and added the *steeple (resembling *Wren's work at St Vedast, Foster Lane, London) to Nering's Parish Church, Potsdam (1695–1703). Thomas Wentworth, Lord Raby (1672–1739), British envoy to Prussia (1703–11), who had also been involved in King William's many military campaigns, obtained designs from Bodt from which the east wing of Stainborough Hall (Wentworth Castle), Yorkshire, was built (*c.*1710–20): the elevation is almost pure Franco-Prussian in style, a considerable rarity in England. Although much of his work in Prussia was concerned with fortifications, he also designed several fine houses, including the Schwerin (1700–2) and Rademacher (1701–4) Palaces, Berlin, and Friedrichstein (1709–14) and Dönhoffstadt (1710–16) Castles, East Prussia. In 1728 Bodt moved to Dresden to take up a position as Superintendent of the Royal Works, and oversaw the construction of Pöppelmann's extensions and restorations of the Dutch (later Japanese) Palace (*c.*1730). He also designed parts of the castle of Königstein, near Dresden (1734–6).

Colvin (1995); Colombier (1955); Hempel (1965); Lorck (1972)

Boehmer (Bomer after 1915), Edward (1861–1940). Pennsylvania-born architect, educated in Stuttgart, Hamburg, and Berlin. He set up a practice in London with Percy Christian Gibbs (1864–1904) in 1889, designing Harley House, Marylebone Road (1904), and Portland Court, 160–200 Great Portland Street (1904–12), both impressive blocks of mansion-flats. 80 Portland Place (1909) has a distinguished Classical *façade with strong French and American influences.

Gray (1985)

Boffrand, Gabriel-Germain (1667–1754). French sculptor turned architect, who made a fortune designing and building Parisian *hôtels on ingenious plans, often incorporating complicated geometries, among them the Hôtels d'Amelot (1712–14) and de Torcy (1713–15). His *Rococo style was of the utmost refinement, and can best be seen in the charming elliptical rooms he created at the Hôtel de Soubise, Paris (1732–9)—now the Archives Nationales: these were decorated by François Boucher (1703–70), Charles-Joseph Natoire, and Charles Andrew van Loo

(1705–65). Boffrand's exteriors are deceptively simple and reticent, influenced by *Bernini's Palazzo Chigi-Odescalchi in Rome, and his frequent use of the ellipse in planning courts and rooms also recalls the great Italian master's work. He was consulted by *Neumann about the plans of the *Residenz* (Seat of the Court) in Würzburg, and made designs for Elector Max Emmanuel of Bavaria. For the Ducal Court of Lorraine he designed the Palais Ducal, Nancy (1715–22), and the château (1702–22) and *chapel at Lunéville (1720–3): the last was influenced by Hardouin-Mansart's chapel at Versailles, and also by *Cordemoy's suggestions for an ideal church with free-standing columns and straight *entablature—its quality of gracious lightness looks forward to *Soufflot's church of Ste-Geneviève in Paris. The enchanting house at St-Ouen, near Paris, with its pavilion in a court surrounded by the guest-wings and offices, was one of his most felicitous creations (1717), but, like much of his work, no longer survives. His *Livre d'architecture contenant les principes généraux de cet art* (Book of Architecture Containing the General Principles of that Art—1745) is an important collection of theoretical essays.

Gallet and Garms (1986); Hautecœur (1950); Kalnein and Levey (1972)

Bofill Levi, Ricardo (1939–). Barcelona-born architect. In 1962 he founded *Taller de Arquitectura*, embracing several disciplines, which became established as a successful creator of inexpensive housing employing traditional materials. The La Fabrica conversion of a cement-factory at Sant-Just Desvern, Barcelona (1973–6), has many historical references, including cathedrals, fortifications, *catacombs, and even *Romanesque revivals, with Venetian arches. A series of enormous *Post-Modern housing-blocks followed, all formal exercises with strong Classical bases: Les Arcades du Lac, St-Quentin-en-Yvelines, and Le Palais d'Abraxas, Marne-la-Vallée, both near Paris (1978–83), are excellent examples of Bofill's monumental stripped *Neoclassical style, with realized works often constructed of prefabricated concrete elements. He published *L'Architecture d'un homme* in 1978.

Emanuel (1994); James (1988)

Bofinger, Helge (1940–). German architect, whose work has a geometrical clarity owing much to 1920s' precedents, including the new offices in the Wilhelmstrasse, Berlin (1992). He designed the BMW Headquarters, Munich (1987), and the Railway Station, Mainz (1988), among many other buildings.

Emanuel (1994)

Bogardus, James (1800–74). Born in Catskill, NY, he established in 1848 a foundry in New York and was a pioneer of cast-iron construction. He invented prefabricated cast-iron structural frames and kits-of-parts that could be quickly assembled on site. He designed the Crystal Palace for the New York Exposition and published *Cast Iron Buildings: Their Construction and Advantages* (both in 1853). His experiments in improving wrought iron led to work with steel, and he is regarded as one of the begetters of prefabrication in building.

Bogardus (1856); Condit (1968)

Bohigas (Guardiola), José Oriol (1925–). *See* MBM Arquitectes.

Böhm, Dominikus (1880–1955). Born in Jettingen, near Ulm, Böhm was an important C20 architect of churches in Germany. His early designs had references to historical styles, but from the 1920s, although his plans remained conventional, his work contained first *Expressionist elements and then abstract *Gothic (as in the Freilingsdorf Parish Church, near Cologne (1926–7)). He experimented with centralized planning in order to bring the congregation nearer the altar, using an elliptical plan. From 1928 his buildings became more Modernist in character, but he fell into disfavour under the Nazis. After 1945 he and his son *Gottfried restored damaged churches and built many new ones.

Hoff, Muck, and Thoma (1962); Maguire and Murray (1965); Stalling (1974)

Böhm, Gottfried (1920–). Son of Dominikus *Böhm, born in Offenbach-am-Main, he joined his father's office in 1952, which he headed after the latter's death. His early work was mostly as a church architect, in which aspects of his father's *Expressionism were reinterpreted. His Pilgrimage Church at Neviges (1963–8), looking like a craggy rock-formation, is a dramatic example of his use of irregular pointed forms, as is his extraordinarily fortress-like *Rathaus* (Town Hall) at Bensberg (1963–9), connected to the ruins of a medieval *Schloss* (castle) and rising above timber-framed houses. Later works, such as the offices for data processing and statistics in Düsseldorf (1969–76) and the Deutsche Bank, Luxembourg (1991), turned away from Expressionism to a more *Rational architecture of steel and glass, while the conversion and restoration of Saarbrücken Schloss (1979–89) demonstrates a sureness of touch in mixing old and new fabric. Other designs include buildings for Bremerhaven University (1982–9) and Mannheim University (1986–8).

Emanuel (1994); Raev (1982); Richardson (1987)

Boileau, Louis-Auguste (1812–96). French architect, an early user of iron in the construction of churches. St-Eugène in Paris (1854–5) and St-Paul, Montluçon, Allier (1863), are examples of his thin *Gothic applied to iron churches (which roused the wrath of critics such as *Daly). He published a project for an iron church in *La nouvelle forme architecturale* (The New Architectural Form—1853), and in 1881 *Les Principes et exemples d'architecture ferronière* (The Principles and Examples of Iron Architecture). With his son, **Louis-Charles** (1837–1910), he built the *Magasins de Bon Marché* (1869), and added an iron-ribbed *dome to the early *reinforced-*concrete Church of St-Eugène Le Vésinet (Yvelines) in 1863, for which *Coignet had designed the frame.

Hartung (1983); Hitchcock (1977); Middleton and Watkin (1987)

boiserie. 1. Wooden panelling, usually from floor to ceiling, on interior walls, embellished with carvings in low relief, gilding, inlay, etc., common in C17 and C18. **2.** *Wainscoting.

Boisserée, Sulpiz (1783–1854). Cologne-born scholar of medieval architecture. In 1808 he began to measure Cologne Cathedral, and in 1813 submitted the results of his survey to Crown Prince Friedrich Wilhelm of Prussia (1795–1861—King Friedrich Wilhelm IV (from 1840)), whose influence promoted the proposals to complete the building, starting with the restoration of the medieval fabric in 1823. Boisserée's *Domwerk* (Cathedral Work) appeared from 1821, showing seductive views of the interior and exterior of Cologne Cathedral as it would look when finished. Sulpiz, his brother **Melchior** (1786–1851), and Georg *Moller found medieval drawings of the building on which he based his proposals, and he himself carried out valuable research into the medieval masons who were responsible for the original designs. In 1833 the architect Ernst *Zwirner was appointed to oversee the works as *Dombaumeister* (Cathedral Architect). Boisserée published *Geschichte Beschreibung des Doms von Köln* (Historical Account of Cologne Cathedral—1823–32) with a text in German and French, as well as sundry works on aspects of medieval architecture, including a paper on the account of the Temple of the Holy Grail. He was an important figure in the history of the *Gothic and *Romanesque Revivals.

Germann (1972)

Boito, Camillo (1836–1914). Italian architect, nationalist, and theorist, much influenced by *Viollet-le-Duc. Among his early works, the best is the cemetery at Gallarate, north of Milan (1865), of brick with stone *dressings, in a round-arched style, and a hospital six years later which is rather sour. More ebullient is his Palazzo delle Debite, Padua (1872–4), in a medieval Venetian round-arched style that, with its richness and modelling, heralded the *Stile Boito*, the Italian equivalent of High Victorian architecture. Also round-arched is the Municipal Museum, Padua (1879), but in Milan he built the *Gothic Il Ricovero pei Musicisti, or Casa Verdi (1899–1913), which includes the colourful tomb-chamber of the composer, whose librettist was Boito's brother. The mixing of elements from several periods and the use of constructional colour point to influences in the *Floreale style. Boito was also responsible for the restoration of the great Church of Sant'Antonio, Padua (1892–6).

Boito (1880, 1882); Meeks (1966); Middleton and Watkin (1987)

bolection, bolexion. Moulding covering a joint between elements where one is recessed, as in a panel set in a door-frame, where the bolection projects beyond the surface of the stile.

bollard. 1. Low robust post, fixed to quays of harbours, in order to secure the moorings of ships. **2.** Street-furniture, often of cast iron, usually in the form of a small column conforming to the *Doric *Order, or resembling a cannon, fixed in a road, footpath, or boundary to prevent vehicles from passing.

bolster. 1. *Baluster-side. **2.** Bellied profile of a *pulvinated *frieze. **3.** *Bolster-*, *cushion-*, or *pillow-work* refers to *rusticated *masonry, each course of which is bowed out, as in

Roman *aqueduct-*piers. **4.** Timber *corbel or *plate supporting a *truss, etc.

Bon *or* **Bono, Bartolomeo** (*c*.1463–1529). Lombard architect (also called Bergamasco) who worked in Venice, where he designed the ground-floor of the early *Renaissance Scuola di San Rocco (1516–24), completed by others. He designed the upper *stages of the *campanile in the Piazza di San Marco (1510–14), rebuilt 1905–11.

Arslan (1971); Howard (1980); Lieberman (1982); McAndrew (1980)

Bon, Bono *or* **Buon, Bartolomeo** (*c*.1405–*c*.1467). Venetian architect and sculptor who worked with his father, **Giovanni** (*c*.1362–1443), on the celebrated *Gothic *palazzo known as the Ca'd'Oro (1421–40), and subsequently on the west wing (facing the Piazzetta) of the Doge's Palace (1424–43) in which their Gothic style reached perfection. The Porta della Carta (1438–43), which lies between the palace and the *basilica, makes a transition between Gothic and early *Renaissance. Bartolomeo was responsible for the west *portals of Santi Giovanni e Páolo (1458–63) and San Cristofero Martire (also known as Madonna dell'Orto), both essentially Classical, as is his east end of the Porta della Carta, known as the Arco Foscari (*c*.1440–64/67). To judge from the lowest *storey of the Ca'del Duca Sforza (now Palazzo Corner), the building (1456–7), had it been finished, would have been a very advanced and early Renaissance palazzo. Also attributed to him is the gateway of the Arsenal (1460), one of the earliest Renaissance structures in Venice.

Arslan (1971); Howard (1980); Lieberman (1982); McAndrew (1980)

Bonatz, Paul (1877–1956). Born in Solgne, Lorraine, he studied in Munich and assisted Theodor *Fischer 1902–6 at the *Technische Hochschule* (Technical High School), Stuttgart, before himself becoming a professor in 1908. In partnership (1913–27) with Friedrich Eugen Scholer (1874–*c*.1940) he designed the City Hall, Hanover (1911–14), and the *Hauptbahnhof* (Main Railway Station), Stuttgart (1911–28), which owes something to *Saarinen's great terminus at Helsinki as well as to the AEG buildings of *Behrens. The partnership also designed locks, bridges, weirs, and other structures on the Neckar Canal (1926–36), the Graf Zeppelin Hotel, Stuttgart (1929–31), the War-Memorial Chapel, Heilbronn (1930–6), and many other buildings, including several private houses. Later, Bonatz was consultant to Fritz *Todt for the design of the *Autobahnen* (motorways) and their handsome bridges (1935–41). He was a signatory of the *Block manifesto, and most of his domestic work was rooted in traditional forms. From 1943 he worked in Turkey—the Nazis regarded him as old-fashioned—returning to Stuttgart in 1953. He published *Leben und Bauen* (Life and Buildings) in 1950, and worked on the reconstruction of the opera-house at Düsseldorf in the 1950s.

Bonatz (1950); Bongartz *et al.* (1977); Graupner (1931); Lane (1985); Rittich (1938)

bond. Placing of bricks, stone, etc., in a construction, breaking joints in every direction, so that each separate brick, stone, tile, etc., holds in and retains its neighbour in its place, and in return is held in the same manner. This arrangement ensures strength and stability, while the pattern of the bond on the face of the wall makes a major contribution to the appearance and aesthetic quality of the building. In *masonry a *bond-header*, *bonder*, *bond-stone*, or *through-stone* (inband in Scots) extends the width of a stone wall, tying it together. (*See* brick.)

Brunskill (1990); Lloyd (1925)

bonnet. **1.** *Cone-* or *curved-hip-tile* used to cover the junctions of plain *tiles on the *hip of a roof. **2.** Chimney-cap.

bonnet-top. Broken, scrolled *pediment.

Bonneuil, Étienne de (*fl.* 1287–8). French architect of the *ambulatory and radiating *chapels at the Cathedral of the Holy Trinity, Uppsala, Sweden (from 1287), the largest church in Scandinavia.

Boëthius and Romdahl (1935)

Bono. *See* Bon.

Bonomi Family. Joseph (1739–1808). Italian-born architect. Educated in Rome, he studied for a period with Antonio *Asprucci and *Clérisseau. In 1767 he came to England to work for the *Adam Brothers, afterwards apparently assisting Thomas *Leverton in the building of Bedford Square, London. For Lord Aylesford he designed the Neoclassical interiors at Packington Hall (1785–8), and the Church of St James, Great Packington, both in Warwickshire (1789–90). A severe brick building with *lunette windows, the church is the only English example of the advanced stripped *Neoclassicism favoured on the Continent. He also designed the pyramidal *mausoleum at Blickling, Norfolk (1794–6). A regular exhibitor at the Royal Academy, he was also a fashionable architect for country-houses (e.g. Lambton Hall, Co. Durham (1796–7)), and is mentioned in chapter 36 of Jane Austen's *Sense and Sensibility* (1811).

His second surviving son, **Ignatius** (1787–1870), built up an extensive practice around Newcastle upon Tyne: he built one of the first railway-bridges in England, at Skerne, near Darlington (1824), and was a competent and prolific designer in many styles. His Burn Hall, Co. Durham (1821–34), was in an advanced French Classical style, while his *Romanesque Revival Oxenhope Church, Yorkshire (1849), had reasonably authentic detail. His pupil and assistant from 1831 to 1841 was J. L. *Pearson. Joseph's youngest son, also **Joseph** (1796–1878), was a distinguished Egyptologist who became curator of Sir John *Soane's Museum: his best works were the Temple Mills, Marshall Street, Leeds (1842), in a scholarly *Egyptian Revival style; the Egyptianizing gate-lodges and gates at Abney Park Cemetery, Stoke Newington, London (1840); and the Egyptian Court, Crystal Palace, Sydenham (with Owen *Jones), completed 1854.

Colvin (1995); Curl (1994); Stillman (1988); Summerson *et al.* (1983)

Borra, Giovanni Battista (1713–70). Piedmontese architect and draughtsman, a pupil of *Vittone, and known as *Il Torquelino*. He accompanied Robert Wood (1716–71) and James Dawkins (1722–57) on their expedition to Asia Minor (1750–1) as a draughtsman: he was in England from 1751 and prepared drawings for *The Ruins of Palmyra* (1753) and *The Ruins of Balbec* (1757). He was probably the designer (1755) of the main rooms in the Duke of Norfolk's house in St James's Square (by *Brettingham) which had motifs derived from the *Antique remains at Palmyra mixed with Italian *Rococo themes. Similar devices occur in the Racconigi Palace, Turin (1756–7), and also in Stratfield Saye, Hampshire, and Stowe, Buckinghamshire. Borra redecorated the State Bedroom and Dressing Room at Stowe and *Neoclassicized several garden-buildings there (he made designs for the Temple of Concord and Victory, and altered the *Rotunda (1752), the Boycott Pavilions (1758), the Oxford Gate (*c*.1760), and the Lake Pavilions (*c*.1761)). He was a member of the expedition (1764–6) that led to the publication of *Ionian Antiquities* in 1769.

Colvin (1995); Harris (1990)

Borromini capital. Type of *Composite capital with incurving *volutes used by the *Bastards at Blandford Forum, Dorset, in the 1730s, and by Thomas *Archer in the 1720s. It was derived from a capital favoured by *Borromini.

Borromini, Francesco (1599–1667). One of the greatest exponents of *Baroque architecture in Rome, he was born Francesco Castello in Bissone, near Como, studied sculpture in Milan (where he probably met the masons working on late-*Gothic forms at the *Duomo*), and was apprenticed to his relative, Carlo *Maderno, from *c*.1620, before assisting *Bernini (of whom he was critical and jealous) at San Pietro, Rome, 1629–33. Borromini was fascinated by the teachings of Galileo, who held that mathematics was the key to Nature, and that geometrical figures were Nature's pictographs. As a result, Borromini developed his architecture through highly complex interlinked geometries, creating powerful, restless, dynamic forms totally different from the *concatenated method of *Renaissance design. His other sources were *Antique buildings such as Hadrian's *villa at Tivoli.

Borromini set up on his own in 1633, and was involved in a number of designs for palazzi and villas, although he is best known for his churches. In 1634 he was commissioned to design the Monastery of San Carlo alle Quattro Fontane (1634–43) in Rome for the Order of Spanish Discalced Trinitarians. In spite of its smallness, the complex of *cloister and church is ingenious in the extreme, illustrating Borromini's concerns with geometrical intricacies. The church has an elliptical, central space that merges with other ellipses, the *Orders being placed on contraflexed curves on plan, so that wall-surfaces bow inwards and outwards. The whole front (from 1665) of the building seems to be in motion, with its concave–convex–concave plan for the lower *Ionic storey and a concave–concave–concave plan for the upper *Composite *façade. The miniature *Orders for the *aedicules recall Borromini's hero, Michelangelo, and his work on the Capitol.

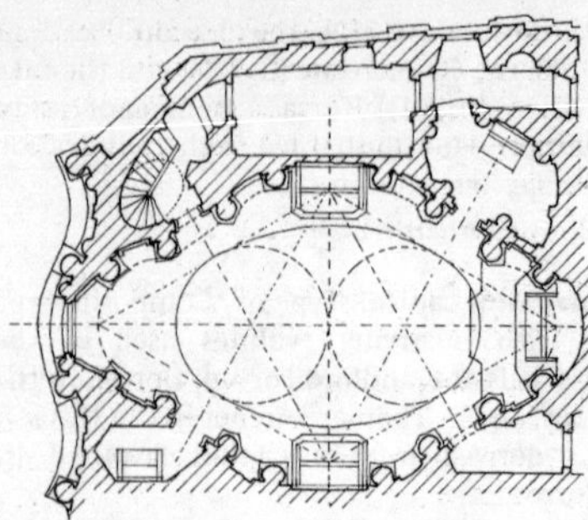

Plan of the Church of San Carlo alle Quattro Fontane, Rome, showing the centres from which arcs describing the circles and ellipse are struck, and the geometrical relationships of those centres to elements within the plan. Note the concave–convex–concave arrangement of the entrance-front.

Shortly after beginning work on San Carlo, Borromini was appointed to design the Casa e Oratorio dei Filippini (1637–50), the façade of which curves slightly, as though it had been bent, but the plan is ingenious and has a wonderful logic. The Monastery of the Oblate Agostiniane, including the Church of Santa Maria dei Sette Dolori (1642–9), remained unfinished, but has several interesting features: vestibule, church, and the space before the concave façade determine each other's shape, for a concave in one creates a convex in the other, giving an impression of almost elastic materials.

The plan of Sant'Ivo alla Sapienza (1642–62) is based on six circles drawn on a six-pointed star evolved from two superimposed equilateral triangles. The resultant space is extraordinary and dynamic, carried up within the dome which is capped by a *lantern (the shape of which resembles the late-Roman temple of Venus at Baalbek), topped by a spiral tower (which may refer to the Tower of Babel) above which is the flame of Truth. The plan resembles the shape of a bee, the heraldic device of Pope Urban VIII (1623–44), who appointed Borromini architect to the ancient University (the *Sapienza*). There are references to the Wisdom of Solomon (and therefore to the Temple) in the Cherubims, palms, pomegranates, and stars within the dome. This eclectic symbolism has no precedent in architecture. The Biblioteca Alessandrina alla Sapienza (1660–6) was the model for many later monastic and university libraries.

The fame that grew from these Baroque masterpieces led to other ecclesiastical commissions (largely through his Pamfili patron, Pope Innocent X (1644–55)), including the renovation and modernization of the ancient *Basilica of San Giovanni in Laterano. There, he clothed the structure of the *nave and *aisles in Baroque garb, with the overlapping *triumphal-arch theme that *Alberti had used at Sant'Andrea in Mantua in C15. The work involved rearranging and adapting the many funerary monuments within the new setting, and this Borromini did with skill, adding *putti and Baroque decorations to give the scheme coherence. However, his intended *vaulting over the nave was never built. He was commissioned to complete *Rainaldi's unfinished Church of Sant'Agnese in Agone in the Piazza Navona (1653–7). The building was a Greek *cross on plan, which Borromini kept in essence, but he raised the drum of the dome and articulated the concave front flanked by two inventive towers. The result is that the onlooker seems to be drawn within the great centralized space, which is the High Baroque version of the centralized plan of San Pietro. This building was influential, especially in Austria (*see* Fischer von Erlach).

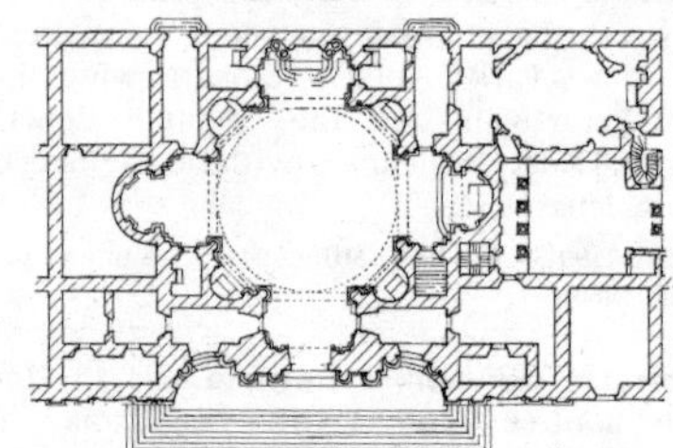

Plan of the Church of Sant'Agnese in Agone, Piazza Navona, Rome, showing the concave front and centralized space.

From 1647 he worked on the Palazzo di Propaganda Fide, the main façade of which has a *Giant *Order of *pilasters (with *capitals reduced to five *flutes) between which strange *Doric *aedicules burst from the plane of the wall. The *cornice, part straight and part swaying, is carried on larger *mutules, and the whole effect is surreal, oppressive, and sinister. Inside the complex is the Cappella dei Re Magi, roofed with rib-vaults connected to the Giant Order of pilasters, giving a *Gothic flavour to what is essentially a Baroque ensemble.

Borromini's commissions dried up on the death of his patron, the Pope, in 1655, and, in spite of a moderately successful decade, he committed suicide in 1667. His style, which fused Gothic and late-Renaissance elements, was unconventional, but his experiments with swaying walls and interpenetrating ellipses were influential in Central Europe in C18. His successful mixing of flowing forms with vigorous sculpture also proved to be a powerful stimulus north of the Alps.

Blunt (1979); Connors (1980); Hempel (1924); Norberg-Schulz (1986, 1986*a*); Portoghesi (1982); Varriano (1986)

bosket, bosquet. 1. Part of a garden enclosed by a *palissade* or high hedgerow of trees to create an interior grassed space, or *cabinet de verdure*, often containing buildings such as summer-houses, or even monuments as mnemonics of ideas, feelings, or people, not uncommon in C18 Continental landscape-design. **2.** Grove or thicket in a park, carefully designed, and often with paths cut through it, also called a *wilderness, intended to give shade and pleasure, and not to be confused with an uncultivated wasteland.

boss *formerly* **boce. 1.** Carved convex block, often richly decorated, at the junction of *vault-ribs, etc., in medieval architecture. **2.** *See* boast **1.**

boss. Medieval Gothic vault boss, Oxford Cathedral, C13. (*After Parker*)

bossage. *See* boast.

Bossan, Pierre-Marie (1814–88). Lyons-born architect, a pupil of *Labrouste. He was appointed Diocesan Architect of Lyons in 1844, and designed several revivalist buildings including the Church of St-Georges (1844). From 1852 he produced a series of churches in a *Byzantinesque *Neo-Grec style, including those at Couzon (1854–6), Ste-Philomène, Ars (1862–5), St-Jean-François Régis, Lalouvesc (1865), and the massive Notre-Dame-de-Fourvière, Lyons (1871–96), completed by Perrin.

Perrin (1889, 1912); Thollier (1891)

bossing. Space under a window where the wall is thinner than on either side.

Botta, Mario (1943–). Swiss architect, who worked with Le *Corbusier and Louis *Kahn in the 1960s, both of whom were influential in the development of his architecture, although *Scarpa's designs also affected his thinking. He established his own practice in Lugano in 1969, and quickly made his name as one of the most influential members of the Ticino or *Ticinese School with a series of private houses set alone in the landscape: these buildings have clear, powerful geometries and display fine craftsmanship. For instance, the house at Riva San Vitale (1971–3) is square on plan, has an asymmetrically placed central staircase, is monumental, and has deep and powerful voids in the elevations; the house at Ligornetto (1975–6) is elongated and boldly striped; while the Casa Rotondo, Stabio (1980–2), is a large drum with *fenestration placed deep in the structure. Other houses at Pregassona (1979–80), Viganello (1980–2), Origlio (1981–2), Morbio Superiore (1982–4), Breganzona (1984–8), Manno (1975–90), and Losone (1987–9), are all brilliant exercises in themes that recall the search for a monumental stripped *Classicism of the late C18 and early C19. His powerful Gothard Bank offices, Lugano (1982–8), which have four linked *pavilions, each with a massive slot notched on its sides, points to his concerns to establish a formal language of *Rational architecture with roots in geometry, order, and careful detail. More recently (1989–95) his Museum of Modern Art, San Francisco, Calif., and the Cathedral, Evry, France (completed 1995), have stark, simple geometries handled with consummate skill.

Botta (1991); Dal Co (1987); Pizzi (1991); Wrede (1986)

Bötticher, Karl (1806–89). German architect and scholar. His *Holzarchitektur des Mittelalters* (1835–40) was an important early study of *timber-framed medieval buildings, while his *Tektonic der Hellenen* (1844–52, and 1869) was of considerable significance in the understanding of *Greek architecture.

Sturgis *et al.* (1901–2)

bouleuterion. Meeting-place or debating-chamber for a senate in a Greek city.

Boullée, Étienne-Louis (1728–99). Parisian architect and teacher (from 1747), whose importance lies in his theoretical writings and visionary drawings, for he taught generations of pupils, including *Chalgrin, *Brongniart, and *Durand. He himself had imbibed the great French Classical traditions of C17 and C18 from *Blondel and Le *Geay, and from 1762 to 1778 he designed several private houses, most of which no longer exist, although the *Hôtel Alexandre, Paris (1763–6), survives. With *Ledoux, *Peyre, and de *Wailly, Boullée pioneered severity in domestic architecture: he monumentalized the main *block with a *Giant *Order and concealed the wings behind trellises or walls to give emphasis to the centrepiece of the composition. In the vanguard of the anti-*Rococo decorators, he won for himself a reputation as an interior designer, exploiting lighting effects with considerable success. From 1778 to 1788 he produced a great range of visionary drawings based on those he used for teaching purposes and those he made to enter architectural competitions. He responded to *Laugier's reductionist themes by stripping all unnecessary ornament from stereometrically pure forms inflated to a megalomaniac scale (influenced by *Piranesi), repeating elements such as columns in huge ranges, and making his architecture expressive of its purpose (*architecture parlante). His most successful (though unrealized) schemes of visionary architecture are those for tombs, *mausolea, *cenotaphs, and cemeteries, including the huge Cenotaph of Newton (a vast sphere set in a circular base topped with cypresses). His treatise, *Architecture. Essai sur l'art*, written in the 1790s, was not published until this century.

Braham (1980); Kaufmann (1952); Pérouse de Montclos (1974); Rosenau (1953, 1976); Rossi (1967); Vogt (1969)

Boumann, Johann A. (1704–76). Amsterdam-born architect whose *Rathaus* (Town Hall), 2 *Am Alten Markt*, Potsdam (1753), is based on *Palladio's Palazzo Angarano, and is a fine example of his very pure *Classicism. He worked with *Büring on St Hedwig's Roman Catholic Cathedral, Berlin (1772–3), but his masterwork is the curved façade of the Royal Library, Forum Fridericianum, Berlin (1774–80). He also designed Schloss Bellevue, Berlin (1785), in the Neoclassical style, now the official residence of the German President.

Watkin and Mellinghoff (1987)

Bourgeau, Victor (1809–88). French-Canadian Diocesan Architect of Montreal, he carried out major renovations to the Church of Notre Dame (1872–80) to create a more convincing *Gothic Revival interior. This was only one of some 23 remodellings of existing churches for which he was responsible, in addition to which he designed over 20 new churches, of which his grandest in the Gothic Revival style is St-Pierre-Apôtre, Montreal (1851–3). Subsequently, his designs became less Gothic, possibly because of the enthusiastic reception of that style by the English Protestant Canadians. His Church of St-Barthélémy, Berthier, Quebec (1866–7), for example, was Classical, with a twin-towered western façade recalling the work of Thomas *Baillargé. In 1854 Montreal Cathedral was destroyed by fire, and the Bishop conceived the idea of building a version of the *basilica of San Pietro, Rome, to replace it. Accordingly, Bourgeau was sent to Europe to study various churches, but returned after only a week in Rome, convinced that a reproduction of the great Roman church would be a mistake. The Bishop then appointed Father Joseph Michaud (1823–1902) to design the replica and construction began in 1870. However, Michaud's lack of expertise led to Bourgeau being reappointed as architect, and the Cathedral-Basilica of Saint-Jacques-le-Majeur (now Marie-Reine-de-la-Monde) was completed in 1894, partly under the direction of Étienne-Alcibiade Leprohon in the latter stages.

Kalman (1994)

Bourgeois, Victor (1897–1962). Born in Charleroi, Belgium, he practised as an architect in Brussels from 1920. He became the leading Belgian disciple of Le *Corbusier. As Vice-President of *CIAM he was an important advocate of *International *Modernism in Belgium. His most celebrated work was the municipal housing-scheme or *Cité Moderne* at Berchem-Ste-Agathe, near Brussels (1922–5), influenced by Tony *Garnier's *Cité Industrielle* and by Frank Lloyd *Wright. Other works include a house at the *Weissenhofsiedlung in Stuttgart (1927). He was active as an architect and planner until his death, designing many industrial buildings.

Bourgeois (1971); Flouquet (1952); Linze (1959)

bow. **1.** Part of a wall projecting from its face, a partial ellipse, semicircle, or segment on *plan, usually with a window set in it or extending the full width, known as a *bow-* or *compass-window*. If the plan is canted (or part of a polygon), or rectangular, it is not called a *bow*, but rather a *bay*, so a projecting window would be a *canted bay-window* or a *rectangular* or *square bay-window*. *See* bay-window. **2.** Arched form, therefore part of a flying *buttress. **3.** *Attribute of the goddess Diana, and therefore associated with hunting.

bower. **1.** Room in medieval houses for the exclusive use of women, therefore the precursor of the *boudoir*. **2.** Small dwelling in the country, or a cottage, therefore a *cottage orné or deliberately rustic building in a Romantic, *Picturesque landscape. **3.** *Gazebo or other similar garden-building. **4.** Shady recess, leafy covert, or place closed in or overarched with branches, deliberately created to look 'natural' in a garden or landscape.

bowl. **1.** Surface of a sloping auditorium floor, sometimes in the form of the surface of an inverted cone for acoustic reasons. **2.** *Basin, as of a fountain. **3.** Plain *capital like a bowl or basin.

bowstring. *See* truss.

bowtell, bowtelle. Also called *boltel*, *bottle*, *boultel*, *boultin*, a plain moulding with a convex *section, such as a *roll-moulding, *ovolo, or *torus. It is larger than an *astragal or *bead, and is sometimes used to describe the *colonnettes or *shafts of medieval *clustered *piers.

box. **1.** Small unpretentious rural house, usually for temporary use, such as a shooting-box for sportsmen. **2.** Compartment, enclosed at the sides and back, with seats for a small number of people in a theatre. **3.** *Box-pew.

box-beam. Rectangular beam constructed of four sheets of wrought iron or steel to form a long box. Also called *box-girder*.

box-frame. **1.** Type of construction resembling a series of boxes, involving structural walls at right angles to the façade (called *cross-walls*): its repetitive nature limits its use to hotel-bedrooms, small flats, hostels, etc. **2.** Type of *timber-framed structure where roof-*trusses are supported on a frame of *posts, tie-beams, and wall-plates.

Alcock, Barley, Dixon, and Meeson (1996)

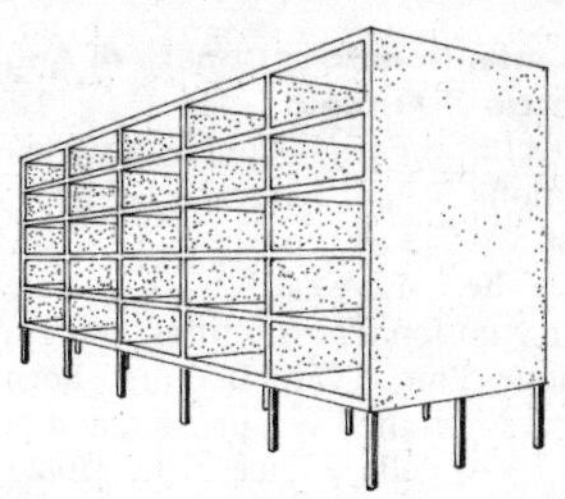

box-frame. Typical C20 box-frame construction, set on pilotis.

Box, John (*fl.* 1333–d. 1375). English mason. He worked on Westminster Palace and the Priory of Christ Church, Canterbury, Kent. He probably designed the fine *chantry-chapel of Archbishop Stratford, Canterbury Cathedral (*c.*1350), and also worked with *Yeveley on the Black Prince's chantry-chapel in the *crypt there (after 1363).

Harvey (1987)

box-pew. Common English (and American) C18 *pew type (some big enough for entire families) surrounded by tall timber-panelled partitions with a hinged door.

Boyle. *See* Burlington.

Boytac, Diogo (*fl.* 1490–1525). French master-mason who worked on the Church of Santa Maria, Belém, Lisbon (begun 1502), one of the first examples of the *Manueline style of Portugal, and also Christ Church at Setúbal (1494–8), which commemorates Portuguese voyages of discovery in its form and detail.

Cruickshank (1996)

brace. **1.** Subsidiary structural timber, curved or straight, placed at an angle between vertical and horizontal members to complete a triangle and thus stiffen a *timber frame. If supporting a rafter, it is called a *strut*. *See* truss. **2.** *See* bracket-moulding.

bracket. **1.** Member (essentially a type of *brace) projecting from the *naked of a wall to support by means of *leverage* an element that overhangs. **2.** *Ancon, *console, *corbel, *modillion, *mutule, or other element expressing a support, or even a *cantilever principle.

bracket moulding. **1.** *Brace in the form of a double *ogee. **2.** Moulding of two ogee-forms joining at a point and supporting e.g. a *finial.

Bramante, Donato *or* **Donato di Angelo di Pascuccio d'Antonio** (1444–1514). The only architect of the High *Renaissance (with the exception of *Raphael) respected by his peers and successors as the equal of the ancients, it was he, above all, who revealed the power, emotional possibilities, and gravity of *Antique Roman architecture. Born near Urbino, he trained as a painter, and perhaps knew Piero della Francesca (*c*.1410/20–1492) and Francesco di *Giorgio at the Court of Federigo da Montefeltro (reigned 1444–82) in that city, but his first documented appearance was as a painter of *frescoes at the Palazzo del Podestà, Bergamo (1477). Around 1479 he entered the service of Ludovico Sforza (1452–1508) in Milan, where he turned his attention to architecture, and met *Leonardo da Vinci, who was to alert him to the problems of designing centralized churches. Bramante's first significant church was Santa Maria presso San Satiro, Milan (begun *c*.1481), where he erected the first *coffered dome since Antiquity, made the shallow east end appear as a deep *chancel by means of theatrical perspective techniques, placed a barrel-vault over the *nave (influenced by *Alberti), and reworked the C9 chapel of San Satiro as a *drum (embellished with *pilasters and *niches). He also planned, with Leonardo, a centralized arrangement at Santa Maria delle Grazie, Milan (1490s), which has a drum with dome on *pendentives rising over it.

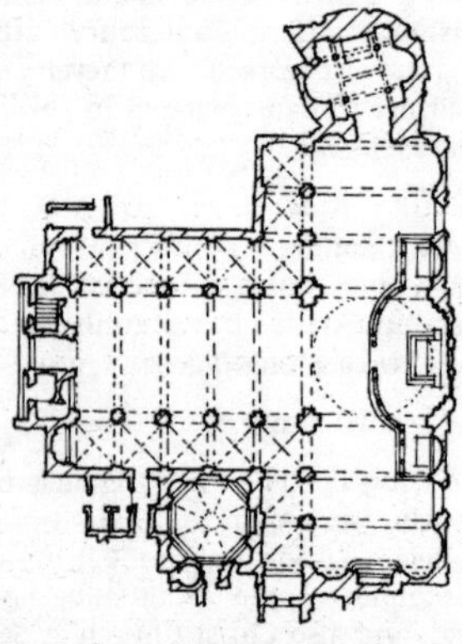

Plan of Church of Santa Maria presso San Satiro, Milan. Note the chapel of San Satiro at the top, and the very shallow chancel in the church itself.

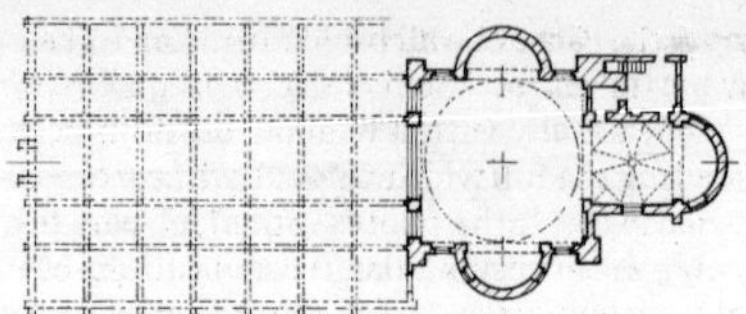

Centralized east end of Santa Maria delle Grazie, Milan.

The fall of the Sforzas forced Bramante to abandon Milan for Rome, where he designed the elegant *cloisters of Santa Maria della Pace (1500–4) which were more refined than his earlier cloisters of Sant'Ambrogio, Milan (1492). The Pace cloisters have *piers with *Ionic *pilasters and *arcades (based on the Colosseum) carrying a continuous *entablature with an inscription on the *frieze, while above is an open *colonnaded gallery with the columns set between piers and situated on the centre-line of each arch. Then (1502–10) came the astonishing *Tempietto* in the *chiostro* (*cloister) of San Pietro in Montorio, a drum surmounted by a dome and surrounded by a *peristyle of *Tuscan columns carrying a Roman *Doric entablature: the effect is graceful, serene, and Antique. Tuscan Doric was used because of its association with the strong masculine character of St Peter, on the supposed site of whose Martyrdom the *Tempietto* was erected. Indeed *Serlio credited Bramante with adapting the Doric temple for Christian purposes, for *Vitruvius, no less, had recommended Doric as appropriate for heroic, masculine deities. Circular plans were based upon Antique temples, but they also have important precedents in the *martyria* of Early Christian churches: thus Bramante, in this tiny building, linked Christian *martyria*, Roman circular temples, and Classical architecture in the first great building of the High *Renaissance.

With the election of Pope Julius II (1503–13) Bramante acquired a patron with ambitions to build, and he drew up a plan for the Vatican and the Basilica of San Pietro. One range of buildings with three superimposed arcades was subsequently incorporated within the Cortile di San Damaso, and then came the vast Cortile del Belvedere of which only the spiral ramp (*c*.1505) remains relatively intact. However, the greatest work was the rebuilding of the Church of San Pietro. The huge Church of Hagia Sophia in Constantinople had fallen to Islam in the mid-C15, and it became politically and symbolically important to replace the Constantinian *basilica (which was really a *martyrium over the tomb of the Apostle) with a great centrally planned church. Bramante proposed a mighty Greek cross (with each arm terminating in an *apse) in the corners of which would be four smaller Greek crosses (each covered by a minor dome), the centre covered by a dome to rival that of the Roman *Pantheon, but carried on a huge colonnaded drum. Bramante's design was derived from the *Tempietto*, and he was designing a martyrium, with reference to Constantine's other foundations (the Church of the Holy Sepulchre and the Church of the Nativity), and to the mathematical perfection of a centralized plan that symbolized the Perfection of God. The building was only partially begun when he and the Pope died, but the great piers of the crossing and the arches carry the dome of the present building.

His other works include the choir of Santa Maria del Pòpolo (1505–9), with a huge coffered vault and apse, and the Palazzo Caprini (House of Raphael) of 1508–9 which had (it has been virtually obliterated) an arcaded and heavily rusticated base, with coupled Tuscan Doric columns above, an arrangement that was greatly admired by *Palladio (who drew the building), and was influential among later generations of architects, notably *Burlington.

Ackerman (1954); Bruschi (1977); Patetta (1987); Serlio (1964); Vasari (1912–15)

Bramantino (*fl.* 1503–36). *See* Suardi.

Branca, Alexander, Freiherr von (1919–). Munich-born architect. He set up his own practice in the Bavarian capital in 1950, and produced many distinguished buildings in which his beliefs in the necessity of continuity through tradition and in the symbolic value of 'supertemporal' architecture are expressed. His religious buildings, including the *mortuary-chapel at the Monastery of Schönstatt (1980–2), are powerful and moving, while his conservation work at Regensburg (from 1981) was sensitive and comprehensive. Two museums stand out for their quality: that at Vaduz, Liechtenstein (from 1978), and the *Neue Pinakothek* picture-gallery, Munich (1973–81), both boldly modelled, with excellent lighting for viewing pictures.

Emanuel (1994)

branch. **1.** *Gothic *rib in a *vault that continues from the top of a *pier without interruption, there being no *capital on the pier. **2.** Any Gothic rib in a vault. *See* tracery.

Brandon, David (1813–97). *See* Wyatt, T. H.

brass. **1.** Mixed metal, an alloy of copper and zinc, capable of taking a high polish. **2.** In the sense of an engraved plate or other design let into a slab of stone or set on top of an altar-tomb, it is not true brass, but an alloy of copper and tin, creating *bronze or *latten, and examples abound with incised figures, *town-canopies, and inscriptions, often with infill of black resin, enamels, and mastic. The monumental or memorial 'brass' once again became popular in the C19 *Gothic Revival, using true brass.

brattice. **1.** *Bartizan. **2.** Timber construction overhanging a wall on a fortification.

brattishing. **1.** Ornamental parapet, especially a *battlement. **2.** Decorative *Gothic *cress on top of a *cornice, parapet, *screen, etc., generally of *openwork consisting of stylized foliate and floral enrichment, often the *Tudor flower.

brattishing (*JJS*)

breastsummer, bressummer, brest summer. Horizontal *beam, *cill, *lintel, or *plate over an opening in an external wall or a fireplace-opening, or set forward from the lower part of a building to support an entire *jettied wall in *timber-framed construction. In the latter case (*jetty-bressummer*) it sometimes rests on the *cantilevered floor-*joists, sometimes is secured to the joists tenoned into it, and is also carried on *jetty-brackets*: in turn, the bressummer supports the *posts of the jettied upper front wall. On occasion the cantilevered *jetty construction is disguised behind an ornamental *fascia-board that is often mistaken for a true bressummer.

Alcock, Barley, Dixon, and Meeson (1996)

Brenna, Vincenzo (1745–*c*.1820). Florence-born architect who settled in Rome by 1767 and, with Franciszek Smuglewicz (1745–1807), produced drawings of Roman wall-paintings and other remains, published as *Vestigia delle Terme di Tito* (Remains of the Baths of Titus—1776–8). In 1777, employed by Count Stanisław Potocki (1755–1821), he moved to Poland, painting *Neoclassical *grotesques for Princess Lubomirska, the Potockis, and King Stanisław Poniatowski (1764–95): some of his best Polish interiors are at Łańcut for *Aigner. He then went on to St Petersburg, where he worked as a decorative painter on schemes by *Cameron, from whom he learned architectural skills, and whom he succeeded as Court Architect in 1796. His main works are at Gatčina, where he designed many Neoclassical interiors, developing a showy Imperial style from his earlier archaeological studies. He moved to Dresden in 1802, where he died.

Lorentz and Rottermund (1984)

bressummer. *See* breastsummer.

bretess, bretesse, bretex, bretise, brettisse, brettys. 1. Battlement, so *bretexed* means *crenellated* or *embattled*. **2.** *Brattice.

Breton, Gilles Le (d. 1553). Master-mason in charge of *François Ier's works at *Fontainebleau. Surviving designs at Fontainebleau include the Porte Dorée, with superimposed *loggie (1528–40), the entrance to the Cour Ovale (from *c*.1531—also with a *portico and staircase by Le Breton), and the north side of the Cour du Cheval-Blanc. His relatively straightforward *Renaissance *Classicism was influenced by *Serlio, and in turn was a precedent for the work of *Lescot.

Blunt (1982); Watkin (1986)

Brettingham Family. Matthew (1699–1769) developed a large East Anglian practice as an architect, builder, and surveyor, and from 1734 supervised the building of *Kent's *Palladian mansion of Holkham Hall, published as *The Plans, Elevations, and Sections of Holkham in Norfolk, the Seat of the late Earl of Leicester* (1761), the plates of which attribute the designs to him as 'Architect', Kent's name being omitted. Holkham led to other commissions, including Norfolk House, St James's Square (1748–52), York House, Pall Mall (1761–3), neither of which survives, and 5 St James's Square (1748–9), which does. One of his most important works was Kedleston Hall, Derbyshire (*c*.1758), another great essay in Palladianism. Only the *wings were built as part of *Paine's revised design, but Paine was in turn replaced by Robert *Adam, who completed the house.

His son, **Matthew** (1725–1803), was responsible for the *Neoclassical work at Charlton House, Wiltshire (1772–6). **Robert William Furze Brettingham** (*c*.1750–1820), grandson of the older Matthew Brettingham, designed several gaols, including the noble front to Downpatrick Gaol, Co. Down (1789–96), and was responsible (with S. Woolley) for the charming *Gothick *choir refurbishment in the Cathedral of the Holy and Undivided Trinity, Downpatrick (1795). For the Marquis of Downshire he carried out enlargements of Hillsborough House, Co. Down (*c*.1795–7), drawings for which were exhibited at the Royal Academy in 1797. George *Smith was trained in his office.

Colvin (1995); Papworth (1852); Summerson (1993)

Breuer, Marcel Lajos (1902–81). Important *Modernist architect and designer, born in Pécs, Hungary. He became Director of the furniture department at the Weimar *Bauhaus in 1924, and invented a series of furniture-designs using structural frames of bent-steel tubes finished in chrome: these were realized as furniture in the Dessau Bauhaus. In 1928 he set up an architectural practice in Berlin, producing the Harnischmacher House at Wiesbaden, and (with the *Roth brothers) the elegant Doldertal Apartments, Zurich (1935–6), for *Giedion. In 1935 he moved to London and a partnership with F. R. S. *Yorke, but crossed the Atlantic to Harvard in 1937, where he became *Gropius's partner (1937–40), and also worked as associate professor with Gropius, numbering among his students Edward *Barnes, John *Johansen, Philip *Johnson, and Paul *Rudolph. After setting up an office in Cambridge, Mass. (1941), in 1946 he moved to New York (he became a citizen of the United States in 1944). His career as an independent architect only really began after 1945, when he designed several private houses in New England (including his own at New Canaan, Connecticut (1947)), in which *rubble and timber played no small part. With *Nervi and *Zehrfuss he worked on the designs of the UNESCO Headquarters in Paris (1952–8) and, with A. Elzas, on the De Bijenkorf Department Store, Rotterdam (1953–7). Stylistically his work became less *International Modernist from this time, as his St John's Abbey and University, Collegeville, Minn. (1953–70, with H. Smith), and the lecture-hall, New York University, University Heights, Bronx (1956–61), demonstrate. His later works included the IBM Research Centre, Le Gaude, Var, France (with Gatje, 1961), and the Whitney Museum of American Art, New York (with H. Smith, 1963–6).

Argan (1957); Blake (1949); Breuer (1955); Jones (1962); Papachristou (1970)

Brewer, Cecil Claude (1871–1918). *See* Smith, Arnold Dunbar.

bric-à-brac. Pejorative term for *Renaissance Revival buildings based on French precedents and overloaded with busy ornament.

brick. Solid, hollow, or indented building element, usually rectangular, but also other shapes for special purposes, manufactured from clay, *concrete, sand, and lime, or other materials, formed in a mould, then burnt, set, or cured. Its advantage over masonry lies in the ease of mass-producing the bricks to standard sizes in the moulds, and in the fact that it can be lifted and laid using one hand, leaving the other free for holding the trowel for manipulation of the mortar. Terms to describe bricks include:

Accrington: see *engineering brick* below;

air-brick: with regular perforations to allow air to pass through a wall;

angle-brick: see *dogleg*;

arch-brick, also called *tapered headers* or *tapered stretchers*: special brick tapered along its length to serve as a *voussoir* in an arch;

bat: *half*, *three-quarter*, *large-bevelled*, or *small-bevelled* part of a brick greater than a quarter-brick, with the cut made across its *width*. It is used as an alternative to a *closer* in *bonding* to make up the dimensions in the courses of a wall;

bird's mouth: with a wide angular notch in one of the header faces;

brick tile: see *mathematical tile* below;

brindle: attractive brown-purple brick, or bricks discoloured with stripes;

bullnose: with a rounded edge instead of an *arris (*single bullnose*, used where arrises are vulnerable) or with two rounded edges (*double bullnose*, for copings);

calcium silicate brick: brick, also called *flint-lime* or *sand-lime* brick made from sand or crushed flint mixed with hydrated lime, then pressed into a mould and permitted to harden, usually in an autoclave;

cant brick: moulded brick with one corner (*single-cant*) or two corners (*double-cant*) cut off with a diagonal;

capping brick: shaped brick laid on edge on the top of a wall but not projecting beyond its faces. It can be a *half-round*, *bull-nosed*, *saddleback* (triangular), or *segmental* type;

circular brick: curved on plan, for curved walls;

closer: brick cut or moulded lengthways, exposing an uncut stretcher-face and a half-header, used to close the course at the return of the wall or at an opening in it, and to keep the *bond. Closers are of various types: *bevelled closer* (with splayed stretcher-face, a half-header at one end, and a whole header at the other), *king-closer* (three-quarter *bat* with concealed splayed corner, and exposed half-header), *mitred closer* (with one end sharply splayed and the header-face removed, leaving a half or three-quarter stretcher, used where adjacent bricks join at an angle), and *queen-closer* (usually next to the first brick in a header-course, consisting of half a brick (*half queen-closer*) or a quarter brick (*quarter queen-closer*));

common brick: cheap bricks used where appearance or strength are not critical;

compass brick: also *radial* or *radiating brick*, it is tapered for use in arches, circular windows, or patterns;

concrete brick: moulded brick made from cement, sand, and crushed stone, etc., used instead of common bricks;

coping bricks: like a *capping-brick*, used for copings, with bullnose, canted, saddle-back, segmental, or semicircular tops, laid on-edge, and made so that the ends project beyond the face of the wall to throw water clear of it;

Cossey white: very pale *gault* brick from Costessey, Norfolk, common in Norwich and environs, around 1830;

course: horizontal layer or row of bricks;

cownose: semicircular at one end only;

cut and rubbed: brick cut to shape with a bolster then rubbed to a fine finish with a *rubber* brick;

cutter: brick made from natural or mixed sandy loams (of uniform texture). When burnt they can be cut and rubbed to precise shapes;

dogleg: *angle-brick* used to ensure a good bond at *quoins which are not right angles. A better job than *mitred closers*;

dry-dipped enamelled brick: moulded, dried, burnt, cooled, coloured, glazed, and reburnt *biscuitware*;

Dutch clinker: small yellowish brick often found in East-Anglian walls and pavements, called *klinkart*;

engineering brick: very dense, durable, strong, and water-resistant, used for bridges, piers, sewers, and other engineering construction. The commonest types are *Accringtons* (bright orange-red, pressed, and smooth), *Hunzikers* (crushed flint and lime), *Southwaters* (pressed and wire-cut), and *Staffordshire Blues* (blue, wire-cut, and handmade, often used for *plinths, as damp-proof courses, and for copings);

facing: superior brick selected to be seen on the exposed face of a wall;

flare: see *vitrified brick*;

Flemish brick: thin brick imported from Flanders or The Netherlands or made to imitate this type;

Fletton: made from Knotts clay found near Peterborough, Cambridgeshire, containing a large proportion of finely distributed combustible matter, with a resulting economy of fuel when being fired. A mass-produced *common* brick;

gault: dense brick made from limy or calcareous clay-beds found between the upper and lower greensands and containing sufficient chalk to render the brick pale yellow or white when burnt, often with bluish tinges;

glass brick: square glass *block, unlike the shape of normal bricks, hollow or solid;

glazed brick: usually of fireclay or shale, and accurate in size and shape, with exceptionally straight arrises, it is waterproof, *enamelled*, or *salt*-glazed. Useful for *dados, *plinths, and other surfaces requiring to be kept clean, or for light-wells where good qualities of clean, reflective surfaces are needed;

header: laid with its short face exposed;

Hitch brick: see *rat-trap bond* below;

hollow brick: clay walling-block, larger than a true brick, useful for quickness of construction and properties of insulation;

Hunziker: see *engineering brick* above;

klinkart: see *Dutch clinker* above;

London stock: yellowish-brown *stock-brick* made from London clay, often with the admixture of clinker from the coal used in previous firings, giving the finished brick dark spots with attractive patches of blue and red;

malm: almost white brick made from marly (limy or calcareous) clay to which chalk is added, common in Cambridgeshire, Lincolnshire, and Suffolk;

mathematical tile: also called *brick tile* or *wall tile*, a tile with one face moulded to resemble the appearance and dimensions of a brick. It was laid in mortar and nailed to battens on a rough wall or timber-frame, then pointed so that the finished work looked like brickwork;

multi-coloured brick: known as a *multi*, used for facing work, it has faces attractively coloured with bright red, dark red, blue, yellow, etc., and is most satisfactory with white pointing;

perforated brick: has several small vertical cylinders of clay taken out from its core, leaving the faces indistinguishable from solid bricks;

Pether's patent moulded brick: pale buff moulded brick with very sharp detail much used in C19, notably by *Butterfield (e.g. at St Augustine's, Queen's Gate, London), and in countless Victorian terraces as *lintels and *string-courses;

Pether's patent brick, from Butterfield's Church of St Augustine, Queen's Gate, London. (*JJS*)

pistol-brick: used to form a smooth curve between wall and floor, especially where good hygiene is necessary and there is regular washing out;

plinth bricks: usually moulded or splayed at the top;

purpose-made brick: *special* brick for unusual or non-standard work;

rubber: also known as a *cutter*, coloured soft red, white, or buff, it is formed from clean clay containing a lot of sand, moulded, then baked (not burnt). It is carved, cut, or rubbed with ease, and used for *gauged* arches, etc., with fine joints of lime-putty;

sand-faced: with sand sprinkled on the clay before firing. Used to enhance the appearance of inferior clays (e.g. *Flettons*) and usually applied to one stretcher- and one header-face only;

sand-lime: see *calcium silicate* above. It is usually employed in internal or below-ground work;

shaped brick: any type of brick other than a normal rectangular unit, such as a *pistol*-brick;

snapped header: broken in half and laid so that its short face only appears in the wall-surface, suggesting a wall thicker than half a brick wide, so deceptive in terms of structural stability;

soldier: with its stretcher-face set vertically;
Southwater: see *engineering brick* above;
special: made specially for a job (*purpose-made*), or a standard *shaped* brick;
splay: with a bevelled top, used for *plinths or *cills;
Staffordshire: see *engineering brick* above;
stock brick: originally hand-made on a *stock-board*, but now machine-moulded. The term is also applied to any characteristic local facing-brick;
stretcher: laid so that its longest face is exposed;
vitrified brick: also a *flare*, it is often a very dark-blue or blue-black colour, usually with a shiny, glazed surface brought about by extremely high temperatures during firing, and is frequently found, often *snapped*, in walls forming *chequer-board*, *diaper*, *lettered*, or *numerical* designs;
and
wire-cut: formed by extruding clay through a rectangular die from the end of which individual bricks are cut off mechanically by serrated wires.

Terms associated with bricks or brickwork are:

arris: sharp edge between two adjacent brick faces;
bed: lower surface. A *bed-joint* is the horizontal mortar joint;
cogging: as *dog-tooth*;
course: complete horizontal layer of bricks—a *brick-on-edge* course has bricks laid on their stretcher-faces, a *brick-on-end* or *soldier* course is one of bricks laid on their header-faces, the stretcher-faces being then vertical, a *heading* or *header course* consists of headers, and a *stretching* or *stretcher*-course of stretchers;
dentilation: alternate projecting headers, also called *toothing*, to carry a projecting *course* or *cornice*. See *dog-tooth* below;
dog-tooth: also *hound's tooth* or *mouse-tooth*, it is a course of projecting bricks laid diagonally to carry a projecting *course* or *cornice*, giving a jagged saw-tooth effect, called *cogging*, achieved by the exposure of one corner. It is an alternative to *dentilation*;
face: exposed surface;
frog: indentation or *kick* on the bed or the uppermost surface or both—one-frog bricks laid with frog down save weight, work, and mortar, but they are usually laid frog up so that mortar fills the frog to ensure that the wall is strong;
gauged: fine, precise brickwork, as in an arch of soft *rubbers*, often a bright red or creamy colour contrasting with the rest of the wall, used around window- and door-openings and for arches;
indentation: see toothing;
lap: horizontal distance between a vertical joint in one course and the joint in the course above or below it;
leaf: thin brick wall forming part of a cavity-wall. There is an inner and outer leaf on either side of the cavity;
nogging: brick infill panel in *timber-framed construction;
perpend: vertical line through superimposed vertical joints;
quoin: external angle of a wall;
sinking: see *toothing*;
stopped end: also *closed end*, a square end of a wall the same thickness as that wall, finished with the aid of *closers*;
toothing: *dentilation*, or projections of alternate courses at the end of a wall to provide a *bond* for a later addition, leaving *indentation* or *sinking* in each alternate course. *Dentilation* is also used in a different sense, as part of a *cornice* support (*see above*).

Brick bonds (the patterns formed by arranging the courses with bricks overlapping the joints to provide a sound structure) are many and varied, and are often confused. The list below is an attempt to establish descriptions of the commonest types:

American bond: US term for a type of *English garden-wall bond*, but with a course of headers to every five or six courses of stretchers;
American with Flemish bond: see *Flemish stretcher bond*;
basket-weave: three soldiers alternating with three stretchers in squares with no bond, forming a *chequerboard* pattern;
bastard bond: also *header bond* or *heading bond*, it has only headers on the wall-surfaces, is very strong, and is useful for engineering work or for curved walls;
block bond: US term for *Flemish bond* or *common bond*;
block bonding: several courses of brick used to join one wall or part of a wall to another, e.g. where facing-bricks are bonded to common bricks of different sizes. The several courses give the effect of *quoins where they interlock with the different brickwork;
chequered bond: bond formed of e.g. *Flemish bond* in which the headers are vitrified (a darker colour than the rest, and glazed), giving a regular chequered pattern. Flint or other materials may be used instead of vitrified headers to give the same effect;
Chinese bond: see *rat-trap bond*;
common bond: see *English garden-wall bond*;

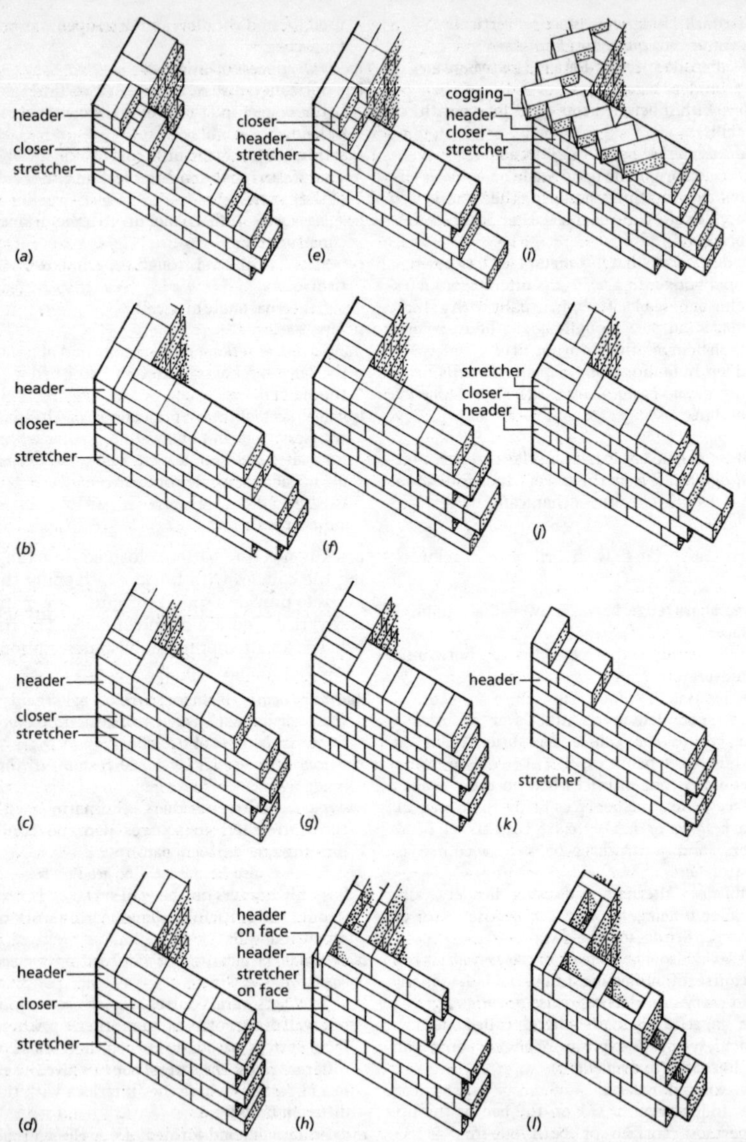

brick bonds. (*a*) Flemish bond. (*b*) Flemish garden-wall bond. (*c*) Flemish stretcher-bond. (*d*) Monk bond. (*e*) English bond. (*f*) English garden-wall bond. (*g*) Header bond. (*h*) Dearne's bond. (*i*) English cross-bond or St Andrew's bond, with upper course of projecting bricks laid diagonally (*cogging* or *dog-tooth*) to support a cornice above. (*j*) Dutch bond. (*k*) Raking stretcher-bond or quarter-bond. (*l*) Rat-trap bond. (*JJS*)

Dearne's bond: variation on *English bond* where stretcher courses are bedded on edge (i.e. on their face) with a cavity between, the header courses laid normally on their beds, bonding the leaves together, and saving bricks by a slight gain in height for every course of stretchers. Dearne's bond is often confused with *rat-trap* or *Silverlock's bond*. Dearne (or Dearn) also designed a bond with a course of headers, then a course of stretchers cut along their lengths giving a final appearance of ordinary English bond, but leaving unseen continuous cavities between the stretchers that could be heated (e.g. by connecting them from a stove to a flue) for use in conservatories;

diaper: bonding involving the creation of patterns using bricks of a different colour set in the wall, such as *vitrified* headers, forming diamond, square, lozenge, and other designs;

Dutch bond: also *staggered Flemish bond*, it is a variation on *Flemish bond*, with alternate headers and stretchers in each course, the courses being moved half a header on each course to left or right, giving a zig-zag effect called *staggered Flemish* in the USA. Another type of Dutch bond is actually a modification of *English bond*, and consists of alternate rows of headers and stretchers, but each stretcher-course begins at the quoin with a three-quarter bat and every alternate stretcher-course has a header placed next to the quoin three-quarter bat, causing the stretchers to break joint in alternate courses, the quoin three-quarter bats rendering the queen-closers of normal English bond redundant;

English bond: strong bond of alternate courses of headers and stretchers;

English cross-bond: also *St Andrew's bond*, it is similar to English bond, with alternate rows of stretchers and headers, and *queen-closers* next to the quoin-headers. Each alternate stretcher-course is moved half a stretcher to right or left to give a stepped effect to the joints. It is sometimes called *Dutch bond*;

English garden-wall bond: also *American bond*, *common bond*, or *Liverpool bond*, it has one course of headers to every three to (usually) five stretcher-courses, with a *queen-closer* introduced next to the quoin-header in the header course. Other variations occur;

facing bond: thin fine bricks employed to face a thicker wall of common bricks;

Flemish bond: alternate headers and stretchers in *each* course with closers next to the header quoins—variants may have three or five stretchers to each header. *Double Flemish bond* shows the bond on both faces of the wall;

Flemish cross-bond: as *Flemish bond*, but with additional headers at intervals instead of stretchers;

Flemish garden-wall bond: also *Scotch* or *Sussex bond*, it has courses of three or five stretchers between each pair of headers, continued along each course and contrived so that the header lies over the central one of the group of stretchers in the course above and below;

Flemish stretcher-bond: also called *American with Flemish bond*, it has courses of alternate headers and stretchers, sandwiching several courses of stretchers. Sometimes there can be anything from one to six courses of stretchers instead of the commoner three courses;

flying bond: see *Monk bond*;

header bond: see *bastard bond*;

heading bond: see *bastard bond*;

herringbone bond: bricks laid in diagonal zig-zag fashion, with each course laid at right angles to the one below;

honeycomb bond: brickwork with the omission (usually) of headers in a pattern to permit ventilation, or for decoration;

hoop-iron bond: reinforced brickwork in which flat iron bars dipped in tar and sanded are laid in every sixth course;

irregular bond: bond using headers, but with no particular or consistent pattern, with broken vertical joints;

lacing bond: one or more courses of bricks or tiles establishing a regular reinforcement and bond in a wall of flint, cobbles, etc.;

Liverpool bond: see *English garden-wall bond* above;

mixed garden bond: also called *mixed garden-wall bond*, it is essentially a variant on *Flemish bond*, but with two to five courses of stretchers, then a course of stretcher-header-stretcher, then three to five more of stretchers. Headers are not placed directly above each other in any regular pattern;

Monk bond: also called *flying bond* or *Yorkshire bond*, it is a variant on *Flemish bond*, with each course consisting of two stretchers rather than one between each pair of headers, each header placed over the joint between pairs of stretchers. Closers are required;

quarter bond: also *quarter bonding* or *raking stretcher bond*, it is a variant on stretcher bond with each brick overlapping the brick below by a quarter-brick;

quetta bond: variant on Flemish bond with continuous vertical gaps left inside the wall thickness filled with reinforcement and mortar;

raking bonds: courses laid alternately in different directions, such as *herringbone*;

raking stretcher bond: see *quarter bond*;

rat-trap bond: also *Chinese*, *rowlock*, or *Silverlock's* bond, it is a variant on Flemish or Sussex bond with courses of alternate headers and stretchers in each course laid on edge rather than on bed, the stretchers forming outer and inner leaves of bricks laid on edge with a cavity between them, and the headers (laid on the centre of each stretcher-on-edge) acting as bonders. Although very economical, it is not watertight, so if used for dwellings has to be rendered on the outside. The main virtue was that its hollow centre could be heated and used for walls against which plants could be grown. In the vicinity of Ware, Hertfordshire, what appears to be rat-trap bond may be a wall of *Hitch* hollow bricks of complex interlocking forms invented by Caleb Hitch in 1828;

Scotch bond: see *Flemish garden-wall bond*;

Silverlock's bond: see *rat-trap bond* above;

single Flemish bond: with the appearance of Flemish bond on the outside face of a wall more than one brick-length thick. *Double Flemish bond* is contrived to look like Flemish bond on both the inner and outer faces;

stack bond: bricks laid on end with continuous vertical joints and no bond, so unsuitable for structural load-bearing walls;

staggered Flemish bond: see *Dutch bond*;

stretcher-bond: stretchers only, each lap being half a stretcher, commonly found in cavity walls;

Sussex bond: also called *Sussex garden-wall bond*, it is the same as *Flemish garden-wall bond*;

and

Yorkshire bond: as *Monk bond*.

Types and colours of pointing (the application of a superior mortar-finish to the raked-out joints (mortar between adjacent bricks, horizontally and vertically)) of ordinary mortar in brickwork are very important for appearance, stability, and weathering. Some common joints are:

bastard tuck-pointing: imitation *tuck-pointing* of mortar only, with a profile similar to that of real tuck-pointing;

bucket-handled joint: see *keyed joint*;

flush joint: mortar flush with the brick faces;

keyed joint: called a *bucket-handled joint*, the mortar is indented with a segmental profile. Also a joint raked out to give a *key* to plaster or *stucco;

overhand struck joint: straight joint struck diagonally downwards, starting flush with the upper course;

raked-out joint: joint cleared of mortar to a depth of 10–15 mm from the face of the brickwork for decorative purposes, to provide a key for plaster, or to permit a different type of pointing;

recessed joint: set back from the face;

rubbed joint: flush joint made by rubbing excess mortar off the surface with a rag, rubber, etc.;

ruled joint: also *scored joint*, in which grooves are ruled by running the point of a trowel against a straight-edge to give the appearance of very precise work;

struck joint: straight joint struck diagonally, the bottom set back, and the top flush with the course below;

tuck-pointing: mortar the same colour as the brickwork is set flush in the joints, and a groove formed along the centre of each joint into which is tucked a precise band of lime-putty to which a small amount of silver sand is added: this putty projects a few millimetres, and the top and bottom edges are trimmed in straight lines. In first-class work the vertical *tucks* are slightly narrower than the horizontal;

vee-jointing: a V-shaped channel formed in a *flush* joint;

weathered joint: straight joint struck diagonally, the top set back, and the bottom flush with the course below.

Brunskill (1990); Lloyd (1925); Lynch (1990, 1994–6); McKay (1957)

bridge. Structure by means of which a path, road, etc., is carried over a ravine, valley, or other depression, or over a river or other water-course, affording passage between two points at a height above the ground level, and allowing a free passage through its one or more open intervals beneath the road, etc. Bridges vary in complexity of structure from a simple plank, log, or slab of stone supported at each end (or a single arch spanning from bank to bank, say), to a far more elaborate structure with architectural pretensions, featuring piers, arches, girders, chains, tubes, and many other elements. Early bridges were made of ropes, while timber bridges of various types have a long ancestry. Arched bridges of brick or stone go back to *Antiquity, and some spectacular Roman bridges survive, such as the Pons Fabricius (62 BC), Pons Milvius (109 BC), and the Pons Aelius (now Ponte Sant'Angelo, completed AD 134), in Rome, but the Puente del Diablo near Martorell in Spain is even earlier (*c*.219 BC), although much restored, and seems to be one of the oldest still in existence. Also in Spain is the celebrated bridge over the Tagus at Alcántara (AD 105), with its six impressive arches. Many fine bridges were erected in medieval times (e.g. the fortified Pont Valentré over the Lot at Cahors, France (1308–80), and London Bridge over the Thames, on which habitable buildings stood: it was erected

1176–1209 to designs by Peter, chaplain of Cole Church, while elegant Classical structures (essentially based on Roman precedents) were built in C17 and C18 (e.g. *Telford's Tay Bridge, Dunkeld, Perthshire (1806–9)). Cast iron was first used for bridge-construction in C18 at Ironbridge, Shropshire (1777–9). The development of canals and railways led to considerable advances in bridge-design, notably the suspension-bridge over the Menai Straits in Wales (1819–26) by Telford, the tubular girder-bridge also over the Menai Straits (1844–50) by Robert Stephenson (1803–59), and the Clifton suspension-bridge, Bristol (1831–64), by the younger *Brunel. Other important designers of C19 bridges were *Eiffel and *Roebling. In C20 *reinforced concrete was used to great effect by many designers, including *Freyssinet, *Hennebique, *Maillart, and other elegant structures were erected by *Ammann, *Arup, and *Bonatz. The main types of bridge are:

aqueduct: for conveying water (such as a canal). Good examples are the Roman Pont du Gard, near Nîmes, France (C1 BC) and Telford's Pont-y-Cysyllte aqueduct (1795–1805);

arch-bridge: carried on arches or *vaults;

bascule: a type of cantilever that can be raised in order to allow ships to pass under, e.g. London's Tower Bridge;

cantilever: arm projecting from a pier, or with two arms projecting from piers and connected in the centre;

clapper: stone bridge of piers with slabs of stone spanning between them;

draw: one that can be drawn up or let down, hinged like a flap;

girder: consisting of straight beam-like elements carried on piers, columns, or other supports;

Palladian: bridge with colonnaded superstructure (e.g. at Wilton, Wiltshire (1735–7));

suspension: hung from chains or cables suspended from elevated piers;

swing: swivelling bridge which revolves horizontally on a pivot;

tubular: essentially a very large hollow-girder, carried on piers, through which traffic passes (e.g. Stephenson's Menai Straits railway-bridge (1844–50));

viaduct: long structure carrying a road or a railway over a valley.

Bennett (1997); Jurecka (1986); Leonhardt (1984); Mainstone (1975)

Bridgeman, Charles (d. 1738). English landscape-architect who had an enormous influence on the design of the informal English garden, introducing features that preceded the looser plans of *Brown and *Kent. He is credited with the introduction of the French *ha-ha to England in 1719 at Stowe, Buckinghamshire, and later used it in the simple form commonly found during C18. He also used the French *pattes d'oie* (literally 'goose-foot', but meaning avenues crossing each other) that drew attention towards various *eye-catchers. Bridgeman first came to notice before 1709 when he appears to have worked under *Vanbrugh and Henry Wise (1653–1738) at Blenheim, Oxfordshire. In 1714 he began to work for Lord Cobham (*c.*1669–1749) at Stowe, Buckinghamshire, the most celebrated landscaped garden of the time, with its 'informal' walks, carefully contrived planting, use of water, and numerous *fabriques, most with literary, mythological, political, or historical allusions. He collaborated with many architects, including *Gibbs and Kent, and worked on many gardens, including those at Claremont, Surrey, Eastbury, Dorset, Rousham, Oxfordshire, and Wimpole Hall, Cambridgeshire (all 1720s). He may have advised Alexander Pope (1688–1744) on his garden at Twickenham, and was possibly involved in the creation of Lord *Burlington's garden at Chiswick. In 1727, with Wise, he began a report on the management of the Royal gardens, and succeeded Wise as Royal Gardener to King George II (1727–60) in 1728, working on numerous gardens, including Hampton Court, Kensington Palace, St James's Park, Richmond Park, and Hyde Park (all *c.*1727–38).

Hadfield, Harling, and Highton (1980); van Vynckt (1993); Willis (1977)

Brierley, Walter Henry (1862–1926). English architect. The leading protagonist of the *Wrenaissance style in the North-East, his fine *Arts-and-Crafts house, The Close, Northallerton, Yorkshire (1895–1904), was mentioned by *Muthesius.

Gray (1985)

Brinkman, Johannes Andreas (1902–49). Rotterdam-born architect, who was in partnership from 1925 to 1936 with Leendert Cornelius van der Vlugt (1894–1936) and, from 1937 to 1948, with van den *Broek. The firm produced the celebrated van Nelle tobacco-factory, Rotterdam (1926–30), on which Mart *Stam also worked. Regarded as one of the purest *Constructivist buildings of the period, as well as a pioneering example of Modern architecture, it was a mushroom-columned *reinforced-*concrete structure with large areas of *curtain-walling, and freely expressed ramped connections crossing backwards and forwards between the factory-block and the warehouse in glazed elevated bridges. Brinkman and van der Vlugt collaborated with Willem van Tijen (1894–1974) on the design of the slab-shaped Bergpolder high-rise residential block in Rotterdam (1933–4), one of the earliest buildings on the *piloti base made fashionable by Le *Corbusier.

Joedicke (1963*a*, 1976); Morgan and Naylor (1987)

brise-soleil (*pl.* **brise-soleils**). Baffle or check of vertical or horizontal *louvres, fixed or swivelling, or other elements attached to or part of a building to protect windows from excessive solar light and heat.

Britannic Order. *See* German Order.

Britton, John (1771–1857). British writer on architecture and topography, whose *Architectural Antiquities of Great Britain* (1807–26) and *Cathedral Antiquities* (1836) were major source-books for the *Gothic Revival. He taught R. W. *Billings. *See* Pugin, A. C.

Britton (1807–26); *DNB* (1917)

broach. 1. To remove the marks of rough scraping from a stone face, thus finishing it as *broached work*. **2.** To drill holes in stone in a quarry and then cut between them to free the *blocks. **3.** *Spire, more particularly one on a tower without parapets, requiring extra masonry to effect the transition between the square tower and the octagonal base of the spire: these partial pyramidal forms are called *broaches*. Broach-spires were usually *First Pointed, and occasionally *Second Pointed. **4.** A pointed ornamental structure, e.g. an *obelisk. **5.** Junction (*broach-stop* or *chamfer*) between a chamfered and squared edge by which the bevel merges into a right angle.

broch. Prehistoric dry-stone circular structure with cells (presumably for habitation) in the wall, surrounding an open space (presumably for livestock), as found in Scotland.

Brodrick, Cuthbert (1822–1905). Hull-born English architect, who won the competition to design Leeds Town Hall in 1852 (the assessor was Charles *Barry). This fine civic building shows pronounced French influence (*Brongniart's Paris *Bourse* (Exchange)) in the ranges of columns. His Corn Exchange in Leeds (1860–3) is Italian *Renaissance in style, with an elliptical plan and an ingeniously arranged roof-structure of iron. Brodrick's Cliffs (now Grand) Hotel, Scarborough (1863–7), is much more overtly French Renaissance, with a massive *Second Empire style roof.

Hitchcock (1977); Linstrum (1978)

Broek, Johannes Hendrik van den. *See* *Bakema.

broken. Signifies interruption of an element, such as *broken arch* (usually segmental with its centre filled by a carved motif), *broken ashlar* (random *masonry laid in irregular courses), *broken column* (with the shaft broken off, symbolizing death, a recurring theme in commemorative art), *broken pediment* (*see* pediment), and *broken rangework* (masonry laid in courses but with *blocks of different heights, thus breaking the horizontal joints).

Brongniart, Alexandre-Théodore (1739–1813). One of the most distinguished exponents of *Neoclassicism in France, born in Paris, a pupil of *Blondel and *Boullée. His Parisian town-houses, such as the *Hôtel de Monaco, Rue St-Dominique (1775–7), Hôtel de Bourbon-Condé, Rue Monsieur (1780–3), and Hôtel de Montesquiou, Rue Monsieur (1782), tend to be in a simple, elegant, Neoclassical style, much influenced by de *Wailly, but he also evolved a severe *primitive type of architecture. He used an unfluted baseless *Doric *colonnade at the *cloister of the Monastery of St-Louis d'Antin, Paris (1779–83), now the Lycée Condorcet, and at the Church of St-Germain l'Auxerrois, Romainville, Paris (1785–7), he was clearly influenced by *Chalgrin's St-Philippe-du-Roule (1768–84), although he used sturdy Doric columns in the *nave. Primitivist, too, was his astonishing stepped *pyramid into which was set a tough Doric tetrastyle *portico carrying a segmental *pediment: he also designed the park, or *Élysée*, at Maupertuis, in which the pyramid stood. From 1804 Brongniart worked on the designs for Père-Lachaise Cemetery, Paris, in which the jardin *anglo-chinois became a burial-ground, a conception that had a profound effect on the design of cemeteries thereafter. His influential *Bourse* (Exchange) in Paris (1807–13), with ranges of *Corinthian columns, satisfied the Napoleonic taste for

Roman Imperial grandeur and embodied many of the theories of *Cordemoy and *Perrault.

Braham (1980); Brongniart (1986); Eriksen (1974); Etlin (1984); Hautecœur (1952–3); Kalnein and Levey (1972); Kaufmann (1955); Middleton and Watkin (1987)

bronze. Alloy of copper and tin used for architectural ornament, doors and door-furniture, funerary monuments, grilles and railings, wall-plaques (commemorative or not), window-frames, etc. It is also used in *masonry for cramps, dowels, etc. *See* brass.

Brooks, James (1825–1901). One of England's most distinguished *Gothic Revival church architects. Born in Berkshire, he set up his own practice in 1851. He favoured *First Pointed Burgundian Gothic of C13, and worked mostly in London, often using brick. Some of his churches follow the ideal of urban *Minsters established by *Butterfield at All Saints', Margaret Street, and include the powerful St Chad (begun 1867) and St Columba, Kingsland Road (1865–74), both in Haggerston: the latter is on a large scale, and light is admitted to the impressive interior through a *clearstorey of plate-traceried windows and lancets at the east and west. Later churches include The Ascension, Lavender Hill (1874), and The Transfiguration, Lewisham (1880s). All Hallows', Gospel Oak (begun 1891), was intended to have stone *vaulting, but the 1914–18 war prevented this; at St John the Baptist, Holland Road, Kensington (1872–1911), however, stone vaulting was erected throughout the church, creating a grand and solemn effect. He was in partnership with his son, **James Martin Brooks** (1852–1903).

Clarke (1966, 1969); Dixon and Muthesius (1985); Eastlake (1970)

Brosse, Salomon de (*c.*1571–1626). French architect, an important figure in the transition from *Mannerism to *Classicism. Born in Verneuil-sur-Oise, he was the son and grandson of architects (his grandfather was J. A. du *Cerceau), settling in Paris in the 1590s. His work tended to eschew Mannerist decorative effects, and was more architectonic, sober, and monumental than that of his immediate predecessors. Of his three *châteaux at Blérancourt, Aisne (1611–19), Coulommiers-en-Brie, Seine-et-Marne (1613), and Luxembourg, Paris (from 1614), only the last and a pavilion at Blérancourt survive. The Luxembourg has *rustication over the whole of the *façades, presumably to emulate the Palazzo Pitti in Florence, the childhood home of de Brosse's client, Maria de' Medici (1573–1642), widow of King Henri IV of France (1589–1610). De Brosse's other surviving works include the Palais de Justice de Bretagne, Rennes (1618), perhaps the very first work of true French Classicism, influenced by work at *Fontainebleau and by *Vignola. The handsome west front of the Church of St-Gervais, Paris (1616–23), with its *superimposed unengaged *Orders, was influenced by Vignola's *Il Gesù* front, Rome, and also by de l'*Orme's *frontispiece at Anet. It has been attributed to de Brosse, but it was probably by J.-C. *Métezeau. De Brosse's Protestant *Temple at Charenton (1623—destroyed) seems to have influenced the design of subsequent Protestant churches in Northern Europe.

Blomfield (1974); Blunt (1982); Coope (1972)

Brown, Joseph (1733–85). American amateur architect who designed several important buildings at Providence, RI, including the First Baptist Meeting House (1774–5), the spire of which is based on the illustrations in *Gibbs's *Book of Architecture* (1728). Among his other works are University Hall (1770–1), the Market House (1773–7), and the Brown House (1786–8).

Cady (1957); Hitchcock (1939)

Brown, Lancelot *called* **Capability** (1716–83). Northumberland-born, he was one of the most influential English landscape-architects who has ever lived, as well as an architect. He became head-gardener at Stowe, Buckinghamshire, in 1741, where, with *Bridgeman and William *Kent, he realized the 'naturalization' of the park. This much-admired work enabled Brown to set up on his own from 1749, and, for the next thirty years, he created many landscapes with artificial lakes, apparently randomly disposed clumps of trees, and expanses of grass that provided an admirable setting for the *Palladian mansions that were such a feature of the period. Country-houses, which had once dominated the park, now tended to nestle in the composed *Picturesque landscape, and Brown's famed 'natural' parks (where untidy Nature was tamed and carefully composed) became enormously popular throughout England as well as influential on the Continent. His nickname is said to have originated in his reputed habit of telling clients that their estates were 'capable' of or had 'capabilities' for improvement. His finest existing landscape-gardens, perhaps, are at Berrington Hall, Herefordshire (1780s), Croome Court, Worcestershire (1751–2), Bowood, Wiltshire (1760s), and Nuneham Park, Oxfordshire (1778–82). Landscapes influenced by his work and ideas are referred to as *Brownian*.

Brown designed buildings, and much of his architectural work was executed by Henry Holland of Fulham (1712–85). In 1771 he took the latter's son Henry *Holland into partnership and gradually handed over the architectural side of his practice. Brown's architectural works include Croome Court, Worcestershire (1751–2), the bridge and chapel at Compton Verney, Warwickshire (1770–8), and Claremont House, Esher, Surrey (1771–4, with Henry Holland).

Colvin (1995); Hadfield, Harling, and Highton (1980); Stroud (1975); Willis (1977)

Brown, Richard (*fl.* 1804–45). Probably from Devon, Brown established an architectural practice, but his main claim to fame was as a teacher of drawing and a writer. His pupils included M. A. *Nicholson, and he wrote *The Principles of Practical Perspective* . . . (1815), the indiscriminately eclectic *Domestic Architecture* (1842), *Sacred Architecture* (1845), and *The Rudiments of Drawing Cabinet and Upholstery Furniture* (1822 and 1835), one of the most handsome of early C19 English furniture pattern-books, in which *Neoclassical taste is well to the fore.

Colvin (1995); Curl (1994)

Browne, George (1811–85). Belfast-born architect who worked in Canada from 1830. His best-known works are the Church of St George, Kingston, Ontario (1859), a variant on *Gibbs's St Martin-in-the-Fields, and the City Hall and Market Building, also in Kingston (1842–4), in a robust mixture of *Neo-classicism and late-*Georgian styles that looks back, perhaps, to the *Baroque of *Hawksmoor and *Vanbrugh, although *Gandon's work in Dublin is called to mind.

Kalman (1994)

Brownian. Resembling 'Capability' *Brown's style of landscape-design.

brownstone. Dark red-brown sandstone much used in the eastern USA in the mid- and late C19, hence the typical *terrace-houses of New York, faced with brownstone.

Bruant *or* **Bruand, Libéral** (*c*.1635–97). Architect of the Hôtel des Invalides, Paris (1670–7), with its severely *Antique arcaded *cour d'honneur*, and long Church of St-Louis des Invalides (the *Dôme* was added later by *Mansart). Bruant was responsible for the Chapel of St-Louis in the Salpêtrière Hospital (*c*.1670), with a *rotunda surrounded by four compartments forming a Greek cross on plan, and four chapels at the angles of the central space. Eight compartments were formed in which the inmates could be separately accommodated.

Blunt (1982); Hautecœur (1948); Reuterswärd (1965)

Bruce, Sir William (*c*.1630–1710). The founder of Classical architecture in Scotland. A Perthshire laird, he became Surveyor-General and Overseer of the King's Buildings in Scotland (1671–8), creating a symmetrical and very French *façade at Holyroodhouse (1671–9). He was consulted by many members of the Scottish aristocracy who wanted to improve their houses. At Kinross House (1686–93) he adopted the highly accomplished manner of *Pratt and *Webb, and the architecture is enhanced by its formal setting. The main vista is terminated by the ruins of Lochleven Castle, so Bruce, like *Vanbrugh, has a position in the history of the *Picturesque. He designed Lauder Church, Berwickshire (1673), Hopetoun House, West Lothian (1699–1710), the Town House, Stirling (1703–5), and (probably) the Hope Aisle, Abercorn Church, West Lothian (1707–8).

Colvin (1995); Dunbar (1970, 1978); Fenwick (1970)

Brückwald, Otto (1841–1904). Saxon Court Architect, and designer of the *Festspielhaus* (Festival Theatre), Bayreuth, Bavaria, for Richard Wagner (1813–83), much influenced by the work of *Semper and Wagner himself. There is a huge stage and the auditorium seating is arranged like a segment of a circle, with the orchestra placed out of sight and partially under the stage. It was an important innovation in theatre design.

Mallgrave (1996)

Brukalski, Stanisław (1894–1967). Polish architect. He and his wife, **Barbara** (1899–1980), were pioneers of *International *Modernism in their country, specializing in public-housing developments, and were members of

*CIAM. They also designed the interiors of passenger-liners, including the *Batory*, *Piłsudski*, *Sobieski*, and *Chrobry* (1927–38). Among their works the Warsaw Housing Co-operative Housing Colony VII, Warsaw-Żoliborz (1930–4), deserves mention.

Leśnikowski (1996); Wisłocka (1968)

Brunel, Isambard Kingdom (1806–59). One of the most distinguished and imaginative engineers of C19, Brunel was born in Portsmouth, son of the French-born engineer **Sir Marc Isambard Brunel** (1769–1849). Educated privately and at the Lycée Henri Quatre in Paris, in 1823 he entered his father's office where he was involved in the construction of the Thames Tunnel from Wapping to Rotherhithe. In 1829 he designed the suspension-bridge over the Avon at Clifton, and an amended conception of 1831 was begun in 1836, completed in 1864 after modification. He was appointed engineer for the Great Western Railway in 1833: he not only surveyed the route, but designed the Box Tunnel between Chippenham and Bath, the bridge over the Thames at Maidenhead, and introduced a limited type of standardization for the designs of station-buildings on the line between London and Bristol. He was responsible for Temple Meads Station, Bristol (1839–40), and Paddington Terminus, London (1850–5—to which M. D. *Wyatt and Owen *Jones contributed), as well as the Royal Albert Bridge over the Tamar at Saltash (1857–9), his most celebrated iron structure. He designed the Railway Company's town at Swindon, Wiltshire (again with Wyatt); the Monkwearmouth Docks (1831), and later similar works at Plymouth and Milford Haven; a prefabricated hospital (complete with tarred wooden sewers and mechanical ventilation, for Renkioi in the Crimea (1855), possibly suggested by the success of the Crystal Palace, for he was a zealous promoter of the Great Exhibition of 1851); and ocean-going steamships (e.g. the *Great Eastern* (1858)) that were larger and more technically advanced than any previously known.

DNB (1917); Pugsley (1980); Rolt (1957)

Brunelleschi, Filippo (1377–1446). Florentine architect, the first and perhaps the most distinguished of the *Renaissance, who trained as a sculptor and goldsmith, learned geometry, and developed the laws and principles of perspective. Gradually he became more interested in architecture, and from 1417 advised on the proposed *cupola for the Cathedral of Santa Maria del Fiore, Florence. His inspiration for his architecture was certainly from earlier buildings, but it came from the Tuscan *Romanesque and *proto-Renaissance buildings rather than from the remains of Imperial Roman architecture, for structures such as San Miniato al Monte and the *baptistery, Florence (both C11 and C12), were thought at the time to be much older than they were. Indeed, he was less of an antiquarian than those who followed him, notably *Alberti and *Michelozzo, and seems to have been more interested in the problems of construction, definition of architectural elements by linear means, and the control and management of volume. In 1420 he began to build the Cathedral cupola (in collaboration with Ghiberti), a vast octagonal structure crowned by an enormous *lantern designed by Brunelleschi alone (1436–67). The octagon, double shell, and pointed profile were settled before Brunelleschi's involvement, but the use of spiralling courses of herringbone brickwork, iron chains and sloping masonry rings to bind the dome together, and ribs joining the shells are his inventions, although owe much to his studies of Roman structures. Brunelleschi's genius lay in his abilities to combine ancient and modern aesthetic, architectural, and engineering principles.

His *Ospedale degli Innocenti* (Hospice for the Innocents, or Foundlings' Hospital), Florence (1419–44), with its elegant *arcades on *Corinthian columns, glazed *terracotta medallions in the *spandrels, *architrave dividing first and second floors, and small rectangular windows over which are *pediments, is reckoned to be the very first truly Renaissance building, but its sources are local. Brunelleschi designed two *basilican churches (San Lorenzo (from 1418) and Santo Spirito (from 1436)): both have *nave-arcades with Classical columns carrying fragmentary *entablatures from which the arches spring, and both have domed crossings with *transepts, although at Santo Spirito the *aisles and semicircular side-chapels carried all round the church give a rhythmic unity not present at San Lorenzo. At the latter Brunelleschi designed the Old Sacristy, also the *Mortuary Chapel of the Medicis, as a cube roofed by a dome with ribs radiating from the central lantern giving an impression of sail-like forms over ribs. The entire interior

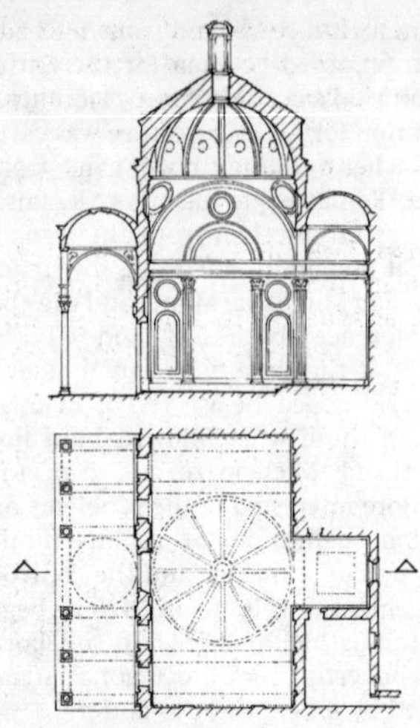
Plan and section of Pazzi Chapel, Florence.

was painted white with bands of grey on the dominant architectural motifs, the first time such a decorative scheme was employed. Brunelleschi may have designed the Pazzi Chapel in the *cloister of Santa Croce, Florence (1429–61), where the Old Sacristy themes are developed with a central domed space flanked on two sides by barrel-vaulted side bays and on the third by a small domed recess set behind an arch. The chapel is approached through an entrance-*loggia consisting of two groups of three Corinthian columns carrying an entablature between which is an arch. Behind the arch is a saucer-dome. The fine interior is articulated by means of *pilasters, entablatures, *archivolts, and other architectural elements, all in local grey stone (*pietra serena*), set against the white walls, while glazed *terracotta *roundels complete the scheme.

The uncompleted oratory of the Camaldulensian convent of Santa Maria degli Angeli (1434–7) is the first truly centrally planned Renaissance building, with a domed octagon set on eight *piers which also provide the divisions between the radiating chapels: it is quite clearly based on Antique precedent, notably the so-called Temple of Minerva Medica, Rome. The *astylar rusticated Palazzo Pitti, Florence, may have been partially designed by Brunelleschi, for its severe *Antique quality and carefully ordered proportions suggest at the very least his influence.

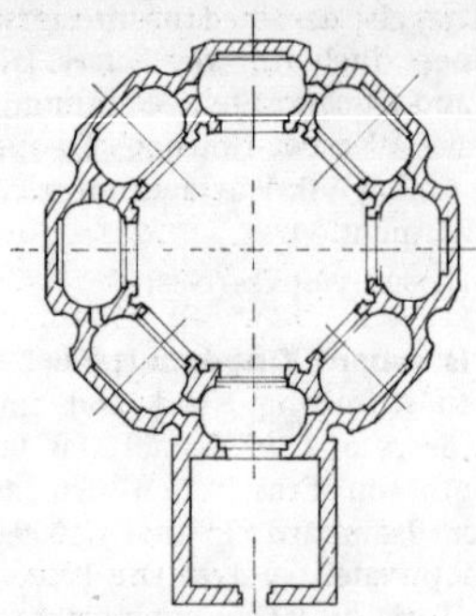
Plan of Santa Maria degli Angeli, Florence.

Brunelleschi used simple proportional relationships throughout his buildings, and this gives his architecture a pleasing harmonious quality that was sought by Renaissance designers.

Argan (1978); Battisti (1981); Braunfels (1981); Doumato (1980); Klotz (1970); Luporini (1964); Placzek (1982—a comprehensive entry and large bibliography); Prager and Scaglia (1970); Saalman (1980)

Brunt, van. *See* Ware & van Brunt.

Brutalism. Style of Le *Corbusier from 1945 in which *béton brut, treated particularly uncompromisingly, with the *formwork patterns not only visible but deliberately emphasized, much admired by the architectural avant-garde from *c.*1954, when the term appears to have been first used in England. Architects influenced by Brutalism included *Mayekawa, *Rudolph, the *Smithsons, *Stirling & *Gowan, and *Tange, but there were very many others as well. *New Brutalism* was particularly associated with British disciples of Le Corbusier, perhaps not unconnected with P. Smithson's nickname, 'Brutus', while also providing an alternative to the 'New Humanist' and 'New Empiricist' architects more influenced by developments in Scandinavia. The Smithsons' austere Secondary Modern School, Hunstanton, Norfolk (1950–3), was described as 'Brutalist', even though it perhaps owed more to *Mies van der Rohe than to Le Corbusier, and its construction was of exposed steelwork with panels of yellow brick and glass: *Pevsner described the building as 'ruthlessly perfect and ruthlessly symmetrical', so the use of the term for a building not made of concrete would appear to refer to rigour, the exposure of structure and services, and work by or influenced by the Smithsons. New Brutalism also encouraged the use of over-sized rough concrete elements, crudely colliding with each other, while aspects of mechanical engineering, such as service-ducts, ventilation-towers, and the like, became overtly displayed. Examples include the Hayward Gallery, Queen Elizabeth Hall, and surrounding walkways, parapets, and stairs at London's South Bank (1968–9).

Banham (1966)

Bryce, David (1803–76). Scots architect, a pupil and assistant of William *Burn. He designed a number of distinguished buildings, including the *Scottish-Baronial Royal Infirmary (1870–9); Fettes College (1863–70); the Head Office of the Bank of Scotland (1864–71); St George's West Church (1867–9); and the British Linen Bank, St Andrew Square (a fine *palazzo of 1846–51), all in Edinburgh. He is best known for his country-houses, most of which are in the Scottish-Baronial style, influenced by *Billings's *Baronial Antiquities* (1845–52): one of his best houses in that style is Kinnaird Castle, Brechin, Angus (1853–7). He designed the enormous Classical Hamilton Palace *mausoleum, Lanarkshire (1848–51), which has a Roman grandeur about it. His brother **John** (1805–51) practised in Glasgow, where he designed monuments in the Necropolis including the McGavin memorial (1830s), and several ranges of Classical houses, including Queen's Crescent (1840).

Colvin (1995); Fiddes and Rowan (1976)

Brydon, John McKean (1840–1901). Dunfermline-born Scots architect, a pupil of David *Bryce. He joined J. J. *Stevenson and Campbell Douglas (1828–1910) in Glasgow (*c.*1863–6) before settling in London where he worked with Eden *Nesfield and Norman *Shaw for three years. In 1880 he set up in practice with William Wallace. He won the 1898 competition to design the new Government Offices at the corner of Parliament Street and Parliament Square, Westminster (1898–1912), a fine ensemble in which *Chambers, *Wren, and *Webb influences can be detected. His more modest Chelsea Town Hall (1885–7) is in a 'Free-Classic' style influenced by the work of Wren. In a series of lectures and articles, Brydon called for the revival of Classical discipline in architecture as an antidote to the free-for-all of late-Victorian times, and promoted a revival of *Palladianism and elements from English *Baroque, as in his Bath Guildhall (1890s).

Gray (1985); Physick and Darby (1973); Stamp and Amery (1980)

Bryggman, Erik (1891–1955). Finnish architect. Born in Turku, he studied architecture in Helsinki, graduating in 1916. He set up his own office in Turku in 1923, where Aino and Alvar *Aalto worked with him for a brief period. The collaboration produced the important design for the 1929 Exhibition to celebrate seven centuries of the city's existence. In 1930 Bryggman won the Grand Prix at the Antwerp World Fair for his Finnish pavilion, an essay in birch plywood, and in 1938 his well-known design for the cemetery chapel at Turku was commenced, though not completed until 1941. Other buildings by him include Vierumäki sports-club (1931–6), the library of Åbo Academy, Turku (1933–6), and the Riihimäki water-tower (1952).

Richards (1978); Wickberg (1962)

Buchsbaum, Hans von (*c.*1390–*c.*1456). German architect who worked in the Danube area, first at Ulm (1418), then at Steyr (1440s), where he built the *Pfarrkirche* (Parish Church). He probably worked at the *Stephansdom* (Cathedral of St Stephen), Vienna, in the 1430s before being appointed Master of the Works there in 1446. He seems to have supervised the construction of the *nave *vaults.

Grimschitz (1947); Koepf (1969)

buckler. 1. *Acrostolium. **2.** *Pelta ornament common on Classical *friezes (especially in the Roman *Doric *Order according to *Vignola), consisting of a wide shield-like form with its extremities on either side returning as heads or scrolls. **3.** Circular shield of small size.

Bucklin, James C. (1801–90). Born in Rhode Island, USA, he is remembered as an architect of monumental buildings in the *Greek Revival style including the Westminster Street front to Providence Arcade (1828) and Manning Hall, Brown University (1833), both in Providence, Rhode Island.

Hitchcock (1939); Pierson and Jordy (1970–86)

bucrane, bucranium. (*pl.* **bucranes, bucrania**). Ornament in the form of an ox-skull or -head frequently associated with *festoons and *garlands, found especially on the *metopes of the Roman *Doric *Order. *See* aegicrane.

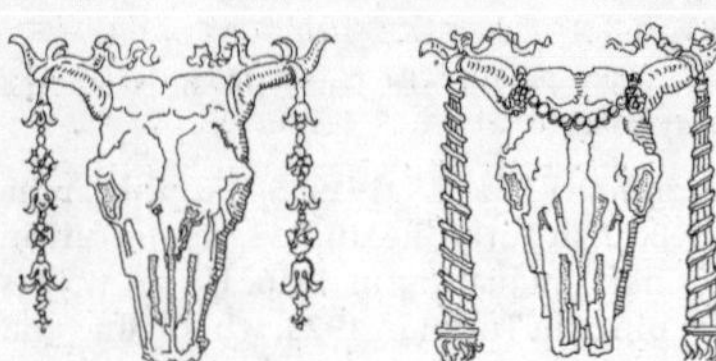

bucranium. (*left*) Hung with bellflower or husk garlands. (*right*) hung with inverted flambeaux.

bud. In the *Corinthian *capital the bud-like form at the top of the stalks out of which the *volutes grow.

Buddhist railing. Stone barrier resembling a timber fence, with the horizontals running through the vertical *posts, usually surrounding a *stupa.

buffet d'eau. Fountain shaped like a stepped cake-stand, with a *basin underneath.

Buffington, Leroy Sunderlund (1847–1931). Born in Cincinnati, Ohio, he set up his own practice in Minneapolis in 1873. His mansion for Charles Pettit (1874) there was much influenced by the style of *Visconti's and *Lefuel's additions to the Louvre in Paris (1852–7), and by *Hunt's house for the Wetmore family, Newport, RI (1872–3). Between 1877 and 1888 he designed several mansions and other buildings including the West Hotel (1881–4) and the Pillsbury 'A' Mill (1880–2), which received national notice. Buffington invented a system of metal *skeleton construction to make the building of *skyscrapers possible. In 1888 he patented the system, but it seems never to have been used by anyone else.

Art Bulletin, 26 (March 1944), 1–12; Handlin (1985); Upjohn (1935)

Bulfinch, Charles (1763–1844). Boston-born, he was one of the USA's first native-born professional architects. His work tended to combine *Colonial *Georgian and *Adam styles in a frugal *Neoclassicism, prompted by his tour of Europe (1785–7). He designed the old State House, Hartford, Conn. (1793–6), followed by the Massachusetts State House, Boston (1795–7), clearly influenced by *Chambers's Somerset House, London (1776–86). He also designed several unified groups of *terrace houses and some churches (including the Church of Christ, Lancaster, Mass. (1816)), but much has been demolished. From 1818 he was architect to the Federal Capitol in Washington, DC, completing his work there in 1830.

Bulfinch (1973); Kirker (1969); Pierson and Jordy (1970–86); Place (1968); Whiffen and Koeper (1983)

Bulgarian architecture. *See* Byzantine architecture.

Bullant, Jean (*c*.1515/20–78). French *Renaissance architect, much influenced by de l'*Orme, who introduced the *Giant *Order to France at the entrance *portico on the south side of the *château at Ecouen, Seine-et-Oise (*c*.1560). He designed the monumental gallery at Fère-en-Tardenois (1552–62) to connect the fortified château to its dependent buildings, placing it on a tall series of arches, giving the impression of a Roman *aqueduct. He designed the small château at Chantilly (*c*.1560), with a *frontispiece featuring a monumental arch carried on *coupled columns, a *Mannerist device to enliven the *façade. He also completed the gallery over de l'Orme's bridge at Chenonceaux (1576–8) for Catherine de' Medici, the Queen Mother; again Mannerist devices and rhythms recur. In terms of style his *Mannerism comes close to that of Jacques Androuet du *Cerceau the Elder. Bullant's publications include *Reigle Générale d'Architecture* (1563) and *Petit Traicté de Géometrie* (1564).

Blomfield (1974); Blunt (1982); Watkin (1986)

Bullet, Pierre (1639–1716). French architect (a pupil of N.-F. *Blondel) who practised in Paris from 1672. His *Hôtels Crozat (now the Ritz) and d'Evreux in the Place Vendôme, Paris (1702–7), were precedents in their interior arrangement for later Parisian houses. He was the author of *Livre Nouveau de Cheminées* and *L'Architecture Pratique* (1691). His son, **Jean-Baptiste Bullet de Chamblain** (1665–1726), assisted his father in the construction of the houses in the Place Vendôme, but on his own he designed the Hôtel Poisson de Bourvalais (1703–7). His Château de Champs (1703–7) had an elliptical salon exposed in a protruding bow on the garden-front, while his Hôtel Dodun, Paris (after 1715), was a fine creation, with *Rococo interiors.

Blunt (1982); Hautecœur (1948, 1950); Kalnein and Levey (1972); Langenskiöld (1959)

bull's-eye. *See* œil-de-bœuf.

bundle. *Gothic *pier resembling a tight bundle of *colonnettes in which the latter are not actually detached, but are formed by the undulating plan-form. *Compare* *clustered or *compound pier.

bungalow. One-storey lightly built detached house, originally a Hindu word for a Bengali temporary single-storey dwelling with a thatched or similar roof.

King (1982); Lancaster (1985)

Bunney, Michael Frank Wharlton (1875–1926). English architect. He became an assistant to Horace *Field before setting up his own practice in 1902, and from 1905 was in partnership with C. C. Makins. Bunney is remembered for his modest houses, especially those he designed for Hampstead *Garden Suburb (1907–14). All were modelled on C17 *vernacular houses of Hertfordshire. Bunney and Field collaborated on *English Domestic Architecture of the XVIIth and XVIIIth Centuries* (1905 and 1928), an invaluable compendium of undervalued buildings.

Gray (1985)

Bunning, James Bunstone (1802–63). London architect who was surveyor to several organizations, including the London Cemetery Company and The Haberdashers' Company. He designed the *Egyptian Revival avenue and other structures at Highgate Cemetery, and the Classical Grecian lodges and gates at Nunhead Cemetery (1839–43). In 1843 he was appointed 'Clerk to the City's Works' (the title was changed to City Architect in 1847), and he was responsible for several street improvements. In 1848 he prepared the first plans for Holborn Viaduct. His masterpiece (demolished 1962) was generally regarded to be the London Coal Exchange (1846–9), an internal top-lit galleried *rotunda of cast iron concealed within an *Italianate Classical exterior. He also designed the handsome Italianate Metropolitan Cattle Market, Caledonian Road (1855)—only the clock-tower and one of the corner pubs survive—and the *castellated Holloway Prison (1849–52), largely demolished. He was the author of *Designs for Tombs and Monuments* (1839).

Curl (1993); *DNB* (1917); Dixon and Muthesius (1985)

Bunshaft, Gordon (1909–90). *See* Skidmore, Owings, & Merrill.

Buon, Bartolomeo (*c*.1405–*c*.1467). *See* Bon, Bartolomeo.

Buonarotti. *See* Michelangelo.

Buontalenti delle Girandole, Bernardo (1531–1608). Florentine architect who also painted and sculpted, as well as designed masques, pyrotechnics (*Girandole* means a Catherine-wheel), and other amusements for his patrons, the Medici Grand Dukes. His *Mannerist detailing is best seen at the idiosyncratic Porta delle Suppliche in the Uffizi, Florence (1580)—where a broken segmental *pediment has its *scrolls reversed to form a wing-like element supporting the bust of Duke Cosimo—and at the new altar-steps for Santa Trinità (1574–6) now in Santo Stefano—where the *trompe l'œil carved steps are unusable, and the real stairs were placed, invisible, on each side. The fantastic *grottoes he designed for the Bóboli Gardens (1583–8), where pumice-stone encrustations submerge the entrance, and the interior, with its hidden sources of light and its eerie figures, are a tour-de-force of theatrical effects. He created the *Tribuna* in the Uffizi (1574–89), the decorations and lavish gardens at the Medici *villa at Pratolino (destroyed), and the Casino Mediceo (Casino di San Marco), Florence (1574). Much more restrained is the *façade of Santa Trinità (1593–4), with four *Giant *pilasters carrying an *entablature, over which is a pedimented *Attic-storey flanked by scrolls. Elegant and simple too is the Fortezza di Belvedere (1590s) set high on a hill to protect the Pitti Palace. Buontalenti designed and built fortifications, engineering works, and a canal. His designs for Mannerist distorted and melting mask decorations anticipate *Auricular ornament.

Berti (1967); Botto (1968); Fara (1979, 1988)

Burges, William (1827–81). London-born architect, one of the least restrained of the *Gothic Revivalists, whose philosophy was strongly influenced by A. W. N. *Pugin. He trained as an engineer and was articled to *Blore (1844) before moving to the office of M. D. *Wyatt (1849). In 1851 he joined Henry *Clutton, later becoming his partner, and assisted in the preparation of *Domestic Architecture of France* (1853). In 1854 the partners won the competition to design the new Cathedral at Lille with an essay in robust C13 *Gothic, but their proposals were not realized. After a quarrel, Burges set up on his own, and won the competition for the Crimea Memorial Church in Constantinople (1857), a fine *polychrome essay in the style of C13, again not executed. From this period he designed much furniture based on C13 French prototypes illustrated in *Viollet-le-Duc's publications, and his work was shown in London at the Architectural Exhibition in 1859, the year in which his remarkable, *muscular, and peculiarly tough east end of Waltham Abbey, Essex, was begun. From 1863 to 1904 his great Anglican Cathedral of St Finbar was erected in Cork, Ireland, with its three *spires, the whole in a convincing French C13 style, with a noble, powerful interior.

From 1866 his alterations, extensions, and additions were designed and built at Cardiff Castle, and from 1872 to 1891 the reconstruction and decoration of Castell Coch, Glamorganshire, Wales, were carried out for the 3rd Marquess of Bute (1847–1900). These works are extraordinary for the richness of their *polychrome decorations and French Gothic style, although the so-called Arab Hall at Cardiff Castle (1881) has a pronounced *Islamic influence. For James McConnochie he designed and built a Gothic house at Park Place, Cardiff (1871–80), and at Melbury Road, Kensington, Burges built his own Tower House (1875–81), a Gothic building of red brick with a circular tower. Decorated and furnished to designs by its architect-owner, it was an instant success, being admired for its medievalism and massive construction. Each room had its own iconography, and symbols and allegories were used throughout. Perhaps partly because of these designs, Burges has a claim to be regarded as a herald of the *Arts-and-Crafts movement.

Massive, tough detail is evident in the two churches he built in Yorkshire: Christ the Consoler, Skelton-on-Ure (1870–6), and St Mary, Aldford-cum-Studley (1870–8). Skelton marked a move from French to English Gothic Revival of *c.*1270, but the French elements are still present, notably in the details of the spire and in the balcony of the organ-loft: the richly beautiful *chancel is one of the most remarkable of the C19. At Studley, French and English sources again mix, and the *piers are derived from English medieval precedents, but the whole is marvellously rich and integrated, with a complicated iconography concerning Paradise Lost and Regained. Burges's ecclesiastical master-work, it is probably the most perfect of his *Muscular Gothic buildings, freely and imaginatively treated, yet backed by genuine scholarship. His designs for Trinity College, Hartford, Conn. (1873–82), were only partly realized, and then in watered-down form. However, his work influenced the executant architect for Trinity College, his American pupil Francis Hatch Kimball (1845–1919), and may also have impressed itself upon H. H. *Richardson.

Crook (1981)

Burgh, Thomas (1630–1730). Irish military engineer, who worked under Surveyor-General William *Robinson, succeeding him in 1700. His buildings in Dublin include the *Custom House (from 1704, demolished 1815), the Library at Trinity College (1709–33), the Royal Barracks (1701–7), various other buildings at Trinity, and Dr Steevens's Hospital (from 1718). His only essay in tentative *Palladianism seems to have been at his own house at Oldtown, Co. Kildare (*c.*1715).

Craig (1982); Loeber (1981)

Burghausen, Hans von (d. 1432). *See* Stethaimer.

Büring, Johann Gottfried (1723–after 1788). Hamburg-born architect, responsible for the *Neues Palais* (New Palace—1763–8), with a main elevation based on *Vanbrugh's Castle Howard, Yorkshire; the Chinese Tea House (1754–7); and No. 5, *Am Neuen Markt* (1753–5), based on *Palladio's Palazzo Thiene, Vicenza, all in Potsdam. He also worked with *Boumann on the building of St Hedwig's Roman-Catholic Cathedral, Berlin (1772–3), and designed the exquisite picture-gallery at Sans Souci, Potsdam (1755–63), one of the first in the history of museums erected solely to exhibit paintings.

Watkin and Mellinghoff (1987)

Burke, Edmund (1729–97). British statesman and writer. His *A Philosophical Enquiry into the Origin of our Ideas of the Sublime and Beautiful* (1756) was of enormous importance in creating a move from *Classicism to *Romanticism, and in the history of aesthetics greatly influenced German philosophers of the Enlightenment, notably Immanuel *Kant. His discussion of the aesthetic categories of the *Beautiful and the *Sublime were especially significant.

Burke (1757); *DNB* (1917)

Bürklein, Georg Christian Friedrich (1813–72). German architect, who assisted *Gärtner in the designs for the Ludwigstrasse, Munich. He designed the *Rathaus* (Town Hall),

Fürth (1840–3), based on the Palazzo Vecchio, Florence, and the *polychromatic *Rundbogenstil *Hauptbahnhof* (Main Railway Station), Munich (1847–9—destroyed). His new architectural style for the Maximilianstrasse was a brick and *terracotta version of English, German, and Italian *Gothic (1852–75).

Hederer (1976, 1976*a*); Nerdinger (1987)

Burle Marx, Roberto (1909–94). Born São Paulo, Brazil, he studied botany at Dahlem, Berlin (1928), and became Director of Parks at Recife, Brazil, from 1934. In 1937 he set up his own practice as a landscape-architect. As a champion of Brazilian flora, he used native species in his designs, composing his palettes of colour with scientific care. He collaborated with *Niemeyer and others in the designs of the gardens of the Ministry of Education and Health, Rio de Janeiro (1938), and with Niemeyer and Lúcio *Costa at Brasília. His bay-front at Glória-Flamengo Park (1961) and the designs for the pavements along Copacabana Beach (1970), both in Rio de Janeiro, demonstrate his use of Brazilian stone and rocks with native plants. His deep interest in ecology is perhaps best demonstrated in his own gardens at Guaratiba, near Rio, but his most celebrated creation is the Odette Monteiro garden, Petropolis (1947–8).

Bardi (1964); Emanuel (1994)

Burlington, Richard Boyle, 3rd Earl of, *and* **4th Earl of Cork** (1694–1753). Succeeding to the Earldom in 1704, Burlington was immensely rich, and from *c*.1716 took up the cudgels on behalf of *Palladianism, a movement of which he was to become the undisputed leader and arbiter of taste. In 1719 he studied *Palladio's work in and around Vicenza, returning later that year with William *Kent, whom he retained as a painter of historical scenes. Burlington had employed *Gibbs to transform his town-house in Piccadilly in 1716, but he replaced him with *Campbell, while Kent was to be responsible for the interiors. From the early 1720s Burlington began to do his own architectural designs, assisted by *Flitcroft, and in 1722 he commenced his first public building, the dormitory of Westminster School, intended as an exemplar in his campaign to restore to England *Vitruvian principles of architecture, as embodied in the works of Palladio, *Scamozzi, and Inigo *Jones. His sources were Palladio's drawings and published works, and drawings by Jones and *Webb. Now Jones's first Palladian Revival was associated with the reigns of the Stuart James I and VI (1603–25) and Charles I (1625–49), so the second Palladian Revival provided an element of continuity after an interruption, perhaps associated with the need to give legitimacy to the Hanoverian succession that was not universally popular, and had received a jolt as a result of the Jacobite Rebellion of 1715. To further his campaign, Burlington produced a collection of drawings by Jones and Webb and arranged for their publication by Kent as *Designs of Inigo Jones* (1727) with some 'few Designs' by Burlington himself. He also published drawings by Palladio in *Fabbriche Antiche disegnate da Andrea Palladio* (1730). In the 1720s and 1730s, virtually all the motifs of English Palladianism recurred in Burlington's designs: at Tottenham Park, Wiltshire (from 1721), the *pavilion-towers based on Wilton were pierced by *serlianas; the *villa (influenced by Palladio's Villa Capra near Vicenza) at Chiswick, Middlesex (*c*.1723–9), had serlianas set in semicircular-headed recesses; and at York, the Vitruvian Palladian *Egyptian Hall was recreated at the Assembly Rooms (1731–2). The *rusticated lower storey, the taller and more important *piano nobile (complete with *portico and windows with *dressings set in large expanses of wall) became common, and not only for country-houses, but in public buildings as well. By the 1730s, in fact, Anglo-Palladian conventions had become *de rigueur* for English country-houses, and Burlington, high-priest of absolute standards and architectural rules, was consulted to ensure that Good Taste was not contravened. His protégés were given influential posts in the Office of Works: for example, Kent became an architect in his own right, designing the Horse Guards Building, the Royal Mews, and the Treasury Buildings, as well as the great Palladian house, Holkham Hall, Norfolk. Burlington was one of the most potent influences on the development of English architecture in its entire history, and was the key figure in the rejection of *Baroque in favour of a more austere *Classicism. As a catalyst for the evolution of English *Neoclassicism he should not be underestimated.

Barnard and Clark (1995); Burlington (1730); Campbell (1967–72); Colvin (1995); Harris (1981); Summerson (1993); Watkin (1979, 1986); Wilson (1984); Wittkower (1974*a*)

Burn, William (1789–1870). Edinburgh-born architect who worked in Robert *Smirke's office in London (1808–11), before returning to Edinburgh to work with his father, **Robert Burn** (1752–1815), the designer of the Nelson Monument on Calton Hill (1807–16). William Burn's earliest commissions were for public buildings (Custom House, Greenock (1817–18), the *Ledoux-like Gasworks at Tanfield, Canonmills (1824, drawn by *Schinkel in 1826), County Hall, Inverness (1834–5), and many others), but his large and phenomenally successful practice consisted mainly of commissions for country-houses. Blairquhan, Ayrshire (*c.*1820–4), is an example of his *Tudor *Gothic style, but by *c.*1825 Burn was designing in a *Jacobethan manner that became his speciality. Scottish *vernacular architecture and *tower-houses were added to his sources from 1829 (Faskally, Perthshire, and Tyninghame House, East Lothian), but, from his completion of *Salvin's great Harlaxton Manor, Lincolnshire (from 1838), his work became more ebullient, leading to his best houses, including Falkland House, Fife (1839–44), Whitehill Hall, Midlothian (1839–44), Stoke Rochford House (1841–3), and Revesby Abbey (1844), both in Lincolnshire, and Dartrey, Co. Monaghan, Ireland (1844–6), all Jacobethan, but including other styles. He also designed in the *Scottish-Baronial manner in which his pupil (and later partner) David *Bryce became adept: Stenhouse, Stirlingshire (1836—demolished) was an example. Although enormously prolific, Burn never rose to great architecture: his work was competent, very often agreeable, but sometimes dull. He took his nephew, J. MacVicar *Anderson, into partnership, who continued the practice after Burn's death, and his pupils included Eden *Nesfield and Norman *Shaw.

Colvin (1995); *DNB* (1917); Macaulay (1975, 1987)

Burnacini, Lodovico Ottavio (1636–1707). Designer (assisted by *Fischer von Erlach) of the *Dreifaltigkeitssäule* (Trinity Column) in the *Graben*, Vienna (erected 1687–93), a *Baroque monument showing the vanquishing of the Plague. He was Architect to the Imperial Court, but most of his work was as a theatrical designer and an engineer.

Aurenhammer (1973)

Burnet, John (1814–1901). Scots architect, born at Kirk of Shotts, he became an architect in 1844, practising in Glasgow. His early work is modestly Classical, including Elgin Place Congregational Church (1856) and the *Italianate 61–3 Miller Street (1854). His later designs include the exuberant Italian *Renaissance Clydesdale Bank, St Vincent Place (1870), and the beautifully restrained Clevedon Crescent (1876). Burnet was responsible for the Italian *Gothic Glasgow Stock Exchange (1874), Woodlands Parish Church (also 1874), and Lanarkshire House, Ingram Street (1876), an *Italianate *Mannerist design of great verve, with an unevenly spaced pilastrade and a *colonnade on the two upper floors.

Gomme and Walker (1987)

Burnet, Sir John James (1857–1938). Glasgow-born son of John *Burnet, educated at the École des *Beaux-Arts in Paris, who joined his father's office in 1878. His Fine Arts Institute, Sauchiehall Street, Glasgow (1879–80—demolished in 1967), was an essay in restrained *Greek Revival, and anticipated the Classical Revival in England by many years. He was commissioned in 1903 to design the extension to the British Museum, the King Edward VII Galleries, which has a *Giant *Order of three-quarters *engaged *Ionic columns that Burnet tilted slightly inwards so that the *flutes ran parallel to the *naked of the wall, avoiding awkward junctions. This Beaux-Arts building, one of the first of the Edwardian *Neoclassical reactions to the *Baroque Revival and *Wrenaissance, made his reputation, and he was knighted in 1914. Apart from a number of works by the Glasgow firm (Burnet, Son, & Campbell), including the Barony Church, Castle Street (1886), modelled on Dunblane Cathedral and the plan of Gerona Cathedral, and the fantastically eclectic Charing Cross Mansions, Sauchiehall Street (1891), Burnet's London office produced a fine essay in Beaux-Arts elevational treatment at 99 Aldwych, London, while his Kodak House, Kingsway, admitted its steel frame and removed all overt references to the *Orders. Adelaide House, London Bridge (1924–5), was one of the first large buildings of the 1920s to be consciously modelled on a monumental Egyptianizing style. By far the most impressive work of the firm (it had become John Burnet, Tait, & Lorne) between the wars was St Andrew's House, Edinburgh (1936–9), to accommodate the Scottish Office: a symmetrical composition in the Beaux-Arts tradition, the building was mainly the work of Burnet's partner Thomas S. *Tait.

Gomme and Walker (1987); Gray (1985); Service (1975, 1977)

Burnham, Daniel Hudson (1846–1912). American architect. A first-class administrator and entrepreneur, he was also gifted in that he could bring out the best in those with whom he collaborated. Born in Henderson, New York, he entered the office of Loring & *Jenney (1867–8) where he acquired some architectural experience, and in 1873 formed a partnership with John Wellborn *Root. As Burnham & Root, the firm was significant in the creation of the *Chicago School: their first *skyscraper was the (demolished) Montauk Building, Chicago (1881–2), and other tall buildings followed in which load-bearing walls were mixed with framed structures. Then came the sixteen-storey Monadnock Building, Chicago (1889–91), with load-bearing walls, tiers of canted *bay-windows, and huge crowning coved *cornice, and then the (demolished) Masonic Temple, Chicago (1890–2), with twenty-two storeys and a steel *skeleton. After Root's early death Burnham set up with *Atwood in 1891, and built up one of the largest practices in the USA. With Atwood the firm produced the Reliance Building, Chicago (1891–4), which further developed architecture using a metal skeleton: a fourteen-storey tower with glass and *terracotta cladding, it looked forward to C20 developments in which structural *frames would be clearly expressed. However, Burnham was appointed the co-ordinator of the World's Columbian Exposition in Chicago (1893), and began to promote a *Beaux-Arts *Classicism which was the favoured style of the Exposition buildings, and had a profound effect on American architecture and planning for many years to come. In Burnham's firm's own work (e.g. Marshall Field's Department Store, Chicago (1893–1902), the Fuller ('Flat-Iron') Building, New York (1902–3), and Wanamaker's Store, Philadelphia (1909)), elements of *Renaissance architecture were grafted on. Burnham's fame, connected with his impressive Beaux-Arts Classicism, caused him to be employed as consultant to Selfridges Store for the new building (1907) in Oxford Street, London (by *Atkinson and *Swales): it was as innovative and as grand as *Burnet's contemporary extension to the British Museum. The Beaux-Arts principles of powerful axes, symmetry, and confident use of Classical motifs were adopted by Burnham for his proposals for the City Beautiful in which he attempted to bring uniformity and an academic approach to urban America: his plan for Washington, DC, attempted to restore the eroded parts of L'*Enfant's design. The firm's Union Station, Washington, DC (1903–7), was its first fully developed Beaux-Arts design, with a *façade of five huge *bays and a triple-arched entrance leading to a *barrel-*vaulted space worthy of Roman *thermae. Burnham's plan for Chicago (1906–9), informed by his success with the Exposition, was influential at the time. His publications include *The World's Columbian Exposition: The Final Report of the Director of Works* (1898), and (with Edward Bennett) *Plan of Chicago* (1909).

Condit (1952, 1961, 1964, 1968); Hines (1974); Hoffmann (1973)

Bürolandschaft. Type of office-planning (literally 'office-landscape') evolved in Germany in the 1950s and 1960s by Eberhard & Wolfgang Schnelle, based on open-plan offices developed in the USA in the 1940s. Freed from partitions, large spaces could be designed that were decently lit and serviced. The informal layouts of such spaces suggested a landscape, an effect enhanced by the fashionable placing of plants in pots.

Boje (1972); Duffy (1969)

Burton, Decimus (1800–81). British architect, who enjoyed success as a designer of *villas, small country-houses, and several distinguished *Greek Revival buildings. He acquired a reputation in the field of iron-and-glass *conservatories. He was the tenth son of **James Burton** (*or* **Haliburton**) (1761–1837), a Scots builder and surveyor who settled in London and became a successful entrepreneur, laying out the new town of St Leonard's-on-Sea, Sussex (1828–32), a development in which advanced *Neoclassical buildings, influenced by French precedents, can be found as well as a full eclectic mixture of styles. Decimus trained in his father's office and then with George Maddox (1760–1843) before entering the Royal Academy Schools in 1817. Under *Nash's supervision he designed Cornwall and Clarence Terraces, Regent's Park. At the age of 23 he designed and built the Colosseum, Regent's Park (1823–7), a vast *Pantheon-like domed structure bigger than the dome of St Paul's Cathedral, with a Greek *Doric *portico. Important commissions followed for the Royal Parks, including the *Ionic *screen at Hyde Park Corner and the lodges at Cumberland, Grosvenor, and Stanhope Gates (1824–5), and then the prestigious Athenaeum Club, Waterloo Place (1827–30), with its fine *frieze and handsome interiors. His dignified arch on Constitution Hill (1827–8), intended as a Royal entrance to Buckingham Palace from the north, was moved to its present position in 1883.

He had considerable success as an architect of villas and modest country-houses. He laid out the Calverley Estate, Tunbridge Wells, Kent (from 1828), in which the Classical and the *Picturesque, clearly derived from the work of Nash, are judiciously mingled. He designed the new town, including St Peter's Church, the North-East Hotel, the Queen's Terrace, the Custom House, and two lighthouses, at Fleetwood, Lancashire (1836–43), which fell on hard times when the railway was extended to Carlisle and then Scotland, passing it by. Burton was interested in the problems of design using iron and glass: his finest essays were the (demolished) Great Stove or *conservatory, Chatsworth (1836–40, with *Paxton); the conservatory (1845–6, with Richard Turner (1798–1881)—demolished) at Regent's Park; and the palm-house (1845–8 again with Turner) at the Royal Botanic Gardens, Kew.

Colvin (1995); *DNB* (1917); Miller (1981); Summerson (1993)

Busby, Charles Augustin (1786–1834). English architect who published *A Series of Designs for Villas and Country Houses* (1808) and *A Collection of Designs for Modern Embellishments* (1810). He designed several villas before building the Commercial Rooms, Bristol (1810), with a Classical *temple-front and an interior lit by means of a lantern supported by *caryatides. In 1817 he went to the USA, and designed a theatre in Virginia before returning to England, where he worked for a time with Francis *Goodwin before settling in Brighton, where he formed a partnership with Amon Henry *Wilds. The firm laid out the Kemp Town and Brunswick Estates there, Busby providing the designs and Wilds acting as contractor. His best work is Sussex Square, Lewes Crescent, Arundel Terrace, and Chichester Terrace (1823–*c*.1850), Kemp Town, and Brunswick Square, Brunswick Terrace, Brunswick Street East and West, Lower Brunswick Place, and Landsdowne Square, Hove (1823–*c*.1834).

Bingham (1991); Busby (1810, 1835); Colvin (1995); Dale (1947)

Buscheto *or* **Busketus** (*fl.* 1063–1110). Architect of the *Romanesque Cathedral at Pisa (*c*.1064–*c*.1115), whose name is recorded in an inscription there.

Sanpaolesi (1975)

bush-hammered. 1. Finish on *concrete (usually *in situ*) made with a mechanical *bush-hammer* fitted with a strong grooved head: the flat plane left after the concrete has set is hammered away to partially reveal the coarser aggregate, leaving a rough-textured surface. **2.** Stone *dressing obtained using a hammer with square ends divided into a number of pyramidal points.

Buszko, Henryk (1924–). Polish architect, who established a partnership with Aleksander Franta (1925–) in Katowice in 1950, designing a wide range of building types. The firm's Roman Catholic Church, Katowice (1993), exploits the possibilities of dramatic curved forms.

Emanuel (1994)

Butler, John Dixon (1861–1920). London architect, who in 1895 was appointed Architect and Surveyor to the Metropolitan Police. He collaborated with Norman *Shaw on the extensions to New Scotland Yard (1904–6), and himself designed the Police Court and Station, Old Street, Shoreditch (1906), a *Mannerist building with a *Baroque centrepiece.

Gray (1985)

Butterfield, William (1814–1900). One of the most prolific and original English *Gothic Revivalists, he was born in London, for a while worked with the *Inwoods, and opened his own practice in 1840. From 1842 he was closely involved with the Cambridge Camden (later Ecclesiological) Society, contributing designs to *The Ecclesiologist* (1842–68) and *Instrumenta Ecclesiastica* (1850–2). His first church and parsonage were at Coalpit Heath, Gloucestershire (St Saviour's, 1844–5), an essay in *Second Pointed much influenced by *Pugin, and decidedly plain. The parsonage is an important precedent for the free domestic compositions of W. E. *Nesfield, Norman *Shaw, and Philip *Webb, for the *fenestration was planned where needed, and all traces of the tyranny of symmetry vanished. Butterfield's mastery of grouping disparate elements together is best seen at the College of the Holy Spirit and Cathedral of the Isles at Millport, Greater Cumbrae, Scotland (1849–51), which demonstrates Pugin's ideal of a 'True Picturesque' composition based on groupings of forms and the function of the plan.

The *Ecclesiologists determined to build a model church that would fulfil the requirements of ritual, and would set standards for Anglican churches in the future. Butterfield was appointed architect, and designed the church, clergy-house, and school of All Saints, Margaret Street, London (1849–59). The buildings were urban in character, of *polychrome brickwork, and considerably influenced by Continental *Gothic precedents. Here was a modern church designed to stand up to the rigorous climate of a Victorian city, a citadel of faith, an urban *Minster. The hard, sharp architecture of the interior was coloured with glazed bricks and tiles, and it marked the beginning of the *High *Victorian Gothic Revival. Many other churches followed, with hard, even violently polychromatic interiors: among them should be mentioned All Saints, Babbacombe, Devon (1865–74), St Augustine, Penarth, Glamorganshire (1864–6), and St Mark's, Dundela, Belfast (1876–91). His Keble College, Oxford, with its riotously polychromatic chapel (1867–83), and Rugby School chapel (completed 1872), the climax of which is the massive tower, are excellent examples of Butterfield's position as a master of the *Sublime. He was *the* High Victorian Goth, using materials with honesty of expression, glorying in harsh structural polychrome effects, expressing his plans in three-dimensional forms, and obeying Pugin's call to build with clarity and truth. His grander houses include Milton Ernest Hall, Bedfordshire (1853–6), a large Gothic pile of startling boldness, anticipating Shaw's Cragside and other examples later in the century: the whole ensemble has a pronounced Continental and un-English air, and the effect is uncompromising, stark, and assured.

Hersey (1972); Hitchcock (1977); Thompson (1971)

butterfly plan. Type of plan popular during the *Arts-and-Crafts period with wings projecting symmetrically at angles from a central core, resembling a butterfly, as in the work of *Prior.

Button, Stephen Decatur (1813–97). Connecticut-born American architect known for his work in Philadelphia, Pennsylvania, and Camden, New Jersey. His State Capitol, Montgomery, Alabama (1847), and Pennsylvania Railroad Building (1856–8) no longer exist. He designed many houses in and around Hoboken, NJ, the Spring Garden Lutheran Church, Philadelphia (*c.*1859), and the City Hall, Camden (1874–5).

Teitelman and Longsteth (1974); Webster (1976)

buttress. *Pier-like projection of brick, *masonry, or other material, built either in close connection with a wall needing extra stability, or standing isolated, to counter the outward thrust of an arch, *vault, or other elements. Types of buttress are:

angle-buttress: one of a pair of buttresses at the corner of a building set at an angle of 90° to each other and to the walls to which they are attached;

Anglo-Saxon: not really a buttress at all, but more a thin freestone *lesene or *pilaster-strip dividing a wall-surface into *rubble panels that were originally intended to be rendered;

arch-buttress: known as an *arc-boutant*. See *flying buttress*;

buttress-tower: tower seeming to function as a buttress, as on either side of a gateway, but mostly for defence;

clasping buttress: massive buttress, square on plan, at the corner of a building, usually of the *First Pointed period;

Decorated buttress: see *Second Pointed buttress*;

diagonal buttress: set at the corner of a building, forming an angle of 135° with the walls, and usually of the *Second Pointed period of *Gothic;

Early English buttress: see *First Pointed buttress*;

First Pointed or *Early English buttress*: C13 type, often of formidable depth, frequently chamfered, and staged, each *stage being defined by *off-sets, and the whole structure surmounted with steep triangular *gables;

flying buttress, also called *arc-boutant* or *arch-buttress*: consists of an arched structure extending from the upper part of a wall to a massive pier in order to convey the outward thrust of (usually) the stone *vault safely to the ground;

hanging buttress: type of slender support, carried on a *corbel;

lateral buttress: attached to a corner of a structure, seeming to be a continuation of one of the walls;

Perpendicular or *Third Pointed buttress*: late-Gothic type with elaborately panelled faces, and, often, crocketed *finials of great elegance;

pier-buttress: detached external pier by which an arch or vault is prevented from spreading, as in the *chapter-house of Lincoln Cathedral, where *flying buttresses* are used. Pier-buttresses are often constructed with a heavy superstructure rising higher than the springing of the flying-buttress arch;

Romanesque buttress: C11 and C12 wide lesene of little projection, it defines *bays;

Second Pointed or *Decorated buttress*: C14 type constructed in stages, frequently elaborately enriched, and surmounted by crocketed gables, pinnacles, finials, and even crocketed spirelets. Many were further embellished with canopied *niches for statuary;

set-back buttress: resembling an *angle-buttress*, but not built immediately at the corner, so does not touch the set-back buttress on the return-wall, thus the quoin of the building remains visible.

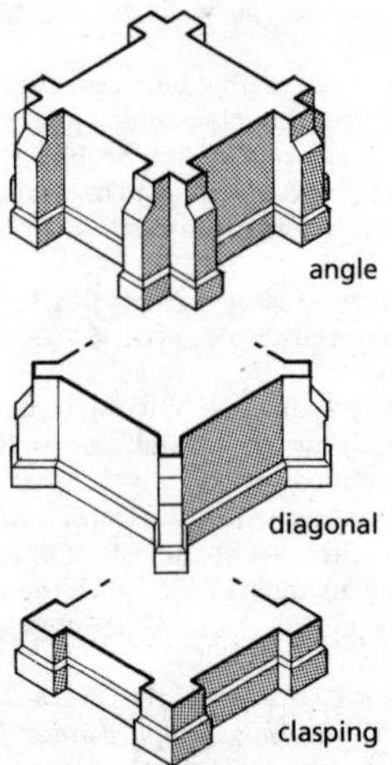

buttress. Typical arrangements at the base of a church-tower. (*JJS*)

Byzantine architecture. The Byzantine, or Eastern Roman, Empire, began with the foundation of Constantinople (formerly Byzantium) in AD 324 and ended with its capture by the Ottoman Turks in 1453. The Byzantine style began in the age of Justinian (527–65), although elements can be found from C4, and continued long after the fall of Constantinople, especially where the Orthodox Church was dominant. When the Roman Emperor Constantine (324–37) established his new Imperial and administrative capital on the Bosphorus, the seeds were sown for a division of the Empire into Eastern and Western parts, with Greek becoming dominant in the former and Latin in the latter. The division was exacerbated in C11 when Christendom suffered its Great Schism, dividing into the Orthodox and Roman Catholic Churches (the latter centred on Rome).

When Constantinople was founded, every effort was made to create a new Rome in the East. Many Roman buildings were plundered to enrich the city, and the Classical *Orders were familiar there, as well as the style of architecture which we call *Early Christian. However, two building-types played an important part in the evolution of a specifically Byzantine church architecture: the *basilica and the circular temple. The latter was known in pagan times, but acquired greater complexity in C4 when circular *clearstoreyed domed structures (as at Santa Costanza, Rome) were developed first as tombs, then centrally planned *martyria* (commemorative or pilgrimage shrines). It is clear that the *martyrium was planned in a different way from an ordinary church, and from C4 *martyria* were known to have been constructed as octagons with radiating arms to produce cruciform plans.

The basilican type of church can be seen at Sant'Apollinare in Classe, Ravenna (534–49), where the clearstorey is carried on *arcades set on rows of columns on rectangular *pedestals and with curiously un-Classical *capitals based on the *Composite type. Above the *abaci are *blocks or *dosserets from which the arches spring. Yet this building is essentially Italian, whereas San Vitale, also in Ravenna (*c*.532–48), is very different: centrally planned, it has a clearstoreyed vaulted octagon carried on *piers, a lower galleried aisle, and an apsidal *chancel. Columns have block-like capitals, making the transition from circular *shafts to square dosseret, and have virtually no connection with Classicism, while the bases are stepped and octagonal. San Vitale appears to have been a *martyrium*, and, architecturally, derives from the Church of Sts Sergios and Bacchos in Constantinople (*c*.525–*c*.536), which has a clearstoreyed octagon. The beautiful lace-like capitals in Sts Sergios and Bacchos have only a suggestion of the Classical about them.

The great achievement of Byzantine architecture was the huge Church of Hagia Sophia (Holy Wisdom) in Constantinople (*c*.532–7),

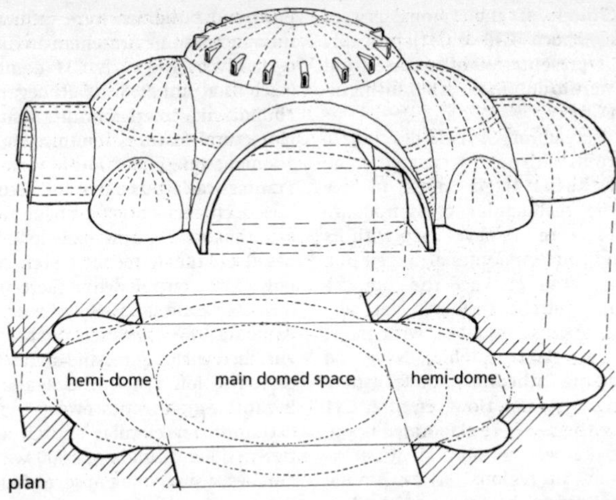

Byzantine architecture. Diagram of geometry and structural system of Hagia Sophia, Constantinople. (*After Rosengarten* et al.)

designed by the scientists and mathematicians *Anthemios of Tralles and *Isidorus of Miletus. Various themes that were familiar at the time were synthesized and combined in one design, and it was rather as though the basic form of Sts Sergios and Bacchos had been cut in two, greatly inflated, and built on either side of a gigantic square space covered with a low saucer-dome carried on *pendentives. Such a huge dome on a square space and constructed thus was unprecedented, and the complete synthesis of the basilican and centralized plan can be found in that great building. The church's interior was enriched with a skin of coloured marbles, porphyry, and other stones, while the vaults and domes were covered with the *mosaics that were such a glorious feature of Byzantine churches.

The next largest church in Constantinople after Hagia Sophia was Hagia Irene (Holy Peace), begun 532, and rebuilt 564 and 740 (the C8 rebuilding included an additional dome over the nave, creating a more longitudinal plan). By C11, the typical Byzantine church-plan was a *Greek *cross within a square, roofed with a central dome flanked by four barrel-vaults and with domed squares in the corners. The plan is also known as the *quincunx, and there were further variations on it (often consisting of three *apses to the east and one or more *narthexes to the west)—a good example is the Church of the Holy Apostles, Thessalonika (early C14), where

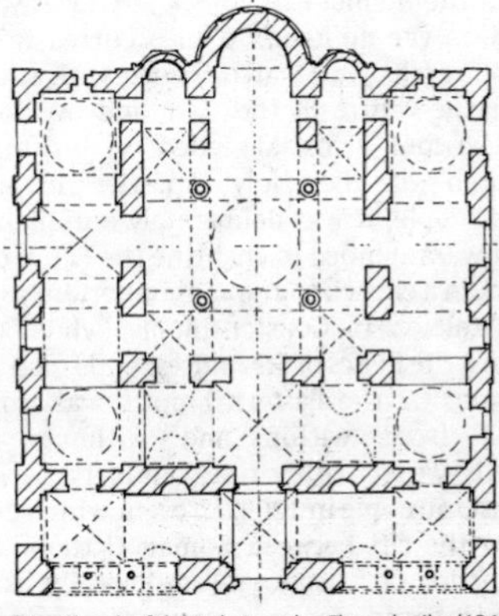

Plan of the Church of the Holy Apostles, Thessalonika (1310–14), a variation on the quincunx and cross-in-square plan.

*cloisonné (stones individually framed horizontally and vertically with bricks), herringbone, and other patterns occur. The exteriors of earlier Byzantine churches often give the impression of having been left to their own devices, as though they were merely the result of the need to encase the rich interiors. Later churches, however, had greater care lavished on their exteriors: clearstoreyed drums of domes are taller, walls are often given the cloisonné treatment, while motifs based on the Kufic alphabet are introduced in bands on the wall-surface. A typical example is the

Theotokos Church of the *monastery of Hosios Loukas, Phocis (C10 or C11), probably the earliest representative of architectural themes that were to dominate in Byzantine architecture in Greece.

With the spread of Christianity northwards, tall drums with domes recurred in the Ukraine and *Russia: Hagia Sophia in Kiev (C11) had the rectangular cross-in-square plan, but there were five naves each with its own apse, and thirteen domes arranged in a pyramidal formation crowned the composition. Byzantine churches in Russia generally consisted of the cross-in-square, with many variants, as at Hagia Sophia, Novgorod (1045–50), and the Cathedral of the Transfiguration, Černigov (*c.*1036). However, after C11 the Byzantine themes were elaborated upon, and architecture became more identified as having national or regional styles. Among characteristic Russian themes are walls subdivided into *bays by means of large blind arcades, and the 'onion' domes that evolved from the helmet-like domes in C13. A variation on the quincunx plan occurred in the C11 Church of San Marco, Venice, with a dome over the centre of the nave and over each of the four arms. Modelled on Justinian's Church of the Holy Apostles in Constantinople, it was deliberately antiquarian, as it was intended to enshrine the Relics of St Mark in a church that was as important as the Apostoleion in Constantinople (which contained the Relics of Sts Andrew and Luke).

From C7 the Eastern Empire was threatened from within and without, and fatally weakened by the Crusaders' sack of Constantinople in 1204, an event which deepened the rift between Roman Catholic and Orthodox Christendom. Paradoxically, as the Empire contracted, missionary activity seems to have increased, and the Byzantine style proliferated over a wide area. In both Armenia and Georgia (Christian from C4), basilican and centralized churches were erected in numbers, although from the end of C6 the domed centralized plan, much influenced by architecture in Syria, began to reach heights of elaboration. In both Armenia and Georgia, a domed interior surrounded by four apses roofed with hemi-domes (the 'tetraconch' arrangement), the whole enclosed in a rectangle, was common. It is best represented by St Ripsime at Echmiadzin, Armenia (618–30), and the Holy Cross, Džvari, Georgia (before 605). It is unclear how certain Western-European buildings were influenced by (or influenced) some Armenian architecture, but certainly by the early C11 domed basilicas (such as at Ani (988–1000)) began to acquire *bundle-like *piers, vaulting systems, and architectural features reminiscent of Western *Romanesque and *Gothic forms. However, Transcaucasia (Armenia and Georgia) developed a characteristic type of church architecture that had a surprisingly long life, usually based on the tetraconch plan with a high polygonal central drum pierced with windows. An example is Holy Cross, Aght'amar, Armenia (915–21), which also has the exterior enriched with figures and stylized ornament carved in low relief. In Bulgaria impressive Byzantine architecture evolved, including the extraordinary circular church at Preslav (a twelve-sided rotunda of *c.*900 with radiating *niches, a projecting apse, a ring of internal columns on which the dome was supported, a western narthex flanked by circular towers, and an *atrium surrounded by columns and with its deep walls enriched with niches). At the Black Sea town of Mesembria (Nesebŭr), known as the 'Bulgarian Ravenna', there are several Byzantine churches, including St John the Baptist (probably C10, a cross-in-square plan with barrel-vaulted aisles).

Serbian churches can be classified in three Schools: Raška (1170–1282); Byzantine Serbia (1282–1355); and the Morava (1355 to the Turkish domination beginning 1459). The first School combined Romanesque elements (notably in the treatment of *gable-tops and *eaves, *fenestration, and *arcading) with Byzantine domes and decorations. Good examples are the Church of the Virgin, Studenica, the Monastery at Sopočani (both C13), and the backward-looking Monastery Church of Dečani (1327–35). Later, the cross-in-square type of church acquired a pyramidal pile-up of domes: for example, the Monastery Church of Gračanica (*c.*1318–21), where the upper array of barrel-vaults has pointed arches. The Morava School may be represented by the Church of the Ascension, Ravanica (*c.*1375)—another five-domed church, the elongated drums of which have deeply recessed arches—and by the church within the fortress of Resava (Manasija) of 1406–18. In Moldavia and Wallachia (Romania), the Byzantine influence acquired a rich exoticism. The Church of the Episcopal Monastery at Curtea de Argeş (C16) is an offspring of the Morava School, where the main body of the church is a trefoil, with a huge narthex given an *ambulatory plan. The Monastic Church of Dealu (1502) is also a descendant of the Morava School, derived from the plan of the Church at Cozia (1386). Moldavian C16 and C17 churches are less overtly Byzantine in inspiration, but are uniquely decorated: among the best was the Monastery Church of Voroneţ (*c*.1488). It had a large rectangular narthex covered by a domical vault, and a trefoil nave with a tall drum in the centre. The three apses of the trefoil plan were treated with tall *blind arcades, and the exterior was decorated with elaborate frescoes protected by wide overhanging eaves. A similar arrangement was given to the Monastery Church at Suceviţa (*c*.1602–4).

A Byzantine Revival was spurred by scholarly publications in C19 following the independence of Greece and the Balkan States. Works include the Greek Orthodox Cathedral of Hagia Sophia, Moscow Road, Bayswater, London (1877–82), by John Oldrid Scott (1841–1913), and Westminster Cathedral (1895–1903), by John Francis *Bentley.

Cruickshank (1996); Hamilton (1983); Krautheimer (1986); Mango (1972, 1986); Peña (1996); Runciman (1975); Watkin (1986)

cabin. 1. Small, single-roomed primitive dwelling. **2.** Contrived rustic retreat in a *Picturesque landscape, often ornamental, but much simpler than a *cottage orné.

cabinet. 1. *Cabin. **2.** Relatively small room used for interviews or private conferences by e.g. a sovereign. **3.** Small room, often richly ornamented, designed for the display of valuable objects. The 'porcelain cabinets' of *Rococo palaces in Germany (e.g. in the *Residenz* (Seat of the Court), Ansbach (1739–40)) are examples. **4.** Garden-compartment or *arbour.

cabinet-window. Projecting shop-window common in early C19, usually with curved sides.

cable. 1. *Rope-moulding* carved to look like a rope, with twisted strands, found in Roman Antiquity (e.g. *Corinthian *Order of the *thermae at Nîmes), but mostly associated with *Romanesque architecture, especially around arches. **2.** *Cabled fluting, cabling, ribbed fluting, rudenture*, or *stopped flute*, consisting of convex mouldings set in the *flutes of Classical column- or *pilaster-*shafts, between the *fillets but not projecting beyond their faces, and seldom carried up higher than a third of the height of the shaft. Cabling occurs occasionally on unfluted shafts, so the cables are in relief, as in *Borromini's Church of Sant'Ivo della Sapienza, Rome (1643–60).

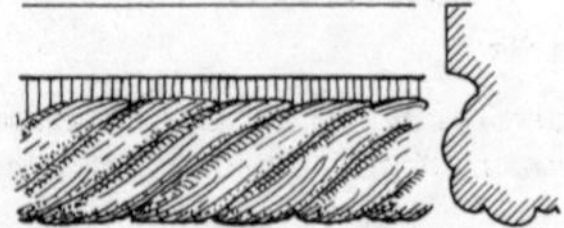

cable. 1. From Romsey Abbey, Hampshire. (*After Parker*)

cabochon. 1. Protruding circular element, notably in *guilloche or *strapwork ornament. **2.** Very small *cartouche and frame.

Cabot, Edward Clark (1818–1901). American architect. He became a leading figure in the Boston architectural world from the time his Athenaeum (1846–9) was built. This, his greatest work, was influenced by Charles *Barry's *Italianate club-houses in London. In the 1850s *Gilman was his associate. During the 1870s he produced several distinguished *Queen Anne houses, and some of his later designs shared affinities with those of H. H. *Richardson.

Placzek (1982)

CAD. *Computer-aided design.

caduceus (*pl.* **caducei**). **1.** Winged rod with two *serpents and leaves wound around it, called the *Wand of Hermes* (of which deity it is an *attribute). *Compare* *Aaron's rod. **2.** Herald's rod, or wreathed olive-branch, originally wingless.

caduceus

Caen. Soft, fine-grained, easily worked limestone from near Caen, Normandy, used in the fabric of a surprising number of English medieval buildings (e.g. Canterbury and Norwich Cathedrals).

Caernarfon. Welsh arch. *See* arch.

cage. 1. Enclosure formed mostly of *tracery, such as the *screen surrounding a *chantry-chapel, as in Winchester Cathedral. **2.** Framework of a building in *timber- or steel-framed construction.

Cagnola, Marchese Luigi (1762–1833). Italian Neoclassical architect, whose work influenced later generations of Italian architects. In Milan he built the *Ionic Porta Ticinese (1801–14) and Arco del Sempione or della Pace (1806–38), the latter a beautifully proportioned and detailed *triumphal arch based on Roman precedents. His own house, the Villa Cagnola at Inverigo (*c.*1813–33), is a severe Neoclassical work with a low domed circular entrance-hall and ranges of Ionic columns outside. His *Pantheon-like Church of San Lorenzo (known as La Rotonda) at Ghisalba (1822–33) is a pure example of the *Antique form. Although he did not design the *campanile at Ghisalba, he was responsible for the free-standing five-stage tower at Urgnano (1824–9) with *caryatides supporting the domed top.

Meeks (1966); Mezzanotte (1966); Middleton and Watkin (1987)

caher. *See* cashel.

cairn. *Tumulus of undressed stones, chamfered or solid, and usually of a sepulchral or commemorative character.

caisson. 1. Watertight chamber in which underwater construction work takes place. **2.** Device for sinking foundations under water or in water-logged conditions, in the form of an air-tight box the size of the *pier to be built, which is sunk to bedrock, or other surface on which it is to remain, then filled with *concrete. **3.** *Coffer in ceilings, *cupolas, *soffits, and *vaults.

Caius, John (1510–73). Refounder of Gonville and Caius College, Cambridge (1557), where he built (1560s and 1570s) the three Gates of Honour, Humility, and Virtue, remarkable for the refinement and correctness of their early *Classical detail, derived from *Serlio, and designed with the assistance of the architect and sculptor Theodore de Have, or Haveus, of Cleve (Clèves), in Germany.

DNB (1917); Roberts (1912); Watkin (1986)

calathus. *See* campana.

Calatrava Valls, Santiago (1951–). Spanish-born architect, engineer, and urbanist, who established an architectural and engineering practice in Zurich (1981) and Paris (1989). His firm has designed numerous distinguished and innovative bridges (Barcelona, Bilbao, Córdoba, Lérida, Mérida, Ripoll, Seville, Valencia, Zurich, and other sites). He has also been responsible for canopies, railway-stations (his Lyons TGV Station (1989–94) and Stadelhofen Station, Zurich (1988–90), are particularly interesting), museums, concert-halls, towers, and works of sculpture, and has been the recipient of many awards. In combining architecture, engineering, and sculpture, he has succeeded in reversing a trend to separate these disciplines that has been one of the legacies of *Modernism. Among his more recent designs (1995) are the Sondica Airport, with its huge wing-like roofs, and the Campo Volantin Bridge, both in Bilbao, Spain.

Blaser (1990); Emanuel (1994); Meyhöfer (1995)

caldarium (*pl.* **caldaria**). Hot- and vapour-baths in Roman balneae and *thermae, or the building in which they were situated.

Calderini, Gugliemo (1837–1916). Architect of the huge, eclectic, and majestic Palazzo di Giustizia, Rome (1888–1910), and other *Renaissance Revival buildings, which drew on many sources, in the decades before the 1914–18 war. He was Director of Monuments for Rome, Aquila, and Chieti, and his restorations, including the *chiostro* of San Giovanni in Laterano, were carried out with great care. Among his buildings may be mentioned the grandiose façade of the *Duomo*, Savona (1880–6), in which the influence of *Alessi can be detected; the *quadriportico* at San Paolo fuori le Mura, Rome (1893–1910); and two *palazzi* in Perugia (Bianchi and Cesaroni). His influence was considerable (e.g. the main Railway Station, Milan (1909)).

Meeks (1966)

calefactory. Artificially heated chamber in a *monastery, usually the common-room.

calf's tongue. Medieval decorative moulding featuring a long continuous series of tongue-like forms with parallel axes, or coinciding with the radii if embellishing an arch.

calidarium. *See* caldarium.

calion, calyon. **1.** *Flint nodule, boulder, or pebble. **2.** Flint panel in *flush-work.

Callicrates. C5 BC Athenian architect, responsible with *Ictinus for the Greek *Doric temple known as the *Parthenon (447–436), and on his own (probably) for the small *Ionic temple of Nikè Apteros (*c*.450–424) on the Bastion outside the *Propylaea. He supervised part of the construction of the walls between Athens and Piraeus, and may have restored the Athenian city-walls themselves.

Carpenter (1970); Dinsmoor (1950)

Callimachus (*c*.430–400 BC). Athenian credited by *Vitruvius with the invention of the *Corinthian *capital. *See* acanthus.

Vitruvius Pollio (1955–6)

calotte. Low segmental dome, circular on plan, without a *drum, so called from its resemblance to a clerical skull-cap.

Calvary. **1.** *Rock-work on which three crosses are erected, or a sculptured and monumental representation of the Crucifixion. **2.** *Rood.

calyon. *See* calion.

calyx (*pl.* **calyces**). Ornament resembling a cup-like (properly *calix*) flower, as in the *Corinthian *capital, or on the neck of the Roman *Doric capital.

camarín. *Chapel or *shrine set above and behind the high-altar in churches in the Iberian peninsula, but still visible from the body of the church.

camber. Very shallow, scarcely perceptible upward curve, often apparent on the underside of *collar-and-*tie beams in a *truss. A *camber-arch* is therefore the *soffit of a 'flat' arch of brick rubbers achieved by using a *camber-strip* as a support for the intrados during construction.

Cambio, Arnolfo di (*c*.1245–*c*.1310). *See* Arnolfo di Cambio.

cambogé. Type of *brise-soleil consisting of a unit or units with transverse openings permitting ventilation but providing shade from direct sunlight.

Cambridge Seven. Architectural and design partnership founded in Cambridge, Mass., and in New York in 1962, by Louis J. Bakanowsky, Peter and Ivan Chermayeff, Alden B. Christie, Paul E. Dietrich, Thomas Geismar, and Terry Rankine. The partnership's best-known works include the United States Pavilion at Expo 67 and other exhibitions, as well as graphic designs and aircraft interiors. More recent works include the North Carolina Museum of History, Raleigh (1992), and the Business Administration Center, University of Maine, Orono (1992).

Emanuel (1994)

came. Cast, extruded, or milled lead rods with a section like an H, also called *lattice*, used in *leaded *lights (e.g. stained-glass windows) to frame and secure the *panes or regular lozenge-shaped *quarrels of glass.

camera, *also* **camara.** Curved or vaulted ceiling. A ceiling or roof looking like a *vault is *camerated*, the term implying a false ceiling with the *appearance* of a vault.

camera lucida. Instrument by which rays of light from an object are refracted by a prism producing an image on paper, thus facilitating an accurate drawing of the object.

camera obscura. Darkened box or chamber into which light is admitted through a double convex lens, thus forming an image of external objects, a view, etc., on a surface placed at the focus of the lens.

Cameron, Charles (1745–1812). London-born architect of Scots ancestry whose importance lies in his accomplished and refined *Neoclassicism and in his introduction to Russia of the *Greek Revival style and the naturalistic English landscape-garden. He was apprenticed to his father in 1760 before becoming a pupil of Isaac *Ware. On the latter's death in 1766 Cameron determined to realize Ware's project for a new edition of *Burlington's *Fabbriche Antiche* (Ancient Buildings—1730), and went to Rome to correct and finish the unsatisfactory drawings of Roman *thermae by *Palladio which Burlington had used. In 1772 he published *The Baths of the Romans Explained and Illustrated, with the Restorations of Palladio Corrected and Improved*, with texts in French and English. An important source for Neoclassical ornament, it went into further editions in 1774 and 1775.

At some time in the 1770s he may have been in Ireland, but by 1779 he was Architect to the Empress Catherine of Russia (1762–96), for whom he made many additions to the Palace of Tsarskoe Selo, near St Petersburg (1779–85), including the colonnaded Cameron Gallery, the Cold Baths, the Agate *Pavilion, the private apartments, and the Church of St Sophia, where he demonstrated his skill as a designer of refined Neoclassical interiors, among the most beautiful of their kind and date in Europe. His use of colour is especially felicitous: in the Agate Pavilion, for example, the red agate columns with gilt-bronze *capitals set against a background of green jasper walls create a stunningly opulent effect. In 1782–5 he designed and built the Palace at Pavlovsk for the Grand Duke Paul as well as many other buildings there, including the theatre, town-hall, and the temples in the English Park. The circular *Doric Temple of Friendship (*c*.1780) is an important pioneering exemplar of the *Greek Revival. Also in the 1780s he produced various designs for the Imperial Palace at Bakhtchi-Serai in the Crimea, including a *triumphal arch, a drawing of which was exhibited at the Royal Academy in London in 1793 by John Linnell Bond (1764–1837).

Cameron fell from favour after Catherine's death (1796), and was superseded as Chief Architect to the Imperial Court by his pupil Vincenzo *Brenna. However, he remained in Russia, and worked for several patrons, including the Razumovskys at Baturin, Ukraine (1799–1802). In 1800 he again was working at Pavlovsk, where he designed the *Ionic Pavilion of the Three Graces. In 1803 he was appointed Architect to the Admiralty and designed various buildings at the Imperial naval-base of Kronstadt, including the barracks and hospital (*c*.1802–5).

In many ways his compositions are essentially Palladian, but his precise knowledge of the *Antique sources of Neoclassicism led him (like *Adam) to design details and furnishings for his buildings.

Cameron (1772); Colvin (1995); Council of Europe (1972); Kuchamov (1976); Loukomski (1943); Rice and Tait (1967–8); Shvidkovsky (1996)

camp. **1.** Ceiling resembling the interior of a truncated *pyramidal form, that is with sloping sides. **2.** Ceiling within a roof-space or *garret with sloping sides formed by the positions of the *rafters. **3.** *Comb* ceiling with sloping convex sides, like the sides of a tent, also called a *tent ceiling*.

Camp. Standing out from the background, or theatrical posturing. Camp taste is concerned with affectation, artificiality, playfulness, and theatricality, and historically is therefore associated with vogues for *Chinoiserie, *Gothick, and the exotic. In C20 Camp taste seems to include *Art Nouveau, *Art Deco, *Baroque, *Kitsch, and *Rococo, as well as the outrageously amusing. Some critics have even detected *High*, *Middle*, or *Low Camp* in architecture. Baroque would be High Camp, for example, while aspects of Kitsch in *Post-Modernism could fall into the Low Camp category.

Booth (1983); Jencks (1973*a*)

campana. *Bell-shaped (*campaniform* or *campanular*) core of a *Corinthian *capital.

campanile (*pl.* **campanili**). Italian bell-tower, usually free-standing.

campanula (*pl.* **campanulae**). Miniature bell-shaped form, such as conic *guttae in the *Doric *Order, or the elements beneath the *eaves of a *pagoda or other building in the style of *Chinoiserie.

Campbell, Colen (1676–1729). Scottish lawyer and landowner who became one of the leaders of *Palladianism and one of the most distinguished figures in English C18 architecture. His metamorphosis into architect is shrouded in obscurity, but he does seem to have had some association with the Scots architect James *Smith, and may have been taught by him. Campbell's first (and most important) house in England was Wanstead, Essex (*c*.1714–20, demolished 1820), the precedent for large Classical country-houses of virtually the whole *Georgian period. In 1715 Campbell published the first volume of *Vitruvius Britannicus*, which promoted the virtues of 'Antique Simplicity' as opposed to 'affected and licentious' *Baroque architecture, lauded the 'renowned Palladio' and the 'famous Inigo Jones', and advertised Campbell's own expertise as an architect, in much the same way as *Palladio had publicized his architecture in *Quattro Libri* (1570).

In 1718 Campbell was appointed Chief Clerk and Deputy Surveyor-General under William *Benson, but in the following year Campbell and Benson were both removed from office, which precluded the possibility of the Palladian Revival being led from within the Office of Works. However, Campbell became architect to George Augustus, Prince of Wales (1683–1760), in 1719, and was also appointed by Lord *Burlington to re-fashion his town-house in Piccadilly in the Palladian style. Subsequently, Burlington transferred his favours to *Flitcroft and *Kent, dropping

Campbell, but the last had no shortage of rich and influential patrons, attracted, no doubt, by his sumptuous *Vitruvius Britannicus*, the second and third volumes of which appeared in 1717 and 1725. They contained illustrations of all his designs, and he addressed many projects to eminent Whigs: he even dedicated volume 1 to King George I (1714–27).

Campbell's patrons included Sir Robert Walpole (1676–1745), for whom he designed Houghton Hall, Norfolk (begun 1722); Henry Hoare (1705–85), for whom he built Stourhead, Wiltshire (*c*.1720–4); and many others. Newby (now Baldersby) Park, Yorkshire (1720–8), was an important precedent for the neo-Palladian villa, while Mereworth Castle, Kent (*c*.1722–5), was a distinguished version of Palladio's Villa Capra at Vicenza. Campbell was the designer of many of the most important buildings of the whole Palladian movement, and in the decade after the publication of volume 1 of *Vitruvius Britannicus* he created many models from which the English Palladian Revival evolved.

In 1726 Campbell was appointed Surveyor of Greenwich Hospital in succession to *Vanbrugh. He brought out a version of the first book of Palladio's *Quattro Libri* in 1728, which was revised in 1729 and published as *The Five Orders of Architecture* with five extra plates featuring some of his own designs.

Campbell (1728–9, 1967–72); Colvin (1995); Colvin and Harris (1970); Harris (1990); Stutchbury (1967); Summerson (1993)

Campen, Jacob van (1595–1657). Chief exponent of *Classicism in The Netherlands. He studied architecture in Italy and was influenced by the work of *Scamozzi and *Palladio. With his Coymans House on the Keizersgracht, Amsterdam (1624), he introduced the *Palladian style to The Netherlands. His most refined work is the *Mauritshuis* in The Hague (1633–5), which has a Palladian plan, elevations featuring a *Giant *Order of *Ionic *pilasters set on a plain base, a *pedimented central section given little emphasis, and a hipped roof. Much grander is the Town Hall (now Royal Palace), Amsterdam (1648–55): it has two internal courtyards separated by a huge central hall, façades with two superimposed Giant Orders of pilasters, and a large projecting pedimented central section over which is a domed *lantern. His *Nieuwe Kerk* (New Church), Haarlem (1645–9), is based on the *quincunx plan (essentially a Greek cross within a square), with square Ionic crossing-piers and a *groin-vault over the *crossing. He was responsible for the Accijnshuis, Amsterdam (1638), the Noordeinde Palace, The Hague (1640), and, with others, the decorations of *Post's Huis-den-Bosch, Maarssen, near Utrecht (*c*.1628). His secular architecture influenced van 's *Gravesande and *Vingboons, and was a precedent for many English buildings. His style was introduced to England by Hugh *May and his contemporaries.

Fremantle (1959); Kuyper (1980); Rosenberg, Slive, and Ter Kuile (1977); Swillens (1961)

Camporese Family. Pietro Camporese (1726–81) and his sons **Giulio** (1754–1840) and **Giuseppe** (1763–1822) were the architects for the remodelling of Santa Scolastica, Subiaco, of the Galleria dei Candelabri (1786–88), and for the completion of the Neoclassical *atrium of the Quattro Cancelli, Museo Pio-Clementino, in Rome (1793). **Pietro the Younger** (1792–1873) was an important scholar of antiquities, and became a member of the Commission formed to study the problems of planning the enlargement of Rome. He was responsible for the *Renaissance Revival work in the Piazza Nicosia *palazzetto*, for the colonnaded Portico di Veio, Palazzo Wedekind, facing the Piazza Colonna (1838), and for the *façade of the Hospital of San Giacomo degli Incurabili (1843), in Rome, among other works.

Meeks (1966); Middleton and Watkin (1987)

campo santo. Italian cemetery, usually surrounded by *arcaded *cloisters or roofed *galleries containing funerary monuments, as in Pisa.

campus. 1. Grounds of a college or university, or a separate, discrete part of such an institution. **2.** Large expanse of parkland containing a series of buildings used for academic purposes. **3.** Arrangement of such buildings around a large open grassed area, as at Downing College, Cambridge (from 1806), by *Wilkins, which replaced the plan featuring the smaller medieval *court or *quad for collegiate buildings. One of the most celebrated campuses is *Jefferson's University of Virginia at Charlottesville (1817–26), the precedent for many others in the USA.

Dober (1992); Turner (1987)

Camus de Mézières, Nicolas Le (1721–89). French architect of the huge circular Halle au

Blé, Paris (1763–7), and author of *Le Génie de l'architecture; ou, l'analogie de cet art avec nos sensations* (The Nature of Architecture; or, the Analogy of that Art with our Feelings—1780) in which the new idea that architecture should be pleasing to the senses and induce elevating impressions on the heart and mind was floated. This led to the notion of *architecture parlante adopted by *Boullée and others, and to the belief that architectural character can be created by the mysterious effects of light, a notion taken up by many important architects, not least *Soane. He also published *Le Guide de ceux qui veulent bâtir* (Handbook for those Wishing to Build—1781) and *Traité de la force des bois* (Treatise on the Strength of Timber—1782). His namesake, **Louis-Denis Le Camus**, designed the *Chinoiserie tower or *pagoda in the gardens of the *chateau at Chanteloup (1775–8), and also the *Colisée*, Champs-Elysées, Paris (1769–71), a vast and complex building, with a huge dome in which spectacular lighting effects were achieved.

Camus de Mézières (1780); Middleton and Watkin (1987); Mosser and Teyssot (1991)

canal. **1.** Channel, gutter, or pipe to convey any liquid, usually water. **2.** Long, narrow, artificially created water-course for the ornamentation of a park, or for inland navigation. **3.** *Flute in the *shaft of a column or *pilaster. **4.** Spiral channel (*canalis*) flanked by small convex mouldings from the eye following the revolutions of the *volute, and carrying over to the other volute between the *abacus and *echinus of the *Ionic *capital.

canaliculus (*pl.* **canaliculi**). Channel or groove on a *triglyph in the *Doric *Order.

cancellus (*pl.* **cancelli**). **1.** *Latticed *screen, especially one (*cancello*) that divides the *sacrarium or *presbyterium from the rest of the church, hence *chancel. **2.** In the plural, *balustrades or railings defining the *choir, usually attached to *ambones, as at San Clemente, Rome (C6).

Candela Outeriño, Félix (1910–97). Madrid-born and -educated naturalized American architect. He was influenced by the structures of *Torroja, and developed a lifelong interest in *shell-vaulting. He emigrated to Mexico in 1939, where he formed the firm of Cubiertas Ala with his brother **Antonio**. His advocacy of shell-vaults brought him commissions, including the Cosmic-Ray Pavilion, University City, Mexico City (1951–2), with its *hyperbolic *paraboloid *concrete roof, much of which is only 15 mm thick, set on legs. His Church of the Miraculous Virgin, Mexico City (1953–5), with Enrique de la Mora, is *Expressionist in style, also influenced by *Gothic and by the work of *Gaudí. He again worked with Mora on the chapel of San Vicente de Paul, Coyoacán, Mexico City (1960), which has an inverted U-shaped canopy set on *rubble walls. He used mushroom-shaped umbrella-like forms at the John Lewis warehouse, Stevenage, Hertfordshire (1963), designed with *Yorke, Rosenberg, & Mardall. He was also involved in the design of the Olympic Stadium, Mexico City (1968).

Emanuel (1994); Faber (1963); Smith (1967)

Candid, Peter, *also* known as **Peter de Wit** *or* **Witte** (1548–1628). Flemish architect and painter. He worked under *Vasari at the Vatican before settling in Munich in 1586, where he worked on the frescoes in the *Grottenhalle* (*grotto-hall) in the *Residenz* (Seat of the Court) that had been designed by *Sustris: indeed, he also appears to have acted as architect. From 1611 he was recognized as the leading painter at the Court, designed many tapestries and *grotesques, and was responsible for painted decorative schemes at the *Altes Schloss* (Old Castle), Schleissheim (1617), and the *Goldener Saal* (Golden Hall) in the *Rathaus* (Town Hall), Augsburg (1619).

Hitchcock (1981); Jervis (1984)

Candilis, Georges (1913–95). Azerbaijan-born, naturalized French architect. He worked in the offices of Le *Corbusier in Paris (1945–8) and Marseilles (1948–50), where he represented Le Corbusier during the construction of the *Unité d'Habitation* (Unit for Living). He entered into partnership with Shadrach Woods (1923–73) and Vladimir Bodiansky (1894–1966) before setting up with Alexis Josic (1921–) as Candilis-Josic-Woods in Paris (1955–63). With Bodiansky and Woods he produced the master-plan for Casablanca (1952–4), and with Woods and Josic he worked on the new towns of Bagnols-sur-Cèze (1956–61) and Toulouse-le-Mirail (1960–77). The firm produced many master-plans, including that for the Free University of Berlin-Dahlem (1963–79). Their work adhered to the propositions of the *Athens Charter and *CIAM.

Candilis (1973, 1977); Woods (1968)

Canella, Guido (1931–). Italian architect responsible for many stark, monumental, and controversial buildings, including the Pieve Emanuele Civic Centre, Milan (1971–81), a complex that expresses his ideas about defence, historical allusions, and composition in a powerful design of towers, massive walls, and stark modelling.

Emanuel (1994—gives a comprehensive list of his works)

canephora (*pl.* **canephorae**). *See* caryatid.

Canevale, Isidore (1730–86). Architect of the Cathedral at Vác, *Hungary (1763–77), an aisleless structure with a bare towered *façade attached to which is a huge *Corinthian *portico. Over the centre of the interior is a large dome, and the *vaults are *coffered. This work of *Neoclassicism is as advanced as anywhere in Europe at the time. He also designed the *Josefinum*, or Military College of Surgery and Medicine, Vienna (1785), in a refined French Classical *Louis-Seize style.

Papworth (1852)

Canina, Luigi (1795–1856). Italian *Neoclassical architect. With *Valadier, he was important as a protagonist of archaeologically correct *Neoclassicism in Rome during the first decades of C19. He succeeded *Asprucci at the Villa Borghese Gardens, where his scholarly Egyptian Gate (completed 1828) with *pylon-towers (the first in Italy, it seems), and *obelisks is a good example of the *Egyptian Revival, and he also designed the archaeologically correct Ionic *in antis* lodges at the Piazza Flaminia entrance, influenced, no doubt, by *Cagnola's Porta Ticinese in Milan (1801–14). His works at the Borghese Gardens included the Fountain of Esculapius and the *astylar *triumphal arch (both 1818–28), the latter recalling *Chalgrin's work in Paris. He produced *Gli edifizi di Roma antica* . . . (Buildings of Ancient Rome—1848–56) and *Le nuove fabbriche della Villa Borghese* . . . (The New Buildings of the Villa Borghese—1828), was an architectural historian of considerable significance, and was responsible for major archaeological excavations in the Forum, Appian Way, and Campagna (1823–46).

Canina (1828, 1846, 1852); Meeks (1966); Raggi (1857)

cannon. **1.** Component of the *Empire and *Federal styles, military decoration, *trophies, etc. **2.** Element of architecture, often found with cannon-balls, powder-kegs, etc. **3.** Cannon-shaped *bollard. **4.** Projecting water-spout shaped like a cannon-barrel.

Cano, Alonso (1601–67). Spanish painter and architect. During the 1620s he assisted his father with the design of altar-pieces, but his west front of Granada Cathedral (from 1667) is stupendous, recalling arched *Romanesque fronts (e.g. Lincoln Cathedral). Consisting of three huge arches, it does not employ the *Orders, but rather species of *pilasters, panels, and layers of planes.

Kubler and Soria (1959); Rosenthal (1961)

Canonica, Luigi (1762–1844). Born in the Ticino, he was trained by *Piermarini. He settled in Milan, where he made his mark by creating spacious layouts, modernizing the street system, and erecting many public buildings in a refined *Neoclassical style, including the Palazzo Brentani-Greppi (1829–31) and the Palazzo Anguissola-Traversi (1829–30), both on the Via Manzoni. His largest work was the Civic Arena near the Castello (1806–13), with a Neoclassical Roman *Doric entrance of 1813, and a battered perimeter-wall pierced at intervals with semicircular arches, the whole effect being powerful, worthy of *Piranesi, but probably influenced by *Fischer von Erlach's *Entwurff* (1721) and by the projects for public spaces by Giovanni Antonio Antolini (1753–1841) and Giuseppe Pistocchi (1744–1841). With Innocenzo Giusti he enlarged La Scala Opera House in 1814.

Meeks (1966); Middleton and Watkin (1987)

Canopus. **1.** Alexandrian town in Ancient Egypt, celebrated for its *canals and beauty. **2.** *Canopic* bulbous ovoid Ancient Egyptian jar, usually of stone, to contain the internal organs of the dead after disembowelling during the mummification process, with the lid shaped like a head. The jar containing the liver had a humanoid head of Imsety, son of Horus, and it was this type that was widely copied for ornaments of the *Neoclassical period and *Egyptian Revival style, though the 'lids' were usually fixed. **3.** Part of the gardens of Hadrian's *villa at Tivoli (*Tibur*), near Rome, laid out AD 134–8 around a *Euripus (canal) lined with Egyptianizing statues and complete with sculptured crocodiles and an elephant, intended as a mnemonic of the Nilotic landscape and of Canopus itself.

Curl (1994); Roullet (1972)

Canopus. Roman Canopic jar in the Egyptian taste. (*After Tatham*)

canopy. **1.** Roof-like ornamented hood surmounting an altar, *doorway, *font, *niche, *pulpit (where it is called a *tester), *stall, statue, *tabernacle, throne, tomb, window-aperture, etc., supported on *brackets, *colonnettes, etc., or suspended. **2.** *Canopy of honour*, *ceele*, *ceilure*, *celure*, *cellure*, or *seele*, is a richly coloured, often gilded, and panelled ceiling above an altar, *chancel, *chantry-chapel, *mortuary-chapel, etc. **3.** *Town canopy* is a structure resembling an arcaded *gabled opening, often with elaborate *pinnacles, *finials, etc., like a model building, set on top of a niche or protecting a statue: the motif was adapted in funerary architecture, often shown in three dimensions, but horizontal (90° from the usual vertical position as a protection from the weather), on *tomb-chests over the heads of *effigies, and was later shown in *incised slabs and funerary *brasses. A canopy over an altar is usually called *baldacchino* or *ciborium*.

cant. **1.** Angle or inclination of a piece, member, or plane to another, especially to the horizontal. **2.** Oblique surface cutting off the corner of a square, or an oblique face of a polygon, hence a polygonal plan is *canted* (e.g. canted *bay-window).

Canterbury, Michael of (*fl.* 1275–1321). Medieval master-mason. He worked at Canterbury Cathedral, and was the architect of St Stephen's *Chapel, Palace of Westminster (from 1292). He was of great importance in the evolution of the *Second Pointed style of *Gothic, especially through his use of the *ogee. He designed the Eleanor Cross at Cheapside, London (1291–4—destroyed); the *canopied tombs of Edmund Crouchback and Aveline of Lancaster in Westminster Abbey (*c.*1296); probably the Chapel of St Etheldreda, Ely Place, London (1290–8); the *Lady Chapel in St Paul's Cathedral, London (*c.*1307–12—destroyed); and the tomb of Bishop William of Louth, Ely Cathedral, Cambridgeshire (*c.*1298). He probably designed the tomb of Archbishop Peckham (d. 1292) in Canterbury Cathedral, Kent.

Harvey (1987)

Canterbury, Thomas of (*fl.* 1323–35). Master-mason who worked under Walter of *Canterbury at the Palace of Westminster and the Tower of London in 1323. Around 1326 he was building the new *chapel at Guildhall, London, and in 1331 was master-mason in charge of the upper chapel at St Stephen's Chapel, Westminster, the epitome of English *Second Pointed *Gothic. He may have been responsible for the tomb of John of Eltham, Westminster Abbey (*c.*1334), and for several works at Canterbury, including the gatehouse of St Augustine's Abbey (*c.*1308), the *parclose-*screens around the *choir in the Cathedral (1304–*c.*1320), the tomb of Archbishop Mepham (d. 1333), and the great window in St Anselm's Chapel (1336).

Harvey (1987)

Canterbury, Walter of (*fl.* 1319–27). Master-mason. He rebuilt the outer *curtain-wall at the Tower of London beside the Traitors' Gate (1324–5), and about the same time he was engaged on work at the lower part of St Stephen's *Chapel, Palace of Westminster, where he probably designed the *vaults and window-*tracery (completed 1327). His masterpiece is the tomb of Aymer de Valance (d. 1323) in Westminster Abbey.

Harvey (1987)

canterius, cantherius. *Principal *rafter in Antiquity.

cantilever. Horizontal member projecting from a wall, etc., without supports at any point in its entire projection, capable of sustaining loads, and prevented from falling by means of a heavy dead-weight at the other end

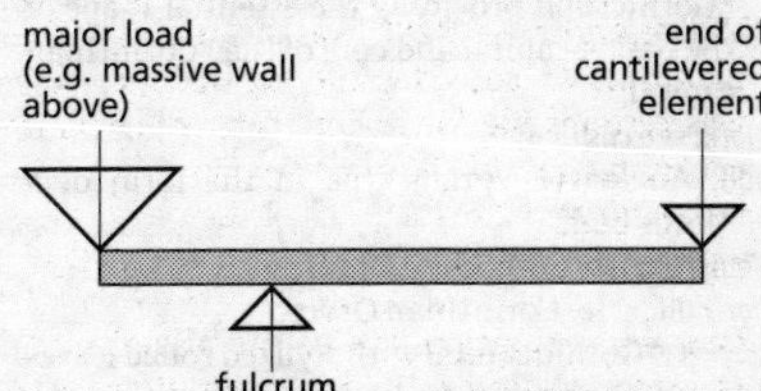

Principle of the cantilever.

to the projection, i.e. on the opposite side of its *fulcrum. Any *bracket, *corbel, *modillion, or *mutule carrying a *canopy, *cornice, or *eaves (for example) is essentially a cantilever.

canton. *Pier or other projection at an angle of a building, such as *antae, columns, *pilasters, or *rusticated quoins. Any work of architecture with this condition is said to be *cantoned*, from the French *cantonné*. A *cantoned pier* (*pilier cantonné*) is found in *Gothic architecture, otherwise a *compound pier* with a massive core and four projecting piers or *shafts connecting to the transverse *vaults over *nave and *aisle and the nave-*arcade.

cantoria. Italian term for a *gallery or *tribune used by the singers, often on the north (*cantoris*) side of the *choir.

cap. **1.** Abbreviation of *capital **2.** Capital, *cope, *cornice, or crowning or terminal feature, fitting closely on any member, or extending beyond it in horizontal dimensions. *Cap-moulding* is the cornice-like finish of a *dado, *pedestal, door-*lintel, handrail, or other architectural feature. **3.** Domical roof on a windmill.

cap-house. Upper enclosed part of a *stair giving access to a walk behind a *parapet or an upper *gallery: in Scotland it is often in the form of a square top to a circular stair-tower, hence its name.

capital. *Chapiter*, head, or topmost member of a *colonnette, column, *pilaster, *pier, etc., defined by distinct architectural treatment, and often ornamented. Types of capital include:

Aeolic: primitive type of *Ionic (*see* Aeolic);

basket: *Byzantine *bell-type, ornamented with carving resembling wicker-work or basket-weave;

bell: inverted bell-like form, found in Ancient *Egyptian architecture and *First Pointed *Gothic, and providing the essential shape of the basket-capital and core of the *Corinthian capital;

block: see *cushion*;

bud: Ancient Egyptian type in the form of a *lotus-bud;

Composite: *see* Composite Order;

Corinthian: *see* Corinthian Order;

crocket: *Gothic capital with stylized rolled leaves resembling small *volutes;

cube: see *cushion*;

cushion, also *block* or *cube* capital: *Byzantine and *Romanesque form, essentially a cube with its lower corners shaved off and rounded in order to accommodate the transition from square *abacus to circular *shaft, its four faces are reduced to semicircular *lunettes*;

Doric: *see* Doric Order;

Hathor-headed: Ancient Egyptian type carved on each face with an image of the goddess Hathor and having a large block-like *abacus, also carved with a variety of images;

Ionic: *see* Ionic Order;

lotus: Ancient Egyptian type in the form of a lotus-bud or decorated with lotus-flowers;

palm: Ancient Egyptian type like the top of a *palm-tree (*palmiform), surrounded by closely arranged vertical palm-fronds and leaves, the column-shaft frequently having vertical bands or large convex reed-like forms. A variant is the Greek *Corinthian capital from the Tower of the Winds, Athens (*c.*50 BC), with one row of *acanthus-leaves and an upper row of palm-leaves under a square abacus;

protomai: with the upper part of figures, mostly animals, projecting from the angles, usually in Romanesque work;

scallop: Romanesque type, like the *cushion*, with the curved lower part further shaped with conical forms resembling trumpets;

stiff-leaf: late-C12 and early C13 Gothic or *Transitional type with stylized leaves, usually with large projections;

Tuscan: *see* Tuscan Order;

water-leaf: late-C12 Transitional or early Gothic type with a big, wide, unribbed leaf growing outwards above the convex moulding on top of the shaft, turning upwards and inwards at the corners to the abacus.

cap-stone. **1.** *Lintel-stone or large flat stone laid horizontally on two or more upright stones in a *dolmen. **2.** *Cap of a *staddle-stone. **3.** Cope.

caracol, caracole. *See* spiral.

Caramuel de Lobkowitz, Juan (1606–82). Spanish-born architectural theorist. He saw architecture as part of a vast system embracing all branches of knowledge, and his major work of theory was *Architectura civil, recta y obliqua, considerada y dibuxada en el Templo de Ierusalem* (1678–81), also published in Latin as *Templum Salomonis*... Solomon's temple was claimed as the fount from which all architecture sprang, and the book included much on mathematical-scientific problems: it was a considerable influence on *Guarini. His only

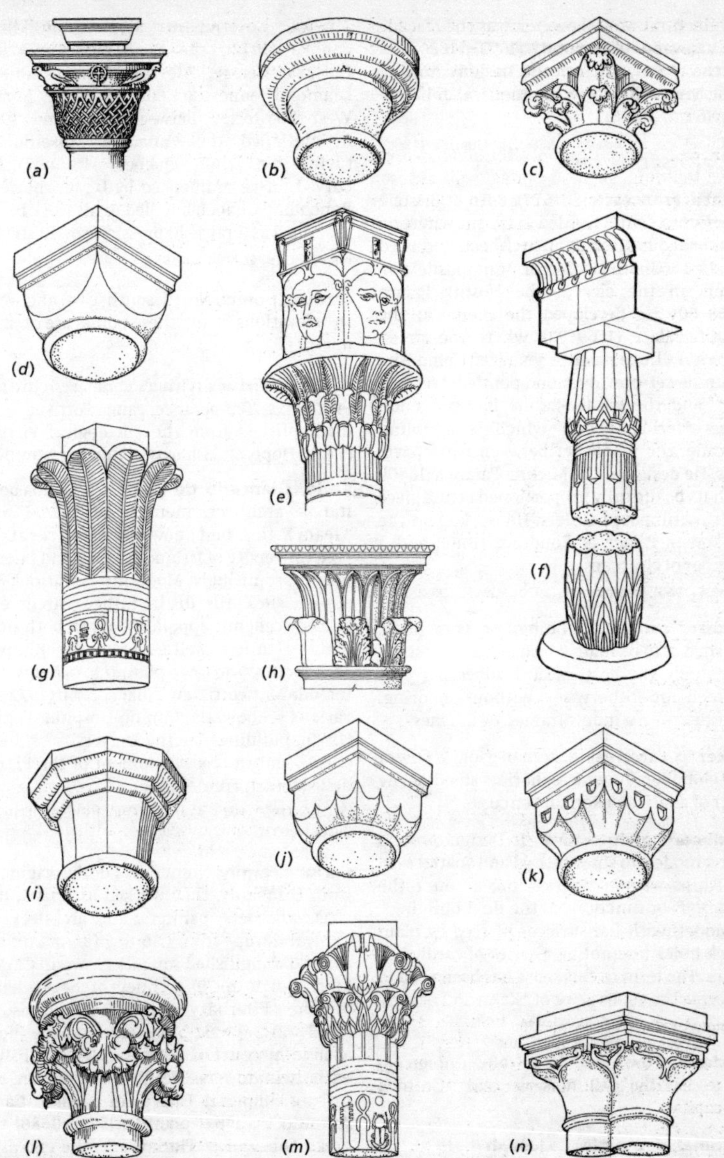

capital. (*a*) Byzantine basket. (*JJS*) (*b*) First Pointed Gothic bell. (*c*) Gothic crocket. (*d*) Romanesque cushion showing lunettes. (*e*) Ancient Egyptian Hathor-headed on bell-capital, from Philae. (*f*) Ancient Egyptian lotus-bud, with column and gorge-cornice. (*g*) Ancient Egyptian palm. (*h*) Ancient Greek Corinthian palm-capital from the Tower of the Winds, Athens. (*i*) Moulded Perpendicular Gothic. (*j*) Romanesque scallop. (*k*) Romanesque trumpet, a variant of the scallop type. (*l*) Gothic First Pointed stiff-leaf, from the Galilee porch, Durham Cathedral. (*m*) Ancient Egyptian volute capital, from Philae. (*n*) Transitional water-leaf, from the Galilee, Durham Cathedral.

architectural work, however, was the *façade of Vigevano Cathedral (1673–*c*.1680) in Northern Italy, an eclectic design showing some virtuosity in its geometrical relationship to the square.

Caramuel de Lobkowitz (1678–81); Guarini (1968); Pastine (1975); Tadisi (1760)

Caratti, Francesco (d. 1677). Born at Bissone near Como, Caratti settled in Prague where he established himself as an architect, and used the first *Giant *Order of *Composite *pilasters in the city at the Nostitz Palace (1658–60). He developed the theme at the Černín Palace (1669–92), where the street-front has a huge range of *engaged Composite columns set over diamond-pointed *rustication, and the garden-façade has two enormous *serlianas over which is a *blind *arcade, the whole set between two *pavilions. He designed the Michna Palace (*c*.1640), with its beautifully proportioned centrepiece of *superimposed Orders. He worked on the Lobkowitz Palace at Roudnice (1665) and a number of churches.

Hempel (1965); Neumann, J. (1970); Powell (1959)

carcase, carcass. Building, or part of it, finished as to its main construction, or *shell, essentially the bare, basic loadbearing part (framed or otherwise) without flooring, roofing-cover, window-frames, or finishes.

carcer (*pl.* **carceres**). **1.** Roman gaol. **2.** One of the chambers in which chariots stood at the start of a race in a Roman *circus.

cardboard architecture. 1. Design process using models to show formal and spatial relationships without taking into account the materials or functions of the final buildings. **2.** Models with flat surfaces pierced by plain black holes resembling a series of cardboard boxes. The term in this sense has been used to describe the 1960s work of *Kahn and others.

Frampton *et al.* (1975); Sharp (1978)

card-cut. Low-relief *fret (but unpierced) in (especially) *Chinoiserie and *Gothick *friezes.

Cardinal, Douglas Joseph (1934–). Canadian architect partly of Native American descent. He was responsible for St Mary's Church, Red Deer, Alberta (1965–8), which has monumental curved forms set in the flat landscape. His works include Grande Prairie Regional College, Alberta (1972–6), the Alberta Government Services Building, Ponoka (1977), the St Albert Civic and Cultural Centre, Alberta (1983), and the Diamond Jenness School, Hay River, North-West Territories. Between 1983 and 1989 he designed the Canadian Museum of Civilization, Hull, Quebec. His powerful curved forms, influenced by Le *Corbusier's Ronchamp Chapel, have led to his work being described as 'Prairie Expressionism' in style.

Emanuel (1994); Kalman (1994)

cardinal points. North, south, east, and west, so *elevations facing these points are *cardinal fronts*.

Cardinal Virtues (*Virtutes Cardinales*). Justice, Prudence, Temperance, and Fortitude, as distinguished from the Theological Virtues (Faith, Hope, and Charity), often *personified.

Carlo, Giancarlo de (1919–). Genoa-born Italian architect, member of *CIAM and *Team X. He is best known for his works at the Free University of Urbino (1973–9 and later)—uncompromisingly Modernist solutions on superb sites. His distinguished career embraced academic appointments on both sides of the Atlantic, as well as a practice combining architecture and town-planning. Other works include Matteotti New Village, Terni (1972–5), various schools, the Mirano Hospital, Venice (1979), buildings for the University of Siena (1982), and the redevelopment of the Piazza della Mostra, Trento (1990).

de Carlo (1965, 1970); Colombo (1964); Emanuel (1994); Zucchi (1993)

Carlone Family. Numerous family, originally from Lombardy, they worked as artists, masons, stuccoers, painters, and architects in Central Europe from C16 to C18. Among the most distinguished members were **Carl(o) Martin(o)** (1616–79), architect of the residence of the Esterházy family at Eisenstadt (1663–72), a vast *Baroque palace built around a *court of honour and embellished with twin towers. He also worked on the *Hofburg* (Imperial Palace) in Vienna. **Carlo Antonio** (d. 1708) planned (from 1686) the great Abbey of St Florian and the exquisite Pilgrimage Chapel at Christkindl (begun 1706), Upper Austria, both completed by his pupil *Prandtauer. **A. Silvestro** (*c*.1610–71) was architect of the *façade of the *Jesuitenkirche* (Jesuit Church) 'Am Hof', or *Neun Chören der Engel* (Nine Choirs of Angels), Vienna

(1662), with its projecting *wings and a central balcony behind which the *Baroque front of the church rises. This arrangement is partially derived from *Mansart's Baroque Minimes Church, Paris, and integrates the front of the church with the flanking palatial façades. The façade is often attributed to Carlo Antonio Carlone.

Bourke (1962); Brucker (1983); Powell (1959)

Carmontelle, Louis Carrogis, *known as* (1717–1806). French dilettante and designer of several gardens, including the jardin *anglo-chinois Parc Monceau, Paris (1773–8), with its many diversions in the form of *fabriques, including 'ruins', a 'Dutch windmill', a 'Tartar tent', and similar conceits. One of its most unusual features was the *Bois des Tombeaux* (Wood of Tombs) containing *fabriques in the form of tombs (pyramids, etc.). Thomas Blaikie (1750–1838), the Scots landscape-gardener, was brought in (*c*.1781) to simplify Carmontelle's somewhat overladen scheme, but the work was an important catalyst in the transformation of the garden, embellished with monuments, to the cemetery.

Adams (1979); Carrogis (1779); Curl (1991); Etlin (1984)

carnel. *See* battlement.

Caröe, William Douglas (1857–1938). Liverpool-born son of a Danish father, he became Senior Architect to the Church Commissioners in England (from 1895), and designed several churches, one of the best of which is St David's, Exeter (1897), with passage-aisles derived from *Bodley's work at Pendlebury. Also fine is St Barnabas's, Walthamstow (1902–23), which forms a felicitous composition with its charming *Queen Anne tile-hung vicarage and adjoining hall. His secular works include the robust 75–83 Duke Street, London (1890–4), and the elegant offices of the Ecclesiastical Commissioners at 1 Millbank, London (1903). His designs for ecclesiastical furnishings and fittings were often exquisite.

Freeman (1990); Gray (1985); Service (1975, 1977)

Carolean. Period of King Charles II (1660–85). *Caroline* refers to the reign of King Charles I (1625–49).

Carolingian. Term describing the style of architecture associated with the reign of Emperor Charlemagne (800–14). Carolingian architecture is generally accepted as dating from late C8 to early C10, and examples were erected in The Netherlands, France, and Germany, especially in the area bounding the Rhine. Stylistically, Carolingian architecture looked back to *Early Christian *basilicas of the time of the Roman Emperor Constantine (324–37), and included the first building of the Abbey Churches of St-Denis (*c*.754–75) and Fulda (790/2–819), the latter based on the Constantinian basilica of San Pietro in Rome (begun *c*.333). At Aachen, the Palatine Chapel (792–805) is based on San Vitale, Ravenna, and was probably designed by Odo of *Metz. At Lorsch in the Rhineland (late C8) is a gate-house and guest-hall with *engaged *Composite columns and arches (a motif derived from Roman Antiquity) above which is a range of fluted *pilasters supporting a series of triangles instead of arches (a theme taken from Roman *sarcophagi). In 790–9 was built the Abbey Church of St-Riquier (Centula), with a *nave, *lean-to *aisles, two sets of *transepts (the west of which had a low entrance-*narthex with a *chapel above called a *west-work), four round towers, an apsidal east end, and towers over each of the *crossings. Although St-Riquier does not survive, similar plans were developed in the *Romanesque period in the Rhineland (Worms, for example), while an impressive west-work can be found at Corvey-on-the-Weser (873–85).

Conant (1979); Watkin (1986)

carolitic, carolytic. Properly *corollitic*, column with foliated *shaft embellished with branches and leaves winding spirally around it.

Carpenter, Richard Cromwell (1812–55). English architect. A friend and admirer of A. W. N. *Pugin, he was one of the first architects of the *Gothic Revival to meet with the approval of the *Ecclesiologists, notably with his Church of St Paul, Brighton (1846–8), and St Mary Magdalene, Munster Square, London (1849–52), both in a sober and scholarly *Middle Pointed style. In 1848 he designed the Anglican College of St Nicholas at Lancing in Sussex, begun in 1854 in a variety of Gothic that owed much to Continental precedent of C13, completed by his son, **Richard Herbert Carpenter** (1841–93), with other work by his pupil and partner William Slater (1818/19–72—who seems to have contributed more to the design than was thought), and, later, S. E. *Dykes Bower.

Clarke (1969); Dixon and Muthesius (1985)

Carpenter's Gothic(k). **1.** Whimsical, unscholarly *Gothick derived from pattern-books of e.g. Batty *Langley. **2.** C19 timber buildings in the USA with Gothicizing tendencies, e.g. in their *barge-boards.

McArdle and Bartlett (1978)

Carr, John (1723–1807). English architect. He was a competent and prolific practitioner in Yorkshire (where he was Surveyor of Bridges, first for the West Riding (1760–73), and then for the North Riding (from 1772)) and the North of England of the *Palladianism he had learned while building Kirby Hall, Ouseburn, Yorkshire, by *Burlington and *Morris (1747–*c*.1755). His reliability gained him favour among the gentry, and many of his works were featured in *Vitruvius Britannicus* (vols. iv and v) and in *New Vitruvius Britannicus*. He was also influenced by Robert *Adam's *Neoclassicism, and could turn his hand to *Gothic when required. Among his works may be mentioned his many bridges, his domestic architecture (e.g. Constable Burton, North Riding (*c*.1762–8), illustrated in *Vitruvius Britannicus*, v), his public buildings, and his churches (e.g. Kirkleatham, North Riding (*c*.1760–3)). The Assize Courts (1773–7) and Prison for Females (1780–3) at York Castle are accomplished *palace-fronted compositions of great refinement, while the Assembly Rooms and Crescent, Buxton, Derbyshire (1780–90), applied an elevational treatment derived from Inigo *Jones's arcaded *piazza at Covent Garden and a variation of the younger *Wood's grand residential Royal *Crescent at Bath. His public buildings include the Palladian Town Hall and Assembly Rooms at Newark, Nottinghamshire (1773–6).

Colvin (1995); Summerson (1993); York Georgian Society (1973)

carrel, carol, carrol. **1.** *Aisle divided into *chapels, or the *screens dividing it, or the divisions themselves. **2.** Small enclosure, room, *niche, compartment, or study in a *cloister or any other small space used for study, as in a library, etc. **3.** *Light in a *Gothic window defined by the *bars of *tracery. **4.** *Bay-window. **5.** Any precinct, or space defined by railings, etc. **6.** Pane of glass secured by *cames in a leaded *light.

Carrère, John Merven (1858–1911). Brazilian-born American architect. He studied at the École des *Beaux-Arts, Paris, before joining *McKim, Mead, & White in New York in 1883. In 1886 he opened an office with Thomas Hastings (1860–1929). The firm of Carrère & Hastings was responsible for many buildings, including the New York Public Library (1902–11), but started with the Ponce de Léon Hotel, St Augustine, Fla. (1886–8), an eclectic mix of *Moorish, Spanish, and *Renaissance elements, constructed of *concrete using shell and coral aggregate. Nearly all the work (and it was extremely varied) of the 1890s was elaborately ornamented with over-scaled embellishments, but gradually turned to more restrained French *Classicism and American *Colonial *Georgian for inspiration. In 1902 the firm built the Blair Building, New York, and in 1905 the Traders' Block, Toronto, Canada, tall buildings influenced by architecture in Chicago. The Royal Bank of Canada retained Carrère & Hastings for their architecture (e.g. Bank, Main Street, Montreal (1909–12), a restrained *Italianate job).

Kalman (1994); van Vynckt (1993)

Carstensen, Georg Johan Bernhard (1812–57). Algerian-born Danish publisher, entrepreneur, the founder of the Tivoli Gardens (1842–3) and the Casino (1845–7—the first commercial theatre in the Danish capital), both in Copenhagen. On both these projects he worked with the architect Harald Conrad *Stilling, although the unique *Chinoiserie fantasy, the Tivoli Pantomime Theatre, was designed by Jens Vilhelm *Dahlerup and Ove *Petersen.

Carstensen resided in New York, USA, from 1852 to 1855, where he designed the *polychrome Crystal Palace (1853–4—burnt down 1858) with the German architect Karl (or Charles) Gildemeister (1820–69).

Arkitekten, 7 (1992), 188–90; Carstensen and Gildemeister (1854); Millech (1951)

Carter, John (1748–1817). English pioneer of scholarly studies of *Gothic. A fine draughtsman, he contributed an imaginative range of designs for *The Builder's Magazine* (1774–86) and drawings of medieval antiquities for several publications, including Gough's *Sepulchral Monuments* (1786). His *The Ancient Architecture of England* (1795–1814) was his major work, which attempted to set out the 'Orders of Architecture during the British, Roman, Saxon, and Norman Æras'. He had a reputation in his lifetime as an antiquarian: his monument to Lord Frederick Campbell in Sundridge Church, Kent (*c*.1810), is an early example of *Gothic Revival based on archaeologically correct precedents. He designed Lea Castle, Worcestershire (1809–16—demolished) in a *castellated sub-*Romanesque style.

Colvin (1995); Crook (1995); *DNB* (1917); Eastlake (1970); Jervis (1984)

Carthusian. Of or belonging to a religious Order of monks founded by St Bruno (*c.*1030–1101) at Chartreuse in Dauphiné in 1084 or 1086 as a more severe interpretation of Benedictine rule. Each monk, devoted to the spirit of contemplation, had individual living-accommodation, generally grouped around courts or cloisters, communal activities being confined to the religious Offices and Holy Days. The architecture was plain and unadorned, and the Order flourished, especially in Germany, France, Italy, and Spain. Good examples of Carthusian monastery-buildings are the Certosa, Pavia (1396–1497), the Certosa di Val d'Ema, near Florence (founded 1341), and the Cartuja de Miraflores, Burgos (C15), built to designs by members of the *Colonia family. In England, a Carthusian establishment was called Charter House, hence the name of the school founded in London on the site of the Carthusian monastery.

Papworth (1852)

Cartilaginous. *See* Oleagenous style.

cartouche. **1.** Carved element resembling a sheet of parchment, with its ends or corners rolled, usually carrying an inscription. **2.** Ornamental or inscribed *tablet, as in a mural funerary memorial, with an elaborate *scroll-like frame resembling curling pieces of parchment, common in *Baroque work. **3.** Any ornament in the form of a scroll, such as a *console or *Ionic *volute. **4.** *Ancon, *console, or *truss supporting an *entablature instead of a column, especially an ornamented key-stone of an arch touching the entablature above. **5.** Ring-like frame around figures or characters expressing Royal or Divine titles in Egyptian *hieroglyphs.

cartouche. C17 funerary cartouche of Sir Walter Curl, Church of Sts Peter and Paul, Soberton, Hampshire.

Carvalho, Eugenio dos Santos de (1711–60). Portuguese architect responsible for the handsome rebuilding, on a regular street plan, of the area between Terreiro do Paço (Praça do Commercio) and O Rocío, Lisbon, after the earthquake of 1755. Buildings were in a sober, restrained French *Neoclassical style, and the works at Lisbon are among the most impressive of all late-C18 town-planning schemes. The work was carried out under the aegis of Sebastião José de Carvalho e Mello, later Marquess of Pombal (1699–1782).

Franca (1965); Kubler and Soria (1959); Smith (1968)

caryatid(e) (*pl.* **caryatid(e)s**). Carved, draped, straight, standing female figure (*cora*), supporting on its head an *astragal (enriched with *bead-and-reel), *ovolo (enriched with

*egg-and-dart), and square *abacus, used as a substitute for a column, and supporting an *entablature. The best-known example of the use of caryatids in Greek Antiquity was the south porch of the Erechtheion, Athens (*c.* 421–407 BC), where six figures supported the roof. A similar draped female figure with a basket-like form over the head instead of the astragal-ovolo-abacus *capital arrangement is a *canephora* (*pl. canephorae*). *See* atlas, herm, Persian, telamon, term.

casemate. **1.** In fortifications, a vaulted and blast-resistant chamber with an *embrasure in the outer wall, used as a gun-emplacement. It is usually within the general constructions comprising the defences. A *casemate* or *casemated wall* is a fortification with a series of casemates between strong outside and inside walls, with massive cross-walls acting as stiffeners between them. **2.** *Cavetto moulding not exceeding a quarter-round.

casement. **1.** Window-frame with hinged or pivoted opening-*lights or *sashes hung from a vertical member of the fixed frame. **2.** *Casemate, or wide hollow moulding, such as in late-*Gothic *jambs or *bundle-piers, not exceeding a quarter-round.

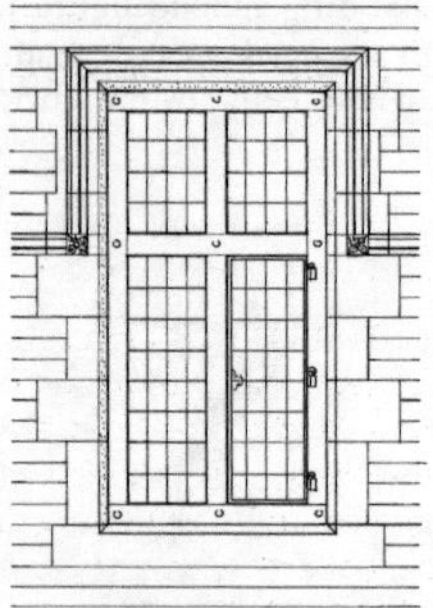

casement. C17 oak cross-casement with leaded lights and one wrought-iron opening sash. It is set in an aperture in a brick wall with stone dressings, protected at the head with a hood-moulding terminating in label-stops.

cashel. Irish ring-fort or enclosure of dry-stone masonry, also called a *caher*.

casino (*pl.* **casinos**). **1.** Small country-house, lightly fortified. **2.** Pleasure-pavilion, *summer-house, *villa, etc., in the grounds of a large country-house. **3.** Place of recreation, public or semi-private, with facilities for various activities (e.g. concerts or dances). **4.** Building or part of a building where gambling takes place. **5.** Dwelling appearing to be one storey high, but not necessarily so.

Gwilt (1903); Papworth (1852); Sturgis *et al.* (1901–2); Symes (1993)

casita. Small *pavilion resembling a *loggia.

Cassels, *also* **Cassel** *or* **Castle, Richard** (*c.*1690–1751). German-born architect who in the 1720s settled in Ireland under the aegis of Sir Gustavus Hume, Bt., and *Pearce (from whom he was to inherit a considerable practice). Reared in the *Baroque tradition, he became a fine exponent of *Palladianism. Cassels's first independent work is the Printing House, Trinity College, Dublin, with a *Doric *temple-front, but his most important Dublin buildings are Tyrone House, Marlborough Street (1740—which incorporates his favourite Palladian motif of a *serliana surmounted by a *blind arch), and Leinster House (1745–7), probably inspired by Burlington House in London. Outside Dublin, Ballyhaise, Co. Cavan (1733), is one of Cassels's earliest country-houses, and has two important features: a stone *frontispiece with superimposed Doric and *Ionic *pilasters; and a semi-elliptical projection or *bow on the rear elevation, suggesting Continental Baroque exemplars, and indicating the elliptical *saloon behind (an innovation for Ireland that anticipated the English fashion for elliptical saloons by some four decades). Russborough, Blessington, Co. Wicklow (1741–50), is one of the most mature of Irish Palladian buildings, with exquisite Baroque and *Rococo plasterwork inside.

Bence-Jones (1988); Craig (1969, 1982); Glin (1964); Summerson (1993)

Casson, Sir Hugh Maxwell (1910–99). English architect. He was Director of Architecture at the *Festival of Britain (1948–51), and with Neville Conder (1922–), formed the Casson Conder Partnership in 1952: he retired in 1985. Works include the Royal College of Art, Kensington Gore (1962—with Henry Thomas Cadbury-Brown (1913–) as principal architect), buildings at Worcester College, Oxford (1963), the Elephant and Rhinoceros House, London Zoo (1964), and the Ismaili Centre, South Kensington, London (1984). Casson was President of the Royal Academy of Arts in the 1970s until 1984, and enjoyed a reputation as a water-colourist of great fluency.

Emanuel (1994); *The Times* (17 Aug. 1999)

cast. Reproduction of the form of any object, usually in a material that hardens after a time. It is essentially an object made by running liquid (such as molten metal) or forcing a plastic substance (such as plaster) into a mould or shape which then sets. Cast-iron kits-of-parts were used to construct entire *façades of buildings in C19, and the material is still widely used for street-furniture, railings, and decorative details, all of which are reproduced from moulds taken from an original model.

Castellamonte, Carlo Conte di (1550/60–1639/40). Trained in Rome, he settled in Turin, working first with *Vitozzi, becoming architect-engineer to the Duke of Savoy on Vitozzi's death in 1615, and taking over responsibilities for fortifications from 1627. Castellamonte made an immense contribution to the development of Turin, where his Churches of San Carlo (1619) and Santa Cristina (1635–8) form a festive entrance to his handsome Piazza San Carlo, a grand square enlivened by elegant *palazzi*. He also designed the Piazza San Giovanni (1630s) and a number of fortresses influenced by developments in France. He was interested in hydraulics and generally in engineering problems. His son, **Amedeo** (1610–80), succeeded him in his Court appointments, and designed the Chapel of the Holy Shroud (SS Sindone), of 1656, completed later by *Guarini. Amedeo was also responsible for the façade of the Palazzo Reale, Turin (1658), and designed the late-*Mannerist Palazzo Beggiono di Sant'Albano (1665), as well as numerous fine church-altars.

Brayda, Coli, and Sesia (1966); Brino *et al.* (1966); Wittkower (1982)

castellated. With *battlements (*crenels, crenelles*). A *castellated* building is one with battlements, *turrets, *balistraria, etc., to give it the appearance of a castle, common in the late C18 and early C19. It was often a *folly.

castle. **1.** Large, strong, fortified structure or complex of buildings used for defence against an attacker. In the Middle Ages the most important part of a castle was the *donjon or *keep (*Bergfried* in German), essentially a strong tower with living quarters. The keep, in France and England, might also include the hall for gatherings, in which case it was called a *hall-keep*. The Tower of London has a hall-keep of great magnificence (1077–97) that also includes an apsidal-ended *Romanesque *chapel. The most usual Continental arrangement was for the hall-range to be separate and not within the keep: perhaps the most impressive C14 hall-ranges are those at Malbork (Marienburg) in Poland, built by the Teutonic Order. The keep was set within the inner *bailey or *ward*, itself protected by walls, either in a corner or the centre of the space. Outside the inner bailey was the *outer bailey*, often containing stables and other offices, so it was a distinct space surrounded by walls. The outer ring of walls had *battlemented tops and walks, with towers at intervals—the walls between towers were called *curtain-walls. Gates leading from the outside to the baileys or from bailey to bailey were protected by towers and *portcullises. An entrance to a castle could also have the extra defence of a *barbican. Around the walls, themselves often raised on sloping embankments or ramparts (*valla*) were usually *fossae* or ditches, sometimes filled with water (*moat), and over the moat was a drawbridge that could be raised. Smaller, less important castles might have the central keep (of modest proportions) set on a *motte surrounded by a bailey contained within palisaded earthworks and surrounded by a ditch. **2.** Country-house, named after a feudal castle, or a large country mansion looking vaguely like a castle. *See* Castle style.

Boase (1967)

Castle. *See* Cassels.

Castle style. Type of C18 architecture employing *battlements, *loop-holes (often false), and *turrets to create the impression of a fortified dwelling, even though the plan might be regular and Classical as in some buildings by Robert *Adam (e.g. Culzean Castle, Ayrshire (1777–92)). Elements derived from medieval military or fortified architecture were also employed for C18 *follies, gateways, *Picturesque cottages, and fake 'ruins', loosely described as *crenellated.

Rowan (1985)

castrum (*pl.* **castra**). Roman fortified camp, rectangular in plan, and standardized throughout the Empire. It had two main thoroughfares at right angles, the *cardo maximus* and *via decumana*, which each joined two gates set in towers with walls and towers around the whole.

catacomb. 1. Single subterranean *crypt, *gallery, or passage cut into and hollowed out of rock and lined with rectangular recesses (*loculi*) or arched *niches (*arcosolia*) for the entombment of corpses. *Catacomb* is properly the name given to the public underground cemetery beneath the *basilica of San Sebastiano, on the Via Appia, outside Rome, but may also relate to the *atrium in front of an early church *portico in which the dead were permitted to be buried. It is also used to describe any built basement used for the entombment of coffined bodies, usually associated with C19 cemeteries or cemetery-chapels. There is a good example of a brick-vaulted catacomb under the Anglican *chapel at the General Cemetery of All Souls, Kensal Green, London (1837). A small underground burial-place with rock-cut loculi, etc., intended for one group or family, was called *hypogeum in Antiquity, while a large chamber (often elaborately decorated) in a public catacomb was called *cubiculum*. **2.** The plural, *catacombs*, is the term for a large subterranean public cemetery of great size, labyrinthine, and on many levels, such as those in the vicinity of Rome.

Krautheimer (1986); Toynbee (1971)

catena d'acqua. Artificial cascade with a series of steps.

catenary. Curve described by e.g. a rope hung from two points on the same horizontal plane. *See* arch.

catenate. 1. To connect like the links of a chain, forming a series, as of linked buildings. **2.** To ornament with suspended chain-like forms.

cathedra. 1. Chair or seat of a Bishop in his church. In Early Christian times it was placed in the *apse of a *basilica behind the altar, but later, in the medieval period, it was situated in the *choir and associated with the *stalls. **2.** Episcopal See or dignity.

cathedral. Church containing the *cathedra, therefore the principal church of the See or Diocese.

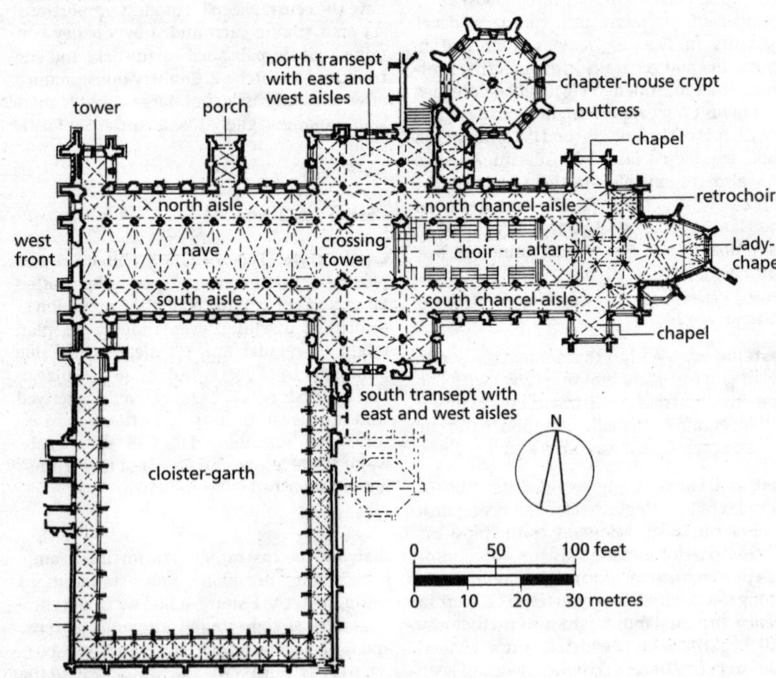

cathedral. Wells Cathedral, Somerset.

Cathedral Style. Early C19 *Gothic Revival (*c.*1810–*c.*1840), in which motifs were used in an unarchaeological unscholarly way before the advent of *Ecclesiology.

Catherine-wheel. Circular *Gothic *marigold- or *wheel-window, resembling a wheel, the radiating *colonnettes suggesting spokes. *See* rose.

cathetus. **1.** Axis of an *Ionic *volute-eye. **2.** Axis of any cylinder or *drum, such as a column-*shaft or *colonnette.

cat-slide. *See* roof.

caul, caulcole, caulicole, cauliculus (*pl.* **cauliculae**), **caulis** (*pl.* **caules**). *Caules* are principal stalks rising behind the upper row of *acanthus-leaves in a *Corinthian *capital. From these *caules* spring lesser branches (*caulicoles* or *cauliculae*) supporting the *volutes or helices.

Caus, *or* **Caux, Isaac de** (*fl.* 1612–55). Born in Dieppe, son or nephew of Salomon de *Caux. He settled in England and was mainly a garden-architect and hydraulics engineer, but was also described as an engineer and architect. He was associated with Inigo *Jones, designed a *grotto in the basement of the Whitehall Banqueting House (1623–4), and supervised the erection of Jones's houses around the 'Piazza' at Covent Garden (1633–4). He designed grottoes at Somerset House (1630–3) and Woburn Abbey, Bedfordshire (1630). De Caux then moved to the service of the Earl of Pembroke, for whom he rebuilt the south front of Wilton House, Wiltshire, and laid out gardens (1635–7). A *Palladianesque composition with *pavilion-towers, it was probably derived from *Scamozzi's *Idea della Architettura Universale* (1615), and Jones was likely involved as a consultant. De Caux also prepared designs for Stalbridge Park, Dorset (1638), and published a book on hydraulics in 1644.

Colvin (1995); Harris and Tait (1979)

Caus, *or* **Caux, Salomon de** (*c.*1577–1626). French hydraulics engineer and designer of gardens. He laid out the gardens at Heidelberg (described in his *Hortus Palatinus* . . . (1620)) for Frederick V, Elector Palatine of the Rhine (d. 1632) and his consort, Princess Elizabeth of Great Britain (1596–1662).

Colvin (1995)

cavaedium. *Cavum aedium*, partially roofed main room or *atrium of a Roman house, with a rectangular opening to the sky (*compluvium*) in the centre, and a pool or cistern (*impluvium*) set in the floor.

cavalier. Elevated platform used as a look-out or a gun-emplacement in a fortress.

cavation, cavazion. **1.** Excavation of earth to form a cellar or basement. **2.** Trench or excavation to accommodate the foundation of a building.

Cave, Walter Frederick (1863–1939). Born in Clifton, Bristol, England, he was articled to A. W. *Blomfield. He set up his own practice in 1889. As Surveyor to the Gunter Estate in Brompton, he laid out the model estate at Tamworth Street, Fulham. He designed several cottage-houses at Walton-on-Thames, Surrey, and built several fine *Arts-and-Crafts houses, two of which were mentioned by *Muthesius in *Das Englische Haus* (The English House (1904–5)). Cave's most celebrated building is Burberry's in the Haymarket, London (1912), with a handsome *Beaux-Arts front and superimposed *Orders applied to a framed structure.

Gray (1985)

cavetto (*pl.* **cavetti**). Concave *chamfer*, *gorge*, *hollow*, *throat*, or *trochilus* moulding the *section of which is a quarter-round, often used on *cornices, distinguished from the *scotia, the section of which is a half-circle, half-ellipse, or more. It normally has a *torus beneath, and, in Ancient Egyptian architecture, was the main element of a cornice, plain or decorated with upright stylized leaf forms.

ceil. **1.** To furnish with a *canopy or *screen. A *ceiling* is therefore the visible covering of the underside of a floor which provides the roofing of a room or other space below. **2.** To cover with a lining of woodwork, e.g. a *wainscot.

ceiling-cornice. *Cavetto *cornice at the junction of the vertical and overhead surfaces of a room.

ceilure. *See* celure.

Celer (*fl.* AD 64). *See* Severus.

cell. **1.** Small apartment of any sort, such as a room in a dormitory or inn, but especially a confined study-bedroom allotted to a monk or nun in a monastery. Also a penitential cell in the Middle Ages in which penitents were immured. **2.** Secure room with bed or beds in a prison. **3.** Any small cavity or room. **4.** *Cella or *naos. **5.** *Web* of a *vault framed by the *ribs*, or one surface of a *groin* vault. **6.** In *timber-framed structures, one room or unit. A *single-cell* plan is one volume, while a *two-cell* plan may have a *cross-entry or *cross-passage, and a *three-cell* plan will have a cross-passage, cross-entry, or *lobby-entry.

cella (*pl.* **cellae**). **1.** *Cell, in the sense of a monastic study-bedroom. **2.** Enclosed part of a Greek or Roman temple including the sacred chamber and vestibule, in fact everything within the walls. In Greek, *naos.

cellar. Subterranean or partly underground room or rooms within a building, normally without windows, for the storage of fuel, provisions, wines, etc., rather than as living-space. *Compare* *basement.

Celtic. Epithet of the peoples now identified as Bretons, Cornish, Irish, Manx, and Scots Gaels, originally Aryans. Early Celtic art seems to have become widespread, or widely influential, from *c.* C5 BC throughout the Rhineland, Central Europe, the Balkans, and Northern Italy, then in France, Ireland, and Britain *c.* C3 BC. Later, during the first millennium AD, its art-forms embraced influences from *Byzantium, *Early Christian, *Etruscan, *Greek, Oriental, and Syrian precedents. Characteristic elements are abstract patterns such as the *triquetrac* (triangular three-lobed form of interlaced crescents), *triskele* (Y-shaped forms), and *trumpet-pattern* (trumpet shapes with sinuous forms between), complex interlaced stalks and ribbons, knots, spirals, and highly stylized flora and fauna. Celtic art influenced other styles, especially *Anglo-Saxon, *Hiberno-Romanesque, and *Romanesque architectural enrichment, and reached its highest architectural development between *c.*650 and *c.*1150 with masterpieces such as the Bewcastle Cross, Cumberland (C7).

Lewis and Darley (1986)

Celtic cross. Monumental carved stone cross consisting of a vertical shaft and horizontal arms with a circlet, its centre at the intersection, linking the blocky forms at the extremities of the arms with the shaft and the base of the shrine-like superstructure with pitched roof that crowns the composition. Also called *wheel-head cross.*

Vallance (1920)

Celtic Revival. C19 revival of *Celtic art, mostly in Britain and Ireland, which sparked the *Hiberno-Romanesque revival in architecture, and influenced the *Arts-and-Crafts movement as well as the development of *Art Nouveau. An example of Celtic Revival ornament can be seen at the Watts Chapel, Compton, Surrey (from 1896).

Larmour (1992)

celure, ceilure, cellure. Part of the roof (especially a wagon-roof) of a church, panelled, decorated, and coloured, immediately above an altar or *Rood. *See* canopy.

cemetery. 1. Burial-ground, especially a large landscaped park or ground laid out expressly for the deposition or interment of the dead, not being a churchyard attached to a place of worship. Grander cemeteries, especially those of C19, contain *chapels, *mausolea, funerary monuments, underground 'vaults' with *loculi*, *colonnades, and entrance-lodges: a good example is the General Cemetery of All Souls, Kensal Green, London (1831–7). **2.** *Catacombs. **3.** Consecrated enclosure for burial of the dead.

Curl (1993); Etlin (1984)

cenotaph. Empty sepulchre, or funerary monument to the dead whose bodies lie elsewhere. *Lutyens's Cenotaph, Whitehall, London (1919–20), is an example of such a symbolic tomb.

centering. Timber framework or mould to support arches or *vaults during construction, removed or *struck* after the setting of the mortar and the completion of the arched form.

centre. Point around which a circle is described, or the middle point of a sphere. A *centrally planned* building is one arranged around a central point, as opposed to an *axial plan*: a *drum or octagonal structure is centrally planned, while a *basilica is axially planned.

centrepiece. Central ornamental element, such as an elaborate doorway and its superstructure in the middle of a façade, or a *rose on a ceiling.

Cerceau, Du, Family. Group of French architects and decorators founded by **Jacques Androuet Du Cerceau the Elder** (1510/12–*c.*1585), whose *Les Trois Livres d'Architecture* (The Three Books of Architecture—1559–72) was very influential. The first volume (1559) was essentially a pattern-book of domestic architecture, some of which was influenced by *Serlio; the second (1561) contained highly decorated features; and the third (1572) followed the treatises of Philibert de L'*Orme and *Palladio. These volumes became important sources of *grotesque ornament and *Mannerist designs in France and Northern Europe. His *Les plus excellents bastiments de France* (The Most Excellent Buildings in France—1576–9) remains a fine record of French *Renaissance *châteaux. He has been credited with the design of the château of Verneuil (1568), clearly inspired by Italian design (an important source of motifs) and also influenced by the Italian Mannerists working at *Fontainebleau.

Du Cerceau's son **Baptiste** (1544/7–90) became a major architect working in Paris at the end of C16, and entered the service of the King in 1575. He succeeded *Lescot as architect at the Louvre in 1578, completing the west part of the south wing of the Square Court (1582). He made designs for the Pont Neuf (1578), but in 1585 he fled Paris as a Protestant refugee. Baptiste's brother **Jacques** (*c*.1550–1614) became architect to King Henri IV (1589–1610) and was very likely responsible for the *pavilions in the Place des Vosges. Baptiste's son, **Jean** (*c*.1585–*c*.1649), was appointed architect to King Louis XIII (1610–43) in 1617 having trained with his cousin, Salomon de *Brosse, with whom he worked on the Palais du Luxembourg, Paris. He was involved in the development of the Marais and Île St-Louis areas (1620s–1640s), and was responsible for the Hôtel Sully (now Béthune-Sully—1625–9) and the Hôtel de Bretonvilliers (1637–43), in Paris, both extraordinary for their cunningly contrived axes and richly carved decorations. Jean also rebuilt de L'Orme's *staircase in the Cour du Cheval Blanc at Fontainebleau with a complicated horseshoe-shaped arrangement.

Androuet du Cerceau (1611); Blunt (1958, 1982); Chevalley (1973); Coope (1972); Geymüller (1887); Hautecœur (1943–57); Ward (1976)

Cerdá, Ildefonso (1815–76). Spanish Catalan architect. Born in Centellas, Barcelona, he studied civil engineering in Madrid (1835–41), and worked as an engineer for the State (1841–9). From 1849 he devoted himself to the theory of urbanization, and planned the expansion of Barcelona on a grid-iron plan (1859) intersected by two diagonal avenues, each block of the grid-iron having *chamfered sides. Originally each block (*c*.100 metres square) was to be built up on two sides only, leaving a central green space, but as a result of increased land-values the remaining areas have been developed. Cerdá influenced Arturo *Soria y Mata in his philosophy of ruralizing the city and urbanizing the countryside, and of integrating both, as in Soria y Mata's Linear City. He was the first to attempt to apply scientific principles to urban and rural planning, and was the author of the important *Teoría general de la urbanización* (1867). His work at Barcelona was the model for other Spanish city enlargements, including Madrid and Bilbao.

Cerdá (1968); Estape (1971); Soria y Puig (1979)

Certosa. *Carthusian monastery in Italy.

chaînes. *Masonry *pier-like elements on a *façade, sometimes with parallel sides, and sometimes with alternating wide and narrow blocks (like the normal arrangement of *quoins), subdividing a façade into panels of brick. Common in C17 French architecture, good examples exist in the Place des Vosges, Paris (early C17). In England they were alluded to in the vertical strips of brickwork differing from the colours of the panels between that became fashionable from the time of *Wren, common in architecture of the *Queen Anne period and its C19 revival.

chair-rail. *Cornice of a continuous *pedestal-like arrangement around the walls of a room, called *dado-rail.

châlet. Wooden dwelling-house of a type common in Switzerland, with a broad, low-pitched roof with wide overhanging *eaves, and often timber balconies and external stairs.

Chalgrin, Jean-François-Thérèse (1739–1811). Paris-born architect who studied with *Servandoni and *Boullée, and worked for a while as Inspecteur des Travaux de la Ville de Paris (from 1763) under *Moreau-Desproux: he erected the Hôtel St-Florentin, Paris (1767–70), to plans by *Gabriel, but he was responsible for the Neoclassical courtyard-screen, portal, and interior décor. An important *Neoclassicist, he designed the *basilican St-Philippe-du-Roule, Paris (1768–74), in a severe *Antique style, much influenced by *Cordemoy, *Laugier, and

*Contant d'Ivry. The interior has free-standing *Ionic columns defining the barrel-*vaulted *nave, and continuing in a curve around the *apse, while the *Tuscan *Order was used for the entrance-portico. The church was contemporary with similar buildings by *Potain and *Trouard. *Quatremère de Quincy praised St-Philippe in 1816 as a model for French architects to follow because it adopted the *Early Christian basilica and avoided *Baroque excesses. While working on St-Philippe, Chalgrin completed Servandoni's great Church of St-Sulpice, building the north tower (1776–8), changing Servandoni's unfluted proposals for the west front to a fluted arrangement, and carrying out other works, including the *baptistry and organ-case. He also designed several gardens, as well as the exquisite Pavillon de Musique, Versailles (1784), with its rotunda containing a *trompe-l'œil painting that suggests the room is set in a garden. He remodelled the Palais du Luxembourg, Paris (1787–1807), creating the impressive Neoclassical Salle du Sénat and grand staircase (1803–7), and designed the enormous Arc de Triomphe de l'Étoile, Paris (1806), completed by *Blouet (1836), which has two main axes instead of just one, and is *astylar.

Braham (1980); Gaehtgens (1974); Gallet (1972); Middleton and Watkin (1987)

Chamberlin, Powell, & Bon. London-based partnership established in 1952 by Peter Hugh Girard Chamberlin (1919–85), Geoffrey C. Hamilton Powell (1920–), and Christoph(er) Bon (1921–), which designed the Bousfield School, South Kensington, London (1955–6), influenced by *Mies van der Rohe's work. The firm won the competition (1952) to create new housing at Golden Lane (1953–7), and later evolved the plan for the Barbican district of London (1955–82), arguably the best example in the British Isles of a high-density urban development, incorporating cultural, residential, and educational uses, influenced by the ideas of Le *Corbusier. The firm was also responsible for buildings at New Hall, Cambridge (1962–6), where the formalism of the hall dome and the circular staircase towers were felt at the time to be a sign of a return to historical allusions. Other works include developments for the University of Leeds, Yorkshire (from 1963), and University of Birmingham (1966).

Emanuel (1994); Webb (1969)

Chambers, Sir William (1723–96). Important British Classical architect. Son of a Scottish merchant, he was born at Göteborg, Sweden, educated in Yorkshire, and travelled in India and China with the Swedish East India Company (1740–9). In 1749 he enrolled in J.-F. *Blondel's École des Arts in Paris and in 1750 he travelled to Italy, where he spent five years and was taught drawing skills by *Clérisseau and others, as well as studying *Antique and contemporary buildings. During his European sojourns he absorbed many of the ideas that were to lead to *Neoclassicism in the second half of C18.

He set up in practice in London in 1755, and in 1756 became architectural tutor to the Prince of Wales (later King George III (1760–1820)). In 1757 he was commissioned to lay out the grounds of the Dowager Princess of Wales's house at Kew, and ornamented the gardens with an exotic array of temples and garden-buildings, including the Chinese Pagoda (1761–2). He published *Designs of Chinese Buildings*... (1757—which was regarded as a source for pictures of Chinese architecture even though by then the fashion for *Chinoiserie had almost ended), and *Treatise on Civil Architecture* (1759) which became an important and standard work dealing with the *Orders and their uses, going into further editions in 1768 and 1791 (when it became *A Treatise on the Decorative Part of Civil Architecture*, much expanded and amended). By 1760 he was established in his practice and became one of the two architects (the other was Robert *Adam) appointed by the Crown in the Office of Works. *Plans, Elevations, Sections, and Perspective Views of the Garden Buildings at Kew in Surrey* came out in 1763, tactfully dedicated to his Royal patroness; he succeeded *Flitcroft as Comptroller of the Works in 1769; and in 1782 was appointed Surveyor-General and Comptroller, in which position he rapidly showed himself to be a first-rate administrator as well as a great official architect.

Chambers's architecture combined English *Palladianism and French Neoclassicism, as can be seen at the Casino, Marino, near Dublin (1758–76), built on a Greek-cross plan, and at his masterpiece, Somerset House, London (1776–96), arguably the grandest official building ever erected in the capital: John *Webb's Queen's Gallery, Somerset House (1662), which had an arched *rusticated ground-floor and a *Giant *Order rising through the first and second floors, was quoted in the new building by Chambers. Duddingston House, Midlothian, a country-house by Chambers near Edinburgh (1763–8), is not unlike *Campbell's Stourhead, Wiltshire, but has no rusticated *basement and the *Corinthian *portico sits on a platform only four steps high. Chambers also designed in 1775 the Theatre (built 1777–86) and Chapel (built 1787–*c*.1800) at Trinity College, Dublin, two of the most distinguished buildings of the College. However, Chambers, it seems, had a blind spot concerning Greek architecture, referring to 'Attic Deformity', but he designed Milton Abbey House, Dorset (1771–6), in the *Gothic style, and indeed seems to have planned a treatise on Gothic for publication. At Kew Gardens he had no stylistic inhibitions, building an Alhambra, Moorish mosque, and buildings in the Chinese style, as well as more conventional Classical structures: he seems to have intended to provide the Gardens with a sort of encyclopedia of architectural styles. It should be remembered that he was the only architect in England at the time who had ever seen real Chinese buildings. In 1772 he published his *Dissertation on Oriental Gardening*, which was in reality an attack on the manner of landscape-design promoted by 'Capability' *Brown, but was misinterpreted as an apology for the Chinese garden as an exemplar, and earned him opprobrium. He may have been responsible for the layout of the model village at Milton Abbas (*c*.1774–80). His pupils included *Gandon, and his influence was important and widespread.

Chambers (1759, 1968, 1969, 1972); Colvin (1995); Harris (1970); Harris and Snodin (1996); McCarthy (1987)

Chambiges, Martin (d. 1532). French *Gothic architect, who designed the *transept *façades at Sens (*c*.1494) and Beauvais (*c*.1499) Cathedrals, and the west front of Troyes Cathedral (*c*.1506). His work consisted of elaborately decorated *screens, and the first signs of Italian *Renaissance influence appear in his designs after 1510. His son, **Pierre** (d. 1544), was associated with his father at Troyes and Beauvais, worked on the old Hôtel de Ville, Paris (1533–4), and built the *Château at St-Germain-en-Laye from 1539.

Berty (1860); Guiffrey (1915); Sanfaçon (1971); Vachon (1907)

chambranle. Frame-like embellishments around apertures such as doors, fireplaces, *niches, and windows, the equivalent of an *architrave, and having the same profile as the *entablature architrave. Its vertical sides are *ascendants* and the *lintel-top is the *transverse*.

chamfer. *Bevel*, *cant*, or oblique surface produced by cutting away an *arris or corner at an angle (usually 45°), not as big as a *splay. Thus a piece of stone or wood (e.g. beam) so treated is *chamfered*. Chamfers can be hollowed out, or concave, called *chamferet*, *chamfret*, or *hollow chamfer*, as in a *flute, and can be *beaded* (with a convex bead-like moulding projecting from the chamfer). When the chamfer does not extend the whole length of the object (e.g. beam or splayed *jamb), it is a *stopped chamfer*, sometimes simply treated, but often ornamented (*chamfer-stop—see* stop). *Rustication includes *chamfered rustication*. *Swelled chamfer* is a *Vitruvian scroll.

Chamoust, Ribart de (*fl.* 1776–83). *See* Ribart de Chamoust.

Champneys, Basil (1842–1935). London-born English architect. He began practice in 1867, and designed many important buildings, including the Selwyn Divinity School, Cambridge (1878–9), in an early *Tudor style, and Mansfield College, Oxford (1887–9), in a *Gothic Revival style. At the Indian Institute, Oxford (1883–96), he mixed early English *Renaissance and Flemish detail. His finest buildings are the John Rylands Library, Manchester (1890–1905), a good example of *Arts-and-Crafts *Second Pointed *Gothic, with tierceron *vaulting, and Newnham College, Cambridge (1874–1910), in red brick, with *Queen Anne and Dutch *Domestic Revival elements.

Champneys (1875, 1901); *DNB* (1949); Gray (1985); Service (1975, 1977)

chancel. Liturgical eastern part of a church, used by those officiating in the services, and often defined by a *cancellus (from which the term is derived) or *screen. It contains the *sanctuary and *altar, and often embraces the *choir, especially in larger churches where the chancel is part of the main body of the building east of the *crossing.

Bond (1916)

chancel-aisle. *Aisle parallel to a *chancel, often continuing behind the high-altar as an *ambulatory, connecting with the chancel-aisle on the other side.

chancel-arch. Arch at the liturgical east of the *nave, carrying a *gabled wall above, separating nave from *chancel. It is often an object of some magnificence and in the Middle Ages sometimes had a representation of the Last Judgement (or Doom) on the surface above the arch facing the nave. Above the roof (usually higher or lower than that of the nave), the gable was often crowned with a *bell- or *Sancte-cote.

chancel-rail. *Balustrade, barrier, *cancelli, or low wall defining or separating the *chancel from the *nave, sometimes doubling as an altar-rail.

chancel-screen. *Screen separating the *chancel from the body of the church. A large stone chancel-screen is a *pulpitum. Many English wooden examples exist with *brattishing on top of elaborately carved, traceried, and vaulted screens: they have *galleries, are approached by narrow stairs (many of which have survived the screens themselves), and originally supported a *Rood, so are often referred to as *Rood-screens.

chandelle. Type of *cable in *flutes of columns, etc., often ornamented with foliage.

channel. 1. *Canal, as in the shaft of a column. **2.** *Canaliculus of a *Doric *triglyph. **3.** Bevelled *channelling* or grooves in *rustication. **4.** Furrow, groove, or gutter sunk for carrying off water from a surface.

Chantrell, Robert Dennis (1793–1872). Southwark-born English architect. He was a pupil of *Soane before settling in Leeds, Yorkshire, in 1819, where he commenced his successful practice with a series of *Greek Revival public buildings, most of which have been demolished. He is of considerable significance as the designer of many important churches erected between 1823 and 1850. St Peter's, Leeds (1837–41), his masterpiece, is a scholarly essay in *Gothic that for its date was unusual in its size and quality, and was recognized as such in *The Ecclesiologist* (1847).

Colvin (1995); Linstrum (1978)

chantry. Establishment, endowment, or foundation for the daily or frequent saying of Masses on behalf of the souls of the founder, founders, or other persons intended. A *chantry-chapel* was therefore a chapel or separate part of a church established for this purpose, often enclosed by a *screen (with or without a *canopy), and frequently erected over the burial-place of the founder, so not unusually incorporated, apart from the altar, a *tomb-chest and *effigy, as in the excellent medieval examples in Winchester Cathedral.

chapel. 1. Building for Christian worship, not a parish-church or *cathedral, often without certain privileges normally those of a parish-church. **2.** Room or building for worship in or attached to a castle, college, great house, monastery, palace, school, or other institution. **3.** *Oratory in a burial-aisle, *mausoleum, *mortuary-chapel, or elsewhere, with an altar where Masses might be chanted (i.e. *chantry-chapel), often with funerary monuments. **4.** Screened compartment in a large church, usually in *aisles, to the east of *transepts, or to the east of the high-altar, with its own altar, separately dedicated, and often of great magnificence (e.g. *Lady-chapels for veneration of the Blessed Virgin Mary, as at Westminster Abbey). **5.** Place of worship subordinate to the parish-church, created for the convenience of parishioners, such as a *chapel-of-ease*, when the parish was very large and distances great, or where populations increased. **6.** Place of Christian worship other than buildings of the Established Church in England, so usually applied to a Nonconformist establishment. In Ireland it refers to a Roman Catholic church, even in the late C20.

chapiter. *See* capital.

chaplet. Moulding resembling a string of beads, as on an *astragal, also called *pearling*.

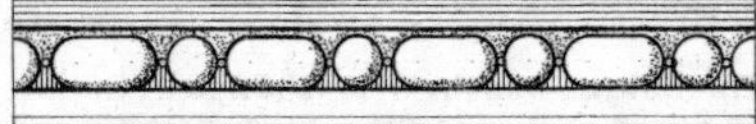

chaplet

chapter-house. Building for assemblies, business, meeting, maintenance of discipline, etc., associated with *cathedral, *collegiate, and conventual churches, often situated on the east side of the *cloisters, but sometimes on the north side of the church with access through a *vestibule or *trisantia. In cathedrals or large churches, chapter-houses in England were often polygonal on plan (e.g. Lincoln and Wells), with or without central *piers supporting the *vaults, with *stalls around the perimeter. Polygonal examples sited on the north side perhaps were suggested by the plan of the Constantinian *basilica of San Pietro, Rome (begun *c.*333).

chaptrel. **1.** *Capital of a *pier supporting the springing or an arch or *vault, or any capital *engaged to a wall, such as those of an *anta or *pilaster. **2.** *Impost.

Chareau, Pierre (1883–1950). Bordeaux-born French architect and furniture-designer. He came to public notice with his remodelling of an apartment in the Rue St-Germain, Paris (1918–19), which included furniture (some of which featured plywood, metal tubing, and ebony), exhibited at the *Salon d'Automne*, 1919. He also showed furniture at the 1924–5 Exposition International des Arts-Décoratifs, and in 1928 designed a house in the Rue St-Guillaume, Paris, in which glass blocks were widely employed (pre-dating Le *Corbusier's use of them), giving the work its name, *Maison de Verre* (completed 1932 in collaboration with Bernard Bijvoet (1889–1979), his associate from 1925 to 1935): it also had an exposed steel structure. In 1940 Chareau emigrated to the USA where he built a house for the painter Robert Motherwell at East Hampton, NY, in the 1940s, but it was of no influence.

Chareau (1929); Vellay (1985)

charnel-house. **1.** Building (sometimes purpose-built), *crypt, *ossuary, or *vault where the bones of disinterred dead are stored as new graves are required in a churchyard. Once very common in medieval England, charnel-houses became less usual from C16 as religious practices concerned with the dead changed with the Reformation, although a three-bay charnel-house of brick with stone dressings was built at the end of C17 in the churchyard of St Nicholas, Deptford Green, London. Charnel-houses may be found on the Continent today, especially where burial-space is limited, as in Alpine churchyards, and several decorative charnel-houses exist, where walls and ceilings are covered with bones arranged in patterns (e.g. Capuchin Church, Rome). **2.** Place of deposit for dead bodies which dry out in certain conditions, as in Palermo, Sicily.

Ariès (1981); Litten (1991)

Charterhouse. *Carthusian monastery, *Certosa, or Chartreuse (French).

château. **1.** French *castle. **2.** Large French country-house, in C16 often retaining allusions to fortifications, as in the deep ditch and corner towers of e.g. Chambord, and various châteaux in the Loire Valley. **3.** Any large French country-house, with allusions to castles or not.

Châteauneuf, Alexis de (1799–1853). Hamburg-born architect of noble French parentage, he trained under *Weinbrenner, *Wimmel, and others. Settling in his native city, he designed buildings in which North-German traditions of brick-built architecture were combined with *Rundbogenstil and *Renaissance elements. His work owed much to *Percier & *Fontaine and *Schinkel, and was itself influential; buildings included the City Post Office (1830s—destroyed), a fine house on the Neu-Jungfernstieg (*c.*1835—destroyed), and an asylum consisting of detached *pavilions in a park near Kiel (1842). He remodelled part of Hamburg around the Alster Lake after the conflagration of 1842, and designed numerous structures, including buildings for the Guild of Cabinetmakers, the Hall for the Guild of Tailors, and the Church of St Peter. With his assistant, W. von Hanno, he built Trinity Church, Oslo, Norway (1850–8), a *Gothic centralized building on an octagonal plan with projecting porch, *transepts, and *chancel. His publications included *Architectura Domestica* and *The Country House* (both 1843). He made several unrealized designs for London, including proposals for the Royal Exchange and the Nelson Memorial.

Châteauneuf (1839, 1860); Lange (1965); Tschudi-Madsen (1965)

château style. C19 revival of the style of architecture of the reign of *François Ier of France (1515–47), epitomized by the *château of Fontainebleau, or a revival incorporating *Gothic and *Renaissance elements derived from Fontainebleau.

chatri. Indian *pavilion consisting of a horizontal slab carried on four *colonnettes, recurring in *Hindoo orientalizing architecture in the West, also called *chavada*, often with an *ogee-shaped roof.

chatta, chattra. Masonry parasol-like form. *See* chat(t)ra.

chat(t)ra. Umbrella-like (from Hindu for umbrella, *chatta*) form on a horizontal slab carried by a post (*chattrayashti*), which, if supporting three umbrellas set each above the other, is termed *chattraval(l)i*. Indian Revival or *Hindoo architecture may have *pavilion-like forms (chavada) on which chatris are set.

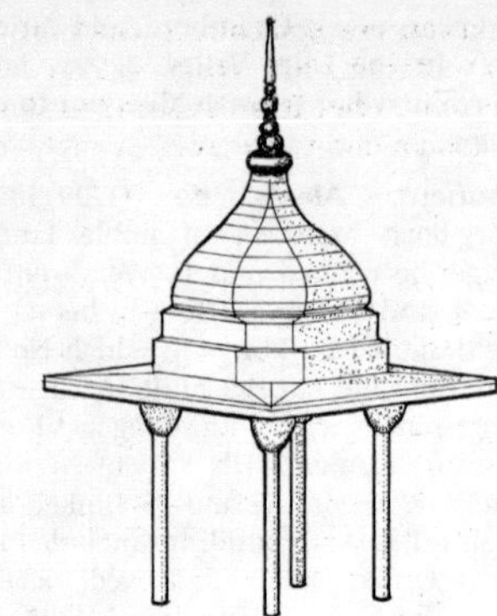

chatri or chavada

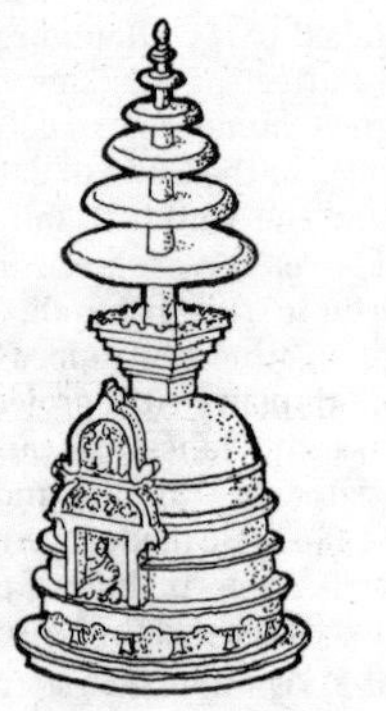

chattravalli. Set on a stupa.

checker. *See* chequer.

Chedanne, Georges (1861–1940). French architect. At the École des *Beaux-Arts, Paris, he came to notice with his drawings for the restoration of the *Pantheon, Rome (1887). As an architect, some of his designs owed something to *Art Nouveau influences, while others exploited the possibilities of exposed iron structures and glass infill (e.g. the elegant Parisien Libéré Office Building, 124 Rue de Réaumur, Paris (1903–4)). His Galeries Lafayettes in Paris was one of the most impressive and elegant of the great department-stores, designed with a framed structure using iron.

Emery (1971); *Byggekunst*, 54/6 (1972), 190–1

chedi. A *stupa in Thailand, rarely occurring in orientalizing architecture in the West.

cheek. Narrow vertical face, usually one of two corresponding opposite faces, as in the sides of an opening or of a projection (e.g. a *buttress, *dormer-window, or *chimney-breast).

Chelles, Jean *and* **Pierre de** (*fl.* C13 and C14). **Jean de Chelles** was the master-mason who built part of the *transepts of Notre Dame, Paris: work on the north transept was carried out in the 1240s and on the south transept in 1258. Pierre de *Montreuil worked with de Chelles and succeeded him as master-mason or architect in 1265. A relative, **Pierre de Chelles**, was master-mason at Notre Dame in the early part of C14, and worked on the Cathedral at Chartres.

Branner (1965); Frankl (1962); Sturgis *et al.* (1901–2)

cheneau. 1. *Eaves-gutter with the profile of an elaborate *cornice. **2.** Ornamented *crest, as on the *ridge of a roof, or associated with a gutter at the eaves.

chequer, checker. 1. Pattern involving the division of a surface into equal squares (*chequers*) treated alternately in different ways, such as in colour or texture: it is commonly found in tile or stone pavements resembling a chess-board and called *chequer-work*. **2.** Type of *diaper-work in which the compartments are all square, as in late-*Romanesque and *Gothic surface-carving.

chequer-set *or* **staggered corbelling.** Row of *corbels or *machicolations placed so that each alternate projection is higher or lower than its neighbour, i.e. set *chequerwise*.

Chermayeff, Serge Ivan (1900–96). Born in Russia, he emigrated to England in 1910. He worked as a designer for a firm of decorators in London (1924–7) before becoming Director of the Modern Furnishings Department, Waring & Gillow (1928), and setting up his architectural practice in 1930. Among his works at that time were the interiors of the Cambridge Theatre (1930), and of the British Broadcasting Corporation (1932), both in London. He formed a partnership with Erich *Mendelsohn (1933–6) which produced several classic *Modern Movement buildings, including the De La Warr Pavilion, Bexhill-on-Sea, Sussex (1934–5), the Nimmo House, Chalfont St Giles, Buckinghamshire (1935), and another house at 64 Old Church Street, Chelsea, London (1935–6). His elegant house at Bentley Wood, Halland, Sussex (1938–9), looked forward to his period in America, and his use of *timber-framed structures. He emigrated to the USA in 1940: his house at New Haven, Conn. (1962–3), is probably his most successful work there.

Chermayeff and Alexander (1963); Chermayeff and Tzonis (1971); Emanuel (1994)

Chersiphron (*fl.* *c*.560 BC). Crete-born architect (with *Theodoros of Samos) of the foundations and *colonnades of the archaic *Ionic temple of Artemis at Ephesus (*c*.565–550 BC). His son, **Metagenes**, continued the work and erected the *entablature. These architects wrote a treatise (now lost) on the building of the temple.

Ashmole (1972); Coulton (1977); Dinsmoor (1950); Lawrence (1983)

chert. Stone resembling *flint.

Cherub. Chubby male infant with wings, or an infant's head with wings, also called *Cupid, similar to the *Antique and *Renaissance *Amorino* or *Love*, found in profusion in *Baroque architecture and decoration. *Compare* *putto.

Cherubim. Figures with wings over the mercy-seat in the Jewish temple, later angels of the second of the *Nine Orders of Angels with attributes of the knowledge and contemplation of Divine things. Thus representations of an adult figure with wings.

Chevakinsky, Savva (1713–*c*.1770). Russian architect. He designed the Nikolsky military-naval Cathedral in St Petersburg, arguably the best late-*Baroque church in Russia (1752). He was also involved from 1745 in the early designs of the development of Tsarskoe Selo before *Rastrelli took over.

Encyclopaedia Britannica (1959); Hamilton (1983)

chevaux de frise. Defensive arrangement of sharp obstacles set in the ground before a fortification to deter or slow a frontal assault.

chevet. Apsidal liturgical east end of a large church, with the *ambulatory around the semicircular end of the *choir off which the *chapels radiate.

chevron. 1. Ornament resembling a V used in series to form a *dancette* or *zig-zag* in *Romanesque architecture, usually on *archivolts and *string-courses. It is mostly of part-circular *section, so-called 'broken sticks' (*bâtons rompus*), but may also be composed of convex and concave elements. **2.** The V-form commonly occurring in *Art Deco design, either alone or in series. It is also found used in series in Roman decorative work, notably in *mosaic.

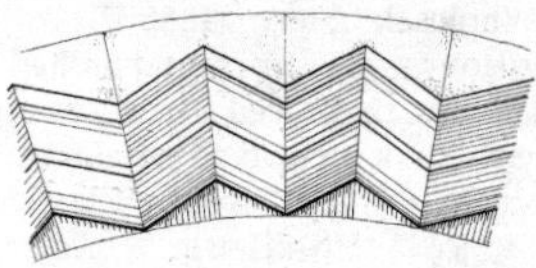

chevron. Romanesque type, as around a doorway. Church of St Lawrence, North Hinksey, Oxfordshire (formerly Berkshire). (*After Parker*)

Chiattone, Mario (1891–1957). Italian architect. He exhibited, with *Sant'Elia, various drawings for a 'modern metropolis' that were among the seminal images of Italian *Futurism. In the 1930s his work was associated with the *Novocento Italiano* group, and he turned increasingly to a stripped *Neoclassicism.

Veronesi (1965)

Chiaveri, Gaetano (1689–1770). Rome-born architect who worked mostly in St Petersburg (1717–27—where he assisted *Trezzini) and in Warsaw and Dresden (*c*.1737–48). His *Katholische Hofkirche* (Roman Catholic Court Church) in Dresden (1737–53) was built as a foil to *Bähr's Lutheran *Frauenkirche* (Church of Our Lady), and is one of the most elegant and accomplished late-*Baroque masterpieces in all Europe (restored after severe war-damage), with a beautiful tower, and elevations influenced by the Royal Chapel at Versailles. Chiaveri also prepared plans for the Vistula frontage of the Royal Palace in Warsaw (1740), and for another Royal Palace (late 1740s) in Dresden, which was not built. Both schemes had a rare refinement of Baroque detail. He published his *Ornamenti Diversi di Porte e Finestre* (Various Ornaments for Doors and Windows—1743–4), in which the influences of *Bernini, *Borromini, and Carlo *Fontana were displayed.

Chiaveri (1743–4); Hempel (1955, 1965)

Chicago School. 1. Group of architects working mostly in Chicago in the last quarter of C19. **2.** Group of high-rise commercial and office-buildings erected in Chicago from *c*.1875 to *c*.1910.

It might be claimed that the *skyscraper was born in Chicago, exploiting the invention of the elevator (lift) and the *metal-framed structure. William Le Baron *Jenney's pioneering use of the steel *skeleton led to other developments, notably those of *Burnham & Root. One of the most important early buildings of the Chicago School was the Marshall Field Wholesale Store (1885–7) by H. H. *Richardson, a massive round-arched building clad in rock-faced *rustication, the precedent for a new type of monumental architecture, freed from Classical or *Renaissance *Historicism. *Adler and *Sullivan's Auditorium Building (1887–9) clearly owed much stylistically to Richardson's model, but the structure was much more innovative. Burnham & Root's Monadnock Building (1889–91) was the last of the tall buildings with *load-bearing outer walls completely devoid of ornament. The metal frame for skyscrapers was first expressed on the elegant exterior in Burnham & Co.'s Reliance Building (1894–5), the designer of which was *Atwood. Sullivan's Schlesinger & Mayer Department Store of 1899 and 1903–4 (now Carson, Pirie, & Scott) was probably one of the most important buildings of the Chicago School expressing the underlying skeleton and exploiting the *Chicago window to the full.

Condit (1952, 1960, 1961, 1964, 1968); Randall (1949); Tallmadge (1941)

Chicago window. Horizontal window consisting of a large square fixed central pane with narrow vertical sliding-sashes on either side, as in the Carson, Pirie, & Scott Store, Chicago, by *Sullivan of 1899–1904. It is usually the full width of a structural *bay.

chien-assis. Medieval miniature pitched-roof *dormer, with unglazed foiled opening, resembling a miniature dog-kennel on a slope of a roof. It permits air and light to enter a roof-space.

chigi. Terminations of *gables on a Japanese roof, like scissors, or projecting *barge-couples, called *forked finials*, occasionally found in orientalizing garden-buildings in the West.

chimney. **1.** Fireplace or hearth. **2.** Fireplace with flue and vent over it, so including the structure rising above a roof or outside the building. A *chimney-stack could be a large structure surrounded by a *timber-framed building, where it helped to stabilize the structure as well as providing heat, could be erected over the *gable-end, or placed in series along a *façade, as in a medieval hospital or *almshouse (e.g. St John's Hospital, Lichfield, Staffordshire (late C15), with its array of stacks). In *Elizabethan and *Jacobethan *prodigy-houses chimney-stacks contributed to the complex *skylines of the composition.

The following terms are associated with chimneys: *fireplace* (opening of a chimney into a room, whether decorated or not); *gathering* (part of the flue that contracts with the ascent); *hearth* (floor of the fireplace); and *inglenook* (small space beside the chimney, often containing seats, sometimes illuminated by means of a small window, and occasionally having a lower ceiling than in the rest of the room, hence its other name, *roofed ingle*).

chimney-arch. Arch over the fireplace-opening, supporting the *chimney-breast.

chimney-back. **1.** *Fireback*, or rear wall of the fireplace, often protected by a decorative cast-iron plate. **2.** Rear of *chimney-stack projecting outwards from the exterior wall of a building.

chimney-bar. Support or *lintel for the *chimney-breast, often a metal flat, H-, or T-section, or a massive timber beam called *mantel-tree*, carried on the *chimney-cheeks.

chimney-breast. **1.** Front wall, from base to top, necessary to house a *chimney, and containing the fireplace. **2.** Wall over the fireplace, whether or not projecting from the wall, carried on the *arch*, *bar*, *mantle*, or *tree*: it is essentially that part of the wall facing the room and forming one side of the chimney.

chimney-can. **1.** Metal pipe set on the top of the flue to increase the up-draught. **2.** Chimney-pot.

chimney-cap. *Abacus or *cornice crowning a *chimney-stack.

chimney-cheek. Side of a fireplace-opening, really the face of a *pier providing the support for the *arch*, *bar*, *mantle*, or *tree*, and the *chimney-breast.

chimney-corner. Corner or side of a large open projecting or retreating fireplace or hearth, or the seat on each end of the fire-grate. Variations include the *inglenook* or *roofed ingle*.

chimney-crane. Swivelling metal bar, hooked at one end, from which cooking-pots may be suspended and swung over the fire, also called *chimney-crook* or *chimney-hook*.

chimney-cricket. Additional protective structure erected over a roof where a *chimney-stack penetrates it, to improve the water-proofing.

chimney-crook *or* **-hook.** *Chimney-crane.

chimney-flue. Hollow part of the *chimney through which smoke can pass. It starts with the *funnel*, tube, or cavity leading upwards from the fireplace.

chimney-head. Top of a *chimney-stack.

chimney-hood. Metal or *masonry hood-like structure projecting from a *chimney-breast over a fireplace to collect the smoke, common in the Middle Ages.

chimney-jamb. Wall projecting from the back to form one side of the enclosure of a fireplace, carrying the *arch*, *bar*, *mantle*, or *tree*.

chimney-mantle. **1.** Horizontal part of the *chimney-piece. **2.** Beam or any horizontal support carrying the *breast*.

chimney-piece. Dressing or surround of a fireplace. The horizontal part is the *mantle-* or *mantel-piece*, and the ensemble can have considerable architectural magnificence.

chimney-pot. Cylindrical, polygonal, or square element of brick, metal, or *terracotta fixed on top of a *chimney-stack to extend the flue and improve the extraction of smoke (draught).

chimney-shaft. As *stalk*, but more often a *chimney-stack containing only one flue.

chimney-stack. Mass of brickwork or masonry containing one or more flues separated by *withs* or *withes*, and projecting above the roof.

chimney-stalk. Any very lofty chimney.

chimney-throat. The part of the *chimney-flue which contracts as it ascends is the *gathering* or *gathering of the wings*, and the part between the gathering and the flue above is the *throat* or *waist* because it is the narrowest part.

chimney-top. The crowning parts of a *chimney-stack or -stalk.

chimney-waist. As *chimney-throat.

chimney-wing. One of the sides or lateral cheeks of the gathering, by which the narrowing towards the *chimney-throat is achieved.

Chinese fret. *Lattice ornament on *balustrades, gates, *friezes, and railings, made of square-sectioned timber, and forming square and rectangular patterns, with diagonals adding triangular and other shapes. It was common in C18 *Chinoiserie-inspired design.

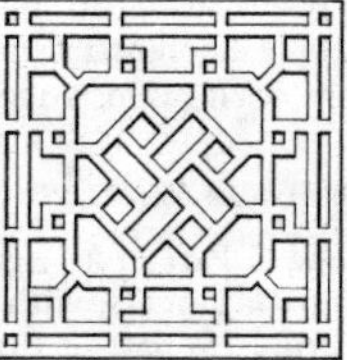

Chinese fret

Chinoiserie. Style of European architecture and artefacts in the Chinese Taste, intended to evoke China, first appearing in C17, and reaching the heights of delicacy and inventiveness in C18 and early C19, notably in Germany. Garden-buildings in the Chinese style include bridges (often with *Chinese fret balustrades), summer- and tea-houses, and *pagodas. The most celebrated examples are the Pagoda in Kew Gardens (1763) by *Chambers (whose *Designs of Chinese Buildings* of 1757 was regarded as a source for pictures of Chinese architecture), the Tea House in the grounds of the palaces at Potsdam (1754–7) designed by King Frederick the Great (1740–86) and *Büring, and the Chinese House, Drottningholm, Sweden, by *Adelcrantz. In the 1750s buildings in the Chinese Taste and the *Gothick style were regarded as relaxations from *Classicism, and were treated almost as a branch of exotic *Rococo. This is made clear in William *Halfpenny's *Chinese and Gothic Architecture* (1752), while William and John Halfpenny's *Rural Architecture in the Chinese Taste* (1752–5) further popularized the style. The interiors of Brighton Pavilion have Chinoiserie elements, including some gaudy decorations by Frederick Crace (1779–1859). The jardin *anglo-chinois was an informal, irregularly planned C18 garden, in which Chinoiserie touches could be found. *See* Sharawadgi.

Conner (1979); Honour (1961)

Chochol, Josef (1880–1956). Influenced by the work of Otto *Wagner through the latter's pupil Jan *Kotěra, Chochol became an important figure in Bohemia and Moravia. Before 1914 he dabbled with *Expressionism, notably in the apartment-block in Neklan Street, Prague (1913), where prismatic shapes and inclined planes predominate. He was a leading practitioner of *Cubism in architecture, as his *villa below Vyšehrad Hill, Prague (1912–14), demonstrates. The applied decoration has no right angles, and virtually no surface is parallel to the outlines of the plan. His elimination of *Historicism and the reduction of façades to elementary shapes led him to experiment with *Constructivism in the 1920s.

Leśnikowski (1996); Vegesack (1992)

choir *or* **quire. 1.** Part of a large church appropriated for the singers, with *stalls, situated to the liturgical east of the *nave, and partially screened. **2.** In a cruciform church that part east of the *crossing, including choir, *presbytery, and *sanctuary around the high-altar, wholly or partially screened.

choir-aisle. *Aisle parallel to and adjoining the *nave of the *choir, sometimes joined at right angles or in a semicircle behind the high-altar, thus becoming an *ambulatory or *deambulatory, often with *chapels to the east.

choir-loft. Balcony in the *choir, or the upper part of a *choir-screen or *pulpitum.

choir-rail. Rail, low *balustrade, or *cancelli separating the *choir from the *nave.

choir-screen *or* **-enclosure.** Partition, railing, screen, or wall of any sort separating the *choir from the *choir-aisles, *ambulatory, *retrochoir, and, sometimes, the *nave, although *chancel-screen, *jubé, *Rood-screen, or *pulpitum were formerly preferred to describe the latter case.

choir-stall. Raised seat, one of a series of fixed *stalls in a *choir, backing on to a *choir-screen (where there are *choir-aisles) and on to a *pulpitum where that exists. In cathedrals choir-stalls have richly embellished canopies of *open-work, enhanced with *pinnacles and much ornament. Seats were usually hinged, with brackets (*misericords) underneath.

choir-wall. As *choir-screen, but a *masonry wall between the *choir and *choir-aisles.

Choisy, Auguste (1841–1904). French archaeologist, architectural historian, and engineer. He was Chief Engineer of the Département des Ponts et Chaussées for several years, but his reputation rests on his considerable published output. His thinking was influenced by the work of *Viollet-le-Duc, and his own analyses of form and structure—not the results of chance or taste but representative of the essence of society—were attractive to later architects such as Le *Corbusier and *Perret. His beautifully illustrated *Histoire de l'Architecture* (1899) emphasized the evolution of construction, and it was that which appealed to the following generation. In this huge book he published a brilliant précis of Viollet-le-Duc's and other architectural theories by boiling them down to neat phrases and diagrams. His arguments supported utilitarian views of architecture as developing from practicalities and analytical investigations best seen in the work of engineers. Effectively, he reduced architecture to structure, and claimed that this was more true of society at a given time than any style or art.

Choisy (1873, 1883, 1883*a*, 1899, 1904, 1910)

choragic. Pertaining to the leader (*choragus*) of a Greek chorus, so a choragic monument (such as that of Lysicrates (334 BC) or Thrasyllus (319–279 BC) in Athens) was one created in honour of a *choragus*, and supported a bronze tripod given as a prize.

chord. 1. Straight line joining two points on an arc. **2.** Span of an arch. **3.** Diameter of an *apse or a semicircular arch. **4.** Principal member of a *truss, usually one of a pair extending along the top and bottom. **5.** Lower straight part of a *Belfast* or *bowstring* truss.

Chrismon. The sacred monogram ☧, an arrangement of the first three Greek letters (*Chi, Rho,* and *Iota*) of ΧΡΙΣΤΟΣ, Christ's name, also called *Christogram*, which suggests the Cross as well as *pax* (peace). Another version is ✳, the initial letters of Ιησούς Χριστος (Jesus Christ) and the first two letters of ιχθύς, the Greek for 'fish', a symbol of the Faith and of Baptism. Other sacred symbols associated with Christ are Α (*Alpha*) and Ω (*Omega*)—the Beginning and the End; INRI (*Iesus Nazarenus Rex Iudaeorum* (Jesus of Nazareth King of the Jews), or *In Nobis Regnat Iesus* (Jesus Reigns In Us), or *Igne Natura Renovatur Integra* (Nature is Regenerated by Fire—referring to the Spirit and to

Redemption)); IHS (variously explained as the first two and last Greek capital letters of ΙΗΣΟΥΣ, Christ's first name (IHC, the *Iota*, *Eta*, and *Sigma*, given as Σ, C, or the Latin S), *Iesus Hominum Salvator* (Jesus the Saviour of Man), *In Hoc Signo* (In This Sign [Thou Shalt Conquer]), and *In Hac Salus* (In This [Cross] is Salvation).

Dirsztay (1978); Ferguson (1961); Whone (1990)

Christian, Ewan (1814–95). British architect, he established his own practice in 1842, and was architect and consultant to the Ecclesiastical Commissioners from 1850. His churches tend to be robust and powerful works of the *Gothic Revival, and include St Mark's, Leicester (1869–72). His best-known building is the National Portrait Gallery, London (1890–5), in an Italian *Renaissance style.

Curl (1995); Dixon and Muthesius (1985)

chryselephantine. 1. Literally, made of gold and ivory, it also described *Antique wooden sculptures overlaid with those materials, the draperies being covered with gold and the nude parts of the figure covered with ivory (e.g. the Athena Parthenos of Phidias). *Quatremère de Quincy made a study of chryselephantine sculpture (1814) which was the starting-point for *Hittorff's work on Classical *polychromy. **2.** The term was sparingly applied to the chaste white-and-gilt colour-schemes of early *Greek Revival interiors before polychromy was introduced.

Dinsmoor (1950); Metcalf (1977)

chujjah, chiyjah. In Indian architecture, or the *Hindoo style, a *cornice with a considerable projection.

church. Edifice for public Christian worship, distinguished from a *chapel or *oratory, which in some respects are not public in the wider sense. Church-plans are of two basic types: the *basilican form with clearstoreyed *nave, lean-to *aisles, apsidal east end, and some kind of porch or *narthex; and the centralized plan derived from *Byzantine domed spaces and from circular or polygonal *mausolea associated with important tombs and *martyria. The simplest type of church-plan (e.g. in *Anglo-Saxon times) consisted of a *nave (for the worshippers) and the smaller *chancel (for the clergy) containing the altar and approached through an arch. Larger, more important churches had several *chapels, two or four *transepts, towers, and other structures such as *cloisters, porches, a *baptistery, and a *chapter-house.

Churriguera Family. Three Catalan architect-brothers, **José Benito de Churriguera** (1665–1725), **Joaquín de Churriguera** (1674–1724), and **Alberto de Churriguera** (1676–1750),

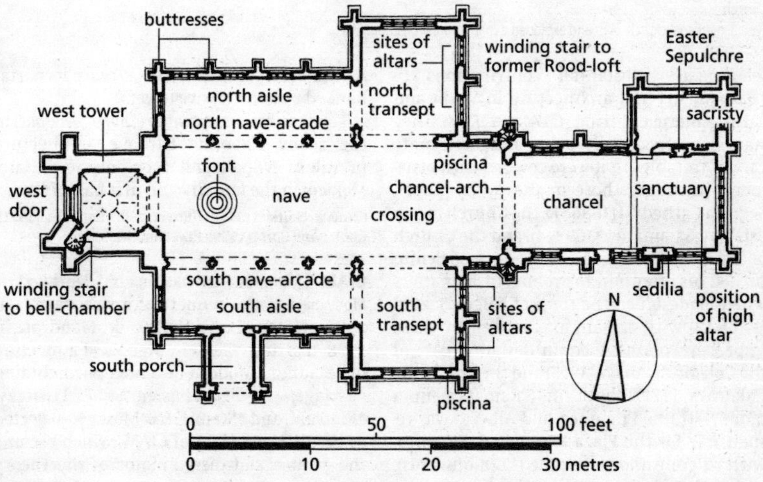

church.
Plan of the Church of St Andrew, Heckington, Lincolnshire (mostly C14).

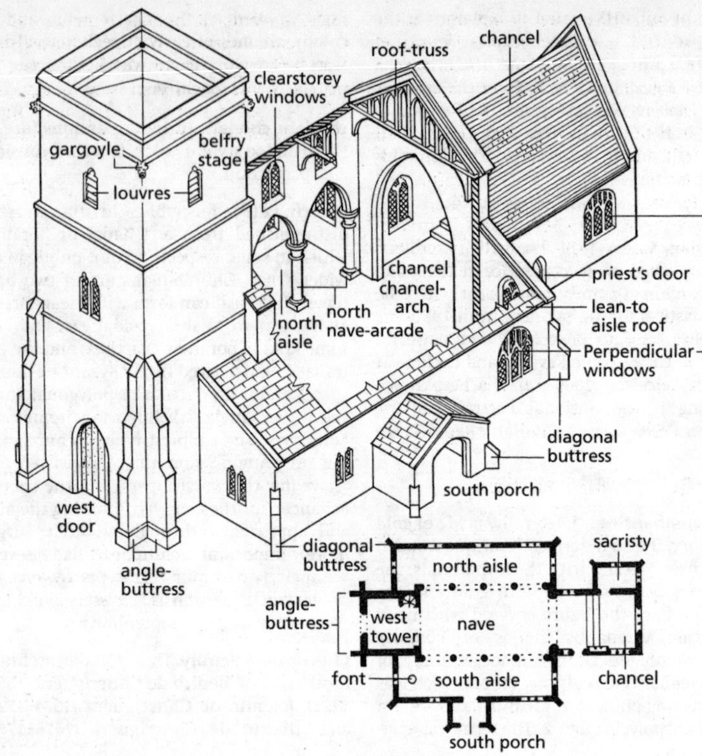

church.
Typical medieval church-plan and exploded axonometric projection. (*JJS*)

who made substantial contributions to *Baroque art and architecture in Spain and Latin America during C17 and C18. They started professionally by creating elaborate carved *retables that were covered with ornament, including those in the Ayala chapel, Segovia Cathedral (1686–7), the Church of San Esteban, Salamanca (1692–4), and the Church of San Salvador, Leganés (1701–4). José Benito turned his attention to architectural matters when he designed the town of Nuevo Baztán (1709–13) with a main axis broken by three impressive plazas. Joaquín designed part of the Colegio de Anaya (1715) and the Colegio de Calatrava (1717)—both in Salamanca—in a more restrained manner, and Alberto was responsible for the Plaza Mayor in Salamanca, with its continuous *arcade (1728 onwards), and the *Rococo church at Orgaz (1738). He designed the main façade of the Church of the Assumption at Rueda (1738–47) with its portal flanked by two massive towers.

The family gave its name (*Churrigueresque*) to the richly elaborate Baroque architecture prevalent in Spain and its colonies (especially Mexico) in the late C17 and first half of C18.

Chueca Goitia (1951); Gutíerrez de Ceballos (1971); Kubler and Soria (1959); Pla Dalmáu (1951)

CIAM (*Congrès Internationaux d'Architecture Moderne*). At the request of a rich patron of architects, Madame Hélène de Mandrot, in 1928, Sigfried *Giedion organized a meeting of leading Modern architects including *Berlage, Le *Corbusier, El *Lissitzky, *Rietveld, and *Stam. Karl *Moser was elected as the first president of CIAM, which became the arbiter and disseminator of the theory and dogma of *International *Modernism until its dissolution in 1959. It promoted

*Functionalism, standardization, and rationalization in the 1930s, when it was dominated first by the Germans, and then by Le Corbusier. In 1933 the *Athens Charter set down the primary functions of urban planning, including rigid functional zones with green belts between, high-rise apartment-blocks for housing, provision for traffic, and space for recreation. *Costa's Brasilia was to be the realization of CIAM's aims in this respect, but rigid adherence to the dogmas of CIAM has been responsible for many problems in planning and architecture since 1945. CIAM held its final meeting in 1959 after which architects such as *Bakema and the *Smithsons attempted to take *Modernism forward on new tracks with *Team X.

Jeanneret-Gris (1973); Lampugnani (1988); Smithson (1968); Smithson and Smithson (1991); Steinmann (1979)

ciborium (*pl.* **ciboria**). Fixed *canopy over a Christian altar, usually supported on four columns. It resembles an inverted cup, or the vessel in which the Eucharist is Reserved, with its domed cover, so the canopy itself has a similar domed top. *Compare* baldacchino.

cill, *or* **sill, sole, sule. 1.** Horizontal timber (usually called a *cill-beam*, *ground-cill*, or *sole-piece* or *-plate*) at the bottom of a *timber-framed wall into which *posts and *studs are tenoned. A *cill-wall* is a low wall of brick or stone supporting the cill-beam. In *timber-framed construction, an *interrupted cill* runs between main posts and is tenoned into them. **2.** Lower horizontal projecting element below an aperture (e.g. doorway or window), to throw water off the *naked of the wall below. **3.** Lower horizontal member of a door- or window-frame.

cima. *See* cyma.

cimbia. 1. *Band or *fillet around a column-shaft. **2.** *Cornice or band formed of fillets.

cimborio. 1. *Lantern set over a roof that permits light to enter. **2.** *Cupola or other device immediately above a high-altar, *choir, etc., or any structure over the *crossing in a Spanish church.

cincture. *Fillet or *list that receives the *apophyge at the extremities of the shaft of a column or *pilaster.

cinerarium (*pl.* **cineraria**). **1.** *Antique *ash-chest or *urn, often of considerable beauty, to hold cremated human remains. Lids of the square box-like types had *horns, so in Neoclassical architecture the *cinerarium lid*, with elements drawn from *sarcophagus-lids, was the model for a type of capping on funerary monuments, gate-piers, and *pedestals.

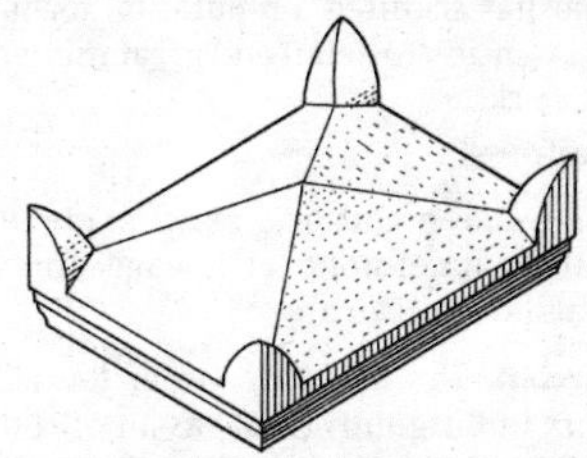

Cinerarium lid capping with cat's-ear horns. (*JJS*)

2. Building to contain ash-chests: a *columbarium.

Toynbee (1971)

Cinquecento. Italian term, literally 'five hundred', applied to C16 *High Renaissance art and architecture, or a C19 revival of it.

cinquefoil. *See* foil.

circus (*pl.* **circuses**). **1.** Oblong roofless enclosure, or *hippodrome, semicircular at one end, having tiered seats for spectators on both sides and round the curved end, and a central barrier (*spina*) on which stood *obelisks, monuments, etc. It was used for Roman chariot-races and other spectacles, so had *carceres* or starting-gates arranged in a curve with its centre a point on the axis of the track the horses would take at the start of the race, thus ensuring each competitor had an equal distance to travel to the centre of the broad route. **2.** Unified group of buildings, with concave façades, fronting a circular open space, as in C18 town-planning schemes by *Wood in Bath and *Nash in London. **3.** Circular road or junction from which streets radiate.

Ciriani, Henri (1936–). Peru-born architect responsible for housing at Marne-la-Vallée (1976–80) and the Cour d'Angle apartments at St-Denis, Paris (1982–3), both large monumental developments owing much to Le *Corbusier.

Emanuel (1994)

Cirici Alomar, Cristián (1941–). Spanish architect, who established Studio PER in

Barcelona with Pep Bonet, Luis Clotet, and Oscar Tusquets in 1964 (dissolved 1992). The firm restored the Casa Thomas by *Domènech i Montaner (1979–80), reconstructed the celebrated pavilion by *Mies van der Rohe (1986), and restored and extended the Zoological Museum (1982), all in Barcelona. Cirici Alomar has acquired a reputation for impeccable attention to detail and great refinement in his work.

Emanuel (1994)

cist. Box-like prehistoric grave made of rectangular slabs of stone set on edge, often concealed under a *cairn.

Cistercian. The monastic Order founded at Cîteaux in Burgundy (1098) as an offshoot of the *Benedictine rules. Cistercian architecture was international, and plans and elevations were severely simple. *Chancels had straight, rather than apsidal, ends, and chapels attached to the *transepts were also squared off. The earliest surviving complete Cistercian church is Fontenay (1139–47), while one of the finest is Pontigny (*c.*1160–1200), both in Burgundy. Impressive ruins of large establishments can be found in England at Byland, Fountains, Kirkstall, and Rievaulx in Yorkshire, and Furness in North Lancashire. Other Cistercian houses include Fossanova (Italy), Heiligenkreuz, and Zwettl (both Austria).

Braunfels (1972); Fergusson (1984); Norton and Park (1986); Stalley (1987)

citadel. Fortress with *bastions (usually four or six) sited within a fortified town, usually on an eminence.

clachan. Small Gaelic settlement of dwellings informally arranged.

cladding. Visible non-structural external finish of a building, such as a thin face of *ashlar, *clap-boarding on a frame, or a *curtain-wall. *Cleading* is rough boarding on a roof.

clair-voie, clairvoyée. Open-work fence, gate, or grille at the end of a vista permitting a view of the landscape beyond. It can occur as a panel in a solid wall.

clap-board. Riven (rather than sawn) horizontal *feather-edged timber boards used for external *cladding, also called *bevel-siding, lap-siding*, or *weather-boarding, although the latter is properly sawn parallel-sided boards.

clapper-bridge. *See* bridge.

Clark, H. Fuller (1869–). *See* Fuller-Clark, Herbert.

Clarke, George (1661–1736). Educated at Oxford, he is mostly remembered as a virtuoso, often consulted by those involved in design and building after the death of Dean *Aldrich. He was involved in the genesis of the Clarendon Building, Oxford, from 1710, and was responsible for revisions to Aldrich's proposals for the south side of Peckwater Quadrangle at Christ Church from 1716: indeed, Christ Church Library, based on Michelangelo's Capitoline Palace, was largely Clarke's design (1717–38). He had a significant role (with *Hawksmoor) in the planning of Queen's College (1710–21), and appears to have provided the designs for the new buildings at Magdalen College, begun by the master-mason *Townesend in 1733. He probably designed and built the Warden's House at All Souls, and proposed a quadrangle that was eventually realized to Hawksmoor's designs (1715–40). Clarke was of great importance as the patron and collaborator of Hawksmoor, and as a collector of architectural drawings: with Aldrich, he can be regarded as an early protagonist of the English *Palladian Revival.

Colvin (1995)

Clarke, George Somers Leigh (1825–82). British architect. A pupil of Charles *Barry, he was an ingenious designer of office buildings on restricted sites. His General Credit and Discount Company Building, Lothbury, London (1866), is an attractive composition in a *Venetian *Gothic style, but he was equally fluent in *Cinquecento, *Elizabethan, *François Ier, and Oriental styles. One of his best houses was Wyfold Court, Oxfordshire (1873–4). His nephew, **George Somers Clarke** (1841–1926), was also an architect: among his works is Holy Trinity Church, Ardington, Berkshire (1887).

Dixon and Muthesius (1985)

Clason, Isak Gustaf (1856–1930). Swedish architect, whose works drew on the *Arts-and-Crafts movement and on *Historicism. His Nordisk Museum, Stockholm (1890–1907), is an essay in the free Northern *Renaissance Revival style. Other works include Östermalms Market Hall (1885–9), the Carpenters' Hall, Stockholm (1915–27), and Mårbacka House, Värmland (1920–2). He influenced *National Romanticism.

Edestrand and Lundberg (1968)

CLASP (Consortium of Local Authorities Special Programme). In 1957 several English local education authorities combined resources to develop a system of prefabricated school-building devised in Nottinghamshire and evolved by *Aslin in Hertfordshire.

Lampugnani (1988)

clasping. *See* buttress.

Classicism. The principles of Greek and Roman art and architecture, so Classical architecture is derived from *Antique precedents that were respected as having some kind of authoritative excellence. Later revivals of Classicism were associated not only with a desire to emulate the magnificence of *Antique architecture, but to establish laws, order, and rules in artistic matters. The first Classical revival is associated with the *Carolingian period (not unconnected with ambitions to re-establish Imperial power), and the next with the Tuscan *proto-*Renaissance of C11, which influenced the early Renaissance, notably the architect *Brunelleschi. From C16 Renaissance architecture and publications had even more of an impact on design than Antique models, for new theoretical writings appeared prompted by the work of *Vitruvius, and there was much published on the canonical nature of the Roman *Orders of architecture. In the late C17 a tendency towards a more severe Classicism was apparent in the works of *Mansart and *Perrault, and in the early C18 a revival of Vitruvian, Antique, and Italian *Renaissance architecture took place, under the aegis of *Burlington, prompted by the works of *Campbell, although the chief models were the works of *Palladio and Inigo *Jones. Burlington and his circle (including *Flitcroft and *Kent) established a veritable tyranny of Taste, with very precise rules about proportions, details, and precedents, called *Palladianism, which was the predominant movement in British architecture for most of C18 from 1714. It was a revolution against the *Baroque of *Wren, *Vanbrugh, and *Hawksmoor. It was no accident that Palladianism (or, more accurately, the second Palladian Revival) coincided with the arrival of the Hanoverian dynasty and the ascendancy of the Whig Oligarchy from 1714, and indeed Burlington's championship of Palladianism may have created a form of architectural continuity from the first Palladian Revival in the reign of King James I and VI (1603–25) after the Baroque interlude of *c.*1660–1714. Some writers have viewed Palladianism as a stylistic cleansing after 'excessive' Baroque exuberance, a notion that was particularly held some 60 years ago, but it should not be forgotten that Baroque architecture was based on Classical precedents, and there were also examples of Antique Roman architecture that displayed similar tendencies to Baroque, especially in C2.

Palladianism has been seen as an early type of *Neoclassicism, but the latter properly started in the mid-C18 when architects and artists began to study original Antique buildings anew rather than derive their Classicism from Renaissance exemplars (as Burlington and Campbell had done). *Piranesi's engravings revealed and exaggerated the grandeur of Roman architecture, while the excavations at *Herculaneum, *Pompeii, and Stabia revealed many aspects of Roman architecture and design that quickly entered into the repertoire of architects. Scholarly archaeology became a primary source for design. Inspired by J. J. *Winckelmann, Greek architecture began to be appreciated, and the tough, rugged, masculine qualities of the powerful *Doric of the temples at *Paestum touched chords in those who thought that architecture, like Mankind, was superior when it was at a stage of primitive simplicity. The search for archaeologically correct motifs from Roman architecture was extended to include Greek exemplars, and so surveys were made of Greek buildings, notably by *Stuart and *Revett, whose *Antiquities of Athens*, one of the prime source-books for the *Greek Revival, began to come out from 1762. Influenced by the writings of *Cordemoy, *Laugier, and *Lodoli, architects sought a cleansed and purified architecture that looked to Antiquity and even to *primitive forms for appropriate precedents, and this led not just to Greece, but to stereometrically pure forms such as the cone, cube, pyramid, and sphere, exploited initially by architects such as *Boullée, *Gilly, and *Ledoux. Simple geometries, clearly expressed, encouraged some extraordinary syntheses of Antique themes, drawing Ancient Egyptian elements into architecture, while decoration became sparse and was sometimes completely avoided. The Orders, if used, were structural, supporting *entablatures or primitive *lintels, and not *engaged. Neoclassicism was severe, even chilly, the antithesis of the Baroque.

By the early C19 Neoclassicism mellowed in favour of a greater opulence, while compositions became more free, drew on the *Picturesque, and had powerful archaeological, emotional, and allusory aspects. Imperial Rome, Greece, and Egypt provided a rich vocabulary for the inventive *Empire style of Napoleonic France and *Regency England. The reaction from 1815 led to a widespread *Greek Revival in Europe and America, producing many distinguished buildings, while in Prussia *Schinkel created an architecture that combined refinement, scholarship, and richness of effect using the simplest of means, though strongly based on Neoclassical principles, including clarity of expression, logic in structural development, truthfulness in the use of materials, and expression of volumes both outside and inside.

In the middle of the century taste again moved towards Renaissance show, expressed in the Paris of the Second Empire (1852–70) and in the Vienna of Kaiser Franz Joseph (1845–1916), followed by a Baroque Revival. In England this was associated with the *Wrenaissance, but in France and the USA with the *Beaux-Arts style, which once more led to a reaction in a C20 Neoclassical Revival in which an architectural language, stripped down to its elements, and free of excess, evolved. This stark Neoclassicism was widespread in the 1920s and 1930s, notably in Scandinavia, France, and the USA, but it was also found in Fascist Italy, Nazi Germany, and the Soviet Union, which gained it opprobrium in spite of the fact that it had many distinguished practitioners in the democracies. In recent times elements of Classicism have reappeared, notably in the work of *Adam, *Bofill, *Botta, *Krier, *Outram, *Rossi, *Stern, *Terry, and others, and in the disparate architecture that has been categorized as anything from *New Classicism to *Post-Modernism.

Curl (1992); Paavilainen (1982); Wiebenson (1969)

clearstor(e)y, clerestor(e)y, overstorey. Upper parts of walls carried on *arcades or *colonnades in the *nave, *choir, or *transepts of a church, rising higher than the *lean-to roofs of the *aisles and pierced with windows to allow light to penetrate.

Clérisseau, Charles-Louis (1721–1820). Paris-born draughtsman, scholar, and architect who studied under *Boffrand, his importance was as a teacher and artist-archaeologist who had a profound effect on the evolution of *Neoclassicism. He instructed James and Robert *Adam in draughtsmanship, and assisted in the survey of Diocletian's Palace at Spalato, later supervising the engraving of the plates for Adam's *Ruins of the Palace of the Emperor Diocletian at Spalatro in Dalmatia* (1764). He also gave lessons in drawing to *Chambers (with whom he quarrelled), and knew or met many important architectural personalities of the time, including *Piranesi and *Erdmannsdorff. More than his relatively few realized works (e.g. the Palais du Gouverneur, Metz, France (1776–89)), his many drawings of *Antique decorative schemes and details, real and imaginary ruins, and designs for buildings in the Ancient style helped to form the language of *Neoclassicism. Later, he produced design-drawings for a 'Roman villa' (unrealized) for the Tsarina Catherine of Russia (1762–96), and also advised *Jefferson on the design of the Virginia State Capitol. He published *Monumens des Nismes* (1778) in Part I of *Antiquités de la France* (1778).

Braham (1980); Clérisseau (1778); Council of Europe (1972); Kalnein and Levey (1972)

Clerk, Sir John (1676–1755). Clerk of Penicuik was a leading figure in learned circles in Edinburgh. With William *Adam he designed a new house for his estate at Mavisbank from 1722, an important precedent for the *Palladian-style *villa in Scotland. In 1727 Clerk visited *Burlington at Chiswick and saw several Palladian houses, after which he published *The Country Seat*, a long poem in which Burlingtonian principles of design were expounded. Indeed, he seems to have become a Caledonian equivalent of Burlington, influencing the design of Arniston, Midlothian (1726–38), and Haddo House, Aberdeenshire (1732–5), both of which were built by William *Adam, and promoting Palladian restraint throughout the land. His son, **Sir James Clerk** (1709–82), was also a cultivated man and an amateur architect, who designed Penicuik House in a Palladian style (1761–9).

Colvin (1995); *DNB* (1917)

Clerk, Simon (*fl.* 1434–d. 1489). English master-mason, who worked on the great Abbey of Bury St Edmunds, Suffolk, from 1445, and later at Eton College (*c.*1453–61). He is known to have been employed at King's College Chapel, Cambridge (1477–85), where he worked with John *Wastell, and was involved in the design of the celebrated fan-*vault. He may have designed the tower of Lavenham Church, Suffolk (*c*.1486–1525), and was probably responsible, with Wastell, for the *naves at Lavenham and at Great St Mary's, Cambridge. He also worked on the church at Saffron Walden, Essex.

Harvey (1987)

clipeus, clypeus. Disc-like ornament resembling a buckler shield fixed to an *architrave or *frieze in Roman architecture.

clochan. Irish circular structure with rings of corbelled stones constructed to form a beehive-shaped building, like a primitive *tholos.

clocher. French bell-tower.

cloisonné. 1. Type of coloured wall-construction consisting of stones of one colour individually framed all round with bricks of another, laid in courses, especially in *Byzantine architecture, such as the Katholikon at Hosios Lukas, Styris (*c*.1020). **2.** Surface formed of coloured enamel panels defined by *fillets.

cloister. Enclosed *court, attached to a monastic or *collegiate church, consisting of a roofed *ambulatory, often (but not always) south of the *nave and west of the *transept, around an open area (*garth*), the walls (*panes*) facing the garth constructed with plain or traceried openings (sometimes glazed or shuttered). It served as a way of communication between different buildings (e.g. *chapter-house, *refectory), and was often equipped with *carrels, seats, and a *lavatorium* in which to perform ablutions before entering the refectory. In *basilican and *Early Christian churches the cloister was at the west end, often with a fountain for washing in the garth, and was called an *atrium, with one side either doubling as or leading to the *narthex. This type of cloister, not intended as a means of communication between conventual buildings, was sometimes used for burial, and in due course became a detached building-type, used as a walled cemetery, such as the *Campo Santo*, Pisa, with memorials set around the walls. *See also* coved vault.

close. 1. *Court, *quad, or yard. **2.** Precinct of a cathedral.

Cluny. By the early part of C12 the great *Benedictine abbey of Cluny in Burgundy (destroyed) had the largest *Romanesque church in Europe, with double *aisles, double *transepts with apsidal *chapels, an *ambulatory with radiating chapels, and a huge barrel-vaulted *nave. This type of plan, devised to permit more altars to be placed in chapels, proved influential. The double transept is known as the *Cluniac transept*.

Conant (1979); Eschapasse (1963); Evans (1972)

cluster. 1. Vertical support, or *cantoned pier (*pilier cantonné*), consisting of a cluster of columns or shafts joined together, *inosculated*, or *engaged with a central pier. **2.** *Annulated, clustered, or compound *pier with *colonnettes or shafts attached to it and each other by means of *bands of a shaft, as distinct (according to some sources) from a *bundle pier. Other sources claim the shafts can be attached or detached, or appear as demi- or engaged shafts against a pier or core: however, the problem arises from the fact that on the Continent the minor shafts were almost always engaged with the central mass, but in English *First Pointed examples they were detached, and often of dark *Purbeck marble, tied together at intervals by bands of a shaft.

cluster-block. Several storeys of apartments grouped around a central service-tower containing stairs, lifts, etc.

Clutton, Henry (1819–93). British architect. A pupil of *Blore (1835–40), he commenced his own practice in 1844. He won first place in the Lille Cathedral competition with William *Burges (his partner from 1851 to 1856). His pupil and assistant was John Francis *Bentley, with whom he built the delightful little Roman Catholic Church of St Francis of Assisi, Notting Hill (1859–60). Clutton was responsible for the heavy *Romanesque *cloister at the Birmingham Oratory (1860).

Dixon and Muthesius (1985); Sheppard (1973)

Clyve, John (*fl*. 1362–92). English mason. He worked at Windsor Castle, Berkshire (1362–3), and was master-mason of Worcester Cathedral Priory (1366–7). He was probably responsible for the tower, north porch, re-casing of the *chapter-house, the east cloister (1386–96), and the south *arcade and *vault of the *nave at Worcester, all in an early *Perpendicular style of the highest quality.

Harvey (1987)

Coade, Mrs Eleanor (1733–1821). Manufacturer and marketer of a type of fine, hard, water-resistant, artificial stone known as *Coade Stone*, made in Lambeth from 1769. Consisting of China clay, sand, and crushed material that had already been fired, it was used for architectural ornaments and components such as *capitals, keystones, and even funerary monuments. The product was also called *Lithodipyra*, meaning twice-fired stone, and its stability during firing enabled the finished size of an artefact to be accurately estimated during modelling.

DNB (1993); Kelly (1990)

Coates, Wells Wintemute (1895–1958). Tokyo-born son of a Canadian missionary, he studied arts, science, and engineering in Canada, and moved to London in 1920. From 1927 he worked on many aspects of design, and was influenced by the work of Le *Corbusier and others. In 1931 he and Jack Pritchard of the Venesta Plywood Company formed the Isokon Company, which was to apply modern design to houses, flats, furniture, and fittings. The Lawn Road flats, Hampstead (1932–4), was a pioneering development of 'minimum dwellings' for tenants who desired few possessions or fittings: among early inhabitants were *Breuer and *Gropius. Wells Coates was one of the founders of the *MARS Group, and was in the vanguard of *International *Modernism in England in the 1930s.

Cantacuzino (1978); Emanuel (1980); Jervis (1984)

cob. Composition containing clay, gravel, sand, straw, and water, thoroughly mixed until it is consistent and plastic, and applied in layers (without *formwork) to make walls, then finished with a roof and several coats of lime-wash. Commonly found in south-west England, it offered a cheap way of building, and, provided it was protected from the rain, was stable. *Compare* *adobe or *pisé-de-terre.

Cockerell, Charles Robert (1788–1863). One of the most gifted and scholarly architects working in England within the Classical tradition in C19, his work was at once bold yet fastidious, thoroughly based on archaeologically proven precedents yet free from dull pedantry, and full of refinements yet achieving a noble monumentality. Born in London, he was the son of S. P. *Cockerell, with whom he trained before moving to Robert *Smirke's office in 1809. He travelled with John *Foster to Athens, where they met the German archaeologists *Haller and Linckh, and together they discovered the Aegina marbles (now in Munich) in 1811, studied the temple of Apollo Epicurius at Bassae in Arcadia (in particular the *Bassae *Order of *Ionic), and found the Phigaleian marbles. With Haller, Cockerell observed the *entasis on Greek column-*shafts (*see* Allason). In 1811–16 he visited several sites in Asia Minor, the Peloponnesos and the Archipelago, Rome, and Florence before returning to London where he set up his own practice in 1817.

In 1819 he succeeded his father to the Surveyorship of St Paul's Cathedral. Receptive to the work of *Wren, he was an early admirer of the compositions of *Hawksmoor and *Vanbrugh. His designs were an eclectic mix of *Greek Revival, *Renaissance, and *Baroque, with a refinement of detail acquired from his archaeological research. A splendid example of his work is the Ashmolean Museum and Taylorian Institution, Oxford (1841–5), where the Bassae Order is much in evidence but the columns stand forward of the *façade in the manner of a Roman *triumphal arch, while the Italian Renaissance influences are strong, notably in the robust *cornice.

In 1833 Cockerell succeeded *Soane as Architect to the Bank of England. He designed much distinguished work, including the branches of the Bank in Bristol (1844–6) and Liverpool (1844–7), where Greek, Roman, and Renaissance features were confidently and intelligently used. He also designed the University Library, Cambridge (1837–40), where the Bassae Order was again incorporated, in conjunction with a *coffered barrel-*vault. Cockerell completed the interiors of both the Fitzwilliam Museum, Cambridge (1845–7), after *Basevi's death, and St George's Hall, Liverpool (1851–64), after the death of *Elmes.

Cockerell was elected to the Royal Academy in 1829, and became Professor of Architecture there in 1840. Awarded the Gold Medal of the RIBA (1840), he was the Institute's first professional President in 1860, and he was honoured by French and many other European academies. His works included *Antiquities of Athens and other Places of Greece, Sicily, etc.* (1830), a supplementary volume to *Stuart and *Revett's *The Antiquities of Athens*; *The Temple of Jupiter Olympius at Agrigentum* (1830); works on William of *Wykeham's contributions to Winchester Cathedral (1845), on the sculptures at Lincoln Cathedral (1848), on the west front of Wells Cathedral (1851 and 1862), and on colour in *Antique architecture (1859); *The Temples of Jupiter Panhellenius at Aegina and of Apollo Epicurius at Bassae* (1860); and the diary of his travels, published as *Travels in Southern Europe and the Levant 1810–1817* (1903).

Cockerell (1830, 1860); Colvin (1995); *DNB* (1917); Watkin (1974—includes a full bibliography)

Cockerell, Samuel Pepys (1753–1827). English architect. A pupil of Sir Robert *Taylor, he held several important official posts from 1774. On Taylor's death, he became Surveyor to the Foundling and Pulteney Estates in London: he was also Surveyor to the Victualling Office (from 1791), to the East India Company (from 1806), to the See of Canterbury, and to St Paul's Cathedral (1811–19).

Cockerell was responsible for laying out the Bloomsbury Estate for the Governors of the Foundling Hospital, London (from 1790), and developed a large and prosperous practice. His pupils included his son, C. R. *Cockerell, *Latrobe, *Porden, and *Tatham. His architecture was eclectic and varied from work of an advanced French Neoclassical type to the exotic. Tickencote Church, Rutland (1792), incorporating a C12 *chancel, is in a harsh *Romanesque style, while his Sezincote House, Gloucestershire (*c.*1805), is a country-house with exotic *Hindoo details, the first example of that style in England.

Colvin (1995); *DNB* (1917); Summerson (1993)

cocking-piece. *See* sprocket.

Coducci *or* **Codussi, Mauro** (*c.*1440–1504). Born at Lenna, near Bergamo, he was the greatest *Quattrocento architect working in Venice from *c.*1469. An inventive technician, he knew the works of *Alberti, clearly revered Venetian *Byzantine architecture, and was largely responsible for introducing a style that was a synthesis of *Renaissance and earlier forms. His San Michele in Isola (1469–78), was the first Renaissance church in Venice, with a *façade influenced by Alberti's San Francesco, Rimini, but with a crowning semicircular *pediment with *volutes and flanking segmental *gables concealing the *aisle roofs. He completed (1480–1500) San Zaccaria, Venice, a church built from 1458 to designs by Antonio Gambella (d. 1481), with a façade topped by paired columns and a huge ornate semicircular *pediment again flanked by volutes. Coducci seems to have been fascinated by the Byzantine *quincunx plan (found at San Marco), and employed it with variations at Santa Maria Formosa (1492–1504), and San Giovanni Crisostomo (1497–1504).

Coducci was probably responsible for the Palazzo Corner-Spinelli (*c.*1493) and Palazzo Véndramin-Calergi (*c.*1500–9), although the latter is said to have been begun by Pietro *Lombardo. Véndramin-Calergi was prototypical of the grander secular architecture of Venice, with a façade of three superimposed *Orders and an array of *Venetian arches. Coducci was the architect of the spectacular double staircase with smooth barrel-*vaults, flights, and domed landings in the Scuola di San Giovanni Evangelista (1498–1504), the *campanile of San Pietro di Castello (1482–8), the great staircase (destroyed) and completion of the façade of the Scuola Grande di San Marco (the crowning storey of semicircular gables), and (probably) of the Torre dell'Orolozio (1496–9), which closes the vista in the Piazzetta San Marco.

Howard (1980); Lieberman (1982); McAndrew (1980); Puppi and Puppi (1977)

coffer. 1. *Caisson or *lacuna, i.e. deep panel sunk in a ceiling, dome, *soffit, or *vault, often decorated in the centre with a stylized flower or similar embellishment, as on the undersides of *Composite and *Corinthian *cornices. A ceiling, etc., with coffers is said to be *coffered*, and *coffering* is an arrangement of coffers. **2.** Cavity in a thick wall, *pier, etc., filled with *rubble and other material, often box-like compartments formed by the facing-stones and cross- or bonding-stones.

coffer-dam. Watertight enclosure constructed of two rows of *piles with clay packed between them used when constructing a bridge-pier, etc., in water.

cogging. Course of projecting bricks laid diagonally to give a saw-like effect in a *cornice or *string-course as a variant on *toothing* (*see* tooth).

Coia, Jack (Giacomo) Antonio (1898–1981). Wolverhampton-born architect of Italian descent, he studied in Glasgow, became the senior partner of Gillespie, Kidd, & Coia (which evolved from *Salmon's office), and carried out several commissions for the Roman Catholic Church. Among the firm's best works were St Anne's, Whitevale Street, Glasgow (completed before 1939), St Paul's, Glenrothes, Fife (1950s), St Bride's, East

Kilbride, and St Peter's College, Cardross (1960s).

DNB (1990); Rogerson (1986)

coign. *See* quoin.

Coignet, François (1814–88). French pioneer of *reinforced-concrete construction, who patented a system of iron tension-rods used to strengthen *concrete in 1856, and later (1863) designed the structural skeleton for the new church of Le Vésinet, Yvelines.

Cruickshank (1996)

coin. 1. Disc used in a series of overlapping coin-like forms, resembling *guilloche, set in horizontal or vertical strips called *coin-mouldings* or *money-patterns*. **2.** *Quoin.

coin-moulding

Coke, Humphrey (*fl.* 1496–d. 1531). English master-carpenter. He worked on the *cloisters at Eton College (1510–11), and on Corpus Christi College, Oxford (1514–18): he seems, with William *Vertue, to have drawn up the plans from which the college was built. He was one of the masters of the works at Cardinal (later Christ Church) College, Oxford, from 1525, where he designed the roof of the Great Hall, the last and one of the finest works of medieval carpentry. There is no doubt that his skills included architectural expertise.

Harvey (1987)

Cola da Caprarola *or* **di Matteucci** (*fl.* 1499–1519). Italian architect. He may have been responsible for the design of the early centralized church of Santa Maria della Consolazione at Todi (*c.*1508), although *Leonardo da Vinci and *Bramante may have been involved.

Heydenreich and Lotz (1974); Pedretti (1985)

colarin, colarino. *See* hypotrachelion.

Colchester, William (*fl.* 1385–d. 1420). English mason. He worked at Southampton Castle (1385–8) before becoming chief mason at Westminster Abbey in 1400, where he worked on the *nave. In 1407 he was appointed to rebuild the fallen *belfry at York *Minster, and remained in charge of the works there until 1419. In 1418 he was appointed King's master-mason at Westminster Palace and the Tower of London. His most notable works are the stone screens at the entrance to the *choir-*aisles, the *buttresses at the eastern *piers of the tower, and the stone altar-*screen, all in York Minster.

Harvey (1987)

Cole, Sir Henry (1808–82). *See* Albert, Prince.

Cole, John (*fl.* 1501–4). English master-mason. He built the elegant *spire at the church in Louth, Lincolnshire (1501–4), and, with *Scune, carried out works there and at Ripon *Minster, Yorkshire.

Harvey (1987)

collar. Transverse horizontal straight, cambered, or cranked timber connecting pairs of *cruck-blades or *rafters in a position above their feet and below the apex of the roof, also called a *collar-beam*, *span-beam*, *spar-piece*, *top-beam*, or *wind-beam*, thus a *collar-beam roof* or *collar-roof* has collars used in its construction. A *collar-* or *arch-brace* is a structural timber to stiffen a roof-*truss. An *extended collar* extends beyond its principal to a gable-wall in roofs with large *gables, often with the lower part of the principal omitted. A *collar-plate*, *collar-purlin*, or *crown-plate* is a horizontal timber *plate resting on collars to tie trusses together, set above a *crown-*post.

collarino. *See* hypotrachelion.

Collcutt, Thomas Edward (1840–1924). Oxford-born English architect who worked in *Street's office before establishing his own London practice in 1869. Collcutt's work was in a free *Renaissance style, of which the *façades of the Royal English Opera House (later Palace Theatre), Cambridge Circus, London (1889), and the Imperial Institute, London (1887–93, demolished except for the handsome tower), were the best examples. He also worked in a relaxed *Arts-and-Crafts style, designing houses at Totteridge, Hertfordshire (1904), and the library, tuck-shop, and Murray Scriptorium at Mill Hill School, London (of the same period). From 1906 he was in partnership with Stanley Hinge Hamp (1877–1968), with whom he designed parts of the Savoy Hotel, London, in a simplified *Renaissance manner much influenced by American precedents.

Dixon and Muthesius (1985); Girouard (1977); Gray (1985); Service (1975, 1977)

Collegiate church. Church endowed for a body corporate, or chapter, of dean and canons, attached to it.

Collegiate Gothic. Secular *Gothic, e.g. that of Oxford and Cambridge colleges, as revived in C19 educational and other institutional foundations, especially *Tudor Gothic.

colombier. *Dovecote or *columbarium.

colonia. Roman farm or farmhouse, also called *colonica*.

Colonia Family. Juan de Colonia (*c*.1410–81), as his name suggests, came from Cologne (he is also known as Hans of Cologne): he settled in Burgos in Spain, where his family was associated with the building of the Cathedral from *c*.1440 to *c*.1540. He built the *spires of the western towers (1442–58), which are of the German *tracery type, and La Cartuja de Miraflores, near Burgos (from 1441). Juan's sculptor-architect son, **Simón** (d. *c*.1511), succeeded his father at Burgos Cathedral in 1481, and designed the spectacular *Plateresque or *Isabellino late-*Gothic Capilla del Condestable (1482–94), with its huge *escutcheons and eight-pointed star-*vault with tracery infill similar to the western spires of the Cathedral. Simón was also responsible for the elaborate *façade of San Pablo, Valladolid (1486–1504), an early example of a church-front designed to look like a *reredos (a type which became common in Spain and in Latin America), and in 1497 was appointed master-mason of Seville Cathedral. His son, **Francisco** (d. *c*.1542) worked with Simón on the decorations of the San Pablo façade, and designed and made the Gothic *retable of San Nicolás, Burgos, (*c*.1503–5), where there are early *Renaissance motifs. Francisco (who succeeded his father as master-mason in 1511) worked with Juan de Vallejo on the *crossing-tower (Gothic) from 1540 and himself made the Puerta de la Pellejería (early Renaissance, 1516), both at Burgos Cathedral. He also worked with Juan de *Álava at the Cathedrals of Plasencia and Salamanca.

Chueca Goitia (1953, 1965); Dezzi Bardeschi (1965); Kubler and Soria (1959)

Colonial. Applied to styles of architecture evolved from that of the motherland in a colony. *American Colonial* is a modification of the English *Georgian or *Queen Anne styles, of particular interest because very often *pattern-book designs were re-interpreted for *timber-framed structures, or otherwise altered, often by very subtle means. Although originally associated with the original thirteen British colonies in America, the essentials of the style were often revived well into C20 all over the USA. American *Colonial Revival* was a late-C19 and C20 variation on Colonial design pioneered by *Peabody & Stearns, later widely employed elsewhere, e.g. by *Lutyens at Hampstead *Garden-Suburb, London (designed 1908–10), and by Louis de *Soissons (from the 1920s) at Welwyn *Garden City, Hertfordshire. *Dutch Colonial* in South Africa and *Spanish Colonial* in Latin America also evolved as separate styles from those of The Netherlands and Spain, and also enjoyed late-C19 and early C20 revivals.

colonial siding. Wide *weather-boarding of pieces of timber the same thickness (unlike *clap-boarding), square-edged, and fixed with each board overlapping that below, often with a roll-moulding along the bottom edge of each board.

Colonna, Fra Francesco (1433–1527). Venetian cleric and author. His *Hypnerotomachia Polifili*, written in 1467 and published by Aldus Manutius (1450–1515) in Venice in 1499, was a work of imagination, but it contains descriptions of *hieroglyphs and many buildings of Classical *Antiquity, clearly drawing on Antique literature (including *Vitruvius) and on contemporary *Renaissance architectural concerns. Manutius's celebrated edition contained fanciful woodcut illustrations that were very influential for long afterwards. *Bernini's elephant carrying an *obelisk and the common theme of an obelisk on top of a *pyramid are but two of the images that recur after 1499. *Hypnerotomachia* is regarded as the first Italian architectural treatise.

Curl (1994); Jervis (1984); Pevsner (1968)

colonnade. Series of columns in a straight line supporting an *entablature: when standing before a building, supports a roof, and serves as a porch, it is a *portico; and if it is carried around three or four sides of a building exterior or round a *court or garden it is a *peristyle. A colonnade is defined in terms of its number of columns (*see* portico) and in terms of spaces between columns (*see* intercolumniation). *See also* temple.

colonnette. Small column, *baluster, or slender circular *shaft, as in an *annulated *pier.

Colossal Order. *See* Giant Order.

Colquhoun & Miller. British firm of architects (Alan Harold Colquhoun (1920–) and John Harmsworth Miller (1930–)), founded in 1961. Among their many works are the Queen's Building, University of East Anglia, Norwich (1993), and the renovation and extension of the Whitechapel Art Gallery, London (1985). Colquhoun retired in 1990, but the firm has continued as John Miller & Partners.

Emanuel (1994)

columbarium (*pl.* **columbaria**). **1.** *Columbier or *dovecote, a substantial building commonly on a circular plan, with *niches (*columbaria*) arranged in tiers around the middle of the structure for nesting doves or pigeons, and an aperture or apertures to allow the birds to fly in and out. **2.** Building or subterranean excavated tomb lined with niches to receive the *cineraria or *urns holding Roman cremated remains, so called from its resemblance to a dovecote, or any C19 or C20 building designed to contain human ashes, as at Père-Lachaise, Paris. **3.** *Putlog-hole, from its resemblance to a niche in a dovecote.

Curl (1993); Toynbee (1971)

columella (*pl.* **columellae**). **1.** *Baluster. **2.** *Colonnette.

column. 1. Detached rather slender vertical structural element, sometimes *monolithic, usually circular (but sometimes square or polygonal) on plan, normally carrying an *entablature or *lintel, but sometimes standing on its own with a statue on top as a monument. In the Classical *Orders, a column consists of a *base, *shaft, and *capital (except for the Greek *Doric *Order, which has no base), and the shaft tapers towards the top in a gentle curve called *entasis. Columns are distinct from *piers and *pillars. **2.** Any relatively slender vertical structural member in compression, supporting a load acting near the direction of its main axis. *See* angular, Antonine, band, barley-sugar, block, carolitic, cluster, colonnade, columniation, Composite, Corinthian, detached, Doric, engaged, grouped, intercolumniation, Ionic, Order, portico, Solomonic, spiral, torso, Trajanic, triumphal, Tuscan, twisted.

columna caelata. Column with shaft, adorned with carving, as in a *carolitic column.

columna cochlis. Large monumental *triumphal column such as the *Antonine or *Trajanic column with an internal spiral staircase and an external *spiral band of continuous sculpture.

columna rostrata (*pl.* **columnae rostratae** *or* **rostral columns**). *Tuscan column on a *pedestal, its *shaft embellished with sculpted prows (*rostra*) of *Antique Roman warships, originally to honour naval victories. The type was revived in C17 and C18.

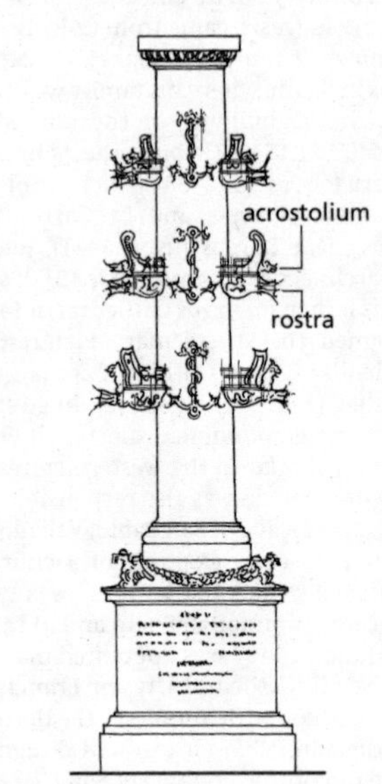

columna rostrata

columna triumphalis. *Triumphal column. As *columna cochlis above.

columnar and trabeated. Type of construction consisting of vertical columns or *posts supporting horizontal *beams or *lintels, as opposed to *arcuated construction.

columniation. Arrangement of columns. *See* intercolumniation, portico, temple.

Colvin, Sir Howard Montagu (1919–). English architectural historian. His meticulous attention to documentary research, rather than a reliance on stylistic attributions, transformed British architectural history. His *Biographical Dictionary of English Architects 1660–1840* (1954), much enlarged as *Biographical Dictionary of British Architects 1600–1840* (1978 and 1995), is the major standard work on British architects of the period. He was general editor and part-author of the *History of the King's Works* (1963–82).

Colvin (1991, 1995)

comb. *See* camp.

Commissioners' churches. Following the Napoleonic Wars, it was feared that England might suffer upheavals similar to those of France, and, faced with irreligion, Nonconformity, and an increasing population (much of it restive and uncivilized), the authorities determined to build Anglican churches, numbers of which (also known as *Waterloo churches*) were erected under the aegis of the Commissioners for Building New Churches appointed under *An Act for Promoting the Building of Additional Churches in Populous Parishes* (58 George III, c. 45), 1818. Most were cheap, utilitarian preaching-boxes, with any architectural pretensions reserved for the west end. Designs were Classical or in a thin, lean, unscholarly *Gothic style, with low-pitched roofs, *galleried interiors, and *Pointed windows set in *bays marked by *buttresses: the last type was known as *Commissioners' Gothic*.

Clarke (1969); Curl (1995); Eastlake (1970)

common ashlar. Hammer- or pick-dressed stone.

common bond. Also *American, English garden-wall*, or *Liverpool bond*, it has four or five courses of stretchers to every one of headers (*see* brick).

common-house. *Calefactory, or heated room in a monastery, also called the *common-room*. Precedent for the university common-room.

common joist. Structural floor-joist spanning from wall to wall.

common rafter. One of a series of *rafters of uniform size regularly spaced along the length of a pitched roof, or placed as intermediates between *principals, with one end attached to the wall-plate and the other to the opposite common rafter at the *ridge. A pair of common rafters is a *couple.

common roof. One consisting of *common rafters only, with or without *purlins, also called *coupled-rafter roof*.

common round. Roll-moulding.

Communion-rail. Altar-rail.

Communion-table. Wooden table in Protestant churches, replacing the stone altar, introduced as a deliberate denial of the doctrine of Transubstantiation.

community architecture. English housing movement involving participation of the users in design and building. The name was probably coined by Charles Knevitt, architectural correspondent of *The Times*, *c.*1975. Walter *Segal pioneered the movement with his system of *timber-framed housing in the 1970s, followed by several instances of rehabilitation of older dwellings as well as new buildings in the 1980s. Christopher *Alexander's arguments for relatively simple labour-intensive housing have been associated with community architecture, as have concepts of public participation in the design process. Ralph *Erskine's Byker housing in Newcastle upon Tyne (1969–80) was built after close consultation with residents. Community architecture was endorsed by the Prince of Wales in the 1980s.

Hackney (1990); Lozano (1991); McKean (1988); Towers (1995); Wates and Knevitt (1987)

compartment. 1. Clearly defined area within a garden, often hedged or walled in. **2.** Room in a building, or an area partitioned off. **3.** Subdivision of a larger division in a building. **4.** *Coffer in a ceiling.

compass-window. *Bay-window.

Comper, Sir John Ninian (1864–1960). Aberdeen-born British architect. Whilst in the office of *Bodley and *Garner (1882–7), he learnt the intricacies and subtleties of late English *Gothic. In partnership with William Bucknall from 1888 to 1905, he designed the exquisite Church of St Cyprian, Clarence Gate, London (1902–3), in which the altar is visible from all parts of the church and the sanctuary is defined using gilded *screens influenced by C14 English prototypes favoured by Bodley. A scholar of *Ecclesiology, Comper revived the 'English' altar with its *riddel-posts at St Wilfrid's Church, Cantley, Yorkshire (1892–4—where he also designed the north *arcade and *aisle, *Rood-screen and loft, *parclose-screens, *reredos, and altar-canopy, all in an archaeologically correct late-Gothic style), and became a prolific designer of and authority on church fittings, furnishings, and, especially, stained glass.

His richest creation is St Mary's, Wellingborough, Northamptonshire (1904–31), in which Classical elements made their appearance, notably in the *ciborium, and the plaster vaulting in the *nave has *pendants. He moved towards giving the altar a new dominance in Anglican church architecture, and was a major influence on the liturgical revival after 1950. One of his last works was the altar and reredos in the Shrine of Our Lady of Walsingham, Norfolk (1959).

Anson (1960); Buckley (1993); Comper (1893, 1897, 1933, 1940, 1950); *DNB* (1971); Symondson (1988)

compluvium. *See* cavaedium.

Composite Order. Grandest of the Roman *Orders, essentially an ornate version of the eight-voluted *Ionic capital known as the *angular capital or *Scamozzi Order under which are added two tiers of *acanthus-leaves. Its *entablature is also very ornate. It bears a resemblance to the *Corinthian Order and is also called the *Compound Order*.

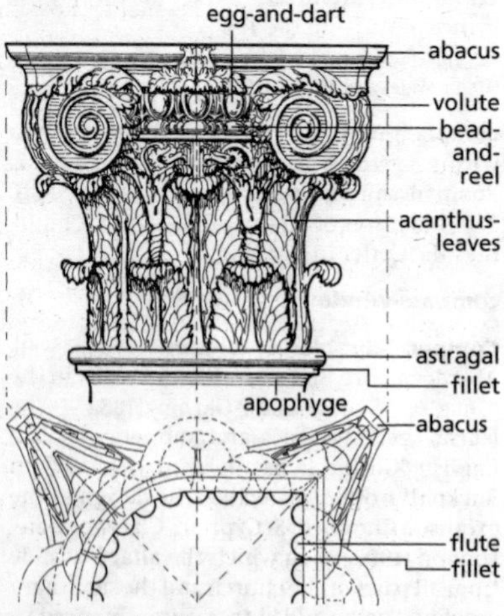

Composite Order. Plan and elevation of circular and square capital of the Order. (*After Langley*)

compound pier. *See* cluster.

computer-aided design. Also CAD or CAM (computer-aided manufacture). From the 1970s computers have been used in design since representations of complicated three-dimensional forms can be easily stored and manipulated. Images can be printed, architectural projections can be produced, and interiors can be explored in virtual reality. Details can be stored for reuse, avoiding the drudgery of repetitive hand-made drawings. To a certain extent the design-process has been changed, but CAD may not be appropriate for all eventualities.

Burger and Gillies (1989); Franke (1985); Jankel and Morton (1984); Lewell (1985); May (1985); Penman (1989); Reynolds (1987)

concatenation. Union by chaining parts together, as with separate architectural elements in a long façade (each with its own roof and separate composition), the fronts being brought forward or recessed, also called *staccato* composition. Concatenated façades were favoured by William *Kent and other *Palladians for purposes of *articulation. *See* additive.

conceit. Agreeable *fabrique in a garden, usually whimsical, such as a bridge not spanning anything but there purely for ornament.

conceptual architecture. Architectural designs that have not been realized are 'conceptual'. Interpretations from the 1960s involved space-defining, simulated images projected into the sky by lasers, and volumes roofed by moving air, with walls of fire and water (e.g. proposals by Yves Klein and Werner Ruhnau). Air-jets instead of structures have been proposed, creating instant forms. Some have held that it is the process that counts in architecture, rather than the final building.

Architectural Design, 45/3 (March 1975), 187–8; *Casabella*, 411 (March 1976), 8–13; *Design Quarterly*, 78, 79 (1970–whole issue)

conch. 1. Quarter-spherical *cupola or dome over an *apse or *niche. **2.** *Pendentive. **3.** Shell motif over a niche or similar.

concrete. Building material made by mixing fragments of hard material (aggregate—usually broken stone) with mortar (fine aggregate—usually sand, water, and a binding-agent—now usually *Portland cement). Historically, concrete was made with lime, sand, and water, with brick-dust, crushed volcanic rock, and other materials added. A type of concrete was used in Roman construction called *opus caementicium, consisting of undressed stones bedded in a mix of lime and *pozzolan, which dried out quickly, so had to be laid in courses. By C1 AD the drying-out process could be slowed, thanks to the evolution of slow-drying mixes, and this facilitated the evolution of huge vaulted structures covering vast spaces. The Romans used types of concrete made of lime, with tufa (porous, light, volcanic rock found around Rome) and other aggregates for these *vaults, often in association with brick or stone reinforcement, and this created an architecture where the inner volumes were more important, perhaps, than the exteriors. Early examples of Roman architecture covered by concrete vaults are the *Domus Aurea* (Golden House) by *Severus, and the enormous *Pantheon in Rome, with its *coffered dome.

Types of concrete were in use for *Byzantine structures but fell from favour until revived in C18, notably in France and England. Concrete was used by *Smirke in the structure of the British Museum, and concrete laid over hollow-brick vaulting was used by Henry *Roberts for fire-proof construction in working-class housing during the 1850s. The discovery of Portland cement made from lime and clay facilitated the development of immensely strong concrete structures as well as the evolution of a scientifically based theory. Strong in compression, concrete is weak in tension, so the weakness has to be eliminated if concrete is to be used in members subjected to tension, such as beams. Reinforcement with metal was experimented with in the early C19, and *Loudon (1832) recorded concrete floors reinforced with interlacing iron bars. Other pioneers include *Coignet, *Monier, and Ward and Hyatt (who published various theoretical works in the USA in the 1870s), but a major advance came when *Hennebique developed concrete reinforced with steel (1892). In the USA advances were made by Ernest L. Ransome (1884–1911) and Albert *Kahn, leading to standardization and the mass-production of building components.

*Baudot's church of St-Jean de Montmartre, Paris (1894–1902), employed steel reinforcement in its brick-and-concrete construction, and *Maillart evolved designs for reinforced-concrete buildings from 1905, developing the theme of unified *pier and *vault known as mushroom slabs. Max *Berg constructed the huge *Jahrhunderthalle* (Century Hall) in Breslau (now Wrocław) of reinforced concrete in 1910–13, and Auguste *Perret began using reinforced concrete almost from the beginning of his career with the Rue Franklin flats, Paris (1903–4). The Royal Liver Building, Liverpool (1908–10), by W. Aubrey Thomas (1859–1934), is an early British example of reinforced-concrete construction on the Hennebique principle, while the same architect's Tower Buildings, near by (1908), expresses the frame more clearly, and is clad in faïence. Reinforced concrete enabled very large *cantilevers to be constructed, but its major advantages were that it was capable of withstanding great compressive *and* tensile loads (as steel can), but with the important advantage of a high degree of fire-resistance. The evolution of complex reinforced-concrete structures was pioneered by *Freyssinet with his bridges and *parabolic vaults. In later times, *Candela and *Nervi further developed reinforced-concrete structures (*see* béton).

Allen (1988); Collins (1959); Davey (1961); Faber and Alsop (1976); McKay (1957); Mainstone (1975)

conditivum, conditorium. Roman sepulchre containing *sarcophagi.

condominium. Large development in which individual units are privately owned, but all owners are bound by certain restrictive covenants. It is usual in major housing schemes, where for aesthetic and social reasons the fabric cannot be altered and communal spaces have to be shared.

Conefroy, Abbé Pierre (1752–1816). French-Canadian Vicar-General for the Montreal region of the Diocese of Quebec. He devised a standardized plan for churches, based on mid-C17 prototypes, in which the apsidal *chancel was narrower than the *nave, and transeptal *chapels were provided. The gabled west front was pierced by a central door, with a smaller door on each side, and single or twin *clochers were provided. Good examples of his work are the Churches of Ste-Marguerite, L'Acadie, Quebec (1800–1), and Ste-Famille, Boucherville (1801). Such conservative (even backward-looking) architecture emphasized cultural and religious identity.

Kalman (1994)

confessio. Place where the body of a Martyr or Confessor is kept, or the *crypt or *shrine under an altar, in which such Relics are placed. By extension, the whole *chapel or church, called *confession*, *confessional*, or *confessionary*.

confessional. Booth, box, or cubicle in which confessions of penitents are heard in a church.

conge. *Echinus or similar moulding (*swelling conge*), or a *cavetto (*hollow conge*).

congé, congee. 1. *Apophyge, scape, or outward concave curves at the top and bottom of a Classical column-*shaft terminating in *fillets. **2.** *Sanitary shoe*, or concave junction between a floor and a wall, used where a right-angled junction would be difficult to clean, as in a toilet.

congelation. *Rustication in the form of icicles, as on *fountains and in *grottoes, also called *frosted*.

Connell, Amyas Douglas (1901–80). New Zealand-born architect. He practised in London from 1929 and entered into partnership with Basil Robert Ward (1902–78) in 1932. From 1933 to 1939 they were in partnership with Colin Anderson Lucas (1906–84), as Connell, Ward, & Lucas, designing a whole series of advanced *International Modern houses in England in the 1930s, much influenced by Le *Corbusier. Connell's most celebrated house was 'High and Over', Amersham, Buckinghamshire (1928), built with a *reinforced-concrete frame on a three-pointed star-shaped plan. 'New Farm', Grayswood, Surrey (1932–3), displayed a series of cubic forms attached to a central circulation area. The firm's later work included the Tarburn House, Temple Gardens, Moor Park, Hertfordshire (1937–8), the Walford House, Frognal, Hampstead (1937), 'Potcraft', Sutton, Surrey (1938), and the Proudman House, Roehampton, London (1938–9).

Emanuel (1994); Sharp (1967*a*)

conoid. Form resembling a cone, as in the springing of a *Gothic *vault where the ribs branch out.

consecration cross. *See* cross.

conservation. Retention of existing buildings or groups of buildings, landscapes, etc., taking care not to alter or destroy character or detail, even though repairs or changes may be necessary. Sensitive conservation (pioneered by *Morris and others connected with the *Arts-and-Crafts movement) is concerned to preserve as much original fabric as possible, and make overt what is new and what is old. Conservation does not necessarily mean preservation: it can involve considerable intervention, even much new building, but the key to success is in respecting existing character, and even enhancing it. A *conservation area* is one designated as of special architectural or historic interest, where all changes should enhance, rather than detract from, its character.

Huxtable (1970, 1986, 1986*a*)

conservative wall. Garden-wall against which glass structures are built to enable plants to be grown.

conservatory. 1. Grander and more ornamental version of a glasshouse or greenhouse used for conserving plants, either a detached structure or one joined to a dwelling, heated and kept humid. Early conservatories were of conventional construction, with large windows, but the finest examples date from C19 when iron-and-glass construction evolved in terms of invention and elegance. While there were early iron-and-glass conservatories in C18, including that at Hohenheim, near Stuttgart, J. C. *Loudon invented a curved bendable sash-bar of iron that made further developments possible, including the Great Stove at Chatsworth (1836–40) by *Burton and *Paxton. **2.** Public building devoted to the cultivation of, and instruction in, any branch of art or science, especially music.

Hix (1996); Kohlmaier and Sartory (1986); Koppelkamm (1981); Loudon (1834); Woods and Warren (1988)

console. Type of Classical bracket or *corbel with parallel sides, usually an *ogee curve terminating in a *volute at the top and bottom surmounted by a horizontal slab, often moulded, fixed upright to a wall with the greater projection at the top. Called *ancon, *crossette, parotis, shoulder, or truss, it is commonly found e.g. on each side of the top of a door- or window-*architrave, supporting the *cornice. In a horizontal position, the curved part downwards and the bigger scroll at the end fixed to a wall, it appears to carry an element, e.g. a *balcony, and thus suggests a *cantilevered form. Horizontal consoles fixed to the *soffits of a building's crowning cornice and appearing to support it are called *modillions. Wedge-shaped (sides not parallel) consoles or *key-stones are called *ancones*.

Constructivism. Anti-aesthetic, anti-art, supposedly pro-technology (in that it favoured the apparently logical use of man-made industrial materials and processes such as weld-

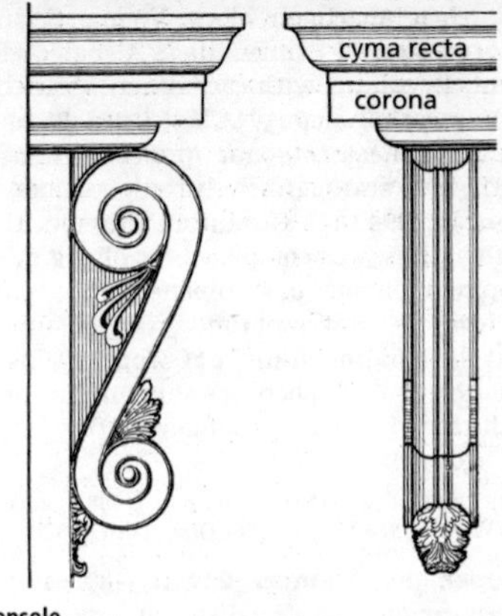

console

ing). Left-wing movement originating in the USSR from *c.*1920, later promoted in the West, notably at the *Bauhaus. Although its scope varied, and was never very clearly defined, many Constructivists insisted that architecture was simply the means of expressing a structure made using industrial processes and machine-made parts, with no hint of craftsmanship, and tended to stress utilitarian aspects, especially the function of elements of the building. The best-known Russian Constructivist projects were V. *Tatlin's huge monument to the Third International (1920), a distorted *frustum in the form of a diminishing spiral; *Melnikov's Rusakov Club, Moscow (1927–8), with *cantilevered *concrete lecture-halls expressed on the main elevation (and yet some commentators would deny that Melnikov was a Constructivist at all, seeing him more as a 'Productivist' (anti-aesthetic technician) concerned with timber structures, as in his pavilions for the Moscow Exhibition of 1923 and the Paris Exposition of 1924–5); and A. *Vesnin's project for the *Leningradskaya Pravda* (Leningrad's Truth) building in Moscow (1923), with advertising signs, clocks, loudspeakers, lifts, and a searchlight all incorporated and expressed as integral elements of the design. One of the key figures was El *Lissitzky, who was the link between Russian Constructivism and Western Europeans such as *Duiker, *Gropius, *Meyer, and *Stam. The last worked on *Brinkman and van der Vlugt's Van Nelle factory in Rotterdam, held by some to be the best example of Constructivism in the West, mostly because of its expression of functional and industrial elements. The movement gave rise to many sub-theories and factions, some more extreme than others, and Constructivist themes have re-emerged in recent years in the work of Richard *Rogers, notably the Centre Pompidou, Paris (1972–7), and Lloyd's Building in London. Russian Constructivism's anti-environmentalist aspects, jagged overlapping diagonal forms, expression of mechanical elements (such as services, lifts, etc.), have proved to be potent precedents for *High Tech architecture, and, more recently, for the followers of *Deconstructivism, notably *Hadid, *Koolhaas, and *Libeskind.

Johnson and Wigley (1988); Khan-Magomedov (1975, 1986, 1987); Kopp (1970); Lampugnani (1988); Lissitzky (1970, 1981); Lissitzky-Küppers (1980); Lodder (1983); Shvidkovsky (1970)

Contant d'Ivry, Pierre (1698–1777). Parisian architect, who was the first to develop *Cordemoy's theories. His Churches of St-Vasnon at Condé-sur-L'Escaut (1751) and St-Vaast at Arras (1775–7—completed 1833) had continuous rows of columns carrying *entablatures from which sprang *vaults, while his Abbaye Royale de Penthémont (104–6 Rue de Grenelle, Paris) of 1747–56 also demonstrates his interest in refined constructional and vaulting techniques. His grand staircase at the Palais Royal, Paris (1756–70), is one of the most elegant of its period, and his only partially executed design for the Madeleine, Paris (1761), exploited columns and entablatures carrying vaults in a manner similar to that adopted by *Soufflot at Ste-Geneviève.

Contant d'Ivry (1769); Kretzschmar (1981); Middleton and Watkin (1987)

Contemporary Style. A style of design prevalent in Britain from 1945 to *c.*1956. In architecture it included the type of light structures of the 1951 *Festival of Britain, and many of that Exhibition's design motifs were adopted as clichés of the period. It evolved from late-1930s styling and the post-war technologies of laminates and alloys.

Banham and Hillier (1976); Sissons and French (1964)

contextual architecture. Also called *Contextualism*, the term suggests an architecture that responds to its surroundings by respecting what is already there, unlike *Constructivism or *Deconstructivism which deliberately work against established geometries and fabric.

Ray (1980); Tugnutt and Robertson (1987)

contractura. *Diminution of a column-shaft from top to bottom, that is tapered, without *entasis, and wider at the top, as in Ancient Crete.

Cook, Peter Frederick Chester (1936–). *See* Archigram.

Cooley, Thomas (*c.*1740–84). English architect. He gained his early professional experience in Robert *Mylne's office, and won the competition to design the Royal Exchange (now City Hall), Dublin (1769–79), which encouraged him to move to the Irish capital. Appointed Clerk and Inspector of Civil Buildings in Dublin in 1775, he was the most important figure in the profession for a few years, and was significant in the creation of Irish *Neoclassicism. He designed Caledon House, Co. Tyrone (1779), later (1812) extended by *Nash, and, with his assistant Francis *Johnston, designed several churches in the Archdiocese of Armagh for Richard Robinson (1709–94), Archbishop of Armagh from 1765, including the exquisite Primate's Chapel, Armagh (1785). He was involved in the design of several country-houses, and was responsible for the Public Offices (1776–84), the *Sublime (now demolished), Newgate Gaol (1775–81), and early plans for the Four Courts (all in Dublin). By 1781 Cooley was overshadowed by *Gandon, who was to build the Four Courts (1786–1802) and many other important public buildings in Dublin.

Craig (1969, 1982)

Coop Himmelblau. Viennese Utopian and activist group of architects, associated with *Deconstructivism. Founded by Rainer Maria Holzer, Wolf D. Prix (1942–), and Helmut Swiczinsky (1944–) in 1968 (Holzer left in 1971), it advocates an exaggeration of tensions, evoking terror, threats, and damage in aggressive designs, and (influenced by *Haus-Rucker-Co and *Hollein), was, in its beginnings, interested in *pneumatic space-structures. Some architectural projects were conceived as bursting into flames, as in *Architektur muss Brennen* (Architecture must Burn—1980). Coop Himmelblau's rooftop remodelling, 6 Falkestrasse, Vienna (1983–8), a renovation of the upper part of a traditional apartment-block, with seemingly unstable wing-like skeletal elements, has been influential. Their apartment-block, Vienna (1986), incorporated 50 living-units in 4 angled elements in conflict with each other, while the Funderwork 3 factory, St Veit (1988–9), and Ronacher-Theater, Vienna (project designed 1987), were also aggressively restless compositions. In 1994 their Groningen Museum, The Netherlands, was completed, involving overlapping montages of steel panel-components that will rust away over time. Prix has claimed that the building fulfils Le *Corbusier's insistence on a parallel between shipbuilding and architecture. It was an example of *computer-aided design.

Coop Himmelblau (1983); Hahn *et al.* (1988); Johnson and Wigley (1988); Klotz (1986); Offermann (1989)

Cooper, Sir Thomas Edwin (1873–1942). Scarborough-born English architect. He entered into partnership with Samuel Bridgman Russell (1864–1955), and together they designed the Guildhall and Law Courts, Hull (1903–14), the Royal Grammar School, Newcastle upon Tyne (1904), and other fine *Edwardian buildings. The partnership ended in 1912, and Cooper went on to design St Marylebone Town Hall and Library, Marylebone Road, London (1914–39); the imposing headquarters of the Port of London Authority, Trinity Square, London (1912–22); and the offices of Lloyd's, Leadenhall Street (1925–8—destroyed), among other buildings. His work was essentially Classical, and sometimes powerfully *Baroque.

DNB (1959); Gray (1985)

cop. Merlon. *See* battlement.

cope, coping. Top course (*capping*) of masonry, brick, etc., usually sloping, of a *chimney, *gable, parapet, or wall, formed of *cap-stones, *copstones*, *copestones*, or *coping-stones* to throw off water. *Feather-edged* coping is thinner on one side than on the other, and *saddle-back* coping has a triangular section with a ridge.

coquillage. Representation of shell-forms in decorative carving, often found at the heads of *niches, or as an important part of *rocaille design.

cora (*pl.* **corae**). Any column in the form of a young woman, as in the *prostasis* of the Erechtheion, Athens, also known as *caryatid.

Corazzi, Antonio (1792–1877). Italian-born, the leading C19 architect in Warsaw. He

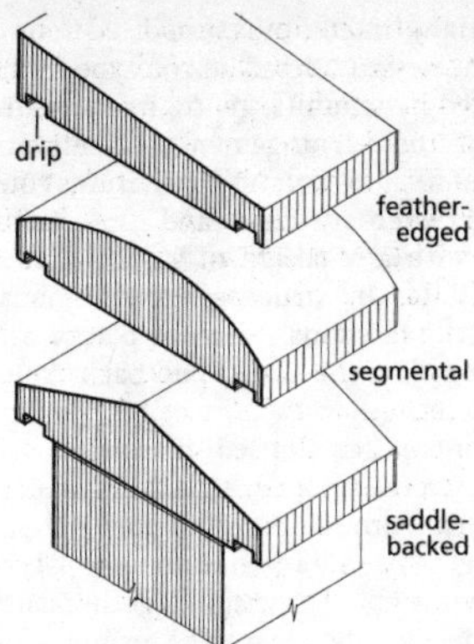

cope

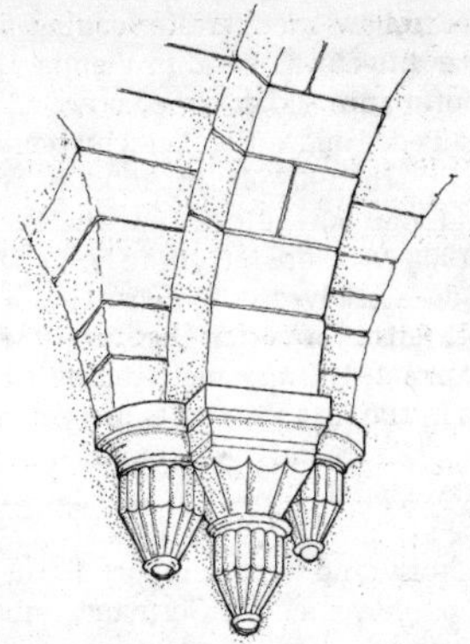

corbel. C12 Romanesque type, Kirkstall Abbey Leeds, Yorkshire. (*After Parker*)

was responsible for many distinguished *Neoclassical buildings, including the Grand Theatre (1826–33), the Stock Exchange, now Polish Bank (1828–30), the Staszic Palace (1820–3), and the County Headquarters at Radom (1822–7).

Lorentz and Rottermund (1984)

corbeil, corbeille. 1. Basket-like architectural member containing flowers and fruit, often in relief or placed on *pedestals as terminal ornaments. **2.** Capital in the form of a basket over the heads of *canephorae* or *corae*, varying in size and type. **3.** *Campana or calathus.

corbel. Projection from the face of a wall, consisting of a *block built into the wall, supporting any superincumbent load such as an arch, beam, parapet, *truss, etc., so essentially a *cantilever. *Corbelling* consists of successive courses of corbels forming a pseudo-*vault or supporting an element projecting over the wall below, such as a *tourelle. *See* chequer-set.

corbel-arch. Pseudo-arch formed of successive *corbels, essentially *cantilevers, anchored back, each projecting over the corbel below.

corbel-course. Continuous uninterrupted course of *corbels forming a projection or projecting moulding.

corbel-gable. Incorrect term for a *crow-stepped *gable.

corbel-piece. *Bolster-work, suggesting a stone projecting face, as in *rustication.

corbel-ring. Old term for *band of a shaft or a *shaft-ring.

corbel-table. Row of *corbels, often with carved heads on them, set at intervals, sometimes carrying connecting arches (*Lombardy frieze), but more often simply supporting a projecting wall, especially a *battlement or parapet.

corbel-vault. *Vault built using the same technique as in a *corbel-arch.

Corbie, Pierre de (*fl.* 1215–50). French master-mason. He was associated with *Villard de Honnecourt in preparing a design for the *choir of Rheims Cathedral (1215), and also worked with him on the building of Cambrai Cathedral (1230–43).

Papworth (1852); Sturgis *et al.* (1901–2)

corbie-step. *See* crow-steps.

Corbusier, Le. Pseudonym from 1920 of the Swiss-born French architect **Charles-Édouard Jeanneret-Gris** (1887–1965), who was probably the most influential figure in C20 architecture. He built (with René Chapallaz) his first house, the Villa Fallet, La Chaux-de-Fonds, Switzerland (1906–7), strongly influenced by the *Arts-and-Crafts movement and by *vernacular architecture, before setting off on one of a series of educational journeys. In 1907 his visit to Italy took him to the medieval *Carthusian monastery (*Certosa di Val d'Ema) which greatly impressed him as an example of how repetitive living-quarters could be organized within one monumental composition. In the winter of 1907–8 he appears to have met certain leading figures of the architectural world in Vienna, including *Hoffmann, and designed more villas for La Chaux-de-Fonds, the Jaquemet and the Stotzer (both 1907–8). In 1908 he visited England and worked briefly with *Perret in Paris (1908–9) before returning home. In 1910 he made a study-visit to Germany, worked in *Behrens's office in Berlin (November 1910–April 1911), and met leading German figures in the Arts-and-Crafts movement and in the *Deutscher Werkbund, including *Muthesius and *Tessenow. At that time he absorbed the works of *Viollet-le-Duc, *Sitte, and *Choisy, and wrote a report on the decorative art movement in Germany, published in 1912, in which his admiration for German organization was expressed. Also in 1911 he travelled down the Danube to Istanbul, returning through Greece and Italy, which profoundly affected his perceptions, and made him more aware of the power of the primitive, the rugged, and the ruined, while awakening his appreciation of the qualities of the southern light. At the end of 1911 he returned to Switzerland, was involved in teaching and in the Swiss equivalent of the Werkbund, but, more especially, designed several buildings, including the Villas Jeanneret (1911–12), Favre-Jacot (1912–13), and Schwob (1916–17). This last was one of his first *reinforced-concrete houses, clearly influenced by Perret and Behrens in its *stripped Neoclassical form: it gained him recognition, and was published. During this period at La Chaux-de-Fonds he evolved the low-cost Maison

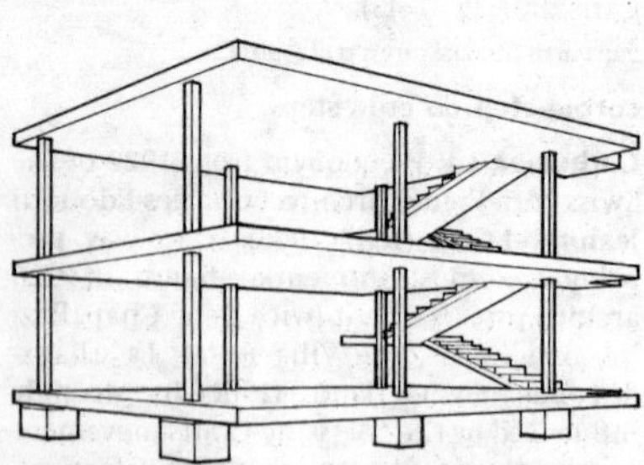

Dom-Ino skeleton showing floor-slabs supported on columns. (*After Le Corbusier*)

Dom-Ino of 1914–15, the name of which evolved from the Latin *domus* (house) and the *innovative* reinforced-concrete column-grid that suggested the patterns of a *domino*-piece. Essentially the columns supported floor-slabs, and the design offered a prototype for industrialized living-units, giving freedom in matters of room-arrangement and elevational treatment: non-structural partitions could be placed where desired, and the elevations filled with any design of glazing and solid uninhibited by structural requirements because the columns were not placed around the edges of the slabs, but back from the perimeters.

Jeanneret-Gris settled in Paris in 1916, where he developed his skills as a self-publicist. Through Perret he met the painter Amedée *Ozenfant, and, having absorbed *Cubism and *Futurism, together they invented *Purism, where the primacy of the objects was insisted upon, disposed on the canvas using a proportioning device based on the *Golden Section, and depicted by means of a limited range of pure colours. Purism was promulgated in the manifesto *Après le Cubisme* (1918) and *L'Esprit Nouveau* (1920–5), a journal edited by Jeanneret-Gris and Ozenfant which also contained ideas on architecture, published under the pseudonym 'Le Corbusier': those contributions were collected in *Vers une architecture* (1923), translated as *Towards a New Architecture* (1927), and became influential texts. Their heady brew of the latest technology, messianic slogans proclaiming the supposed moral and hygienic virtues of the architectural language, and claims that the ideas derived from Antiquity found many devotees. In his writings Le Corbusier defined architecture as a play of masses brought together in light, and advocated that buildings should be as practically constructed as a modern machine (an idea perhaps derived from *Alberti), with rational planning, and capable of being erected using mass-produced components.

Another study-visit to Italy in 1922 was followed by the exhibition of his *Maison Citrohan* which he had begun to evolve in 1919: it started as a box-like form with the structural walls along the long sides, but evolved with the introduction of *pilotis or columns to raise the building from the ground. The name suggests the Citroën motor-car, with its connotations of mass-production and industrialization, logical evolution, economy, and efficiency. From 1921 Le Corbusier collaborated with his cousin, A.-A.-P. *Jeanneret-Gris, and their Paris office attracted many architects, for from it flowed *Modernist polemics

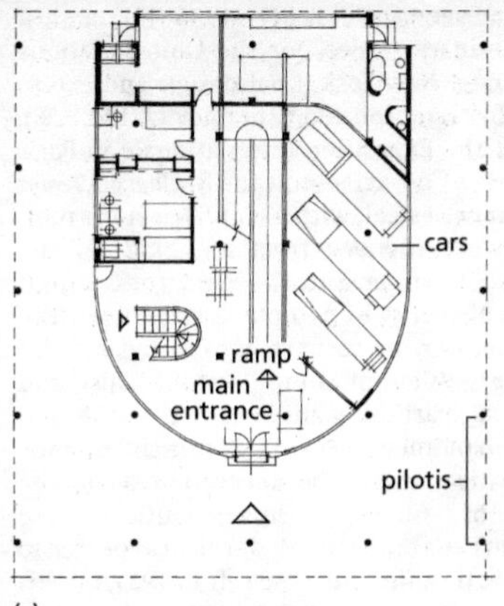

(*a*)

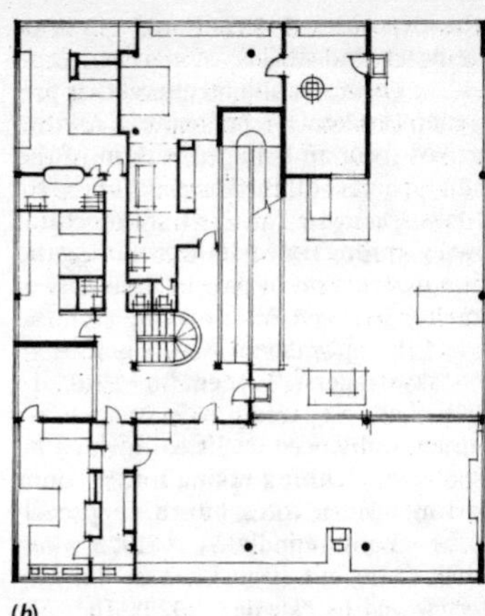

(*b*)

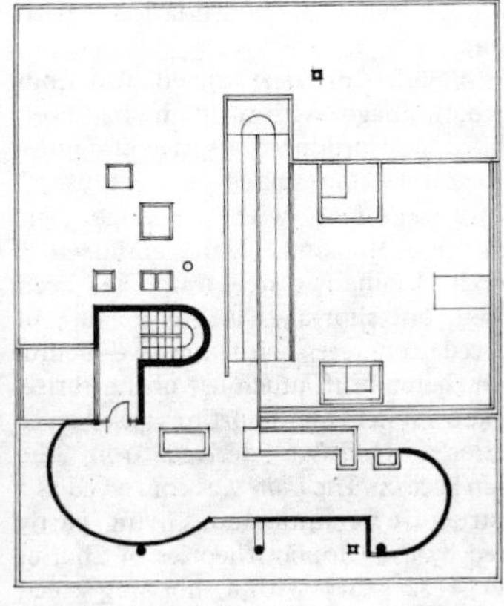

(*c*)

Corbusier.
Plans of Villa Savoie (Savoye), Poissy, near Paris. (*After Le Corbusier*)
(*a*) Ground-floor plan showing pilotis, car-parking arrangements, entrance, central ramp, and stair.
(*b*) First-floor plan.
(*c*) Second-floor plan.

and designs for experimental housing in which simple forms and smooth surfaces were expressed. The Citrohan houses were published in *L'Esprit Nouveau* and *Vers une architecture*, and were the precedents for the realized designs at the Villa Besnus, Vaucresson (1922–3), followed by many more, including the influential Villa Stein at Garches (1927), two houses at the *Weissenhofsiedlung, Stuttgart (1927), and the Villa Savoie, Poissy (1928–31). The last was the definitive exemplar of the famous *Five Points for a New Architecture*, and, with its formal architectural language, pilotis, linkage of external and internal spaces, long strip-windows, and crisp, uncompromising lines, became a powerful paradigm for C20 *Rationalism in architecture. The *cinq points*, with other ideas, were expounded in Alfred *Roth's *Zwei Wohnhäuser von Le Corbusier und Pierre Jeanneret* (Two Houses by Le Corbusier and Pierre Jeanneret–1927): they were, in essence, the use of pilotis as structural elements, lifting the building and leaving a space under it; columnar-and-slab construction enabling floor-plans to be left as free and adaptable as possible, partitions (if required) not being structural; the creation of a roof-garden at the top, affording better light and air than on the ground; the mode of construction facilitating long continuous strips of windows; and complete freedom of façade-design.

At the Exposition International des Arts-Décoratifs et Industriels Modernes, Paris (1924–5), Le Corbusier and Jeanneret-Gris presented their *Pavillon de l'Esprit Nouveau*. A white box derived from an L-shaped variant of the Citrohan type, it contained a model of the so-called *Plan Voisin* for Paris, an architectural and town-planning time-bomb, proposing the complete destruction of part of Paris east of the Louvre, between Montmartre and the Seine, and its replacement with eighteen gigantic *skyscrapers. Earlier, in 1910, Le Corbusier had prepared *La Construction des Villes*, much influenced by Sitte, in which he analysed town-planning taking into account the existing historic cores, but this approach was to be wholly repudiated by 1925 when *Urbanisme* came out (translated as *The City of Tomorrow and Its Planning*, 1929). The *Ville Contemporaine*, a design for a city of 3 million inhabitants (1922), and the *Plan Voisin* provided the imagery for redevelopment and new towns that was to be almost universally adopted (largely through the influence of *CIAM, with which Le Corbusier and Jeanneret-Gris were to be intimately connected from its beginnings in 1928) after the 1939–45 war with such unfortunate results for countless towns and cities.

His book *La Ville Radieuse* (The Radiant City) of 1935 contains proposals for a Utopian city in which buildings conforming to his aesthetic would be erected. In the 1930s, indeed, he was able to build paradigmatic structures in Paris, including the Pavillon Suisse, Cité Universitaire (1930–3), and the Cité de Refuge (Salvation Army Hostel—1929–33). These slab-blocks of framed construction were designed with large areas of glass (the *curtain-wall) that caused problems of solar-heat gain and glare as well as heat-loss, yet were to be the models for countless slab-blocks thereafter. Such facts can only be explained by the preoccupation with glass (perhaps derived from the slogans of *Taut) as an indicator of 'modernity', 'progressiveness', and 'cleanliness'.

Large-scale projects also occupied Le Corbusier from the late 1920s, including the competition designs for the League of Nations Palace, Geneva (1927), and the Palace of the Soviets, Moscow (1931). From 1929 to 1934 he built the Centrosoyus Building, Moscow, and prepared other designs, including the Ministry of Education and Health, Rio de Janeiro, Brazil (executed by *Costa, *Niemeyer, and *Reidy, 1936–43), and a preliminary project for the United Nations Building, New York (final design and execution by *Harrison and *Abramovitz, 1947–50).

For the Exposition Internationale in Paris (1937) Le Corbusier built the *Pavillon des Temps Nouveaux* of steel, with a tent-like canvas roof, the whole derived from an image of the Jewish Tabernacle in the Wilderness mixed with elements of aeroplane structures. The slogan over the rostrum evoked the Popular Front (a union of Communist, Socialist, and Radical parties), and inside, like the Ten Commandments, were CIAM principles, some of which would be incorporated in the *Athens Charter. Thus, politically, Le Corbusier's brand of *Modernism appeared to be overtly allied with the Left in 1937, but his position throughout the 1930s was ambivalent, for he was also involved with the Syndicalists (who had affiliations with Fascism).

After 1945 Le Corbusier turned away from the smooth images with which he had been associated, and produced a series of aggressive, massively constructed, and sculptural buildings beginning with the huge *Unité d'Habitation* (Housing Unit), Marseilles (1946–52). Originally a steel frame had been proposed, but shortages led to the use of reinforced concrete, with massive board-marked *béton-brut, much use of the *brise-soleil, and a system of proportions based on Le Corbusier's *Modulor, derived from the *Golden Section. The *Unité* was conceived as a huge structure for autonomous living, partly inspired by the Utopian theories of Charles Fourier (1772–1837), with a shopping-street, hotel, gymnasium, crèche, community services, and running-track. Other *Unités* were built at Nantes-Rezé (1952–7), Berlin (1956–8), Meaux (1957–9), Briey-en-Fôret (1957–60), and Firminy-Vert (1962–8): apartments within them were two-storey living-units with double-height living-space. The images of the *Unités* were copied in a scaled-down form at Roehampton Park by the London County Council's Department of Architecture (1952–5), but the immediate international influence was in the use of raw, unfaced concrete in countless buildings, giving rise to the style known as New *Brutalism. Powerful, chunky forms of béton-brut recurred at the Dominican Monastery of Ste-Marie-de-la-Tourette at Eveux-sur-Arbresle, near Lyons (1953–9).

Le Corbusier's Pilgrimage Church of Notre-Dame-du-Haut at Ronchamp (1950–4), with its *battered walls filled with rubble and sprayed with Gunnite (a patent rough-cast finish), silo-like tower, windows of many shapes and sizes piercing the walls at random, and distorted boat-like roof apparently floating over the walls, seemed to suggest a complete shift towards anti-*Rationalism (and caused consternation in CIAM). At the Maisons Jaoul, Neuilly-sur-Seine (1952–6), coarsely laid brickwork, oversized concrete beams, and segmental *vaults influenced architects such as *Spence and *Stirling.

In the 1950s Le Corbusier, with *Drew, *Fry, and others, laid out Chandigarh as the administrative capital of the Punjab, India, and built several gigantic public buildings (using excessively heavy, over-sized, chunky, raw concrete) that have been influential, notably in Japan, and were (like the *Unités*) attempts to create monumentality. Le Corbusier had many British and American architectural disciples who espoused *Ville Radieuse* principles and countless designs inspired by his work were realized. One of his last significant buildings was the Carpenter Center for the Visual Arts, Harvard University, Cambridge, Mass. (1960–3).

Boesiger (1966–70, 1972); Brooks (1982, 1987*a*); Choay (1960); Curtis (1996*a*); Etlin (1994); Franclieu (1981–2); Jeanneret-Gris (from 1964 and 1973–7); Jencks (1973); Ozenfant and Jeanneret-Gris (1975); Placzek (1982—contains a large bibliography); Raeburn and Wilson (1987); Tafuri and Dal Co (1986)

Cordemoy, Abbé Jean-Louis de (1631–1713). French priest and architectural theorist (not to be confused with L.-G. de Cordemoy (1651–1722)). His *Nouveau Traité de Toute l'Architecture* (New Treatise on the Whole of Architecture—1706) was an important influence on the search for truth, simplicity, and honest expression of form, drawing on the works of *Perrault, and demonstrating an early understanding of the sophistication of *Gothic structures. His argument was essentially in favour of Classical clarity with the *Orders used structurally, all unnecessary ornament eschewed, design that drew upon Nature and Antiquity, and buildings that expressed their purpose. He was an important precursor of *Neoclassicism, and an influence on *Laugier.

Cordemoy (1714); Herrmann (1962); *Journal of the Warburg and Courtauld Institutes*, 25 (1962), 278–320, and 26 (1963), 90–123; Rykwert (1980)

cordon. 1. *String- or belt-course, usually a *band, projecting slightly from a wall, normally used in connection with fortifications. **2.** Slightly projecting step or riser at the lower edge of each part of a stepped ramp so that each section between steps has less of an inclination than the ramp as a whole (called *scala cordonata* or *scala a cordoni*), for surer footing. It is essentially a step-division in an inclined plane.

coretti. Galleries resembling theatre-boxes in the *choirs of *Baroque churches (e.g. *Frauenkirche*, Dresden, by *Bähr).

Corinthian Order. Classical *Order of architecture, the third of the Greek Orders and the fourth of the Roman. Slender and elegant, it consists of a *base (usually of the *Attic type, often with further enrichment, or a more elaborately moulded variety, called *spira*) on a *plinth; a tall *shaft (fluted or plain); a *capital (the distinguishing feature, consisting of two rows of *acanthus-leaves over the *astragal, with *caules rising from the acanthus-leaves and sprouting *helices or *volutes from each *calyx with *bud) with concave-sided *abacus (with chamfered or pointed corners) in the centre of each face of which is a *fleuron in the Roman version and sometimes an *anthemion or *palmette in the Greek; and an *entablature, often of great magnificence, with *bead-and-reel between *fasciae of the *architrave, *frieze ornamented with continuous sculpture, and *cornice with ornate *coffers and richly carved *modillions.

Supposedly invented by *Callimachus, the capital is essentially a bell-like core (*campana) from which the acanthus-leaves, caules, helices, etc., sprout, reflecting its origin as vegetation growing from a basket capped with a slab. Among the earliest examples of the Greek Corinthian Order were the three (or possibly only one) at the end of the *naos of the temple of Apollo Epicurius at *Bassae (*c.*429–*c.*400 BC), but the beautiful capitals of the *Choragic Monument of Lysicrates, Athens (334 BC), were among the most elegant ever designed (and probably the first to be used externally): they were much admired and copied after being recorded by *Stuart and *Revett in *The Antiquities of Athens* from 1762. The Lysicrates capital is taller than most other examples of the Order, with the shaft *fillets terminating in leaf- or tongue-like forms over which is a recessed band (probably once filled with a metal collar), then a row of tongue-like leaves above which is a row of acanthus-leaves between each pair of which is a flower, and finally the exquisite volutes with an anthemion in the centre of each concave face of the moulded abacus. A simpler type of capital, often found in C18 work in Britain, was that of the Tower of the Winds (or Horologium of Andronicus Cyrrhus) in Athens (*c*.50 BC), consisting of a row of acanthus-leaves then a row of palm-leaves, and finally a square abacus, with no volutes.

Greek column-shafts of this Order were invariably fluted. Not surprisingly, the Order has always been associated with Beauty. Taken as a whole, it was developed by the Romans into an expression of the grandest architectural show.

Normand (1852)

Cormier, Ernest (1885–1980). Perhaps the most versatile of architects working in Canada in the first half of C20. Not only an accomplished planner, he was a master of joining disparate masses, creating impressive spaces, and incorporating beautiful orna-

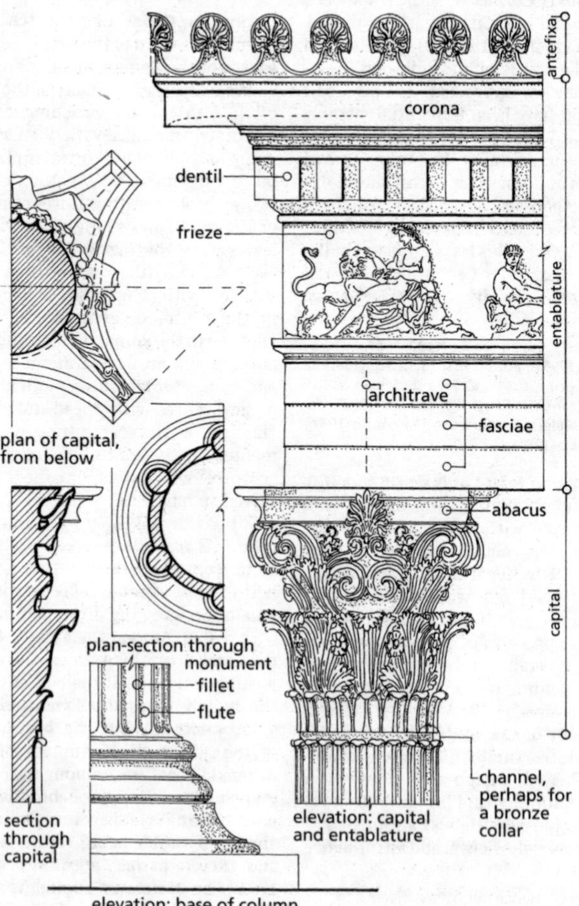

Corinthian Order. Greek Corinthian Order from the Choragic Monument of Lysicrates (334 BC). (*After Normand*)

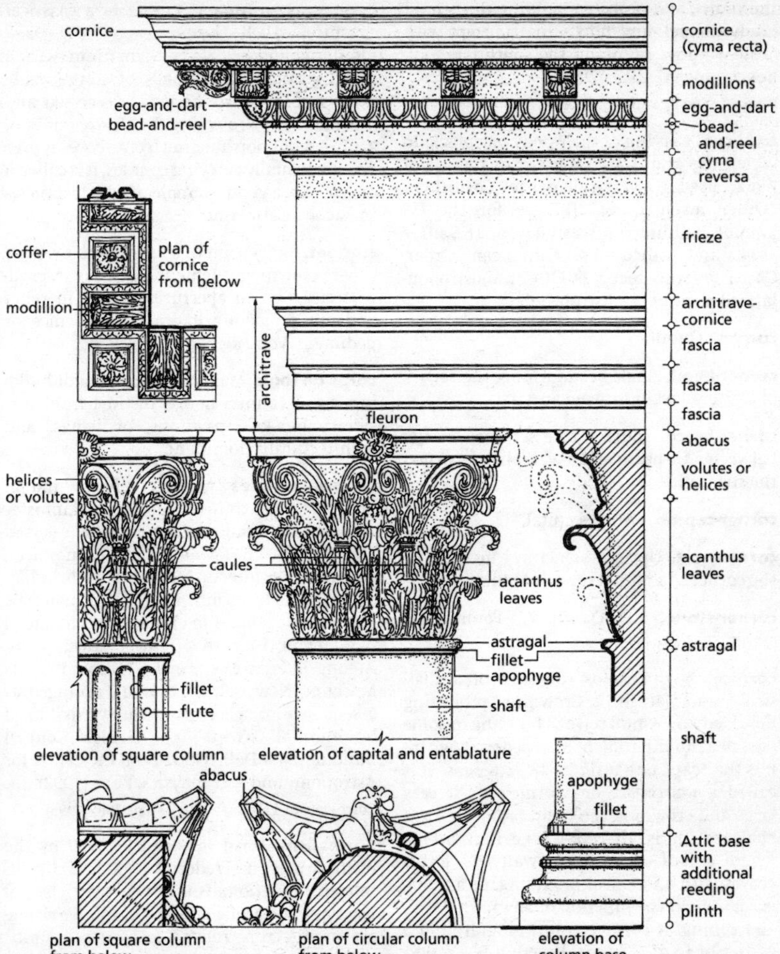

Corinthian Order. Roman Corinthian Order from the Pantheon, Rome, probably recycled from an early C1 temple and re-erected in the early C2. (*After Normand*)

ment within his designs. His *Art Deco building for the University of Montreal (1928–35) is probably his greatest work, planned on *Beaux-Arts principles, but his Supreme Court Building, Ottawa (1938–50), draws on stripped *Classicism and French C17 precedents, notably in its steeply pitched roofs. Cormier's own house in Montreal (1930–1) was influenced by contemporary European *Modernism, with Art Deco-inspired interiors, while his National Printing Bureau, Hull, Quebec (1950–8), incorporated technical innovations such as the *curtain-wall.

Kalman (1994)

Cormont, Thomas de (d. 1228). French master-mason. He assisted *Luzarches in the building of Amiens Cathedral, succeeding him as architect in 1223, and supervised the construction of the *nave up to the springing of the *vaults. His son, **Regnault** or **Reynaud**, succeeded him in 1228 at Amiens, completing the vaults, and probably building the *choir, *Lady Chapel, and northern *transept with *rose-window. He began the south transept, not completed until 1296.

Papworth (1852); Sturgis *et al.* (1901–2)

corn-cob. Carving of the woody receptacle to which the grains are attached in the ear of maize, used in a variation of the *Corinthian *Order invented by *Latrobe for the US Capitol Building in Washington, DC, after 1814, and called the *American Order. Corn-cobs also recur as C19 *finials, popularized no doubt by Latrobe's design.

corner. *Quoin.

corner-bead. Angle-bead forming the corner of plastered walls to avoid an *arris.

corner-brace. Short *brace set horizontally between a tie-beam and a wall-plate to stiffen the structure.

corner-capital. *Angle-capital.

corner-post. Upright structural member at the corner of a *timber-framed building.

corner-stone. **1.** *Quoin. **2.** Foundation-stone.

cornice. **1.** Uppermost division of a Classical *entablature. **2.** Crowning projecting moulded horizontal top of a building or some part of a building, such as a *pedestal (where it is the *cap), or a wall. In the latter case it is called a *wall-cornice* or *cornicione (if very large and crowning the main façade of e.g. a *palazzo). It is an *eaves-cornice* if it occurs where a roof overhangs a wall and forms *eaves with a Classical moulding, or a *crown-moulding* if at the junction of an internal wall and ceiling. A cornice continuing around a corner or in a different direction is a *cornice return*, and one faced with e.g. *terracotta or some other material is an *encased* cornice. On a *pediment the cornices are differentiated as *raking* if on the sloping sides. A *block-cornice* is a wall-cornice with very simple blocks instead of *modillions projecting from rudimentary *bed-mouldings.

cornicione. Italian *Renaissance *wall-cornice* proportioned to be a suitable crowning feature of the entire *façade and mass of a large building, usually *astylar, such as a *palazzo, e.g. Palazzo Strozzi, Florence (begun 1489).

corona (*pl.* **coronae**). **1.** Part of a Classical *cornice, called *larmier, above the *bed-moulding and below the *cymatium, with a broad vertical face, usually of considerable projection, with its underside recessed and forming a *drip* protecting the *frieze under it. **2.** Circlet or hoop hanging from above, as over an altar: usually carrying candles, it is called a *corona lucis*, a good example of which survives in Aachen Cathedral.

coronet. Suggestion of a *pediment or some other crowning element such as *scroll-patterns over an aperture, usually in relief and not projecting like a true *cornice or pediment. Von *Klenze employed it.

corps de logis. Main *block of a major building, e.g. a country-house, distinct from subsidiary blocks, *pavilions, or wings, and architecturally dominant.

Correa, Charles Mark (1930–). Indian architect. He trained under Buckminster *Fuller and *Yamasaki, and then rejected *Modernism in favour of an economical, adaptable architecture derived from Indian *vernacular traditions using local materials in order to respond to climatic and financial parameters. He also produced town plans. Among later works are the National Crafts Museum, New Delhi (1975–91), arranged as a sequence of spaces and courtyards linked by internal 'streets'; the British Council Building, New Delhi (1992); and the Centre for Astronomy and Astrophysics, Pune (1992).

Correa (1996); Emanuel (1994); Khan (1987, 1995)

Correalism. Term invented in 1939 by the Austro-American Frederick J. *Kiesler. He dismissed *Functionalism as the 'mysticism of hygiene', and argued for an alternative visionary architecture related to spirals, infinity, and eternity. Forms he perceived as points where apparent known forces met invisible, secret, spiritual ones, and that reality was really the interaction of these forces. The nature of their relationships and of the connections between humans, forms, space, time, and the world he called *Correalism*.

Conrads (1970); Kiesler (1964, 1966); Phillips (1989)

corsa. **1.** *Fascia of a Classical *architrave. **2.** *String-course higher than its projection.

cortile (*pl.* **cortili**). Internal area (*cortis*) or courtyard of a *palazzo, often with *arcades or *colonnades rising several storeys, and open to the sky (as in various Florentine *palazzi*) or roofed (as in *Barry's Reform Club, London (1837–41)).

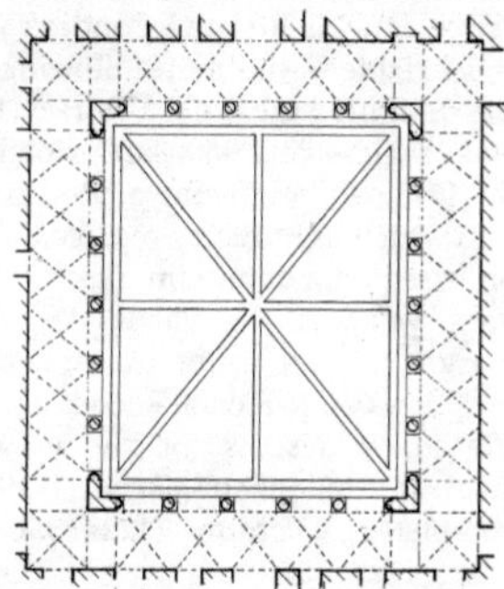

cortile. Palazzo Ducale, Urbino (C15), showing the Renaissance attention to geometry and detail in providing an arcaded walk around the open space.

Cortona, Pietro Berrettini da (1596–1669). With *Bernini and *Borromini, one of the great masters of Roman *Baroque. Trained as a painter, Cortona settled in Rome around 1611, where he was patronized by the Sacchettis, for whom he designed the Palazzetto del Pigneto (1626–36). Although the building no longer exists, it made his reputation at the time, for it was approached through a series of ramps and terraces leading up to the entrance *exedra, a design influenced, no doubt, by the Roman temple of Fortuna at Palestrina (Praeneste), and containing other *Antique allusions, including semicircular apses screened by columns and derived from Roman *thermae. The *façade was one of the first curved fronts in Rome. He came to the notice of Cardinal Francesco Barberini, for whom he created the sensational Baroque ceiling-*fresco (completed 1639) in the *saloon of the Palazzo Barberini. His first church was Sts Luca e Martina (1634–69) in the Forum: the central part of the front has a convex plan, and columns are sunk into the wall in the manner of *Michelangelo's Laurentian library-vestibule in Florence. Inside the church (a Greek *cross on plan) the walls are articulated by means of *Ionic columns and *pilasters (the capitals are of the *angular type), giving a unity to the entire composition enhanced by the lack of colour (the interior is painted white).

Under Pope Alexander VII (1655–67) da Cortona built two of the finest Baroque church façades in Rome. The front of Santa Maria della Pace (1656–9) has a half-elliptical porch of paired *Tuscan columns and an upper storey with a recessed convex central section: the plastic qualities recall Michelangelo at his *Mannerist best. Da Cortona carried the main elements of the façade over the adjacent buildings, creating a unified piazza resembling a theatre with boxes, with the church-front appearing as the backdrop. With the façade of Santa Maria in Via Lata (1658–62) in the Corso, da Cortona achieved a deceptive simplicity and grandeur with an *in antis* (*see* anta) porch and an upper storey featuring an arch continuing the profile of the *entablature. The design was reminiscent of elements from Diocletian's Palace at Spalato and the temples at Baalbek.

Briganti (1962); Norberg-Schulz (1986); Placzek (1982—substantial article with bibliography); Varriano (1986); Wittkower (1982)

Cosmati. Family of C12 and C13 *marmorarii* (workers in marble) in Rome, taking their name from the leading member, Cosma, or Cosmatus. *Cosmati-work*, known as *Cosmatesca* or *Cosmatesque*, consists of inlaid geometrical *polychrome patterns of stone, glass, mosaic, and gilding set in marble. Good examples survive in Westminster Abbey: the pavements of the *presbytery (1268) and *feretory (1267–8), the base of the *shrine of the Confessor (1270), and the *tomb-chest of King Henry III (*c.*1280). Cosmatesque is also a style of architectural decoration deriving from southern Italian, Sicilian, and *Byzantine work.

Hutton (1950)

cosmic architecture. Term coined by the Japanese architect Monta Mozuna (1941–) to describe his own architecture from the 1970s onwards, supposedly inspired by cosmology.

Bognar (1985, 1990–2)

Costa, Lúcio (1902–98). One of Brazil's most influential architects and planners. Born in France, he settled in Brazil, and was influenced by Gregori *Warchavchik, with whom he worked for a time. He was in the vanguard of *International *Modernism in Brazil, and headed a team of young architects (all disciples of Le *Corbusier) designing the building for the Ministry of Education and Health in Rio de Janeiro (1936–43), for which Le Corbusier was consultant architect and *Burle Marx was landscape-architect. Costa and *Niemeyer designed the Brazilian Pavilion at the World's Fair, New York (1939), and he himself was responsible for the Eduardo Guinle apartment-block in Rio (1948–54) and the Brazilian Pavilion at the Cité Universitaire, Paris (1955). In 1956 the imagination of the world was captured by his plan for the new capital, Brasília, and construction moved rapidly ahead. The plan is formal, in the shape of a bow and arrow, and it encapsulates many of the principles laid down by *CIAM in the *Athens Charter.

Bullrich (1969); Costa (1962); Gazeneo and Scarone (1959)

cot. **1.** Very humble small rural cottage, especially with wattled sides and a thatched roof, or a structure in a garden or park in imitation of it, but used as a retreat, summer-house, or similar. **2.** *Dovecote.

cottage orné. Small late-C18 or early C19 dwelling in the country or a park. It was often asymmetrical, with small leaded windows, thatched roofs, fretted *barge-boards, large ornamental chimneys, and rough timber *verandahs supported by tree trunks, and was part of the cult of the *Picturesque. The fashion for the *cottage orné* was promoted in many pattern-books (including those by *Plaw, who seems to have been the first to use the term, in 1795), largely in *Regency Britain, but it also influenced *Carpenter's Gothic in the USA. Sources of Picturesque designs for such cottages include James Malton's (d. 1803) *An Essay on British Cottage Architecture* . . . (1798 and 1804), his *Collection of Designs for Rural Retreats* . . . (1802), and J. B. *Papworth's *Rural Residences* . . . (1818 and 1832). Good examples of the *cottage orné*, designed by *Nash, survive at Blaise Hamlet, near Bristol (1811). A larger structure, in character resembling the *cottage orné*, set in parkland, and used as a real working farm, is a *ferme ornée*.

Hussey (1967, 1967*a*); Lyall (1988); Watkin (1982*a*)

Cotte, Robert de (1657–1735). French architect. Brother-in-law and pupil-assistant of J. *Hardouin-Mansart, he promoted French architecture throughout Europe, notably in the German-speaking lands, where he was in demand as a designer in the *Régence style. He was consulted about Schloss Brühl, Schloss Schleissheim, the Thurn und Taxis Palace at Frankfurt, and the *Residenz* (Seat of the Court) at Würzburg; designed extensions to the Electoral Palace, Bonn (1715–23); and was entirely responsible for Poppelsdorfer Schloss, also in Bonn (1715–18). He succeeded Hardouin-Mansart as *Premier Architecte* in 1709, and carried out his first independent work, the Hôtel du Lude, Paris, in the following year. As well as designing the Hôtel d'Éstrées (1713), he remodelled François *Mansart's Hôtel de la Vrillière (1713–19), producing a *Rococo confection in which asymmetry replaced a composition based on a dominant axis. His most important work is the Palais de Rohan, Strasbourg (1728–42), a fine example of the noble *simplicité* of C18 French Rococo architecture. He made designs for the episcopal residences at Châlons-sur-Marne (1719–20—not completed), Verdun (1724–35), and Strasbourg (1727–35).

Blondel (1752–6); Kalnein and Levey (1972); Neuman (1994)

Cottingham, Lewis Nockalls (1787–1847). English architect and antiquary. He was a pioneer of the *Gothic Revival, and carried out numerous works of restoration to medieval churches, notably at Theberton, Suffolk (1836—where his sensitive colouring and detailing of the south *aisle deserve respect), Ashbourne, Derbyshire (1839–40), and St Mary's, Bury St Edmunds, Suffolk (1840–3). He refitted Magdalen College Chapel, Oxford (1830–2), virtually rebuilt St Patrick's Cathedral, Armagh (1834–7), and carried out careful restorations at Hereford Cathedral (from 1841). Among his buildings were Snelston Hall, Derbyshire, a Gothic house (1828—demolished), the former Savings Bank in Crown Street, Bury St Edmunds (1846—*Tudor Gothic), and an extensive estate at Waterloo Bridge Road, London (from 1825). He established a fine collection of medieval architectural details (a descriptive memoir of which was published in 1850) that was later incorporated into the collections of the South Kensington Museum. He published several books, including *Plans, etc. of Westminster Hall* (1822), *Plans, etc. of King Henry VII's Chapel* (1822–9), *The Ornamental Metal Worker's Director* (1823—with later editions), *Working Drawings of Gothic Ornaments* (1824), and *Grecian and Roman Architecture* (1820). He deserves to be better known as one of the first scholarly architects working in the Gothic style, and his work at Magdalen College, Oxford, is very fine for its date.

Colvin (1995); *DNB* (1917); Myles (1996)

counter. Opposite, or against, hence used as a noun for a long narrow flat-topped construction to separate staff from customers in a bank, inn, or shop.

counter-apse. Apse opposite another apse, as in the east and west ends of German churches (e.g. the Cathedrals of Speier, Trier, and Worms).

counter-arch. Arch opposing another arch's outward force, the principle of a flying *buttress.

counter-change. Pattern formed by repetitive figures but alternating in colour or texture, the basic type of which is the *chequer.

counter-fort. 1. *Buttress or other projection (e.g. *spur-wall or *pier), built against a wall in order to prevent it from moving or bulging. **2.** *Sconce.

counter-mure. 1. In fortifications, a wall (*contramure*) behind another as a reserve defence, in case of the first wall being breached, or an outer wall to prevent an attacker from getting at the first wall. **2.** Breakwater.

counter-scarp. 1. Outer wall or slope of the ditch in a fortification. **2.** Area between the parapet and *glacis, also in a fortification. **3.** The term sometimes includes the glacis.

counter-vault. Inverted arch or *vault, used e.g. in foundations.

couple. Pair of common *rafters. A *couple-roof* therefore consists of couples resting on *wall-plates and pitched together at the *ridge, with or without *purlins. A *close-couple* roof has couples with *ties above their feet, thus forming triangles, preventing the feet from spreading.

coupled columns. *Accouplement, or columns placed in a *colonnade (or *arcade) in line in very closely spaced pairs, as in the east front of the Louvre, Paris, or in pairs at 90° to the line of the *entablature.

cour d'honneur. Principal *court, often the forecourt, of a grand house or palace, often enclosed between the principal front of the *corps de logis, the projecting wings and *colonnades, and the fourth side composed of very low buildings, lodges, etc., or a wall or railing. A good example is at Burley-on-the-Hill, Rutland (1696–1704).

course. Any horizontal level range of bricks, stones, etc., placed according to some rule or order in the construction of a wall, laid evenly. *Coursed* *rubble, for example, is roughly dressed stones of the same height laid in courses, unlike *random* rubble, which is uncoursed and requires ingenuity in getting the stones to bond. Thus *coursed* masonry has courses of dressed stones (*ashlar) of the same height, yet each course may vary in height. Courses may be described by position or function: *base* or *plinth*, *blocking* (plain course above a *cornice weighing down the ends of the cantilevered sections of stone), *bond* (with every stone, or stones at regular intervals, bonding a wall), *lacing* (as *bond*, but with continuous ranges of brick or tile, and with *piers every two metres or so, used in a *flint wall for bonding, levelling, and strengthening), and *string-courses are some examples.

court. 1. Clear area enclosed by walls or surrounded by buildings, such as a space left for the admission of light and air, an area around a castle *keep, a forecourt or *cour d'honneur in front of a grand house, a *cortile, a Cambridge college quadrangle, or a *cloister. **2.** Princely or Royal residence (as at Hampton Court Palace). **3.** Building where legal tribunals sit.

Court style. Earliest phase of the *Rayonnant style of French *Gothic, closely associated with the reign of King Louis IX (1227–70). It was characterized by the dissolution of walls in favour of huge areas of windows subdivided by thin, wire-like *tracery, the piercing of the wall of the *triforium-gallery with windows, and the introduction of masses of *colonnettes corresponding to the ribs in the *vault. The most glorious examples of the Court style are Ste-Chapelle, Paris (1243–8), the *Collegiate Church of St-Urbain, Troyes (begun 1262), and the east end of Sées Cathedral, Normandy (*c*.1270).

Branner (1965); Grodecki (1986); Watkin (1986)

Courtonne, Jean (1671–1739). French architect. His Hôtel de Noirmoutier and Hôtel de Matignon, Paris (both 1720–4), are models of elegance and restraint. They have continuous *astylar wall-surfaces punctuated by tall windows (some with semicircular and others with segmental heads). His chief importance lies in his treatise on architectural perspective, published in 1725, which also contained numerous remarks on architecture, including his insistence that the exterior of a building should be derived from the forms of the interior.

Courtonne (1725); Hautecœur (1950); Kalnein and Levey (1972)

coussinet. **1.** Cushion of the *Ionic *capital, including the two *volutes and their connecting bands, like a rolled mattress. **2.** Lowest *voussoir of an arch resting on the *impost.

Covarrubias, Alonso de (1488–1570). Spanish mason and sculptor. He worked at Salamanca Cathedral (1512) before carrying out decorations at Sigüenza. His most important work was El Alcázar, Toledo (1537–53—badly damaged during the Civil War, 1936–9), where the top storey is rusticated and the two lower storeys plain (an inversion of the normal Classical arrangement), and Italian forms were applied to a large plain *ashlar *façade for decorative purposes. As master-mason to Toledo Cathedral, he was responsible for the *Chapel of the New Kings (1531–4).

Chueca Goitia (1953); Kubler and Soria (1959)

cove, coving. **1.** Surface of concave, more or less quarter-cylindrical form, usually applied to the *cavetto moulding between a wall and *coved ceiling*, called *coving*. In many cases the coving is heavily ornamented. **2.** Large concave part of a *chancel-*screen under the *gallery, often with the appearance of *vaulting. **3.** Curved transition between an exterior wall and the *eaves, called *coved eaves*.

coved vault. *Cloistered* arch or *vault, composed of four triangular *coves rising from a square plan in *corbelled *courses to an apex and meeting in vertical diagonal planes, the axial *sections being arcs, but actually pseudo-vaults.

cover. Anything finishing a join, e.g. a *cover-fillet*, *cover-moulding*, or *cover-strip* moulding concealing a joint in panelling, or the part of a tile or slate covered by the overlap of the course above.

coving. *See* cove.

cowl. Cap, hood, etc. for covering the open top of a chimney-flue and improving the draught, often with a wind-vane to permit it to rotate.

Cowlishaw, William Harrison (1869–1957). English *Arts-and-Crafts architect and disciple of William *Morris. He is remembered for two buildings: The Cearne, Kent Hatch, Crockham Hill, Kent (1896), a charming house for Edward and Constance Garnett, and the summer-school known as The Cloisters, Barrington Road, Letchworth *Garden City, Hertfordshire (1908), an eclectic and romantic building. He worked for the Imperial War Graves Commission, and later for Charles *Holden.

Gray (1985); Miller (1989)

Cowper, John (*fl.* 1453–84). English mason. He worked at Eton College in the 1450s, Tattershall Church, Lincolnshire, in 1478, and around the same time built Kirby Muxloe Castle, Leicestershire, where the resident mason or clerk of the works was Robert Steynforth (*fl.* 1480s). Cowper may also have been responsible for the gatehouse-tower at Esher, Surrey (*c.*1475–80), the school at Wainfleet, Lincolnshire (1484), and the great tower at the Bishop's Palace, Buckden, Huntingdonshire (also 1480s). Cowper is important in the development of *Tudor brick-built architecture which was to become fashionable. He appears to have finished his career in the service of King James IV of Scotland (1488–1513), for a John Cowper was in charge of the works at Rothesay Castle, Bute, in 1512, where he was paid handsomely, so must have enjoyed considerable status.

Harvey (1987)

coyn. *See* quoin.

Crabtree, William (1905–91). English architect. His reputation rests mainly on his Peter Jones Department Store, Sloane Square, London (1932–7), designed for Spedan Lewis (1885–1963—founder of the John Lewis Partnership) in collaboration with Slater & Moberly, with C. H. *Reilly (Crabtree's former mentor at Liverpool University) as consultant. It was one of the first C20 uses of the glass *curtain-wall in England, was influenced by the work of *Mendelsohn (Schocken department-stores in Chemnitz and Stuttgart), and is one of the most distinguished *Modern Movement buildings in Britain. He subsequently worked with *Abercrombie on the reconstruction of Plymouth and Southampton after the 1939–45 war, and designed several buildings in Basildon and Harlow New Towns, Essex, and elsewhere, but never again was he to build anything to match in quality the Peter Jones store.

Architectural Review, 85 (June 1939), 291–8; *Architectural Review*, 187/1115 (Jan. 1990), 75–9

cradle. 1. Light structure or framework (*cradling*) to support a plaster *cornice or *vault. **2.** *Corbeil. **3.** *Caisson.

cradle-roof. Form of timber roof more or less arched on the underside, as when *braces were used.

cradle-vault. Improper term for a *barrel-*vault.

Craig, James (1744–95). Edinburgh-born architect who achieved fame with his design for Edinburgh New Town (1766). In 1786 he published *Plan for improving the City of Edinburgh*. He was the architect of St James Square (1773—demolished), the *Palladian Physicians' Hall, George Street (1775—demolished), and the Old Observatory, Calton Hill (1776–92).

Colvin (1995); Craig (1786); Youngson (1966)

Cram, Ralph Adams (1863–1942). Leading *Gothic Revivalist in the USA, much influenced by the works of *Bodley, *Morris, and *Ruskin. He went into partnership with Charles Francis Wentworth (1861–97) in 1889, and together they built the Episcopalian Church of All Saints, Ashmont, Dorchester, Boston, Mass. (1891–1913). This brought them fame and attracted the gifted Bertram Grosvenor Goodhue (1869–1924) to join them as a partner in the firm, renamed Cram, Wentworth, & Goodhue (1892–1914). After Wentworth's early death Frank Ferguson (1861–1926) joined the partnership, and Cram, Goodhue, & Ferguson rose to national pre-eminence with two important commissions: the master-plan and chapel for the US Military Academy, West Point, NY (1903–14), and the Church of St Thomas, Fifth Avenue, New York (1906–14). The church is one of the finest works of the *Arts-and-Crafts and *Gothic Revival styles in America. The Graduate School Complex and Chapel at Princeton University (1911–29) were sophisticated designs, but Cram's greatest achievement (1915–41) is undoubtedly the project for the completion and Gothicizing of the Cathedral of St John the Divine, Morningside Heights, New York, begun in a *Byzantine *Romanesque style in 1892 to designs by *Heins and Lafarge. A respected scholar, Cram was the author of *Church Building* (1901) and *The Substance of Gothic* (1917) among other important works.

Cram (1924, 1925, 1930, 1966, 1967, 1969); Daniel (1980); Muccigrosso (1980); North (1931); Shand-Tucci (1975, 1994); Watkin (1986)

cramp. Piece of metal used to hold stones together in the same *course.

Cranbrook. The Cranbrook Academy of Art, Bloomfield Hills, Michigan, was founded in the 1920s under the influence of the *Arts-and-Crafts movement. Buildings for its *campus were designed by the *Saarinens. Its importance lies in its promotion of modern design, many practitioners having been associated with it over the years.

Gaidos (1972)

credence. Table or shelf (called *prothesis*) on the south side of the *sanctuary of a church, near the altar (where the Sacred Elements were placed before the Oblation), often given architectural treatment, and sometimes associated with the *piscina.

cremone, cremorne. *Casement bolts with a rack-and-pinion mechanism controlled by a rotary handle: two sliding rods, fixed to one leaf of e.g. a *French window, are moved up and down in opposite directions into sockets in a frame in order to lock it. A variant is called the *espagnolette*, where the bolt-rods have hooks on the ends that engage in slots at the top and bottom of the main frame, locking and tightening the opening-light.

crenel, crenelle. *See* battlement.

crepido. 1. Any elevated base on which e.g. an *obelisk, altar, or temple is supported or built. *See* crepidoma. **2.** Raised footpath parallel to a Roman street. **3.** Projecting ornamental parts of a Classical building, such as a *cornice.

crepidoma. 1. Greek foundation of a building. **2.** Platform, *crepis*, or *crepido on which a Greek temple stood, normally of three tall steps, the topmost platform surface of which was termed *stylobate.

crescent. 1. Building or series of buildings of which the frontage stands in plan on the concave arc of a circle or of an ellipse, generally facing a garden or promenade. The earliest examples are the Royal Crescent, Bath (1767–75), by *Wood the Younger, and the semicircular Crescent at Buxton, Derbyshire (1780–90), by *Carr of York. Camden Crescent (*c.*1788) by John Eveleigh (*fl.* 1756–1800) and Lansdown Crescent (1789–93) by John Palmer (*c.*1738–1817), both in Bath, are two further examples of a type of development that became common in C19. A range of buildings with the front on a convex arch is called a *quadrant*. **2.** Type of arch, also called a *horseshoe-arch*.

cress, crest, cresting. 1. Ornament or series of ornamental elements, often perforated, used to form a decorative finish on top of an architectural element, e.g. a *canopy, *ridge, *screen, or wall. A *crest-table* is a medieval term for a *cope. **2.** A *finial.

Creswell, Harry Bulkeley (1869–1960). British architect. He was articled to Aston *Webb before setting up his own practice in 1899. In addition to his work as Inspecting Engineer for the Crown Agents for the Colonies, he designed the turbine-factory at Queensferry, Flint (1901–6), with its huge *pylon-like tower and *battered Egyptianizing *piers articulating each *bay. Creswell was a contributor to the *Architectural Review*, and the author of *The Honeywood File* (1929) and *The Honeywood Settlement* (1930), both witty and humorous 'fictional' correspondence between architect, client, quantity surveyor, and builder.

Creswell (1929, 1930, 1931, 1935, 1942, 1943); Gray (1985)

Cret, Paul Philippe (1876–1945). French-born American architect. He trained at the Écoles des Beaux-Arts in Lyons and Paris, before emigrating to the United States in 1903 where he taught at the University of Pennsylvania and set up his own practice in 1907. Under his aegis Penn's School of Architecture achieved an outstanding reputation, and produced many graduates of distinction, including Louis I. *Kahn. Cret's monumental Pan-American Union Building, Washington, DC (1907–10), reveals his *Beaux-Arts training. The Public Library, Indianapolis, Ind. (1914–17), has massive blocky *pavilions on either side of a severe *Doric *colonnade, but with the Folger Shakespeare Library, Washington, DC (1928–32), Cret's style became more stripped and powerful. His most moving works in a simplified Classical idiom are the memorials he designed to the dead of the 1914–18 war: a good example is the Aisne-Marne Memorial, near Château-Thierry, France (1926–33).

Gossman (1996); Hoak and Church (1930); White (1973)

Cretan architecture. Large palace complexes, designed in the second millennium BC and later replaced with even grander structures planned on asymmetrical lines, with vast corridors, many chambers, *courts, and columned halls, are known to have been built at Knossos and Phaestos in Crete. At the 'Palace of King Minos' at Knossos there was a formal axially planned arrangement with a great stair leading to the state rooms (so-called 'Minoan' architecture). Painted decorations were plentiful, vigorous, and strongly coloured, while *contractura columns (often of cypress-wood) were set with the smaller diameter at the base, so the taper was downwards, without *entasis, a curious reversal of natural form. The *primitive character of Cretan architectural detail attracted some C20 architects, notably *Plečnik.

Cruickshank (1996); Dinsmoor (1950)

Crewe, Bertie (*c.*1860–1937). Essex-born English architect. He became an important and prolific designer, responsible for over 100 theatres and music-halls as well as several early cinemas. His buildings include the New Prince's (later Shaftesbury) Theatre, London (1911), the Hippodrome, Golders Green (1910), and the first 'super-cinema' in England, the New Tivoli, Strand (1923—demolished 1957).

Gray (1985)

Crickmer, Courtenay Melville (1879–1971). London-born architect. In 1907 he began work at Letchworth *Garden City, then being developed by *Parker & *Unwin, where he designed and built groups of houses, single houses, schools, and other buildings, all in a restrained *vernacular style. He also designed a number of houses at Hampstead *Garden Suburb, and was appointed resident architect at the new munitions town of Gretna, Scotland.

Gray (1985); Miller and Gray (1992)

crinkle-crankle, crinkum-crankum. Garden-wall, usually aligned east–west so that one side faces south, on a plan of elongated S-shaped curves joined in a continuous *ribbon* or *serpentine* form that stiffens the wall, enabling it to be less thick than a straight wall would have to be for stability, and removing the need for any *buttresses.

criosphinx. Ancient Egyptian *sphinx-like form, but with the head of a ram on a lion's body.

Critical Regionalism. A strategy for achieving a more humane architecture in the face of universally held abstractions and international clichés. Coined by A. Tzonis and L. Lefaivre in 1981, the term was seized upon by the critic Kenneth Frampton, who argued that architects should seek regional variations in their buildings instead of continuing to design in a style of global uniformity using 'consumerist iconography masquerading as culture', and should 'mediate the impact' of universal civilization with themes drawn indirectly from the individual 'peculiarities of a particular place'. While appreciating the dangers of industrialization and technology, he did not advocate revivals of either the great historical styles or a humbler *vernacular type of building. In essence, he sought the deconstruction of global *Modernism, criticized *post-Modernism for reducing architecture to a mere 'communicative or instrumental sign', and proposed the introduction of alien paradigms to the indigenous *genius loci*. He cited the work of *Aalto and *Utzon as offering examples of Critical Regionalism in which the local and the general were synthesized.

Curtis (1996); Foster (1983)

crocket. **1.** *Gothic ornament, generally a bud, flower, leaf, or bunch of foliage, placed at regular intervals on the external edges of *canopies, *gables, gablets, *hood-moulds, *pinnacles, *spires, etc. The largest bunches at the top, standing on an upright stem (*finial), are properly called *crops. **2.** Crockets also occur on the corners of foliated *Gothic *capitals, based, no doubt, on the *Corinthian *Order. **3.** *Foil, as in a *crocket-arch* with foils on the intrados.

croft. *See* crypt.

croisée. *See* French window.

croisette. *See* crossette.

cromlech. *See* dolmen.

Cronaca, Simone del Pollaiuolo *called* **Il** (1457–1508). Florentine architect. He worked with Giuliano da *Sangallo on the octagonal *sacristy of Santo Spirito, and with Benedetto da *Maiano on the Palazzo Strozzi, where he was responsible for the grand *cornicione (*c.*1489–1504). He completed the monastery-church of San Salvatore (or San Francesco) al Monte in 1504, the chaste proportions of which were admired by *Michelangelo. Cronaca has been credited with the design of the Palazzo Guadagni (1504–6).

Goldthwaite (1980); Heydenreich and Lotz (1974)

Crook, Joseph Mordaunt (1937–). English architectural historian. He made a considerable contribution to the study of *Neoclassicism in Britain with his work on *Smirke, the British Museum, and the *Greek Revival. His elegant book on William *Burges is one of the most substantial studies of any Victorian architect, while his investigations of styles have added to his reputation. A monograph on John *Carter has shed new light on aspects of antiquarianism and the *Gothic Revival, He co-edited part of the *History of the King's Works* (1973–6).

Crook (1964, 1972, 1972*a*, 1981, 1987, 1995); Crook and Port (1973); personal knowledge

crop, crope. *Gothic *knop* of sculptured unfolding leaf-like forms surmounting a *finial, *gable, *spire, etc. A more rounded, less leafy, ball-like finial is a *pommel.

cross. Very ancient ornamental form consisting primarily of two straight or nearly straight members, set at 90° to each other, one vertical and the other horizontal, but also with many variations. Varieties of cross include:

alisée patée: like a circle with four curved, spear-headed slices taken out of it;

Ankh: Ancient Egyptian T-form topped by a halo-like loop, signifying Life and Resurrection, and therefore a prototype of a Crucifixion symbol. With *serif*-like (splayed) ends to the three arms (instead of being *sans-serif*), the Ankh-form becomes a *crux ansata*;

bottonée: *Greek* cross with each arm terminating in a trefoil-like form resembling a clover-leaf;

Calvary: large stone cross erected on three steps representing Faith, Hope, and Charity;

cantonée: *Greek* cross with four small Greek crosses in each of the areas bounded by the arms;

churchyard: large stone cross standing on a stepped base in a churchyard to indicate the ground was consecrated, and from the base of which itinerant friars would preach;

city: see *market* below;

clover-leaf: as *bottonée* above;

consecration: cross painted or carved on a church wall indicating where chrism was to be applied during the consecration of the building. There were 12 in all, and many have survived as permanent interior decoration;

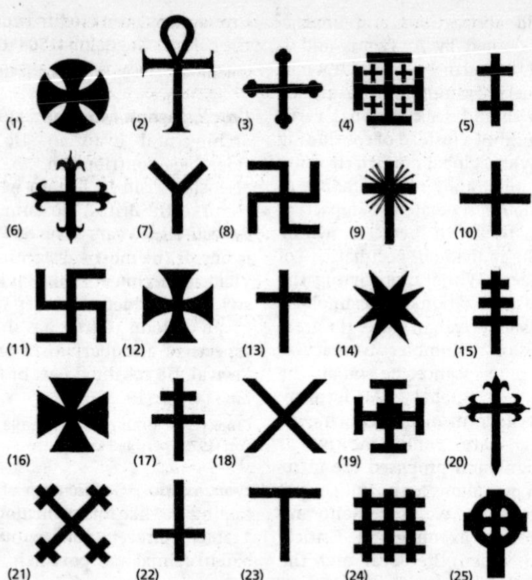

cross. (1) Alisée patée or pattée. (2) Ancient Egyptian *Ankh.* (3) Bottonée or clover-leaf. (4) Crusader's or Jerusalem. Without the four small crosses it is a *potent* cross. (5) Double. (6) Fleurée or fleury. If the centre-leaf of each arm is omitted, it becomes a *moline.* (7) Forked. (8) Fylfot or swastika. (9) Glory. (10) Greek. (11) Hakenkreuz or potent rotated. (12) Iron or Eisenkreuz of Prussia. (13) Latin. (14) Maltese. (15) Papal. (16) Patée formée. (17) Patriarchal. (18) St Andrew's or saltire. (19) St Chad's. (20) St James's. (21) St Julian's. (22) St Peter's. (23) Tau or St Anthony's. (24) Triparted. (25) Wheel-head or Celtic.

Crusader's: *potent* cross with four *Greek* crosses added to the areas bounded by the arms;

crux ansata: see *Ankh* above;

double: two *Greek* crosses, one set above the other, with the lower arm of one joined to the upper arm of the other;

Eisenkreuz: Prussian *iron* cross, designed by *Schinkel as a form of *patée* cross, but with the ends of the arms straight, so like a square from which four wide curved-sided sections like spear-heads have been taken out of the diagonals;

Eleanor: one of the 12 tall *Gothic memorial structures resembling a variety of ornate *spire set over a stepped base, erected to commemorate the funeral route of Queen Eleanor (d. 1290), consort of King Edward I of England. Three survive (Geddington, Northamptonshire, Northampton, and Waltham Cross, Hertfordshire). The monument at Charing Cross, London, is a C19 revival of the type;

fleury or *fleurée*: *Greek* cross with each arm terminating in three leaves resembling the *fleur-de-lys. If the centre-leaf of each termination is missing, it is a *moline* cross;

forked: Y-shaped;

fylfot: *Greek* cross, with the arms cranked at 90°, the ends pointing anti-clockwise, an ancient symbol associated with good fortune and the sun, called *swastika*, related to the *Greek-key, *fret, or *labyrinth, and to the *potent* cross;

glory: *Latin* cross with radiating lines like a *sunburst projecting from the centre of the cross where the two arms intersect, symbolizing glory;

Greek: with arms of equal length, representing the miraculous powers of Christ, and used as the basic form of *Byzantine and some *Renaissance church-plans;

Hakenkreuz: *potent rotated* cross, like the *fylfot* or *swastika*, but with the cranked arms pointing clockwise, anciently associated with misfortune and with dark forces. It was used by the National Socialist German Workers' Party (Nazis);

iron: see *Eisenkreuz* above;

Jerusalem: as *Crusader's* cross above;

Latin: with three equally long topmost arms, though sometimes the vertical arm may be shorter than the two horizontals, and a much longer bottom arm. Used as the basic form for many Western *cruciform* church-plans from the *Romanesque period;

Latin cross fleurée: as *Latin* cross above, but with a

three-leafed termination to each arm resembling the fleur-de-lys;

Lorraine: resembles the *patriarchal* cross, but the lower, longer arm is set further down the vertical element;

Maltese: like four identical acute-angled triangles or arrow-heads meeting at their most acute points, with V-shaped notches taken out of the ends of each equal arm;

market: large structure in the principal market-place of a town, consisting of a raised platform with a high and elaborate superstructure, sometimes acting as a *canopy over the platform. A good example is the *Gothic *city-* or *market*-cross, Chichester, Sussex (1501);

moline: see *fleury* above;

papal: like a *Latin* cross, but with three horizontals set across the vertical, the lowest longer than the one above, which is in turn longer than the topmost member. If the lowest arm is set diagonally, it is a *Russian Orthodox* cross;

patée or pattée: see *alisée patée* above;

patée formée: like a square from which four sharp straight-sided triangular notches have been removed from the diagonals, so like the *Eisenkreuz* but with straight-sided triangular arms;

patriarchal: like a *Latin* cross but with two horizontals set across the vertical, the lower longer than the top and set roughly half-way up the vertical;

pommée: *Greek* cross with each arm terminating in a circular blob;

potent: *Greek* cross with each arm a T;

potent rotated: see *Hakenkreuz*;

Rood: cross set above the western entrance to a *chancel, sometimes on a *screen, sometimes on a *Rood-beam, and sometimes suspended. Roods often have a representation of the Crucifixion with Sts Mary and John on either side;

St Andrew: X or *saltire* cross;

St Anthony: T or *Tau* cross;

St James: *Latin* cross *fleurée*, with each arm terminating in three leaves, like the fleur-de-lys, although the base is usually pointed;

St Julian: X or *saltire* cross with each arm terminating in a *Latin* cross;

St Peter: Latin cross set upside-down;

saltire: X-shaped cross, also known as *St Andrew's* cross. If each arm terminates in a *Latin* cross, it is a *St Julian's* cross;

Tau: T-shaped cross, also known as *St Anthony's* cross.

The Cross is the emblem of the Christian religion, and is employed architecturally, not merely in the plan of *cruciform* churches with *transepts, but on grave-slabs and tombs and on crowning features on *cupolas, *gables, *spires, etc. It was also placed surmounting a monument, such as a *churchyard-*, *Eleanor-*, or *market*-cross (see above).

Dirsztay (1978); Ferguson (1961); Seymour (1898)

cross-aisle. 1. *Transept. **2.** Clear passage between rows of *pews. **3.** Clear way to exits set parallel to rows of seats in a theatre.

cross-banded. Veneered, with the grain at right angles to the length of an object, especially the handrail of a *stair-*balustrade.

cross-bar. *Transom.

cross-beam. Transverse *beam spanning from wall to wall.

cross-church. Cruciform church with *transepts.

cross-domed. Type of *Early Christian or *Byzantine church on a cruciform plan with a dome over the *crossing and four barrel-*vaults over the arms, also known as an *ambulatory* church. The centre had galleried *aisles on three sides.

cross-entry. *See* entry.

crossette. Also *croisette* or *crosette*. **1.** Projection on each side of the top of a Classical *architrave around an aperture at the junction of the *lintel and *jamb, where the *supercilium projects beyond the *ante-pagments, and the mouldings return, forming ears, elbows, knees, lugs, or shoulders. **2.** *Console set on each flank at the top of an architrave around an aperture, supporting a *cornice: consoles are also called *ancones, ears, elbows, hawksbills (or beaks), knees, lugs, prothyrides, or *trusses. **3.** *Shoulder*, *ledged* projection, ear, *joggle, or lug in a *voussoir of a flat arch, segmental arch, or architrave constructed of voussoirs, fitting into a recess in the adjacent voussoir for stability. **4.** Ledged or joggled voussoir resting on a neighbouring voussoir, as in *rusticated

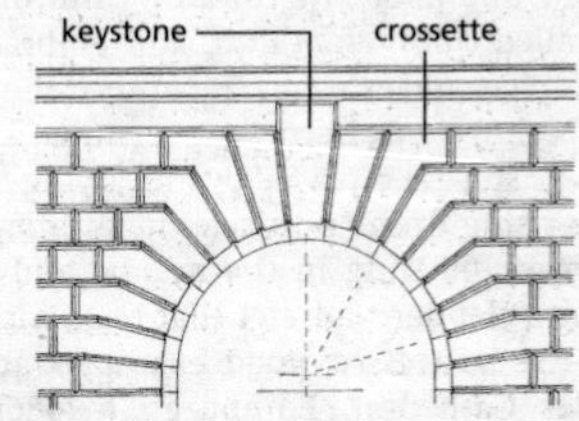

Crossettes in V-jointed rusticated stonework.

*ashlar over an aperture or in an *arcade on *piers.

cross-gable. One parallel to the roof-ridge of the main part of a building, as on a *cross-wing.

crossing. Volume formed on a square plan by the intersection of *chancel, *nave, and *transepts of a *cruciform church, often with a tower, *flèche, or other architectural feature, such as a *cupola, over it.

cross-in-square. Common *Byzantine church-plan consisting of a large central domed square (with the dome supported on four *piers or columns), four corner (domed or barrel-vaulted) squares, and four rectangular barrel-vaulted *bays, the whole called a *cross-inscribed*, *croix inscrite*, or *quincunx* arrangement.

cross-passage. *See* entry.

cross-quarter. Quatrefoil (*see* foil), its lobes set diagonally, usually in series as a *band.

cross-rail. In *timber-framed construction, the main horizontal mid-rail parallel to the *cill and wall-*plate.

cross-rib. Transverse rib in a *vault, i.e. at right angles to the main axis of a *nave or *aisle.

cross-springer. Diagonal rib in a *vault.

cross-vault. Intersecting barrel-vaults forming a groin-vault.

cross-window. Window with *lights defined by a *mullion and *transom forming a cross.

cross-wing. Wing attached to the hall-range of a medieval house, its axis at right angles to the hall-range, and often gabled.

croud, croude, crowd, crowde. *See* crypt.

crown. **1.** Head of any part of a building, especially of an arch or *vault (including the keystone and about the middle third of the arc), called *crown of an arch*, and embracing both *intrados* and *extrados*. **2.** *Apse at the east end of a church. **3.** Decorative termination in which a *spire is replaced by four flying *buttresses rising from *pinnacles at the corners of a tower, meeting in the middle and supporting a slender *spirelet that rests entirely upon the buttresses: good examples are at St Giles Cathedral, Edinburgh (*c.*1486), St Nicholas, Newcastle upon Tyne (*c.*1475), and St Dunstan-in-the-East, London (1697—based on a medieval precedent at St Mary-le-Bow, London (destroyed)).

crown cornice. **1.** Main *cornice and *frieze defining the top of a *façade, such as a *cornicione. **2.** Upper part of a *cornice, including the *corona and anything over it.

crown glass. Fine English window-glass with a brilliant, fine-finish lustre, in general use until the mid-C19. *See* glass.

crown-moulding. Any moulding that crowns anything, e.g. the *corona of a *cornice.

crown-plate. Longitudinal timber in a *crown-post roof, supported on crown-posts and bearing the *collars, also called a *collar-purlin* or *collar-plate*.

crown-post. Upright timber set on a *tie-beam, or occasionally on a *collar, supporting the *crown-plate and not rising above a collar.

crown-steeple. *Spirelet on a tower carried on flying *buttresses, looking like a *crown.

crown-strut. Upright timber resembling a *crown-post, but not supporting a *plate.

crown-tile. *Ridge-tile or -cresting.

crow-steps. *Corbel-, *craw-*, or *corbie-*steps forming the stepped tops of a *gable, the *crow-stone* being the topmost stone at the apex. Crow-stepped (or cat-stepped) gables were common in Flemish, Netherlandish, North-German, and Scandinavian architecture, and influenced the design of buildings in East Anglia and Eastern Scotland.

Croxton, John (*fl.* 1411–47). English mason. He worked at Guildhall, London, in 1411, when that structure was begun, and was associated with it for most of his career. He was undoubtedly the architect, and the *crypt and porch appear to have been fine examples of the *Perpendicular style.

Harvey (1987)

Croyland, William de (*fl.* 1392–1427). English master-mason. He was responsible for most of the *Perpendicular work at Croyland Abbey, Lincolnshire, including the existing north *aisle, tower, and *nave-*screen. His other very considerable buildings there have all been destroyed, but he was clearly a competent designer.

Harvey (1987)

cruciform. *Cross-shaped; e.g. a church with *transepts.

cruck. *Blade or inclined curved timber, meeting a similar timber to form an approximately triangular frame on which the subsidiary structure rests. A *full* or *true cruck* has two blades serving as the *principals of a roof, rising from near ground level to the *ridge, and supporting both walls and roof. A *cruck-truss* has two blades with a transverse timber that could be a *tie-beam (at or below the top level of the walls), a *collar (at high level), a *saddle (just under the apex), or a *yoke (just below the apex). A *cruck-framed* structure is therefore one constructed of crucks instead of box-frames.

Types of cruck include:

base-cruck: rises from just above ground level to just under the first transverse member, and provides the main upright for the wall;

end-cruck: cruck-blade in the centre of a *gable-wall of a cruck-framed building supporting the ridge-timber;

jointed cruck: cruck-truss made of two or more pieces of timber, the lowest of which rises from just above ground level and doubles as a wall-post at the top of which the cruck is jointed and changes direction to follow the slope of the roof;

middle-cruck: the same as a *raised cruck* below;

raised cruck: cruck with its feet set in solid walls, with the blades reaching down the walls (if the blades reach half-way down the walls, they are *middle-crucks*);

two-tier cruck: supporting a small pair of cruck-shaped blades over the collar;

upper cruck: cruck with its feet resting on a first-floor *ceiling-beam* that is not a *tie-beam*.

Alcock (1981); Alcock, Barley, Dixon, and Meeson (1996)

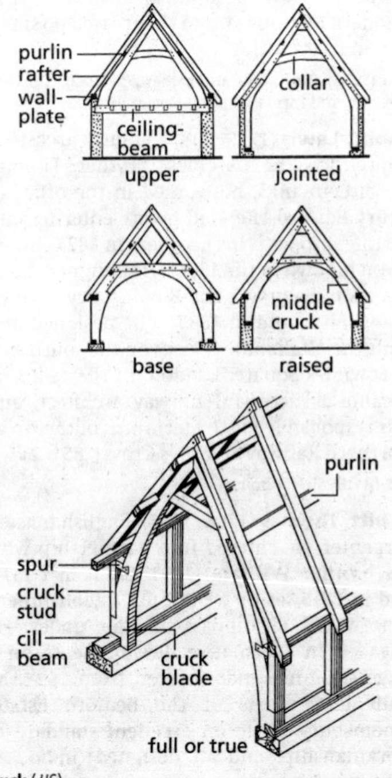

cruck (*JJS*)

Crucy, Mathurin (1749–1826). Architect-Surveyor of Nantes, he created many fine buildings and public spaces, including the Grand Théâtre and Place Graslin (1784–7), Place d'Armes (1786–90), Place Royale (1787), Bourse (1790–1814), and Textile Exchange (1821). His civic designs were conceived on a grand scale, and are among the supreme examples of Greek-inspired *Neoclassicism by a Frenchman.

Lelievre (1988)

Crundale, Richard (*fl.* 1281–d. 1293). English master-mason. He worked under Robert of *Beverley at the Tower of London (1281–3), and in 1284–5 was at Westminster Abbey, where he succeeded Beverley as King's Chief Mason for London Works. He designed the Eleanor Cross at Charing Cross (1290—replaced by the later work by E. M. *Barry), and the beautiful tomb of Queen Eleanor (d. 1290) in Westminster Abbey. His brother, **Roger** (*fl.* 1290–8), completed the Charing Cross, and worked with Nicholas Dyminge de Reyns (*fl.* 1290s) on the designs and making of the tomb of Queen Eleanor's viscera in Lincoln Cathedral (1291–4—destroyed) and the Eleanor Cross at Waltham, Hertfordshire (which survives).

Harvey (1987)

Crunden, John (*c.*1741–1835). English architect. He is known for his *pattern-books, one of which, *Convenient and Ornamental Architecture, consisting of Original Designs (from) the Farm House . . . to the Most Grand and Magnificent Villa* (1767), went into seven later editions, and was the most successful of its type, containing designs for a range of Palladianesque buildings. He collaborated with J. H. Morris to produce *The Carpenter's*

Companion . . . for . . . Chinese Railing and Gates (1765), and also designed in the *Gothick style, including a garden-pavilion illustrated in Krafft's *Plans des plus beaux jardins pittoresques* (1809). His architectural works are not numerous, but include Boodle's Club, St James's Street, London (1775–6), which is influenced by the work of Robert *Adam. In turn, his pattern-books were influential, notably in America.

Colvin (1995); Crunden (1767); Harris (1990)

crypt. **1.** Large vaulted chamber (*croft, croud, croude, crowd, crowde, shroud*, or *undercroft*) beneath a church, wholly or partly underground, usually under the *chancel, often divided into *nave, *aisles, and *chapels, equipped with altars, and used for religious services and burials beneath the floor. They often had some degree of natural light, and were generally bigger than a *confessio, though very small crypts, such as the *Anglo-Saxon example at Hexham (C7) were little more than Relic-chambers. *Ring-crypts* were semicircular crypts inside and below an *apse, originating with the *basilica of San Pietro, Rome, in *c.*590: outer ring-crypts (called *ambulatories) were characteristic of the *Carolingian and *Ottonian periods, but a very early example, pre-dating those on the Continent, existed at All Saints Church, Brixworth, Northamptonshire (*c.* C8). **2.** Burial-chamber.

crypta. **1.** Long narrow *vault, wholly or partly underground, associated with a Roman farm, used for storage. **2.** Long narrow *gallery with windows on each side, the larger openings being on the side next to the sea or an especially fine view, used for walking and conversation, attached to a Roman *villa, called *cryptoporticus*.

C-scroll. C- and S-scrolls were essential elements of *Rococo ornament, especially in frames around *cartouches or inscriptions.

cubiculum (*pl.* **cubicula**). *See* catacomb.

Cubism. Movement in art originating with the work of Pablo Picasso (1881–1973) and Georges Braque (1882–1963), and mainly dating from *c.*1905 to 1914. Cubism departed from the notion of art as an imitation of Nature that had been paramount in Europe from *Renaissance times, and also retreated from traditional *perspective. Instead it attempted to achieve the illusion of three-dimensionsal forms in a different way by showing solids and volumes in two-dimensional flat planes to suggest space. To do this, many aspects of familiar objects were represented all at once, their forms shown on various geometrical planes redrawn from many vantage-points to create new combinations. Thus it claimed to be a new way of seeing, and tried to indicate that which was visible as well as everything known about the item depicted.

The relationship of Cubism and architecture was tentative, often involving the application of Cubist decorations to *stripped Neoclassical buildings. Hints of Cubist themes are found in *Art Deco and *Modernist work: however, even in Prague, the Czech Cubist group (Čapek, *Chochol, *Gočár, Hofman, Janák, and Novotny) did little more than treat façades with prismatic ornament not unlike that of *Expressionism. The fundamentals of Cubism, however, including asymmetrical composition, interpenetration of volumes, transparency, and perception simultaneously from various points of view, became enshrined in the *Modern Movement, and they played no small part in its evolution.

Barr (1936); Burkhardt and Lamarová (1982); Chilvers, Osborne, and Farr (1988); von Vegesack (1992)

Cubitt, Lewis (1799–1883). English architect. Apprenticed to his eldest brother, Thomas *Cubitt, in 1815, he worked in the office of Henry Edward *Kendall before entering into partnership with his brothers in 1824. He set up on his own in the 1830s. He designed many houses in Belgravia and Bloomsbury built by the Cubitts, and in 1837–9 he designed and built the *Italianate houses on the south side of Lowndes Square, London. In the 1840s he became a successful railway architect, and was responsible for the terminus of the Great Northern Railway at King's Cross (1851–2).

Colvin (1995); Hobhouse (1995)

Cubitt, Thomas (1788–1855). English master-carpenter. He entered into partnership with his brother **William** (1791–1863) in *c.*1814, and in 1815 set up a building establishment that would encompass all the trades. He engaged in speculative developments on a huge scale in London. Later, from 1824, he built large parts of the Bedford Estate, Bloomsbury, all to an excellent standard of workmanship, and all designed 'in-house', largely by his brother, Lewis *Cubitt. He developed huge tracts of Belgravia and Pimlico, and much of Kemp Town, Brighton. He also erected several large, substantial, and well-built houses to his own designs. These buildings were sub-*Palladian or *Italianate, and the most celebrated is Osborne House, Isle of Wight (1845–8), to which Prince *Albert also contributed. Cubitt was active in promoting public hygiene, public parks, better building regulations, and smoke abatement.

Colvin (1995); *DNB* (1917); Hobhouse (1995); Summerson (1988)

Cuijpers *or* **Cuypers, Petrus Josephus Hubertus** (1827–1921). Roermond-born Dutch architect. He designed many *Neo-Gothic churches in The Netherlands, and in the Church of St Willibrordus-buiten-de-Veste, Amsterdam (1864), demonstrated his interest in honesty of materials and construction derived from his readings of *Viollet-le-Duc. As a Roman Catholic from the province of Limburg he was ideally placed when the Roman Catholic episcopal hierarchy was restored in 1853, and an ambitious programme of church-building was set in motion. His best-known works are the *Rijksmuseum* (State Museum—1877–85) and the Central Station (1881–9), in Amsterdam, both powerfully symmetrical, in a free style, and with lively skylines. The *Rijksmuseum* was much influenced by the University Museum, Oxford, even in respect of its iron roofs and interior galleries. His *Picturesque compositions and principles of truth to materials and expression were important influences on several generations of architects including the *Amsterdam School.

Cuypers (1917); Fanelli (1968); Hitchcock (1977); Rosenberg (1972)

cul-de-four. 1. Half-dome, as used over an *apse or a *niche. **2.** Incorrectly held to mean a hemispherical vault on a circular or elliptical plan.

cul-de-lampe. 1. Pendent ornament shaped like a *pyramid or a cone. **2.** *Corbel formed like a half-cone.

cul-de-sac. Alley, lane, passage, street, etc., closed at one end, with no exit except the entrance.

Cullinan, Edward (1931–). British architect. His practice has produced a large number of schemes in which the conflict of discrepancies is expressed. Some critics have detected *vernacular themes in his work, but this does not stand up to serious examination. His best-known work is perhaps the Fountains Abbey and Studley Royal Visitors' Centre, Yorkshire (1987–92).

Emanuel (1994); Powell (1995)

culver-hole. Aperture in a wall to receive the end of a timber-member. *Putlog-hole.

culver-house. *Columbarium in the sense of a *dovecote.

Cumberland, Frederick William (1820–81). Canadian architect, one of the most accomplished *Gothic Revivalists working in Canada. He designed St James's Cathedral, Toronto (1852–3), in the *Gothic style, working in partnership with William G. Storm (1826–92) during the construction of the church. With Storm he also designed University College, University of Toronto (1856), a demonstration of *Ruskinian principles of design that is arguably a superior composition to *Deane & Woodward's University Museum, Oxford. The Toronto building has central and corner towers, and is a fine example of the *High Victorian *Picturesque manner.

Kalman (1994)

Cundy, Thomas (1765–1825). Cornwall-born architect, who became Surveyor to Lord Grosvenor's Estates in Belgravia and Pimlico, London, in 1821. He designed numerous country-houses in a *Picturesque *Gothic style, e.g. Wytham Abbey, Berkshire (1809–10), and Middleton Stoney Rectory, Oxfordshire (1816–17).

Colvin (1995); *DNB* (1917)

Cundy, Thomas, Junior II (1790–1867). London-born architect. He worked in his father's office and succeeded him to the practice and the Surveyorship of the Grosvenor Estate. He oversaw the development of Belgravia and Pimlico, largely by Thomas *Cubitt. His Normanton Church, Rutland (1826), has a tower derived from *Archer's *Baroque towers at St John's, Smith Square, Westminster. From the late 1840s Cundy was joined by *his* son, **Thomas III** (1820–95), who eventually succeeded to the practice and Surveyorship. Thomas II and III seem to have been jointly responsible for a number of *Gothic Revival churches, including St Barnabas, Pimlico (1847–50—said by the St Paul's Ecclesiological Society to be the 'most sumptuous and correctly fitted church erected in England since the Reformation'). Thomas III was also the architect for some of the tall *stucco-fronted terraces in Kensington, in a free *Italianate manner that was widely imitated. His best houses are arguably 22–4 Queen's Gate (1858–60), and Cornwall Gardens (1866–79).

Colvin (1995); *DNB* (1917); Hobhouse (1986)

cuneus. **1.** Wedge or *voussoir. **2.** Part of a Classical theatre auditorium, shaped like a wedge, containing seating and defined by the gangways, passages, etc. **3.** Species of *zig-zag or fret painted on flat *bands, a variation on *Greek key.

Cupid. God of Love, usually depicted as a winged male child with bow and arrow, as distinct from an unarmed *Cherub or wingless *putto. *See* Amorino.

cupola. **1.** Bowl-shaped *vault on a circular, elliptical, or polygonal plan. **2.** Underside or *soffit of a *dome. **3.** Bowl-shaped element carried on columns set as a *canopy over a tomb, etc., or a *ciborium. **4.** Small dome on the *lantern over the eye of a large dome, or the dome plus lantern, or any diminutive domed form, visible above a roof. **5.** Revolving dome of an observatory, or an armoured revolving dome over the guns of a fortress.

curb-roof. *Mansard roof.

curtail. In a *stair, the outward curving or *scroll-shaped part of the handrail, and the outer end of the lowest step. In grander stairs the first flight, detached from a wall, may have a *curtail-* or *scroll*-step with curved parts at each end of the *balustrades and lowest step, often curving around the centre-line of the *newels.

curtain-wall. **1.** Part of a straight wall constructed between two advancing structures, such as *bastions, *buttresses, or *piers. In a fortification it is the weakest element, and in a church it is pierced with large windows, as in a *Perpendicular *Gothic *aisle. **2.** Any plain enclosing screen-wall not supporting a roof. **3.** Partition between two rooms, or subdividing a space. **4.** In modern construction, a thin subordinate wall between piers or other structural members, the curtain being a filling, having no share in the support of other parts of the building. This principle was extended to the provision of entire external non-loadbearing skins, supported by the structure, and usually made of metal, glass, or some other type of *cladding.

Hart, Henn, and Sontag (1985)

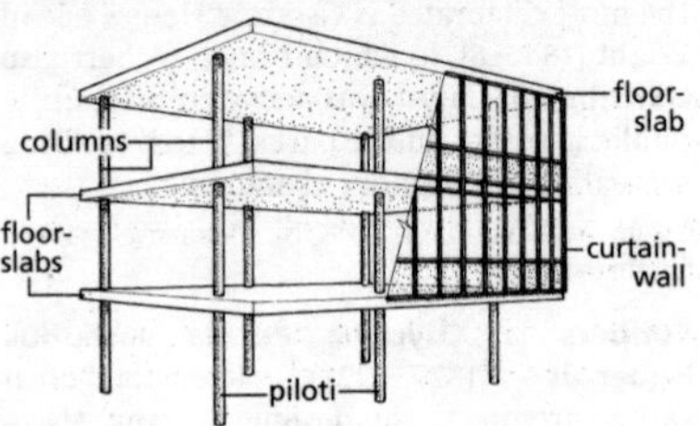

curtain-wall. On column-and-slab construction.

Curvilinear. *See* tracery.

cushion. **1.** Convex projection (*pulvinus*) of part of a building, e.g. a *frieze apparently bulging outwards as if under pressure, called *cushion-course*, *cushioned*, or *pulvinated* frieze, or even a *bolster* or *pulvin*. **2.** Stone block on an *impost, being the springer of an arch. **3.** *Corbel or *pad-stone.

cushion-capital. *See* capital.

cushion-course. *Pulvinated *frieze.

cusp. Point made by the intersection of two curved lines or members, e.g. the projecting point between the small arcs or *foils in *Gothic *tracery, or the enrichment on the intrados of a Gothic arch provided by foliation, the curves of which touch the inner edge of the main arch (*cusped* arch).

cuspidation. Series of *cusps, as on the intrados of a *Gothic arch.

cussom(e). Large heavy slate, or stone slab, bedded in mortar and laid as part of a course, slightly inclined, immediately above the *eaves of a pitched roof above the gutter, thus providing an overhanging *soffit and avoiding the necessity of *sprockets, timber *fasciae, or soffit-linings.

cut brackets. **1.** Piece of board cut with a profile resembling a *corbel or *console, used to support a shelf, or a larger timber cut similarly used to support overhanging *eaves. **2.** Similar board, sometimes further carved, under the returned nosing of each step on the outer string of a stair, sometimes resembling the sides of *consoles or *modillions.

cut-roof. Roof with the appearance of having the part above the *collars removed, i.e. flattened.

cut splay. Obliquely cut corners of *bricks in walling, as in *gables before the placing of *copes, or the reveals of apertures.

cut-string stairs. *Open-string* stairs in which the outer string is cut to accommodate the steps, with the treads on top of the string, the nosings mitred and returned, and the risers mitred to the string.

cut-water. *Starling, or sharply pointed bridge-*pier to reduce the pressure on it when a river is in flood.

Cuvilliés, Jean-François-Vincent-Joseph (1695–1768). *Rococo architect of the utmost refinement. Born in Soignies-en-Hainaut, near Brussels, as Court Dwarf he entered (1708) the service of Max Emanuel, Elector of Bavaria (1679–1726), who was then in exile in France. As a member of the Electoral household, Cuvilliés was exposed to the latest French tastes in architecture. When the Court returned to Munich in 1715, Cuvilliés worked under *Effner, who had been a pupil of *Boffrand, and, in due course, the budding architect Cuvilliés was also sent to Paris, where he studied briefly under Jean-François Blondel (1683–1756). When he came back to the Bavarian capital he worked with Effner, and, when Karl Albrecht succeeded as Elector (1726–45), seems to have been treated as the older architect's equal, although the prize of *Oberhofbaumeister* (Chief Court Architect) eluded him until 1763. For the new Elector's brother, Clemens August (d. 1761), Elector and Prince-Archbishop of Cologne, Cuvilliés designed Rococo interiors (1728–30) at Schloss Brühl near Cologne (newly built to designs by *Schlaun), as well as the charming hunting-lodge of Falkenlust (1729–37), with its interiors gaily decorated with *Chinoiserie and other orientalizing motifs judiciously mingled with Rococo ornament. Cuvilliés also may have been responsible for the *chinesisches Haus* for the Pheasantry in the Park (*c.*1730).

Cuvilliés was recalled to Munich, where he was to carry out his finest works, prompting the dissemination of the Rococo style throughout Bavaria, including the *Reiche Zimmer* (State Room) in the Munich *Residenz* (Seat of the Court), executed from 1730 to 1737, and acclaimed as among the finest of European Rococo achievements before being badly damaged during the 1939–45 war. From 1733 he was involved in the building of the Archiepiscopal Palais Königsfeld (or Holnstein), Munich (completed 1737), and, at the same time, in preparing the plans of the Premonstratensian Abbey of Schäftlarn, south of Munich. However, his finest creation is unquestionably the Amalienburg in the grounds of Schloss Nymphenburg (1734–9): this is an exquisite single-storey hunting-*pavilion with a balcony (a *tir aux faisans* from which pheasants could be shot) over the central circular *saloon, part of which extends outwards in a *bow in the centre of the entrance-façade. The enchanting Rococo interior decorations, with blue, yellow, and straw-coloured walls enriched with refined silvered embellishments, and enlivened with mirrors and Chinoiserie motifs, are outstanding, although J. B. *Zimmermann was responsible for the *stucco-work.

Cuvilliés was called in as a consultant by the Archbishop-Elector of Cologne to advise on the building of the *Collegiate Church of St Michael, at Berg-am-Laim, Munich (1738–51), J. M. *Fischer being the architect, and, around 1737, designed the lovely high-altar for the former Augustinian (now Parish) Church at Diessen, also by Fischer.

The *Livre de Cartouches* (Book of Cartouches) marked the start of a series of publications by Cuvilliés from 1738 featuring illustrations of ornamental designs for *cartouches, ceilings, frames, and entire rooms, with furnishings and panels. Other publications, featuring designs for mirrors, chandeliers, and a great deal more, followed from 1745, and from 1756 yet another series, this time featuring architectural designs, came out. These works were hugely influential in Central Europe. By the mid-1740s his advice was being sought by many patrons, and he was involved in the designs for *Schlösser* at Haimhausen, near Munich (from 1747), and Wilhelmstal, near Kassel (from 1750—a restrained Classical design), but his finest works were in and around Munich. His *Residenz-Theater*, Munich (1750–3), is one of the most beautiful small theatres in the world, bursting with the type of ornament he had published in various *Livres*: it was badly damaged in 1944, but was reconstructed in 1958, albeit on a different site within the *Residenz* complex. His appointment as *Oberhofbaumeister* by the Elector Maximilian III Joseph (1745–77) came late in his career, after he had rebuilt the central room at Schloss Nymphenburg (1756–7), and he did not live long after. His last work was the completion of the *façade of the *Theatinerkirche* (St Kajetan, the church of the Theatine Order) in Munich (1767). His son, **François-Joseph-Ludwig** (1731–77), produced many of the illustrations for his father's publications, and seems to have been largely responsible for the third series of the 1750s in which Rococo and *Neoclassicism merged. He reissued many of his father's designs in his *École de l'Architecture Bavaroise* (from 1770).

Bourke (1962); Braunfels (1938, 1986); Hitchcock (1968*a*); Jervis (1984); Lieb (1992); Wolf (1967)

Cuypers. *See* Cuijpers.

cyclopean. 1. Masonry composed of irregularly shaped very large blocks, sometimes approximating to polygons, dressed sufficiently for them to fit tightly together, without mortar, called *Megalithic* or *Pelasgic*. Found in Antiquity, it was also occasionally used by later architects to suggest very early origins, or rock-like foundations, as in the *plinth of Alexander 'Greek' *Thomson's Caledonia Road Church, Glasgow (1856). **2.** *Rock-faced* masonry, intended to appear like roughly quarried stones, but in fact dressed with rough surfaces for effect.

cyclostyle. Circular *peristyle of columns surrounding a wall-less volume, i.e. a *monopteral temple, often found in C18 parks.

cyma, cima (*pl.* **cymae**). Projecting moulding, common in Classical architecture, with an *ogee *section, usually of equal convex and concave arcs, with a plain *fillet above and below it. There are two main types: the *cyma recta*, or *Doric cyma*, usually found at the top of a *cornice, with the concave part uppermost (called *cymatium), and the *cyma reversa*, *Lesbian cymatium*, or *reverse ogee*, with the convex part uppermost, usually part of the bed-mouldings of a cornice or the exterior moulding of *architraves.

cymatium. *Crown-moulding of a Classical *cornice, commonly of the *cyma type, but sometimes an *ovolo (in some *Tuscan *Orders) and sometimes a *cavetto (in the *Doric Order).

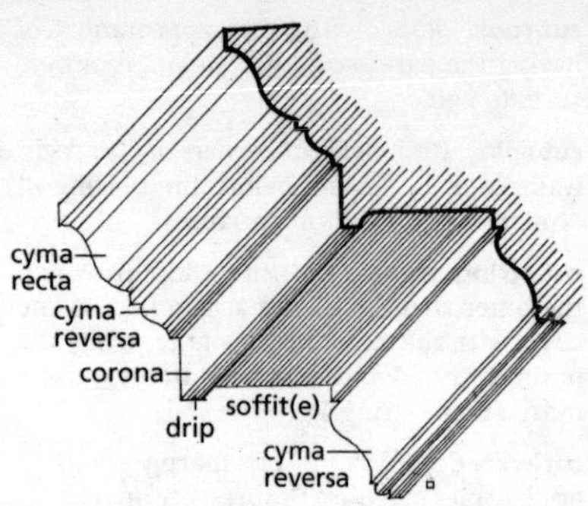

cyma. Cornice with cyma recta and cyma reversa profiles.

cynocephalus. Beast with the body of an ape, and a dog-like head, probably derived from baboons, found in Ancient Egyptian and Roman work.

cynocephalus. Roman statuette in the Egyptian taste.

cypher. Capital letters of the alphabet interwoven in one symmetrical design, or two capitals together, one reversed (e.g. ⅃ L) and surrounded by wreaths, etc., commonly found in schemes of architectural decoration, especially from the time of *Louis Quatorze.

cyrtostyle. 1. *Portico on a semicircular plan projecting from a *façade. **2.** Curved *colonnade.

cyzicene hall. *Oecus Cyzicenus*, or large hall overlooking a garden in an Ancient Greek house.

dado. **1.** *Die or flat-faced plain block of a Classical *pedestal between the *base and *cap. **2.** Surface of an internal wall like an extended pedestal all the way round a room between a *chair-rail (*cornice), and skirting (base or *plinth). A panelled timber dado is called a *wainscot. *Dado* is not used to describe an external pedestal-course. **3.** To cut or form with a groove of rectangular section, so the rectangular groove itself is also called a *dado*.

Daedalus. The 'cunning artificer' of Greek mythology, he was an inventor, artist, and architect, responsible for creating the *labyrinth at Knossos, Crete. Medieval architects identified with Daedalus as his heirs, and his legends are closely associated with those of Freemasonry.

Curl (1991); Hornblower and Spawforth (1996)

dagger. *Light shaped like an *ogee-ended elongated lozenge resembling a dagger in *Second Pointed *tracery. It is distinct from a *mouchette*, which is shaped like a tadpole.

dagoba. *Stupa, consisting of a low drum surmounted by a bell-shaped or dome-like form above which is a square platform or *tee*, or several umbrella-forms. It is associated with Buddhist architecture, and its name may have been the origin of the curious corrupt word *pagoda.

Dahinden, Justus (1925–). Swiss architect. His works have been influenced by *Archigram and *Metabolism, as well as by his own Christian beliefs. They include many churches and parish-centres (e.g. *Heilige Geist* (Holy Ghost) Church, Weingarten, Germany (1977), and Migros Centre, Ostermundingen, Switzerland (1988)), in which he has attempted to incorporate a sensitivity to 'biotechnics' (life and all its processes), 'geometrics' (the expression of order and form), 'psycho-logics' (the spiritual and reasoned processes that inform the environment), and 'cosmics' (the universal forces of order). He has evolved a modular constructional system (the Trigon) based on the triangular prism, of which the village at Doldertal, near Zurich, is an example (1969).

Emanuel (1994)

Dahlerup, Jens Vilhelm (1836–1907). Danish architect. A pupil of *Hetsch and *Nebelong, he was also influenced by the works of T. von *Hansen and *Schinkel, but turned more to a rich Italian *Renaissance style, persuaded in that direction by the works of *Semper. His reputation was quickly established, and he designed numerous important buildings: among them the Agriculture School at Lyngby, the Royal Theatre, Copenhagen (1872–4—with Ove *Petersen), the Pantomime Theatre, Tivoli Gardens, Copenhagen (1870s), the New Carlsberg Brewery Building (1880–3), the Jesuskirken at Valby, the Royal Museum of Art (1888–95—with Georg Møller), the Glyptoteket (1891–5), and many private houses in and around Copenhagen. The Vejlefjord Sanatorium (1899) was also built to his designs. He was one of the last of the academic architects of *Historicism in Denmark, but something of a virtuoso in his use of that architectural language.

Saur (1991–); Weilbach (1947)

daïs. **1.** *Estrade*, *footpace*, *halpace*, or platform in a banqueting-hall on which a high table is situated. **2.** Any similar platform, as in a lecture-theatre. **3.** The high table itself. **4.** Canopy over such a table or platform. **5.** *Tester or protective top over a throne, etc.

Dakin, James Harrison (1806–52). Born in New York, he became one of the most distinguished American architects of his time, equally fluent in *Egyptian, *Greek, or *Gothic styles. He joined *Town & *Davis in

1829, becoming a partner in 1832, and, with Ithiel Town, he designed New York University (1833–7), one of the first examples of *Collegiate Gothic in America. He set up an independent practice in 1833, and designed several distinguished *Greek Revival buildings, including the First Presbyterian Church, Troy, NY (1834), Bank of Louisville, Ky. (1834–6), and University of Louisiana (1847–55), later Tulane University. His Louisiana State Capitol, Baton Rouge (1847–52), is a daring *Gothic Revival essay. He influenced Minard *Lafever and produced drawings for several plates in two of the latter's books.

Lafever (1968, 1969); Patrick (1980); Placzek (1982); Scully (1973)

Dalton, John (1927–). Yorkshire-born Australian architect. He contributed to the creation of an architecture drawing on simple, unpretentious forms and responsive to the climatic conditions of Queensland, by controlling solar-heat gain and providing cross-ventilation to counteract the problems of humidity. His University House, Griffith University (1975), and Halls of Residence, Kelvin Grove College of Technology and Further Education (1977), both in Brisbane, are among his larger works, but many of his houses, with their *louvres, *verandahs, and other features that reflect the climate, deserve notice. Among his houses the Mount Manning Homestead, Darling Downs (1982), and the Beach House, Point Lookout (1988), both in Queensland, reflect his architectural philosophy.

Emanuel (1994); Freeland (1968); McKay and Boyd (1971); Tanner (1976)

Daly, César-Denis (1811–93). The most important French architectural editor and journalist of the second half of C19. He was brought up in England, studied architecture under *Duban, and later directed the *Revue Générale de L'Architecture et des Travaux Publics* (1839–90), France's first illustrated architectural journal, and *La Semaine des Constructeurs* (1876–97). His most influential work was *L'Architecture privée au XIX*me *siècle* (1864–77), a many-volumed pattern-book of domestic architecture in the era of Napoleon III and after. *L'Architecture Funéraire Contemporaine* (1871) is a richly illustrated record of French cemetery art of the period. He was responsible for the restoration of Albi Cathedral (1844–77). During his career, he gave critical support to *Barry, *Duc, *Garnier, *Labrouste, and *Vaudoyer, among others, and he was an admirer of François-Marie-Charles Fourier (1772–1885), the social theorist, who had an affection for the ellipse, also espoused by Daly. Indeed, Daly had been involved with the Fourierists since the 1830s, and had contributed articles and money to *La Phalange*, *La Démocratie Pacifique*, and other journals. As early as 1833 he had proposed a scheme for communal *phalanstères* for 400 children. During 1849 plans were made to found a Fourierist colony in Texas, and La Réunion, near Dallas, was founded in 1855: Daly travelled to Texas, and was a member of the Board of Directors, but did not remain long, probably because of internal dissent. In 1856 he visited Central America where he discovered important pre-Columbian ruins, and returned to Paris in 1857 a changed man, his pro-Fourierist notions dissipated. Thereafter he promoted the single-family suburban villa as the ideal home rather than the *phalanstère*. He and *Viollet-le-Duc were founding members of the Société d'Ethnographie Americaine et Orientale (1858), charged with encouraging pre-Columbian archaeology in Mexico.

Becherer (1984); Daly (1840–90, 1864, 1869, 1871, 1871*a*, 1877, 1880, n.d.); Lipstadt and Mendelsohn (1980)

Damascene-work. Designs incised into metal and filled with gold, silver, or copper, often of the *arabesque type.

Damesme *or* **Damême, Louis-Emmanuel-Aimé** (1757–1822). French architect. He supervised the erection of *Ledoux's *barrières* (toll-collecting offices) in Paris in the 1780s, and followed the master's severe *Neoclassical style. He designed several mansions and apartment-blocks in Paris and the theatre of the Société Olympique which so impressed Tsar Alexander I of Russia (1801–25) that he requested a set of the drawings for it. He also designed the Théâtre Royale de la Monnaie, Brussels (1813–18), with its handsome *portico of eight *Ionic columns. This and other works are illustrated in Goetgheuber's *Délices* (1819).

Gallet (1972); Krafft (1801–3)

Dammartin Family. French architects. **Guy**, **Gui**, or **Guiot de Dammartin** (d. 1398) worked with Raymond du *Temple on the Louvre, Paris (1362–72), and from 1367 to 1372 was employed by Jean de France, Duc de Berry (1340–1416), to oversee his ambitious building plans. He designed the Palace of Bourges (1375–85) with an *enfilade system of planning, an innovative arrangement for the time in an *hôtel. He designed two Saintes-Chapelles, at Riom (1382–8) and Bourges (1392–8), and remodelled the *châteaux of Mehun-sur-Yèvre, Riom, and Poitiers as grand mansions, excising *battlements and constructing *dormers, windows, and architectural embellishments, all in the 1380s. His brother, **Drouet de Dammartin** (d. 1413), also contributed to building operations at the Louvre and the Hôtel de Nesle (the latter for the Duc de Berry), Paris. Later, in the 1380s, he became Master of the Works for the Duc de Bourgogne, and built the Sainte-Chapelle, Dijon (1387), as well as a *Carthusian monastery. Drouet's son, **Jean de Dammartin** (d. 1454), was supervising architect at the Cathedral of St Julian, Le Mans, from 1421, where he built the north *transept and *rose-window. In 1432 he was appointed Master of the Works at Tours Cathedral, where he completed the *nave and the west portal.

Champeaux and Gauchery (1894); Lehoux (1966–8)

Damon, Isaac (*fl.* 1812–40). American architect. A pupil of Ithiel *Town, he was the leading architect in Western Massachusetts for over three decades. He designed the First Churches of Northampton (1811—destroyed) and Springfield (1818), and the Church and Court House in Lenox (*c.*1814).

Sturgis *et al.* (1901–2)

Dance, George, sen. (1695–1768). London mason, monumental sculptor, builder, and architect. He collaborated with his father-in-law, James Gould (d. 1734), in the erection of St Botolph's Church, Bishopsgate, London (1725–8). In 1735 he was appointed Clerk of the Works to the City of London, and designed the Mansion House (1739–42) with its grand *Egyptian Hall, probably his best work. His other buildings have influences from *Gibbs, *Palladianism, and *Wren, of which St Leonard's Church, Shoreditch (1736–40), with a *steeple design clearly based on the precedent of Wren's St Mary-le-Bow (completed 1680), is the best example. He also rebuilt the *nave of St Mary's Church, Faversham, Kent (1754–5), and designed the Market House, Coleraine, Co. Londonderry, for The Honourable The Irish Society (*c.*1740–3—demolished).

Colvin (1995); Curl (1986); Geffrye Museum (1972); Perks (1922); Stroud (1971)

Dance, George, jun. (1741–1825). Youngest son of George *Dance, sen. He set off for Italy in 1758, met up with his brother Nathaniel (1735–1811) in Florence, and arrived in Rome in 1759, where he acquired his skills as a draughtsman and absorbed the essentials of the new *Neoclassicism, returning to England in 1764. His first commission was All Hallows Church, London Wall (1765–7), an advanced Neoclassical building with a barrel-vaulted interior and a bare exterior that perhaps shows influences of *Laugier and other French writers. In 1768 he succeeded his father as Clerk of the Works, and designed the outstandingly fine Newgate Gaol (1768–85—demolished 1902), a powerful and *Sublime composition with massive windowless *rusticated walls based on precedents by *Palladio and Giulio *Romano, and certain elements reminiscent of *Piranesi's imaginary prisons. It was one of the few works of architecture by an Englishman to be illustrated in *Durand's *Recueil et parallèle des édifices* (1799), and was architecture expressive of its purpose (*architecture parlante), in this case retribution. Dance effected various town-planning improvements that altered many of the medieval street-plans of London, and, with Sir Robert *Taylor, drafted the *Building Act* (1774), which had a profound effect on the character of the London street-façade for the subsequent seven decades by setting down the thickness of front walls and ensuring no timbers such as *sash-frames were exposed but set back behind the brickwork. He remodelled part of the Mansion House, roofing over the *cortile, removing the grand staircase, lowering the roof of the *Egyptian Hall and erecting a coffered ceiling (1795–6). In 1788–9 he rebuilt the south façade of Guildhall in a *Hindoo *Gothic style with Greek detailing, later to be lampooned by A. W. N. *Pugin. His most distinguished pupil was *Soane, some of whose work was influenced by Dance's designs (e.g. the low dome of the Council Chamber at Guildhall (1737–8—demolished 1908)). Some of Dance's work anticipated the *Greek Revival, e.g. the severe *portico at Stratton Park, Hampshire (1803–6), and the Royal College of Surgeons, Lincoln's Inn Fields, London (1806–13), where the portico is all that survives the rebuilding by *Barry, who fluted the columns (1835–7).

Colvin (1995); Geffrye Museum (1972); Pugin (1973); Stroud (1971); Summerson (1963)

dancer. **1.** Curved or spiral *stair. **2.** Wedge-shaped step in a curved stair with the narrow end widened, also known as *danced* or *dancing step*, or *balanced winder*.

dancette. *Romanesque *chevron.

Daniell, Thomas (1749–1840). English artist. His views of topographical subjects in India, produced in collaboration with his nephew, **William Daniell** (1769–1837), were published in *Oriental Scenery* (1808) and *Picturesque Voyage to India* (1810) which greatly influenced the *Hindoo and *Indian styles during C19.

DNB (1917)

Danish knot. Complicated intertwining tendrils of foliate *Anglo-Saxon and *Celtic ornament. Also called *Runic knot*.

Dannatt, James Trevor (1920–). English *Modernist architect. He worked under Leslie *Martin on the Royal Festival Hall (completed 1951), and set up his own practice in 1952. With Martin he designed student residences for the University of Leicester (1960), and in 1962 he designed Vaughan College, Leicester, on two sides of the Roman remains there. In 1993 he built the entrance-gates and visitors' centre at Kew Gardens, Surrey.

Emanuel (1994)

Dantesque. C19 revival of the austere *Gothic styles prevalent in Italy during the lifetime of Dante Alighieri (1265–1321).

Danyell, Thomas (*fl.* 1461–87). English mason. In 1492 he was appointed King's Master-Mason. He carried out works at London Bridge, Deptford, Greenwich, and The Mote, Maidstone, Kent, where he seems to have been involved in major construction in 1482.

Harvey (1987)

Daphnis of Miletus (d. *c*.300 BC). Architect (with *Paeonius of Ephesus) of the huge *Ionic temple of Apollo at Didyma (begun *c*.313 BC), one of the largest temples in Asia Minor.

Dinsmoor (1950); Vitruvius Pollio (1955–6)

Darbishire, Henry Astley (1825–99). English architect mostly associated with philanthropic schemes, including the *Gothic Columbia Market (1866) and the Gothic working-class housing-scheme at Columbia Square (1857–60), both in Bethnal Green, London, financed by Miss Angela Georgina (later Baroness) Burdett-Coutts (1814–1906), but both demolished. For the same client he designed the *Picturesque Gothic Holly Village, Highgate, London (1865), a group of modest houses round a green, influenced no doubt by *Nash's Blaise Hamlet in Somerset. Darbishire produced a standard design for five-storey apartment-blocks (the planning of which was derived from Henry *Roberts's pioneering schemes of the 1850s) for the Peabody Trust (set up in 1862 to ameliorate the condition of the London poor). Many of these *Italianate blocks survive in London.

Curl (1983); Dixon and Muthesius (1985); Tarn (1971)

Darling, Frank (1850–1923). Canadian architect. He trained with *Street and Arthur *Blomfield in London before setting up in practice in Toronto. His early works, including his Anglican churches, were influenced by *Pearson and Street, but he is best remembered for his fine *Beaux-Arts Classical Banks (designed with his partner (from 1895) John A. Pearson), notably the Canadian Bank of Commerce, Winnipeg, Manitoba (1910–11), and a whole series of prefabricated timber banks that could be erected on site in a day. The firm also designed the Sun Life Assurance Company Building, Montreal (1914–31), one of the tallest buildings in the British Empire at the time.

Kalman (1994)

D'Aronco, Raimondo (1857–1932). *See* Aronco.

dart. Part of the *egg-and-dart or egg-and-anchor ornament.

David, Charles (1552–1650). French architect and son-in-law of **Nicholas Lemercier** (*see* Lemercier, Pierre), he succeeded his father-in-law as architect of St-Eustache, Paris, in 1585, and was involved in the construction of the *choir and *nave (completed 1637).

Sturgis *et al.* (1901–2)

Davioud, Gabriel-Jean-Antoine (1823–81). French architect. He studied with *Viollet-le-Duc and *Vaudoyer, then worked with *Baltard on the *Halles Centrales*, Paris, who recommended him for the post of *Inspecteur des Promenades*. He built many *pavilions and *lodges in the *Picturesque style for the Bois de Boulogne (1855–9), and designed structures for other Parisian parks, including the Parc Monceau, where the railings and gates, suggested by *Héré de Corny's work at Nancy, show him at his best. He designed the circus and *panorama for the Champs Élysées, and four large fountains for Paris (Saint-Michel, Boulevard Saint-Michel (1858—much praised by *Daly); Château d'Eau (1867–74); l'Observatoire (1870–5); and Place du Théâtre-Français (1872–4)). He was also responsible for the Théâtre du Châtelet (1860–2) and Théâtre Lyrique (1860–2, now Théâtre de la Ville). He was the architect of the *Magasins Réunis* Department Store, Place de la République (1865–7), the *Mairie du XIX*[e] (1876–8), and the Trocadéro for the 1878 Paris Exhibition (1876–8). His mixing of styles (especially in theatre design) is identified with the *Rageur style.

Daly (1840–90); Daly and Davioud (1874); Middleton and Watkin (1987)

Davis, Alexander Jackson (1803–92). American architect, one of the most imaginative of his generation. His first important design was Highwood, a house at New Haven, Conn. (1829–31), which brought him recognition, and, as a result, Ithiel *Town invited him to become a partner in his office. Town & Davis evolved a bold *Greek Revival style, and designed a series of public buildings that are among the most distinguished Greek-inspired works of architecture in the USA: a good example is the Indiana State Capitol, Indianapolis (1831–5), with its *octastyle Greek *Doric *porticoes, long side elevations of *antae-piers, and domed drum set over the centre of the roof. The firm also designed the State Capitol of North Carolina, Raleigh (1833–40), and several Greek Revival churches with distyle *in antis* fronts. The powerful range of antae-piers was used again at the New York Custom House (1833–42). Davis invented a variety of multi-storey *fenestration in which the windows were set in recesses with panels between them at floor-levels, anticipating later developments. This *Davisean window* (as he called it) appears to have been used first between the antae-piers at the Lyceum of Natural History, New York (1835–6).

The partnership was dissolved in 1835, after which Davis mostly practised on his own. He designed several *Picturesque houses, such as the influential *cottage orné at Blithewood, Barrytown, NY (1836). In 1836 he started writing *Rural Residences*, the first American book on the subject that really marks the birth of the Picturesque movement in the USA: it was illustrated with ingeniously planned eclectic designs, although only two parts were published (1838). From 1838 to 1850 he also provided illustrations for A. J. *Downing's works. Thereafter, for some twenty years, Davis ran a successful practice, designing Picturesque houses, generally favouring the *Gothic and *Italianate styles. His first large villa was Lyndhurst, Tarrytown, NY (1838–42—later expanded (1865–7)), which, with its asymmetry and Gothic style, was widely admired. In his many commissions Davis also re-interpreted the English 'cottage' style, although he returned to Neoclassicism for Montgomery Place, Barrytown, NY (1843–67), and the refined and beautiful Greek Revival John Cox Stevens House, New York (1845–8). Davis was interested in the possibilities of cast-iron construction and kits-of-parts (he designed a cast-iron shop-front in 1835). Among his other works the *Tuscan Town Hall and Court House, Bridgeport, Conn. (1853–4), and the estate of villas and cottages at Llewellyn Park, West Orange, NJ (1857–66), deserve mention.

Andrews (1955); Davis (1980); Downing (1967, 1967*a*, 1968); Newton (1942); Pierson and Jordy (1970–86)

Davis, Arthur Joseph (1878–1951). London-born English architect. Trained at the École des *Beaux-Arts, he joined the practice of the Parisian Charles F. *Mewès in 1900. Mewès & Davis brought Parisian Beaux-Arts *Classicism to London with their Ritz Hotel, Piccadilly (1903–9), the first steel-framed building in the capital. Their next work was Inveresk House, Aldwych, Strand (1906–8), followed by the Royal Automobile Club, Pall Mall (1908–11). After Mewès's death in 1914, Davis and others designed the *palazzo of the Cunard Building, Pier Head, Liverpool (1914–16), which was a foretaste of his Italian *Renaissance buildings in London, including the London County and Westminster Bank, Threadneedle Street (1922).

Gray (1985); Montgomery-Massingberd and Watkin (1980); Service (1975, 1977)

Dawber, Sir Edward Guy (1861–1938). Norfolk-born English architect. He worked with *George & Peto from 1882 before establishing his own practice in 1890. He earned his reputation as a designer of small well-mannered country-houses, some of which were published in *Muthesius's *Das Englische Haus* (The English House—1904–5). Among his designs Conkwell Grange, Bradford-on-Avon, Wiltshire (1907), deserves note. He wrote *Old*

Cottages and Farmhouses in Kent and Sussex (1900) and *Old Cottages, Farmhouses, and Other Stone Buildings in the Cotswolds* (1905).

Gray (1985)

Dawson, Matthew James (1875–1943). British architect. He designed several houses at Hampstead *Garden Suburb, London (1909–14), all quietly individual variations on *vernacular themes, including 87–9 Hampstead Way.

Gray (1985); Miller and Gray (1992)

day. *See* light.

dead. 1. Without variety or features, such as a *blank unrelieved wall. **2.** Aperture that is *blind, that is sealed up, such as a blocked-up window, or an opening looking like a window, but actually blind. **3.** Flat or dull, without brilliance, as in finishes. **4.** Useless, or not used for its original purpose, such as a *chimney-flue.

dead-house. 1. *Mortuary, in the sense of a building for the temporary accommodation of corpses before disposal. **2.** *Ossuary.

dead-light. 1. Window or part of a window that does not open. **2.** *Blank or *blind window, sealed up or designed to look like a window but actually blocked up.

deambulatory. 1. Covered walk, especially a continuous walk around something, such as a *cloister around a *garth. **2.** *Aisle or *ambulatory joining the liturgical east ends of *chancel-aisles behind the high-altar, especially in an apsidal arrangement with radiating *chapels on one side.

Deane, Sir Thomas Newenham (1828–99). Irish architect. He was the son of **Sir Thomas Deane** (1792–1871), who founded one of the most successful architectural practices in Ireland, designing the Commercial Buildings, Cork (1811–13), and the castellated *Tudor-style Dromore Castle, Kenmare (1831–6). Sir Thomas Deane was joined by Benjamin Woodward (1815–61) in 1841, and the latter, a disciple of *Pugin, seems to have been the moving force behind the *Ruskin-inspired buildings for which the firm (Deane & Woodward) is mainly known: they designed The Queen's College (now University College), Cork (1845–9). T. N. Deane became active in the partnership from 1850: soon afterwards, Deane & Woodward designed the beautiful Trinity College Museum, Dublin (1852–7), which established their reputation and, moreover, gained the approval of Ruskin, who admired the vigorous carvings of the O'Shea brothers that enriched the detail. The Oxford University Museum (1855–61) followed, their most celebrated work, a monumental secular *Gothic edifice with pronounced Continental features: it has a *cortile, roofed with a structure of iron, timber, and glass, surrounded by Venetian Gothic *cloisters. The firm also designed the Debating Room of the Oxford Union Society (1857), the Kildare Street Club, Dublin (1858–61), and, after Woodward's death, T. N. Deane built the Meadow Buildings, Christ Church, Oxford (1862–6). Deane & Woodward were important in the history of the *Gothic Revival in England, and were the first significant followers of Ruskin's ideas. From 1871, T. N. Deane continued in practice, and was joined by his son, **Thomas Manby Deane** (1851–1933), in 1876. They designed the National Library and Museum, Dublin (1885–90), which earned T. N. Deane his knighthood, and that forms part of the handsome group of buildings (also designed by the firm) around Leinster House. T. N. Deane was active in preserving Ireland's ancient buildings. T. M. Deane, a pupil of *Burges, was in partnership with his father from 1884, and then with Aston *Webb from 1899. He, too, was knighted, in 1911.

Acland and Ruskin (1859); Blau (1982); Dixon and Muthesius (1985); Eastlake (1970); Hersey (1972); Hitchcock (1954); Muthesius (1972); O'Dwyer (1997)

de Bodt, Jean (1670–1745). *See* Bodt.

Debret, François (1777–1850). French architect. A pupil of *Percier, he in turn became an important teacher of many architects who were destined to transform Paris under *Haussmann. He was a controversial and over-zealous restorer of historic buildings: he had worked on the *basilica of St-Denis for many years when he started his dramatic transformation of the west front in 1839, adding details to the north tower unsupported by *archaeology. When the tower began to collapse in 1846, Debret was dismissed, to the delight of those protagonists of the *Gothic Revival who saw him as a reactionary in favour of academic *Classicism. The disputes that raged at the time greatly promoted the cause of scholarly Gothic Revival in France, notably with the building of Ste-Clotilde, Paris (1846–57) by *Gau and *Ballu.

Middleton and Watkin (1987)

de Brosse, Salomon (*c.*1571–1626). *See* Brosse.

Decalogue. Parts of a *reredos in a church on which the Ten Commandments are set out, commonly found in England from the C17. It may also be in the form of separate framed panels set up on a wall in a church.

de Carlo, Giancarlo (1919–). *See* Carlo.

decastyle. *See* portico.

de Caus, Isaac (*fl.* 1612–55). *See* Caus.

Decker, Paul (1677–1713). Born in Nuremberg, he worked under *Schlüter during the building of the *Schloss* in Berlin and in 1707 become Court Architect at Bayreuth. He is remembered as an architectural theorist and for his imaginative and grand *Baroque designs, published in his *Fürstlicher Baumeister* (Princely Architect—1711–16), which had a considerable influence on the building of German aristocratic residences in C18, and on certain architects, notably *Fischer von Erlach. A second edition was published in 1885.

Decker (1711–16); Schneider (1937)

declination. Angle formed between the *naked of a wall and the inclined *mutules of the *Doric *Order.

Deconstructivism. Late-C20 tendency in architecture having certain formal similarities to some aspects of Russian *Constructivism, such as diagonal overlappings of rectangular or trapezoidal elements, and the use of warped planes, as in the works of *Lissitzky, *Malevich, and *Tatlin, although many critics and protagonists have denied those similarities, and the connections are only tentative in the case of some claimed to be Deconstructivists. Deconstructivist architecture has been held to embrace the works of *Coop Himmelblau, *Eisenman, *Gehry, *Hadid, *Koolhaas, *Libeskind, and *Tschumi, among others. Deconstructivism tends to produce a sense of dislocation both within the forms of projects and between the forms and their contexts. By breaking continuity, disturbing relationships between interior and exterior, fracturing connections between exterior and context, Deconstructivism undermines conventional notions of harmony, unity, and apparent stability. However, Deconstructivism is hardly a new movement, nor is it a coherent stylistic development agreed upon by some independent architects: rather it is a fragmentary, rather devious, series of architectural episodes in which forms are distorted to reveal forms anew. It perhaps exposes the unfamiliar and the disturbing by means of deformity, distortion, fragmentation, and the awkward superimposition of jarring, disparate grids all themselves derived from familiar and traditional forms, so it disturbs rather than overthrows conventional elements, abandoning serenity for unease, and subverting from the core, rather than attacking from the perimeter.

Broadbent (1991); Johnson and Wigley (1988); Norris (1982); Norris and Benjamin (1988)

Decorated style. *See* Second Pointed.

de Cotte, Robert (1656–1735). *See* Cotte.

dedication cross. Consecration *cross.

defensive architecture. 1. Military architecture, such as castles, city walls, and fortifications. **2.** Architecture that looks inwards, away from the hostile urban environment, such as a Greek or Roman house in Antiquity, or some of the works of Japanese architects (e.g. *Ando).

dégagement. 1. Restricted space forming a connection between two rooms, or between a room and a passage, for privacy, the equivalent of a lobby or *vestibule. **2.** The opposite of *engaged, so applied to free-standing columns.

Deilmann, Harald (1920–). German architect. He did much to re-establish *Modernism in Germany after the 1939–45 war, and strove for informality in his designs, notably with his Municipal Theatre, Münster (1954–6). His subsequent work included hospitals, cultural buildings, and many office-blocks. His Spielbank Building, Dortmund-Hohensyburg (1981), is a good example of his crisp, hard style.

Emanuel (1994)

Deinocrates (*fl.* mid-C4 BC). *Hellenistic architect, supposedly the designer of the city of Alexandria, laid out on the most lavish lines. He was reported by *Vitruvius to have proposed reconstructing Mount Athos into a gigantic carved image of Alexander the Great. He may have been (with *Paeonius) the architect of the last great *Ionic temple of Artemis at Ephesus (from 356 BC).

Martin (1956); Vitruvius Pollio (1955–6)

de Key, Lieven (*c*.1560–1627). *See* Key.

de Keyser, Hendrick (1565–1621). *See* Keyser.

de Klerk, Michel (1884–1923). *See* Klerk.

Delafosse, Jean-Charles (1734–91). French architect, one of the creators of the *Louis Seize style, as the ornament in his *Iconologie*, featuring *Greek keys, *garlands, and much other Classical ornament, demonstrates. He also published a treatise on the five *Orders, and designed two *hôtels at 58–60 Rue du Faubourg Poissonnière, Paris (1776–83).

Braham (1980); *Gazette des Beaux-Arts*, 6/61 (1963–4), 157; Kaufmann (1955)

del Duca, Giacomo (*c*.1520–1604). *See* Duca.

della Porta, Giacomo (1533–1602). *See* Porta.

Delorme. *See* Orme.

de L'Orme, Philibert (*c*.1510–70). *See* Orme.

demi-column. *Engaged half-column, not to be confused with a *pilaster.

demilune. *Ravelin, or projecting outwork of a fortification beyond the *bastions and *curtain-wall, semicircular or segmental on *plan rather than the more usual triangular arrangement, to facilitate the turning of guns.

demi-metope. Fragmentary or half *metope at the external angle (and sometimes of a *re-entrant internal angle) of a Roman *Doric *frieze, commonly found in *Renaissance and C18 work.

Demmler, Georg Adolph (1804–86). German architect. A pupil of *Schinkel, he was Court Architect to the Grand Dukes of Mecklenburg-Schwerin, for whom he transformed the *Schloss* at Schwerin into a *Picturesque pile of the Northern *Renaissance Revival (1844–57), although *Stüler and *Strack were responsible for the interiors and completing the building, and the overall scheme owed something to an earlier project by *Semper of 1842. Like his master, Schinkel, Demmler cunningly mixed medieval and Classical elements in some of his designs, notably the *Rathaus* (Town Hall—1835) and the *Zeughaus* (Arsenal—1840–4), both in Schwerin.

Ende (1971); Ohle (1960); Stüler, Prosche, and Willebrand (1869)

Denby, Elizabeth (1893–1965). *See* Fry, Edwin Maxwell.

Denham, Sir John (1615–69). English poet, courtier, and administrator. He was Surveyor-General of the King's Works (1660–9), with John *Webb as his deputy at Greenwich Palace. In 1669 *Wren was appointed Denham's sole deputy, and Wren succeeded him on Denham's death two weeks later. Although he does not appear to have designed anything, Denham was probably a competent administrator, and, as the holder of the same position as Inigo *Jones and Wren, deserves mention.

Colvin (1995); *DNB* (1917)

Denon, Baron Dominique Vivant (1747–1825). French *savant*, he accompanied the Napoleonic expedition to Egypt (1798) as leader of the learned Commission on the Sciences and Arts that was to study Ancient Egyptian buildings and architecture and herald the birth of modern Egyptology. In 1802 he published his *Voyage dans la Basse et la Haute Égypte pendant les campagnes du général Bonaparte* (Journey in Lower and Upper Egypt during the campaigns of General Bonaparte). An accurate source-book of Ancient Egyptian architecture, it had an extraordinary impact, triggering the C19 *Egyptian Revival that at first was correctly described as 'Egyptomania', and was a major influence on *Neoclassicism. Denon was Director-General of Museums, and was in charge of the Musée Napoléon (now the Louvre). He supervised the design and production of the Sèvres *Service Égyptien* (a dinner-service sumptuously decorated with Ancient Egyptian themes and motifs), one of the high points of the Egyptian Revival, and was a major influence on the *Empire style and on the work of *Percier and *Fontaine.

Carrott (1978); Curl (1994); Denon (1802); Humbert (1989, 1996); Humbert, Pantazzi, and Ziegler (1994)

dentil. Small block forming one of a long horizontal series, closely set, under the *cornices, associated with the *bed-mouldings of the *Composite, *Corinthian, *Ionic, and (sometimes) Roman *Doric *Orders. An *entablature with dentils is said to be *dentilated* or *denticulated*. Early Greek dentils include those of the *caryatid porch of the Erechtheion (C5 BC) and the *Choragic Monument of Lysicrates (C4 BC), both in Athens. In better work dentils should stop at the angle of a building, forming a *re-entrant, and there should not be a dentil at the angle itself. They should also be arranged so that the dentil above a column should be on the centre-line.

dentilation. 1. With, or an arrangement of, *dentils. **2.** *Toothing.

dentil-band. Plain moulding of square or rectangular section forming part of the *bed-mouldings of an *entablature, that could be cut to form *dentils, but is left as a *band, as on *Scamozzi's version of the *Ionic *Order.

depressed. *See* arch.

Dereham *or* **Durham, Elias of** (*fl.* 1188–d. 1245). A Canon of Salisbury and Wells, he may have designed the *shrine of St Thomas à Becket (*c.*1118–70) in Canterbury Cathedral, Kent (completed 1220), which, by all accounts, was of great magnificence. He seems to have been involved in the building of Salisbury Cathedral, Wiltshire, from *c.*1220, where he was described as being the director of the new fabric, and supervised at least the building of the *Lady Chapel (1225) and the eastern arm of the Cathedral (1237). In 1233 he was in charge of the King's Works at Winchester Castle, Hampshire. Reading between the lines he was probably an informed amateur, a forerunner of the C18 dilettante architect, perhaps a kind of C13 *Burlington.

Harvey (1987)

Derneford, Nicholas de (*fl.* 1309–31). English mason. He seems to have been a specialist in military architecture and fortification, was master-mason at Beaumaris Castle (from 1316), and Master of the Works at Caernarfon, Conway, Criccieth, and Harlech Castles in Wales from 1323. In 1327 he was also put in charge of the castles at Aberystwyth, Cardigan, and Carmarthen. In addition, he may have designed the exquisite *choir at St Augustine's Church, Bristol (now the Cathedral), built 1298–1340, in which case he was an architect of great originality.

Harvey (1987)

de Rossi, Giovanni Antonio (1616–95). *See* Rossi.

de Sanctis, Francesco (1693–1740). *See* Sanctis.

desert. C18 landscape *designed* to look wild, forsaken, uninhabited, and uncultivated, with 'ruined' buildings, giving the impression of having been abandoned, and conducive to melancholy. A good example is the *Désert de Retz*, Chambourcy, Yvelines, France (1770s), with its *folly in the form of a huge overscaled ruined column with an interior of three floors of apartments arranged around a central spiral stair. The rooms on the fourth floor were illuminated by means of top-lighting behind the 'column'-shaft's broken top and through jagged glazed 'cracks' in the 'flutes'.

Adams (1979); Mosser and Teyssot (1991)

Desgodets *or* **Desgodetz, Antoine Babuty** (1653–1728). Paris-born architect, he recorded many ancient structures in Rome, which he published in *Les Édifices Antiques de Rome* (1682), later brought out in an English version (1771–95). The book made his reputation, for it was the most accurate printed source for *Antique Roman architecture to date. It was a source for the detail of many significant C18 buildings (e.g. *Kent's entrance-hall at Holkham Hall, Norfolk), and was an important influence on C18 styles, especially *Neoclassicism.

Desgodetz (1771–95); Hautecœur (1948–50); Kalnein and Levey (1972); Wiebenson (1969)

Desornamentado. Austere style of Spanish *Renaissance architecture typical of the reign of King Philip II (1556–98), of which *Herrera's Escorial, near Madrid (1559–84) is a good example.

Kubler (1982); Kubler and Soria (1959)

Desprez, Jean-Louis (1743–1804). French architect, illustrator, and stage-designer. He settled in Sweden in 1784 and produced severe Neoclassical and Egyptianizing designs for tombs. His buildings include the Uppsala Botanicum (1788), with its low octastyle Greek *Doric *portico, and Egyptianesque *capitals.

Curl (1994); Humbert, Pantazzi, and Ziegler (1994); Rosenblum (1967)

Destailleur, Hippolyte-Alexandre-Gabriel-Walter (1822–93). Paris-born architect. He built a number of town- and country-houses in a *Renaissance Revival style, including the *Château du Duc de Massa, Franconville, Oise (1880–5), Waddesdon Manor, near Aylesbury, Buckinghamshire (1888–90), and the Palais d'Albert de Rothschild, Prinz Eugen Strasse, Vienna (1876–82). He designed the priory and *mausoleum for Napoleon III and his family at Farnborough, Hampshire (1887–9—in a *Flamboyant *Gothic style), and various mausolea and memorials, including the Hersent tomb, Père-Lachaise Cemetery (1861), and the Collard tomb, Montparnasse Cemetery (1864), both in Paris. His published works include

Recueil d'estampes relatives à l'ornamentation des appartements aux XVIe, XVIIe, and XVIIIe siècles (Collection of Engravings Relative to the Ornamentation of Rooms of C16, 17, and 18—1858–71), and he was much sought-after as a designer of furniture and interiors.

Berckenhagen (1976); Dixon and Muthesius (1985); *Hampshire: The County Magazine*, 23/9 (1983), 36–9

De Stijl. *See* Stijl.

detached. *Insulated or free-standing, the opposite of *engaged, as with a column.

Deutscher Werkbund. Organization founded in Munich in 1907 to improve the design of products through the joint efforts of artists, craftsmen, and manufacturers, its leading lights were Peter *Behrens, Theodor *Fischer, Hermann *Muthesius, and Fritz Schumacher (1869–1947). In 1914 it organized a major exhibition in Cologne, with buildings by *Gropius, *Taut, and van de *Velde, but a debate was sparked in which Muthesius argued for industrialized design while van de Velde spoke up for the creative artist and craftsman. After the 1914–18 war the Werkbund moved away from anything redolent of an *Arts-and-Crafts position towards the *Modern Movement, as is clear from the journal *Die Form* (Design) published from 1925 until 1934. It held a housing exhibition in Stuttgart, the *Weissenhofsiedlung, in 1927, under the directorship of *Mies van der Rohe, which included influential designs by Le *Corbusier, *Oud, and *Stam. Further exhibitions were held in Paris (1930) and Berlin (1931), but it disbanded in 1934. It was revived after the 1939–45 war, largely to promote *Modernist ideology, and published *Werk und Zeit* (Work and Time) from 1952. The Werkbund inspired further organizations in Austria (1912), Switzerland (1913), Sweden (1913), and England (Design and Industries Association of 1915).

Burckhardt (1980); Lampugnani (1988); Pommer and Otto (1991); Schwartz (1997)

Devětsil Group. Founded in 1920, the group was the focus for the avant-garde of the new Czechoslovak Republic after 1918, and embraced *International *Modernism. It promoted work by Josef *Chochol, Jaromír Krejcar (1895–1949), and Karel *Teige, evolved close relations with German and Austrian Modernists, and promoted ideas from the Soviet Union.

Leśnikowski (1996)

Devey, George (1820–86). London-born architect. He promoted the *Domestic Revival with the use of *vernacular elements in his buildings. His first commission was at Penshurst, Kent, where he designed cottages and various estate buildings from 1850 in a C15 style. His larger buildings, which often look as though they were developed and added to over a long period, include Betteshanger House (1856–82), St Alban's Court, Nonington (1874–8), and Denne Hill (1871–5), all in Kent. A good example of his *additive style is Smithills Hall, Bolton, South Lancashire (1874–86), a medieval house which he extended. He influenced his pupil, *Voysey, and was an important precursor of the *Arts-and-Crafts movement.

Allibone (1991); Girouard (1979)

de Wailly, Charles (1730–98). *See* Wailly.

diaconicon. *Sacristy in or near an *Early Christian or *Byzantine church used as a treasury and library.

diagonal. *See* buttress *and* vault.

diameter. *See* module.

Diamond, Abel Joseph (1932–). South-African-born, 'Jack' Diamond became one of Canada's most distinguished and influential architects. His buildings are exemplary in their detail and finishes. He and his partner (from 1969 to 1974), Barton *Myers, became known as enemies of badly sited high-rise developments. The firm designed the Wolf House, Toronto (1975), conceived as a prototype for a row- or terrace-house unit; the Citadel Theatre, Edmonton (1976); and the Housing Union Building, University of Alberta (1972), all of which are impeccably detailed and crisply planned. Among recent works is the Richmond Hill Central Library, Ontario (1993).

Emanuel (1994); Kalman (1994)

diamond-faced. *See* rustication.

diamond-fret. *Lozenge-fret consisting of intersecting *fillets or thin beads forming lozenge- or diamond-shaped patterns repeated in series. It occurs in *Romanesque work as a variation on *chevron or *zig-zag mouldings (using round rod-like elements) and in C18 *Chinoiserie and *Gothick (using flat strips, fillets, or square sections).

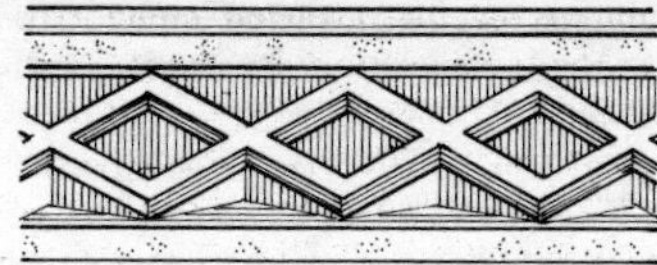

diamond fret. Church of Sts Peter and Paul, Tickencote, Rutland. (*After Parker*)

diaper. Decorative pattern on a plain, flat, unbroken surface consisting of the constant repetition of simple figures (such as squares, lozenges, or polygons) closely connected with each other, sometimes with embellishments in the form of stylized flowers. It may be lightly carved, as on the *Gothic *pulpitum (*c*.1320–40) in Southwell *Minster, Nottinghamshire; painted on a wall; or formed of dark bricks laid in diagonal patterns on a lighter brick wall, commonly found in *Tudor brickwork and in the works of *Butterfield.

diaper. Tudor brick diaper-work with vitrified bricks the darker hue.

diaphragm. *See* arch.

diastyle. *See* intercolumniation.

Dickenson, Christopher (*fl.* 1528–d. 1540). English freemason. In 1528 he was appointed master-mason at Windsor Castle, Berkshire, on the death of Henry *Redman. In 1531 he was master-bricklayer at Westminster (Whitehall) Palace, and in 1536 was in charge of the works at Hampton Court Palace. In 1539 he was appointed to work on the three castles at Deal, Sandown, and Walmer, Kent, all remarkable examples of *Tudor military architecture.

Harvey (1987)

die. 1. *Dado. **2.** *Abacus.

Dientzenhofer Family. Master-masons and architects originally from Bad Aibling, near Rosenheim, Bavaria, they made an enormous contribution to the complexities of *Baroque architecture in Germany and Bohemia. **Georg** (1643–89) built the Cistercian Abbey Church at Waldsassen (1682–1704) to designs by *Leuthner (who seems to have given the Dientzenhofer clan their chance to rise above artisan status, possibly for family reasons, as he married Anna Dientzenhofer in 1678). Georg also designed the Pilgrimage Church (*Wallfahrtskirche*) of the Holy Trinity at Kappel, near Waldsassen (1684–9), with a triapsidal plan and three slender cylindrical towers, an unusual arrangement clearly intended to symbolize the Trinity. It was completed by his brother **Christoph** (1655–1722), who was strongly influenced by the geometries of *Guarini (published in 1686), and who designed several churches of great splendour in Bohemia, including St Joseph, Obořiště (1699–1712), the Chapel in the Castle, Smiřice (1700–11), Sv Mikuláš (St Nicholas), Malá Strana, Prague (1703–11), and Sv Markéta (St Margaret), Břevnov, near Prague (1708–15). Christoph's uses of ellipses mixed with the *Wandpfeiler arrangement made his interiors particularly complex, and demonstrate how he synthesized motifs drawn from *Borromini and Guarini. His beautiful façade of the monastery of Our Lady of Loreto, Hradčany, Prague (1717–23), has a central belfry, one of the most elegant in Central Europe.

Wolfgang (1648–1706) is remembered for several buildings, notably the Abbey Church of Speinshart (1691–1706) and the Pilgrimage Church at Straubing (1705–7), while **Leonhard** (1660–1707) was responsible for the abbeys at Ebrach (1686–1704) and Banz (1695–1705). However, **Johann** (1663–1726) completed Banz, designing the Abbey Church there (1710–19) in which complex interlocking ellipses (not unlike Christoph's scheme at Obořiště) again feature, contributing to an interior of great beauty, arguably the finest design by any Dientzenhofer. Johann's first great church was the *Stiftskirche* (Monastery Church now *Dom* (Cathedral)) at Fulda (1704–12), with echoes of St Peter's, *Il Gesù*, Sant'Ignazio, and (especially) Borromini's remodelling of San Giovanni in Laterano, all in Rome. Johann Dientzenhofer worked at Pommersfelden, near Bamberg, in 1711, and there, for Lothar Franz, Graf von Schönborn (1655–1729), Elector-Archbishop of Mainz and

Prince-Bishop of Bamberg, built Schloss Weissenstein, one of the noblest Baroque palaces in Franconia (1711–18), with a stupendous symmetrical *Treppenhaus* (staircase—partly designed by *Hildebrandt and von Schönborn himself) rising in a vast galleried hall the full height of the building.

Christoph's son, **Kilian Ignaz** (1689–1751), trained with his father and with Hildebrandt. He may have been partly responsible for completing the latter's stunning Church of Maria Treu, Vienna, but the first building for which he was solely responsible was the Villa Amerika, Prague (1715–20), which has obvious Hildebrandtian echoes. He collaborated with his father in the building of the Prague Loreto, Hradčany (1721–4). His Ursuline Church of St Johann Nepomuk, Hradčany (1720) and the Pilgrimage Church at Nitzau (Nicov—1720–6) represent his earliest independently designed churches, but in both buildings Hildebrandt's plan for St Lawrence at Gabel (influenced by Guarini) is synthesized with the Dientzenhofer family's much-used *Wandpfeiler* theme. At the noble Church of St Johann Nepomuk am Felsen (Sv Jan na Scalce), Prague (1729–39), Kilian Ignaz's mastery of Baroque rhetoric, drama, and plastic modelling is admirably expressed. His Church of Sv Mikuláš (St Nicholas, Staré Město, Prague (1732–7)), has astonishing originality and fluency, with a complex central space surrounded by ellipses: the twin-towered façade is parallel to the long axis. Elliptical elements again form the basis of the plan of Sv Majdaléna (St Magdalena), Karlovy Vary (1732–6). He added the beautiful *cupola (1750–2) and tower (1755) to his father's Church of Sv Mikuláš, Malá Strana, Prague. Among his last churches, St Florian, Kladno (1746–8), and St John the Baptist, Paštiky (1748–51), show a tendency towards restraint and simplification.

Bourke (1962); Büchner (1964); Franz (1942, 1943, 1943*a*, 1962); Hegemann (1943); Hempel (1965); Kreisel (1953); Norberg-Schulz (1968, 1986, 1986*a*); Swoboda (1964); Vilímková and Brucker (1989)

Dietterlin, Wendel (1551–99). German *Renaissance architect. His fame rests on his *Architectura und Ausztheilung/Symmetria und Proportion der Fünff Seulen* (Architecture and Divisional Arrangement/Symmetry and Proportion of the Five Columns—1593–4), an exotic collection of plates showing architectural features derived from Flemish *Mannerist details involving much *strap-work and fantastic ornament, called *Ditterling.

Dietterlin (1598); Jervis (1984); Lewis and Darley (1986); Pirr (1940); Placzek (1968)

diglyph. *Doric *triglyph with only two vertical channels, omitting the two half-grooves at its sides, regarded by some as an *abuse.

dike. *See* dyke.

Dilettanti, Society of. Originally a convivial gathering of rich young men who had been on the *Grand Tour, it met in London from 1732, and developed as a serious supporter of architectural and archaeological explorations of Greece, the Middle East, and Italy, thereby laying the foundation for a systematic scholarly study of Classical antiquities. The Society financed a series of expeditions and published the results. Notable successes were *The Antiquities of Athens* (1762–1814) and *Antiquities of Ionia* (1769–1814). It was a powerful stimulus for the *Neoclassicism of the late C18, and especially for the *Greek Revival.

Chilvers, Osborne, and Farr (1988); Crook (1972*a*); Dilettanti (1814)

diminished. 1. For *diminished* arch, *see* arch. **2.** In a sash-window, a *diminished bar* is a glazing-bar moulded or shaped to present a finer, thinner appearance inside a room than it would appear if unshaped. **3.** *Diminishing* or *graduated courses* are layers or rows of slates that are of the same length in each course, but diminishing in height with each course from *eaves to *ridge.

diminution. *Contractura or reduction of the diameter of a column-shaft with height: in Antiquity it began from the lowest part of the shaft, but C18 practice began it from about a third of the height. It is associated with *entasis.

Dinkeloo, John (Gerard) (1918–81). *See* Roche.

Dinocrates. *See* Deinocrates.

Diocletian window. Semicircular opening (usually a window) subdivided by two plain *mullions into three compartments. Named after its use in the *thermae (baths) of Diocletian, Rome (AD 306), its alternative name is a *thermal* window, commonly found in Palladian and *Neoclassical architecture.

diorama. 1. Large picture given additional reality by optical illusions and illumination,

Diocletian *or* thermal window

and viewed through an aperture in a dark room. It underwent repeated changes by the operation of modified light on its transparent and semi-transparent surface. **2.** Building specially constructed for such a picture, sometimes with a revolving circular room for spectators.

Diotisalvi (*fl.* C12). Probable architect of the circular *Romanesque *baptistery at Pisa (1153–1265). He also seems to have been responsible for the octagonal Church of San Sepolcro, Pisa (from 1153), and worked at Santa Maria Maggiore, Florence. His likely name was Diotisalvi de Petroni.

Papworth (1852); Sturgis *et al.* (1901–2)

dipteral. Classical temple with two rows of columns forming the *peristyle around the *cella, so with a minimum of eight columns (octastyle) beneath the *pedimented ends.

Directoire. Austere, simplified *Neoclassicism favoured during the *Directoire* (1795–9) in France sparingly ornamented with motifs associated with the French Revolution (e.g. Phrygian cap), and after 1798 including Egyptian elements (e.g. *lotus and *sphinx). Taste demanded more opulent decoration by 1800, and the following *Empire style embraced more Egyptianizing detail, especially after the publication of *Denon's account of Egypt and Nubia (1802). The *Directoire* style provided the inspiration for the *American Directory* style (*c*.1805–30) in general terms, except that the favoured motifs in the USA were those of Freemasonry. *American Directory* was a sub-species of the USA *Federal style (1776–*c*.1830).

Chilvers, Osborne, and Farr (1988); Curl (1994); Lewis and Darley (1986)

Directory. *See* Directoire.

disc. 1. Flat, circular, raised ornament, like a small slice of a pole, carved as a series of discs adjacent to each other, found in *Romanesque work (e.g. Canterbury Cathedral, *c*.1100). **2.** Any disc-like ornament.

discharging. *See* arch.

distyle. *See* portico.

ditriglyph. *See* intercolumniation.

Ditterling. Northern European Mannerist fantastic ornament based on the *grotesques and *strapwork found in the publications of *Dietterlin, and occurring in England and the Low Countries in the late C16 and early C17.

Dixon, Jeremy (1939–). English exponent of *Post-Modernism, and architect of several housing schemes in London, including St Mark's Road, North Kensington (1975–80), Lanark Road, Maida Vale (1982), and Dudgeon Wharf, Isle of Dogs (1986–8), which all contain paraphrases of C19 London housing (especially the work of John Booth (1759–1843) for the Lloyd-Baker Estate, Clerkenwell, London (*c*.1819–40)).

Watkin (1986)

Dobson, John (1787–1865). The most gifted and prolific architect, engineer, and surveyor working in north-east England in the first half of C19, his best architecture was in a restrained *Neoclassical style. With the builder Richard Grainger (1797–1861) he was responsible for the area bounded by Grey, Market, and Grainger Streets (*c*.1835–7), Newcastle upon Tyne, one of the most distinguished urban developments in the England of King William IV (1830–7). His Central Railway Station, Newcastle (1847–50), built on a gently curving plan, combined *Greek Revival architecture with a station roof of iron and glass, while his entrances to Jesmond Old Cemetery (1836) are as severe and stark as any Continental architecture of the period. His best country-houses are Nunnykirk (1825) and Meldon Park (1832) in Northumberland. He advised *Monck on the building of Belsay Castle (1807–17).

Colvin (1995); Dobson (1885); Faulkner and Greg (1987); Wilkes (1980); Wilkes and Dodds (1964)

dodecastyle. *See* portico.

Dodington, John (*fl.* 1412–27). English mason. He was in charge of the works during the construction of many new buildings at King's Hall (now Trinity College), Cambridge, including the range of buildings projecting north behind the Great Court (1417–22), and known as the King's Hostel. In 1427 work began on the new Gate Tower (completed 1432) forming the south entrance to the

College, but later (1600) taken down and re-created on the north side of the Great Court west of the Chapel. Known as King Edward's Gate, it is the prototype of the Cambridge college gate-tower with corner *turrets.

Harvey (1987)

Doesburg, Theo van (1883–1931). Born Christian Emil Maries Küpper in Utrecht, Netherlands. Though not an architect, he had considerable influence on modern architecture. With *Oud and others he established the periodical *De Stijl* (*see* Stijl, De), taught at the *Bauhaus in Weimar (1921–4), and, with van *Eesteren, designed houses for a De Stijl exhibition in Paris (1923). He designed a studio and house at Meudon, near Paris (1929–31), based on Le *Corbusier's *Citrohan* houses of the early 1920s. He influenced *Rietveld's designs for the Schroeder House, Utrecht.

Chilvers, Osborne, and Farr (1988)

dog-ear. Old term for an *acroterion.

dog-kennel. *See* chien-assis.

dog-leg. *See* stair.

dog-tooth. 1. Pyramidal ornament consisting of four leaf-like forms radiating from the apex or resembling a pyramid with V-shaped notches pointing towards the apex, forming one of a closely spaced series within a *cavetto moulding. It is characteristic of *First Pointed *Gothic, and is also found enriched with stylized foliage. **2.** Brick laid diagonally with a corner corbelled out and projecting from the *naked of a wall below, forming one of a series of adjacent similar bricks to create a continuous saw-toothed *band on a *string-course or as part of a *cornice.

dog-tooth. C13 First Pointed example, Lincoln Cathedral.

dog-wheel. Cylinder, *spit*, or *treadwheel*, turned by a dog treading inside it, commonly used to turn a spit in a kitchen.

Doll, Charles Fitzroy (1850–1929). English architect, educated in Germany and in the office of Sir Matthew Digby *Wyatt, where he worked on the drawings for the India Office, Whitehall, London (1866–8). He was appointed Surveyor to the Bedford Estates in Bloomsbury and Covent Garden, London (1885). He designed the Hotel Russell (1898), a luxuriant essay in the *François Ier style, based on the *Château de Madrid, Paris (1528–1785), clad in *thé-au-lait *terracotta, and the Imperial Hotel, of a few years later, which *Pevsner described as a 'vicious mixture of Art Nouveau Gothic and Art Nouveau Tudor', to which he might have added 'Bavarian spires'. It was demolished in the late 1960s, and, like the Hotel Russell, stood in Russell Square. Its replacement is banal. Doll was also responsible for the exquisitely detailed Flemish Franco-*Gothic terrace of shops with apartments over them in Torrington Place (1907). His practice continued under his son, **C. C. T. Doll** (1880–1955), who was partly responsible for reconstructing the grand staircase of the Palace of King Minos, Knossos, Crete.

Gray (1985); Pevsner, *Buildings of England, London 2* (1952)

dolmen. Prehistoric enclosure (usually a tomb-chamber) formed by three or more upright *megaliths supporting a large flat horizontal stone usually covered with earth to form a tumulus. Also known as a *cromlech*.

dome. *Cupola, essentially a species of *vault, constructed on a circular, elliptical, or polygonal *plan, bulbous, segmental, semicircular, or pointed in vertical *section. It can be built on top of a structure the plan of which is identical to that of the dome: if that wall is circular or elliptical it is a *drum* (often pierced with windows) as in a *rotunda. However, domes usually provide a covering for a square- or rectangular-planned building or compartment, so there have to be adjustments to make the transition from the square to the circular, elliptical, or polygonal base of the cupola or dome. This can be achieved by means of *pendentives* (fragments of a *sail-vault* resembling a species of concave, distorted, almost triangular *spandrels, rising up from the corner at the top of the right-angled compartment to the circular or elliptical base of the drum or cupola) or *squinches* (small arch or series of parallel arches of increasing radius spanning the angle of the square compartment). Both the drum and cupola will have a diameter the same dimension as the side of the square on which the whole structure stands.

Types of drum include:

calotte: low cupola or saucer-dome of segmental vertical section;

cloister-vault: as *domical vault* below;
domical vault: *cloister-vault*, not a true dome, but formed of four or more (depending on the shape of the base) *cells* or *webs* forming *groins* where they touch vertically and rising to a point;
melon: as *parachute* below;
Pantheon: low dome on the exterior, often stepped, resembling that of the *Pantheon in Rome, and coffered on the interior, widely copied by Neoclassical architects;
parachute: *melon*, *pumpkin*, or *umbrella* dome standing on a scalloped circular base and formed of individual *webs*, segmental on plan, joining in *groins* or *ribs*. Each web has a concave interior and convex exterior so it resembles a parachute, rather than an umbrella;
pumpkin: as *parachute* above;
sail-dome: dome resembling a billowing sail over a square compartment with its diameter the same dimension as the *diagonal* instead of the side of the square below, enabling the structure to rise as though on *pendentives* but continuing without interruption. Pendentives are really parts of a sail-dome and themselves are a species of *sail-vault*;
umbrella: as *parachute* above.

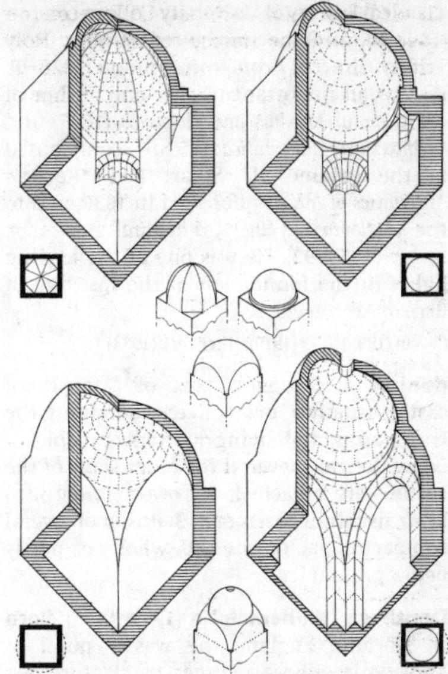

dome. Plans, large exploded axonometric projections from below, and smaller isometric projections from above, showing the different types of dome. (*JJS*) (*top left*) Octagonal domical vault on a square compartment, partly supported on squinches. (*top right*) True hemispherical dome on a square compartment, partly supported on squinches. (*bottom left*) Sail-dome. (*bottom right*) Hemispherical dome on pendentives.

Domènech i Montaner, Lluís (1850–1923). With *Gaudí the most inventive practitioner of *Modernisme, the Catalan variant on *Art Nouveau at the turn of C19 in Spain. He drew on *Romanesque and *Gothic themes as well as the ideas of *Viollet-le-Duc, and as early as 1878 published an article in which he argued for a specifically national Catalan architecture that would be a transformation of eclecticism into something new, yet distinctive, clearly an early manifestation of *Critical Regionalism. His café-restaurant for the Barcelona Universal Exposition (1887–8) drew on medieval models, but in the Palau de la Música Catalana (1905–8), Barcelona, he drew on modern technology with a structure of interlaced iron to produce his master-work.

Bohigas (1968, 1991); Borràs (1970); Pevsner and Richards (1973); Sack (1995); Tschudi-Madsen (1967)

Domenig, Günther (1934–). Austrian architect and leader of the Graz School, which counters *Historicist traditions and promotes individualistic buildings no matter what the context. His *Zentralsparkasse* Regional Headquarters, Favoritenstrasse, Vienna (1974–9), was designed with a front that seemed to be folding and crumpling. His individualism was influential on younger Austrian architects.

Emanuel (1994)

Domestic Revival. Offshoot of the cult of the *Picturesque and the *Gothic Revival, it was essentially a style of domestic architecture that incorporated forms, details, and materials found in English *vernacular buildings, including steeply pitched tile roofs, *dormers, *timber-framing and jettied construction, small-paned *mullioned and *transomed windows (often with leaded *lights), tile-hung walls, tall chimneys (often of the *Tudor type in carved and moulded brick), and carefully contrived asymmetrical compositions. Also called *Old English style.

Curl (1990); Dixon and Muthesius (1985)

domical vault. *See* vault.

domus. Roman house for a single wealthy family. *See* Roman architecture, atrium.

Donaldson, Thomas Leverton (1795–1885). London-born architect and first Professor of Architecture at University College London (1842–65). His work includes the noble

Classical Library of University College London (1848–9), and the uninspired *Gothic Holy Trinity Church, Brompton, London (1826–9). He was an important teacher and author of *Architectural Maxims and Theorems* (1847) and *Architectura Numismatica* (1859). He contributed to the volume of *Stuart and *Revett's *Antiquities of Athens* published in 1830, and to the *Dictionary of the Architectural Publication Society* (1853–92). He was one of the leading lights in the foundation of the Institute of British Architects.

Colvin (1995); *DNB* (1917); Hitchcock (1954)

donjon. 1. Strongest part of a medieval castle, usually a tower or *keep* containing the best rooms and living-quarters, capable of being defended even if the outer walls of the castle were breached. **2.** Lowest storey in a keep, usually a basement. **3.** Prison of several compartments, or one cell, wholly or partly below ground level.

Donthorn, William John (1799–1859). Born in Norfolk, England, he was a pupil of *Wyatville, whose manner of *Picturesque composition he developed. He established an extensive practice, designing country-houses and parsonages, but most of his Neoclassical works recalling the designs of *Dance the Younger and *Soane have been demolished. His very severe *Neoclassicism can best be appreciated from his drawings in the RIBA British Architectural Library Drawings Collection, and from a handful of buildings (e.g. the stable-block, High House, West Acre, Norfolk (*c*.1823–9), and Upton Hall, near Southwell, Nottinghamshire (*c*.1830). He designed the Leicester Testimonial at Holkham, Norfolk, a column of the *Agricultural Order (with mangel-wurzel and turnip-leaves instead of *acanthus), and the romantic *Gothic Highcliffe Castle, Hampshire (1830–4), which incorporated medieval fragments from the Grande Manoir des Andelys (C15) and the *Romanesque Abbey of Jumièges, both in Normandy, while the interiors contained *Louis Quinze panelling and *Empire décor. His output of *Tudor Gothic was prolific, and he made forays into Norman Revival (e.g. Gaol and Session House, Peterborough, of 1841–2). He was a founder member of the Institute of British Architects.

Architectural History, 21 (1978), 83–92; Colvin (1995)

Doom. Pictorial representation of the Last Judgement in the Middle Ages. In a church it often took the form of a mural painting over the *chancel-arch, with Christ in the middle, Hell and the damned on His left (the south or right when seen from the *nave), and the Blessed on the left (north). It was also a subject for stained-glass windows: a spectacular glass Doom survives in St Mary's Church, Fairford, Gloucestershire (late C15 and early C16).

Duffy (1992)

door. Movable lockable barrier of wood or other material consisting of one piece, or of several pieces framed together, usually turning on hinges or sliding in a groove, serving to permit or bar access through a *doorway. Commonly supported on hinges secured to the *door-post* or *door-frame*, a door may also turn on pivots at the top and bottom (an arrangement usual in Antiquity), slide or roll up horizontally or vertically, and itself can be divided into more folds, or *valves*, hinged to the frame or each other. In traditional timber-*framed* (see below) doors the horizontal timbers are called *rails*, the verticals at the sides *stiles*, and the vertical in the centre *muntin*.

Types of traditional door include:

batten: see *ledged* below;
bivalve: door with two leaves meeting in the middle;
blind: door with fixed or movable slats having the character of, and serving as, a *blind. Also a *sham* door;
casement: door with a glazed part above the middle rail, usually with *diminishing stiles* on either side of the glazed part (itself subdivided with glazing-bars);
crapaudine: door turning on a pivot at top and bottom;
double: door divided into two folds or valves;
double margin: door looking as though it has two leaves with a *muntin* looking like a *stile* in the centre, twice as wide as the side stiles, but with its centre beaded or otherwise finished to make it resemble two stiles, therefore showing a double margin;
Dutch: divided horizontally into two pieces so that the lower part can be kept shut, also called *half-door*;
false: immovable, imitation door;
flap: small vertical door hinged at the bottom to open downwards, or one placed horizontally and opening up;
flush: with its construction concealed behind plain flush faces, usually plywood;
folding: door divided into two or more valves hinged to the frame or to each other, properly called *bivalve*, *quadrivalve*, etc. In larger heavier

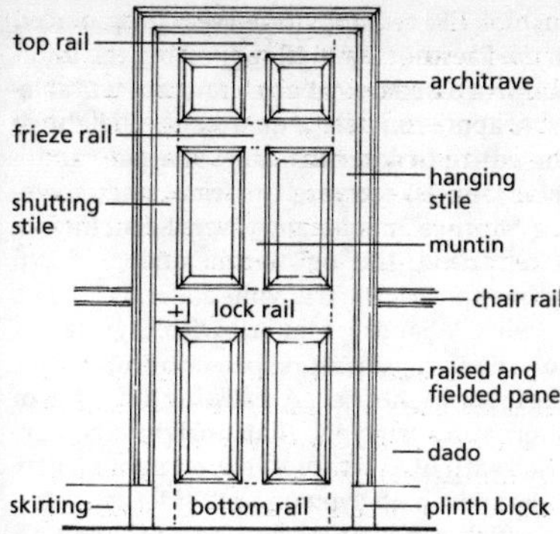

door. Framed door.

doors, the valves should be supported on wheels;

framed: with a timber frame all round, consisting of vertical *stiles* (one of which is the *hanging* stile to which the hinges are fixed) and horizontal rails top and bottom. An additional *middle* or *lock* rail (in which the locks are fixed) is usual, while in panelled doors a central vertical element, the *muntin*, is found;

framed, ledged, braced, and battened: with top, middle, and bottom *rail* mortised and tenoned into two *stiles*, and two braces housed into the rails rising diagonally from the hinged side, clad on the outside with vertical boards or battens;

half: one half of a *Dutch* door, or the entire Dutch door, or a door less high than the doorway, with an opening top and bottom;

Holy: door to the *iconostasis in a church;

jib: hinged *flush* door set in a wall or panelling without a visible frame, designed to be almost invisible to preserve the appearance of a wall, etc., where a visible door would be unacceptable;

ledged and battened: with horizontal rails or ledges (to which hinges and other ironmongery can be fixed), clad with vertical boards or battens outside;

ledged, braced, and battened: as *ledged and battened*, but stiffened by means of braces or struts set diagonally (in better work mortised and tenoned into the ledges) and rising from the hanging side;

overhung: hinged at the top and swinging outwards;

panelled: *framed* door with a frame and one or more *panels. As with a *framed* door (see above) the frame consists of horizontal *top* and *bottom* rails (for one panel), a *middle* or *lock* rail (for four or more panels) to which the handles, locks, etc. are fixed, and a *frieze* rail (where there are six panels) near the top, with vertical *stiles* (one *hanging* (to which the hinges are fixed) and the other *shutting*). Where there are four or more panels a central vertical *muntin* is placed between the rails. In panelled doors the frame is exposed and expressed, surrounding the panels, which can be *plain, decorated, raised*, or *fielded*;

revolving: four flaps or valves fixed at right angles to each other and hung from a central pivot at the axis of a cylinder within which the doors revolve. The outer edges of the valves are finished with rubber or other materials so that close contact is maintained with the cylindrical shell. Access is like a turnstile. It helps to conserve energy and prevent draughts;

rolling: type of shutter consisting of slats joined together and rolling on a suspended axle;

sash: see *casement* above;

sham: finished on one side and set into a wall or partition to look like a door for reasons of appearance or symmetry, really a kind of *blind* door;

sliding: one sliding horizontally on tracks, often suspended from wheeled brackets, and sometimes designed to be housed within a wall;

storm: door or pair of doors, commonly extra outer doors to give added protection in cold weather;

swing: with no striking piece, commonly with double-action spring hinges, used e.g. for doors between kitchen and dining-room in a restaurant.

trap: fitted to a horizontal surface to give access to a cellar or roof;

wicket: small door forming part of a very large one, as in a big church-door.

McKay (1957); Papworth (1852)

door-case. Case or frame lining a door-opening, from which a door is hung, consisting of *architraves, *panels, etc., and sometimes with a *cill.

door-frame. Frame to which a *door is hung set in a *reveal in a *doorway. The verticals of the frame are the *door-checks, -jambs*, or *-posts*, and the top part is the *door-head*. Frames can sometimes include *cills. Door-frames are often associated with a **door-case*.

doorway. Opening for an entrance to a building, part of a building, or an enclosure, together with its immediate structure and surroundings, often of considerable architectural magnificence. Classical *Antique doorways were mostly rectangular (occasionally *battered), surrounded by mouldings, normally the *architrave, conforming with the architrave of the *entablature in *section, and often with *ears, *lugs, or *tabs. Above the architrave there was sometimes a *cornice supported on *ancones or *consoles. A Classical doorway could also be framed by an arrangement of columns, *pilasters, and entablature (often with a *pediment), in which case the opening would be said to be *aediculated. *Renaissance doorways were sometimes arched.

A doorway can often be treated architecturally to enhance its importance in a façade, as in a church, where symbolic aspects play a great part in the design. *Romanesque doorways, for example, usually have semicircular heads, and may consist of several parallel arched layers, each with its own *Order of *colonnettes, *chevron, *beak-head, *billet, or other mouldings. *Gothic doorways have pointed heads, and grander types have several Orders, lush ornament (e.g. *dog-tooth), *Purbeck marble colonnettes, and, in the centre of the opening, a vertical post (*trumeau) dividing it into two parts, with an elaborate sculptured *tympanum above, framed by the pointed arch.

Doric Order. Classical *Order of architecture found in distinct *Greek and *Roman varieties, probably evolved from timber prototypes before C6 BC, as suggested by the *frieze with its *triglyphs perhaps representing beam-ends, *guttae the constructional dowels, and *metopes the spaces between beams, but this interpretation is by no means accepted as gospel. Ancient Egyptian columns, especially those at the Beni-Hasan rock-cut tombs (*c.*1950 BC) and the sixteen-sided columns at the Temple of Queen Hatshepsut, Deïr-el-Bahari (*c.*1480 BC), also have been seen as prototypes of the Doric column. The Greek Doric Order comprises a baseless shaft (normally cut with *flutes separated by *arrises, but occasionally unfluted, as in the temple of Apollo, Delos (*c.*325–300 BC)), rising directly from the *stylobate, diminishing in diameter from bottom to top (*diminution) in a delicate outward curve called *entasis (very pronounced in the Orders used at *Paestum (*c.*565–*c.*450 BC)), terminating in the *trachelion (part of the shaft between the horizontal grooves circumscribing the shaft (*hypotrachelion) and the *annulets); a *capital consisting of 3–5 *annulets (rings) that stop the shaft and its flutes and form the base of the cushion-like *echinus (often very pronounced in the Paestum temples) supporting the unornamented square *abacus; and an *entablature, approximately a quarter the height of the entire Order, consisting of a flat *architrave (*lintel) carrying the frieze and crowning *cornice. Immediately over the architrave is a plain *band or *taenia under which, lining up with the triglyphs above, is a series of narrow bands (*regulae) with 6 guttae or cone-like drops hanging beneath them. Over the taenia is the frieze, consisting of a series of alternating triglyphs (flat upright slabs, incised with two vertical V-shaped glyphs (channels) and a half-glyph on each side, at the top of which is a plain projecting band) and approximately square metopes set back from the face of the triglyphs and often embellished with sculpture in *relief (earlier with painted *terracotta panels). Triglyphs are normally set over the centre-line of each column and over the centre-line of each *intercolumniation in *Hellenic buildings (where one triglyph only is set between each column centre-line), but in *Hellenistic buildings the intercolumniation is usually wider, so two or more triglyphs occurred. However, the Athenian *propylaea (C5 BC) had two triglyphs over the centre intercolumniation. In Greek Doric the triglyphs invariably terminate a frieze, so touch at the angle of a building: as a column set on the centre-line of the triglyph would have an unacceptably clumsy projection at a corner it is therefore set back, and the centre-line rule is broken at the angle, resulting in narrower intercolumniations between the corner-columns and their immediate neighbours. Set over the frieze is the cornice with inclined projecting *mutules on the *soffit placed over the triglyphs and centre-lines of the metopes, so there is insufficient space for ornamentation of the soffit except for the guttae on the undersides of the mutules and (sometimes) an *anthemion or other enrichment at the corner of the soffit, where there are no mutules. The paradigm of Greek Doric is held by some to be the Athenian *Parthenon (447–438 BC), although the type is established by the temple of Aphaia at Aegina (*c.*495 BC).

In the Roman version of Doric, there may be a rudimentary *base, but the shaft is generally more slenderly proportioned, and the entablature is only an eighth the height of the Order (as at the *prostyle tetrastyle temple at Cori in Latium (C1 BC)), giving a somewhat

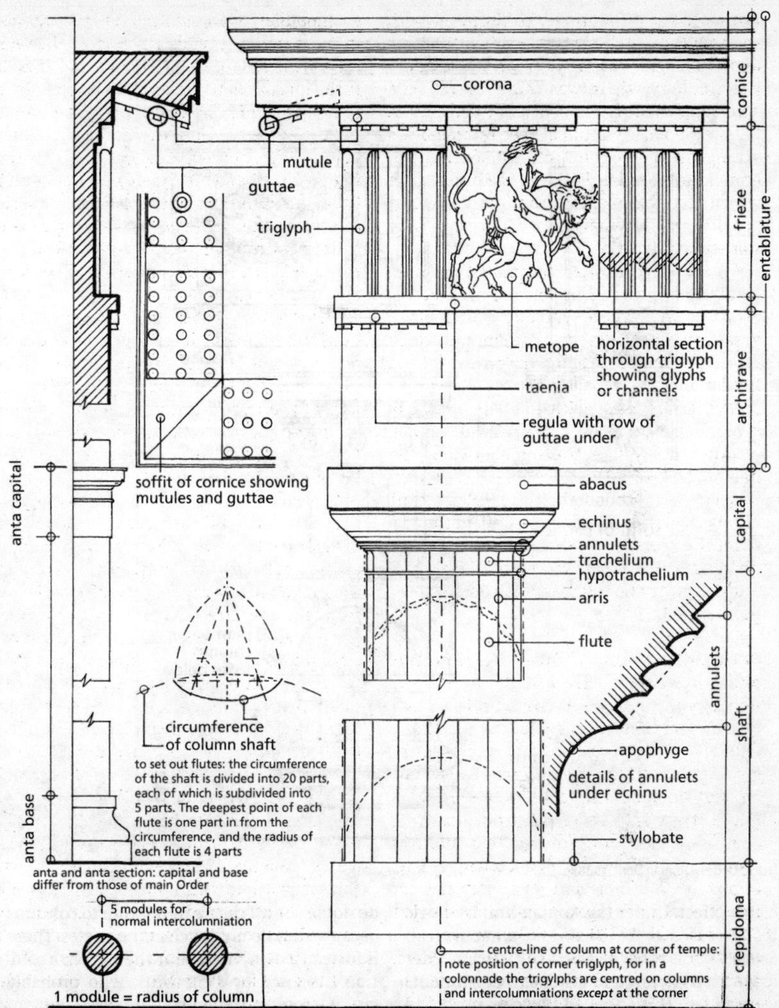

Doric Order. C5 BC Greek Doric Order from the Temple of 'Theseus', Athens. (*After Normand*)

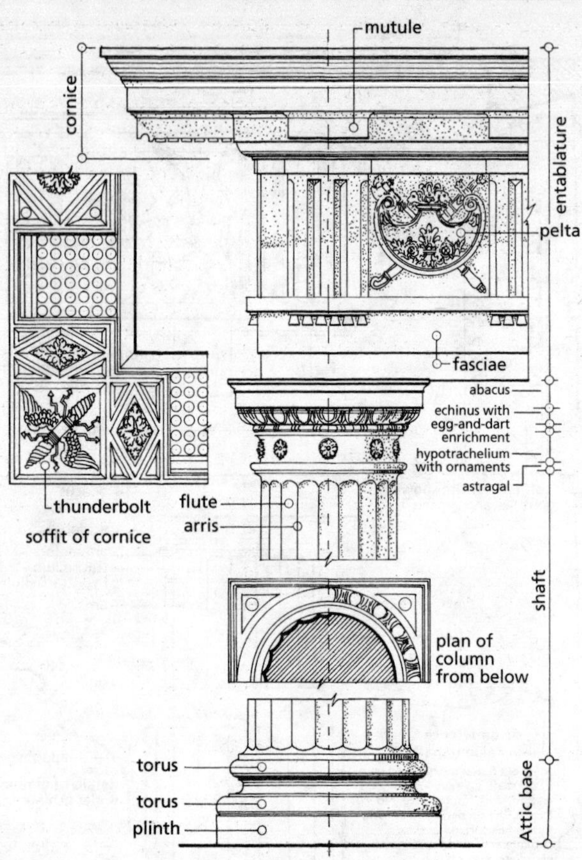

Doric Order. Roman Doric 'mutule' Order of Vignola. (*After Normand*)

feeble effect. Under the Roman Empire Doric really ceased to be used, and what we call *Roman Doric* is really a variety of *Tuscan Order to which triglyphs and other embellishments were added. This so-called Doric was codified and developed during the *Renaissance, and consists of a base, a shaft (fluted or unfluted) more slenderly proportioned than in Greek Doric, and a capital consisting of an *astragal (sometimes ornamented with *bead-and-reel) joined to the shaft by an *apophyge, a frieze-like hypotrachelium (often ornamented), an echinus (sometimes enriched with *egg-and-dart), and a square abacus with a crowning moulding. Architraves are sometimes plain, but usually have two *fasciae separated by mouldings, and the frieze has triglyphs that do not occur off-centre in relation to columns because they do not touch at the angles. There is instead a demi-metope at the corner, a solution proposed by *Vitruvius, who probably got it from a Hellenistic theorist: Roman Doric columns are therefore always equidistant, with identical intercolumniations, even at the corners, though the spacing is invariably wide, with two or more triglyphs over each intercolumniation although there are some exceptions, such as *Hawksmoor's Mausoleum at Castle Howard, Yorkshire (1729–36), where the intercolumniation is deliberately narrow, to add to the *gravitas* of the architecture. Metopes are often ornamented with *bucrania and other devices derived from Hellenistic models, especially from Asia

Minor. Mutules are usually set over the triglyphs only, giving scope for additional inventive ornamentation on the soffit, and have a slight slope and very modest projection (usually only the guttae) below the cornice. The powerful Mutule Order of *Vignola has horizontal mutules that do project, giving a highly modelled soffit additionally ornamented with lozenges and thunderbolts. *Scamozzi and Vignola both used *dentils associated with the *bed-mouldings of their versions, clearly derived from the *Antique Order of the *thermae of Diocletian, Rome (AD 306), which has a continuous band of *fret-like ornament suggesting *dentils.

Curl (1992); Dinsmoor (1950); Hersey (1988); Normand (1852); Onians (1988)

Doric Revival. Until *c.*1570 the Greek *Doric *Order was virtually unknown, and, even when the Greek temples at *Paestum began to be taken seriously by *Winckelmann and others in C18, aroused controversy, as they were perceived to be deformed, crude, and ugly by eyes accustomed to *Palladian refinements. Only when tough, primitive, *Antique themes began to be explored did Doric begin to be appreciated, and it became a powerful element in *Neoclassicism and in the *Greek Revival.

Pevsner (1968)

dorman, dormant. **1.** Large horizontal structural timber or *summer-tree*. **2.** Main beam supporting smaller ones. **3.** *Dormer-window.

dormer. Projecting framed structure set vertically on the *rafters of a pitched roof, with its own roof (pitched or flat), sides (*dormer cheeks*), and a window set vertically in the front. It will often have a small *gable or *pediment (*dormer-head*) over the window if the roof is pitched at right angles to the main roof, but if the roof is a *cat-slide it will have a flat top. Not to be confused with a *lucarne rising directly over the *eaves from the *naked of the main wall below.

dorse. Canopy or *dorsel.

dorsel, dossal, dossel. **1.** *Reredos. **2.** Embroidered cloth suspended over the rear of an altar. **3.** Ornamental hanging suspended at the backs of *sedilia or elsewhere at the sides of a *chancel. **4.** Stall with a back to it, as in a *Collegiate church or cathedral. **5.** High *wainscoting or panelling in a room.

dorter, dortour. Sleeping-room, bedchamber, or dormitory, especially in a *monastery or college.

Dortsman, Adriaan *or* **Adriaen** (1625–82). Dutch architect and military engineer. Born in Vlissingen, he practised in Amsterdam from 1665, and designed the Nieuwe Lutherse Kerk (1668–71), a domed *rotunda with an *ambulatory around half its circumference. He supervised the construction of the defences at Amsterdam and Naarden, and built several groups of houses on the Heerengracht and Keizersgracht, Amsterdam (1665–72), in a refined, plain, stripped style, the only architectural emphases being on door-cases, balconies, and crowning elements.

Kuyper (1980); Landale-Drummond (1934); Rosenberg, Slive, and Ter Kuile (1977)

Doshi, Balkrishna Vithaldas (1927–). Indian architect, designer of the Centre for Environmental Planning and Technology, Ahmedabad (1967–81), one of the most successful *Modernist buildings of its time in the Subcontinent. Influenced by Le *Corbusier (with whom he worked), his own studio at Sangath, Ahmedabad (1979–81), and the Gandhi Institute of Labour Studies, Ahmedabad (1980–4), show his debt to the Franco-Swiss architect.

Curtis (1996); Emanuel (1994)

dossal, dossel. *See* dorsel.

dosseret. **1.** Supplementary cubical block or *super-abacus*, often taller than the *capital itself, placed over an *abacus of *Early Christian, *Byzantine, and *Romanesque capitals, really an *impost-block* from which arches spring. **2.** Block formed like a section of *entablature over a column or pier. **3.** Small projection on a *jamb, forming a *pilaster-like member supporting e.g. a *lintel.

Dotti, Carlo Francesco (1670–1759). Born in Como, he settled in Bologna, where he became the leading *Baroque architect. His most celebrated designs are the dramatically sited Pilgrimage Church of the Madonna di San Luca, near Bologna (1723–57), a vast domed church on an elliptical plan, and the Meloncello arch (1722).

Matteucci (1969); *Zeitschrift für Kunstgeschichte*, 34/3 (1971), 208–39

double. Mirror-image of a motif (e.g. *double cone), or twofold, forming a pair.

double arch. Arch erected from two centres, with radii shorter than half the span, sometimes occurring in *Romanesque work.

double bead. Two beads parallel to each other, one of which is generally smaller, with *quirks.

double-bellied. *Baluster shaped like two long-bows (weapons, as in archery), one mirroring the other, identical above and below its middle and on either side of its centre-line.

double church. 1. Two-storeyed church, i.e. with a church on each storey, as in the *Romanesque Church of Schwarz-Rheindorf, Rhineland, Germany (C12). **2.** Church with two distinct *naves joined together at a centre point, as at the L-shaped Lutheran Church, Freudenstadt, Germany (1601–8).

double cloister. *Ambulatory divided in two by a range of columns or *piers.

double cone. *Romanesque moulding consisting of a series of truncated cones laid on their sides, set with bases joined and truncated tops together, forming a continuous horizontal ornament in a *cavetto.

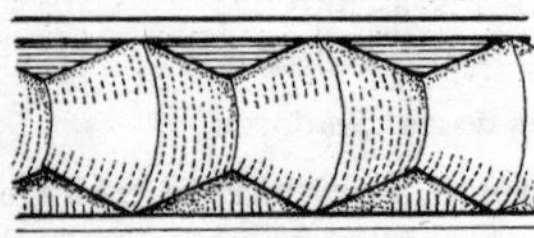

double cone. Church of St Mary, Stoneleigh, Warwickshire (C12).

double floor. One consisting of three horizontal ranges of timbers: boards laid on flooring- or bridging-joists which are carried on binding-joists, to the underside of which the ceiling-joists are fixed.

double-framed roof. *See* roof.

double-fronted. House with a centre door, its front symmetrical about an axis through the door (e.g. houses in Pembridge Square and Holland Park, Northern Kensington, London (1857–79)).

double hammer-beam. *See* truss.

double-hung sashes. Window with two *sashes hung with pulleys, lines, and weights, each capable of being moved up and down in the same frame.

double lancet. 1. *Gothic window consisting of two *lancet-lights separated by a *mullion, often with a small circular or lozenge-shaped light above. **2.** Two lancets placed close together in a wall.

double-margin door. *Door looking like a pair of doors with its central *muntin divided vertically by a *bead.

double-pile house. A *pile* is a row of rooms: a *single-pile* house is therefore one with a single row of rooms; a *double-pile* house is two rooms thick, sometimes, but not always, with a corridor between the two rows. According to some authorities, one of the earliest double-pile houses to survive is Whitehall, Shrewsbury, Shropshire (1578–82), although Inigo *Jones's Queen's House, Greenwich (1616–35), was somewhat grander, anticipating a not uncommon type of English C17 plan.

double ressaunt. Moulding consisting of two *ogees meeting in a *fillet.

double-return stair. *See* stair.

double vault. Two *vaults carried up with a space between them, as in the dome at San Pietro, Rome (1546–90).

double window. Window with two *lights within one architectural entity, as in *Gothic work, the lights separated by a *mullion.

doucine. *Cyma recta.

Douglas, John (1829–1911). English architect. He set up in Chester and influenced a regional style of *vernacular architecture, featuring timber-framing. His best works (as Douglas and Fordham (with J. P. Fordham (1843–99)) are the cottages, houses, and model farms on the Westminster Estates at Eaton Hall, Cheshire, and several fine buildings at Port Sunlight, including the Lyceum (1894–6). He designed the Church of St Chad, Hopwas, Staffordshire (1881), in which he introduced *timber-framed construction, giving the building a domestic air.

Darley (1975); Davison (1916); Gray (1985); Hubbard (1991)

Doultonware. High-fired vitrified non-porous salt-glazed ceramic made of a hard grey-brown material (stoneware) on which designs were drawn, a part or the whole then being richly coloured. Produced in the Doulton Works, Lambeth, London, founded by John Doulton (1793–1873), it was invented and patented by Sir Henry Doulton (1820–97), and exhibited in 1871 as *sgraffito*-ware. He then developed *Lambeth faïence* (brightly coloured glazed blocks) and *Doulton impasto* (glazed earthenware, the colour applied thickly). Both products were used for festive façades, such as the fronts of public-houses, bar-fronts, and the like. Hardwearing and easily washed, Doultonware's heyday was the late C19 to *c*.1914.

DNB (1917)

dovecot(e). Circular, polygonal, rectangular, or square building, like a short tower, called *columbier* or *columbarium, the interior of which is fitted with small niches (*columbaria) all round the walls for nesting pigeons or doves.

dovetail. *See* swallowtail.

Dow, Alden Ball (1904–83). American architect. He worked with F. L. *Wright in 1933 before setting up his own prolific practice. Most of his works are in or near Midland, Michigan, and have been noted for their influences from or rejection of Wright's designs. Midland Country Club (1930), built before he moved to work with Wright; his own studio, Midland (1935), much influenced by Wright; and the Midland Center for the Arts (1970), which represents the complete rejection of Wright, may be cited.

Dow (1965, 1970, *c*.1970); Emanuel (1994); Robinson (1983)

dowel(l). Headless peg, pin, or bolt of wood, metal or other material, used to fasten two members together by being set into each part. *See* cramp.

Dowland, Thomas (*fl*. 1490s). English mason. He built the west tower of the Holy Cross Guild Chapel at Stratford-on-Avon, Warwickshire (begun 1496), and may have been responsible for the *chancel and *clearstorey of the Parish Church in the same town (*c*.1465–*c*.1495). To judge from the stylistic similarities he seems to have worked on several churches in Warwickshire and Worcestershire, especially towers.

Harvey (1987)

Downes, Kerry John (1930–). English architectural historian. Specializing in English *Baroque architecture, he made a significant contribution to scholarship with his works on *Hawksmoor, *Vanbrugh, and *Wren. He has also written perceptively on Sir Peter Paul Rubens (1577–1640), the great Flemish painter. Downes's productivity seems to run counter to his claim that procrastination is one of his recreations.

Downes (1966, 1977, 1980, 1982, 1987, 1988, 1988*a*); personal knowledge

Downing, Andrew Jackson (1815–52). Leading American writer and rural architect of the first half of C19. His *A Treatise on the Theory and Practice of Landscape Gardening Adapted to North America* (1841) drew generously on *Loudon's and *Repton's work, while his *Cottage Residences* (1842) and *The Architecture of Country Houses* (1850) helped to disseminate his ideas and designs, which owed much to the skills of A. J. *Davis (who made professional drawings for Downing's publications from 1839 to 1850), but, when his proposals to form a professional relationship with Davis failed, he took the Englishman Calvert *Vaux, a pupil of *Cottingham, on as his partner (1850). Through his editorials in *The Horticulturist* (the 'Journal of Rural Art and Rural Taste') he had a profound effect on architecture and landscape design, and can be compared with Loudon (from whom he derived many of his ideas) in his importance. He was the father of the American public park, and his visions were given substance by Vaux and *Olmsted in Central Park, New York (1857–60).

Downing (1967, 1967*a*, 1968); Hitchcock (1977); Placzek (1982)

Dowson, Sir Philip Manning (1924–). South-African-born architect, he worked with Ove *Arup from 1953, becoming a founder of Arup Associates in 1963. Among the works of Arup Associates are the Maltings Concert Hall, Snape, Suffolk (1965–7—with Derek Sugden), the IBM Process Assembly Plant, Havant, Hampshire (1966–72), Sir Thomas White Building, St John's College, Oxford (1970–6—with an elegant precast concrete frame), and part of the Broadgate Development, London (1983). He designed the important *Modernist Long Wall House, Long Melford, Suffolk (1962–4).

Emanuel (1994)

Doxiadis, Constantinos Apostolos (1913–75). Greek architect, engineer, and town-planner, born in Bulgaria, he became influential in Greece, and formed the Office for National, Regional, and Town Planning

Studies and Research in 1939. He was intimately involved with the reconstruction of Greece after the 1939–45 war, and founded his own architectural, consulting, and engineering firm in 1951, which quickly won an international reputation. He is remembered primarily for the evolution of the theory of *Ekistics, notably through the Graduate School of Ekistics and the Ekistic Centre in Athens, and through his book *Ekistics: Introduction to the Science of Human Settlements* (1968).

Deane (1965); Doxiadis (1963, 1966); Emanuel (1994)

Doyle, Albert Ernest (1877–1928). California-born, he founded his architectural firm in Oregon with William B. Patterson as his partner in 1907, and designed a ten-storey extension to the Meier and Frank Department Store in Portland. The firm's commercial designs were eclectic, largely in Revival styles, but its simpler seaside houses (e.g. Wantz Studio House, Neahkahnie, Oregon (1916)), were inspirations for *Belluschi and others who worked with Doyle.

Architect and Engineer, 8/1 (1919), 38–96

Doyle, John Francis (1840–1913). Influential Liverpool architect, his churches were in a scholarly *Gothic Revival, but his commercial buildings, notably the Royal Insurance Offices, Dale Street, Liverpool (1897–1903), were assured *Baroque compositions. His White Star Building, Pier Head (with Norman *Shaw), of 1894–6, resembled Shaw's New Scotland Yard in London. He also designed a number of houses for the prosperous classes of the area, but most have been demolished or unsympathetically altered.

Gray (1985)

draft, draught. Regular *dressed *drafted margin* the width of the chisel, also called a *border*, along the edges of the face of a squared stone.

dragon-beam. In *timber-framed construction, a beam set diagonally to support *jetties on two adjacent façades at an angle of an upper storey, or to carry the foot of a hip-*rafter in a building with a hipped roof.

dragon-bracket. Bracket, often shaped or curved, supporting the corner of a *jetty and set at an angle of 135° from a corner-post.

dragon-piece, dragging-piece. Short length of horizontal timber (really a shortened *dragon-beam) set diagonally at an angle, one end on the junction of two adjacent wall-plates and the other on a *dragon-tie, to support the foot of a hip-*rafter.

Dragon style. Style of decoration influenced by Scandinavian Viking art, a revival of which took place in the second half of C19 in Norway. Certain motifs were incorporated within the *Celtic Revival and *Art Nouveau.

Tschudi-Madsen (1967)

dragon-tie. **1.** Horizontal timber *angle-brace* between a tie-beam and a wall-plate. **2.** The same, but between adjacent wall-plates at the angle of a hipped roof, especially when it supports one end of a *dragon-piece, the other supported on the angle of the wall-plates.

drapery. *Swag of drapery instead of a *festoon, suspended from an object, e.g. *bucranium, in Classical ornament.

drapery panel. As *linenfold.

Dravidian architecture. Architecture in the southern part of the Indian Subcontinent.

drawbridge. **1.** Bridge over a moat, ditch, river, etc., hinged at one end, like a flap, fixed to chains at the other end, capable of being raised and lowered to prevent or permit passage over it, especially in fortifications. **2.** The same, but over a waterway, raised to permit the passage of ships beneath it. In such cases the flap is often matched with an identical flap on the other side, and each rotates about an axis, counterweighted at the other side of the axis. This type is a *bascule bridge*.

dressed. Describes the operation a stone has undergone before it is built into a wall. A *dressed stone* is therefore one finished.

Dresser, Christopher (1834–1904). Glasgow-born, one of the most distinguished and inventive industrial designers of C19. His publications include *Botany as Adapted to the Arts and Art Manufactures* (1857–8), *The Art of Decorative Design* (1862), *The Principles of Decorative Design* (1873), *Japan, its Architecture, Art, and Art Manufactures* (1882), and *Modern Ornamentation* (1886). Many of his designs for incised ornament and cast-iron artefacts were widely copied. He was profoundly influenced by the natural world, by A. W. N. *Pugin, by Owen *Jones, and by Japanese artefacts.

Dennis and Jesse (1972); *DNB* (1994); Dresser (1862, 1873, 1882)

dressings. **1.** General term for all finishes, mouldings, ornaments, *dressed stones, and the like (often projecting) around an aperture such as a door or window, and distinguished from the rest of the plain surface of the *naked of a wall. **2.** Dressed stone: a façade of brick with stone dressings has most of the wall-surface (naked) of brick, but *quoins, *architraves, and the like are of dressed stone.

Drew, (Dame) Jane (Joyce) Beverley (1911–96). British *Modernist architect, who founded an all-women firm in 1940. Later, she was a founder-partner with E. Maxwell *Fry (her husband from 1942) of Fry, Drew, & Partners, London (1945), of which *Lasdun became a partner in 1951. The firm worked extensively in West Africa, designing educational buildings in Nigeria, the Gold Coast, Sierra Leone, and The Gambia, and was the force behind the establishment of the first School of Tropical Architecture by the Architectural Association of London. From the 1950s Drew and her colleagues worked on the designs for the new capital of the Punjab, India, at Chandigarh, in association with Le *Corbusier (with whom she became emotionally involved) and Pierre *Jeanneret: Corbusier redesigned the original master-plan, and Drew was involved in the genesis of colleges, health-centres, housing, shopping areas, and schools. She also designed buildings in Iran, Ceylon, and Ghana, as well as housing for Harlow (Essex), Welwyn, and Hatfield (both Hertfordshire) in the 1960s which was much admired at the time. She was responsible for the Open University buildings at Milton Keynes, Buckinghamshire (1969–77). A member of the *MARS group, she also published various works including *Architecture for Children* (1944) and *Kitchen Planning* (1945), as well as several books on tropical architecture in collaboration with Fry.

Brockman (1978); Fry and Drew (1947, 1956, 1964, 1976); *The Times*, 1 August 1996

Drew, Sir Thomas (1838–1910). Irish architect. Born in Belfast, he trained under *Lanyon from 1854, and set up in practice in Dublin in 1875. He gained a reputation as a writer and antiquarian (he was President of the Royal Society of the Antiquaries of Ireland), and was noted for his robustly virile *Gothic. His best work is the nave of St Anne's Anglican Cathedral, Belfast (from 1898), in a tough *Romanesque Revival. As Diocesan Architect for Down, Connor, and Dromore, he designed many churches, including the fine Kilmore Church, Crossgar, Co. Down (1866–8), Drumbeg Parish Church, Co. Down (1868–70), St Jude's Church, Ormeau Road (1869–75), Belfast, and St Donard's Church, Dundrum, Co. Down (1886). He carried out major restorations at St Patrick's Cathedral, Dublin (1899–1904).

DNB (1917); Larmour (1987); *Journal of the Royal Society of Ulster Architects*, 4/5 (May/June 1996), 61–3

drift. Thrust or outward pressure of an arch or *vault requiring the counter-thrust of a *buttress.

drip. **1.** Any projection so shaped as to throw rainwater off and stop it running back to the wall, usually with a channel or throat underneath. **2.** *Head- or hood-mould, *label, or weather-moulding over the head of an aperture.

drip-cap. Horizontal *head-moulding or *label over an opening to divert rainwater, causing it to drip on either side.

drip-channel. Throat under the *drip.

drip-course, dripstone-course. Continuous horizontal *drip-moulding on a wall.

drip-mould, drip-moulding. Moulding or *hood performing as a *drip.

dripping eaves. *Eaves without gutters, overhanging a wall, throwing rainwater to the ground.

dripstone. *Hood-moulding or *label, especially in *Gothic work on an exterior, convex on top and returning to the wall underneath by deep hollows or *throatings*. If used inside a building *label* or *hood-mould* would be the preferred terms.

dromos. **1.** Long, narrow passage, partly open and partly within a mound, giving access to Aegean chamber- or *tholos-tombs. **2.** Straight, formal entrance-avenue of great magnificence, lined on each side by columns, *sphinxes, statues, *obelisks, etc., as existed in the Serapeion (Temple of Serapis) at Delos (C1 BC), and especially at the huge Isaeum Campense (Temple of Isis), Rome (AD C1–C4). This long axial formal plan leading to a Holy of Holies and associated with courts, *porticoes, and *colonnades got its name from a Greek race-course. A *dromic* or *dromical* church was a term for an Eastern *basilican church, the plan of which resembled the Greek dromos arrangement of Isaea. **3.** Open space with room to move freely, such as a forecourt.

Dinsmoor (1950); Roullet (1972)

drop. **1.** Type of arch. **2.** *Gutta, *campanula, droplet, or lachryma (tear-drop) in the *Doric *Order, or any small pendant. **3.** Pendent ornament hanging from the base of a *newel-post or beneath a *jetty in *timber-framed construction. **4.** Outlet from an eaves-gutter to a downspout.

drop-ornament. Pendent ornamental form like a tear-drop on the intrados of *Gothic arches, really an enriched *cusp.

drop-point slating. Diagonal slating, i.e. roof laid with slates turned so that their diagonals are horizontal, and one sharp corner faces downwards.

drop-tracery. Fragmental *Gothic *tracery suspended from the *soffit of an arch.

drum. **1.** One of the nearly cylindrical pieces of which a column-shaft is constructed. **2.** Vertical wall constructed on a circular or polygonal plan, usually carrying a *cupola or *dome, and often pierced with windows. **3.** *Bell or core of a *Composite or *Corinthian *capital.

dry area. **1.** Gap excavated between a basement-wall of a building (lower than the floor-level) and the adjacent soil to prevent water-penetration and allow light and air to enter. **2.** Space between a retaining-wall and the wall of a basement commencing at least as low as the foundations, drained and ventilated to prevent moisture seeping through into the building.

dry masonry. Stones (usually *rubble) laid without mortar in a wall (*dry-stone walling*).

Dryopic. Pertaining to the Dryopians, held to be one of the earliest settlers in Ancient Greece, hence prehistoric columnar structures pre-dating Classical Antiquity, such as those of Euboea.

Duban, Félix-Louis-Jacques (1797–1870). Paris-born French architect, he was in the vanguard (with *Duc, *Labrouste, and *Vaudoyer) of the younger generation that came to eminence in the 1830s, and he won a reputation as a restorer of lavish interiors. Appointed architect to the École des *Beaux-Arts in 1832, he incorporated *Picturesque techniques in his composition, and his details were refined. With *Lassus and *Viollet-le-Duc he restored the C13 Sainte-Chapelle, with its powerful colouring attracting the favour of *Pugin, although he seems to have been more at ease with Italian *Classicism. His best work is probably the Salle de Melpomène (1860–3) at the École des Beaux-Arts, and the richly opulent resuscitation of the salons in the Louvre. From 1845 he worked on the restorations of the *Châteaux at Blois, Chantilly, Dampierre, and Fontainebleau.

Middleton (1982); Middleton and Watkin (1987); Placzek (1982)

Duc, Gabriel Le (d. 1704). French architect. He designed several houses in Paris, mostly destroyed, but he is best known for his work at the Val-de-Grâce, Paris, in *c.*1658, where, with Le *Muet, he constructed (*c.*1654–65) the *vaults, *dome, and other upper parts of the church, refining and improving the designs of *Mansart and *Lemercier.

Papworth (1852); Sturgis *et al.* (1901–2)

Duc, Louis-Joseph (1802–79). Paris-born French architect, he restored and extended the Palais de Justice, Paris (1840–79): the Cour des Assises, Salles des Pas Perdus, and the façade on the Rue de Harlay (1857–68) are particularly robust, anticipating *Beaux-Arts *Classicism of forty years later. With *Duban, *Labrouste, and *Vaudoyer he was one of the more radical architects of the 1830s. He was responsible for completing the Colonne de Juillet, Place de la Bastille, Paris (1835–40—originally designed by J.-A. *Alavoine), which is an eclectic mix of *Egyptian, *Greek, *Roman, and *Renaissance motifs. He also designed the Lycée Michelet, Vanves (1862), in a *Lombardic *Gothic style.

Daly (1840–90); Delaborde (1879); Middleton and Watkin (1987)

Duca, Giacomo del (*c.*1520–1604). Known also as Jacopo Siciliano *or* Ciciliano, he was born in Cefalù, Sicily, and eventually became a pupil of *Michelangelo in Rome. He completed the Master's Porta Pia (1562–5), and designed the Porta San Giovanni (1573–4). He also completed the *drum, dome, and *lantern of Santa Maria di Loreto (1573–7), near Trajan's column, and designed parts of the *piazza before the Palazzo Farnese, Caprarola (1584–6), including the curved ramps, as well as the upper garden with its elaborate water-chain of contorted dolphins.

Benedetti (1973); Papworth (1852)

Du Cerceau Family. *See* Cerceau.

Dudok, Willem Marinus (1884–1974). Amsterdam-born Dutch military engineer, he became one of the most influential architects working in The Netherlands between the two World Wars. In 1915 he was appointed Director of Public Works at Hilversum, near Amsterdam, where he designed around 250 buildings, most of some distinction, and drew up the expansion-plan inspired by the English *Garden City movement. Initially, he was influenced by *Berlage, then by the *Amsterdam School, and, from *c*.1920, by De *Stijl. His masterpiece is Hilversum Town Hall (1924–30), which has certain similarities with the work of F. L. *Wright, and was particularly admired in Britain in the 1930s.

Country Life Annual (1972), 104–7; Cramer, Grieken, and Pronk (1981); Langmead (1996); Magnée (1954); Oosterman (1995); personal knowledge

Duff, Thomas (*c*.1792–1848). Irish architect who designed and built the first scholarly *Gothic Revival buildings in that country. He practised from Newry, Co. Down, and formed a partnership with Thomas *Jackson of Belfast. His masterpiece is the Roman Catholic Pro-Cathedral of St Patrick, Dundalk, Co. Louth (1835–47), in the English *Perpendicular style. In 1838 he prepared designs for St Patrick's Cathedral, Armagh (also Perpendicular), but *McCarthy completed the building in the *Second Pointed style, leaving Duff's incongruous Perpendicular *nave-*piers supporting stylistically earlier elements. With *Jackson, he designed the *Greek Revival Old Museum, College Square North, Belfast (1830–1). He was also responsible for a number of Classical (e.g. extensions to Hillsborough Castle, Co. Down (*c*.1830–40)) and *Tudorbethan (e.g. Parkanaur, Castlecaulfeild, Co. Tyrone (1839–48); Narrow Water Castle, Warrenpoint, Co. Down (*c*.1831–7)) country-houses, as well as court- and market-houses, the latter usually in a sober Classical style (e.g. Hilltown (1828) and Newry (1841), Co. Down). His assistant was W. J. *Barre.

Bence-Jones (1988); Brett (1967, 1973); Casey and Rowan (1993); Larmour (1987); Sheehy (1977)

Duiker, Johannes (1890–1935). Dutch architect, influenced first by F. L. *Wright and then by De *Stijl. He was editor of, and a regular contributor to, the architectural journal *De 8 en Opbouw* (The Eight and Reconstruction—1932–5), and was one of the leading Modernists of the inter-war period. The Zonnestraal Sanatorium, Hilversum (1926–8), was a good example of *International *Modernism, and his Handelsblad-Cineac Cinema, Amsterdam (1934–6), with its huge *sky-sign, owed much to *Constructivism and to Le *Corbusier. His last work, completed by his partner, Bernard Bijvoet (1889–1979), was the Grand Hotel Gooiland, Hilversum (1934–6).

Architectural Review, 102 (1947), 128–30; Duiker (1930); van Vynckt (1993)

Dülfer, Martin (1859–1942). German architect. He taught in Dresden and acquired a formidable reputation as a theatre-designer. His works include the Dortmund Municipal Theatre (1903), the Dresdner Bank, Leipzig (1910–12), and the Technische Hochschule, Dresden (1912–14). He used massive rock-faced *masonry, certain motifs derived from *Jugendstil, and powerful, blocky forms in his compositions that stand comparison with those of *Bonatz and *Kreis.

Dülfer (1914); Licht (1910)

dungeon. *See* donjon.

Dunn, William Newton (1859–1934). British architect and early advocate of *reinforced concrete. With Robert Watson (1865–1916), he continued James Marjoribanks *MacLaren's practice after the latter's death. The firm designed competent *Arts-and-Crafts *vernacular-revival buildings, but could also produce excellent essays in *Classicism. A good example of the latter is the Scottish Provident Institution's Building, 16–17 Pall Mall, London (partly designed by Curtis *Green, who became a partner in 1900), which incorporated Michelangeloesque Mannerist devices derived from the New Sacristy at San Lorenzo, Florence.

Gray (1985)

Dupérac, Étienne (*c*.1525–1604). Paris-born French architect, painter, engraver, and landscape-architect. He is mostly remembered for his drawings of *Antique objects made during his stay in Rome (1573–5), where he also prepared archaeologically based reconstructions. He designed the garden at Anet (*c*.1580) and St-Germain-en-Laye (1595). He may have been involved in the design of parts of the Tuileries, Paris, in the early C17 (destroyed).

Dupérac (1973); Ehrle (1908)

Durand, Jean-Nicolas-Louis (1760–1834). Paris-born architect, one of the most important theorists and teachers of the early C19. He worked for *Boullée, and became Professor of Architecture at the École Polytechnique in 1795. His lectures were published as *Précis des leçons d'architecture données à l'école polytechnique* (Summary of Lectures on Architecture Given at the École Polytechnique—1802–5), and were widely influential, notably in Prussia, and his *Recueil et parallèle des édifices de tout genre* (Compendium and Parallel of Buildings of all Kinds—1800) was the first book organized by building type to deal with historical architecture, and with illustrations reproduced to the same scale. He was an important figure in *Neoclassicism, and his system of design using simplified, repetitive, modular elements anticipated *industrialized building components.

Braham (1980); Durand (1802–9, 1809); Hautecœur (1953); Hitchcock (1977); Middleton and Watkin (1987); Szambien (1984); Villari (1990); Watkin (1986)

Durham. *See* Dereham.

durn. 1. Timber cut from a piece with a grown angle from which e.g. a door-frame with a shaped arched head can be formed: a symmetrical arched frame was usually made from paired durns sawn from a single baulk. **2.** Door-post made of solid timber.

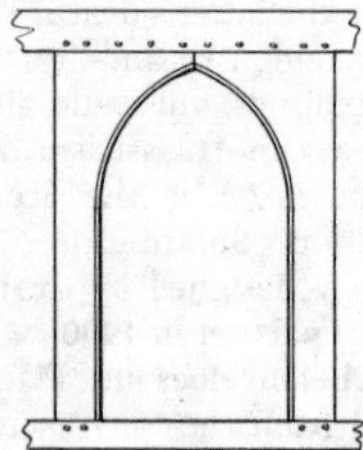

durn. Doorway of opposed durns. (*JJS*)

Du Ry, Paul (1640–1714). *See* Ry.

Dutch gable. Tall *gable with sweeping curved sides, often *ogees with *volutes, crowned by a triangular *pediment. Not to be confused with a *shaped gable.

Dutert, Charles-Louis-Ferdinand (1845–1906). French architect of the *Galerie des Machines* at the International Exposition in Paris (1889, but demolished 1905), a huge development of the metal-and-glass structures that proliferated in C19, designed in collaboration with the engineer Victor Contamin (1840–93). It had an unprecedented span of 114 metres, with the principal trusses in the form of four-centred arches (*see* arch) hinged at the apices and bases. He designed the new galleries for the Museum of Natural History, Paris (1896), which had its metal structure expressed.

Middleton and Watkin (1987)

Duthoit, Edmond-Armand-Marie (1837–89). French architect. A pupil of *Viollet-le-Duc, he acquired a formidable architectural eclectic vocabulary from his studies of historic buildings. His most celebrated design is the colourful *basilica of Notre-Dame-de-Brebières, at Albert, Somme (1884–96). His Château du Roquetaillade, near Langon, in the Gironde (1864–70), continued work begun by Viollet-le-Duc, but it is mostly Duthoit's: it is an exotic confection of *Gothic, but leavened with Arabic and *Byzantine themes, continuing a trend he had evolved at the reconstruction of the C15 Château d'Arragori, near Hendaye, Basses-Pyrénées (*c*.1864–79). It is almost as luxuriant as contemporary work by *Burges.

Middleton (1982); Middleton and Watkin (1987)

Düttmann, Werner (1921–83). German architect. As City Architect of Berlin in the 1960s he was a leading light in the *conservation movement to save Berlin's heritage of stucco-fronted C19 apartments, but he was also a prime mover in the campaign to persuade *Mies van der Rohe to return to Berlin and build the *Nationalgalerie*, which, arguably, with the *Philharmonie* by *Scharoun, ignored the historic plan of the city in that area. He was responsible for some major developments, including low-density housing at Heiligensee (1975) and apartment-blocks at Märkisches Viertel, Wittenau, both in Berlin (1970).

Emanuel (1994)

dwarf gallery. External covered passage or *ambulatory with an *arcade on one side, as at the *Romanesque church at Schwarz-Rheindorf, Germany (C12), where it ran virtually all round the upper church.

Sturgis *et al.* (1901–2)

dwarf wainscoting. *Dado.

dwarf wall. Low perforated wall giving intermediate support to floor-joists that would otherwise be liable to deflect.

dyke. *Dry-stone *rubble wall.

Dykes Bower, Stephen Ernest (1903–94). English architect. He continued the traditions of the *Gothic Revival, and was in the front rank of church architects and decorators. He rebuilt All Saints, Hockerill, near Bishops Stortford, Hertfordshire (1936), in Modern Gothic, and designed St John's Church, Newbury, Berkshire (1955–7), a robust essay in the *Rundbogenstil, probably his best work. Other designs include the vigorous *Baroque high-altar and *ciborium at St Paul's Cathedral, London (1949–58). He restored St Vedast's, Foster Lane, London (1953–60), Westminster Abbey (from 1951—where he was Surveyor of the Fabric for 22 years), and *Bodley's *polychrome interior of St John's, Tue Brook, Liverpool (from 1967—a particularly felicitous achievement). He designed distinguished extensions for the Cathedral at Bury St Edmunds, Suffolk, from 1956. In 1979 R. C. *Carpenter's Lancing College Chapel, Sussex, was completed to Dykes Bower's designs: it has the largest *rose-window to be built in England since those medieval examples in the *transepts of Westminster Abbey.

Obituary by Fr. Anthony Symondson, SJ: *Independent* (14 Nov. 1994), 14; personal knowledge

dyostyle. **1.** As distyle. *See* portico. **2.** Having coupled columns.

Eads, James Buchanan (1820–87). American engineer. He pioneered the use of structural steel for a major building with the Eads Bridge, St Louis, Mo. (1867–74). He also invented tests for compression and tension in steel, and devised ironclad ships for the Union side in the Civil War.

Scott and Miller (1979); Vollmar (1974)

eagle. 1. *Pediment of a temple, or, more especially, *tympanum from the Greek ἀετός, ἀέτωμα. **2.** *Gable. **3.** Reading-desk or lectern in a church, often in the form of an eagle, symbol of the Word and St John the Evangelist.

Eames, Charles Ormond (1907–78). American designer, one of the most significant and versatile of his time. His reputation as an architect rests on his own dwelling and the John Entenza House (both 1945–9) at Pacific Palisades, Calif., steel-framed pavilions owing something to the work of *Mies van der Rohe. They were important works of *industrialized building. He was even better known as a designer of moulded plywood chairs and other furniture, especially the Eames Chair (1940–1), produced with Eero *Saarinen (whom he met while at *Cranbook Academy). With his second wife, Ray Kaiser, he founded an influential design team.

Curtis (1996); Drexler (1973); Emanuel (1994); Kirkham (1995)

ear. 1. *Acroter or *horn of an altar, *sarcophagus, or *stele. **2.** *Crossette. **3.** *Lug or *tab.

Early Christian architecture. An integral part of the architecture of the Roman Empire, the most important buildings are of three types: churches, commemorative structures, and covered cemeteries. The exemplar of churches after the recognition of Christianity in C4 was the Roman *basilica, of which San Pietro, Rome (*c.*320–30—demolished early C16), was an influential example because seen by countless pilgrims. The form reached its standard in Santa Maria Maggiore, Rome (423–40), with the *clearstoreyed *nave, lean-to *aisles, and apsidal end. The old St Peter's was built over a cemetery, and its funereal character was emphasized by the large mausolea attached to the tall *transeptal structure on one side. Another circular *mausoleum, that of Santa Costanza, Rome (*c.*350), is a clearstoreyed domed structure surrounded by an *annular *barrel-vault. Originally it was attached to the covered cemetery of Santa Agnese (*c.*340). Early Christian basilicas had nave-*arcades incorporating columns taken from early buildings, or even nave-*colonnades where the *entablatures were recycled. Openings were almost invariably semicircular-headed.

Aspects of Early Christian architecture were revived in C19, especially as part of the *Rundbogenstil pioneered by von *Klenze, *Gärtner, and others. Good examples can be found in England too (e.g. *Wild's Christ Church, Streatham Hill, London (1840–2), and *Losh's St Mary, Wreay, Cumberland (begun 1842)).

Colvin (1991); Krautheimer (1986); Mango (1986)

Early English. *See* First Pointed.

earth *and* **earth-work architecture.** There are long traditions of buildings made of earth or mud (*see* adobe, cob, pisé de terre). In the 1960s proposals were mooted to create buildings by pouring concrete on to mounds of earth which would be excavated once the concrete had set, thus creating cave-like forms called *earth-work architecture*.

Dethier (1983)

earth-table. *Grass-* or *ground-table*, or *foot-stall*, meaning the base-course or *plinth of a building in *Gothic work, or the lowest visible course of stone above the ground projecting in front of the *naked of a wall.

earthwork. **1.** Mound, rampart, etc., of earth, as in fortifications. **2.** Work done in removing earth, etc.

Easter Sepulchre. The ritual 'burial' of Christ was a most solemn observance in medieval times, and required a 'tomb'. At the end of the liturgies of Good Friday (including the strange Creeping to and Adoration of the Cross), the Priest, in bare feet and clad in his surplice, carried a *Pyx containing the third Host (consecrated on Maundy Thursday) and the Cross, both wrapped in linen, to the north side of the *chancel, where a temporary 'sepulchre' (usually of timber, draped with a pall) was made ready, and laid them within. The 'sepulchre' was censed, and numerous candles glowed before it, a continuous watch being kept to protect both the Host and the Pyx (which was usually of high quality). Early on Easter Morning, the church was illuminated with candles; clergy processed to the 'sepulchre', which was censed; the Host was removed to the Pyx above the high-altar; and the Cross was raised from the 'sepulchre' and carried in procession round the church while bells chimed and the Resurrection was celebrated. The Cross was then set on an altar on the north side of the church, where it was again venerated. The now empty 'sepulchre' remained an object of devotion (being censed, having illuminated candles in front of it, etc.) for the days after Holy Week. The Easter Sepulcre often found more permanent architectural expression as a recess, usually canopied, over a tomb-chest. Wealthy patrons, desiring association with the annual Easter mysteries, often built tombs for themselves that doubled as Easter Sepulchres (e.g. Clopton tomb, Long Melford, Suffolk (*c*.1497), and Sackville tomb, Westhampnett, Sussex (*c*.1535). Other Easter Sepulchres were just that, not associated with human tombs: a richly decorated example survives at Heckington, Lincolnshire (*c*.1330), complete with somnolent soldiers, the three Marys and the Angel, and, above, the Risen Christ, the whole exquisitely carved.

Brooks (1921); Duffy (1992); Pevsner, *Buildings of England, Lincolnshire* (1989); *Suffolk* (1975); *Sussex* (1965)

Eastlake, Charles Locke (1836–1906). English architect, better known for his work as a journalist and writer. His *Hints on Household Taste in Furniture, Upholstery, and Other Details* (1868) popularized design derived from the work of *Seddon, *Shaw, and *Street, especially in the USA where a style of *Gothic domestic architecture with oversized elements, rich ornament, and a general toughness is called the Eastlake or *Stick style. His *A History of the Gothic Revival* (1872) is an important and perceptive study.

DNB (1917); Eastlake (1970)

eaves. Lowest portion of a pitched roof projecting beyond the *naked of the wall beneath.

eaves-cornice. Classical *cornice forming the transition between the *naked of a wall and the edge of the *eaves of a pitched roof above.

Ecclesiology. The study of churches, church-history, traditions, decorations, and furnishings. The Ecclesiological Society was a powerful force in the English *Gothic Revival, and its journal, *The Ecclesiologist* (1841–68), was influential, especially in the making (or breaking) of architectural reputations.

Cambridge Camden Society (1842–68, 1847); Curl (1995); Eastlake (1970)

echal. Enclosure for the Ark containing the scrolls in a *synagogue.

échauguette. *Turret, watch-tower, etc., corbelled out from a *curtain-wall or a *salient angle, open or roofed. A *bartizan or angle-turret.

echinus. Plain circular cushion-like convex moulding between the *abacus and *annulets of the Greek *Doric *capital, between the abacus and *hypotrachelium of the *Tuscan and Roman Doric Orders, and beneath the *pulvinus joining the *volutes of the *Ionic capital where it is enriched with *egg-and-dart (so it also occurs in the upper part of a *Composite capital, always enriched).

eclecticism. **1.** Design drawing freely on forms, motifs, and details selected from historical styles and different periods. **2.** The practice of selecting from a wide range of sources what elements, styles, motifs, details, etc., that may appear to be sound, acceptable, functional, and beautiful, in order to create an architectural effect.

Porphyrios (1982)

École des Beaux-Arts. *See* Beaux-Arts.

ecological architecture. Aims to respond to declining energy resources, e.g. using energy conservation, efficient insulation, rainwater, solar radiation, and wind-power, and recycling as much as possible. The term was coined in the 1970s.

Architectural Design, 44/11 (1974), 681–9; Goldstein (1977)

ecphora. Projection of one part over another, e.g. a Classical column-*base projecting beyond the shaft; or a *plinth before the *naked of a wall.

edge-moulding. Medieval moulding often used on *string-courses, with a convex top and a *cavetto underneath, often with a sharp edge at the junction.

edge-roll. Convex moulding, such as a *bowtell, *ovolo, or *torus.

edge-shaft. Common *Romanesque arrangement of an *engaged half-shaft attached to a *pier, usually the element from which an arch springs.

edicula. *See* aedicule.

Edis, Sir Robert William (1839–1927). English architect. He is best known as a protagonist of the *Queen Anne style. His works included houses at 31–3 Tite Street, Chelsea (1879–81), additions to Sandringham House, Norfolk (1891–2), the Constitutional Club, Northumberland Avenue, London (1884–6), and the Great Central Railway Hotel, Marylebone Station, London (1897–9).

Edis (1973); Girouard (1977)

Edwardian architecture. Architecture of the British Empire in the reign of King Edward VII (1901–10), often characterized by an opulent *Baroque revival or *Wrenaissance, as in *Belcher's Ashton Memorial, Lancaster (1906). However, another aspect was the enormous amount of fine domestic design, including much influenced by the *Arts-and-Crafts movement, that was greatly admired on the Continent, notably as a result of the work of *Muthesius.

Muthesius (1979); Service (1975, 1977)

Edwardine. Of the time of King Edward VI (1547–53).

Eesteren, Cor(nelis) van (1897–1988). Dutch architect much influenced by *Bauhaus ideas and by Theo van *Doesburg, with whom he drew up the architectural principles of *Neo-Plasticism as well as the manifesto *Vers une construction collective* (Towards a Collective Construction—1924—also signed by *Rietveld). He was involved in the De *Stijl movement, and by 1929 was firmly within the Modernist camp that envisaged high-rise blocks and huge traffic arteries to replace traditional cities. He was responsible for the General Extension plan for Amsterdam (1936), where he was Chief Architect of the Town Planning Department for nearly half a century. He was president of *CIAM (1930–47).

Blijstra (1962, 1971); Lampugnani (1988)

effigy. Sculptured representation of a figure, normally shown clothed or in armour, lying on its back on a tomb-chest.

Papworth (1852)

Effner, Joseph (1687–1745). Court Architect of Bavaria, he introduced fashionable French styles of architecture and decoration to that country, having studied in Paris, probably under *Boffrand, during the Elector Max Emanuel's (1662–1726) exile there. He worked on the Electoral palaces of Nymphenburg (1715–23), adding the wing-pavilions to *Barelli's existing building, and Schleissheim (1719–25), begun by *Zuccalli. He designed the *Chinoiserie Pagodenburg (1716–19), Roman Badenburg (1718–21), and *Picturesque Magdalenklause (1725–8), all *pavilions in the park at Nymphenburg. He worked with J. B. *Zimmermann and *Cuvilliés on several of his projects, making a major contribution to the evolution of Bavarian *Rococo, but was gradually eclipsed by the latter.

Frank (1985); Hager (1955); Hager and Hojer (1976); Hauttmann (1913); Hempel (1965); Hitchcock (1968*a*); Schmid (1987); Thon (1977); Vits (1973)

Egas, Enrique de (d. *c.*1534). Important Castilian architect, his style was a synthesis of late *Gothic and *Plateresque. As Master of the Works at Toledo Cathedral, he redesigned the sanctuary (*Capilla Major*—1500–4) and built the *Capilla Mozárabe* (1519). His most celebrated designs are the cruciform hospitals of Santiago de Compostela (1501–11) and Holy Cross, Toledo (1504–15), two buildings where Italian *Renaissance influences are evident. He was involved in work at Plasencia (1490s), Seville (1512–15), Malaga (1528), Salamanca (1523–34), and Segovia (1529) Cathedrals. He contributed to the design of the Royal Chapel,

Granada, from 1506, as well as the Cathedral there from 1523.

Azcárate (1958); Chueca Goitia (1951, 1953); Gallego y Burin (1952); Kubler and Soria (1959); Rosenthal (1961)

egg-and-dart. Classical ornament applied to convex rounded moulding (such as the *echinus or other *ovolos) consisting of a series of vertical oviform elements (with their tops cut off) surrounded by a groove and raised rim, between which rims are inserted, one between each pair of 'eggs', a sharply pointed dart-like or anchor form, sometimes resembling a tongue. Thus the egg and dart alternate in series. Also called, depending on the shape of the 'dart', *egg-and-anchor*, *egg-and-tongue*, or *nut-and-husk*.

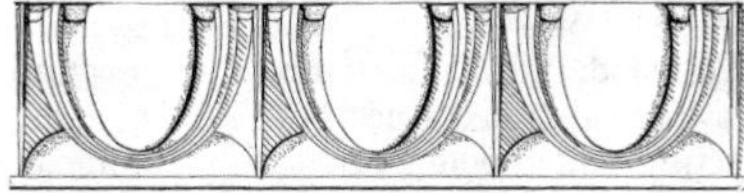

egg-and-dart

Eginhard (*fl.* *c.*800–20). German abbot and architect. He has been credited with the famous plan of the *monastery of St Gall in Switzerland, with its double-apsed *basilican church and highly organized disposition of parts.

Papworth (1852); Sturgis *et al.* (1901–2)

Egyptian architecture. Ancient Egyptian architecture was mostly that of the monumental temple and tomb, and featured *obelisks, *battered walls, *pylon-towers, *pyramids, *cavetto (or *gorge*) *cornices, large columns with *lotus, papyrus, palm, and other *capitals, *hypostyle halls, courts, vast processional axes (called *dromos) flanked by *sphinxes, stylized sculpture, and *hieroglyphs. It was an architecture of the *columnar and *trabeated type. The early stone-built funerary complex at Saqqara (*c.* 2778–*c.* 2600 BC) had many buildings including a stepped pyramid, processional hall with reeded and fluted *engaged columns, courts, and a vast wall containing the whole: it was designed by *Imhotep. Stepped pyramids were superseded by the smooth-sided type, of which the Gizeh pyramids (mid-third millennium BC) are exemplars. The big temple complex at Deïr-el-Bahari (middle of the second millennium BC) was designed with three main levels approached by ramps and having long façades of plain square columns that were greatly influential in C20 *Neoclassicism and *Rational architecture. The temple-groups of Karnak and Luxor were also started around the same time, and their remaining ruins are still impressive. There are many surviving buildings of the Ptolemaic period (323–30 BC), including the Philae and Edfu temples.

Egyptian architecture influenced other styles: the rock-cut tombs at Beni-Hasan, for example, have *proto-*Doric columns; very many Egyptian motifs were absorbed by the *Hellenistic Greek cultures and by the Roman Empire; and Neoclassicism, *Art Deco, Rational architecture, and *Post-Modernism drew on Ancient Egyptian motifs.

Cruickshank (1996); Curl (1994); Lloyd and Müller (1986)

Egyptian gorge. *Cavetto cornice between a flat horizontal slab-like element at the top and a *torus, often enriched, below.

Egyptian hall. Type of grand rectangular public room, neither its style nor form having any connection with Egypt. It was evolved by *Palladio based on descriptions in *Vitruvius, its essential elements being an internal *peristyle carrying a smaller upper *Order or *pilastered *clearstorey above the *entablature. The Order used was *Corinthian, and the form was referred to as an *oecus. A good Palladian example is the Assembly Rooms, York (1731–2), designed by *Burlington.

Curl (1993*b*)

Egyptian Revival. Elements of Ancient Egyptian architecture were found in *Hellenistic and *Roman architecture in Antiquity. After Egypt became part of the Roman Empire and Egyptian deities (especially the goddess Isis and her consort Osiris, whom the Greeks and Romans called Serapis) were venerated by the Romans the process accelerated: not only were many Egyptian artefacts, including *obelisks, brought to Rome and re-erected to embellish Roman buildings, but countless objects in the style of Egyptian art were made in Europe. Ancient obelisks were again set up in *Renaissance Rome, where they can be seen in several locations today, and huge numbers of Egyptian and Egyptianizing artefacts re-emerged to grace the collections in the Vatican and elsewhere. During the latter half of C18, Egyptian motifs began to intrigue designers in the West. *Piranesi designed an 'Egyptian' interior for the *Caffeè degl'Inglesi*, Piazza di Spagna, Rome (*c*.1768), which he published together with a number of fireplaces in an 'Egyptian' style, in *Diverse Maniere d'adornare i Cammini* (Different Ways of Decorating Chimneypieces, 1769). This work included illustrations of the Roman *telamones and figure of Antinoüs from the *Villa Adriana*, Tivoli (all C2), bogus *hieroglyphs, Apis bulls, various Nilotic motifs, and also corbelled pseudo-arches of stepped form which passed into Western artistic consciousness as 'Egyptian'. At the time, many architects, influenced by French theorists such as *Laugier, began to discard architectural ornament deemed to be inessential, and, prompted by a growing admiration for the primitive, explored the possibilities of simple, basic geometries that would bring clarity, severity, and integrity to their compositions. Ancient Egyptian forms such as *battered rectilinear buildings, obelisks, and *pyramids, were combined with cubes, spheres, etc., in the developing language of *Neoclassicism. C18 archaeological activity that encouraged a scholarly and accurate approach to Antiquity, especially the study of buildings in Rome, *Pompeii, Herculaneum, Greece, Sicily, and *Paestum, encouraged by *Winckelmann among others, also turned to Egypt. The Napoleonic investigations of Egyptian architecture, published from 1802 by *Denon and the Commission des Sciences et Arts d'Égypte from 1809 to 1829, did for Egyptian architecture what *Stuart and *Revett had done for Greek. *Empire and *Regency designs were permeated with Egyptianizing influences after the Franco-British campaigns in Egypt (1798–1801) and the subsequent division of information and objects: so great was the enthusiasm for Egypt that *l'Égyptomanie* (Egyptomania) played an enormous role in early C19 taste in both France and Britain.

The Egyptian style was used for several buildings in France, notably a series of fountains (e.g. Place du Châtelet, Paris (1807)), while elsewhere the Egyptian Revival spawned progeny (P. F. *Robinson's Egyptian Hall, Piccadilly, London (1811–12), *Canina's Egyptian Gate, Borghese Gardens, Rome (*c*.1825–8), J. *Haviland's 'Tombs' Gaol, New York (1835–8), and the same architect's New Jersey State Penitentiary, Trenton (1843–6), the entrance-gates and lodges of Abney Park Cemetery, London (1840), by William Hosking (1800–61) and *Bonomi, and the last's Temple Mills, Marshall Street, Leeds, Yorkshire (1842) are examples). Egyptianizing motifs are common in European and American design: they include battered square chimney-pots with Egyptian cornices, lotus-buds and leaves, obelisks, pyramids, and *sphinxes. Battered towers resembling those flanking Egyptian temple *pylons were ideally suited for suspension-bridges, while battered retaining-walls and dams often had *sections derived from Ancient Egyptian precedents. Funerary architecture was often in the Egyptian style, especially in the period 1820–50. C20 Egyptology, including the discovery of Tutankhamun's tomb in 1922, influenced a further revival of the Egyptian style that was spurred by the 1925 Paris exhibition in which Egyptian and Aztec archaeology influenced the burgeoning *Art Deco style, though many elements were derived from *Piranesi. More recently both *Post-Modernism and *Rational architecture have incorporated aspects of Egyptian architecture, and its potency remains undimmed.

Carrott (1978); Clayton (1982); Commission des Sciences et Arts d'Égypte (1820–30); Curl (1994—which includes a comprehensive Bibliography); Denon (1802); Humbert (1989, 1996); Humbert, Pantazzi, and Ziegler (1994); Piranesi (1769); Roullet (1972)

Egyptian triangle. The 3–4–5 triangle, fundamental to architecture and surveying because it enables a right angle to be constructed.

Curl (1991); Jones (1956)

Ehn, Karl (1884–1957). Austrian architect. He studied under *Wagner, became City Architect of Vienna, and was responsible for many public housing-schemes in the 1920s and 1930s. Initially he was attracted by the English *Garden City movement, as his development at Hermeswiese shows (1923), but at the Lindenhof project (1924) he was influenced by housing in Amsterdam. His most celebrated works are the Bebelhof (1925), the huge *Expressionist Karl-Marx-Hof, Heiligenstadt (1927), and the more *Modernist Adelheid-Popp-Hof (1932). The housing-block at Heiligenstadt is nearly half a mile long, designed with 1,382 apartments, offices, laundries, a library, and a clinic, so is a *Unité d'Habitation*, a forerunner of works by Le *Corbusier, and a descendant of C19 ideas, such as those of Charles Fourier (1772–1837). It has simplified façades, powerful cubic, blocky masses, and highly organized geometries.

Hautmann and Hautmann (1980); Mang (1977)

Ehrenkrantz, Ezra David (1932–). American architect and inventor of a system using standardized prefabricated components for low-cost school buildings with adaptable plans, of which the School Construction System Development, Pilot Unit, Stanford, Calif. (1964), is an example. He restored the *Art Deco Woolworth Tower, New York (1980), and designed many educational buildings, including Canaday Hall, Harvard University, Cambridge, Mass. (1974), and the Henle Student Village, Georgetown University, Washington, DC (1980).

Emanuel (1994)

Ehrensvärd, Carl August (1745–1800). Swedish Neoclassical architect. His storehouse at the dockyard at Karlskrona (1784) is one of the most severe buildings of the late C18. After a visit to *Paestum in the 1780s (recorded in his *Journey to Italy 1780, 1781, 1782* (1786)) he designed a primitivist *Doric project for an entrance-gate to the dockyard that influenced *Stirling in his *Staatsgalerie*, Stuttgart (1977–84). His architectural designs, including a pyramid and an extremely squat Doric Order, were as advanced as any at the time, and his polemical works promoted something remarkably like C20 *Functionalism.

Council of Europe (1972); Curl (1994); Ehrensvärd (1786, 1922–5, 1948); Frykenstedt (1965); Josephson (1963); *Konsthistorisk Tidskrift*, 33 (1964), 1–20; Rosenblum (1967); Warburg (1893)

Eidlitz, Cyrus Lazelle Warner (1853–1921). American architect, the son of Leopold *Eidlitz. He made his reputation with Dearborn Station, Chicago (1885), the *Rundbogenstil New York Public Library, Buffalo, NY (1884–7), and the *New York Times* Building (1903).

Wodehouse (1976)

Eidlitz, Leopold (1823–1908). Prague-born American *Romanesque and *Gothic Revivalist. He was much influenced by the work of von *Gärtner in Munich and by the writings of *Pugin and *Ruskin. St George's Church, New York (1846–8), was his first major commission, for which he designed a large *Rundbogenstil galleried hall, clearly influenced by developments in Munich. His later Gothic work is of the *muscular type, best seen in the Albany State Capitol Assembly Chamber, Albany, NY (1875–85), designed with *Richardson and *Olmsted. His *The Nature and Function of Art* (1881) was influential, notably on *Furness and Richardson, and he published many papers in sundry journals.

Eidlitz (1977); Jordy and Coe (1961); Placzek (1982)

Eiermann, Egon (1904–70). German architect. A pupil of *Poelzig and *Tessenow, his architecture was always firmly within *Rationalism. Before the 1939–45 war he worked on the exhibition and propaganda film *Gebt mir vier Jahre Zeit* (Give me Four Years—1936–7), and built many administrative and industrial buildings, notably for Dega AG, Berlin (1937–9). After the war he designed several major buildings, including the handkerchief-factory at Blumberg (1949–51), the Burda-Moden Buildings, Offenburg (1953–5), and the Neckermann KG Mail Order Building, Frankfurt (1958–61), all in collaboration with Robert Hilgers. His best-known buildings were the German Pavilion at the Brussels World's Fair (1958, with Sep Ruf), the German Embassy in Washington, DC (1958–64), and the *Kaiser Wilhelm Gedächtniskirche* (Emperor William Memorial Church), Berlin (1957–63), a polygonal structure, named the 'egg-crate' by Berliners, that stands next to the ruins of the Neo-Romanesque church by *Schwechten. His administrative-building for Olivetti in Frankfurt (1968–72) was more elegantly modelled.

Lampugnani (1988); Placzek (1982); Schirmer (1984); van Vynckt (1993)

Eiffel, Gustave (1832–1923). French engineer, he is best known for the iron tower bearing his name erected for the Paris Exhibition of 1889. While the Eiffel Tower was an important step in the use of exposed metal for architectural purposes, Eiffel made other significant contributions, notably in bridge-building throughout Europe, South America, and Indo-China. His railway-bridge over the Truyère at Garabit, France (1880–4), was an example of his technical mastery. He was consultant for the Paris Exhibitions of 1867 and 1878, and devised a theory of how wrought-iron construction performed that enabled precision of design to be achieved. He worked with *Boileau on the Bon Marché Department Store, Paris (1876), and designed the internal structural framework for the Statue of Liberty, New York (1885).

Besset (1957); Harriss (1989); Lemoine (1984, 1986); Poncetton (1939); Prevost (1929)

Eigtved, Nils, Niels, *or* **Nicolai** (1701–54). Danish architect. He trained under Carl Friedrich Pöppelmann (d. 1750) in Dresden and Warsaw before returning to Copenhagen, where he became Court Architect and was largely responsible for laying out the Frederiksstaden Quarter, with its octagonal Amalienborg Square (1750–5), the finest and most noble composition of its time in Denmark, influenced by the work of *Juvarra and by Parisian *hôtels. He also designed the Royal Theatre (1750), Frederik Hospital (1752), and several *Rococo interiors and other works at Christiansborg Palace (1755–6—destroyed by fire in 1794, apart from the charming entrance-pavilions and bridge). His work was exquisitely refined and delicate.

Norberg-Schulz (1986*a*); Voss (1971)

Einhart (*fl.* early C9). German architect. He appears to have worked in some kind of overseeing capacity on the *Carolingian palace and chapel at Aachen, in which case he was of considerable importance as an influential designer.

Sturgis *et al.* (1901–2)

Eisenman, Peter D. (1932–). American architect. He founded the Institute of Architecture and Urban Studies, New York (1967), co-edited the architectural journal *Oppositions* (1973–82), and was associated with the *New York Five from 1972. His work derived partially from the *Rationalism of *Terragni and others, while some of his earlier designs for family houses (Barenholtz House, Princeton, NJ (1967–8), and Falk House, Hardwick, Vt. (1969–70)) perhaps had aspirations towards *cardboard architecture. With his Miller House, Lekeville, Conn. (1969–70), he created a plan grid with walls placed at an angle to it, thus creating tensions in the geometries, and his superimposition or layering theme was developed further in his designs for the Biocentrum, J. W. Goethe University, Frankfurt, Germany (1987–8). Eisenman demonstrated his contempt for function in the Frank House, Cornwall, Conn. (1972), with its stair too low to descend without stooping, extremely narrow door, and column to the side of the dining-room table, and his name has been closely associated with *Deconstructivism. His flexible, sculptural approach created a dramatic castle-like composition at the Wexner Center for the Visual Arts, Ohio State University, Columbus, Ohio (1989). Other works include Kolzumi Sangyo Corporation Headquarters, Tokyo, Japan (1990), the Aronoff Center for Design and Art, Cincinnati, Ohio (1988–96), a hotel and office-development, Madrid, Spain (1990), and the Arts Center, Emory University, Atlanta (1990). He published *House of Cards* (1978).

Frampton *et al.* (1975); Jencks (1988); Johnson and Wigley (1988); Klotz (1988)

Eisenmann, John (1851–1924). American architect, best known for the Cleveland Arcade, Ohio (1882–90), with its two nine-storey round-arched blocks flanking a galleried iron-and-glass arcade.

Journal of the Society of Architectural Historians, 25 (1966), 281–91

Ekistics. The science and study of human settlements, invented by *Doxiadis.

Doxiadis (1963, 1966)

elbow. *See* crossette.

electrographic architecture. Term coined by the American Tom Wolfe in *c.* 1969 to describe structures supporting electric advertising signs or *sky-signs.

Architectural Design, 39/7 (1969), 379–82; Proulx (1977)

elevation. 1. Accurate geometrical projection, drawn to scale, of a building's façade or any other visible external or internal part on a plane vertical (at a right angle) to the horizon. **2.** Any external *façade.

Fraser Reekie (1946)

Elias of Dereham *or* **Durham** (d. 1245). *See* Dereham.

elision. Omission of part of an architectural element. If a *frieze is *elided* from an *entablature, an *architrave-cornice* is created.

Elizabethan architecture. Architecture of the reign of Queen Elizabeth I of England (1558–1603), regarded as within the last phase of the *Tudor period, but showing the influence of European *Renaissance styles, though often somewhat provincial in treatment. Elizabethan England was relatively isolated from mainstream developments on the Continent, partly because of religious schism, but essentially because the Queen's legitimacy and rights to the Throne were not accepted by the major European Roman Catholic powers. Architectural trends were therefore slow in arriving, and were mostly disseminated through publications. Initially,

Renaissance motifs were largely treated as surface decoration. The first major building to incorporate reasonably accurate French Renaissance elements, old Somerset House, London, was not built until 1547–52, and was derived from work by Philibert de l'*Orme and Jean *Bullant. In 1550 John *Shute was sent to Italy to study *Antique and modern architecture, after which he published *The First and Chief Groundes of Architecture* (1563), derived from *Serlio and *Vignola, and the first book on the Classical *Orders in English. Thereafter, several great *prodigy-houses were built, including Burghley House, Northamptonshire (1550s–1580s), Longleat, Wiltshire (1572–80), and Hardwick Hall, Derbyshire (1590–6). Late-*Gothic features, such as large *mullioned and *transomed windows, the *E-shaped late-Tudor plan, elaborate upperworks such as arrays of tall chimneys, *turrets, etc., and even the occasional *spire, were mixed promiscuously with the *Orders (often used as an *assemblage or even as chimneys), much *strapwork, *grotesque ornament, and *obelisks (upright and inverted, often with *herms). Sources were often French, especially the school of *Fontainebleau's *Mannerism which had such a profound influence on North-European Renaissance and Mannerist designs, notably those of *Dietterlin and de *Vries: indeed, the so-called *ditterling ornament was often strongly represented. The Gate of Honour, Gonville and *Caius College, Cambridge (1572–3), has an arch derived in form from late-Tudor examples, but set within a Classical ensemble of Roman *Doric over which is an *engaged *temple-front flanked by obelisks, the whole crowned by a hexagonal superstructure with a domical vaulted top. It is clearly derived from Serlio, and from Flemish Renaissance designs: indeed its architect was Theodore de Have, or Haveus, a Fleming or German from Cleve (Cleves), who settled in England in 1562. However, van *Paesschen, who was involved in the design of Burghley House, Theobald's Palace (Hertfordshire), Bach-y-Graig (Flintshire), and the Royal Exchange (London) in the 1560s, has a claim to be regarded as the first architect to design buildings in England that were Italian rather than French in style.

Elizabethan architecture was often ebullient, notably in *chimney-pieces, *frontispieces, and funerary monuments (the last often with spectacular structural *polychromy, i.e. the colour provided by the materials used in the construction e.g. Kelway monument (1580s), Church of Sts Peter and Paul, Exton, Rutland, and the Cecil tomb (late C16), perhaps by Cornelius Cure, in the Church of St Martin, Stamford, Lincolnshire). The essence of the Elizabethan style continued into *Jacobean architecture, and there was a C19 revival.

Cruickshank (1996); Girouard (1966, 1983); Pevsner, *Buildings of England* (1951–); Summerson (1993); Watkin (1986)

Elizabethan Revival. During the 1830s *Elizabethan architecture provided attractive precedents for those in search of a national style: it was associated with a period of great creativity, wealth, and naval and military power, and, unlike *Gothic, had no connections with pre-Reformation religion. In 1835 the recommendations for the rebuilding of the Palace of Westminster stipulated that the designs should be either Elizabethan or Gothic, and the accession of Queen Victoria in 1837 prompted hopes of a new 'Elizabethan' age. The revival of the style therefore dates from these times: Harlaxton Manor, Lincolnshire (1831–7), Highclere Castle, Hampshire (1842–9), and Mentmore Towers, Buckinghamshire (1851–4), are good examples of the Revival, which also had occasional manifestations in the USA. A second revival occurred in the 1920s and 1930s, although it drew more on *timber-framed and *vernacular exemplars for domestic architecture and public-houses.

Curl (1990); Dixon and Muthesius (1985); Girouard (1979); Hitchcock (1954)

ell. 1. Measure of length, in England once 45 inches. **2.** Extension or wing added at right angles to the principal direction of the original building.

Ellerton, Henry de (*fl.* 1304–22). English mason, he became Master of the Works at Caernarfon Castle, Wales, in 1309, and in 1318 Master and Surveyor of the King's Works in the castles of North Wales. He designed the King's Gate at Caernarfon as well as the northern walls.

Harvey (1987)

Elliot, Archibald (1760–1823). Scots architect. With his brother, **James** (1770–1810), he formed one of the leading Edinburgh practices of the early C19. He designed the Regent Bridge (1815–19) in the *Greek Revival style, but his country-houses were usually *castellated with *Gothic detail (e.g. Taymouth Castle, Perthshire (1806–10)). His Grecian Forbes *mausoleum, Callendar House, Stirlingshire (1816), is a distinguished variation on the circular temple theme, while Waterloo Place, Edinburgh (1815–19), demonstrates his expertise in civic design. The practice continued under his son, **Archibald Junior** (d. 1843), architect of the handsome Greek Revival Royal Bank of Scotland, Glasgow (1827).

Colvin (1995); Gifford, McWilliam, and Walker (1984); Gomme and Walker (1987); Williamson, Riches, and Higgs (1990)

Elliot, James (1770–1810). *See* Elliot, Archibald.

ellipse. Figure formed by *section made by a plane passing obliquely through the axis of a regular cone. Unlike an oval, it is identical at each end, i.e. on both sides of its dividing axes. *See* arch.

Ellis, Harvey (1852–1904). American architect. His *eclecticism was typical of the period, but his chief claim to importance lies in his drawings, especially perspectives published in *American Architect and Building News* and elsewhere: he produced illustrations for L. S. *Buffington that helped the latter's claims as a pioneer of the steel-framed *skyscraper. From 1902 until his death he was editor of *The Craftsman*.

Placzek (1982); Rochester (1972)

Ellis, Peter (1804–84). English architect, known for two office-buildings in Liverpool. Oriel Chambers, Water Street (1864), has a cast-iron frame supporting shallow brick-vaulted floors and stone-faced elevations with canted *oriel-windows of metal and glass. The office-building at 16 Cook Street (1866) has a rear elevation of iron and glass with a spiral staircase set within an iron-and-glass *curtain-wall that is remarkably advanced for its time.

Hitchcock (1977); Hughes (1964)

Ellwood, Craig (1922–92). American architect who made his name with the Courtyard Apartments, Hollywood, Calif. (1951–2), in which he demonstrated how standardization could be applied to house-designs. The Daphne House, Hillsborough, Calif. (1960), and the Rosen House, Brentwood, Los Angeles (1961), developed the *parti of *Mies van der Rohe into a new refinement and elegance. In his later buildings he exploited exposed trusses, notably at the Arts Center College of Design, Pasadena, Calif. (1970–5).

Emanuel (1994); McCoy (1968)

Elmes, Harvey Lonsdale (1814–47). English architect, son of James *Elmes. He won the competition to design St George's Hall, Liverpool (1839), extended the following year to include the Assize Courts. Arguably the finest Neoclassical building in England, it was completed (1847–54) by Robert *Rawlinson and C. R. *Cockerell. The design may have been influenced in part by published works of von *Klenze and *Schinkel, some of whose monumental buildings Elmes saw during a study-visit in 1842. Other works by him include the façades of houses in Ennismore Gardens and Prince's Gate, Kensington, London (*c.*1843–6), some houses in Wallasey, Cheshire (*c.*1845), and the Lancashire County Lunatic Asylum, Rainhill (1847–51).

Colvin (1995); Sheppard (1975); Watkin (1974)

Elmes, James (1782–1862). Father of H. L. *Elmes, he is known for his writings, especially as editor of T. H. Shepherd's *Metropolitan Improvements* (1827–9) and for *Memoirs of the Life and Works of Sir Chr. Wren* (1823). Other works included *Hints for the Improvement of Prisons* (1817) and *A Topographical Dictionary of London and its Environs* (1831). He also practised as an architect and surveyor: a list of his works is given by Colvin.

Colvin (1995)

Elmslie, George Grant (1871–1952). *See* Purcell & Elmslie.

Elsaesser, Martin (1884–1957). German architect. He studied under *Bonatz and Theodor *Fischer, from whom he gained his interest in historical styles. He was an important educator, and published *Einführung in das Entwerfen* (Introduction to Design—1950) and *Wohnung und Lebensgefühl* (Dwelling and Living Sense—1955). Many of his designs for houses, schools, churches, and hospitals were published in 1933: most have simple forms, pitched roofs, and agreeable proportions.

Placzek (1982)

Ely, Reginald *or* **Reynold of** (*fl.*1438–d. 1471). English master-mason. As one of the masons working at King's College Chapel, Cambridge, from its commencement, he is a likely candidate as its architect, and must be regarded as one of the greatest English architects of C15. His name is first associated with Peterhouse, Cambridge, in 1438, where he built the stair to the library at the west side of the medieval *court and may have worked on the kitchen-wing at the west end of the Hall. In 1444 he was commissioned to find craftsmen for the building of works at King's College, and in 1446 work began on the Chapel, King Henry VI (1422–71) laying the foundation-stone. Reginald Ely seems to have been the man on the spot, and was involved at the Chapel until work stopped in 1461. He was probably the designer of the *elevations, but it is doubtful if he was responsible for the *tracery patterns except for the east window of the easternmost chapel on the north side, unusual for its *Curvilinear design differing from the tracery of the rest of the chapels which is all firmly *Perpendicular. King's Chapel was designed to have a lierne rather than a fan-vaulted ceiling, as is clear from the design of the piers in the *choir. He may have designed Burwell Church, Cambridgeshire (1454–64), and Queen's College, Cambridge (from 1446).

Harvey (1987)

Elysium, Elyzium. **1.** Land of the dead in Classical Antiquity. **2.** Place where a state of ideal or perfect happiness may be achieved, so, by extension, a charming, exquisitely beautiful, tenderly elegiac landscaped garden, often embellished with monuments and even real tombs, as at C18 *Elysées* of Maupertuis and Ermenonville in France. **3.** Landscaped *Picturesque cemetery, such as Père-Lachaise, Paris (from 1804), and Mount Auburn, Cambridge, Mass. (1831).

Bazin (1990); Etlin (1984); Symes (1993)

embattled. *See* battlement.

Emberton, Joseph (1890–1956). English architect. He worked with *Burnet and *Tait from 1918 to 1922, when he established a practice with P. J. Westwood. The firm introduced a vaguely Islamic style to the various kiosks for the British Empire Exhibition, Wembley, Middlesex (1924–5—demolished). They also designed Summit House, Holborn (1925), for Austin Reed, which showed Burnet & Tait's influence. He refaced and extended the exhibition-halls at Olympia, Hammersmith Road, London, in a 'grim and sensational' *Modernistic style in 1929–30, as *Pevsner put it, which looks like *concrete, but is, in fact, of steel and rendered brick, the details 'borrowed from progressive Continental buildings such as the Einstein Tower' by *Mendelsohn in Potsdam. To the rear, the new entrance-hall towards Sinclair Road (1936) is 'quieter' and 'well-proportioned'. This tendency towards conventional *International *Modernism continued with the Royal Corinthian Yacht Club, Burnham-on-Crouch, Essex (1930–1), an early example of the style in England, and this was followed by Simpson's Department Store, Picadilly, London (1935–6), which Pevsner pronounced 'progressive', with the 'new idiom' handled 'with conviction': the building has a pioneering welded-steel frame. Clearly Mendelsohn was the main influence on Emberton, as can be seen from 363–7 Oxford Street, London (1938–9), and the Casino, South Shore, Blackpool, North Lancashire (1937–8).

Architectural Association Quarterly, 8/3 (1976), 51–9; *DNB* (1994); Ind (1983); Pevsner, *Buildings of England*, *London 1* (1973), *London 3* (1991)

emblem. **1.** Picture, sign, or device expressing a moral allegory. **2.** Picture of an object serving as a symbolic representation of an abstraction. **3.** Device used as a badge of a person, family, Saint, etc. Emblems were often connected with hidden meanings in C16 and C17, and books of emblematic designs were important sources of architectural decoration.

embrasure. **1.** Space between cops in a *battlement. **2.** Splayed enlargement of an aperture creating a larger opening on the inside of a wall than outside, thus affording an extended range of vision from within the wall while keeping the aperture smaller. This allowed more light in as well as improving the defensive aspect of a wall.

Emerson, Sir William (1843–1924). English architect. He designed (from 1909) the epitome of *Edwardian *Baroque magnificence (even grander than Brumwell *Thomas's Belfast City Hall), the Queen Victoria Memorial, Calcutta, India, opened in 1921. He was President of the RIBA (1899–1902), and prepared the master-plan for Waterloo Place, London (1910).

Gray (1985)

Emerson, William Ralph (1833–1917). American architect. His late-C19 domestic architecture, especially in the *Shingle and *Stick styles, was significant, although he produced elegant designs in versions of *Queen Anne and *Colonial Revival. The Forbes House, Milton, Mass. (1876), is reckoned to be his finest building in the Stick style, while his earliest building in the Shingle style was the C. J. Morrill House, Bar Harbor, Me. (1879). His Loring House, Pride's Crossing, Mass. (1881), was his most remarkable developed work in the Shingle style.

Scully (1971, 1974, 1989); Zaitzevsky (1969)

Emler, Lawrence (*fl.* 1492–1506). German carver and designer. He made the exquisite head of the funerary *effigy of Queen Elizabeth of York (1503) in Westminster Abbey, and may have designed the bronze *screen around the tomb of King Henry VII (1485–1509) and his Queen in the *Lady Chapel, one of the finest screens of its period.

Harvey (1987)

Empire. Neoclassical style of decoration and interior design that evolved in the Napoleonic period in France in the first fifteen years of C19, corresponding to British *Regency and American *Directory styles. It was largely the creation of *Percier and *Fontaine, and it drew on *Egyptian, *Etruscan, *Greek, *Pompeian, and *Roman motifs, treated with extraordinary verve, synthesized in a satisfactory whole. Motifs such as eagles, the letter N, wreaths, lotuses, winged discs, and other ornaments, gilded, were set against fine, rich woods. The style had a profound effect on taste in Britain, Prussia, Russia, and the USA, although in the last-named country Greek forms and Freemasonic symbols played more of a role.

Council of Europe (1972); Lewis and Darley (1986)

encarpus. Sculptured *festoons of fruit, flowers, leaves, and drapery in Classical architecture.

encaustic. 1. Fixed by heat, with reference to e.g. painting with wax colours and fixing them during firing so that the colours are burnt in. **2.** Type of tile decorated with patterns formed with different coloured clay inlaid in the tile made of another colour, then fired, and usually glazed. Encaustic tiles with yellowish patterns on a dark red ground were commonly used in medieval and *Gothic Revival churches.

enceinte. 1. Wall or rampart surrounding a fortified enclosure. **2.** Area bounded or defined by such a wall or rampart. **3.** Central, best-defended part of a fortification in the middle.

end. Term used to denote the distinctions between private and service rooms in a medieval *timber-framed house, with the *upper* or *high end* the private part of a hall and the *lower end* containing the *entry and near the services.

en délit. *Gothic detached stone shaft or *colonnette with its grain vertical.

Endell, Ernst Moritz August (1871–1925). German *Arts-and-Crafts architect and designer, connected with the Munich *Sezession. His first significant architectural work was the Elvira Photographic Studio, Munich (1896–7), the façade of which was decorated with swirling masses of marine-like forms of *stucco set beneath an *Egyptian *gorge-cornice: it was one of the most celebrated of *Jugendstil designs. He developed a successful Berlin practice from 1901, and argued for sensitivity to spiritual values in *Die Schönheit der grossen Stadt* (The Beauty of the Large City—1908). He was a supporter of van de *Velde's stance in favour of individualism in design against *Muthesius's arguments for standardization in the 1914 debate within the *Deutscher Werkbund. He moved to Breslau (now Wrocław) in 1918 to head the Academy of Art.

Benton *et al.* (1975); Endell (1896); Killy, Pfankuch, and Scheper (1965)

end lobby-entry. *See* entry.

Enfant, Pierre-Charles L' (1754–1825). A Frenchman, he served as a volunteer with the American forces during the War of Independence from 1777, and designed a large Neoclassical *pavilion in Philadelphia to commemorate the birth of the Dauphin (1782). He remodelled the City Hall in New York as the Congress or Federal Hall of the USA (1788–9—demolished 1812). From 1789 he was involved in the design of the new Federal Capital of Washington, DC, where the plan was on the grandest lines, owing something to *Baroque precedents, especially Versailles.

Caemmerer (1970); Kite (1929); Reiff (1977); Reps (1967); Whiffen and Koeper (1983)

enfilade. French *Baroque alignment of all the doorways in a series or suite of rooms so as to create a vista when the doors were open, as in a palace. Doorways were usually placed near the window-walls. The system avoided corridors, any privacy required being provided by e.g. the hangings around a bed.

engaged. Applied, attached, semi-engaged, *inserted, or seemingly partly buried in a wall or *pier, such as a column with half or more of its shaft visible, quite distinct from a *pilaster. A fluted engaged column with more or less than half its shaft exposed creates difficulties at the junction with the wall because of the *entasis unless the whole shaft is tilted back towards the wall, as *Burnet did with the *Ionic columns at the *Edwardian extension to the British Museum, London (1904–14).

Engel, Carl Ludvig (1778–1840). German architect. He trained under Friedrich *Gilly and further developed his *Neoclassicism in St Petersburg, Russia. He settled in Helsinki, Finland, in 1816, having been appointed architect for the new capital of the then Grand Duchy, and designed many important buildings there, including the Senate House (1818–22), Lutheran Cathedral (1830–40), the University Library (1836–45), and City Hall (1827–33). In 1824 he was appointed Controller of Public Works, leading to the dissemination of his Neoclassical language throughout Finland. His architectural output was prolific and usually distinguished.

Engel (1990); Lilius (1990); Middleton and Watkin (1987); Suolahti (1973); Wickberg (1962)

Engelberger, Burkhard (*fl.* 1469–d. 1512). German architect. He completed the *choir of the *Kilianskirche* (Church of St Kilian), Heilbronn, in 1480, and was consultant architect at Ulm *Minster in 1492–4, where he strengthened the tower. He seems to have carried out major works at the Church of Sts Ulrich and Afra, Augsburg, including *vaults and the tower (1475–1506). His gravestone records that he was the master who built the Great Church of St Ulrich, and he probably designed most of the main fabric.

Papworth (1852); Sturgis *et al.* (1901–2)

English altar. Type of late-medieval altar arrangement with *riddells, riddell-posts, and, sometimes, a *tester. *See* Comper.

English bond. *See* brick.

English cottage. *Picturesque rural cottage, also called *cottage orné.

English Extremists. Title of 1988 book dealing with the work of the British architects Nick Campbell, Roger Zogolovitch, Rex Wilkinson, and Piers Gough (CZWG), who formed a practice in 1977. Their 'extremism' derives from their extravagant *eclecticism and startling, jarring geometries. Their work includes 'Cascades', a tower-block in London's Docklands (1988).

Sudjic, Meade, and Cook (1988)

English garden. Informal, asymmetrical, 'natural' type of landscape evolved in C18, associated with L. *Brown, H. *Repton, and others, and widely copied in Europe, where it was called *jardin *anglo-chinois* because of its apparent haphazard design. It was associated with the *Picturesque and *Sharawadgi.

Coffin (1994)

Englishman, William the (*fl.* 1174–d. *c.*1214). English master-mason. He worked under William of *Sens on the rebuilding of Canterbury Cathedral, Kent, from 1174, and continued the works after 1177 (when Sens was injured) until 1184. He was responsible for innovations at Canterbury, as the Trinity Chapel and the Corona (circular chapel at the east) show. He may also have been involved at Chichester Cathedral (1187–99), and perhaps the Abbey of St Radigund, Dover, Kent.

Harvey (1987)

English style. Term coined in 1984 to describe a type of English and North-American late C20 interior design in which antique and modern, the odd and the familiar, the permanent and the ephemeral, and above all, fine quality, were synthesized.

Dickson (1989); Slesin and Cliff (1984)

Enlightenment. C18 French intellectual climate in which belief in reason as a means to ensure human progress was combined with a questioning of tradition and authority, the systematic collection and categorizing of facts, and the study of nature on a scientific basis. In German-speaking countries it was called the *Aufklärung*. Its architectural manifestations were a reaction to *Baroque and *Rococo, the adoption of *Rationalism and therefore a return to the principles of *Classicism. International *Neoclassicism began to be established in the French Academy in Rome, and led to a growing severity, prompted by writers such as *Laugier: it was also sustained by the growth of *archaeology, which gave a solid basis upon which it could develop. *Winckelmann and others drew attention to the art of Ancient Greece, while French scholars argued for even greater severity which led to the beginnings of Egyptology after 1798. In addition, C18 investigations and explorations encouraged sympathetic appropriations of other than European cultures, made manifest in a growing *eclecticism, often expressed in the design of *fabriques in landscaped gardens, one of the finest being Wörlitz in Sachsen-Anhalt (late C18), by *Erdmannsdorff, *Eyserbeck, and others. So the Enlightenment also influenced the design of *Picturesque gardens, and the jardin *anglo-chinois was more than fashion, for it suggested an admiration for English resistance to Absolutism, and the cultivation of a civilized, ironic detachment, leading to an attempt to give visual expression to a wide range of ideas and themes.

enneastyle. *Portico with nine columns in a line.

enrichment. Any ornamentation on mouldings, such as the *egg-and-dart on *ovolos.

Ensingen, Ulrich von (*c.*1350–1419). One of the greatest German medieval master-masons. He worked for many years at the *Minster, Ulm (from 1392), where he designed the beautiful *Sondergotik tower and west porch, though the upper stages were built by *Böblinger. He was also the architect of the elegant octagonal stage of the tower at Strasbourg Cathedral, France, with its cage of intricate *tracery (from 1399). He worked at the *Frauenkirche* (Church of Our Lady), Esslingen (from 1398), and the convent at Pforzheim (from 1409). He, or his son, also **Ulrich**, appears to have acted as a consultant at Milan Cathedral in 1394.

Frankl (1962); Mojon (1967); Recht (1989); Wortmann (1977)

Ensinger, Matthäus (*c.*1390–1463). Son of Ulrich von *Ensingen, he worked under his father at Strasbourg and Ulm before moving to Berne, Switzerland, where he designed the Cathedral (begun 1421). He also became master-mason for the *Frauenkirche* (Church of Our Lady), Esslingen (1429) and the *Minster, Ulm (from 1446). Like his father, he ranks high among German medieval master-masons.

Frankl (1962); Mojon (1967); Recht (1989); Wortmann (1977)

entablature. In Classical *Orders the entire horizontal mass of material carried on columns and *pilasters above the *abaci. Normally it consists of three main horizontal divisions, the *architrave (essentially the *lintel spanning between the columns), the *frieze (occasionally elided (omitted), as in certain examples of the *Ionic Order, especially *Hellenistic versions), and *cornice. An entablature on the top of an *astylar (without columns or pilasters) façade, as in a Florentine *Renaissance *palazzo, is called *cornicione. Entablatures are also found at the tops of Classical rooms, between ceiling and wall.

entasis. In Classical architecture shafts of columns have a greater diameter at the bottom than at the top: the *diminution does not result in slightly *battered straight inclining slides, but a subtly convex curved swelling called *entasis*. In the Greek *Doric Order from *Paestum the shafts are much smaller at the tops than the bases, and the entasis is very obvious. Entasis can also be found on walls, *spires, and towers. Entasis may have been noticed first by *Allason in *c.*1814, but it was subsequently confirmed by C. R. *Cockerell and *Haller von Hallerstein. Allason published a paper in the *Quarterly Journal of Science and Arts* (1821) on the subject (but was indebted to Cockerell for material), and F. C. *Penrose followed with detailed discussions in the 1850s.

entresol. *See* mezzanine.

entry. Term used to describe the position of the main entrance to a medieval *timber-framed house. Types of entry include:

baffle-entry: entry to a lobby in front of an axial chimney-stack, without doors;
cross-entry: entry to a hall through opposite doors, without any partition;
cross-passage: similar to a cross-entry, but with a partition forming a passage and screening the hall;
end lobby-entry: like a lobby-entry but at the end of a side-wall, with access to one room only;
gable-entry: situated in a gable-wall;
lobby-entry: with door leading to a lobby at the rear of which is the axial chimney-stack, with doors on either side.

Alcock, Barley, Dixon, and Meeson (1996)

envelope. 1. Outer part of a building enclosing the interior volumes. **2.** Light waterproof protective *cladding, e.g. glass and metal frames, protecting the structure, as in *curtain-walling. **3.** In geometry, the covering of a solid with a thin pliable substance.

Eosander, Johann Friedrich, Freiherr von Göthe (1670–1729). Scandinavian-born, he became Court Architect in Berlin, succeeding *Schlüter as architect to the Berlin *Schloss*: from 1707 to 1713 he worked there, adding the west side with the great *triumphal-arch portal and part of the frontage facing the *Lustgarten* (all destroyed). He designed part of the main wing, the *cupola with *drum, and the chapel at Charlottenburg Palace, Berlin, from 1702. He also designed the Royal *Schloss* at Schönhausen, near Berlin (from 1704), carried out works at the *Schloss*, Oranienburg, also near Berlin (1706–9), and designed the central block of the Garden Palace Monbijou, Berlin (from 1708). He built a mansion at Altlandsberg, near Frankfurt-on-the-Oder (1709—destroyed), and the *Schloss* at Übigau, near Dresden (1724–6).

Biederstedt (1961); Hempel (1965)

épi. *Spire-shaped termination, as on a hipped roof.

epinaos. In a Greek temple, the rear open vestibule to the *naos.

Epistle side. South side of a church or altar.

E-plan. English country-house plan shaped like an E, formed of a principal range attached to two parallel wings extending at right angles to it, and with a central projecting porch. Barrington Court, Somerset (from 1514), is a good example.

equilateral. 1. *See* arch. **2.** An *equilateral roof* has 60° pitches, and thus in *section the timbers form an equilateral triangle.

Erdmannsdorff, Friedrich Wilhelm, Freiherr von (1736–1800). German Neoclassical architect. He travelled with his friend and patron, Prince Leopold Friedrich Franz of Anhalt-Dessau (1740–1817), in the British Isles (1763–4—where he imbibed *Palladianism and aspects of the *Picturesque (especially from English landscaped gardens)), and Italy (1761–3, 1765–6, and 1770–1—where he absorbed *Neoclassicism (notably from *Winckelmann and *Clérisseau)). His English experiences stood him in good stead when designing the Neo-Palladian *Schloss* at Wörlitz, near Dessau (1769–73—which resembles Claremont in Surrey (1771–4) by Capability *Brown and *Holland), and some of the *fabriques in the park there. The interiors of the *Schloss* include some Pompeian elements, while the park itself (laid out by J. F. *Eyserbeck, Ludwig Schoch (1728–93), and Johann Georg Schoch (1758–1826)) has many allusions to England (e.g. the Iron Bridge (a quarter-scale version of *Pritchard's original of 1775–9 at Coalbrookdale, Shropshire), the Gothic House (an allusion to *Walpole's Strawberry Hill, Twickenham, Middlesex, of 1750–76), the Temple of Flora (derived from *Chambers's Casino at Wilton, Wiltshire (*c.*1759), and much else). In fact, the park incorporates many influences from Kew, near Richmond, Rousham (Oxfordshire), Stourhead (Wiltshire), and Stowe (Buckinghamshire), and was an attempt to create England-by-the-Elbe, not just out of caprice, but as an exemplary and educational programme to raise the tone of the Principality to one of *Enlightenment and Progress. Erdmannsdorff also designed Schloss Luisium, near Dessau (1775–80), the Court Theatre, Dessau (1777), and many other buildings in the *Gartenreich* (Garden Kingdom) created by the Prince. In 1786 he was called to Berlin to contribute to the new Royal Academy there, and designed Neoclassical interiors at Sanssouci, Potsdam, and the *Schloss*, Berlin. In 1787 he designed the new cemetery and portal in Dessau, and between 1791 and his death contributed further to the fabric of Dessau, Magdeburg, and Wörlitz.

Alex (1986, 1988); Harksen (1973); Hempel (1987); Kadatz (1986)

ergonomics. Study of the relationships between working humans and e.g. tools, machinery, and instrument panels to ensure the efficiency and usability of designs.

Murrell (1965)

Erickson, Arthur Charles (1924–). Canadian architect. He gained international recognition with his plan and central covered mall for the Simon Fraser University, Burnaby, Vancouver (1963–5), designed with Geoffrey Massey (1924–), and influenced by the work of Le *Corbusier, *Kahn, and *Rudolph. Erickson's expression of *columnar and trabeated architecture is best seen at the Smith House, West Vancouver (1965), and the Museum of Anthropology, University of British Columbia (1973–6). His Provincial Government Offices and Court House complex, Robson Square, Vancouver (1973–9), is a formal essay in urban design, imaginatively landscaped with trees and water.

The Canadian Chancery, Washington, DC (1983–9), demonstrates a response to aspects of Washington's *Classicism, with its huge courtyard and *rotunda.

Erickson (1988); Iglauer (1981); Kalman (1994)

Erith, Raymond Charles (1904–73). English traditionalist and Classical architect. In partnership (1929–39) with Bertram Stewart Hume (1901–77), he designed a house at Dedham, Essex, in the idiom of *c.*1800, followed by lodges at the approach to Royal Lodge, Windsor, Berkshire (1939), in the same style. He started his own practice in 1946 and designed the Classical Provost's Lodging, The Queen's College, Oxford (1955), followed by the new library and residential block at Lady Margaret Hall, Oxford (1960–6). He reconstructed 10 and 11 and rebuilt 12 Downing Street, London (1958–63). His *Gothick Jack Straw's Castle, Hampstead (a large public-house of 1963–4), the common-room building at Gray's Inn (1971–2), and various residential buildings (e.g. the Palladian *villa at Wivenhoe New Park, Essex, of 1962–4) demonstrate his mastery of English historical styles. He took Quinlan *Terry into partnership in 1962.

DNB (1986)

Erlach, Johann Bernhard Fischer von (1656–1723). *See* Fischer.

Ersatz architecture. Indiscriminately eclectic architecture with motifs taken from many sources (not copied with exactitude, understanding, or scholarship), and verging on *Kitsch, as in many examples of *Post-Modernism. The term seems to be one of many inventions of Charles *Jencks (*c.*1973).

Architectural Design, 43/9 (1973), 596–601

Erskine, Ralph (1914–). British architect. He emigrated to Sweden in 1939, where he began to specialize in the design of low-cost housing, notably at Gyttorp (1945–55), Fors in Dalecarlia (1950–3—with cardboard-factory of modelled brickwork), and Tibro (1959–64). His housing-scheme at Byker, Newcastle upon Tyne (1969–82), is arranged behind a huge eight-storey wall a kilometre long, and was designed with the participation of the residents. He also designed the Postgraduate College, Clare Hall, Cambridge (1867–9), a housing-estate at Killingworth, near Newcastle upon Tyne (1969–72), and the Eaglestone Estate, Milton Keynes, Buckinghamshire (1973–7). The Larson Office Building (called 'The Ark'), Hammersmith, London (1988–91—with Vernon Gracie) is a major development near the Hammersmith flyover. He was a member of *Team X from 1959.

Collymore (1982); Egelius (1988); Emanuel (1994); Lasdun (1984); Ray (1978)

Ervi, Aarne Adrian (1910–77). Finnish architect. He worked for *Aalto before setting up his own practice in 1938, designing a large number of works, including power-stations, industrial, and university buildings. Ervi won the competition to design Tapiola *Garden City, Espoo, and from 1954–64 realized his projects for the town centre, houses, and apartments there, making use of the natural features of the site.

Richards (1978); Salokorpi (1970); Tempel (1968); van Vynckt (1993); Wickberg (1962)

Erwin von Steinbach (d. 1318). *See* Steinbach.

escape. *Apophyge.

escarp, escarpment. 1. In fortification, a steep bank or wall immediately in front of and below the *rampart. **2.** Ground formed like an escarp as a feature in a garden.

escoinson. 1. Corner of a *jamb, essentially to accommodate something, especially in medieval work, sometimes enriched with a shaft or *colonnette. **2.** *Squinch. **3.** Arch over a window-opening with splayed reveals. **4.** Part of the reveal of an aperture where a window is set.

Eseler, *or* **Essler, Nikolaus** (*c.*1400–92). German architect, involved in the building of the fine *Gothic *hall-churches (*Hallenkirchen*) at Nördlingen (from 1427) and Dinkelsbühl (from 1448). He and his son (also **Nikolaus**) contributed to other works in churches at Rothenburg-ob-der-Tauber and Augsburg.

Papworth (1852)

esonarthex. *Narthex within a church, separated from *nave and *aisles by columns or some other means.

espagnolette. *See* cremone.

espalier. 1. Lattice-work trellis upon which tree-branches are trained in horizontal directions. **2.** Row of trees so trained, without the trellis.

esquillage. *See* shell.

Essenwein, August Ottmar (1831–92). German architect and historian. He enlarged the *Germanisches Nationalmuseum* (German National Museum), Nuremberg (1860s), and restored churches in Nuremberg, Cologne, Bonn, and elsewhere. He acquired a reputation as an expert on *Romanesque architecture, and published extensively. Among his works were *Die mittelalterlichen Kunstdenkmäler der Stadt Krakau* (Medieval Historic Buildings in Kraków—1869) and *Nord-Deutschlands Backsteinbau im Mittelalter* (North-German Brick Architecture of the Middle Ages—1877).

Sturgis *et al.* (1901–2)

Essex, James (1722–84). English architect, one of the best of the early *Gothic Revivalists. He designed many works in a Classical style in Cambridge, but is important as among the very first to understand the structural properties of *Gothic buildings, publishing several pioneering papers on medieval architecture in the *Journal* of the Society of Antiquaries of London, and writing an (unpublished) history of Gothic architecture in England. He designed the Beauclerk Tower and Gothic Gate at Strawberry Hill, Twickenham, Middlesex (1776), for Horace *Walpole, and carried out restorations at Lincoln (1762–5) and Ely (1757–62) Cathedrals that were far more scholarly than anything attempted by his contemporaries (or some of his successors).

Colvin (1995); *DNB* (1917); Mowl (1996)

Estilo Modernista. Spanish *Art Nouveau.

estípite. *Pilaster or square column, often tapered so that it is smaller at the bottom than the top, lavishly enriched with geometrical patterns, low reliefs, intermediate *capital-like mouldings, and *cartouches derived from pattern-books such as those of *Dietterlin and North-European Mannerists. It occurs in Spanish *Baroque and *Churrigueresque architecture.

Pla Dalmáu (1951)

estrade. Low raised platform or daïs in a room, usually with a *balustrade.

Etchells, Frederick (1886–1973). English architect and painter. He was a pioneer of *International *Modernism, as is evident from his Crawford's Advertising Building, 223 High Holborn, London (1929–30). With chamfered corners, long uninterrupted bands of windows subdivided by steel *mullions, and white cement-rendered walls, it was one of the earliest paradigms of the style to be built in England. Etchells also designed 38 Chapel Street, Westminster (1934), and several buildings on the Grosvenor Estate, Westminster. He is best remembered for translating Le *Corbusier's *Vers une architecture* into English as *Towards a New Architecture* (1927) and *Urbanisme* as *The City of Tomorrow and Its Planning* (1929): the changes of titles enhanced the messianic and polemical nature of the texts. With the Dean of Chester, G. W. O. Addleshaw, he wrote *The Architectural Setting of Anglican Worship* (1948), a thoughtful book that became a classic. He was also a publisher and typographer (Etchells & Macdonald, Haslewood Books).

Etchells (1947, 1989); Etchells and Addleshaw (1948)

Etruscan. The surviving buildings of Etruria (now approximating to Tuscany and part of central Italy) are not numerous, but Etruscan design is important for the part it played in the evolution of *Roman architecture. Buildings were mostly of wood, clay, *rubble, and *terracotta, stone being reserved for temple-bases, fortifications, and tombs. The finest surviving Etruscan architecture consists of city walls and *rock-cut tombs (of which the best examples are at Cervéteri, Chiusi, Corneto Tarquinia, and Perugia) dating from C6 to C4 BC. A few arched town-gateways still stand, e.g. Falerium Novum (Fáleri—*c.*250 BC) and Perugia (*c.*300 BC). From C5 BC a temple type evolved consisting of a central *cella flanked by two *alae and a very deep *portico, often tetrastyle, and with widely spaced timber columns (normally short and without *flutes) carrying a low-pitched wooden roof structure. These columns were the prototypes of the Roman *Tuscan *Order, and the very wide *intercolumniation made possible by the timber construction clearly influenced Roman column-spacing. The timber superstructure was often enriched with terracotta *claddings. Tombs were richly decorated and coloured, and constitute the most substantial Etruscan architectural legacy.

Boëthius and Ward-Perkins (1970); Robertson (1945); Toynbee (1971)

Etruscan style. In C18, widespread archaeological activity associated with *Neoclassicism (e.g. at Herculaneum and *Pompeii) led to many collections being made of black and red vases then thought to be *Etruscan (but actually Greek), and greatly admired for their elegance, shape, decorations, and, not least, for the priapic and ithyphallic aspects of many of the figures. The vases were widely illustrated, notably by Francesco Bartoli (*fl.* 1706–30), the Comte de Caylus (1692–1765), and Bernard de Montfaucon (1655–1741). In particular de Caylus's *Recueil d'antiquités égyptiennes, étrusques, grecques, romaines et gauloises* (Collection of Egyptian, Etruscan, Greek, Roman, and Gaulish Antiquities—1752–67) had an enormous influence on the development of Neoclassicism and on the evolution of the *Egyptian and *Greek Revivals as well as the creation of the Etruscan style of interior decoration, involving the use of much red, black, and white, with griffins, harpies, lions, *sphinxes, medallions, *festoons, *bell-flowers, tripods, urns, chimeras, and very light, delicate details derived from *Antique sources. The C18 Etruscan style first emerged in France in the reign of *Louis Seize, and was used by Robert *Adam for the Etruscan Room, Osterley House, Middlesex (1775). By then, what was known as the *style étrusque* owed much to Pompeii and Herculaneum, with some Greek influences: the actual Etruscan influence was tenuous.

Chilvers, Osborne, and Farr (1988); Lewis and Darley (1986); Osborne (1970)

eucharistic window. *Hagioscope or *lychnoscope.

Papworth (1852); Sturgis *et al.* (1901–2)

Eulalius (*fl.* C6). Possible inventor of the *Byzantine cross-plan or *quincunx with five domes, at the Church of the Holy Apostles, Constantinople (536–45—destroyed), the prototype of San Marco, Venice (begun *c.*1063).

Drachmann (1963); Mango (1986)

Eupolemos of Argos (*fl.* 430–410 BC). Architect of the *Doric Heraion, Argos, Greece (*c.*416 BC), of which only the foundations survive.

Dinsmoor (1950)

Euripus. 1. Formal stretch of water in a Roman garden, often flanked by architectural constructions, statuary, etc., as at the *Canopus of the *Villa Adriana*, Tivoli (134–8). **2.** Ditch or *canal around an arena in a Roman *amphitheatre to deter the escape of wild animals and to separate spectacle from spectators.

Curl (1994); Roullet (1972)

eustyle. *See* intercolumniation.

Everard, Robert (*fl.* 1440–85). English master-mason. He seems to have succeeded James *Woderofe at Norwich Cathedral *c.*1453, where he designed the stone *spire and the *nave *vault (*c.*1463–72). His *Perpendicular lierne vaults are widely regarded as among the finest of their type.

Harvey (1987)

excubitorium. 1. Roman dormitory for *vigiles* or night-watchmen. **2.** As *watching-loft.

exedra, exhedra. 1. Passage, *colonnade, *portico, or other outdoor element, often fitted with seats, or where debate and conversation could occur. **2.** Large semicircular *niche-like building with stone seats ranged around the walls, sometimes with a hemidome over, resembling a large *apse, often arranged on an axis related to a larger space. **3.** Semicircular low wall with seats on the concave side so that the wall acts as the seat-backs. **4.** Place in a garden partially enclosed by a semicircular hedge, walls, etc.

exonarthex. *Narthex outside the main façade of a church, usually part of a colonnaded or arcaded *atrium or *quadriporticus*.

Experimental architecture. Architecture that questions concepts and limitations and is committed to experimentation with form, materials, technology, constructional methodology, and even social structure. It was the title of a book by Peter *Cook (1971), who identified certain architects, including *Friedman, *Goff, *Otto, *Price, the *Smithsons, *Soleri, and *Tange, and groups, such as *Archigram, *Haus-Rucker Co., and the *Metabolists, as involved in Experimental architecture.

Cook (1971)

Expressionism. Artistic movement in Northern Europe, especially in Germany and The Netherlands, from *c.*1905 to *c.*1930, it was concerned in architecture not to emphasize function, but to create free and powerful sculptural forms, often crystalline, sometimes sharply angular, and occasionally stalactitic. In The Netherlands the most important protagonists were members of the *Amsterdam School, and the characteristic works housing by Michel de *Klerk and the *Scheepvaarthuis* (Navigation House—1913–17) in Amsterdam. In Denmark the greatest work of Expressionism (with a pronounced *Gothic flavour) was the Grundtvig Church,

Copenhagen (1913–26), by *Jensen-Klint. In Germany, however, there were several outstanding examples: the water-tower and exhibition-hall at Posen (now Poznań) of 1911, with a polygonal steel structure resembling crystalline hexagonal forms, by *Poelzig; the glass pavilion, Werkbund Exhibition, Cologne (1914), by Bruno *Taut; the *Grosses Schauspielhaus* (Great Playhouse), Berlin (1918–19), with its interior resembling a cave of stalactites, by Poelzig; the Einstein Tower, Potsdam (1919–21), by *Mendelsohn; the Chile-Haus, Hamburg (1922–3), by Fritz *Höger; the administrative-building of the Hoechst Dyeworks (1920–5), by *Behrens; the Liebknecht-Luxemburg Monument, Berlin (1926—destroyed), by *Mies van der Rohe; the churches of *Bartning; some churches by Dominikus *Böhm; and the farm buildings, Gut Garkau, by *Häring. The Goetheanum, Dornach, Switzerland (1924–8), by Rudolf *Steiner, was one of the greatest works of the movement. Some of Gottfried *Böhm's architectural language derived from Expressionism.

Chilvers, Osborne, and Farr (1988); Lampugnani (1988); Pehnt (1973); Sharp (1967)

external angle. When two lines meet at an angle an *internal (*re-entrant) angle and an *external* angle (*salient) are formed.

extrados. *See* arch.

extruded corner. Projection from the inner corner of a *court or at the junction of a main block and a projecting wing, often containing a *stair, and carried above the roof-line. Also called an *angle-tower*, and common in C16 and C17 architecture.

Eyck, Aldo van (1918–99). Dutch architect. He worked in the Public Works Department, Amsterdam (1946–50), set up his own practice in 1952, and entered into partnership (1971–82) with Theo Bosch. In his work he insisted on structural and practical adaptability, and was a committed *Modernist (he was a member of *Team X). His Municipal Orphanage, Amsterdam (1957–60), embraced forms of various sizes flowing into each other within a quadrangular frame, creating a complex mnemonic of various urban spaces. Other works include the Arnhem Sculpture Pavilion, in which the circular plan was subdivided by straight and semicircular partitions (1966), the Pastoor van Arskerk, The Hague (1968–70), and a Conference Centre and Restaurant, Noordwijk (1984–9). His work has been classified within *Structuralism, and he published many articles and polemics.

Blijstra (1962); Curtis (1996); Jencks (1973*a*)

eye. 1. *Oculus, or any circular element placed in the centre of something, e.g. a bull's-eye circular window in the middle of the *tympanum of a *pediment. **2.** Circular or nearly circular central part of a *volute, as in an *Ionic *capital. **3.** Very small, more or less triangular, light in *Gothic *tracery. **4.** Circular base or rim of a *cupola, i.e. the circle from which the domed part springs.

eyebrow. 1. *Fillet. **2.** Low *dormer with no cheeks or sides on a pitched roof, the roof-covering rising in a concave curve, then convex over its top, then falling away in a concave curve on the other side, like an eyebrow.

eyebrow window. 1. Window in an *eyebrow dormer. **2.** Window-light hinged at the bottom in a semicircular-topped opening.

eye-catcher. *Folly, ruin, temple, or other structure in a landscape, such as a *gloriette*, drawing the eye to a desired point.

eye-form. **Vesica piscis* or fish-bladder form serving as small *lights in *Gothic *tracery of the *Second Pointed *Curvilinear and *Flamboyant styles.

eyelet. Small aperture in a wall, such as a miniature *loop-hole.

Eynsham, Henry de (*fl.* 1301–45). English mason. He worked at Caernarfon Castle, Wales, in the first years of C14, and was in charge of important repairs at Clarendon Palace (1316–17) before building a great tower at Pontefract Castle, Yorkshire (1323–6). He was engaged in building at Spalding Priory, Lincolnshire, from *c.*1328, and seems to have remained there for the rest of his life. He was versatile, being engaged in architectural work for military, civil, and ecclesiastical buildings. He probably began his career carrying out construction at the Benedictine Abbey of Eynsham, Oxfordshire, in the early 1290s, hence his surname.

Harvey (1987)

Eyserbeck, Johann Friedrich (1734–1818). German landscape-gardener. He is known primarily for his work at the Park of Schloss Wörlitz, near Dessau, one of the most important and beautiful gardens of allusion of the C18 *Enlightenment, designed for Prince Leopold Friedrich Franz of Anhalt-Dessau (1740–1817) in collaboration with *Erdmannsdorff, and the gardeners Ludwig Schoch (1728–93) and Johann Georg Schoch (1758–1826). The Park with its *fabriques was exemplary and mnemonic in intention, with its series of allusions, including an iron bridge based on the original by T. F. *Pritchard in Shropshire (1775–9), a *Rousseauinsel* (Rousseau-Island) based on the *Île des Peupliers* (Isle of Poplars) at Ermenonville, France, and a *Synagogue (to demonstrate freedom from bigotry).

Alex (1986, 1988); *Garden History*, 24/2 (1996), 221–36

Eyton, William de (*fl.* *c.*1310–36). English master-mason. He worked at Lichfield Cathedral, Staffordshire, at least from *c.*1310 when the *Lady Chapel was designed, with its *vault and the eastern *bays of the *chancel-*aisles.

Harvey (1987)

Fabiani, Max (1865–1962). Slovenian architect. A pupil of Otto *Wagner in Vienna, from 1899 he was a senior member of Wagner's office, and was mostly responsible for the Portois & Fix Department Store (1899) and the Artaria Apartment Block (1900), both in Vienna. As personal architectural adviser to the heir to the throne, the Archduke Franz Ferdinand (1863–1914), he had considerable influence. Most of his important buildings, however, were designed after the 1914–18 war in Ljubljana and Trieste, and he prepared master-plans for Ljubljana, Gorizia (near Trieste), and elsewhere.

Pozzetto (1966, 1979)

fabric. Structural parts of a building, as opposed to furniture or movable fittings.

fabrique. Building in a landscaped garden, such as an *eye-catcher, *folly, or temple.

façade. External *face or *elevation of a building, especially the principal front.

face. Dressed or finished external plane of a wall, piece of *masonry, brick, etc., intended to be seen.

face-work *or* **facing.** Better type of material and finish masking an inferior one. It is generally applied in a thin layer, such as *ashlar (known as *bastard ashlar*) fixed to brickwork, etc.

factable. Erroneous term for *fractable.

Fahrenkamp, Emil (1885–1966). German architect. He assisted and then succeeded Wilhelm *Kreis at the School of Applied Arts and the Academy of Arts, Düsseldorf. He designed the factories and administration buildings for the Rhine Steel Corporation in several cities (1920s), the I. G. Farben power-station, Frankfurt-am-Main (1945–56), and several churches, including those for the Lutherans at Düsseldorf (1926) and Essen (1927).

Hoff (1928); Rittich (1938)

faïence. Earthenware covered with an opaque coating called *enamel*, usually coloured, and glazed, used for *face-work. It is essentially a type of *terracotta, but coloured and glazed, and usually twice fired.

Falconetto, Giovanni Maria (1468–1535). Verona-born architect and painter. His work suggests the Roman *Classicism of *Bramante and *Raphael, and he was an important practitioner of the style in Northern Italy. His garden-houses, the *Loggia Cornaro and Odeon (1524), now part of the Palazzo Giustiniani, Padua, pre-date designs by *Palladio and *Sansovino, yet have architectural characteristics of the later masters' works. He may have been the first to design a formal country *villa, with his Villa dei Vescovi, Luvigliano, near Padua (*c*.1529–35), which has a sophisticated arched loggia of remarkable architectural quality. He designed the handsome town-gates (Porta di San Giovanni (1528) and Porta di Savonarola (1530)) and worked on the Cappella del Santo (from 1533) in the Church of Sant'Antonio, all in Padua.

Heydenreich and Lotz (1974); Murray (1986)

false. Anything that seems to be what it is not, such as a false or *pseudo-arch, false *Attic (wall concealing a roof, but not containing rooms), false door, or false front (*façade extending beyond the side walls and/or roof of the building to make a building seem grander than it is).

fan. *See* vault.

fane. 1. Pagan temple, therefore a *fabrique in a C18 garden. **2.** *Weather-cock or -vane.

fanlight. 1. Glazed *light over a door, often with a semicircular or other type of curved top, with radiating glazing-bars suggesting the shape of an open fan, also called *sunburst-light*, common in British C18 houses. From *c*.1800 *batswing and tear-drop designs were introduced. **2.** Any glazed light over a door, fan-shaped or not, or any upper part of a window hinged to open.

Sambrook (1989)

fanlight. (*top*) Typical fanlight. (*bottom left*) Tear-drop pattern. (*bottom right*) Bat's-wing pattern. All *c*.1820. (*JJS*)

Fantastic architecture. Eccentric, imaginative architecture, such as the later work of *Gaudí, Bruno *Taut, or Hans *Poelzig; futuristic high-technology megastructures (*see* High Tech); *follies of an outlandish sort; or irrational structures, defying logic or considerations of use.

Conrads and Sperlich (1960, 1962); Schuyt and Elffers (1980); Vostell and Higgins (1969)

fan tracery. *See* tracery.

fan-vaulting. *See* vault.

Fanzago, Cosimo (1591–1678). Born in Clusone, near Bergamo, he became the most important exponent of *Baroque architecture in Naples from 1612, especially in his designs for altars. He created a series of exuberant *façades for existing churches, notably the Certosa di San Martino (1623–56), with its *triumphal arch, Santa Maria della Sapienza (1638–53), with its triple-arched *loggia, and San Giuseppe degli Scalzi at Pontecorvo (1643–60). His huge unfinished but very original Palazzo Donn'Anna, Posilipo, near Naples (1642–4) is a gigantic *belvedere of three stories of *loggie*, and has bevelled corners. His elaborate Guglia di San Gennaro monument (1637–60) is typical of his confidently triumphalist style.

Blunt (1975); Fogaccia (1945); Winther (1973); Wittkower (1982)

Farleigh, Richard of (*fl.* 1332–65). English mason. He was in charge of work at the Abbeys of Reading, Berkshire, and Bath, Somerset, before 1334, when he was appointed Master-Mason of Salisbury Cathedral. He probably built the great tower and *spire at Salisbury, and it is likely he was also responsible for the tower of Pershore Abbey, Worcestershire. Farleigh may have designed St Anne's Gate and *Chapel at the Close, Salisbury (1350–4). For around a year (1352–3) he was Master of the Works at Exeter Cathedral, Devon.

Harvey (1987)

Farnham, Richard de (*fl.* 1242–7). Probably the master-mason of the Chapel of the Nine Altars, Durham Cathedral (begun 1242), the design of which is attributed to Elias de *Dereham. He is described as *architector nove fabrice Dunelm* (architect of the new fabric of Durham) in a contemporary document, which points to his considerable importance.

Harvey (1987)

Farrell, Terry (1938–). British architect. With *Grimshaw, he founded the Farrell/Grimshaw Partnership in 1965, but set up his own practice in 1980. Among his early works were designs for Clifton Nurseries in Bayswater (1979–80) and Covent Garden (1980–1), both in London, in which Classical references appeared. His large developments, e.g. Embankment Place, Charing Cross (1987–90), over the railway-tracks of the railway-terminus, and a similar bridged solution at Alban Gate, over London Wall, in the City (1987–92), make powerful contributions to the urban fabric of London. One of his most felicitous buildings is the headquarters of the Henley Royal Regatta, Henley-on-Thames, Oxfordshire (1983–5). Other works include the TV AM Television Studios, Camden Town, London (1981–2), Government Buildings, Vauxhall Cross, London (1988–93), and Kowloon Railway Station, China (completed 1998), the largest of its kind in the world.

Emanuel (1994); information provided by Terry Farrell and Partners

fasces. Bundle of straight rods bound together, often around an axe. A Roman emblem of legal power, it was frequently used in *Empire and *Neoclassical design, and was revived as an emblem of Fascism (which gets its name from fasces) in Italy in the 1920s.

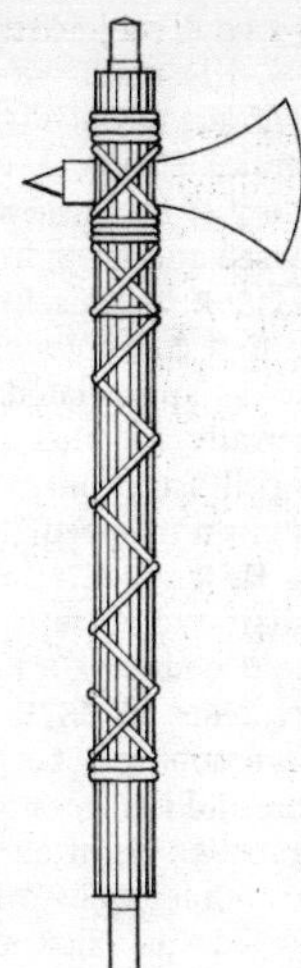

fasces

fascia (*pl.* **fasciae**). **1.** One of two or three *bands on a Classical *architrave, each projecting slightly beyond the one below, often separated by enriched mouldings. **2.** Any band or belt with a plain vertical *face, such as a fascia-board at *eaves-level. **3.** Deep board over a shop-front on which lettering is placed.

fastigium. **1.** Slope or fall of any surface or plane. **2.** *Gable or *pediment. **3.** Raking mouldings, especially the *cyma, of a pediment. **4.** *Canopy carried on four columns, especially with a pedimented top. **5.** *Ridge on a pitched roof. **6.** *Acroterion block.

Fathy, Hassan (1900–89). Egyptian architect. He used traditional materials, means of construction, and *vernacular styles in his search for an inexpensive architecture for the poor. At New Gourna, Luxor (from 1945), he created a model village made of sun-dried bricks, and exploited traditional methods to encourage the natural convection of cool air. He founded the International Institute for Appropriate Technology, Cairo (1977), intended to develop his ideas. His writings include *Architecture for the Poor* (1973) and *Natural Energy and Vernacular Architecture* (1986).

Richards, Serageldin, and Rastorfer (1985); Steele (1994*a*)

feather-edged. **1.** Horizontal timber board thicker at the bottom than at the top, i.e. tapered in *section, normally used for *clap-boarding. **2.** Type of *coping with one edge thicker than the other, so it drains in one direction.

feathering. Arrangement of small *foils separated by *cusps, usually on the inner mouldings of *Gothic arches.

Federal style. Style of architecture and decoration prevalent in the USA from the Declaration of Independence (1776) to *c.*1830. It drew on aspects of *Palladianism, *Georgian architecture, the work of Robert *Adam, Freemasonic symbolism, and French styles (especially the *Directoire and *Empire styles), and, promoted by *Jefferson, *Neo-classicism. *American Directoire* or *Directory* is a useful term to describe the styles from *c.*1805–30 that were influenced by French *Directoire* and *Empire* taste.

Craig (1978); Franco (1976); Lewis and Darley (1986)

Fehling, Hermann (1909–). German architect. He established a practice with Daniel Gogel (1927–) in 1953 in Berlin. Their Max Planck Institute for Educational Research, Berlin-Dahlem (1965–74), and European Southern Observatory, Garching, near Munich (1976–80), suggest aspects of *Expressionism and certain influences from *Scharoun, but the firm's work is stylistically varied and individual.

Emanuel (1994); Pehnt (1970)

Félibien des Avaux, André (1619–95). French architect and writer. His *Des Principes de l'architecture . . . avec un dictionnaire des termes propres . . .* (Principles of Architecture . . . with a Dictionary of Correct Terms—1676) was one of the most important reference works of its time. His son, **Jean-François Félibien des Avaux** (*c.*1656–1733), published a somewhat unreliable work on the lives and works of celebrated architects in 1687 which, nevertheless, contained a synoptic discussion of *Gothic architecture, one of the very first printed attempts to do so.

Félibien (1687, 1699); Hautecœur (1948)

Fellner, Ferdinand (1847–1916). Viennese architect and critic. Much influenced by *Semper, he specialized in theatre-design, using *Renaissance and *Baroque languages, and, later, *Jugendstil. He designed and built some fifty theatres and concert-halls, including the *Deutsches Volkstheater*, Vienna (1887–9), the *Stadttheater*, Graz (1898–9), the *Jubiläums-Stadttheater*, Baden-bei-Wien (1908–9), and the *Stadttheater*, Klagenfurt (1909–10), all in Austria, and all with Hermann Gottlieb Helmer (1849–1919).

Hoffmann (1966); Wurm-Arnkreuz (1919)

femerall, femerell, fomerell, fumerell. *Louvred *lantern or other device placed on a roof over a hall for ventilation or to permit the escape of smoke. It was a common arrangement for a medieval building before *chimneys became usual.

femme-fleur. The *dream-maiden* with long strands of hair resembling vegetation tendrils, often intertwined with marine-like plant-forms, found in *Art Nouveau designs.

Tschudi-Madsen (1967)

femur. Flat vertical *face of a *Doric *triglyph between pairs of channels (*glyphs).

fenestella. 1. Small opening (*cataracta* or *foramen*) in an altar or *shrine affording a view of the Relics within. **2.** *Niche in the south wall of a *chancel containing the *piscina and (sometimes) *credence-table. **3.** Opening for a bell in a *bell-cote over a *gable.

fenestration. Pattern formed by windows in a building *façade.

fereter. 1. Permanent *shrine in a church for Relics. **2.** Portable shrine containing Relics. **3.** Construction of a funerary type or association, such as a *catafalque or *tomb-chest.

feretory. Place in a church or chapel, usually defined in some way, e.g. with a *screen, containing a *fereter.

Fergusson, James (1808–86). Scots architectural writer. His first book was *Picturesque Illustrations of Ancient Architecture in Hindustan* (1847). A skilled draughtsman, he prepared his own illustrations and carried out the measured drawings of Indian buildings, many of which he published, establishing a name for himself as an authority on Indian architecture. In 1849 he published his *Historical Inquiry into the True Principles of Beauty in Art*, which he always held to be his best work, although it was not commercially successful. It included some of the earliest expositions of themes he was later to develop, such as the means by which Greek temples were illuminated. In the 1840s and 1850s he brought out various papers on fortifications as well as his views on the topography of Jerusalem which prompted various surveys of the city: later, in 1878, he was to publish a book on Jewish temples and other buildings. His major work, however, was *A History of Architecture in All Countries*. This began as *Illustrated Handbook of Architecture* (1855) and *History of the Modern Style* (1862), which were revised and brought out as the 3-volume *History* (1862–7). A useful text for students, and the first comprehensive study of the subject, it was appreciated for its accuracy, and especially for the quality of its many excellent illustrations, even though Fergusson was given to speculation and dogmatic opinions. He later (1876) added another volume on Indian and Eastern architecture. Awarded the Gold Medal of the Royal Institute of British Architects in 1871, by the end of his life Fergusson was being compared with *Vitruvius, and his work was respected in many countries. Heinrich Schliemann (1822–90), the archaeologist and discoverer of Troy, dedicated his book on Tiryns to Fergusson.

DNB (1917); Fergusson (1847, 1847*a*, 1849, 1851, 1855, 1862, 1862–7, 1874, 1876, 1878, 1883); MacLeod (1971)

ferme ornée. Farm designed for both utility and beauty, the buildings treated decoratively and contributing to the aesthetic effect within a *Picturesque landscape.

Ferrey, Benjamin (1810–80). English architect. He became a zealous pioneer of the *Gothic Revival, much influenced by A. W. N. *Pugin, having been articled to A. C. *Pugin in 1825. His Church of St Stephen, Westminster (1847–50), was one of the most significant ecclesiastical buildings of the early Revival, its hard interior a model for later work, and was justly appreciated by *The Ecclesiologist*. Soon he was recognized as one of the ablest pioneers of scholarly Gothic Revival. St Michael's, Chetwynd, Shropshire (1865–7), demonstrated his *archaeological approach, drawing on elements derived from several historic buildings. He wrote *Recollections of A. W. N. Pugin* (1861). His son, **Edmund Benjamin Ferrey** (*c*.1845–1900), worked in his office from 1862 to 1869 before joining Sir George Gilbert *Scott and then establishing his own practice.

Clarke (1969); Dixon and Muthesius (1985); Eastlake (1970); Felstead, Franklin, and Pinfield (1993)

Ferriss, Hugh (1889–1962). Distinguished American architectural draughtsman and visionary, his images of *skyscrapers in which ornament was suppressed were influential, and best seen in *The Metropolis of Tomorrow*

(1929). His *Power in Buildings: An Artist's View of Contemporary Architecture* (1953) was an important record of some of his later work. His impact on the development of architecture in the USA in the 1920s was considerable.

Ferriss (1929, 1953); Leich (1980)

ferro-concrete. *See* reinforced concrete.

Ferstel, Heinrich, Freiherr von (1828–83). Prolific Austrian architect. He designed the twin-towered *Gothic Revival *Votivkirche* (1856–82) and various other *Historicist buildings, including the vast Italian *Renaissance Revival University (1873–84) in Vienna. Much of his important work (where the influence of *Semper is often clear) was done for the area adjoining the *Ringstrasse*, but he also designed many buildings throughout the Austro-Hungarian Empire. An advocate of housing reform, he admired English low-density developments, which influenced the *Cottageverein* (Cottage Association), Vienna (1872–4), responsible for building small single-family houses. Ferstel also promoted the laying out of the *Türkenschanzpark*, a public park on English lines (from 1883). Among his publications, *Über Styl und Mode* (On Style and Fashion—1883) is revealing of his attitudes.

Eitelberger and Ferstel (1860); Wagner-Rieger (1970); Wibiral and Mikula (1974)

Festival of Britain. National celebratory event throughout the United Kingdom in 1951. Plans were laid by the then Labour Government, and (Sir) Gerald Reid Barry (1898–1968) was appointed Director-General. Partly inspired by the success of the Great Exhibition of 1851, the Festival was later said to be a 'manifestation of gaiety and ordered imagination in a world . . . short of both'. The centrepiece of the Festival was a major exhibition on the South Bank of the Thames in London housed in various purpose-built structures, the whole architectural development under the direction of Hugh *Casson. While the exhibition was intended to encourage national achievements, inventions, and so on, attracting custom from abroad, thereby improving morale and the economy after the economic doldrums following the 1939–45 war, it also offered a great opportunity to show off modern architecture, design, and planning principles. Of all the structures on the site, only the Royal Festival Hall (by Leslie *Martin, Robert *Matthew, and a large team) remains, although the river-front was later extended and altered. The main buildings were the Dome of Discovery (Ralph Tubbs (1912–96)), the administrative block (*Fry, *Drew, and Edward David Mills (1915–98)), the Skylon (*Powell & Moya with Felix Samuely (1905–59)), the Minerals and Land Pavilion (*Architects' Co-Partnership), the Natural Scene and the Country (Brian *O'Rourke and Frederick Henri Kay Henrion (1914–90)), the Power and Production Pavilion (George Grenfell Baines (1908–) and Heinz J. Reifenberg (1894–1968)), the Sea and Ships Pavilion (Basil *Spence), the Transport exhibit (Arcon), the Lion and Unicorn Pavilion (Robert Yorke Goodden (1909–) and R. D. Russell), and the Land of Britain (Henry Thomas Cadbury-Brown (1913–)).

The Festival brought *Modernism to the attention of the public, popularizing certain aspects and motifs that recurred in design over the following decade.

Banham and Hillier (1976)

festoon. Classical ornament representing drapes, flowers, fruit, and foliage, depicted as a *swag hanging in a natural *catenary curve from two points on the same horizontal plane, and tied at each end with ribbons. It is light and narrow at the points of suspension and thick and heavy in the middle of the swag. It was common in Antiquity, during the *Renaissance, and in *Neoclassicism.

Feszl, Frigyes (1821–84). Hungarian architect. A pupil of von *Klenze and *Gärtner (1839–41), he returned to Hungary where he built several houses in Budapest (e.g. Glosz House (1847)). He seems to have favoured an exotic version of the *Rundbogenstil he had absorbed when in Munich, mingling it with *Moorish and other elements, as in the Municipal Concert Hall, Budapest (1859–64).

Merényi (1970); Rados (1975)

Feuerstein, Bedřich (1892–1936). Czech architect. Educated in Prague, he designed several important buildings after the formation of Czechoslovakia, including the Military Geographic Institute, Prague-Bubenec (1921–2), a somewhat heavy version of vaguely stripped *Classicism. Feuerstein was associated with *Behne, *Chochol, and other members of the Prague avant-garde. His Nymburk Crematorium (1921–3) is regarded as one of his best buildings, reminiscent of the severe, stripped stereometrically pure forms advocated in the late C18. He later worked with

*Perret in Paris and *Raymond in Tokyo (where he designed the Soviet Embassy (1928) and St Lucas Hospital (1928–30)).

Leśnikowski (1996); Masaryková (1967)

Field, Horace (1861–1948). London-born English architect. His work was often in a refined *Wrenaissance manner, e.g. Lloyd's Bank, Rosslyn Hill, London (1891), and the offices for the North Eastern Railway Company, York (1904). With *Bunney, he compiled *English Domestic Architecture of the XVIIth and XVIIIth Centuries* (1905, 1928). With Charles Evelyn Simmons (1879–1952) he designed houses at Letchworth *Garden City and Hampstead *Garden Suburb, as well as churches at Eastriggs and Gretna in Scotland.

Gray (1985); Miller (1989); Miller and Gray (1992)

fielded. Flat central raised part of a *panel thicker than the edges or margin.

fieldstone. US term for *rubble.

Figini, Luigi (1903–84). Italian architect. He formed a partnership with Gino Pollini (1903–91) in 1929, and, with *Terragni and others, founded *Gruppo 7 in 1926. He was a leading figure in Italian *Rationalism. From 1934 to 1957 he and Pollini were involved in the design and extension of the Olivetti Factory, Ivrea, where *Modern Movement principles were applied. Their Church of the Madonna dei Poveri (1952–4), Milan, in which themes drawn from industrial and administrative architecture were adapted to a basilican arrangement, was influential.

Blasi (1963); Emanuel (1994); Savi (1980); Seta (1972)

Figueroa, Leonardo de (1650–1730). *Baroque architect. All his known buildings are in Seville, Spain, and feature yellow or white cut brickwork framed with red, glazed tiles. He favoured *Solomonic columns, *estípites, elaborately contorted *cornices, and much statuary and carved decoration, all mingled in unbridled freedom, with occasional touches of *mudéjar ornament. Examples of his designs include the Hospital de Venerables Sacerdotes (1687–97) and the Churches of the Magdalena (1691–1709) and San Salvador (1696–1711). He was responsible for the west door of San Telmo (1724–34), and may have designed the outstandingly ornate Church of San Luis (1699–1731). His son, **Ambrosio** (1700–75), also worked in an ornate Baroque style in Seville (he designed Santa Catalina (1732)), and his grandson, **Antonio Matías** (*c.*1734–*c.*96), was responsible for the *campanile of La Palma del Condado (*c.*1780).

Bazin (1964); Kubler and Soria (1959)

Figurative architecture. Term apparently coined by Paolo *Portoghesi in the late 1970s to describe architectural design from the 1970s, influenced by *Graves, *Rossi, and others, in which attempts were made to restore the obscured meaning of *types found in traditional architecture, as in walls, columns, door-cases, *pediments, etc., after the jettisoning of so much by the *Modern Movement. It was regarded as part of *Post-Modernism.

MacDonald (1986); Portoghesi (1983)

Filarete, Il (**Antonio di Pietro Averlino** (*c.*1400–69)). Florentine sculptor and architect, his pseudonym, by which he is known, means 'Lover of Virtue' (or *Virtù*). His importance lies in his promotion of the early *Renaissance style, and in his *Trattato d'architettura* or *Libro architettonico* (1461–4), which was widely circulated, though not published until C19: *Vasari had no high opinion of it. It includes plans for ideal cities (Sforzinda and Plousiapolis) as well as an ingenious ten-storey House of Vice and Virtue complete with whore-house and observatory. It also proposed (perhaps taking the basic idea from *Vitruvius) using the Greek *Orders to suggest social classes, a form of associationism. He seems to have designed Bergamo Cathedral (from 1457), but his major architectural work was the Ospedale Maggiore (Cà Granda), Milan, designed on a complex symmetrical plan, only part of which was built, including arcades (1456) rather coarser than *Brunelleschi's work in Florence. However, the idea of designing for the isolation of patients into wards probably makes the Milan building the first scientific modern hospital of our era, and was influential in the following centuries. He may have been involved in the design of the Cà del Duca, Venice (1445–61).

Filarete (1965); Heydenreich and Lotz (1974); *Journal of the Warburg and Courtauld Institutes*, 34 (1971), 96–114, 35 (1972), 391–7; Murray (1986); Onians (1988); Patetta (1987); Tigler (1963)

fillet. Small, narrow, flat moulding, usually a plain *band in a group of mouldings, either of projecting rectangular *section or simply a flat surface between other mouldings, such as *flutes of a *column-*shaft, or one of the elements of an *Attic base between the *torus and *scotia. It often defines, emphasizes, and clarifies mouldings, as at the top of a *cornice, above the *cyma recta, where it is termed *list* or *listel*. A very small fillet, e.g. between the channels under the *echinus of a *Doric *capital, is an *annulet.

finial. *Boss, *crop, crope, *knob, or *pommel at the top of e.g. a bench-end, canopy, *gable, *pinnacle, or *spire, usually decorated.

Gothic C14 finial from Wimborne, Dorset.

(*left*) Pine-cone finial. (*right*) Acorn finial.

finial.

Finsterlin, Hermann (1887–1973). German designer of visionary buildings, many of which were published by Bruno *Taut and promoted by *Arbeitsrat für Kunst. Interest in his work was revived in the 1960s, but he did not erect any permanent structures.

Frülicht, 3 (1922), 73 ff.; Placzek (1982)

Fioravanti, Aristotele (*c*.1415–86). Bolognese architect and engineer. He worked on many engineering problems in Bologna, Mantua, Venice, Rome, and Naples, and was in the service of the Sforzas in Milan (1458–64). In 1467 he was in Hungary, and spent the last decade of his life in Russia, working on various projects, including the Cathedral of the Dormition (or Assumption), Kremlin, Moscow (1475–9), in the *Byzantine style.

Beltrami (1912)

First Pointed. First of the *Gothic styles of architecture from the end of C12 to the end of C13, known in England as the *Early English* style. Good examples include much of Wells (from 1180), Lincoln (from 1192), and Salisbury (from 1220) Cathedrals. Gothic is characterized by the pointed arch and *vault. Windows started as apertures in a wall of the *lancet type, often very sharply pointed, or with blunter heads formed of equilateral arches. *Foil arches occurred in some locations, and grander doorways, with numerous *Orders, often had the doorway divided in two with a central *pier or shaft (*trumeau) supporting a *tympanum ornamented with sculpture and associated with an almond-shaped (*mandala) or quatrefoil panel. Mouldings of arches were often composed of contrasting concave and convex forms in *section, sometimes with *fillets, giving emphasis to light and shade, while detached *colonnettes or shafts of black or grey marble, secured to piers at vertical intervals by *bands of a shaft, enriched the architectural effect and accentuated verticality. Common ornament of horizontal mouldings (often on *capitals) was *nail-head, consisting of a series of small pyramids touching at their bases, while the larger, sharper *dog-tooth ornament usually occurred in *cavetto mouldings around doorways, windows, *niches, etc. *Capitals, in their simplest form, were shaped like an inverted bell, but more frequently were ornamented with vigorous stylized foliage of the stiff-leaf, trefoil-leaf, or *volute type, deeply under-cut. *Bases of colonnettes or piers consisted of cylindrical forms with *torus mouldings and the occasional *cavetto, displaying a debt to Classical architecture, just as the bell- and volute-capitals clearly were derived from *Antique Roman precedents. *Vaulting was often employed for ceilings, ribbed vaults first occurring probably at Durham or in Lombardy: the pointed vault overcame the problems of vaulting rectangular areas using semicircular arches because the curved forms meeting at an apex were far more flexible and adaptable, the pointed apex being effectively

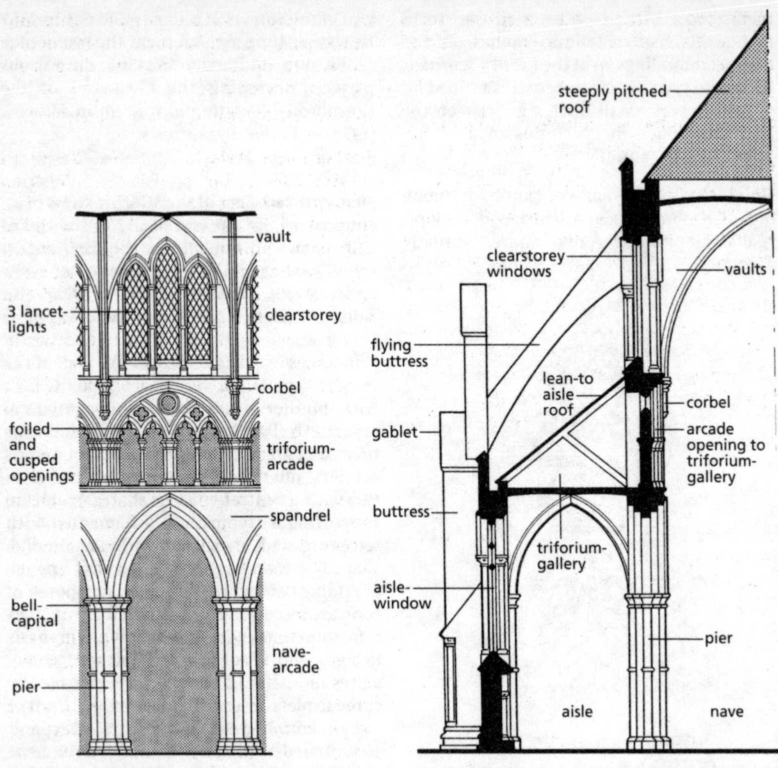

First Pointed. (*left*) Internal elevation of a typical bay, derived from C13 Salisbury Cathedral, Wiltshire. (*JJS*) (*right*) Section through half the nave and an aisle, Salisbury. (*JJS*)

the 'hinge', enabling arches to span from apex to springing without the awkward geometry and junctions inevitable when the *Romanesque semicircular arch was used. *Bosses were the usual ornament at the intersection of ribs. The outward-thrusting forces of heavy vaults had to be counteracted by means of deep *buttresses, which divided *façades into *bays, and were themselves capped by *gablets or *pinnacles designed as *clustered piers. Roofs, like Romanesque roofs, were steeply pitched, and in some cases (e.g. Lincoln Cathedral) increased in pitch to 70° or thereabouts. Circular windows of the wheel type were used, especially in gables (e.g. north and south *transept walls), while other windows started out as the lancet, then evolved as two lancet-lights with a *roundel over, as in early plate-*tracery. Starting with Rheims Cathedral (1211), the moulded *bar *mullion was used to separate *lights, with the bars forming decorative patterns above, beginning with the simple *Geometrical type featuring circles, foils, and approximately triangular elements. By the time Geometrical bar-tracery was fully developed, the style merges with *Middle Pointed.

Grodecki (1986); Parker (1850); Rickman (1848)

Fischer, Heinrich Karl von (1782–1820). German architect. He settled in Munich in 1796, where he designed the Prinz-Karl-Palais (1803–6), the first great Neoclassical building in the Bavarian capital, with a fine *portico. He contributed to the considerable improvements in the planning of the city under King Maximilian I (1808–25), including the Karolinenplatz (1808–12), and the *Hoftheater* (Court Theatre, 1810–18—destroyed 1823 and rebuilt by von *Klenze, who retained parts of the exterior, then destroyed again in the 1939–45 war, and rebuilt as the *Nationaltheater*).

Hederer (1960); Nerdinger (1987)

Fischer, Johann Michael (1692–1766). Important architect responsible for thirty-two churches, twenty-three monasteries, and many secular buildings in Bavaria in the *Rococo style. His Benedictine Abbey Churches of Zwiefalten (1741–64) and Ottobeuren (1748–68) are his masterworks, with two of the most frothy and exquisite Rococo interiors in all Germany (*stucco-work by J. M. Feichtmayr (1709–72)), but each shows a powerful command of architectural form that is not lost in a welter of ornament. He fused longitudinal axes with central spaces at Rott-am-Inn (1759–63) and Berg-am-Laim (1738–51), and created a series of interpenetrating volumes each formed on elliptical or circular plans at Ottobeuren. At Zwiefalten, wall-piers define the chapels, *transepts flank the crossing-dome, and *choir and sanctuary are set in an elongated space beyond the crossing: galleries sway out into the nave between the pairs of *engaged *scagliola columns. Other works include the churches at Altomünster (1763–6); Diessen (1732–9—with high-altar by *Cuvilliés); Fürstenzell (1739–48); and Osterhofen (1726–40—with decorations by the *Asam brothers). Without exception, his churches are worthy of the closest study.

Bourke (1962); Hitchcock (1968*a*); Lieb (1982)

Fischer, Theodor (1862–1938). German architect and teacher, a founding member of the *Werkbund* (1907). His architecture often drew on *vernacular forms, as in the housing at Gmindersdorf (1903–8), and he insisted that the local landscapes and indigenous architectural character should be respected and enhanced. In this his ideas were related to those of *Sitte, and wholly repudiated by the *Modern Movement. He carried out expansion plans for several German cities, including Mannheim (1916) and Augsburg (1926), and designed workers' housing for various sites, including Weberstrasse, Stuttgart (1904–6), Langensalza (1907–8), and Neu-Westend, Munich (1909–10). He influenced *Bonatz, Bruno *Taut, *Mendelsohn, and *Oud. In his *Für die deutsche Baukunst* (For German Architecture—1917) he advocated the study of construction and crafts, and denounced the excessive emphasis on mathematics, natural sciences, draughtsmanship, and 'design' in architectural education as it failed to inculcate any understanding of the handling of volumes.

Fischer (1903, 1917); Karlinger (1932); Pfister (1968)

Fischer von Erlach, Johann Bernhard (1656–1723). Distinguished Austrian *Baroque architect. He studied in Rome from 1671, where he became acquainted with the work of *Bernini and Carlo *Fontana, and developed an interest in *Antique objects and architecture. After the defeat of the Turks in 1683 and the rise of Austria as a European power, Fischer settled in Vienna. He designed Schloss Frain, Moravia (1688–95), with its elliptical hall clearly influenced by his Roman stay, and shortly afterwards he developed the theme in his three Salzburg churches. At the elliptical *Dreifaltigkeitskirche* (Holy Trinity Church—1694–1702) the long axis is that of the entrance-high-altar, while (owing a debt to *Guarini) twin towers flank a concave front (a theme derived from *Borromini's church of Santa Agnese, Rome, although the middle of the façade was influenced by the work of *Hardouin-Mansart, and the basic plan by *Vignola's Santa Anna dei Palafrenieri, Rome). His mastery of synthesis was demonstrated, and he may also have been influenced by *Zuccalli's Salzburg churches. Then came the *Kollegienkirche* (College or University Church—1694–1707—a mixture of the longitudinal and central church-plan, with a soaring *cupola over the central space) and the *Johannesspitalkirche* (St John's Hospital Church—1699–1704—where influences from Borromini are again apparent). While in Salzburg he designed the exquisite high-altar (1709) for the *Franziskanerkirche* (Franciscan Church). The *Ursulinenkirche* (Ursuline Church—1699–1705) is also attributed to him. These Salzburg buildings, in a sense, were trial runs for the *Karlskirche* (Church of St Charles), Vienna (from 1715), with its Antique Roman *portico, biblical allusions to the Temple of Solomon (enhanced by the twin *Trajanic columns doubling as the Pillars of Hercules and Jachin and Boaz), elliptical central space crowned by a cupola, and wide front, one of the most original and powerful designs of the entire Baroque period. Mention should also be made of his Electoral Chapel next to the *choir of Breslau (now Wrocław) Cathedral (1715–24): it mixes Palladian and Borrominiesque themes, again exploiting the ellipse.

His secular architecture includes the Town Palace of Prince Eugen of Savoy (1663–1736) in Vienna (1696–1700), influenced by Bernini and Le *Vau, the Palais Clam-Gallas, Prague (1713–*c*.25), designs (only partly realized, and much altered) for Schönbrunn Palace, Vienna (from 1696), and the *Hofbibliothek* (Court Library), Vienna (1722–30), one of the finest Baroque rooms in Europe. At both the *Karlskirche* and the *Hofburg* (Imperial Palace) much of the work was carried out by his son, **Joseph Emanuel Fischer von Erlach** (1695–1742). Johann Bernhard's *Entwurff einer historischen Architektur* (Outline of Historical Architecture—1721) appeared in English as *A Plan of Civil and Historical Architecture* in 1730, and was among the first books to include illustrations of Egyptian and Oriental buildings, although the images were fanciful in the extreme. Nevertheless, they had a profound influence on later generations, and especially on *Boullée.

Aurenhammer (1973); Bourke (1962); Brucker (1983); Fischer von Erlach (1964); Fuhrmann (1950); Polleross (1995); Powell (1959); Sedlmayr (1976)

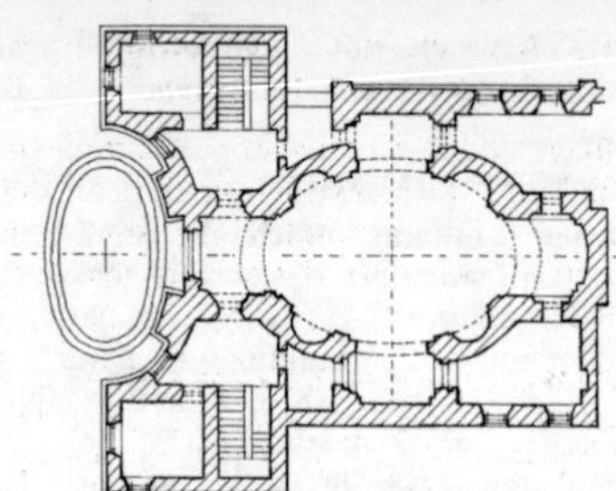

Plan of *Dreifaltigkeitskirche*, Salzburg, showing the concave front and elliptical body of the church.

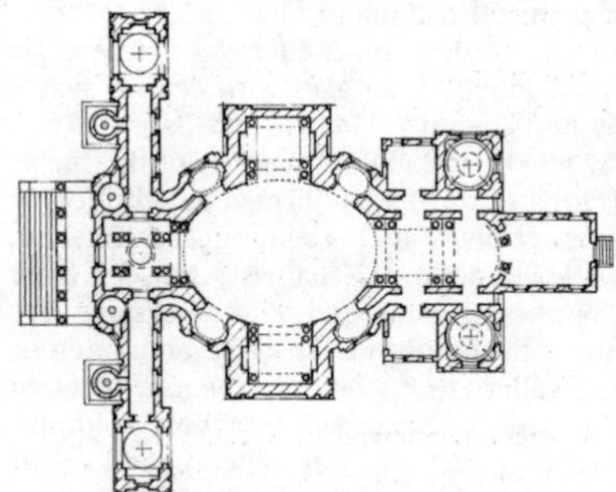

Plan of the *Karlskirche*, Vienna, showing the wide front with towers and Solomonic/Trajanic columns, prostyle hexastyle portico on a podium, and central ellipse.

Fischer von Erlach.

fish-bladder. Form found in *Second Pointed *Curvilinear *tracery looking like a tadpole, with a round or pointed head and a curving pointed tail, also called *mouchette. Apparently from the German *Fischblase*, referring to comma shapes in *Sondergotik tracery.

Fisker, Kay (1893–1965). Danish architect. His inspiration came from Danish *vernacular buildings and from German *Modernism. He was best known for Aarhus University (with Povl *Stegmann and Christian Frederik *Møller—1932–45), in which traditional materials (e.g. bricks) and simple forms were used. He had a considerable reputation as a designer of public and private housing, notably the Co-operative Building Society Housing, Borups Allé and Stefansgade, Copenhagen (1918–21); the Voldparken Housing and School, Husum (1945); and many other schemes, including Interbau Housing, Berlin (1956–7). His *Modern Danish Architecture* (with F. R. Yerbury—1927) disseminated Danish achievements in Britain and America.

Faber (1966); Fisker and Yerbury (1927); Lankilde (1960)

Five Points. *See* Le Corbusier.

Flagg, Ernest (1857–1947). American architect. He promoted French *Beaux-Arts ideals in the USA, and is best known for the Singer Loft Building (1902–4), and the Singer Tower (1906–8—demolished), both in New York. In those works he promoted the idea of structural rationality he had absorbed from his studies of *Viollet-le-Duc. He was interested in the problems of designing housing for the urban poor, and published *Small Houses: Their Economic Design and Construction* (1922), in which ingenious planning and inexpensive construction techniques were promoted.

DAB (1974); Handlin (1985); Placzek (1982)

Flamboyant. Late style of Continental *Gothic (*c*.1375–mid-C16) that evolved from *Second Pointed *Curvilinear work, especially the flowing forms of the *tracery: it gets its name from the flame-like shapes bounded by the curved *bars. In France its most outstanding manifestations were at the west porch of St-Maclou, Rouen (*c*.1500–14), and the west front of Troyes Cathedral (early C16) by *Chambiges. Flamboyant tracery occurs elsewhere, including the British Isles (e.g. west window of York *Minster).

flank. **1.** Lateral *face of a structure: an end or side as distinguished from the front or back (e.g. side of a *bastion). **2.** Party-wall between terrace-houses. **3.** Haunch of an arch. **4.** *Valley of a roof.

flanker. One of several (3 or 4) circular, polygonal, or square projections at the corner of a *bawn (enclosure) to help to defend the straight *curtain-wall linking them.

flanking window. Framed *margin-, *side-, or *wing-*light on either side of a door or window.

flashing. Metal (usually lead) set into brickwork joints, or *raglets in masonry, where e.g. a pitched roof is pierced by a *chimney-stack. It provides a watertight joint.

flèche. **1.** *Spire. **2.** *Spirelet surmounting a roof, especially over the *crossing of a French *Gothic cathedral.

Flemish bond. *See* brick.

Flemish Mannerism. North-European mutation and mélange of *Flamboyant *Gothic, *High *Renaissance Italian *Mannerist, and French Renaissance *Fontainebleau styles. It exploited *cartouches, *caryatides, *grotesque ornament, *herms, *banded *pilasters, *obelisks, and *strapwork, composed with a freedom bordering on licentiousness. The style was disseminated in pattern-books by *Dietterlin, de *Vries, and others, notably in England and C18 Spain, where it had a profound effect on *Baroque details such as the *estípite. Examples of the style include some of the guild-houses in the Grand' Place, Brussels (from the 1690s), the Town Hall, Leiden (1597), and the doorway of the Huis Rockox, Keizerstraat, Antwerp (mid-C16).

Flemish Revival. *See* Pont-Street Dutch.

Fletcher, Banister (1833–99). English architect and surveyor. He designed several industrial buildings in Newcastle upon Tyne before settling in London in 1870, where he published *Model Houses for the Industrial Classes* (1871) in which the influence of Henry *Roberts can be detected. He built up an extensive architectural and surveying practice in which he was assisted by his sons, **Banister Flight** (see below) and **Herbert Phillips Fletcher** (1872–1916). In 1890 he was appointed to a Chair at King's College, London, in which capacity he did much to further architectural education. He was indefatigably industrious, publishing many works, including *Dilapidations* (1872), *Compensations* (1874), *Arbitrations* (1875), *Quantities* (1877), *Light and Air* (1879), *The Metropolitan Building Acts* (1882), and, with his son Banister, his celebrated *A History of Architecture* (1896), which rapidly went into further editions, and became the standard work for generations of students.

Cruickshank (1996); *DNB* (1917)

Fletcher, Sir Banister Flight (1866–1953). British architect, barrister-at-law, and architectural historian. The son of Banister *Fletcher, he joined his father's office in 1884. His early work was noted for its quality: it included 111–25 Oxford Street, London (1887); part of King's College School, Wimbledon (1899); 20 and 46 Harley Street and 30 Wimpole Street, London (1890); Goslett's, 127–31 Charing Cross Road, London (1897); the charming monument to his father in Hampstead Cemetery (*c.*1900); St Ann's Vestry Hall, Carter Lane, City of London (1905); 'Seldowns', 23 The Avenue, and 'Tiverton', pleasant houses in Potters Bar, Hertfordshire (1909); and the handsome former Westminster Bank, Hythe, Kent (1912). After the 1914–18 war the works at Roan School, Greenwich (1926–8); the extensions to Morden College, Blackheath (1933); and the monumental Gillette Factory, Osterley (1936–7—which *Pevsner described as having an 'incongruous, timidly modernistic grandeur') deserve note. On the whole, however, Pevsner adopted a respectful tone when commenting on Banister Fletcher's work.

Accomplished though his architecture was, Fletcher is better known as an author (jointly, with his father), of *A History of Architecture on the Comparative Method* (1896). The 1921 edition was rewritten by him and his first wife, **Alice Maud Mary** (d. 1932), and illustrated with the famous line-drawings by George G. Woodward and others. This edition remained the basis for subsequent editions of 1924 and 1928, and underwent some textual revisions for the 1931 edition. The tenth edition of 1938, with its successors (essentially only slightly revised versions), was definitive until R. A. Cordingley's revision of 1961, followed by others (1975, 1987, and 1996). This extraordinarily informative book, of vast scope (described by Pevsner as the 'indispensable historical compilation of architectural history'), has been used by countless students of architecture since it first appeared, and has been translated into various languages. Other works by Fletcher include a much-criticized study of *Palladio (1902), and books written with his brother, **Herbert Phillips Fletcher** (1872–1916)—*Architectural Hygiene* (1899), and *Carpentry and Joinery* (1898). The last volume and his own *Architectural Work* (1934) were illustrated with his accomplished sketches. He did much to further the profession and education, and gave generously to the RIBA and the University of London. He was knighted in 1919.

DNB (1971); Gray (1985)

Flettner *or* **Flötner, Peter** (*c.*1485–1546). German *Renaissance architect and sculptor. He designed the fountain, Marktplatz, Mainz (1526), and the *Hirschvogelsaal*, Nuremberg (1534—destroyed). His *Kunstbuch* (Art Book—1549) contained elaborate and masterly designs for *arabesques and one design for *grotesque ornament that remained influential long after his death.

Angerer (1986); Hitchcock (1981); Jervis (1984)

fleur-de-lis *or* **-lys.** Ornament consisting of three leaf-like pointed members above and three or one below a horizontal cross-bar. It is essentially a stylized lily, often found in late-*Gothic *tracery and as a poppy-head *finial on a medieval *bench-end.

fleuron. 1. Ornamental termination of the apex of a roof, such as a *crop, *finial, or *épi. **2.** Stylized four-leafed square floral ornament, used in late-*Gothic cresting, *tiles, *crockets, and *cavetto mouldings. **3.** Ornament in the middle of each concave *face of the *Corinthian *abacus. **4.** *Anthemion.

fleuron. Also called *tablet-flower*, C14 Lady Chapel, Wells Cathedral, Somerset. (*After Parker*)

flight. Continuous straight series of steps, uninterrupted by landings, in a *stair, e.g. from landing to landing.

flint. Hard steely-grey stone occurring in nodules of a varying size, usually covered with a white encrustation. It is used for building in combination with brick or stone *dressings. It is easily split, or *knapped, and is used in *flush-work with *freestone dressings.

Flitcroft, Henry (1697–1769). English architect. He became draughtsman to Lord *Burlington, and produced drawings for *Kent's *The Designs of Inigo Jones* (1727). Burlington had him installed in the Office of Works, and for the rest of his life 'Burlington Harry' was made, becoming Master-Mason and Deputy Surveyor in succession to Kent, then Comptroller of the Works in succession to *Ripley. He was a competent practitioner of *Palladianism, and his designs for decorative features showed he had made a careful study of Inigo *Jones. His Church of St Giles-in-the-Fields, London (1731–4), follows the *type established by *Gibbs at St Martin-in-the-Fields. He designed the east front and wings of Wentworth Woodhouse, Yorkshire (*c.*1735–*c.*1770), the longest Palladian composition in England, and Woburn Abbey, Bedfordshire (1747–61).

Colvin (1995); *DNB* (1917)

Flockhart, William (1854–1913). Scots architect. He set up a practice in London in 1881, and produced a number of competent and well-designed buildings. His Lansdowne House, Flats, and Studios at 11 and 13 Lansdowne Road, London, were in a free *Renaissance style. His best work was probably Rosehaugh, Avoch, Ross and Cromarty (1890s), a vast house, the site architect for which was the young *Adshead. His 108 and 110 Old Brompton Road (1885–6) are finely crafted buildings.

Gray (1985)

floor-slab. Stone funerary *monument in a church in the form of a coffin-lid or a flat slab, inscribed and sometimes incised, set in the floor.

Floreale. Style of exuberant decorative architecture used particularly for the dwellings of the prosperous Italian *bourgeoisie*, and essentially a branch of *Art Nouveau, derived from America, Belgium, Britain, France (notably *Viollet-le-Duc), and (especially) Austria. It featured distorted mouldings, ribbons like tapeworms, and luxuriant plant-forms. It reached its apogee in the 1902 Turin Exposition of Decorative Arts, in the works of Raimondo d'*Aronco, and its legacy was ubiquitous, Italian architecture from *c.*1898 to 1914 being often ornamented with lushly decorated *bands, garlands, and growths of flowers and fruit. *Sommaruga's Palazzo Castiglioni, Milan (1901–3), is generally regarded as the apotheosis of the *Stile Floreale*. *Basile's dining-room in the Villa Igiea, Palermo (1901), was a fine example of the style too, with ornament in such abundance it seemed almost sinister, in danger of consuming room and diners.

Meeks (1966)

Florentine arch. *See* arch.

floriate. Type of ornament resembling flowers or leaves and foliage.

Floris, Cornelis (1514–75). Cornelis Floris II *or* Floris de Vriendt was born in Antwerp, and made his name as a designer and sculptor of funerary monuments, notably that of Duke Albrecht I of Prussia in the Cathedral, Königsberg (now Kaliningrad—1570–3). After a visit to Rome he became the most influential designer of *Renaissance and Mannerist ornament in Flanders. The Town Hall in Antwerp (1561–6) was an important step in the assimilation of Italian sources into Northern Europe, and incorporated features derived from *Bramante and *Serlio such as coupled columns and *triumphal arches in its six-storey frontispiece. However, there is some doubt as to whether Floris himself was the architect of the building, as he was primarily a sculptor. The real architect appears to have been Hans Hendrick van *Paesschen, who also may have designed the *Hanseatenhuis* (Hanseatic House), Antwerp (1564–6), attributed to Floris de Vriendt. The latter designed and made the *Rood-screen in Tournai Cathedral (1573–4). His decorative style was much disseminated by de *Vries.

Gelder and Duverger (1954); Gerson and Ter Kuile (1960); Hedicke (1913); Millar (1987); Tafuri (1966)

Flötner. *See* Flettner.

flowing. *See* tracery.

Flügelaltar. *See* triptych.

flush. **1.** Even with or in the same plane as something else, such as a *panel with its surface on the same plane with its surrounding frame, or flush *pointing on the same plane as the face of the brickwork. **2.** Stones or bricks bedded closely in mortar with very small joints.

flush bead moulding. Double-*quirked *bead with its face level with the plane of the surfaces on either side, as in panelling.

flush-pointing. Mortar on the same plane as (flush with) the *face of brickwork.

flushwork. Knapped *flint, with the split (*spaultered*) dark sides of the flint facing outwards, built into finely jointed panels framed by *freestone *dressings resembling *tracery, all the finished faces of flint and stone in the same plane.

flushwork. Typical East Anglian knapped flint with limestone dressings.

flute. Channel (*stria*) of semicircular, segmental, or partially elliptical *section, one of many set parallel (or nearly so) to each other, as in Classical column-*shafts, where they occur in all save the *Tuscan *Order. In the Greek *Doric Order segmental flutes are separated by *arrises and stopped by *annulets, while those in other Orders are deeper, separated by *fillets, and terminate in quarter-spherical forms. In some instances flutes may have convex mouldings or beads (*cables) set within them to one-third the height of the shaft. Small horizontal flutes, as on the *Asiatic *base of the *Ionic Order, are *reeds. If ornamenting a flat *band, set vertically, flutes are *strigils, while flutes cut in elongated S-shapes (as on the sides of Roman *sarcophagi) are collectively referred to as *strigillation.

flying buttress. *See* buttress.

flying façade. As *false façade.

foil. In *Gothic *tracery any circular *lobe tangent to the inner side of a larger arc or arch, meeting other lobes in points called *cusps projecting inwards from the arch: prefixes are used to describe how many foils occur—*tre*foil (3), *quatre*foil (4), *cinque*foil (5), *sex*foil (6), *multi*foil, etc. A *quatrefoil*, therefore, has four lobes, separated by cusps, in the shape of a flower with four leaves the axes of which are vertical and horizontal. Bands of quatrefoils were much used for *enrichment during the *Perpendicular period. When placed with the axes set diagonally, quatrefoils are called cross-*quarters.

foliate. 1. Made or adorned with foils, as in *Gothic *tracery. **2.** Ornament resembling leaves, as on a *capital.

foliated. 1. Decorated with leaf ornament. **2.** With *foils separated by cusps in apertures or *tracery.

foliate mask. Sculptured human face or mask (called *Green Man, masque feuillu*, or *tête de feuilles*), amid foliage, some of which sprouts from the mouth and nose.

folly. *Eyecatcher, usually a building in a contrived landscape, often otherwise useless. It might be in the form of a sham ruin, a Classical temple, oriental tent, *Chinoiserie *pagoda, or other charming *fabrique set in a *Picturesque garden. It can also provide seats and shelter from which an agreeable view can be enjoyed, but more often it simply demands attention and gives pleasure by its eccentricity. One of the oddest follies in Britain is the giant pineapple at Dunmore Park, Stirlingshire, Scotland (1761). More recently the term has been given to buildings that are out of the ordinary, do not conform to any of the recognized styles, and are not necessarily placed in a landscape. The delightful King's Coffee House, King Street, Knutsford, Cheshire (1907–8), built by Richard Harding *Watt to designs by W. Longworth, could be regarded as a folly, as could the complex of open-work turrets of steel covered with broken pottery and glass, seashells, and other detritus by Simon (Sam) Rodia (1879–1965), known as Watts Towers, Los Angeles, Calif. Other C20 follies include the Bottle Village, Simo, Santa Susana, Calif. (*c.*1950–70s), built by Tressa Prisbrey (1895–*c.*1985) of bottles set in concrete to house her curious collection scavenged from rubbish-dumps. Esther *McCoy wrote lovingly about 'Grandma's Bottle Village' in 1974. Mention should also be made of the *Palais Ideal*, Hauterives, Drôme, France (1879–1905), a fantastic dream-like castle of concrete and stone embellished with much decoration, built to a plan of great complexity by Facteur Ferdinand Cheval (1836–1924), who also designed and built his own *mausoleum in Hauterives Cemetery (1913–15). There are other marvellous inventions that show the folly is more than whimsical, but the result of the creative longing of the human spirit, often coming within the category of *Fantastic architecture.

Art and Architecture, 68 (July 1951), 23–5; Hawley (1993); Headley and Meulenkamp (1986); Jones (1974); Mosser and Teyssot (1991); Prisbrey (1967); Schuyt and Elffers (1980); Walker Art Center (1974)

Fonoyll, Raynard (*fl.* 1331–62). English master-mason. He built the south *cloister of the *Monastery of Santes Creus in Catalonia, Spain (1331–41), and the Church of Santa Maria, Montblanch, Spain (from 1352). He also seems to have worked at the Cathedrals of Tarragona and Lérida, the Royal Monasteries of Pedralbes at Barcelona and Poblet, and the Town Church of Morella. He is of considerable importance in the history of Spanish architecture because his work is the earliest-known *Curvilinear *Gothic in the Iberian peninsula.

Harvey (1987)

font. Baptismal basin for the consecrated water used during the Sacrament of Baptism. It is commonly formed from a large block of stone, hollowed out and elaborately carved with Christian symbols, supported on a short *pier or cluster of *colonnettes that are set on a stepped plinth or platform. *Font-covers* adorned with *pinnacles and *finials, raised on ropes and pulleys, and sometimes coloured, were not unusual in the medieval period.

Fontaine, Pierre-François-Léonard (1762–1853). French architect and interior designer. He studied under *Peyre, in whose *atélier* he met *Percier, with whose name his was to be so intimately linked. He went to Rome in 1786, where he was joined by Percier, and absorbed the principles of *Neoclassicism while there. In 1792 they worked together on decorations for the Opéra, and in 1793 designed furniture for the Convention. Drawing on their Roman experiences, they produced their first book, *Recueil des palais, maisons, et autres édifices modernes dessinés à Rome* (Compendium of Palaces, Houses, and Other Modern Buildings drawn in Rome—1798). By that time Fontaine had established a reputation as a designer of fine furniture, and his contacts led to an introduction to Napoleon: Percier and Fontaine were appointed to design the interiors of Malmaison (1800–2), in which exquisite work they effectively created the *Empire style. From that time, they were virtually Napoleon's official architects, and their influence was widespread, especially after their *Recueil de décorations intérieures* (Compendium of Interior Decorations) was published in 1801, in which their developed eclectic Neoclassical style, embracing Egyptian, Greek, Roman, and Renaissance ornament, was enticingly displayed. It was reissued in 1812 and 1827, and in an enlarged Italian edition of 1843. They restored many palaces (e.g. Saint-Cloud and the Tuileries) that had been vandalized at the time of the Revolution, and designed the settings and trappings for two great Napoleonic public events: the Coronation (1804) and the Emperor's second marriage to Marie Louise of Habsburg-Lorraine (1791–1847) in 1810.

Fontaine seems to have been the entrepreneur, with Percier as the designer of fine detail. However, the partners did not confine their activities to providing rich *Empire* interiors, for their buildings (though few) were also beautifully proportioned and elegant: they include the Arc du Carrousel, Paris (1806–8—modelled on the Arch of Septimius Severus, Rome, but treated polychromatically); a whole series of transformations of Paris, of which the Rue de Rivoli and Place des Pyramides (1802–3) are the best-known, although they prepared a huge scheme including a Palais de Chaillot, larger than Versailles, linked on a vast *axis to a huge complex of buildings, including a University, École des *Beaux-Arts, and Archives, not executed.

After Napoleon's fall, Fontaine became architect to King Louis XVIII (1814–24), for whom he built the *Chapelle Expiatoire*, Paris (1815–26), on the site of the burial of King Louis XVI and Queen Marie Antoinette. He also restored the Palais Royal (1814–31) and the Hôtel-Dieu, Pontoise (1823–7). He published *Le Palais-Royal* (1829) and *Résidences de Souverains* (1833). In the words of obituarists, Percier and Fontaine 'never married', and are buried in the same grave in Père-Lachaise Cemetery, Paris.

Biver (1964); Braham (1980); Middleton and Watkin (1987); Watkin (1986)

Fontainebleau. Style of architectural decoration at the French Royal *Château created by Italian (notably Rosso Fiorentino (1495–1540), Francesco Primaticcio (1504/5–70), *Serlio, and *Vignola), French, and Flemish artists for *François Ier from 1528 to 1558. It was an eclectic mutation of *High *Renaissance design into a distinct form of *Mannerism featuring lavish *cartouches, *caryatides, *grotesques, *scrolls, *strapwork, and etiolated *stucco figures. Fontainebleau influenced French design until the end of C16, but the style was widely disseminated through printed sources emanating from Antwerp, and had a great impact on *Flemish Mannerism and architecture in England, Germany, and The Netherlands.

Blunt (1982); Chilvers, Osborne, and Farr (1988); Shearman (1967)

Fontana, Carlo (1638–1714). Italian *Baroque architect. Born near Como, he lived in Rome from the early 1650s, and assisted *Cortona, *Rainaldi, and *Bernini. For the last he worked on the design of the Piazza di San Pietro, the Scala Regia, and other projects, and was to succeed the master as architect of St Peter's in 1697. Fontana was a prolific architect, and his fame was based on the series of works starting in 1671: the Cappella Ginetti, Sant'Andrea della Valle, has a rich interior of coloured marble, and there were other chapels, but the Cappella Cibo, Santa Maria del Pòpolo (1682–4), is perhaps the finest of them. At the same time he built the concave façade of San Marcello al Corso. His remodelling of the Baptismal Chapel in St Peter's (1692–8) involved ingenious high-level lighting. He transformed and enlarged the Palazzo di Montecitorio (1694–6), left unfinished by Bernini, made additions to the Ospizio di San Michele (1700–11), and remodelled the façade and porch of Santa Maria in Trastévere (1702). Fontana also published books on St Peter's (1694), the Baptismal Chapel (1697), and other subjects. As the leading architect in Rome towards the end of his long life, he was highly influential, not least because he taught men of genius who carried his ideas far and wide: those pupils numbered among them *Fischer von Erlach, *Hildebrandt, and *Gibbs.

Braham and Hager (1977); Norberg-Schulz (1986, 1986*a*); Wittkower (1982)

Fontana, Domenico (1543–1607). Architect and engineer, born in the Ticino, Switzerland. He settled in Rome, where he worked for Cardinal Montalto, the future Pope Sixtus V (1585–90), for whom he designed the villa on the Quirinal (1576–88). In 1585–6 he made his name by re-erecting the huge Egyptian red-granite *obelisk from the Circus Gai et Neronis (but originally in Alexandria), in the centre of the piazza in front of St Peter's *basilica, and also re-erected the ancient obelisks at Santa Maria Maggiore (1587), San Giovanni in Laterano (1587–8), and Piazza del Pòpolo (1589). Thereafter he built the Lateran Palace (1585–9), the Vatican Library (1587–90), and supervised the erection of the dome of St Peter's under della *Porta (1588–90). His other major contributions in Rome were the laying out of new streets, including the Via Felice (1585–9), and other town-planning improvements ordered by Sixtus V. In 1593 he moved to Naples, where he built the Palazzo Reale (1600–2).

Architectural Review, 111 (1952), 217–26; Fontana (1604); Muñoz (1944); Roullet (1972); Wittkower (1982)

Fontana, Giacomo (1710–73). Italian architect. He made a major contribution in Poland during the reign of King Stanisław Augustus Poniatowski (1764–95), working in a refined early Neoclassical style. He designed the façade of the Church of the Holy Cross (1756), and the interiors of the Krasiński Palace, both in Warsaw (1766–73).

Lorentz and Rottermund (1984)

Förderer, Walter-Maria (1928–). Swiss architect. His works include the Commercial High School, St Gallen (with Rolf Georg Otto and Hans Zwimpfer—1957–63), in which powerful forms of concrete are boldly expressed. His Church Centre at Hérémence (1963–71) has been admired for its late-flowering *Expressionism, and was perhaps his most adventurous essay in freely treated volumes.

Burckhardt and Förderer (1968); Förderer (1964, 1975)

fore. Situated in front of something else, and usually used as a prefix. Examples include:

fore-choir: *ante-choir;

fore-church: *ante-church, like a *narthex, but with *nave and *aisles;

fore-court: outer court of a large building or assemblage of buildings, in grander ensembles a *cour d'honneur;

fore-front: principal façade or entrance-front of a building.

Forman, John (*fl.* 1515–d. 1558). English mason. He worked under *Lebons at Hampton Court Palace, and in *c.*1523 was appointed master-mason at York *Minster. From 1525 he built the Church of St Michael-le-Belfry, York (completed 1536). He was involved in the redecoration of York Minster when Roman Catholicism was restored in 1557 in the reign of Queen Mary I (1553–8).

Harvey (1987)

formeret. *Gothic arch-rib in a *vault *engaged with the wall, called a *wall-rib*, smaller than the rest of the ribs of the vault-compartment.

form-piece. Piece of stone from which *Gothic *tracery is constructed.

formwork. Temporary metal or timber *shuttering* constructed as the mould for *concrete. When removed (*struck*) after the concrete has set, the imprint of the formwork is left on the face of the concrete, and so the timber boarding can be designed to leave a rugged *board-marked* finish on the concrete, much sought after in the 1950s and 1960s as part of *Brutalism.

Förster, Christian Friedrich Ludwig von (1797–1863). Bavarian-born architect. He designed the *Ringstrasse* (begun 1858) and the *Romanesque *Byzantine Revival Arsenal (with Theophil von *Hansen) of 1850–6, both in Vienna. He was Professor at the Vienna Academy (1843–6), and influenced the following generation of Viennese architects through the *Allgemeine Bauzeitung* (Universal Building Journal—founded 1836) and his own studio. His son, **Emil von Förster** (1838–1909), worked with him for a time, and then for the State, remodelling the *Hofburg* (Imperial Palace) and the *Burgtheater* (Court Theatre) (1895–7), designing the *Allgemeine Österreichische Baugesellschaft* (Universal Austrian Building Corporation—1872–4) and the *Dorotheum* (1898–1901), all in Vienna.

Eggert (1976); Niemann and Feldegg (1893); Wagner-Rieger (1970, 1980)

fort. 1. Fortified camp or base for an army. **2.** *Folly or *fabrique like a sham castle in a garden.

fortress. 1. *Castle, or strong defensive military structure of *bastions, earthworks, *ramparts, *walls, etc., far grander than a *fort. **2.** Town or city with a *citadel and surrounded by fortifications.

forum (*pl.* **fora**). Public market-place, open square, or place of assembly for judicial and other public business in a Roman town or city. It was surrounded by important buildings, *colonnades, and *porticoes, and ornamented with monuments. The Imperial fora were symmetrical, formal, and axially planned, owing much to *Hellenistic precedent.

foss, fosse. Defensive wet or dry ditch.

fosse communale. Common grave in a *cemetery, usually cleared every seven years or so and re-used.

Foster, John (*c.*1759–1827). English architect. As Surveyor to the Corporation of Liverpool from 1790, he became a powerful figure in that city's architectural concerns, especially after he added the Surveyorship of the Docks to his portfolio. He built many well-mannered houses in Liverpool as well as most of the late-Georgian public buildings, including the Exchange (now Town Hall) with James *Wyatt from 1789 to 1811, his most impressive work. Foster's achievements have been eclipsed somewhat by those of his second son, **John Foster** (*c.*1787–1846), a pupil of Jeffry and (probably) James *Wyatt. In 1809 he travelled abroad, and worked with *Haller, Linckh, and C. R. *Cockerell on excavations in Greece before returning to Liverpool in 1816. In 1824 he succeeded his father as Architect and Surveyor to Liverpool Corporation, designing many of the most significant buildings in that city, mostly in a competent *Greek Revival style, many of which have been destroyed. St James's Cemetery, Liverpool (1823–4—partly cleared, and comprehensively vandalized), laid out in a disused quarry, was one of his most distinguished designs, and included the surviving *Doric *mortuary-chapel, entrance arch, superintendent's house, and *mausoleum (1834) of William Huskisson, MP (1770–1830), who was killed at the opening of the Liverpool and Manchester Railway (15 September 1830). His greatest work was Liverpool Custom House (1828–35—destroyed in the 1939–45 war).

Colvin (1995); Papworth (1852); Picton (1875)

Foster of Thames Bank, Norman Robert, The Lord (1935–). English architect, one of the most distinguished practitioners of the *High Tech style. With his first wife (d. 1989) and Richard *Rogers he formed Team 4 (1963–7), and designed the Reliance Controls Factory, Swindon, Wiltshire (1966), with an exposed steel frame and light industrial cladding. When Team 4 split up, Foster established his own reputation with the Willis Faber Offices, Ipswich, Suffolk (1975), and the Sainsbury Centre for the Visual Arts, University of East Anglia, Norwich (1978), both uncompromisingly *Modernist buildings. His largest commission was the Hong Kong and Shanghai Bank, Hong Kong (1979–86), an assured and finely detailed tower with the structure clearly expressed. His Renault Distribution Centre, Swindon (1981–3), Passenger Terminal, Stansted Airport, Essex (1981–91), Sackler Gallery, Royal Academy of Arts, London (1985–92), the *Carré d'Art* Gallery, Nîmes, France, beside the 16 BC Roman temple (1985–93), the *Torre de Collserola*, Barcelona (1988–92), and remodelling of *Wallot's *Reichstag* (Parliament Building), Berlin (1992–9), have consolidated his position as a leading late-C20 architect. In 1995 he began to move away from *High Tech design with proposals for an office-block in Düsseldorf for the German insurance giant ARAG. The building was designed in collaboration with Rhode Kellerman Wawrosky & Partners. His designs for the Metropolitan Railway Stations, Bilbao, Spain (1988–95), are crisply detailed, and part of a major regeneration scheme for the transport infrastructure of that city. More recently, Foster & Partners' Hong Kong International Airport, said to be the largest enclosed space in the world, was completed (1998).

Emanuel (1994); Lambot (1989–91); Sudjic (1986); van Vynckt (1993)

Fouilhoux, Jacques-André (1879–1945). Paris-born French architect. He was in the USA *c.*1904 and became a partner of Raymond *Hood in 1924, with whom he designed the St Vincent de Paul Asylum, Tarrytown, NY (1924), the Masonic Temple, Scranton, Pa. (1929), the McGraw-Hill *skyscraper, New York (1930–2), and other buildings. He was also partly responsible for the Rockefeller

Center, New York (1931–4). When Hood died in 1934 Fouilhoux joined Wallace K. *Harrison, and continued working on the Rockefeller Center. He also contributed to the New York World's Fair (1938–9) and worked on the Fort Greene and Clinton Hill housing-schemes, New York, in the 1940s.

Architectural Forum, 83/2 (1945), 86; Krinsky (1978)

Foulston, John (1772–1842). English architect. He established himself in Plymouth, Devon, where he became the leading practitioner. His Royal Hotel, Assembly Rooms, and Theatre (1811–22—demolished) employed much cast and wrought iron in its construction, and was made all the more interesting for the grouping of three buildings into one coherent composition. Most of his work was in the Classical manner of the *Regency period, with Greek *Orders and detail applied to *stucco terraces, but at Ker Street, Devonport, Plymouth, he created an eclectic *Picturesque group of buildings, including an *Egyptian Revival Library (1823), a Baptist Chapel in the *Hindoo style (1824), a Greek *Doric Town Hall (1821–3), and a Doric Column (1824). He published *The Public Buildings erected in the West of England, as designed by J. Foulston* (1838), and was in partnership with George *Wightwick from *c.*1830.

Colvin (1995); Crook (1987); Curl (1994); Nettleton (1836)

four-centred. *See* arch.

four-leafed flower. *See* fleuron.

Fowke, Captain Francis (1823–65). Ulster-born military engineer. He designed the Raglan Barracks, Devonport, Plymouth (1853–5—demolished), to an advanced hygienic specification. Ingenious and inventive, his ideas were usually blocked by a conservative military and naval establishment, but his opportunity arrived when he was appointed Superintendent of Buildings for 'Albertopolis', the cultural complex in South Kensington, London, from 1856 until his death. His buildings, of brick and *terracotta, were in the *Rundbogenstil, influenced by German precedents (notably by von *Gärtner and *Semper), and include the galleries, courts, and lecture-theatre of the South Kensington (now Victoria & Albert) Museum (1856–65—with Godfrey Sykes (1824–66)), the buildings for the International Exhibition, South Kensington, London (1862—demolished), and the Royal Albert Hall (1867–71—with Lt.-Col. Henry *Scott). He also designed the handsome Royal Scottish Museum, Edinburgh (1861), a grand essay in the Lombardic Renaissance style, with an elegant galleried Great Hall of iron and glass, and improved and enlarged the National Gallery, Dublin (also 1860s). His designs have been underrated, but there can be little argument about his finesse in building large-scale structures and impressive public buildings. *See also* Albert, Prince.

DNB (1917); Gifford, McWilliam, and Walker (1984); Physick and Darby (1973); Sheppard (1975)

Fowler, Charles (1792–1867). English architect from Devonshire. He settled in London, establishing his practice in 1818. His Covent Garden Market Buildings (1828–30) and masterly iron-and-glass conservatory at Syon House, Isleworth, Middlesex (1827–30), established his reputation. Hungerford Market, London (1831–3), and Lower Market, Exeter, Devon (1835–7)—both demolished—demonstrated his understanding of elegant iron structures as well as his grasp of a simplified straightforward *Neoclassicism derived from *Durand. He also designed Totnes Bridge, Devon (1826–8). *Loudon praised his work for its rational qualities and freedom from slavish adherence to antiquated rules and precedents. His pupils included Henry *Roberts.

Colvin (1995); *DNB* (1993)

foyer. **1.** Lobby or entrance-hall of a theatre or other public building. **2.** Area outside the auditorium for the audience to meet, promenade, mingle, talk, etc. It acts as a sound-barrier between the exterior and the auditorium. **3.** Any public area in a large public or civic building between the exterior and the main parts of the building, i.e. an extended entrance-hall. **4.** Room for gatherings or meetings. **5.** Room for meetings, especially of actors and performers, in a theatre.

fractable. *Cope on a *gable-wall carried up as a parapet. The term is especially appropriate for scrolled, shaped, or stepped gables: the horizontal part at the base of the gable is the *foot*-table; the curved parts are *boltels* or *bottles*; and a step is a *square*.

frame. **1.** Skeletal structure of *concrete, steel, or timber on which floors, roof, and external *cladding are placed to form the building, as opposed to a structure of heavy *load-bearing walls. **2.** Frame of a door. **3.** Surround of an opening, usually an *architrave, trim, or border.

Francesco Maurizio di Giorgio Martini (1439–1501/2). *See* Giorgio.

Francke, Paul (1538–1615). Important German architect of the late-*Renaissance period. He designed the University Buildings, Helmstedt (1592–7), and the Protestant *Marienkirche* (Church of St Mary), Wolfenbüttel (1604–26).

Fink and Appuhn (1965); Hempel (1965)

François Ier**,** *or* **François Premier.** King of France (1515–47), he gave his name to the style of *High *Renaissance and *Mannerist architecture and decoration that emerged at *Fontainebleau. It enjoyed a C19 revival sometimes called the *Château* style.

frater, fratery, fraterhouse. Monastic *refectory.

Fréart de Chambray, Roland (1606–76). French exponent of *Classicism, his *Parallèle de l'Architecture Antique et de la Moderne* (Parallel of Ancient and Modern Architecture—1650) was an important source for students of the works of *Palladio, *Scamozzi, *Serlio, *Vignola, and others. It appeared in English in a translation by John Evelyn (1620–1706) as *A Parallel of the Ancient Architecture with the Modern* (1664).

Fréart de Chambray (1650)

Free Classicism. Late-C19 English style, essentially a mixture of *Classical, *Mannerist, *Renaissance, and *Baroque motifs. Examples include John McKean Brydon's (1840–1901) Chelsea Town Hall, London (1885–7), and Government Offices, Whitehall, London (1898–1912), the latter perhaps more *Baroque.

Free Gothic. 1. Revival of *Gothic forms and motifs, freely used in an eclectic mix, as in the Midland Grand Hotel, St Pancras Station, London (1868–74), by George Gilbert *Scott. **2.** Late-C19 style, in which *Arts-and-Crafts and other influences were mingled, creating a non-archaeological, scholarly, yet highly individual style. Examples include work by *Caröe, Temple *Moore, Charles *Nicholson, *Sedding, *Shaw, and others.

Freemason. 1. Craftsman capable of hewing, dressing, and setting *freestones. **2.** Person 'Free' of the Masons' Guilds, i.e. a Freeman. **3.** Itinerant mason, emancipated, so able to travel widely to carry out work, enjoying an élite status among craftsmen. **4.** Member of a secret or tacit Brotherhood organized into groups (Lodges) as a system of morality illustrated by symbols, allegories, and rituals, probably originating in the late C16 in Scotland.

Curl (1991); Knoop and Jones (1949); Stevenson (1988)

freestone. Stone that can be easily cut and worked in any direction, such as a fine limestone or sandstone.

Free style. Late-C19 style in which *Classical, *Domestic Revival, *Gothic, *Queen Anne, and *vernacular themes, motifs, and elements were mingled promiscuously in eclectic compositions, sometimes with additional *Elizabethan or *Renaissance allusions added, as in the works of Philip *Webb (especially 'Clouds', East Knoyle, Wiltshire (1879–91)).

Free Tudor. Style in which late-*Perpendicular, *Tudor, or *Elizabethan forms were mingled in a free manner in the late C19 and early C20, as in the work of Leonard *Stokes.

Frémin, Michel de (*fl.* early C18). French critic, the author of *Mémoires critiques d'architecture* (1702), which argued for a rational approach to design, drawing attention to restrictions suggested by the site, materials, costs, and needs of the users. He stated that the *Orders and rules of *Classicism were of no great significance, and viewed medieval *Gothic buildings such as Sainte-Chapelle and Notre Dame in Paris as more logical works of architecture than Classical buildings such as the Church of St-Sulpice, Paris. He was an influence on *Neoclassicism. *See* Primitive Hut.

Middleton and Watkin (1987); Watkin (1986)

French Order. 1. *Corinthian *capital featuring the cock and *fleur-de-lys. **2.** Type of *Order invented by Philibert de l'*Orme with *bands of sculptured leaves concealing the drums of the *shafts. **3.** Classical Order consisting of three columns set at the points of an equilateral triangular plan (∴), with creepers trailing in spiral forms around the column-shafts (reminiscent of *Solomonic or spiral columns), invented by *Ribart de Chamoust (1783).

Curl (1991); Lewis and Darley (1986)

French Renaissance Revival. C19 revival of C16 styles, exemplars of which are the enlargements to the Louvre, Paris (from 1853).

French roof. *See* roof.

French Second Empire style. Eclectic mixture of *Baroque, *Empire, *François Ier, *Louis Quatorze, *Louis Seize, *Neoclassical, and *Renaissance styles prevalent in the France of Napoleon III (1852–70).

Lewis and Darley (1986)

French window. *Casement-window, also called *croisée*, carried down to floor-level, and opening like two-leafed glazed doors to a garden, *verandah, or terrace.

fresco. Mural painting, carried out while the plaster is still wet and fresh (*buon fresco*). A wall-painting on dry plaster (*secco*) is a poor substitute, for the paint peels and the pigments fade.

fret, frette, fretwork. 1. *Meander, or *band-like ornament of shallow short *fillets touching each other at right angles, called variously angular *guilloche, *Greek key, or *lattice, depending on the type. If some fillets are set diagonally it is called *Chinese fret*, found in *Chinoiserie and *Regency work. **2.** *Trellis-work. **3.** Any interlacing raised work. **4.** Complex patterns of ribs on a *Gothic *vault. **5.** Net-like forms, as in *tracery.

Freysinnet, Eugène (1879–1962). French engineer and pioneer of *reinforced-concrete construction. He designed several bridges, including Plougastel (1924–30), five bridges over the Marne (1947–51), and the Saint-Michel Bridge, Toulouse (1959–62). During the 1914–18 war he designed industrial buildings with reinforced-concrete roofs, followed by two huge parabolic-arched airship-hangars at Orly (1916–24). He developed *prestressed concrete (which he patented in 1928), and published much on his ideas and methods from 1921 until 1954, including *Une Révolution dans les techniques du béton* (A Revolution in the Techniques of Concrete—1935).

Fernández Ordóñez (1978); Günschel (1966); *Journal of the Prestressed Concrete Institution*, 21/5 (1976), 48–71

Frézier, Amédée-François (1682–1773). French military engineer. He is known primarily for his championship of *arcuated rather than *columnar and trabeated structures, and for his perceptive writings on *Gothic architecture, especially his *La Théorie et la pratique de la coupe des pierres et des bois pour la construction des voûtes . . . ou, traité de stéréotomie, à l'usage de l'architecture* (Theory and Practice of the Cutting of Stones and Woods for the Construction of Vaults . . . or, Treatise on Stone-Cutting for Use in Architecture), first published 1738–9. He noted that Gothic structures were accurately conceived, depending upon carefully balanced systems of thrust and counter-thrust, and in his formal analysis he revealed the principles of order and construction in Gothic architecture, although he did not favour reintroducing its forms into contemporary work. He opposed *Cordemoy's views, and can be said to have been a prophet of *Romantic Classicism. He published a book on the *Orders of Architecture in 1738, and designed the high-altar and *baldacchino for the Church of St-Louis, Brest (1742–58—destroyed).

Frézier (1716, 1737–9, 1738, 1747; Hoefer (1857); *Journal of the Warburg and Courtauld Institutes*, 25 (1962), 278–320, 26 (1963), 90–123

Friedman, Yona (1923–). Hungarian-born, he moved to Paris in 1957, and made his reputation as an architectural theorist and visionary designer. With Frei *Otto and others he founded the *Groupe d'Étude d'Architecture Mobile* (*GEAM—Group for the Study of Mobile Architecture), and evolved the notion of the city as a primary permanent infrastructure or framework with a changeable impermanent secondary structure determined by the users and erected using simple technologies. He published several books expounding his ideas, including *L'Architecture Mobile* (1970) and *Alternatives Énergétiques* (1980). He has been considered as contributing to *Experimental architecture, and is associated with *Megastructures and *Mobile architecture.

Cook (1970); Emanuel (1994); Friedman (1970, 1975); Lampugnani (1988)

frieze. 1. Horizontal central *band of a Classical *entablature below the *cornice and over the *architrave, occasionally omitted in the Greek *Ionic *Order. It is a flat unornamented band in the *Tuscan Order; it is broken up into *metopes and *triglyphs in the *Doric Order; and is plain or enriched with sculptured reliefs in the Ionic, *Corinthian, and *Composite Orders. It can have a convex profile (i.e. be *pulvinated*), usually in variations of the Ionic and Composite orders. **2.** *Hypotrachelion of some Ionic Orders resembling a frieze under the *capital. **3.** Strip or *band under the cornice of an internal wall over the picture-rail.

frieze-rail. Intermediate rail below the top-rail of a six-panelled framed door.

Frisoni, Donato Giuseppe (1683–1735). North-Italian architect. He worked in Germany, where he laid out Ludwigsburg, Württemberg (1715–35), with its regular streets and gardens. He remodelled the Ducal Palace (Schloss Ludwigsburg—1714–35) carefully integrating it with the planned town, having taken over from the previous architect, Johann Friedrich Nette (1672–1714). He also designed the Favorite Banqueting Hall at Ludwigsburg (from 1718). He designed the *façade, *gable, dome, upper storeys of the towers, and some altars of the great Benedictine Abbey of Weingarten (1715–24), decisively shaping it to its present form.

Bourke (1962); Hempel (1965); Lieb (1992)

front. **1.** *Façade of a building, as in *garden-front*, but especially the most important façade, e.g. the street-front. **2.** East end of a church.

frontal. **1.** *Antependium, movable or fixed, in front of a church-altar from the table downwards. It is often an embroidered cloth, but can be carved or painted. **2.** Small *pediment or other decorative top to a door-case, *niche, etc., but this usage may be a corruption of *fronton.

Frontinus, Sextus Julius (*c*.35–105). Roman author of a major, clearly written, uncluttered treatise (*De Aquæductibus Urbis Romae*) on the water-supply of the city as well as another on surveying (which survives in fragments). He provided useful descriptions of the *aqueducts, as well as of the methods used to provide the linings for the conduits.

Hornblower and Spawforth (1996)

frontispiece. **1.** Principal *front or façade of a building. **2.** Elaborate entrance, centrepiece, or gateway embellishing the centre of a main façade.

fronton. *Frontal, in the sense of a small *pediment or similar element over a doorway, *niche, *dormer, etc.

frosted. *See* rustication.

frustum. **1.** Slice of a solid body, especially a form produced by cutting through a cone or pyramid between the base and a parallel plane, or between any two planes. **2.** Drum of a column-*shaft.

Fry, Edwin Maxwell (1899–1987). Leading English *Modernist architect. Encouraged by Wells *Coates he gradually abandoned the *Classicism he had absorbed at the Liverpool School under *Reilly, and followed the example of Le *Corbusier, becoming involved in *MARS, the English branch of *CIAM. He established his own practice in London in 1934, demonstrating his final acceptance of *International *Modernism with Sassoon House, Peckham (a block of working-class flats—1934), and two private dwellings that made his name—the Sun House, Frognal Lane, Hampstead (1936), and Miramonte, Kingston upon Thames (1937), where the influence of *Mies van der Rohe's Tugendhat House, Brno, was evident. With Elizabeth Denby (1893–1965) he designed Kensal House, Ladbroke Grove, London (1936–7), a *Modern Movement block of workers' flats, much publicized for its progressiveness by Fry's clients, The Gas Light and Coke Company. Fry helped *Gropius when he arrived in England in 1934, and revised the German's designs for Impington Village College, Cambridgeshire (1936–7), overseeing its construction. Fry was responsible for the MARS Group Exhibition (1937) which promoted CIAM ideas and publicized International Modernism. In 1942 he married Joyce Beverley 'Jane' *Drew with whom he wrote several books, including *Tropical Architecture in the Dry and Humid Zones* (1966). A Fry–Drew partnership was established in 1945, later joined by *Lasdun: among its works were the Passfield Flats, Lewisham (1949), the Riverside Restaurant for the *Festival of Britain South Bank Exhibition site (1951), and numerous projects in Ghana and Nigeria, including University College, Ibadan, Nigeria (1953–9). In 1951 Fry and Drew were appointed to the design team for the building of the new capital of the Punjab at Chandigarh, and were largely responsible for the appointment of Le Corbusier and Pierre *Jeanneret-Gris as architects for some of the major buildings. In later years Fry designed the headquarters of Pilkington Brothers in St Helen's, Lancashire (1959–65), and a crematorium in Mid-Glamorgan, Wales (1966). He wrote *Autobiographical Sketches* (1975).

Brockman (1978); *DNB* (1996); Fry (1944, 1969, 1975); Fry and Drew (1947, 1956, 1964, 1976); personal knowledge

Fuchs, Bohuslav (1895–1972). One of the most talented pupils of *Kotěra, he became leader of the avant-garde in Brno, Moravia, Czechoslovakia, where he settled in 1923, and designed the influential *Modernist Avion Hotel (1927–8). At the Czechoslovak *Werkbund* Exhibition, Brno (1928), he and Josef Štěpánek built a 'triple house' which received acclaim. He designed a house for himself in Brno (1928–9); the Special School for Girls, Brno-Pisarky (with Josef Polášek, 1929–30), held to be a paradigm of the *International Modern style; the Moravská Bank, Brno (1930–1); and the elegant Green Frog Thermal Bath Building, Trenčianske Teplice (1936–7).

Kubinszky (1977); Kuděkka (1966); Leśnikowski (1996)

Fuga, Ferdinando (1699–1781). Florence-born architect. His early works were in Rome, where he designed the ingeniously planned Palazzo della Consulta (1732–7) at the Quirinal, the Palazzo Corsini (1736–54), the handsome, even ebullient, façade of Santa Maria Maggiore (1741–3), and the Church of Sant'Apollinare (1742–8). In 1750 he left Rome for Naples, where his huge Albergo de'Poveri (1751–81), a gigantic poor-house for 8,000 inhabitants, was one of the grandest architectural projects of C18, and one that anticipated the boldest *Neoclassicism of *Boullée, in its sparse Classical dignity. In Naples he also designed the façade of the Chiesa dei Gerolomini, and the Palazzo Giordano (both *c.*1780).

Bianchi (1955); Blunt (1975); Borsi (1975); Kieven (1988); Matthiae (1952); Pane (1956)

fulcrum. A prop, support, or fixed point on which a lever moves, i.e. about which rotation can take place. It is the point beyond which a *cantilever extends into space, its other end anchored on the opposite side of the fulcrum.

Fuller, Richard Buckminster (1895–1983). American inventor of the Dymaxion House (1927), evolved from aircraft and motor-car construction techniques, intended for mass-production, and of the prefabricated modular bathroom (1929—patented 1936). While he was much concerned with the design of cheap, industrialized living-units, he also developed means of covering large areas by means of *geodesic domes constructed on the *space-frame principle, using timber, plywood, metal, *concrete, and other materials. These domes did not require elaborate foundations as their structural integrity was such that they only needed to be anchored to the ground. His US Pavilion at the International Exposition, Montreal, Canada (1967), was an exemplar. This system could enable huge clear-span structures to be made, and therefore whole cities could be roofed over, with considerable possibilities for environmental control and saving of energy. A collection of his somewhat breathless writings was published in 1970.

Fuller (1971, 1975, 1979, 1981); Hatch (1974); Marks (1973); Robertson (1974); Ward and Tomkins (1984)

Fuller, Thomas (1822–98). English architect. He settled in Canada (1857), where he formed a partnership with Canadian-born Chilion Jones (1835–1912). They designed St Stephen's-in-the-Fields, Toronto (1858), in the *Gothic style, before building their grandest work, the Parliament Building, Ottawa (1859–67), the Gothic Revival style of which emphasized the connection between the traditions of Great Britain and British Canada. Only the library-block (reminiscent of a medieval *chapter-house) survives, as the building was destroyed by the tragic fire of 1916 and reconstructed on simpler lines by J. Omar Marchand (1873–1936) and John A. Pearson (1867–1940). Fuller won the competition to design the New York State Capitol in Albany in 1867, later altered by *Eidlitz and *Richardson after Fuller and his then partner Augustus Laver (1834–98) left in disgrace after major problems arose. Fuller and Laver won the competition to design the San Francisco City House and Law Courts (1871), but its construction also went badly, and Fuller returned to Canada in 1881 as Chief Architect of the Department of Public Works, and under his aegis some 140 buildings were designed and erected, including post-offices in a variety of styles, all substantial works of architecture.

Kalman (1994); Roseberry (1964)

Fuller-Clark, Herbert (1869–after 1912). English *Arts-and-Crafts architect. He was responsible for the rich interior of the ground-floor of the *Black Friar* public-house at Blackfriars, London (1905), with Henry Poole (1878–1928). He also designed Boulting's Offices at Riding House Street, a remarkably original and free composition, and 40 and 41a Foley Street, both in London (*c.*1908). He appears to have been in Jamaica, West Indies, in 1912.

Gray (1985)

Functionalism. Theory that good design results from or is identical with functional efficiency, i.e. architecture should be determined by function alone. It is of considerable antiquity, and it was promoted by *Viollet-le-Duc and other C19 architects before Louis *Sullivan coined his 'form follows function' slogan (1896).

Banham (1960); Lampugnani (1988); Richards (1958); Sartoris (1936); Zurko (1957)

Furness, Frank (1839–1912). American architect. He was the dominant figure in Philadelphia's architectural world from 1866, when he settled there, having worked in *Hunt's office. He designed almost 400 buildings, mostly in and around Philadelphia, many of which are memorable, rather fierce, and full of character. For a brief period *Sullivan worked in his office, and some of Furness's inventiveness rubbed off on the young man. Furness's first success was the Philadelphia Academy of Fine Arts (1871–6), in which Continental *polychrome *Gothic is treated with rumbustious zest, demonstrating his penchant for elephantine eclectic motifs that almost puts him in the category of a *Rogue Goth like *Keeling or *Teulon. Influenced by *Ruskin and *Viollet-le-Duc, Furness eagerly absorbed their lessons, and transformed them in works of bold and aggressive creativity. Apart from the synthesis of architectural influences, he adapted detail and geometrical ornament from many published sources, notably the works of Christopher *Dresser, who reached Philadelphia *en route* for Japan in 1876, and returned there the following year with a collection of artefacts for Tiffany & Co. of New York and Londros & Co. of London. A series of banks, designed in the 1870s and 1880s, brought in new clients, and when Allen Evans became his partner in 1881, the firm (now Furness & Evans) enjoyed considerable success, thanks to Evans's sociability. One of the more vigorous products of the partnership was the National Bank of the Republic, Philadelphia (1883–4—demolished), with the front divided by a circular stair-tower expressed on the *elevation, and massive, over-sized detailing reminiscent of *Viollet-le-Duc's and *Burges's work. At the Provident Life and Trust Company, Philadelphia (1876–9, 1888–90, and 1902—demolished), he over-sized lintels and cills, giving the building an overwhelmingly powerful personality. His Library for the University of Pennsylvania (1888–91), intelligently planned and boldly detailed, is perhaps the crowning achievement of his career. It is now the Furness Library.

Handlin (1985); Hitchcock (1977); O'Gorman (1987); van Vynckt (1993)

Furttenbach, Josef (1591–1667). German architect. He prepared a guide-book for Italy (1626) and made his base in Ulm, where he wrote several books on architecture, including *Architectura Civilis* (1628), *Architectura Navalis* (1629), *Architectura Martialis* (1630), *Architectura Universalis* (1635), and *Architectura Recreationis* (1640). He became director of the *Stadtbauamt* (City Building Office), Ulm, and designed the *Brechhaus* (1634), a hospital designed on the latest Italian lines, and a theatre with seats for 1,000 people (1641). He was responsible for introducing *High Renaissance architecture to Germany.

Hempel (1965); Hewitt (1958); Hitchcock (1981); Papworth (1852)

fusarole. Ring of semicircular *section under the *echinus of the Roman *Doric, *Ionic, and *Composite *Orders, often ornamented.

fust. 1. Column-*shaft or *pilaster-trunk. **2.** Ridge of a roof.

Future Systems. Anglo-American architectural consultancy founded by Jan Kaplicky and David Nixon in 1979 to synthesize ecology, popular architecture, and technology in projects such as low-cost shelters, lightweight homes capable of being moved from site to site, and 'green' environmentally friendly office-blocks. They designed crew-quarters for NASA, the US Space Agency, in the 1980s. From 1989 Future Systems has been based in London, with Prague-born Kaplicky (1937–) and London-born Amanda Levete (1955–) as partners.

Pawley (1994)

Futurism. Italian architectural movement founded by Filippo Tommaso Marinetti (1876–1944) in 1909. It exploited images derived from industrial buildings (dams, hydro-electric schemes, silos, etc), *skyscrapers, multi-level highways, and factories with curved ends, and it glorified machines, speed, and violence leading to world war. The chief architectural exponents were Antonio Sant'Elia (1888–1916) and Mario Chiattone (1891–1957), who produced visions of the metropolis of the future, with forms reminiscent of some of those designed by the Vienna *Sezessionists and *Mendelsohn. The movement became closely associated with Fascism, and many of its ideas were absorbed by the avant-garde, notably Russian *Constructivism, Le *Corbusier, *Archigram, and many others.

Banham (1960); Caramel and Longatti (1988); Meyer (1995); Tisdall and Bozzolla (1977)

fylfot. *See* cross.

Gabio, Jean-Michel del *also* **Dalgabio** (1788–after 1828). French architect. A pupil of *Vaudoyer, he subscribed to the rational views held by his master. As Town Architect of St-Étienne, Loire, he taught at the School of Architecture there and designed several buildings, including the Cemetery Chapel, Abattoirs, Exchange (1820), Town Hall and other municipal buildings (1821–8), and the Prison, Corn Market, and Barracks (1823). He also restored the churches of Ste-Marie and St-Thomas.

Papworth (1852)

gable, gavel. Wall (*gable-end*), of a building, closing the end of a pitched roof: its top may be bounded by the two slopes of the roof forming *parged verges* or overhangs with *barge-boards*, or it may be a parapet following (more or less) the slopes of the roof behind. Thus *Romanesque gables were steep, and often ornamented (as at Southwell *Minster, Nottinghamshire), while *First Pointed gables (e.g. Lincoln Cathedral) were extremely steep and pierced with windows to illuminate the space behind. Later medieval gables were usually very steep on domestic architecture, but in churches were almost invariably very slightly sloped, and had *battlemented parapets, often richly decorated. Brick gables are sometimes finished with *tumbling courses, and the *cope or tumbling course is usually prevented from sliding or moving by means of a *gable-springer*, also called *gable-shoulder*, *kneeler*, *skew-block*, or *skew-butt*, at the *foot* of the gable. Not all gables are triangular. Other types of gable include:

crow-stepped: with a stepped top, also called *corbie-stepped*;
Dutch: with curved (often scrolled) sides and a *pediment on top;
hipped: with the top crowned by a small hipped roof;
shaped: with the sides composed of convex and concave curves, usually with steps between them, and a semicircular or segmental top.

Elaborate gables with windows were features of North-European (especially Flemish and German) C16 and C17 domestic architecture, revived in C19.

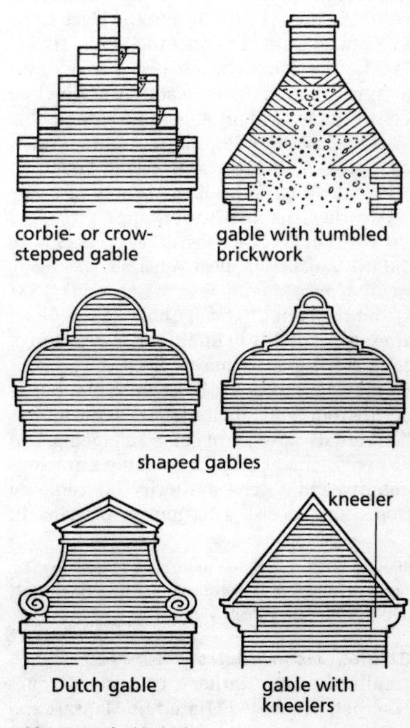

gable. Types of gable. (*JJS*)

gable-entry. *See* entry.

gable-shoulder. *See* gable.

gablet. 1. Small *gable-shaped top to e.g. a *buttress, common in early *Gothic architecture. **2.** Type of roof (*gambrel-* or *gablet-roof*) with a small gable rising up from a hipped roof.

Gabriel, Ange-Jacques (1698–1782). One of the greatest French C18 architects. He trained under his father, whom he succeeded as *Contrôleur* of Versailles (1735) and as *Premier Architecte* and Director of the Academy (1742). He was responsible for some of the most refined Classical buildings of the *Louis Quinze period, continuing and further refining the architectural language established by François *Mansart as in the Grand Pavillon, Fontainebleau (1749). As Architect to the King, Gabriel carried out extensive alterations and extensions to the Royal Palaces, notably the Opera House at Versailles (1761–8). His largest schemes were for the École Militaire, Paris (1750–68), and the Place Louis XV (now Place de la Concorde), Paris (1755–74): in the latter he created two elegant Classical monumental façades (the Hôtel de Coislin (now Crillon) and the Gardemeuble (now the Ministère de la Marine)) with screens set between end-pavilions owing much to *Perrault's east front of the Louvre of a century earlier. His smaller buildings, including the Pavillon Français, Versailles (1749–50), Le Butard, Vaucresson, near Versailles (1749–50), Pavillon de la Muette, near St-Germain (1753–4) and the Petit Château, Choisy (1754–6), all attest to his ability in finding an expression of *noble simplicité*. His masterpiece is the Petit Trianon, Versailles (1761–8), which may partly derive from *Palladianism, but its continuous horizontals, absence of curved elements, and ultra-refinement give the building a gracious nobility and serene authority far removed from the *Rococo, a harbinger, perhaps, of *Neoclassicism.

Blondel (1752–6, 1771–7); Bottineau (1962); Braham (1980); Gallet and Bottineau (1982); Hautecœur (1943–57); Tadgell (1978)

Gabriel, Jacques-Jules (1667–1742). French architect. The father of Ange-Jacques *Gabriel, he assisted *Hardouin-Mansart and succeeded de *Cotte as *Premier Architecte* (1734) and Director of the Academy (1735). He designed several *hôtels in Paris (including the Hôtel Peyrenne de Moras—now Musée Rodin), the Place d'Armes in Rennes, and the Place Royale, Bordeaux (from 1728), which is probably one of his finest achievements.

Hautecœur (1943–57); Tadgell (1978)

Gaddi, Taddeo (*c.*1297–after *c.*1366). Consultant architect to the Cathedral in Florence (where he probably completed *Giotto's *campanile from 1337), he also appears to have been responsible for the rebuilding of the Ponte Vecchio (1333–45). He may also have worked at the Palazzo Vecchio (*c.*1333). **Agnolo Gaddi** (*fl.* second half of C14), presumably Taddeo's son, may have designed several Florentine buildings, but the evidence is confused.

Papworth (1852); Sturgis *et al.* (1901–2); Vasari (1568)

gadroon, godroon. One of a series of *thumb-mouldings* like fat fingers joined side by side on the upper surface of a convex moulding. *Gadrooning* (also *knulled* or *lobed decoration*) means ornamented with convex rods or *lobes*.

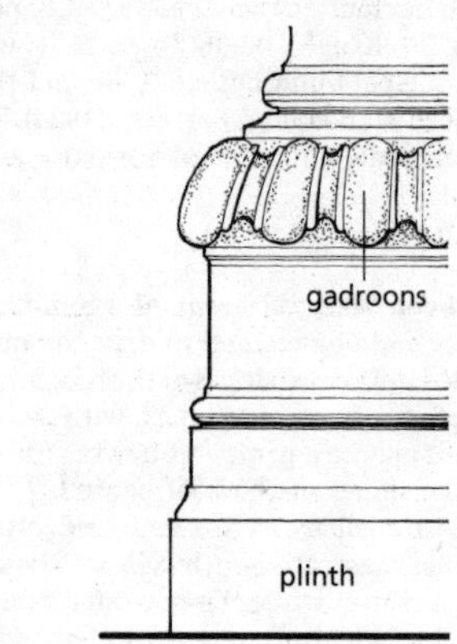

gadroon

gaine. *Pedestal or *herm (but usually the lower part).

Galilee. *Narthex or large room between the exterior and the west end of the *nave where penitents and women were admitted, corpses laid out before burial, and where monks collected before or after processions. At Durham Cathedral the Galilee is divided into *aisles. It is also called a *Paradise.

Galilei, Alessandro Maria Gaetano (1691–1737). One of a number of gifted Italian architects active in the first half of C18 whose work moved away from *Baroque towards *Neoclassicism. He arrived in the British Isles as the chosen architect of the 'New Junta for Architecture', a group of connoisseurs who wished to encourage a Classical style. He designed (1718–19) the palazzo-like country-house of Castletown, Celbridge, Co. Kildare, for Speaker William Conolly (d. 1729)—begun 1722 under the direction of *Pearce—and the *Doric *portico (1718–19) on the east front of Kimbolton Castle, Huntingdonshire, for Charles, 1st Duke of Manchester (*c.*1660–1722). He returned to Italy in 1719, and was responsible for the splendid façade of San Giovanni in Laterano, Rome (1732–6), and for the lavish Corsini Chapel in the same church (1731–3). He also designed the front of the Church of San Giovanni dei Fiorentini (1733–5), Rome.

Colvin (1995); *Country Life*, 145 (1969), 722–6, 798–802, 882–5; Wittkower (1982)

gallery. 1. Large internal passage, often a grand room on the upper floor of an *Elizabethan or *Jacobean house, called *long gallery*, extending the full length of a façade, and used to display pictures and tapestries, for recreation, and as a connecting corridor. Good examples exist at Hardwick Hall and Haddon Hall, both in Derbyshire. **2.** Large room in which pictures, etc., are hung so that they can be viewed to advantage, often with plain walls and illumination from above, hence a building containing such rooms. **3.***Arcade, *passage* or *galerie*, in the French sense, top-lit, with shops on either side, also serving as a pedestrian way from street to street. **4.** Passage leading to a burial chamber (*gallery-grave*) within a *tumulus, the equivalent of the *dromos. **5.** *Tribune over the *aisles in a large church above the *nave *arcade. **6.** *Scaffold* or extra floor for seating in a church placed at the west end and over the aisles. **7.** *Mezzanine at the end of a large hall or room for access between rooms or to accommodate musicians, etc. **8.** Upper level of seating in a theatre. **9.** Passage on top of a *Rood-screen, *choir-screen, or *pulpitum. **10.** Any narrow passage intimately connected with the *fabric of a large building, especially a church. *See* dwarf gallery. **11.** Any *arcaded or *colonnaded long passage, not wide or deep, such as an *ambulatory in a *cloister or a passage leading from one building to another.

gallet. One of several slivers of stone, splinters of flint, spalls, or small pebbles inserted in the mortar-joints of a *rubble wall to fill the gaps between stones and leave less mortar exposed. Hence *galleting* or *garreting*.

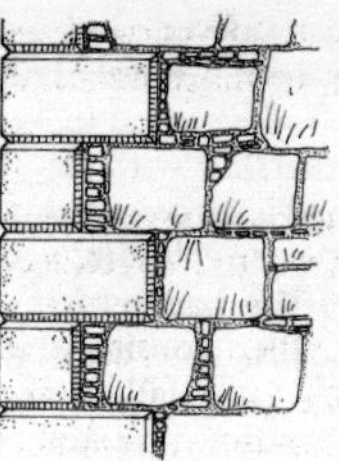

gallet. Galleting with roughly squared rubble and dressed quoins with chamfered joints.

Galli da Bibiena Family. Important Italian *quadratura painters, theatrical designers, and architects. **Ferdinando** (1657–1743) was architect of Sant'Antonio Abbate, Parma (1712–60), and author of *L'Architettura civile . . .* (Civil Architecture . . . —1711), a text that describes various means of creating spatial illusion. **Francesco** (1659–1739), Ferdinando's brother, designed several theatres (none has survived intact), but **Giuseppe** (1695–1747), Ferdinando's son, designed the enchanting *Rococo interior of the *Markgräfliches Opernhaus* (Margrave's Opera House), Bayreuth, Bavaria (1745–8), one of the loveliest auditoria in Europe, completed under the direction of Giuseppe's son, **Carlo Ignazio** (1728–87). Another son of Ferdinando, **Antonio** (1697–*c.*1774), designed the Nuovo Teatro Pubblico (now Teatro Communale), Bologna (1755–63), the Teatro Scientifico, Mantua (1767–9—inspired by *Palladio's Teatro Olimpico, Vicenza), and the Church, Villa Pasquali, near Sabbioneta (1765–84), with its delicate trellis-like stucco-work under the dome. A third son, **Alessandro** (1686–1748), became Court Architect to the Electors Palatinate at Mannheim, in which capacity he designed the *Jesuitenkirche* (Jesuit Church—1738–48), one of the most important *Baroque churches in South-West Germany before it was badly damaged in the 1939–45 war.

Galli da Bibiena (1703–8, 1711); Hadamowsky (1962); Mayor (1945); Muraro and Povoledo (1970); Wittkower (1982)

Gallier, James, sen. (1798–1868). Irish-born architect, he designed the 'Chinese Bridge' at Godmanchester, near Huntingdon, England (1827), and several houses in South Street, Mayfair, London, before emigrating to the USA in 1832 where he worked for a while in New York, formed a short-lived partnership with Minard *Lafever, and published *The American Builder's General Price Book and Estimator* (1833). He settled in New Orleans in 1834, in partnership with Charles B. Dakin, and established a successful practice, designing many important buildings, all in a *Greek Revival style. The partnership broke up in 1836, and Gallier continued on his own, designing the City Hall, New Orleans, La. (1845–50), a handsome building with a Greek *Ionic *portico. He published his autobiography in 1864.

Christovich *et al.* (1972–7); Colvin (1995); Gallier (1973)

gambrel. *See* roof.

Gameren, Tilman *or* **Tylman van** (*c.*1630–1706). Dutch architect and painter, he became the foremost C17 *Baroque architect in Poland, having been invited (*c.*1660) to settle there, and took the surname Gamerski. He designed the villa at Puławy (1671–2), the first with a *pediment on an *Order in Poland. Three rooms designed by him for the pavilion within the Ujazdów area survive in the Łazienki Palace, and he was also responsible for the Church of the Nuns of the Holy Sacrament in Warsaw's New Town (1688–92—one of the most perfect centralized churches in Europe), and for the Bernardine Church at Czerniaków, Warsaw (1687–92—on a Greek-cross plan with octagonal sanctuary). His Krasiński Palace, Warsaw (1688–95), was an outstanding achievement, and incorporated a *Giant Order for the first time in Poland. He designed some 75 buildings in all, including the remodelling of the Palace at Nieborów (1695–7).

Karpowicz (1991); Mossakowski (1973); *Zeitschrift für Kunstgeschichte*, 57/2 (1994), 201–18

Gandon, James (1743–1823). London-born English architect. He was apprenticed to *Chambers and established his own practice *c.*1765. With John Woolfe (d. 1793) he produced the fourth and fifth volumes of *Vitruvius Britannicus* (1767 and 1771), and also published *Six Designs of Frizes* (1767) and two volumes on ornament (1778). He designed Nottingham County Hall (1770), and went to Dublin in 1781 to oversee the erection of his Custom House, the design of which owes much to Chambers's Somerset House in London. His excellent contacts ensured he had plenty of work, including the Four Courts (1786–1802) and the new *portico and screen-wall for the Parliament House (1785–9), Dublin. His architecture was influenced by French *Neoclassicism (through Chambers), but he also admired *Wren. He created some of Ireland's most outstanding buildings.

Colvin (1995); Craig (1969, 1982); Gandon (1969); McParland (1985); Mulvaney (1969); Summerson (1993)

Gandy Brothers. English architects and draughtsmen. **Joseph Michael** (1771–1843), who was the eldest, travelled to Italy (1794–7) with C. H. *Tatham, and became a draughtsman in *Soane's office. Thereafter, even though he established his own practice in 1801, he undertook work for Soane from time to time (especially fine renderings of Soane's designs), and produced a large number of accomplished and eclectic architectural fantasies from 1789 to 1838. He published *The Rural Architect* and *Designs for Cottages, Cottage Farms and other Rural Buildings* in 1805. As an architect, Gandy perhaps lacked the discipline to make a success of practice, but he produced some competent work, including the completion of *Harrison's Courts and Gaol, Lancaster (1802–21), the 'Doric House', Sion Hill, Bath (*c.*1810–12—a remarkable severe Grecian building), and Storrs Hall and Boat House, Windermere, Westmorland (1804–11).

Michael (1778–1862) studied under his brother and became James *Wyatt's assistant before travelling in India and China. He was later employed as a draughtsman by *Wyatville, and, with *Baud and *Britton, published *Architectural Illustrations of Windsor Castle* (1842). **John Peter** (1787–1850)—who changed his name to **Deering** in 1828—was a pupil of James Wyatt, and in 1811–13 travelled to Greece and Asia Minor with Sir William *Gell and Francis Octavius *Bedford for the Society of *Dilettanti: the results of the journey were published as *Unedited Antiquities of Attica* (1817) and Volume III of *Antiquities of Ionia* (1840). He co-authored (with Gell) *Pompeiana* (1817–19), an important work on the excavations. He was regarded as an authority on Greek architecture, and designed the handsome St Mark's Church, North Audley Street, London (1825–8), which was typical of his scholarly approach. Other works by him include the *Tudor Gothic Infirmary, Stamford, Lincolnshire (1826–8), the County Gaol, Cardiff, Glamorgan (1827–32), and houses in South Street, Mayfair, London (*c.*1828–30).

Colvin (1995); Liscombe (1980); Summerson (1963)

Ganghofer, Jörg (d. 1488). German architect, also known as **Jörg von Halspach** or as the

Mason (*Maurer*) **von Polling**. In *c*.1468 he became City Architect of Munich, where he designed and built the *Gothic *Frauenkirche* (Church of Our Lady). He also contributed to the works at the *Rathaus* (Town Hall) in the same city.

Frankl (1962)

gantry. Stand for barrels, shelves, racks, etc., often treated with elaborate architectural enrichment and mirrors, behind a *bar in a public-house.

Garbett, Edward Lacy (d. 1900). English architectural theorist. The author of *Rudimentary Architecture for the Use of Beginners and Students, the Principles of Design in Architecture as Deducible from Nature and Exemplified in the Works of the Greek and Gothic Architects* (1850), he argued that style was linked to construction, and saw that modern methods of building would lead to a new non-*Historicist style.

Architectural Review, 152 (1972), 239–41; *Journal of the Society of Architectural Historians*, 17 (1958), 25–30

Gardella, Ignazio (1905–). Italian architect. His work was steeped in *Rationalism, and he made his name with the Anti-Tuberculosis Dispensary, Alessandria (1936–8). His Regina Isabella Thermal Baths, Lacco Ameno, Ischia (1950–3), and Gallery of Contemporary Art, Villa Reale, Milan (1951–4), were admired for their rigour and clarity. More recently, the School of Architecture, University of Genoa (1990), drew on traditional forms.

Emanuel (1994)

Garden City *and* **Garden Suburb.** The concept of the Garden City was devised in England by Ebenezer *Howard in order to combine the benefits of town and country, and involved the creation of a town built in the countryside with all facilities, places of work, etc. Influenced by the Garden Suburbs (low-density developments that were essentially derived from the *Picturesque tradition of houses in gardens evolved by *Nash and others at e.g. Blaise Hamlet near Bristol), the first Garden City was at Letchworth, Hertfordshire (begun 1903), designed by *Parker and *Unwin. The *vernacular-revival style of houses at Letchworth was influenced by the earlier Garden Suburb at Bedford Park, Chiswick, London (from 1877), and by housing developments and settlements such as Port Sunlight (from 1888) and Bournville, Birmingham (from 1879). The Hampstead Garden Suburb (from 1906) was an excellent example of low-density development in which the *Domestic Revival featured prominently, but it was essentially a dormitory suburb as opposed to a Garden City, which was, in theory, largely self-contained.

Beevers (1988); Benoît-Lévy (1911, 1932); Creese (1967, 1992); Darley (1975); Fishman (1977); Howard (1898, 1902, 1946, 1965); Miller (1989, 1992); Miller and Gray (1992)

garderobe. 1. Place where garments were stored. **2.** Medieval latrine.

gargoyle. Water-spout to take water from a gutter behind a *parapet away from a wall to spew it on the ground. Medieval gargoyles (sometimes mere ornaments rather than spouts) are frequently of stone, imaginatively sculpted in the form of devils, composite animals, etc.

garland. 1. Wreath-like ornament of flowers, leaves, etc. **2.** *Festoon. **3.** Ornamental band around a *Gothic *spire etc.

Garner, Thomas (1839–1906). English *Gothic Revival architect. He was a pupil of the elder *Scott. In partnership (1869–97) with G. F. *Bodley, he made a major contribution to the work of the firm, notably at St Augustine, Pendlebury, Manchester (1870–4), and the exquisite Holy Angels, Hoar Cross, Staffordshire (1872–6). After the partnership was dissolved, Garner carried out works at Yarnton Manor, Oxfordshire, and Moreton House, Hampstead, among other commissions. *Bentley considered him a designer of genius, and there is certainly a warmth in the buildings he erected in collaboration with Bodley that is lacking when the latter worked on his own. He wrote *The Domestic Architecture of England during the Tudor Period* (1908–11), with Arthur James Stratton (1872–1955).

Dixon and Muthesius (1985); Fawcett (1976); *RIBA Journal*, 17 (1910), 305–40

Garnier, Jean-Louis-Charles (1825–98). French architect, a student of *Lebas. During his time as a *pensionnaire* in Rome (1848–54) he visited Greece and Turkey, and seems to have been more enchanted with *Byzantine and other styles than he was with Ancient Greek architecture, although he investigated the Temple of Aphaia at Aegina, largely from the point of view of its colouring in Antiquity. When he returned to Paris he worked for a period under *Ballu, but took on what private commissions he could obtain. He made his name with his designs (won in competition) for the *Opéra* in Paris (1861–75), the most luxuriant building of the Second Empire and of the *Beaux-Arts style, yet one in which the disposition of the main elements is immediately clear from the exterior. Garnier drew his inspiration from the Italian *Renaissance, notably the architectural visions of Paolo Veronese (1528–88), the Venetian painter, while echoes of *Sansovino are detectable. The lavish staircase mingled *Baroque and Venetian Renaissance themes. The *Opéra* was immensely successful and influential, its confident brashness finally laying the drier aspects of French *Rationalism to rest, and setting the agenda for public architectural style in France until 1914. The *Opéra* has tended to overshadow Garnier's many other architectural achievements. His ebullient interpretation of Italian and French Renaissance styles can be seen in a number of his works, including the Cercle de la Librairie (1878–9), 117 Boulevard St-Germain, the Maison Hachette apartment-block at 195 on the same Boulevard (1878–80), and, especially, the Casino, Monte Carlo (1876/8–9). The last, a lushly festive concoction, influenced the style of buildings along the Riviera and in other seaside resorts. In the 1890s, however, the Casino theatre was altered to enable large-scale operatic performances to take place, and in 1897 Garnier protested, in vain, to the architect Henri Schmit (1851–1904) about the changes to his work.

He published his theory of theatre design in *Le Théâtre* (1871) and *Nouvel Opéra de Paris* (1878–81). His reconstruction of the temple at Aegina (complete with *polychrome decorations) was published in *Le Temple de Jupiter panhellenique à Egine* (1884), and he also published works on domestic architecture in *Constructions élevées aux Champs de Mars* (1890) and *L'Habitation humaine* (1892).

Drexler (1977); Garnier (1871, 1878–81); Mead (1991); Steinhauser (1970)

Garnier, Tony (1869–1948). French architect. Born in Lyons, France, he was City Architect there (1905–19) before setting up his own practice. He designed the huge Abattoirs de la Mouche, Lyons (1909–13), with a gigantic top-lit open hall constructed of large steel trusses recalling *Dutert's *Galerie des Machines* in Paris (1889). He is remembered primarily for his unrealized *Cité Industrielle*, a design for a model town of 35,000 people, which he mostly conceived while a student in Rome: it was exhibited in 1904, and published in 1918. While the idea for the *Cité* owed something to English ideas (low density, zoning of function, etc.) and the Utopian notions of Fourier and others, the architecture was to be uncompromisingly non-derivative, most of the structure was to be of *reinforced concrete, and the town-planning principles as taught by the École des *Beaux-Arts were jettisoned. The *Cité Industrielle* influenced Le *Corbusier and other Modernists. Garnier continued to build monuments, schools, and other buildings until the 1939–45 war, but his chief legacy was in forming C20 ideas about architecture and planning.

Garnier (1920, 1932, 1938, 1951); Hitchcock (1977); Jullian (1989); Pawlowski (1967); Veronesi (1947); Wiebenson (1970)

garret. Space in a building beneath the roof-covering and above the uppermost storey of flat-ceilinged rooms, therefore with sloping sides. It may be unlit, or illuminated with roof-lights, *dormers, etc. Not to be confused with an *Attic.

Garrett, Daniel (d. 1753). English builder and architect. A protégé of *Burlington, he acted as clerk of works for many projects before establishing his own practice in *c*.1735, designing numerous schemes in the North of England. He added the steps, balustrades, and outer court to *Hawksmoor's great *mausoleum at Castle Howard, Yorkshire (1737–42), which had Burlingtonian influences from the celebrated Villa at Chiswick. He was not averse to using *Rococo plasterwork or to designing in the *Gothick taste (e.g. Banqueting House, Gibside, Co. Durham (1751)). He brought out the first book ever published on farm-buildings, *Designs and Estimates of Farm-Houses, etc. . . .* (1747). He may have been related to, or had business connections with, James *Paine, who succeeded him as architect in many locations (e.g. Gibside).

Colvin (1995)

garth. 1. Planted enclosure. **2.** Open area surrounded by the *ambulatory of a *cloister.

Gärtner, Friedrich von (1792–1847). German Romantic Neoclassical architect. Alongside von *Klenze, he was the most distinguished practitioner working in Munich in the first half of C19, and had a powerful influence on later generations. He trained under K. von *Fischer in Munich (1808–12), *Weinbrenner in Karlsruhe (1812–13), and *Percier and *Fontaine in Paris (1814), before making the obligatory tour of Italy (1814–17) followed by a visit to The Netherlands and England, where he was fascinated by industrial architecture and the problems of industrialization. He then settled in the Bavarian capital and taught at the Academy. He published his *Ansichten der am meisten erhalten griechischen Monumente Siciliens* (Views of the Best-preserved Greek Monuments in Sicily) in 1819. Not until after he had met the future King Ludwig I (reigned 1825–48) in 1827 was he commissioned to design buildings, starting with the Court and State Library (1827–43) and Ludwigskirche (1829–44) in the Ludwigstrasse, both in the *Rundbogenstil derived from Florentine palazzi and Italian *Early Christian and *Romanesque architecture. Semicircular arched Florentine Renaissance was used for the Institute for the Blind (1835), the Women's Charitable Foundation (1835–9), and the Offices of the Salt Works (1838–43), all in the Ludwigstrasse. At the Salt Works building Gärtner employed exposed brickwork, suggested by buildings in Bologna which he had seen on his Italian tour. He also designed the Universitätsplatz, including the University (1835–40), Georgianum (1835–40), and Girls' School (1837). This rich urban scheme was further embellished by the *Siegestor* (Victory Gate—1843–54), a *triumphal arch derived from the Arch of Constantine, Rome. For the other end of the Ludwigstrasse Gärtner designed the *Feldherrnhalle* (Commanders' Hall—1841–3), a copy of the Loggia dei Lanzi, Florence. This mix of Florentine medieval and Romanesque architecture with Classical elements was not accidental, but was a component of the King of Bavaria's policy to make Munich a cultural and national capital of European significance. Perhaps Gärtner's finest composition was the Pompeian House, Aschaffenburg (1842–6), based on the house of Castor and Pollux, Pompeii, which inventively alludes to Antiquity. He also designed the Villa Ludwigshöhe, near Edenkoben, Palatinate—an Italianate villa that has reminiscences of *Palladio's Palazzo Chiericati, Vicenza—and the *Kursaal*, Bad Kissingen (1834).

When Prince Otto of Bavaria, Ludwig's son, became King Othon of Greece (reigned 1833–62), Gärtner travelled to that country in order to design the new Royal Palace in Athens (1836–41), a Neoclassical building with fine interiors, many in the *Pompeian style. Gärtner also planned part of the new Athens that was to acquire so many distinguished Neoclassical buildings by the *Hansens and others.

Eggert (1963); Hederer (1976); Hitchcock (1977); Nerdinger (1987); Watkin and Mellinghoff (1987)

Gau, Franz Christian (1790–1853). German-born architect. He settled in Paris from 1810, travelled in Italy and Egypt, and published his *Antiquités de la Nubie* (Antiquities of Nubia—1822–7) as well as important work on Pompeii (1829 and 1838). In 1839 he was appointed architect for the distinguished and scholarly *Gothic Revival Church of Ste-Clotilde, Paris (begun 1846), completed by *Ballu.

Gau (1822–7, 1829–38); Middleton and Watkin (1987)

Gaudí y Cornet, Antonio (1852–1926). Catalan architect, he worked all his life in and around Barcelona, where he was part of the *Renaixensa* or renascence of Catalan patriotism, expressed in a strange and wilful architecture drawing on the Islamic and *Gothic monuments of Spain. His first important work was the Casa Vicens (1878–85), Barcelona, a riotously *polychrome villa in which the Gothic and *Moorish themes were overtly expressed. This was followed by *El Capricho* (1883–5), a summer villa at Comillas, near Santander, again uninhibited in its exploitation of geometry and colour. His patron from the early 1880s was the industrialist Güell, for whom Gaudí designed the Palacio Güell in Barcelona (1885–9), an extraordinary and complex building with a street façade reminiscent of a vaguely Venetian Gothic prototype, with parabolic arches and a roof embellished with tile-encrusted chimneys and ventilators. Tile-encrusted too were the serpentine seats of the Parque Güell (from 1900).

From 1883 Gaudí worked on the design of the Expiatory Church of the Sagrada Familia, which started as a Gothic structure, but was gradually transformed into a very free composition owing something to Gothic, but more to an imagination fired by *Art Nouveau tendencies and the structural possibilities of parabolic forms and inclined piers. In order to evolve a structure in equilibrium, Gaudí designed *catenary cord models with weights that transformed the hanging curves into funicular polygonal elements from which the masons could take measurements. Even more startling was the *Modernismo apartment-block, the Caso Batlló (1904–6), a remodelling of an earlier structure, with a façade of bony stone uprights carrying free arched openings over which is a ceramic-faced front from which project mask-like balconies resembling human pelvic bones. More extreme is the Casa Milá (1906–10), a layered pile-up of inwardly inclining stone piers carrying I-beams between which spring tile vaults, the whole capped by a strange, surreal collection of tiled chimneys and ventilators. The internal planning avoids right-angled rooms, and the block is one of the most extraordinary creations of its time.

In, 1998 it was proposed that Gaudí should be beatified, an unusual honour for an architect.

Bassegoda Nonell (1977, 1979); Bohigas (1968, 1991); Casanelles (1968); Collins (1960, 1973); Collins and Bassegoda Nonell (1983); Descharnes (1982); Martinell (1975); Pane (1964); Placzek (1982); Sweeney and Sert (1970); Tschudi-Madsen (1967)

gavel. *See* gable.

gazebo. 1. Garden-house built at the corner of a garden-wall with windows on all sides commanding views. **2.** *Turret, *lantern, or look-out on the roof of a house or a *belvedere or summer-house in a garden commanding an extensive prospect. **3.** Projecting *balcony or window with a view.

GEAM (*Groupe d'Étude d'Architecture Mobile*). Architectural association formed in 1957 by Yona *Friedman, Frei *Otto, and others to investigate possible responses to demographic, social, and technological changes.

Cimaise, 79 (Jan./Mar. 1967), 42–51

Geary, Stephen (*c*.1797–1854). English architect, civil engineer, and inventor. He designed King's Cross, Battle Bridge, London (1830–6, lampooned by A. W. N. *Pugin in 1836, demolished 1845), but is best known as the original architect for Highgate Cemetery, London (from 1837), with its *Egyptian Revival *catacombs. He published *Designs for Tombs and Cenotaphs* (1840) in which he was credited with the founding of other cemeteries in the London area. He is supposed to have designed the first *gin-palace in London (*c*.1829).

Colvin (1995); Curl (1993, 1994); Pugin (1836)

Geay, Jean-Laurent Le (*c*.1710–*c*.1786). French architect. He won the Grand Prix d'Architecture in 1732, and worked at the French Academy in Rome (1738–42), returning to Paris, where he gained a reputation as one of the chief protagonists of *Neoclassicism. With *Knobelsdorff he prepared plans (1747–8) for St Hedwig's Roman Catholic Cathedral Church, Berlin (executed with modifications by *Boumann and *Bühring, 1772–3). After a spell as Architect to Duke Christian Ludwig II (d. 1756) of Mecklenburg-Schwerin from 1748 (where he designed a water-garden at Schwerin and a larger (unexecuted) project for Ludwigslust), he was appointed *Premier Architecte* to King Frederick the Great of Prussia (reigned 1740–86) in 1756, for whom he designed the elegant *Communs* (or service-wing), in the form of semicircular *colonnades flanked by domed and porticoed *pavilions, standing before the *Neues Palais* (New Palace) in Potsdam, realized later to slightly altered designs by *Gontard. After quarrelling with the King in 1763, he seems to have built little, but published etchings of fountains, ruins, tombs, and vases collected as *Collection de Divers Sujets de Vases, Tombeaux, Ruines, et Fontaines Utiles aux Artistes Inventée et Gravée par J.-L. Le Geay, Architecte* (1770), providing a large array of Neoclassical motifs, many of which were based on the work of *Piranesi. Le Geay taught *Boullée, *Moreaux-Desproux, *Peyre, and de *Wailly, and through them spread the Neoclassical gospel.

Jervis (1984); Watkin and Mellinghoff (1987)

Geddes, Norman Bel (1893–1958). American designer, he became identified with the style known as 'streamlining', based on aerodynamics. He designed the General Motors Pavilion at the New York World's Fair (1939), and published *Magic Motorways* (1940). He was responsible for many interiors, designed the Toledo Scale Company Building, Ohio (1929), and produced a scheme of prefabricated housing systems for the Housing Corporation of America (1940).

Geddes (1932, 1940, 1940*a*); Kelley (1960)

Geddes, Sir Patrick (1854–1932). Scots town-planning theorist. He gave emphasis to preliminary surveys and analysis (including sociological research) before any action should be taken. His study of Dunfermline, described by *Abercrombie as the first town-planning report ever undertaken, was published as *City Development* (1904). He organized a huge 'Cities and Town-Planning Exhibition' in London (1910) that was influential, and later he prepared numerous reports on cities in India. His designs included the first hall of residence for students at Edinburgh University (1892) and the Outlook Tower (1895) in the same city.

Boardman (1978); *DNB* (1949); Geddes (1918, 1973); Tyrwhitt (1947)

Gehry, Frank O. (1929–). Canadian-born American architect. He settled in California, where he built several single-family houses from which most traditional forms were expunged. Examples are the Wosk House, Beverly Hills (1982–4), and the Gehry House, Santa Monica (1978–88): in the latter the rectangular form of the house is distorted, a tilted cube emerges from the façade, and layers of the house are peeled away to reveal the structure. He has specialized in using ordinary materials in an unusual way, in destroying structural logic, in playing down the problems caused by weather, and in disdaining gravity as a determinant of form. Other works include the Californian Aerospace Museum, Santa Monica (1982–4), the Iowa Laser Laboratory, Iowa City (1987), the Walt Disney Concert Hall, Los Angeles (1989), the Schnabel House, Brentwood (1990), the University of Toledo Art Building, Toledo, Ohio (1990–2), the EMR Offices, Hanover, Germany (1992), the Vitra Headquarters, Basle, Switzerland (1988–94), the American Center, Paris (1988), the Weisman Center, Venice, Calif. (1988), the University of Minnesota Art Museum, Minneapolis (1989–90), the Minden-Ravensberg Electric Company Offices, Bad Oeynhausen, Germany (1991–5), and the fragmented Guggenheim Museum, Bilbao, Spain (1991–7). In the last building several volumes project from a central mass, and cladding includes titanium (for the gallery spaces), sandstone (public spaces), blue rendered walls (administration), and glass. The much-publicized and praised Guggenheim Museum resembles a large steel sculpture to which cladding has been attached. His work is closely identified with *Deconstructivism.

Bletter (1996); Curtis (1996); Dal Co and Forster (1998); Diamonstein (1980, 1985); van Vynckt (1993)

geison. 1. Block of stone forming part of a Classical *cornice and its subordinate mouldings. **2.** *Cope projecting from a wall. **3.** Horizontal cornice of a *pediment, often with a very deep shelf-like top to permit statuary to be placed in the *tympanum (in the *Parthenon the geison is nearly a metre deep).

Gell, Sir William (1777–1836). English archaeologist and antiquarian. His publications include *Topography of Troy* (1804), *Geography and Antiquities of Ithaca* (1807), *Itinerary of Greece* (1810), *Itinerary of the Morea* (1817), and other works. With John Peter *Gandy (later Deering) he published *Pompeiana* (1817), and later (1832) *Pompeiana: the Topography, Ornaments, etc.*, showing the results of excavations at *Pompeii since 1819. His work is of particular interest because he drew the excavations and artefacts with the aid of a *camera lucida*, so the images are remarkably accurate. His work influenced late *Neoclassicism, the *Neo-Grec style, and many designers, e.g. Owen *Jones.

DNB (1917); Gell and Gandy (1852)

Genelli, Hans Christian (1763–1823). German architect and archaeologist. He was a pioneer of the *Greek Revival, and proposed (1786) a severe Greek *Doric temple as a monument to King Frederick the Great of Prussia (reigned 1740–86), an idea that influenced F. *Gilly when designing his later monument in Berlin in 1797. Genelli's unrealized work was the first example of a Greek Doric temple to be produced in Germany. He also published a reconstruction of the Mausoleum at Halicarnassus in an edition of *Vitruvius (1801), a commentary on Vitruvius (1801–4), and a study of the theatre in Athens (1818). He designed Haus Ziebingen near Frankfurt-on-the-Oder (*c.*1800), one of the most severe of all Neoclassical villas of the period.

Watkin and Mellinghoff (1987)

Genga, Girolamo (*c.*1476–1551). Born in Urbino, where he spent most of his life, his architecture was influenced by *Bramante and *Raphael, notably at the Monte dei Imperiale villa, Pesaro (begun 1530), which in turn influenced the design of the Villa Giulia, Rome. He carried out alterations and additions to the Ducal Palace, Urbino, from 1523, and designed the Churches of Santa Maria delle Grazie, Sinigaglia (from 1535), and San Giovanni Battista, Pesaro (from 1543).

Müntz (1889); Pinelli (1971); Tafuri (1966)

Gentz, Heinrich (1766–1811). German architect, he studied under *Gontard, and was a leading light of spartan Franco-Prussian *Neoclassicism. He became *Hofbaumeister* (Court Architect) in Berlin (1795), and won praise for his entry to the 1797 competition for a monument to King Frederick the Great of Prussia (reigned 1740–86). His severe, uncompromising style was demonstrated in the New Mint, Berlin (1798–1800), which also contained (1799–1806) the *Bauakademie* (Building Academy or School of Architecture), where both Gentz and Friedrich *Gilly, his brother-in-law, taught. At the *Schloss* (Castle or Palace), Weimar, Gentz designed some fine Neoclassical interiors, including the staircase of the East Wing (an early example of the *Greek Revival), the *Festsaal* (Banqueting Hall), Cedar Room, and Falcon Gallery (1800–3). He also designed an extension to the *Prinzessinpalais* (Princess's Palace), Berlin (1810), and (with *Schinkel) the Greek *Doric *mausoleum for the beloved Queen Luise of Prussia (1797–1810), Charlottenburg (also 1810).

Doebber (1911, 1916); Jericke and Dolgner (1975); Watkin and Mellinghoff (1987)

geode. Piece of rock having a *druse*, or cavity lined with crystals, or a rounded hollow ironstone nodule used e.g. in *rock-rash facings.

geodesic dome. Half-spherical *space-frame made of linked lightweight elements arranged in hexagonal figures. It was evolved by Buckminster *Fuller.

Geoffrey de Noiers (*fl. c.*1200). *See* Noiers.

geometric. *See* stair.

Geometrical. *See* stair and tracery.

George, Sir Ernest (1839–1922). English architect. He set up a practice first (1861–71) with Thomas Vaughan (1836–74), then (1876–90) with Harold Ainsworth Peto (1854–1933), and last (1892–1919) with Alfred Bowman Yeates (1867–1944). The firm specialized in expensive domestic architecture, often of brick with *terracotta dressings, in a *Free style derived from North-European late-*Gothic and *Renaissance architecture. Good examples include Harrington Gardens and Collingham Gardens, South Kensington (1880–90), and houses on the Cadogan Estate, London, notably in Pont Street, which gave the style the name *Pont Street Dutch. Herbert *Baker, *Lutyens, and Weir *Schultz all worked in his prestigious office. Other buildings include Golders Green Crematorium (1901–5—in a Lombardic style), and the Ossington Coffee Palace, Newark, Nottinghamshire (1882—a charming building with gables and a variety of *Ipswich window).

DNB (1937); Gray (1985); Hobhouse (1986)

Georgian architecture. English architecture during the reigns of the first four Georges (1714–1830), which saw the rise of *Palladianism, the varied and elegant styles of Robert *Adam, and the fashions for *Rococo, *Chinoiserie, *Gothick, and *Hindoo. It also embraced the early *Gothic and *Greek Revivals, the *Picturesque, *eclecticism, *Neoclassicism, and the taste for *Etruscan and *Pompeian design, as well as the new, unadorned, powerful architecture of the canals, railways, and industry, so it included much that was *Sublime. 'Georgian' often describes a type of C18 and early C19 domestic architecture with unadorned window-apertures, double-hung *sashes, and *door-cases, the latter often with *fanlights, and sometimes given ambitious architectural features such as columns, *pilasters, *entablatures, *pediments, and *consoles.

Clarke (1963); Cruickshank (1985); Curl (1993*b*); Summerson (1980*a*, 1986, 1988, 1993); Summerson *et al.* (1983)

Gerbier, Sir Balthazar (1592–1663). Born in Middelburg, Netherlands, he was descended from French Huguenots, and settled in England in 1616, becoming naturalized in 1629. He became adviser to George Villiers, 1st Duke of Buckingham (1592–1628), for whom he carried out extensive alterations at York House, Strand, London, and New Hall, Essex, in 1624–5 (both destroyed). The Water Gate on Embankment Gardens, London (formerly at York House), has been attributed to him, but *Jones and Nicholas *Stone perhaps have stronger claims. Gerbier appears to have been responsible for introducing Netherlandish *Baroque and *Mannerist themes to England, but these were somewhat overshadowed by the *Palladianism of Inigo Jones. He published *A Brief Discourse concerning the Three Chief Principles of Magnificent Building* (1662) and *Counsel and Advise to All Builders* (1663). The large *Jacobean house at Hampstead Marshall, Berkshire (started 1662, and completed in 1688 by William *Winde), was remodelled by him (destroyed).

Colvin (1995); Croft-Murray and Hulton (1960); Summerson (1993); Williamson (1949)

Gerlach, Philipp (1679–1748). Born in Spandau, Brandenburg, he became head of the State Building Administration in 1720, and laid out the Berlin district of Friedrichstadt (1732–6), complete with square, octagonal, and circular urban spaces. He designed a number of the most important buildings for this quarter, including the Palais von Marschall (1735–6—destroyed), and the *Kammergericht* (Supreme Court—1733–5), where the dominant influence was French. His Garrison Church, Potsdam (1731–5), had the finest *Baroque tower in Northern Germany before its destruction in the 1939–45 war.

Hempel (1965); Reuther (1969); Zucker (1959)

German Order. Type of C18 British *Corinthian *Order, the *volutes replaced by winged lions and unicorns and the *fleuron superseded by the Crown. Its incorporation of Royal emblems led to its association with the House of Hanover, hence its name, but it was also called the *Britannic Order*.

Gesellius, Herman (1874–1916). Finnish architect. He designed (with Eliel *Saarinen) the Helsinki and Viipuri Railway Stations (from 1904). His work was in the *National Romantic style, of which the Villa at Hvitträsk (1901–3) and National Museum, Helsinki (1902–5), both designed with *Lindgren and Saarinen, are good examples, drawing on stylistic aspects from Britain, the USA, and Vienna. His work was also influenced by *Jugendstil tendencies, but his Wuorio Office Building, Helsinki (1908–10), designed independently, was free from both Jugendstil and National Romanticism.

Curtis (1996); Richards (1978); Salokorpi (1970); Smith (1975)

gesso. Plaster of Paris, or gypsum, mixed with glue and whiting (ground chalk) used to prepare a flat surface for painting, or to raise parts of the surface to enhance enrichment of a painting, as in the exquisite late-medieval panels of the *chancel-screen in St Edmund's Church, Southwold, Suffolk. *Gesso duro* is of superior quality, used for making bas-reliefs which are then painted to resemble *terracotta or *faïence.

Nicholson (1835)

Gherardi, Antonio (1644–1702). Italian painter and architect, he remodelled the Avila Chapel, Santa Maria in Trastévere, Rome (*c*.1686), in which space is magically extended in all directions, notably upwards, where angels carry a ring under the *cupola. Even richer is his Chapel of Santa Cecilia, San Carlo ai Catinari (1691–1702). The influences of *Bernini, *Borromini, and *Guarini were strong in his work.

Portoghesi (1970); Wittkower (1982)

Ghiberti, Lorenzo (*c*.1378–1455). Florentine goldsmith, he designed bronze doors for the Baptistery, Florence (1403–24 and 1424–32), and from 1420 was appointed supervisor (with *Brunelleschi and Battista d'Antonio) for the building of the great dome at Florence Cathedral, a position he held until 1436. He claimed in his autobiographical *Commentaries* to have executed the dome with Brunelleschi and at the same salary.

Ghiberti (1947); Heydenreich and Lotz (1974); Krautheimer and Krautheimer-Hess (1956)

Giant Order. Classical *Order of architecture, the *pilasters or columns of which rise from the ground or *plinth through more than one *storey. Also called a *Colossal Order*. *See* Gigantic Order.

gib *or* **jib.** Door with the same continuity of surface as that of the partition or wall in which it is set, i.e. in panelling, to preserve uniformity or symmetry that would be destroyed if the door were to be overtly displayed.

Gibberd, Sir Frederick Ernest (1908–84). English architect, town-planner, and landscape-architect, whose work was influenced by Le *Corbusier, *Mies van der Rohe, and F. R. S. *Yorke. He set up in practice in 1930, designing Pulman Court, Streatham, London (1934–6), a low-cost housing development which established his reputation. After the 1939–45 war, he designed (1949–51) the Lansbury Shopping Centre and Market, Poplar, London (curiously described as 'dainty' by *Pevsner), in the style promoted at the South Bank Exhibition of the *Festival of Britain (1951). He was also appointed (1946) Architect and Planner of Harlow New Town, Essex, a post he held until 1972. Other buildings by him include Heathrow Airport, London (1950–69), Didcot Power Station, Berkshire (1964–8), the Ulster Hospital, Belfast (1953–61), the Roman Catholic Cathedral of Christ the King, Liverpool (1960–7), and Coutts Bank, The Strand, London (1966–75). While most of his work was conventionally *Modernist, the Liverpool

Cathedral design was influenced by *Niemeyer's Cathedral in Brasilia. He also designed the London Central Mosque, Regent's Park (1969–70), and the Inter-Continental Hotel, Hyde Park Corner, London (1968–75).

DNB (1990); Emanuel (1994); Gibberd (1952, 1968, 1970, 1980); Gibberd and Yorke (1978)

Gibbs, James (1662–1754). A Scots Roman Catholic, he turned to architecture in 1704 while training for the priesthood in Rome, and became a pupil of Carlo *Fontana. He returned to Britain in 1709, having acquired a thorough knowledge of Roman *Baroque. Partly through the good offices of *Wren, he became one of the two Surveyors to the Commissioners for Building Fifty New Churches in London in 1713, and designed the masterly St Mary-le-Strand (1714–24), with its powerfully Roman side elevations and modelling recalling works by *Cortona and *Borromini, which made his reputation. With Queen Anne's death in 1714 and the new regime of King George I (1714–27) and Whiggery, Gibbs, who, as a Tory, Scot, and Papist, was suspect, was dismissed. He was then patronized by *Burlington, but shortly afterwards superseded by *Campbell as architect of Burlington House. Campbell's machinations also led to the omission of any mention of Gibbs from *Vitruvius Britannicus*. Through John Campbell, 2nd Duke of Argyll (1680–1743), he was employed to design Sudbrooke House, Petersham, Surrey (*c*.1717–20), and in 1720 designed St Martin-in-the-Fields (1722–6), with its Roman *temple-front, steeple derived from the works of Wren, and galleried rectangular body with two rows of windows, which became the prototype for urban Anglican churches for the next century, being widely copied even across the Atlantic. He also designed Derby Cathedral (1723–5), the *mausoleum at Kirkleatham Church, Yorkshire (1740), and St Nicholas Church West, Aberdeen (1741–55).

His secular buildings were many, and his training in Italy gave him an advantage over his rivals, compensating for his difficulties of birth and religion. He designed the Senate House, Cambridge (1722–30), Fellows' Building, King's College, Cambridge (1724–49), and the Radcliffe Library, Oxford (1737–8). The last owes much to earlier designs by *Hawksmoor, but as completed shows an Italian influence unthinkable in Hawksmoor.

Among other works are the *cupolas at Houghton Hall, Norfolk (1725–8), various *fabriques at Stowe, Buckinghamshire, including the *Gothic Temple of Liberty (1741–4), Temple of Friendship (1739), and Belvedere (1726–8—demolished). He also designed numerous monuments, including several in Westminster Abbey (e.g. Dryden, 1720). Gibbs advertised his work in *A Book of Architecture* (1728—2nd edn. 1739), which spread his influence far and wide, and was probably the most widely used architectural book of C18. He also published *Rules for Drawing the Several Parts of Architecture* (1732—with further editions of 1736, 1738, and 1753).

Colvin (1995); Friedman (1984); Gibbs (1728, 1732, 1747); Harris (1990); Little (1955); Summerson (1993)

Gibbs surround. *Banded architrave around a *door-case, *niche, or window, usually with a massive keystone and *voussoirs breaking into the top of the architrave. Named after *Gibbs (who illustrated and often employed it) the surround was widely used by other C18 and later architects.

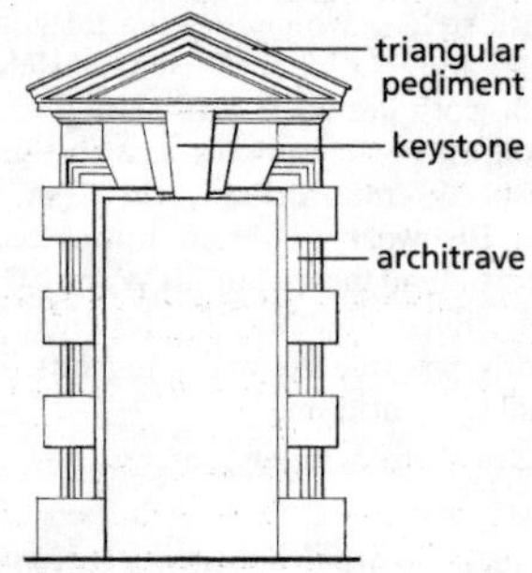

Gibbs surround

Gibson, Jesse (*c*.1748–1828). English architect. He was District Surveyor of the Eastern Division of the City of London (1774–1828), and Surveyor to The Saddlers' Company (from 1774) and Drapers' Company (from 1797). For The Vintners' Company he designed the almshouses, Mile End Road, London (1802—demolished), and for The Drapers' Company he designed many buildings at Moneymore, Co. Londonderry (1818–23), including the Lancasterian Schools, Inn, Court House, and other structures in the village and elsewhere on The Drapers' Company Estate in Ireland.

Colvin (1995); Curl (1986)

Gibson, John (1817–92). Prolific English architect. He trained with *Hansom and Charles *Barry, and most of his work was for bank buildings, using the *Italianate palazzo treatment he had learnt from Barry. Typical of his work was the National Provincial Bank, Bishopsgate, London (1864–5). He designed the impressive Todmorden Town Hall, Yorkshire (1860–75—essentially a Roman temple with an *engaged *Composite *Order set on a *podium) and the *Rundbogenstil Central Baptist Chapel, Bloomsbury, London (1845–8).

Curl (1990); Dixon and Muthesius (1985)

Giedion, Sigfried (1888–1968). Swiss art-historian, he became a powerful advocate of the *Modern Movement, and, with Le *Corbusier, was a leading light in the founding of *CIAM, for which he served as Secretary-General until 1956. His influence was considerable and widespread, and his *Space, Time, and Architecture* (1941) was *de rigueur* in Schools of Architecture from the 1940s. He also wrote *Mechanization Takes Command* (1948), *The Eternal Present* (1964), and *Architecture and the Phenomena of Transition* (1970).

Giedion (1922, 1928, 1954, 1954*a*, 1958, 1962–4, 1967, 1969, 1971)

Gigantic Order. *Tuscan *Order, according to *Scamozzi. Not to be confused with the Colossal or *Giant Order.

Gigliardi, *or* **Gilardi,** *or* **Giliardi,** *or* **Zhilyardi, Domenico** (1788–1845). Italian-born architect, he settled in Moscow with his father, **Giacomo**. They built the Widows' House (1809–18—with its impressive octastyle *portico of unfluted Greek *Doric columns) and the Guardianship Council Building (1823–6—with its portico of *Ionic columns and its vaulted staircase-hall with two tiers of unfluted columns). Probably his finest work is the Lunin House (1818–23), but his largest commission was the reconstruction (1817–19) of *Kazakov's Moscow University, where he replaced the Ionic Order on the entrance-portico with a tougher Greek Doric Order, and remodelled the side-*pavilions to render them more severe. He designed the Khruschev (1814) and Lopukhin (1817–22) Houses, both essentially *Palladian, but with *Empire enrichments. His main importance lies in the bold *Neoclassicism he promoted, and in his influence on Russian architecture that, to some extent, paralleled that of *Gilly in Prussia. He altered Kazakov's Music Pavilion of the Equerry on the Kuzminki Estate (1819), and completed Kazakov's and *Quarenghi's Suburban Palace, begun in 1788, in the 1820s.

Hamilton (1983); Middleton and Watkin (1987)

Gil de Hontañon Family. *See* Hontañon.

Gilbert, Cass (1859–1934). American architect. He designed the Minnesota State Capitol, St Paul, Minn. (1895–1903), a vast *Beaux-Arts pile with a dome based on *Michelangelo's at San Pietro, Rome, which made his reputation, gaining him commissions to design the US Custom House (1901–7) and the Florentine *palazzo of the Union Club (1902), both in New York. He later built a *Gothic *skyscraper on West Street, New York (1905–7), the trial run for the huge Woolworth Building, New York (1911–13), that was clad in light-weight fire-resistant *faïence. The pyramidal composition of the New York Life Insurance Building (1925–8) was crowned with a vaguely Gothic spire. His later buildings were nearly all Classical.

Handlin (1985); Kaufmann (1970); Pierson and Jordy (1970–86)

Gilbert, Émile-Jacques (1793–1874). French architect. A pupil of *Durand, he became an expert on the design of hospitals, asylums, and prisons. He was influenced by *Hittorff, as can be seen in his severe Greek *Doric chapel with *polychrome interior at the enormous lunatic asylum (*Asile d'Aliénés*) at Charenton (1838–45—consisting of a series of elongated blocks linked by colonnaded walkways). His buildings were the expression of humanitarian reform and its administration. They include the *Préfecture de la Police*, Île de la Cité, Paris (1862–76), and the impressive *Hôtel-Dieu* (hospital) near by, designed with his son-in-law, Arthur-Stanislas Diet (1827–90), and built 1864–76.

Middleton and Watkin (1987)

Gill, Irving John (1870–1936). American architect. He trained under *Sullivan and worked with *Wright before setting up on his own in 1893. His early buildings owed much to the *Arts-and-Crafts, *Shingle, and *vernacular styles, but he began to experiment with *concrete construction from 1907, perfecting a system by 1912, and by 1915 inventing an insulation core to concrete panels to elminate condensation and heat-loss. His Laughlin House, Los Angeles (1907), employed concrete construction, while his Dodge House, Los Angeles (1914–16—demolished), and Horatio West Court, Santa Monica (1919), were in a crisp, cubic style owing nothing to period precedent, and were remarkably advanced for their time, showing that *Modernism was manifest in the USA at least as early as in Europe, and in Gill's case his buildings look as though they ought to date from the 1920s, so he was unquestionably a pioneer of Modern Architecture and of building using concrete.

Gebhard (1965); Kamerling (1979); Kaplan (1987); McCoy (1975); Pierson and Jordy (1970–86); Starr (1973)

Gilles le Breton (d. 1553). *See* Breton.

Gilly, David (1748–1808). German architect. His French Huguenot forebears established the family in Pomerania in 1689. He was successful in the new State Examination in architecture (1770), and eventually became Director of Building in Pomerania, founding a private architectural academy in Stettin (now Szczecin) in 1783. In 1788, with *Erdmannsdorff and *Langhans, he was called to Berlin by King Friedrich Wilhelm II of Prussia (reigned 1786–97) to help establish a new style of architecture removed from the Francophilia of Frederick the Great (reigned 1740–86). He founded the Building School in Berlin (1793), re-established as the *Bauakademie* in 1793, which became one of the most important architectural schools in Europe, numbering *Schinkel, von *Klenze, *Weinbrenner, *Engel, and *Haller von Hallerstein among its most illustrious students. Gilly also founded *Sammlung nützlicher Aufsätze und Nachrichten, die Baukunst betreffend* (Collection of Useful Essays and Reports concerning Architecture), one of the first German architectural journals, published in Berlin from 1797 to 1806. He designed Schloss Paretz (1796–1800) and Schloss Freienwalde (1798–9), both near Potsdam, and Vieweg House, Brunswick (1800–7), all in a severe Neoclassical style.

Gilly (1797, 1797–8, 1797–1806); Lammert (1964); Watkin and Mellinghoff (1987)

Gilly, Friedrich (1772–1800). Son of David *Gilly, he learned practice and theory with his father in Stettin (now Szczecin), and in 1788 settled in Berlin. He developed his skills while also acting as Inspector in the Royal Buildings Department aged only 16, where he worked under *Erdmannsdorff and *Langhans. His own designs began to experiment with stereometrically pure forms and primitivist, elemental architecture, while his studies (1794) of the medieval Marienburg (now Malbork, Poland) fortress in East Prussia led to the beginnings of a conservation programme for that *Sublime building as well as to a growing appreciation of the *Backsteingotik of North Germany.

In 1796 the Academy of Fine Arts, Berlin, announced a competition for a monument to King Frederick the Great (reigned 1740–86), and in 1797 Gilly's design, set in a re-ordered Leipzigerplatz, and incorporating a powerful monumental gate, sarcophagi-lids, *obelisks, and a *Doric temple (suggested by a design of 1786 by Hans Christian *Genelli) on a massive *podium, was exhibited. With this seductive image, Gilly won the admiration of younger architects and affected many of them, including von *Klenze, *Schinkel, *Strack, and *Stüler. Gilly was profoundly influenced by French theories and buildings (notably those of *Bélanger), and was closely associated with his brother-in-law, *Gentz, whose Mint (1798–1800) had a *frieze designed by Gilly. His later unrealized designs, such as those for a National Theatre, Berlin, with its primitive Doric portico, *Diocletian windows, and clearly defined bare masses, were among the most advanced of the period, influenced by *Legrand and *Molinos, and eventually influencing *Semper in turn. His stark (also unrealized) designs for a Stonehenge-like *mausoleum are unprecedented in their stripped severity. He was Professor of Optics and Perspective at the new *Bauakademie* (Building Academy or School of Architecture) until his untimely death.

Gilly (1994); Gilly and Frick (1965); Hederer (1976*a*); Herrmann (1977); Horn-Oncken (1981); Kaufmann (1952); Middleton and Watkin (1987); Oncken (1935); Simson (1976); Watkin and Mellinghoff (1987)

Gilman, Arthur Delavan (1821–82). American architect. Much influenced by contemporary trends in England and France, he first rose to prominence with a series of articles in the *North American Review* in the 1840s. A friend of Charles *Barry, he may have influenced E. C. *Cabot in the designs for Boston's Athenaeum (1846–9), and indeed was an Associate in Cabot's firm in 1857. His best known work is Arlington Street Church, Boston (1859–61—derived from *Gibbs's Church of St Martin-in-the-Fields, London), a late example of Gibbs's potent and long-lived influence, especially in the USA. He was prominent in early moves to conserve Boston's architectural heritage. His Equitable Life Assurance Company Building, New York (1867), was one of the world's first *skyscrapers. He collaborated with Gridley James Fox Bryant (1816–99) on the design of Boston City Hall (1861–5), where the architectural style of the French *Second Empire was employed with much élan.

Dictionary of American Biography (1943); Hitchcock and Seale (1976); Whitehill (1968)

Gimson, Ernest William (1864–1919). Leicester-born English architect and designer, he was an admirer of William *Morris and worked (1885–8) with *Sedding. Gimson formed an association with the *Barnsley brothers (1893), and moved to Sapperton, Gloucestershire, where he designed the village hall in a C17 gabled style, as well as The Leasowes Cottage (*c*.1901) and various artefacts. He was a convinced follower of the *Arts-and-Crafts movement: his houses include Inglewood, Ratcliffe Road (1892), and The White House, North Avenue (1897), both in Leicester, and Stoneywell and Lea Cottages, Charnwood Forest, Leicestershire, two remarkable essays in the *vernacular cottage style. He designed the Hall and War Memorial Library, Bedales School, Steep, Hampshire, after 1919.

DNB (1994); Dixon and Muthesius (1985); Gray (1985); Jervis (1984)

gingang, gin-case, gin-house, gin-rink. Farm-building, circular or polygonal on plan, containing a horse-engine to operate the threshing-mill. Also called *mill-course*, *mill-gang*, or *mill-rink*.

gin-palace. Ornate public-house evolved in Britain in the 1830s, featuring plate- and mirror-glass, a *bar, *gantry, showy elaborate fittings, and illuminated by gas-flares and lights. Thompson & Fearon's gin-palace, Holborn, London (1829–31), seems to have been among the earliest, and Stephen *Geary had a reputation as a designer of the type.

Girouard (1979*a*); Loudon (1834)

Ginsburg, Moisei Yakovlevich (1892–1946). Born in Minsk, he was a pioneer Russian *Constructivist and engineer. The author of *Ritm v Arkhitektura* (Rhythm in Architecture—1923) and *Stil' i Epokha* (Style and Epoch—1924), among other works, he founded with *Vesnin the influential Soviet architectural journal *Sovremenia Arkhitektura* (Contemporary Architecture) in 1926. From 1927 he specialized in mass-housing, building experimental blocks in Moscow (1928–9) and Sverdlovsk (1928–9). He was involved in avant-garde planning, notably the proposal for a linear Green City, Moscow (1930), and remained active in architecture and planning until his death.

Ginsburg (1982); Khan-Magomedov (1975, 1986, 1987); Kopp (1970); Lissitzky (1970); Shvidkovsky (1970)

Giocondo, Fra Giovanni (1433–1515). Verona-born architect and engineer, he made his name with an early woodcut-illustrated edition of *Vitruvius' *Ten Books of Architecture* (1511). He succeeded *Maiano as supervising architect at Poggioreale, Naples, completing it in 1485, and from 1495 to 1505 he worked for the Kings of France, designing the Pont Notre Dame over the Seine (*c*.1499–1512—destroyed). On his return to Italy he designed the fortifications at Treviso (1509–11) with rounded (rather than canted) gun-platform bastions. He worked with da *Sangallo and *Raphael on St Peter's, Rome, from 1514.

Croix (1972); Fontana (1988); Heydenreich and Lotz (1974); Vagnetti (1978)

Giorgio di Martini, Francesco di (1439–1501/2). Sienese architect, theorist, and engineer. His architectural tracts of 1475–92 and his version of *Vitruvius were influential in C16. He proposed a complete theory for *Renaissance architecture based on that of Antiquity, argued for the placing of altars in centralized church-plans, gave a rational explanation of ecclesiastical symbolism, and invented fortifications that were a defence against gunfire. On moving to Urbino (1476) he contributed (possibly the refined *loggia) to the design of the Palazzo Ducale (1476–82) and other works. In 1484 he designed Santa Maria della Grazie al Calcinaio, near Cortona (finished 1516), an accomplished harmonious Renaissance building; (probably) the Palazzo degli Anziani, Ancona (completed 1493—destroyed), and the severe Palazzo del Comune, Iesi (completed 1503). Many other buildings have been attributed to him, including Santo Spirito, Siena (1498–1509), which has a barrel-vault penetrated by *lunettes, but his architectural career is not well documented. *Vasari held him in high regard.

Croix (1972); Giorgio di Martini (1967); Heydenreich and Lotz (1974); Papini (1946); Rotondi (1950–1, 1970); van Vynckt (1993); Weller (1943)

Giotto di Bondone (*c*.1266–1337). Florentine painter and architect. He probably designed the *Gothic *campanile beside the Cathedral (from 1334), completed by *Gaddi, *Pisano, and *Talenti. Only the first stage of the *base or *socle appears to have been completed by the time of his death.

Gioseffi (1963); Trachtenberg (1971); White (1987)

Girault, Charles-Louis (1851–1932). French *Beaux-Arts Classical architect. His work is among the most splendid, festive, and rich late-C19 and early C20 Neo-*Baroque architecture. He designed the Petit Palais, Paris (1897–1900), for the 1900 International Exhibition, the triumphal Arc du Cinquantenaire, Palais du Cinquantenaire, Brussels (1905), and the Musée du Congo Belge, Tervueren, Belgium (1904–11). One of his richest and most colourful designs is the tomb of Louis Pasteur (1822–95) in the Pasteur Institute, Paris (1896), embellished with *mosaics in the *Early Christian style.

L'Architecture, 46 (1933), 253–62; Baedeker, *Belgium* (1931)

girder. Beam built up for additional strength to support a floor, road, etc. A *plate-girder* is constructed of plates of rolled iron or steel, consisting of vertical *webs* with flat plates fixed to the upper and lower parts.

Gisel, Ernst (1922–). One of the most successful Swiss architects of the second half of C20, he has designed a wide variety of buildings. Interested in flexibility and technology, his Park Theatre, Grenchen (1949–55), demonstrates this. Working from first principles, his compositions are often made up of colliding and disparate forms, notably in the Reformed Church, Effretikon, Zurich (1956–61). Other works include the Gisel House and Studio, Zurich (1972–5), the High School, Liechtenstein (1969–73), and Town Hall and Centre, Fellbach, near Stuttgart, Germany (1979–82). His new building inserted in a courtyard at the University, Zurich (1991), is clearly expressed as such, floating above the space, and his *Regierungsgebäude* (Government Offices), Vaduz, Liechtenstein (1992), is a comprehensive development.

Blaser (1982); Emanuel (1994)

Giuliano da Maiano (1432–90). *See* Maiano.

Giulio Romano (*c*.1499–1546). Italian architect, he was one of the major figures of the late Renaissance. Called Giulio Pippi *or* Giuliano Giannuzzi, he was born in Rome, became the pupil of *Raphael, and trained amidst the *High *Renaissance reverence for Classical antiquities. He completed Raphael's Villa Lante al Gianicolo, Rome (1523), and designed the Palazzo Maccarani, Piazza Sant'Eustachio, Rome (*c*.1520–4), where his originality was demonstrated in the ambiguous capital-less *pilasters and the windows that rest uneasily on a string-course. His bending of the rules of Classical propriety led him to extremes, and he became one of the most interesting Mannerist architects, especially after he settled in Mantua (1524), where he worked for Prince (later Duke Federigo II) Gonzaga (1519–40).

His extraordinary Palazzo del Tè (1525–32), Mantua, one of the first Mannerist buildings, is a single-storey building around a courtyard. The vestibule of the main entrance mixes elements from the Basilica of Maxentius, Rome, and a plan taken from *Giocondo's edition of *Vitruvius (1511). In the courtyard finely finished ashlar is contrasted with deliberately 'unfinished' work, and on two elevations some of the *triglyphs are designed to appear to 'drop' from the *entablature, giving a feeling of instability, probably suggested to the architect by Roman ruins in which the frieze had broken up: such a ruin (the Basilica Aemilia in the *Forum Romanum*) had been drawn by *Sangallo. The garden-front is composed of overlaid *serlianas and the garden itself is enclosed, terminating in a semicircular pilastered *colonnade. The plan is a clever mixture of an *Antique villa and Raphael's Villa Madama (itself influenced by Roman *thermae*).

As a result of his success with the Palazzo del Tè, Giulio was ennobled and presented with a house in Mantua, on the façade of which (1538–44) he reworked the themes of the House of Raphael (Palazzo Caprini) by *Bramante. His Cortile della Mostra (or Cavallerizza) in the Palazzo Ducale, Mantua (1538–9), employs tortured, engaged, irregular spiral columns on pedestals carried on chunky rusticated consoles, while the rusticated façades have arches that are not quite semicircles, nor are they segments of circles. It is a distortion of themes from Bramante's House of Raphael and the Colosseum, with allusions to the *Solomonic columns in San Pietro, Rome. Such preoccupations with Antiquity and with the *gravitas* of the great Bramante suggest that, far from acting with a disregard for *Classicism, as some have suggested, Giulio was scholarly and witty, drawing on many sources to give his buildings authority.

He prepared designs for the market-square in Vicenza from 1542: the Palazzo Thiene, Vicenza, with its overt quotations from Ancient Rome, may owe more to him than to *Palladio, who completed it. He restored the Abbey of San Benedetto al Polirone, near Mantua (1540–6), and remodelled the Cathedral, Mantua (1544–6), with double aisles incorporating massive *Corinthian columns. The *Residenz* (Seat of the Court), Landshut, Bavaria (begun 1536), was influenced by his architecture, but was not by him. He was also a famous painter: his *frescoes in the Vatican (Stanza dell'Incendio di Borgo of 1514–17) and at Mantua helped to make him celebrated in his lifetime.

Frommel (1973); Frommel *et al.* (1989); Hartt (1958); Heydenreich and Lotz (1974); *Journal of the Society of Architectural Historians*, 30 (1974), 267–93; Kaufmann (1995); Verheyen (1977)

Giurgola, Romualdo (1920–). *See* Mitchell & Giurgola.

glacis. 1. Steep slope of ground falling from one level to another in a landscaped garden. **2.** The same, sloping from the bottom of a fortress wall or from the top of a trench, so that it presents a clear view for defenders and gunners. **3.** Sloping upper surface of a *battlement, *cope, *cornice, or *parapet to promote the descent of rainwater.

Gläserne Kette. German group (*The Glass Chain*) founded by Bruno *Taut in 1919, including *Gropius and *Scharoun, that favoured fundamental forms derived from crystals, shells, and plants, with glass, steel, and concrete as materials. Several members later joined the *Ring.

Boyd Whyte (1982)

Glasgow School. Name given to contemporary architects and designers in Glasgow in the 1890s and early 1900s, especially C. R. *Mackintosh, Margaret (1865–1933) and Frances (1874–1921) Macdonald, and Herbert McNair (1868–1953). They employed calligraphic elements of *Art Nouveau, including the *femme-fleur, *rose-ball, and long, flowing tendrils, earning them the collective title of 'Glasgow Spook School'. They exhibited on the Continent, and had a considerable impact on the *Sezession, especially in Vienna, where *Hoffmann particularly admired their work. In architecture Art Nouveau was synthesized with aspects of *vernacular buildings and the English *Arts-and-Crafts movement, perhaps best seen at Mackintosh's Hill House, Helensburgh, and the Willow Tea Rooms, Sauchiehall Street, Glasgow.

Lewis and Darley (1986); Steele (1994)

glass. Semi- or fully transparent hard, brittle, lustrous material made by igneous fusion of silica (usually sand) with an alkaline sodium or potassium salt and added ingredients, such as lime, alumina, lead oxide, etc. Colour may be added by the addition of metallic oxides. It appears to have come into use for glazing the windows of grander buildings during the Roman Empire. In the Middle Ages coloured and painted glass, used in small pieces because of the difficulties of manufacturing larger expanses, was set in lead *cames, commonly in churches: surviving examples (e.g. Chartres Cathedral, King's College Chapel, Cambridge, and Fairford, Gloucestershire) are among the glories of medieval art. Glass used for domestic architecture also had to be set in lead cames or in *sashes subdivided by glazing-bars.

Types of glass include:

acid-etched: glass treated with wax or a similar substance into which a design is cut, then subjected to action by hydrofluoric acid which etches into the unprotected surface to create a design. Much used from Victorian times for decorative windows for public-houses, etc.;

armourplate: thick toughened polished plate glass used for large windows, doors, etc.;

broad: glass blown in cylinders which are then cut open and flattened, called *muff* or *window-glass*;

Crown: blown from a glass tube into a bulb then opened and spun rapidly, the outer part thin, clear, and lustrous, but the centre or hub of thick glass (*bottle*, *bullion*, or *bull's eye*) largely opaque and never used for good work. It was the commonest type of glass found in British domestic architecture until the mid-1830s;

flint: made from white sand, potash, nitre, red lead, and ground window-glass, used where refraction is desired, as on decorative *altar-pieces, etc.;

ground: with a rough surface, usually ground, to make it lose transparency;

iridescent: with a coating to give it the appearance of the surface of a soap-bubble with rainbow colours;

jealous: glass roughened to allow the light to pass through, but with a loss of transparency;
laminated: toughened glass made by a laminated process;
plate: poured on to a cast-iron table, rolled with a heavy roller, and polished on both sides;
sheet: made by blowing into a cylinder of glass which increases in diameter before being cut lengthways, flattened, and polished. It was a refinement of *broad* or *muff* glass, invented by Messrs. Chance, near Birmingham (1832–8), and had a finish comparable to that of *Crown* glass, but cheaper and capable of being made in larger sheets, thus making glazing-bars in sashes obsolete;
stained: coloured throughout its mass or with the colour applied or *flashed*. Crimson is produced with oxides of copper or tin, blue with cobalt, purple with manganese, and other colours using various combinations of chemicals;
toughened: thick glass made in a variety of ways;
wire: with a network of wire enclosed within it to improve security.

Glass was used as a major component of external walls first in *conservatories and greenhouses, and then as a roofing material with glazing-bars of wood and, later, of iron. The evolution of railway termini and major exhibition buildings (such as *Paxton's Crystal Palace, London (1851)) developed the architectural possibilities of glass, leading to *Dutert's *Galerie des Machines*, Paris (1889). Glazed *curtain-walls were suggested by conservatories and used by architects such as *Ellis, later developed by *Behrens, *Gropius, and others. Later developments have included solar-reflective and tinted glass for large expanses (as in Norman *Foster's work), while blocks of glass, glass tubes, and glass slabs have been used widely in C20.

Blaser (1980); Hix (1996); Kohlmaier and Sartory (1986); Koppelkamm (1981); Korn (1967); Papworth (1852); Parissien (1997); Sturgis *et al.* (1901–2); Wigginton (1996)

glazed brick. Brick with a ceramic coating or finish applied then fixed in a second firing. Earthenware so treated can be brightly coloured and useful in decorative *façades. *Polychrome glazed bricks were used in Assyrian and Babylonian architecture, notably at Khorsabad (C8 BC), Babylon itself (C6 BC), and Susa (C5 BC).

Andrae (1925); Brunskill (1990); Lloyd and Müller (1986); McKay (1957)

gloriette. *Eye-catcher, or *pavilion in a garden from which views may be enjoyed. A good example is *Hohenburg's *Gloriette* at Schönbrunn, Vienna (1775).

Gloucester, John of (*fl.* *c.*1245–d. 1260). English mason. From 1255 he carried out works at the Tower of London and Windsor Castle, Berkshire, and at the same time appears to have been in charge of the works at Westminster Abbey. He was a man of some substance, and his activities and responsibilities ranged far and wide, especially in regard to the Royal Castles, for he was involved at Oxford, Winchester, Gloucester, Porchester, and Salisbury Castles.

Harvey (1987)

glyph. Channel, *flute, or groove, normally vertical, as in a *Doric *frieze, where the blocks framing *metopes are the *triglyphs so called because they each have two glyphs and two half-glyphs.

glyptotheca. Sculpture-gallery.

Gočár, Josef (1880–1945). Czech architect. He experimented with *Cubism and with attempts to introduce a National style into his work, as at the Czechoslovak Legion Bank, Prague (1921–3), heavily decorated with cubes, cylinders, and squares, giving the building a backward-looking appearance for its date. His High School, Hradec Králové (1924), owed much to stripped *Classicism and to Dutch brick architecture, but his Czechoslovak Pavilion at the *Exposition International des Arts-Décoratifs*, Paris (1924–5), attempted to use the architectural language of *Modernism, somewhat uneasily mixed with decorative elements. With the Baba Hill housing development exhibition of the Czechoslovak Werkbund, Prague (1932–3), however, Gočár's work became more *International *Modern in style (Mauk and Glücklich Houses, 1932), and he went further with the Sochor House, Dvůr Králové (*c.*1934). He was also an influential teacher.

Benešová (1971); Gočár (1930); Leśnikowski (1996)

Goddard, Henry Langton (1866–1944). English architect from Leicester, the son of Joseph *Goddard. His most distinguished work was the basilican Church of St James the Greater, London Road, Leicester (1899–1914), a splendidly noble essay in the Italian *Renaissance style. He designed many of the charming *Arts-and-Crafts *vernacular-revival houses at Horninghold, Leicestershire

(1903–14), and was responsible for Gilroes Cemetery and Crematorium, Leicester (1901–2). He also designed the Carnegie Library, Kettering, Northamptonshire (1903), and many commercial buildings in the Midlands of England.

Gray (1985)

Goddard, Joseph (1839/40–1900). English architect, the most distinguished of the *Gothic Revival working in Leicester in the second half of C19. He designed the *polychrome brick church of St Andrew, Tur Langton, Leicestershire (1865–6), the Leicestershire (now Midland) Bank, Granby Street, Leicester—in a Continental Gothic polychrome manner—(1872–4), the ornate Gothic clock-tower, Leicester (1868), and numerous houses and other buildings in and around Leicester.

Pevsner, *Buildings of England, Leicestershire and Rutland* (1984)

Godde, Étienne-Hippolyte (1781–1869). French architect. As Chief Architect of the City of Paris (1813–48) he carried out many restorations and alterations, notably at the Hôtel de Ville (with Jean-Baptiste-Ciceron Lesueur (1794–1883)) in 1840–5. He improved the layouts of the Cemeteries of Père-Lachaise (where he designed the mortuary-chapel) and Montparnasse (1840–5). Other works by him include the Chapel and Seminary, St-Sulpice (1820–8), and the basilican Churches of St-Pierre-du-Gros-Caillou (1822), Notre-Dame-de-Bonne-Nouvelle (1823–30), St-Denis-du-Saint-Sacrement (1823–35), and St-Pierre-de Chaillot (1823–35), all in Paris.

Baedeker: *Paris* (1904); Middleton and Watkin (1987)

Godefroy, Maximilien (*c*.1765–1840). French architect, he, with *Latrobe, introduced the latest *Neoclassicism to the USA, where he settled (1805–19). Most of his work was in Baltimore, and included the *Gothic St Mary's Chapel (1806–8), the Commercial and Farmers' Bank (1812–13—destroyed), the Unitarian Church (1817–18), and the Egyptianizing Battle Monument (1810–27), the first civic monument to be erected in the USA. He returned to France by 1827 after a few years (from 1819) in London (where he designed the Roman Catholic Charities School, Clarendon Square (1825–6—demolished)). His later works included the *Hospice des Aliénés*, Nayenne (1829–36), and a new wing to the Palais de Justice (1829–33) and the Préfecture (1831–40), both at Laval. His work was influenced by *Blondel and *Durand.

Alexander (1974); Carrott (1978); Colvin (1995); van Vynckt (1993)

Godwin, Edward William (1833–86). English architect from Bristol, he designed a huge round-arched warehouse at Merchant Street there (1862) and the impressive Jacob Street Brewery (1865), before moving to London. He made his name with Northampton Town Hall (1861–4), an accomplished Anglo-Franco-Italian *Gothic Revival essay influenced by *Ruskin, and designed the less substantial Congleton Town Hall, Cheshire (1864–6), also Gothic. His Dromore Castle, Co. Limerick, Ireland (1867–70—ruined), was a composition of exceptional quality, not only archaeologically correct, but beautifully composed and partly designed for defence (the period of building was the time of the Fenian disturbances). He also designed Glenbeigh Towers, Co. Kerry (1867–71—burnt 1922), a fortress-house in the form of a massive keep; St Baithan's Church, St Johnstown, Co. Donegal (1857–60), in the *First Pointed *Gothic style, the interior of which was unsympathetically modernized in the 1970s; and the 'Twelve Apostles', a handsome terrace of houses at Castlerock, Co. Londonderry (1882).

From *c*.1870 he became closely associated with the *Aesthetic movement, designing 'art furniture', much of it inspired by Japanese work, that was very influential, especially in Germany, Austria, and the USA. Thereafter his architecture became very free, and almost style-less, including several remarkable houses in Chelsea, among them the White House, Tite Street (1877–9—demolished) for James Abbott McNeill Whistler (1834–1903), and 44 Tite Street (1878). He designed the interiors of Oscar Wilde's (1854–1900) house at 16 Tite Street (1884).

Aslin (1969); Bence-Jones (1988); Harbron (1949); Hitchcock (1977)

Godwin, George (1813–88). English architect. The son of the architect **George Godwin** (1789–1863), he is remembered as the editor of *The Builder* (1844–83), the most important British architectural journal of C19. He also practised with his brothers **Sidney** (1828–1916) and **Henry** ((1831–1917), designing the Churches of St Mary Boltons (1849–50), St Luke's, Redcliffe Square (1872–4), and St Jude's, Courtfield Gardens (1870–9), as well as Redcliffe Mansions (1871), all in

Kensington, London). He published important papers on concrete (1835), *The Churches of London* (1838–9), and *History in Ruins* (1853). He was also active in attempts to ameliorate the housing conditions of the working classes.

DNB (1917); Dixon and Muthesius (1985); Hobhouse (1986)

Goff, Bruce Alonzo (1904–82). One of the most idiosyncratic architects the USA has ever produced, he was originally influenced by F. L. *Wright, but gradually evolved a free style of his own, using materials such as coal, ropes, objects retrieved from rubbish-dumps, and bits of aircraft in his buildings. At the Bavinger House, Norman, Okla. (1950–5), he created a spiral *rubble stone wall enclosing a volume illuminated from above, while subsidiary volumes were hung from a central mast. Other works include the Ford House, Aurora, Ill. (1948–50), the Price House, Bartlesville, Okla. (1956–8), the Glen Harder House, near Mountain Lake, Minn. (1970–2), the Barby House, Tucson, Ariz. (1974–6), and many other projects, all of which are treated with great individuality and verve. He was identified by Peter *Cook as an exponent of *Experimental architecture.

J. Cook (1978); P. Cook (1970); Futagawa (1975); Long (1977, 1988); Mohri (1970); Murphy and Muller (1970); Saliga and Woolever (1995)

Gogel, Daniel (1927–). *See* Fehling.

Golden House. *Domus Aurea* built by Nero to designs by *Severus (mid-C1) on the Esquiline Hill, Rome. It was a large palace with landscaped gardens, and was remarkable for its complex plan with rooms of different geometrical shapes, many of them *vaulted and sumptuously decorated.

Sturgis *et al.* (1901–2)

golden rectangle. The basis of standardized sizes of components, in which the ratio of width to length is the same as that of length to the sum of the width and length.

golden section. Proportion resulting from the division of a straight line into two parts so that the ratio of the whole to the larger part is the same as the ratio of the larger part to the smaller. It is constructed in geometry by creating a rectangle (2 × 1) composed of two squares of 1 × 1 each: from the diagonal add or subtract one (1) and place the remainder against the longer side of the rectangle. It is expressed as $(\frac{1}{2}(\sqrt{5} \pm 1)$, and produces a ratio of approximately 5 : 8. It was held to be divine by Luca Paccioli (*c.*1445–*c.*1514) in *Divina Proportione* (1509), but the idea is probably much older, for the proportional relationships have been known at least since Euclid's time (*c.*325–*c.*250 BC).

Ghyka (1976); *OED* (1972); Osborne (1970)

Goldfinger, Ernö (1902–87). Hungarian-born British architect. He worked in Paris before settling in England in 1934. His best-known building is 1–3 Willow Road, Hampstead, London (1937), a terrace of three houses, one of which was his own dwelling, the first *Modern Movement house to be taken over by the National Trust, and opened to the public in the 1990s. With Charlotte *Perriand he designed the French Government Tourist Offices in London at 66 Haymarket (1958) and 177 Piccadilly (1963). Other works by him include the office-building at 45–6 Albemarle Street (1956), Alexander Fleming House, Elephant and Castle (1962–6), Rowlett Street Housing, St Leonard's Road (1966–78), and Edenham Street Housing, Cheltenham Estate, Golborne Road (1968–9), all in London.

Emanuel (1994)

Goldie, Edward (1856–1921). English Roman Catholic architect. Born in Sheffield, Yorkshire, he was articled to his father, **George**, and designed several important buildings for the Church, including (with Charles Edwin Child (1843–1911)) St James's, Spanish Place, London (1885–90), a very serious and learned work of the *Gothic Revival, much influenced by Continental precedents, and especially by *Pearson. Other works include Ashorne Hill House, Newbold Pacey, Warwickshire (1895–7), St Alban's, Larkhill, Blackburn, Lancashire (1900–1), and St Mary's Priory, Storrington, Sussex (1904). He was in partnership with his son, **Joseph** (1882–1953), until his death.

Dixon and Muthesius (1985); Gray (1985)

Goldie, George (1828–87). English architect. The grandson of Joseph *Bonomi, he was articled to, and later a partner of, the Roman Catholic architects *Hadfield & *Weightman in Sheffield before setting up his own practice from 1861, later joined by Charles Edwin Child (1843–1911) and his son **Edward**. His Churches include the heavy *Gothic Revival St Wilfred's, York (1862–4), the Abbey of St Scholastica, Teignmouth, Devon (1863), St Augustine's, Stamford, Lincolnshire (1864), the Assumption, Kensington Square, London (1875), and St Joseph's, Durban, South Africa (1878), in all of which Continental, rather than English, Gothic was dominant.

Dixon and Muthesius (1985); Eastlake (1970)

Golgotha. 1. Burial-ground or *charnel-house. **2.** Carved timber base of a *Rood from which the figures of the Crucified Christ, St Mary, and St John rise, as at St Andrew's Church, Cullompton, Devon.

Gollins, Melvin, Ward. Partnership established in London in 1947 by Frank Gollins (1910–), James Melvin (1912–), and Edmund Ward (1912–98). In 1957 it built offices at New Cavendish Street, London, incorporating one of the most sophisticated and early uses of *curtain-walling in England at the time. Castrol House, Marylebone Road, London (1960), was an even more confident example of curtain-walling. The firm designed additions to the Royal Opera House, Corent Garden, London (1975), and was responsible for many office-buildings throughout its history. GMW Partnership (as it became) designed the St Enoch Centre, Glasgow (1988), and the headquarters of Barclays Bank, Lombard Street, London (1993).

Emanuel (1994); Gollins, Melvin, and Ward (1974)

Golosov, Ilya Aleksandrovich (1883–1945). Moscow architect, he worked with his brother, **Pantelemon** (1882–1945), who was first a Neoclassicist and then a Constructivist. Ilya's Zuyev Workers' Club, Moscow (1926–8), was one of the bolder essays in *Constructivism. When the Stalinist era insisted on 'Socialist Realism' and a return to *Neoclassicism, Ilya designed in that mode. He was in charge of the redevelopment of Moscow from 1933, responsible for numerous housing-schemes and public buildings. His work includes the Theatre, Minsk (1934), the Hydro-Electric Station, Gorky (1936–40), and collective housing on the Yausky Boulevard, Moscow (1934). His monumental designs for battle memorials of the 1940s were firmly traditionalist, drawing on historical allusions: a good example was the Monument to the Defence of Moscow (1941—unrealized).

Council of Europe (1995); Kopp (1970); Shvidkovsky (1970)

Gómez de Mora, Juan (*c.*1580–1648). Leading C17 Spanish architect. He designed the Church of the Royal Convent of the Encarnación, Madrid (1611–16), an important prototype for monastic churches in Spain and Latin America. He planned the *Clerecía*, or Jesuit College and Church (Seminario Conciliar), Salamanca (1616–1750), based on *Il Gesù*, Rome. Much influenced by the work of Juan de *Herrera, he succeeded his uncle, **Francisco de Mora** (d. 1611) as architect to the Escorial and as Court Architect. He worked on the development of the Plaza Mayor, Madrid (1617–19), designing the ground-level arcades and façades.

Norberg-Schulz (1986); Papworth (1852); van Vynckt (1993)

Gondoin *or* **Gondouin, Jacques** (1737–1818). French architect. Trained under J.-F. *Blondel, he designed the École de Chirurgie (now École de Médecine), Paris (1769–75), one of the most important and influential buildings of French *Neoclassicism. It has an *Ionic *colonnade on the street elevation with a *triumphal arch in the centre leading to a court off which is a semicircular top-lit anatomy-theatre roofed with a coffered hemi-dome resembling that of the *Pantheon, Rome. The severe *Antique character of the theatre was the precedent for the Chamber of Deputies, Paris (1795–7), and for aspects of *Latrobe's interiors in the Capitol, Washington, DC. With Jean-Baptiste Lepère (1761–1844) he designed the Colonne Vendôme, Paris (1806–10), based on *Antonine and *Trajanic exemplars.

Braham (1980); Middleton and Watkin (1987)

Gontard, Karl von (1731–91). German architect. He studied under J.-F. *Blondel in Paris, and travelled in Italy (1754–5) with the Margrave and Margravine of Bayreuth. In 1763 he was called to Potsdam by the Margravine's brother, King Frederick the Great of Prussia (reigned 1740–86), and became Director of the Building Office with responsibility for all Royal buildings. He built the *Communs* in front of the *Neues Palais* (New Palace) to designs by Le *Geay, as well as the Temples of Friendship and Antiquity (1768–70) in the Sanssouci Park. With G. C. *Unger he designed the handsome Brandenburg Gate, Potsdam (1770), a Frenchified version of the *triumphal arch reminiscent of the works of *Perrault. His most important contributions to the urban fabric of Berlin were the tall cupolas he added to the French Protestant Church (by Louis Cayart of 1701–5) and the New Church (by Giovanni Simonetti to designs by Martin Grünberg of 1701–8) in the *Gendarmenmarkt*, while his works at the *Marmorpalais* (Marble Palace), Potsdam, and Berlin *Schloss* (both 1786–9) were influenced by English *Neoclassicism.

Borrmann (1893); Hempel (1965); Watkin and Mellinghoff (1987); Zieler (1913)

González de León, Teodoro (1926–). Mexican architect, he entered into partnership with the Polish-born Mexican architect Abraham Zabludovsky (1924–). Their State Auditorium, Guanajuato, Mexico (1991), is typical of their powerful, sculptural work, with the forms clearly expressed, and they have built up an impressive practice.

Emanuel (1994)

Goodhart-Rendel, Harry Stuart (1887–1959). English architect of great originality, whose best work is arguably the *Art Deco Hay's Wharf Building, Tooley Street, London (1929–31). Other works include Broad Oak End, Bramfield, Hertfordshire (1921–3), and the Churches of St Wilfrid, Brighton, Sussex (1932–4), St John the Evangelist, St Leonards, Sussex (1946–58), Holy Trinity, Dockhead, Bermondsey, London (1957–9), and Our Lady of the Rosary, Marylebone Road, London (1958). He was an accomplished writer, publishing *Nicholas Hawksmoor* (1924), *Vitruvian Nights* (1932), and *English Architecture since the Regency* (1953). He coined the term *Rogue Goths.

Architectural Design, 49/10–11 (1979), 44–51; *Architectural Review*, 138 (1965), 259–64; *DNB* (1971); Goodhart-Rendel (1924, 1949, 1989)

Goodhue, Bertram Grosvenor (1869–1924). American architect. In partnership with *Cram from 1892 to 1913, they designed All Saints' Church, Ashmont, Mass. (1892–1941), a robust and scholarly work that established their reputation, consolidated with the US Military Academy, West Point, NY (1903–10), and St Thomas's Church, New York (1906–13—a distinguished work of the *Gothic Revival). In 1913 the partnership was dissolved, and Goodhue designed the Cathedral of the Incarnation, Baltimore (1911–24—partly influenced by Giles Gilbert *Scott's Anglican Cathedral, Liverpool, which Goodhue saw being built in 1913), St Vincent Ferrer Church, New York (1914–19), and St Bartholomew's Church, New York (1914–18), the last in a *Byzantine *Romanesque style influenced by *Bentley's Westminster Cathedral, London. Probably his greatest work is the Nebraska State Capitol, Lincoln (1920–32), in a free style, vigorously composed, and with a central tower reminiscent of *skyscraper designs. He designed the National Academy of Sciences, Washington, DC (1919–24), in a simplified Classical style.

Baker (1915); Handlin (1985); Oliver (1983); Whitaker (1925)

Goodwin, Francis (1784–1835). English architect. He established a practice in 1819 and designed a number of churches in a late-*Gothic style as well as several Classical buildings of which the *Greek Revival Town Hall at Manchester (1822–5—demolished) was the most accomplished. He published *Domestic Architecture* (1833–4), reissued in 1835 as *Rural Architecture*. His unrealized designs for a 'Grand National Cemetery' for London (1830) were in a spectacular and monumental Greek Revival style.

Architectural History, 1 (1958), 60–72; Colvin (1995); Curl (1993*b*)

gopura. Tall, ornate *gateway to a Hindu temple-enclosure.

gorge. 1. Shallow part-elliptical *cavetto. **2.** *Neck (*gorgerin) of a column-shaft at the top, as in the *Tuscan and *Roman *Doric *Orders. **3.** *Cyma. **4.** *Apophyge.

gorge-cornice. Large *cavetto as used on Ancient Egyptian *pylon-towers as a *cornice.

gorge-cornice. Gorge-cornice of Ancient Egyptian and Egyptian Revival type, ornamented with *winged globe* and rearing *uraei*, with torus beneath.

gorgerin. Collarino, *gorge, *hypotrachelium, or *neck separating a *capital from a *shaft, such as the *frieze-like collar above the *astragal and below the *annulets and *echinus of the *Roman *Doric *Order.

Gospel side. North side of an altar or a church.

Göthe. *See* Eosander von Göthe.

Gothic. Architectural style, properly called *Pointed, that evolved in Europe (starting with France) from the late C12 until C16, even lingering until C17 in some places (e.g.

Oxford). As its correct name suggests, it is the architecture of the pointed arch, pointed rib-*vaults, *piers with *clusters of *shafts, deep *buttresses (some of the *flying* type), window-*tracery, *pinnacles, *spires, *battlements, and a soaring verticality. While Ancient *Egyptian and *Greek architecture is *columnar and *trabeated, Gothic is *arcuated, giving an impression of dynamic thrust and counter-thrust. Certain elements of Gothic church architecture, such as the *triforium, *clearstorey, and *Orders found in doorways, had developed in *Romanesque architecture. Pointed rib-vaults had been used in Burgundy and Durham, while half-arches or half-barrel-vaults used as buttresses were exploited by English and French Romanesque builders. Fully developed Gothic, however, was not a matter of eclectic motifs being gathered together: it was a remarkably coherent style of logical arcuated forms in which forces were expressed and resisted, and non-structural walls were dissolved into huge areas of glazed window.

*First Pointed (Early English) Gothic was used from the end of C12 to the end of C13, though most of its characteristics were present in the lower part of the *chevet of the Abbey Church of St-Denis, near Paris (*c*.1135–44). Windows were first of all *lancets, but later contained elementary tracery of the *plate* type (*see* tracery), then got larger, divided into *lights by means of *Geometrical* *bar-tracery. Once First Pointed evolved with Geometrical tracery it became known as *Middle Pointed. *Second Pointed work of C14 saw an ever-increasing invention in bar-tracery of the *Curvilinear*, *Flowing*, and *Reticulated* type, where the possibilities of the *ogee form were fully exploited in canopies, tracery, and *niches, culminating in the *Flamboyant style (from *c*.1375) of the Continent. Second Pointed was relatively short-lived in England, and was superseded by *Perpendicular (or *Third Pointed*) from *c*.1332, although the two styles overlapped for some time. On the Continent, however (where Perpendicular Gothic was unknown), lace-like patterns of tracery evolved, and churches of great height were erected with highly complex vaulting, as at the Church of St Barbara, Kutná Hora, Bohemia (1512). The Gothic style embraced a complete system of dynamic structure with developed geometries and daring experiments with stone, especially in the final flowering of *Flamboyant* in Central Europe. Although Gothic was superseded by a revival of interest in the language of *Classicism from the *Renaissance period, it enjoyed a widespread and scholarly revival in C19. *See* Gothic Revival.

Branner (1965); Frankl (1960, 1962); Grodecki (1986); Osborne (1970); Parker (1850); Rickman (1848); Viollet-le-Duc (1875)

Gothic cornice. C18 *Gothick *cornice or *frieze consisting of a series of interlacing pointed arches not carried on anything, but with *pendants hanging from where the arches would normally spring. A curious C20 use of the motif was under the cornice of Ideal (Palladium) House, Great Marlborough Street, London (1928), by Raymond *Hood.

Gothic Revival. Conscious movement that began in England to revive Gothic forms, mostly in the second half of C18 and throughout C19. It was, arguably, the most influential artistic movement ever to spring from England, and from it grew the *Domestic Revival, the *Arts-and-Crafts and *Aesthetic movements, and many other developments in art and architecture. *Hawksmoor's All Souls' College, Oxford (1716–35) and western towers at Westminster Abbey (1734), were among the earliest *Georgian examples, followed by *Gibbs's *Gothick Temple, Stowe, Buckinghamshire (1741–4), Sanderson *Miller's work (1740s), and *Keene's designs (1760s). Miller and Keene both advised Sir Roger Newdigate, Bt. (1719–1806), about the Gothic work at Arbury Hall, Warwickshire (*c*.1750–2), which, with Horace *Walpole's (1717–97) Strawberry Hill, Twickenham (*c*.1760–76), made the style fashionable, and it was adopted in Germany, France, Italy, Russia, America, and elsewhere. While many 'Gothic' churches were built in the early C19, they were often unconvincing in archaeological terms, and do not resemble medieval buildings: the Friedrich Werdersche Kirche, Berlin (1821–31), by *Schinkel, is one example, and in England there were many simple Georgian *Commissioners' churches with rudimentary *Perpendicular or *First Pointed windows that only purported to be Gothic. What might be called the archaeological phase of the Gothic Revival in which real medieval buildings provided the precedents for design began in England with *Rickman and *Pugin, and was triggered partly by *Ecclesiology and partly by the popular success of the Palace of Westminster by *Barry and Pugin (from

1836). From that time a growing body of scholarship informed the Gothic Revival, and the ambitious programme of Victorian church-building was served by architects thoroughly immersed in the style. The building industry, manufacturers, and craftsmen had to be trained too, for all manner of artefacts, carvings, stained-glass, and the like had to be provided. In France the main protagonist of the Revival was *Viollet-le-Duc, whose restoration of Sainte Chapelle, Paris (1840–9—with *Duban and *Lassus), had such an influence on Pugin. Indeed, the very considerable C19 programme of restoration of medieval buildings throughout Europe (especially in the UK, France, and Germany), prompted partly by national pride and partly by the religious revival after the *Enlightenment experiment, had a powerful impact, encouraging scholarship, archaeological investigations, accurate surveys of extant buildings, and the production of illustrated books. Experience gained in restoration increased confidence in the use of the style for modern buildings. Very soon the Revival was embraced throughout Europe and America. The C19 main Gothic Revival in Britain began with a resurrection of Perpendicular; turned to *Second Pointed (English first, then Continental) in the 1840s, largely due to the arguments of Pugin and the Ecclesiologists who perceived C14 Gothic as fully developed with advantages over both the 'undeveloped' *lancet style and the 'decadent' Perpendicular; then embraced Continental Gothic, especially that of Italy, where the possibility of structural *polychromy had attracted many commentators, the most effective of which were *Ruskin and *Street. The 'High Victorian' Gothic Revival of the 1850s and early 1860s was thus often coloured, incorporating polished granites, marbles, many-coloured brick- and tile-work, becoming more free in expression and less archaeologically derivative in the process. As with *Neoclassicism's search for the *primitive early forms, Gothic Revivalists also sought a more robust and 'primitive' Gothic, and so turned to the powerful First Pointed Burgundian precedents of C13, giving birth to the *muscular Gothic of *Brooks, Street, and *Pearson. George Gilbert *Scott drew on eclectic elements of Continental Gothic for his Midland Grand Hotel, St Pancras, London (1868–74), *Waterhouse also paraphrased European precedents for Manchester Town Hall (1868–76), and there were many other examples. Towards the end of the British and American Revivals *Bodley and other architects once more used Second Pointed sources, and Perpendicular was also restored to favour, as in *Sedding's Holy Trinity, Sloane Street, London (1888–90). Other major buildings of the Revival include *Gau's and *Ballu's Ste-Clotilde, Paris (1846–57), von *Schmidt's *Rathaus* (Town Hall), Vienna (1872–83), *Steindl's Hungarian Parliament Building, Budapest (1883–1902), Giles Gilbert *Scott's Liverpool Anglican Cathedral (from 1902), and *Cram's Cathedral of St John the Divine, New York (begun 1911).

Aldrich (1994); Andrews (1975); Baur (1981); Clark (1974); Clarke (1958, 1969); Curl (1995); Dixon and Muthesius (1985); Eastlake (1970); Frankl (1960, 1962); Germann (1972); Hersey (1972); Macaulay (1975); McCarthy (1987)

Gothic Survival. Continuation of Gothic elements in architecture in C16 and C17, of which St-Eustache, Paris (1532–1640), the Chapel at Lincoln's Inn, London (*c.*1619–23), the Cathedral of St Columb, Londonderry (1628–33), and the Hall staircase, Christ Church, Oxford (*c.*1640), are important examples.

Curl (1986); Eastlake (1970)

Gothick. C18 style only vaguely based on archaeologically correct Gothic, and more connected with a taste for the exotic, so really a branch of *Rococo frivolity. It was largely associated with Sanderson *Miller's work, with Horace *Walpole's Strawberry Hill (1750–70), and especially with Batty *Langley's pattern books, *Ancient Architecture Restored* . . . (1741–2) and *Gothic Architecture* . . . (1747). Gothick, sometimes curiously intermingled with *Chinoiserie motifs, was an aspect of *Georgian *eclecticism, and was often treated with great delicacy, so it was pretty, ideal for interiors, *fabriques in gardens, and built *ruins. It was a significant part of the *Picturesque. Although originating in England, Gothick influenced architecture in Germany (the Gothic House at Wörlitz (*c.*1773)), Poland (the *fabrique at Arkadia (1797)), and in other European countries.

Curl (1993*b*); Clark (1974); Cruickshank (1985); Davis (1974); Eastlake (1970); Langley (1747); Macaulay (1975); McCarthy (1987)

Gough, Alexander Dick (1804–71). English architect. Partner of R. L. *Roumieu, he designed the curiously sinister Milner Square, Islington (*c.*1840), in a stripped, vaguely

Classical style. His son, **Hugh Roumieu Gough** (1843–1904), designed St Paul's, Hammersmith, London (1882–7—with J. P. *Seddon), and, his masterpiece, the *Gothic Revival St Cuthbert's, Philbeach Gardens, Kensington, London (1884–8).

Curl (1995); Dixon and Muthesius (1985)

Gowan, James (1923–). Scots architect, born in Glasgow. He entered into partnership with *Stirling (1956–63) with whom he built the much-admired Engineering Building, University of Leicester (1963—which triggered the departure of British architecture from the influences of Le *Corbusier and *Mies van der Rohe), and the sub-*Brutalist housing at Ham Common, Richmond, Surrey (1958). His career as an independent architect has been marked by work that is difficult to classify. His large house at West Heath Road, Hampstead, London (1964–8, with Frank Newby), had its devotees, and was finely detailed.

Curtis (1996); Emanuel (1994)

Graham, James Gillespie (1776–1855). Scots architect. He had a large practice, specializing in *castellated country-houses and *Gothic churches. The former were essentially symmetrical, with a nod to the *Picturesque by means of round towers to one side, but had plainish exteriors, although interiors frequently had impressive Gothic treatments. Among his houses Achnacarry, Inverness-shire (1802–5), Armadale Castle, Skye (1814–22), Duns Castle, Berwickshire (1818–22), and Dunninald, Craig, Angus (1823–4), may be mentioned. His best Gothic works are probably the R. C. Cathedral, Glasgow (1814–22), and the*steeple at Montrose, Angus (1832–4—based on a precedent at Louth, Lincolnshire). His most distinguished Classical essays are Gray's Hospital, Elgin, Morayshire (1812–5), the layout and design of the Moray Estate, Edinburgh New Town (1821–8—with the polygonal Moray Place), and a street-plan for Birkenhead, Cheshire (1825–8), of which only Hamilton Square appears to have been developed according to his designs (1825–44). He was probably the first to use the term *Baronial (1813, 1846).

Colvin (1995); *DNB* (1917); Macaulay (1975); Youngson (1966)

Grandjean de Montigny, Auguste-Henri-Victor (1776–1850). French architect. He settled in Brazil as part of the artistic mission introduced by King John VI (1816–26) to elevate public taste. A Neoclassicist, he studied with *Percier and *Fontaine, and was architect to Napoleon's brother, Jérôme (King of Westphalia from 1807 to 1813), until 1808. He designed the Roman Arch (1816), Customs House (1819–26), and many eclectically *Classical buildings in Rio de Janeiro. The first Professor of Architecture at the Imperial Academy of Fine Arts in Rio, he introduced a *Beaux-Arts curriculum there. He wrote *Recueil des plus beaux Tombeaux exécutés en Italie pendant les XVe et XVIe siècles* (1813), and *Architecture de la Toscane* (1815).

Castedo (1969); Morales de Los Rios Filho (1942)

Grand Tour. Obligatory Continental journey, especially taking in Italy and France, regarded as an essential part of the education of a young gentleman from the British Isles in the C18. It encouraged a sophisticated taste among the aristocracy and landed gentry, led to the formation of many great collections, gave much work to the compilers and publishers of guide-books, and promoted the cause of *Palladianism and *Neoclassicism. It frequently lasted a year or more.

Osborne (1970)

grapevine. *See* trail.

Grassi, Giorgio (1935–). Italian architect, born in Milan, he was influenced by the work of *Rossi and *Tessenow, and has been classified as an Italian *Neo-Rationalist. His student residential hostel, Chietí (1976), in the form of a long colonnaded street, recalls the C19 proposals of *Weinbrenner for the Lange Strasse, Karlsruhe (1808), in its severely stripped *Classicism. His works include *La Costruzione logica dell'architettura* (1967) and *Architettura: lingua morta* (Architecture: Dead Language—1988). He has insisted that architecture is made up of fundamental elements expressive of their purpose and responsive to social conditions, and that the architect's job is to clarify. He distils his architecture from primary forms.

Bonfanti (1973); Grassi (1982, 1989); Klotz (1986, 1988); Lampugnani (1988); Moschini (1984)

Graves, Michael (1934–). One of the most controversial US architects. He was identified as one of the *New York Five, and first came to prominence with a series of private houses in which themes of Le *Corbusier were reworked (e.g. Benacerraf House addition, Princeton, NJ (1969), where reminiscences of De *Stijl also occur). From the 1970s his work became classified as *Post-Modernist, as his architecture assimilated historical images and quotations. The Public Services Building, Portland, Oreg. (1980–3), and the Humana Tower, Louisville, Ky. (1982–6), are celebrated examples of his work. Other buildings by him include the Environmental Education Center, Liberty State Park, Jersey City, NJ (1981–3), the Graves Residence, Princeton, NJ (1986–93), the Detroit Institute of Arts, Mich. (1990), the Mega Corporation, Sony Building, Tokyo (1991), and the Federal Court House, Trenton, NJ (1992).

Frampton *et al.* (1975); Nichols, Burke, and Burke (1995); Nichols, Burke, and Hancock (1990); van Vynckt (1993); Wheeler, Arnell, and Bickford (1982)

Gravesande, Arent van 's (*c.*1600–62). Municipal architect to several Netherlandish towns, including The Hague, Leiden, and Middelburg, he was a leading Classicist and disciple of van *Campen. His best work is in Leiden, including the Bibliotheca Thysiana (1655), Laeckenhalle (1639–40), and octagonal Marekerk (1639–49—with Ionic columns carrying the dome). He completed the Oostkerk, Middelburg (1646—a variation on the Marekerk), and designed the Sebastiansdoelen, The Hague (1636).

Kuyper (1980)

Gray, Eileen (1879–1976). Irish-born designer. Her *International Modernist architectural work included the 'E-1027' House, Roquebrune, France (1926–9), the *Badovici Apartment, Paris (1930–1), the Tempe à Pailla House, Castellar, France (1932–4), and a cultural centre exhibited at the Paris Exhibition of 1937 by Le *Corbusier in his Pavillon des Temps Nouveaux. She was also a gifted furniture-designer, starting with her lacquer work, influenced by Japanese precedents. After the 1914–18 war she became an interior designer, anticipating aspects of De *Stijl themes, and designing furniture using chromed steel, aluminium, and mirror-glass.

Jervis (1984); Johnson, J. S. (1980)

Grayson, George Enoch (*c.*1833–1912). Liverpool architect. He was in partnership with Edward Augustus Lyle Ould (1852–1909) and built up a successful practice, later joined by **George Hastwell Grayson** (1871–1951) in 1897. The firm designed several distinguished groups of houses at Port Sunlight, Cheshire, including those with stepped gables in Wood Street (1895) and the Gothic houses of hard *terracotta and brick (1896). At Cambridge, Grayson & Ould designed the Hall at Selwyn College (1907) and buildings at Trinity Hall (1910).

Davison (1916); Gray (1985)

Greek architecture. The cradle of *Classicism, Greece perfected and refined *columnar and *trabeated architecture, each part of which was expressive of a long tradition of such construction, and related to the whole by subtle systems of proportion. Greek architecture was related to human scale, and expressive of its essential structural elements, yet was perfected in the temples, the greatest achievements of Greek architects, as habitations for the deities. The three Greek *Orders (*Doric, *Ionic, and *Corinthian) were evolved, each with its own characteristics and rules, refinements of detail and appropriate ornament, and these Orders were adapted by the Romans, providing the essentials of everything known as Classical architecture thereafter. The Corinthian Order is often thought to be no more than a variant of Ionic with a different capital, but there are, in fact, subtle differences.

Greek architecture was essentially a petrified and ultra-refined development of timber construction from the period after C6 BC, so much of the ornament of the Orders that appears merely decorative had its origins in carpentry, *triglyphs suggesting the ends of beams, *guttae the dowels, and *metopes the planes between the beams. It appears to have derived much from Ancient Egyptian architecture, notably the columnar and trabeated elements, but also the basic forms of the Doric Order have precedents of sorts in the Egyptian rock-cut tombs at Beni-Hasan (end of third to early second millennium BC) and in the Mortuary Temple of Queen Hatshepsut at Deïr-el-Bahari (*c.*1480 BC). However, the Greek Doric temple, which may have been derived partly from the Mycenaean *megaron and partly from Egyptian columnar and trabeated models, was a unified, original, and entirely Greek invention, and was established in C7 BC. Among early Doric temples may be mentioned the Temple of Apollo, Thermum (*c.*640 BC); the Heraeum, Olympia (before 600 BC—and *originally* with timber columns later replaced with stone); the fragmentary Temple of Artemis at Corcyra (Corfu) of *c.*580–570 BC (which was lavishly embellished with sculpture); the first Temple of Hera at *Paestum (*c.*550 BC), the Temple of

Aphaia at Aegina (*c*.500–495 BC), and the huge Temple of Zeus Olympios at Acragas (Agrigentum), Sicily (*c*.510–409 BC). These temples had sturdy, even stocky, columns, and, at Paestum especially, the columns had an exaggerated *entasis and very wide overhanging capitals much admired for their powerful, even *primitive, evocations by C18 Neoclassicists. Indeed, the severity, toughness, roughness (emphasized by the loss of the smooth *stucco rendering that covered the heavily textured stone), and sturdiness of Paestum Doric suggested masculine strength, and was used for expressive purposes by C18 and C19 Neoclassical architects. Much more refined were the Hephaesteion ('Theseion'), Athens (449–444 BC), and the *Parthenon, Athens (447–438 BC), regarded by many commentators as one of the finest works of architecture ever created because of its elegant proportions, equilibrium between sculpture and structure, and subtle optical corrections to ensure serenity and repose (although there are many details such as the relationships of columns to *soffits that are less than satisfactory). Mention should also be made of the *Propylaea, the plural name given to the whole structure of formal gateway to the Acropolis with its wings, designed by *Mnesicles and constructed 437–432 BC: the central *intercolumniation of the Doric Order was wider than the others to facilitate the passage of processions and sacrificial beasts, and the Ionic Order was used to flank the central roadway inside the structure.

The Ionic Temples of Athene Nikè (Nikè Apteros—*c*.448–421 BC) and the Erechtheion (421–405 BC), both on the Athenian Acropolis, were among the most refined inventions, and are therefore important exemplars. The latter Temple, with its *caryatid porch and exquisite Order incorporating a *frieze around the neck of the columns, was widely admired during the *Greek Revival: its asymmetrical composition was of particular interest. Among other important Ionic buildings were the Temples of Artemis at Ephesus in Asia Minor (*c*.560–450 BC and *c*.356–236 BC) and the Mausoleum at Halicarnassus (355–330 BC).

All three Orders were used in the Temple of Apollo Epicurius at *Bassae (*c*.450–425 BC): the external Order was Doric; the internal Ionic Order was unusual in that it had a unique *capital with adjoining *volutes, columns were attached to or *engaged with *piers or spur-walls along the inner walls of the naos: and at the southern end one isolated Corinthian column stood between two spur-walls that had an engaged Ionic, or, some authorities say, an engaged Corinthian, Order attached to each of them. The use of a Corinthian Order for interiors only as at Bassae was normal until the *Hellenistic period: examples include the *Tholos at Epidaurus (*c*.350 BC) and the Temple of Athena Alea at Tegea (*c*.350 BC). However, a refined Corinthian was used on the exterior of the exquisite little *Choragic Monument of Lysicrates, Athens (334 BC), and was much admired in C18, as the many quotations from it demonstrate.

Apart from temples, monuments, and tombs, the Greeks perfected the design of theatres, of which those of Dionysus, Athens (C5 BC), and Epidaurus (C4 BC) were the most impressive, and were influential, notably in Asia Minor. The Greeks also evolved designs for the *stadium, the *stoa, and other building-types. Elaborate public monuments were also vehicles for Greek architecture: a distinguished example was the Great Altar of Zeus, Pergamon (early C2 BC), with its vigorous sculpted *podium and Ionic superstructure. It is now in Berlin.

Curl (1992); Dinsmoor (1950); Fyfe (1936); Normand (1852); Robertson (1945)

Greek cross. *See* cross.

Greek key. Geometrical ornament consisting of horizontal and vertical *fillets joining at angles, a variety of *fret called *grecque* or *labyrinthine*, like a series of key-like shapes on *bands (usually *friezes and *string-courses).

Greek key. Two types of Greek key or labyrinthine fret.

Greek Revival. Style of architecture in which accurate copies of Ancient *Greek motifs were incorporated in the design of buildings from the 1750s. It was essentially part of *Neoclassicism in that it drew upon scholarly studies of *Antique buildings, especially the work of *Stuart (who designed the early *Doric garden-temple at Hagley, Worcestershire (1758), the first example of the Doric Revival) and *Revett in the *Antiquities of Athens* (from 1762). In the mid-C18 Greece and most of what had been Greek territories were part of the Ottoman Empire, and therefore relatively unknown in the West. Curiously, the accessible Greek temples at *Paestum in Italy and in Sicily had never really been studied, and were not taken seriously until relatively late, because baseless Greek Doric was seen as *primitive and uncouth. Early admirers of Greek architecture included *Winckelmann, *Ledoux, and *Soane, but the Revival was not universally adopted until after the Napoleonic wars, when it was associated with national aspirations. Unlike older styles, it was not tainted with discredited ideas or regimes, and was widely used in the USA, the British Isles, Prussia, and Bavaria. Among its most accomplished practitioners were *Hamilton, *Hansen, von *Klenze, *Playfair, Schinkel, *Smirke, *Strickland, *Thomson, and *Wilkins.

Crook (1972*a*); Curl (1992, 1993*b*); Honour (1977, 1979); Kennedy (1989); Liscombe (1980); Middleton and Watkin (1987)

Green, John (1787–1852). English architect and civil engineer. His two sons, **John** (*c*.1807–68) and **Benjamin** (1813–58) were also architects, and Benjamin, a pupil of A. C. *Pugin, worked with his father from *c*.1831 until 1852. They designed numerous undistinguished churches and altered medieval fabric in a destructive and unscholarly way. Their best work was for the railways, and includes the wrought-iron suspension-bridge, Whorlton, near Barnard Castle, Co. Durham (1829–31), and Tynemouth Railway Station, Northumberland (1847). In Newcastle upon Tyne they designed the Literary and Philosophical Society's Library (1822–5), the Theatre (1836–7), the Grey Column (1837–8), the Corn Exchange and Cloth Market (1838–9—demolished 1854 and 1972), the Corn Warehouse (1848), and the United Secession Meeting House (1821–2). One of their best works was the Greek *Doric temple, Penshaw Hill (1840).

Colvin (1995); *DNB* (1993)

Green, Leslie William (1875–1908). English architect. He made his name as Architect to the Underground Electric Railways Company of London Ltd., working with Harry Wharton Ford (1875–1947), Staff Architect to the Company (1899–1911). He designed stations for the Baker Street and Waterloo Railway, the Great Northern, Piccadilly, and Brompton Railway, and the Charing Cross, Euston, and Hampstead Railway, all in a clean, clear, functional manner, using glazed bricks and tiles in a simple, uncomplicated way.

Gray (1985)

Green, William Curtis (1875–1960). English architect. A pupil of *Belcher, he set up a practice in 1898 and designed a number of electricity-generating stations, houses, and cottages (notably at Letchworth *Garden City and Hampstead *Garden Suburb). He became a partner in the London firm of *Dunn and Watson (1912), responsible for several accomplished Classical buildings, including Wolseley House of 1921 (later Barclays Bank) and the National Westminster Bank (with details derived from *Peruzzi), both in Piccadilly, and the Scottish Provident Institution, Pall Mall (with elements derived from Michelangelo's New Sacristy, San Lorenzo, Florence). In the 1930s he designed the exterior and interiors of the Dorchester Hotel, London, the structure of which was by Owen *Williams. He also designed churches (e.g. St Christopher, Cove, Hampshire (1934)).

DNB (1971); Gray (1985); Lloyd (1978); Miller (1989, 1992); Miller and Gray (1992); Reilly (1931)

Green architecture. 1. Formal, *Picturesque gardens that are closely related to buildings, or where landscape and architecture coalesce. **2.** Buildings designed according to energy-saving criteria and the reduction of pollution.

Architectural Review, 187/1123 (Sept. 1990), whole issue; Solomon (1988); Vale and Vale (1991)

Greenberg, Allan (1938–). Born in South Africa, he became a citizen of the USA in 1973. His confident rejection of *Modernism led him to a re-appraisal of *Classicism, of which he has been one of the most distinguished practitioners. His News Building, Athens, Ga. (1992), has an unfluted Greek *Doric portico, and an overall authority worthy of earlier Neoclassicists.

Emanuel (1994)

Greene, Colonel Godfrey T. (1807–86). Director of Engineering and Architectural Works for the British Admiralty (1850–64), he was responsible for the factory, smithy, foundry, ship-fitting shop, and boat-store at

Sheerness, Kent (1856–7), all remarkably straightforward well-crafted buildings within the functional tradition, with no stylistic pretensions. The boat-store appears to be the very first four-storeyed lightly clad iron-framed structure.

Cruickshank (1996); Pevsner, *Buildings of England, North East and East Kent* (1976)

Greene & Greene. Charles Sumner (1868–1957) and **Henry Matthew** (1870–1954) Greene were important American *Arts-and-Crafts architects who established their practice in Pasadena, Calif., exciting attention with their Kinney-Kendall Building (1896): it had simplified façades of *mullions, wide *friezes, and a crowning *entablature. Thereafter, however, their work was almost entirely in the field of domestic architecture, with low-pitched roofs reminiscent of Swiss chalet architecture, the *Italianate style of *Schinkel and *Thomson, and the *Prairie houses of F. L. *Wright. Good examples of their work were the Robert C. Blacker House (1907), the David B. Gamble House (1908), and the S. S. Crow House (1909), all in Pasadena. In all three, massive over-sized timbers, overhanging roofs, and a careful relationship with the landscape were hallmarks of their style.

Current (1974); Greene and Greene (1977); McCoy (1975); Makinson (1974, 1977–9)

greenhouse. *See* conservatory.

Greenway, Francis Howard (1777–1837). English architect. A pupil of *Nash, he set up in business in Bristol with his builder and stonemason brothers (*c*.1805), himself providing the architectural expertise. The firm built the Hotel and Assembly Rooms in The Mall, Clifton, and erected many housing developments. He was found guilty of forgery in connection with a contract to complete a house, and was transported to Australia in 1812. In 1816 he became Civil Architect to the Government of New South Wales, and designed many public buildings in Sydney, including St James's Church (1819–24), the Barracks (1817–19), the Macquarie Tower, and the stables of Government House. The last were in the *castellated style, but most of his other buildings were competent and well-proportioned essays in *Classicism. He also designed St Matthew's Church, Windsor (1817–20), and St Luke's Church, Liverpool (1818), both in New South Wales.

Colvin (1995); Ellis (1966); Herman (1954)

Greeves, Thomas Affleck (1917–97). British architectural conservationist and draughtsman. A founder-member of the Victorian Society (1957) he was an active pioneer in resisting wholesale demolition of buildings of quality, and was particularly involved in the *conservation of Bedford Park, Chiswick, West London, the C19 *Arts-and-Crafts development by Norman *Shaw and others. He appreciated Victorian urban fabric before it became fashionable, and at a time when the Great and the Good were involved in plans for its wholesale destruction. Influenced by visions of *Piranesi and by his own experiences viewing the decaying buildings of the British Raj in India, he began to produce beautifully drawn architectural fantasies of great power and imagination, often showing Victorian buildings in a state of decay, composed in the form of the C18 *capriccio*. His publications include *Bedford Park* (1975) and *Ruined Cities of the Imagination* (1994).

Greeves (1975); personal knowledge; *The Times* (27 Sept. 1997), 25; *Daily Telegraph* (29 Sept. 1997), 23

Gregotti, Vittorio (b. 1927). *Neo-Rationalist Italian architect, at one time (1950s) influenced by the *Neo-Liberty movement. His architecture has grown increasingly stereometrically pure, culminating in the Belém Cultural Centre, Lisbon, Portugal (1993), a terraced structure that evokes Ancient Egypt, Greece, and much early architecture. Other works include the ENEA Research Centre, Rome (1985), and the University of Calabria, Cosenza (1973–85), the latter a linear development 3 km long based on a huge bridge structure. His *Territorio dell'architettura* (1966) and *La Città Visibile* (1993) helped to establish his reputation.

Amsoneit (1994); Emanuel (1994); Gregotti (1968); Lampugnani (1988); Tafuri and Dal Co (1986)

grid, gridiron. 1. Network of one lot of equidistant parallel lines laid at right angles over a similar set forming squares, thus establishing the pattern for a plan, e.g. of a building using, say, a *columnar and *trabeated framework, the columns placed at the intersections, or of a city with streets regularly spaced and crossing each other at right angles. **2.** *Mullioned and *transomed window (grid-*tracery), or a *grille of metal or wood in a screen.

griffe. *See* spur.

Griffin, Walter Burley (1876–1937). Illinois-born American architect. He worked in *Chicago (1899–1901) and for F. L. *Wright (1901–5), before being appointed Director for the design and construction of the Federal Capital at Canberra, Australia, in 1913. The formal geometry of his plan was successfully imposed upon a natural landscape of great beauty, perhaps reflecting Griffin's interest in the Rudolf *Steiner movement of Anthroposophy. Among his best designs are Newman College, University of Melbourne (1917), the Capitol Theatre, Melbourne (1924), and several houses in Australia. He designed and patented a system of construction involving interlocking components he called Knitlock. He produced an enormous number of designs for his adopted country, many of which were realized. Griffin's wife was Marion Lucy Mahony (1871–1961), who worked in Wright's Oak Park Studio, Chicago (1898–1909), and was responsible for many drawings in the influential *Ausgeführte Bauten und Entwürfe von Frank Lloyd Wright* (Executed Buildings and Projects by Frank Lloyd Wright), published by Wasmuth (1910).

Birrell (1964); Brooks (1972); Emanuel (1980); Johnson (1977); Peisch (1964); van Zanten (1970)

grille. *Lattice or *screen of open-work, usually metal.

Grimshaw, Nicholas (1939–). British architect, he set up his own practice in London in 1980 having worked with *Farrell from 1965. The firm has tended to specialize in the design of *High Tech metallic buildings, finely crafted, as in the Waterloo International Railway Terminal, London (1990–3), the *Financial Times* Printing Plant, Docklands, London (1986–8), the British Pavilion, Seville Expo (1992), the IGUS factory and offices, Cologne (1993), and the Western Morning News building, Plymouth, Devon (1993).

Amery (1995); Emanuel (1994); Jodidio (1995*a*); Meyhöfer (1995); Moore (1995)

grisaille. 1. Style of painting in grey monochrome to represent solid objects in *relief, the objects being supposedly white and the shadows they project properly depicted by various grey tints. It was used on the external leaves of medieval *triptych altarpieces. In Neoclassical schemes of decoration it represents e.g. figures in *Etruscan or *Pompeian interiors. **2.** Grey-tinted stained glass.

groin. *Arris formed by the *salient between two intersecting *vaults, as in two barrel-vaults crossing each other at right angles.

Gropius, Georg Walter Adolf (1883–1969). German-born naturalized American architect, best known for promoting *International Modernism both as practitioner and educator. He worked with *Behrens in Berlin (1907–10) before setting up his own practice. His earliest significant work (with A. *Meyer) was the Fagus Factory, Alfeld-an-der-Leine (1911), a three-storeyed steel-framed structure with glass *curtain-walls, one of the first buildings in which the beginnings of the *International Modern style were displayed. For the *Deutscher Werkbund Exhibition, Cologne (1914—again with Meyer), he designed the administrative building with curved glazed towers enclosing the staircases (an influential motif throughout the 1920s and 1930s), but otherwise the building had a stripped Neoclassical simplicity, certain aspects of it were reminiscent of *Wright's work, and its plan resembled the Ptolemaïc temple of Horus, Edfu, Egypt. Through van de *Velde, Gropius was given the opportunity in 1915 to direct the *Grossherzoglich-Sächsische Kunstgewerbeschule* (Grand-Ducal Saxon School of Arts and Crafts) at Weimar, but was prevented by the war from taking this up. In 1918 Gropius joined in the euphoria following the collapse of the monarchial system, and, with *Taut, was active in promoting Modernist and left-wing ideas: he was involved in the *Novembergruppe and *Arbeitsrat für Kunst which combined efforts, out of which grew Die *Gläserne Kette. Seeing the Weimar possibilities as a means by which he could promote Leftist ideology, he sought those who might be able to confirm the 1915 offer, and in 1919 became Director not only of the former Grand-Ducal *Kunstgewerbeschule*, but of the *Hochschule für Bildende Kunst* (High School for Fine Arts), which he amalgamated under the new title of *Das Staatliche Bauhaus Weimar* (the Weimar State House of Building). Influenced by the De *Stijl movement and by his own belief in industrialization and mass-production, the Bauhaus moved inexorably away from a craft-oriented ethos to one of industrial design.

When the *Bauhaus moved to Dessau, Gropius designed the buildings (completed in 1926) that became a paradigm for the International Modernist style. Even while at the Bauhaus, Gropius continued in practice with Meyer, designing the Sommerfeld House, Berlin-Dahlem (1921–2), made of teak from a scrapped warship, an *Expressionist memorial at Weimar (1922), and the Jena State Theatre (1923). In 1927 he designed buildings for the Werkbund Housing Exhibition at Stuttgart, the *Weissenhofsiedlung. He resigned as Bauhaus Director in 1928, and laid out the Siemensstadt Housing Estate, Berlin (1929–30), designing two of the apartment-blocks himself: with long strip-windows set in smooth rendered walls, they were widely imitated. As an active member of *CIAM his proposals for high-rise housing in green areas were disseminated, and became part of Modernist orthodoxy. His own moderate left-wing views and the more overtly Communist political stance adopted by Hannes *Meyer at the Bauhaus had repercussions, and even though he registered with the Nazi-created *Reichskulturkammer* (State Chamber of Culture) and designed a recreational and cultural centre (unrealized) for the *Kraft durch Freude* (Strength through Joy) Nazi movement (a project that invoked images of gigantic Party junketings worthy of a Nuremberg Rally), he failed to get anywhere.

In 1934 he settled in England where he lived in Lawn Road Flats, Hampstead, designed by Wells *Coates, was involved in the *MARS group, and worked with Maxwell *Fry, designing the film laboratories at Denham, Buckinghamshire (1936), Wood House, Shipbourne, Kent (1937), 66 Old Church Street, Chelsea (1935–6), and Impington Village College, Cambridgeshire (1936), the latter his main contribution to architecture in England. In 1937, however, Gropius accepted the offer of a post at Harvard in the Graduate School of Design, and in 1938 became Chairman of the Department of Architecture there, at once expunging all *Beaux-Arts traditions, an event followed at architectural schools throughout the USA. With *Breuer he designed the Gropius House, Lincoln, Mass. (1937), the first monument of International Modernism in New England, which was followed by several more private houses, culminating in the Frank House, near Pittsburg, Pa. (1939). With *Wachsmann, Gropius evolved systems for constructing prefabricated houses (1943–5).

After the 1939–45 war Gropius went into partnership with several younger architects, forming The Architects Collaborative (TAC), which produced the Graduate Center, Harvard University, Cambridge, Mass. (1949–50). For the *Hansaviertel* (Hansa Quarter), Berlin, Gropius designed an apartment-block (1957), and in the 1960s the new town of Britz-Buckow-Rudow, Berlin, was laid out to plans by him. He was probably the most influential architectural pedagogue of all time.

Fitch (1960); Franciscono (1971); Gropius (1945, 1952, 1962, 1965, 1968); Gropius and Harkness (1966); Hesse (1964); Hüter (1976); Isaacs (1983–4); Lane (1985); O'Neal (1966); Probst and Schädlich (1986–8); Weber (1961); Wingler (1969)

Gropius, Martin (1824–80). Influential German architect and teacher. He studied at the *Bauakademie* (Building Academy or School of Architecture) in Berlin, where he became familiar with the Grecianized *Classicism evolved by *Schinkel. He later became Professor at the *Bauakademie*, Director of the Art School in Berlin, and supervisor of all Prussian Art Schools. He designed the Lunatic Asylum at Neustadt-Eberswalde (1862–3), the hospitals at Friedrichshain (1867–71) and Tempelhof (1875–8), and the Art-Industrial Museum, one of his best buildings, now the *Martin-Gropius-Bau* (Martin Gropius Building—1881), Berlin. The clarity of his planning and structural systems owes much to Schinkel, while the *terracotta and red and yellow brick he favoured created an opulent *polychrome architecture. From 1866 he was in partnership with Heino Schmieden.

Schliepmann (1892)

Grosch, Christian Henrik (1801–65). Danish architect, of German descent, he made a significant contribution to North-European *Neoclassicism. He worked under C. F. *Hansen, from whom he acquired his severe Neoclassical style. In *c.*1825 he settled in Christiana (Oslo), Norway, where he assisted *Linstow in connection with the building of the Royal Palace (1824–7), taught for a while at the Royal Drawing School, and became City Architect (1828) then Inspector for Buildings (1833). He produced a huge amount of architecture, including the Greek *Doric Børs (Exchange—1826–52), the Norwegian Bank (1826–30), Immanuel Church, Halden in Østfold (1827–33—influenced by Hansen's *Vor Frue Kirke* in Copenhagen), and the monumental Oslo University (1838), plans of which were sent to *Schinkel for comment, with the result that the finished buildings were more refined and less severe than Grosch's earlier works. Grosch also designed the Market Halls (1840–59) and Fire Station (1854–6), Oslo, in a red-brick *Rundbogenstil. Fifty-nine churches were built after his designs, together with many houses and other buildings. He also designed numerous timber buildings based on Norwegian *vernacular architecture.

Cruickshank (1996); Middleton and Watkin (1987); Weilbach (1947)

grotesque. **1.** Capricious Classical ornament consisting of animals, figures, flowers, foliage, fruits, and sphinxes, all connected together, and distinct from *arabesques which do not have animal or humanoid representations. It is so called after the *Antique decorations rediscovered (1488) during the *Renaissance period in buried ruins of Roman buildings called *grotte*. Grotesques as a type of decoration were revived by *Raphael (so sometimes called *Raphaelesques*), and were used at the Vatican *Loggie* (from *c*.1515) and the Villa Madama, Rome (1520–1). Designs for grotesques were made available in publications, and, with *strapwork, were common in *Renaissance and *Mannerist schemes of decoration, especially in Northern Europe. **2.** *Picturesque irregular landscape, often with *grottoes.

Chastel (1988); Dacos (1969); Lewis and Darley (1986); Ward-Jackson (1967, 1967*a*)

grotto. **1.** Cave or cavern, especially one that is a pleasant retreat in a *Picturesque landscape. **2.** Built structure of *rock-work, or an excavation imitating a rocky cavern, often adorned with broken pottery and shells arrayed in patterns, sometimes with fountains and cascades of water, and serving as a cool retreat. Grottoes were not unknown in *Antique Roman gardens, and were often revived during the *Renaissance, *Mannerist, and *Baroque periods (in the last period they were sometimes features of the lowest or entrance-floor of palaces, such as Schloss Weissenstein, Pommersfelden, Germany (1711–20)). Some grottoes were further embellished with *congelated* *rustication.

Bazin (1990); Coffin (1994); Heydenreich and Lotz (1974); Jones (1974); Mosser and Teyssot (1991)

ground-plan. *See* plan.

Grounds, Sir Roy (1905–81). Australian architect. He made *Modernism acceptable in that country with his early houses (1950s) and the Academy of Science Building, Canberra (1958–9). Among his later works, the Arts Centre, Melbourne (1961–85), may be mentioned.

Cruickshank (1996)

grouped. **1.** Two columns or *pilasters used in pairs are *coupled (as on the east front of the Louvre, Paris). More than two closely placed on one *base, pedestal, or *plinth are *grouped*. **2.** *Clustered *pier.

Gruen, Victor David (1903–80). Viennese architect, born **Grünbaum**, he settled in the USA in 1938. He established his own firm in Los Angeles (1951), specializing in out-of-town shopping-centres including the Northland Center, Detroit, Mich. (1954), the Southdale Center, Minneapolis, Minn. (1956), and the first inner-city enclosed shopping-mall at Midtown Plaza, Rochester, NY (1962). He also designed The Mall, Fresno, Calif. (1968). His interest in the revitalization of cities is encapsulated in his *The Heart of Our Cities* (1964).

Fitch (1961); Gruen (1964, 1973); Gruen and Smith (1960); Jacobs (1961); Tunnard and Pushkarev (1981)

Gruppo 7. Association of seven Italian architects (Ubaldo Castagnoli (soon replaced by A. *Libera), L. *Figini, Guido Frette (1901–), Sebastiano Larco (1901–), G. *Pollini, Carlo Enrico Rava (1903–85), and G. *Terragni) formed in 1926, which, in their exhibition at Monza in 1927 and their manifesto of 1926–7 in *La Rassegna Italiana* (The Italian Review), promoted a national modern *Rationalism in which the Classical heritage of Italy and a *machine aesthetic derived from Le *Corbusier were balanced. The Movimento Italiano per L'Architettura Razionale (*MIAR) developed from Gruppo 7 (1930). Works associated with the group include Terragni's Novocomum Apartment Block, Como (1927–9), Libera's façade for the Exhibition of the Fascist Revolution, Rome (1932), and the Città Universitaria, Rome (1930s). Most Gruppo 7 members were closely associated with support for Mussolini's Fascists.

Architectural Design, 51 (1981), 5–8; *Oppositions*, 6 (1976), 85–8; Savi (1980); van Vynckt (1993)

Guadet, Julien (1834–1908). French architect and writer. A pupil of *Labrouste, he was associated with the École des *Beaux-Arts for virtually all his life. Among his few buildings the Hôtel des Postes, Rue du Louvre, Paris (1881–6), a stone-faced work with a partly metallic structure behind, may be mentioned. As a theorist he is regarded as of some importance because of his promotion of rationalist approaches to architecture, as expounded in his *Éléments et théories de l'Architecture* (1901–4, with later editions): this work covered an enormous range of problems and solutions that students might encounter in their careers, and included a comprehensive study of building-types from many periods in history. He argued that the architect should always establish the content from which he would arrive at the design of the container of that content. Taken out of context this remark gave his writings a spurious position in the canon of *Functionalism, but he also advocated clothing buildings in any historical garb demanded by the client (a fact that tends to be overlooked by most commentators). His pupils included Tony *Garnier and *Perret. The latter collaborated with Guadet's son, **Paul** (1873–1931), in the building of a pioneering *concrete house in Paris (1912).

Banham (1960); Collins (1965); Egbert (1980)

Guarini, Guarino (1624–83). Born in Modena, where he was baptized Camillo, he became a mathematician, Theatine priest, and one of the most original architects of the late C17. Indeed, he was a sophisticated geometrician, and a pioneer of projective and descriptive geometry, as is clear from his *Euclides Adauctus* (1671) and *Architettura Civile* (1686), anticipating the work of Gaspard Monge (1746–1818), who is usually credited with the invention of descriptive geometry. His work on *stereotomy doubtless helps to explain the great complexity of his buildings. His main architectural influences derived from *Bernini, *Borromini, and *Cortona: the deeply modelled façades of the Collegio di Nobili, Turin (1679–83), clearly owe a debt to Borromini; while the Palazzo Carignano (also 1679–83) was influenced by Bernini's proposals for the Louvre, Paris (1665), with elements drawn from Borromini's San Carlo alle Quattro Fontane, Rome. All his most interesting surviving work is in Turin, where he developed openwork systems of intersecting ribs instead of solid domes, derived, perhaps, from Borromini's Oratory and Propaganda Fide chapels in Rome. At Turin Cathedral Guarini built the Cappella della SS Sindone to house the Holy Shroud, with a cone-shaped dome (1667–90) composed of diminishing tiers of segmental rib-arches piled up upon one another and framing windows (severely damaged 1997). His Church of San Lorenzo, Turin (1668–80), has an approximately octagonal central space each side of which curves inwards and is composed of a *serliana motif, while the dome above is formed of interlocking semicircular ribs disposed to form an eight-pointed star with an open octagon in the centre. The parallel to these arrangements can be found in the *Moorish architecture of Spain, such as the Mosque at Córdoba (*c*.965), and in French *Gothic cathedrals. Indeed, his *Architettura Civile* (1737) contains an intelligent appraisal of Gothic architecture, and his work seems to have exercised a considerable influence in Central Europe, notably on von *Hildebrandt, the *Dientzenhofers, *Fischer von Erlach, *Neumann, J. M. *Fischer, and, above all, *Santini-Aichel, for he made designs for St Maria, Altötting, Prague (1679), while his project for Santa Maria della Divina Providenza, Lisbon (1679 or 1681), has a plan remarkably similar to that of Neumann's Pilgrimage Church of *Vierzehnheiligen* (Fourteen Saints), Franconia, Germany (1740s).

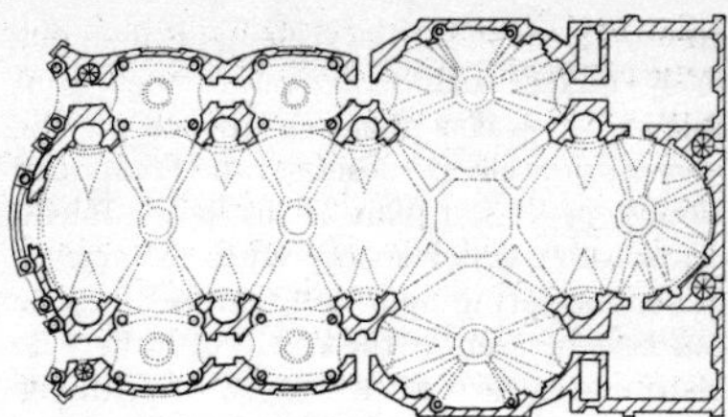

Guarini. Plan of Church of Santa Maria della Divina Providenza. (*After Guarini*)

Brinckmann (1931, 1932); Guarini (1660, 1665, 1671, 1674, 1675, 1676, 1678, 1683, 1966, 1968); Meek (1988); Norberg-Schulz (1986, 1986*a*); Oechslin (1970); Pommer (1967); Portoghesi (1956); Wittkower (1982)

Guas, Juan (*c*.1433–96). One of the greatest architects working in late-*Gothic Spain, he drew on Flemish medieval elements imaginatively mixed with *Moorish themes from Toledo. He was a major influence on the *Isabelline style. He designed the Franciscan Monastery of San Juan de los Reyes, Toledo (from 1477), which incorporates *muqarnas under the springing of the *vaults. His style can best be seen at the castle of El Real de Manzanares, near Madrid (1475–9), with vigorously modelled muqarnas *cornice, and at the Palace of El Infantado, Guadalajara (1480–3), where the façade is enriched with projecting diamond-shaped stones arranged in a rhomboid grid all over the wall: above is an arcaded gallery with corbelled balconies. He worked at the Cathedrals of Segovia and Toledo, and designed the Chapel of the Dominican College of San Gregorio, Valladolid (1487–9).

Chueca Goitia (1965); Herrera Casado (1975); Kubler and Soria (1959); Layna Serrano (1941)

Gucewicz, Wawrzyniec (1753–98). Polish Neoclassicist, he prepared designs for the monumental Wilno (now Vilnius) Cathedral (1777–1801), with a huge Roman *Doric *portico and long side *colonnades: it was as impressive an exercise in Neoclassical clarity as anywhere else in Europe. For the same city he designed a Town Hall with a vast *Tuscan column as its tower (1785–6), and the Bishop's Palace (also 1780s).

Lorentz and Rottermund (1984); Watkin (1986)

Guedes, Amancio d'Alpoim Miranda (1925–). Portuguese architect, trained in South Africa. He was responsible for much work in Mozambique and Angola (1949–75), influenced by many sources, including works by Le *Corbusier, *Gaudí, *Kahn, and African art. His buildings include the Prometheus Apartments (1951–3), the Tonelli Condominiums (1954–7), and the Church of the Sagrada Familia, Machava (1962–4), all in Lourenço Marques. His later work includes the Cohen House, Forest Town, Johannesburg (1987), and the Guedes House, Calhandriz, Portugal (1993).

Emanuel (1994); Guedes (1977)

Guedes, Joaquim (1932–). Brazilian architect. Critical of the stranglehold of Le *Corbusier's dogmas in Brazil ever since the late 1930s, he advocated an architecture that was more attuned to climatic and economic realities in his plan for the new town of Caraiba (from 1976) which drew on traditional urban models and a study of vehicle and pedestrian circulation-patterns. His own house at São Paulo (1974) has a series of crisp planes and an elegantly minimal structure. Recent work includes the State Primary and High School, Jandira, São Paulo (1991), the Botanical Gardens Pavilions, Rio de Janeiro (1993), and the Mesquita House, São Paulo (1994).

Emanuel (1994)

Guelphic crenellation. *See* battlement.

Guêpière, Pierre-Louis-Philippe de la (*c.*1715–73). French architect. With *Pigage he introduced the *Louis Seize style to Germany. He worked on the *Neues Schloss* (New Castle), Stuttgart, with Leopoldo Retti (d. 1751), built 1746–68 (destroyed), and designed Schloss Solitude (with Johann Friedrich Weyhing (1716–81)), above Stuttgart (1763–7), a charming single-storey building with two wings extending from a central elliptical domed element. He was also responsible for Monrepos (1760–7), an enchanting Classical lakeside building near Ludwigsburg. All three buildings were for Duke Karl Eugen of Württemberg (ruled 1744–93). Following his retirement to France in 1768, he designed the Hôtel de Ville, Montbéliard, erected in modified form after his death in the late 1770s. He published *Recueil de projets d'architecture* (Compendium of Architectural Projects—1750) and *Recueil d'esquisses d'architecture* (Compendium of Architectural Designs—1759).

Colombier (1955); Guêpière (1759); Hautecœur (1950); Klaiber (1959); Watkin and Mellinghoff (1987); Wörner (1979)

guilloche. 1. Classical ornament, or *plait-band*, usually composed of a series of equidistant circular elements all of the same diameter surrounded by curved bands, enriched with single or double *fillets, that overlap each other in a continuous strip. Each

guilloche. Two types of guilloche.

circle can also be enriched with a flower or can be plain. It is related to a *fret, but with curves instead of right angles. **2.** Inaccurate term for a fret.

Guimard, Héctor (1867–1942). French *Art Nouveau architect, he was influenced by *Viollet-le-Duc and *Horta. He designed Castel Béranger, 16 Rue de la Fontaine, Paris (1894–9), an apartment-block of *rubble, coloured brick, stone, and *faïence, with an entrance in a fully developed Art Nouveau style, causing the building to be christened *Castel Dérangé* (Mad Castle). His Paris *Métro*-Station entrances (1899–1913), featuring metal that seemed to grow from the stone, modular prefabricated construction, and bizarre, almost surreal lamps, made his works familiar, although many have been destroyed. The decorations of his own house, the Hôtel Guimard, Avenue Mozart, Paris (1912), perhaps were his most exquisite creations.

Brunhammer *et al.* (1975); Brunhammer and Naylor (1978); Graham (1970); Guimard (1907); Rheims and Vigne (1988); Tschudi-Madsen (1967).

Gumpp, Johann Martin (1643–1729). Son of **Christoph Gumpp the Younger** (1600–72), Court Architect to the Tyrolean Habsburgs and designer of the *Jesuitenkirche* (Jesuit Church, from 1627) and the centrally planned *Mariahilfkirche* (1647–9), both in Innsbruck. J. M. Gumpp designed the Fugger-Taxis Palace (1679–80), reworked Government House (1690–2), and designed the *Spitalkirche* (1700–5), all in Innsbruck. He, his father, and his son (**Georg Anton** (1682–1754)) all contributed to the transformation of the great Abbey of Stams with *Baroque overlays (1719–25 and 1729–32), while Georg Anton alone designed the adjoining *Heiligenblutkapelle* (Holy Blood Chapel—1715–17), the distinguished Church of St Johann am Innrain (1729–35), and the *Landhaus* of the Tyrolean Estates (1724–8). The Gumpps were pioneers of the Baroque style in the Tyrol, working on a number of projects in the area, including the *Stiftskirche* (Monastery Church), Wilten (from 1649). **Johann Martin Gumpp** the Younger (1686–1765) designed the south wing of the Hofburg, Innsbruck (1754–6).

Bourke (1962); Frodl-Kraft (1955); Hempel (1965); Krapf (1979)

gun-loop. Aperture, often of horizontal elliptical form, in a wall to enable fire to be directed over a wide angle, found in Scots architecture, even in C19 revivals.

Gurlitt, Cornelius (1850–1938). German architect and architectural historian. He wrote nearly 100 books and many more articles, but he is remembered as the first effective champion of *Baroque art and architecture which, in C19, had been out of favour. Rejecting the language of *Schinkel and his followers, he favoured *Semper, *Wallot, and others who turned to a richer, less restrained architecture. His *magnum opus* was the influential *Geschichte des Barockstiles, des Rococo und des Klassizismus* (History of the Baroque, Rococo, and Classical Styles—published in Stuttgart in 1887–9).

Mallgrave (1996); Placzek (1982)

gutta (*pl.* **guttae**). Pendent ornament resembling a truncated cone under the *soffits of the *mutules and *regulae of the Greek *Doric *Order. In *Renaissance and later versions of Doric, guttae are often cylindrical, or like truncated pyramids. There are usually 18 under each mutule, set in three rows, and 6 under the regula, but the number may vary. In the Athenian *Choragic Monument of Thrasyllus (319 BC) a continuous series of guttae was set above the *architrave under the *taenia, with no regulae at all: this was often revived in C19 during the *Greek Revival, notably by *Schinkel at Charlottenhof, Potsdam (1826), and the *Neue Wache* (New Guard House), *Unter den Linden*, Berlin (1816–18). Guttae are also called *campanulae*, *drops*, *lachrymae*, *nails*, or *trunnels*.

guttae band. *Regula or listel from which the guttae are suspended in the *Doric *Order, directly under the *taenia and lining up with the *triglyph above.

Gwathmey, Charles (1938–). American architect, identified as one of the *New York Five. He established (1966) a practice with Richard Henderson in New York, later (1971) forming a partnership with Robert Siegel. Most of his best works are private houses (e.g. Gwathmey House, Amagansett (1965–7), Steel House, Bridgehampton (1968–9), Cogan House, East Hampton (1971–2), De Menil House, East Hampton (1979–84), all NY, and the Garey House, Kent, Conn. (1982–3)). Larger projects include East Campus Housing and Academic Center, Columbia University, New York (1976–81), Fogg Art Museum, Harvard University, Cambridge, Mass.

(1989–90), Disney World Convention Center, Orlando, Fl. (1990–1), and the Guggenheim Museum Extension and Refurbishment, New York (1991–2). The Gwathmey/Siegel design for the Chen Residence, Taipei, Taiwan (1992–4), is a distillation of the Modernist architectural vocabulary.

Emanuel (1994); Frampton *et al.* (1975); Jodidio (1993)

Gwilt, Joseph (1784–1863). English architect, he was the younger son of **George Gwilt** (1746–1807), and designed in various eclectic styles, but is better known as a writer. His works include *A Treatise on the Equilibrium of Arches* (1811), an edition of *Chambers's *Treatise on the Decorative Part of Civil Architecture* (1825), which included a new section on Greek architecture, a translation of *Vitruvius (1826), and the very important expanded version of his *Rudiments of Architecture* of 1826, *An Encyclopaedia of Architecture, Historical, Theoretical, and Practical* (1842—work on which was partly carried out by his son, **John Sebastian Gwilt** (1811–90)), with many subsequent editions, the last three of which were enlarged by Wyatt *Papworth. His brother, **George Gwilt** (1775–1856), rebuilt the *steeple of *Wren's Church of St Mary-le-Bow, London (1818–20), and carried out works at Southwark Cathedral (then the Church of St Mary Overie) in 1818–33.

Colvin (1995); *DNB* (1917); Gwilt (1811, 1818, 1822, 1825, 1826, 1826*a*, 1837, 1848, 1903); Pevsner (1972)

gymnasium. Place for physical exercise and teaching in Ancient Greece, also known as *palaestra.

Delorme (1960); Dinsmoor (1950)

Habershon, Matthew (1789–1852). English architect. He published a pioneering study of C16 and C17 buildings, *The Ancient Half-Timbered Houses of England* (1836), in which year he gave A. W. N. *Pugin's *Contrasts* a hostile reception. In 1842 he went to Jerusalem to superintend the erection of the Anglican Cathedral, designed by James Wood Johns (*c.*1810–63), and designed St Peter's Church, Belper, Derbyshire (1824), the County Courts, Derby (1828–9), the Town Hall and Market, Derby (1828–30—partially destroyed), model cottages at Brampton, Huntingdonshire (*c.*1837), and Burbage Church, Leicestershire (1842). Among his pupils were Ewan *Christian and his son, **William Gilbee Habershon** (1818/19–91), who was in partnership with Alfred Robert Pite (1832–1911) from 1863 to 1878.

Colvin (1995)

Hablik, Wenzel August (1881–1934). Bohemian *Arts-and-Crafts designer. He finished an influential series of drawings of crystalline structures in 1909 (exhibited in 1912), and produced several powerful architectural fantasies after the 1914–18 war, some in association with *Arbeitsrat für Kunst and Die *Gläserne Kette. He envisaged airborne settlements in the future, as in *Cyklus Architektur* (1925). His work had some influence on German *Expressionism.

Architectural Association Quarterly, 12/3 (1980), 18–24; Collins (1979); Rossow (1980); Ungers (1963); Urban (1960)

Hadfield, George (1763–1826). English architect. Born in Italy, he became a pupil of James *Wyatt, and in 1795 settled in the USA to superintend the building of the Capitol in Washington, DC, in succession to *Hallet, but was dismissed in 1798, having fought a losing battle against the ignorance and incompetence of the officials and workmen. He designed several Neoclassical buildings in Washington, including City Hall (1820–6—now the District of Columbia Court House), the unfluted *Paestum *Doric *portico of the Custis-Lee Mansion, Arlington (1818), the Assembly Rooms (1822), and the J. P. van Ness *mausoleum, Oak Hill Cemetery, Georgetown (1826). With *Godefroy and *Latrobe, he can be credited with introducing the *Greek Revival to the USA.

Colvin (1995); Goode (1979); Maddex (1973); Reiff (1977); Whiffen and Koeper (1983)

Hadfield, Matthew Ellison (1812–85). *See* Weightman, John Grey (1801–72).

Hadid, Zaha (1950–). Iraqi architect, trained at the Architectural Association, London, under *Koolhaas, and working in the UK. She has long been associated with *Deconstructivism. Her work often seems restless, even fragmented, with surfaces apparently slashed as though with a knife, and bereft of visual stability, but some commentators have noted strengths in her designs based on an apparent expansion of energy-charged space, extending outwards into infinity. Typical of her rather jagged style are the designs for The Peak Club, Kowloon, Hong Kong (1982–3—Competition drawings), the realized Monsoon Bar, Sapporo, Japan (1988–9), the Vitra Fire Station, Weil-am-Rhein (1991–3), and the Cardiff Opera House (1993–5—Competition drawings). Other works include extensions to the Dutch Parliament buildings, The Hague (1978–9), IBA housing, Berlin (1983), various office-buildings, exhibitions, and proposals for residential developments, but most of her designs have remained on paper.

Emanuel (1994); Johnson and Wigley (1988); Meyhöfer (1995)

Haesler, Otto (1880–1962). German pioneer of industrialized housing construction and member of Der *Ring from 1926. He designed buildings on the Dammerstock Estate, Karlsruhe (1927–8), collaborating with *Gropius, and also designed numerous *Modern Movement developments at Celle (1920–31), Kassel (1929–31), Misburg (1931) and Rathenow (1946–51).

Haesler (1930, 1957); Lane (1985)

hagioscope. *Squint, loricula, or aperture cut obliquely in a wall (usually of a *chancel), affording a visual connection between the high-altar and the *aisles or side-*chapels. One of its functions was to enable the celebrant at a side-altar (e.g. in a *chantry-chapel) to see if the Priest at the high-altar had reached the sacring, to ensure sacrings would not occur simultaneously.

Bloxham (1882); Duffy (1992); Parker (1850)

ha-ha. In landscape-gardening, a boundary to a garden designed not to interrupt a view from e.g. a country-house. It consists of a ditch with side or *revetment nearest the viewpoint perpendicular (or slightly *battered), faced with brick or stone, and the other side sloped and turfed. It kept animals away from the area contiguous to the house, yet was concealed. It appears to have been a French invention called *ah, ah*, and described as having *un fosse sec au pied* in d'Argenville's *La Théorie et la Pratique du Jardinage* (1709).

Hadfield, Harling, and Highton (1980); Symes (1993)

Hakewill, Henry (1771–1830). English architect. He designed two distinguished *Greek Revival buildings: Coed Coch, Denbighshire, Wales (1804), a country-house with a diagonally placed *portico (demolished) and *stair; and St Peter's Church, Eaton Square, London (1824–7—rebuilt after a fire in 1987). He had a large and flourishing practice, mostly concerned with country-houses, and he published an account of the Roman villa at Northleigh, Oxfordshire (1823). His brother, **James** (1778–1843), is known primarily for his many architectural and topographical publications, including a work on the abattoirs of Paris (1828) and *Views . . . in the Regent's Park, laid out from the Designs of Decimus Burton* (1831), although he designed buildings, all architecturally competent.

Colvin (1995); *DNB* (1917)

half. If applied to a *baluster or a column, it means *engaged.

half-bat. Snapped header (*see* brick).

half-column. *See* half.

half-figure. *Term.

half-moon. *See* demi-lune.

half-pace. **1.** Landing where two flights of a *stair meet at 180°. **2.** *Daïs or step forming the floor in a bay-window.

Halfpenny, William (d. 1755). English architect and carpenter (*alias* **Michael Hoare**), he is known as the author of several successful pattern-books for domestic buildings, among the first of which was *Practical Architecture* (*c.*1724), a cheap, clear guide to the *Orders and various architectural elements drawing on *Campbell's *Vitruvius Britannicus* (1715). He disseminated *Gothick and *Chinoiserie designs in his *Rural Architecture in the Gothic Taste*, *Chinese and Gothic Architecture properly ornamented* (both 1752 and both with his son, **John Halfpenny**), and *Rural Architecture in the Chinese Taste* (1752–5, parts of which were by John). With these, *Improvements in Architecture and Carpentry* (1754), *The Art of Sound Building* (1725), and other publications, he and *Langley dominated the pattern-book market of the time. In his *A New and Compleat System of Architecture* (1749–59) there are indications he may have known the Irish *Palladian architect *Pearce, and indeed he seems to have been involved in designing in Ireland, notably at Hillsborough, Co. Down (1732), and Waterford (1739). In spite of his debt to Campbell, Halfpenny was never a polished Palladian, and his work drew on *Baroque elements. His publications clearly had a profound effect on the appearance of many cathedral- and market-towns throughout England, while his *Twelve Beautiful Designs for Farm Houses* (1750) and other publications showed he was capable of designing for the countryside as well. From *c.*1730 he settled in Bristol (whence he probably travelled to Ireland), and designed several buildings there, although none is particularly distinguished. He or his son may have been responsible for the charming Gothick orangery at Frampton-on-Severn, Gloucestershire (*c.*1750).

Colvin (1995); Cruickshank (1985); Curl (1993*b*); Halfpenny (1731, 1747, 1748, 1749, 1752, 1752*a*, 1752*b*, 1757, 1774, 1965, 1968, 1968*a*, 1968*b*, 1968*c*); Harris (1990); Summerson (1993)

half-timbering. **1.** Obsolete term for a *timber-framed building, the gaps between the members of the frame filled with some other material, e.g. brick *nogging or plaster on *wattles or laths. **2.** Building with the lower storey of stone or brick and the upper storeys, or parts of them, such as *gables, timber-framed, and visible as such. **3.** Building constructed of brick, block, etc., with timber applied to it in parts suggesting timber-framing, but in fact false.

hall. **1.** Main room of a medieval house or the large, communal room of a college, etc., often an *open-hall, open to the roof, and sometimes with an open hearth. **2.** Large room or building for the transaction of public business, the holding of courts of justice, or any public assembly, meeting, or entertainment (e.g. *music-hall*). **3.** Building for a guild or fraternity, such as a London Livery-Company Hall (e.g. Hall of The Fishmongers' Company), or for a municipal body (e.g. city- or town-hall). **4.** Principal messuage of a manor, i.e. the residence of a territorial proprietor. **5.** University building set aside for the residence or instruction of students. **6.** Common-room in a mansion in which servants dined. **7.** Any large roofed volume.

Alcock, Barley, Dixon, and Meeson (1996); Gwilt (1903); Papworth (1852)

hall-church. Church with *aisles but without a *clearstorey, the interior of which is of approximately uniform height throughout, i.e. the *nave and *aisles are of the same or about the same height. It is a characteristic German *Gothic type, called *Hallenkirche*, with very tall windows illuminating the aisles, no *transepts, and, sometimes, with the *chancel defined only by the furnishings rather than by a separate architectural compartment. Examples include the churches at Nördlingen (1427–1505), Dinkelsbühl (1444–92), and Pirna (consecrated 1546).

Sturgis *et al.* (1901–2)

Hallenkirche. *See* hall-church.

Haller, Fritz (1924–). Swiss architect, he established his reputation with his system of building in steel, notably the *Maxi* system for large spans, as well as for his skeletal systems for furniture (USM). His fully developed system for medium-span structuring (*Midi*) was first used for the Swiss Railways Training Centre, Löwenberg, near Murten (1978–82). Other buildings include the USM, Münsingen (1960–4), Wagsenring School, Basle (1951, 1962), Canton School, Baden (1958–64), and Higher Technical Training Centre, Brugg-Windisch (1961–6).

Bauen & Wohnen 36/7/8 (1981); Blaser (1982)

Haller, Karl Christoph Joachim, Freiherr von Hallerstein (1774–1817). German architect. A pupil of David *Gilly, he was one of the first (with T. *Allason and C. R. *Cockerell) to discover the *entasis on Greek columns. With *Foster, Linckh, and Cockerell he discovered the Aegina marbles (1811), and helped to survey the temple of Apollo Epicurius at Bassae. He submitted a design for the Walhalla, near Regensburg (1814–15), consisting of a massive series of battered platforms, a *propylaeum with three *pylon-towers, and a *Greek Revival temple on top, obviously inspired by F. *Gilly's monument to Frederick the Great (1797). His unrealized proposals for the Munich *Glyptothek* (Sculpture Gallery—1814) combined Greek and Egyptian elements. Leo von *Klenze built both projects to his own designs, retaining Haller's platform idea at Walhalla.

Colvin (1995); Watkin and Mellinghoff (1987)

Hallerstein. *See* Haller, Karl Christoph Joachim, Freiherr von.

Hallet, Étienne-Sulpice, *also called* **Stephen** (*c.*1760–1825). French architect, he settled in the USA from 1786, and from 1793 was employed to supervise the building of the Capitol in Washington, DC, to *Thornton's designs, which he modified slightly in building, but was dismissed in 1794 and succeeded by *Hadfield.

Art Studies, 1 (1923), 76–92; Brown (1970); *DAB* (1932); Padover (1946)

hall-house. Obsolete term for an *open hall.

Hamilton, David (1768–1843). Leading Glasgow architect of the early C19. He designed the Neoclassical Hutcheson's Hospital, Ingram Street (1802–5), and became adept at the *Greek Revival style. His former Royal Exchange (1829–30) is in sumptuous Graeco-Roman *Corinthian, while his Western Club, Buchanan Street (1840), is *Italianate. He designed the 'Bridge of Sighs' at the Glasgow Necropolis (1833–9). His country-houses were eclectic, and he designed in *Jacobean (e.g. Dunlop House, Ayrshire, 1832–4), *Gothic (e.g. Castle House, Dunoon, Argyll, 1823–4), and even *Romanesque (e.g. Lennox Castle, Lennoxtown, Stirlingshire, 1838–41) with some facility. His son **James** (1818–61) contributed to many of the designs.

Colvin (1995); *DNB* (1917); Gomme and Walker (1987); Williamson, Riches, and Higgs (1990)

Hamilton, Thomas (1784–1858). Distinguished Scots Neoclassical architect. He worked mostly in Edinburgh, and in 1818 won the competition to design the Burns Monument, Alloway, freely adapted from Greek sources. His Royal High School, Edinburgh (1825–9), one of the most brilliant essays in the *Greek Revival style, is of international importance, with its Theseion-like temple, flanking *colonnades, pylon-like pavilions, and stepped platforms recalling *Haller's designs for Walhalla. He designed the George IV Bridge, providing the southern approach to the city of Edinburgh (1827–34), the *Doric John Knox Memorial, Glasgow Necropolis (1825), the Municipal Buildings and Steeple, Ayr (1828–30), and the elegant Neoclassical Royal College of Physicians, Queen Street, Edinburgh (1844–6). His essays in the *Gothic, *Romanesque, and *Jacobethan styles, however, are relatively undistinguished.

Colvin (1995); Crook (1972*a*); *DNB* (1917); Gifford, McWilliam, and Walker (1984); Rock (1984); Summerson (1993); Youngson (1966)

hammer-beam. Transverse timber in the position of a tie-beam, but short, not spanning the space, essentially a bracket supported on a wall and brace and carrying the *hammer-post. A *false hammer-beam* is like a true hammer-beam, but does not have the hammer-post above: rather it is braced below and supports the base of the principal or collar.

hammer-post. Upright timber *post set on the end of a *hammer-beam and forming one side of a triangle with the principal and hammer-beam.

hanging. Tapestry, paper, or other material for covering and decorating the walls of a room.

hanging-buttress. Not a true *buttress, but put there to maintain a sequence or series, and carried on a *corbel. It might also help in the construction of a *vault, and in such a case will have elements responding to the *ribs.

hanging-post. Post from which a *door or gate is hung.

hanging step. Step with one end built into a wall and *cantilevered, or perhaps resting on the step underneath.

Hankar, Paul (1859–1901). Belgian architect. Influenced by *Beyaert and *Viollet-le-Duc, he later became one of the most important protagonists of *Art Nouveau. His buildings were exquisitely detailed, and include the Hôtel Zegers-Regnard (1888), Hôtel Hankar (1893), and the superbly crafted Hôtel Ciamberlani (1897), all in Brussels. Influenced by Japanese art, his work in turn influenced Otto *Wagner, who saw some of Hankar's lushly inventive interiors in 1897.

Borsi and Wieser (1971); Loyer (1991); Maeyer (1963); Tschudi-Madsen (1967)

Hansen, Christian Frederik (1756–1845). Leading architect of the *Greek Revival in Denmark. Trained under *Harsdorff, he assisted the latter at Frederik V's Chapel (which he eventually completed 1821–5), Roskilde Cathedral, before visiting Italy (1782–4). His finest work is *Vor Frue Kirke* (Church of Our Lady), Copenhagen (designed 1808–10 and built 1811–29), with a *portico in which the primitive *Doric *Order from *Paestum was adapted. He also designed the splendid Law Courts, Prison, and Town Hall, with archways (1803–16), in the same city, which were in the severe Neoclassical style also developed by *Gilly and others in Germany. In his official capacity as Surveyor for Holstein, he designed the Mental Hospital in Schleswig (1818–20), a serene, symmetrical complex of buildings in a rural setting that aroused much interest. From 1784 until 1844 he was the chief arbiter in matters of architectural taste in Denmark. His works include various delightful Classical buildings in Altona, Hamburg (e.g. his own house at 116 Palmaille, of 1803–4), and along the banks of the Elbe (e.g. Hirschparkhaus, *c.*1798), as well as the churches at Husum (1828–33) and Neumünster, Germany (1828–34).

Langberg (1950); Lund and Küster (1968); Lund and Thygesen (1995); Watkin and Mellinghoff (1987)

Hansen, Hans Christian (1803–83). Distinguished Danish Neoclassicist, the brother of T. E. *Hansen, he was influenced early in his career by C. F. *Hansen (to whom he was not related), and by G. F. *Hetsch, who brought the influence of *Schinkel to the architectural world of Denmark. Hansen completed his studies by travelling in Italy and Greece, and in 1834 became Architect to the Greek Court in Athens, where he remained for eighteen years, making archaeological investigations (he reconstructed the Temple of Niké Apteros and, with Eduard Schaubert (1804–60) and Joseph Hoffer (*c*.1810–before 1851), compiled the material for Hoffer's account of horizontal curvature and optical corrections in Greek temples (1838)), and designing many important buildings, including the Mint (1834–6), and the University (1839–50), in a refined *Greek Revival style influenced by Schinkel. With C. R. *Cockerell and others he designed the Anglican Church of St Paul, Athens (1841). He designed the *Rundbogenstil Arsenal and Dockyards at Trieste (1852–6), and the City Hospital, Copenhagen (1856–63), in a Byzantino-Rundbogenstil. Other works include the Observatory (1859–61) and the Zoological Museum, Copenhagen (1863–70). He was a pioneer in the study and application of *polychromy in architecture.

Middleton and Watkin (1987); Placzek (1982); van Vynckt (1993); Weilbach (1947)

Hansen, Theophilus Edvard von (1813–91). Brother of H. C. *Hansen (by whom his work was influenced), he was trained in Copenhagen, where the dominant figures were C. F. *Hansen (no relation) and G. F. *Hetsch, who imparted a robust *Neoclassicism to the aspiring architect. In 1838 Hansen went to Greece, where he joined his brother in Athens, designing the Demetrios House (1842–3—later a hotel, but demolished 1958), and later the Academy of Sciences (1859–87) and the National Library (1859–91). In 1846 he settled in Vienna at the invitation of *Förster, whose daughter he later (1851) married. Influenced by French *Neoclassicism, by the architecture of *Schinkel, and by his studies of Greek *Antique and *Byzantine architecture, he created many of the most distinguished buildings of his time in Vienna. He collaborated with Förster on Byzantino-*Rundbogenstil designs for the Army Museum in the Arsenal (1850–6), and contributed to the developments on the *Ringstrasse*, including his masterpiece, the *Parliamentsgebäude* (Parliament Building—1874–83), a handsome composition in the spirit of Greek Antiquity with some of the finest *Greek Revival interiors ever conceived. After a visit to Italy in 1856 his style turned to a luxuriant Italian *Renaissance (e.g. Protestant School, Karlsplatz (1859), and the *Heinrichshof* on the *Ringstrasse* (1861), which set the *Cinquecento flavour of many apartment-blocks on the *Ringstrasse* over the following years). However, Hansen also became a leader in the use of *polychromy, influenced no doubt by *Semper, and synthesized Greek and *Renaissance themes in his beautiful *Musikvereinsgebäude* (Hall of the Music Society—1869–70) and Academy of Fine Arts (1872–7), Vienna.

Anzeiger der österreichischen Akademie der Wissenschaften, 114 (1977), 260–76; Lhotsky (1941); Middleton and Watkin (1987); Niemann and Feldegg (1893); Russack (1942); Strobl (1961); Traulos (1967); Wagner-Rieger (1970, 1980)

Hansom, Joseph Aloysius (1803–82). English architect, he entered into partnership with Edward Welch (1806–68), and designed Birmingham Town Hall (1830–4), a large *peripteral *Corinthian Roman temple on a high rusticated *podium, completed in 1849 by Charles Edge (*c*.1801–67), who went on to become a leading Birminghan architect (although his only important design was The Crescent, Filey, Yorkshire (1835–8)). Bankrupted by the Birmingham venture (1834), the partnership was dissolved and Hansom turned to invention (he designed the Hansom Cab) and business (he founded *The Builder* in 1842). Welch practised in Liverpool (1837–49), and patented various heating-systems for houses (1850 and 1865). Hansom resumed architectural practice, designing the robustly Classical Particular Baptist Chapel, Belvoir Street, Leicester (1845), now in secular use and known as the 'Pork-Pie', but is better known for his *Gothic Roman Catholic churches, including St Walburga, Preston, Lancashire (1850), the Holy Name of Jesus, Manchester (1869–71), and St Philip Neri, now the Cathedral of Our Lady and St Philip Howard, Arundel, Sussex (1870–3).

Curl (1995); Dixon and Muthesius (1985)

Hara, Hiroshi (1936–). Japanese architect. His spectacular buildings, including the Yamato International Building, Ota-ku, Tokyo (1985–6), the Umeda Sky City, Osaka (1988–93), and the Kyoto JR Station, Shimogyo, Kyoto (1991–7), demonstrate his skills in handling enormous structures based on sophisticated technologies. They have influenced younger architects.

Jodidio (1997*a*)

Hard architecture. Tough, impersonal, windowless buildings with *graffiti*-resistant walls, usually associated with prisons, mental-hospitals, and other secure structures.

Sommer (1974, 1983)

Hardouin-Mansart, Jules (1646–1708). French architect. His great-uncle was F. *Mansart, who trained him. He was the master of the *Louis Quatorze style, imbibing architectural ideas from Le *Vau and *Bruant, and was eventually appointed to the important State offices associated with building, becoming *Premier Architecte* (1685) and *Superintendant des Bâtiments du Roi* (1699). He worked with Bruant on the Church of St-Louis, Invalides, Paris, in the 1670s, but himself designed and built the noble Dôme des Invalides (*c.*1677–91), where *Baroque and Classical tendencies are serenely balanced, the whole constructedon a Greek-cross plan and influenced by F. Mansart's unexecuted designs for the Bourbon *mortuary-chapel at St-Denis. From 1673 he worked at Versailles, taking charge in 1678, and filling in Le Vau's Garden-Court to form the *Galerie des Glâces* (Hall of Mirrors—1678–89), the epitome of the grand Louis Quatorze style. He also designed the Grand Trianon (again 1678–89), several fountains in the grounds, and the Chapel (1688–after 1708). The last, with its steeply pitched roof, looks like a Classicized medieval building, but the beautiful interior, with its arcade carrying an elegant screen of *Corinthian columns, is almost a harbinger of *Neoclassicism, and was completed by de *Cotte. In much of his work he was also assisted by *Lassurance and Pierre Le Pautre (*c.*1643–1716)—who was the leading interior decorator at Versailles, responsible for the *Salon de l'Œil de Bœuf* (1701), and the finishings of the Chapel. Hardouin-Mansart's Place Vendôme (from 1698) has handsome, unified façades on an arcaded *rez-de-chaussée*, and is one of the French capital's most distinguished urban spaces. His circular Place des Victoires only partially survives. His grandson, **Jean Hardouin-Mansart de Jouy** (1700–   ), rebuilt the west façade of St-Eustache, Paris (1733–88).

Blunt (1982); Bourget and Cattaui (1960); Braham and Smith (1973); Hautecœur (1948); Marie and Marie (1972)

Hardouin-Mansart de Levi, Jacques, Comte de Sagonne (1703–58). French architect, grandson of Jules *Hardouin-Mansart. He became *Architecte du Roi* in 1742. His domestic designs include the Maison des Dames de Saint-Chaumont (1734) and the Hôtel Mansart de Sagonne (1743), both in Paris, both of which were essentially *Rococo in style. His masterpiece is the elegant *Cathedral Church of St-Louis, Versailles (1743–54), with its noble *cupola and assured architectural enrichment. He also designed a hospital at Marseilles (1753). Given to high living, he eventually fled from France and may have settled in Lisbon, Portugal, after the earthquake of 1755.

Papworth (1852); Sturgis *et al.* (1901–2)

Hardwick, Philip (1792–1870). English architect, he commenced practice with his father **Thomas** (1752–1829), who had been a pupil of *Chambers and later designed St Marylebone Parish Church, London (1813–17). Philip held several official posts, and was a competent and eclectic designer in various styles. He is best known for the nobly monumental *Doric *propylaeum at Euston Station, London (1836–40—needlessly demolished 1962), but he was capable of a remarkably plain, robust *Neoclassicism, as in his utilitarian brick St Katharine's Docks and Warehouses, London (1827–9). His *Tuscan Dock Traffic Office, Albert Dock, Liverpool (1846–7), is a powerful design, and he also collaborated with Jesse *Hartley on the designs of the warehouses there. His Goldsmiths' Hall, Foster Lane (1829–35), and City Club, Old Broad Street (1833–4), both in London, are typical of his robust *Baroque and Classical styles. With his son, P. C. *Hardwick, he was responsible for the *Tudor *Gothic Hall and Library, Lincoln's Inn, London (1843–5), an accomplished design for its date, on which the young *Pearson also worked.

Colvin (1995); *DNB* (1917); Dixon and Muthesius (1985); Smithson (1968)

Hardwick, Philip Charles (1822–92). Son of Philip *Hardwick, he was a pupil of *Blore and joined his father in practice in 1843. He designed the majestic Great Hall at Euston Station, London (1846–9—demolished), the huge Great Western Hotel, Paddington Station (1851–3), and the exquisite *Gothic Revival Beauchamp Almshouses and Chapel, Newland, Worcestershire (1862–4).

Curl (1995); Dixon and Muthesius (1985)

Hardy, Hugh Gelston (b. 1932). American architect, he formed a partnership with Malcolm Holzman and Norman Pfeiffer (Hardy Holzman Pfeiffer Associates, or HHPA in New York (1967). The firm's work includes the Olmsted Theater, Adelphi University, Garden City, NY (1974), and the Los Angeles County Museum of Art (from 1987). HHPA became known for its use of familiar roadside structures, signs, and collages. The firm has insisted on creating buildings of disparate parts, seemingly thrown together, giving an impression of incompleteness that some might argue is not architecture at all. The bunker-like WCCO-TV building, Minneapolis (1983) is a good example of their work.

Emanuel (1994); Lampugnani (1988)

Hare, Henry Thomas (1861–1921). English architect, he designed several distinguished buildings, including the *Renaissance Revival Town Hall, Oxford (1893–7), with *Elizabethan gables derived from Kirby Hall, Northamptonshire. At University College, Bangor, Wales (1907–10), and Westminster College, Cambridge (1897–9), he used a late-*Tudor *Gothic style, but he was also capable of powerful *Mannerist and *Baroque essays, as in his stupendous United Kingdom Provident Institution, Strand, London (1906–7—with fine sculpture and internal paintings—but demolished in 1961), and Central Library, Islington (1905–8).

Dixon and Muthesius (1985); Gray (1985)

Häring, Hugo (1882–1958). German architect, a pupil of Theodor *Fischer. He became Secretary of Der *Ring, and an early participant in *CIAM. He designed Modernist buildings for Berlin-Zehlendorf (1926–7) and Berlin-Siemensstadt (1929–31). Later, he gradually evolved theories concerning *Organic architecture, which in his terms seems to have meant fitness for purpose and an abandonment of preconceived aesthetic ideas or forms, although some of his works had a flavour of *Expressionism. Among his works were the complex of farm-buildings, Gut Garkau, near Lübeck (1923–5), the Tobacco Goods Factory, Neustadt, Holstein (1925), the Behrendt House, Berlin (1930), the von Prittwitz Building, Tutzing (1937–41), the Kunst und Werk School, Berlin (1942), and the Schmitz House, Biberach (1949–50).

Lampugnani (1988); Morgan and Naylor (1987); van Vynckt (1993)

Hårleman, Carl (1700–52). Swedish architect, son of the landscape-architect **Johan Hårleman** (1662–1707), he assisted *Tessin the Younger in building the Royal Palace, Stockholm, and introduced the French *Rococo style in his works in Stockholm and Drottningholm. He designed various country-houses based on *Blondel's ideas that were influences on *Adelcrantz and others. In the 1740s he carried out sensitive works at the Carolinian *Mortuary Chapel (*Karolinska Grafkoret*), Riddarholms Church, Stockholm, originally designed by *Tessin the Elder. Among his other works were the exquisite *maison de plaisance* at Svartsjö (1735–9) and the East India Company warehouse, Göteborg (*c*.1740), a four-storey industrial building with *Sublime qualities.

Stavenow (1927)

harling. Rough-cast render on a wall, made with sand, lime, water, and small gravel.

harmonic division *or* **proportion.** Relation of successive numbers in a series, the reciprocals of which are in arithmetical progression, the numbers being proportional to the lengths of twanged cords that sound harmonious. Rooms with measurements 1:2, 2:3, and 3:4 were held by *Renaissance theorists to be harmonious: some, including *Alberti, argued that this was the basis for satisfactory relationships of dimension and form in Classical architecture, and indeed the key to understanding Nature and the Universe. *Palladio and others evolved further complex proportions including ratios of 5:6 and others.

OED (1933); Wittkower (1988)

Harris, Emanuel Vincent (1879–1971). English architect, his finest works were the extension to *Waterhouse's Town Hall, Manchester, and the circular Municipal Library beside it, a truly masterly sequence of buildings in terms of style and scale (1927–38). His Civic Hall, Leeds, Yorkshire (1930–3), and Central Library, Kensington, London (1958–60), are good examples of his confident Classicism. Among his largest works are County Hall, Trent Bridge, Nottingham (1935–50), Bristol Council House (1937–9), and Government Offices, Whitehall, London (1951–9).

Gray (1985)

Harrison, Peter (1716–76). Born in York, England, he settled in America in 1740 and designed various distinguished buildings of the *Colonial period. He was a practitioner of *Palladianism, presumably gleaned from various standard works sponsored by

*Burlington which he had in his own library. He drew on *Gibbs for his King's Chapel, Boston (1749–58), and Christ Church, Cambridge (1760–1), both in Massachusetts, and on Gibbs and *Kent for the Touro Synagogue, Newport, Rhode Island (1759–63). For his Brick Market, Newport, Rhode Island (1761–73), he was influenced by *Jones's Old Somerset House, illustrated in *Campbell's *Vitruvius Britannicus* (vol. 1). The clarity of his remarkably advanced Redwood Library, Newport, RI (1748–50), points to *Neoclassicism, and appears to have inspired *Jefferson. He was the most talented architect working in America at the time, and it is known he possessed a fine architectural library, destroyed by an anti-Loyalist mob in 1775.

Bridenbaugh (1949); *DAB* (1943); Downing and Scully (1967); Placzek (1982)

Harrison, Thomas (1744–1829). English provincial architect, he was nevertheless among the most advanced Neoclassicists of his time, designing the Lycaeum, Bold Street, Liverpool (1800–3), the Portico Library, Mosley Street, Manchester (1802–6), and his masterpiece, the Castle, County Courts, Prison, Armoury, Barracks, Exchequer, and *Propylaeum, Chester (1788–1822), in all of which he demonstrated his talents as a creator of the most monumental Neoclassical buildings. The Chester Castle group is arguably the finest *Greek Revival ensemble in the British Isles. He also designed two huge *Doric memorial columns: one commemorating Rowland, 1st Viscount Hill (1772–1842), in Shrewsbury, Shropshire (1814–16), and the other celebrating Herry William Paget, 1st Marquis of Anglesey (1768–1854), at Llanfairpwll, Anglesey (1816). Hill and Paget were distinguished soldiers during the Napoleonic Wars. As a designer in the *Gothic style, however, Harrison was less impressive, although at Lancaster Castle (1788–99) he composed some fine buildings, notably the polygonal Shire Hall. His engineering abilities were formidable: his Skerton Bridge, Lancaster (1783–8), was the first large masonry bridge in Britain carrying a flat road from bank to bank, while his Grosvenor Bridge, Chester (1827–9), his largest such structure, was the biggest stone arch in the world when it was built. He also designed some visionary national monuments as severe as any of the time, and he was highly regarded in his lifetime, notably by C. R. *Cockerell. Among his many works of domestic architecture may be mentioned Broomhall, Fife (1796–9), and The Citadel, Hawkstone, Shropshire (1824–5). Had he not lived in relative isolation in Chester he would conceivably have outshone *Soane and *Smirke.

Colvin (1995); *Country Life*, 149 (1971), 876–9, 944–7, 1088–91, 1539; Crook (1972*a*); *DNB* (1917); Placzek (1982); Summerson (1993)

Harrison, Wallace Kirkman (1895–1981). American architect, he formed one of the most successful practices in the USA. With Raymond *Hood and others he worked on the Rockefeller Center, New York (1929–33), and was joined by *Abramovitz in 1941. As Harrison, André *Fouilhoux, and Abramovitz, the firm expanded the Rockefeller Center, work continuing until 1974. After Fouilhoux's death (1945), the firm became Harrison and Abramovitz and, with Le *Corbusier, *Niemeyer, and *Markelius, designed the United Nations Headquarters, New York (1947–53), with the Secretariat, one of the city's first *curtain-walled *skyscrapers. Then came the Corning Glass Center and Administrative Building, Corning, NY (1955–6), followed by the Phoenix Mutual Life Insurance Building, Hartford, Conn. (1960–4). A much more formal style was adopted for the Lincoln Center, New York (1962–8), with its Metropolitan Opera House and Philharmonic (now Avery Fisher) Hall: the building is clad in travertine, and the style is an extremely stripped minimalist type that cannot really be called Neoclassical. The gigantic South Mall, Albany, NY (1963–78), was supposedly influenced by the Dalai Lama's Palace at Lhasa, Tibet.

Koolhaas (1978); Krinsky (1978); Newhouse (1989); Young (1980)

Harsdorff, Caspar Frederik (1733–99). Danish architect. A pupil of N.-H. *Jardin and J.-F. *Blondel, he was an accomplished designer in the Neoclassical style. He was responsible for the *Mortuary Chapel of King Frederik V (1746–66) in Roskilde Cathedral (1768–78), one of the purest works of *Neoclassicism in Europe for its date, with octagonal coffering derived from the *basilica of Maxentius in Rome. For this project he was assisted by C. F. *Hansen, his pupil for several years, who completed the work (1821–5). He also designed the *propylaea between the Royal Palaces, the *Doric Hercules pavilion, and a house in Kongens Nytorv, all of the 1770s, and all in Copenhagen. The house, intended as an exemplar of Neoclassicism, is extraordinary for its *engaged *Ionic *capitals that show not the usual fronts of the *volutes on the *façade, but the *pulvins or *baluster-sides.

Cruickshank (1996); Middleton and Watkin (1987)

Hartley, Jesse (1780–1860). English Surveyor to the Liverpool Dock Trustees (1824–60), in which capacity he designed (with contributions from P. C. *Hardwick) the Albert Dock (1843–5), a powerful exercise in utilitarian brick carried on massive unfluted cast-iron *Doric columns. It is as *Sublime an ensemble as anywhere in Europe. He also designed the Brunswick (1832), Waterloo (1834), Stanley (1850–7), Wapping (1855), and West Canada (1858) Docks, all in Liverpool.

Colvin (1995); Curl (1990); Dixon and Muthesius (1985)

Hartung, Hugo (1855–1932). German architect, he was primarily a designer of domestic architecture, much of it with medieval *vernacular motifs, steep roofs, and *turrets. His *Motive der mittelalterlichen Baukunst in Deutschland* (Themes in Medieval Architecture in Germany—1896–1902) and *Ziele und Ergebnisse der italienischen Gotik* (Italian Gothic Objectives and Influences—1912) prompted some early C20 architects into exploring how medieval architecture might be a starting-point for contemporary design. His drawings of buildings in Egypt and the Middle East (published 1907) had an impact on *Behrens and others who sought to simplify design into blocky cubic forms. Among his buildings his own house and others at the Villencolonie, Grünewald, Berlin, of the early 1900s, deserve mention.

Hartung (1896–1902, 1902, 1912); *Zentralblatt der Bauverwaltung*, 20 (1900), 4–6, 16–17, 27 (1907), 566–9, 578–80

Harvard architecture. The work of architects trained in *Bauhaus principles by *Gropius and *Breuer at Harvard University's Graduate School of Design in the 1940s and 1950s. Its practitioners included E. L. *Barnes, Philip *Johnson, I. M. *Pei, and Paul *Rudolph, who promoted *Modernism throughout the USA.

Herdeg (1985)

Harvey, John Hooper (1911–97). English architectural and garden historian. A prolific writer and distinguished scholar, he made a major contribution over many years to several aspects of garden history, but his greatest achievement by far was his magisterial *English Mediaeval Architects: A Biographical Dictionary down to 1550*, first published in 1954, and subsequently revised. Based on documentary sources, it illumines the English medieval architectural world with gracefully presented facts.

Garden History 26/1 (Summer 1998), 102–5; Harvey (1987); personal knowledge.

Haschenperg, Stephan von (*fl.* 1539–43). German military engineer. He was employed by King Henry VIII of England (1509–47) to design part of the new coastal defences, including Sandgate, Deal, and Walmer Castles in Kent, all remarkably coherent geometrical examples of C16 military architecture. He carried out surveys at Calais (completed 1540), and was in charge of the works at St Mawes Castle, Cornwall. He also fortified Carlisle against the Scots before returning to Central Europe, where he worked for the Bishop of Olmütz.

Harvey (1987)

Hasegawa, Itsuko (1941–). Japanese architect. One of the first Japanese women to establish a major architectural reputation, her work includes the Shonandai Cultural Centre, Fijisawa, Kanagawa (1987–90—a reduced model of the Universe), the Oshima-machi Picture-Book Museum, Imizu, Toyama (1992–4), the Sumida Culture Factory, Sumida, Tokyo (1991–4), and the Museum of Fruit, Yamanashi-shi, Yamanashi (1993–5—a highly sophisticated development of the conservatory, with added symbolic aspects in the evocative forms used).

Jodidio (1997*a*)

Hasenauer, Karl, Freiherr von (1833–94). Austrian architect, he was involved with the building of *Semper's Museums of Art and Natural History in Vienna (1872–9), and realized the gigantic proposals of van der *Nüll and *Siccard von Siccardsburg for the Great Exhibition in Vienna (1873), a huge rectangle with central *rotunda and, on both sides, 32 *pavilions. He built the *Burgtheater*, Vienna (1874–8), to Semper's designs, and supervised the Imperial Forum complex after Semper's death, including the grandiose New Hofburg (completed 1913). He also designed the Villa

Zang, Neidling (1864), the Lützow Palace (1870), and the Hermesvilla, Lainz (1882–6), all in or near Vienna, and all on cunningly contrived plans, with *Renaissance-inspired interior decorations.

Beetz (1929); Bernhard (1992); Eggert (1976); Lhotsky (1941); Mallgrave (1996)

hatchment. *See* Achievement of Arms.

haunch. **1.** Indefinite roughly triangular portion or *flank* between the *crown* and *abutments of an arch, i.e. between the crown and the *springing* on the *piers. **2.** Timber slightly arched or concave on its underside under a *lintel. **3.** Part of a beam projecting below a floor, usually slightly cambered.

Haus-Rucker-Co (House-Mover Company). Viennese architectural and design group founded in 1967 by Laurids and Manfred Ortner, Günter Zamp Kelp, and Klaus Pinter, with others representing different disciplines. The group opened offices in Düsseldorf (1970) and New York (1971), so quickly became international. Specializing in 'disposable architecture', pneumatic structures, air-mattresses, and life-support systems, its projects (often featuring plastics) have included Balloon for Two (1967), the external shell around the Haus Lange Museum, Krefeld (1971), and the Oasis 5 in Kassel (1972). Among unrealized projects that have received attention are the Pneumacosm pneumatic-cell expansion of New York (1967) and an artificial cloud with a huge ladder for access (the Big Piano—1972). *Cook has identified Haus-Rucker-Co as contributing to *Experimental architecture.

Burns (1972); Cook (1971); *Design Quarterly*, 78/79 (1970), 29–33; Haus-Rucker-Co (1984)

Haussmann, Baron Georges-Eugène (1808–91). French Préfect of the Département of the Seine from 1853, he directed the improvements of the City of Paris during the Second Empire of Napoleon III (1852–70). His models were those established by Henri IV (1589–1610), Louis XIV (1643–1715), Napoleon I (1804–14), and the late-C18 type of Classical layout involving straight avenues meeting at circular spaces (*rond-points*), while his brief was to make Paris a capital-city suitable for an Imperial power; to modernize it for an expanding population and the needs of industrialization; to solve the problems of traffic (especially by connecting the railway-termini by means of wide streets and boulevards); and to create vistas of Roman grandeur terminating in monumental buildings. In a mere 17 years of wholesale clearance and rebuilding Paris got nearly 100 miles of brand-new streets, thousands of buildings, over 4,000 acres of parks, nearly 400 miles of sewers, and means by which millions of gallons of clean water flowed daily to the city. He encouraged modern methods of construction, such as the use of iron and glass by *Baltard and others, and he managed to ensure the erection of a homogeneous *Classical *Renaissance Revival urban fabric. His *Mémoires* (1890–3) are a valuable record of his career and ideas, while under his patronage several monumental works on the history and architecture of Paris were published, including *Histoire générale de Paris*, *Paris dans sa splendeur*, and *Promenades de Paris* (1867–73). Some critics have been harsh about his destruction of old buildings and whole quarters, while others have seen his work as inimical to the urban proletariat. Nevertheless, he created an elegant and beautiful city, laid out on principles established at the École des *Beaux-Arts, which can still be admired, and his systems of streets worked well until excessive numbers of motor-vehicles created such immense problems of traffic-jams and pollution from the 1960s. His work was influential, especially in France and the USA, and had a profound effect on the planning of Vienna.

Chapman and Chapman (1957); Gaillard (1977); Haussmann (1890–3); Lavedan (1975); Loyer (1987); Malet (1973); Middleton and Watkin (1987); Pinkney (1958); Reau, Lavedan, *et al.* (1954); Saalman (1971); van Vynckt (1993)

Haviland, John (1792–1852). Born in Somerset, England, he became a pupil of James *Elmes. He settled in the USA in 1816, where he designed several buildings, including the Franklin Institute, Philadelphia, Pa. (1825–6), with a severe *Greek Revival front based on the *Choragic Monument of Thrasyllus, Athens. He published *The Builder's Assistant* (1818–21), intended, like his other publishing and teaching activities, to augment his meagre earnings as an architect: it was the first American publication in which the Greek *Orders were depicted, and was reissued in four volumes in 1830. He designed the first prison in the USA built in accordance with the ideas of English reformers, the Eastern State Penitentiary, Philadelphia

(1821–37), using a *Gothic castellated style. He brought out a new edition of Owen Biddle's *Young Carpenter's Assistant* (first published in 1805) in 1830, embellished with new plates, including an illustration of his Miner's Bank, Pottsville, Pa. (1830–1—demolished), with its façade covered with iron plates made in such a way to look like *ashlar. His many churches and private houses were mostly in the Greek Revival style, but his building housing the New York City Halls of Justice and House of Detention, known as the 'Tombs' (1835–8), was in the *Egyptian Revival style, calculated to instil awe and terror in all who saw it. He first used Egyptianizing details at the New Jersey State Penitentiary, near Trenton (1832–6), partly for reasons of economy, but partly to suggest the 'misery which awaits the unhappy being' unfortunate enough to be incarcerated, for the building was Sublimely robust and terrifying, with its large areas of blank walls and sinister *portico set between two *pylons. Egyptianesque, too, was his Essex County Court House and Gaol, Newark, NJ (1836–8). Haviland has been called the greatest of the American Egyptian Revival architects.

Carrott (1978); Curl (1994); Hamlin (1964); Haviland (1830, 1830*a*); Hitchcock (1976); *Journal of the Society of Architectural Historians*, 23 (1964), 101–5, 25 (1966), 197–208, 26 (1967), 307–9; Kennedy (1989); Teeters and Shearer (1957); Whiffen and Koeper (1983)

Havlíček, Josef (1899–1961). Czechoslovak avant-garde architect who vigorously promoted the ideas of *CIAM and Le *Corbusier. With Karel Honzík (1900–66) he designed the *International *Modernist Ministry of Pensions, Prague (1926–35). His proposal (1950s), in line with CIAM orthodoxy, to demolish the New Town, Prague, replacing it with pyramidal *skyscrapers, was not realized. His apartment-block, Prague-Letná (1937–8), was probably his most elegant design.

Havlíček (1964); Leśnikowski (1996); Roth (1946)

hawksbeak, hawksbill. 1. *Romanesque *ovolo moulding enriched with sculpted *beak-heads. **2.** Any moulding with a convex top and a concave underside meeting at a point, in *section resembling the beak of a bird of prey, as on a *string-course. **3.** *Doric moulding related to the *cyma recta. **4.** *Crossette in the sense of a *volute at the upper corner of a door- or window-*architrave.

hawksbell. *Ballflower ornament.

Hawksmoor, Nicholas (1661–1736). One of the two most imaginative English *Baroque architects (the other was *Vanbrugh), he worked with *Wren, notably on the Chelsea Hospital, St Paul's Cathedral, and the City Churches, all in London. From 1689 to 1715 he was Clerk of Works at Kensington Palace (where he designed the Orangery (1704–5), with revisions by Vanbrugh), and from 1698 to 1735 Clerk of Works at Greenwich Hospital, where he seems to have played a major role in the design of the east range of Queen Anne's Court and the dormitories in King William's Court. In 1715 he also became Clerk of the Works at Whitehall, Westminster, and St James's, as well as Secretary to the Board of Works, which made him a senior official of the Royal Works. Vanbrugh engaged his services at Castle Howard, Yorkshire, and Blenheim Palace, Oxfordshire, and it is now clear that the skills Hawksmoor had acquired under Wren enabled the architecturally untrained Vanbrugh's schemes to come to fruition. By 1700 Hawksmoor had evolved his original style, as is evident from Easton Neston, Northamptonshire (*c*.1695–1702), a large country-house, and over the next decades demonstrated his assured understanding of the Classical vocabulary as well as its imaginative application. In particular, he understood the tensions and possibilities of the juxtaposition of masses of masonry, while the drama and power of modelling, light, and dark were exploited to the full in his vigorous designs (e.g. the Orangery, Kensington Palace, London (1704–5)).

Hawksmoor was appointed one of the two Surveyors (the other was *Gibbs) to the Commissioners for Building Fifty New Churches in London under the Act of 1711 and in that capacity he designed six of the most original churches in and near the capital: the body of St Alphege, Greenwich (1712–14), St Anne, Limehouse (1714–30), St George-in-the East, Wapping (1714–29), Christ Church, Spitalfields (1714–29), St Mary Woolnoth, City of London (1716–24), and St George, Bloomsbury (1716–31). St Alphege's is in the form of a temple, with a huge *serliana at the east end; St Anne's has a powerful tower with a crowning *lantern like a medieval element in Classical clothes; St George-in-the-East has four pepper-pot staircase-towers and a curious top to the western tower formed of altar-like drums; Christ Church, Spitalfields, has a *broach spire set above a gigantic serliana porch; St Mary Woolnoth has powerful Baroque modelling; while St George Bloomsbury has an immense Roman temple *portico and a tower crowned with a stepped *pyramid derived from descriptions of the *Mausoleum at Halicarnassus. From these buildings the interests of Hawksmoor may be deduced. He was bookish (he had a considerable library), steeped in a love of Antiquity, fascinated by English medieval architecture, and intrigued by the possibilities of freely interpreting the great buildings of the past from descriptions. Some of his work is derived from earlier French publications showing images of supposedly *Antique buildings, which partially explains the element of fantasy in his designs.

Hawksmoor often introduced powerful emotional contents: at the Mausoleum, Castle Howard (1729–42), for example, the *peristyle of his circular Roman-temple form is a *Doric Order, but the unfluted columns have only one *triglyph over each *intercolumniation, giving a brooding solemnity to the architecture, influenced perhaps by *Bramante's *tempietto* at San Pietro in Montorio, Rome. The Clarendon Building, Oxford (1712–65), also employs closely packed unfluted Roman Doric columns as well as inventively oversized keystones and oddly placed *guttae. He also designed in the *Gothic style, as at All Souls College, Oxford (1716–35), and the western towers at Westminster Abbey, London (designed 1734 and completed by J. *James (*c*.1745)). Some of his inventions, such as the Carrmire Gate, Castle Howard (*c*.1730), with its steep pyramids, powerful modelling derived from *Serlio, and emphatic qualities, combine the *primitive, allusions to Antiquity, and a fascination with geometry, anticipating the most robust and stripped language of late-C18 *Neoclassicism. He also designed the Pyramid *eyecatcher at Castle Howard (1728), the *obelisk in the Market Place, Ripon, Yorkshire (1702), and (with James) the Church of St Luke, Old Street, London (1727–33), with its obelisk-spire. In its essentials, however, Hawksmoor's architecture is primarily a demonstration that in geometry lies the key to all order, all creation. One of his last designs to be realized (with modifications by its builder, *Townesend) was the screen-wall and entrance at Queen's College, Oxford (1733–6), on the High Street.

Colvin (1995); Colvin (ed.) (1976); Downes (1966, 1980); Goodhart-Rendel (1924); Placzek (1982); Summerson (1993)

Hayberger, Johann Gotthard (1699–1764). With *Hueber, Hayberger is credited with the design of the *Baroque library of the Benedictine Abbey of Admont (*c*.1745–66). He was also responsible for the library of the Benedictine Abbey of St Florian (1744–50), and designed the *Rathaus* (Town Hall), Steyr (1765–78), a *Rococo palace with a handsome tower.

Blunt (1978); Hempel (1965); Powell (1959)

head. 1. Top or upper part of anything, e.g. a *doorway or window-aperture. **2.** Roofing-tile forming part of the first course of a roof at the *eaves. **3.** Any stone so finished as to have one end exposed on the face of a wall as a *header in brickwork. **4.** Upper part of a chimney-stack. **5.** Small cistern at the top of a rainwater-pipe receiving water from the gutter called a *rainwater- or hopper-head.

header. Brick or stone with its longer dimension buried within the wall and the smaller *face exposed.

head-mould. *Hood-mould, *drip-stone, *label, or weather-moulding set above the *head of any aperture.

head-stone. 1. Upright inscribed memorial stone at the head of a grave in a burial-ground. **2.** Corner- or foundation-stone. **3.** Keystone in an arch.

hearse, herce, herse. 1. Falling door of grated construction, i.e. *portcullis. **2.** Horizontal grating, flat or curved, fixed with *prickets for candles to commemorate the dead. **3.** Open metal framework over a sepulchral memorial, usually to support the pall, as in the Beauchamp chapel, St Mary's Church, Warwick. An iron hearse, with prickets, survives over the Marmion tomb in St Nicholas's Church, West Tanfield, Yorkshire (*c*.1387).

Hegemann, Werner (1881–1936). German architect and planner, he designed (in association with Elbert Peets (1881–1936)) several *Garden Suburbs in the USA, and (again with Peets), published *The American Vitruvius: An Architects' Handbook of Civic Art* (1922), an important work in city-planning literature in which *Beaux-Arts ideas and the influence of *Sitte are clear. In Berlin he edited *Wasmuths Monatshefte für Baukunst und*

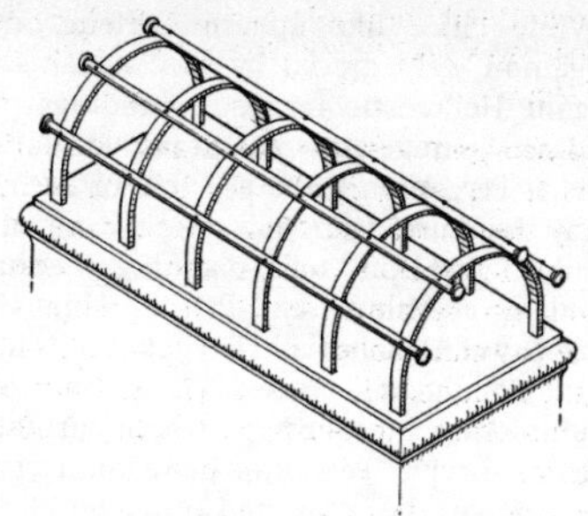

hearse. 3. Based on the Beauchamp hearse, Warwick. (*JJS*)

Städtebau (Wasmuth's Monthly Periodicals for Architecture and Town Planning) from 1922, and wrote prolifically on architecture and planning. He was a major influence in the USA, especially after he returned to the USA having fallen foul of Nazism, which he denounced in a volume published in 1933.

Hegemann (1911, 1911–13, 1923, 1929, 1929*a*, 1936–8, 1976); Hegemann and Peets (1972)

Heideloff, Karl Alexander von (1788–1865). German architect. He was Professor at the *Polytechnische Schule* (Polytechnic School) in Nuremberg from 1822, and wrote several important studies, including *Bauhütte des Mittelalters in Deutschland* (Masonic Lodges of the Middle Ages in Germany—1844) and *Kunst des Mittelalters in Schwaben* (Art of the Middle Ages in Swabia—1855). He carried out numerous restorations of medieval buildings, including Bamberg Cathedral (1831–4), and St Jakob, Rothenburg-ob-der-Tauber (1854–7). Among his designs for new churches, based on late-*Gothic and geometrical principles owing much to *Neoclassicism, St Peter's, Sonneberg, in the former Dukedom of Saxe-Meiningen (1843–4), is probably the best surviving example.

Heideloff (1838–55, 1844, 1855, 1855*a*); Hensoldt (1845); Mittig and Plagemann (1972)

Heins & La Farge. The American architects George Louis Heins (1860–1907) and Christopher Grant La Farge (1862–1938) formed a partnership in 1886. The firm won the competition (1888) to design the Cathedral of St John the Divine in New York with an entry mixing a round-arched style influenced by the work of H. H. *Richardson and *Byzantine architecture. From 1911, *Cram, Goodhue, & Ferguson took over and transformed the building into a masterpiece of *Gothic Revival, the original style having fallen from favour. Heins & La Farge also designed St Matthew's Roman Catholic Cathedral, Washington, DC (from 1893), the subway stations for the New York Rapid Transit Commission (from 1904), and buildings in the New York Zoological Park (from 1899). La Farge continued to practise after Heins's death, and, with Benjamin Wistar Morris (1870–1944), designed St James's Cathedral, Seattle, Wash., and St Patrick's Church, Philadelphia, Pa. (both from 1915).

Muccigrosso (1980); Wickersham (1977); Wodehouse (1976)

Heinzelmann, Konrad (*c*.1390–1454). Important German late-*Gothic architect, he worked at Ulm *Minster in the 1420s before devoting his energies to the building of the great *hall-church of St Georg, Nördlingen, Bavaria, from 1427 to 1438. He was in Rothenburg-ob-der-Tauber, overseeing works at the Church of St Jakob, in 1438, and from 1439 until his death was building the *choir of St Lorenz, Nuremberg (completed by *Roriczer).

Frankl (1962)

Hejduk, John Quentin (1929–). American architect. With *Graves, *Eisenman, *Meier, and *Gwathmey one of the *New York Five. He established his practice in 1965, and his works include the Demlin House, Locust Valley, Long Island, NY (1960), the Hommel Apartment, New York (1969), and the Cooper Union Foundation Building restoration, New York (1974–5). Later, he designed the Tegel Development and Kreuzberg Tower and Wings, IBA Social Housing, Berlin (1987–8), and the Tower of Cards project, Groningen, The Netherlands (1990). Hejduk is best known through his writings, theories, and projects, including the *Lancaster/Hanover Masque* (1982–3), an experiment in town-planning containing 'dwellings' for a variety of inhabitants: these include the House of the Suicide and the House of the Mother of the Suicide, in which his theoretical and didactic strivings to push space to the limits are exhibited.

Architecture and Urbanism, 53 (1975), 73–154; Diamonstein (1985); Emanuel (1994); Frampton *et al.* (1975); *Hejduk*, Le Corbusier Foundation (1972); *Journal of the Society of Architectural Historians*, 38/2 (1979), 205–7; van Vynckt (1993)

helioscene. Type of external blind with *louvres, ensuring adequate ventilation, yet keeping out the rays of the sun.

helix (*pl.* **helices**). **1.** Small *volute or *urilla under the *abacus of the *Corinthian *capital, of which there are 16 (2 at each angle, and 2 on each face) connected to the stalks. According to some authorities the 8 inner spiral forms are the helices, while those at the angles are volutes. **2.** Any volute, as on an *Ionic or *Composite capital, a *console, or a *modillion. **3.** Handrail of a stair balustrade forming a helix over the newel.

Hellenic. *Greek architecture and culture from C11 BC to *c.*323 BC.

Wycherley (1962)

Hellenistic. *Greek architecture and culture from the consolidation of Macedonian supremacy under Alexander the Great (356–323 BC) to the foundation of the Roman Empire under Augustus in 27 BC and after in the Eastern Mediterranean. The Hellenistic period therefore coincided with the relative decline of Greece and the evolution of centres of art and patronage in the Greek Kingdoms of Asia Minor and Egypt. Hellenistic architecture is characterized by a greater variation of influence than was apparent in *Hellenic architecture, and was often more opulent, elegant, and graceful. Furthermore, Hellenistic buildings often gained in lightness of effect through a wider *intercolumniation than that found in Hellenic work. The *Doric *Order, for example, became more attenuated and less severe (often with two or more *triglyphs over each intercolumniation), becoming less 'pure' in the process and acquiring certain features from the *Ionic Order: an example was the Temple of Hera Basileia, Pergamon (mid-C2 BC), with very slender columns ($7\frac{1}{2}$ diameters high) and a relatively low *entablature. Among the finest Hellenistic buildings incorporating the Ionic Order, much embellished with vigorous sculpture, were the Mausoleum at Halicarnassus and the Temple of Artemis at Ephesus (both mid-C4 BC, and both 'Wonders' of the Ancient World). Features of the Hellenistic Ionic Order included the *Asiatic base and the omission of the *frieze, as in the Temple of Athena Polias, Priene (from *c.*335 BC). The *Corinthian Order was represented by the *Choragic Monument of Lysicrates, Athens (a very beautiful and delicate version of this Order—334 BC), and by the Temple of Zeus Olympios (later the Olympeion), Athens (started 174 BC), the latter the first external use of that Order for a major building.

While cities like Ephesus, Priene, and Pergamon were graced by spectacular and elegant Hellenistic religious buildings (including the huge and opulent public altar of Zeus at Pergamon (*c.*180 BC—now in Berlin), many structures were of a civic nature, and regular grid-iron town-planning became usual, as at Miletus and Priene, while the huge city of Alexandria in Egypt not only had a grid plan but vast processional avenues and monumental buildings of which virtually nothing survives. Pergamon had a library, theatre, palace, the altar, and other buildings composed as a sequence (C2 BC), and the monumental effects of vistas of *scenography anticipated Imperial Roman planning. Among the most elaborate civic buildings was the *Bouleuterion at Miletus (175–164 BC), with its seating arranged like that of a theatre.

Hellenistic fortifications, gates, public buildings, and monuments drew on eclectic motifs and themes, and often displayed dazzling technique and bravura. Dwelling-houses were often of considerable magnificence, anticipating the luxurious Roman *villa. Arches and *vaults were also employed, notably for tombs and subterranean structures, again pointing the way for Roman architecture. Roman architecture absorbed many aspects of Hellenistic design, as is demonstrated by the temple-complex of Baalbek, Lebanon (AD C1 and 2).

Dinsmoor (1950); Fyfe (1936); Onians (1979); Robertson (1945); Wycherley (1962)

helm. **1.** *Spire on a square tower each side of which is crowned with a *gable. **2.** Bulbous termination of a tower or turret, commonly occurring in Central and Eastern Europe.

Helmer, Hermann Gottlieb (1849–1919), *See* Fellner, Ferdinand.

Helpeston, William de (*fl.* 1319–75). English mason. He worked at Caernarfon Castle, Wales (1319–20), and built 12 chapels at the east end of Vale Royal Abbey, Delamere, Cheshire, from 1359, the plans of which were similar to aspects of Toledo Cathedral, Spain. Helpeston was also in charge of the walls at Chester.

Harvey (1987)

hemi-. Greek word meaning 'half'. It prefixes other words in architectural terminology. Examples include:

hemi-cycle: semicircular room, part of a room, or area off a *court, *forum, garden, etc. A large *exedra. Also a semicircular *vault or arch;
hemi-dome: half-dome, as over an *apse or *niche;
hemi-glyph: half-glyph or chamfer on each side of a *triglyph in the *Doric *Order;
hemi-sphaerium: *dome;
hemi-triglyph: half-triglyph-block as in an internal corner of a *frieze, touching another.

Hénard, Eugène-Alfred (1849–1923). French architect, he made an important contribution to the City of Paris. He was involved in planning the Expositions of 1889 and 1900, and throughout his career worked to conserve the best of the historic fabric, helping to formulate legislation to facilitate the preservation of whole areas, such as the banks of the Seine and the various squares. He also headed the Commission for the extension and improvement of Paris (1908–12). He is regarded as one of the founding-fathers of *urbanism.

Bardet (1978); Hénard (1903–9); Wolf (1969)

Hennebique, François (1842–1921). French pioneer who developed a complete system of *concrete reinforced with steel bars and hooked connections in 1892, evolving earlier patents by *Monier. His first experiment seems to have been proposals for a house at Lombartzyde, Belgium (1879), in which an iron frame was replaced by one of steel bars encased in concrete. He called his system *ferro-concrete, and used it for the first reinforced-concrete *bridge at Viggen, Switzerland (1894), followed by grain-elevators and factories built of the same material from 1894. His Charles Six spinning-mill, Tourcoing, France (1895), was an early use of a framed structure in ferro-concrete, and he gained further publicity with his *cantilevered concrete structure for an exhibition in Geneva (1896), followed by staircases at the Petit Palais, Paris (1897–1900). He revolutionized *theatre-design with the use of cantilevered galleries at Morges (1899): his *Schauspielhaus* (theatre) in Munich (1901–3) was one of the first buildings to have an exposed concrete *frame, while his own house at Bourg-la-Reine (1904) was a remarkable example of the sculptural possibilities of the material. He designed the structure of the Imperial Palace Hotel, Nice (1900), the first use of reinforced concrete for a hotel. His in-house journal, *Le Béton Armé* (1898–1921) is an important record of his designs.

Christophe (1902); Collins (1959); Hennebique (1908); Pevsner (1976); van Vynckt (1993)

Henri II (Deux). Architecture in France from 1547 to 1559 following the reign of *François Ier. Italian *Renaissance influences became stronger, and *arabesques were much favoured, although *Gothic traces were never entirely eliminated. Philibert de L'*Orme was an active protagonist of the period, notably at Anet, while *Bullant also contributed. The *style Henri-Deux* was revived in C19.

Lewis and Darley (1986); Watkin (1986)

Henri IV (Quatre). Architectural style in France from 1589 to 1610 of which the *Place des Vosges* in Paris (1605–12) is a good example, with its private houses set over uniform vaulted *arcades (a theme derived from Italian precedents), brick *façades with limestone *dressings and *chaînes, and tall hipped roofs like *pavilions with *lucarnes. Another fine example of the style is the Château de Grosbois, Seine-et-Marne (*c.*1600), with brick chaînes and stone dressings. The *style Henri-Quatre* was revived in C19.

Cruickshank (1996); Sturgis *et al.* (1901–2)

Henry of Reyns (*fl.* mid-C13). *See* Reyns.

Hentrich, Helmut (1905–). German architect and principal of Hentrich-Petschnigg & Partners (HPP) of Düsseldorf, responsible for many gigantic buildings for large corporations, all in the style of *International Modernism. The best-known works of the firm are the Thyssenhaus, Düsseldorf (1957–60); the Europa Centre, Berlin (1964); the standard façade components for the department-store firm, Horten AG; the Dietrich-Bonhoeffer Church, Düsseldorf-Garath (1964–5); the Finnlandhaus, Hamburg (the first high block in Europe constructed on the suspension system (1966)); the Standard Bank Centre, Johannesburg, South Africa (with Ove *Arup (1967–70)); the *Konzerthalle*, Düsseldorf (1978); and various large office-buildings in Düsseldorf, Cologne, and other cities in Western Germany.

Adams (1989); Emanuel (1994); Hentrich-Petschnigg (1969, 1975)

heptastyle. *See* portico.

herald's rod. *See* caduceus.

Herbert, Henry, 9th Earl of Pembroke (*c.*1689–1750). Owner of Wilton House, Wiltshire, he studied at Christ Church

College, Oxford, in the time of *Aldrich, and was active in promoting the *Palladianism that Inigo *Jones had introduced, and which was being revived in Herbert's lifetime under the aegis of *Burlington. He became an important amateur, probably more faithful to Palladian principles than either Burlington or *Kent. He and Roger *Morris appear to have designed the elegant bridge at Wilton (1736–7), Marble Hill, Twickenham (1724–9), White Lodge, Richmond New Park (1727–8), and other works. *Campbell also worked for or with Herbert, notably in connection with the latter's house in Whitehall, London (1724), and, it seems, Marble Hill. It is probable that Herbert, lacking practical architectural skills, worked with Morris as his amanuensis.

Colvin (1995); *DNB* (1917)

Herculaneum. Roman city near Naples, buried after the eruption of Vesuvius in AD 79. Its rediscovery in C18 and excavation (from 1738) proved to be a potent catalyst in *Neoclassicism, especially as the finds were documented in *Le Antichità di Ercolano* (The Antiquities of Herculaneum—1757–92) and sumptuously illustrated. The artefacts were particularly influential because they revealed much about domestic furnishings and the lives of ordinary Romans. As with *Pompeii (which was actually found later than Herculaneum), the excavations gave countless motifs to designers that were ingredients of Neoclassical schemes, notably the *Etruscan, *Pompeian, *Adam, *Empire, and *Regency styles. *Die schönsten Ornamente und merkwürdigsten Gemälde aus Pompeji, Herkulanum und Stabiae* (The Most Beautiful and Remarkable Paintings from Pompeii, Herculaneum, and Stabia—1828–59) by Wilhelm Zahn (1800–71) provided a rich and accurate source for C19 designers, with its many chromolithographed plates.

Hornblower and Spawforth (1996); Lewis and Darley (1986)

Héré de Corny, Emmanuel (1705–63). French architect (from 1738) to Stanisław Leszczyński (1677–1766), King of Poland (1704–9 and again 1733–4), and Duke of Lorraine and Bar (1736–66). For the Duke, Héré de Corny produced many elegant designs for châteaux and garden-buildings in Lorraine, but his masterpiece is the sequence of urban spaces in Nancy—the Place Royale (now Place Stanislaus), the promenade or Place de la Carrière, and the Hemicycle (1752–6), that together form the most exquisite and impressive work of *Rococo urban planning in the world. Héré published his designs in *Recueil* (1753–6) and *Plans et élévations de la place royale de Nancy & des autres edifices à l'environment bâtis par les ordres du Roy de Pologne duc de Lorraine* (1753). Earlier, he designed Notre Dame de Bon-Secours, Nancy (1738–41), as a mortuary-church for the Duke and his family. He also designed a series of gardens and *fabriques at the Duke's estates of Chanteheux, Commercy, Einville, Lunéville, and Malgrange: Héré was among the first designers to build exotic fabriques, including the influential Turkish and Chinese Kiosks at Lunéville (1737 and 1740). At Lunéville he also built a *Rocher* or *rock-work structure (1742–52) that was early for its type, and completed the Church of St-Jacques (1743–7).

Boyé (1910); Conner (1979); France-Lanord (1984); Héré de Corny (1753, 1753–6); Marot (1954, 1966); Rau (1973); Wiebenson (1978)

Hereford, Walter of (*fl.* 1277–d. 1309). English mason. He was Master of the Works at Vale Royal Abbey, Delamere, Cheshire (1278–90), was in charge of building operations at Caernarfon Castle, Wales, from 1304, and was the principal master-architect employed by the Crown between 1285 and 1309. He designed Grey Friars' Church, Newgate, London (from 1306), and probably influenced the design of St Thomas's, Winchelsea, Sussex, and Holy Trinity, Hull (1295–1300). He may have planned Denbigh Castle, including the gate-house, begun *c.*1300.

Harvey (1987)

Herholdt, Johan Daniel (1818–1902). Danish architect. A pupil of *Bindesbøll and *Hetsch, he also studied old brick buildings in Denmark and *Renaissance architecture in Northern Italy, amalgamating aspects of both in his designs. It was partly through his influence that brickwork became fashionable for grander C19 Danish buildings, and he was a pioneer in the use of exposed structural cast-iron members. His most celebrated work is the University Library, Copenhagen (1857–61), in a robust brick *Rundbogenstil with exposed and elegant ironwork inside. The Main Railway Station, Copenhagen (1863–4), was also fine, but was demolished in 1917. Perhaps his most significant building is the National Bank (1865–70) in which the influence of C15 Florentine Renaissance architecture was strong. In Odense he designed the Town Hall (1881–3—with Carl William Frederik Lendorf (1839–1918)). In his many villas and other private houses he was influenced by developments in England, especially the *Domestic Revival, and he in turn influenced the following generation, notably Martin *Nyrop.

Faber (1963); Millech (1951); Rasmussen (1940); Weilbach (1947)

Herland, Hugh (*c*.1330–*c*.1411). English carpenter, possibly the son of William *Herland. He worked on the *stalls for the *Chapel at Windsor Castle, Berkshire, in 1350, and in the 1360s was employed at Westminster Palace and the Tower of London. He designed and made the *tester over the tomb of Queen Philippa (consort of King Edward III, 1328–69) in Westminster Abbey. In 1375 he was put in charge of the King's Works 'touching the art or mastery of carpentry', and in 1378 was in command of building operations at Rochester Castle, Kent. Around this time he designed the tester over the tomb of King Edward III (reigned 1327–77), foreshadowing his design for the ceiling of Winchester College Chapel, Hampshire, ten years later. In the 1380s he was working at Rochester, Leeds, and Portchester Castles, and worked for William of *Wykeham at New College, Oxford, *c*.1384. In the 1390s he was engaged on building work at Westminster Hall, where he designed and built the outstanding *hammer-beam roof, one of the greatest achievements of medieval carpentry. Herland may also have designed the ceiling of the Fitzalan Chapel, Arundel, Sussex (*c*.1380–1400).

Harvey (1987)

Herland, William (*fl*. 1332–d. 1375). English carpenter. In 1332 he was making moulds for St Stephen's Chapel, Westminster. He worked at Eltham and Windsor Castles in 1350, and seems to have been appointed the King's Chief Carpenter in 1354. He supervised carpentry works at the Tower of London and Westminster Palace, and designed the Great Hall roof and other works at Windsor Castle, Berkshire (1355–7). He was also involved at Hadleigh Castle, Essex, Rotherhithe Manor, near London, Rochester Castle, Kent, and the Tower of London.

Harvey (1987)

herm, hermes. Statue composed of a head and neck or head and shoulders (often representing Hermes or Mercury) joined to a quadrangular shaft proportioned to be the same height as a human body and slightly tapered downwards, found in *Antiquity, frequently with the male reproductive organs protruding from the front face of the shaft. The form was revived from *Renaissance times, often used for garden-ornaments (e.g. at the Palazzo Farnese, Caprarola (1547–9)), and from C18 became a common motif, often with female head and frequently with the feet showing at the base (since Antiquity the phallic imagery has normally been avoided). Herms are distinct from *terms in that they do not have torsos or waists, and are without arms, but may have volute-like forms instead of shoulders.

Curl (1992); Lewis and Darley (1986)

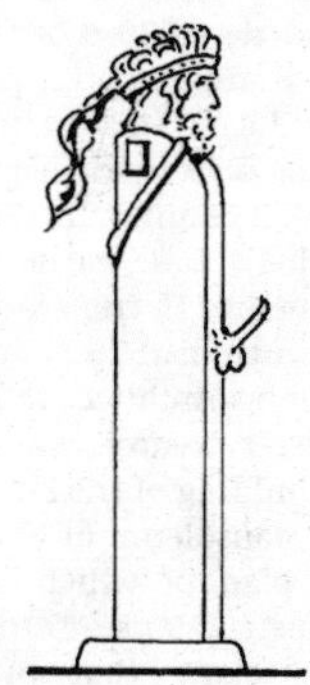

herm. Greek ithyphallic type.

hermitage. 1. Dwelling of a hermit or religious recluse, in the medieval period often associated with religious foundations, endowed for an *anchorite* in a churchyard or some other place, often attached to a monastery, and frequently associated with an *oratory. **2.** Habitation in a lonely situation, often in a landscaped park, occupied by a paid 'hermit' in C18. **3.** *Cottage orné, *primitive hut, or rustic residence in a landscape intended as a mnemonic of a hermit's house. **4.** *Bower, *gazebo, or secluded place, often associated with a *grotto or cave, artificial *rock-work, or some other such construction in a C18 elegiac landscape.

Gwilt (1903); Papworth (1852); Symes (1993)

Hermogenes (*fl*. *c*.220–190 BC). *Hellenistic architect and theorist, he was mentioned by *Vitruvius, and designed the temples of Dionysus, Teos (*c*.220–205 BC), and Artemis,

Magnesia on the Meander (*c*.205–190 BC). He favoured the *Ionic Order, objecting to *Doric because of the problem of combining equal *intercolumniation with the *triglyph *frieze at the corners. He seems to have promoted the pseudodipteral plan (large temples in Ionia had been built with two rows of columns surrounding the cell, but Hermogenes omitted the inner *colonnade, providing a very wide, open, airy space, surrounded by the *peristyle). He also promoted the *eustyle* intercolumniation (with space between columns equal to $2\frac{1}{4}$ column diameters), giving a stable yet elegant appearance to the colonnade.

Dinsmoor (1950); Gerkan (1929); Humann (1904); Lawrence (1983); Onians (1979); Placzek (1982)

Herrera, Juan de (1530–97). The most celebrated Spanish architectural practitioner of C16, he introduced an austere *Classicism (known as *éstilo desornamentado* because of its bareness) to that country. In 1563 he became assistant to Juan Bautista de *Toledo, and when the latter died Herrera rose to a position of eminence until in 1579 he was confirmed in his position as Architect to King Philip II (1556–98). Herrera's career was closely bound up with the building of the Royal Monastery, Palace, and *Mausoleum of El Escorial, near Madrid, the plan of which is not unlike various reconstructions of the Temple of Solomon, especially that of the Jesuits Hieronymo Prado (1547–95) and Juan Bautista Villalpando (1552–1608), and has various astrological, magical, religious, geometrical, and symbolic allusions that cannot be discussed here. The form of the complex, with its grid-iron plan and four angle-towers, may be an allusion to the martyrdom of St Laurence: Pope Gregory XIII (1572–85) presented some of that Saint's melted fat to the King, and the Escorial Church is dedicated to St Laurence. Herrera's other Royal buildings include the completion of the Alcázar, Toledo (1585), work on the Palace at Aranjuez (1571–86) which has many of the Escorial motifs, the elegant Lonja (Exchange), Seville (1582–98), and part of the Cathedral of Valladolid (1585–97). The last, though incomplete when Herrera died, was widely copied, notably at Salamanca, Mexico City, Puebla, and Lima Cathedrals.

Chueca Goitia (1953); Curl (1991); Fraser, Hibbard, and Lewine (1967); Kubler (1982); Kubler and Soria (1959); Placzek (1982); Ruiz de Arcaute (1936)

herring-bone. Bricks, stones, tiles, or wood-blocks laid aslant in alternate rows or courses at 45° to the general direction of the course or row, and at 90° to the adjoining courses or rows, thus each course or row slopes in a different direction to those on either side or above and below, forming a zig-zag pattern.

Herron, Ronald (Ron) James (1930–). London-born architect, associated with *Archigram in the 1960s. He was partly responsible, when working for the Greater London Council, for the conception of the South Bank Arts Complex, London (early 1960s). His best-known work is probably the refurbishment of an existing office-building in Store Street, Bloomsbury, London (1989), for Imagination Ltd., a design involving covering a courtyard with a stretched-fabric roof. He has also designed buildings for the Toyama Prefecture, Japan (1992–3).

Cook (1991); Emanuel (1994)

Hertfordshire spike. *Flèche or short *spire rising from a church-tower, its base concealed by a *parapet, common in Hertfordshire, England.

Pevsner, *Buildings of England, Hertfordshire* (1977)

Hertzberger, Herman (1932–). Dutch architect, much influenced by van *Eyck. One of the leaders of *Structuralism in The Netherlands, he developed a theory that the architect's job is to provide a structure and envelope based on a regular *grid, to be fitted out later by the users of the building: this is best seen at the Centraal Beheer Insurance Offices, Apeldoorn (1970–2). Other buildings include the Ministry of Social Welfare, The Hague (1979–90), the experimental housing (Diagoon), Gebenlaan, Delft (1971), the Vredenburg Music Centre, Utrecht (1973–8), and the Artistic Education Library and Amsterdam Theatre, both in Breda (1993).

Curtis (1996); Emanuel (1994); Lampugnani (1988)

Hesse, Ludwig Ferdinand (1795–1876). German architect, he worked under *Schinkel in Berlin, where he detailed and supervised the building of the *Gothic Friedrich Werderschekirche (1825–31). He became *Hofbaumeister* (Court Architect) in Potsdam (1831), and worked with *Persius, whose *villas were models for his own buildings. He designed the extension to the *mausoleum of Queen Luise, Charlottenburg, Berlin (1841), the Teehaus (1847), the

Belvedere, Pfingstenberg (1847–52), and the Orangery and Terraces (1851–60), all at Sanssouci. The last two projects (designed with *Stüler) were derived from C16 *Renaissance precedents (e.g. Villa Madama and Villa Pamphili, Rome).

Börsch-Supan (1977); Dehio (1961); Hesse (1854–5, 1854–6); Placzek (1982)

Hetsch, Gustav Friedrich (1788–1864). German architect. He trained in Germany and in Paris (with *Percier and *Fontaine) before settling in Copenhagen, Denmark, in 1815, where he worked with C. F. *Hansen, whose daughter he married. He designed the Roman Catholic Church of St Ansgar (1840–1) and the Synagogue (1829–33), both in Copenhagen. He is better known for his work in the applied arts, for he designed furniture, metal-work, ceramics, and published many patterns that proved influential. As a representative of late *Classicism, his work was severe and rational, with refined detailing. Among his many pupils was *Herholdt.

Weilbach (1947)

hewn. Cut, prepared, dressed stone, or *ashlar.

hexastyle. *See* portico.

Hiberno-Romanesque. Style of ecclesiastical buildings in Ireland from C10 to C12 characterized by very simple rectangular buildings, tall detached circular towers with conical roofs, semicircular-headed openings, and the usual array of *Romanesque ornament, with such structures as *Celtic crosses sumptuously carved (e.g. Monasterboice, Co. Louth (C9 or C10)). Some of the most outstanding buildings are those at Devenish, Co. Fermanagh (C10–C12), and Cormac's Chapel, Cashel, Co. Tipperary (1127–34). The style was resurrected in C19 as part of the *Celtic Revival, its most common manifestations being carved *high crosses in *cemeteries, used as memorials, and numerous churches, including many erected in C20. Aspects of Hiberno-Romanesque and Celtic design played a part in the evolution of *Art Nouveau, and were associated with the *Arts-and-Crafts movement. It is also called *Hiberno-Saxon* as there were similarities between aspects of Irish and *Anglo-Saxon decoration.

Casey and Rowan (1993); Cruickshank (1996); Lewis and Darley (1986); Rowan (1979)

high-altar. Main altar of a church sited on the main axis at the east of the *choir or *chancel.

high cross. Free-standing detached sculpted stone cross, usually *Celtic or *Anglo-Saxon. There are many examples in Ireland (e.g. Monasterboice, Co. Louth (C9 or C10)), and Scotland (e.g. Ruthwell, near Dumfries (C7)), while England also has several, including the magnificent Bewcastle Cross, Cumberland (C7).

Casey and Rowan (1993); Pevsner, *Buildings of England, Cumberland and Westmorland* (1967)

High Gothic. *Second Pointed style of C14.

high relief. *Alto-rilievo*, i.e. sculpture in relief projecting more than half its form from its background.

High Renaissance. Early C16 Italian *Renaissance style at the height of its development, called *Cinquecento.

high-rise. Tall structure of several floors, or a *skyscraper.

High Tech. Style expressive of structures, technologies, and services by exposing and even emphasizing them, or appearing to do so. Some hold that High Tech originated in C19 iron-and-glass structures such as *Paxton's Crystal Palace (1851), but its aggressive imagery owes more, perhaps, to Buckminster *Fuller, Frei *Otto, *Archigram, and even *Futurism and New *Brutalism. The Centre Pompidou, Paris (1977), by *Piano and *Rogers; the Sainsbury Centre, University of East Anglia, Norwich (1977), by Norman *Foster; the Lloyd's Building, London (1986), by Rogers; the Hong Kong and Shanghai Bank, Hong Kong (1986), by Foster; Schlumberger Research Laboratories, Cambridge (1985), by *Hopkins; and the *Financial Times* Printing Works, Docklands, London (1988), by *Grimshaw are among the most paradigmatic High Tech structures.

Davies (1988); Forester (1987); Jencks (1988); Kron and Slesin (1979)

High Victorian. Style of the somewhat harsh *polychrome structures of the *Gothic Revival in the 1850s and 1860s when *Ruskin held sway as the arbiter of taste.

Hersey (1972); Jervis (1983)

Hilbersheimer, Ludwig Karl (1885–1967). German-born American architect, he taught at the *Bauhaus, and was involved with *Arbeitsrat für Kunst and other avant-garde groups, including the *Expressionist Der *Sturm and Der *Ring. He joined *CIAM and in 1931 was Director of the *Deutscher Werkbund, so his *International Modernist credentials were impeccable, and indeed he was one of the founders of that style. His project for a 'skyscraper city' (1924) evolved from Le *Corbusier's ideas, and he built a house for the *Weissenhofsiedlung, Stuttgart (1927). He was closely associated with *Mies van der Rohe, and joined the latter at the Illinois Institute of Technology (then the Armour Institute) in 1938. He published *Grossstadtbauten* (Metropolitan Buildings—1925), *Grossstadt Architektur* (Metropolitan Architecture—1927), *Contemporary Architecture: Its Roots and Trends* (1964), and many other polemical works intended to further International Modernism. He was responsible for many development plans in the USA from 1938 until his death.

Hilbersheimer (1925, 1927, 1927*a*, 1929, 1944, 1949, 1955, 1956, 1963, 1963*a*); Lampugnani (1988); Pommer (1988)

Hild, József (1789–1867). Hungarian Romantic-Classicist architect (with J. *Packh) of the Cathedral, Esztergom (Gran), Hungary (1822–56), with its centralized plan and octastyle *portico. It was originally designed by Kühnel in 1821.

Cruickshank (1996); Papworth (1852)

Hildebrandt, Johann Lukas von (1668–1745). Born in Genoa, Italy, he trained as a military engineer, later becoming one of Austria's most distinguished and inventive early C18 *Baroque architects (with *Fischer von Erlach). He studied in Rome with Carlo *Fontana, and absorbed much from the works of *Borromini and *Guarini, notably the possibilities of using interpenetrating elliptical plans, and undulating façades. During military campaigns in the 1690s he met his future patron, the great commander Prince Eugen of Savoy (1663–1736), and settled in Vienna in 1696, becoming Court Architect in 1700. From 1697 to 1715 he was concerned with the design of the Mansfeld-Fondi (later Schwarzenberg) Palace in Vienna, where influences from Borromini and Guarini are overt, notably in the two-storey elliptical salon that bows outwards on the garden-front. The axial garden-layout, with ramps, changes of level, and terraces, derives from Italian prototypes, especially the Villa Giulia, Rome, and, with the Palace, demonstrates the synthesis of Italian, French, and German sources that was such a feature of Hildebrandt's style, for there are traces of Le *Vau's Vaux-le-Vicomte Palace, Guarini's Palazzo Carignano, and *Bernini's project for the east wing of the Louvre, Paris. Hildebrandt's admiration for Guarini was even clearer at the Dominican Chapel of St Laurenz, Gabel, North Bohemia (1699–1711),

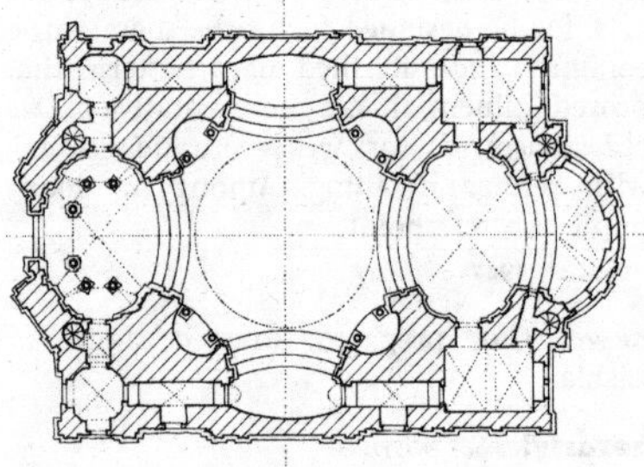

Laurenzkirche, Gabel.

with its concave corners, convex balconies, and plan of a circle flanked by two ellipses with chapels placed on the diagonals. This church-plan was to be influential, especially on the work of the *Dientzenhofers in Bohemia.

Hildebrandt designed the Church of St Peter, Vienna (1702–8), on an elliptical plan crowned by a *cupola, flanked by two rectangular compartments and an apsidal *choir. The tall entrance-front is flanked by twin towers set at angles, giving great drama to the composition. A variant of the plan of the *Peterskirche* was used again for the *Seminarkirche* (Seminary Church), Linz (1717–25). From 1698 he worked on the Borrominiesque *Piaristenkirche* (Piarist Church) of Maria Treu, Vienna (built 1714–46), which has a similar plan to that of the Gabel church. Completed by Mathias Gerl (possibly with a contribution from K. I. Dientzenhofer), the church is by far the lightest and most joyous in a city where the Baroque tends to be sombre.

Hildebrandt's greatest work is arguably the Belvedere, Vienna (1700–24), the dream-palace of Prince Eugen, with almost oriental roofs and frothy façades with shaped pediments and corner towers. There are, in fact, two buildings—the Upper and Lower (1714–15) Belvedere—linked by a series of terraced gardens, with statuary and planting. The Upper Palace contains the most celebrated of Hildebrandt's staircases where massive, struggling *atlantes carry heavy vaulting. He also designed the staircase with urns and *putti* at Schloss Mirabell, Salzburg (1721–7). Other fine staircases can be found at the Palais Daun-Kinsky, Vienna (1713–16), and Schloss Weissenstein, Pommersfelden (1711–15)—where he also designed the central pavilion. From 1720 to 1723 and again from 1729 to 1744 he collaborated with *Neumann on the *Residenz* of the Prince-Bishop at Würzburg: his hand is evident in the shaped pediments of the central pavilion as well as in the *Kaisersaal* (Emperor's Hall) and Chapel. He was involved in the rebuilding of the *Stift* (Monastery) of Göttweig from 1719: his plans were ambitious but never fully realized, although the building containing the *Kaiserstiege* (Emperor's Stair) of 1738 is as fine as anything he conceived.

Aurenhammer, G. (1969); Aurenhammer, H. (1973); Brucker (1983); Franz (1942, 1943, 1943*a*, 1962); Freeden (1952, 1981); Grimschitz (1959); Hempel (1965); Hoffmann (1968); Kerber (1947); Kreisel (1953); Placzek (1982); Sedlmayer (1930); *Wiener Jahrbuch für Kunstgeschichte*, 17 (1955), 49–62

Hindoo. Style of exotic orientalizing architecture that was part of the *eclecticism associated with the C18 cult of the *Picturesque. One of its earliest manifestations was the Hindoo *Gothick façade of Guildhall, London (1788–9), by *Dance. The Hindoo or *Indian style gained momentum with the publication of the various views of India by *Hodges and the *Daniells. Sezincote, Gloucestershire (*c*.1805), a country-house by S. P. *Cockerell, is perhaps the finest example of the style.

Conner (1979); Lewis and Darley (1986)

Hiorne Family. Francis (1744–89) was an architect and builder based in Warwick who created a number of buildings in the *Gothick taste including the fine Church of St Mary, Tetbury, Gloucestershire (1771–81), with its elegant *piers of timber containing iron cores. He was the architect of the Classical Church of St Anne, Belfast (1772–6—demolished 1900). His father, **William** (*c*.1712–76), and his uncle, **David** (1715–58), worked for William *Smith whom they succeeded in business, and designed numerous works in the English Midlands. William Hiorne was the executant architect for Sir Roger Newdigate's (1719–1806) Gothick Arbury Hall, Warwickshire, from *c*.1748, and the brothers designed and built the Church of the Holy Cross, Daventry, Northamptonshire (1752–8), in a Classical style. They also erected several buildings to Sanderson *Miller's designs, including Shire Hall, Warwick (1754–8), and the stable-block, Packington Hall, Warwickshire (1756–8).

Brown (1985); Colvin (1995)

hip. 1. Sloping *salient angle of a roof where two sides (*skirts*) join. **2.** The rafter at this angle.

hip-bevel. 1. Angle between two slopes of a roof separated by a *hip. **2.** Bevel on the end of a *hip-rafter.

hip-knob. *Finial where the *ridge and *hips of a roof meet.

hippocamp. Sea-horse, with the upper body of a horse and lower of a fish-like creature, often used in Classical decorations.

Hippodamus of Miletus (*fl*. *c*.500–440 BC). Greek architect and town-planner, he proposed that the layout of a town could express social order, be rational and geometrically clear, and employ the grid-pattern. He may have designed Miletus, Asia Minor (from *c*.475 BC), Piraeus, near Athens (*c*.470 BC), and Thurii (Thourioi), Italy (*c*.443 BC), but he is remembered as one of the earliest theorists of the *Ideal City, and through Aristotle's writings influenced later thinkers, notably from the *Renaissance period.

Castagnoli (1956, 1971); Martin (1956); Placzek (1982); Ward-Perkins (1974); Wycherley (1962)

hippodrome. Place used by the Greeks for horse- and chariot-races, or for equestrian exercises.

hip-rafter. Rafter at the angle of a hipped roof to which the upper ends of the rafter are fixed.

hip-roll. Long rounded piece of timber fixed above the *hip-rafter over which lead or other metal can be dressed to render the *hip watertight.

hip-roof. Roof with all sides sloping and meeting at *hips.

hip-tile. One of several curved or angled tiles laid in series over the *hips.

Hirsau style. Type of *Romanesque architecture in Germany and Austria derived from the great Abbey of Cluny in France, and developed at Hirsau in Germany (from 1082). Hirsau-type churches had antechurches, two west towers, nave-arcades with columnar *piers rather than massive square structures, plain block-*capitals, and slender towers over the eastern bays of the *aisles.

Conant (1979)

Hispano-Moresque. Architectural style based upon that of *Moorish buildings in the Iberian peninsula from C8 to C15. Earlier work was contemporary with *Romanesque and was called *Mozarabic. Later architecture infused with *Gothic is known as *Mudéjar. The Alhambra, Granada (mostly 1338–90), is a fine example of the style, which was revived elsewhere in Europe in C19 and C20, often for *synagogues. It was also an ingredient of Catalan *Modernisme.

Lewis and Darley (1986)

Historicism. Architecture strongly influenced by the past, especially Revivalist architecture (*Greek, *Gothic, *Early Christian, *Romanesque, *Italianate, *Renaissance, the various *Henri and *Louis styles, *Rundbogenstil, *Elizabethan, *Jacobethan, *Tudor, and other revivals). Revivals were facilitated by the many lavish and scholarly publications, notably those based on measured drawings and archaeology that were such a feature of the late C18 and C19, collections of architectural castings and details, and the desire to enter into the essence of a style or styles. Virtually all the way through the C19 concerns to find a style appropriate to the time were voiced (notably by *Hübsch), and by the time *Shaw, *Webb, and others were working in the 1870s the theory evolved that by mixing styles in a free, eclectic way, some kind of new style would emerge from the mélange. Although conventional wisdom holds that the so-called *Queen Anne and *Free styles were relatively free from Historicism, such a view is demonstrably false, while *Art Nouveau, supposedly a reaction against historical revivals, was really too firmly embedded in the late Gothic and *Celtic Revivals, and even in *Rococo, to be regarded as such, in spite of the claims of its protagonists.

Crook (1987); Döhmer (1976)

Hitchcock, Henry-Russell (1903–87). American architectural critic and historian. In 1929 he published *Modern Architecture*, the first English-language book on the subject, and in 1932 he and Philip *Johnson organized the celebrated exhibition at the Museum of Modern Art in New York entitled 'The *International Style', a term which he and Alfred H. Barr (1902–81) coined, and which was also used as the title of a book (by Hitchcock and Johnson) issued at the same time as the Exhibition. Having written about H. H. *Richardson (1936) and Frank Lloyd Wright (1942) he turned his attention to C19 architecture with the magnificent *Early Victorian Architecture* (1954) and *Architecture: Nineteenth and Twentieth Centuries* (1958). Later still he wrote perceptively about South-German *Rococo, especially the practitioners, the *Zimmermann Brothers (1968), and near the end of his life his first book on German *Renaissance architecture was published (1981). The scope of his scholarship and interests was vast, and his output enormous. In 1983 *In Search of Modern Architecture: A Tribute to Henry-Russell Hitchcock* was published, edited by Helen Searing. He was a pioneer of research into C19 architecture, and impressive, both as a man and a scholar.

Hitchcock (1931, 1938, 1939, 1954, 1955, 1966, 1966*a*, 1966*b*, 1968, 1968*a*, 1973, 1976, 1977, 1981, 1993); Hitchcock and Johnson (1966); Hitchcock and Seale (1976)

Hittorff, Jakob Ignaz, *known as* **Jacques-Ignace** (1792–1867). German-born architect and scholar. He settled in Paris (1811), and studied under *Percier from whom he acquired his 'liberal' *Classicism and eclectic philosophy. He worked with *Bélanger on the creation of the iron-and-glass dome of the Halle au Blé, Paris (1808–13), during which he met Joseph Lecointe (1783–1858), which led to the two men being appointed Architects for all ceremonial occasions after Bélanger's death in 1818. They quickly became fashionable architects, designing many interiors for wealthy patrons. Hittorff travelled in England, Germany, and Italy (1820–4) during which he became interested in the problem of *polychromy in Ancient Greek architecture and, with Ludwig *Zanth, published

Architecture antique de la Sicile (1827) in which his record of traces of painted decorations on the Greek temples was publicly attacked by scholars in 1830. However, he became one of the leaders of the Société Libre des Beaux-Arts, publicized his ideas, and obtained various important commissions, including alterations to the Place de la Concorde (1832–40) and the Champs-Élysées (1834–40). His first great Parisian building was the Church of St-Vincent-de-Paul, sketched out first by Jean-Baptiste Lepère (1761–1844) in 1824, but completely redesigned and built by Hittorff (1830–48). It is a particularly beautiful *basilica in the *Early Christian style, with two rows of superimposed *colonnades carrying the timber *trusses of the roof, an apsidal *chancel, and the whole interior strongly coloured in a manner Hittorff insisted was a modern expression of Greek Antiquity. The exterior has an *Ionic *portico set against a plain façade flanked by two square towers. The building is not only important for its use of colour, but because its exterior anticipates the *Beaux-Arts *Classicism of the late C19. Hittorff wished to extend polychromy to the exterior, proposing enamelled panels for the wall of the portico as well as lavish colour elsewhere, but the plans were blocked by *Haussmann after he inspected a trial section. *Lave emaillée* (enamelled fired sheets) was the material Hittorff intended to use (it had been invented in 1827 and was manufactured by Hachette et Cie from 1833 for fire-surrounds, table-tops, and even altar-frontals), but the ideas for the church were not implemented. Nevertheless, St-Vincent-de-Paul was an important landmark in the development of a free *eclecticism drawing on many sources that was to be of such significance in C19 French architecture. His most innovative structures, however, were Rotonde les Panoramas with its suspended roof, the Cirque National with elegant lattice-trusses (both 1834–40), and the Cirque Napoléon (Cirque d'Hiver) also with lattice-trusses (1852), which established his reputation as an innovative architect.

A renewal of interest in polychromy in the 1850s encouraged Hittorff to bring out his *Architecture polychrome chez les Grecs* (1851), which was successful, and silenced his enemies. He enjoyed favour under the new regime of Napoleon III (1852–70), designing a series of handsome houses in Paris in the vicinity of the Place de l'Étoile (1852–5), the *Mairie* of the First Arondissement (1855–61), the Grand Hôtel du Louvre, Place du Théâtre Français (1856–9—with Alfred Armand (1805–88), J.-A.-F.-A. Pellechet (1829–1903), and C. *Rohault de Fleury), and, finally, his best-known building, the Gare du Nord (1859–66), where his main contribution appears to have been a 'tidying-up' of what was essentially a design by the Railway Company's engineers. Nevertheless, it is an excellent example of how the new Beaux-Arts Classicism could be used in conjunction with iron-and-glass structures: some of the trusses were designed by Antoine-Rémi Polonceau (1778–1847), and all the castings done in Glasgow.

Hammer (1968); Hitchcock (1977); Hittorff (1851, 1987); Hittorff and Lecointe (1827); Hittorff and Zanth (1827, 1835); Schneider (1977)

Hitzig, Georg Heinrich Friedrich (1811–81). German architect. A pupil of *Schinkel, he also spent some time in Paris where he absorbed influences from the works of *Percier and *Fontaine. With *Knoblauch and others he helped to consolidate the style of Berlin's domestic architecture in a series of exquisite villas built in the 1840s and 1850s. He also used brick to considerable effect, taking his cue from Schinkel's *Bauakademie* (1831). Most of his buildings have been destroyed, including the Kronenberg Palace, Warsaw (1866–70—on which he published a monograph in 1875), and the Börse, Berlin (1859–64—also the subject of a monograph, in 1867).

Börsch-Supan (1977); Hitzig (1850–9, 1867, 1875)

Hoban, James (*c*.1762–1831). Irish-born, he emigrated to America in 1785. He won the competition to design the President's House, Washington, DC, with a proposal (1792) originally based on Leinster House, Dublin, but altered at the request of Washington and *Jefferson. As built, the White House, (1793–1801, rebuilt 1814–29) was derived from plate 41 of *Gibbs's *A Book of Architecture* (1728). His other Washington buildings (hotels, houses, and Government buildings) no longer exist.

Architecture, 11 (1981), 66–82; *Dictionary of American Biography* (1932); Goode (1979); Maddex (1973); Reiff (1977); Ryan and Guinness (1980); Summerson (1993)

Hodges, William (1744–97). English painter. He specialized in topographical views, and accompanied Captain James Cook (1728–79) on his expedition to the South Seas (1722–5) as draughtsman. Under the aegis of Warren

Hastings (1732–1818) he went to India in 1778 and published *Selected Views of India* (1785–8) followed by *Travels in India* (1793) which had a considerable impact, popularizing *Hindoo and *Indian architecture.

DNB (1917)

Hoff, Robert van 't (1887–1979). Dutch architect, he studied in England and visited the USA in 1914, where he admired buildings by Frank Lloyd *Wright. At Huis ter Heide, near Utrecht, he designed a couple of symmetrical houses (1915–16), with flat roofs and wide overhanging eaves and fenestration very closely derived from Wright's work, notably the Unity Temple, Oak Park, Illinois (1905–7). He became a contributor to the journal *De Stijl* (1917–20).

Bouw, 12 (1979), 6–8, 13 (1979), 17–23; Fanelli (1968); Rijksmuseum (1975); Zevi (1974)

Hoffmann, Josef Franz Maria (1870–1956). Austro-Hungarian designer and architect. Born in Moravia, he studied with *Hasenauer and *Wagner in Vienna. He became involved in the Vienna *Sezession (he greatly admired, and was friendly with, C. R. *Mackintosh) and, with Koloman Moser (1868–1918) and Fritz Wärndorfer (1868–), founded the *Wiener Werkstätte in 1903. He absorbed the *Beaux-Arts method of composition, the Classically inspired style of Wagner, the freer style of the British *Arts-and-Crafts movement, and early in the C20 began to simplify and purify his architecture, moving away from the *Art Nouveau of the early Sezession. His white cubic building at the Purkersdorf Sanatorium (from 1903) led to a blocky style, the most developed example of which was the Adolphe Stoclet House, Brussels (1904–11): for this Hoffmann and other artists of the Werkstätte designed virtually everything. The Stoclet House was sumptuously finished in panels of marble framed with bronze, while some of the interiors (notably the dining-room) were also finished in marble, with glittering mosaics designed by Gustav Klimt (1862–1918). His Ast (1909–11) and Skywa-Primavesi (1913–15) Houses, both in Vienna, showed a profound shift towards *Neoclassicism that was a general tendency of the time. Later works were never again of such distinction: they included the Austrian Pavilion, Exposition Internationale des Arts-Décoratifs, Paris (1924–5), an asymmetrical composition with strong horizontal bandings on the walls; the Ast House, Velden, Austria (1924), and the Austrian Pavilion, Venice Biennale (1934–5). In 1953–4 he designed housing on the Heiligenstädterstrasse, Vienna.

Kleiner (1927); Placzek (1982); Rochowanski (1950); Sekler (1985); Veronesi (1956); Weiser (1930)

Höger, Johann Friedrich, *called* **Fritz** (1877–1949). German architect and protagonist of *Expressionism, he was a student of the *Backstein* (brick) architecture of North Germany, particularly interested in the decorative traditions of brickwork and the effects of light and shade on brick buildings. He helped to evolve the Hamburg *Kontorhaus* (office-building) style, notably with his *Klostertorhof Kontorhaus* (1910–11), and (especially) the *Chilehaus* (1923–4), a vast 12-storey block with curved façades and a ship-like form. He also designed the *Sprinkenhof Kontorhaus*, Hamburg (1927–43), the *Rathaus* (Town Hall), Wilhelmshaven-Rüstringen (1928–9), the Evangelischekirche, Hohenzollernplatz, Wilmersdorf, Berlin (1929–30), the City Hospital, Delmenhorst (1930), and the Siebetsburg Housing, Wilhelmshaven (1935–8).

Berckenhagen (1977); Pehnt (1973); Westphal (1938)

Hohenburg, Johann Ferdinand Hetzendorf von (1732–1816). Architect of the arcaded *Gloriette*, the celebrated *eye-catcher in the park at Schönbrunn, Vienna (1775), an early revival of the Italian *Cinquecento style. He also contributed to the design of the landscaped gardens at Schönbrunn, and is credited with the interior of the theatre at Schönbrunn Palace.

Papworth (1852); Powell (1959)

Holabird & Roche. American architects. William Holabird (1854–1923) settled in Chicago where he worked in William le Baron *Jenney's office in 1875 before setting up in practice with Martin Roche (1853–1927) from 1881. In 1886 the firm was commissioned to design the 12-storey Tacoma Building (completed 1889—demolished 1929), with a structure of cast-iron columns and wrought-iron beams as well as brickwork and concrete and steel, the whole clad in *terracotta and glass. This established a skeletal structure for *skyscrapers and the *Chicago School style. The firm's numerous office-buildings in Chicago had external walls employing the *Chicago window, continuous piers, recessed panels, and terracotta ornament. A good example is the Marquette Building (1894–5), economically planned, and highly efficient. Other works included the Cable Building (1898–9—demolished 1961), the Republic Building (1905–9—demolished 1961), the Brooks Building (1909–10), and the McClurg Building (1899–1900), which anticipated the design of later skyscrapers.

Bruegmann (1991); Condit (1968, 1973); Mujica (1929); Zukowsky (1987, 1993)

Holden, Charles Henry (1875–1960). English architect. Born in Bolton, Lancashire, Holden worked for a while with *Ashbee before joining Henry Percy *Adams in 1899 as an assistant. Among their earliest buildings was the Belgrave Hospital for Children, Clapham Road, Lambeth, London (1900–3), a complex composition on a tight site, with elevations in an *Arts-and-Crafts style influenced by Philip *Webb and Henry *Wilson. Their Central Reference Library, Deanery Street, Bristol (1906), avoided fashionable *Neo-Baroque for stripped *Neo-Tudor, and at the new Library for the Incorporated Law Society (1902–4) in Chancery Lane, London, an assured understanding of *Mannerism was displayed. The King Edward VII Sanatorium, Midhurst, Sussex (1903–6), followed, by which time Lionel Godfrey Pearson (1879–1953) had joined the firm. Holden became Adams's partner in 1907.

Adams & Holden's Headquarters for the British Medical Association (now Zimbabwe House) in The Strand (1906–8) developed Mannerist themes in an assured composition, with, at the time, controversial nude sculptured figures (now mutilated) by (Sir) Jacob Epstein (1880–1959—with whom Holden also collaborated in the design of Oscar Wilde's tomb in Père-Lachaise Cemetery, Paris, of *c.*1912). The firm became Adams, Holden, & Pearson in 1913, and Holden was appointed one of the four principal architects of the Imperial War Graves Commission for which he designed 67 cemeteries. From 1924 Holden worked with Frank Pick (1878–1941) to design more than 50 London Underground Railway Stations that represent a high peak of rational English design. Much influenced by modern architecture in Scandinavia and The Netherlands, they have a clear, uncluttered geometry, and include Arnos Grove (1932), Boston Manor (1934), Southgate (1935), and Sudbury Town (1930–1). Holden also designed shelters, signs, lamp-standards, platforms, and much else for the London Passenger Transport Board.

The firm could always be relied upon to create a monumental effect by piling up blocky, cubic masses, as in Pearson's designs for the powerful Royal Artillery Memorial, Hyde Park Corner (1921–5), with sculptures by Charles Sergeant Jagger (1885–1934), but Holden's Headquarters Building for London Transport at 55 Broadway, Westminster (1927–9), is an even more sophisticated essay in massing. Epstein, Eric Gill (1882–1940), and Henry Moore (1898–1986) were responsible for the external sculpture. From 1931 he designed new buildings for the University of London, including the Senate House (which lacks the sculpture intended for it), and from the 1939–45 war was involved in redevelopment plans for London, working with William (later Lord) *Holford.

Architectural Review, 158 (1975), 349–56; *DNB* (1971); Gray (1985); Pevsner (1968); Placzek (1982); Stamp (1977); van Vynckt (1993)

Holford, William Graham, Lord (1907–75). South-African born, he trained under Charles *Reilly at Liverpool. During the 1939–45 war he helped to create the framework of British town-planning legislation, and was involved with *Abercrombie in creating the County and Greater London Plans. He proposed development plans for the Universities of Liverpool (1949–54), Exeter (1955–75), and Kent (1958), and, with *Holden, the Plan for the City of London (1946–7). His designs for the precinct of St Paul's Cathedral, London (1956), perhaps have not stood the test of time. His influence as an architect and planner, however, was widespread, especially in the United Kingdom during the first three decades after 1945.

Cherry (1986); *DNB* (1986); Emanuel (1994)

Holl, Elias (1573–1646). Born in Augsburg, he became the leading *Renaissance architect in Germany after a visit to Italy (1600–1). He was responsible for the city of Augsburg's official buildings from 1602, designing the *Giesshaus* (Foundry—1601), *Zeughaus* (Arsenal—1602–7), *Siegelhaus* (Municipal Seal office—1605), *Metzge* (Slaughterhouse—1609), and many other structures. His most important building was the *Rathaus* (Town Hall—1614–20), the central section of which has all the verticality of a gabled German house, but on either side the elevations are more Classical and serene. His *Heilige Geist Spital* (Hospital of the Holy Ghost—1626–30) is marked by clear cubic forms, a separation of individual elements, the subordination of decoration, and a two-storey arcade around a court. Among his works outside Augsburg, his designs for the Willibaldsburg, Eichstätt, are the most architecturally significant.

Hempel (1965); Hieber (1923); Hitchcock (1981); Roeck (1985); Schürer (1938); Walter (1972)

Holland, Henry (1745–1806). Leading English *Georgian architect. He became the partner of Lancelot 'Capability' *Brown in 1771, whose daughter he married, and with whom he built Claremont House, Esher, Surrey (1771–4). He evolved an elegant Neoclassical style to rival that of the *Adams, as can be seen at Brooks's Club House, 60 St James's Street, London (1776–8). The success of this building made his name known in aristocratic circles, and he designed a number of pleasing country-houses, including Berrington Hall, near Leominster, Herefordshire (1778–81); the remodelling of Woburn Abbey, Bedfordshire (1787–1802), including the entrance *portico (demolished), conservatory (later sculpture-gallery), and Chinese dairy; the remodelling of Althorp, Northamptonshire (1787–9—including *cladding the building with *mathematical tiles); and alterations at Broadlands, Hampshire (1788–92). His greatest work was probably the remodelling of Carlton House, Pall Mall, London (1783–96), including the *Corinthian portico and *Ionic screen (all demolished, 1827–8). He also designed The Albany, Piccadilly, London (1803–4).

Holland developed Hans Town, Chelsea, from 1771, including Sloane Street, Cadogan Place, and the polygonal Hans Place, but the fabric has been mostly redeveloped. As an architect he was influenced by French sources, notably *Gondouin, *Patte, and *Peyre, but, unlike *Chambers, he did use *Greek elements in his designs.

Colvin (1995); Stroud (1950, 1966); Summerson (1993); van Vynckt (1993)

Hollein, Hans (1934–). Austrian architect. He established his reputation with small, well-crafted shops, including the Retti Candle Shop (1964–5), Schullin Jewellery Shop with its 'cracked' front (1972–4), and the Austrian State Travel Agency with its palm-tree supports (1976–8), all in Vienna, which employ materials such as marble, brass, stainless steel, and chrome, detailed with meticulous care. Less happy, however, is the relationship of the new fronts with the existing façades into which they are set, while the use of themes such as the apparently haphazard crack suggests tension and disruption of perfection. Much admired have been the Städtisches Museum, Abteiberg, Mönchengladbach (1972–82), with a grid-structure that breaks down in the corner, and the Museum of Modern Art, Frankfurt (1987–91). The Haas House, near the Cathedral in Vienna (1987–90), might suggest that ideas that work on the scale of a shop-front are less successful on a large, prominent building on a key site within a historic urban centre. His proposals for a Museum cut into the Mönschberg rock, Salzburg (1990), were ingenious, and included dramatic interiors.

Amsoneit (1994); Emanuel (1994); Klotz (1988); Pettena (1988); van Vynckt (1993)

hollow gorge. *Cavetto or *Egyptian *gorge.

hollow moulding. *Trochilus, *cavetto, or *scotia.

hollow square. *Romanesque moulding consisting of a series of indented pyramids, the base coinciding with the *face.

hollow walls. *See* brick.

Holy Loft. *Rood-loft, -beam, or -screen.

Holy Sepulchre. The Church of the Holy Sepulchre, or Anastasis (Resurrection), Jerusalem, was Emperor Constantine's most important church foundation (C4). It was essentially a domed *rotunda with an inner ring of columns and *piers carrying the dome and an *annular *ambulatory contained by a wall from which three *apses projected, so was not unlike Imperial *mausolea such as 'Santa Costanza', Rome. It contained a tiny temple-like structure encasing the tomb itself. Both church and shrine were destroyed in 1009, but rebuilt (C11) in a *Byzantino-*Romanesque style, the plan remaining similar. The basic form was the precedent for many cemetery-chapels, *martyria, and churches (notably the round churches at Cambridge, the Temple (London), and Northampton), while the shrine inspired numerous progeny, including *Alberti's Rucellai Chapel, San Pancrazio, Florence (1460–7).

Holzbauer, Wilhelm (1930–). Austrian architect. A pupil of *Holzmeister, he was a founding-member (with Friedrich Kurrent (1931–), Otto Leitner, and Johannes Spalt (1920–)) of *Arbeitsgruppe* (Work Group) 4, which promoted 'constructive functionalism', supposedly an updating of the theories of *Loos. He was partly responsible for the design of the St Joseph Seminary, Salzburg-Aigen (1960–4), where the forms were dictated wholly by the construction, indicating the influence of *Wachsmann. He opened his own office in Vienna in 1964, having moved away from *Arbeitsgruppe 4* and towards a position influenced by Le *Corbusier, as can be seen in his St Virgil School, Salzburg-Aigen (1966–76). His railway-stations for the Vienna underground system (from 1971), carried out with others, are models of clarity. In The Netherlands he designed the De Bijenkorf Department Store, Utrecht (1978–82), and the City Hall and Opera House, Amsterdam (1979–88).

Emanuel (1994); Lampugnani (1988)

Holzmeister, Clemens (1886–1983). Austrian architect, he was an influential teacher, numbering among his pupils *Hollein, *Holzbauer, and *Peichl, while building many works throughout his career. Much of his design drew on historical precedent, even when he was attracted to *Expressionism, as in the City Crematorium, Vienna (1921–3). His Eichmann Country House, Litzelberg, Seewalchen (1926–8), was almost Arcadian in its relation to nature, but his more monumental buildings, such as those for the Government in Ankara, Turkey (1931–4), show his grasp of a tradition based on *Classicism. He was responsible for developing the *Festspielhaus* (Festival Theatre), Hofstallgasse, in Salzburg (1926–60), tucked in between a rocky eminence and *Fischer von Erlach's *Kollegienskirche* (College or University Church), and built many churches, among which the Maria Hilf, Bregenz-Vorkloster (1924–31), Judas Thaddeus in der Krim, Vienna (1924–32), St Adalbert, Berlin (1933), Seipel-Dollfuss Memorial, Vienna (1933–4), and the Evangelical Church, Kitzbühel (1960–2), may be mentioned. His output was prodigious.

Becker (1966); Emanuel (1994); Gregor (1953); Holzmeister (1937, 1976); Weiser (1927)

Honeyman, John (1831–1914). Scots architect. He practised in Glasgow from 1854, later joined by John Keppie (1862–1945) in 1885 and C. R. *Mackintosh in 1904. The firm became Keppie & Henderson in 1945. Honeyman's best works include the *First Pointed Landsdowne United Presbyterian Church, Great Western Road, Glasgow, with an extremely tall, thin spire (1863), Smith's Warehouse, now the Ca d'Oro, Gordon and Union Streets (with its upper façade of iron and glass—1872), Westbourne Church (1881), the refronting of the Mitchell Street façade of the *Glasgow Herald* Building (with Keppie and Mackintosh—1893–5), and many other fine buildings, including the Martyr's Public School (1896–8—with Keppie and Mackintosh). He published *Open Spaces in Towns* (1883) and works on municipal improvements and working-class housing.

Gomme and Walker (1987); Williamson, Riches, and Higgs (1990)

honeysuckle. Common Greek enrichment resembling a honeysuckle flower, and called *anthemion or *palmette.

Hontañon Family. Father and son, they worked on some of the last *Gothic buildings in Spain. **Juan Gil de Hontañon** (d. 1526) worked on Siguenza Cathedral, and designed and built *mortuary-chapels in the *hall-church of San Antolin, Medina del Campo, Valladolid, and the Church of Santa Clara, Briviesca, Burgos (both *c*.1503–*c*.1523). He worked on the *cloister and *chapter-house of Palencia Cathedral (1505–16). In 1512 he was appointed Master-Mason at Salamanca Cathedral, and by 1520 the building had risen to the *vaults of the side-chapels. He designed the new *crossing-lantern at Seville Cathedral with its complicated rib-vaults (1513–19) to replace *Colonia's structure that had collapsed. From 1524 he was engaged on the design of Segovia Cathedral, the building of which was carried out by his son, **Rodrigo Gil de Hontañon** (*c*.1500–77).

Rodrigo seems to have worked at Santiago, probably with Álava, in 1521, and was consulted at Valladolid before becoming Master-Mason (1530) at Astorga Cathedral, where he probably built the *nave. He then worked on the *transepts at Salamanca from 1537, and then, or simultaneously, at the cloisters of Santiago. He also contributed at Plasencia and designed the *chevet of Segovia Cathedral (from *c*.1560). At Salamanca he introduced *Renaissance ideas, and at the façade of the College of San Ildefonso, Alcalá de Henares, near Madrid (1537–53), the style is entirely *Renaissance, of the *Plateresque type. He designed Monterey Palace (1539–41), the Monasterio de Bernardas de Jesús (from 1542), both in Salamanca, and the Church of La

Magdalena, Valladolid (1566–72). He wrote *Compendio de Arquitectura y Simetria* in *c.* the 1560s, which exists in a distorted copy made by one Simon Garcia in 1681.

Aznar (1941); Chueca Goitia (1951, 1953); *Journal of the Society of Architectural Historians*, 41 (1982), 281–93; Kubler and Soria (1959); Pereda de la Reguera (1951)

hood. **1.** Projecting cover to a fireplace to increase the draught and remove smoke, attached to the wall behind. **2.** Canopy or cover above an aperture, such as a *doorway, to protect it from the weather. **3.** *Drip-stone or *label over the *heads of apertures, arched or rectangular, usually with *label-stops* at each end.

Hood, Raymond Mathewson (1881–1934). American architect. Together with John Mead *Howells he won the competition in 1922 to design the *Chicago Tribune* Tower, Chicago, Ill. (built 1923–5), a high point of *Beaux-Arts *eclecticism with a *Gothic superstructure (Hood had studied (1905–6 and 1908–10) in Paris). From 1924 he was in partnership with Frederick A. Godley (1886–1961) and *Fouilhoux, and from 1931 with Fouilhoux only. The *Tribune* Building was followed by the American Radiator Company Building, Chicago (1924), with a black exterior and gilded *pinnacles and trims, and the Masonic Temple, Scranton, Pa. (1929), again Gothic. With Stanley Gordon Jeeves (*c.*1888–1964) he designed Ideal (now Palladium) House, at the corner of Argyll and Great Marlborough Streets, London (1929), a building completely clad in black Swedish granite with cast-bronze gilded and enamelled *Art Deco detailing. The *Daily News* Building, New York (1929—with Howells), was devoid of any historical references, and was a *skyscraper with vertical window-strips set between continuous vertical solid strips, a design that was to be influential for the next three decades, notably at the Rockefeller Center, New York (1931–4), for which he and his partner Fouilhoux acted as consultants. The McGraw-Hill Building, New York (1930–2) (with Fouilhoux and others), combined bold horizontal bands with central vertical strips, paving the way for lighter cladding and the *International style in skyscraper design.

Curl (1994); Hood (1931); Kilham (1974); Placzek (1982); Schwartzmann (1962); Stern (1982)

Hooke, Robert (1635–1703). English scientist and colleague of *Wren, he became one of the three Surveyors (the others were Edward *Jerman and Peter *Mills) for the reconstruction of the City of London after the Great Fire of 1666, and was the author of a plan (now lost) for a new layout (not implemented). He seems, with Wren, to have designed the Monument (1671–6), and collaborated on some of the City churches (he was probably responsible for St Benet, Paul's Wharf (1678–84)). He designed Bethlehem Hospital, Moorfields, London (1675–6—demolished), Escot House, Devonshire (1677–88 demolished, illustrated in vol. 1 of *Vitruvius Britannicus*); the Royal College of Physicians, Warwick Lane, London (1672–8—demolished); Ragley Hall, Warwickshire (1679–83), subsequently altered by *Gibbs (1750–5) and James *Wyatt (*c.*1780); and many other buildings, most of which have been demolished or altered beyond recognition. His planning was strongly influenced by French precedents. He was one of the first to assert the true principles of *arcuated construction, notably in relation to *catenary curves and ellipses.

Colvin (1995); *DNB* (1917); Downes (1966); 'Espinasse (1962); Keynes (1960); Pevsner, *Buildings of England, London 1: The City of London* (1997); Summerson (1993)

Hope, Thomas (1769–1831). British connoisseur and virtuoso, he was born in Amsterdam, where his family, of Scots descent, had resided and worked as merchants and bankers for several generations. An avid collector of antiques as well as modern Neoclassical sculpture, he became an arbiter of taste by exhibiting his collections and publishing books on architecture and furniture including *Household Furniture and Interior Decoration* (1807), *Costumes of the Ancients* (1809), *An Historical Essay on Architecture* (1835), and *Anastasius, or Memoirs of a Modern Greek, written at the Close of the Eighteenth Century* (1819). A member of the Society of *Dilettanti, he was asked to comment on James *Wyatt's designs for Downing College, Cambridge, and published his opinions in *Observations on the Plans and Elevations . . . for Downing College . . .* (1804) which had the effect of discrediting the Roman *Doric proposals in favour of the *Greek Revival. The result was the building of *Wilkins's College in a suitably Greek style, and Hope was established as a champion of modernity and judge of architecture.

Hope designed two remarkable houses for his collections. At Duchess Street, Portland Place, London, he altered and enlarged

(1799–1804, and 1819) a house designed by Robert *Adam (demolished 1851), adding a picture-gallery decorated in a Neoclassical style, a sculpture gallery, another picture-gallery in the Greek style, a *Hindoo room, an *Egyptian Revival room (with furniture in an extraordinarily powerful Graeco-Egyptian style designed by Hope), a Flaxman room, and various other rooms for the display of Greek vases. These interiors were published in *Household Furniture* (1807). Like *Soane's house, the building was open to the public, and played no small part in popularizing *Neoclassicism. The other house was The Deepdene, near Dorking, Surrey, enlarged with the assistance of William Atkinson (*c*.1773–1839) in 1818–19 and 1823 in an asymmetrical *Picturesque yet Classical manner, and containing much Egyptian ornament, including a bed derived from published French sources. Many of Hope's designs were related to the *Empire style of *Percier and *Fontaine. One of his sons was **Alexander James Beresford Hope** (1820–87), *Ecclesiologist and *Gothic Revivalist.

Colvin (1995); Curl (1994); *DNB* (1917); Hope (1804, 1835, 1962, 1971); Watkin (1968)

Hopkins, Sir Michael (1935–). English architect, he worked with N. *Foster before setting up a practice with his wife, Patricia (1942–), in 1976. Their own house in Hampstead, London (1976), was designed with a steel frame, much glass, and two walls of corrugated metal, classified as a *High Tech building. The bottling-plant, Greene King Brewery, Bury St Edmunds, Suffolk (1981), followed, while the Mound Stand, Lord's Cricket Ground, London (1987), with its load-bearing brick arches, mild-steel seating areas, and tent-like fabric roof, was much acclaimed. Hopkins was responsible for other designs, including major works at Sir Albert *Richardson's Bracken House, City of London, retaining parts of the older building and slotting in a new structure (1990–2); the new Opera House at Glyndebourne, Sussex (1992–4); and the Inland Revenue Buildings, Nottingham (1992–4).

Architecture in Detail series (Phaidon); Davies (1988, 1995); Emanuel (1994)

Hopper, Thomas (1776–1856). English eclectic *Regency architect, his extensive works at Craven Cottage, Fulham, London (1806—demolished), included an exotically vulgar *Egyptian Revival room and a *Gothic dining-room. He designed the Gothic conservatory at Carlton House, Pall Mall (1807—demolished), in the manner of Henry VII's chapel at Westminster Abbey, but with the *tracery panels of the bogus fan-vaulting filled with coloured glass. Thereafter he had a successful practice as a country-house architect, designing fluently in a great number of styles: the buildings include Leigh Court, near Bristol, Somerset (1814—Greek *Ionic), Gosford Castle, Co. Armagh (1819–21—*Romanesque Revival), Penrhyn Castle, Caernarfonshire (*c*.1819–*c*.1844—again Romanesque Revival), Margam Abbey, Glamorgan (1830–5—*Tudor Gothic), Wivenhoe Park, Essex (1846–9—*Jacobethan), and Amesbury House, Wiltshire (1834–40—*Palladian).

Brown (1985); Colvin (1995); Crook and Port (1973); Curl (1994); Hussey (1958)

hopper-head. *See* rainwater-head.

Horeau, Héctor (1801–72). French architect, he built little, but published designs for urban improvements, including many iron-and-glass structures, early proposals for the markets in Paris (1844), a *jardin d'hiver* at Lyons (1846–7), and a design for a vast iron glazed building for London's 1851 exhibition in 1849, which pre-dates *Paxton's realized scheme. Most of his buildings have been demolished. He designed Pippingford Park, Nutley, Sussex (1857–8), and published the spectacular coloured *Panorama d'Égypte et de Nubie* (1841–6).

Boudon, Loyer, and Dufournet (1979); Dufournet (1981); Hix (1996); Horeau (1841–6); Koppelkamm (1981); Middleton and Watkin (1987); Pevsner (1976)

horizontal cornice. Lower, *unraked* *cornice of a *pediment.

horn. **1.** *Ionic, *Composite, or *Corinthian *volute, but especially Ionic. **2.** Strong-stemmed projections ending in stiff leaves commonly found on C13 *Gothic *capitals or *crockets. **3.** Projection at each corner of an *altar, ash-chest, *sarcophagus, or *stele, also called *acroterium or *ear. **4.** Each of four projecting portions of any *abacus curved on plan. **5.** *Cornucopia* or Horn of Plenty. **6.** Projection of one member in framed work, as in the head of a door-frame, or the horn of a C19 *sash-window.

horn-work. In fortifications, an outer defence of two half-*bastions linked to the main fortress.

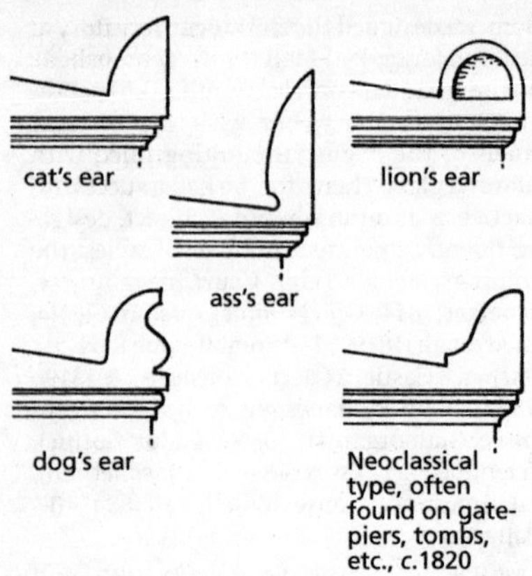

horn. 3. (*JJS*)

horseshoe. *See* arch.

Horta, Baron Victor (1861–1947). Belgian architect, one of the most brilliant protagonists of *Art Nouveau. He absorbed *Viollet-le-Duc's theories, admired the works of *Eiffel and *Boileau, and learned much about iron-and-glass from his mentor *Balat. He made his name with the exquisite Tassel House, Brussels (1892), in which the exposed iron-work and curvaceous decorations showed Art Nouveau at its most inventive and refined. The success of the Tassel House brought many commissions, including the ingenious and beautiful Solvay House, Brussels (1894–1900), and the brilliant *Maison du Peuple*, Brussels (1895–9—demolished), with its curved iron, glass and masonry façade, and a light-filled interior with exposed ironwork and much fine detailing. Both his own house (1898–1911) and the Aubecq House (1899) were beautifully planned and again marvellously detailed, with metal and masonry effortlessly joined. Thereafter, Horta's work became more pedestrian: his Central Railway Station (1911–37), and his Palais des Beaux-Arts (1920–8), both in Brussels, have reinforced-concrete structures, and lack all the grace and charm of the Art Nouveau work. He designed numerous funerary and other monuments.

Borsi (1969); Delevoy (1958); Dernie and Carew-Cox (1995); Hoppenbrouwers *et al.* (1975); Loyer (1986); Placzek (1982); Tschudi-Madsen (1967)

Hosking, William (1800–61). English architect. With John Jenkins (d. 1844) he published *A Selection of Architectural and Other Ornaments, Greek, Roman, and Italian* (1827). In 1834 he became Engineer to the Birmingham, Bristol, and Thames Junction Railway Company, and in 1840 he was appointed Professor at King's College, London. He published *The Principles and Practice of Architecture* (1842) and (with J. Hann) *The Theory, Practice, and Architecture of Bridges* (1843), which became the standard work. He also issued publications connected with building regulations in towns. He is best remembered as the architect of Abney Park Cemetery, Stoke Newington, London (1839–43), for which Joseph *Bonomi was brought in as the consultant for the *Egyptian Revival entrance-gates and lodges. Conceived as an arboretum as well as a cemetery, Abney Park had an educational agenda, and its scheme of planting was influenced by *Loudon. In 1849 he proposed filling in the quadrangle of the British Museum with a circular *Pantheon-like building (published 1850), which may have prompted the realized circular reading-room (1854–7) by S. *Smirke.

Colvin (1995); Curl (1993, 1994); *DNB* (1917)

hôtel. 1. Large private residence, or town-house in France. **2.** Official residence of a public figure or official. **3.** University hostel. **4.** Building for accommodation of strangers, really a superior inn, since the C19 a very large and luxurious establishment with bedrooms, dining-rooms, and other facilities, usually spelled without the circumflex accent.

hôtel de ville. Town-hall in Francophone countries.

hôtel-Dieu. French hospital.

hôtel particulier. French town-house of considerable grandeur, the basic form of which was invented by *Serlio and consisted of a *corps de logis flanked by lower projecting wings on either side forming a *court enclosed on the street side by a wall in which was the entrance-gate, often with an enclosed garden on the other side of the main block. The plans of the Hôtel Carnavalet (*c.*1545 and later additions) by *Lescot, remodelled by *Mansart (1660–1), and Mansart's Hôtel de la Vrillière (1635–45—destroyed), both in Paris, are good examples.

Contet (1914–34); Gallet (1964, 1972, 1972*a*); Loyer (1987); Sturgis *et al.* (1901–2)

Houghton, Thomas de (*fl.* 1288–1318). English carpenter and engineer. In 1288 he was involved in building works at Westminster Palace, and in 1292 made the carved timber *screen and canopy for the tomb of Queen Eleanor (d. 1291) in Westminster Abbey. For the rest of his career he was in the King's service, working at Beaumaris, Edinburgh, Linlithgow, Dover, and Carlisle Castles, as well as the Tower of London. He was with the English army from 1298 to 1318, and was closely involved not only with building-work, but with the supply, transportation, and building of military equipment for the wars against the Scots.

Harvey (1987)

Howard, Sir Ebenezer (1850–1928). English begetter of the *Garden City movement. Inspired by Edward Bellamy's (1850–98) Utopian book *Looking Backward 2000–1887* (1888) which prophesied a transformation of society in an industrial age made possible by co-operative ventures, he wrote *To-morrow: A Peaceful Path to Real Reform* (1898), later republished as *Garden Cities of Tomorrow* (1902). Howard envisaged curing the ills of densely packed urban living and rural decline by merging the best of town and country into Garden Cities of limited size. His ideas were taken up, and the Garden City Association was formed in 1899 which led to the creation of Letchworth Garden City, Hertfordshire (from 1903), and the second experiment, Welwyn Garden City, also in Hertfordshire (from 1919). Low densities, separation of housing and industries, and the provision of all amenities were essential ingredients. Howard's ideas led to the *New Town policy adopted in Britain after the 1939–45 war.

Bellamy (1967); *DNB* (1937); Fishman (1977); Howard (1898, 1902, 1946, 1965); Lampugnani (1988); MacFadyen (1970); Miller (1989, 1992); Miller and Gray (1992)

Howe, George (1886–1955). American architect. He designed High Hollow, Chestnut Hill, Philadelphia, Pa. (1914–17), which evidenced influences from his *Beaux-Arts training in Paris (1908–13), his European travels (notably Italy), and the *vernacular architecture of Pennsylvania. From 1915 until 1928 he was a partner in the firm of Mellor, Meigs, & Howe, specializing in houses much influenced by the work of *Lutyens and by English *Arts-and-Crafts movement. A monograph of 1923 contains illustrations of the houses designed at that time (also illustrated in Arthur Meigs's *An American Country-House* (1925). Following a visit to the Exposition Internationale des Arts-Décoratifs in Paris (1924–5), Howe began to abandon his architectural stance, adopting the language of *International Modernism, and, with *Lescaze, designed the Philadelphia Saving Fund Society Office (1929–32), the paradigm of an International Modernist *skyscraper. Howe promoted Modernism in the USA throughout the 1930s, but broke with Lescaze in 1935 and returned to designing private houses, merging traditional plans with Modernist forms and local materials (e.g. Square Shadows, Whitemarsh, Pa. (1932–4), and Fortune Rock, Mount Desert Island, Me. (1937–9). In 1940 he entered into partnership with Louis I. *Kahn, and in 1950 became Chairman of the Department of Architecture, Yale University.

Lampugnani (1988); Placzek (1982); Stern (1975); van Vynckt (1993)

Howell, Killick, Partridge, & Amis. British architectural firm established in 1959 by William Gough Howell (1922–74), John Alexander Wentzel Killick (1924–72), John Albert Partridge (1924–), and Stanley Frederick Amis (1924–). With the London County Council Architects' Department they designed the Roehampton Lane Housing, London (1951–60), with blocks based on scaled-down images of Le *Corbusier's *Unités*. Work included buildings at St Anne's College, Oxford, using precast concrete elements (1960–9), the new Hall and Common Rooms, St Antony's College, Oxford (1966–71), and various building in Cambridge, including the combination-room, hall, and kitchens at Downing College (1965–70). Later works include the Warrington Crown and County Court House, Cheshire (1992).

Emanuel (1994); Jencks (1980); Lampugnani (1988)

Howells, John Mead (1868–1959). American architect. He worked with *McKim, Mead, & White before establishing an office with Isaac Newton Phelps Stokes (1867–1944) in New York (1897). The firm designed the Madison Square Church Mission House, New York (1898), and Woodbridge Hall, Yale University, New Haven, Conn. (1901), the latter resembling an C18 Parisian *hôtel. Generally, their work was restrained, eclectic, and sensitive to context. The First Congregationalist Church, Danbury, Conn. (1909), reflected Howells's interest in American *Colonial C18 architecture. Stokes developed interests in philanthropic work, notably the housing of the working classes, and published *The Iconography of Manhattan Island, 1498–1909* (1915–28). The partnership was dissolved in 1917, but Howells designed (with Raymond *Hood) the *Chicago Tribune* Tower (1922–5), drawing on French *Flamboyant *Gothic precedents. Howells and Hood collaborated on the *Daily News* Building, New York (1929–30), and Howells himself was responsible for the Panhellenic (later Beekman) Tower, New York (1928), with *Art Deco modelling. He was a sensitive restorer of early American architecture, and wrote much, including *Lost Examples of Colonial Architecture* (1931) and *The Architectural Heritage of the Merrimack* (1941).

Bunting and Nylander (1973); Goldstone and Dalrymple (1974); Kaufmann (1970); van Vynckt (1993)

H-plan. *Plan shaped like an H, as in *Elizabethan houses such as Montacute House, Somerset (finished 1599). It was a variation on the *E-plan in that it was like two Es placed back to back, with the wings extending symmetrically in both directions.

Hübsch, Heinrich (1795–1863). Accomplished German practitioner of the *Rundbogenstil, and author of the theoretical book *In welchem Stil sollen wir bauen?* (In What Style Shall We Build?) of 1828, which created a climate of opinion antagonistic to the *Neoclassicism dominant in Baden and Prussia. Prompted by rational French arguments, notably those of *Durand, Hübsch argued that style should be derived from carefully considered structural methods and a realistic approach to cost. His plumping for *Byzantine *Romanesque round-arched forms was based less on style than on the qualities of brick as a building material. His best work of architecture is arguably the elegant *Trinkhalle* (Spa Pump Room), Baden-Baden (1837–40), with its segmental arcades. He succeeded *Weinbrenner as *Baurat* (Building Inspector) at Karlsruhe, Baden, in 1827.

Döhmer (1976); Valdenaire (1926); Watkin (1986); Watkin and Mellinghoff (1987)

Hueber, Joseph (d. 1787). Austrian architect, probably the designer of the great *Baroque Library at *Stift* (Monastery) Admont, Austria (*c*.1745–74), the plan of which (also credited to *Hayberger) resembles *Fischer von Erlach's *Hofbibliothek* (Court Library) in Vienna. He also designed the elegant towers of the *Mariahilfkirche*, Graz (1742–4), and two pilgrimage-churches.

Blunt (1978); Hempel (1965); Powell (1959)

Hulle, Robert (*fl*. 1400–d. 1442). English mason. In 1400 he was engaged on works at Winchester College and St Cross Hospital, Winchester, Hampshire, and in 1411/12 he was Master-Mason of Winchester Cathedral. He carried out works on the *Rood-loft at St John's, Glastonbury, Somerset, and supervised the works at St John's Hospital, Sherborne, Dorset (1439–40).

Harvey (1987)

Hültz, Johann (d. 1449). Architect of the north tower of Strasbourg Cathedral after the death of Ulrich von *Ensingen (1419). Hültz designed the *tracery spire and spiral staircase rising from the octagonal *stage (completed 1439).

Frankl (1962)

Hungarian Activism. Movement associated with *Constructivism, *Cubism, *Expressionism, and *Bauhaus ideas, influenced also by *Futurism and Leftist ideologies. It published *MA* (Today) in Budapest (1916–19) and in Vienna (1920–5), which influenced architects such as *Breuer. Among those loosely associated with the movement were El *Lissitzky, *Oud, *Molnár, *Tatlin, the *Tauts, and other *Modernists.

Lampugnani (1988)

hungry. Deeply recessed raked-out mortar joints in brickwork leaving the outline of each brick clearly defined. It weathers badly and is not recommended.

Hunt, Richard Morris (1827–95). American architect, the first to be trained at the École des *Beaux-Arts, Paris (from 1846). He worked in the office of *Lefuel, and assisted during construction at the Louvre from 1854, designing the Pavillon de la Bibliothèque. In 1855 he settled in the USA where he used his knowledge of French Renaissance Revival architecture to great effect. His works included the Studio Building (1857–8—demolished), Lenox Library (1870–7—demolished), and the Tribune Building (1873–6—one of the first tall buildings equipped with 'elevators'—demolished), all in New York, and a series of grand private houses, including the French *Gothic Vanderbilt Mansion (Biltmore House), Asheville, NC (1888–95), and several at Newport, RI, including the *Stick-style

Griswold House (1861–3), and the Neoclassical Vanderbilt Mansion (Marble House, 1888–92). Even though he was the most nationally and internationally honoured American architect of the time, a great many of his buildings have been demolished. His grand *Beaux-Arts Classical entrance-wing of the Metropolitan Museum of Art, New York (1894–1902), was completed by his son, **Richard Howland Hunt** (1862–1931).

Baker (1980); Hitchcock (1977); Placzek (1982); Stein (1986); van Vynckt (1993)

Hurley, William (*fl.* 1319–d. 1354). English carpenter. He was involved in a consultancy capacity at Ely Cathedral, Cambridgeshire, in 1323–4, where he designed the octagon over the *crossing, making him one of the most outstanding inventors of structure of the medieval period. He was also an accomplished designer of *stalls: his works at Windsor and St Stephen's Chapel, Westminster, have not survived, but the stalls at Ely still exist. He was also active at the Tower of London (1324), Caerphilly Castle, Wales, and Guildhall, London (where he was in charge of the works until its completion in 1337). He may also have designed the roof of the Great Hall at Penshurst Place, Kent (1341–9).

Harvey (1987)

Hurtado Izquierdo, Francisco de (1669–1725). Spanish *Baroque architect responsible for some of the most ornate church-interiors of the period. Most of his works are in Córdoba and Granada, including the Sagrario Chapel of the Cartuja (1702–20), Granada, with a *polychrome central tabernacle on *Solomonic columns. Also remarkable is the Sagrario of the Cartuja of Nuestra Señora del Paular, near Segovia (from 1718), with a capricious marble and lapis lazuli *camarín. Even more imposing is the Sacristy of the Cartuja, Granada (1724–64), the masterwork of Spanish Baroque with *piers encrusted with 45 different motifs, giving a rich, jewel-like effect: the building was completed under the direction of Luís de Arévalo, and contains exquisite inlaid *cómodas* (cabinets) by José or F. Manuel Vázquez (1730–64).

Archivo Español de Arte, 35 (1962), 135–73; *Art Bulletin*, 32 (1950), 25–61; Gallego y Burín (1956); Kubler and Soria (1959); Schubert (1924); van Vynckt (1993)

husk. Classical ornament in the form of a stylized *bell-flower*, *nut-shell*, or *wheat-ear*, usually in series, linked together in *drops, *festoons, *garlands, or *strings. When composed to form a *husk-garland*, the vertical parts 'hanging' on each side often have nut-shells diminishing in size towards the bottom, although, like festoons, they increase in size towards the centre of the *catenary curve.

husk (*JJS*)

Husly, Jacob Otten (1738–96). Dutch architect and teacher, his work was influenced by *Palladianism, and then by *Neoclassicism, of which he appears to have been among the earliest practitioners in The Netherlands. He designed the Town Halls at Weesp (1771–6) and Groningen (1793–1810), van Teyler's Museum interiors, Haarlem (1780), and the Felix Meritis Society Building, Amsterdam (1781–8), all in The Netherlands.

Rosenberg, Slive, and Ter Kuile (1977); Vriend (1949)

hut. *See* hermitage *and* Primitive Hut.

Huvé, Jean-Jacques-Marie (1783–1852). French architect. A pupil of his father, **Jean-Jacques Huvé** (1742–1808), and *Percier, he later worked with *Vignon at the Temple de la Gloire, Paris, and later became sole architect, completing it (1817–42) as the Madeleine, a grand Roman temple of the most sumptuous kind. He was Architect to the Paris *hospices* and to the postal service.

Middleton and Watkin (1987); Watkin (1986)

Huxtable, Ada Louise Landman (1921–). American architectural critic. She established her reputation with a series of trenchant articles in the *New York Times* from 1963, but before then had published her monograph on Pier Luigi *Nervi (1960) and many articles in various journals. Her love of her native city was expressed in *Classic New York: Georgian Gentility to Greek Elegance* (1964), and her forthright writings have assailed the insupportable hideousness of many aspects of American cities: indeed, her *Will They Ever Finish Bruckner Boulevard?* (1970) has been described as a 'Primer on Urbicide'. A passionate conservationist, she was a major figure in the creation of a Landmarks Preservation Commission for New York City in 1965 to resist the 'blind mutilation', as she called it, 'in the name of urban renewal'. She also championed excellence in contemporary architecture, denouncing the 'big, the expedient, and the deathlessly ordinary', and making plain her exasperation with the General Services Administration (the body in charge of all Federal construction in the USA) for proliferating banality. She made her admiration for *Mies van der Rohe clear, and has called the *skyscraper one of the 'great technological and architectural achievements of our civilization'. Her *The Tall Building Artistically Considered: The Search for a Skyscraper Style* (1982, 1984) is a major study of the subject. *Pevsner described her as 'the best architectural critic' of his time.

Huxtable (1960, 1960*a*, 1961, 1964, 1970, 1976, 1984, 1986, 1986*a*, 1997)

Hyndeley, Thomas (*fl.* 1401–33). English mason. He worked at Durham Cathedral Priory from 1401, including the *cloisters, and in 1416 became chief mason. He designed an octagonal lavatory in the centre of the cloister (1433), and in the 1420s was in charge of works at Scarborough Castle, Yorkshire.

Harvey (1987)

Hyndeley, William (*fl.* 1466–d. 1505). English mason. He became Master-Mason at York *Minster in 1473, where he constructed the *battlements on the south side. He seems to have been greatly esteemed, in spite of having spent some time in gaol on suspicion of murdering a tiler, one John Partrik, and was buried in the Minster under one of the towers.

Harvey (1987)

hypaethral. Structure without a roof, or partly open to the sky.

hypaethron. **1.** Open *court or enclosure. **2.** Part of a building open to the sky.

hypaethros, hypaethrus. **1.** Building open to the sky, but especially a promenade between *porticoes or *colonnades in a garden. **2.** *Antique temple with its middle part unroofed. **3.** Antique temple with a two-storey *peristyle in the middle, often of superimposed *Orders.

hypaethrum. Roman *fanlight of *latticework over a door and within a *doorway *architrave. It is more properly *hypaethri lumen*.

hyperbola. Conic *section formed by the intersection of a plane with both branches of a double cone (two identical cones on either side of the same vertex or pointed top).

hyperboloid. Solid figure, some of the plane *sections of which are *hyperbolas.

hyperbolic parabola. Continuous flowing double-curved form, used for *concrete shell-roofs, wing-like in *elevation, starting from a parabolic arch and progressing to an upside-down *parabola of similar size, often doubled, as a mirror-image. Its geometry, although seemingly complex, is actually very simple, and its construction is largely dependent on straight lines. It was pioneered by *Nowicki.

Mainstone (1975); *OED* (1933)

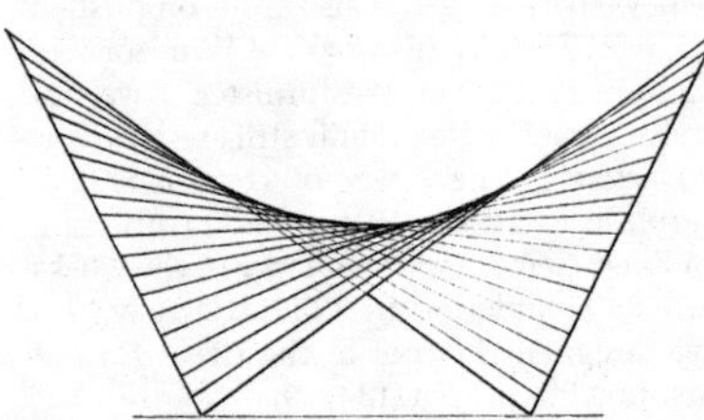

hyperbolic parabola

hyperthyris. *Lintel or *supercilium of an *architrave in a Classical *doorway or other aperture.

hyperthyrum. *Frieze between the *architrave and *cornice over a *doorway or other aperture in Classical architecture.

hypocaust. Hollow space under the floor of a Roman building through which hot air passes by convection to heat the rooms.

hypogaeum, hypogeum. **1.** Antique *building or part of a building below ground, i.e. a cellar, basement, etc. **2.** Underground rock-cut or built tomb with *niches for cremated remains or *loculi for bodies. Smaller than *catacombs, it was usually intended for one family or group.

Toynbee (1971)

hypophyge. *Apophyge.

hypopodium. Lower *podium when the latter is very high, defined horizontally by architectural means (e.g. *strings, *bands, etc.).

hypostyle. Any roofed *colonnade, or series of colonnades, as in an Ancient Egyptian temple.

hypostyle hall. Large room with a flat roof carried on many columns in rows, the middle rows often having taller columns to accommodate a *clearstorey. Examples are those of the cult-temples of Ancient *Egypt, including the temple of Amun at Karnak (*c*.1570–*c*.1200 BC, with additions to *c*.323 BC).

Cruickshank (1996); Papworth (1852)

hypotrachelion(um). In Classical architecture, a member or part between the *capital proper and the *shaft of an *Order, meaning literally 'below the neck' or the 'lower part of the neck'. Its exact meaning seems to have varied slightly according to the source consulted or the Order used. *Vitruvius appears to suggest it refers to the *apophyge, but *Renaissance commentators on Vitruvius, while accepting the apophyge/apophysis connection, also apply it to the lower part of the capital between the *astragal and the *echinus, so it meant the *frieze-like *collarino*, *gorgerin, or *neck of the Tuscan, Roman *Doric, and Greek *Ionic (Erechtheion) Orders. In the Greek Doric Order it meant the horizontal grooves, *reeds, or *fillets encircling the column, the part of the column above, with *flutes, terminating in the *annulets under the echinus being the *trachelion(um). However, in certain archaic Greek Doric Orders (e.g. the C6 BC 'Basilica' at *Paestum) the hollow 'necklace' of vertical stylized leaf-like forms is defined as the hypotrachelion(um).

Curl (1992); Dinsmoor (1950)

ice-house. 1. Building for the storage of ice collected during the winter for use in summer, usually wholly or partly underground, often of two walls insulated with sawdust or other material, fitted with a drain at the base, and frequently of circular *vaulted form. They were not uncommon on larger estates in C18 and C19. An advanced design by J. B. *Papworth was published in his *Rural Residences* (1818). **2.** Eskimo igloo (*iglugeak*), a circular domed or pseudo-domed structure built of ice, often of complex plan.

Nicholson (1835); Papworth (1852)

icicle. 1. Representation of icicles or falling water occurs in *rustication and is known as *congelation: it is often a feature of fountains, *grottoes, *hermitages, *nymphaea, etc. **2.** Motif in *Rococo ornament, often associated with *Chinoiserie, resembling icicles.

iconography. Branch of knowledge dealing with representations of people or objects in art and design, hence the symbolism in a design. Christian iconography, for example, is immense and complex, and informed virtually every aspect of Western art and architecture until comparatively recently.

iconostasis. In the Greek and Russian Orthodox churches, a *screen between the *sanctuary and the body of the church, with three *doorways. It is often hung with icons and other images, hence its name.

Ictinus, *or* **Iktinos** (*fl.* C5 BC). Distinguished architect active in Periclean Athens, he (with *Callicrates) designed the *Parthenon (447–432 BC), and wrote a description of the building (with Carpion) that has not survived. He prepared a scheme for the Telesterion, Eleusis (*c.*440 BC), and may have designed the temple of Apollo Epicurius, Bassae (*c.*429–*c.*400 BC), which was remarkable in that it had a *Doric *Order outside, an Ionic *engaged Order (*see* Bassae Order) inside, and a *Corinthian Order at the end of the *naos.

Berve and Gruben (1963); Carpenter (1970); Dinsmoor (1950); Placzek (1982); Robertson (1945)

ideal. Concept of something perfect, sometimes equated with works that attempt to reproduce the best of natural forms but improve upon them, ironing out imperfections. In Europe since the *Renaissance the ideal has been the art of Classical Antiquity.

Ideal City. City existing as an idea or an archetype, conceived as perfect, or as an object to be aimed at as a standard of excellence. The term suggests something whole and complete, as in many of the geometrical symmetrical plans for such cities in the *Renaissance period, all of which are variants on patterns established by *Vitruvius, who in turn may have derived his typology from earlier sources, now lost. Renaissance designers of the *città ideale* froze the elements into formal patterns as an expression of order in which Man imposed ideals and heroic dimensions, often with a central structure as an expression of the social order. Such perfect geometrical plans also symbolized the yearning for Utopia, the perfect state, and even the City of God, the New Jerusalem.

Rosenau (1975)

IHS. *See* Chrismon.

imbrex (*pl.* **imbrices**). Bent or curved tile like a half-cylinder used for gutters or for covering the junction of adjacent concave or flat tiles with upstands.

imbrication. Scale-pattern, or petal-diaper ornament resembling a surface covered with scale-like curved roofing-tiles, found on *Antique *sarcophagi-lids and on the roof of the *Choragic Monument of Lysicrates, Athens (334 BC). It is also used on *terracotta panels, *screens, *tracery, etc., and resembles a construction of imbrices (*see* imbrex) piled on top of each other.

Imhotep (*fl. c.*2778 or *c.*2650 BC). Ancient Egyptian courtier, priest, and architect to King Zoser (Djoser). He was deified later as Architect of the Universe, and one of the Trinity, with Horus and Isis. He was 'son of Ptah', and identified with Asclepius. As designer of the huge and sophisticated step-pyramid and complex at Saqqara, he must be regarded as one of the greatest architects of all time, and an important innovator in the development of masonry construction.

Curl (1991); Hurry (1928); Sethe (1902); Smith and Simpson (1992); Wildung (1977)

impluvium. *See* atrium.

impost. *See* arch.

in antis. *See* anta.

in cavetto. Impressed ornament, like *relief in reverse.

incised slab. Slab of stone with a design cut into its surface, commonly a funerary monument featuring human figures representing *effigies, inscriptions, emblems, etc., the incised work often enhanced with black or coloured filling. A variation is a more comprehensive series of *indents filled with *brass or *latten sheets cut to fit and themselves incised and inlaid.

indent. Shape cut out in a stone slab to receive *brass or *latten *inlaid work, such as an *effigy or inscription.

Indian style. The architecture of India influenced the West in a lesser way than did the architecture of China (*see* Chinoiserie), and was most evident during the *Regency and *Victorian periods as a variation on the theme of *Picturesque eclectic orientalism. The vogue for the *Hindoo style was partly prompted by Thomas *Daniell, his nephew William Daniell (1769–1837), and William *Hodges, who published views of India. Hodges's *Travels in India* (1780–3) also came out in a French edition, while his *Dissertation on the Prototypes of Architecture, Hindoo, Moorish, and Gothic* (1787), and *Select Views in India* (1785–8) revealed the 'Barbaric Splendour' of Indian buildings to the West. Hodges proposed that *Egyptian, Hindoo, *Moorish, and *Gothic all derived from a common visual memory of stalactite and rock formations. His theory suggests the longing for the *Primitive and the Natural that was a feature of late-C18 Romantic sensibility. One of the first fruits of the linking of Indian and Gothic forms was *Dance the Younger's south façade of the Guildhall, City of London (1788–9). The Hindoo style appeared in Sezincote, Gloucestershire (early 1800s), complete with onion-domes, *chattra-topped *pinnacles, and multifoil arches, while *Porden introduced the Hindoo style into the stables, riding-school, and coach house, the Pavilion, Brighton, Sussex (1804–8). *Nash's Royal Pavilion, Brighton (1815–21), promiscuously mixed *Chinoiserie and Hindoo styles. Daniell produced a *capriccio* of Hindu and *Islamic architecture for *Hope's 'Indian' room at Duchess Street, London. After the Great Exhibition of 1851 the Indian style became influential, given the importance of the Subcontinent in the British Empire, and Owen *Jones in his *Grammar of Ornament* (1856) praised the contribution of India. The style was used in numerous interiors, including smoking-rooms and Turkish baths, especially after Queen Victoria was declared Empress of India (1877). A good example is the Indian Hall, Elveden Hall, Suffolk (1890s), by William *Young and his son Clyde Francis Young (1871–1948), added to the house designed by John Norton (1823–1904), who had also incorporated certain Indian features in the work of 1863–70.

Earlier, the Indian style had appeared in the USA, notably at P. T. Barnum's house at Bridgeport, Conn. (1846–8), designed by Leopold *Eidlitz and based on Nash's work at Brighton. This clearly influenced Henry *Austin when designing the New Haven Railroad Station (1851). Samuel *Sloan's *The Model Architect* (1852–3) included designs with Indian flavours (e.g. the 'Oriental Villa'), clearly the model for his Longwood Villa (Nutt's Folly), Natchez, Miss. (1854–61), a polygonal house crowned with an onion-dome. The published design may have influenced the New York Crystal Palace (1853–4) by *Carstensen and Gildemeister, a *polychrome structure of iron and glass.

In the C20 *Lutyens's Viceroy's House, New Delhi (1912–31), combined an essential *Classicism with many themes derived from Indian architecture.

Conner (1979); Handlin (1985); Lewis and Darley (1986)

industrial architecture. Architecture to house manufactories, such as mills, engineering works, potteries, etc.

industrialized building. Architecture and constructional techniques dependent on *prefabrication. Mass-produced building components were available from C18, while the iron-foundries made many and varied artefacts (e.g. balcony-fronts, *balusters, *crests, railings, etc.). Cast-iron *Greek *Doric columns (far cheaper than stone and easy to make because repetitive) were used by *Nash at Carlton House Terrace, London (1827–33), *Barry employed mass-produced metal window-frames and cast-iron roof-panels at the Palace of Westminster (1839–60), and *Paxton's Crystal Palace, London (1851), was almost entirely built of prefabricated parts assembled within a *modular system. *Curtain-walling designs, panel systems, *precast concrete, and many other aspects of industrialized building have speeded C20 building processes. Charles *Eames, E. D. *Ehrenkrantz, Buckminster *Fuller, *Gropius, *Nervi, *Perret, *Prouvé, and *Wachsmann were in the forefront of developments in C20 industrialized building. In England, *Aslin and *CLASP evolved systems for building, while *Arup, *Foster, *Grimshaw, *Rogers, and others have raised industrialized building techniques to some degree of refinement.

Herbert (1984); Hix (1996); Klotz (1986); Pevsner (1976)

ingle-nook. 1. Corner of a large fireplace where the opening of the *chimney was far larger than needed, and there was space where persons could sit. **2.** Area off a room, containing the fireplace, often with a small window, fitted with seats between the *chimney-breast and the wall.

ingo, ingoing. *Reveal or return face of a wall in a recess, such as a *niche, door, or window.

inlaid work. Decoration made by inserting one material within an incision, *indent, or depression cut into another material to the same depth and finished flush. This may be accomplished using hard materials, such as black marble set in white, wood of one colour laid in wood of another colour (*marquetry*), one metal set in another, e.g. gold in steel (*damascening*), or *brass set in polished tortoiseshell (*boule* or *buhl* work). Surfaces made up of very small pieces fitted together are properly *mosaics because they are laid *on* and not *in* the background, although wood of various colours laid within a surface in Italian *Renaissance designs does qualify as inlaid work and is called *intarsia*, *intarstatura*, or *tarsia*. Soft materials, such as paint, mastic, or coloured pastes, which harden after a while, really fall into the category of *incised rather than inlaid work.

inosculating column. *Cluster column.

INRI. *See* Chrismon.

inserted. *Engaged.

insula. 1. Group of buildings in a Roman town bounded by four streets, so essentially an isolated block containing one large structure or several smaller ones joined together. **2.** Detached house in Antiquity.

insulated. 1. Building, column, or other work standing *detached so that all sides of it are visible, as in the *peristyles of *Greek temples, but unlike a pseudo-*peripteral Roman temple where the columns around the *cella are *engaged. **2.** Kept apart and separate, to assist sound-proofing, retention of heat, prevent contamination, etc.

intercolumniation. Space between the lower parts of the *shafts of adjacent columns in a Classical *colonnade or *portico defined by *modules the same size as the shaft diameters (*d* below). Vitruvius described its commonest varieties:

$1\frac{1}{2}d$: *pycnostyle* (used only with the *Ionic and *Corinthian *Orders);
$2d$: *systyle*;
$2\frac{1}{4}d$: *eustyle* (usual Roman and *Renaissance spacing, with $3d$ used for the wider central intercolumniation of a portico);
$3d$: *diastyle*;
more than $3d$: *araeostyle*.

*Perrault is supposed to have invented *araeosystyle*, an arrangement with two columns $\frac{1}{2}d$ apart followed by a space of $3\frac{1}{2}d$ used at the east front of the Louvre, Paris, and also by *Wren at St Paul's Cathedral, London. *Doric intercolumniation is not controlled by diameters, but by the relationships of *triglyphs and *metopes. *Greek *Doric *Hellenic intercolumniation normally had one triglyph over the space between columns (therefore of the *monotriglyph* type), and, of course, one on the centre-line of each column, although the *Propylaea in Athens has two over the entrance. *Hellenistic intercolumniation was generally wider (even in Doric), often with two (*ditriglyph*) or more triglyphs above, giving a lighter, more elegant appearance. At the angles of Greek Doric porticoes, however, because the end triglyphs must terminate each *frieze and therefore touch at the corner, the corner-columns cannot be placed on the centre-line of the triglyphs, and have to be moved inwards, so that the adjoining intercolumniations are smaller than usual. This problem does not exist in Roman or Renaissance Doric, as the triglyphs do not touch at the corners, so the corner-columns can be on the centre-lines of both corner-triglyphs, and a half-metope is set on each face of the angle.

Curl (1992); Dinsmoor (1950); Gwilt (1903); Robertson (1945); Vitruvius Pollio (1955–6)

interlace. Carved ornament of crossed and re-crossed cords or bands arranged like a single piece of flexible material returning upon itself, like unravelled knots. Called *entrelacs*, it is common in *Anglo-Saxon, *Celtic, and some *Romanesque art.

Glazier (1926); Jones (1868); Lewis and Darley (1986)

interlacement *or* **interlacing band.** *Guilloche ornament.

interlacing arch. *See* arch.

internal angle. Figure formed when two walls meet each other at an angle, as in the corner of a room, called a *re-entrant.

International Modern *or* **International style.** C20 architectural style which began just before the 1914–18 war. The term appears to have been coined by Alfred H. Barr (1902–81), later publicized by H.-R. *Hitchcock and Philip *Johnson *c.*1932. It is generally accepted as having originated in Germany with the work of W. *Gropius and others, and, because its image was free from *Historicism and indeed from most allusions to the past, it was eagerly embraced by the avant-garde after 1918, first in Central Europe, then elsewhere. Its main themes were asymmetry; severe, blocky, cubic shapes; smooth flat plain undecorated surfaces (often painted white); the complete elimination of all mouldings and ornament; 'flat' roofs; large expanses of glass held in steel frames (often in the form of long horizontal bands or *curtain-walling); and very free planning made possible by the adoption of steel-framed or *reinforced-concrete post-and-slab construction (with a series of flat slab-floors and a flat roof-slab carried on concrete columns or posts) thus enabling partitions to be erected where desired as they played no part in the structure.

Paradigms of the International Modern style include Gropius's *Bauhaus building, Dessau (1925–6), Le *Corbusier's Salvation Army Hostel (from 1929) and Pavillon Suisse (1930–2), both in Paris, and *Mies van der Rohe's housing-blocks at the *Weissenhofsiedlung, Stuttgart, Germany (1926–7). Regarded as indicative of progressive, Leftist ideologies, its so-called *Machine Aesthetic was used in both the Fascist headquarters by *Terragni at Como, Italy, and the Soviet Union in the 1920s. It was adopted universally after 1945, especially in Western Europe, Britain, and the USA.

Hitchcock (1993); Hitchcock and Johnson (1966); Korn (1967); Lampugnani (1988)

interrupted. Architectural element from which part has been elided (*see* elision). A *pediment *broken or *open is interrupted.

intersecting. *See* arch, tracery.

intersectio. Space between the *dentils or the *triglyphs (i.e. *metope) in a Classical *entablature.

intertriglyph. *Metope.

intrados. *See* arch.

Inwood, William (*c.*1771–1843), English surveyor and architect. He was the author of *Tables for the Purchasing of Estates* (1811 and several editions thereafter). He designed many houses, barracks, and warehouses in collaboration with his son, **Henry William** (1794–1843), who brought his scholarly understanding of the *Greek Revival to their buildings. There were two other sons, both architects: **Charles Frederick** (*c.*1799–1840), designer of the Church of All Saints, Marlow, Buckinghamshire (1832–5), and **Edward** (1802–). Henry William travelled in Italy and Greece (1818–19), and published *The Erechtheion at Athens: Fragments of Athenian Architecture and a few remains in Attica, Megara, and Epirus* (1827), the standard work on the great Greek temple. His undoubted scholarship was displayed in St Pancras New Church, London (1819), one of the finest monuments of the Greek Revival, which adapted *Gibbs's type of the Anglican church using Greek motifs (*portico, *caryatides, and windows from the Erechtheion, and a *steeple derived from the Tower of the Winds). It was designed in collaboration with his father, with whom he also built All Saints, Camden Town (1822–4), and St Peter's, Regent Square (1822–5, demolished). They designed St Mary's Chapel, Somers Town (1824–7), a thin and unscholarly *Gothic effort lampooned by A. W. N. *Pugin in *Contrasts* (1836). W. H. Inwood also published *The Resources of Design in the Architecture of Greece, Egypt, and other Countries* (1834).

Crook (1972*a*); Colvin (1995); *DNB* (1917); Inwood (1827, 1834); Summerson (1988, 1993)

Ionic Order. Classical *Order of architecture, the second *Greek and the third *Roman. It is primarily identified by its *capital, with its rolled-up cushion-like form on either side creating the distinctive *volutes. The Ionic Order has a base of the *Asiatic or *Attic type (the latter being favoured by the Romans), and the *shaft is more slender in proportion than in the *Doric Order: Greek shafts are almost invariably fluted with *fillets separating the flutes (although *Hellenistic columns often have the lower part of the shaft faceted or plain, as in the stoa, Priene (*c*.158–156 BC)), but Roman shafts are often wholly unfluted. The *astragal, *echinus, and fillet occur in both Greek and Roman capitals, the echinus is enriched with *egg-and-dart, and sometimes (e.g. Erechtheion, Athens) the astragal is embellished with *bead-and-reel. The particularly elegant and beautiful capitals of the Erechtheion (*c*.421–407 BC) also have a *hypotrachelion enriched with a continuous *frieze of *anthemion motifs, while the astragal below has bead-and-reel and the moulded *abacus is ornamented with egg-and-dart. Indeed, abaci are always moulded, much smaller than Doric abaci, and usually plain, but sometimes enriched. *Entablatures consist of *architrave (usually divided into *fasciae), frieze (sometimes omitted, particularly in *Hellenistic buildings), and *cornice. The frieze has no *metopes or *triglyphs, so the *inter-columniation discipline inherent in Doric does not exist, and spacing can be wider. Furthermore, the Ionic frieze may be a plain *band, can be richly ornamented with continuous sculpture either in relief (as with Roman work), or as applied in different coloured stone (e.g. Erechtheion), and may also be *pulvinated (as in the *thermae of Diocletian, Rome). Cornice-mouldings can be very rich, with bed-mouldings including *dentil-courses, egg-and-dart, or other ornament, as in the temple of Fortuna Virilis, Rome (*c*.40 BC). Additional mouldings of bead-and-reel occur between the architrave fasciae in richer versions of the Order. One of the main problems when using the Ionic Order is the capital, with its two distinct *elevations—one with the two volutes (desirable on a front), and the 'side' with the *baluster side or *pulvinus (not desirable on a façade). In Greek temples, therefore, a 'special' had to be designed so that two adjacent volutes would appear on two faces at the external angle of a *portico by pulling the corner volutes out with concave curved faces at 45° (135° to each façade). This *angle-capital also had two adjacent partial volutes at the inner angle within the portico. This somewhat clumsy arrangement was superseded by the Romans, who invented a capital with four identical faces, the eight volutes projecting under the four corners of the abacus thus doing away with the need for a 'special' as all the capitals were the same on all four sides. This *angular capital (also known as the *Scamozzi Order) was used at the temple of Saturn, Rome (*c*.42 BC, rebuilt *c*. AD 320), and was the basis for the upper part of the *Composite capital. *See also* Ammonite.

Curl (1992); Dinsmoor (1950); Normand (1852)

Ipswich window. C17 *oriel window, with convex sides between the wall and *mullions, *transoms two-thirds of the height of the convex side-*lights, and an arched centre-light with small lights on either side of an elaborate *ancon, the lights leaded, and the mullions and panels beneath the cills heavily encrusted with ornament. Good examples survive at Sparrowe's House, Buttermarket, Ipswich, Suffolk (*c*.1670). The Ipswich window was the inspiration for R. N. *Shaw, who used it at New Zealand Chambers, London (1871–3—demolished), and elsewhere.

Ireland. *See* Celtic, Hiberno-Romanesque.

iron. Widely used in architecture. There are two basic types: *cast iron*, which is strong in compression, but weak in tension, so is used for columns, bollards, railings, and decorative features; and *wrought iron*, which is employed for gates, ornamental scrolls, filigree-work, and the like. Some fine medieval ironwork survives, notably associated with English tombs and *chantry-chapels in cathedrals and churches. Later, iron was widely used for balcony-fronts, railings, etc., in C18. Exposed cast iron was used for components in whole façades in C19, notably by John *Baird in Glasgow, and wrought iron was used to

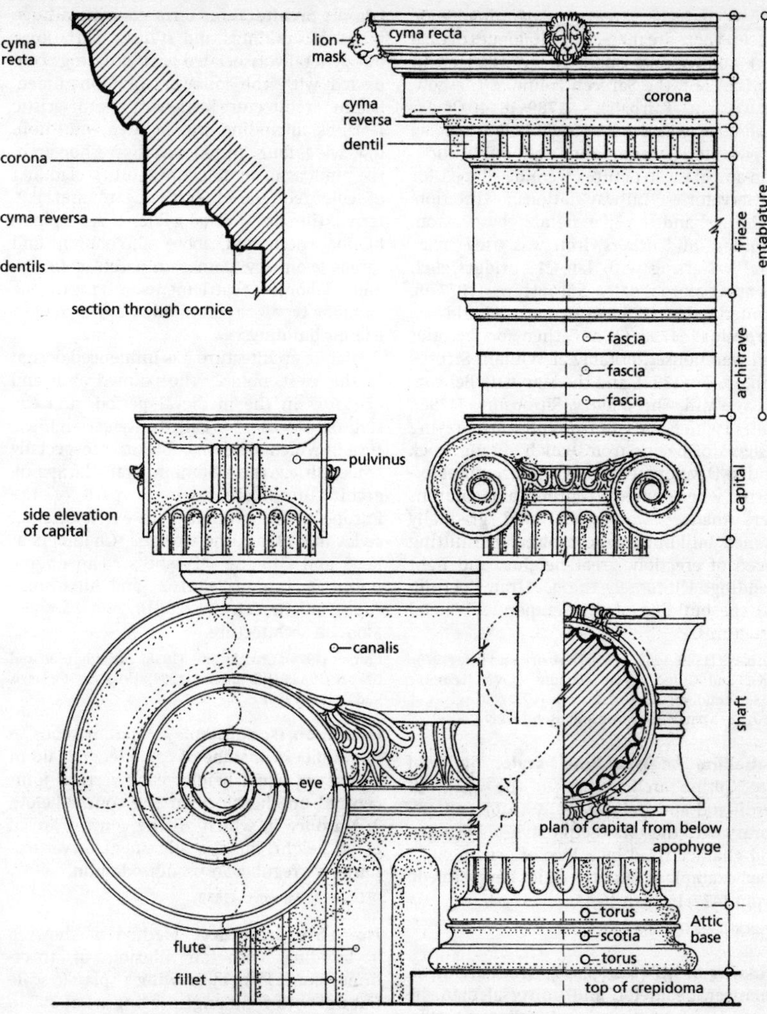

Ionic Order. Greek Ionic Order from Eleusis. (*After Normand*)

construct large *trusses spanning wide spaces. There are many C19 catalogues of cast-iron components, notably by *Badger in the USA and the Saracen Foundry, Glasgow. Sir William Fairbairn's (1789–1874) *On the Application of Cast and Wrought Iron to Building Purposes* (1854) was an important publication. Iron-and-glass structures were developed for conservatories, railway-stations, exhibition-buildings, and the like, notably by *Paxton, *Loudon, and others. Iron was used structurally, starting with late-C18 bridges such as at Coalbrookdale, Shropshire (1777–9), Sunderland (1793–6), and Buildwas, Shropshire (1795–6), and then for factories and warehouses, notably at William Strutt's Mill, Derby (1792), and the Marshall, Benyon, & Bage Mill, Shrewsbury, Shropshire (1796), both of which had cast-iron columns carrying systems of beams from which sprang brick vaults. Developments in iron structures occurred when composite girders and columns were made, using rivets, and gradually framed buildings were evolved, permitting speed of erection, great heights, and light claddings. Ultimately, the steel frame permitted the building of *skyscrapers. *See* metal structures.

Fairbairn (1849, 1869, 1870); Fairbairn and Pole (1970); Gayle and Gillon (1974); Hartung (1983); Lemoine (1986); Loudon (1834); Mainstone (1975); Sturgis *et al.* (1901–2—a particularly full and useful essay)

Isabelline *or* **Isabellino style.** Style of late-*Gothic architecture in the Spain of Ferdinand and Isabella (1474–1516), contemporary with the *Manueline style of Portugal, and characterized by a love of ornament. A good example is San Juan de los Reyes, Toledo (from 1477) by Juan *Guas.

Cruickshank (1996)

Isidorus of Miletus (*fl.* C6). Greek architect, engineer, geometer, and universal man, he worked with *Anthemios of Tralles on the design and construction of the great *Byzantine Church of Hagia Sophia (Holy Wisdom), Constantinople (532–7). They may also have worked on the Church of the Holy Apostles, Constantinople (*c.*536–550—destroyed), the model for the Church of San Marco, Venice (begun 1063). When the dome of Hagia Sophia collapsed in 558, it was rebuilt to a modified design by **Isidorus the Younger**, also from Miletus, probably the elder man's nephew.

Krautheimer (1986); Mango (1972, 1986); Watkin (1986)

Islamic architecture. Term covering a huge range of buildings and stylistic variations, but generally associated with buildings connected with the followers of Mohammed. Islamic architecture has several characteristic features, including the pointed, multifoil, low, wide, four-centred, and horseshoe arch, the *muqarna or stalactite *corbel, cladding of coloured glazed earthenware and patterned tilework, fretted gables of stone, marble, or stucco, and, above all, coherent and serene geometry. Domes, minarets, cloisters, and elaborate *battlements, often of the *almena type, are commonly associated with Islamic buildings.

Islamic architecture has influenced design in the West, notably the pointed arch and *cusping in the medieval period, and the stylistic aspects of so-called *Moresque* architecture in which elements of Islamic, especially *Moorish (e.g. the Alhambra, Granada, Spain), architecture were used as part of the European enchantment with exotic oriental styles in C18 (e.g. the work of *Chambers at Kew) and C19 (e.g. *Persius's steam-engine house at Potsdam (1841–2), and Aitchison's Arab Hall in Kensington (1877–9)). *See also* Moorish architecture.

Conner (1979); Cruickshank (1996); Ettinghausen and Grabar (1988); Hillenbrand (1994); Hoag (1986); Lewis and Darley (1986)

isodomon, isodomum. **1.** *Masonry consisting of blocks of stone of equal length laid in courses of equal height, each vertical joint centred on the block in the course below. **2.** Masonry in which all the courses are of equal height, but the alignment of vertical joints is irregular. *See* pseudisodomon.

OED (1933); Papworth (1852)

isometric projection. Method of showing a building with an illusion of three-dimensional form by drawing a *plan to scale but not with right angles (being set at 30° to the horizontal), and projecting the vertical axes to scale. Thus the plan is slightly distorted, but the effect is more realistic than in an *axonometric projection, although diagonals and curved lines are not accurately depicted.

Fraser Reekie (1946)

Isozaki, Arata (1931–). Japanese architect. He has drawn on a wide range of sources, believing that anything in the history of architecture is open to quotation. His syntheses of

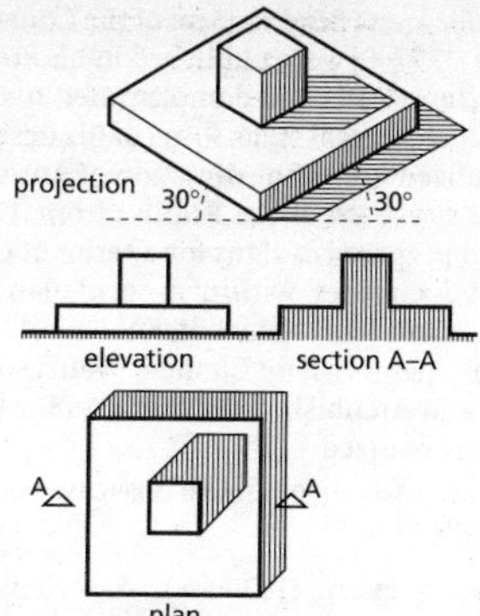

isometric projection

Western and Japanese themes, concentrating on the clarity of geometry and stereometrically pure forms, have been impressive. He established his reputation with the Oita branch of the Fukuoka Mutual Bank (1966–7), followed by the Fujimi Country Club House, Oita (1973–4). His more recent work includes the Tsukuba Civic Centre, Ibaragi (1978–83), the Museum of Contemporary Art, Los Angeles, Calif. (1981–6), Team Disney Headquarters, Buena Vista, Fla. (1990–1), the Museum Nagi MoCA, Nagi-cho, Okayama, Japan (1992–4), the Concert Hall, Kyoto (1992–5), and Domus: La Casa del Hombre, La Coruña, Spain (1993–5).

Barratucci and Russo (1983); Drew (1982); Emanuel (1994); Jodidio (1997*a*); Yatsuka and Stewart (1991)

Italianate. Style of C19 architecture modelled on a type of *astylar Italian *palazzo, represented by the Palazzo Farnese, Rome (1517–89), by da *Sangallo the Younger and *Michelangelo. The plain façade had window-apertures framed by *aedicules, *quoins were emphasized and the whole front was held down by a large *cornicione*. Typical of this style are *Barry's Travellers' (1829–32) and Reform (1837–41) Clubs, Pall Mall, London, the Northern (formerly Belfast) Bank Head Office, Belfast, by *Lanyon (1845), and Osborne House, Isle of Wight, by Thomas *Cubitt and Prince *Albert (1845–51). Following such a Royal *imprimatur* Italianate *stucco ornament was widely used to enrich the façades of terrace-houses in areas such as Kensington, London, from the mid-C19. The style was widely used in Germany (especially Berlin, Dresden, and Munich) and in the USA.

Curl (1990, 1995); Dixon and Muthesius (1985); Lever and Harris (1993); Middleton and Watkin (1987); Sheppard (1973)

Italian roof. Low-pitched *hip-roof covered with *pan-and-roll tiles.

Italian Villa style. Eclectic style used for C19 domestic buildings originating with *Nash and other architects. Its main characteristics were very low-pitched roofs (sometimes hipped) with wide overhanging *eaves (often supported on ornamented brackets or *mutules), asymmetrical compositions, windows that were sometimes treated as *aedicules but just as often had semicircular heads influenced by the fashionable *Rundbogenstil, square towers, often with a *loggia, and an *arcaded or *colonnaded element connecting it with the garden. Nash's Cronkhill, Shropshire (*c*.1802), *Schinkel's and *Persius's Court Gardener's House, Potsdam (1829–33), and 'Greek' *Thomson's villas in and around Glasgow are good examples.

Gomme and Walker (1987); Watkin and Mellinghoff (1987)

Ittar, Henryk (1773–1850). Polish Neoclassical architect of Italian extraction. He designed several of the *fabriques in the garden of allusions at Arkadia, near Nieborów, Poland, including the Circus (1801) and Amphitheatre (*c*.1805) influenced by *Piranesi's visionary engravings. The Circus perhaps alluded to the Imperial Palace on the Palatine Hill, Rome (AD C1), but was otherwise unprecedented in European gardens. He was also responsible for the Isle of Poplars (complete with Rousseauesque 'tomb') on the axis of the Circus. Some of his designs for buildings at Arkadia are among the most advanced severe conceptions of their time.

Garden History, 23/1 (1995), 91–112; Lorentz and Rottermund (1984)

Ivanov-Shits, Illarion Aleksandrovich (1865–1937). Russian architect. By the 1890s he was one of the most fashionable designers in Moscow, where he was responsible for the Morosov Children's Clinic (1903–5), the Merchants' Club (1907–8), the Soldatenkovskaya Hospital (1908–13), and the Shanyavsky People's University (1910–13), among other buildings. His work was strongly influenced by that of Otto *Wagner (especially at the Merchants' Club, Chekhov Street).

Raeburn (1991)

iwan. Porch or short entrance-hall roofed with a half-elliptical barrel-*vault often found in *Islamic architecture. An impressive pre-Islamic example was the Sassanian Palace, Ctesiphon, Iraq (C4 or C6).

Cruickshank (1996)

Ixnard, Pierre-Michel d' (1723–95). French architect, he was an early protagonist of *Neoclassicism in Germany from 1764 after he became Court Architect to the Elector of Trier. He designed the great domed *Klosterkirche* (Monastery Church) St Blasien, Black Forest (*c*.1768–84). He rebuilt the Church of Sts Cornelius and Cyprian, Bad Buchau (1773–6) and another at Hechingen (1776), both in a plain Neoclassical style. His designs for a vast *Residenz* (Seat of the Court) at Koblenz (1777–9) were published in his *Recueil d'Architecture* (1791) and demonstrated his advanced Neoclassical style: some of his designs were realized under the direction of Antoine-François Peyre (*see* Peyre Family) from 1779. D'Ixnard prepared designs for a series of crescents and circuses within a *grid-plan for Clemensstadt, later Neustadt, Koblenz (1777), a spacious new town for Clemens Wenzeslaus, Elector and Archbishop of Trier (1768–94): it was partly realized.

Franz (1985); Ixnard (1791); Powell (1959); Watkin and Mellinghoff (1987)

Izenour, Steven (1930–). *See* Venturi, Robert.

jack. **1.** *Rafter set obliquely where two roofs meet (e.g. in *dormers or *valleys). **2.** Short *common rafter*, such as those between the *eaves and a *hip.

Jackson, John (*c*.1602–63). English master-mason active in Oxford. He oversaw the building of Canterbury Quadrangle, St John's College (from 1634). The unusual south porch at the Church of St Mary the Virgin (1637), with *Solomonic columns and other *Baroque effects curiously co-existing with the *Perpendicular *Gothic fan-vaulting of the ceiling, is a tour-de-force, and is known to have been built by him, although the name of Nicholas *Stone has also been associated with the design. He was consulted about the tower and gateway of University College (1635–6), and superintended the building of the new Chapel and Library of Brasenose College (1656–66), where late-Gothic and *Renaissance elements are again mixed with great élan. He may have designed Welford Park, Berkshire (*c*.1660—later remodelled).

Colvin (1995)

Jackson, Thomas (1806–90). Accomplished Irish architect. He was in partnership with Thomas *Duff of Newry, Co. Down, with whom he designed the Old Museum, College Square North, Belfast (1830–1), an essay in the *Greek-Revival style. He settled in Belfast where he laid out an estate of Grecian villas on the Cliftonville Road, Belfast (1831–2), and designed several fine Neoclassical houses, including Graymount (1835), the pair of villas at Mount Charles (1842), and Clonard House (1843). He was probably responsible for 4–30 University Square, but his masterpiece is the charming *Tudor Gothic Roman Catholic Church of St Malachy (1840–4), with its fine plaster fan-vaulting. He designed a series of ambitious *Italianate villas, including Glenmachan Tower (1860s), Altona (1864), and Craigavon (1870), all in Belfast. He took his son, **Anthony T. Jackson** (d. 1910) into practice as Thomas Jackson & Son, and together they designed the first purpose-made insurance-offices in Belfast in the form of a Venetian *palazzo at 10 Victoria Street (1863) as well as the round-arched Town Hall, Victoria Street (1869–71).

Brett (1967, 1996); Larmour (1987)

Jackson, Sir Thomas Graham (1835–1924). English architect. A pupil of George Gilbert *Scott, he commenced practice in 1862. His works include the *Jacobethan Examination Schools (1876–82), the vaguely *Gothic New Buildings, Brasenose College (1909–11), the Girls' High School, Banbury Road (1879), the Boys' High School, George Street (1880–1), and the new buildings for Hertford College (1887–1914—including the chapel and the 'bridge of sighs', in a style Jackson himself called 'refined English Renaissance'), all in Oxford. Other works include the Science Block, Uppingham School, Rutland (1894–7), extensions (including the Chapel) to Radley College, Berkshire (1891–1910), and the Chapel at Giggleswick, Yorkshire (1897). He published many books, including *Modern Gothic Architecture* (1873), *Reason in Architecture* (1906), *Byzantine and Romanesque Architecture* (1913), and *Gothic Architecture in France, England, and Italy* (1915).

Dixon and Muthesius (1985); Gray (1985)

Jacobean architecture. Style of English architecture of the reign of King James I and VI (1603–25), not greatly differing from *Elizabethan architecture, and largely continuing into the reign of Charles I (1625–49). It was essentially a mélange of Flemish, French, and Italian *Renaissance influences, with pronounced emphases on themes drawn from Flemish *Mannerism, including *jewelled *strapwork and *grotesque ornament.

*Assemblages of Orders, emblems, heraldic devices, *herms, and *obelisks abounded, while curved and Dutch *gables were also favoured. Traces of *Gothic, especially *Perpendicular, architecture remained, notably the continuing use of mullioned and transomed windows, and the late-medieval E- and H-plans were also used. Good examples of Jacobean architecture are Hatfield House, Hertfordshire (1607–12), Bramshill, Surrey (1605–12), and Audley End, Essex (1603–16). However, Inigo *Jones's contributions also took place in the reigns of James I and VI and Charles I, but his sophisticated Italian style is not described as 'Jacobean'. There was a *Jacobean Revival* in C19, notably in country-houses, and it was also mixed with the *Queen Anne style to produce a singularly curious hybrid (e.g. R. N. *Shaw's New Zealand Chambers, London (1872–3—demolished)).

Cruickshank (1996); Lewis and Darley (1986); Pevsner, *Buildings of England* (1951–); Sturgis *et al.* (1901–2)

Jacobethan. Revivalist architecture of C19 and early C20, in which *Elizabethan and *Jacobean elements were freely mixed. William *Burn specialized in the style for his country-houses, and many other architects used it.

Colvin (1995); Lever and Harris (1993)

Jacobs, Jane Butzner (1916–). American city planner and critic. Believing cities provide the foundation for civilization, she made her name with *The Death and Life of Great American Cities* (1961), a sustained attack on the 'urban renewal' being promoted by architects and centralized agencies, arguing that such policies were killing the living organism that was the city, and demanding a new respect for self-generating urban forces to create social and economic diversity and well-being. She began her career as a critic with *Architectural Forum* in 1952, and her realization that the orthodoxies of *CIAM and the *Athens Charter (e.g. zoning and a free-for-all for motor-cars), which had permeated Government and professional circles, were strangling cities and ruining their diversity. She contributed an important chapter to *The Exploding Metropolis* (1958) in which she argued that 'Downtown is for People' at a time when traditional urban centres were dying. Her studies convinced her that when the principles advocated by Le *Corbusier and Ebenezer *Howard were applied (as they almost invariably were), they not only failed to stop decay, but actually made matters worse, causing immense social and economic problems as well. Drabness and uniformity were imposed where once there was charm and diversity. She rightly saw that cities were far more complex, like living organisms, than the simplistic notions of planners and architects would allow, and she advocated that the forces advancing social and economic diversity should be encouraged rather than destroyed. Claiming to investigate the 'real life' of the city (which she said orthodox planners ignored), she illustrated her points with many real case-histories, pointing out that high density was not necessarily the same thing as overcrowding, and drawing attention to why certain areas were pleasant to live and work in, while others were not.

In her *The Economy of Cities* (1969) she emphasized the manufacturing and trade side of cities, and showed how they helped the development of rural areas, and how some cities flourished and others stagnated. Again she emphasized the importance of diversity, stressing that economic well-being rests with the many small, innovative, diverse businesses rather than with grand conglomerations and monopolies.

While her work became accepted and widely read, she herself complained that very little had changed and that the same mistakes were being 'compulsively repeated', not least because of the application of 'urban studies' and the use of myriad statistics to justify the same old panaceas, which were nothing of the sort. However, her work undoubtedly encouraged the *conservation movement, and in time many of her heretical ideas were adopted.

Jacobs (1961, 1969, 1984, 1992, 1996)

Jacobsen, Arne Emil (1902–71). Danish architect, he was influenced by *International Modernism in the 1920s, as is demonstrated in his own house (1928) and in the Bellavista Estate, Klampenborg (1934), both in Copenhagen, where he embraced the style of the Stuttgart *Weissenhofsiedlung. In the 1930s Jacobsen was influenced by *Asplund in his designs for Aarhus (1937–42—with Erik Møller (1909–)) and Søllerød (1940–2—with Flemming Lassen (1902–84)) Town Halls. He used *curtain-walls of the utmost refinement from the 1950s, good examples of which were the Jespersen Building (1955), and Rødovre Town Hall (1955), both in Copenhagen.

Attention to detail was clear in St Catherine's College, Oxford (1960–4—with Knud Helmuth Holscher (1930–)), where the brickwork and *precast concrete were meticulously detailed in every respect. Jacobsen also designed all the furnishings and fittings for the College. He was responsible for the Danish Embassy, Sloane Street, London (1969–77), which, like his *Rathaus* (Town Hall), Mainz, Germany (1970–3), was completed by his colleagues Hans Oluf Dissing (1926–) and Otto Weitling (1930–).

Dyssegaard (1971–2); Emanuel (1994); Faber (1964); Kastholm (1968); Skriver *et al.* (1971); Thau and Vindum (1998)

Jacobsen, Holger Alfred (1876–1960). Danish architect. He designed Bispebjerg Crematorium, Copenhagen (1905–7), drawing on eclectic motifs, which made his name. Later he worked on the Police Headquarters, Copenhagen (1918–24—with Anton Frederiksen (1884–1967), Hack *Kampmann, and Aage *Rafn), an important C20 Neoclassical building. His most significant work was the Nye Scene, a major extension to the Royal Theatre, Copenhagen, designed in 1919 and completed in 1930, in which *Mannerism and stripped *Neoclassicism are evident, although the interior has touches of colourful *Art Deco, without parallel in Denmark. His Neoclassical villas of the 1920s (including his own house, Copenhagen, of 1926) combined a rational approach to planning with a scholarly refinement of detail.

Paavilainen (1982); Weilbach (1949)

Jacobsen, Theodore (d. 1772). English architect of German descent, he worked in London, where his best-known building was the Foundling Hospital (1742–52—demolished 1928). He is remembered today for the main quadrangle, Trinity College, Dublin (1752–9).

Colvin (1995); *DNB* (1917)

Jadot de Ville Issy, Jean-Nicolas (1710–61). French architect. Trained by *Boffrand, he settled in Vienna under the aegis of Francis Stephen, Duke of Lorraine (1708–65) and consort of Maria Theresia (reigned 1740–80). Jadot designed the Arco San Gallo, Florence, to commemorate Francis Stephen's accession to the Grand Duchy of Tuscany (1739), and, after he arrived in Vienna, was the architect of the Alte Aula, or Old University (later Akademie der Wissenschaften—1753–5), and the Schönbrunn Menagerie, both in the *Louis Quinze style. He may have been the author of the plan for the Royal Palace in Budapest (1749).

Baedeker, *Austria* (1929); Kalnein and Levey (1972)

Jahn, Helmut (1940–). German-born architect. He joined (1967) the Chicago, USA, firm of architects founded by C. F. *Murphy, among others, in 1937, having studied in Munich and then under *Mies van der Rohe at the Illinois Institute of Technology. In 1973 he became Partner, Vice-President, and Director of the Design Section, and the firm was renamed Murphy/Jahn in 1981. Under Jahn's leadership the firm designed the Kemper Arena, Kansas City (1974), the Sports Hall, St Mary's College, Notre Dame, Ind. (1977), the Xerox Center, Chicago (1980), the Agricultural Engineering Science Building, University of Illinois (1984), the State of Illinois Center, Chicago (1985), the vast *Messeturm* block, Frankfurt, Germany (1985–91), extensions to O'Hare International Airport, Chicago (1983–7), the Sony Centre, Berlin (1995–7), and an enormous range of very large projects too numerous to be listed here. His style moved away from the severity of Mies's work to a new richness of expression drawing on aspects of *Art Deco, notably for the Frankfurt *Messeturm*.

Emanuel (1994); Jodidio (1993); Klotz (1986); Lampugnani (1988); Miller (1986)

jalousie. **1.** External slatted or *louvred shutter. **2.** Grille protecting a *gallery in a church.

jamb. Vertical side of an aperture, such as a window or doorway, essentially that part on which a superincumbent load is sustained. That part of the jamb between the *outer* wall and the door- or window-frame is the *reveal*.

jamb-shaft. *Colonnette or *shaft, often *detached, set against or part of the junction of a *jamb and an internal or external wall in medieval architecture.

James, John (*c.*1672–1746). English architect. He was joint Clerk of the Works at Greenwich with *Hawksmoor, and in 1715 became Assistant Surveyor to *Wren at St Paul's Cathedral, London, succeeding to the Surveyorship on Wren's death (1723). In 1716 he became Hawksmoor's colleague as Surveyor to the Commissioners for Building Fifty New Churches when *Gibbs was dismissed, and James designed St George's, Hanover Square, London (1720–5), with its handsome

*Corinthian *portico that was the precedent for Gibbs's St Martin-in-the-Fields. With Hawskmoor he designed St Luke's, Old Street, London, with its very original *obelisk-spire (1727–33—partly derelict), and St John's, Horselydown, Southwark (1727–33—demolished). On Hawksmoor's death (1736) James became Surveyor to the Dean and Chapter of Westminster, and completed the western towers of Westminster Abbey to Hawksmoor's designs. He also added the not entirely satisfactory steeple to Hawksmoor's otherwise robust Church of St Alphege, Greenwich (1730). He published several works, including *Rules and Examples of Perspective* (1707 and 1725) translated from *Pozzo's original (1693) and *A Treatise on the Five Orders of Columns* (1708) from *Perrault's original (1683).

Colvin (1995); *DNB* (1917); Downes (1980); Harris (1990); Lees-Milne (1970); Summerson (1993)

Janyns, Henry (*fl.* 1453–83). English mason, son of Robert *Janyns. He was appointed Chief Mason of the Works at the Chapel of St George, Windsor Castle, Berkshire, in *c.*1475, and so was responsible for the foundations and early stages of the building. He may have designed the tomb of Cardinal Bourchier (d. 1486) in Canterbury Cathedral (*c.*1480) and the monument of King Edward IV (reigned 1461–83) in Windsor.

Harvey (1987)

Janyns, Robert (*fl.* 1438–64). English mason. He was Warden of the Masons during the building of All Souls College, Oxford (1438–43). He became master-mason during the building of the bell-tower at Merton College, Oxford (1448–51), before becoming Warden of the Masons at Eton College. He was also involved in the building of the Divinity Schools, Oxford (1452–3). He made and fixed the carving above the *gateway of Merton College (1463–4).

Harvey (1987)

Janyns, Robert, jun. (*fl.* 1499–1506). English mason, son of Robert *Janyns. He was chief mason during the building of King Henry VII's (reigned 1485–1509) polygonal tower at Windsor Castle, Berkshire (1499), where he remained until 1505. He was probably responsible for the *Lady Chapel at Burford Church, Oxfordshire (1490s), the four-centred windows of which resemble those at St George's Chapel, Windsor. He was probably in charge of the building of the Royal Palace at Richmond, Surrey, after 1497 (destroyed).

Harvey (1987)

Japelli, *or* **Jappelli, Giuseppe** (1783–1852). Unusually eclectic Italian early C19 architect, he trained under *Selva before designing his most celebrated work, the Caffé Pedrocchi, Padua (1816–31), reckoned by H.-R. *Hitchcock to be the 'handsomest C19 café in the world' and the 'finest Romantic Classical edifice in Italy'. It is an essay in *Neoclassicism with Greek *Doric, *Corinthian, *Empire, *Palladian, *Gothic, *Moorish, and *Egyptianesque themes. *Il Pedrocchino*, an extension of 1837, was designed in the Venetian *Gothic style. From 1816 he worked on the Villa dei Conti Cittadella Vigodarsere, Saonara, near Padua, with a *Pantheon-like dome over the chapel, and a strong whiff of *Palladianism throughout. The gardens of the villa were in the English style, complete with *Picturesque compositions and *fabriques in several styles. He also designed the garden for the Villa dei Baroni Treves de' Bonfili, Padua (late 1810s). Jappelli designed the severe *Greek Revival Meat Market, Padua (1819–24), the *Moorish conservatory, Villa Torlonia, Rome (1840s—where the park was also in the *giardino inglesi* style), and the Neo-*Empire *Rococo Teatro Nuovo, Padua (1847).

Fiocco (1931); Hitchcock (1977); Lavagnino (1961); Mazzi (1982); Meeks (1966); Middleton and Watkin (1987); Puppi (1980*a*)

Japonaiserie. Until the mid-C19 Japan was largely a closed book to the West. After 1858, when the USA signed a trade agreement with that country (followed by European nations), Japanese artefacts became more familiar, and greatly influenced Western designers of furniture and buildings, especially those of the *Aesthetic and *Arts-and-Crafts movements. Among architects to draw inspiration from Japanese design were E. W. *Godwin. *Art Nouveau also was influenced by aspects of Japanese art. Fashionable taste appreciated the simplicity of Japanese objects after various exhibitions (e.g. London (1862) and Paris (1867)), and by the 1870s *Japonaiserie*, or design influenced by the arts of Japan, permeated art and architecture, especially in Britain, France, and the USA. Various publications helped to make the style familiar, including Rutherford Alcock's *Art and Art Industries of Japan* (1878), T. W. Cutler's *Grammar of Japanese Ornament and Design* (1880), Louis Gonse's *L'Art*

Japonais (1883), and Siegfried (not Samuel) Bing's (1838–1905) *Artistic Japan* (1888–91—with French and German editions). Bing's shops in Paris helped to popularize Japonaiserie, while his connections with Tiffany in New York contributed to the spread of the style to the USA. A further catalyst was provided by Christopher *Dresser, who not only knew Japan and supplied Tiffany & Co. with Japanese *objets d'art*, but married a Japanese woman, and published *Japan, its Architecture, Art, and Manufactures* (1882).

Jervis (1984); Lewis and Darley (1986)

Jardin, Nicolas-Henri (1720–99). French Neoclassical architect, he moved to Denmark in 1754, where, as Professor at the Royal Academy, he was influential. He continued the Frederikskirke, Copenhagen (1749–1894), a fine, domed Neoclassical essay, begun by *Eigtved, completing the lower part and the eastern portal: the church was finished by *Harsdorff, *Meldahl, and others. Jardin's dining-room (1755–7) in the Amalienborg Palace, Copenhagen, was described by Eriksen as probably the 'earliest surviving room decorated entirely in the Neoclassical style by a French architect'.

Eriksen (1974); Hautecœur (1946); Høller (1973); Middleton and Watkin (1987); Redslob (1922)

jardin anglais. English garden. Term used on the Continent to describe the 'natural' type of C18 garden with winding paths, clumps of trees, etc.

Parreaux and Plaisant (1977); Symes (1993)

jardin anglo-chinois. French term for the informal type of 'natural' garden. *See* Sharawadgi.

Mosser and Teyssot (1991); Parreaux and Plaisant (1977); Symes (1993)

jaspé now *jaspered*. Marbled, mottled, veined, and coloured paint finish to represent marble, as on a *dado or column-*shaft.

Jean de Chelles (*fl.* C13). *See* Chelles.

Jean d'Orbais (*fl.* C13). *See* Orbais.

Jeanneret-Gris, Arnold-André-Pierre (1896–1967). Swiss architect, arguably one of the most important protagonists of the *International *Modern Movement. A relative of Le *Corbusier, he joined the office of *Perret in Paris, and, from 1921 to 1940 worked with Le Corbusier on architectural designs, town-planning schemes, and ideas for furniture and other artefacts. Their office was a magnet for the aspiring young, not only because of the well-publicized *Modern Movement designs produced there, but because of the Modernist polemics (a few of which were signed jointly by both men, including the Five Points of Architecture, the basis for their theory of design), which were published at the time. Their combined efforts produced paradigms of the Modern Movement, including the Villa Besnus, Vaucresson (1922), the *Pavillon de L'Esprit Nouveau* for the Exposition Internationale des Arts-Décoratifs et Industriels Modernes, Paris (1924–5), the houses for the *Weissenhofsiedlung, Stuttgart (1927), the unrealized project for the League of Nations Building, Geneva (1927), the Maison Stein, Garches (1927–9), the Villa Savoie, Poissy (1928–31), the Centrosoyus Building, Moscow (1929–33), the Cité de Refuge, Paris (1929–33), the Maison Suisse, Cité Universitaire, Paris (1930–3), and the Apartment House Clarté, Geneva (1930–2). These designs were jointly produced, although Jeanneret-Gris seems to have been more closely involved in resolving details and supervising construction. Both men participated in debate and in meetings and events that helped to form the ideology of Modernism, such as *CIAM (from 1928) where Jeanneret-Gris was always vocal, but the latter was deeply interested in *Rationalism and *industrialized building, while Le Corbusier seems to have esteemed them more for emotional or symbolic reasons.

After the Fall of France in 1940 the two men went their separate ways, Jeanneret-Gris establishing an office in Grenoble where he designed prefabricated systems for buildings to be erected in the Free Zone. He returned to Paris in 1944, and designed (1946–7—unrealized) a large apartment-building which anticipated Le Corbusier's *Unités d'Habitation*, although the apartments were planned to permit more daylight to enter the interior than Le Corbusier was able to achieve. However, his collaboration with Le Corbusier was re-established when he began to work with him, *Fry, and *Drew (1951) on plans for a new capital of the Punjab at Chandigarh, India, and supervised the construction of the monumental designs by Le Corbusier, including the Supreme Court. He himself designed numerous buildings there, including hospitals, housing, offices, schools, and shops, as well as the grander State Library, City Hall,

Governor's Palace, and much else, often working with Indian colleagues. From 1961 he worked on the new University of the Punjab. In particular, he experimented with non-mechanical methods of environmental control.

Jeanneret-Gris's achievements have been obscured by those of Le Corbusier, who was the more charismatic publicist, but it is clear that he was of enormous importance in the genesis of the paradigms with which the name of Le Corbusier is solely and unfairly associated in the popular mind.

Design, 8/9 (1964), 17–24; Emanuel (1994); Placzek (1982); *Progressive Architecture*, 45/2 (1964), 148–53; Roth (1977); *Werk*, 55/6 (1968), 377–96; *see also* Further Reading after the entry on Le Corbusier

Jeeves, Stanley Gordon (*c.*1888–1964). *See* Hood, Raymond Mathewson.

Jefferson, Thomas (1743–1826). Able native-born American self-taught architect of the late C18, he excelled in many things, and became third President of the USA (1801–9). It is known he had a fine library of architectural books, and it was largely from these that he acquired his skills. One of his first buildings was Monticello, his own house near Charlottesville, Va. (1768–82—remodelled 1796–1809), the plans of which were a variation on a design in Robert *Morris's *Select Architecture* (1755), with additional elements derived from *Gibbs, and a dash of *Palladio taken from *Leoni's edition of the *Quattro Libri*. Indeed, Monticello was Palladian in layout, intelligently altered to accommodate the most convenient internal arrangements, but in its final version it suggested the *Antique villa transformed by French *Neoclassicism (e.g. Hôtel de Salm, Paris, of 1783).

In 1784 Jefferson was appointed Second American Minister to Paris, a stroke of good luck enabling him to absorb up-to-date architectural ideas at first hand. He was also conveniently placed to visit England, which he did in 1786, expressly to study *Picturesque gardens that attracted the admiration of Europe at that time. In France he admired the top-lighting at the Château de Chaville (1764–6—destroyed) by *Boullée, as well as *Legrand and *Molinos's dome of the Halle au Blé, Paris (1782–3).

When it was decided to build a State Capitol in Richmond, Va., Jefferson chaired the Committee charged with arranging for this, and he himself proposed a building based on the *Corinthian Roman temple, the Maison Carrée, Nîmes (16 BC): thus he was the first to reintroduce the rectangular temple-form into public architecture (as opposed to small garden *fabriques, e.g. at Stowe, Buckinghamshire) in the West since Classical Antiquity. In the event, the State Capitol (1785–99), which was designed by Jefferson with *Clérisseau as adviser, employed the *Ionic *Order with *angular capitals of the *Scamozzi type, and had *pilasters rather than *engaged columns as on the *cella of the Maison Carrée.

From 1789, when he returned to the USA, becoming Secretary of State in Washington's Government, he involved himself in the planning and architecture of the new Federal capital, promoting French ideas when he could. Jefferson's greatest architectural achievement, however, was the University of Virginia, Charlottesville (1817–26), a series of porticoed pavilions (each with an Order from a different Roman building) linked by *colonnades, on either side of a long rectangular lawn (the first *campus plan) with a scaled-down version of the *Pantheon in Rome on the long axis at one end. While *Latrobe helped Jefferson with this design, the main scheme was Jefferson's own, though possibly based on Marly-le-Roi, the *château of Louis XIV. The *Rotunda at the University contained the most remarkable elliptical rooms in America, an arrangement possibly derived from the Doric column-base in the Désert de Retz near Paris, which Jefferson had seen. The University is arguably the most beautiful architectural ensemble in the American Continent. Like Monticello and the Virginia Capitol, it was more than a fine work of Classical architecture: all three were intended as exemplars from which Americans would learn the rules of architecture and design.

Adams (1976, 1983); Boyd (from 1950); Kimball (1966, 1968); Lehman (1980); Malone (1948–74); Mayo (1970); Nichols (1978); Nichols and Bear (1967); O'Neal (1960); Placzek (1982)

Jellicoe, Sir Geoffrey Alan (1900–96). English landscape-architect. His work included designs for industrial installations, including the Calverton Colliery, Nottinghamshire (1937–40), where he demonstrated that industry need not damage the landscape. He was responsible for very many conversions of clay and gravel excavations into well-landscaped recreation amenities, notably in Derbyshire. He made major contributions to the planning of Guildford, Surrey, Hemel Hempstead, Hertfordshire, Wellington, Shropshire, and Plymouth, Devon. He carried out commissions for gardens at many sites, including *Gibbs's Ditchley Park, Oxfordshire (1935). Among his publications, *Baroque Gardens of Austria* (1931), *Motopia* (1961—a visionary design for a town where cars would travel on high-level roads and helicopters would be the prime method of travel), *Modern Private Gardens* (1968), *The Use of Water in Landscape Architecture* (1938), and *Studies in Landscape Design* (1959–70) may be mentioned. Some of his writings were produced in collaboration with his wife, Ursula. Perhaps his best book was *Italian Gardens in the Renaissance* (1925), which was widely admired. Towards the end of his life he claimed not to know about plants, and that he 'loathed' gardens.

Emanuel (1994)

Jencks, Charles Alexander (1939–). American architect, architectural critic, and historian. His works include many studies in which he defined a range of categories and terms, including *Abstract Representation, *Action Architecture, *Adhocism, *Camp, *Cardboard Architecture, *Ersatz Architecture, the evolution of *High Tech which he termed 'Slick Tech', *Late-Modern Architecture, the *Modern Movement, *Neo-Vernacular, *New Classicism, *Pop Architecture, *Post-Modernism, *Rational Architecture, the *Semiological School, *Supersensualists, *Symbolic Architecture, counterfeit *Trompe l'Œil (which he called 'Superdeception'), and much else. Among his influential books may be mentioned *The Language of Post-Modern Architecture* (1987), *Architecture Today* (1988), and *Post-Modern Architecture: The New Classicism in Art and Architecture* (1988).

Jencks (1968, 1971, 1972, 1973, 1973*a*, 1977, 1979, 1980, 1980*a*, 1982, 1982*a*, 1983, 1985, 1987, 1988, 1988*a*, 1990); Jencks and Baird (1969)

Jenney, William Le Baron (1832–1907). American architect. He studied in Paris and opened his practice in Chicago in 1868. With the Leiter Building, Chicago (1879), he gave expression to the framed structure, but in the Home Insurance Building, Chicago (1884–5—demolished), he used columns of cast and wrought iron, girders and floor-beams of wrought iron up to the sixth floor, and girders of steel above that, the first major use of structural steel in a building (as opposed to a bridge or other work of pure engineering). Thus Jenney created a skeleton-frame appropriate for a high building, and his design was a proto-*skyscraper, an important step in the evolution of constructional principles leading to the achievements of the *Chicago School, although the building also contained brick walls and massive stone *piers, so it cannot be regarded as having a true structural frame: rather it was a prototypical *form* or image for later developments. He taught *Sullivan, *Holabird, *Roche, and *Burnham, and published important papers on the problems of building tall buildings.

Condit (1952, 1968); Mujica (1929); Placzek (1982); Randall (1949); Turak (1986); Zukowsky (1987)

Jensen, Albert Christian (1847–1913). Danish architect responsible, usually in collaboration with Ferdinand *Meldahl, for several important buildings in Copenhagen. They completed the Frederikskirke (or Marble Church) begun by *Eigtved and *Jardin, in 1874–94. He designed the Charlottenborg Art Gallery (1880–3), Hagemanns Kollegium (1908), and the Magasin du Nord Department Store on the Kongens Nytorv which emulated Parisian prototypes even to the extent of having pavilion-roofs. Active in the Society of Architects, he was instrumental in starting the Society's journal *Architekten*.

Weilbach (1995)

Jensen-Klint, Peder Vilhelm (1853–1930). Danish architect, a pupil of *Herholdt. His most celebrated building is Grundtvig's Church, Bispebjerg, Copenhagen, designed 1913, built 1919–26, and soundly based on configurations found in the brick *Gothic churches of Northern Europe. It has a steep, stepped, gabled brick front, rather like organ-pipes, and its style is balanced between C19 *Historicism and C20 *Expressionism. The surrounding buildings form one composition with the church, and were completed by Jensen-Klint's son, **Kaare** (1888–1954), in 1940. Jensen-Klint, who was informed in his work by traditional Danish brick architecture, was an important influence on architectural education.

Jørgensen (1979); Millech (1951); Weilbach (1947)

jerkinhead. Hipped roof above a part-gable. The *gable-wall is *clipped* about half-way up its raked part, the pitched roof terminating in *barge-boards and then becoming a hipped roof, the *verges merging with *eaves. Also called *shread-head*.

Jerman *or* **Jarman, Edward** (d. 1668). London surveyor and carpenter, he was one of the three Surveyors appointed to control the rebuilding of the City after the fire of 1666, the other two being *Hooke and *Mills. He designed several Livery-Company Halls and the Royal Exchange (1667–71—demolished), a handsome building with a tower rising from a *triumphal arch.

Colvin (1995)

Jerusalem. 1. *See* cross. **2.** The Ideal or Holy City, a symbol of Paradise as the goal of a pilgrim (or indeed of any Christian), and therefore represented by the centre of a medieval *labyrinth or *maze cut in turf or inlaid in a church floor (as in the *nave of Chartres Cathedral, France) used for ritual pilgrimages and penances.

Jesse. Genealogical tree depicting the genealogy of Christ, a common medieval motif. It is usually in the form of a winding trunk of a tree or vine springing out of the recumbent body of the patriarch Jesse, with figures denoting his descendants (as given in the Bible) standing on the ends of its branches, the Virgin and Child forming the fruit at the top. A good example survives in the *tracery of the Abbey Church of Sts Peter and Paul, Dorchester, Oxfordshire (*c*.1340).

jetty, jettie, jutty. 1. Projection of a *timber-framed upper storey overhanging a wall beneath, usually formed by the *cantilevered floor-joists and beams supporting the *bressummer from which the projecting timber-framed wall rises. Associated with the jetty are:

hewn jetty: wall-post thickened above the lower storey.

jetty-bracket: curved bracket under a jetty, usually associated with a support for the bressummer or *dragon-beam;

jetty-bressummer: *cill-beam on the ends of jettied beams or joists, often given additional support by jetty-brackets;

jetty-plate: wall-plate of the storey on which the jetty rests;

2. Construction carried out from land into deep water to protect a harbour and act as a landing-stage.

Alcock, Barley, Dixon, and Meeson (1996)

Jewell, Richard Roach (1810–96). English-born architect, he settled in Western Australia (1852), where he became foreman then Supervisor of Public Works. He designed many public buildings in Perth, including the Court House and Gaol (1854), Pensioner's Barracks (1863), Trinity Church (1864), Town Hall (1867), the Old Treasury (1874), and the Girls' School (1877).

Morison and White (1979); Oldham and Oldham (1978)

jewelled. Late-C16 and early C17 complex *strapwork enriched with half-spheres or *lozenges (*prismatic ornament) formed to suggest jewels.

jib. *See* gib.

Joass, John James (1868–1952). Scots architect, he worked with *Burnet, Son, &

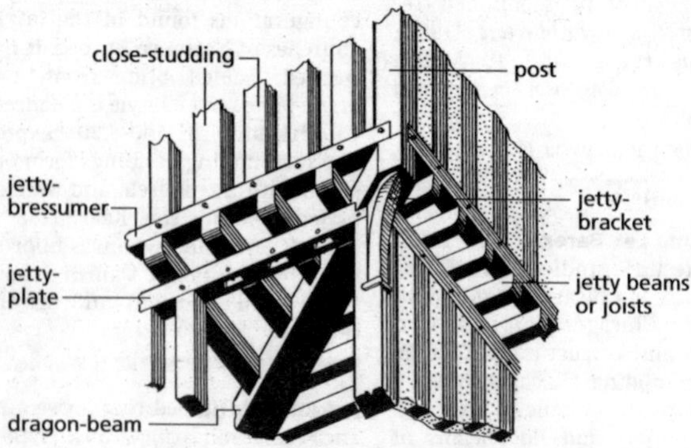

jetty (*JJS*)

Campbell in Glasgow, and then (1889) in Rowand *Anderson's office in Edinburgh. In 1893 he joined the progressive office of Sir Ernest *George, but left to work with *Belcher in 1896, becoming the latter's partner (1905–13). One of the most distinguished buildings of the partnership was the Royal Insurance Office at the corner of Piccadilly and St James's Street, London (1907–9), a robust essay in C20 *Mannerism. Other Joass/Belcher buildings included the former Mappin & Webb Building, Oxford Street, London (1906–8), and the opulent *Wrenaissance Ashton Memorial, Williamson Park, Lancaster (1907–9).

Gray (1985)

joggle, joggling. 1. Joint at the meeting of two adjacent pieces of stone to prevent them from sliding: it consists of a projection in one piece fitting into a notch in another, and is especially used in flat *arches or built-up *lintels made of several pieces, sometimes called *crossette. **2.** Rebated joints in timber construction, especially braces joining an upright *post.

Johann, Meister (*fl.* C14). Designer of the hall-choir of the *Cistercian Abbey of Zwettl in Lower Austria (1343–83), which has the *chevet arrangement of *ambulatory and radiating chapels, probably influenced by the work of the *Parler family.

Baedeker, *Austria* (1929); Grodecki (1986)

Johansen, John MacLane (1916–). American architect. He worked with *Breuer and *Skidmore, Owings, & Merrill before establishing an office in 1948. At the circular Chancellery for the US Embassy, Dublin (1958–64), he employed the geometry of a continuous wave made of elegant precast concrete frames. Around the same time he experimented with the fragmentation of form, the climax of which was the Mummers' Theater, Oklahoma City (1970), actually three theatres loosely linked together by tubes containing passages and services, perhaps influenced by images of *Archigram, *Constructivism, and *Brutalism. Other works include the Johansen House, Stamfordville, NY (1974), the Ellsworth House, Salisbury, Conn. (1976), and the Barna House, Bedford, NY (1979).

Emanuel (1994); Heyer (1978); Lampugnani (1988)

John of Ramsey (*fl.* early C14). *See* Ramsey.

Johnson, Francis (1911–95). English architect. He established his practice in Bridlington, Yorkshire, in 1934, specializing in scholarly restorations of C18 buildings. Notable successes included Fairfax House, Castlegate, York, by John *Carr (1975–80), and the Long Gallery, Burton Agnes, Yorkshire (1975). He carried out important works at York and Howden *Minsters, Belton House, Lincolnshire, and Heath Hall, Wakefield, during his long career, and built new houses, including several in Yorkshire, and Strathconan, Muir of Ord, Ross and Cromarty, Scotland (1980s). He designed the Church of St Margaret, Hilston, Yorkshire (1956–7), in a style reminiscent of the Free *Romanesque of Scandinavia. He had an unrivalled knowledge of C18 architectural *pattern-books.

Powers (1987); *The Times* obituary, 13 Oct. 1995

Johnson, John (1732–1814). English architect, he built up a considerable practice. In 1782 he became Surveyor to Essex County, and in that capacity designed Shire Hall, Chelmsford (1789–91). He was responsible for the handsome County Rooms (formerly a hotel), Hotel Street, Leicester (1792–1800).

Briggs (1991); Colvin (1995)

Johnson, Philip Cortelyou (1906–). American architect and critic, he was a convert to the *International style in the 1920s, and indeed may, with Alfred H. Barr (1902–81) and H.-R. *Hitchcock, have coined, or at least disseminated, the term with the publication of their *The International Style: Architecture since 1922* (1932) and the exhibition 'Modern Architecture' at the Museum of Modern Art, New York (where he was in charge of the Department of Architecture from 1932 to 1934), in the same year which publicized work by Le *Corbusier, *Gropius, *Mies van der Rohe, and others. In 1942 he built the Johnson House in Cambridge, Mass., influenced by Mies's work, and published a monograph on the German architect in 1947.

He made his name with his own Glass House, New Canaan, Conn. (1949), clearly influenced by Mies's projects, and crisply detailed: with Mies's Farnsworth House (1945–50), Plano, Ill., it was a key building of the period. During the early 1950s Johnson remained influenced by Mies, and was associated with the latter during the erection of the Seagram Building, New York (1956–8), even though in the guest-house at New Canaan

(1952) he introduced *vaults with more than a touch of *Soane about them. Thereafter his work turned to stripped Neoclassical formulae, including the New York State Theater, Lincoln Center, New York (1964), and a developing tendency to monumentality was displayed in his extension to the Boston Public Library (1964–73). In the late 1970s Johnson sent shock-waves through the world of orthodox *Modernism with his American Telephone and Telegraph *skyscraper, New York (1978–83), a masonry-clad building with powerful *mullions set on a stripped variation of a *serliana-cum-triumphal-arch and capped by a paraphrase of an open-topped *pediment: it has been described as the first major *Post-Modern building. For the AT & T building and other projects of the 1970s and 1980s Johnson worked with John Henry Burgee (1933–). In the 1980s he again surprised his critics by turning to *Deconstructivism, helping to organize a major exhibition at the Museum of Modern Art, New York, and contributing to the catalogue (1988). He designed the Gate House, New Canaan (1995), a pavilion without any right angles, and the Cathedral of Hope, Dallas, Texas (1996–9). Johnson published *Writings* in 1979, edited by R. A. M. *Stern.

Hitchcock (1966*a*); Hitchcock and Johnson (1966); Jacobus (1962); Jodidio (1997); Johnson and Wigley (1988); Lampugnani (1988); Miller (1979); Schulze (1994); Stern (1979)

Johnson, Thomas (d. 1800). English architect, he designed the County Gaol, Warwick—now the County Council offices—(1779–82), one of the earliest uses of Greek *Doric in an English public building. He also built the Church of St Nicholas, Warwick (1778–9), and rebuilt St Mary's, Hanbury, Worcestershire (1792–5), both in the *Gothic style. The Warwick church was reputedly designed by his son, **John Lees Johnson** (1762–), who was then not 16 years old, but who seems to have predeceased his father.

Colvin (1995)

Johnston, Francis (1760–1829). Irish architect, he trained under *Cooley and worked for Richard Robinson, Archbishop of Armagh (1765–94). He was appointed Architect to the Board of Works and Civil Buildings in Dublin (1805). Influenced by James *Wyatt and *Gandon, his work was eclectic, and includes St George's Church, Dublin (1802–17—which has echoes of work by *Gibbs), the austere but beautifully proportioned Neoclassical Townley Hall, Drogheda, Co. Louth (from 1793), and the grim Richmond Penitentiary, Grange Gorman Lane (1812–20). He was largely responsible for converting *Pearce's Parliament House, Dublin, to the Bank of Ireland (1804–8), built the Chapel Royal, Dublin Castle (1807–14), and designed the Court House, Armagh (from 1809). His handsome *Greek Revival General Post Office, Dublin (1814–18), was probably his best work, although the very pretty Strawberry Hill *Gothick house, Charleville Forest, Tullamore, Co. Offaly (1800–12), is the finest early C19 *Picturesque house in Ireland. He completed King's Inns, Dublin, by Gandon in 1817, and built the Royal Hibernian Academy (1824–6).

Bence-Jones (1988); Craig (1982)

jointing. Completion of joints in brickwork or *masonry while the mortar is still soft, in contrast to *pointing.

Brunskill (1990)

joist. One of a series of horizontal timbers, spanning the space between walls, beams, etc., supporting a floor-finish and a ceiling. Types of joist include:

cogged: joist supported and held in a notch in a transverse beam;

cross: one of a series of joists in a section of floor running at right angles to the direction of joists in other sections of the same floor;

lodged: joist resting on a beam;

trimmer: also *trimmed* joist, spanning between two joists and supporting the ends of short joists, e.g. to permit an opening to be formed in a floor.

Alcock, Barley, Dixon, and Meeson (1996); McKay (1957)

Joly, Jules-Jean-Baptiste de (1788–1865). French architect. A pupil of *Percier and *Fontaine, he designed the Chambre des Députés, vestibule, Salon du Roi, and sumptuous Library (1821–33) in the Palais Bourbon, Paris, which he published in 1840 as *Plans, coupes, élévations et détails de la restauration de la Chambre des Députés*.

Middleton and Watkin (1987)

Jones, Edward (1939–). English-born architect (with M. Kirkland (1943–)) of the memorable City Hall and Civic Square, Mississauga, Toronto, Canada (1986–8), in a *Post-Modern style of great severity that is reminiscent of French C18 *Neoclassicism at its simplest.

Kalman (1994)

Jones, Sir Horace (1819–87). English Architect and Surveyor to the Corporation of the City of London from 1864, his best works were Smithfield Meat Market (1866–75), Guildhall Library and Museum (1872–6), Leadenhall Market (1881–2), Guildhall School of Music, Embankment (1886–8), and, with Sir John Wolfe-Barry (1836–1918), Tower Bridge (1886–94).

DNB (1917); Dixon and Muthesius (1985)

Jones, Inigo (1573–1652). London-born architect of Welsh origin, he was largely responsible for introducing the Classical *Palladian style to *Jacobean England, and indeed for begetting the first Palladian Revival. From 1605 to 1640 he staged over 50 masques, plays, etc. (often in collaboration with Ben Jonson (1572–1637)) for the Courts of Kings James I and VI (1603–25) and Charles I (1625–49), the surviving drawings for which show that he was well acquainted with the most up-to-date Italian designs by 1609. From *c.*1606 he produced a number of designs for structures in which his partially digested understanding of *Classicism taken from sources such as *Palladio, *Sangallo, and *Serlio was apparent. In 1610 he was appointed Surveyor to Henry, Prince of Wales (d. 1612), and in 1613 was granted the reversion of the place of Surveyor of the King's Works. He had visited Italy before 1603, but his second visit to that country (1613–14) was important in forming his architectural tastes, for he met *Scamozzi and visited a great number of buildings illustrated in Palladio's *Quattro Libri*. In 1615, armed at last with the necessary architectural expertise, he became Surveyor of the King's Works, and built the Queen's House, Greenwich (1616–35), the Banqueting House, Whitehall (1619–22), and the Queen's Chapel, St James's (1623–5), all of which survive as a testimony of his careful study of the work of the Italian masters and of his own understanding of the principles of Classical design. Nothing resembling them had ever been built in England before, and indeed in a Europe dominated at the time by the *Baroque style they had no contemporary exemplars in France or Italy. Although they were not immediately influential, and were perhaps oddities when Jacobean *Mannerism was *de rigueur*, they became exemplars for a type of *astylar house that came into favour after 1660, and indeed led to the second Palladian Revival of *Campbell, *Burlington, and their contemporaries in C18. He also designed the Prince's Lodgings, Newmarket, Cambridgeshire (1619–22—destroyed), which influenced the design of many red-brick houses with stone *dressings and hipped roofs throughout the second half of C17.

From 1625 to 1640 Jones worked on the Classicization of the old St Paul's Cathedral, London, clothing the medieval fabric in a new garb, and adding a huge prostyle *Corinthian *portico, the grandest north of the Alps at that time, which showed Englishmen the power, scale, and possibilities inherent in Roman architecture, and provided an important precedent for *Wren when rebuilding the Cathedral after 1666. For Francis Russell, 4th Earl of Bedford (1539–1641), he designed and laid out the Piazza, Covent Garden (1631–7), the first London Square, with unified façades consisting of arcaded ground floors over which was a *Giant Order of *pilasters, perhaps suggested partly by the *piazza and church in Livorno (Leghorn) and partly by the *Henri Quatre Place des Vosges, Paris (1605–12). It was an enormously influential development, anticipating much C18 British urban planning and domestic architecture in towns. He designed St Paul's Church, Covent Garden (1631–3), the first complete Classical church in England, with a *Tuscan portico taken from Barbaro's version of *Vitruvius. His design for a huge new palace at Whitehall (*c.*1638) reveals that he was not, however, impressive as an architect of large complexes, although his work influenced developments at Whitehall until the end of C17.

Jones seems to have acted as a consultant for the south front of Wilton House, Wiltshire (*c.*1636), designed by Isaac de *Caus, but his supposedly prolific activities as a country-house architect (a hare apparently started by Colen *Campbell) are now, through modern research, largely exploded as myths. Among works attributed to him were Byfleet House, Surrey (*c.*1617), Coleshill House, Berkshire (from 1647), Houghton House, Houghton Conquest, Bedfordshire (after 1615), and Stoke Park, Stoke Bruern, Northamptonshire (*c.*1630), but the documentation is inadequate. He did, however, design a very handsome Classical choir-screen for Winchester

Cathedral, Hampshire (1637–8), during the episcopacy (1632–45) of Walter Curl (1575–1647), who made it his business to decorate and improve the interior: the screen was dismantled in 1820, but the central part is now in the Museum of Archaeology, University of Cambridge. He was an important influence on his pupil and nephew, John *Webb, through whom Jones's collection of drawings were passed down to subsequent generations. Many of the drawings in Burlington's collection were published in *Kent's *The Designs of Inigo Jones* (1727), *Ware's *Designs of Inigo Jones and Others* (1731), and *Vardy's *Designs of Mr. Inigo Jones and Mr. William Kent* (1744). All Jones's known drawings were listed in John Harris's and Gordon Higgott's *Inigo Jones: Complete Architectural Drawings* (1989). *See* Paesschen.

Colvin (1995); Harris (1990); Harris and Higgott (1989); Harris, Orgel, and Strong (1973); Harris and Tait (1979); Millar (1987); Placzek (1982); Summerson (1966, 1993)

Jones, Owen (1809–74). London-born architect and designer of Welsh descent, he is celebrated as an expert on colour and ornament. He travelled extensively, afterwards producing *Views on the Nile* (1843) and (with Jules Goury) *Plans, Elevations, Sections, and Details of the Alhambra* (1836–45), which established him as an authority on *Moorish architecture and colour in architecture. He was in demand as a designer of tiles, and published *Designs for Mosaics and Tessellated Pavements* (1842) and *Encaustic Tiles* (1843). As well as designing two Moresque houses at 8 and 24 Kensington Palace Gardens, London (1845–7), he was appointed (1850) joint architect of the Great Exhibition in Hyde Park, and was responsible for the colour-scheme of red, blue, and yellow in *Paxton's Crystal Palace (1851). The success of this led to his employment as director of decorations for the new Crystal Palace at Sydenham (opened 1854). With *Semper, Digby *Wyatt, and Joseph *Bonomi jun., Jones was involved in the creation of 'Courts' illustrating various historical architectural styles as part of a permanent exhibition there. The Egyptian Court (1854), designed with Bonomi, was spectacular, polychrome, and scholarly. Jones was very influential in his own lifetime, especially in the evolution of *polychromatic ornament: he decorated the interior of *Wild's Christ Church, Streatham (1841), and the apse of All Saints' Ennismore Gardens (1850). He taught at the Department of Science and Art in the South Kensington Museum, London, from 1852. His *Grammar of Ornament* (1856), based on his theories and lectures, illustrated all the known historical styles of ornament in colour, became a source-book of international importance, and showed the potential of non-European, particularly Islamic, schemes of decoration.

Curl (1994); Physick and Darby (1973); Jervis (1984); Jones (1843, 1854, 1863, 1868); Jones and Bonomi (1854); Jones and Goury (1836–45); Placzek (1982); Sheppard (1973)

Jones, William (d. 1757). Minor British *Georgian architect remembered for one outstanding building, the Rotunda in Ranelagh Gardens, Chelsea, London (1742, demolished 1805). It was a large circular structure with a very pretty, light galleried interior, really a glorified concert-hall and place for drinking tea, and its design showed rare originality for the period. He published designs for doors, gateways, and other architectural elements in 1739. Much of his built work has also been demolished, although Alresford House, Hampshire (1749–51), survives.

Colvin (1995)

Jourdain, Frantz (1847–1935). Antwerp-born architect and writer. He was influential as the designer of the *Art Nouveau *La Samaritaine* Department Store in Paris (1907), extended by him in 1914 and 1926–8. He saw Art Nouveau as the C19 equivalent of C18 French *Rococo, and argued for gracious ornament to bring elegance to buildings. His fulminations against a slavish adherence to *Beaux-Arts *Classicism before 1914 were influential at the time, and were associated with the search for a renewal of French culture. His son, **Francis** (1876–1958), was an important interior designer of the *Modern Movement, exhibiting at the Paris exhibitions of 1925 and 1937.

Borsi and Godoli (1978); Clausen (1987); Jervis (1984); Jourdain (1893, 1895, 1902, 1914); Rey (1923)

jowl. Part of a *post in *timber-framed construction at the top or bottom, wider than the rest of the post on one face, to house *tie-beams, *wall-plates, etc. Tops of *crown-posts are often *jowled*.

Joy, William (*fl.* 1329–47). English mason. He was appointed Master-Mason at Wells Cathedral, Somerset, in 1329, where he appears to have been responsible for the substantial building-works at the eastern arm of the church, including the refashioning of the *First Pointed *choir, the building of the *presbytery and new *vaults, the *retrochoir, *pulpitum, and the celebrated strainer-arches of the *crossing-tower. He also carried out works at the gate-houses and wards of the Close at Wells in the 1340s, and may have designed the works at the *Collegiate Church at Ottery St Mary, Devon (1337–45). Joy's work has affinity with aspects of St Augustine's Abbey, Bristol (now the Cathedral), and indeed he probably came from that area.

Harvey (1987)

Juan de Álava (d. 1537). *See* Álava, Juan de.

Juan de Colonia (d. *c.*1511). *See* Colonia Family.

jube, jubé. 1. *Pulpitum, or *screen at the west end of the *choir in a French church. **2.** *Rood-loft or *gallery in the same position, often forming part of the screen. One of the most celebrated surviving jubés is in the church of St-Étienne-du-Mont, Paris (*c.*1545), with its twin spiral stairs winding round the *piers.

Jugendstil. Literally 'youth-style', the German version of *Art Nouveau, it was named after the journal *Die Jugend* (1896–1914) which publicized the style. It tended to be more angular and less curvaceous than its French or Belgian counterparts, and was associated with the various *Sezession movements, notably in Vienna (where it was called *Sezessionstil*), Munich, and Dresden. It had a considerable influence on Scandinavia. Its chief architectural protagonists were *Endell, *Hoffmann, *Kotěra, *Olbrich, and O. *Wagner.

Wiener Sezession (1972)

Jussow, Heinrich Christoph (1754–1825). German Neoclassical architect. He trained under S.-L. du *Ry from whom he acquired a *Palladianism derived from England, but he had a taste for a simpler, more severe style that developed during his time with C. de *Wailly in Paris (1784). He is known for his completion of du Ry's work at Schloss Wilhelmshöhe, Kassel (1791–8), including the massive central block and the creation of the *Picturesque garden complete with water-works and *fabriques in various exotic styles. Also at Kassel he designed Schloss Löwenburg (1793–8—an early example of the *Gothic Revival in Germany, much influenced by English precedents and Picturesquely composed) and many other buildings, including the charming *mausoleum of Kurfürstin (Electress) Wilhelmine Karoline von Hessen, Luther Cemetery, Kassel (1820).

Biehn (1965); Mosser and Teyssot (1991); Paetow (1929); Vogel (1958–9); Watkin and Mellinghoff (1987)

Juvarra, Filippo (1678–1736). A pupil of Carlo *Fontana, he was arguably the most gifted architect of his time in Italy, and carried on a late-*Baroque tradition evolved by *Bernini. His architecture is characterized by its pellucid forms, sustained invention, and perfectly balanced massing, while his command of decorative devices was extensive and inventive.

He was appointed Architect to Duke Vittorio Amedeo II of Savoy (1675–1730) in 1714 (the Duke having assumed the title of King of Sicily and Piedmont in 1713), and proceeded to realize the monarch's ambition to elevate Turin into a Royal capital by designing and building a vast range of churches, lodges, palaces, and villas, as well as planning large new areas of the expanding city. His masterpiece is the Church and Monastery of Superga, Turin (1716–31), with its temple-portico, tall, elegant *cupola, and delightful twin *campanili, but the church of San Filippo Neri (1717 and 1730–6—a variation on *Alberti's Sant'Andrea, Mantua) and the emphatic façade added to *Castellamonte's Church of Santa Cristina (1715) are also demonstrative of his mastery of the Baroque style.

Juvarra designed the Castello at Venaria Reale (1714–26), with its spectacular chapel (1716–21), the Palazzo Birago di Borgaro (1716), the Palazzo Madama (1718–21), and the Castello Reale, Rivoli (1718–21), among others. His greatest palace for the King was the Palazzina di Stupinigi, near Turin (1729–33), with an elliptical nucleus and four radiating wings: it is the grandest hunting-lodge in Europe, with its remarkably rich *salone* decorated in the richest possible fashion. Juvarra also designed the garden-front of the La Granja Palace at San Ildefonso, near Segovia in Spain, and was working on the Royal Palace, Madrid, when he died. This last owed much to Bernini's third design for the Louvre in Paris, and was completed by Giovanni Battista *Sacchetti.

Boscarino (1973); Carboneri (1979); Gritella (1992); Hager (1970); Millon (1984); Placzek (1982); Pommer (1967); Rovere, Viale, and Brinckmann (1973); Viale (1966); Wittkower (1982)

Kahn, Albert (1869–1942). German-born American architect. He founded (1902) the most prolific architectural practice of its time in the USA with his brothers **Julius** and **Moritz**. Their Packard Motor Car Company Plant, Detroit, Mich. (1903–10) was an early example of an overt *reinforced-concrete structure. From 1905 the firm pioneered systems of standardization and modularization for factory design. The Ford River Rouge Plant, Dearborn, Mich. (1917–39) was a significant new type, a single-storey building for the assembly-line production technique evolved by Henry Ford (1836–1947). It had a steel frame, a plan devised to accommodate the assembly-line, top-lighting, curtain-walling, was made of standard prefabricated components, and was erected with remarkable speed. The Kahns continued to develop their designs for mass-produced goods: the Chrysler Half-Ton Truck Plant, Warren, Mich. (1938), was the logical conclusion of their methods. Their Clements Library, University of Michigan at Ann Arbor (1922), however, was in the Neoclassical style, and their non-industrial work was often not undistinguished: it included the Hill Auditorium (1913), the Engineering Building (1903), and Angell Hall (1922), all at Ann Arbor. A pragmatist, he had no time for *International *Modernism, which he found unintelligent, doubting if it was architecture at all.

Ferry (1987); Hildebrand (1974); Kahn, A. (1948); Roth (1980)

Kahn, Ely Jacques (1884–1972). American architect. Trained in Paris, he designed several *Art Deco *skyscrapers in New York in the 1920s and 1930s. Among his best-known works were the Insurance Center Building (1926–7), the Bergdorf Goodman Store (1927), the Film Center Building (1929), and the Squibb Building (1929). He designed the Mile High Center Building, Denver, Colo. (1955—with I. M. *Pei & Associates), and published widely, notably *Designs in Art and Industry* (1935), *A Building Goes Up* (1969), and various papers on tall buildings in New York.

Emanuel (1994); Kahn, E. J. (1935, 1969); van Vynckt (1993)

Kahn, Louis Isadore (1901–74). Born in Estonia, he settled in the USA in 1905, only becoming an internationally renowned architect in the 1950s, starting with the Yale Art Gallery, New Haven (1951–3). Then in 1957–64 came the influential Alfred Newton Richards Medical Research Building, University of Pennsylvania, Philadelphia, where the laboratories were clearly separated from the services stacked in slim towers, giving the whole composition a powerful monumentality. Kahn's insistence that there should be a distinction between served and serving volumes was taken a stage further with the Salk Institute Laboratories, La Jolla, Calif. (1959–65), where the ducts were placed horizontally in the structure spanning the laboratory, while the towers housed study-areas. For the Performing Arts Theater, Fort Wayne, Ind. (1965–74), Kahn used segmental brick arches springing from concrete blocks, a traditional image that signified his return to an architecture that was more humane and expressive than much that the *Modern Movement produced. Highly controlled geometries and meticulous detailing gave the Phillips Exeter Academy Library, New Hampshire (1967–72), a sense of order and dignity that marked Kahn's later work. His use of traditional brick detailing in his Indian Institute of Management Studies, Ahmadabad (1962–74), drew on Roman and other precedents to produce a work of rare quality. Other buildings by Kahn include the Erdman Dormitory Block, Bryn Mawr College, Pa. (1960–5), the Kimbell Art Museum, Fort Worth, Tex. (1967–72), and the Mellon Center for British Art and Studies, Yale University (1969–77). At the end of his life he built the National Assembly of Bangladesh, Dacca (1962–83), an emotive work that drew on many historical and traditional allusions, but for which he had problems in getting paid, with the result that his office ran into severe financial difficulties. His work marked a significant move away from *International *Modernism towards new directions in architecture.

Giurgola and Mehta (1975); Kahn, L. I. (1969, 1973, 1975, 1977); Klotz (1988); Placzek (1982); Ronner (1987); Scully (1962); Tafuri (1980); Tyng (1984); Wurman (1986)

Kallikrates. *See* Callicrates.

Kampen. *See* Campen.

Kampmann, Hack (1856–1920). Danish architect. He was a protagonist of the *National Romantic movement that drew on traditional and *vernacular forms as well as on themes from the *Rundbogenstil. He designed the Regional Archives, Viborg (1889), and the Custom House (1897), Theatre (1900—with touches of *Jugendstil), and State Library (1902), all in Aarhus. Influenced by the strong Danish tradition of *Neoclassicism, he was responsible for the New Carlsberg Glyptotek, Copenhagen (1901–6—with a stepped pyramidal roof over the centrepiece), and, with Anton Frederiksen (1884–1967), Holger *Jacobsen, and Aage *Rafn, designed the Copenhagen Police Headquarters (1919–24), one of the finest C20 Neoclassical essays in Scandinavia. His son, **Christian Peter Georg Kampmann** (1890–1955), designed the distinguished State School, Viborg (1918–26), combining Neoclassicism with aspects of *Modernism. He was also responsible for the Railway Station, Teheran, Iran (*c.*1935).

Paavilainen (1982); Weilbach (1995)

Kamsetzer, Jan Chrystian (1753–95). Important Neoclassical architect. He worked in the Poland of King Stanisław Poniatowski (1764–95), designing a number of stylish interiors at the Royal Palace, Warsaw (1777–82), and Mielżyńskich Palace, Pawłowice (1789–92), and collaborated with *Merlini on the exquisite Łazienki Palace, Warsaw (1784–93). Kamsetzer designed the austere Roman *Doric Guard-House, Poznań (1787), the Tyszkiewicz Palace, Warsaw (1785–92), and the robust and severe Church of St Dorothy, Petrykozy (1791–5).

Lorentz and Rottermund (1984)

Kant, Immanuel (1724–1804). German philosopher. His *Observations on the Feeling of the Beautiful and Sublime* (1764) and *Critique of Judgement* (1790) laid the foundations of much aesthetic theory, especially in relation to the *Beautiful and the *Sublime discussed earlier by Edmund *Burke in 1756.

Chilvers, Osborne, and Farr (1988); Osborne (1970)

Karfík, Vladimír (1901–85). Czechoslovak Modernist architect. He worked for *Holabird & Root and F. L. *Wright in the USA (1926–9), became influenced by Le *Corbusier, and later became a member of *CIAM. Head of the Architecture Department of the Bat'a Company from 1930, he designed new settlements on the *Garden City principle at Zlín, Partizánske, and Otrokovice, but with the Modernist aesthetic well to the fore. Other designs for Bat'a included a hotel (1932) and 17-storey office-building in Zlín (1937–8—with a *reinforced-concrete frame influenced by his work in Chicago), department-stores in Brno (1930) and elsewhere, and housing at Belcamp, Md., and East Tilbury, Thurrock, Essex (1932–8). He designed the first prefabricated residential buildings in post-war Bratislava.

Leśnikowski (1996); van Vynckt (1993)

Kay, Joseph (1775–1847). English architect. A pupil of S. P. *Cockerell, he later travelled on the Continent (for part of the time with Robert *Smirke), and in 1807 married the eldest daughter of *Porden, for whom he acted as assistant during the building of the *Gothic Revival Eaton Hall, Cheshire (1804–12—demolished). He designed the handsome range of houses on the east side of Mecklenburgh Square, London (1810–21), the Post Office, Waterloo Place, Edinburgh (1818–19), and Nelson Street and the Market, Greenwich, London (1829). His masterpiece is the elegant Pelham Crescent with the Church of St Mary-in-the-Castle in the centre, in Hastings, Sussex (1824–8). The church is top-lit and has an *Ionic *prostyle *portico, while beneath the terrace in front of the whole composition is an ingenious structure intended for shops and services. His eldest son, **William Porden Kay** (1809–97) emigrated to Australia in 1842 where he was Director of Public Works.

Colvin (1995)

Kazakov, Matvei Feodorovich (1733–1812). Russian Neoclassical architect, who was influential in giving a Classical character to late-C18 and early C19 Moscow. He studied with D. V. Ukhtomski, later assisting *Bazhenov on the enormous Kremlin Palace project (1767–74) and (probably) the Pashkov Palace, Moscow (1784–6—a boldly articulated Classical design) before setting up on his own in Moscow, creating palaces, hospitals, official buildings, and churches in a pure Classical style. His Senate Building, Kremlin, Moscow (1771–85), was designed with a *Doric *rotunda containing an internal *Corinthian Order. Kazakov travelled in France and Italy, and developed a taste for the works of *Palladio, as is evident in his Golitsyn Hospital (1796–1801), Demidov House (1789–91), and Batashev House (1798–1802). Other works include the Churches of St Philip the Metropolitan (1777–88—a rotunda), Sts Cosmas and Damian (1780s), and the Ascension (1780s), the 'Old' University (1786—later remodelled), and the impressive Hall of the Noblemen's Assembly (Hall of Columns—1784–6).

Kazakov collaborated with *Quarengi and others on the Sheremetev Palace, Ostankino (1791–8), one of the grandest houses of the time, with an opulent theatre and various pavilions in the grounds, including 'Italian' and even 'Egyptian' *fabriques. As a Goth he produced curious effects, as in the Petrovsky Palace, near Moscow (1775–82).

Cruickshank (1996); Hamilton (1983); Middleton and Watkin (1987)

keel. Common *First and *Second Pointed moulding on *vault-ribs and elsewhere, resembling the keel of a ship, in section consisting of two *ogees or convex curves meeting at an arris, and sometimes at a *fillet. Some authorities hold that a *keel-moulding* consists of two curves meeting at an arris rather than a fillet.

keel-arch. *Ogee arch.

Keeling, Enoch Bassett (1837–86). English *High Victorian *Rogue *Gothic Revival architect. He built several churches in London with violent *polychrome brick interiors, but none survives intact. His most extraordinary creation was the eclectic, eccentric, and outrageous Strand Music Hall, London (1864—demolished).

Architectural History, 16 (1973), 60–9; 42 (1999), 307–15

Keene, Henry (1726–76). English architect. He was Surveyor to the Dean and Chapter of Westminster from 1746 and Surveyor to the Fabric of Westminster Abbey from 1752. He may have refined *Jacobsen's designs for the west front of Trinity College, Dublin. One of the first exponents of C18 *Gothic Revival, as early as 1749 Keene assisted Sanderson *Miller to prepare drawings for Hagley, Worcestershire, and in *c.*1750 he fitted out the chapel at Hartlebury Castle, Worcestershire, in the *Gothick style. He designed the exquisite octagonal Hartwell Church, Buckinghamshire (1753–5), and Sir Roger Newdigate, Bt. (1719–1806), employed him on the remodelling of Arbury Hall, Warwickshire, from 1761, where some of the details were copied from Westminster Abbey. He was also responsible for the handsome Classical Guildhall, High Wycombe, Buckinghamshire (1757), and the Provost's Lodgings, Worcester College, Oxford (1773–6).

Brown (1985); Colvin (1995); *DNB* (1917); McCarthy (1987)

Keene's cement. Gypsum (sulphate of lime or *plaster of Paris) steeped in a solution of alum (double sulphate of aluminium and potassium) then subjected to intense heat, ground to a powder, and sifted. Invented around 1840, and also called *Martin's* or *Parian cement*, it was exceptionally hard when dry, took a high polish, and could also be coloured. Easily cleaned, it was often used for skirtings, *dados, mouldings, and even floor-surfaces. It was combined with marble for parts of the interior of *Butterfield's Church of All Saints, Margaret Street, London (1848–59).

Architects' Journal, 191/25 (20 June 1990), 36–55; Papworth (1852)

keep. Inner and strongest portion (*donjon) of a medieval *castle or citadel, also the residence of the lord.

Kelderman van Mansdale *or* **Keldermans.** Important family of C15 and C16 architects from Mechelen (Malines), Belgium. The most distinguished members were **Anthonis I**, the Elder (1450–1512) and **Rombout II** (*c.*1460–1531). Anthonis designed the Town Hall in Middelburg, The Netherlands (1507–12), and worked on the *choir of St Lawrence's Church, Alkmaar (1497–1512), while Rombout worked with *Waghemakere on the Town Hall at Ghent (Gent), Belgium (1517–33). Rombout designed the *Flamboyant *Gothic Hôtel de Savoie in Mechelen (1515–17) to which Guyot de Beauregard (d. 1551) applied the first *Renaissance façade in Belgium (1517–26). **Matthieu I** (1425/50–*c*.1503) worked on Antwerp Cathedral north *transept (1487–98).

Papworth (1852); Placzek (1982); Sturgis *et al.* (1901–2)

Kellum, John (1809–71). American architect best known for his iron buildings in New York. These included the cast-iron ferry-houses for Fulton Ferry and South Ferry (1864—demolished), and the boldly modelled A. T. Stewart (later Wanamaker's) Department Store, Broadway (1859–62—demolished). He designed Stewart's Model Town, or *Garden City, New York (from 1870).

Architectural Record, 120/3 (1956), 273–9; Francis (1980); Gayle and Gillon (1974); Placzek (1982)

Kemp, George Meikle (1795–1844). Scots self-taught *Gothic Revival architect. He worked for William *Burn from 1826, and in 1834 prepared drawings for the restoration of St Mungo's Cathedral, Glasgow, that formed the basis for J. Gillespie *Graham's scheme published in *Plans and Elevations of the Proposed Restorations and Additions to the Cathedral of Glasgow* (1836), though Graham failed to acknowledge Kemp at all. In the event, *Blore got the job. In 1838 Kemp won the second competition to design the monument to Sir Walter Scott (1771–1832), Princes Street, Edinburgh, with proposals derived from his studies of late-*Gothic churches on the Continent and in Scotland, and built 1840–6. It is one of the finest and earliest Gothic Revival canopied monuments, of which George Gilbert *Scott's Albert Memorial, London (1863–72), is the most famous example. Kemp was responsible for Maybole West Church, Ayrshire (1836–40), and the south wing of Woodhouselee, Midlothian (1843—demolished). The success of the Scott monument augured well for a career in architecture, but Kemp was drowned in 1844 while the building was under construction.

Bonnar (1892); Colston (1881); Colvin (1995); Gifford, McWilliam, and Walker (1984)

Kendall, Henry Edward (1776–1875). English architect. A pupil of Thomas *Leverton and (probably) John *Nash, he had a successful and varied practice. His Sessions-House and House of Correction, Spilsby, Lincolnshire (1824–6), is a handsome essay in the *Greek Revival, but he was equally at home with *Tudor Gothic, as at the Carr's Hospital, Sleaford, Lincolnshire (1830–46), and his winning (but unrealized) designs for Kensal Green Cemetery, London (1832). His son, **Henry Edward Kendall** (1805–85), was also a successful architect, among whose works were Shuckburgh Hall, Warwickshire (1844), the *Tudor Gothic 'Pope's Villa', Crossdeep, Twickenham, Middlesex (*c*.1845), the round-arched church of St John, Harrow Road, Kensal Green (1844—described by *Pevsner as 'atrocious'), and the splendid *Egyptian Revival *mausoleum of the 2nd Earl of Kilmorey (1787–1880) and his mistress, at Gordon House, Isleworth, Middlesex, originally built in Brompton Cemetery, London, in 1854, then in 1862 moved to Woburn Park, Chertsey, and finally brought to Isleworth in 1870.

Colvin (1995); Curl (1993); Pevsner, *Buildings of England, Lincolnshire* (1989), and *London 3: North West* (1991)

Kent, William (*c*.1685–1748). English painter, designer, landscape-architect, and architect. He was taken up by the nobility early in his career, and travelled to Rome (from 1709), where he made the acquaintance of many English grandees, including Thomas Coke, the future (1744) Earl of Leicester (d. 1759), and Lord *Burlington, whose protégé he became. Kent edited the *Designs of Inigo Jones with some Additional Designs* (1727), the 'additions' being by Burlington and himself, and drawn by *Flitcroft. Kent did not practise as an architect until the 1730s, at a time when the second *Palladian Revival was in full swing, but he was not stylistically restricted, for some of his schemes of interior decorations (and his furniture-designs) are sumptuous, looking back towards the *Baroque he had admired in Italy; 22 Arlington Street (1741) and 44 Berkeley Square (1742–4—with a noble staircase), both in London, contained some of his most successful interiors. Burlington got his man into the Office of Works in 1726, and in 1735 Kent became Master-Mason and Deputy Surveyor. His best-known works are the Treasury Buildings (1733–7) and the Horse Guards Building (1748–59—completed by *Vardy), both in Whitehall, London, but he also designed several *fabriques at Stowe, Buckinghamshire (including the Temple of Venus (before 1732), the Temple of Ancient Virtue (*c*.1734), the celebrated Temple of British Worthies (*c*.1735), Congreve's Monument (1736), and other buildings). Of considerable significance in the history of

Palladianism was Holkham Hall, Norfolk (1734–65), for which M. *Brettingham was the executive architect. Holkham is the most splendid Palladian house in England (Burlington had a hand in its design): its lavish marble apsidal entrance-hall (an amalgam of a Roman *basilica and a Vitruvian *Egyptian Hall), with a coffered ceiling and a magnificent stair leading to the *piano-nobile level, is one of the grandest rooms of the period. The exterior of the house is an excellent example of *concatenation, of which Kent was a master (e.g. Horse Guards Building, London).

Kent was an important figure in garden-history, for he was in the vanguard of the revolution against the formal gardens of the C17, and combined Palladian architecture with the contrived 'naturalness' of the park. He created landscapes that were comparable to the pictures of Claude or Poussin (as at Rousham, Oxfordshire (1738–41)), and so must be regarded as a pioneer of the *Picturesque. He also designed in the *Gothick style, notably the choir-screen, Gloucester Cathedral (1741—destroyed), and the pulpit at York *Minster (1741—burned, 1829), published by John *Vardy (1744), which may have been the source of some of the Gothick elements in St John's Church, Shobdon, Herefordshire (1746–56).

Kent's mastery of the Baroque style may best be seen in his funerary monuments, e.g. the huge memorial to John Churchill, 1st Duke of Marlborough (1650–1722), in Blenheim Palace Chapel, Oxfordshire, carved by John Michael Rysbrack (1694–1770), of 1730.

Colvin (1995); Cruickshank (1985); Curl (1993*b*); Gunnis (1968); Hunt (1987); McCarthy (1987); Placzek (1982); Summerson (1993); Wilson (1984)

Kentish rag. Very hard compact grey-white limestone used in polygonal *rubble rough- or close-pitched walling, often on *Gothic Revival London churches, where it was usually a facing to common brick walls. Its irregular forms create a network of mortar-joints.

Kentish tracery. *See* tracery.

Keppie, John (1863–1945). Glasgow architect, he joined John *Honeyman in 1889, and, with C. R. *Mackintosh, became a partner when Honeyman retired in 1900. Keppie worked on the remodelling of the *Glasgow Herald* Building, Mitchell Street (1893–5), and remained with Keppie, Henderson, & Partners until 1937.

Gomme and Walker (1987); Gray (1985); Williamson, Riches, and Higgs (1990)

key. Rough surface of brick, stone, etc., the interstices of which, being entered by plaster or *stucco, cause a sound adherence of one material to the other.

Key, Lieven de (*c.*1560–1627). Born in Ghent (Gent), Belgium, he settled in Haarlem, The Netherlands, in 1590, where he became Town Mason and Architect. With Hendrick de *Keyser he was the most prominent architect working in the *Renaissance style in that part of Europe. He designed the façade of the Town Hall in Leiden (1594–7), the scrolled *strap-work gables, downward tapering *pilasters, and *obelisks of which show a pronounced influence from the pattern-books of Vredeman de *Vries. He also designed the spectacular stepped-gabled Meat Hall, Haarlem (1601–5), with an exterior of brick with stone *dressings, the whole much decorated with *scrolls, *festoons, and *cartouches derived from de Vries, used with skill and originality. He built the exotic tower for the Nieuwe Kerk of St Anna, Haarlem (1613).

Cruickshank (1996); Rosenberg, Slive, and Ter Kuile (1966); Vermeulen (1941); van Vynckt (1993)

key-block. *Keystone or *sagitta*. (*See* arch).

key-brick. Tapered brick or *voussoir (*see* arch), not to be confused with a *keyed* brick, i.e. one with a stretcher-surface indented to act as a key for plaster or *stucco.

Brunskill (1990)

key-console. *Console-shaped *keystone (properly an *ancon) sometimes also functioning as a base for a statue, etc.

key-course. More than one *keystone in an arch of great depth, or the stones in the crown of a barrel-*vault.

key pattern. *Greek key, *labyrinthine *fret, or *meander.

Keyser, Hendrick de (1565–1621). One of two important early C17 architects working in The Netherlands, the other being Lieven de *Key. De Keyser was appointed Municipal Mason and Sculptor to Amsterdam in 1594, where he built the Zuiderkerk (1606–14) and the Westerkerk (1620–31), both models for Protestant churches in The Netherlands and Northern Germany, partly through their publication in *Architectura Moderna* (1631) by Salomon de Bray. Both have handsome *steeples that may have had some influence, disseminated through the publication, on *Wren's designs for the London City churches. At the Westerkerk, built on a Greek-cross plan, his style reached maturity, moving away from Dutch *Mannerism towards the *Classicism of van *Campen. His most important secular work was the handsome Town Hall in Delft (1618), and he invented a type of gable for Amsterdam houses (e.g. on the Herengracht) that was less busy and more Classical than earlier examples. His son-in-law and pupil was Nicholas *Stone, with whom de Keyser's son, **Willem** (1603–78), worked when living in London.

Landale-Drummond (1934); Rosenberg, Slive, and Ter Kuile (1966); van Vynckt (1993)

keystone. Wedge-shaped *key-block at the crown of an arch to consolidate a structure.

Kiesler, Frederick John (1890–1965). Vienna-born American visionary architect. In the 1920s he worked for a while with *Loos and joined De *Stijl, later producing designs in which endless curves and continuous wall- and ceiling-planes contrasted with the grid, rectangle, and flat wall generally favoured at that time. His Endless House (from 1923, with revisions as late as the 1960s) encapsulated his ideas of improving the human condition by means of an architecture derived from organic forms. Believing that forms are the 'visible trading-posts' of visible as well as invisible forces, and that reality consists of the two forms inter-acting in a way he dubbed *Correalism, he argued that humans react continuously with their environment, and that space and time are continuous, endless, and capable of expanding architectural possibilities. He published *Inside the Endless House: Art, People, and Architecture* in 1966. Described by *Huxtable in 1960 as the 'greatest non-building architect' of his time, his Shrine of the Book, Hebrew University, Jerusalem (1959–65), is perhaps his most impressive realized work, although his stage-designs for the theatre from the 1920s to the 1940s were of innovative importance.

Architectural Record, 86 (Sept. 1939), 60–75; Conrads and Sperlich (1962); Emanuel (1994); Huxtable (*New York Times*, 27 Mar. 1960, 2, 13); Kiesler (1964, 1966)

Kikutake, Kiyonori (1928–). Japanese architect, a leading light in *Metabolism, committed to adaptability, as expressed in his visionary designs for cities. His Sky House, Tokyo (1958–9—a single volume elevated on *piers with scope for hanging future rooms when needed below it), made his reputation, while in the 1960s his Tower Shaped Community (1958), with a main spine-like element for services to which cylinders containing the living-apartments could be fixed, was publicized in *Metabolism: Proposals for a New Urbanism* (1960), a document which also proposed Marine City, an extension of Tokyo into the sea. Arguing that elements most likely to change should be designed for ease of replacement, he disposed the services around the open living-space of the Sky-House, and attached the bathroom-units to the external walls of the Pacific Hotel, Chigasaki (1966). At Aquapolis, Okinawa (1975), the concept of extending cities into the sea was partially realized. Other works include Miyakonoyo Civic Hall (1966—with a light, collapsible roof-structure), the Administration Building, Shrine of Izumo (1963), and the Tokoen Hotel, Yonago (1964). Like their *Archigram colleagues in Britain, the Metabolists proposed prefabricated pods and cells which could be fixed to frames or some kind of central structure, often of monumental character, the pods (as variables) being given insubstantial architectural treatment. In 1978 he published *Kiyonori Kikutake: Concepts and Planning*.

Boyd (1968); Curtis (1996); Emanuel (1994); Kikutake (1973); Kurokawa (1977, 1988, 1992); Placzek (1982)

Kinetic architecture. Architecture evolved in the belief that the static, permanent forms of traditional architecture were no longer suitable for use in times of major social and technological change. Kinetic architecture was supposed to be dynamic, adaptable, capable of being added to or reduced, and even disposable. *Archigram, *Futurism, *Metabolism, and the work of *Friedman and *Fuller have been suggested as examples of Kinetic architecture.

Zuk and Clark (1971)

king-pendant. Vertical timber in a *truss between the ridge and projecting below the lowest transverse member.

king-post. *See* truss.

kiosk. **1.** Oriental summer-palace or *pavilion for temporary resort. **2.** Small open or partly open free-standing structure, the roof (often tent-like) carried on posts or a light *colonnade, used as a garden-*pavilion, bandstand, or summer-house, often with an orientalizing character, in the *Moorish, *Hindoo, or other exotic style. **3.** Public telephone-box or a small stall for the sale of newspapers, etc.

Kitsch. Rubbish or trash. The term suggests work in any of the arts that is pretentious, shoddy, tawdry, inferior, and in bad taste, aping styles without understanding them, and vulgarizing them beyond redemption. It has been described as the cultural revenge of the lower classes, but it has also been seen as a part of *Camp taste that values the outrageously hideous or the worst excesses of populist commercial atrocities. The term embraces both abstraction and false appearance. Much *Post-Modernism in architecture has tendencies to Kitsch-like aspects, notably in the allusions to *Classicism or *Historicism made without any evidence of scholarship, rationality, or intellect, but some groups, including *Archizoom, have deliberately reflected Kitsch and vulgar culture in their work.

Brown (1976); Dorfles (1969); Giesz (1971); Saisselin (1985); Steinberg (1975); Sternberg (1971); Ward (1991)

Kleihues, Josef Paul (1933–). German architect. His early work was influenced by New *Brutalism and by *Structuralism, but in the 1960s *Neo-Rationalism began to change his architecture. His buildings include the Main Workshops of the Berlin Sanitation Service, Berlin-Tempelhof (1969–83), the Hospital in Berlin Neukölln (from 1973), and the Museum Complex at Solingen, near Düsseldorf (1981–5). With *Ungers, he is probably the chief protagonist of an architecture of severe clarity, pure geometry and reason working in Germany.

Emanuel (1994)

Klenze, Leo von (1784–1864). German architect. He created some of the finest C19 buildings in Bavaria, notably in Munich, which he helped to transform into a sophisticated and beautiful Court and Capital City. Trained in Berlin (1800–3—where he was influenced by the elder *Gilly and designs by the younger), he worked with *Percier and *Fontaine in Paris (where he also absorbed much of *Durand's approach), and then became Court Architect to Jérôme (1784–1860), Napoleon's brother, King of Westphalia from 1807 to 1813. For Jérôme he designed the Court Theatre, Wilhelmshöhe, Kassel (1812), and in 1816 was called to Munich at the behest of Crown Prince Ludwig of Bavaria, who was to reign as King Ludwig I (1825–48). Under Ludwig's aegis Klenze created many of Munich's noblest buildings, starting with the *Glyptothek* (Sculpture Gallery—1816–31), built to house *Antique sculptures, including parts of the Greek temple at Aegina, discovered by *Haller von Hallerstein and others in 1811. Although Haller had produced a ravishing Graeco-Egyptian design, and *Fischer a severe project with a *Pantheon-dome, Klenze's realized building is a synthesis of Greek, Roman, and Italian *Renaissance styles. Originally the vaulted interiors (destroyed in the 1939–45 war and unhappily not reinstated) had mural and ceiling decorations in the manner of *Raphael's *grotesques, and provided an explanatory *iconography for the collection.

Also in 1816 Klenze designed the Leuchtenberg Palace (the first scholarly *Italianate building in C19 Germany) on the wide, straight, new Ludwigstrasse running north from the *Residenz* (Royal Palace). Klenze designed several façades for the Ludwigstrasse, many of which had Florentine Renaissance allusions. Then in 1822 he designed the Neo-Renaissance *Pinakothek* (Picture Gallery), built 1826–36, to display the Royal Collection: the architecture drew on the Palazzo Cancellaria, Rome, and on the Belvedere *cortile* in the Vatican, but its clear, logical plan and top-lit galleries were influential, and the building was expressive of its purpose. When Ludwig ascended the Throne in 1825, Klenze was commissioned to add various buildings to the *Residenz*. These were the *Königsbau* (King's Building—1826–35), in which elements of the Palazzo Pitti and Palazzo Rucellai, both in Florence, were mixed; the *Allerheiligenhofkirche* (Court Church of All Saints—1826–37), an important essay in the *Rundbogenstil, with quotations from the Palatine Chapel, Palermo, San Marco, Venice, and Lombardic *Romanesque; and the remodelling of the north front, the *Festsaalbau* (Festive Assembly Room building—1832–42).

Klenze's greatest buildings are his public monuments, which testify to his deep feeling for the architecture of Greek Antiquity. Walhalla, near Regensburg (1830–42), is a *Greek Revival temple, based on the *Parthenon and set on a high stepped platform derived partly from the image of F. *Gilly's proposed monument to Frederick the Great (1797), and partly from an earlier scheme for the site by Haller von Hallerstein (1814–15). The rich *polychrome interior, illuminated from above, is not unlike C. R. *Cockerell's sensitive and scholarly drawings of the Temple of Apollo Epicurius at Bassae, while the exposed decorated roof-trusses recall *Hittorff's work at St-Vincent-de-Paul, Paris, which was contemporary. Then came the *Propyläen* (Propylaeum), Königsplatz, Munich (1846–60), with Graeco-Egyptian *pylon-towers flanking the Greek *Doric *porticoes; the *Ruhmeshalle* (Hall of Fame), Munich (1843–54), a Greek Doric *stoa-like *colonnade terminating at each end in projecting pedimented wings, essentially a shelter for portrait-busts of eminent Bavarians; and the *Befreiungshalle* (Liberation Hall), near Kelheim (1842–63), a drum surrounded by buttresses, with a Roman Doric colonnade around the upper part. These four monuments are among the noblest works of C19 architecture in all Europe.

When Prince Otto of Bavaria (1815–67), second son of King Ludwig I, was chosen as King of Greece in 1832, Klenze prepared an ambitious plan for Athens, including a vast new museum and elaborate proposals for the protection of ancient monuments, but only the Roman Catholic Cathedral of St Dionysus (1844–53), a Neo-Renaissance basilica, was built. Klenze was more fortunate in his dealings with the Russians, for whom he demonstrated his skills in the huge Neoclassical addition he designed for the Hermitage Museum, St Petersburg (1839–51), one of the noblest buildings of the European Classical Revival. He was a master of synthesis of styles, and was equally at home with most of them. As a Neoclassicist, however, he was in the first rank.

Hederer (1964); Honour (1979); Klenze (1830, 1833, 1843); Lieb and Hufnagel (1979); Nerdinger (1980); Watkin and Mellinghoff (1987)

Klerk, Michel de (1884–1923). Dutch architect and member of the *Amsterdam School, he is best known for his *Expressionist designs carried out in collaboration with Pieter Lodewijk *Kramer, notably the *Scheepvaarthuis* (Navigation House), Amsterdam (with van der Mey, 1911–16), and the De Dageraad Housing Estate, Amstellaan (1920–2). His Eigen Haard Housing Estate, Spaarndammerbuurt, Amsterdam West (1913–20), in which towers, turrets, different types of windows, and finely crafted brickwork suggested the richness of a medieval town, reflects the architect's aim to avoid barrack-like tenements for working-class Socialist housing.

Bock (1997); Fanelli (1968); Frank (1984); Millon and Nochlin (1978); Pehnt (1973); Placzek (1982); Sharp (1967)

Klint. *See* Jensen-Klint.

knap. To snap or break stones, so split flint is *knapped* and laid with the smooth dark surfaces exposed on the surface of the wall, set *flush with freestone patterns of *tracery, initials, etc., as in medieval *flushwork*.

knee. 1. Short *brace or bracket between a *post and a *tie-beam, post and rafter, or any stiffener in a similar position in a *timber frame. **2.** *Corbel or other projection supporting a beam. **3.** Bend of 90° such as that at the top of a Classical *architrave round a *doorway suggesting the ends of a *lintel, called *ear*, *elbow*, *lug*, etc. *See* crossette. **4.** *Label-stop, especially if the label or hood-mould is cranked at 90°. **5.** *Kneeler. **6.** Length of *stair-*balustrade handrail bent in a convex curve where a flight arrives at a landing: opposite of the concave *ramp*.

knee-brace. *See* knee **1**.

kneeler, knee-stone. 1. Large, approximately triangular stone at the foot of a *gable, cut to have a horizontal bed and a top conforming, wholly or in part, to the slope of the gable. This *foot-stone*, *gable-springer*, or *skew-table* provides a securely anchored stop for the *raked *cope. **2.** Similarly, a stone securely bedded with one side cut at an angle or *skew* forming the *springing of an arch or *vault. **3.** *Cop* in a *battlement. **4.** Square return of a *label over a late-*Gothic aperture.

Knight, Richard Payne (1750–1824). English landscape theorist, member of the Society of *Dilettanti, and connoisseur. He designed (with some initial help from T. F. *Pritchard) Downton Castle, Herefordshire (1772–8), a *Picturesque composition in the *Gothic style (though *Neoclassicism dominated the interiors) in which symmetry was avoided in the overall planning, but not in the individual rooms. It was the anti-symmetry of the plan that made it revolutionary, and it had a profound influence on English and Continental architects. Knight claimed that the house was designed to resemble buildings in landscapes by Claude Gellée (1600–82). His tastes and experiences led him to question 'Capability' *Brown's style of landscape-design in *The Landscape—A Didactic Poem* (1794), helping to create a climate in which the asymmetrical, serene, reposeful, and informal aspects of much architecture and landscape-design developed in C19. His *Analytical Enquiry into the Principles of Taste* (1805) contained important discussions on contemporary architectural ideas, notably the Picturesque. When Lord Elgin (1766–1841) had the sculptures from the Parthenon exhibited in London Knight made a fool of himself by dogmatically declaring they were Roman of the time of Hadrian, and led other members of the Dilettanti in the controversy about their artistic worth.

Ballantyne (1997); Chilvers, Osborne, and Farr (1988); Colvin and Harris (1970); Knight (1794, 1972); Pevsner (1968)

knob, knop. *Finial or *boss.

Knobelsdorff, Georg Wenzeslaus, Freiherr von (1699–1753). Prussian aristocrat, architect, and soldier. He was a friend of Crown Prince Frederick of Prussia (1712–86—later King Frederick II (the Great)), and built for him the circular *Tuscan temple of Apollo in the gardens of Amalthée at Neu-Ruppin, Brandenburg (1735). After a journey in Italy (1736–7), Knobelsdorff enlarged Schloss Rheinsberg, near Neu-Ruppin, introducing a pronounced French note with coupled columns on the water front derived from *Perrault's east front of the Louvre. When Frederick became King in 1740, Knobelsdorff was appointed *Oberintendant* (Director) of Buildings and Gardens. He added a new wing to Schloss Monbijou, Berlin (1740–2), and another at Schloss Charlottenburg, Berlin (1740–3), with a sumptuous *Rococo interior, and designed the new Opera House on the *Unter den Linden*, Berlin (1740–3). The last was the first example of a *Palladian Revival in Prussia, with a design closely derived from Colen *Campbell's Wanstead House, Essex, illustrated in *Vitruvius Britannicus* (1715 and 1725).

When the King moved his Court to Potsdam, Knobelsdorff remodelled the *Stadtschloss* there (1744–51), with Rococo interiors (destroyed). The enchanting Schloss Sanssouci—also known as the Weinberg-Schloss because it stands above a series of glazed terraces forming conservatories for growing vines—Potsdam (1745–7), survives, one of the most charming masterpieces of Rococo ever erected. A single-storey building with an elliptical Neoclassical *Marmorsaal* (Marble Hall) in the centre, it has paired *terms instead of *pilasters on the exterior. He also designed St Hedwig's Cathedral, Berlin, built by *Boumann and *Büring (1742–73), and renovated the Schloss at Dessau, Anhalt (1747–51).

Hempel (1965); Kadatz (1983); Streichhan (1932); van Vynckt (1993); Watkin and Mellinghoff (1987)

Knoblauch, Carl Heinrich Eduard (1801–65). German architect. A pupil of *Schinkel, he designed a number of houses in Berlin, and indeed, with *Hitzig and *Stüler, evolved a refined *Italianate style for mid-C19 domestic architecture in the Prussian capital. He also designed country-houses, some in the castellated style of Schinkel's Babelsberg. The Berlin Synagogue (1859–66—in a *Moorish-medieval style) was by him, but completed by his son, **Gustav** (1833–1916), and Stüler (destroyed). He edited the *Zeitschrift für Bauwesen* (Journal for Building) for many years.

Börsch-Supan (1977); Knoblauch and Hollen (1878)

Knöffel, Johann Christoph (1686–1752). German architect, much influenced by French *Classicism. A pupil of *Longuelune, he spent most of his professional life in Dresden, where he became *Oberlandbaumeister* (Senior State Architect—1734). Nearly all his fine and considerable work has been destroyed, but he completed *Chiaveri's exquisite *Hofkirche* (Court Church), Dresden, after 1748 (restored after severe damage in 1945), and finished Longuelune's *Blockhaus* (Log House—so called because a timber customs-house once stood on the site), or Guard House, Dresden (1749).

Hempel (1965); Hentschel and May (1973); Watkin and Mellinghoff (1987)

knop. *Finial or swelling termination to anything.

knot. 1. *Boss or *finial. **2.** Ornament resembling a bunch of leaves or flowers. **3.** Architectural treatment resembling tied ropes, as in a *knotted shaft. **4.** *Strapwork.

Knott, Ralph (1879–1929). London-born English architect. He assisted Aston *Webb and in 1908 won the competition to design London's County Hall, a massive building in which *Baroque, *Neoclassicism, and even *Mannerism play their parts. Shortly afterwards Knott took Ernest Stone

Collins (1874–1942) into partnership, and together they produced several well-mannered buildings, including 21 Upper Grosvenor Street, London (1913). Knott collaborated with Arnold *Thornely on the designs for the *Greek Revival Parliament Buildings, Stormont, Northern Ireland, and he and Collins designed the Speaker's House, Stormont (1926) in the years preceding his early death.

Gray (1985)

knotted shaft. *Romanesque column-shaft carved to look as though tied in a knot. Good C12 or C13 examples survive in Würzburg Cathedral, Germany, and similar knotted shafts can be found at the east end of the *Broletto*, Como, Italy (*c*.1215).

Cruickshank (1996); Curl (1991)

knotwork. *Interlacing carved cord or ribbon ornament, occurring at many times and in many styles. Obvious examples are the intricate patterns in *Anglo-Saxon and *Celtic design, but it also occurs in *arabesque, *Art Nouveau, *Moorish architecture, and *strapwork, to name but a few examples.

Lewis and Darley (1986)

Knowles, James Thomas, sen. (1806–84). English architect. He designed a great number of competently composed houses, including the handsome *Italianate *palazzo at 15 Kensington Palace Gardens, London (1854). Together with his son, **(Sir) James Thomas Knowles** (1831–1908), he was responsible for the Grosvenor Hotel, Victoria Station, London (1860–2). Knowles jun. laid out the Cedars Estate, Clapham, London (1860), the Park Town Estate, Battersea, London (1863–6), and other developments. He also edited the *Contemporary Review* and founded *The Nineteenth Century*.

DNB (1920); Dixon and Muthesius (1985); Metcalf (1978, 1980); Sheppard (1973)

knull. 1. Type of *gadroon. **2.** Variety of *bead-and-reel with the components apparently squashed, so that they are very thin and close together.

Koch, Alexander (1848–1911). Swiss architect and architectural writer. He studied and worked under *Semper, contributing to the first projected designs for the exteriors to the Hofburg, for the Burgtheater, and for the museums on the *Ringstrasse*, Vienna. After further studies in Berlin (1870–1), he set up in practice with Heinrich Ernst in Zurich, where they designed numerous buildings, including a children's hospital, several mansions on the Alpenquai, and other works. He settled in London in 1885, attending the South Kensington Schools, and in 1889 began his outstanding career as a publisher, beginning with *Academy Architecture and Architectural Review* (1889–1931), which is an invaluable record of the period. He was closely involved in promoting new architecture and design from the 1880s, and was responsible for organizing the famous competition of 1900 for a *Haus eines Kunstfreundes* (House for an Art Lover) which he announced in the journal *Zeitschrift für Innendekoration* (Journal for Interior Decoration). In 1901 Baillie *Scott was given a prize, but *Mackintosh was awarded a special award for his radical scheme. He also published *British Competitions in Architecture* from 1905, which continued for five years, and is another useful record. Koch submitted an entry to the 1905 Palace of Peace competition in The Hague. One of his sons, also **Alexander**, continued the publishing interests in Germany.

Gray (1985); Koch (1889–1931, 1901, 1902, 1907, 1908); Saur (from 1991)

Koch, Gaetano (1849–1910). Italian architect, he designed mostly in a refined *Cinquecento style, and built mostly in Rome. His works include the Palazzo Voghera, Via Nazionale (1870s), the splendid Piazza dell'Esedra (1880), with its quadrant façades, the Palazzo Boncompagni, Largo Goldoni (1886–90), the tiny Museo Barracco (from 1902), and his masterpiece, the Palazzo Margherita, Via Veneto (1886). He helped to complete *Sacconi's monument to King Victor Emmanuel II (1885–1911).

Hitchcock (1977); Meeks (1966); Portoghesi (1968)

Koenig, Pierre (1925–). American architect. Known for his assured use of the steel frame and industrialized building techniques, he made his name with the Case Study House 21, Hollywood, Calif. (1958). More recently the Koenig House, Los Angeles (1984–5), and the Schwartz House, Santa Monica, Calif. (1991), have confirmed him as a sophisticated designer.

Emanuel (1994)

Konstantinidis, Aris (1913–93). Greek architect. He sought to harness tradition, technology, and simplicity in his work, employing clear geometries. His works include the Ciné-News Cinema, Athens (1940), various housing developments in Greece, Hotel Xenia, Mykonos (1960), a holiday house, Anavyssos, near Athens (1962), and the Museum, Komotini (1967).

Emanuel (1994)

Koolhaas, Rem (1944–). Dutch architect, he formed OMA (Office for Metropolitan Architecture) in 1975 with Madelon Vriesendorp and Elia and Zoe Zenghelis, producing a number of visionary and theoretical projects, including 'Delirious New York' (1972–6), later published as a book (1978), in which overlapping themes and ideas produced a collage-like effect. Koolhaas and his colleagues have been successful publicists for *Deconstructivism and winners of competitions, notably for the National Dance Theatre, The Hague (1981), and for several sites in Berlin. His high-rise apartment-block with communal facilities and observation-tower, Rotterdam, The Netherlands (1982), demonstrated his fondness for distorting, engulfing, and twisting form, for it is essentially a row of towers distorted by a slab. Among later works, the Kunsthal, Rotterdam (1987–92), a vast exhibition-building bisected by an entrance-ramp, and featuring deliberately rough concrete on some façades, may be mentioned. The gigantic Grand Palais and master-plan for Euralille (a shopping-centre, conference, concert and exhibition-halls, and many other facilities at Lille, France (1989–96)), on a major station of the Eurostar rail-link between London, Brussels, and Paris, is one of his largest projects.

Emanuel (1994); Jodidio (1995*a*); Johnson and Wigley (1988); Lampugnani (1988); Office for Metropolitan Architecture, Koolhaus and Mau (1995)

Korb, Hermann (1656–1735). German architect and carpenter to the Duke of Brunswick-Wolfenbüttel, he supervised the building of a huge, largely timber *Schloss* (Palace or Castle), designed by Johann Balthasar Lauterbach (1660–94—demolished), with certain architectural motifs that anticipated the work of *Hildebrandt at the Belvedere, Vienna. He also appears to have designed the elliptical library at Wolfenbüttel (1706–10), but his only remaining work is the *Dreifaltigkeitskirche* (Church of the Holy Trinity), Wolfenbüttel (1705), with its tiers of galleries opening to an octagonal space, an arrangement not unlike *Bähr's *Frauenkirche* (Church of Our Lady), Dresden, but less impressive.

Gerkens (1974); Hempel (1965)

Korn, Arthur (1891–1978). German-born architect. He worked with *Mendelsohn in Berlin (from 1919) before setting up in partnership with Sigfried Weitzmann in 1922, with whom he built the Villa Goldstein, Grünewald, Berlin (1922), the Kopp and Joseph Shops, Berlin (1922–30), the Ullstein Building, Berlin (1930), the Fromm Factory, Köpenick, Berlin (1928), and the Intourist Shop, Unter den Linden, Berlin (1929), among other works. The Fromm Factory had a steel frame, painted red, exposed, and emphasized, and it was this building, more than any other, that was the spark for *Mies van der Rohe's development of the theme. In 1929 he published *Glas im Bau und als Gebrauchsgegenstand* (Glass in Building and as an Item of Practical Use), which was influential, but his most important years were arguably spent in England. He chaired the *MARS Group, which produced a plan for London that encapsulated his Hegelian and Marxist ideas, and worked with *Fry and *Yorke (1938–41). As a teacher, first at the Oxford School of Architecture (1941–5) and then at the Architectural Association (1945–65), he had a powerful influence on determining the course of architecture and town-planning until well into the 1980s.

Emanuel (1994); personal knowledge

Korsmo, Arne (1900–86). Norwegian architect, one of the first to build in the *International Modern style, his Dammann (1930–2) and Hansen (1936) Houses in Oslo were influenced by the work of *Mendelsohn and *Dudok. He had a strong influence on architecture in Norway after 1945. His later works included the von der Fehr Summer House, Larkollen (1947), the Girls' Home, Tåsen, Oslo (1951), Terrace Houses, Planetveien, Oslo (1952–5—with C. Norberg-Schulz), and the Britannia Hotel, Trondheim (1962—with Terje Moe).

Emanuel (1980)

Kotěra, Jan (1871–1923). Born in Brno, he studied with Otto *Wagner in Vienna. From around 1898 until 1905 he was profoundly influenced by the *Sezession, actively designing with *Jugendstil themes well to the fore, while also taking a lively interest in the folk art of his native land and drawing upon ideas and themes connected with the English *Arts-

and-Crafts movement. His early work was published in *Meine und meiner Schüler Arbeiten: 1898–1901* (Works of Mine and My Students—1902), dominant flavours of which were Arts-and-Crafts and Jugendstil. Typical of his designs at that time were the Peterka House, Wenceslas Square, Prague (1899–1900), and the National House, Prostějov (1905–7). A journey to the USA (1903) brought him into contact with the work of Frank Lloyd *Wright, and visits to The Netherlands and England led him to introduce an architecture of brick to Bohemia, as well as Wrightian ideas of space as in the Hradec Králové Town Museum (1906–12). He was an influential teacher, numbering *Fuchs, *Gočár, and *Krejcar among his pupils.

Kotěra (1902); Mádl (1922); Russell (1979); van Vynckt (1993)

Kramer, Piet(er) Lodewijk (1881–1961). Dutch architect of the *Amsterdam School. He worked with van der *Mey and de *Klerk on the *Scheepvaarthuis* (Navigation House), Amsterdam (1911–16), and collaborated with de Klerk at the De Dageraad housing complex, Amsterdam South (1925–6), in which the brick walls were modelled in flowing curved forms regarded as important examples of *Expressionism. He designed the De Bijenkorf Store, The Hague (1924–6), again with a carefully modelled façade. Most of his works were bridges for the Amsterdam Department of Public Works (1917–28).

Cruickshank (1996); Retera (1928); Vriend (1949–50)

Krebs, Konrad (1491–1540). German architect, he designed the *Johann-Friedrichs-Bau* (Johann Friedrich Building—1533–6) at Schloss Hartenfels, Torgau, one of the earliest and finest *Renaissance ensembles in Saxony, with a central open stair-tower.

Cruickshank (1996)

Kreis, Wilhelm (1873–1953). German architect. Influenced by a growing taste in Wilhelmian Germany for national monuments of powerful, elemental, aggressive character (e.g. the work of *Schmitz), he rose to the occasion with the many towers commemorating Bismarck erected to his designs. He was responsible for the Provincial Museum of Prehistory, Halle (1911–16), complete with massive cyclopean masonry and corner-towers slightly resembling the Roman *Porta Nigra* at Trier. After the 1914–18 war some of his work leant towards *Expressionism, such as the exhibition-buildings and art-museum by the banks of the Rhine at Düsseldorf (1925–6), including the circular *Rheinhalle* (Rhine Hall) with its lozenge-patterned brick-work, *buttresses, openings topped by inverted Vs, and a *stalactite vault inside recalling *Poelzig's work. In the 1930s Kreis turned to a monumental stripped Neoclassical style for buildings proposed for *Speer's new plan for Berlin, and he looked to *Boullée and *Gilly for precedents for his gigantic smoking cones and other memorials (*Totenburgen*, or Fortresses of the Dead) designed (but never realized—see Kreis's *Soldatengräber und Gedenkstätten* (War Graves and Commemorative Sites—1944)) to commemorate the German 'sacrifice and victory' of the 1939–45 war.

Ellenius (1971); Kreis (1927); Krier (1985); Lane (1985); Larsson (1983); Mayer and Rehder (1953); Meissner (1925); Stephan (1944)

Krejcar, Jaromír (1895–1949). Czechoslovakian Modernist architect. With Karel *Teige, he was one of the protagonists of the *Devětsil group, and edited *Život II* (1922), which promoted *Constructivism and Purism. His works include the Olympic Department Store, Prague (1924–6—one of the first *reinforced-concrete framed structures in Czechoslovakia), the Machnáč Sanatorium, Trenčianské Teplice (1929–32—a paradigm of *International *Modernism), and the Czechoslovak Pavilion, Paris International Exhibition (1937—destroyed).

Krejcar (1928); Leśnikowski (1996); Teige (1933)

Kremlin. Russian fortress or citadel within a town, especially that in Moscow, established 1156, more strongly fortified with stone walls from 1367 and brick walls and towers (1489–95), and beautified with many fine buildings from C15.

Krier, Léon (1946–). Luxembourg-born architect and theorist, he has championed *Rational architecture, influenced, perhaps, by *Durand, and has seen early C19 *Neoclassicism as a suitable means of recovering the civilized aspects of the European City before industrialization. His seductive graphics and powerful polemical writings have aroused new interest in the qualities of street, square, and urban district, and his work might be said to be a series of meditations on urban themes in a world where so much has been devalued. His view of the city as a document of intelligence, memory, and pleasure is the antithesis of the concept of the disposable, adaptable, plug-in city of *Archigram, *Metabolism, and other advocates, and he has been critical of *Post-Modernism and stylistic pluralism, condemning both as unserious, unintellectual *Kitsch. He has seen de-zoning of activities in cities to be essential and is fundamentally opposed to the views of Le *Corbusier, *CIAM, and the *Athens Charter that seem to be firmly embedded virtually everywhere, despite efforts by Jane *Jacobs and many others to excise them. He was involved in the creation of the master-plan for the Duchy of Cornwall development at Poundbury, Dorset, England (1988–91). Among his most ravishing visions is his version of Pliny's villa (1982).

Emanuel (1994); Klotz (1988); Krier (1978, 1981); Ruffinière du Prey (1994); van Vynckt (1993); Watkin (1986)

Krier, Rob(ert) (1938–). Luxembourg-born Austrian architect, the brother of Léon *Krier, with whom he has shared an interest in giving the contemporary city qualities enjoyed prior to industrialization. Influenced by Camillo *Sitte's ideas, he has been concerned to develop types of urban spaces derived from, but not copies of, historical exemplars. Many of his housing projects have been built, notably at Ritterstrasse, Berlin-Kreuzberg (1978–80—reminiscent of *Terragni's Italian *Rationalism), Rauchstrasse, Berlin-Tiergarten (1981–5), and Schinkelplatz, Berlin-Kreuzberg (1986–8). His Dickes House, Bridel, Luxembourg (1974–6), is a large cube from which volumes have been removed, and has parallels with the works of the *Ticino School. He has been dubbed a devotee of *Neo-Rationalism.

Emanuel (1994); Hertz and Klein (1990); Krier (1979); van Vynckt (1993)

Kroll, Lucien (1927–). Belgian architect. He set up his own practice in Brussels in 1957. He advocated 'creative participation' in building, by which the users would contribute to the design, in the belief that *Functionalism no longer functions and that *Modernism is essentially totalitarian barbarism. His work has been called 'controlled anarchy'. His most important building is the Medical Faculty Housing at the Université Catholique, Woluvé-St-Lambert, Brussels (1970–7), perhaps an example of *Adhocism, and certainly of improvisation.

Emanuel (1994); Jencks (1972, 1977); Lampugnani (1988); Mikellides (1980); Tafuri and Dal Co (1986)

Krubsacius, Friedrich August (1718–89). German architect and theorist. He studied under *Longuelune and *Bodt, and in 1764 he was appointed Professor at the Academy of Arts, and in 1776 *Oberhofbaumeister* (Chief Court Architect) in Dresden. In his book, *Betrachtungen über den wahren Geschmack der Alten in der Baukunst* (Considerations on the Taste of the Ancients in Architecture—1747), he proposed (drawing on French sources) that the proportions of the human body should be the basis of architectural invention, and in another book of 1759 that the *Baroque style should be replaced by something more pure. In spite of this his own designs in and around Dresden were largely Baroque in flavour, but nearly all his work has been destroyed or damaged, although the *Landhaus* (Chamber of Deputies), Dresden (1770–6), has been partly restored and contains a fine *Rococo *staircase. He also carried out works at the *Schlösser* of Neschwitz and Otterwisch in the 1760s, little of which has survived. He published the interesting studies of *Pliny the Younger's villas in *Warscheinlicher Entwurf von des jüngern Plinius Landhause, Laurens gennant* (Probable Designs of Pliny the Younger's Villa at Laurentum—1760) and a further (1763) volume on the Tuscan villa.

Lüttichau (1983); Ruffinière du Prey (1994); Watkin and Mellinghoff (1987)

Krumpper, Hans (*c*.1570–1635). Architect of the somewhat ungainly *Renaissance façade of *Sustris's *Hofkirche* (Court Church) of St Michael, Munich (1583–97).

Cruickshank (1996)

Kufic. Characters employed in stonework and tile inscriptions in *Islamic architecture. Kufic inscriptions were sometimes used decoratively (and meaninglessly) in *Hispano-Moresque architecture in much the same way as Egyptian *hieroglyphs were used before they could be read and understood by C18 and C19 designers. They were widely employed in C19 revivalist architecture of the *Moorish or orientalizing type.

Lewis and Darley (1986)

Kurokawa, Kisho Noriaki (1934–). Japanese architect and prominent force in *Metabolism, his buildings and publications have been influential. He was among the first Japanese architects to question the basis of the *International *Modern Movement, and promoted the Metabolists' argument that life-sciences had more relevance to architecture than the *Machine Aesthetic. The Nagakin Capsule Tower, Tokyo (1972), demonstrated his concept of sophisticated buildings incorporating the latest technology yet capable of being changed. He is active in fusing Eastern and Western cultural currents, and his search for an inter-cultural architecture has led him to an *eclecticism ranging from the Neoclassical extension to the Japanese Embassy, Berlin (1988), to the gigantic Pacific Tower, La Défense, Paris (1991).

Drew (1972); Emanuel (1994); Kurokawa (1977, 1988, 1990, 1992); Lampugnani (1988)

Kympton, Hugh (*fl.* 1343–88). English master-mason. He was involved in building at Windsor, Berkshire, Porchester, Hampshire, and Southampton, Hampshire, Castles. At Porchester he took his instructions from *Yeveley.

Harvey (1987)

label. **1.** *Hood-moulding extending horizontally across the top of a late-*Gothic *Perpendicular or *Tudor aperture, returning downwards vertically on each side and terminating in *label-stops, often elaborately carved. While the term is mostly applied to rectangular drip-mouldings (often forming *spandrels between a low four-centred or Tudor arch and the label), it can also be applied to certain curved hood-mouldings. **2.** Rectangular tablet, framed or plain, with wedge-shaped tab-projections on each side, commonly found in Neoclassical architecture, but having its origins in Roman architecture, where it was used for inscriptions.

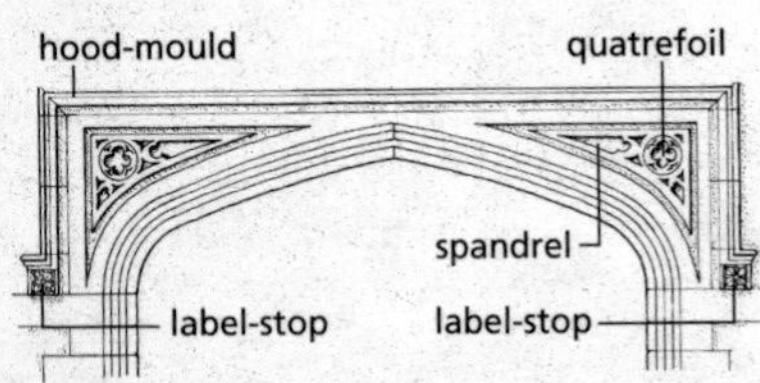

1. Typical late-Gothic arch with spandrels, hood-mould and label-stops.

2. Classical label, often associated with an inscription.

label.

label-stop. **1.** *Knee, or termination of a drip-stone, *hood-mould, or *label by cranking the moulding horizontally for a short length. **2.** Decorative feature as a termination of a label, hood-mould, or *string-course. If carved to resemble a human head, it is called a *head-stop*.

Labrouste, Pierre-François-Henri (1801–75). French architect, he studied under A.-L.-T. *Vaudoyer and L.-H. *Lebas, and then at the French Academy in Rome, where he mixed with the future leaders of the profession in France. His theoretical reconstruction (though based on accurate site-surveys) of the *Doric temples at *Paestum (1829) was described later by *Viollet-le-Duc as a 'revolution on several folio sheets of paper' because it proposed a re-ordering of the accepted historical sequence of the temples and suggested that the architectural *type was adapted to new environmental, social, and political conditions in a colonial setting, thereby upsetting the accepted opinions of French academics. Indeed, this work (which included the application of colour) is considered to be a watershed in French architecture, heralding a new order to challenge the supremacy of *Classicism. When he returned to Paris he opened an *atelier* (architectural studio and office) in 1830 which promoted rationalist ideas. His reputation rests on his Bibliothèque Ste-Geneviève, Paris (1838–50), a superbly clear design in which an elegant iron structure seems to have been slotted into the cage of masonry: it was one of the first monumental (rather than utilitarian) public buildings to have an exposed iron frame. The masonry exterior is a powerful *Cinquecento essay employing a range of semicircular-headed windows to illuminate the great library space, but it has mnemonic aspects too, for there are allusions to *Alberti's Tempio Malatestiano, Rimini, *Sansovino's Biblioteca Marciano, Venice, and *Wren's Trinity College Library, Cambridge. The Bibliothèque placed him in the highest echelons of French Government architects, and between 1854 and 1875 he created the iron-and-glass interior of the Reading-Room at the Bibliothèque Nationale, Rue Richelieu, Paris, and built the stack-rooms, again employing iron. He published his work on Paestum in 1877, and designed several other buildings, including tombs in Montmartre and Montparnasse Cemeteries, Paris.

His brother, **François-Marie-Théodore** (1799–1885), was also an architect, again trained under Vaudoyer and Lebas. He was architect-in-chief to the hospitals of Paris in succession to *Gau from 1845.

Drexler (1977); Hitchcock (1977); Labrouste, H. (1877); Labrouste, L. (1885, 1902); Middleton and Watkin (1987); Saddy (1977); van Zanten (1987)

labyrinth. **1.** *Key-pattern, *maze, or *meander. **2.** Planting in a garden arranged as hedges between labyrinthine paths leading to a centre. **3.** Place laid out for ritual pilgrimage, e.g. the *inlaid maze in the *nave-floor of Chartres Cathedral, France, or the turf labyrinth at Wing, Rutland, England: the centre of such a labyrinth was the *Jerusalem or *Paradise, the Holy City of God to which the pilgrim aspired.

labyrinthine fret. *Key-pattern, *Greek key, or *meander, resembling a *labyrinth pattern.

laced valley. Valley formed of tiles or slates without a valley-gutter where two sloping roofs meet at an angle.

laced windows. Vertical series of window-apertures in a line with *dressings, such as bright red brick rubbers contrasting with the rest of the wall, common in early C18 England.

laceria. In *Islamic architecture ordered regular patterns formed by straight lines crossing and intersecting in various ways.

lacertine. *Celtic *interlacing scrolling ornament, with dragon-like head biting its tail.

lacing-course. Course of brick or tile, or several such courses collectively, built, often at regular intervals, in rough or *rubble walls as a bond- or bonding-course, and to assist the creation of level horizontals. In walls of *knapped or ordinary unknapped flint pebbles lacing-courses are essential for stability, and are usually combined with *piers of brick, tile, or stone to secure panels of facings bound to the core of a wall.

Brunskill (1990)

lacuna (*pl.* **lacunae**). Literally a gap, applied to a Classical coffer in a ceiling, *cornice-*soffit, or any flat, level horizontal underside, a coffer under a *cupola being a *caisson. Lacunae are often elaborately ornamented with *egg-and-dart, *bead-and-reel, etc., and *laquear* is used to express the effect of mouldings separating the margins of panels in coffering.

lacunar. **1.** *Coffer in a flat *soffit, ceiling, etc. **2.** Ceiling with coffers. **3.** Soffit, as under a *cornice, with coffers or *lacunae. **4.** Beams enclosing a coffer.

lacunarium (*pl.* **lacunaria**). System of *lacunae or *coffers. The plural, *lacunaria*, is given to the coffered ceiling of an *ambulatory or *peridrome* between the *peristyle and the *cell-walls of an *Antique temple, as well as to the *soffit of the main *cornice, presumably because they had many lacunae.

Lady-chapel. *Chapel in a larger church, expressly for venerating the Virgin Mary, often situated to the east of the *chancel or *choir, as in Westminster Abbey (1503–*c.*1512) and Hereford Cathedral (*c.*1220–40), but in parish or other churches often to the east of one or other chancel-*aisle. At Long Melford, Suffolk, the Lady Chapel (1496) is virtually a separate building to the east of the church proper. Even grander is the chapel at Ely Cathedral, Cambridgeshire (*c.*1321–53), a huge rectangular *Second Pointed building to the north of the choir, mostly free-standing, but entered via the north *transept.

Lafever, Minard (1798–1854). American architect. His New York practice produced a wide range of buildings in a variety of styles, but his chief importance lies in his dissemination of *Greek and *Gothic Revivals through his many publications, including *The Young Builder's General Instructor* (1829), *The Modern Builder's Guide* (1833), *The Beauties of Modern Architecture* (1835), *The Modern Practice of Staircase and Handrail Construction* (1838), and *The Architectural Instructor* (1856). Lafever himself drew heavily on *Stuart and *Revett's *Antiquities of Athens* and the various publications of Peter *Nicholson, but his own Grecian work was inventive, going far beyond archaeological exactness, and there are interesting parallels with some of Alexander 'Greek' *Thomson's details and those of Lafever (which came first). His major New York buildings were Gothic Revival churches, including the handsome Holy Trinity (1844–7) and the Church of the Saviour (First Unitarian Church, 1842–4), both in Brooklyn Heights.

He also designed in the *Egyptian Revival (Shields *obelisk, Greenwood Cemetery, Brooklyn, 1845, and the Whalers' First Presbyterian Church, Sag Harbour, Long Island, 1843–4), *Italianate, and *Renaissance styles.

Carrott (1978); Hamlin (1964); Lafever (1829, 1838, 1856, 1968, 1969); Landy (1970); Stamp and McKinstry (1994)

Laing, David (1774–1856). London-born architect. He was articled to *Soane before publishing *Hints for Dwellings* (1800) that contained original designs for various types of house, and in 1810 became Surveyor to the Customs, designing the Custom House, Plymouth, Devon (1810), a refined Neoclassical building clearly derived from a study of French architecture. His vast London Custom House (1813–17), on the bank of the Thames, was also Neoclassical, but the collapse of the central portion in 1825 ruined him, and R. *Smirke was called in to reconstruct the building.

Architectural History, 6 (1963), 91–101; Colvin (1995)

Laloux, Victor-Alexandre-Frédéric (1850–1937). French architect. Early in his career he published a book on Greek architecture (1888), and with Paul Monceaux, another tome on Olympia (1889). Perhaps, as a result of these studies, his *Beaux-Arts *Classicism was dignified and serious, avoiding the *Baroque extravagances of C. *Garnier and his followers. He designed the Gare du Quai d'Orsay, Paris (1896–1900), and the Station at Tours (1895–8): both are scholarly, handsome, and competent works. Some of his most distinguished work was in Tours, his birthplace, including the Byzantino-*Romanesque Basilique St-Martin (1887–1924—his first major building, reminiscent of designs by *Abadie) and the Hôtel de Ville (1896–1904).

Laloux (1888); Lemaresquier (1938)

Lamb, Edward Buckton (1806–69). English *Rogue *Gothic Revivalist, his elephantine churches tend to have centralized plans and frenetically busy timber roofs: examples are St Margaret's, Leiston, Suffolk (1853), and St Mary Magdalene, Canning Road, Addiscombe, Croydon, Surrey (1868–70). His work attracted opprobrium, notably in *The Ecclesiologist*, and he seems to have been untouched by more conventional tastes of the time. He produced many drawings for J. C. *Loudon's publications and refashioned Hughenden Manor, Buckinghamshire (1863–6), the residence of Benjamin Disraeli (1804–81). He published books on Gothic ornament (1830); *Ancient Domestic Architecture* (1846); and many articles in *Architectural Magazine* (1834–8), as well as a memoir of Loudon (1843).

Curl (1995); Dixon and Muthesius (1985); Girouard (1979); *RIBA Journal*, ser. 3, 56/6 (1949), 251–9; Summerson (1970)

lambrequin. Horizontal ornamental *band, fringed, lobed, and notched on the underside, like a series of aprons and tassels, often found under *cornices.

Lewis and Darley (1986)

lamb's tongue. **1.** Regency glazing-bar with a *section of two long *ogees separated by a *fillet, very fine and deep compared with its width. **2.** Tapering tongue-like end to a *stair handrail rising in a concave curve and joining the handrail in a convex sweep.

lancet. *First Pointed *Gothic tall, narrow window-aperture with a pointed arched *head, either a single insert in a wall or one of several *lights of similar shape in a window.

Lancet style. *First Pointed *Gothic of the late C12 before the introduction of *tracery.

Lanchester, Henry Vaughan (1863–1953). English architect. He set up in practice in 1887, and in 1896 took James S. Stewart (1865–1904) and E. A. *Rickards into partnership. They won the competition to design the City Hall and Law Courts, Cathays Park, Cardiff (1898–1906), with *Beaux-Arts planning and exuberant *Baroque façades, and followed this success with the even more splendid Wesleyan Central Hall, Westminster (1905–11). In 1919 Thomas Geoffrey Lucas (1872–1947), who had built several houses at Letchworth *Garden City and Hampstead *Garden Suburb, joined the partnership, followed by Thomas A. Lodge (1879–1967) in 1923. As Lanchester, Lucas, and Lodge, the firm enjoyed great success, and when Lucas retired, it continued as Lanchester & Lodge, designing many university buildings, hospitals, and other major works.

Gray (1985)

Langhans, Carl Gotthard (1732–1808). German architect from Silesia (now in Poland), he became *Oberbaurat* (Chief Building Officer) in Breslau (now Wrocław), designing a number of Palladianesque buildings influenced by *Erdmannsdorff's work at

Schloss Wörlitz. These included a new wing for the Palais Hatzfeld, Breslau (1766–86); the Samotwór Palace (1776–81), with a *serliana as the frontispiece-porch; the noble Mielżyński Palace, Pawłowice (1779–87), with its *corps-de-logis linked to the handsome *service-wings by arcaded *quadrants; and several elliptical Protestant churches. In 1788 King Friedrich Wilhelm II of Prussia (1786–97) summoned Langhans to Berlin (with David *Gilly and Erdmannsdorff) in order to make the capital a major cultural centre. There, Langhans created one of the pioneering monuments of the *Greek Revival, the Brandenburg Gate (1789–94), inspired by Le *Roy's reconstruction of the Athenian *Propylaea in *Ruines des plus beaux monuments de la Grèce* (1758), and the first building based on the *Antique prototype. The gate was greatly admired by all who saw it, and influenced Thomas *Hope when he argued for a Greek Revival design for Downing College, Cambridge. It was also the model for Thomas *Harrison's propylaeum at Chester Castle (1811–13), and von *Klenze's *Propyläen, Königsplatz* (King's Square), Munich (1817, built 1846–60).

Langhans designed several theatres, including the State Theatre, Potsdam (1795), which had a severely Neoclassical façade, and the unadventurous Royal Theatre, *Gendarmenmarkt*, Berlin (1800–2—which burned down in 1817 and was replaced by *Schinkel's *Schauspielhaus* (play-house)). He designed the *Gothick top for the tower of the *Marienkirche* (Church of St Mary), Berlin (1787).

Bauch (1966); Hinrichs (1909); Lorentz and Rottermund (1984); Watkin and Mellinghoff (1987)

Langhans, Karl Ferdinand (1781–1869). Son of C. G. *Langhans, he studied in Berlin under his father and David *Gilly, and settled in Breslau (now Wrocław) in 1815. His own dwelling and other buildings there were clearly influenced by the austere *Neoclassicism of *Gentz and F. *Gilly. He published works on theatre design, and was among the first to examine the science of acoustics as an influence on the planning of auditoria, outlined in a book on the subject (1810). He designed several theatres, including Breslau (1838–41), Liegnitz (now Legnica, 1841–2), Stettin (now Szczecin, 1846–9), Dessau (1855–6), and Leipzig (1864–8). He was responsible for several buildings in Berlin, including the Palace of Prince Wilhelm, *Unter den Linden* (1834–6). Much of his work, however, no longer exists.

Börsch-Supan (1977); Langhans (1810); Rohe (1934); Schneider and Langhans (1845)

Langley, Batty (1696–1751). English landscape-gardener, architect, and prolific producer of architectural books. His works included *Practical Geometry* (1726), *The Builder's Chest Book* (1727 and 1739), *New Principles of Gardening* (1728), *The Landed Gentleman's Useful Companion* (1741), *A Sure Guide to Builders* (1729), *The Young Builder's Rudiments* (1730 and 1734), *The City and Country Builder's and Workman's Treasury of Designs* (1740 and further editions). His grandest book, with 500 or so plates (most looted from other sources), probably the largest English pattern-book, was *Ancient Masonry* (1736). His publications are full of sensible advice on how to set about drawing and constructing various elements. He is remembered today primarily for *Ancient Architecture Restored and Improved by a Great Variety of Grand and Usefull Designs, Entirely New in the Gothick Mode* (1741–2), reissued as *Gothic Architecture, Improved by Rules and Proportions in Many Grand Designs* (1747), an attempt to systematize *Gothic on the lines of five Classical *Orders. There was virtually nothing of real Gothic in the books, for Langley's sources were more an early *Georgian *Gothick invented by people like *Kent, so his work was ridiculed. However, 'Langley', 'Carpenter's', or 'Sham Gothick' had considerable success, and his designs were widely copied. Sanderson *Miller and Horace *Walpole were indebted to Langley for some of their Gothick, though they were reluctant to say so. A pioneer of what he described as the *Artinatural, or 'regular irregularities', he must be counted as one of the earliest to espouse the 'natural' landscape that was to be such a feature of C18, and he was also an advocate of the *Rococo, presumably as an antidote to *Palladianism. A veil should be drawn over his own architectural efforts, but his importance as an influence on *Georgian architecture cannot be overestimated.

Colvin (1995); Curl (1993*b*); Harris (1990); Langley (1724, 1726, 1728, 1729, 1729*a*, 1734, 1736, 1738, 1739, 1742, 1745, 1747, 1756, 1970, 1970*a*, 1971)

languet. Tongue-shaped upright ornament like a U reproduced in series on Classical enrichment, e.g. *frieze.

lantern. 1. Any structure rising above the roof of a building and having apertures in its sides by which the interior of the building is ventilated or illuminated, e.g. the octagonal lantern at Ely Cathedral (1322–*c*.1344). **2.** Any such structure whether lighting an interior or not, such as the upper part of cathedral- or church-towers, especially those treated in a light, almost transparent way, usually octagonal uppermost stages (e.g. St Botolph, Boston, Lincolnshire (*c*.1510–20), St Mary and All Saints, Fotheringhay, Northamptonshire (late C15), All Saints, York (late C15), and the *crossing-tower of St-Ouen, Rouen, France (C15)). **3.** By extension, the upper structure on top of a *cupola (e.g. Florence Cathedral (C15), San Pietro, Rome (C16), and St Paul's Cathedral, London (C17)).

lantern-cross. Medieval stone churchyard-cross with a top carved to resemble a lantern, in the sense of a structure surrounding and protecting an artificial light.

lantern-light. *Lantern **1.**

lantern-tower. Tall *crossing-tower with *lights or any tower with an elegant, usually octagonal, upper storey, as in St Botolph, Boston, Lincolnshire (*c*.1510–20).

Lanyon, Sir Charles (1812–89). English-born architect, engineer, and surveyor. He settled in Ireland, where he became County Surveyor of Antrim (1836–60). His Palm House, Botanic Gardens, Belfast (1839), built with Richard Turner (1798–1881) of Dublin, was an elegant early iron-and-glass structure, pre-dating Turner's collaborations with Decimus *Burton at Regent's Park and Kew Gardens, London. Lanyon established a successful practice, designing the powerful Crumlin Road Gaol (1843–50), the noble Classical Court House opposite the Gaol (1848–50), the Union Theological College near The Queen's University (1852–3), the Head Office of the Northern Bank (1851–2), and the *Tudor Gothic Queen's College (now The Queen's University) (1849), all in Belfast.

He also remodelled Sir Robert *Taylor's Exchange and Assembly Rooms as the Head Office of the Belfast Bank in an *Italianate *palazzo style derived from Barry (1845), and reworked Killyleagh Castle, Co. Down, in a robust Franco-Scottish style (1849–51). In 1854 he took William Henry *Lynn of Co. Down into partnership, and, as Lanyon & Lynn, designed many of Belfast's finest Victorian buildings including the Italian *Renaissance Custom House (1854–7) and the beautiful Lombardic Gothic Sinclair Seamen's Church, Corporation Square (1856–7). Lanyon's son **John** (d. 1900) joined the firm (it became Lanyon, Lynn, & Lanyon in 1860), and they produced the Italian Gothic warehouse of Richardson, Sons, & Owden (1867–9), the *polychrome Venetian Gothic Clarence Place Hall (1865–6), both in Belfast, and the charming *Hiberno-Romanesque St Patrick's Church, Jordanstown, Co. Antrim, complete with round tower (1865–8). The spectacular Gothic Revival Carlisle Memorial Church, Belfast (1872–5), was completed by Lanyon & Lanyon, Lynn having left the firm in 1872.

Brett (1967); Curl (1990); *DNB* (1917); Larmour (1987)

La Padula, Ernesto Bruno (1902–69). *See* Padula.

laquear. *See* lacuna. Also perhaps a net-like form of decoration used on ceilings, etc., maybe in *Antique *grottoes. Passages in Virgil suggest chain-like forms, but other Classical sources, although using the term, are vague.

lararium (*pl.* **lararia**). **1.** Small room or *niche in a Roman house used as a type of private chapel or *shrine where images of the *lares* and *penates* (household deities) were placed for devotional observances. Emperor Alexander Severus (222–35) furnished his lararia with an eclectic collection of the principal Roman deities to which he added Abraham, Achilles, Alexander the Great, Christ, Cicero, Orpheus, and Virgil. **2.** Place or a room set aside solely for the display of *Antique statuettes, as in Thomas *Hope's celebrated house in Duchess Street, London (1799–1819).

larmier. 1. Classical *corona or similar horizontal moulding acting as a drip, also called *lorimer*. **2.** Medieval moulding curved on top with a deep concave underside, called *ressaunt lorymer*, acting as a drip or based on a drip-stone.

Larsen, Henning (1925–). Danish architect. He established his practice in Copenhagen in 1956, and built the Primary School, Søllerød (1958) with each classroom a separate pavilion with its own courtyard. He developed an approach to architecture based on flexibility, to allow change and adaptation. Among his works are the Høje Tåstrup Grammar School, near Copenhagen (1978–82), the Genofte Library, Copenhagen (1979–84), the Danish

Embassy, Riyadh, Saudi Arabia (1982–6), the Faculty Building, Free University, Berlin (1982–8), the Conference Centre, Churchill College, Cambridge (1994), and a Congress Centre, Esbjerg (1982–8). He won the competition to design the Opera House, Compton Verney, near Kineton, Warwickshire (1989), an interesting proposal so far unrealized.

Emanuel (1994)

Lasdun, Sir Denys Louis (1914–). British, he became one of the leading architects in England after the 1939–45 war. He worked with Wells *Coates (1935–7), then joined *Tecton, remaining there until 1948, when he founded his own practice. Clearly influenced by *Lubetkin and Le *Corbusier, he designed a house at 32 Newton Road, Paddington, London (1937–8), which was indebted to Le Corbusier's Maison Cook of over a decade earlier. In 1952–5 he built *cluster-blocks of flats in Bethnal Green, the living-apartments joined to a central core for circulation and services. Then, in 1958, came the apartment-block at 26 St James's Place, one side of which overlooks Green Park: it is also Corbusian, but with smooth, fine materials, unlike the exposed concrete of the Bethnal Green blocks. The Royal College of Physicians (1960) also has a sensitive position, overlooking Regent's Park, London. In the 1960s Lasdun's firm designed several major projects, including the University of East Anglia, Norwich (1962–8); the Charles Wilson Building, University of Leicester (1963); the School of Oriental and African Studies, the Institute of Education, and Institute of Advanced Legal Studies, University of London, Bloomsbury (1965); the National Theatre, by Waterloo Bridge (1967–76); the IBM Central London Marketing Centre, South Bank (1978–84); and the City of London Real Property Company Offices, Fenchurch Street (1980–5).

Curtis (1995, 1996); Emanuel (1994); Lasdun (1976, 1984)

Lassurance, Pierre Cailleteau, *known as* (1650–1724). Assistant to J. *Hardouin-Mansart, he worked at Versailles (1684–1700), where he seems to have been behind the effective disposition of mirrors as part of the interior decoration. In Paris he designed several *hôtels, illustrated by *Blondel, with many features that influenced *Boffrand and de *Cotte. Among his essays of the *hôtel particulier type were the Hôtel des Marets, Rue de St-Marc (1704), Hôtel de Montbazon, Rue St-Honoré (1719), and Hôtel de Roquelaure, Rue St-Dominique (1722).

Blondel (1752–6); Hautecœur (1950); Kalnein (1995); Kalnein and Levey (1972); Kimball (1980)

Lassus, Jean-Baptiste-Antoine (1807–57). French architect. A pupil of *Lebas and *Labrouste, he was an early student of *Gothic. He worked on the restoration of Sainte-Chapelle, Paris (from 1838), especially its influential *polychrome decorations (hailed in 1844 by A. W. N. *Pugin as 'glorious'), with *Duban and *Viollet-le-Duc. From 1849 he was in sole charge, and designed the elegant *flèche. From 1844 he collaborated with Viollet on the huge programme of restoration at the Cathedral of Notre-Dame, Paris, where many significant French Gothic Revivalists acquired their skills. He was an active conservator, working in the Dioceses of Paris, Le Mans, and Chartres (where he restored the Cathedral *spires). A scholarly Ecclesiologist, he contributed numerous learned papers to various publications, including *The Ecclesiologist* (1856). Although his designs for the Lille Cathedral competition (1855) were placed third, they were the ones partially realized. He designed several other Gothic Revival churches, including Sacré-Cœur, Moulins (from 1849), St-Jean-Baptiste-de-Belleville, Paris (1854–9), and St-Pierre, Dijon (1853–8).

Germann (1972); Lassus (1842–67, 1858); Léon (1951); Middleton and Watkin (1987); Troche (1857)

Last Judgement. *See* Doom.

Late-Modern architecture. Architecture in which the images, ideas, and motifs of the *Modern Movement were taken to extremes, structure, technology, and services being grossly overstated at a time when Modernism was being questioned. The work of *Piano and *Rogers at the Pompidou Centre, Paris (1971–7), has been cited as an example, although it has also been seen as *High Tech.

Jencks (1980, 1990)

lath. 1. Narrow, thin strip of wood used as a base for a plaster finish. **2.** Slightly larger timber, more a *batten* or *firring-strip* secured to beams, rafters, studs, etc., as a fixing for tiles, slates, or other finish.

Latin cross. *See* cross.

Latrobe, Benjamin Henry Boneval (1764–1820). English-born Moravian architect of French descent, educated in England and

Saxony (where he absorbed many advanced ideas, partly through Freemasonry), who introduced an advanced, austere *Neo-classicism to the USA. He was a pupil of S. P. *Cockerell before setting up his own office in 1790 from which he designed Hammerwood Lodge, East Grinstead, Sussex (1792), an essay in Neoclassicism with an unfluted version of the 'primitive' *Paestum *Order of *Doric, much influenced by French architects such as *Ledoux. He also designed Ashdown House, Forest Row, Sussex (1793), a beautiful building having a projecting Greek *Ionic circular porch with *Coade-stone details. These are two of the most remarkable houses for their date in the British Isles, and show Latrobe to have been in the vanguard of Neoclassicism, far more adventurous than any of his better-known contemporaries in England.

He emigrated to America in 1796, where, through his Freemasonic connections, he met George Washington and acquired a wide circle of influential friends. He made his mark with the very advanced Richmond Penitentiary (1797), which incorporated many of *Jefferson's ideas, and then with the Bank of Pennsylvania, Philadelphia (1798), the first great monument of the *Greek Revival in the USA. In the following year he designed Sedgeley, a house for William Crammond on the banks of the River Schuylkill, the first *Gothic Revival domestic building in the USA (destroyed). In 1803 he was appointed Surveyor of Public Buildings by Jefferson, and worked on the Capitol in Washington, DC, creating some of the finest Neoclassical rooms in America, and inventing *American Classical *Orders such as the *corn-cob and tobacco *capitals. He also advised Jefferson on the design of the University of Virginia (1817–26), and should be given credit for what is one of the most beautiful architectural ensembles in the USA. His best complete work is the Roman Catholic Cathedral, Baltimore (1804–18), with segmental coffered *vaults, minimalist *Classicism, and shallow-domed ceilings as severe as any of their date. The Louisiana State Bank, New Orleans (1820), was his last building, but it was still faithful to the dignified polished Classicism he had introduced to his adopted country. His pupils included *Mills and *Strickland.

Brown (1970); Carter (1977, 1980); Colvin (1995); Hamlin (1955, 1964); Hitchcock (1977); Kennedy (1989); Norton (1977); Padover (1946); Whiffen and Koeper (1983)

latten. Pale yellow metal resembling *brass, actually an alloy of copper and tin, much used for medieval funerary monuments (the so-called 'brasses' in churches, which are *incised, coloured, and *inlaid in stone slabs).

lattice. **1.** A *came. **2.** System of small, light bars crossing each other at intervals, often made of *laths, or light slips of wood forming regular square- or *lozenge-shaped openings. Lattices formed of square-sectioned wood arranged in square, rectangular, and diagonal patterns were a common feature of C18 and C19 *Chinoiserie. **3.** Undivided part of a C18 theatre auditorium between the boxes and the pit.

lattice-girder. Metal *girder with webs uniting the flanges by means of a trellis of diagonal braces crossing each other, or with a web of a single series of braces arranged in a zig-zag pattern.

lattice-moulding. Reticulated or net-like arrangements of diagonal *fillets or other straight mouldings crossing each other diagonally and resembling a *lattice.

lattice-window. Any window, fixed or with an opening *sash, the *lights filled with *lozenge-shaped glass panes set in lead *cames.

Laudian rails. Altar- or communion-rails, often with *balusters, and usually of oak, dating from the time (1633–40) when William Laud (1573–1645) was Archbishop of Canterbury, and endeavoured to restore something of dignity to Anglican worship.

Laugier, Abbé Marc-Antoine (1713–69). French Jesuit, he became one of the earliest and most important theorists of *Neo-classicism. His *Essai sur l'Architecture* (1753) was profoundly influential, setting out a rational interpretation of *Classicism as a logical, straightforward expression of the need for shelter, derived from the *Primitive Hut of tree-trunks supporting a structure. He extolled the need for columns as opposed to those of the *engaged variety or *pilasters, and argued for a return to *Antique principles as an antidote to all the accretions from the *Renaissance period onwards that had hidden the essence of the origins of *columnar and *trabeated construction. The immediate influence of his views was on *Soufflot, but translations into English and German carried them throughout Europe. In his *Observations* *sur l'Architecture* (1765) he recognized the grace of *Gothic.

Braham (1980); Fichet (1979); Herrmann (1962); Laugier (1753, 1753*a*, 1765); Middleton and Watkin (1987); Placzek (1982); Rykwert (1980)

Laurana, Luciano (*c*.1420–79). Born in Dalmatia, he was a key figure in the transition from *Renaissance to the *High Renaissance of *Leonardo and *Bramante. In 1465 he provided a design for the Palazzo Ducale, Urbino, and built the elegant arcaded *cortile (1465–79). Many of the exquisite details (e.g. door-cases, chimney-pieces, etc.) in the palace were also by him.

Heydenreich and Lotz (1974); Placzek (1982); Rotondi (1950–1)

Lautner, John (1911–94). American architect, a pupil of Frank Lloyd *Wright (1933–9). He established his own practice in Los Angeles, designing some remarkably original private houses, including the Arango House, Acapulco, Mexico, of 1973 (where terraces exploit the views over the bay below), and the Sheats Goldstein House, Beverley Hills, Calif., of 1960–3 (which seems to grow out of the rocks and is covered with a massive folded concrete roof). Perhaps his best-known buildings are the Malin House, or 'Chemosphere', Torreyson Drive, Los Angeles (1960), with the entire structure carried on one *pier, and the Elrod House, Palm Springs (1968), with a concrete wheel-like roof of massive 'spokes' framing wedge-shaped windows. Esther *McCoy called him a 'lyrical technologist'.

Emanuel (1994); Escher (1994)

Lauweriks, J. L. Mathieu (1864–1932). Dutch theorist, he evolved a proportional system that he connected with his occult beliefs, and produced intricate designs of cubes, squares, and rectangles that influenced *Behrens, notably in his design for the crematorium at Hagen (1906–7), and later Le *Corbusier in his *Modulor system. The journal *Der Ring* (1909) published his designs.

Placzek (1982); Tummers (1968)

Laves, Georg Ludwig Friedrich (1788–1864). German architect, one of the most distinguished Neoclassicists of his generation. A pupil of *Jussow, he became Court Architect in Hanover in 1814 where he remodelled the Leineschloss (1817–35), and designed the Bibliothek-Pavillon, Herrenhausen (1818–19), Wangenheim Palais (1829–33), Waterloo Column (1825–32), Opera House (1845–52—his greatest work), and *Mausoleum at Herrenhausen (1842–6). He specialized in a Neoclassical style derived from the work of *Schinkel and *Persius and in a half-century he transformed Hanover into a fine Neoclassical capital-city to rival Berlin, but much of his work was destroyed in the 1939–45 war. He was also involved in iron-and-glass construction, and made several designs for 'crystal palaces', including a proposal (1850) for a prefabricated structure at the London Exhibition of 1851 made out of old railway-lines. He invented (1839) a type of *trussed beam that involved cutting a timber beam in two along its length, fixing each end together with straps, and placing blocks between the two parts so that the beam-truss ended up as convex on the top and bottom. Its advantage was that it was much stronger than it was before treatment, did not deflect much, and was extremely economical.

Architectural Review, 148 (Oct. 1970), 257; Dolgner (1971, 1993); Hoeljte (1964); Papworth (1852); Watkin and Mellinghoff (1987)

Layens, Matthieu de (*fl.* C15). Architect and Master-Mason of the *Flamboyant *Gothic Town Hall at Louvain (Leuven), Belgium (1448–63), one of the most perfect of late-Gothic secular buildings in Northern Europe. His work was particularly harmonious and controlled in its use of Gothic ornament and motifs, and resembles contemporary architecture at Bruges, Ghent, Brussels, and Oudenarde, but surpasses in its richness of detail. He also designed the *choir of St Waudru, Mons, Belgium (1450–1502), and other works.

Papworth (1852)

Layer, William (*fl.* 1419–d. 1444). English mason. He was involved in repairs to the *Lady Chapel at Ely Cathedral (1439–40), and he may have designed the fine *nave of St Mary's Church, Bury St Edmunds (1424–44), as well as the tower of Rougham Church, both in Suffolk.

Harvey (1987)

lazaretto. Originally a *lazar-house* where lepers were confined, but later any hospital for contagious diseases.

leaded lights. Any windows, fixed or opening, in which the panes or *quarrels (quarries) of glass are secured in lead *cames, often arranged in *lattice patterns, usually lozenges.

leaf. **1.** Part of a door, panel, or shutter that folds, i.e. is hung on hinges or pivoted. **2.** One of two skins of brick or block forming a cavity-wall. **3.** Ornament derived from the leaves of plants, such as the *acanthus, *bay, laurel, olive, *palm, or other plant. *See* water-leaf. **4.** Very thin finish, such as a veneer, or *gilding*.

leaf and dart moulding

lean-to. Structure with a monopitch roof sloping from a taller building or wall, e.g. an *aisle of a *basilica, leaving the *clearstorey rising above. *See* pent.

Lebas, Louis-Hippolyte (1782–1867). French architect trained by A.-L.-T. *Vaudoyer and *Percier and *Fontaine. He designed Notre-Dame-de-Lorette, Paris (1823–36), on a *basilican plan with a noble *portico of the *Corinthian Order and an interior entirely *Early Christian in style, multi-coloured. The *clearstorey is carried on an *Ionic *colonnade, the ceiling is *coffered, and the east end is *apsidal. In 1825 he won the competition to design a model prison on the site of La Roquette, Paris, in the form of a huge hexagon with six wings linked to the central chapel. Among his pupils were the *Labrouste brothers and Charles *Garnier.

Middleton and Watkin (1987)

Le Blond, Jean-Baptiste-Alexandre (1679–1719). *See* Blond.

Lebons, John (*fl.* 1506–29). English master-mason. With *Janyns and *Vertue he was involved in preparing estimates for the new *Lady Chapel at Westminster Abbey for King Henry VII (1485–1509). He was employed by Cardinal Wolsey (*c.*1475–1530) at Hampton Court from 1515, and by 1525 was resident master-mason at Cardinal (now Christ Church) College, Oxford. He also carried out works at Balliol College, Oxford, and Windsor Castle, Berkshire. There is evidence that he was a designer, as paper for 'platts' (i.e. plans) was accounted for his use in 1515.

Harvey (1987)

Le Breton, Gilles (d. 1553). *See* Breton.

Lechner, Ödön (1845–1914). Austro-Hungarian architect. He was a master of the exotic national version of *Jugendstil, with strong injections of Hungarian folk-art and certain *Gothic *Moorish *Rundbogenstil themes reminiscent of *Gaudí's work and *Modernisme generally in Barcelona. His most celebrated buildings are the Museum of Applied Arts (1891–6), Institute of Geology (1898–9), Post Office Savings Bank (1899–1901), and György Zala studio (1905), all in Budapest.

Bakonyi and Kubinszky (1981); Éri and Jobbágyi (1990); Kismarty-Lechner (1961)

Lecointe, Jean-François-Joseph (1783–1858). French architect. An early associate of *Hittorff, he worked with *Gilbert on the design of La Nouvelle Force, the prison at Mazas (commenced 1843), and designed several villas and theatres, including the Salle-Favart (1825) and Ambigù-Comique (both destroyed).

Hautecœur (1955); Papworth (1852)

Le Corbusier, Charles-Édouard (1887–1965). *See* Corbusier.

lectern. **1.** High sloping reading-desk, especially in a church, placed on the *Epistle side, often consisting of a columnar or *pedestal arrangement supporting a globe on which stands an eagle with outstretched wings, a symbol of St John the Evangelist. **2.** *Ambo.

ledge. *Course of stone, etc., especially one projecting, as a *plinth. **2.** Structural timber placed horizontally on the inner side of a wooden *door, as in *ledged*, *braced*, and *battened* door.

ledger. **1.** Large flat stone slab used as the top of a structure, e.g. an altar-tomb, or covering a brick-lined grave, usually *incised or *inlaid with e.g. *brasses. **2.** Any member intended to occupy a horizontal position, as in scaffolding or a *door.

Ledoux, Claude-Nicolas (1736–1806). Prolific French Neoclassicist, he is regarded as one of the greatest architects of his time, although very few of his works survive. He studied under J.-F. *Blondel, and his earliest works were elegant paradigms of the *Louis XVI style. These include the Hôtel d'Hallwyl, Rue Michael-le-Comte, Paris (1766), the Château de Bénouville, Normandy (*c.*1764–*c.*1770), the exquisite Hôtel d'Uzès, Rue Montmartre, Paris (1768), and the ingenious Hôtel de Montmorency, facing the Boulevard Montmartre and the Chaussée d'Antin

(1769–71—with a diagonal axis and elliptical *salon*). From 1771, however, he worked for Madame du Barry (1746–93) for whom he built the charming Pavillon de Louveciennes (1771–3), one of his first essays in a pure Neoclassical style, with interior decorations perfect examples of their time. At the Hôtel Thélusson, between the Rue de Provence and Rue de Chantereine, Paris (1778–83—demolished), he created an approach via a gigantic rusticated *astylar *Doric arch, and surrounded the house with an informal garden in the 'English' style, complete with *rock-work constructions. His command of stark geometry evolved further at the semicircular theatre at Besançon (1775–80—burnt 1957), with its Greek Doric *colonnade inside, and at the extraordinarily tough *Salines* (Salt-Works) *d'Arc-et-Senans* (1775–80), built in his role as *Inspecteur des Salines de la Franche-Comté*. Banded columns, simplified rigid geometry, and *primitivist qualities emphasized by the unfluted *Greek *Doric columns were something new. The complex formed the centrepiece for his Utopian town of Chaux (published in *L'architecture considerée sous le rapport de l'art, des mœurs, et de la législation* (Architecture Considered in Relation to Art, Standards, and Legislation—1804 and 1847)), in which simplified, stripped *Neoclassicism was the language, with allusions to all sorts of stereometrically pure geometries, including Egyptian *pyramids, a phallus-shaped brothel, a hoop-shaped house for a cooper, and even spherical structures. Allied to this were routes passing through various mnemonic devices, clearly Freemasonic in origin and intent. Although Chaux (meaning 'lime', the binding agency of *masonry and therefore an allusion to a programme of Freemasonic connections) remained mostly a strange and wonderful dream, Ledoux was able to realize many of his most advanced ideas in the series of *Barrières* or toll-houses erected around Paris (1785–9), including the Rotonde de la Villette, with its mighty drum on unfluted Greek Doric *serlianas, set over a square plan to each elevation of which are attached square Doric columns, and the grimly powerful Barrières of Passy, Longchamp, l'Observation, and Chopinette. Here was 'primitive' Neoclassicism at its starkest and most sophisticated, among the greatest architectural creations of C18.

Gallet (1980); Kaufmann (1952); Middleton and Watkin (1987); Placzek (1982); Vidler (1987, 1990)

Lee *or* **Alee, John** (*fl.* 1487–d. 1522). English master-mason. With *Wastell he was involved in the final phase of building at King's College Chapel, Cambridge, from 1506. He probably designed the Ramryge *Chantry Chapel in St Alban's Cathedral, Hertfordshire (*c*.1521).

Harvey (1987)

Lee, Richard (*fl.* 1525–35). English master-mason, probably the son of John *Lee. He designed the tomb of Fisher, Bishop of Rochester, intended for St John's College Chapel, Cambridge, but now destroyed. It had early *Renaissance features, like those of Bishop West's *Chantry Chapel, Ely Cathedral. He was therefore among the first to use Renaissance motifs in England.

Harvey (1987)

Lee, Sir Richard (*c*.1513–75). English architect and military engineer. He was probably the grandson of John *Lee, and was the first English architect to be knighted. He was Surveyor of Fortifications at Calais from 1536 to 1542, and from 1558 to 1565 worked on the impressive fortifications at Berwick-on-Tweed. He seems to have designed Sandown Castle, Isle of Wight (1540s) and Upnor Castle on the River Medway, Kent (1560s).

Harvey (1987)

Leeds, William Henry (1786–1866). English architectural critic, his essays on public improvements in the *Companion to the Almanac* (1838–50) were important. He published *Moller's Memorials of German Gothic* (1836), a Supplement in *Britton and A. C. *Pugin's *Illustrations of the Public Buildings of London* (1838), *The Travellers' Club House . . . and the Revival of the Italian Style* (1839), *Railway Architecture* (1848), and edited *A Treatise on the Decorative Part of Civil Architecture by William Chambers* (1862). His work on *The Travellers' Club* did much to publicize the *Italianate style of *Barry, and he introduced words such as *cornicione to the architectural vocabulary.

Colvin (1995); Hitchcock (1954); Leeds (1836, 1839, 1862, 1904)

Lefuel, Hector-Martin (1810–80). French architect, he succeeded L. *Visconti as architect of the Louvre and Tuileries (1854–80), where he was assisted by R. M. *Hunt. His tall *mansard roofs and rich (even excessive) *Renaissance Revival decorations were the epitome of the *Second Empire style, and influential. He also designed the theatre at

*Fontainebleau (1853) in an C18 style, and the buildings for the 1855 Paris International Exhibition.

Hautecœur (1957); Hitchcock (1977); Middleton and Watkin (1987)

Legeay, Jean-Laurent (*c*.1710–*c*.1786). *See* Geay.

Legorreta Vilchis, Ricardo (1931–). Mexican architect, after the death of *Barragán regarded as one of the most distinguished working in that country at the end of C20. Best known for his adaptations of *vernacular and other styles, as in his Camino Real hotels at Baja, California, Mexico City (1972), Cancun, Quintana Roo (1975–9), and Ixtapa, Guerrero (1981), his work extends to other concerns, notably his expression of walls as major architectural elements (with emphasis on solids rather than voids) reflecting Mexican architecture before the invasion of *International *Modernism and its ubiquitous Corbusian *pilotis. Good examples of his work are the Contemporary Art Museum, Paloma, Mexico (1991), and the series of buildings for the Westlake/Southlake Development, Solana, near Dallas, Tex., including the Village Center, the Real Estate Office Building, the IBM Offices, and the Marriot Hotel (1987–90).

Emanuel (1994)

Legrand, Jacques-Guillaume (1743–1808). French architect. He was a student of J.-F. *Blondel and became *Clérisseau's son-in-law. With *Molinos he built the dome, using timber construction, over the central court of the Halle au Blé, Paris (1782–3), by Le *Camus de Mézières. This was likened to the Roman *Pantheon at the time, and was greatly admired for its bold geometry. He re-sited and remodelled Goujon and *Lescot's Fontaine des Innocents (1788) when the cemetery closed, and published several books, including *Parallèle de l'architecture* (1789).

Etlin (1984); Middleton and Watkin (1987)

Leicester, John (*fl*. 1349–51). English mason. He built a *postern at the Tower of London (1349–51), and was ordainer of all the King's Works there.

Harvey (1987)

Leith, George Esslemont Gordon (1885–1965). Eminent South African architect working in the Classical language established in that country by Herbert *Baker for whom he worked. He was assistant architect to the Imperial War Graves Commission (1918–20) in England before returning to South Africa where he set up his practice. His works include the Calais Southern War Cemetery, France (1918–20), the Central Railway Station, Johannesburg (1927–32), the Town Hall, Bloemfontein (1920–40), and the South-African Reserve Bank, Johannesburg (1938), all in a stripped Neoclassical style derived partly from Scandinavia, reminiscent of *Holden's work.

Placzek (1982); Stamp (1977)

Lemercier, Jacques (*c*.1585–1654). Important mid-C17 French architect. He worked on the Square Court of the Louvre in Paris, begun by *Lescot, and was responsible for the Pavillon de l'Horloge (completed 1641) in which he introduced an *Order of *caryatids above the *Attic carrying a triangular *pediment, containing smaller triangular and segmental pediments, derived from della *Porta's façade of *Il Gesù*, Rome. Lemercier was architect to Cardinal Richelieu (1585–1642) for whom he built the Palais Cardinal (later Royal) in Paris (1624–36—destroyed, apart from a piece of external wall), and the domed Church of the Sorbonne, Paris (begun 1626—probably based on the Church of San Carlo ai Catinari, Rome), with a fine *Corinthian *portico on the courtyard side. He designed the handsome dome at the Val-de-Grâce Church (from 1646), with its drum surrounded by powerful *buttresses, treated as Classical *Orders, giving it lively modelling. From 1631 he designed and laid out the Château (mostly demolished) and Town of Richelieu near Chinon, the latter a strict essay in formal rectilinear planning (which survives virtually intact). Also for Richelieu he enlarged the Château, laid out the superb formal gardens, and built the Church at Rueil (from 1633). Lemercier is also remembered as the architect of some *hôtels particuliers in Paris, including the Hôtel de Liancourt (1623—destroyed), which Marot published in 1655.

Babelon (1991); Blomfield (1974); Blunt (1982); Cramail (1888); Marot (1969, 1970)

Lemercier, Pierre (*fl*. early and mid-C16). French architect, supposedly the designer of the Church of St-Eustache, Paris (begun 1532), an interesting building on a typical French *Gothic plan with apsidal east end, *ambulatory, *radiating chapels, and *transepts, but almost entirely *Renaissance in its detail, including the *tracery, which, though superficially Gothic, is transformed by the patterns and ornament. In 1552 he was commissioned to complete the tower of the Church of St-Maclou, Pontoise. His works at St-Eustache and St-Maclou were continued by his son, **Nicholas Lemercier** (*fl.* 1570–1600), who worked mainly on the *nave of the Paris church, dated 1578–80. Nicholas's son is supposed to be the great Jacques *Lemercier.

Sturgis *et al.* (1901–2)

Le Muet, Pierre (1591–1669). *See* Muet.

Lemyinge *or* **Liminge, Robert** (d. 1628). Carpenter employed to design and supervise the building of Hatfield House, Hertfordshire (1607–12), for which Inigo *Jones was consulted about the south front. Lemyinge also designed another *Jacobean house, Blickling Hall, Norfolk (1616–17).

Colvin (1995)

L'Enfant, Pierre-Charles (1754–1825). *See* Enfant.

Lenginour, Richard (*fl.* 1272–d. 1315). English military engineer. He was involved in the building of Flint and Rhuddlan Castles (1277–*c.*1282), but his greatest works were the Castle and fortifications at Conway, Wales. He carried out major building operations at Chester Castle (1290–1312), and probably designed the *choir of Chester Cathedral (*c.*1305–15). He was an important figure in the creation and upkeep of the military architecture of Edward I (reigned 1274–1307).

Harvey (1987)

Lengynour, Robert (*fl.* 1308–27). English master-mason. He worked at Glastonbury Abbey, Somerset, for some 19 years, where he was in charge of (and probably designed) the major part of the great *Gothic church (mostly destroyed).

Harvey (1987)

Lenné, Peter Joseph (1789–1866). Prussian Court Landscape Gardener. He collaborated with *Schinkel on numerous schemes, notably the grounds of Schloss Glienecke and the gardens contiguous to Charlottenhof and Schloss Babelsberg, all in the vicinity of Potsdam and the Havel Lake. He prepared an ambitious scheme for the landscaping and general improvement of the whole Potsdam-Havel-Sanssouci district (1833) that transformed it into one of the most enchanting regions in Europe, with reciprocal vistas, panoramic views, and intimate enclosures. Adopting the English landscape style, his work was very influential in C19 Germany, and was followed by his ardent disciple, Hermann, Fürst von Pückler-Muskau (1785–1871), who sought to revive the spirit of *Antique architecture and its relationship with Nature. Lenné's designs must be considered with the architecture of Schinkel, his contemporaries, and pupils, and played no small part in *Romantic Classicism.

Bergdoll (1994); Giersberg and Schendel (1982); personal knowledge

Lennox, Edward James (1854–1933). Canadian architect. In 1911 he was still designing in a vaguely late-Victorian manner, as with his *Scottish Baronial Casa Loma, Toronto, but drew on themes from the USA for his earlier Toronto City Hall and Court House (1887–99), much influenced by *Richardson's round-arched Allegheny County Court House and Gaol, Pittsburgh (1884–8). His work therefore mixed British and American influences, but he was also capable of impressive *Beaux-Arts *Classicism, as with the Toronto Power Generating Station, Niagara Falls, Ontario (1903–13).

Kalman (1994)

Le Nôtre, André (1613–1700). *See* Nôtre.

Leonardo da Vinci (1452–1519). *Uomo Universale* of the Italian *Renaissance, he made important contributions to architectural theory and town-planning. He was involved in preliminary studies for the *crossing of Milan Cathedral (*c.*1487) and, with Francesco di *Giorgio, was consulted about the building of Pavia Cathedral in *c.*1490. He provided plans for Milan's urban renewal and expansion (1490s), and produced sketches in which his interest in relating buildings geometrically to streets, squares, and gardens using axes is demonstrated. Like others of his time, he was fascinated by the possibilities of centrally planned domed buildings, and in this respect his relationship with *Bramante in Milan is important, for the two men developed their ideas under the aegis of the Sforza family. Leonardo was involved with Bramante in the design of the domed crossing and chancel of Santa Maria delle Grazie, Milan (1490s), intended as a *mausoleum for the Sforzas, and painted his beautiful *Last Supper* (which contains an architectural setting of remarkable modernity for its date, almost anticipating *Palladio) in the refectory (*c*.1495). It would seem that the maturing of Bramante's style to the *gravitas* of his *Tempietto* at San Pietro in Montorio, Rome, and his development of centralized geometries at the *basilica of San Pietro, Rome, may be due in no small part to Leonardo's influence.

Leonardo's notebooks give a fascinating glimpse of his architectural interests. Apart from his important scientific and mechanical drawings, his lively mind often experimented with the Classical vocabulary in a way that looked forward to developments much later. Fortifications, centralized plans, and technology were all his concerns, but there are also studies of designs for *villas (*c*.1506) that anticipate *Palladianism, and even *Mannerism, with columns *inserted* in recesses, something *Michelangelo was to do years later. With Bramante, he seems to have acted as some kind of adviser for the Church of Santa Maria della Consolazione at Todi (1508), begun by *Cola da Caprarola. In his last years Leonardo worked in France, planning a vast Royal residence and settlement at Romorantin (*c*.1517–19), complete with huge canals linking the English Channel to the Mediterranean.

Arata (1953); Firpo (1963); Heydenreich and Lotz (1974); Murray (1969, 1986); Pedretti (1985); Placzek (1982)

Leoni, Giacomo (*c*.1686–1746). Venetian architect, he spent most of his life in England from *c*.1713. Before that he was in Düsseldorf, where he assisted in the design of Schloss Bensberg, near Cologne (1705–16). While in Germany he worked on a treatise on the Five Roman *Orders of architecture which indicates that the idea of publishing a version of *Palladio's *Quattro Libri* was already in his mind before he settled in England and did just that. The translator of the texts was Nicholas Dubois, and Leoni prepared the drawings on which the engravings were based: the results of these labours appeared as *The Architecture of A. Palladio, Revis'd, Design'd and Publish'd by Giacomo Leoni, a Venetian: Architect to his most Serene Highness, the Elector Palatine* with texts in English, French, and Italian (1715–20). It was the first English edition, illustrated with large engraved plates instead of the rather crude woodcuts used by Palladio himself, and was an outstanding and immediate success, helping to promote *Palladianism and probably helping to spark *Burlington's interest in the cause. In 1726–9 he published *The Architecture of L. B. Alberti*.

Leoni designed a number of houses including Queensberry House, Burlington Gardens, London (1721—an important prototypical Palladian town-house), Lyme Park, Cheshire (*c*.1725–35), Argyll House, King's Road, Chelsea, London (1723), Clandon Park, Surrey (*c*.1730–3), and Alkrington Hall, Lancashire (1735–6). All had borrowings from Inigo *Jones and Palladio, but he was not a purist, and there is more than an echo of the *Baroque in his work, suggesting a position closer to that of *Gibbs than of *Campbell.

Brown (1985); Colvin (1995); Harris (1990); Leoni (1742, 1755); Papworth (1852); Summerson (1993)

Leonidov, Ivan Ilich (1902–59). Russian architect, he was influenced by *Vesnin, and was a figure in *Constructivism. His unrealized project for a Lenin Institute, with glass-clad suspended elements and an elevated monorail communications network, looked forward to the kind of adaptable open-ended structures envisaged by *Archigram, *Koolhaas, and other late-C20 architects. His only significant built work was the landscaped *amphitheatre and stairway for Ordjonikidze Sanatorium, Kislovodsk (1932).

Curtis (1996); Gozak and Leonidov (1988); Kopp (1970); Quilici and Scolari (1975); Shvidkovsky (1970)

Le Pautre, Antoine (1621–81). *See* Pautre.

leper window, *also called* **leper's squint.** *See* lychnoscope.

Lepère, Jean-Baptiste (1761–1844). One of the scholars who accompanied Napoleon to Egypt in 1798, he was involved in the preparation of the great *Description de l'Égypte*, one of the most important source-books of C19 Egyptology. He designed the exquisite *surtout* of the Sèvres *Service Égyptien* (1811–12) representing the Kiosk at Philae, obelisks from Luxor, and the *pylon-towers of the temple at Edfu. He also designed many of the medals struck to glorify episodes in the history of the *Empire of Napoleon I. In 1802, with *Percier and *Fontaine, he was involved in the design of Malmaison, and, with *Gondouin, was responsible for the Colonne Vendôme, Paris (1806–10), based on the *Trajanic exemplar. He prepared the earliest designs for the Church of St-Vincent-de-Paul, Paris (1824), in the style of *Chalgrin's St-Philippe-du-Roule (1768–84). He was *Hittorff's father-in-law.

Curl (1994); Hautecœur (1952, 1957); Hitchcock (1977); Middleton and Watkin (1987); Schneider (1977)

Lequeu, Jean-Jacques (1757–*c*.1825). French visionary Neoclassicist, he is known for the extraordinary drawings that survive in the Bibliothèque Nationale, Paris. These include a weird 'Gothic House' that has nothing Gothic about it, but is in fact a design for a route for Freemasonic trials by Fire, Water, Earth, and Air, clearly derived from descriptions in the Abbé Jean Terrasson's (1670–1750) prolix novel *Séthos* (1731) which were also the sources for the text of *Die Zauberflöte* (The Magic Flute, the 1791 *Singspiel* by Mozart, Giesecke, and Schikaneder). Other designs include Egyptianizing temples, *fabriques, spherical buildings, phallic erections, and even a dairy in the shape of a gigantic cow. His grotesque and obscene drawings (*figures lascives*) suggest that he was at least very odd. None of his buildings survives, but he built a country-house known as the Temple of Silence (1786), actually a Roman temple with *engaged columns along the side, but embellished with dogs, turtles, owls and much else. Inside was what appears to have been a Freemasonic Lodge.

Braham (1980); Curl (1991); Duboy (1987)

Leroy, Julien-David (1724–1803). *See* Roy.

Lesbian cymatium. *See* cyma.

Lescaze, William Edmond (1896–1969). Swiss-born architect, he was an important figure in bringing the *International Modern style to the USA, where he established his practice in New York in 1923. His early work included essays in *Neoclassicism and *Art Deco before he went into partnership with George *Howe in 1929. The firm designed the Philadelphia Saving Fund Society Bank and Office (1931), regarded as the pioneering International Modern *skyscraper of the time. The partnership was dissolved in 1933, but Lescaze continued to work under the joint names until 1935 when he once again set up in independent practice. Among his works of that period were the Headmaster's House at Dartington Hall, Totnes, Devon, England (1930–2), the Churston Estate Housing Development, Devon (1932–6), and the Lescaze House, New York (1933–4—which A. L. *Huxtable said was the first modern house built in the USA. Its success led to further commissions). In 1939 his Longfellow Building was commenced, completed in 1941—it was the first International style work in Washington, DC. During the 1939–45 war Lescaze designed prefabricated buildings using experimental materials, and later produced several large public, office-, and apartment-buildings, including the Swiss Embassy Chancellery, Washington, DC (1959), the Christian Peace Building, United Nations, New York (1961), and the Chatham Center, Pittsburgh (1964).

Emanuel (1994); Lescaze (1942); Pierson and Jordy (1970–86); Stern (1975)

Lescot, Pierre (1510/15–78). French architect, possibly of Scots descent, credited with introducing *Renaissance *Classicism to France. He collaborated with the sculptor/architect Jean Goujon (*c*.1510–*c*.1568) for nearly 20 years. One of their earliest works is the Fontaine des Innocents, Paris (1547–9), wholly rebuilt (1788) and re-worked by *Legrand and others. He also collaborated with Jean *Bullant at the Hôtel de Ligneris (now Carnavalet—*c*.1545–50). Lescot was appointed in 1546 to design part of the Louvre, and he was responsible for the south-western corner of the Square Court there (1546–51, with Goujon), with façades of great refinement, lacking the monumental quality of Italian work, but introducing a delicate ornamental quality that was peculiarly French. However, Goujon may have been responsible for the entire architectural embellishments of the Louvre façades, with Lescot primarily in charge of the planning and disposition of the main elements.

Androuet du Cerceau (1972); Blunt (1982); Colombier (1949); Hautecœur (1943); van Vynckt (1993)

lesene. Vertical strip resembling a *pilaster, but without a *base or *capital. It is a feature of *Anglo-Saxon (e.g. Earls Barton church-tower, Northamptonshire (early C10)) and *Romanesque architecture. Anglo-Saxon lesenes were composed of bonding-stones (often *long-and-short work) in *rubble walls, and subdivided wall-surfaces into framed plastered panels.

Lesyngham, Robert (*fl.* 1376–94). English master-mason, he designed the *cloisters (destroyed), the upper part of the screen on the west front, and the great east window at Exeter Cathedral, Devon (1376–94). He may have designed the cloisters at Gloucester Cathedral.

Harvey (1987)

Lethaby, William Richard (1857–1931). English architect, educator, and theorist. He trained with Norman *Shaw before establishing his own office (1889). Influenced by William *Morris, *Ruskin, and Philip *Webb, he was an important figure in the *Arts-and-Crafts movement, being a founder-member of the Art-Workers' Guild (1884). He built in a *Free style, not without historical references, and among his houses are Avon Tyrrell, Christchurch, Hampshire (1891–2), High Coxlease, Lyndhurst, Hampshire (1898), and the fine Melsetter, Hoy, Orkney (1898–1900). His All Saints' Church, Brockhampton, Herefordshire (1901–2), while having *Gothic allusions, is a free Arts-and-Crafts interpretation of church architecture of great beauty, while the Eagle Insurance Building, Colmore Row, Birmingham (1899–1900), shows Webb's influence, although it is boldly personal.

Lethaby helped to found the Central School of Arts and Crafts, London (1894), and was its first Principal. It was the earliest such school to have craft-teaching facilities and workshops. He was a leading member of the Society for the Protection of Ancient Buildings and wrote several books including *Architecture, Mysticism, and Myth* (1892), *Mediaeval Art* (1904), *Architecture* (1912), *Form in Civilization* (1922), and *Westminster Abbey* (1906, 1925).

Backemeyer and Gronberg (1984); *DNB* (1949); Garnham (1994); Gray (1985); Hitchcock (1977); Lethaby (1935); Muthesius (1979); Rubens (1986)

Leuthner *or* **Leitner von Grund, Abraham** (*c*.1639–1700/1). Born in Upper Austria, he became active as an architect in Prague when the influence of the Italians was in decline. He built the Černín Palace, Prague (1669–92), to designs by *Caratti, and designed the Cistercian Abbey Church of Waldsassen, Bavaria (1681–1704), although Georg and Christoph *Dientzenhofer (whose sister Anna was married to Leuthner) seem to have had more than a little influence in shaping the final design. From the 1680s Leuthner supervised the fortifications in Bohemia. He published an architectural treatise containing many designs of fountains, portals, etc., that appears to have been used by the Dientzenhofers and *Fischer von Erlach. Leuthner was instrumental in promoting the careers of the Dientzenhofers.

Bourke (1962); Knox (1962); Leutheusser (1993); Morper (1940); Neumann, J. (1970); Placzek (1982); Powell (1959); Wackernagel (1915)

Levasseur Family. Noël (1680–1740) and his cousin **Pierre-Noël Levasseur** (1690–1770) were French designers and craftsmen working in Quebec, Canada. They carried out the altars, retables, and architectural sculptures for the Chapel of the Ursuline Convent in Quebec (1726–36), for which the architect was the Parisian François de Lajoüe (*c*.1656–*c*.1719). The high-altar of the Church of St-François-de-Sales, Île d'Orléans, Quebec (1734–6), was designed and made by **François-Noël Levasseur** (1703–94).

Kalman (1994)

Le Vau, Louis (1612–70). *See* Vau.

Leverton, Thomas (1743–1824). English builder and architect, he was a successful developer in late-C18 London. There is no evidence that he planned Bedford Square, Bloomsbury, London (1775–80), but he certainly decorated some of the houses there (1, 6, 10, and 13). Leverton's style was influenced by that of the fashionable *Adam brothers, as the Neoclassical interiors of Watton Wood Hall (now Woodhall Park), Hertfordshire (1777–81), and Plaistow Lodge, Bromley, Kent (1780), demonstrated. Leverton built 65 Lincoln's Inn Fields, London (1772), for Henry Kendall, who had originally enabled Leverton to perfect his knowledge of architecture. In turn, Leverton took on Kendall's son, Henry Edward *Kendall, as a pupil. He laid out Hamilton Place, Piccadilly, London (1806), for the Crown.

Colvin (1995); *DNB* (1917); Papworth (1852); Summerson (1988, 1993)

Levi, Rino (1901–65). Brazilian Modernist architect. He designed the first large *International style apartment-building, the Columbus block, São Paulo, in 1928. Later works include the UFA Art Palacio Cinema (1936), and the Central Cancer Hospital (1948), both in São Paulo. He adopted *Brutalism in the 1960s, as in the Parahyba Dairies, São João dos Campos (1963–7), and the Santo André Civic Centre, São Paulo (1965).

Levi (1974); Morgan and Naylor (1987)

Lewerentz, Sigurd (1885–1975). Swedish architect. At the beginning of his career he worked with *Fischer, *Möhring, and *Riemerschmid in Germany (1908–10), where he absorbed the new rational attitude. His work was within the camp of *National

Romanticism, as with his influential but unrealized project for the Hälsingborg Crematorium (1913–14), and indeed it was in cemetery and crematorium design that he was to make his name. In the Hälsingborg project the relationships of building, water, and landscape were carefully and sensitively designed, and this was to be true of his later works. For the Hälsingborg project and the various houses he designed around the time of the 1914–18 war he worked with Torsten Stubelius (1883–1963). In 1915 he began a long collaboration with *Asplund in the design of the Woodland Cemetery, Stockholm, which was to last until his death. There he designed the landscapes and the exquisite Neoclassical Resurrection Chapel (1922–6), one of Sweden's finest and most subtle essays in C20 *Neoclassicism. Other major commissions for cemeteries included that for Malmö's Eastern Cemetery, work on which likewise extended from the 1920s until the end of his life. There, the buildings, with their severe geometries, recall Roman Antiquity and late-C18 Neoclassicism. The mortuary-chapel, Stora Tuna (1928), employs the simplest of means for its tenderly conceived dignity.

In 1930 Lewerentz designed the sans-serif lettering, posters, and many pavilions for the Stockholm Exhibition of 1930, marking a change of direction in his style. For his two late churches, St Mark's at Skarpnäck, Stockholm (1956–60), and St Peter's, Klippan (1963–6), he used naked, unadorned brick to great effect, and virtually all historical references are absent.

Emanuel (1994); Paavilainen (1982); *Svenskt Biografiskt Lexikon* (1979)

Lewyn, John (*fl.* 1364–*c.*1398). English master-mason. He was principal mason at Durham Cathedral in the latter part of C14, and carried out many works in the North, including the great kitchen at Durham (completed 1374), repairs to Bamburgh Castle (1368–72), the new *keep at Durham Castle, works at Carlisle and Roxburgh Castles (from 1378), various structures at Bolton Castle, Yorkshire, and major alterations to Dunstanburgh Castle (1380–7). He was unquestionably the most important provincial architect working in the North of England at the time.

Harvey (1987)

Libera, Adalberto (1903–63). Italian architect, he joined *Gruppo 7 in 1927, and was from the first involved with *Rationalism which he sought to promote as the official Fascist architectural language. He exhibited at *Mies van der Rohe's *Weissenhofsiedlung, Stuttgart (1927), and organized the first exposition of Rationalism in architecture in Rome (1928). The Malaparte Villa, Capri (1938), was an interesting attempt to marry architecture to its natural rocky site. While he designed the Olympic Village, Rome, with others (1959–60), and a few buildings (e.g. Palazzo della Regione Trentina, Trento (1954)), nothing of his later years compares with the designs for the monumental *Mostra della Rivoluzione Fascisto* (Exhibition of the Fascist Revolution) held in Rome in 1932 and intended by Mussolini to promote a 'contemporary style, very modern and audacious, without melancholy references to the decorative styles of the past'. The exhibition was influenced by *Futurism and *Constructivism as well as by *Stripped Classicism, and had considerable influence thereafter, even into the post-war years.

Argan (1976); Placzek (1982); Seta (1972)

Libergié *or* **Libergier, Hue** *or* **Hugues** (d. 1263). French master-mason. He designed the Benedictine Abbey Church of St-Nicaise, Rheims (1231–63—destroyed), with an exquisite west front incorporating a *tracery screen and a gigantic twin-*lancet with oculus rather than the rose-window usual at that time. He is commemorated by an *incised slab in Rheims Cathedral, on which he is shown holding a model and a staff of office, while a square and compasses are drawn on either side of his feet.

Branner (1965); Givelet (1897); Svanberg (1983)

Liberty. 1. Allegorical female figure frequently depicted by French Revolutionary artists, complete with flaming torch and Phrygian cap. **2.** Italian *Art Nouveau, called *Stile Liberty.

Libeskind, Daniel (1946–). Polish-born American architect. He studied with John *Hejduk (*see also* New York Five) and enjoyed a varied career in architectural academe where, it has been said, he was essentially 'isolated from the practicalities and resultant compromise inherent in building'. He designed the City Edge project, Berlin (1987), an influential proposal that ripped through established geometries of urban fabric, responding to the logic of the Berlin Wall by slicing up territory, so his approach is the antithesis of that of Léon *Krier and others who have rediscovered the city and argued for the repair and restoration of traditional forms, spaces, volumes, and streets. He also designed the extension to the Berlin Museum to house the artefacts relating to the city's Jewish history (1989–93), a proposal to develop an office complex in Wiesbaden (1993), and the stark Felix Nussbaum Museum, Osnabrück, Germany (opened 1998). His work has been associated with *Deconstructivism, notably with his proposals for the jagged proposals for an extension to the Victoria & Albert Museum, London (1996).

Emanuel (1994); Johnson and Wigley (1988)

lich-gate. *See* lych-gate.

Licht, Hugo (1841–1923). German architect. He trained in Berlin and under von *Ferstel in Vienna and became Director of Municipal Building in Leipzig (1879–1906), where he built a series of monumental buildings including the Music Conservatory (1885–7), the Police Headquarters (1889–90), Grassi Museum (1892–5), and the new City Hall (1898–1912). The latter, a massive structure, is eclectic, drawing on aspects of medieval architecture, and with the masonry treated in a deliberately powerful, oversized way recalling the work of *Richardson in the USA. Licht was important for his many publications, notably those produced for the great publishing-house Wasmuth, which include *Die Architektur des XX. Jahrhunderts: Zeitschrift für moderne Baukunst* (The Architecture of the Twentieth Century: Journal of Modern Architecture—1901–14), a lavishly illustrated journal he edited which is a mine of information of the period, and which promoted the careers of many younger architects.

Licht (1877, 1879–82, 1882, 1886–1900, 1900, 1901–6, 1901–14)

Lienau, Detlef (1818–87). Born in Schleswig-Holstein, he was trained in Germany and in Paris under *Labrouste (from whom he derived his *Classicism). After settling in the USA in 1848, he developed a thriving practice in New York. His architecture was eclectic, ranging through *Rundbogenstil, *Gothic, French *Second Empire, *Italianate, *Picturesque asymmetrical, to a nondescript, even dour manner from which French influences, however, were not entirely obliterated. He designed several large blocks of town-houses in New York, including the Rebecca Jones group, Fifth Avenue and 55th Street (1868–70), which were influential. In the 1870s and 1880s his career was closely bound up with the most spectacular growth of Manhattan.

Journal of the Society of Architectural Historians, 14 (Mar. 1955), 18–25; Placzek (1982); van Vynckt (1993)

lierne. *See* vault.

light. Aperture (called *day*) through which daylight may pass, such as a pane of glass, an area around which are *mullions or *transoms, or an opening defined by the bars of *tracery.

Light, Colonel William (1784–1838). Surveyor-General of South Australia, he founded and laid out Adelaide from 1837 on a generous plan with six large squares, the whole development surrounded with a vast green belt of parkland, the first to be realized on any scale.

DNB (1917)

light-well. Unroofed space in a building, really a small *court with high buildings around it, providing light and air to the windows that open to it.

Ligorio, Pirro (*c*.1510–83). Italian architect, archaeologist, and painter, he settled in Rome in 1534 after which he explored and recorded antiquities and remains, and began to collect material for his huge encylopedias of Classical artefacts. He brought out a volume on Roman antiquities in 1553, the only publication in his lifetime disseminating his vast knowledge. In this respect, his work is an invaluable source of information on what Antique remains were known at the time. In 1549 he was appointed archaeologist to Cardinal Ippolito d'Este of Ferrara, and for him carried out major works at the old Franciscan monastery, Tivoli, creating the Villa d'Este and its gardens (1550–72), greatly influenced by the nearby Villa Adriana which Ligorio had recorded. The fountains, cascades, and waterworks at the Villa d'Este contributed to the making of one of the finest C16 European gardens. In 1558 he began work on a summer-house for Pope Paul IV (1555–9) in the Vatican Gardens: work on this resumed in 1560 after the election of Pope Pius IV (1559–65), and by 1562 the exquisite Casino di Pio IV, one of the most affecting creations of

*Mannerism, was complete. Jacob Burckhardt (1818–97), the Swiss art-historian, called it the most beautiful 'afternoon retreat' ever created. It drew on the *type of the *Antique *diaeta*, or auxiliary building used for the *otium* (rest or leisure time). At the same time Ligorio began work on *Bramante's Belvedere Court at the Vatican, with the addition of curved seating at the lower terrace's south side, making changes to the *exedra to the north so that it formed an enormous *niche. He also designed the *astylar rusticated Lancellotti Palace (*c.*1560), restored the *Pantheon (1561), and built the Cenci Palace (*c.*1564), all in Rome. He succeeded *Michelangelo as Architect of San Pietro in 1564, but in the following year was accused of fraud and theft, thus ending his Papal career. Once more he turned his attention to the gardens at Tivoli, supervising the works and designing several fountains. In 1569 he moved to Ferrara, where he was placed in charge of the important collection of antiquities belonging to the Duke.

Ackerman (1954); Coffin (1960, 1979); Dernie and Carew-Cox (1996); Heydenreich and Lotz (1974); Mandowsky and Mitchell (1963); Placzek (1982); Smith, G. (1977)

Liminge. *See* Lemyinge.

Lindgren, Armas (1874–1929). Finnish architect, he formed a partnership with Herman *Gesellius and Eliel *Saarinen. The firm's work was eclectic, drawing on *Arts-and-Crafts, medieval, *vernacular, and *Art Nouveau styles, and was regarded as part of *National Romanticism. It includes the Pohjola Insurance Building, Helsinki (1900–1), the Studio and House, Kirkkonummi (1902–3), and the National Museum, Helsinki (1902–5). The partnership was dissolved in 1905, and he established a new one with one of Finland's first female architects, Wivi Lönn (1872–1966), designing the Vanemuinen Theatre, Tartu (1906), and the Estonia Theatre, Tallinn (1912), both in Estonia, and both in a *Jugendstil manner. Some of his other works merged *Renaissance elements with a subdued Jugendstil, as in the Suomi (1911) and Kaleva (1913) Insurance Companies' buildings in Helsinki. His later work drew on medieval precedents, notably in his restoration of Turku Cathedral (1923–8), and in the churches at Säynätsalo and Valkeala (both with Bertel Liljeqvist, 1926). He also designed housing, mostly in Helsinki.

Richards (1978); Salokorpi (1970); Smith (1975)

linenfold. *Parchemin plié or *linen-pattern*, a late-*Gothic ornamental finish to a panel, resembling linen with vertical loose folds. It evolved in Flanders from C15, and is very common in architecture of the *Tudor period. Linenfold was revived in C19.

linenfold. C16 example, Layer Marney Hall, Essex. (*After Parker*)

Linstow, Hans Ditler Frants (1787–1851). Architect of the Neoclassical Royal Palace, Oslo, Norway (1824–48), one of the most distinguished of Greek-inspired buildings in that country, with an impressive *Ionic *portico. The building was influenced by German exemplars, especially the works of *Schinkel, who advised on the design, and from 1824 to 1827 Linstow was assisted by the Danish architect *Grosch, who was to make Oslo his home from 1825.

Weilbach (1995)

lintel. Beam over an aperture carrying the wall above and spanning between *jambs.

lintel-course. *String-course or *band continuing the lines of a *lintel along a *façade.

lion. 1. Carved representation of lions' masks in Classical architecture, especially on *cornices (e.g. temple of Aphaia, Aegina (*c.* 490 BC)). **2.** Emblem of St Mark, so common in Christian *iconography.

Lisboa, António Francisco (1730–1814). *See* Aleijadinho.

Lissitzky, Eleazar Markevich *called* **El** (1890–1941). Russian architect, graphic designer, painter, and polemicist, he was an early devotee of *Suprematism before becoming a protagonist of *Constructivism. He studied at Darmstadt from 1909, travelled, and graduated in architecture at Riga in 1916, after which he worked with Marc Chagall (1887–1985) at the Vitebsk School of Art, where he evolved the idea of a work of art as an 'interchange station' between painting and architecture. This he termed *Proun* (an acronym for the Russian meaning 'Project for the Affirmation of the New'), and his paintings of the time have a resemblance to plans for three-dimensional structures. Influenced to some extent by the painter Kasimir Malevich (1878–1935) and *Tatlin, Lissitzky helped to organize Malevich's *New System of Art* (1919), the manifesto of Suprematism, and later designed the Lenin Tribune project (1920), which was a precedent for *Vesnin's *Pravda* (Truth) Building in Leningrad (1923). Through his Western contacts van *Doesburg, *Stam, and others, his ideas were disseminated within the De *Stijl group and at the *Bauhaus. He designed several rooms for exhibitions, including the Proun Room for the Greater Berlin Art Exhibition (1923—reconstructed at the Stedelijk Museum, Eindhoven, Netherlands) and the Exhibition Cabinet (room) for the International Art Exhibition, Dresden (1926), and Hanover (1928—recreated at the *Landesmuseum*, Hanover). His images and, especially, his graphics, have been widely influential, especially in the late C20.

Architects' Year Book, 12 (1968), 253–68; Jervis (1984); Lissitzky (1970, 1981); Lissitzky-Küppers (1980); Placzek (1982); Richter (1958)

list, listel, listella. *Annulet or *fillet crowning or separating other mouldings.

liturgical orientation. *See* orientation.

liwan. *See* iwan.

load-bearing. Type of construction in which walls, blank or punctuated with openings, support the floors, roofs, etc., as opposed to a structure based on the *frame principle, as in *timber-framed construction.

lobby-entry. *See* entry.

lobe. **1.** Small arch, arc, or *foil in medieval architecture, separated by a *cusp from another lobe or foil. Thus *lobed* describes anything such as an arch or *tracery with lobes and cusps. **2.** *Gadroon.

Lock, Adam (*fl.* 1215–29). English master-mason, known for his work at Wells Cathedral, Somerset. He was in charge of the building of the second work of the *nave, west of the north porch, and he probably carved the detail of the first *Lady Chapel at St Augustine's Abbey (now Cathedral), Bristol (1218–20).

Harvey (1987)

Lockwood, Henry Francis (1811–78). English architect. He was articled to P. F. *Robinson and set up his own office in Hull, Yorkshire, in 1834. In 1849 he moved to Bradford, Yorkshire, then a rapidly expanding town, where he formed a partnership with Richard (1834–1904) and William (1828–89) Mawson. As Lockwood & Mawson they designed some of the most distinguished buildings in Bradford, including St George's Hall (1851–2), the impressive Venetian *Gothic Wool Exchange (1864–7), and the very fine C13 Continental *Gothic Revival Town Hall (1869–73). They also laid out and designed the Mill, Model Town, and Church at Saltaire, near Bradford (1851–76), one of the most important examples of a philanthropic industrial and housing development in the world for its date, all in an *Italianate Classical style. Lockwood trained Cuthbert *Brodrick. When the partnership was dissolved in 1874 Lockwood moved to London, where he built the Methodist City Temple, Holborn Viaduct, London (1873–4), and the Church of St Stephen, Cowbridge Park, East Twickenham, Middlesex (1874).

Curl (1990); Dixon and Muthesius (1985); Hitchcock (1954); Physick and Darby (1973)

loculus (*pl.* **loculi**). **1.** In a *catacomb, *hypogeum, *mausoleum, or other place of entombment, a recess large enough to receive a human corpse, with or without a coffin or *sarcophagus, or a *cinerarium or *ollarium of impressive dimensions. Should the recess be arched, it is termed *arcosolium. **2.** *Sarcophagus.

lodge. **1.** Medieval masons' workshop, refectory, tracing-house, and living-quarters erected during the building of a great work. In very large projects, such as a cathedral, it was often a permanent structure, with a resident master-mason, associated with the building and maintainance of the fabric. **2.** Place where Freemasons assemble, representing the lost Temple of Solomon and an ideal. **3.**

Small, usually decorative, building at the gateway to an estate or park, serving as the accommodation and office for a gatekeeper or porter. **4.** Dwelling in the grounds of a large country-house, usually substantial, granted as a permanent residence for e.g. minor Royalty. **5.** Quarters for the porter, as in the entrance to a collegiate establishment or a club.

Booz (1956); Bucher (1979); Colombier (1953); Curl (1991); Gwilt (1903); Mowl and Earnshaw (1985); Papworth (1852); Sturgis *et al.* (1901–2); Svanberg (1983)

Lodoli, Fra Carlo (1690–1761). Venetian Franciscan and architectural theorist. His theories had some bearing on *Neoclassicism from the time they were (rather inaccurately) propounded in *Algarotti's *Saggio sopra l'Architettura* (1753). Later, Andrea Memmo (1729–93) published *Elementi d'architettura Lodoliana* (1786), but it was incomplete until Lucia Mocenigo, Memmo's daughter, organized a fuller edition of *Elementi*, including other hitherto unpublished texts by Lodoli, in 1833–4. Among other things, Lodoli insisted that 'proper function and form are the only final, scientific aims of civil architecture', merged in an 'indivisible entity', and that when a *fully* suitable material is *openly* used in accordance with its characteristics and the purpose of the building, a strong, well-proportioned, and convenient building will *always* result. He designed the Pilgrim's Quarters at the Monastery of San Francesco della Vigna, Venice (n.d.), with curiously carved *cills and plain utilitarian raking *hoods, but its significance is perhaps overrated, and Lodoli, as an architect, seems to have had no influence, as his one known design was unpublished and unvisited.

Art Bulletin, 46/2 (1964), 159–75; Council of Europe (1972); Grassi (1966); Herrmann (1962); Kaufmann (1955); Memmo (1973); Rykwert (1980); Torcellan (1963); Wittkower (1982)

Lods, Marcel-Gabriel (1891–1978). French architect. He was in partnership with Eugène *Beaudouin from 1925 to 1940, and thereafter practised on his own from 1945 in Paris. The Lods–Beaudouin partnership was responsible for building early prefabricated housing schemes at the Cité de la Muette, Drancy, Paris (1934—unfortunately remembered mostly as the transit-centre for French Jews on their way 'to the East'), and (with Vladimir Boliansky (1894–1966) and *Prouvé) the Maison du Peuple, Clichy (1939). It also designed the layout of the World's Fair, Paris (1937). After the 1939–45 war Lods argued for the planning of all land and towns on the principles advocated by *CIAM.

Emanuel (1994); Morgan and Naylor (1987)

Loewy, Raymond Fernand (1893–1986). French-born American industrial designer. After a chequered career he was retained by the Gestetner firm in 1929 to restyle their products, and his success prompted other firms to employ him (e.g. BP, the Co-op, Exxon, Lockheed, Shell, Studebaker). He designed automobile bodies, railway-engines and passenger-cars, refrigerators, the famous Greyhound buses, and the celebrated Coca-Cola bottle. He and his firm designed various corporate identity packages. Among his later works were the interiors of the *Skylab* for NASA (1967–73). He published *Never Leave Well Enough Alone* (1951), and must be regarded as a considerable influence on the late-C20 Western environment.

L'architecture d'aujourd'hui, 247 (Oct. 1986), 96–8; Jodard (1994); Loewy (1937, 1951, 1975, 1988); Schönberger (1990)

loft. **1.** Formerly, any upper floor, but now the volume contained by the pitched roof of a building and the supports for the ceiling of the topmost floor bounded by the walls. Essentially a *garret, but used for storage, without any finishes. **2.** Elevated platform, staging, or *gallery within a larger room or hall, such as an *excubitorium* or *watching-loft* (e.g. the example in St Alban's Abbey, Hertfordshire), *Rood-loft, or organ-loft in a church.

log. Type of construction in which walls are formed of straight tree-trunks each placed horizontally on top of another, overlapping at the corners of the building.

Hansen (1971); Jordan (1985); Sturgis *et al.* (1901–2)

loggia (*pl.* **loggie**). **1.** Roofed structure, open on at least one side, essentially a gallery, an *arcade, or *colonnade, affording a protected seating-place with a view, common in Italy, and often with architectural pretensions. It is usually part of a building, and subsidiary to the whole, although there are some *loggie* that have immense scale and overwhelming presence, such as the *Sala Terrena*, Valdštejn Gardens, Prague (C17). **2.** *Lodge, in the sense of a building in a park.

Loire-château *or* **Touraine style.** Type of C19 architecture based on the French *Renaissance C16 châteaux of the Loire valley in the time of *François Ier. Examples include *Destailleur's Waddesdon Manor, Buckinghamshire (1874–90), and William Henry Crossland's (1823–1909) Royal Holloway College, Egham, Surrey (1879–87).

Dixon and Muthesius (1985); Pevsner, *Buildings of England, Buckinghamshire* (1960) and *Surrey* (1962)

Lomax-Simpson, James (1882–1977). British architect. His finest works are the late-*Arts-and-Crafts *Domestic Revival houses he designed at Port Sunlight, Cheshire, from 1910 as Architect to Lever Brothers, including virtually all the buildings facing The Diamond (1–22 King George's Drive, 8–12 The Causeway, 25–50 Queen Mary's Drive, and 13–17 The Causeway) of 1913; those in The Ginnel, 60–2 Bolton Road, and 2–4 Water Street (*c*.1914); the Duke of York's Cottages (1933); Jubilee Crescent (*c*.1938); and many other houses and structures (e.g. the Social Centre, King George's Drive (1913), the Rose Garden and Arch (*c*.1937), and the axial vista at Windy Bank). Other works are St George's Church (1906–7), handsome additions to Thornton House (1906), the Smithy (1905), and houses, all at Thornton Hough, Cheshire. With Sir John *Burnet, *Tait, & Lorne, he designed the Unilever Building, New Bridge Street, London (1930–1).

Pevsner, *Buildings of England, Cheshire* (1971); personal knowledge

Lombardo, Pietro Solari, *called* (*c*.1435–1515). One of the most important sculptors and architects working in Venice in the late C15 from *c*.1467. From 1471 he worked on embellishments for the *chancel of the Church of San Giobbe, which has certain stylistic affinities with the work of *Brunelleschi in Florence. Florentine too are the large funerary monuments he designed for the Church of Santi Giovanni e Paolo: conceived as architectural compositions in the *Renaissance style, the tomb of Doge Pietro Mocenigo (1481) is his finest achievement in this genre. He designed and built Santa Maria dei Miracoli (1481–9), an aisleless *nave with a barrel-vaulted timber ceiling and a raised chancel set under a *cupola on *pendentives, the whole exterior treated with a two-storey arrangement of *engaged *Orders, the uppermost carrying a *blind *arcade. Inside is marble panelling, and the combination of rich Byzantinesque wall-decorations and Renaissance detailing is impressive. The chancel-arch is approached from a flight of steps, and this creates the appearance of greater size. *Trompe l'œil effects were also employed on the façade of Lombardo's Scuola di San Marco (from 1487), built as a confraternity hall: on the ground floor are panels treated as perspective views of architectonic spaces. The upper parts of the front were completed by *Coducci. Lombardo's name is associated with various Venetian palazzi, notably the beginnings of Véndramin-Calergi (*c*.1500), and the Ca' Dario (*c*.1488), the decorative work of which is not unlike that of Santa Maria dei Miracoli. In much of his work Lombardo was assisted by his sons **Antonio** (*c*.1485–1516) and **Tullio** (*c*.1455–1532).

Howard (1980); Luciani (1987); McAndrew (1980); van Vynckt (1993)

Lombard style. Style of architecture, essentially an amalgam of *Early Christian and *Romanesque, that flourished in Northern Italy in and around Como (e.g. Sant'Abbondio, Como (C11)). It was revived in C19 as part of the *Rundbogenstil, and enjoyed a further American Revival, especially for churches.

Lombardy frieze. Arched *corbel-*table or series of small arches under *eaves and supported on corbels, as on the church of Sant'Abbondio, Como (C11).

Long, Robert Cary (1810–49). American architect, he set up in Baltimore, Md. (1835–6), where he made designs in the Classical, *Egyptian, and *Gothic styles. He was responsible for Greenmount Cemetery, Baltimore, where he built the Gothic entrance (1840) and an Egyptian Revival *mausoleum. Among his works, the Perine House, Baltimore (1839), Institution for the Deaf, Dumb, and Blind, Staunton, Va. (1839–44), and Jérôme Bonaparte Town House, Baltimore (1844), deserve mention. Some of his *Greek Revival work was distinguished, such as the *Doric Church of St Peter the Apostle, Baltimore (1843–4). He published many articles on aspects of architecture, as well as a volume on *The Ancient Architecture of America* (1849).

Carrott (1978); Howland and Spencer (1953); Placzek (1982); Stanton (1968)

long-and-short work. *Anglo-Saxon masonry consisting of tall thin verticals and short lengths of horizontal blocks, both of *freestone, used as *dressings in *rubble walls, set alternately one on the other as *quoins and *lesenes, the shorts set deep into the wall to help bind the wall together. Lesenes were formed by creating a raised vertical strip on the long-and-short work which, with the raised quoins, provided a frame for the rendering that concealed the rubble walls.

long gallery. Room or *gallery in a great *Elizabethan or *Jacobean house of the *prodigy type, sometimes the width of a *façade, as at Hatfield House, Hertfordshire (1607–11), and Hardwick Hall, Derbyshire (1590–7), well lit by means of lavish windows and sumptuously appointed with chimney-surrounds, panelling, moulded ceilings, etc., used to hang tapestries and pictures, and for entertainment.

Longhena, Baldassare (1596/9–1682). The most distinguished Venetian architect of the *Baroque period. He is said to have trained under *Scamozzi. Early in his career he designed the Palazzo Giustinian-Lolin on the Grand Canal (1620–3), which was a taste of things to come in its lively invention. In 1630 Longhena won the competition to design the splendid votive Church of Santa Maria della Salute on which he was to work for the remainder of his life. Its plan is an octagonal domed space surrounded by lower *aisles off which are six rectangular chapels illuminated by *Diocletian windows, with a domed *chancel on either side of which are apses. The *clearstorey carrying the dome is linked to the radiating chapels by means of vast *buttresses in the form of *scrolls, and a *triumphal-arch motif is used on the entrance-façade. The Church is sited at the entrance to the Grand Canal opposite the Piazzetta and Doge's Palace and on the axes of *Palladio's Churches of San Giorgio Maggiore and *Il Redentore*. The connection with *scenography is continued inside with telescoping views from the great central space, creating an architectural experience at once powerful and satisfying. Almost identical in plan is the Philippine Church, Gostyń, Poland (from 1679), for which Longhena provided drawings, realized by Andrea and Giorgio Catenazzi and completed by Pompeo Ferrari (*c*.1660–1736) in 1728. Longhena's mastery of theatrical effects was also demonstrated in the influential double staircase he designed for the Benedictine Monastery of San Giorgio Maggiore (1643–5).

His domestic designs were many, but his finest achievements in the field were the Palazzo Pésaro (1649/52–82—completed by his disciple, Antonio Gaspari (*c*.1658–1738)), with its diamond-rusticated *plinth, two superimposed *Orders, and an arrangement of arched windows carried on subsidiary Orders. It is arguably one of the most carefully composed of all Venetian palazzi, with a deeply layered façade, the main Orders standing in front of the 'real' structural wall. He also began the Palazzo Bon (later Rezzonico) in 1666, with a façade (completed by Giorgio *Massari, 1759) regularly arranged as wall and pier over a plinth derived from *Sanmicheli's Porta Palio, Verona (1548–9), the upper part evolved from *Sansovino's Biblioteca Marciana (1536–60), and a total composition with a precedent in Sansovino's Palazzo Corner della Ca' Grande (begun 1537). His façade of the Chapel of the Ospedaletto (1670–4) was elaborately embellished, a precursor of late-Baroque tendencies. Apart from the scenographic triumph of Santa Maria della Salute, his greatest town-planning achievement was the completion of Scamozzi's Procuratie Nuove, Piazza di San Marco (1640–63).

Cristinelli (1978); Howard (1980); Karpowicz (1991); Lewis (1979); Puppi *et al.* (1982); van Vynckt (1993); Wittkower (1982)

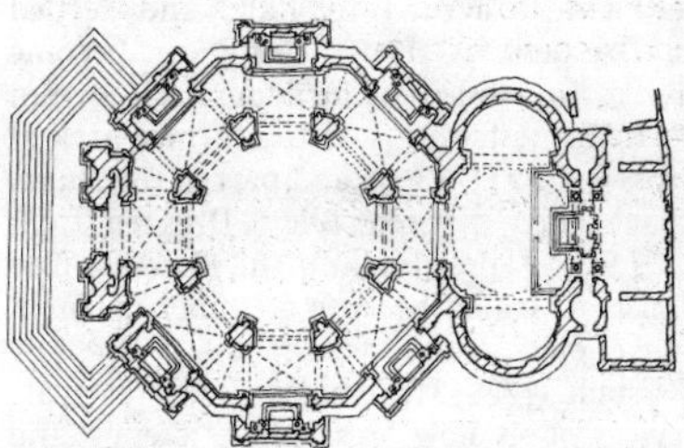

Longhena. Plan of Santa Maria della Salute, Venice.

Longhi Family. Group of architects who worked mostly in Rome in C16 and C17. **Martino Longhi the Elder** (*c*.1540–91) appears to have settled in Rome *c*.1569, where he worked for the Papacy, notably at the Vatican and Quirinal Palaces, the rebuilding of the *portico of Santa Maria Maggiore (1575), and the new *campanile on the Palazzo del Senatore (1578). He designed the well-mannered but unadventurous façade of San Girolamo degli Schiavoni (1588–9). His son, **Onorio** (*c*.1569–1619), who seems to have been an odd character, fled Rome in 1606 for his part in a murder, and returned in 1611 after a Papal Pardon. He designed the huge Church of Santi Ambrogio e Carlo al Corso (1612–19), completed by his son, **Martino the Younger** (1602–60), the most gifted of the tribe, who designed Sant'Antonio dei Portoghesi (1630–8), with its lively façade. It was as a designer of church-fronts that the younger Martino excelled, and his masterpiece is the façade of Santi Vincenzo ed Anastasio (1646–50). He introduced three new features to Roman *Mannerism: detached columns accentuating unhesitant verticality; the mixing of triangular, segmental, open-topped, and open-bedded pediments; and the layering of planes, with the scrolls merging with other sculpture as part of *scenographic effects. The assured rhetoric of Roman *Baroque had arrived.

Arco (1972); Hess (1934); Koksa (1971); Pascoli (1965); Placzek (1982); Varriano (1986); Wittkower (1982)

long-house. Domestic building including living-quarters, byres, etc., under one roof, with access by a single *entry-passage.

Alcock, Barley, Dixon, and Meeson (1996)

Longuelune, Zacharias (1669–1748). French artist and architect. He worked on the *Zeughaus* (Arsenal), Berlin (*c.*1698), under de *Bodt, travelled in Italy, and settled in Dresden in 1715, rising to become *Oberlandbaumeister* (Senior State Architect) in 1731. His best work was the formal park at Gross-Sedlitz (1723–6), and part of the Dutch Palace (later *Japanisches Palais*), Dresden (from 1729 with *Pöppelmann). The *Blockhaus* (Log House—so called because a timber customs-house once stood on the site), Dresden-Neustadt (1728–31), employed his favourite devices of shallow *ressaults, *lesenes, and horizontal *bands: it was completed by *Knöffel. His designs in a rather dry French Classical style had some influence in Saxony and Poland, and he proposed schemes for an enormous Saxon Palace in Warsaw (1717– with Pöppelmann) and for Schloss Pillnitz, near Dresden.

Colombier (1955); Franz (1953)

look-out. *See* prospect tower.

loop. **1.** Long, narrow, vertical aperture with splayed *jambs set in a parapet (sometimes in the *merlon of a *battlement) or wall for the discharge of arrows, etc., also called *arrow-loop*, *loop-window*, or *loophole*, occasionally with a shorter horizontal aperture across it forming a cruciform opening. The terminations of the apertures (little more than slits in the wall) were often widened into circular holes, and occasionally the point at which the slits crossed was enlarged to a circular opening as well. *See* gun-loop. **2.** Merlon.

loop-hole. Vertical series of doors each set above the other in a warehouse wall in tiers, usually with hinged drop-platforms and with a pulley above the series so that goods could be hoisted up and swung into storage through the doors.

Loos, Adolf (1870–1933). Influential Austro-Hungarian architect and polemicist. Born in Brno, Moravia, he studied in Dresden, where *Semper's ideas made a great impression on him, and in 1893 visited the USA, where he absorbed the lessons of the *Chicago School, and was influenced especially by an essay of *Sullivan (1892) in which the latter advocated refraining from all ornament for a period, so that architects could concentrate on the design of buildings 'well-formed and comely in the nude'. He was also influenced by the work of F. L. *Wright (whom he also met), by the English *Arts-and-Crafts movement, and by the designs of Otto *Wagner. Loos settled in Vienna, and in a series of articles denounced the ornamenting tendencies of *Jugendstil, notably in the works of *Hoffmann and *Olbrich, so he was opposed to aspects of the *Sezession. He likened extravagance and dishonesty in architecture to the fake fronts of streets in towns erected for show by Grigory Aleksandrovich Potemkin (1739–91) in Russia, publishing his views in the important journal *Ver Sacrum* (Sacred Spring) in 1898.

In 1908 came the publication of *Ornament und Verbrechen* (Ornament and Crime), in which he claimed that lack of ornament was a sign of spiritual strength: this has led to his beatification as a 'pioneer' of the *Modern Movement, but he was nothing of the sort, for his designs of the period are almost entirely Neoclassical in spirit, reflecting his admiration for Greek architecture and for *Schinkel. A prime example of this stripped Classicizing tendency is the Goldman & Salatsch block on the *Michaelerplatz*, Vienna (1909–11), with its simplified *Tuscan columns and unornamented façades using the finest materials, but nearly two years before, in 1907–8, his Kärntner Bar, Vienna, had demonstrated a type of stripped *Classicism, but using fine materials. The Steiner House, St-Veit-Gasse, Vienna (1910) is usually shown in a view from the garden, but the street-front, an almost single-storey symmetrical composition with a great curved roof, is hardly ever illustrated because it shows how Loos was deeply rooted in tradition, as it is an interpretation of a small *Baroque building stripped of ornament and with its curved roof simplified.

In both the Steiner and Scheu (Larochegasse 3, Hietzing—1912–13) Houses, Loos suggested exposed timber beams (they were not always structural), and drew heavily on the Arts-and-Crafts tradition of England (a country he greatly admired), with *inglenooks, brick fireplaces, and wooden panelling. His reverence for Greek architecture was expressed in his competition entry (1923) for the Chicago Tribune Building: his design was a *skyscraper shaped like a gigantic Greek *Doric column. For a brief period (1920–2) he was the Chief Architect for the City of Vienna's Housing Department, and produced several schemes, including proposals for a model estate at Heuberg. He designed a 'rowhouse with one wall' which he patented.

He spent the next five years in Paris, where he made contact with the leading figures of the avant-garde and built the celebrated house for Tristan Tzara (Avenue Junot 15, Paris XVIII—1925–6), which, like the *Michaelerplatz* building, had an innovative plan with the volumes divided up to form rooms of differing heights, but the architectural language was more stark, and followed Modernist tendencies. After he returned to Vienna in 1928 Loos designed a few houses, including the Moller House, Starkfriedgasse 19, Pötzleinsdorf, Vienna (1927–8), and the Müller House, Střešovická 33, Prague (1929–30), both of which had complex interiors with ingenious spatial planning, and had smooth rendered walls that were very much *de rigueur* as *International *Modernism acquired its essential language. In 1931, he designed houses for the Werkbund at Woinovichgasse 13–15–17–19, Vienna, also with stark geometries and white rendered walls. These late works appear to have influenced the younger generation of architects. Both *Neutra and *Schindler were among those who were profoundly affected by Loos's ideas before the 1914–18 war. His early writings on architecture and design (1897–1900) were collected as *Ins Leere Gesprochen* (Spoken into the Void—1921) and his later works (1900–30) as *Trotzdem* (In Spite Of—1931).

Arts Council of Great Britain (1985); Banham (1960); Gravagnuolo (1982); Hitchcock (1977); Kulka (1931); Leśnikowski (1996); Loos (1962); Münz and Künstler (1966); Safran and Wang (1985)

loricula. *See* hagioscope.

lorimer. *See* larmier.

Lorimer, Sir Robert Stodart (1864–1929). Scots architect. Articled to Rowand *Anderson, he later worked with *Bodley and *MacLaren. He commenced practice in Edinburgh in 1893 and established his reputation with a series of cottages in the *vernacular style, so much so that he was recognized by Hermann *Muthesius as one of the most significant architects of his time, doing for Scotland what R. N. *Shaw and his contemporaries had done for England a generation before. His interest in the *Arts-and-Crafts movement led him to design several distinguished country-houses (e.g. Rowallan, Ayrshire (1903), and Ardkinglass, Argyll (1906)), and by 1905 he was unassailable as the top architect in Scotland for restorations, renovations, garden design, and new houses. In 1906 he designed his first important church, St Peter's, Morningside, Edinburgh (completed 1929), followed by the Chapel of the Knights of the Thistle, St Giles's Cathedral, Edinburgh (1909—an exquisite work, earning him his Knighthood in 1911). He designed several memorials and war cemeteries, but his undisputed masterpiece is the Free *Gothic Scottish National War Memorial Chapel, Castle Rock, Edinburgh (1922–7).

Curl (1993); *DNB* (1937); Gray (1985); Gifford, McWilliam, and Walker (1984); Hussey (1931); Jervis (1984); Placzek (1982); Savage (1980)

L'Orme, Philibert de (1500/15–70). *See* Orme.

Lote, Stephen (*fl.* 1381–d. 1417 or 1418). English mason. He was warden under *Yeveley of the *lodge of St Paul's Cathedral, London (1381–2). He worked with Yeveley on the tombs of King Richard II (reigned 1377–deposed 1399) and his first Queen (Anne of Bohemia (1366–94)) in Westminster Abbey (1394–5). In 1400 he became the King's Master-Mason at Westminster and the Tower of London, and worked at Canterbury Cathedral, Kent, where he completed the *nave, built the *cloisters, continued work on the *transepts, and probably designed the *pulpitum (*c.*1410) and tomb of King Henry IV (reigned 1399–1413). He carried out works at Maidstone Church, Kent, and Rochester Bridge in the same county. He may have designed the *choir (destroyed) of Fotheringhay Church, Northamptonshire. Lote made the tomb of Edward, Duke of York (killed at Agincourt, 1415), for Fotheringhay (destroyed), and also, with Yeveley, the tomb of Simon Langham, Archbishop of Canterbury (d. 1376), in Westminster Abbey (1390s). He is also referred to as a 'latoner', indicating he made monumental funerary *brasses as well as stone tombs.

Harvey (1987)

lotus. Ornament based on one of several water-plants, including the Egyptian water-lily, the source of much architectural enrichment of the stylized, bud, flower, and leaf type. Ancient Egyptian *capitals decorated with both bud and flower motifs were common, and were revived in *Egyptian Revival design. The lotus is related to a great number of common decorative devices, including the *fleur-de-lys, the *palmette, and sundry Classical and medieval motifs.

Glazier (1926); Jones (1868)

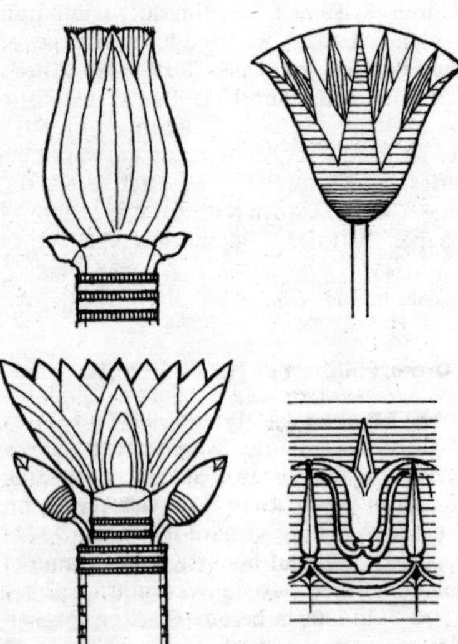

lotus. (*top left*) Ancient Egyptian lotus-bud. (*top right*) Ancient Egyptian stylized lotus flower. (*bottom left*) Ancient Egyptian lotus flower. (*bottom right*) Ancient Greek lotus ornament consisting of stylized flower and buds.

Loudon, John Claudius (1783–1843). Scots agriculturist, encyclopedist, landscape-gardener, horticulturist, editor of journals, expert on cemeteries, architect, and influential critic. He settled in London in 1803 and began a career of frenetic literary activity. His first book, *Observations on the Formation and Management of Useful and Ornamental Plantations, on the Theory and Practice of Landscape Gardening* . . . etc. came out in 1804, followed by *A Short Treatise on Several Improvements Recently Made in Hothouses* (1805), and *A Treatise on Forming, Improving, and Managing Country Residences* (1806), in which he revealed a passionate interest in architecture. About that time he began to do architectural work. On the death of his father he designed a Neoclassical monument in Pinner churchyard, Middlesex (1809), a vertical mass with two battered sides from which a *sarcophagus projects, as advanced as any architectural scheme could be for its date, *primitive, severe, and stripped.

In 1811 he invented an iron glazing-bar that made curved glazing possible and erected various prototype hot-houses incorporating his structural and other practical ideas. In 1817 he published *Remarks on the Construction of Hothouses* and in 1818 *Sketches of Curvilinear Hothouses* and *A Comparative View of the Common and Curvilinear Modes of Roofing Hothouses*. The principles that Loudon developed became the basis of the more famous works by *Paxton at Chatsworth (and ultimately at the Great Exhibition of 1851), of *Lanyon and Turner at Belfast, and Turner and *Burton at Kew, and were applied to countless conservatories and exhibition-buildings throughout C19 Europe and America.

Work then began on the enormous and immediately successful *Encylopaedia of Gardening* (1822), which enabled Loudon to design and build the 'double detached villa' for himself at 3 and 5 Porchester Terrace, London (1823–4), an advanced and convenient building of *Italianate Classical appearance. In 1826 he established *The Gardener's Magazine*, which had a profound effect on taste and expertise. In 1829 he proposed a Green Belt half-a-mile broad around London, the formation of national schools for compulsory education, and the beneficial use of sewage for agricultural purposes. In 1830 he brought out the first part of *Illustrations of Landscape-Gardening and Garden Architecture*, laid out the Botanic Gardens in Birmingham, and married the remarkable Jane Webb (1807–58), author of a futuristic novel (1827) about an England in C21, complete with universal air-travel, world-wide instant communication systems, intolerable burdens of taxation, and endemic inflation. John and Jane Loudon worked together on the *Encylopaedia of Cottage, Farm, and Villa Architecture* (1833). With its numerous illustrations (many by E. B. *Lamb) it played an important part in the formation of *Victorian suburban architectural taste as well as recording much that has proved ephemeral. From 1834 to 1838 the Loudons published *The Architectural Magazine*, the first British periodical solely devoted to architecture. As a landscape architect Loudon was influenced by Payne *Knight, *Repton, and Uvedale *Price, and himself advocated *Picturesque compositions. He invented the 'Gardenesque' style in which the Picturesque was combined with the display of trees and plants chosen for their botanical, scientific, and horticultural qualities. More than anyone he established the character of the Victorian garden, public park, and arboretum, and his design for the Derby Arboretum (1839–41) was a good example of his style.

His *On the Laying Out, Planting, and Managing of Cemeteries; and on the Improvement of Churchyards* (1843) is the most exhaustive book ever written on the subject, and includes detailed ideas for the landscaping of cemeteries that were very widely followed. Loudon's idea of the cemetery as a landscaped garden and arboretum, with all plants labelled, was part of his concept of mass-education and improvement of society. He produced designs for three cemeteries: Histon Road, Cambridge, the Bath Abbey Cemetery, and Southampton Cemetery (all 1842–3).

Curl (1993); Jervis (1984); Loudon (1834, 1981); MacDougall (1980); Simo (1988)

Loudon's hollow wall. Brick wall of two *leaves each of *Flemish bond* (*see* brick), the *stretchers* of which have a gap between them two inches (5.08 cm) apart, so the *headers* require a two-inch *closer* brick to make up the full width of the wall. A variant was to lay the headers without the closers, or to lay them so that they were only one inch back from each face, thus providing excellent *keys for plaster or *stucco rendering. The hollow could be heated for horticultural purposes. *Loudon also invented variations on other types of hollow wall, including improvements to *Dearn's* and *Silverlock's* bonds.

Brunskill (1990)

Louis, Louis-Nicolas-Victor (1731–1800). French Neoclassical architect. He designed several interiors in the *Louis Quinze style for the Royal Palace, Warsaw, in 1765, after which he returned to France and built the Governor's Residence, Besançon (1770–6), and several hôtels. His most influential building was the Grand Théâtre, Bordeaux (1773–80), with a huge *colonnade of the *Corinthian *Order running the width of the façade and a high foyer with symmetrical staircase, the grandest in any theatre to that date. The auditorium was a truncated circle on plan, surrounded by a *Giant *Composite Order, and there was an elliptical concert-room over the vestibule. There was much in the design that influenced the planning of later theatres, notably *Garnier's Opéra, Paris. He built several town- and country-houses, and designed the elegant colonnades and enclosing buildings for the Palais Royal Gardens, Paris (1780–5). His Théâtre du Palais Royal, later the Comédie-Française (1786–90—rebuilt), had wrought-iron trusses and hollow-clay-pot floors set in concrete, an early use of fire-resistant structure.

Braham (1980); Hautecœur (1952); Kalnein and Levey (1972); Lorentz and Rottermund (1984); Middleton and Watkin (1987); Pariset (1980)

Louis Quatorze. Style of French *Baroque and Classical architecture of the reign of King Louis XIV (1643–1715), beginning in the 1660s. Its great monuments are the Churches of the Sorbonne and the Val-de-Grâce, the Institut de France, and the east front of the Louvre, all in Paris, and, of course, the great *Château of Versailles.

Louis Quinze. Style of French Classical, *Rococo and early Neoclassical architecture of the reign of King Louis XV (1715–74), characterized by its extreme charm, lightness, and elegance. Apart from several exquisite schemes of Rococo interior decoration the characteristic buildings are the interior of the *Chapel at Versailles, the Châteaux at Nancy and Lunéville, the Panthéon, Paris, and the fine *palace-fronted buildings of the Place de la Concorde, Paris.

Louis Revivals. There were revivals of all four *Louis styles in C19 and C20.

Louis Seize. Style of Neoclassical architecture that really began during the reign of Louis XV, but evolved in that of Louis XVI (1774–92). It was marked by simplicity, even severity, manifest in its more extreme forms in the *barrières* of *Ledoux and in the same architect's *Salines* (Salt Works) *d'Arc-et-Senans* (1775–80). It also included exquisitely refined detail in schemes of interior design, much less exuberant in its use of ornament than during the previous reign.

Louis Treize. Style of French *Renaissance architecture coinciding with the reign of King Louis XIII (1610–43), but continuing until the 1660s, as *Le style* *Louis Quartorze did not really evolve until then. The best-known buildings of the period are the Luxembourg Palace and the west front of the Church of St-Gervais, both in Paris.

louvre, louver, luffer. **1.** Outlet for smoke in a roof. **2.** *Lantern or *femerell over such an outlet with openings at its sides. **3.** Structure on a roof for ventilation fitted with horizontal fixed *lever-*, *louvre-*, or *luffer-boards* sloping downwards and outwards, each board lapping over the one below, with a space between to exclude rain but allow the passage of air. **4.** Any opening fitted with sloping boards or *louvres*, especially the *belfry-stage of a church-tower.

low-side window. *See* lychnoscope.

Low Tech. Antithesis of *High Tech, it involves the recycling of materials and components and the use of traditional construction, insulation, and natural means of heating and ventilation. Low Tech recognizes the environmental damage done by High Tech through excessive use of resources, and has been applied to the circumstances of poverty-stricken areas, where it has been termed 'alternative', 'intermediate' and even 'utopian' technology. It might involve the harnessing of solar energy or the use of human wastes to generate energy and nutrient for the soil.

Ball and Cox (1982); Dickson (1974); Papanek (1985)

lozenge. *Diamond-* or *rhomboid*-shaped equilateral parallelogram with two opposite angles more acute than the other two. Lozenges occur in mouldings, on *diaper-patterns, in *jewelled *strapwork, in window-*lights subdivided by lead *cames (*see* lattice), and as small lights over *Gothic *lancet-lights in *tracery, in net-*vaults, and in many other instances.

lozenge-fret. *Diamond-fret*, or moulding of repeated lozenges, like a double *chevron occurring in *Romanesque or *Romanesque Revival work.

Lubetkin, Berthold (1901–90). Russian-born, he was the most influential Socialist architectural immigrant to Britain in the 1930s, bringing *International Modernism with him. He studied in Russia in the 1920s, then in Berlin and Warsaw, and finally with *Perret in Paris (1925–7). He worked with Jean Ernest Ginsberg (1905–83) in Paris (1927–30), where the apartment-block at 25 Avenue de Versailles, with its aggressive horizontal bands of windows, attracted hostility. Nevertheless, it was the prototype of Lubetkin's style in the 1930s.

He settled in London in 1931, and in 1932 became senior partner of *Tecton, a firm composed of former Architectural Association students. A founder-member of the *MARS Group, he was also involved with *CIAM. In 1932–3 Tecton built the Gorilla House, London Zoo, followed by the elegant Penguin Pool with its spiral concrete ramps designed in conjunction with Ove *Arup (1934). Other Zoo buildings at Whipsnade, Bedfordshire (1933–6), and Dudley, Worcestershire (1936–7), followed. The influential apartment-block, again designed with Arup, Highpoint I (1933–5), Highgate, London, was a paradigm for similar developments, followed by Highpoint II (1936–8), which, with elevations of patterns of brick, glass, and tile, suggested Tecton realized the white-painted flat surfaces of the International Modernist style were unsuited to London. The entrance-canopy seemed to be supported by a cast of one of the *caryatids from the Erechtheion in Athens, which some saw as a witty reference to *Classicism, but to others was either a vulgar manifestation of *Kitsch or a betrayal of Modernism.

Tecton's most celebrated building of the period was the Finsbury Health Centre, London (1935–8), an axially planned building that was widely photographed in a way that disguised its very small size. Both the Priory Green (1937–51) and Spa Green (1938–46) Estates in London were early paradigmatic slab-blocks. In 1948 Lubetkin was appointed Chief Architect to Peterlee New Town Development Corporation, Co. Durham, but his ideas for a high-density development were not realized and he resigned in 1950.

Coe and Reading (1981); Emanuel (1994); van Vynckt (1993)

lucarne, luthern. **1.** Elliptical, rectangular, segmental-headed, or semicircular-headed window, to illuminate a volume within a pitched roof. Its front is usually built of the same material as the wall of the building's main façade, is constructed on that wall, lines up with the *naked of the wall, and is positioned over the *entablature. It is distinct from a *dormer, which rises from the slope of a roof and is normally of light construction. **2.** Small gabled aperture on the sloping sides of a *Gothic *spire, constructed of the same material.

Lucas, Colin Anderson (1906–84). English architect and pioneer of *reinforced-concrete construction. He formed a company to build concrete structures in the style of *International Modernism, including Noah's House at Spade Oak Reach, Bourne End, Buckinghamshire (1930), and Hop Field House, St Mary's Platt, Wrotham, Kent (1933—with Amyas *Connell and Basil Ward (1902–76)). In 1933 he joined Connell and Ward to form Connell, Ward, & Lucas, and brought his expertise to the creation of a whole series of International Modernist houses (e.g. four houses, High and Over Estate, Amersham, Buckinghamshire (1934), the Gunn House, The Ridgeway, Westbury-on-Trym, Bristol (1936), the Tarburn House, Temple Gardens, Moor Park, Hertfordshire (1937–8), Walford House, 66 Frognal, Hampstead, London (1937) and Potcraft, Thomas House, Sutton, Surrey (1938)) unparalleled elsewhere in the country. After the 1939–45 war he worked in the Architects' Department of the London County Council, heading a team of young Modernists who designed, among much else, the Le *Corbusier-inspired Alton Estate West at Roehampton, London (1951–78), where the slab-blocks are on a very small scale yet superficially modelled on Le Corbusier's *Unités d'Habitation*.

Emanuel (1994)

Lucas, Thomas Geoffrey (1872–1947). *See* Lanchester, Mountford.

Luckhardt Brothers. Hans (1890–1954) and **Wassili** (1889–1972) worked mostly in Berlin where they were born, and were associated with Bruno *Taut in the 1920s and 1930s. After the 1914–18 war they shared their theoretical, *Expressionist ideas with others through the *Gläserne Kette (Glass Chain) circle, and from 1921 to 1954 practised as architects. They designed one of the first *Modern Movement housing estates at Dahlem-Berlin (1924), rapidly evolving an architecture of rectangular blocks with bands of horizontal windows that were such a feature of the *International Modern style. Their houses at Schorlemerallee, Berlin (1925–8), and three houses at Rupenhorn (1928) were constructed with steel frames and large areas of glazing. Some of their ideas were publicized in *Zur neuen Wohnform* (Towards New Design for Living—1930). Their Berlin Pavilion at the *Constructa* exhibition, Hanover (1951), was built of steel and glass in the manner of *Mies van der Rohe. After the death of Hans, his brother continued in practice, building the Bavarian Social Welfare Administration Centre, Munich (1957), the Plant Physiology and Veterinary Medicine Institute, Free University of Berlin (1962–70), and the Deputies' Assembly Hall, Bremen (1962–9).

Kliemann (1973); Kulturmann (1958)

Ludovice, João Frederico (*born* **Johann Friedrich Ludwig** (*c.*1670–1752)). German-born, he brought Italian *Baroque to Portugal, and became the leading C18 architect in that country. His greatest work was the Convent Palace at Mafra, near Lisbon (1717–30). The plan resembles that of the Escorial, Madrid, and, of course, reconstructions of Solomon's Temple in Jerusalem, but there are echoes of Central-European designs in the scheme, notably the Monasteries of Weingarten, Einsiedeln, and Göttweig. The Church at Mafra influenced other designs in Lisbon and Rio de Janeiro. He was also responsible for the sumptuously beautiful Library at the University of Coimbra (1716–23), and for the *apse at Évora Cathedral (1716–29), both in Portugal.

Carvalho (1960–2); Cruickshank (1996); Kubler and Soria (1959); van Vynckt (1993)

luffer. *See* louvre.

lug. **1.** Projecting plate, *ear, or *tab on either side of a pipe for fixing it to a wall. **2.** *Crossette.

Lundy, Victor Alfred (1923–). American architect, he trained under *Gropius and worked with *Breuer. He set up his practice in

New York in 1953. His best-known work was the I. Miller Shoe Salon, Fifth Avenue, New York (1961), where timber ribs and many mirrors were liberally employed. His various churches, such as the Westminster Unitarian, East Greenwich, RI (1964), relied on bold and simple elements. The US Tax Court, Washington, DC (1976), has a huge block cantilevered out to an uneasy extent.

Emanuel (1994)

lunette. 1. Portion of a vertical plane beneath a segmental or semicircular *vault running into it, bounded by the intrados and springing-line. **2.** Similar-shaped aperture bounded by an arch or vault, e.g. in a wall at the end of a barrel-vault or above a door set in an arched opening, possibly a *fanlight. **3.** *Tympanum in a segmental or semicircular *pediment. **4.** In a fortification a detached *bastion, usually shaped like a half-moon. **5.** Semicircular face of a *Romanesque *cushion-*capital formed by the shaping of its lower part to fit the circular *shaft.

Lurago, Rocco (1501–90). Italian architect, he spent most of his life in Genoa, where he was influenced by *Alessi. He built the Palazzo del Municipio (1564–6) on Alessi's Strada Nuova, cleverly planned as a series of terraces built on the steep hillside joined by grand staircases. *Bianco derived benefit from this scheme when designing his Jesuit College, now the University (1634–6).

Brinckmann (1915–19); Heydenreich and Lotz (1974); Watkin (1986)

Lurçat, André (1894–1970). French architect, he embraced the doctrines promoted by Le *Corbusier and others, and was a founding-member of *CIAM. He designed several villas and studios, including the Huggler House, Cité Seurat, Paris (1925–6), the Villa Michel, Versailles (1926), and the Guggenbuhl House, Paris (1927), all pioneering *Modern Movement works. A prolific polemicist, he promoted both Communism and Modernism with zeal, and at the École Karl-Marx, Villejuif (1931–3), attempted to associate architectural forms with the revolutionary workers' movement. Invited to Moscow in 1934, he carried the *Bauhaus and *CIAM positions there, only to find they did not fit into the Stalinist stance of Socialist Realism in which powerful, stripped *Neoclassicism loomed large. He accepted the need for monumentality in architecture imposed during the Stalin era (1925–53), as his later works, including his many buildings at St-Denis and Maubeuge (1946–50), demonstrate.

Giedion (1928); Lurçat (1929, 1953–7); Piccinato (1965); Sartoris (1936); Tafuri and Dal Co (1986); van Vynckt (1993)

luthern. *See* lucarne.

Lutyens, Sir Edwin Landseer (1869–1944). English architect. He began his career in the office of *George and *Peto, where he met Herbert *Baker. In 1889 he set up his own practice, and designed the house, gardens, and stables at Crooksbury, Surrey, influenced by works of George, Norman *Shaw, and Philip *Webb. Indeed, his early houses were pleasant *Arts-and-Crafts buildings incorporating Surrey *vernacular elements, e.g. steeply pitched tiled roofs, tall brick chimneys, and *casement-windows with *leaded *lights, but he began to achieve real distinction shortly after he met and began to collaborate with Gertrude Jekyll (1843–1932), the artist and gardener, who was to work with him on the design of many gardens over the next two decades. Jekyll commissioned Munstead Wood, Munstead, Surrey (1896–9), where Lutyens's use of finely crafted traditional building-materials and the subtle relationship between house and garden demonstrate a new sensitivity prompted by Jekyll's *Ruskin-inspired beliefs. Among his best houses of the late-Victorian period are Fulbrook, near Elstead (1897–9), Orchards, Munstead, near Godalming (1897–9), both in Surrey, and Roseneath, Dumbartonshire, Scotland (1898). At Les Bois des Moutiers, Varengeville-sur-Mer, France (1897–8), certain elements, such as the tall windows, pre-empted some of *Mackintosh's work, notably the Library windows at the Glasgow School of Art (1907–9).

With Tigbourne Court, Witley, Surrey (1899–1901), a new theme of Classically composed formal symmetry began to emerge. He again used vernacular motifs at Deanery Garden, Sonning, Berkshire (1899–1902), but the prominent axes connecting elements inside and outside the building had a similarity to ideas then being pursued by F. L. *Wright. For the same client, Edward Hudson (d. 1936), founder (1897) of *Country Life*, Lutyens reconstructed and reworked Lindisfarne Castle, Holy Island, Northumberland (1903–4). From around this time his work began to draw on a wider range of styles. At Little Thakeham,

Sussex (1902), for example, the exterior continued the vernacular late-*Tudor manner, but the interior, with its double-height hall and stair, contains Classical Mannerist elements. Classical *pilasters graced Homewood, Knebworth, Hertfordshire (1901), and aspects of *Mannerism were explored at Overstrand Hall, Cromer, Norfolk (1899–1901).

Then, with Heathcote, Ilkley, Yorkshire (1906), came a change of direction. The house is a *palazzo, with the *Doric *Order as used by *Sanmicheli at the Porta Palio, Verona (*c*.1545), but Lutyens made the *antae of the Order disappear into the walls, re-emerging only as *base and *capital (a device also used with *pilasters on many of his buildings, including the Midland Bank, Poultry, London (1924–39)). Heathcote marked the period when Lutyens was fired with enthusiasm for what he called the 'big game, the high game', of Classical architecture. He employed a *William-and-Mary style at Folly Farm, Sulhampstead, Berkshire (1906), while Nashdom, Taplow, Buckinghamshire (1905–8), was a vast pile in the early *Neo-Georgian style, and William-and-Mary was used with great sensitivity at The Salutation, Sandwich, Kent (1911), one of his most serene creations. Castle Drogo, Drewsteignton, Devon (1910–32), however, is an allusion to medieval domestic architecture, built of granite, with mullioned and transomed windows and powerfully composed interiors and stairs. For Hudson's *Country Life* offices at Tavistock Street, Covent Garden, London (1904), Lutyens drew on *Wren's work at Hampton Court Palace for the façade, and at Hampstead *Garden Suburb, London (1908–10), he designed the formal centre with two Churches, the Institute, and surrounding houses.

In 1912 Lutyens was appointed architect for the planning of New Delhi, India, and was joined by Baker, who was to design several of the buildings there. Together they created a magnificent *Beaux-Arts-inspired work of civic design centred on the huge Viceroy's House by Lutyens (1912–31): the latter, with its Private and State Rooms, planned with unerring skill, is an eloquent testament of Lutyens's greatness as an architect. Certain Indian architectural elements were incorporated, such as the *chatris and *chujjah; the dome was derived from a *stupa; and Lutyens invented a 'Delhi Order', a version of Roman Doric of different heights, the capitals all at one level, but the bases not. The gardens, too, were an ingenious synthesis of Eastern and Western themes.

Lutyens became one of the chief architects (with Baker, Reginald *Blomfield, and *Holden) to the Imperial War Graves Commission (from 1917). He designed many of the Cemeteries, including that at Étaples, France (1923–4), with twin arched pavilions carrying stone sculptured military standards and *cenotaphs on high *catafalques. He was also responsible for the Cenotaph, Whitehall, London (1919–20—a tall podium with subtle *entasis carrying a tomb-chest); for the Stone of Remembrance to be erected in the War Cemeteries; and for Memorials to the Missing, including that to the Missing of the Somme, at Thiepval (1927–32), a metamorphosis of the *triumphal arch with its subordinate sides also triumphal arches.

During the 1920s Lutyens's practice changed direction towards commercial buildings. His works included the Midland Bank, Piccadilly, London (1921–5); Britannic House, Finsbury Circus, London (1920–4); the Midland Bank, Manchester (late 1920s); and Offices in Pall Mall, London (1929). For the British Embassy, Washington, DC (1927–8), he employed an American Colonial Georgian style, and designed subtly detailed buildings at Magdalene College, Cambridge (1928–32), and Campion Hall, Oxford (1935–42). His later years were devoted to the design of the Roman Catholic Cathedral, Liverpool (from 1929), to be a huge building based on similar ideas to those of the Thiepval Memorial, the whole composition crowned by an enormous dome larger than that of St Peter's, Rome. Only part of the crypt was built (1933–41), but the *Sublime dark-brick vaults, inventive Orders, and Mannerist detail (including a keystone 'bending' a *transome) are impressive. Lutyens's greatest design was abandoned after the 1939–45 war, and *Gibberd's circular structure was erected instead. Lutyens also designed the Beatty and Jellicoe Memorial Fountains, Trafalgar Square, London (1937–9), and the Irish National War Memorial, Phoenix Park, Dublin (1930).

After his death Lutyens's reputation declined with the rise of *International Modernism, but began to revive after major exhibitions in New York (1978) and London (1981).

Amery *et al.* (1982); Brown (1982); Butler (1950); Gradidge (1981); Hussey (1989); Inskip (1979); Placzek (1982); Stamp (1977); Weaver (1981)

Luzarches, Robert de (d. *c*.1236). Master-mason, and presumably architect, of Amiens Cathedral from 1220. He started the *nave, and was succeeded (*c*.1235) by **Thomas de Cormont**, who designed the west front and the upper parts of the nave. In turn, he was succeeded by his son, **Regnault de Cormont** (master-mason *c*.1240–88), who was responsible for the *choir above the *tribune, crossing-vault, and *transept elevations, all in the *Rayonnant style of *Gothic.

Branner (1965); Sturgis *et al.* (1901–2)

lych-gate. Gateway, usually protected by a wide spreading pitched roof, sited at the main entrance to a burial-ground. It was customary for bearers carrying the coffin to rest beneath the gate while awaiting the officiating clergy.

lychnoscope. *Leper's squint, low-side window*, or *offertory-window*, an aperture set low in the south side of a *chancel-wall of a church near its west end, or sometimes on both sides of the chancel, or even occasionally in an *aisle-wall. Lychnoscopes are found in a great variety of shape and form, but there is no evidence that any were ever glazed. Instead, they were *shuttered from within and often protected by an iron grille without. The *cill of the opening on the inside was sometimes adapted as a seat (e.g. at Elsfield, Oxfordshire). They very often commanded a view of a *chantry-altar. Various explanations have been given as to the use of a lychnoscope: hearing confessions and giving Communion to lepers or other persons not permitted for whatever reason to enter the church; distributing alms; for sounding a bell during the Manifestation of the Host; and even for ventilation.

Lyming. *See* Lemyinge.

Lynn, William Henry (1829–1915). Irish architect, born in County Down. He was apprenticed to *Lanyon, and later (1854–72) became his partner. A gifted and assured *Gothic Revivalist, he was responsible for the Town Halls of Chester, Cheshire (1864–9), and Barrow-in-Furness, North Lancashire (1878–87). He favoured Italian Gothic, as both these buildings showed, and he used Venetian Gothic for the charming Banks he designed at Newtownards, Co. Down, and Dungannon, Co. Tyrone (both *c*.1855). Many of the Italian Gothic buildings built by Lanyon & Lynn and Lanyon, Lynn, & Lanyon owed much to his skills (notably the *polychrome Clarence Place Hall, May Street (1865–6), and Sinclair Seamen's Church, Corporation Square (1856–7), both in Belfast). He continued the work of construction at St Anne's Cathedral, Belfast, after *Drew's illness and death.

Brett (1967); Larmour (1987)

Lyons, Eric Alfred (1912–78). English *Modern Movement architect, he worked with many professionals, including *Gropius and *Fry, before setting up an office with Geoffrey Paulson Townsend (1911–) in 1945, a partnership that lasted until 1950, after which Lyons practised in London on his own before taking Ivor Richard Cunningham (1928–) into partnership in 1963. The firm specialized in designing speculative housing developments in a modern idiom, including the landscaping and planning of entire estates, e.g. the SPAN housing at Blackheath, London (1959–63), and Weybridge, Surrey (1964–5).

Emanuel (1994)

Macartney, Sir Mervyn Edmund (1853–1932). Son of a Co. Armagh, Ireland, family, he was born in London, was a pupil of Norman *Shaw, and a founder of the *Art-Workers' Guild. He began practice in 1882, his work showing Shaw's influence with a strong dash of late-C17 and early C18 architectural elements. Among his buildings, 169 Queen's Gate (1899), 1–6 Egerton Place (1893), and the Public Library, Essex Road, Islington (1916), all in London, may be mentioned, but he was better known for his publications, including *The Practical Exemplar of Architecture* (1908–27) and (with *Belcher) *Later Renaissance Architecture in England* (1898–1901), which celebrated the riches of English architecture in the age of *Wren. He was Editor of *The Architectural Review* (1905–20), and, as Surveyor to St Paul's Cathedral, London, carried out important works of *conservation on Wren's building (1906–31), including the strengthening of the *dome.

Davey (1980); Gray (1985); Macartney (1907–27, 1908); Macartney and Belcher (1901)

McCarthy, James Joseph (1817–82). Arguably Ireland's greatest *Gothic Revival architect, called the 'Irish Pugin'. Dublin-born, he flourished during the impressive building-programme of the Irish Roman Catholic Church after 'Catholic Emancipation' (1829), designing in a robust *First and *Second Pointed style, following the lead of Pugin and the Ecclesiologists in England.

He may have been in England during the early 1840s, but in 1846 work started on his Church of St Kevin, Glendalough, Co. Wicklow. In a severe *First Pointed style, it was the first attempt by a native-born Irish architect to build a church on *Ecclesiological principles. McCarthy was one of the three joint-secretaries of the Irish Ecclesiological Society, founded in 1849, and he published *Suggestions on the Arrangement and Characteristics of Parish Churches* (1851). In 1853 he was appointed Architect to the Armagh Roman Catholic Cathedral in succession to Thomas *Duff of Newry, Co. Down. Although the building was well advanced, McCarthy changed Duff's *Perpendicular to *Second Pointed in accordance with Ecclesiological preferences, added the two western *steeples, omitted the *crossing-tower, and increased the pitch of the roof. In the process he changed the character from English Perpendicular to a pronouncedly French Gothic, reflecting his growing Irish Nationalism by adopting non-English exemplars. He built many churches in Dublin (St Saviour's, Dominic Street, is the finest) and Co. Kerry, drawing on the great wealth of Irish ecclesiastical remains for the elements of his designs. Occasionally he made forays into *Romanesque revival, as at the *chapel, Glasnevin Cemetery, Dublin (finished 1878), but most of his work is assured Continental Gothic, as at St Patrick's, Dungannon, Co. Tyrone (1870–6), the Chapel, Maynooth College, Co. Kildare (1875–1903), and St Macartan's Cathedral, Monaghan (1861–92).

Sheehy (1977)

McCormick, William (Liam) Henry Dunlevy (1916–96). Irish architect. He made his reputation with a series of *Modernist churches for the Roman Catholic Church, including the circular St Aengus, Burt (1964–7), the fan-shaped St Michael, Creeslough (1970–1), both in Co. Donegal, the circular St Patrick, Clogher, Co. Tyrone (1979), and the rectangularly planned St Conal, Glenties, Co. Donegal (1974–5).

Journal of the Royal Society of Ulster Architects, 5/2 (Nov./Dec. 1996), 30–43

McCoy, Esther (1904–89). American self-taught architectural historian and critic. She worked in *Schindler's office, which gave her insights about the architectural world, before publishing *Five California Architects* and *Richard Neutra* in 1960, which established her name, encouraging her to produce further work on the California avant-garde from the early C20. She was also a novelist, and contributed hundreds of articles to various books, journals, and exhibition catalogues, all demonstrating her mastery of taut prose. She was successful in relating social history to architecture, and she was emboldened to argue that the *Modern Movement developed in America at least as early as in Europe. In her work on Californian architecture she succeeded in revealing the significance in ordinary and familiar things, and her analyses showed how important modest architecture can be.

McCoy (1960, 1962, 1968, 1974, 1975, 1977, 1979, 1983, 1989, 1990); McCoy and Goldstein (1982); *Progressive Architecture*, 71/2 (Feb. 1990), 118–19

McGrath, Raymond (1903–77). Australian architect. He designed the *Modernist interior of Fischer's Restaurant, New Bond Street, London (1932), and, with *Chermayeff and *Coates, the interiors of BBC Broadcasting House, London. He published *Twentieth Century Houses* (1934—which promoted *International Modernism for domestic architecture), and, with Al Frost, *Glass in Architecture and Decoration* (1937). His best houses are St Anne's Hill, Chertsey, Surrey, a *reinforced-concrete building (1937–8), and Carrygate, Galby, Leicestershire (1938–42). In 1940 he joined the Office of Public Works, Dublin, becoming Principal Architect (1948–68), after which he returned to private practice. He designed a house, St Anne's, Carrickmines, Co. Dublin (1974), and the new Headquarters of the Royal Hibernian Academy, Dublin (1979).

Architectural Review, 162 (July 1977), 58–64; *Architecture Australia*, 67 (May 1978) 72; McGrath (1934); McGrath and Frost (1937); O'Donovan (1998)

machicolation. Space between the *corbels carrying a parapet that is set in front of the *naked of a fortified wall or tower to enable missiles to be dropped on any attacker below.

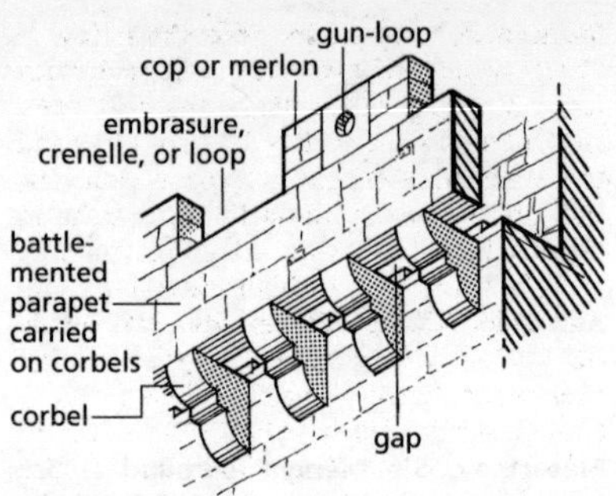

machicolation (*JJS*)

Machine Aesthetic. Architecture that suggested something machine-made, acknowledging industrialization, mass-production, and engineering, or that used elements of metal structures (ships, aeroplanes, motor-cars, etc.) in an eclectic fashion, more a matter of arriving at an *appearance* than of actually *being* what it seemed, a fact that contradicted demands for honesty and truth in architecture, and denied the logic of structural principles. *International Modernism tended to use smooth wall-finishes and long strips of metal-framed windows suggested by ocean-going liners of the *Titanic* vintage, but the walls were often of rendered brickwork.

Architectural Review, 78 (Dec. 1935), 211–18; Banham (1960); Giedion (1969); Johnson (1969); Sparke (1981); Wilson *et al.* (1986)

Machuca, Pedro (*c.*1485–1550). Spanish architect, he designed the great Palace of Charles V (Emperor 1519–55, d. 1558) in the Alhambra, Granada (1527–68), in an accomplished Italian *Renaissance style worthy of *Raphael or *Bramante. The circular colonnaded court is especially fine.

Chueca Goitia (1953); Rosenthal (1985)

McIntire, Samuel (1757–1811). American architect and builder, he worked in and near Salem, Massachusetts, producing a number of well-mannered houses in an elegant late-*Georgian style, mostly of three storeys. His sources appear to have been pattern-books, including those of *Langley and *Ware, and he was certainly familiar with *Palladianism, for he used that style at the Peirce-Nichols House (1782). The influence of *Bulfinch, from whose work he seems to have been introduced to the *Adam style, was evident in many of his domestic designs (e.g. the John Gardner House (1804–5), a refined composition with an entrance-porch bowing outwards).

Kimball (1966*a*); Labaree (1957); Whiffen and Koeper (1983)

Mackay, David John (1933–). *See* MBM Arquitectes.

Mackenzie, Alexander Marshall (1847–1933). Scots architect. He practised with James Matthews (1820–98) in Aberdeen from 1877, designing Greyfriars Church (1906) and the Marischal College (1904–6) in that city, the latter an extraordinarily hard essay in *Perpendicular *Gothic, all in granite. In 1903 he was joined by his Paris-trained son, **Alexander George Robertson Mackenzie** (1879–1963) with whom he designed the fine *Beaux-Arts Classical Waldorf Hotel (1906–7) and Australia House (1913–18), both in Aldwych, London. The latter was in the Imperial-Classical style that was widely used throughout the Empire, notably by *Palmer & Turner.

Gray (1985)

McKim, Mead, & White. American architectural partnership, the most distinguished of its time, based in New York. Charles Follen McKim (1847–1933), William Rutherford Mead (1846–1928), and Stanford White (1853–1906) were in the vanguard of a return to *Classicism in the USA. McKim and White had worked in *Richardson's office, and McKim had attended the École des *Beaux-Arts in Paris. At first the firm's work drew on American *Colonial architecture and then Italian High *Renaissance was added to the palette of styles, as was evidenced by the six houses for Henry Villard, Madison Avenue, New York (1882–5). However, White's taste for the *Picturesque and for variety in colour and texture led to the creation of a great number of buildings in the *Shingle style, partly derived from American Colonial prototypes, and influenced by the English *Domestic Revival of the *Arts-and-Crafts movement, with a dash of rural French medieval buildings. The study of Renaissance buildings led to geometries becoming more formal, as in the beautiful William G. Low House, Bristol, RI (1886–7).

Then came the Boston Public Library (1887–8), with a façade treatment derived from *Labrouste's Bibliothèque Ste-Geneviève, Paris, but given a more Italian Roman flavour. This celebrated design made the firm's reputation. Madison Square Garden, New York (1887–91—demolished), had a pronounced Sevillian flavour in its tall tower, but the Rhode Island State Capitol, Providence (1891–1903), was influenced by the Federal Capitol in Washington, DC, with a *Wrenaissance dome. At Columbia University, New York (1893–4), both the New Sorbonne in Paris and *Jefferson's University of Virginia, Charlottesville, were precedents for the plan, and the Library Building, with its *Pantheon dome and long *portico of *Ionic columns, entered the language of *Neoclassicism. This growing interest in Antiquity reached its apogee in the enormous and brilliant Pennsylvania Station, New York (1902–11—destroyed), with the gigantic hall based on the *thermae of Caracalla, Rome. It not only worked extremely well, but was the most *Sublime work of architecture in the USA—its destruction was a grievous loss, as was the demolition of the perfect Madison Square Presbyterian Church, New York (1904–6), another variant on the Pantheon theme, but with *polychrome enrichment. The *Georgian Revival Symphony Hall, Boston (1892–1901), was much more subdued, but the series of great works of the three decades 1880–1910 (including the very fine J. Pierpont Morgan Library, New York (1902–7)) put McKim, Mead, & White in the forefront of world architects of their time.

Stanford White was shot dead in 1906 in public in Madison Square Garden by a jealous husband. The ensuing publicity did enormous damage, and McKim died in 1909. However, the firm itself survived well into the second half of C20, and its achievements were celebrated in *A Monograph of the Works of McKim, Mead, & White, 1879–1915* (1915 and 1973).

Architectural Record, 20 (1906), 153–246; Baldwin (1976); Hitchcock (1977); Placzek (1982); Reilly (1972); Roth (1973, 1983); Wilson (1983); Wodehouse (1988)

Mackintosh, Charles Rennie (1868–1928). Scots architect, interior designer, and watercolourist, he worked mostly in and around Glasgow. In 1889 he joined *Honeyman & *Keppie and studied at the Glasgow School of Art. In 1891 he travelled in Italy, and in the following year, with Margaret (1865–1933) and Frances (1874–1921) Macdonald and Herbert J. McNair (1868–1953), began to produce watercolours, posters, and artefacts. The friends became known as 'The Four', 'The Mac Group', the *Glasgow School, or the 'Spook School' (the last because of the attenuated *femme-fleur, long tendrils, *rose-balls, and other slightly sinister elements that were an integral part of their *Art Nouveau-inspired style). In 1897 they gained recognition in *The Studio*, which made their work known to the avant-garde in America, Austria, and Germany.

Mackintosh's first built work for Honeyman & Keppie seems to have been the tower of the *Glasgow Herald* Building, Mitchell Street, Glasgow (1893). This was followed by Queen Margaret's Medical College (1894–6) and the Martyr's Public School (1895), both essentially traditionally constructed, but in a free style. Mackintosh began to draw on Scottish *vernacular buildings for his inspiration, often looking to medieval tower-houses and fortified dwellings (which he misnamed *Scottish Baronial) for his themes. His sources were not exclusively Scottish, however, and in later buildings his *eclecticism ranged more widely. In essence, Mackintosh was an *Arts-and-Crafts designer who used Art Nouveau decorative devices, but always employed traditional forms of construction of his native land.

In 1896 Honeyman & Keppie won the competition for the new Glasgow School of Art, but the design was Mackintosh's. The plan worked well, and the studios were lit by large north-facing windows, while the centrepiece had vernacular canted bay-windows derived from Dorset (or perhaps from *Voysey's work), Art Nouveau elements, and an arched feature paraphrasing certain English *Wrenaissance motifs. While the School was being built (1897–9), Mackintosh was commissioned to design fittings and decorations for Miss Cranston's Tea Rooms, and this was followed by Queen's Cross Church, Garscube Road (1897–1900), in a free Arts-and-Crafts *Gothic style with touches of Art Nouveau. In 1899–1902 came his first important house, Windy Hill, Kilmacolm, Renfrewshire, and some of his furniture designs were published in *Dekorative Kunst* (Decorative Art—1898 and 1899). In 1900 Mackintosh married Margaret Macdonald, and the couple decorated their apartment at 120 Mains (now Blythswood) Street, Glasgow, with white, elegant furniture and all fittings designed by themselves (now in the Hunterian Art Gallery, University of Glasgow). Together, they participated in the *Sezession Exhibition in Vienna, where their work was well received, and they became friendly with *Hoffmann and other Sezessionists. Indeed, in 1901 the Sezession journal *Ver Sacrum* (Sacred Spring) publicized Glasgow and Mackintosh, and the latter won a special prize for his *Haus eines Kunstfreundes* (House for an Art-Lover) in a competition organized in 1900 by *Koch, publisher of *Zeitschrift für Innen-Dekoration* (Journal of Interior Design): this design (to which Margaret Macdonald contributed) was published (1902), and built at Bellahouston Park, Glasgow, in the 1980s and 1990s.

In 1902, having designed the Scottish section at the International Exhibition of Decorative Art in Turin, Mackintosh was commissioned to design Hill House, Helensburgh, probably his finest achievement in domestic architecture. The exterior is completely harled (finished with a rough rendering), and beautiful interiors have panelled or stencilled walls: the white bedroom is one of Mackintosh's most felicitous creations. Then came the Willow Tea Rooms of Miss Cranston, the first of which (1903–19) was in Sauchiehall Street, Glasgow. Mackintosh's domestic work was featured in *Muthesius's *Das Englische Haus* (The English House—1904–5 and 1908–11), while Muthesius and other commentators wrote up Mackintosh's designs in *Deutsche Kunst und Dekoration* (German Art and Decoration) and *Dekorative Kunst*, all of which made his name and the Glasgow School widely known.

Perhaps influenced by the Germans and Austrians, Mackintosh began to adopt a more formal, angular geometry from around 1904, gradually discarding the curving lines of Art Nouveau. For example, his Scotland Street School, Glasgow (1904), was influenced by castle architecture, and is a symmetrical building with two conical-roofed staircase-towers flanking the stone front: the traditional arrangement is reversed, however, for the *curtain-wall is solid, pierced by windows, and the towers are glazed. In 1906 it was decided to complete the Glasgow School of Art, and Mackintosh revised the original design for the west end, with tall vertical *oriel windows perhaps suggested by *Lutyens's Les-Bois-des-Moutiers (1898), while on the south side the windows were recessed, and a cantilevered conservatory was introduced, suggested, no doubt, by Scottish *bartizans on castles such as Claypotts. This western extension contains Mackintosh's library, where his angular style is eloquently exhibited in the galleried timber construction, suggesting an almost Japanese economy of means.

Mackintosh became a partner in the firm, probably in 1902, although this was not made public until 1904 when Honeyman, Keppie, & Mackintosh was established, but by 1909 his career as an architect was foundering, not least because his criticism of the profession alienated his colleagues. He was also suspect among English Arts-and-Crafts architects because his work was tainted with 'decadent' Art Nouveau, and because he does not appear to have been overly concerned with honesty or soundness in construction, and so offended purists who held to the views promoted by A. W. N. *Pugin, William *Morris, and others. He left the practice in 1913, and after a period in Walberswick, Suffolk (1914–15), the Mackintoshes settled in Chelsea, London.

In 1916 'CRM' was commissioned by Wenman Joseph Bassett-Lowke (1877–1953) to alter and furnish his house at 78 Derngate, Northampton, which he did, introducing a repeated triangular motif suggested by trends in Viennese design. The guest bedroom (*c*.1919—now in the Hunterian Art Gallery, Glasgow), with its startling linear, striped, and black-white-ultramarine colour-scheme, was illustrated in *The Ideal Home* (1920), and had affinities with designs by *Loos and *Behrens. Some of the triangular stencilled patterns for Derngate may have been suggested by F. L. *Wright's Dana House, Springfield, Ill. (1903), published in Berlin (1911). From 1914 Mackintosh had been producing exquisite drawings and watercolours, and from 1923 to 1927 concentrated on painting.

He has been proclaimed since the 1930s as a kind of proto-Modernist, but this does not stand up to serious examination. He had far more in common with fin-de-siècle *Jugendstil and the Sezessionists in Vienna, Berlin, and Munich, and it was there that his work was best appreciated.

Billcliffe (1977); Cooper (1984); Ferguson (1995); Howarth (1977); MacLeod (1983); Nuttgens (1988); Phaidon, *Architecture in Detail, Glasgow School of Art* (1992); Placzek (1982); Robertson (1995); Steele (1994); van Vynckt (1993); Wilhide (1995); Young (1968)

Mackmurdo, Arthur Heygate (1851–1942). London-born architect and designer. His first work was influenced by Norman *Shaw but he also drew on Italian *Renaissance, *Queen Anne, and *Wrenaissance styles. He founded the Century Guild, based on *Arts-and-Crafts principles (1882), which made well-designed artefacts, including furniture. These were featured in *The Hobby Horse* from 1884, which influenced *Voysey and *Mackintosh. In some of his designs, notably the title-page of *Wren's City Churches* (1883), early *Art Nouveau forms were overt. His buildings include 6 and 8 Private Road, Enfield, Middlesex (1872–7), and 109–13, Charterhouse Street, London (1900).

Lambourne (1980); Pevsner (1968); Pevsner and Richards (1973); Stansky (1996)

MacLaren, James Marjoribanks (1853–90). Scots *Arts-and-Crafts architect. He established a London practice in 1886 with Richard Coad (1825–1900), following a short stay in E. W. *Godwin's office. After a new wing for Stirling High School, Scotland (1887–8), MacLaren designed several farm-buildings and cottages at Fortingall, Perthshire (1889–90—including the tenant-farmer's house), and Aberfeldy Town Hall, in all of which the Scottish *vernacular roots of the designs were clear, and provided precedents for *Mackintosh's domestic work. He designed some original houses, including 10–12 Palace Court, Bayswater, London (1889–90), and Heatherwood, Crawley Down, Sussex (1890–1). W. N. *Dunn and Robert Watson (1865–1916) continued the practice as Dunn & Watson, later taking W. Curtis *Green into partnership (1900).

Dixon and Muthesius (1985); Service (1975, 1977)

Maclure, Samuel (1867–1929). Canadian architect. He designed a large number of interesting houses in the *Shingle style in and around Victoria, British Columbia, from 1890 until his death. He later favoured Tudoresque *Arts-and-Crafts detailing, and the best examples that survive include the Biggerstaff-Wilson House (1905–6), with its natural materials, careful siting, and plan of two axes meeting in the stairway and hall. With Cecil Croker Fox (1879–1916), who had worked in *Voysey's office, he designed several successful houses, including the Huntting House, Vancouver, British Columbia (1911). After the 1914–18 war he was influenced by the Classical work of *Lutyens.

Kalman (1994)

McMorran & Whitby. British firm of architects (Donald Hanks McMorran (1904–65) and George Whitby (1916–73)) which produced work of real architectural distinction after the 1939–45 war. Influenced partly by Vincent *Harris (for whom McMorran worked from 1927 to 1935) and mostly by *Lutyens, the firm's architecture could best be described as undoctrinaire *Classicism. Good examples include Devon County Hall, Exeter (1957–64), and the extension to Shire Hall, Bury St Edmunds, Suffolk (1968). Their housing estate at Lammas Green, Sydenham Hill (1957), London, used traditional materials and had a village-like character totally different from that of contemporary local-authority estates elsewhere in London, while their Holloway Estate, Parkhurst Road (late 1950s), London, was also far more successful than the much-publicized *Modern Movement estates of the time, both socially and architecturally. Among McMorran & Whitby's works of the 1950s were the designs for the University of Nottingham (Cripps and Lenton Halls and the Education Block for Social Sciences), which employ a *stripped Classical manner inspired by *Soane, with a baseless *Ionic Order at the entrance to the internal courtyard, and a fine bell-tower with Lutyensian echoes over the Refectory. Other buildings include those in the City of London: the Police Station, Wood Street (1966), and the extension to the Central Criminal Court in the Old Bailey (1972). Although their work of late has been largely ignored by architectural historians, they were masters of a progressive Classicism that is beginning to be admired.

Modern Painters, 4/4 (1991), 56–61; information from Dr Gavin Stamp

Maderno, Carlo (*c*.1556–1629). Leading architect working in Rome from the mid-1570s, before *Bernini, *Borromini, and *Cortona developed the *Baroque style to its greatest potential. He started under D. *Fontana, his uncle, and was involved in the re-erection of the Ancient Egyptian *obelisks at Piazza di San Pietro (1586), Piazza dell'Esquilino (1587), Piazza di San Giovanni in Laterano (1588), and Piazza del Pòpolo (1589). He worked on a number of engineering projects before designing his masterpiece, the remodelling of the Church of Santa Susanna on the Quirinal Hill (1593–1603), with a dramatic *façade based on that of *Il Gesù*, but with an *engaged lower *Order and *scrolls linking the narrower upper pilaster façade to the wider front below. Emphasis was more decisive and vertical than at *Il Gesù*. After the election of Pope Paul V (1605–21) Maderno was appointed Architect to St Peter's, where he constructed the *nave (1609–16), began work on the decorations of the *crossing, built the curving stairs leading to the *confessio, designed the façade facing the Piazza (its great width was occasioned by the enforced requirement to add two *campanili of which only the first two stages were built), and created the fountain (later moved to the cross-axis of the obelisk and duplicated with a twin by Bernini).

At the Mother-Church of the Theatines, Sant'Andrea della Valle, Maderno completed the nave, added the *transepts and *chancel, and constructed the distinguished and beautiful dome with *lantern (1608–*c*.1628). He also designed the façade, begun in the mid-1620s, and completed with modifications by *Rainaldi in the 1660s. He was responsible for the Palazzo Mattei di Giove, Rome (1598–1617), and the Villa Aldobrandini, Frascati (1603–*c*.1620), including the superb semicircular water-theatre featuring arched *niches with *grottoes and fountains fed by a chain of stepped cascades at the top of which is a pair of spiral columns. One of his last works was the Palazzo Barberini, Rome (1626–8), completed by Bernini.

Hibbard (1971); Murray (1969, 1986); Placzek (1982); van Vynckt (1993)

Maekawa *or* **Mayekawa, Kunio** (1905–86). Japanese architect. He worked for Le *Corbusier and *Raymond before setting up on his own in 1935. He brought *International Modernism to Japan, and was a pioneer there of *reinforced-concrete construction, prompted by the ideas of *Nervi. His work was strongly modelled, including Kyoto Cultural Hall (1958–60) and Tokyo Metropolitan Festival Hall (1958–61), and influenced later generations including *Tange. Other buildings include the City Museum, Fukuoka (1979), the Prefectural Museum, Miyagi (1980), and the Concert Hall, Kunitachi College (1983).

Curtis (1996); Emanuel (1994); Lampugnani (1988); van Vynckt (1993)

Maher, George Washington (1864–1926). American architect of the *Prairie School, influenced by the English *Arts-and-Crafts movement. His work, mostly domestic, was refined, well made, and decently composed, some reminiscent of *Greene & Greene, and some of Frank Lloyd *Wright.

Brooks (1972); Kaplan (1987)

Maiano Brothers. C15 Florentine architects. **Giuliano da Maiano** (1432–90) designed the Chapel of Santa Fina in the Collegiata, San Gimignano (1466), where he was influenced by *Brunelleschi and *Michelozzo, and the Palazzo Spannocchi, Siena (1473), where the watered-down themes derived from *Alberti's

Palazzo Rucellai, Florence. In Florence itself he probably designed the *portico of Brunelleschi's Pazzi Chapel (1472), and in 1474 was called to Faenza where he designed the Cathedral. From 1485 he worked in Naples and built the Porta Capuana and the Villa di Poggio Reale (*c*.1488—destroyed), one of the most important early *Renaissance villas derived from Classical sources which later influenced *Peruzzi at the Villa Farnesina, Rome (1509–11).

Giuliano had two brothers, **Giovanni** (1438–78) and **Benedetto** (1442–97). The latter collaborated with Giuliano at the Gimignano Chapel, may have designed the portico of Santa Maria delle Grazie, Arezzo (1490–1), and was involved in the construction of the Palazzo Strozzi, Florence, which was mostly *Cronaca's work.

Heydenreich and Lotz (1974); Pampaloni (1963); Placzek (1982); van Vynckt (1993)

Maillart, Robert (1872–1940). Swiss engineer who evolved designs for bridges using curved *reinforced-concrete members. He also designed columns with mushroom-shaped tops to support floor-slabs which he used in the Giesshübel Warehouse, Zurich (1910). It is for his bridges that he will be remembered, notably the Valtschielbach, Donath (1925), and Salginatobel, Schiers (1930), bridges, both in Switzerland, where elegance of form and economy of means combine.

Abel *et al.* (1973); Bill (1969); Billington (1990); Collins (1973*a*); Morgan and Naylor (1987)

Maillou, *called* **Desmoulins, Jean-Baptiste** (1668–1753). French-Canadian, he became the principal architect, with the title of King's Architect of New France, working in Quebec in the first half of C18. His buildings included the Hôpital-Général, Quebec (1710–12), the façade of St-Laurent, Île d'Orléans (1708), the Church and Vestry of St-Nicolas, Quebec (*c*.1720), and many fortifications and other buildings.

Gowans (1955); Kalman (1994)

Maitani, Lorenzo (*c*.1270–1330). Sienese architect, he worked under *Pisano at the Cathedral there before being called to Orvieto Cathedral in 1310, where he enlarged the *transepts and designed the west front, a fine example of Italian *Gothic. He carried out other commissions, and was to all intents and purposes City Architect of Orvieto.

White (1987)

Majewski, Hilary (1837–97). Polish architect of most of the vast and extraordinary Poznański cotton-factory and housing complex, Łódź, Poland (from 1872). The adjacent palace (by A. Seligson) was in a *Beaux-Arts *Renaissance style, while the factory and houses were in a mixture of *Rundbogenstil and *Gothic. The entrance-gates had stunted, massive, deformed, vaguely *Tuscan columns carrying the pointed arches over which were brick *battlements and other decorations.

Cruickshank (1996)

majolica. 1. Fine Italian pottery coated with opaque white enamel ornamented with metallic colours. **2.** Any kind of glazed coloured earthenware or *faïence, also called *Raffaella* ware.

Maki, Fumihiko (1928–). Japanese architect. Like many of his generation, he experimented with aspects of Western *Modernism. He was associated with the start of *Metabolism in 1960. The National Museum of Modern Art, Kyoto (1978–86), was typical of his work during the 1960s and 1970s, with its powerful sculptural forms and formal language, clearly influenced by American architects, notably *Sert. Japanese conceptual ideas played an increasing role in his work, such as the intersection of two different grid-systems to express incompleteness, found in the Toyota Memorial Museum, Kuragaike, Toyota (1974). Later works include the Center for the Arts, Yerba Buena Gardens, San Francisco, Calif. (1991–3), YKK Research Centre, Sumida-ku, Tokyo (1993), the Kinishima Concert Hall, Aira, Kagoshima (1993–4), the Isar Büro Park, Munich, Germany (1993–5), and the Shonan Fujisawa Campus, Keio University (1994).

Emanuel (1994); Jodidio (1997*a*); Kurokawa (1977); Maki (1972)

Makovecz, Imre (1935–). Hungarian architect, he has been influenced by the work of F. L. *Wright and by the ideas of Rudolf *Steiner. The Roman Catholic Church, Paks, Hungary (1987–9), seems to grow from the earth within a huge *ogee-shaped roof pierced by pointed windows. Three spires, carrying a crescent, a symbol of the sun, and a Latin cross, rise up from the almost animal-like shape. His work draws on primitive shapes, forms, and naturally occurring elements, and includes the Naturata Shop Restaurant, Überlingen, Germany (1992), and the Hungarian Pavilion, Expo 92, Seville, Spain (1992—with seven church-like spires rising through the roof).

Emanuel (1994); Meyhöfer (1995)

Malevich, Kasimir Severinovich (1878–1935). Russian artist, he built many architectural models of projects that would have been difficult to show graphically, and was a pioneer of *Suprematism. He influenced El *Lissitzky and activities in the *Bauhaus.

Malevich (1959); Zhadova (1982)

Mallet-Stevens, Rob(ert) (1886–1945). French architect. He collaborated with *Bourgeois, *Chareau, and *Jourdain on various projects before setting up his own practice in 1920. He was influenced by *Hoffmann and *Mackintosh before the 1914–18 war, but the Pavilion of Tourism at the Paris Exposition International des Arts-Décoratifs (1924–5) gained him a position as one of the leading exponents of *Art Deco. He is best known for his apartments and other buildings in the Rue Mallet-Stevens, Paris (1926–7), where certain *Cubist elements occurred, and later he was a pioneer of *International Modernism.

Emanuel (1994); Jervis (1984); Mallet-Stevens (1922, 1929, 1937)

Mallows, Charles Edward (1864–1915). English *Arts-and-Crafts architect practising from 1892 in Bedford. A gifted draughtsman, he produced many architectural perspectives, and in 1898 he took George H. Grocock (*fl.* 1892–1904) into partnership. His finest work was for houses and gardens, including Three Gables, King's Corner, and White Cottage, all at Biddenham, Bedford (1899–1900), and Tirley Garth, Tarporley, Cheshire (1907).

Gray (1985)

Maltese cross. *See* cross.

Malton, William de (*fl.* 1335–8). English mason. He was master-mason at Beverley *Minster, Yorkshire, from 1335, where he supervised the completion of the *nave. He appears to have designed the tomb of Lady Eleanor Percy there (1340), reckoned to be one of the finest creations of English C14 funerary architecture of its type before the Black Death. He built the north *aisle and wall-*arcade at Beverley, and may also have worked at York Minster and Bainton Church, Yorkshire, in the 1320s.

mandala, mandorla. 1. Almond-shaped figure composed of two vertical arcs each passing through the other's centre, enclosing a panel, called *aureole, *halo, or *vesica piscis, and often found in a *Gothic *tympanum of a *doorway. **2.** Geometrical figure with a centre, such as a circle, polygon, or square, usually in the form of a *labyrinth or *maze with symbolic meanings.

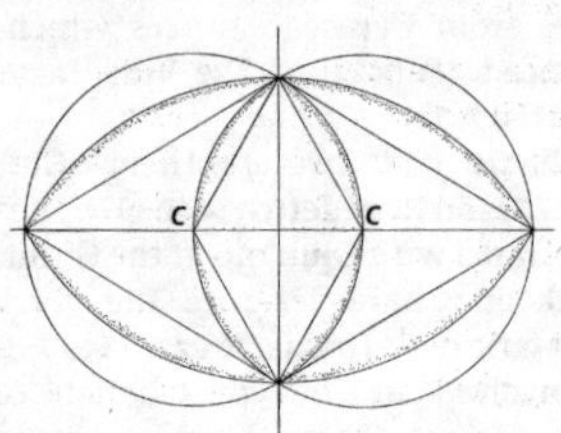

mandala. Diagram showing how almond-shaped form (related to equilateral triangles) is described. *c*: centres of two circles passing through each other.

Mangiarotti, Angelo (1921–). Italian architect. Much influenced by *Mies van der Rohe and *Nervi, he evolved refined systems for building using prefabricated concrete units. With Bruno Morassutti (1920–) he designed the starkly simple Mater Misericordiae Church, Baranzate (1957), and on his own the Marmi and Machine Offices and Exhibition Building, Carrara (1989–92).

Emanuel (1994)

Mannerism. C16 style of architecture from the period of *Michelangelo identified by the employment of Classical elements in a strange or abnormal way, or out of context, such as slipping *triglyphs or keystones, columns *inserted in deep apertures in walls and seemingly supported on *consoles, and distortion of *aedicules and other features, as in *Giulio Romano's buildings in Mantua or *Michelangelo's work at San Lorenzo, Florence. In Northern Europe the works carried out by the School of *Fontainebleau contributed to a peculiarly inventive Mannerism evolved in the Low Countries (especially in Antwerp and Flanders generally), where *cartouches, *grotesque decoration, *herms, *swags, and *terms were used in abundance, and examples published in pattern-books, influencing design in Germany, the British Isles, and elsewhere.

Heydenreich and Lotz (1974); Jervis (1984); Lewis and Darley (1986); Mowl and Earnshaw (1995); Shearman (1967); Wüsten (1951)

manor-house. House in a district in medieval England over which the Court of the Lord of the Manor had authority, or on the land belonging to that nobleman: it was usually unfortified, of medium size, and architecturally unpretentious.

Wood (1965)

mansard. *See* roof.

Mansart, François (1598–1666). Leading French Classical architect. Establishing his own practice by 1624, he evolved a style influenced by de *Brosse and du *Cerceau. One of his most important works was the Church of the Val-de-Grâce, Paris (from 1645), completed by *Lemercier and others when building had reached the *nave *entablature: the original design was probably a derivation of *Palladio's *Il Redentore*, Venice. One of his earliest works was the Château de Balleroy, near Bayeux, Calvados (*c.*1626), with single-storey pavilion-wings set in front of a massive central block, the whole composed with assurance. With the Orléans wing, Château de Blois (1635–8), Mansart reached a mature architectural style derived from de Brosse but distinguished by purity of detail giving the building an unfussy Classical dignity. Later elevations were modelled more elaborately, as in his Château de Maisons, near Paris (1642–51), a serene, very French composition, with elliptical rooms set in the projecting wings. Elevations are treated as a regular grid with planes defined by *pilasters, unengaged columns, *entablatures, and *architraves. The centrepiece has three superimposed *Orders.

He also designed Ste-Marie-de-la-Visitation, Paris (1632–4), a circular domed church surrounded by small chapels, and prepared designs for a huge domed *mausoleum for the Bourbons at St-Denis (1665), complete with chapels set around the main circular space, but this was not realized. However, the design demonstrates that Mansart was an architect of genius: it influenced J. *Hardouin-Mansart's dome of the Invalides. Ingenuity and assured geometries were also demonstrated in Mansart's Parisian *hôtels, although most of his work has been destroyed. However, his remodelling of the Hôtel Carnavalet (1660–1) survives in part: there he placed rooms all round the court, eliminating the usual wall with gate on the street-frontage. His ambitious schemes for the Louvre (1660s) survive only on paper.

Blunt (1941, 1982); Braham and Smith (1973); Hautecœur (1948); Watkin (1986)

Mansart, Jules Hardouin (1646–1708). *See* Hardouin-Mansart.

manse. Ecclesiastical residence, especially a dwelling of a Presbyterian Minister.

mantel. 1. Structure supporting the masonry above a fireplace-opening, either arched or a beam (*mantel-tree*). **2.** Projecting *hood above a fireplace to collect the smoke. **3.** Finish to the outer *face of a wall, covering the structure, and of a material differing from that of the wall itself.

mantelpiece. 1. *Mantel with its supports, i.e. the fireplace *jambs. **2.** Shelf in front of the mantel. **3.** Ornamental structure and frame around a fireplace-opening, including the shelf, concealing the mantel and structure, and often surmounted by an *over-mantel*.

Manueline. Portuguese late-*Gothic style of the reign of King Manuel I (1495–1521). Highly decorative, it included *ropes, corals, twisted *piers, and the Cross of the Military Order of Christ, best seen at the Cristo Monastery at Tomar (from 1510).

Cruickshank (1996); Lewis and Darley (1986); Watkin (1986)

Mapilton, Thomas (*fl.* 1408–d. 1438). English master-mason. He built the cloisters at Durham Cathedral (1408–16), and from 1416 to 1418 was employed at Westminster Abbey and the Tower of London. In 1420 he may have been in Florence, acting as one of the consultants for the design of the *dome of the Cathedral there, and in 1421 was promoted to the office of King's Master-Mason in London. He designed the south-west tower of Canterbury Cathedral (1423–34), and may have been responsible for the Lollards' Tower at Lambeth Palace, London (begun 1434). He built the Church of St Stephen, Walbrook, London (1429–39—replaced by *Wren's church after the Great Fire of 1666). He gave advice at the great Abbey of Bury St Edmunds, Suffolk (1429–30—destroyed), and may have been involved in the early planning of St Bernard's (now St John's) and All Souls Colleges, Oxford, just before his death.

Harvey (1987)

March, Otto (1845–1913). German architect, he became *Regierungsbaumeister* (Official or

Government Architect) in Berlin from 1878, and was responsible for several Government buildings, theatres, and private houses (he also built up a prosperous practice). The Municipal Theatre, Worms (1889), had hefty structural forms, and the Neue Friedrichstrasse Store, Berlin (1895), with its three-storey bays of iron and glass, anticipated work by *Gropius. His private houses usually had steep roofs, projecting bays, and a plan grouped around a double-height hall: the best examples were the Landhaus Vörster, Cologne (1891), Landhaus Holtz, Eisenach (1894), and Twin House, Villenkolonie, Grünewald, Berlin (1894). He also designed the Schillertheater, Charlottenburg (*c.*1895), and the Siemens Residence, Potsdam (*c.*1900).

Placzek (1982); Muthesius (1974)

March, Werner (1894–1976). German architect, the son of Otto *March. He designed in a powerful, stripped Neoclassical style. He is remembered for his masterpiece, the impressive stadium, grounds, and various buildings of the *Reichssportfeld*, Berlin, created for the 1936 Olympic Games from the earlier Grünewald Stadium (1925–8), which March and his brother **Walter** had designed. He was the architect of *Karinhall*, in Prussia (1935–6), for Hermann Goering (1893–1946).

Adam (1992); Petsch (1978); Rittich (1938); *Wasmuths Monatshefte für Baukunst*, 12 (1928), 187–91 and 14 (1930), 13–21

Marchi, Virgilio (1895–1960). Italian *Futurist architect and polemicist, he wrote *Architettura Futurista* (Futurist Architecture—1924) and *Italia Nuova, Architettura Nuova* (New Italy, New Architecture—1931), which extolled speed, modern techniques, and the 'formal exaltation' of machinery. He conceived architecture as sculpture to be inhabited, in visions of gigantic spaces and megalomaniac perspectives. He designed the Casa d'arte Bragaglia e Teatro degli Indipendenti, Rome (1921), probably the first Futurist work of architecture, and Il Teatro dei Piccoli di Vittoria Prodecca at the Teatro Odescalchi, Rome (1924–5).

Amico and Damesi (1977); Clough (1961); Marchi (1924, 1931); Pehnt (1973)

Marchionni, Carlo (1702–86). Italian architect and decorator, he is best known for his work at the Villa Albani, Rome (from 1746), including the *casino, coffee-house, temples, and fountains, which demonstrate his mastery of scenographic effects. While the casino's arcaded front owes much to *Michelangelo's Palazzo dei Conservatori, Rome, the temples show the influence of *Winckelmann's *Neoclassicism, especially the Tempietto Diruto (1751–67), an artificial ruin composed of *Antique fragments. He designed the new Sacristy, St Peter's, Rome (1776–83).

Debenedetti (1988); van Vynckt (1993); Watkin (1986); Wittkower (1982)

margent. Ornament of vertical flowers and leaves suspended from a bow, mask, *patera, ring, or rosette, usually derived from the *festoon (with which it is often found), on either side of an aperture or in the centre of a panel.

margent. Husk type. (*After JJS*)

margin-draft. *Dressed band the width of a chisel all around the *face of a block of *ashlar, contrasting with the rest of the exposed stone.

margin-light. 1. Tall, narrow flanking-window or wing-light on either side of a wider door or window, often found in late-C18 and early C19 British houses of the grander sort. **2.** Narrow *lights defined by glazing-bars around the edges of a *sash-window, often with coloured glass, and common in C19 *Greek Revival architecture or that influenced by a taste for a wider, squatter proportion of rectangular window that became fashionable *c.*1810.

marigold. Formalized circular floral decoration in *Greek architecture, resembling a *rosette, but more like a chrysanthemum or marigold, repeated in series, e.g. on the *architrave of the north *portico of the Erechtheion, Athens.

marigold window. Medieval circular window, its area subdivided into segments by radiating *bars of *tracery, sometimes resembling a marigold, and sometimes more like a rose, if more complicated, so called a *rose-window.

marine decoration. Classical architectural ornament suggesting the sea or navigation, including anchors, the *columna rostrata, dolphins, fish, *hippocamps, mermaids, Neptune with his *attribute (the trident), nets, ropes, sea-shells, and tritons, often associated with *grottoes.

Markelius, Sven Gottfrid (1889–1972). Swedish architect and town-planner, he worked for *Östberg before becoming influenced by Le *Corbusier. He won the competition to design a Concert Hall at Hälsingborg (1925, built 1932–4), and made his reputation with the Swedish Pavilion at the New York World's Fair (1939). From 1944 to 1954 he was Director of the Stockholm Planning Commission and implemented a policy of building 'town-sections' (really new towns) fully integrated with the city, including Vällingby (from 1953) with its central pedestrian zone. He was consulting architect for the United Nations Building, New York, and the UNESCO Building, Paris.

Emanuel (1994); Ray (1969)

Marot, Daniel (1661–1752). Son of **Jean Marot** (*c.*1619–79—who produced *L'Architecture Française* (*c.*1660) and *Recueils d'Architecture* (*c.*1670)), he was born in Paris, but fled to The Netherlands after the Revocation (1685) of the Edict of Nantes (1598) of the reign of King Henri IV (1589–1610) that had guaranteed the rights and citizenship of French Protestants (Huguenots). He introduced the *Baroque *Louis Quatorze style to England and The Netherlands. His engravings, published as *Livre d'Ornemens, Nouveau Livre de Placfond*, and *Livre d'Appartement* over some 15 years from 1687, and subsequently collected as *Œuvres du Sieur D. Marot* (1703, 1713, and later), are a complete record of the Louis Quatorze style. His work was influential in The Netherlands, Germany, Austria, Denmark, Sweden, and England.

Marot settled in The Hague and collaborated with the Leiden architect Jacob *Roman on the design of William and Mary's palace and garden, Het Loo, near Apeldoorn in the 1690s, and remodelled the audience-chamber in the Binnenhof, The Hague (1695–8). He accompanied William and Mary to England in 1688, where he appears to have designed the Grand Parterre and some of the interiors of the old Water Gallery at Hampton Court Palace, Middlesex (1689–98). His name has been associated with work at Boughton House, Northamptonshire, Montagu House, London, and Petworth House, Sussex (all *c.*1689–96), while Schomberg House, Pall Mall, London (*c.*1698), appears to owe much to his style, although documentary evidence is lacking. He enlarged Huis ten Bosch, near The Hague (1734–9), and built the Huis Schuylenburch (1715), Huis Wassenaar-Obdam (1716–17), a new wing of the *Stadhuis* (Town Hall) (1734–5), and Huis Huguetan (1734–7), all in The Hague. He was assisted for many years by his son, **Daniel Marot the Younger** (1695–1769).

Jessen (1892); Kuyper (1980); Ozinga (1939); Placzek (1982); Rosenberg, Slive, and Ter Kuile (1966)

MARS (Modern Architectural Research) Group. Group of architects (including *Arup, *Coates, and *Lubetkin) founded in 1933 to promote *International Modernism and *Rationalism in the United Kingdom (it was really the UK branch of *CIAM). Taking its cue from Le *Corbusier's *Plan Voisin* and other theoretical ideas, it proposed (1942) the complete reconstruction of London.

Tafuri and Dal Co (1986)

Martellange, Étienne (d. 1641). French architect who designed the Jesuit Novitiate, Paris (1630), and followed (with *Lemercier) the refined *Classicism later illustrated in *Parallèle de l'Architecture* (1650) by Roland *Fréart de Chambray (1606–76).

Babelon (1991); Blunt (1982)

Martello tower. One of a number of *battered two-storeyed circular or elliptical fortified towers built on the coasts of the British Isles from 1804 as a precaution against invasion by the French, named after Cape Mortella, Corsica, where a watch-tower of similar form was occupied by a British garrison in 1794. Good examples can be seen on the Suffolk coast between Aldeburgh and Bawdsey. Most were constructed under the direction of General William Twiss (1745–1827) and a Captain Ford.

Sutcliffe (1973)

Martienssen, Rex (1905–42). South African pioneer of *International Modernism, who quoted liberally from the works of Le *Corbusier, *Gropius, and *Mies van der Rohe. He published numerous articles in the *South African Architectural Record* (1931–3). His buildings include the Stern House, Houghton, Johannesburg (1934–5), and the Martienssen House, Greenside, Johannesburg (1940). In 1956 he published *The Idea of Space in Greek Architecture: with Special Reference to the Doric Temple and its Setting*, a book that seems to have influenced American writers, notably Vincent Scully in *The Earth, the Temple, and the Gods* (1979—revised from 1962 edn.).

Emanuel (1980)

Martin, Leonard (1869–1935). English architect, he practised in London with H. J. *Treadwell from 1890 to 1910, producing many elaborately modelled buildings in the West End, notably in New Bond Street and Jermyn Street. *Tudor, *Baroque, and *Art Nouveau styles were used very freely. After Treadwell's death Martin practised on his own, designing houses in Ilchester Place, Kensington, and many other places.

Gray (1985)

Martin, Sir (John) Leslie (1908–). English architect. He taught at Manchester and Hull before working as an assistant architect for the LMS Railway. As Deputy Architect of the London County Council he designed his best-known work, the Royal Festival Hall (1948–51—with Robert *Matthew, Peter *Moro, and Edwin Williams (1896–1976)), after which he was recognized as a leading *Modern Movement architect. He set up his own practice in 1956. He designed Harvey Court, Gonville and Caius College, Cambridge (1957–62), and the Library at Manor Road, Oxford (1959–64—with Colin St John *Wilson and Patrick Hodgkinson (1930–)), the William Stone Building, Peterhouse, Cambridge (1960–4—also with Wilson), the Zoology/Psychology Building, Oxford (1964–70), and the Royal Concert Hall, Glasgow (1983–90—with Ivor Richards (1943–)). Professor of Architecture (1956–72) and Emeritus Professor (from 1973) at Cambridge University, he exercised enormous influence on architecture and planning.

Emanuel (1994)

Martinelli, Domenico (1650–1718). Italian architect. He worked with Carlo *Fontana in Rome from 1678. His importance lies in his influence on the *Baroque style in Central Europe, notably with the *Stadtpalais* (Town Palace) Liechtenstein, Vienna (1684–1705), which includes an elaborate staircase, and was as a whole derived from *Bernini's Chigi-Odescalchi Palace, Rome. He probably designed the Palais Harrach (*c.*1690), the *Gartenpalais* (Garden Palace) Liechtenstein, Vienna (1691–1711), the Kaunitz Palace, Slavkov (Austerlitz), where he introduced the *cour d'honneur (from 1701), and the *Invalidenhaus*, Pest (built 1721–37).

Grimschitz (1947*a*); Lorenz (1991); Neumann, J. (1970); Powell (1959)

Martorell, Codina Josep Maria (1925–). *See* MBM Arquitectes.

Martorell y Montells, Joan (1833–1906). Catalan disciple of *Viollet-le-Duc and one of the most distinguished architects of the eclectic Barcelona school. His *Gothic work was influenced by English architects, especially *Butterfield. His most outstanding building is the Church of the Salesas (1882–5), where Gothic, *Romanesque, and *Mudéjar styles merge. His Mercantile Credit Society Building, Barcelona (1896–1900), was influenced by *Neoclassicism and other trends of the time. He taught *Gaudí.

Bohigas (1968)

martyrium (*pl.* **martyria**). **1.** Structure, usually circular or polygonal, built over the tomb of a Christian martyr, so essentially a *mausoleum. Hundreds of Christian churches owe their existence to martyria, which took their form from well-established Roman funerary types (*exedrae, octagons, rotundas, etc.). The complex martyrium at Hierapolis in Phrygia, Turkey (early C5), had a plan derived from Nero's Golden House, Rome (C1). **2.** Place in a church where Relics are deposited.

Colvin (1991); Cruickshank (1996); Grabar (1972)

Maruscelli, Paolo (1596–1694). Italian *Baroque architect of the time of *Bernini, *Borromini, and *Cortona. He designed the Chiesa Nuova, Perugia (1629–49), and the Casa dei Filippini, Rome (1622–36), which Borromini transformed after 1637. At the Palazzo Medici-Madama, Rome (1642), he enlarged the building and composed the impressive façade, loosely derived from the Palazzo Farnese.

Connors (1980)

Marvuglia, Giuseppe Venanzio (1729–1814). Sicilian architect. He designed the tepidarium and caldarium (1789) in a stripped Neoclassical style at the Botanic Gardens, Palermo, using the Greek *Doric *Order. Other designs incorporated *Baroque and Classical elements, e.g. the Monastery of San Martino delle Scale, Palermo (1762–74), and the Palladian Villa Belmonte all'Acquasanta, Palermo (from 1801). His most extraordinary building is La Favorita (Palazzina Cinese—1799–1802), a partly Classical and partly *Chinoiserie confection, which may have been partly designed by Giuseppe Patricola. Marvuglia also designed the *Doric Hercules Fountain at the Villa della Favorita, Palermo (*c.*1814).

Blunt (1968); Meeks (1966); Middleton and Watkin (1987)

mascaron. Representation of a human or partly human face, more or less caricatured, used as an architectural ornament, e.g. on a keystone over an arch.

Mascherino, Ottaviano (1536–1606). Bolognese by birth, he settled in Rome in 1574, where he made additions to *Bramante's Cortile di Belvedere (1578–85), built the Church of San Salvatore in Lauro (1591–1600), and planned the Palazzo del Quirinale (1583–5). He designed the façades of Santa Maria della Scala (1592) and Santo Spirito dei Napoletani (1593), both in Rome.

Ackerman (1954); Wittkower (1982)

mask. Representation of a face, human, animal, or fantastic beast, used in architectural ornament, often part of *grotesque decoration. *See* mascaron.

masonry. **1.** Art, craft, and practice of building with natural or artificial stone, involving its quarrying, cutting, *dressing, jointing, and laying. **2.** Work produced by a mason, such as an *ashlar wall, stone dressings, and the like. Types of masonry include:

ashlar: stone cut and dressed to accurate shapes with right-angled corners, laid in true courses with mortar on flat beds, and with fine joints, carefully bonded;

cyclopean: **1.** any polygonal masonry, but especially masonry of large irregularly shaped stones; **2.** rusticated masonry dressed to appear it is naturally rough *rock-faced work straight from the quarry;

rubble: stonework of undressed or roughly dressed stones including *coursed rubble* (stones laid in courses, so requiring some preparation to ensure that joints are horizontal and stones properly bedded), *dry-stone* (rough stones laid without mortar), *random rubble* (very rough stones, uncoursed), and *squared rubble* (stones cut roughly to have verticals at right angles to the horizontals);

rusticated: masonry laid with joints exaggerated by chamfering, etc., the surface projecting beyond the joints. *See* rustication.

3. Brickwork or any load-bearing structure such as blockwork, but the term is not recommended in this sense.

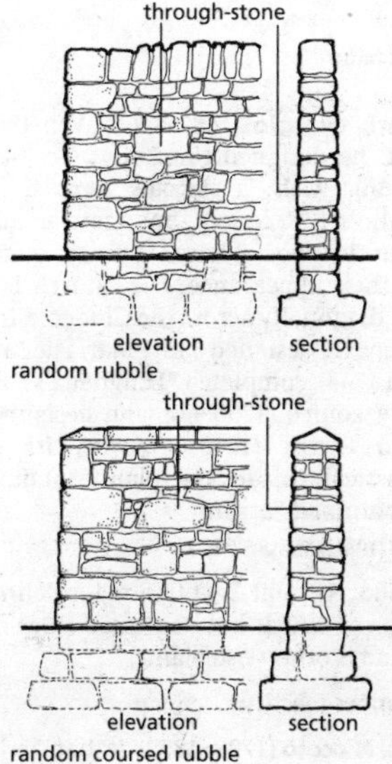

masonry

mason's lodge. *See* lodge.

mason's mark. Device carved in stones by a mason to identify his work, often found in medieval buildings.

Jones (1956)

mason's mitre. When stone mouldings, *cills, *string-courses, etc., are continued around an external angle, the point where they change direction must not coincide with the joint because an acutely angled piece of stone is subject to damage and easily snapped off. The joint, therefore, is formed at right angles to the *naked of the wall at a distance from the angle, the change of direction of the moulding effected by cutting it to shape.

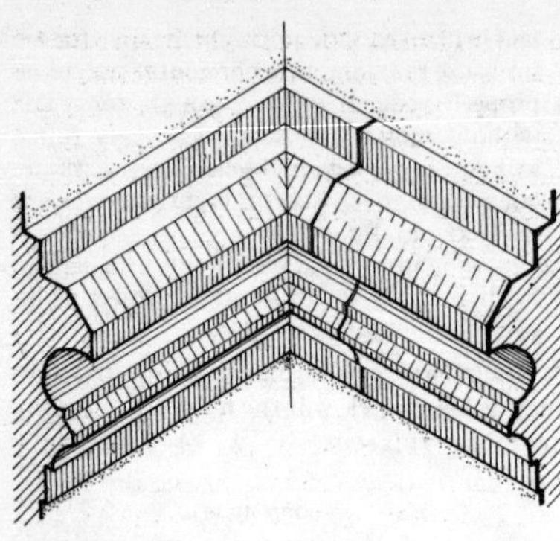
mason's mitre

Massari, Giorgio (1687–1766). Venetian architect, he designed the Chiesa dei Gesuati (1725–36) with a façade derived from *Palladio's *Il Redentore*, but more ebullient, and an interior where *Rococo elements made their appearance. The Church is positioned diagonally across the Giudecca from *Il Redentore*. He designed Santa Maria della Pietà (begun 1744), completed *Longhena's Palazzo (Ca') Rezzonico (1750–66), and designed the Palazzo Grassi (1748–60) with its sober Neoclassical façade and plan containing a four-columned *atrium.

Howard (1980); Massari (1971)

mastaba. Ancient Egyptian mausoleum, the exterior of which has *battered sides, a flat roof, and is otherwise plain.

mastin. *See* mestling.

Matas, Niccolò (1798–1872). Italian architect of the *polychrome *Gothic façade of Santa Croce, Florence (1857–63). He worked on several other buildings in Florence, and contributed to the design of the cemetery at San Miniato al Monte.

Baedeker, *Northern Italy* (1913)

Matcham, Frank (1854–1920). Leading English theatre and music-hall architect of the late-*Victorian and *Edwardian periods. His designs are festive, often elephantine, and have distorted *Orders and ornament. His best-known works are the Grand Opera House, Belfast (1895), the London Coliseum (1904), and the London Palladium (1910).

Gray (1985)

mathematical tiles. Small facing-tiles designed to look like *brick headers with joints, used to clad *timber-framed fronts to give the appearance of top-quality brickwork. Excellent C18 examples abound in Lewes, Sussex.

Brunskill (1990)

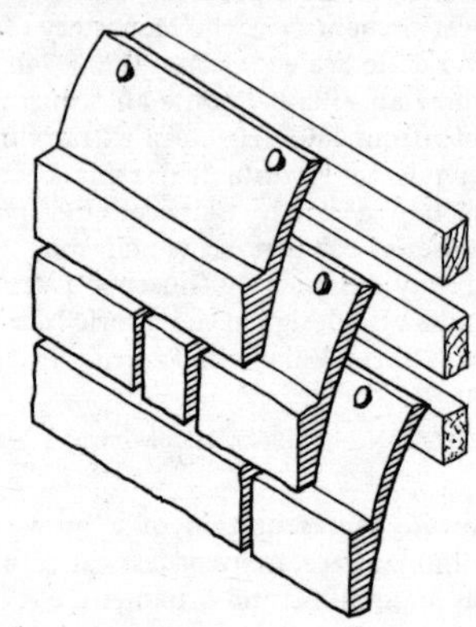
mathematical tiles (*JJS*)

Mathey, Jean-Baptiste (*c*.1630–95). Born in Dijon, France, Mathey worked in Prague (1675–94), and designed the Troja Palace there (1679–96), with its central *block and *perron, and two wings linking the main building to symmetrically disposed *pavilions: it combines French ideas about the planning of châteaux with Italian detailing. He designed the *Kreuzherrenkirche* (Church of the Crusader Knights—1679–88) and the Toskana Palace (1689–90), both in Prague. His church architecture influenced *Fischer von Erlach.

Hempel (1965); Neumann, J. (1970); Powell (1959)

Matthew, Sir Robert Hogg (1906–75). A Scot, he was Architect to the London County Council (1946–53) and was responsible for the Royal Festival Hall, London (1948–51, with J. L. *Martin, Peter *Moro, and Edwin Williams (1896–1976)), as well as for the housing developments of that era. He established Robert Matthew, Johnson-Marshall, & Partners in 1953, designing the University of York (1963) and many other major projects throughout the United Kingdom, including the University buildings, Coleraine, Co. Londonderry (1970s). The *Neo-Vernacular Hillingdon Civic Centre, Uxbridge, near London (1973–8), was a significant change of direction for the firm.

DNB (1986); van Vynckt (1993)

Matthias of Arras (d. 1352). *See* Arras.

Maufe, Sir Edward Brantwood (1883–1974). English architect of simplified *Gothic churches influenced by developments in Scandinavia, he is best known for Guildford Cathedral, Surrey (1932–66). Other works include Kelling Hall, Norfolk (1912–14), an *Arts-and-Crafts house with flint walls, St Bede's Church, Clapham, London (1922–3), St Saviour's Church, Acton, London (1924—which had reminiscences of *Tengbom's Högalid Church, Stockholm (1917–23), much admired by Maufe), Yaffle Hill, Broadstone, Dorset (a house of 1929), the Playhouse Theatre, Oxford (1937–8), and Chapel Court and North Court, St John's College, Cambridge (1937–9). He rebuilt Gray's Inn and the Middle Temple, London, in a *Neo-Georgian style after the 1939–45 war. With John McGeagh he designed the Sir William Whitla Hall, The Queen's University of Belfast (designed 1937, built 1938–49). From 1943 to 1969 he was involved with the Imperial (later Commonwealth) War Graves Commission, and designed many memorials (e.g. the Royal Air Force Memorial, Coopers Hill, Runnymede, Surrey (1949–51)).

DNB (1986)

mausoleum (*pl.* **mausolea**). Any roofed building used as a tomb, detached or joined to another building (e.g. a church), containing coffins, *sarcophagi, or *urns, often on shelves. The term originated with the C4 BC *Hellenistic *Ionic tomb of King Mausolos of Caria at Halicarnassus, one of the *Seven Wonders of the Ancient World.

Colvin (1991); Curl (1993); Toynbee (1971)

Mawson. *See* Lockwood.

Maxwell, Edward (1867–1923). Canadian architect. He was skilled at mixing the round-arched and *Italianate styles (e.g. Henry Birks Store, Montreal, 1893–4). He entered into partnership with his brother, **William Sutherland Maxwell** (1874–1952—who had trained at the École des *Beaux-Arts, Paris), in 1902, and together they produced many confident *Classical designs (e.g. the Saskatchewan Legislative Building, Regina (1907–10), the J. K. L. Ross House, Montreal (1908–9), and the Montreal Art Association Gallery (1910–12)). Their additions to Bruce Price's (1845–1903) Château Frontenac Hotel, Quebec (1892–3), included the St-Louis Wing and Tower Block (1920–4), in which a mixture of the French *château style and elements derived from Scots fortified houses encapsulated the importance of Scots settlers and French colonization in the history of Canada. The firm had an enormous and successful practice, designing many commercial and other building-types.

Kalman (1968, 1994)

May, Edward John (1853–1941). A pupil of Decimus *Burton, he worked for Eden *Nesfield and Norman *Shaw, for whom he designed several buildings at the Bedford Park Estate, Chiswick, near London in the 1870s and 1880s, including the Vicarage (*c.*1882), the Club House (1879), Hogg House, Priory Gardens (1883), and Queen Anne's Grove (1883).

Gray (1985); Hitchcock (1977)

May, Ernst (1886–1970). German architect and disciple of the *Garden City movement, he studied first in London (1907–8), then in Darmstadt (1908–10), before working with *Unwin (1910–12). He completed his studies in Munich under *Fischer and *Thiersch (1912–13). Director of the Silesian Building Department, Breslau (now Wrocław), from 1919 to 1925, he produced the Development Plan for the City, and had to deal with the huge influx of German refugees from Poland. From 1925 to 1930 he was *Stadtbaurat* (Director of Town Planning and Building) at Frankfurt-am-Main, where he designed the famous Römerstadt Housing Development (1926–30) and other schemes incorporating English low-density ideas with the architectural language of the *International Modernist style, using prefabricated *industrialized systems. From 1926 to 1930 he edited *Das neue Frankfurt* (New Frankfurt) and promoted his ideas about housing, transport, and pollution as well as publishing proposals for Berlin and planning generally. He moved to the Soviet Union in 1930, where he planned a series of new towns (the 'May' towns). From 1934 until 1945 he was in Africa, farming in Tanganyika and practising as an architect-planner in Kenya, but was interned as an enemy alien in 1942–5. Returning to Europe in 1945, he carried out many housing developments in Hamburg and elsewhere in West Germany. He edited *Das schlesische Heim* (The Silesian Home—1919–25) and *Die Neue Heimat* (The New Homeland—1954–60).

Buekschmitt (1963); Emanuel (1994); Korn (1953); Miller (1992)

May, Hugh (1621–84). English architect of the period between the first Palladian Revival of Inigo *Jones and the *Baroque style of *Vanbrugh and *Hawksmoor. He became Comptroller of the Works in 1668 and held several other official posts. He seems to have been responsible for introducing well-mannered Dutch *Palladianism into England and, with *Pratt, for establishing what became known (inaccurately) as the *Wren style. Apart from the *double-pile Eltham Lodge, Kent (1664—apparently influenced by the work of *Vingboons), however, his only major surviving works are the east front, stables, and chapel at Cornbury House, Oxfordshire (1663–8). He remodelled the Upper Ward, St George's Hall, and the King's Chapel at Windsor Castle, Berkshire (1675–84), with paintings by Antonio Verrio (*c*.1639–1707) and carvings by Grinling Gibbons (1648–1721), creating what was once the most complete Baroque ensemble in England, now virtually obliterated.

Colvin (1995); Downes (1966); Hill and Cornforth (1966); van Vynckt (1993)

Mayan architecture. A *Meso-American people, the Maya built (*c*. C2 BC–*c*. AD 900) very steep *battered platforms on which monumental structures were created. The remains of many such temples have *corbelled *vaults inside (*c*. C4), but most openings have *lintels or triangular *heads. Mayan and *Aztec architecture influenced European *Art Deco in the 1920s and 1930s.

Cruickshank (1996)

Maybeck, Bernard Ralph (1862–1957). American eclectic architect, he made a distinctive contribution to domestic design. Educated in Paris, he was influenced by *Viollet-le-Duc's theories, and in 1886 returned to New York to work with *Carrère & Hastings before setting up on his own in California, where he worked mostly in the *Stick style. In his First Church of Christ Scientist, Berkeley, California (1910–12), he mixed *Gothic, *vernacular, the Stick style, and more than a hint of Japanese-inspired timber-work. His many houses had similar qualities, but at the A. C. Lawson House, Berkeley (1907), he also used *reinforced concrete, an early example of this material. He employed *Classicism too, notably in the Palace of Fine Arts, San Francisco (1913–15), built for the International Exposition.

Architectural Record, 103 (1948), 72–9; Cardwell (1977); Longstreth (1983); McCoy (1975); Placzek (1982)

Mayekawa, Kunio (1905–86). *See* Maekawa.

maze. *Fret, *Greek key, *labyrinth, *meander, but especially labyrinthine figures in churches and gardens.

MBM Arquitectes. Martorell-Bohigas-Mackay Arquitectes was established in Barcelona, Spain (1962), by Josep Maria Martorell i Codina (1925–), Oriol Bohigas i Guardiola (1925–), and David John Mackay (1933–), joined in 1985 by Albert Puigdomenech i Alonso (1944–). An influential firm, it was largely responsible for the transformation of that city up to and beyond the Olympic Games (1992). Among significant designs were the Pavilion of the Future, Expo 92, Seville (1992), and the Harbourmaster's House and Sailing School, Olympic Port, Barcelona (1989–91). In the Mollet City Block, Barcelona (1983–7), many typologies were explored, while the high-level street, so usually a disaster, was made to work. Other buildings include the Villa Escarrer, Palma de Mallorca (1985–8), in which certain geometries derived from *Palladio were explored, and the earlier Santa Agueda development, Benicassim, Castelló (1966–7).

Amsoneit (1994); Emanuel (1994); Lampugnani (1988)

Mead, William Rutherford (1846–1928). *See* McKim, Mead, & White.

meander. *Band-like progressive ornament composed of straight lines joining at right angles or cut diagonally (as in the *fret and *key patterns), or curving (as in the *Vitruvian scroll, *running-dog, or *wave-scroll). It is used on *friezes, *string-courses, etc.

Mebes, Paul (1872–1938). Important C20 German housing architect and theorist, whose designs for apartments were influential. He published *Um 1800. Architektur und Kunsthandwerke im letzten Jahrhundert ihrer traditionellen Entwicklung* (Around 1800. Architecture and Art Work in the Last Century in its Traditional Development—1908) which dealt with German *Biedermeier architecture, and argued that simple, stripped *Neoclassicism was more adaptable for modern needs than *Jugendstil or any of the other styles in vogue at the time. His views influenced *Behrens, *Bonatz, and *Troost, among others.

Lane (1985); Mebes and Behrendt (1920); Meyer (1972)

medallion. **1.** Panel or tablet, usually circular, elliptical, oval, or sometimes square, bearing a portrait or figures in *relief, really like a large medal, used for Classical architectural decoration. **2.** Repeated circular ornament, e.g. in a *frieze (especially in *Romanesque work).

medieval architecture. Architecture of Europe in the Middle Ages from the end of C8 to the first half of C16, thus including the *Romanesque and *Gothic (or *Pointed) styles.

meeting-house. Building for Nonconformist (usually Presbyterian or Quaker) religious observances.

megalith. Large block of undressed or partially dressed stone used singly or with other megaliths as prehistoric monuments in *c*.4000–*c*.1000 BC. A single standing-stone is a *menhir*, sometimes arranged in regular rows (as at Carnac, Brittany). Megaliths are also found set in a circle, as at Stonehenge, Wiltshire (*c*.1800 BC), with *lintels forming a continuous band around the tops. Structures formed of uprights supporting a large flat slab were usually chamber-tombs, known as cromlechs or *dolmens.

Burl (1976); Daniel (1972)

megaron. **1.** Principal men's room or hall in an Ancient Greek house, or a room in a temple where only the priest could enter. **2.** Square or rectangular room often with a raised central hearth, and four columns supporting the roof. The side walls projected beyond the front wall and partly enclosed a columned porch, probably the precedent for a *Doric temple.

Dinsmoor (1950); Robertson (1945)

megastructure. Gigantic entirely enclosed complex of buildings, usually with many functions under one or several roofs. Examples include work by *Andrews and *Soleri's *Arcology.

Banham (1976)

Meier, Richard Alan (1934–). One of the top late-C20 American architects, he worked with *Breuer and *Skidmore, Owings, & Merrill before setting up on his own in New York (1963). The most prolific of the *New York Five, his persistent use of white in his buildings (e.g. the Saltzman House, East Hampton, NY (1967–9), and the beautifully sited Douglas House, Harbor Springs, Mich. (1971–3)), led to the group's nickname 'The Whites'. His public buildings attracted much attention, including the Atheneum, New Harmony, Ind. (1975–9); the Museum für Kunsthandwerk, Frankfurt-am-Main (1979–84); the High Museum of Art, Atlanta, Ga. (1980–3); the City Hall and Central Library, The Hague, The Netherlands (1986–95); the Museum of Contemporary Art, Barcelona (1987–95); and the huge Getty Center for the History of Art and the Humanities, Los Angeles, Calif. (1984–97). The last, likened in complexity to the *Villa Adriana*, Tivoli, is one of the most ambitious of his projects.

Emanuel (1994); Jodidio (1993, 1996, 1997); Klotz (1988); Meier (1984); Meier *et al.* (1996); Pettera (1981)

Meissonnier, Juste-Aurèle (1695–1750). Born in Turin, Italy, of French descent, he settled in Paris *c*.1718, where he established himself as an interior designer and architect, eschewing straight lines, symmetry, and blandness in his polished *Rococo designs. The ingenious house for Léon de Bréthous, Bayonne, France (1733), demonstrated his mastery of irregular plans and his fondness for sweeping curves. Most of his work has been destroyed, but can be studied in *Œuvre de Juste-Aurèle Meissonnier*, published by Gabriel Huquier (1695–1772) in *c*.1750.

Fitzgerald (1963); Hautecœur (1950); Jervis (1984); Kalnein and Levey (1972); Kimball (1980); Nyberg (1969)

Meldahl, Ferdinand (1827–1908). Danish architect. Influenced especially by the work of *Persius, *Schinkel, and *Semper, he became the leading proponent of *Historicism in Denmark. At the Manor House, Pederstrup, Lolland (1859–62), he drew on French *Renaissance prototypes, and at the School for Navigation (later Life Assurance Institution), Copenhagen (1864–5), he quoted the façade of *Lombardo's Palazzo Véndramin-Calergi, Venice (*c*.1500–9). Other works include the Royal Mint (1872–3) and the completion (1878–94) of the *Baroque *Frederikskirke* or Marble Church, Copenhagen, originally designed by *Jardin and *Eigtved, with its noble *cupola.

Millech (1951); Weilbach (1995)

Melnikov, Konstantin Stepanovich (1890–1974). Russian architect who rose to eminence in the Soviet Union in the 1920s. His early work was influenced by *Tatlin, and he evolved an architecture partly informed by traditional rural timber buildings using roughly sawn members (e.g. the USSR Pavilion at the Exposition in Paris of 1925, a split rectangle slashed by powerful diagonals (perhaps anticipating aspects of *Deconstructivism), which gained him international celebrity among the avant-garde). Although his work has been associated by some with *Constructivism, he was more connected with the Productivists, who saw themselves as anti-artistic Constructivist technicians. He is best known for his Workers' Factory Clubs in Moscow, including the Frunze (1927), Rubber (1927), Rusakov (1927), Svoboda (1927–8), and Stormy Petrel (1929). The Rusakov Club has auditoria and circulation-spaces externally expressed in strong elemental forms. His own house in Moscow essentially consisted of two interlocking cylinders (1927–9), a theme he explored in other buildings.

Khan-Magomedov (1987); Starr (1978)

melon-dome. *See* dome.

Mendelsohn, Eric(h) (1887–1953). German-born naturalized American architect. He started as an *Expressionist, producing many images of structures with streamlined curves while serving in the German Imperial Army (1914–18). His Einstein Tower, Potsdam (1919–24), resembles aspects of the early typological sketches: built of brick and block and rendered, it had the appearance of being made of *reinforced concrete, and is popularly believed to be so constructed. The plan owed much to South-German *Baroque staircase designs of C18. Expressionist, too, was the Steinberg-Herrmann Hat Factory, Luckenwalde (1921–3), with its jagged, angular forms, but curved walls were also used in some of his other buildings, notably the WOGA Complex with Universum Cinema, Berlin (1925–8), and the Schocken Department Stores at Stuttgart (1926) and Chemnitz (1928–9). The cinema was the precedent for many such buildings in Europe and America in the 1930s, while the long strips of horizontal windows at the stores made a considerable impact.

*International Modernism impinged more and more on Mendelsohn's work, and in 1933 he settled in England where he joined *Chermayeff, designing the celebrated de la Warr Pavilion, Bexhill-on-Sea, Sussex (1933–5), which has bands of windows and a streamlined curved glass enclosure for the staircase derived from the Schocken Store, Stuttgart. In the late 1930s he moved to Palestine, where he designed buildings for the Hebrew University, Jerusalem (1937–9), and in 1941 emigrated to the USA, where his work lacked the power of his German designs. The Russell House, Pacific Heights, San Francisco (1950–1), was probably his best work in America.

Aschenbach (1987); Eckardt (1960); Hitchcock (1977); Pehnt (1973); Whittick (1956); Zevi (1985, 1999)

Mengoni, Giuseppe (1829–77). Italian architect. His best work is the cruciform Galleria Vittorio Emanuele, Milan (1861–77), one of the largest and most impressive iron-and-glass covered *arcades of C19, in the Italian *Renaissance style, with an important elevation facing the Piazza del Duomo. He also designed the handsome Palazzo della Cassa di Risparmio (1868–76) and the impressive Classical arcades of the Campo Santo (1860s), both in Bologna.

Geist (1983); Meeks (1966)

menhir. *See* megalith.

mensa. Upper slab of stone forming the top of an altar in a church.

mensole. Keystone.

Merlini, Domenico (1730–97). Italian-born Court Architect to King Stanisław August Poniatowski (1764–95) of Poland from 1773. He collaborated with *Kamsetzer in creating the lovely *Louis Seize interiors of the Royal Palace, Warsaw (1776–85), and various buildings in the Royal Park of Ujazdów, Warsaw. Among these are the remodelling of the exquisite lakeside Łazienki Palace (1775–93). Merlini designed the Orangery Theatre (1784–8) with Jan Bogumił Plersch (1737–1817) as his collaborator, and the little Lodge in the Park (*c*.1765–74). More *Baroque are his Myślewicki Palace (1775–6—with a curved front, end pavilions, and a two-storey apsidal entrance), Jabłonna Palace (1775–9), and Królikarnia Palace (1782–6—with *Ionic *portico and domed *rotunda), all in Warsaw. His Jabłonowski Palace, Racot (*c*.1785), is almost *Palladian in composition, but given a rustic flavour.

Lorentz and Rottermund (1984); Watkin (1986)

merlon. Cop. *See* battlement.

meros, merus. Plain surface of a *triglyph between the *glyphs.

Merovingian architecture. Architecture of the first dynasty of Frankish Kings in Gaul (*c.*500–751/2), derived from *Early Christian Roman prototypes, and usually taken to mean buildings of C5 to the end of C8. Among the C5 buildings are the *baptisteries of Aix, Fréjus, and Mélas, similar to such structures in Italy, and clearly derived from Roman precedents. Surviving buildings include the *crypt of Jouarre near Meaux and the baptistery of St-Jean, Poitiers (both essentially C7).

Merrill, John O. (1896–1975). *See* Skidmore, Owings, & Merrill.

Meso-American architecture. Architecture of the *Aztec, *Mayan, and other Central-American civilizations of the first millennium BC until the Spanish Conquest of C16. Most surviving structures had a ritualistic function, and included flat-topped pyramidal platforms with ramps and/or steps leading to the summit. Many buildings had sculpted *friezes, borders, and panels, and the simple rectilinear blocky forms of the temples bore a resemblance to European *stripped Classical buildings of C18 and later, while the formal symmetrical geometry of layouts and complexes (including settlements such as the great city of Teotihuacán (*c.* C1–C8), near Mexico City) had ceremonial roads and a grid-iron plan. Meso-American architecture had a considerable influence on aspects of *Art Deco.

Mesopotamian architecture. *See* Assyrian, Babylonian, Sumerian architecture.

mestling. *Mastin*, *mastline*, or yellow metal, such as *brass or *latten, used in medieval sepulchral brasses.

Metabolism. Japanese architectural movement founded in 1960 by *Tange. With members including *Kikutake, *Kurokawa, and *Maki, it was concerned with the nature and expression of private and public spaces. Prefabrication, advanced technology, and industrialization were employed to create small capsules or living-units for private spaces, connected to service-towers and circulation-areas, as in Kurokawa's Nagakin Capsule Tower, Tokyo (1972).

Kurokawa (1977, 1992); Lampugnani (1988)

Metagenes. There were two Ancient Greek architects of that name. *Metagenes of Athens* (*fl. c.* late C5 BC) was involved with others in the building of the Periclean Telesterion, or Hall of the Mysteries, Eleusis (*c.*430 BC). **Metagenes of Knossos**, son of *Chersiphron, worked on the great C6 BC *Ionic Temple of Artemis, Ephesus, and contributed to an architectural treatise (now lost).

Dinsmoor (1950); Vitruvius Pollio (1955–6, 1960), vii, 12

metal structures. The first were bridges, such as the *iron structure at Coalbrookdale designed by *Pritchard (1777–9), and various industrial and storage buildings where cast-iron columns carried beams from which low segmental brick vaults sprang. *Schinkel designed cast-iron monuments (e.g. to Queen Luise of Prussia, Gransee (*Gothic *sarcophagus and canopy—1811), the war-memorial at Grossbeeren (Gothic *pinnacle—1817), and the Kreuzberg monument, Berlin (tall Gothic *spire-like cross—1818–21)) and a cast-iron formal interior staircase (at Prince Albert's Palace, Berlin (1830–2)), while iron was also used by many C19 designers including *Baltard, *Bélanger, *Burton, *Fontaine, *Labrouste, *Lanyon, and *Paxton. *Loudon was a pioneer in the evolution of iron-and-glass *conservatories. Whole cast-iron fronts were designed by John *Baird in Glasgow, and *Badger, *Bogardus, and *Kellum, among others, in the USA. Early iron-and-glass walls were used by *Ellis in Liverpool. Paxton's Crystal Palace, London (1850–1), was the prototype for many C19 exhibition buildings, and there were many conservatories, railway-stations, and other structures using iron and glass. Fairbairn's book *On the Application of Cast and Wrought Iron to Building Purposes* (1854) was an important publication, while Badger's illustrated *Catalogue of Cast-Iron Architecture* (1865) was a remarkable compendium. Prefabricated iron structures, such as churches, were designed, and kits-of-parts widely available for *industrialized buildings. Metal-framed buildings were evolved, starting with wrought-iron, and then the steel skeleton was developed for tall buildings, including *skyscrapers, notably in Chicago and New York. Then came the use of steel as an element in *reinforced concrete, and the concept of the completely framed building with a light *envelope of metal and glass, the *curtain-wall. Later structures have included *space-frames, light *trusses, and various developments allowing speed of erection as well as prefabrication, lightness, and adaptability.

Gayle and Gillon (1974); Hartung (1983); Jodice (1988); Lemoine (1986); Loudon (1834); Mainstone (1975)

Métezeau, Jacques-Clément (1581–1652). French architect. The brother of Louis *Métezeau, he was involved in town-planning and architectural schemes for the Paris of *Henri IV (1589–1610). His designs looked forward to the style of le *Vau, and derive from that of de *Brosse, with whom he worked on the Luxembourg Palace, Paris (1615). Other buildings include the Place Ducale, Charleville (1610), the Orangerie du Louvre (1617), the Hôtel de Brienne, Paris (1630–2), and the Château de la Meilleraye (*c*.1630). He was probably responsible for the handsome west front of St-Gervais, Paris (1616–23), with an *assemblage of *Orders placed on a tall *Gothic church therefore requiring three orders instead of the two on *Il Gesù*, Rome, by *Vignola and della *Porta. St-Gervais has been attributed to de Brosse.

Babelon (1991); Berty (1860); Blunt (1982)

Métezeau, Louis (*c*.1562–1615). French architect, brother of Jacques-Clément *Métezeau. He contributed to the design of the Place des Vosges from *c*.1603 and, like his brother, designed other town-planning schemes for the Paris of *Henri IV with du *Cerceau. He may have been responsible for the south façade of the Grande Galerie, and contributed to the interiors of the Petite Galerie and Salle des Antiques, all at the Louvre, Paris (1601–8). He worked with *Dupérac on the interiors of the Hôtel de Jean de Fourcy, Paris (1601–10).

Babelon (1991); Berty (1860); Blunt (1982)

metope. 1. Plain or enriched slab on the *frieze of the *Doric *Order between *triglyphs. **2.** *Intersectio*, *metoche*, or space between *dentils.

Metz, Odo of (*fl. c*.792–805). Architect of the Palatine *Chapel or *Minster at Aachen, Germany, begun by Charlemagne *c*.790, that was modelled on San Vitale, Ravenna, but toughened and made more robust in the process. It may also have been derived from the C6 *Chrysotriclinion* (Hall of State) in Constantinople in order to suggest Imperial splendour.

Cruickshank (1996); Watkin (1986)

meurtrière. *Gun-loop.

Mewès, Charles (1860–1914). French architect. Trained in Paris, he worked in an elegant Classical (often *Louis Seize) style. He developed a large international practice from the 1890s, in association with architects in several countries. In England his colleague was Arthur Joseph *Davis (1878–1951), who had worked with him in Paris. Mewès designed the Ritz Hotel in Paris (1898) and in 1900 the interiors of the Carlton Hotel, London, by Henry Louis Florence (1843–1916). Mewès and Davis designed the Ritz Hotel, Piccadilly, London (1906–9), a steel-framed building with an elegant Frenchified façade and tall roofs reminiscent of the architecture of the Paris Boulevards. Other joint projects were the Royal Automobile Club, Pall Mall (1908–11), which has a façade reminiscent of *Gabriel's work, and the *Morning Post* Building, Aldwych, Strand (1905–6). Mewès was responsible for the luxurious interiors of the German liners *Amerika* (1905), *Kaiserin Auguste Victoria* (1907–8), *Imperator* (1911–12), *Vaterland* (1913), and *Bismarck* (1914). He also designed the décor in the Cunard liner *Aquitania* (1914).

Architectural Review, 14 (1907), 137–48; Gray (1985); Hamlin (1953)

mews. 1. *Court, street, or yard with stables, coach-houses, and accommodation for servants, at the rear of London town-houses. **2.** Group of small terrace-houses, set close together in a court or cul-de-sac, not on a main street-frontage.

Mey, Johann Melchior van der (1878–1949). Dutch architect, he worked with de *Klerk and *Kramer on the *Expressionist *Scheepvaarthuis* (Navigation House), Amsterdam (1912–16), and designed housing in the Titiaanstraat (1925) and Hoofdorpplein (1928–30), Amsterdam.

Fanelli (1968); Zuydewijn (1969)

Meyer, Adolf (1881–1929). German architect, he worked with *Lauweriks (before 1907), *Behrens (1907–8), *Paul (1909–10), and *Gropius (1911–14 and 1919–25). With the last he designed the Fagus Shoe Factory, Alfeld-an-der-Leine, Germany (1910–11), housing at Wittemberg, Frankfurt-an-der-Oder (1913–14), the Kleffel Cotton Factory, Dramburg (1913–14), and the Model Factory and Office Building for the Werkbund Exhibition, Cologne (1914), all of which are more controlled and elegant than anything Gropius was to produce later on his own. The Fagus *curtain-walling and the Cologne curved glazed cases for the stairs were to be enormously influential on *International Modernism. In 1925 he designed part of the Zeiss Factory, Jena. He taught at the *Bauhaus (1919–25).

Meyer (1925); Tafuri and Dal Co (1986)

Meyer, Hannes (1889–1954). Swiss-born Marxist architect, he began teaching at the Dessau *Bauhaus in 1927 and succeeded *Gropius as Director (1928–30). Meyer's Collectivist approach alienated many people (he made Marxism and Leninism essential studies), and his insistence that architecture had nothing to do with formal aesthetics caused friction with other teachers. Dismissed in 1930, he went to the Soviet Union where he was heaped with honour and privilege until the Stalinist insistence on a return to *Classicism made him return to Switzerland (1936–9), after which he spent a decade in Mexico before retiring to Switzerland (1949). His best-known works are the Trade Union School, Bernau, near Berlin (1928–30), and the Toerten Housing, Dessau (1928–30).

Schnaidt (1965)

mezzanine. Partial low storey (*entresol* if immediately over the ground-floor) introduced in the height of a principal storey, or any subordinate storey intermediate between two main storeys.

MIAR (***Movimento Italiano per l'Architettura Razionale***). Italian *Rationalism was promoted at an exhibition in Rome (1928) organized by *Libera and *Gruppo 7. A new movement, MAR (*Movimento Architettura Razionale*) was then formed to bring all Italy's Rationalist architects together and to promote another exhibition, this time in 1931, where the event was celebrated by the publication of *Manifesto per l'Architettura Razionale* supported energetically by the Fascist leader, Benito Mussolini (1883–1945).

Danesi and Patetta (1976)

Michael of Canterbury (*fl.* 1300–36). *See* Canterbury.

Michaud, Joseph (1822–1902). *See* Bourgeau.

Michela, Costanzo (1689–1754). Italian architect. Influenced by *Guarini, he designed several churches in the vicinity of Turin, including the Parish Church at Barone (1729–39), San Giacomo, Rivarolo Canavese (1728–33), and Santa Marta in Agliè (1739–60). The last is an extraordinary example of complex geometries with three internal volumes (a hexagon contained by convexes and concaves instead of straight lines, a square contained by convex shapes, and a circle), and is an exceptional late-*Baroque masterpiece.

Art Bulletin 50 (1968), 169–83; Norberg-Schulz (1986*a*)

Michelangelo Buonarroti (1475–1564). Italian poet, painter, and sculptor of the first half of C16, he was also the most original, inventive, and influential architect of the time. His architectural career did not really start until he began work on the façade of the Chapel of Pope Leo X (1513–21), Castel Sant'Angelo, Rome (1514), followed by his connection with San Lorenzo, Florence, starting in 1516, when he prepared designs for the façade of the Church (never realized). His first actual building was the New Sacristy (1519–34), the *Mortuary Chapel of the Medici, the shell of which already was built. For this interior he modelled the wall-surfaces with *cornices and *pediments resting on *consoles without *friezes or *architraves, panels breaking through open-bedded segmental pediments, and other *abuses of architecture. These *elisions and distortions created a dynamic tension unknown in the Early *Renaissance. *Aedicules seem to press down on the architectural elements below, and each many-layered wall is framed by a *triumphal arch (defined by *pietra-serena *Orders) over which the *coffered *dome rises on *pendentives that only begin above the cornice over the great arches, with an extra storey slotted in at pendentive level. The darker pietra-serena work is conventional, resembling treatment by *Brunelleschi, but Michelangelo erected the walls of white marble, seeming to crowd and break out of the areas framed by the Orders.

He was commissioned to design the Biblioteca Laurenziana (1524–71), in which *pilasters seemed to carry the structure of the ceiling, the pattern of which was repeated in the design of the floor, unifying the room in a manner not previously seen. In the vestibule, columns were set in recesses and appeared to sit on consoles, while the *blind aedicules in the wall-panels between the Orders were designed with shafts tapering towards the bases. The vestibule stair (completed by *Ammannati after 1559) is extraordinary, with two external flights and a curious arrangement of steps. The whole structure occupies the centre of the vestibule, and was the very first grand stair of the Renaissance period to be treated as a major feature of architectural design. Both the New Sacristy and the Laurentian Library vestibule are examples of *Mannerism.

In 1534 Michelangelo departed from Florence and settled in Rome, where he painted the Sistine Chapel ceiling for Pope Paul III (1534–49). His Florentine architecture had been mostly interiors, with *Quattrocento treatments of colour, but in Rome his architecture was public, grand, and on a huge scale. He set up the *Antique statue of Emperor Marcus Aurelius (161–80) on a new base in the centre of a space in front of the Palazzo del Senatore on the Capitoline Hill in 1539, and designed the genesis of the trapezoidal Piazza del Campidoglio as a setting for the statue, though this was not completed until the mid-C17 by the *Rainaldis. He planned a new façade for the Palazzo dei Conservatori (completed 1584) which was set at an angle to that of the Palazzo del Senatore, and, to balance it, an identical façade on the other side of the Piazza that became the front of the Capitoline Museum (completed 1654). In these façades he used a *Giant Order, a device that was to be widely employed thereafter, with a smaller Order carrying the first floor, and an even smaller one in the aedicules. The piazza itself was designed to look like a rectangular space, and in the centre is an elliptical pattern around the statue: both devices are read as a circle and square, and the elliptical element is the first use of this figure in Renaissance design. Both the trapezium and ellipse were precedents for the area in front of the basilica of San Pietro in Rome.

In 1546 Michelangelo was appointed to complete *Sangallo's Palazzo Farnese, and he first designed the huge *cornicione over the *astylar façade and redesigned the upper storeys of the *cortile, introducing some of his perverse Mannerist devices (such as consoles with pendent *guttae that seem to have slipped down the window-architraves). In the same year Michelangelo was appointed to complete St Peter's in succession to Sangallo and *Giulio Romano, and immediately began to undo some of Sangallo's work in an attempt to return to *Bramante's Greek-cross plan, but in a much more powerful version. His work was largely confined to the outer and upper parts of the building, although he simplified and clarified the basic geometry. For the exterior he unified the façades with a Giant Order based on the one he had used at the Capitol and designed a sixteen-sided drum with paired columns. As built by della *Porta in 1588–90 the dome is higher and more pointed, and the vertical lines of the paired columns are continued in the ribs of the dome and the *lantern. Michelangelo's proposal for a giant *portico was never realized, as *Maderno built the nave and façade that muddied the clarity of the great architect's design.

At the Porta Pia, Rome (1561–4), named after Pope Pius IV (1559–65), Michelangelo's Mannerist tendencies became more extreme: a broken segmental scrolled pediment with *swag was set inside a triangular pediment, while oversized guttae hung below blocks on either side of the *tympanum; *Ionic capitals, freely interpreted, became copings for the *battlements; aedicules and frames around openings were deliberately oversized and blocky; and panels had broken scrolled pediments holding broken segmental pediments between them. The gate, which faces towards the city at the end of a newly straightened street leading from the Quirinal, anticipates the beginning of *Baroque town-planning.

Pius IV also commissioned Michelangelo to remodel the *tepidarium of the *thermae of Diocletian as a church, using the ancient vaulting and eight monolithic granite columns of the Roman building. It was called Santa Maria degli Angeli, and was begun in 1561, remodelled in C18.

Ackerman (1986); Heydenreich and Lotz (1974); Millon and Smyth (1988)

Michelozzo di Bartolommeo *called* **Michelozzo Michelozzi** (1396–1472). Florentine architect and sculptor of the Early *Renaissance, a contemporary of *Brunelleschi. He worked first with Ghiberti (1417–24) and later with Donatello (*c.*1425–32), with whom he designed and made a series of architectural funerary monuments. Around 1427 he designed the *loggia and court for the Medici *villa at Careggi, near Florence, having already remodelled the villa at Trebbio (*c.*1422). The influence of the essentials of Renaissance architecture and Brunelleschi's work is clear from his reconstruction of the *cloister, refectory, cells, and public rooms at the Church and Monastery of San Marco, Florence (*c.*1437–52), including

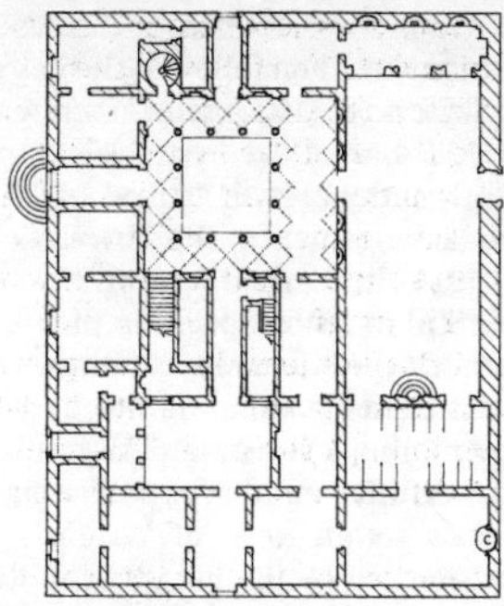

Plan of Palazzo Medici, Florence, showing central *cortile*.

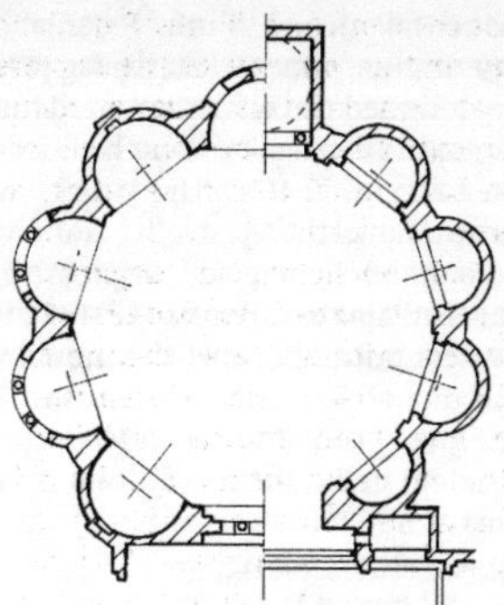

(*left*) Temple of 'Minerva Medica', Rome (*c.* AD 250). (*right*) East end of the Church of Santissima Annunziata, Florence, by Michelozzo di Bartolommeo, begun 1444. A Renaissance solution to the problem by direct reference to Roman Antiquity.

the light, elegant, triple-aisled, vaulted library. Michelozzi's best-known work is the enormous *astylar Palazzo Medici (later Riccardi), Florence (1444–59), which has the lowest storey faced with rock-faced *rustication and pierced with arched openings, channel-rusticated *piano-nobile with regularly spaced semicircular Florentine arches, and a top storey of smooth *ashlar, the whole held down under a massive *cornicione. Behind this powerful exterior he designed an arcaded *cortile (with echoes of Brunelleschi's Foundling's Hospital) that was to be enormously influential. Michelozzo was also responsible for the remarkable *tribune in Santissima Annunziata, Florence (1444–55), one of the first centrally planned domed spaces of the Renaissance, with a polygonal plan off which are radiating apsidal chapels. Inspired by Brunelleschi's unfinished Santa Maria degli Angeli, Florence (1434), it is even more strongly related to the *Antique Roman temple of 'Minerva Medica', of *c.* AD 250, and was completed by *Alberti. At Santa Maria delle Grazie, Pistoia (from 1452), he used the cross-in-square plan of central and four subsidiary domed spaces.

Michelozzi was *capomaestro* of Florence Cathedral (1446–55) and supervised the building of the *lantern on the great dome. He designed the fortress-like villa at Cafaggiolo, Mugello (*c.*1452), the much more elegant Villa Medici, Fiesole (*c.*1458–61), remodelled the Palazzo Comunale, Montepulciano (1440), and designed the Hospital of San Paolo dei Convalescenti, Florence (1459). Although he was credited with introducing Florentine Brunelleschian ideas to Lombardy in the Portinari Chapel, Sant'Eustorgio, Milan (1460s), based on the Old Sacristy in San Lorenzo, Florence, this attribution is now rejected, as is his authorship of the Medici Bank, Milan.

Caplow (1977); Ferrara and Quinterio (1984); Heydenreich and Lotz (1974); Morisani (1951); van Vynckt (1993)

Michelucci, Giovanni (1891–1991). Italian architect. He met *Piacentini in the 1920s, who influenced him towards the stripped *Neoclassicism of the University City, Rome, where Michelucci later designed the Physiology, Psychology, and Anthropology Building, as well as the Institute of Mineralogy, Geology, and Palaeontology (1935). He collaborated with the *MIAR Tuscan Group in the design of the Santa Maria Novella Railway Station, Florence (1935–6), the most significant large example of Italian *Rationalism. His Government Building, Arezzo (1939), was an essay in sober Classicism. After the 1939–45 war, he abandoned the earlier architectural languages. The Church of San Giovanni Battista, Autostrada del Sole, near Florence (1960–3) verges towards *Expressionism.

Belluzzi and Conforti (1986); Emanuel (1994); Michelucci (1978); Quaroni (1980)

Michetti, Nicola *or* **Niccolò** (*c.*1675–1758). Italian architect. A pupil of Carlo *Fontana, he carried Roman *Baroque design well into C18. His elliptical church of San Pietro, Zagarolo, Italy (1717–23), is a conception comparable with designs by *Juvarra. From 1718 to 1723 he worked for Tsar Peter the Great (1682–1725) in Russia and built the Summer Palaces of

Katherinental, near Tallinn, Estonia (1718–20), and Strelna, near St Petersburg (1720–3). He also designed the enormous gardens with fountains (influenced by French precedents) at Peterhof (1719–23). His work was a significant model for *Rastrelli to follow. Back in Rome he designed the impressive west front of the Palazzo Colonna (1731–2), with a pavilion containing one of the most impressive C18 non-ecclesiastical interiors in Rome. He designed the Theatine Monastery of Sant'Andrea della Valle, with its splendid staircase (1755–7).

Millon (1980); Placzek (1982)

Middle Pointed. The *Second Pointed or *Decorated *Gothic style of the late C13. It seems to refer more to early Second Pointed of the *Geometrical* variety rather than to the later *Flowing* or *Curvilinear* type, so comes just after the *First Pointed so-called *Lancet style.

Mies van der Rohe, Ludwig (1886–1969). German architect, one of the most influential of *International Modernism. His earliest buildings (e.g. Riehl House, Neubabelsberg, near Berlin (1907)) drew on late-C18 German houses mingled with influences from the works of *Behrens, whose office he joined in 1908 and where he met *Gropius and Adolf *Meyer. His designs from 1911 were influenced by Behrens's interest in *Schinkel, as displayed at Behrens's Imperial German Embassy, St Petersburg (1911–12). Mies worked on a project for the Kröller-Müller House and Gallery, The Hague, The Netherlands, the 1912 version of which (produced independently of Behrens) was influenced by Schinkel's work at Potsdam and by designs of F. L. *Wright, whose buildings were known through Wasmuth's publications (notably of 1910) and the 1911 exhibition. In 1912 he established his own Berlin practice (even though the Kröller-Müller project fell through) and designed three houses in a stripped Neoclassical style. His Kempner House, Berlin (1919–21), had similarities to the pre-war houses but had a flat roof and an arched *loggia, again influenced by Schinkel's *Italianate round-arched style.

The changed political climate after the 1914–18 war led Mies to join the *Novembergruppe (1922), becoming its President in 1923. His 'Five Projects' of this period (1921–3) included the glass-clad Friedrichstrasse Office Block, published by Bruno *Taut, which had affinities with *Expressionism. Then followed the design for a Glass Skyscraper (1922), the Concrete Office Block (1922—one of the first designs to have the *International-style strip- or ribbon-window arrangement), the Brick Country House (1923—influenced by van *Doesburg and De *Stijl in its composition of cubic volumes), and the Concrete Country House (1923—designed for a sloping site, and with a plan resembling a swastika). The last project had powerfully emphasized overhanging horizontals reminiscent of Wright's work, counterbalanced by the big vertical block of the chimney, while the configuration of the L and T plan-shapes of the walls of the Brick Country House is one of the first instances of walls being disposed according to the principles of De Stijl composition. The connection with van Doesburg, Mies's admiration of *Berlage's work and ideas, and his sense of rapport with The Netherlands led him to add his mother's maiden-name, Rohe, to his own surname, joining the two by means of the slightly affected 'van der'. In 1923 he exhibited at the exhibition of De Stijl work in Paris, and made contact with the protagonists of Russian *Constructivism and *Suprematism. He also exhibited in Berlin and Weimar (in the latter case at the invitation of Gropius).

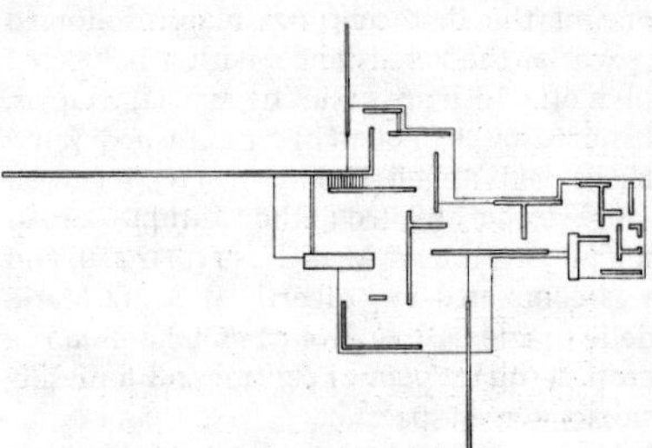

Plan of a proposed brick villa (1923), showing the influence of Mondrian and De Stijl.

With *Bartning, *Behrendt, *Häring, *Mendelsohn, *Poelzig, the *Tauts, and others, he formed Der *Ring, which rapidly became a nationwide organization to reject historical forms and styles and prepare the ground for an architecture of the new epoch based on contemporary technology. In 1926 Mies designed the monument to the Socialist and Spartacist Karl Liebknecht (1871–1919) and the Polish Communist Rosa Luxemburg (1870–1919) in Berlin: of brick projecting and receding planes on which the hammer and sickle were prominently displayed, it was nevertheless based on a steel-framed construction. In the same year he designed the Wolf House, Guben, where blocky masses of brick were pierced with windows and all *Historicist references were expunged.

Mies and other members of Der Ring were elected to the *Deutscher Werkbund in 1926, which, as a result, shifted ground from its historical mission to promote good industrial design and crafts to become a pressure-group promoting the new architecture. As Vice-President of the Werkbund and Director of the proposed *Weissenhofsiedlung Exhibition in Stuttgart (1927), he enhanced his reputation as leader of the avant-garde. The exhibition, for which he designed the master-plan and the long apartment-block on the highest land, contained temporary structures as well as over twenty permanent buildings, including villas, designed by leading German and other Modernists, including *Bourgeois, Le *Corbusier, *Oud, and *Stam. Predominant motifs were long horizontal strips of windows, smooth white walls, and flat roofs: the language of International Modernism had been found, and its influence was worldwide. Mies was also able to exhibit his famous tubular-steel chair, the earliest of several later variations that were to place him in the forefront of furniture-design.

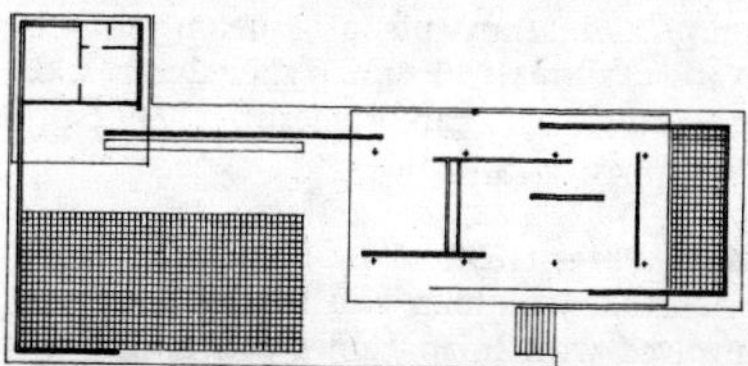

Plan of the Barcelona Pavilion showing structural columns and spaces defined by screen-walls.

For the International Exposition, Barcelona (1928–9), Mies designed the German Pavilion, with a flat roof supported on steel columns clad in chromium-plated casing and walls of onyx and marble (some of which projected beyond the roof into the space beyond). This little building, exquisitely and expensively detailed, won immediate approval and became one of the most admired paradigms of the late 1920s. It was furnished with Mies's famous 'Barcelona Chair', consisting of a chromium-plated frame with black leather upholstered back and seat. Then followed the Tugendhat House, Brno, Czechoslovakia (1930), with a single storey on the street frontage and two storeys facing the garden. The living-room was a continuous space with chromium-cased steel columns and free-standing panels, derived from the Barcelona design, while the full-height windows could be fully lowered out of sight, enabling the interior space to extend into the garden-terrace. Every detail of the house was purpose-made, designed by the architect.

In 1930 Mies was appointed to direct the *Bauhaus on Gropius's recommendation following the dismissal of Hannes *Meyer, and emphasized instruction within a more defined pedagogic structure, but in 1932 the National Socialist majority on the Dessau Town Council closed the institution. Mies attempted to reconstitute the Bauhaus in Berlin, but there it was threatened, and Mies closed it in 1933, although he tried to continue teaching in Switzerland until 1934.

In 1937, having attempted a futile accommodation with the new German regime, he emigrated to the USA, becoming an American citizen in 1944. He taught at the Armour Institute (later Illinois Institute of Technology), Chicago, from 1938, and from 1940 redesigned the campus and buildings, placing rectangular blocks on an overall grid, exposing the steel frames, and designing all the junctions with his customary meticulous care (he claimed 'God is in the detail'). He invented a sophisticated language of metal-and-glass architecture, shown to best effect at the Farnsworth House, Fox River, Plano, Ill. (1946–50), in which the terrace-slab, floor-slab, and roof-slab were all raised from the ground and carried on steel stanchions of I section. This open glass-sided pavilion idea with impeccable detailing was used by Mies on several occasions, e.g. Crown Hall, IIT, Chicago (1952–6), and the National Gallery, Berlin (1962–8). The Lake Shore Drive Apartments, Chicago (1950–1) had steel frames, while the huge Seagram Skyscraper, New York (1954–8—with Philip *Johnson), was clad in bronze and glass.

Mies's influence cannot be overstated and, with Le Corbusier and Gropius, he completed the Trinity of Modernism. His impact worldwide is clear, and his metal-and-glass-fronted buildings have been widely copied.

Bill (1955); Blaser (1977, 1996); Carter (1974); Drexler (1960); Glaeser (1977); Hilbersheimer (1956); Johnson (1978); Schulze (1985); Zukowsky (1986, 1994)

Milesian plan. Town laid out on a regular grid-iron plan, derived from the Greek colonial city of Miletus, and promoted by *Hippodamus, who only publicized rather than invented it.

Wycherley (1962)

Miletus. *See* Hippodamus *and* Isidorus.

military decoration. Architectural ornament representing an arrangement of armour, flags, guns, helmets, swords, etc., known as a *trophy, often used on arsenals, barracks, and the like, as well as on funerary monuments and memorials commemorating military men or war.

Millar, John (*fl.* *c*.1816–*c*.1856). ?Irish architect trained by *Hopper. Having worked on Hopper's prodigious *Romanesque Revival Gosford Castle, Co. Armagh (1819–21), he settled in Belfast. He designed some remarkable Presbyterian churches (1830s) in an advanced, austerely noble *Greek Revival style, including the First Presbyterian Church, Antrim (1834—with *Doric columns based on those from the Temple of Apollo at Delos published by *Stuart and *Revett (1794)) and the splendid Portaferry Church, Co. Down (a Greek Temple of the same severe Order on a high *podium). At Crumlin, Co. Antrim, he designed the pretty *Gothic Revival Presbyterian Church (inscribed *Ecclesia Scotia* and signed by Millar—1839), and other churches in Belfast and Castlereagh. In 1849 he was called on to report on progress at Garron Tower, near Carnlough, Co. Antrim, apparently designed by Lewis *Vulliamy and Charles Campbell of Newtownards (who also worked at Mount Stewart, Co. Down). In 1856, Millar emigrated to the Antipodes.

Brett (1996); Colvin (1995)

Miller, James (1860–1947). Scots architect. He designed Belmont Parish Church, Hillhead, Glasgow (1893), and the charming *Arts-and-Crafts Free *Scottish Baronial building in St Enoch's Square, Glasgow, for the Underground Railway (1896). He won the competition to design the Glasgow International Exhibition (1898–1901), designed the Glasgow Royal Infirmary (1907), and the powerful Classical (with Mannerist touches) Institute of Civil Engineers, Great George Street, London (1910). One of the most important commercial architects working in Glasgow after 1900, his houses were also very attractive: Lowther Terrace, Glasgow, and the Village Estate at Forteviot, Perthshire (1908), are among his best. The Peebles Hydro, Borders, the Turnberry Hotel, Ayrshire, and the Village Hall, Bournville, Birmingham (all 1908), were also by him.

Gray (1985); Williamson, Riches, and Higgs (1990)

Miller, Sanderson (1716–80). English amateur architect and connoisseur, he was an important figure in the *Georgian *Gothic Revival (*see also* Gothick). He embellished his Manor House at Radway Grange, Warwickshire, with Gothic features in 1744–6, and erected an octagonal *battlemented and *machicolated Gothic Tower at Edgehill, Warwickshire (1745–7). At Hagley Park, Worcestershire (1747–8), he designed a 'ruined' castle that to contemporaries had the 'true rust of the Barons' Wars', and very soon the Squire of Radway was being consulted as an expert by many anxious to embrace fashionable Gothicizing for their properties. The motif of a two-storey *bay-window was used at a number of sites, including Radway, Arbury Hall, Warwickshire (*c*.1750–2), Adlestrop Park, Gloucestershire (1750–62), and Rockingham Hall, Hagley, Worcestershire (1751). The number of buildings where he was involved was considerable, including Lacock Abbey, Wiltshire (1754–5—where he advised on the Great Hall and Gothic Gateway), the *nave and *transepts of Kineton Church, Warwickshire (1755–6), and the *sham Castle at Wimpole Hall, Cambridgeshire (1749–51).

Colvin (1995); McCarthy (1987)

Mills, Peter (1598–1670). English architect, brickmaker, builder, and surveyor. He was involved with Inigo *Jones concerning the Church of St Michael-le-Querne, London (1638), and appears to have designed houses on the south side of Great Queen Street, Lincoln's Inn Fields, London (*c*.1640—an early example of uniform elevations for a group of London houses—demolished), and elsewhere in the capital. His greatest work was Thorpe Hall, Peterborough, Northamptonshire (1653–6), a major monument of *astylar *Artisan Mannerism and the *Protectorate style. He may also have designed Wisbech Castle, Cambridgeshire (*c*.1658—demolished). With *May, *Pratt, and *Wren he was one of the Surveyors employed to supervise the rebuilding of the City of London after the Great Fire (1666). His later work has something of the style of May and Pratt: at Cobham Hall, Kent (1661–3), for example, there was hardly a trace of Artisan Mannerism.

Colvin (1995); Papworth (1852)

Mills, Robert (1781–1855). American architect, a protégé of *Jefferson, he worked with *Hoban and assisted *Latrobe on the Capitol, Washington, DC (1803–8). After Latrobe sent him to Philadelphia to oversee the building of some houses and the Bank of Philadelphia in 1807–8, Mills set up his own practice there. Washington Hall, Philadelphia (1809–16), was in a severe Neoclassical style worthy of *Ledoux, while the circular Sansom Street Baptist Church (1811–12) and Octagon Unitarian Church (1812–13) drew on an eclectic collection of sources. At the Monumental Church, Richmond, Va. (1812–17), there was a centralized octagonal plan with a massive porch featuring distyle *in antis* (*see* anta) unfluted Greek *Doric columns based on those of the temple of Apollo at Delos, a robust design worthy of Latrobe. This Doric *Order was again used for the Washington Monument, Baltimore, Md. (1814–42), where he designed many buildings.

Mills is best known for his monumental architecture in Washington, DC. These include the vast *obelisk of the Washington National Monument (1833–84), the great *stoa-fronted *Ionic Treasury Building (1836–42), the Doric Patent Office Building (1836–40—now the National Portrait Gallery), and the *Corinthian Old Post Office (1839–42). It is clear he was a competent *Greek Revivalist. One of his best buildings was the Lunatic Asylum, Columbia, SC (1821–7), in the Greek Doric style with south-facing wards and a complete absence of the forbidding severity usually associated with such institutions. He designed several customs-houses and was a pioneer of fire-resistant construction.

Bryan (1976); Gallagher (1935); Hamlin (1964); Hitchcock (1977); Liscombe (1985, 1994); Pierson and Jordy (1970–86); Placzek (1982); Whiffen and Koeper (1983)

minaret. Tall, slender tower (circular, rectangular, or polygonal on plan), usually attached to a *mosque, with one or more projecting balconies from which Muslims are called to prayer.

Bloom (1989)

Minimalism. Style inspired by severe Modern architecture (such as the purest of *Mies van der Rohe's work or the bare images of Barragán's designs), traditional Japanese architecture, and Zen Buddhist gardens. Minimalism seeks to avoid clutter, ornament, and even colour, while possessions were stored away. It has sometimes been adopted to suggest exclusiveness and luxury. A feature of the *Modern Movement since the 1920s, it re-emerged in the 1960s and 1980s.

Pawson (1996); Tate and Smith (1986)

Minoan architecture. The architecture of Ancient Crete, of which the palace at Knossos (C15 BC) is an outstanding example. *See* Cretan architecture.

Dinsmoor (1950)

minster. **1.** A *monastery or its church. **2.** Abbey- or priory-church, or, more properly, a large *collegiate or conventual church, distinguished from a parish-church or a cathedral.

minstrel gallery. Balcony, gallery or loft for musicians, also called a *musician's gallery*, e.g. in a church or hall.

minute. **1.** Subdivision of a *module, sometimes a sixtieth part of a column-shaft diameter at its base if two modules are equivalent to that diameter, so a minute in this case would be a thirtieth part of a module. **2.** Sixtieth part of a degree by which angles are measured.

Mique, Richard (1728–94). One of the creators of the *Louis Seize style in C18 France, he was trained under J.-F. *Blondel, and worked for a while at Nancy for Stanisław Leszczyński (1677–1766), exiled King of Poland (1704–9 and 1733–4). In 1766 he was called to Versailles by Leszczyński's daughter, Marie, Queen of King Louis XV (reigned 1715–74), where he designed the Ursuline Convent with its Church (completed 1772) derived from *Palladio's Villa Capra near Vicenza. He also designed the Church of the Carmelites, St-Denis (1775), and the Chapel of the Hospice of St-Cloud (1788). In 1775 he succeeded *Gabriel as *premier architecte du Roi* and, collaborating with Hubert *Robert, designed the master-plan (1777) for the development of the Trianon at Versailles in the 'English Taste'. He built the Temple de l'Amour, the Theatre, the Grotto with Cascade, the Belvedere, and the *Picturesque *Hameau du Trianon* with its exposed timbers and rustic roofs (1778–82) that was a precedent for *Nash's Blaise Hamlet, near Bristol (1811). The interiors of the *petits appartements* at Versailles (1779) were designed for Queen Marie Antoinette (Méridienne, two Libraries, and the *Cabinet Intérieur* or *Petit Salon*), all in the Neoclassical style. He fell victim to the Guillotine during the Terror.

Braham (1980); Kalnein and Levey (1972); Morey (1868)

Miralles, Enric (1955–). Spanish (Catalan) architect, he established his practice in Barcelona in 1984, collaborating (1983–92) with Carme Pinós (1954–). Their works included the Igualada Cemetery, near Barcelona (1985–92—with monumental banks of concrete *loculi); the Olympic Archery Range, Barcelona (1992); Els Hostalets de Balenyá Civic Centre, near Barcelona (1988–94—which some commentators have seen as linked to *Deconstructivism); and the National Training Centre for Rhythmic Gymnastics, Alicante (1989–93). In 1998 Miralles won the competition to design the new Scottish Parliament Building, sited at the foot of the Royal Mile, Edinburgh, in partnership with RMJM Scotland (successors of Robert *Matthew, Johnson-Marshall, & Partners).

Curtis (1996); Jodidio (1995*a*); Meyhöfer (1995)

miserere, misericord. 1. *Mercy-seat*, *subsellium*, or miniature ledge on the underside of hinged medieval choir-stall seats, so that, when the seats were folded upright, the misericords could give support to a person standing up. It had a carved *corbel-like element under the ledge, frequently representing everyday life, comic episodes, fantastic creatures, fables, and even indecencies. Excellent carved medieval misericords survive, e.g. in the Parish Church of St Laurence, Ludlow, Shropshire. **2.** Room where monastic regulations were relaxed.

Anderson (1954); Bond (1910, 1912); Parker (1850); Remnant (1969)

Mitchell, Arnold Bidlake (1864–1944). Gifted English *Arts-and-Crafts architect. He began practice in 1886, specializing in parish-halls, houses, and schools. His best works include St Felix School, Southwold, Suffolk (1902), the School of Agriculture, Cambridge (1909–10), and University College School, Frognal, Hampstead, London (1905–7), the last in a full-blown, robust *Wrenaissance style. His domestic works include the fine 1 Meadway Close (1910) and 34 and 36 Temple Fortune Lane (1908), Hampstead *Garden Suburb, and the outstanding houses in Basil Street, Brompton, London (1900s), with long ranges of *mullioned and *transomed windows and tall gables (mutilated in the 1939–45 war).

Gray (1985); Miller and Gray (1992)

Mitchell & Giurgola. American architectural firm founded (1958) by Rome-born Romaldo Giurgola (1920–), and Pennsylvania-born Ehrman Burkman Mitchell (1924–). Their work has been consistently admired for its sense of continuity and freedom from stylistic quotation, influenced mostly by the work of *Kahn. Among their buildings are the Volvo Headquarters, Göteborg, Sweden (1984), the Parliament House of Australia, Canberra (1988), and the IBM Offices, Darling Park, Sydney, Australia (1993).

Emanuel (1994); Placzek (1982)

Mithraeum. Building dedicated to the cult of Mithras, popular during the Roman Empire, often partly underground and planned on an *axis between shelves or *loculi on which followers reclined during the mysteries, and with an *apse at one end. A good example was discovered in 1870 under the Church of San Clemente, Rome.

mitre. Junction of two members at right angles involving chamfers or mouldings meeting at a diagonal line. *See* arch, mason's mitre.

mitre-head. Type of *ogee-headed bulbous top of a *pinnacle or *turret of late *Perpendicular *Tudor *Gothic, as in Henry VII's *Chapel at Westminster Abbey, London. The name is derived from its resemblance to a Bishop's head-dress.

mitre-leaf. C18 and early C19 moulding enrichment featuring a leaf spliced at its base, often found with *beading as *bead-and-leaf* moulding.

Mixed style. Eclectic architectural style incorporating hybrid elements from different periods, styles, and even cultures in order to attempt the creation of a new style. Sometimes called *Synthetic Eclecticism* or *Syncretism*. Although much discussed in the 1970s, 1980s, and 1990s, it was also a phenomenon of other periods notably during the *Regency and late C19.

Crook (1987); Dixon and Muthesius (1985); Walker (1992)

Mixtec architecture. A *Meso-American people, the Mixtecs lived in a region in modern Mexico alongside the Pacific shore-line. Unlike the *Aztecs they did not build pyramidal structures. At Mitla, one of their major settlements, there are the remains of large houses, including the Palace of the Columns (*c.*1000) embellished with fine geometrical patterns, suggesting a sophisticated culture capable of producing impressive architecture.

Cruickshank (1996); Kubler (1984)

Mnesicles (*fl.* 437–420 BC). Athenian architect of the time of Pericles (460–429 BC), he designed the monumental *Doric *Propylaea, or entrance-gate to the *Acropolis (437–432 BC). It was a precedent for numerous Neoclassical gates, including *Langhans's Brandenburg Gate, Berlin, and von *Klenze's *Propyläen*, Munich. Mnesicles has been credited with the design of the *stoa of Zeus Eleutherios (*c.*430 BC) in the north-west corner of the *agora in Athens, which had projecting wings at each end. His name has also been associated with the Erechtheion (421–405 BC), but the evidence is lacking.

Bungaard (1957); Dinsmoor (1950); Placzek (1982); Tiberi (1964)

moat. Large steep-sided trench around a town or building for defensive purposes, sometimes filled with water.

Mobile architecture. Concept promoted by Yona *Friedman and others, which held that users of buildings and settlements should have a say in plans and changes to them. Architecture would consist of structural frameworks, infrastructures, and services raised above the ground that would be infinitely adaptable. Such views influenced thinking in the 1960s and 1970s.

Friedman (1970, 1975)

Moderne. The *Art Deco style.

Modernism. 1. *See* Modern Movement. **2.** Style of the 1920s and 1930s described as *Modernist.

Weston (1996)

Modernisme. Cultural movement in Catalonia, Spain, from *c.*1880 to *c.*1920, divided into conservative *National Romanticism (La Renaixença—which promoted and celebrated Catalonian culture and language) and Progressivism (which tended to embrace many European tendencies, including the *Arts-and-Crafts movement, *Art Nouveau, and faith in the benefits of scientific investigation, technological advances, and industrialization). Catalan intellectuals saw Progressivism as a release from the stifling centralist structures of Madrid, and so Modernisme was associated with an assertion of regional (even nationalist) pride and identity. Its architectural expression lay in the incorporation of eclectic elements derived from historic styles, notably the *Moorish and *Gothic architecture of Spain; exploitation of materials (especially brick and tile) to express structure as well as to embellish every visible part of the fabric; and the exuberant use of enrichment, applied or integral to the structure. Its most celebrated protagonists were *Domènech i Montaner, *Gaudí, and *Puig i Cadafalch.

Bohigas (1968, 1991); Freixa (1991); Lampugnani (1988); Marfany (1975)

Modernismo. Spanish *Art Nouveau, also called *Estilo Modernista*.

Tschudi-Madsen (1967)

Modernist. 1. Architectural style of the 1920s and 1930s incorporating decorative devices that owed not a little to *Art Deco, *Aztec, and Ancient Egyptian styles, prompted by the 1925 Paris Exhibition. Among the commoner motifs were *chevrons, canted and *corbelled 'arches', *medallions, wave-scrolls, flutings, mouldings stepped over surfaces, and geometrical patterns. Colours were vivid, influenced by artefacts discovered in Tutankhamun's tomb in 1922, so blacks, vermilions, greens, yellows, blues, and lots of gilt and chrome were *de rigueur*, often in enamels and even glazed openings. *Modernistic* buildings (as they are often called) also incorporated streamlining and curved walls. A good example of a Modernistic building is the former Hoover Building, Great West Road, London (1931–8), by *Wallis, Gilbert, & Partners. **2.** Person subscribing to the doctrine and principles of the *Modern Movement.

Lewis and Darley (1986); Hitchmough (1992)

Modern Movement. C20 architectural movement (also called *Modernism*) that sought to sunder all stylistic and historic links with the past. While C19 theorists sought to find a style suitable for the times, the methods attempted to achieve this involved *eclecticism and mingling of styles to produce so-called *Free or

*Mixed styles, the idea being that a new style might emerge from the mélange. There were also some for whom function, honest expression of structure and materials, and a rational approach to design problems from first principles offered the way forward.

Early C20 movements such as *Futurism and *Constructivism sought answers in machinery, technology, and the expression of industrialized power, while the search for a *Machine Aesthetic became at times an end in itself. To some (notably Le *Corbusier), grain silos, trans-Atlantic liners of the *Mauritania* and *Titanic* vintage, motor-cars, and aeroplanes were paradigms of a desirable new aesthetic, while others held that all art, all aesthetics, and all refinement were bourgeois affectations and therefore should be rejected. The aims of Modernism were radical, concerned with the suppression of all ornament, historical allusions, and styles, counterbalanced by the elevation of *Sachlichkeit* (objectivity) and the evolution of *industrialized methods of building. Some groups within the Modern Movement, such as De *Stijl, advocated abstractions and purity of expression, and there were various emphases within the overall Movement, but virtually all were agreed on the need for rational responses to contemporary needs using modern materials, mass-produced building components, and experimental, industrial methods of construction. While idealistic iconoclasm, allied with leftist attitudes, was endemic, the more extreme protagonists advocated violence and revolutions to achieve their objectives, but slogan-making and polemics all too often replaced rational argument. *Functionalism was widely held to be ground on which all agreed, but even that faced objections in the search for an architecture freed from the constraints not only of the past and aesthetics, but from use as well. Some elements within the Modern Movement advocated that the purest architecture was that which remained on paper, or even in the mind, uncorrupted by the processes of being built, let alone used by untidy humanity.

By 1927 *International Modernism had arrived, and the white rectilinear flat-roofed building with strip-windows in metal frames (as in the exhibits at the *Weissenhofsiedlung, Stuttgart (1927), and Le Corbusier's designs) became the exemplar of what Modern Movement architecture should aim to be. So the Movement that sought to abolish style had simply created a new image, with its own pressures on members to conform. Devoted to the destruction of academic architecture and institutions, it constructed its own theories, dogmas, and pedagogic establishment: the *Bauhaus became the model for education; *CIAM (1928) set the agenda and laid down the creeds; and historians (e.g. *Giedion and *Pevsner) evolved theories of a continuous, logical, and inevitable development of Modernism from C18 and C19 'Functional' buildings by the so-called 'pioneers' of design. Architecture that did not fit neatly into this seamless 'history' was ignored, a chilling parallel to C20 political totalitarianism and its methods. After the 1939–45 war, 'Modernismus', as Reginald *Blomfield called it in the 1930s (a reference to its Teutonic origins), became the doctrine of the architectural establishment until new challenges arose from Modernist apostates (such as Philip *Johnson), advocates of contrast and contradiction (such as *Venturi), the protagonists of *Neo-Rationalist architecture (in particular the *Ticino School), and the critiques of academics some of whom have identified many strands within a Movement that has not been as coherent, logical, objective, or homogeneous as some of its apologists apparently have believed.

Blake (1977); Brolin (1976); Curtis (1996); Drexler (1980); Frampton (1980); Jencks (1973*a*); Jervis (1984); Pevsner (1960, 1974*a*); Riseboro (1983); Rowland (1973); Tafuri and Dal Co (1986); Watkin (1977); Wilenski (1957); Wolfe (1981)

Modern style. *Art Nouveau.

modillion. Projecting bracket resembling a horizontal rather than vertical *console fixed in series under the *soffit of the *cornice of the *Composite, *Corinthian, and (occasionally) Roman *Ionic *Orders, expressive of a *cantilever. Modillions are regularly spaced, their centre-lines relating to the vertical axes of columns, and have *coffers set between them under the *corona. A plain rectangular block in the same position is a *block* or *uncut* modillion, or a variety of *mutule.

modinature. Arrangement, positions, and types of mouldings appropriate to any building, part of a building, or an *Order.

modular design. Based on *modules, or certain standard sizes and multiples of those sizes, often associated with *industrialized buildings and prefabrication.

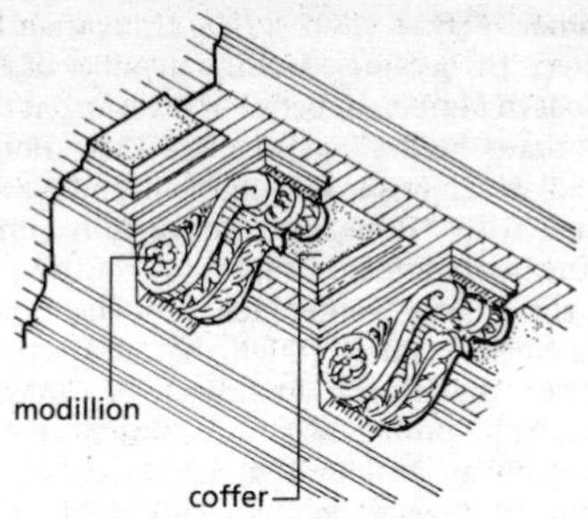

modillion. Modillions supporting a cornice with coffers between them.

module. 1. Unit of length used in multiples to determine proportion, in *Classicism the module is reckoned to be the diameter or the radius of a column-shaft at its base, subdivided into 60 or 30 *minutes. **2.** In *modular design a unit of measurement in prefabricated construction, or *industrialized building enabling ease of reproduction of repetitive standard components.

Modulor. Le *Corbusier's system of proportion, in *Le Modulor* (1948), based on the *golden section and on the male human figure (183 cm) with arm raised (total height 226 cm).

Jeanneret-Gris (1964, 1968, 1973–7)

Moffatt, William Bonython (1812–87). English architect in partnership with George Gilbert *Scott the Elder from 1835 to 1844. He was an expert on workhouses, designing around 50 (e.g. Old Windsor, Berkshire (1835), and Great Dunmow, Essex (1840)).

Dixon and Muthesius (1985)

Moghul, Mogul, *or* **Mughal architecture.** C16 to C18 Indian *Islamic architecture of which the Tâj Mahal (1630–53) is an outstanding exemplar, designed by Ustad Ahmad Lahori (*c*.1580–1649). Characterized by strict symmetry, the use of the flattened four-centred arch, *chatris, bulbous domes, and exquisite, regular decorations, it inspired the so-called *Hindoo style (really an amalgam of Moghul and Hindu styles) in the West, of which *Nash's Brighton Pavilion (1815–22) and S. P. *Cockerell's Sezincote, Gloucestershire (*c*.1805–20), are examples.

Conner (1979); Cruickshank (1996); Lewis and Darley (1986)

Möhring, Bruno (1863–1929). German architect. He was involved in the design of several international exhibitions (e.g. St Louis, Mo., 1904), but he is remembered primarily as an authority on town-planning. A disciple of *Sitte, he proposed plans for Greater Berlin (1910), and, with *Gurlitt, founded *Stadtbaukunst alter und neuer Zeit* (Ancient and Modern Civic Design—from 1919).

Stadtbaukunst alter und neuer Zeit, 10 (1929), 1–4

molecular structure. Building of tubes and balls arranged to resemble a diagram of a molecule, as in the *Atomium* erected for the Brussels Exposition (1958).

Lewis and Darley (1986)

Molinos, Jacques (1743–1813). French architect. He collaborated with J.-G. *Legrand on a number of projects, including the erection of the huge timber dome over the central court of the Halle au Blé, Paris, in 1782–3 (destroyed 1803), which was regarded as very progressive at the time. Also with Legrand he designed the Julien Garden at Épinay, and the Théâtre Feydeau which influenced F. *Gilly. On his own he built the Château of Puisieux, near Villers-Cotterets (1780–5). As Architect and Inspector of Civil Buildings for the Department of the Seine he produced some experimental but unrealized Neoclassical designs for cemeteries and crematoria, including the original proposals for Montmartre Cemetery, Paris (1799). His son, **Auguste-Isidore Molinos** (1795–1850) became an architect in Paris, designing the Churches of St-Jean, Neuilly (1827–31), and Ste-Marie, Batignolles (1828–9).

Delaire (1907); Etlin (1984); Gallet (1972); Hautecœur (1955); Middleton and Watkin (1987)

Møller, Christian Frederik (1898–1988). Danish architect. Taught by Kay *Fisker, he was with the latter from 1928 to 1943. With Povl Stegmann (1888–1944) they designed Aarhus University (begun 1932), influenced by Hannes *Meyer's Trade Union School at Bernau, Berlin. Construction (from 1943 solely the responsibility of Møller) went on until 1965, the various buildings (in a yellow brick) being placed in the undulating landscape for which C. T. Sørensen was consultant. He also designed the Museum of Modern Art, Aarhus (1963–5), and the Carl-Henning Pedersen Museum, Herning, Denmark (1973).

Weilbach (1995)

Moller, Georg (1784–1852). German architect. After training under *Weinbrenner in Karlsruhe (1802–7), he became in 1810 Director of Architecture for the Grand Duchy of Hesse-Darmstadt, and created a Neo-classical town-centre in Darmstadt itself. His architecture was austerely impressive: it included many houses (1811–25), the Freemasons' Hall (1817–20), the Court Theatre and Opera House (1818–20), and New Chancellery (1826–31). The Roman Catholic *Ludwigskirche* (1820–7—a drum with an internal *peristyle of *Corinthian columns carrying the *dome), the chaste Palace for Prince Carl (1837–41), the *Greek Revival *mausoleum on the Rosenhöhe (1826–31), the *Doric Victory Column (1841–4), and Kasino (1812) were all very fine buildings, but Darmstadt was severely damaged in the 1939–45 war, so his work only survives in part.

Outside Darmstadt Moller designed several works of considerable importance, including the Gothic House (1823–4), and the remodelling of the *Schloss* (Palace or Castle—1825–41), both in Homburg, while at Wiesbaden he rebuilt the *Schloss* (1837–41—now the *Hessischer Landtag* (State Parliament of Hesse)). At Mainz the Theatre (1829–33), with its clearly expressed auditorium and blocky fly-tower, was derived from *Durand's *Précis* (1802–5), and was reminiscent of F. *Gilly's unexecuted design for a National Theatre for Berlin (1799): with its external arcades the building influenced *Semper's celebrated Opera Houses in Dresden.

While Moller was one of the greatest of German Neoclassicists, he was also a pioneering student of medieval architecture. With Sulpiz *Boisserée (1783–1854) he discovered (1814) the original plans for Cologne Cathedral that were used as the basis of that building's completion. He published *Denkmäler der deutschen Baukunst* (Monuments of German Architecture—1815–21) which came out in English as *Moller's Memorial of German Gothic Architecture* (1836), and was of immense importance as a source-book for the *Gothic Revival. He was interested in constructional advances, using iron to reconstruct a dome at Mainz Cathedral, and bringing out publications, including *Beiträge zu der Lehre von den Construktion* (Contribution on the Theory of Construction—1832–44).

Fröhlich and Sperlich (1959); Haupt (1952–4); Krimmel (1978); Moller (1815–44); Watkin and Mellinghoff (1987)

Molnár, Farkas (1897–1945). Hungarian architect. He became a leading member of the *Modern Movement between the wars. At the *Bauhaus he designed his Red Cube House (1922) which was to be published, and is associated with *Hungarian Activism. In 1929, at the invitation of *Gropius, he contributed to the *CIAM conference on 'The Small Apartment', after which he and others formed the Hungarian branch of CIAM. A powerful protagonist of *International *Modernism, Molnár designed several white-rendered blocky houses, with bold *cantilevers and deep terraces, set in the hills around Budapest, clearly influenced by De *Stijl. Some of his designs (e.g. Houses on Cserje (1931) and Lejtö (1932) Streets, Budapest) are paradigms of the International Style that gelled at the *Weissenhofsiedlung, Stuttgart, in 1927. His Budapest apartment-blocks on Lotz Károly Street (1933) and Pasaréti Avenue (1937) are also significant. For a brief period in 1933 he collaborated with *Breuer before the latter emigrated to America. Molnár was killed during the Soviet siege of Budapest (1945).

Leśnikowski (1996)

Molton, John (*fl.* 1524–d. 1547). English master-mason. He worked at Westminster (1524–8) and Bath (1526–39) Abbeys, and succeeded Henry *Redman as master-mason to the King and to Westminster Abbey in 1528. He probably designed the *chantry-chapel of Abbot John Islip (d. 1532) in Westminster Abbey (1530s), and he worked on Cardinal (now Christ Church) College, Oxford, the Palace of Westminster, and, from 1532, Hampton Court Palace, where he designed the Great Hall. He seems to have been responsible for works at all the major buildings for King Henry VIII (1509–47), including the Palaces of St James, Bridewell, and Nonsuch, and the Forts of Deal, Walmer, and Sandown in Kent, although the last three buildings were designed by von *Haschenperg, with probable contributions from Richard *Lee. He was probably the last of the great English medieval architects before *Renaissance influences brought the *Gothic tradition to an end.

Harvey (1987)

monastery. Building or group of buildings arranged for the occupancy of members of a religious Order, or of persons desiring religious seclusion. European medieval monastic architecture derives from C6 types evolved under the rules of the Order founded by St Benedict, of which the C9 plan of St Gall, Switzerland, is the earliest surviving drawn example, with *cloister, *chapter-house and *dorter, *refectory, and infirmary set well away to the south-east. In terms of architectural organization the Benedictine plan was of a high order, and was the basis for the *Cistercian monastic plan, of which Fountains Abbey, Studley Royal, Yorkshire (mostly C12 and C13), is a fine example.

Braunfels (1972); Horn and Born (1979)

Moneo Valles, José Rafael (1937–). Spanish architect, he worked with *Utzon before establishing his practice in Madrid (1965). His work drew upon Classical traditions of proportion and composition, and many of his best buildings were of brick. His works include the Diestre Factory, Zaragoza (1965–7), the Town Hall, Logroño (1973–81), and the National Museum of Roman Art, Mérida (1980–6—employing massive brick arches reminiscent of Ancient Rome), the Previsión Española Building, Seville (1982–7), the Bank of Spain, Jaén (1983–8), and the Davis Museum, Wellesley College, Massachusetts, USA (1989–93).

Amsoneit (1994); Emanuel (1994); Jodidio (1995*a*)

money pattern. *See* coin.

Moneypenny, George (1768–*c*.1830). Architect who succeeded *Blackburn as the leading designer of English prisons. His work was often distinguished, and even, according to a contemporary, 'terrific', meaning striking *Sublime terror into the beholder. His Sessions House and House of Correction, Knutsford, Cheshire (1817–19), was almost as good as anything by *Harrison, and his County Gaol, Leicester (1790–2—demolished), had the distinction of being sketched by *Schinkel in 1826. He and Ignatius *Bonomi completed (1811) the Durham County Courts and Gaol after *Sandys's dismissal.

Bindmann and Riemann (1993); Colvin (1995)

Monier, Joseph (1823–1906). Pioneer of *reinforced-concrete construction, he patented designs in the 1860s, and later (1877) his system for manufacturing beams and columns, developed by the German firm Wayss, which published its theoretical work *Das System Monier* (1887).

Christophe (1902); Collins (1959)

monolith. Anything made of one piece of stone, e.g. an *obelisk or column-*shaft.

monolithic. **1.** Made of one piece of stone. **2.** Architecture appearing blocky, huge, and uniform. **3.** Building constructed of concrete poured and cast *in situ*. **4.** Rock-cut buildings.

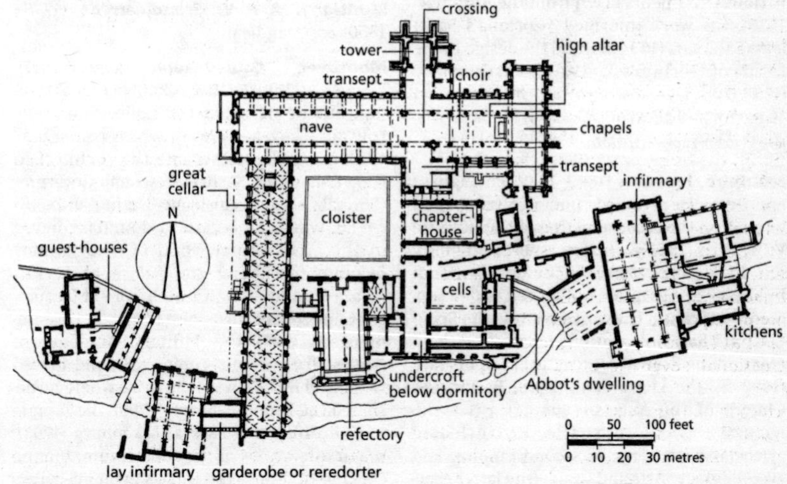

monastery. Fountains Abbey, Yorkshire.

monopteron *or* **monopteros.** Circular *colonnade supporting a roof, but without walls. *Soane called a *monopteral* building one without walls but with columns, but did not confine it to circular buildings, as he used the term to describe part of his own *mausoleum in the burial-ground of St Giles-in-the-Fields, Old St Pancras, London (1816), which has a square plan.

monotriglyphic. *Intercolumniation with one *triglyph on the *frieze between the centre-lines of two adjacent *Doric columns.

Montano, Giovanni Battista (1534–1621). Italian architect, of primary importance as a recorder of *Antique Roman architectural remains. Engravings were made of his drawings by his pupil G. B. *Soria, the first volume published as *Scelta di varii tempietti antichi* (Selection of Various Antique Temples—1624). Montano recorded *grottoes, caverns, and much else, but augmenting what he had surveyed with elevations and sections evolved from his imaginings, with reality 'corrected' for subjective aesthetic reasons. He seems to have understood Roman *concrete structures, and recorded *vaults and complicated stairs. His other works include *Diversi ornamenti capricciosi per depositi o altari* (Different Capricious Ornaments for Reliquaries or Altars—1625), *Tabernacoli diversi* (Various *Shrines—1628), and *Architettura con diversi ornamenti cavati dall' antico* (Architecture with Various Ornaments taken from the Antique—1636). His work informed *Cortona's Santi Luca e Martina (1634–69) and the design of the façade of *Bernini's Sant'Andrea al Quirinale (1658–70). He was also an influence on *Guarini and *Borromini.

Jervis (1984); Papworth (1852)

Monteiro, José Luis (1849–1942). Portuguese architect. He studied under *Pascal and worked on the reconstruction of the Hôtel de Ville, Paris (1874–8), before establishing himself in Lisbon, where he designed several public buildings much influenced by developments in France. His works include the Rocío Central Railway Station (1886–7—with a *Manueline Revival façade), the Hotel Palace (1890–2), the Liceu Central (1887), and the Church of the Angels (1908–11). His architectural styles were eclectic, including *Neoclassicism, French Second Empire, and even English *Arts-and-Crafts (the latter especially for his private houses). He used metal for the interior of the Railway Station and the Sala de Portugal, Sociedade de Geografia, Lisbon (1897). He was Professor of Architecture, Escola de Belas Letras, Lisbon (1881–1920), and therefore an influence on later Portuguese architects.

Smith (1968); Turner (1996)

Montereau, Pierre de (d. 1267). *See* Montreuil, Pierre de.

Montferrand, Auguste-Ricard de (1786–1858). French architect, he worked on the Madeleine, Paris, under *Vignon in Paris before emigrating to Russia in 1816. He designed St Isaac's Cathedral, St Petersburg (1818–58), based on *Soufflot's Ste-Geneviève, Paris, with an iron-framed dome the exterior of which was modelled on *Wren's dome at St Paul's Cathedral, London. This important early use of iron was a precedent for the later dome of the Federal Capitol, Washington, DC. He also designed the huge Alexander Column, St Petersburg (1830–4).

Butikov (1980); Hamilton (1983); Montferrand (1845); Watkin (1986)

Montfort, John (*fl.* 1376–d. *c.*1405). English military architect. He was responsible for works at the Castle, Elmley, Worcestershire (1391–6), and Warwick Castle, where he built Guy's Tower (1390s) and parts of the East Range.

Harvey (1987)

Montigny, A.-H.-V. Grandjean de (1776–1850). *See* Grandjean.

Montoyer, Louis-Joseph (*c.*1749–1811). Flemish architect. Little is known of his training, but he designed the Collège du Pape, Louvain (Leuven—1776–8), which is in a late-*Baroque style. He became the Architect to Duke Albert of Sachsen-Teschen, Governor-General of the Austrian Netherlands, in *c.*1780, where he became a dominant figure in the architectural world of what is now Belgium, designing the Palace at Laeken (1782–4) and the Church of St-Jacques-sur-Coudenberg, Brussels (1776–85). He commenced (1791) the Military Academy of Ixelles, Brussels (not completed), and moved to Central Europe with the Duke where he designed the Redoute, Baden (1799), the Temple of Concord in the Park at Laxenburg (1795), major alterations at the Albertinum, Vienna (1801–4—to house the Duke's great art-collections), and the Classical Great Hall of the

Hofburg, Vienna (1804–7). He was responsible for the saloon in the Palais Rohan, Prague (1807), one of the best examples of *Neo-classicism in Bohemia.

Baedeker, *Austria* (1929); Gerson and Ter Kuile (1960); Thieme and Becker (1932)

Montreuil *or* **Montereau, Pierre de** (d. 1267). French architect active in C13 Paris. Probably trained at Amiens, his first recorded works were a refectory (1239) and a *Lady Chapel (1245) at St-Germain-des-Prés (both destroyed) in Paris. He was recorded as *caementarius* (mason) at St-Denis (1247), and may have worked at Sainte-Chapelle, Paris. The higher parts of the south *transept at Notre Dame, Paris (1258–67), were designed and built by him following the death of Jean de *Chelles. His tombstone (no longer extant) at St-Germain-des-Prés acknowledged his status as a Doctor of Masons.

Eudes de Montreuil (*fl. c.*1250–87), perhaps Pierre's son, was a *Magister Caementarius Operum Domini Regis* (Master-Mason of the King's Works), and may have been involved in building fortifications at Jaffa, Palestine. Part of Beauvais Cathedral was attributed to him, but the evidence for this, and for his involvement at the Aigues-Mortes town fortifications, is virtually non-existent.

Branner (1965); Papworth (1852)

Montuori, Eugenio (1907–). Italian architect best known for the Stazione Termini, Rome (from 1947). With other Italian architects associated with *Terragni, he won the competition to design the new town of Sabaudia, one of five towns planned by the Fascist regime as part of the reclamation of the Pontine Marshes near Rome. The architecture, which was stark and tough, was firmly embedded in the *Rationalism and *Neo-classicism that evolved in Italy during the 1930s. Montuori designed the concourse for the Railway Station, Venice (1934), the town-plans of Bolzano (1936) and Carbonia (1940), and various Classicizing buildings at the University of Rome (1935) and the Piazza Imperiale, Rome (1940s).

van Vynckt (1993)

monument. 1. Building or memorial intended to perpetuate the memory of an event or an individual, such as a public memorial or funerary monument. **2.** Structure considered to be an object of historic or architectural interest.

monumental. 1. Building intended as a *monument, or looking like one. **2.** Building that is formal, impressive, very large, and permanent, probably intended to overawe.

monumental brass. Plate of *brass or *latten *incised with a formalized image and inscription, let into a slab of stone as a funerary monument.

Moore, Charles Willard (1925–93). American architect, a leading figure of *Post-Modernism. He founded his own firm in 1970, subsequently forming associations with other professionals. His work was varied, full of allusions, and *scenographic. His early buildings included his own house, Orinda, Calif. (1962), where the living-areas were identified by means of historical references, and this set the agenda for later work in which knowledge of architectural history played no small part, for his architecture was often tempered with fancy, myth, and mnemonic associations. Other schemes included the Athletic Club, Sea Ranch, near San Francisco (1964–6—where the buildings recall summer-cottage and sea-shore architecture); Kresge College, University of California, Santa Cruz (1973–4); and the Piazza d'Italia, New Orleans, Louisiana (1975–80—a stagey composition (almost a collage) of reminiscences from *Classicism that *International Modernists found profoundly shocking). More recent buildings included the Humboldt Library and housing, Tegel Harbour, Berlin (1987–8); the Church of the Nativity, Rancho Santa Fé, Calif. (1989), and the University of Oregon Science Complex, Eugene, Oreg. (1990), all of which had historical references. Moore's influence was considerable, and his use of evocative motifs powerfully polemical.

Bloomer and Moore (1977); Emanuel (1994); Jodidio (1993); Klotz (1988); Littlejohn (1984); Stern (1977)

Moore, Temple Lushington (1856–1920). Church architect with Ulster connections, he was articled to George Gilbert *Scott Junior before setting up on his own in 1879. His work, a mixture of scholarly *Gothic Revival and ingenious invention, was a link between *Bodley's style and the final phase of the Revival as epitomized in the work of Moore's pupil, Giles Gilbert *Scott. His buildings include St Peter's Church, Barnsley, Yorkshire (1893–1911), All Saints' Church, Tooting, London (1904–6), St Wilfrid's Church, Harrogate, Yorkshire (1905–14), and Pusey

House, Oxford (1911–14—one of his finest and most sensitive works).

Brandwood (1997); *DNB* (1927); Gray (1985)

Moorish arch. *See* arch.

Moorish architecture. *Islamic architecture of North Africa and regions of the Iberian peninsula where the Moors were dominant (711–1492). The most perfect examples were the exquisite Alhambra, Granada (mostly 1338–90), and La Mezquita at Córdoba (785–987). *Moresque* is architecture like or derived from that of the Moors (see *Hispano-Moresque), or, more loosely, from Islamic architecture, and the term is especially associated with formal foliate ornament of an interlacing type, also known as *arabesque. Moorish influences had a considerable effect during the C19 enthusiasm for exotic *Picturesque buildings, and they were exploited by many designers, such as Owen *Jones.

Conner (1979); Lewis and Darley (1986); Papworth (1852); Sturgis *et al.* (1901–2)

Moosbrugger, Caspar Andreas (1656–1723). Benedictine monk who, with the *Beers and *Thumbs, was among the most important contributors to what is known as the *Vorarlberg School of *Baroque and *Rococo architects working in and around the eastern shores of the Bodensee (Lake Constance). He was one of the first (1680s) Central-European architects to alter the *basilican plan by introducing circular, elliptical, or polygonal volumes. His grandest work was the huge Benedictine Abbey Church of Einsiedeln, south of Lake Zürich, Switzerland (1674–1723). The Abbey's plan, as rebuilt from 1702 by Moosbrugger's designs, has a resemblance to the Escorial, Madrid, and the Church itself has an interior arrangement that marks its architect as a great original. In *c.*1617 Santino *Solari had designed a shrine for the Black Virgin of Einsiedeln (destroyed in 1798 and rebuilt in reduced form to plans by Jakob Natter (1735–1815) and Luigi *Cagnola) to the east of which was a C17 *chancel: Moosbrugger's solution was to unify these elements by placing the shrine within an approximately octagonal volume with a two-bay nave flanked by aisles separated by wall-piers to the east. The western volume, accommodating the shrine and pilgrims, has, rising from the shrine, two piers carrying vault-arches, creating complex geometries. Eastwards lie the *choir and high-altar, and the entire interior seems to be very long, an effect enhanced by refinements of *scenography and by the rich frothiness of the *stucco and other decorations by the *Asam brothers (from 1724).

Moosbrugger had previously remodelled the *Romanesque Church at Muri, Switzerland (1684–97), and prepared schemes for the Benedictine Abbey Church of St Gallen, Switzerland, where the great central space is probably his idea. His early advice (1684) on the design of the great Abbey Church at Weingarten (built 1714–24) does not appear to have borne fruit, but his influence may be detected at Rheinau (1702), Lachen (1703), and Solothurn (1711). He was also involved in the design of the Benedictine Abbey of Disentis (1683–99) and the Convent of Seedorf (from 1695). Other members of the family, **Andreas** and **Peter Anton I Moosbrugger**, were designing Rococo stucco-work in the 1780s; **J. S. Moosbrugger** designed the Neoclassical high-altar at St Gallen (1810); and in the 1840s **Hieronymus Moosbrugger** was working in a Neo-Baroque style in Vienna.

Birchler (1924); Böck (1989); Bourke (1962); Hempel (1965); Hitchcock (1968*a*); Lieb and Dieth (1976); Oechslin (1973)

Morandi, Riccardo (1902–89). Italian civil engineer, renowned for his *reinforced-concrete structures, notably the Maracaibo Bridge, Venezuela (1957–62), the Polcevera autostrada viaduct, near Genoa (1960–7), the huge sail-roof of the maintenance hangar, Fiumicino Airport, Rome (1970), and the subterranean car-showroom, Valencia Park, Turin (1959).

Boaga (1984); Emanuel (1994); Imbesi *et al.* (1991); Masini (1974)

Morava School. *See* Byzantine architecture.

More, Edmund (*fl.* 1523–d. 1536). English Freemason. Between 1523 and 1533 he worked on Bishop West's exquisite *Chantry Chapel in Ely Cathedral, Cambridgeshire, a sumptuous work in which late-*Perpendicular *Gothic and early *Renaissance (especially the vaulted ceiling) merge. Virtually all the images he carved have been destroyed, but if he and his assistant, Peter Cleyft (probably a German from Cleves), had anything to do with the architectural treatment (which seems likely), they were a remarkable team, creating one of the loveliest early C16 spaces in all England.

Harvey (1987)

Moreau-Desproux, Pierre-Louis (1727–93). French architect. He designed the Hôtel de Chavannes, Boulevard du Temple, Paris (1756–8), which was praised by *Laugier as an example of the new 'Greek' fashion, although there was precious little Grecian about it apart from the bands of key frets under the first-floor windows. He refronted the Palais Royal, Paris, when he reconstructed the Théâtre de l'Opéra there (1763–70—destroyed 1781). He was guillotined in 1793.

Braham (1980); Middleton and Watkin (1987)

Moresque. *See* Moorish architecture.

Moretti, Luigi Walter (1907–73). Italian architect. His early works were in the stripped Neoclassical style of *Rationalist architecture under Fascism, epitomized by the buildings and the plan for the Foro Mussolini, Rome (1927–32), developing by the late 1930s to acquire Grecian references. After the 1939–45 war his buildings became marked by strong horizontals and verticals, and an almost violent juxtaposition of elements. His strong individuality was marked in the Astrea Co-operative Building, Monteverde Nuovo (1949), and Il Girasole House (1950), both in Rome, and the Villa la Saracena, Santa Marinella (1954). He was an important and influential writer in the 1940s and 1950s, being especially critical of *International Modernism and opposed to the fundamental principles of *Mies van der Rohe and his disciples. He designed the Watergate Complex, Washington, DC (1960–3), which is better known for other than architectural reasons.

Emanuel (1994)

Morgan, Julia (1872–1957). American architect and engineer, she was the first woman to study at the École des *Beaux-Arts, Paris, and became California's first licensed woman architect. Her works include several buildings for Mills College, Oakland, Calif., including the *reinforced-concrete *campanile (1903–4), library (1905–6), and gymnasium (1907–8). She was responsible for many private houses in the San Francisco area and her responses to client-needs were realized drawing on eclectic motifs, often building with local materials, and always displaying the assurance in design acquired in Paris. Her Conference Center for the Young Women's Christian Association at Asilomar-Pacific Grove, Calif. (1913–28), is now a State Monument and National Conference Center. Insisting on fine detailing and sensitivity to human beings and sites, she was capable on occasion of creating eclectic fantasies of extraordinary power, among which must be mentioned San Simeon, Calif. (1919–38), a vigorously composed collection of cultural references at Enchanted Hill, for William Randolph Hearst (1863–1951).

Beach (1976); Longstreth (1977); Torre (1977); Winslow (1980)

Moro, Peter (1911–98). German-born architect of the *Modern Movement. He settled in England in 1936 (naturalized 1947) and worked with *Tecton (1937–9). He joined the Architect's team of the London County Council, and was responsible for the interior of the Royal Festival Hall, London (1948–51). Establishing his own practice in London in 1952, he designed several buildings including Moro House, Blackheath Park, London (1957), the Playhouse, Nottingham (1964), a Hall of Residence, University of Leicester (1965), the Gulbenkian Centre, University of Hull, Yorkshire (1969), and the Theatre Royal, Plymouth, Devon (1982).

Emanuel (1994); Obituary, *The Times* (15.x.98), 21

Morphew, Reginald (1874–1971). English architect, he designed 111–12 Jermyn Street, London (1901–3), described at the time as a 'Florentine Palazzo'. In 1902 he designed 7–12 Jermyn Street, which had *Art Nouveau details on a building in a free, vaguely Tyrolean, style. His work was eclectic, and always interesting.

Gray (1985)

Morphosis. Californian firm of architects, led by Thom Mayne (1944–) and Michael Rotondi (1949–), established in 1979, that aims to search for the 'ability to absorb the idiosyncratic' by drawing on the more terrifying aspects of technology. The Crawford House, Montecito, Calif. (1987–92), is derived from overlaying the contradictory geometries of the global Mercator grid with functional and experiential axes. The broken grids and fragmented walls establish their own highly complex geometries, but suggest change, impermanence, and incompleteness. The Venice III house, Venice, Calif. (1982), has a system of weights and pulleys controlling sun-sails that change the appearance of the building from an unfinished structure to a temporary tent. Covering a wide range of building types, their architecture is about possibilities of change. Works include the Mantilini Restaurant, Beverly Hills (1986), Cedar's Sinai Comprehensive Cancer Care Center, Beverly Hills (1987), and the Blades House, Goleta, Calif. (1992–4).

Jodidio (1993, 1995)

Morris, Robert (*c*.1702–54). English theorist of the second *Palladian Revival, his *Essay in Defence of Ancient Architecture* (1728), *Lectures on Architecture* (1734), *Essay on Harmony* (1739), *Art of Architecture* (1742), *Rural Architecture* (1750), and *Architectural Remembrancer* (1751) were significant in augmenting Palladio's work with an aesthetic theory powerful enough to command attention and respect (e.g. from *Jefferson). As an architect he was of small importance, but may have designed the south front of Culverthorpe, Lincolnshire (*c*.1730–5).

Colvin (1995); *DNB* (1917); Harris (1990); Kaufmann (1955); Summerson (1993)

Morris, Roger (1695–1749). London-born architect, an important figure in the history of *Palladianism, the *Gothic Revival, and *Castle style. A kinsman of Robert *Morris, he was associated with Colen *Campbell and Henry *Herbert, 9th Earl of Pembroke, functioning as the last's amanuensis and interpreter of his architectural designs. He appears to have assisted Campbell, notably on the designs for Goodwood House, Sussex, before collaborating with Herbert on a number of projects including Marble Hill, Twickenham, Middlesex (1724–9), the White Lodge, Richmond New Park (1727–8), the Column of Victory, Blenheim Palace, Oxfordshire (1730–1), the Palladian Bridge at Wilton, Wiltshire (1736–7), and Westcombe House, Blackheath, Kent (*c*.1730—demolished). He enlarged Adderbury House, Oxfordshire (1831), for the 2nd Duke of Argyll (1678–1743), designed the stable-block at Althorp House, Northamptonshire (*c*.1732–3), with a *Tuscan *portico based on Inigo *Jones's St Paul's, Covent Garden, London (itself derived from *Palladio), and produced his masterpiece, Inveraray Castle, Argyll (1745–60), for the 3rd Duke of Argyll (1682–1761). Earlier, he built Clearwell Castle, Gloucestershire (*c*.1728) in a castellated *Gothic style, but Inveraray was the precedent for a series of symmetrical *Georgian 'castles', and may itself be derived from a sketch by *Vanbrugh.

Colvin (1995); *DNB* (1993); Kaufmann (1955); Lindsay and Cosh (1973); Summerson (1993)

Morris, William (1834–96). English artist, poet, craftsman, medievalist, and printer, who had a profound effect on architecture. Early in his career he studied the medieval churches of England and France. Working briefly (1856) in *Street's office, he met Philip *Webb, with whom he became friendly, and was influenced by the ideas of *Ruskin. Disappointed by contemporary architecture and design, he commissioned Webb to build his own dwelling, the Red House, Bexleyheath, Kent (1859–60): with its unpretentious brick walls, fenestration arranged where needed, and tiled roof, it drew on *vernacular, *Gothic, and other traditions, treated in a very free way, and was influential, especially in the search for a style-less architecture. The difficulties of finding furniture and furnishings for the house led Morris to found Morris, Marshall, Faulkner, & Co., 'Fine Art Workmen in Painting, Carving, Furniture, and the Metals' in London (1861—after 1874 Morris & Co.).

Morris founded the Society for the Protection of Ancient Buildings (1877) in response to the over-zealous and destructive ideas of church-'restorers'. He was anxious to publicize not only the concept of *conservation (as opposed to wholesale renovation) but the qualities of hitherto unappreciated *vernacular buildings, all of which led him to be regarded as a founding-father of the *Arts-and-Crafts movement, the *Domestic Revival, conservation, and the search for a society in which work would be a joy. His was the inspiration behind the establishment of the Art-Workers' Guild (1884), the first Arts and Crafts Exhibition Society exhibition (1888), and many other late-C19 organizations intended to improve design, craftsmanship, and the appreciation of art. His published works include *The Earthly Paradise* (1868–70), various beautifully produced volumes from his Kelmscott Press (which had a great influence on typography), and the Utopian *News from Nowhere* (1891) in which by the end of C21 London was rebuilt in a way inspired by medieval architecture.

DNB (1917); Henderson (1967); Morris (1966); Pevsner (1968, 1972, 1974*a*); Stansky (1996); Thompson (1993)

Morrison, Sir Richard (1767–1849). Irish architect, he specialized in country-houses, drawing on types established by *Cassels and *Pearce. His *Useful and Ornamental Designs in Architecture composed in the manner of the Antique* (1793), was the first work of its kind to be attempted in Ireland. His houses include the charming Bearforest, Mallow, Co. Cork (1807–8—complete with elliptical entrance-hall expressed on the main front), the castellated *Tudor Gothic Castle Freke, Rosscarbery, Co. Cork (*c*.1814–20—ruined), and Castlegar, Ahascragh, Co. Galway (from 1803—again with elliptical entrance-hall). He designed several handsome Classical public buildings, including the County Court House, Clonmel, Co. Tipperary (*c*.1800), Sir Patrick Dun's Hospital, Dublin (1803–16), the County Gaol, Enniskillen, Co. Fermanagh (1812), and the County Court House, Galway (1812–15). He collaborated with his son, W. V. *Morrison, on a number of country-houses, notably Ballyfin, Mountrath, Co. Leix (1822—the grandest C19 Classical country-house in Ireland), Baronscourt, Newtownstewart, Co. Tyrone (1835—to which *Steuart, *Soane, and others had contributed), Borris House, Borris, Co. Carlow (*c*.1813), Fota Island, Carrigtwohill, Co. Cork (*c*.1825—with very handsome Grecian entrance-hall) and the *Gothic Shelton Abbey, Co. Wicklow (*c*.1819—with vaulted gallery).

Bence-Jones (1988); *DNB* (1917); McParland, Rowan, and Rowan (1989)

Morrison, William Vitruvius (1794–1838). Irish architect, son and collaborator of Richard *Morrison. His work was more Neoclassical than his father's, but he also carried out a number of *Tudorbethan designs. Apart from the distinguished buildings they designed together (e.g. Baronscourt, Co. Tyrone (1835)), W. V. Morrison produced many houses of great interest, including Clontarf Castle, Clontarf, Co. Dublin (1836–7—Tudorbethan), Glenarm Castle and 'Barbican', Glenarm, Co. Antrim (1823–4—*Tudor *Gothic—not unlike his work at Borris, Co. Carlow), Hollybrooke House, Bray, Co. Wicklow (*c*.1835—Tudor Gothic), and Mount Stewart, Newtownards, Co. Down (1825–8—Neoclassical, essentially alterations and additions to the house by George *Dance of 1803–6, with later changes by Charles Campbell). His public buildings include Carlow County Court House (1828—with handsome *Ionic portico and two semicircular court-rooms separated by the entrance and stairs), and Tralee County Court House, Co. Kerry (1828—the plan of which is related to Carlow Court House). His Ross Monument, Rostrevor, Co. Down (1826), a massive *obelisk on an Egyptianizing base, is one of the noblest memorials in Ireland, commemorating Major-General Robert Ross (1766–1814).

Bence-Jones (1988); Curl (1994); *DNB* (1917); McParland, Rowan, and Rowan (1989)

mortar. Plastic material to bond stones and bricks together. Before C20 it was usually made from crushed burnt limestone mixed with sand and water, often with additional brick- or stone-dust. Today, Portland cement is used with sand and water, sometimes with lime or other additives.

Nicholson (1835); Papworth (1852); Sturgis *et al.* (1901–2)

mortice and tenon. A *mortice* (or *mortise*) is a volume hollowed out to receive something, such as a lock or the *tenon* (projection at the end) of another piece of timber.

mort-safe. Protective iron railings completely surrounding and covering a grave or vault.

Curl (1993)

mortuary. 1. Building where corpses are temporarily accommodated, for identification, or autopsies. **2.** Burial-place or sepulchre. **3.** *Dead-house.

mortuary-chapel. 1. Free-standing or attached to a church, under which is a sepulchre or tomb, often built and used for interment by one family. **2.** Chapel in a cemetery, or attached to a building (e.g. a hospital), where coffined bodies briefly lie before disposal.

Colvin (1991); Curl (1993)

mosaic. Patterned surface on floors, *vaults, walls, etc., consisting of regular squares (*tesserae*) of glass, stone, pottery, marble, etc., embedded in a cement or plaster matrix.

Anthony (1968)

Mosbrugger. *See* Moosbrugger.

Moser, Karl (1860–1936). Pioneer of the *Modern Movement in Switzerland, and first President of *CIAM (1928). He designed the *Antoniuskirche* (Church of St Anthony), Basle (1925–31), the first *concrete church in

Switzerland. His earlier work is less well known, but in its use of round-arched forms it was influenced by the work of *Richardson in America (e.g. Pauluskirche, Basle (1897–1901)). At the *Kunsthaus* (Art-House), Zurich (1907–10), however, the language was stripped *Neoclassicism. The main building of the University of Zurich (1911–14) combined round-arched themes with paraphrases of Greek *Doric, and this gives the key to Moser's eclectic approach. His son, **Werner Max Moser** (1896–1970), also had a successful architectural career. His works include several early *Modern Movement buildings with Emil Roth (1893–1980)—e.g. Hagmann Boat-House, Erlenbach, Zurich (1929), the Eglisee Housing, Basle (1930), and the Neubühl Housing, Zurich (1932). He also designed an Old People's Home near Frankfurt (with Mart *Stam—1930), and the Kornfeld Church, Riehen, Basle (1962).

Emanuel (1994); Kienzle (1937); *Schweizer Rundschau*, 36/8 (1936), 633–9; van Vynckt (1993)

mosque. *Islamic building for communal prayer and exhortation, usually with at least one *minaret, and often domed. A good example is the Suleymaniye Mosque, Istanbul (1551–8).

Papworth (1852); Sturgis *et al.* (1901–2)

moss hut. *Fabrique in a primitive, rustic style, usually made of branches of trees with the interstices filled with moss, and sometimes clad with *thatch or bark. It could be a mnemonic of the *Primitive Hut, or be a simpler *cottage orné.

Symes (1993)

Mothe, Jean-Baptiste-Michel Vallin de la (1729–1800). *See* Vallin.

motte. Steep artificial earthen mound or tumulus on which a *keep or fortress stood in a C11 or C12 military structure, usually associated with the Anglo-Normans in the British Isles. It was sometimes surrounded by a ditch, but more often with an enclosed space. *Motte-and-bailey* was a defensive structure consisting of a tower (often of timber) on a motte, sited inside a *bailey enclosed by a ditch, bank, and palisade.

mouchette. C14 *light (often *ogee on at least one side), resembling a curving dagger-like form with *foils at one end in *Second Pointed *Curvilinear or *Flowing *Gothic *tracery.

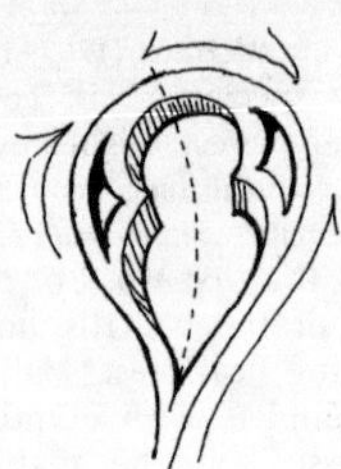

mouchette

moulding. Any continuous projecting or inset architectural member with a contoured profile. It defines, casts shadows, enriches, emphasizes, and separates, and is usually horizontal or vertical, although it occurs around arches and *vaults. It is an essential part of *architraves, *bases, *entablatures, and *string-courses, and is found in virtually all periods of architecture except the *International *Modern Movement from which it was expunged. It occurs in many forms in the Classical *Orders (e.g. *astragal, *bead, *cavetto, *cyma, *fillet, *flute, *ovolo, *scotia, and *torus), *Romanesque work (e.g. *beak-head, *billet, *chevron, hollows, rounds, and splays), and *Gothic (e.g. deep rounds, and hollows, *ball-flower, *dog-tooth, *keels, *nail-head, etc.). *See* bead, beak-head, bolection, bowtell, cable, cant, cavetto, chaplet, chevron, dancette, dog-tooth, dovetail, echinus, edge-roll, fascia, gadroon, gorge, hood, label, nail-head, nebule, ogee, ovolo, pellet, ressault, roll, running dog, wave. *See also* Orders.

Mountford, Edward William (1855–1908). English architect who designed several *Gothic Revival churches, but is best known for his public buildings, including the Free Renaissance-style Sheffield Town Hall (1890–7—with elements culled from Spain, France, England, and The Netherlands), and the *Gibbs Revival-style Lancaster Town Hall (1907—with Thomas Geoffrey Lucas (1872–1947)). He designed the Northampton Institute, Finsbury, London (1893–6), again in a Free Renaissance style. The Central Criminal Court, Old Bailey, London (1900–7), is in a grandly *Edwardian *Baroque style, with a *cupola derived from the work of *Wren.

Dixon and Muthesius (1985); Gray (1985)

mourner. *See* weeper.

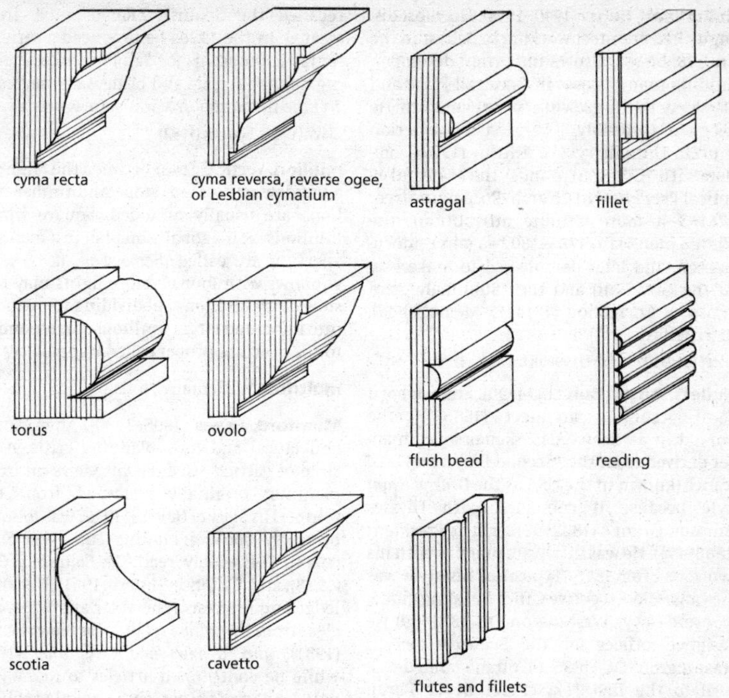

mouldings

Moya, John Hidalgo (1920–94). *See* Powell & Moya.

Mozarabic. C9–early C11 style of Spanish Christian architecture under *Moorish rule. It included horseshoe-shaped arches, but was essentially an amalgam of *Romanesque and *Islamic elements, as in San Miguel de la Escalada, near Léon (913).

Fernandez Arenas (1972)

mud-and-stud. *Timber-framed wall construction filled in with staves or battens as a base for a mud finish, also called *clam-staff and daub* or *raddle and daub*.

Alcock, Barley, Dixon, and Meeson (1996)

Mudéjar. Style of architecture and decorative art, partly *Islamic (from the *Moorish and *Mozarabic traditions) and partly *Gothic, that evolved in the Iberian peninsula C12–C16. It incorporated horseshoe-shaped arches, *Kufic inscriptions, *arabesques, *stalactite work or *muqarna, and ceramic tiles. It can be seen at the C14 Alcázar, Seville. The style persisted well into *Plateresque C16 buildings, and aspects of it were revived in C19 and early C20.

King (1927); Kubler and Soria (1959)

Muet, Pierre Le (1591–1669). French Mannerist architect, his most important work was *Manière de bien bastir pour toutes sortes de personnes* (Manner of Building Well for All Sorts of People—1623), based on Du *Cerceau's first book of architecture. He designed the *Hôtels de l'Aigle (1649) and Tubeuf (1650), in Paris, both of which are Classical but tinged with more than a trace of *Mannerism. The Hôtel Duret de Chevry-Tubeuf (1635–41) was attributed to him, but was probably by Jean Thiriot (1590–1647). He carried out works at the Val-de-Grâce, Paris (*c*.1654–65), above the lower cornice, with Le *Duc to complete the building. *See* Lemercier.

Blunt (1982); Papworth (1852); Placzek (1982)

Mulholland, Roger (1740–1818). The most distinguished architect working in Belfast in the late C18, he was also an important developer, building many houses in Donegall Place and elsewhere in the growing *Georgian town. He designed (probably) the First Presbyterian Church, Dunmurry, Co. Antrim (1779—complete with *Gibbs surrounds), the beautiful elliptical Presbyterian Church, Rosemary Street (1781–3—a more definite attribution), the White Linen Hall (1785–1802—again undocumented, and later demolished to make way for the City Hall) and the *Sublimely grim House of Correction (1814–18—demolished), all in Belfast.

Brett (1967, 1976); Curl (1993*b*); Larmour (1987)

Mullett, Alfred Bult (1834–90). English-born US Government architect (1865–74), he worked in a *Beaux-Arts *Renaissance manner derived from the *Second Empire style of France (known in the USA as the *General Grant* style because it coincided with Ulysses Simpson Grant's (1822–95) term as President (1868–77)). He was in private practice with his two sons after 1875. Typical of his style was the huge Old Executive Office Building (State, War, and Navy), Washington, DC (1871–89). He designed offices for the *Baltimore Sun* in Washington, DC (1885–6), often claimed as a rival to the first *skyscraper by Le Baron *Jenney. Like many architects before him (e.g. *Latrobe) he was treated appallingly by a parsimonious US Government: facing ruin, he shot himself.

Condit (1968); Fitch (1973); Jordy (1976); Maddex (1973); Placzek (1982)

Mullgardt, Louis Christian (1866–1942). American architect of German descent. He was influenced by the *Arts-and-Crafts movement after a visit to England (1903–4). Establishing his own office in San Francisco, Calif., in 1906, he designed a *timber-framed house around a brick chimney-core at Mill Valley, Calif. (1907), that had an Alpine flavour, but over the next few years the houses that made his name had stuccoed walls, low-pitched roofs, and long bands of *mullioned windows, all in a style strongly reminiscent of *Schinkel and 'Greek' *Thomson. One of his most spectacular designs was the Henry W. Taylor House, Berkeley, Calif. (1908–10—destroyed). Later works were inventively and freely eclectic, such as the Theodore H. Davies Building, Honolulu, Hawaii (1917–21), a vast concrete structure faced with *faïence that recalled the Spanish *Renaissance, freely treated. In the 1920s he produced a series of fantastic proposals for San Francisco, including habitable piers and bridges connected by 24-lane tiered motorways. None was realized.

Clark (1966); Placzek (1982)

mullion. Vertical *post between the *lights of a window or *screen. Stone and timber mullions are usually moulded. Square timber mullions set diagonally on plan in a medieval aperture are called *diamond mullions*, while windows with four or more lights may have subsidiary mullions subdividing the window into lights and larger mullions corresponding to the aperture proper called *king-mullions*.

multifoil. With many *foils.

Mumford, Lewis (1895–1990). American architectural and town-planning critic. A disciple of Patrick *Geddes, his views on urban planning originally stemmed from that source. His *Story of Utopias* (1922) was followed by many books including *Sticks and Stones* (1924), the widely read *The Culture of Cities* (1938), and *The City in History* (1961). His knowledge and interests ranged far and wide, as is clear from *The Culture of Cities*, *The Brown Decades* (1931), and *Technics and Civilization* (1961), while he contributed articles to many journals, and wrote a perceptive regular column on architecture and the environment for *The New Yorker* entitled 'The Skyline' (1930s–1950s). A critic of the dehumanizing effects of technology, he nevertheless believed in the need for large-scale regional, even national, plans, and was a founding-member of the Regional Planning Association that sponsored the *Garden City complex of Sunnyside Gardens, Queens, New York, and also worked for the New York Housing and Planning Commission. He belonged to the low-density decentralist tradition of Ebenezer *Howard, *Abercrombie, and *Unwin, yet, because of his belief in the need for large-scale planning, found his philosophical position confused. In his *New Yorker* articles he prophesied the roles that the motor-car and urban motorways would play in the decay of the city as early as 1943, but his support for large-scale centralized intervention was challenged by others, notably Jane *Jacobs, with whose views on *urban renewal he agreed, but when her *The Death and Life of Great American Cities* came out in 1961 he was obliged to attack her thesis regarding urban densities. He insisted that architecture and planning had to be socially responsible, and he emphasized the plight of the individual in the face of threats from militarism and the destruction of the environment in *The Myth of the Machine* (1967) and *The Pentagon of Power* (1971).

Architectural Review, 187 (Mar. 1990), 9; Mumford (1922, 1924, 1931, 1934, 1938, 1944, 1946, 1952, 1952*a*, 1961, 1963, 1967, 1970, 1975); Pile (1994); *Progressive Architecture*, 71 (Mar. 1990), 24; Wojtowicz (1996)

Munday, Richard (d. 1740). American *Classical architect, working in the *Georgian style, he designed Colony House, Newport, RI (1739), an accomplished and pretty work with a *Baroque centrepiece. He also designed Trinity Church (1726) and many of the most substantial houses in Newport.

Downing (1937); Downing and Scully (1967); Hitchcock (1939); Ware (1923)

Munggenast, Josef (1680–1741). Tyrolean architect, a kinsman of *Prandtauer, he completed *Stift* (Abbey) Melk on the Danube, designing the graceful upper parts of the western towers (1738). With Matthias Steinl *or* Steindl (1644–1727), he worked in Lower Austria on the tower of Zwettl (1723) and on the lovely Augustinian Church at Dürnstein, which has the most handsome *Baroque tower in all Austria (1721–7). On his own he reconstructed *Stift* Altenburg, Upper Austria (1730–3), casing the medieval Church in a sumptuous Baroque crust, and creating one of the most felicitous of all libraries of the period (1730–3—influenced by *Fischer von Erlach's *Hofbibliothek*, Vienna).

Bourke (1962); Brucker (1983); Hempel (1965); Karl (1991); Mungenast (1963); Powell (1959)

munnion. *Mullion or *muntin.

muntin. 1. Vertical intermediate timbers or *mullions between the *panels of a door and the outer *stiles, fixed top and bottom to the horizontal *rails. **2.** Glazing-bar in a window-sash. **3.** Window-mullion.

Müntz, Johann Heinrich (1727–98). German-Swiss architect. He arrived in England in 1755 and was taken up by Horace *Walpole, for whom he painted a ceiling at Strawberry Hill, Middlesex, and designed several *Gothick elements. He created an octagonal *Gothick room for Richard Bateman (d. 1774) at Old Windsor, Berkshire (1761–2), and a Gothick room with Egyptianizing features for James Caulfeild, 1st Earl of Charlemont (1728–99), at Marino, near Dublin (1762). At Kew Gardens, Surrey, he was responsible for the 'Gothic Cathedral' and provided *Chambers with drawings for the *Moorish 'Alhambra' (1759). A pioneer of the *Gothic Revival and a master of the exotic, he proposed to publish *A Course of Gothic Architecture* (1760), which, if it had come out, would have been one of the earliest books on the subject. He designed a villa for Prince Poniatowski when in Poland (1780–3), and finally settled in Kassel, Germany, where he died.

Colvin (1995); Harris (1970); McCarthy (1987); Mowl (1996)

muqarna. *Islamic ornament, usually on the *soffits of arches and *vaults, constructed of corbelled brick *squinches with scalloped surfaces leaving forms resembling *stalactites.

Murcutt, Glenn Marcus (1936–). English-born architect of Australian parents, he settled in Australia, forming his own practice in 1969. He attempted to create an original Australian architectural typology in his Local History Museum and Tourist Information Centre, South Kempsey, New South Wales (1981–2), having until then been a follower of *International Modernism of the *Mies van der Rohe school. He experimented with mixing Miesian pavilions with the Australian *verandah, and produced a house-type sheathed in corrugated iron, of which the best examples are probably the Ball-Eastaway House, Glenorie, Sydney (1980–3), Neville Fredericks Farm House, Jamberoo, New South Wales (1981–2), and the Moruya House, Bingi Point, New South Wales (1985). He also designed several town-houses of which the Ken Done House, Mosman (1988–92), and the Richard Pratt House, Kew, Melbourne (1988–92), are probably the most interesting.

Emanuel (1994); Fromonot (1995)

Murphy/Jahn. Leading Chicago architectural practice founded in 1959 by Charles Franklin Murphy (1890–1985), Chicago, who through his work with *Burnham had a direct connection with the *Chicago School. The German architect Helmut *Jahn joined the firm in 1967, and in 1973 became a Partner. The practice was renamed Murphy/Jahn in 1981. In the 1960s the office produced several Chicago buildings much influenced by the work of *Mies van der Rohe, including the Continental Insurance Building (1962), the O'Hare International Airport (1965), the Chicago Civic Center (1965), and the Exhibition Building, McCormick Place (1971). After Jahn became a leading member of the firm, its buildings began to incorporate historical references, including *Art Deco elements. Jahn has been associated with *High Tech architecture, and his *skyscrapers have been admired, including the *Messeturm*, Frankfurt-am-Main, 1991. Jahn also designed a series of buildings for the *Kurfürstendamm*, Berlin, including a steel-and-glass block at the junction with *Adenauer-Platz* and *Brandenburgische Strasse* (1995).

Emanuel (1994); Jodidio (1993); Klotz (1986); Lampugnani (1988); Miller (1986)

muscular Gothic. Phase of the *Gothic Revival that embraced a primitive, early *First Pointed style derived from Burgundian Gothic of C13: it employed brickwork, massive, cylindrical *piers, and chunky elements, and was bold, broad, strong, stern, and robust. Some of the work of *Street and *Brooks could be described as 'muscular Gothic' in style.

Clarke (1969); Curl (1995); Dixon and Muthesius (1985); Eastlake (1970); Smart (1990)

mushrabeyeh. Timber *lattice-work in the upper-storey windows of *Islamic houses. The term is usually applied to a projecting balcony or bay on an upper floor protected by such a screen so that those inside can see without being seen.

Sturgis *et al.* (1901–2)

Muthesius, Hermann (1861–1927). Attaché at the Imperial German Embassy, London (1896–1903), he surveyed British architecture and design on behalf of the German Government, and his work was published in *Die Englische Baukunst der Gegenwart* (English Architecture Now—1900–2) and *Die Neuere Kirchliche Baukunst in England* (New Church Architecture in England—1903) by Wasmuth, the German publishers of F. L. *Wright's work. His greatest contribution was *Das Englische Haus* (The English House—1904–5), which described elements, history, plans, styles, and types of English domestic architecture, as well as publicizing works by many architects and extolling the *Arts-and-Crafts movement. The book had a profound influence on Continental (especially German) domestic architecture, and the 'English style' for houses became as fashionable as the English landscaped park had been for the C18 garden. Furthermore, Muthesius's admiration for the simplicity and utility of English domestic buildings and artefacts led to the concept of *Sachlichkeit* (objectivity) and to the foundation of the *Deutscher Werkbund (1907). By 1914 Muthesius (who had been a powerful official in the Prussian Government for at least a decade, and was to remain influential until his death) was advocating mass-production, standardization, and the development of industrialization for architecture, notions which were completely the opposite of the Arts-and-Crafts position: his stance was opposed by van de *Velde and others, but became an article of faith in the 1920s among those who were to be the protagonists of the *Modern Movement.

Muthesius designed some houses, including the Haus Freudenberg, Berlin (1907–8), which suggests variations on a theme by Baillie *Scott, and the Cramer House, Berlin (1911–12). He published some of his own work in *Die Schöne Wohnung* (The House Beautiful—1922 and 1926).

Frampton (1980); Muthesius (1902, 1979)

mutilated. Broken or discontinued, as in a *pediment.

mutule. Flat inclined block on the *soffit of the *Doric *cornice, with several *guttae on the underside, placed in line with the *triglyphs and centre-lines of *metopes in the *frieze below. *Tuscan mutules are plain and horizontal. *See* *modillion.

Muzio, Giovanni (1893–1983). Italian architect. His *Neoclassicism was exemplified by the Ca' Brutta apartment-block, Via Turati and Via Moscova, Milan (1919–23), with its simplified triumphal arch set between vaguely *Mannerist blocks that responded with great success to the urban context and drew on historical references. His other works include the Catholic University of Milan (1926–36), Palazzo del Governo, Sondrio (1935), the Church of Sant'Antonio, Cremona (1936), and the Basilica of the Annunciation, Nazareth, Israel (1969). His early work was associated with the Metaphysical movement in art, of which Georgio de Chirico (1888–1978), with his juxtaposition of the commonplace and the fantastic, was the main exponent.

Danesi and Patetta (1976); Seta (1972)

Mycenaean architecture. Architecture in and around Mycenae on the Greek mainland of *c*.1500–1200 BC, of which the *megaron, *propylaeum, *in antis* (*see* anta) *portico, *court, and *tholos were features of monumental building. At Tiryns there were two propylaea leading to the fortified palace complex: the outer gateway was the model for all the great Greek gateways, including that on the Athenian Acropolis, while in the centre of the palace was a large and impressive megaron with distyle *in antis* porticoes. The finest existing tholos of Mycenaean design is the so-called Treasury of Atreus (*c*. C15 BC), approached by a *dromos or open passage lined with masonry, and constructed of *courses of stone laid on a circular plan, each course a slightly smaller diameter, so that a *corbelled or pseudo-*vault was constructed. At the end of the dromos the entrance to the tholos was framed by two tapering columns with zig-zags cut in the *shafts. With Mycenaean architecture ordered planning reached a high degree of sophistication.

Cruickshank (1996); Dinsmoor (1950); Robertson (1945)

Myers, Barton (1934–). American architect, he settled in Canada in 1968 and established Barton Myers Associates. His own house at Yorkville, Toronto (1970), created an exemplar for the small family house sensitively placed within an established urban context. Well adapted to the Canadian climate, his work includes the University of Alberta Students' Union, Edmonton (1972–4), designed with the South-African-born Canadian Abel Joseph *Diamond: it contains large interior circulation-spaces and sophisticated environmental controls. More recent work included the Concert Hall, Alberta (1991), and the School of Architecture, University of Nevada, Las Vegas (1991).

Emanuel (1994); Kalman (1994)

Mylne, Robert (1733–1811). Scots architect, member of a family working as master-masons and architects at least as far back as the beginning of C17. He trained in France and Italy with his brother **William** (1734–90), met *Piranesi, achieved recognition at St Luke's Academy, Rome, and made useful aristocratic contacts. He drew some studies of the Greek temples in Sicily which he allowed Piranesi and *Winckelmann to use (1757). Reaching London in 1759, he won the competition to build the new bridge over the Thames at Blackfriars (1760, opened 1769, demolished 1868), with a handsome and economical design employing elliptical arches. Thereafter, bridges and canal works became a significant part of his practice. With Robert *Adam and James *Wyatt as contemporaries, Mylne found it difficult to become a fashionable country-house architect, but nevertheless designed several houses, including Woodhouse, near Whittington, Shropshire (1773–4), which have a refinement and restraint that pre-empt the *Neoclassicism of the 1790s. His interiors have a delicate decorative manner not unlike that of Adam, which may be explained by the fact that he paid Adam's draughtsman, George *Richardson, for drawings on occasion. His finest work is arguably at Inveraray, Argyll, Scotland, where he built the elegant Aray (1774–6) and Dubh Loch (1786–7) bridges, the Church (1795–1800), two groups of tenements, Arkland and Relief Land (1774–6), and the arched screen-wall that is such a memorable frontage to Loch Fyne, and many more structures, all of which are pleasingly well mannered. He carried out extensive redecoration of the principal rooms at the Castle (1782–9), having earlier made alterations to *Morris's windows (1777). Amongst several memorials he designed is the urn in memory of Sir Hugh Myddelton (*c*.1560–1631—projector of the New River to bring fresh water to London) on an island in the New River at Great Amwell, Hertfordshire (1800), perhaps suggested by Rousseau's tomb at Ermenonville.

Colvin (1995); *DNB* (1917); Harris (1990); Lindsay and Cosh (1973); Papworth (1852); Summerson (1993)

Mylne, William Chadwell (1781–1863). Son of Robert *Mylne, he gained early experience with his father and in 1811 succeeded him as Surveyor to the New River Company. He laid out the Company's property in Clerkenwell, London, including the pleasant late-*Georgian Myddelton Square, and Amwell, Inglebert, River, and Chadwell Streets, begun 1819. In order to raise the tone of the area, St Mark's Church, Myddelton Square, was built, designed by him (1826–8) in a *Gothic style of the pre-ecclesiological type.

Colvin (1995); *DNB* (1917); Papworth (1852)

nail-head. Late-*Romanesque and *First Pointed *Gothic moulding featuring a series of small contiguous projecting pyramids, so called from their resemblance to medieval wrought-iron nail-heads.

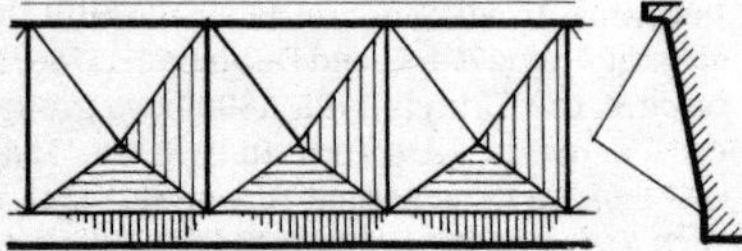

nail-head. Church of St Leonard, Upton St Leonard, Gloucestershire.

naked. Unadorned plain surface of anything, but especially the main plane of a building's *façade.

naos. 1. Inner cell or sanctuary of a Greek temple, equivalent to the Roman *cella, containing the statue of the deity. **2.** Sanctuary of a centrally planned *Byzantine church. **3.** Small shrine, often portable, e.g. the *battered-sided Egyptian type, carried by a Naöphorus figure.

naos. 3.

Curl (1994); Dinsmoor (1950)

narthex. 1. Church vestibule, in *Byzantine churches of two kinds: an *esonarthex or inner narthex, between the outer porch and the body of the church proper separated from the *nave and *aisles by a wall, *arcade, *colonnade, or screen; or an *exonarthex or outer narthex outside the main wall, sometimes also serving as the *portico or part of the cloistered *atrium or quadriporticus. **2.** Medieval *ante-church often with nave and aisles, sometimes referred to as a *Galilee porch, as at Durham Cathedral.

Mango (1986); Parker (1850); Watkin (1986)

Nash, John (1752–1835). English architect, master of *scenography, urban designer, and important architect of the *Picturesque. He trained in the office of Sir Robert *Taylor before setting up on his own in 1775 as a designer and builder of *stucco-fronted houses. Bankrupted in 1783, he moved to Wales, where he met Uvedale *Price and was initiated into the cult of the Picturesque. While there he designed the County Gaol, Carmarthen (1789–92—demolished), and other buildings, and became so busy he had to take on A. C. *Pugin, then a refugee, as a draughtsman. He returned to London in 1796 and formed a partnership with Humphry *Repton, the fashionable landscape-gardener, who had ample opportunities to pick up architectural commissions. Between them they remodelled many country seats and grounds, enhancing their Picturesque qualities, before the partnership was dissolved in 1802. Nash went from strength to strength, designing many houses and villas, including Killymoon Castle, Co. Tyrone (*c.*1801–3—castellated with round arches), the very pretty Cronkhill, Shropshire (*c.*1802—*Italianate and asymmetrical), and Caerhayes Castle, Cornwall (*c.*1808—castellated). These asymmetrical compositions were influenced by Payne *Knight's important house, Downton Castle, Herefordshire (begun 1772). Nash built an estate of cottages at Blaise Hamlet, near Bristol (1810–11), the prototype of the Picturesque village, with a heady brew of thatch, *leaded lights, elaborate chimneys, asymmetry, and 'rustic' architecture loosely based on *vernacular forms.

Nash was appointed architect to the Office of Woods and Forests (1806), and from this time was in favour with the Prince of Wales (later Prince Regent and King George IV (reigned 1820–30)). He laid out Marylebone Park, London, an estate that reverted to the Crown in 1811, with proposals that became (1819) Regent's Park, an agreeably planted area around which were huge stucco-fronted palatial terraces and private villas. The façades of Cornwall and Clarence Terraces were designed by Decimus *Burton, and Cumberland Gate and Terrace were built under James *Thomson. Nash himself designed Ulster, York, Hanover, Kent, Chester, Cambridge, and St Andrew's Terraces, York Gate, Sussex Place, and Park Square (1821–30). Park Crescent was built 1812–22. Of the villas, Nash designed Hanover Lodge, and was responsible for the layout and many of the designs of the Park Villages (begun 1824), really a model suburb, completed by *Pennethorne, and including Italianate and Picturesque barge-boarded inventions. So that the Park should be connected to Westminster, Nash proposed a new street (Regent Street), designing many of the buildings, including The Quadrant, Piccadilly Circus, and the Church of All Souls, Langham Place (1822–5), all of which were clever devices to change the direction of the street, while the palatial blocks along the street were designed as scenographic events (begun 1813, but all redeveloped). Regent Street was linked to the existing Portland Place (1776–90—by James and Robert *Adam) by means of a curved thoroughfare laid out around the ingenious *portico and *steeple of the Langham Place Church.

Nash became personal architect to the Regent and remodelled the Royal Pavilion, Brighton, Sussex (1815–21), in the *Hindoo and Chinese styles, exotically intermingled. Once the Prince became King in 1820, Nash was ordered to reconstruct Buckingham House (later Palace) on the most lavish scale: much of his work there (1820–30) survives, although the Mall front was twice changed, first by *Blore and then by Aston *Webb. Other designs include the Royal Opera Arcade, Haymarket (1816–18), the Haymarket Theatre (1820–1), Suffolk Street and Suffolk Place (1820s), Clarence House, St James's (1825–8), the United Services Club, Pall Mall (1826–8), the West Strand improvements opposite Charing Cross (1830–2), and Carlton House Terrace, the Mall (1827–33), which has a row of cast-iron Greek *Doric columns on the Mall front. One of his most exquisite designs was Marble Arch, originally designed to stand in front of Buckingham Palace, but moved to its present site in 1851.

Nash's works have suffered greatly from demolitions and alterations, and of his brilliant scheme linking Waterloo Place to Regent's Park very little remains. His eclecticism, charm, scenographic effects, and widespread use of stucco did not find favour with younger architects, concerned as they were with purity, morality, expression of structure and materials, and the *Gothic Revival. Yet he was the most successful civic designer London has ever had.

Ballantyne (1997); Colvin (1973, 1995); Davis (1973); Hobhouse (1975); Middleton and Watkin (1987); Musgrave (1959); Placzek (1982); Roberts (1939); Summerson (1980*a*); Temple (1979)

Nasoni, *or* **Nazzoni, Niccolò** (d. 1773). Italian architect, he settled in Oporto, Portugal (1723–73), where he introduced the lush forms of late *Baroque and *Rococo. His greatest work is São Pedro dos Clérigos, Oporto (1732–50), built on an elliptical plan, with a lavishly decorated and energetic front, complete with spectacular stairs.

Kubler and Soria (1959); Nasoni (1991); Smith (1968)

National Romanticism. Late-C19 and early C20 movement, particularly in Sweden and Catalonia (*see* Modernisme), in which aspects of national or regional historical architecture, including *vernacular sources, were brought together in a fusion. Probably the best-known examples are *Östberg's impressive City Hall (1909–23) and *Wahlman's Engelbrekt Church (1906–14), both in Stockholm.

Cornell (1965)

Naturalism. Art in which the artist represents objects as they are, rather than in a *stylized* manner.

Chilvers, Osborne, and Farr (1988); Jervis (1984)

nave. Central *clearstoreyed *aisle of a *basilican church, or the main body of the church between the western wall and the *chancel, whether aisled or not, used by the laity. The nave was often separated from the *choir by a screen, and from the aisles by *nave-arcades* which support the clearstorey.

Nazi architecture. Architecture of the Hitlerian Third Reich in Germany (1933–45), basically of three types: a stripped *Neoclassicism, as in works by *Kreis and *Speer; a *vernacular style drawing on rural and especially Alpine types; and a simple, utilitarian, industrialized type for factories. Speer's megalomaniac master-plan for the north–south axis of Berlin (1937–45) was unrealized, although his New Chancellery, Berlin (1938–9—demolished), was a fine essay in *stripped *Classicism with an ingenious plan. *March's impressive Olympic Stadium, Berlin (1934–6), was a fresh adaptation of a Classical theme. *Bonatz's *Autobahn* (motorway) bridges were monumental, with elegant geometries. Apartment-blocks (of which many examples survive) were generally of a standardized type, with *casement windows, grey-rendered walls, and pitched roofs. However, it should be emphasized that the National Socialist German Workers' Party had a pluralistic attitude to architecture, and saw no reason to object to the use of steel and glass in factory design.

Adam (1992); Krier (1985); Larsson (1983); Speer (1970); Taylor (1974)

Nebelong, Niels Sigfried (1806–71). Danish architect. A pupil of *Hetsch and *Labrouste, he was an exponent of *Schinkelesque *Neoclassicism (e.g. J. C. Jacobsen's *villa at Carlsberg, Copenhagen (1852–4)), but later turned to other aspects of *Historicism. He used a *Gothic Revival style for the new *cloister at Slagelse (1857–8). His social commitment led to his philanthropic housing for the working classes at Christianshavn (1851), influenced by the work of Henry *Roberts in England.

His brother, **Johan Henrik Nebelong** (1817–71) followed his stylistic development. Resident in Norway (1840–53), he designed the Royal Summer Residence, Oscarshall in Bygdøy, Oslo (1847–52—Neo-Gothic with Classical interiors), and many public and private buildings. After he returned to Denmark he collaborated with *Bindesbøll in the design of the mental-hospital at Oringe (1853–7).

Millech (1951); Weilbach (1995)

nebule, nebulé, nebuly. *Romanesque ornament, slightly resembling an undulating rounded *chevron moulding, the lower part of which forms a continuous waving overhang, usually found on *corbel-tables.

nebule. Church of St Peter at Gowts, Lincoln.

neck. Upper cylindrical element forming a circular *band at the top of a Roman *Doric or *Tuscan column defined by the *astragal between it and the top of the shaft and the mouldings under the *echinus of the *capital. It also occurs in some versions of the Greek *Ionic *Order, as in the Erechtheion, Athens (*c*.421–407 BC), where it is exquisitely ornamented with *anthemion and *palmette. *See* hypotrachelion.

necking. Moulding on a column defining the top of the shaft, dividing it from the *capital.

necking-course. Any horizontal moulding like a *band coinciding with a *neck (e.g. at the union of the *finial with a *pinnacle) or continuing along a wall linking necks or *necking.

necropolis (*pl.* **necropoleis**). City of the dead, or *cemetery, often partly built above ground, as in the Staglieno, Genoa (1844–51), or other Southern-European C19 cemeteries.

Colvin (1991); Curl (1993)

Nedeham, James (*fl.* 1514–d. 1544). English carpenter and surveyor. He worked on York Place for Cardinal Wolsey (*c*.1475–1530) and King Henry VIII (from 1528 to 1530), and on the Tower of London, where he reconstructed the Traitors' Gate (1532). He designed the roof of the Great Hall at Hampton Court Palace, and was involved in works at Greenwich and Whitehall Palaces as well as being responsible for the extensive building-works during the last 15 years of King Henry's reign (1509–47) in his position as Clerk and Surveyor of the King's Works in England.

Harvey (1987)

needle. *See* spire.

Nehring, Johann Arnold (1659–95). *See* Nering.

Neill, John McBride (1905–74). Irish architect. He commenced practice in Belfast in

1928. One of his first important projects was the remodelling of the Savoy Hotel, Bangor, Co. Down (1933), in a *Modernist style with horizontal bands of windows and streamlined mouldings. He made his name with a series of cinemas, starting with the *Apollo*, Belfast (1933), with an *Art Deco façade, followed by the *Picturedrome* (1934—again Art Deco with much use of *chevrons). With the *Strand* (1935), *Majestic* (1936), *Troxy* (1936), and *Curzon* (1936) cinemas in Belfast, and the *Tonic* in Bangor (1936), he was influenced by the *International style. The *Tonic* was perhaps his finest cinema (and, with a capacity of 2,250, the largest), as accomplished an essay in Modernism as could be found anywhere in the British Isles at that time. Its interior was a superb example of the latest in cinema auditorium design. The *Troxy*, *Curzon*, and *Regal*, Larne, Co. Antrim (1937), cinemas all owed something to *Mendelsohn's Universum Cinema, Berlin (1928), which had been widely published.

Most of Neill's buildings have been demolished or converted, but his work was as good as any in that genre at the time.

Journal of the Royal Society of Ulster Architects, 5/4 (Mar./Apr. 1997), 26–37

Nelson, Paul Daniel (1895–1979). Chicago-born American architect. He worked in Paris with *Perret and befriended Le *Corbusier. By 1928 he had established his own office there, pioneering research in hospital design. The Petite Maison de Santé, near Paris (1930–2), was one of his first independent designs. In 1946–50, with others, he built the France/USA Memorial Hospital, Sant-Lô, using his invention of the flexible *curtain-wall. He developed an egg-shaped operating-theatre for hospitals that permitted better asepsis (not having angles that were difficult to clean) and lighting. His best-known project was the *Maison Suspendue* (Suspended House) of prefabricated units hung from a steel cage (1936–8), which was widely exhibited in Europe and the USA. He also designed hospitals at Dinan (1963–8) and Arles (1965–74).

Emanuel (1994)

Nénot, Henri-Paul (1853–1934). French *Beaux-Arts trained architect. A pupil of Charles *Garnier, *Pascal, and *Questel, he designed one of the biggest buildings of his time, the Nouvelle Sorbonne, Paris (1885–1901), a splendid display of Beaux-Arts ideals that was influential in America, especially on the work of *McKim, Mead, & White. He also designed the Palace of the League of Nations, Geneva (1927–37), and the Oceanographic Institute, Paris (1911).

Architect and Building News, 140 (1934), 351 and 149 (1937), 118–21; Middleton and Watkin (1987); Nénot (1895, 1903)

Neo-Baroque. Revival of *Baroque architecture, or of elements drawn from such architecture, especially towards the end of C19 and the beginning of C20. Examples include Brumwell *Thomas's City Hall, Belfast (1898–1906), *Belcher and *Joass's Ashton Memorial, Lancaster (1907–9), *Wallot's *Reichstag* (Parliament) Building, Berlin (1889–98), and Cass *Gilbert's gaudy Festival Hall for the St Louis, Mo., Purchase Exhibition (1904).

Gray (1985); Pevsner (1976)

Neo-Byzantine. *Byzantine Revival, or a style incorporating certain Byzantine features, as in the C19 *Rundbogenstil. Good examples of the Neo-Byzantine style are Beresford *Pite's Christ Church, Brixton Road, Lambeth, London (1898–1903), and S. H. *Barnsley's St Sophia, Lower Kingswood, Surrey (1891).

Curl (1995); Dixon and Muthesius (1985)

Neoclassicism. Dominant styles in European and American art and architecture in the late C18 and early C19, essentially a return to the *Classicism of Antiquity as the Italian *Renaissance began to be perceived as offering architectural paradigms that were untrue to the *Antique. Taste was also turning away from *Baroque and *Rococo, and moving towards a greater appreciation of the importance of *archaeology and scholarship to arrive at an architecture that was more true to the spirit of Antiquity. Bodies such as the Society of *Dilettanti of London began to sponsor scholarly and accurate publications dealing with architecture and antiquities, of which *The Antiquities of Athens* (from 1762) was one of the most important, and a major catalyst of that branch of Neoclassicism we call the *Greek Revival. Comprehensive excavations led to a huge number of publications dealing not only with Rome and Athens, but with the important Roman sites at *Herculaneum and *Pompeii, leading to the so-called *Etruscan style, and contributing in no small measure to the *Adam and *Empire styles. Appreciation of the architecture of ancient and modern Rome was enhanced by *Piranesi's engraved views published in

Antichità Romane (1748), *Della Magnificenza ed Architettura de' Romani* (1761), and other works, and also promoted a taste for the *Sublime because Piranesi made his subjects more impressive than they really were by greatly exaggerating their size. The *primitive and the severe began to be explored, especially the baseless *Doric *Order of Ancient *Greek architecture, which looked strange to eyes accustomed to the refinements of *Palladianism. Promoted by *Winckelmann, Greek art began to be taken seriously, first in studies of the temples at *Paestum and Sicily, and then in Greece itself under the aegis of the Dilettanti by *Stuart, *Revett, and others, leading to the *Doric *Revival and the use of bold primitive forms in architectural composition. Theorists such as *Cordemoy, *Laugier, and *Lodoli argued for a return to simplicity, rational design free from clutter and unnecessary ornament, and the use of the Orders for *structural* rather than decorative reasons. Furthermore, geometry was to be used for expressive purposes, enabling volumes, parts of buildings, and elements to be clearly seen and understood. Charles-Nicholas Cochin (1715–90) published his *Observations sur les antiquités de la ville d'Herculaneum* (1753, 1754, 1756, 1757—with illustrations by J.-C. Bellicard (1726–86)) while writers such as Le *Roy and *Peyre moved French architecture towards Ancient Greece for its inspiration and away from Rome. Robert *Adam and *Clérisseau published *Ruins of the Palace of the Emperor Diocletian at Spalatro* (1768), drawing further attention to late-Roman Antique remains. While certain aspects of Neoclassicism involved scholarly reproductions of Antique buildings and elements, as in the Greek Revival works by Stuart, *Smirke, and *Wilkins, the movement as a whole was not confined to copying (though accurate quotation was an integral part of it), but favoured clarity, stereometrical purity of form, and a lack of superfluous ornament or fussiness to *evoke* the Antique. This tendency can best be seen in the works of architects such as *Boullée, *Durand, *Ehrensvärd, *Gilly, *Latrobe, *Ledoux, and *Soane. The publication of accurate surveys of Ancient Egyptian buildings from 1802 by *Denon and the Commission des Monuments d'Égypte from 1809 brought further elements into the vocabulary of architects seeking stark, tough, forms (*see* Egyptian Revival). Neoclassicism reached peaks of refinement in the hands of *Empire designers such as *Percier and *Fontaine, and in architecture in the hands of von *Klenze and *Schinkel: it also enjoyed a C20 revival as a reaction to *Neo-Baroque and *Art Nouveau styles, often in very stripped, simplified form, notably in Scandinavia, Germany, and the USA (e.g. work by *Asplund, *Behrens, *Burnham, Tony *Garnier, *Kampmann, *Lewerentz, *Loos, *McKim, Mead, & White, *Muzio, *Perret, *Petersen, *Piacentini, *Plečnik, *Speer, *Tessenow, and many others).

Council of Europe (1972); Crook (1972*a*); Curl (1992, 1994); Honour (1977); Jervis (1984); Lewis and Darley (1986); Larsson (1983); Lampugnani (1988); Watkin and Mellinghoff (1987)

Neo-Georgian. Late-C19 and early C20 English and American architecture inspired by C18 *Georgian domestic architecture, usually featuring brick façades with rubbed-brick *dressings, *sash-windows, and *door-cases with *fanlights. Sometimes the inspiration was more *Colonial than English, on both sides of the Atlantic, and *vernacular elements were mixed with the underlying *Classicism. It was especially used to describe architecture of the reign of King George V (1910–36).

Gray (1985); Lewis and Darley (1986); Pevsner, *Buildings of England* (1951–)

Neo-Gothic. 1. *See* Gothic Revival. **2.** Neoclassical style (also called *Neo-Grec*) of the *Second Empire in France (1852–70) in which Graeco-Roman, *Louis Quinze, *Louis Seize, *Pompeian, *Adam, *Egyptian Revival, and other motifs were disposed in a richly eclectic *polychromatic mélange. It enjoyed a vogue in the USA, and had a short-lived impact on interior design in England and elsewhere in Europe.

Turner (1996)

Neo-Grec *or* **-Greek. 1.** *See* Greek Revival. **2.** Neoclassical style (also called *Neo-Grec*) of the *Second Empire in France (1852–70).

Neo-Liberty. Revival of elements of Italian *Art Nouveau in the 1950s.

Architectural Review, 125/747 (Apr. 1959), 231–5, and 126/754 (Dec. 1959), 341–4

Neo-Norman. *Romanesque Revival, especially from *c*.1820, e.g. work by *Hopper.

Lewis and Darley (1986)

Neo-Palladianism. 1. C18 revival of *Palladian architecture by *Burlington and his circle. **2.** Late-C20 revival based on earlier revivals.

Whitehill and Nichols (1976)

Neo-Picturesque. Revival of elements of the *Picturesque in Britain in the 1940s, particularly associated with the retention of *ruins after war-time bombing (e.g. *Spence's Coventry Cathedral (1950)).

Mellor (1987); *Studio*, 164/832 (Aug. 1962), 54–7

Neo-Plasticism. Associated with Piet Mondrian's (1872–1944) austere abstractions after 1914, the term suggests art freed from any naturalistic tendencies. To this end he confined his designs to straight vertical and horizontal lines and primary colours, with black, grey, and white, reducing three-dimensional forms to simplified, elemental plans which he thought the bases of plastic shapes. Neo-Plasticism was adopted as an aesthetic by De *Stijl, notably by *Rietveld, and had a profound effect on architectural plans of the 1920s.

Chilvers, Osborne, and Farr (1988); Lampugnani (1988)

Neo-Rationalism. 1. Italian movement, also called *Tendenza, of the 1960s and 1970s. Opposed to the dogmas of *International Modernism and to the prevalent tendency to treat architecture only as a commodity, it stressed the autonomy of architecture and the need to redefine it in terms of *types with rules for the rational combination of all its elements. Rejecting the notion that architecture ends and begins in technology, it insisted on the social and cultural importance of existing urban structures, and reasserted that the huge vocabulary of historical forms was a fecund source for fertile creation. Important texts of Neo-Rationalism were *Rossi's *Architettura della città* (Architecture of the City—1966), *Grassi's *La costruzione logica dell'architettura* (Logical Construction in Architecture—1967), and *Gregotti's *Il territorio dell'architettura* (The Realm of Architecture—1966). Rossi's great cemetery at Modena is the movement's most celebrated work (1971–85). The *Krier brothers have been associated with Neo-Rationalism. **2.** To confuse matters, the same label has been applied to those who (like the *New York Five) have been seen to return to the 'white' architecture of International Modernism and the *Weissenhofsiedlung of the 1920s.

Bonfanti (1973); Klotz (1986, 1988)

Neo-Romanesque. *Romanesque or Norman Revival, especially from the 1820s, notably in the works of *Hopper. Aspects of Romanesque occurred in the *Rundbogenstil, and also in the work of *Richardson in the USA.

Lewis and Darley (1986); Pevsner, *Buildings of England* (from 1951)

Neo-Tudor. C19 revival of late-English medieval architecture of the period 1485–1547. Tudor *vernacular architecture was also revived in the 1920s and 1930s.

Dixon and Muthesius (1985); Pevsner, *Buildings of England* (from 1951)

Neo-Vernacular. Architecture that drew on brick, tile, and other traditional materials and even on *vernacular forms in a general reaction against *International Modernism in the 1960s and 1970s. It was called the *Neo-Shingle style* or the *Shed Aesthetic* in the USA.

Jencks (1988)

Nering, *or* **Nehring, Johann Arnold** (1659–95). German architect and military engineer of Dutch descent, he settled in Berlin where he worked on the *Schloss* (Royal Palace) from 1679, designing *Baroque and *Palladian interiors, all of which have been destroyed. He built the Chapel at Schloss Köpenick, near Berlin (1684–5), extended Schloss Oranienburg (1689–95), and worked on the laying out of Friedrichstadt, Berlin, from 1688. His grandest surviving building is the Baroque *Zeughaus* (Arsenal), Berlin (from 1695), evolved from a plan by N.-F. *Blondel, and completed by *Schlüter and Jean de *Bodt. He commenced Schloss Lützenburg, near Berlin (1695), later altered by *Eosander von Göthe and renamed Schloss Charlottenburg. In Saxony he seems to have had a hand in designs for the Schloss at Barby (*c.*1687).

Borrmann (1893); Geyer (1936); Hempel (1965); Reuther (1969)

Nervi, Pier Luigi (1891–1979). Italian civil engineer, he made his reputation as one of the most gifted designers of *reinforced-concrete structures of C20. Although influenced by Italian *Rationalism, notably by *Terragni, he remained stylistically independent of fashion. His Florence Stadium (1930–2), with its huge cantilevered roof-structure and projecting spiral stairs, was the first of his many buildings to gain international acclaim. From 1932 he headed his own company, and invented a *vault of diagonally intersecting concrete arched forms, the whole resting on leaning columns like flying *buttresses, which he realized in the huge aircraft hangars at Orvieto (1935–42—destroyed) and elsewhere. He then evolved a system of superimposed steel meshes encased in concrete that enabled him to create prefabricated corrugated elements with high tensile capacity at the Great Hall B, Exhibition Hall, Turin (1947–9). Variations on these techniques were used in Rome at the Palazzetto dello Sport (1956–7—with Vitellozzi), and the huge Palazzo dello Sport (1958–9—with *Piacentini), where an immense dome seems to float over the space. Nervi designed the structure for *Ponti's Pirelli *skyscraper, Milan (1955–8), and, with *Breuer, *Zehrfuss, and others, the UNESCO Buildings, Paris (1953–7), where he was responsible for the Congress Hall, with its roof formed of folded ferroconcrete plates. He published *Aesthetics and Technology in Building* (1965) and other works.

Collins (1959); Desideri *et al.* (1979); Emanuel (1994); Huxtable (1960); Lampugnani (1988); Nervi (1956, 1965); Pica (1969)

Nesfield, William Eden (1835–88). English *Arts-and-Crafts architect. Articled to William *Burn (1851), he soon moved to *Salvin's office and later published *Specimens of Mediaeval Architecture* (1862—the result of several Continental journeys). In 1863 he set up an office with Norman *Shaw, but practised independently. Many of his finest domestic buildings were in the *Queen Anne style, which he appears to have inaugurated, starting with the C17-style Lodge at Regent's Park, London (1864—destroyed), followed by his masterpiece, Kinmel Park, Denbighshire (1866–74), and then Bodrhyddan, Flintshire, (1872–4), both in Wales. His importance lies in his influence on the evolution of the English *Domestic Revival, and in the charm of his Queen Anne buildings. One of his finest designs was Cloverley Hall, Whitchurch, Shropshire (1862–8—destroyed), which featured *mullioned-and-transomed windows, and a free use of *Gothic and C17 features.

Dixon and Muthesius (1985); Eastlake (1970); Girouard (1977); Jervis (1984)

Netherlands Grotesque. C16 *grotesque ornament combined with *strapwork, entwined with human figures, invented by Flemish Mannerists such as de *Vries.

Lewis and Darley (1986)

net tracery. *See* tracery.

Neue Sachlichkeit. Term coined in 1923 to describe the 'New Objectivity' in art and architecture, especially in the Weimar Republic in Germany. A reaction to *Expressionism, it was associated with the development of *Rationalism and the *International Modernist style.

Chilvers, Osborne, and Farr (1988); Lampugnani (1988)

Neues Bauen. Avant-garde architecture in Germany in the 1920s and 1930s, originally associated with the *Arbeitsrat für Kunst, then with *Häring, and later with new architecture in general, especially of the *International Modernist style.

Lampugnani (1988)

Neufforge, Jean-François (1714–91). Born near Liège, he settled in Paris (1738). His *Recueil élémentaire d'Architecture* (Elemental Compendium of Architecture—1757–80—the greatest collection of designs in the early Neoclassical style of the period), with over 900 plates, reinforced his reputation as an archaeological Classicist, so that he was called the *Vignola of the age of *Louis Seize. He also helped with the production of plates for Le *Roy's important *Les Ruines des plus beaux monuments de la Grèce* (Ruins of the Most Beautiful Monuments of Greece—1758), one of the early significant influences on *Neoclassicism and the *Greek Revival.

Jervis (1984); Lewis and Darley (1986); Middleton and Watkin (1987)

Neumann, Johann Balthasar (1687–1753). German architect and military engineer, one of the greatest of the late-*Baroque and *Rococo eras. He worked mainly in Franconia under the aegis of the Schönborn Prince-Bishops in the areas around Bamberg and Würzburg, where his brief covered responsibility for all military, religious, and secular architecture. His first significant major architectural work was on the new *Residenz* (Seat of the Court) at Würzburg from 1719, although Johann *Dientzenhofer, *Hildebrandt, de *Cotte, *Boffrand, and von *Welsch were all consulted about the design. Hildebrandt's influence is clear in the great central *pavilion (the roof and *pediments resemble his Belvedere in Vienna), the *Kaisersaal* (Emperor's Hall), the Chapel, and the great *Treppenhaus* (stair), although Neumann seems to have finalized the designs about 1735. With its ceiling painted (1750–3) by Giovanni Battista Tiepolo (1696–1770), the stair at Würzburg is one of the most splendid of the Baroque period, comparable with Neumann's other ceremonial stairs at the St Damiansburg Palais, Bruchsal (1728–50), and Schloss Augustusburg, Brühl, near Cologne (1740–8). All three are spacious, breathtakingly beautiful, and elegant.

Neumann's churches are many and invariably interesting. His first was the Schönborn *Mortuary Chapel attached to the *Romanesque Cathedral, Würzburg (1721–6), an adaptation of a building begun to designs by von Welsch. Among other ecclesiastical works were the Parish and Pilgrimage Church, Gössweinstein (1729–39), the *Residenz* Chapel (*Hofkirche*), Würzburg (1730–43), the *Collegiate Church of St Paulinus, Trier (1734–54), the Pilgrimage Church of the Visitation of Mary (called the Käppele), Würzburg (1740–81), and the Parish and Mortuary Church of Sts Cecilia and Barbara, Heusenstamm, near Offenbach, Hesse (1739–56).

His celebrated Pilgrimage Church (*Wallfahrtskirche*) of the Assumption of Mary, *Vierzehnheiligen* (Fourteen Saints), Franconia (1742–72), had been started on site, but the spot where the Fourteen Helper Saints are said to have appeared was left in the middle of the *nave rather than in the *chancel as intended. Neumann turned this error to advantage, creating a large elliptical space around the *Nothelfer* (Helper in Time of Need) *shrine, within a basically cruciform-basilican plan, and making the nave and chancel five overlapping ellipses, three of which had their long axes on the centre-line of the church, and two at right angles to the main axis. The transeptal arrangement consisted of one of the two ellipses at the *crossing, with intersecting circles at either end. The resultant interlocking vaults have almost a *Gothic flavour about them, but this is disguised by the sumptuously joyous Rococo decorations, nearly all the work of Franz Xaver Feichtmayr (1705–64), Johann Michael Feichtmayr (1709–72), and Johann Georg Üblhör (1700–63). The lovely *Gnadenaltar* (Altar of Grace), a Rococo tour-de-force resembling a sedan-chair covered in marine encrustations and standing within an elliptical space to the west of the *crossing, was designed by Neumann's assistant, Johann Jakob

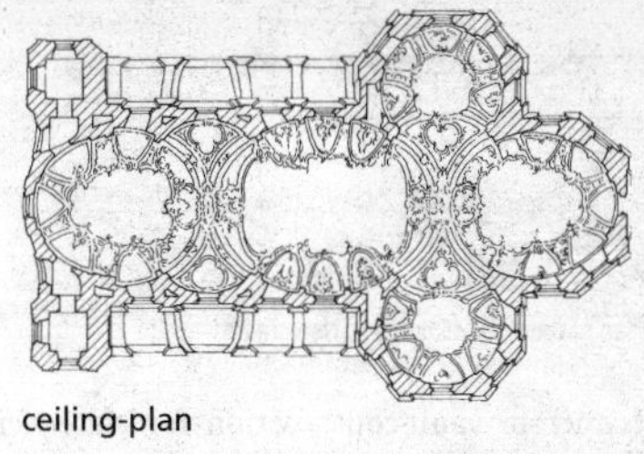

ceiling-plan

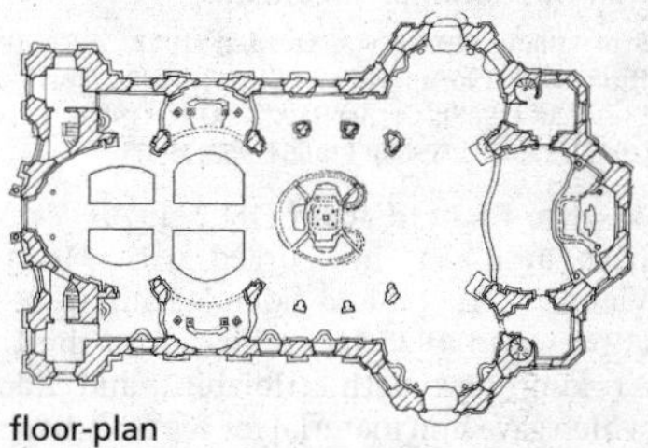

floor-plan

Plans of *Wallfahrtskirche Vierzehnheiligen*, Franconia, showing interpenetrating ellipses, ovals, and circles. Note position of *Nothelfer* shrine in the centre of the largest ellipse to the liturgical west of the crossing.

Michael Küchel (1703–69), to whom some of the credit for the building should be given, for he was the man on the spot from 1744. Neumann has been praised to the skies for this lovely building (notably by *Pevsner), but the beauty of the interior owes much to the Feichtmayrs, Küchel, and Üblhör, and the plan itself resembles *Guarini's Santa Maria della Divina Providenza, Lisbon (1656–*c.*59), published in the latter's *Architettura Civile* (1737). However, Neumann may have evolved his plan by way of Dientzenhofer's churches in Prague, which he had visited in 1738.

Larger and grander was the huge Benedictine Abbey Church at Neresheim, near Nördlingen (1745–92), completed after Neumann's death by Dominikus and Johann Baptist *Wiedemann. It is a *Wandpfeiler church, but with seven ellipses, two each in nave and choir, one in each transept, and a large one over a vast space at the 'crossing'. In Neresheim spatial interpenetration is eloquently demonstrated, as it is in many of Neumann's creations, especially his three great stairs and, perhaps most effectively of all, at *Vierzehnheiligen*. His son, **Franz Ignaz Michael von Neumann** (1733–88) was a pioneer of fire-resistant roof-construction, and proposed an early system of stiffened

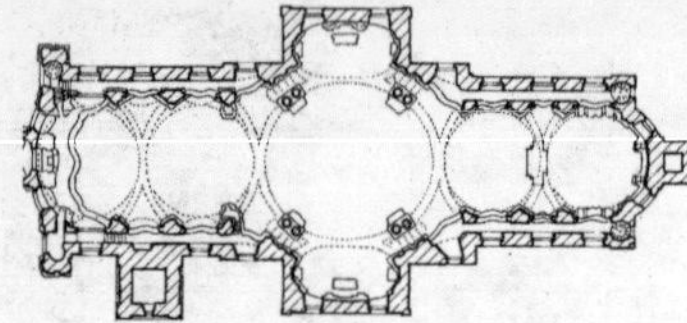

Plan of the Abbey Church of Neresheim.

*concrete vault-construction for Neresheim that was not implemented.

Brinckmann (1932); von Freeden (1952, 1963, 1981); Hitchcock (1968*a*); Hubala (1987, 1989); Korth and Poeschke (1987); Ortner (1978); Otto (1979); Pevsner (1960); Reuther (1960); Teufel (1953, 1957)

Neutra, Richard Josef (1892–1970). Vienna-born architect, he worked with *Loos in Vienna (1912–14) and *Mendelsohn in Berlin (1921–3). In 1923 he emigrated to the USA, working first with *Holabird and Roche, which gave him material for *Wie Baut Amerika?* (How Does America Build?—1927). He met *Sullivan and F. L. *Wright, and in 1925 formed an association in Los Angeles with *Schindler. Together they built the Jardinette Apartments (1927), using *reinforced concrete, cantilevered balconies, and horizontal strips of metal-framed windows. It was one of the first *International Modernist buildings in America, and was followed by the steel-framed Lovell 'Health House', Hollywood Hills, Los Angeles (1927–9), largely made of components selected from catalogues. It made Neutra's name.

He became a visiting critic at the *Bauhaus and represented America at *CIAM. His most productive years as an architect were the 1930s and 1940s, when he designed several houses for famous Hollywood names (e.g. Josef von Sternberg House, San Fernando Valley, Calif., 1935–6). The Kaufmann House, Palm Springs, Calif. (1946–7), was influenced by *Mies van der Rohe. Later works included the US Embassy, Karachi, Pakistan (1959), his own house, Silverlake, Los Angeles (1932–3 and 1963–4), and the Los Angeles Hall of Records (1961). He published *Survival Through Design* (1954) and *Life and Shape* (1962).

Boesiger (1966); Drexler and Hines (1982); Hines (1994); McCoy (1960); Neutra (1954, 1962); Spade (1971*b*)

New Brutalism. *See* Brutalism.

New Classicism. Classical architecture has played a hugely important role, starting with Antiquity, then resurfacing in the *Renaissance, and gaining new attention and respect with C18 *Classicism and *Neoclassicism. As a reaction to *Beaux-Arts, *Neo-Baroque, and *Art Nouveau, there was a further Classical Revival before the 1914–18 war, leading to the Neoclassicism and *stripped Classicism that was so widespread in the 1920s and 1930s. Certain Classical elements were used in *Post-Modernism, such as *pediments, the *Orders, *porticoes, and *aedicules, but that in itself does not constitute the New Classicism, which is concerned with recovering the language of Classicism, suppressed by the *Modern Movement. Among the most effective publicists for New Classicism are *Jencks, Léon *Krier, and *Stern.

Jencks (1980*a*, 1982*a*, 1988*a*); Krier (1978, 1981); Kuspit *et al.* (1986); Papadakis and Watson (1990); Powers (1987); Searing and Reed (1981); Stern (1988)

newel. 1. Continuous vertical member forming the axis of a circular stair. **2.** Upright member set at any turning-point of a stair, or at the top or bottom of a flight, commonly forming part of the framing of the stair, and serving to connect and support the *strings and handrails at a turn or end.

New Empiricism. Swedish architecture of the 1940s by *Erskine, *Markelius, and others, perceived as the 'New Humanism' and 'Welfare-State' architecture. Its somewhat bland imagery was opposed by New *Brutalism.

Architectural Review, 101/606 (June 1947), 199–204, and 103/613 (Jan. 1948), 8–22

New Georgians. 1. Pejorative term for those who restore run-down C18 houses in inner cities. **2.** Anti-*Modernists who sought a revival of *Georgian *Classicism.

Robinson and Artley (1985)

New Objectivity. *See* Neue Sachlichkeit.

New Sensualism. Architecture by e.g. *Candela, Le *Corbusier, *Nervi, *Rudolph, *Saarinen, *Utzon, *Yamasaki and others, who, after the 1939–45 war, exploited plastic form and created buildings quite unlike the style adopted for *International Modernism from the time of the *Weissenhofsiedlung (1927).

Progressive Architecture, 40/9 (Sept. 1959), 141–7, and 40/10 (Oct. 1959), 180–7

Newsom Brothers. Samuel (1854–1908) and **Joseph Cather** (1858–1930) **Newsom** were prolific designers and builders of late-C19 domestic architecture in the USA. Their most celebrated house is the William Carson Residence, Eureka, Calif. (1884–5), a composition featuring barge-boarded *gables, gouty *colonnettes and extreme ornamentation in what can only be described as an exuberant free style. Many designs were published in the *California Architect and Building News*, and Joseph Cather produced a large number of pattern-books, including *Artistic Buildings and Homes of Los Angeles* (1888), *California Low Priced Cottages* (1888), and *Picturesque and Artistic Homes and Buildings of California* (1890). At the beginning of their partnership (1878) they were building in the *Eastlake or *Stick style, then they turned to *Colonial *Queen Anne, followed by much cribbing from *Richardson, then a flirtation with the Colonial Revival or *Shingle style, the *château style, the *Georgian Colonial Revival, and *Beaux-Arts Classicism. Clearly all was grist to their architectural mill. Later they turned to regional Mission Revival (based on Spanish Colonial architecture) and around 1900 to the *Arts-and-Crafts style. Whatever style they used, they were never guilty of restraint.

Gebhard *et al.* (1979); Newsom (1859*a*, 1888, 1890, 1893, 1895, 1897–9, 1981); Newsom and Newson (1978); Placzek (1982)

Newton, Ernest (1856–1922). One of the most successful and influential domestic architects in England of his generation. London-born, he was articled to Norman *Shaw in 1873 before establishing his own practice in 1897. Red Court, Scotland Lane, near Haslemere, Surrey (1894–5), drew on canted *bays, sash-windows, and other features that led *Pevsner to describe it as an 'ominous house with sterile Neo-Georgianism just round the corner'. He published *A Book of Houses* (1890) and *A Book of Country Houses* (1903). His son, **William Godfrey Newton**, published *The Work of Ernest Newton R.A.* (1925).

Gray (1985); Pevsner, *Buildings of England, Surrey* (1971)

New Towns. After the 1939–45 war some of the ideas of Ebenezer *Howard were adopted by the new Socialist Government of the United Kingdom, and various new towns were planned and built to take the pressure off large existing cities. London acquired eight (Stevenage was the first), and there were others in England, Scotland, Wales, and Northern Ireland.

Whittick (1974)

New York Five. Known as the 'Whites' because of their predominantly white buildings (notably those of *Meier), they were a loose grouping of American architects (the others were Peter *Eisenman, Michael *Graves, Charles *Gwathmey, and John *Hejduk) who exhibited in New York in 1969, and were perceived as producing revisions of *International Modernist white buildings of the 1920s influenced by the works of *Rietveld and *Terragni in particular. They have been described as *Neo-Rationalists.

Frampton *et al.* (1975); Klotz (1988)

Niccolini, Antonio (1772–1850). Italian Neoclassical architect and stage-designer. Much influenced by French work, he designed the stupendous façade for Medrano's Teatro San Carlo, Naples (1810–12), with a robust, rusticated, arched lower storey and an *Ionic *colonnade on the upper floor beneath a huge *entablature. Six years later, after a fire, he built a new theatre behind the façade. He also built the Teatro Piccini and the Church of San Ferdinando at Bari, and for the Bourbon Royal Family he built the Villa Floridiana (1817–19) and the Villa Lucia (1818).

Meeks (1966); Middleton and Watkin (1987)

niche. Shallow ornamental recess in a wall or *pier, usually to contain a statue, *urn, or other ornament. Classical niches are usually arched, sometimes with a quarter-spherical *head if semicircular on plan, and often with the half-dome carved to resemble a scallop-shell. Some niches are set within *aedicules, and *Gothic niches (called *tabernacles) have *gablets or canopies over them.

Nicholson, Sir Charles Archibald, Bt. (1867–1949). British architect. He was articled to *Sedding, after whose death he continued to practise with Henry *Wilson. In 1893 he set up on his own and in 1895 was joined by the Australian Hubert Christian Corlette (1869–1956), who had trained with *Belcher. Their first church was St Alban, Westcliffe-on-Sea, Essex (1895–1908), and they published important papers on the furnishing of ecclesiastical buildings (1907–12). They designed one of the first extensive *reinforced-concrete complexes, Government Buildings and House, Kingston, Jamaica (1910), an extraordinary work with *bays defined by massive *buttresses. Their finest church is arguably St Matthew's, Chelston, Torquay, Devon (1895–1904), where *Arts-and-Crafts influences merged with *Gothic Revival. Nicholson contributed to the design of St Anne's Cathedral, Belfast, where he was consultant architect from 1924 to 1948.

DNB (1959); Gray (1985); Larmour (1987); Pevsner, *Buildings of England, Devon* (1989)

Nicholson, Peter (1765–1844). Scots architect. Settling in London, he published *The New Carpenter's Guide* (1792), which described new methods of constructing vaults and niches. This was followed by *The Principles of Architecture* (1795–8) and *The Carpenter's and Joiner's Assistant* (1797). He practised as an architect in Glasgow from 1800, building Carlton Place, Laurieston (1802–18), other buildings in Scotland and Cumberland (he was Surveyor to that County from 1808), and laying out the town of Ardrossan, Ayrshire (1800–8—although the harbour was constructed by *Telford). Back in London (1810) he published *The Architectural Dictionary* (1812–19), and *The School of Architecture and Engineering* (from 1825, but abandoned). He was assisted in some of his publications by his son, **Michael Angelo Nicholson** (1796–1842), who also brought out several books: their prodigious output constitutes an important repository of architectural and building knowledge, and includes *An Architectural and Engineering Dictionary* (1835, revised 1852). One of M. A. Nicholson's two daughters married 'Greek' *Thomson.

Colvin (1995); *DNB* (1917); Nicholson (1823, 1835, 1852); Papworth (1852)

Niemeyer, Oscar (1907–). Brazilian architect who joined the group working with Le *Corbusier on the Ministry of Education and Health Building, Rio de Janeiro (1936–45). Although an early devotee of *International Modernism, he moved away from rectilinear forms with his Casino, Yacht Club, and Restaurant, and São Francisco Chapel, in Pampúlha, Belo Horizonte (1942–7). Such departures from *Modernist orthodoxy led to hostility from critics such as Max *Bill, but nevertheless in 1957 Niemeyer was appointed Chief Architect to the new City of Brasília, the layout of which had been devised by *Costa. The main buildings, including the centrally planned Cathedral, Palaces of the Three Powers (Presidential, Supreme Court, and Congress), and Government Buildings, were all by Niemeyer (1957–64). He designed the Communist Party Headquarters, Paris (1968–75), and the Mondadori Headquarters, Milan (1968–75), which many consider to be among his most distinguished buildings. He brought out a volume on his life in Brazil (1961) as well as other works.

Fils (1988); Hornig (1981); Lampugnani (1988); Niemeyer (1975, 1978); Papadaki (1960); Sodré (1978); Spade (1971*a*)

nimbus. *See* aureole.

nine altars. According to tradition there are Nine Choirs or Orders of Angels, mediating between God and Man, nine squaring the Trinity. This is reflected in the design of certain *retrochoirs (e.g. Fountains Abbey, Yorkshire (*c.*1205–47), and Durham Cathedral (1242–1280s)).

Whone (1990)

Nobile, Pietro (Peter) von (1774–1854). Born in the Ticino area of Switzerland, he trained in Rome, and became established in Trieste, where he designed the Fontana House (1813–16, built 1827–30), and the Accademia di Commercio e Nautica (1817). His fine Church of Sant'Antonio Nuovo, Trieste (1825–49), is a powerful Neoclassical design with a severe hexastyle *Ionic *portico set against the plain blocky mass of the domed building behind. In 1817 he built the *Theseustempel* (Temple of Theseus) in the *Volksgarten* (People's Garden—1822) and the *Burgtor* (Fortress Gate) in the *Heldenplatz* (Place of Heroes—1821–4), both in Vienna, the former a miniature version of the Temple of Hephaestus, Athens, built to contain Antonio Canova's (1757–1822) Theseus sculpture (1819), and the latter based on a severe design by *Cagnola.

Hitchcock (1977); Meeks (1966); Middleton and Watkin (1987)

nodding ogee. *Ogee *canopy-head. Its *apex projects beyond the springing-line of the canopy, i.e. it is an ogee form in *section as well as in *elevation.

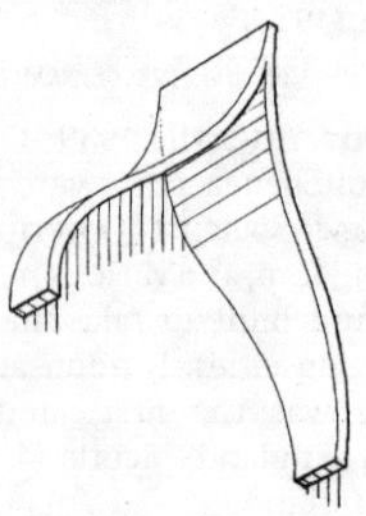

nodding ogee (*JJS*)

nogging. Brickwork infill-*panel set in a timber *frame.

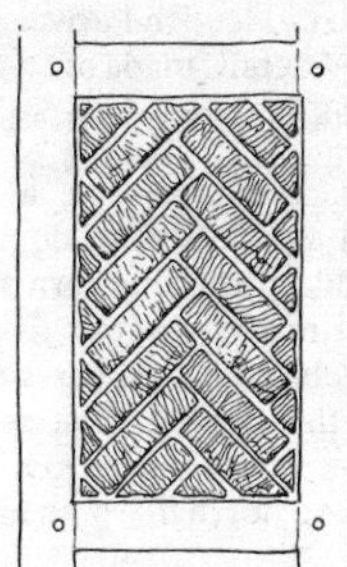

nogging (*JJS*)

nogging-piece. Horizontal timber between the *posts in a *timber-framed structure forming part of the frame of an infill-*panel, e.g. of brick *nogging.

Noiers, Geoffrey de (*fl.* 1189–*c.*1200). Probably the Norman-French master-mason responsible for part of the rebuilding of the *Gothic Lincoln Cathedral from 1192. The vault of St Hugh's *Choir (1192–1200), by him, is probably the first case in Gothic Europe where the emphasis was on decorative rather than structural ribs, and he was perhaps also responsible for the three-dimensional blind overlaid arcading on the walls of St Hugh's Choir. However, *Richard the Mason (*fl.* 1190s) was also involved, and the original design of the Gothic Cathedral may be his.

Harvey (1987)

Nolli, Giovanni Battista (*c.*1692–1756). Italian surveyor, typographer, and architect, he prepared the plan of Rome that was an accurate and full survey of *Antique remains. He designed Santa Dorotea in Trastévere (1751–6), with a concave façade of monumental gravity, and interior of deceptive simplicity.

Ehrle (1932)

nook. 1. Corner of a room, i.e. interior angle formed by the meeting of two walls. **2.** Piece taken out of an angle, e.g. where a *reveal meets the exterior *face of a wall and a re-entrant angle is formed, giving two *arrises instead of one. **3.** Part of the corner of a room beside a fireplace, often with its own window, called an *ingle-nook, sometimes treated as an alcove off a room providing a more intimate space.

Harris (1983); *OED* (1933)

nook-rib. Rib in the corner of a *Gothic *vault.

nook-shaft. *Colonnette set in a *nook (**2**), i.e. in the external angle of a building or where the *reveal of an aperture joins the external *face of the wall.

nook-window. Window in an *ingle-nook, i.e. in the corner of the room next to the fireplace, often recessed.

Norman architecture. *Romanesque architecture in Normandy and the British Isles C11–end of C12, generally with massive walls pierced by semicircular-headed windows and doors. There was a short-lived C19 **Norman Revival.**

Normand, Alfred-Nicolas (1822–1909). French architect and writer, son of **Louis-Eléonor Normand** (1780–1862), also an architect. After sustained study abroad, he settled in Paris in 1852 and became an important designer during the *Second Empire. A confirmed Classicist, he avoided all medieval allusions in his work. His greatest achievement was the *Maison Pompéienne*, Avenue Montaigne, Paris (designed 1855, destroyed 1891), influenced by Roman *villa plans, with a central glazed *atrium. Interiors were revivals of Graeco-Roman, *Pompeian, *Empire, *Islamic, and other styles, juxtaposed in a rich and fruity mélange. The house, for Prince Napoléon-Joseph-Charles-Paul (Plon-Plon) Bonaparte (1822–91), was the paradign of the *Neo-Grec style. Normand also designed the women's prison, Rennes (1867–76), a vast establishment for 1,000 inmates. Among his other works were the C17 Revival Château at Liancourt-St-Pierre, near Paris (1862–8), the restoration of the Colonne Vendôme and the Arc de Triomphe, Paris (1871–8), and the Hospital at St-Germain-en-Laye (1878–81). He was the editor of *Le Moniteur des Architectes* (Gazette of Architects) (1866–8) and published illustrations of the pavilions erected for the Exposition Universelle (1867). His sons, **Charles-Nicolas** (1858–) and **Paul** (1861–) were architects too.

Gary (1979); *Gazette des Beaux-Arts* NS 5/87 (1976), 127–34; Turner (ed.) (1996)

Normand, Charles-Pierre-Joseph (1764–1840). French architect, engineer, and engraver, whose plates for *Percier and *Fontaine's *Recueil* . . . (1801) encapsulated the *Empire style. His *Nouveau Recueil en Divers Genres d'Ornemens* (New Compendium of Different Types of Ornament—1803) contained many *Directoire and Empire themes, and he collaborated with Pierre-Nicolas Beauvallet (1749–1828) on *Décorations intérieures et extérieurs* (Interior and Exterior Decorations—1803). His most celebrated work was *Nouveau Parallèle des Ordres* (New Parallel of the Orders—1819), an accurate and exquisitely engraved book of the *Orders of architecture that remains one of the best sources for the Orders. His son, **Louis-Marie** (1789–1874), published important engravings of funerary monuments and mausolea in the new cemeteries of Paris in 1832.

Jervis (1984); Lewis and Darley (1986); Middleton and Watkin (1987); Normand, C. (1852); Normand, L.-M. (1832); Papworth (1852)

Norse. Viking ornament, consisting of *interlacing forms linked to zoomorphic forms in continuous complex designs (*Jellinge* style—late C10), frantic foliate ornament, sometimes with dragon-like forms (*Ringerike* style), ribbon-patterns and *lacertine work (*Urnes* style—late C11). It influenced *Celtic, *Hiberno-Romanesque, and *Anglo-Saxon designs. An excellent example of the *Ringerike* Norse or Viking style is the carving of the south *doorway of the church of Sts Mary and David, Kilpeck, Herefordshire (*c.*1140–5). Norse ornament was revived in C19 and C20, and, mingled with Celtic motifs, occurred in *Art Nouveau and *Jugendstil design.

Glazier (1926); Jones (1868); Lewis and Darley (1986); Tschudi-Madsen (1967)

North, Roger (*c.*1653–1743). Aristocratic English amateur architect, he played an important role in negotiations with *Barbon for the rebuilding of The Temple, London, after the fire of 1678/9. He designed the Great Gateway from Fleet Street to The Temple (1683–4), and was responsible for a number of other competent Classical designs, including Wroxton Abbey, Oxfordshire (1680–5), and a house at Rougham, Norfolk (1690s—destroyed). An essay, entitled 'Of Building' by him survives in the British Library.

British Library Add. MSS 23005, 32510, 32540; Colvin (1995); *DNB* (1917)

Northern Renaissance Revival. Late-C19 revival (especially in England) of the *Renaissance and *Mannerist styles of Flanders, The Netherlands, and Northern Germany, notably by Sir Ernest *George and other contemporaries, also termed *Pont-Street Dutch or Flemish Revival. It frequently incorporated details made of *terracotta.

Dixon and Muthesius (1985); Gray (1985)

north-light. 1. Glazing in a roof facing north, with a pitched roof sloping from the window-head on the southern side. In e.g. a factory, a series of north-lights is often formed with valleys between the bases of the north-lights and the sloping roof, so in *section the roof resembles a jagged saw. **2.** Any large window facing north in e.g. an artist's studio.

north side. Side of a church facing north, regarded as the source of cold winds and the haunt of the Devil (hence *Devil's door*, meaning a north door).

nose. Projecting edge.

nosing. Projection formed by a horizontal rounded edge extending beyond an upright *face below, such as the edge of a tread in a stair, a *cill, or a drip-stone or *label.

notch ornament. Ornament produced by cutting notches in series along the edges of a *band, *fillet, etc.

Notman, John (1810–65). Scots-born architect, he worked with W. H. *Playfair before emigrating to the USA in 1831. He designed Laurel Hill Cemetery, Philadelphia, Pa. (1836–9), one of the finest of all C19 cemeteries of the *Picturesque landscaped type. He followed this with Hollywood Cemetery, Richmond, Va. (1848), and Capitol Square, Richmond (1850–*c.*1860), one of the USA's first public parks laid out in the informal style. His houses included Nathan Dunn's Cottage, Mount Holly (1837–8—in the *Regency exotic eclectic style), and Riverside, Burlington (1839—in the *Italianate style), in New Jersey; neither survives, but both were published in A. J. *Downing's *A Treatise on the Theory and Practice of Landscape Gardening* (1841). His Prospect Villa, Princeton, NJ (1851–2), was a sophisticated Italianate asymmetrical villa that could easily have been transported from the Edinburgh suburbs. Among his large and always competent buildings were the New Jersey State House, Trenton (1845–6), the New Jersey State Lunatic Asylum (1845–8), and the Philadelphia Athenaeum (1845–7), the last a *palazzo no doubt prompted by *Barry's

Clubs in London. His best *Gothic Revival works were St Mark's Church, Philadelphia (1847–52), and the Cathedral of St John, Wilmington, Del. (1857–8), but he was equally fluent in the round-arched styles (e.g. St Clement's Church, Philadelphia (1855–9)). He embraced new techniques and at the rebuilding of Nassau Hall, Princeton (1855–9), employed rolled-iron beams, one of the first such instances in the USA. His practice declined from *c*.1860, and the Demon Drink may have played its part in this, as well as in his comparatively early death.

Downing (1967, 1967*a*); Greiff (1979); Placzek (1982)

Nôtre, André Le (1613–1700). Creative designer of formal gardens in C17 France, his greatest work was the Park at Versailles, with fountains, canals, avenues, and *parterres (1662–90). His work for *Louis XIV was enormously influential throughout Europe. In 1657 he was appointed *Contrôleur Général des Bâtiments, Jardins, Tapisseries, et Manufactures de France* after he had begun work on the design of the gardens at Vaux-le-Vicomte (laid out 1656–61) for Nicolas Fouquet (1656–61), his first master-work. It was followed by the redesigning of the gardens at Fontainebleau (1662–87). For the newly restored King Charles II (1660–85) of Great Britain he designed the park at Greenwich (1662—much decayed). He carried out works at Chantilly (1663–8), St-Germain-en-Laye (1663–73), and the Tuileries, Paris. The gardens at Clagny (1674–6), Maintenon (1675–8), Meudon (1679–80), the Palais Royal (1674), St-Cloud (1665–78), and Sceaux (1673–7), were also his work. In 1698 he designed a garden at Windsor, Berkshire, for King William III (1688–1702).

Adams (1979); Fox (1962); Ganay (1962); Hazlehurst (1980)

Nouvel, Jean (1945–). French architect. His works include the huge Institut du Monde Arabe (with *Architecture Studio), Paris (1981–7—where the whole building seems to revolve around a transparent lift-shaft), a block of flats called *Nemausis*, Nîmes (1987—with flexible internal plans), the Hôtel des Thermes, Dax (1992), the Opera House, Lyons (1987–93—a new building constructed inside the Classical stone shell of the 1831 design by Chenevard and Pollet), the Palais des Congrès, Tours (1989–93), and the Fondation Cartier, Paris (1991–4). His Concert-Hall, Lucerne, Switzerland (opened 1998), beautifully sited by the lake, has been acclaimed as one of C20's finest musical venues. He has been one of the most relentless and uncompromising protagonists of *Modernism, expressing his ideas almost polemically through his buildings. Many of his projects have been carried out with Emmanuel Cattani and Associates.

Emanuel (1994); Goulet (1994); Jodidio (1995*a*); Meyhöfer (1995)

Novembergruppe. Association of German artists and architects founded immediately after their nation's defeat in the 1914–18 war. It included *Bartning, *Gropius, *Häring, *Hilbersheimer, the *Luckhardts, *Mendelsohn, *Mies van der Rohe, and the *Tauts. Many members were also active in *Arbeitsrat für Kunst, and the group exhibited and argued in favour of what was to become the *Modern Movement. It ceased to be a force by 1931 and was banned by the National Socialists in 1933.

Berlin Exhibition Catalogue, *Die Novembergruppe* (1977)

Nowicki, Matthew (Maciej) (1910–51). Polish architect, influenced by Le *Corbusier and *Perret. He designed the Dorton Arena, North Carolina State Fair, Raleigh (1948–53), with two intersecting *hyperbolic parabolas, and is regarded as a pioneer of such structural design. He worked with *Saarinen on the Master Plan for Brandeis University, Waltham, Mass. (1948–9), and was engaged on the Master Plan for Chandigarh, India (1948–51), when he was killed in an aeroplane crash.

Mainstone (1975); Morgan and Naylor (1987); Shafer (1973)

Noyes, Eliot Fette (1910–77). American architect and industrial designer. He worked with *Gropius and *Breuer (1938–41) and made his reputation as a designer of many houses, office-buildings, interiors, and work for IBM, Mobil Oil, and Westinghouse. Buildings include the Bubble Houses, Hobe Sound, Fla. (1953—made by spraying concrete on to a large balloon), the Noyes House, New Canaan, Conn. (1955), the United Nations Pavilion, Expo 67, Montreal (1967), and the IBM Management Development Center, Armonk, NY (1980). He published *Organic Design and Home Furnishing* (1941).

Emanuel (1994)

Nüll, Eduard van der (1812–68). Austrian architect, involved in the *Rundbogenstil fashion of the 1840s, who assisted Georg Müller in the design and erection of the Altlerchenfeld Church, Vienna (1848–61), a brick structure in a pronounced and convincing Italian round-arched style with two western towers and an octagonal *cupola. He teamed up with August Siccard von *Siccardsburg to design the *Kommandantur-Gebäude* (Commandant's Building) at the Vienna *Zeughaus* (Arsenal), another Rundbogenstil essay of *polychrome brick (1849–55), as well as other works for the military establishment. Their largest building, the Opera House on Vienna's *Ringstrasse*, an uninspired concoction in a free French Renaissance style (1861–9), was severely criticized during its construction, and this may have led to van der Nüll's suicide. They also proposed the Vienna International Exhibition of 1873, which was realized by *Hasenauer.

Auer (1885); Baedeker, *Austria* (1929); Pevsner (1976)

nuraghi. *See* beehive.

nutmeg. *First Pointed Northern-English ornament consisting of a series of projections, with a gap between each pair, resembling half-nutmegs, of which good examples occur at St Mary's Church, Nun Monkton, Yorkshire.

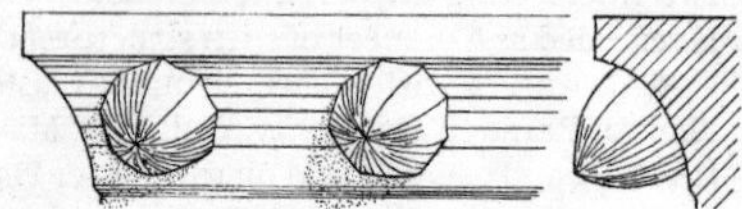

nutmeg. Church of St Mary, Nun Monkton, Yorkshire. (*After Parker*)

nymphaeum. Temple, sanctuary, or *grotto of nymphs, often a feature of *Renaissance and later gardens, incorporating statuary, pools, and fountains, or suggesting water by means of congelated *rustication in a formal Classical garden-building. A good example is at the *Zwinger Palace, Dresden, Saxony (1710–32), by *Pöppelmann.

Nyrop, Martin (1849–1921). Danish architect. His first independent work seems to have been the *rotunda for Østre Gasværk (Gas Works), Copenhagen (1881—now a theatre), the dome of which is almost the same size as that of the *Pantheon in Rome. Influenced by *Dahlerup, *Herholdt, and his travels, his work began to draw on historical precedents. His buildings include the Vallekilde Training College (1884—with later extensions of 1889), the *Landsarkivet*, Copenhagen (Zealand Public Records Office—1891–2), and a series of country-houses (e.g. those at Gisselfeld (1894) and Vallekilde (1889)). He also designed churches (e.g. Stenderup (1903–4), the *Eliaskirke*, Copenhagen (1905–8), and the *Lutherkirke*, Copenhagen (1914–18)), but made his name with the Nordic Exhibition (1888) which established his credentials as a major figure of *National Romanticism. His greatest building, however, is the City Hall, Copenhagen (1892–1905), inspired by the Palazzo Pubblico and Square in Siena. One of the internal courts was designed with a glazed roof, possibly a precedent for *Berlage's Stock Exchange in Amsterdam, and the building had an immense influence on Northern-European public architecture. His Bispebjerg Hospital (1906–13) drew on the *timber-framed tradition in Denmark, and it was designed on the *pavilion principle.

Millech (1951); Rasmussen (1940); van Vynckt (1993); Weilbach (from 1994)

obelisk. Lofty, four-sided, often *monolithic shaft, on a square plan, tapering (i.e. diminishing) upwards, usually covered with *hieroglyphs, with a pyramidal top. An Ancient Egyptian form, obelisks were found in pairs, flanking axes, such as a temple *dromos, but on their introduction to Europe from the time of Augustus (27 BC–AD 14), when the first Egyptian obelisks were re-erected in Rome from 10 BC, they were usually treated as single free-standing objects. They were again set up singly in *Renaissance Rome, this time on *pedestals, where they stand today as the centrepieces of major urban spaces (e.g. Piazza di San Pietro, Piazza del Pòpolo), and were widely copied as a form in Northern-European Mannerist work. Subsequently, obelisks were used as *eye-catchers, memorials, and the like, such as *Morrison's Ross Monument, Rostrevor, Co. Down (1826): it (like many C19 European and American obelisks) is not a monolith, but constructed of *ashlar.

Curl (1994); Habachi (1984); Iversen (1968); Roullet (1972)

Obrist, Hermann (1863–1927). Swiss *Arts-and-Crafts designer influential in art and architecture before the 1914–18 war. He was the major figure in the establishment of the *Vereinigte Werkstätten* (United Workshops) in Munich (1897), and his designs helped to promote *Art Nouveau. He was a particular influence on *Behrens and *Endell. He published *Neue Möglichkeiten in der bildenden Kunst* (New Possibilities in the Graphic Arts—1903) and several significant contributions to the journals *Dekorative Kunst* (Decorative Art). His designs for tombs and monuments from *c.*1900 were early examples of *Expressionism.

Jervis (1984); Tschudi-Madsen (1967); Wichmann (1968)

obtuse. *See* arch.

octagon. Eight equal-sided polygonal figure often found as the plan-form for *Antique Classical and later buildings, such as cathedral *chapter-houses.

octastyle. *See* portico.

octopus-leaf. *See* orchid.

oculus (*pl.* **oculi**). **1.** Roundel, circular opening or recess, bull's-eye, or *œil-de-bœuf, as in a window in the *tympanum of a *pediment or at the top of a dome (e.g. the *Pantheon, Rome). **2.** Button, disc, or *eye from which the spirals of a *volute progress, e.g. the *Ionic *capital or a Classical *console or *modillion.

odeion, odeon, odeum. Small, roofed, Ancient Greek theatre for musical performances or recitations.

O'Donnell, James (1774–1830). Irish-born architect. Emigrating to New York in 1812, he designed *Federal-style houses, the Bloomingdale Asylum (1817–21), Fulton Street Market (1821–2), and some churches (including Christ Church (1820–1). He was responsible for one of the North-American Continent's largest and earliest *Gothic Revival churches, that of Notre-Dame, Place d'Armes, Montreal, Canada (1823–9): it was to have a considerable influence on Canadian church architecture.

Journal of the Society of Architectural Historians, 29/2 (May 1970), 132–43; Kalman (1994)

Odo of Metz (*fl. c.*792–805). *See* Metz.

oecus. Hall or large room in a Roman house, usually with columns around the interior, like an *atrium without *compluvium* or *impluvium*. There were four types of oecus:

oecus Aegyptus: with columns round the sides (an internal *peristyle) supporting a smaller superimposed peristyle between the columns of which light could enter (so a type of *clearstorey), and with a walkway over the lower area. Also called an *Egyptian hall;

oecus Corinthius: with an *Order carrying a vaulted roof;

oecus Cyzicenus: with a view over gardens and the countryside, usually with folding doors;

oecus tetrastylos or *-us*: with four columns carrying the roof-structure.

œil-de-bœuf (*pl.* œils-de-bœuf). **1.** Elliptical ox-eye window, often with four key-stones among the *dressings, and frequently associated with *mansard roofs. **2.** Loosely, *oculus, but only of elliptical, not circular, form.

œillet. **1.** *Loophole, especially if circular, in medieval fortified walls through which missiles could be discharged. **2.** Triangular sinking at the back of each *cusp-point, in *Gothic *tracery, produced by the intersection of the mouldings.

Oesterlen, Dieter (1911–). German architect. Some of his work is powerfully monumental and jagged, such as at the German Military Cemetery, Passo della Futa, near Florence (1961–7). Other designs include the Filmstudio Cinema, Hanover (1951–3), Christ Church, Bochum (1957–9), the Twelve Apostles Church, Hildesheim (1964–7), the Bischof Stahlin Geriatric Centre, Oldenburg (1974–5), the Post Office Headquarters, Bremen (1979–95), the German Embassy, Buenos Aires, Argentina (1980–3), and the Elia Church Community Centre, Langenhagen, near Hanover (1987–8).

Emanuel (1994)

offertory-window. *Lychnoscope.

off-set *also* **set-off.** Top of a wall, *buttress, etc., created where the wall or buttress above is smaller, usually appearing as a sloping ledge in medieval buttresses or *plinths, and called *weather-table*.

ogee. Upright double curve, concave at the top and convex at the bottom, as in the *cyma recta (a *cyma reversa or *Lesbian cymatium, with the convex curve at the top and the concave below, is called a *reverse ogee*). A moulding with an ogee profile is called *ogee moulding*, *ressant*, *ressaunt*, or *ressaut*. Reverse ogee-headed canopies or openings are characteristic of *Second Pointed work, especially over funerary monuments, *niches, *sedilia, and shrines, as well as in *tracery, where it continued well into the *Perpendicular period. A *nodding ogee is a canopy of two ogee arches joined at the apex and bowing outwards from the wall in another ogee double curve, so ogee in *elevation as well as in *section.

ogive. Diagonal *rib of a *Gothic *vault, or any arch made up of two arcs meeting at a point. *Ogival* architecture is therefore *Pointed or Gothic architecture.

O'Gorman, Juan (1905–82). Mexican architect. He designed houses and schools, influenced by Le *Corbusier, regarded as paradigms of *Functionalism in the 1920s and 1930s. In the 1950s, he had a very public change of heart concerning *International Modernism, and began to incorporate Pre-Columbian and *vernacular motifs into his designs (e.g. the National Library, State University of Mexico, Mexico City (1952–3—covered with colourful *mosaics), and the O'Gorman House II, Mexico City (1953–6—destroyed)).

Emanuel (1994); Smith (1967)

Olbrich, Joseph Maria (1867–1908). Austro-Hungarian architect, one of the leading figures of the Vienna *Sezession. A pupil of *Hasenauer and *Sitte, he worked in Otto *Wagner's Vienna office (1894–8), contributing designs for the Vienna *Stadtbahn* (City Railway) stations. Gradually his style moved away from Wagner's dignified and simplified *Neoclassicism and began to incorporate *Art Nouveau motifs. He made his reputation with the Club House and Exhibition Gallery he designed for the artists associated with the Sezession (1897–8). The building had something of Wagner's Neoclassicism on the outside, but with *Jugendstil decorative effects and a gilded wrought-iron dome-like ornament held between four *battered *pylon-like forms crowning the composition, a motif suggesting the *Ver Sacrum* (Sacred Spring—the title of an influential Sezessionist publication) heralding a new era of art. For the Max Friedmann House, Hinterbrühl (1898–9), Olbrich, influenced by the English *Arts-and-Crafts movement, designed not only the building but all the furnishings and fittings.

In 1899 the artistic Ernst Ludwig Charles Albert William, reigning Grand Duke of Hesse (1892–1918), invited Olbrich to the new artists' colony at *Mathildenhöhe* (Matilda's Hill), Darmstadt. There, Olbrich designed the communal studios, the Ernst-Ludwig-Haus (1899–1901), with a pronounced Art Nouveau entrance flanked by two large Neoclassical figures looking forward to the 1930s in style. For his own house (1900–1) Olbrich drew on Austro-German *vernacular forms, but enlivened with blue-and-white tile squares (a motif used by Wagner and *Mackintosh) set in the elevations. Seven of his houses and one by *Behrens (all fully furnished) at *Mathildenhöhe* were ready for public inspection in 1901, the intention being to awaken a sense of modern design in Hesse: it was the first exhibition of its kind. He added further buildings to the *Mathildenhöhe* complex, including the *Hochzeitsturm* (Wedding Tower—erected partly to celebrate the Grand Duke's second marriage (1905) to Princess Eleonore Ernestine Marie of Solms) and Exhibition Building (1905–8). The tower had a top reminiscent of North-German medieval stepped *gables but with semicircular upper parts to the 'steps'.

In 1907 Olbrich became a founder of the *Deutscher Werkbund, and his work became more severe and Classically inspired, including the handsome Leonhard Tietz Department Store, Düsseldorf (1906–9), now the *Kaufhof*. His Joseph Feinhals House, Cologne (1908–9—destroyed), showed the way in which his architecture might have evolved had he lived: it was a powerful Neoclassical composition with two severe wings between which was a Greek *Doric *colonnade, the whole topped by a *mansard roof. Wasmuth published a sumptuous set of volumes, *Architektur von Olbrich* (1901–14).

Haiko and Krimmel (1988); Latham (1980); Lux (1919); Schreyl (1972); Tschudi-Madsen (1967); Veronesi (1948)

Old English. Architectural style involving the revival of *vernacular elements from Sussex and the Kent Weald, essentially one of the threads of the C19 *Domestic *Revival, *Queen Anne style, and the *Arts-and-Crafts movement. It was characterized by tile-hung walls (often in patterns), diaper patterns on brickwork, *leaded windows of the *casement type, *timber-framing (sometimes not real, but merely decorative) of elements (often *gables and *jetties), *barge-boards cut with fretwork, rubbed brick *dressings, steep tiled roofs, and tall ornamental chimney-stacks of moulded brick or *terracotta. Planning was informal and *additive, while composition was *Picturesque. In the USA the *Colonial Revival had similar trends, and led to the *Shingle style.

Dixon and Muthesius (1985)

Old French. C19 *Rococo Revival.

Oleaginous style. C17 precursor of *Rococo, called *Auricular, *Cartilaginous*, *Dutch Grotesque*, *Kwabornament* (Lobed Ornament), or *Lobate* style, a branch of *Mannerism. It consisted of smooth flowing lines, folding in on each other, like human ears, intestines, or marine plants. It was invented in The Netherlands, was disseminated in a series of illustrated books, e.g. *Veelderhande Nieuwe Compartemente* (Many Kinds of New Ornamental Parts—1653), a set of engravings after Gerbrand van den Eeckhout (1621–74), and *Cartouches de différentes inventions* (Cartouches of Different Designs—*c*.1620–30), by Daniel Rabel (*c*.1578–1637). Its chief protagonists were Paulus (d. 1613), Adam (*c*.1565–1627), and Christiaen (*fl.* 1628–66) van Vianen, and Jan Lutma the Elder (*c*.1585–1669) and Younger (1624–85 or 89).

Jervis (1984); Lewis and Darley (1986); Osborne (1970, 1975)

olive. Classical ornament, similar to *bay-leaf, laurel, and myrtle, used in wreaths and garlands.

Oliveira, Mateus Vicente de (1710–86). Portuguese *Rococo architect, who worked under *Ludovice at first, adopting the latter's grand manner, and then evolved a much more exquisite style, of which the Palácio Nacional, Queluz, near Lisbon (1747–92), is a good example, with its swagged and garlanded window-heads. He was responsible for the Basilica da Estrêla, Lisbon (1778).

Cruickshank (1996); Kubler and Soria (1959); Smith (1968)

ollarium (*pl.* **ollaria**). Recess, often arched, in a *columbarium or *hypogeum in which pairs of *cinerary *urns, or ash-chests were placed.

Glare (1982); Toynbee (1971)

Olmec architecture. *Meso-American architecture, of which La Venta, a ceremonial platform in the form of a truncated cone, is an early example (*c.* early C8 BC), situated on an island in the Tonalà River Delta. Important buildings were laid formally out on axes.

Cruickshank (1996); Kubler (1984)

Olmsted, Frederick Law (1822–1903). One of the most important landscape-architects of C19 after *Downing's death, he developed the C18 English *Picturesque style of landscape, and was an innovator in the design of public parks, much influenced by *Paxton's

Birkenhead Park, Cheshire (1847), as is clear from his admiration for English landscape-design, expressed in his *Walks and Talks of an American Farmer in England* (1852).

With Calvert *Vaux (who had been associated with Downing) he created Central Park, New York (1858), an ingenious scheme with a wide variety of types of landscape, including *rock-work with cascades, meadows and water, and traffic-routes sunk from view, with paths over and under them as the grade required. He designed the *campus for the College of California at Berkeley, Mountain View Cemetery, Oakland, Calif. (1864), and proposed creating a nature-reserve in the Yosemite Valley, a precedent for the National Parks movement. Again with Vaux he designed Prospect Park, Brooklyn (1866), resumed work on Central Park, and planned Riverside, near Chicago, Ill. (1868), which proposed dwellings around common land, parks, and the beginnings of a scheme that anticipated pedestrian routes. He began the landscaping around the Federal Capitol, Washington, DC (1874), his work being completed by **F. L. Olmsted, jun.** (1870–1957), in the 1920s, who continued to practise with his cousin, **John Charles Olmsted** (1852–1920).

Persuaded to settle in Massachusetts by H. H. *Richardson (with whom Olmsted had collaborated on the design of the State Asylum for the Insane, Buffalo, NY (1871), and on other projects) in 1881, Olmsted had commenced designs for the system of parks in Boston in 1878, a brilliant scheme forming a meandering trail of greenery and water connecting Charles River to Franklin Park. He contributed to the designs of the campus of Stanford University, Palo Alto, Calif. (1886), worked with Vaux on the Niagara Falls Reservation, NY (1887), and designed the Louisville Park system, Ky. (1891). His last large scheme was the World's Columbian Exposition, Chicago (1893), where he created a sylvan setting for the Neoclassical buildings of *McKim, Mead, & White, Daniel *Burnham, and others. Olmsted's system of transport, roads, and jetties for water-borne visitors was, like most of his work, forward-looking, imaginative, and inventive. He was a prolific writer, and published numerous works of considerable importance.

Beveridge (1995); Cook (1972); Hall (1995); McLaughlin (from 1977); Olmsted and Hubbard (1973); Roper (1973); Sutton (1979); Todd (1982)

OMA (Office for Metropolitan Architecture). Architectural firm founded by Rem *Koolhaas in 1975.

onion-dome. Pointed bulbous structure on top of a tower, resembling an onion, common in Central- and Eastern-European architecture as well as in The Netherlands. It is usually an ornamented top, made of a timber substructure covered with lead, copper, or tiles, and is not a true *dome.

Opbergen, Antonius van (1543–1611). Flemish architect who worked at the Royal Palace of Kronborg, Helsingør, Denmark (1574–85), and designed the Arsenal in Danzig (now Gdańsk, Poland), one of the great buildings in the Flemish *Renaissance style (1602–5). He also designed several fine houses in Gdańsk with J. Strakowski, built 1597–8.

Cruickshank (1996); Karpowicz (1991)

open cornice *or* **eaves.** Overhanging *eaves with exposed rafters, visible from below, the ends of which are sometimes shaped to look like attractive brackets.

open hall. Main living-room of a medieval house, open to the roof, usually with an *open hearth or chimney-stack. An *open-hall house* contained such a hall, and was formerly called a *hall-house.*

Alcock, Barley, Dixon, and Meeson (1996)

open hearth. Hearth, usually sited clear of the walls, without a chimney-stack or hood above it, therefore requiring a *femerall, *lantern, or *louvre on the roof.

open-heart moulding. *Romanesque moulding consisting of a series of overlapping pointed shapes like hearts or spades, with the points upwards, formed of strap-like elements draped over a roll-moulding.

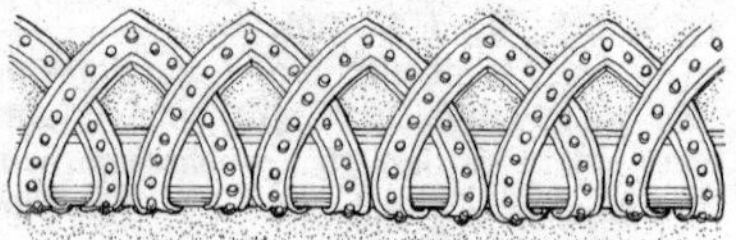

open-heart moulding. 'The Jew's House', Lincoln. (*After Parker*)

open-newel *or* **open-well stair.** Stair built round a well (i.e. with a void between the outer *strings), unlike a well-less *dog-leg.

open pediment. *See* pediment.

open roof. *Open-timbered* roof with its rafters visible from beneath (i.e. with no ceiling).

open stair. *Open-string stair with treads visible at the ends, often ornamented below with scrolls resembling *consoles.

open-string. *Open-stringer* or *cut-string* stair with the top of its *string notched so that the *treads and *risers can fit within the notches.

open-timbered. 1. Exposed *timber frame unconcealed by *pargetting. **2.** *Open-roof. **3.** Floor with *joists exposed on the *soffit.

openwork. 1. Elaborate perforated ornament, like *tracery, common on *Gothic *canopies, *gables, *parapets, and *choir-stalls. **2.** Unprotected part of a fortification, such as a narrow entry into a *bastion.

opisthodomos, opisthodomus. Recessed porch or *epinaos* at the rear of a Greek temple, sometimes enclosed with bronze grilles and used as a treasury. If a porch, it balances the *pronaos at the other end.

Dinsmoor (1950)

Oppenord, Gilles-Marie (1672–1742). French architect and decorator of Flemish descent of the *Régence period, influenced by the work of *Bernini and *Borromini, he had a considerable role in the evolution of the *Rococo or *Louis Quinze style. He designed several altarpieces (e.g. at St-Germain-des-Prés (1704)), but his most influential work included interiors in Bonn, Brühl, and Falkenlust (under de *Cotte), Rhineland, and the Palais Royal (1716–20) and Hôtel Crozat (1721–30), Rue de Richelieu, Paris. From 1719 he was engaged on work at the Church of St-Sulpice, Paris, completing the building except for the west portal (which he designed, but which was eventually finished, in greatly modified form, by *Servandoni and *Chalgrin), and designing the high-altar. Three volumes of engravings (*Livre de Fragments d'Architecture*, *Livre de différents morceaux*, and *Œuvres*) based on his work were published by Gabriel Huquier in 1737–51, thus making his work widely known. By 1755 devotees of *Neoclassicism (e.g. Charles-Nicolas Cochin (1715–90)) saw him as one of those who had debauched Classical architecture. His work also informed the Rococo Revival of the 1880s.

Jervis (1984); Lewis and Darley (1986); Placzek (1982); Sturgis *et al.* (1901–2)

Oppler, Edwin (1831–80). Architect active in C19 Hanover, he published influential *Gothic Revival furniture designs in the journal *Die Kunst im Gewerbe* (Art in Industry—1872), of which he was editor 1872–8.

Jervis (1984)

optical corrections. Alterations to planes or surfaces to correct possible perceptions of distortion. They include *entasis, increasing the height of stone courses with the height of a wall so that the courses appear identical in height, and the slight convex surface of a *stylobate.

opus. Latin for 'work', as intended to designate construction, or arrangement of materials in construction.

opus albarium. 1. Species of *opus tectorium* (a thin coat of burnt powdered marble, lime, sand and water, well mixed) covering a wall and polished after it was quite set so that it had a sheen. **2.** Coating or coatings of pure lime on a wall.

opus Alexandrinum. Type of church paving found from C4 to C13 consisting of black, porphyry, serpentine, and other marble slabs, cut to simple geometrical shapes and inlaid in paving-slabs of a light colour in repetitive geometrical patterns, sometimes with *guilloche, and occasionally including *opus sectile.

opus antiquum. Type of Roman *masonry, called also *opus incertum*, the *face of which has irregularly placed stones of different sizes (*rubble-work, uncoursed), and *bands of brick or tile laid in *courses to provide horizontal levelling courses and to bind the wall together.

opus caementicium, opus caementum. Roman wall constructed of rough undressed stones placed in a *concrete mix of lime, *pozzolan, sand, and water, also known as *opus structile* or *structura caementicia*.

opus incertum. *See* opus antiquum.

opus isodomum. Regular coursed *masonry, the *courses being of equal height and the *blocks being of equal length, laid with their vertical joints centred on the blocks above and below.

opus latericium *or* **lateritium.** Wall built of thin bricks or tiles, or of *concrete faced with bricks, tiles, or a mixture of both, giving the impression that the wall is constructed of these materials rather than merely faced.

opus lateritum. Roman brickwork. *See* opus latericium.

opus listatum. Roman wall constructed of alternating *courses of masonry and brickwork or tiles.

opus lithostrotum. Any type of ornamental paving, such as *mosaic, with pictures or abstract geometrical patterns.

opus marmoratum. Plaster or *stucco of calcined gypsum mixed with powdered marble and water, rubbed and polished to a fine marble-like surface when dry.

opus mixtum. Wall-facing of brick (or tile) and squared tufa (porous cellular stone) blocks, laid in alternate *courses.

opus musivum *or* **museum.** *Mosaic-work made of coloured glass or enamelled pieces.

opus polygonum. Polygonal masonry.

opus pseudisodomum. *Ashlar with the stone *blocks of each *course alike, but differing from the stones of other courses in height, length, or thickness, so that while continuous horizontal joints were maintained they varied in height, resulting in masonry laid in regular courses of alternating broad and narrow *bands. Alexander 'Greek' *Thomson used *pseudisodomic* masonry at the Caledonia Road Church, Glasgow (1856), with the narrow bands projecting slightly from the face of the wider bands, emphasizing the horizontal qualities of the building. *See* isodomon, pseudisodomon.

McFadzean (1979); Papworth (1852)

opus quadratum. Squared *ashlar laid in regular *courses.

opus reticulatum. *Concrete wall faced with small squared stones (sometimes the bases of small pyramids) set diagonally all over the *face creating a network or *lattice of *lozenge-shaped interconnected joints.

opus scalpturatum *or* **sculpturatum.** *Inlaid work consisting of a pattern chiselled out of a solid ground, then filled in with thin leaves of coloured marble. A variant was a marble surface with a pattern cut out and filled with coloured cement or *stucco.

opus sectile. Pavement or wall-covering of differently coloured pieces (larger than *tesserae in *mosaics) of marble, stone, and, sometimes, glass, cut into regular pieces of a few uniform sizes, laid in geometrical patterns.

opus signinum. Type of *terrazzo made by mixing fragments of broken pottery or tiles with lime-mortar, then smoothing it off.

opus spicatum. Masonry faced with stones or tiles arranged in herringbone patterns, usually with horizontal *courses at various heights to provide *bands and to bond the wall together.

opus tectorium. *See* opus albarium.

opus tessellatum. Pavement or facing of regular-shaped pieces of differently coloured material (e.g. marbles) in larger pieces than *mosaic *tesserae, laid in cement in geometrical patterns.

opus testacaeum *or* **testaceum.** Wall of *rubble and *concrete faced with whole or broken tiles, usually on both sides.

opus topiarum. *Antique mural-painting or *fresco depicting gardens with *trellis-work, trees, shrubs, etc.

opus vermiculatum. Very fine and delicate *Antique *mosaic, its *tesserae carefully laid in curving serpentine lines, sometimes with emphasis added by darker tesserae suggesting shadow-projections.

orangery. Building of the nature of a *conservatory used for the storage in winter of trees in tubs. It usually had large, south-facing windows, and often had architectural pretensions.

Woods and Warren (1988)

oratory. **1.** Domestic *chapel or a room in a private house for prayer. **2.** Small chapel of any sort, more particularly one for private solitary devotion. **3.** Church and buildings belonging to the Congregation of St Philip Neri (1515–95), constituted *c.*1550 and approved by Pope Gregory XIII (1572–85) in 1575, and called the *Oratorians*.

orb. **1.** Globe surmounted by a cross, an emblem of power and sovereignty, often placed on top of the *lantern of a *cupola, *pinnacle, or *spire. **2.** Spherical termination or *finial on a *pedestal or *pier. **3.** Circular knot of flowers or herbs (*boss) fixed at the intersection of *ribs in a *Gothic *vault, serving to conceal the junction of the mouldings and act as an *abutment to them. **4.** Medieval term for a *blind panel in *tracery, especially in *Perpendicular work.

Orbais, Jean d' (*fl.* C13). With Jean de or le Loup, Gaucher de Rheims, Bernard de Soissons, Robert de Coucy, and Adam de Rheims, he appears to have been one of the architects responsible for Rheims Cathedral from 1211. He probably drew up the original plan, as he was Master-Mason from *c.*1211 to 1229.

Bony (1982); Frankl (1962); Grodecki (1986)

Orbay, François d' (1631–97). Paris-born architect. He assisted Le *Vau at the Château de Vincennes (1654–61), and after Le Vau's death executed the designs for the *Escalier des Ambassadeurs* (Ambassadors' Stair), Versailles (1674–80), and the Collège des Quatre Nations, Paris (1662–74—now the Institut de France). He became *Hardouin-Mansart's draughtsman at Versailles and, according to some, he designed the garden elevations of the Palace there (begun 1668) as well as the Louvre *colonnade, Paris (begun 1667), in which case he was a major figure in the evolution of the French Classical style of *Louis Quatorze. On his own account he designed the Arc de Triomphe du Peyrou, Montpellier (1690–2—built in modified form by Charles Daviler (1653–1700)), and the Cathedral of Mountauban (1691–1739).

Blunt (1982); Hautecœur (1949); Laprade (1960)

Orcagna, Andrea di Cione, *called* (*c.*1308–68). Florentine *Gothic architect. *Capomaestro* of the *oratory of Or San Michele, Florence, from 1355, he designed the exquisite gabled domed *tabernacle (*c.*1352–9). At Orvieto Cathedral in 1358 he supervised the construction of the façade *rose-window and may have contributed to the decorations of the front. He was involved as a consultant at the Florence *Duomo* (Cathedral) from 1350 and was probably an influence on the final design.

Steinweg (1929); White (1987)

orchaestra, orchestra. **1.** Circular space for the chorus and dancers in an Ancient Greek theatre. **2.** In a Roman theatre, the semicircular level space between the stage and *proscenium and the first semicircular row of seats. **3.** In a modern theatre the space reserved for the musicians. **4.** In the USA the main floor, *parquet, or *stalls of a theatre.

Orchard, William (*fl.* 1468–d. 1504). English master-mason. He designed Magdalen College, Oxford (from 1467), the beautiful vaults of the Divinity School (1480–3), and (on stylistic grounds) probably the *chancel-vaults (*c.*1478–1503) and the *cloisters (*c.*1489–99) at Oxford Cathedral. Both the vaulting schemes have elaborate pendants that look as though they are supports for the structure, the piers, as it were, having been removed: it is a curious and interesting type of design. He was also responsible for Waterstock Church, Oxfordshire (*c.*1500–2), and built part of the Cistercian College of St Bernard (now St John's College), Oxford (from 1502). He designed the Harcourt Aisle in Stanton Harcourt Church (*c.*1470), and he may be regarded as one of the most distinguished architects of his time.

Harvey (1987)

orchid. *Romanesque *octopus-leaf*, a leaf-like form with pronounced round fleshy *lobes.

Order. **1.** In Classical architecture the elements making up the essential expression of a *columnar and *trabeated structure, including a column with (usually) *base and *capital, and *entablature. There are eight distinct types of Classical Order: *Greek *Doric, *Roman *Doric, Greek *Ionic, Roman Ionic, Greek *Corinthian, Roman Corinthian, *Tuscan (also known as the *Gigantic Order), and *Composite, although before the systematic rediscovery of Greek architecture in C18 the canonical *5 Orders* (Tuscan, Roman Doric, Roman Ionic, Roman Corinthian, and Composite) were accepted, codified by *Alberti, and illustrated by *Serlio in 1537. The Greek Doric Order has no base, and sometimes (as in the *Paestum Orders of Doric) the *entasis is exaggerated and the capital is very large, with a wide projection over the *shaft; the Ionic Order has variations in the design of its base (*Asiatic and *Attic types) and capital (especially in relation to *angle, *angular, and *Bassae capitals where the problem of the corner *volute is dealt with in different ways); and the Greek Corinthian capital (e.g. C4 BC *Choragic Monument of Lysicrates, Athens) is taller and more elegant than its Roman counterpart. In London, Kent, and Sussex there is a unique type of English Ionic capital known as the *Ammonite Order. *See* Agricultural, American, Ammonite, Britannic, Composite, Corinthian, Doric, Giant, Ionic, and Tuscan Orders. **2.** *Romanesque and *Gothic arched opening consisting of several layers of arched openings usually with *colonnettes, each smaller than the layer in front, and forming an *Order Arch*.

Chitham (1985); Curl (1992); Lewis and Darley (1986); Normand (1852)

Ordish, Rowland Mason (1824–86). English civil engineer. He made most of the working-drawings for Charles (later Sir Charles) Fox (1810–74), who was responsible for the construction of *Paxton's Crystal Palace in Hyde Park, London (1851), and supervised the re-erection of the Palace at Sydenham. He patented a type of suspension-bridge with the roadway consisting of a rigid girder suspended by inclined straight chains, known as 'Ordish's straight-chain suspension system' (1858). His works include Farringdon Street Bridge, Holborn Viaduct, London (1863–9), St Pancras Train-Shed roof, London (1866–8—with W. H. *Barlow), the Albert Hall roof, London (1867–71), the Franz-Josef Suspension Bridge, Prague (1868), and the Albert Bridge, Chelsea, London (1872–3).

DNB (1917); Dixon and Muthesius (1985)

ordonnance. 1. Proper disposition of parts of a building. **2.** Selection and application of an *Order of architecture suitable for a building and its *type.

Organic architecture. C20 term used in so many ways it is virtually meaningless. *Organic* suggests organization formed as if by some natural process, so organic architecture may mean governed in its evolution by natural factors rather than by an imposed predetermined plan. F. L. *Wright, taking his cue from *Sullivan, who insisted form and function should be one, suggested that the relationship of parts to the whole, and the special relationship of parts, whole, and site, whereby a sense of natural growth was given, constituted organic architecture. *Häring proposed that architecture implied a search, allowing forms to develop during the searching, and that the very discovery of forms was associated with harmony in nature. *Aalto rejected the determination of form by geometrical means, used natural materials in unusual ways (not always successfully), and claimed to respond to the qualities of the sites. *Scharoun's buildings have also been claimed as 'organic' because their design-treatment was not unlike that practised by Häring. Curved *reinforced-concrete shell-structures and tent-shapes (e.g. the work of Frei *Otto) have been perceived as organic, while there are those who would claim the use of natural materials, especially those indigenous to an area, leads to organic buildings. 'Organic architecture' also seems to imply the opposite of rational, geometrical architecture, and is probably associated with intuition, irregularity, and a blurring of the man-made artefact with what is natural. The work of *Makovecz has been described as 'Organic', probably because it is difficult to see where rocks, earth, and plants end and structure begins in some of the designs, while *Kroll's buildings, evolving slowly as they are required, and altered by their users, have been labelled 'Organic'.

Jencks (1988); Lampugnani (1988); Wright (1939); Zevi (1950)

Organic Modernism. Architecture employing, for example, asymmetrical blob-like forms and multi-directional curves. Organic Modernism was mostly a feature of fabric- and furniture-design in the 1940s and early 1950s (e.g. table-tops).

Lewis and Darley (1986)

oriel, oriole, oryel. Large *bay-window projecting from the *naked of a wall on an upper storey, supported on brackets, *corbels, a *pier, or *engaged column.

Orientalism. Architecture and design drawing on Islamic, Chinese, Japanese, Ottoman and the Eastern styles, such as *Chinoiserie or the *Hindoo style.

Conner (1979); Honour (1961)

orientation. Planning, siting, and arrangement of a building with reference to any special point of the compass, especially in relation to the rising and setting of the sun. It was significant in church architecture, where the altars were usually sited to the east. Churches arranged with the *chancel not to the east are nevertheless described as though orientated correctly (*liturgical orientation*).

orle, orlet, orlo. 1. Narrow *band or series of small *fillets forming a border. Specifically, the fillet beneath the *ovolo of a *capital. **2.** *Cincture or fillet at the upper and lower extremities of a column-*shaft, terminating the *apophyge. **3.** *Plinth under the moulded base of a column or its *pedestal. **4.** Face of the fillet between parallel *flutes of e.g. a shaft.

Orme, Philibert de L', *also given as* **Delorme, De L'Orme,** *or* **de l'Orme** (*c*.1510–70). French architect who influenced later generations largely through his books. In Rome from 1533 to 1536, he became acquainted with *Classicism, before returning to Paris where he designed several buildings (all very un-Italian), most of which have been mutilated or destroyed. He was responsible (with others) for the tomb of *François Ier (1515–47) in St-Denis (1547–58), inspired by the *triumphal arch of Septimius Severus, Rome, but with an *Ionic *Order substituted. The Château of Anet, Dreux (1547–55), was probably his finest building, of which the *frontispiece of the central *corps-de-logis (now in the École des Beaux-Arts, Paris) survives, as do the entrance-gate and chapel. The frontispiece has an *assemblage of Orders, its severity and restraint making the contemporary work of *Lescot at the Louvre seem over-elaborate and fussy. The gate (*c*.1522) is an interesting variation on the Roman triumphal arch, with a Mannerist *Attic storey surmounted by a stag and hounds, motifs that give a foretaste of the complete scheme of iconography related to the hunt and Diana that ran through the château, for de L'Orme designed it for Diane de Poitiers (1499–1566), mistress (from *c*.1533) of King Henri II (reigned 1547–59). The chapel at Anet (1549–52) is a variation on the circular form, with coffering in the dome shaped like bent *lozenges echoed in the design of the marble floor: it is a master-work of *stereotomy. The celebrated *jubé in the Church of St-Étienne-du-Mont, Paris (*c*.1545), are no longer attributed to him. He designed the stone bridge and gallery at Chenonceau (1556–9), completed (1576–8) by *Bullant.

De L'Orme established a French version of Classicism that was influential until C18, and his work was followed closely by Bullant, Salomon de *Brosse, and F. *Mansart. His published works include *Nouvelles inventions pour bien bastir* (New Inventions to Build Well—1561) and *Le premier Tome de l'Architecture* (The First Book of Architecture—1567 and later editions). Apart from useful practical considerations, some of the published designs for buildings are extraordinary, and include a *basilica with a great arched wooden roof that looks like a C19 train-shed; there are also references to Divine systems of proportion and measurement and the importance of the Temple of Solomon in Jerusalem in tempering the rules of Classicism. He produced his own versions of the Orders, including a column with a pruned tree as the shaft, but his 'French Orders' had decorated *bands to disguise the joints in the drums of the shaft, and this motif he used in his work at the Tuileries Palace, Paris (1564–70—mostly destroyed). French rationalism owed much to de L'Orme, and his system of timber trusses to span great widths was revived by *Legrand and *Molinos for the dome of the Halle au Blé, Paris (1782–3). His work inspired *Jefferson in the USA and David *Gilly in Prussia. *Viollet-le-Duc recognized his importance in his *Entretiens* (1858–72).

Berty (1860); Blunt (1958, 1982); Brion-Guerry (1960); Hautecœur (1943); Mayer (1953); Orme (1567); Placzek (1982); Prévost (1948); Watkin (1986)

Ornamentalism. Revival of architectural ornament marking a reaction against the so-called *Machine Aesthetic of *International Modernism from the 1960s. It was one of the many aspects of *Post-Modernism.

Brolin (1985); Jensen and Conway (1983)

O'Rorke, Brian (1901–74). New Zealand-born architect, he was best known for his *Modernist interiors from the 1930s, including the liner *Orion* (1934–5) and the Mayor Gallery, London (1933). He was appointed Architect of the National Theatre to be erected in London, but the project was abandoned (*Lasdun's National Theatre was erected on a different site and to a much expanded brief). At Derby Hall, University of Nottingham (early 1950s), however, he used a stripped-down Classical manner derived from the work of *Soane that influenced *McMorran & Whitby in their work for the same University.

Personal knowledge; Pevsner, *Buildings of England, Nottinghamshire* (1979)

orthography. *Elevations of a building or any part of it, showing correct relative proportions.

orthostata (*pl.* **orthostatae**). One of several vertical stone posts set in the base of a wall to form part of the facing, sometimes carved, e.g. forming part of the *revetment at the base of a temple *cella, or as a form of *dado.

orthostyle. Series of columns in a straight row.

Osiride. *Pier supporting an *entablature or other load, with an *engaged figure of the Ancient Egyptian god Osiris attached to it, which, unlike a *caryatid or a *telamon, does not itself act as a support.

Curl (1994)

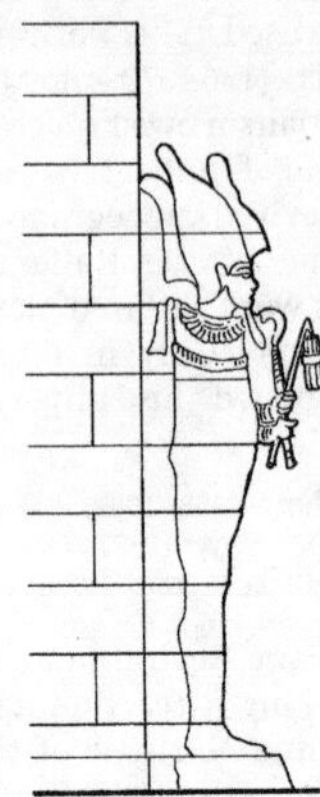

Osiride

ossature. Skeleton of a building, such as a frame or the ribs of a *vault.

ossuary. 1. Bone- or charnel-house (*ossuarium*) for the deposit and preservation of remains of the dead disinterred from churchyard grounds to be re-used for burial. **2.** Container for the skeletal remains of an individual, e.g. a King or Saint.

Östberg, Ragnar (1866–1945). Swedish architect who enjoyed international celebrity in the first three decades of C20 because of the success of his Stockholm City Hall (1908–23), a building of memorable personality with beautifully crafted interiors. Drawing on *Romanesque and *Renaissance elements and certain ideas from Venice (Doge's Palace and *Campanile), perhaps suggested by the marvellous waterside site, Östberg combined them in a wholly convincing synthesis of *Arts-and-Crafts architecture, and created a masterpiece of *National Romanticism, drawing on many mnemonics of Sweden's history for the interiors. His first important building was Östermalms Läroverk School, Stockholm (1910), where powerful forms, red brick, and finely crafted details combined in a satisfying whole. The Swedish Patent and Registration Office, Stockholm (1921), began to show Neoclassical tendencies, while his National Maritime Museum, Stockholm (1936), was more austere, yet reflects Östberg's strivings to create a truly National architecture.

Cornell (1965); Östberg (1908)

Otaka, Masato (1923–). Japanese architect and member of the *Metabolist group, his work has been associated with the search for 'group form', as in the Chiba Prefectural Centre (1967), but later turned to more conventional designs with a hint of traditional styles in them, an example of which is the Fukushima Museum of Art (1984).

Emanuel (1994)

Otani, Sachio (1924–). Japanese architect. He was an early collaborator of *Tange, whose influence can be detected at the Kyoto International Conference Hall (1963–6), with its aggressive display of structure, bold modelling of the masses, and an expression of function. However, the repetition of trapezoidal sections—the result of his use of slanting columns and precast wall-panels—did not create the most serene of internal arrangements. Among later works, the Bunkyo Ward Sports Centre, Tokyo (1986), also exploits angles.

Emanuel (1994)

Ottmer, Carl Theodor (1800–43). German architect. Appointed Court Architect in Brunswick (1829), he brought a robust *Neoclassicism (he had trained under *Schinkel in Berlin) to that city. He designed several villas (e.g. Villa Bülow, Cellerstrasse (1839), and 29 Wilhelmtorwall (1841), but his grandest work, the *Residenz* (Seat of the Court—1831–8) was a casualty of the 1939–45 war: it had a stunning staircase-hall with squat Greek *Doric columns and massive *coffering. The Railway Station (1843–5—now a Bank) was a fine conception in the *Italianate style.

Watkin and Mellinghoff (1987)

Otto, Frei (1925–). German architect and pioneer of the suspended tent-like roof. He was initially influenced by *Expressionism especially the crystalline fantasies of Bruno *Taut, and later by *Candela and *Fuller among others, as well as by the possibilities of lightweight aircraft construction (he was in the German Air-Force in the 1939–45 war). His structures were based on traditional tents but infinitely expanded in terms of shapes and materials. He used cable-nets for the Restaurant Pavilion at the Swiss National

Exhibition, Lausanne (1964), and developed the idea (with Rolf Gutbrod and Fritz Leonhardt) for the West-German Pavilion, Expo 67, Montreal (1967), in which prestressed cable-net roofs were used. With Günter *Behnisch he designed the Olympiapark, Munich (1967–72), using mathematical methods for determining the structure. His adaptable roof-covering for the Open Air Theatre, Bad Hersfeld, Hesse (1967–8—with Romberg & Bubner), demonstrated how the roof-membrane could easily be moved. Later projects include the Wilkhahn Furniture Factory, Bad Münder (1987–8), a school for Woodland Industries, Hooke Park, Dorset, England (1988—with *Ahrends, Burton, & Koralek; Happold; and Dickson), and the *Fachhochschule* (High School), Ulm (1991). In 1962–6 he published *Tensile Structures*.

Drew (1976); Emanuel (1994); Glaeser (1972); Klotz (1986); Otto (1961, 1963); Roland (1970); Wilhelm (1985)

Ottoman architecture. *Islamic architecture, mainly in Asia Minor, that developed from C14, characterized by domes, thin *minarets, tile-work, and decorations in relief cut in stone. Typical of early Ottoman buildings was the Yeshil *Mosque, Iznik (1378–92). After the conquest of Constantinople by the Ottoman Turks (1453), Ottoman architecture absorbed *Byzantine influences, notably in the buildings of *Sinan (1489–*c*.1588), including the Mosque of Sokollu Mehmet Pasha (1570–4) and the Süleymaniye Mosque (1551–8), both in Istanbul. Later architecture of great magnificence was produced, notably the impressive Mosque of Sultan Ahmed, Istanbul (1610–16). The lovely *kiosk of Chinli, Istanbul (1472), has arcaded tile-encrusted elevations of great beauty. Ottoman motifs influenced aspects of C18 and C19 Western design, including some of the orientalizing buildings erected in gardens, e.g. by *Chambers and others.

Conner (1979); Cruickshank (1996); Lewis and Darley (1986)

Ottonian architecture. Style evolved in the reign of Emperor Otto the Great (936–75), and found in Germany from mid-C10 to mid-C11. The finest Ottonian *Romanesque churches that survive are Ste-Gertrude, Nivelles (Nijvel), in Belgium (consecrated 1046), St Michael, Hildesheim (1010–33), and the Abbey Church of Gernrode (begun 959–63), both in Germany. The last building was apparently one of the first in Europe to have the *tribune gallery.

Conant (1979); Cruickshank (1996); Watkin (1986)

Otzen, Johannes (1839–1911). German church architect, whose *Gothic Revival buildings were influential throughout Northern Germany. His best work was the *Johanneskirche* (Church of St John), Hamburg-Altona (1869–83). He also designed the *Bergkirche* (Hill Church), Wiesbaden (1877), the *Jakobikirche* (Church of St James), Kiel (1885), and the *Heiligkreuzkirche* (Holy Cross Church), Berlin (1888).

Bahns (1971)

oubliette. 1. Hidden medieval place of imprisonment excavated in the masonry or foundations of a castle, into which unfortunate captives could be dropped. **2.** Secret pit where a person could be thrown or his body hidden.

Oud, Jacobus Johannes Pieter (1890–1963). Dutch architect. After collaborating with *Dudok on working-class housing at Leiderdorp, Leiden (1914–16), he became a member of De *Stijl and developed an interest in *Cubism and *Futurism under the influence of van *Doesburg. As City Architect to Rotterdam (1918–33), he became more concerned with functional, economic planning and design. The Café de Unie, Rotterdam (1924—destroyed), was composed on the principles of De Stijl, and had affinities with the paintings of Piet Mondrian (1872–1944).

Perhaps Oud's most significant designs were the housing schemes where his growing involvement with *International Modernism was expressed: the terraces of houses at Hook of Holland (1924–7) and Kiefhoek, Rotterdam (1925–9), had the long bands of windows and clean white plain wall-surfaces that formed a non-structural protective skin, while the curved ends of the blocks suggested aerodynamic forms and contemporary ship construction. He designed a row of houses for the *Weissenhofsiedlung Exhibition, Stuttgart (1927), which brought him even more international recognition. However, ten years later, his Bataafsche Import Maatschappij (now Shell) Office Building, The Hague (1938–42), with its symmetry, crude monumentality, and skin of brick and carved sandstone hiding the *reinforced-concrete frame seemed like retrogression. This, the Utrecht Life Insurance Company Office, Rotterdam (1954–61), and the Convention Centre, The Hague (1957–63), suggest that he became disenchanted with the aesthetic of the International style, but was unsuccessful in finding a satisfactory solution to his dilemma. His Bio-Children's Convalescent Home, near Arnhem (1952–60) attempted a return to the architectural language of the 1920s.

Hitchcock (1931); Lampugnani (1988); Morgan and Naylor (1987); Placzek (1982); Stamm (1984); Veronesi (1953*a*)

Ould, Edward Augustus Lyle (1853–1909). *See* Grayson.

oundy, undy. *Vitruvian scroll, *string-course decorated with a wave-like undulating motif, *zig-zag, or the like.

Ouradou, Maurice-Augustin-Gabriel (1822–84). French architect. He studied with *Lebas and *Viollet-le-Duc (whose daughter he married), and worked with him on Notre-Dame Cathedral, Paris, and on the Château of Pierrefonds, where he carried out a major reconstruction. He was Diocesan Architect of Châlons.

Middleton and Watkin (1987); Sturgis *et al.* (1901–2)

Outram, John (1934–). British architect. He established a practice in London in 1973 and produced a series of robust buildings in which *polychromy and Classical allusions were well to the fore. Among his best works were the temple-like Storm Water Pumping Station, Isle of Dogs, London (1985–8), and the New House, Sussex (1978–86), the latter a country-house in which colour was used with great subtlety. The extension and refurbishing of Digby *Wyatt's Addenbrooke's Old Hospital as the Judge Institute of Management Studies, Cambridge (1993–5), is boldly imaginative, disciplined, scholarly, and tough, combining the *trabeated language of Classical architecture with the engineering components necessary in a modern building. Services were incorporated within what Outram has called the 'Robot Order' (*Ordine Robotico*), not coyly hidden away, but expressed as a new *Order visible throughout the building as the columns and beams were large enough to contain the services. Responding to Wyatt's polychromy, Outram created his own colourful architecture, intellectually and theoretically based on precedent, while incorporating late-C20 technology.

Emanuel (1994); personal knowledge

overdoor. 1. Wall-surface over a *door-case, whether decorated or not. **2.** The *sopraporta, only used for internal positions: an exterior sopraporta is a *coronet. **3.** *Fanlight.

overhang. 1. Projection of part of a structure beyond the portion below, e.g. an *oriel or *jetty projecting beyond the *naked of the wall below. **2.** Wall not upright, but with its naked sloping outwards and upwards, i.e. the opposite of *batter. **3.** *Corbel.

overlight. Square or rectangular equivalent of a *fanlight.

overmantel. Decorative framed panel or the architectural arrangement above a *mantel-shelf.

oversail. Element projecting over another, so courses of masonry, each *cantilevered out beyond the *face of the course beneath it, are *corbelled or oversailing courses, as in a *cornice or *eaves.

overshot. *Jetty.

overstorey. 1. *Clearstorey. **2.** Upper storey.

overthrow. 1. Ornamental iron structure set between upright gate-piers or standards and over the gates. **2.** Arched iron support for a lamp between gate-piers or standards.

ovolo. Convex Classical moulding, often enriched with *egg-and-dart or similar motifs. Greek ovolos were more egg-like in profile, while Roman ovolos were normally quarter-rounds.

ovum. Egg-shaped form in Classical mouldings, e.g. *egg-and-dart.

Owen, Segar (1874–1929). English architect. He was articled to and later (1896) was in partnership with his father, **William Owen** (1850–1910), architect, of Warrington, Cheshire. In 1895–6 he worked with G. E. *Street. At Port Sunlight, Cheshire, William refined William Hesketh Lever's (1851–1925) plan for the layout of the town, and designed the first 28 cottages and entrance-lodge. W. & S. Owen's designs for houses at Port Sunlight often quoted the *half-timbered gabled *vernacular style of Cheshire but also employed *ogee gables, vitrified *diaper-work, and walls of brick and terracotta. Among other buildings at Port Sunlight are Hulme Hall (1901) and the very distinguished Gothic Christ Church (1902–4), where the *Perpendicular style was made more four-square and robust. Segar Owen designed the severe Neoclassical Art Gallery at Port Sunlight (1914–22).

Davison (1916); Gray (1985); Pevsner, *Buildings of England, Cheshire* (1971)

Owen, William (1850–1910). *See* Owen, Segar.

Owings, Nathaniel A. (1903–84). *See* Skidmore, Owings, & Merrill.

ox-eye. *See* œil-de-bœuf.

ox-head. *See* bucranium.

Ozenfant, Amédée (1886–1966). French co-founder, with Le *Corbusier, of *Purism and *L'Esprit Nouveau* (1920–5), the first periodical dedicated to the C20 Modernist aesthetic in 'all its manifestations'. He contributed to articles with Le Corbusier (on whom he was a formative influence), published in *Vers une Architecture* (1923).

Golding (1973); Ozenfant (1968); Ozenfant and Jeanneret-Gris (1975)

P. *See* Chrismon.

Pabenham, Simon I (*fl. c.*1262–d. 1280). English master-mason. He was in charge of the building of the Church of St Mary's Abbey, York (1270–94). He, or a relative, may also have been involved in building-works at Lincoln Cathedral and York *Minster.

Harvey (1987)

Pabenham, Simon II (*fl.* 1282–d. 1334). English master-mason. He worked at the Tower of London in the 1280s, and in 1293, with John de Bataile, he built the Eleanor *Crosses at Northampton and St Albans. He became Master-Mason at the Tower of London (1307–11), and was involved in the implementation and enforcement of building-codes in the City of London from 1313.

Harvey (1987)

pace. 1. Part of a floor raised above the general level; a daïs. **2.** Broad raised step around a *tomb-structure, altar, etc. **3.** Landing in a *stair, especially the area where the stair turns. A *half-pace* is a landing where one flight ends and another begins, involving a turn of 180°. A *quarter-pace* is a landing between two flights involving a turn of 90°.

Pacioli, Luca (*c.*1445–*c.*1514). Italian mathematician. His *Summa de Arithmetica, Geometria, Proportioni, etc.* (The Totality of Arithmetic, Geometry, Proportions, etc.—1494) and *Divina Proportione* (Divine Proportion—1496, published 1509) set out the mathematical bases of architecture embraced by *Alberti and others, and described the *Golden Section.

Chilvers, Osborne, and Farr (1988); Osborne (1970)

Packh, János (1796–1839). Hungarian Neoclassical architect, trained in Vienna. He assisted his uncle, **Pál** or **Paul von Kühnel** (d. 1824), in the design and erection of the monumental Cathedral of St Stephen, Esztergom. Packh was responsible for the *crypt (1823), and after his uncle's death he took over as sole architect to oversee the building of the greatest architectural project within the Habsburg domains at the time. The Cathedral was completed (1840–56) by József *Hild, and has a vast *polychrome dome and a huge *portico. Among Packh's other designs the additions (tower of 1828–32) and extension to the Library (1833–6) at the Abbey of Pannonhalma and his unrealized proposals for Eger Cathedral (1829), again Neoclassical, should be cited.

Papworth (1852); Turner (ed.) (1996)

packing. Filling of interstices with small broken stones embedded in the mortar between bigger stones in *rubble walls.

packing-piece. 1. Element, e.g. block of wood, to raise e.g. a beam to the required height. **2.** Timber at the back of a *cruck-*blade to carry a *purlin.

Alcock, Barley, Dixon, and Meeson (1996)

pad. 1. Block (also called a *template*) built into a wall or fixed to the top of a *pier on which a beam or *truss rests. **2.** *Kneeler at the lowest point of a *gable at the *eaves to hold the *cope in place and stop it sliding off, also called *knee-stone* or *skew*. **3.** Short timber across the top of a wall to support a wall-plate or the foot of a common *rafter. **4.** Any large block carrying a load.

Padula, Ernesto Bruno La (1902–69). Italian architect, he became a member of the Italian Movement for Rationalist Architecture (*MIAR). He designed the Knights of Columbus Foundation (1934) and the Palace of Italian Civilization (1938–9—known as the 'Square Colosseum'), both in Rome, two of the most powerful examples of *Rationalism of the Fascist era.

Cennamo (1976)

Paeonius *or* **Paionios of Ephesus** (*fl.* 350–310 BC). Ancient Greek architect, he was partly responsible (with *Demetrius and, possibly, *Deinocrates) for the great Temple of Artemis, Ephesus (*c.*356–236 BC), and, with *Daphnis of Miletus, built the Temple of Apollo at Didyma from *c.*313 BC. Both were huge buildings: the Temple of Artemis employed an elegant *Ionic *Order, and the temple of Apollo was the only Greek Ionic decastyle temple, but also had *engaged *Corinthian columns at the entrance to the steps leading to the oracular *shrine.

Dinsmoor (1950); Lawrence (1983)

Paesschen, Hans Hendrik van (*c.*1515–*c.*1582). Flemish architect from Antwerp, he introduced Italian *Classicism to a Northern Europe where *Mannerism was pre-eminent. A contemporary of *Palladio and de L'*Orme, his reputation has suffered because much of his work has been attributed to Cornelis *Floris de Vriendt, and he is known by many names (e.g. Hendrik Fleming, Henry Passe, etc.). He appears to have been selected by Floris to prepare drawings for Antwerp Town Hall (1561–6), while Floris carved the sculptures and dealt with the clients. The *Raadhuis* (Town Hall) contains many Italian themes and motifs, as does the *Hanseatenhuis* (Hanseatic House), Antwerp (1564–6—also attributed to Floris, but probably by Paesschen). If, as seems likely, he was involved in the design of the Royal Exchange, London (1566–8), Burghley House, near Stamford, Lincolnshire (1564), and Theobald's Palace, Hertfordshire (1560s), he must be credited with the introduction of Italian *Renaissance architecture to England before Inigo *Jones was born. He also seems to have designed Bach-y-Graig, Tremeirchion, Flintshire, Wales (1567–9—demolished), in which case he was a Renaissance pioneer there too. His connections with England and Wales were made through Sir Thomas Gresham (*c.*1519–79), founder of the Royal Exchange, friend of the powerful Cecil family, and English agent in Antwerp. He may have had a hand in the design of Osterley, just outside London, in Middlesex. He began Kronborg Castle, Helsingør, Denmark (1574). Later he designed Uraniborg, Hven Island, Denmark (1576), for the astronomer Tycho Brahe (1546–1601); the house was crowned with a dome to aid astronomical observation.

Hubbard (1986); Millar (1987); van Vynckt (1993)

Paestum. Greek colony in Italy, south of Naples, of which a group of ruined *Doric temples survives (*c.*530 BC–*c.*460 BC). This Doric *Order has the most exaggerated *entasis of any *Antique example, and the very wide squat *capitals on top of the shafts emphasize the *primitive effect. The Paestum Order was much admired by Neoclassical architects in C18 and C19, and was used where powerful effects were sought.

Curl (1992); Dinsmoor (1950)

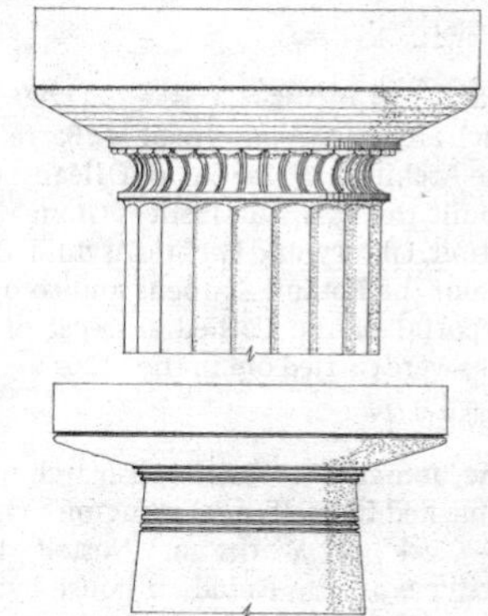

Paestum. Primitive Paestum Doric capitals. (*After Normand*)

Pagano Pogatschnig, Giuseppe (1896–1945). Italian architect, Fascist, and polemicist, who was a leading player in the arguments about the renaissance of Italian architecture in the 1930s, largely through his leadership (from 1931) of the influential architectural journal *Casabella*. His early works had a suggestion of *Perret, *Behrens, and the Vienna *Sezession about them, but in 1928, with Gino Levi-Montalcini (1902–74), he designed one of the first monuments of Italian *Rationalism, the Gualino Office Building, Turin (1928–9). He prepared a plan for the Via Roma, Turin (1931—with the Turin branch of *MIAR), designed a standardized industrialized system for building housing (1933) for the Fifth Triennale, and in 1932–5 built the Istituto di Fisica, University of Rome (destroyed). The Università Commerciale Bocconi (1937–41—destroyed) was remarkable for its adherence to geometry and schemes of proportion throughout the design. He died in Mauthausen concentration-camp, Austria, having renounced Fascism in 1942.

Melograni (1955); Placzek (1982); Seta (1972, 1976, 1979); Veronesi (1953)

pagoda. European term for a tall structure, often polygonal on plan, of several separately roofed stories marked by upturned *eaves, fretwork brackets, and, often, ornaments resembling bells (*campanulae) suspended from the eaves. Based on Chinese temple-towers, pagodas were used as garden-buildings in the C18 *Chinoiserie manner (e.g. *Chambers's Pagoda at Kew Gardens, London).

Lewis and Darley (1986)

Pagot, François-Narcisse (1780–1844). French architect. A pupil of de la *Barre, he became Architect to the City of Orléans, where he built the Palais de Justice, Grain-Market, Abattoir, Library, and Lunatic Asylum. He also laid out the Botanic Gardens and completed the portal of the Cathedral. Most of these works were carried out in the 1820s.

Sturgis *et al.* (1901–2)

Paine, James (1717–89). English architect. He established himself in *Burlington's circle as the Clerk of Works at Nostell Priory, Yorkshire, a large Palladian house by James Moyser (*c.*1688–1751) probably based on designs by Colen *Campbell. In the 1750s Paine succeeded to the practice of Daniel *Garrett and designed or made alterations to a great number of country-houses. It was said that he and Sir Robert *Taylor 'nearly divided the practice' of architecture between them, for they had few rivals until Robert *Adam appeared on the scene. His architecture was essentially Palladian in that he planned competent, sensible villas consisting of a central building (often containing a fine stair) with wings. At Kedleston Hall, Derbyshire (1759–60), he superseded Matthew *Brettingham (who built the east wing) and designed a great central block connected to the wings by *quadrants. His greatest innovation was his proposal for a reconstruction of a *Vitruvian 'Egyptian' colonnaded hall behind the *Corinthian *portico. This would lead to a symmetrically disposed staircase beyond which was a circular *saloon projecting from the south front like a Roman round temple; however, Adam (who, in turn, superseded him) moved the stair to one side and placed a *rotunda in a square block faced on the south front by a *triumphal arch. Paine was no Neoclassicist: he was scornful of the pursuit of the *Antique, felt foreign travel to be less valuable than practical experience, and considered Greek buildings to be 'despicable ruins'. At Wardour Castle, Wiltshire (1770–6), however, he designed a fine staircase under a *Pantheon-like dome. In interior decoration he was one of the first in England to be attracted to *Rococo forms. Much of his work was illustrated in his *Plans, Elevations, and Sections of Noblemen and Gentlemen's Houses* (two volumes, 1767 and 1783). From the 1770s his practice declined as the Adam star rose.

Colvin (1995); Curl (1993*b*); *DNB* (1917); Harris (1990); Leach (1988)

Paionios. *See* Paeonius.

pair. Flight or series of flights in a *stair from one floor to the next.

pala. Altarpiece.

palace. 1. Official residence of any noble, monarch, or high dignitary, or any grand house of exceptional magnificence. The term derives from the Palatium, the Imperial residence on the Palatine hill in Rome. **2.** Large public building, such as a Palais de Justice. **3.** Place of entertainment, usually with architectural pretensions, such as a picture-palace or palais de danse.

palace-front. Classical symmetrical main elevation of a large building or, as in the work of *Wood in Bath (from 1729), where several houses appear to be one palatial composition with emphasis given to the centre and ends by means of *engaged *porticoes, *temple-fronts, end-pavilions, and the like.

palaestra. *Antique wrestling-school or building for athletics, often an open area surrounded by *colonnades, etc.

palatial Italian. *Italianate style applied to C19 clubs, banks, offices, making them look like Italian astylar *palazzi, as in *Barry's Travellers' Club, Pall Mall, London (1829).

palazzo (*pl.* **palazzi**). Italian *palace, corresponding to a town-house (*hôtel), or to a palace in the sense of a large official residence or municipal building. *See* Italianate.

palazzo style. *See* Italianate, palatial Italian.

Paley, Edward Graham (1823–95). With Hubert James Austin (1841–1915) he founded Paley & Austin (1868), one of the most distinguished English architectural practices of the time, specializing in work for the Anglican

Church in the North and the North Midlands. They tended to follow *Bodley & Garner's rich late-*Second Pointed and early *Perpendicular English *Gothic Revival. Their masterpiece is St George's, Buxton Road, Stockport, Cheshire (1893–7), by which time **Harry Anderson Paley** (1859–1946) and **Henry Austin** (1865–1946) had joined the firm, later renamed Austin & Paley.

Curl (1995); Dixon and Muthesius (1985)

paliotto. Altar-covering, hanging on all four sides, unlike an *antependium which covers the front alone.

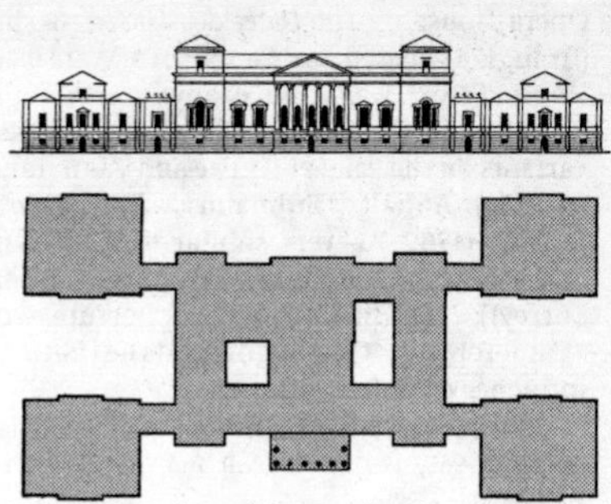

Palladianism. Plan and elevation of Holkham Hall, Norfolk (from 1734), by Lord Burlington and William Kent, with Matthew Brettingham as executant architect. An example of *concatenation*. (*JJS*)

Palladianism. Classical style based on the architecture of the C16 Italian architect Andrea *Palladio, disseminated primarily by his *Quattro Libri dell'Architettura* (The Four Books of Architecture—1570), which contained illustrations of his designs, described them and his ideas, and promoted his work. The first *Palladian Revival* was instigated by Inigo *Jones in England in the reigns of James I and VI (1603–25) and Charles I (1625–49), having studied Palladio's buildings in Vicenza and its vicinity in 1613–14 as well as his publications, notably *Le antichità di Roma* (1554). Key buildings were the Queen's House, Greenwich (1616–35), the Banqueting House, Whitehall, London (1619–22), and the Queen's Chapel, St James's (1623–5). Certain features derived from Palladio's buildings appeared in the works of van *Campen in The Netherlands (e.g. the plan reminiscent of Italian villas at the Mauritshuis, The Hague (1633–5)), and *Holl in Germany (e.g. the restrained severity of the Town Hall, Augsburg (1615–20)), but the main source for these architects seems to have been *Scamozzi. The second *Palladian Revival* of the early C18 began in Venetia (where it was evident in ecclesiastical and secular buildings) and in England (where it was mostly overt in domestic architecture, especially the grand country-house). The key figures of the English Revival were Colen *Campbell and Lord *Burlington, who also promoted a re-appraisal of the first Revival led by Jones. As the high-priest of English Palladianism, Burlington not only designed exemplary buildings but promoted the interests of architects sympathetic to the cause and encouraged publications that established the architectural vocabulary and language that were to dominate (even tyrannize) taste for most of the century. Important in disseminating such elements as the *temple-front and the *serliana were *Vitruvius Britannicus* (1715–25) and *Leoni's *The Architecture of A. Palladio* (1715–20) which remained the standard text-book until *Ware's more scholarly tome of 1738. English Palladian ideals were exported, notably to Prussia (*Knobelsdorff's

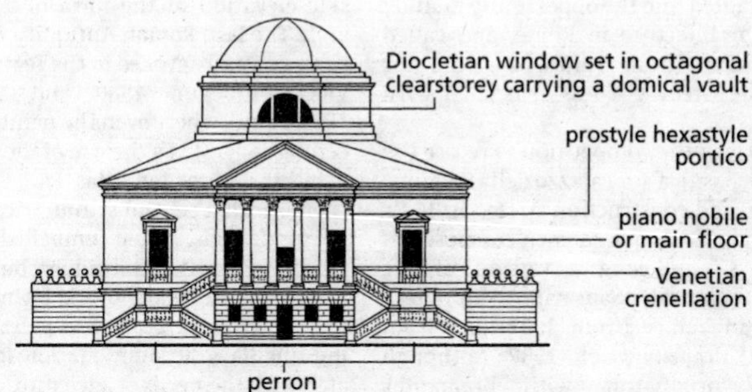

Palladianism. Elevation of Burlington's villa at Chiswick (*JJS*).

Opera House on the *Unter den Linden*, Berlin (from 1741—based on Campbell's Wanstead House, Essex), was a fine example, although, influenced by *Algarotti, Potsdam acquired variants on the Palazzi Thiene and Valmarana in 1750), Anhalt (*Erdmannsdorff's Schloss Wörlitz (1769–73—very similar to L. *Brown and *Holland's Claremont House, Esher, Surrey)), Russia (the architecture of *Cameron and *Quarenghi), and the USA (the influence of *Jefferson).

Ackerman (1967, 1977); Harris (1981); Köster (1990); Palladio (1965, 1997); Whitehill and Nichols (1976); Wittkower (1974*a*)

Palladian window. *See* serliana.

Palladio, Andrea (1508–80). One of the most gifted, professional, and intelligent of architects working in Italy in C16, whose work provided the models for the Palladian style (*Palladianism) and had a profound effect on Western architectural thinking. Palladio's studies of the architectural remains of ancient Rome led him to attempt to emulate its nobility and grandeur. Interpreting the texts of *Vitruvius in his architecture and theories, he further explored the potential of symmetry in design, and developed various other concerns of the *Renaissance, including the theory of *harmonic proportions. He also drew on precedents provided by Italian architects, notably *Bramante, *Raphael, *Giulio Romano, *Sanmicheli, and *Sansovino.

Born Andrea di Pietro della Gondola in Padua, Palladio began his career as a stonemason, and joined the Guild of Masons and Stonecutters of Vicenza in 1524. Around 1536 he became the protégé of Count Giangiorgio Trissino (1478–1550), the leading intellectual in Vicenza, who stimulated the young man to appreciate the arts, sciences, and Classical literature, granted him the opportunity to study *Antique architecture in Rome, and called him 'Palladio' (from Pallas, a name for Athene, the Greek goddess associated with Wisdom).

Palladio won the competition to recase the municipal 'Basilica' (or Palazzo della Ragione) in Vicenza, and construction started in 1549. The design consists of a *screen composed of two storeys employing a version of the arcuated theme at *Sansovino's Biblioteca Marciana in Venice (from 1537) and from *Serlio's *L'Architettura* of 1537 (although ultimately originating with Bramante). Consisting of arches flanked by smaller rectangular openings beneath the *entablatures from which the arches spring, the motif is in essence the *serliana, also called *Palladian* or *Venetian* window. An elegant tour-de-force of Classical elements put together with verve and *élan*, the Basilica made Palladio's name, and from 1550 he was fully employed as a designer of churches, *palazzi, and *villas.

His first grand house in Vicenza was the Palazzo Thiene (commenced 1542 to designs probably by Giulio Romano), in which the *Mannerism of the heavily rusticated exterior is combined with an interior plan drawing on themes from Antiquity (e.g. the sequence of rectangular rooms with an apsidal-ended hall and octagonal spaces with *niches, clearly derived from the precedents of *Antique Roman *thermae). For the Palazzo Iseppo Porto (*c*.1548–52), Palladio planned two identical blocks on each side of a central *court around which was to be a *Giant *Order of columns, evoking the *atrium of a Roman house and the Capitoline palaces of *Michelangelo in Rome. The symmetry and the sequence of rooms (each in proportion to the adjoining) were to become features of Palladio's work. Of the other Vicentine buildings, the Palazzo Chiericati (1550, but not completed until late in C17) deserves mention as it was designed to be a side of a great 'forum', with *loggie as public amenities arranged as two storeys of *colonnades, an unusual and highly original design for C16. The Loggia del Capitaniato (begun 1571), opposite the 'Basilica' in Vicenza, again employed a Giant Order, giving the impression that the building was constructed within surviving remains of a Roman temple, and there are Mannerist touches, including windows breaking into the *entablature, *triglyphs acting as brackets carrying balconies, and the side elevation in the form of a *triumphal arch. The last, Roman Antiquity, and tricks of perspective are evoked in the Teatro Olimpico, Vicenza (begun 1580 and finished by *Scamozzi), where even the painted sky of the ceiling suggested a theatre of the ancients.

In his designs for villas, Palladio devised a theme with a central symmetrically planned *corps-de-logis, often embellished with a *prostyle *portico. Subsidiary buildings were linked to the main block by means of extended wings or curved *quadrants containing ancillary accommodation (often associated with the needs of agriculture). Agreeably sited to revive the idea of the Roman love of country life and gardens, the spirit of *Pliny was never far removed from the villas. One of Palladio's most enchanting designs was the Villa Barbaro at Maser (*c.*1560), with a *temple-fronted two-storeyed centrepiece and symmetrical wings on either side consisting of five-bay *arcades terminating in end-*pavilions crowned with *pediments, a fine example of the *villa rustica. Palladio devised many permutations of his villa theme, including the powerful, almost Neoclassical boldness of the Villa Poiana (*c.*1549–60); the deceptive simplicity of the Villa Foscari, Malcontenta di Mira, near Mestre (*c.*1558–60); and the remarkable Villa Capra (known as *La Rotonda*), a *villa suburbana, near Vicenza (*c.*1566–70), with identical hexastyle *Ionic porticoes (temple-fronts) on each of the four elevations and a central circular two-storey room capped with a *cupola. This employment of temple-fronts or porticoes on villas was based on Palladio's erroneous belief that Antique Roman houses had them: nevertheless, the relationships of porticoes to elements of the composition, including room dimensions, were governed by the concept of harmonic proportion. The Villa Capra's only function was as a pleasure-pavilion or *belvedere from where beautiful views could be enjoyed.

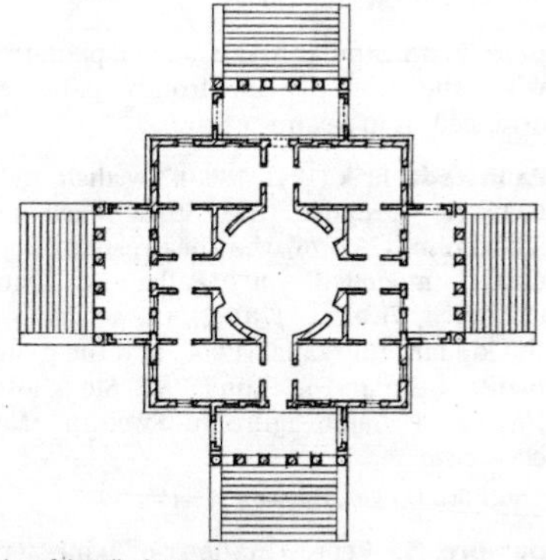
Plan of the Villa Capra, Vicenza.

The façades of Palladio's Venetian Churches of San Francesco della Vigna (1562–70), San Giorgio Maggiore (1564–80), and *Il Redentore* (1576–80) show ingenious solutions to the problems of placing Classical temple-fronts on to the *basilican arrangement of *clear-storeyed *nave with lean-to *aisles. High, narrow temple-fronts are placed at the ends of the naves, complete with *pediments, with a wider, lower, pedimented front set 'behind' so that its extremities provide the façades to the aisles. The interior spatial effects in San Giorgio and *Il Redentore* have a *gravitas* and complexity unlike other churches of the time.

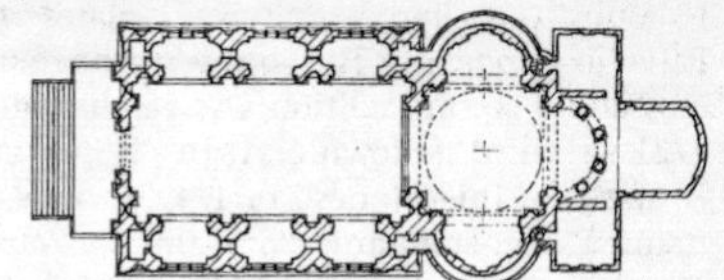
Plan of *Il Redentore*, Venice, with chapels between the sculpted wall-piers.

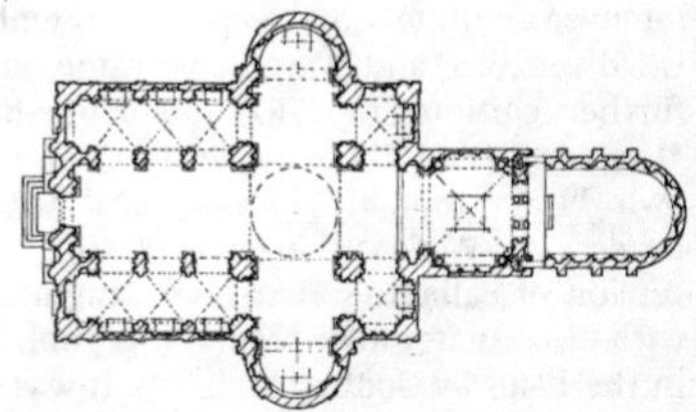
Plan of San Giorgio Maggiore, Venice, with monastic choir in the space behind the high-altar.

Palladio published *Le antichità di Roma* (valued as a gazetteer for two centuries), and *Descrizione delle chiese . . . di Roma* (Description of the Churches of Rome) in 1554. He also provided important illustrations for Barbaro's edition of Vitruvius (1556). In 1570 he brought out *I Quattro Libri dell'Architettura* (The Four Books of Architecture), which publicized his own works, set out his theories, and illustrated and described various important buildings (mostly Roman, including Bramante's circular Tempietto at San Pietro in Montorio). It also illustrated canonical versions of the Roman *Orders of architecture and a range of his own buildings in *plan, *elevation, and *section, with measurements and descriptive text. Thus the work put his designs on a par with the great buildings of the past, and helped to enhance his reputation. The *Quattro libri*, a more accurate treatise than those by Serlio or *Vignola, appeared in several subsequent editions, but that of *Leoni (1715–20—translated as *The Architecture of A. Palladio . . .*) appeared in English, French, and Italian, the first adequate edition since 1642, and the first to substitute large engraved plates for Palladio's woodcuts. The book was a huge success and a second edition was published in 1721, a third following, with 'Notes and Remarks of Inigo Jones', in 1742. Leoni's remained the standard work until *Ware's more scholarly edition of 1738, and it is the latter that has found most favour, republished in facsimile in 1965 with an introduction by Adolf K. Placzek. The plates, by Ware, were a lot more accurate than Leoni's rather embellished versions, and Ware's *opus* came out in further editions in 1767 and 1768. Batty *Langley looted these publications for his own books (notably his *City and Country Builder's and Workman's Treasury* (1740)), and a version of Palladio's First Book, augmented with other material by *Muet, was published in the 1740s by Godfrey Richards. It was this Franco-English edition that seems to have introduced Palladianism to America. *See* Palladianism.

Ackerman (1967, 1977); Burns (1975); Palladio (1715–20, 1965, 1997); Placzek (1982); Puppi (1975, 1980); Tavernor (1991); Wittkower (1974*a*); Zorzi (from 1959)

palm. Palm-leaves occur in Ancient Egyptian decoration (especially palmiform *capitals). Flat palm-fronds with curved ends appear in a unique type of *Corinthian capital at the Tower of the Winds, Athens (*c*.50 BC), often copied on C18 capitals, *friezes, and other mouldings.

palmate. With fan-like lobes or leaves, as in the *anthemion or *palmette, or with the leaves of a palm-tree, as in a *palmiform *capital.

Palmer, Clement (1857–1952). China-based British architect. With his partner, Arthur Turner (1858–*c*.1945), he built several important *Beaux-Arts-inspired buildings, including the Hong Kong and Shanghai Banking Corporation Building (1921–3). Palmer & Turner also designed many other Classically influenced banks, as well as the Sassoon House (now Peace Hotel), Shanghai (1926–8—a vast building clad in granite and embellished with *Art Deco motifs), and the Sassoon Villa, Shanghai (1930—an essay in the *Domestic Revival emulating timber-framed *Tudor precedents).

Cruickshank (1996)

Palmer, John (*c*.1738–1817). English builder and architect. In partnership for a time with Thomas Jelly (d. 1781), he built several buildings in and around Bath. The most important was Lansdown Crescent, Bath (1789–93), convex–concave–convex on plan, responding to the contours of the landscape, and combining the Classical and the *Picturesque.

Colvin (1995)

palmette. Stylized fan-shaped *palmate leaf (called *palmetto*), one type resembling a honeysuckle flower and the other a *raceme arrangement, often used in bands with the *anthemion or the *lotus in Classical *friezes, but also on its own to embellish certain elements. It is found incised, in relief, or painted.

palm-house. *Conservatory in which palm-trees, etc., are given an environment conducive to growth.

palmiform. Similar to the top of a palm-tree, with the ribs of the fronds palmately arranged, as in a palm-*capital.

Palmstedt, Erik (1741–1803). Swedish architect. He designed the Stock Exchange, Stockholm (1767–76), the Theatre, Gripsholm Castle (modelled on *Palladio's Teatro Olympico, Vicenza—1781–2), the bridge over the Riddarholmskanal (1784), and the monumental German Fountain (1785), Stockholm. He was a major figure in Swedish *Neo-classicism.

Cruickshank (1996); Thieme and Becker (1932)

pampre. 1. Representation of vine-stems with grapes, often found draped in spirals around columns, suggesting the twisted *Trajanic or *Solomonic form. **2.** Grapes, leaves, and vine-stems as running undercut ornament in *cavettos and other continuous hollows at the tops of *Perpendicular *Gothic *screens called *trail.

Bond and Camm (1909)

pan. 1. Wall-plate. **2.** Part of an exterior wall, especially the *panel between the structural horizontal and verticals in a *timber-framed building.

panache. Approximately triangular surface of a *pendentive.

pan-and-roll. Tile roof composed of repeated patterns formed by two adjacent flat tiles with upturned flanges on each side, the joint covered by tapering semicircular-profiled tiles fitting neatly over the upstanding flanges.

McKay (1957)

pancarpi. Classical enrichments consisting of *garlands or *festoons of fruit, flowers, and leaves.

pane. **1.** *Light in a window, or a piece of glass in a frame forming part of a light. **2.** Side of any large object, such as one face of a *spire or tower. **3.** Space between the structural members of a *timber frame. **4.** Pierced walls of a *cloister facing the *garth.

panel. **1.** Flat plane surface surrounded by mouldings or channels, or by other surfaces in different planes. Architectural panels are generally rectangular, but can be circular, square, quatrefoiled, or other shapes. *Blind *tracery is really a type of panelling. The sunken surface of the panel is often *charged* with ornament, e.g. *parchemin. Panels are commonly found in ceilings, doors, *wainscots, etc., and are separated by frames, etc., called *panel-dividers*, while the *beads and other mouldings holding them in their frames are *panel-mouldings* and can be of various types (e.g. *bolection, *ogee, etc). Types of panel include:

fielded: with a flat central portion projecting above the edges of the panel, and sometimes beyond the frame;
flush: with the face in the same plane as the frame around it, often with a flush *bead on the edges next to the panel to mask the joint;
linen-fold: decorated with *parchemin plié;
lying: with its greater dimension horizontal;
raised and fielded: as *fielded* above, i.e. with a flat raised surface, but surrounded by a sunken, moulded, or bevelled edge;
sunk: with the face recessed from the frame.

2. Subdivision of a *bay of a *timber-framed wall defined by *studs* and *rails*, called a *pane.

Alcock, Barley, Dixon, and Meeson (1996); McKay (1957); Parker (1850); Sturgis *et al.* (1901–2)

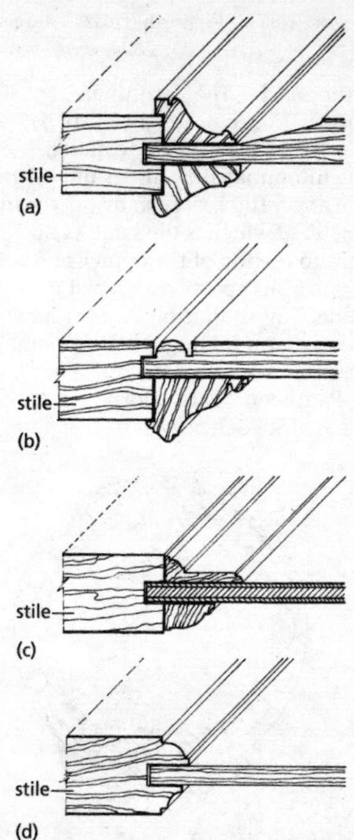

panel. Selection of panels and panel-mouldings. (*a*) Raised and fielded panel secured with two variations of bolection moulding. (*b*) Flush panel with beaded edge secured with bolection moulding. (*c*) Flush ply panel secured with two varieties of planted mouldings. (*d*) Flush panel held in stile with solid or struck ovolo upper moulding and cavetto lower moulding.

panel tracery. *Perpendicular *tracery.

pane-work. Division of an external wall into *panes or *panels, as in a *timber-framed structure.

panier. **1.** As *corbeil. **2.** Bracket or *corbel supporting a *beam or *truss shaped to soften the angle between them, resembling a basket-shape.

panoply. Sculpted representation of the parts of a suit of armour, with various weapons, arranged decoratively in a heap, in schemes of *military decoration.

Panopticon. **1.** Building, especially a gaol, planned on the radiating principle, with wings branching from a central control-point, invented by Jeremy Bentham (1748–1832). **2.** Exhibition-room or show-room for novelties, etc.

panorama. Building containing a large picture, either arranged on the inside of a cylindrical surface around the spectator at the centre (*cyclorama*) or unrolled or unfolded and made to pass before the spectator so as to show the various parts in succession. If the picture (some parts of which are translucent) is viewed through an aperture, its sides continuing towards the picture, it is called a *diorama*, which can show weather-changes. One of the most celebrated was the *Panorama National*, Paris (1859).

Nicholson (1835); Papworth (1852); Sturgis *et al.* (1901–2)

Pantheon. 1. The *rotunda erected by Emperor Hadrian (reigned AD 117–38) in Rome (AD 118–28), with *coffered *concrete dome (illuminated by an *oculus at the top) set on a very thick circular drum (the internal diameter of which is the same as the internal height to the top of the dome), and octastyle *temple-front *portico attached to the drum outside. Any similar building is known as a Pantheon. **2.** Building for the general burial-place of or memorial to the great dead, such as the Panthéon, Paris (formerly *Soufflot's Church of Ste-Geneviève).

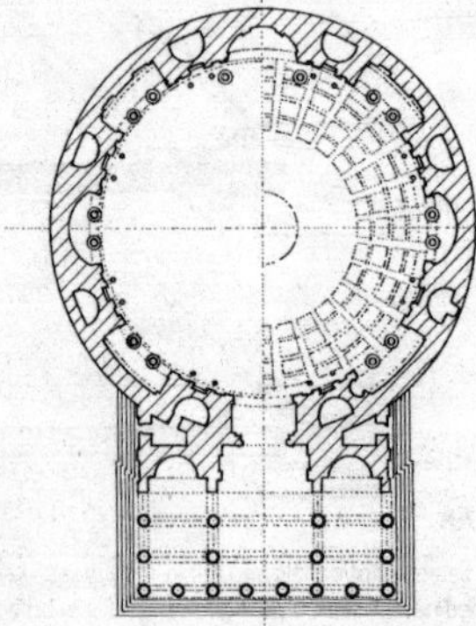

Plan of Pantheon.

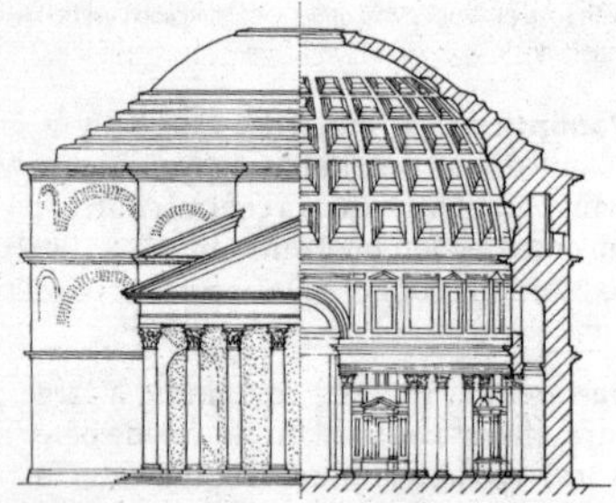

(*left*) Half-elevation showing portico and low stepped dome, a type admired during the Neoclassical period. (*right*) Half-section showing oculus at the top and the coffering of the dome.

Pantheon

Pantheon-dome. Internally *coffered dome, with a low, plain, severe, segmental-sectioned exterior surrounded by rings of concentric steps, resembling that of the *Pantheon in Rome, much used in C18 and early C19 as part of the vocabulary of *Neoclassicism, and not necessarily with an *oculus.

pan-tile. Plain roofing-tile with a profile resembling an S on its side (∽) giving a corrugated effect when laid on the roof.

papier-mâché. Substance consisting of paper-pulp mixed with resin and glue, or consisting of shreds of paper glued together and pressed into a mould, used to make ornament or wall-coverings.

Papworth (1852)

Papworth, John Buonarotti (1775–1847). London-born English architect, designer of landscapes, and town-planner. He laid out the Montpellier (1825–30) and Lansdowne (1825–8) Estates in Cheltenham, Gloucestershire, and was one of the most prolific architects of his generation as well as a designer of a wide range of artefacts, including furniture, textiles, fireplaces, and much else.

The second son of **John Papworth** (1750–99), a master stuccoer, he worked in John *Plaw's office for two years, exhibited beautiful drawings and water-colours at the Royal Academy from 1794, and was a promoter of new ideas and technologies. By 1800 he had his own practice (largely concerned with domestic architecture), was able to take on pupils, and began to write and produce designs for publication. In 1815 his drawing of a *Tropheum* to celebrate Wellington and Blücher's victory at Waterloo caused him to be acclaimed by his circle as a second *Michelangelo, and he modestly took 'Buonarotti' as his second name.

He designed conservatories, entrance-gates, coach-houses, stables, and the *Gothic summer-house at Claremont, Surrey (1816), for Prince Leopold of Saxe-Coburg (1795–1865) and Princess Charlotte Augusta (1796–1817). The latter's untimely death caused the summer-house to be adapted as her memorial. From 1817 to 1820 he prepared designs for the Park and Palace at Bad Cannstadt, near Stuttgart, for King Wilhelm I (1816–64): only part of the Park (in the English style) was realized, but Papworth was honoured with the title of 'Architect to the King of Württemberg'. He designed (1819) the famous *Egyptian Revival gallery in P. F. *Robinson's Egyptian Halls, Piccadilly, London (1811–12—

demolished). For William Bullock (*fl. c.*1795–1826), builder and owner of the Egyptian Halls, he designed (1825–7) a model new town intended to be built on the bank of the River Ohio facing Cincinnati: named *Hygeia*, it never materialized. Papworth was responsible for many London shop-fronts and other buildings, and was a pioneer in the use of *iron for construction purposes. His monument to Lieutenent-Colonel Sir Alexander Gordon (1786–1815) on the field at Waterloo, Belgium (1815), was an early (if not the first) example of a broken column used as a memorial. He directed the Government School of Design (1836–7), and was a founder (1834) of the Institute of British Architects.

He contributed frequently to Rudolph Ackermann's (1764–1834) *Repository of Arts* (1809–28). Papers, entitled *Architectural Hints* (1813, 1814, 1816, and 1817), were republished as *Rural Residences, consisting of a Series of Designs for Cottages, Small Villas, and other Ornamental Buildings* (1818 and 1832), and in 1823 he published designs for garden-buildings as *Hints on Ornamental Gardening*. *Rural Residences* was far more influential than most commentators have suggested: it appears to have been a stimulant for designs by *Schinkel and *Persius, notably the Court Gardener's House and Roman Bath complex at Potsdam (1829–37) and the *Gothic Hunting Lodge at the park at Glienecke (1827–8). In fact, he helped to create the rational Greek style that was so ubiquitous in the period 1815–40, yet his importance has not receieved the recognition it deserves. Papworth helped (1818–19) William Henry Pyne (1769–1843) with the descriptions of Marlborough House, St James's, and Kensington Palace, published as *Royal Residences* (1820), contributed to *Britton and *Pugin's *Public Buildings in London* (1825–8), and edited the fourth edition of *Chambers's *Treatise* (1826), adding much new material; he also wrote the important *Essay on the Causes of Dry Rot in Timber* (1803). Many designs in *Loudon's *Encyclopaedia* (1833) appear to have originated with Papworth.

His elder son, **John Woody Papworth** (1820–70), architect and antiquary, was the author of *Ordinary of British Armorials*, an important book on heraldry, and his younger son, **Wyatt Angelicus van Sandau Papworth** (1822–94) founded the Architectural Publication Society and edited its great *Dictionary of Architecture* (1852–92). His pupils included his brother, **George** (1781–1855), who practised in Ireland (he designed the famous cast-iron bridge over the Liffey in Dublin), and James *Thomson.

Colvin (1995); *DNB* (1917); J. B. Papworth (1832); Papworth (1852, 1879); Summerson (1993)

papyrus. Decoration based on stylized versions of the flowers and leaves of the paper-reed (*Cyperus papyrus*), often found in Ancient Egyptian architecture, notably on *capitals.

parabema. Room or area associated with the *bema of a *basilica.

parabola. Curve based on a conic section, that is the intersection of a cone with a plane parallel to its side. It resembles a three-centred arch, vertically emphasized.

Nicholson (1835)

Paradise. 1. Cloistered *atrium, *court, or *garth at the west end of a church. **2.** West or south porch of a church, including space above it, sometimes corruptly called a *parvise. **3.** Burial-ground of a conventual establishment. **4.** *Jerusalem, or innermost part of a *labyrinth or maze.

parapet. Low wall or barrier at the edge of a balcony, bridge, roof, terrace, or anywhere there is a drop, and therefore danger of persons falling. Originally a feature of defensive architecture on castles and town-walls, it often retained *battlements and other features, even when used for non-defensive purposes, e.g. on churches. Parapets can be ornamented, pierced, or plain. A *parapet gutter* lies behind the wall, with holes in the wall through which water is discharged.

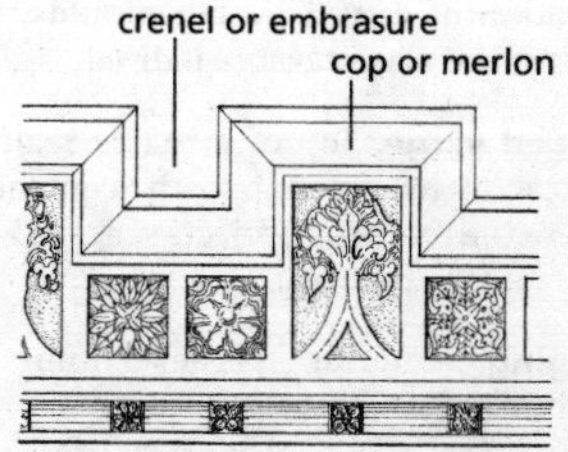

parapet. Pierced parapet with moulded battlements or crenellations, typical of English Perpendicular churches. (*After JJS*)

parastas. 1. Part of the flanking wall of a Greek temple porch projecting beyond the front wall, finished with an *anta. **2.** The space between two such flanking walls, outside the *naos, also called the *pronaos, so applied to a *vestibule. **3.** *Parastata. **4.** Element like a massive *pedestal at the termination of a grand formal stairway.

parastata, parastatica. 1. *Synonymous with *anta with only very small parts of the return face exposed. **2.** *Pilaster, again with small return-faces.

parchemin. C16 development of *linenfold incorporating vines, foliage, etc.

parchemin plié. As *linenfold.

parclose. 1. *Screen marking off *chapels or tombs from the rest of a church, e.g. between a *chancel and the chapel to its side. **2.** Front of a gallery, open or closed.

Bond (1908*a*)

parekklesion. *Byzantine chapel.

Parent, Claude (1923–). French architect who worked with Le *Corbusier and was a contributor to *L'Architecture d'aujourd'hui*. His works include *Vivre à l'Oblique*, *L'Aventure Urbaine* (1970) and *Cinq Réflexions sur l'Architecture* (1972). He was responsible for the Commercial Centre, Sens (1970).

Collins (1979)

parge. To plaster.

parge *or* **parget work.** *Pargetting*, or external plasterwork on *timber-framed buildings, commonly used in England from the late-*Tudor period, often decorated with patterns (indented or in low relief) produced by the application of carved timber moulds, pressed against the plaster before it dried.

parged verge. Top of a *gable sealed with mortar at its junction with a pitched roof where the roof only projects very slightly over the *naked of the wall.

parging. Interior plaster lining of a *chimney-flue.

Pâris, Pierre-Adrien (1745–1819). French architect and pupil of Louis-François *Trouard (whom he succeeded as Architect to the Cathedral of Ste-Croix, Orléans, where he worked on the west front (1787–90)), he made his reputation with his drawings of *Antique remains in Italy. He designed the interiors of the Hôtel Crillon, Paris (1774), and an extraordinary but unrealized palace for the Prince-Bishop of Basle, Porrentruy (1776). His Neuchâtel Town Hall, Switzerland (1784–90), a severe essay in *Neoclassicism, has an entrance-hall containing baseless Greek *Doric columns supporting low *vaults, a powerful combination. His taste for the exotic and for archaeology influenced his students *Percier and *Fontaine. He directed some important archaeological surveys in Rome (1806–17), including work at the Colosseum.

Middleton and Watkin (1987)

Parker, Richard Barry (1867–1941). English *Arts-and-Crafts architect, remembered primarily for the work with his brother-in-law, Raymond *Unwin, with whom he practised from 1896 until the dissolution of their partnership in 1914. An early work was 'Woodcote', a house at Church Stretton, Shropshire (1896–7), which incorporated motifs from English *vernacular architecture, and established his stylistic preferences. Parker & Unwin's first major commission was to build the model village of New Earswick, near York (begun 1902), based on the precedents of Bournville and Port Sunlight, with low-density housing based on *vernacular forms. In 1903 they won the competition to design the first *Garden City at Letchworth, Hertfordshire, inspired by the ideas of Ebenezer *Howard, and from 1906 Unwin undertook the planning of Hampstead *Garden Suburb, while Parker contributed designs for several houses there. They published *The Art of Building a Home* (1901), but tended to go their own ways after the 1914–18 war. Parker was involved in the new town of Pacaembu, São Paulo, Brazil (1917–20), and in England was responsible for the Wythenshawe Estate outside Manchester (from 1927) and the smaller Shelthorpe Road Estate at Loughborough, Leicestershire (1926–39).

Darley (1975); Gray (1985); Miller (1989, 1992); Miller and Gray (1992)

Parker's cement. Patented in 1796, sometimes known as *Roman* or *Sheppey cement*, it was a grey-brown *stucco rendering composed of burnt clay nodules crushed to powder and mixed with lime, sand, and water. It hardened quickly and was commonly applied to inferior brickwork façades as a substitute for *ashlar, the 'joints' suggested by scores made before the cement had dried. It was also used (without the addition of lime) for construction under water, as it had the peculiar property of hardening in such conditions: it was superseded by *Portland cement.

Gwilt (1903); Papworth (1852)

Parkin, John Burnett (1922–). Canadian *Modernist architect. He founded John B. Parkin Associates with his brother, **Edmund T. Parkin**, and John Cresswell Parkin (1922–88—no relation)—who trained with *Gropius. Among the firm's works are Toronto International Airport (1963–6), Toronto City Hall (1965—with Viljo *Revell), the Union Railway Station, Ottawa (1967–9), and the Trade Centre and Arena, Hamilton, Ontario (1985).

Emanuel (1994); Kalman (1994)

Parler Family. German master-masons working in Swabia and Bohemia in C14 and early C15. **Heinrich I** (b. *c*.1300) was *Parlier* (foreman with responsibility for a *Mason's *lodge) at Cologne Cathedral, when the *choir was completed *c*.1322, but other works proceeded very slowly. He moved to Schwäbisch-Gmünd where he built the *nave (from *c*.1330) and (probably) the *choir (designed on *hall-church principles) of the *Stadtkirche zum Heiligen Kreuz* (Town Church of Holy Cross), one of the most influential buildings of the *Sondergotik style. He may have worked on the choir of the Cathedral at Augsburg, the *Frauenkirche* (Church of Our Lady) at Nuremberg, and the *Minster at Ulm.

Peter Parler (1333/5–99), son of Heinrich, is the most celebrated of the tribe. He worked at Schwäbisch-Gmünd, Cologne Cathedral (possibly), and the *Frauenkirche* at Nuremberg before being summoned to Prague *c*.1350 by Kaiser Karl IV (1346–78) to work on the Cathedral of St Vitus (Veit), begun in 1344 by Matthias of *Arras. Master of the Works at St Vitus by 1356, he completed the choir (1385) and later the south *transept. He also designed and built the Charles Bridge over the River Vltava (Moldau), Prague (begun 1357), added the choir to the Church of St Bartholomew, Kolín (1360–78), and carried out works at St Barbara, Kutná Hora (begun 1388), and was responsible for various tombs, shrines, and sculptures.

Johann, Heinrich's eldest son, settled in Freiburg-im-Breisgau and became Master of the Works at the Minster from 1359 (he may have designed the *chancel). Johann's son, **Michael II** of Gmünd, who was Master of the Works at Strasbourg Cathedral from 1383, may have been responsible for modifying Erwin von *Steinbach's designs for the west front. He was also involved in the building of the Minsters at Freiburg and Ulm. His brother, **Heinrich II** of Gmünd and Freiburg (d. *c*.1392), worked at Augsburg, Vienna, Cologne, and Prague, and succeeded Michael II at Ulm from 1387 to 1391. He also acted as a consultant for Milan Cathedral (1391–2), a job he probably got through his father-in-law, **Michael of Savoy**, who worked at Cologne.

Wenzel or **Wenceslaus** Parler (d. *c*.1404), Peter's second son, worked on the south tower of St Vitus's Cathedral in Prague from *c*.1375 to 1398. Settling in Vienna *c*.1399, he became Master of the Works at the *Stephensdom* (Cathedral of St Stephen), and seems to have been responsible for the lower stages of the south tower. His brother, **Johann the Younger**, of Prague (d. *c*.1405), succeeded his father and brother as Master of the Works at St Vitus in 1398, proceeding with the erection of the south tower, and completing parts of the south transept. He was also involved at Kutná Hora.

The Parlers were masters of elegant, flowing *tracery, complex vaulting, and fine carving; their works had a profound influence throughout Germany, Austria, and Bohemia in C15 and C16.

Legner (1978–80); Neuwirth (1890, 1891), Nussbaum (1994); Placzek (1982); Recht (1989); Swoboda (1943)

parotis. *Ancon, *bracket, or *console resembling the human ear.

parpend. Bond- or through-stone visible on both sides of a wall, and therefore dressed or faced at both ends, as in *parpend ashlar*.

parquet. **1.** Floor finish of hardwood blocks laid in patterns (often herringbone) on a firm base and polished. **2.** Orchestra-stalls of a theatre.

parquetry. Patterned floor-surface of thin wood veneers, called *inlaid* or *plated* *parquet.

parterre. **1.** Flat terrace near a house laid out with flower-beds or decorative planting in a regular formation to be read from above. Types include:

parterre à l'anglaise: *plat* or turfed lawn with a design cut into it;

parterre de broderie: *embroidered* parterre with the patterns formed of trimmed box planting bordering beds of coloured earth, occasionally with bands of turf;

parterre de compartiment: embroidered parterre symmetrical about two axes.

2. Orchestra-stalls of a theatre (*see* parquet).

Sturgis *et al.* (1901–2); Symes (1993)

Parthenon. The C5 BC Greek Temple of Athena Parthenos on the *Acropolis in Athens, widely regarded as the most refined building featuring Greek *Hellenic *Doric architecture, and the model for much *Greek Revival work. The Parthenon had a *peristyle surrounding the *naos and Virgin's chamber, with seventeen columns on the flanks and eight at each pedimented end. The *metopes contained exquisite sculptures, as did the *pediments (much is now in the British Museum, London), while subtle optical refinements such as *entasis and curved *stylobates further contributed to its stature as a canonic work. Within the Virgin Goddess's chamber were four elegant *Ionic columns, so in some respects it was a synthesis of Doric and Ionic architecture.

Dinsmoor (1950)

parti. Choice, means, or method. *Parti pris* means a bias or a mind made up, so in architectural criticism the *parti* is the assumption made that informs a design as well as the choice of approach when realizing the scheme. *Prendre le parti* is to take a decision, or a certain course, as in architectural design.

Participatory Design. During the 1960s and 1970s architects and planners, mostly in the public sector, began to involve the public in consultations concerning housing and the environment. In the USA and the UK there were many such experiments.

Becker (1977); Cross (1972)

partition. 1. *Screen. **2.** Non-loadbearing wall.

parvis(e). 1. Corruption of *Paradise, often, but incorrectly, applied to a room over a church porch. **2.** Open area, *court, or *atrium in front of a church, or the entire space around a church, especially in France.

Pascal, Jean-Louis (1837–1920). French architect who worked with C. *Garnier on the Paris Opéra and, from 1870, with *Labrouste. His buildings include various *mausolea in Père-Lachaise Cemetery and additions to the Bibliothèque Nationale (1878–81—Rue Colbert Stack Rooms—and 1906–17—Rue Vivienne Periodicals Reading Room and Stacks), in Paris. His most significant building was the Faculté de Médecine et de Pharmacie, Place de la Victoire, Bordeaux (1880–8). An important teacher, he promoted an impeccable *Beaux-Arts *Classicism that had a profound influence from the 1870s through to 1914.

RIBA Journal, 21 (1914), 543–4

Pasqualini, Alessandro (1485–1558). Bolognese architect. He designed the tower of IJsselstein Church, near Utrecht, The Netherlands (1532–5), with its vertical sequence of *Orders. The *Residenz* (Seat of the Court) at Jülich (1548–*c*.71), which introduced *High Renaissance motifs to Germany, shows that he was familiar with *Bramante's work.

Cruickshank (1996)

pasticcio. As *pastiche.

pastiche. 1. Work produced in deliberate imitation of another or others, hence a composition incorporating imitations of earlier styles. **2.** Transfer to another medium of a design, such as a book-cover as a *pasticcio* of a *mosaic.

pastophorium. One of two rooms on either side of the *chancel of an *Early Christian or *Byzantine church.

pastoral column. Column resembling a tree-trunk, with branch-stumps and bark, associated with the *cottage orné.

patand. 1. Column or *pier-*base. **2.** *Plinth supporting columns, piers, or *pilasters. **3.** Bottom-rail, *cill, *sleeper, or sole-plate of a *timber-framed wall.

patent-glazing. Metal glazing-bars supporting glass without putty, employed in roofs and walls. Its dry construction enables speed of erection.

patera (*pl.* **paterae**). Circular or elliptical dish-like Classical ornament in bas-relief, like a shallow medallion with a raised decorated centre, often incorporating *flutes. When further enriched to represent a flower, it is termed *rosette. It occurs in *coffers, on *friezes, and as punctuations on walls, especially in C18.

paternoster. 1. Row of bead-like ornament on *astragals, etc. **2.** Passenger-lift composed of platforms in series fixed to a continuous loop of chains and constantly in motion.

patio. **1.** Spanish roofless courtyard, often with furniture or pools. **2.** Paved area adjoining a house.

Patrington, Robert (*fl.* 1352–85). English master-mason. In 1368 he was appointed Master-Mason at York *Minster, where he completed the *presbytery. He was probably responsible for the later parts of St Patrick's Church, Patrington, Yorkshire (1368–71), in which case he was one of the most accomplished designers of his time, for the building is unusually beautiful and uncommonly homogeneous.

Harvey (1987)

Patte, Pierre (1723–1814). Influential French architect, editor, and critic. He continued J.-F. *Blondel's *Cours d'architecture* (1771–7), responsible for many texts and plates dealing with building materials and construction. His most impressive publication, *Monuments érigés en France à la Gloire de Louis XV* (Monuments Erected in France to the Glory of Louis XV—1765), included proposals for sophisticated civic designs for Paris. *Discours sur l'Architecture* (Discourse on Architecture—1754), *Études d'Architecture* (Studies of Architecture—1755), *Mémoires* on street-planning (1766), on the building of the west front of St-Sulpice (1767), and *Essai sur l'Architecture Théâtrale* (Essay on Theatre Architecture—1782), among others, were highly analytical works, and had a powerful effect on late-C18 French rationalist architecture of the *Neoclassical period. He analysed *Gothic architecture with great intelligence, showing that *buttresses, *pinnacles, *ribs, *piers, and so on were part of a logical structural system, using Notre-Dame at Dijon as his exemplar.

Middleton and Watkin (1987); Sturgis *et al.* (1901–2)

pattée. *See* cross.

pattern-books. Collections of published designs from which builders and craftsmen could copy architectural details. They were largely the means by which Classical architecture, as well as *Chinoiserie and the *Gothick tastes, became widespread, notably in C18 and the early C19.

Paul, Bruno (1874–1968). German member of the *Deutscher Werkbund, designer of machine-made furniture, the *Typen-Möbel*. His achievements in standardization impressed Le *Corbusier. Stylistically his architectural work was influenced by the Italian *Renaissance, then the *Sezession, *Art Deco, and finally *International Modernism. He designed the *Jugendstil hunting-room for the Paris Exposition Universelle (1900—which made such an impression it was shown again at the 1901 Munich and 1902 Turin Exhibitions), the interiors of the liner *Kronprinzessin Cecilie* (Crown-Princess Cecilie—1907), the beer-hall, restaurant, and other public rooms for the Werkbund Exhibition, Cologne (1914), and *Das Plattenhaus* (Standard House), Hellerau, near Dresden (1925). In 1929 he formed an association with *Mies van der Rohe.

Campbell (1978); Jervis (1984); Popp (1916)

Pautre, Antoine Le (1621–81). After Le *Vau and *Mansart, the most inventive French architect of C17. He designed the Chapelle de Port-Royal, Paris (1646–8), but his most celebrated work was the Hôtel de Beauvais, Paris (1654–60), on an impossibly irregular site with two street-frontages. He imposed order, creating an internal *court on a strong axis, with an impressive variety of invention there and in the staircases. He published *Desseins de plusieurs palais* (Designs of Many Palaces—1652–3) and *Les œuvres d'architecture d'Anthoine Le Pautre* (Works in Architecture of Antoine Le Pautre—1681), which included designs for enormous country-houses and palaces even more Baroquely exuberant than those of Le Vau; these publications seem to have influenced *Wren and *Schlüter. His *Baroque cascade at Saint-Cloud (early 1660s) was one of his finest creations. His nephew, **Pierre Le Pautre** (1659–1716) worked at Versailles under *Hardouin-Mansart, where he decorated the Salon de l'Œil de Bœuf (1701) and chapel (1709–10), significant works in the beginnings of the *Rococo style.

Berger (1969); Blunt (1982); Hautecœur (1948); Jervis (1984); Kalnein and Levey (1972); Kimball (1980)

pave. To lay a surface underfoot with bricks, paving-stones, tiles, etc. *Pavé* consists of small blocks of stone in regular patterns to form a paved surface, common in Northern France and Belgium.

pavement. Path with a surface of stones or other materials, including cement, cobbles, flags, *rag-stones, square-setts, tarmacadam, etc.

pavement-light. Solid glass blocks set in a cast-iron frame or cast in a *reinforced-concrete grid bedded in a *pavement, permitting light to penetrate a *basement.

pavilion. 1. Central, flanking, or intermediate projecting subdivision of a monumental building or façade, accented architecturally by more elaborate decoration (e.g. *Orders, *pediments, or *palace-fronts), or by greater height and distinction of *skyline, as in the Louvre, Paris. **2.** Feature at the angle of a building, or terminating feature of a wing of a larger structure, as in a symmetrical Palladian composition. **3.** One of several distinct buildings or blocks, linked by e.g. corridors, as in a hospital or gaol, for reasons of hygiene or security. **4.** Detached ornamental building, such as a *gazebo or a summer-house, often, but not always, dependent on a larger or principal building. **5.** Building with a *verandah in a sports-ground, e.g. cricket-pavilion. **6.** Temporary building. **7.** Covering or canopy, so a tent-like structure, such as a canopied litter or the *velarium over an *amphitheatre.

pavilion roof. *See* roof.

pavior, paviour. Brick or stone used in pavements, also called a *paver*.

Paxton, Sir Joseph (1803–65). English gardener. Discovered by the 6th Duke of Devonshire (1790–1858), he was appointed Head Gardener at Chatsworth, Derbyshire (1826), where he remained for 30 years, cultivating plants, tending and improving the gardens, and designing buildings. Entirely self-taught, his main influences were *Loudon and Payne *Knight. Encouraged by the Duke, he published *The Horticultural Register* (1831–5) and *Paxton's Magazine of Botany and Flowering Plants* (1834–49).

In 1831 he began constructing *conservatories at Chatsworth, and used the ridge-and-furrow system of glazed roofs invented by Loudon (1817), patenting his own variation in 1850. As a designer he made his reputation with the elegant 'Great Stove' conservatory at Chatsworth (1836–40), then the biggest glass-house in Europe. The curved ridge-and-furrow glazed timber roof was carried on arched laminated-timber frames supported on cast-iron columns and buttressed by the side arches over the flanking *aisles. Although Decimus *Burton was involved in a consultative capacity, the basic conception was Paxton's, who was to turn more and more to designing buildings.

He created the village of Edensor, near Chatsworth (1838–48), drawing on a range of styles, mostly *Italianate, for the houses, and designed Prince's Park, Liverpool (1842–4), and Birkenhead Park, Cheshire (1843–7), the latter one of the first English municipal parks, the layout of which was an influence on F. L. *Olmsted. In 1849 he constructed a special conservatory for the *Victoria Regia* lily, which flowered for the first time in England in its Paxton-designed glass-house. The structural advances in the lily-house helped in the creation of the Crystal Palace for the Great Exhibition, London (designed and built 1850–1), for which Paxton drew on his experiences of greenhouses at Chatsworth. That vast building was remarkable for several reasons: it was designed so that all its constituent parts could be prefabricated, erected, and dismantled on site, the first example of a very large scale *industrialized building; it only took just over six months to build; and it was the model for a series of huge C19 exhibition buildings. It earned Paxton his knighthood in 1851.

He entered into partnership in 1847 with his son-in-law, **George Henry Stokes** (1827–74), and together they laid out the gardens beside the re-erected and enlarged (1852–4) Crystal Palace at Sydenham, South London, which were widely admired. From 1851 Paxton concentrated on his work as an architect, and he and Stokes designed Mentmore Towers, Buckinghamshire (1851–4), a sumptuous country-house in the *Jacobethan style for the Rothschild family. He carried out extensive alterations to the Devonshires' Lismore Castle, Co. Waterford, Ireland (1850–8), and designed the house and gardens at Ferrières, near Paris (1853–9), again for the Rothschilds, in a French *Renaissance style.

Architectural History, 4 (1961), 77–92; Chadwick (1961); *DNB* (1917); Hitchcock (1977); Hix (1996); Pevsner (1976)

Peabody & Stearns. Boston architectural firm founded by **Robert Swain Peabody** (1845–1917) and **John Goddard Stearns** (1843–1917), whose work was of national importance throughout the USA from *c.*1880 until 1914. They pioneered the American *Colonial Revival but also influenced *Cram and others with their *Gothic Revival work. Kragsyde, Manchester-by-the-Sea, Mass. (1883–5—destroyed), combined the *Shingle style with elements drawn from English *Arts-and-Crafts work, and was one of their best houses. By the 1890s the firm had adopted *Classicism, as in their work for the World's Columbian Exposition, Chicago (1892–3), but several houses drew on the *Federal and Colonial *Georgian styles. All in all, Peabody & Stearns created some of the most significant buildings in New England at the turn of the century. They also designed railway-stations including Boston, Mass. (1872–4—destroyed), Jersey City, NJ (1889–90), and Union Station, Duluth, Minn. (1890–1).

Downing and Scully (1967); *Journal of the Society of Architectural Historians*, 32/2 (1973), 114–31; Meeks (1964); Scully (1971, 1974, 1989); Sturgis (1971)

Peach, Charles Stanley (1858–1934). British architect. He worked with H. R. *Gough in London from 1882 before setting up on his own in *c*.1885. Specializing in the design of electricity generating-stations, he advised on the design of several in London and elsewhere, showing considerable ingenuity, such as the raised garden over the electricity transformer station in Brown Hart Gardens, London, with a splendid *Mannerist domed *pavilion at each end (1904). He designed 127 Stamford Street, London (1915), with Egyptianizing detail. Responsible for the Centre Court for the Lawn Tennis Association at Wimbledon, he used 'board-finished' *reinforced-concrete earlier than Owen *Williams's Wembley Stadium (1934).

Gray (1985)

pearc, pearch. *See* perch.

Pearce, Sir Edward Lovett (*c*.1699–1733). A relative of *Vanbrugh, from whom he appears to have gained some architectural knowledge, Pearce was one of the most important *Palladian architects working in Ireland in C18. Pearce's first important commission seems to have been the interior and wings at Castletown, Co. Kildare (*c*.1726–7), begun by *Galilei. The handsome entrance-hall was the precedent for several later designs for Irish country-houses. In 1731 he was appointed Surveyor of Works and Fortifications in Ireland in succession to *Burgh, and was knighted in 1732. Pearce designed Bellamont Forest, Co. Cavan (*c*.1730), Ireland's first mature Palladian *villa, but his masterpiece is unquestionably the Parliament House (now Bank of Ireland) in Dublin (1729), with its massive *Ionic *portico and projecting wings. He designed the *obelisk and *grotto at Stillorgan, Co. Dublin (*c*.1733), derived from *Bernini's fountain in the Piazza Navona, Rome. His German assistant, *Cassels, took over his practice after his death.

Colvin (1995); Craig (1969, 1982); *DNB* (1917); Hall (1949); Summerson (1993)

pearling. Also *beading*. Moulding consisting of repetitive beads resembling pearls.

Pearson, John Andrew (1867–1940). English architect who settled in Toronto in 1888 and trained under *Darling, becoming his partner in 1892. He rebuilt the central block of the Parliament, Ottawa (1916–24), and the Bank of Commerce, Toronto (1929–31).

Kalman (1994)

Pearson, John Loughborough (1817–97). One of the most distinguished English *Gothic Revival architects. He trained with Ignatius *Bonomi and worked with *Salvin and P. C. *Hardwick before establishing his own practice. At first influenced by A. W. N. *Pugin, by the 1850s he began to draw on Continental Gothic for his precedents. His first significant church was St Peter's, Vauxhall, London (1859–65), a robust essay in early French *First Pointed, with *vaults of brick and stone ribs, plate-*tracery, an apsidal *chancel, and proportions based on the *Golden Section. His greatest works are arguably among the finest Gothic Revival churches in the world, including his soaring St Augustine's, Kilburn, London (1870–97), with a tower and *spire derived from St-Étienne, Caen, Normandy, and internal *buttresses dividing the *aisles into *bays in the manner of Albi Cathedral in France. His Truro Cathedral, Cornwall (1880–1910), again drew on Franco-English sources, and his understanding of Gothic vaulting was nowhere better demonstrated. He designed what is one of the noblest Victorian buildings in North-West England: Sts Agnes and Pancras, Ullet Road, Sefton Park, Liverpool (1883–5). With his son, **Frank Loughborough Pearson** (1864–1947), he designed St John's Cathedral, Brisbane, Australia (from 1887).

Curl (1995); Dixon and Muthesius (1985); Quiney (1979)

pebble-dash. External wall-rendering made by casting small pebbles on a second coat of rendering before it sets, also called *rough-cast or *harling.

pebble-wall. Wall faced with pebbles bedded in mortar or constructed of pebbles or uncut flints.

pecking. As *picked.

pectinated. Ornamented with narrow parallel elements, resembling the teeth of a comb, as on *friezes, *string-courses, etc.

Pede *or* **Peede, Hendrik van** (*fl.* 1527–30). Architect of the *Flamboyant *Gothic Town Hall, Oudenaarde, Belgium (1525–36). He also worked in Brussels from 1516, especially on the *Broodhuis* (1516–36), and remodelled the chapel at the Castle of Louvain (Leuven), Belgium (1531–2). He was one of the last of the great Gothic architects working in the region.

Baedeker, *Belgium* (1931)

pedestal. Substructure, consisting of a *plinth, *dado (or *die), and *cornice, beneath a column-*base in Classical architecture; used as a support for an *obelisk, statue, *urn, etc.; or found in *balustrades, terminating rows of *balusters, and supporting vases etc. A Classical *podium is a continuous elongated external pedestal, while inside a building it is expressed as a chair-rail, dado, and skirting. *Orders used on *triumphal arches have pedestals for reasons of composition and massing in the combination of *arcuated and *columnar and trabeated forms.

pediment. Low-pitched triangular gable following the roof-slopes over a *portico or *façade in Classical architecture, formed with raked *cornices of the same section as that of the horizontal *entablature at its base and mitring with it in part. *Doric examples often omit the *mutules under the sloping cornices. The triangular *tympanum framed by the raking and horizontal cornices was the field left plain or embellished with sculpture in high relief. *Greek or *Greek Revival pediments were lower in pitch than Roman examples. Pediments may crown subordinate features such as *door-ways, niches, windows, etc., and in such cases are termed *fronton*. The triangular pediment is the most usual, but the *segmental* pediment was evolved in *Antique Roman architecture in AD C1, and found on buildings connected with the worship of Isis, a goddess associated with the crescent-moon. Types of pediment include:

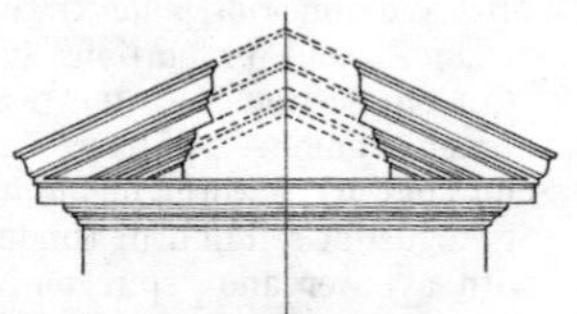

triangular pediment (shown with broken lines)

open-topped or broken-apex triangular pediment (shown with solid lines only)

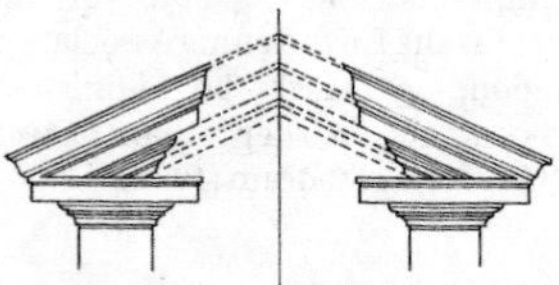

open-bed or broken-base triangular pediment (shown with broken lines

true broken or open triangular pediment (shown with solid lines only)

In both cases the entablature at an angle is *raking*

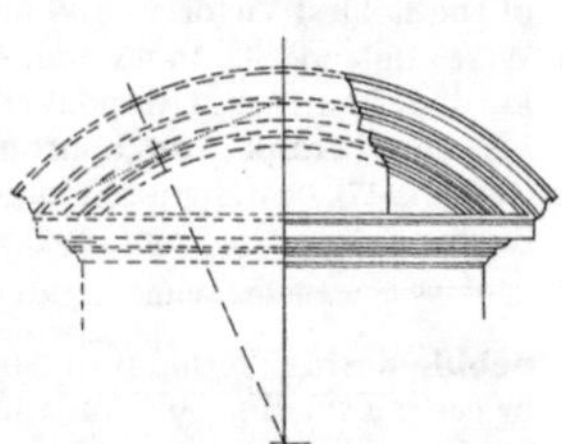

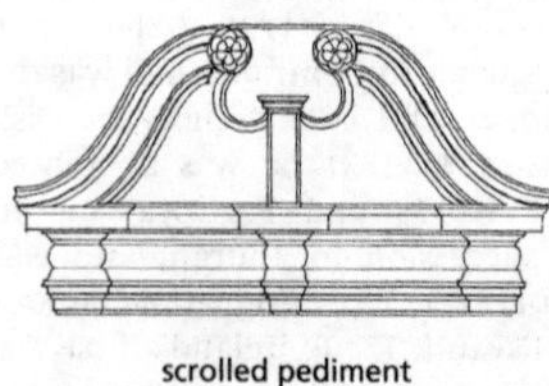

scrolled pediment

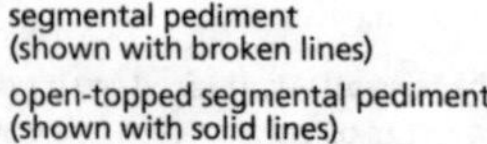

segmental pediment (shown with broken lines)

open-topped segmental pediment (shown with solid lines)

pediment

broken: with gap in the middle of the lower horizontal cornice and with raking cornices stopping before they can meet, so having no apex;

broken-apex: with raking sides too short to meet at the apex, also called *open* or *open-topped*;

broken-base: with the horizontal base lacking a middle section, also called *open-bed*, often occurring in C18 door-cases with *fanlights breaking upwards into the lower cornice;

scrolled: *open-topped* segmental pediment with segmental tops curling inwards as *scrolls, or with the tops in the form of two *ogees ending in scrolls, called *bonnet*-scroll, *goose-neck*, or *swan-neck*.

Curl (1992, 1994)

pediment-arch. *See* arch.

peel, pele. Fortified tower-house with vaulted ground-floor for cattle or storage, found especially in the Border-country between Scotland and England.

Pei, Ieoh Ming (1917–). Chinese-born American architect. He studied with *Gropius at Harvard before working for the architectural section of William Zeckendorf's contracting firm (Webb & Knapp, Inc.). Among his many large projects for Zeckendorf was the Mile High Center, Denver, Colo. (1952–6): consisting of a low transportation building, with cylindrical lifts rising in the centre of a vaulted space, and an office-tower with black-faced frames and exposed services, it made Pei's name. He collaborated with *Affleck on the design of the Place Ville Marie, Montreal (1956–65), an office-building that brought a new sophistication to the building type in Canada. He opened his own office in the late 1950s, drawing on the work of *Mies van der Rohe for most of his paradigms, but he turned to the triangle as a major motif in his designs in the 1970s, notably the extension to the National Gallery, Washington, DC (1971–8), the Morton H. Myerson Symphony Center, Dallas, Texas (1981–9), the Bank of China, Hong Kong (1982–9), and the huge extension to the Musée du Louvre, Paris (1983–93), the concourse of which is illuminated by a metal-and-glass pyramid, an extension of the triangular theme, the latter designed in collaboration with Peter Roman Rice (1935–92). Other works include the Rock and Roll Hall of Fame, Cleveland, Ohio (1993–5).

Emanuel (1994); Jodidio (1993, 1996); Suner (1988); Wiseman (1990)

Peichl, Gustav (1928–). Leading Austrian architect. His early work made references to the *International Modernism of the 1930s but in the 1960s he embraced *Brutalism, as in the Rehabilitation Centre for the Mentally Retarded at Vienna-Meidling (1965–7). His best-known buildings are the regional studios of the Austrian State Radio (ÖRF), where the various elements are grouped around large tall entrance-halls through which shiny metalwork is exposed. Good examples are the ÖRF studios at Salzburg (1968–72) and Eisenstadt (1981–3) which exploit the *Machine Aesthetic. Later still, he appears to have become more interested in *contextual design, as with the extension to the Städel Museum, Frankfurt (1987–90). Throughout his career he has been well known as the caricaturist 'Ironimus'.

Amsoneit (1994); Emanuel (1994); Lampugnani (1988)

pele. *See* peel.

pelican. *Gothic sculpture of the bird piercing her breast with her beak to draw blood to feed her young, symbolic of piety and the Eucharist.

Pellegrini, Pellegrino (1537–90). *See* Tibaldi.

pellet. *Band enriched with a series of closely spaced discs or half-balls found in *Romanesque architecture.

Pelli, Cesar (1926–). Argentine-born American architect. He worked with Eero *Saarinen from 1954 to 1964 before moving to Los Angeles where he was Director of Design for Daniel, Mann, Johnson, & Mendenhall (1964–8) and then Design Partner, Gruen Associates (1968–77). He established his own office in New Haven, Conn., in 1977. The Pacific Design Center, Los Angeles (1971), brought Pelli's name to notice: it drew on C19 iron-and-glass exhibition-halls for some of its themes, though the external cladding derived from *Mies van der Rohe's paradigms. The *Paxtonian Crystal Palace idea recurred in the winter-garden attached to Pelli's huge skyscraper and plaza at the World Financial Center, New York (1981), where his skill in designing the external skin of his buildings was demonstrated. Even simpler in form, with a pyramid roof, was the enormous Canary Wharf Tower, Isle of Dogs, London (1986), regrettably not quite aligned on the axis running through the finest *Baroque composition in England at Greenwich. Other works include the House for an Anonymous Patron, Western USA (1990–3), and the huge Petronas Twin Towers, Kuala Lumpur, Malaysia (1991–7).

Emanuel (1994); Futagawa (1981); Jodidio (1996, 1997)

pelta. Form resembling a wide shield, with sides swooping up and returning as eagle- or ram-heads, often found in *Neoclassical design.

Pembroke, 9th Earl of (*c*.1689–1750). *See* Herbert, Henry.

pencilling. Mortar-joints in brickwork painted to emphasize them.

pencil-rounded. *Arris blunted by rubbing to form a slightly rounded edge.

pendant. Fixed hanging ornament, resembling an elongated *boss suspended from *Perpendicular fan-*vaulting, *Jacobean ceilings, *posts of timber roof-*trusses, *staircase *newels, or at the mitring of *barge-boards at the apex of a gable. It often resembles an inverted *finial.

pendant-post. Upright post set against a wall, the lower end resting on a *corbel or *capital, with a hammer-beam or tie-beam fixed to its upper end, as in a *hammer-beam *truss.

pendent frieze. *Gothic *cornice, or open-work series of pendants arranged as interlacing C18 *Gothick arches.

pendentive. *See* dome.

pendill. Base of a vertical post in e.g. a *jetty or a *newel in a *stair, ornamentally carved. A *pendant or *pendicle*.

Pennethorne, Sir James (1801–71). English architect and planner, most of whose work was for *Nash or the Government. Brought up in Nash's household, he entered Nash's office in 1820 and worked with A. C. *Pugin. Later he completed the *Picturesque Park Villages, Regent's Park. In 1832 he was employed by the Commissioners of Woods and Forests and in 1843 became Architect to the Commissioners. He designed Victoria Park, Bethnal Green, Kennington Park, and Battersea Park, and prepared many schemes for urban improvements. His best-known public building is the Public Records Office, Chancery Lane, London (1851–96), in which the *module was arrived at by cells made of iron with shallow brick *vaults, the whole of fire-resistant construction. He also designed the sumptuous State Ball Room, Buckingham Palace (1853–5), the Duchy of Cornwall Offices, Buckingham Gate (1854), and what is now the Museum of Mankind, London (1866–70). His brother **John Pennethorne** (1808–88), was also a pupil of Nash, and made detailed studies of the *optical corrections at the Parthenon, Athens, which he published in 1844, and which prompted *Penrose to pursue the matter.

DNB (1917); Tyack (1992)

Penrose, Francis Cranmer (1817–1903). English architect and archaeologist. He worked for *Blore before travelling extensively in Europe. He realized the significance of John *Pennethorne's paper (1844) on *optical corrections in Ancient Greek architecture, and under the aegis of the Society of *Dilettanti made accurate records of the Periclean monuments of Athens (1846–7), working with Thomas John Willson (1824–1903). The results of the survey were published first in 1847, and in 1851 his vast tome *Principles of Athenian Architecture* was published, a later expanded edition coming out in 1888. He designed the entrance-gate to Magdalene College, Cambridge, and the severe Cornish porphyry *sarcophagus of Wellington in the *crypt of St Paul's Cathedral, London (1858), among other works.

DNB (1920)

pent. Sloping lean-to roof such as a canopy over a door, or over a low building set against a higher one. A pent carried round a building or across its main façade is termed a *skirt, and a skirt supported on slender columns and carried round the house is a *verandah.

pentastyle. *See* portico.

penthouse. **1.** Structure erected against the sides of another building as a lean-to, that is with a mono-pitched or *pent roof. **2.** Covered walkway set against a larger building or buildings. **3.** Structure occupying part of the area of a roof of a building used as a select separate dwelling. **4.** Protection from the weather over a door or window (i.e. the same as pent).

pepperpot. Small circular *turret or *tourelle with a conical roof, called a *pepper-box turret*.

perch. Small *bracket or *corbel such as those found near an altar in a church to carry a reliquary, statue, etc. Also called *pearc* or *pearch*.

Percier, Charles (1764–1838). French *Neoclassical architect who studied with A.-F. *Peyre and in Rome before establishing an architectural practice with *Fontaine in Paris in 1794. As Percier and Fontaine the firm became the leading architects of the Napoleonic period, and was largely responsible for the creation of the *Empire style, the epitome of which was at Malmaison, with its celebrated *tent-room and other ravishing interiors (1799–1803). In 1801 the two men were appointed Architects to the Government, designed the interiors of the Tuileries and St-Cloud Palaces, and extended the Louvre, Paris. They also laid out the Rue de Rivoli, Paris, with its arcaded ground-floors, and carried out extensive works at Fontainebleau, Compiègne, and Versailles. Their Arc de Triomphe du Carrousel (1806–8) shows their mastery of Roman *Antique *Classicism and refinement of detail. Their *Palais, maisons, et autres édifices modernes dessinés à Rome* (Palaces, Houses, and Other Modern Buildings Designed in Rome—1798) and *Receuil de décorations intérieures, comprenant tout ce qui a rapport à l'ameublement* (Compendium of Interior Decorations, Comprising all that Relates to Furnishing—1801) were influential throughout Europe and America, and ensured the *Empire* style was widely disseminated.

Biver (1963, 1964); Duportal (1931); Jervis (1984); Middleton and Watkin (1987); Watkin (1986)

Peressutti, Enrico (1908–75). *See* BBPR.

perforate. To form openings in something. A *perforated wall* is therefore one with openings, often arranged in patterns.

pergola. Two parallel rows of columns or *piers carrying beams and a structure for climbing plants, flanking a path, set in a garden and often attached to a dwelling.

peribolus. Wall or *colonnade around a Greek temple or a sacred space, or the space itself.

peridrome. *See* peristyle.

peripteral. Of a building surrounded by a single range of columns known as the *periptery or *peristyle.

periptery. Row of columns around a temple, also called *peristyle. A *peripteral building, such as a Greek temple, has a continuous *colonnade around it.

peristyle. *Periptery, peristasis*, or *colonnades surrounding a building or *court. The *peridrome* is the space between the columns and the solid wall of the cell behind them, such as in a Greek temple. A *peristylium* is an inner court surrounded by a colonnade.

perithyrides. The same as *ancones.

Perpendicular. Third and latest of the English *Gothic architectural styles, also known as *Third Pointed* or *Rectilinear*, it followed from the previous *Decorated* or *Second Pointed style. The Perpendicular style first emerged in designs of *c*.1332 for the *chapter-house and *cloisters of old St Paul's Cathedral, London (destroyed), by William de *Ramsey: key Perpendicular details, including *mullions extending to the *soffits of window-arches; extensive use of the *bowtell; developed employment of the double-*ogee; quatrefoils set in squares; bases with circular rolls, bells, and cushions over octagonal sub-bases of bell form; four-centred arches with flattened upper arcs; and square-framed arches with cusped blind *spandrels were all evident. So the Perpendicular style emerged in the first half of C14 in London, and was further developed at Gloucester Cathedral, where the *chancel (*c*.1337–57) displays many of its attributes, including the *panel-like effect created by vertical and horizontal elements. An English style, it has no Continental, Irish, or Scottish equivalent, and survived for around three centuries (the fan-vaulted hall staircase at Christ Church, Oxford, is *c*.1640). It was the first of the Gothic styles to be revived in C18.

Perpendicular is immediately recognizable by its pronounced verticals and horizontals in *blind panels covering wall surfaces and in *tracery (where the *transoms are often ornamented with miniature *battlements, and mullions rise straight up to the soffits of window-openings). Apertures gradually acquired flatter tops, with arches of the four-centred type. *Vaults evolved from the complicated varieties involving *liernes* into the *fan-vaults* first found at the Chapter House of Hereford Cathedral (destroyed 1769) and the Cloisters of Gloucester Cathedral (both second half of C14), and developing into the spectacular fan-vaulting of King's College Chapel, Cambridge (early C16), and the *Lady Chapel (or Chapel of King Henry VII (reigned

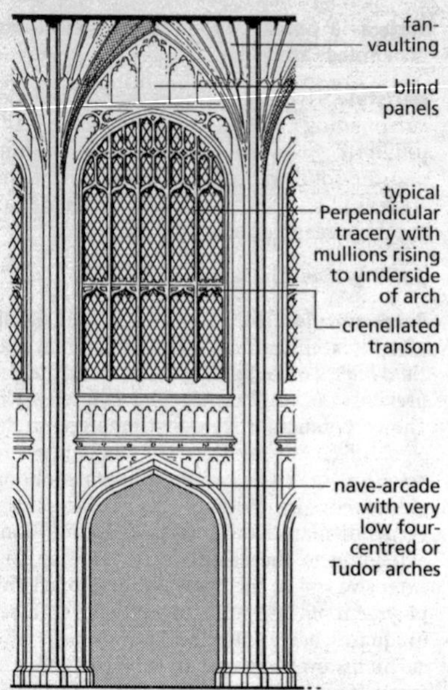

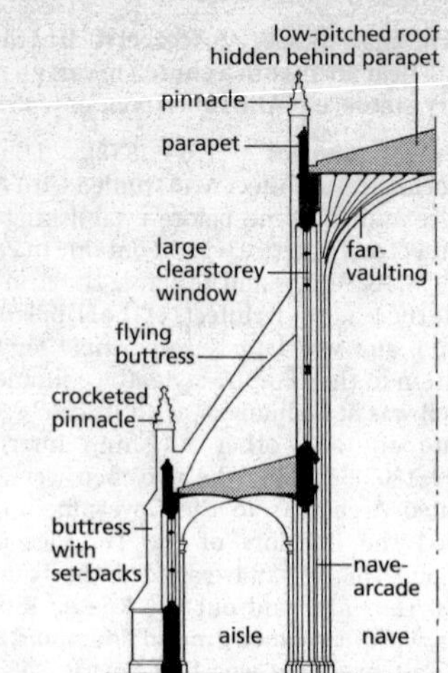

Perpendicular. (*left*) Internal elevation of typical bay of Perpendicular church. (*JJS*)
(*right*) Section through typical Perpendicular aisle and nave. (*JJS*)

1485–1509)) at Westminster Abbey (1503–19). Rectangular mouldings framing door- or window-openings formed *spandrels (often ornamented) reinforcing the controlled panel-like appearance: those *hood-mouldings terminated in carved *label-stops. Indeed, the panel motif is one of the most recognizable features of the style, each framed panel having an arched top, often cusped, and is repeated in rows in tracery and over the walls as *blind panels. Windows got larger, composed of many *lights (repeating the panel-like forms), and often filled the entire wall between *buttresses.

The Perpendicular style is commonly found in parish-churches, especially in East Anglia, the Cotswolds, and Somerset, where great wealth was created by the wool trade. *Clearstoreys were added to existing churches, and they often were vast, airy, and light: as *naves were increased in height to accommodate ranges of large Perpendicular windows in their clearstoreys, roofs were flattened, and disappeared behind crenellated decorative *parapets. In East Anglia, especially, *chancels were not distinctly compartmented, being part of the main volume of the church, but demarcated by means of elaborate timber *screens, often sumptuously decorated and coloured. Mouldings tended to become mechanical, and foliage less deeply cut than previously: a common moulding was the grapevine or *trail, often found on screens and *canopies.

The use of hood-mouldings, the flattening of roofs and arches, the adoption of widespread crenellations, and the elaboration of lierne- and later fan-vaulting gave the Perpendicular style its predominant flavour. Perpendicular architecture from the end of C15 to the beginnings of the *Elizabethan style is often called *Tudor, and frequently featured brick walls ornamented with *diaper-work, very flattened arches, and prominent hood-mouldings. The Tudor style was revived in C19, often for schools, workhouses, and collegiate buildings.

Papworth (1852); Parker (1850)

Perrault, Claude (1613–88). French physician and amateur architect whose fine translation of *Vitruvius (1673) achieved fame, and still commands respect. He played some part (with Le *Vau and Le Brun) in the design of the celebrated east front of the Louvre in Paris, of 1665–74, an astonishingly 'modern' Classical building for its date, with *coupled *Corinthian columns set on a plain *podium, but he was not solely responsible. The noble *façade, which was partly influenced by a design of *Bernini, impressed *Wren sufficiently for him also to use twinned columns on the west front of St Paul's Cathedral, London. Perrault published *Ordonnance des Cinq Espèces de Colonnes* (Regulation of the Five Sorts of Columns—1683—translated into other languages later) in which he expressed doubts that proportions could determine beauty, which attracted the opprobrium of N.-F. *Blondel. Perrault was an important figure in the evolution of French rationalism, and indeed one of the fathers of the *Enlightenment.

Blunt (1982); Hautecœur (1948); Herrmann (1973); Middleton and Watkin (1987); Perrault (1683); Picon (1988); Soriano (1972)

Perrault, Dominique (1953–). French architect. He entered many architectural competitions, including that for the École Supérieure d'Ingénieurs en Électronique, Marne-la-Vallée (won in 1984 and completed in 1987), and the Hôtel Industriel Berlier, Paris (won in 1986 and completed in 1989). In the latter year he crowned his success by winning the competition to design the huge Bibliothèque Nationale de France in Paris, one of the *Grands Projets* of the late President François Mitterrand, and consisting of four huge L-shaped towers linked by lower blocks (1989–1996).

Emanuel (1994); Jodidio (1996*a*)

Perret, Auguste (1874–1954). French architect and building contractor. He and his brother **Gustave** (1876–1952) were among the first to exploit the architectural possibilities of *reinforced concrete as evolved by *Hennebique. Perret Frères's first reinforced-concrete multistorey building was the celebrated apartment-block at 25b Rue Franklin, Paris (1903–4), which has *faïence patterns in the panels. They built the Théâtre des Champs Élysées, Paris (1911–13), loosely based on designs by Roger Bouvard and Henri van de *Velde. Perret and his engineer, Louis Gellusseau, evolved reinforced-concrete technology so that the surface of the material itself would be exposed and sufficient thickness of concrete (theoretically) provided to ensure the internal steelwork was protected from damp. With the war-memorial Church of Notre Dame, Le Raincy (1922–4), a truly monumental work of architecture was created, with all the concrete unclad and exposed: the building received widespread publicity and established the reputation of the firm (although by 1985 the steel was rusting, and surfaces of the concrete were crumbling). At the apartment-block, 51–5 Rue Raynouard, Paris (1929–32), some of the concrete was finished with *bouchardage* (bush-hammering) to remove the cement film and expose the coarser aggregate within the concrete, one of the first instances of this technique. Perret also designed the Mobilier National (1934–5) and the Musée des Travaux Publics (1936–57), both in Paris, and both concrete buildings. His last works were the master-plan for the rebuilding of Le Havre (1949–56), which had been destroyed in the 1939–45 war, and the central square and centrally planned Church of St Joseph (1952). In all his works the discipline of *Classicism, even in an extreme, stripped form, was rarely absent. He published *Une Contribution à une théorie de l'architecture* (A Contribution to a Theory of Architecture—1952).

Champigneulle (1959); Collins (1959); Jamot (1927) Perret (1959); Zahar (1959)

Perriand, Charlotte (1903–). French architect and furniture designer, she was one of the most influential creators of interiors of her time. She collaborated with Le *Corbusier and Pierre *Jeanneret on the Salon d'Automne Exhibition, Paris (1928), and later with Jean *Prouvé on the design of 'serial' furniture (modular wall-units, etc.) in the 1950s. She also designed kitchen prototypes for Le Corbusier's *Unité d'Habitation* at Marseilles (1950), and her output of designs during the period was prodigious. With Ernö *Goldfinger she designed the interiors of the French Government Tourist Offices at 66 Haymarket (1958–60) and 177 Piccadilly (1963–4), both in London. At her châlet, Méribel-les-Allues, Savoie, France (1960–3), she married traditional and Japanese design to the *International Modernist style.

Architectural Design, 33 (1963), 601–3; Emanuel (1994); Jervis (1984); Perriand (1985)

perron. 1. External platform-landing reached by symmetrical flights of steps, leading to the *piano nobile of a building, a feature of *Palladian architecture. **2.** The steps leading to the platform.

Perronet, Jean-Rodolphe (1708–94). French architect and military engineer. In 1745 he rebuilt the *choir of the Cathedral of Alençon, and in 1747 was appointed Director of the École des Ponts et Chaussées where engineers and architects were instructed in bridge-, embankment-, and road-construction. He is important because he developed bridge-design in which each arch thrust against its neighbour, enabling spans to be increased, arches flattened, and structures lightened, essentially a principle of *Gothic design. His theories influenced *Telford, among others. He designed Pont de Mantes (over the Seine—1757–65), Pont de Château-Thierry (over the Marne—1765–86), Pont de Neuilly, Paris (over the Seine—1768–74), Pont des Fontaines, Chantilly (1770–1), the Pont de Sainte-Maxence, Oise (over the Oise—1771–86—destroyed), Pont Biais, near Lagny (over the Bicheret—1775), the Ponts de Brunoy and de Rozoy (over the Yères—1785–7), and the Pont Louis Seize (now Concorde—over the Seine in Paris—1787–91). He also designed the Canal de Bourgogne (1775–1832). He wrote *Description des projets et de la construction des ponts de Neuilly, de Mantes, d'Orléans et autres* (Description of Projects and of the Construction of the Bridges of Neuilly, Mantes, Orléans, and others—1782–9). He was a champion of *Soufflot and his ideas, so is a founding-father of *Neoclassicism. With his pupil, Émiliand-Marie Gauthey (1732–1808), he sought the best building-stones in France, subjecting them to scientific tests to ensure the Church of Ste-Geneviève would be structurally stable. Perronet is therefore of great importance in the development of structural theory, experiment, and calculations.

Lesage (1806); Middleton and Watkin (1987); Riche de Prony (1829)

Persian. **1.** *Telamon sculpted with clothes suggestive of a Persian origin. *Persae* occur e.g. on the portal of the *Friedrichsbau*, Heidelberg Castle (1601–7). **2.** The C19 *Persian style* embraced a range of motifs associated with *Islamic and *Moorish architecture.

Persic. Column with bell-shaped *capital and similarly sized *base, ornamented with *lotus-like forms, derived from *Achaemenian prototypes from Persepolis. It was fashionable in early C19 *Egyptian Revival schemes of decoration.

Persico, Edoardo (1900–36). Italian architect and critic. He was invited (1929) by *Pagano to work as an editor for *Casabella*, the architectural journal, which he helped to transform into one of the leading journals of its era. He also published polemics in other magazines, including the influential and widely read *Domus*. He saw the identification of the Rationalists and Traditionalists with Fascism as potentially dangerous, and he was scathing about certain aspects of the *Modern Movement. Modern architecture, he decided, was not a mere engineering solution to an architectural problem (as many Americans thought) nor was its direction to be determined by Le *Corbusier's dogmatic approach, nor by Bruno *Taut's claims for social concerns. Instead, he perceived it as a means of liberating the human spirit, with no doctrinaire overtones. His best works were probably the two Parker Stores, Milan, both of which he carried out with Marcello Nizzoli (1934–5), and the various displays he designed for important international exhibitions.

Emanuel (1980); Veronesi (1964)

persienne. Type of slatted window-shutter either hinged at the side or fixed at the top and hanging loosely.

Persius, Friedrich Ludwig (1803–45). Prussian architect from Potsdam. The most able of *Schinkel's pupils, he supervised the building of the master's Schloss Glienicke on the Havel (1824–6) and the exquisite Charlottenhof, Potsdam (1826–7). He built the *Römische Bäder* (Roman Baths), Potsdam (1834–5), to Schinkel's designs. His masterpieces were the *Rundbogenstil *Early Christian-basilica-style *Friedenskirche* (Church of Peace), Potsdam (1845–87), and the *Heilandskirche* (Church of the Redeemer) Sakrow (1841–4—completed by *Stüler and others), but he also designed a number of charming *villas finished in *stucco and based on a rural Tuscan *vernacular style pioneered by Schinkel, but probably partly derived from *Papworth. He was responsible for the exotic orientalizing Steam-Engine House, Sanssouci, Potsdam, and he constructed the *dome and *turrets of Schinkel's *Nikolaikirche* (Church of St Nicholas), Potsdam (1843–50). Under King Friedrich Wilhelm IV (1840–58), with *Lenné, he co-ordinated the transformation of the landscape in the vicinity of the Havel, Potsdam, into one of the most enchanting creations of the first half of C19.

Börsch-Supan (1977, 1980); Dehio (1961); Giersberg and Schendel (1982); Persius (1843–9); Poensgen (1930); Watkin and Mellinghoff (1987)

persona. 1. *Gargoyle carved as a grotesque mask. **2.** *Antefix, or stop to the ends of the joint tiles of an Antique temple, appearing at the *cymatium or *corona of the *cornice.

personification. Representation of a human figure with *attributes to suggest an abstraction, such as Hope with Anchor. Cesare Ripa's *Iconologia* (1593) was an important source-book for personification.

Lewis and Darley (1986)

perspective. Method of representing graphically an object as it appears to the eye, suggesting three dimensions.

Fraser Reekie (1946); Nicholson (1835)

Peruzzi, Baldassare (1481–1536). Italian *uomo universale* of the *High Renaissance, influenced by *Bramante and *Raphael. His first great building was the Palazzo della Farnesina, Rome (1505–11), an exquisite house (sometimes referred to as a *villa) with *frescoes by Ugo da Carpi (d. 1532), Peruzzi himself, Raphael, *Giulio Romano, and Giovanni Antonio Bazzi (1477–1549—known as *Il Sodoma* (the Sodomite)). Essentially a square on plan, it has a *loggia between two projecting wings on the garden-front. In 1520 he was appointed Architect (with *Sangallo) at St Peter's, but fled the city after the Sack of Rome (1527), settling in Siena, where until 1532 he was engaged on strengthening the fortifications, and remodelled the Church of San Domenico (1531–3). From 1531 he was again working at St Peter's, Rome, and was appointed Architect to the *basilica in 1534. The Palazzo Massimi alle Colonne, Rome (1532–7), however, is reckoned to be his masterpiece: an ingeniously planned building on a difficult site, it has a curved *façade to the street with *Tuscan columns and *pilasters on the ground-floor arranged in pairs. The whole front is rusticated, and the *piano nobile is separated from the ground-floor by an *entablature. Above the piano nobile are two rows of small windows—the lower has architraves with elaborate frames, the patterns of which were to be developed as *strapwork by *Serlio and disseminated through his publications all over Europe. The courts which are arranged to be similar to Roman *atria are on two different axes. Certain details of this *palazzo (such as the frames of the second-floor windows and the freedom with which the Orders are used) suggest proto-*Mannerism.

Adams (1980); Frommel (1973); Heydenreich and Lotz (1974); Lotz (1977); Placzek (1982); Tessari (1995); Wurm (1984)

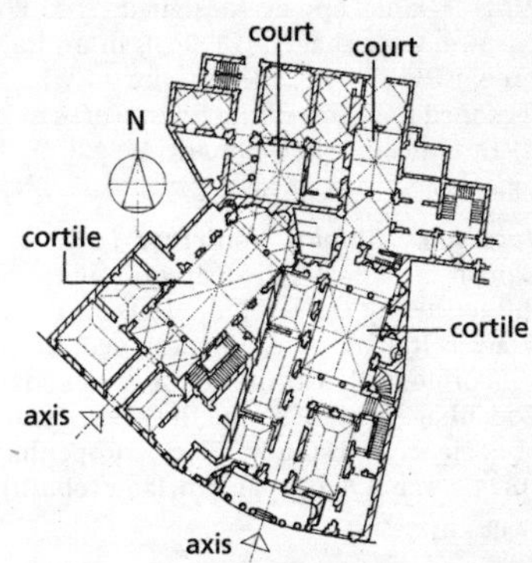

Peruzzi. Palazzo Massimi alle Colonne, Rome, 1532. A highly ingenious plan on a difficult site, with internal courtyards. Note how the axes are set up on two separate entrances, one for each palace: on the left is the Palazzo Angelo Massimi, and on the right is that of Pietro Massimi.

petal. *Imbrication*, *petal-diaper*, or *scale-pattern* ornament suggesting overlapping scale-like shapes. It represents roofing-tiles, as on the top of the *Choragic Monument of Lysicrates, Athens (C4 BC), and was often found in Roman work, e.g. *sarcophagi. Petal-diaper patterns occur in roofing and tile-hanging.

Petersen, Johan Carl Christian (1874–1923). Danish architect and ceramic artist who was prominent in the Neoclassical trend in that country from *c.*1910. He made an especial study of the works of C. F. *Hansen and M. G. *Bindesbøll. His best work is the exquisite Faaborg Museum, Funen (1912–15—with furniture by Kaare Klint (1888–1954)), in which the influence of the earlier masters is clear, and was a manifestation of the return to *Neoclassicism. He was a vigorous polemicist and prolific writer on architecture, notably in the journal *Architekten*. Some of his projects (e.g. the unrealized proposals for the old railway-station area of Copenhagen (1919—with Ivar Bentsen (1876–1943)) anticipate the *Neo-Rationalism of *Rossi and others in the 1970s.

Paavilainen (1982); van Vynckt (1993); Weilbach (1995)

Petersen, Ove (1830–92). Danish architect. Influenced by *Herholdt and *Meldahl, he worked in a free Historicist style, and was a powerful force in the revival of interest in

Danish brick buildings (e.g. his Hirschsprung Tobacco Factory, Copenhagen, of 1866, with round arches and ornamental brickwork). With *Dahlerup he designed the Royal Theatre, Copenhagen (1872–4), in an Italian *Renaissance style, the interior of which is reckoned to be one of the finest works of late-C19 architecture in Denmark.

Millech (1951); Weilbach (1995)

Petersen, Vilhelm Valdemar (1830–1913). Danish architect. His early designs were influenced by the work of *Hetsch, but in a heavier Italian style. He designed the Old Meteorological Institute on the Esplanaden in Copenhagen (1872–3), and the Royal Academy of Sciences, Dante's Place, Copenhagen (1894–8—an Italian *palazzo, later rebuilt).

Weilbach (1995)

Peto, Harold Ainsworth (1854–1933). *See* George, Sir Ernest.

Petschnigg, Hubert (1913–). Partner of Helmut *Hentrich from 1953.

Emanuel (1994)

Pevsner, Sir Nikolaus Bernhard Leon (1902–83). German-born British art-historian. He was a strong supporter of the *Modern Movement, which gave some of his early writings an undoubted bias, notably the very influential *Pioneers of the Modern Movement from William Morris to Walter Gropius* (1936, later re-issued as *Pioneers of Modern Design*) and the enormously successful (and again influential) *An Outline of European Architecture* (1942 with many subsequent editions). He had a powerful impact on *The Architectural Review* in the 1940s, when it became a pro-Modern-Movement force, and changed the architectural climate of Britain. He originated and edited the *Pelican History of Art* (from 1953), one of the most impressive series on art and architecture published in C20. His greatest achievement was arguably the county-by-county guides of *The Buildings of England* (from 1951), much of which he wrote himself, although some of his highly subjective comments have been toned down in later editions. His distinguished collections of essays and papers published as *Studies in Art, Architecture, and Design* (1968) and *A History of Building Types* (1976) are mines of information. He was devoted to the study of the architecture (especially churches) of his adopted country, and made an incalculable contribution to scholarship.

DNB (1990); Pevsner (1969, 1974*a*)

pew. Fixed wooden seat with a back and *bench-ends (the latter often elaborately carved with *blind *tracery and finished with *poppy-head *finials) in use in churches from *c.* C13. *Box-pews* were enclosed with high panelled partitions and a door, commonly dating from C18.

Parker (1850)

Peyre Family. French architects active from the reign of *Louis Quinze (1715–74) to that of Louis-Philippe (1830–48). The most distinguished members were **Marie-Joseph** (1730–85) and his younger brother **Antoine-François** (1739–1823). Marie-Joseph, a pupil of *Blondel, was an influential innovator who shot to fame with his *Œuvres d'architecture* (1765), which featured several vast *Neoclassical schemes that had an immense effect on architecture for the next few decades. In particular, his studies of *Antique Roman remains (with de *Wailly and *Moreau-Desproux) had prompted his advocacy of ingenious internal planning with top-lit rooms, something that was to influence *Adam, the younger *Dance, and *Gondouin, among others. His Hôtel Leprêtre de Neubourg, Clos Payen, near Paris (1762), was one of the first Neoclassical buildings in France, and a highly original, compact, modest composition applicable to quite ordinary houses. With de Wailly he designed (1768–82) the Théâtre-Français (later Théâtre de l'Odéon), a severe Neoclassical building (rebuilt by *Chalgrin after a fire of 1799). A.-F. Peyre, who taught *Percier, *Fontaine, and A.-L.-T. *Vaudoyer, designed the Electoral Palace and Chapel at Koblenz, Germany (1780–92), for Clemens Wenzeslaus, Elector and Archbishop of Trier (1768–94): it was a simplified version of the grand scheme of 1777 by d'*Ixnard. Peyre also excavated the Roman antiquities at Trier, publishing his findings in 1785. He designed the noble *Akademiesaal* in the Electoral Palace at Mainz (1786–7), and was responsible for part of the new Neoclassical Clemensstadt (later Neustadt), Koblenz (1782–3).

M.-J. Peyre's son, **Antoine-Marie Peyre** (1770–1843), was for a time aide-de-camp to General M.-J.-P.-Y. Roch Gilbert du Motier, Marquis de La Fayette (1757–1834), and subsequently had a career as an architect in Paris.

Middleton and Watkin (1987); Watkin and Mellinghoff (1987)

pharos. **1.** *Antique lighthouse, such as that at the harbour of Alexandria. **2.** Symbol for a lighthouse. **3.** Any conspicuous beacon or light.

Philander *or* **Philandrier, Guillaume** (1505–65). French architect whose translation of and annotations on *Vitruvius (1543 and later editions) were greatly respected in C16 as major sources for architectural theory and precedent. He is said to have studied under *Serlio, and designed the tomb of Cardinal d'Armagnac in Toulouse Cathedral.

Hautecœur (1948); Papworth (1852)

Philo *or* **Philon** (*fl.* C4 BC). Athenian architect. He designed the dodecastyle *portico of the great Hall of the Mysteries (Telesterion) at Eleusis (330–310 BC) and the huge Arsenal of the Piraeus, near Athens (*c.*346–328 BC), intended as a store for the sails, ropes, etc., of the Athenian navy. He was the author of books on proportion and prepared a description of the Arsenal. Another **Philo of Byzantium** wrote on mechanics and architecture *c.* C2 BC.

Coulton (1977); Dinsmoor (1950); Lawrence (1983)

Piacentini, Marcello (1881–1960). Italian architect, the son of **Pio Piacentini** (1846–1928), who was one of the leading architects in Rome in the first fifty years after Italian Unification (1861–71). Pio's works included the Palazzo delle Exposizioni (1880–2), Palazzo Sforza Cesarini (1886–8), and the Ministero di Grazia e Giustizia (1913–20), all in Rome, and all thoroughly competent buildings.

Marcello established his reputation with the Villa Allegri, Rome (1915–17), the Cinema 'al Corso', Rome (1915–17), the Palace of Justice, Messina (1921–8), and the centre of the *Garden City Garbatella, Rome (1920). His designs of that time were academically sound and eclectically based. He became Professor of Architecture at Rome in 1920, and, in 1921, with Gustavo Giovannoni (1873–1947), founded the journal *L'Architettura* of which he was Chief Editor (1922–43) and was influential in promoting the work of younger architects, including those associated with *Rationalism. When Benito Mussolini (1883–1945) came to power (1922), Piacentini became the leading protagonist of a *stripped *Neoclassicism that was to be virtually the style of State Architecture under Fascism. In fact, he rose to such a position of influence that he has been called 'Mussolini's Albert *Speer'. He was no mean architect, as his Hotel Ambasciatori, Rome (1926–7), shows in its powerful *Mannerist façade. Other significant works of the time include the remodelling of the Piazza della Vittoria (1927–32) and the completion of the Via Elena Regina (1932). In 1933 he commenced (with Attilio Spaccarelli (*c.*1890–1975)) the Via della Conciliazione that opened up the vista from *Bernini's Piazza di San Pietro, and has been criticized since for its insensitivity to Bernini's intentions as well as for the destruction of historic buildings to facilitate its construction (completed 1950). Piacentini was responsible for the general plan of the Città Universitaria, Rome (1932–5), and designed the stripped Classical Administration Building (1932–3). He worked with *Pagano, *Piccinato, and others on the planning of the Esposizione Universale di Roma (EUR) for the projected E42 exhibition (which did not occur because of the 1939–45 war) and worked with *Nervi on the Palazzo dello Sport, Rome (1958–9). His *Architettura d'oggi* (Architecture Today—1930) was admired at the time, and he also published a work on the buildings of Rome from 1870 until the post-1939–45 war period (1952).

Accasto, Fraticelli, and Niccolini (1971); Meeks (1966); Patetta (1972); Piacentini (1930); Pica (1936); Placzek (1982); Portoghesi (1968); Seta (1972); Zevi (1973)

Piano, Renzo (1937–). Italian architect. Working in partnership with Richard *Rogers (1970–7), he built the *High Tech Centre Pompidou, Paris (1971–7), much influenced by *Futurism, *Constructivism, and *Archigram. After establishing a separate practice he worked with Peter Roman Rice (1935–92) on a number of projects, including the Menil Collection Exhibition Building, Houston, Texas (1981–6), and the Football Stadium, Bari, Italy (1987–90). More recently his huge Cité Internationale, Lyons, a conference-centre, offices, museum of contemporary art, cinema, and a hotel, has been developed (from 1985), with *pavilions clad in *terracotta panels. Other works include the Kansai Airport, Osaka, Japan (1988–94), built on an artificial island in Osaka Bay.

Buchanan (1996–7); Emanuel (1994); Dini (1984); Jodidio (1995*a*); Piano (1989)

piano nobile. Principal storey of a building containing the apartments of ceremony and reception, usually set over a lower floor, and approached by a flight of steps from the ground level, often expressed as a *perron. The piano nobile was often of greater height than the storeys above and below, and the architectural embellishments of e.g. windows usually emphasized its significance.

Ackerman (1967, 1977, 1990)

piazza. **1.** Open space, square, or market-place, surrounded by buildings and approached by various streets. **2.** In C17 and C18 a roofed *arcade or *colonnade with buildings above, as at Covent Garden, London, (1631–3), by Inigo *Jones. **3.** Any covered way, colonnaded walk, or *pentice. **4.** Open *porch or *verandah (US).

Piccinato, Luigi (1899–1983). Italian architect and town-planner. Active as a member of the Rationalist tendency in the inter-war period, he worked with *Pagano, *Piacentini, and others on the plans for the Esposizione Universale di Roma (EUR) for the E42 exhibition (not realized because of the 1939–1945 war). His town-planning work included schemes for Sabaudia (1936–8) and Catania (1960–2).

Cennamo (1973)

picked. Masonry faced with a multitude of small crevices, like rock-faced work on a small scale (*see* rustication).

picnostyle, pycnostle. *See* intercolumniation.

picture-rail. Moulding from which pictures are hung in a room. It defines the lower part of a *frieze.

Picturesque. C18 English aesthetic category that was hugely influential throughout Europe. It was a standard of taste, largely concerned with landscape, and with emotional responses to associations evocative of passions or events. From *Pittoresco* ('in the manner of the painters'), it was also associated with carefully contrived landscape paintings, particularly those of Claude Lorraine (1600–82), Salvator Rosa (1615–73), and the two Poussins (1615–75 and 1593–1665). It was essentially an anti-urban aesthetic concerned with sensibility, linked to notions of pleasing the eye with compositions reminiscent of those in paintings. To Sir Uvedale *Price the Picturesque comprised all the qualities of nature and art that could be discerned in paintings executed since the time of Titian (*c.*1485–1576), and he argued in his *Essay on the Picturesque* (1794) in favour of 'natural' beauty, deploring contemporary fashions, such as those established by 'Capability' *Brown for laying out grounds, because they were at variance with all the principles of landscape-painting. Price's arguments were set out by Richard Payne *Knight in his didactic poem *The Landscape* (1794), and both men had considerable influence over the design of gardens and landscapes in later years, helping to create a climate in which the asymmetrical and informal aspects of much architectural and landscape design developed in C19. However, Price and Knight also conceded that there was always a place in a Picturesque landscape for formal and symmetrical composition, just as could be seen in many paintings. Picturesque scenes were full of variety, interesting detail, and elements drawn from any sources, so were neither serene (like the *Beautiful) nor awe-inspiring (like the *Sublime).

In architectural terms, the asymmetrical *villas of John *Nash, for example, were a product of the Picturesque, and the freeing of architectural composition from the tyranny of symmetry was undoubtedly due to ideas of the Picturesque, a term that suggested variety, smallness, irregularity, roughness of texture, and an association with the power to stimulate imagination. Thus the Picturesque led to *eclecticism and, by its appreciation of variety and asymmetry, to the *Gothic and other Revivals.

Ballantyne (1997); Chilvers, Osborne, and Farr (1988); Colvin and Harris (1970); Crook (1987); Hussey (1967*a*); Knight (1794, 1972); Osborne (1970); Parreaux and Plaisant (1977); Pevsner (1968, 1974); Price (1810); Watkin (1982*a*)

picture-window. Large window containing a single undivided pane of glass.

pie. Ornament resembling a stylized chrysanthemum, or the *rosette.

piecrust. *Rococo scalloped, scrolled, raised border around e.g. a mirror.

piedroit. *Lesene, or species of *pilaster without any *base or *capital.

pien, piend. **1.** Apex, arris, ridge, or salient angle. **2.** Hip-rafter in a roof. **3.** *Coping. **4.** Horizontal and sloping joint in a stone geometrical *stair where one step fits into another to prevent it slipping.

pier. **1.** A detached mass of construction, generally acting as a support, such as the solid part of a wall between two openings, or a massive element from which arches spring, as in a bridge. **2.** Support, such as a pier in a repetitive medieval *nave-*arcade varying from sturdy, oversized *Romanesque examples to the lighter, taller, more slender, multi-moulded *Perpendicular types. Piers are therefore very much more massive than columns. **3.** Vertical formation in brickwork on the face of a *flint or *rag-stone wall, serving to strengthen it. **4.** Stone, concrete, metal-work, or timber construction jutting out into the sea or other water as a break-water, landing-stage, or promenade. **5.** Jetty or wharf.

pier-arch. Arch springing from a *pier.

pier-buttress. *Pier so constructed to resist the thrust of a flying *buttress, thus giving the latter support.

Piermarini, Giuseppe (1734–1808). Italian architect who worked in Milan from 1769 to 1796 as City Architect, where he not only designed many buildings but was the arbiter of all matters relating to the work of other architects. He built the enormous Palazzo Belgioioso (1772–81), followed by other houses, including the Palazzo Greppi (1772–8), the Palazzo Moriggia (1770s), and the Casa Casnedi (*c.*1776), all in Milan. He designed the Palazzo Ducale (from 1773—with interior decorations by Giocondo Albertolli (1742–1839)), and the Villa Ducale, Monza (1776–80—again collaborating with Albertolli). He was responsible for several theatres including the Teatro alla Scala, Milan (1776–9), the Teatro Canobbiana, Milan (1777–80), and others at Novara (1777), Monza (1778), Mantua (1782–3), Crema (1783–5), and Matelica (1803–12), all in a refined *Neoclassical style. His work was widely imitated.

Cesarini (1983); Meeks (1966); Mezzanotte (1966); Middleton and Watkin (1987)

Pieroni, Giovanni Battista (*fl.* 1620s). Architect of the *Sala Terrena*, a huge triple-arched *loggia on the Valdštejn Palace, Prague (1624–7), which faces the *Baroque garden designed by Pieroni and Nicolo Sebregondi. This loggia cannot be matched in grandeur and sophistication by anything of contemporary date in Vienna.

Neumann, J. (1970)

Pierre de Chelles. *See* Chelles.

Pierre de Montreuil. *See* Montreuil.

Pietilä, Reima (1923–93) and **Raili** (1926–). Finnish husband-and-wife team of architects responsible for the Kaleva Church, Tampere (1966), with its inward canted walls and tall window-strips. Among other buildings were the Congregational Centre, Leisure Centre, and Shopping Hall, Hervanta New Town, Tampere (1979) and the President's House, Mantyniemi (1984–93).

Emanuel (1994); Richards (1978); Salokorpi (1970); Tempel (1968)

pietra dura. Inlaid work with hard stones (agate, jasper, marble, etc.) later used from C16 for *mosaics, also called *Florentine mosaic*, *opera commesso*, *pietra commesse*, and *lavoro di commesso*. The *capella dei principi* (Chapel of the Princes), San Lorenzo, Florence, is decorated with such work (from 1604).

Baldini (1979); Papworth (1852)

pietra serena. Dark, slippery, greenish-grey Florentine *Macigno* stone from Fiesole used for the interior *pilasters, *entablatures, and architectural elements by *Brunelleschi at the Pazzi *Chapel and *Michelangelo in the Medici Chapel, both in Florence.

Papworth (1852)

Pigage, Nicolas de (1723–96). French architect, a pupil of J.-F. *Blondel. Called to the Court of Karl Theodor, Elector Palatine (1743–99), in 1749 as a landscape-architect, he became Court Architect in 1752. He adorned the enchanting gardens at Schwetzingen, near Mannheim (1752–95), with the sumptuous Court Theatre (1752), Temples of Minerva and Apollo (1761), Bath-House (1766–73—with exquisite Louis *Seize interiors), serpentine bird-bath, water-spouting birds, water-castle, ruined *aqueduct, 'Mosque' (1778–95), and Classical Temple of Mercury. These constitute a collection of some of the finest *fabriques in Europe. He created the beautiful interiors of the Electoral Palace, Mannheim (1752–96), and built his greatest work, the charming Schloss Benrath and gardens, near Düsseldorf (1755–65), where a restrained *Rococo merges with nascent *Classicism.

Colombier (1955); Heber (1986); Pigage (1805); Powell (1959); Watkin and Mellinghoff (1987).

Pikionis, Dimitrios A. (1887–1968). Greek architect who had a considerable influence on contemporary Greek architecture. His work included the Experimental School, University of Salonika (1933–5), the Hotel Xenia, Delphi (1953), the Town Hall, Volos (1961), and St Paul's Church, Ethniki, Estia (1960–8). He designed a number of tombs, but is probably best known for his master-plan and landscape-design for the Acropolis, Hill of Philopappou, and surrounding area, Athens (1950–7).

Curtis (1996); Emanuel (1994)

pila. **1.** Plain, unmoulded, undecorated, detached rectangular or square masonry *pier, square or rectangular on plan, with no allusions to the *Orders whatsoever, also termed *pillar. **2.** *Font on a free-standing *shaft, as opposed to one fixed to a wall or a bracket. **3.** Plain block set on a column, etc., supporting a roof. **4.** *Antique mortar or plastered finish.

pilaster. Roman version of the *anta, except that generally it conforms to the *Order used elsewhere, with column, *shaft, and *base, and supports an *entablature. It is attached to a wall from which it projects only slightly, and is rectangular on plan, so does not conform to the circular plans of columns, and should not be confused with an *engaged column. In most cases, and correctly, unlike antae, pilaster-shafts have *entasis. Unlike a *pier, a pilaster has no structural purpose, and is used to respond to columns or the design of the *soffit of a ceiling for purely architectural and decorative reasons.

Normand (1852)

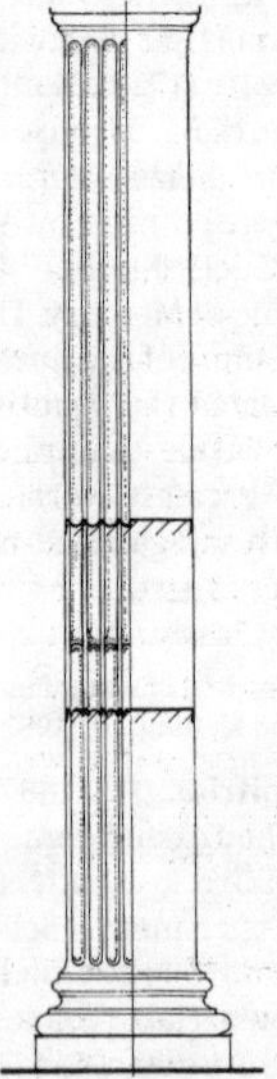

pilaster. Typical Classical example (*left*) with flutes and cabling, and (*right*) plain, with Attic base.

pilaster-face. Longest exposed surface of a *pilaster, parallel to the wall behind.

pilaster-mass. **1.** *Pier to which a *pilaster is attached. **2.** Pier or mass of wall with *impost mouldings. **3.** As *pilaster-strip but more massive.

pilaster-side. Exposed part of a *pilaster at 90° to the wall to which it is attached.

pilaster-strip. *Lesene or *piedroit which, unlike an *anta or *pilaster, has no base or capital, has no *entasis, and is not a true pilaster: it is a feature of *Anglo-Saxon work, and with the *plinths and *corbel-table, frames the panels of *Romanesque bays. It is more slender than a *pilaster-mass.

pilastrade, pilastra. Continuous row of *pilasters in series.

pile. **1.** Any building with architectural pretensions, such as a castle or a country-house. **2.** Mole or *pier in the sea. **3.** *Pier e.g. of a bridge. **4.** Large upright timber post hammered into marshy or uncertain ground to support a superstructure. Later piles were cylindrical or other hollow forms of iron or steel, and more recently piles are of *reinforced concrete. **5.** Row of rooms, hence a *double-pile house is two rooms deep, with or without a corridor between them.

Pilgram, Anton (*c*.1455–1515). Master-mason and architect, born probably in Brno, Moravia. His first work was the Church of St Kilian, Heilbronn (*c*.1482–90), much influenced by the work of *Buchsbaum. He was involved in the building of the Parish Church, Wimpfen (*c*.1493–7), and then worked on the Church of St James, Brno (1502). He designed the *Judentor* (Jews' Gate—1508) and the staircase to St James's School (1510), also in Brno, both destroyed in C19. He moved to Vienna, where he carved the organ base (1513) and the *pulpit (1514–15), containing self-portraits, in the *Stephansdom* (St Stephen's Cathedral). He designed rooms in the *Niederösterreichisches Landhaus* (Building of the Lower Austrian Diet), Vienna (1513–15), and may have been responsible for the *choir of the Parish Church, Freistadt, Austria (1513–15).

Feuchtmüller (1951, 1978); Oettinger (1951)

pilier cantonné. *Gothic *pier consisting of a large central core with four attached *colonnettes associated with the springing of the *nave-arcade and the *vaults over the *aisle and nave.

Viollet-le-Duc (1875)

Pilkington, Frederick Thomas (1832–98). Scots High Victorian *Rogue *Gothic architect. His best works were the Church of the Trinity, Irvine, Ayrshire (1861–3), and the Barclay Church, Edinburgh (1862–3), both of which are powerful compositions, with deliberately over-emphatic elements.

Dixon and Muthesius (1985); Gifford, McWilliam, and Walker (1984)

Pilkington, William (1758–1848). English architect, a pupil and assistant of Sir Robert *Taylor. He supervised the building of Taylor's design for the Council House, Salisbury, Wiltshire (1788–95), and then built a number of houses in *Neoclassical and *Tudor styles. His buildings included Otterden Place, Kent (1802—Tudor), Clermont Lodge (now Hall), Norfolk (1812), and Calverton Church, Buckinghamshire (1818–24—*Gothic, with Neo-Norman tower). His younger son, **Redmond William Pilkington** (1785–1844), succeeded his father as Surveyor to the Charterhouse, London, where he built the Preacher's and Pensioners' Courts (1825–30), to the designs of which *Blore contributed.

Colvin (1995); *DNB* (1917)

pillar. **1.** Free-standing unadorned *pila or *pier, *monolithic or built up, usually on a rectangular or square plan. **2.** Incorrect term for a free-standing memorial column, such as *Railton's Nelson Column in Trafalgar Square, London (1840–3), and such usage should be avoided. **3.** Pier, as in a *nave-arcade in a church, although some commentators find such usage obsolete and confusing.

pillow capital. *Capital resembling a cushion, or a cubic capital with the lower angles rounded off, as in *Romanesque architecture.

pillowed. *Pulvinated, like a cushion, as in a pulvinated *frieze bowing outwards in section.

piloti. One of several columns or *piers supporting a building over the ground, thereby elevating the lowest floor to the first-floor level and leaving an open space below the building. It was a favourite device of Le *Corbusier.

Jeanneret-Gris (1973–7)

pinacotheca. Building or room in which pictures are exhibited.

pine. *Finials and *pendants in the form of pine-cones, commonly found in Classical architecture. They sometimes resemble the skins of pineapples.

Pineau, Nicolas (1684–1754). French architect. He trained under *Boffrand and *Hardouin-Mansart and settled in Russia where he worked for Tsar Peter the Great (1672–1725), for whom he designed a richly decorated *cabinet in Peterhof (1721) and his tomb (1725). Returning to Paris in 1726, he designed several *hôtels (e.g. Hôtel Mazarin (1740)). He was best known as a creator of exquisite *Rococo interiors, for which many drawings survive, some being publicized in J.-F. *Blondel's *De la distribution des maisons de plaisance et de la décoration des édifices en général* (1737–8), while Batty *Langley also reproduced some of his designs for console-tables.

Deshairs (1914); Gallet (1972); Hautecœur (1950); Jervis (1984); Kalnein and Levey (1972); Kimball (1980); Lewis and Darley (1986)

Pingusson, Georges-Henri (1894–1980). French architect and town-planner. After a period with Le *Corbusier he evolved his *Style Paquebot* (Packet-Boat style) based on Corbusier's ideas likening a passenger-ship to a floating apartment-block. His main achievements were in the reconstruction of war-damaged areas in the Moselle, Lorraine, and Saar regions, where he planned various industrial towns. He designed the Hôtel Latitude 43, St-Tropez (1931–2), the Pavillon des Artistes Modernes, Paris Exposition (1937—destroyed), and (with Corbusier), the satellite town of Briey-en-Forêt (1953–9). His masterpiece is the Mémorial des Martyrs de la Déportation, at the east end of the Île de la Cité, Paris (completed 1962), a severe underground crypt of great emotional impact, commemorating French victims of the Nazi terror.

Curl (1993); personal knowledge

pinnacle. Ornamental pyramid or cone, the terminating feature of a *buttress, *parapet-angle, *spire, *turret, etc., often ornamented with *crockets.

Piper, Fredrik Magnus (1746–1824). Swedish architect who introduced the English *Picturesque movement (having made studies of Stourhead and other gardens) to Sweden in his landscaped gardens at Haga and

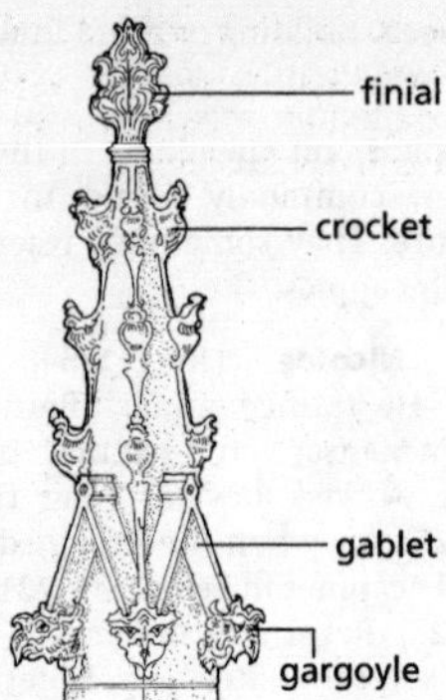

pinnacle. Second Pointed crocketed type with finial. (*After JJS*)

Drottningholm, near Stockholm, with their exotic *fabriques (1780–1820).

Woods (1996)

Piranesi, Giovanni Battista (1720–78). Venetian engineer, architect, and engraver of genius, he had a profound effect on *Neoclassicism with his *Sublime images of Rome. He produced a series of *Invenzioni* (Inventions or Imaginary Views) featuring *Carceri* (Prisons) in *c*.1745 that were powerful images of vast spaces and huge structures, the whole drawn to a terrifyingly megalomaniac *scale. Then came the first of the *Vedute di Roma* (Views of Rome—*c*.1749) that revealed a Rome so overpoweringly Sublime that the plates became influential throughout Europe, but especially among the young architects of the French Academy in Rome. His speculative archaeology led him to design fantasies of considerable originality. Appearing in the *Opere Varie* (Various Works—1750), they had a great influence on architects like de *Wailly and the *Peyres. His antiquarian studies led to the *Antichità Romane* (collected in four volumes in 1756), which made his reputation: it was designed to illustrate constructional techniques and the Roman ornamental vocabulary. He took sides in the Graeco-Roman controversy, assuming leadership of the pro-Roman cause against the pro-Greek camp of *Winckelmann. In 1761 he published *Della Magnificenza ed Architettura de' Romani* (On the Magnificence and Architecture of the Romans) designed to show the supremacy of Roman architecture, followed by *Il Campo Marzio dell' Antica Roma* (The Campus Martius of Ancient Rome—1762), dedicated to Robert *Adam, containing a complex fantasy of urban buildings purporting to show Rome under Constantine, but far grander than anything created by Ancient Romans.

In *c*.1760 he reissued the *Carceri* plates, reworked, and with some new images, that struck chords among advanced Neoclassicists, notably George *Dance the Younger, *Desprez, and others. The *Parere su l'Architettura* (Thoughts on Architecture—1765) argued for a free use of Roman exemplars for the creation of a new style. In 1763, Pope Clement XIII (1759–69) commissioned him to design a new Papal high-altar for the Church of San Giovanni in Laterano, Rome. Piranesi developed his scheme to include the replacement of the whole structure to the liturgical east of the *transept by a gigantic top-lit apsidal sanctuary, but it was never implemented. Around this time he remodelled the Church and Headquarters of the Knights of Malta, redesigning the façade of Santa Maria Aventina (1764–6—for which detailed account-books have survived), Rome, and creating a formal *piazza one wall of which was embellished with a series of decorative *stelai. The altar and lighting inside the church were elaborately contrived. This Aventine commission was Piranesi's only building, but it is one of the most powerful and original of C18.

His *Diverse Maniere d'adornare i cammini* (Different Ways of Decorating Chimney-Pieces—1769) was his most important publication for interior design and the applied arts. It was to be significant in the development of Adam's chimney-pieces and *Etruscan style, and also provided *Bélanger and other French architects with motifs. The book contained a series of chimney-pieces in the 'Egyptian' style that provided many ideas for the *Egyptian Revival and indeed influenced aspects of the *Art Deco style of the 1920s and 1930s. The book also illustrated Piranesi's Egyptianizing painted interiors of the *Caffè degl'Inglesi* (English Café), Rome (*c*.1768). *Vasi, Candelabri, Cippi, Sarcophagi* (Vases, Candelabras, Markers, and Sarcophagi) was brought out between 1778 and 1791 and had an enormous following among designers of the *Empire and *Regency periods. It publicized many of the artefacts he had been designing and making since at least the 1760s, as well as Piranesi's activities as a restorer of Antiquities. In spite of his antipathy towards all things Greek, he made superb drawings of the Greek *Doric temple at *Paestum, which were acquired by *Soane. The engravings made from these, published in 1778 as *Différentes Vues... de Pesto*, had a tremendous impact on the *Doric and *Greek Revivals, and were brought out partly under the aegis of Piranesi's son, **Francesco** (1758–1810), who played an important part in completing his father's later works, notably the *Vasi*... Francesco Piranesi published a map of the Villa Adriana, Tivoli (1781), and added new plates to further editions of the *Vedute*, *Antichità*, and other works. Most importantly, he issued a massive collection of graphic works in 27 volumes (1800–7) as well as a three-volume set of *Antiquités de la Grande Grèce* (1804–7) based on his father's work at Pompeii.

Calvesi (1967); Curl (1994); Focillon (1967); Fraser, Hibbard, and Lewine (1967); Nyberg and Mitchell (1975); Placzek (1982); Reudenbach (1979); Rykwert (1980); Scott (1975); Wilton-Ely (1972, 1978, 1978*a*); Wittkower (1975)

Pisano, Andrea (d. 1348/9). Master-Mason of the *Duomo* (Cathedral), Florence, from *c.*1337, where he probably designed the *niche *stage of the *campanile. He was Master-Mason at Orvieto Cathedral from 1347.

Trachtenberg (1971); White (1987)

Pisano, Nicola (*c.*1225–*c.*1280). Tuscan sculptor and architect, he influenced the evolution of *Gothic architecture in Italy. He made the hexagonal Pisa *Baptistery *pulpit (1255–9) and may have designed the second-storey arcade of the Pisa Baptistery (1260–85). Responsible for the large octagonal pulpit in Siena Cathedral (1265–8), he may have played some part in the design of the west front, commenced by his son, **Giovanni Pisano** (*c.*1248–*c.*1314), Master-Mason there, who built the lower section of the west front (1287–96). Giovanni became *capomaestro* (master-builder) of Pisa Cathedral in 1299, where he designed the pulpit (1302–11).

White (1987)

piscina. (*pl.* **piscinae**). Stone basin connected with a drainage channel for carrying away the water used in rinsing the vessels employed at Mass and washing the hands of the Priest. It was usually set in a *niche in the south wall of a *chancel in a church to be near the altar, though it was sometimes carried on a short *colonnette or projected from the face of a wall. Piscinae, which were often equipped with a *credence-table for the vessels, were frequently ornamented with an elaborate canopy, sometimes designed as part of the *sedilia installation, in which case the ensemble was called *prismatory*.

piscina. C14 example, Church of St Michael, Cumnor, near Oxford. (*After Parker*)

pisé. Type of wall-construction using stiff clay or earth (*pisé de terre*), kneaded, sometimes mixed with gravel, rammed between two lines of wicker-work or boards that are removed as the material hardens.

pitch. **1.** Amount of slope given to any part of a roof. **2.** Tenacious black resinous substance, hard when cold, becoming a thick viscid semi-liquid when heated: it is obtained as a residue from the boiling or distillation of tar. It is used in its melted form to protect external timbers, e.g. *clap-boarding or *weather-boarding, and, if mixed with ground chalk, sand, and tar, for surfacing roads, etc.

pitched stone. Stone with its rough face framed by bevelled edges, so a type of *rustication.

pitch-faced. Piece of stone with all the edges of the face trimmed down to true *arrises all round so that joints are tight and fine, the remaining part of the face projecting from the margins and left rough. A type of *rustication.

Pite, Arthur Beresford (1861–1934). English architect and draughtsman who is remembered for several distinguished buildings and his architectural fantasies. He worked with John *Belcher for 14 years, also carrying on his own practice and making drawings for *The Builder*. With Belcher he designed the Hall of the Incorporated Chartered Accountants, Great Swan Alley, City of London (1889–90), where sculpture (by Harry Bates (1850–99), Sir William Hamo Thorneycroft (1850–1925), and others) was fully integrated with the Mannerist *Baroque architecture. The building was to be influential, mainly in Great Britain and Germany, mostly Berlin. Pite's *Mannerism was best seen at 44 and 82 Mortimer Street, London (1890s), where the precedents were in the work of *Michelangelo in Florence.

On his own account, Pite travelled in the Middle East, and, influenced perhaps by *Bentley's designs for Westminster Cathedral, London (1895–1903), designed the Parish Hall and Christ Church, North Brixton, London (1901–5), in which *Byzantine, Mannerist, and *serliana motifs are synthesized in one centralized composition. He also designed the Anglican Cathedral at Kampala, Uganda (1913–18), and churches at Entebbe, Uganda, Bucharest, and Warsaw, among other places.

Like other architects of the period, Pite turned to *Neoclassicism, and his office for the London, Edinburgh, and Glasgow Assurance Company, Euston Square, London (1906–19), was the first scholarly *Greek Revival building in London since the 1850s, using a variation on the *Bassae Order of C. R. *Cockerell. One of his most interesting works, Pagani's Restaurant, Great Portland Street, London (1904–5), with its ceramic-covered *façade, was destroyed in the 1939–45 war. He also designed the rumbustious Piccadilly entrance to Burlington Arcade, London (1911–30).

Dixon and Muthesius (1985); Gray (1985); Service (1975, 1977)

plain tile. Roofing-tile of burnt clay or *concrete, called a *common* or *flat* tile.

plaisance, pleasance. Secluded part of a landscaped garden laid out with lawns, shady walks, trees, and shrubs, as well as architectural elements such as statues on *pedestals, *urns, arches, fountains, pools, *gazebos and seats.

plaiting. Intertwining ornament like a plait, such as the *guilloche on a *band, hence *plait-band*.

plan. Horizontal *section through a building showing the arrangement of rooms, etc. It is a drawing that represents an object in horizontal projection, to *scale, as distinct from those representing vertical sections or *elevations, and might show an exterior of an object as seen from above, as in a roof-plan. *See* axial, bay, cell, centre, double pile, end, entry, F-plan, H-plan, hall, longhouse, open-hall, solar, Wealden.

Fraser Reekie (1946)

planceer. **1.** Underside of any projecting member, e.g. a *cornice. **2.** Any *soffit.

plank. Long flat piece of timber, thicker than a *board*. *Plank-walling* is a *timber-framed structure, the spaces filled by planks. *See* stave.

Alcock, Barley, Dixon, and Meeson (1996)

plantain. Architectural ornament consisting of a wide flat leaf.

planted. Anything wrought on a separate piece of stuff, then attached by gluing, nailing, etc., as a moulding round a *panel.

plaque. Metal plate, stone *slab, or any kind of tablet, usually inscribed, fixed to (*planted) or inserted in a wall-surface, pavement, etc., as a memorial, ornament, etc.

plaster. Pasty composition of soft and plastic consistency spread or daubed on a surface where it hardens. It was traditionally made of burnt limestone (quicklime or calcium oxide) mixed with sand, water, and hair to provide a smooth surface fit to receive decorations. *Plaster of Paris* is lime sulphate (gypsum) deprived of its natural water-content by heat, ground to a fine powder and mixed with water to form a paste: it sets quickly, expanding at the time of setting, a peculiarity that not only makes it useful for filling cracks, but causes it to take sharp and delicate impressions from a mould. *See* stucco.

McKay (1957); Nicholson (1835); Papworth (1852)

plat. Plan, drawing, or instructions for building.

platband. **1.** Flat, square-faced *band, *fascia, or *string, with a projection less than its height, e.g. *architrave or *fasciae. **2.** Actual or ornamental *lintel. **3.** *Fillet or *stria separating the *flutes on the *shaft of a Classical column. **4.** Broad step. **5.** *Stair-landing. **6.** 'Flat' arch or soldier arch. *See* arch.

plate. Any timber, e.g. a wall-plate, laid horizontally on *posts or walls serving as the support for other timbers above, its main functions being to provide fixings and to distribute the loads. Types include:

aisle-plate: *wall-plate* of a *timber-framed *aisled building;

arcade-plate: plate on top of the *posts of an arcade in an aisled building;
collar-plate: plate resting on collars. Called *collar-purlin*;
crown-plate: plate in a *crown-post* roof, carried on the *crown-posts* and bearing the *collars*. Also called *collar-purlin*;
head-plate: beam at the top of a timber-framed wall or internal partition;
jetty-plate: wall-plate of a lower timber-framed storey on which the joists of the jettied floor above rest, really a type of *head-plate*;
sole-plate: short piece of timber (*sole-piece*) set at 90° to the face of a wall, supporting the foot of a rafter and *ashlar-piece;
wall-plate: plate on top of a timber frame or load-bearing wall on which the roof-timbers rest.

Alcock, Barley, Dixon, and Meeson (1996); Sturgis *et al.* (1901–2)

plated parquet. *Parquet floor with pieces of contrasting wood laid in patterns.

plate-girder. *See* girder.

plate-glass. High-quality, strong, thick glass cast in sheets and polished, widely available after the 1830s.

plate-rail. Narrow grooved shelf *planted high on the walls of a room to support and display china plates.

Plateresque. Intricate highly decorative style of early C16 Spanish architecture, supposedly resembling fine silversmith's work, with enrichments derived from Classical, *Gothic, *Moorish, and *Renaissance sources, extravagantly applied to the walls of late-Gothic buildings and generally unrelated to any expression of construction.

Kubler and Soria (1959); Lewis and Darley (1986); Osborne (1970)

plate-tracery. *See* tracery.

Platt, Charles Adams (1861–1933). American architect and landscape-designer. His *Italianate gardens of the 1890s and early 1900s were famous. He advised on the designs of the *campuses of Dartmouth, Johns Hopkins, and Rochester Universities, and was architect of the Freer Gallery, Washington, DC (1913–18). His earlier architectural work was informed by *Classicism, and especially by Italian exemplars, but he also designed in a restrained *Georgian *Colonial style, as with the John T. Pratt House and Garden, Glen Cove, NY (1910–13). He designed the campus and buildings for the University of Illinois, Champaign-Urbana, Ill. (1919–30—a particularly fine work in which axes, symmetry, and composed vistas are fully developed), the Coolidge Auditorium, Library of Congress, Washington, DC (1925), and the Deerfield Academy, Conn. (1930–2), among many other distinguished works. He published *Italian Gardens* in 1894, based on his travels in 1892, and a monograph on his work in 1913.

Platt (1913); van Vynckt (1993)

Plaw, John (*c*.1745–1820). British architect and artist. He is remembered primarily for *Rural Architecture: or Designs for the Simple Cottage to the Decorative Villa* (1785 and five other editions), *Ferme Ornée or Rural Improvements* (1795, 1813), and *Sketches for Country Houses, Villas, and Rural Dwellings* (1800, 1803). These publications were among the first of the cottage and villa pattern-books that were so influential in the early part of C19. He designed a remarkable circular house on Belle Isle, Windermere, Westmorland (1774–5—burned 1996), based on the *Pantheon; St Mary's Church, Paddington (1788–91); and several buildings in Charlottetown, Prince Edward Island, Canada, where he settled from 1809 (e.g. the Legislative Building and Court-House (1811)).

Colvin (1995); Darley (1975); *DNB* (1917); Kalman (1994)

Playfair, James (1755–94). Scots architect, noted as the author of *A Method of Constructing Vapour Baths* (1783). The latest *Neoclassicism was evident in the powerful Graham *mausoleum at Methven, Perthshire (1793), a Greek temple-front *engaged to *rusticated masonry. At Cairness House, Aberdeenshire (1791–7), his interesting design included a hemicycle of offices, *primitive *Doric columns, and an extraordinary *Egyptian Revival Billiard Room. He also designed Farnell Church, Angus (1789–1806), in a precocious *Gothic style.

Colvin (1995); Crook (1972*a*); Curl (1994)

Playfair, William Henry (1790–1857). Younger son of James *Playfair, he was a pupil of William *Stark, and later worked in the offices of '*Wyatt and *Smirke' (probably Benjamin Dean and Robert, respectively) before returning to Scotland (1818) to plan the Calton Hill Estate, Edinburgh, where he built Blenheim Place, Brunswick Street, Brunton Place, Carlton Terrace, Elm Row, Hillside Crescent, Leopold Place, Montgomery Street, Regent Terrace, Royal Terrace, and Windsor Street.

From 1820 he also designed Royal Circus, Circus Place, and Circus Gardens (1821–3).

For the next three decades, with *Burn and Gillespie *Graham, he was a leading architect in Scotland and gave Edinburgh some of its finest buildings. These include the splendid *Greek Revival (with slight Egyptianesque touches) Royal Institution (1822–35—now Royal Scottish Academy), the unfinished Greek *Doric National Monument, Calton Hill, based on the *Parthenon (1824–9—with C. R. *Cockerell), the Surgeons' Hall, Nicolson Street (1830–2), the *Greek Revival Dugald Stewart Monument, Calton Hill (1831—based on the *Choragic Monument of Lysicrates, Athens), the *Jacobethan Donaldson's Hospital (1842–54), the scenographic *Gothic Free Church College (1846–50), and the Neoclassical National Gallery of Scotland (1850–7). He also designed a number of monuments, including those to Ferguson of Raith, Kensal Green Cemetery, London (1842), the pyramidal Rutherford Tomb, Dean Cemetery, Edinburgh (*c.*1852), and his own tomb in the Dean Cemetery (*c.*1857). Many of his drawings survive in Edinburgh University Library.

Colvin (1995); Crook (1972*a*); *DNB* (1917); Gifford, McWilliam, and Walker (1984); Macaulay (1975); Youngson (1966)

Plečnik, Jože (1872–1957). Slovenian architect who was one of the most distinguished and imaginative designers working in the Classical tradition in C20. Born in Ljubljana, he trained under Otto *Wagner in Vienna from 1895 and became friendly with *Kotěra. He was appointed Secretary of the *Sezession in 1901, having established his own office in the Austrian capital in 1900, where he designed the Weidmann House, Hietzing (1902), and an office and apartment-block for the wealthy Johannes Zacherl in Vienna (1903–5), both of which showed strong Wagnerian influences.

His greatest work of the Vienna years was the *Heiliggeist* (Holy Spirit) Church, Herbststrasse (1908–13), where he used *reinforced concrete, and created a stripped Neoclassical exterior and a *crypt employing crystalline, almost *Expressionist forms. He was nominated by the Vienna Academy to become Professor of Architecture in succession to Wagner (1911), but his appointment was blocked at Court on the grounds that the 'first school' of the Austro-Hungarian Empire should not be headed by a Slovene. Plečnik was invited to head the Prague School of Applied Arts (1911), and with the independence of Czechoslovakia (1918), began work on the restoration, adaptation, and gardens of Prague Castle as the Presidential Residence (1920–30), where his free use of Classical motifs and allusions constitutes one of the loveliest ensembles in all Europe. He also designed the Presidential *Villa at Lány (1920–30), and the powerful Neoclassical Church of the Sacred Heart, Prague (1928–31).

In 1920 Plečnik accepted the Headship of the Architecture Department of the University of Ljubljana, Slovenia (newly part of Yugoslavia), retaining a post as Honorary Architect to the City of Prague. He created a series of masterpieces of *Neoclassicism in Ljubljana, including the Church of St Francis, Šiška (1926–7), various structures along the river, including bridges and *colonnades in the Markets Area (1930s), the Slovene National Cemetery, Žale (1937–40), National and University Library (1939–42), and various other buildings. The Church of the Ascension, Bogojina (1925–7), employs the toughest of *primitive *Doric columns inside, and the Church of St Michael in Barje, Ljubljana (1937–40), has a powerful *campanile and a most elegant interior featuring much timberwork. Throughout his designs from 1920 until his death are free interpretations of the Greek *Orders, including derivations from the *Aeolian and *Ionic forms, suggesting an archaic quality of great power. Unlike those who used the Classical language with literalness, Plečnik demonstrated what infinite variety and emotional expressiveness could be achieved by developing and extending possibilities. He deserves to be ranked among the greatest architects of C20.

Achleitner (1986); Andrews, Bentley, and Gržan-Butina (1983, 1986); Borsi and Godoli (1986); Burkhardt, Eveno, and Podrecca (1989); Krečic (1993); Prelovšek (1979, 1997); Svácha (1995)

plinth. **1.** Plain, continuous projecting surface under the *base-moulding of a wall, *pedestal, or *podium *quadra, connecting the architectural member with the ground or floor. **2.** In the Classical *Orders, the low plain block under the base-mouldings of a column, pedestal, or *pilaster. **3.** Any monumental support for a statue, etc. **4.** Base-course of a wall supporting an *off-set, as when a wall diminishes in thickness. **5.**

*Eaves-course. **6.** *Abacus (*plinthus) of the Greek *Doric Order.

plinth-block. Simple rectangular base-block against which *architrave, *plinth, *skirting, etc., stop to avoid awkward junctions. It is set e.g. between the floor or ground and the architrave, and is the same height as the plinth or skirting.

plinth-course. Top, moulded course of a *plinth, or the continuous course of masonry comprising the plinth.

plinthus. Term used by *Vitruvius for the *abacus of the Greek *Doric *Order.

Pliny (Plinius) the Younger (Caius Plinius Caecilius Secundus) (AD 62–*c*.116). Roman politician, orator, and writer. From AD 106 he was superintendent of *aqueducts, but his chief importance in architecture lies in his descriptions of his Laurentine and Tuscan *villas that have exercised the imaginations of scholars ever since.

Ruffinière du Prey (1994)

ploughshare twist. Warped *web of a *Gothic *vault framed by a diagonal rib and stilted wall-rib, occurring when the wall-ribs are sprung from a higher level than the diagonal ribs, as when accommodating *clear-storey *lights. As the web is distorted, twisted like a ploughshare, it is also called a *plowshare vault*.

Plumet, Charles (1861–1928). French architect. He drew on medieval and early French *Renaissance themes for his architecture, but used *Art Nouveau forms in his shop interiors and furniture design. He often employed *polychromy, *loggie, and *bay-windows in his façades. His apartment-blocks at 67 Avenue Malakoff (1895), 50 Avenue Victor Hugo (1900), and 15 and 21 Boulevard Lannes (1906), all in Paris, are typical of his work. He designed the Château de Chênemoireau, Loire-et-Cher, France (1901), and an office block at 33 Rue du Louvre, Paris (1913–14). Chief Architect of the Exposition International des Arts-Décoratifs, Paris (1924–5), he had an influence on the *Art Deco style.

Badovici (1923); Borsi and Godoli (1978); Tschudi-Madsen (1967)

Pluralism. 1970s' term defining aspects of *Post-Modernism, and suggesting the drawing on various styles and motifs in eclectic compositions.

Jencks (1973*a*); Papadakis (1989); Robins (1985)

pluteus. Low wall closing the gap between Classical columns, about one-third the height of the columns, in a *colonnade.

pneumatic architecture. Inflatable structures such as balloons and airships have been known for many years, but not until 1917 was the first patent for *pneumatic architecture* taken out by Frederick William Lanchester (1868–1946), brother of H. V. *Lanchester, and manufacturer of the Lanchester motor car. With the development (1940s) of the *Radome* (Radar Dome) to provide protection for microwave antennae, the manufacture of pneumatic structures evolved further, structural stability being achieved by air or gas pressure on some kind of membrane or bag, so pneumatic structures are usually curved, often domes or cylinders, or some other form compatible with pressurized construction. Pneumatic buildings have been used for exhibitions, covering stadia, and even formwork for *concrete structures. Pneumatic architecture has been proposed by Cedric *Price, *Haus-Rucker-Co, and the *Utopie Group, among others.

Dent (1971); Herzog (1977); Price (1971)

Poccianti, Francesco Gurrieri Pasquale (1774–1858). Italian architect. He worked with Giuseppe Cacialli (1778–1828) and Gaspare Maria Paoletti (1727–1813) in the rebuilding of the Villa del Poggio Imperiale, near Florence (begun 1806), with its strong *Neoclassical façade. He designed the circular Sala d'Elci, Biblioteca Laurenziana, Florence (1816–41), and also the huge system of *aqueducts, filters, and water-works in and around Livorno for which he built his masterpiece, the Cisternone (1829–42), one of the most successful realizations of the severe *Neoclassicism of *Ledoux and his contemporaries. A plain façade is fronted by an octastyle unpedimented *portico, and over is half a *Pantheon dome, built in section, as it were, with the interior *coffers showing.

Meeks (1966); Middleton and Watkin (1987)

podium. **1.** Continuous *pedestal with *base, *plinth, *die, and *cornice, such as used to support an *Order of Classical columns high above ground level in a monumental building. In Classical architecture it is essentially the platform on which stood a Roman temple or a *peristyle of columns supporting a dome. **2.** Platform around the arena of a Roman *amphitheatre over which the seats of the nobility were placed.

Poelaert, Joseph (1817–79). Belgian architect, influenced by *Schinkel and *Visconti, who became Brussels City Architect in 1856. He designed the Colonne du Congrès (1850–9) and other buildings in Brussels, but his greatest work was the *Sublime *Beaux-Arts *Baroque Palais de Justice (1866–83), a vast *pile of pyramidal composition crowned by a massive *dome. Some of the internal public spaces have an *Antique Roman grandeur worthy of *Piranesi. He also designed the *Neo-Gothic Notre-Dame de Laeken, Brussels (1854–72), completed by von *Schmidt of Munich.

Hitchcock (1977); Watkin (1986)

Poelzig, Hans (1869–1936). Berlin-born German architect. After working under *Häring in the 1890s, early in the new century he was appointed (through the influence of *Muthesius) Professor (and Director from 1903) at the Academy of Arts and Crafts in Breslau (now Wrocław), where he also had his own office until 1916. While in Breslau he designed the *Expressionist Water Tower and Exhibition Hall, Posen (now Poznań), Silesia (1910–11), a heptagonal steel-framed structure filled with panes of *herringbone brickwork. Other buildings included an office-block in Breslau (1911–12), with horizontal window-strips (anticipating the *International Modernism of the following decades), and a Chemical Factory and Workers' Housing at Luban (now Luboń, Poland—1912).

He became City Architect of Dresden (1916–20) and Professor at the Technische Hochschule there, where he produced several fantastic Expressionist designs (unrealized), including a proposal for the *Festspielhaus* (Festival Theatre), Salzburg (1919–20), but built the Dresden Gasworks (1916). In 1918 he joined the *Novembergruppe, followed by *Arbeitsrat für Kunst, became Chairman of the *Deutscher Werkbund in 1919, and was an active participant of Der *Ring. In 1919, for Max Reinhardt (1873–1943), he converted the Schumann Circus into the Expressionist *Grosses Schauspielhaus* (Great Playhouse), Berlin, with stalactite vaults in the auditorium. By 1920 he had moved to Berlin, heading a studio in the Academy of Arts there and, from 1923, teaching at Berlin-Charlottenburg: his pupils included *Eiermann and *Wachsmann. Among his other buildings the Capitol Cinema, Berlin (1925), the Sigmund Goeritz Factory, Chemnitz (1927), a house for the *Weissenhofsiedlung, Stuttgart (1927), Broadcasting House, Berlin (1930), and the gigantic I. G. Farben Administrative Building, Frankfurt-am-Main (1928–31), the last showing certain tendencies towards a *stripped *Neoclassicism, deserve mention.

Heuss (1939); Killy, Pfankuch, and Scheper (1965); Lampugnani (1988); Lane (1985); Poelzig (1954); Posener (1970, 1992); Sharp (1967); Tafuri and Dal Co (1986)

point. To fill up and carefully finish, as in the mortar joints in brickwork or masonry. Its purpose is to preserve the material from the weather as well as create an aesthetically pleasing effect.

Brunskill (1990)

point-block. High apartment-building with the circulation and services in the central core and the residential areas grouped around it on several storeys.

pointed. 1. Type of rough masonry finish made by a pick or pointing tool, with a *picked face (i.e. with only the coarsest projections removed) also called *pecking*. **2.** Type of arch. **3.** With a capital P, 'Pointed' refers to the *Gothic style, divided into *First, *Middle, *Second, and *Third Pointed, the last most commonly called *Perpendicular in England. **4.** Brickwork or masonry the joints of which have been raked out and *pointed* with mortar.

pointel, poyntell *or* **poyntill. 1.** Pavement formed of small tiles laid diagonally in patterns rather than forming a picture, as in *mosaic. **2.** Pavement of lozenge-shaped tiles.

pointing. Process, material, or completed finish of mortar-joints in brickwork or masonry. *See* brick, pointed.

Brunskill (1990)

polis. Ancient Greek city (πόλις) or city-state. It is commonly found combined with other words as a nickname for a town, e.g. Linenopolis for C19 Belfast, and with prefixes such as *metro-* it means a capital, mother-city, chief centre, or major city. *See* acropolis, necropolis.

Wycherley (1962)

Polish parapet. Type of *Renaissance *parapet ornamented with *blind *arcades, *aedicules, *pilasters, *pedestals, *pediments, *pyramids, etc., concealing the roof, commonly found in Poland. Good examples are the Cloth Hall, Kraków (1555–8), the Town Hall, Chełmno on the Vistula (1567–72), and two remarkable façades in the Market Square of Kazimierz Dolny (1615 and 1635).

Zachwatowicz *et al.* (1952)

Polish parapet. Based on an example from Kazimierz Dolny. (*After JJS*)

Polk, Willis Jefferson (1867–1924). American architect. He worked for several architects (including van *Brunt) before establishing himself in San Francisco in 1890, from which he produced a rich array of architecture, the best of which was influenced by the work of *McKim, Mead, & White. He assisted *Burnham in preparing the plan for San Francisco (1904–5), and in the years up to the 1914–18 war his buildings were modelled on Burnham's polished Classical manner. However, Hallidie Building, San Francisco (1917–18), was different, having a fully glazed *curtain-wall hung from the main framed structure, reckoned to be among the very first examples of its kind, although ornamented in the manner of *Sullivan with vaguely *Art Nouveau details.

Journal of Architectural Historians 30 (1971) 323–9; Longstreth (1979); Woodbridge (1976)

Pollack, Johann Michael *called* **Mihály** (1773–1855). Step-brother of Leopoldo *Pollack, he settled in Budapest in 1798 where he had a successful career as a *Neoclassical architect, making occasional forays into *Gothic as in Pécs Cathedral (from 1805). He designed the Theatre and Assembly Room, Budapest (finished 1832), the Ludoviceum (1828–36), and the National Museum (1836–45).

Baedeker, *Austria* (1929); Middleton and Watkin (1987); Zádor (1960, 1985)

Pollack, Leopoldo (1751–1806). Vienna-born architect who settled in Milan in 1775 and assisted *Piermarini on the Palazzo Ducale. He designed the Villa Casati, Muggiò, and the Villa Villani Rocca-Saporini, called La Rotonda, Borgovico, each of which has an elliptical salon. His greatest work was the Villa-Reale Belgioioso, Milan (1790–6), the elevations of which are derived from *Gabriel's frontages to the Place de la Concorde, Paris (1753–75), although the *Order used by Pollack was *Ionic rather than *Corinthian. He also laid out the gardens in a *Picturesque style.

Meeks (1966); Mezzanotte (1966); Middleton and Watkin (1987)

Pollini, Gino (1903–91). *See* Figini.

polos. 1. Cylindrical headdress of a *caryatid. **2.** Greek centring-pin or dowel used when jointing the drums of the column-shafts.

Dinsmoor (1950)

polychromy. Elaborate architectural decoration using many colours, as in Ancient Greek architecture, and revived by *Hittorff, *Bindesbøll, and others. *Structural polychromy* is where the colour is not applied after construction, but is provided by the brick, stones, or tiles used in the building: it was a feature of the mature *Gothic Revival.

Gwilt (1903); Papworth (1852); Sturgis *et al.* (1901–2); van Zanten (1977)

Polyclitus the Younger (*fl.* 370–336 BC). Ancient Greek architect and sculptor. He designed the theatre and *tholos (*c.* 350 BC) at Epidaurus, which had very beautiful *Corinthian capitals on the internal circle of fourteen columns, and a *Doric *Order for the external *peristyle.

Burford (1969); Dinsmoor (1950); Lawrence (1983)

polyfoil. With many *foils, also *multifoil*.

polygonal masonry. Made of smooth many-sided (i.e. with more than four angles or sides) stone blocks closely fitted together. In Antiquity called *opus polygonum. It is also known as *cyclopean* or *pelasgic* masonry.

polystyle. Composed of many columns.

polytriglyphal. *Doric *frieze with more than one *triglyph per *intercolumniation.

pomel. *See* pommel.

Pomerance, Ralph (1907–95). American architect. He founded his New York practice in 1933 and was responsible for a great number of buildings, including several much-admired houses in the *International Modernist style, notably his own house at Cos Cob, Conn. (1940). He built the Swedish Pavilion at the New York World's Fair (1939) in collaboration with *Markelius. A single-storey house at Croton-on-Hudson, NY (1940–1), received acclaim, and he later built many hospitals, research centres, and university buildings. Also interested in housing, he was involved in several housing-authority schemes at Greenwich, NY.

Information provided by Mrs Pamela Pomerance Steiner

pommel, pomel. 1. As *crop. **2.** Ball, boss, knob, or knot terminal used as a *finial for *pinnacles, pyramidal roofs, etc.

Pompeian. The Roman town of Pompeii was buried by deposits of volcanic ash when Mount Vesuvius erupted in AD 79, thus partially preserving it for posterity. Rediscovered in 1748, it began to be excavated from 1755, and the architecture, artefacts, interior decorations, motifs, and details uncovered there and at *Herculaneum and Stabia had a profound effect on *Neoclassical design after they began to appear in publications. Pompeian schemes of *frescoed wall-decorations were to provide the main themes, including the bold blacks, greens, reds, and yellows, with finely drawn borders and *grotesques that became an important part of the *Etruscan or *Pompeian* style in C18. *Gell and *Gandy's *Pompeiana* (1817–19 with later editions) was an important source, as were *Die schönsten Ornamente und merkwürdigsten Gemälde aus Pompeji, Herkulaneum und Stabiae* (The Finest Ornaments and Remarkable Paintings from Pompeii, Herculaneum, and Stabia—1828–59) by Wilhelm Zahn (1800–71), and *Les Ruines de Pompeii* (1809–38) by Charles-François Mazois (1783–1826). Among architects who used the Pompeian style were Joseph *Bonomi at Great Packington, Warwickshire (*c.*1782), and *Schinkel at Schloss Glienecke, near Berlin (1824–9), but these are only two examples of many. *See* Neo-Grec.

Gell and Gandy (1852); Lewis and Darley (1986); Osborne (1970)

Pontelli, Baccio (1450–92). Florentine architect, sculptor, and engineer celebrated for his impressive fortifications, e.g. those at Ostia, with massive *machicolations (1483–6). He worked on the Ducal Palace at Urbino with F. di *Giorgio Martini and *Laurana from 1479, and settled in Rome *c.*1481, where he may have designed (or influenced the design of) San Pietro in Montorio (1481–94) and the Palazzo della Cancellaria (1480s). The enormous body of work attributed to him by *Vasari seems to be spurious.

Fiore (1963); Heydenreich and Lotz (1974)

Ponti, Gio (1891–1979). Italian architect and designer. His earliest work was first influenced by the *Sezession movement and then by the clear rational architecture of Otto *Wagner. He was founder-director of the influential architectural journal *Domus* (1928–79), which is perhaps his greatest legacy, and demonstrated his *Rationalist and Classicist credentials with the School of Mathematics, University of Rome (1934). In 1936–9 he built the Montecatini Building, Milan, in which standardization played a major role (a second block was completed in 1951). His work after the 1939–45 war abandoned all traces of Classical formalism, as in the Pirelli Tower, Milan (1956–8—with *Nervi and others), one of the first *skyscrapers to deviate from the rectangular slab-form common in *International Modernism. Other buildings include the Bijenkorf Shopping Centre, Eindhoven, The Netherlands (1967—with others), and the Museum of Modern Art, Denver, Colo. (1972—with others).

Emanuel (1994); Piacentini (1930); Ponti (1990); van Vynckt (1993)

Ponting, Charles Edwin (1850–1932). English church architect, who also designed several secular buildings, including the *Caroléan *Edwardian Town Hall, Marlborough, Wiltshire (1901–2), with a prominent use of the *Ipswich window. He designed the handsome St Mary's Church, West Fordington, Dorchester, Dorset (1910–12), probably his best work.

Gray (1985)

Pont Street Dutch. Revival of Flemish and North-German *Renaissance architecture in the 1870s and 1880s featuring high, stepped, shaped, and ornamented *gables, rubbed and moulded brickwork, *terracotta, and other elements derived from a similar revival in Belgium and The Netherlands, but given particular opulence in England by Sir Ernest

*George and his firm in the Kensington and Knightsbridge areas of London, hence the reference to Pont Street. Also called *Northern Renaissance Revival.

Curl (1990); Gray (1985); Lever and Harris (1993); Lewis and Darley (1986)

Ponzio, Flaminio (*c*.1559–1613). From Lombardy, he settled in Rome in the mid-1580s, where he designed a number of late-*Mannerist buildings. The Pauline Chapel at Santa Maria Maggiore (1605–11) is much enriched with coloured marbles, gilded *stucco, and inlaid work. He reconstructed part of the Palazzo Borghese, where the long elevation is probably his (1605–13), and designed the noble Acqua Paola fountain on the Janiculum (1612). Further reconstruction was planned by him at San Sebastiano fuori le Mura, including the elegant west front (1609–13), and at *Raphael and *Peruzzi's Sant'Eligio degli Orefici (1602).

Hibbard (1962, 1971)

Pop architecture. 1. Architecture *popular* with the public. **2.** Buildings the forms of which suggest their function, such as a shoe-shaped shoe-shop; also called 'bizarre', 'illegitimate', 'programmatic', or 'roadside' architecture. *Venturi has included 'autoscape' architecture of the large illuminated advertisements common in the USA in the pop-architecture category. **3.** Work influenced by popular architecture, or responding to *High Tech and *Archigram-promoted images.

Andrews (1985); *Architectural Review*, 132/785 (July 1962), 43–6; Jencks (1979); *RIBA Journal*, 72/3 (Mar. 1965), 142–3; Venturi, R. (1966, 1996); Venturi, R., Scott Brown, and Izenour (1977); Vostell and Higgins (1969)

Pope, John Russell (1874–1937). American architect. A disciple of *McKim, Mead, & White, he trained at the École des *Beaux-Arts, Paris (1897–9), began practice in 1903, and produced some fine Neoclassical buildings of national and international importance, including the Temple of the Scottish Rite, Washington, DC (1910—a vast pyramidal composition alluding to the *Mausoleum at Halicarnassus), and his two best-known works, the Jefferson Memorial (1937–43) and the National Gallery of Art (1937–41), both in Washington, DC (and both completed by Otto Eggers (1882–1964) and Daniel Paul Higgins (1886–1953)). He also designed the Sculpture Hall, Tate Gallery, London (1937–8), and the Duveen Sculpture Gallery, British Museum, London (1937–8). The latter contains the sculpture from the Parthenon in Athens (the 'Elgin Marbles').

Bedford (1998); van Vynckt (1993)

Pope, Richard (*fl. c*.1442). English freemason. He designed the tower of Dunster Church, Somerset, and was probably master-mason at St John's Hospital and Sherborne Abbey, Sherborne, Dorset (1440s): if this is the case, he was responsible for the design of the noble *choir at the Abbey. **Thomas** and **Walter** Pope (probably related) worked at Exeter Cathedral in the first half of C15.

Harvey (1987)

Pöppelmann, Matthäus Daniel (1662–1736). Born in Herford, Westphalia, he settled in Dresden in 1686, and from 1704 was in charge of palace rebuildings for Friedrich Augustus II (the Strong), Elector of Saxony (1694–1733) and King of Poland (1697–1704 and 1709–33). His masterpiece is the *Zwinger, Dresden (1711–20), a space surrounded by single-storey galleries linking two-storey *pavilions and a gateway of extraordinary inventive *Rococo vitality. Part *orangery, part grandstand, part *nymphaeum, and part gallery, it was intended to enhance Augustus's status by allusions to Roman *theatres, *fora, and *thermae. Richly embellished with architectural sculpture by Balthasar Permoser (1651–1732), the Zwinger was to be part of a vast new palace designed by Pöppelmann that showed influences from *Hildebrandt and Carlo *Fontana, but the *Kronentor* (crown-gate) (1713) of the Zwinger was derived from plates 60 and 100 in *Pozzo's *Prattica della Perspettiva*, published in a German edition in 1708.

The 'Indian' Schloss Pillnitz, upstream on the Elbe (1720–3), has charming *Chinoiserie elements, including the roofs, and is one of the largest C18 European buildings in an oriental style. Pöppelmann was in charge of the alterations at the Dutch (later Japanese) Palace, Dresden, from 1715, but was gradually edged out by *Longuelune whose flat elevations were a marked contrast to Pöppelmann's work, and the job was completed by de *Bodt. From 1722 Pöppelmann worked on the alterations and rebuilding of the hunting-lodge, Moritzburg, again completed by Longuelune, and widened the C12 bridge over the Elbe at Dresden by cantilevering raised footpaths from the edges of the old structure. Iron railings were used to reduce the weight. The bridge (1727) is seen to best advantage in Bernardo Bellotto's (1720–80) views of the city. Pöppelmann designed the *Dreikönigskirche* (Three Kings Church), Dresden-Neustadt (1731–9), built by Georg *Bähr, who altered the project as it was under construction. His last works were with Longuelune, preparing designs for a huge palace in Warsaw, not realized.

Asche (1978); Gurlitt (1924); Heckmann (1972, 1986); Hempel (1965); Marx (1989); Pevsner (1960); Sponsel (1924)

poppy. Long recognized as an opiate, the seed-pods and flowers of the poppy were commonly used in *Neoclassicism as ornaments in bedrooms and funerary architecture, being associated with the twin brothers, children of Night, Sleep and Death. Poppy motifs were much used by *Percier and *Fontaine in *Empire design, and they were common elements of *Art Nouveau.

poppy-head. Carved *finial of a C15 or early C16 *Gothic *bench- or *pew-end, resembling the *fleur-de-lys, but often richly decorated with figures, foliage, fruits, and flowers. The term derives from the French *poupée*, meaning a bunch of hemp or flax tied to a staff, and has nothing to do with the *poppy.

Parker (1850); Sturgis *et al.* (1901–2)

porch. 1. Covered place of entrance and exit attached to a building and projecting in front of its main mass, such as the south porch of a medieval church, often with a room over it. **2.** Interior volume serving as a vestibule. **3.** *Transept or side-*chapel in a church. **4.** *Cloister, *colonnade, *Galilee, *narthex, *portico, *stoa, or *verandah (all with columns). A columned porch or portico usually has a *pediment and resembles a *temple-front.

Porden, William (*c.*1755–1822). English architect, he trained under James *Wyatt. He was employed by the Prince of Wales (later King George IV (1820–30)), for whom he designed the stables, riding-house, tennis-court, and other buildings at the Royal Pavilion, Brighton, Sussex (1804–8), where he introduced the *Hindoo style (he is said to have worked with S. P. *Cockerell). He had a reputation as an architect of *Gothic buildings, and he built the competent Eaton Hall, Cheshire (1804–12—demolished in the 1870s).

Colvin (1995); Conner (1979); Roberts (1939)

Porphyrios, Demetri (1949–). Greek-born architect. Believing that architecture must be firmly grounded in building technology and craftsmanship, using sustainable natural materials, he has not been afraid of returning to the ancient principles of 'firmness, commodity, and delight' as essentials. Among his major works is Pitiousa Village, Spetses, Greece (completed 1993), where he created a built environment firmly based on traditional European urban patterns, with a series of two-storey compact houses drawing on Neoclassical precedents, including the works of *Schinkel. His mastery of architectural language based on developing tradition has been further demonstrated in Chepstow Villas, London (1988), Belvedere Village, Ascot, Berkshire (1989), and the Residential Buildings, Theatre, and Library, Selwyn College, Cambridge (1995). At Magdalen College, Oxford, his accommodation block (1991–6) uses a C17 architectural language, but the adjoining theatre (1995–9) is crisply Neoclassical.

Active in the academic world, he has published several books dealing with architectural history, *Classicism, *Rational architecture, and his own work.

Personal communication

porta. Monumental gate of a Roman city or fortress, or any grand entrance (e.g. to a church).

Porta, Giacomo della (*c.*1533–1602). After *Vignola's death (1573) this Lombardy-born architect became the leading exponent of *Mannerism in Rome. He supervised the building of *Michelangelo's buildings on the Capitoline Hill, completing (with some changes) the Palazzo dei Conservatori (1561–84) and building the Palazzo del Senatore (1573–1602). His intervention also included modifications to the Piazza and to the great flight of steps. He finished Vignola's noble church of *Il Gesù*, designing the façade (1571–84) which was to be of enormous importance as a precedent for Jesuit churches in Italy, Central Europe, and Latin America. The great barrel-*vault (1577) was his design too. As Architect of St Peter's from 1573, he built the western arm of the *crossing, the minor domes (1578–85), and Michelangelo's designs for the elevation to the garden. He collaborated with Domenico *Fontana on the building of the great dome (1586–92) to which he gave a more pointed profile (like that at Florence Cathedral) than that intended by

Michelangelo. He also completed the chapels of Gregory XIII (1574–8) and Clement VIII (1594–1601).

He designed the north and south fountains in the Piazza Navona (1574–8) and many other Roman fountains, the Church of Santa Maria ai Monti (from 1580), the façades of San Luigi de' Francesi (1580–4) and (probably) Santissima Trinità de' Monti (*c.*1583), the naves of San Giovanni de' Fiorentini (1582–1602) and Sant'Andrea della Valle (1591—completed by *Maderno, 1608–23), and the Villa Aldobrandini, Frascati (1594–1603—completed by Maderno and G. *Fontana). His output was enormous, and he is of singular importance as a transitional figure between the *Cinquecento and the evolution of *Baroque.

Ackerman (1986); Heydenreich and Lotz (1974); Murray (1969); Onofrio (1957, 1963); Tiberia (1974); Wittkower (1964)

portal. **1.** Entrance doorway or gateway of monumental character, especially if emphasized by a stately architectural treatment making it the principal architectural motif of a façade. **2.** Lesser doorway to a gateway-tower. **3.** *Portico. **4.** Arch over a gateway or doorway. **5.** Structural frame consisting of two stanchions connected to beams that are fixed at angles corresponding to the roof-pitch and rigidly joined at the apex and the tops of the stanchions. **6.** Frame of a gate. **7.** Small lobby in a room defined and separated off from the rest of the apartment by *wainscoting.

portcullis. Strong door in a fortified medieval gateway, sliding vertically, normally a grating heavily framed of wood strengthened with iron, with pointed iron bars at the bottom. Usually kept in the raised position, it could be dropped suddenly when required for reasons of defence. *See* yett.

porte-cochère. **1.** Doorway to a house or *court, often very grand, large enough to permit wheeled vehicles to enter from the street. **2.** Erroneous term for a projecting canopy or porch large enough to admit carriages.

Porter, John (*fl.* 1423–d. 1465). English master-mason. He worked at Lincoln Cathedral before being called to York *Minster by *c.*1542. He was the architect of the handsome *steeple of the Parish Church at Louth, Lincolnshire (*c.*1431).

Harvey (1987)

portico. Covered *ambulatory consisting of a series of columns placed at regular intervals supporting a roof, normally attached as a colonnaded *porch to a building, but sometimes forming a separate structure (e.g. James *Stuart's *Doric Temple at Hagley, Worcestershire (1758)). The volume so created can be open or partly enclosed at the sides, stand before a building such as a temple, and often have a *pediment over the front, in which case it is described as a *temple-front. A Classical portico can be defined with precision. The main types are:

engaged: with the portico not standing in front of the building but with the ensemble of columns, entablature, and pediment embedded in the front wall, i.e. *engaged;

in antis: with the columns set in a line between the projecting walls enclosing the sides of the portico, i.e. between the *antae* (see anta) of the walls;

prostyle: with the columns set in a line standing before and detached from the front wall of the building behind.

In both *in antis* and *prostyle* porticoes the design is further defined by the number of columns visible on the front *elevation: the commonest varieties are *distyle* (2, usually *in antis*); *tristyle* (3); *tetrastyle* (4); *pentastyle* (5); *hexastyle* (6); *heptastyle* (7); *octastyle* (8); *enneastyle* (9); *decastyle* (10); and *dodecastyle* (12). Even numbers of columns are usual to ensure a void on the central axis for the door. A portico with 4 columns standing in front of the main wall of the building behind it is *prostyle tetrastyle*, and if it has 2 set between the antae of flanking walls it is *distyle in antis*. *See* colonnade, intercolumniation.

Curl (1992)

Portland. Type of white oölitic limestone from Portland, Dorset, often quarried to provide the *ashlar façades of public buildings from the time of *Wren. *Portland cement*, which is made from chalk or limestone and clay, has a light grey colour, is classed as an *artificial hydraulic cement*, and was invented in *c.*1821. It is very strong and can be used under water.

Gwilt (1903); Nicholson (1835); Papworth (1852)

Portland, Nicholas (*fl.*1394–*c.*1406). English master-mason. He worked at Salisbury Cathedral from 1394, where he stabilized the *crossing-tower, and from 1396 to 1405 he was engaged on the rebuilding of St John's

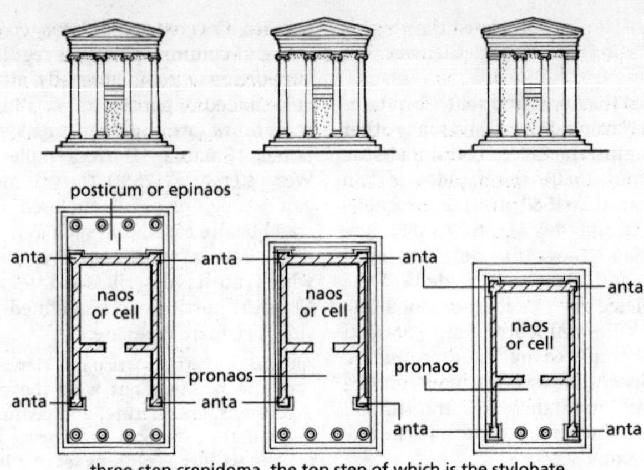

portico. Column arrangements in temples. (*left*) Amphi-prostyle tetrastyle, or amphi tetra-prostyle, i.e. with four columns standing in front of and at each end of the cell. (*middle*) Prostyle tetrastyle, or tetra-prostyle, i.e. with four columns standing in front of the cell. (*right*) Distyle *in antis*, i.e. with two columns standing in front of the cell set between the antae terminating the projecting cell walls. It is an arrangement found only in small temples, tombs, or shrines.

Hospital, Winchester, Hampshire, where he seems to have been responsible for the main block, apart from the chapels.

Harvey (1987)

Portman, John Calvin, jun. (1924–). American architect/developer known for his huge urban buildings, including the Peachtree Center, Atlanta, Ga. (from 1961), with the Hyatt Regency Hotel (1967–71) and the revolving 'Polaris' restaurant on top. He created a new type of hotel with large interior *atria, containing shops, and employed glass-enclosed capsule-like lifts that ran up and down the façades. Ample use of planting, water, and lighting effects have made his work popular.

Emanuel (1994); Portman and Barnett (1976)

Portoghesi, Paolo (1931–). Italian architect who established his practice in Rome in 1958 and formed a partnership with Vittorio Gigliotti in 1964. He was among the first modern Italian architects to turn to historical precedents and away from so-called *Rationalism, drawing on *Gothic, *Baroque, *Art Nouveau, and various other styles to influence his buildings, though without direct quotations. The Church of the Sacra Famiglia, Salerno (1968–74), incorporated complex interlocking circular elements, while the Thermal Bath, Montecatini (1989), has *ogee-shaped structural elements like trees supporting the roof, a motif he also employed at the Mosque and Islamic Centre, Rome (1976). Other works include the Civic Square, Poggioreale, Sicily (1986–91), the vigorous Casa Baldi, Rome (1959), and the elliptical staircase, Palazzo Corrodi, Rome, which acknowledges Baroque precedents. Recognizing the inhibiting effects of *International Modernism, he has been identified with *Post-Modernism, and has stated he is in search of a lost architecture. No mean scholar, he has published many works on *Renaissance, Baroque, and C19 periods: his books include studies of *Borromini, *Guarini, *Michelangelo, *eclecticism, and Post-Modernism.

Emanuel (1994); Meyhöfer (1995); Portoghesi (1956, 1960, 1964, 1966, 1968, 1970, 1982, 1983, 1990)

Portzamparc, Christian de (1944–). French architect responsible for the Cité de la Musique Ouest, La Villette, Paris (1984–95), won in competition in 1985, reckoned by some to be one of the better late-C20 buildings in the capital. Other works include the Paris Opéra Dance School, Nanterre (1983–7), the tower at Lille-Europe Railway Station, an extension to the Palais des Congrès, Paris, and a Court House, Grasse, France (all early 1990s).

Amsoneit (1994); Curtis (1996); Jodidio (1995*a*)

Posener, Julius (1904–96). German-born architect. He moved to Paris in 1929 where he became an architectural critic for the influential journal *L'architecture d'Aujourd'hui* before emigrating to Palestine in 1935 where he worked in *Mendelsohn's office. He returned to Berlin in 1961 and produced many books on architecture as well as making a reputation as a lecturer and promoter of architecture. He was an authority on *Expressionism and especially on *Poelzig.

Posener (1970, 1979, 1992)

post. Any vertical structural timber supporting a *lintel or providing a firm point of lateral attachment, as in a gate or fence. The term is usually applied to a main vertical member in *timber-framed construction or in roof-*trusses. Types of post include:

aisle-post: as *arcade-post*;
arcade-post: post in an arcade, in the sense of a division in a *timber-framed building consisting of a series or row of posts;
crown-post: vertical timber on a *tie-beam*, or sometimes on a *collar*, supporting the *crown-plate*;
king-post: vertical timber on a *tie-beam* or *collar* rising to the roof apex to support a *ridge*-piece: without a ridge-piece it is a *king-strut*;
queen-post: one of two posts on a *tie-beam* supporting *plates* or *purlins*.

Alcock, Barley, Dixon, and Meeson (1996); Sturgis *et al.* (1901–2)

Post, George Browne (1837–1913). American architect and engineer who contributed to the origin and development of the early *skyscraper from *c.*1870. Architecturally eclectic and competent, he was more noted for his grasp of planning and structural principles. He designed many hotels, and evolved the modern hotel-plan with a bath in each room (e.g. Statler Hotel, Buffalo, NY (1911–12)). He contributed to the design of the Equitable Life Assurance Building, New York (1868–70), one of the very first structures designed with a lift or elevator, thus helping to develop the planning and organization of tall buildings. The Western Union Building, New York (1873–5—demolished), was, with *Hunt's Tribune Building, one of the earliest skyscrapers, essentially Classical in its arrangement of a *base, middle section (*shaft), and crowning element (*cornice). His Stock Exchange, New York (1901–4), probably his best-known building, has a handsome *Corinthian pedimented front typical of his early C20 Classical style. Other works included the Vanderbilt House (1882–93), *New York Times* Building (1888–90), Pulitzer Building (1889–90), and St Paul Building (1897–9), all in New York. The New York Produce Exchange (1881–5) was constructed with a complete metal structure within outer load-bearing walls.

Condit (1961); Placzek (1982); Sturgis (1971a); Whiffen and Koeper (1983)

Post, Pieter (1608–69). Dutch architect. He assisted van *Campen at the Mauritshuis, The Hague (1630s), the Town Hall, Amsterdam (1648–55), and supervised the building of the Noordeinde Palace, The Hague (1640s), a dignified and serene building. Post designed the Huis ten Bosch, The Hague (1645–7—influenced by *Palladio's Villa Capra, Vicenza), with its cruciform domed *Oranjezaal* (Orange Hall); the *Waaghuis* (Weigh-House) for Leiden (1657–9), with a *Tuscan *Order on the rusticated base; and the handsome Town Hall, Maastricht (1656–64). His refined Palladian style can also be seen at the De Onbeschaamde House, 123–5 Wijnstraat, Dordrecht (1650–3). He may have designed the town-plan and several buildings at Mauritsstad, Brazil (1630s). His style had considerable influence on English architects, notably *May, and he also built in Germany.

Blok (1937); van den Boogaart (1979); Kuyper (1980); Placzek (1982); Rosenberg, Slive, and Ter Kuile (1966)

post-and-beam. *Timber frame consisting of *posts supporting horizontal *beams.

post-and-lintel. Simple form of construction involving *posts carrying horizontal *beams or *lintels, as in *timber-framed work or in *columnar and *trabeated architecture. Ancient Egyptian and Ancient Greek architecture was of this type, using stone.

post-and-pane, post-and-pan. *Timber-framed building with exposed *posts, the intervals between them (*panes) filled with plaster, bricks, etc. Obsolete term for *box-frame construction.

postern. **1.** Subsidiary door or gate, as in military architecture, where it is very modest and remote from the main gate. **2.** In domestic architecture, it is set near a larger one, such as a door for pedestrians next to a *porte-cochère. **3.** Rear gate in a city wall used for sorties in war.

postiche. Addition to a work of architecture after it has been finished; especially something inappropriate.

posticum. **1.** Open vestibule in an *Antique Classical temple, to the rear of the *cella or *naos, also called epinaos or *opisthodomus, corresponding to the *pronaos, really part of a back *portico. **2.** Inferior, subsidiary, or rear door in an Antique Roman house.

Post-Modernism. Style or styles in architecture and the decorative arts that were a reaction to the *Modern Movement, *Modernism, *International Modernism, and the dogmas developed especially at the *Bauhaus. Some have held it began in 1972 when *Yamasaki's Pruitt-Igoe Modernist housing, St Louis (1958), was destroyed after its inhabitants refused to live there any more. Essentially, Post-Modernism (known variously as *P-M*, *PoMo*, or *the Post*) has been connected with a loss of faith in what were once regarded as certainties (e.g. progress, rationality, science) and with a growing acceptance of a bewilderingly large palette of images, signs, and products promoted on a scale never experienced before in the history of the world, which some (e.g. *Venturi) have welcomed as offering 'complexity' and 'contradiction' in design. In the 1960s *Pop architecture began a tendency away from so-called *Rationalism towards *Pluralism, and later architecture drew on elements that were not themselves archaeologically or historically accurate, but made vague references to once-familiar motifs such as the *Orders, *cornices, *pediments, etc., often brashly and crudely used. Post-Modernism seems to have heralded a major change in Western culture, even a new condition permeating every walk of life, involving cynicism, fragmentation, ill-digested *eclecticism, and what some (e.g. F. Jameson) have called the 'cultural logic of late capitalism'. The label has been loosely stuck to various architects moving away from the Modern Movement and *High Tech architecture, even though their various responses widely differ. Among architects identified with Post-Modernism are *Bofill, *Farrell, *Graves, *Hollein, Philip *Johnson, Charles *Moore, and *Stern, but these have all produced work of great individuality, and the label is far too comprehensive to have much meaning other than to refer to architecture of the late C20 that has rejected the certainties of the International Modern style.

Appignanesi (1986); Jencks (1977, 1980, 1980*a*, 1987, 1988*a*); Klotz (1988); Lampugnani (1988); Lyotard (1984); Portoghesi (1983); Rowe and Koetter (1984); Venturi, R. (1966, 1996); Venturi, R., Scott Brown, and Izenour (1977)

Potain, Nicolas-Marie (1713–96). French architect. He worked under *Gabriel, and between 1754 and 1770 helped to lay out the Place Louis XV (now Place de la Concorde), Paris. He published a work on the *Orders of Architecture in 1767, and designed the *basilican church of St-Louis, St-Germain-en-Laye in 1764, completed 1823–4, as well as the Cathedral at Rennes (1764–1844), both of which were important examples of *Neoclassicism in church design.

Braham (1980); Middleton and Watkin (1987)

potence. **1.** T- or Γ-shaped element like a crutch, used as a gibbet, support, etc. **2.** Type of cross, known more correctly as *a potent cross* (*see* cross). **3.** Revolving structure inside a circular *columbier, *columbarium, or *dovecote, to enable all the niches to be reached with ease. **4.** Any *stud supporting a bearing.

Potter, Edward Tuckerman (1831–1904). American architect. He was influenced by *Viollet-le-Duc's arguments for using iron in architecture, and by English *High Victorian *Gothic. Indeed, his First Dutch Reformed Church, Schenectady, NY (1861–3), demonstrates how far *Ruskin's writings had affected him, and has certain aspects reminiscent of *Deane & *Woodward's Oxford Museum (1855–60). The Church of the Good Shepherd, Hartford, Conn. (1867–9), was a good example of his *polychrome style. One of his most interesting designs was the polygonal Nott Memorial, Schenectady, NY (1858–78), with its exposed iron interior structure, domed *clearstorey, and *Moorish Gothic polychrome exterior. He often employed cast-iron *piers in his churches which resemble the work of English *Rogue Goths. His Mark Twain House, Hartford (1873–81), was much influenced by Northern-French domestic architecture, and by the *Stick style, designed with polychromy well to the fore.

Landau (1979); Placzek (1982); Summerson (1968)

Potter, William Appleton (1842–1909). American architect, the half-brother of E. T. *Potter, he designed several outstanding US equivalents of *High Victorian *Gothic, including the Chancellor Green Library, Princeton University (1871–3), the South Congregational Church, Springfield, Mass. (1872–5—with bold *polychrome treatment and a vast *wheel-window of plate-*tracery, probably his finest work), and the Custom

House, Evansville, Ind. (1875–9). He took Robert Henderson Robertson (1849–1919) into partnership in 1875, and thereafter the firm's work was strongly influenced by that of H. H. *Richardson, notably at the round-arched Alexander Hall, Princeton University (1891–4). The Pyne Library at Princeton (1896–7) and the First Reformed Dutch Church, Somerville, NJ (1895–7), are *Gothic Revival. For his houses he drew on the English *Domestic Revival as well as on American *Colonial exemplars.

Landau (1979); Placzek (1982); Summerson (1968)

poupée. *See* poppy-head.

Powell & Moya. British architectural firm established by (Sir) Arnold Joseph Philip Powell (1921–) and John Hidalgo Moya (1920–94) in 1946 to carry out the Pimlico Housing Scheme (now Churchill Gardens), London (1946–62), much influenced by the *International Modernist style. Their 'Skylon' vertical monument for the *Festival of Britain (1951—destroyed) received much publicity at the time. Subsequently they designed hospitals, swimming-baths, and other buildings including the Chichester Festival Theatre (1961–2). The firm's much-admired work at Oxford and Cambridge included a building at Brasenose College, Oxford (1962), the Cripps Building, St John's College, Cambridge (1965–7), Blue Boar *Quad and Picture Gallery, Christ Church, Oxford (1966–8), Magpie Lane Annexe, Corpus Christi College, Oxford (1968–9), Wolfson College, Oxford (1972–4), and New Buildings, Queen's College, Cambridge (1976–8). They were also responsible for the Museum of London, London Wall, Barbican, London (1974–6), the Queen Elizabeth II Conference Centre, Broad Sanctuary, Westminster, London (1985), and major redevelopment of the Great Ormond Street Hospital, London (1994).

Booth and Taylor (1970); Emanuel (1994); Maxwell (1972); Mills (1953)

Poyet, Bernard (1742–1824). French architect who studied with de *Wailly. He designed the vast circular Hôpital Ste-Anne, Paris (1788), heavily influenced by *Durand's theories, but never completed, and the huge *portico to the Palais Bourbon, now the Chambre des Députés, Paris (1806–8). He was involved in the urban design schemes around the rebuilt and modified Fontaine des Innocents, Paris, in the 1790s, and also in the proposals for the Rue des Colonnes, eventually built to designs by *Vestier (1793–5).

Braham (1980); Etlin (1984); Middleton and Watkin (1987)

Pozzo, Andrea (1642–1709). Italian lay Jesuit who was one of the greatest *Baroque painters of ceilings that exploited illusion and high drama. His best works were in Sant'Ignazio, Rome (1684–94—perhaps the finest ceiling of *quadratura ever created), San Francesco Saverio, Mondovi (1676–9), and the Palais Liechtenstein, Vienna (1704–8). In 1702 he settled in Vienna, where he created a sumptuous *Baroque interior at the *Universitätskirche* (University Church—1703–9). His work was influential in disseminating the Baroque style in Central Europe, especially through his *Perspectiva pictorum et architectorum* (Perspective in drawing and architecture—1693–1700), which was translated into several languages, including Chinese. He designed several churches and altars, e.g. the stupendous altar of Sant'Ignazio, *Il Gesù*, Rome (1695–9), the high-altar of the *Franziskanerkirche* (Franciscan Church), Vienna (1706), the Church of Sant'Ignazio, Dubrovnik, Croatia (1699–1725), and the Cathedral, Ljubljana, Slovenia (1700–5).

Carboneri (1961); Feo (1988); Kerber (1971); Marini (1959); Placzek (1982); Portoghesi (1970); Wittkower (1982)

pozzolan, pozzolana, pozzuolana, puzzolana. Variety of volcanic sand with burnt granules resembling powdered brick: it is a siliceous or siliceous and aluminous material which, when mixed with hydraulic limes and water, becomes a cement-like compound capable of setting under water. It was used in Antiquity. Artificial pozzolan was made by calcining fire clay and adding lime, sand, and water, with fine brick dust.

Gwilt (1903); Nicholson (1835); Papworth (1852); Sturgis *et al.* (1901–2)

Prachatitz, Hans von (*fl.* C15). Architect who completed the south tower and handsome spire of the *Stephansdom* (St Stephen's Cathedral), Vienna (1349–1433), one of the most perfect of German *Gothic *steeples. He may also have designed the stone altar-canopy in the north aisle (*c.*1437).

Baedeker, *Austria* (1929)

Prairie School *or* **style.** Architectural style in the Mid-West USA named after a design of

Frank Lloyd *Wright published in *The Ladies' Home Journal* (1901). Typical of the Prairie style are Wright's Robie House, Oak Park, Chicago, Ill. (1909), and *Greene & Greene's Gamble House, Pasadena, Calif. (1908–9). It was characterized by low-pitched roofs with very wide overhanging *eaves, a strongly emphasized horizontality, large hearths separating parts of the living area, and the use of traditional materials.

Brooks (1972, 1984)

Prandtauer, Jakob (1660–1726). One of the greatest of Austrian *Baroque architects, related to *Munggenast, he designed the huge Benedictine Abbey of Melk (1702–38), high on a cliff-top on the south bank of the Danube, some 50 miles west of Vienna. *Pevsner called it the 'Durham of the Baroque', a judgement with which there can be full agreement, for the architectural composition vigorously exploits the splendours of its site and makes a *Sublime impact. The handsome Abbey Church, with its twin towers and high *cupola, is placed between two wings of the Abbey buildings (in which are the Library and *Kaisersaal* (Emperor's Hall)) projecting in front of its façade and converging towards the cliff-edge. Set on a *podium, these wings are linked in front of the Church by a mighty arch (its form derived from a *serliana), and appear to embrace the *court before the church.

Prandtauer and Munggenast built the Parish and Pilgrimage Church (*Wallfahrtskirche*) of Sonntagberg (1706–32), with a façade perhaps influenced by *Fischer von Erlach's *Dreifaltigkeitskirche* (Holy Trinity Church), Salzburg. He designed the *Marmorsaal* (Marble Hall) and very fine open stair at C. A. *Carlone's Monastery of St Florian (1718–24), completed Carlone's Pilgrimage Church of Christkindl near Steyr (1788–9), collaborated with Matthias Steinl and Munggenast at the Church at Dürnstein (from 1717), and transformed the Cathedral of St Pölten (from 1722) into a Baroque building. He also built several houses in St Pölten.

Bourke (1962); Brucker (1983); Feuchtmüller (1960); Hempel (1965); Millon (1961); Pevsner (1960); Sedlmayr (1930)

Pratt, Sir Roger (1620–85). English gentleman-architect. He was one of the C17 pioneers of *Classicism in England, having studied Continental architecture during extended tours and a period of residence in Rome, and was one of the Commissioners appointed to supervise the rebuilding of the City of London after the fire of 1666. He seems to have intended to write an architectural treatise, for his notebooks contain some rules for the guidance of architects as well as on the building of country-houses. He designed four *astylar country-houses: Coleshill, Berkshire (*c*.1650–62—demolished 1952), Kingston Lacy, Dorset (1663–5—altered by *Barry 1835–9), Horseheath Hall, Cambridgeshire (1663–5—demolished 1792), and Ryston Hall, Norfolk (1669–72—altered by *Soane 1786–8). The first truly Classical house in London, Clarendon House, Piccadilly (1664—destroyed), was also by him. All his houses were planned on the *double-pile system with a hall and saloon on the central axis. His work influenced later designs, notably Belton House, Lincolnshire (1685), and Denham Place, Buckinghamshire (1688).

Colvin (1995); *DNB* (1917); Gunther (1928); Summerson (1993)

precast concrete. *Concrete cast in moulds before being incorporated in a building.

Pre-Columbian architecture. Architecture of the Americas before their discovery by Columbus in C15.

predella. 1. *Gradino* or step at the top of an altar supporting the altar-piece. It may have panels describing events in the lives of Saints and be associated with a *triptych. **2.** Platform or steps on which an altar stands. **3.** Ledge or ledges surmounting an altar to hold the Crucifix, painting, etc.

prefabrication. Manufacture of parts of a building in a factory before they are brought to the site for incorporation in the finished structure. *Industrialized buildings have as many prefabricated parts as possible.

Klotz (1986)

Prentice, Martin (*fl.* 1459–87). English carpenter. He worked at King's College Chapel, Cambridge (1459–62), and became Master-Carpenter there in 1480, when construction was resumed. He was responsible for the design of the timber roof above the vaulting.

Harvey (1987)

presbytery. 1. Part of a church in which the high-altar stands, at the east of the *choir. It is often raised above floor-level, and is used exclusively by those who minister in the services of the altar. **2.** Priest's house.

prestressed concrete. Type of *reinforced *concrete, in which steel bars are replaced by steel cables within ducts disposed to enable the tension areas of the concrete to be compressed by stretching them before loading. It allows for accuracy as well as economical use of both concrete and steel.

Preti, Francesco Maria (1701–84). Italian architect, he developed *Palladio's laws of *harmonic proportion by further elaborating upon the system. He also numbered among his works the completion of the huge Palladian Villa Pisani, Strà, Italy, and various outbuildings, begun in 1720 to designs by Count Giovanni Frigimelica (1653–1732).

Baedeker, *Northern Italy* (1913)

Price, Bruce (1843–1903). American architect. He designed around 40 vigorous *Shingle-style houses at Tuxedo Park, Rockland County, NY (1885–90), with pronounced axes, which influenced Frank Lloyd *Wright and the *Prairie School. His Windsor Station, Montreal, Canada (1888–9), was in a round-arched style strongly influenced by the work of H. H. *Richardson, but his Banff Springs Hotel, Alberta (1886–8), and Château Frontenac Hotel, Quebec (1892–3), drew on wider ranges of eclecticism (especially from French and Scots exemplars) for their highly effective compositions. One of his last works was the Gould House, Lakewood, NJ (1897–8), a magnificent essay in *Classicism.

Kalman (1994); Scully (1971); Sturgis (1977)

Price, Cedric (1934–). English architect, in practice in London since 1960. With Frank Newby (1926–) and Lord Snowdon (1930–) he designed the Aviary at London Zoo (1961), and himself projected the Fun Palace for Joan Edensor Littlewood (1885–1977) at Stratford East, London, one of the most influential (though unrealized) *High Tech projects. Indeed, Price's influence has been widespread, and he has been an important figure in the ideological debate through his ideas and writings. He has advocated that buildings should be constructed of light-weight, easily dismountable parts in the interests of flexibility and ease of demolition, and he has taken an anti-aesthetic stance, believing that permanence, monumentality, and preservation in architecture are indefensible. An enthusiastic believer in the benefits of technology, he has been an important influence on many architects, notably *Archigram and *Rogers. *See* Pneumatic architecture.

Anderson (1968); Emanuel (1994); Landau (1968); Price (1971, 1984)

Price, Sir Uvedale (1747–1829). Author of *Essay on the Picturesque* (1794) and important influence on the cult of the *Picturesque (which he defined as a separate aesthetic category, identifiable as distinct as *Burke's categories of the *Beautiful and the *Sublime). He also influenced the development of 'natural' English landscape-design, as well as R. Payne *Knight, *Nash, and *Repton.

Ballantyne (1997); *DNB* (1917); Hussey (1967*a*); Summerson (1993); Watkin (1982*a*)

pricket. 1. Metal spike on which to stick a candle, as on a *hearse, with a rimmed plate fixed below it into which the wax could run. **2.** Top of a *spire.

prick-post. 1. A secondary *post in a *timber-framed structure or a *truss, e.g. queen-post. **2.** Short post in a post-and-rail fence between the two standards into which the horizontal rails are mortised: it is pointed and driven into the ground, giving additional stiffness.

priest's door. Entrance to the *chancel of a church, usually on the south side.

Primaticcio, Francesco (1504/5–70). Italian painter, sculptor, and architect who was important as a bringer of *High Renaissance and *Mannerist design to Northern Europe. He worked with *Giulio Romano in Mantua (1526–31), and then at *Fontainebleau from 1532 for *François Ier where he designed the Aile de la Belle Cheminée (1568) and other parts, including the heavily rusticated *Grotte de Pins* (*c.*1543) in a style reminiscent of Giulio Romano's work. He also designed the Valois *mortuary-chapel at St-Denis with obvious influences from *Bramante, da *Sangallo, and *Vignola (1563—destroyed). *Vasari credited him with the first *stucco ornament and the first frescoes of any account in France: certainly his combination of paintings with stucco decorations was very influential.

Blunt (1982); Chilvers, Osborne, and Farr (1988)

primitive. Type of architecture mnemonic of the very beginning, the earliest, original, crude, or fundamental. Suggested by roughness and squatness (as in the primitive *Doric from *Paestum with its exaggerated *entasis), it was a feature of advanced late-C18 *Neoclassicism.

Curl (1992); Vidler (1990)

Primitive Hut. During C18 many architectural theorists, notably M. de *Frémin (1702), J.-L. de *Cordemoy (1706), and M.-A. *Laugier (1753), argued for a greater rationalism in architectural design, and especially for the structural and honest use of the Classical *Orders, avoiding superfluous fripperies and excessive surface-decoration. Laugier, notably, proposed a cleansing of design, a re-examination of first principles, and a study of the origins and sources of architecture which he saw as evolving from a simple structure of four tree-trunks, still growing and rooted in place, with *lintels composed of sawn logs, and branches providing an elementary pitched roof. This was perceived as the prototype for all great architecture, including the Classical temple, so leading to archaeological endeavours to find the earliest and original exemplars of Classical buildings where the Orders were used for construction rather than applied or *engaged for decorative effects. Inevitably this led to studies of *Antique remains, notably those of Ancient Greek architecture: *Paestum, for example, provided models of tough, uncompromisingly *primitive architecture, and the Primitive Hut was regarded as the original form, a *type, so a potent ideal in *Neoclassicism.

Council of Europe (1972); Curl (1992); Middleton and Watkin (1987); Vidler (1990)

principal. Inclined timber in a roof-*truss supporting a *purlin but not functioning as a common *rafter.

principal beam. Main tie-beam of a roof-*truss supporting the smaller inclined structural timbers.

principal brace. Brace under the *principal rafter.

principal rafter. *Principal serving as a common *rafter.

principals of a hearse. *Turrets or *pinnacles on the central *posts of a *hearse.

print room. Interior decorated with prints (topographical engravings, etc.) arranged and stuck to the walls, surrounded by decorative painted or printed frames of wallpaper.

Prior, Edward Schroeder (1852–1932). English *Arts-and-Crafts architect. Articled to Norman *Shaw, he was a founder-member of the *Art-Workers' Guild. The Barn, Exmouth, Devon (1895), was the first of a series of houses on X-shaped plans (*butterfly plans) that were widely copied at the time. He designed St Andrew's, Roker, Monkwearmouth, Sunderland (1906–7), one of the best churches of the Arts-and-Crafts movement, containing work by Burne-Jones, Ernest *Gimson, and others. A. Randall *Wells assisted Prior at St Andrew's, and also at Voewood (later Home Place), Kelling, Holt, Norfolk (1904), a pioneering house constructed of *concrete faced with *flints, and with in-situ concrete on which the boards of the *formwork are expressed. Prior published *History of Gothic Art in England* (1900) and other works.

Garnham (1995); Gray (1985); Pevsner, *Buildings of England, Devon* (1989), *County Durham* (1985), and *North-East Norfolk and Norwich* (1962)

prismatic billet. *Billet-moulding resembling rows of prisms in series, alternate rows staggered, in *Romanesque architecture.

prismatic ornament. C16 and C17 ornament consisting of simple geometric repetitive forms in low relief, including pyramidal and chamfered *rustication, *jewelled *strap-work, and *lozenges. It returned in favour in the early C20.

Lewis & Darley (1986)

prismatic rustication. *See* rustication.

prismatory. *See* sedile.

prison. Gaol, jail, or place for confining criminals and segregating them from society. Prisons provided scope for rational planning to ensure efficient control over inmates, and many fine designs date from the later decades of C18 and the first half of C19. *Piranesi's images of phantasy prisons (*carceri*), with their *Sublime volumes, had considerable influence on Neoclassical architecture and stage-sets. *See* Panopticon.

Nicholson (1835); Papworth (1852); Pevsner (1976); Sturgis *et al.* (1901–2)

Prisse d'Avennes, Achille-Constant-Théodore-Émile (1807–79). French artist, designer, and engineer. His publications include *Les Monuments Égyptiens* (The Egyptian Monuments—1847) and *L'Histoire de l'Art Égyptien, d'apres les Monuments* (History of Egyptian Art, after the Monuments—1878–9), the latter a sumptuous two-volume set illustrated with chromo-lithographs. He also published *L'Art*

Arabe d'après les monuments de Caire (Arab Art after the Monuments of Cairo—1869–77), a scholarly work that is still a marvellous source for *Islamic decorations, and which influenced *Burges when designing the Arab Hall, Cardiff Castle, Wales (1881).

Clayton (1982); Curl (1994); Lewis and Darley (1986)

Pritchard, Thomas Farnolls (1723–77). English architect. Competent in *Rococo and *Gothick styles, he practised mainly in his native Shropshire, where he designed an enormous number of buildings and other structures, including the first cast-iron bridge in the world, at Coalbrookdale over the Severn (1775). Built by Abraham Darby (1750–91) in 1777–9, the bridge was illustrated in *The Philosophical Magazine and Annals of Philosophy* (1832) and in John White's *On Cementitious Architecture as applicable to the Construction of Bridges, with a Prefatory Notice of the First Introduction of Iron as the Constituent Material for Arches of Large Span, by Thomas Farnolls Pritchard in 1773* (1832). Among his other works are Hosyer's Almshouses (1758–9), and The Guildhall, Mill Street (1774–6), both in Ludlow, Shropshire. He made early designs for Payne *Knight's Downton Castle, Herefordshire (1772), one of the key buildings of the *Picturesque, but the Castle as realized was mostly Knight's work.

Ballantyne (1997); Colvin (1995); Curl (1993*b*); Ionides (1999); Pevsner, *Buildings of England, Shropshire* (1958)

Pritchett, James Pigott (1789–1868). Welsh-born architect. He had an extensive practice in Yorkshire, where he was responsible for many competent buildings. He designed York Cemetery, including the *Greek Revival Chapel (1836–7), Huddersfield Railway Station (1846–7), and the *portico of the Assembly Rooms, York (1828).

Colvin (1995); *DNB* (1917)

Prix, Wolf D. (1942–). *See* Coop Himmelblau.

processional way. Monumental roadway of great grandeur used for ritual processions, as a *dromos before the *pylons of an Ancient Egyptian temple.

procession path. 1. In monastic churches a line of paving for the marshalling of those participating in the daily processions associated with religious observance. **2.** *Ambulatory, or *aisle to the east of the high-altar and its *reredos in cathedrals and monastic churches.

prodigy-house. Large, showy, late-*Elizabethan or *Jacobean house with North-European *Renaissance detailing and certain post-*Gothic features, such as *mullioned-and-*transomed windows, e.g. Wollaton Hall, Nottingham (1580–8).

Summerson (1993)

prodomus *or* **prodomos.** Open vestibule at the entrance to the *cella or *naos of a temple, set behind the *portico proper. Also called *anticum or *pronaos.

profile. 1. Contour or *section of an architectural member, e.g. a *cornice. **2.** Outline of a building showing heights, projections, etc.

projection. 1. Representation of a design in *perspective, *axonometric or *isometric projection, or *orthographical means, in order to explain it. **2.** Element or elements of a building projecting before the *naked of the main wall of the façade, such as a *jetty, *cantilever, *oriel, etc.

Fraser Reekie (1946)

pronaos. *Vestibule flanked by three walls and one row of columns between the front *portico and the *cella or *naos of an *Antique temple, or the space between the *colonnade of a portico and the front wall of the cell. Also called *anticum or *prodomus.

proportion. In architecture, a system of relationships of parts to each other and to the whole, often governed by a standard unit of length called a *module based e.g. on half the diameter of a Classical column.

Scholfield (1958)

propylaeum, propylon (*pl.* **propylaea, propyla**). Imposing monumental entrance gateway leading to a temple, sacred court, or enclosure, such as a *battered gateway in front of Ancient Egyptian temple *pylon-towers, or the large *Doric gateway leading to the Athenian *acropolis.

proscenium. 1. Stage, or part of an *Antique *theatre whereon actors performed in front of the *scena*. **2.** In later theatres, the portion of the stage between the curtain and the orchestra.

prospect tower. Tall building on high ground commanding a view, called a *look-out* or *standing tower*. *See* belvedere, gazebo.

Prost, Léon-Henri (1874–1959). French architect and town-planner who won the competition to design the infrastructure plan for Antwerp, Belgium (1910), in which he exploited the canal encircling the old city to make a connection with the engineering complex of Berchem. He also prepared plans for Casablanca, Fez, and Marrakesh, all in Morocco (1913–17), and for the Paris Regional Plan (1928–39) and Istanbul Master Plan (1939–58).

Académie d'Architecture (1960)

prostyle. Building with a *colonnade in front of it, usually a *portico. A temple with a portico at each end is *amphi-prostyle.

Protectorate. The period of the Commonwealth (1649–60) in the British Isles when Oliver (1599–1658) and then Richard (1626–1712) Cromwell held the title of Lord Protector (1653–60). It gave its name to the *Protectorate style* of architecture found in several country-houses of the period, notably Thorpe Hall, Peterborough (1653–6), built by Peter *Mills. The style was influenced by the architecture of The Netherlands, notably the works of *Vingboons, and also by *Artisan Mannerism that evolved from *c.*1630.

Mowl and Earnshaw (1995); Summerson (1993)

prothesis. Recess on the north side of the *bema or *apse in a basilican church out of which the Bread and Wine were taken for consecration, or a *chapel containing the recess.

proto-. *Primitive, first, early, or precursor of something. Proto-*Doric was an early primitive harbinger of the Doric *Order, as in the rock-cut tombs at Beni-Hasan, Egypt (*c.* 2133–1786 BC). Proto-*Ionic refers to precursors of aspects of the Ionic *Order, especially the *Aeolic type of *capital and certain features from Mesopotamia. Proto-*Romanesque is a term embracing various round-arched styles that evolved from *Early Christian and *Byzantine exemplars including *Carolingian, *Lombardic, and *Ottonian architecture. Proto-*Renaissance was a late-C11 style in which *Antique elements were copied: examples include the *baptistery, Church of San Miniato, and Santi Apostoli, Florence, and the late-C13 *façades of Cività Castellana Cathedral and San Lorenzo fuori le Mura, Rome.

protoma (*pl.* **protomai**). Foremost or upper part of a figure, such as those on the angles of some *Romanesque *capitals.

proudwork. *Masonry, found occasionally in *Tudor *Gothic work, similar to *flushwork, except that the *freestone patterns and *tracery stand in higher relief than the *flint *panels. From *proud*, meaning projecting from a plane surface—probably only used in limited geographical areas.

Prouvé, Jean (1901–84). French pioneer of *prefabrication and *industrialized building, he worked with Le *Corbusier, Tony *Garnier, Pierre *Jeanneret, and Charlotte *Perriand, among others. He developed the concept of the *curtain-wall, metal *cladding systems, and infill panels for walls (e.g. Roland Garros Aero-Club, Buc (1936–7—destroyed). His adaptable Maison du Peuple, Clichy (1937–9—with *Beaudouin and *Lods), and aluminium houses at Meudon (1949–50) were very advanced for their time. He constructed the pump-room at Évian Spa (1956–7—Maurice Novarina, architect), and evolved the 'Sahara' prefabricated housing-units (1958). It is perhaps revealing that he referred to himself as a *constructeur*, emphasizing his role as inventor, master-builder, engineer, and designer.

Clayssen (1983); Emanuel (1994); Huber & Steinegger (1971); Jervis (1984); Placzek (1982); van Vynckt (1993)

prow. Essential embellishment of the *columna rostrata, consisting of three sets of prows (*rostra*) and rams of *Antique warships projecting on either side of the column. *Rostra* are also found as sculpture on keystones or buildings associated with commerce or trade.

pseudisodomon. *Antique *ashlar *masonry consisting of low bonding and high unbonded courses, thus the taller courses consisted of stones thinner than the lower. *Pseudisodomous* or *pseudisodomic* describes this condition. *See* isodomon.

pseudo-. False, counterfeit, pretended, or deceptively resembling something. *Pseudodipteral* refers to a Classical building with the appearance of being a dipteral temple (with two rows of columns along the longer sides), but with no inner row, leaving a wide passage between *cella and *peristyle. *Pseudo-Gothic* is a term for C18 *sham *Gothic, and *pseudo-* is also applied to any style used falsely, e.g. *pseudo-Georgian*. *Pseudoperipteral* is applied to a Classical temple with the 'peristyle' *engaged with the cell wall. *Pseudoprostyle* describes a *prostyle temple without a *pronaos, the *portico *colonnade set closer than an *intercolumniation from or engaged with the cella wall behind. *Pseudothyrum* is a false or secret door.

pteroma, pteromata. In an Ancient Greek temple, the area between the *naos or cell walls and the *peristyle *colonnade.

pteron. External *peripteral *colonnade of a Greek temple.

Pugin, Augustus Charles (1769–1832). French-born, he came to Wales during the French Revolution. He became an assistant to *Nash, and made his reputation as a draughtsman, drawing and etching plates for Rudolph Ackermann (1764–1834), John Britton (1771–1857), Edward Wedlake Brayley (1773–1854), and other publishers. He produced some of the first archaeologically accurate images of medieval architecture in *Specimens of Gothic Architecture . . . at Oxford* (1816), *Specimens of Gothic Architecture* (1821–3), *Gothic Furniture* (1827), *Specimens of the Architectural Antiquities of Normandy* (1827–8), *Examples of Gothic Architecture* (1828–36), *Gothic Ornaments from Ancient Buildings in England and France* (1828–31), and *A Series of Ornamental Timber Gables, from Existing Examples in England and Wales* (1831). These works were as important for the *Gothic Revival as *Stuart and *Revett's were for the *Greek Revival. With Charles Heath (1785–1848) he produced *Paris and its Environs* (1829–31). He made designs for cemeteries, including a layout for Kensal Green Cemetery, London (1830). His pupils included *Ferrey, *Pennethorne, and his son, A. W. N. *Pugin.

Colvin (1995); *DNB* (1917); Ferrey (1861); Jervis (1984); Placzek (1982)

Pugin, Augustus Welby Northmore (1812–52). English architect and polemicist, the son of A. C. *Pugin, he was one of the key personalities of the *Gothic Revival. After his conversion to Roman Catholicism in *c.*1835 he became a leading figure in *Ecclesiology.

In 1836 he published *Contrasts; or, a Parallel between the Noble Edifices of the Fourteenth and Fifteenth Centuries, and Similar Buildings of the Present Day; Shewing the Present Decay of Taste*. He claimed that *Pointed architecture (*Gothic) was produced by the Roman Catholic faith, that Classical architecture was pagan, that the Reformation was a dreadful scourge, and that medieval architecture was greatly superior to anything produced by the *Renaissance or Classical Revivals. The great test of architectural beauty was the fitness of the design to the purpose for which it was intended, and the style of a building should tell the spectator at once what its purpose was. Buildings of C19 (especially those of the leading architects of the day) were weighed in the balance against those of C14 and found wanting. His other main works, *The True Principles of Pointed or Christian Architecture set forth* (1841), *The Present State of Ecclesiastical Architecture in England* (1843), and *An Apology for the Revival of Christian Architecture in England* (1843), made it clear that Gothic was not a style, but a principle, a moral crusade, and the only mode of building possible for a Christian nation. His arguments and his very deep knowledge of all aspects of Gothic design had an immense impact on Anglican church-architects, however. George Gilbert *Scott was to write that he was 'awakened' from his 'slumbers by the thunder of Pugin's writings'.

Pugin assisted Charles *Barry with the details and furnishings of the Palace of Westminster (built 1840–70) and indeed it was Pugin, rather than Barry, who designed the exquisite architectural enrichments and confident colour-scheme for what is one of the great monuments of the Gothic Revival. As a church-architect, however, Pugin was unfortunate. Most of his churches have a mean and pinched look owing to a shortage of funds, and the Roman Catholic hierarchy was not always convinced by the furious arguments of its recent convert, but at St Giles's, Cheadle, Cheshire (1840–6), where his patron, John Talbot, 16th Earl of Shrewsbury and Earl of Waterford (1791–1852), paid handsomely (against his better judgement), Pugin was able to create a scholarly and sumptuous revival of a parish-church of the time of King Edward I (1272–1307), with a glowing *polychrome interior, complete with *chancel-*screen, all in the *Second Pointed style. Other works by him include St Chad's Cathedral, Birmingham (1939–41), St Alban's Church, Macclesfield, Cheshire (1838–41), St Barnabas's Cathedral, Nottingham (1841–4), and St Mary's (or Marie's), Derby (1837–9).

His secular architecture and his polemics were of great importance because he demonstrated by historical argument (e.g. Haddon Hall, Derbyshire (C12–C17)) and by his own example (e.g. Alton Castle, Staffordshire (1840–52); the complex of the Grange and St Augustine's, Ramsgate, Kent (1843–52—where he is buried); and Scarisbrick Hall, Ormskirk, Lancashire (1836–47)) that the three-dimensional form of the building should grow naturally out of the plan. This he called the 'true Picturesque', while many houses he criticized were sham *Picturesque with 'donjon keeps . . . nothing but drawing rooms', 'watch-towers . . . where the house-maids sleep', and bastions 'where the butler keeps his plate'. Such buildings (e.g. G. L. Taylor's Hadlow Tower, Kent (*c*.1840)) were 'mere masks' and 'ill-conceived lies', whereas beauty should grow from necessity. *Pattern-books and illustrations of historical architecture, to Pugin, were dangerous because they were mindlessly copied, and bits jumbled together in new concoctions. Such publications, in the possession of architects and builders, were as 'bad as the Scriptures in the hands of Protestants'. His arguments led to the adoption of freely composed asymmetrical buildings (e.g. the vicarages of *Butterfield) and to the *Domestic Revival, the *Queen Anne, and *Free styles.

Aldrich (1994); Atterbury and Wainwright (1994); Crook (1987); Curl (1995); *DNB* (1917); Dixon and Muthesius (1985); Eastlake (1970); Ferrey (1861); Germann (1972); Hitchcock (1977); Pevsner (1972); Placzek (1982); Port (1976); Pugin (1841, 1843, 1843*a* 1973); Scott (1995); Stanton (1971)

Pugin, Edward Welby (1834–75). Son and pupil of A. W. N. *Pugin, he was a gifted *Gothic Revivalist, whose works were robust and Continental in influence. They included the Church of the Immaculate Conception, Dadizeele, Belgium (1857–9), Queenstown (now Cobh) Cathedral, Ireland (1868–1919), as well as several Roman Catholic churches in England (e.g. St Francis, Gorton, Manchester (1864–72)).

Curl (1995); *DNB* (1917); Dixon and Muthesius (1985); Ferrey (1861)

Puig i Cadafalch, Josep *or* **José** (1867–1957). Catalan architect. He worked mostly in and around Barcelona, Spain, and was a pupil of *Domènech i Montaner. His Casa Amatller, Barcelona (1898–1900), drew on German *Gothic exemplars, even to the quotation of a stepped *gable. Later, he paraphrased *vernacular Catalan architecture for his *Modernisme (*see* Art Nouveau) houses, Casa Garí, Argentona (1898), and Casa Macaya, Barcelona (1901). From *c*.1904 his work became more influenced by the Vienna *Sezession, and the Casa Pich i Pon, Barcelona (1921), had a flavour of *Sullivan's designs in the USA. His Fábrica Casarramona (1911–12) is one of his best works. He published a comprehensive study of Catalan *Romanesque art (1909–18).

Bohigas (1968, 1991)

pulpit. Partially enclosed elevated desk of wood, masonry, etc., in a church (usually on the north-east side of the *nave) for a preacher. Often ornate, a pulpit may have a canopy over (called *tester) functioning partly as a sound-reflector. The Anglican *three-decker* pulpit contains at the bottom level a clerk's stall, a reading-desk above, and at the top the pulpit proper, designed as a whole.

pulpitum. **1.** Stone *screen in a monastic church between the *nave and *choir, acting as the back of part of the choir-*stalls, over which is a *gallery, *Rood, or organ. **2.** In an *Antique *theatre the part of the stage used by the actors, also called *proscenium.

pulvin, pulvinata, pulvinus (*pl.* **pulvins, pulvinatae, pulvini**). **1.** Form resembling a cushion or pillow, such as the *baluster-like side of an *Ionic *volute, called *balteus. *Pulvination* is therefore a swelling, as though a cushion was being squashed. *Friezes in some of the Roman Classical *Orders are occasionally *pulvinated*, or bulging out with a convex profile, also called *cushioned* or *swelled*. **2.** Impost-block or *dosseret between the *capital and arch in a *Byzantine or *Rundbogenstil arcade. **3.** *Pulvinus et gradus inferior* were the seat and step below around a warm-water bath in Roman times.

punched. First operation to a block of stone before it is finely worked, usually with a pointed chisel.

puncheon. *Stud, or vertical timber shorter and lighter than a *post in a *timber frame.

Purbeck. Dark-grey or grey-greenish hard limestone, called a marble, originating in the Isle of Purbeck, Dorset, England, and almost entirely composed of univalve and bivalve remains fossilized and bound together. It was extensively employed by English medieval architects for *colonnettes, *shafts, monuments, *effigies, and *tombs because of its attractive properties, being capable of taking a spectacular polish. Patterned with fossils, the dark shiny marble shafts set against ordinary limestone contribute to the sumptuous richness of *First Pointed *Gothic interiors such as those of Lincoln, Salisbury, and Winchester Cathedrals, where *clustered or compound piers may be found featuring the material.

Purcell & Elmslie. American architectural partnership of William Gray Purcell (1880–1965) and George Grant Elmslie (1871–1952), famous first for the various fine houses of the *Prairie School. Elmslie, originally from Scotland, worked for a while with Adler & *Sullivan and was responsible for the ornament on e.g. the Cage Building (1898–9) and the Carson Pirie Scott Store (1899–1904), both in Chicago, Ill. Purcell & Elmslie designed several small Banks for the Mid-West, e.g. First State Bank, Le Roy, Minn. (1914), which were similar to some of Sullivan's Banks. Their best work was in the field of private houses (e.g. Bradley House, Woods Hole, Mass. (1911), Owre House, Minneapolis (1911–12), Decker House, Holdridge, Lake Minnetonka, Minn. (1912–13), Purcell House, Minneapolis (1913), Backus House, Minneapolis (1915), and Purcell Bungalow, Rose Valley, Pa. (1918)). Their Woodbury County Court House, Sioux City, Iowa (1915–17), was in a robust *stripped Classical style, with certain details reminiscent of *Wright's work in the brick façade.

Andrews (1955); Brooks (1972); Condit (1968); Gebhard (1953, 1965*a*); Placzek (1982); Spencer (1979)

Purism. French artistic movement of *c.*1918–25 linked to the *Machine Aesthetic and founded by *Ozenfant and Le *Corbusier. It claimed *Cubism was becoming concerned with mere decoration, that art needed to reflect the 'spirit of the age', exclude emotionalism and expression, and learn lessons inherent in the precision of machinery. Advocated in *Après le Cubisme* (1918), *L'Esprit Nouveau* (1920–5), and *La Peinture Moderne* (1925), it influenced the architectural theories of *Constructivism and the teachings of the *Bauhaus.

Chilvers, Osborne, and Farr (1988)

purlin. Horizontal beam also called *bridging*, *rib*, *side-timber*, or *side-waver*, carried on roof-*trusses in order to give intermediate support to the common *rafters.

putlog hole. Hole in a wall to enable the cross-timbers or horizontal *putlogs* of scaffolding to be supported. The scaffold-boards were supported on the putlogs.

putto (*pl.* **putti**). Unwinged, often obese, male child found in Classical and *Baroque sculpture (frequently on funerary monuments), not to be confused with the winged *Amorino, *Cherub, *Cupid, or Love.

pycnostyle. *See* intercolumniation.

pylon. 1. *Portal of an Ancient Egyptian temple composed of two huge *battered towers, usually decorated with bas-relief sculptured figures and *hieroglyphs, flanking a lower framed gateway which, like the towers, was crowned by a *cavetto or *gorge-*cornice. The towers had the corners finished with *torus mouldings that were continued horizontally at the tops of the battered walls under the gorge-cornices. Some authorities use the terms *pylon*, *propylon*, *pylône* for the gateway, but others prefer *pylon* for the gateway and *propyla* for the towers. A *pylon-form* resembles one of the towers, and indeed the term *pylon* is now usually given to the towers, following the precedent set by the editors of the *Description de l'Égypte* (1820s). Pylon-forms (often found in C19 chimney-pots) lent themselves to the towers of suspension-bridges, such as *Brunel's structure over the gorge at Clifton, Bristol (1831–64), and the battered *section was widely employed in C19 dams and retaining-walls. **2.** Tall structure erected as a support, especially a lattice-work metal tower to carry overhead electricity-lines.

Curl (1994); Cruickshank (1996); Gwilt (1903); Lloyd and Müller (1986)

pynun- *or* **pignon-table.** Sloping stones of a *gable.

pyramid. Monumental structure with a square base and steep *battered triangular sides terminating in an apex. The form was used in Ancient Egypt for funerary structures: celebrated examples are the pyramids at Giza, near Cairo, Egypt (*c.*2723–2563 BC). Other types of pyramid include the stepped form found in both Ancient Egyptian and *Meso-American *Pre-Columbian architecture, but in the latter region the buildings were temple-platforms rather than tombs. The best-known stepped pyramids are the Ancient Egyptian pyramid at Saqqara, built by *Imhotep for King Zoser (*c.*2778–*c.*2650 BC), and the temple-pyramids of the *Meso-American *Aztec and Maya cultures (*c.* C6–C16). Pyramids often featured in Neoclassical architecture, and appealed to designers for their stereometrical purity of form, thus responding to *Laugier's admiration for an architecture that was *primitive and pure. Pyramidal compositions were common in funerary monuments from the time of *Bernini, and countless C18 examples exist.

Curl (1994); Cruickshank (1996); Edwards (1985); Gunnis (1968); Lloyd and Müller (1986)

pyramidal hipped roof. *See* roof.

pyramidal rustication. *See* rustication.

pyramidion. Small pyramid, such as that on the top of an *obelisk.

Pythius *or* **Pytheos** (*fl.* 353–334 BC). *Hellenistic architect, who, with Satyros, designed and wrote about the *Mausoleum at Halicarnassus (begun *c.*354 BC), one of the *Seven Wonders of the Ancient World. His Temple of Athena at Priene (334 BC) is one of the finest *Ionic temples and therefore he is credited with bringing the Ionic Order to canonical perfection. His writings, known to *Vitruvius, no longer exist.

Dinsmoor (1950); Fyfe (1936); Lawrence (1983); Robertson (1945)

pyx, pyxis. Box, casket, *shrine or *tabernacle to hold the consecrated Host in a church.

Duffy (1992)

quad. Abbreviation of *quadrangle, used in Oxford to describe a college *court surrounded by buildings on all four sides and approached through a gateway (often set in a tower).

quadra. 1. Plain *plinth or *socle of a *pedestal, *podium, etc. **2.** *Fillet or *list on either side of the *scotia in an Attic *base, and especially if used with the *Ionic *Order. **3.** Square architectural moulding framing a sculptured relief, panel, plaque, inscription, etc.

quadrangle. 1. Figure with four sides in the same plane. **2.** Large rectangular inner court around which buildings are erected, such as in Oxford colleges, where it is called *quad, and in Cambridge, called *court.

quadrangular style. Building erected in square form around a court, or on an H-plan.

quadrant. 1. The fourth part of a circle, hence an object or a street with a plan-form based on a fourth of the circumference of a circle. *Quadrant* was the name given to part of Regent Street, London, designed 1813–16 by John *Nash, laid out on a plan conforming with that shape. A series of buildings the façades of which form a convex curve is called a *quadrant*, as opposed to that on a concave curve, called *crescent. Quadrants were important in Classical composition as e.g. a means of joining a *corps-de-logis to *pavilions or *wings, as in *Palladian compositions (Villa Mocenigo (1544–64) by *Palladio and Kedleston, Derbyshire, as designed by *Paine (1757–9)) **2.** Medieval term for a *quadrangle or *quad. **3.** Octagonal part of a *spire.

quadratum. *See* opus.

quadratura. Painted perspectives of architecture in Roman, *Renaissance, and (especially) *Baroque ceilings and walls, often very realistic, and frequently (in C17 and C18) extending the actual interior architecture as *trompe l'œil work of breathtaking technical brilliance, as in the works of *quadraturisti* such as A. *Pozzo.

Chilvers, Osborne, and Farr (1988)

quadrel. 1. Artificial stone, perfectly square, made in Italy of a chalky white pliable earth, dried in shady conditions for at least two years. **2.** Square *quarrel, or *tile.

quadrifores. Roman folding doors divided in height into two parts, so there were two hinged or pivoted leaves on either side.

quadrifrons. 1. Sculptured form, such as an Ancient Egyptian Hathor-headed *capital, with four heads of the goddess joined at the sides and backs, facing outwards in four directions at the top of the shaft and under the *abacus, or any other object with four outward-facing heads. **2.** *Tetrapylon, i.e. with four equal gates on four identical *façades, perhaps a structure erected over the intersection of two avenues.

quadriga. Sculptured group representing a two-wheeled chariot, with driver, drawn by four horses harnessed abreast, often associated with victory monuments, *triumphal arches, etc. With two horses drawing the chariot it is a *biriga*, while the three-horse type is a *tririga*. A Graeco-Roman motif, it was revived and enjoyed a new lease of life in the Neoclassical period (e.g. the Arco del Sempione, Milan (1806–38), by *Cagnola).

quadripartite. Divided by the system of construction used into four parts, e.g. a *Gothic *vault on a rectangular plan, with the rectangle divided into four parts by means of intersecting diagonal ribs.

quadriporticus. *Quadrangle with covered *ambulatory, *gallery, or *portico on each side, as in the *atrium of San Clemente, Rome, which has *arcades and *colonnades supporting the roofs of the structures surrounding the atrium.

quadro riportato. Ceiling-painting without foreshortening illusionistic effects, designed as though it is to be seen at normal eye-level. It was a Neoclassical reaction against *Baroque *quadratura and *trompe l'œil work.

Chilvers, Osborne, and Farr (1988)

Quaglio Family. Italo-Swiss family who designed operatic and theatrical stage-sets for the Electoral Courts of Mannheim and Munich and the Imperial Court of Vienna from C17 to C19. Some Quaglios were also architects. **Lorenzo** (1730–1804) designed some theatres, including the reconstruction of the *Schlosstheater* (1768) and the building of the *Nationaltheater* (1777–8), both in Mannheim, as well as (probably) Schloss Wain, Laupheim, Württemberg (1780), and the *Rathaus* (Town Hall), Lauingen (1783–90). **Angelo** (1778–1815) introduced *Neo-Gothic designs, while **Simon** (1795–1878) produced a series of very fine *Egyptian Revival sets for the 1818 production of Mozart's *Die Zauberflöte* (The Magic Flute) at Munich, equal in authority to Schinkel's 1816 designs for Berlin. **Giulio** (1764–1801) decorated the Court Theatre, Dessau (1798), and **Domenico** (1787–1837) was a pioneer of the *Gothic Revival, publishing some views of old Munich in 1812 and *Denkwürdige Gebäude des Mittelalters* (Memorable Buildings of the Middle Ages), an important work on German medieval art (1818–23). He rebuilt Schloss Hohenschwangau, near Füssen, Bavaria, in a charming Neo-Gothic style (1832–7). **Giovanni Maria**, also called **Johann Maria von** (1772–1813) published *Praktische Anleitung zur Perspektive mit Anwendung auf die Baukunst* (Practical Guidance on Perspective with Application to Architecture—1811, 1823).

Council of Europe (1972); Curl (1994); Quaglio (1823); Trost (1973)

Quaint style. Pejorative term used for *Art Nouveau in its last phases in the early C20.

Quarenghi, Giacomo Antonio Domenico (1744–1817). Bergamo-born architect, working in *Russia from 1779, who united developing Russian *Classicism, *Palladianism, and burgeoning *Neoclassicism. His first significant known work, the reconstruction of the Benedictine Church of Santa Scolastica, Subiaco, near Rome (1769–77), is a clever variant on the interior of *Palladio's *Il Redentore*. After a spell designing for English clients (e.g. an altar for the chapel at Wardour Castle, Wiltshire (*c*.1774–6)), Quarenghi left for Russia (where he was patronized by Empress Catherine II (1729–96)): there he became a prolific designer, working on the grandest of scales in an impressive Neoclassical style, and creating a series of important buildings in and around St Petersburg. At the English Palace, Peterhof (1781–9—destroyed), and the Hermitage Theatre (1782–7), for example, he employed a monumental Palladianism, and in both the State Bank (1783–90) and Academy of Sciences (1783–9), St Petersburg, he exploited monumental *colonnades set against simple unadorned stark *elevations. Precision, clarity, and severity were to predominate as his French-inspired Neoclassicism developed: examples include the Imperial Pharmacy, St Petersburg (1789–96), Jusopov Fontanka Palace (1789–92—with semicircular courtyard), and Alexandrovsky Palace, Tsarskoe Selo (1792–6—with small courtyard embellished with two elegant Corinthian colonnades set within the main courtyard). With M. F. *Kasakov and Ivan Petrovich Argunov (1727–1802) he designed the Sheremetev Palace, Ostankino (1791–8), in which Palladianism and the grandest Neoclassicism merge.

Quarenghi used Greek *Doric for his Horse Guards Building (1804–7), and Roman Imperial architecture for his Narva *triumphal arch (1814), which draws on the Antique Roman arches of Titus and Constantine and the refinements of *Percier and *Fontaine's *Arc du Carrousel* in Paris. His work, which defined the heroic and severe character of early C19 St Petersburg, laid down the direction for the development of Russian Neoclassicism. Many of his designs were published in 1810 and 1821.

Council of Europe (1972); Hamilton (1983); Meeks (1966); Middleton and Watkin (1987); Quarenghi (1821); Zanella (1988)

Quarini, Mario Ludovico (1736–*c*.1800). Italian architect. He collaborated with *Vittone on the latter's buildings and architectural treatises. He designed the *façade of the Church of San Filippo (1759), the side elevation of the Palazzo Comunale (1771), and the façade of San Bernardino (1792), all in

Chieri. His later works at Fossano (Annunziata (1777), Palazzo Comunale (1779–80), and Cathedral (1779–81)) were more Neoclassical, although he never quite shed the *Baroque influence of Vittone.

Atti e rassegna tecnica della Soc. degli ing. e degli archit. in Torino, 12 (1958), 153–94

Quaroni, Ludovico (1911–87). Italian architect, teacher, and town-planner, he was a distinguished Neoclassicist during the Fascist era. He designed a group of small villas, Gaeta Region, Latina (1936), and the Piazza della Nuova Stazione Urban Plan, Ostia Lido, near Rome (1937—with E. Fuselli). Other works included the Church of Santa Maria Maggiore (later San Franco), Francavilla al Mare (1948–58), a housing development, in which a Roman *vernacular style was attempted, at the Tiburtino Quarter, Rome (1950—with C. *Aymonino, Mario *Ridolfi, and others), and La Martella Housing and Church, Matera (1951–2—with others). He published numerous works, including *La Torre de Babele* (The Tower of Babel—1967), *Immagine di Roma* (Image of Rome—1976), and *La città fisica* (The Physical City—1981).

Emanuel (1994); Tafuri (1964); Tafuri and Dal Co (1986)

quarrel, quarry. **1.** Lozenge-shaped or square piece of glass held in the *cames of leaded *lights. **2.** Approximately lozenge- or square-shaped *light in *Gothic *tracery. **3.** Any floor-*tile, lozenge-shaped or square.

quarry-faced. *Masonry appearing to be very rough, as though it had not received much attention since being quarried, but squared for the joints, used in *rustication. Also called *rock-faced* masonry.

quarter. **1.** *Quatrefoil. **2.** Timber *post or *stud in a *timber-framed wall or partition. A series of such posts or studs is called *quartering*.

quarter-hollow. Concave moulding or *cavetto, the opposite of a *quarter-round.

quarter-pace. Landing in a stair between two flights at 90°, so usually square on plan.

quarter-round. Convex moulding or *ovolo, its *section the *quadrant of a circle.

quatrefoil. *See* foil, quarter.

Quatremère de Quincy, Antoine-Chrysostôme (1755–1849). French Freemason, architectural theorist, and author of *De l'Architecture Égyptienne* (written 1785 and published 1803)—an important influence on *Neoclassicism and the *Egyptian Revival. He wrote much of the architectural content in the *Encylopédie Méthodique* (1788–1825) and many other significant works, including *Dictionnaire Historique d'Architecture* (1832–3). He was also a key figure in the formation of the first landscaped cemeteries, and was responsible for the conversion of the Church of Ste-Geneviève in Paris (under the direction of *Rondelet) into the Panthéon by blocking up the windows, not to strengthen the structure, as is erroneously supposed, but to give it the character of a *mausoleum (1791–2). As permanent secretary to the Académie des Beaux-Arts (1816–39) he had an enormous influence on virtually all French official architecture.

Curl (1994); Etlin (1984); Middleton and Watkin (1987); Quatremère de Quincy (1788–1825, 1803, 1814, 1823, 1828, 1830, 1832, 1834); Schneider (1910, 1910*a*)

Quattrocento. Literally 'four hundred', it is the term for *Renaissance art and architecture in Italy of C15.

Queen Anne. **1.** Period of English architecture during the reign of Queen Anne (1702–14), when the English *Baroque style of *Wren, *Vanbrugh, *Archer, and *Hawksmoor came to maturity, notably with Vanbrugh's Blenheim Palace, Oxfordshire (1705–25), and Hawksmoor's London churches (e.g. Christ Church, Spitalfields of 1714–29). Domestic architecture of the time was derived from *Caroline and Dutch precedents: in London, for example, houses were mainly faced with red brick, had tall *sash-windows and canopy-like timber door-cases, while roofs became flatter and hidden behind parapets. Plainness and dignified restraint marked the domestic architecture in Britain and the American Colonies, and were influential virtues appreciated by later generations, especially from *c.*1860 to *c.*1890 and again in C20. **2.** The *Queen Anne style* or *Revival* evolved from the 1860s, and was not really what its label suggests. Some details were derived from C17 and C18 English and Flemish domestic architecture, but eclectic motifs were drawn from many sources: they included tall white-painted small-paned sash-windows with *rubbed-brick arches and *dressings over and around openings, *terracotta embellishments, open-bed and broken *pediments, steeply pitched roofs (often rising from *eaves-cornices), monumental *chimneys, shaped and *Dutch *gables, white-painted *balustrades, *balconies, and *bay-windows. Such architectural elements were combined with a new freedom of asymmetrical and informal planning derived from the *Gothic Revival and the ideas of A. W. N. *Pugin. In the hands of architects such as G. F. *Bodley, W. E. *Nesfield, R. N. *Shaw, J. J. *Stevenson, and Philip *Webb, the style evolved and began to incorporate elements from *vernacular architecture (e.g. tile-hung gabled walls with *barge-boards, *clap-boarding, and *casement-windows with *leaded *lights). Such developments led to the adoption of the term *Domestic Revival, while buildings in which Classical motifs predominated were referred to as examples of *Free Classicism or the *Northern Renaissance Revival. It should be emphasized that the so-called Queen Anne style was not a purist scholarly revival, as aspects of the *Gothic and *Greek Revivals had been, but essentially eclectic, drawing on a wide range of motifs from various periods and regions. It affected domestic architecture in the USA as well, often merging with the *Colonial Revival. Professor Crook has called it 'a flexible urban argot', which is as close a description as one can get to capture its flavour.

Crook (1987); Dixon and Muthesius (1985); Girouard (1977); Gray (1985)

Queen Anne arch. Type of arch formed of a central semicircular arch flanked by two 'flat' arches constructed of brick *rubbers* set over tall thin side-lights on either side of a wider semicircular-headed window, a variation on the *Palladian or *Venetian window known as a *serliana (e.g. 39 Broad Street, Ludlow, Shropshire, *c.*1765). It is actually more common in the *Georgian period than in the Queen Anne.

Cruickshank (1985); Pevsner, *Buildings of England, Shropshire* (1958)

queen-post. *See* roof.

querelle. Square space forming a division or compartment of an *arcade or *colonnade defined by the columns, beams, structure, and (sometimes) pavement pattern.

Questel, Charles-Auguste (1807–88). French architect, he studied under Antoine-Marie Peyre (*fl.* 1790–1832—*see* Peyre Family), *Blouet, and *Duban, and began his career with a competent, tough, *Neo-Romanesque design for the Church of St-Paul, Place de la Madeleine, Nîmes (1835–49). Also in Nîmes the handsome Classical Palais de Justice (begun 1838) is by him. His restoration of St-Martin-d'Ainay, Lyons, and the furnishings he designed for the same church were much admired when they were exhibited in 1855. Later work was much influenced by the *Quattrocento. He designed the Hospital, Gisors, Eure (1859–61), the Hôtel de la Préfecture (1862–7), and the Musée Bibliothèque (1864–70), the last two both in Grenoble, Isère.

Delaborde (1890); Middleton and Watkin (1987); Placzek (1982)

quincunx. Arrangement or disposition of five objects so placed that four occupy the corners of a square and the fifth the centre. Common in schemes of planting, it is also the basis of the plan of many *Byzantine churches on a Greek-*cross plan with four barrel-vaulted bays, central dome, and the corner bays supporting small domes over the angles of the cross (the cross-in-square plan).

Mango (1986); Symes (1993); Watkin (1986)

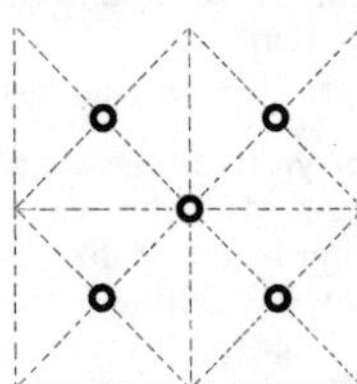

quincunx. Diagram of typical quincunx arrangement in architecture and planting.

quire. *See* choir.

quirk. 1. Small acute-angled channel, groove, or deep indent by which a moulding stands out from its ground, commonly found in *Gothic work. Any deep groove separating one moulding from another or from a flat plane or ground. In the latter case a *quirk-bead* would have a quirk on each or one side so that it would be flush with both planes or one. **2.** Re-entrant angle, such as a piece taken out of a regular figure. A rectangular room with a corner boxed in for e.g. a staircase would be classed as having a quirk. **3.** *Quarrel **1**.

quodlibet. Fanciful type of *trompe l'œil of oddments, often showing letters, paper-knives, playing-cards, ribbons, and scissors, in apparently accidental array, painted on walls, etc.

quoin (*also* **coign, coin, coyn**). **1.** Any external angle or corner of a structure. **2.** Angular courses of stone, etc., at the corner of a building, usually laid as alternate quoin *headers and quoin *stretchers, often dressed with *channels around them so they project from the *naked of the wall (*rustic quoins). **3.** One of the dressed stones used to dress and strengthen the corner of a building. *See* long-and-short work.

rabbet, rebate. Long rectangular piece removed from the edge of wood, stone, etc., to receive the edge or end of another element, e.g. door in a frame.

Rabirius (*fl.* late AD C1). Roman architect, known only from the *Epigrams* of the poet Martial (*c.*39–*c.*102), who designed for Emperor Domitian (81–96) a new Imperial Palace on the Palatine, Rome, to the south of earlier buildings erected for Domitian's predecessors. Still occupied as late as C6, it was the origin of the word 'palace', and was enormously influential. A huge complex, it included enclosed gardens, a *hippodrome, libraries, and many grandly formal rooms for State occasions as well as private apartments. *Vaults and domed constructions of concrete were used throughout, and the brick-faced concrete walls were clad in coloured marbles. Rabirius seems to have been partly responsible for the assured application of the *Orders to the new type of vaulted structure in order to create an opulence of unparalleled richness. Throughout the plan, formal axes were handled with deftness, and *apses, octagons, and segments were employed with square and rectangular plan-forms. Rabirius has been linked with architectural works of the period such as the Colosseum, *thermae of Titus, Domitian's Villa near Albano, and others, but documentary evidence is lacking.

MacDonald (1965–86); Placzek (1982); Ward-Perkins (1981)

raceme. Ornament based on a plant where flowers or leaves are borne in succession in the direction of the tip of the plant on an unbranched main stalk (as in *anthemion or *palmette).

Radburn. Planning principle developed at Radburn, NJ, on lines suggested originally by Ebenezer *Howard and promoted by Lewis *Mumford, Clarence *Stein, and others. The proposed town (which was transmogrified as a commuter-suburb) was designed in 1929 to segregate pedestrians and traffic by having *cul-de-sac feeder-roads and paths on bridges or in under-passes. This principle of segregation, known as *Radburn planning*, was also used in various New Towns created in Britain and on the Continent after the 1939–45 war.

Schaffer (1982)

radial brick. 1. *Voussoir. **2.** Special brick used for walls curved on plan.

radial step. Winder in a stair.

radiating chapels. In a church, projecting chapels arranged radially around the *ambulatory of a semicircular or polygonal liturgical east end. *See* chevet.

radiating principle. Planning system applied to certain building-types, especially gaols and hospitals, in which, from a central block or core, wings radiate in several directions. *See* Panopticon.

Radical architecture. Term often used in the 1960s and 1970s to suggest some extreme of shape, structure, or (more usually) the Leftist political position of its creators. The notion was propounded largely by the Italian architectural journal *Casabella*. In reality Radical architecture was often drawn or collage presentation of projects by certain groups (e.g. *Archizoom) questioning what constitutes architecture, usually involving assaults on architecture conceived as a formal language.

Navone and Orlandini (1974); Sparke (1988)

raffle-leaf. 1. Serrated, indented, or crumpled leaf-like enrichment with waving indented frond-like (or *raffled*) edges. *Raffling* is applied to the notched edges of carved foliage in architectural ornament, e.g. the *acanthus-leaf. **2.** Asymmetrically disposed curving flowing *scrolling serrated foliage arranged in *ogee and C forms, characteristic of *Rococo decorations, especially round frames or *cartouches.

Rafn, Aage (1890–1953). Danish architect. One of the most accomplished of C20 Neoclassicists, he designed the circular courtyard of *Kampmann's Police Headquarters, Copenhagen (1919–24), and, with Hans Jørgen Kampmann (1889–1966), Christian Kampmann (1890–1955), Holger *Jacobsen, and Anton Frederiksen (1884–1967), completed the great work. He was responsible for other Neoclassical buildings in Denmark (e.g. 22 Gl. Vartowej, Copenhagen (1919–20)—in a very simplified style). His unrealized but ravishing design for a crematorium (1921) won him the Gold Medal of the Royal Academy of Fine Arts. He was Principal of the School of Arts and Crafts in Copenhagen (1925–30), and designed some fine furniture.

Millech (1951); Paavilainen (1982); Weilbach (1947)

rafter. One of several long, inclined, rectangular timbers used in the construction of pitched roofs, supporting the roof-covering, e.g. laths and tiles. Types of rafter include:

angle rafter: principal rafter under the hip rafter carrying the *purlins on which the common rafters rest. In the USA any rafter at the angle of a roof, whether principal or not, hence either a hip- or jack-rafter in a valley;

auxiliary rafter: in a *truss, a rafter used to stiffen the *principal by doubling it;

binding rafter: purlin;

common rafter: of uniform dimensions, placed at regular intervals along the sloping section of a roof, sometimes as intermediate members between principals. A pair of common rafters is a *couple*;

compass rafter: one curved on the lower side, or wholly curved, as in a truss;

compound rafter: two rafters, one set over the other, separated by cleats, distance-pieces, or spacers, the inner rafters being *secondary rafters*;

hip rafter: one set diagonally at the hip of a roof where two slopes at 90° join, supporting the upper ends of the common rafters;

jack-rafter: **1.** One set diagonally at the valley of a roof where two slopes join, such as at a *dormer-window roof, supporting the lower ends of common rafters. **2.** Shorter common rafter between wall-plate and hip-rafter, or between a valley and the ridge;

principal rafter: large rectangular inclined timber in a sloping roof supporting a purlin and also serving as a common rafter. A principal rafter *not* serving as a common rafter is a *principal*;

valley rafter: one set diagonally where two roof-slopes meet in a valley, e.g. at a dormer-window, as in *jack-rafter* **1**;

verge rafter: common rafter set beyond a *gable to support the roof-covering beyond the *naked of the wall, itself supported on the ends of projecting wall-plates and purlins.

Alcock, Barley, Dixon, and Meeson (1996); McKay (1957)

rafter-plate. Timber by which *rafters are supported, e.g. *wall-plate.

Sturgis *et al.* (1901–2)

rag. Piece of hard, coarse-textured stone, capable of being broken into thick, flattish pieces, the commonest types being *Kentish rag* (tough, hard limestone, readily broken into usable pieces), *Rowley rag* (a basaltic stone from Staffordshire), and other stones, notably in the USA. Rag-stones are not laid in regular *courses, and mostly used as *facings* to brick or other types of stone wall. The appearance of a rag-stone wall is net-like, formed of a pattern of approximate polygons, with the mortar joints coarse (*rough-picked*) or fine (*close-picked*). Kentish rag is commonly found in C19 *Gothic Revival churches in London and the south-eastern counties of England. Rag is also used in *rubble walls.

McKay (1957); Parker (1850)

Rageur. Style of French C19 architecture in which *Classicism, *Louis Quatorze, *Italianate, *Renaissance, and *Gothic themes were promiscuously mixed. A *rageur*, in French, is a bad-tempered person, and there are aspects of the Rageur style that are certainly overstated, over-emphatic, and outlandishly proportioned: an example is *Viollet-le-Duc's tomb for the Duc de Morny, Père-Lachaise Cemetery, Paris (1865–6). *See also* Raguer.

Papworth (1887)

raggle. Groove or *raglet in *masonry.

Raghton, Ivo de (*fl.* 1317–*c.*1339). English master-mason. He appears to have designed the west front of York *Minster including the great west window (1338–9) in the *Curvilinear style of *Second Pointed *Gothic. He may have designed, or influenced the design of, the east front of Carlisle Cathedral (1318–22), the *reredos at Beverley Minster, Yorkshire (1324–34), the east window of Selby Abbey, Yorkshire (begun *c.*1330), the *pulpitum at Southwell Minster, Nottinghamshire, and the south *rose-window at Lincoln Cathedral.

Harvey (1987)

raglet. Continuous *raggle or groove in *masonry, mortar-joints, etc., into which lead flashing can be set.

Raguer. French for to chafe or irritate, so applied to a phase of the mid-C19 *Gothic Revival in France characterized by perversity, discordance, and aggressive originality owing little to precedent. It had much in common with English and American *Rogue Gothic by *Keeling and others. *See* Rageur.

Raguzzini, Filippo (*c*.1680–1771). The most celebrated architect working in the *Rococo style in Rome during the Pontificate of Benedict XIII (1724–30). He designed the Ospedale di San Gallicano (1725–6), with a well-considered sytem of ventilation, but he is celebrated for the Piazza di Sant'Ignazio (1727–36), in which five apartment-blocks have façades rising from plans that are segments of ellipses to enclose the space in front of the huge Church of Sant'Ignazio. Among his many other works, the façades of the Churches of Santa Maria della Quercia (1727-31), San Filippo Neri (1728), and Santi Quirico e Giulitta (1728–30), and his restoration of the Spanish Steps (1731), all in Rome, may be mentioned.

Albisinni (1984); Rotili (1951, 1982); *Town Planning Review*, 13/3 (1929), 139–48; *Zeitschrift für Geschichte der Baukunst*, 11 (1981), 31–65

rail. 1. Horizontal member of a wall-frame between the *posts or *studs in *timber-framed construction. **2.** Horizontal timber in a door, panelling, *wainscot, etc. Types of rail include:

chair-rail: *cornice at the top of a *dado around a room;

clamp rail: rebated timber to receive the ends of boards, as in a ceiling, etc., called *batten* or *cleat* in the USA;

dado-rail: as *chair-rail* above;

frieze rail: rail in a panelled door corresponding to the *frieze in position;

hanging-rail: rail to which hinges are fixed in a door, window, etc. A rail with hinges at the side of a panelled door is a *stile;

lock-rail: rail in a framed door into which the lock is fitted, usually corresponding to the top of a dado;

mid-rail: horizontal timber in a wall-frame placed half-way in a storey, or between a *cill and a wall-plate.

Alcock, Barley, Dixon, and Meeson (1996); Gwilt (1903); McKay (1957)

Railton, William (*c*.1801–77). British architect. He was Architect to the Ecclesiastical Commissioners (1838–48), but his economical parsonages and *Gothic Revival churches (such as St Paul's, Woodhouse Eaves, Leicestershire (1836–7)) did not win the approval of the ecclesiologically-minded. He is best known for the Nelson Memorial, Trafalgar Square, London (1839–43), a *Corinthian column on a *pedestal carrying a statue of the Admiral. The four lions by Sir Edwin Landseer (1802–73) which were added later (1867) were not part of his design. His account of the 'Temple at Cadachio, in Corfu' was published in the supplementary volume of *Stuart and *Revett's *Antiquities of Athens* in 1830.

Colvin (1995); *DNB* (1917)

Rainaldi, Carlo (1611–91). Rome-born architect who adopted aspects of late *Mannerism and *Baroque. The son of **Girolamo Rainaldi** (1570–1655—the architect of the Church of Santa Teresa, Caprarola (from 1621), and the Palazzo Pamphili, Piazza Navona, Rome (1645–50)), he worked with his father (Chief Papal Architect, appointed in 1644 by Innocent X (1644–55)) on the Church of Sant'Agnese in Agone, Piazza Navona, Rome (from 1652). *Borromini took over in 1653, but was sacked in 1657, after which Carlo Rainaldi was recalled, although *Bernini and *Cortona were consultants. To Rainaldi the plan, front, and huge *piers are credited. Other buildings include Santa Maria in Campitelli (1663–8), the front of Sant'Andrea della Valle (1656–65), and the apparently twin churches (1662–79) flanking the axis of the Corso in the Piazza del Pòpolo (one church (Santa Maria in Monte Santo—Bernini replaced Rainaldi in 1673) has an elliptical dome to make it appear the same diameter as the dome of its 'twin' because the sites are of different size).

Eimer (1970–1); Fagiolo and Carandini (1977–8); Fasolo (1961); Norberg-Schulz (1986); Wittkower (1982)

rain-conductor. Downspout, leader, or pipe to conduct rainwater from a gutter or hopper-head.

Rainer, Roland (1910–). Austrian architect and town-planner. His influence since the 1939–45 war has been considerable, not only as a practitioner, but as a teacher. In his role as Director of Planning for the City of Vienna (1958–63) he argued for an ecologically aware approach to design. He (with others) was responsible for the Veitingergasse Housing Estate, Vienna (1953–4), and the Puchenau *Garden City near Linz, Austria (1969–93), both of which demonstrated his opposition to the high-density housing promoted in Vienna in the 1920s by e.g. *Ehn, as well as his advocacy of decentralized developments. He designed Municipal buildings in Vienna (1958), Bremen, Germany (1964), and Ludwigshafen, Germany (1965), and housing developments at Kassel, Germany (1980), Tamariskengasse, Vienna (1985–93), and Auwiesen, Linz (1990–3). He published many books, including *Livable Environments* (1972).

Emanuel (1994); Kamm (1973); Placzek (1982)

rainwater-head. Small cistern or tank of cast-iron, lead, etc., also called *hopper-head*, frequently ornamented, to collect rainwater from e.g. a gutter behind a parapet, before it is discharged to a *rain-conductor. Elaborate cast-lead rainwater-heads are often of great significance on façades of buildings, especially of the C17 and C18.

raised moulding. Anything raised above its surroundings, such as a *bolection moulding, or a raised *panel with its centre higher than its edges.

rake. Inclination or slope of anything, such as the top of a triangular *pediment or a pitched roof.

raking arch. Rampant arch. *See* arch.

raking coping. *Cope on a sloping surface, e.g. a *gable.

raking cornice. *Cornice on the inclined tops of a triangular *pediment.

raking course. *Course of bricks laid diagonally between two normally laid faces of a wall, called *diagonal* (for walls 3 to 4 bricks thick) or *herring-bone* (for walls at least 4 bricks thick) bond.

McKay (1957)

raking flashing. *Flashing of metal (usually lead, but sometimes copper or zinc), following the slope of a pitched roof where it abuts a chimney, gable-parapet, wall, etc., set in a straight line with a *raglet where stepped flashings (as would be usual with brickwork) are not possible (as with *ashlar masonry).

McKay (1957)

raking moulding. Moulding on an inclined plane, e.g. the *raking cornice of a *pediment.

raking out. Removal of mortar before pointing.

raking riser. In a *stair, an inclined or *overhung *riser (upright front of a step), making a deeper tread than would be possible with a vertical riser.

ram. 1. Ram's head or skull on a Classical *frieze: a variation on the more usual *aegicrane or *bucranium. **2.** *Criosphinx. **3.** Reinforced prow or beak (*rostrum*) of an *Antique warship for *ramming* and holing an enemy ship, featured on the *columna rostrata. **4.** To beat down earth, clay, etc., with a heavy implement, to make it hard and firm. *See* rammed.

Ramírez Vázquez, Pedro (1919–). Mexican architect. He designed the School of Medicine, Mexico City (1953), but his museum work is best known, notably the National Museum of Anthropology, Mexico City, with a huge forecourt featuring much masonry (1963–4). He designed the Guadalupe *Shrine, Mexico City (1975–6), a tent-like structure for 10,000 people inside and 30,000 in the outside court, and the National Parliament, including the House of Representatives and the Senate (1976–80). He was responsible for the Mexican Pavilion, Universal Exposition, Seville (1991–2).

Emanuel (1994)

rammed. Structure, e.g. wall, made by beating down earth contained between *formwork or *shuttering with a heavy implement. If cement and other strengthening ingredients are added, the rammed earth is *pisé de terre*. *See* cob.

ramp. 1. Inclined plane connecting two different levels. **2.** Part of the handrail of a *stair *balustrade with a steep concave upward bend occurring where there is a landing, or where the stair has *winders. Opposite of *knee.

rampant. *See* arch.

rampart. 1. Thick wall in fortifications for defence, with a walkway or platform on top for the defenders, and a *battlemented parapet. **2.** Defensive mound of earth, with an inclined slope on the outside, its top flat and wide enough for guns and troop-movements, protected by a parapet.

ramping. **1.** To ascend or descend from one level to another. **2.** Asymmetrical *rampant* arches associated with the rake of a *ramp or *stair. *See* arch.

Ramsey, John de (*fl.* 1304–39). English master-mason. He was the son of Richard Curteys (*fl. c.*1300—probably Richard Le Machun, mason, of Norwich Cathedral from 1285 to 1290), and was Master of the Works at Norwich in 1304, when he was working on the detached *belfry. He worked on (and may have designed) the south part of the *cloisters at Norwich (1324–30), and was probably in charge of the works at Ely Cathedral (1322–*c.*1326). He is likely to have been the master-mason of that name (d. 1349) who settled in London, where the de Ramseys worked on several important projects.

Harvey (1987)

Ramsey, William de (*fl.* 1323–d. 1349). English master-mason. He worked at Norwich Cathedral on the *cloisters under John de *Ramsey in the 1320s, and probably on St Ethelbert's Chapel over the gate to the *precincts. However, he is of major importance for his work in London, where in 1323 he was employed at St Stephen's Chapel, Westminster, and from 1326 to 1331 he was Visiting Master (i.e. consultant) at Norwich Cathedral. By 1332 he was Master-Mason at St Paul's Cathedral, London, where he worked on the *chapter-house and *cloister. In 1335 he was a member of a four-mason Commission charged with reporting on the fabric of the Tower of London, and in 1336 he was appointed Chief Mason at the Tower and Chief Surveyor of the King's Works in the Tower and other castles south of the River Trent for life. In 1337 he was consulted about the works at Lichfield Cathedral, Staffordshire, where the *presbytery was being built, and in the same year was put in charge of building at St Stephen's Chapel, Westminster. He was probably involved in the design of the Hall and other buildings at Penshurst, Kent (1341–8).

Ramsey is of great importance in the evolution of the *Perpendicular style of *Gothic, for surviving illustrations and fragments of masonry suggest that the chapter-house at St Paul's (destroyed) was in that style, which first emerged there and at St Stephen's Chapel, Westminster. He was therefore probably one of the inventors of that style, and if this was so, he was one of the most influential architects England ever produced.

Harvey (1987)

rand. Border, *fillet, margin, or rim, especially in connection with landscape-gardening.

random ashlar. *Masonry of *ashlars not laid in continuous regular courses, but formed of dressed stones of different heights and widths fitted closely together, otherwise called *broken ashlar*, *random bond*, or *random range* ashlar.

random bond. *See* random ashlar.

random course. Masonry course of stones of the same height, set in a wall where the courses are of differing heights.

random range. *See* random ashlar.

random rubble. *See* rubble.

random tooled. *Ashlar wrought to a surface with irregular tooling, called random *droving* in Scotland.

range. **1.** Course of stone in a straight line. **2.** Several bodies standing in a given plane, such as columns forming a *colonnade.

ranged masonry. Coursed regular *ashlar in a straight line, called *rangework*.

ranged rubble. *See* rubble.

rangework. *As* ranged masonry.

Raphael (**Raffaello Sanzio** (1483–1520)). *High *Renaissance Urbino-born architect and painter of great distinction. Trained by his father, **Giovanni Santi** (d. 1494), and Pietro Perugino (1445/50–1523), whom he later assisted and soon surpassed, one of his early paintings, *The Marriage of the Virgin* (1504—far superior to Perugino's version of the same subject), depicts a polygonal domed building indicating a mature understanding of architecture, notably centrally planned buildings. Moving to Rome in 1508, he was commissioned by Pope Julius II (1503–13) to decorate the Stanza della Segnatura in the Vatican, including *The School of Athens* showing the ancient philosophers in an architectural setting that is a masterpiece of *perspective, and evokes *Antique *Classicism.

His first architectural foray was the Church of Sant'Eligio degli Orefici, Rome (from *c.*1511, with later dome by *Peruzzi, the whole rebuilt by *Ponzio in C17). This was followed by the *Mortuary Chapel of Agostino Chigi in Santa Maria del Pòpolo, Rome (from 1512), a centrally planned work of great authority owing its present appearance to *Bernini, who completed it (1652–6). The Palazzo Pandolfini, Florence (begun *c.*1518), merged the Florentine style of the Palazzo Strozzi with the Roman style as epitomized in *Bramante's 'House of Raphael' (Palazzo Caprini), and indeed it was from Bramante that Raphael took his precedents. In turn, his own buildings, though few in number, were soon recognized as exemplars as significant as Antique remains and the works of Bramante. Appointed Superintendent of Roman Antiquities by the Medici Pope Leo X (1513–21), in 1515, he may have been behind proposals to record all Roman ruins and restore some. The Villa Madama, which he began building near Rome (*c.*1516) for Cardinal Giulio de' Medici, the future Pope Clement VII (1523–34), is ample evidence of his feeling for Antiquity, notably in the *loggia facing the garden, and aspects of the villa were derived from recently discovered vaults of the *Domus Aurea* (Golden House) of Nero and the so-called *thermae of Titus, as well as from *Pliny's description of his Laurentine villa. Embellished with reliefs of *stucco and painted *grotesques by Raphael's assistants (including *Giulio Romano), the ensemble (though only partly completed) was an authoritative evocation of Antique interior décor. After Bramante's death Raphael was appointed *magister operis* (Master of the Works) of St Peter's, and proposed a basilican version of Bramante's plan.

Chastel (1959, 1988); Frommel *et al.* (1984); Heydenreich and Lotz (1974); Placzek (1982); Ray (1974); Tafuri (1966); Weiss (1969); Wittkower (1988)

Raphaelesque. *Antique type of ornament, the *grotesque, revived by *Raphael and others during the *Renaissance period.

Papworth (1887)

Raschdorff, Julius Karl (1823–1914). German architect. As City Architect of Cologne (1854–72) he restored many of that city's churches and other buildings. He evolved an opulent *Renaissance style in which French and German elements were mixed. From 1878 he was Professor at the *Bauakademie* (Academy of Architecture), Berlin. He designed the *mausoleum of Kaiser Friedrich III (1831–88—reigned 1888), Kaiserin (1888) Victoria, Princess Royal of England (1840–1901), and two of their children, Princes Sigismund (1864–6) and Waldemar (1868–79), at the *Friedenskirche* (Church of Peace), Potsdam (1884–9), and built the Lutheran Cathedral in the *Lustgarten* (Pleasure Garden), Berlin (1890–1905), which replaced an earlier structure altered by *Schinkel. He published *Rheinische Holz- und Fachwerkbauten des XVI. und XVII. Jahrhunderts* (Rhenish Timber and Half-timbered Buildings of the Sixteenth and Seventeenth Centuries—1895), *Der Dom zu Berlin* (Berlin Cathedral—1896), *Kaiser Friedrich Mausoleum zu Potsdam* (Emperor Friedrich's Mausoleum in Potsdam—1899), and other works.

Börsch-Supan (1977); Curl (1991); Raschdorff (1879, 1886–1922)

Rastrelli, Count Bartolomeo Francesco (1700–71). Italian architect. He was the most distinguished practitioner in mid-C18 Russia, having settled there when his father **Bartolomeo Carlo** (*c.*1675–1744), sculptor and architect, was called to St Petersburg in 1715. In the 1720s he may have studied with de *Cotte in Paris, and then travelled in Germany and Italy before returning to Russia in 1730. Under the aegis of Empress Anna Ivanovna (1730–40) and her 'favourite', Ernst Johann Biren (Biron or Bühren—1690–1772), Duke of Courland, he rose in the architectural world, designing several important buildings including the Biron Palace at Mitau (Jelgava), Latvia (1736–40). His position as Court Architect continued under Empress Elisabeth Petrovna (1741–62), and it was during her reign that he created many influential buildings in a *Baroque style of great magnificence yet delicacy. His works include the Andreas Church, Kiev (1747–68), renovations and extensions to the Summer Palace, Peterhof (1747–52), the Vorontsov (1743–57) and Stroganov (1750–4) Palaces, St Petersburg, the Smolny Cathedral and Convent, St Petersburg (1748–59), the Grand Palace, Tsarskoe Selo (1749–56), and the fourth Winter Palace, St Petersburg (1754–62), the last probably his finest achievement.

His work often synthesized French, Italian, South-German, and Russian styles, and his sources were many. He was accomplished in creating very long façades broken up by emphatic vertical punctuations, best seen in the charming *scenographic Winter Palace. At the Andreas Church, Kiev, and the Smolny Convent, St Petersburg, he drew on C17 Russian church architecture for his

Greek-cross plans, dominant central *cupola, and lesser domes. His highly individual style created buildings of great charm. Most of his *Rococo interiors have been destroyed or altered.

Hamilton (1983); Norberg-Schulz (1986*a*); Ousiannikov (1982)

ratch(e)ment. Curved member resembling a sort of flying *buttress rising from the corner uprights of a *hearse, meeting a similar member at a central upright. Ratchements supported the hangings, valancing, and palls, and often carried *prickets for candles.

Parker (1850)

rath. Earth or stone enclosure, often circular on plan, serving as a fortified enclosure, found in Ireland.

Rational architecture. Movement in late-C20 architecture that proposed reasonable and buildable responses to design problems drawing on order in urban fabric and on architectural typology. It evolved from the 1960s, prompted by Aldo *Rossi's *L'Architettura delle città* (Architecture of the City—1966 and 1982) and *Architettura Razionale*, by Rossi and others, published during the XVth Milan Triennale (1973). Rational architecture embraced *Renaissance theory, the bold *Neoclassicism of the C18 *Enlightenment, and some of the architectural arguments of the 1920s. Its apologists insisted that its essentials, its laws, and its historical continuity confirmed it as an independent legitimate discipline. Unlike the theorists of C20 *Rationalism and of the *Modern Movement, the protagonists of Rational architecture saw the European historical city as a repository of great riches, composed of *types that were primary, unchangeable, historical essentials in architecture incapable of reduction or subdivision. By rediscovering and redefining the formal vocabulary and language of architecture that had been so thoroughly disrupted (and even corrupted) from the 1920s they sought to reconcile Architecture, the City, and Mankind, for they argued that humans had become alienated by *Functionalism, *International Modernism, and the Modern Movement as a whole.

Examples of Rational architecture include Rossi's Apartment Building in the Gallaratese 2 Complex, Amiata Estate, Milan (1969–73), and *Grassi's Students' Residence, Chieti (1976–84). Among the chief protagonists of Rational architecture were *Botta, the *Kriers (Léon being one of its most powerful polemicists), *Reichlin, and *Ungers. Some critics prefer to call Rational architecture *Neo-Rationalism or the *Tendenza.

Lampugnani (1988); Rossi (1982); Rossi *et al.* (1973)

Rationalism. Term employed to mean different things at different times by various groups in the history of C20 architecture, but mostly applied to mean the architectural principles behind the *International *Modern Movement led by such personalities as *Gropius and *Mies van der Rohe subscribing to the so-called *Machine Aesthetic and to *Functionalism. However, the word has been so loosely used that some expanded explanations are necessary.

Classical and *Renaissance architectural treatises argued that architecture was a science with principles that could be understood on a rational basis. C18 and C19 theorists, notably J.-N.-L. *Durand, *Viollet-le-Duc, *Semper, and others also argued for reasonable approaches to design derived from the culture of the European *Enlightenment. Those arguing for C20 Rationalism did not have any one coherent theory, but made assumptions that architectural and urban problems could be solved primarily through an abandonment of *Historicism and of movements such as the *Arts-and-Crafts, *Art Nouveau, and *Expressionism (which they regarded as dead-ends), thus creating a *tabula rasa* on which to start again. They tended to be messianic in their desire for a new world, better architecture, Socialist structures, and a belief in the inherent rightness of what they were seeking, drawing on a Machine Aesthetic to achieve the appropriate image.

Advocates of Rationalism evolved certain principles by which their aims were to be met. First, architecture, industrial design, and planning could be used for social engineering and educational purposes, and so design had a moral meaning (a notion drawn partly from the writings of A. W. N. *Pugin and *Ruskin). Second, strict economy, cheap *industrialized building methods, and a total absence of ornament were to be employed to achieve a minimum standard for everyone's habitation. Third, *prefabrication, industrial technologies, and mass-production at all levels were to be used in the making of the new environment, but, even if traditional methods of construction were employed (bricks, after all, are mass-produced, standardized, prefabricated building-components), buildings should *look* machine-made in their pristine state (so brickwork was disguised by being covered with smooth *render). Fourth, wholesale clearances, demolitions, and the destruction of existing urban fabric were deemed to be essential so that vast housing-estates could be erected. Lastly, form itself should be evolved for constructional, economic, functional, political, and social reasons, and so was not (in theory) subject to individual fancy (but in fact was largely determined by a few paradigms).

In practice, Rationalism encouraged an approved *International style from which all historical and decorative elements were expunged, drawing on influences from e.g. *Constructivism and de *Stijl. Among key buildings were *Gropius's *Bauhaus, Dessau (1925–6), Le *Corbusier's Maison Stein, Garches (1927), and houses at the *Weissenhofsiedlung, Stuttgart (1927), while theoretical and unifying bases were provided by *CIAM and certain writers, notably *Giedion and *Pevsner.

It is one of the curiosities of Rationalism that it flourished in Italy under Benito Mussolini's Fascist regime (1922–43), and in fact *International Modernism was also called Rationalism by *Gruppo 7. *Terragni was perhaps the most distinguished Italian Rationalist, with his Fascist Party Headquarters, Como (1932–6). Gruppo 7 expanded to form the Movimento Italiano per l'Architettura Razionale (*MIAR), inspired partly by *Futurism. After the 1939–45 war Rationalism was adopted, virtually as the *de rigueur* style of Western Europe and America. Looked at objectively, it was just another style, drawing its motifs from a limited range of features approved in the 1920s, and owing very little to rationalism at all, but more to the desire for images thought to be appropriate for the times, and that, in any case, were usually only *metaphors* of mass-production, modernity, and industrialization.

Behne (1926); Etlin (1991); Giedion (1967, 1969); Gropius (1952, 1962, 1965); Hilbersheimer (1925, 1927*a*); Koulermos (1995); Lampugnani (1988); Mantero (1984); Pevsner (1960, 1974*a*); Pevsner and Richards (1973); Schumacher (1991); Watkin (1977)

Rattenbury, Francis Mawson (1867–1935). English architect. He won the competition for the British Columbia Legislature, Victoria, Canada (1893–8), with a handsome design in which English *Renaissance elements were mixed with massive arches similar to those employed by *Richardson. He also designed in the *Beaux-Arts and *château styles. Notable buildings include the Empress Hotel, Victoria, British Columbia (1903–8), and the Bank of Montreal (1907). He was the victim of a notorious murder in Bournemouth, England, after he retired.

Barrett and Liscombe (1983); Kalman (1994)

Rauch, John (1930–   ). *See* Venturi.

ravelin. In a fortification, an outwork consisting of two *battered faces forming a *salient angle, constructed beyond the *counter-scarp or slope of the main ditch in front of the *curtain-wall of the fortifications. It was a common feature in *Renaissance and later military architecture.

Rawlinson, Sir Robert (1810–98). English civil engineer. In 1831 he joined Jesse *Hartley and worked on the construction of docks and harbour works until he entered the employment of Robert *Stephenson, and was engaged on the building of the London and Birmingham railway. In 1840 he returned to Liverpool as Assistant Surveyor to the Corporation, where he was primarily concerned with public health: his proposals to supply the city with water drawn from Wales were eventually implemented. He is best remembered as head of the Commission charged with ameliorating the deplorable sanitary conditions of the British army during the Crimean war. Thereafter he was mostly involved in improving public health, especially in regard to water-supply and sewerage: for his contributions he was knighted in 1883. He published numerous books and papers on drainage, hygiene, and public works. Apart from his undoubted national and international importance in this respect, his architectural activities included responsibility for the construction of *Elmes's St George's Hall, Liverpool, from 1841: the structure of this, probably the finest Neoclassical building in the British Isles, was completed by Rawlinson in 1851, after which C. R. *Cockerell finished the interiors, largely to his own designs (1851–4).

Colvin (1995); *DNB* (1917)

Raymond, Antonin (1889–1976). Bohemia-born American architect. He assisted Cass *Gilbert when designing the Woolworth Building, New York (1910–12), and then joined

F. L. *Wright in 1912, later collaborating in the building of the Imperial Hotel, Tokyo (1919–20). He practised in Tokyo on his own account (1923–37), designing several buildings, including his own houses at Reinanzaka (1923—an early example of *International Modernism) and Karuizawa (1932–3), the Akaboshi House (1932), and the Kawasaki House (1934), all in Tokyo. In the 1930s he began to experiment with pitched roofs, but in 1937 left Japan, and after a brief stay in India set up an office in New York, specializing in Federal, State, and Local-Government work. In 1949 he returned to Japan to build the *Reader's Digest* Building, Tokyo (1947–50), which incorporated Japanese elements such as *louvres, and in 1953, with his house at Azubu, he introduced traditional Japanese construction. Among his last works were the *campus of the Nanzan University, Nagoya (1960–6), and the Pan-Pacific Forum, University of Hawaii, Honolulu (1966–9). He was a considerable influence on those Japanese architects who pioneered the *Modern Movement after the 1939–45 war.

Emanuel (1994); Raymond (1973); van Vynckt (1993)

Raymond, Jean-Arnaud (1742–1811). French architect. A pupil of J.-F. *Blondel and *Soufflot, he supervised the erection of some of *Ledoux's *Barrières* around Paris from 1785, and designed the *hôtel and gallery for Elisabeth Vigée-Lebrun (1755–1842), the celebrated portrait-painter (1784–6). He became architect to the Louvre, Paris, in 1798, rendering parts of it suitably magnificent to provide a setting for the treasures looted by Napoleon from the rest of Europe, and was succeeded by *Percier and *Fontaine (1805). His main claim to fame was his association with *Chalgrin in the early designs of the Arc de Triomphe de l'Étoile, Paris (1805–6—engraved by L.-M. *Normand), but he also contributed to works at the Bibliothèque Nationale and the Opéra, little of which has survived.

Gazette des Beaux-Arts, ser. 6, 56 (1960), 275–84; Papworth (1887); Sturgis *et al.* (1901–2)

Raymond du Temple (*fl. c.*1360–1405). French master-mason to Kings Charles V (1364–80) and VI (1380–1422) of France. He was involved in work at Notre Dame, Paris, from 1363. Employed at the Louvre, Paris, in 1364, he built the external spiral staircase and made other extensive additions. He was also a consultant at Troyes Cathedral, *c.*1401, and has been credited with the design of the *Château and Chapel of Vincennes (1370s). He designed and built the Chapelle des Célestins (1367–70) and the Collège de Beauvais, Paris (1387), including the *chapel.

Papworth (1887); Sturgis *et al.* (1901–2)

Rayonnant. Style of *Gothic prevalent in France from *c.*1227 to the mid-C14. Its first phase is called the *Court style, from its association with the reign of Louis IX (1227–70), of which the rebuilt Abbey of St-Denis, Troyes Cathedral, and the Chapel at St-Germain-en-Laye are good examples (all 1230s). The Rayonnant style takes its name from the shapes formed by *tracery-*bars and from the vault-ribs radiating from *piers shaped with masses of shafts corresponding to the ribs.

Branner (1965); Papworth (1887); Watkin (1996)

Read, Herbert (*c.*1861–1935). British architect. Articled to *George & Peto, he set up in partnership with Robert Falconer Macdonald (1862–1913) in 1891. They carried out numerous well-crafted designs for the Cadogan and Grosvenor Estates in London. Typical of their work was the group of buildings at the corner of 57–9 Piccadilly (1904), and 45–6 Old Bond Street, both in London.

Gray (1985)

Read, Sir Herbert Edward (1893–1968). British critic and writer. He was a leading supporter of *Modernism in the 1930s, and edited *Unit One: The Modern Movement in English Architecture, Painting and Sculpture* (1934). His *The Meaning of Art* (1931), *Art Now* (1933), *Art and Industry* (1934), *Surrealism* (1936), *Art and Society* (1936), and *Education Through Art* (1943) were reprinted several times, and were very influential in spreading the gospel of Modernism in the English-speaking world. His *Concise History of Modern Painting* (1959) and *Concise History of Modern Sculpture* (1964) further enhanced his reputation. He edited the *Burlington Magazine* (1933–9).

Chilvers, Osborne, and Farr (1988); *DNB* (1981)

rear arch. *See* arch.

rear *or* **rere vault.** Internal arch or *vault (called *arrière voussure* or *scoinson arch*) at the head of a splayed *Gothic aperture springing from the *jambs, *corbels, or attached shafts (*escoinsons*) at the angles of jambs and interior walls.

Re/architecture. The reuse and refurbishment of old buildings of quality that no longer function as originally intended (e.g. *Hartley's Albert Docks, Liverpool).

Cantacuzino (1989)

rebate. *See* rabbet.

Rebecca, John Biagio (d. 1847). English architect of Italian descent. The son of **Biagio Rebecca** (1735–1808), the decorative painter, he practised in London and Sussex. He designed Castle Goring, near Arundel, Sussex (*c*.1795–1815), *Neoclassical on one side and *castellated on the other. He seems to have specialized in *Tudor *Gothic, but could turn his hand to Greek *Doric to some effect.

Colvin (1995)

rebus. Enigmatical representation of a name, or graphic pun on the name of a person connected with a building, usually in the carved ornamentation, as in the Alcock *Chantry Chapel in Ely Cathedral, Cambridgeshire (1488–1501), with its many representations of cockerels.

Rectilinear. *See* Perpendicular, tracery.

Rectory. Province or residence of the parson (Rector) serving the parochial or common church, who had the right to the great tithes and who was the holder of a perpetual curacy.

redan. 1. Small *ravelin or fieldwork with two faces forming a *salient angle. **2.** Projection or break at the angle of a panel. **3.** Step in a wall built on rising ground.

Redman *or* **Redmayne, Henry** (*fl.* 1495–d. 1528). Leading English master-mason. A son of **Thomas Redman** (*fl.* 1490–d. 1516), he worked at Westminster Abbey from 1495 to 1497. With William *Vertue he was consulted about King's College Chapel, Cambridge, visiting the building in 1509, and succeeded his father as Master-Mason at Westminster Abbey in 1515/16, working on the *nave. He rebuilt the *chancel of St Margaret's Church, Westminster (1516–23), where he also designed the tower and porch (1516–22). From 1516 he worked with Vertue on the designs for the new work at Eton College, Buckinghamshire, including the west side of the court and Lupton's Tower (1516–20). He became architect to Cardinal Wolsey (*c*.1475–1530), with power of supervision over His Eminence's enormous range of building-projects, including Hampton Court Palace, and by 1525 was at work with John *Lebons at Cardinal (now Christ Church) College, Oxford, where they laid out the plan and built the south range and most of the east and west ranges. Among his last works were the *cloister and cloister-chapel of St Stephen's College, Westminster Palace, begun *c*.1526. He was a pioneer in the use of brick in late-*Gothic architecture of the *Tudor period, and his works had a lasting influence.

Harvey (1987)

redoubt. 1. Inner last retreat in a fortification. **2.** Fieldwork or outwork enclosed on all sides, of square or polygonal shape, set beyond the *glacis, known as a *detached redoubt*. **3.** Small work projecting from or within a *bastion or *ravelin. **4.** Public assembly-hall, especially in Germany (e.g. *Redoutensaal*, Vienna).

reed. Small, convex moulding, smaller than an *ovolo or bead, usually found with several others parallel to it, called *reeding.

reeding. Decorative moulding of several parallel *reeds in a continuous line. It is an important element of the *Asiatic base of the *Ionic *Order.

reel. *See* bead.

re-entrant. Two faces of a building meeting at an *external angle form a *salient, while two walls meeting at an *internal angle form a re-entrant. An external angle or salient with an internal angle formed in it, as though, on plan, a small square had been removed from the angle of the building, is a re-entrant.

refectory. Frater-house or dining-hall of a college, *monastery, etc.

Régence. Style in the period (1715–23) of the minority of King *Louis XV of France associated with *Rococo.

Regency. Strictly speaking, the style of English architecture and decoration fashionable during the illness of King George III (1810–20), when George, Prince of Wales (1762–1830), was Regent, but loosely applied to the period from the late 1790s to the accession of King William IV (1830–7). It was essentially Neoclassical, embracing *Egyptian, *Greek, and *Pompeian motifs, and was much influenced by the *Empire style of France. Regency taste was showy, eclectic, and opulent, uninhibitedly drawing on Oriental themes such as *Chinoiserie and the *Hindoo style, *Gothick, and a host of diverting styles. It was particularly associated with the *Picturesque and with the architecture of *Nash.

Lewis and Darley (1986); Osborne (1975)

Reginald of Ely (d. 1471). *See* Ely.

reglet. *Fillet-moulding such as that in a *Chinese fret or *guilloche ornament. Used mostly in compartments and panels, it defines and separates parts from each other, or covers joints.

regula (*pl.* **regulae**). **1.** *Fillet beneath the *taenia, in line with the *triglyph above, from which the *guttae hang in the *Doric *entablature. **2.** *Plinth under the base of a column. **3.** *Pedestal under a column.

Reichlin, Bruno (1941–). Swiss architect, associated with the *Ticinese School and the *Tendenza. He practised from 1970 with Fabio Reinhart (1942–), and both men taught under *Rossi at the *Eidgenössische Technische Hochschule* (Confederate Technical High School), Zurich (1972–4). They designed the Casa Tonini, Torricella (1972–4), a variant on *Palladio's *Villa Capra*, and built other villas, including the Casa Sartori, Riveo (1976–7), where *Classicism is stripped and bared to its most essential elemental forms. They have been distinguished exponents of *Rational architecture, or *Neo-Rationalism. In 1976 Marie-Claude Bétrix and Eraldo Consolascio joined the partnership, and among their works is the Sferax Factory, Cortaillod (1978–81).

Blaser (1982); Steinmann and Boga (1975)

Reid, Robert (1774–1856). Chief Government Architect in Scotland in the first half of C19. Influenced by the style of the *Adam brothers, his public buildings are less attenuated than theirs. Although castigated by some of his contemporaries for dullness, his contributions do much for the urban fabric of Edinburgh, and include the Law Courts, Parliament Square (1804–40), the Bank of Scotland on The Mound (1802–6—with Richard Crichton, *c.*1771–1817), the exterior of the Signet and Advocates' Houses, Parliament Square (1810–12), St George's Church, Charlotte Square (1811–14—the *cupola of which resembles those by *Gontard in the *Gendarmenmarkt*, Berlin (1780–5), a fact noted by *Schinkel when he visited Edinburgh in 1826), the handsome Custom House, Leith (1811–12), and the layout of the northern extension of Edinburgh New Town, including Cumberland, Dublin, Dundas, Dundonald, Great King, India, Nelson, Northumberland, and Scotland Streets, as well as Abercromby Place, Drummond Place, Fettes Row, Gloucester Place, Heriot Row, Mansfield Place, and Royal Crescent (from 1802). This New Town layout was prepared with William *Sibbald, but Reid designed the main elevations. He was also responsible for 33–46 Charlotte Square, Edinburgh (1807–15), the Academy, Perth (1803–7), the Prison, Perth (1810–12), and part of Downpatrick Gaol, Co. Down, Ireland (1824–30). The Library and Picture Gallery he designed at Paxton House, Berwickshire (1812–13), is arguably his best work. In 1809 he published *Observations on the Structure of Hospitals for the Treatment of Lunatics*, and designed the Lunatic Asylum, Morningside, Edinburgh (1809–10—demolished).

Colvin (1995); *DNB* (1917); Youngson (1966)

Reidy, Affonso Eduardo (1909–64). Brazilian Paris-born architect. A disciple of *Warchavchik and Le *Corbusier, he worked with others on the Ministry of Health and Education Building, Rio de Janeiro (1936–49). In 1947 he was appointed to the Department of Public Housing, and designed Pedregulho, a large low-income housing project in Rio de Janeiro (1947–52), followed by the similar residential project at Gávea, also in Rio (1950–2). His best-known work is the Museum of Modern Art, Rio de Janeiro (1954–60), a variation on Le Corbusier's 1937 design for the Pavillon des Temps Nouveau.

Franck (1960); Morgan and Naylor (1987)

Reilly, Sir Charles Herbert (1874–1948). London-born British architect, important as a pedagogue and author. He gained his early experience in *Belcher's office before working with *Peach, with whom he designed the Power Station, Ipswich, Suffolk (1900–4) and the Grove Road Power Station, London (1902–4—demolished). He built up the School of Architecture at the University of Liverpool, where he was Professor from 1904 until 1933, adopting American *Beaux-Arts principles. Under his direction it acquired an international reputation. At first, the School promoted the Neoclassical (or *Neo-Grec) style, with a pronounced American flavour (e.g.

Reilly's Student-Union Building (1908) and Gilmour Hall (1910–12), both in Liverpool), but later, as a consultant, he encouraged *International Modernism in London with the Peter Jones Department Store, Sloane Square, London, designed by his former students, *Crabtree, Slater, & Moberley (1934–9). Reilly himself designed few buildings, but those that were realized were of interest: they include the Church of St Barnabas, Shacklewell, Hackney, London (1909–29), a crescent of houses in the South-African *Colonial style at Port Sunlight, Cheshire (designed before 1914), the Accrington War Memorial, Lancashire, and Durham County War Memorial (both 1920). His books include *Some Liverpool Streets and their Buildings* (1921), *McKim, Mead, & White* (1924), *Some Manchester Streets and their Buildings* (1924), *Representative British Architects of Today* (1931), and *The Theory and Practice of Architecture* (1932).

DNB (1959); Gray (1985); Stamp and Harte

reinforced concrete. *Concrete once set will take a superimposed load that compresses it, but, if used, say, as a beam, will fail if heavily loaded, because it is weak in tension. Steel, on the other hand, is strong in tension, so the two materials are combined to enable the concrete to perform well in tension as well as in compression by casting steel rods in the positions where reinforcing is necessary to improve tensile strength, especially in beams, *lintels, etc. Reinforced concrete can be used to construct entire skeletal *frames, floor-slabs, walls, etc., either *pre-cast* in a factory or *in situ* (on site, i.e. where it will be permanently). Also called *ferro-concrete* it lends itself to the creation of complex curved forms that may get their stability partly from shape, permitting its use in bridges and *shell-roofs.

Allen (1988); Faber and Alsop (1976)

Reinhart, Fabio (1942–). *See* Reichlin.

relief. Projection of a design, or parts of it, from a plane surface in order to give a natural and solid appearance, called *rilievo*. The three main types in architecture are *alto-rilievo* (ornament in high relief, almost detached from its ground); *mezzo-rilievo* (ornament standing out roughly half its three-dimensional form from the ground); and *basso-rilievo* (ornament with a projection less than half its three-dimensional form).

relieving arch. *See* arch.

relieving triangle. Approximate triangle above a *lintel where masonry courses in a wall are corbelled over each other so avoiding any loading on the lintel (e.g. in Mycenaean construction).

Renaissance, Renascence. From the French *renaître* (to be born again) and the Italian *Rinascimento* (rebirth), the term is given to the great revival of arts and letters under the influence of Classical precedents which began in Italy in C14 and continued during the following two centuries, spreading to virtually all parts of Europe. It is also a convenient label for the style of architecture that developed in, and was characteristic of, that period from the time of *Brunelleschi in Florence (early C15) to the beginnings of *Mannerism (*c.*1520), and which was based on the architecture of Roman Antiquity. Indeed, it was referred to as *maniera all'antica*, and the style was codified by *Alberti in *De re aedificatoria* (begun around 1450), drawing on the exemplary work of *Vitruvius. In architecture the Renaissance includes the *High Renaissance (*c.*1500–*c.*1520) in which *Leonardo, *Michelangelo, and *Raphael flourished, but it does not include the *Baroque. Elsewhere in Europe, Renaissance architecture tended to acquire Italian Renaissance motifs, either from printed sources or from the observations of travellers, but each country or region produced buildings that looked un-Italian: German, French, Flemish, Spanish, and English (the latter associated with *Elizabethan and *Jacobean architecture) Renaissance styles all had distinct flavours. English, Flemish, German, Polish, and Scandinavian Renaissance buildings of C16 and early C17 fall into the Northern Renaissance category, but the infusion of Mannerism gave French Renaissance architecture a different flavour. Only in the early C17 was uncorrupted Renaissance architecture, firmly based on Italian prototypes, introduced in England (*see* Paesschen) by Inigo *Jones, an event that was enormously influential in C18, first in England, and then elsewhere. There were various national Renaissance Revivals in C19 once *Neoclassicism had become wearisome.

Chilvers, Osborne, and Farr (1988); Lewis and Darley (1986); Osborne (1970)

render, rendering. 1. Finish or finishing applied to a surface not intended to be exposed. The term was given historically to the first coat, the second the *float*, and the final the *set*.

Common renders are with *pebble-dash, plaster, and *stucco. **2.** Architectural drawing enlivened by water-colour washes and *sciagraphy to make it more realistic.

Rennie, John (1761–1821). Scots architect and engineer. He made his reputation with the design and installation of machinery at the Albion Flour Mills, Southwark, London (1784—destroyed 1791), and he established his own business in 1791, designing bridges, canals, systems of land-drainage, harbours, light-houses, and docks, all of which are admirable both in their architecture and engineering. They include the Tweed Bridge, Kelso, Roxburghshire (1800–3), the Dundas Aqueduct, Limpley Stoke, Wiltshire (*c.*1795–7), and London Bridge (1824–31—rebuilt at Lake Havasu City, Ariz., USA, 1963–71). London Bridge was constructed under the direction of his sons, **George** (1791–1866) and **John** (1794–1874). The latter, who was knighted on the completion of the bridge in 1831, designed various works in the Royal Dockyards, including the Royal William Victualling Yard, Stonehouse, near Plymouth (completed 1832), one of the most impressive architectural ensembles ever constructed in England. J. *Britton, in *The Original Picture of London*, claimed John Rennie jun. was the architect of the Stamford Street Unitarian Chapel, Blackfriars, London (1823), the fine Greek *Doric *portico of which alone survives. However, Charles Parker (1799–1881) has also been credited with the authorship of this building.

Boucher (1963); Colvin (1995); *DNB* (1917); Reyburn (1972); Smiles (1862); Summerson (1993)

Renwick, James (1818–95). American architect, mostly active in New York. He is best remembered for Grace Church, Broadway (1843–6—one of the first in the USA in which a scholarly feeling for *Gothic Revival of the *Second Pointed variety was demonstrated), and St Patrick's Cathedral (1858–79). The original design (1853–7) of St Patrick's, the most important building for Roman Catholics in the USA at the time, was an eclectic tour-de-force made possible after Renwick augmented his knowledge of Continental Gothic during a study-visit to France in 1855. It drew on architectural themes from Rheims, Amiens, and Cologne Cathedrals for the exterior, and York *Minster, Exeter Cathedral, and Westminster Abbey for the interior, but, as built, was severely modified and skimped, even to the loss of the proposed octagonal *crossing-tower. He also designed the Smithsonian Institution, Washington, DC (1847–55), a *Picturesque composition incorporating aspects of English, French, and German *Romanesque exemplars, and Vassar College, Poughkeepsie, NY (1861–5), a simplified version of the French *Renaissance Palace of the Tuileries, Paris, with other Renaissance influences.

DAB (1943); Hitchcock (1977); Pierson and Jordy (1970–86); Placzek (1982); Whiffen and Koeper (1983)

repeating ornament. Pattern capable of being infinitely extended, e.g. *chequer-board and *diaper-work.

Repton, Humphry (1752–1818). Leading English landscape-designer after the death of 'Capability' *Brown (1783). Repton responded to the fashion of the 1780s for a more truly 'natural' *Picturesque approach than Brown's, and his abilities as a water-colourist enabled him to make his intentions clear to clients by means of 'before' and 'after' views which he presented in his famous 'red books', of which over 70 are recorded. His plantations were more dense than Brown's, and he introduced unfamiliar imported varieties of trees and shrubs. In 1795 he formed an association with John *Nash, and carried out works at Burley-on-the-Hill, Rutland (1795), Corsham, Wiltshire (1796–1800), Southgate Grove, London (1797), Attingham Park, Shropshire (1798), Luscombe, Devon (1799), and other places. There is no doubt that Repton's ideas had a profound influence on Nash, as can be seen at the latter's Blaise Hamlet, near Bristol (1810–11), and developments at Regent's Park Villages, London, completed by *Pennethorne. Repton had been on good terms with those high-priests of the Picturesque, Payne *Knight and Uvedale *Price, but Knight poured scorn on Repton's red book for Tatton Park, Cheshire, to which Repton responded by defending his approach to design in *Sketches and Hints on Landscaping Gardening* (1795). He later published *Observations on Landscape Gardening* (1803) and *An Inquiry into the Changes of Taste* (1806). *Fragments on the Theory and Practice of Landscape Gardening* (1818) was his last publication.

Although not trained as an architect, he saw architecture as an 'inseparable and indispensable auxiliary' to landscape-gardening, and often introduced architectural arrangements around the houses for which he was preparing landscape-designs, including terraces with steps, *conservatories, and 'winter-corridors' (for perambulation during inclement weather). He prepared a *Hindoo design for Brighton Pavilion, Sussex (1806), but was not a little put out when his former colleague, Nash, supplanted him. With Nash, however, Repton was a pioneer of the cottage style that was to be such an important part of the Picturesque movement. In 1840 Repton's disciple, J. C. *Loudon, reprinted his main publications, with a memoir and reproductions of the Brighton Pavilion designs, in *The Landscape Gardening and Landscape Architecture of the late Humphry Repton*. Repton collaborated with his son **John** on the landscapes of Sheringham Hall, Norfolk (1812–19), and Ashridge, Hertfordshire (*c*.1814). His reintroduction of terraces and *parterres, and his designs for rose-gardens and aviaries had a profound effect on *Victorian garden-design.

Colvin (1995); *DNB* (1917); Hussey (1967*a*); Stroud (1962); Watkin (1982*a*)

Repton, John Adey (1775–1860). Eldest son of Humphry *Repton, he collaborated with his father on a number of projects, especially after the latter was severely disabled in 1811. J. A. Repton studied with William *Wilkins, Senior, in Norwich, from whom he acquired a love of medieval architecture. In 1796 he entered *Nash's office where he carried out alterations at Corsham Court, Wiltshire (1797–8), but Nash appears to have exploited the young man (who was totally deaf from infancy), so he joined his father in 1802, and carried out many alterations to country-houses where Humphry was improving the gardens. He made extensive changes to a number of Continental estates, including that of Prince Hermann Pückler-Muskau (1785–1871—author of *Andeutungen über Landschaftgärtnerei* (Hints on Landscape Gardening—1834)) at Neu-Hardenberg, near Frankfurt/Oder (1822), and Schloss Glienicke, near Potsdam (also 1822, but begun by Peter Joseph *Lenné in 1816). Architecturally he favoured an *Elizabethan style, but he also used the Classical style (Sheringham Hall, Norfolk (1813–19)), and the *Romanesque Revival (at Holy Trinity Church, Springfield, near Chelmsford, Essex (1842–3)).

Colvin (1995); *DNB* (1917); Hussey (1958); Stroud (1962)

rere. *See* rear.

reredorter. Privy at the back of a dormitory in a *monastery.

reredos. Ornamental facing or *screen behind an altar in a church, free-standing or forming part of the *retable. In larger churches it separates the *choir from the *retrochoir, *Lady-chapel, and other parts to the liturgical east, and is often found enriched with statues in *niches, *pinnacles, etc. Another form of medieval reredos was the *triptych.

respond. *Corbel, half-pier, or other architectural element *engaged to a wall at the end of an *arcade from which the first arch springs. In Classical architecture, an *anta or *pilaster-like motif where arcades or *colonnades engage with a wall.

ressant, ressaunt. *Ogee.

ressault, ressaut. 1. Projection, as of a *chimney-breast, *pilaster, or any member or part of a building before a wall or another, e.g. a moulding projecting in front of another moulding. **2.** In Classical architecture the breaking out of a length of *entablature with two returns, with a column and pilaster, or pair of columns supporting the projection. **3.** *Roll-moulding.

ressaunt. *See* ressant.

restoration. Process of carrying on alterations and repairs to a building with the intention of restoring it to its original form, often involving reinstatement of missing or badly damaged parts, so it usually includes replication, that is new work in an old style. While often necessary after a disaster, it is generally regarded as more drastic than *conservation, which suggests retention, repair, and maintenance.

Restoration. The re-establishment of the Stuart Monarchy in Great Britain and Ireland in 1660, so the period following this event, later in the reign of King Charles II (1660–85) referred to as the *Caroline period. Restoration architecture was strongly influenced by Continental fashion, the dominant style being *Baroque derived from French and Netherlandish precedents. Typical Restoration buildings were the symmetrical houses of *Pratt and Hugh *May, the grander works of *Talman, and the great contribution of *Wren, whose chief sources were French and Italian.

retable. 1. Screen to the rear of an altar, rising up behind it, often richly decorated and carved, including the *reredos. **2.** Shelf or ornamental setting for panels behind an altar. **3.** Frame around painted or other decorated panels of a reredos.

retaining-wall. **1.** Wall, often *battered, also called a *revetment, preventing a bank of earth, etc., from slipping: it is found in the form of battered arched *piers at the back of which are segmental concave walls (like *vaults) to resist the pressure behind them, often associated with C19 railway architecture. **2.** A dam.

reticulated. **1.** Constructed or arranged to resemble a net, with the repetition of the same figure all over the surface or plane, as in a *screen or *lattice, or a wall made of polygonal masonry, such as *ragstone, or constructed of square stones placed diagonally. **2.** With a capital R (*Reticulated*), the term refers to a type of Curvilinear *Gothic *tracery consisting of a net-like mesh of interweaving *ogees forming a pattern. *See also* *opus reticulatum.

retrochoir. Portion of a large church behind the *retable or *reredos of the high-altar, in apsidal arrangements including parts of the north and south *chancel-aisles on either side as well as the area to the east. It is essentially the volume bounded by the sanctuary and the *chapels to the east, as in Winchester Cathedral, Hampshire.

return. Any part of a building that turns at an angle (usually 90°) from its principal face, such as the side of a *pilaster or the *jamb of an aperture. A return forming an oblique angle is a *splayed return*. If a moulding is continued in a different direction from its main direction, as with a *hood-moulding over a medieval window or door returning downwards to a *label-stop, it is referred to as a *returned moulding*. Similarly, the *stalls in a church *choir set against *screens between the choir and choir-aisles and returning at an angle of 90° at the back of the *pulpitum or choir-screen are called *returned stalls*.

reveal, revel. Vertical *return or side of an aperture in a wall between the *naked of the wall and e.g. a door-frame. It is generally set square with the face, the return inwards from the reveal for the door- or window-frame being the *rebate*, and the inside return the *jamb, often splayed, hence a *splayed reveal*.

reveal lining. Panelling, shutter-cases, etc., as a finish on the inner *reveal of a window, etc.

Reveley, Henry Willey (1788–1875). English architect, the son of Willey *Reveley. He was civil engineer at Cape Town, Cape Colony, South Africa from 1826 where he built the *Doric St Andrew's Presbyterian Church (1827) and the *Ionic St George's Church (1828). He then settled in Western Australia, where he designed the Gaol, Fremantle (1830), and the Court House (1837), and erected other public buildings in Perth. He returned to England in 1838.

Colvin (1995); Lewcock (1963)

Reveley, Willey (1760–99). English architect. He assisted *Chambers in the building of Somerset House, London, and from 1784 to 1789 he travelled in Italy, Greece, and Egypt with the antiquary Sir Richard Worsley, Bt. (1751–1805), as an architect and draughtsman. On his return to England he established a reputation as an expert on Greek architecture. He designed the Neoclassical All Saints' Church, Southampton (1792–5—destroyed), and a mansion at Windmill Hill, Sussex (1796–8), illustrated in *New Vitruvius Britannicus* (1810). His chief claim to fame is that he edited and prepared the third volume of *Stuart and *Revett's *The Antiquities of Athens* (1794), and made drawings of the pyramids at Giza (now lost).

Colvin (1995); *DNB* (1917); Papworth (1887)

Revell, Viljo Gabriel (1910–64). Finnish architect. He made his name with the 'glass palace' office-building, Helsinki (1935—with Niilo Kokko and Heimo Riihimäki). He assisted *Aalto on the Finnish Pavilion for the 1937 Paris Exposition, and after the 1939–45 war his frequent use of horizontal strip-windows and *pilotis in many of his buildings (such as the Teollisuuskeskus office-building, Helsinki (1952), designed with Keijo Petäjä) established his credentials as an *International Modernist. In 1958, with Heikki Castrén, Bengt Lundsten, and Seppo Valjus, he won the competition to design the City Hall, Toronto, Canada, with a design incorporating two curved towers embracing a domed hall (completed 1964): the building was realized in conjunction with John B. *Parkin Associates. He was influential in promoting *industrialized building and standardization.

Ålander (1996); Hertzen and Speiregen (1973); Kalman (1994); Morgan and Naylor (1987)

reversed zig-zag. *Chevron moulding overlapping another in the opposite direction, forming a series of Z-shapes instead of V-shapes.

reverse ogee. *See* cyma.

revetment. 1. In masonry, a thin facing to hide the surface or construction behind, such as the marble *cladding of *Terragni's Casa del Fascio, Como (1932–6). **2.** *Retaining-wall.

Revett, Nicholas (1720–1804). English architect and painter, and a leading figure in the dissemination of knowledge of Ancient Greek architecture. With James *Stuart he measured all the principal monuments of Athens (1751–3), and was responsible for the architectural parts of the drawings from which the plates of *The Antiquities of Athens, Measured and Delineated by James Stuart, F.R.S. and F.S.A., and Nicholas Revett, Painters and Architects* were made (the first volume appeared in 1762). This was one of the key publications leading to the *Greek Revival. Stuart bought out Revett's interest even before the first volume appeared, but Revett went on to measure antiquities in Asia Minor (1764–6) under the aegis of The Society of *Dilettanti, and under his editorship *The Antiquities of Ionia* appeared (1769–97).

Revett was sufficiently well-off not to have to earn his living, but he turned his hand to architecture on occasion. Among his works are the *Ionic *portico (based on the Temple of Bacchus at Teos) of West Wycombe Park, Buckinghamshire (1771), and Ayot St Lawrence Church, Hertfordshire (1778–9), with a *Doric Order based on the Temple of Apollo at Delos. He seems also to have designed a portico in the garden at Brandeston, Suffolk, which, if Greek in style, must have been one of the earliest examples of the Greek Revival anywhere (1757).

Colvin (1995); Crook (1972*a*); *DNB* (1917); Wiebenson (1969)

Revival. Resuscitation of any previous style, properly founded on archaeological studies and scholarship, as with the *Egyptian, *Gothic, or *Greek Revivals.

Reynolds-Stephens, Sir William Ernest (1862–1943). British *Art Nouveau and *Arts-and-Crafts designer, born in the USA. His finest work is the interior of the Church of St Mary the Virgin, Great Warley, Essex (1901–5), with an exquisite Art Nouveau *Rood-screen and other furnishings, described by *Pevsner as an 'orgy of the English Arts-and-Crafts variety of the international Art Nouveau'. Harrison *Townsend designed the building.

Gray (1985); Pevsner, *Buildings of England, Essex* (1954); Tschudi-Madsen (1967)

Reyns, Henry de (*fl.* 1243–*c.*1253). Master-mason, probably from Rheims in France, but possibly an Englishman who had worked there. He was probably Master of the King's Masons at Windsor Castle in 1243, and advised on the defences of York Castle in 1244–5. His chief importance, however, lies in his connection with Westminster Abbey. Demolition of the east end of Edward the Confessor's (d. 1066) church began in 1245, and work began on the new, grander building, with which Henry was to be intimately connected, beginning with the *crypt of the new polygonal *chapter-house (1246), and proceeding with the *cloister, the *chancel, and *transept. Progress was rapid, for by 1251 the *piers were ready to receive their marble shafts or *colonnettes, and by the next year timber was arriving for the roof and *stalls. In 1253 the *vaults and pavements were being completed, and all window *tracery was ready. Henry's work ensured that the eastern parts of Westminster Abbey are French in style, resembling Rheims and Amiens Cathedrals in many aspects of the architecture, although many commentators hold that the details are English, which would be expected, as most of the masons working on the job would have been natives rather than French.

Harvey (1987); Webb (1965)

rez-de-chaussée. Ground-floor of a building.

rib. Moulding on a flat or vaulted ceiling. In medieval work a raised moulding forming part of the *vault, framing the panels or *webs*, often with elaborate *sections, and with their crowning intersections adorned with sculptured *bosses. Types of *Gothic rib include:

diagonal rib: main ribs running diagonally across a compartment square or rectangular on plan;
lierne rib: subordinate rib between the main ribs, or between the apex (or *clef*) of the vault and the junction of two *tierceron* ribs;
ridge rib: rib at the apex of a medieval vault, i.e. horizontal and coincident with the main axis of *nave or *aisle;
tierceron rib: secondary rib springing e.g. from the *pier to the *ridge rib*;
transverse rib: rib rising from a pier and set at right angles to the main axis of the nave or aisle, i.e. spanning either of the latter;
wall-rib: *formeret* or rib *engaged to the wall of a vault compartment.

Ribart de Chamoust (*fl.* 1776–83). French architectural writer, author of *L'Ordre François trouvé dans la Nature* (1776), which contains a curious *French Order consisting of three columns set at the points of an equilateral triangular plan (∴) with creepers trailing in spirals around the shafts, *capitals similar to those of the *Corinthian Order, and a *pedestal with three *volutes resembling a compressed and inverted *Ionic capital. The analogy with a tree (capital = foliage, shaft = trunk, and pedestal with volutes = roots visible above ground) suggests an extension of ideas from *Laugier. Ribart's first names may have been **Charles-François**, who was author of some works on finance, or (more likely) **François-Joseph**, who was probably the author of *Architecture Singulière* (1758) and *Lettre de M. Ribart* (*c.*1770): this latter Ribart was an 'Ingénieur'.

Architectural Design 52/1–2 (1982), 110–20; Curl (1991); information kindly provided by Miss Claudia Merrick and Mr Paul Nash of the RIBA

ribbed arch. Arch comprising several *ribs, or moulded to look like a collection of ribs.

ribbed dome. Type of *vault giving the effect of a dome, or where the under-surface of a dome or *cupola is subdivided by radiating *ribs.

ribbed fluting. **1.** Flutes separated by *fillets, as in the shaft of a Classical column. **2.** *Cabled fluting.

ribbed vault. Any vault with an under-surface subdivided by *ribs framing the *severies or *webs.

ribbon. **1.** Any ribbon-like strip of decoration, or a *riband*. **2.** Lead *came around the pieces of glass in a leaded window. **3.** Representations of ribbons binding *festoons, *garlands, *trophies, wreaths, etc. **4.** Light timber fixed to the faces of studs forming a continuous tie around the building and supporting the ends of beams in US balloon-frame timber construction.

ribbon development. Houses built in series along main roads.

ribbon-moulding. Ornament in the form of a ribbon loosely spiralling around a thin cylindrical element (*ribbon-and-stick*), often *reeded, and found with knots, *labels, *rosettes, etc.

ribbon-wall. *Crinkle-crankle wall.

Ribera, Pedro de (*c.*1683–1742). Castilian architect. He worked mostly in Madrid (where he was employed by the municipality from 1719). His late-*Baroque designs included much *Churrigueresque decoration. Typical of his style was the elaborate main portal of the San Fernando Hospital, Madrid (from 1722), in which *festoons, *estípites, flame-like forms, urns, and other motifs tumble over each other in abundance. It was said by Neoclassicists that he 'filled Madrid with a number of designs that have become the opprobrium of Europe', and his buildings were catalogued as a dire warning to students of architecture: as a result, we know quite a lot about his output, which was remarkably old-fashioned for its date.

Kubler and Soria (1959); Papworth (1887)

Ricardo, Halsey Ralph (1854–1928). English architect of Portuguese-Dutch Jewish descent. He established his practice in 1878, and from 1888 to 1898 was in partnership with William Frend de Morgan (1839–1917), for whom he designed relief tiles, vases, and other artefacts. Ricardo advocated the use of *faïence and other glazed materials to resist the depredations of the polluted atmospheres of the C19 city, suggesting that coloured materials would supply the equivalents of shadows and half-tones provided by *cornices, *pilasters, and mouldings. In this, he anticipated the designs of Otto *Wagner in Vienna, who used coloured tiles set in the same planes as walls and *piers to suggest architectural features. He designed several buildings, of which the best were the Howrah Station, Calcutta, India (1901—with a glowing exterior of brick and coloured tiles), and 8 Addison Road, Kensington (1905–8), completely faced with impervious glazed materials, even the roof-tiles. He was an *Arts-and-Crafts architect, whose work was extraordinarily sensitive, imaginative, and original. Among his works his own house, 'Woodside', Graffham, near Petworth, Sussex (1905), deserves note.

Gray (1985); *DNB* (1927); Jervis (1984); Sheppard (1973)

Ricardo of Burgos (*fl. c.*1180–1226). Probably an English master-mason. He designed and built the Monastery of Las Huelgas, near Burgos, Spain, and may have settled in Castile through his connections with Queen Eleanor of Castile (1162–1214), daughter of King Henry II of England (reigned 1154–89). It is likely that he was also responsible for the Monastery of Santa Maria, Aguilar de Campóo (finished 1222), and his designs remained influential for several years.

Harvey (1987)

Ricchino, Francesco Maria (1583–1658). Leading Lombard architect of the early *Baroque period. His Church of San Giuseppe, Milan (1607–30), was designed with a main octagonal space, a square *presbytery, and an *aediculated *façade, all of which anticipate later churches in Central Europe. The concave façade he designed for the Collegio Elvetico, Milan (1627), is one of the first in Italy, while the *cortile of the Palazzo di Brera, Milan (1651–86) is also a distinguished design.

Norberg-Schulz (1986); Wittkower (1982)

Richardson, Sir Albert Edward (1880–1964). Influential English architect, teacher, and writer. His *Monumental Classic Architecture in Great Britain and Ireland during the Eighteenth and Nineteenth Centuries* (1914) helped to foster an appreciation of C. R. *Cockerell and of *Neoclassicism generally. His own work began by being influenced by *Soane, but then became more a form of understated *stripped *Classicism that was reminiscent of *Perret's work in Paris. Many of his domestic commissions were in a refined late-*Georgian style. He was Professor at the Bartlett School of Architecture, University of London (1919–46), but in his later years in the 1950s and 1960s he was increasingly reviled by those who supported *International *Modernism. He himself was contemptuous of the intellectual pretensions of the *Modern Movement, especially of the work of Le *Corbusier and *Gropius. Nevertheless, he produced many fine buildings that have stood the test of time, including the *Financial Times* Building, Bracken House, London (1955–9—with a new core by *Hopkins (1988–91)), the restoration and enlargement of Trinity House, Trinity Square, London (1950–3), and many other distinguished and well-composed works. Other books by him include *An Introduction to Georgian Architecture* (1949), *Robert Mylne, Architect and Engineer, 1733 to 1811* (1955), and (with Hector Corfiato (1893–1963)) *The Art of Architecture* (1938).

Architectural Review, 140/835 (Sept. 1966), 199–205; *DNB* (1981); Houfe (1980); *RIBA Journal*, ser. 3, 31/8 (1924), 267–74; Richardson (1914)

Richardson, Charles James (1809–71). English architect. A pupil of *Soane, he seems to have imbibed very little in terms of style or refinement from his master. He designed 13 Kensington Palace Gardens, London (1851–3—now the Russian Embassy—in a coarse quasi-*Tudor style), and various houses in Queen's Gate, Kensington, London, including 'Albert Houses' (nos. 47–52) of *c.*1860, in a lavish Classical style. He collected architectural drawings, including work by *Adam, *Tatham, *Thorpe, and *Vanbrugh (now in the Victoria & Albert Museum), and published *Observations on the Architecture of England During the Reigns of Queen Elizabeth and King James I* (1838), *Architectural Remains of the Reigns of Elizabeth and James I* (1840), *Studies from Old English Mansions* (1841–8), *Studies of Ornamental Design* (1848 and 1852), *Picturesque Designs for Mansions, Villas, Lodges, etc.* (1870), and *The Englishman's Home from a Cottage to a Mansion* (1871), some plates of which resemble the *Tudorbethan St Ann's Villas, Norland Estate, North Kensington (1840s). His books gained him a reputation as an expert on *Jacobethan architecture.

DNB (1917); Jervis (1984); Papworth (1887); Sheppard (1973, 1975)

Richardson, George (d. *c.*1813). Influential British draughtsman, writer, and designer. He worked for John *Adam and accompanied James *Adam on the *Grand Tour (1760–3), during which he became familiar with the *Antique sources of the Adam style. He appears to have suffered from Adam's parsimoniousness, but nevertheless worked in the London office as he had little hope of establishing his own career. Among the works for which he made drawings were Kedleston, Derbyshire, and it would seem that he played more than a draughtsman's role there, for designs for several ceilings, etc., were signed by him, and survive. By 1765, however, he appears to have set himself up as a draughtsman, and exhibited under his own name. He probably designed the pretty *Georgian *Gothick churches at Stapleford, Leicestershire (1789), and Teigh, Rutland (1782), as well as (possibly) the Classical church at Saxby, Leicestershire (1789).

Richardson published several books, including *Aedes Pembrochianae* (1774), *A Book of Ceilings composed in the Stile of the Antique Grotesque* (1774, 1776, 1793), *A New Collection of Chimney Pieces* (1781), *A Treatise on the Five Orders of Architecture* (1760–3), *New Designs in Architecture* (1792), *Original Designs for Country*

Seats or Villas (1795), and the very important *New Vitruvius Britannicus* (1802–8 and 1808–10), which promoted fine late-C18 English architecture just as *Campbell, *Woolfe, and *Gandon had promoted earlier designs.

Colvin (1995); Curl (1993*b*); *DNB* (1917); Fleming (1962); Harris (1990)

Richardson, Henry Hobson (1838–86). Influential and brilliantly gifted American architect. He studied and worked in Paris under *Labrouste's elder brother, Théodore (1799–1885), and then *Hittorff, before returning to the USA (1865). With his Brattle Square (1870–2) and Trinity (1872–7) Churches, Boston, Mass., he established his reputation as an architect of great power, scholarship, and originality. Trinity Church is an assured essay in freely treated *Romanesque Revival, with a monumental *crossing-tower, apsidal *chancel, and gritty exterior, clearly influenced by contemporary French round-arched churches such as St-Augustin, Paris, and the works of *Vaudremer, but the massiveness and strength also suggest an influence from *Burges, some of whose publications Richardson had in his collection. With the geometrical emphases inherent in using the semicircular arch, Richardson gradually moved towards evolving his own style, using rock-faced *rustication to give added weight to his buildings, as in the 7-storey Marshall Field Wholesale Warehouse, Chicago (1885–7—demolished). Round-arched too was his Allegheny County Court House and Gaol (1883–8), the staircase of which was ingenious and thrilling in terms of spatial interpenetration. At the Gaol, the massive oversized *voussoirs, clearly derived from Florentine precedents, suggest the *Sublime.

Richardson was also attracted to the *Arts-and-Crafts movement, and designed many fine and original houses, some of which were in the *Shingle style, but all were ingenious, beautifully crafted, and organized with great sensitivity to their sites, especially those on the New England coast. Among his best domestic buildings were the Watts Sherman House, Newport, RI (1874–5), the Paine House, Waltham, Mass. (1884–6), the Glessner House, Chicago (1885–7), and the Stoughton House, Cambridge, Mass. (1882–3). His work influenced *McKim, Mead, & White, *Root, and *Sullivan, among others.

Hitchcock (1966, 1966*b*, 1977); Mumford (1924, 1931); Ochsner (1982); Placzek (1982—includes comprehensive bibliography); Rensselaer (1969); Scully (1971, 1974)

Richard the Mason (*fl. c.*1195). English master-mason. He seems to be the most likely progenitor of the original *Gothic designs for Lincoln Cathedral, his portrait probably being a carved head in the south-east *transept.

Harvey (1987)

Rickards, Edwin Alfred (1872–1920). English architect. He formed a partnership (1896) with Henry Vaughan Lanchester (1863–1953) and James Stewart (1860–1904), and, as Lanchester, Stewart, & Rickards entered a number of competitions, as a result of which they built the new City Hall and Law Courts, Cardiff, Wales (from 1898), the first planned civic-centre in Great Britain, with buildings in an exuberant *Edwardian *Baroque style with sculptures by Henry Poole (1873–1928), who also collaborated with the partnership on Deptford Town Hall, London (1908), again Baroque, but leaning towards C17 Anglo-Dutch work of the time of *Wren. After Stewart's death Lanchester and Rickards won the competition to design the Wesleyan Central Convocation Hall, Westminster (1907), one of the finest monuments of the Edwardian era in England. A contemporary critic referred to Rickards's work as 'combining opulence and taste with a touch of refined swagger', and that describes his work to perfection.

Gray (1985); Newman (1995); Service (1975, 1977)

Rickman, Thomas (1776–1841). English architect. He was of great importance in the history of the *Gothic *Revival as he was the first (as early as 1811) to subdivide the medieval styles into 'Norman', 'Early English', 'Decorated English', and 'Perpendicular English'. He wrote an architectural history of Chester Cathedral (1812), and published his observations on medieval architecture as *An Attempt to Discriminate the Styles of English Architecture from the Conquest to the Reformation* (1817, with many subsequent editions). He applied simple scientific methodologies to a subject that had, up to then, been treated with vagueness, and Rickman's grasp of detail enabled him to come to conclusions about stylistic progressions that were reasonably sound.

With the iron-master John Cragg (*c.*1767–*c.*1854) he built St George's Church, Everton,

Liverpool (1813–14), a Gothic Revival church with a cast-iron interior, followed by two more churches, St Michael's, Toxteth (1814–15), and St Philip's, Hardman Street (1815–16), both in Liverpool. His early churches were really *Georgian preaching-boxes with Gothic details of the *Perpendicular style, but his later churches are more robust, including St Andrew's, Ombersley, Worcestershire (1825–9), and St Peter's, Hampton Lucy, Warwickshire (1822–6). He developed his practice in Liverpool, remodelling Scarisbrick Hall, Lancashire (1812–16—later gone over by A. W. N. *Pugin), and building a great number of churches under the aegis of the Church Building *Commissioners in Lancashire and the West Midlands. He opened another office in Birmingham (1820), took (1821) Henry Hutchinson (1800–31) and then (1835) Richard Charles Hussey (1802–87) into partnership, and built up one of the most prolific practices in England. One of his prettiest buildings was the Gothic New Court, St John's College, Cambridge (1827–31), with its charming 'bridge of sighs' designed by Hutchinson. His grasp of the *Picturesque was also demonstrated at the village of Great Tew, Oxfordshire (1820–1), where he designed some of the buildings. His son, **Thomas Miller Rickman** (1827–1912), also became an architect, and compiled a list of his father's works for *Papworth's great *Dictionary*.

Colvin (1995); *DNB* (1917); Hitchcock (1977); Port (1961); Rickman (1848)

riddel(l) *or* **riddle.** In a church, the curtains suspended around an altar, sometimes from rods fixed into the wall behind, but more often from some means of hanging spanning between *riddel-posts*: there were normally four of the last, polygonal on *plan, coloured and gilded, and crowned by angels, often supporting candelabra. Arrangements of riddels behind and around altars seem to have been not uncommon in England towards the end of the *Gothic period, in the decades immediately before the iconoclasm of C16, and were revived in the early C20 during the late flowering of the *Gothic Revival, notably by *Comper and Temple *Moore.

Dirsztay (1978)

Riddle, Theodate Pope (1868–1946). One of the first (and most distinguished) female architects to practise in the USA. She used materials with great intelligence, and her work included housing and educational establishments. Her finest work was the Avon Old Farms School, Avon, Conn. (1920–9), which drew on English *vernacular prototypes, synthesized with considerable panache.

Andrews (1955); Paine (1979); Torre (1977)

ridge. 1. Apex of a pitched roof where the two slopes meet, especially the horizontal edge thus formed, often decorated with a *ridge-crest. **2.** Structural top of a pitched roof, including the timber, or *ridge-piece, against which the upper ends of *rafters abut or pitch. **3.** Internal apex of a *Pointed *Gothic *vault, often covered by a *ridge-rib.

ridge-and-furrow. 1. Roof composed of a series of *ridges and furrows, e.g. as used by *Paxton at the Crystal Palace, London (1851). **2.** Pan-tile roof.

ridge-beam. Obsolete term for timber against which the upper ends of the *rafters below pitch. *See* ridge-piece, -plate, and -purlin.

ridge-cap. Cover of metal, tile, etc., over the *ridge, sealing the joint between the two sides of a pitched roof.

ridge-course. Uppermost course of shingles, slates, or tiles immediately below the *ridge-cap or *ridge-crest of a pitched roof.

ridge-crest. Ornamental *ridge-cap or some kind of ornamental *crest fixed above the *ridge of a pitched roof.

ridge-fillet. *Fillet between two depressions, such as the *flutes in a Classical column-shaft.

ridge-piece. General term for the longitudinal timber or *ridge-plate at the apex of a pitched roof where the rafters pitch against it. It may be rectangular, thin, and upright (*ridge-plank), square, set square (*ridge-plate), or square and set diagonally (*ridge-purlin).

Alcock, Barley, Dixon, and Meeson (1996)

ridge-plank. Thin *ridge-piece set upright.

Alcock, Barley, Dixon, and Meeson (1996)

ridge-plate. Square-sectioned timber *ridge-piece set square under the *ridge.

ridge-pole. Obsolete term for a *ridge-piece.

ridge-purlin. Square-sectioned *ridge-piece set at an angle under the *ridge.

Alcock, Barley, Dixon, and Meeson (1996)

ridge-rib. *Rib at the apex of a *Gothic *vault running horizontally coincident with the main longitudinal axis of a *nave or *aisle.

ridge-roll. **1.** Timber roll over which metal is dressed at the ridge, or the metal covering itself. **2.** *Ridge-tile or a metal covering over a roll at the *ridge.

ridge-roof. Any roof with sloping sides and *gable-ends, the *rafters pitching against a *ridge-piece.

ridge-saddle. *See* yelm.

ridge-tile. Tile, often like a half-cylinder, but sometimes angular and decorated with *cresting. Also called a *crown-tile* or a *ridge-roll, it is used to cover the joints between pitched roofs at a *ridge or *hip. In the latter case it is called a *hip-roll* or *hip-tile*.

Ridinger, *or* **Riedinger, Georg** (1568–*c*.1616). German *Renaissance architect. His greatest work was Schloss Johannesburg, Aschaffenburg (1605–14), built round a central courtyard with four massive towers at the corners, an arrangement possibly prompted by Du *Cerceau's publications. The *gables were decorated with Mannerist devices reminiscent of aspects of *Dietterlin's works. The building was influential throughout Germany for the next century.

Bachmann (1970); Hitchcock (1981); Kreisel (1932)

Ridolfi, Mario (1904–84). Italian architect, a member of *MIAR. He designed the Post Office in the Piazza Bologna, Quartiere Nomentano, Rome (1932–3), influenced partly by German *Expressionism and partly by Italian *Rationalism, but soon shed all traces of the former, especially after he formed a professional association with the German engineer Wolfgang Frankl (1907–94) that lasted from the 1930s until Ridolfi's death. The Rea Mansion, Via di Villa Massimo, Rome (1934–7), for example, designed with Frankl, was entirely Rationalist Modernist in style. After the 1939–45 war he published *Manuale dell'architetto* (1946) that seemed to favour stylistic *Pluralism, and, with *Aymonino, *Quaroni, and others, designed the INA-Casa in the Tiburtino Quarter, Rome, where Pluralist leanings became apparent (1949–54). Yet, in the same period, he designed (with Frankl), the Casa a Torre, Viale Etiopia, Rome (1950–4), that was unequivocally *Modernist and from which Pluralism was absent. By the 1960s his work became very coarse in its detailing, and almost wilfully crude (e.g. Infants' School, Poggibonsi (1960–1)). He died by drowning.

Cellini, d'Amato, and Valeriani (1979); Emanuel (1994); Lampugnani (1988)

Ried, *or* **Rieth, von Piesting, Benedikt** (*c*.1454–1534). German architect. He was Master of the King's Works in Bohemia, and the greatest figure in the final phases of *Sondergotik in Bohemia and Moravia. He designed the extraordinary vaulting, the ribs of which rise from the *piers and flow and undulate to describe elegant panels framed by their gently curving forms (begun by M. Rajsek and completed 1540–8), in the Church of St Barbara, Kutńa Hora, and, even stranger, the very elegant double-curved branch rib-vaulting that seems to grow out of the walls of the Vladislav Hall in Hradčany Castle, Prague (1487–1502)—where the *fenestration is almost entirely *Renaissance in style. Ried also designed the vault with stumps or cut-off ribs of the equestrian staircase (*c*.1500) leading to the Hall, and (probably) the stunning *oratory in Prague Cathedral, with its ribs of decorated branches and twigs (1480–93), although Rajsek has also been proposed as its architect.

Fehr (1961); Hitchcock (1981); Seibt (1985); Watkin (1986)

Riemerschmid, Richard (1868–1957). German *Arts-and-Crafts architect, a founding member (with *Behrens and others) of the Munich *Vereinigten Werkstätten für Kunst und Handwerk* (United Workshops for Arts and Crafts—1896) and of the *Deutscher Werkbund (1907), who was an influential designer in Germany from the turn of the century until the mid-1920s. His works include the *Jugendstil *Kammertheater* (Chamber Theatre) in the *Schauspielhaus* (Play House), Munich (1901), and he planned the *Garden City, Hellerau, near Dresden (1907). German *vernacular styles and English Arts-and-Crafts influences were often synthesized in his architecture, as in his own house at Pasing (1896). By the time he was designing buildings at Hellerau (1910) his work was turning to stripped *Neoclassicism.

Deutsche Kunst und Dekoration, 27 (1910–11), 447–65; Jervis (1984); Nerdinger (1982)

Rieth. *See* Ried.

Rietveld, Gerrit Thomas (1888–1964). Dutch designer and important De *Stijl architect. He designed several items of furniture in which the elements of the structure were unequivocally expressed (e.g. the Red-Blue Chair (1918)). From 1921 he began to work with the designer Truus Schröder-Schräder (1889–1985) on the planning of the celebrated Schröder House, Prins Hendriklaan, Utrecht (completed 1924), a paradigm of *International Modernism with its adaptable interior spaces, removable partitions, asymmetry, white slabs, and large areas of glass. Like his furniture, the house seems to be put together from pieces of card-like elements, with planes overlapping, but it is constructed almost entirely of traditional materials, and expressed its 'modernity' largely by metaphor. He also designed terrace-houses, Erasmuslaan (1934), and the Vreeburg Cinema (1936), both in Utrecht. With others he designed the Rijksmuseum Vincent van Gogh, Amsterdam (1963–72). He was a founder-member of *CIAM.

Brown (1958); Buffinga (1971); Fanelli (1968); Jaffé (1956); Mulder (1975); Overy (1969); Overy *et al.* (1988)

Riley, William Edward (1852–1937). English architect. In 1899 he succeeded Thomas Blashill (1831–1905) as Architect to the London County Council, and under their direction two major programmes of slum-clearance and rebuilding took place at Boundary Street, Shoreditch (from 1893), and Millbank (from 1897), London. Both were triumphs of humane, well-designed housing, in an eclectic *Queen Anne style. Riley took over the London School Board's building programme begun by E. R. *Robson in 1904. Some of his team's best works include the London Fire Brigade Stations, including the fine composition opposite St Pancras's Church on the Euston Road, London (1902).

Gray (1985)

Rinaldi, Antonio (*c.*1709–94). Italian architect, he became an important figure in Russia, designing in late-*Rococo and early Neo-classical styles. His works include the Marble Palace, St Petersburg (1768–85), where influences from *Juvarra are apparent: it is named because its façade is clad in granite and marble. It was one of the first buildings in the world to use iron beams. He was responsible for palaces at Oranienbaum (Lomonossow), including some *Chinoiserie interiors and a blue-and-white pavilion.

Cruickshank (1996); Hamilton (1983)

rinceau. Classical ornament on a *band consisting of a continuous wave of scrolling foliage, often vine. *See* trail.

Ring, Der. Architectural pressure-group founded in 1923–4 as the 'Ring of Ten' representing *Neues Bauen. In 1926 membership was extended to include *Bartning, *Behrens, *Gropius, *Häring, *Haesler, *Hilbersheimer, *Korn, the *Luckhardts, E. *May, *Mendelsohn, A. *Meyer, *Mies van der Rohe, *Poelzig, *Scharoun, the *Tauts, *Tessenow, and Martin *Wagner, among others, and it acquired its name. It promoted the 'new architecture' (which, in effect, became *International Modernism) in order to solve contemporary problems, to reject forms based on *Historicism, and to design for the 'new scientific and social' epoch. The *Modernist elements in Der Ring, who were in the majority, grouped with Mies to establish the architectural images of the *Weissenhofsiedlung (1927), causing an opposition (Der *Block) to be formed by *Bonatz and others.

Lane (1985)

riparene. Classical ornament associated with water. Motifs include *personifications of rivers, vases pouring water, Neptune, tritons and mermaids, dolphins, fish, reeds and seaweed, frogs, etc. The term is named after Cesare Ripa (*c.*1560–before 1625), author of *Iconologia* (1593 with later editions, notably 1603 and 1779–80), an immensely influential source-book of personifications, emblems, and decorative motifs.

Lewis and Darley (1986)

Ripley, Thomas (*c.*1683–1758). English carpenter, he succeeded *Vanbrugh, no less, as Comptroller of the Works (1726). His meteoric rise was due to the patronage of Sir Robert Walpole (1676–1745), whose seat, Houghton Hall, Norfolk, Ripley constructed according to *Campbell's and *Kent's designs (1722–5). He also acquired the Surveyorships of Greenwich Hospital (1729) and the King's Private Roads (1737), which, for one so untalented, was remarkable. His architecture was unloved by his contemporaries, and has not risen much in estimation since. In particular, his *portico for the Admiralty, Whitehall, London (1723–6), earned him well-deserved opprobrium, and occasioned the building of a *colonnaded *screen to Robert *Adam's design (1760) to hide it. Wolterton Hall, Norfolk (1727–41), however, was not an ungainly house, suggesting that something of *Palladian grace had rubbed off on him after his work at Houghton. Alexander Pope (1688–1744) thought Ripley a model of 'Dulness' compared with *Burlington, *Jones, and *Wren, while Vanbrugh laughed so much when he came across Ripley's name in the public prints that he 'had like to Beshit' himself.

Colvin (1995); *DNB* (1917)

rise. 1. Vertical measurement from the springing-line to the *soffit of an arch or vault. **2.** Vertical distance between two consecutive *treads in a *stair, or that between landing and landing.

riser. 1. Vertical piece between the *treads of a *stair. **2.** Whole vertical part of a step of a stair between treads. **3.** Stone in *rubble-work, usually a *bonder* or *through-stone*, also called a *jumper*.

Robe, Sir William (1765–1820). British military engineer and soldier. He was architect of Holy Trinity Church, Quebec, Canada (1803), a variant on *Gibbs's St Martin-in-the-Fields. His work was competent and solid, and he was involved in several improvements and administration in the Province of Quebec in the early years of C19.

DNB (1917); Kalman (1994)

Robert, Hubert (1733–1808). French landscape-painter and designer of gardens. He was fascinated by *Antique ruins, often using them as central elements of his pictures. He sometimes incorporated Egyptian and Egyptianizing motifs in his paintings, and played a minor role in the *Egyptian Revival. He worked on the gardens at Ermenonville (1770s) for René-Louis, Marquis de Girardin (1735–1808), and contributed to the design of one of the most enduring images of the period: the *Île des Peupliers* (Isle of Poplars) and the tomb of J.-J. Rousseau (1712–78). From 1786 he worked on designs for the gardens at Méréville for Jean-Joseph, Marquis de Laborde (1724–94), in succession to *Bélanger. He was a key figure in the transformation of the landscaped garden into a *Picturesque place of allusions where sentimental, mnemonic, and moral associations informed the design.

Curl (1994); Mosser and Teyssot (1991); Nolhac (1910)

Robert de Luzarches (d. *c.*1236). *See* Luzarches.

Robert the Mason (*fl.* *c.*1077–1119). Master-mason, responsible for the *transepts, eastern part of the *nave, and the tower of the *Romanesque Abbey Church of St Alban (now the Cathedral), Hertfordshire.

Harvey (1987)

Roberto Brothers. Marcelo (1908–64), **Milton** (1914–53), and **Mauricio** (1921–) were Brazilian architects, much influenced by Le *Corbusier. Their Brazilian Press Association building (1935–6) made their reputation. Their designs have been successful in controlling the intense sunlight of Brazil, notably in their Seguradores Office Building, Rio de Janeiro (1949).

Emanuel (1994)

Roberts, Henry (1803–76). British architect, born in Philadelphia, Pa. He worked in *Fowler's and R. *Smirke's office before setting up his London practice in 1830, and in 1832 won the competition to design the new Hall of The Fishmongers' Company beside *Rennie's new London Bridge. It was a masterly composition in the *Greek Revival style with more than a touch of Smirke's influence (Roberts had assisted Smirke on the working-drawings for the British Museum), and included many interesting features such as an ingenious plan, the use of cast and wrought iron in the construction, the inclusion of four unfluted Greek *Doric columns of polished Peterhead granite in the entrance-hall and stair (among the first instances of this material being used for such a situation and object), the employment of a huge *concrete raft for the foundation, and quotations from the refined Greek *Corinthian *Order of the *Choragic Monument of Lysicrates in Athens in the main Hall itself. His pupil and assistant at the time was George Gilbert *Scott.

Roberts developed a successful practice, designing country-houses for members of the aristocracy with liberal and Evangelical tendencies. These buildings were in a *Jacobethan, *Tudor Gothic (Norton Manor, Norton Fitzwarren, Somerset (1843)), or pleasing *Italianate (Escot House, Devon (1838)) style. His essays in *Gothic Revival churches, however (e.g. St Paul's, Dock Street, Whitechapel (1846)) did not meet with the approval of the *Ecclesiologists.

However, it is as the architect of a number of philanthropic buildings that Roberts is of world importance. His Evangelical leanings brought him into contact with those who wished to improve society by example. His first essay was the Destitute Sailors' Asylum, Whitechapel (1835), but in 1844 he became Honorary Architect to the Society for Improving the Condition of the Labouring Classes, with which Lord Shaftesbury (1801–85) and Prince *Albert were to be so intimately involved. For the Society Roberts designed a great variety of exemplary buildings, including houses in Lower Road, Pentonville, London (1844—demolished), various lodging-houses, and the epoch-making Model Dwellings, Streatham Street, Bloomsbury (1849–51). The last provided very advanced standards of accommodation, fire-resistant construction using vaulted floors and concrete, and gallery access which Roberts argued were elevated streets to individual houses, thus avoiding window-tax which would have been imposed on a large building. As a result of this building and Roberts's arguments the Government was obliged to abolish both window-tax and other enactments, making it more economical for philanthropic organizations and private individuals to provide dwellings for the labouring classes. Roberts developed the plan of a typical apartment evolved at Streatham Street for his 'Model Houses for Four Families Erected in Hyde Park at the Industrial Exhibition of 1851' paid for by the philanthropically motivated Prince Consort to further the aims of the Society for Improving the Condition of the Labouring Classes of which he was President. This brilliant design had four self-contained apartments, each with its own toilet facilities, access from an open stair, excellent insulation and fire-proof construction, and with a standard of accommodation far in advance of its time. The exhibit (the first of its kind in the world, long before the much-trumpeted *Weissenhofsiedlung of 1927) was visited by thousands of people, and the Society published the detailed plans and elevations. Roberts's designs were influential throughout Europe and the USA, and versions of his plans were still being used in Amsterdam South in the 1920s and 1930s. His designs for model cottages for the country were also published, and built in numbers throughout the United Kingdom from 1851: most were in a vaguely C17 style, but this could be varied according to local circumstances and taste. An entire estate of his model dwellings, with a version of the Great Exhibition (or Prince Albert's) model dwellings, was built at Windsor, Berkshire (1852), and survives virtually intact.

Roberts was not only a pioneer in the design of accommodation for the less fortunate members of society, but an influential theoretician in the field. His publications include *The Dwellings of the Labouring Classes* (1850 with a revised edition of 1867 also published in French), *The Improvement of the Dwellings of the Labouring Classes through the Operation of Government Measures* (1859), *The Essentials of a Healthy Dwelling and the Extension of its Benefits to the Labouring Population* (1862), *The Physical Condition of the Labouring Classes, Resulting from the State of their Dwellings* (1866), and *Efforts on the Continent for Improving the Dwellings of the Labouring Classes* (1874). In these works he laid the foundations for later experiments such as those at Port Sunlight, Bournville, and Letchworth *Garden City, and, in particular, drew attention to the fact that the State and Municipalities would have to intervene to provide housing for those who would never be able to afford to build their own housing. He was opposed to the expansion of Building Societies as he foresaw the effect of easier loans would be to inflate costs, as the price of a dwelling would depend, not on its value, but on the amount of money available for loans. In his analyses he has been proved abundantly right.

Colvin (1995); Curl (1983)

Robertson, Daniel (*fl.* 1812–43). Scots architect, probably related to the *Adam family, and seemingly a contributing factor creating the financial difficulties that beset William Adam in the 1820s. Robertson and his (presumably) brother, **Alexander**, were involved in speculative developments in London in 1812 which seem to have contributed to their bankruptcy in 1817. However, in the 1820s Daniel worked in Oxford, where he designed the Graeco-Roman Clarendon Press, Walton Street (1826–7), restored the *Gothic High Street front of All Souls College (1827), rebuilt the west side of the North *Quad, Oriel College (1826), and designed St Clement's Church (1827–8—in an unconvincing *Romanesque style). He left Oxford under a cloud and settled in Ireland where he designed several country-houses, including the castellated Johnstown Castle, Co. Wexford (*c.*1833–6), and the *Tudor Carrigglas, Co. Longford (1837–8). He was working on the upper terrace at Powerscourt, Enniskerry, Co. Wicklow (1843), where he had to direct the works from a wheelbarrow in a state of inebriation. Thereafter his fate eludes discovery. He has been confused with the Irish architect **William Robertson** (1770–1850), of Kilkenny, to whom he does not seem to have been related.

Colvin (1995)

Robertson, Sir Howard Morley (1888–1963). American-born British architect. He trained in Paris and the USA and formed a partnership (1919–31) with John Murray Easton (1889–1975), which became Easton & Robertson. Their Royal Horticultural Hall, London (1925) exploited the parabolic arch, and the whole ensemble, including the stepped arrangement of windows, recalling *Berg's *Jahrhunderthalle* (Century Hall), Breslau (Wrocław), was as advanced an interior for its date as can be found anywhere. Robertson's admiration for *Mendelsohn was demonstrated in his Metropolitan Water Board Laboratories, New River Head, Rosebery Avenue, London (1938). The firm also carried out the remodelling of the Savoy Hotel (1930–9), Claridge's Hotel (1935–9), and Sadler's Wells Theatre (1939), all in London. One of their best works was the Bank of England Printing Works, Loughton, Essex (1956), for which *Arup was the consultant. One of Robertson's last buildings was the Shell Centre, York Road, Waterloo, London (1961), a lumpish tower that did not add to his reputation. He published widely: among his books were *The Principles of Architectural Composition* (1924), *Architecture Explained* (1926), *Modern Architectural Design* (1932), and *Architecture Arising* (1944). He was Principal of the Architectural Association School of Architecture (1920–35).

Architectural Review, 114/681 (Sept. 1953) 160–8; *DNB* (1981); Morgan and Naylor (1987); Robertson (1924)

Robinson, Peter Frederick (1776–1858). English architect. He was a pupil of *Porden and later assisted *Holland with the enlargement of Brighton Pavilion (1801–2). He became a prolific provider of eclectic designs suitable for *Regency taste, and could turn his hand to most styles without a qualm. He designed the 'Egyptian Hall' in Piccadilly, London (1811–12—demolished), a curious concoction of somewhat unscholarly Egyptianizing elements on a façade intended to advertise William Bullock's (*fl.* *c.*1795–1826) Museum (*Papworth later added an equally unscholarly interior in the same style). He carried out developments around Beauchamp Square, Leamington Spa, Warwickshire (1825–6), and designed the original Swiss Cottage, Regent's Park, London (*c.*1828—demolished). One of his best buildings (attributed) is probably Seaforde House, Co. Down (1816–20—with *Greek Revival interiors and entrance-arch to the Park—the latter 1833). He is best known today as the author of *Rural Architecture* (1823 with subsequent editions), *Designs for Ornamental Villas* (1825–7 and later editions), *Designs for Village Architecture . . . illustrating the Observations contained in an Essay on the Picturesque by Sir Uvedale Price* (1830 and later editions), *Designs for Farm Buildings* (1830, etc.), *Designs for Lodges and Park Entrances* (1833, etc.), and other works that were responsible for disseminating his somewhat ungainly ideas of *Picturesque buildings throughout the land and the USA.

Bence-Jones (1988); Colvin (1995); Curl (1994); *DNB* (1917)

Robinson, Sir Thomas, Bt. (*c.*1702–77). English amateur architect. He was a devoted disciple of Burlington's *Palladianism, and rebuilt his mansion at Rokeby, Yorkshire (1725–30), to conform to the Palladian style (though it also acquired a *portico of baseless *Doric columns which must have been a very early example of the use of such an *Order). This expense, together with a somewhat extravagant lifestyle, obliged him to accept the Governorship of Barbados in 1742, where he was carried away with his love of building, erecting the Arsenal and Armoury at Pilgrim, which further financially embarrassed him. Among his works are the landscaped Park and Church (1776) at Rokeby, the west wing of Castle Howard, Yorkshire (1753–9—which did little for the composition), Claydon House, Buckinghamshire (1760–*c.*1780—of which one wing of Robinson's design remains), the powerful and original *Gothick gateway at Bishop Auckland Castle, Co. Durham (1760), and the Classical Church at Glynde, Sussex (1763–5).

Colvin (1995); *DNB* (1917); McCarthy (1987)

Robinson, William (*c.*1720–75). English architect. With *Vardy he supervised the building of *Kent's Horse Guards Building, Whitehall (from 1748). He designed the Excise Office in Old Broad Street, London (1769–75—demolished), in a *Palladian style. He is best remembered for making the first alterations at Strawberry Hill, Twickenham (1748), and for the *Georgian *Gothick church at Stone, Staffordshire (1754–8).

Colvin (1995); Papworth (1887)

Robinson, Sir William (*c*.1643–1712). English architect and engineer. After becoming Surveyor-General of the Fortifications and Buildings in Ireland in 1671, his main works were the redesigning of Dublin Castle from 1684 (completed by Thomas *Burgh), the building of the Royal Hospital, Kilmainham, Co. Dublin (1679–87), and several forts, including Charlemont, Co. Armagh (1673), and Charles, Kinsale, Co. Cork (1677–81). He seems to have played a significant part in the development of *Classicism in Ireland, for the *Baroque features at the Royal Hospital were of fine quality. After the Williamite wars (1688–91) he designed St Mary's Church (1701–5) and Marsh's Library (1703–4), both in Dublin. He acquired so many official positions in Ireland and amassed such a fortune that the suspicion of corruption on an enormous scale is difficult to avoid, the more so when the Privy Council was obliged to pass an enactment to relieve his creditors in 1724, long after his death.

Loeber (1981)

Robson, Edward Robert (1836–1917). English architect. He was articled to *Dobson and worked in G. G. *Scott's office before setting up on his own. He was appointed Architect to the London School Board in 1871, and worked with J. J. *Stevenson from that time until 1876. Robson's designs for schools (1872–89) drew on the brick-built architectural style that Stevenson and others were promoting at the time. So successful were these robustly conceived schools that they gave their name to the London School Board style. Among his works are Berger Road School, Hackney (1878), and the People's Palace, Stepney (1886). Robson published his influential *School Architecture* in 1874.

Dixon and Muthesius (1985); Gray (1985); Robson (1972)

Robson, Philip Appleby (1871–1951). English architect, the son of E. R. *Robson. He was articled to *Pearson, assisting the latter at Truro Cathedral, before joining his father. He later worked for various Government Departments before establishing his own practice. Like his father he built many London schools, but his planning on tight urban sites was even more ingenious. He was responsible for a whole series of handsome *Queen Anne style tall-windowed brick and *terracotta buildings that enliven parts of London. Among his works are St George's School, South Street (1898–9), St Gabriel's College, Camberwell (1899–1903), both in London, and the Eastbourne School of Art, Sussex (1903–4).

Gray (1985)

Rocaille. **1.** System of decoration derived from *rock-work, ornamented with pebbles and shells found in *follies and, especially, *grottoes, often associated with water, fountains, cascades, etc. **2.** Type of *Rococo *scroll-like ornament, not unlike *Auricular forms, arranged asymmetrically, notably around frames etc., suggesting seaweed and other marine flora.

Bauer (1962); Kimball (1980); Lewis and Darley (1986)

Roche & Dinkeloo. American architectural firm founded by the Irish-born **Eamonn Kevin Roche** (1922–) and US-born **John Gerard Dinkeloo** (1918–81). Roche and Dinkeloo worked with Eero *Saarinen in the 1950s before establishing their partnership after Saarinen's death in 1961. Their first work was the Oakland Museum, Calif. (1961–8), a huge building covering four city blocks and constructed of sand-blasted *concrete both inside and out, with a series of gardens contained within the complex. The Cummins Engine Plant, Darlington, Co. Durham, England (1963–5), constructed of steel with the H-sections exposed externally, was a paradigm for its day, and exposed steelwork was again used at the Ford Foundation Headquarters, 42nd Street, New York (1963–8), with a 12-storey indoor garden or office *atrium that became immensely influential. In 1967–85 came the huge extensions to the Metropolitan Museum of Art, New York, including the Pavilion for the Ancient Egyptian temple of Dendur. After Dinkeloo's death Roche followed the reaction against the *Modern Movement, designing the E. F. Hutton Building, New York (1980—with a stone *colonnade and *mansard roofs), and other works with Classical references. More recently the firm has built the enormous World Headquarters of Merck & Company, Whitehouse Station, New Jersey (1993).

Dal Co (1985); Emanuel (1994); Futagawa (1975*a*); Stern (1977)

rock-cut. Building excavated from solid rock, such as an Ancient Egyptian temple or tomb.

rock-faced. **1.** *Quarry-faced *ashlar with a dressed projecting rough face, as though recently taken from the quarry, also called *cyclopean* masonry or rock-faced *rustication. **2.** Used erroneously for *rock-work.

rock rash. Stone facing composed of a mosaic of irregularly shaped and sized stones, frequently with cobbles, *flints, and *geodes.

rock-work. **1.** Erroneous term for *rock-faced or *quarry-faced *ashlar. **2.** Correct term for a structure in a garden constructed of large fragments of rock, imitation rocks, broken bricks, and other materials, held together with mortar, the cavities further filled with earth, pebbles, and plants, intended to look 'natural'. Sometimes it was contrived to look like very large rocks, or even natural cliff-like faces as though a path had been cut through rock (but entirely artificial). Rock-work was often associated with *grottoes, fountains, *hermitages, and *labyrinths in C18 landscaped gardens. Good examples exist at Wörlitz, Anhalt, by *Eyserbeck and von *Erdmannsdorff.

Rococo. C18 style originating in France, and coinciding with the *Régence and *Louis Quinze periods, that rapidly spread throughout Europe. It was elegant and frothy, deriving from *Auricular, *Rocaille, and *Baroque themes, drawing on the marine and shell motifs found in *grottoes, and incorporating *ogee and C-*scrolls, asymmetrically disposed around frames, *cartouches, etc., like a mixture of coral, seaweed, and stylized foliage. Colours were light and pale, often incorporating gold and silver, while the exotic was never far away, for Rococo designs included aspects of *Chinoiserie, *Gothick, and even, in its late phase, *Hindoo decorations. Rococo decorations included *bandwork, *diaper-patterns, *espagnolettes, scallop-shells, and scroll-work, incorporated in schemes of decoration of unsurpassed grace and beauty, perhaps achieving their greatest heights in France and Southern Germany. In Southern Bavaria and Franconia Rococo reached its finest expression with the interiors of the Amalienburg, Schloss Nymphenburg, Munich, by *Cuvilliés and *Zimmermann, and the Pilgrimage Church of *Vierzehnheiligen* (Fourteen Saints), Franconia, by *Neumann, Franz Xaver Feichtmayr (1705–64) Johann Michael Feichtmayr (1709–72), and Johann Georg Üblhör (1700–65). Rococo enjoyed a revival in France during C19, while in America, Britain, and Germany aspects of Rococo re-emerged from the 1820s to the 1860s, and in the late 1880s and 1890s there was another revival which was transmogrified into a synthesis of design in *Art Nouveau.

Chilvers, Osborne, and Farr (1988); Hitchcock (1968*a*); Kimball (1980); Lewis and Darley (1986); Powell (1959); Zürchner (1977)

Rode. A *Rood.

Rod of Aesculapius. Vertical staff or torch round which two snakes are twined, common in Neoclassical and French *Empire design. An emblem of healing and medicine, it is associated with apothecaries and hospitals. It resembles the *caduceus without the wings.

Rodríguez Tizón, Ventura (1717–85). Spanish architect of the late-*Baroque period, whose work veered strongly in the direction of *Neoclassicism. He worked under *Sacchetti on the Royal Palace, Madrid (1735–50), and then designed the Church of San Marcos, Madrid (1749–53), which bears a resemblance in plan to *Bernini's Sant'Andrea al Quirinale, Rome, notably in its elliptical domed form and the disposition of the *façade. He also fused Baroque and Neoclassical themes at Pamplona Cathedral (designed 1783), but his College of Surgery, Barcelona (1761–4), was severe and stripped, much influenced by French Neoclassical theory.

Kubler and Soria (1959); Reese (1976)

Roebling, John Augustus (1806–69). German-born American engineer. In 1841–9 he perfected the manufacture of twisted-wire cables which he employed to suspend the Pennsylvania State Canal aqueduct above the Allegheny River (1844–5), a work that won him recognition. With his son, **Washington Augustus Roebling** (1837–1926), he designed the Brooklyn Bridge, New York (1869–93), then the longest suspension-bridge in the world. J. A. Roebling published *Long and Short Span Railway Bridges* (1869).

Condit (1960, 1968); Schuyler (1931); Trachtenberg (1965); Vogel (1971)

Roger the Mason (*fl.* 1296–d.1310). English master-mason. He was in charge of the works at Exeter Cathedral, Devon, by 1280, and probably designed the *presbytery (completed 1299) and the *choir (1310) there.

Harvey (1987)

Rogers, Ernesto Nathan (1909–69). Italian architect. Founder, with Banfi, Belgiojoso, and Peressutti, of *BBPR, whose Torre Velasca, Milan (1957–60) created much controversy at the time of its building because it did not conform to the accepted image of *International *Modernism. Rogers co-edited *Domus* (1946–7) and *Casabella-continuità* (1953–64). The latter became one of Europe's most influential architectural journals during his tenure.

Morgan and Naylor (1987)

Rogers, Isaiah (1800–69). American architect, best known for his hotels, the first of which, Tremont House, Boston, Mass. (1828–9), was very advanced for its time and established the USA's pre-eminence in this building-type. He formed his own practice in 1826, specializing in the *Greek Revival style, of which his *Ionic Merchants' Exchange, New York (1836–42), was his masterpiece, inspired by *Schinkel's *Altes Museum*, Berlin. The great *Pantheon-like dome over the *rotunda was destroyed when *McKim, Mead, & White drastically altered the building in 1907, adding four more storeys. He used the *Egyptian Revival style for the gates of the Old Granary Burial Ground, Boston (1840), and the almost identical gates at Touro Cemetery, Newport, RI (1843). Thereafter, he began to favour the *Italianate style, although St John's Episcopal Church, Cincinnati, Ohio (1849–52), was *Neo-*Romanesque, and the Tyler Davidson Store, also in Cincinnati (1849–50), had a *Gothic *cast-iron front. Posterity has not been kind to Rogers: many of his most distinguished buildings have been demolished or altered beyond recognition, many works by him have been misattributed, and some have been attributed to him that were not by his hand.

Carrott (1978); Hamlin (1964); Hitchcock (1977); Kennedy (1989)

Rogers, John (*fl.* 1473–5). English Freemason. He probably designed Thornbury Castle, Gloucestershire (1511–22). He built the upper parts of the tower at Lavenham Church, Suffolk (*c.*1523), and worked at Hampton Court Palace (1533–5). In 1541 he was the King's Master-Mason at Calais and Guisnes, and in the following year was inspector of the fortifications at Hull and Berwick-on-Tweed. If actually responsible for the impressive *Tudor military architecture at Berwick, he was the most important designer of such works in the land.

Harvey (1987)

Rogers of Riverside, Richard George, The Lord (1933–). Florence-born British architect. He was associated with (Sir) Norman *Foster in Team 4 (1964–6) and built the Reliance Controls Ltd Factory, Swindon, Wiltshire (1965–7), with its diagonal braces announcing its construction. From the beginning of his career Rogers has used the image of advanced technology overtly expressed as his main theme, and has been called a *High Tech architect as a result. High Tech too was the Centre Georges Pompidou, Paris (1971–7), inspired by *Archigram, which he designed with Renzo *Piano and the Ove *Arup team to display not only its structure but its services as well, some might say in an aggressively demonstrative manner. In 1971 he formed the Richard Rogers Partnership, and designed the Headquarters of Lloyd's of London (1978–86), another example of his emphatic display of services, circulation, and structure, as was his Inmos Microprocessor Factory, Newport, Wales (1982). He refurbished Sir Horace *Jones's Billingsgate Market Building, London (1985–8), and most recently built the Channel 4 Television Headquarters, London (1990–4), and the European Court of Human Rights, Strasbourg, France (1989–95), both of which were polished performances in his chosen idiom, that of emphasizing the *Modern Movement's obsession with a 'truthful' approach to structure, function, and materials going back to *Viollet-le-Duc and A. W. N. *Pugin.

Appleyard (1986); Burdett (1996); Emanuel (1994); Jodidio (1996*a*); Sudjic (1995)

Rogue architecture. Term used by H. S. *Goodhart-Rendel to describe works by those *Gothic-Revival architects whose works were not marked by scholarship, serenity, or tact. Among the more celebrated 'Rogues' were E. Bassett *Keeling, E. B. *Lamb, S. S. *Teulon, and George Truefitt (1824–1902), all practitioners, and Thomas Harris (1830–1900), whose *Victorian Architecture* (1860) and *Examples of the Architecture of the Victorian Age* (1862) earned him some opprobrium. Keeling and Lamb designed churches for the Evangelical persuasion—both gloried in repetitive notchings and chamferings, expressed their roof-structures in an outlandish, restless way, and seemed to want to jar the eye with saw-toothed arrises, scissor-shaped *trusses, and harsh, barbaric *polychromy. Their almost frantic originality, debauched acrobatic Gothic, and elephantine compositions brought the wrath of the *Ecclesiologists on their heads, and few have taken their work seriously ever since. *See* Rageur, Raguer.

Architectural History, 16 (1973), 60–9; Curl (1995); *RIBA Journal*, ser. 3, 56/6 (1949), 251–9

Rohault de Fleury, Charles (1801–75). French Neoclassical architect, the son of **Hubert Rohault de Fleury** (1777–1846), a fine draughtsman who designed much but built little. Charles designed in a variety of other styles as well, including *Moorish (the Hippodrome, Paris (1844–5)—destroyed) and *Renaissance (Pavillon de Rohan (1853)). A pioneer of iron-and-glass structures, his Musée d'Histoire Naturelle (1833–4) was studied by *Paxton. He designed many villas and commercial buildings, was responsible for the plan of the Place de l'Opéra, surrounding streets, and many buildings, and built the Grand Hôtel du Louvre (1855) with *Hittorff and J.-A.-F.-A. Pellechet (1829–1903). Although he developed plans for a new opera-house, much influenced by *Semper's work, and was appointed Architect for the new Opéra in 1859, the Empress Eugénie (1826–1920) called for a competition in 1859, which was won by C. *Garnier. Embittered, Rohault de Fleury then abandoned architecture and devoted himself to the production of religious writings, including *Le Sainte Vièrge: Études archéologiques et iconographiques* (The Holy Virgin: Archaeological and Iconographical Studies—1878). His son, **Georges** (1835–1905), wrote on medieval architecture and published a memoir of his father's work in 1884.

Gourlier, Tardieu, and Tardieu (1825–50); Hix (1996); Middleton and Watkin (1987); Placzek (1982)

Rohe. *See* Mies van der Rohe.

roll. 1. *Bowtell* or common nearly cylindrical moulding, semicircular or more than semicircular in *section. **2.** Rounded piece of wood along a *ridge or hip over which metal is dressed as a *ridge-cap.

roll-and-fillet. *Roll-moulding with a *fillet running along its length emphasizing it by means of the extra shadows and lines of the fillet, common in *Gothic work.

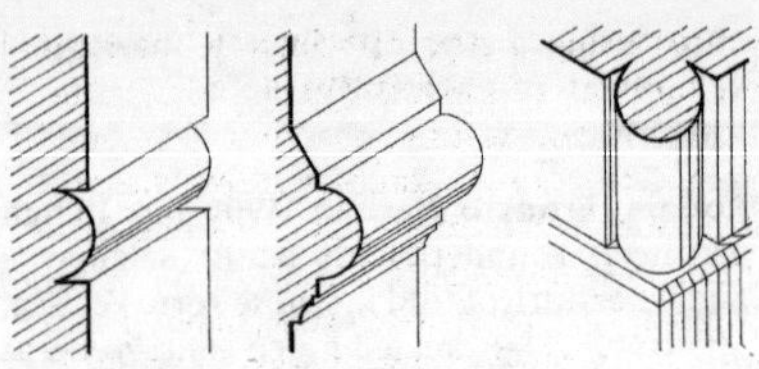

roll. (*left*) Flush bead moulding. (*middle*) Torus or half-round. (*right*) Angle-bead or bowtell.

roll-billet. One of a series of short *rolls like dowels with spaces between each short length set in *cavetto mouldings. Type of *billet, as in *Romanesque ornament.

roll-moulding. 1. As *roll. **2.** *Drip-stone, basically partly cylindrical in *section, but with a *fillet forming a *throat under it to shed water, so found in *hood-moulds or *labels.

roll-work. 1. *Strap-work. **2.** *Cartouche. **3.** *Volute.

Roman, Jacob (1640–*c*.1716). Netherlandish architect and sculptor. He designed the late-C17 Town Halls at Deventer and de Voorst, typical of Dutch *Renaissance design of the period, and also worked on the Palace of Het Loo.

Kuyper (1980)

Roman arch. Semicircular arch of wedge-shaped *voussoirs or thin tile-like bricks.

Roman architecture. Knowledge of the architecture of Ancient Rome during the Republic (509–27 BC) is limited, although the Sanctuary and Temple of Fortuna, Primigenia, Palestrina (Praeneste—perhaps late C2 BC, but more likely *c*.80 BC), has been investigated. It consisted of several terraces, connected by steps and ramps, rising up a steep hillside above the temple, with a semicircular double *portico surrounding a theatre. The climax of the composition was the circular temple at the top of the terraces. It is undoubtedly the finest partly surviving Republican composition, and was clearly of great magnificence. We know more, however, about the architecture of the Roman Empire from the time of Augustus (Emperor 27 BC–AD 14) to the foundation of Constantinople (AD 330). Not only was Roman architecture of great significance in itself in the history of *Classicism, the evolution of complex geometries, advances in constructional techniques of the *arcuated type (including *domes and *vaults) using a type of *concrete, and the development of engineering (roads, *aqueducts, bridges, heating, etc.), but it inspired *Early Christian, *Byzantine, *Romanesque, *Renaissance, *Baroque, and *Neoclassical design up to the end of C20.

Roman architecture, even that of the Empire at its most advanced, was derived from *Hellenistic prototypes, yet in *Hellenic and Hellenistic architecture the column of an *Order was fully exploited in design, while in Roman work was often reduced in status, becoming *engaged or used *decoratively, as in the pseudo-peripteral Temples of Fortuna Virilis, Rome (C2 BC or probably *c*.40), and the *Maison Carrée*, Nîmes, France (16 BC), both of which are set on high *podia, have deep *porticoes based on the *prostyle *Etruscan type, but with the rest of the surrounding *colonnade or *peristyle usual in a Greek temple engaged with the *cella walls. From the Greeks, too, came the Orders, but developed as distinctive Roman types of *Doric, *Ionic, and *Corinthian. Roman Doric, as at the Republican Temple at Cori (*c*.80 BC), was taller and more slender than Greek Doric (with the upper two-thirds of the column-shafts fluted with 18 flutes in the Hellenistic style, the lower thirds cut as 18-sided polygons), and its *entablature was much less high (with 3 *triglyphs over each *intercolumniation), while the distinctive type of Roman Tuscan Doric (amalgamating the *Tuscan Order (derived from Etruscan prototypes)) only shared triglyphs, *guttae, and *mutules with the Hellenic Order. Roman Ionic was less elegant than Hellenic or Hellenistic precedents, and included the eight-voluted *angular *capital as at the Temple of Saturn, Rome (AD C3 or AD C4), that removed the need for a special *angle capital at the corners of the portico. Such 'diagonal' capitals occurred at *Pompeii, and were in widespread use before AD 79.

The Greeks had used the Corinthian Order sparingly (e.g. *Choragic Monument of Lysicrates, Athens (334 BC)), but the Romans adopted it as an all-purpose Order, greatly elaborating the *entablature and applying lavish enrichment with an almost uninhibited zest. To the range of Orders the Romans added the *Composite Order, which was really a type of Corinthian, but with a capital consisting of a luxurious version of the Ionic angular capital set over two rows of acanthus-leaves. Greek Ionic and Corinthian shafts were always fluted, but in Roman Ionic, Corinthian, and Composite Orders the shafts could be fluted or unfluted. In addition to the range of Greek ornament the Romans added a great repertoire of their own. There was also the simple and robust Tuscan Order among the five Roman Orders.

Another influence on Roman design from Hellenistic architecture was the tendency to a much wider intercolumniation than that of Hellenic buildings, something that was no doubt partly due to the widely spaced columns of Etruscan porticoes. Wall-surfaces, too, were given considerable attention, not only with finishes (e.g. coloured marbles, etc.), but by means of the engaged columns and *pilasters so typical of Roman work. One of the most influential Roman innovations was the synthesis of arches (set in substantial blocky structures) and the *columnar and trabeated forms of the Orders (applied with very wide intercolumniations), an example of which was the *triumphal arch of Titus (*c*. AD 90) in Rome. This combination was further developed as the *assemblage of Orders applied to several storeys of arcuated walls, as in the Colosseum, Rome (*c*. AD 75–82). The impact of these inventions cannot be overstated, as the history of Classical architecture demonstrates. In particular, they were used in various combinations and transformations from Renaissance times.

Roman developments in the use of brick, *concrete, and stone for building led to the construction of enormous arched and vaulted monumental buildings in which interpenetration of volumes based on complexities of plan-form were explored. Rough surfaces were then clad with *stucco, coloured marbles, and other materials, and internal décor of great magnificence was achieved. Good examples of vaulted and domed structures were those at Pompeii in C2 BC, the Roman *Tabularium* with its half-engaged columns (78 BC), *Nero's *Domus Aurea* (Golden House—AD mid-C1) attributed to *Severus, and the huge complex of Severan buildings on the Palatine by *Rabirius (AD late C1). Vaulted structures with ingenious geometries in the planning include the *thermae of Caracalla (*c*.215) and Diocletian (306) and the *basilica of Maxentius (310–313) in Rome. Highly organized monumental Roman buildings such as the thermae, *Domus Aurea*, *Villa Adriana* (Hadrian's Villa) at Tivoli (from *c*.123), and the gigantic Palace of Emperor Diocletian at Spalato (Salona), Dalmatia (*c*.300), differ greatly from the architecture of Ancient Greece, yet can be described as 'Classical'. In fact, they can also be seen as having tendencies that in a curious way anticipated some designs of the Baroque period (although cannot be described as truly Baroque themselves), not only in the geometrical complexities of their plans, but in the elevational treatment, such as the segmental arch rising into the *pediment (called an arcuated lintel) in the forecourt of Diocletian's Palace. Furthermore, vast developments such as the *Villa Adriana* at Tivoli had different areas and parts intended as mnemonics of various regions within the Empire (such as the *Canopus with its Nilotic references), and so were not only important precedents for the C18 garden of allusions, intended to trigger associations, improving thoughts, and sentiments in the visitor, but were forerunners of the eclectic cult of the *Picturesque.

Temples with porticoes at one end only, set on high podia, derive from Etruscan precedents, while temples related to colonnaded forecourts were Hellenistic in origin, and reached heights of magnificence in the Imperial fora at the Baalbek complex, Lebanon (formerly Heliopolis—AD C1–3). The Romans also built circular temples (e.g. 'Temple of Vesta' (probably Hercules Victor) in the Forum Boarium (*c.* C1 BC) and the 'Temple of Vesta' or 'Sybil' at Tivoli (probably of the same period). The latter temple was influential, especially in C18. At Baalbek there was a circular temple around which columns carried an entablature consisting of five prototypes, circular *mausolea, e.g. the Tomb of Caecilia Metella, Rome (C1 BC), derived from Etruscan tumuli which were precedents for Imperial mausolea and other circular structures. Possibly the best-known Roman circular building is the Hadrianic *Pantheon (*c.*120), a thick drum from which rises a *coffered dome with a central *oculus. The height of the drum is the same as the radius of the dome (the low, stepped exterior was an inspiration to Neoclassical architects), and the diameter of the drum is the same as the dimension from the floor to the oculus. Attached to the drum is a large deep octastyle pedimented portico. Another familiar Roman building-type is the basilica which, with its *clearstoreyed *nave, *lean-to *aisles, and apsidal end, was one of the most influential of all forms and the precedent for countless churches and halls for the best part of two millennia. Other important Roman buildings included *amphitheatres (of which the Colosseum was the grandest and most influential representative); thermae (mentioned above, and including many rooms of different shapes and sizes all combined within one ingenious plan); *circuses and *hippodromes (huge structures, clearly influences in the design of C20 sports stadia, race-courses, and running-tracks); commemorative columns, e.g. Trajan's Column, Rome (early C2); triumphal arches; and Imperial fora, such as Trajan's *forum, Rome (*c.*113), designed by *Apollodorus (which were the models for many civic spaces).

Structural and uninhibited use of the arch made great engineering works possible, such as aqueducts and *bridges. Good examples of aqueducts include the Pont du Gard, Nîmes (AD C1), which carried the aqueduct of Nîmes over the river-gorge, and the Aqua Claudia, Rome (AD 38–52), with its *Sublime array of arches carried on massive stone piers. Surviving bridges include the Pons Mulvius (*c.*109 BC), which crosses the Tiber near Rome and carries the Via Flaminia. Such a command of structure also enabled multi-storey apartment-blocks called *insulae* to be built, with identical floor-plans throughout, and fire-resistant construction of brick with concrete vaults (e.g. *insulae* at the Roman port of Ostia, near Rome). From C1 insulae often had arcaded ground-floors.

The better type of dwelling-house in towns (*domus*) had its origins in Greek and Hellenistic models, and was usually of one or two storeys. Internal planning was based on axes and symmetry, with the main rooms placed around the *atrium and perhaps other internal *courts (often with peristyles). The domus presented blank walls to the street, or backed on to shops that faced the street, as at Pompeii, so it was an intensely private place, keeping the outside world at bay. Bigger houses also had walled gardens attached to them.

Country or suburban houses were called *villas, the plans of which were looser and often of some complexity, designed to exploit views of the countryside or the sea: the most celebrated example was *Pliny's villa at Laurentum, an elusive building described by its owner that has exercised the imaginations of many who have attempted a reconstruction. However, it must be regarded primarily as a literary phenomenon, and does not represent an archaeological datum, whereas many other Roman villas have been excavated in Italy, France, Tunisia, and England. The villa, unlike the *domus*, was therefore outward- rather than inward-looking, and had rooms of various shapes and sizes, including internal galleries. External *colonnades, connected to the gardens, enabled the pleasures of nature to be enjoyed.

Whereas Greek temples tended to be set on an *acropolis (e.g. the *Parthenon, Athens), remote from the city below, Roman temples, on the other hand, were usually sited near or in public places (e.g. *Maison Carrée*, Nîmes, and Temple of Fortuna Virilis, Rome). The triumphalism of Roman architecture was influential in Early Christian basilican churches, while Roman constructional techniques were passed to the Eastern Empire, and were continued and developed by Byzantine architects.

Finally, there was the architecture of Death, including the underground cemetries (*catacombs), private *hypogea, and *columbaria, linear cemeteries (roads lined with family and individual tombs, often set in funerary gardens (e.g. the Appian Way)), vast Imperial mausolea, cemetries with built tombs in clusters (e.g. at Ostia), and circular tomb-structures (e.g. Santa Costanza, Rome (mid-C4)) that were important models for *martyria and other Christian buildings.

Boëthius (1960); Boëthius and Ward-Perkins (1970); Colvin (1991); Curl (1992, 1993); Macdonald (1965–86); MacDonald and Pinto (1995); Robertson (1945); Toynbee (1971); Ward-Perkins (1974, 1981, 1986); Watkin (1986); Wheeler (1964)

Roman brick. Long, thin brick (*later*), much larger than modern bricks, requiring approximately 6 courses for 300 mm wall-height, but even this varies.

Robertson (1945)

Roman bronze. Alloy of copper, tin, and zinc.

Roman cement. 1. Cement or hydraulic mortar made by mixing lime with reactive siliceous material (in the form of crushed tiles or volcanic ash), later developing superior strength and water-resistance, used by the Romans. **2.** *Parker's or *Sheppey* hydraulic cement, manufactured from *c.*1796 using *septaria* (nodules containing networks of mineral-filled cracks) from Harwich, Essex, and the Isle of Sheppey. The calcareous clay nodules were crushed and burnt, then mixed with lime, sand, and water. Setting quickly and hard, it was brownish in colour, and was much used in C19 as a *render for walls, often scored to resemble *ashlar joints. *See* pozzolan.

Gwilt (1903); Papworth (1887)

Romanesque. Architectural style of buildings erected in Romanized Western Europe from C7 to the end of C12 having certain characteristics similar to those in *Early Christian, late-*Roman, and *Byzantine architecture, notably the semicircular-headed arch, the use of the *basilican form for churches, and the survival of design elements such as the Classical *capital (though much coarsened and transformed). Opinion, however, is divided about when the Romanesque style began: some accept C7, drawing *Carolingian and *Anglo-Saxon architecture within the Romanesque umbrella; others hold that true Romanesque began with the *Ottonian Empire in Germany and the evolution of architecture at *Cluny in Burgundy from 910 and the subsequent rise of the Cluniac branch of the *Benedictine Order. The latter view tends to regard Romanesque as arriving in England with the Norman Conquest in 1066, but this therefore denies the qualities of such unquestionably sophisticated structures as the *crypt of St Wystan's Church, Repton, Derbyshire (*c.*827–40—with vaulted roof carried on columns with spiral shafts (clearly associated with the tomb of St Peter in the Basilica of San Pietro in Rome) and *pilasters (obviously derived from Classical precedents), and the Old and New *Minsters, Winchester, Hampshire (C7–C11—with evident Carolingian prototypes).

Mature Romanesque architecture, mostly surviving in churches and castles, had thick walls and sturdy *piers (often cylindrical); the semicircular arch, as mentioned above; *vaults based on semicircles, often simple barrel-vaults, but frequently groin- and rib-vaults; *plans that were simple in their geometry, including *apses and circular buildings (such as Holy Sepulchre Church, Cambridge (*c.*1130)); and clearly defined *bays, square or rectangular on plan, making the construction of vaulted ceilings relatively simple. Bays were often delineated outside the building by means of pilaster-like *lesenes marking each division between bays, and inside by shafts rising up to the tops of the walls, or associated with the springing of arches. Romanesque architecture was therefore clear and logical, the forms and subdivisions comprehensible with ease, both inside and out: this inherent geometrical simplicity also made it powerful and impressive.

Grander churches had *ambulatories at the apsidal east end, with *radiating *chapels around them (as at Cluny). Barrel- or tunnel-vaults were employed in France (e.g. Notre Dame, Clermont-Ferrand, and St-Austremoine, Issoire (C12)) and in Spain; groin-vaults were common in Germany (e.g. the *nave of Speier Cathedral (1082–1106)); domes in parts of France (e.g. Angoulême (1105–30) and Cahors (1119) Cathedrals and St-Front, Périgeux (1120)); and rib-vaults in England (e.g. Durham Cathedral (end of C11–*c*.1130)) and Italy (e.g. San Michele, Pavia (*c*.1117)). In England and Northern France (where Romanesque is called *Norman*) the western fronts of larger churches usually had two towers with a tower over the *crossing (as at Southwell Minster, Nottinghamshire, and St-Étienne, Caen, Normandy). In Italy the basilican clearstoreyed-nave-and-aisles shape of the west end is often expressed and decorated with ranges of *arcades (as at Pisa and Pistoia); in Southern France the west ends often have *screen-façades (as at St-Gilles-du-Gard, near Arles, where the Roman *triumphal arch is clearly a precedent); and in Germany there may be several towers as well as structures (often octagonal) over the crossings (as at Speier Cathedral (1030–1106) and Maria Laach Abbey (1093–1156)). In Northern Europe roofs were invariably steeply pitched. In terms of rigid, powerful geometries, German Romanesque was unsurpassed: plans were often composed of a series of square bays in the nave, *transepts, and *chancels, with square bays a quarter of the main nave-bays in

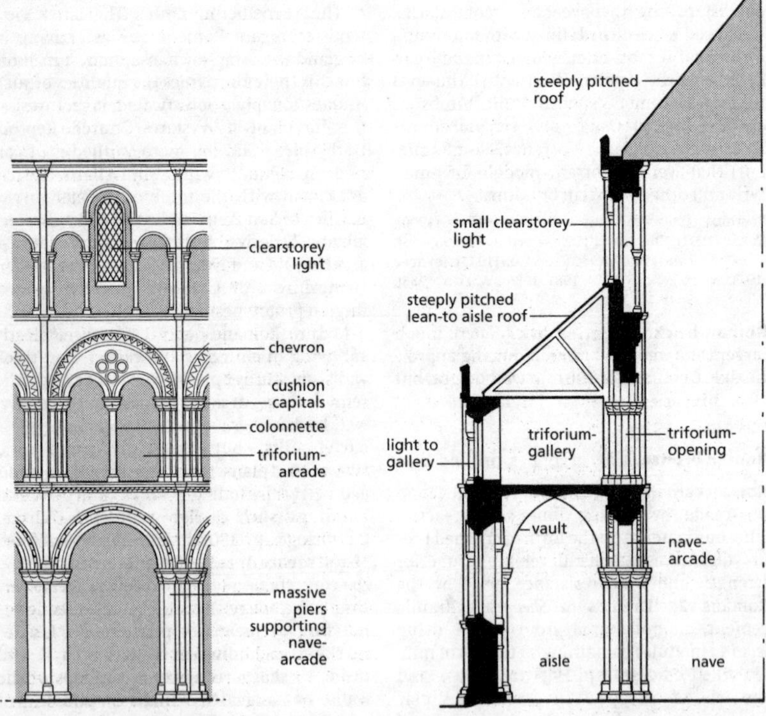

Romanesque. (*left*) Typical internal bay of large Romanesque church, paraphrased from Peterborough Cathedral, Cambridgeshire. (*JJS*)
(*right*) Section through aisle and nave. (*JJS*)

the *aisles (e.g. Worms Cathedral (1110–81) and the Church of the Apostles, Cologne (1035–1220)), the three-dimensional compartments of each bay emphasizing the rigidity more than in other parts of Europe.

Architectural detail was fairly limited in range, but distinctive. Capitals were often clearly derived from Roman and Byzantine prototypes, but simplified, as with certain examples where the *Corinthian volutes are still visible (e.g. the *cloisters of Monreale Cathedral (C12)). Basic Romanesque capitals include the *cushion and *scalloped type. Mouldings and ornaments, too, were simple, and straightforward, including the *beak-head, *billet, *cable, *chevron, *double cone, *nebule, and *reversed zig-zag.

Romanesque enjoyed a revival in the early C19 connected with a general trend towards *Historicism. In Germany the style was mingled with Early Christian and Byzantine elements to produce the *Rundbogenstil that was to be widely influential especially in Munich. In England there were some attempts to create a C19 untainted Romanesque, including *Cottingham's Church of St Helen, Thorney, Nottinghamshire (1846), and some buildings by *Donthorn and Thomas *Hopper. Serious archaeological revival of the style was rare, however, but was a phenomenon in France (with the work of *Abadie and others—e.g. basilica of Sacré-Coeur, Paris (1874–1919)), and in Ireland, where it enjoyed considerable success as *Hiberno-Romanesque continuing well into the 1960s (e.g. St Oliver Plunket, Blackrock, Co. Louth (1923), by Patrick Byrne). Perhaps the most impressive work of Romanesque Revival in Ireland was Sir Thomas *Drew's Cathedral of St Anne, Belfast (from 1898, with work continued (1924–86) under Charles *Nicholson, Thomas J. Rushton, John McGeagh, and Robert McKinstry).

Conant (1979); Cruickshank (1996); Kubach (1986); Pevsner (1960); Watkin (1986)

Roman mosaic. *Mosaic with small *tesserae laid in mortar to form geometrical or other decorative patterns.

Romano. *See* Giulio Romano.

Roman Order. The *Composite Order.

Romantic Classicism. *See* Romanticism.

Romanticism. Late-C18 and early C19 artistic movement, its many variations and strands defying any neat definition. The one characteristic found throughout its sundry manifestations was the insistence on individual experience, intuition, instinct, and emotion. Commonly perceived as a reaction against the rationalism of the *Enlightenment, *Classicism, and *Neoclassicism, it nevertheless shared with Classicism reverence for the *ideal, transcending reality, hence the term *Romantic Classicism* applied to works displaying a Romantic response to the *Antique. A perfect Ancient Greek temple in its pristine state would be Classical, but a ruined Greek temple, though Classical in one sense, cannot be Classical in another because it is broken, incomplete, partial, and in ruins. Such a ruin might, however, be perceived as beautiful, and so a Classical building constructed as a 'ruin' in an C18 garden could be described as an example of *Romantic Classicism*. Asymmetrical compositions set in the context of the *Picturesque often are purely Classical in detail, such as *Schinkel's exquisite buildings at Potsdam (Charlottenhof and the Roman Baths complex), and so can be classed as examples of Romantic Classicism.

Form, in Romantic art, was determined by the inner idea within the subject represented, and the yearning for spirituality and inner meaning allied Romanticism with medievalism, *Historicism, the Picturesque, the *Gothic Revival, and the *Sublime. A new tenderness towards the dead, a love of melancholy, and the cultivation of feelings were characteristics of Romanticism, creating elegiac gardens, the first cemeteries, and fuelling the religious revival that was such an important part of C19 European and American culture.

Chilvers, Osborne, and Farr (1988); Clay (1981); Honour (1979); Osborne (1970)

Roman tile. There are various types, including *Single Roman* (rectangular with an upstand on one side and a slightly tapered roll on the other that fits over the narrower part of the roll of the tile below as well as covering the upstand of the adjacent tile); *Double Roman* (large rectangle with an upstand on one side and two tapered rolls, one on the other side and the second in the centre, laid with 'break joints', or staggered, but requiring special tiles at the *verges to complete the bond); and *Old Roman, basilican,* or *Italian* (flat tapered *under* tile with upstands on both sides, the joints at the upstands being covered by convex tapering *over* or *top* rolls, that resemble half truncated cones).

McKay (1957)

rondel. **1.** Circular window-opening (i.e. *roundel) or a circular glazed *light. **2.** *Bead-moulding of a *capital around the top of a shaft. **3.** Tower circular on plan.

Rondelet, Jean-Baptiste (1743–1829). French architect and theoretician. He studied under J.-F. *Blondel and assisted *Soufflot during the construction of Ste-Geneviève, Paris, afterwards being responsible for the construction of the dome. He altered the building (1791–1812) under *Quatremère de Quincy when it was converted into the Panthéon. He is best known for his *Traité théorique et pratique de l'art de bâtir* (Theoretical and Practical Treatise on the Art of Building—1802–17), although he also published a *Mémoire sur l'Architecture* (1789), and other works, including well over 100 entries on construction for the *Encylopédie Méthodique* (1788–1820).

Chevalier and Rabreau (1977); Middleton and Watkin (1987); Rondelet, A.-J.-B. (1852); Rondelet (1790, 1802–17)

Rood. Term, derived from the Anglo-Saxon and Middle-English word for a cross, now used to describe the large Crucifixion set above the entrance to the *chancel of a church, sometimes suspended, sometimes supported on a *Rood-beam* spanning from wall to wall, and sometimes rising from the *Rood-loft* over the *Rood-screen*. During the Middle Ages, Rood-, chancel-, or choir-screens were erected in churches where the *nave ended and the *choir began: in cathedrals and larger churches they are usually of stone and called *pulpitum, while in smaller churches simply *screens. The top of screens had a gallery or loft, approached from a stair, used for readings and chantings.

Roods themselves, usually of wood but sometimes of stone, consisted of a carving of Christ crucified on the Cross, often flanked by figures of the Blessed Virgin Mary and St John on either side. The two figures and Crucifixion were occasionally supported on a base carved with rocks and skulls to represent Golgotha (a unique example survives in the Church of St Andrew, Cullompton, Devon).

Timber screens (of which many survive, especially in Devon) are often richly decorated with *tracery, painted panels (excellent examples can be found in St Edmund's Church, Southwold, Suffolk), and enrichment, the loft or gallery supported on a coved vaulted structure projecting over the screen proper. Most surviving English Rood-screens are C15 or C16 in date, though many were erected during the *Gothic Revival, some of the most beautiful by *Bodley, *Comper, and A. W. N. *Pugin.

Bond and Camm (1909); Parker (1850); Vallance (1947)

Rood-altar. **1.** *Nave-altar erected under a *Rood. **2.** Altar physically attached to a Rood-screen, facing the nave, as in the remarkable altar-bases of the *pulpitum in the Cathedral Church of St Kentigern (or Mungo), Glasgow, added by Archbishop Blackadder (1483–1508).

Bond and Camm (1909); Williamson, Riches, and Higgs (1990)

Rood-arch. **1.** Central opening or arch in a *Rood-screen. **2.** *Chancel-arch, if associated with a *Rood.

Rood-beam. *See* Rood.

Rood-loft. *See* Rood.

Rood-screen. *See* Rood.

Rood-spire. *Flèche or *spire over a *crossing in a church.

Rood-tower. Tower over a *crossing.

roof. Covering of any building by which its fabric and habitants are protected from the inclemencies of the weather. Roofs are here considered as to their form or type and finish, the structure of roofs being dealt with elsewhere. *Cladding of roofs may be of metal (especially aluminium, copper, lead, iron, steel, and zinc), glass, slate, stone, thatch, tile, turf, wood, or other materials. Greek temples had marble roofs, the slabs worked to prevent leaks; the Romans used tiles; medieval churches were clad in lead, tiles, or thatched; and since C19 a variety of materials has been used. *Barry's Palace of Westminster, for example, is clad in cast-iron panels.

Types of roof include:

appentice: see *lean-to*;

barrel: roof with internal appearance of a barrel-vault, like a cylinder;

catslide: *pitched* roof covering one side of a roof and continuing at the same pitch over a rear extension, commonly found in *Colonial architecture in New England (USA), where it is referred to as a *saltbox*. A catslide can also be the roof of a *dormer pitching in the same direction but less steeply than the main roof;

cradle: shaped like a half-cylinder or barrel-vault, common in the Middle Ages, where the rafters, collar-beams, and braces of each *truss

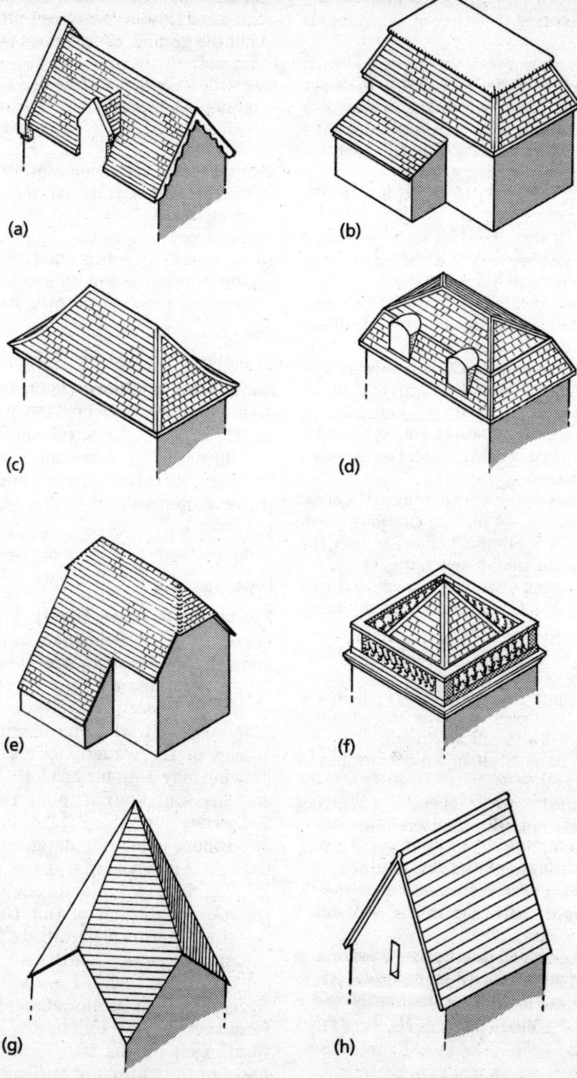

roof. (*a*) Common pitched roof with gable-ends terminating in a barge-board (*right*) and raised gable (*left*), and with a gablet or lucarne rising from the naked of the wall. (*b*) Pie-ended platform on a hipped roof with lean-to extension. (*c*) Hipped roof with sprocketed eaves. (*d*) Mansard roof with segmental-headed dormers. (*e*) Half-hipped roof with catslide. (*f*) Pyramid roof surrounded by balustrade. (*g*) Helm roof, as on a church-tower. (*h*) Saddleback roof. (*JJS*) were combined into an arched form on the *soffit, producing the effect of a continuous *barrel*;

curb: *pitched gable*-roof with the slopes broken to form two sets of planes on each side, the outer planes being steeper in pitch. Similar to a *mansard* roof, but with a *curb* or horizontal band with a vertical face at the junction between the two pitches;

cut: truncated, with the part of a truss over the collar-beams flattened off;

French: *curb*-roof with the sides set at very steep angles (almost vertical) and the pitched top part (*gabled* or *hipped*) almost flat;

gable or *pitched*: commonest type with sloping sides meeting at a *ridge and with a *gable at each end;

gambrel: in the USA *curb* roof with only the two sides sloping (i.e. a *gabled curb*-roof), but in Britain a *hipped* roof with a small gable or *gablet under the ridge at one or both ends;

half-hipped: pitched roof with gables terminating in hipped roofs;

helm: with four sloping sides joining at the apex, like a *pyramid, set on a square tower with gables the tops of which coincide with the lines of the junctions between the sides of the roof. The sloping sides sweep downwards over the raking tops of the gables, and terminate in points where the gables join;

hipped: with four pitched slopes joining at *hips*, and without gables;

lean-to: monopitched *appentice*, set against a higher wall, as over an *aisle and against a *clearstorey of a *basilican church;

M: with two parallel pitched roofs meeting in a valley or gutter;

mansard: named after F. *Mansart, a *curb*-roof with steeply pitched or curved lower slopes and pitched or hipped roof over, almost invariably with *dormer-windows. Distinguished from the *French* roof in having a more steeply pitched upper part, and in the USA called *gambrel*;

pavilion: hipped on all sides to have a pyramidal or almost pyramidal form, as *pyramid*-roof;

penthouse: as *lean-to*, but not necessarily associated with a church, so a simple *monopitched* roof;

pitched: as *gable*;

pyramid: shaped like a pyramid or a *hipped* roof with a very short *ridge* so that the slopes almost meet at a point, as *pavilion*;

ridge: any *pitched* roof with the sloping sides meeting at a ridge;

saddleback: ordinary *gable*-roof on top of a tower;

shed: as *penthouse*;

span: *ridge* roof of two equal slopes as distinct from a *lean-to* or *penthouse*-roof;

suspended: web or webs hung on cable-nets stretched between heavy cables fixed to masts and the ground, as in *Otto's work, called a *tent-roof*;

tent: with a concave surface like a *camp roof, or sloping inwards with a convex surface, such as the roof of a *Regency *balcony or a *verandah;

terrace: flat roof with imperceptible slope or *fall*, waterproofed, and permitting free use for sitting, etc.;

trough: *M*-roof;

valley: *M*-roof, or roof covering a building with projecting wings requiring valleys where the subsidiary roofs join the main roof.

See cruck, truss.

Papworth (1887); Sturgis *et al.* (1901–2)

Root, John Wellborn (1850–91). American architect educated in England and New York. In 1873 he formed a partnership with Daniel H. *Burnham as Burnham & Root, which became a successful practice and influenced the development of the *Chicago School. *See* Burnham.

Hoffmann, D. (1967, 1973); Monroe (1966);

rope. *See* cable.

Roriczer, *or* **Roritzer, Family** (*fl.* C15). Family of German or Bohemian master-masons. **Wenzel**, who seems to have been trained in the *Parler Lodge in Prague, became Architect of the Cathedral of St Peter, Regensburg, Bavaria, in 1411, where he designed the lower *stages of the western towers: a surviving drawing may be in his hand. He died in 1419, and his son, **Konrad**, built the *choir of St Lorenz, Nuremberg (1454–66), worked at Regensburg (where he designed the elegant triangular porch of *c.*1474), was a consultant in Vienna (1462), and advised on the *Frauenkirche* (Church of Our Lady), Munich (1474). He appears to have died *c.*1477.

Konrad's son, **Matthäus** or **Mathes** (*c.*1430–*c.*1495), worked with his father at Nuremberg, and became Master-Mason at the *Lorenzkirche* (1463–6), having worked at Nördlingen on his father's design for the tower of the Church of St Georg. From 1468 to 1472 he was again connected with Regensburg, and worked with *Böblinger on the *Frauenkirche* at Esslingen, designing the tabernacle there. He built the sacristy at Eichstätt, and in 1473 he was in Munich, working on the *Frauenkirche*, before returning to Regensburg in 1476 and succeeding his father as Master-Mason for the Cathedral. He built the upper part of the west façade, the pulpit (1482), the third stage of the north tower (1487–8), the tabernacle (1493), the Eichel turret, and, perhaps, the Three Kings altar. His brother, **Wolfgang**, completed the west front, added further stages to the towers, and designed the font and baldachin. He backed the losing side in a political dispute, and paid with his head in 1514.

Matthäus is particularly important as the author of a surviving tract on the design of Gothic *finials (*Das Büchlein von der Fialen Gerechtigkeit* (Little Book of Correct Finials—1486)) as well as a treatise on geometrical procedures relating to the resolution of certain constructional problems published as *Geometria Deutsch* (1486–90). His other surviving publication is a tract on gables (*c.*1488–9).

Geldner (1965); Recht (1989); Shelby (1977)

rosace. 1. Circular aperture or window. **2.** Rose. **3.** Rose-window. **4.** *Rosette.

rose. 1. Conventional representation of a flower (e.g. *fleuron in the centre of an *abacus-face on a *Corinthian capital). **2.** Circular ornament resembling a *patera, used to decorate ceilings, etc., hence *ceiling-rose* in the centre from which a chandelier or light-fitting is suspended. It is frequently found ornamented with stylized leaves, and according to its size is termed *rosace or *rosette. **3.** *Rose-window.

Rose, Peter (1943–). Canadian architect, a pupil of Charles *Moore. He evoked the *Shingle style in many of the houses he designed in and around Quebec, notably the Bradley House, North Hatley (1977–9). His Canadian Centre for Architecture, Montreal (1984–9—with Phyllis Lambert (1927–) as patron and consultant architect), has enjoyed international acclaim: it is a large museum and study-centre, rigorously ordered and finely detailed, owing much to Rose's understanding of *Classicism in its composition and to Lambert's understanding of detail. Other works include Brookside School, *Cranbrook Educational Community, Bloomfield Hills, Mich. (1991), and the Lower Canada College, Montreal (1992). He has made many contributions to the debates concerning the nature of architecture.

Emanuel (1994); Jencks (1977); Kalman (1994); Stern (1988)

rose-ball. Stylized tightly petalled rose-flower adopted by C. R. *Mackintosh and his wife for systems of decoration such as stencilled *friezes. It was an *Art Nouveau motif also favoured by the Vienna *Sezessionists.

Steele (1994); Tschudi-Madsen (1967)

Rosenberg, Eugene (1907–90). British architect, born in Moravia. Educated in Czechoslovakia, he worked with Le *Corbusier from 1929. He settled in England in 1939, forming a partnership with F. R. S. *Yorke and Cyril Mardall (1909–94) in 1944 which became Yorke, Rosenberg, & Mardall (YRM). Rosenberg's credentials were firmly established within *International Modernism, and he quickly became part of the English Modernist circle with *Fry, *Gibberd, and others. Among his works with YRM were the Cowley Peachey Housing Development, Middlesex (1947), the Sigmund Pumps Factory, Gateshead, Co. Durham (1948), Barclay Secondary School, Stevenage, Hertfordshire (1950), Warwick University (1965–71), and St Thomas's Hospital, London (1966–74).

Emanuel (1994); Yorke, Rosenberg, and Mardall (1972)

rosette. Circular stylized ornament, essentially a *patera with floral enrichment, associated with Classical architecture, and occurring on the *soffits of *coffers, and as the *fleuron of the *Corinthian *abacus. It is therefore generally smaller than a *rose.

Sturgis *et al.* (1901–2)

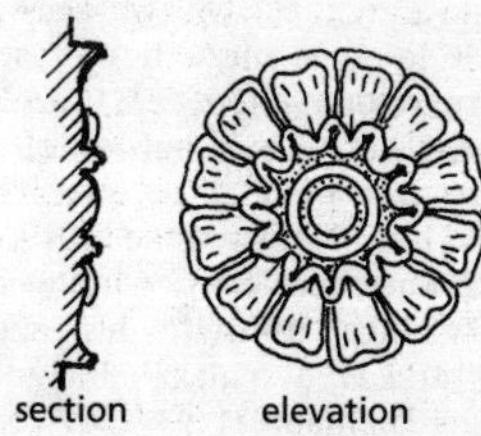

rosette

rose-window. *Gothic circular or *marigold window subdivided by complex *tracery radiating from the centre and joining in *foils to form a stylized floral design of great intricacy and beauty. It is often found combined with the tracery of a large *Pointed window as well as isolated within a circular aperture. It is distinguished as a *Catherine-wheel or *Wheel-window, both of which have *colonnettes coincident with the radii, like spokes.

Parker (1850); Sturgis *et al.* (1901–2)

Rossellino, Bernardo di Matteo Gambarelli *called* (1409–64). Florentine sculptor and architect. He completed the façade of the Fraternità di Santa Maria della Misericordia, Arezzo (1433–5), designed the Spinelli *cloister at Santa Croce, Florence (1448–52), and supervised the completion of *Alberti's Palazzo Rucellai, Florence (1448–62), including the façade. His masterpiece was the town-centre of Pienza (from 1459), the first *Renaissance *ideal city, which he realized for Aeneas Silvius Piccolomini, Pope Pius II (1458–64). It consists of the *piazza containing the Cathedral, Palazzo Piccolomini, Palazzo Vescovile, and Palazzo del Pretorio, and other palazzi and houses. The palazzi on either side of the *duomo* are set at angles to its main axis, like stage wings, and the Palazzo Piccolomini has elevational treatments derived from that of the Palazzo Rucellai, although the three-storey garden façade has tiers of *porticoes from which views of the countryside may be had, a concept clearly derived from *Pliny's description of his villa in Tuscany. Some scholars hold that it was Rossellino who designed the façade of the Palazzo Rucellai in its final form, and indeed it is almost exactly contemporary with the Palazzo Piccolomini in Pienza.

Carli (1966); Heydenreich and Lotz (1974); Mack (1987); Murray (1969); Tyszkiewicz (1928); Watkin (1986)

Rossetti, Biagio (*c*.1447–1516). Important *Renaissance architect, who worked mostly in Ferrara. He designed one of the most spectacular urban developments of C15, the Addizione Erculea, the northern extension of the city that more than doubled its area, complete with the Piazza Nuova and the intersection of the Via Prione and Via degli Angeli (from 1492). Rossetti himself designed four churches and eight palazzi, including the Palazzo dei Diamanti (1493–1567), so called because of the diamond-pointed *rustication of its façades. In the Piazza Nuova he designed the Palazzo Rondinelli and the Palazzo Strozzi-Bevilacqua (both from 1494), with arcaded ground-floors. He also designed the Church of San Francesco in the old city (from 1494) on a plan based on *Brunelleschi's San Lorenzo, Florence, with a nave ceiling consisting of transverse arches supporting shallow domes on pendentives. In the Addizione he also designed the aisleless vaulted San Cristofero alla Certosa (from 1498), with a dome over the *crossing.

Heydenreich and Lotz (1974); Placzek (1982); Zevi (1960)

Rossi, Aldo (1931–97). Italian architect, the most eminent protagonist of *Rational architecture (also called *Neo-Rationalism* or *Tendenza), the theoretical bases of which he set out in *L'architettura della città* (Architecture of the City—1966) in direct contradiction of the tenets of the *Modern Movement. Yet in the early 1960s his work had seemed to embrace aspects of *International Modernism, late-C18 *Neoclassicism of the stereometrically pure type advocated by *Boullée, and a proto-Surrealism reminiscent of the paintings of Giorgio de Chirico (1888–1978). Something of the Surreal atmosphere in Chirico's work could be found in Rossi's apartment-blocks for *Aymonino's Gallaretese 2 Complex, Monte Amiata, Milan (1969–74). With Gianni Braghieri he designed the San Cataldo Cemetery, Modena (1971–6 and 1980–8), a master-work of stripped Neoclassical geometry as severe as any late-C18 or C20 essay, which became a paradigm of Neo-Rationalist architecture. Other important works include the School at Fagnano di Olona (1972–6), apartments in the *Rauchstrasse*, Berlin (1983), housing blocks for the *Internationale Bauaustellung* (International Building Exhibition) Berlin (1984–7), the School of Architecture, University of Miami, Coral Gables, Fla. (1986), the *Il Palazzo* Hotel, Fukuoka, Japan (1987–9—with Morris Adjmi), the Carlo Felice New Theatre, Genoa (1983–93—with Ignazio Gardella), and the Bonnefanten Museum, Maastricht, The Netherlands (1990–4). His *A Scientific Autobiography* (1982) and *Selected Writings and Projects* (1983) set out many of his ideas regarding building typologies and urban morphologies.

Adjmi (1991); Amsoneit (1994); Arnell and Bickford (1985); Emanuel (1994); Ferlenga (1987, 1992); Jodidio (1996*a*); Klotz (1988); Moschini (1979); obituary in *The Times* (18 Sept. 1997) 25; Savi (1976)

Rossi, Domenico (1657–1737). A pupil of *Longhena, he made his name as a designer of firework displays and as an expert on explosives before he turned to the less ephemeral pursuit of architecture after winning the competition to design the façade of the Church of San'Staë (Sant'Eustachio), Venice (1709–22), a handsome *engaged *temple-fronted composition on the Grand Canal. Thereafter his output was prolific, and included palazzi (e.g. Palazzo Corner della

Regina, Venice (1723–*c.*1730)), churches, and *villas. Among his many works the Archiepiscopal Palace, Udine (1708–25), and the Church of Santa Maria Assunta (Jesuit Church), Venice (1714–29—with others), may be cited.

Howard (1980); Lewis (1979)

Rossi, Giovanni Antonio de (1616–95). Roman *Baroque architect. He designed the Church of Santa Maria in Publicolis, Rome (1641–3), in which *scenographic aspects are well to the fore. His Santa Maria in Campomarzio (1676–86) and Cappella Lancellotti in San Giovanni in Laterano (1674–80), both in Rome, deserve mention for their splendour. His best-known work is the Palazzo Altieri, Rome (1650–76), with its spectacular four-flight staircase, although his finest work is arguably the Palazzo d'Aste-Bonaparte (1658–65), influenced by *Borromini.

Coudenhove-Erthal (1930); Fagiolo dell'Arco and Carandini (1977–8); Hibbard (1971); Portoghesi (1970); Spagnesi (1964); Wittkower (1982)

Rossi, Karl Ivanovich (1775–1849). Russian architect, the most important working in St Petersburg from 1816, largely responsible for giving the city-centre its monumental *Neoclassical character. He designed the noble arch of the Winter Palace (1819–29—later the General Staff Arch) with the flanking hemicycle of administrative buildings, the gigantic range of the Senate and Synod (1829–34), the impressive Mikhailovsky Palace (1819–33—later the Russian Museum), and the Alexandrinsky (later Pushkin) Theatre (1827–32). He created formal spaces, an urban fabric of great grandeur, and a *Sublime architectural effect by repetition of *colonnades and huge scale.

Egorov (1969); Hamilton (1983); Middleton and Watkin (1987); Taranovskaia (1980)

Rossi, Marcantonio de (1607–61). Italian architect and military engineer. His greatest work was the replanning of San Martino al Cimino near Viterbo (1648–54), a remarkable early instance of comprehensive order and system being imposed on an urban fabric. He fortified the Janiculum, Rome, for Pope Urban VIII (1623–44), building the Porta di San Pancrazio and the Porta Portese in Trastévere (both 1643). He was responsible for the Acqua Acetosa, Rome (1661).

Bentivoglio and Valtieri (1973); Heimbürger Ravalli (1971, 1977); Onofrio (1978)

Rossi, Mattia de (1637–95). The son of Marcantonio de *Rossi, he assisted *Bernini, notably at Sant'Andrea al Quirinale, Rome (1670s). Among his best works are the Church and Hospice of Santa Galla, Rome (1684–6—with an elliptical interior to the church), the Palazzo Muti Bussi, Piazza della Pilotta (1675), and the Collegiate Church of Santa Maria dell'Assunta, Valmontone (1686–98—with concave *portico flanked by light, airy, *belfries). He also designed numerous altars, funerary monuments, and chapels.

Coudenhove-Erthal (1930); Fagiolo d'Arco and Carandini (1977–8); Hibbard (1965, 1971); Wittkower (1982)

Rosso, Giovanni Battista *called* **Rosso Fiorentino** (1495–1540). Florentine painter and decorative artist. From 1530 he worked at *Fontainebleau for King *François Ier (1494–1547), and, with Francesco Primaticcio (1504/5–70), can be credited with the creation of the Fontainebleau School of decoration (as in the Galerie François Ier).

Chilvers, Osborne, and Farr (1988)

rostral column. *See* columna rostrata.

rostrum. 1. Bow section of an *Antique Roman warship, resembling a beak, ornamented with an animal-head, buckler, or helmet (*acrostolium*), forming the projections on *columnae rostrata. **2.** *Daïs or platform raised above the general level.

Roth, Alfred (1903–). Swiss architect. He established his position within *International Modernism by collaborating with Le *Corbusier and *Jeanneret-Gris on two houses for the *Weissenhofsiedlung (1927), described in *Zwei Wohnhäuser von Le Corbusier und Pierre Jeanneret* (Two Houses by Le Corbusier and Pierre Jeanneret—1927), and later published his reminiscences in *Begegnung mit Pionieren* (Meeting with Pioneers—1973). He was a member of the Swiss *CIAM group, through which he obtained his celebrated commission for the Doldertal Apartment Block, Zurich (1935–6), designed with his cousin **Emil Roth** (1893–1980) and Marcel *Breuer for *Giedion. From 1934 he edited the CIAM journal, *Weiterbauen*, published *The New Architecture* (1939), and edited *Werk* from 1942 to 1956. He was influential in making modern Swiss architecture and the International style well known.

Gubler (1975); Roth (1946, 1973, 1977)

rotunda. 1. Building shaped like a cylinder both inside and outside, especially one covered with a dome, such as the *Pantheon in Rome. It may have a *peristyle around the exterior (e.g. the drum of the Panthéon *crossing-dome in Paris by Soufflot) or within it, or both inside and outside (e.g. *tholos at Epidaurus). **2.** Hall or room shaped like a cylinder contained within a larger building so that the drum is not expressed externally as a totality, but may appear partially as a *bow, with or without a *cupola over it.

roughcast. Species of external plastering or *render composed of lime, sand, water, and small particles of gravel, pebbles, or crushed stones, thrown on to an undercoat of render before the latter has dried, also called *pebble-dash* rendering.

round. Anything circular, or almost circular, such as a round (i.e. semicircular) arch, round-arched style (*Rundbogenstil), round (as opposed to prismatic) *billet, round church (i.e. circular on plan), round moulding (e.g. *torus), round *pediment (i.e. segmental or semicircular), round *ridge (i.e. with a half-cylindrical *crest or ridge-tile), round tower (as in Irish round towers with conical caps and certain other bell-towers in England and Italy), and round window (as in a *Catherine-wheel or *rose-window).

roundel. 1. Small circular panel or window, specifically a deep circular *niche containing a bust. **2.** Bull's eye (*œil-de-bœuf) window or *oculus. **3.** *Astragal or large *bead.

Rousseau, Pierre (1751–1810). French architect, much influenced by *Peyre. His masterpiece is the Hôtel de Salm (Palais de la Légion d'Honneur, 64 Rue de Lille, Paris (1782–5)), with its *colonnaded *Ionic screen containing a central monumental arch. He designed a number of apartment-blocks, including those at 25 Quai Voltaire, the Rue Royale, and the Rue de Bellechasse (1770s and early 1780s). He also designed the *Chinoiserie pavilion of the Hôtel de Montmorency, Boulevard Montmartre, Paris. He was appointed Architect for the town of Clermont-Ferrand and also had responsibilities for the *Département* of Puy-de-Dôme, in which capacity he designed the market-buildings at Issoire and the gaol at Riom.

Braham (1980); Middleton and Watkin (1987); Papworth (1887)

Rowe, Colin (1920–). English architectural critic and teacher. He established his reputation in the 1940s with a series of papers in which he explored Classical continuity within *Modernism and probed ideas that lay behind forms. He was to point out that Le *Corbusier's proportional systems regulating the structural grid and the façade of the Villa Stein at Garches (1926–8) were the same as those used by *Palladio, e.g. at the Villa Malcontenta. He seems to have held that much International Modern architecture of the 1920s offered paradigms for the second half of C20.

His works include *The Architecture of Good Intentions* (1994), *As I Was Saying: Recollections and Miscellaneous Essays* (1996), and *The Mathematics of the Ideal Villa and Other Essays* (1976). Rowe gave his disciples metaphors and historical references as generators of modern forms, and his belief that there was a direct architectural relevance between the Classical past and the protagonists of the Modern Movement had profound effects on late-C20 theory and design. He collaborated with Fred Koetter for *Collage City* (1978) in which he advocated the use of collage and mixed historical references, which influenced the work of *Stirling, among others. By proposing a wide-ranging *eclecticism, he appeared to view collage as a method for using things and simultaneously disbelieving in them. It would seem that a manipulation of themes used as collage in design might be a means of enjoyment without depth, for conviction and belief were no longer possible.

Curtis (1996); Rowe (1976, 1994, 1996); Rowe and Koetter (1984)

Roy *also* **Leroy, Julien-David Le** (1724–1803). French architectural historian, who succeeded J.-F. *Blondel as Professor of Architecture at the Academy, and succeeded in preventing the abolition of the School of Architecture when the Revolutionaries closed the Royal Academies during the Terror. His studies of Ancient Greek buildings had a profound effect on *Neoclassicism and on the *Greek Revival, although his surveys were not always accurate and attracted adverse criticism as a result. His *Les Ruines des plus beaux monuments de la Grèce, ouvrage divisé en deux parties, où l'on considére dans la première, ces monuments du côté de l'histoire et, dans la seconde du côté de l'architecture* (Ruins of the Most Beautiful Monuments of Greece, etc.) appeared in 1758, and he also published *Histoire de la Disposition et des Formes Différentes que les chrétiens ont données à leurs temples depuis le règne de Constantin le Grand jusqu'à nous* (History of the Disposition and Different Forms that the Christians Gave to their Temples since the Reign of Constantine the Great to our Own Day—1764), and *Observations sur les édifices des anciens peuples* (Observations on the Buildings of Ancient Peoples—1767) which also contained reflections on criticisms of his *Ruines... de la Grèce* published in *Stuart and *Revett's *Antiquities of Athens*, the first volume of which had appeared in 1762. His 'reconstruction' of the Athenian *propylaea was the model for *Langhans's masterpiece, the Brandenburg Gate, Berlin.

Braham (1980); Egbert (1980); Eriksen (1974); Middleton and Watkin (1987); Rykwert (1980); Wiebenson (1969)

rubbed, rubber. *Rubbed brick*, *brick rubber*, *cutter*, or *malm* is a soft brick made of special well-mixed fine loamy clay containing a lot of sand and baked (not burnt) in a kiln, readily sawn and rubbed to the required shape. It is used for making *gauged* brick arches, etc., the extremely fine joints between the rubbers being formed of lime-putty rather than conventional mortar, which would be too coarse.

Brunskill (1990); Lloyd (1925); McKay (1957)

rubble. Rough stones of irregular shapes and sizes used in the construction of *rubble-work* walls with the mortar-joints fairly large, often requiring small pieces of stone (*gallets) to be set into the mortar if the stones are especially irregular and difficult to fit reasonably closely together. Types of rubble-work include:

random rubble: constructed of stones not of uniform size or shape laid in apparently random patterns, with no courses, needing great skill in its bonding so that continuous (and therefore weakening) vertical jointing can be eliminated, and requiring the wall to be sound by means of *bonders* (*bond-stones*), *headers*, or *through-stones* providing the transverse bond by extending through the thickness of the wall. Random rubble is also used without mortar (called *dry-rubble* or *dry-stone* walling) for field boundary-walls, the stability of which is entirely dependent on the careful interlocking and bonding of the stones;

random rubble built to courses: similar to random uncoursed rubble in basic construction, except that the work is roughly levelled up to form courses the heights of which coincide with the *quoin or *jamb-stones of a *reveal (which can also be of brick). Thus courses may be composed of one large irregular stone, then two or three stones set over each other, then two, then one, all laid to form a level upper surface;

squared coursed rubble: rubble roughly formed of rectangular blocks, laid in courses, with the individual stones in a course all the same height, although the heights of courses themselves may vary, also called *regular coursed rubble* or *ranged* rubble;

squared uncoursed rubble: roughly squared stones of different sizes placed in an uncoursed arrangement, with *levellers* (stones of low height), *jumpers* or *risers* as *bond-* or *through-stones*, and checks or snecks to fill in the areas left by the larger stones. It is also called *square-snecked rubble*.

In addition there are variations of walling which can be classed under rubble-work. They include:

flint-walling: flints or cobbles in panels framed by *lacing-courses* of brick or stone to bond the wall together;

knapped-flint walls: flints split to expose the hard dark interiors and dressed in pieces roughly square, which are then laid very closely together so that little, if any, mortar joints are visible. Panels of knapped flint are commonly found with dressed stone around them, especially in East Anglian churches of the *Perpendicular period, and the material always has to be used in conjunction with brick or stone for stability;

Lake District masonry: slate from Cumberland and Westmorland in flat rough-faced or square-faced blocks dressed and laid in courses bedded in mortar set back from the faces on both sides of the wall, the centre of the wall being packed with dry stones without mortar. Blocks are closely fitted together, spalls being used to pack gaps, and laid tilted (*watershot*) towards the external wall to prevent water-penetration. *Quoins are usually of dressed limestone;

polygonal walling: usually found as a facing using stones such as *ragstone set so that the joints form a net-like pattern all over the wall.

Gwilt (1903); McKay (1957); Papworth (1887); Sturgis *et al.* (1901–2)

rudenture. Cabling. *See* cable.

Rudnev, Lev Vladimirovich (1885–1956). Architect in the former Soviet Union. He was one of the team responsible for the gigantic University Complex, Moscow (1948–53), typical of the overblown coarse stripped *Classicism favoured in the Stalinist era. Similar buildings, with vast towers, were erected in several places in the Soviet bloc during the 1950s.

Council of Europe (1995)

Rudolph, Paul Marvin (1918–97). American architect. He studied with *Gropius at Harvard before setting up in practice in 1947. He was Chairman of the Department of Architecture, Yale University (1958–65), and designed the monumental Art and Architecture Building at New Haven (1958–63), which was fairly typical of his *Brutalist architecture, with its massive towers, many levels joined by stairs and bridges, colliding forms, powerful textured surfaces, and dramatic interiors. The building was partly burned in 1969 during student unrest, an episode Rudolph found too painful to discuss. The architecture was influential, however, and aspects of its geometries recurred in *Lasdun's work in England. Rudolph's State Service Center, Boston, Mass. (1962–72), a composition of terraced wings and a powerfully modelled tower arranged around a public square, was supposedly inspired by the Campio, Siena, but is arguably less successful than its model. Other works include Sarasota High School, Fla. (1958–9), the Endo Laboratories, Garden City, NY (1960–4), and the Science Building, Southeastern Massachusetts University, Boston (1984).

Emanuel (1994); Moholy-Nagy (1970); obituary in *Daily Telegraph* (13 Aug. 1997); Placzek (1982); Spade (1971*c*); Stern (1977)

ruin. Carefully contrived specially constructed 'ruins' (sometimes called *folly) or real ruins (e.g. of a castle or abbey) were often incorporated within C18 English *Picturesque landscapes, a fashion that spread to Europe. Some architects (e.g *Chambers and *Soane) established their architectural works as worthy of the best Classical *Antique models by arranging for them to be depicted as imaginary ruins, inspired by the *Grand Tour and the influential engravings of *Piranesi.

Coffin (1994); Jacques (1983); Mosser and Teyssot (1991)

Rundbogenstil. German for *round-arched style, it was essentially eclectic, drawing on *Byzantine, *Early Christian, Italian *Romanesque (especially North-Italian buildings in and around Como), and Florentine (e.g. the round-arched *palazzi) *Renaissance precedents. As the name suggests, it developed in C19 Germany, notably in Bavaria, where its chief practitioners were von *Klenze (*Königsbau* (King's Building) and *Allerheiligenhofkirche* (Court Church of All Saints), Munich (1826–37)) and von *Gärtner (Court and State Library (1827–43), *Ludwigskirche* (1829–44), and other Munich buildings), and in Prussia, where *Schinkel and *Persius created some distinguished buildings in the style (e.g. *Friedenskirche* (Church of Peace), Potsdam (completed 1850)). The style, promoted by *Hübsch, had considerable success in England, where it was emulated under the aegis of Professor Ludwig Grüner (1801–82) and Prince *Albert. Among works of English Rundbogenstil were those of *Wild (Christ Church, Streatham Hill, London (1840–2), and T. M. *Wyatt and Brandon's Sts Mary and Nicholas, Wilton, Wiltshire (1840–6).

Nerdinger (1987); Schinkel (1989)

runic cross. *Celtic cross.

runic knot. Type of intricate interlacing ornament associated with *Anglo-Saxon and *Celtic work, especially *high crosses, but also found in *Romanesque design.

Rickman (1848)

running. Term describing anything linked in a smooth continuous progression or repeating asymmetrical flowing motifs, set on a *band, each apparently leaning to one side or the other. Types of *running ornament* are:

running dog: Classical *Vitruvian scroll or *wave-scroll, like a repeated stylized wave on a band;

running vine: grapevine, *trail, or vignette, common on the upper parts of *Perpendicular *Gothic *screens.

rural architecture. Buildings associated with the countryside, but especially C18 and C19 *cottages ornés and *fermes ornées or other buildings designed to suggest the rural ideal, as in a *Picturesque landscape, using free compositions, asymmetry, *vernacular detail, and materials such as *roughcast, *thatch, *rubble, etc. *See* rustic.

Rusconi Sassi, Ludovico (1678–1736). Roman *Baroque architect. His works include the Aedicula, Via del Pellegrino (1715–16), and the Odescalchi Chapel, Santissimi Apostoli (1719–22), both in Rome, in which the influence of *Borromini was apparent. He also designed the Chapels of the Holy Sacrament in the Churches of San Lorenzo in

Damasco, Rome (1732–6), and Santa Lucia, Porto Fiumicino (1735).

Fasolo (1949); Grioni (1975); *Journal of the Warburg and Courtauld Institutes*, 37 (1974), 218–48; Zocca (1959)

Ruskin, John (1819–1900). English academic and critic, who had an enormous influence not only on architectural style but on the ways in which standards of aesthetics were judged. He used an Evangelical and polemical tone in his writings that not only reached a mass audience but received the approval of the *Ecclesiologists. Initially encouraged by J. C. *Loudon, he contributed to some of Loudon's publications, but his key works date from the late 1840s and 1850s. The *Gothic Revival was well established when Ruskin published *The Seven Lamps of Architecture* (1849), which was an immediate success, encapsulating the mood of the period rather than creating new ideas. He argued that architecture should be true, with no hidden structure, no veneers or finishes, and no carvings made by machines, and that Beauty in architecture was only possible if inspired by nature. As exemplars worthy of imitation (he argued that the styles known to Man were quite sufficient, and that no new style was necessary) he selected Pisan *Romanesque, early *Gothic of Western Italy, Venetian Gothic, and English early *Second Pointed. In the choice of the last, the style of the late C13 and early C14, he was echoing A. W. N. *Pugin's preferences as well as that of most ecclesiologically minded Gothic Revivalists such as G. G. *Scott.

The Stones of Venice (1851–3) helped to promote that phase of the Gothic Revival in which Continental (especially Venetian) Gothic predominated. *Deane and *Woodward's University Museum, Oxford (1854–60), is an example of Venetian or *Ruskinian Gothic*. In particular, structural *polychromy, featuring colour in the material used, rather than applied, was popularized by Ruskin's writings. The *Stones* also contained a section on the nature of Gothic in which Ruskin argued that the admirable qualities of medieval architecture were related to the commitment, creative pride, and freedom of the craftsmen who worked on the buildings. From this idea *Morris developed his theories, and the *Arts-and-Crafts movement began to evolve.

Ruskin found certain styles (e.g. *Baroque) unacceptable because they exploited illusions, and therefore were not 'truthful'. This use of moral disapprobation of justify an aesthetic stance has been a potent weapon in the hands of *International Modernists. *Gropius, for example, claimed to have been influenced by Ruskin's writings.

Bell (1978); Blau (1982); Brooks, M. W. (1987); *DNB* (1917); Hewison (1976); Hitchcock (1954); Pevsner (1972); Ruskin (1903–12); Swenarton (1989); Watkin (1977)

rustic, rustick. **1.** Species of *masonry characterized by surfaces artificially roughened or left rough-hewn, or by having the joints, notably the horizontal ones, emphasized by being deeply sunk or chamfered. *See* rustication. **2.** Simple, plain, unrefined, and made of rough materials (e.g. roughly hewn tree-trunks), to suggest *rural architecture or the *Picturesque.

rustic arch. Arch constructed of *rubble in e.g. *rock-work.

rusticated column. **1.** Column with blocks of plain ashlar at intervals the length of the shaft, called a *banded* column. **2.** The same, but with the blocks treated with *rustication.

rustication. In *masonry, stone cut in such a way that the joints are sunk in some sort of channel, the faces of the stones projecting beyond them. In addition, the faces of the stones are usually roughened to form a contrast with ordinary dressed *ashlar. Rusticated masonry enhances the visual impact of *keystones, *plinths, *quoins, and even entire storeys, while its application to whole façades can suggest power, solidity, and even the *Sublime. *Rusticating* is the carving or creation of rustication, or the making of a texture on a face. Types of rustication include:

banded: plain or textured ashlar with the horizontal joints only grooved, giving the impression of a series of *bands;

chamfered: with each ashlar chamfered to create V-shaped joints, either all round each stone or, if at the tops and bottoms, to create *banded* rustication with chamfers;

channelled: with a rectangular sunken channel at the joints, formed horizontally only or round each stone;

congelated: see *frosted* below;

cyclopean: *rock-faced or *quarry-faced ashlar with dressed projecting rough faces, as though recently taken from the quarry, giving a massive, powerful, impregnable effect particularly useful for plinths, *piers of viaducts, etc.;

diamond-pointed: with ashlar blocks cut with chamfered faces giving the effect in a wall of a

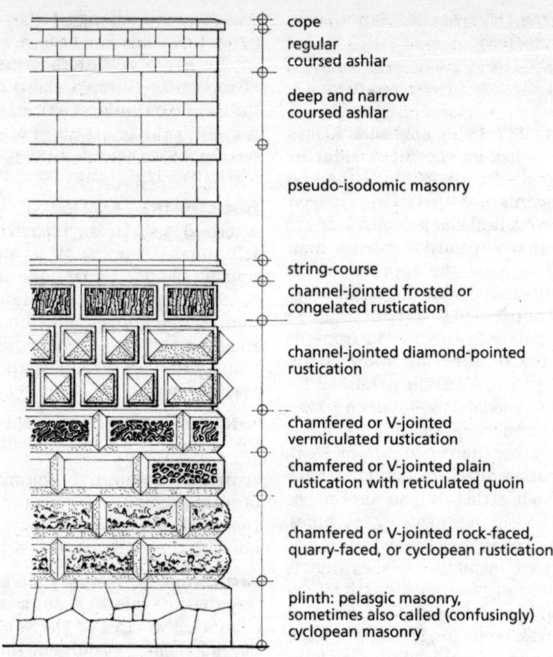

rustication. Varieties of ashlar and rusticated masonry.

series of small pyramids or hipped roofs set on their sides, also called *prismatic* or *pyramidal* rustication;

frosted: carved to look like icicles or stalactites, also called *congelated* rustication, normally found on fountains, in *grottoes, or other situations associated with water;

reticulated: carved with indentations leaving the surface connected in an irregular net-like pattern;

rock-faced: as *cyclopean* above;

smooth: with joints clearly shown by some means (e.g. channels or V-joints) but the faces flat and plain;

V-jointed: as *chamfered* above;

vermiculated: with the face carved as though eaten away in parts, with irregular worm-like tracks and holes all over it, reminiscent of wood or sand.

rustic brick. Facing-brick with surfaces improved by a sand covering or with a scratched texture applied before firing, often with variegated colouring.

Brunskill (1990); McKay (1957)

rustic joint. In masonry a joint emphasized by the chamfering of the arrises of the stones.

rustic quoin. At the external angle of a building, one of several stone quoins with its face roughened and raised (e.g. by chamfering or simply by having a *rock-faced surface surrounded by chamfers) so that it projects beyond the *naked of the wall.

rustic slate. One of many slates of different thickness imparting a varied uneven appearance to a roof or wall.

rustic stone. *Rubble.

rustic woodwork. Poles and roughly sawn timber with the bark adhering to it used in timber buildings intended to look like humble *rural architecture such as *cottages ornés, *gazebos, etc., often with decorative touches such as *lattice-windows, twisted *chimneys, thatched roofs, and ornamental fencing and *barge-boards.

Ruusuvuori, Aarno Emil (1925–92). Finnish architect. His work was at first firmly established in *International Modernism and in the 1960s continued in *Rationalism and became more ascetic as *Brutalism was embraced. He often favoured stereometrically pure shapes, such as cubes and pyramids, as in his Hyvinkää Church and Parish Centre (1961). Other works include the extensions and renovations of the City Hall, Helsinki (1970–84), and the ingenious proposals for extending the National Museum, Helsinki (1987). He was an influential teacher and practitioner.

Emanuel (1994); Kidder-Smith (1964); Richards (1978); Salokorpi (1970); Tempel (1968)

Ruysbroeck, Jan van (*fl.* C15). Flemish architect of the tower (1444–63) of Brussels Town Hall, one of the most elegant creations of late-medieval *Gothic secular European architecture. Other works include the fountain, Hospital of Our Lady, Oudenaarde (1443–5); the tower of the Church of Ste-Gertrude, Leuven (Louvain), (completed 1453); and part of the Church of St-Pierre, Anderlecht, Brussels (1479–85). He worked on the great Church of Ste-Gudule, Brussels (1470–85), probably on the tower. To confuse matters, he is also known as **Jan van den Berghe**.

Baedeker, *Belgium* (1905); Białostocki (1972); Duverger (1933)

Ry, Paul du (1640–1714). Member of a family of French Huguenot architects. His grandfather, **Charles** (*fl.* 1610–36), was related to and worked with de *Brosse, and his father, **Mathurin**, was Court Architect in Paris. Paul trained with N.-F. *Blondel, worked as a military engineer on the fortifications of Maastricht, The Netherlands (from 1665), and finally left France in 1685 after the Revocation of the Edict of Nantes. He became Court Architect to Landgrave Karl of Hesse-Kassel (1670–1730), and designed the *Oberneustadt* (Upper New Town), Kassel, where other Huguenot refugees settled under the benevolent rule of the Landgrave. This modest and humanely scaled new town in *Baroque and Classical styles had the octagonal *Karlskirche* (Charles Church—1698–1710) as one of its main foci. He also built the *Gartenpalais* (Garden Palace) and the Palace of Prince Wilhelm, and designed Karlshafen, Hesse (1699–1720). His son, **Charles-Louis** (1692–1757), succeeded his father as *Oberhofbaumeister* (Chief Court Architect) and continued the development of the *Oberneustadt*, Kassel, designing the canal system (1739). All his buildings have been destroyed.

Colombier (1955); Gerland (1895); Hempel (1965); Watkin and Mellinghoff (1987)

Ry, Simon-Louis du (1726–99). Son of **Charles-Louis du Ry**, he studied with *Hårleman and J.-F. *Blondel before settling in Kassel, where he worked first for Landgrave Wilhelm VIII (1730–60) and then for the enlightened Landgrave Friedrich II (1760–85), creating an urban fabric that survived until its destruction in the 1939–45 war. He further developed the *Oberneustadt* (Upper New Town) originally designed by his grandfather (completed 1776), and linked it (by means of handsome urban spaces (*places*) on the French model) to the *Altstadt* (Old Town) after the fortifications were demolished in 1767. He designed the Museum Fridericianum and observatory (1769–79—the first purpose-built library/museum of C18), in which French and Anglo-Palladian influences were strong, and a great many other buildings, all of them of quality. In short, he made of Kassel a charming German Court Residence, and so it largely survived until 1945. For Landgrave Wilhelm IX (1785–1821), he designed Schloss Weissenstein (later Wilhelmshöhe), near Kassel (1786–90), the side wings of which were set diagonally, responding to the landscape beyond: it is a great work of *Classicism inspired by English and French exemplars, but the over-monumental *corps-de-logis was by *Jussow. He may have designed some of the *fabriques in the park, and was responsible for the *Ionic *monopteron marking the spring at Bad Hofgeismar, Hessen (1792).

Although much of his work no longer exists, the elegance of du Ry's Neo-*Palladianism may be savoured at the charming Schloss Mont-Chéri, near Hofgeismar (1787–9).

Boehlke (1958, 1980); Both and Vogel (1973); Keller (1971); Paetow (1929); Placzek (1982); Watkin and Mellinghoff (1987)

Saarinen, Eero (1910–61). Finnish-born American architect, the son of G. E. *Saarinen. He studied in Paris, then Yale, and worked with Charles *Eames at Kingswood, *Cranbrook, Mich., G. E. Saarinen's Academy. With Eames he designed moulded plywood chairs in the late 1930s and produced numerous other pieces of furniture until he became more closely involved with architecture after the 1939–45 war. He worked with his father at Ann Arbor, Mich., from 1937, and from 1941 was in partnership with him before setting up his own practice as Eero Saarinen & Associates in 1950. At first, his architecture was in the *International Modern style of *Mies van der Rohe, notably his General Motors Technical Center, Warren, Mich. (1947–56), designed in collaboration with his father and others, but later, as with many American architects, he became concerned with the enriching of modern architecture that would still leave the buildings valid in terms of *Functionalism. For the Kresge Auditorium Building at the Massachusetts Institute of Technology (MIT), Cambridge, Mass. (1952–6), he created a roof based on a triangular segment of a sphere: the whole ensemble was criticized for straying from *Modernist principles and not going far enough to create a paradigm of architectural freedom of expression. It was too tentative. Certainly the exemplars of Le *Corbusier's chapel at Ronchamp (1950–5) had created a desire towards a greater expression of emotion in architecture, and Saarinen was in the vanguard of this tendency in the USA.

For MIT he had experimented with massive brick walls at the circular chapel (1952–6), and at Concordia Senior College, Fort Wayne, Ind., he also designed the chapel, this time with a pointed roof (1953–8). At the David S. Ingalls Ice Hockey Rink, Yale University, New Haven, Conn. (1953–9), he spanned the length of the building with a great central arch carrying the curved roof-structure. This was followed by his celebrated TWA Terminal Building at Kennedy International Airport, New York (1956–62), with its huge sail-like vaulted roofs rising from dynamically shaped *piers, expressive of wings and flight. The Thomas J. Watson Research Center, Yorktown, NY (1957–61), also exploited curves, to be used again at Dulles International Airport, Chantilly, Va., near Washington, DC (1958–63).

With the Ezra Stiles and Morse Colleges, Yale University (1958–62), the composition is stepped on *plan and vertical *section, and he used a fragmented, layered geometry for the treatment of the façades of the US Embassy, Grosvenor Square, London (1955–60—built in collaboration with *Yorke, Rosenberg, & Mardall). His practice was continued by *Roche and *Dinkeloo.

Gaidos (1972); Kuhner (1975); Saarinen (1968); Spade (1971); Temko (1962)

Saarinen, Gottlieb Eliel (1873–1950). Finnish-born American architect. He practised with Herman *Gesellius and Armas *Lindgren from 1896 to 1905, and with Gesellius only until 1907, when he worked on his own, emigrating to the USA in 1923. He established his first American office at Evanston, Ill. (1923–4), later (1924) moving to Ann Arbor, Mich., where he also taught at the School of Architecture, University of Michigan. The firm was joined by his son, Eero *Saarinen, in 1937, and then by J. Robert Swanson, who was a partner from 1941 to 1947. His early work in Finland was in the *National Romantic style to express Finnish identity (when *Neoclassicism was perceived as the architectural language of Tsarist Russia), and was influenced by late *Gothic Revival, English *Arts-and-Crafts architecture, and contemporary work in the USA, notably the round-arched buildings of H. H. *Richardson. Saarinen, Gesellius, and

Lindgren designed the Finnish Pavilion for the Exposition Universelle, Paris, of 1900, adding touches of vaguely oriental exoticism. Influences from the Vienna *Sezession were apparent in the Hvitträsk Studio House, Kirkkonummi, near Helsinki (begun 1902), designed for the firm as an idealistic variation on English Arts-and-Crafts themes, with a strong input of American *vernacular, *Shingle style, *Jugendstil, and national Finnish elements.

In 1904 Saarinen himself won the competition to design the Helsinki Central Railway Station (erected 1910–14), one of the finest termini of the period, comparable with Leipzig (1905) and Stuttgart (1911—which was influenced by the Helsinki exemplar), having massive masonry walls and a noble composition strongly influenced by the school of Otto *Wagner and the work of the *Wiener Werkstätte, notably *Hoffmann. He came second in the competition to design the *Chicago Tribune* Building (1922), which made his name in the USA and led to the commission to design the *Cranbrook Academy of Art, Bloomfield Hills, Mich. Saarinen designed the Cranbrook School for Boys (1926–30) and the Kingswood School for Girls (1929–30) there, followed by the Institute of Science (1931–3), and Museum and Library (1940–3). This beautiful series of *Picturesque buildings was evolved in collaboration with his second wife, Louise (Loja) Gesellius (1879–1968), and is freely eclectic, incorporating Expressionist, round-arched, and vernacular elements. He was President of the Cranbrook Academy of Art from 1932 to 1942, and was joined by his son, Eero, and by Charles *Eames, who both taught there. His published works include *The Cranbrook Development* (1931), *The City: Its Growth, Its Decay, Its Future* (1943), *Search for Form* (1948), and *The Search for Form in Art and Architecture* (1985).

Christ-Janer (1979); Gaidos (1972); Lampugnani (1988); Placzek (1982); Saarinen (1931)

Sacchetti, Giovanni Battista (1700–64). Italian architect. Taught by *Juvarra, he assisted his master by building models, preparing drawings, and compiling an important list of his works. He designed several temporary funerary structures for the House of Savoy, and oversaw (from 1734), the building of San Filippo, Turin, designed by Juvarra. In 1736 Sacchetti settled in Spain where he continued Juvarra's work on the garden-front of the Palacio Granja, San Ildefonso, Segovia (1736–42). Sacchetti also worked on the Royal Palace, Madrid, where he expanded Juvarra's proposals, influenced in part by *Bernini's unrealized designs for the Louvre, Paris. The work was completed in 1764, and the final composition must be ranked among the greatest architectural achievements of the period.

Brayda, Coli, and Sesia (1966); Ferrero (1970); Kubler and Soria (1959); Pommer (1967)

Sacconi, Count Giuseppe (1853–1905). Italian architect. He designed the elegant façade of the Palazzo delle Assicurazioni Generale, Piazza Venezia, Rome (1902–7), and, as Superintendent of Monuments in Ascoli Piceno and Umbria (1891–1905), he carried out many works of preservation and renovation in those regions and in Rome itself. He reconstructed the Church of San Francesco, Force, Ascoli Piceno (1878–83), and restored the Cathedral of Sant'Emidio, Ascoli Piceno (1888–90), among many other buildings. He is remembered primarily for the gigantic Neoclassical monument to King Vittorio Emanuele II (1884–1911), a huge pile-up of masonry (known by irreverent Romans as 'The Typewriter') dwarfing the Capitoline Hill in Rome, much altered after Sacconi's death by others, including G. *Koch and P. *Piacentini.

Accasto, Fraticelli, and Niccolini (1971); Acciaresi (1911); Maranesi (1929); Meeks (1966); Morosini (1929); Portoghesi (1968)

sacellum. **1.** Small enclosed space or *chapel in *Antique Rome where the household deities (*Lares* and *Penates*) were venerated, often treated as an *aedicule, also called *lararium. **2.** *Chantry-, *mortuary-, or any other small chapel in a church defined by a *screen. **3.** Unroofed enclosed space associated with an Ancient Egyptian temple, or found in Roman architecture in connection with religious rites.

sacrarium. **1.** *Antique *chapel, *sacellum, or *shrine. **2.** *Cella or *adytum of a Roman temple. **3.** That part of the *chancel or *choir in the vicinity of the high-altar, normally defined by the altar-rails, i.e. the *sanctuary. **4.** *Piscina in a church. **5.** *Sacristy.

sacristry *or* **sacristy.** Church *vestry near the *chancel in which ecclesiastical garments, utensils used in the services, etc., are stored. It may also be used for meetings.

saddle. **1.** Cap of a door-*cill or the bottom part of a door-frame. **2.** Thin timber board, or threshold, sloping slightly on each side, fixed on the floor between the *jambs. **3.** Short length of structural timber fixed to the tops of two *cruck *blades, forming the flattened top to a ∧ shape, and providing a support for the *ridge-piece. **4.** Any ∧-shaped form suggesting a saddle in *section, usually a splayed capping for a *ridge or a *cope-stone.

saddle-back. **1.** *Pack-saddle* roof, or ordinary roof with two pitches and *gable-ends on a church-tower. **2.** *Cope of triangular *section with a central *ridge and slopes on either side.

saddle-bar. Iron bar fixed horizontally in window-openings to which the *cames of stained-glass windows are fixed to help to support the structure of the leaded *lights.

saddle-board. *Comb-* or *ridge-board* at the *ridge of a pitched roof.

saddle-coping. *Saddle-back *cope.

saddle-stone. Upper or crowning piece of the *cope of a *gable.

Saénz de Oíza, Francisco Javier (1918–). Spanish architect. He won the competition for the Aránzazu *basilica (1949—with Laorga). Shortly afterwards he began to move towards acceptance of the *Modern Movement, and in the 1950s his work became openly eclectic, drawing on the works of *Aalto, L. I. *Kahn, and Frank Lloyd *Wright, leading to his Torres Blancas apartments, Madrid (1959–68). His chapel on the Camino de Santiago (1954—with Romaní y Oteiza), was influenced by *Mies van der Rohe, and sophisticated technology was employed in his Banco de Bilbao Vizcayano, Azca, Madrid (1972–80).

Domenech (1968); Emanuel (1994)

Safdie, Moshe (1938–). Israeli-Canadian architect. He worked with L. I. *Kahn before setting up his own practice in Montreal, Canada, in 1964. He established his reputation with the 'Habitat' housing-scheme at Expo 67, Montreal, in which the parts were given expression and composed like a pile of building-blocks to form the whole. The antithesis of the *Corbusian insistence on slab-like forms, it drew on Mediterranean *vernacular architecture to create a new paradigmatic *mega-structure built of prefabricated parts. His subsequent works also explored vernacular elements at the Habitat for San Juan, Puerto Rico (1968–72), the Yeshivat Porat Yosef Rabbinical College, Jerusalem (1971–9), and the Mamilah Central Business District masterplan, Jerusalem (1972–80), in all of which cubic geometry was exploited, clearly influenced by Kahn. He designed (with *Parkin Associates) the National Gallery of Canada, Ottawa (1988), and many other buildings. Among his publications may be mentioned *Beyond Habitat* (1970), *For Everyone a Garden* (1974), *Form and Purpose* (1982), and *Jerusalem: The Future of the Past* (1989).

Drew (1972); Emanuel (1994); Kalman (1994); Kohn (1996)

sagitta. Keystone in an arch.

sail-dome. *See* dome, vault.

sail-over. *Jetty or element projecting beyond the *naked of the wall below.

sail-vault. *See* dome, vault.

Saint-George, James of (*fl.* 1261–d. 1309). Master-mason, probably from Piedmont, in charge of the construction of King Edward I's (reigned 1272–1307) chain of fortresses in North Wales. Saint-George superintended the building of Flint and Rhuddlan Castles, and probably designed Aberystwyth and Builth Castles (1277–82). He then designed the town walls of Conway, Caernarfon, and Denbigh (begun 1282–3), and the Castles of Conway and Harlech. To judge from his rates of pay, he was obviously held in high esteem, and in the 1290s he began to build Beaumaris Castle, Anglesea. By 1302 he was involved in securing the English stronghold of Linlithgow, Scotland, and may have designed the gatehouse at Kildrummy Castle (1303). He was probably in the service of the Counts of Savoy in the 1260s before coming to England.

Harvey (1987)

Sakakura, Junzo (1904–69). Japanese architect. He designed the Japanese Pavilion at the Exposition, Paris (1937), but his devotion to Le *Corbusier (in whose office he worked from 1931 to 1936) later led to massive concrete structures, often heavily over-emphasized. Among his works thus influenced may be mentioned the City Hall, Hashima, Gifu Prefecture, Japan (1959).

Morgan and Naylor (1987)

sala terrena. Large, formal room with direct access to a garden gained by one side being open to that garden, especially in C17 and C18 grand houses, frequently embellished with *trompe l'œil and other decorations to suggest a *grotto. One of the finest examples is that at the Valdštejn garden, Prague (1624–7), by *Pieroni.

Neumann, J. (1970)

salient, saliant. **1.** Projection, *jetty, or *sail-over. **2.** Angle pointing outwards, i.e. opposite of a *re-entrant, e.g. gun-emplacement in a fortification.

sally. **1.** As *salient. **2.** Notch cut in the end of a piece of timber used at the lower ends of inclined timbers, e.g. *rafters.

sally-port. *Postern- or side-gate, or a subterranean passage, between the inner and outer works of a fortification, used for the defenders to sally from or pass through.

Salmon, James (1873–1924). Scots architect. A pupil of William Leiper (1839–1916), he was in partnership in Glasgow with his father, **William Forrest Salmon** (1843–1911) from *c.*1890. The firm was joined by John Gaff Gillespie (1870–1926), and became Salmon, Son, & Gillespie until 1913. His work had more in common with Continental *Art Nouveau than any of his contemporaries in Scotland (including *Mackintosh). While with Leiper, he worked under William James Anderson (1864–1900) on the Italian *Gothic Templeton Carpet Factory, Glasgow Green (1888–92), and the *François Ier Sun Life Assurance Building, 38–42 Renfield Street, Glasgow (1889–93). Salmon's best building on his own account was the Mercantile Chambers, Bothwell Street (1896–7), at the time one of the largest steel-framed office-blocks in the city, with sculpture by Francis Derwent Wood (1871–1926). He is best remembered for 142–4 St Vincent Street (1898–1900), known as the 'Hatrack' because of the peg-like forms of its exterior: in this remarkably complex building, the entire façade of which is *cantilevered from an internal steel frame, the external stone *dressings are reduced to a minimum, and most of the details are Art Nouveau in style. Other works include elegant restorations at 79 West Regent Street (1900–4). His Lion Chambers, 170–2 Hope Street (1904–6), used *reinforced-concrete construction based on the *Hennebique system. The firm eventually transmogrified into Gillespie, Kidd, and *Coia.

Gray (1985); Gomme and Walker (1987); *RIBA Journal*, 97/8 (Aug. 1990), 35–40; Service (1975, 1977)

Salomónica. *See* Solomonic.

salon, saloon. **1.** Large, high room, frequently with a vaulted ceiling, and often of double height (i.e. rising the equivalent of two storeys), serving as one of the principal reception-rooms in a palace or great house, or as a means of communication through which the main rooms can be reached. Sometimes it was circular or elliptical on plan. **2.** Large apartment or hall, especially in a hotel or other place frequented by the public, adapted for assemblies, entertainments, exhibitions, etc. **3.** Public room for a specific purpose, e.g. billiards, dancing, or drinking (*saloon-bar*) **4.** A drawing-room in a house.

Salvart, Jehan (*fl.* 1390s–1447). French master-mason. In 1398 he was appointed Master at the Cathedral of Rouen, reconstructed the west portal in 1407, and enlarged the *choir windows (1430). In 1432 he became City Architect of Rouen.

Sturgis *et al.* (1901–2)

Salvi, Nicola (1697–1751). Italian architect. In the 1730s he entered the architectural competitions arranged by Pope Clement XII (1730–40), and won that to build the Trevi Fountain (1732–7), his masterpiece, based on a *triumphal arch, the whole composition set on a *rock-work base. He remodelled the interior of the Church of Santa Maria dei Gradi, Viterbo (1737), designed the Chapel of St John, St Roch, Lisbon, Portugal (1742), and extended *Bernini's Palazzo Chigi-Odescalchi, Rome (1745). He was accomplished in *scenography.

Onofrio (1957); Pinto (1986); Schavo (1956)

Salvin, Anthony (1799–1881). English architect. He is said to have worked in *Nash's office. In the 1820s he designed a mansion in the *Tudor style, Mamhead, Devon (1826–38), and established a reputation as an architect of country-houses. His masterpiece is undoubtedly Harlaxton Manor, Lincolnshire (1831–8), a lavish pile in the *Jacobethan style, at once learned yet inventive, with a heavy *Baroque staircase inside designed by William *Burn. Scotney Castle, Lamberhurst, Kent (1837–44), was a reinterpretation of a more modest C17 manor-house type with a cunningly contrived massing that made the building look as though it had been added to at various times for the sake of convenience. His enchanting Peckforton Castle, Cheshire (1844–50), was a brilliant evocation of a C13 castle, conveniently planned, and truly *Picturesque. He took part in the important redecorations of Christ Church, Kilndown, Kent (from 1839), which transformed the *chancel in accordance with the ideals of *Ecclesiology, and indeed was one of the first of its kind in England. He was an authority on English medieval military architecture, and worked on the Tower of London and various castles, including Alnwick, Caernarfon, Durham, Rockingham, Warwick, and Windsor. He built many churches as well as country-houses, ending with the fanciful *Jacobethan Thoresby Hall, Nottinghamshire (1864–75). His pupils included Eden *Nesfield, J. L. *Pearson, and R. N. *Shaw.

Allibone (1988); Dixon and Muthesius (1985); Eastlake (1970); Hussey (1958); White (1962)

Salvisberg, Otto Rudolf (1882–1940). Swiss-born architect. He settled in Berlin in 1908, where he designed the vaguely Expressionist *concrete office-building the *Lindenhaus*, Berlin-Kreuzberg (1912–13). Some of his early works, however, contained eclectic references influenced, perhaps, by the ideas of Camillo *Sitte. Many of his *villas in and around Berlin were influenced by *Jugendstil and *Expressionism, as well as by the *Arts-and-Crafts movement publicized by *Muthesius. In the mid-1920s he became influenced by the *Modern Movement, designing several houses on the Berlin-Zehlendorf housing estate under the overall direction of Bruno *Taut (1926–31). One of his most luxurious houses was the Flechtheim Villa, Berlin-Grünewald (1928–9). He also designed the *Gross-Siedlung Schillerpromenade*, Weisse-Stadt (White City) development, Berlin-Reinickendorf (1929–31).

In 1930 he succeeded Karl *Moser as Professor at the Eidgenössische Technische Hochschule (Confederate Technical High School—ETH), Zurich, Switzerland, and designed numerous works, including university buildings, Berne (1930–1), the Machine Laboratory and Heating Plant, ETH (1930–3), and the Hoffman-La Roche Administration Building and Factories, Basle (1936–40), all in a severely rational manner. He was responsible for the Roche Products Factory, Welwyn *Garden City, Hertfordshire, England (1939).

Platz (1927); Wertheim (1927)

Sambin, Hugues (*c*.1520–*c*.1602). French architect, sculptor, and engineer. He was familiar with the works of du *Cerceau and *Vredeman de Vries, as is clear from his portals on the Palais de Justice, Dijon (1583). Other works attributed to him include the Maison Milsand, Rue des Forges (1561), the Maison Chasseret, 8 Rue Stephen-Liègeard (1560), and the Hôtel le Compasseur, 66 Rue Vannerie (1560s), all in Dijon, and the Palais de Justice, Besançon. He was a master of French *Mannerism, and his work was influential. He published *Œuvre de la Diversité des Termes* (dealing with types of *term—1572).

Blunt (1982); Castan (1891); Hautecœur (1948)

Samonà, Giuseppe (1898–1983). Italian architect and town-planner. His output was prolific, and embraced *Expressionism, *eclecticism, *International Modernism, Italian *Rationalism, and much else. He won many architectural competitions during the Fascist era, including that for the Post Office in the Appio Quarter of Rome (1933–6). He was Director of the Istituto Universitario di Architettura, Venice, from 1945 to 1971, and published much on urban planning. He prepared housing-schemes for several Italian cities including Mestre (1951–6) and Palermo (1956–8), and designed the Banco d'Italia, Padua (1968), and the Theatre, Sciacca, Sicily (1974–9).

Aymonino (1975*a*); Emanuel (1994); Lovero (1975)

Sancte-cote. *See* bell-cote.

sanctuary. **1.** Especially holy place within a church or temple **2.** *Sacrarium, or part of a church in the vicinity of the high-altar. **3.** *Chancel or *presbytery.

Sanctus bell-cote. *See* bell-cote.

Sandys, Francis (*fl.* 1788–1814). Irish-born architect. He was in the service of Frederick Augustus Hervey, 4th Earl of Bristol and Bishop of Derry (1730–1803), at whose expense he travelled in Italy (1791–6). He built the Earl-Bishop's Palace at Ickworth, Suffolk, in 1796, consisting of a *Pantheon-domed elliptical *rotunda connected to wings by *quadrants, and apparently based on a design by Mario Asprucci (presumably father of Antonio *Asprucci). Ickworth had a predecessor in the Earl-Bishop's great house at Ballyscullion, Co. Londonderry (begun 1787, and designed, probably, by Michael Shanahan, Sandys, and Sandys's brother **Joseph**), influenced by *Plaw's Belle Isle, Windermere (1774–5). The *portico of

Ballyscullion now forms the front of St George's Parish Church, High Street, Belfast. Ickworth was a more Neoclassical version of Ballyscullion.

Sandys remained in Suffolk, in Bury St Edmunds, where he built up his practice, designing Finborough Hall, Suffolk (1795), the entrance-lodges at Chippenham Park, Cambridgeshire (*c*.1800), the Assembly Rooms (now Athenaeum), Bury St Edmunds (1804), the County Gaol, Worcester (1809–13—demolished), Dorchester Bridge, Oxfordshire (1813–15), and the County Courts and Gaol, Durham (begun 1809 and completed by George *Moneypenny and Ignatius *Bonomi in 1811 after Sandys was dismissed following his loss of a legal action by the Durham Magistrates). This event seems to have ended his architectural practice by 1814.

Colvin (1995); Rankin (1972)

Sanfelice, Ferdinando (1675–1748). Neapolitan architect. He was celebrated for *scenographic effects, especially in his staircases, as at the Palazzo Sanfelice, Naples (1725–8), a late-*Baroque arcuated structure between the *cortile and the garden. He designed the *scalinata* (flight of steps) in front of the Church of San Giovanni a Carbonara, Naples (1708—probably a prototype of the Spanish Steps in Rome), and the Palazzo Serra di Cassano (1720–38—a very free and original composition).

Norberg-Schulz (1986*a*); Ward (1988); Wittkower (1982)

Sangallo, Antonio da, the Elder (*c*.1455–1534). Florentine *Renaissance architect, military engineer, and sculptor, also known as **Antonio Giamberti**. The son of the wood-carver and decorator **Francesco Giamberti** (1404–80), he re-fortified the Castel Sant'Angelo, Rome (formerly the *mausoleum of Emperor Hadrian (reigned 117–38)), in 1493, and carried out many works of military architecture, including the Papal fortress of Cività Castellana (1494–7). He built the Loggia de' Servi, Florence (1517–29), giving unity to the Piazza della Santissima Annunziata opposite *Brunelleschi's Ospedale degli Innocenti. His finest architectural work was the Church of the Madonna di San Biagio, Montepulciano (1518–34), a domed building on a Greek-cross plan resembling *Bramante's designs for St Peter's in Rome, originally intended to have a tower in each of the four *re-entrants formed by the arms of the cross, but only one tower was built. Each arm of the cross is barrel-vaulted, and the dome over the *crossing is carried on a drum supported by *pendentives. It may also have been influenced by Giuliano da *Sangallo's Santa Maria delle Carceri at Prato (begun 1485). For its date it has remarkable clarity, grandeur, integrity, and rigour.

Heydenreich and Lotz (1974); Lotz (1977)

Sangallo, Antonio da, the Younger (1483–1546). Also known as **Antonio Cordiani**, he was born in Florence and became one of the most distinguished architects of the *High *Renaissance in Rome in the second quarter of C16 after the death of *Raphael. He received his early training with his uncles **Giuliano** and **Antonio the Elder** before entering the studio of *Bramante, where he worked on St Peter's. He also assisted Raphael at St Peter's and at the Villa Madama (1517–18). He became architect to Cardinal Alessandro Farnese (later Pope Paul III (1534–49)), designing his monumental palazzo in Rome from *c*.1515, a vast block with *astylar external *façades and noble cortile with an *assemblage of *Orders based on *Antique prototypes. The palazzo was completed (1546) by *Michelangelo and della *Porta, and was influential, especially during the vogue for C19 *Italianate architecture begun by Charles *Barry. Among his other secular works the Palazzi Baldassini (*c*.1515–46) and Sacchetti (1542–6), both in Rome, deserve notice.

When Raphael died in 1520 da Sangallo shared the responsibilities of St Peter's with *Peruzzi, becoming sole architect in 1536. His ideas for the building are clear from the model of 1538–43, with a rather busy multistorey façade flanked by tall towers, not executed. There is no doubt that it was aesthetically unsatisfactory, and lacked the sense of Roman grandeur implicit in the Bramante and later Michelangelo schemes. He carried out many works for fortifications in the Roman region, much ecclesiastical design (e.g. the Cesi Chapel, Santa Maria della Pace, Rome (1530)), and various schemes for the Vatican (including the Pauline Chapel (1540–6)).

Frommel (1973, 1994); Giovannoni (1959); Heydenreich and Lotz (1974); Lotz (1977)

Sangallo, Giuliano da (1445–1516). Florentine architect, military engineer, and sculptor, born **Giuliano Giamberti**, son of

Francesco Giamberti (1404–80), and brother of Antonio da *Sangallo the Elder. Influenced by the work of *Brunelleschi, he continued to work in that master's early *Renaissance style well into the period dominated by *Bramante and *Raphael. He was in Rome in 1465 working on fortifications where he made a series of studies of *Antique remains (now in the Vatican Library and in Siena). He returned to Florence in the 1470s, and built the Villa Medici, Poggio a Caiano (*c*.1480–*c*.1497), one of the very first *Renaissance *villas designed with conscious emulation of Antiquity in mind, notably in its arcaded terrace-platform, *Ionic pedimented porch like a *temple-front embedded in the façade, symmetrical arrangement, and barrel-vaulted hall. He designed the Church of Santa Maria delle Carceri, Prato (1484–91), the first realized Renaissance church constructed on a Greek-cross plan with barrel-vaulted arms and domed drum on pendentives over the *crossing, although the interior owed much to Brunelleschi: it influenced Antonio da Sangallo's designs for the Church of the Madonna di San Biagio, Montepulciano (1518–34). Also influenced by Brunelleschi was the *atrium of Santa Maria Maddelena dei Pazzi (*c*.1491–5), and the octagonal *sacristy with adjoining vestibule of Santo Spirito (1489–95—with *Cronaca), both in Florence. He designed the Palazzo Gondi (1490–1501), the façade of which is an elaboration on the Palazzo Medici-Riccardi, and constructed a model of the Palazzo Strozzi (1489–90), later realized by da *Maiano and Cronaca: that palace was very likely partly da Sangallo's design. Also by him was the Palazzo Rovere (or *Ateneo*), Savona (*c*.1494), but his hopes of preferment when his patron, Cardinal Rovere, became Pope Julius II (1503–13), came to nothing, the plum job of St Peter's going to Bramante. Under Pope Leo X (1513–21), however, he shared the responsibility for organizing the building-works at St Peter's with Raphael and Fra *Giocondo, and seems to have had an influence on *Michelangelo's architectural development. He made several unrealized designs that demonstrate a sound knowledge of Antique Classical composition, including plans for a Papal palace for Leo X in the Piazza Navona, Rome (1513).

Bardazzi and Castellani (1981); Heydenreich and Lotz (1974); Huelsen (1910); Lotz (1977); Marchini (1943); Morselli and Corti (1982); Murray (1969, 1986)

Sanmicheli, Michele (*c*.1484–1559). Italian architect and military engineer. Born in Verona, he studied the *Antique remains there, and went to Rome in the early 1500s where he fell under the influence of *Bramante's work which demonstrated how *Classicism might suggest something of the grandeur of Ancient Rome. In 1509 he became Superintendent of the Works at Orvieto Cathedral and built fortifications at Parma and Piacenza in 1526 before returning to Verona. With the *Sangallos he is credited with the evolution of massive triangular *bastions and enormous *curtain-walls in military architecture. He applied his expertise to fortifying Verona, where he constructed the bastion of the Maddalene and many other impressive structures including the *rusticated gateways with the *Doric Order much in evidence. The best examples of these gates are the Porta Nuova (1533–51), Porta San Zeno (1547–50), and the Porta del Palio (1548–59), the last a masterpiece of *Mannerism, with its severe Roman Doric Order *in antis* *engaged with a rusticated wall-layer behind which are three recessed rusticated walls into which the gateways are set. The influence of *Giulio Romano's Palazzo del Tè, Mantua, is clear. He also designed the Forte di Sant'Andrea di Lido, Venice (1535–71). All these works were not only strong, but looked impregnable, as did the façade of his Church of Santa Maria in Organo, Verona (1547–59).

Sanmicheli's early palazzi show influences from Bramante, *Raphael, and *Serlio. The Palazzo Pompei, Verona (*c*.1527–57), for example, has a rusticated ground-floor acting as a *podium for the engaged Doric Order of the *piano nobile, a variant on Bramante's 'House of Raphael' in Rome, but with the central bay wider and *pier-*pilasters terminating the façade at both ends, thus giving the design greater serenity. At the Palazzo Canossa, Verona (begun *c*.1533), the Palazzo del Tè was again the influence in the rusticated base, with its triple arched openings in the centre, while Bramante's work affected the piano nobile with its paired pilasters and paraphrased *serlianas. Much richer is the Palazzo Bevilacqua, Verona (late 1530s), with a rusticated Doric podium, the *triglyphs of which project forward as brackets supporting the piano-nobile balcony over which is an elaborately complex façade designed as a series of three overlapping *triumphal arches. His Palazzo Grimani, Venice (from 1557, completed by others), employed the triumphal-arch motif in the centre of the lowest storey, while above, the perceived *naked of the wall was virtually dissolved, and the areas framed by columns and *entablatures contained complicated systems of *fenestration.

He did some ecclesiastical work, including the charming circular domed Cappella Pellegrini (begun 1527) at the Church of San Bernardino, Verona, clearly influenced by the *Pantheon in Rome. It features columns with twisted or spiral fluting which he also employed at the Palazzo Bevilacqua. Outside Verona he designed the circular Pilgrimage Church of the Madonna di Campagna (from 1559), the drum pierced by a rhythm of 3 windows, 2 *blind arches, then 1 window, then 2 blind arches, and then 3 windows, demonstrating Sanmicheli's ability to surprise.

Frommel (1995); Gazzola (1960); Heydenreich and Lotz (1974); Langenskiöld (1938); Lotz (1977); Murray (1969, 1986); Puppi (1971)

Sansovino, Jacopo d'Antonio Tatti, *called* (1486–1570). Florentine architect and sculptor, he spent most of his working life in Venice, where he created some of the greatest buildings of the *High *Renaissance, although *Mannerism was not entirely absent from his designs. His finest works were the Biblioteca Marciana (begun 1537 and completed by *Scamozzi in 1588—a powerful composition featuring superimposed *Ionic and *Doric *Orders between the columns of which are arcuated arrangements of great sophistication); the Zecca (Mint—of 1535–47); and the Loggetta (1537–40—a composition of three overlayered triumphal arches), all near the Doge's Palace, and contributing to the brilliant urban scenery of Venice. The Biblioteca (Library of St Mark) was the first Venetian building in which the Orders were used in a thoroughly scholarly way, and was recognized by *Palladio as one of the most authoritative buildings erected since Antiquity, and indeed drew on the exemplar of the Theatre of Marcellus in Rome for its arrangement of Orders.

Sansovino also designed the Church of San Francesco della Vigna (1534—completed by Palladio), and built the influential Palazzo Corner della Ca' Grande (begun 1537), with a *rusticated ground-floor slightly reminiscent of *Sanmicheli's Palazzo Canossa, Verona, but with curiously placed Mannerist *consoles over the openings on either side of the triple-arched centre. Above, the façade has superimposed Orders with arched windows set back behind the plane of the Orders. He also designed the Villa Garzoni, Pontecasale, near Padua (designed *c.*1540), with a five-bay arcaded *loggia in the centre over the entrance, a composition of grave serenity worthy of the Ancients.

Howard (1975, 1980); Lotz (1977); Murray (1969, 1986); Tafuri (1972)

Sant'Elia, Antonio (1888–1916). *See* Futurism.

Santini-Aichel, Jan Blažej (1667–1723). Born in Prague, he was one of the most original and inventive architects of C18 Bohemia. He mingled *Baroque and *Gothic styles, as at the Church of the Assumption at Sedlec (1701–6), the Cloister Church, Kladruby (1712–26—where he was influenced by *Ried's Gothic vaulting), the Church of the Virgin, Želiv (1713–20), and the Pilgrimage Church of St John Nepomuk, Zelená Hora, near Žd'ár nad Sazavou (1720–2). Some of his centrally planned churches recall the geometries of *Borromini and *Guarini, and *Pevsner called him a 'Bohemian *Hawksmoor'. His palaces have more affinity with the work of *Fischer von Erlach: a good example is Karlová Koruna, Chlumec nad Cidlinov (1721–3). His work does not appear to have stimulated further experiment or development.

Architectural Review, 121/71 (Feb. 1957), 113–14; Franz (1962); Hempel (1965); Neumann, J. (1970); Norberg-Schulz (1986*a*); Queysanna (1986)

SAR (Stichting Architecten Research). Dutch foundation for architectural research and design that sought to give the inhabitants of urban housing a collective and individual say in its control and evolution. It was formed in Eindhoven in 1965 by Nicholas John Habraken (1928–), and was influential in the so-called *community-architecture movement.

Habraken (1972)

Saracenic architecture. Term given to an exotic style that evolved in Western Europe in C18, and was derived from *Moorish and *Islamic sources. Until recently, it was applied to all Islamic architecture.

sarcophagus (*pl.* **sarcophagi**). Stone or *terracotta sepulchral chest to contain a corpse, with or without a coffin, often enriched with sculpture or given architectural form (e.g. Tomb of the Weepers, Sidon, looking like a miniature *Hellenistic temple). A common *Antique type had a pitched roof-like lid with *horns at the angles. Sarcophagi forms were often employed as architectural elements in *Neoclassicism, especially by *Soane.

Sartoris, Alberto (1901–98). Italian architect. Early in his career he was associated with *Futurism, and in 1928 was a founder-member of *CIAM. In the late 1920s he became closely involved with Italian *Rationalism, and built numerous structures, mostly in Switzerland. In 1938 he was associated with *Terragni in the design of a *satellite city at Rebbio, Como (1938–9). Among his works the Moreur Pasteur house, Saillon, Valais (1933–8), earned acclaim for its *International style aesthetic. A devotee of *Functionalism, he published *Gli Elementi dell' architettura funzionale* (1932, 1936, 1941) and *Encyclopédie de l'architecture nouvelle* (1948–54).

Emanuel (1994); Gubler (1978); obituary, *The Times* (23 Apr. 1998), 25; Sartoris (1936, 1948–51)

sash. Rebated frame, fixed or opening, fitted with one or more panes of glass forming a window-*light, set in a larger frame placed in the whole window-opening or aperture. Opening sashes can be of the vertical or horizontal sliding type in grooves, or can be hinged or pivoted at the sides, tops, bottoms, or centres. Thus *casements have sashes. A sash capable of being moved up and down is a *hung sash*, suspended from cords or chains and pulleys fixed in the linings of the sash-frame, and counterbalanced by weights attached to the concealed ends of the cords or chains within the *sash-box* of the main window-frame. If only one sash moves, the window is said to be a *single-hung* sash-window, and if both sashes can be moved, it is *double-hung*. *Yorkshire* sliding-sashes are moved horizontally.

Sassanian architecture. Architecture in Persia in the period AD 226–641, usually of brick, with much use of arches and *vaults, covered with *stucco. Surviving examples are the palaces at Ctesiphon (probably C4), Sarvistan (*c*.350—with a dome on squinch arches), and Feruz-Abad (*c*.230s).

Cruickshank (1996)

satellite town. Town, self-contained and limited in size, built in the vicinity of a large town or city to house and employ those who would otherwise create a demand for expansion of the existing settlement, but dependent on the parent-city to a certain extent for population and major services. Although not to be confused with *Garden Cities, satellite towns were influenced by Ebenezer *Howard's theories.

Howard (1898, 1902, 1946, 1965); Miller (1989)

Satyros (*fl*. mid-C4 BC). Joint architect, with *Pythios, or Pythius, of the celebrated *Hellenistic *Ionic *mausoleum of Mausolus at Halicarnassus (begun *c*.353 BC), one of the finest buildings of Antiquity, embellished with sculpture of supremely vigorous quality, much of which is in the British Museum, London.

Dinsmoor (1950)

saucer-dome. *See* dome.

Saulnier, Jules (1828–1900). French architect. His most celebrated work is the Menier Chocolate Factory, Noisiel-sur-Marne (1869–72), constructed on an iron frame spanning between *piers set in the River Marne. The panels between the metal frame were of *polychrome brick over which iron diagonals ensuring structural rigidity were expressed. It was influenced by the ideas of *Viollet-le-Duc.

Middleton and Watkin (1987)

Sauvage, Frédéric-Henri (1873–1932). French architect. He trained at the École des *Beaux-Arts, Paris, where he met the *Jourdains (father and son). His early work was in the *Art Nouveau style, much influenced by his partnership with the Majorelle family, for whom he designed the Villa Majorelle, Nancy (1898–1901), one of the finest example of the Art Nouveau 'École de Nancy'. He designed numerous interiors, fabrics, wallpapers, ceramics, and jewellery in the early years of the C20, but gradually moved more towards architectural design from the time of the building of his glazed Galerie Argentine, Avenue Victor Hugo, Paris (*c*.1900). This was followed by an inexpensive apartment-block, 1 Rue Fernand Flocon, Paris (1901), a building-type which he evolved as founder (with his partner from 1898 to 1912, Charles Sarazin (1873–1950)) of a company (the Société Anonyme de Logements Hygiéniques à Bon Marché) to build hygienic model dwellings in 1903. He designed various exemplary blocks, including that at 26 Rue Vavin (1912), where he exploited stepped terraces, and treated the walls in a manner derived from the work of *Wagner and his colleagues in Vienna. The Gambetta (1920) and Les Sèvres (1922) cinemas were built to Sauvage's designs, followed by sundry pavilions for the Exposition Internationale des Arts-Décoratifs (1924–5), after which his work had a pronounced *Art Deco flavour. In 1926 he designed the huge garage at the Rue Campagne-Première and, with Frantz *Jourdain, the new department-store *La Samaritaine*, Rue du Pont Neuf, in Paris. His Magasins Decré, Nantes, had an overtly expressed steel frame (1931—destroyed).

Borsi and Godoli (1978); Emanuel (1980); Sauvage and Sarazin (1904); Tschudi-Madsen (1967)

Savage, James (1779–1852). English architect. He built Richmond Bridge, Dublin (1813–16), and Tempsford Bridge, Bedfordshire (1815–20), both of which demonstrated his command of construction. He is remembered today for the Church of St Luke, Chelsea (1820–4), remarkable for its scholarly (and very early) *Gothic Revival style incorporating a real stone *vault supported by flying *buttresses. He designed several other churches, including the Classical St James, Bermondsey, London (1827–9), and the *Gothic Holy Trinity, Tottenham Green, Middlesex (1828–9). He was responsible for the Tenterden Union Workhouse, Kent (1843–7), and other workhouse buildings. He published *Observations on Style in Architecture* . . . (1836) and other works.

Colvin (1995); *DNB* (1917); Eastlake (1970)

Saxon. *See* Anglo-Saxon.

scabellum (*pl.* **scabella**). High pedestal for the support of a bust, usually shaped like the lower part of a *gaine or *herm.

scagliola. Imitation marble, known since Antiquity, and much used in C17 and C18 for column- and pilaster-shafts, etc. It is made of crushed gypsum (or selenite), calcined, then reduced to powder or plaster of Paris, mixed with isinglass (gelatine) or similar (Flanders glue or size was commonly used), and then having colours added. Veined marbles were imitated by mixing the different hues in separately. The prepared mix was applied to the intended surface (usually a coat of lime and hair), smoothed, then rubbed down with a pumice-stone and a wet sponge before being polished with tripoli (diotomite) and charcoal using fine soft linen, then rubbed with felt dipped in linseed oil and tripoli, then finally finished off with a rubbing of pure linseed oil. It was also called *stucco lustro*. It should not be confused with *Florentine mosaic* or *opere di commasso* made with thin veneers of marble.

Nicholson (1835); Papworth (1887)

scale. 1. In architecture, the proportions of a building or its parts with reference to a *module or unit of measurement. **2.** In architectural drawing, the size of the *plans, *elevations, *sections, etc., in relation to the actual size of the object delineated.

Fraser Reekie (1946)

scale moulding. *Imbrication* or *petal diaper*, i.e. ornament resembling shaped roof-tiles or the scales of fish, often found on *Antique *sarcophagi-lids. The best-known example is the top of the *Choragic Monument of Lysicrates, Athens (334 BC). In its simplest form it is a pattern of several series of semicircular forms, each row staggered with the centres of each semicircle on the junction of vertical lines struck from the points on which the semicircles spring and other horizontal lines drawn across the top of each arc.

Lewis and Darley (1986)

scallop. 1. Classical architectural enrichment derived from the shell of a scallop with many applications including the decoration of the quarter-spherical heads of arched *apses and *niches. **2.** *Romanesque moulding consisting of a series of convex lobes similar to a *scale moulding, but in one series only, like the edge of an apron. A variety of it to a very large *scale was used by Neoclassical architects, often for *friezes.

scallop *or* **scalloped capital.** *See* capital.

Scamozzi, Ottavio Bertotti (1719–90). *See* Bertotti-Scamozzi.

Scamozzi, Vincenzo (1552–1616). Italian architect, remembered primarily as a disciple of *Palladio and as the author of one of the great *Renaissance treatises on architecture, *L'Idea dell'Architettura Universale* (The Idea of Universal Architecture—1615), which included an analysis and codification of the Classical Roman *Orders that remained influential for many years. Early in his career he designed the Vettor Pisani Villa or *Rocca* (rock or stronghold), Lonigo (1576–9), a variant of Palladio's Villa Capra (Rotonda), near Vicenza, which

Scamozzi completed in *c*.1592. The *Rocca* was planned with a *serliana on three elevations, and on the fourth a *loggia behind a *colonnade carrying a *pediment, the four openings giving access to a circular hall illuminated by an *oculus set in a dome, the whole conceived as an enchanting summer retreat, filled with light and air. *Burlington drew on this building as well as on the Villa Capra for his villa at Chiswick in C18. Scamozzi's Villa Molin, Mandria, near Padua (1597), also has a great central hall. His finest town-house was the Palazzo Trissino, Vicenza (1592–1616), in which influences from *Peruzzi and Palladio are clear.

In the late 1570s he travelled to Rome and Southern Italy, visiting Rome on at least three more occasions in 1585–6 and the 1590s. In 1580 he published engravings of Roman *thermae, and later prepared commentaries for various topographical prints of Rome as *Discorsi sopra le Antichità di Roma* (Discourses on the Antiquities of Rome—1582 and 1583). Around this time he produced designs for the Theatine Church of San Gaetano, Padua, and won the design competition for the *Procuratie Nuove*, Piazza San Marco, Venice (1592—completed in 1663 by *Longhena). The vast *Procuratie* elevation is based on *Sansovino's Library of St Mark (which Scamozzi was at that time completing), but it has an extra storey based on a design by Palladio. He also worked on Palladio's Church of San Giorgio Maggiore, Venice, and designed the fixed architectural stage-sets for Palladio's Teatro Olimpico, Vicenza (1584–5), an elaborate construction using tricks of perspective and illusion. He designed a similar theatre at Sabbioneta in 1588, and wrote a treatise on *perspective and *scenography (*Dei Teatri e delle Scene*—*c*.1574), which does not appear to have survived.

Scamozzi toured Central Europe and France (1599–1600), making an unexecuted design for the Cathedral of Sts Rupert and Virgil at Salzburg. Santino *Solari retained the apsidal *transepts and certain other features derived from Palladio's *Il Redentore* and San Giorgio Maggiore in the realized scheme (commenced 1614). Scamozzi designed and built the Hospital and Church of San Lazzaro dei Mendicanti (1601–36), and the Palazzo Contarini on the Grand Canal (1609–16), both in Venice.

Barbieri (1952); Howard (1980); Muraro (1986); Scamozzi (1615)

scarf. Type of joint between two timbers meeting end-to-end and designed to appear as one continuous piece. Types include *face-halved* (with a rectangular notch taken out of each face); *side-halved* (with a rectangular notch taken out of each side); *splayed* (with each piece ending in a splay slanted across its length); *splayed and tabled* (with a splay broken by a step); and *stop-splayed* (with a partial splay leaving perpendicular elements at each end of the splay, often with further refinements). These joints are very complex, and are in the specialist realm of *timber-framed buildings.

Alcock, Barley, Dixon, and Meeson (1996)

scarp, escarp. **1.** Pitch or *batter of a bank. **2.** Steep slope below and away from a fortress-wall. **3.** Inner wall or bank of the *fosse.

Scarpa, Carlo (1906–78). Italian architect. He set up his practice in Venice from 1927 and later directed the Istituto Universitario di Architettura in that city (1972–8). In the Fascist era he was both a devotee of Italian *Rationalism as well and a subscriber to *Modern Movement. He made his post-war reputation as a designer of exhibitions, galleries, and museums, starting with the renovation of the Galleria Nazionale della Sicilia, Palermo (1953–4). Other works include the extension to the Gipsoteca Canoviana, Possagno, near Treviso (1956–7), and interior of the Museo Castelvecchio, Verona (1964). His invention, sense of drama, fine detailing, and use of materials created remarkably successful designs of great intensity. Various works, including the Villa Zoppas, Conegliano (1948), the Olivetti Building, Venice (1957–61), and the Casa Veritti, Udine (1955–61), demonstrated aspects of his command of volumetric juxtapositions. One of his most successful designs is the Brion Cemetery, San Vito d'Altivole, near Treviso (1970–2), where powerful geometries and stark *concrete are combined.

Crippa (1986); Dal Co and Mazzariol (1985); Kahn and Cantacuzino (1974); *Progressive Architecture*, 62/5 (1981)

Scarpagnino, Antonio Abbondi, *called*. *See* Bon or Bono.

scenography. Perspective drawing or scene-painting. The representation of a building in perspective. *Nash's composition of Regent Street, London, was an exercise in *scenographic composition* as his *palace-fronts were designed to be seen in perspective as a series of episodes.

Schädel, Gottfried (*c*.1680–1752). German *Baroque architect. He accompanied *Schlüter when the latter was called to St Petersburg in 1713, and appears to have been responsible for the design of Prince Alexander Menshikov's (1673–1729) Palace at Oranienbaum (completed *c*.1725), the first great palace in Russia in the Western-European style, situated overlooking the Gulf of Finland, west of the city. He later worked in Kiev, Ukraine, where he did ecclesiastical jobs, including the design of the Church of St Andrew (1744–67), a confection in which Baroque and *Byzantine elements coalesce.

Hamilton (1983)

Scharoun, Hans (1893–1972). German architect. Sometimes described as influenced by *Expressionism, he was actually more eclectic, drawing on ideas of 'new building' promoted by *Häring and on the tenets of the *Modern Movement. During the 1914–18 war he worked on reconstruction projects in East Prussia until 1918, and later practised in that area of Germany (1919–25). His association with the *Gläserne Kette and Der *Ring led to his building a house at the *Weissenhofsiedlung, Stuttgart (1927). From 1925 to 1932 he taught at the *Staatliche Akademie für Kunst und Kunstgewerbe* (State Academy for Art and Applied Art), Breslau (now Wrocław), and built a residential hall for the *Deutscher Werkbund exhibition in that city devoted to the theme of living- and work-spaces (1929). He prepared plans for the Siemensstadt and other housing schemes in Berlin (1929–30): at Siemensstadt he was associated with *Bartning, *Gropius, Häring, and others. During the 1930s he produced several Modernist houses, including the Schminke House, Löbau, Saxony (1933), with huge *cantilevered balconies, much glass, and steel construction. After the 1939–45 war he directed the Building and Housing Department for Greater Berlin, and prepared (with others) plans for the rebuilding of the shattered city. He was also appointed to the Chair of Urban Planning, Technical University of Berlin, which he occupied until 1958, exercising great influence.

He designed a series of residential schemes ('Romeo' and 'Juliet' apartments, Stuttgart-Zuffenhausen (1954–9), 'Salute' block, Stuttgart-Möhringen (1961–3), and dwellings at Charlottenburg-Nord, Berlin (1956–61)), schools, and other structures. His most celebrated building, however, is the *Philharmonie* (Hall for the Berlin Philharmonic Orchestra), Berlin (1956–63), where the auditorium is surrounded by foyers and offices, the whole freely composed in a way some have seen as a late flowering of Expressionism, or even as evidence of Scharoun's commitment to *organic architecture. He also designed the Prussian State Library, Berlin (1964–78), sited on the *Kulturforum* that includes the *Philharmonie* and *Mies van der Rohe's National Gallery, but it has to be said that these structures relate neither to each other nor to the city as a place of memory, and ignore one of the most significant historical axes. He also designed the German Embassy in Brasilia (1963–71), the Maritime Museum, Bremerhaven (1970–5), and the Town Theatre, Wolfsburg (1965–73), among other projects.

Blundell Jones (1995); Conrads and Sperlich (1960); Janofske (1984); Messina, Taut, and Lauterbach (1969); Pehnt (1973); Pfankuch (1974)

Schattner, Karl-Josef (1924–). German architect. Most of his works were carried out in his capacity as Architect to the Diocese of Eichstätt, and he built up his own *Dombauhütte* (Cathedral Workshop) employing a team of craftsmen. The founding of the University at Eichstätt enabled Schattner to conserve and adapt the many historic buildings, while most of his new works were uncompromisingly radical and modern, erected within the historical context. Influenced by William *Morris's philosophies, he was one of the more sensitive architects working on old buildings in a Germany that rather often favoured wholesale reconstructions. His works include the Archives Building (1989–93), the conversion and extension of Schloss Hirschberg (1987–92), and the Episcopal Seminary (1981–93). His rational approach has much in common with that of the *Ticinese School and his Italian contemporary *Scarpa.

Emanuel (1994)

Scheerbart, Paul (1863–1915). German writer and fantasist, the high-priest of *Expressionism. He was the mentor of Bruno *Taut and *Tatlin. In his writings he frequently alluded to an imaginative architecture of glass as an instrument of social change, and indeed his most celebrated work was *Glass Architecture* (1914 and 1972), dedicated to Taut, whose famous Glass Pavilion at the Werkbund Exhibition, Cologne (1914), was dedicated to Scheerbart. His work was an important influence on *Gropius, *Mies van der Rohe, and the evolution of *International Modernism.

Journal of the Society of Architectural Historians, 34 (1975), 83–97; Sharp (1967, 1972)

Schickhardt, Heinrich (1558–1635). German architect, one of the earliest of the *Renaissance period, and therefore of importance in spite of the fact that very little of his work survives. In his capacity as Architect to the Duke of Württemberg (from 1590), he travelled in Italy to gather ideas for his addition to the *Schloss* in Stuttgart (1600–9—destroyed). It was symmetrical, and employed many *Tuscan columns. Of even greater importance was his layout for the new town of Freudenstadt (Town of Gladness), originally founded for Protestant refugees from Salzburg in 1599, and rebuilt after a fire in 1632. It was laid out around a huge square, partly occupied by gardens and surrounded by houses on arcades, and was based on C16 plans for *Ideal Cities, notably one by Albrecht Dürer (1471–1528). A similar design occurred in *Christianopolis* (1619) by the scholar and humanist Johann Valentin Andrea (1568–1654). Freudenstadt's Protestant church consisted of two *naves at right angles to each other (one for males and one for females), on an L plan, with the pulpit and altar in the corner, and a tower at the end of each nave. The town was burned in April 1945 and subsequently rebuilt.

Hitchcock (1981); van Vynckt (1993)

Schindler, Rudolph Michael (1887–1953). Vienna-born American architect. Early influences were *Loos, Otto *Wagner, and Frank Lloyd *Wright (in whose Chicago office he worked from 1918). He established his own practice in Los Angeles in 1921, and collaborated in the mid-1920s with *Neutra. Most of his work was in the field of domestic architecture, for which, in the 1920s, he used systems of *concrete construction. His Schindler House, North Kings Road, Hollywood, Calif. (1921–2), was freely composed, with two L-shaped plans containing studios and giving access to external living-areas, but his most celebrated building of the period (influenced by the De *Stijl movement and by *Constructivism) was the Lovell Beach House, Newport Beach, Calif. (1922–6), supported on five exposed concrete frames, with spaces enclosed by prefabricated elements. His work then became more blocky, as in the Buck House, Los Angeles (1934), and he gradually ceased using concrete as his main building material, turning to *timber frames and *stucco finishes in the 1930s, and to plywood panels in the 1940s. He began to express roofs, as in the van Dekker House, Canoga Park, Calif. (1940), and then evolved an architecture that appeared increasingly fragmented, as in the Janson House, Los Angeles (1949). His individuality, humour, and dislike of the totalitarianism inherent in the *International *Modern Movement led to his comparative neglect, but he was later perceived as a designer of pioneering Modernist buildings.

Andrews (1955); Banham (1971); Gebhard (1980); McCoy (1975); March and Sheine (1993); Morgan and Naylor (1987); Sarnitz (1988)

Schinkel, Karl Friedrich (1781–1841). Prussian architect, the greatest in Germany in the first half of C19. He was not only an architect of genius, but a civil servant, intellectual, painter, stage-designer, producer of *panoramas, and gifted draughtsman. His output was prodigious, and his stylistically eclectic work was lyrical and logical. He designed many buildings that became paradigms of excellence in the period during which he served his country and King as Prussian State Architect, and he established standards that influenced generations of architects throughout Germany.

Friedrich *Gilly's Graeco-Roman Egyptian design for a monument to King Friedrich II (the 'Great'—reigned 1740–86), exhibited in Berlin in 1797, fuelled the young Schinkel's ambition to become an architect, and in 1798 he entered the studio and household of Gilly's father, David *Gilly, enrolling at the *Bauakademie* (Building Academy or School of Architecture), where he received a rigorous training in practical matters as well as absorbing the theoretical bases of *Classicism as expounded by Alois Hirt (1759–1834). Other teachers included *Gentz and *Langhans, and the ethos of the *Bauakademie* included much derived from the teachings of *Blondel and the École Polytechnique in Paris, so the young Schinkel absorbed the elements of a rational approach to architecture from which Franco-Prussian *Neoclassicism evolved.

During his tour of Italy and France (1803–5) he studied *vernacular and medieval architecture and was particularly interested in the structural principles of apartment-blocks in Naples and the *Gothic *vaults of Milan Cathedral. He was less enthusiastic about *Antique remains than about their *Picturesque qualities, and studied *Romanesque and other structures as well as brick buildings (e.g. those in Bologna). On his return to Berlin he found lean times, and with the defeat of Prussia by the French in 1806 and the occupation of the capital there were no prospects of architectural commissions, so Schinkel occupied himself by producing panoramas and dioramas as well as numerous idealized landscapes and other pictures. These works made Schinkel well known, and attracted the attention of Queen Luise (1776–1810), recently returned (1809) from exile in Königsberg, who commissioned him to redecorate several palace-interiors in Berlin and Charlottenburg. In 1810 he was appointed to a post in the Department of Public Works (partly through the influence of (Karl) Wilhelm von Humboldt (1767–1835)—Minister of Public Instruction and Education) with responsibility of assessing the aesthetic content of all buildings erected or owned by the State, and began his meteoric rise through the bureaucracy that would later enable him to create architecture to ennoble all human relationships and to express Prussia's aspirations. The death of the greatly loved Queen in 1810 focused patriotic sentiments, and Schinkel, with Gentz and King Friedrich Wilhelm III (1797–1840), designed the Queen's Greek *Doric *mausoleum at Charlottenburg. He also exhibited an alternative (and enchanting) Romantic Gothic design in which the supposed 'natural' origins of Gothic were alluded to in the palm-fronds on the ribs of the vaults, like a canopy of peace over the dead Queen, and at that time began to see Gothic as an embodiment of the Germanic soul. It was his synthesis of the Classical and Gothic that gave much of his later work an especial interest. In 1811 he designed the cast-iron Gothic memorial at Gransee on the spot where the Queen's coffin had rested on its way to Charlottenburg, a concept suggested by the medieval 'Eleanor crosses' in C13 England. A series of *Sublime paintings followed in which were depicted vast Gothic cathedrals, bathed in light, comparable with aspects of work by the Romantic painter Caspar David Friedrich (1774–1840), whose work was exhibited in Berlin in 1810.

With the galvanizing of the national spirit, the King's proclamation to his people, the collection of gold jewellery for the *Freiheitskrieg* (War of Liberation), and Schinkel's design of the *Eisenkreuz* (Iron Cross) military decoration in 1813, the idea of the Prussian State became associated with economy, fortitude, and self-sacrifice. For the rest of his life Schinkel was to use iron with sensitivity, and indeed his attitudes to new technologies and industrialization were judicious. Napoleon's eventual defeat encouraged a great upsurge of Prussian national pride, partly to be expressed in architecture. In 1815 Schinkel was promoted as *Geheimer Baurat* (Privy Building Officer) with special powers to plan Berlin and oversee all State and Royal building-commissions. He also initiated an influential report on the preservation of national monuments that led to State protection of historic buildings throughout Prussia. Among his more important concerns at the time was the commencement of the restoration of Cologne Cathedral (1816) and his investigation of the Marienburg fortress (1309–98), once the seat of the Grand Masters of the Teutonic Order: his recommendations for the latter complex (now Malbork, Poland) were realized after 1845, and the programme he set in motion continued well into C20. His work as a painter and creator of dioramas and panoramas inevitably brought commissions to design for the theatre, and his scenes for Mozart's *Die Zauberflöte* (The Magic Flute—1815–16) were among the finest conceived, with their *Egyptian Revival architecture, derived partly from the Napoleonic publications, and exotic Meso-American-tropical landscapes inspired by Friedrich Heinrich Alexander von Humboldt's (1769–1859) travels to South America and Mexico (1799–1804), published in 1807.

Schinkel's major buildings were designed from 1816, starting with the *Neue Wache* (New Guard House) on the *Unter den Linden*, Berlin (1816–18), with a free Greek Doric for the portico (there are no *triglyphs and there is a continuous row of *guttae-like elements under the *frieze) set against a plain fortress-like block. This was followed by the monument to the dead of the Napoleonic Wars, Spandau (1816), the Gothic monument on the Templower Berg (now Kreuzberg—1818–21) and the *pinnacle-monument in the churchyard at Grossbeeren (1817), all of cast iron. A master-plan for Berlin and series of splendid buildings came next. After the destruction of Langhans's *Nationaltheater*, Schinkel replaced it with the *Schauspielhaus* (Play House—

1818–21), a brilliant design with an *Ionic portico and a *mullioned and *trabeated system derived from the Ancient Greek *Choragic Monument of Thrasyllus, Athens, and the square columns of Ancient Egyptian temples. This theatre, with the twin churches in the *Gendarmenmarkt*, forms one of the noblest urban ensembles in Berlin. He prepared comprehensive proposals for the *Lustgarten* (Pleasure Garden) in front of the Royal Palace, including the reorganization of the waterways, the remodelling of the Cathedral, the construction of various buildings, and the creation of a new bridge linking the *Lustgarten* and the *Unter den Linden*. As part of the scheme he worked on the idea of building a new museum, accepted by the King in 1823. This, his masterpiece (very badly damaged in the 1939–45 war, and indifferently treated thereafter), was part of the high-minded programme to raise the tone of society, and consists of a long Ionic *colonnade like a *Hellenistic *stoa behind which a double staircase leads to an open gallery-landing from which views may be enjoyed. Influenced by French theorists such as *Durand, the plan had a clarity and purity worthy of the high ideals of its creator, but in the reconstructed building those qualities are barely discernible. Behind the stair and entrance is a *Pantheon-like *rotunda inside a cubic form.

Meanwhile, he had also built two other great buildings: Humboldt's Schloss Tegel (1820–4—west of Berlin, in which he mingled the mullion-and-trabeated style of the *Schauspielhaus*, themes from the Villa Trissino near Vicenza, elements from English *Palladianism, and various allusions to Antiquity); and the hunting-lodge of Antonin (for Prince Radziwiłł (1775–1833)), Ostrow, near Poznań, Poland (1822–4—a five-storey timber-framed and timber-clad octagon with four square wings, the central area galleried and with a huge Doric column rising in the centre containing the fireplaces and chimney). In addition, he designed the tomb-marker of General Gerhard Johann David von Scharnhorst (1755–1813) in the *Invaliden-Friedhof*, Berlin (1820–4).

During the building of the *Lustgarten* Museum (1824–30) Schinkel obtained approval for his Neo-Gothic *Friedrich-Werderschekirche*, Berlin (1824–30), an important example of his work in the Gothic style, after which he set out on a tour of Germany, France, England, Scotland, and Wales, accompanied by Peter Christian Wilhelm Beuth (1781–1853), Prussian civil servant. His diaries describe his impressions, notably his interest in English industrial architecture (e.g. the London Docks, building construction, the Staffordshire Potteries, gas-works, etc.). On his return to Berlin he incorporated aspects of fire-resistant construction he had seen at *Smirke's British Museum, and he was instrumental in getting gaslight installed by an English firm in Berlin (1826–7).

Then followed an essay in Gothic with the Town Hall of Kolberg (Kołobrzeg), built 1827–32, and the exquisite series of buildings in the park at Potsdam: Charlottenhof (1826–7), the Court-Gardener's House (1829–33—evocative of the *vernacular architecture in Tuscany), and the 'Roman Baths' (1830). The last three buildings, beautifully integrated with the gardens, drew on ideas of asymmetrical *Picturesque composition pioneered in England, notably by *Nash and *Papworth. With the *Nikolaikirche* (Church of St Nicholas), Potsdam (1830–7), Schinkel realized the ideals of stereometrical purity advocated by C18 French theorists with a great cube surmounted by a drum and dome, an apsidal *chancel, and an *Antique portico. It demonstrates its designer's complete mastery of Greek, Roman, Italianate, and Neoclassical languages.

An interest in *terracotta and brick, fuelled perhaps by his visit to England, was realized (1828) in the structural *polychrome treatment of the house for Tobias Christoph Feilner (1773–1839), a forward-looking design anticipating the ideas of *Hittorff and others. This also led to the *Bauakademie*, Berlin (1831–6), a polychrome brick and terracotta structure influenced by Classical rigour, Gothic systems of *piers and *buttresses, and English industrial architecture. The *Bauakademie* housed the School of Architecture, Schinkel's living-quarters, and the *Oberbaudeputation* (State Building Directorate). Until its wholly unwarranted destruction by the Communist authorities (1961), it remained one of his finest creations. Other masterly works in the Classical style by Schinkel include the exquisite New Pavilion, Schloss Charlottenburg (1824–5), the Casino, Schloss Glienicke (1824–5), Schloss Glienicke itself (1824–32), the *Hauptwache* (Main Guard House), Dresden, Saxony (1831–3), and the *Grosse Neugierde* (Great Curiosity), Schloss Glienicke (1835–7), the last in a Greek Revival style of enchanting beauty, quoting elements of the Choragic Monument of Lysicrates, Athens (334 BC).

Schloss Babelsberg, near the Havel (1832–49), was conceived in a Romantic *castellated style, based on English exemplars, as was the little-known but charming Schloss Kurnik (now Kórnik, Poland), a remodelling of an earlier building (1830s), but Schinkel's other great Picturesque Romantic-Classical dream-palaces were never built. These were Schloss Orianda, Crimea, Russia (1838—in which the spirit of *Pliny is detectable), and a palace on the Athenian Acropolis (1834): both are among his most imaginative and beautiful designs. With the *Bauakademie* they represent the last phase of Schinkel's career in which eclecticism, mature Classicism, syncretism, and influences from many countries, styles, and periods coalesced. From 1831 to 1837, as *Oberbaudirektor* (State Director of Building), he was placed in charge of all State building schemes in Prussia, and advised on the conservation of historic monuments, and in 1838 he became *Geheimer Oberlandesbaudirektor*, the top post within the State bureaucracy.

Schinkel's funeral in 1841 was a national event. He was buried in the Dorotheenstädtischer-Friedhof, Berlin, his grave marked by a Greek stele modelled on his own design (1833) for Siegmund F. Hermbstaedt's memorial. In 1842 his friend King Friedrich Wilhelm IV (reigned 1840–61) decreed that all his works should be purchased by the State. Called the 'last great architect' by *Loos, his publications included *Sammlung Architektonischer Entwürfe* (Collection of Architectural Designs—1819–40), *Werke der höheren Baukunst für die Ausführung entworfen* (Works of Higher Architecture designed for execution—1840–8), and (with Beuth) *Vorbilder für Fabrikanten und Handwerker* (Models for Manufacturers and Craftsmen—1821–7). His most gifted pupils included *Persius, *Strack, and *Stüler.

Architects' Journal, 193/25 (19 June 1991), 5, 30–49, and 194/4, 5 (24 and 31 July 1991), 22–39; Bergdoll (1994); Bindmann and Riemann (1993); Börsch-Supan and Grisebach (1981); Council of Europe (1972); Curl (1991, 1992, 1994); Forsmann (1981); Placzek (1982); Riemann (1981); Schinkel (1989); Snodin (1991); Watkin and Mellinghoff (1987); Zukowsky (1994*a*)

Schlaun, Johann Conrad von (1695–1773). German *Baroque architect, most of whose works, mixing local and cosmopolitan styles in free compositions, are in Westphalia. His earliest buildings were uncomplicated churches, but after a year working with *Neumann in Würzburg (1720–1) he travelled in Italy and France to broaden his understanding of architecture. In 1725 he became Architect to the Prince-Bishop Clemens August, Elector of Cologne (d. 1761), for whom he designed Schloss Brühl (1725–8—later much changed by Neumann, *Cuvilliés, and others) in a Franco-German Baroque style, and the enchanting brick *Rococo hunting-lodge of Clemenswerth (1736–50), with a two-storey building at the centre and a ring of eight detached pavilions, one of which contained a convent and chapel. Among his most successful palaces were the *Erbdrostenhof*, Münster (1755–7), on a triangular urban site with a concave façade fronting the *cour d'honneur and with a convex garden-elevation, the whole on an ingenious plan with irregularly shaped rooms. The Bishop's Palace, called the *Schloss*, Münster (1767–73), contained elements derived from designs by Neumann, notably the curved frontispiece and rounded corners, and made use of rose-coloured brick with stone dressings. Schlaun's own dwellings, the *Rüschhaus*, near Münster (1745–8), and the *Schlaunhaus* Münster (1753–5) both employ brick, the former looking like a Westphalian rural farm-building with a Rococo centrepiece, and the latter with a massive two-storey *rusticated arch in the middle. His *Clemenskirche*, Münster (1745–53), is a rotunda on a triangular site constructed on a six-pointed star of superimposed triangles, clearly based on *Borromini's church of Sant'Ivo in Rome.

Boer, Lechtape, and Buske (1995); Hempel (1965); Kalnein (1956); Norberg-Schulz (1986*a*); Powell (1959)

Schlüter, Andreas (*c*.1659–1714). Born in Danzig (now Gdańsk, Poland), he is claimed as a major *Baroque sculptor and architect by both Germany and Poland. His first works included decorations at the Royal Chapel, Gdańsk (1681), the high-altar, Oliva Cathedral, near Gdańsk (1688), and various commissions in Warsaw, to which city he was called in 1683 to execute the sculptured decorations of the Krasiński Palace. He also carved the monument of Canon Adam Konarski for Frombork Cathedral (1686), made the high-altar for the Czerniaków Church in Warsaw (1690), and the shockingly powerful crucifix for the Church of the Reformati, Węgrów, which was a model for the style of the 22 'heads of dying warriors' at the *Zeughaus* (Arsenal), Berlin (1696–8). He made four funerary monuments at Wilanów (1692–4). In 1694 he moved to Berlin, and was sent by Elector Friedrich III of Brandenburg (1688–1713) on a study-tour to France and Italy. On his return he carved the elaborate heads and *trophies at *Nering's *Zeughaus*, succeeding Nering as architect in 1698, the year in which he was appointed to direct building works at the *Schloss* in Berlin, to transform it from an Electoral *Residenz* into a Royal Palace. He also created the equestrian statue of the Great Elector (Friedrich Wilhelm (1640–88)), now at Charlottenburg Palace, Berlin. The *Schloss* was Schlüter's masterpiece, and showed the influences of his former Warsaw colleague, van *Gameren, as well as of *Bernini and Le *Pautre. This great Baroque Palace was mostly finished when the Elector became King of Prussia in 1701, was completed by *Eosander, badly damaged in 1945, and demolished in 1950 (an ideologically inspired act that makes nonsense of the historic fabric of the city). From 1701 to 1704, as Director of the Academy of Arts, Schlüter had an immense influence on artistic life in Berlin, and designed the Wartenburg Palace, Berlin (1702–4—later the Post Office—demolished 1889), and Villa Kamecke, Dorotheenstadt, Berlin (1711–12—destroyed). Following the collapse of the *Münzturm* (Mint Tower), Berlin (1704), he began to fall from favour, was removed as *Schlossbaudirektor* in 1707, and resigned from the Academy in 1710. In 1713 he went to St Petersburg where he made a major contribution to the planning of the new capital, and prepared designs for the grotto near the Summer Palace, the Peterhof, and Monplaisir. His work in Berlin influenced *Fischer von Erlach, M. D. *Pöppelmann, and G. W. von *Knobelsdorff.

Gurlitt (1891); Hager (1942); Hempel (1965); Iwicki (1980); Karpowicz (1991); Ladendorff (1935); Mossakowski (1973); Peschken and Klünner (1982)

Schmidt, Friedrich, Freiherr von (1825–91). Architect of the *Neo-Gothic *Rathaus* (Town Hall) in Vienna (1872–82), which resembles a Flemish Cloth or Town Hall. Schmidt established himself as an important exponent of the *Gothic Revival in Austria with his *Fünfhaus Pfarrkirche*, Maria vom Siege (1868–75), built on an aisled octagonal plan, with medievalizing detail. He worked on the continuation of Cologne Cathedral from 1843 (he was an expert on *stereotomy), and taught architecture at Brera, Italy (1857–9). He restored the Church of Sant'Ambrogio, Milan. Among his other buildings is the Church of St Stephan, Krefeld, Germany (1854–81).

Germann (1972); Haiko (1991); Meeks (1966); Sturgis *et al.* (1901–2)

Schmidtz, Bruno (1858–1916). German architect, remembered primarily for his heroic monuments, including that to Kaiser Wilhelm I (1871–88) at Deutsches Eck, where the River Mosel joins the Rhine at Koblenz (1896–7—destroyed in the 1939–45 war, but reconstructed in the early 1990s). On the Kyffhäuser Hills, Thuringia, he designed the huge monument (1890–6) to Emperor Friedrich I Barbarossa (*c*.1123–90). His gigantic *Völkerschlachtsdenkmal* (Battle of the Nations Memorial), near Leipzig (1896–1913), is the epitome of the glorification of German history, and is the greatest and most menacingly monumental national memorial of the early C20, built of *reinforced concrete faced with massive granite blocks: it represents the power of the German peoples who rose in 1813 to drive the French from their lands. Schmidtz's brooding work was a considerable influence on Wilhelm *Kreis.

Meeks (1966); Pevsner (1976); Spitzner (1913); Watkin (1986)

Schmu(t)zer, Joseph (1683–1752). One of a family of Bavarian architects and workers in *stucco from Wessobrunn. He built the *Wandpfeiler *Heiligenkreuzkirche* (Church of the Holy Cross), Donauwörth (1717–22), designed by Franz *Beer, and carried out the exquisite *Rococo decorations in the Benedictine Abbey Church of Ettal (1744–52), and in the Parish Churches of Rottenbuch (1737–47), Mittenwald (1738–40), and Oberammergau (1736–42). His father, **Johann** (1642–1701) was probably responsible for the *Baroque decorations in the Pilgrimage Chapel at Ilgen, Steingaden (1670–6), designed the cruciform Church at Vilgertshofen (1686–92), and worked on the Church at Obermarchtal (1689). **Franz Xaver** (1676–1741) carried out fine stucco-work at Weingarten (1718), designed altars at Obermarchtal (erected 1759), modelled the stucco-work at Weissenau (*c*.1711), did the stucco in the nave at Steingaden (1740s), and also worked at Oberammergau, Rheinau, and elsewhere.

Bourke (1962); Dischinger (1977); Hauttmann (1921); Hitchcock (1968*a*); Powell (1959)

Schnebli, Dolf (1928–). Swiss architect. Although influenced by Le *Corbusier, *Gropius, and others, his work produced in his office in Ticino tended to move towards the formal language of the *Ticinese School, notably with his severe Villa Meyer, Zurich (1986–7), which owes something to Classical symmetry and formalism. His designs for houses at Campione d'Italia and Carabbia, Ticino, aroused considerable interest in the 1960s, and made his reputation. Other works include Ruopigen Primary School, Littau (1975–6).

Blaser (1982); Emanuel (1994)

Schoch, Johannes, *called* **Hans** (*c*.1550–1631). German architect. His most celebrated work is the *Friedrichsbau*, Heidelberg Castle (1601–7), an early and vigorous essay in *Renaissance architecture, designed for the Elector Frederick IV Palatine of the Rhine (reigned 1592–1610). He probably worked on the *Neuer Bau* (New Building—1582–5) and *Grosse Metzig* (Great Shambles—1586–8), Strasbourg. His work may have influenced other early Renaissance buildings in Germany, notably the *Zeughaus* (Arsenal), Amberg (1604), and the *Fleischhalle* (Meat Market), Heilbronn (*c*.1600), both of which have been attributed to him.

Hitchcock (1981)

Schultes, Axel (1943–). German architect. His best-known buildings are museums, many of which explore the possibilities of spatial depth and complexity, as in the *Kunstmuseum* (Art Museum), Bonn (1985–92). He was very successful as a winner of architectural competitions, notably the Government Buildings on the Spree, Berlin (1993—with Charlotte Frank (1959–)), the *Altmarkt*, Dresden (1991), and the German Pavilion, Expo 92, Seville (1990).

Emanuel (1994); Jodidio (1995*a*)

Schultz, Robert Weir (1861–1951). *See* Weir, Robert Weir Schultz.

Schultze-Naumburg, Paul (1869–1949). German architect and theorist. His work before the 1914–18 war was mostly in historical styles, including *Schloss Cecilienhof*, Potsdam (1913–17), in a free half-timbered English *Arts-and-Crafts style, influenced by *Muthesius's publications, that manages nonetheless to look stolidly German. His books were important, starting with *Kulturarbeiten* (Creative Works—1902–17), *Das ABC des Bauens* (The ABC of Building—1927), *Kunst und Rasse* (Art and Race—1928 and 1938), *Das Gesicht des deutschen Hauses* (The Appearance of the German House—1929), *Kampf von die Kunst* (Struggle around Art—1932), *Kunst aus Blut und Boden* (Art from Blood and Soil—1934), and *Bauten Schultze-Naumburg* (Buildings by Schultze-Naumburg—1940). He argued that architecture was expressive of race, and that German architecture was being corrupted by non-Teutonic influences, notably through the *International *Modern Movement. This enabled him to rise to some degree of influence during the Nazi period (1933–45), and during his brief tenure as Director of the Weimar School that had been the *Bauhaus he removed all Modernists from their posts.

Adam (1992); Hinz (1979); Lane (1985)

Schumacher, Fritz (1869–1947). German architect. He directed the German *Arts-and-Crafts exhibition in Dresden (1906) and was a founding-member of the *Deutscher Werkbund (1907). He built many houses while in Dresden before becoming City Architect of Hamburg (1909–33). His work there was influenced by the North-German traditional brick buildings with steeply pitched tile roofs, but after the 1914–18 war his designs became angular, hard, and flat-roofed. He published *Die Kleinwohnung* (The Small Dwelling—1917) in which he argued for industrialized mass-production. Other books include *Probleme der Grossstadt* (Problems of the Large City—1910) and many works dealing with questions of architecture, planning, politics, and style. He was a pioneer of regional planning, notably at Hamburg. His best work is probably the Hamburg Stadtpark (1910–24).

Architekten und Ingenieur-Verein (1929); Fischer (1977); Kallmorgen (1969); Placzek (1982—contains a useful bibliography)

Schuricht, Christian Friedrich (1753–1832). German architect. A pupil of *Krubsacius, he travelled in Italy and England, and collaborated with the garden theorist Christian Cajus Lorenz Hirschfeld (1742–92), author of the influential *Theorie der Gartenkunst* (Theory of the Art of Gardening—1779–85). Chief among his works is the Palladian house at Kačina, near Prague (1802), in which Neoclassical themes became dominant. Earlier (1794), he designed the beautiful domed blue room and other Neoclassical interiors in the 'Roman House' in the Schloss Park, Weimar, erected to plans by *Arens. He was appointed Court Architect at Dresden (1812), and designed the *Neues Palais*, Schloss Pillnitz (1818–26), the roof of which echoed the oriental theme established by *Pöppelmann in the 1720s, but the building itself was plain, in the manner of *Schinkel, and with primitive Greek *Doric columns flanking the entrances. He also designed the Belvedere on the *Brühlsche Terrasse* by the Elbe, Dresden (1812–14—destroyed), influenced by the Franco-Prussian style of F. *Gilly.

Watkin and Mellinghoff (1987)

Schwarz, Rudolf (1897–1961). German church-architect. He studied under *Poelzig in Berlin. He worked with Dominikus *Böhm on the prize-winning unexecuted design for a church in Frankfurt (1926–7), and Böhm's influence is clear in Schwarz's Corpus Christi Church, Aachen (1928–30), a simple white building with a black altar on a platform reached by a flight of steps. He published a work on church-design in 1938 in which he discussed the relationships of plans, structures, and congregations. After the 1939–45 war he designed a great number of churches, many with *reinforced-concrete frames, the spaces filled with brick, glass, and stone. Chief among his works are St Anna, Düren (1951–6), St Michael, Frankfurt (1953–4), and the Church of the Holy Family, Oberhausen (1956–8). In 1960 he published *Kirchenbau* (Church Building) in which he emphasized the desirability of bringing the congregation into a more intimate relationship with the altar.

Emanuel (1994); Hammond (1962); Kidder-Smith (1964); Schwarz (1958, 1960); Schwarz and Conrads (1979)

Schwechten, Franz Heinrich (1841–1924). German architect. A pupil of Martin *Gropius, F. A. *Stüler, and J. A. *Raschdorff, he established his practice in Berlin in 1869, specializing in buildings for the railways. He was greatly influenced by the *polychromy of *Schinkel and M. Gropius in his designs for the *Anhalter Bahnhof* (Anhalt Station), Berlin (1875–80—destroyed). He also designed the railway-stations at Dessau and Wittenberg (both 1875–80). His best-known work was the *Romanesque-revival *Kaiser-Wilhelm Gedächtniskirche* (Emperor Wilhelm Memorial Church), Berlin (1891–5—of which part remains), and he also designed the Church of the Redeemer, Essen (1905–9). He had a successful career, building all over the German Empire.

Deutsche Bauzeitung, 58 (1924), 427–8; Posener (1979)

Schwitters, Kurt (1887–1948). German artist. In 1917 he made collages from detritus collected from dumps and streets which he called *Merz* (Cast-Off). He then created *Merzbau* (Cast-Off Building) which virtually took over his entire dwelling in Hanover (1923–32—destroyed). The *Merzbau* was wholly unfunctional, and was really an essay in which *Expressionism and *Constructivism merged. He built a *Merz* mural in Ambleside, English Lake District (1947–8), later moved to King's College, Newcastle upon Tyne.

Chilvers, Osborne, and Farr (1988); Schmalenbach (1970); Steinitz (1968)

sciagraph. Representation of a *section.

sciagraphy. Branch of the science of *perspective dealing with the projection of shadows.

Fraser Reekie (1946)

scissor-truss. *See* truss.

scoinson. Interior edge of a window-side, so *scoinson-arch* is that over the interior of a window-aperture on the inside, often much larger than on the outside if the *jambs are splayed.

Scoles, Joseph John (1798–1863). English Roman Catholic architect. He became interested in medieval architecture through the influence of John *Carter. He travelled in Sicily, Greece, Egypt, and Syria with Joseph *Bonomi jun. before setting up in practice in 1826. He planned Gloucester Terrace, Regent's Park, London, with the basic elevational treatment by *Nash. He is best known for his Roman Catholic churches, which were mostly in the *Gothic style, although some were *Romanesque, and a few were Classical. His churches include St Peter, Stonyhurst College, Lancashire (1832–5—Gothic), St Ignatius, Preston, Lancashire (1833–6—Gothic), St James, Colchester, Essex (1837—Romanesque), St John, Duncan Terrace, Islington, London (1841–3—Romanesque), Prior Park College Church, Bath, Somerset (1844–6—Classical), St Francis Xavier, Liverpool (1845–9—Gothic), and his masterpiece, the Church of the Immaculate Conception, Farm Street, Mayfair, London (1846–9—Gothic). He also designed the residential buildings for the

Oratory, Brompton, London (1849–53), and the chapel, Ince Blundell Hall, Lancashire (1858–9—Classical).

Colvin (1995); Curl (1995); *DNB* (1917); Dixon and Muthesius (1985); Papworth (1887)

sconce. 1. Earthwork or fort, especially in front of a gate or the main defences. **2.** Protective *screen or shelter. **3.** Screen in the sense of a partition, e.g. to define a *chapel, etc. **4.** Squinch (*see* dome), in the sense of a small arch across the angle of a square room carrying a superimposed mass (e.g. in a church-tower carrying an octagonal *spire). **5.** Decorative lamp-bracket attached to a wall. **6.** Seat or bench fixed in a screen-wall near a fireplace.

scoop pattern. *Band or *frieze ornamented by a series of closely spaced vertical *flutes, normally with the upper ends curved, common in Classical work of C18.

scotia (*pl.* **scotiae**). *Trochilus, or hollow concave moulding, in e.g. an *Attic *base of a Classical column sandwiched between the *fillets above and below the *torus Mouldings.

Scott, Sir George Gilbert (1811–78). Prolific English *Gothic Revival architect. He was articled to James Edmeston (1791–1867) in 1827, who was better known as a writer of hymns ('Lead us, Heavenly Father, lead us' (1821) was one of his efforts) than as an architect, and later joined the office of Henry *Roberts in 1832, where he worked on the new Fishmongers' Hall, London, and on a school at Camberwell (1834). Early in 1835 he assisted Sampson Kempthorne (1809–73), Architect to the Poor Law Commissioners, who produced several designs for workhouses and schools that were published and widely copied in the 1830s and 1840s. By the end of 1835 Scott was practising on his own, but had also formed a working relationship with William Bonython Moffatt (1812–87) that developed into a partnership (1838) which was responsible for over 50 workhouses and many other buildings. In 1838 Scott designed the little Gothic church of St Mary Magdalene at Flaunden, Hertfordshire (1838), and thereafter, possibly through the influence of *Blore, greatly expanded his architectural practice. The first real success was when Scott & Moffatt won the competition to design the Church of St Giles, Camberwell (1841), an important and reasonably scholarly essay in Gothic that gained the approval of the *Ecclesiologists. Scott also won the competition for the Martyrs' Memorial, Oxford (1841–2), with a design based on the C13 'Eleanor Crosses'. In 1841 Scott started to read A. W. N. *Pugin's writings, which excited him, and he began to contribute to *The Ecclesiologist*, the influential journal of the Cambridge Camden (later Ecclesiological) Society. Scott & Moffatt entered the competition to design the Church of St Nikolaus, Hamburg, in 1844, and came third, but through the influence of *Zwirner, their scholarly *German Gothic design (with its handsome *steeple which survived the 1939–45 war) was accepted and realized (but, as it was to be a Lutheran Church, gained the architects no credit with the Ecclesiologists, who did not recognize the validity of Lutheran Orders). The 1840s also saw Scott developing a career as a restorer of ecclesiastical buildings, starting with Chesterfield, and continuing with several major churches, including Ely, Peterborough, and Westminster Abbey. Moffatt's extravagance and financial recklessness led to a dissolution of the partnership in 1845, the year in which the firm's Reading Gaol, Berkshire, was completed.

In the 1850s, in common with many of his peers, Scott developed an interest in Continental Gothic. His designs for the War and Foreign Office, London (1856), drew on Flemish Gothic, but he was requested to revise the designs in a Classical style, and produced a handsome essay in a florid *Renaissance manner (1862–73). Meanwhile he had built the handsome Parish Church of St George at Doncaster, Yorkshire (1853–8—one of his best buildings), the Chapel at Exeter College, Oxford (1856–9—based on Sainte-Chapelle, Paris), the huge *Middle Pointed All Souls, Haley Hill, Halifax (1855–9), and St Mary Abbots, Kensington, London (1869–72).

In 1861, *Albert, Prince Consort, died, and Scott's design for his memorial in London (drawn by his son, **George Gilbert, jun.**) was chosen. Like *Worthington's Albert Memorial in Manchester (1862–3), it was in the form of a canopied *shrine, but Scott's version was in the Italian Gothic style, glowing with colour and richness (1862–72). For this, the epitome of *High Victorian Gothic Revival, Scott was knighted in 1872.

He also enjoyed considerable success as a secular architect. His Kelham Hall, Nottinghamshire (1858–62), and Midland Grand Hotel, St Pancras, London (1868–74) have much in common: both are self-confident eclectic brick structures, based on Continental Gothic sources from Ypres (Ieper), Louvain (Leuven), and Venice, with a dash of English and French Gothic, and both were almost outrageously opulent and extravagant. He designed the University, Gilmore Hill, Glasgow (1866–70), including Scots *tourelles to give the building a regional flavour, although J. O. *Scott added the Germanic *tracery *spire in 1887. His Albert Institute, Dundee (1865–7), also employed Scots features such as *crow-step *gables and circular *turrets of the *Scottish Baronial style. Among his other works the Chapel at St John's College, Cambridge (1863–9), and the Episcopal Cathedral of St Mary, Edinburgh (1874–9), may be mentioned, the latter a noble composition with three spires.

As a church architect, Scott had his drawbacks. In his *A Plea for the Faithful Restoration of Our Ancient Churches* (1850) and other writings he argued for a sensitivity in dealing with ancient fabric he rarely showed in practice. Indeed, his work at St Mary de Castro, Leicester, was not only drastic, but very destructive. The Society for the Protection of Ancient Buildings (SPAB) was founded by William *Morris in 1877 as a direct result of Scott's draconian proposals for the 'restoration' of Tewkesbury Abbey, Gloucestershire. He was a tireless advocate of Gothic as the only style in which to build, as in his *Remarks on Secular & Domestic Architecture Present and Future* (1857). His *Personal and Professional Recollections* (1879) is entertaining and interesting, but it demonstrates Scott had a higher opinion of his own abilities than posterity has granted him. Indeed, whilst he was industrious and professionally competent, he lacked the spark of real originality and verve, and many of his restorations demonstrated a negation of the very qualities of scholarship and care that he himself advocated. His *Gleanings from Westminster Abbey* (1860), however, was not unscholarly, and demonstrates a love for medieval architecture he was perhaps unable to sustain in practice.

Architectural History, 19 (1976), 54–73; Clarke (1958, 1966, 1969); Cole (1980); Curl (1990, 1995); *DNB* (1917); Eastlake (1970); Fisher *et al.* (1981); Hitchcock (1954); Howell and Sutton (1989); Pevsner (1972); Physick and Darby (1973); Port (1961); Scott (1995); Toplis (1987); Victoria & Albert Museum (1971, 1978)

Scott, George Gilbert, jun. (1839–97). English architect. The eldest son of Sir George Gilbert *Scott, he was a much more gifted church architect, and championed English *Perpendicular *Gothic. He was articled to his father (1857–60), and commenced practice in 1863. His restorations were infinitely more sensitive than those of his father, and his new work often reached heights of excellence. Among his best works were the Hall and Combination Room, Peterhouse, Cambridge (1868–70); the Church, School, and Vicarage of St Agnes, Kennington, London (1874–91—destroyed); and the *First Pointed English Gothic church of St John the Baptist (now the Roman Catholic Cathedral), Norwich (1884–1910—completed by J. O. *Scott in 1910), a scholarly and satisfying essay in the C13 style. He also designed the Church of St Mary Magdalene, Eastmoors, Yorkshire (1879–82), and the new building for St John's College, Oxford (1880–2). He published *An Essay on the History of English Church Architecture Prior to the Separation of England from the Roman Obedience* in 1881, the year after he became a Roman Catholic himself. In 1884 his increasingly erratic behaviour led to his being declared as of unsound mind.

Architectural Review, 5 (Dec. 1898), 58–66, and 5 (May 1899), 124–32; *British Architect*, 15 (7 Jan. 1881), 1–3; Curl (1995); Scott (1995)

Scott, Sir Giles Gilbert (1880–1960). English architect, one of the most eminent of the first half of C20. The son of George Gilbert *Scott, jun., he was articled to the latter's pupil, Temple *Moore, and was profoundly affected by the work of both men. In his early twenties (1903) he won the second competition to design the Anglican Cathedral in Liverpool (1903–80) which occupied him for the rest of his life. Until 1907 he had an association with *Bodley, and something of the latter's extremely delicate and sensitive interpretation of *Gothic can be seen in the *Lady Chapel at Liverpool, although the architectural language owes much to German Gothic of the late-medieval period. As the work on the Cathedral progressed, Scott changed the design, and created a *Sublime monument with breathtaking internal volumes, quite unlike any other work of the *Gothic Revival. At Liverpool Scott demonstrated an inventiveness and an original genius lacking in the work of his grandfather. Among his other churches may be mentioned The Annunciation, Bournemouth (1905–6), the *nave at Downside Abbey, Somerset

(1917–39), the Chapel at Charterhouse School, Godalming, Surrey (1922–7), Ampleforth Abbey and College, Yorkshire (1922–60), St Alban, Golders Green, London (1930–2), the Roman Catholic Cathedral, Oban, Scotland (1931–51), and the Carmelite Church, Kensington, London (1954–9).

His sense of the monumental in composition and his control of massing were demonstrated at his University Library, Cambridge, and Battersea Power Station, London (both 1930–4). Among his best-known designs were the 1924 and 1935 versions of the Post Office telephone-kiosk, based on *Soane's tomb in London. He rebuilt the House of Commons, Westminster, after war damage (1944–51), and designed Waterloo Bridge, London (1934–45), the New Bodleian Library, Oxford (1935–46), and Bankside Power Station, London (1947–60). After the 1939–45 war, however, his work was not appreciated in the climate in which *International Modernism was enthusiastically embraced. In some of his early work he was assisted by his brother, **Adrian Gilbert Scott** (1882–1963), who later, on his own account, designed Cairo Cathedral, Egypt (1918–38), the tower of *Hansom's Church of the Holy Name, Manchester (1928), and many churches.

Architectural Design, 69/10–11 (1979), 72–83; Cotton (1964); *DNB* (1971); Reilly (1931); Stamp and Harte (1979)

Scott, Major-General Henry Young Darracott (1822–83). English military engineer. He became Secretary to the Commissioners for the Great Exhibition on the retirement of Sir Henry Cole (1808–62), and served in the Department of Science and Art in succession to *Fowke. With *Wild and others he designed the Science Schools (Huxley Building), Exhibition Road, Kensington (1867–71), a red-brick and *terracotta-faced *Rundbogenstil building. With Fowke he designed the Royal Albert Hall, London (1867–71), in which the *Antique, *Renaissance, and Rundbogenstil combine. He rendered considerable services to the Great Exhibition, London (1862), and other international exhibitions. He contributed papers on types of cement and on the construction of the Albert Hall as well as preparing plans for the completion of the South Kensington Museum.

DNB (1917); Dixon and Muthesius (1985)

Scott, John Oldrid (1841–1913). English architect. The second son of Sir George Gilbert *Scott, he carried out various works with his brother, George Gilbert *Scott, jun., including the spectacular Church of St John the Baptist (now the Roman Catholic Cathedral), Norwich (1884–1910). He added the German *Gothic *tracery spire to his father's Glasgow University (1887). Scott was responsible for the Church of St John the Baptist, Hythe, Kent (1869), but his masterpiece is the Greek Orthodox Cathedral of Western Europe, St Sophia, Moscow Road, Bayswater, London (1874–82), an essay in the *Byzantine style.

Dixon and Muthesius (1985)

Scott, Mackay Hugh Baillie (1865–1945). British architect. He was articled to Charles Edward Davis (1827–1902), City Architect of Bath. In 1889 he moved to Douglas, Isle of Man, and in 1893 established his own practice, specializing in domestic architecture that used *vernacular motifs, influenced partly by American work, notably in the *Shingle style, and partly by *Voysey. In 1895 he began to publish articles on house-design in *The Studio* which brought him to public notice, and his work caught the attention of Ernst Ludwig, reigning Grand Duke of Hesse from 1892 to 1918, who employed Scott to decorate and furnish the main rooms of his house at Darmstadt (1897). In 1901 he won the highest award in the House of an Art-Lover competition organized by *Koch, and published in *Meister der Innenkunst* (Master of Interior Design—1902)—*Mackintosh was awarded a special prize in the same competition. More commissions followed, including Blackwell, Bowness, Westmorland (1898–9), the White Lodge, Wantage, Berkshire (1898–9), and the White House, Helensburgh, Scotland (1899–1900). He built several model dwellings at Letchworth *Garden City, Hertfordshire, Hampstead *Garden Suburb, London, and Gidea Park, Essex, and his work was published and praised by *Muthesius in 1904. Other designs include Bill House, Selsey-on-Sea, Sussex (1907), Undershaw, Guildford, Surrey (1908–9), and Home Close, Sibford Ferris, Oxfordshire (1910).

Scott was essentially an *Arts-and-Crafts architect, drawing on the domestic vernacular architecture of England, and his best works were probably those produced between 1901 and 1911, when he seems to have been influenced by *Lutyens. His planning was ingenious, with spaces freely flowing into each other, and he designed fitted furniture to reduce clutter. This, with his tendency to simplify the exterior treatment of his buildings, gained him a spurious reputation as a proto-Modernist, but this is nonsense, as is clear from his *Houses and Gardens* (1906 and 1933) in which his ideas are cogently expressed. From 1919 he worked in partnership with Arthur Edgar Beresford (1880–1952), with whom he collaborated on the second edition of *Houses and Gardens* that specifically denounces the *International *Modernism *Pevsner and others claim he 'pioneered'.

Creese (1992); *DNB* (1993); Dixon and Muthesius (1985); Haigh (1995); Jervis (1984); Koch (1902); Kornwolf (1972); Miller (1989, 1992); Miller and Gray (1992); Muthesius (1979); Scott (1906, 1910, 1933); Slater (1995)

Scott, Michael John (1905–89). Irish architect. A devotee of *International Modernism since the 1930s, he was one of the first to build in the style of *Gropius and his associates in Ireland, as with St Lawrence's Community School, Drogheda, Co. Louth (1934), and the Scott House, Sandycove Point, Dunlaoghaire, Co. Dublin (1938). Among his large buildings were the Laois County Hospital, Portlaoise (1936–7), the Offaly County Hospital, Tullamore (1937), the Ritz Cinema, Athlone, Co. Westmeath (1940), the Central Bus Station, Store Street, Dublin (1950–3), the Radio Telefís Éireann Studios, Dublin (1959–61), and the Brown & Polson factory, Dublin (1959). From 1959 his style became influenced by that of *Mies van der Rohe, as with the Carroll Factory, Dundalk, Co. Louth (1970), and the Bank of Ireland Building, Baggot Street, Dublin (1968–73). From 1966 his firm became Scott, Tallon, Walker.

Casey and Rowan (1993); Emanuel (1994)

Scott Brown, Denise (1931–). Zambian-born American architect (née Lakofski). Educated in South Africa, London, and the USA, she worked with numerous architects, and married Robert *Venturi in 1967 with whom she had collaborated since 1965. As a partner of Venturi, Rauch, & Scott Brown from 1980, and principal in charge of urban planning and design, Venturi, Scott Brown, & Associates, since 1989, she made a considerable contribution to the success of the firm, and has had a distinguished academic career. She influenced Venturi's *Learning from Las Vegas* (1972) in which the idea was promulgated that simple sheds with applied decorations and large signs were more appropriate exemplars for the time than *International Modernism.

Emanuel (1994)

Scottish Baronial. C19 style evolved during the *Jacobethan Revival in England, with a distinctly Scottish flavour, incorporating *battlements, *tourelles, *machicolations and conical roofs. It was derived from medieval fortified tower-houses and castles, and among its instigators were William *Burn and his pupil David *Bryce. It was essentially an eclectic amalgam of the traditional fortified domestic architecture of Scotland and the asymmetrical compositions common during the vogue for the *Picturesque. The style was popular in Ulster, as in Scrabo Tower, Newtownards, Co. Down (1858), by *Lanyon & *Lynn, and several larger houses.

MacGibbon and Ross (1887–92)

scraped. 1. *See* sgraffito. **2.** Building from which all additions have been removed. The term was current during the *Gothic Revival when over-enthusiastic 'restorers' such as Sir George Gilbert *Scott would remove virtually everything so that a homogeneous *Middle Pointed building could be created. In the process, all *Perpendicular, *Jacobean, and *Georgian work would be ruthlessly ripped out. This widespread C19 tendency led William *Morris to found the Society for the Protection of Ancient Buildings (SPAB) in 1877 when Scott proposed to 'restore' Tewkesbury Abbey within an inch of its life. SPAB was known affectionately as 'Anti-Scrape'.

scratchwork. *See* sgraffito.

screen. 1. Partition of timber, stone, or metal, not part of the main structure of a church, to separate the *nave from the *choir (called variously *chancel-, *choir-, *Rood-screen, or *pulpitum), nave from choir- or chancel-*aisle (called *parclose screen), or to define a *chantry- or *mortuary-chapel, etc. **2.** Any other such screen, as in a medieval *hall, defining the *screens passage. **3.** Open *colonnade or *arcade around a *court, e.g. in a *cloister.

screen-façade. Non-structural façade disguising the realities of form, size, and structure of a building behind, as in the C13 screens on the west fronts of Lincoln and Salisbury Cathedrals.

screens passage. Space at one end of a medieval *hall between the *buttery and kitchen-doors and the *screen (placed to conceal activity behind), often with a *gallery over it. It is a common arrangement in Oxford and Cambridge colleges.

screen-wall. **1.** Solid unperforated wall hiding something, e.g. a court in front of a house. **2.** Retaining-wall in a garden, often decorated with *niches, etc. **3.** Wall carried up between columns, as in an Ancient Egyptian temple.

screw stair. Any *newel-, *vice, or circular stair wound about a newel or *pier.

scriptorium. Room assigned in a medieval conventual establishment for the copying and storage of texts.

scroll. **1.** Ornament composed of curved lines like *volutes, often of double flexure passing from one volute to another in series on a *band or *frieze, as in *Vitruvian or *wave*-scroll, but sometimes used as a terminal feature, e.g. handrail of a stair *balustrade. **2.** *Volute of a *console, *modillion, or *capital (e.g. in the *Composite, *Corinthian, and *Ionic *Orders). **3.** Type of *Gothic moulding with a deep scroll-like indentation under a hood-like top occurring on *hood-moulds, *labels, and *string-courses. **4.** *Torsade or spiral scroll.

scrolled heart. Classical ornament consisting of a repeated heart-shaped form in series formed by two parallel *bands of *wave-scrolls, often occurring on *friezes and borders.

scrolled pediment. Open-topped curved *pediment, its two S-shaped sides ending in *scrolls, also called *bonnet-scroll*, *bonnet-top*, *goose-neck*, or *swan-neck.

scrolling foliage. Architectural ornament of many types, usually combining naturalistic foliage and stems with stylized or even abstract patterns.

scroll-step. Bottom *curtail-step in a flight of stairs, having rounded ends or ends scrolled around the *newel-post, often echoing the *scroll of the handrail.

scroll-work. Any complex ornamental element composed of *scrolls or scroll-like forms, such as the C- and S-shapes found in *Baroque, *Celtic, *Jacobean, and *Rococo designs.

Scune, Christopher (*fl.* 1505–21). English mason. He succeeded John *Cole as Master-Mason at Louth, Lincolnshire, from 1505, and worked on the *steeple until it was almost finished (*c.*1512). Around 1508 he was appointed Master of the Masons at Durham Cathedral. From *c.*1514 he was at Ripon, Yorkshire, where he carried out all the new works at the *nave of the *Minster (now Cathedral), completed in 1520. He was presumably also responsible for the tower and tower-arch at Fountains Abbey, Yorkshire (1494–1526).

Harvey (1987)

Searles, Michael (1751–1813). English architect and surveyor. He had a large London practice devoted mostly to the design and building of residential developments south of the River Thames, where he was Surveyor to the Rolls Estate from 1783. His architecture was in a late-*Georgian style, distinguished by his originality of massing and simplicity of detail. His masterpiece is The Paragon, Blackheath (*c.*1793–1807), a series of semi-detached dwellings linked by *colonnades and set out on a *crescent. He also designed Clare House, East Malling, Kent (1793), with a complex series of circular, elliptical, and octagonal rooms. He was responsible for Surrey Square, Southwark, London (1792–3), and The Circus, Greenwich, London (1790–3).

Bonwitt (1987); Colvin (1995); Cruickshank (1985); Summerson (1988)

Secession. *See* Sezession.

Second Empire. Describes characteristic styles of Bonapartist France in 1852–70 during the reign of Emperor Napoleon III, or styles influenced by them. Essentially eclectic, the Second Empire was a period of revivals, especially *Baroque, *Empire, *François Ier, *Louis Seize, *Neo-Grec, and *Renaissance styles. The École des *Beaux-Arts encouraged *Historicism, as can be seen in the Paris created by *Haussmann for Napoleon III, and especially in the extensions to the Louvre, from 1853. High roofs, *lucarnes, and lush ornament gave French architecture of the period an opulent flavour that was widely appreciated and copied in the USA.

Second Pointed. Style of *Gothic architecture that emerged in the late C13, known in England as the *Decorated* style, and developed in C14, during which enrichment became more elaborate, with *diaper-work covering surfaces, and widespread use of the *ogee form. At the end of C13 *First Pointed period *plate-tracery* had evolved, then *bar-tracery* arranged in *Middle Pointed *Geometrical* patterns. *Nail-head and *dog-tooth ornaments were superseded by *fleuron and *ball-flower enrichment, while *crockets on *pinnacles and *canopies became profuse. Floral and foliate ornament were given naturalistic treatment, nowhere more so than in the enchanting leaves of the *Chapter House of Southwell *Minster, Nottinghamshire (*c*.1290—damaged in the late C20). The later phase of Second Pointed saw the development of *Curvilinear* or *Flowing* *tracery, the almost universal adoption of ogee or S-shaped curves, the appearance of *mouchette* or *dagger*-forms in tracery, and the invention of *Reticulated* or net-like tracery patterns formed by ogees. Windows became very large, and the flame-like forms of the *lights in the upper parts of traceried windows gave the name *Flamboyant to late (C15) elaborate (especially Continental) Gothic (which continued until the early C16). *Vaults acquired *intermediate* or *lierne* ribs, enabling very complex patterns (some star-shaped) to be created. Celebrated examples of Second Pointed work include the octagon and *Lady Chapel at Ely Cathedral (first half of C14) and the Percy tomb at Beverley, Yorkshire (with its elaborate canopy). Roofs remained steeply pitched.

Bony (1979); Parker (1850); Rickman (1848)

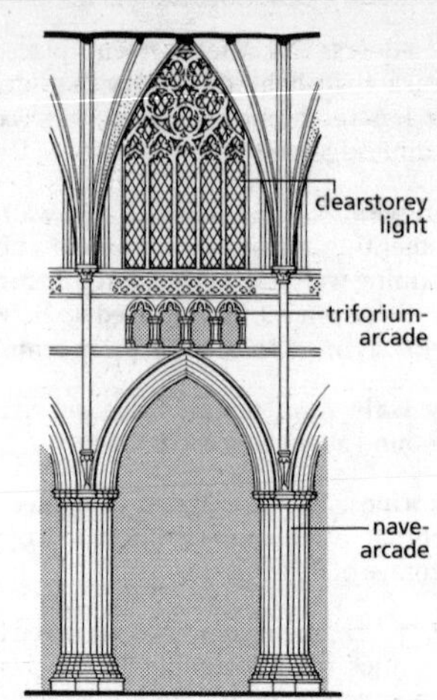

Second Pointed. Typical Second Pointed bay. (*JJS*)

secos, sekos. *Adytum, *cella, *naos, or *sanctuary in an Ancient *Egyptian temple.

section. Surface or portion obtained by a cut made through a structure or any part of a structure to reveal its profile, and/or interior. It may therefore show the outline of a moulding, and a drawing of an imaginary vertical cut through a building will show the *elevations of the walls of internal rooms, the convention being that all beyond the plane made by the intersection of the section is depicted in elevation. A *plan is therefore a section, the section-plane being horizontal, and shows the floors in elevation.

Sedding, John Dando (1838–91). English architect, one of the most inventive of his time. Trained by *Street, he later became much influenced by *Ruskin and *Morris, and his London office became a magnet for all those interested in the *Arts-and-Crafts movement. His assistant, Henry *Wilson, contributed much to his later designs. Among his early works are St Clement's Church, Boscombe, Bournemouth, Hampshire (1871—designed with his brother, **Edmund Sedding** (1836–68)), but his greatest buildings are in London. His Church of the Holy Redeemer, Exmouth Market, Clerkenwell, London (1887–8), is a remarkable *Italianate early *Renaissance Revival building, starkly simple, with a west front crowned by a *Tuscan *pediment. Henry Wilson added the *Early Christian Italian *Romanesque *campanile. Sedding and Wilson also designed St Peter's, Mount Park Road, Ealing, London (1889–93), an essay using the curvaceous forms of late *Gothic with originality and virtuosity. Their masterpiece is undoubtedly Holy Trinity, Sloane Street, London (1888–90), a work in which late-*Perpendicular Gothic, *Byzantine, *Second Pointed *tracery, Renaissance, *Art Nouveau, and Arts-and-Crafts elements are found. His nephew, **Edmund Harold Sedding** (d. 1921), was also an architect.

DNB (1917); Dixon and Muthesius (1985); Howell and Sutton (1989); Naylor (1971); Sedding (1891, 1893); Wilson *et al*. (1892)

Seddon, John Pollard (1827–1906). English *Gothic Revival architect who trained with T. L. *Donaldson. He was in partnership with John Prichard (1817–86) from 1853 to 1869, and with John Coates Carter (1859–1927) from

1884 to 1894. With Prichard he designed the *High Victorian *Gothic Ettington Park, Warwickshire (*c*.1856–62). Other works include University College, Aberystwyth, Wales (1864–90), the Powell Almshouses, Fulham, London (1869–70), St Peter's Church, Ayot St Peter, Hertfordshire (1874–5), St Paul's Church, Hammersmith, London (1880–8—with H. R. *Gough), and the lovely Church of St Catherine, Hoarwithy, Herefordshire (*c*.1874–85—in an Italian *Romanesque style with *Byzantine detail).

Darby (1983); Dixon and Muthesius (1985); Eastlake (1970)

sedile (*pl.* **sedilia**). Seat. The plural term is used to describe the series of stone seats (usually three) in a church set in the south wall of the *chancel, often crowned with elaborate *canopies and *pinnacles, used by officiating clergy. Sedilia, collectively known as the *prismatory*, may include the *piscina within a series of arched *niches.

sedilia. C14 Second Pointed *prismatory* type incorporating piscina and credence shelf, Church of St Swithun, Merton, Oxfordshire. (*After Parker*)

Segal, Walter (1907–85). Swiss-born architect of Romanian descent. He studied architecture at Delft, Zurich, and Berlin, where he met Bruno *Taut and became interested in *Expressionism. He settled in London, where he established a practice, publishing work in the 1940s and 1950s. His buildings include the Casa Piccolo, Ascona, Switzerland (1932), a housing estate, St Anne's Close, Highgate, London (1950), and a house at Rugby Road, Twickenham, Middlesex (1961). During the 1960s he became interested in low-cost housing, specializing in cheap *timber-framed construction. His Timber House, Main Street, Yelling, Huntingdonshire (1970), led to experiments in *community architecture for the Lewisham Self-Build Housing Association, London (1977–80), and it was in the field of cheap, easily constructed housing that he became famous.

Emanuel (1994); McKean (1988); Placzek (1982); *RIBA Journal*, ser. 3, 84 (1977), 284–95

segment. Plane figure contained by a straight line and part of the circumference of a circle. A *segmental arch* is therefore the shape of a segment, formed by its centre far below the springing-line of the arch.

Seidler, Harry (1923–). Vienna-born architect. He studied in Canada and at Harvard (under *Breuer and *Gropius), settled in Sydney, Australia, in 1948, and brought aspects of Breuer's style with him, as in the Rose Seidler House, Sydney (1949), and other designs firmly embedded in pre-War *International *Modernism in conformity with *Bauhaus principles. His work includes the Australia Square Tower, Sydney (1960–7), MLC Centre Tower, Sydney (1971), the Australian Embassy, Paris (1973–7), Hong Kong Club and Offices (1981), Riverside Centre, Brisbane (1983–6), Grosvenor Place, Sydney (1982), and the Shell Headquarters, Melbourne (1985). He also designed a large public housing-development in Vienna (1992–7), and a proposal for a 120-storey tower in Melbourne (1996).

Blake (1973); Emanuel (1994); Frampton and Drew (1992); Johnson, D. L. (1980); Seidler (1954, 1963)

Sellars, James (1843–88). Scots architect. He practised in Glasgow, and was in partnership (1872–88) with Campbell Douglas (1828–1910) after the latter's partnership (1860–9) with J. J. *Stevenson ended. Their finest works were the *Greek Revival St Andrew's Halls (1873), Belmont and Hillhead Church (1875), Belhaven Church (1877), and Kelvinside Academy (1877), all in Glasgow, the last influenced by the work of Alexander *Thomson. His work was either Grecian, *Free *Renaissance, or French *Gothic in style. His Glasgow International Exhibition Buildings (1887–8) were exotic and oriental, with a strong whiff of *Saracenic influence.

Gomme and Walker (1987); *Scottish Art Review*, 9/1 (1967), 16–19, and 9/2 (1967), 21–4; Williamson, Riches, and Higgs (1990); information from Prof. David Walker

Selva, Giovanni Antonio (1753–1819). Important Venetian architect. A pupil of *Temanza, he travelled in Italy, France, Austria, The Netherlands, and England before establishing a practice in Venice where he became a leading Neoclassicist, much influenced by Antonio Canova (1757–1822), the Neoclassical sculptor. His early works show a pronounced *Palladian influence, notably the Teatro La Fenice, Venice (1788–92—burnt 1996), but his later designs were powerful essays in *Neoclassicism, and include the grandly Roman Duomo, Cologna Veneta (1806–17), and Santissima Nome di Gesù, Venice (1815–34). He prepared works by *Chambers, *Perrault, and *Scamozzi for publication, wrote *Sulla voluta ionica* (On the *Ionic *Volute—1814), and taught *Jappelli.

Bassi (1936); Howard (1980); Meeks (1966); Mezzanotte (1966); Milizia (1785)

Semark, Henry (*fl.* 1482–d. 1534). English mason. From 1508 to 1515 he was one of the wardens of the masons at King's College *Chapel, Cambridge, and worked with *Wastell on the high *vault from 1512. He also contributed to the eastern chapels at Peterborough Cathedral, Cambridgeshire, and the Abbey and St James's Church, Bury St Edmunds, Suffolk. It has also been suggested he built the fan-vault under the tower of Fotheringhay Church, Northamptonshire (1528).

Harvey (1987)

semi-arch. Half-arch, e.g. flying *buttress.

semicircular arch. Arch with its head a half-circle.

semicircular dome. *Dome with a half-circular *section on its greatest diameter, i.e. half a sphere.

semi-column. *Engaged column.

semi-dome. *Hemi-dome, or quarter-sphere over *apses and *niches.

semi-elliptical arch. 1. Arch in the form of a half-ellipse. **2.** Three- or five-centred arch (*See* arch).

Semiological *or* **Semiotic School.** Semiotics (the science of signs and the study of how signs work) has been perceived as of major significance in architecture, for the built environment may be seen as a communicating system of signs and symbols. The school of thought that recognizes contemporary signs and symbols in design has been termed the Semiological or Semiotic School, and its protagonists include *Sert and *Venturi. It was influenced by *Semper.

Broadbent *et al.* (1980); Jencks (1971); Jencks and Baird (1969); Preziosi (1979)

Semper, Gottfried (1803–79). Hamburg-born German architect. He is said to have studied his subject under von *Gärtner in Munich (1825), though this is doubtful, but he definitely worked under *Gau in Paris from 1826, where he became acquainted with *Hittorff's theories of *polychromy in Ancient Greek architecture. From 1830 to 1834 he travelled widely, and in Berlin (1833) met *Schinkel who was enthralled by some of the new theories of polychromy. In 1834 Semper himself published *Vorläufige Bemerkungen über bemalte Architectur und Plastik bei den Alten* (Preliminary Remarks on Polychrome Architecture and Sculpture in Antiquity), a pamphlet dedicated to Gau, which created quite a stir. Partly as a result of this publication he was appointed Professor at the Dresden Academy of Fine Arts the same year. While at Dresden (1834–49) he designed some of his best buildings, including the *Hoftheater* (Court Theatre—1838–41, destroyed), a *Cinquecento Revival building with an exterior that made clear what were the internal arrangements, not uninfluenced by F. *Gilly's design for a National Theatre of the 1790s. This structure was replaced after a fire with the celebrated Opera House, also designed by Semper, and built 1871–8 under the direction of Semper's son, Manfred (1838–*c.*1914). It was destroyed in 1945 but rebuilt in the 1980s. It is arguably his greatest achievement, one of the most beautiful theatres in the world. He also designed the eclectic Synagogue (1838–40—destroyed) in a mix of *Byzantine, *Lombardic, *Moorish, and *Romanesque styles, with a polychrome interior of great richness; the Villa Rosa in a *Quattrocento manner (1839—destroyed); the sumptuous Oppenheim Palais in *Cinquecento Revival (1845–8—destroyed); and the *Gemäldegalerie* (Picture Gallery) attached to the *Zwinger (1847–54—restored). In 1835 he designed the polychrome 'Antique' rooms in the Japanese Palace, Dresden, which caused a sensation because of their vivid Classical beauty.

Having fallen foul of the Saxon authorities after the 1848–9 revolution, Semper went first to Paris and then to London, where he met

Henry Cole (1808–82), the energetic member of the 1851 Exhibition committee, in 1850. Semper gained valuable introductions through Cole, and designed the Canadian, Danish, Swedish, and Turkish sections for the 1851 Exhibition in the Crystal Palace. His connections and his book, *Wissenschaft, Industrie, und Kunst* (Science, Industry, and Art—1852) brought him to the attention of Prince *Albert, who was greatly interested in Semper's ideas about the relationship between architecture, design, industry, and education. Semper taught design while in London, but his most remarkable achievement was his detailing of the great funeral-car for the Duke of Wellington's exequies (1852). In 1855 Semper went to Zurich, teaching at the Polytechnic there until 1871. While there he designed the fine Zurich Polytechnikum building (1858–63—now ETH, Zurich), and made designs for the composer Richard Wagner's (1813–83) proposed (but unrealized) *Festspielhaus* (Festival Theatre—1864–7) for Munich which influenced the building (1876) designed by Otto Brückwald (1841–1904) that Wagner eventually succeeded in erecting in Bayreuth. Semper won the competition to design the Town Hall at Winterthur, Switzerland (1862), which was built 1865–70.

In 1851 Semper published *The Four Elements of Architecture* identified as hearth; platform; roof and its supports; and non-structured enclosure of textiles, etc. (keeping out the weather).

His *Der Stil in den technischen und tektonischen Künsten, oder praktische Ästhetik* (Style in the Technical and Structural Arts, or Practical Aesthetics—1861–3) proposed that artefacts and architecture acquire meaning from the ways in which they are made and from their functions, so Semper described materials and their uses, investigating how design motifs appeared and how those motifs were transferred from one material or context to others. In architecture, he noted how traditional and familiar forms retained traces of very early, primitive uses. In Semper's theory he conceived four essential categories of making artefacts: weaving (producing textiles and patterns); moulding (creating pottery from clay); carpentry (providing essential structures of timber, especially walls, partitions, and roofs); and masonry (involving building with stone for hearth, walls, piers, etc.). To the four processes he added working with metal, and came to the conclusion that the greater part of the forms used in architecture actually originated in those processes (now five) themselves. From these he derived his theory of style, and argued that architecture was reducible to the materials and processes associated with their uses. Semper believed that long before Man made a building he evolved patterns (e.g. in weaving, which he called *Urkunst*, or original art, meaning the source of art, providing prototypical models), and that these preceded the evolution of structural form, so ornament, far from being an afterthought, was actually more basic and symbolic than structure. He further developed his theory to postulate how political, religious, and social institutions create conditions by which appropriate and poetic expression is given to architectural forms. Thus architecture should be expressive of its purpose and the parts of a building easily distinguished. This is very far from the 'materialist' and 'functionalist' position he is often held to have adopted: in fact he stated that his conception of basic forms and their origins was the antithesis of the view which held that architecture was nothing more than evolved construction, a demonstration of statics and mechanics, and a pure revelation of material. For example, he noted that the patterns and ornaments used in producing textiles might reappear on walls constructed of other materials, while swags or garlands on several buildings often reappear as sculpted or painted elements on friezes, and in their transformations the materials used are of no great importance. Claims for Semper as a proto-Modernist are exaggerated, for he derided *Viollet-le-Duc as a materialist, and could not accept that monumental architecture could be created using iron structures (he did not approve of *Paxton's Crystal Palace). He was, however, an influence on Semiotics (*see* Semiological School).

The final years of Semper's architectural life were spent in Vienna, where his style became more florid than in his Dresden period. He collaborated with Karl von *Hasenauer on the design of the *Kunsthistorisches Museum* (Art History Museum) and the Natural History Museum (1872–81), which face each other across *Maria-Theresien-Platz*: they are fine essays in the Italian High Renaissance Revival, and were built under the direction of von Hasenauer. Semper and Hasenauer also worked on the *Burgtheater* (Castle Theatre), in an assured Renaissance Revival style

(1872–86) with a curved front reminiscent of the Dresden Opera House. The grandiose and triumphal *Neue Hofburg* (New Palace—1870–94), where the double columns of the east front of the Louvre, a Roman triumphal arch, and various Renaissance Revival motifs are quoted, was planned to harmonize the Imperial Palace with the new Museums, and formed part of a great Forum, the plan of which was essentially Semper's, although von Hasenauer was mostly responsible for the realization of the buildings.

Bernhard (1992); Ettlinger (1937); Fröhlich (1974); Herrmann (1984); Mallgrave (1996); Mallgrave and Herrmann (1988); Middleton and Watkin (1987); Pevsner (1972); Placzek (1982); Rykwert (1973); Semper (1851, 1860–3, 1884, 1966).

Senmut (*fl.* *c.*1520 BC–*c.*1480 BC). Ancient Egyptian architect and courtier. His career was associated with the reign of Queen Hatshepsut (1503 BC–1482 BC), and his masterpiece is the huge Mortuary Temple at Deïr-el-Bahari (*c.*1520 BC–*c.*1480 BC), with its great ranges of square columns, massive ramps joining the three main levels, and powerful symmetry. The complex includes columns that are seen by some as proto-*Doric, *Osiride features and numerous sphinxes. It is one of the finest and most original of all the buildings of the New Kingdom (1570–1085 BC), and has had a considerable impact on the *stripped *Classicism of C20, notably some of the works of *Speer and the *Rational architecture of *Grassi and *Rossi.

Cruickshank (1996); *Journal of the American Research Center in Egypt*, 6 (1967), 113–18; Lloyd and Müller (1986); Werbrouck (1949)

Sens, William of (*fl.* 1174–d. *c.*1180). French architect of the *Gothic *choir from the main *crossing eastwards, including the western *transept, Canterbury Cathedral, Kent (1174–84). As his name suggests, he had worked at Sens Cathedral (begun *c.*1140), which had some elements similar to those used at Canterbury, and he knew Notre-Dame, Paris, and other Gothic buildings in Rheims, Soissons, Arras, Cambrai, and elsewhere in North-West France, notably Notre-Dame-la-Grande at Valenciennes (1171). After he fell from the scaffolding in 1177 he was incapacitated and was succeeded by William the *Englishman who completed the choir *vaults, eastern transept, Trinity Chapel, circular chapel at the end of the choir called 'Becket's Crown' or the 'Corona' (1184), and introduced the *triforium-gallery previously used at Laon. Among influential motifs used by William of Sens were shafts of *Purbeck marble set against light Caen limestone, and *sexpartite vaults which draw the *bays into pairs. The prestige of Canterbury ensured the swift adoption of the new style throughout England.

Harvey (1987); *Journal of the Warburg and Courtauld Institutes*, 12 (1949), 1–15; Pevsner, *Buildings of England, North East and East Kent* (1976); Stubbs (1879); Webb (1965)

sepulchre. **1.** *Tomb, burial-place, building, vault, or excavation made for the interment of a human corpse. **2.** Receptacle for Relics in a Christian altar. **3.** *Easter sepulchre. **4.** *Holy Sepulchre.

serial. *See* additive.

serliana. Tripartite window, door, or *blind architectural feature consisting of a central opening with a *semicircular arch over it springing from two *entablatures each supported by two columns or *pilasters flanking narrower flat-topped openings on either side. Called a *Palladian* or *Venetian* window, it was a common motif in the works of *Palladio and was a feature much used in *Palladianism in C17 and C18 British architecture. It got its name as it was published in *Serlio's *L'Architettura* (1537–75), but probably originated with *Bramante.

serliana

Serlio, Sebastiano (1475–1554). Italian architect, theorist, and painter. He is remembered primarily as the compiler of *L'Architettura* (published in instalments (1537–75) and collected in one volume in 1584). The first part to appear was actually Book IV, called *Regole generale*

(1537), which outlined the later books, but, most significantly, codified and illustrated the five Roman *Orders of architecture. *L'Architettura* was an enormously important treatise, not only in terms of *Renaissance theory, but because it was a useful tome for architects, essentially because of its excellent illustrations and the fact that it was in a modern language. It was also a model for *Palladio's *Quattro Libri*. Book III (1540) disseminated the architecture of *Bramante and *Raphael, but in the work as a whole Serlio covered a huge range of Classical details (including *grotesques and *rustication), discussed the meaning and emotive power of Classical architecture, and, in *Livre extraordinaire* (published in French in 1551), provided illustrations of doorways, many of which were richly inventive fantasies, and influenced *Mannerism in Northern Europe.

In *c.*1514 he had been in Rome, where he worked under *Peruzzi, his principal tutor, from whom he acquired many drawings used subsequently in *L'Architettura*. Following the Sack of Rome (1527) he settled in Venice, then a major publishing centre, and an obvious place to live for someone engaged on writing a treatise on architecture. While in Venice he may have designed a few buildings. It is known he participated in the competition to renovate the 'basilica', Vicenza (1539), won by Palladio, whose design was not unlike that submitted by Serlio, and featured motifs similar to the *serliana, which is named after him.

He was called to *Fontainebleau, France, in 1541, where he advised on the design of the considerable building works at the château and designed the Salle du Bal there (1541–8—completed by de L'*Orme) in which the influence of Raphael is clear. His Grand Ferrare, the house for the Papal Legate to France at Fontainebleau (1541–8—mostly destroyed), was an important prototype of the *hôtel (town-house) in France for the next century, while his château of Ancy-le-Franc in Burgundy (1541–50), with its corner towers and central *court, shows the influence of *Maiano. Serlio's work undoubtedly informed Palladio, while his books had a considerable effect on many generations of designers, initially through the editions of Pieter Coeck (1502–50) in Northern Europe, and through the 1611 English edition of Robert Peake (*The Five Books of Architecture*), which was a major source from the time of Inigo *Jones to the flowering of the second Palladian Revival of *Burlington and *Campbell.

Art Bulletin, 24 (1942), 55–91, 115–55; Harris (1990); Heydenreich and Lotz (1974); Lewis and Darley (1986); Onians (1988); Placzek (1982); Rosenfeld (1978); Serlio (1584, 1611, 1663, 1964, 1996)

serpent. 1. In *Classical architecture, an emblem of healing, wisdom, and the Messenger (Hermes, St John, etc.), so part of the winged baton or *caduceus. **2.** Arranged in a circle, with tail in mouth, a serpent suggests immortality.

serpentine wall. *See* crinkle-crankle.

Sert, Josep Lluís (1902–83). Catalonian architect. He worked with Le *Corbusier and *Jeanneret-Gris (1929–32) before returning to Barcelona, where he built several structures, including an apartment-block (1931) and other works. He was involved in the organization of local groups associated with *CIAM, and designed the Spanish Pavilion at the Paris Exposition of 1937 in the *International Modern style. He settled in the USA in 1939 where he worked on numerous town-planning schemes (mostly in Latin America) using Le Corbusier's principles. Through the influence of *Gropius he was appointed Dean of the Faculty of the Graduate School of Design and Chairman and Professor of Architecture at Harvard (1953–69), founded a successful architectural practice in Cambridge, Mass., in 1955, and designed numerous buildings, including the Peabody Housing, Harvard (1963–5). He was responsible for the US Embassy, Baghdad, Iraq (1955–8), the Museum (Fondation Maeght) at St-Paul-de-Vence, Nice, France (1959–64), the Carmelite Convent, Cluny, France (1968–9), and the Miró Foundation Building, Barcelona (1972–5).

Borràs (ed.) (1975*a*); Emanuel (1994); Freixa (1979); van Vynckt (1993)

Servandoni, Giovanni Niccolò Geronimo (1695–1766). Florentine architect and painter, he trained under Giovanni Paolo Pannini (1691–1765), the pre-eminent C18 painter of real and imaginary views of Rome. He settled in Paris in 1724, where he designed stage-sets, firework-displays, and fêtes, and was also in demand for these skills in a number of European cities, including London, where he designed the fireworks in Green Park to celebrate the Peace of Aix-la-Chapelle (1749). In 1732 he won the competition to design the west front of the Church of St-Sulpice, Paris, based on an earlier project by Gilles-Marie *Oppenord. This colonnaded façade of two superimposed *Orders (perhaps influenced by the west front of St Paul's Cathedral in London) was nobler and more severe than anything contemporary built in France, and was recognized at the time as having affinities with the *Antique. It was certainly an early example of the Neoclassical reaction against *Rococo. He designed numerous altars and other fittings in various churches, and the interior of the sculpture-gallery at Brandenburg House, Hammersmith, London (*c.*1751—demolished—but illustrated in *Vitruvius Britannicus*, iv (1767), 28–9). His pupils included *Chalgrin and de *Wailly.

Colvin (1995); Hautecœur (1952); *Revue Universelle des Arts*, 12 (1860–1), 115–18; Rykwert (1980)

set-back. *See* buttress.

Seven Wonders of the Ancient World. Pyramids at Giza, Mausoleum at Halicarnassus, Temple of Artemis at Ephesus, Hanging Gardens and Walls of Babylon, Colossus of Rhodes, Pharos at Alexandria, and statue of Zeus at Olympia.

Severus (*fl.* AD 64). Supposedly the designer (with the engineer **Celer**) of Nero's *Domus Aurea* (Golden House), a complex only rediscovered early in C20 buried within the substructures of the *Thermae of Trajan on the slopes of the Oppian Hill, Rome (64–8). This huge palace contained a series of interior volumes of contrasting geometrical shapes illuminated by indirect and top lighting. It is unclear, however, if *columnar and trabeated forms were expunged from the interiors of the vaulted, domed, and *arcuated compartments, as many C20 commentators have claimed they were. Doubtless beguiled by the surviving bare walls and powerful, clear geometries, they have seen the octagonal hall and its ancillary spaces as original and as heralding a new aesthetic. *Concrete was used for the basic structure, *Orders were employed for the exterior, and it seems highly probable that Orders were used inside as well, as was the case in the vestibule of the 'Piazza d'Oro' at Hadrian's Villa at Tivoli (118–34). The fact that the rich marble and *stucco finishes have long since disappeared, and with them other internal embellishments (including Orders) does not mean they did not exist. There is no trace of stucco or marble finishes to the dome itself (though there is evidence that such finishes were employed on the walls and elsewhere), but it is likely that the space was covered by a ribbed structure, perhaps of bronze, from which fabric panels were suspended. As David Hemsoll has convincingly shown, the octagonal hall of the Golden House, 'far from representing a "revolution" in architecture', seems 'to have been a design that actually was deeply rooted in tradition . . . Modernist aesthetic criteria', such as efforts to define the design as 'an heroic attempt to come to terms with advances in building technology and to free architecture from the constraints of the past', are 'inaccurate and misleading'. Nero and his architects bettered their predecessors by exploiting tradition and established forms, and taking advantage of technological developments. After all, halls and dining-rooms with sophisticated geometries and spatial elaboration were known before Nero's time, and there is evidence from tombs and other building-types of similar ingenious geometrical arrangements before the *Domus Aurea* was built. Severus and Celer may also have played roles in the rebuilding of Rome after the fire of AD 64 and the drawing up of the building regulations that set the agenda. They also proposed a vast canal (begun but unfinished *c.* AD 60) linking Lake Avernus near the Bay of Naples to the Tiber. Severus and Celer's works are described by Tacitus (*c.* AD 55–*c.*117) and Suetonius (*c.* AD 70–*c.*160), neither of whom was particulary sympathetic to Imperial idea, yet both were impressed by the *Domus Aurea*, its grandeur, its rich interior décor, the bathing facilities, and the enchanting gardens.

Antiquity, 30 (1956), 209–19; *Architectural History*, 32 (1989), 1–17; Boëthius (1960); MacDonald (1965–86); Ward-Perkins (1981, 1986)

severy. 1. Structural *bay of a building, especially a *vault. **2.** Top of a *ciborium.

sex-. In composition, six. *Sexfid* is six-cleft; *sexfoil* is a window, opening, or panel with six *lobes or leaves; and *sexpartite* is parted in six, a term usually applied to vaulting. *See* vault.

Sezession. Term adopted by several groups of artists in Germany and Austria-Hungary in the 1890s, who seceded from the traditional, conservative academies to show their works. The first group was formed in Munich in 1892, but the most celebrated of the *Sezessionen* was founded in Vienna in 1897, and included the artist Gustav Klimt (1862–1918) and the architect Joseph Maria *Olbrich (1867–1908): the latter designed the exhibition-gallery and premises for the Vienna Sezession which made his reputation. The Sezessionists' enthusiasm for *Art Nouveau gave the name *Sezessionstil* to that style in Austria-Hungary.

Wiener Sezession (1972)

sgraffito. *Scratchwork* made by covering a wall with coloured plaster on top of which a white coat was applied on which a design was drawn then *scraped or scratched while wet to expose the colour below.

shaft. **1.** Body, fust, or trunk of a *colonnette or column extending from the top of the *base to the bottom of the *capital, in the Classical *Orders diminishing in size as it rises (*see* diminution, entasis). **2.** Slim cylindrical tall element, one of several clustered around a *pier and tied to it by *shaft-rings, often made of *Purbeck marble or some other material to contrast with the lighter stone of the pier. **3.** *Colonnette set at an angle of a building, e.g. junction of a *jamb with a wall, or framing a *reveal.

shaft-ring. *Annulet, *band of a *shaft, band-ring, bracelet, or corbel-ring.

sham. C18 term for a fake 'ruin' or other building erected for effect, e.g. the 'Sham Gothic' of Batty *Langley.

Clark (1974)

shaped gable. *Gable with sides formed of convex and concave curves, with a semi-circular top.

Sharawadgi, *also* **Sharawaggi.** First used by Sir William Temple (1628–99) in his *Upon the Gardens of Epicurus* (1685) to describe the Chinese way of planting in an apparently haphazard manner 'without any Order of Disposition of Parts', the term was popularized in mid-C18 England to describe irregularity, asymmetry, and the *Picturesque qualities of being surprising through graceful disorder, and so was applied to irregular gardens, known as Chinese, or as *les jardins anglo-chinois*, embellished with Chinese bridges with *fretwork railings and vermilion-painted *pagodas shaded by weeping willows. *Sharawadgi* was also used to describe irregular, asymmetrical, informal designs in town-planning circles in the 1940s.

Pevsner (1968)

Shaw, John (1776–1832). English architect. He was apprenticed to the elder *Gwilt before setting up his London practice in 1798. In 1803 he became Surveyor to the Eyre Estate in St John's Wood, and exhibited a proposal (unrealized) for a 'British Circus' of detached and semi-detached houses arranged on either side of a circular road a mile in circumference. Thereafter he and his son, **John Shaw** (1803–70), became developers of suburbs set out on irregular winding roads. He carried out *Gothic additions at Christ's Hospital, London (1820–32—demolished), a style he also employed at Newstead Abbey, Nottingham, which he remodelled (1818–*c.*1830). He is best remembered for the Church of St Dunstan-in-the-West, Fleet Street, London (1831–2), completed by his son. The detail is an early example of archaeologically correct *Gothic Revival. The younger Shaw became Surveyor to Eton College in *c.*1825 and designed the *Tudor Gothic buildings at Weston's Yard there, also developing the Chalcots Estate, Chalk Farm, London (1840–5), including Adelaide Road and Eton College Road. He was employed by the Church Building Commissioners and published *A Letter on Ecclesiastical Architecture* . . . (1839) in which he proposed the *Romanesque style should be used for churches because it would be cheaper than the Gothic or Classical styles. His work in 'Norman Revival' included Holy Trinity, Gough Square, London (1837–8—demolished), Christ Church, Watney Street, Stepney, London (1840–1—demolished), and St Peter's, Woodford, New Road, Walthamstow, Essex (1840), although the last was a vaguely *Early Christian *Italianate *Rundbogenstil. He designed a number of buildings in a revived *Renaissance style that pre-empted the *Wrenaissance of the end of the century. His best buildings are at Wellington College, near Sandhurst, Berkshire (1855–9—a mixture of *Louis XIII, *Wren's work at Hampton Court Palace, and other Anglo-Dutch elements pre-empting *Nesfield's *Queen Anne style at Kinmel Park, Denbighshire some 12 years later), and Goldsmith's College, formerly the Royal Naval School, Lewisham Way, Deptford, London (1843—an astonishing, restrained design of decidedly Italian character that would easily pass for a building of *c.*1900).

Clarke (1966); Colvin (1995); *DNB* (1917); Dixon and Muthesius (1985); Summerson (1988)

Shaw, Richard Norman (1831–1912). Scots-born architect, the son of an Irish father and a Scots mother. A pupil of William *Burn from 1849, he later travelled (1854–6) and published *Architectural Sketches from the Continent* (1858). He joined *Salvin's office in 1856 before accepting (1858) a position with *Street in succession to Philip *Webb. He was influenced by A. W. N. *Pugin's writings, but most of all by Street: he acknowledged the latter as his mentor. In 1862–3 he set up in practice with Eden *Nesfield, specializing in domestic and commercial work, each influencing, but working independently of, the other.

Shaw's early work included the Church of Holy Trinity, Bingley, Yorkshire (1866–8), a tough essay in the *Gothic Revival, much influenced by Street's designs, but the most important aspect of Shaw's output was his domestic work, in which the Gothic Revival, the *Picturesque, *vernacular architecture, and the *Domestic Revival played their parts, influenced by designs of *Butterfield, *Devey, Nesfield, and Street. Shaw was most successful in refining and applying elements derived from traditional houses of the Sussex Weald (including tall brick chimneys, much tile-hanging, and mullioned windows with leaded lights) to large country-houses. His early work includes Glen Andred (1866–8) and Leys Wood (1868–9—mostly destroyed), both near Groombridge, Sussex, Grim's Dyke, Harrow Weald (1870–2—perhaps Shaw's finest interpretation of the *Old-English version of the Domestic Revival), and the enormous and eclectic Cragside, Rothbury, Northumberland (1870–84). These buildings, with their use of local materials and vernacular details had a profound effect on the evolution of domestic architecture and on the *Arts-and-Crafts movement in general. Shaw's houses were published in *The Building News*, thus making his work widely known on both sides of the Atlantic, and influencing development of the *Shingle style in the USA.

Both Shaw and Nesfield drew on C17 domestic architecture of The Netherlands and the William and Mary period in England (1688–1702), so their work of the 1870s began to be called the *Queen Anne style. Shaw's chief works in this style were New Zealand Chambers, Leadenhall Street, London (1871–3—demolished), Lowther Lodge, Kensington (1873), 6 Ellerdale Road, Hampstead (1875–6—Shaw's house), Cheyne and Swan Houses, Chelsea (1875–7), and the celebrated Artists' Houses, 8 Melbury Road (1875–6), 118 Campden Hill Road (1876–8), and 31 Melbury Road (1876–7), Northern Kensington. Shaw also worked at Bedford Park, Turnham Green, Chiswick, London, where he designed the church, a club, an inn, shops, and several small houses (1877–80). The Church of St Michael and All Angels, Bedford Park (1879–80), was eclectic, mixing late Gothic Revival with Arts-and-Crafts detail, and in the commercial architecture of the period (New Zealand Chambers and some of the buildings at Bedford Park), Shaw used the device of the *Ipswich window that was to be widely copied and paraphrased. Around this time he published *Sketches of Cottages and Other Buildings* (1878).

Between 1879 and 1889 Shaw was assisted by *Lethaby, and the character of his work began to change, as in the huge Albert Hall Mansions, Kensington Gore, London (1879–86), the first block of flats in the new red-brick free style that was to be so influential for this type of development. Then there was the very refined 170 Queen's Gate, Kensington, London (1888–90), with early C18 features (such as the *eaves-cornice and tall *sash-windows) and a *Wrenaissance doorcase, the whole ensemble looking forward to a type of *Colonial *Georgian revival. At the Alliance Assurance Offices, St James's Street, London (1881–8), he introduced a hybrid style incorporating *Renaissance scrolled gables, mullioned and transomed windows, and brick façades with bands of stone. Striped too were the elevations of New Scotland Yard, London (1887–90 and 1901–7), in which many eclectic elements were mixed, including the *tourelles of smaller French châteaux, *Scottish Baronial architecture, and, a new note, the *Baroque doorcases and *aedicules in the gables. Similar themes occur at the offices for the White Star Line, Liverpool (1895–8—with J. F. *Doyle). Later, the grand manner of *Classicism became more pronounced, as with Bryanston House, Dorset (1889–94—with its great columns and Baroque details), Chesters, Northumberland (1890s), the Alliance Assurance Office, St James's (1901–5—opposite the earlier block mentioned above), and the huge Piccadilly Hotel, Piccadilly, London (early 1900s).

Two other churches by him deserve mention: All Saints', Compton, Leek, Staffordshire (1885–7—a wide, broad, church incorporating much personal interpretation of *Second Pointed and *Perpendicular detail, *nave-arcades similar to those of the Bedford Park church, and some furnishings by Lethaby), and All Saints', Batchcott, Richard's Castle, Shropshire (1890–3—again interpreting Second Pointed and Perpendicular detail, some of which was derived from local examples, the whole composed to give the impression of having been established and altered over a period). In both these works the influences of *Bodley and of George Gilbert *Scott jun. were apparent.

When he retired in 1896, Shaw was hailed as the leading British architect. In 1892 he co-edited (with T. J. *Jackson) *Architecture: A Profession or an Art*, in which the proposals to make the registration of architects compulsory were denounced. His last works were Portland House, London (1907–8—one of the first buildings with a *reinforced-concrete frame in England), and studies for the new elevations for the Quadrant, Regent Street, London (1905–8—most unrealized, but finally built to designs by *Blomfield and others).

Blomfield (1940); Dixon and Muthesius (1985); Gray (1985); Saint (1976); Sheppard (1973, 1975)

Shchusev, Aleksei Viktorovich (1873–1949). Russian architect and scholar. Trained in St Petersburg and Paris, he established his practice in St Petersburg, specializing in ecclesiastical work. He designed the Russian Pavilion at the International Exposition, Venice (1913–14), and the Kazan Railway Station, Moscow (1912–48), in both of which he employed *vernacular themes and plentiful embellishments derived from C17 *Baroque styles. After the Revolution he settled in Moscow, where he had a successful academic career. In 1924–30 he designed his best-known work, the powerful stripped Neoclassical *mausoleum of Lenin, reminiscent of stark Ancient Egyptian architecture, with its unadorned *columnar and *trabeated architecture set on blocky *podia, the whole forming a stepped pyramidal composition.

Shchusev was an important promoter of the official architectural style of the Stalin era, and his architectural style set precedents for many buildings throughout the Soviet Union. A good example of his work is the Hotel Moskva, Moscow (1930–5).

Kopp (1978); Placzek (1982); Sokolov (1952); van Vynckt (1993)

shed-roof. *Lean-to or monopitch roof abutting a higher element, as in the case of an *aisle-roof and a *clearstorey.

Shekhtel', Fedor Osipovich (1859–1926). Russian architect. He was an important designer of buildings in the *Art Nouveau style, and also exploited iron, glass, and *reinforced concrete in his works which include the sumptuous *Gothic Revival house for Z. G. Morozova, Spiridonovka Street, Moscow (1893–6—very badly damaged by fire, 1995). He was responsible for the Russian Pavilions (which drew on traditional roof-forms to some extent, and were regarded as 'barbaric' by those who saw them) for the International Exhibition in Glasgow (1901), and the following year he was the leading light behind the 'New Style' Exhibition in Moscow (1902–3), where designs by *Mackintosh and *Olbrich (among others) were shown. At the same time he designed the Yaroslavl' Railway Station, Moscow (1902–3), a curious mixture of Art Nouveau details, vaguely *Historicist roof-forms, and *Classicism, that was rather ungainly taken as a whole. His Mansions for S. P. Ryabushinsky, Malaya Nikitskaya (1900–2), and A. I. Derozhinkaya, Shtatny Lane (1901–2), both in Moscow, stand favourable comparison with any other comparable European work of the time. The former has an extraordinary Art Nouveau staircase and hall around which the house is planned, and the latter has elements drawn from Gothic, the Vienna *Sezession, and especially motifs favoured by Otto *Wagner and his circle. The last influence was overt in the Villa Kshesinskaya, St Petersburg (1904–6). The newspaper offices for *Utro Rossii*, Moscow (1907), also had Viennese flavours. Much of his work immediately before the 1914–18 war was elegant and sometimes austere, while around 1910 he began to introduce a severe *Neoclassicism to Moscow (e.g. his own house, Bol'shaya Sadovaya (1909–10) and the headquarters of the Trading Society (1909–11). More than 50 fine buildings by him survived the Soviet regime, but are now under threat from the pressures caused by the need for office-accommodation in Moscow in the late C20.

Borisova and Kazhdan (1971); Kirichenko (1975); *Perspectives on Architecture*, 24 (Aug.–Sept. 1996), 58–61; Raeburn (1991)

shell. 1. *Concrete structure evolved from work by *Candela, *Freyssinet, *Maillart, *Nervi, *Nowicki, *Saarinen, and *Torroja, and derived from the exemplar of an egg-shell. The *stressed skin or shell operates with the frame to form a strong structural system. **2.** Scallop. **3.** Ornament called *coquillage in which shells and mother-of-pearl pieces are used for effect in *grottoes, *marine ornament, *nymphaea, etc.

Joedicke (1963); Lewis and Darley (1986); Papworth (1887)

Shepherd, Edward (d. 1747). English architect and builder. He completed Cannons, the great house for James Brydges, 1st Duke of Chandos (1673–1744), in Middlesex (1723–5—demolished). He carried out building operations for the Duke in London and elsewhere, and appears to have attempted to build a *palace-fronted range in Grosvenor Square, London (*c*.1728–30—demolished). He built houses in Cavendish Square (1724–8), Brook Street (1725–9), St James's Square (1726–8), and South Audley Street (1736–7), and developed Shepherd's Market and adjoining streets in Mayfair (*c*.1735), all in London, but little of his work survives. Other works by him include Great Stanmore Rectory, Middlesex (1725), and monuments in the De Grey Mausoleum, Church of St John the Baptist, Flitton, Bedfordshire (1739–40).

Collins Baker (1949); Colvin (1995)

Sheppard, Richard Herbert (1910–92). British architect. He established Richard Sheppard, Robson, & Partners with Geoffrey Robson (1918–91) in London. The firm's work includes Churchill College, Cambridge (1959–73), the School of Navigation, University of Southampton (1959–66), buildings for Loughborough University, Leicestershire (1961–6), Digby Hall, University of Leicester (1958–62), West Midlands College of Education, Gorway, Walsall, Staffordshire (1964–72), buildings for Imperial College, South Kensington, London (1964–8), the City University, St John Street, Clerkenwell, London (1969–76), and the Lymington Road Housing Development, Hampstead, London (1978).

Emanuel (1994); personal information

Shereff, John (*fl.* 1528–35). English master-mason who completed the upper two stages of the Great Gate, Trinity College, Cambridge (1528–35). He may have undertaken other works in Cambridgeshire and London, but evidence is lacking.

Harvey (1987)

shingle. 1. Thin timber (normally oak or cedarwood) slab cut to standard sizes, with parallel sides and one end thicker than the other, used instead of slates or tiles to cover roofs or clad walls. Called *scandulae* by the Romans. **2.** In the plural, small stones for rough-cast rendering, gravel paths, or aggregate in a *concrete mix.

Shingle style. USA version of the *Old English style of the *vernacular or *Domestic Revival of the 1870s. In England, tile-hung walls and *gables were commonly incorporated in designs of the period, and in America *shingles were substituted. In 1876 the centenary of the American Revolution encouraged a revival of *Colonial *Georgian domestic architecture, with shingle *cladding, *gambrel roofs, and other features which were mixed with the *dormers, *oriels, and elements of the *Queen Anne style popular in England. The result was the Shingle style. Good examples include the Sherman House, Newport, RI (1874–5), and Stoughton House, Cambridge, Mass. (1892–3), both by H. H. *Richardson, and Low House, Bristol, RI (1886–7), by *McKim, Mead, & White. Many houses in the Shingle style had ingenious open planning inside, anticipating later work by Frank Lloyd *Wright and *Greene & Greene.

Harmon (1983); Scully (1971, 1974, 1989)

Shinohara, Kazuo (1925–). Japanese architect. His best-known works are the house in Uehara, Tokyo (1975–6), with its massive *truss-like structure inside, a development of the free-standing columnar theme first used in the 'House in White', Tokyo (1966). His designs are characterized by a powerful expression of architectural elements which he uses in symbolic ways, as in the 'Unfinished House', Tokyo (1970). His work gradually became more expressive and extreme, as in the fractured *segments of the Karuizawa house (1975). He has attempted to obliterate all sentimentality from his designs, and moved away from his early interest in Japanese *vernacular traditions (e.g. the Tokyo Institute of Technology Centennial Hall (1987)). He published *Residential Architecture* (1964), *Theories on*

Residences (1970), *16 Houses and Architectural Theory* (1971), and much else.

Emanuel (1994); Shinohara (1976); van Vynckt (1993)

shoulder. **1.** *Bracket or *console, also called *shoulder-* or *shouldering-piece*. **2.** *Crossette. **3.** Projection narrowing the top of an aperture, as in a *shouldered* arch (*see* arch).

Shreve, Raymond (1877–1946). *See* skyscraper.

shrine. **1.** *Fereter, often of great architectural magnificence, for Relics. **2.** Building, *feretory*, or *shrine-chapel* in which the Relics are deposited.

Shute, John (d. 1563). Author of the first treatise on architecture in English, *The First and Chief Groundes of Architecture* (1563), based on his travels in Italy in the 1550s, and drawing heavily on *Serlio and *Vitruvius. Primarily dealing with the *Orders, its illustrations (probably by Shute himself) are important for their clarity and originality, and the book went into further editions (1579, 1584, 1587). It is difficult to assess its influence, but it was probably a source for many details.

Harris (1990); Lewis and Darley (1986); Shute (1563); Summerson (1993)

shutter. Sliding, rolling, or folding door to close a window on the outside or the inside.

shuttering. *See* formwork.

Shutze, Philip Trammell (1890–1982). American architect. He was a partner in the firm of Hentz, Adler, & Shutze, New York, from 1926. His works included the English Chambers House, Atlanta, Ga. (1930), the Hebrew Benevolent Congregation Temple, Atlanta (1931–2), and the Whitehead Memorial Annex, Emory University, Atlanta (1945). His masterpiece was the Citizen's and Southern National Bank, Atlanta (1929), with a stunning interior of Roman grandness. Shutze was called 'America's Greatest Living Classical Architect' in 1977. His work deserves more attention than it has been given hitherto.

Dowling (1989)

Sibbald, William (d. 1809). Scots architect and builder. He was Superintendent of Public Works in Edinburgh from 1790 until his death. He worked with Robert *Reid on the layout of the first extension to the New Town. He designed Lady Yester's Church, Edinburgh (1803), in an early version of the *Jacobean style. His son, **William Sibbald** (d. 1823), built the Bank of Scotland on The Mound, Edinburgh (1802–6), to designs by Reid and Richard Crichton (*c*.1771–1817).

Colvin (1995); Gifford, McWilliam, and Walker (1984); Youngson (1966)

Siccard von Siccardsburg, August (1813–68). Austrian architect. He studied in Vienna, where he met Eduard van der *Nüll, with whom he later travelled to Italy, France, Germany, and England. They were appointed Professors at the Akademie in Vienna (1844), and thus influenced later Viennese architects. With van der Nüll he designed several Viennese buildings, including the Arsenal and *Kommandantur-Gebäude* (1848–55), but they are best known for the Opera House on the *Ringstrasse* (1861–9) in a free *Renaissance style. They planned a huge complex for the Vienna International Exhibition of 1873, eventually realized with buildings designed by *Hasenauer. Siccard died shortly after van der Nüll took his own life.

Auer (1885); Pevsner (1976)

side. *Horn of an altar, that on the south being the *Epistle side and that on the north the *Gospel side.

side-chapel. Chapel to the side of an *aisle or *choir in a church.

side-light. *Margin-light or window to the side of a door or window, usually very narrow.

sill. *See* cill.

Siloé, Diego de (*c*.1495–1563). Spanish *Renaissance architect and sculptor of Flemish descent. He travelled in Italy before returning to Burgos in 1519 where he designed a number of works including the symmetrical *Escalera Dorada* (Golden Staircase) in the Cathedral (1515–23) derived in part from *Bramante's work at the Belvedere Court in the Vatican (begun 1505), although much encrusted in a plethora of *grotesque ornament, probably influenced by the works of *Michelangelo and *Raphael. In 1528 he was called to Granada to complete the Church of San Jéronimo, and then to design the Cathedral in the Renaissance style, with its huge domed *chancel, which, with *ambulatory and chapels, suggests a *martyrium or sepulchre (probably based on the Church of the Holy Sepulchre in Jerusalem), the ensemble cleverly joined to a five-aisled *basilica. This brilliant design was to be influential.

Other works by Siloé include the arcaded courtyard of the Colegio Fonseca, Salamanca (1529–34), and the plans for San Salvador, Ubeda (1536—built by Andrés de Vandelvira (*fl.* 1536–60) with a *rotunda owing much to the precedent of Siloé's work at Granada Cathedral). He is regarded as a master of the *Plateresque style.

Chueca Goitia (1953); Kubler and Soria (1959); Placzek (1982); Rosenthal (1961); van Vynckt (1993)

Silva, Domingos Parente da (1836–1901). Portuguese architect. He was the designer of the fine Municipal Chambers, Lisbon (1865–80), in a *Renaissance style with a strong French influence, and built other important buildings in the capital.

Baedeker, *Spain and Portugal* (1913)

Silvani, Gherardo (1579–1675). Prolific Florentine architect and sculptor. He designed the interior of the Salviati Chapel, Santa Croce, Florence (1611), one of the finest examples of late-*Renaissance architecture in the city. He also designed the assured *cloister at the Church of San Frediano in Castello (1628) and the interior of the Church of San Gaetano (from 1628), including the *sacristy (1633–48) in which the influence of his master *Buontalenti is clear. For San Gaetano he also designed the robust and assured *Baroque façade (1628–49).

Paatz and Paatz (1940–54); Papworth (1887); Placzek (1982); Venturi (1967)

sima. *See* cyma.

simatium. *See* cymatium.

Simmons, Charles Evelyn (1879–1952). *See* Field, Horace.

Simón de Colonia (*c.*1450–1511). *See* Colonia Family.

Simonetti, Michelangelo (1724–81). Italian architect. He worked at the Vatican where he redesigned (with *Camporese) the Venetian Museum and Museo Pio Clementino as a master-work of *Neoclassicism. His use of exposed brickwork, *Antique elements, and clearly expressed structure gave his work great authority comparable to the architecture of *Piermarini in Milan. The Sala Rotonda in the Museum (from 1776) is especially fine.

Meeks (1966); Middleton and Watkin (1987)

Simon the Mason (*fl.* 1301–d. 1322). English master-mason. He was probably in charge of the building of the *nave at York *Minster from 1291, so had control of this virtually from start to finish.

Harvey (1987)

Simpson, Archibald (1790–1847). Scots architect. He was responsible for many distinguished buildings in Aberdeenshire. His *Greek Revival designs include the Aberdeen Music Hall or County Assembly Rooms (1820–2) and Crimonmogate, a country-house at Lonmay (*c.*1825), both built of fine granite masonry that gives them a monumental severity. Thainston House, near Kintore (*c.*1847), was in a simplified Classical style, and he also experimented with *castellated architecture (Castle Forbes (1814–15)), *Gothic (Old Aberdeen Free Church (1845–6)), and *Tudor Gothic (The Gordon Schools, Huntly (1839)). Other works include the handsome Greek Revival Church of St Giles, Elgin, Morayshire (1827–8).

Colvin (1995)

Simpson, John Anthony (1954–). English architect. Having rejected *International Modernism he sought to show how the Classical language of architecture could be used in buildings that satisfied contemporary economic, technical, and functional requirements. His work is derived largely from late-*Georgian sources, and he made his name with Ashfold House, West Sussex (1991), influenced by *Soane's architecture. Simpson had considerable influence in making the public aware of the *New Classicism in the 1980s, especially with the exhibition *Real Architecture* at the Building Centre, London (1988). His works at Gonville and Caius College, Cambridge (1993–8), including a dining-hall and reading-rooms for the Fellows, have added lustre to his reputation. In 1998 his firm won the competition to redevelop the Queen's Gallery and Kitchens at Buckingham Palace, London (due for completion 2000).

Emanuel (1994); Powers (1987); personal knowledge

Sinan (1489–1578 *or* 1588). Prolific and brilliant master-architect of the Ottoman Empire, holding responsibilities for an enormous range of public works. One of his greatest buildings was the Süleymaniye *Mosque in Istanbul (1550–7) which shows how much he had absorbed of *Byzantine forms and construction, especially those of the Church of Hagia Sophia, but Sinan improved and rationalized the system of buttressing for the central dome, and clarified the subsidiary elements. However, the huge complex at Selimiye, Edirne, Turkey (1569–74), in which domed structures and rigorous geometry are thoroughly exploited, is even more successful as a solution to the problem of providing a large domed centralized volume, for the secondary volumes are more closely related to the large domed space, with a logic and clarity carried to their ultimate conclusions. Sinan is credited with around 460 buildings, including mosques, hospitals, schools, public buildings, baths, palaces, bridges, tombs, and grand houses. Among his finest tombs are the *mausoleum of Selim II (1577) and Süleyman I (the latter an octagonal domed structure, exquisitely decorated with tiles, in the Süleymaniye complex). His work was an extraordinary felicitous synthesis of styles in which Byzantine and Turkish themes merged, and demonstrates his mastery of complicated planning problems, notably in the larger developments.

Egli (1976, 1997); Goodwin (1971); Gurlitt (1907–12); Kuran (1987); Placzek (1982—contains a very comprehensive bibliography); Stratton (1972); Strazzullo (1972); Vogt-Göknil (1993)

singing-gallery. 1. Elevated choir-loft, *tribune-gallery, or *cantoria for the singers in a church. **2.** *Rood-loft.

single frame. Floor of one tier of common joists, without girders or binding-beams, or roof with one tier of common rafters, without principals, but stiffened with collar-beams, diagonal braces, etc.

single-hung. Window having only one opening *sash.

single-pile house. Type of house-plan one room deep, contrasted with a *double-pile plan.

Sirén, Heikki (1918–). Finnish architect, in partnership with his wife, Kaija (1920–), since 1949. Their work has been seen as offering paradigms of Scandinavian Modernism, characterized by simplicity and formality. Their Chapel at the Technical College, Otaniemi (1957), was much admired when completed, with its minimalist altar and cross set against a large window with a background of pine-trees. Other works include the Otsonpesä Linked Houses, Tapiola (1959), Brucknerhaus Concert Hall, Linz, Austria (1974), and the Granite House, KOP Kamppi Offices, Helsinki (1985).

His father, **Johan Sigfrid Sirén** (1889–1961), was a distinguished architect. Among his buildings the extension to *Engel's University of 1810 (completed 1931) and the Parliament Building (also completed 1931), both in Helsinki, confirmed him as a leader of Nordic *Neoclassicism between 1918 and 1939. His Bank of Finland, Vaasa (1943–52), is a noble work of *stripped *Classicism.

Bruun and Popovits (1978); Doumato (1980, 1980*a*); *Monatshefte für Baukunst und Städtebau*, 22/1 (1938), 33–40; Paavilainen (1982)

SITE (Sculpture in the Environment). American multi-disciplinary architectural group launched in 1969 by James *Wines, and best known for the Best Products chain of stores, including the Peel Project, Richmond, Va. (1971–2), the Indeterminate Façade, Houston, Tex. (1974–5), the Tilt Showroom, Towson, Md. (1976–8), and the Inside/Outside Showroom, Milwaukee, Wis. (1984). In these, 'broken' walls, whole fronts lifted as though they are cardboard, and other curious elements have made their buildings notorious. Other works include Avenue 5, Expo 92, Seville, Spain (1992), and several projects in which ecology was well to the fore.

Jodidio (1993, 1996); SITE *et al.* (1980); Wines (1987); Wines *et al.* (1989)

Sitte, Camillo (1843–1903). Austro-Hungarian architect and town-planner, a pupil of *Ferstel, and an admirer of William *Morris and Gottfried *Semper. His importance lies in one work, his well-illustrated *Der Städtebau nach seinen künstlerischen Grundsätzen* (Town-Planning according to Artistic Principles—1889), which emphasized the need to design the urban fabric with aesthetics and composition in mind, and ran into several editions, with translations in French (1902), Russian (1925), Spanish (1926), English (1945 and 1965), and Italian (1953). It was one of the first major books to analyse what became known as *townscape. His work was rediscovered in the 1960s when the reaction against the destruction of towns as a result of the dogmas of Le *Corbusier, *CIAM, and *International Modernism gained momentum. He designed the *Renaissance Revival *Mechitaristenkirche*, Vienna (1873–4), and a few other buildings in other parts of the Austro-Hungarian Empire.

Collins and Collins (1986); Placzek (1982); Sitte (1965); van Vynckt (1993)

Sixdeniers, C. (*fl.* 1530s). Builder of the *Ancien Greffe* (Old Registry), Brugge (Bruges), Belgium, of 1535–7, in which *Gothic elements were freely mixed with *Renaissance motifs.

Baedeker, *Belgium* (1931)

Sixteen Principles of Urbanism. Agreed with Moscow in 1948, the Sixteen Principles were drawn up in Communist East Germany as a radical alternative to the Le *Corbusier-*CIAM-*Athens-Charter dogmas so widely accepted in the West after 1945. Among the Principles were the rejection of urban motorways cutting swathes through the urban fabric, the abandonment of zoning that played havoc in Western cities, and the re-establishment of the urban block and traditional street as essentials, all of which are being reassessed at the end of C20.

Kostof (1995); Personal knowledge from the Ministry of Culture of the former DDR

Siza (Vieira), Alvaro Joaquim de Melo (1933–). Portuguese architect. He commenced practice in 1958, and designed the Boa Nova Seaside Restaurant and the Swimming-Pool, Matosinhos (1958–65). Responding to the topography, he designed several well-publicized houses, including the Alcino Cardoso House, Moledo do Minho (1971), and the Beires House, Póvoa dó Varzim (1973–6). His Banks (e.g. the Banco Borges e Irmao, Succursal de Vila do Conde (1978–86)), display aspects of *International Modernism and Italian *Rationalism. His housing complexes in Oporto, including the São Victor scheme (1974–7), have been admired for their simplicity. More recently, his granite-clad Galician Centre for Contemporary Art, Santiago de Compostela, Spain (1988–95), set on a triangular site in the Convent of Santa Domingo de Boneval, has attracted critical acclaim.

Emanuel (1994); Jodidio (1996*a*); Lampugnani (1988)

skeleton. *Personification of Death, common in funerary architecture.

Weber (1914)

skeleton-frame. Structural *frame of *concrete, metal, or timber supporting the floors, roof, and exterior treatment. The spaces are filled with a lighter material or the entire structure is protected by an external *cladding or *curtain-wall, fixed inside or outside the frame. *See* skyscraper.

Blaser (1980)

skew. Anything that slopes or is set obliquely, e.g. top of a medieval *buttress or the *cope of a *gable.

skew-arch. *See* arch.

skew-back. Sloping bed, line, sommering, or surface of an *abutment from which a segmental arch springs. *See* arch.

skew-block, skew-butt, skew-corbel, skew-put, skew-table. Large stone at the bottom end of the raking top of a *gable to hold the *cope and stop it sliding off, also called gable-springer, *kneeler, *springer, or *summer-stone.

skew-butt. 1. As *skew-block. **2.** *Rising hinge.*

skew-corbel. As *skew-block, but especially one projecting beyond the *naked of the return wall of the *gable, terminating the *eaves, any *cornice, and the gutter.

skew-table. *Skew-block.

Skidmore, Owings, & Merrill (SOM). American architectural firm founded by Louis Skidmore (1897–1962) and Nathaniel Alexander Owings (1903–84) in Chicago (1936) and New York (1937), later (1939) joined by John Ogden Merrill (1896–1975) and (1945) Gordon Bunshaft (1909–90). It was organized on teamwork principles and incorporated ideas from American business practice. SOM won fame with Lever House, Park Avenue, New York (completed 1952), a 21-storey *curtain-walled *skyscraper slab set on a lower *podium-like building, influenced by the *International Modern Movement and *Mies van der Rohe, and designed largely by Bunshaft. Their work had a profound effect on the development of architecture in the USA, notably with buildings in landscaped settings (e.g. Connecticut General Life Insurance Company, Bloomfield, Conn. (1953–7), and the United Airlines Building, Des Plaines, Ill. (1962)). With the John Hancock Center, Chicago (1970), SOM evolved a multi-functional complex (with offices, residential accommodation, and shops), and more recently the firm designed a series of office buildings with large, covered *atrium-halls, including the Fourth Financial Center

Wichita, Kan. (1974), and the First Wisconsin Plaza Building, Madison, Wis. (1974). The National Commercial Bank, Jeddah, Saudi Arabia (1982), set new standards for tall office-blocks in very hot climates, while the Broadgate and Canary Wharf developments in London (1990s) have kept the firm well in the public eye.

Bush-Brown (1984); Danz (1962); Emanuel (1994); Krinsky (1988); Menges (1974); Woodward (1970)

Skillyngton, Robert (*fl.* 1391–1400). English mason. He was in charge of the works at Kenilworth Castle, Warwickshire, from 1391, including the great hall, towers, and state apartments. He probably designed the *choir of St Mary's *Collegiate Church, Warwick (1381–96), and the tower of St Michael's Church, Coventry (1373–94). From 1397 to 1400 he was in charge of the College of St Mary in the Newark, Leicester, and in 1400 was master-mason at Tutbury Castle, Staffordshire, where he built a new tower and part of the *curtain-wall.

Harvey (1987)

skirt. **1.** Projection of the *eaves. **2.** *Apron-piece under a window. **3.** Plane sides of a room.

skirting. Timber facing fixed to the base of the walls of a room as a finish between the plaster and the floor, corresponding to a Classical *plinth.

skirt-roof. Roof around a building, e.g. over a *verandah, between storeys.

skull. **1.** Of an animal, an *aegicrane or *bucranium, on *friezes, etc. **2.** If human, represents mortality, transitory life, and vanity, so occurs in funerary architecture, notably as supports for *obelisks.

skylight. Glazed opening in a roof or ceiling.

skyline. Arrangement of roofs, *chimney-stacks, *spires, and other architectural accessories, creating a pattern against the sky, often *Picturesque.

skyscraper. High multi-storey building based on a *steel- or *concrete-*framed or *skeleton structure, evolved in the USA in the late 1880s after the limitations of traditional *load-bearing construction had been reached with ten- or twelve-storey buildings. While it would be possible to build higher load-bearing walls, the huge amounts of material needed would be uneconomic. Important in the evolution of the skyscraper was William Le Baron *Jenney's Home Insurance Building in Chicago (1883–5—demolished), which incorporated iron columns, *lintels, girders, and steel beams, and was the model for the later architecture of the *Chicago School. Steel and iron, with traditional loadbearing brick, were also used by *Holabird & Roche in the 22-storey Tacoma Building in Chicago (1887–8—demolished 1929), although L. S. *Buffington claimed to have originated the whole system on which skyscraper construction was based, and there were earlier experiments by *Loudon, *Paxton, *Saulnier, and others that pointed the way forward. Of great significance in the evolution of the skyscraper was the invention of the passenger-lift (elevator) in the late 1850s: from *c.*1880 the speed and reliability of lifts or elevators were greatly improved, enabling the building-type to develop further. Later important skyscrapers include Cass *Gilbert's Woolworth Building (1913), Shreve, Lamb, & Harmon's Empire State Building (1930–2), and *Yamasaki's World Trade Center (1970–4), all in New York.

Bletter and Robinson (1975); Condit (1952, 1960, 1961, 1964, 1968, 1973); Goldberger (1981); Hart, Henn, and Sontag (1985); Landau and Condit (1996); van Leeuwen (1988); Willis (1995); Yeang (1997); Zukowsky (1987)

sky-sign. Lettering or other advertising material on a metal frame, free-standing or mounted on top of a building, so that it is seen against the sky. It was a feature of *Constructivism and De *Stijl, and was extolled by *Venturi and others.

Shvidkovsky (1970)

slab. Large flat but not very thick portion of any material. Slabs of stone are used for pavements, the *mensa of an altar, *cladding, grave-covers, tomb-stones, etc.

slab-house. Building *clad in rough-hewn timber planks.

slab-roof. 'Flat' roof of *concrete or other material resembling a *slab.

slate. Sedimentary stone readily divisible into thin plates or *slabs used for *cladding, roofing, paving, tomb-stones etc.

slate-hanging, *also* **slate-boarding,** *or* **weather-slating.** *Cladding of a wall with slates.

sleeper. Any piece of timber employed to support other timbers, e.g. large horizontal beam (*patand) from which the *posts and *studs of a *timber-framed wall rise from just above ground level, or any beam under a ground-floor surface supporting the *joists of a larger span.

sleeper-wall. 1. Wall, usually perforated to allow free passage of air, supporting the *joists of a timber ground-floor in the case of heavy loads or wide spans between the walls of the room. **2.** Wall between two structural elements (e.g. *piers) to prevent movement. **3.** Wall supporting a *sleeper.

Sloan, Samuel (1815–84). American architect. He worked mostly in Philadelphia, Pa., where he established an office in 1849. Among his first works were Bartram Hall, West Philadelphia (1851), a luxurious *villa in the *Italianate *Rundbogenstil, several schools, and the Masonic Temple (1853). He published *The Model Architect* (1852–3), containing designs for cottages, villas, and suburban residences, and thereafter brought out many books, including *City and Suburban Architecture* (1859 and 1867), *Sloan's Constructive Architecture* (1859 and 1867), *American Houses* (1861 and 1868), and much else to publicize his work. He also edited (with Charles J. Lukens) *The Architectural Review and American Builder's Journal* (1868–70), the first periodical in the USA devoted wholly to architecture. One of his most extraordinary buildings was Longwood, Natchez, Miss. (1854–61), an octagonal domed house in the *Indian style. He was uninhibitedly eclectic in his tastes, capable of designing buildings in the *Gothic, *Italianate, and many other styles.

Handlin (1985); Sloan (1867, 1868, 1870, 1873, 1873*a*); Sloan and Lukens (1868–70); van Vynckt (1993); Whitwell (1975)

SLOAP (Space Left Over After Planning). Useless bits of ground left between streets and rigidly rectilinear buildings of *International Modernism (which rarely followed traditional street- or urban-patterns).

slurb. Combination of 'slum' and 'suburb', the USA equivalent of *subtopia.

slype. Narrow passage (*slip*) between the *transept and *chapter-house with access from the *cloister in a monastic establishment.

Smeaton, John (1724–92). English civil engineer and inventor of Scots descent. He travelled on the Continent in 1754 to study canals and harbours, and in 1755–6 he designed his Eddystone Lighthouse, near Plymouth, Devon, using a system of dovetailing the stones together, including the courses and the foundations in the rock. The building was completed in 1759, but was replaced in 1877–82. He designed several bridges, the best of which are in Scotland, including those at Banff, Coldstream, and Perth, using *segmental arches, and with circular perforations in the *spandrels. He also designed the Forth and Clyde Canal (begun 1768, completed 1790).

DNB (1917); Skempton (1981); Smeaton (1813, 1837)

Smirke, Sir Robert (1780–1867). English architect. He trained briefly with *Soane (with whom he quarrelled) and the younger *Dance before travelling in France, Greece, Italy, and Sicily (1801–5), publishing *Specimens of Continental Architecture* (1806) after his return in 1805. He set up in practice in London, and found favour with the Establishment. Among his first works were the *castellated Lowther Castle, Westmorland (1806–11), and Eastnor Castle (also castellated), Herefordshire (1812–20), but he made his reputation with Covent Garden Theatre, London (1808–9—destroyed, and rebuilt 1856–8 by E. M. *Barry), the first public building in the capital to have a pure *Greek *Doric *portico. Thereafter he became an important protagonist of the *Greek Revival. In 1813, with *Nash and *Soane, he was appointed as one of the three Architects to the Office of Works, and he gained several important London commissions including the General Post Office, St Martin's Le Grand (1824–9—demolished), the Custom House (1825–7—a rebuilding after the failure of the foundations of *Laing's building), King's College, The Strand (1830–5), and his masterpiece, the prestigious British Museum, Bloomsbury (1823–46). He also designed the Royal College of Physicians (now Canada House), Trafalgar Square (1822–5), and the Oxford and Cambridge Club, Pall Mall (1835–8—with his brother **Sydney**).

He built or altered around 30 country-houses, and designed 8 county-halls, including those at Bristol, Carlisle, Gloucester, Hereford, Lincoln, Maidstone, Perth, and Shrewsbury, all buildings of some personality and presence, but it is as a Greek Revivalist that he produced his best work. The British Museum is one of the greatest buildings in that style in England, with its noble Greek *Ionic *Order, the *capitals based on those of the Temple of Athena Polias, Priene (338 BC and later), and the *bases on those of the Temple of Dionysus, Teos (*c.*130 BC), and King's Library (arguably the finest Neoclassical interior in England). Greek Revival was admirably suited to Smirke's taste for geometrical simplicity and rationalism: a tendency to simplify further and create crisply cubical compositions was apparent at his Kinmount, Dumfriesshire (1812), The Homend, Stretton Grandison, Herefordshire (1814–21), and Worthy House, Hampshire (1816). He was innovative in construction, pioneering *concrete foundations, fireproof hollow-clay *vaults, and the use of iron in architecture. Among his successful pupils and assistants were William *Burn, C. R. *Cockerell, Henry *Roberts, Lewis *Vulliamy, and his own brother, Sydney *Smirke. Although a conventional designer, his office was regarded as the most progressive of its time, certainly in the 1820s and early 1830s.

Architectural History, 6 (1963), 91–102; *Architectural Review*, 142/847 (Sept. 1967), 208–10; Colvin (1995); Crook (1972, 1972*a*); Crook and Port (1973); *DNB* (1917); *Transactions of the Newcomen Society*, 38 (1965–6), 5–22

Smirke, Sydney (1798–1877). English architect. He was perhaps overshadowed by his older and more famous brother, Robert *Smirke, but nevertheless designed several important buildings. Among his works in London were the *portico and dome of the Bethlehem Hospital (now the Imperial War Museum—1838–46), and the two luxurious clubs, the *Palladian Conservative in St James's (1843–5—with *Basevi), and the Carlton, Pall Mall (1854–6—demolished), an essay in Venetian *Renaissance Revival with elevations (in which polished granite columns were used in the façade) based on *Sansovino's Library of St Mark. He also assisted his brother with the Oxford and Cambridge Club, Pall Mall (1835–8). His most celebrated building is the domed Reading Room in the British Museum (1854–7), in which the structure was of cast iron, and he also completed his brother's work at the Museum. He designed the exhibition galleries for the Royal Academy, Burlington House, Piccadilly, London (1866–70), and was Architect to Brookwood Cemetery, Woking, Surrey (1854–6).

DNB (1917); Fawcett (1976); Papworth (1887)

Smith, Arnold Dunbar (1866–1933). English architect. He entered into partnership with Cecil Claude Brewer (1871–1918) in 1895, and they won the competition to design the Passmore Edwards Settlement (now Mary Ward Centre), Tavistock Place, London (1896–8). It is a delightful building, with influences from *Voysey in the *cornice and roof, Harrison *Townsend in the vaguely *Sezessionist porch, and *Shaw in the fenestration. Smith & Brewer designed Little Barley End, Tring, Hertfordshire (1899), and were pioneers of the Neoclassical Revival with their severe National Museum of Wales, Cathays Park, Cardiff (1910), which played an important role in establishing the American *Beaux-Arts style of *Classicism in England. Their best-known work was Heal's, Tottenham Court Road, London (1916), a reticent *stripped Classical design described by *Pevsner as the 'best commercial front of its date'.

Gray (1985); Newman (1995); Pevsner, *Buildings of England, London 2* (1952)

Smith, George (1783–1869). English architect. He was Surveyor to The Mercers' Company (from 1814), for which he designed many buildings and layouts, including the Estate in Stepney, London, with York Square and surrounding areas (*c.*1820–35), and the Company's lands in Co. Londonderry, where he was assisted by his partner (from 1836 to 1842), William Barnes (1807–68). With Barnes he designed the *Romanesque Revival Parish Church, Kilrea (1841–2), and other buildings on the Co. Londonderry Estate. His most important works were the *Gothic Whittington Almshouses, Highgate, London (1822—demolished 1966), the handsome *Greek Revival St Alban's Court House and Town Hall, Hertfordshire (1829–33), the *Greek Doric Corn Exchange, Mark Lane, London (1827–8—demolished 1941), and the Grammar School, Horsham, Sussex (1840–1). He also designed the Italianate London Bridge Railway Terminus with Henry *Roberts (1841–4—demolished). He laid out the Morden Estate, Greenwich, where he designed houses in a variety of styles.

Colvin (1995); Curl (1986); Papworth (1887)

Smith, James (*c.*1645–1731). Scots architect. As a young man he travelled on the Continent, but by 1679 was settled in Edinburgh, married to a daughter of Robert Mylne (1633–1710), architect and builder. Smith was appointed

Surveyor or Overseer of the Royal Works (1683). He built Drumlanrig Castle, Dumfriesshire (*c*.1680–90—probably designed by Mylne), designed Hamilton Palace, Lanarkshire (1693–1701—demolished), Melville House, Fife (1697–1700), and Yester House, East Lothian (*c*.1700–15), remodelled Dalkeith House, Midlothian (1702–10), and constructed the handsome domed Mackenzie *mausoleum in Greyfriars churchyard, Edinburgh (*c*.1690–2), among much else. He was responsible for disseminating the Classical style introduced by *Bruce to Scotland, but in his surviving drawings it is clear he was familiar with the works of *Palladio, and he may have been an early and formative influence on Colen *Campbell and therefore on English *Palladianism. In his realized buildings, however, any Palladian tendencies were decidedly muted, and virtually non-existent. His works pre-date any *Palladian essays of the *Burlington Palladian Revival which therefore may have originated in Scotland.

Architectural History, 17 (1974), 5–13; Colvin (1995)

Smith, John (1781–1852). Scots architect. He established himself in Aberdeen where he became City Architect in 1824. He directed building works in the city for some 30 years, his only rival being Archibald *Simpson. He designed some distinguished *Greek Revival buildings, including the Schools in Little Belmont Street (1841), but he also carried out many designs in C16 and C17 *vernacular styles that caused him to be referred to as 'Tudor Johnny'. He designed the handsome *Ionic *screen in St Nicholas churchyard, Union Street (1830), and the *Tudor Gothic Trinity Hall, Union Street (1845–6). His son, **William Smith** (1817–91), designed Balmoral Castle with Prince *Albert in the *Scottish Baronial style (1853–5).

Colvin (1995); Papworth (1887)

Smith Brothers. Francis (1672–1738) and **William** (1661–1724) were important master-builders and architects in the English Midlands in the first quarter of C18. Francis, known as 'Smith of Warwick', was based in that town, and was largely responsible for its rebuilding after the fire of 1694. The brothers rebuilt (1698–1704) the *Collegiate Church of St Mary to designs by Sir William Wilson (1641–1710) in an airy, vaguely *Gothic style of considerable originality. They carried out numerous ecclesiastical commissions in the Midlands, Francis being responsible for Gainsborough Church, Lincolnshire (1736–44). William designed Stanford Hall, Leicestershire (1697–1700), and the brothers were active over a wide geographical area. Sir Howard *Colvin gives an impressive list of their works in his *Dictionary* (1995). Francis designed Stoneleigh Abbey, Warwickshire (1714–26), in a *Baroque style, but many of his houses are plain. His Court House, Warwick (1725–30), is in a refined *Palladian style.

Francis's son, **William Smith** (1705–47), was also an architect and builder, specializing in a competent *Palladianism. Among his works are Catton Hall, Derbyshire (*c*.1742–5), Kirtlington Park, Oxfordshire (1742–7), and Thame Park, also Oxfordshire (*c*.1745).

Architectural History, 35 (1992), 183–8; Colvin (1995); Downes (1966); Hussey (1965); Lees-Milne (1970); *Warwickshire History*, 2/2 (1972–3), 3–13

Smithson, Alison (1928–93) **and Peter Denham** (1923–). British architects and polemicists. A husband-and-wife team (married 1949), they formed a partnership in London (1950). As members of *Team X (10) and *CIAM they established themselves as leaders of the *Modern Movement in Britain during the 1950s and 1960s. Their steel-framed Secondary School at Hunstanton, Norfolk (1949–54), the panels filled with bricks and glass, owed much to the style of *Mies van der Rohe, and, with its exposed internal services, was seen to be an honest expression of *Functionalism. Their *Economist* Building, St James's, London (1962–4), was perceived as architecture of high quality in an established setting. With developments such as the Robin Hood Gardens Estate, London (1972), their use of exposed raw concrete derived from Le *Corbusier's work confirmed them as exponents of 'New *Brutalism', not unconnected with P. D. Smithson's nickname 'Brutus'. The high-level corridor-streets, making a spurious connection with streets of terrace-housing, together with the character of the buildings, have not been universally admired. Prolific writers, they published *Urban Structuring* (1967), *Without Rhetoric: An Architectural Aesthetic 1955–72* (1973), and *The Heroic Age of Modern Architecture* (1981), all of which seem curiously dated, yet were influential at the time.

Architectural Design, 41/8 (Aug. 1971), 479–81; 43/8 (Aug. 1973), 524–9 and 621–3; 44/9 (Sept. 1974), 573–90; 46/6

(June 1976), 331–54; *Domus*, 534 (1974), 1–8; Emanuel (1994); Smithson (1968); Smithson and Smithson (1967, 1968, 1975, 1981, 1991); van Vynckt (1993)

Smyth, Henry (*fl.* 1506–d. 1517). English mason. He worked with *Vertue and *Lee at King's College *Chapel, Cambridge, from at least 1506, and in 1508 began work at the hospital of the Savoy, London, where he was engaged when he died. He seems to have worked as Master-Mason at Richmond Palace, Surrey, from 1505 to 1509.

Harvey (1987)

Smyth, John (*fl.* 1429–d. *c.*1460). English mason. He was a *lodge-mason at Canterbury in 1429, and Warden of the Masons at Eton College, Buckinghamshire, in 1441, before being appointed Master-Mason at Westminster Abbey in 1453.

Harvey (1987)

Smyth, William (*fl. c.*1465-d. 1490). English mason. He carried out works at St John's Church, Glastonbury, Somerset, *c.*1465, and was Master-Mason at Wells Cathedral, Somerset, before 1480. He may have designed the *crossing *vault under the tower, the Sugar *Chantry Chapel (1489), and other parts of the Cathedral. He was probably the architect of Crewkerne Church, Somerset (*c.*1475–90), and may have worked on the vaults of Sherbourne (*c.*1486–93) and Milton (after 1481) Abbeys, both in Dorset.

Harvey (1987)

Smythson, Robert (*c.*1535–1614). Distinguished English architect of the *Elizabethan period. He worked at Longleat, Wiltshire, from 1568 to 1575, a great house disposed almost symmetrically about both axes, and with very large windows, both features of Smythson's first known independent work, the dramatic *prodigy house of Wollaton Hall, Nottinghamshire (1580–8), a powerful composition (possibly indebted in part to *Serlio) with much Flemish-derived ornament (probably from de *Vries), tall corner towers, and a central *clearstoreyed hall (rather than the internal *courts of Longleat) rising high above the surrounding structure. He also designed Worksop Manor, Nottinghamshire (*c.*1585—destroyed), his masterpiece, Hardwick Hall, Derbyshire (1590–7—a less frenetic composition than Wollaton), and (probably) Burton Agnes Hall, Yorkshire (1601–10). His son, **John Smythson** (d. 1634), assisted Robert, but then worked for the Cavendish family at Bolsover Castle, Derbyshire (*c.*1612–34), Welbeck Abbey, Nottinghamshire (1622–3), and (possibly) Slingsby Castle, Yorkshire (*c.*1630). Bolsover is an extraordinary building, very consciously medieval in appearance, and may be classified as an early prototype of the *sham castle so popular in C18. John's son, **Huntingdon** (d. 1648), and *his* son, **John** (1640–1717), were also architects.

Airs (1975, 1995); *Architectural History*, 5 (1962), 21–184; Colvin (1995); Girouard (1966, 1983); Lees-Milne (1951); Summerson (1993)

sneck. 1. Lifting-lever of a latch lock. **2.** In squared uncoursed *rubble, a small stone set in the interstices between larger stones preserving the horizontal and vertical *bonds.

snecked harling. *Rendered or *harled wall leaving some stones exposed for effect.

Soane, Sir John (1753–1837). English architect, arguably one of the greatest since *Vanbrugh and *Hawksmoor. Trained in the office of the younger *Dance and at the Royal Academy Schools, he joined the office of Henry *Holland (1772), where he gained valuable experience. In 1778, having been awarded the King's Travelling Studentship, he went to Italy where he met several influential Englishmen on the *Grand Tour. Led to expect employment by the erratic and enormously rich Lord Frederick Augustus Hervey, Bishop of Derry and later Earl of Bristol (1730–1803), he foolishly ended (1780) his stay in Rome to travel to Ireland where he hoped to design the Bishop's house at Downhill, Co. Londonderry, but this came to nothing. He spent the next four years making good his losses by carrying out small works, some in East Anglia, helped by acquaintances who had heard of his disappointment. Among his designs at this time were lodges and a rustic dairy at Hamels Park, Buntingford, Hertfordshire (1781–3), and a new house, Letton Hall, Norfolk (1783–9). He built up a reputation for probity and competence, exhibited at the Royal Academy, made a good marriage, and carried out alterations and additions to Holwood House, Kent (1786–95), for William Pitt (1759–1806), cousin of one of Soane's friends from his Roman trip, and Prime Minister (1783–1801). In 1788, the year in which he intended to publish *Plans, Elevations, and Sections of Buildings Erected in the Counties of Norfolk, Suffolk*, etc. (it appeared in 1789), Soane, through his connection with Pitt, gained the Surveyorship of the Bank of England after the death of Sir Robert *Taylor. This appointment gave him status and security, and set him up as one of the leading English architects. The death of his wife's uncle in 1790 brought a legacy that enabled him to build a house at 12 Lincoln's Inn Fields, London (1792–4), and start the great collection of works of art and books that form the contents of his Museum today. Other important official appointments followed.

Security also enabled him to evolve an individual style that, while rooted in *Classicism, was yet original, and consisted of certain original themes. These included the extensive use of segmental arches; shallow saucer-domed ceilings on segmental arches carried on *piers and sometimes lit from above; cross-vaults carried on piers; top-lit volumes rising through two floors; a *primitive, *stripped language of architecture, sometimes featuring *Orders such as the *Paestum *Doric, but more often the replacement of the Orders by a series of incised ornaments cut into unadorned simple elements; very careful attention to lighting, often involving mirrors (plain and convex) and tinted glass; and, above all, an obsession with the furniture of death in the form of *sarcophagi, cinerary *urns, oppressive vaulted spaces, and the like.

Among his greatest works was the Bank of England in London, with the Stock Office (1792–3—reconstructed by Higgins Gardner, 1986–8) and the Rotunda (begun 1796) two of the most remarkable spaces within the complex, both treated without reference to the Orders, but with the *Classicism reduced to simple grooves. The exterior was largely a blank wall, enlivened by recesses and *colonnades of the *Corinthian Order from the Temple of Vesta at Tivoli. Virtually nothing of his work at the Bank survived within the exterior wall after the drastic alterations by *Baker in the 1920s and 1930s.

After 1800 his work became more intensely personal, as with Pitzhanger Place, Ealing, Middlesex (1800–3), the Dulwich Picture Gallery and *Mausoleum (1811–14, restored 1953—where his architectural language reached a new simplicity and refinement), and his own house, 13 Lincoln's Inn Fields, London (1812–13—now Sir John Soane's Museum), one of the most complex, intricate, and ingenious series of interiors ever conceived, with much top lighting (using coloured glass), mirrors, folding walls, double-height spaces, and parts where the extraordinary obsession with death and the *Antique almost overwhelm. The exterior, with its plain ashlar incised front, shows how far Soane had moved in abstracting his *Neoclassicism. *Schinkel saw the building in 1826, and described the internal spaces as resembling cemeteries and catacombs, with everywhere 'little deceptions'. Schinkel also found Soane's ornamentation at the Bank of England 'strangely simple'.

In 1806 Soane became Professor of Architecture at the Royal Academy, and gave a series of meticulously prepared lectures. He demanded the highest professional standards, was passionately interested in architectural education, and was very well-read, having one of the finest architectural libraries ever collected. He was clearly influenced by French theorists, notably *Laugier, and by certain architects, including the younger *Dance, *Ledoux, and *Peyre. The impact of Paestum Doric was clear from the entrance-hall at Tyringham Hall, Buckinghamshire (1793–*c*.1800), and the primitive 'barn à la Paestum' he designed at 936 Warwick Road, Solihull, Warwickshire (1798). He owned the original drawings of the Paestum temples by *Piranesi, still in the Museum.

One of his most beautiful creations was the Council Chamber, Freemasons' Hall, Great Queen street, London (1828—demolished), in which his uses of top-lit saucer-domes, segmental arches, simple incised ornament, and a rigorous unification of walls and ceilings were demonstrated. In spite of the fact that Soane was a convinced Freemason (a portrait of him in his Freemasonic regalia survives), his biographies have been unaccountably reticent about this, yet much of his personal style can only be explained with reference to Freemasonic concerns with Ancient Egypt, death, and the moral meaning of architecture. The *mausoleum he designed for himself and his wife in the overspill burial-ground of St Giles-in-the-Fields (now St Pancras Gardens), London, of 1816, with its segmental pediments and much curiously original treatment is indubitably Freemasonic, and was the model for Giles Gilbert *Scott's C20 GPO telephone-kiosks. His other tombs were severe and dignified, and some works, including the stables at Chelsea Hospital, London (1804–17), and the farmhouse at Butterton Grange, Staffordshire (1816–17), were even more minimalist, of plain brick treated with the utmost simplicity.

Although Soane had many pupils, including *Basevi, J. M. *Gandy, and *Wightwick, he does not seem to have exercised any lasting influence on English architecture, and indeed his own work was lampooned by A. W. N. *Pugin, who did considerable damage to his reputation. Earlier, an anonymous attack on his work in *The Champion* (1815) turned out to be by his son, **George** (1790–1860), from whom he was thereafter estranged. Although knighted in 1831, Soane is said to have declined a Baronetcy to prevent his son from inheriting the title. His exacting personality cannot have made him an easy man to deal with, and his struggle to evolve a new type of Classicism that was a synthesis of Greek, Roman, Italian, Egyptian, and French Neoclassicism, handled with scholarship, sensitivity, and originality, did not lead anywhere after his death, although his architecture aroused new interest in the late C20.

Architectural Review 163/973 (March 1978), 147–55; Bindmann and Riemann (1993); Bolton (1927, 1929); Colvin (1995); Crook (1972*a*); Crook and Port (1973); *DNB* (1917); Harris (1990); Middleton and Watkin (1987); Placzek (1982); Ruffinière du Prey (1982); Schumann-Bacia (1989, 1990); Soane (1830); Stroud (1984); Summerson (1952); Summerson *et al.* (1983); Watkin (1979, 1986, 1996); Waterfield (1996)

Social architecture. 1. Architecture intended for use by the mass of people as social beings as a reaction against architecture concerned with form and style supposedly for the dominant members of society. **2.** Schools and other buildings erected after the 1939–45 war in England incorporating scientific method, *prefabrication, and *industrialized building as part of the *Modern Movement.

Hatch (1984); Saint (1987); Sommer (1983)

Socialist Realism. Offically approved styles of art, architecture, literature, etc., in the former Soviet Union and some other Communist countries. In architecture it usually involved a type of coarse *stripped Classicism.

Council of Europe (1995)

socle, zocle. 1. Block of less height than horizontal dimension, without *base or *cornice, serving as a support for a *pedestal, bust, *urn, etc., really an unornamented *plinth. **2.** Base-course of a wall.

soffit(a) *or* **(e). 1.** Ceiling. **2.** Visible underside of an arch, *balcony, *beam, *corona, *cornice, *vault, or any exposed architectural element.

soffit-cusp. *Gothic *cusp springing from a flat *soffit or *intrados rather than from a chamfered side, looking like additions.

Soft architecture. 1. Living-spaces with few fixed items or partitions. They would be instantly controlled by computers as required. **2.** Low-energy self-build dwellings.

Boyd (1968); Negroponte (1974); Spoerry (1989)

Soissons, Bernard de (*fl.* C13). One of the master-masons of Rheims Cathedral recorded in the *maze (destroyed) on the floor. He seems to have been active from *c.*1253 until *c.*1290, but his contribution is never likely to be established with any certainty.

Svanberg (1983)

Soissons, Comte d'Ostel, Baron Longroy. Louis-Emmanuel-Jean-Guy de Savoie-Carignan de (1890–1962). Canadian-born architect, he studied at the École des *Beaux-Arts, Paris, and at the Royal Academy in London. He designed several buildings in England including houses at Bagshot, Surrey (1914), the Earl Haig Memorial Homes, Meadow Head, Sheffield, Yorkshire (1928–9), Broom Park and Huxhams Cross Houses, Dartington Hall, Devon (1932–3), and much else, but he is best known for the many buildings he designed at Welwyn *Garden City, Hertfordshire (1919–60), where he introduced a pleasing *Neo-Georgian style with a *Colonial flavour to the second English Garden City.

Architectural Review, 66/392 (July 1929), 7–16; *DNB* (1981); *RIBA Journal*, ser. 3, 43 (1936), 975–84

solar, soler. 1. *Garret, *loft, or *Rood-loft. **2.** Private upper chamber on the first floor, often in a cross-wing, of a medieval house. **3.** *Bay-window, almost the size of a small room, at the side of the high-table end of a medieval hall, or attached to a late-medieval withdrawing-room or dining-room.

Alcock, Barley, Dixon, and Meeson (1996); Gwilt (1903)

solar glass. Tinted glass to reduce glare from sunlight.

solar house. Dwelling heated using energy from the sun's rays.

Solari, Guiniforte (1429–81). Milanese architect. He completed the Ospedale Maggiore, Milan, designed by *Filarete, in the *Gothic style and was responsible for the Gothic *nave of Santa Maria delle Grazie in the same city (1463–90) to which *Bramante added a domed *crossing and *choir (from 1493). He also seems to have carried out works at the Duomo, Milan, and at the *Certosa, Pavia.

Heydenreich and Lotz (1974); Papworth (1887)

Solari, Santino (1576–1646). Italian architect from the Como area. He was one of the first to bring a mature Italian Classical style north of the Alps into the German-speaking lands. His masterpiece is the Cathedral of Sts Rupert and Virgil, Salzburg (1614–28), with its apsidal *transepts clearly influenced by *Palladio's *Il Redentore* and San Giorgio Maggiore, Venice, probably suggested by an earlier design by *Scamozzi. He also designed Schloss Hellbrunn, near Salzburg (1613–15), in the early *Baroque style, and the *Sanctum Sanctorum*, the *shrine of the *Gnadenbild*, or picture of the Black Virgin, at the Benedictine Abbey of Einsiedeln, Switzerland (*c.*1617–20—destroyed and rebuilt in modified form).

Bourke (1962); Fuhrmann (1950); Hempel (1965); Powell (1959)

solarium. 1. Flat roof, balcony, or terrace exposed to the sun. **2.** Room on an upper floor, often opening to a terrace facing east to catch the morning sun. **3.** *Solar. **4.** *Loggia. **5.** Sun-dial, often with architectural pretensions.

sole. 1. *Cill. **2.** Base-plate supporting a *post, e.g. *timber-framed construction. **3.** Part of anything touching the ground and sustaining a load.

Alcock, Barley, Dixon, and Meeson (1996)

solea. 1. Elevated *podium in an *Early Christian or *Byzantine church linking an *ambo to a *bema. **2.** Step on which stood the *balustrade separating *choir and *sanctuary in a *basilica.

sole-piece. 1. Horizontal timber carrying the *posts in *timber-framed structures. **2.** Short timber (also called *sole-plate*) laid across a wall (i.e. with its length at 90° to the *naked of the wall), supporting the foot of a *rafter and an ashlar-piece in a timber roof.

Alcock, Barley, Dixon, and Meeson (1996)

Soleri, Paolo (1919–). Italian-born American architect. He worked for Frank Lloyd *Wright (1947–9) before going back to Italy to build the Ceramics Factory, Vietri-sul-Mare, Salerno (1953). As a visionary designer, he returned to the USA where he established the Cosanti Foundation, Scottsdale, Ariz. (1955), building the Earth House (1956–8) there to demonstrate the possibilities of alternative technologies. He evolved the concept of *Arcology in which architecture and ecology are merged, and designed many *megastructures, one of which, called Arcosanti, near Scottsdale, intended to demonstrate his ideas, was commenced in 1970. He published *Arcology: The City in the Image of Man* (1969).

Banham (1976); Casper (1988); Emanuel (1994); Sky and Stone (1976); Soleri (1969, 1971); Wall (1971)

Solomonic column. *Barley-sugar, Salomonic, Salomónica, *spiral, torso or twisted column, with a contorted or twisted *shaft, unlike the *Antonine, *triumphal, or *Trajanic column with its spiral *band of sculpture wound around it. The form was based on the *Antique precedents from the Herodian Temple in Jerusalem in the first century AD, thought to be from the Temple of Solomon. These and others were set up over the tomb of the Apostle in the Constantinian *basilica of San Pietro, Rome, and so copies or columns inspired by them became familiar throughout Europe, being often used on altarpieces, *shrines, and the like, because they were associated with the gates of Paradise. The earliest English examples are the columns (half-way between the Solomonic and Trajanic type) supporting the *vaults in the *crypt of St Wystan's Church, Repton, Derbyshire (C9), but the spiral column was often used in *Romanesque *cloisters, and in *Baroque funerary monuments. The form became widely known in C17 through engravings of the tapestry cartoons by *Raphael showing Christ at the Temple which were brought to England in the reign of King Charles I (1625–49).

Curl (1991, 1992); Lewis and Darley (1986); Papworth (1887)

SOM. *See* Skidmore, Owings, & Merrill.

Sommaruga, Giuseppe (1867–1917). Milanese architect. With *Basile and d'*Aronco he was a major *Art Nouveau designer in Italy. His works include the spectacular Palazzo Castiglione, Milan (1901–3), one of the most important *Stile-Liberty* buildings, elaborately ornamented. He also designed the Aletti tomb, Varese (1898), the Italian Pavilion, International Exposition, St Louis, Mo. (1903–4), the Palazzino Comi, Milan

(1906), the Hotel Tre Crocí, Campo di Fiori, Varese (1908–12), and the Faccanoni *mausoleum, Sarnico (1907). Many of his works have accomplished Stile *Floreale ornamentation (*see* Stile).

Meeks (1966); Monneret de Villard (1908); Nicoletti (1978); Pevsner and Richards (1973)

sommering. *Skew-back, or the radiating joint between the *voussoirs of an arch. *See* arch.

Sonck, Lars Eliel (1870–1956). Finnish architect. His early work, combining contemporary European styles and *vernacular idioms, was associated with *National Romanticism. His Villa Sonck, Finström, Åland Islands (1894), and other houses of the period, drew on traditions of log-construction. He designed St Michael's Church, Turku (1894), much influenced by German brick churches, and St John's Cathedral, Tampere (1902–7), in which rough-textured stone and sculpted details were successfully integrated. His monumental Stock Exchange (1911) and Mortgage Society Building (1908), both in Helsinki, showed a tendency towards *Neoclassicism. In his town-planning work he was influenced by *Sitte. He laid out Kulosaari, a Helsinki suburb (1907–9), and parts of Töölö district (1903).

Journal of the Society of Architectural Historians, 30/3 (1971), 228–37; Richards (1978); van Vynckt (1993)

Sondergotik. German late-*Gothic from *c.*1380, characterized by *hall-churches of immense height, complicated *vaults, fine portrait-sculpture, and highly complex filigree *tracery.

Grodecki (1986)

sopraporta. *Overdoor*, really a kind of *Attic-storey over the *cornice of a *doorway, often with *scrolls, and other architectural enrichment, sometimes forming a panel containing a picture or sculpture.

Soria, Giovanni Battista (1581–1651). Roman architect. He studied with *Montana, and arranged for the publication of the latter's drawings, including *Scielta di varij tempietti antichi* (Selection of Various Small *Antique Temples—1624). In the mid-1620s he began to practise architecture, designing the façades of the Churches of Santa Maria della Vittoria, near the Baths of Diocletian (1625–7), San Crisógono, Trastévere (1626), and San Gregorio Magno, Monte Celio (1629–33), the last a more sophisticated exercise than the previous two, with a two-storey arrangement featuring three arches below and pedimented windows above. He designed the *nave of the Duomo, Monte Compatri (1630), the Library of the Palazzo Barberini (1635–8), and the façade of Santa Caterina da Siena (1638–40), the last two in Rome.

Hibbard (1962, 1971); Ortolani (1927); Papworth (1887)

Soria y Mata, Arturo (1844–1920). Spanish inventor, civil servant, and town-planner. He devised the linear city-plan along a 'spine' devoted to tracked transport (he ran one of Madrid's tramways), and in 1894 inaugurated the Ciudad Lineal, Madrid, a linear low-density suburban development that pre-dated Letchworth *Garden City. Soria published the journal *La Ciudad Lineal* (1897–1932) which influenced a number of people including Frank Lloyd *Wright and (initially) Le *Corbusier.

Collins *et al.* (1968); *Newsletter* of the Urban History Group, 29 (1970), 1–12

Sosnowski, Oskar (1880–1939). Polish architect, one of the leading designers of the inter-war period. His masterpiece is the Church of St Jakob (James), Warsaw (1909–23), in a type of severe monumental cubic Neo-Romanesque, much influenced by Finnish, Russian, and Swedish *National Romantic architecture. He restored the Garrison Church (1923–33), the Neoclassical Paca Palace (1920s), and the Church of St Wenceslas (1916–23), all in Warsaw. His *reinforced-concrete Church of St Roch, Białystok (1927–46), was almost an essay in *Expressionism, but also incorported late-*Gothic forms.

Chrościcki and Rottermund (1977); Leśnikowski (1996)

Sostres (Maluquer), Josep Maria (1915–84). Catalan architect. He and others formed Grupo R in 1952 to resurrect and promote the *Modern Movement, while he also (an apparent contradiction) galvanized interest in the works of the 'anti-Rationalist' *Gaudí. His architectural output was small, but included admired buildings including the Agustí House, Sitges (1953–5), the Casa M. M. I., Barcelona (1955–8), the Hotel Maria Victoria, Puigcerdà (1956–7), the *El Noticiero Universal* Newspaper Offices, Barcelona (1963–5), and the Xampeny and Campana Houses, Ventola, Gerona (1971–3), all in Spain.

Emanuel (1994); Lampugnani (1988)

Sottsass, Ettore (1917–). Italian architect. He established his own firm in Milan (1947), designing artefacts, exhibitions, and interiors. Among his works were office-machines for Olivetti, but he gradually turned away from conventional *Modernism on the grounds that the only design *not* valid for today is that which claims to be 'timeless' and has pretensions to some sort of moral mission, e.g. the *Bauhaus philosophy. As a result, his work has become eclectic, drawing on many styles and periods, as his rejection of *Rationalism became more complete, especially by the time he founded the Memphis Design Co-op, Milan, 1981. As the name might suggest, Egyptianizing, Neoclassical, and aspects of *Art Deco are brought together in a synthesis, a hybrid, that even draws on trashier elements of popular 'culture' (e.g. Rock 'n' Roll) that could be described as parody or as *Kitsch, so he has been classed as a Post-Modernist. Sottsass has been successful in merging consumer and popular culture with High Design. Among his works the INA-CASA housing development at Carmagnola, near Turin, and Meina, Lake Maggiore (1952–4); the Galleria del Cavallino, Venice (1956); the Memphis furniture (from 1981); and the various projects for Nonsense Architecture and Pornographic Architecture (1973–7) deserve note. Sparke, in her critiques, has detected 'anti-design' and a 'blurring of the boundaries between design practice and design criticism' giving birth to something new she terms 'meta-design' in Sottsass's output. *Jencks (1971) has identified Sottsass as one of the *Supersensualists.

Architectural Design, 41/6 (June 1971), 345–7, and 42/1 (Jan. 1972), 18–21; Bure (1987); Burney (1994); Cable (1985); Emanuel (1994); Radice (1993); Sottsass (1976, 1983, 1985, 1987, 1988, 1993, 1993*a*, 1994, 1995); Sparke (1982)

Soufflot, Jacques-Germain (1713–80). French Neoclassical architect. He studied in Rome (1731–8) before settling in Lyons where he built the Hôtel-Dieu (1739–48), the Loge des Changes (1748–50), and the Théâtre (1753–6) which made his reputation. The last, with its relationship between stage and auditorium, was an important paradigm for later developments. He was a respected theorist too, and after a further nine-month visit to Italy (1750–1), he was able to demonstrate his knowledge of Classical antiquities, notably with his up-to-date reports on the latest archaeological discoveries at Herculaneum and elsewhere. This important Italian study-visit, which he undertook as part of the entourage of Abel-François Poisson de Vandières (1727–81), later Marquis de Marigny, and brother of Madame de Pompadour (1721–64), was highly significant in the history of French architecture, for it marked a change away from the *Rococo of *Louis Quinze to the *Neoclassicism of *Louis Seize. Marigny (*Directeur-Général des Bâtiments du Roi* from 1751 to 1773) called Soufflot to Paris in 1755, where he was made *Contrôleur des Bâtiments du Roi au Département de Paris*, and given the task of building the new Church of Ste-Geneviève, the first great building of French Neoclassicism. A Greek *cross on plan, the *nave and *aisles were defined by rows of *Corinthian columns carrying a continuous *entablature over which light domes and *vaults rose. Soufflot's pupil, Maximilien Brébion (1716–96—who carried out Soufflot's designs for the drum and dome over the *crossing from 1780), wrote that in building the church Soufflot had reunited, under one of the most beautiful forms, the lightness of construction found in *Gothic churches with the purity and magnificence of Greek architecture. With its great Roman *temple-front, elegant columned drum and dome over the crossing, and rational geometry it made a great impact, and was much admired by *Laugier as a seminal example of perfection in architecture. The *gravitas* of the *Antique was eloquently expressed, especially in the severe *crypt, where the impact of the Greek *Doric Order from *Paestum is clear. The Church was secularized in 1791, and altered under *Quatremère de Quincy to become the *Panthéon*, with the character of a *mausoleum. Soufflot also designed de Marigny's own house in the Faubourg du Roule (from 1769), and various *fabriques (including a fine *nymphaeum) at the Château de Ménars (from 1764), in a dessicated Neoclassical style. He also designed the *sacristy at the Cathedral of Notre Dame, Paris (1756–60).

Braham (1980); Caisse Nationale (1980); Etlin (1984); Gallet (1964); Gallet *et al.* (1980); Hautecœur (1952); Middleton and Watkin (1987); Petzet (1961); Rykwert (1980); Ternois and Pérez (1982); Watkin (1986)

sounding-board. *See* tester.

space-frame. Complex three-dimensional structural framework, capable of spanning and containing very large volumes, con-

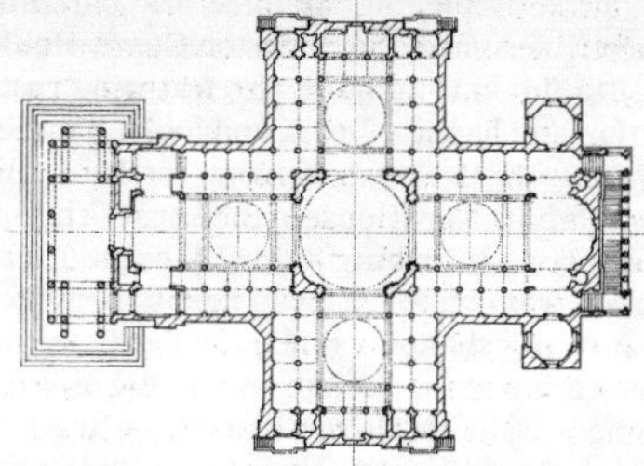

Soufflot. Plan of the Panthéon, Paris, formerly the Church of Ste-Geneviève.

structed using pyramidal, hexagonal, and other geometrical figures, often made of lightweight tubing. It has further advantages of behaving as a single integral unit, and can resist loads in any direction. Space-frame designers include Buckminster *Fuller, Bruno *Taut, and Konrad *Wachsmann.

Makowski (1965)

span. Distance apart of two supports, especially as applied to the opening of an *arch or the width of a space covered by a beam, *lintel, *truss, etc.

spandrel. 1. Quasi-triangular plane, the *hanse* or *haunch, framed by the extrados of an arch, a horizontal line projected from the crown, and a vertical line rising from the springing, often decorated. **2.** Similar plane between two arches in an *arcade. **3.** Web of a vault between two ribs. **4.** Triangle formed between the string of a *stair and the floor. **5.** In a framed structure the panel between the *cill of a window and the top of the window below. **6.** Approximately triangular space between the curve of a brace and a *post and beam in a medieval timber *truss.

spandrel-bracket. 1. Infilling of the *spandrel (**6**) of a medieval *truss, to strengthen it. **2.** One of several brackets, set in a vertical plane, fixed between one or more curves and the circumference of a circle set in a horizontal plane: it is used to construct *cornices, coves, etc., for plasterer's work.

Nicholson (1835); Papworth (1887)

spandrel-panel. 1. Part of a wall between the head of a window-aperture and the *cill of the window above in a building of two or more storeys, especially in a *curtain-wall. **2.** As *spandrel-bracket (**1**). **3.** Any panel filling a *spandrel (**1**, **2**, **4**, **6**).

spandrel-step. Step with an approximately triangular *section, the hypotenuse of which is part of the *soffit of a stone *stair.

spandrel-strut. Short timber placed diagonally between an arch-brace and the corner of the main *timber-frame.

Alcock, Barley, Dixon, and Meeson (1996)

spandrel-wall. Wall built over an arch, forming the *spandrel (**1**, **2**).

Spanish Order. *Corinthian *Order with the *abacus embellished with lions' masks rather than *fleurons.

span-piece. *Collar-beam.

span-roof. Roof with two inclined sides as opposed to a *shed-roof* which only has one.

Speer, Albert (1905–81). German architect of the Nazi period (1933–45). He studied under *Bestelmeyer, *Billing, and *Tessenow, and rose to prominence on the death of *Troost, becoming Adolf Hitler's (1889–1945) friend, confidant, and architect from 1934. His interest in archaeology led him to evolve a style of architecture that would be as expressive as anything left by Ancient Rome, and his main influences were *Boullée (for megalomaniac scale) and *Schinkel (for a *columnar and trabeated Neoclassical architecture). He became known for his theatrical staging of Nazi Party rallies, using searchlights to suggest 'cathedrals of light' in the night skies, massed flags, and blocky forms for buildings. His Party Congress-Grounds at Nuremberg, with a vast grandstand and other structures (from 1934—partly destroyed), were impressive in their simplified *Neoclassicism, drawing on paraphrases from Queen Hatshepsut's Ancient Egyptian Mortuary Temple at Deïr-el-Bahari, Roman architecture, and themes derived from the work of Schinkel and Boullée. He designed the German Pavilion, World's Fair, Paris (1937), which was much admired at the time, but his masterpiece was the Chancellery, Berlin (1938–9), the plan of which was ingenious and the architecture designed to awe the visitor by suggesting stability, opulence, and power. He remodelled the interior of the German Embassy in *Nash's Carlton House Terrace, London, at the same period: his work there (since 1967 The Royal Society) survives virtually intact. He was in charge of a team to re-plan Berlin with a huge north–south axis joining a gigantic domed hall to a new railway terminus, the whole lined by enormous official buildings, all in a *stripped Neoclassical style, but vast in scale.

In 1942 Fritz *Todt was killed in an air-crash, and Speer succeeded him as head of the Organization Todt, which carried out the most ambitious and vast construction programme since the Roman Empire, employing one and a half million men. He was also Minister for Armaments and Munitions (1942–3), and in 1943 was given responsibility (as Reich Minister for Armaments and War Production) for the direction of the Reich's war economy, which expanded threefold in two years under the Speer Plan. The organizational abilities Speer had demonstrated as architect of the Chancellery were now channelled throughout the Reich and occupied territories. In particular, his planning of the production of synthetic oil enabled the German war effort to continue long after access to naturally occurring fuels had been stopped. He was sentenced to 20 years in prison at the Nuremberg Trials, and afterwards published his memoirs, *Inside the Third Reich* (1970), and *Spandau: The Secret Diaries* (1976).

Adam (1992); Arnst, Koch, and Larsson (1978); Krier (1985); Lane (1985); Larsson (1983); Petsch (1978); Sereny (1995); Speer (1970, 1976, 1981); Stephan (1939); Teut (1967)

Speeth, Peter (1772–1831). German architect. He worked under *Pigage at Frankfurt (1788–94), and from 1804 at Amorbach for the Prince of Leiningen before moving to Würzburg, then the capital of the ephemeral (1806–14) Grand Duchy of the Rhenish Confederation under Ferdinand III of Tuscany (1769–1824). In Würzburg Speeth designed the St Burkhardt Gaol (1811, built 1826–7), originally the Guards Barracks, one of the most radical and startling works of Franco-German *Neoclassicism, standing below the slopes rising to the impressive Marienberg fortress of the Prince-Bishops. It has a *rusticated base of immensely impressive power punctuated by three semicircular arches, and above the central entrance-arch is a colonnade of *primitive unfluted Greek *Doric columns set within a Graeco-Egyptian *battered element with a plain *pediment over it. The blank wall above, the over-scaled lion's mask, and the curiously forbidding character of the building give it tremendous authority as an example of *architecture parlante. Speeth designed the Zellertor Guard House (*c.*1813–14) in Würzburg, also featuring rustication and baseless Doric, and looking rather like one of *Ledoux's *barrières* for Paris. His *Gerichtsdienerhaus* (House of the Court Usher), 9 Turmgasse, Würzburg (1811–13—but much altered), was conceived as an Egyptian *pylon-tower in shallow relief, with powerful rustication at the bottom and highly original *fenestration. He also designed the Church of St John the Baptist, Unterhohenried, near Hassfurt (1812–17), and the Metropolitan Church, Kishinev, Russia (begun 1826).

Nerdinger (1980); Watkin and Mellinghoff (1987)

Spence, Sir Basil Urwin (1907–76). British architect, born in India and educated in Scotland and London. He worked in the office of *Lutyens for a brief period. He made his name when he won the competition for the rebuilding of Coventry Cathedral, Warwickshire (1950–1), regarded as a symbol of Britain's reconstruction after the 1939–45 war. Spence had been Architect for the 'Britain Can Make It' Exhibition (1947) and for the Scottish Industries Exhibition (1949). He also designed the Sea and Ships Pavilion for the *Festival of Britain South Bank Exhibition, London (1951). From that time he was able to build up a large and successful practice. Among his works were Undergraduate Residences, Queen's College, Cambridge (completed 1960), buildings for Liverpool and Southampton Universities (1960s), and the layout and first phase of Sussex University (1962–72). For the last he designed Falmer House, where he used *arcuated forms derived from Le *Corbusier's Maison Jaoul. He also designed the Library and Swimming-Centre, Hampstead Civic Centre, Swiss Cottage, London (1964), the Household-Cavalry Barracks, Knightsbridge, London (1970), and the British Embassy, Rome (1971), in all of which he tried to create a degree of monumentality. Spence's work brought contemporary architecture before the public, and his Coventry Cathedral enjoyed a degree of popularity. His work, however, seems hesitant in retrospect, owing something to Scandinavian sources, yet striving for a grandeur that eluded him, possibly because of reasons of *scale, but perhaps more due to the poverty of the *Modern Movement's architectural language. He was a gifted draughtsman and artist.

DNB (1986); Edwards (1995); Emanuel (1994); Spence (1964, 1973); Spence *et al.* (1964); Spence and Snoek (1963)

spere, speer, spier, spure. 1. *Screen, usually treated decoratively, and with one or two doorways, at the lower end of a medieval *hall defining the *screens passage between hall and kitchen, or separating the cross-entry from the hall. Its top often coincided with the *tie-beam of a roof-truss above, in which case the screen and *truss were termed the *speer-* or *spere-truss*. **2.** Short screen, check, or heck between a doorway and a fireplace, acting as a baffle.

Alcock, Barley, Dixon, and Meeson (1996)

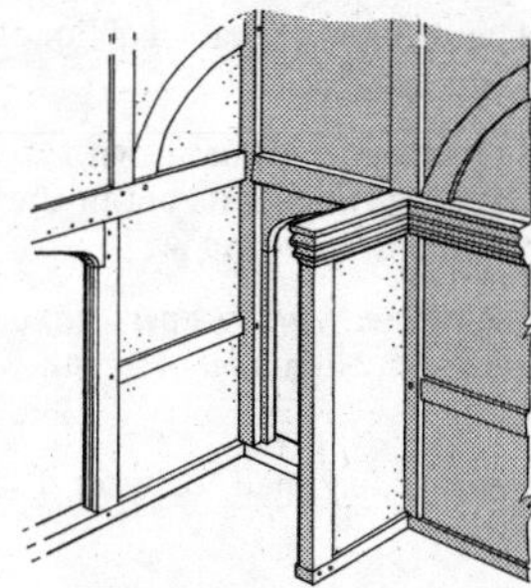

Free-standing draught spere. (*JJS*)

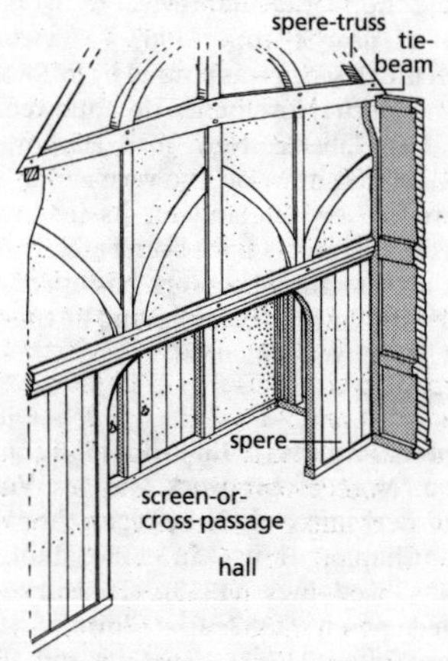

Spere and spere-truss. (*JJS*)

spere.

Spezza, Andrea (d. 1628). Architect of the *Baroque Valdštejn Palace, Prague (1624–34), for Albrecht Wenzel Eusebius (1583–1634), Graf von Waldstein (Wallenstein), the famous commander of the Imperial forces during the Thirty Years War. This monumental building, with its five courts and gigantic gardens, was projected by Spezza and realized by G. B. *Pieroni and others, but it was Pieroni who created the enchanting and monumental *Sala Terrena* there, facing the gardens.

Neumann, J. (1970)

sphinx. Ancient Egyptian sculptured figure of a recumbent lion's body with a male human head (*androsphinx*), often with the *Nemes* head-dress. Sphinxes in the Egyptian style were often made by the Romans, and the form was revived in the *Renaissance, though by then they were female as often as male, and were commonly used in Neoclassical architecture, especially during the *Egyptian Revival. Other types include the Egyptian *criosphinx* (ram-headed) and *hieracosphinx* (hawk-headed), and the seated winged Greek sphinx on upright front legs, with the head and breasts of a woman.

Curl (1994); Roullet (1972)

spike. *See* flèche, pricket, spire.

spina. Wall or barrier along the middle of a Roman *circus around the ends of which the contestants turned. It was decorated with obelisks and other monuments.

spiral column. *Barley-sugar, Salomonic, Salomónica, *Solomonic, torso, or twisted column.

spiral stair. *See* stair.

spire. Tall structure, circular, polygonal, or square on *plan, rising from a roof, tower, etc., terminating in a slender point, especially the tapering part of a church-*steeple. Often of stone, and occasionally of brick, it was also built as a *timber-framed structure *clad with copper, lead, shingles, slates, tiles, or thin stone *slabs. If square, a spire rises directly from the tower, but octagonal spires required the top of the tower not covered to be occupied by *pinnacles or by an arrangement (*broach) forming a transition between the square and octagon resembling part of a pyramid and sloping towards the spire (*broach-spire*). Other types of spire include:

crown spire: spire carried on *buttress-like elements, i.e. with the structure fully exposed, resembling the arched forms at the top of a crown;

Hertfordshire spike: small needle-spire rising from a tower behind a parapet;
needle-spire: very tall slender spire rising from a tower behind a parapet, like a *Hertfordshire spike but much bigger, taller, and finer;
spike: short spire, *flèche, or *spirelet*;
splay-foot: spire with a base opening out at a flatter pitch and forming *eaves over the tower.

Gwilt (1903); Papworth (1887); Parker (1850); Sturgis *et al.* (1901–2)

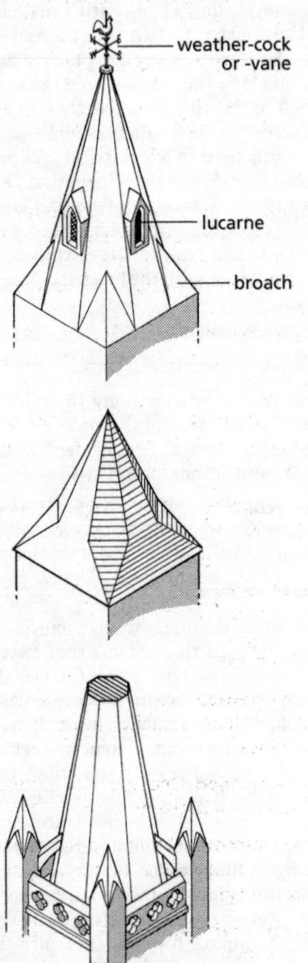

spire. (*top*) Broach with lucarnes and weather-cock or -vane. (*JJS*) (*middle*) Splay-foot spire. (*bottom*) Needle-spire behind a pierced parapet and attached to pinnacled clasping buttresses by flying buttresses. (*JJS*)

spirelet. Small *spire, spike, or flèche.

spire-light. *Gabled *lucarne.

splay. **1.** Any surface, larger than a bevel or *chamfer, making an oblique angle with another surface, such as a *jamb of an aperture permitting more light to enter. **2.** *Embrasure.

splayed arch. Arch over an aperture with splayed *jambs, i.e. with a larger span on the inside wall than on the exterior.

splayed coping. Feather-edged *cope sloping or pitched in one direction.

splayed-foot. *See* spire.

splayed jamb. *Jamb set at an oblique angle to the face of a wall.

splayed mullion. *Mullion with splayed sides separating two *lights not in the same plane in a canted *bay-window.

splayed window. Window-aperture containing a frame with *lights set obliquely within it.

split. *Engaged, e.g. half-*baluster attached to a *pedestal.

Spoerry, François (1912–). French architect. He startled the architectural world by designing the *vernacular-revival resort of Port Grimaud, near St-Tropez (1967–75), a work on which much scorn was poured by followers of the *Modern Movement. He followed this with Port Liberté, New York Harbor, USA (1984), which drew on the vernacular architecture of New England for its inspiration. Both developments have been categorized as *Soft architecture. His work has encouraged others to follow his example, and he therefore must be seen as influential.

Spoerry (1989)

Sponlee, John de (*fl.* 1350–d. *c.*1386). English mason. Most of his work was at Windsor Castle, Berkshire, where he began the *Vestry and *Chapter House in 1350, built the Canons' Lodgings (1353), Treasury with vaulted porch (1353–4), *Cloisters (1356), Spicery Gate (1357–8), New Gate and *Belfry Tower (1359–60), and the Royal Lodgings (1358–65). Although William de *Ramsey drew up plans for St George's Chapel in 1348–9, it was Sponlee who carried the work upwards, constructing the chapel in one of the first examples of the fully developed *Perpendicular style.

Harvey (1987)

Spreckelsen, Johan Otto von (1929–87). Danish architect. He often used stereometrically pure forms (including the cylinder, pyramid, and sphere) in his work. Among his places of worship St Nicolai Church, Hvidovre (1960), Vangede Church, north of Copenhagen (1974), and Stavnsholt Church, Farum (1981), deserve mention. He is perhaps best known for *La Grande Arche de la Défense*, Paris (1981–9), a vast structure that is essentially a hollowed-out cube, and terminates the axis that runs from the Tuileries Gardens in the east, through the Arc de Triomphe in the Place de l'Étoile, to the La Défense District in the west.

Curtis (1996); *Denmark: An Official Handbook* (1974)

spring, springing. Plane at which an *arch or *vault unites with its impost. *See* abutment, skew-back.

springer. 1. Lowest stone of an arch on the impost. **2.** *Kneeler or *skew-block at the lowest end of the raking top of a *gable.

springing-course. Impost.

springing-line. Horizontal plane from which an arch begins to leave its *impost by rising upwards.

springing wall. *Buttress.

sprocket. Small triangular- or wedge-shaped timber cocking-piece attached to the upper face of a *rafter near its foot to reduce the slope above the *eaves, which are said to be *sprocketed*.

spur. 1. Short horizontal timber, one end fixed to a *cruck *blade about a third of the height of the blade, and the other fixed to a cruck-stud, to carry the wall-plate. **2.** Short diagonal strut. **3.** Strengthening *pier or sloping *buttress. **4.** Ornamental timber bracket by the sides of doors to support a projecting upper floor (e.g. C14 examples in York). **5.** *Salient outwork of a fortress. **6.** Prow-shaped bridge-pier, or *cut-water. **7.** Carved claw, leaf, or *griffe* on the corners of a square *plinth under a medieval pier. **8.** *Spere.

spur-beam. Horizontal timber over the thickness of a wall (i.e. set with its length at 90° to the *naked of the wall), forming a triangle with the *rafters and ashlering and fixed to

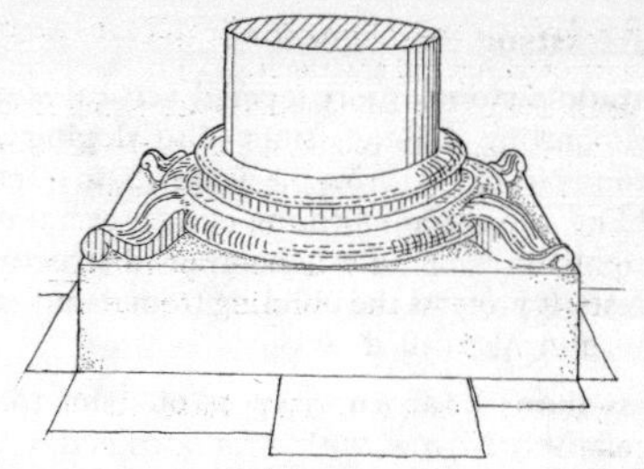

spur. 7. C13 example, Church of St Mary Magdalen, Stockbury, Kent. (*After Parker*)

the wall-plate. As *sole-piece (**2**).

spur-stone. Upright stone, often circular on plan, like a *bollard, fixed in the road at an angle of a building or on each side of a vehicle-entrance to protect the corners.

square. 1. Angle of 90°. **2.** Figure of four equal sides and angles of 90°. **3.** Open space, generally more or less rectangular, in a town, formed at the junction of two or more streets, and surrounded by buildings, as in the *Georgian squares of Britain, often with gardens in the middle. **4.** *Fillet in a series of mouldings.

square billet. Small cube placed in series, often with a parallel row, forming a moulding in *Romanesque architecture.

square dome. *Cloister vault* formed on a square plan from which four curved *vaults rise, joined by groins (not a true *dome).

square end. East end of a church, with a rectangular plan, common in the British Isles, unlike the Continental *apsidal arrangement.

square-framed. With all angles square, e.g. a panelled *door with stiles, etc., square, and no mouldings.

square-headed. Opening with vertical parallel sides and a horizontal top.

square-turned. Member not carved on a lathe, but shaped on four sides, e.g. *baluster square on *plan.

squared rubble. *Rubble with roughly squared stones.

squinch. *See* dome.

squint. *See* hagioscope.

staccato. *See* concatenation.

stackstand. *See* staddle-stone.

staddle-stone. Short tapered vertical stone supporting a rough stone disc sloping all round its top to throw the water off, so resembling a toadstool, forming one of several uprights on which a *timber-framed structure rests. It protects the building from damp and vermin. Also called *stackstand*.

stadium. 1. Large open space, often long and relatively narrow, with a rounded end, used for foot-racing in Classical Antiquity. **2.** Modern sports arena or football stadium.

stage. *See* tower.

Stainefield, Oliver de (*fl.* 1305–10). English master-mason. He was at Beverley *Minster, Yorkshire, from 1305, and was the probable architect of the *nave, begun 1308.

Harvey (1987)

stair. Series of *treads* and *risers*, the two making a *step*, in a *flight* of stairs, usually enclosed in a structure or cage (*staircase), providing access from one storey or floor to another. Common parts of a stair are:

baluster: one of a series of upright supports for a *handrail*, also providing protection, and also called *banister*;
balustrade: ensemble including the *balusters*, *handrail*, and *newels*, also called *banisters*, providing a barrier at the side and a grip for those ascending or descending;
cap: top of a *newel*;
drop: lower end of a *newel* if visible;
easing: junction between *strings* when the *flight* changes direction;
flight: series of steps between *landings*, or from floor to floor, or from floor to landing;
going or *run*: of a step, horizontal distance between two *risers*, and of a *flight*, horizontal distance between the faces of the top and bottom riser;
half-space: *landing* the width of two parallel *flights*, one going up and the other down, involving a turn of 180° (*see* pace (**3**));
headroom: vertical distance from the *line of the nosings* to the *soffit of the flight over;
landing: small floor between *flights*;
line of the nosings: line drawn through the extremities of all the *nosings*, so parallel to the *string*;
newel: central *pier of a circular stair carrying the narrower ends of each wedge-shaped *step*, or upright member supporting the *bearer*, *handrail*, *string*, and *trimmer* at the end of a *flight*;
nosing: projecting front edge of a *tread*, often rounded, overhanging the *riser*;
pitch: angle formed by the *line of the nosings* and a horizontal;
quarter-space: *landing* half the size of a *half-space*, where flights are set at 90° to each other (*see* pace);
rise: vertical dimension between the tops of consecutive *treads*, or between floors, or between landings, or between floor and landing, defined as *rise of a step* or *rise of a flight*;
riser: face of a step, sometimes sloping back to the *tread* under it (thus increasing the size of the tread);
scotia: concave moulding beneath the *nosing*;
soffit: sloping surface under a *flight*;
spandrel: triangular figure formed between *string* and floor;
string: inclined support for the *steps*, really a raking *beam*;
tread: horizontal upper surface of a step;
tread-end: smaller dimension of a *tread* projecting over the *string* in a *cut-string* stair, often with a carved *console- or *modillion-like bracket below;
well: void between the outer *strings* of *flights*, or the volume within which the stair rises, its inner strings against the walls of the well, as in a *half-turn* stair;
winder: *tread* wider at one end than the other, used when a stair turns.

Types of stair include:

bifurcated: dividing into two *flights* or *branches*;
closed-string: with *strings* from which rise identical balusters, the rake being parallel to the handrail;
cockle: see *winding* below;
cut- or *open-string*: with *strings* notched to accommodate the *treads* from which *balusters* of differing lengths rise, the *tread-ends* not being parallel to the handrail, and often having decorative console-like ornaments under them;
dog-leg: two parallel *flights*, each rising half a storey, with a *half-landing* joining them but no *well* between the strings;
double-return: stair starting with one *flight* and returning in two from a *landing*;
flying: with stone steps *cantilevered from the *stair-well* wall without *newels* at the angles or turning points, each step resting on that below. Handrails are usually joined by means of short curved portions called *wreaths*;
geometrical: *flying* stair, usually circular or elliptical on plan, the ends of the cantilevered steps forming a curve:
half-turn: stair with *flights* on three sides of the *stair-well* with *landings* at the corners;
Imperial: starts with one straight flight, and then, after the landing, turning by 180°, with two flights parallel to the first flight, leading to the

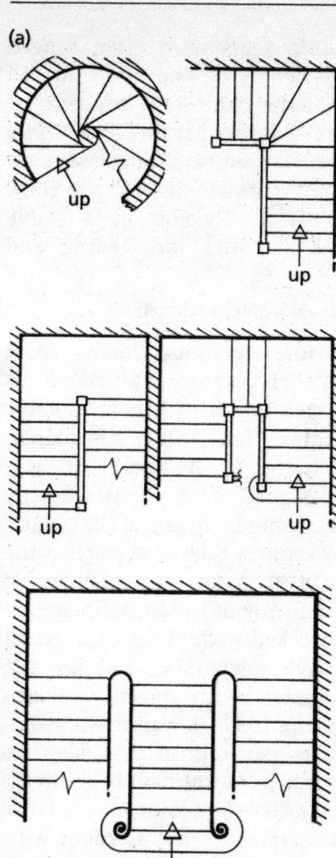

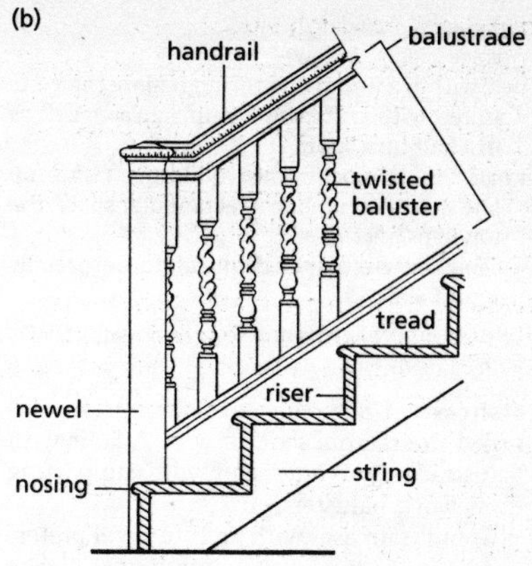

stair.
(*a*) Plans of stairs. (*top left*) Spiral stair with winders and central newel. (*top right*) Quarter-turn with winders at the turn. (*middle left*) Dog-leg with half-pace landing. (*middle right*) Open-well with quarter-pace landings. (*bottom*) Geometrical Imperial with scrolled handrail. (*JJS*)
(*b*) Closed-string stair.
(*c*) (*left*) Timber stair with cut string and carved console-like brackets below the ends of the treads, and with plain balusters. (*right*) Stone geometrical or flying stair with each step resting on that below, and with metal balusters and moulded handrail. (*JJS*)

upper floor. It probably first occurred at the Escorial, near Madrid (1563–84), and spectacular later examples include the staircases at Schloss Brühl (1740s) and the *Residenz*, Würzburg (1734);

newel: circular stair winding around a solid central *pier or *newel* which carries the narrower ends of the steps, or a rectangular stair with newels at the angles to receive the ends of the *strings*;

open-newel: *half-turn* or other stair around a *well*, as distinguished from a *dog-leg*;

open-riser: with no *risers*; the space between *treads* left open;

open-well: resembling a *dog-leg* but with a gap or *well* between the outer strings, more especially with a larger well, each flight terminating in a *quarter-landing*;

perron: unenclosed *flight* of external steps before the entrance to a *piano-nobile level, or the balcony-landing at the top of a double flight of steps meeting at each end of such a landing;

spiral: see *winding* below;

straight-flight: with one flight;

turngrece: see *winding* below;

turning: with flights of different directions, so including *bifurcated*, *half-turn*, *quarter-turn*, and *three-quarters turn* stairs;

turnpiece: see *winding* below;
vice: see *winding* below;
well: within a well rising through more than one storey, with *newel-posts* forming an *open well*, as in a half-turn stair;
winder: in *timber-framed buildings rising up one storey, occupying a rectangular space, the top steps *winders*;
winding: any circular or elliptical stair, especially a *newel* stair.

Centre d'Études Supérieures de la Renaissance (1985); Templer (1992)

staircase. **1.** Structure enclosing a *stair, also called the *staircase-shell*, or *well*. **2.** Stair with balustrade. **3.** Whole stair with supporting framework, balusters, etc.

Grand staircases with architectural pretensions are of considerable antiquity and were known in ancient Crete and Mesopotamia. In Classical Antiquity, curiously enough, staircases were not often exploited as architectural elements, and it was only with the *Renaissance that staircases began to be developed architecturally, notably with *Bramante's staircase at the Belvedere Court, Vatican, and the Imperial staircase at the Escorial, near Madrid, by Juan Bautista de *Toledo and de *Herrera (1563–84). *Palladio seems to have been responsible for the *flying* or *geometrical* stair, much used in C18. During the *Baroque period staircase-design progressed to such masterpieces as the *Treppenhaus* in the *Residenz* (Seat of the Court) at Würzburg by *Neumann. Staircases were often expressed as powerful architectural elements, notably by *Gropius, *Mendelsohn, and others in C20.

Baldon and Melchior (1989); Pevsner (1960); Templer (1992)

stalactite. **1.** System of corbelling, called *muqarna, really brick squinches (*see* dome) and *vaults with the *soffits elaborately carved to resemble a series of stalactites, in *Islamic, particularly *Moorish, architecture. **2.** Stone or *stucco forms resembling stalactites or icicles, called *congelation, found in *grottoes.

stalk. In the *Corinthian *capital, the representation of a stem, sometimes with *flutes, from which the *volutes rise.

stall. **1.** Fixed seat in a *chancel or *choir, one of a number, generally elevated, enclosed at the back and sides, arranged in rows on the north and south sides, and often, in grander churches, surmounted by lofty canopies of *tabernacle-work. Seats were often hinged and had *misericords on the underside. In larger churches the choir-stalls returned at the west end of each row, parallel to the *pulpitum or choir-screen. **2.** Theatre-seat in the part of the *parquet nearest the stage (*orchestra-stalls). **3.** Division in a stable equipped with facilities for feeding and drainage.

Bond (1910, 1912, 1913, 1916); Parker (1850)

Stam, Martinus Adrianus, *called* **Mart** (1899–1986). Dutch architect. Much of his work was carried out with others, notably *Poelzig and Max *Taut (1922), *Brinkman and van der Vlugt (1925–8), and Ernst *May (1930–4). He designed terrace-houses for the *Weissenhofsiedlung in Stuttgart (1927), and was invited by Hannes *Meyer to teach at the *Bauhaus (1928–9). A founding-member of *CIAM, he was firmly of Leftist political persuasion, and worked with May in the Soviet Union on the New Towns. With El *Lissitzky, he was associated with *Constructivism (1924–5). After the 1939–45 war he worked in Dresden and East Berlin until 1952 when he settled for a while in Amsterdam before retiring to Switzerland. His best-known work is the van Nelle Tobacco Factory in Rotterdam, with Brinkman and van der Vlugt (1926–30).

Blijstra *et al.* (1970); Joedicke (1963*a*, 1976); Joedicke and Plath (1968); Oorthuys and Moller (1995)

stanchion. **1.** *Post, or vertical support, such as a structural steel upright in a framed structure. **2.** *Mullion. **3.** *Stud of a *timber-framed wall. **4.** Vertical iron bar between mullions of a *Gothic window.

standing-tower. *See* prospect tower.

Stanley, Thomas (*fl.* 1429–d. 1462). English mason. He built the tower at Lydd Church, Kent (1442–6), and for some time from at least 1429 was a senior mason at Canterbury Cathedral. He may have designed the towers of Tenterden (1449–61) and Ashford Churches, Kent (1460–90).

Harvey (1987)

Stark, William (1770–1813). Scots architect, exponent of a refined *Neoclassicism. He worked in St Petersburg, Russia, in some capacity now unknown (1798), but most of his professional career was spent in Glasgow. Highly regarded in his own lifetime (by Sir Walter Scott (1771–1832), no less, among others), his buildings were distinguished, and included St George's Church, Buchanan Street (1807–8), the Court House, Gaol, and Public Offices, Saltmarket (1810–11—later rebuilt retaining the Greek *Doric *portico, one of the earliest on any public building in Britain), the handsome interiors of the Signet Library (1812–15—now Lower Signet Library) and Advocates' Library (1812–16—now Upper Signet Library), Parliament Square, Edinburgh, and other refined works. His sensitive *Report* on the planning of lands between Edinburgh and Leith was published in 1814, and contains analyses of what was later called *townscape, as well as the *Picturesque aspects of composition. His pupil, W. H. *Playfair, later realized a plan influenced by Stark's *Report*.

Colvin ((1995); Council of Europe (1972); *DNB* (1993); Gifford, McWilliam, and Walker (1984); Gomme and Walker (1987); Williamson, Riches, and Higgs (1990)

starling. **1.** Protective *piles round the *piers of a river-bridge, or a pointed projection of the pier called *cut-water. **2.** Breakwater formed of piles driven closely side by side in hydraulic constructions.

Starov, Ivan Yegorovich (1743–1808). Russian architect. A pupil of de *Wailly (1762–8), he introduced a sophisticated French *Neoclassicism to his native land, notably with his church and belfry at Nikolskoe (1774–6—partly destroyed) and the Tauride Palace, St Petersburg (from 1783), with its grand Catherine Hall flanked by *Ionic columns. Among his other works the Alexander Nevsky Monastery, St Petersburg (1776–90), and the great house at Pella (1785) deserve mention. Throughout the 1770s, 1780s, and 1790s, he was involved in town-planning improvements and in laying out new towns.

Hamilton (1983); Middleton and Watkin (1987); Papworth (1887)

starved Classicism. Mean, thin, ill-proportioned, non-style, loosely based on *Classicism but displaying little feeling for rules, proportions, details, and finesse, and lacking all verve and *élan*. It is not to be confused with *stripped Classicism, which is usually robust, confident, powerful, and often *Sublime.

Stasov, Vasily Petrovich (1769–1848). Russian architect. A pupil of *Bazhenov and *Kazakov, he later travelled in France, England, and Italy, returning to Russia in 1808. He designed numerous buildings, some of which were clearly influenced by the severe *Neoclassicism of *Ledoux. His Victualling-Store, Moscow (1821–35), was understated and plain, but his interesting cast-iron Moscow Gate, St Petersburg (1834–8), was a Greek *Doric *propylaeum of great nobility and power. He built several structures at Gruzino in the 1820s, including various towers and a church: the church-*belfry (1822), not unlike Zakharov's Admiralty *spire in St Petersburg, was destroyed in the 1939–45 war.

Hamilton (1983); Pilyavski (1970)

Statham, Henry Heathcote (1839–1924). English architect. He became Editor of *The Builder* (then one of the most important influences on architecture throughout the British Empire) in 1884, and contributed to numerous journals as well as to *Grove's Dictionary of Music* (he was an accomplished musician). Among the many talented men he encouraged in architecture were Curtis *Green and Beresford *Pite. He designed the fronts of *The Builder* office and those of its neighbours in Catherine Street in 1903. He wrote *A History of Architecture* (1912) which, with its many excellent illustrations, was once widely used as a textbook by students (revised 1927, 1950).

Gray (1985)

stave. **1.** Upright cleft thick timber, usually with a groove for vertical jointing, used for walls and load-bearing, rather than infilling. **2.** One of several small vertical timbers with pointed ends set between *studs in a *timber frame, placed far enough apart to accommodate interweaving rods or other backing for infill panels. **3.** Small vertical cylindrical bar used to form hay-racks to feed horses in stables. **4.** One of many timbers shaped to form wooden barrels.

stave-church. Timber-framed and timber-walled Scandinavian church type (from early C11), built of *staves. Later examples have elaborate tiered roofs.

steel. Following the use of cast and wrought iron in buildings, steel was employed for tall structures, notably *skyscrapers in America from the 1880s. One of the first to have a full skeletal frame, supporting all the floors, etc., without the help of brick or masonry stiffeners, was *Jenney's Manhattan Building, Chicago (1889–90), but the frame was not entirely of steel, and consisted of cast and wrought iron as well as steel. Jenney had used steel in the upper storeys of the Home Insurance Company Building, Chicago (1884–5), which was really a prototypical skyscraper, but the structure was a hybrid, and did not have a true steel skeleton. Steel, strong and capable of being assembled quickly, had been proved in bridge construction and elsewhere, so its potential for *industrialized building and skyscrapers became apparent in the closing years of C19, although full expression of steel structure had to wait until C20. Steel is liable to fail at high temperatures, so it has to be protected against fire, and this seems to have inhibited designers at first, who disguised the frames behind masonry and other façades. Elegant uses of steel structures were demonstrated by *Mies van der Rohe much later.

Hartung (1983); Mainstone (1975)

Steenwinckel Family. Dutch *Renaissance architects. They worked for the Royal House of Denmark. **Hans van Steenwinckel the Elder** (*c*.1545–1601) rebuilt (from 1629) the Castle of Kronborg, Helsingør, while **Hans van Steenwinckel the Younger** (1587–1639) and **Lourens van Steenwinckel** (*c*.1585–1619) designed Frederiksborg, a huge complex of buildings with elaborate towers and *spires, much influenced by contemporary architecture in The Netherlands. Hans the Younger's masterpiece is reckoned to be the exquisite Stock Exchange in Copenhagen (1619–25) with its curious spire formed of three entwined dragons' tails, long repetitive façade pierced by large mullioned and transomed windows, and elaborate *lucarnes.

Cruickshank (1996)

steeple. Collective term embracing a church-tower and *spire together.

Steffann, Emil (1899–1968). German architect. He carried out various works in Lorraine from 1941 and directed the design of housing for the Archdiocese of Cologne from 1947. He made his name with the reconstruction of the Franciscan Monastery, Cologne (1950), and designed many churches, including the St Elisabeth Parish Centre, Oplanden (1953–8), and the round-arched Carthusian Monastery of Marienau, Seibranz (1962–4—with Gisberth Hülsmann). He was a close friend of Rudolf *Schwarz, who influenced his thinking.

Bauwelt, 70/19 (18 May 1979), 766–87

Stegmann, Povl (1888–1944). Danish architect. A pioneer of Danish Modernism, he designed Aarhus University (with Kay *Fisker and C. F. *Møller—1931–3). He was an influential teacher at Aarhus (1924–37) and Aalborg (1937–44).

Weilbach (1952)

Stein, Clarence S. (1883–1975). American architect and planner. He founded the Regional Planning Association to promote solutions to urban overcrowding and applied Ebenezer *Howard's *Garden City ideas to two important developments: Sunnyside Gardens, Queens, NY (from 1924), and Radburn, NJ (from 1926), both with Henry Wright (1878–1936). The separation of pedestrians from vehicular traffic and the large communal gardens of Radburn were influential, and Stein later promoted these in his *Towards New Towns for America* (1951). He advised on the creation of Chatham Village, Pittsburgh (from 1930), and Baldwin Hills Village, Los Angeles (from 1941). He was associated with *Mumford and others in his work.

Journal of the American Institute of Architects, 65/12 (1976), 19–29; *Journal of the American Planning Association*, 46/4 (Oct. 1980), 424–39

Steinbach, Erwin von (d. 1318). German architect. His greatest work was the west front (which survives) and Chapel of the Virgin (destroyed), Cathedral of Our Lady, Strasbourg, France (*c*.1275–1318). In documents he is referred to as *Meister Erwin Werkmeister* (meaning Erwin, Master of the Works). Erwin's name may derive from the small village of Steinbach in Baden, and was celebrated by Johann Wolfgang von Goethe (1749–1832) in *Von deutscher Baukunst* (Concerning German Architecture—1770–3). The drawing, known as *Dessin B*, which survives in the Musée de L'Œuvre de Notre-Dame, Strasbourg, dates from *c*.1275, and is probably in Erwin's hand. The Strasbourg façade, with its exquisite tracery over the portals, influenced many late-German *Gothic designs.

Frankl (1960, 1962); Holt (1958); Recht (1989)

Steindl, Imre (1839–1902). Austro-Hungarian architect. His masterpiece is the *Gothic Revival Parliament Building in Budapest (1883–1902), situated by the Danube, clearly influenced by Charles *Barry's Palace of Westminster, London, although the style is not English *Perpendicular but a symmetrically composed essay in Continental Gothic, with a great and somewhat incongruous dome probably derived from George Gilbert and John Oldrid *Scott's entry to the *Reichstag* (German Parliament-Building) competition, Berlin (1872).

Éri and Jobbágyi (1990); Pevsner (1976)

Steiner, Rudolf (1861–1925). Austro-Hungarian philosopher, artist, scientist, founder of Anthroposophy (knowledge produced by the Higher Self in Man), and architect. Much influenced by the writings of Johann Wolfgang von Goethe (1749–1832), he began designing objects in 1907, guided by ideas of empathy, natural philosophy, *Expressionism, and *Symbolism. He believed that spiritual laws and values could be expressed in architecture, and designed seven columns to be set up in sequence within the assembly-hall of the Theosophical Congress, Munich (1907): these represented the seven ancient planetary spheres of influence believed to regulate human development. In 1910 he designed an underground chamber for the Theosophical Society in Stuttgart, a windowless elliptical space with two rows of columns supporting arches and *vaults bearing astral and Zodiac signs with a polyhedral glass centrepiece. In 1912 he began to plan a domed auditorium and theatre in which all the forms would relate harmoniously to each other and have a mnemonic content. This was realized eventually at the Goetheanum, Dornach, Switzerland (1913–20), a domed structure that was the epitome of Expressionism with a strong Symbolist and *Jugendstil flavour. This 'temple of spiritual wisdom' burned down in 1922, and was replaced by his second Goetheanum (1924, completed 1964), a remarkable Expressionist structure of *reinforced concrete.

Architectural Association Journal, 79/873 (June 1963), 371–83; Biesantz, Klingborn, and Fant (1980); Fant, Klingborn, and Wilkes (1969); Kemper (1966); Pehnt (1991); Placzek (1982); Zimmer (1971)

stele, stela (*pl.* **stelai**). Ancient Greek monument consisting of a vertical stone carved with reliefs, inscriptions, and ornament, often a crowning *anthemion, and commonly used as a gravestone. It was a form often used during the *Greek Revival, and a fine example stands over *Schinkel's grave in Berlin.

Kurtz and Boardman (1971)

Stella, Paolo della (d. 1552). Italian architect of the beautiful Belvedere (Queen Anne's Pavilion), Hradčany, Prague (1535–63), completed by Hans Tirol (*c.*1505–*c.*1575) and Bonifaz Wohlmut (*fl.* 1522–before 1579). It is an essay in pure *Cinquecento, consisting of a rectangular block surrounded by an elegant *Ionic *arcade, and is uniquely sophisticated for its time and location.

Landisch (1968); Watkin (1986)

stellar vault. *See* vault.

Stephenson, Robert (1803–59). English railway engineer. The son of the pioneering railway-builder and designer of locomotives, **George Stephenson** (1781–1848), Robert was mostly responsible for the construction of the main lines from London to Birmingham (1833–8), in the North-East of England, and elsewhere. His greatest works were bridges, e.g. spanning the Tyne at Newcastle and the Tweed at Berwick (1846–9), but his masterpiece was the Britannia Bridge (1845–50), a tubular-girder structure carrying the Chester to Holyhead line over the Menai Straits. In the detailed design of the last Stephenson was assisted by *Fairbairn and others. He also designed the tubular bridge at Conway, Wales (1845–50). His Victoria Bridge over the St Lawrence, Montreal (1854–9), was for some time the longest bridge in the world.

DNB (1917); Rolt (1960); Smiles (1862)

Stephenson, Stephen (*fl.* *c.*1387–1400). English mason. He worked at the great Abbey at Batalha, Portugal (begun 1388), under Affonso Domingues (*fl.* 1387–d. 1402). There are so many English influences in the architecture that Stephenson must have made a major contribution to the design.

Harvey (1987)

Stephen the Mason (*fl.* 1180–1228). English? mason. He made the wall of the King's Forge at Winchester, Hampshire (1180–1), became Master of the King's Works at Corfe Castle, Dorset (1213), and built part of the Great Hall at Winchester Castle (1220s). He probably contributed to the design of the *retrochoirs of Winchester Cathedral (1202–*c.*1235) and St Mary Overie (now Southwark Cathedral—1208–35).

Harvey (1987)

stereobata, stereobate (*pl.* **stereobatae, stereobates**). **1.** Top of a foundation or substructure, forming a solid platform on which a Classical temple stands. It is therefore the top of a *crepidoma, or the *stylobate.

2. Walls of a Roman *podium supporting a *colonnade. **3.** *Pedestal.

stereometry. Art or science of measuring solids. Branch of geometry dealing with solid figures. *Stereometric* therefore pertains to stereometry or solid geometry. Stereometrically pure forms would include the cone, cube, pyramid, and sphere, and were important elements in *Neoclassicism.

Nicholson (1835)

stereotomy. 1. Craft of cutting and dressing complicated blocks of *masonry such as those for an arch, *vault, or *spiral staircase. **2.** The art of making sections of solids.

Stern, Raffaello (1774–1820). Roman architect. An important figure in *Neoclassicism, he designed the Braccio Nuovo (1817–22) which, with the Sala delle Muse and the Sala a Croce Greca (by *Camporese and *Simonetti) in the Vatican Museum, makes up a memorable sequence of spaces based on *Antique precedents.

Meeks (1966)

Stern, Robert A. M. (1939–). American architect. After graduating, he worked with *Meier before setting up his own office in 1977. He has been seen as one of the greatest influences in *Post-Modernism and a formidable critic of *International Modernism. Advocating an architecture of associations, prompting mnemonic perceptions, and firmly rooted in culture, he has argued robustly for a study of history, and for an eclectic use of forms to give buildings meaning. His works include the Lang House, Washington, Conn. (1974), the Ehrman House, Armonk, NY (1975), and Point West Place, Framingham, Mass. (1983–5—with a powerful *portico of *primitive square columns with a *pediment like a section through a *sarcophagus-lid, the whole reminiscent of the work of Ledoux). Stern has, in fact, been successful in reviving something of the severe French *Neoclassicism of the late C18 and early C19. Other works include the Norman Rockwell Museum, Stockbridge, Mass. (1987–93), the Observatory Hill Dining Hall, University of Virginia, Charlottesville, Va. (1982–4), the Kol Israel Synagogue, Brooklyn, New York (1985–9), the Ohrstrom Library, St Paul's School, Concorde, NH (1987–91), and the Darden School of Business, University of Virginia, Charlottesville, Va. (1992–6), all finely detailed and crafted. He has published widely, his contributions including *New Directions in American Architecture* (1969) and much else.

Emanuel (1994); Funari (1990); Stern (1977, 1988, 1996); Stern *et al.* (1995); van Vynckt (1993)

Stethaimer, *or* **Stettheimer, Hans** (d. 1432). Also called **Hans von Burghausen**, he seems to have worked first on the immensely tall *Pfarrkirche* (Parish Church) in Landshut, Bavaria (1387), a fine example of a *hall-church. He was among the most distinguished of German late-*Gothic architects, and was the designer of the beautiful hall-choir of the *Franziskanerkirche* (Franciscan Church), Salzburg (begun 1408), completed by Stefan Krumenauer (*c*.1460): it has vaulting, the ribs of which are arranged in net-like forms, with star-shaped patterns immediately bursting from the very tall cylindrical *piers, one of which is set on the axis at the east end. Burghausen may also have designed the *Spitalkirche*, Landshut (1407–61), and other churches at Neu-Ötting, Straubing, and Wasserburg.

Frankl (1962); Fuhrmann (1950); Grodecki (1986); Liedke, Nussbaum, and Puchta (1986); Watkin (1986)

Steuart, George (*c*.1730–1806). Gaelic-speaking Highland-Scots architect. He worked for the 3rd and 4th Dukes of Atholl, for whom he designed a house in Grosvenor Place, London (1770—demolished). Most of his significant works are in Shropshire, where he designed in a refined and attenuated Neoclassical style. His masterpieces are Attingham Park, near Shrewsbury (1783–5), and the ingenious Church of St Chad, Shrewsbury (1790–2), the latter with a circular galleried *nave, an intermediate vestib-ule, a large and noble *steeple, and an unfluted Roman *Doric *portico. It is one of the most original and pleasing of all *Georgian churches. He also designed the *Ionic temple at Millichope Park, Shropshire (1770), Baronscourt, Co. Tyrone (1779–82—subsequently remodelled by *Soane and *Morrison), All Saints' Parish Church, Wellington, Shropshire (1787–9), the Court House, Ramsey, Isle of Man (1798—demolished), and Castle Mona, Douglas, Isle of Man (1801–6).

Colvin (1995); *Journal of the Manx Museum*, 6 (1962–3), 177–9; Papworth (1887)

Stevenson, John James (1831–1908). Scots architect. He worked in the offices of *Bryce and George Gilbert *Scott, and was later (1860–9) a partner of Campbell Douglas (1828–1910), and (1871–6) E. R. *Robson. He settled in London in 1869 where he worked with Robson on several schools for the London School Board. His Red House, 140 Bayswater Road, London (1871—demolished), was one of the earliest examples of the *Queen Anne style, and was a catalyst in the move away from *stucco to brick for London houses. Among other works were houses at 42–8, Pont Street, Knightsbridge (1876–8), Lowther Gardens, South Kensington (1878), 14 Melbury Road (1876–8—demolished), all in London, and Ken Hill, Snettisham, Norfolk (1879–80). He also designed the first 'Queen Anne' houses in Oxford at 27 and 29 Banbury Road, a fine pair of 1880–1 featuring red brick, richer red-brick *dressings, balconies, and white-painted window-frames. He wrote *House Architecture* (begun 1869–70, and published 1880).

Aslin (1969); Dixon and Muthesius (1985); Girouard (1977, 1979); Sheppard (1973); Stevenson (1880)

Stick style. Late-C19 style of domestic architecture in the USA, partially evolved from *Carpenter's Gothic. While many examples were *timber-framed, the name of the style was also given to buildings in which thin struts or 'sticks' were fixed (sometimes over *clap-boarding) to suggest a timber-framed structure. The elements were often very hard, jagged, and angular, and overhanging *eaves and wide *verandahs were frequently employed. It was more influenced by French and Swiss than by English timber buildings. *Hunt's Griswold House, Newport, RI (1861–3), is a good example.

Handlin (1985); Scully (1971, 1974, 1989)

Stieglitz, Christian Ludwig (1756–1836). German architectural historian. He published many important books including *Encyklopaedie der bürgerlichen Baukunst* (Encylopaedia of Civil Architecture—1792–8), *Zeichnungen aus der schönen Baukunst* (Drawings of Fine Architecture—1804), *Denkmäler der Baukunst der Mittelalters in Sachsen* (Medieval Historic Buildings in Saxony—1836–52), *Von altdeutscher Baukunst* (Old German Architecture—1820), and many other works.

Papworth (1887)

stiff-leaf. 1. *Gothic late-C12 and C13 stylized three-lobed carved foliage, usually an enrichment of *bosses and *capitals evolved from *crocketed capital designs, mostly English rather than Continental, and is characteristic of *First Pointed work. **2.** In Neoclassical ornament, a vertical leaf- or feather-form repeated in series on e.g. *friezes.

Lewis and Darley (1986); Parker (1850); Rickman (1848)

Stijl, De. Literally The Style. Derived from *Semper's *Der Stil* (1861–3), erroneously believed to advocate Materialism and *Functionalism, it was a Dutch artistic movement and name of a journal founded by van *Doesburg in 1917. Other members included the painter Piet Mondrian (1872–1944), *Rietveld, *Oud, and van 't *Hoff. It was influenced by *Cubism, by *Neo-Plasticism, and by a Calvinistic concern with objectivity, simplicity, and truth, and, like many C20 movements, was anti-historical and antagonistic to tradition. It proposed an abstracted clarity of expression, wholly divorced from Nature, advocated straight lines, pure planes, right angles, primary colours, and decomposed cubes, and was one of the most powerful influences on architecture between the World Wars, especially on the *Bauhaus and the *International Modern Movement. Early architectural works of the De Stijl group included van 't Hoff's Huis ter Heide, Utrecht (1916—clearly influenced by Frank Lloyd *Wright's work), Oud's projected but unrealized distillery at Purmerend (1919), and van *Eesteren's and van *Doesburg's axonometric studies for a house (1923). However, the paradigm of De Stijl architecture was the celebrated Schröder House, Utrecht, by Rietveld (1921–4), with its slab-like elements, flat roof, primary colours, and angular construction. Other architects influenced by De Stijl were *Mies van der Rohe (especially his Barcelona Pavilion of 1928–9), *Eisenman, and *Portoghesi.

Friedman (1982); Jaffé (1956); Overy (1969); Overy *et al.* (1988); Petersen (1968); Troy (1983); Zevi (1974)

stile. Upright framing of a *door into which the ends of the horizontal *rails are fixed: they are *hanging* (if fixed with hinges), *middle* or *mounting* (abbreviated to *muntin), and *shutting* stiles.

McKay (1957)

Stile. *Stile floreale* is the Italian term for early *Art Nouveau, but *Stile Liberty* (after the Regent Street, London, store which did much to popularize the style) is the more usual Italian label.

Meeks (1966)

Stilling, Harald Conrad (1815–91). Danish architect. A pupil of *Hetsch, he designed the

Concert Hall, Bazaar, and other graceful late-Classical buildings at the Tivoli Gardens, Copenhagen (1843), for the entrepreneur *Carstensen. He also designed the Casino (1845–7), later Copenhagen's first commercial theatre (1848), but intended by Carstensen as a 'Winter Tivoli'. Stilling's Boutique Schwartz, 3 Svaertegade, Copenhagen, was strongly influenced by *Schinkel's work. Stilling wrote a history of Church Architecture (1870).

Millech (1951); Weilbach (1952)

stilted. Raised higher than normal, a term almost entirely confined to the arch. *See* arch.

Stirling, James Frazer (1926–92). Scots architect. Educated at Liverpool, he was in partnership (1956–63) with James *Gowan with whom he designed several influential buildings. Their flats at Ham Common (1955–8) featured exposed concrete beams with brick infill which were widely copied, though influenced by the work of Le *Corbusier, and fell into the category of early *Brutalism. The Engineering Building, University of Leicester (1959–63—a collage of quotations influenced by *Melnikor and *Constructivism), with its angular chamfered forms and hard red brick contrasted with much glazing, attracted much attention. Thereafter Stirling, practising alone, designed the History Faculty wing, University of Cambridge (1964–7), Student Residences, University of St Andrews (1964–8), the Florey Building, Queen's College, Oxford (1966–71), housing for Runcorn New Town (1967–76), and other projects.

In the 1970s he was joined in partnership in 1971 by Michael *Wilford. The firm carried out work in Germany, including the *Staatsgalerie*, Stuttgart (from 1977, opened 1984), which paraphrases elements from the work of Ehrensvärd, Ancient Egyptian architecture, the primitive, and *Schinkel's Museum in Berlin, but in an apparently whimsical way, owing something, perhaps, to techniques of collage discussed by Colin *Rowe and others. Later works include the Clore Gallery, Tate Gallery, London (from 1980–7), and a development at No. 1 Poultry, London (1985–97). His later architecture became increasingly eclectic and expressive, containing allusions to historical themes.

Arnell and Bickford (1984); Emanuel (1994); Girouard (1998); Jencks (1973*a*); Maxwell (1972); Sudjic (1986)

stoa. 1. Type of Ancient Greek *portico of limited depth but great length, with a long wall at the back and a *colonnade on the front, usually facing a public space, used for promenades, meetings, etc. Some were of two storeys, e.g. Stoa of Attalus, Athens (C2 BC—restored), with *Doric columns on the lower storey and *Ionic above. **2.** Temple portico with the front columns so much in advance that an extra column is needed between the colonnade in front and the structure behind, i.e. a deep *prostyle portico. **3.** *Byzantine *hall with its roof supported on one or more parallel rows of columns.

Coulton (1976); Cruickshank (1996); Dinsmoor (1950); Robertson (1945); Sturgis *et al.* (1901–2); Wycherley (1962)

stoep, stoop. Dutch or *South African *verandah.

Stokes, Isaac Newton Phelps (1867–1944). *See* Howells, John Mead.

Stokes, Leonard Aloysius Scott (1858–1925). English architect. He was articled (1871–4) to the Roman Catholic church-architect Samuel Joseph Nicholl (1826–1905), before gaining further experience with *Street, *Collcutt, and *Bodley. He established his own practice in 1882, and designed many buildings for the Roman Catholic Church in a free *Arts-and-Crafts style. His masterpiece is St Clare's Church, Sefton Park, Liverpool (1888), a fine composition with traceried windows set in powerfully modelled walls, with internal *buttresses resembling those used by Bodley at St Augustine's, Pendlebury, Manchester (1870–4). He favoured long, low, solid compositions on complex plans, as at All Saints' Convent, London Colney, Hertfordshire (1899–1903). He also designed Downside School, near Bath, Somerset (1910–12), and the North Court, Emmanuel College, Cambridge (1913–15). His domestic architecture was refined and often impressive: Yew Tree Lodge, West Drive, Streatham, London (1898–9), Thirteover House, Cold Ash, Berkshire (1898), and, Littleshaw, Woldingham, Surrey (1902–4), were mentioned by *Muthesius in *Das englische Haus*. His designs were rooted in tradition yet were innovatory and imaginative.

Architectural Review, 100/600 (Dec. 1946), 173–7; Dixon and Muthesius (1985); Gray (1985); *RIBA Journal*, ser. 3, 34/5 (1927), 163–77; Service (1975)

Stone, Edward Durell (1902–78). American architect. He absorbed the lessons of the *Modern Movement in the 1920s, working on the Rockefeller Center, New York (1929), where he designed the interior of the Radio City Music Hall. His best *International Modernist buildings were the Mandel House, Mount Kisco, NY (1932–3), and (with Philip Lippincott Goodwin (1885–1958)) the building for the Museum of Modern Art, New York (1936–9). After the 1939–45 war his work became rather more personal and formal as he moved away from International Modernism, and turned to regional influences. His US Embassy, New Delhi, India (1954), and Kennedy Center for the Performing Arts, Washington, DC (1961–71), were axial, symmetrical, and paraphrases of *Classicism.

Emanuel (1994); Stone (1962, 1967); van Vynckt (1993)

Stone, Nicholas (1587–1647). English sculptor and architect. He worked for Isaac James, sculptor, of Southwark, London, and then Hendrick de *Keyser in Amsterdam from 1606, whose daughter he married. He settled in London in 1613 and established his reputation as a monumental sculptor, much influenced by the *Antique. He was also a master-mason, and was employed by Inigo *Jones to build the Palladian Banqueting House, Whitehall (1619–22). In 1626 Stone was appointed Master-Mason and Architect at Windsor Castle, and in 1632 Master-Mason to the Crown. His works include the impressive gateways at the Botanic Gardens, Oxford (1632–3), and the remodelling of the north front of Kirby Hall, Northamptonshire (1638–40). He may have designed the York Water Gate on the Embankment, London (1626), but his connection with the *Baroque south porch of St Mary's Church, Oxford (1637), is tenuous, as it is now known to be by John *Jackson. His primary sources came from the works of *Serlio. He possibly designed Lindsey House, Lincoln's Inn Fields, London (*c*.1640). He made the punning monument of William Curl, Auditor of the Court of Wards to Queen Elizabeth I, shown curled up in his shroud in the Church of St Etheldreda, Hatfield, Hertfordshire (1617).

Architectural History, 14 (1971), 30–9; Bullock (1908); Colvin (1995); Harris, Orgel, and Strong (1973); *Walpole Society*, 7 (1918–19); Whinney (1964)

stop. 1. Anything serving to keep a door or opening-*sash from swinging past its proper plane, such as a rebate, stop-*bead, or strip. **2.** Continuous strip or moulding serving to keep a sliding-sash in its place (*stop-bead*). **3.** Termination of any moulding, e.g. *architrave, *hood-moulding, *label, *skirting, or *string-course. A medieval label over a window, for example, terminates in a label-stop.

stop-chamfer. *Broach-stop*, the position of transition between an *arris and a bevel or *chamfer on a medieval timber *beam, often decoratively carved. The term is also applied to the triangular plane, like an inverted *broach*, where an octagonal *pier is transformed into a square block.

Alcock, Barley, Dixon, and Meeson (1996)

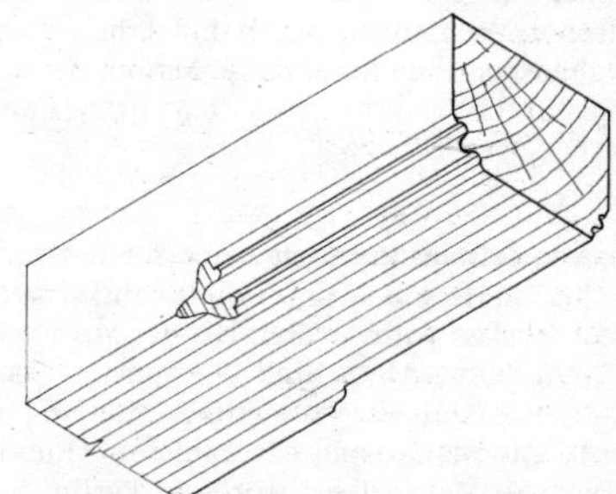

stop-chamfer

stopped flute. *Flute cut in the upper two-thirds of the *shaft of a *Classical column, below which the shaft is faceted (i.e. polygonal), smooth, or the flutes contain *cabling.

storey, story. Volume between the floors of a building or between its floor and roof. Storeys are defined as *basement* (wholly or partly underground), *ground* (in the USA *first* and in France *rez-de-chaussée*), *first* (or *piano nobile if containing the principal rooms), *second*, *third*, etc., then *Attic (over the *entablature of the principal façade). The volume within a roof-space is the *garret rather than the Attic. Entresols and *mezzanines are intermediate floors between the main storeys. Towers have stages rather than storeys, and, like storeys, are often identified by horizontal *bands of mouldings, *string-courses, cornices, etc.

stoup. Fixed basin for Holy Water in a *niche, *corbelled out from a *pier or wall, or free-standing on a *pedestal or similar construction, near the entrance to a church. Also called a *Holy-Water stone*, it can be shaped like a *scallop-shell.

Stow, Richard de (*fl*. *c*.1270–1307). English mason. He was master-mason at the erection of the Eleanor Cross at Lincoln (1291–3—destroyed), and Master of the Fabric at Lincoln

Cathedral from 1291. He built the *belfry-stage of the Cathedral's *crossing-tower from 1306/7 (completed 1311), one of the greatest *Gothic structures in England.

Harvey (1987)

Stowell, Robert (*fl.* 1452–d. 1505). English mason. He was Master of the Stonemasons at Windsor Castle, Berkshire from 1452, and worked at Westminster Abbey from 1468, becoming Master-Mason in 1471. He probably designed the *nave and *aisles of St Margaret's Church, Westminster (1488–1504), by which time he was the King's Master-Mason. He carried out the *vaults of three *bays in the nave of the Abbey in 1488–9.

Harvey (1987)

Strack, Johann Heinrich (1805–80). German architect. He was a pupil of *Schinkel and later worked with *Stüler. His designs were often influenced by Schinkel's exquisite *Neo-classicism, but were sometimes *Italianate, and occasionally explored a confident *Rundbogenstil. Many of his works in Berlin did not survive the 1939–45 war, including the fine Rundbogenstil Borsig Factory (1858–60) and Italianate Villa for the same family (1868–70). With *Persius he altered and completed Schinkel's *Nash-inspired Schloss Babelsberg, near Potsdam (1844–9). For Crown Prince Friedrich Wilhelm (1831–88—reigned as Kaiser Friedrich III (1888)) and his wife, Victoria, Princess Royal of Great Britain (1840–1901), he remodelled the *Kronprinzenpalais* (Palace of the Crown Prince), *Unter den Linden*, Berlin (1856–8), and with Stüler he designed the handsome National Gallery, Berlin (1866–76). He added the two pavilions and wings to the Brandenburg Gate (1868), and designed the Victory Column (1869–73), both in Berlin. He was a sensitive colourist and interior decorator, and published several works including a book of architectural details (1858) and a study of Greek theatres (1843).

Börsch-Supan (1977); Strack (1843, 1858); Strack and Gottgetreu (1857); Strack and Kugler (1833); Watkin and Mellinghoff (1987)

straight arch. *See* arch.

strainer. *See* arch.

straining-piece. Piece of timber acting in opposition to two equal and opposite forces at its extremities to keep those forces apart, essentially a strut.

strapwork. Common Northern-European C16 and C17 ornament in the form of narrow *bands or *fillets, folded, crossed, cut, and interlaced, resembling narrow leather-straps or thongs. It occurred in an early guise in *Mudejar decoration in C15 Spain, but evolved in its most usual forms in early C16 decorations in *Tudor England and, especially, at *Fontainebleau, France (1533–5). Strapwork became common in Flanders, where complex *Mannerist designs were developed, later published by *Dietterlin, *Floris, de *Vries, and in sundry pattern-books, and was much used in English *Elizabethan and *Jacobean architecture, especially on funerary monuments in churches. It was often decorated with *jewels, *lozenges, and *roundels.

Ward-Jackson (1967)

strapwork. Carolean strapwork from Crewe Hall, Cheshire.

streamlining. Aerodynamic design in the 1920s and 1930s in which curving walls, long strips of windows (often curved around elements of a building), and thin flat roofs with pronounced overhangs were used, often in factories to suggest cleanliness and modernity. It was a characteristic of *Modernism, and was promoted by designers such as *Loewy and *Teague.

Street, George Edmund (1824–81). English *High Victorian *Gothic Revival architect. A pupil of Owen Browne Carter (1806–59), of Winchester, Hampshire (1841–4), he later worked in George Gilbert *Scott the Elder's office in the 1840s with G. F. *Bodley and William *White. His first buildings included churches in Cornwall (e.g. St Mary's, Par (1847)) and a vicarage in Wantage, Berkshire (1847–50). Almost from the beginning his work was robust, assured, and satisfying, and he played an important role in the evolution of *muscular Gothic, turning back to a *primitive *First Pointed style derived from exemplars in Burgundy, not uninfluenced by *Viollet-le-Duc. In 1849 he established his own office and became Architect to the Diocese of Oxford (1852), where he designed some of his best work (the Theological College, Cuddesdon (1852–75), Sts Simon and Jude, Milton-under-Wychwood (from 1854), St Mary, Wheatley (1855–68), St Peter, Filkins (1855–7), all in Oxfordshire, and Sts Philip and James, Oxford (1858–66). In the last building the Gothic Revival moved emphatically away from English roots to early French exemplars. He was assisted for a brief period by William *Morris (1855–6) and Philip *Webb (1852–9), and, having built up a national reputation, moved his practice to London in 1856.

Street made several journeys to the Continent, publishing some of his observations on medieval architecture in *The Ecclesiologist* (1850–3), and bringing out his important and influential *Brick and Marble Architecture in the Middle Ages: Notes on Tours in the North of Italy* (1855 and 1874) which argued for a rational approach to design, and drew attention to the wide range of Continental precedent available to architects. His best works thereafter included All Saints', Boyne Hill, Maidenhead, Berkshire (1854–65), St Peter's, Bournemouth, Hampshire (now Dorset) (1854–79), St James-the-Less, Westminster (1859–61—with a powerful brick polychrome interior and plate-*tracery), St John the Evangelist, Torquay, Devon (1861–5—First Pointed), St Mary Magdalene, Paddington, London (1867–73—again First Pointed, with structural *polychromy in the tower), the Crimean Memorial Church, Istanbul, Turkey (1863–8), St Paul's, Rome (1872–6—First Pointed Italian Gothic), and All Saints', also in Rome (1880–1937—completed by **Arthur Edmund Street** (1855–1938)). Both Roman churches employed the striped effects Street admired in his *Brick and Marble*. If Sts Philip and James, Oxford, had demonstrated Street's interest in French First Pointed Gothic of the Burgundian type, his magisterial and cleverly planned Royal Courts of Justice, The Strand, London (1866–81), was an accomplished synthesis of Burgundian French, English, and Italian Gothic, one of the last great monuments of the Gothic Revival containing the grandest secular room of the style, the Great Hall.

His many publications include not only *Brick and Marble* referred to above, but an important essay on the 'proper characteristics' of a town church (1850—which set the scene for those 'citadels of faith' by *Brooks and others), a paper in the *Ecclesiologist* on the true principles of architecture and its development (1852), *An Urgent Plea for the Revival of True Principles of Architecture in the Public Buildings of the University of Oxford* (1853), an essay (in *The Ecclesiologist*) on the revival of the 'Ancient Style of Domestic Architecture' (1853—which was a milestone in the *vernacular and *Domestic Revivals), and *Some Account of Gothic Architecture in Spain* (1865).

Architectural History, 23 (1980), 86–94; Brownlee (1984); Clarke (1966, 1969); *Ecclesiologist*, 11 (1850), 227, 233, 13 (1852), 247–62, and 14 (1853), 70–80; Martley and Urbin (1867); Meeks (1966); *RIBA Journal*, ser. 3, 77/1 (1970), 11–18; Street, A. E. (1972); Street, G. E. (1867, 1874, 1969); Summerson (1970)

street-furniture. Anything erected on pavements or streets, including bollards, iron railings, lamp-posts, post-boxes, street-signs, and telephone-kiosks, often of cast iron.

Design Council (1974); Glancey (1989*a*); Stamp (1989)

stressed-skin. Type of complex structure involving curves and bendings, where the outer skin combines with a *frame to produce a sound, strong, bent, curved structure.

Joedicke (1963)

stretcher. *See* brickwork.

stria (*pl.* **striae**). **1.** Flat facet in lieu of a *flute on a column-*shaft. *See* stopped flute. **2.** *Fillet between flutes of a Classical column. **3.** Rib in *Gothic *vaults. **4.** Any small channel, flute, or indentation in a series, separated by fillets, etc.

Strickland, William (1788–1854). A pupil of *Latrobe, he was among the most accomplished of USA-born architects. He is remembered primarily for his designs in the *Greek Revival style, although two of his earliest buildings, the Masonic Hall (1808–11—demolished) and Temple of the New Jerusalem (1816–17—demolished), both in Philadelphia, were a rather uncertain *Gothick. He made his reputation with the handsome Second Bank of the United States, Philadelphia (1818–24—with a *portico modelled on the Athenian *Parthenon), and followed this with the US Naval Asylum, Philadelphia (1826–33—with an octastyle *Ionic portico), the US Mint, Philadelphia (1829–33—demolished), and the very beautiful Merchants' Exchange, Philadelphia (1832–4—with the Greek *Corinthian Order from the *Choragic Monument of Lysicrates in Athens wrapped round a drum crowned by a replica of the Monument). Indeed, it is clear that Strickland used *Stuart and *Revett's *Antiquities of Athens* (1762–1830) as his main source-book, but with considerable verve and imagination. He again incorporated the Lysicrates Monument as a crowning feature of his otherwise Ionic State Capitol, Nashville, Tenn. (1845–59).

A gifted Neo-Greek designer, Strickland also used the *Egyptian Revival style for the Mikveh-Israel Synagogue, Philadelphia (1822–5—demolished), and the First Presbyterian Church, Nashville, Tenn. (1848–51—with a stunning *polychrome interior based on the Napoleonic and other publications showing Ancient Egyptian architecture). It seems that the Nashville church's style was supposed to suggest the Temple of Solomon in Jerusalem. He designed St Mary's Roman Catholic Cathedral, Nashville (1845–7), and may have been responsible for several *Italianate houses in the same city.

Carrott (1978); Gilchrist (1969); Hamlin (1964); Hitchcock (1977); Kennedy (1989); Pierson and Jordy (1970–86); Placzek (1982); Stanton (1968)

strigil. *Flute, usually curved, like an elongated S, often found on Classical and Neoclassical *sarcophagi, urns, etc.

strigillation. 1. Repeated upright flutes or reeds on a flat *band such as a *fascia or *frieze. **2.** Repeated closely spaced S-shaped flutes, commonly enriching the sides of Classical or Neoclassical *sarcophagi.

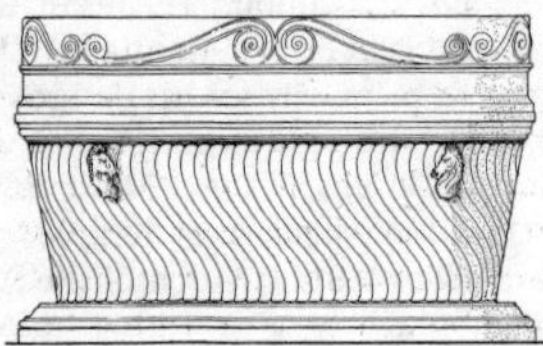

strigillation. Roman sarcophagus.

string. 1. One of two inclined beams (*stringers*) supporting the steps of a *stair. **2.** Horizontal projecting *band or moulding on a façade. **3.** Horizontal tie in e.g. a *truss.

stripped Classicism. Classical architecture from which mouldings, ornament, and details have been elided, leaving visible only the structural and proportional systems. *Boullée, J. J. *Burnet, F. *Gilly, L. *Krier, *Ledoux, *Speer, *Speeth, *Stern, and *Troost, among many others, experimented with stripped *Classicism. It is a feature of late-C18 and early C19 *Neoclassicism, as well as of the *Rational architecture of C20, notably works by *Grassi and *Rossi. Sometimes Classical ornament is merely suggested or implied, as when incisions are used instead of mouldings. With most *stripped* or *diagrammatic* Classicism the *Orders are only alluded to in the most subtle way, but could be added, as the proportions and dispositions of elements would permit this. *Soane's Dulwich Picture Gallery and *Mausoleum, London, is an example. Not to be confused with *starved Classicism.

Council of Europe (1972); Curl (1992); Middleton and Watkin (1987); Powers (1987); Watkin (1996); Watkin and Mellinghoff (1987)

strix. *Canalis* (*see* canal), *flute, or *strigil.

Structuralism. Architecture derived from 'archeforms' (meaning archetypal or original forms), supposedly involving a creative searching for those archetypes, sign-systems, and indicators that determine, in theory, the history of architecture. Elements of Structuralism have been detected by some in early designs by Le *Corbusier involving an overlay on a pronounced circulation-pattern, and in works by *Kahn and the *Smithsons. It seems to have evolved from discussions by *Team X and *CIAM, and has been used to describe certain Dutch buildings, notably by *Blom, van *Eyck, and *Hertzberger.

Bauen + Wohnen, 31/1 (1976), 5–40; Ehrmann (1970); Jencks and Baird (1969); Lévi-Strauss (1963)

strut. Any member in compression that keeps two others apart. It is found, for example, in roof structures between a tie-beam and a collar. Types of strut include:

king-strut: vertical timber set on a collar or tie-beam extending to the apex of a pitched roof (with a ridge-piece, -plate, or -purlin);
queen-strut: one of two vertical members framed between a tie-beam and a collar;
rafter-strut: as *raking-strut* but vertical;
raking-strut: one of a pair of straight or curved members set at an angle on the tie-beam and framed into a principal rafter, often supporting a *purlin.

Alcock, Barley, Dixon, and Meeson (1996)

Stuart, James 'Athenian' (1713–88). British architect of Scots descent, a key figure in the *Greek Revival. He travelled to Rome in 1742, probably supporting himself by acting as a guide and producing drawings and paintings. In 1748 he travelled with M. *Brettingham, Gavin Hamilton (1723–98), and Nicholas *Revett to Naples, an expedition on which a scheme to visit Athens (then part of the Ottoman Empire, and difficult to visit) was mooted. Stuart and Revett announced proposals for publishing reliable surveys of the antiquities of Athens in 1748 which was taken up by various noblemen and gentry then on the *Grand Tour. Finance was raised and the two young men were elected to the Society of *Dilettanti in 1751 under the aegis of which they travelled to Greece. After a dangerous sojourn they returned to England in 1755 to prepare their drawings for publication, and the first volume of *The Antiquities of Athens Measured and Delineated by James Stuart, F.R.S. and F.S.A., and Nicholas Revett, Painters and Architects*, duly appeared in 1762, some time after Le *Roy's *Les Ruines . . .* (1758), which Stuart criticized for inaccuracy: Le Roy and Stuart continued to castigate each other's efforts for some time thereafter. *The Antiquities of Athens* was the first reliable source-book of Greek architecture and was at once recognized as a work of importance. Stuart bought Revett's interest out, but, being of an indolent disposition, the second volume did not appear until 1789. The third was edited by Willey *Reveley and came out in 1795, while the fourth, issued by Joshua Taylor, was published in 1816, and C. R. *Cockerell saw to the last volume in 1830.

Stuart designed the garden-buildings at Hagley, Worcestershire (1758), and Shugborough, Staffordshire (1760s), that were apparently the first buildings in C18 Europe to have the Greek *Orders. He designed a *Palladian house with Grecian details at 15 St James's Square, London (1763–6—later altered). He was also responsible for the exquisite interiors (including some of the earliest C18 uses of *Pompeian motifs) of Spencer House, Green Park, London (1759–65), Holdernesse (later Londonderry) House, Hertford Street, London (*c*.1760–5—demolished), the beautiful Chapel at Greenwich Hospital, London (1780–8—assisted by William Newton (1735–90)), and the Tower of the Winds, Mount Stewart, Co. Down (1782–3). Had he not been so idle, his command of *Neoclassicism, including his knowledge of Greek and Roman decorations, together with his flair for synthesizing various schemes of ornament, could have made him a dangerous rival to the *Adam brothers.

Architectural History, 22 (1979), 72–7; Colvin (1995); Crook (1972*a*); *DNB* (1917); Stuart and Revett (1762–1816); Watkin (1982); Wiebenson (1969)

Stuart architecture. Architecture of the C17, especially *Jacobean and *Carolean, but also applied to the period of the Stuart dynasty in Great Britain from James I and VI (1603–25) to Queen Anne (1702–14). However, the architecture of the reign of Charles II (1660–85) is usually referred to as *Restoration or Carolean, followed by the *William and Mary (1688–1702), then *Queen Anne styles.

Stubbins, Hugh Asher (1912–). American architect. In 1939 he became assistant to *Gropius at Harvard, established his own practice in Cambridge, Mass. (1940), and succeeded Gropius as Chairman of the Department of Architecture (1953). His work was influenced by Gropius, *Aalto, and *Breuer, and included houses, churches, offices, and schools. Among his buildings may be mentioned the Loeb Drama Center, Cambridge, Mass. (1957–60), and the Citicorp Center, New York (1978). His MM21 *skyscraper, Yokohama (1988–92), was the tallest building in Japan at the time of its completion. His Congress Hall, Berlin (1957), with its saddle-shaped catenary roof, was hailed when built, but irreverently referred to by Berliners as the 'pregnant oyster'. He published *Architecture: The Design Experience* in 1976.

Doumato (1987); Emanuel (1994)

stucco *also* **stuc.** Slow-setting plaster known from Antiquity, and made of various ingredients. There are basically two types of stucco: one made from limes and the other from plaster, the former often classed under cements. As an external rendering, *common stucco* is a plastered finish of lime, sand, brick-dust, stone-dust, or powdered burnt clay nodules, mixed with water, used as a finish instead of stone, often lined to resemble *ashlar-work, and moulded to form architectural features such as *string-courses, *cornices, etc. Internal stucco, widely used in C18, and elaborately modelled, was made of very fine sand, pulverized white Carrara marble, gypsum (hydrated calcium sulphate), alabaster-dust, and water, often with other additions, such as colouring, provided by mixing in metallic oxides etc. It was sometimes mixed with size or gum dissolved in lukewarm water, often with the colour also dissolved in the size water. When the stucco was perfectly dry it was rubbed and polished.

Historically, stucco was widely used by the Romans and in *Islamic architecture, but it reached new heights during the *Renaissance, *Baroque, and *Rococo periods, especially in Southern Germany, where the great masters included members of the *Wessobrunn School (notably J. G. Üblhör (1700–63) and J. M. Feichtmayr (1709–72)), and *Zimmermann.

Beard (1983); Blunt (1978); Garstang (1984); Gwilt (1903); Nicholson (1835); Papworth (1887); Schnell and Schedler (1988); Sturgis *et al.* (1901–2); Vance (1983)

stucco lustro. *Scagliola.

stud. In *timber-framing, a subsidiary vertical member in a framed wall (e.g. *herringbone-studding* set at an angle (usually 45°) i.e. the space framed by the *posts and *rails). In *close-studding* the spaces between studs are about the same in width as the studs themselves, a profligate use of material intended for show rather than for any practical purpose. A *cruck-stud* is set outside a *cruck blade and fixed to it.

Alcock, Barley, Dixon, and Meeson (1996)

stud-and-panel. Partition or wall made of *studs with panels of vertical planks or *staves slotted into grooves, called also *post-and-plank* or *plank-and-muntin*.

Alcock, Barley, Dixon, and Meeson (1996)

Studio PER. Architectural partnership in Barcelona established in 1965 by Pep Bonet (1941–), Christian Cirici (1941–), Lluís Clotet (1941–), and Oscar Tusquets (1941–). Work is characterized by fine detailing and a critical, questioning attitude to established notions and forms, as in the triangular, partly excavated Casa Penina, Cardedeu (1968), and the *Belvedere 'Georgina' at Llofriu (1972), a *Post-Modernist temple dedicated to the motor-car. At the Casa Vittoria, Pantelleria, Italy (1974), the column is used to relate the external spaces to the house. Other works include the Profitos Factory, Polinya (1973), and the Tokyo housing-block, Barcelona (1974).

Lampugnani (1988)

Stüler, Friedrich August (1800–65). German architect. Educated at the *Bauakademie* (School of Architecture) Berlin, he was one of the most gifted of *Schinkel's students, and continued designing in a manner reminiscent of the master's style. He supervised the remodelling of Prince Karl's Palace, Berlin (1827), and his first independent work was the inventive *polychrome Stock Exchange (*Börse*), Frankfurt-am-Main (1839–44—demolished). In 1841 he made a design to transform the island in the River Spree behind Schinkel's *Lustgarten* (now *Altes* (Old)) Museum as a Cultural Centre with Museums, and the *Neuesmuseum* (New Museum) was completed to his designs (1843–50) in a Neoclassical style harmonizing with Schinkel's great building. With *Strack he designed the *Nationalgalerie* near by (1865–76), a Graeco-Roman temple on a high *podium. He designed, with Albert Dietrich Schadow (1797–1869—*Hofbaumeister* (Court Architect) in Potsdam), the Russian-style Church of Sts Peter and Paul, Nikolskoë, *Pfaueninsel* (Peacock Island), Berlin (1833–7), several *Rundbogenstil Berlin churches, the *Quattrocento Revival National Museum, Stockholm, Sweden (1850–66), the Officers' Barracks, Charlottenburg, Berlin (1851–9—opposite the Charlottenburg Palace—now the Egyptian Museum), and many other buildings. He was responsible for the interiors of the lavish *Renaissance Revival *Schloss* at Schwerin, erected to plans by *Demmler (1851–7), and for several charming villas in and around Berlin and Potsdam from 1845.

Börsch-Supan (1977); Dehio (1961); *Kunst im Deutschen Reich*, 7 (1943), 74–89; Plagemann (1967); Stüler (1853–66, 1861); Stüler, Prosche, and Willebrand (1869); Watkin and Mellinghoff (1987); *Zeitschrift für Bauwesen*, 15 (1865), 507–12

stump tracery. *See* tracery.

stupa. Buddhist funerary mound in the form of a hemisphere of earth and *rubble. The earliest (C3–C1 BC) are raised on low drums faced with brick or stone. Stupas are sometimes of bell-like form with a platform at the top (surrounded by stone railings) carrying a mast-like stone upright with one or more canopies resembling umbrellas (*chattra*). Stupa-like elements sometimes occur as ornaments in the *Indian style.

Cruickshank (1996); Snodgrass (1985)

Sturgis, John Hubbard (1834–88). American architect, educated in England and the Continent where he absorbed ideas associated with the *Gothic Revival and the *Arts-and-Crafts movement. He started practising architecture in Boston, Mass., in 1861, and in 1870 won the competition for the Museum of Fine Arts, Boston, the first public art museum in the USA, with a design based on Continental-Gothic exemplars possibly influenced by the

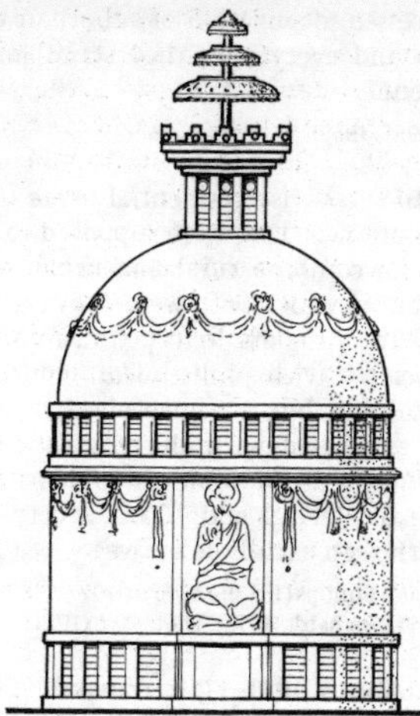

stupa. Surmounted by a *chattravalli.*

University of Oxford Museum by *Deane & Woodward in England. He employed English *terracotta in the design, heralding other *polychrome essays, including the Church of the Advent, Boston (1874–8), in which the influences of *Brooks, *Pearson, and *Street can be detected. He also designed a large number of interesting seaside and country-houses which, after 1870, were influenced by the English *Domestic Revival and the works of Eden *Nesfield and Norman *Shaw, especially those buildings in which the *Queen Anne style emerged. Sturgis drew on American *Colonial and *Federal styles to create new and original works. Among his finest domestic designs was the Ames House, 306 Dartmouth Street, Boston (1882). He was also responsible for the beautiful interiors of the Gardner House, 152–4 Beacon Street, Boston (1882).

Journal of the Society of Architectural Historians, 32 (1973), 83–103; *Proceedings of the American Institute of Architects*, 5 (1871), 39–43; van Vynckt (1993); Whitehill (1970)

Sturgis, Russell (1838–1909). American architect. He worked for *Eidlitz before a period of study in Munich (from 1859), where he absorbed the essences of various medieval styles as well as acquiring a sound grasp of constructional principles. Setting up in practice in New York (1863), his works included Farnam Hall, Yale University, New Haven, Conn. (1869–70), a well-composed essay in *High Victorian *Gothic Revival, and the Farnam House, New Haven (1884), in the *Queen Anne style. His assistants included G. F. *Babb , C. F. *McKim, and W. R. Mead (of *McKim, Mead, & White). He compiled the important *Dictionary of Architecture and Building, Biographical, Historical, and Descriptive* (1901–2), and built up the Avery Library, Columbia University.

Architectural Record, 25 (1909), 146, 220, 404–10, 26 (1909), 123–31, 393–416; Sturgis (1970, 1970*a*); van Vynckt (1993)

Sturm, Der. Literally The Assault *or* The Storm. Title of a Berlin art-gallery (1912–14) and a journal (1910–32) devoted to the avant-garde in Germany, founded by Herwarth Walden (1878–1941). Through *Der Sturm* *Futurism and *Expressionism were promoted.

Chilvers, Osborne, and Farr (1988)

Sturm, Leonhard Christian (1669–1719). German mathematician and architect. He published a treatise on Solomon's Temple in Jerusalem (1694) in which he endeavoured to prove the building's Divinely inspired dimensions and proportions were the basis for Classical architecture (a notion that resurfaces every so often). He designed parts of the *Lustschloss* (Pleasure Palace) of Salzdahlum, near Brunswick (1694–1702), with its celebrated picture-gallery. Later, he completed the Church of St Nikolai auf dem Schelfe, Schwerin, from 1710, after which he published *Architektonisches Bedenken von der protestantischen Klein Kirchen Figur und Einrichtung* (Architectural Reflections on the Form and Arrangement of Protestant Churches—1712 and 1718). His main importance lies in his theoretical writings, of which there are many.

Berckenhagen (1966); Papworth (1887); Sturm (1694, 1712); Wackernagel (1915)

Style 1925. *Art Deco.

Style Moderne. *Art Deco.

Style Rayonnant. *See* Rayonnant.

stylobate. 1. Upper step of a three-stepped *crepidoma* (*see* crepido) forming the platform on which a Greek temple, any *colonnade, or *peristyle stands. **2.** In Classical architecture any continuous base, *plinth, or *pedestal on which a row of columns is set, properly the uppermost part of a *stereobate.

Suardi, Bartolomeo, *called* **Bramantino** (*c*.1455–1536). Milanese painter and architect.

He was influenced by *Bramante and *Leonardo da Vinci, took part in works at Milan Cathedral in 1503, and worked in Rome (1508–13) where he studied antiquities. He later made a study of old buildings in Milan. While his paintings often feature architectural backgrounds, his only surviving building is the octagonal Trivulzio *mortuary-chapel, San Nazaro Maggiore, Milan (begun 1512), an early and remarkable example of refined *Classicism.

Chilvers, Osborne, and Farr (1988); Suida (1953)

sub-arch. *See* arch.

sub-base. Lowest part of a *base set under the base proper in *Gothic architecture, e.g. piers.

Sublime. C18 aesthetic category associated with ideas of awe, intensity, power, ruggedness, terror, and vastness emphasizing Man's relative insignificance in the face of Nature, arousing emotions, and stimulating the imagination. It was therefore distinct from the *Beautiful and the *Picturesque, and was of profound importance in relation to an appreciation of the grandeur, power, and violence of natural phenomena. Its chief apologists were Edmund Burke (1729–97), with his *A Philosophical Enquiry into the Origin of our Ideas of the Sublime and Beautiful* (1756), and Immanuel Kant (1724–1804), with his *Observations on the Feeling of the Beautiful and Sublime* (1764). In architecture the Sublime was associated with great size, overwhelming *scale, the *primitive (especially the unadorned *Doric *Order), and stereometrical purity (as in much *Neoclassicism, e.g. *Boullée's work, and the visions of gaols by *Piranesi).

Chilvers, Osborne, and Farr (1988)

sub-Order. **1.** *Order of architecture inferior to the dominant structural Order, as in *Palladio's Basilica, Vicenza, where the subsidiary Order forms part of a *serliana, and the dominant Orders carry the intermediate and crowning *entablatures. **2.** In *Romanesque and *Gothic doorways, with a series of Orders, the smaller or inferior Orders.

sub-plinth. Second lower *plinth under the main one, as in column-bases or *pedestals.

Subtopia. **1.** Pejorative term derived from 'suburb' and 'utopia', meaning an area with a character that is neither urban nor rural. *See* slurb. **2.** An idealization of suburban urban fringes and everything they stand for and represent.

Nairn (1955, 1959)

Suburbia. Low-rise residential areas on the fringes of towns that were supposed to be attempts to combine rural and urban advantages, but in which both were so diluted they became meaningless. In its pejorative sense it is associated with philistinism, conformity, and dullness, but in fact evolved from C19 ideals associated with the *Arts-and-Crafts and *Aesthetic Movements and with the *Domestic Revival and *Garden City movement, though usually as a travesty.

Barrett and Phillips (1987); Fishman (1977, 1987); Oliver *et al.* (1981); Richards (1973); Thompson (1981)

Suger, Abbot (1081–1151). Abbot of St-Denis, near Paris (from 1122), when the great church there was being rebuilt (*c*.1135–44) in the new *Gothic style. There is no evidence that he was in any way responsible for the design, but he presided over, and wrote about (1144–7), the new buildings which were the earliest in which a mature and consistent Pointed style was used.

Crosby (1987); Panofsky (1979)

Sullivan, Louis Henry (1856–1924). American architect of Irish and German descent. He worked briefly with F. *Furness in Philadelphia (1872–3) before moving to Chicago and the office of W. Le Baron *Jenney (1873–4). He was in Paris in 1874 at the École des *Beaux-Arts under *Vaudremer before returning to Chicago in 1875. He entered the office of Dankmar Adler (1844–1900—the German-born engineer who had settled in the USA in 1854), in *c*.1879, and became a full partner in the firm of Adler & Sullivan in 1883. Their first joint work was the Auditorium Building, Chicago (1886–90) containing a 4,000-seat theatre, hotel, and office-building, the exterior showing the influence of H. H. *Richardson and the interior an eclectic mix of flowing foliate forms containing elements of *Arts-and-Crafts invention as well as *Art Nouveau themes. Even more Richardsonian was the powerful St Nicholas Hotel, St Louis, Mo. (1892–4—destroyed), with its massive round arches.

From 1888 to 1893 Adler & Sullivan employed the young Frank Lloyd *Wright, who was devoted to Sullivan, calling him *Lieber*

Meister (Dear Master), but designed work on his own account in violation of his contract while working for the firm, which led to his leaving to establish his own practice. However, Adler & Sullivan continued to prosper. Their two best-known *skyscrapers, the Wainwright Building, St Louis, Mo. (1890–1), and the Guaranty Building, Buffalo, NY (1894–5), adhere to Classical principles in that each has a plain *plinth-like base; a series of identical floors above expressed by bands of windows and panels set within recessed strips between *piers, with large corner-piers acting as *antae; and crowning *cornices (the Wainwright Building cornice is particularly lushly enriched). Some critics, however, have seen these buildings as expressing the framed structures behind the external skins.

In 1899–1904 Sullivan (having set up on his own after the partnership with Adler was dissolved in 1895) built the Schlesinger & Mayer (later Carson, Pirie, Scott, & Co.) Store, Chicago, which marked a change of direction, in that it did not emphasize the vertical, but created a series of horizontal openings framed by the *skeleton structure of floors and vertical supports. However, he still treated the two lower storeys as a massive plinth enriched with ornament, clad the upper storeys with white *faïence, filled the voids in with *Chicago windows, and capped the whole with an overhanging cornice-like roof. It is the paradigm of the *Chicago School (*but see* Purcell & Elmslie).

In spite of his *de rigueur* remarks in the *Engineering Magazine* (1892) suggesting that ornament should be eschewed for a while, he was an inventive and uninhibited user of architectural enrichment combined with powerful simple geometries and blocky masses, as in the Getty *Mausoleum, Graceland Cemetery, Chicago (1890), and the Wainwright Tomb, Bellefontaine Cemetery, St Louis, Mo. (1891–2). At the Getty Mausoleum the arch motif looks back to Richardson's work, and strong, simple geometrical forms with well-integrated ornament were themes Sullivan explored in the elegant and colourful series of Banks he designed (e.g. National Farmers' Bank, Owatonna, Minn. (1906–8), Merchants' National Bank, Grinnell, Iowa (1913–14), People's Savings & Loan Association Bank, Sidney, Ohio (1919), and Farmers' & Merchants' Union Bank, Columbus, Wis. (1919)).

Sullivan was a prolific writer, his output covering the period 1885–1924, but his prolix texts lack clarity, and his obfuscatory style has been seen as evidence of his profound thought. In 1896, in his 'The Tall Building Artistically Considered', published in *Lippincott's Magazine*, he announced that 'form follows function', a dictum eagerly grasped by the protagonists of the *International *Modern Movement. However, a careful reading of Sullivan's own texts makes clear that his concept of *Functionalism embraces and calls for emotional, expressive, spiritual, and creative values that later Modernists wholly rejected. His built work shows very clearly that it had virtually nothing in common with the teachings of the *Bauhaus or with the apologists for the style that was to be almost universally embraced after 1945.

Bush-Brown (1960); Condit (1952, 1964); Connely (1960); Elia (1996); *Engineering Magazine*, 3 (1892), 633–44; *Journal of Architectural Historians*, 26 (1967), 259–68, and 39 (1980), 297–303; Kaufmann (1956); *Lippincott's Magazine*, 57 (1896), 403–9; Manieri-Elia (1997); Paul (1962); Pierson and Jordy (1970–86); Placzek (1982—contains a useful bibliography); Schuyler (1961); Sprague (1979); Sullivan (1956, 1967, 1980); Twombly (1986); Zukowsky (1987, 1993)

Sumerian architecture. The Sumerians of Mesopotamia were creating sophisticated works of architecture in the fourth millennium BC, almost wholly constructed of brick, and used arches, *domes, and *vaults. The huge Eanna temple precinct at Uruk (Erech in the Old Testament), the greatest of the Sumerian cities, had two groups of temples connected by a mighty *portico of huge circular columns of brick facing a court the walls of which were embellished with *engaged columns. Interior wall-faces were decorated with a geometrical pattern of small *terracotta cones of different colours. Other features of buildings were the *buttress-like projections used to articulate walls, a type of wall-treatment that was to extend well into the last centuries BC. By the mid-third millennium BC painted and *relief ornamental schemes were in widespread use, as in the elevated shrine of Al 'Ubaid, where *friezes, free-standing columns covered in *mosaics, copper sculptures, and other enrichment occurred in profusion. The huge *ziggurat at Ur (C22 BC) had enormous battered walls, monumental flights of stairs, and a temple on the summit of the platform. The basic principles of Sumerian architecture were absorbed by their successors, the

*Assyrians from Northern Mesopotamia, around 2000 BC.

Cruickshank (1996); Lloyd and Müller (1986)

summer. **1.** *Lintel, e.g. over a fireplace. **2.** Beam, also called *breastsummer or bressumer, set on the extremities of *cantilevered joists (*jetty) and supporting the posts of a wall above in *timber-framed construction. **3.** Main beam or girder in a floor, or any large beam, called a *summer-beam* supporting floor-joists. **4.** Large stone, the beginning of a *vault, or at the extremity of a *gable. **5.** Stone at the top of a *pier or *jamb supporting a *lintel or arch.

summer-beam. *See* summer.

summer-house. Primitive or rustic structure in a garden or park to provide shaded seating during hot weather. It may be an *eyecatcher.

Summerson, Sir John Newenham (1904–92). Anglo-Irish architectural historian. He began work as an architect in the office of (Sir) Giles Gilbert *Scott in 1926, later assisting the younger Adrian Scott on the working-drawings for the upper stage of the noble tower of *Hansom's Church of the Holy Name, Manchester. He also worked for W. D. *Caröe before becoming an architectural journalist. As assistant editor of the *Architect and Building News* (1834–41) he developed his cool, even icy, style of criticism, as well as cultivating his support for *International Modernism (in his 1957 lecture 'The Case for a Theory of Modern Architecture', he attempted to promote a solid philosophical base for Modernism, recognizing that Classical architecture had always had just that, but in time he recognized that his efforts were not entirely successful).

He made his name with his biography of John *Nash (1935, 1949, 1980), yet after the 1939–45 war argued that only a fraction of Nash's *scenographic architecture around Regent's Park should be preserved. A founder-member of the Georgian Group (1937), he was also not in favour of anything but highly selective retention of C18 and early C19 buildings. During the war he established, and was Deputy Director of, the National Buildings Record (1941–5), and made extensive photographic records of London buildings: with James Maude Richards (1907–92) he was responsible for *The Bombed Buildings of Britain: A Record of Architectural Casualties 1940–41* (1942, 1947). He brought out his magisterial *Georgian London* in 1945, the year he was appointed Curator of Sir John *Soane's Museum, a position he held until 1984. He wrote several perceptive essays on Soane's work, but never produced a major study, probably because he found Soane's architecture and personality uncongenial. On the other hand, he pioneered studies of John *Thorpe, and, under *Colvin's rigorous editorship, contributed much material on C16 and C17 architecture to the *History of the King's Works* (1975, 1982). In 1953 he made a valuable contribution to the Pelican History of Art series of volumes with his *Architecture in Britain 1530–1830*, which went into several editions: in that formidable work of scholarship his appreciation of the earlier periods (including the designs of Inigo *Jones, *Wren, and others) as well as his ambivalence towards figures such as Nash and Soane were made overt. His attempts to produce a Victorian sequel to *Georgian London* resulted in *Victorian Architecture: Four Studies in Evaluation* (1970), *The London Building World of the Eighteen-Sixties* (1973), and *The Architecture of Victorian London* (1976), with other articles collected as *The Unromantic Castle* (1990). Clearly Summerson was uncomfortable with much of Victorian architecture, finding its variety (and, one suspects, its rumbustiousness) unpalatable, but his scholarly essays on Inigo Jones, Wren, *Viollet-le-Duc, and others reveal areas he found more to his taste. In 1963 he published *The Classical Language of Architecture* to introduce and accompany the six broadcasts he made on the subject for the BBC: a revised and enlarged edition came out in 1980.

Towards the end of his life he modified some of his earlier acerbic judgements, and seems to have become disillusioned with aspects of the Modern Movement. Nevertheless, he supported the demolition of Victorian fabric in the City of London to enable new buildings to go ahead, in spite of having admitted that 'cheap modern' was all Britain ever had (a view from which it would be hard to dissent).

Architectural Review, 192/1151 (Jan. 1993), 9–10; *Burlington Magazine*, 135 (Apr. 1993), 277–9; *RIBA Journal*, 100/2 (Feb. 1993), 63; Summerson (1948, 1952, 1963, 1965, 1966, 1968, 1970, 1976, 1980, 1980*a*, 1986, 1988, 1990, 1993); Summerson *et al.* (1983)

summer-stone. Lowest stone, or raked *skew-block, of a *gable at the end of the *eaves against which the first *cope-stone of the tabling is set to prevent it sliding off. *See* kneeler.

sunburst. **1.** Any collection of rods, normally gilded, representing sunbeams, radiating from a centre. In religious contexts it is common in *Baroque architecture, surrounding e.g. a dove, representing the Holy Spirit. **2.** In a secular context, the rods occur around the head of e.g. Apollo, in *Apolline ornament of the *Louis Quatorze style. **3.** *Fanlight.

sunburst

sun-disc. Ancient Egyptian motif of a disc or globe flanked by rearing *uraei (snakes) and outstretched wings commonly found on the *gorge *cornice.

sunk draft. Margin round a piece of *ashlar leaving the face framed by it raised.

sunk face. Panel surrounded by a raised margin or frame.

sunk fence. *Ha-ha.

sunk moulding. One recessed behind the main surface or *naked of a wall.

sunk panel. Recessed framed panel.

sunk relief. Carved relief not projecting beyond the *naked of the surface on which it is carved, called *cavo rilievo* or *intaglio rilevato*.

super-abacus. *Impost-block, *dosseret, or super-capital set on top of an *abacus, common in *Byzantine architecture.

Mango (1986)

super-altar. **1.** Consecrated altar-stone, -slab, or *mensa*. **2.** Shelf or ledge let into the east wall above and behind the altar.

super-capital. *See* super-abacus.

supercilium. **1.** *Lintel above an aperture (*see* antepagment). **2.** *Fillet above a *cyma on a *cornice forming the topmost member of the *entablature. **3.** Fillets above and below the *scotia of an *Attic *base. **2.** and **3.** are of doubtful authenticity.

supercolumniation. *See* assemblage of Orders.

superimposed Orders. *See* assemblage of Orders.

Supermannerism. American style of interior decoration dating from the 1960s employing odd optical tricks, synthetic materials that were either shiny and mirror-like, or transparent, and over-sized elements, so it was referred to as 'mega-decoration', and owed more to images in 'Superman' comics than to *Mannerism. The term was applied in the 1970s to some large buildings falling into the category of *Post-Modernism.

Progressive Architecture, 10 (Oct. 1968), 148–208; Smith, C. R. (1977)

Supersensualism. Label given by *Jencks to works by certain designers of the 1970s (including *Archizoom, *Hollein, *Haus-Rucker-Co, and *Sottsass) which he identified as having excessive sensuality, warped beauty, fantasy, tortured meaning, and technological sophistication, all taken to extremes.

Architectural Design, 41 (June 1971), 345–7, and 42 (Jan. 1972), 18–21

Superstudio. Italian group founded by Adolfo Natalini and Cristiano Toraldo di Francia in 1966 to produce experimental architecture, but dissolved in 1978. Among projects were the 'Continuous Monument' (*Il Monumento Continuo*), an endless framework structure to cover the world's entire surface (1969), cities built in space, conveyor-belt cities, and other extravagant ideas, including permanently flooding Florence leaving only the Cathedral dome partly above water, and therefore cocking a snook at the *conservation movement. Its work has been seen as an 'alternative' or 'conceptual' architecture with a radical programme antipathetic to capitalist system, and has been categorized as part of *Supersensualism.

Pettena (1982)

Suprematism. Russian artistic movement founded (1915) by Kasimir Malevich (1878–1935), who produced paintings limited to basic geometric shapes using a sparse range of colour. His *White Square on a White Ground* (1918) was regarded as the paradigm of the movement, and had considerable influence on the West, notably on the *International Modern Movement and De *Stijl, though Suprematism was *passé* by 1919.

Chilvers, Osborne, and Farr (1988)

surbase. Topmost moulding of a *dado, *pedestal, or *stereobate.

surbased arch. *See* arch.

surmounted. **1.** *See* arch. **2.** Element placed over another part, such as a *door-case *surmounted* by a *sopraporta.

surround. Frame of an architectural feature, such as an *architrave around an aperture or a *chimney-piece in front of a fireplace.

suspended. Used to describe a structure supported from higher points, such as a bridge *suspended* from *piers or a building or floors hung from a separate structure. A *suspended ceiling* is one hung from the structure above to lower the ceiling and conceal services, etc., and a *suspended floor* is one supported only by its ends.

Sussex bond. *See* brick.

Sustris, Friedrich (1524–*c*.1599). Flemish architect. He worked for the Court at Munich, Bavaria, and was a contemporary of *Candid. He seems to have visited Italy, and was an accomplished designer within the style known as *Mannerism. He was responsible for the *chancel and *transept of the huge *Jesuitenkirche* (Jesuit Church) of St Michael, Munich (1590s—the first large Jesuit church in Northern Europe), and for the *Grottenhof* (Grotto Court) in the Munich *Residenz* (Court Palace—1580–8), a lively composition with statue-filled *niches rather Florentine in style. He carried out alterations at the *Residenz* in Landshut, Bavaria (1570s), and may have designed the former Jesuit College, Munich (now the *Akademie der Wissenschaften* (Academy of Sciences)), built 1585–90.

Baedeker, *Southern Germany* (1929); Hitchcock (1981); Papworth (1887); Pevsner (1960); Powell (1959)

swag. *Festoon on two supports with the suspended element resembling drapery.

Swales, Francis S. (1878–1962). American architect. Educated in the USA and at the Atelier Jean-Louis Pascal and the École des *Beaux-Arts, he was imbued with a sound training in the *Classicism promoted in Chicago and Paris. He set up in practice in Chiswick, London, in 1906. His best-known work (carried out with R. F. *Atkinson with *Burnham as consultant) is Selfridges' Store, Oxford Street, London (1907–9), a massive essay in Beaux-Arts *Neoclassicism, much influenced by Franco-American architecture, and with a *Giant *Ionic *Order rising from a massive *plinth to carry an *entablature in which windows are inserted in the *frieze. Swales provided the original drawing. The Order is derived from Philibert de L'*Orme's Palais des Tuileries, Paris, but with *angular capitals. The building was constructed on a steel frame designed by the Swedish engineer Sven Bylander (1877–1943), who also designed the steel frames for *Mewès & Davis's RAC Club, Pall Mall, and their Ritz Hotel, both in London, and both firmly in French Beaux-Arts Classical styles. Other buildings by Swales included works at le Touquet, Paris Plage, and Boulogne, a hotel in Sandwich, Kent, and the His Master's Voice Pavilion for the Gramophone Company at the Franco-British Exhibition, White City (1908). He settled in Canada shortly afterwards, where he worked for the Canadian Pacific Railway, notably on the Hotel Vancouver, Canada (1912–16—demolished), with Walter S. Painter (1877–1957).

Gray (1985); Kalman (1994)

swallowtail. **1.** *Dovetail moulding* or *triangular fret* moulding consisting of a series of adjacent equilateral triangles, each set alternately with apex and base uppermost, the series framed by a system of *fillets joining at acute angles, and decorating a *band. **2.** Guelphic crenellation. *See* battlement.

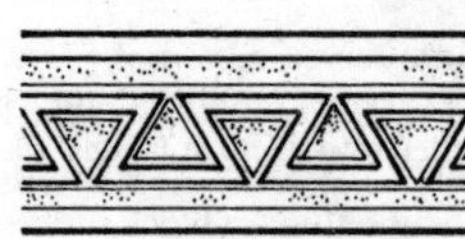

swallowtail. Romanesque swallow- or dovetail moulding, also called *triangular fret*, from Ely Cathedral, Cambridgeshire. (*After Parker*)

swan-neck. **1.** Any member constructed on a double curve, e.g. a *stair handrail with a concave curve then bending into a convex curve before straightening out to join a newel-post.

2. Form of a rainwater-pipe connecting a gutter to a downpipe under the *eaves. **3.** *Scrolled *pediment.

Swastika. *See* cross.

swelled chamfer. *Vitruvian scroll.

swelled frieze. *See* pulvin.

Symbolic architecture. Term coined by Charles *Jencks in the 1980s to describe architecture with a strong degree of *personification or with allusions to cultural ideas, historical references, and other pre-Modernist themes, or in which there were visual jokes, puns, and mnemonic motifs.

Jencks (1985)

symbolism. Representation of acts, persons, ideas, or anything by means of familiar objects, e.g. Christianity by the Cross, a Saint by the means of his/her Martyrdom (St Lawrence/grid-iron), or the Holy Spirit by a dove.

Ferguson (1961)

Symbolism. Artistic movement that flourished in the late C19 as a reaction to French Impressionism and Realism in painting. The poet Jean Moréas (1856–1910) published a manifesto in 1886 in which he stated the essential aim of art was to clothe ideas in sensual forms and to resolve the dichotomy between the real and the spiritual world. In painting this often gave expression to mysticism and occultism and the idea that line and colour could express ideas by suggestion and evolution rather than by depiction or description. Symbolist painting was often full of *femme-fatale* and death imagery, the erotic, the occult, the diseased, and the decadent. Among Symbolist painters may be mentioned Arnold Böcklin (1827–1901), Ferdinand Hodler (1853–1918), Gustave Moreau (1826–1980), and Franz von Stuck (1863–1928). In architecture it was associated with *Art Nouveau and *Expressionism. Perhaps its greatest architectural exponents were Rudolf *Steiner and Henry van de *Velde.

Cassou (1984); Chilvers, Osborne, and Farr (1988)

symmetry. 1. Exact correspondence of parts on either side of an axis, e.g. Greek temple. **2.** Harmony, proportion, or uniformity between the parts of a building and its whole.

Synagogue. Building or place of meeting for Jewish worship and religious instruction. Early surviving examples have affinities with Roman *basilicas, with the Ark of the Covenant containing the Scrolls of the Law placed in a *niche or an *apse. Stylistically, Western synagogues conformed to the period and place where they were erected, although late-C19 examples tended to favour a round-arched *Byzantine *Romanesque style, sometimes with orientalizing detail, especially in Germany and England (e.g. Prince's Road, Toxteth, Liverpool, Synagogue (1874–82) by George Ashdowne Audsley (1838–1925)). Many fine examples of *timber-framed synagogues existed in Poland before the 1939–45 war, but the architectural losses of synagogues during the Nazi domination of Europe were catastrophic.

Chiat (1982); Krinsky (1996); Papworth (1887); Sturgis *et al.* (1901–2)

synclastic. Refers to a surface with the same kind of convex or concave curvature in all directions through all points as in a hemispherical dome. *See* anticlastic.

synthronus (*pl.* **synthroni**). Joint throne of the Bishop and Presbyters, usually a semicircular row of seats with the *cathedra in the middle behind the altar in the *apse of an *Early Christian or *Byzantine church, or disposed on the *bema.

Syrian arch. *See* arch.

Systems architecture. 1. Architecture based on prefabricated systems and components variously arranged. **2.** Architecture derived from logical, rational, analytical procedures related to computerized design. **3.** Architecture designed as part of greater (e.g. cultural, social, and urban) systems. In this sense it has been related to *performance design* based on an analysis of function as well as on the aesthetic, physical, and psychological needs of the users. Fashionable in the 1960s, it has not proved to be the all-purpose solution hoped for by its protagonists.

Ehrenkrantz (1989); Finnimore (1989); Handler (1970)

systyle. *See* intercolumniation.

t'a *or* **taa.** Chinese name for a *pagoda, probably derived from a *stupa, and occurring in *Chinoiserie decoration and buildings.

tab. *Ear, or means of securing a rainwater-pipe to a wall.

tabby. Gravel, lime, and crushed oyster- or mussel-shells mixed with water, forming a type of *concrete.

tabernacle. **1.** Portable *shrine, originally a curtained tent, containing the Jewish Ark of the Covenant. **2.** Cupboard with doors containing the consecrated Host on an altar. **3.** *Pyx. **4.** Any canopied *niche containing an image. **5.** Shrine or canopied tomb. **6.** *Baldacchino or ciborium. **7.** Place of worship distinguished from a church, e.g. meeting-house, especially one with no architectural pretensions, for Nonconformist Protestants.

tabernacle-work. **1.** *Openwork canopy over *niches, *shrines, church-*stalls, or a *cathedra. **2.** Ornate Gothic canopy over a funerary monument.

tabia, tapia, tappia. Wall-construction of earth *rammed in *formwork, often with added lime and gravel, finished with several coats of limewash.

table. **1.** Flat broad slab, as on a medieval altar where it forms the *mensa* or top. **2.** Any flat, distinctive, rectangular surface or panel on a wall, often charged with inscriptions, painting, or sculpture. **3.** Altar-frontal or -retable. **4.** Protestant *communion-table. **5.** Any horizontal moulding, e.g. *band, *cornice, or *string-course, usually with a defining word, e.g. *base-table, *corbel-table, etc.

tabled. **1.** With a flat smooth surface. **2.** *Coped or provided with any horizontal moulding (*see* table).

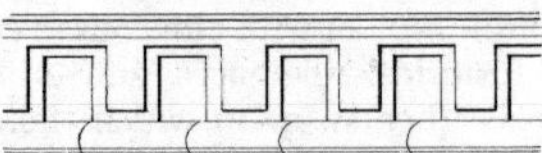

table. 5. Romanesque label-table, Church of St Julian (mostly destroyed), Norwich. (*After Parker*)

table-stone. Large, flat stone, as on a *dolmen or *table-tomb.

tablet. **1.** Small slab or *panel set into or attached to a wall or other large mass, often framed, and carrying an inscription, usually commemorative. **2.** Horizontal capping or *coping. *See* tabling.

tablet-flower. *Second Pointed ornament like a four-petalled flower, probably a variant on *ballflower.

table-tomb. **1.** Funerary monument consisting of a stone slab supported on e.g. *colonnettes, common in C17 and C18. **2.** *Dolmen.

tablet-tomb. *Loculus in a *catacomb or *hypogeum sealed with a *tablet.

tabling. *Cope.

tablinum, tabulinum. Large room in a Roman house connected to the *atrium, often serving as a vestibule.

tabula. **1.** *Niche or cupboard. **2.** Altar-frontal of metal or wood.

tabulatum. **1.** Floor or storey of a building. **2.** Timber floor, *wainscot, ceiling, etc. **3.** Balcony or other projection.

TAC (The Architects' Collaborative). Firm founded in the USA by Walter *Gropius in 1945 to foster teamwork. Its works included the Harvard Graduate Center, Cambridge, Mass. (1949).

Gropius and Harkness (1966)

Taché, Eugène-Étienne (1836–1912). Architect of the Hôtel du Parlement, Quebec

City, Canada (1876–87), based on a plan derived from *Fuller's Ottawa Parliament Building, but with elevations in a French *Second Empire style. The same architect's Military Riding School, Quebec (1888), is a work in the *Gothic Revival style influenced by *Viollet-le-Duc.

Kalman (1994)

taenia, tenia. *See* Doric Order.

tailloir. *Abacus, especially in the *Ionic *Order.

Tait, Thomas Smith (1882–1954). Scots architect. Educated in Glasgow, he became chief draughtsman to J. J. *Burnet in 1904, with whom he worked on Kodak House, Kingsway, London (1910–12), a spectacular and important essay in *stripped Classicism, and the noble Neoclassical extension to the British Museum (completed 1914). Burnet made him his partner in 1918, and the firm designed several important buildings, including the Graeco-Egyptian *Art Deco Adelaide House, London Bridge (1920–5), the Royal Masonic Hospital, Ravenscourt Park, London (1933), and the very fine St Andrew's House, Edinburgh (1930–9). Tait was consultant architect for the *Daily Telegraph* Building, Fleet Street, London (1928), where the detail was again Graeco-Egyptian. He designed some of the earliest British housing in the *International Modern style at Silver End, near Braintree, Essex (1926–8), influenced partly by *Behrens's house for Wenman Joseph Bassett-Lowke (1877–1953) at Northampton, and partly by the work of *Dudok.

Gifford, McWilliam, and Walker (1984); Pevsner, *Buildings of England, Essex* (1954); Williamson, Riches, and Higgs (1990)

Takeyama, Minoru (1934–86). Japanese architect. Educated in Japan and the USA, he worked with, among others, *Harrison & Abramovitz, Arne *Jacobsen, H. *Larsen, *Sert, and *Utzon. He established his reputation with certain buildings incorporating aspects of popular culture in his designs, becoming a member of *Architext in 1971, and developing an interest in architecture as a system of signs and language. His most highly acclaimed buildings were the 'Renaissance' Cultural and Commercial Complex, Kyoto (1983–6), and Tokyo International Port Terminal Building (1989–91).

Emanuel (1994)

Talenti, Francesco (*c*.1300–69). Florentine architect. He worked at Orvieto Cathedral in the 1320s, and succeeded *Pisano at Florence Cathedral in *c*.1343. He completed the upper stages of the *campanile from that time, and continued working at the Duomo (1351–64 and 1366–8), building the *nave and helping to finalize the design of the east end, including the great octagon. His son, **Simone di Francesco Talenti** (*c*.1341–81), also worked at the Duomo, and designed the ground-floor *arcade of the Church of Or San Michele (1360s), but his most celebrated building is the Loggia dei Lanzi, Piazza della Signoria, Florence (1376–81), with Benci di Cione and others.

Kreytenberg (1974); Placzek (1982); Trachtenberg (1971); White (1987)

tall buildings. *See* skyscraper.

Taller de Arquitectura. International multidisciplinary workshop established by Ricardo *Bofill in 1962. Its works include the Calle J. S. Bach Flats, Barcelona (1964–5), the Barrio Gaudí Quarter, Reus (1964–7), both in Spain, the important Les Arcades du Lac, St-Quentin-en-Yvelines (1975–6), in France, a monumental work in a simplified Neoclassical style, and the Palais d'Abraxas Housing Development, Marne-la-Vallée, France (1978–83).

Emanuel (1994); Guedes (1981); James (1988)

tallet, tallot, tallus, tallut, talus, talut. 1. *Batter. **2.** Any space beneath the pitched roof of a building. **3.** Hay-loft.

tallus wall. Battered retaining-wall.

Talman, John (1677–1726). English architect and artist. The son of William *Talman, he spent much of his life travelling to visit buildings and make topographical drawings. On one of his expeditions (1709) to Italy he was accompanied by William *Kent, and made a large collection of drawings, while developing his contacts with connoisseurs and *virtuosi*. He seems to have supplied images of Italian buildings to several personages, including Dean *Aldrich, and so may have played some part in the second English Palladian Revival (*see* Palladianism).

Colvin (1995); *DNB* (1917); Papworth (1892)

Talman, William (1650–1719). English gentleman-architect. He rose to eminence during the *Restoration period and became Comptroller of the Works to King William III

(1688–1702) in 1689. He designed several large *Baroque country-houses in which both French and Italian influences were apparent, favouring *Giant Orders of *pilasters and *entablatures to frame his elevations. Chatsworth House, Derbyshire, where Talman rebuilt (1687–96) the south and east fronts for William Cavendish, 4th Earl (later (1694) 1st Duke) of Devonshire (1640–1707), heralded a majestic series of houses, including the Baroque redecoration of the interior of Burghley House, Stamford (*c*.1688–90), Uppark, Sussex (*c*.1690—restored 1990–3), the east front of Dyrham Park, Gloucestershire (1698–1704), the interiors of the State Apartments and layout of gardens at Hampton Court Palace, Middlesex (1699–1702—where he attempted to undermine *Wren's position), and the south front of Drayton House, Northamptonshire (1702). In the last building he almost achieved greatness with an exquisite and beautifully articulated design. In 1702 Talman was dismissed from his official posts and fell out of favour with the rise of *Vanbrugh and *Hawksmoor.

Colvin (1995); *DNB* (1917); Harris (1982); *Journal of the Warburg and Courtauld Institutes*, 18 (1955), 123–39

talus, tallus. **1.** Retaining-wall. **2.** *Battered wall, especially in fortifications.

tambour. **1.** Section of column-*shaft when the latter is composed of *drums. **2.** *Bell, ground, or *vase of a *Composite or *Corinthian *capital. **3.** *Rotunda, or any circular building, e.g. drum supporting a *cupola. **4.** Wall of any circular structure.

Tange, Kenzo (1913–). Japanese architect. After graduating from Tokyo University (1938) he joined Mayekawa's office (*see* Maekawa), where he absorbed the influences of Le *Corbusier. In the early 1940s he began to draw on themes from and allusions to traditional Japanese architecture, and in 1949 won the competition for the Hiroshima Peace Centre Community Centre and Museum (1949–56), his first major building, which was presented to *CIAM in 1951 and announced his arrival on the international architectural scene. Then followed several buildings in which Tange developed forms using up-to-date technology, and quickly achieved status as a leader of the *Modern Movement in his country, arguing for a synthesis between Japanese and Western design. His Kagawa Prefectural Offices, Takamatsu (1955–8), relied for its effect on the expression of posts and beams, but the Sports Arena, Takamatsu (1962–4), and St Mary's Roman Catholic Cathedral, Tokyo (1961–4), were more dynamic, the last with a basic cruciform plan and paraboloids superimposed. This forceful dynamism was developed further in the National Gymnasium, Tokyo (1961–4), seating 15,000 people protected by a gigantic tensile *catenary roof-structure.

Tange's work has involved much research into town-planning, including a remarkable design for the expansion of Tokyo based on rapid-transit systems, areas of high-density housing, and a major extension of the urban fabric into the sea at Tokyo Bay (published as *A Plan for Tokyo, 1960*). He also developed schemes for multi-purpose blocks linked in various ways. His Yamanashi Press and Broadcasting Centre, Kofu (1964–7), has 16 cylindrical services- and stair-towers acting as huge columns, with floors spanning between them according to their functional requirements. This, and the Tokyo plan, were potent influences on *Metabolism. In the 1970s his designs became much more international in character, with strong affinities to developments in Europe and the USA. More recently, the lively dynamism of his earlier work was superseded by a refinement of precise detailing, as in the Tokyo Prince Hotel (1983–7). He has obliquely criticized *Functionalism, stating that only the beautiful can be functional.

Altherr (1968); Banham (1976); Borràs (1975); Boyd (1962); Emanuel (1994); Kulturmann (1970); Tange (1960, 1970); White (1990)

taper. Gradual *diminution in width or thickness in any elongated object towards one extremity or another, e.g. *herm, *obelisk, *spire, or *term. Column-*shafts properly do not taper, as they diminish with height not in a straight taper but a curved *entasis.

tapia. *See* tabia.

Tapper, Sir Walter John (1861–1935). English architect. He worked with Basil *Champneys and then *Bodley & Garner. Although he opened an office in London in 1893 he did not leave Bodley until 1901, specializing in ecclesiastical work. His churches include the Ascension, Malvern Link, Worcestershire (1903), St Mary's, Harrogate, Yorkshire (1904), St Erkenwald, Southend-on-Sea, Essex (1905–10), and a large extension to St Michael's,

Little Coates, Grimsby, Lincolnshire (1913). Much of his work was in brick, handled with great integrity, and his style was generally *Arts-and-Crafts *Gothic. He designed some exquisite church furnishings, including the beautiful additions to Sir Arthur *Blomfield's 1883 reredos in St Wulfram's, Grantham, Lincolnshire (1901), but in later life he became more of a Classicist, as with the screen at Christchurch Priory, Hampshire (1920s), and the Memorial Carillon Tower, Loughborough, Leicestershire (1921).

Gray (1985); Pevsner, *Buildings of England* (1951–)

tarsia. *Inlaid wood, usually light on dark, common in the *Renaissance period, and featuring *arabesque or *scroll-work, but especially representing paintings in *perspective, e.g. in Santa Maria Organo, Verona (C15).

tas-de-charge. **1.** Lowest *courses of a group of *Gothic *vault-*ribs, bonded with the wall, forming a solid mass, and receiving the weight of the ribs and panel-work above. **2.** In an arch or vault, the lowest *voussoir.

Tatham, Charles Heathcote (1772–1842). English architect. He worked for S. P. *Cockerell and then for Henry *Holland who helped him to visit Italy in 1794. There, he met many aristocrats and gentry on the *Grand Tour, including Frederick Howard, 5th Earl of Carlisle (1748–1825), who became one of his main patrons. He made a study of *Antique remains and ornament, later published as *Etchings of Ancient Ornamental Architecture*, etc (1799–1800) and *Etchings Representing Fragments of Grecian and Roman Ornaments* (1806) which enjoyed considerable success and were used internationally as source-books for Neoclassical design, notably by *Hope, *Percier, and *Fontaine. His sculpture-gallery at Castle Howard, Yorkshire (1800–2), was an early exercise in his severe *Neoclassicism, but his masterpiece is the *primitive Graeco-Egyptian *mausoleum at Trentham, Staffordshire (1807–8), one of the most formidable Neoclassical essays in England. He also designed a mausoleum at Ochtertyre, Perthshire (1809—*Gothic).

Colvin (1995); *Country Life* 151/3905 (1972), 918–21, 151/3912, 1481–6; Curl (1994); *DNB* (1917); Papworth (1892)

Tatlin, Vladimir Evgrafovich. (1885–1953). Russian painter and sculptor. Influenced by *Cubism and *Futurism he became one of the main protagonists of *Constructivism from 1913. His project (only realized as a large model) for a monument to the Third International (1919–20) consisted of a steel double-helical structure over 400 metres high, containing rotating glass buildings containing administrative, legislative, and propaganda facilities for the Komintern. Intended as a symbol of progress and technology (based on images of fairground structures and oil-derricks, and painted bright red), this proposal became a paradigm for architects such as *Leonidov, El *Lissitzky, and *Vesnin, and was admired in avant-garde circles in the West. It has also been a potent image for those associated with *Deconstructivism.

Andersen (1968); Milner (1983); Placzek (1982); Zhadova (1988)

tauriform. *Bucranium.

Taut, Bruno (1880–1938). German architect. He worked with Theodor *Fischer (1904–8), then practised with Franz Hoffmann (d. 1950), designing several works before gaining critical attention with his Steel Industry Pavilion at the International Building Trades Exhibition, Leipzig (1913). In that year he met Adolf *Behne and Paul *Scheerbart, whose ideas about glass in architecture influenced Taut, notably in his *Expressionism, and in 1914 his brother, **Max**, joined the firm, which became Brothers Taut & Hoffmann. Taut also became adviser to the German *Garden City movement. At the Werkbund Exhibition in Cologne (1914) his polygonal Glass Pavilion with dome-like roof (constructed of a *space-frame with diamond-shaped glass panels) employed glass of various forms and colours, and water cascades as well. It caused something of a sensation, and is his most celebrated work, a paradigm of *Expressionism.

During the 1914–18 war he published Pacifist polemical works, some of which came out as *Alpin Architektur* (Alpine Architecture—1919), showing the Alps redesigned, as a gigantic task of construction, the antithesis of destructive war. He was a founding-member of *Arbeitsrat für Kunst and the *Novembergruppe in the aftermath of war, and became a leading light of the avant-garde, exercising influence through various writings and bodies including the *Gläserne Kette. However, his utopian and Expressionist tendencies withered as he turned more to *Rationalism from 1921, when he became Director of Building and Planning in Magdeburg. In 1924 he returned to Berlin, where he designed many huge *Modern Movement Housing Schemes, including the 'Uncle Tom Cabin' development, set among pine-forests at Berlin-Zehlendorf (with *Häring and others—1926–31) and the *Hufeisensiedlung* (Horse Shoe Estate, so called after its plan-form), Britz, Berlin-Neukölln (with Martin *Wagner—1925–30).

Taut left Germany in 1932, settling first in the Soviet Union (until 1933), then Japan (where he wrote *Houses and People of Japan* (1937) among other works), and finally (1937) Turkey, where he designed various buildings, his own house, and schools in Ankara (1938). His publications were many.

Akademie der Künste (1963, 1980); Bletter (1979); Boyd Whyte (1982); Conrads (1970); Conrads and Sperlich (1960); Curtis (1996); Junghanns (1970); Lane (1985); Offermann (1993); Pehnt (1973); Pitz and Brenne (1980); Sharp (1967); Taut (1920, 1924, 1927, 1929, 1929*a*, 1930, 1934, 1939, 1958, 1963, 1972, 1977); Taut *et al.* (1919)

Taut, Max (1884–1967). German architect. He joined Franz Hoffmann (d. 1950) and his brother, **Bruno**, in partnership in 1914, and remained with Hoffmann until the latter's death. He designed various buildings before 1914, including a Pavilion for the International Building Trades Exhibition, Leipzig (1913), and in 1918 became a founder of various left-wing groups, including *Arbeitsrat für Kunst, *Novembergruppe, and later Der *Ring. He contributed to Bruno Taut's *Gläserne Kette group and built the extraordinary Wissinger family-vault, Stahnsdorf, Berlin (1920), one of the few *Glass-Chain* designs ever realized. He built a formidable reputation as an architect with the offices for the *Allgemeiner Deutscher Gewerkschaftsbund* (Federation of German Labour Unions—1923) and other works for trade-unions and similar organizations, one of which (the *Verband der Deutschen Buchdrucker*—Headquarters of the German Printers' Union—1922–5) he designed with Mart *Stam, where the concrete frame was expressed. Other works in the *International Modernist style by him included two houses at the *Weissenhofsiedlung, Stuttgart (1927), the German Trade Union Building, Frankfurt-am-Main (1931), and the Co-operative Department Store, Berlin (1932). After the 1939–45 war he was active as an architect and teacher, designing the Reuter Housing, Bonn (1949–52), the August-Thiessen Siedlung, Duisburg (1955–64), and an extension to his brother's *Hufeisensiedlung* (Horse Shoe Estate), Berlin-Neukölln (1954). He was an important figure in the evolution of the *Neue Sachlichkeit.

Akademie der Künste (1964); Taut, M. (1927); *Wasmuths Monatshefte für Baukunst*, 16 (1932), 257–69

Taylor, George Ledwell (1788–1873). English architect. Articled to James T. Parkinson (*fl. c.*1800–*c.*1840) in 1804, he was involved in the building of Montague and Bryanston Squares and other parts of the Portman Estate in London. In 1816–19 he and Edward Cresy (1792–1858) travelled in England, France, Italy, Greece, Malta, and Sicily, after which they published *The Architectural Antiquities of Rome* . . . (1821–2 and 1874) and *The Architecture of the Middle Ages in Italy* . . . (1829), an early work extolling Italian medieval architecture. In 1824 Taylor was appointed Civil Architect to the Navy, and carried out robust and virile works at the dockyards of Chatham, Sheerness, and Woolwich. He was responsible for the fine Clarence Victualling Yard, Gosport, Hampshire (1828–32). In the 1840s he laid out a large part of the Bishop of London's Estate in Paddington (e.g. Chester Place and parts of Hyde Park and Gloucester Squares). He published *Stones of Etruria and Marbles of Ancient Rome* (1859). His most extraordinary work is the huge *Gothic Revival tower of Hadlow Castle, Kent (*c.*1840), a *folly to almost rival *Wyatt's Fonthill in extravagance, and he pioneered the modern use of concrete as a building material in the Proprietary School, Lee, Kent (1836), modelled on the Propylaea in Athens.

Colvin (1995); *DNB* (1917); Papworth (1892)

Taylor, Sir Robert (1714–88). English architect, with *Chambers and *Paine one of the most gifted of his generation between *Burlington's *Palladianism and the meteoric rise of Robert *Adam. After an apprenticeship with Henry Cheere (1703–81), the sculptor, Taylor travelled to Italy before establishing himself as a sculptor in the 1740s, but began practising architecture in the 1750s with almost immediate success, thanks to a happy mixture of talent and extremely hard work. It was said that Taylor and Paine divided the practice of architecture between them until Adam 'entered the lists'. He was Surveyor to the Bank of England from *c.*1764 and in 1769 became one of the two Architects of the Office of Works. As a designer of villas and country-houses his work was original and compact, the plans incorporating ellipses, octagons, and his favourite motif, the *canted bay (he also favoured octagonal door-panels and window-lights). A good example of his work is Asgill House, Richmond, Surrey (1761–4), with bold *eaves on shaped *mutules and ingeniously shaped rooms inside. At Purbrook House, Portsdown Hill, Hampshire (1770—demolished), he designed the first revival of a Roman *atrium in an English house, and so has a place in the history of *Neoclassicism. His finest country-houses were Heveningham Hall, Suffolk (1778–*c*.1780—completed by James *Wyatt, but severely damaged in the 1980s), Gorhambury, Hertfordshire (1777–90—later altered), and Sharpham House, Devon (*c*.1770—with a large domed elliptical stair-well). His major works at the Bank of England had segmental arches and side-lit *cupolas that clearly influenced *Soane's later works there, but Taylor's contribution to the Bank was much altered by Soane and obliterated by Herbert *Baker (in 1921–37), apart from the Court Room (1767–70), which was reconstructed. He designed the Stone Buildings, Lincoln's Inn, London (1775–7), and the Assembly-Rooms in the Old Exchange, Belfast, Northern Ireland (1776—later altered by *Lanyon and *Lynn when the building became a Bank). Among other works he designed Osney Bridge, Oxfordshire (1767), Maidenhead Bridge, Berkshire (1772–7), and the *Gothick spire of St Peter's Church, Wallingford, Berkshire (1776–7). He made many designs for funerary monuments which survive, together with other material, in the Taylorian Institute, Oxford. The latter was established through Taylor's bequests to the University of Oxford. His pupils included S. P. *Cockerell and John *Nash.

Binney (1984); Colvin (1995); *Country Life*, 142/3670 (6 July 1967), 17–21, 142/3671 (13 July 1967), 78–82; *DNB* (1917); Gunnis (1968)

Teague, Walter Dorwin (1883–1960). Pioneering American industrial designer. He settled in New York in 1903 and established his own office in 1911, specializing in typographical design for books and advertisements. In 1926 he renamed his office an industrial-design firm, and in 1927 acquired Kodak Eastman as his client, for which he designed the Baby Brownie camera (1933). Other projects followed, including the Marmon Car (designed with his son, **Walter Dorwin Teague, jun.**), and several Pavilions for the 1939 New York World's Fair. Other works included a vast range of designs, from Schaefer beer-labels to the VIP interiors of the Boeing 707 jet. He also developed quality-control for the assembly of complex firing-mechanisms used for the US Navy's Bureau of Ordnance in its missiles, including the well-known Polaris. His *Design this Day: The Technique of Order in the Machine Age* (1946) analysed modern industrial civilization and the role of contemporary industrial design.

Industrial Design, 8 (Jan. 1961), 25–9; Teague (1946)

Team X (10). Mid-C20 alliance of architects so called because they combined to organize the tenth *CIAM conference in 1956. Believing CIAM had become too big and too vague in its aims, they argued for a revitalization of the *International *Modern Movement to be pursued with even greater zeal. Members included van *Eyck and the *Smithsons.

Architectural Design, 32/12 (Dec. 1962), 559–602; Banham (1966); Smithson, *Team 10* (1968)

tebam. *Rostrum or *daïs in a *synagogue.

Tecton. Association of London architects established by *Lubetkin in 1932, arguably the most influential promoter of *International Modernism in the UK until it broke up in 1948. Its best-known works are various structures for London Zoo, Regent's Park (1932–7), including the Gorilla House (1932) and Penguin Pool (1933–4); the apartment-blocks at Highgate, London, known as Highpoint I (1933–5) and II (1936–8); the slab-blocks of flats at Spa Fields, Clerkenwell, London (1939–49); and the much-praised Finsbury Health Centre, London (1935–8). Tecton also designed several significant private houses as well as various buildings for Whipsnade Zoo, Bedfordshire, and Dudley Zoo, Worcestershire.

Coe and Reading (1981); Gould (1977); Hancocks (1971); Yorke (1947)

Teige, Karel (1900–51). Czechoslovak Communist architect, critic, and polemicist. With others he founded the anti-academic *Devětsil Group (1920) which promoted *Constructivism and other aspects of *Modernism. Teige was opposed to any aesthetic considerations predetermining construction, believing the 'New Architecture' had to be hygienic, and that medical science should dictate layout, structure, and urban planning. From 1922 to 1928 he edited the avant-garde journal *Stavba* (Building), and developed relations between Czech Modernists and leading figures abroad (e.g. *Behne, Hannes *Meyer, Le *Corbusier, and the *Vesnins). He promoted new housing-schemes for the working-classes, advocating 'dwelling-cabins' for each individual grouped into large 'dwelling-hives', also arguing for the abolition of family households (no permanent living together of two persons in one unit was to be possible) and for the complete socializing of children's education (1932). He prepared and edited the general report *Die Wohnung für das Existenzminimum* (Minimum Existence Housing) for the third *CIAM Congress in Brussels. He chaired the Prague-based Left Front, which he argued was the Czech CIAM group, but its extreme and intolerant views caused dissent within Czechoslovakia and with CIAM as a whole. Nevertheless the municipal authorities of Prague and Brno determined to construct apartments taking into account Teige's anti-family views. However, by 1935, with Czechoslovak architects isolated, and Teige's opinion of architecture as a branch of science no longer fashionable, his influence, so strong for fifteen years or so, waned. Opposed to Stalinist Socialist Realism, he soon became a marginal figure.

Curtis (1996); Leśnikowski (1996)

telamon (*pl.* **telamones**). Straight, unbowed male whole figure acting as a column supporting an *entablature on its head. *See also* atlas, canephora, caryatid, from which it is distinct.

Telford, Thomas (1757–1834). Scots mason, surveyor, architect, and engineer of genius. He was employed on the building of Edinburgh New Town before he moved to London in 1782. Through the good offices of (Sir) William Pulteney (d. 1805), MP for Shrewsbury, Shropshire, he was employed to carry out certain works in that town, including alterations to the Castle (1787). He built (1787–93) the County Gaol there to designs by John Hiram Haycock (1759–1830) with modifications by John Howard (*c*.1726–90), the prison reformer. He designed the robust Neoclassical Church of St Mary, Bridgnorth, Shropshire (1792–4), the utilitarian octagonal Church at Madeley, Shropshire (1794–6), and pioneered the use of iron for the construction of bridges (he was Surveyor of Bridges to the County of Shropshire) with his handsome structure at Buildwas, Shropshire (1795–6—demolished). His canal *aqueducts at Longdon, Shropshire (1793–4), Pont-y-Cysyllte, near Llangollen, Wales (1795–1805), and Chirk, Denbighshire (1796–1801), are among the finest and most dignified of such structures in the world. Telford designed more than 1,000 bridges, including the Menai (1819–26) and Conway (1821–6) *suspension bridges, Caernarfonshire, Wales, Craigellachie iron bridge, Banffshire, Scotland (1814–15), and arched bridges at Bewdley, Worcestershire (1797–9), Dunkeld, Perthshire, Scotland (1806–9), and Dean, Edinburgh (1829–31). His works as a road- and canal-builder and his designs for harbours and docks (including works at Wick, Caithness (from 1808), Aberdeen, Peterhead, Banff, Leith, and the very important St Katherine Docks, London (1825–8—with severe brick warehouses by *Hardwick (mostly demolished)), were among the most accomplished designs for such buildings ever made. He was responsible for over 30 churches and manses in the Scottish Highlands (1825–34), including those at Acharacle, Ardgour, Portnahaven, and Strontian (all in Argyll), and Ullapool (Ross-shire). He laid out Pulteney Model Town, near Wick, Caithness (1808).

Colvin (1995); *DNB* (1917); Nicholson (1835); Penfold (1980); Rolt (1958); Smiles (1862); Telford (1838); Thorne (1990)

Temanza, Tommaso (1705–89). Venetian architect. His work was firmly in the style of *Palladianism, including the façade of the Church of Santa Margarita, Padua (*c*.1740s), and the exquisite Santa Maria Maddalena, Venice (from 1763—in which influences from the *Pantheon in Rome and *Palladio's chapel at Maser can be discerned). He is better remembered as a writer, with his *Delle antichità di Rimini* (1741) and the lives of various architects, collected later as *Vite dei Più Celebri Architetti e Scultori Veneziani* (1778), a scholarly work on Venetian architecture and sculpture. He was a promoter of the principles of *Neoclassicism, as is clear from his *Antica pianta dell'inclita città di Venezia* (Ancient Plan of the Illustrious City of Venice—1781), and his work was influential.

Howard (1980); Meeks (1966); Placzek (1982); Wittkower (1982)

tempietto. Small *Renaissance temple, often circular, e.g. *Bramante's *tempietto* in the *cloisters of San Pietro in Montorio, Rome (*c.*1510).

template, templet. 1. *Pad-stone or any block of timber or stone, or a metal plate, placed beneath the end of a *girder, *truss, etc., to distribute the load, especially the timber block placed under the foot of a *cruck-*blade. **2.** Mould, outline, or pattern to ensure accuracy when forming a profile or moulding. **3.** *Beam or *lintel.

temple. 1. Building for pagan religious observances, or the dwelling-place of a deity. The word was applied to sacred buildings of the Ancient Egyptians, Greeks, Romans, and others. The *Antique Classical temple was usually rectangular, and consisted of a *cella (*naos in Greek), *sanctuary, and *portico. Greek temples were commonly surrounded by columns (*peristyle) supporting an *entablature, with a *pediment at each end (e.g. C5 BC *Parthenon, Athens), but sometimes had a portico at each end (amphi-prostyle) with plain walls (e.g. C5 BC temple of Nikè Apteros, Athens). Roman temples usually had a deep portico at one end (derived from Etruscan exemplars), a plain cella (sometimes with *engaged columns, e.g. C1 BC Maison Carrée, Nîmes), and were built on high *podia. Circular buildings of the *tholos type were built by both the Greeks and Romans (e.g. C1 BC temple of Vesta, Tivoli). Terms used to describe arrangements of columns are described elsewhere (*see* anta, colonnade, intercolumniation, portico). **2.** *Synagogue. **3.** French Protestant church, or any building for public worship by Nonconformist Protestant sects, especially a large or grand structure. **4.** Mormon place of worship. **5.** Sacred edifice in Jerusalem, seat of the Jewish worship of Jehovah, especially the Temple of Solomon. **6.** Headquarters of the Knights Templars, or a place once occupied by a preceptory of the Knights Templars (as in London and Paris). **7.** Building with architectural pretensions for special ritual use, as a Freemasonic *Lodge, related to the Temple of Solomon.

Temple, Raymond du (*fl.* *c.*1360–1405). French master-mason under Kings Charles V and VI (1364–1422) of France. He became Master-Mason at Notre Dame, Paris, in 1363, was in charge of the building of the Célestins Chapel (1367–70—fragments survive), and built in the 1370s the celebrated Vis du Louvre, an external spiral *stair, one of the first monumental stairs in Western Europe. He was involved in the design and building of the Collège de Beauvais, Paris (from 1387), but little of his work survives. He appears to have enjoyed exceptional Royal favour.

Papworth (1892); Sturgis *et al.* (1901–2)

temple-front. Element of a façade resembling the front of a Classical temple, with columns or *pilasters carrying an *entablature and *pediment, applied to an *elevation, as in a *Palladian composition with *portico (e.g. *Aldrich's Peckwater *Quad, Christ Church, Oxford (1707–14)).

temple-tower. High platform, often stepped, with a temple on top, e.g. in *Meso-American architecture or the Mesopotamian *ziggurat.

Tendenza. Italian *Neo-Rationalist architectural movement of the 1960s that rose to eminence in the 1970s, led by *Aymonino, *Botta, *Grassi, *Reichlin, *Reinhart, and Aldo *Rossi, and associated with the Canton of Ticino in Switzerland. It recognized the social and cultural significance of established urban fabric, the importance of historical forms and elements as a resource, and the need for architecture to be redefined in terms of rules and *types. *See* Rational architecture, Ticinese School.

Brown-Manrique (1989); Grassi (1982, 1989); Pizzi (1991); Steinmann and Boga (1975)

tendril. Very common architectural ornament resembling plant-like tendrils. In Classical architecture it is associated with *acanthus, *anthemion, and *palmette, and occurs in *Celtic and *Anglo-Saxon ornament, medieval grapevine or *trail, *Renaissance and *Mannerist *arabesque and *grotesque, *Art Nouveau *whiplash and derivations from Celtic and *Norse ornament, and many other styles in various guises and variations.

Tschudi-Madsen (1967)

tenement. 1. Land or real property, e.g. a building. **2.** Dwelling. **3.** Portion of a house, or an apartment or flat tenanted separately. **4.** Block of purpose-built flats.

Tengbom, Ivar Justus (1878–1968). Swedish architect. One of the most influential of his time, he was the chief protagonist in the evolution of a simplified *Neoclassicism in the inter-war period, as exemplified in his

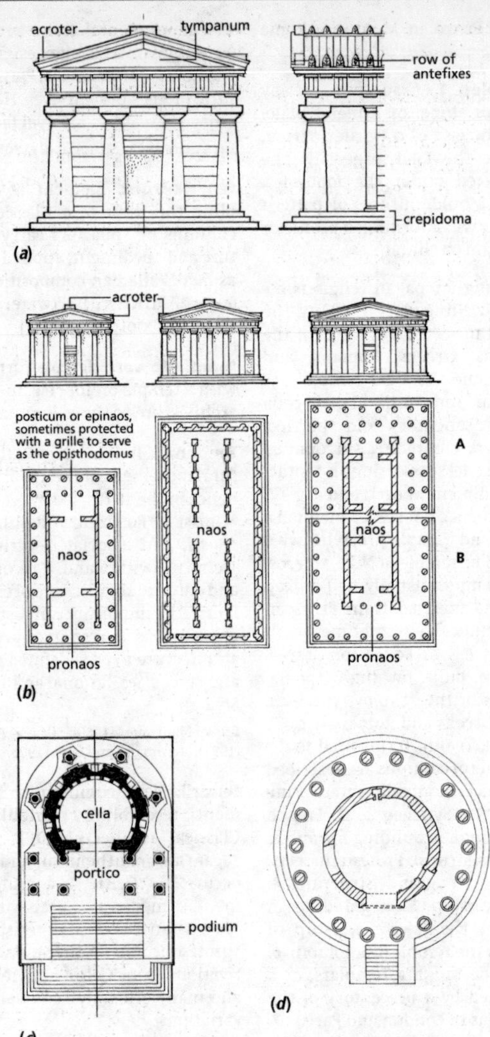

temple.
(*a*) Greek Doric prostyle tetrastyle temple-front. Note the anta terminating the cell wall.
(*b*) Various types of Greek Doric temple plans. (*left*) Peripteral hexastyle, i.e. with colonnades surrounding the cell, and six columns at each end forming the porticoes and carrying the pediments. (*middle*) Pseudo-peripteral septostyle (or heptastyle), i.e. with all columns *engaged* with the temple walls, and with seven engaged columns at each end, resulting in entrances off-centre. (*right*) **A** Half-plan, dipteral octastyle, i.e. with two rows of columns surrounding the cell, and eight at each end forming the porticoes and carrying the pediments. **B** Half-plan, pseudo-dipteral octastyle, i.e. with a wider space between the walls of the cell and the peristyle, and with eight columns at each end forming the porticoes and carrying the pediments. This wide space suggests that further colonnades ought to stand behind the outer ones.
(*c*) Plan of Roman 'Temple of Venus', Baalbek, Lebanon (AD C3), showing typical arrangement of podium, portico, and steps, used for a circular structure.
(*d*) Plan of Temple of Vesta, Tivol: (*c*.80 BC), showing circular peristyle.

Concert House, Stockholm (1923–6), in which the building became a blocky mass fronted by a huge *portico of stripped columns, the whole reminiscent of the work of *Behrens. A prolific designer, his early works, such as the Högalid Church, Stockholm (1911–23), were often in the *National Romantic style inaugurated by Östberg at the Stockholm City Hall (1909), but Tengbom himself was more influenced by *Nyrop and *Wahlman. Other important buildings by Tengbom include the School of Economics (1925–6) and the Match Company Offices (1926–8), both in Stockholm, and the Swedish Institute of Classical Studies, Rome (1937–40).

Ahlberg (1925); *American Architect*, 140/2598 (1931), 32–7, 98–100; *Byggmästeren*, 6 (1941), 69–75, 14 (1944), 239–60; Hall (1981); Östberg (1908); Paavilainen (1982); Rasmussen (1940)

tenia. *See* Doric Order.

tenon. **1.** Projection at the end of a timber, of smaller transverse *section than the timber, so with a shoulder, fitted into a corresponding hole or *mortise in another piece, e.g. timber *door. **2.** Projecting stone at the end of a wall. *See* toothing-stones.

Tensile architecture. Rigid structures formed of cables and rods in tension. Based on the principle of the tent, it evolved in the 1950s and 1960s, notably in the hands of Frei *Otto, who used steel netting in tension. Otto's pioneering and influential work included the German Pavilion, Expo 69, Montreal, Canada, and buildings for the Munich Olympic Games (1972). Other examples include the Aviary at London Zoo (1961–2—by *Price, Lord Snowdon (1930–), and Frank Newby (1926–)), and the Mound Stand, Lord's Cricket Ground, London (1987—by *Hopkins).

Architectural Association Quarterly, 1/2 (Apr. 1969), 56–74; *Architectural Design*, 38/4 (Apr. 1968), 179–82; *Architectural Review*, 134/801 (Nov. 1963), 324–34; Drew (1976); Glaeser (1972); Glancey (1989)

tent ceiling. *Camp ceiling. The inward-sagging curved form was frequently found in late C18 garden-buildings, especially those in *Chinoiserie or oriental styles, e.g. Turkish Tent, Painshill, Surrey (*c*.1760—recently (1990s) restored), and also occurred on *Regency canopies and *verandahs. A fine example of a tent-ceiling in fabric was conceived for the blue-and-white *Zeltzimmer* (Tent Room) at Charlottenhof, Potsdam, by *Schinkel (*c*.1830).

tepidarium. Room of intermediate temperature in Roman *thermae.

term, terminal. Classical head and bust (often with torso) merging with the top of a downward-tapering *pedestal resembling an inverted *obelisk, sometimes with feet appearing under the base of the pedestal (which is proportioned like the lower part of a human figure). A *terminal pedestal* is like that of a term, but is separate, and a bust stands on it. *Compare* herm.

terminal. **1.** *Term. **2.** Ornamental finish, or termination, of an object, e.g. a *finial, *bench-end in a church, or *knob.

terminal figure, terminus. Bust or top part of a *term.

termination. **1.** *Label-stop or anything stopping a moulding. **2.** *Terminal, e.g. *finial on a *pinnacle or *urn on a *pedestal.

terminus. *See* term, terminal figure.

terrace. **1.** Embankment or prepared and levelled mass of earth in e.g. a garden. **2.** Any artificial or built level platform for promenading, with a vertical or sloping front or sides faced with masonry, turf, etc., and sometimes having a *balustrade, often adjacent to a country-house. **3.** One of several platforms, as on a hillside or in a *stadium, furnished with seats. **4.** *Loggia or external usable space, e.g. roof-garden. **5.** Series of houses joined together in one row, as in the *Georgian terraces of the British Isles.

terracotta. Hard unglazed pottery of which decorative tiles, architectural enrichment, statuary, *urns, etc., are made.

Terragni, Giuseppe (1904–43). Italian architect. He was primarily associated with *Rationalism, *Gruppo 7, and *Movimento Italiano per l'architettura Razionale* (*MIAR), inspired partly by *Futurism, and was active in *CIAM. His first important building (one of the earliest manifestations of *International Modernism in Italy) was the Novocomum Apartment Block, Como (1927–8), but his Casa del Fascio, Como (1932–6) is regarded as his finest work. With its open grid-like elevation leading to a glass-roofed *atrium surrounded by four storeys of galleries and offices, it demonstrates that the Fascist Party could patronize *Modern Movement buildings. He designed the Sant'Elia Nursery School (1936–7) and the Giuliani-Frigerio Apartment Block

(1939–40), both in Como. He was also responsible for the Villa Bianco, Seveso (1936–7), and the Casa del Fascio, Lissone (with Antonio Carminati—1938–9). A convinced Fascist (a fact often ignored by commentators who find it inconvenient when admiring the impeccable *Modernist credentials of some of his buildings), his unrealized design for the Dante Memorial, Museum, and Study Centre, Rome (1937), sums up the essence of architectural expression as favoured by the Party, with its stripped, severe monumentality and dramatic impact. His work influenced *Rational architecture in the 1960s (especially the work of *Rossi), and also had a powerful effect on the *New York Five, notably *Eisenman.

Art Bulletin, 62 (1980), 466–78; *Casabella*, 34 (1970), 38–41; Etlin (1991); Germer and Preiss (1991); Labò (1947); Mantero (1969, 1984); Marcianò (1987); Schumacher (1991); Veronesi (1953); Zevi (1980*a*)

terrazzo. *In situ* or *precast finish for floors, *dados, etc., made of small pieces of marble beaten down into a fairly stiff cement or lime-mortar, rubbed down, and polished.

Terry, Quinlan (1937–). English architect. He joined R. *Erith in 1962, becoming a partner in 1966, and from 1973 worked under his own name. He has been primarily associated with the *New Classicism in England. Among his works are the Howard Building (1983–6) and the *Greek Revival Maitland Robinson Library (1989–93), both at Downing College, Cambridge. His *Ionic *Villa (1987), Veneto Villa (1988), and *Gothick Villa (1988), all in Regent's Park, London, are scholarly evocations of *Georgian buildings. Earlier, he was attracted to C17 Palladian models, as with Waverton House, Gloucestershire (1979–80), and Newfield Park, Yorkshire (1980–1), but in the 1980s he entered the world of major office developments, popularizing *Classicism at the same time, as in his building in Soho and at Richmond Riverside Development (1986–8), allying himself with the architectural theorist Léon *Krier. Since then Terry has become internationally known.

Aslet (1986); Emanuel (1994); Powers (1987)

tessella (*pl.* **tessellae**). Small *tessera.

Tessenow, Heinrich (1876–1950). German architect. A prominent member of the German *Arts-and-Crafts movement, he was also influenced by the work of *Schinkel and *Thiersch. He published *Der Wohnhausbau* (The Dwelling House—1909, with later editions), illustrated with his own designs, and laid out several housing-schemes with pitched roofs, modelled on traditional types (e.g. State Electricity Company Workers' Housing, Trier (1906–7), and housing, Am Schänkenberg, at the *Garden City, Hellerau, Dresden (1910–11)). His best-known work is the Dalcroze Institute for Physical Education, Hellerau (1910–11), where he employed a rigorous, severe, *stripped *Classicism, especially in the forbidding tetrastyle *in antis* *portico. With the Heinrich-Schütz School, Kassel (1927–30), Tessenow showed a tendency to move nearer the prevailing *Rationalism of the period.

He was an important and influential teacher, and the 1914–18 war affected him deeply, moving his interests towards the creation of small towns and communities and drawing on craft-orientated buildings. In 1930–1 he converted Schinkel's guard-house (*Neue Wache*) on the *Unter den Linden*, Berlin, into a memorial to the dead of the 1914–18 war. He found it difficult to practise under the Nazi regime, but after the 1939–45 war he resumed teaching in Berlin and concerned himself with the reconstruction of old town centres, notably Lübeck (1947). He was a prolific writer, and interest in his architecture has grown since a major exhibition devoted to him in 1961, influencing *Grassi and other protagonists of *Rational architecture. Among his pupils was *Speer.

Campbell (1978); *Kunst und Künstler*, 15 (1917), 32–6, 24 (1925), 55–60; Tessenow (1919, 1921, 1927); Wangerin and Weiss (1976); *Wasmuths Monatshefte für Baukunst*, 9 (1925), 365–81

tessera (*pl.* **tesserae**). One of a great number of small square (almost cubical) pieces of glass, marble, pottery, stone, tile, etc., called in the singular *abaculus, *abacisus, or, if very small, *tessella, embedded in mortar forming a *mosaic.

Tessin, Nicodemus, the Elder (1615–81). Swedish architect and military engineer of French origins. After its successes in the Thirty Years War (1618–48) Sweden became a magnet for artists, and enjoyed a period of considerable activity in creative spheres. In 1646, during the reign of Queen Christina (1644–54), Tessin was appointed Royal Architect, travelled to improve his taste and knowledge, and returned to Sweden in 165[illegible] armed with the necessary experience, books and drawings to become the country's foremost *Baroque architect. Influenced by

French designs, he created the gardens at the Royal Palace of Drottningholm as well as the Palace itself, with its system of *pavilions, monumental staircase, and composition in which precedents from France, The Netherlands, and Italy can be detected (1660s). He also designed Kalmar Cathedral (begun 1660), partly influenced by the Roman *Cinquecento and built on a Greek-cross plan with corner turrets, but with the east and west arms lengthened and with *apses. He was City Architect of Stockholm from 1661 until his death. Among his other works were the noble *Karolinska Grafkoret* (Carolinian *Mausoleum) at the *Riddarholms-Kyrka* (Riddarholms Church—1671–1740), many houses in Stockholm, and the Bank of Sweden, Stockholm (1676).

Kommer (1974); Paulsson (1958); Placzek (1982)

Tessin, Nicodemus, the Younger (1654–1728). Swedish architect, the son of *Tessin the Elder. Trained by his father and partly educated in Rome (1673–8) and Paris (1678–80), he thoroughly absorbed Italian and French *Classicism, especially after a second study-tour in Rome and Paris (1687–8). When in Rome he was introduced to *Bernini and Carlo *Fontana under the aegis of the exiled Queen Christina of Sweden (1626–89). He succeeded his father at Drottningholm and as Stockholm City Architect, and built a fine house for himself in Stockholm (1692–1700) that served as a clever advertisement for his skills as an inventive, eclectic architect, demonstrating his mastery of contemporary French and Roman *Baroque, especially with the garden-front. In 1697 fire consumed the old Royal Castle in Stockholm, and Tessin lost no time in producing designs for the great Palace that stands there today. Building took a long time as Sweden was bankrupted by the disastrous wars against Denmark, Poland, and Russia under King Charles XII (1697–1718), and the Palace was not completed until 1753 by Tessin's son, **Carl Gustav Tessin** (1695–1770), and Carl *Hårleman. Nicodemus Tessin the Younger was also responsible for Steninge Castle, Sweden (1694–8), a country house in the French style much influenced by Vaux-le-Vicomte, and designed a huge Palace for the Amalienborg Gardens, Copenhagen, Denmark (1694–7—unrealized).

Josephson (1930, 1930–1); Kommer (1974); Weilbach (1947–52); Wrangel (1912)

Testa, Clorindo (1923–   ). Argentinian architect, born in Italy. He designed the Civic Centre and Bus Station, Santa Rosa, La Pampa (1955–63), the first essay in *Brutalism in Argentina. Other works include the Bank of London and South America (1960–6), the National Library (1962–84), and the Bank of Holland (1970–5), all in Buenos Aires. His work was firmly in the *International Modernist style.

Bullrich (1969); Emanuel (1994); van Vynckt (1993)

tester. Canopy over a *pulpit (called *abat-voix) or *tomb.

tetraprostyle. Classical *portico of four columns set before the *cella.

tetrapylon. 1. With four gateways. **2.** Building with four identical (or almost identical) arched façades set on two intersecting axes (e.g. Arco di Giano, or Arch of Janus, near the Church of San Giorgio in Velabro, Rome (C4)).

tetrastyle. With four columns. *See* portico.

tetrastyle atrium. *Atrium with a column at each of the four corners of the *compluvium*, supporting the roof around the opening.

Teulon, Samuel Sanders (1812–73). English *High Victorian *Gothic Revival architect of French Huguenot descent. He commenced practice in 1838 and designed a very large number of startlingly original churches and other buildings. His masterpiece was St Stephen's, Rosslyn Hill, Hampstead, London (1868–71), with a *polychrome brick interior, powerful roof construction, and a general inventiveness that won admiration from *Eastlake, no less. Ingenious too is St Mary's, St Mary's Road, Ealing, London (1866–74), with an elephantine tower and a galleried interior incorporating a riotously complex roof structure. More serene and impressive is St John the Baptist, Huntley, Gloucestershire (1861–3), with its fine *polychrome interior. Of his great houses, Tortworth Court, Gloucestershire (1849–52), and the wildly exuberant Shadwell Park, Norfolk (1856–60), deserve especial mention. Teulon is regarded as a *Rogue Goth. His brother, **William Milford Teulon** (1823–1900), also an architect, founded the City Church and Churchyard Protection Society.

Brown (1985); *DNB* (1993); Dixon and Muthesius (1985); Eastlake (1970); Goodhart-Rendel (1949); Muthesius (1972); Saunders (1982)

thatch. Thick roof-covering of reed, rushes, or straw, used in *vernacular buildings, sometimes on medieval churches, and often on structures intended to fit within a *Picturesque landscape, e.g. *cottage orné.

Davey (1961); West (1988)

theatre. Building for the public enjoyment of drama, etc. *Antique Classical theatres were planned as segments of a circle, the seats rising in concentric tiers above and behind one another around the *orchaestra separating the auditorium from the stage. *See* amphitheatre.

thé-au-lait. Colour resembling tea with milk often used to describe *terracotta-faced buildings.

Theodorus of Samos (d. 540 BC). Greek architect. He designed (with Rhoecus) the great *Ionic temple of the Heraion, Samos (from *c.*575 BC), and wrote an architectural treatise, now lost, one of the earliest of Classical Antiquity. He was also involved in the building of the fourth temple of Artemis at Ephesus (*c.*565 BC) with *Chersiphron.

Dinsmoor (1950); Lawrence (1983)

Theodotos (d. *c.*360 BC). Greek architect. He designed the *Doric temple of Asclepius, Epidaurus (*c.*375 BC), celebrated for its sculptures in the *pediments and for the *chryselephantine statue within, and also for the curious fact that the expense-accounts for the building survive.

Burford (1969); Dinsmoor (1950); Lawrence (1983)

thermae. Public bathing-establishment in Classical Antiquity. The vast Roman *thermae* of the Imperial era embraced not only hot, medium, and cold baths, but luxuriously appointed places for exercise, athletics, and recreation, as well as formal gardens. Furthermore, the *plans included room-shapes of various geometries that were influential on *Renaissance and Neoclassical planning.

Cruickshank (1996); Robertson (1945)

thermal window. *See* Diocletian window.

Thibault, Jean-Thomas (1757–1826). French architect. A pupil of *Boullée, he became a partner of J.-N.-L. *Durand, winning several prizes for Government-sponsored projects in the 1790s. He renovated several important buildings, including the Elysée and Neuilly Palaces, and worked for a time in The Netherlands, where he adapted the Town Hall, Amsterdam, as a Royal Residence. He published *Application de la Perspective linéaire aux arts du dessin* (Application of Linear Perspective to the Arts of Design—1827, 1831, 1833–4).

Papworth (1892)

Thibault, Louis-Michel (1750–1815). French architect. He studied under A.-J. *Gabriel, and in 1785 became Architect to the Dutch East India Company at the Cape in South Africa. His works include a number of Neoclassical buildings in and around Cape Town, including the Supreme Court and Government Offices (1811–15). With *Anreith he brought advanced European architectural ideas to South Africa.

Fransen and Cook (1978); Lewcock (1963); Puyfontaine (1972)

Thibiage, —— De (*fl.* 1840s). French author, probably a pseudonym. His *Histoire pittoresque et anecdotique des anciens châteax*, etc. (1846), was a significant catalyst in the *Gothic Revival in France and, especially, Germany, where the book was published as *Geschichte der berühmtesten Ritterburgen und Schlösser Frankreichs, Englands, Deutschlands, der Schweiz, etc.* (History of the Most Celebrated French, English, German, Swiss, etc., Fortresses and Castles—1846).

Library of Congress Catalogue; Thibiage (1846, 1846*a*)

Thienen, Jacob van (*fl.* early C15). Flemish architect. He designed the *Gothic Town Hall in Brussels, Belgium (begun 1402), one of the masterpieces of secular medieval architecture in Northern Europe, although the *belfry was designed by Jan van *Ruysbroeck, built 1448–63. He may have built the south *aisle of the Church of Ste-Gudule, Brussels (*c.*1400).

Duverger (1933)

Thiersch, Friedrich von (1852–1921). German architect and teacher, much affected by *Semper's ideas. He was one of the most influential architects in Southern Germany, designing many important buildings, some in a *Rundbogenstil, and others in a Classical style combining the *Neoclassicism and *Renaissance influences so common in C19 Germany. Among his works are the Munich Palace of Justice (1887–97), the remodelling of the *Kurhaus* (Cure House for the Spa), Wiesbaden (1904–7), originally designed by

Johann Christian Zais (1770–1820) in a simplified *Palladian style, and the *Festhalle*, Frankfurt-am-Main (1909). His pupils included *Bonatz, Theodor *Fischer, W. *Gropius, Ernst *May, and *Tessenow.

Eitel (1952); Marschall (1981); Thiersch (1925)

Third Pointed. *See* Perpendicular.

Thirsk, John (*fl.* 1420–d. 1452). English master-mason. He worked at Westminster Abbey, notably on the *nave, and designed the beautiful *Chantry Chapel of King Henry V (reigned 1413–22) as well as the great altar-screen (completed 1441). In 1449 he was appointed Master-Mason at Windsor Castle.

Harvey (1987)

thole. 1. *Boss or escutcheon at the apex of a timber *vault, where the *ribs meet. **2.** *Niche or recess to receive votive offerings in medieval times.

tholobate. 1. Substructure for a Greek *tholos, really a circular version of the *crepidoma or *stylobate. **2.** Circular substructure of a *cupola.

tholos. 1. Circular building with a conical, domed, or vaulted roof, e.g. a circular tomb roofed with a pseudo-dome of *corbelled rings, such as the 'Treasury of Atreus', Mycenae (*c.*1300 BC). **2.** Ancient *Greek circular building, often with a *peristyle, e.g. the Tholos of Epidaurus (*c.*350 BC).

Dinsmoor (1950)

Thomas, Sir Alfred Brumwell (1868–1948). English architect. He commenced practice in 1894, and in 1898 won the competition to design the new Belfast City Hall, the grandest of all late-Victorian and Edwardian examples of the *Baroque Revival or *Wrenaissance. The interiors, notably the monumental stair, are as splendid as the exterior, with its great dome and corner towers modelled on those of *Wren's St Paul's Cathedral in London. The building was opened in 1906 and gained Thomas his knighthood in the same year. Thomas followed this triumph with other competition successes, including Stockport Town Hall, Cheshire (1903–8), in which a *Beaux-Arts influence is clear, although Wren's themes are not entirely absent. Among his other fine town-halls, all of which are competent, confident, and redolent of civic pride, are Plumstead (now Woolwich) Town Hall (1903–6—in a florid Baroque style with open-bedded segmental pediments, a tower placed asymmetrically, and a long entrance-hall of great magnificence), the Library, Lewisham Way, Deptford, London (1914—again Baroque), and the Town Hall, Clacton-on-Sea, Essex (1931—in a *Neo-Georgian style, but with a large central pedimented *portico).

Gray (1985); Pevsner, *Buildings of England, Cheshire* (1971), *Essex* (1954), *London* (1952); Service (1975, 1977)

Thomas, William (1799–1860). English architect. He practised in Leamington Spa, Warwickshire, from 1831, and built many villas and houses there, including Lansdowne Crescent and Circus (1835–8). He also designed the Baptist Chapel, Warwick Street (1833–4), and the Victoria Terrace, Pump-Room, and Baths (1837), all in Leamington. He suffered bankruptcy after the Leamington Bank failed in 1837, and in 1843, the year his *Designs for Monuments and Chimney Pieces* was published, emigrated to Canada, where he built up a flourishing architectural practice, designing around 30 churches, many town-halls, gaols, and other public buildings, as well as numerous mansions and villas in all the principal towns of Ontario. Among his works were the Commercial Bank, Toronto (1844–5), St Paul's Anglican Cathedral, London, Ontario (1844–6), the District Court House, Town Hall, and Market, Niagara, Ontario (1846–8), St Michael's Roman Catholic Cathedral, Toronto (1845–8), and the handsome Brock Monument, Queenston, Ontario (1853–6—a monumental *Composite column on a high *pedestal).

His sons, **Cyrus Pole Thomas** (1833–1911) and **William Tutin Thomas** (1829–92), were also architects. The latter designed the *Gothic St George's Church, Dominion Square, Montreal (1870), and the sumptuous *Italianate Mount Stephen Residence, Drummond Street, Montreal (1881–4).

Colvin (1995); Kalman (1994); Macrae and Adamson (1963, 1975)

Thomas of Canterbury (*fl.* 1324–31). *See* Canterbury.

Thomon, Thomas de (1754–1813). Swiss-born Neoclassical architect. He studied in Paris under *Ledoux and in Italy, where the Greek *Doric temples at *Paestum had a considerable impact on his sensibilities. He settled in Russia in 1799 where he became Court Architect to Tsar Alexander I (reigned

1801–25) in St Petersburg in 1802 and designed several buildings, including the Grand Theatre (1802–5—demolished). His most outstanding work is the *Bourse* (Exchange—1801–16), a powerful Neoclassical barrel-vaulted hall surrounded by a *peristyle of Greek Doric columns of the unfluted type, not unlike *Ledoux's designs for the Stock Exchange and Discount Bank at his imaginary town of Chaux. With its severe unadorned treatment, clear expression of elements, huge *Diocletian windows set within great arches of rusticated *voussoirs, and platform of ramps and podia, it was a major essay in *Neoclassicism as advanced as anywhere in the world for its date, and also shows some affinity with *Boullée's designs. Among his other buildings are warehouses on the Salni Embankment, St Petersburg (1804–5), the Doric *Mausoleum of Tsar Paul I (reigned 1796–1801) at Pavlovsk (1805–8), and the Column of Glory, Poltava (1805–11). He published *Recueil de plans et façades des principaux monuments construits à Saint-Pétersbourg et dans les différentes provinces de l'Empire de Russie* (Compendium of Plans and Elevations of Principal Buildings Erected in St Petersburg and in the Different Provinces of the Russian Empire—1809) and a treatise on painting. His own watercolours were much influenced by the work of *Piranesi.

Berckenhagen (1975); Grabar, Lazarev, and Kemenov (1963); Hamilton (1983); Middleton and Watkin (1987); van Vynckt (1993); Vogt (1974)

Thomson, Alexander 'Greek' (1817–75). Scots Neoclassical architect, the greatest of his time, and a formidable and original designer apparently influenced by the works of *Schinkel. He lived and worked for most of his life in Glasgow, starting with a period (1836–49) with John *Baird before he established his own practice in partnership with another John Baird (1816–93) until 1857, then with his brother, **George Thomson** (*c*.1819–78), from 1857 to 1871, and finally with Robert Turnbull (*c*.1839–1905) from 1874 until Thomson's death.

Thomson earned his nickname because of the frequent allusions to the *Greek Revival in his buildings, but his work was very eclectic and inventive, drawing on a variety of sources, including Ancient Egyptian, Persian, and even vaguely Indian architecture, put together with enormous verve and sureness of touch. His best works were designed between 1857 and 1871, and included individual *villas, *terrace houses, *tenement-blocks, churches, warehouses, and offices for the rapidly expanding city of Glasgow. Among his individual houses, the most outstanding are the Double Villa (25 and 25a Mansion-house Road, Langside (1856–7—illustrated in Blackie's *Villa and Cottage Architecture* (1868)), combining two medium-sized houses in one large asymmetrical composition, with low-pitched roofs and glazing well set back from the stone *mullions; Holmwood, Cathcart (1856–8—also illustrated in *Villa and Cottage Architecture*), a sumptuous villa with an *engaged circular bay-window featuring a peristyle of inventive columns; and Ellisland, 200 Nithsdale Road, Pollokshields (1871—a single-storey symmetrical villa with Graeco-Egyptian detail).

He also designed several terraces of houses. Moray Place, Strathbungo (1857–9), is unquestionably his finest achievement in this respect, and is arguably the most distinguished Greek-inspired group of terrace-houses anywhere. It is a symmetrical design with projecting pedimented ends (featuring *Giant Orders of square columns), between which is a long façade with first-floor windows set behind a regular row of square mullions reminiscent of Schinkel's use of the same motif at the Berlin *Schauspielhaus* (Play House) of 1818–21. The form of the building recalls von Klenze's *Ruhmeshalle* (Hall of Fame), Munich (1850s), and the great *Hellenistic altar of Pergamon (*c*.180 BC—now in the Pergamon-Museum, Berlin). Other Thomson terraces include Great Western Terrace (1867–9) and Northpark Terrace, Hamilton Drive (1866), the latter again with a top storey treated with a row of square mullions derived from the Berlin *Schauspielhaus* and ultimately from a synthesis of the *Choragic Monument of Thrasyllus, Athens (319 BC), and the long rows of square columns found in Ancient Egyptian temples at Elephantine and Deïr-el-Bahari. The very severe columnar and trabeated Walmer Crescent, Paisley Road (1857), a tenement block, again uses the Schinkel *Schauspielhaus* motif, the whole composition, with its projecting rectangular bay-windows, handled with absolute rigour.

Thomson's three United Presbyterian Churches, Caledonia Road (1856—mostly destroyed by fire), St Vincent Street (1859), and Queen's Park (1869—destroyed in the 1939–45 war), were among the most original inventions of their time. Queen's Park had pronounced Egyptian elements and a hollow *stupa-like top to the crowning element of the composition. At Caledonia Road the *Schauspielhaus* *clearstorey row of square mullions was again used, but at St Vincent Street a complex system of *pylon-forms, high-level *Ionic *porticoes set on tall blocky *podia, and a strangely inventive tower with two Neoclassical heads facing each other in each T-shaped recess over an H-shaped lower stage, with much else, suggests some kind of mnemonic system perhaps connecting the building with the Temple of Solomon (*Templum Hierosolymae*). The platform system also suggests von Klenze's *Walhalla*, near Regensburg (1830–42), a building that may also have influenced Thomson's brilliant but unrealized designs for the South Kensington Museum, London (1864). Furthermore, von Klenze employed *cyclopean (or pelasgic) and *pseudisodomic masonry on some of his designs, and Thomson also used these at the Caledonia Road Church, possibly for symbolic purposes (e.g. the Rock on which the Church is built). The St Vincent Street Church also has interior cast-iron columns rising from the basement hall to carry the gallery and the clearstorey, while the inventive *capitals employing sharp claws, *acanthus, and stars suggest something exotic and Eastern, perhaps the Solomonic Temple itself.

Among Thomson's designs for commercial buildings are two important buildings, the Grecian Chambers, Sauchiehall Street (1865—with squat Egyptianesque columns along the top storey and an *Attic storey vaguely derived from the Thrasyllus Monument), and the Egyptian Halls, Union Street (1871–3—with a highly complex façade of paraphrases and variations on Graeco-Egyptian themes, and a suggestion of a *Renaissance *cornicone anchoring the whole *Sublime composition).

In 1874 Thomson gave a series of lectures in Glasgow in which he argued for the superiority of *columnar and trabeated construction over *arcuated forms, castigated *Ruskin for his highly selective arguments, demanded that architects should follow the example of the Greeks rather than imitate their work, and extolled the 'mysterious power of the horizontal element in carrying the mind away into space and into speculation upon infinity'. The contents of the lectures demonstrate that Thomson was widely read and had a deep understanding of architectural styles of all periods as well as their principles. In particular, he analysed the Thrasyllus Monument which was so important in his own architecture. It has become clear that, although he does not appear to have travelled, and built in a small geographical area, he was an architect deserving of international fame.

Architects' Journal, 183/8 (19 Feb. 1986), 36–53; *Architectural Review*, 15/90 (May 1904), 183–95, 115/689 (May 1954), 307–16; *British Architect*, 1 (1 May 1874), 274–8, (5 June 1874), 354–7; 2 (24 July 1874), 50–2, (7 Aug. 1874), 82–4, (30 Oct. 1874), 272–4, (6 Nov. 1874), 288–9, (20 Nov. 1874), 317–18; *Builder*, 24/1215 (19 May 1866), 368–71; Crook (1972*a*); *DNB* (1917); Gomme and Walker (1987); McFadzean (1979); Stamp and McKinstry (1994); Summerson (1993); Williamson, Riches, and Higgs (1990)

Thon. *See* Ton.

Thornely, Sir Arnold (1870–1953). English architect. Articled and educated in Liverpool, he commenced practice in 1898. With Gilbert Wilson Fraser (1873–1954) he designed the Presbyterian Church, Warren Road, Blundellsands, near Liverpool (1898–1905), in a free *Perpendicular style of *Gothic. He entered into partnership with Frank Gatley Briggs (1862–1921) and Henry Vernon Wolstenholme (1863–1936) in Liverpool. Among the firm's works are the *Wrenaissance Bluecoat School, Wavertree (1903–6), the very showy *Baroque Wrenaissance domed and towered Mersey Docks and Harbour Board Offices, Pier Head, Liverpool (1907), extensions to the Walker Art Gallery, Liverpool (1931–3), and the Geology Department, University of Liverpool (1929). His masterpiece is the Northern Ireland Parliament Building, Stormont, Belfast (1927–32), an outstanding, if late, essay in the *Greek Revival style, with an *Ionic *temple-front in the centre and magnificent scholarly interiors (although some were lost in a fire of 1995). Ralph *Knott contributed to the designs. Also at Stormont, Thornely was responsible for the handsome gateways and lodges, and for the former Provincial Bank at the Massey Avenue entrance to the grounds (1932).

Felstead, Franklin, and Pinfield (1993); *Journal of the Royal Society of Ulster Architects*, 6/2 (Nov./Dec. 1997), 24–35; Larmour (1987); Pevsner, *Buildings of England, South Lancashire* (1969)

Thornton, William (1759–1828). Born in the British West Indies, he studied medicine at Edinburgh and became an American citizen in 1788. He designed the Library Company Building, Philadelphia (1789–90—destroyed), based on a plate in volume 2 of Abraham Swan's (*fl.*1745–*c.*1770) *Collection of Designs in Architecture* (1757), and in 1792 prepared drawings for the competition to design the US Capitol in Washington, DC, loosely based on plates in Colen *Campbell's *Vitruvius Britannicus* (1715–25). His second design, drawn up (rather unsportingly) after he had been able to peruse some of the entries and submitted after the deadline, was accepted in 1793, but, having major flaws as a realizable proposition, was revised by *Hallet, who changed Thornton's plans to conform more to his own ideas. Thornton again produced a third design in 1795 when *Hadfield was dismissed as supervising architect, and it is that which forms the basis of the final version, with the central pedimented *portico and rather French *Louis Quinze elevations (although the Capitol went through several further transformations in the course of its history). He designed the Octagon, a town-house in Washington (1797–1800—which, like his Capitol designs, demonstrates his fascination for elliptical and circular interior spaces), and also a house at Tudor Place, Georgetown, Washington (*c.*1805–10, probably his best work, perhaps influenced by a design by *Soane in *New Vitruvius Britannicus* (1802–3)). He also designed Pavilion VII, University of Virginia, Charlottesville (1817–21). *See also* Bulfinch, Hoban, Latrobe, and Walter.

Brown (1970); *Dictionary of American Biography* (1936); McCue (1976); Maddex (1973); Peterson (1976); Placzek (1982); Reiff (1977); Stearns and Yerkes (1976)

Thorpe, John (*c.*1565–*c.*1655). English land- and building-surveyor, who also appears to have designed (though rarely supervised) buildings. He produced a book of plans (preserved in Sir John *Soane's Museum, London) containing surveys and projects for country-houses. He probably designed Thornton College, Lincolnshire (*c.*1607–10), the outer court at Audley End, Essex (*c.*1615), Aston Hall, Warwickshire (1618–35), perhaps Dowsby Hall, Lincolnshire (after 1610), and Somerhill, near Tonbridge, Kent (*c.*1610–13), all showy *Jacobean houses with plans reminiscent of works by *Palladio, but with detail derived from French sources, notably du *Cerceau. A gallery between the Rosse and Stanton Towers, Belvoir Castle, Leicestershire, for which drawings survive, was by him (1625–7). He was probably responsible for the English version of Hans Blum's treatise (1550) on the *Orders, which appeared as *The Booke of Five Collumnes of Architecture* (1601 and 1608), and also prepared an English version of du Cerceau's work on perspective. His father was **Thomas Thorpe**, master-mason, who was involved in building at Kirby Hall, Northamptonshire.

Architectural Review, 106/635 (Nov. 1949), 291–300; Colvin (1995); Lees-Milne (1951); *Lincolnshire History and Archaeology*, 8 (1973), 13–34; Summerson (1993); *Walpole Society*, 40 (1966)

three-centred. *See* arch.

throat. Contraction of the flue of a *chimney over the fireplace.

throating. Continuous groove or *drip under a *coping or *string-course to prevent water running back towards the wall.

throughstane. **1.** Flat grave-stone or *slab, also called *thruch*. **2.** *Table-tomb.

Parker (1850); Pride (1996)

through-stone. **1.** Bond-stone or *parpend passing through the whole thickness of a wall, binding the *ashlar or facing-stone with the inner or backing-course. **2.** *Throughstane.

thrust. Outward pressure of any arch or *vault. It has to be resisted by a counter-thrust provided by another arch, *buttress, etc.

Thumb Family. German architects and craftsmen, one of several dynasties from the Bregenz district comprising the *Vorarlberg School. Indeed the Thumb family intermarried with the *Beers. **Michael Thumb** (*c.*1640–90) was responsible for several important *Baroque designs, including the Priory Church of Wettenhausen (1670–97), the Pilgrimage Church (*Wallfahrtskirche*) of Schönenberg, Ellwangen (1682–92), and the Premonstratensian *Klosterkirche* (Monastery Church) of Obermarchtal (1686–92). At Schönenberg he introduced the *Wandpfeilerkirche arrangement, in which deep internal *buttresses divide the *aisles into side-chapels, the *nave face of each buttress being enriched with *pilasters. Outside, the position of each wall-pier is marked by a pilaster. Both Schönenberg and Obermarchtal were precedents for other *Wandpfeilerkirchen* of the Vorarlberg School incorporating what became known as the *Vorarlberger Münsterschema* (Vorarlberg large-church arrangement), in which galleries connect the wall-piers and form the ceilings of each chapel.

Peter II Thumb (1681–1766), so called to distinguish him from his grandfather, was Michael's son, and in 1707 married Maria Anna Beer, having supervised the building of Franz Beer's Church at Rheinau, Switzerland (1704–11). He designed the Church and Library of the Benedictine Church of St Peter in the Black Forest, near Freiburg (1724–53). His greatest work is the exquisite Cistercian Monastery and Pilgrimage Church of Neu-Birnau (1745–51) on the north shores of Lake Constance (*Bodensee*). The church has a large open interior, like a prayer-hall (it does not have the *Wandpfeiler* arrangement but the gallery continues all round the volume), with curved eastern corners and diagonals at the west, vestigial *transepts, flattened *vaults, and a partial ellipse for the *sanctuary: its internal decorations are *Rococo, among the loveliest in all Germany, mostly white, but enlivened by subtle colouring. *Stucco-work (1747–50) of the frothiest, lightest kind, was by Josef Anton Feuchtmayr *or* Feuchtmayer (1696–1770), who also designed and made the enchanting statuary, including the celebrated *Honigschlecker* (honey-sucker, a figure suggestive of the *Antique Harpocrates), and the frescoes are by Gottfried Bernhard Götz (or Göz—1708–74). Thumb contributed to one of the biggest and most sumptuous churches of the period, the Benedictine Abbey of St Gallen, Switzerland, where he also designed the fine Library. *Moosbrugger had already begun the Church (1720–1), but Thumb was probably responsible for the nave and domed area, developing the *Wandpfeilerkirche* type further, opening it up with an impressive centralized volume.

Other members of the family include **Christian Thumb** (1683–1726), who worked with Michael at Schönenberg and Obermarchtal, designed the *Schlosskirche* (Castle Church) at Friedrichshafen (1695–1700) with stucco-work by the *Schmutzers, and was also active at Weingarten Abbey Church (1716–24). **Gabriel Thumb** (1671–) worked on the *Pfarrkirche* (Parish Church) at Lachen, Lake of Zurich, Switzerland (1707–10), based on a plan by Moosbrugger. Again it was a *Wandpfeilerkirche*. **Michael Peter Franz Xaver Thumb** (1725–69) superintended the completion of his father's Library at St Gallen as well as the nave and rotunda of the same Church.

Bourke (1962); Gubler (1972); Hitchcock (1968*a*); Lieb and Dieth (1976); Powell (1959)

thumb-moulding. *See* gadroon.

thunderbolt. Classical ornament, an *attribute of Jupiter, in the form of a spiral roll, pointed at both ends, often held in the talons of an eagle, or shown winged, with arrow-headed, forked, or zig-zag lightning-flashes. It occurs on the *soffits of Classical *cornices (e.g. *Vignola's *mutule *Doric *Order) and in *Empire schemes of decoration.

Thura(h), Laurids (Lauritz) Lauridsen (1706–59). Danish architect. He became Architect to the Danish Court in 1733, after a tour of Europe (1729–31), and developed an enviable reputation as the finest late-*Baroque architect of his time in Denmark. He designed the exquisite Hunting Lodge, the *Erimitage* (1734–6), in the Deer Park north of Copenhagen, the interiors of which are among the finest of the period in Scandinavia. In 1749–50 he added the *steeple to the Church of Our Saviour, Copenhagen, built in 1696 without a spire. The unusual external staircase (gilded to contrast with the copper roof), was probably inspired by *Borromini's Sapienza Church in Rome. He published the Danish *Vitruvius I–II* (1746, 1749), and produced a manuscript of Vitruvius III, complete with *cartouches.

Cruickshank (1996); *Denmark: An Official Handbook* (Copenhagen, 1974); Weilbach (1947–52)

Tibaldi, Marchese di Valsolda, Pellegrino *or* **Pellegrini** (1527–96). Bolognese architect and painter. His earliest building appears to have been the Cappella Poggi in San Giacomo Maggiore, Bologna (*c.*1555), after which he worked on the fortifications at Ancona. Around 1562 he moved to Milan under the aegis of St Charles Borromeo (1538–84), Archbishop of Milan (from 1564), canonized 1610. He designed the Collegio Borromeo, Pavia (1564—with its elegant two-storeyed *cortile, a more austere and lighter version of *Alessi's Palazzo Marino), and the Cortile della Canonica in the Archiepiscopal Palace, Milan (1565–75). Other works include the circular Votive Church of San Sebastiano (from 1577), the Jesuit Church of San Fedele (from 1569), the *choir-crypt and screens in the Cathedral (1567), all in Milan, and the powerfully articulated façade of the Sanctuario della Madonna dei Miracoli, Saronno (1583).

Heydenreich and Lotz (1974); Murray (1986); Panizza and Mazzottas (1990); Torre (1994)

Ticinese School. Group of architects working in the Ticino region of Switzerland from the 1960s, concerned with a reconsideration of architectural style and a greater historical awareness. Among the more influential members were *Botta, *Reichlin, and *Rossi. The School promoted *Rational architecture. *See* Tendenza.

Brown-Manrique (1989); Grassi (1982, 1989); Pizzi (1991); Steinmann and Boga (1975)

tie. Any member that resists a pull, as to prevent the spreading of two sides of a sloping roof. In e.g. a *truss, the tie-beam is the main transverse timber connecting the feet of the principal *rafters or the *blades of a *cruck truss.

Alcock, Barley, Dixon, and Meeson (1996)

tierceron. *See* vault.

Tiffany, Louis Comfort (1864–1933). American designer, best known for his work in the *Art Nouveau style. He evolved interiors for *McKim, Mead, & White and *Carrère & Hastings, among others. His works include the Chapel for the Columbian Exposition in Chicago (1893), parts of which survive, the *loggia of Laurelton Hall, New York (1903–5—re-erected in the American Wing of the Metropolitan Museum of Art), and the Hanley House, Oyster Bay, NY (1921). He designed many fine artefacts in glass, and his work has been favourably compared with the best French Art Nouveau works of the period.

Johnson (1979); Koch (1966); McKean (1980); Tschudi-Madsen (1967)

Tigerman, Stanley (1930–). American architect. He opened his office in Chicago in 1964 and produced designs reminiscent of the works of *Mies van der Rohe and *Skidmore, Owings, & Merrill (for which firm he previously had worked). Later he became interested in metaphors expressed in architecture, as in the Daisy House, Porter, Ind. (1975–7), built for the owner of a striptease-club and suggesting something of *Ledoux's phallic imagery. His growing eclecticism reflects his acknowledgement of the pluralist nature of the USA, and his *The Architecture of Exile* (1988) revealed his interest in reconstructions of the Temple of Solomon and in Judaeo-Christian architectural traditions. His Powerhouse Museum for the Commonwealth Eddison Electric Company, Zion, Ill. (1988–92), evokes the basilican form as well as many-layered imagery giving a host of meanings to the structure. His controversial architecture has been much debated.

Architecture and Urbanism, 67 (1976), 71–120; Banham (1976); Dahinden (1972); Emanuel (1994); Sky and Stone (1976); Stern (1977); Underhill (1989); van Vynckt (1993)

tile. Plate of burnt clay. Thin flat tiles are termed *plain* tiles, and are commonly used to clad roofs or walls: in the latter case the wall is referred to as being *tile-hung*. Thicker tiles, often of the *encaustic type, are used for paving. Glazed coloured tiles for wall-finishes were employed in Ancient Mesopotamian architecture, and that tradition continued in *Islamic architecture. In Spain, *Moorish architecture was often decorated with glazed tilework of great beauty (*alicatado) formed of uniformly shaped *azulejos. Glazed tiles were often employed in France and The Netherlands from C15 to C17, and during C19 were widely used throughout Europe and America, especially in the 1890s and 1900s.

McKay (1957); Parker (1850); Vallet (1982)

tile-creasing. Two or more courses of *tiles laid to protect the surface of a wall below, e.g. in a *cill or *string-course, and, very often, where a tile roof joins a *gable, and does not overhang, the roof ending almost flush with the *naked of the gable wall.

McKay (1957)

timber frame. Type of building construction sometimes called *half-timbering*, where walls and partitions are made of a wooden skeleton, set on a foundation, with the spaces filled with brick *nogging, plaster, *wattle-and-daub, etc. Timber-framed buildings are frequently *tile-hung, plastered, weather-boarded or otherwise protected from the weather, as with *mathematical tiles. *See* beam, brace, breastsummer, cill, collar, cross-rail, cruck, dragon-beam, jetty, joist, post, principal, purlin, rafter, rail, stud, truss, Wealden house.

Alcock, Barley, Dixon, and Meeson (1996); Brown (1986); Brunskill (1994)

Tirol, Hans (*c*.1505–*c*.1575). *See* Stella, Paolo della.

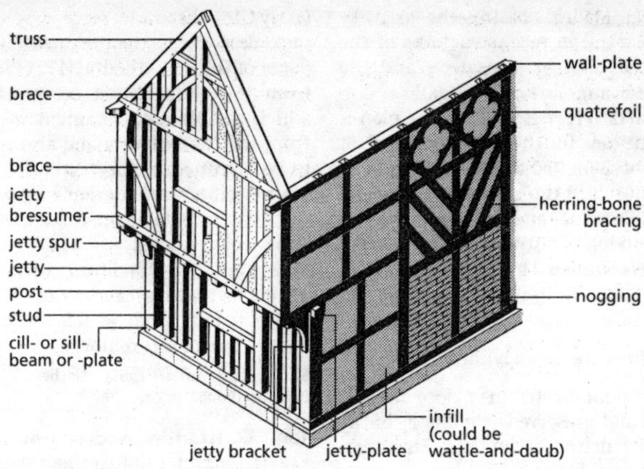

timber frame (*JJS*)

Tite, Sir William (1798–1873). English architect. He began his career by designing the Classical Mill Hill School, Middlesex (1825–7), and later laid out the South Metropolitan Cemetery, Norwood, London (1838), with *Gothic Revival chapels (demolished) and gates. He is best known for the Royal Exchange, City of London (1842–4), an opulent, perhaps rather coarsely detailed building, with a massive *Corinthian *portico. He designed many railway-stations, including the very handsome Classical one at Gosport, Hampshire (1840–2). His *Rundbogenstil *Byzantine polychrome Church of St James, Gerrard's Cross, Buckinghamshire (1858–9), is one of his best buildings, and shows that he was an accomplished eclectic designer. His *Gothic railway-stations at Carlisle, Cumberland (1847), and Perth, Scotland (1848), are more successful architecturally than his churches in that style. He laid out the London Necropolis Cemetery, Brookwood, Surrey (1853–4), and built most of the stations on the railway-lines on the Caledonian and Scottish Central Railways and on the line from Le Havre to Paris, France. He designed Government House, Termonbacca, Co. Londonderry, Ireland (1846–8—the headquarters of The Honourable The Irish Society of the City of London), and, as a member of the Metropolitan Board of Works, was involved in the construction of the Thames Embankment (1862–70).

Biddle (1973); Binney and Pearce (1979); Colvin (1995); Curl (1986, 1993); *DNB* (1917); Hitchcock (1954)

tithe barn. Large medieval *barn for the storage of the tithe-corn, that quota (a tenth part) of the annual produce of agriculture to support the priesthood.

Tivoli window. Type of window-opening based on a Roman example in the Temple of Vesta at Tivoli (*c*.80 BC), published by *Palladio. It is less wide at the top than at the bottom (i.e. with sloping sides), has an *architrave with *crossettes crowned with a *cornice, and is sometimes called a *Vitruvian opening.

Todt, Fritz (1891–1942). German engineer. He designed many bridges and roads, becoming under the Nazis director of the construction of *Autobahnen* (motorways). Not a few motorway *viaducts carrying the system are *Sublime constructions, some by *Bonatz. He quickly acquired control at all waterways, power-plants, military installations, and many other aspects of construction-works and production in the Reich, so by 1940, when he was appointed Minister of Armaments, he had enormous influence. After he was killed in an air-crash he was succeeded by Albert *Speer.

Adam (1992); Council of Europe (1995); Speer (1970, 1976, 1981); Stockhorst (1967)

Toledo, Juan Bautista de (d. 1567). Spanish architect, mathematician, and philosopher. He lived in Italy for some time, where he absorbed the essence of *Renaissance architecture. In 1562 he became Architect to the

Escorial, near Madrid, basing the grid-like ground-floor plan on reconstructions of the Temple of Solomon in Jerusalem, and the Court of the Evangelists on *Sangallo's *cortile in the Palazzo Farnese, Rome. The plan is also an allusion to the *attribute of St Laurence, whose melted fat was enshrined in the great Church in the centre of the whole ensemble. El Escorial's enormous external elevations are models of restraint. After his death the work was completed by Juan de *Herrera.

Cruickshank (1996); Curl (1991); Fraser, Hibbard, and Lewine (1967); Kubler (1982); Kubler and Soria (1959)

Toltec architecture. *See* Aztec architecture.

tomb. Monument erected to enclose or cover a dead body and preserve the memory of the dead, so a sepulchral or funerary structure. *See* mausoleum, table-tomb.

Colvin (1991); Crossley (1921); Curl (1993)

tomb-canopy. Canopy above an *altar-tomb or *tomb-chest, as though protecting the *effigies that lie beneath, and often forming a very grand ensemble.

Blore (1826); Crossley (1921); Curl (1993); Sturgis *et al.* (1901–2)

tomb-chest. Rectangular stone funerary monument above a *tomb, often found in churches, with recumbent *effigies on top or suggested by figures outlined (incised) on the top *slab or cut into inserts of metal (*brasses). The sides of the chest were often enriched with *quatrefoils, etc., or with *niches containing *weepers (upright or kneeling figures). Canopies and railings often completed the ensemble. Tomb-chests were sometimes associated with *chantry- or *mortuary-chapels. Simplified tomb-chests without weapons, effigies, or canopies were often employed as funerary monuments in churchyards and cemeteries in C18, C19, and C20.

Crossley (1921); Curl (1993)

tombstone. Vertical or horizontal inscribed grave-marker or memorial set up over a tomb.

Weaver (1915)

tombstone-light. Small window with lights resembling *tombstones with curved tops, often over a doorway.

Tomé, Narciso (*c*.1694–1742). Spanish architect and sculptor. He worked with his father and brothers on the decorations of the sumptuous front of the University at Valladolid (early C18). His masterpiece, described as a *fricassée de marbre*, is the *Trasparente* in the *capilla mayor* of Toledo Cathedral (1721–32), so called from the glass-fronted receptacle through which the Blessed Sacrament could be seen from the *ambulatory and also permit light to be admitted to the *camarín behind the altar itself within the *capilla mayor*. Around the glass receptacle on the ambulatory side Tomé constructed a wildly extravagant *Baroque confection illuminated from a kind of *dormer set high above the *Gothic ambulatory *vaults from which the masonry between the ribs was removed.

Kubler and Soria (1959); Norberg-Schulz (1986*a*); Pevsner (1960); Watkin (1996)

Ton, Konstantin Andreevich (1794–1881). Russian architect of German extraction. He was a leading figure in the revival of traditional Russian church-architecture, and was closely associated with official Government buildings. His work is variously referred to as 'Russian Byzantine' or the 'Russian style'. His earliest buildings in St Petersburg, including the Main Halls and Chapel of the Academy of Arts (1829–37), were firmly within the Classical tradition, while the monumental Dock in front of the Academy building was an essay in *Neoclassicism. His first building consciously drawing on five-domed C15 and C16 precedents was the Church of St Catherine, St Petersburg (1830–7), followed by several other churches in the 'National' style. His designs for centralized five-domed churches based on old Muscovite sources were published, proved influential, and were widely copied. He was also a pioneer in the study of traditional timber *vernacular domestic architecture. His most important buildings were the Bolshoi Kremlin Palace (1838–49) and the gigantic Church of Christ the Redeemer (1839–83) in Moscow. The last, like many of his buildings, was destroyed during the Soviet period (1934), but was reconstructed (1994–7). Ton also designed several railway-stations (1844–51) drawing on *Renaissance themes.

van Vynckt (1993)

tondo. Circular medallion or plaque, often set in *spandrels.

tooth. Late-*Romanesque and *First Pointed *Gothic ornament consisting of a series of projecting hollow pierced *pyramids, also known as *dog-tooth, or tooth ornament, sometimes with the points and bases of the pyramidal form transformed into stylized flowers.

toothing. **1.** Projecting course of alternate *header bricks under *eaves, *cornice, or *string-course like large *dentils, called *dentilation. **2.** As *toothing-stones.

toothing-stones. Projecting stones or *tenons at the end of a wall so that, when required, another building or wall can be bonded into it to make a continuous surface.

torana. Richly ornamented Indian gateway associated with the enclosure of a *stupa.

torch. Motif, also known as a *flambeau*, often used in Classical ornament. If inverted, it represents the extinguishing of life and therefore occurs in funerary architecture.

Torralva, Diogo de (*c*.1500–*c*.1566). Portuguese architect, perhaps of Spanish extraction. The son-in-law of *Arruda, he nevertheless moved away from the *Manueline style to a more Italian *Renaissance manner, as in the great *cloister of the Convent of Christ, Tomar (begun 1557), where influences from *Bramante, *Palladio, and *Serlio are clearly displayed in the highly articulated treatment of the façades. He designed the main chapel at the Jeronymite Monastery, Belém, near Lisbon (1560s). Other works have been attributed to him.

Kubler and Soria (1959); Smith (1968); van Vynckt (1993)

Torrigiano, Pietro (1472–1528). Italian sculptor. In 1510 he was working in England on the tomb of Margaret, Countess of Richmond and Derby (1443–1509), mother of King Henry VII (reigned 1485–1509), and in 1512 contracted to build the funerary monument of the King and Elizabeth of York (1465–1503) in the *Lady Chapel (now *Mortuary Chapel of Henry VII), Westminster Abbey, completed 1518. He also carried out various other works while in England, much of it portrait-sculpture. His importance lies in the fact that his work was the first mature Italian *Renaissance design to be created and realized in England.

Chilvers, Osborne, and Farr (1988); Papworth (1892)

Torroja y Miret, Eduardo (1899–1961). Spanish architect, engineer, and designer of *concrete structures, including *shells. His first large project was the Tempul *aqueduct, Guadalete, Jerez de la Frontera, in which he used *prestressed *girders, and he made his name with the concrete shell-roof at the Algeciras Market Hall (1933) and the *cantilevered grandstand roofs in the form of giant *flutes at the Zarzuela Racecourse, near Madrid (1935). He also used steel with great *élan*, as at the roof of the Football Stadium, Barcelona (1943). He designed innovative structures in numerous parts of the world, including Morocco and Latin America. His books include *The Philosophy of Structure* (1951, 1958) and *The Structures of Eduardo Torroja* (1958).

Bohigas (1970); Bozal (1978); Joedicke (1963); Lampugnani (1988); Morgan and Naylor (1987); Torroja (1958)

torsade. Twisted *cable-moulding.

torso. Twisted column-*shaft.

torus (*pl.* **tori**). Bold projecting convex moulding of semicircular *section, e.g. on either side of the *scotia in an *Attic base. Larger *tori*, e.g. on the base of a *triumphal column, are often enriched with *bay-leaf garlands.

Total architecture. Advocated by Walter *Gropius and Bruno *Taut in the 1920s, it suggested a synthesis of all the arts and crafts in a new architecture (based on the composer Wilhelm Richard Wagner's (1813–83) idea of *Gesamtkunstwerke* (Total Work of Art)), but did the opposite by sundering the arts and crafts from architecture. In spite of this manifest failure of the *International Modern Movement, Gropius published *The Scope of Total Architecture* in 1955 (revised edition 1962).

Bildende Kunst, 36/7 (1988), 298–9; Gropius (1962)

Totalitarian architecture. Supposedly the officially approved architecture of dictatorships, over-centralized governments, or political groups intolerant of opposition, especially that of Fascist Italy, Nazi Germany, Stalinist Soviet Union, Communist China, etc. As an international style, it drew on simplified *Neoclassicism, and sculpture based on C19 realism and *Classicism for massive oversized State monuments.

Adam (1992); Council of Europe (1995)

touch. **1.** Black basalt or basanite, capable of being carved, used for *fonts and *tombs, e.g. the Tournai fonts of Hampshire. **2.** Compact dark-coloured stone, such as Petworth or *Purbeck marble, capable of taking a high polish, used for *Gothic *shafts, tombs, etc.

tourelle. *Corbelled *turret, circular on plan, cone-roofed, sometimes containing a circular stair, set at the angle of a tower or wall at high level, and common in *Scottish Baronial architecture.

MacGibbon and Ross (1887–92)

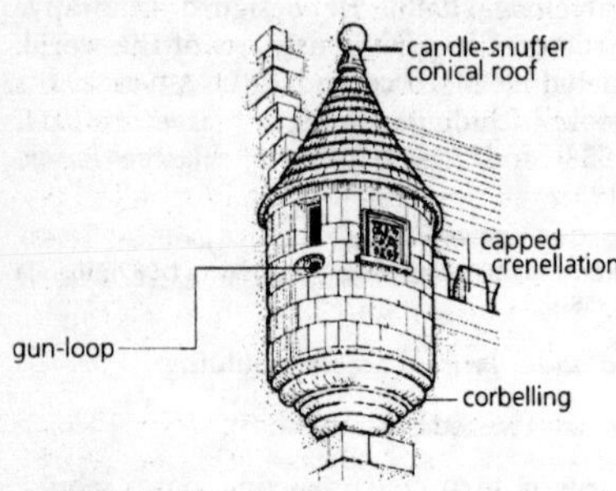

tourelle. Typical Scots tourelle.

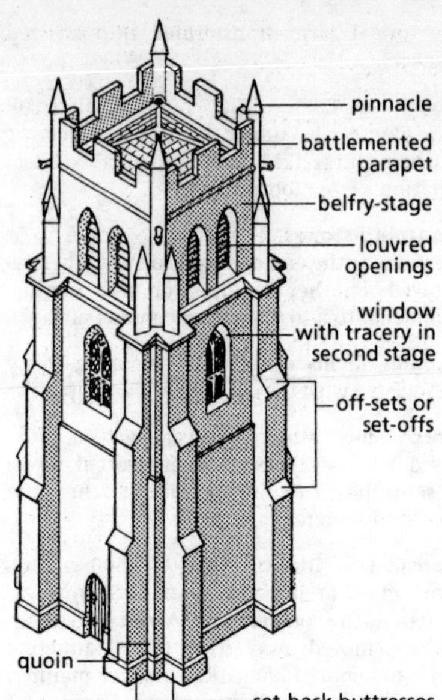

tower. Typical medieval three-stage church-tower with set-back buttresses. (*JJS*)

tower. Tall structure of any form on *plan, high in proportion to its lateral dimensions, often rising in *stages (rather than *storeys), free-standing or part of another building, used in fortifications, as points of reference in the landscape, or as a *belfry attached to a church. Church-towers often have *buttresses, are crowned with *battlements, or support *spires, and have important architectural features.

tower-house. Compact fortified house of several storeys with its main chamber or *hall on an upper storey, usually over *vaulted lower floors. Common in Scotland (where many spectacular examples survive) and Ireland, tower-houses were still being built in C17.

Town, Ithiel (1784–1844). Prolific and influential American architect and engineer, he was a significant figure in the *Greek and *Gothic Revivals in the USA. He studied with Asher *Benjamin and in 1810 built the Botanic Garden House, Harvard University, Cambridge, Mass., in the *Federal style. In *c.*1813 he moved to New Haven, Conn., where he built the Center (1812–15) and Trinity (1813–16) Churches, the former a variation on *Gibbs's design for St Martin-in-the-Fields, London (1722–6), and the latter an early example of the Gothic Revival. From 1816 he designed many bridges and developed a *lattice-*truss or *girder, patented in 1820, which brought him fame and fortune. He employed latticed scissor-trusses in his Gothic Christ Church Cathedral, Hartford, Conn. (1827–8—designed with Nathaniel S. Wheaton). He turned to the Greek Revival around 1820 with several buildings in New Haven, Conn., including the *Doric State House (1827–31—destroyed). In 1825 he moved to New York and carried out work of national importance, mainly in an austere Greek Revival style, often incorporating massive *anta-like *piers. From 1829 to 1835 he was in partnership with Alexander J. *Davis, practising as Town & Davis, producing such outstanding monumental work as the State Capitols at Indianapolis, Ind. (1831–5—destroyed), and Raleigh, NC (1833–40), and the Custom House, New York (1833–42). The firm also produced the first large asymmetrical Gothic house in the USA at Glen Ellen, Towson, Md. (1832–4—demolished). Town published a book on the forming of an Academy of the Fine Arts in 1835. He built up an important architectural library during his career which he was obliged to sell in the Depression of the 1840s. Among his last works was the main front of the Wadsworth Athenaeum, Hartford, Conn. (1842–4).

Hamlin (1964); Hitchcock and Seale (1976); Kelly (1948); Kennedy (1989); Newton (1942); Pierson and Jordy (1970, 1978); Placzek (1982); Town (1835, 1842); van Vynckt (1993)

town canopy. *See* canopy.

Townesend, William (1676–1739). English master-mason and architect who worked in Oxford. He probably designed, and certainly built, the Fellows' Building and Cloister (1706–12) and the Gentleman Commoners' Building (1737), Corpus Christi College, and was the contractor (1706–14) for Peckwater Quadrangle, Christ Church, erected to *Aldrich's designs, the first *palace-fronted English *Palladian composition of C18. He built (under Dr *Clarke's supervision) the front quadrangle, hall, and chapel (1710–21), as well as the entrance-screen with *cupola (1733–6), modifying *Hawksmoor's designs in the process, at Queen's College. Other buildings erected by him to designs by others include the north-east block of the Garden Quadrangle, New College (1707), Hawksmoor's Clarendon Building (1712–15), the Bristol Buildings, Balliol College (1716–20), Hawksmoor's North Quadrangle, Hall, Buttery, and Codrington Library, All Souls College (1716–35), and (again under Dr Clarke's direction) the Radcliffe Quadrangle, University College (1717–19). He designed and built the Robinson Buildings, Oriel College (1719–20), and arrived at the final design for New Buildings, Magdalen College (built 1733–4). He carried out many works at Blenheim Palace, Oxfordshire, including the Woodstock Gate (1722–3), and the Column of Victory (1727–30), and built Christ Church Library, Oxford, to Dr Clarke's designs (1717–38). In short, he had a hand in the building of almost every important work of architecture erected in Oxford between 1720 and 1740. He was also a sculptor and made several funerary monuments, including that to his father, **John Townesend** (1648–1728), Mayor of Oxford (1682–3 and 1720–1) also a master-mason, in St Giles's churchyard, Oxford (*c.*1728).

Colvin (1995)

townscape. Portion of the urban fabric that can be viewed at once. It was a term much used from the 1940s, analogous to *landscape*, associated with a series of studies in the *Architectural Review* intended to encourage the enhancement of the urban environment in Britain. Many historic towns have pleasing townscapes revealed as the pedestrian moves through sequences of spaces, and the *AR's* campaign proposed that the study of townscape (pioneered by *Geddes, *Parker, *Sitte, and *Unwin) would provide precedents for the enormous amount of urban redevelopment as well as for the new towns that were planned in Britain after the 1939–45 war. However, protagonists of *International *Modernism rejected the concept as *Picturesque, leading to the failure of its application since 1945.

Architectural Design, 46/9 (Sept. 1976), 534–6; Burke (1976); Collins and Collins (1986); Cullen (1973); Miller (1992); Tugnutt and Robertson (1987)

Townsend, Charles Harrison (1851–1928). English architect. He worked in the offices of Walter Scott of Liverpool (*fl.* 1843–71) from 1867 to 1872, Charles Barry jun. (1823–1900) from 1873 to 1875, and E. R. *Robson from 1875–1877, before commencing independent practice. From 1884 to 1886 he was in partnership with Thomas Lewis Banks (1842–1920), but by 1887 he was on his own. His designs were firmly within the *Arts-and-Crafts tradition, and most were for minor domestic and church work, but in 1892 he won the competition to design the Bishopsgate Institute, the first of three fine public buildings in London on which his reputation largely rests, the other two being the Whitechapel Art Gallery and the Horniman Museum (1898–1901). *Muthesius drew attention to these buildings in 1900 as among the most significant European works of architecture at the time, with their architect as one of the two English 'prophets' of the 'new style' (the other was *Voysey). All three show an American influence, notably derived from the works of H. H. *Richardson, as well as *Art Nouveau, *Renaissance, and even *Gothic traces. Townsend used artificial stone, *mosaic, and *terracotta to face these buildings, and the overt use of Art Nouveau motifs for the exteriors is unusual for an English architect. His masterpiece is arguably the enchanting Church of St Mary the Virgin, Great Warley, Essex (consecrated 1904), with a complete Arts-and-Crafts and Art Nouveau interior, including the *chancel-screen by Sir William Reynolds-Stephens (1862–1943), the *stalls and *pews being by Townsend himself. His best domestic work, inclining to the style of *Devey and Eden *Nesfield, was at Blackheath, Chilworth, Surrey, where he designed several houses, St Martin's Church (1892–5—much embellished with *frescoes), the Congregational Church (1893), and the Village Hall (1897).

DNB (1993); Dixon and Muthesius (1985); Felstead, Franklin, and Pinfield (1993); Gray (1985); Pevsner, *Buildings of England, Essex* (1965); Pevsner and Richards (1973); Russell (1979); Service (1975, 1977)

trabeated. Constructed on the column-and-*lintel system, as opposed to *arcuated. *See* columnar and trabeated.

tracery. Arrangement by which panels, *screens, *vaults, or windows are divided into parts of different shapes or sizes by means of moulded stone *bars* or *ribs*, called *form-pieces* or *forms* in the medieval period. Early *Gothic windows with more than one *light did not have bars, but had the flat stone *spandrel above the main lights (usually two) pierced with a quatrefoil, *roundel, or other figure: this type of tracery is the late-*First Pointed *plate* variety, consisting of a thin flat panel of *ashlar pierced, like simple fretwork, with lights. Starting with early C13 examples, the flat plate was abandoned, and the large lights were divided by moulded *mullions, the *section of which continued at the heads of the window-apertures to describe circular and other lights, leaving the spandrels open and divided into small lights of various shapes and sizes: this type of subdivision, termed *bar-tracery*, first occurred at Rheims, was introduced to England *c.*1240, and was one of the most important decorative elements of Gothic architecture, with definite stylistic connotations. The possibilities of bar-tracery helped to create the *Rayonnant style of Gothic on the Continent (*c.*1230–*c.*1350), so called from the radiating ray-like arrangement of lights in rose-windows. Simple bartracery formed patterns of early *Middle Pointed *Geometrical* tracery, consisting of circles and foiled arches, with roughly triangular lights between the major elements: mullions in Geometrical tracery usually had *capitals from which the curved bars sprang. After the late-C13 Geometrical tracery came *Intersecting* tracery in which each mullion of the window branched (without capitals) equidistant to the window-head formed of two equal curves meeting at a point: the Intersecting tracery-bars were struck from the same centres as the window-head, with different radii. Mullions therefore continued in curved Y-branches (often found in two-light windows of *c.*1300 and known as *Y-tracery*) to meet the head of the window-opening, thus describing a series of lozenge-shaped lights: the bars and main arches of the window-opening were subdivided into two or (usually) more main lights, each forming a pointed, *lancet-shaped arch. *Cusps and other embellishments were often added to Intersecting tracery, which was common around 1300. *Curvilinear, Flowing*, or *Undulating* tracery of *Second Pointed work dominated C14, when *ogees were applied to a basic arrangement derived from the geometry of Intersecting tracery, thus creating elaborate net-like constructions of bars at the tops of windows: this type of tracery is called *Reticulated*, because it looks like a net, and was commonly found in work of the first half of C14. Curvilinear or Flowing tracery was then developed further and more freely, to exploit the ogee curves and create dagger- or flame-shaped lights called *daggers, fish-bladders*, and *mouchettes*: such designs evolved further throughout C15 in Europe, and became known as *Flamboyant because of the flame-like forms enclosed by the tracery-bars. From the late C14 England began to develop *Perpendicular or *Third Pointed* tracery, in which the main mullions (often joined by *transoms) continued as straight verticals to the undersides of the main window-arch head, with some mullions branching to form subsidiary arches: this system created *panel-like lights, and so the tracery became known as *Rectilinear* or *panel-tracery*. Later still, in C15 and early C16, window-heads became much flatter *four-centred* arches, while ever-larger openings (often filling the entire walls between *buttresses) were subdivided into panels of lights by means of *crenellated transoms, the crenellations really miniature *battlements, each panel having a flattened four-centred arch at its top. Other types of tracery include:

branch tracery: with ribs that flow from *piers or walls into *vaults without any interruption of a *capital, evolved from *intersecting* tracery. On the Continent, especially in Central Europe, it means tracery fashioned to resemble tree-branches, as in St Vitus Cathedral, Prague;

drop-tracery: pendent tracery unsupported by mullions, often found on *tabernacle-work, canopied *niches, etc., but also on e.g. the ceilings of the Divinity Schools (finished 1483) and Cathedral (*c.*1478–1503), Oxford;

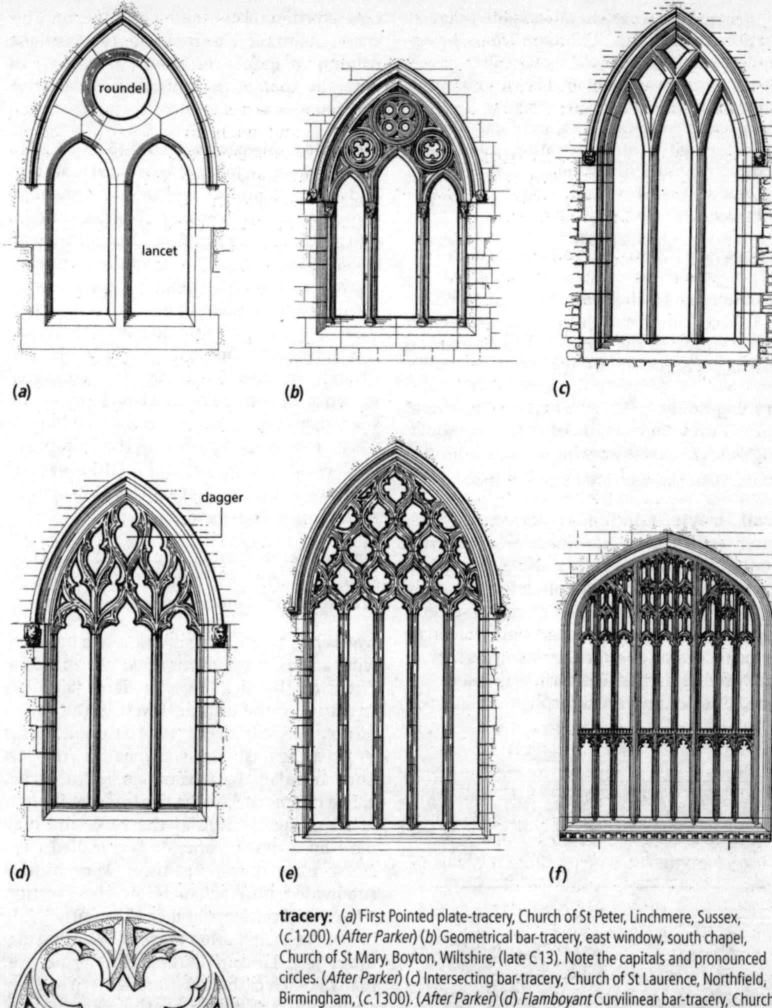

tracery: (*a*) First Pointed plate-tracery, Church of St Peter, Linchmere, Sussex, (*c*.1200). (*After Parker*) (*b*) Geometrical bar-tracery, east window, south chapel, Church of St Mary, Boyton, Wiltshire, (late C13). Note the capitals and pronounced circles. (*After Parker*) (*c*) Intersecting bar-tracery, Church of St Laurence, Northfield, Birmingham, (*c*.1300). (*After Parker*) (*d*) *Flamboyant* Curvilinear bar-tracery, Church of St Matthew, Salford Priors, Warwickshire (C14). Note the flame-like lights (from which *Flamboyant* is named) called *daggers*. (*After Parker*) (*e*) Reticulated, flowing bar-tracery, Greyfriars, Reading, Berkshire (C14). The net-like form gives the tracery its name. (*After Parker*) (*f*) Perpendicular or panel-tracery (early C16), King's College Chapel, Cambridge. Note the miniature battlements, or crenellations, over the transom, and the mullions rising straight to the low four-centred arch. (*After Parker*) (*g*) Kentish tracery: quatrefoil with Kentish cusps. (*After JJS*)

fan-tracery or *fanwork*: tracery on the *soffit of a vault with ribs radiating like those of a fan, an invention of English Perpendicular, culminating in the ceiling of King's College Chapel, Cambridge (1508–15). Medieval fan-tracery only occurs in England;

grid-tracery: with a grid of mullions and transoms, common in late-Gothic and early

*Renaissance windows, often found in grand *Elizabethan and *Jacobean houses, e.g. Hardwick Hall, Derbyshire (1590–6);

Kentish tracery: with barbs or split cusps between the foils;

stump-tracery: late-Gothic tracery in Central Europe with interpenetrating intertwined bars truncated like stumps, as in Benedikt *Ried's Vladislav Hall, Hradčany Castle, Prague (1487–1502).

Gwilt (1903); Papworth (1892); Parker (1850); Rickman (1848); Sturgis *et al.* (1901–2)

trachelion, trachelium. Neck of a Greek *Doric column between the *hypotrachelion grooves around the top of the shaft and the *annulets under the *echinus.

tracing-house. Place where a medieval mason drew out details of *tracery, mouldings, etc., for those working to his direction.

Booz (1956); Colombier (1953); Papworth (1892)

trail, trayle. Continuous horizontal *running enrichment of vine-leaves, tendrils, stalks, and grapes, called also *grapevine*, *vignette*, *vine-scroll*, or *vinette*, often found enriching *Perpendicular canopies and *screens, e.g. in funerary architecture and *chancel-screens. Several spectacular examples survive in Devon churches. The form was essentially late *Gothic, and recurs throughout Europe.

Bond (1908*a*); Bond and Camm (1909)

trail, trayle.
(*top*) Wells Cathedral, Somerset (second half of C15). (*After Parker*)
(*bottom*) Church of St Mary, Oxford (late C15). (*After Parker*)

Trajanic column. Large commemorative single free-standing column, essentially of the *Tuscan *Order, also called a *Gigantic Order, with internal winding-stair, spiral *bands of relief sculpture winding around the shaft, a large *pedestal-base, and a commemorative statue on top. It is named after the *Antique column of Emperor Trajan (AD 98–117) in Rome (*c.* AD 112). *See* Antonine column, triumphal column.

Tramello, Alessio (*c.*1460–*c.*1529). Italian *Renaissance architect who worked mainly in and around Piacenza, and was strongly influenced by the architecture of *Bramante. He designed the Piacenza Churches of San Sisto (1499–1514—with a barrel-vaulted coffered *nave resembling *Alberti's Sant'Andrea, Mantua) and San Sepolcro (*c.*1510—with alternate square and rectangular nave-*bays). He was responsible for the centrally planned Church of the Madonna di Campagna, Piacenza (begun 1522), on a Greek-cross plan, with forms clearly derived from *Bramante's work. He was also involved in the building of the Steccata, Parma (begun 1521) to designs by Giovanni Francesco Zaccagni (*fl.* 1510–25).

Heydenreich and Lotz (1974); Placzek (1982)

transenna. 1. Roman cross-beam. **2.** *Transom. **3.** *Early Christian *lattice-work of marble or metal enclosing a *shrine.

transept. 1. Any large division of a building lying across its main axis at 90°. In an *Early Christian *basilica it was the large and high structure to the liturgical west of the *apse, on occasion so high that the *nave and *aisles stopped against its wall, as in the C4 Constantinian *basilica of San Pietro, Rome. **2.** In a cruciform church the transept is often of the same *section as the nave, and may have no aisles, or one, or two (called *cross-aisles*): eastern transept-aisles were usually subdivided into *chapels. At the position where the transepts branched on either side of the *crossing, often marked by a crossing-tower (e.g. Lincoln Cathedral), *flèche (e.g. many French cathedrals), or *lantern (e.g. Ely Cathedral), the *choir continued eastwards, often divided immediately to the east of the crossing by a *pulpitum or choir-*screen. Larger medieval cathedrals (e.g. Lincoln) sometimes had secondary transepts at the west end of the nave (really a form of *narthex), and to the east of the crossing, on either side of the *sanctuary and choir-aisles: in both cases they would have had eastern chapels.

transept-aisle. *Aisle on the east or west or both sides of a *transept.

transept-chapel. Chapel on the eastern side of a *transept, usually set in a *transept-aisle, but sometimes projecting from it in apsidal arrangements (e.g. Lincoln Cathedral).

Transitional architecture. Term used to denote the merging of one style with another, especially the C12 transition from *Romanesque to *Gothic, but sometimes applied to other styles.

Architectural History, 30 (1987), 1–30

transom(e). **1.** Cross-bar or beam. **2.** Horizontal element framed across a window, generally used during the *Perpendicular period, and commonly found in the grid-*tracery of *Elizabethan and *Jacobean houses, dividing the window-aperture into *lights framed by *bars forming the *mullions and transoms. **3.** Horizontal piece in a *doorway forming part of the frame, above which is a *fanlight.

transverse arch *or* **rib.** Arch or rib at 90° to the main axis of the vaulted space or outside wall, separating one *bay of a *vault from another.

Trasparente. *See* Tomé, Narciso.

trave, travis. **1.** Cross-beam. **2.** Division or *bay, as in a ceiling (thus said to be *travated* or *traviated*) formed by cross-beams. **3.** Division between *stalls in a *choir or stable.

traverse. **1.** *Screen or barrier, usually a baffle, or to allow a passage from one part to another in privacy. **2.** *Transom or horizontal part of an *architrave or door-frame. **3.** *Gallery or *loft, usually screened, for communication between two apartments, e.g. across a *hall.

trayle. *See* trail.

tread. *See* stair.

Treadwell, Henry John (1861–1910). English architect. With Leonard Martin (1869–1935) he practised in London from 1890 to 1910, specializing in developing small, narrow-fronted sites in London's West End. Stylistically, their work was an eclectic mix of *Art Nouveau, *Baroque, late-Continental *Gothic, and dashes of other styles, used in a very free way. Among their best buildings are 23 Woodstock Street, 7 Dering Street, 7 Hanover Street, 74 New Bond Street, 20 Conduit Street, 78 Wigmore Street, 106 Jermyn Street, and 61 St James's Street (all early 1900s), and 78–81 Fetter Lane, in the City. They designed the *Rising Sun* Public House, 46 Tottenham Court Road (1897), St John's Hospital, Lisle Street, Leicester Square (1904), the *White Hart*, Windsor, Berkshire, and St John's Church, Herne Hill (1910).

Gray (1985)

tree. Any large piece of timber, e.g. *beam, *lintel, *Rood-beam, bressummer. *See* tree-trunk.

Tree of Jesse. *See* Jesse.

tree-nail. **1.** *Gutta. **2.** Dowel, or wooden pin, used to join timbers together.

tree-trunk. Pieces of trunks of trees, the branches lopped off, were sometimes used in *Picturesque or *rustic* buildings, e.g. *cottage orné, where a particularly *primitive effect was sought for columns. The form was carved in stone for some *Renaissance and *Mannerist designs.

trefoil. *See* foil.

trellis. **1.** Any *screen-work made of thin strips (usually timber laths) crossing each other, either at 90° or set diagonally, forming a *lattice of lozenge-shapes, as in an *arbour or any framework supporting vines or other plants. **2.** Stone enrichment of the *Romanesque period resembling a wooden trellis composed of *fillets, giving the appearance of continuous overlapping *chevrons set between two horizontal framing mouldings. The chevron-strips are frequently decorated with stud-like elements perhaps suggesting nails.

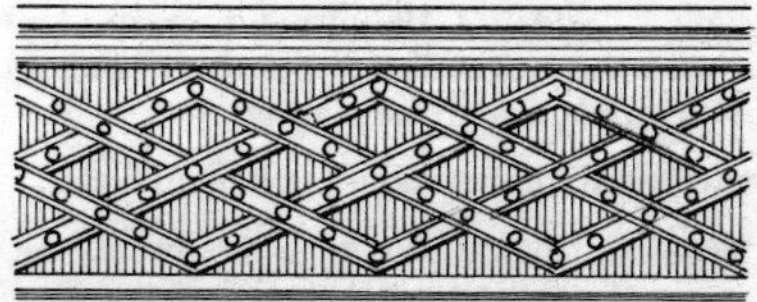

trellis. Romanesque studded trellis moulding from Malmesbury Abbey, Wiltshire (early C12). (*After Parker*)

Tresk, Simon de (*fl.* *c.*1255–*c.*1291). English master-mason. He supervised the construction of the Angel Choir at Lincoln Cathedral (1256–80), and thus must be regarded as one of the most important designers of that period.

Harvey (1987)

tresse. *Interlacing ornament resembling overlapping *guilloches, usually on a *torus moulding, but also occurring on flat horizontal *bands or *string-courses.

Tressini. *See* Trezzini.

Trezini. *See* Trezzini.

Trezzini, *or* **Tressini,** *or* **Trezini, Domenico** (1670–1734). Swiss-Italian architect. He settled in Russia, having been called by Tsar Peter the Great (1682–1725) from Copenhagen at the foundation of St Petersburg (1703). He established an office there, designing the Summer Palace (1712–33), the Cathedral of Sts Peter and Paul in the Fortress (1712–33), and the Government Ministries in a series of buildings linked by a huge open gallery. His relative **Pietro Antonio** (*fl.* 1726–51) reintroduced the *quincunx church-plan to ecclesiastical buildings in St Petersburg.

Hamilton (1983)

triangular arch. Two flat stones set at an angle of 45° or thereabouts, mitred at the top, and touching each other at the apex of a triangular-headed opening. It occurs in *Anglo-Saxon architecture and is not an arch at all.

triangular fret. *See* swallowtail.

triangulation. **1.** Construction in which rigidity is assured by means of *struts and *ties disposed to form triangles in one or more planes. **2.** Setting out of a series or network of triangles from a base-line in order to survey land.

tribune. **1.** Apsidal part of a *basilica. **2.** *Bema, raised platform, or seat in a basilican building. **3.** Eastern part of a church, especially if apsidal. **4.** *Pulpitum or *ambo, and therefore, by extension, a *pulpit. **5.** *Gallery in a church, usually for seating.

triclinium. Dining-room in a Roman house.

triconch. *Plan in the form of a trefoil, e.g. space off which there are three *apses.

triforium, triforium-gallery. In larger *Romanesque and *Gothic churches, an upper *aisle with its own *arcade forming an important part of the *elevation of a nave interior above the *nave-arcade and below the *clearstorey. Gervase (*fl.* late C12), in his account of Canterbury Cathedral, used 'triforium' to mean the clearstorey-gallery or any upper passage or thoroughfare, and his usage does not in any way indicate 'three openings', as those at Canterbury were two or four, so the term does not seem to apply to the arcade through which the triforium-gallery is visible from the nave. Probably the most accurate way of describing the arcade would be *triforium-arcade*, or *arcade opening to the triforium-gallery*.

Bond (1913)

triglyph. One of the upright blocks occurring in series in a *Doric *frieze on either side of the *metopes, possibly suggesting the outer ends of timber beams. Each plain face of the triglyph has two vertical V-shaped channels cut in it, called *glyphs, and the edges are chamfered with half-glyphs, hence the three glyphs in all. In some versions of the Doric *Order the half-glyphs do not occur, so each block is referred to as a *diglyph.

trilith, trilithon. Prehistoric structure composed of two massive upright stones supporting another set horizontally as a *lintel.

trim. **1.** Frame around an aperture or any architectural feature. **2.** To construct such a frame. **3.** To fit to anything. **4.** Visible timber finish to a building.

trimmer. Short timber, also called *trimmer-joist*, fixed to the ends of joists, and spanning between *trimming-joists*, when an opening is formed in a floor.

tripartite. *See* vault.

triptych. 'Picture or carving in three compartments side by side, the lateral ones being usually subordinate', though connected in subject, 'and hinged so as to fold over the central one', often forming a late-medieval altarpiece, called *Flügelaltar* in Germany (where some of the finest carved and painted examples can be found). When closed, the part visible (i.e. the backs of the folding leaves) often displayed *grisaille paintings.

Chilvers, Osborne, and Farr (1988); Gwilt (1903); *OED* (1933)

trisantia, *also* **transyte, tresantia, tresauns, tressaunte.** *Vestibule or narrow passage between the *chapter-house and the *transept, or behind the *screen in a hall.

tristyle. *See* colonnade.

triumphal arch. Type of formal gateway set over an axis to commemorate a victory or individual. In Roman Antiquity there were two basic kinds: a tall rectangular structure with a single arch (e.g. Arch of Titus, Rome (after AD

81)); and an even grander building containing a large arch flanked by two smaller and lower arches (e.g. Arch of Septimius Severus, Rome (AD 203)). In the history of architecture triumphal arches are important not only because they were precedents for many later such structures, but because they combined the *arcuated and *columnar and trabeated methods of construction. The *Antique Roman type consisted of a large rectangular mass of masonry pierced by one or three parallel arches cut through the wider sides, with an *engaged or applied *Order, invariably set on *pedestals, and a large *Attic-storey over the *entablature usually carrying a grandiose inscription. In the Titus arch the panel with inscription was set on the Attic over the single wide arch, but in the Septimius Severus arch the inscription stretched almost the full width of the Attic. Other arches of the three-arched type include the 'Arch of Tiberius', Orange, France (late C1 BC), and the Arch of Constantine, Rome (*c.*312–15).

The triumphal arch was quoted by *Alberti for the front of the Church of San Francesco, Rimini (from 1446), and for the inside and west front of the Church of Sant'Andrea, Mantua (designed 1470): it was used on countless *Renaissance façades in various combinations and transformations as it offered almost limitless possibilities for enrichment. It was often used as a centrepiece (e.g. the south front of Kedleston, Derbyshire, by Robert *Adam (1759–70), and the Avenue d'Antin entrance to the Grand Palais, Paris, by Deglane, Louvet, and Thomas (1900)), but was also revived as a free-standing monument during the Neoclassical period (e.g. Arc de Triomphe du Carrousel, Paris, by *Percier and *Fontaine (1805–9)). Some later triumphal arches were designed to have extra arches at 90° to the main axis (e.g. Arc de Triomphe de l'Étoile, Paris, by *Chalgrin and others (1806–36), and the Thiepval Arch, Somme, by *Lutyens (1920s)).

Curl (1992); Mansuelli *et al.* (1979); Meeks (1966); Nilsson (1932); Watkin (1986); Westfehling (1977)

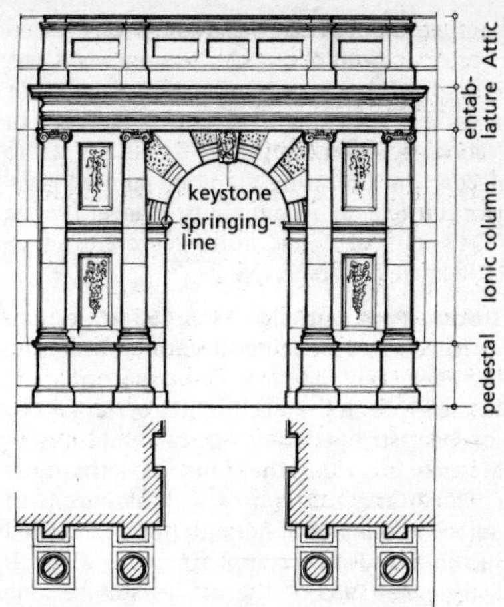

triumphal arch. Plan and elevation of C18 triumphal arch. (*After Langley*)

triumphal column. Very large free-standing column, usually of the *Tuscan *Order (called *Gigantic Order), on a *pedestal, intended as a monument commemorating an individual and events. An example is Trajan's Column, Rome (*c.* AD 112–13), with a continuous spiral *frieze wrapped around the shaft narrating the Emperor's Dacian wars (AD 101–2, 105–6), and formerly with a statue of Trajan (Emperor AD 98–117) on top: the pedestal was Trajan's tomb-chamber. Very similar is the column of Marcus Aurelius (Emperor AD 161–80), formerly called the *Antonine column. The form was used by *Fischer von Erlach for the twin columns of the *Karlskirche*, Vienna (1715–25), the spirals recording events in the life of St Charles Borromeo (1538–84), and the columns themselves suggesting the entry to Paradise, the Temple of Solomon, and the *emblems of the Habsburgs. C19 examples include the Vendôme Column, Paris, by *Gondoin and *Lepère (1806–10, destroyed 1831, and re-erected 1874). Many commemorative columns, however, have plain or fluted shafts, omitting the spiral (e.g. The Monument (1671–7), and the Nelson Column (1839–42), both in London).

Becatti (1960); Hornblower and Spawforth (1996)

trochilus. *Scotia.

trompe. *Vaulted structure over an external angle of a building that has been removed, as when an entrance or *niche is placed at the corner. Thus the vault is really a type of *pendentive or *corbel and carries a load above, e.g. a *tourelle, etc.

trompe l'œil. **1.** Literally a deception or trick of the eye, it is usually two-dimensional painting showing an arrangement of objects that look disconcertingly real, often used to suggest architectural elements. **2.** Painted representations of marble, grained wood, etc. **3.** Applied decoration imitating a surface or texture, such as *grisaille figures in Neoclassical work imitating reliefs, *sgraffito decoration imitating diamond-pointed *rustication (e.g. Schwarzenburg Palace, Prague (1543–63)), or *quadratura representing architecture in perspective.

Troost, Paul Ludwig (1878–1934). German architect. He was a skilled decorator, designing the interiors of the North-German Lloyd liners in the 1920s and 1930s, but he is better known for his *stripped Neoclassical buildings in Munich, including the House of German Art (1933–7) and the two office-buildings with adjacent 'temples of honour' (for Nazis killed in the 1923 *Putsch*) completing von *Klenze's *Königsplatz* (1933–7—the offices survive (one of them the *Führerbau*) but the *Ehrentempel* structures have been destroyed). His severe square-columned stripped Classicism was a considerable influence on Albert *Speer.

Adam (1992); Lane (1985); *Monatshefte für Baukunst und Städtebau*, 18 (1934), 205–12; Speer (1970); Troost (1941)

trophy. 1. Arms and armour hung in an orderly fashion on a tree-trunk and branches to celebrate a victory in Antiquity. **2.** Sculpted representation of **1.** in Classical architecture, not to be confused with a *panoply.

Lewis and Darley (1986)

Trouard, Louis-François (1729–94). French architect. He is important as the designer of the Church of St-Symphorien de Montreuil, Versailles (1764), the earliest and most austere of the *Neoclassical *basilican churches erected in and around Paris at the time, with Roman *Doric *nave-*colonnades carrying a coffered barrel-vault. The tetrastyle *portico is of the severe *Tuscan Order. He also designed the Chapelle des Catéchismes, Church of St-Louis, Versailles (1764–70), using an *Ionic Order with straight *entablatures. He was also a pioneer of a severe, stripped, Grecian style, as in the town-houses, Faubourg-Poissonnière, Paris (1758), and *Gothic Revival, as in the work he carried out at the medieval Cathedral of Ste-Croix, Orléans (1766–73). He taught *Ledoux.

Braham (1980); Middleton and Watkin (1987); Papworth (1892)

trullo (*pl* **trulli**). In Southern Italy, a rough dry-stone building, circular on *plan, with a cone-shaped *corbel-vaulted roof.

Trumbauer, Horace (1868–1938). American architect. In practice from 1890, he designed numerous houses (Harrison House, Glenside, Pa. (1892–3), and several others in Philadelphia, New York, and Washington). He was an accomplished *Beaux-Arts *Renaissance Revival architect, and could turn his hand to scholarly *Gothic. His best works were the two main *campuses of Duke University, Durham, North California (1927–38), and the Philadelphia Free Library, Pennsylvania (1917–27). Virtually all his buildings were well crafted and soundly based on precedent.

Maher (1975); Placzek (1982); van Vynckt (1993)

trumeau. Stone *mullion or *pier supporting the *tympanum of a wide *doorway, as in medieval *Gothic churches.

trumpet-arch. *See* arch.

truss. 1. Rigid structural framework of timbers bridging a space, each end resting on supports at regular intervals (often defining *bays), to provide support for the longitudinal timbers (e.g. purlins) that carry the common *rafters and the roof-covering. Its stability, dependent on e.g. *triangulation, also prevents the roof from spreading. Types of truss include:

aisle: in *timber-framed work a complete aisled structure set over the tie-beams;

Belfast or *bowstring*: of timber, for spans of up to 15 metres, with a segmental top member joined to a horizontal lower *chord, *string, or *tie (sometimes slightly cambered) by inclined *lattice-members;

box-framed: complete cross-frame the entire height of the building in a *box-framed* structure;

closed: with the spaces between its members filled in (e.g. between rooms or at *gable-ends);

common rafter: pair of common rafters held together with a *collar or tie-beam;

cruck: pair of *cruck *blades with transverse members (e.g. tie-beam, collar, saddle, yoke, or spur);

double arch-braced: with two pairs of arch-braces forming a continuous curve from where the braces are supported to where they join in the middle of the collar;

false hammer-beam: with a transverse timber like a *hammer-beam, but braced to a principal or collar without a hammer-post;

hammer-beam: with transverse timbers, like a tie-beam from which the middle section has been removed, supported on braces and carrying hammer-posts and braces that carry the open structure of the roof;

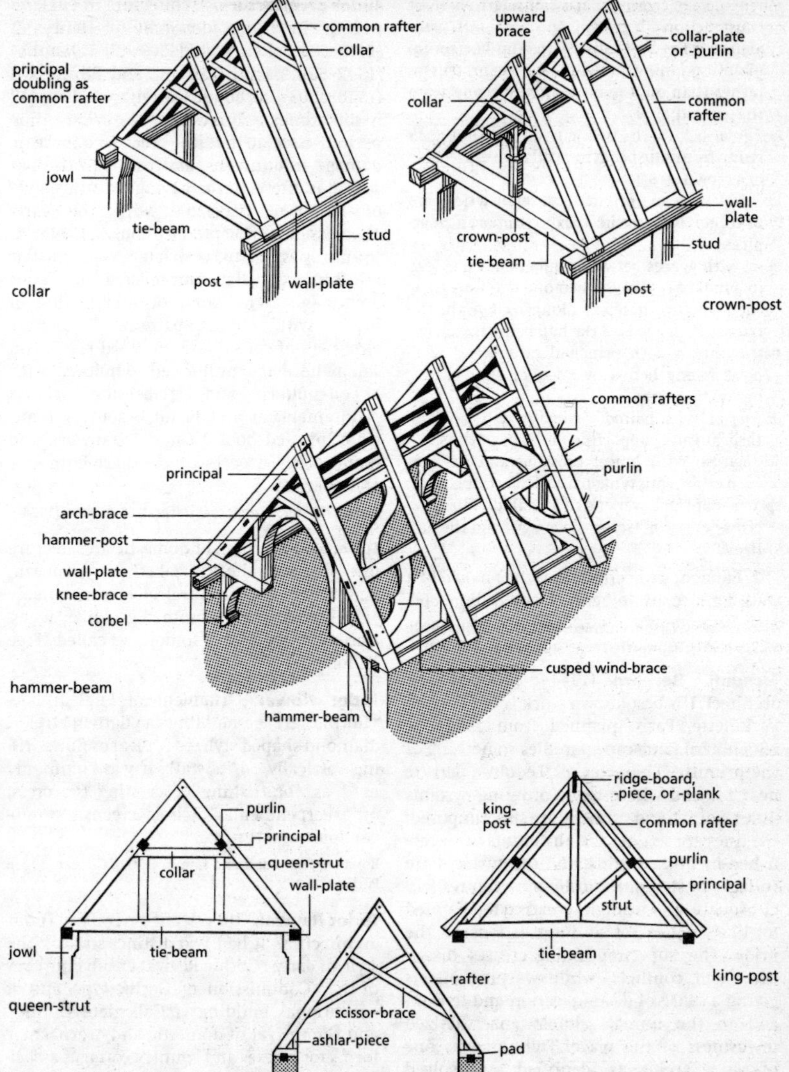

truss. (*top left*) Typical arrangement of common rafters connected by collars. (*top right*) Crown-post. (*middle*) Hammer-beam. (*bottom left*) Queen-post, properly a queen-strut truss. (*bottom middle*) Scissor-truss. (*bottom right*) King-post. (*JJS*) *intermediate* or *secondary*: truss of relatively light construction between the main trusses (defining the bays) and carried on horizontal plates spanning between the main trusses rather than on a main structure rising from the ground;

kerb-principal: with two curved *kerb-principals* rising from a tie-beam to a collar on either side of a crown strut;

king-post: with an upright *post set on a tie-beam or collar rising to the apex to support a ridge-piece;

open: with spaces between timbers unfilled (e.g. in a hall of two bays when one truss supports the structure half-way along its length, the trusses at the ends of the hall being *closed*);

post-and-rafter: with principal rafters and wall-posts strengthened by knee- or sling-braces, but no tie-beams;

queen-post: with paired vertical posts set on the tie-beam and supporting plates or purlins;

scissor-truss: with braces crossing and fixed to each other, thus tying pairs of rafters together;

spere: set at the lower end of a *hall dividing the cross-*entry or *screens passage from the hall itself.

2. Element projecting from the *naked of a wall, e.g. a *console, *corbel, *modillion, etc.

Alcock, Barley, Dixon, and Meeson (1996); Gwilt (1903); McKay (1957); Papworth (1892); Sturgis *et al.* (1901–2)

Tschumi, Bernard (1944–). Swiss-born architect. His best-known work is the Parc de la Villette, Paris (planned from 1982), in which hard landscape parodies something of the primitive character of *Ledoux's *Barrière* near by, and where three ordering systems (lines, points, and surfaces) are superimposed: the lines are sets of axes; the points are established by broken grids; and the surfaces are collages of stereometrically pure figures (circle, square, and triangle) creating red-painted toy-like *follies set at intersections of the grids. The superimposition creates distortions and conflicts, while warping effects giving a sense of decomposition and tension add to the unreal, almost anaesthetized uneasiness of the place. Tschumi was one of seven architects identified as involved in *Deconstructivism in the New York Exhibition of 1988. His publications include *Architectural Manifestoes* (1979), *Architectural Writings* (1988); *Manhattan Transcripts* (1981), and *Questions of Space* (1990).

Architectural Design, 60/9–10 (1990), 32–49; Curtis (1996); Johnson and Wigley (1988); van Vynckt (1993)

Tudor arch. *See* arch.

Tudor architecture. Architecture in England during the Tudor monarchy (of Henry VII (1485–1509), Henry VIII (1509–47), Edward VI (1547–53), Mary I (1553–8), and Elizabeth I (1558–1603)), although the reign of Edward VI is sometimes referred to as the *Edwardine period associated with much iconoclastic damage to churches, and the *Elizabethan period is often seen as having a distinct style of its own associated with the early *Renaissance and *prodigy houses. 'Tudor' is primarily associated with late-*Perpendicular *Gothic, very flat four-centred or Tudor arches (*see* arch), domestic architecture of brick with *diaper-patterns, elaborate chimneys of carved and moulded brick, and square-headed *mullioned windows with *hood-moulds and *label-stops. From *Fontainebleau and Flemish sources (especially printed books) came *strapwork and many other aspects of Northern-European *Mannerism.

Brunskill (1990); Lewis and Darley (1986); Lloyd (1925)

Tudorbethan. Style of domestic architecture involving revival of *Elizabethan, *Jacobean, and *Tudor architectural elements, notably *mullioned and *transomed grid-like *fenestration, freely mixed, sometimes called *Free Tudor.

Tudor flower. Ornament of English late-*Gothic art resembling a flattish trefoil diamond-shaped stylized ivy-leaf or flower rising vertically on its stalk. It was commonly used as *brattishing or cresting (*see* cress) on *Perpendicular *choir-screens, *tomb-canopies, and the like.

Bond (1908*a*); Bond and Camm (1909); Glazier (1926); Parker (1850)

Tudor Revival. C19 eclectic revival of *Tudor architecture. It had two distinct strands: the style of early *Gothic Revival cheap churches of the *Commissioners' Gothic type, and of educational buildings (*Collegiate Gothic); and the revival of domestic and *vernacular forms for houses and country cottages associated with the *Picturesque. As Tudor architecture was often of brick, the Revival lent itself to the construction of schools, workhouses, *chapels, gate-lodges, and model cottages, often with *diaper-patterns, small *casement-windows with leaded *lights, moulded-brick chimneys, and even partially *timber-framed structures. Many books of designs were published that featured such domestic buildings.

Later C19 Tudor Revival was part of the *Arts-and-Crafts movement and the *Domestic Revival, and at its best could produce masterpieces, such as the housing in Port Sunlight (1880s–1914) and Thornton Hough (1890s), both in Cheshire, and both containing brilliant designs by *Grayson & Ould, *Douglas & Fordham, and William & Segar *Owen. A further, not often successful revival occurred in C20, especially in public-house and domestic architecture of the 1920s and 1930s.

Hubbard (1991); Lewis and Darley (1986)

tumbling-course, tumbling-in. Courses of brickwork laid at 90° to the slope of a *buttress, *chimney, *gable, or other feature, and tapering into the horizontal courses. It was often employed by C19 architects during the *Muscular phase of the *Gothic revival, using dense bricks of an engineering type, instead of a *cope.

Brunskill (1990); Clifton-Taylor (1987); Lloyd (1925)

tumulus. Artificial mound of earth erected over a prehistoric tomb, etc. If it is made of stones it is called a *cairn*, An elongated mound is a *barrow.

tunnel-vault. *See* vault.

Turin 1902 Exhibition. Important international *Arts-and-Crafts exhibition in Turin, Italy, that marked the apotheosis of *Art Nouveau as a widely used style in that country (called *Stile Liberty*). The main building, by Raimondo d'*Aronco, was a tour-de-force of Art Nouveau, much influenced by the Vienna *Sezession.

Meeks (1966)

Turner, Thackeray H. (1853–1937). English *Arts-and-Crafts architect. Articled to Sir George Gilbert *Scott, he later assisted John Oldrid *Scott and George Gilbert *Scott jun. before setting up in practice in 1885 with Eustace James Anthony Balfour (1854–1911), the brother of the future Prime Minister, Arthur James Balfour (1848–1930). E. J. A. Balfour was Surveyor to the Grosvenor Estate in London from 1890, and it was in that capacity that Balfour & Turner designed Balfour Place, Balfour Mews, and buildings in Mount and Aldford Streets, Mayfair, as well as many other works of distinction for the Estate. They also refaced Wilton Crescent, Belgravia. Turner designed Westbrook, Godalming, Surrey (1902); the impressive *Lethaby-influenced Phillips memorial *cloister, Church of Sts Peter and Paul, Godalming (1913—in memory of the wireless operator who went down with the *Titanic* in 1912); and Wycliffe Buildings (1894), Mead Cottage (1895), and The Court (1902), Guildford, Surrey, among other works of quality.

Gray (1985); Pevsner, *Buildings of England, Surrey* (1971)

turnpike. *See* stair.

turret. 1. Small or subordinate tower normally forming part of a larger structure, especially a rounded addition to the angle of a building, sometimes commencing on *corbels at some height from the ground, and usually containing a spiral *stair. **2.** Round tower of great height in proportion to its diameter. **3.** Small circular tower on the top of a large tower, often at the corners, called *tourelle, usually with a conical or domical roof, so known as a *pepper-pot turret*. Such subsidiary turrets are found in *crenellated and *Scottish Baronial architecture, and may also be capped by *spires, *pinnacles, or *ogee-headed tops.

MacGibbon and Ross (1887–92); Papworth (1892)

turret-step. Piece of stone with a plan resembling the outline of a keyhole. The circular end forms part of the central *pier or *newel of a circular or winding newel-stair, and the fan-tailed part is the step.

turriculated. Building furnished with *turrets.

Tuscan architecture. *See* Etruscan architecture.

Tuscan Order. One of the five *Roman *Orders of architecture identified during the *Renaissance, and the simplest, also sometimes called the *Gigantic Order after *Scamozzi, probably because a variety of Tuscan column was used for *triumphal columns of the *Antonine or *Trajanic type in Antiquity. It resembles Roman *Doric, but has no *triglyphs on its unadorned *frieze. Its *base is very plain, consisting of a square *plinth-block supporting a large *torus over which is the *fillet and *apophyge creating the transition to the plain unfluted *shaft (often with an *entasis more pronounced than in the other Orders). At the top of the shaft is another apophyge and fillet, then an unadorned *astragal over which is a *neck or *hypotrachelium, then another fillet or fillets, a plain *echinus, and a square *abacus, usually with a simple fillet at the top, but sometimes an unmoulded block. The *entablature has a plain *architrave, plain *frieze, and crowning *cornice of simple bed-moulds, and a *cyma recta on top, and there are no *modillions, *dentils, *mutules, or enrichment of any sort. However, in a much more severe version of the Order codified by *Palladio based on *Vitruvius and used by Inigo *Jones at St Paul's Church, Covent Garden, London (1631–3), the conventional frieze and cornice are omitted: instead, there is a very wide overhanging *eaves-cornice supported on long, plain, bracket-like mutules, immediately over the architrave.

Chambers (1759); Chitham (1985); Curl (1992); Normand (1852); Spiers (1893)

Tuscher, Carl Marcus (1705–51). German architect and painter. He worked in Italy (1728–41), where he was influenced by *Juvarra, and designed the Palazzo Ferretti, Cortona. After a brief period in London (1741–3), he was called to Copenhagen by King Christian VI of Denmark (1730–46) in 1743, where he worked mostly as a painter. Impressed by Tuscher's *Abecedario dell'Architettura Civile* (Primer of Civil Architecture—1743), the King asked him to present plans for the Amalienborg, and it is probably because of Tuscher that the Amalienborg Plads acquired its octagonal form and that the four palaces were broken up into pavilions and galleries.

Weilbach (1952)

tusk, tuss. Projecting *tenon or *toothing-stone left in a wall to enable another wall to be joined and bonded to it.

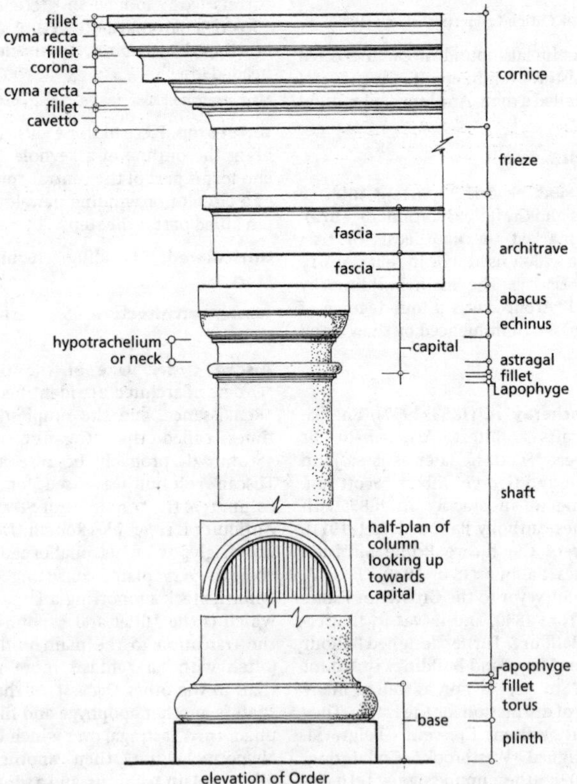

Tuscan Order. (*After Palladio*)

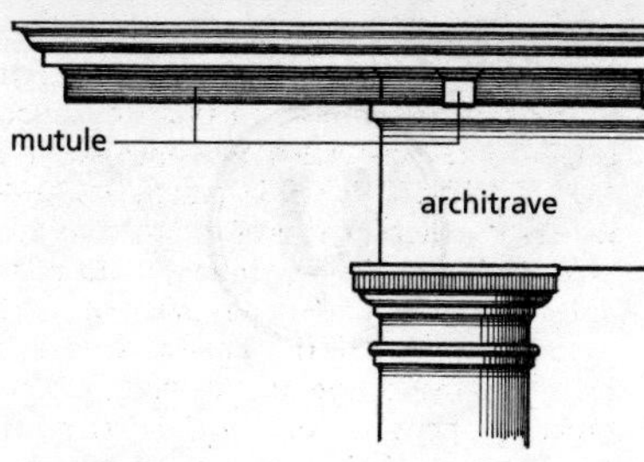

Tuscan Order. (*After Inigo Jones*)

tuss. *See* tenon, toothing-stones.

twining stem, twisted stem. Moulding resembling a long, thin, cylindrical rod with a stem wrapped around it, forming a spiral ornament set in a *cavetto between two continuous plain *bowtells, common in *Romanesque work.

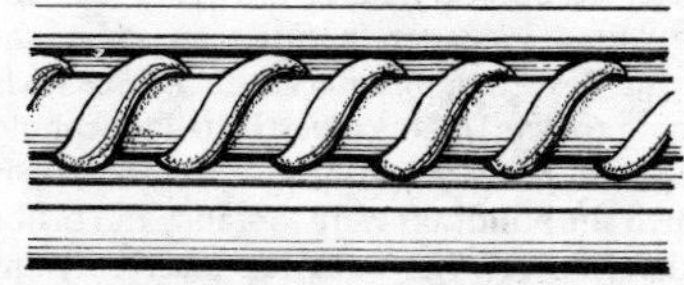

twining stem. Church of St Mary, Wimbotsham, Norfolk. (*After Parker*)

twisted column. *Torso.

two-light window. Window of two *lights separated by a *mullion or (rarely) a *transom, called a *coupled* or *gemel* window.

Tylman van Gameren (*c*.1630–1706). *See* Gameren.

tympan, tympanum (*pl.* **tympana**). **1.** Triangular or segmental face of a *pediment contained between the horizontal and *raking *cornices or horizontal and segmental cornices, often enriched with relief sculpture. **2.** Area above a *lintel over an opening contained by an arch set above it, e.g. in the west doors of the Churches of St-Gilles-du-Gard, near Arles (C12), and the Madeleine, Vézelay (C12), both in France.

type. 1. Exemplar, pattern, prototype, or original work serving as a model after which a building or buildings are copied. **2.** Something exemplifying the ideal characteristics of, say, a temple, so some would hold that the *Parthenon is the very *type* of a Greek *Doric temple. **3.** *Tester. **4.** Top of a small *cupola or *turret, e.g. the crowning part of a *Tudor turret, such as those of the White Tower, Tower of London (1532). **5.** Form or character that distinguishes a class or group of buildings (building-type), e.g. church, *mausoleum, town-hall, temple.

umbraculum. *Baldachin.

umbrella. **1.** *Chattra, normally on a *stupa but used on its own, in *Hindoo architecture. **2.** Type of *dome.

umbrella dome. *See* dome.

umbrello. *Fabrique in a garden, essentially a small structure protecting a seat.

Langley (1747)

uncut modillion. *Mutule, as in variants of the *Tuscan *Order, or a *modillion resembling a bracket or simple cantilevered block.

undé, undy. *Wave-scroll, or *oundy*, like a *Vitruvian scroll, or any *undulating repeated *running wave-like ornament, especially in Classical architecture (from *undy*, meaning wavy), but also a late-*Gothic ornament (e.g. *trail).

undercroft. *Crypt or vaulted space under a church or other building, wholly or partly underground.

undulating. **1.** *Curvilinear* or *Flowing* *tracery. **2.** Undulate *band moulding, *guilloche, oundy, *undé, undy, wave-scroll or *Vitruvian scroll.

Unger, Georg Christian (1743–1812). German architect. He was a pupil of *Gontard, with whom he worked. Together they designed the very fine *triumphal arch at Potsdam (1770), and with *Boumann the Royal Library with its curved façade to the Forum Fridericianum, Berlin (1774–80). He designed 26–7 Breiterstrasse, Potsdam (1769), based on Inigo *Jones's proposals for the Palace of Whitehall published in *Vitruvius Britannicus*.

Papworth (1892); Watkin and Mellinghoff (1987)

Ungers, Oswald Mathias (1926–). German architect. Among his buildings his own house at Belvederestrasse, Köln-Müngersdorf (1959), stands out as an unusually crisp and rigorous essay in simple blocky geometrical forms for its time. He became one of the more influential architects of the late C20, as a theorist and a builder of exemplars, and, more especially, as a forceful opponent of *International Modernism. His mature works include the German Architecture Museum, Schaumainkai, Frankfurt-am-Main (1979–84), the Baden State Library, Karlsruhe (1979–84), and the Alfred Wegener Institute for Polar and Ocean Research, Bremerhaven (1980–4). In these projects Ungers investigated morphologies and transformations, the contexts in which the buildings were to stand, and historical references. His work has a serenity and a geometrical integrity unusual in post-war German architecture. He and *Kleihues have been two of the most influential exponents of *Rational architecture or *Neo-Rationalism in Germany. Ungers has published extensively, including *Quadratische Häuser* (Quadratic Houses—1983). In his belief that architecture must reflect the *genius loci*, history, and evolution, he displays a rare sensitivity.

Baumeister, 64 (1967), 557–72; *Casabella*, 244 (1960), 22–35; Conrads (1970); Conrads and Marschall (1962); *Das Kunstwerk*, 32/2–3 (1979), 132–41; Emanuel (1994); Jencks (1988*a*); Klotz (1977); *Lotus*, 11 (1976), 12, 14–41; Pehnt (1970); Ungers (1963); van Vynckt (1993)

Ungewitter, Georg Gottlob (1820–64). German architect, a pioneer of the *Gothic Revival in his homeland. In 1842 he established a practice in Hamburg, where his domestic architecture was influenced by *Chateauneuf, but in 1845 he became convinced that *Gothic could be applied to all building-types, and his attitudes to structure and use of materials drew on arguments advocated by A. W. N. *Pugin and *Viollet-le-Duc. He was also interested in German *timber-framed construction. His publications, including *Entwürfe zu Stadt- und Landhäusern*

(Projects for Town and Country Houses—1858–64), *Lehrbuch der gotischen Konstruction* (Textbook of Gothic Construction—1859–64), *Sammlung mittelalterlicher Ornamentik in geschichtlicher und systematischer Anordnung* (Collection of Medieval Ornamentation in Historical and Systematic Arrangement—1866), and works on medieval town- and country-houses (1889–90) were influential. His *Gotisches Musterbuch* (Gothic Pattern Book—1856—with Vincenz Statz (1818–98)) appeared in an English edition in 1858 and a French edition was published 1855–6. He designed churches at Neustadt, Marburg (1859–64), Bockenheim, Frankfurt-am-Main (1862), and elsewhere in Germany, and his studies of German *timber-framed buildings were published posthumously as folios in Berlin (1889–90).

Germann (1972); Muthesius (1974); Reichensperger (1866); Sturgis *et al.* (1901–2)

Unwin, Sir Raymond (1863–1940). English town-planner, the most influential of his time. Influenced by William *Morris and by Socialist ideas, he was later drawn to the theories of Ebenezer *Howard concerning planning and cities. He formed a partnership (1896–1914) with his brother-in-law, Barry *Parker: as Parker & Unwin they designed St Andrew's Church, Barrow Hill, Derbyshire (1893), and several houses in the *Arts-and-Crafts style before establishing their reputation by planning New Earswick Village near York for the Joseph Rowntree (1836–1925) Village Trust (from 1901). This was followed by the realization of Ebenezer Howard's proposals, the layout of Letchworth, Hertfordshire, the first *Garden City (from 1903), where Parker & Unwin also built several houses and other structures. Progress at Letchworth was slow, but at the next project, Hampstead *Garden Suburb, it was rapid (from 1905). Unwin settled in Hampstead, while Parker stayed on at Letchworth. The Suburb was a successful example of the ideals of low-density housing derived from the pioneering development at Bedford Park, Chiswick, and was the prototype for many inter-war suburban developments. The very grand, formal centre at Hampstead, however, consisting of two churches, several houses, and an institute, were designed by *Lutyens (from 1908).

Unwin published *Town Planning in Practice: An Introduction to the Art of Designing Cities and Suburbs* in 1909, an important text that had a considerable effect on town-planning for the next three decades. Appointed Chief Inspector of Town Planning at the Local Government Board (later Ministry of Health) in 1914, and then Director of Housing for the Ministry of Munitions during the 1914–18 war, he influenced a number of developments, including the settlements at Gretna, Scotland, and Mancot Royal (Queensferry), near Chester. He was a member of the Tudor-Walters Committee on Housing (1918), was consulted for the New York Regional Plan in the USA (1922), and remained a senior civil servant with the Ministry of Health until 1928. He advised on the planning of the Manchester satellite development of Wythenshawe, for which Parker was the main consultant (1927–41): it was one of the most ambitious local-authority housing-schemes of the time, and anticipated the first-generation New Towns after the 1939–45 war. He was also involved in the proposals for London, the fruits of which were the Greater London Plans of the 1940s. He was one of the founders of the Town Planning Institute (1913) and was President of the Royal Institute of British Architects (1931–3). His other works included *Cottage Plans and Common Sense* (1902—with a later edition of 1908), *Nothing Gained by Overcrowding: How the Garden City Type of Development May Benefit Both Owner and Occupier* (1912), and many contributions to journals, etc.

Architectural Review, 163/976 (June 1978), 325–32, 366–75; Ashworth (1954); Creese (1967, 1992); *DNB* (1949); Jackson (1985); Miller (1989, 1992); Mumford (1961); Swenarton (1981); Unwin (1908, 1909, 1918, 1971)

Upjohn, Richard (1802–78). English-born architect, he emigrated to the USA in 1829, and settled in Boston, Mass., where he established a practice in 1834. His earliest works were the serene and pleasing *Greek Revival houses in Bangor, Me. (1833–6), and a *Gothic Revival house in Gardiner, Me. (1835), but he is remembered primarily as a church-architect and as a Gothic Revivalist. His masterpiece was the *Second Pointed Trinity Church, New York (1841–6), which shows the influence of A. W. N. *Pugin (it resembles the church depicted in Plate H of *The True Principles of Pointed or Christian Architecture* (1841)), and gained critical acclaim. St Mary's, Burlington, NJ (1846), with its handsome *crossing-tower and *broach-spire, was derived from the English medieval Church of St John the

Baptist, Shottesbrooke, Berkshire, illustrations of which, from drawings by *Butterfield, had been published by the Oxford Society for Promoting the Study of Gothic Architecture (later called the Oxford Architectural Society). Upjohn's Trinity Chapel, New York (1846), was also Anglo-Gothic in style.

Upjohn produced some buildings in the *Romanesque style, e.g. the Church of the Pilgrims, Brooklyn, New York (1844–6), Bowdoin College Chapel and Library, Brunswick, Me. (1845–55), and St Paul's Church, Baltimore, Md. (1854–6), the last more like a true *Rundbogenstil building based on Lombardic exemplars. He built an enormous number of churches, many of some distinction, and also designed other building types, a fact often obscured by his reputation as a church-architect. He published *Upjohn's Rural Architecture* in 1852 which shows something of his grasp of composition and style. He was first President of the American Institute of Architects which he helped to found.

Pierson and Jordy (1978); Placzek (1982—a very full accound by Phoebe B. Stanton); Stanton (1968); Upjohn, E. M. (1939); Upjohn, R. (1975)

Upjohn, Richard Michell (1828–1903). English-born American architect, the son of Richard *Upjohn. He worked closely with his father, becoming a junior partner in 1853. The earliest building for which he alone appears to have been responsible was Madison Square Presbyterian Church, New York (1853–4). He introduced an almost *Rogue *High *Victorian *Gothic style to the USA, as at the Grace Church, Manchester, NH (1860), and the spiky, rather frantic north gates of Greenwood Cemetery, Brooklyn, New York (1861–5). The Connecticut State Capitol, Hartford (1872–8), a showy American interpretation of Continental *Gothic Revival, with many *gables, crested roofs, and an extraordinary (and somewhat incongruous) high *cupola, is his most famous work. He published an influential paper on *Colonial architecture in New York and the New England States in 1869.

Curry and Pierce (1979); *Dictionary of American Biography* (1948); Placzek (1982); *Proceedings of the Third Annual Convention of the American Institute of Architects* (Nov. 1869), 47–51; Upjohn, E. M. (1939)

Urabe, Shizutaro (1909–91). Japanese architect. Much of his work was carried out in Kurashiki (his birthplace), near Okayama, the *vernacular architecture of which was largely constructed of beaten earth and brick, to which he responded with sensitivity, reorganizing traditional warehouses and other buildings. His most celebrated work was Kurashiki Ivy Square (1970–4), a conversion of some brick-built industrial buildings into a Cultural Centre for Youth, complete with exhibition areas, refreshment facilities, and lecture-rooms. Other works included the Historical Archives Building, Yokohama (1981), and the Kanagawa Prefectural Archives of Modern Literature, Yokohama Women's University (1984).

Emanuel (1994)

uraeus (*pl.* **uraei**). Representation of the sacred asp, cobra, or serpent, e.g. on the *Nemes* headdress of Ancient Egyptian divinities and sovereigns, or on either side of winged discs or globes on the *gorge-cornice of Egyptian architecture.

Curl (1994); Roullet (1972)

Urban, Joseph (1872–1933). Austrian architect, he studied in Vienna under *Hasenauer, settling in the USA in 1911. His best-known building is the New School for Social Research, New York (1929–30), but became primarily a designer of interiors and theatres (about which he published a book in 1929).

Architecture 69 (1934), 250–6, 275–90; Urban (1929)

urbanism. 1. Term much used in the 1980s, based on Le *Corbusier's ideas concerning town-planning. **2.** Urban way of life compared with life in the country. **3.** Approach to urban design taking into account the need to respond with sensitivity to urban morphologies: the *Kriers have been in the vanguard of the movement to respond to urban history and fabric in a more positive and less destructive way than was propounded by *International *Modernism, the *Athens Charter, and *CIAM. The Kriers and their colleagues argued that context was important where sites were being redeveloped, and that it was not just a question of one building, but streets, urban spaces, and, ultimately, whole towns that needed careful design to avoid the visual chaos imposed so destructively on so many cities since 1945: they argued in favour of a sensitivity to *townscape that had been so thoroughly rejected by Modernists. Urbanism (3) also rejects the concept of zoning advocated by Le Corbusier (for the pleasures of urban life suggest a plurality of activities), and accepts the necessity of keeping the motor-car at bay. According to Jane *Jacobs and others, people should live in cities, use them, and walk in them, not clutter and pollute them with cars and other vehicles. Urbanism implies recapturing quality, beauty, pleasure, and civilized living in cities. *See* Sixteen Principles of Urbanism.

Architectural Design, 56/9 (Sept. 1986); Choay (1965); Collins and Collins (1986); Glancey (1989); Hertz and Klein (1990); Jacobs (1961); Jencks (1988*a*); Krier (1979); Lavedan (1952–60, 1975)

urban renewal. Fashionable American term of the 1950s, which really meant large-scale redevelopment of urban areas. It was adopted in the United Kingdom to mean the replanning of towns or urban centres to modernize them and provide access for traffic. More recently it has tended to imply a renewal of urban fabric damaged through neglect or inappropriate intervention.

Huxtable (1970, 1976, 1986, 1986*a*); Jacobs (1961, 1969, 1984)

urilla (*pl.* **urillae**). *Helix or *volute of a *Corinthian *capital.

urn. Lidded ovaloid *vase on a circular *plan used in Classical Antiquity to contain cremated remains. It was a form later revived for purposes of architectural decoration, on *balustrade *pedestals, set in *niches, used as garden-ornaments, employed in funerary monuments (often draped, or with a portrait-medallion of the deceased on its side, especially in Neoclassical examples), shown in relief on *friezes, etc., and sometimes with representations of flames issuing from the lid.

Utopian architecture. Designs for buildings and cities providing an ideal, or supposedly ideal, environment for their users, usually implying development where none previously existed, or where wholesale destruction of built fabric is envisaged to provide a site. It is associated with social engineering.

Architectural Review, 140/834 (Aug. 1966), 87–91; Choay (1965); Fishman (1977, 1987); Jencks (1971); Tafuri (1976)

Utopie group. French architectural group established in 1967 in Paris to promote expendable, inflatable, pneumatic, temporary, transportable structures. It often used *collage* in its publications.

Architectural Design, 38/6 (June 1968), 255, 273–7

Utzon, Jørn (1918–). Danish architect. He studied with *Fisker and worked briefly with *Aalto and F. L. *Wright (who influenced his conception of architecture) before setting up on his own. His work often includes the platform or *plinth, a feature of *Meso-American architecture, as in the Utzon House, Hellebaek, Copenhagen (1952–3), and always employs very clear geometries. In 1956 he won the competition to design the Sydney Opera House and Concert Hall, Australia, where the platform theme provides a base for the huge sail-like *shell-vaults that rise above the harbour. The firm of Ove *Arup collaborated on the construction of these. Utzon did not design the interiors, however, as he had to withdraw during construction in 1966 when political arguments made his position impossible. Other projects by Utzon include the School at Højstrup (1958), the Melli Bank, Teheran, Iran (1959–63), and the National Assembly Building, Kuwait (1972–85—severely damaged in the Gulf War). He also designed residential complexes: the Kingo Houses, Helsingør (1956–60), and the development at Fredensborg (1962–3), in both of which units, designed on an *additive principle and responding to the contours of the site, were subtly disposed round courts. In addition, he explored the possibilities of *industrialized building, employing prefabricated parts that could be easily arranged in various permutations and combinations, leading to the evolution of his 'Espansiva' system (1969). In 1977 his Bagsvaerd Church, near Copenhagen, was completed, a highly controlled complex of simple geometries. He was also responsible for Paustian's Furniture Store, Nordhavn, Copenhagen (1987), and for his own house at Porto Petro, Mallorca, Spain (1971–3).

Architects' Yearbook, 6 (1955), 173–81; *Architectural Design*, 30 (30 Sept. 1960), 347–8; *Architectural Record*, 141/5 (1967), 189–92; *Architectural Review*, 165/985 (1979), 146–9; *Bauen und Wohnen*, 20 (Sept. 1966), 10–14; Curtis (1996); Doumato (1983); Drew (1972); Drexler (1980); Emanuel (1994); Lampugnani (1982, 1988); *Zodiac*, 5 (1959), 70–105, 10 (1962), 112–40, 14 (1965), 36–93

Uytenbogaart, Roelof Sarel (1933–). South-African architect. His early works (Welkom Church, Orange Free State (1964), and Bonwit Clothing Factory, Cape Town (1967)) were influenced by *Kahn, and during the 1970s (Werdmuller Centre, Claremont, Cape Town (1973), and University of Cape Town Sports Centre (1977)) looked to Le

*Corbusier for precedents. His own house at Kommetjie, Cape (1992), featured brick and wide overhanging *eaves, handled with great *élan*. He published (with others) *A Comparative Analysis of Urbanism in Cape Town* (1977), and several articles on aspects of South-African urbanization.

Emanuel (1994)

Vaccarini, Giovanni Battista (1702–68). Prolific Sicilian architect, influenced by *Borromini, Carlo *Fontana, and (to a lesser extent), aspects of French *Classicism then beginning to percolate into Italy. His appointment (1730) as City Architect of Catania heralded the introduction of Roman *Baroque, as in his Church of San Giuliano (1739–51), derived from Carlo *Rainaldi's Santa Maria in Monte Santo on the Piazza del Pòpolo, Rome, while the Convent Church of Sant'Agata (1735–67) owes something to Sant'Agnese in Agone, Piazza Navona, with a façade slightly reminiscent of that of San Carlo alle Quattro Fontane, both in Rome. Sant'Agata's façade is also embellished with carved *valancing like that on *Bernini's *baldacchino in St Peter's, Rome, and has *pilaster-*capitals decorated with palms, lilies, and crowns, symbols of the Saint's martyrdom. Vaccarini designed the façade of the Cathedral (1733–58), the elephant fountain bearing an *obelisk (1735—a motif also used by Bernini), and many other buildings in Catania, also completing the Town Hall in the Piazza del Duomo (1735). Later works, e.g. Palazzo del Principe di Reburdone (*c.*1740–50) and the Collegio Cutelli (1748–54), owed less to Baroque and more to Classicism.

Blunt (1968); Boscarino (1961); Fichera (1934); Giuliana Alajmo (1950); Norberg-Schulz (1986*a*); Pisano (1958); Watkin (1986)

Vaccaro, Domenico Antonio (1681–1750). Neapolitan architect. His cleverly planned churches, combining octagonal and rectangular volumes, include the Monastery Church of the Concezione at Montecalvario (1718–24) and Santa Maria delle Grazie, Calvizzano, Naples (*c.*1743). In the latter the junctions between the *drum and the *cupola are blurred by much frothy *stucco. His loveliest creation is the majolica *cloister at Santa Chiara, Naples (1739–42), in which are vine-clad *pergolas on octagonal majolica-clad *piers linked by seats (also majolica-faced).

Blunt (1975); Papworth (1892); Watkin (1986)

vagina. Lower part of a *term *pedestal with which the bust merges.

Vago, Pierre (1910–). Hungarian-born French architect, whose father, **József Vágó** (1877–1947), and uncle, **László** (1875–1933), were distinguished Austro-Hurgarian architects influenced by Otto *Wagner and by *Neoclassicism. As a pupil of *Perret, construction and its expression was always a strong component in his work. He was editor of the influential journal *L'Architecture d'aujourd'hui* in the 1930s which publicized *International Modernism. He set up his own practice in 1934 and exhibited a prefabricated steel house at the Exposition de l'Habitation in Paris that year. He prepared master-plans for several towns, including Arles, Avignon, and Beaucaire (1945–7), and Le Mans (1947–8). His buildings included churches, houses, *villas, and much else. He collaborated with Eugène *Freyssinet on the design and construction of the Basilica of St Pius, Lourdes (1958), a vast *reinforced-concrete structure. In 1932 he founded the *Réunions Internationales des Architectes*, an important forum which evolved into the *Union Internationale des Architectes* (UIA) after the 1939–45 war, with Vago as its Secretary-General.

Emanuel (1994)

Valadier, Giuseppe (1762–1839). Rome-born architect, urban designer, and archaeologist of French descent. He designed the Villa Pianciani, Terraja, between Spoleto and Todi (1784), and carried out major works of restoration and reconstruction at the Cathedral, Urbino (from 1789), where he drew on *Palladian precedents, but his rigorous attention to architectural unity was influenced by *Neoclassicism. From 1800 he worked for

Prince Stanisław Poniatowski (1757–1833), for whom he built the *villa (and laid out the gardens) on the Via Flaminia, Rome (completed 1818), later remodelled (1824–44) by his pupil *Canina. Around the same time he rebuilt the severe gate at the Ponte Milvio (1805), carried out works at the Palazzo Braschi, Rome (1790–1804), and designed the façade of San Pantaleo, Rome (1806), robustly Neoclassical in style, opposite the Palazzo Braschi. His most significant work, however, was the reorganization of the Piazza del Pòpolo (designed 1794–1811 and built 1816–24), where he created two huge hemicycles (with walls decorated with *sphinxes and other Neoclassical devices) around the Ancient Egyptian red-granite *obelisk which Augustus had brought to Rome in 10 BC, and which Pope Sixtus V (1585–90) caused to be re-erected on its present site in 1589. Steps and ramps ascend to Valadier's triple-arched *Loggiato* (1816–20) and the terraced garden on the Pincio at the top of which he built the Casinò Valadier (1813–17), an original design with different elevations on all four sides. This work of eclectic *Picturesque *Classicism, as remarkable as anything by *Jappelli, has Greek *Doric *loggie surmounted by *Ionic columns, a curved entrance-*portico with Ionic columns carrying a Doric *frieze, and vaulted interiors decorated with Neo-*Antique frescoes.

He also carried out extensive restoration works on various Ancient Roman buildings, including the arch of Titus, the Colosseum, the Temple of Fortuna Virilis, and Trajan's column. He designed the circular Church of Santa Cristina, Césena (1814–22), and re-worked Palladian themes for church-fronts for his new façade for the Church of San Rocco, Rome (1833–4), drawing on San Giorgio Maggiore, Venice, for his precedent. He published *Progetti* (1807), *Opere d'Architettura e di Ornamente* (1833), and many other works, some of which deal with his multifarious activities as a restorer.

Debenedetti (1979); Giedion (1967); Hoffmann (1967); Lapadula (1969); Marconi (1964); Meeks (1966); Schulze-Battman (1939)

valance. 1. Fall or edging of hanging drapery, e.g. around a *baldacchino, canopy, or *tester, really a pendent border, as that hung in front of curtain-rails in a room to conceal them and give a suitable finish. It is often simulated, as in the bronze valancing of *Bernini's celebrated baldacchino in San Pietro, Rome (1624–33). **2.** Vertical timber boards, often pointed or curved at the lower ends, finishing the *eaves of the roofs above C19 railway-platforms.

Valle, Gino (1923–). Italian architect. His main output was in the field of industrial buildings, a typical example of which was the Zanussi Electrical Appliances Factory, Pordenone (1956–61), in which the aggressive terdencies of movements such as New *Brutalism are expressed. He designed the monument to the Resistance, Udine (1969—with D. Balsadella and F. Marconi), and the formal Town Hall, Casarza (1974), the Valdadige Prefabricated Schools, Udine and Venice (1978), Public Housing, Udine (1979), and the Banca Commerciale Italiana, New York (1983).

Emanuel (1994); *Zodiac*, 20 (1970), 82–115

Vallée, Simon de la (d. 1642). French architect. In 1639 he was appointed Royal Architect to the Court of Queen Christina of Sweden (1632–54) in Stockholm, and trained his son **Jean de la Vallée** (1620–96) and Nicodemus *Tessin the Elder, both of whom were to exercise considerable influence on the development of *Baroque architecture in Sweden. He designed the exquisite *Riddarhus* (House of the Nobility), Stockholm (*c*.1641–74—completed by his son and *Vingboons). Jean also gained experience in France and Italy before returning to Sweden in 1650. He was responsible for the Axel Oxenstierna Palace, Stockholm (*c*.1650–4—influenced by the *Renaissance Roman *palazzi of *Raphael and *Peruzzi), the octagonal Hedvig Eleonora Church, Stockholm (begun 1656), and the Palladian *Villa Mariedal, Västergötland (1666), among other fine buildings.

Cruickshank (1996); Nordberg (1970); Papworth (1892)

valley. Internal angle formed by the meeting of two roof slopes, the opposite of a *hip.

Vallin de la Mothe, Jean-Baptiste-Michel (1729–1800). French architect. He settled in Russia in 1759, introduced French *Classicism influenced by *Palladio, A.-J. *Gabriel, and J.-F. *Blondel (to whom he was related), and taught at the new Academy of Arts in St Petersburg. He designed Gostiny Dvor (Merchants' Court), a pioneering work of *Neoclassicism (1762–5), the Old Hermitage (1764–7), the Classical New Holland Port Gateway and Warehouses (1765), and the

Academy of Fine Arts (1765–72), all in St Petersburg. In the last building (originally planned by Blondel) he collaborated with A. F. Kokorinov (1726–72), Director of the Academy of Arts, and himself no mean architect.

L'Architecture, 35 (1922), 173–80; Braham (1980); Gallet *et al.* (1980); Hamilton (1983); Hautecœur (1912, 1952); Middleton and Watkin (1987)

vallum. **1.** Wall or rampart of earth or stone with palisades, e.g. Hadrian's Wall in Northern England. **2.** Roman palisaded bank constructed from material cast up from its surrounding ditch, as in a camp or fortress.

valva, valve. One or other of the halves or leaves of a double- or folding-door, e.g. a *French window.

Valvassori, Gabriele (1683–1761). Architect born in Rome, and much influenced by *Borromini. He designed the ingeniously planned Church of the Madonna della Luce (formerly San Salvatore della Corte), Rome (1730–68), but his most brilliant work was the Corso Wing of the Palazzo Doria-Pamphili, Rome (1730–5), one of the few *Rococo palaces where the exterior, abounding in quirky detail, is almost as decorative as the interior. He was also responsible for the Gate at the Villa Pamphili, Porta San Pancrazio (1732), and the Convent of Santi Quirico e Giulitta (1750–3), in Rome. C19 commentators often found his work 'depraved'.

Fasolo (1949); *L'illustrazione vaticana*, 4 (1933), 303–4, 428–9; Mallory (1977); Norberg-Schulz (1986*a*); Portoghesi (1970)

van Alen, William (1882–1954). *See* Alen.

van Baurscheit, Jan Pieter (1699–1768). *See* Baurscheit.

Vanbrugh, Sir John (1664–1726). English architect of Flemish descent, author of *risqué* plays (including *The Provok'd Wife* (1697) sketched while languishing in French gaols), herald, soldier, and wit. Architecture became his prime interest around 1699 when he made designs for Castle Howard, Yorkshire, for Charles Howard, 3rd Earl of Carlisle (1674–1738—to whom he was distantly related), supplanting *Talman, who had prepared an earlier scheme. Castle Howard (1699–1726) was a virtuoso performance in the *Baroque style, more Continental than English, all the more extraordinary as the work of an inexperienced amateur. The powerful, virile, and confident designs were realized with the assistance of *Hawksmoor, who was appointed Draughtsman and Clerk of Works in 1700. Partly as a result of this success (and through his connections), Vanbrugh superseded Talman as Comptroller of the Works in 1702, and thus became *Wren's colleague on the Board of Works. Quickly perceived as an architect of genius (though apparently without any formal training or experience), the agreeable, clubbable Vanbrugh lost no time in getting himself appointed architect to members of the Whig Oligarchy, replacing the quarrelsome Talman whenever possible. For a decade, as Comptroller of Her Majesty's Works, he enjoyed not only power but perquisites as well, and made the most of his opportunities. The Tories removed him from his post in 1713, but when the Whigs returned to power and George Lewis, Elector of Hanover, became King George I (reigned 1714–27) in 1714 he was not only restored to the Comptrollership but knighted as well, and in 1715 was also appointed Surveyor of Gardens and Waters. He was a strong personality within the Office of Works, but failed to succeed Wren as Surveyor in 1718, the job going to *Benson, and towards the end of his life his Baroque style was out of favour, being superseded by *Burlington's *Palladianism.

In 1704 Vanbrugh gained his most important commission to design Blenheim Palace, Oxfordshire, a great house intended as a symbol of the Nation's and the Queen's gratitude to John Churchill, 1st Duke of Marlborough (1650–1722), for his victories over the French. There he was able to build on a vast scale, unhampered by penny-pinching, and with Blenheim English Baroque achieved its climax, though it was a Baroque that had no exact Continental equivalent despite the fact that its sources were French, Italian (the arcaded *belvederes at the corner are reminiscent of *Borromini's work), and English (notably the works of Talman and Wren). There was another aspect too, that of Vanbrugh's interest in medieval and *Elizabethan architecture. Something of the dramatic skyline of *prodigy houses can be seen at Blenheim and at other creations by one of England's greatest architects. Blenheim was completed by a cabinet-maker, James Moore, and by Hawksmoor.

Other houses by Vanbrugh were Kimbolton Castle, Huntingdonshire (1707–10—with later additions by *Galilei), King's Weston, near Bristol (*c.*1710–19); Eastbury Park, Dorset (begun 1718—demolished except for one wing); the *Sublime Seaton Delaval, Northumberland (1720–8), and the north front of Grimsthorpe Castle, Lincolnshire (1722–6). He evoked something of the 'Castle Air' (as he termed it), medieval, and Elizabethan architecture without overt quotation. Seaton Delaval, with a plan combining Classical formalism and a reminiscence of medieval corner-towers, is one of Vanbrugh's most remarkable, powerful, memorable, and massive creations, with its insistent *banding and *rustication. Vanbrugh's sensitivity towards the past led him to attempt to retain the remains of Woodstock Manor in the grounds of Blenheim, for he recognized the importance of ruins in a landscape. Indeed, he contributed to the making of the gardens at Stowe, Buckinghamshire (where he designed the Lake *Pavilions, the *Rotunda, the Temples of Bacchus and Sleep, the Cold Bath, and the Pyramid (*c.*1719–24—nearly all demolished or altered)), and at Castle Howard, where he was responsible for the *Obelisk (1714), Pyramid Gate (1719), and Belvedere Temple (1725–8), and must therefore be regarded as an important pioneering creator of *Picturesque landscapes. Some of his architecture also had Picturesque qualities, notably his own house at Greenwich (Vanbrugh Castle, from 1718), with crenellated towers and bogus *machicolations, the composition anticipating the *Gothic Revival later in the century.

Architectural History, 10 (1967), 7–88; Beard (1986); Campbell (1967–72); Colvin (1995); Colvin (ed.) (1976); Colvin and Craig (1964); *DNB* (1917); Downes (1966, 1977, 1987); Hussey (1967*a*); Saumarez Smith (1990); Summerson (1993); Vanbrugh (1927–8); Whistler (1954)

van Brunt, Henry (1832–1930). *See* Ware & van Brunt.

van Campen, Jacob (1595–1657). *See* Campen.

van den Broek, Johannes Hendrik (1898–1978). *See* Bakema.

van der Nüll, Eduard (1812–68). *See* Nüll.

van der Rohe, Ludwig Mies (1886–1969). *See* Mies.

van de Velde, Henri (*or* **Henry**) (1863–1957). *See* Velde.

van Doesburg, Theo (1883–1931). *See* Doesburg.

vane. Banner-shaped plate of metal, or a weather-cock or -vane, placed on a pivot on a high part of a building, to point towards the direction from which the wind comes.

van Eesteren, Cor(nelis) (1897–1988). *See* Eesteren.

van Eyck, Aldo (1918–). *See* Eyck.

Vanvitelli, Luigi (1700–73). Neapolitan architect of Dutch descent. He came to public attention with his entry for the competition to design a new *façade for San Giovanni in Laterano, Rome (1732), won by *Galilei. As a result, he was commissioned to design the new *lazaretto* (hospital) in Ancona, a polygonal fortress-like building (1737–8), and also built the *Gesù* Church (1743) and the austere Arco Clementino (1735–8) in the same city. He added wings to the Odescalchi Palace (1750), enlarged *Michelangelo's Church of Santa Maria degli Angeli (1749), and designed the *cloister of Sant'Agostino (1746–50—where *Borromini's influence is overt), all in Rome.

In 1751 he was called to Naples to build a new Royal Palace of great splendour at Caserta for Carlo III di Borbone, King of the Two Sicilies (1738–59). With its vast internal and external *scenographic vistas and octagonal entrance *vestibule it had *Baroque qualities, but many of the interiors leant towards *Neoclassicism. The building (the main fabric of which was completed in 1774) resembled Robert de *Cotte's unexecuted visionary designs for the Royal Palace of Buenretiro near Madrid (1714–15), while Versailles proved another precedent. Associated with the palace were gardens, with elaborate waterworks and ancillary structures designed by Vanvitelli, who was responsible for the *aqueduct system (including the 25-mile-long Acquedotto Carolino (1752–64)). The Church of the Annunziata (1761—completed by his son **Carlo** (d. 1821)) and the Piazza Dante (1755–67—influenced by *Bernini's Piazza di San Pietro, Rome) were also designed by him.

Blunt (1975); Defilippis (1968); Fagiolo dell'Arco (1863); Fusco (1973); Meeks (1966); Strazzullo (1976–7); Vanvitelli (1975); Wittkower (1982)

Vardy, John (1718–65). English Palladian architect. He enjoyed a long association with the Office of Works and worked with *Kent, whose Horse-Guards Building, Whitehall, London, he built from 1748 with William *Robinson. He published a volume of engravings entitled *Some Designs of Mr. Inigo Jones and Mr. William Kent* (1744). His greatest work was Spencer House, Green Park, London

(1756–65), some of the finest rooms in which were designed by James *Stuart, and he produced several designs in the *Rococo style as well as an essay in *Gothick (Milton Abbey, Dorset, of *c.*1754–5).

Brown (1985); Colvin (1995); Colvin (ed.) (1976); *DNB* (1917); Friedman (1993); Summerson (1993)

Vasanzio, Giovanni (*c.*1550–1621). Born Jan van Santen in Utrecht, The Netherlands, he settled in Rome *c.*1595 where he practised architecture, specializing in fountains, gardens, and *villas. He completed *Ponzio's *façade of San Sebastiano fuori le mura (1612), but his best-known work is the Villa Borghese on the Pincio (1613–15), with a main elevation enlivened with niches and statuary owing much to *Mannerism. He enlarged the Villa Mondragone, Frascati (1614), begun by *Longhi, and designed the Fontane dell'Acqua Paola (1613) and del Galera (1620).

Hibbard (1971); Onofrio (1957); Papworth (1892)

Vasari, Giorgio (1511–74). Italian architect, author, and painter. His *Le Vite de' più eccellenti architetti, pittori, e scultori italiani* (Lives of the Most Eminent Italian Architects, Painters, and Sculptors) was published in 1550 and is a prime source of information on *Renaissance architecture as well as having been a key document in creating perceptions about the period. An expanded edition came out in 1568. As an architect he made an important contribution to the designs for the Villa Giulia, Rome (1551–5), vetted by *Michelangelo and realized by *Vignola and *Ammannati. In 1555 he settled in Florence to work for Duke Cosimo I de' Medici (1519–74). There, he created his masterpiece, the Uffizi, the Government Offices of the Tuscan State (1560–80s), with façades influenced by *Bramante's Belvedere in the Vatican, Michelangelo's Biblioteca Laurenziana, Florence, and *Peruzzi's Palazzo Massimo alle Colonne, Rome. The Uffizi buildings enclose a long piazzetta terminated at the river end by a *loggia incorporating a *serliana, and was completed by *Buontalenti, who designed several *Mannerist details, including the Porta delle Suppliche.

At Arezzo Vasari designed the Church of Santi Fiora e Lucilla (1564–86) on a plan resembling that of San Marco, Venice, and the handsome loggia in the Piazza Grande (1570–96). He also carried out several major alterations of church interiors following the Council of Trent (1545–63) which required unimpeded views of the high-altar. His drastic work at Santa Croce (1565–84) and Santa Maria Novella (1565–72), Florence, gave the interiors architectural unity, but also removed many medieval features.

Boase (1979); Hall (1979); Heydenreich and Lotz (1974); Satkowski (1979, 1993); Vasari (1912–15)

vase. 1. Hollow vessel, unlidded, of decorative character and various forms, with or without handles. **2.** Representation of this for architectural ornament, often in gardens, in *niches, on *pedestals, etc., but distinct from an *urn, commonly found in Neoclassical designs. Vases were promoted as architectural ornaments by Enea Vico (1523–67) in a series of publications, collected in 1543, Matthias Darly (*fl.* 1741–80) in *The Ornamental Architect* (1770), d'Hancarville (P. F. Hugues (1729–1805)) in *Antiquités Étrusques, Grecques, et Romaines* (1766–7), *Piranesi in *Vasi, Candelabri, Cippi, Sarcofagi* (1778), Johann Heinrich Wilhelm Tischbein (1751–1829) in *Collection of Engravings from Ancient Vases* (1791–3), and many other authors. **3.** *Bell or core of the *Corinthian *capital.

Jervis (1984); Lewis and Darley (1986)

Vásquez *or* **Vázquez, Lorenzo** (*fl.* 1489–1512). Spanish master-mason and architect responsible for some of the first *Renaissance buildings in the Iberian peninsula. He designed the *Quattrocento *frontispiece at the College of Santa Cruz, Valladolid (1489–91), the heavily rusticated Medinaceli Palace, Cogolludo (1492–5—modelled on Quattrocento Florentine prototypes, though with late-*Gothic *fenestration), and the Mendoza Palace, Guadalajara (before 1507). He may also have designed the castle of La Calahorra, Granada (1509–12).

Chueca Goitia (1953); Kubler and Soria (1959); van Vynckt (1993)

Vau, Louis Le (1612–70). French *Baroque architect. With a team of decorators, sculptors, gardeners, and painters he was largely responsible for creating the *Louis Quatorze style at the great palace of Versailles from 1667. His earliest buildings were Parisian *hôtels particuliers, notably the fine Hôtel Lambert on the Île-St-Louis (1640–4), where he created a formal staircase leading to a landing flanked by an octagonal vestibule on one side, and, on the other, an elliptical vestibule leading to a long gallery terminating in a bow-window affording views over the Seine. In

1656 he began Vaux-le-Vicomte, a great *château for Nicolas Fouquet (1615–80), with interiors decorated by Charles Lebrun (1619–90) and others. It incorporated a grand vestibule and stair, with a domed saloon behind partly projecting on the garden-front, the whole set in formal gardens designed by André le Nôtre (1613–1700). Le Vau and Lebrun rebuilt the Galerie d'Apollon in the Louvre, Paris (1661–4), and, with *Perrault, designed the celebrated east front of the Louvre (1665–74—a harbinger of C18 Classicism) so admired by *Wren and others. At the Collège des Quatre Nations, Paris (1661–74—now the Institut de France), with a pedimented front (behind which rises a tall *cupola) flanked by two *quadrants terminating in *pavilions facing the Seine (so the composition has a concave façade contained by the *wings), Le Vau demonstrated a strong affinity with Italian Baroque, and possible influences from *Bernini and *Borromini. The front and pavilions are graced by *Giant Orders, and the quadrants by subservient superimposed Orders. His most ambitious work, however, was at Versailles, where he remodelled and expanded the château. Le Vau's new garden-front can still be seen, although considerably altered and extended by *Hardouin-Mansart. At Versailles and the Collège des Quatre Nations he was assisted by François d'*Orbay, who may have made a major contribution to the overall design.

Architectura, 6/1 (1976), 36–46; Blunt (1982); Hautecœur (1948); Laprade (1960); Placzek (1982); Watkin (1986)

Vauban, Sébastien le Prestre, Maréchal de (1633–1707). French military engineer, architect, and urban designer. He has been credited with the design of over 120 fortresses, and protected France's borders with a series of powerful strongholds, notably those of Lille (1668–74), Maubeuge (1678–81), and Neuf-Brisach (1696–1708). Responsible for planning several new towns, including Sarrelouis (1681–3), Longwy (from 1679), and Neuf-Brisach (1689–99), using regular geometrical layouts, he also designed several monumental gateways including the *Baroque Porte de Paris, Lille (1668–70), complete with *trophies, and the massively severe Porte de Mons, Maubeuge (1681). He was the author of *Mémoire pour servir à l'instruction dans la conduite des sièges* (drawn up 1669, published in 1740 with a memorandum on the defence of fortresses, apparently by another hand) (1667–72), *Traité de l'attaque des places* (1737), *De de la défense des places* (published with the *Traité de l'attaque*, 1828–9), *Véritable manière de bien fortifier* (1702), *Plusieurs maximes bonnes*, etc. (a treatise on building), and a proposal for a fairer system of taxation in France (*Projet d'une dix^{me} royale*, 1707), which was instantly suppressed. He designed the aqueduct of Maintenon (1684–5) that supplied Versailles with water.

Blomfield (1938); Halévy (1925); Lazard (1934); Parent and Verroust (1971); Rébelliau (1962); Rochas d'Aiglun (1910); Sauliol (1931); Toudouze (1954)

Vaudoyer, Antoine-Laurent-Thomas (1756–1846). French architect. A pupil of A.-F. *Peyre, his early unexecuted designs demonstrated a concern for stereometrical purity that was a feature of late-C18 French *Neoclassicism, perhaps influenced by *Boullée and anticipating works by *Ledoux. In 1793, with L.-P. *Baltard and J.-D. *Leroy he founded a special School of Architecture that was to evolve into the École des *Beaux-Arts. He was an important and influential teacher and began the conversion of the Priory of St-Martin-des-Champs, Paris, into the Conservatoire des Arts et Métiers (1845). With Baltard and others he published designs for the Grands Prix (1806–34), and he himself published many works.

Architectural History, 3 (1960), 17–180; Bergdoll (1994*a*) Middleton and Watkin (1987); Papworth (1892); Sturgis *et al.* (1901–2)

Vaudoyer, Léon (1803–72). French architect, the son of A.-L.-T. *Vaudoyer. With *Duban, *Duc, and *Labrouste he became a leading light in architectural circles in the 1830s, and continued work on the Conservatoire des Arts et Métiers, Paris (1845–72), in which he synthesized Graeco-Roman and *Renaissance elements (the conversion of St-Martin-des-Champs into the Conservatoire had been started by his father). He tried to demonstrate that the Greek Classical ideal was central to all subsequent architecture in Southern Europe, and attempted in his own designs to demonstrate a further transformation for modern times, as in his Cathedral-Church of Ste-Marie-Majeure, Marseilles (1855–72), the overall stylistic effect of which is that of a *Byzantine *Romanesque *basilica with *polychrome strips recalling the Duomo at Siena. He also designed the elegant Greek *Doric monument of Général Maximilien-Sébastien Foy (1775–1825), Père-Lachaise Cemetery (1825–32), and the Vaudoyer *mausoleum, Montparnasse Cemetery (1846), both in Paris. He published several important works including perceptive articles on *Ledoux in the 1850s in which he referred to *architecture parlante (architecture expressive of its purpose).

Bergdoll (1994*a*); Drexler (1977); Hitchcock (1977); Middleton and Watkin (1987); van Zanten (1987)

Vaudremer, Joseph-Auguste-Émile (1829–1914). French architect. He trained in the *Blouet-*Gilbert atelier, worked with *Baltard and *Duban, and was appointed Architect to the XIII and XIV *Arondissements* of Paris. He designed the Santé Gaol, Paris (1862–85), in the rational manner of Blouet, but his masterpiece is the powerful freely treated *Romanesque Revival Church of St-Pierre-de-Montrouge, Place Victor Basch, Paris (1864–72), a building of great presence and dignity that may have influenced H. H. *Richardson. He also designed Notre-Dame d'Auteuil, Place d'Auteuil, Paris (1876–80), with stone *vaults possibly inspired by work of *Abadie. His St-Antoine-des-Quinze-Vingts, Avenue Ledru-Rollin, Paris (1901–3), is an interesting asymmetrical composition of some originality.

Drexler (1977); Egbert (1980); Hautecœur (1957); Hitchcock (1977); Middleton and Watkin (1987); Vaudremer (1871)

vault. **1.** Arch the depth of which exceeds the span, i.e. an elongated arch covering a space, or a structure composed of various curved elements in various combinations, built of brick, concrete, stone, etc., and sometimes of plaster and wood to suggest something heavier. It is primarily a ceiling over a space, but may also be a roof, and it may carry a floor or roof. As with an arch, it is constructed so that the stones or other materials of which it is composed support and keep each other in their places. Any volume covered by means of a vault or voussure is said to be *vaulted*, while a system of vaults on a ceiling is called *vaulting*. A vault *bay is defined by transverse ribs.

Types of vault include:

annular: barrel-vault springing from two concentric walls. *See* annular;

barrel, *cylindrical*, *tunnel*, or *wagon*: simplest variety of vault, really an elongated or continuous arch like half a cylinder (i.e. with a semicircular *section and a uniform concave *soffit), spanning the distance between parallel walls or other supports. It can also be segmental in section, or with a profile like a half-ellipse;

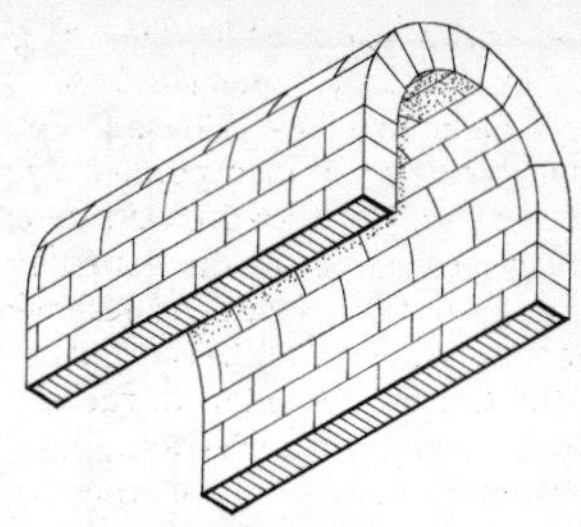

Annular- or barrel-vault. (*After JJS*)

cloister: see *domical*-vault below;

cross: see *groin*-vault below;

cylindrical: see *barrel* above;

domical: rises from a polygonal or square base, and is not a true dome, having curved surfaces (*cells, *severies, or *webs) meeting at precise lines (*groins). Also called a *cloister*-vault (USA);

fan: late-*Gothic form of the *Perpendicular style, only known in England during the Middle Ages (though widely copied later), and consists of inverted half-cones or funnel-shapes with concave sides, their rims touching at the top of the vault and their visible surfaces covered with *blind *panel-*tracery rising from a *capital or *corbel and diverging like the folds of a fan over the entire surface of the distorted cones. The areas between the circular tops of the fans are flat and form concave-sided lozenge-shapes. At King's College Chapel, Cambridge (1508–15), there are large pendent *bosses in the centres of the distorted lozenges, and at Henry VII's Chapel, Westminster Abbey (1503–*c*.1512), the distorted lozenges are covered with blind panel-tracery and there are pendants under the points of each cone as well as in the centres of the lozenges;

groin: formed by the intersection at 90° of two identical *barrel-vaults* (also called *cross-vaults*) creating *groins where they join;

handkerchief: *see* dome;

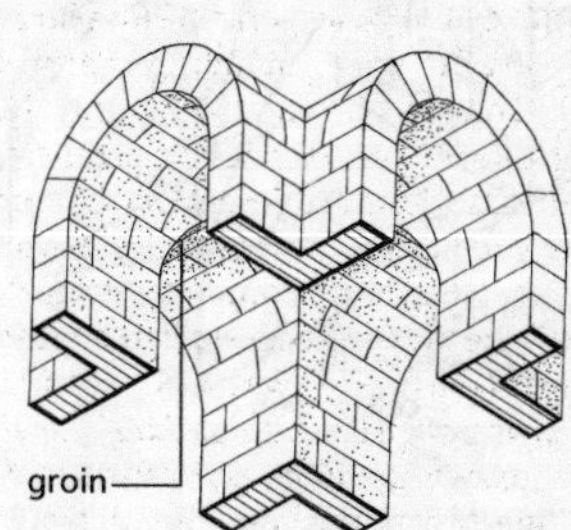

Intersecting barrel-vaults forming groin-vaults. (*After JJS*)

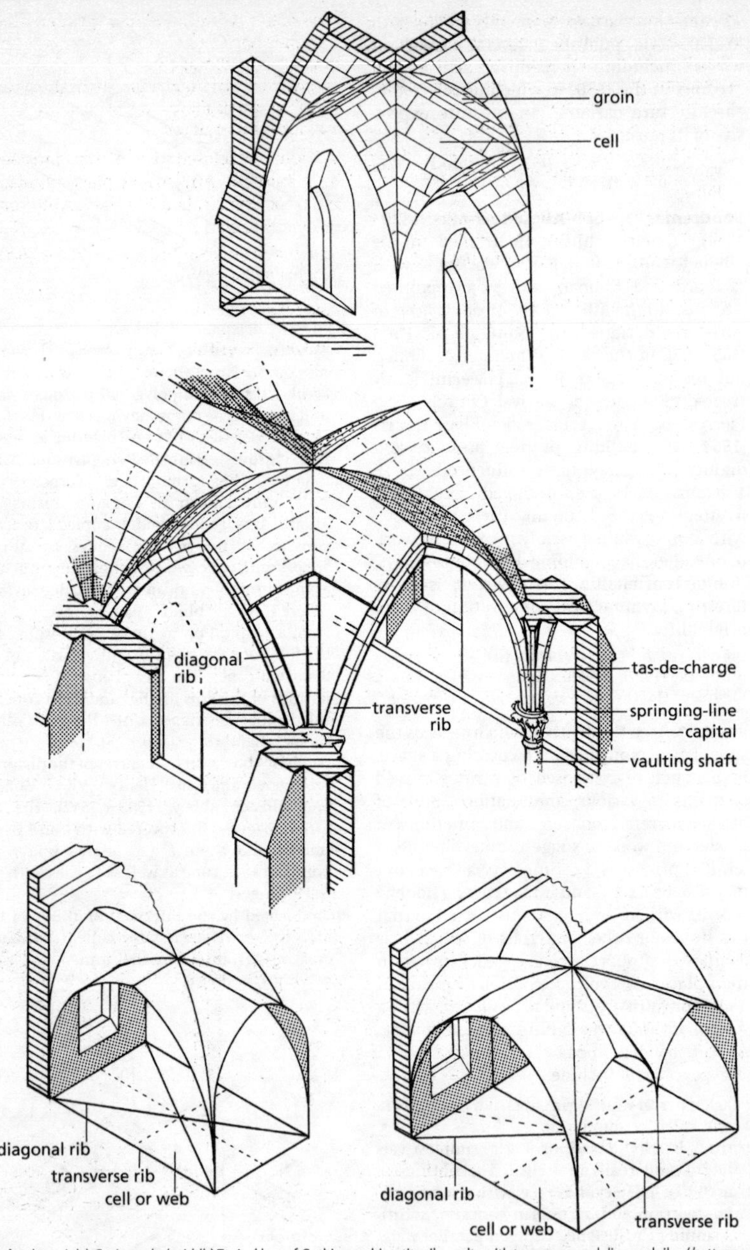

vault. (*top right*) Groin vault. (*middle*) Typical bay of Gothic quadripartite rib-vaults with transverse and diagonal ribs. (*bottom left*) Quadripartite rib-vault. (*bottom right*) Sexpartite rib-vault. (*JJS*)

hyperbolic paraboloid: *see* hyperbolic paraboloid;
lierne: *ribbed* vault with some ribs (*tertiaries* or *liernes*) not running from one of the main springing-points, but from rib to rib, usually joined to them at *bosses;
net: *rib*-vault with the ribs forming a net of distorted lozenges all over the surface of the vault, common in late-Gothic work in Central Europe;
parabolic: vault of parabolic *section, resembling a cone cut along a line parallel to its surface angle, usually constructed of a light *shell of *reinforced concrete;
ploughshare: with wall-ribs springing from points higher than those of the diagonal ribs (therefore called a *stilted* vault) so that more light can be admitted from a *clearstorey window, thus distorted and twisted;
quadripartite: bay divided by diagonal and transverse ribs into four cells or webs;
rampant: barrel-vault with one springing-line higher than the other;
rib: with ribs framing the webs and concealing the groins;
sail: *see* dome;
sexpartite: bay resembling that of a *quadripartite* vault, but further divided by an extra transverse rib so that there are six cells instead of four;
shell: thin self-supporting structure. *See* shell;
stellar: with ribs, including *liernes* (ribs running from rib to rib) and *tiercerons* (rib rising from one of the main springing-points to a position on the *ridge*-rib), forming a star-shaped pattern of ribs;
stilted: see *ploughshare* above;
surbased: with a section less than a semicircle (i.e. a segment);
surmounted: with a section greater than a semicircle;
tierceron: see *stellar* above;
tripartite: on a triangular plan with three parts;
tunnel: see *barrel* above;
wagon: see *barrel* above.

2. Room or enclosed space of any kind covered by a vault. **3.** Any strong place or place of safety. **4.** Burial-chamber or *crypt, vaulted or not. **5.** Cellar.

Gwilt (1903); Nicholson (1835); Papworth (1892); Parker (1850); Sturgis *et al.* (1901–2)

vaulting. *See* vault.

vaulting capital. *Capital of a *pier or *colonnette (or even *corbel) from which a *vault or *rib springs.

vaulting cell. Area or *web framed by the ribs of a *vault.

vaulting shaft. Small shaft or *colonnette which supports a *vault *rib or group of ribs at their springing. It may rise from the ground or from a *corbel set in the masonry.

Vauthier, Louis-Léger (1815–1901). French architect and engineer. He settled in Recife, Brazil, in 1840, designing the layout for the town's development as well as several buildings, including the Santa Isabel Theatre (1840–6). He returned to Paris in 1846.

Freyre (1940)

Vaux, Calvert (1824–95). London-born American architect and landscape-designer, he assisted A. J. *Downing in laying out

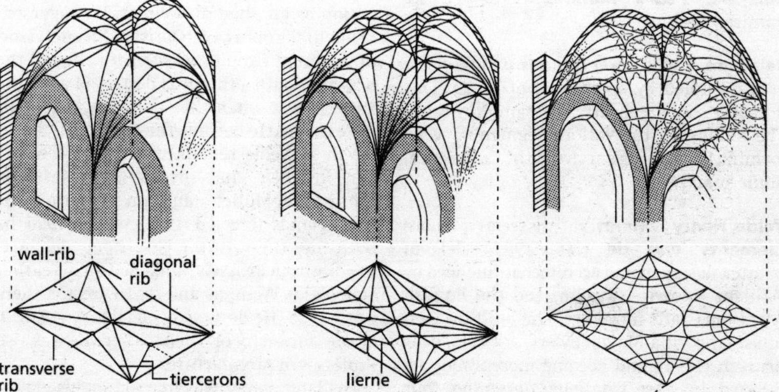

vault. (*left*) Tierceron rib-vault with bosses. (*middle*) Lierne vault. (*JJS*) (*right*) Typical Perpendicular fan-vault. (*JJS*)

the grounds of the Capitol, Smithsonian Institution, and White House, Washington, DC (1850–2). In 1857 he published his much-admired *Villas and Cottages* prompted by Downing's successful *pattern-books, and in the same year approached F. L. *Olmsted to work with him to prepare an entry for the competition to design Central Park, New York, which they won in 1858. Their plan, combining aspects of the English *Picturesque style with ideas taken from *Loudon and *Paxton, and embracing ingenious segregation between vehicles and pedestrians, was very influential. Following this success, Vaux prepared further plans for landscapes (including Prospect Park, Brooklyn, New York (1866–73)), and was assisted by the English-born Jacob Wrey Mould (1825–86), a pupil of Owen *Jones. It was Mould who designed many of the architectural features in Vaux's parks, including the *Ruskinian *Gothic Terrace (1858–71) at Central Park. Vaux and Mould worked together on designs for the Metropolitan Museum of Art (1874–80) and the Museum of Natural History (1874–7), both in New York, but only part of each was realized. Although Vaux's greatest achievements were in the field of landscape-design, he was an accomplished domestic architect. He designed the *Gothic Revival Tilden House, New York (1881–4), later the National Arts Club.

American Association of Architectural Bibliographers: Papers, 5 (1968), 69–106; Cook (1972); Francis (1980); *Journal of the Society of Architectural Historians*, 6 (Jan.–June 1947),1–12; Placzek (1982—contains a comprehensive list of works); Reed and Duckworth (1967); Roper (1973); Schuyler and Censer (1992); van Vynckt (1993); Vaux (1970)

Vázquez, Pedro Ramírez (1919–). *See* Ramírez Vásquez.

velarium. Awning over the *cavea* (whole of the area occupied by spectators) of an Ancient Roman *court, *theatre, or *amphitheatre. The fixings for the various segments (*vela) forming the awning survive at the Colosseum, Rome (*c.* AD 75–82).

Velde, Henry (*or* **Henri**, but this seems spurious) **Clements van de** (1863–1957). Belgian painter, designer, and architect. Influenced by William *Morris, *Ruskin, and the English *Arts-and-Crafts movement, he built his own house, the Villa Bloemenwerf, at Uccle, near Brussels (1895), and became increasingly interested in *Art Nouveau, designing four rooms for Siegfried Bing's (1838–1905) celebrated gallery, the *Maison de l'Art Nouveau*, Paris (1895–6), and achieved international recognition for the interiors and furniture he exhibited at Dresden in 1897. His success in Germany (e.g. interiors for the Havana Cigar Company, Berlin (1899–1901), and for the Kaiser's barber, Haby (1901), also in Berlin) encouraged him to move there, in 1900, where he served (from 1901) as art-adviser to the reigning Grand Duke Wilhelm Ernst (1901–18) of Saxe-Weimar-Eisenach and published his *Die Renaissance im moderne Kunstgewerbe* (The Renaissance of Contemporary Arts and Crafts—1901, 1903). He designed exquisite interiors for the art-loving Graf Harry Kessler (1868–1937) in Weimar (1903), and the new Grand-Ducal Saxon Schools of Art and Arts and Crafts (1904–11), also in Weimar, directing the latter School from 1908. A founder-member of the *Deutscher Werkbund (1907), he consolidated his position as a leading designer with the sumptuous decorations for the Folkwang Museum (now Karl Ernst Osthaus Museum), Hagen (1900–12), his finest creations in the curvilinear Art Nouveau style. He prepared proposals for the Théatre des Champs-Élysées, Paris, in 1910, but *Perret's realized building was more severe. Van de Velde's use of curved forms in his buildings (e.g. the Weimar School and the rather eerie Theatre for the Deutscher Werkbund Exhibition, Cologne (1914—destroyed)), led to a fundamental disagreement within the Werkbund, *Muthesius stressing *industrialized building, standardization, and the machine, while van de Velde objected to the restrictions this would place on the individual designer. War in 1914 led to his resignation as an alien at Weimar. He suggested *Endell, *Gropius, or *Obrist as his successor: in the event Gropius was appointed, and the Arts-and-Crafts ethos was destroyed after the 1914–18 war when the Grand-Ducal Schools were merged to become the *Bauhaus.

Van de Velde remained active as a writer and teacher, and from 1923 designed the Kröller-Müller Museum, Otterlo, The Netherlands (erected 1937–54). In 1926 he built up the Institut Supérieur des Arts Décoratifs in Brussels, modelled on his earlier Schools at Weimar, and was Director there until 1935. He designed the Library (1936–9) at the University of Ghent, where he was also Professor of Architecture.

His later career was marked by his claims to have been an early protagonist of the

*Modern Movement, and his attitude towards the important retrospective 1952 Art Nouveau Exhibition in Zurich was equivocal, if not hostile, as it seems he feared it would draw attention to his skills in a style he had repudiated, even though from the end of C20 it is clear that his best work was carried out before 1914. He published *Déblaiement d'art* (Clearing (i.e. Purifying) of Art—1894), *Aperçus en vue d'une synthèse d'art* (Prospects for a Synthesis of Art—1895), *Vom neuen Stil* (Concerning the New Style—1907), and *Geschichte meines Lebens* (Story of my Life—1962).

Architectural Review, 133/793 (Mar. 1963), 165–8; Curjel (1955); Delevoy *et al.* (1963); Hammacher (1967); Hüter (1967); Jervis (1984); Lenning (1951); Sembach (1989); Tschudi-Madsen (1967); van de Velde (1903, 1962)

vellar cupola. Dome like a *sail-vault*, i.e. with its diameter equal to the diagonal of the square from which it rises, the arched forms between the springing-lines creating an impression of a floating awning or sail billowing upwards. It is really a semicircular dome with four sides sliced off, coinciding with the sides of the square.

velum (*pl.* **vela**). Segment of the awning (*velarium) of a Roman *amphitheatre, etc.

Venetian arch. *See* arch.

Venetian blind. *Jalousie, or sun-blind formed of horizontal laths or slats that can be drawn up or down, and swivelled.

Venetian crenellation. *Palladian type of *crenellation with balls set on a series of curved cops (*see* battlement) resembling a row of pawns in a game of Chess. A good example is at the *piano-nobile level of *Burlington's *Villa at Chiswick, near London (1726–9).

Venetian dentil. Common medieval moulding in Venice consisting of a projecting *band with its upper and lower parts cut alternately into notches sloping to the middle of the band, producing the effect of a double row of staggered *dentils.

Venetian door. *Serliana used as a door.

Venetian Gothic Revival. Phase of the *Gothic Revival that drew on exemplars from Venice, featuring *polychrome brickwork, plate-*tracery, and elaborately patterned *arcades. It was promoted by *Street's *Brick and Marble in the Middle Ages: Notes of a Tour in the North of Italy* (1855) and popularized by *Ruskin's *Stones of Venice* (1851–3).

Venetian window. *See* serliana.

Vennecool, Steven Jacobs (1657–1719). Dutch architect. He designed the *astylar Town Hall at Enkhuizen, one of the best late-C17 buildings in The Netherlands (1686–8), and the Manor House of Middachten, De Steeg (1695), with its *battered *basement rising from the moat.

Cruickshank (1996); Gelder and Duverger (1954); Rosenberg, Slive, and Ter Kuile (1977)

Venturi, Robert Charles (1925–). American *Post-Modern architect. He set up his own practice with John Rauch (1930–) in 1964, later (1967) joined by his wife, Denise *Scott Brown (1931–), and later still by Steven Izenour (1930–). His early buildings include the Vanna Venturi House, Chestnut Hill, Pa. (1961–5). In 1966 his *Complexity and Contradictions in Architecture* proposed (among much else) that ambiguity, tensions, and intricate complexities should replace the blandness of *International Modernism (getting in a dig at *Mies van der Rohe's pronouncement that 'less is more' by stating 'less is a bore'), and the book made his reputation. He drew attention to the sources of *meaning* in architecture, insisted that architecture should deal in allusion and symbolism, and was critical of *Functionalist dogma. With his wife and Izenour he wrote *Learning from Las Vegas* (1972, 1977) which suggested that architects should draw on what ordinary people like rather than impose pre-determined forms on the public.

Among the paradigmatic buildings of the firm, Guild House Retirement Home, Philadelphia, Pa. (1960–4), the Humanities Building of the State University of New York at Purchase (1968–73), the Dixwell Fire Station, New Haven, Conn. (1970–4), Franklin Court, Philadelphia (1972–6), the Allen Art Museum, Oberlin College, Ohio (1973–6), the Brant-Johnson House, Vail, Colo. (1975–7), the Gordon Wu Hall, Butler College, Princeton University, NJ (1980–3), and the Seattle Art Museum, Seattle, Wash. (1984–91), may be mentioned. In 1986 the firm won the competition to design the Sainsbury Wing, National Gallery, London (completed 1991), a building with a partial continuation of the Classical *Order of *Wilkins's original *elevation facing Trafalgar Square. Other recent works include the Museum of Contemporary Art, San Diego, La Jolla, Calif. (1986–96).

Diamonstein (1985); Drew (1972); Drexler (1980); Emanuel (1994); Jodidio (1993, 1997); Klotz (1988); Mead (1989); Stern (1977); Venturi (1966, 1996); Venturi and Rauch (1978); Venturi, Scott Brown, and Izenour (1977)

veranda, verandah. Light external open gallery, or covered way, with a sloping or *lean-to roof carried by slender (usually metal) columns or posts, attached to a building, often in front of the windows of the principal rooms, affording shelter from the sun as well as a pleasant external seating area with access from French windows. Sometimes it can be very decorative, with *trellis-work and plants, and may extend all round a house, forming a *skirt-roof. It was a feature that became popular from the early C19.

verge. 1. Slight projection formed by a pitched roof over the *naked of a *gable-wall. The junction between the tiles on the roof and the top of the wall has to be watertight, and this is achieved by creating a tight joint, using tiles and mortar (*parged verge*), *tumbled brickwork, etc. If the roof is extended beyond the naked of the wall, with a board fixed under the edge of the roof-covering, that board (often decorated, carved, and cut with *fret-work) is termed *barge- or verge-board. **2.** *Shaft of a Classical column. **3.** Small ornamental shaft of a medieval *colonnette, e.g. the *Purbeck-marble shafts on *piers of the *First Pointed style of English Gothic.

Verge, John (1782–1862). British architect. He settled in Australia in the 1820s and designed in a competent, eclectic manner; his buildings were freely *Greek Revival, *castellated, *Tudor *Revival, and even *Chinoiserie in style. His best work was probably Elizabeth Bay House, Sydney (1832), which incorporated an elliptical staircase and hall, but he also created many fine late-*Georgian houses with very wide *verandahs (often with the roofs carried on Classical (usually *Doric) columns). Other works include Camden Park, Menangle (1831–2), Tusculum, Potts Point, Sydney (1824), and the Homestead, Braidwood, near Canberra (*c*.1838).

Cruickshank (1996)

Verity, Francis (Frank) Thomas (1864–1937). English architect. He studied in London and in Paris at the Atelier *Blouet, and became a partner in the practice of his father, Thomas *Verity in 1889, specializing in theatre design. His grandest contributions to the urban fabric of London were his *astylar apartment-blocks in the style of the Champs-Élysées *façades in Paris, of which Cleveland House, opposite St James's Palace (1906), 12 Hyde Park Place, Marble Arch (1908), and 25 and 26 Berkeley Square (1906) were the most distinguished.

Gray (1985)

Verity, Thomas (1837–91). English architect. Early in his career he assisted *Fowke and H. Y. D. *Scott at the South Kensington Museum and the Albert Hall. He designed the Neo-Renaissance Criterion Theatre and Restaurant, Piccadilly Circus (1870–4—mutilated), the Comedy Theatre (1881), and, with his son, F. T. *Verity, 96–7 Piccadilly (1891) and the Imperial Theatre (1901), all in London.

Dixon and Muthesius (1985); Felstead, Franklin, and Pinfield (1993)

vermiculation. Decoration of a surface by means of random channels resembling worm-tracks. *See* rustication.

vernacular architecture. Unpretentious, simple, indigenous, traditional structures made of local materials and following well-tried forms and *types, normally considered in three categories: agricultural (barns, farms, etc.), domestic, and industrial (foundries, potteries, smithies, etc.). In England and Germany the great range of *timber-framed medieval and later buildings would largely be classed as vernacular architecture, while humble rural structures, such as cottages, would also fall into the category. It was first taken seriously in the late C18 when attempts were made to re-create it as part of the *Picturesque movement, and it provided exemplars for C19 architects, especially those of the *Gothic and *Domestic Revivals and the *Arts-and-Crafts movement. In the USA *Colonial and simple *clap-boarded buildings provided models for designers, especially for the *Stick and *Shingle styles. It has been contrasted with *polite* architecture, and even classed as *architecture without architects*, but this is not really true, as most vernacular architecture drew on more sophisticated designs somewhere in its development, while architects such as *Devey, *Lutyens, and *Webb derived much of their styles from vernacular buildings, so it was never really an isolated phenomenon, an architecture of the proletariat, rural or urban.

Alcock, Barley, Dixon, and Meeson (1996); Brunskill (1987, 1990, 1994); Clifton-Taylor (1987); Kemp (1987); Oliver (1997)

Vertue, Robert (*fl.* 1475–d. 1506). English master-mason. He was at Westminster Abbey in a junior capacity from 1475 to 1480, and in a more senior one from 1482. He was appointed King's Master-Mason (*c.*1487) and carried out works at Greenwich. With his brother William *Vertue, he designed the Abbey Church at Bath, Somerset (begun 1501), with its beautiful fan-*vault.

Vertue was involved in several works, but among his most important activities was the design of the *Lady Chapel, now King Henry VII's (reigned 1485–1509) Chapel, Westminster Abbey, the foundation-stone for which was laid in 1502/3. Furthermore, Vertue, *Lebons, and *Janyns were involved in the preparation of the sepulchre of the King. He was also engaged at St George's Chapel, Windsor, Berkshire, including the fan-vaults. In his will he gave directions that he should be buried in the Abbey Church of St Augustine, Canterbury, Kent, with which he seems to have had connections, probably as Master-Mason. He may have designed the new bell-tower there (1461–1516). His son, **Robert Vertue jun.** (*fl.* 1506–55), was Master of the Works at Evesham Abbey, Worcestershire, where he designed the splendid buildings for Abbot Clement Lichfield (1514–39), including the spectacular *Perpendicular free-standing bell-tower. For Abbot Lichfield he also designed the *Mortuary Chapel in the Church of All Saints, Evesham, shortly before 1513, with a fan-vault resembling the work at King Henry VII's Chapel, Westminster Abbey, which suggests the younger Vertue either had a hand in the Westminster work, had his father's drawings, or knew the fabric well. Also in the Westminster style is the exquisite *Chantry Chapel of St Clement in St Lawrence's Church, Evesham (*c.*1520), also built for Abbot Lichfield.

Harvey (1987); Pevsner, *Buildings of England, Worcestershire* (1968)

Vertue, William (*fl.* 1501–d. 1527). English master-mason, the brother of Robert *Vertue sen. He worked with his brother on Bath Abbey Church, Somerset, from 1501. From *c.*1502/3 the *vaults of the *nave, *aisles, and *transepts of St George's Chapel, Windsor, Berkshire, were under construction, and it is known William Vertue and John *Aylmer contracted to vault seven *bays of the *choir of the Chapel to follow the design of the nave-vault. They also contracted to build the flying *buttresses, *parapets, *pinnacles, and all carvings.

Vertue visited King's College Chapel, Cambridge, on at least three occasions, and in 1507 there are records he was at a meeting in Cambridge with Henry *Smyth and others to discuss the resumption of the works there. In 1509 Vertue again visited Cambridge with Henry *Redman, probably to act as advisers on the fan-vault, and in 1512 Vertue and *Wastell are known to have dined in Hall shortly after Wastell signed the contract to build the vault, so it is reasonable to surmise that Vertue, as one of the great masters of the design of fan-vaults, was called in as consultant.

He became King's Master-Mason at the Tower of London in 1510, but his main work at the time was at King Henry VII's (reigned 1485–1509) Chapel, Westminster Abbey, where he was in charge after the death of his brother in 1506. He also designed buildings at Corpus Christi College, Oxford (1512–18), and visited the site on several occasions. He may have supplied designs for Thornbury Castle, Gloucestershire (*c.*1511), and probably designed the Church of St Peter ad Vincula, Tower of London, to replace the earlier structure destroyed in a fire (1512). He and Henry Redman designed the west side of the *Court of Eton College, Buckinghamshire, including Lupton's Tower, and Vertue probably was responsible for Lupton's *Chantry Chapel in Eton College Chapel (1515). Humphrey *Coke was also involved in the works at Eton. Vertue designed the *cloister and fan-vaulted cloister-chapel of St Stephen in the Palace of Westminster (1526).

Vertue must be regarded as one of England's greatest architects. His mastery of the techniques and intricacies of fan-vault construction enriched the architectural heritage of late-*Gothic England, and his work at Windsor and Westminster is unparalleled for its beauty. It is fair to say it was the culmination of English medieval architecture.

Harvey (1987)

vesica piscis. **1.** *Glory*, *mandala, or *mandorla* of the upright almond-shaped type produced by the geometrical process of placing two equilateral triangles above and below a base-line as mirror-images and striking arcs from each end of the base-line passing through the other points of the triangle. This creates two pointed arches base-to-base, commonly found as a vertical *aureole enclosing of figure of e.g. Christ in Majesty. Its resemblance to a fish, or to a fish's bladder, relates it to the *Chrismon. The shape is also found in windows, e.g. the *rose-window in the south *transept of Lincoln Cathedral. **2.** *Light in *Second Pointed Curvilinear or Flowing *tracery resembling a tadpole or the air-bladder of a fish.

Vesnin Brothers. Three Russian architects, **Leonid Aleksandrovich** (1880–1933), **Viktor Aleksandrovich** (1882–1950), and **Aleksandr Aleksandrovich** (1883–1959), they worked together on various projects during the period when *Constructivism was fashionable. Aleksandr co-edited the journal *Sovremenia Arkhitektura* (Contemporary Architecture) with Moisei Yakovlevich *Ginsburg. The Brothers' design for a Palace of Labour (1923), although not built, was a paradigm of Constructivism, as was the project (by A. and V. Vesnin) for the *Leningradskaya Pravda* (Leningrad Truth) Building, Moscow (1923), which exposed the lifts (elevators), loudspeakers, searchlights, and digital clock on the exterior of the overtly framed structure. Their largest realized works were the *curtain-walled Mostorg Department Store, Moscow (1926–7), the Cultural Palace, Vostochnaya Ulitsa, Moscow (1931–7—later called ZIL—a building that looked to *International Modernism for its style), and the Dnieper Dam and Hydro-Electric Station, Dneprostoi (1929–31).

Khan-Magomedov (1986, 1987); Kopp (1970); Kroha and Hrüza (1973); Lissitzky (1970); Shvidkovsky (1970)

vestibule. 1. Enclosed or partly enclosed space (*vestibulum*) in front of the main entrance of a *Greek or *Roman house or building, i.e. an entrance-court or fore-court. **2.** Entrance-lobby or hall immediately between the entrance-door and the interior of a building. **3.** Ante-chamber acting as a baffle between e.g. a corridor and a room, really a communication-lobby.

Vestier, Nicolas-Jacques-Antoine (1765–1816). French *Neoclassical architect. He designed the Rue des Colonnes, Paris (1793–5), including the *primitive unfluted *Paestum *Doric *arcades, one of the most remarkable designs of the French Revolutionary period. He also designed houses in the Rue Mont-Blanc and Rue Caumartin, the Théâtre Gymnase (after 1795), the apartment-block at 1 Rue de Helder, (in which, as in the Rue des Colonnes, miniature Doric columns are used for the balustrades at first-floor level), the Passage Delorme (1808), proposals for a church at Meslay-le-Vidame (1810–16—where square Paestum Doric columns featured), and the Orphanage, Mont-Valérien (1812–14). Two of his sons, the appropriately named **Archimède** (1794–1859) and **Phidias** (1796–1874), also became Neoclassical architects. Archimède designed railway-stations (e.g. Brest) and grand country-houses in Touraine, while Phidias did the railway-station in Tours (1851) and became Inspector of Historic Monuments for Indre-et-Loire.

Architects' Journal, 190/2 (12 July 1989), 32–41; *Archives de l'Art Français*, 24 (1969), 309–21; Curl (1992); Thieme and Becker (1940)

vestry. 1. Room adjoining the *chancel in a church where the vestments are kept and the clergy are vested. **2.** *Sacristy, often large, where books, sacred vessels, and vestments are stored, and where meetings may be held.

via. 1. Roman paved street or road. **2.** Gap between the *mutules of a Roman *Doric or *Tuscan *Order.

viaduct. Structure, often a series of arches, carrying a road, railway, etc., over a valley.

vice, vis, vyse. Spiral *stair constructed round a central *newel or *pier.

Vicente de Oliveira, Mateus (1706–86). Portuguese architect. He worked under *Ludovice and then established himself in practice. He designed the exquisite *Rococo Palácio Nacional, Queluz, near Lisbon (1747–60), completed by J.-B. Robillion (d. 1768), who also designed the gardens. The Estrêla Church, Lisbon (1777–82) was built to his designs.

Cruickshank (1996); Kubler and Soria (1959); Smith (1968); Watkin (1986)

Vicenzo, Antonio di (*c.*1350–1401/2). Italian architect. He designed the gigantic brick *Gothic church of San Petronio, Bologna (from 1390), and around the same time produced drawings for Milan Cathedral showing a main vault some 23 metres higher than that realized, although the basic design remained unchanged. He appears to have been one of the great masters of the Gothic style in Italy.

Cruickshank (1996)

Victorian. Of the period in which Queen Victoria reigned (1837–1901).

Vienna Sezession. *See* Sezession.

vignette, vinette. 1. *See* trail. **2.** Low ornamental metal railing on a window-*cill or *balconet, to prevent flower-pots, etc., from falling.

Vignola, Giacomo *or* **Jacopo Barozzi da** (1507–73). Born in Vignola, near Modena, he became the most important architect working in Rome immediately after the death of *Michelangelo. With *Ammannati, Michelangelo (as consultant), and *Vasari he designed (for Pope Julius III (1550–5)) the Villa Giulia, Rome (1551–5), one of the great works of *Mannerism in which *villa, *terraces, hemicycles, and gardens were composed as a whole. It was intended as an elegant retreat for the Pope, the hemicycle clearly intended to be a reflection of *Bramante's Belvedere Court in the Vatican (begun 1505). Around the same time he built the Church of Sant'Andrea, Via Flaminia, Rome (1550–4), the earliest example of the use of an elliptical *drum and dome set on a rectangular base: the building's external appearance was derived from Roman tombs and the *Pantheon, while the body of the church had an applied *temple-front of *pilasters carrying a *pediment. His later Church of Sant'Anna dei Palafrenieri, Vatican, Rome (begun 1572), has an elliptical plan with a dome over it. Both buildings were influential on architects of the *Baroque period, for the ellipse was to become a favoured device, especially in Rome and Central Europe.

In 1559 Vignola was appointed by Cardinal Alessandro Farnese (1520–89) as Architect of the Palazzo Farnese at Caprarola, near Rome, already begun on a pentagonal plan to designs (1520s) by *Peruzzi and *Sangallo the Younger for Pope Paul III (1534–49). It has a circular *cortile in which *rustication and overlapping *triumphal arches feature, and an ingenious, very beautiful spiral staircase with *Tuscan columns and a winding Roman *Doric *string. With its ramps, huge flights of external stairs, and formal gardens, it is one of the most majestic ensembles of C16, brilliantly connected to the adjoining village. The building's great *cornice, with its plain vertical *consoles, was widely copied, notably in C19. Vignola designed the Mother Church of the Jesuits in Rome, *Il Gesù*, begun in 1568 (also for Cardinal Farnese). The plan has similarities to that of *Alberti's Sant'Andrea, Mantua, with a tall, tunnel-vaulted *nave, a series of *chapels instead of *aisles, and a *façade (begun 1571 by della *Porta) consisting of two storeys of *Orders of pilasters and columns, with the *buttresses hidden behind *scrolls, a device used earlier at Alberti's Church of Santa Maria Novella, Florence. The Baroque decorations of the interior were added in 1668–73. Churches derived from the exemplar of *Il Gesù* were built all over Roman Catholic Europe and Latin America, so the Roman church was Vignola's most influential building.

Vignola was Architect to the Basilica of San Pietro, Rome (1567–73), where he carried on Michelangelo's designs. He wrote *La Regola delli Cinque Ordini d'Architettura* (The Rule for the Five Orders of Architecture—1562) in which (clearly influenced by *Serlio) he established paradigms of the *Orders based on *Antique examples, with clear guidance for setting them out based on a simple modular system. It was an enormously useful and influential book, especially in France, and appeared in many editions and in several countries.

Harris (1990); Heydenreich and Lotz (1974); Lotz (1977); Murray (1969, 1986); Orazi (1982); Patetta (1990); Vignola (1596); Walcher Casotti (1960); Watkin (1986)

Vignon, Alexandre-Pierre (1762–1828). French architect of the Revolutionary and Napoleonic periods. A pupil of *Leroy and *Ledoux, he was commissioned to build the *Temple de la Gloire* (after 1813 the Madeleine), Paris, in 1806 to be erected on the foundations of an earlier church (1746) begun by *Contant d'Ivry, and revised by G.-M. Couture (1732–99) in the 1770s. It is a grand octastyle *Corinthian building on a high *podium resembling a rectangular Roman temple (a *type only revived from C18), with an interior (1828–40) by Jean-Jacques-Marie Huvé (1783–1852) derived from Roman *thermae.

Biver (1963); Hautecœur (1953); Kriéger (1937); Middleton and Watkin (1987); Vignon (1806, 1816)

villa. 1. *Antique Roman country-house or farmstead of three basic types:

villa rustica: house in the country with spacious accommodation for the owner and his family, and quarters for staff and workers, stores, and animals (the latter called *villa fructuaria*). It was really a grand farmhouse with refinements;

villa suburbana: house near a town, lacking service buildings (e.g. *Palladio's Villa Capra, Vicenza (*c*.1566–70));

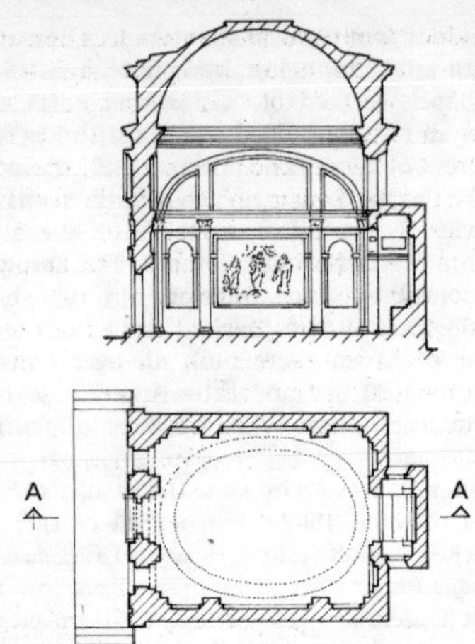

Plan and section of the Church of Sant'Andrea, Via Flaminia, Rome.

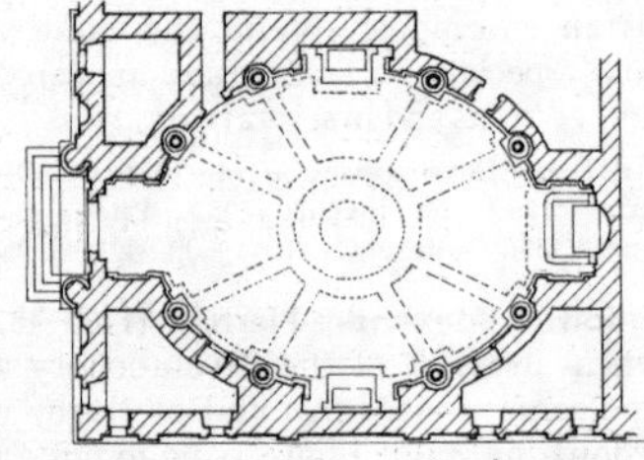

Plan of the Church of Sant'Anna dei Palafrenieri, Rome.

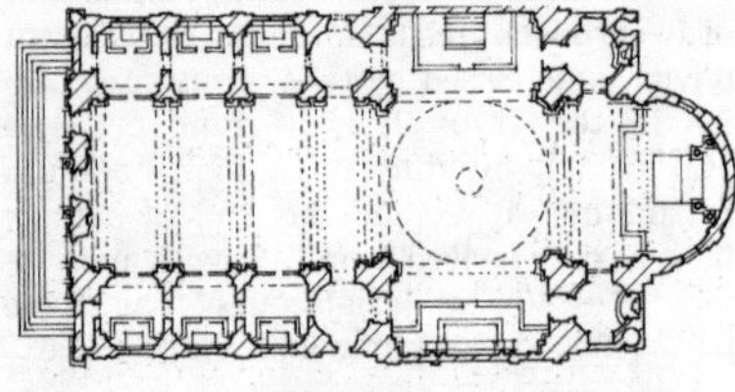

Plan of the Church of *Il Gesù*, Rome, showing the wall-pier arrangement with side-chapels between the piers instead of aisles.

Vignola.

villa urbana: essentially a retreat, with spacious rooms, access to agreeable gardens, fine views over the landscape and the sea (if possible), galleries, and parts suitable for summer and winter use. *Pliny's villas were paradigms of this type, which contained all the conveniences, and more, of a town or city mansion.

2. *Renaissance country-house that was almost a cultural centre, where the like-minded could enjoy civilized life in beautiful surroundings, with fine gardens, works of art, and pleasant views. *Palladio's designs for villas were important exemplars for C18, and led to the creation of some grand country-houses, e.g. Kent's Holkham Hall, Norfolk, and *Paine and *Adam's Kedleston Hall, Derbyshire. **3.** Detached C19 house set in its own grounds on the fringes of a town, often with outbuildings and wings. **4.** Small detached house in a modest garden in the suburbs in the late C19 and C20.

Ackerman (1967, 1990); Arnold (1996); Coffin (1979); Mansuelli (1958); Robertson (1945); Ruffinière du Prey (1994)

Villagrán García, José (1901–82). Mexican architect and teacher. In 1923 he was appointed Chief Architect to the Department of Public Health, in which capacity he designed the Hygiene Institute, Popotla, Mexico City (1925). Regarded as the father of modern *Functionalism and *Rationalism in his country, his massive Instituto Nacional de Cardiologia, Mexico City (1937—with later additions), and sundry other works, including the Architectural School at the Universidad Nacional de México (1951), demonstrated his debt to *International Modernism, and especially the influence of Le *Corbusier and *Gropius.

Arquitectura México, 12/55 (Sept. 1956); Born (1937); Cetto (1961); Emanuel (1994)

Villanueva, Carlos Raúl (1900–75). Venezuelan architect, born in England. He was Architect to the Venezuelan Ministry of Public Works (1929–39), and was a tireless promoter of *International Modernism in his country. He designed the enormous housing-estates known as Dos de Diciembre (1943–5—with J. M. Mijares, José Hoffman, and C. Branco) and the El Paraiso development (1954—with Mijares and C. Celis), both in Caracas. His bold, even brutal expression of structure gave the buildings a forbidding character. He designed several works for University City, Caracas, including the Olympic Stadium with its *shell-concrete *cantilevered elements (1950–2), the Auditorium (Aula Magna—1952), and the Covered Square (Plaza Cubierta—also 1952). He founded the School of Architecture in the University of Venezuela in 1944 and taught there for the rest of his life, designing new buildings for the school (1950–7), and influencing succeeding generations of Latin-American architects.

Emanuel (1994); Hitchcock (1955); Moholy-Nagy (1964); van Vynckt (1993)

Villanueva, Juan de (1739–1811). Spanish architect. He worked in the *Churrigueresque and *Baroque styles before visiting Rome (1759–65) when he adopted *Neoclassicism. He and his brother **Diego** (1715–74) published a collection of critical papers on architecture (1766) in which they promoted a purer form of *Classicism than that currently being practised in Spain. Appointed to work at El Escorial by the Jeronymite Order, he soon came to the notice of the Spanish Royal House. King Carlos III (1759–88) and his son, the future Carlos IV (1788–1819), became his patrons. He designed the Palafox Chapel, Burgo de Osma Cathedral (1770–83), the Casita de Arriba in the Escorial (1773), the Casita del Príncipe, El Pardo (1784), and his masterpiece, the Prado Museum, Madrid (1787–9), a powerful Neoclassical composition, the finest of its type in all Spain. He also designed the cemetery and *chapel, Puerta da Fuencarral, Madrid (1809).

Chueca Goitia and Miguel (1949); Gaya Nuño (1966); Kubler and Soria (1959); Papworth (1892); Schubert (1924)

Villard *or* **Wilars de Honnecourt** *or* **Honecort** (*c*.1175–*c*.1240). French master-mason and author of the most important and wide-ranging medieval architectural treatise to survive, the so-called Lodge Book, apparently designed to assist apprentices and others. It includes sections on architecture, machinery, figures, sculpture, theory, and drawings of animals. Now in the Bibliothèque Nationale, Paris, the Lodge Book contains plans of actual buildings as well as unrealized designs. He seems to have worked at Cambrai, Lausanne, Meaux, St-Quentin, and the Cistercian Church at Vaucelles, and also ventured into Central Europe, where he may have taken part in design-work at Pilis, near Esztergom, Hungary (*c*.1220). During his travels he recorded buildings and details he had seen, including works at Chartres, Laon, and Rheims. Paul Frankl has gone so far as to dub Villard the 'Gothic Vitruvius'.

Barnes (1982); Bowie (1968); Bucher (1979); Frankl (1960, 1962); Hahnloser (1937); Recht (1989)

Vinci, Leonardo da (1452–1519). *See* Leonardo.

Vincidor, Tommaso (*also known as* **Thomas Vincenz**, *c*.1495–1560). Bolognese architect who had worked in *Raphael's studio in Rome. He designed the courtyard of Breda Castle, The Netherlands (from 1536), one of the first early *Renaissance buildings in that country. He was also responsible for the design of the imposing monument to Count Engelbert II of Nassau-Dillenburg (d. 1504) in the Hervormde Kerk, Breda: this work of funerary architecture was the model for the monument of Sir Francis Vere (1560–1609) in Westminster Abbey, London (1614).

Baedeker, *Belgium and Holland* (1905); Murray (1986)

vine. *See* vignette.

vinette. *See* vignette.

Vingboons, *or* **Vinckeboons, Philip(pu)s** (1607/8–78). Dutch domestic architect who is known primarily from two volumes of his works published in 1648 and 1674 which proved influential, notably in England. He designed in a Classical style derived from the work of van *Campen. Typical of his work are 168 Herengracht (1638), 319 Keizersgracht (1639), and 364–70 Herengracht (1662), all in Amsterdam. His brother **Justus (Joost) Vingboons** (*fl.* 1650–70) designed the handsome Trippenhuis, Amsterdam (1662), with a *Giant *Order of *pilasters rising 2½ storeys. He completed Jean de la *Vallée's *Riddarhus* (House of the Nobility), Stockholm (*c*.1641–74), with a *Giant Order reminiscent of Dutch *Palladianism.

Gelder and Duverger (1954); Kuyper (1980); Ottenheym (1989)

Viollet-le-Duc, Eugène-Emmanuel (1814–79). French architect, archaeologist, rationalist, scholar, and theorist, author of the influential *Dictionnaire raisonné de l'architecture française du XIe au XVIe siècle* (published 1854–68, with a definitive edition of 1875) and the important *Entretiens* (Discourses) on architecture (1858–72). The *Dictionary* helped to consolidate the course of the *Gothic Revival in France (one of its aims was to promote Gothic through logical exposition), and it was scoured for details in England and Germany: *Burges noted that all the English Gothic Revivalists of his generation 'cribbed' from Viollet-le-Duc, though probably not one in ten ever read the text. The fine illustrations helped to create an international taste for French Gothic, especially of the early period.

Under the aegis of Prosper Mérimée (1803–70), dramatist, wit, and Inspector-General of Historic Monuments, Viollet-le-Duc established a reputation as a restorer of medieval buildings, notably the Madeleine, Vézelay (1840–59), Sainte-Chapelle, Paris (from 1840—with *Duban), and Notre Dame Cathedral, Paris (1844–64—with J.-B.-A. *Lassus). It was primarily through the study and restoration of historic buildings such as these that the Gothic Revival gained momentum in France, not least through a system of training instigated by Viollet and his colleagues. From 1844 he restored Carcassonne, including the walls and fortifications, but this, and especially his work on the Château de Pierrefonds, Oise (1858–70), drew criticism for their dominant, drastic, and conjectural natures.

His interpretation of Gothic was as a rational style, the construction clearly defined by *buttresses and flying buttresses supporting *ribs and *vaults, the whole essentially a *skeletal system, with *curtain-walls and *webs really non-structural infill. Forces were transferred to the ground by these systems, and this notion of Gothic became widely accepted, especially by apologists for the much later *Modern Movement (even though surviving ruined Gothic buildings might sometimes have prompted different conclusions). In his *Entretiens* he suggested similarities between iron structures and Gothic systems, and proposed new techniques to design *framed buildings that would be a modern equivalent of Gothic. His ideas had a profound effect on many architects, including *Perret and Frank Lloyd *Wright, especially his insistence on the importance of structure, purpose, dynamics, techniques, and the visible expression of these. In particular he saw parallels between the giving of form to myths in Antiquity and the possibilities in C19 to express mechanical power. Such views made some critics see him as a proto-Modernist, and there can be no doubt about his influence on the architectural worlds of the Continent and the USA.

He published *Dictionnaire raisonné du mobilier français de l'époque carolingienne à la renaissance* (Analytical Dictionary of French Furniture from the *Carolingian Period to the *Renaissance—1858–75), *Histoire de l'habitation humaine depuis les temps préhistoriques jusqu'à nos jours* (History of the Human Dwelling-Place from Prehistoric Times to the Present—1875), and many other works, including *L'art russe, ses origins, ses éléments constitutifs, son apogée, son avenir* (Russian Art, its Origins, its Constituent Elements, its Zenith, its Future—1877), translated into Russian (1879), which may have had some influence on *Constructivism. As an architect, his work was often aesthetically somewhat coarse, even clumsy, as in the elephantine Morny Tomb, Père-Lachaise Cemetery, Paris (1865–6), and the ungainly Church at Aillant-sur-Tholon, Yonne (1864–7), while his somewhat drastic reconstructions of historic fabric helped to spur William *Morris to found the Society for the Protection of Ancient Buildings (SPAB) and encourage the beginnings of the *conservation movement.

Auzas (1965); Bercé and Foucart (1988); Crook (1981, 1987); Foucart (1980); Middleton and Watkin (1987); Pevsner (1972); Placzek (1982—a very comprehensive entry giving a list of works); Summerson (1963); Viollet-le-Duc (1874, 1875, 1876, 1877, 1959); Viollet-le-Duc and Narjoux (1979); Vogt, Reble, and Frohlich (1976); van Zanten (1987)

Viscardi, Giovanni Antonio (1647–1713). A Ticinese, he settled in Munich where he became Court Architect in 1685. From 1702 he enlarged Schloss Nymphenburg by adding the pavilions and began the saloon. He was involved with E. *Zuccalli (his rival) in the building of the *Theatinerkirche* (Church of the Theatines) St Kajetan, Munich, in the 1680s, and designed the *Dreifaltigkeitskirche* (Church of the Holy Trinity) in the same city (1711–14). Probably his best work is *Wallfahrtskirche* (Pilgrimage Church) Mariahilf, Freystadt, near Nuremberg (1700–8), a high-domed centrally planned building, incorporating circle, cross, and octagon, that was to influence *Bähr in his design for the *Frauenkirche* (Church of Our Lady), Dresden. Other buildings by him include the Cistercian Monastery Church at Fürstenfeldbruck (1701–6), one of the largest and grandest of Bavarian *Baroque churches, a larger version of his Premonstratensian (now Parish) Church of Sts Peter and Paul, Freising-Neustift (1700–15).

Bourke (1962); Hempel (1965); Lippert (1969); Powell (1959)

Visconti, Louis (Ludovico)-Tullius (Tullio)-Joachim (1791–1853). French architect of Italian ancestry. He trained under *Percier, and designed some Parisian fountains in a robust *Renaissance style, including the Fontaines Gaillon (1828), Louvois (1839),

Molière (1844), Quatre Evèques (1844), and Saint-Sulpice (1848). He built several large houses, including the Hôtel Pontalba (1828). He is best known for two works: the New Louvre, Paris (begun 1852 but redesigned and completed by H.-M. *Lefuel after Visconti's death); and the serene, magnificent, yet dramatic tomb of Emperor Napoleon I (1769–1821, reigned 1804–14 and 1815) under the Dôme of the Invalides (1841–53), one of the finest *Neoclassical creations in Paris. He designed a number of handsome tombs in Père-Lachaise Cemetery, Paris, notably the elevated *sarcophagus of the Duc Decrès (1761–1821), Vice-Admiral of France.

Aulanier (1953); Hamon and MacCallum (1991–contains very full information); Lassalle (1846)

Visionary architecture. Describes especially the work of certain Neoclassical architects, notably *Boullée, *Ledoux, and *Lequeu. Boullée's gigantic schemes for *cenotaphs and monuments were noted for their scale and stereometrical purity, while Ledoux's proposals for an ideal city, Chaux, contained many buildings that were expressive of their purpose (*architecture parlante). It was later applied to any imaginary scheme featuring fantastic futuristic structures, of which there have been many in C20.

Architectural Design, 31/5 (May 1961), 181–2; Belov *et al.* (1988); Feuerstein (1988); Kaufmann (1952); Lampugnani (1982); Rosenau (1976); Sky and Stone (1976); Vidler (1990)

Vitozzi, Ascanio (*c.*1539–1615). Italian architect, military engineer, and soldier. In 1584 he was called to Turin to serve as architect and engineer to Carlo Emanuele I, Duke of Savoy (reigned 1580–1630). He designed the Churches of Santa Maria del Monte (or dei Cappuccini) (1585–96), Santissima Trinità (begun 1598), and Corpus Domini (1607), in Turin. Santissima Trinità has a plan based on a star within a hexagon, pre-empting *Borromini's later Church of Sant'Ivo in Rome (1643–60). His greatest work was the huge centrally planned domed Santuario di Vico, Mondovì, Piedmont (also called Vicoforte di Mondovì—1596–1736), based on an ellipse and anticipating C17 *Baroque plans. He made a contribution to the urban design of Turin, including the façades of the Piazza Castello (1606) and the adjoining Contrada Nova (1615), both of which served as models for subsequent developments in the city. He fortified the town of Cherasco from 1610, and wrote a treatise on fortifications (1589).

Carboneri (1966); Papworth (1892); Placzek (1982); *Römisches Jahrbuch für Kunstgeschichte*, 7 (1955), 9–99; Scotti (1969); Wittkower (1982)

vitrified. Converted into a glassy substance by exposure to intense heat, as with certain bricks used as headers in *diaper-work.

Brunskill (1990)

Vitruvian opening. Aperture, wider at the bottom than at the top (i.e. with sloping sides), in Classical architecture and *Neoclassicism. It was described by *Vitruvius.

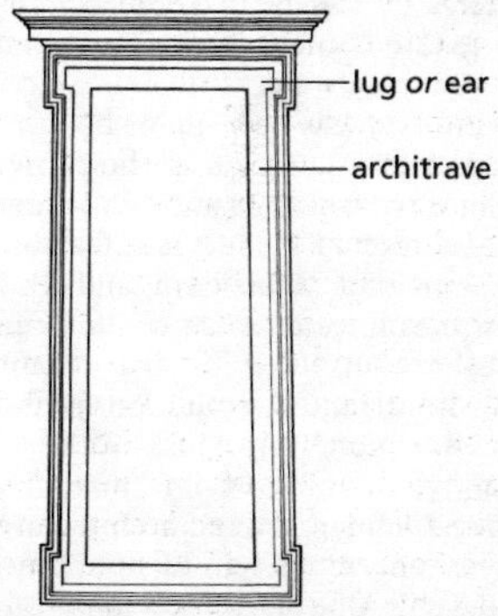

Vitruvian opening. With lugged architrave, based on the example from the interior of the 'Temple of Vesta', Tivoli (*c.* 80 BC), also called the *Tivoli window*. If was described by Vitruvius and published by Palladio.

Vitruvian scroll. Repeated pattern consisting of convolved undulations in Classical *bands, *friezes, *string-courses, etc., resembling a series of scrolls joined together by a wave-like form, also called *running-dog or *wave-scroll.

Vitruvian scroll

Vitruvius Pollio, Marcus (*fl.* 46–30 BC). Roman architect, engineer, and architectural theorist, author of the only substantial *Antique treatise on architecture to survive. Entitled simply *De Architectura*, it was dedicated to Emperor Augustus (reigned 27 BC–AD 14), and is subdivided into ten 'books' or main sections. Although known and copied in manuscript form during the Middle Ages, from 1414, when Poggio Bracciolini (1380–1459) publicized the existence of the fine manuscript in the Abbey of St Gallen, Switzerland, *De Architectura* began to be taken very seriously, and was the basis for *Alberti's important treatise. The first printed edition (by Fra Giovanni Sulpitius) came out in 1486, an influential illustrated version by Fra Giovanni Giocondo (1435–1515) appeared in 1511, and Italian translations were published from the 1520s, starting with the important edition of 1521 with copious illustrations and notes by Cesare di Lorenzo Cesariano (1483–1543). Daniele Barbaro's edition of 1556 had plates by *Palladio. Since C15, Vitruvius' text has been published in many forms and translations (e.g. the Nuremberg German version of 1528 and *Philander's annotated edition of 1544). It is still an authoritative source for *Classicism, and while the precise meanings of some of its terms and phrases are disputed, it has acquired a wholly unwarranted reputation for dullness and obfuscation. Vitruvius' work, on the contrary, is a mine of information about Greek and Roman art and architecture, and has been enormously influential since the *Renaissance. One of the most important and encylopedic editions of Vitruvius was that by *Perrault (1673). The first English version of the first five books of *De Architectura* was that of William Newton (1735–90), published in 1771, and in 1791 all ten books appeared in English, translated by Newton and edited by his brother, James Newton. However, a potted Vitruvius in English had been published in 1692, but it was so abridged that its usefulness was limited. Newton's edition was superseded by that of *Gwilt in 1826, although William *Wilkins had published *The Civil Architecture of Vitruvius* in 1812, with commentaries, but it was incomplete.

As an architect, Vitruvius designed (*c*.27 BC) a *basilica (destroyed) for Colonia Iulia Fanestris (modern Fano), a new town for army veterans.

Harris (1990); Knell and Wessenberg (1984); MacDonald (1965–86); Placzek (1982); Vitruvius Pollio (1567, 1955–6); Ward-Perkins (1981)

Vittone, Bernardo Antonio (1702–70). One of the supreme masters of Piedmontese *Baroque. He edited *Guarini's *Architettura Civile* for publication by the Theatine Order (1737), but is known primarily for his churches in which the influences of Guarini, *Juvarra (his teacher), and French *Rococo were manifest. From 1737 to 1742 he created three of his masterpieces, the little hexagonal Cappella della Visitazione, Vallinotto, near Carignano (1738–9), the octagonal-domed San Bernardino, Chieri (1740–4), and Santa Chiara, Brà (1742). At Santa Maria di Piazza, Turin (1750–4), one of his structural inventions may be seen to advantage: the gouged-out pendentive or inverted squinch (which opens the form to extra light). This recurred in his Santi Pietro e Paolo, Mondovì (1755), and Santa Croce (later Santa Caterina), Villanova di Mondovì (1755), where the pendentives were virtually eliminated. He experimented with circular, elliptical, octagonal, hexagonal, and longitudinal plans, all ingeniously and assuredly handled, and occasionally threw three *vaults over the space to create a type of domical vault in which the geometries were unusually subtle and complex, creating light and airy effects. His Church of San Michele, Borgo d'Ale (1770), combined themes from *Borromini (the convex wall-plans and convex porch) with elements from Guarini.

Vittone published *Istruzione Elementari per indirizzo de'giovani allo studio dell' Architettura Civile* (Elementary Instructions Addressed to the Young for the Study of Civil Architecture) and *Istruzione diverse concernanti l'officio dell'Architetto Civile* (Diverse Instructions Concerning the Duty of a Civil Architect)—both 1760.

Brinckmann (1931); Carboneri and Viale (1967); Oechslin (1972); Olivero (1920); Placzek (1982—contains a comprehensive bibliography); Pommer (1967); Portoghesi (1960, 1966); Varriano (1986); Viale (1972); Wittkower (1982)

vivo. **1.** *Shaft or *fust* of a column. **2.** *Naked of any part of a building, but especially a column or *pilaster.

volute. Spiral *scroll, of which there are normally four on the *Ionic capital, eight on the *angular and *Composite capitals, and smaller types, sometimes called *helix, on the *Corinthian capital. It is also a distinctive element of the *ancon, *console, and *modillion, where, like the Ionic capital, it resembles a rolled-up mattress.

Vorarlberg School. Term describing several families of architects, stuccoers, painters, and craftsmen, all related, in the Vorarlberg of Austria, west of the Tyrol towards the *Bodensee* (Lake Constance). The main families were the *Beers, *Moosbruggers, and *Thumbs, and they made an enormous contribution to late-C17 and C18 *Baroque architecture in South Germany and Switzerland. The main general characteristics of churches by the Vorarlberg School were longitudinal plans, often with centralized spaces associated with the *transepts, the *Wandpfeiler arrangement, vestigial 'aisles' the same height as the nave set between wall-piers (as in medieval Hallenkirchen (*hall-churches)), *nave-*arcades almost as high as the *vaults, *galleries between the *piers (often with significant elements placed to draw the eye towards the high-altar), slight transeptal projections, *choirs narrower than naves, twin-towered *façades, and decoration subordinated to the architecture.

Bourke (1962); Lieb and Dieth (1976); Oechslin (1973); Powell (1959)

Voronikhin, Andrei Nikiforovich (1760–1814). Born a serf on the Stroganov Estates near Perm, Russia, he was fortunate to receive the patronage of his master, who arranged for his formal education and travel. A pupil of de *Wailly, he became one of Russia's most distinguished *Neoclassical architects after his return to his motherland in the 1790s. His main works include the Stroganov Dacha, near St Petersburg (1790s), the remodelling of the State-Rooms of the Stroganov Palace (1790s), the Cathedral of the Virgin of Kazan, St Petersburg (influenced by *Soufflot's Panthéon in Paris—1801–11), and the severe Academy of Mines, with its huge dodecastyle *Paestum *Doric *portico, also in St Petersburg (1806–11).

Berckenhagen (1975); Grabar, Lazarev, and Kemenov (1963); Hamilton (1983); Middleton and Watkin (1987)

voussoir. *Cuneus, or block (normally of stone, brick, or terracotta), shaped on two opposite long sides to converging planes in what is normally the shape of a wedge, forming part of the structure of an *arch or *vault, its sides coinciding with the radii of the arch.

voussure. *Vault.

Voysey, Charles Francis Annesley (1857–1941). English *Arts-and-Crafts architect and designer, much influenced by *Mackmurdo and *Morris. Apprenticed to *Seddon in 1874, he later (1880) worked with *Devey before establishing his own practice in 1882. From then until the 1914–18 war he designed many medium-sized country-houses, all beautifully sited, informally and asymmetrically composed with exteriors rendered in *pebble-dash, and nearly all with bands of windows subdivided by square unmoulded *mullions. *Battered *buttresses, wide overhanging *eaves, and steeply pitched roofs often featured in his buildings, which were largely based on *vernacular C16 and early C17 traditions, and also influenced by the work of Devey. His fireplaces, furniture, and details were influenced by Mackmurdo, and in turn were precedents for *Mackintosh. Typical of his country-houses that were widely admired at the time were Perrycroft, Colwell, Herefordshire (1893–4), Broadleys (1898) and Moor Crag (1898–1900), near Windermere, Westmorland, in the English Lake District, and Pastures House, North Luffenham, Rutland (1901). Forster House, 14 South Parade, Bedford Park, Chiswick (1888–91 and 1894), owed something to *Art Nouveau, but also to mullioned vernacular architecture and *Regency metal *verandah roofs. His only house in Ireland, 'Dallas', 149 Malone Road, Belfast (1911–12), is very similar to his English domestic work. Voysey's designs were widely publicized in *The Studio* magazine and by *Muthesius in *Das englische Haus* (1904–5), but in the British Isles tended to be parodied in countless speculative houses built in the 1920s and 1930s, although Voysey himself had virtually no commissions after 1918. One of his most interesting designs is the Sanderson Wallpaper Factory, Chiswick (1902), with its bold *piers and glazed-brick walls. *Pevsner greatly admired The Orchard, Chorley Wood, Hertfordshire (1899–1901), Voysey's own house, unaccountably seeing in it and his other houses, with their bold 'bare walls and long horizontal bands of windows', precedents for the *International *Modern Movement, and made what seem to be spurious claims for Voysey (who was Master of the *Art Workers' Guild in 1924) as a 'pioneer' of modern design (1937), notably at Broadleys, where Pevsner detected Voysey coming 'amazingly close' to a C20 'concrete and glass grid', which is perhaps an excessive claim. While Voysey had no qualms about using machinery (e.g. to reproduce his wallpaper designs), he actually detested the International style, claiming it could not last and that its Godless creators knew nothing of spirituality and of that which was exalted.

Brandon-Jones *et al.* (1978); *DNB* (1959); Gebhard (1975); Gray (1985); Mitchmough (1995); Pevsner (1960, 1968); Richardson (1983); Simpson (1979)

Vredeman. *See* Vries.

Vriendt, Cornelis Floris de (1514–75). *See* Floris.

Vries, Hans Vredeman de (1526/7–1606). Flemish architect, painter, decorator, and prolific writer. His engravings were widely distributed throughout Europe, and his architectural devices, derived from *Serlio, made the style evolved at *Fontainebleau familiar. His treatises on architecture (1565) and his *pattern-books were hugely influential throughout Northern Europe, notably in England, where direct quotations of *strapwork and much else informed much *Elizabethan and *Jacobean architecture. His published work demonstrates how important was the Flemish and Dutch contribution to *Mannerism, and includes *Architectura* (1563 and later editions), *Variae Architecturae Formae* (1601), and many other books, e.g. *Perspectiva* (1604).

Gerson and Ter Kuile (1960); Jervis (1984); Lewis and Darley (1986); Vries (1617, 1651)

Vulliamy, Lewis (1791–1871). English architect of French descent. He was articled to R. *Smirke before establishing a large and lucrative London practice. He designed the sumptuous Italian *Renaissance Dorchester House, Park Lane, London (1850–63—demolished 1929), and the *Jacobethan Westonbirt House, Gloucestershire (1863–70—with *Renaissance interiors) for the wealthy Robert Stayner Holford (1808–92). An eclectic designer, he was competent in any style required of him. Among his churches, St Barnabas, Addison Road, Kensington (1828–9), St Michael, Highgate (1830–2), and St James, Norlands, Kensington (1844–5), are typical of his *Commissioners' *Gothic style, but he also designed All Saints', Ennismore Gardens, Kensington (1848–9—*Italianate), and the Church of St Peter, Glasbury, Breconshire, Wales (1836–7—*Neo-Norman). The handsome *Greek Revival Law Institution, Chancery Lane (1828–32), and the *Corinthian frontage of The Royal Institution, Albemarle Street (1838), both in London, were by him. He designed a number of imposing elevations for speculative buildings in Bloomsbury, including the north and west ranges in Tavistock Square (1827) and Gordon (now Endsleigh) Place (1827), and built or altered many country-houses. He published *The Bridge of The Sta. Trinita at Florence* (1822) and *Examples of Ornamental Sculpture in Architecture, Drawn from the Originals in Greece, Asia Minor, and Italy in the years 1818, 1819, 1820, 1821* (1823). His pupils included Owen *Jones, and his nephew, **George John Vulliamy** (1817–86), worked in his office until 1861, when he joined the Metropolitan Board of Works as its Superintending Architect, in which capacity he designed the base, ornaments, and bronze *sphinxes associated with 'Cleopatra's Needle' (*c.*1468 BC) on the Embankment, London (1878–80).

Colvin (1995); *DNB* (1917); Felstead, Franklin, and Pinfield (1993)

vulne window. *See* lychnoscope.

vyse. *See* vice.

Wachsmann, Konrad Ludwig (1901–80). German-born American architect. Trained as a cabinet-maker, later studying architecture (1920–4) under *Poelzig and *Tessenow, he worked briefly (1924–5) in Le *Corbusier's studio before joining (1925) Christoph and Unmack, makers of timber buildings and building components, as draughtsman-designer, becoming Chief Architect (1926–8). He then established his own practice in Berlin (1928–32), where he numbered Albert Einstein (1879–1955) among his clients (e.g. the Einstein House, near Potsdam (1928–9)). He exhibited and published several designs for timber buildings (e.g. for the *Deutscher Werkbund Exhibition, 1931), and evolved *reinforced-concrete building systems having set up a practice in Rome, where he erected several structures (1935–8). In France in 1938–9 (where he had a very short-lived association with Le Corbusier) he designed tubular steel and plywood-panel construction systems before emigrating to the USA where he joined *Gropius (1941–8), designing prefabricated building-components for the General Panel Corporation. In the late 1940s he evolved the 'Mobilar' system of tubular steel construction for aircraft hangars, making his speciality the design of connecting joints used in cellular structures.

He was appointed Professor of Design and Director of the Department of Advanced Building Research at the Institute of Design, Illinois Institute of Technology (1949–56), and further developed his 'Mobilar' system with joints capable of receiving up to 20 tubular members enabling enormous *cantilevers to be constructed so that large areas could be roofed with minimal vertical supports. His work anticipated many later developments, and influenced designers including Buckminster *Fuller. He published *Holzhausbau: Technik und Gestaltung* (House Building in Timber: Technique and Construction—1931), *Holz im Bau* (Wood in Building—1957), *Wendepunkt im Bauen* (Turning Point in Building—1959, with an English translation of 1961), and various other works on prefabrication and industrialization in building.

Emanuel (1994); Herbert (1984); Klotz (1986); Wachsmann (1961, 1988)

Waghemakere Family. Flemish architects based in Antwerp. **Herman de Waghemakere** (*c*.1430–1503) was Master of the Works at Antwerp Cathedral, where, in 1474, he was engaged in building the north-western tower to the second stage, and other works, including the completion of the *nave, north *aisle, and *chapel of the Holy Circumcision (1473–1503). His masterpiece is the Church of St Jakob, Antwerp, begun 1491, but he was also responsible for much of the fabric of St Gommarius, Lier (*ambulatory, *choir, and *Lady Chapel—1473–85), St Willibrord, Hulst, The Netherlands (1482–7), and the butchery (*Vleeshuis*), Antwerp (1501). His son, **Domien** or **Dominikus de Waghemakere** (*c*.1460–1542), assisted Herman at St Gommarius, Lier (1494), completed the upper stages of the north-western tower of Antwerp Cathedral (1502–42), completed the Church of St Jakob, Antwerp (1502–42), and, with Rombout *Keldermans, built the Maison du Roi, Brussels (1514–23), the Town Hall, Ghent (1517–33), and the *Handelsbeurs* (Exchange), Antwerp (1531—destroyed).

Baedeker, *Belgium and Holland* (1905); Białostocki (1972); *Deutsche Kunst und Denkmalpflege*, 2/11 (1909), 81–4; Leemans (1972); Papworth (1892); Vlaamse Toeristen-Bond (1977)

Wagner, Martin (1885–1957). German architect and planner. His reputation was made in the field of low-cost industrialized housing in Berlin, where he headed the Building Department (1926–33). A member of Der *Ring and active in the *Deutscher

Werkbund, he collaborated with several *Modern Movement architects, including *Gropius, *Häring, *Mies van der Rohe, *Poelzig, and *Scharoun, and was a pioneer of the *International Modern style. His best-known housing schemes were the Lindenhof Estate, Berlin-Schöneberg (1918–21), and the Britz, known as the *Hufeisensiedlung* (Horse Shoe Estate) at Berlin-Neukölln (1925–30—with Bruno *Taut). He also worked with *Bartning, Häring, and Gropius on the Siemensstadt Housing Development, Berlin (1927). He left Germany for Turkey in 1935, and in 1938, through Gropius's influence, joined the staff of Harvard University, USA, where he taught planning until 1950. He published many (usually polemical) works on architecture and planning throughout his career, promoting his left-wing views.

Wagner (1918, 1923, 1925, 1929, 1932)

Wagner, Otto (1841–1918). Austrian architect of great distriction. Born in Penzing, near Vienna, he studied in that city and in Berlin (where he absorbed something of *Schinkel's *Classicism), and began practice in Vienna as a competent architect of many *Historicist buildings, drawing heavily on the *Renaissance and *Baroque traditions (influenced by van der *Null and *Siccard von Siccardsburg). In 1890 he was appointed to prepare proposals for replanning the city: the only part to be realized was the *Stadtbahn* (City Railway—1894–1901), with its series of remarkable and beautiful buildings (stations, bridges, and other structures) in a restrained, economical style, tending to *Neoclassicism (but where even *Ionic capitals are transformed into machine-like elements), and openly exploiting the possibilities of metal and glass in architecture. The elegant stations at Schönbrunn (*Hofpavillon* (Court Pavilion)) outside the city and in the Karlsplatz in the centre both displayed Baroque and *fin-de-siècle* *Art Nouveau tendencies.

Among his finest creations in an Art Nouveau style are the *Majolikahaus* (faced with ceramic tiles), and adjacent apartment-block (with Art Nouveau *stucco ornament), on the Linke Wienzeile, Vienna (1898–9), while the second Villa Wagner, 28 Hüttelbergstrasse, Vienna (1912–13), anticipated aspects of C20 Neoclassicism and even *Art Deco. As a practitioner and Professor of Architecture at the Academy, Wagner influenced the younger generation, including *Hoffmann, *Kotěra, *Olbrich, and *Plečnik, and in his influential *Moderne Architektur* (1896) he argued for forms, style, structures, and materials that would be suitable for the times. His *stripped Classical Post Office Savings Bank, Vienna (1904–6), has a façade clad in stone fixed with metal bolts, the heads of which are exposed, and the interior of the banking-hall is treated without historical references in a fresh and confident manner, using metal and glass. His mastery of combining new technology and materials with traditional forms is best seen at the Church of St Leopold, Am Steinhof (1905–7), on a hill in the grounds of the Vienna State Mental Asylum: there, aspects of *Jugendstil, *Neoclassicism, and *Baroque combine in a masterly synthesized whole. Wagner's influence extended after his death to the successor-states of the Austro-Hungarian Empire through his many pupils and assistants.

Asenbaum *et al.* (1984); Borsi and Godoli (1986); Geretsegger and Peintner (1983); Graf (1985); Lux (1914); Ostwald (1948); Ouvrard, Bouniort, and Huet (1986); Pintarić (1989); Trevisiol (1990); Wagner (1914, 1988)

wagon-chamfer. Type of *chamfer consisting of a series of small scoops, like bites, removed from the arrises of a timber of rectangular section, favoured in *Arts-and-Crafts work. A good example is the *balustrade of the Library at the Glasgow School of Art (1907–9) by C. R. *Mackintosh, where the scoops are accentuated with colour.

wagon-headed. Having a continuous round-arched ceiling or *vault, as in *barrel-vaulting*.

wagon-roof. *Cradle-roof* constructed of a closely spaced series of double arch-braced *trusses, suggesting the shape of a covered wagon or barrel-*vault. It may be exposed, plastered, or finished with panels.

wagon-vault. As barrel- or tunnel-*vault.

Wahlman, Lars Israel (1870–1952). Swedish architect. Much influenced by the English *Arts-and-Crafts movement, especially the work of William *Morris and R. N. *Shaw, he also derived aspects of his work from *Berlage, *Nyrop, and H. H. *Richardson's designs. Drawing especially on *vernacular architecture, he became celebrated as a designer of houses and churches, and his buildings were important influences on *National Romantics such as Östberg. His most celebrated religious work is the powerful Engelbrekt Parish Church, Stockholm

(1906–14), and among his houses the Villa Widmark, Lysekil (1902–4), is a good example of his style.

Ahlberg (1925); Lind, Romans, and Sterner (1950)

Wailly, Charles de (1730–98). French architect and painter, one of the most distinguished and influential of the *Louis Seize and Revolutionary periods. He studied under J.-F. *Blondel, Le *Geay, and *Servandoni, and at the French Academy in Rome (1754–6), where he fell under the spell of *Piranesi. His numerous surviving drawings compare favourably with those of Hubert *Robert, and he acquired a formidable reputation as an interior decorator and stage-designer before becoming an urban planner and architect of several buildings of real distinction, including the austere Théâtre de l'Odéon, Paris (1769–82—with M.-J. *Peyre—but subsequently altered), and the *Château de Montmusard, near Dijon (1764–9—only partly realized). The latter, with an ingenious plan and rigorous geometry, was the first country-house in France in which the *Antique flavour was dominant, heralding a severe later *Neoclassicism of which *Boullée and *Ledoux were the most celebrated protagonists. His town-houses in the Rue de la Pépinière, Paris (1776–8), were resourceful designs, but, like most of his work, no longer exist. For the crypt of the Church of St-Leu-St-Gilles, Paris (1773–80), he employed sturdy columns derived from the Greek temples at *Paestum (but with *reeds instead of *flutes) supporting arches and vaults, a very advanced design for its date. He also designed the luxurious Gran' Salone, Palazzo Spinola, Genoa (1772–3), and a theatrical pulpit for the Church of St-Sulpice, Paris (1789), for which building he also redecorated the Chapelle de la Vierge (1777–8). In 1785 Landgrave Friedrich II of Hesse Kassel invited de Wailly to submit designs for a Neoclassical palace at Kassel, but died that year. In the event, Landgrave Wilhelm IX (1785–1803—when he became Elector of Hesse, 1803–21) built (1786–92) the Palace to designs by du *Ry and de Wailly's pupil *Jussow. Through his pupils (e.g. *Voronikhin) his influence spread to Russia, especially St Petersburg.

Braham (1980); Gallet (1964); Middleton and Watkin (1987); Mosser and Rabreau (1979); Watkin (1986); Watkin and Mellinghoff (1987)

wainscot. 1. Fine oak panel-work for walls. **2.** Timber *dado (USA). **3.** Panelled *box-pews.

Walker, Ralph Thomas (1889–1973). American architect best known for his *Art Deco *skyscrapers, including the Barclay-Vesey Telephone Building (1923–6) and the Irving Trust Building (1929–32), both in New York. He was an innovative designer of laboratories and of scientific research-centres, including the Argonne National Laboratory, Chicago (1952). He published *A Fly in the Amber* (1957).

Bosserman (1968); Placzek (1982)

wall. Structure of stone, brick, etc., serving to enclose a room, house, or other space, and, in most cases, *load-bearing, i.e. supporting the floors, roof, etc. It may also be a *screen-wall for privacy or enclosure. Types of wall include:

cavity: with an air-gap between two *leaves to improve insulation and prevent water-penetration;
hollow: as cavity above, but *see* brick;
partition: wall dividing a space, not usually load-bearing;
party: between adjoining properties, usually load-bearing and fire-resistant;
retaining: prevents earth from slipping, so used in gardens and in excavations;
springing: *buttress;
sustaining: load-bearing or retaining wall, unlike one serving merely as a partition or screen.

McKay (1957)

Wallace, William (d. 1631). Scottish architect. He was Master-Mason to the Scottish Crown from 1617 until his death, and carried out works including the King's Lodging, Edinburgh Castle (1615–17), the north quarter of Linlithgow Palace, West Lothian (1618–21), and parts of Stirling Castle. He was responsible for Heriot's Hospital, Edinburgh (1628–59), a showy work with Anglo-Flemish *Mannerist decorations. Indeed, he was a major figure in the introduction of this style to Scotland. Among his other designs were Wintoun Castle, East Lothian (*c*.1620–30), and the monument of John Byres of Coates (d. 1629) in the Greyfriars Cemetery, Edinburgh, in which exuberant *strapwork abounds.

Colvin (1995); Dunbar (1966, 1978); Gifford, McWilliam, and Walker (1984); Mylne (1893)

wall-base. *Plinth, *skirting, or *socle.

wall-column. *Engaged column.

wall-dormer. *Lucarne with a front continuous with and above the *naked of the main wall below it.

wall-garden. Wall with plants growing out of the joints or from specially created hollows, *niches, etc.

Wallot, Paul (1841–1912). German architect. A pupil of Martin *Gropius, he began his career by designing numerous houses in Frankfurt-am-Main, but made his name with the *Reichstag* (Imperial Parliament Building), Berlin 1884–94—gutted 1933, reconstructed with major modifications *c.*1975–99), which he followed with the *Ständehaus* (later *Landtag*—Building for the Saxon Parliament), Dresden (1901–7), and a house at the artists' colony, Darmstadt (*c.*1901). His official buildings were in an opulent *Renaissance Revival style. Later, he taught at the Academy of Art in Dresden.

Mackowsky (1912); Schliepmann (1913); Schmädecke (1970)

wall-piece. 1. *Wall-plate, also called *pan-piece* or *raising piece*. **2.** Wall-painting or *fresco with the figures adjusted to fit the shape of the wall.

wall-pier. *Wandpfeiler.

wall-plate. Longitudinal timber set on top of a *timber frame or a brick or masonry wall on which roof-*trusses, *joists, *rafters, etc., rest. *See* wall-piece.

wall-press. Cupboard or shelving recessed into a wall.

wall-rib. *Gothic *formeret, i.e. *vault-rib set against the outer wall of a *vault-compartment or *bay.

wall-shaft. *Colonnette or projecting part of a *pier, like an *engaged column, from which a *Gothic *vault springs.

wall-string. Raking support (*string*) of a stair nearest the wall.

Walpole, Horace, 4th Earl of Orford (1717–97). English virtuoso and wit. His importance in the realm of architecture lies in his creation of Strawberry Hill, Twickenham, Middlesex (from 1750), one of the earliest key buildings of the *Gothic Revival, publicized in his *A Description of the Villa of Horace Walpole at Strawberry Hill* (1774 and 1778). This asymmetrical house set precedents for *Picturesque composition. He also helped to make *Gothic fashionable when he published his *The Castle of Otranto*, a 'Gothic Romance' (1764), an early work of *Romanticism. He included notes on the works of architects in his *Anecdotes of Painting in England* (1762–71), and he furthered the study of medieval architecture by encouraging James *Essex in his researches.

Aldrich (1994); *DNB* (1917); Germann (1972); Lewis (1960, 1973); McCarthy (1987); Mowl (1996)

Walsingham, Alan of (*fl.* 1314–d. 1364). Sacristan of Ely Cathedral, Cambridgeshire, from 1321 during the erection of the exquisite *Second Pointed *Lady Chapel (1321–49—which, before iconoclastic damage in C16, must have been one of the most stunning Gothic ensembles in England) and the building of the octagon and *lantern (1322–42) over the *crossing after the Cathedral's central tower collapsed (1322). It would appear that the genesis of the design of the octagon came from him, and the works were carried out by the Ely masons John the Mason (Cementarius—*fl.* 1322–6) and John atte Grene (*fl.* 1334–d. 1350), the timber superstructure (1334–50) being by William *Hurle(y).

Harvey (1987)

Walter of Canterbury (*fl.* *c.*1322). *See* Canterbury.

Walter, Thomas Ustick (1804–87). American architect of German descent. A pupil of *Strickland and John *Haviland, he began to practise on his own from 1831, building (1831–5) the *Gothic Moyamensing Gaol (Philadelphia County Prison), and making his reputation with the *peripteral temple-like Girard College for Orphans, Philadelphia (1833–48), one of the finest monuments of the *Greek Revival in the USA, although inspired by the Madeleine in Paris, and employing the *Corinthian *Order of the *Choragic Monument of Lysicrates in Athens (334 BC). Thereafter, he designed a vast number of buildings in a variety of styles, including the *Egyptian Revival Debtors' Apartment, Moyamensing (1836), influenced by Haviland's New Jersey Penitentiary, Trenton (1833–6). In 1843–5 he built the breakwater at La Guaria, Venezuela, and in 1846 published (with John Jay Smith) *Guide to Workers in Metal and Stone* and *Two Hundred Designs for Cottages and Villas*. In 1850 he prepared designs for the extension of the Capitol in Washington, DC, and until 1865 worked on the building. His greatest contributions were the wings and the elegant dome on its cast-iron frame (influenced by *Montferrand's St Isaac's Cathedral, St Petersburg, Russia (completed and publicized 1857)). He was assisted by August Gottlieb Schoenborn (*fl.* 1850–65) in this work. While in Washington Walter also extended the Treasury (1852), Patent Office (1850), Post Office (1856), and Hospital for the Insane (1852). He was responsible for Marine Barracks at Pensacola, Fla. (1857), and Brooklyn, New York (1858–9).

Brown (1970); Ennis (1982); Hamlin (1964); Hitchcock (1977); *Journal of the Society of Architectural Historians*, 7/1, 2 (1948), 1–31, 39, 7/4 (1980), 307–11; Placzek (1982); Whiffen and Koeper (1983)

Walton, Walter *or* **Watkin** (*fl.* 1381–d. 1418). English mason. He was *Yeveley's deputy during the rebuilding of Westminster Hall (1394–5). He worked at Porchester Castle, Hampshire, from 1396, and probably designed the *pulpitum and *cloisters at Chichester Cathedral, Sussex (*c.*1400–10). He may have been responsible for the detached bell-tower at Chichester as well. In 1397 he was appointed Chief Surveyor of all stonecutters and masons for the King's Works in England.

Harvey (1987)

Wandpfeiler. Literally a *wall-pier* or *-column*, the term is given to internal *buttresses forming the walls of side-chapels or pierced with arches to form *aisles in South-German *Baroque churches, especially those of the *Vorarlberg School.

Bourke (1962)

Wank, Roland Anthony (1898–1970). Austrian-born architect, he was one of the most important designers of the *International Modern style working in the USA. The series of dams and power-houses he produced for the Tennessee Valley Authority (1933–44) are recognized as his finest works. He also concerned himself with public housing: his Grand Street Housing, New York (1929–30), is his best-known achievement in this field.

van Vynckt (1993)

Warchavchik, Gregori (1896–1972). Born in Odessa, Russia, he studied in Rome and worked with *Piacentini before emigrating to Brazil in 1923, where he became one of the leaders of *International *Modernism. He published his manifesto on architecture in 1925, and designed several houses from 1927 that were much influenced by the blocky cubic forms fashionable in Europe at that time, including his own house in São Paulo (1927–8—the first example of Modernism in Brazil (with some *Art Deco touches)), and the First Modern House Exhibition, São Paulo (1930). His works were mostly houses and apartments, and he worked for a time with *Costa.

Correio de Manha (1 Nov. 1925); Emanuel (1994); Ferraz (1965); Mindlin (1956); Sartoris (1936)

ward. 1. *Bailey or *court of a castle, protected by a wall, towers, etc. **2.** Large apartment in a gaol or hospital.

Wardell, William Wilkinson (1823–99). London-born architect, engineer, and surveyor, who emigrated to Australia in 1858, where he became Chief Architect to the Victoria Department of Works, and subsequently Inspector-General of Public Buildings in Victoria (1869–78). His *Italianate Government House, Melbourne (1872–6), was influenced by Osborne House on the Isle of Wight, but his two Roman Catholic Cathedrals (St Patrick's, Melbourne (1857–1927), and St Mary's, Sydney (1865–1940)) were competent *Gothic Revival in style. He also designed the Church of St John the Evangelist, Toorak, Melbourne (1860–73), St John's College, Sydney University (1858), and St Mary's Cathedral, Hobart, Tasmania (1876).

Cruickshank (1996); Herman (1954)

Ware & van Brunt. Leading architectural firm in the USA from 1863 to 1881, formed by **William Robert Ware** (1832–1915) and **Henry van Brunt** (1832–1930), both pupils of Richard Morris *Hunt in New York, having studied at Harvard. Their best work was for ecclesiastical and institutional buildings, notably First Church, Boston, Mass. (1865–7), the Memorial Hall, Harvard (1865–80—perhaps the finest *Gothic Revival building ever erected in the USA), the Episcopal Theological School, Cambridge, Mass. (1869–80), Weld Hall, Harvard (1871–2), Third Universalist Church, Cambridge, Mass. (1875), the stack addition to Gore Hall, Harvard University Library (1876–7—the first example of such book-storage in the USA), and St Stephen's Church, Lynn, Mass. (1881–2). Their Gothic work was much influenced by *Ruskin, but they designed in the *Queen Anne and North-European *Renaissance styles with considerable flair.

Ware was appointed Professor and Head of the first US School of Architecture at the

Massachusetts Institute of Technology (1865) and later (1881) set up the School at Columbia, New York, based on *Beaux-Arts principles. He designed the American School of Classical Studies, Athens, Greece (1886–8), a scholarly essay of considerable distinction. Van Brunt continued to practise, taking Frank Howe into partnership, and moved the firm to Kansas, Missouri, from where they designed many railway-stations for the Union Pacific railroad (Ware and van Brunt's Union Station, Worcester, Massachusetts of 1873–5—destroyed—was an example). Their Electricity Building, World's Columbian Exposition, Chicago (1892–3), was firmly Classical in style.

Ware and van Brunt were committed to high standards of professionalism, and both were distinguished writers and critics. Van Brunt was the first to translate *Viollet-le-Duc's *Entretiens* into English as *Discourses on Architecture* (1875–81), while Ware published several works, including *Greek Ornament* (1878) and *The American Vignola* (1901).

Hitchcock (1977); Placzek (1982); Ware (1866, 1878, 1900, 1912–13, 1977); Whiffen and Koeper (1983)

Ware, Isaac (1704–66). English architect. Apprenticed to *Ripley, he later became under *Burlington's aegis an able devotee of *Palladianism. He published *Designs of Inigo Jones and Others* (1731 and 1743—which included many drawings from *Burlington's collection), *The Plans, Elevations, and Sections of Houghton in Norfolk* (1735), and the celebrated scholarly translation (and immaculate edition) of *Palladio's *Four Books of Architecture*, dedicated to Burlington (1738). His most important book was *A Complete Body of Architecture*, which came out in weekly parts between 1756 and 1757, with a second edition of 1767, re-issued in 1768: it became a standard work on *Georgian architectural practice and theory. Encylopedic and lavishly illustrated, it remained one of the most influential architectural publications well into the following century. Among his buildings were Clifton Hill House, Bristol (1746–50), Chesterfield House, South Audley Street, London (1748–9—demolished), and Wrotham Park, Middlesex (1754), the last illustrated in *Vitruvius Britannicus* (vol. v, plates 45–6), and clearly derived from Colen *Campbell's Wanstead III. His pupil, *Cameron, carried his influence to Russia.

Colvin (1995); *DNB* (1917); Harris (1990); Summerson (1993); Ware (1756–7); Wittkower (1974)

Warren, Edward Prioleau (1856–1937). English architect. Articled to *Bodley, he later wrote the latter's biography. He designed a number of distinguished buildings, including the Warren Building, Balliol College, Oxford (1906–8). Perhaps his best work is the range of mansion-flats at Hanover Lodge, St John's Wood High Street, London (1903–4). Other designs include 5 Palace Green (1904), Shelley House, Chelsea Embankment (1912), both in London, and the Fishermen's Institute, Newlyn, Cornwall (1911). Among his churches may be mentioned St Mary, Bishopstoke (1890–1), and St Michael and All Angels, Bassett, Southampton (1897–1910), both in Hampshire. The latter was described by *Pevsner as 'intriguing and distinguished', and the former contains an iron *chancel-screen (1903) by W. Bainbridge Reynolds (1845–1935).

Gray (1985); Pevsner, *Buildings of England, Hampshire* (1967)

Warren & Wetmore. Successful American firm of architects practising in New York from the 1890s to *c.*1930, founded by **Whitney Warren** (1864–1943) and **Charles D. Wetmore** (1867–1941). Warren's Paris *Beaux-Arts training was apparent in the New York Yacht Club (1898) and the Grand Central Terminal, New York (with Charles A. Reed (1857–1911) and Allen H. Stem (1856–1931)—1903–13).

Fitch and Waite (1974); Meeks (1964)

Wastell, John (*c.*1460–*c.*1515). English master-mason, perhaps one of the greatest of the last phase of English *Gothic architecture. He worked under Simon *Clerk at the Abbey of Bury St Edmunds, Suffolk (demolished), Saffron Walden Church, Essex (1485), and King's College Chapel, Cambridge, where he was active from 1486, by which time he appears to have been Clerk's partner. However, Bury was his normal place of residence, and he probably spent most of his time in the 1480s working on the Abbey there.

From 1490 his name recurs in the records of King's College, and he was also called by Cardinal-Archbishop John Morton (*c.*1420–1500) to Canterbury Cathedral, Kent, where he designed and built the *crossing-tower (1494–1505), one of the great works of the *Perpendicular style (known as 'Bell Harry'), with fan-*vaults (*c.*1503) almost identical to the patterns of those at King's College Chapel, Cambridge. He carried out other works for Morton, and was involved in designing buildings at King's Hall, Cambridge, now part of the east range of the Great *Court of Trinity College, and including the lower stages of the Great Gate Tower. He was also engaged in works at Great St Mary's Church, Cambridge (1491–1514), and, on stylistic grounds, at Dedham Church, Essex (1494), and the lower stages of the tower at Soham Church, Cambridgeshire. It has also been suggested that he worked on the *nave at Lavenham Church, Suffolk (1495–1515), and St James's Church (now the Cathedral), Bury St Edmunds (1503–21). Dr Harvey confidently attributed the latter to Wastell. He may also have designed the eastern chapels and *retrochoir at Peterborough Cathedral, Cambridgeshire (1496–*c.*1528), the fan-vaults of which are similar in design to those at King's College Chapel.

Wastell's greatest surviving work was the completion of the latter from 1506, and building operations began in 1508, finishing in 1515. He is known to have consulted William *Vertue, John *Smyth, and Henry *Redman about the design and construction, but it must also be remembered that he had had plenty of experience planning and erecting fan-vaults at Bury St Edmunds and Peterborough. Wastell was responsible for building the *ante-chapel from just above ground level and for completing the *choir, five *bays of which had been roofed in *Clerk's time. He and Henry *Semark contracted to build the vaults in 1512, and those and most of the decorative elements, including the *Tudor badges, were made under Wastell's direction. The latter (who was clearly the senior partner in the contract) designed the great west window, the *buttress *pinnacles, and the tops of the corner-*turrets. The entire ensemble at King's is of such high quality that Wastell must be named as among the most gifted architects England ever produced.

DNB (1993); Harvey (1987)

Watanabe, Hitoshi (1887–1973). Japanese traditionalist architect responsible for many buildings in the inter-War years. His best-known work is the National Museum, Tokyo (1931–8), in which European *stripped Classicism mingled with elements taken from native buildings.

Cruickshank (1996); Turner (ed.) (1996)

watching-chamber *or* **-loft. 1.** Elevated *gallery in a church from which the monks could watch over a holy *shrine, e.g. the beautiful surviving timber example in St Alban's Cathedral, Hertfordshire (early C15). **2.** Place from which monks could be summoned to the services, appropriately called *excubitorium*.

Bond (1908*a*); Bond and Camm (1909)

watch-tower. Tower or station from which observation is kept of the approach of danger, as on a city wall.

water. Classical ornament such as the *Vitruvian scroll may represent waves, while the Ancient Egyptians used parallel zig-zag lines to suggest water. Sculpted representations of flowing water are associated with *grottoes, *nymphaea, and the like, and are found in *rustication, often frozen, or *congelated.

water-bar. Small strip, usually of metal, fixed in a *cill so that a door will shut against it, thus stopping the ingress of water.

water-holding base. Type of early *Gothic *pier or *colonnette *base with a hollow channel at the top bounded by two roll-mouldings, as though it could hold water (but not for this purpose).

Waterhouse, Alfred (1830–1905). English architect. A master of rational planning, he made his reputation as the designer of several important secular buildings, starting with the *Gothic Revival Assize Courts, Manchester (demolished), which he won in competition (1858–9), and gained the approbation of *Ruskin. He consolidated his position by almost winning the competition to design the Royal Courts of Justice, London (1866–7—the buildings were erected to designs by *Street), and by his success in the competition (1867–8) to design the brilliantly planned Gothic Revival Town Hall in Manchester (1869–77). Waterhouse designed numerous university buildings including the Master's Lodge and Broad-Street Front, Balliol College, Oxford (1866–9—Gothic Revival), the French *Renaissance Revival Tree Court, Gonville and Caius College, Cambridge (1868–70), and the Gothic Owen's College (now the University), Manchester (1869–88). Interested in experimentation, he used hard *terracottas, bricks, and *faïences, as in the Natural History Museum, London (1873–81—much influenced by German (especially Rhineland) *Romanesque architecture), the Gothic Prudential Assurance Building,

Holborn, London (1878–1906), and the Free *Rundbogenstil Congregationalist Churches at Lyndhurst Road, Hampstead (1883), and King's Weigh House, Duke Street, Mayfair, London (1889–91). His National Liberal Club, London (1885–7), was in a mixture of Romanesque and Italian and French *Renaissance styles, said at the time to reflect the uneasy *pot-pourri* of disparate opinions within the Liberal Party. The spectacular Eaton Hall, Cheshire (1870–83), seat of the Dukes of Westminster, was demolished in 1961, and was his largest country-house. He also designed the *Tudor Revival Blackmoor House and Gothic Revival Church, Blackmoor, Hampshire (1868–72). His son, **Paul** (1861–1924), studied with him, became his partner in 1891, completed his father's University College Hospital, Gower Street, London, and added the Medical School and Nurses' Home (1905). Paul Waterhouse's other works included the Whitworth Hall, University of Manchester (1902) and New Buildings, College Road, University of Leeds (1907–8). Paul Waterhouse was succeeded in the practice by his son, **Michael** (1889–1968).

Axon (1878); Curl (1990); *DNB* (1920); Dixon and Muthesius (1985); Eastlake (1970); Fawcett (1976); Girouard (1990); Gray (1985); Hitchcock (1977); Maltby, Macdonald, and Cunningham (1983); Sheppard (1975); Waterhouse (1867)

water-leaf. 1. *Transitional early *Gothic C12 carved ornament on each angle of a *capital, essentially a large, broad, plain leaf resembling a water-lily or lily-pad, flowing out from above the astragal in a concave curve, then returning upwards in a convex curve, turning inwards at each angle under the *abacus. **2.** Classical ornament, often on a *cyma reversa moulding, resembling a series of pointed tongue-like forms pointing downwards, with darts between them, also called *hart's tongue*, *Lesbian*, or *lily-leaf*, each tongue-form divided vertically by an incision. It is probably related to the *lotus-leaf, or to ivy-leaves. **3.** Long, feather-like unserrated leaf used by *Palladio in his enrichment of the *Ionic, *Corinthian, and *Composite *Orders, also called *stiff-leaf, and used as a series of vertical ornaments on *friezes, etc.

Papworth (1892); Sturgis *et al.* (1901–2)

Waterloo church. *See* Commissioners' Gothic.

water-shot. Dry-stone wall without mortar in which the stones are laid to a slope so that water is less likely to penetrate. It is common in the English Lake District where such walls are often constructed of slate.

McKay (1957)

water-table. Inclined surface on a projection, such as a *plinth or a *buttress *off-set, also called *weathering*.

Watkin, David John (1941–). English architectural historian. His *Morality and Architecture* (1977), a critique of arguments and criteria of judgement prevalent from the time of A. W. N. *Pugin to that of *Pevsner, exposed the populist fallacies of an inevitable unfolding logic in architectural evolution leading to the *Modern Movement. Among his publications *Thomas Hope 1769–1831 and the Neo-Classical Idea* (1968), *The Life and Work of C. R. Cockerell R.A.* (1974), *German Architecture and the Classical Ideal (1740–1840)* (1987—with Tilman Mellinghoff), and *Sir John Soane: Enlightenment Thought and the Royal Academy Lectures* (1996) may be cited.

Middleton and Watkin (1987); personal knowledge; Watkin (1968, 1974, 1977, 1979, 1982, 1982*a*, 1986, 1996); Watkin and Mellinghoff (1987)

Watt, Richard Harding (1842–1913). English creator of buildings out of architectural features collected from demolition contractors. He worked with clay models to convey his ideas to executive architects (including Walter Aston (1861–1905), John Brooke (1853–1914), Harry Smith Fairhurst (1868–1945), J. H. France (*fl.* early C20), and W. Longworth (*fl.* early C20)), and created a series of very remarkable and original eclectic buildings in Knutsford, Cheshire, in the years before the 1914–18 war. Among his most extraordinary works are the Gaskell Memorial Tower with the adjacent King's Coffee House (1907–8), the Old Croft (1895—with tower of 1907), Moorgarth (1898), the Ruskin Rooms and Cottages (1899–1902), Swinton Square (1902), cottages in Drury Lane, houses in Legh Road, and the laundry in Knutsford Mere (all *c.*1904). Stylistically, the buildings tend to the *Italianate, with touches of *Moorish, Classical, and the exotic about them.

Gray (1985); Pevsner, *Buildings of England, Cheshire* (1971)

wattle-and-daub *or* **-dab.** Interwoven *staves and twigs used to fill a panel in a *timber frame, providing a backing for a finish of daub (clay, dung, or mud) or plaster (usually on straw or hair), which is then lime-washed. It is also used in roofs beneath *thatch, in which case it is *under-thatch wattling*.

Alcock, Barley, Dixon, and Meeson (1996); Brunskill (1987, 1994)

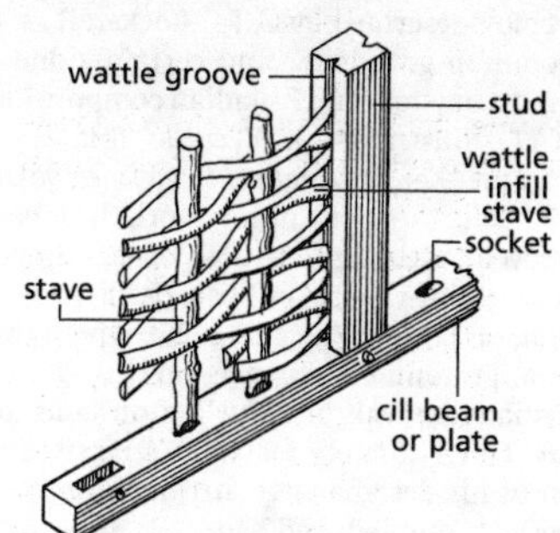

wattle-and-daub. Typical arrangement in a timber-framed construction. (*JJS*)

wave-moulding. *Gothic *Second Pointed moulding consisting of two roll-mouldings following one another, as at the base of a *pier, i.e. in profile looking like a wave.

wave-scroll. Classical ornament consisting of a series of repeated *scrolls or waves, sometimes like the side-view of a series of overlapping *consoles or long S-shapes on their sides, known also as *running-dog or *Vitruvian scroll.

Wealden house. Medieval *timber-framed dwelling type found mainly in the South-East of England, and named after the Weald, a district, once forested, between the North and South Downs. It consists of an open *hall the full height of the structure with a two-storey *bay on each side of the hall, having a single roof in one direction over the whole, the *ridge of the pitched roof (sometimes hipped) following the length. The upper floors of the end-bays project on *jetties on the front elevation, but the *eaves are continuous, so that part of the roof over the set-back hall wall rests on a flying *wall-plate supported on diagonal (often curved) *braces in line with the front of the jettied first-floor wall. A *single-ended* or *half-Wealden* house is similar, but has only one jettied bay.

Alcock, Barley, Dixon, and Meeson (1996); Brunskill (1987); Pevsner, *Buildings of England*, especially volumes dealing with the South-East of England (Hampshire, Kent, Surrey, Sussex)

weather-boarding. **1.** Any external wall-cladding of overlapping horizontal timber boards. **2.** True weather-boarding consists of sawn boards of rectangular section (i.e. with

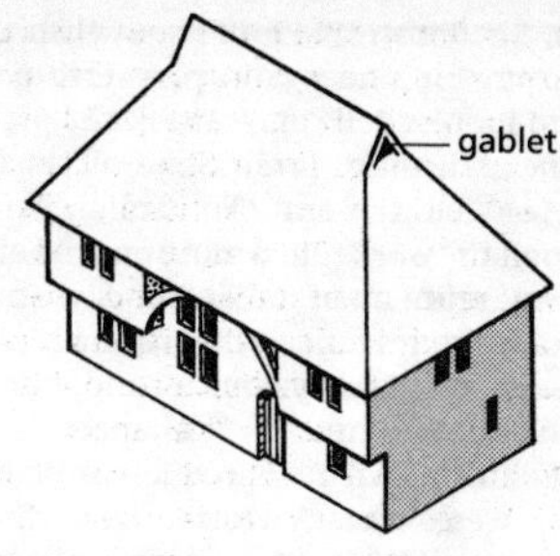

Wealden house (*JJS*)

parallel sides), as distinct from riven *clapboards of triangular section.

Alcock, Barley, Dixon, and Meeson (1996)

weather-cock. *See* weather-vane.

weathered. **1.** Changed by exposure, so it can mean anything from satisfactorily toned down so as not to appear garish and new, to badly worn, damaged, and eroded. **2.** *Weathering.

weathering. **1.** Inclination given to any upper surface, e.g. *off-set. **2.** Process of undergoing change caused by action of weather. In some instances the effect of time on a building may be beneficial, giving the surface a beauty that cannot be artificially applied (e.g. limestone *ashlar).

weather-moulding. Moulding projecting from the face of a wall to cast off water, e.g. *label, or anything similar with a sloping top for that purpose.

weather-struck. *Pointing in brickwork with the mortar sloping outwards from the underside of one brick to the face of the one underneath so that water does not lie on the top surface of any brick.

Brunskill (1990)

weather-tiling. Wall-finish of hung tiles.

weather-vane. Swivelling *vane, often combined with crossed rods to show the compass points, and frequently in the form of a cock, hence *weather-cock*.

web. **1.** *Cell, compartment, infill, or *severy between the ribs of a *Gothic *vault. **2.** Vertical plate connecting two horizontal flanges or plates in a steel or iron I-beam. **3.** Sheet of lead, e.g. on a roof.

Webb, Sir Aston (1849–1930). English architect. From 1882 he was in partnership with Edward Ingress Bell (1837–1914). The practice was one of the most prolific and successful of the late-*Victorian and *Edwardian periods, although the work relied more on bold effects than on refinement of detail. Stylistically, Webb favoured *François Ier early in his career, but later mixed *Byzantine and *Gothic, *Renaissance and *Italianate, and *Palladianism with *Baroque. Among his works were the Victoria Law Courts, Birmingham (1885–91), Christ's Hospital, Horsham, Sussex (1893–1904), and the Royal Naval College, Dartmouth (1899–1904), the last two in a *Wrenaissance style. His free eclecticism is perhaps best expressed by the Byzantine Gothic University of Birmingham (1901) and the Gothic Venetian François Ier Renaissance *Romanesque mix at the Victoria & Albert Museum main front, South Kensington (1899–1903). He also designed the Admiralty Arch between Trafalgar Square and The Mall (1903–10), the familiar Mall front of Buckingham Palace (1912–13), and the Royal College of Science, Dublin (1906—with Thomas N. *Deane), the last three demonstrating his mastery of the Classical language of architecture.

DNB (1937); Gray (1985); Service (1975, 1977)

Webb, John (1611–72). English architect. A pupil and relative (by marriage) of Inigo *Jones, he assisted the latter when working on St Paul's Cathedral, London, in the 1630s. He made many drawings for the unrealized Whitehall Palace, and rebuilt (1648–50) the interior (notably the celebrated double-cube room once thought to be by Jones) of Wilton House, Wiltshire, after a fire (1647–8). After Jones's death (1652) Webb was the unrivalled master of Classical architecture in England, steeped as he was in knowledge of the works of *Palladio, *Scamozzi, and *Serlio, although he seems never to have visited Italy (but may have travelled in France in 1656). His finest surviving works are the *Corinthian *portico and north front of The Vyne, Hampshire (1654–6), the earliest domestic portico in England (a motif derived from Palladio's Villa Barbaro at Maser), and the King Charles Block, Greenwich Palace (1664–9), the last a masterly composition in which *Baroque devices such as the *Giant Order and the overhanging keystone were employed to great effect. Probably his finest country-house was Amesbury Abbey, Wiltshire (1659–61—rebuilt by *Hopper, 1834–40), described by C. R. *Cockerell as 'of uncommon grandeur', and certainly one of the most outstanding Palladian compositions of C17 (illustrated in *Vitruvius Britannicus*, 1725, and *Kent's *Designs of Inigo Jones*, vol. ii, 1727). Much of his other work has been destroyed, although several of his important buildings were published in *Vitruvius Britannicus* (1715, 1717, and 1725), where they had a profound influence on the second Palladian Revival of *Burlington and his circle. Unfortunately for Webb's reputation, most of his designs were attributed to Inigo Jones by *Campbell and Kent.

Bold (1989); Colvin (1995); *DNB* (1917); Harris and Tait (1979); Summerson (1993)

Webb, Philip Speakman (1831–1915). Influential English *Arts-and-Crafts architect, specializing in houses. With Norman *Shaw he was one of the leaders of the English *Domestic Revival. His style from the first was deliberately eclectic, drawing on elements from *Gothic, *Queen Anne, and *vernacular architecture. Initially, his fame grew from his association (dating from his time (1852–9) in the office of G. E. *Street) with William *Morris, for whom he designed the Red House, Bexley Heath, Kent (1859–60), and many artefacts for Morris's firm. Later, he was involved with Morris in the setting up of the Society for the Protection of Ancient Buildings (1877). At the Red House the influence of *Butterfield and *Street is clear, especially in relation to the clear expression of materials and the very free asymmetrical composition: with this building and Benfleet Hall, Fairmile, near Cobham, Surrey (1860), he established his reputation. His best town buildings are the Prinsep House, 14 (formerly 1) Holland Park Road, Kensington (1864–92), 1 Palace Green, Kensington (1868–73—with interior decorations by Edward Coley Burne-Jones (1833–98), Walter Crane (1845–1915), and William Morris), and 19 Lincoln's Inn Fields (1868–9), all in London, in which steep gables, Queen Anne *sash-windows, and a few Gothic features are used in free compositions. His country-houses include Joldwynds, near Dorking, Surrey (1872–3—destroyed), Smeaton Manor, Great Smeaton, North Riding, Yorkshire (1876–9—much altered), and Standen, East Grinstead, Surrey (1891–4), all *gabled and freely composed. Clouds, East Knoyle, Wiltshire (1876–91), is perhaps his most eclectic composition, with a veritable jumble of styles making the building almost style-less. His one church, St Martin's, Brampton, Cumberland (1874–8), is certainly Gothic, but treated very freely, with ceilings that are more domestic than ecclesiastical in character. Claims that Webb was a pioneer of the *Modern Movement do not stand up to serious examination, for his work showed too much of an understanding of traditional materials and vernacular architecture, and his sources lay in historical exemplars.

DNB (1927); Dixon and Muthesius (1985); Ferriday (1963); Lethaby (1935); McLeod (1971); Naylor (1971); Richardson (1983); Swenarton (1989)

weeper. One of a series of mourning figures set around a *tomb-chest, usually in *niches, in funerary architecture, common in medieval work (e.g. Beauchamp Chapel, St Mary's Church, Warwick).

Weightman, John Grey (1801–72). English architect. Trained in the offices of Charles *Barry and C. R. *Cockerell, he commenced practising in Sheffield in *c*.1832, and was in partnership with **Matthew Ellison Hadfield** (1812–85) from *c*.1838 to 1858. As **Weightman & Hadfield**, the firm designed many Roman Catholic churches, including the archaeologically derivative Cathedral at Salford (1844–8), based on medieval exemplars at Newark, Howden, and Selby. Among the firm's pupils was George *Goldie.

Dixon and Muthesius (1985); Felstead, Franklin, and Pinfield (1993)

Weinbrenner, Friedrich (1766–1826). The most important architect working in South-West Germany in the first quarter of the C19. Having met *Genelli, David *Gilly, and *Langhans in Berlin in the early 1790s, he was introduced to the severe Franco-Prussian *Neoclassicism that was to inform his work for the rest of his life. After a period in Rome (1792–7) he studied the ruins of the Greek temples at *Paestum and Sicily, and later prepared the illustrations for *Die Baukunst nach den Grundsätzen der Alten* (Architecture According to the Principles of the Ancients) by Alois Hirt (1759–1834) of 1809. Most of his buildings were erected in Karlsruhe, which he transformed into the Neoclassical Grand-Ducal capital of Baden from the time he was engaged as a State official in 1797 until his death. He superimposed a sequence of urban spaces over the existing town-plan, including the *Marktplatz* (Market Place—1797–1826) with a pyramid at its centre, the whole modelled on urban spaces in Antiquity. His *Schloss-strasse* (Castle Street—begun 1799) led to the severely *Doric *Ettlinger Tor* (Ettlinger Gate) of 1803, and was composed as a series of episodes, asymmetrically disposed, giving a *Picturesque effect more varied than that of *Nash's Regent Street in London. All Weinbrenner's buildings in Karlsruhe were of an impressively grand, if severe, quality, especially the Roman Catholic Church of St Stephen (1804–14), which was inspired by the *Pantheon and the Imperial *thermae in Rome, and by the Graeco-Egyptian Gothic Synagogue (1798—destroyed), one of his most eclectic compositions. His startlingly bold scheme for the *Langestrasse* (1808), with both sides lined by a continuous *colonnade of plain arches carried on slender undecorated *piers, was not realized, but was an inspiration for certain C20 *Neo-Rationalists (notably *Grassi). He was responsible for six of the major public buildings, including the Sculpture Gallery (1804), and *Kurhaus* (Assembly Rooms (1821–4)) at Baden-Baden. Weinbrenner published *Architektonisches Lehrbuch* (Architectural Textbook—1810–17) and *Ausgeführte und projektierte Gebäude* (Executed and Projected Buildings—1822–35). His ideas for Karlsruhe and his style were effectively ended by his successor *Hübsch.

Brownlee (1986); Elbert (1988); Valdenaire (1919, 1926, 1976); Watkin and Mellinghoff (1987)

Weir, Robert Weir Schultz (**Robert Weir Schultz** until 1915) (1860–1951). Scots-born *Arts-and-Crafts architect. Articled to Rowand *Anderson, he later joined the office of Norman *Shaw, where he met *Lethaby, with whom he formed a lasting friendship. After a period in the office of Ernest *George and Peto, he set up his own practice in London and worked on several buildings for the 3rd (1847–1900) and 4th (1881–1947) Marquesses of Bute, including the reconstruction of Wester Kames Tower, Isle of Bute (1897–1900). Weir studied *Byzantine architecture with Lethaby and Sidney *Barnsley (with whom he collaborated on *The Monastery of St Luke . . . in Phocis* (1901)), and was a leading light in the Byzantine Revival. His Byzantine studies led to the creation of the Chapel of St Andrew and the Saints of Scotland in *Bentley's

Westminster Cathedral (1910–15). His greatest work is probably the Anglican Cathedral Church of All Saints, Khartoum, Sudan (1906–13), which deserves to be considered, with Lethaby's Brockhampton, *Prior and A. R. *Wells's Roker, and *Bellot's Quarr Abbey, as among the most successful C20 church buildings. One of its most interesting features is the *clearstorey, consisting of a series of *triangular arches based on *Anglo-Saxon exemplars. He had a thriving country-house practice before 1914, but he also designed economical housing at Gretna Green, Scotland (1914–18—under the general direction of *Unwin), and built an extension to a barn at Hartley Wintney, Hampshire (1903–12), as his own home. Like many Arts-and-Crafts architects, he worked with several styles, drawing on many sources, and his smaller domestic buildings were invariably agreeable.

Architectural History, 22 (1979), 88–116; Clarke (1958); Gray (1985); Placzek (1982); Stamp (1981)

Weissenhofsiedlung. Literally the 'white house estate', it was the name given to the development by the *Deutscher Werkbund intended as an exhibition of workers' housing in Stuttgart, Württemberg (1927). Directed by *Mies van der Rohe, it included buildings by Le *Corbusier, *Gropius, and others, and got its name from the flat-roofed, white-painted minimalist *International Modern style of the houses which established paradigms for many years to come.

Welch, Edward (1806–68). *See* Hansom.

Welch, Herbert Arthur (1884–1953). English architect. He made a major contribution to the development of Hampstead *Garden Suburb, London, from 1908, where he designed many houses, including gabled work in Denman Drive. He also designed the handsome curved terraces of shops and apartments in Golders Green Road that demonstrate the early C20 change of style from *vernacular revival to *Neo-Georgian. In collaboration with Frederick *Etchells (the translator of Le *Corbusier's works into English), Welch, with Nugent Francis Cachemaille-Day (1896–1976) and Felix J. Lander (1898–1960), designed the pioneering *International Modern Crawford's Office Building, High Holborn, London (1930), with long bands of windows subdivided by steel *mullions, much influenced by the *Weissenhofsiedlung.

Gray (1985); Miller and Gray (1992)

Wells, Arthur Randall (1877–1942). English *Arts-and-Crafts architect. As Clerk of Works for *Lethaby's Church of All Saints, Brockhampton, Herefordshire (1902), he absorbed much of the elder man's style, as is clear from his own Church of St Edward the Confessor and St Mary, Kempley, Gloucestershire, with its charming *Rood and exquisite furnishings (1904). He built Voewood (later Home Place), Kelling, near Holt, Norfolk (1903–4), and St Andrew's, Roker, Sunderland, Co. Durham (1906–7—arguably the finest church of the Arts-and-Crafts movement), for E. S. *Prior. Both buildings employed *concrete structure, in the case of the church *reinforced, and at the house mass-concrete faced with *flints and thin tile-like bricks (there are also areas where the *in situ* concrete is simply left with the board-marks of the form-work exposed as the finish, many years earlier than fashionable *Brutalism). Wells also designed a prize-winning cottage for Letchworth *Garden City, Hertfordshire.

Garnham (1995); Gray (1985); Miller (1989); Pevsner, *Buildings of England, County Durham* (1985), *Gloucestershire: The Vale and the Forest of Dean* (1970)

Wells, Joseph Merrill (d. 1890). Member of the office of *McKim, Mead, & White, responsible for introducing a revival of the Italian High *Renaissance style to the firm from 1879. Early examples include the Villard Houses, Madison Avenue, New York (1882), and the Public Library, Boston, Mass. (1888–95).

Roth, L. M. (1973, 1983); Wilson (1983)

Wells, The Master of (*fl.* *c.*1175–*c.*1215). The part of Wells Cathedral in Somerset between the west front and the eastern arm (*choir) is unusually of a piece and unified in terms of design and style. Unfortunately the identity of the architect is not known, but he was probably English, for his style has no affinities with French *Gothic, being horizontally emphasized, the *triforium-*arcade treated as a long band and the springing of the *vaults pushed upwards to just below *clearstorey level, quite unlike anything on the Continent. In addition, the *First Pointed *stiff-leaf *capitals are among the finest and most vigorous in England. The architect is called The Master of Wells, perhaps a Master Thomas who worked at Bath Abbey in the late C12.

Harvey (1987); Pevsner, *Buildings of England, North Somerset and Bristol* (1958)

Wells, Simon de (*fl.* 1240–57). English sculptor. He was very likely the carver of the statues on the west front of Wells Cathedral, Somerset, and was in Westminster in 1257 making a design for the tomb of Katherine, King Henry III's (1220–72) daughter, in the Abbey there.

Harvey (1987)

Wells Coates, Wintemute (1895–1958). *See* Coates.

Welsch, Johann Maximilian von (1671–1745). German architect and military engineer. In the service (from 1704) of Lothar Franz, Graf von Schönborn (1655–1729), Prince-Bishop of Bamberg and Elector of Mainz, he contributed to the flowering of *Baroque architecture in Franconia. With *Neumann, von *Hildebrandt, and others, he was involved in the planning of Schloss Weissenstein, Pommersfelden (1711–18), the Palace at Bruchsal (1720–52), and the *Residenz* (Seat of the Court) in Würzburg (1719–79). He designed numerous gardens, garden-buildings, and small houses for the German nobility. Among his other works were the Schönborn *Mortuary Chapel, Würzburg Cathedral (1720–1), the Court Chapel, the *Residenz*, Würzburg (1720–3), and the *Abteikirche* (Abbey Church), Amorbach (1742–7), all of which had major contributions from others.

Bourke (1962); Lohmeyer (1931); Meintzschel (1963); Powell (1959)

Welsh. *See* arch.

Werkbund. *See* Deutscher Werkbund.

Werkstätte. *See* Wiener Werkstätte.

Westerley, Robert (*fl.* 1421–61). English master-mason. He and 30 other English masons went to Rouen in Normandy in 1421 to work on the castle there, and he was employed as deputy mason at Westminster Abbey when construction on the *nave was resumed in 1423/4. Appointed King's Master-Mason in 1438/9 on the death of *Mapilton, he worked at the Palace of Sheen, near London, and from 1442 was in charge of the works at Tutbury Castle, Staffordshire, where the south tower at the east end of the hall range was being built. He also supervised the early works at Eton College, Buckinghamshire, from its foundation in 1441, and was the architect of the original layout. He made a design for a bell-tower at King's College Chapel, Cambridge (shortly after 1448, but not realized), which seems to have been the model for the tower of the Church of St Mary Aldermary, London (begun 1510—destroyed).

Harvey (1987)

Westphalen (*or* **Westfalen**), **Arnold von** (*fl.* C15). German architect. He was called to the Wettin Court at Meissen in 1470, and was responsible for many of the late-*Gothic buildings in Saxony. Among his works are Albrechtsburg (from 1471), the *Rathaus* (Town Hall—from 1472), and the Cathedral (1472–6), all in Meissen, and part of the *Schloss* in Dresden (from 1471). His influence spread into Eastern Europe, especially to Bohemia.

Białostocki (1972); Hubala and Schweikhart (1978); Mrusek (1972)

west-work. *Westwerk* in German, i.e. massive, wide, tower-like west front of an early *Romanesque or *Carolingian church containing an entrance-vestibule with a chapel and other rooms over it opening to the upper part of the *nave. A good surviving example is the Abbey Church of Corvey-on-the-Weser, Germany (873–5), which has a low entrance-hall with massive *piers and circular columns carrying the *vaults over which is a two-storey upper church surrounded by *arcades and *aisles.

Conant (1979); Cruickshank (1996); Pevsner (1960); Watkin (1986)

wheeler. 1. Winder in a *stair, especially a *newel or spiral stair. **2.** Lower part of a *battlement. *Wheelers* (embrasures) and *kneelers* (merlons or cops) therefore refer to *crenellation.

wheel-head cross. *Celtic cross.

wheel-step. *Wheeler (**1**).

wheel-window. 1. Circular window-aperture with spoke-like *colonnettes or *bars radiating from the centre, e.g. west front of Chartres Cathedral, France (late C12). **2.** Circular part of an early *Middle Pointed Geometrical window with bar-*tracery.

whelmer and kneeler. The former is a *dripstone, the latter its return.

whiplash. Common decorative element in *Art Nouveau ornament, a whip-like, flowing, curved line.

Tschudi-Madsen (1967)

White, Stanford (1853–1906). *See* McKim, Mead, & White.

White, William (1825–1900). English *High Victorian *Gothic architect. He trained in George Gilbert *Scott's office (where he met *Bodley and *Street) before establishing (1847) a practice in Cornwall. His works include the Church of All Saints, Notting Hill (from 1852), and St Saviour's, Aberdeen Park, both in London (1865—with a *polychrome brick interior), but his master-work is St Michael's, Lyndhurst, Hampshire (1858–70), a big red- and yellow-brick structure in the *First Pointed style, with odd *tracery, strange cross-gables, and a sumptuous polychrome interior that contains work by Edward Coley Burne-Jones (1833–98), *Morris, Lord Leighton (1830–96), and Street. He also designed several houses, including the Old Rectory, St Columb Major, Cornwall (1849–50), the Vicarage, Little Baddow, Essex (1858), and Humewood, Co. Wicklow, Ireland (1873–7).

Curl (1995); Dixon and Muthesius (1985); Eastlake (1970); Sheppard (1973)

Whitfield, Sir William (1920–). English architect. His design-method is largely dependent on separating functions (e.g. 'served' and 'serving' areas), expressing them as architectural forms. Among his works are the Library and Hunterian Museum and Art Gallery Extension, University of Glasgow (1962–81), expressed as a series of powerful verticals finished in rectilinear bush-hammered concrete. Within the Gallery is a re-creation of *Mackintosh's house at 78 Southpark Avenue (1906), demolished by the University in 1963. He also designed the extension (1964–70) to the fine Institute of Chartered Accountants Building by Beresford *Pite and John *Belcher (1892), including a new entrance based on the Pite–Belcher idiom. His Department of Health, Richmond Terrace, Whitehall, London (1987), with its striped exterior and carefully modelled vertical elements, responds to Norman *Shaw's New Scotland Yard (1890) near by, and also suggests something of the *Gothic, an allusion, perhaps, to the lost *Tudor buildings of Whitehall Palace. Whitfield has often favoured load-bearing construction to create a sense of permanence and monumentality, as in his powerful brick Chapter House at St Alban's Cathedral, Hertfordshire (1975–83), and the massive block at Bessborough Street, Pimlico, London (1980–4), both of which successfully exploit the segmental arch. More recently (1995), his masterly red sandstone Cathedral Library at Hereford has enhanced his reputation as a sensitive contextual designer. Like *Scarpa, *Schattner, and other Continental architects, Whitfield can respond intelligently to existing buildings in historic settings and create new architecture that is vigorous yet well mannered.

Perspectives on Architecture, 2/20 (Dec. 1995/Jan. 1996), 32–9; personal knowledge; Williamson, Riches, and Higgs (1990)

wicket. Small door or gate forming part of a larger door or gate, essentially a door within a door.

Wiedemann Family. C18 German master-builders. **Dominikus** and **Johann Baptist Wiedemann** realized J. B. *Neumann's designs for the great Benedictine Abbey Church at Neresheim after the latter's death in 1753, one of the finest late-*Baroque churches in all Europe. **Christian Wiedemann** began the Benedictine Abbey Church at Wiblingen (1732), continued after 1750 by J. M. *Fischer, and completed by Johann G. Specht (1721–83): he also contributed to the design of the beautiful Baroque Library at Wiblingen.

Bourke (1962); Hitchcock (1968); Powell (1959)

Wiener Werkstätte. Literally 'Vienna Workshop', founded in 1903 to emulate English *Arts-and-Crafts workshops, such as the Guild of Handicrafts of C. R. *Ashbee. It grew partly from the *Sezession exhibition of 1900 that included designs by *Mackintosh and Ashbee. By 1905 the Werkstätte was employing over 100 people, most of the artefacts being designed by Josef *Hoffmann and Koloman Moser (1868–1918). It became the centre for progressive design in Austria-Hungary, promoting a severe rectilinear style. It ceased operations in 1932.

Jervis (1984); Ouvrard, Bouniort, and Huet (1986)

Wightwick, George (1802–72). English architect. He assisted the elderly *Soane, and in 1827 published *Select Views of Roman Antiquities* based on a visit to Italy in 1825. In 1829 he established himself in practice in Plymouth, Devon, joined *Foulston (who was about to retire) in partnership, and became the leading architect in the West of England. He designed a formidable range of buildings in a variety of styles, but his essays in *Gothic did not meet with the approval of the *Ecclesiologists, who were particularly strong in the Diocese of Exeter from the time the High Churchman Henry Philpotts became Bishop (1831–69). Wightwick was a successful architectural journalist, much of his writing being agreeable and light (in his early years he had contemplated a career as an actor), but he also contributed a weighty essay on the use of iron in architecture to J. C. *Loudon's *Architectural Magazine* (1837), and published an eccentric quasi-Masonic book entitled *The Palace of Architecture: A Romance of Art and History* (1840), among much else.

Colvin (1995); *DNB* (1917); Papworth (1892)

Wijdeveld, Hendrik Theodor (1886–1987). Dutch architect and writer. As Editor of the journal *Wendingen* (Turnings—published 1918–31) he encouraged innovatory typography and design, and was a central figure in promoting the *Amsterdam School. He formed links between German and Dutch exponents of *Expressionism, and publicized work by Eileen *Gray and Frank Lloyd *Wright. As an architect he was influenced by *Mendelsohn, *Wright, and *Futurism. He designed several housing projects for Amsterdam South in the 1920s, and a large development on the Hoofdweg (1925–6) with tortuously curving complex *façades. He published *My First Century* shortly before he died.

Jervis (1984); Pehnt (1973)

Wild, James William (1814–92). English architect. Articled to *Basevi, he travelled widely, was Owen *Jones's brother-in-law, worked on the decorations of the 1851 Great Exhibition, and was Curator of Sir John *Soane's Museum from 1878 until his death. His most distinguished works include the *Rundbogenstil Christ Church, Streatham (1840–2), a reworking of the *Early Christian *basilica type, but influenced by C19 German precedents, with decorations (now largely obliterated) by Owen Jones. If the *campanile of the latter is tall, assured, and handsome, it is put in the shade by the gigantic dock-tower, Grimsby, Lincolnshire (1851–2), based on the tower of the Town Hall in Siena, Italy, but with a crowning *minaret influenced by Wild's travels in Egypt and Syria in the 1840s. He contributed to the design of the Huxley Building, Exhibition Road, Kensington, London (1867–71), and was responsible for the exterior of the Bethnal Green Museum, London (1873), around the re-sited 'Brompton Boilers', the prefabricated iron structure (by Charles D. Young of Edinburgh) originally erected (1855–6) in South Kensington to house the Museum of Science and Art.

Curl (1990, 1995); Dixon and Muthesius (1985); Sheppard (1975)

wilderness. 1. Ornamental and agreeable landscape, neither wild nor deserted, carefully planned and tended, planted with trees to form a grove or wood with paths cut through it, often designed in a fantastic way, frequently with a *maze. **2.** *Bosket. **3.** Land giving the appearance of being wild or uncultivated, a variant on the idea of the *desert. **4.** Informally laid out woodland of mixed species, with paths and open areas running through it.

Coffin (1994); *OED* (1933); Symes (1993)

Wilds, Amon (*c*.1762–1833). English builder and architect. He designed and erected a number of houses in Brighton and Lewes, Sussex, featuring the *Ammonite capital, which seems to have been his firm's trademark. His son, **Amon Henry Wilds** (1748–1857), laid out the Kemp Town Estate, Brighton, and erected many *stucco-faced terraces and crescents there in a style reminiscent of that of *Nash, including Sussex Square, Lewes Crescent, Arundel Terrace, and Chichester Terrace (1823–*c*.1850). Like his father, he employed the Ammonite capital on his buildings.

Colvin (1995); Dale (1947)

Wilford, Michael (1938–). English architect. He assisted *Stirling & *Gowan (1960–3) before working with Stirling only, becoming a partner in James Stirling Michael Wilford & Associates (1971–92), and since 1993 has been senior partner in Michael Wilford & Partners. He worked with Stirling & Gowan on the University of Leicester Engineering Building (1959–63), and with Stirling on many projects, including the *Staatsgalerie* (State Gallery), Stuttgart, Germany (1977–84), No. 1 Poultry, City of London (from 1986), and the Lowry Centre, Salford, Manchester (from 1991). Since Stirling's death his practice has developed, especially in Germany, and his work has attracted considerable critical attention. In 1997 the Stuttgart Music-School (1987–95) was acclaimed, winning the Stirling Prize.

Information from Michael Wilford & Partners

Wilkins, William (1751–1815). English plasterer and architect. He carried out many architectural commissions for *Repton, and was an antiquarian with an interest in medieval architecture. Among his works may be mentioned Donington Hall, Leicestershire (*c.*1790–7—in the *Gothic style), alterations, including the addition of the *portico, to Calke Abbey, Derbyshire (1793–1808), and two houses in Cambridge (38 Newmarket Road, *c.*1795, and Newnham Cottage, Queen's Road, *c.*1800).

Colvin (1995); Papworth (1892); Stroud (1962)

Wilkins, William (1778–1839). English architect, son of William *Wilkins. Educated at Cambridge, he became acquainted with Greek and Italian architecture during his travels (1801–4). He set up his office in London in 1809 and quickly established himself as a leading figure of the *Greek Revival. He designed the first pure Greek *Doric *portico for any English country-house at Osberton House, Nottinghamshire (*c.*1805—demolished). This was followed by the East India (now Haileybury) College, Hertfordshire (1806–9), and then Downing College, Cambridge (1807–20), both early and important buildings of the Greek Revival. In the latter case, where Wilkins's scheme was selected instead of James *Wyatt's Neoclassical design, Thomas *Hope was the chief protagonist in promoting the Grecian style. Downing was the first of all university *campuses, or separate buildings disposed around a grassed area. Wilkins followed these important schemes with University College, London (1827–8), the Philosophical Society's Museum, York (1827–30), St George's Hospital, Hyde Park Corner, London (1828–9), and the National Gallery, Trafalgar Square, London (1834–8), all in the Grecian style, although the last had a disastrous effect on his reputation for its lack of distinction. One of his most handsome creations in the Greek Revival style, the Nelson 'pillar' (i.e. *column), Sackville (later O'Connell) Street, Dublin (1808–9), was destroyed in 1966.

At Grange Park, Hampshire (from 1809), he used Greek Revival for an English country-house, and created one of England's noblest buildings in that style. Elsewhere he succumbed to fashion and designed in *Tudor Gothic, including Dalmeny House, West Lothian (1814–17), Dunmore Park, Stirlingshire (1820–2), and New Court, Trinity College, Cambridge (1823–5). At King's College, Cambridge, however, he responded brilliantly to the great medieval *chapel by designing the entrance-*screen, gateway, and new buildings (1824–8), in a *Tudor Gothic of great charm, inventiveness, and delicacy. However, as a Classical (and especially Greek Revival) architect, Wilkins could be somewhat prissy and feeble, for, with the exception of Grange Park, his buildings tend to lack any sense of power in massing, although his detailing was always scholarly, if constricted by his inhibitions as a designer. However, he was among the first to note the optical corrections used by the Greeks in their buildings, and his *The Antiquities of Magna Graecia* (1807) contained accurate illustrations of the Greek temples at Agrigentum, *Paestum, Segesta, and Syracuse. He also published *Atheniensia, or Remarks on the Topography and Buildings of Athens* (1816), as well as *The Civil Architecture of Vitruvius* (1812—an incomplete translation), and *Prolusiones Architectonicae* (1837—essays on Greek and Roman architecture probably based on his lectures as Professor of Architecture at the Royal Academy), among other works.

Burlington Magazine, 113 (1971), 318–29; Colvin (1995); Colvin and Harris (1970); Crook (1964, 1972*a*); *DNB* (1917); Liscombe (1980); Middleton and Watkin (1987); Watkin (1968); Wiebenson (1969); Wilkins (1807, 1816, 1817, 1836, 1837)

Willard, Solomon (1783–1861). American architect. Influenced by the work of *Latrobe, Willard brought the *Greek Revival to Boston. He designed the United States Branch Bank, Boston (1822–4), the Norfolk County Court House, Dedham (1824–6), and the Suffolk County Court House, Boston (1835), all in Greek *Doric, and all in Massachusetts. He was also responsible for the Town Hall, Quincy, Mass. (1844). From 1824 to 1842 he concerned himself with the Bunker Hill Monument, Charlestown, Mass., a vast *obelisk with an *Egyptian Revival base: he published *Plans and Sections of the Obelisk on Bunker's Hill* in 1843.

Bjelajac (1997); Carrott (1978); Edwards (1954); Hamlin (1964); Kennedy (1989); Wheildon (1865); Whiffen and Koeper (1983); Willard (1843)

William and Mary. Architectural style of the reigns of William III (reigned 1688–1702) and Queen Mary II (reigned 1688–94) in Great Britain, coming mid-way between the French-inspired *Baroque of the *Restoration and the *Queen Anne period. It embraced influences from William's own country, The Netherlands, and was leavened by themes from France brought over by Huguenot refugees after the Revocation (1685) of the Edict of Nantes (1598—which had given French Protestants equality of citizenship). It also included an exotic thread in that it had a taste for oriental motifs from China which led to the beginnings of *Chinoiserie.

William of Ramsey (*fl.* 1323–d. 1349). *See* Ramsey.

William of Sens (*fl.* 1174–d. 1180). *See* Sens.

William of Wykeham (1324–1404). *See* Wykeham.

William of Wynford (*fl.* 1360–d. 1405). *See* Wynford.

William the Englishman (*fl.* 1174–d. *c.*1214). *See* Sens.

Williams, Sir (Evan) Owen (1890–1969). British engineer. In the 1930s he designed some of the most celebrated contemporary buildings in England, using *reinforced-concrete construction. At the Boots Factory, Beeston, Nottingham (1930–2), he used the *pier system with a mushroom-like top invented by *Maillart. He was consulting engineer for the *Daily Express* Building, Fleet Street, London (1932—in association with Ellis and Clarke), in which a *curtain-wall with black 'Vitrolite' glass panels was used. He was largely responsible for the Pioneer Health Centre, Peckham, London (1934–6), and for the Dorchester Hotel, London (1929–30—with William Curtis *Green). Once seen as a pioneer of *Functionalism and of the *Modern Movement, his designs for the M1 Motorway, including the very heavy concrete bridges (1951–9—some of which have the canted arches of the 1920s *Art Deco style) dimmed his reputation.

Architectural Design, 39/7 (July 1969), 348; Emanuel (1994); *Zodiac*, 18 (1968), 11–30

Williams-Ellis, Sir (Bertram) Clough (1883–1978). British architect. Main influences on his work were the *Picturesque, aspects of the *Arts-and-Crafts movement, the Italian *Renaissance, and Mediterranean and English *vernacular architecture. In the years before and after the 1914–18 war, Williams-Ellis had a flourishing practice, designing houses (among which was the remarkably precocious Llangoed Castle, Breconshire (1913–19)) and other buildings, but he was also involved in the campaign to build cheap cottages, and was much influenced by Patrick *Geddes. In 1919 he published *Cottage Building in Cob, Pisé, Chalk, and Clay* (later reissued in a revised edition of 1947). Among his most felicitous designs of the period were Glenmona House, Maud Cottages, and other additions to the village of Cushendun, and the McNaughton Memorial Hall and School, Giant's Causeway, all in Co. Antrim, Northern Ireland. In 1925 he began his most famous creation, the village of Portmeirion, Merioneth, Wales, a Picturesque composition of individual buildings incorporating Classical details, salvaged fragments, and vernacular elements. Several of the themes explored in Portmeirion were elaborated upon in *The Pleasures of Architecture* (1924, 1954), written with his wife, Mary Annabel Nassau (Amabel) Strachey (1894–1984).

He began to campaign for effective town-and country-planning, working with (Sir) Charles *Reilly, (Sir) Patrick *Abercrombie, and others. Among his polemics of the time were *England and the Octopus* (1928) and *Britain and the Beast* (1937), and he worked tirelessly for the Councils for the Preservation of Rural England and Wales, the National Trust, and the National Parks. After the 1939–45 war, Williams-Ellis was appointed Chairman of Stevenage New Town Development Corporation, but a growing disillusion with the *Modern Movement (which he had once supported in *Architecture Here and Now* (1934—with John *Summerson)) and his independence of mind led to a short-lived association with 'Silkingrad', as wags called the New Town (after Lewis Silkin (1889–1972), the Socialist Minister of Town and Country Planning who had promoted the New Towns Act (1946)). In his architectural works his handling of internal and external volumes was masterly, and his buildings are invariably pleasant, helped by his innate understanding of scale and materials. One of his most delightful creations was the garden at Plas Brondanw, Merioneth (begun *c.*1913). His last written works included *Architect Errant* (1971) and *Around the World in Ninety Years* (1979).

Brett (1996); *DNB* (1986); Emanuel (1994); Haslam (1979, 1995); personal knowledge

Willmott, Ernest (Ernest Willmott Sloper until 1907) (1871–1916). English architect. He worked with Herbert *Baker in South Africa, notably on the Government Offices at Bloemfontein and Pretoria. He returned to England and established his own practice in 1907, much of his work at the time showing a pronounced Dutch *Colonial style. He published *English Shopfronts Old and New* (1907) and the useful *English House Design* (1911). His contributions to Hampstead *Garden Suburb were exceptionally fine (79 and 81 Hampstead Way).

Gray (1985); Miller and Gray (1992)

Wilson, Sir Colin St John (1922–). English architect. With J. L. *Martin he was very influential at the School of Architecture, University of Cambridge (where he and Martin designed the brick and raw-concrete blocky Extension of 1958–9—influenced by Le *Corbusier), and, with Martin, designed several university buildings, including the inward-looking, remorselessly hard terraced brick-built Harvey Court, Gonville and Caius College, Cambridge (1960–2—influenced by *Aalto and *Kahn), and the Law, Economics, and Statistics Libraries, Manor Road, Oxford (1961–4), which explored the themes of the fragmented courtyard and the stepped terrace. Their eight-storey brick William Stone Residential Building, Peterhouse, Cambridge (1962–4), shows influences again from Aalto. Other designs (by Wilson alone) include two houses, 2 and 2a Grantchester Road (1963–4—described by *Pevsner as 'memorable'), and Spring House, Conduit Head Road (1967—about which Pevsner was less enthusiastic), both in Cambridge. In 1962 Wilson and Martin were commissioned to design the British Library opposite the British Museum in Bloomsbury, but Conservationists opposed the destruction of so much earlier fabric in the area. In 1977–9, Wilson designed the West Wing Extension to the Museum, an uncompromisingly Modernist solution grafted on to *Smirke's great building, and in due course was commissioned to design the new British Library on a different site on the Euston Road, London, beside *Scott's huge frontage to St Pancras Railway Station. Begun in 1982 and completed in 1998, the Library is his largest work, displaying affinities with some of his earlier designs. The hard red-brick exterior perhaps is a rather dour neighbour of Scott's great pile, demonstrating the Modern Movement's chronic problems with context, but some of the interiors rise to the occasion. He has published many articles, and in 1994 his book, *Architectural Reflections*, appeared.

Architectural Review, 126/750 (1959), 42–8, 164, 126/982 (1978), 336–44; *RIBA Journal*, 86/3 (1979), 107–15; Emanuel (1994)

Wilson, Henry (1864–1934). English architect. He worked in the offices of *Belcher, J. O. *Scott, and J. D. *Sedding (whose partner he became and with whom he collaborated on the designs for Holy Trinity Church, Sloane Street, London, where he was responsible for the metal-work, screens, bas-reliefs, and much of the beautiful detail of the interior (1888–*c*.1901)). He completed Sedding's *Italianate *Renaissance Revival Church of the Holy Redeemer, Exmouth Market, London (1887–8), where he added the *campanile, and (again with Sedding) designed the Church of St Peter, Mount Park Road, Ealing, London (1889–93), where curvaceous *Gothic forms are used with great power and originality.

Wilson's chief claim to fame is as an *Arts-and-Crafts designer of exquisite enamel- and metal-work, jewellery, and sculpture (he was Master of the *Art Workers Guild in 1917 and President of the Arts and Crafts Exhibition Society (1915–22)), and had a distinguished career designing church-furnishings, including the decorations (1895–1910) for Edmund Evan Scott's (d. 1895) *Sublime Church of St Bartholomew, Ann Street, Brighton, Sussex (built 1872–4), all of the finest Arts-and-Crafts quality, ample and rich. One of his loveliest creations is the monument to Canon E. D. Tinling (d. 1897) in Gloucester Cathedral. He also designed the sculpted *frieze over the entrance to Leonard *Stokes's Church of All Saints, London Colney, Hertfordshire (1899), and the monument to Bishop William Elphinstone (1431–1514), King's College, Aberdeen. His work was exhibited and greatly admired before the 1914–18 war in Germany, notably by *Muthesius. He published *Silverwork and Jewellery: a text-book for students and workers in metal* (1903) which went into further editions (1912, 1966, 1978), and was Editor of the *Architectural Review* (1896–1901).

Gray (1985); *RIBA Journal*, ser. 3, 41/10 (24 Mar. 1934), 539; Service (1975, 1977); Thieme and Becker (1932)

Wimmel, Carl Ludwig (1786–1845). German architect. A pupil of Christian Friedrich Lange (1768–1833), *Langhans, and *Weinbrenner, he worked in Hamburg from 1814, becoming Director of the Building Department in 1841. His earliest buildings for the City included the Greek *Doric *Steintor* and *Millerntor* (1818–19—both destroyed), and the *arcuated General Hospital (1815–23—destroyed). For the Municipal Theatre (1826–7—destroyed) and the dignified terrace-houses at the Esplanade (1827–30) he chose a refined *Classicism, but his best building, the Johanneum (two schools and a library grouped around a court, of 1837–40—destroyed), was in the rusticated Florentine round-arched style made fashionable by *Gärtner and von *Klenze in Munich. He chose a Neo-*Cinquecento style for the Exchange (1837–41), designed, like the Johanneum, in collaboration with Franz Gustav Joachim Forsmann (1795–1878), whose finest work on his own account, the Jenisch House at Flottbeck, near Hamburg (1828–34), survives, a taut Grecian *villa strongly influenced by the work of *Schinkel.

Grundmann (1957); Hannmann (1975); Watkin and Mellinghoff (1987)

Winchcombe, Richard (*fl.* 1398–1440). English mason. He worked at Porchester Castle, Hampshire in the 1390s, and thereafter mostly in Oxfordshire. He seems to have designed the *tithe-barn at Swalcliffe (1403–6), the *chancel of Adderbury Church (1408–18), and carried out various jobs at New College, Oxford. Although employed by New College, he seems to have run some kind of private practice, and his hand has been detected in various churches, including Bloxham (Milcombe Chapel), Broughton, Deddington, Enstone, North Leigh (Wilcote Chapel), and Thame (*transept), all in Oxfordshire. He may have carried out works at Northleach Church, Gloucestershire, but his main claim to fame is the Divinity School, Oxford, begun 1424, later vaulted by William *Orchard.

Harvey (1987)

Winckelmann, Johann Joachim (1717–68). German art-historian and archaeologist. He settled in Rome, became librarian to Cardinal Alessandro Albani (1692–1779), and established himself as a scholar and antiquarian, advising on the acquisition of the Cardinal's great collection of *Antique sculpture (many items of which are now in the *Glyptothek*, Munich). He was an important influence on *Neoclassicism, and especially on the *Greek Revival. His two great books, *Gedanken über die Nachahmung der griechischen Werke in der Malerei und Bildhauerkunst* (1755—published in English in 1765 as *Reflections on the Painting and Sculpture of the Greeks*) and *Geschichte der Kunst des Altertums* (History of Ancient Art—1764), proclaimed the superiority of Greek art and subjected it to analysis. His art-historical method and his interpretation of Classical Antiquity informed education, especially in Germany, well into the present century. His notion of the best of Classical art imbued with 'noble simplicity and calm grandeur' became deeply embedded in Western thought, and he influenced many artists and architects, notably the painter Anton Raffael Mengs (1728–79—whose ceiling *fresco, *Parnassus*, in the Villa Albani, Rome (1761), was one of the key works of Neoclassicism), *Schinkel, and von *Klenze.

Chilvers, Osborne, and Farr (1988); Gaehtgens (1986); Watkin and Mellinghoff (1987)

wind. The winds are often shown personified, as in the Tower of the Winds (Horologium of Andronicus of Cyrrhus), Athens (*c.*50 BC), published by *Stuart and *Revett and copied widely in C18.

wind-beam. Collar-beam tying rafters or *crucks.

wind-brace. *Brace, usually arched or curved, set in the plane of a roof, tying a *principal to a *purlin, or otherwise stiffening a roof-structure to prevent it falling sideways along its length.

Alcock, Barley, Dixon, and Meeson (1996)

Winde, William (*c.*1640–1722). English architect, soldier, and military engineer. He appears to have been trained by *Gerbier, and succeeded the latter as architect at Hampstead Marshall, Berkshire (*c.*1663–*c.*1688), when Gerbier died. With *Hooke, *May, *Pratt, and *Talman, Winde was one of the most important country-house architects working in England in the later part of C17. He rebuilt Combe Abbey, Warwickshire (1682–8), drawing on Pratt's work, and probably designed part of Dingley Hall, Northamptonshire (*c.*1684–8), and Belton House, Lincolnshire (1685–8). He may also have carried out works at Cliveden House, Buckinghamshire (*c.*1676–8), and Buckingham House, St James's,

London (1702–5—destroyed), both of which had balustraded *Attics instead of steeply pitched roofs. Buckingham House, with its *colonnaded *quadrants and wings, was an influential design, and was the prototype for a formula applied to many C18 country-houses.

Colvin (1995); Summerson (1993)

winder. *See* stair.

winding stair. *See* stair.

window. **1.** Aperture in a wall to allow light and air to enter a building. If a window-aperture is divided into compartments by means of, say, *mullions and *transoms, those compartments are *lights. In its simplest form, a window is a mere hole in a wall, with an arch or *lintel at its head. Some Greek windows on important buildings were narrower at the top than at the bottom (*see* Tivoli and Vitruvian opening), and had *architraves, often with *crossettes, as in the Philippeion at Olympia (begun 339 BC).

Roman windows were much larger and more varied in type especially after glazing was readily available by *c.* AD 65, although other materials were in use until the early C18. Thin parchment stretched on a frame, then painted and varnished; parchment painted and coated with linseed-oil; linen painted and coated with white of egg and gum-water and varnished; paper soaked in poppy-oil, mutton suet, or wax; and linen dipped or coated in beeswax were employed. In many cases glazing was found only in the upper part of the window, the lower part having wooden shutters, and this arrangement was commonly found even in Scotland's Royal palaces until comparatively recently (C18). In Classical architecture, windows not only had architraves, but were crowned with *entablatures with or without *pediments. In grander window-openings, columns or *pilasters may be found on either side supporting an entablature, *gable, pediment, etc., in which case they are said to be *aediculated* (*see* aedicule).

Early medieval windows were small and narrow, often with *splays on *cills and *reveals of *jambs to improve the ingress of light, and this type of construction seems to be of considerable antiquity. It was as much controlled by questions of security as by the problems of keeping rain out. *Anglo-Saxon windows were of this type, frequently crudely arched, or with lintels at their heads shaped on the *soffits to look like small arched openings, or having two stones set diagonally at the top to form triangular heads: in towers of the period, apertures often consisted of two distinct openings between which were turned *baluster-*colonnettes with exaggerated *entasis. *Romanesque windows were larger, but were still of the hole-in-the-wall type, splayed, semicircular-headed, and often decorated with *billet or *chevron mouldings. Romanesque semicircular-headed lights were occasionally paired, separated by a *shaft, and contained within a bigger semicircular-headed opening. Circular window-apertures were common, often in *gables, but sometimes elsewhere, e.g. the *clearstorey lights of Southwell *Minster, Nottinghamshire. In *First Pointed *Gothic, early window-apertures were tall and narrow (*lancets), almost invariably with splayed jambs, having sharply pointed heads, used singly or sometimes in groups of three or five (as in the eastern gables of *chancels (e.g. the *Lady Chapel of Hereford Cathedral (*c.*1220–40)), but circles, quatrefoils, and other simple figures were used, especially in plate-*tracery. With the transition to early *Middle Pointed came *Geometrical* *bar-tracery and Y-tracery. *Second Pointed work introduced *Curvilinear, Flowing, Intersecting*, and *Reticulated* tracery, the various lights framed by *mullions and bar-tracery. In England, *Perpendicular windows had mullions and *transoms subdividing ever-larger windows into panel-like lights, the design often continuing repeated as *blind panels over the adjacent walls: the main mullions rose from the cill to the head which, towards the end of the medieval period, was usually a very depressed arch, and transoms were often ornamented with miniature *battlements. *Tudor Gothic window-heads frequently were four-centred arches, but were also fitted within rectangular apertures subdivided by mullions and framed at the top by a pronounced *hood-mould dropping down on either side and terminating in *label-stops. This was the usual arrangement in late-medieval domestic architecture. *Elizabethan and *Jacobean windows in grander houses were often vast, subdivided by mullions and transoms, called *grid-tracery*.

2. Filling of a window-opening with glass fixd in a frame or *sash of wood or metal, with accessories. The frame usually takes two forms: the *casement and the *sash. The latter is a frame holding the glass, fixed or opening, set in a large frame encompassing the whole window-opening or aperture: if opening, the operation is effected by a vertical or horizontal sliding movement or by hinges or pivots at the side, top, bottom, or centre. A casement-window, therefore, has a sash or sashes. Sashes moving up and down are called *boxed sliding*, *double-hung*, or *vertical sliding*. In C17, window-frames were often cruciform, with the lights held in frames within each opening, the pieces or *quarries of glass secured in lead *cames stiffened by *saddle-bars* fixed to the main frame. One or more of the rectangular sashes were hinged so that they could open in or out, so were referred to as casements.

With the advent of larger panes of crown *glass in C17, the design of windows changed, and the sashes were subdivided into rectangular squares or rectangles formed by wooden glazing-bars into which the glass was set. One sash slid vertically in front of the other in grooves formed on robustly constructed frames, and suspended on cords over pulleys, counter-balanced by means of weights free to move up and down inside the boxes within the main frame. This *boxed sliding* or *double-hung* sash-window appears to have been an English invention of the 1670s (although some have claimed it originated in The Netherlands), and was employed when earlier windows were replaced in the *Palladian Banqueting House, Whitehall, London (1685). From then, double-hung sash-windows gained in popularity, often replacing earlier types. However, the limitations of techniques of manufacturing glass ensured that individual panes remained relatively small, so glazing-bars were universal in better work, and somewhat obtrusive, being thick. During C18, glazing-bars (called *astragals in Scotland) were refined and acquired moulded profiles, reducing their visual impact. This elegance of *section and improvements in the methods of making glass enabled larger panes to be made, so that in the finest *Georgian sliding sash-windows the obtrusiveness of glazing-bars was minimal, and the bars themselves contributed to the overall appearance of refinement and well-proportioned artefacts. During the first decades of C19, proportions of window-openings changed: C18 apertures had generally been tall and narrow, but with the advent of *Neoclassicism and, especially, the *Greek Revival, became wider in proportion to height. Extra glazing was introduced at the sides of sashes in narrow strips, often with tinted glass: these were called *margin-panes*. Continuing improvements of manufacturing techniques made large panes of glass available at reasonable cost from the 1830s, and this again encouraged a change of proportion as windows could become wider still and glazing-bars dispensed with. In many cases glazing-bars were removed from earlier windows, changing the geometry and destroying the vertical emphasis created by repeated vertical rectangular panes. C18 relationships between pane, sash, window, and façade that had been so important in establishing the proportions of *Georgian domestic architecture was destroyed. Furthermore, tax changes in England (e.g. repeal of window-tax (1851)) tended to encourage more and larger windows, further freeing design from the earlier constraints. Historically, window-widths were determined by the size and strength of the lintel or the stability of the arch. With the evolution of structural frames, the various changes outlined above, and C19 stylistic eclecticism, traditional relationships of window-openings to solid walls changed. Many contemporary buildings have external *cladding (consisting of glass in some kind of light frame as the *curtain-wall) forming the enclosing envelope around the internal volumes.

3. Types of window include *bay; *bow; *casement; *Catherine-wheel; *Chicago; *clearstor(e)y; *cross; *Diocletian or thermal; *dormer; *fanlight; *French (or *croisée*); *Ipswich; *laced; *lancet; *lattice; leper; low-side; *lucarne; *lychnoscope; *marigold; *oculus; *œil-de-bœuf; *oriel; *Palladian; *picture; *rose; *sash; *serliana; *skylight; *tracery; *Venetian; *wheel; *Wyatt; and *Yorkshire light.

Gwilt (1903); Nicholson (1835); Papworth (1892); Parker (1850); Sturgis *et al.* (1901–2)

window-back. Framing between the bottom of a window-aperture and the floor.

window-bar. 1. *Mullion. **2.** Any division between *lights.

window-board. Inner *cill, usually of timber.

window-bossing. Recess beneath a window, often used for a seat.

window-case. Window-frame for hung *sashes.

window-frame. Frame set in a window-aperture for sliding-sashes or rebated as in a *casement window.

window-guard. 1. Small *balcony, *balconet*, or *vignette, fitted with a low railing so that flower-pots, etc., do not fall. **2.** Grate or bars, protecting a window, especially at ground-floor level.

window-head. 1. *Soffit of an arched top or of a *lintel above a window-aperture. **2.** Architectural enrichment above a window-aperture.

window-lead. Lead *came subdividing the *quarries of glass and holding them in place in a leaded *light.

window-ledge. *Cill, inside or outside.

window-post. *Post in a *timber-framed building on either side of the window-aperture into which the *window-frame is to be set.

window-screen. 1. Pierced *lattice-screen or *shutter. **2.** Any form of closure, e.g. to prevent insects from entering a room through a window-aperture, or to obstruct a view into a room.

window-seat. Seat in the recess of a window-aperture between the inner *jambs, floor, and *cill.

window-shutter. Hinged leaf hung on either side of a window-opening, inside or outside, in one or more folds, to secure the aperture.

Wines, James (1932–). American architect and sculptor. Founder of the design team *SITE (Sculpture in the Environment), in 1969, he was concerned to fuse art and architecture, integrating both. The firm is best known for the Best Products Retail Stores, such as the Indeterminate Façade, Houston, Tex. (1974–5), and the Tilt Showroom, Towson, Md. (1976–8), the latter with a front resembling a sheet of material lifted up to display the showroom behind. The suggestion of instability in apparently crumbling façades or irrational elements in SITE's work attracted much attention in the 1970s and 1980s. More recently Wines has been concerned with environmental problems, e.g. the decommissioning of Nuclear Power Stations.

Emanuel (1994); Jodidio (1993, 1996); SITE *et al.* (1980); Wines (1987); Wines *et al.* (1989)

Winford, William de. *See* Wynford.

wing. 1. Part of a building, or any feature of a building, projecting from and subordinate to the main, central part. In Classical and especially *Palladian compositions the wings are smaller buildings on either side of the *corps de logis, perhaps joined to it by means of *quadrants or *colonnades, and projecting forward to partially enclose a *court or *cour d'honneur. **2.** Part of a building with its roof at right angles to the adjacent main range, as in a *hall-and-cross-wing* medieval *timber-framed house, with the hall-range flanked by one or two wings. **3.** *Fillet on a moulding. **4.** Straight or curved projecting wall at each side and end of a bridge, also the retaining-wall at each end of a bridge to sustain the bank. **5.** One of the folds of a double door or screen. **6.** Lateral wall of a rectangular Classical temple, or the space between the *cell walls and the *peristyle.

Alcock, Barley, Dixon, and Meeson (1996); Gwilt (1903); Papworth (1892); Sturgis *et al.* (1901–2)

winged globe. Disc or representation of a globe, usually flanked by rearing *uraei (snakes), associated with Ancient Egyptian architecture, and often occurring on the *cavetto or *gorge *cornice.

Curl (1994)

wing-light. *Side-light.

Wintringham, William (*fl.* 1361–d. 1392). English carpenter. He supervised the construction of the Great Hall roof at Windsor Castle, Berkshire (1361–5), probably designed in general form by William *Herland. He worked with *Yeveley on John of Gaunt's Palace of the Savoy, London (1375), and carried out various tasks at Westminster Abbey, including the roof of the Abbot's Hall. Other projects included a new chapel and houses at Hertford Castle, Hertfordshire (1380s), various roofs and other structures at Kenilworth Castle, Warwickshire, including the roof of the Great Hall, then the widest trussed roof before Westminster Hall eclipsed it. Virtually everything he designed or made has been destroyed.

Harvey (1987)

Wit, *or* **Witte, Peter de** (1548–1628). *See* Candid.

Witney, Thomas of (*fl.* 1292–1342). English mason. He was engaged on the first building of St Stephen's Chapel, Westminster, in the 1290s, but by 1311 was living in Winchester,

Hampshire, and working on the Cathedral. He carried out alterations to the eastern arm of the church (*presbytery) before being called to Exeter Cathedral in 1313, where he was in charge by 1316, completing the *crossing, building the *nave, and creating the *reredos and *sedilia (1316–26) as well as the *pulpitum, all of which are in an advanced *Second Pointed style. The *piers and other aspects of the architecture at the presbytery of Winchester resemble the style of the works at Exeter. He may have designed the *Lady Chapel and associated parts of the *retrochoir at Wells Cathedral, Somerset (completed by 1326), and the crossing at Merton College Chapel, Oxford (1330–2). He was one of the most outstanding architects of the period.

Harvey (1987)

Wittkower, Rudolf (1901–71). German-born architectural historian. Educated in Berlin and Munich, he spent from 1923 to 1933 at the Bibliotheca Hertziana, Rome, where he worked with the Director, E. Steinmann, on an annotated bibliography of *Michelangelo (1927) and acquired his unrivalled knowledge of Italian art and architecture. As a result of his studies he published (with Heinrich Brauer) the important catalogue of *Bernini's drawings (1931), which was to prepare the ground for his *Gian Lorenzo Bernini* (1955—with subsequent editions). It was while working on Bernini that he turned his attention to the study of architecture, publishing a learned paper on Michelangelo's dome of St Peter's (1933, 1964), and followed this with a study of the Laurentian Library, Florence (1934, 1978), in which he discussed *Mannerism and architecture. He became a British citizen in 1934, co-editing (1937–56) the *Warburg Journal*, publishing many papers, and producing a study of *Rainaldi (1937), which discussed centralized Roman *Baroque church architecture. Further work on *Alberti (1941) and *Palladio (1944) gathered material that led to his *Architectural Principles in the Age of Humanism* (1949), which made an immediate and lasting impact on future studies. It showed (among other things) the importance of modular systems during the *Renaissance, and especially in the works of Palladio. It also examined centrally planned *Renaissance churches and their meaning in Christian symbolism, as well as the system known as *Harmonic Proportion in architecture. For the Pelican History of Art series he wrote *Art and Architecture in Italy* (1958, with subsequent editions). Having shed new light on *Baroque art with his *Gian Lorenzo Bernini* (mentioned above), he added to knowledge of the period with *Baroque Art: The Jesuit Contribution* (1972—which he edited with Irma B. Jaffé) and *Studies in Italian Baroque* (1975). With Friedrich 'Fritz' Saxl (1890–1948) he wrote *British Art and the Mediterranean*, first published by the Warburg Institute (1948), which showed the debt owed to Italy and France by British art and architecture. His *Palladio and English Palladianism* (1974) was a tantalizing foretaste of what might have been his greatest book, a study of *Burlington, which he never finished. He was Professor at Columbia University, New York (1956–69), where, in the words of * Pevsner, his regime was exacting but generous.

Architectural Review, 151/899 (Jan. 1972), 63; *DNB* (1986); Wittkower (1964, 1974, 1975, 1978, 1981, 1982, 1988); Wittkower and Brauer (1970); Wittkower and Jaffé (1972); Wittkower and Saxl (1969)

Wodehirst, Robert de (*fl.* 1351–d. 1401). English mason. He worked at Westminster Palace in the 1350s, but by 1361 was at work at Norwich Cathedral, where he rebuilt the *clearstorey of the *presbytery (1361–9), and was Master of the Works for the *cloisters (1385–6). From 1387 to 1393 he was at Ely Cathedral, Cambridgeshire, where he built the *reredos of the high-altar and (probably) the *lantern over the great western tower.

Harvey (1987)

Woderofe, James (*fl.* 1415–51). English mason. He and his brother, **John**, worked at Norwich Cathedral in the 1410s and 1420s, where they vaulted some of the *bays of the *cloister and carried out other tasks. He seems to have designed the Erpingham Gate (1416–25), the remodelled west front of the Cathedral, Norwich (*c*.1426–50), and the west tower of Wymondham Abbey, Norfolk (from 1445). His expertise must have carried some weight, because he was called to Eton College, Buckinghamshire, in 1449, but on what pretext is unclear.

Harvey (1987)

Wohlmut, Bonifaz (d. 1579). *See* Stella, Paolo della.

Wolff, Jacob, the Elder (*c*.1546–1612). German architect and master-mason. His most significant buildings were those he designed and built in Nuremberg, but he seems (from records of 1572) to have begun his career as Master-Mason at Bamberg Cathedral. He made alterations and additions to the Marienberg fortress above Würzburg (1600–7), linking the two *wings to create an enormous court. He and one Peter Carl erected (1602–7) the splendid Peller House in Nuremberg that incorporated a *Renaissance *rusticated façade inspired by Venetian exemplars crowned with an elaborate three-storey gabled confection. The internal *court had superimposed *arcades and much Renaissance enrichment. The *Pellerhaus* was a casualty of the 1939–45 war, but has been partly rebuilt. Wolff's son, **Jacob the Younger** (1571–1620), travelled (early C17) in Italy, acquiring a knowledge of Italian Renaissance architecture which he employed in the extension to the Nuremberg *Rathaus* (Town Hall) with its long façade incorporating three festive portals (1616–20). After his death the work was completed by his brother, **Hans** (*fl.* 1620s), but was destroyed in the 1939–45 war. It has since been rebuilt.

Cruickshank (1996); Hempel (1965); Hitchcock (1981)

Wolveston, Richard de (*fl.* 1170–d. *c.*1182). English engineer and architect. He designed the remarkable *Galilee porch at Durham Cathedral (*c.*1170) and part of Durham Castle, including the fine west doorway of the Great Hall. As an employee of the Bishop of Durham until *c.*1182 he must have been one of the ablest professionals of his time. He built the keep of Bowes Castle, Yorkshire (1170–4).

Harvey (1987)

Wolvey, Thomas (*fl.* 1397–d. 1428). English mason. He built the south *chancel-*chapel of the Church of Henley-on-Thames, Oxfordshire (1397), and Westminster Hall (1398), where he built the upper parts of two towers at the north end of the Hall, complete with *battlements, designed by *Yeveley. He appears to have been master-mason of St Alban's Abbey, Hertfordshire, for some 30 years, and worked on a number of churches in that county, including St Peter's in St Alban's, Newnham St Vincent, and King's Langley.

Harvey (1987)

Wood, Edgar (1860–1935). English architect. He designed a great number of houses, churches, and schools, most of which incorporate *Arts-and-Crafts and *vernacular influences. Works include Halecroft, Hale Road, Hale, Cheshire, 37–9 Rochdale Road, Middleton, and Westdene, Archer Road, Middleton, Manchester (all 1890s). Some of his designs were noted by *Muthesius. His First Church of Christ Scientist, Daisybank Road, Victoria Park, Manchester (1903), is an idiosyncratic free composition with a circular tower, *buttresses, and inventive fenestration. With James Henry Sellers (1861–1954) he designed several important buildings, including Elm Street and Durnsford Street Schools, both in Middleton (1909–10).

Gray (1985); Pevsner, *Buildings of England, Cheshire* (1971), *South Lancashire* (1969)

Wood, Thomas (*c.*1644–95). Oxford master-mason. He designed the old Ashmolean Museum, Broad Street, now the Museum of the History of Science (1679–83), the first public museum in England, one of the most advanced Classical buildings for its date in Oxford. He rebuilt the tower of Deddington Parish Church, Oxfordshire (1683–5), in a convincing *Gothic style, so he deserves mention as a versatile and competent designer.

Colvin (1995)

Wood Family. English architects and builders. **John Wood the Elder** (1704–54) was one of the developers of the Cavendish-Harley Estates in London, building houses in Oxford, Margaret, and Edward Streets, as well as in Cavendish Square. He was also employed at Bramham Park, Yorkshire, where he laid out the grounds (1722–4). His experience stood him in good stead when he returned to his birthplace, Bath, Somerset, then (1727) about to enjoy a building-boom. Between 1728 and 1736 he developed Queen Square, based on London exemplars, sub-leasing the sites of individual houses, but controlling the development so that the contractors had to comply with his *elevations. The result was a unified *Palladian *palace-fronted composition on the north side. Wood followed this with further schemes for Wood, John, and Old King Streets (1729–31), the North and South Parades, with Pierrepont and Duke Streets (1740–3), and then Gay Street (from *c.*1750) and the Circus (begun 1754). The last was an important innovation in English town-planning, with unified façades featuring an *assemblage of *Orders, the whole resembling the design of the Colosseum in Rome, but on a concave instead of convex plan. His proposals for a Royal Forum were not realized, but the general idea was to re-create a mnemonic of a Roman city.

Wood's publications are more interesting for their curiosity value than for their scholarship, and indeed they stray into the realms of bizarre, even insane, speculation. They include *The Origin of Building, or the Plagiarism of the Heathens Detected* (1741) in which he proposed that the three main Roman Orders had been the result of Divine revelation and had been first used in Solomon's Temple in Jerusalem, a notion recurring in Freemasonry and in Juan Bautista Villalpando's *Ezechielem Explanationes ...* (1596–1631). Behind this was the desire to cleanse Classical architecture of any pagan origins. Wood further fantasized about the origins of Bath in *An Essay towards a Description of Bath* (1742, 1749, and 1765), and also published *A Description of the Exchange of Bristol* (1745), *Choir Gaure, vulgarly called Stonehenge ...* (1747), and *Dissertation Upon the Orders of Columns and their Appendages* (1750). His meanderings drew on a curiously dotty volume (*Chronology of Ancient Kingdoms Amended* (1728)) by none other than Sir Isaac Newton (1642–1727).

Other buildings by Wood included a Classical church within the ruined *nave of Llandaff Cathedral, Glamorgan (1734–5—demolished *c.*1850), the handsome Palladian Prior Park, near Bath (1735–48), Lilliput Castle, Lansdown, near Bath (1738), the Exchange and Market, Corn Street, Bristol (1741–3), and the Exchange (now Town Hall), Liverpool (1749–54—much altered).

The development of Bath was continued by his son, **John Wood the Younger** (1728–81), who supervised the building of the Liverpool Exchange and completed the building of the Circus in Bath. His greatest contribution was Royal Crescent, Bath, the climax of the handsome sequence of residential developments begun in 1727. The Crescent (1767–75), with its *Giant *Ionic Order rising from a *plinth, was both original and influential, and was widely imitated thereafter. His new Assembly Rooms (1769–71) and Hot Bath (now Old Royal Baths) of 1773–7 were fine examples of Palladian architecture. He also designed Buckland House, Berkshire (1755–8), the Infirmary, Salisbury, Wiltshire (1767–71), and the *castellated Tregenna Castle, St Ives, Cornwall (1773–4). He published *Description of the Hot-Bath at Bath ...* (1777) and *A Series of Plans, for Cottages or Habitations for the Labourer* (1781, 1792, 1806, and 1837). In the latter volume he demonstrated a concerned attitude to housing for the working classes unusual for the time.

Colvin (1995); Curl (1991); *DNB* (1917); Harris (1990); Ison (1969); Mowl and Earnshaw (1988); Placzek (1982); Summerson (1963, 1993)

wood-mosaic. Marquetry or parquetry.

Woodroffe, Edward (*c.*1622–75). English architect and surveyor. After the Great Fire of London (1666) he was appointed (with *Hooke and *Wren) as one of the three Surveyors to rebuild the City churches. He assisted Wren from 1668 in the rebuilding of St Paul's Cathedral and in 1670 designed houses in Amen Court, St Paul's, for the Residentiary Canons.

Colvin (1995)

Woods, Shadrach (1923–73). *See* Candilis, Georges.

Woodward, Benjamin (1816–61). *See* Deane, Sir Thomas Newenham.

Woodyer, Henry (1816–96). English *Gothic Revival architect. Briefly a colleague of *Butterfield (1844), his work featured sharp angles, inventive *tracery, and imaginative use of materials. His best works are perhaps the House of Mercy, Clewer, Hatch Lane, Windsor, Berkshire (1853–96), St Michael's College, Tenbury Wells, Worcestershire (1854–6—an idiosyncratic building with very thin spiky *dormers), and his masterpiece, the Church of the Holy Innocents, Highnam, Gloucestershire (1847–52), with a painted *polychrome interior (by Thomas Gambier Parry (1816–88)) rivalling *Pugin's work at Cheadle, Staffordshire. He carried out numerous church restorations and erected vicarages, among them the red-brick and stone one at Toot Baldon, Oxfordshire (1860).

Architectural History, 38 (1995), 192–219—by far the most complete account (by Prof. Quiney); Curl (1995); Dixon and Muthesius (1985); Howell and Sutton (1989)

Worlich, John (*fl.* 1443–76). English mason. He worked as master-mason at King's College Chapel, Cambridge, before Simon *Clerk took over in 1477. Before that, he was at All Souls College, Oxford, working under Reginald *Ely on the Chapel. He seems to have been employed at Bury St Edmunds, Suffolk, and had connections with that county. A **Robert Worlich** (*fl.* 1492–1524) of Bury St Edmunds, perhaps a son or grandson of John, was one of the Wardens of Masons at King's College Chapel under *Wastell from 1508 to 1515.

Harvey (1987)

Worthington, Thomas (1826–1909). English architect. He designed numerous buildings in Manchester including the canopied *Gothic Albert Memorial (1862–7), the Mayfield Baths, Ardwick (1857), the Towers, Didsbury (1868), and the handsome *First Pointed Brookfield Unitarian Church, Hyde Road, Gorton (1869–71), with a fine interior. With his son, (Sir) **Percy Scott Worthington** (1864–1939), who became a partner in the firm in 1889, he designed Manchester College, Mansfield Road, Oxford (1891–3), and the Unitarian Church, Ullett Road, Sefton Park, Liverpool (1896–1902), the last with much excellent *Arts-and-Crafts detail. Sir Percy Scott Worthington was later joined by his half-brother **Sir John Hubert Worthington** (1886–1963), and his son, **Thomas Shirley Scott Worthington** (1900–81). Sir Hubert was responsible for the Radcliffe Science Library (1933–4), Linacre College (1936), Rose Lane Buildings, Merton College (1939–40), New College Library (1939), the History Faculty Library, Merton Street (1938–56), Lincoln House, Turl Street (1939), Dolphin Gate, St Giles's (1947–8), and the twin block for the Departments of Forestry and Botany (1947–50), all in Oxford.

Curl (1995); *DNB* (1949, 1981); Dixon and Muthesius (1985); Gray (1985); Hague and Hague (1986)

wreath. 1. Curved portion of the handrail following a turn around each angle of a geometrical *stair (which has no *newels), or the continuous turn of the handrail in such a circular or elliptical stair. **2.** Circular or elliptical *garland of flowers, leaves, or ribbons, used for decorative purposes in Classical architecture.

wreathed column. 1. Column with its *shaft cut with a spiral sinking, generally as a flat band, sometimes with an *annulet or two annulets between which mosaics are set, as in C13 *Cosmati work. **2.** Column-shaft with a spiral of leaved tendrils wound around it.

wreathed stair. Geometrical *stair.

Wren, Sir Christopher (1632–1723). One of the greatest English architects. His father was the High Church Rector of Knoyle, Wiltshire, and he was well connected, but he was also exposed to a spirit of enquiry, and became a pioneer of experimental learning. While at Oxford, he assisted Dr Charles Scarburgh (1616–94), the physician, mathematician, and anatomist, and himself developed an interest in anatomy and astronomy. He invented a model (the *Panorganum Astronomicum*) to demonstrate various periodical positions of the earth, sun, and moon, and became a skilled maker of models and diagrams. Made a Fellow of All Souls, Oxford, in 1653, in 1657 he was appointed Professor of Astronomy at Gresham College, London. In 1661 he returned to Oxford as Savilian Professor of Astronomy, and, although only 28, was highly regarded as a scientist by his peers. By that time he was becoming interested in architectural matters, and in 1663 his advice was sought by the Commission appointed to repair St Paul's Cathedral in London. In the same year he designed the new *Chapel for Pembroke College, Cambridge, a pleasant, if unstartling Classical building. This was followed by the Sheldonian Theatre, Oxford (1664–9), based on *Antique exemplars noted in Italian architectural publications. To roof the considerable span, Wren evolved a timber *truss which gained him approbation as an architect, although the *Baroque façade opposite the medieval Divinity Schools is somewhat hesitant, and clumsy in the sum of its parts. In 1665 he made an important visit to Paris to see 'esteem'd Fabricks', which influenced his future work.

After the Great Fire of London (1666) he prepared a plan for rebuilding the City that was not adopted, but he was appointed (with *Pratt and *May) as one of the Commissioners to survey and determine how best to proceed with the work. He was also appointed (with *Hooke and *Woodroffe) to rebuild the City churches, and for this task Wren had overall control, although claims that he personally designed each building are exaggerated, and in nearly all cases the furnishings and architectural details were designed by craftsmen, Wren and his colleagues acting in supervisory roles. Designs for the 50 or so City churches either originated in or were vetted by his office, and in most cases accorded with Wren's idea of how ecclesiastical designs should be adapted for Protestant worship. The inventive towers, however, including that of St Dunstan-in-the-East (1697–9—*Gothic), all seem to have originated in, or were modified by, Wren's office. Plans were also varied and interesting, notably the domed St Stephen, Walbrook (1672–9), and St Mary Abchurch (1681–6), a single-volume domed space. The galleried *auditory church was ideally suited to Protestant worship, and the type was perfected at St Peter's, Cornhill (1675–81), St Clement Danes (from 1680), and St James, Piccadilly (1676–84). Wren's greatest achievement was the new St Paul's Cathedral (begun 1675), although he himself wanted a centrally planned church on the lines of the 'great model' of 1673. As built, St Paul's was essentially a medieval plan, adapted with a *drum and *dome over the *crossing, and with western towers owing much to Roman Baroque prototypes. The western *façade, with its coupled columns, echoes the east front of the Louvre, Paris, and the great drum and dome were a triumphant affirmation of Wren's intellect, invention, and ability. The design of the Cathedral's exterior includes features such as *aedicules with windows below in the *pedestals, and a screening upper storey on the sides that serves only to hide the nave *buttresses, both of which have been the subject of adverse criticism for their alleged 'falseness'.

In 1668/9 Wren became Surveyor-General of the King's Works, succeeded *May as Comptroller at Windsor in 1684, was appointed Surveyor at Greenwich Palace in 1696, and was Architect in charge of the building of the Military Hospital at Chelsea. The last, with its bold and severe Roman *Doric *Order (1682–9), was suggested by the Invalides in Paris, and also by *Webb's plan for the Palace at Greenwich. When Wren prepared designs for the completion of Greenwich Palace as a Naval Hospital, the need to retain Inigo *Jones's Queen's House led to the solution of building two tall *cupolas on either side of the central axis (from 1696) and the making of the grandest Baroque composition in England, including the handsome Hall (1698), decorated by Sir James Thornhill (1675–1734), 1708–27. He prepared major schemes for the Palaces of Whitehall (destroyed 1698), Winchester (destroyed 1894), and Hampton Court (south and east ranges (1689–94)) and interior of the King's apartments (completed by *Talman (1699)).

Other works include the Garden Quadrangle, Trinity College, Oxford (1668–1728—much altered), the Gothic Tom Tower, Christ Church, Oxford (1681–2), and the very grand Library at Trinity College, Cambridge (1676–84), one of the noblest buildings of its time. He designed Marlborough House, St James's, London (1709–11—later altered on numerous occasions), in which work he was assisted by his son, **Christopher** (1675–1747), who collected the papers that led to *Parentalia, or Memoirs of the Family of the Wrens*, published by Christopher jun.'s son, **Stephen**, in 1750. Sir Christopher Wren's work was influenced by French architecture, notably that of *Mansart and Le *Vau, and by Netherlands *Classicism and Roman Baroque. He in turn influenced *Vanbrugh, Christopher Kempster (1627–1715—the master-mason who built the City Churches of St Stephen, Walbrook, St James, Garlickhythe (1764–87), and St Mary Abchurch, and who was responsible for the Town Hall, Abingdon, Berkshire (1678–80)), and *Hawksmoor, who was his assistant and pupil.

Architectural History, 15 (1972), 5–22; Colvin (1995); *DNB* (1917); Downes (1982, 1986); Placzek (1982); Sekler (1956); Summerson (1965, 1993); Webb (1937); Whinney (1971)

Wrenaissance. Revival of late-C17 architecture in the period *c.*1890–1914 in which themes from designs by *Wren were prominent. Its chief protagonists were John *Belcher, Sir Mervyn Edmund *Macartney, and Sir Alfred Brumwell *Thomas.

Wright, Frank Lloyd (1869–1959). American architect, some say the greatest of C20. He learned the rudiments of his art from Joseph Lyman Silsbee (1845–1913), whose essays in the *Queen Anne and *Shingle styles were competent. He later (1888) became assistant to Louis H. *Sullivan, and remained with the firm of Adler & Sullivan until 1893. While revering Sullivan, Wright was also influenced by Owen *Jones, the English *Arts-and-Crafts movement, *Ruskin, and *Viollet-le-Duc (or rather by what Viollet was said to have written), interlocking forms (perhaps suggested by the Froebel blocks with which he played when a child), and Japanese architecture (prompted by the Japanese pavilion at the Chicago Exposition of 1893). In 1889 he designed his first independent building, his own house and studio at Oak Park, Chicago, Illinois, an eclectic work, with a shingled exterior (altered and extended 1889–1911), and in 1894 became a founder-member of the Arts-and-Crafts Society in Chicago. At this time he began to evolve his *Prairie House type, with volumes developing from a central core, long, low roofs that appeared to float over the structure, corners treated as voids, and enclosing walls that were treated more as independent *screens (techniques he called 'breaking the box'). Furthermore, the main axes within the houses were continued into the gardens and terraces, suggested in the schemes Wright published in the *Ladies' Home Journal* (1901), and developed in the series of houses he designed from that time until just before the 1914–18 war. Yet *Lutyens had also been moving in this direction, as with the Deanery, Sonning, Berkshire (1899–1902), while *Schinkel had also brought gardens, water, and terraces within his profoundly ordered geometries, as at the Court Gardener's House and Roman Baths complex, Potsdam (1820s). Wright's finest essays in the Prairie House style were the Willitts House, Highland Park, Ill. (1962), Robie House, Chicago (1908), and Coonley House, Riverside, Ill. (1908–12).

With the Unity Temple (Unitarian Church), Oak Park (1906), and the Larkin Building, Buffalo, NY (1904—demolished), a severe, monumental architecture evolved, in which a powerful grid-like geometry was well to the fore, while the architectural language seemed to owe something to a *stripped *Classicism reminiscent of aspects of the work of Schinkel, Otto *Wagner, and others (especially the rows of square columns at Unity Temple which recall the Berlin *Schauspielhaus* (Play House) by Schinkel and some of the Vienna Metropolitan Railway Stations by Wagner).

Wright's work had been widely publicized, and in 1910 Wasmuth of Berlin published *Ausgeführte Bauten und Entwürfe von Frank Lloyd Wright* (Realized Buildings and Projects of Frank Lloyd Wright) as a handsome pair of portfolios, followed in 1911 by a paperback volume of illustrations and plans. The introduction was by C. R. *Ashbee, the prominent English Arts-and-Craftsman, and these publications helped to promote Wright's work. His designs seem to have enjoyed considerable favour in Germany (*Gropius and *Mies van der Rohe were two architects affected) and in The Netherlands, in particular, where Robert van 't *Hoff, *Dudok, and some members of De *Stijl were undoubtedly influenced by his work, and it shows. In 1911 he moved to the Wisconsin countryside, where he built his Prairie House-based home and studios at Taliesin (burnt down 1914, but rebuilt and extended during the 1920s). There he was the Master with his pupils, a pose he developed further at Taliesin West, mentioned below.

In spite of a scandalous private life he gained two important major commissions: the Midway Gardens, Chicago (1913—demolished); and the Imperial Hotel, Tokyo, Japan (1915–22—with Antonin *Raymond—also demolished). Both had highly organized plans in which axes featured prominently, and both were lavishly decorated with polygonal, triangular, and other sharp-angled forms, including *chevrons, that had already begun to appear on the lead *cames of some of the Chicago houses, and that anticipated *Art Deco ornament. With the Hollyhock (or Barnsdall) House (1916–21), Los Angeles, Calif., he experimented with repetitive stylized motifs (abstractions of hollyhock forms) cast in moulds (the whole house was cement-rendered), and created a building faintly reminiscent of pre-Columbian American architecture, a theme more pronounced in the Ennis House, Los Angeles (1923–4), constructed of decorated concrete blocks, and featuring battered walls set on terraces. He again used concrete blocks in e.g. the Millard House, Pasadena, Calif. (1923), and Freeman House, Los Angeles (1923–4), but for the rest of the decade his work did not attract the attention his earlier designs had enjoyed. In the 1930s, however, Wright's buildings were once more widely publicized.

At the Kaufmann House (1935–48), 'Falling Water', Connelsville, Pa. (1935–48), he gave full expression to horizontals and verticals in a tour-de-force constructed over a stream called Bear Run, a design that had superficial resemblances to the *International Modernism of the time, but, with its coursed *rubble walls and hand-crafted detail, owed more, perhaps, to the Arts-and-Crafts tradition, while the disposition of elements derived from his Prairie House type. In 1936–9 he designed and built the Johnson Wax Factory, Racine, Wis., with a tall interior the roof of which was supported by tapered mushroom-shaped columns, the walls being of brick with glass tubes forming the light-sources. At the same time he developed his low-cost *Usonian* houses, based on vernacular American buildings, that explored the possibilities of prefabrication. The prototype was the Jacobs House, Madison, Wis. (1936–7), and Wright publicized his ideas in *Architectural Forum* of 1938. He also evolved proposals for Broadacre City, a low-density plan in which

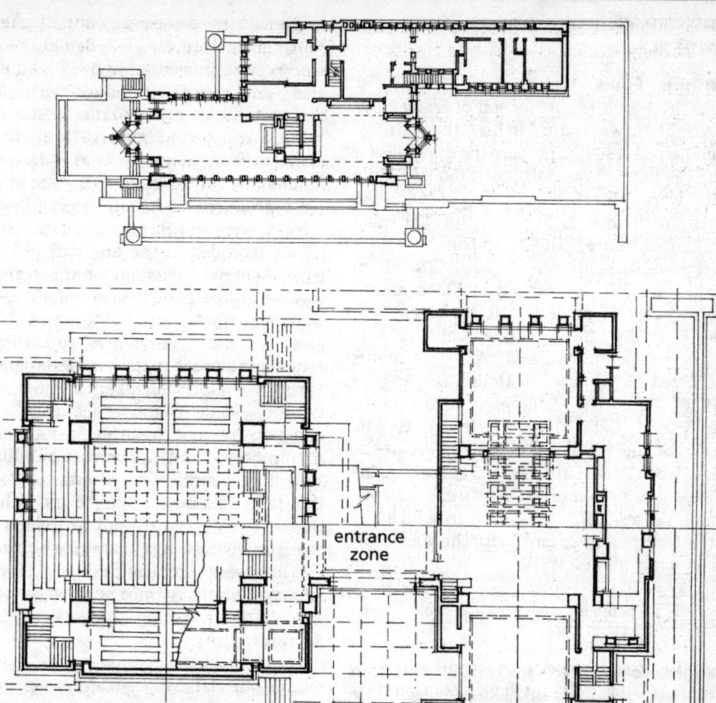

Wright, Frank Lloyd.
(*Top*) Plan of Robie House.
(*Bottom*) Plan of Unity Temple.

the Usonian house would feature large. In 1937 he designed Taliesin West, winter quarters for himself and his disciples, which he built at Scottsdale, Ariz. From 1942 he prepared designs for the Guggenheim Museum, New York (completed 1960), a spiral ramp that proved to be an inappropriate form for viewing works of art, but as an exercise in formal geometry was remarkable for its time. At Bartlesville, Okla., he designed the Price Tower (1953–6), a tall block rather more elegant than the slabs so prevalent during that period, demonstrating Wright's interest in the acute angles he had also employed at Taliesin West. Among his last works the Marin County Civic Center, San Rafael, Calif. (1957–66), and the Beth Sholom Synagogue, Elkins Park, Pa. (1958–9), deserve note.

Wright has been seen as an exponent of *organic architecture, by which he seems to have meant design that proceeds from the nature of Mankind and his circumstances as they both change. Although his writings suffer from rather obvious conceit, prolixity, and dense obfuscation (e.g. *An Autobiography* (1943), *An Organic Architecture* (1939), and *When Democracy Builds* (1945)), they were collected and published as *Frank Lloyd Wright on Architecture: Selected Writings 1894–1940* (1941) and *In the Cause of Architecture: Essays by Frank Lloyd Wright for the* Architectural Review *1908–1952* (1975).

Etlin (1994); Gill (1987); Gubitosi and Izzo (1981); Heinz (1982); Hitchcock (1973); Levine (1996); Long (1996); McCarter (1997); Placzek (1982); Storrer (1974, 1993); Sweeney (1978); Twombly (1979); Wright (1939, 1943,

1945); van Vynckt (1993—includes a large bibliography); Zevi (1979)

Wright, Frank Lloyd, jun. (1890–1978). American architect, elder son of Frank Lloyd *Wright. He was trained in his father's studio, and helped (1909) to prepare the drawings for the celebrated Wasmuth portfolio (1910). He later worked for the Boston firm of *Olmsted, then with his father on the Barnsdall Hollyhock House (1916–21) and on the various concrete-block houses of the 1920s, all in California. His own output included houses constructed of precast concrete blocks (e.g. Derby House, Chevy Chase, Calif. (1926)), while pre-Columbian and *Art Deco motifs occurred in the Sowden House, Los Angeles (1926), and the Samuel-Navarro House, Hollywood, Calif. (1926–8). He was responsible for the *shell-concrete structure at the Hollywood Bowl, Calif. (1924–5 and 1928). The Swedenborg Memorial Wayfarer's Chapel, Palos Verdes, Calif. (1946–71), in which the architecture is integrated with the landscape, is arguably his best work.

Arts and Architecture, 83 (1966), 22–6; Emanuel (1994—includes a very full list of his works); Gebhard and von Breton (1971); Long (1996)

Wright, John Lloyd (1893–1973). American architect, son of Frank Lloyd *Wright. He trained in his father's studio at Oak Park, Chicago, Ill., and designed an early *reinforced-concrete structure, the Golden West Hotel, San Diego, Calif. (1912). His Woods House, Escondido, Calif. (1912), was a version of his father's *Prairie House designed for the *Ladies' Home Journal* (1901). He assisted his father during the building of the Imperial Hotel, Tokyo (1915–22). Established in his own practice by 1926, he designed several buildings in which aspects of *Art Deco and *Expressionism were well to the fore. From 1945 he developed some of the ideas in his father's *Usonian* houses, and published some thoughts on the nature of ornament, derived from lichens.

Journal of the American Institute of Architects, 18 (Oct. 1952), 187–8; Long (1996); Placzek (1982); *Prairie School Review*, 7/2 (1970), 16–19

Wright, Thomas (1711–86). English architect, antiquary, astronomer (he was the first to explain the Milky Way), and landscape-designer. In 1748 he published *Louthiana, or an Introduction to the Antiquities of Ireland*, a pioneering work anticipating many C18 studies. He designed Nuthall Temple, Nottinghamshire (1754–7—demolished, but see *Vitruvius Britannicus*, iv (1767)), an elaborated version of *Palladio's Villa Capra, Vincenza, and *Scamozzi's Vettor Pisani *villa, called Rocca Pisana (1575–8). His main claim to fame, however, is as a designer of remarkable garden-buildings, some of which are reproduced in his *Six Original Designs of Arbours* (1755) and *Six Original Designs of Grottos* (1758), intended as the first part of his projected *Universal Architecture* which, regrettably, was never completed. Many of his designs were for *sham castles, *Gothick *follies, gateways, and *eye-catchers, constructed of *rubble and rough materials. He designed the *primitive *Doric 'Shepherd's Grave', a *fabrique of elegiac character featuring a relief based on Poussin's painting *Et in Arcadia Ego*. A number of Gothick garden-buildings at Tollymore Park, Co. Down (*c.*1740–80), Dundalk, Co. Louth (1746–7), and Belvedere House, Co. Westmeath, all in Ireland, were based on his drawings, many of which survive in the Avery Architectural and Fine Arts Library, Columbia University, New York. He was therefore among the earliest *Gothic Revivalists.

Colvin (1995); Harris, E. (1979); *Journal of Garden History*, 1/1 (Jan.–Mar. 1981), 55–66; McCarthy (1987)

Wurster, William Wilson (1895–1973). American architect with a strong belief that architecture should respond to local conditions. As principal of Wurster, Bernardi, & Emmons, he was responsible for a great number of 'Regional' buildings in California, many having *timber frames with pitched roofs, *shingle or *clapboard-covered walls, and rough carpenter's detailing, collectively called the 'Bay Region School'. Good examples of his work were the Gregory Farmhouse, Scotts Valley near Santa Cruz (1927), the Butler House, Pasatiempo (1934–6), and the Reynolds House, San Francisco (1946), all in California. He also designed Stern Hall, University of California, Berkeley (1942), the Medical Plaza, Stanford University, Palo Alto (1959), the Woodlake Residential Community, San Mateo (1965), and the award-winning Ghirardelli Square, San Francisco (1962–7), all in California. With *Belluschi and *Skidmore, Owings, & Merrill the firm designed the Bank of America World Headquarters, San Francisco, Calif. (1970–1).

Cruickshank (1996); Emanuel (1994)

Wyatt, Benjamin Dean (1775–1855). English architect, eldest son of James *Wyatt. In 1811 he won the competition to rebuild the Drury Lane Theatre, London (later altered by *Beazley and others), which he published as *Observations on the Design for the Theatre Royal, Drury Lane, as Executed in the Year 1812* (1813). He succeeded his father as Surveyor of Westminster Abbey in 1813, and built up a flourishing London practice. With his brother, **Philip William** (d. 1835), he designed Crockford's Club, 50–3 St James's Street (1827—since altered), Londonderry House, Park Lane (1825–8—demolished), York (later Stafford, and later still Lancaster) House, St James's (1825–7), the Oriental Club, 18 Hanover Square (1827–8—demolished), and the addition of the *portico and remodelling of the interiors of Apsley House (1828–9), all in London. He was particularly adept at re-creating the *Louis Quatorze style which he first used at Crockford's Club. He redecorated the principal rooms at Belvoir Castle, Leicestershire, and built a *Romanesque *mausoleum in the grounds (*c*.1820–30), in collaboration with his brother, **Matthew Cotes Wyatt** (1777–1862). He designed the Duke of York's Column, Carlton Gardens, London (1831–4), and carried out extensive alterations at Stratfield Saye, Hampshire (1838–40). He was declared bankrupt in 1833 and died in obscurity in Camden Town.

Architectural Review, 155/926 (April 1974), 217–23; Colvin (1995); Papworth (1892); Robinson (1979)

Wyatt, James (1746–1813). English architect, one of the most outstanding, prolific, and successful of his time. He spent six years in Italy from 1762 before returning to England where he worked for the family firm, mostly with his brother **Samuel.** He evolved an elegant *Neoclassicism, possibly derived not only from his time in Italy, but from studies of the work of *Adam at Kedleston, Derbyshire. Indeed his first architecturally significant house was Heaton Hall, Lancashire (*c*.1772–8), loosely based on a simplified and refined version of *Paine's designs for Kedleston, complete with a central *bow. He made his name, however, with The Pantheon, Oxford Street, London (1769–72—with Samuel), a Neoclassical domed assembly-room given the *imprimatur* of that arbiter of taste, Horace *Walpole, who declared it the 'most beautiful edifice in England'.

At 26 Wyatt had arrived. He became Surveyor to Westminster Abbey (1776), Architect to the Board of Ordnance (1782), and Surveyor-General and Comptroller of the Office of Works (1796), designed or altered several Royal residences, and carried out many other commissions, including well over 100 country-houses. However, his interventions with medieval buildings were not universally admired, and he made drastic, even irresponsible, and certainly controversial alterations to five cathedrals (his work at Salisbury, Wiltshire (1789–92), and Hereford (1786–96) earned him the nickname 'The Destroyer', as his approach to medieval fabric was cavalier, speculative, and unarchaeological), and at Durham Cathedral his proposals to demolish the *Galilee and commit other acts of vandalism roused ferocious opposition led by John *Carter.

His Radcliffe Observatory, Oxford (1776–94), drew on the Tower of the Winds in Athens (*c*.50 BC) for its inspiration, and he completed the interior of Sir Robert *Taylor's Heveningham Hall, Suffolk (*c*.1780–4), in an elegant Neoclassical style (damaged in the 1980s). His finest houses are Heaton Hall (mentioned above), Castle Coole, Co. Fermanagh, Northern Ireland (1790–7—with an elliptical *saloon expressed as a *bow on one of the fronts), and the severe Dodington Park, Gloucestershire (1798–1813). Two of his best designs were for *mausolea: that for the 4th Earl of Darnley at Cobham, Kent (*c*.1783–4—in ruins), was a noble and severe Neoclassical work, while that for the 1st Earl of Yarborough at Brocklesby Park, Lincolnshire (1786–94), is a refined interpretation of the *Antique Roman Temples of Vesta at Tivoli and Rome, a work of rare beauty that unquestionably is his masterpiece.

As a *Gothic architect Wyatt was fashionably successful, his most *Sublime house in that style being Fonthill Abbey, Wiltshire (1796–1812—destroyed), which was much admired when new. Ashridge Park, Hertfordshire (1802–13), and the additions to Wilton House, Wiltshire, including the *cloister (1801–11), were also Gothic. One room for his Gothic Lee Priory, Ickham, Kent (*c*.1785–90—demolished), survives in the Victoria & Albert Museum, London. He provided plans for the Earl-Bishop of Derry's great house, Downhill, Co. Londonderry, Northern Ireland (*c*.1776–9—in ruins), and remodelled Belvoir Castle, Leicestershire (1801–13) in a castellated Gothic style.

His output was enormous and embraced country-houses, public buildings, ecclesiastical works, and almost every type of architecture, although there is evidence that he accepted more commissions than he was capable of carrying out, and he persistently neglected his official duties to the point of incompetence. Nevertheless, he began to eclipse the *Adam brothers quite early in his career, and some of his interiors are as delicate as anything they achieved. Particularly felicitous are those of Heaton Hall, near Manchester, and the enchanting Brocklesby Mausoleum, Lincolnshire.

Colvin (1995); Crook and Port (1973); Curl (1993); Dale (1956); *DNB* (1917); Robinson (1979); Summerson (1993)

Wyatt, Lewis William (1777–1853). English architect. He trained with his uncles **Samuel** and **James**, and set up in practice *c.*1805. He published *A Collection of Architectural Designs, rural and ornamental, executed . . . upon the Estates of the Right Hon. Lord Penrhyn in Caernarvonshire and Cheshire* (1800–1), but he is best known as a designer of country-houses. He completed Tatton Park, Cheshire (1807–18), begun by Samuel *Wyatt, and built Willey Hall, Shropshire (1813–15—probably his best work), both in a *Neoclassical style. He used the *Tudor style at Cranage Hall, Cheshire (1828–9), and *Jacobean at Eaton Hall, Congleton, Cheshire (1829–31—demolished). At Sherborne House, Gloucestershire (1829–34), he emulated a C16 house complete with an *assemblage of *Orders. In 1816 he published *Prospectus of a Design for Various Improvements in the Metropolis* in which he argued for a development plan for London, especially the West End.

Colvin (1995); Papworth (1892); Robinson (1979)

Wyatt, Sir Matthew (1805–86). English architect and speculative builder. He was the son of the sculptor **Matthew Cotes Wyatt** (1772–1862) and the grandson of James *Wyatt. He built and designed Victoria Square, London (1838–40), created houses in Stanhope Terrace, Westbourne and Bathurst Streets, and developed land bounded by Connaught, Southwick, and Hyde Park Streets and Hyde Park Square (1830s and 1840s). Many houses were put up in collaboration with his brother **George** (d. 1880).

Colvin (1995); Robinson (1979)

Wyatt, Sir Matthew Digby (1820–77). Prolific English architect, the younger brother of T. H. *Wyatt, distantly connected to the rest of the fecund *Wyatt dynasty. He was Secretary to the Executive Committee for the Great Exhibition (1851), and carried out orientalizing architectural detailing at Paddington Station, London (1852–4), for *Brunel. He designed the *polychrome Addenbrooke's Hospital, Cambridge (1863–5), collaborated with Brunel on Temple Meads Railway Station, Bristol (1865–78), and designed (with George Gilbert *Scott) the interior and Durbar Court, India Office, Whitehall (1867–8—perhaps one of the finest examples of Victorian *Renaissance Revival). He wrote *Geometrical Mosaics of the Middle Ages* (1848—finely illustrated with chromolithographic plates), edited *Industrial Arts of the Nineteenth Century* (1851–3), and published many other works. When the Crystal Palace was re-erected at Sydenham, Wyatt acted as Superintendent of the Fine Arts Department, and, with Owen *Jones, designed the various 'Courts' demonstrating the main characteristics of various periods and styles. One of his most exotic interiors was the spectacular billiard-room at 12 Kensington Palace Gardens, London (1864), in the *Moorish style. He was a pioneer of the *Renaissance Revival, the first Slade Professor of Fine Arts at Cambridge (1869), and a prolific author. His Rothschild *Mausoleum in the Jewish Cemetery, Buckingham Road, West Ham, Essex (1866), is a domed building on a circular plan with *Renaissance and *Baroque detail, an example of his 'mixed style'.

DNB (1917); Dixon and Muthesius (1985); Jervis (1984); Sheppard (1973)

Wyatt, Samuel (1737–1807). English architect, the third son of **Benjamin Wyatt** (1709–72). As master-carpenter and later clerk of works at Kedleston, Derbyshire, he gained first-hand experience of working on a major work of architecture for an important architect, Robert *Adam. He worked with his younger brother **James** on the design and construction of The Pantheon, Oxford Street, London (1769–72), which made James *Wyatt's name. After this, he designed several country-houses in a *Neoclassical style, often with elliptical or circular rooms expressed as bowed projections. Good examples of his work include Doddington Hall (1777–98), Delamere House (1784—demolished), and Tatton Park (1785–9—constructed by his nephew, L. W. *Wyatt), all in Cheshire. He designed numerous model farm-buildings, lodges, and cottages, including nearly 50 at Holkham, Norfolk (1780–1807), and he was a pioneer in the use of cast-iron construction. He designed the Albion Mills, Blackfriars, London (1783–6—destroyed 1791), the first mill in the world to be powered by steam-engines, and also one of the first to be constructed on a raft-foundation. He also patented designs for cast-iron bridges, warehouses, and other structures in 1800, and designed systems for constructing prefabricated timber hospitals for use abroad. Other works include lighthouses at Dungeness, Kent (1791), Flamborough Head, Yorkshire (1806), and elsewhere, and he built Trinity House, Tower Hill, London (1793–6—bombed 1940, and restored by Sir Albert *Richardson in 1953). Towards the end of his life he was occupied with major works at Ramsgate Harbour, Kent (1794–1804—all demolished).

Colvin (1995); Placzek (1982); Robinson (1979)

Wyatt, Thomas Henry (1807–80). English architect, elder brother of Sir Matthew Digby *Wyatt, distantly connected to the other architectural *Wyatts. He trained in Philip *Hardwick's office, and entered into partnership with David Brandon (1813–97) in 1838. Their masterpiece was the Church of SS Mary and Nicholas, Wilton, Wiltshire (1840–6), a convincing *Italianate *basilica with detached *campanile, recognized at the time as a major exercise in the *Rundbogenstil, even in the Viennese journal *Allgemeine Bauzeitung* (Universal Building Journal). It is a remarkable and beautiful building, and contains *Antique black columns (*c*.2 BC) as well as examples of *Cosmati work from Santa Maria Maggiore, Rome. They also designed the Churches of St Andrew, Bethnal Green, London (1841–in a cheaper, less successful Rundbogenstil), and St Mary, Atherstone, Warwickshire (1849–*Gothic). On his own, Wyatt designed Orchardleigh Park, Somerset (1855–8), in a vaguely *Jacobean style. With **M. D. Wyatt**, he designed the *polychrome Rundbogenstil Garrison Church of St George, Grand Depot Road, Woolwich (1862–3—gutted in the 1939–45 war and only partially preserved).

Dixon and Muthesius (1985); Eastlake (1970); Hitchcock (1954); Pevsner (1972)

Wyatt window. Tripartite window resembling a *serliana, but with the arch over the centre omitted and the *entablature carried over the wider central window, named after its inventor, James *Wyatt. It may be placed in a segmental-headed recess, or may be capped by a *pediment (as at the Radcliffe Observatory, Oxford (1776–94)).

Wyatville, Sir Jeffry (1766–1840). English architect, born **Wyatt**. He was apprenticed to his uncle, **Samuel**, and showed early promise as a draughtsman. In 1792 he joined the office of his uncle **James**, leaving in 1799 to set up in partnership with John Armstrong (d. 1803), a building-contractor in Pimlico, London. By the 1820s he had become a highly successful country-house architect (unlike his Uncle James he was thorough, reliable, and highly professional), and in 1824 began work for King George IV (1820–30) at Windsor Castle, Berkshire, not completed until 1837. He raised the *keep, battlemented and *machicolated the towers, and converted the old fortress into a residence for the Sovereign. He virtually rebuilt the Upper Ward with a new George IV Gateway, reconstructed the State Apartments on the north side around a new staircase (replaced by *Salvin in 1866), and built new apartments on the east (garden) side. The *Picturesque appearance of the Castle today is largely due to Wyatville, who was knighted in 1828 (he had been permitted to call himself 'Wyatville' from 1824). An account of his works at Windsor (in which he was assisted by *Baud) was published in *Illustrations of Windsor Castle by the Late Sir Jeffry Wyatville* (1841).

Most of his country-houses were in Picturesque *Tudor Gothic or *Tudorbethan modes, and he could design in the Grecian style. Among his works were the County Gaol, Abingdon, Berkshire (1805–11), the completion of and additions to Ashridge Park, Hertfordshire (*c*.1814–17—*Gothic), the Brownlow *Mortuary Chapel at Belton Church, Lincolnshire (1816), major alterations and additions, including the library, north wing, tower, and various estate buildings at Chatsworth, Derbyshire (1820–41), the remodelling of Sidney Sussex College, Cambridge (1821–2 and 1831–2—Tudor Gothic), extensions to the castellated Fort Belvedere, Windsor Great Park, Berkshire (1828–9), and many other building works.

Colvin (1995); *DNB* (1917); Linstrum (1972); Robinson (1979)

Wykeham, William of (1324–1404). English ecclesiastic and builder. In 1356 he was named as Clerk of the Royal Works at Henley and Easthampstead, and later Surveyor of the Royal Castles at Windsor, Leeds, Dover, and Hadleigh. He superintended the erection of the Royal apartments east of the *keep at Windsor Castle (1360–9), and built a new castle on the Isle of Sheppey, called Queenborough (1361–7), known from plans drawn by Hollar, but destroyed. In the 1360s his rise as an ecclesiastic was meteoric, and he was showered with livings. He was responsible for the foundations of New College, Oxford (1379) and Winchester College, Hampshire (1382). Both were erected on similar plans, with hall, chapel, and sets. They were the models for later colleges including Eton and King's, Cambridge. Wykeham does not appear to have been an architect, however, and obtained the services of William of *Wynford to act in that capacity. Wykeham's name is primarily associated with major works at Winchester, where he was Bishop from 1366. There, using Wynford, he remodelled the *Romanesque *nave from 1394 in the *Perpendicular style of *Gothic, which explains the abnormally substantial *piers for that style.

DNB (1917); Harvey (1987); Hayter (1970)

Wynford, William of (*fl.* 1360–d. 1405). English master-mason. In 1360 he was working at Windsor Castle, Berkshire, under *Sponlee and William of *Wykeham (then Clerk of the Works there), and probably built the Great Gate and Royal Lodgings. In 1364/5 he was appointed Master-Mason at Wells Cathedral, Somerset (where Wykeham had been Provost since 1363): there, he built the south-west tower (after 1386) and carried out other works. He may have designed the handsome tower of St Cuthbert's Church, Wells (*c.*1385–1400), and sundry ecclesiastical structures in the county, including the church-towers at Banwell, Cheddar, and Shepton Mallet. He favoured set-back *buttresses, and seems to have established a pattern for handsome C15 towers in the South-West of England. In 1375–6 he was working at Abingdon Abbey, Berkshire, in 1377–8 on Corfe Castle, Dorset, and in 1378–9 he strengthened the fortifications at Southampton. With Hugh *Herland and Henry *Yeveley he supervised the building of parts of Carisbrooke Castle, Isle of Wight (1384–5).

For Wykeham he designed New College, Oxford (begun 1379/80), and Winchester College, Hampshire (begun 1387), on a similar plan. With Herland and Yeveley he repaired and strengthened Winchester Castle (1390s), and it is known he worked at Orford Harbour, Suffolk, in the 1370s, so he obviously had a comprehensive grasp of engineering and military architecture as well as other building-types. In 1394 he began the great work of transforming the *Romanesque *nave of Winchester Cathedral into a *Perpendicular space without actually rebuilding it, creating a high lierne-*vault, leaving the steeply pitched early medieval roof, and casing-in the huge *piers, thus creating a curiously chunky type of architecture for the period. He probably had a considerable part in the design of the exquisite Perpendicular *chantry-chapel and tomb of Wykeham in Winchester Cathedral, with its cusped lierne-vault (early C15).

Harvey (1987); Papworth (1892)

X. **1.** Mnemonic of Christ, the first letter of ΧΡΙΣΤΟΣ. *See* Chrismon. **2.** Roman numeral symbol for 10. *See* Team X.

xenodocheion, xenodochium. Guest-house in a monastery, etc.

Xylonite. Fibrous vegetable matter (e.g. cotton and flax waste and old rags), dissolved in acid and neutralized, which produced a substance called *Parkesine*, named after its inventor, Alexander Parkes, of Birmingham. In its liquid state it was used as a waterproofing agent, in its plastic form for insulation, and, with the addition of oils, glues, and colour, for making objects, e.g. tubes and architectural enrichment. Capable of being coloured, and susceptible to a high polish, it was first exhibited at the International Exhibition, South Kensington, London (1862). In the 1890s it was developed as a substitute for plaster *cornices, *friezes, *mouldings, and other decorations in rooms, and was supplied in accurately moulded prefabricated 3-metre lengths which were then fixed to timber grounds by means of screws. Its extreme light weight made it easy to handle and fix.

Papworth (1892)

Xylotechnigraphy. Decoration of wood by staining, graining, and finishing to resemble a more expensive and finer wood, patented in England *c*.1871.

xystum. **1.** Open path, wall, promenade, or alley. **2.** *Ambulacrum, *atrium, or *parvis in front of a *basilica.

xystus. **1.** Roman garden planted with groves of plane-trees, usually laid out with flower-beds and surrounded with a *colonnaded *ambulatory, like a *cloister. **2.** Long covered *portico, open-sided colonnade, or *court used for athletic exercises in Ancient Greece. **3.** Covered promenade. **4.** Church ambulatory. **5.** Long *loggia or *verandah. **6.** Hypaethral walk, shaded by trees. **7.** Part of a Roman house, bigger than an *atrium, surrounded by a *peristyle, and planted in the middle.

Y. *See* tracery.

Yamasaki, Minoru (1912–86). American architect of Japanese descent. He and his partners George Hellmuth and Joseph Leinweber made their names with the Lambert Airport Terminal Building, St Louis, Mo. (1953–6), the main concourses of which are covered by intersecting *concrete-shell barrel-*vaults. His public housing, Pruitt-Igoe, St Louis (1950–8), won several architectural awards, but made history by being detested by those living there (it suffered several arson attacks), and was demolished in 1972, an event many have seen as the beginning of *Post-Modernism as a reaction against the *Modern Movement. Later buildings tended to have *screen-like elements in the *façades that disguised the structural grids. Profiled concrete blocks were used for this purpose at the American Concrete Institute, Detroit (1958), and metal grilles at the Reynolds Metals Regional Sales Office, Southfields, Mich. (1959). His Michigan Consolidated Gas Company Office Building, Woodward Avenue, Detroit (1963), a rigorous concrete tower, was admired for its detailing. With Emery Roth & Sons he designed the twin-towered World Trade Center, New York (1966–74). He wrote *A Life in Architecture* (1979).

Curtis (1996); Emanuel (1994); Heyer (1978); van Vynckt (1993); Yamasaki (1979)

yard. Uncovered piece of ground, surrounded by walls or buildings, without the architectural pretensions of a *court or *quadrangle.

Ybl, Miklós, *or* **Nikolaus von** (1814–91). Austro-Hungarian architect. A pupil of von *Gärtner, he designed many buildings, including the richly *Renaissance Revival Opera House of Budapest, Hungary (1875–84), much influenced by developments at the *Ringstrasse*, Vienna. He rebuilt part of the sumptuous Church of St Stephen, Budapest (1983–9), following the collapse of the dome designed by *Hild in 1851.

Baedeker, *Austria* (1929); Papworth (1892); Sturgis *et al.* (1901–2)

Yeates, Alfred Bowman (1867–1944). *See* George, Sir Ernest.

yellow metal. Alloy of three parts of copper to two of zinc, often used for covering domes, roofs, etc., because of its malleability.

yelm. Straight bundle of reeds or straw for thatch.

Yenn, John (1750–1821). English architect. A pupil of *Chambers, he was employed by the latter as Clerk of Works at Somerset House, London, from 1776. He was a fine draughtsman, probably the best among any C18 English architects. He designed the Temple of Health (1789) at Blenheim Palace, Oxfordshire, and, with Henry Hake Seward (*c.*1778–1848), rebuilt the west *façade of the King Charles Block, Greenwich Hospital, London (1811–14), having succeeded Sir Robert *Taylor as Surveyor of the Hospital.

Colvin (1995); Papworth (1892)

yett. Grated iron door, *portcullis, or *screen, its horizontals passing through alternate vertical bars, and its verticals passing through alternate horizontal bars, thus creating a very strong grid.

Yeveley *or* **Yevele, Henry** (*c.*1320/30–1400). English master-mason, possibly hailing from Yeaveley, Derbyshire. He may have learned his craft at one of the many building-projects of the Midlands, perhaps Lichfield Cathedral, Staffordshire, but was in London in 1353 and rose rapidly in fame and fortune. Around 1357 he was employed by Edward, the Black Prince (1330–76), at Kennington Manor, and worked at St Alban's Abbey, Hertfordshire, around the same time. By 1360 he was active at Westminster Palace, the Tower of London, Queenborough Castle, Kent (1361–7), and various other castles and properties of the Crown. In the 1370s, for example, he worked with *Sponlee and *Wynford on the fortifications at Southampton.

He designed a number of funerary monuments, including the magnificent tomb (1374–8—destroyed) for John of Gaunt, Duke of Lancaster (1340–99), and his first wife, Blanche of Lancaster (d. 1369), which stood in old St Paul's Cathedral, London. It appears to have been enclosed in a very grand canopied *chantry-chapel. He was also responsible for the noble tomb of the Black Prince, Canterbury Cathedral, Kent (1375–6). When King Edward III (reigned 1327–77) died, it was most likely Yeveley who designed his monument (1386) in Westminster Abbey, closely resembling the tombs of King Richard II (reigned 1377–1400) and Cardinal-Archbishop Langham (d. 1376), also in the Abbey, which we know were by him. He may also have designed the canopied tomb of Prior Rahere (d. 1144) in the Church of St Bartholomew-the-Great, Smithfield, London, or his work may have influenced the finished artefact.

In the early 1370s he probably designed the great Neville *screen of *Caen stone for Durham Cathedral, which was made in London and shipped north. Stylistically it is similar to work at John of Gaunt's destroyed chantry-chapel mentioned above. James *Wyatt wanted to remove the Neville screen in the 1790s. By 1378 Yeveley had developed his connections with Canterbury, designing the West Gate of the city, and in 1381 was involved with Wynford as a consultant for some of William of *Wykeham's architectural projects. As he had begun building the Charterhouse in London in 1371, he was well placed to advise on collegiate establishments, and it seems likely he was consulted about the design of New College, Oxford. By 1385 he was spending much time in Canterbury, where he designed the great *nave of the Cathedral (*c.*1380–1405), one of the most beautifully proportioned of any in England. While in Kent he may have provided designs for Meopham Church (1381–96), the gate-house of Saltwood Castle (*c.*1383), and the new Church and College at Maidstone (founded 1395).

At Westminster Abbey he worked on the nave, generally following the (by then rather old-fashioned) lines set down by Henry of *Reyns. In 1394 he commenced work on Westminster Hall, one of the grandest secular rooms of the Middle Ages, with a great timber roof by Hugh *Herland (completed 1400). He also acted as a consultant on numerous works, including Leeds Castle, Kent, Rochester Castle, Kent, Winchester Castle, Hampshire (with Wynford and Herland), Orford harbour, Suffolk, and many other places.

Yeveley was an important medieval architect (some have called him the *Wren of C14, and Dr Harvey has claimed he was the 'greatest English architect'), whose output was prodigious. Fortunate in having the patronage of Kings Edward III and Richard II, he was able to bring English *Perpendicular to maturity. As a designer of funerary architecture he was in the premier division.

Crossley (1921); Harvey (1987)

ymage. Medieval term for a statue.

yoke. 1. Short timber linking two other timbers, especially the tops of *cruck *blades. **2.** Horizontal timber forming the top of a frame for a *double-hung* *sash-window.

Yorke, Francis Reginald Stevens (1906–62). English architect. He was one of a handful devoted to the *Modern Movement in England in the 1930s (he was a founder of the *MARS Group (1932) and his use (from 1933) of *reinforced concrete testified to his *Modernist credentials). He became well known with *The Modern House* (1934) that publicized Continental *International Modernism. With A. Adam, W. *Holford, and G. Stephenson he designed (1933) a pair of houses (conventional in plan but conforming in image to the paradigms promoted at the *Weissenhofsiedlung of 1927) for the Modern Homes Exhibition at Gidea Park, East London (held 1934), and in 1935 built a more sophisticated house with reinforced concrete at Nast Hyde, Hatfield, Hertfordshire (destroyed 1980s). In the same year he formed a partnership that lasted until 1938 with the former *Bauhaus teacher, *Breuer, designing an exhibition house for the Royal Show, Bristol (1936), and Sea Lane House, East Preston, Sussex (1937—in the *International Modern style, with *pilotis). With another emigré, Arthur *Korn, he built some flats in Camberwell, London (1940). He published *The Modern House in England* (1937), *The Modern Flat* (1937—with Frederick

*Gibberd), *A Key to Modern Architecture* (1939—with Colin Penn), and *The New Small House* (1951 and 1954—with Penelope Whiting) all of which were immensely influential and had a powerful effect on British architecture after 1945.

In 1944 he entered into partnership with Eugene *Rosenberg and Cyril Sjostrom Mardall (1909–), forming one of the most successful practices in England after the 1939–45 war as Yorke, Rosenberg, Mardall (YRM). Their many schools (e.g. Barclay Secondary, Stevenage, Hertfordshire—1950), housing-schemes, factories (e.g. Sigmund Pumps, Gateshead, Co. Durham—1948), offices, and hospitals were fairly typical of architecture in Britain in the 1950s and 1960s, but with their own offices at Greystoke Place, London (1960–1), St Thomas's Hospital, London (from 1966), and University of Warwick (also 1960s) they introduced an architecture clad in white tiles. At Gatwick Airport (from 1967) a style reminiscent to that of *Mies van der Rohe was chosen.

DNB (1981); Emanuel (1994); van Vynckt (1993); Yorke (1947, 1951); Yorke and Penn (1939); Yorke, Rosenberg, and Mardall (1972); Yorke and Whiting (1954)

Yorkshire lights. *Mullioned two-*light window, one light fixed and the other a sash sliding in grooves in a horizontal direction.

Yoshida, Isoya (1894–1974). Japanese architect. He made his name as a designer of timber houses, often discarding the logic of historical types, e.g. when creating windows in the corners of the buildings where traditionally they would have *posts. From the 1950s he designed several public buildings, using concrete. Among his works the Sekiya House (1931), Shinkiraku Restaurant (1940–62), Ryuzaburo Umeharo Studio-House (1951–8), Suzuki House (1957), Inomata House (1967), Mangan-ji Temple (1969), Mikiya House (1971), and Prince Chichibu House (1972), all in Tokyo, may be cited. He sought to create a truly modern Japanese architecture, freed from *International *Modernism and other non-Japanese influences.

Emanuel (1994); Placzek (1982)

Yoshizaka, Takamasa (1917–80). Japanese architect. He worked in Le *Corbusier's studio in Paris (1950–2), and subsequently designed in a manner suggestive of the latter's *Brutalism at the Maisons Jaoul (e.g. Yoshizaka House, Tokyo (1955)), although he moved away from that tendency in later years. Among his works were the City Hall, Gozu (1961—in which the office-block was supported on trellis-like forms so resembled a large bridge), and the Kosizuka House, Tokyo (1976).

Emanuel (1994)

Young, Ammi Burnham (1798–1874). American architect. His early work was in a restrained *Federal style, but his Vermont State House, Montpelier (1833–6), with a Greek *Doric *portico and a low *Pantheon-like dome (destroyed), was an essay in modestly advanced *Neoclassicism. He turned to the *Gothic Revival for St Paul's Church, Burlington, Vermont (1832), then back to Greek Doric and a Pantheon dome for the Custom House, Boston, Mass. (1837–47—overwhelmed by extensions carried out by *Peabody & Stearns in 1915). In 1852 he was appointed First Supervising Architect of the Office of Construction of the Treasury Department, and designed numerous Federal buildings, notably custom-houses, post-offices, and federal-courts, many of which are in *Italianate styles. A good example is the Custom House and Post Office, Windsor, Vt. (1856–8), where iron was used structurally as well as for external and internal ornament. Many of his designs were published in *Plans of Public Buildings in Course of Construction for the United States of America under the Direction of the Secretary of the Treasury* (1855–6).

Hamlin (1964); *Journal of the Society of Architectural Historians*, 19 (1960), 119–23, 25 (1966), 268–80; Kennedy (1989); *Vermont History*, 36 (1968), 55–60

Young, William (1843–1900). Scots architect, he made designs for many town- and country-houses throughout the United Kingdom. One of his most resplendent interventions was at Robert *Adam's Gosford House, near Longniddry, East Lothian, Scotland (completed 1891), while at Elveden Hall, Suffolk, he enlarged the already extravagant house in a lavish *Italianate *Baroque style (1899–1903). He is remembered primarily for the Glasgow Municipal Chambers, George Square (1883–9), an opulent pile of French, Flemish, Venetian, and Spanish *Renaissance styles, with a bewildering array of eclectic influences from *Sansovino to 'Greek' *Thomson. This building made his reputation, and he was commissioned to design the New (now Old) War Office, Whitehall, London (1899–1906), a confident amalgam in which *Palladian, *Mannerist, and *Baroque styles were evident, with corner *cupolas, the whole reminiscent of the work of *Wren. The ensemble made such an impression at the time that it was virtually copied by Samuel Stevenson (1859–1924) for the exterior of the Belfast College of Technology (1900–7), and was a good example of the *Wrenaissance style. The War Office was completed by Young's son, **Clyde Francis Young** (1871–1948), after William's early death. William Young was responsible for the proposal to create Kingsway and Aldwych to connect The Strand to Holborn, London.

Curl (1990); Dixon and Muthesius (1985); Gray (1985); McWilliam (1978); Pevsner, *Buildings of England, Suffolk* (1974); Williamson, Riches, and Higgs (1990)

Y-tracery. *See* tracery.

Zabłocki, Wojciech (1930–). Polish architect. He designed the Sports Centre, Warsaw (1974), and many other sports-stadia, often with bold geometrical forms, such as the Stadium, Latakia, Syria (1987).

Emanuel (1994)

Zachwatowicz, Jan (1900–83). Polish architect and architectural historian, a graduate of the School of Architecture, Warsaw (1930). In 1939 he became Director of the Department of Architecture, teaching students clandestinely throughout the Nazi occupation and terror, always in great personal danger. In 1945 he was nominated General Conservator of Historical Monuments, and appointed to the Chair of Polish Architecture, Warsaw Polytechnic. Not only did he organize a national *conservation structure, but evolved a strategy for the reconstitution of buildings and historic town-centres that had been reduced to rubble, all the more difficult when Nazi barbarism had been replaced by Stalinist repression.

The 'Polish School of Conservation' (a term for which he did not care), of which, nevertheless, he was the leading light, held that reconstruction should be based as much as possible on reliable historical evidence, documentary, architectural, and archaeological. Under Zachwatowicz's guidance the impressive achievements of reconstruction in Poland began to be internationally recognized. The entire Old Town of Warsaw was painstakingly and brilliantly reconstructed, together with its churches, and the rebuilding of the Royal Palace (completed 1981—with others, including Professor Stanisław Lorentz) can only be regarded as a triumph (especially as the Communist authorities proposed erecting a large *Modernist building on the site to obliterate all historical references). Other historic centres (e.g. Gdańsk, Poznań, and Wrocław) were also repaired and rebuilt according to principles established by Zachwatowicz and his team. Among his other achievements was the rebuilding of St John's Cathedral, Warsaw (1960). He was an outstanding scholar, with over 200 major publications to his credit.

Personal information from Pani Katarzyna Zachwatowicz-Jasieńska; Puget (1994)

Zakharov, Andreyan, *or* **Adrian Dmitrievich** (1761–1811). Russian architect. He trained in St Petersburg and then, in 1782–6, under *Chalgrin in Paris. His reputation rests on the massive *Neoclassical buildings he designed for St Petersburg, including the New Admiralty (1806–23). A huge structure, probably the largest Neoclassical building in the world, it was influenced by *Rousseau's arch at the Hôtel de Salm, Paris (1782–5), as well as by designs of *Boullée and *Ledoux. The entrance-block is capped by a massive *Ionic *peristyle (based on descriptions of the Mausoleum at Halicarnassus) supporting a very tall gilded needle-spire. The severe end-*pavilions with arched cubic blocks surmounted by *drums and flanked by Roman *Doric *colonnades are among the most *Sublime buildings derived from French Neoclassical designs of the late C18. He also designed the Church of St Andrew, Kronstadt (1806–11), standardized administrative buildings for the Russian provinces, and a range of warehouses facing the River Neva on Proviantsky Island territory. He was also involved (with *Voronikhin) in the planning of the handsome *Bourse* (Exchange) in St Petersburg (1801–16), designed by de *Thomon.

Auty and Oblensky (1980); Grabar, Lazarev, and Kemenov (1963); Grimm (1940); Hamilton (1983); Middleton and Watkin (1987); van Vynckt (1993)

Zanth, Karl Ludwig Wilhelm von (1796–1857). Born Zanik, the son of the Jewish doctor to Jérôme Bonaparte (1784–1860—King of Westphalia from 1807 to 1813), he studied in Paris with *Percier and *Hittorff, collaborating with the latter (1822–30) on *Architecture antique de la Sicile* (1827) and *Architecture moderne de la Sicile* (1835) in which Hittorff's work on *polychromy was published. Later, Zanth received his Doctorate from the University of Tübingen for his work on *Pompeian domestic architecture. Settling in Stuttgart in *c.*1830 as Court Architect, he enjoyed the patronage of King Wilhelm I of Württemberg (1816–64), for whom he built the Villa Wilhelma (1837–51) below the hill in the Royal Park of Rosenstein. An asymmetrical composition, with very rich structural polychromy in the *Moorish style (the designs of which Zanth published as *La Wilhelma* in colour in 1855), it was his best work. He designed several town- and country-houses in and around Stuttgart, taught Christian Friedrich Leins (1814–92), who built the *Königsbau* (King's Building—1857–60), Stuttgart, designed earlier (*c.*1857) by Johann Michael Knapp (1793–1861). Leins also designed (for Crown Prince Karl of Württemberg, who later reigned as King Karl I (1864–91)) the charming Villa Berg, near Stuttgart (1844–53), an *Italianate building with influences from the works of *Schinkel.

Hittorff and Zanth (1827, 1835); Papworth (1892); Watkin and Mellinghoff (1987)

Zanuso, Marco (1916–). Italian architect. He designed the Olivetti Office Buildings in Buenos Aires, Argentina, and São Paulo, Brazil (1955–7), the latter with a thin *shell-vault covering central element. His Vacation-House, Arzachena, Sardinia (1963–4), was constructed of local red, yellow, and white granite, giving it a fortress-like appearance that seemed to grow naturally from the rock. Among later works the IBM Italian Factory, Santo Palomba, Rome (1979–82) and the Water Tower, Reggio Emilia (1985), may be mentioned. He was Chief Editor of *Casabella* (1947–9), and designed furniture and much else.

Emanuel (1994); Jervis (1984)

Zapotec architecture. The Zapotec civilization of *Meso-America produced buildings that were similar to those of the *Maya, Toltec, *Aztec, and other groups, with a clear distinction between the substructure and superstructure. The religious centre of the Mixtec-Zapotec peoples in the valley of Oaxaca, Mexico, was the Palace of the Columns, Mitla (*c.*1000), with an impressive platform the walls of which were decorated with elaborate geometrical patterns.

Cruickshank (1996); Kubler (1984)

zecca. Italian mint for making coins, e.g. the fine C16 example in Venice by *Sansovino.

Zehrfuss, Bernard-Louis (1911–). French architect. From 1943 to 1948 he designed public buildings, including housing, schools, hospitals, and a hippodrome in Tunisia, and, with a team of architects, was responsible for planning much that was subsequently realized in that country. Back in France he designed the Mame Printing Works, Tours (1950), and the Renault Factory, Flins (1952). Then, with *Breuer and *Nervi, he built the UNESCO Headquarters, Paris (1953–8), which made his name. Thereafter he designed the Danish Embassy, Paris (1968), the French Embassy, Warsaw (1970), the Siemens Company Headquarters, St-Denis, near Paris (1972—with Burckhardt), and the Gallo-Roman Museum, Lyons, France (1975). The National Centre for Industry and Technology, La Défense, Paris (1955—with Robert Camelot, *Prouvé, and Jean de Mailly, with a large vault by Nicolas Esquillan), was severely (and justly) criticized for its siting and impact on the Parisian skyline.

Emanuel (1994)

Zeidler, Eberhard H. (1926–). German-born architect, trained at the *Bauhaus after it reopened in Weimar after 1945, he settled in Canada in 1951 (naturalized 1956). From the late 1960s his work turned away from *International Modernism and began to show tentative references to a wider range of architectural expression. Best known for the enormous Eaton Centre, Toronto (1969–81—with Bregman and Hamann), essentially a gigantic variation on the C19 shopping *arcade expanded on several levels, he also designed Ontario Place, Toronto (1968–71), and Canada Place, Vancouver (1983–6—with others). His work includes churches, houses, hospitals, community centres, schools, and hotels. Among his other buildings the Mackenzie Health Sciences Centre, University of Alberta, Edmonton (1980–2), Queens Quay Terminal Warehouse, Toronto (1981–3), and the Raymond F. Kravis Center for the Performing Arts, West Palm Beach, Fla. (1985), may be mentioned. He published *Healing the Hospital*

(1974) and *Multi-Use Architecture in the Urban Context* (1984).

Emanuel (1994); Kalman (1994)

zeta. 1. Upper storey. **2.** Watch-tower. **3.** Summer-house in a garden. **4.** Small upper chamber above the porch of a church.

Zettervall, Helgo Nikolaus (1831–1907). Important Swedish architect of the 1870s and 1880s, strongly influenced by *Viollet-le-Duc. He was best known for his restorations of Lund Cathedral (1868–80), but at Uppsala Cathedral his faith in *concrete mixes as an alternative to traditional masonry of free-stones was misplaced. As Chief of the National Board of Public Building in Stockholm, he produced many works, all eclectic, and all interesting. As a church architect he also restored the Cathedral of Skara (1886–94), and built All Saints, Lund (1877–91), St Matthew's, Norrköping (completed 1892), and the Oscar Fredrik Church, Göteborg (completed 1893). He published an influential book on church-restoration, and also designed many ecclesiastical furnishings and fittings (those at All Saints, Lund, are especially fine).

Åman (1966); Jervis (1984); Placzek (1982)

Zevi, Bruno (1918–). Italian architectural theorist. He studied at Harvard University, USA (1939–43), before returning to Italy. His works included *Towards an Organic Architecture* (1945 and 1955), *Architecture as Space: How to Look at Architecture* (1948 and 1980), *Storia dell' architettura moderna* (1950 and 1973), and *The Modern Language of Architecture* (1973 and 1978). Opposed to *International Modernism, *Post-Modernism, *Classicism, and *Neoclassicism, he advocated a vaguely defined *organic architecture, apparently partly influenced by F. L. *Wright and a return to drawing on natural forms: he stated that architecture can only be called organic when it aims at human happiness, and seems to have advocated a popular idiom that would be contemporary and unindebted to past styles to achieve this. He also contributed major publications on *Michelangelo (1964), *Mendelsohn (1970), and F. L. Wright (1979).

Curtis (1996); Zevi (1950, 1960, 1973, 1974, 1978, 1979, 1980, 1980*a*, 1985)

Zhilyardi, Domenico (1788–1845). *See* Gigliardi.

Zholtovsky, Ivan Vladislavovich (1867–1959). Belorussian architect. He practised in Moscow from 1900, and was devoted to *Classicism, translating *Palladio's *Quattro Libri* into Russian (1936). He saw the *Neoclassicism of St Petersburg as the Russian style, but his fine Tarasov House, Moscow (1909–10), looked back to Palladio's Palazzo Thiene, Vicenza (*c*.1550). He designed the All-Russian Exhibition for Agriculture and Home Industries, Moscow (1922–3), firmly Classical in form; the Residence, Mokhovaya Street, Moscow (1932–4), based on the *Giant Order arrangement of Palladio's Loggia del Capitaniato, Vicenza (1571–2); the Housing Complex, Bolshoi Kaluzhskoi, Moscow (1940–9); and the huge Apartment Block, Smolensk Square, Moscow (1947–53), a powerful Neoclassical composition, the style of which was identified with *Socialist Realism. After the death of Stalin (1953), Zholtovsky was denounced for his adherence to Classicism, but some of his works, especially the earlier buildings, were not without distinction.

Cruickshank (1996); Kopp (1978); Musgrove (1987); Oschepkov (1955)

Ziebland, Georg Friedrich (1800–73). German architect, a pupil of Karl von *Fischer. He completed *Quaglio's charming *Gothic Hohenschwangau, near Füssen, Bavaria (1839–50), but his chief importance lies in his contribution to the *Rundbogenstil, notably his splendid brick and *terracotta (with stone dressings) fusion of *Early Christian and *Byzantine architecture at the St Boniface *basilica, Munich (1828–50), which drew on exemplars in Ravenna and Rome (e.g. San Paolo fuori le Mura). He also designed the *Corinthian exhibition-building opposite von *Klenze's more lively *Glyptothek* (Sculpture Gallery) in the *Königsplatz*, Munich (1816–31).

Nerdinger (1987); Papworth (1892); Reidelbach (1888); Stubenvoll (1875)

ziggurat. Ancient Mesopotamian staged temple-tower of pyramidal form in which each successive stage is smaller than that below it, leaving a terrace all around it. Each stage was connected by formal ramps.

Cruickshank (1996); Lloyd and Müller (1986)

zig-zag. 1. *Romanesque decorative Z- or V- and inverted V-(Λ) shaped device (*chevron or *dancette), either incised or in relief, occurring in a continuous *band or *string (as at Southwell *Minster, Nottinghamshire), as an ornament around an arch or series of arches (*see* Order), or cut into the drum of a *pier (as at Durham Cathedral). This architectural ornament has several variations **2.** Plan-form of fortifications with gun-emplacements built outwards with *salient angles.

Ziller, Karl H. Ernst (1837–1923). German architect. He studied with T. von *Hansen in Vienna, and exhibited designs in Berlin in 1856. He established himself in Athens in 1861, where he worked with Hansen on the Academy of Sciences (1859–87), the Zappeion (1870s), and the National Library (1859–91), all distinguished essays in *Neoclassicism, and among the best of C19. Ziller himself was responsible for several buildings in Athens, including the house of Heinrich Schliemann (1822–90—the archaeologist and discoverer of Troy), which became the building of the Greek Supreme Court. He was one of the best practitioners of his generation working within a free Neoclassical idiom.

Middleton and Watkin (1987); Thieme and Becker (1932)

Zimbalo, Giuseppe (*fl.* 1659–86). Italian *Baroque architect of the Prefettura (1659–95), Cathedral (1659–82), Sant'Agostino (*c.*1660–3), and the Rosary Church (1689–91), all in Lecce. His somewhat overblown style was continued into C18 by his pupil, Giuseppe Cino (1645–1722).

Calvesi and Manieri-Elia (1970)

Zimmermann Brothers. Bavarian artists, they were masters of the South-German *Rococo style, creating several masterpieces. Born near Wessobrunn, where the Abbey was the centre of one of the most important and innovative schools of workers in *stucco, they were trained by Johann *Schmu(t)zer, the leading C17 Wessobrunn architect and stuccoer. The Zimmermanns usually worked independently, but joined forces to create some of their best work (e.g. the Pilgrimage Churches of Steinhausen and Die Wies). They acquired and evolved a light, delicate, and elegant style perhaps influenced by French exemplars, but certainly far removed from the heavy C17 German *Baroque of some of Schmu(t)zer's creations. **Dominikus Zimmermann** (1685–1766) was a stuccoer and *scagliola worker before emerging as one of the most gifted architects of the first half of C18 in Southern Germany. His older brother, **Johann Baptist Zimmermann** (1680–1758), was not only a stuccoer and worker in scagliola, but a fine *fresco-painter as well. J. B. Zimmermann's exquisitely delicate stucco decorations in the Amalienburg (1734–9), Nymphenburg (1755–7), and *Residenz* (1733–7), all in Munich, were among the most beautiful of their kind in Europe.

Dominikus's first church was at Mödingen, near Dillingen (1716–21), for which he also carried out stucco decorations, while his brother did the frescoes and other parts of the stucco-work. The fully developed Rococo style of the Zimmermanns, however, was first evident at the Pilgrimage Church

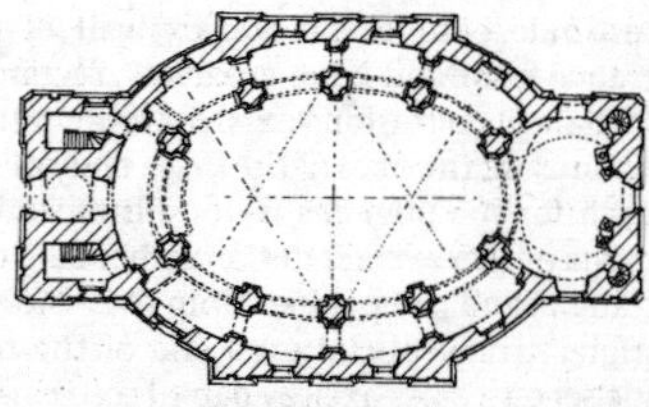

Plan of *Wallfahrtskirche* Steinhausen.

(*Wallfahrtskirche*) of Our Lady of Sorrows, Steinhausen, near Biberach, Württemberg (1727–35—signed by Dominikus as architect and stuccoer in an inscription beneath the organ-gallery), a large elliptical volume surrounded by a continuous *aisle, with the high-altar and tower placed at either end of the long axis (an arrangement perhaps suggested by an earlier proposal by *Moosbrugger, and probably by C. D. *Asam's design for Weltenburg). Colouring is predominantly white and gold, with a superb ceiling-fresco by J. B. Zimmermann, while Marian imagery and colouring are found throughout the church, all marvellously integrated within the total design. Steinhausen has been called the first true Rococo church.

Dominikus Zimmermann's next important solo work was the *Frauenkirche* (Church of Our Lady), Günzburg on the Danube (1736–41), downstream from Ulm: from outside the nave appears to be rectangular, but the positions of columns and curving elements produce an elliptical space further defined by the siting of the side-altars. The Günzburg church, however, lacks the *élan* of Steinhausen, but at the Pilgrimage Church of Christ Scourged (1744–54), set in charming meadows (hence the popular name, *Die Wies*) not far from Füssen near the Bavarian Alps, Dominikus

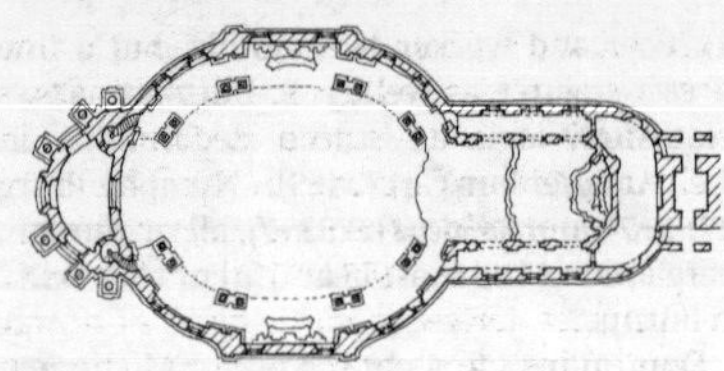
Plan of *'Die Wies'*.

Zimmermann again achieved greatness. Many writers hold *Die Wies* in high esteem as the triumph of South-German Rococo. Like Steinhausen, it consists of a large, almost elliptical, space surrounded by an aisle, but has a vestibule behind the convex wall of the entrance-front and a long, narrow, rectangular *chancel on the long axis. However, unlike Steinhausen, the plan of the main body of the church for the pilgrims is not elliptical, but consists of two semicircles on either side of a rectangle, and is separated from the aisle and vestigial *transepts (at each end of the rectangle set on a cross-axis) by paired columns instead of piers, enhancing the delicacy and elegance of the interior. Above the central congregational volume is a ceiling-fresco by J. B. Zimmermann, a vision of the Heavens depicting the moment just before the Last Judgement, with Christ on the Rainbow prior to being seated on the Throne. Christ's Scourging is symbolized by the columns of white and blood-red scagliola in the *choir, and the Evangelists by the high-altar have their Gospels open at the passages describing that event. Otherwise, *Wieskirche* is mostly white, colouring being confined to altars, the remarkable *pulpit (one of D. Zimmermann's most effervescent creations), and the ceilings. The architectural arrangements permit generous lighting, enhancing the extraordinary brilliance and delicacy of the interior, a joyous ensemble that is essentially an outpouring of creative energy to astound, delight, and enchant.

The Zimmermanns, with some of their contemporaries, the brothers Franz Xaver (1705–64) and Johann Michael (1709–72) Feichtmayr and Johann Georg Üblhör(r) (1700–63), invented a regional Rococo that was one of the most delicious and elegant styles ever evolved.

Bauer and Bauer (1985); Bourke (1962); Hager (1955); Hitchcock (1968, 1968*a*); Kasper and Strache (1957); Lampl (1979); Rupprecht (1959); Schnell (1981); Schnell and Schedler (1988); Thon (1977)

Zítek, Josef (1832–1909). Bohemian architect. He designed the National Theatre (*Národni Divadlo*), Prague (1868–81), an essay in the *Renaissance Revival style much influenced by the *Ringstrasse* buildings in Vienna. He was also responsible for a number of other distinguished buildings in his native country, including the *Rudolfinum*, Prague (1884).

Baedeker, *Austria* (1929); Landisch (1968)

zocco, zoccolo, zocle. *Socle, *plinth, or any square support (less in height than breadth) under the mouldings of the bases of *pedestals, etc.

zoömorph. Representation of an animal form. *Zoömorphic ornament* is anything featuring stylized animal forms (e.g. in *Art Nouveau, *Celtic, and *Romanesque design).

zoöphoric column. Column supporting an animal form, e.g. that in the Piazzetta, Venice.

zoöphorus, zophorus. Continuous Classical *frieze, especially (but not always) embellished with reliefs of human and animal forms.

Zopf und Perücke. German pejorative term (literally Pigtail and Periwig) for a style of late *Rococo architecture of C18, sometimes called *Zopfstil*.

zotheca. 1. *Alcove or *niche, especially one containing a statue or an *urn. **2.** Small day-room or study, usually entered from a larger room, so a kind of large alcove or *carrel.

Zuazo Ugalde, Secundino (1887–1971). Spanish architect and town-planner. His work was stylistically eclectic, and included several post-offices (e.g. Bilbao, Madrid, and Santander—1924–7), where Viennese influences may be detected, perhaps even more strongly expressed in the Casa de las Flores housing, Madrid (1930–2). A distinguished town-planner, much influenced by his studies of the organization and geometry of El Escorial, near Madrid, he reorganized the inner-city of Bilbao, prepared plans for Greater Seville, and provided designs for the new stretch of the Avenue Castellana, Madrid (opened 1933), on which new Government Ministries were to be erected (1930–7). However, Zuazo's vision of a 'hymn to the soberness and nobility' of stone-built architecture was not shared by the architects of the realized buildings which were in a bleak *stripped-Classical style reminiscent of the

1930s' official architecture in Fascist Italy and Nazi Germany. A competent Classicist himself, he designed the Palacio de la Música (1924–6), and the Casa Domingo Ortega (1946–7), both in Madrid, in that style.

Arquitectura, 146 (1971—contains a comprehensive list of works); Flores Lopez (1961); Placzek (1982); Tafuri and Dal Co (1986)

Zuccalli, Enrico (1642–1724). Member of a family of architects from the Italian-Swiss Canton of Grisons. He was appointed (1673) Court Architect to Elector Ferdinand Maria of Bavaria (1651–79) in Munich in succession to *Barelli, and enjoyed the favour of Elector Maximilian II Emmanuel (1679–1704) so that he was the pre-eminent architect working in Munich for around a quarter of a century. His significance lies primarily in his success at transplanting Italian, French, and Austrian *Baroque styles to Bavaria. He took over from Barelli (1674) the building of the *Theatinerkirche* (Church of the Order of Theatines) St Kajetan, Munich, designing the twin-towered façade (completed 1765–8 by *Cuvilliés, who made changes to it during its building), the tall *cupola over the *crossing, and the interior. His greatest work was Schloss Schleissheim, near Munich (1684–1704). The layout there began with Schloss Lustheim (1684–9), set in gardens, and continued with the main palace (completed by *Effner) which stands at one end of a long canal, Schloss Lustheim being sited at the other. Zuccalli supervised the making of some interiors of the *Residenz* (Seat of the Court—1679–1701—destroyed in the 1939–45 war, but partly restored) in Munich, including the *Kaiserzimmer* (Emperor's Room), *Alexanderzimmer* (Alexander Room), and *Sommerzimmer* (Summer Room). He built the Palais Fugger-Portia, Munich (1693–4), and extended the *Residenz* in Bonn, completed by de *Cotte after 1702. His last major commission was the rebuilding of *Kloster* (Monastery) Ettal, near Oberammergau (1709–26), including the design of the curved *façade and the domed space of the church itself.

Bourke (1962); Brucker (1983); Hager (1955); Hager and Hojer (1976); Hauttmann (1921); Hempel (1965); Heym (1984); Lieb (1941, 1976, 1992); Paulus (1912); Placzek (1982); Riedl (1977)

Zuccalli, Giovanni Gaspare *or* **Johann Kaspar** (*c*.1667–1717). A kinsman of Enrico *Zuccalli, he designed two centrally planned *Baroque Salzburg churches: the *Erhardskirche* (St Erhard's Church—1685–9), on a Greek-*cross plan (derived from *Cortona's Church of Santi Luca e Martina in Rome) with a circular *drum carrying the *cupola; and the more interesting Theatine *Kajetanerkirche* (St Kajetan's Church—1685–1711), with its elliptical cupola derived from *Bernini's Church of Sant'Andrea al Quirinale, Rome. These two buildings may have influenced the design of *Fischer von Erlach's *Dreifaltigkeitskirche* (Church of the Holy Trinity), Salzburg (1694–1702), and his later *Karlskirche* (Charles Church), Vienna (from 1716). The *Schloss* (Castle) at Aurolzmünster (1691–1711), near Ried-im-Innkreis, Austria, is also probably by him.

Bourke (1962); Ebhardt (1975); Fuhrmann (1950)

Zucker, Paul (1888–1971). German-born American architect, architectural historian, and theorist. In the 1920s he was involved with *Arbeitsrat für Kunst and the *Novembergruppe, and taught at various institutions, including the *Staatliche Hochschule für Bildende Kunst* (State College for Fine Art), Berlin. Among his many works were the shops for the Etam (1921–2) and Festa (1928) chains, the Bankhaus Lewinsky, Taubenstrasse (1924), the Henkel House, Hagenstrasse, Grünewald (1927), and the Posnansky Studio-cum-Boathouse, Kleiner Wannsee (1930), all in Berlin, but his best works were probably the villas in the western suburbs of that city. Zucker's copious writings include *Town and Square: From the Agora to the Village Green* (1959) and numerous contributions on architectural theory in various journals, mostly dealing with aspects of space in the urban context.

American Association of Architectural Biographers Papers, 12 (1977), 53–145; *Journal of the Society of Architectural Historians*, 2/3 (1942), 6–13, 10/3 (1951), 8–14; Placzek (1982); Ven (1980); *Wasmuths Monatshefte für Baukunst*, 4 (1919–20), 83–6; Zucker (1959)

Zug, Simon Gottlieb *or* **Szymon Bogumił** (1733–1807). Saxon architect, born in Dresden. He settled in Poland where he designed many distinguished *Neoclassical buildings. He was responsible for the Guardhouse of the Wilanów Palace, Warsaw (1775–6), and the circular domed Protestant Church, Warsaw (1777–81), with its severe *Doric *portico, the first example of a Neoclassical church in Poland. For Princess Izabela Czartoryska (1746–1835) he laid out the *jardin anglais* at Powązki, near Warsaw (1770s—now the Cemetery), with Jan Piotr

Norblin (the French landscape-painter Jean-Pierre Norblin de la Gourdaine (1745–1830)), and contributed an article on Polish gardens to Christian Cajus Lorenz Hirschfeld's (1742–92) *Theorie der Gartenkunst* (Theory of the Art of Gardening—1785), one of the seminal works on late-C18 gardens in Europe. At Natolin, near Warsaw, he designed the beautiful *pavilion (1780–2), with its main elliptical domed room half-open to the garden through a screen of *Ionic columns, an idea perhaps derived from de *Wailly's Montmusard (1764). His most interesting work (again with Norblin) is Arkadia, near Nieborów (1777–98), the *Picturesque garden laid out for Princess Helena Radziwiłł (1745–1821): it has a lake, various *fabriques, including a *Gothic House, an eclectic 'high priest's sanctuary', a megalithic grotto of the Sybil, *arcades, a 'Greek' arch, an *aqueduct, an *Île des Peupliers* complete with *cenotaph as a mnemonic of Rousseau's tomb at Ermenonville in France, and a Temple of Diana with a curious interior of curved rooms. He also designed a block in Warsaw (1784–5) with a ground-floor featuring *primitive unfluted Greek *Doric columns supporting arches, reminiscent of the work of *Ledoux.

Garden History, 23/1 (Summer 1995), 91–112; Lorentz and Rottermund (1984); Mosser and Teyssot (1991)

Zwinger. **1.** *Bailey or outer *court, as in a castle. **2.** Place for dog-kennels etc., attached to a grand house. **3.** Large arena for entertainment, e.g. for jousting, processions, etc., or bear-baiting, usually a formally designed space with grandstands around it for spectators. Hence the C18 *Zwinger* Palace, Dresden, Saxony, by *Pöppelmann, an extraordinary composition, with a festive gate (*Kronentor*), *pavilions, galleries, *orangeries, and a *nymphaeum grouped around a large court.

Zwirner, Ernst Friedrich (1802–61). German architect. A pupil of *Schinkel (who demonstrated his confidence in the young man by supporting his appointment (1833) as *Dombaumeister* (Cathedral Architect) for the then unfinished medieval Cathedral of Cologne in the Rhineland), he carried out major works of restoration there. Building on preliminary research by *Boisserée, he prepared designs for the Cathedral's completion before the momentous decision was taken to do so in 1842, and thus was in an excellent position to realize what was to be his greatest achievement. His proposals were published in César Daly's *Revue Générale* (1856), although the building was not completed until 1888 (under the aegis of Vincent (or Vincenz) Statz (1819–98) and others). He also designed several important new structures, including the *Gothic Church on the St Apollinarisberg, near Remagen (1839–43), the Drachenfels Monument (1857), and the Cologne *Synagogue (1859–61—before its destruction one of the finest essays in *Moorish *Byzantine *Rundbogenstil of C19). Several of his other churches were in a Rhenish *Romanesque style.

Zwirner argued for the accurate reproduction of Gothic detail, and was a key figure in the German *Gothic Revival not only because of the exemplary nature of his own work, but because he trained several successful practitioners, including Statz (who became Diocesan Architect of Cologne in 1863) and Friedrich von *Schmidt. Zwirner was called in to advise on the competition to design the *Nikolaikirche* (Church of St Nicholas), Hamburg (1844). He recommended that George Gilbert *Scott's design (placed third by the jury, with schemes by *Semper and *Strack winning first and second places respectively) should be declared the winner, and that Scott should be appointed architect. As this is what happened, it is clear that his views carried considerable weight. He published *Vergangenheit und Zukunft des Kölner Dombaues* (Past and Future of Cologne Cathedral—1842) and contributed regular reports on progress in *Kölner Domblatt* which were published in translation in *The Ecclesiologist*, and thus aroused considerable interest in Great Britain and the USA.

Borger (1980); Germann (1972—a particularly informative source); Hoster and Mann (1973); *Rheinische Lebensbilder*, 3 (1968), 173–89; Weyres and Mann (1968); Zwirner (1842)

zystos. *See* xystus.

Bibliography

Abel, John F., Billington, David P., and Mark, Robert (eds.) (1973), *The Maillart Papers* (Princeton: Princeton UP).

Abercrombie, Patrick (1926), *The Preservation of Rural England* (Liverpool: Liverpool UP).

—(1933, 1959), *Town and Country Planning* (London: Oxford UP).

Abramovitz, Max (1963), *The Architecture of Max Abramovitz* (Chicago: College of Architecture and Art, University at Congress Centre, Krannert Art Museum).

Académie d'Architecture (1960), *L'Œuvre de Henri Prost* (Paris: Académie d'Architecture).

Accasto, Gianni, Fraticelli, Vanna, and Niccolini, Renato (1971), *L'architettura di Roma Capitale: 1870–1970* (Rome: Golem).

Acciaresi, Primo (1911), *Giuseppe Sacconi e l'opera sua massima* (Rome: Tipografia dell'Unione Editrice).

Achleitner, Friedrich, *et al.* (1986), *Jože Plečnik, Architecte, 1872–1957* (Paris: Centre Pompidou).

Ackerman, James S. (1954), *The Cortile del Belvedere* (Vatican: Biblioteca Apostolica).

—(1966), *Palladio* (Harmondsworth: Penguin; 2nd edition of 1977).

—(1967), *Palladio's Villas* (Locust Valley, NY: Inst. of Fine Arts, New York University, Augustin).

—(1986), *The Architecture of Michelangelo* (Chicago: University of Chicago Press).

—(1990), *The Villa: Form and Ideology of Country Houses* (Princeton: Princeton UP).

Acland, Henry, and Ruskin, John (1859), *The Oxford Museum* (London: Smith, Elder).

Adam, Peter (1992), *The Arts of the Third Reich* (London: Thames & Hudson).

Adam, Robert, and Adam, James (1975), *The Works in Architecture of Robert and James Adam*, ed. Robert Oresko (London: Academy Editions).

Adam, William (1980), *Vitruvius Scoticus* (Edinburgh and New York: Harris and AMS).

Adams, Hans-B. (ed.) (1989), *Hentrich-Petschnigg & Partner, Architekten* (Munich: Prestel).

Adams, Maurice Bingham (1883), *Artists' Homes* (London: Batsford).

—(1904), *Modern Cottage Architecture* (London: Batsford).

Adams, Robert William (1980), *Baldassare Peruzzi, Architect to the Republic of Siena* (Ann Arbor: University of Michigan Press).

Adams, William Howard (1976), *The Eye of Thomas Jefferson* (Washington: National Gallery of Art).

—(1979), *The French Garden 1500–1800* (London: Scolar).

—(1983), *Jefferson's Monticello* (New York: Abbeville).

Adjmi, Morris (ed.) (1991), *Aldo Rossi: Architecture, 1981–1991* (New York: Princeton Architectural Press).

Ahlberg, Hakon (1925), *Swedish Architecture of the Twentieth Century* (London: Benn).

—(1943), *Gunnar Asplund Arkitekt, 1885–1940* (Stockholm: Byggmästeren).

Airs, Malcolm (1975), *The Making of the English Country House 1500–1640* (London: Architectural Press).

—(1995), *The Tudor and Jacobean Country House—A Building History* (Stroud: Alan Sutton).

Akademie der Künste (1963), *Die Gläserne Kette* (Berlin: Akademie der Künste).

—(1964), *Max Taut* (Berlin: Akademie der Künste).

—(1980), *Bruno Taut: 1880–1938* (Berlin: Akademie der Künste).

Ålander, Kyösti (ed.) (1966), *Viljo Revell: Works & Projects* (New York: Praeger).

Alberti, Leon Battista (1988), *De Re Ædificatoria* (Florence: Lorenzo Alamani, 1486); see the version entitled *On the Art of Building in Ten Books*, tr. Joseph Rykwert, Neil Leach, and Robert Tavernor (Cambridge, Mass., and London: MIT Press).

Albini, Franco (1981), *Franco Albini, 1930–1970* (New York: Rizzoli).

Albisinni, P., *et al.* (1984), *Piazza S. Ignazio: la regola ritrovata* (Rome: Kappa).

Alcock, Nathaniel Warren (1981), *Cruck Construction: an introduction and catalogue* (London: Council for British Archaeology).

—Barley, M. W., Dixon, P. W., and Meeson, R. A. (1996), *Recording Timber-Framed Buildings: An Illustrated Glossary. Practical Handbooks in Archaeology No. 5* (York: Council for British Archaeology).

Aldrich, Henry (1789), *The Elements of Civil Architecture, according to Vitruvius and Other Ancients, and the most approved Practice of Modern Authors, especially Palladio* (Oxford: Prince & Cooke, and London: Payne *et al.*).

Aldrich, Megan (1994), *Gothic Revival* (London: Phaidon).

Alessi, Galeazzo (1974), *Libro dei Misteri: Progetto di pianificazione urbanistica, architettonica e figurativa del Sacro Monte di Varallo in Valsesia (1565–1569)* (Bologna: Forni).

Alex, Reinhard (ed.) (1986), *Friedrich Wilhelm von Erdmannsdorff, 1736–1800* (Wörlitz: Staatliche Schlösser und Gärten).
—(1988), *Schlösser und Gärten um Wörlitz* (Leipzig: VEB E. A. Seemann Buch- und Kunstverlag).
Alexander, Robert L. (1974), *The Architecture of Maximilien Godefroy* (Baltimore: Johns Hopkins UP).
Allen, Arthur Horace (1988), *Reinforced Concrete Design to BS 8110: Simply Explained* (London: Spon).
Allibone, Jill (1988), *Anthony Salvin, 1799–1881* (Columbia, Mo.: University of Missouri Press, and Cambridge: Lutterworth Press).
—(1991), *George Devey, Architect, 1820–1886* (Cambridge: Lutterworth Press).
Altherr, Alfred (1968), *Three Japanese Architects: Mayekawa, Tange, Sakakura* (Teufen: Niggli).
Åman, Anders (1966), *Helgo Zettervall: 1831–1907* (Stockholm: Swedish Architectural Museum).
Ambasz, Emilio (1976), *The Architecture of Luis Barragán* (New York: Museum of Modern Art).
Amery, Colin (ed.) (1981), *Lutyens: The work of the English architect Sir Edwin Lutyens (1869–1944)* (London: Arts Council).
—(1995), *Architecture, Industry, and Innovation: The Early Work of Nicholas Grimshaw & Partners* (London: Phaidon).
Ames, Winslow (1967), *Prince Albert and Victorian Taste* (London: Chapman & Hall).
Amico, Alessandro D', and Damesi, Silvia (eds.) (1977), *Virgilio Marchi: Architetto scenografo futurista* (Venice: Editrice).
Amsoneit, Wolfgang (1994), *Contemporary European Architects*, i (Cologne: Taschen).
Andersen, Troels (ed.) (1968), *Vladimir Tatlin* (Stockholm: Moderna Museet).
Anderson, Mary Désirée (1954), *Misericords: Medieval Life in English Woodcarving* (Harmondsworth: Penguin).
Anderson, Stanford (ed.) (1968), *Planning for Diversity and Change* (Cambridge, Mass.: MIT Press).
Ando, Tadao (1989), *The Yale Studio and Current Works*, with essays by Ando, Eisenman, and Kunihiro (New York: Rizzoli).
Andrae, Walter (1925), *Coloured Ceramics from Ashur* (London: Paul, Trench & Trubner).
Andrews, J. J. C. (1985), *The Well-built Elephant and Other Roadside Attractions* (New York: Congdon & Weel).
Andrews, Richard M., Bentley, Ian, and Gržan-Butina, Đurđa (eds.) (1983), *Jože Plečnik 1872–1957: Architecture and the City* (Oxford: Urban Design, Oxford Polytechnic; *see also* the Spanish version, Bilbao: Cenicacelaya, Saloña, 1986).
Andrews, Wayne (1955), *Architecture, Ambition, and Americans: A History of American Architecture . . .* (New York: Harper).
—(1975), *American Gothic: Its Origins, its Trials, its Triumphs* (New York: Vintage).
Androuet du Cerceau, Jacques (1611), *Livre d'Architecture . . . contenant les plans et dessaings de cinquante bastimens tous differens . . .* (Paris: Jean Berjon).
—(1972), *Les plus excellents Bâtiments de France* (Farnborough: Gregg; reprint of 1576–9 edn.).
Angerer, Martin, *et al.* (1986), *Gothic and Renaissance Art in Nuremberg 1300–1550* (Nuremberg: Germanisches National-museum).
Ansell, Peter F. (1960), *Fashions in Church Furnishings 1840–1940* (London: Faith Press).
Anthony, Edgar Waterman (1968), *A History of Mosaics* (New York: Hacker Art).
Antolini, Giovanni Antonio (1806), *Descrizione del Foro Bonaparte* (Milan and Parma: Tipi Bodoniani).
Appignanesi, L. (ed.) (1986), *Post-Modernism* (London: ICA Documents).
Appleyard, Bryan (1986), *Richard Rogers: A Biography* (Boston: Faber & Faber).
Arata, Giulio Ulisse (1953), *Leonardo Architetto e Urbanistica* (Milan: Museo Nationale della Scienza e della Tecnica).
Architectural Publication Society, *The Dictionary of Architecture*: *see* Papworth, Wyatt.
Architekten und Ingenieur-Verein (1929), *Hamburg und seine Bauten: 1918–29* (Hamburg: Boysen & Maasch).
Architext (1976), 'Architext', *Japan Architect*, 232/51/6: 19–80.
Arco, M. Fagiolo dell' (ed.) (1972), *Architettura barocca a Roma* (Rome: Bulzoni).
Arets, W., and Bergh, W. van der (1990), *Luis Barragán (1902–88), Architect* (Rotterdam: Uitgeverij Publishers).
Argan, Giulio Carlo (1957), *Marcel Breuer: Disegno industriale e architettura* (Milan: Görlich).
—(1975), *Walter Gropius e la Bauhaus* (Turin: Einaudi).
—(1976), *Adalberto Libera* (Rome: Editalia).
—(1978), *Brunelleschi* (Milan: Mondadori).
Ariès, Philippe (1981), *The Hour of Our Death* (London: Allen Lane).
Arnell, Peter, and Bickford, Ted (eds.) (1984), *James Stirling: Buildings and Projects* (New York: Rizzoli).
——(1985), *Aldo Rossi: Buildings and Projects* (New York: Rizzoli).
Arnold, Dana (ed.) (1996), *The Georgian Villa* (Stroud: Alan Sutton).
Arnst, Karl, Koch, Georg F., and Larsson, Lars Olof (1978), *Albert Speer: Arbeiten 1933–1942* (Berlin, Frankfurt, and Vienna: Ullstein).

Arslan, Edouardo (1971), *Gothic Architecture in Venice* (London: Phaidon).
Arts Council of Great Britain (1985), *The Architecture of Adolf Loos* (London: Arts Council).
—(1987), *see* Raeburn and Wilson (1987).
Asche, Sigfried (1978), *Balthaser Permoser und die Barockskulptur des Dresdner Zwinger* (Berlin: Deutscher Verlag für Kunstwissenschaft).
Aschenbach, Sigrid (ed.) (1987), *Erich Mendelsohn, 1887–1953: Ideen, Bauten, Projekte* (Berlin: W. Arenhövel).
Asenbaum, Paul, *et al.* (1984), *Otto Wagner: Möbel und Innenräume* (Salzburg: Residenz-Verlag).
Ashmole, Bernard (1972), *Architect and Sculptor in Ancient Greece* (New York: New York UP).
Ashworth, William (1954), *The Genesis of Modern British Town Planning* (London: Routledge & Kegan Paul).
Aslet, Clive (1986), *Quinlan Terry: The Revival of Architecture* (Harmondsworth: Viking).
Aslin, Elizabeth (1969), *The Æsthetic Movement* (London: Paul Elek).
Asplund, Erik Gunnar (1985), *Asplund, 1885–1940* (Stockholm: Arkitekturmuseet).
—(1988), *Gunnar Asplund, 1895–1940: The Dilemma of Classicism* (London: Architectural Association, 1988).
—*et al.* (1931), *Acceptera* (Stockholm: Bokförlagsaktiebolaget Tiden).
Atterbury, Paul, and Wainwright, Clive (1994), *Pugin: A Gothic Passion* (New Haven and London: Yale UP and The Victoria & Albert Museum).
Auer, Hans (1885), *Das k. k. Hof-Opernhaus in Wien* (Vienna: Lehmann).
Aulanier, Christiane (1953), *Le Nouveau Louvre de Napoléon*, vol. iii of *Histoire du Palais et du Musée du Louvre* (Paris: Éditions des Musées Nationaux).
Aurenhammer, Gertrude (ed.) (1969), *Das Belvedere in Wien* (Graz: Akad. Druck und Verlagsanstalt).
Aurenhammer, Hans (1973), *J. B. Fischer von Erlach* (London: Allen Lane).
Auty, Robert, and Oblensky, Dimitri (eds.) (1980), *An Introduction to Russian Art and Architecture* (Cambridge: Cambridge UP).
Auzas, P. M. (ed.) (1965), *Eugène Viollet-le-Duc—1814–1879* (Paris: Caisse Nationale des Monuments Historiques).
Axon, William E. A. (1878), *An Architectural and General Description of the Town Hall, Manchester* (London and Manchester: Heywood).
Aymonino, Carlo (1971), *Origine e sviluppo della città moderne* (Padua: Marsilio).
—(1975), *Il significato della città* (Rome-Bari: Laterza).
—(ed.) (1975*a*), *Giuseppe Samonà: 1923–1975* (Rome: Officina).
Azcárete, José María de (1958), *La Arquitectura Gótica Toledana del Siglo XV* (Madrid: Instituto Diego Velasquez).
Aznar, José Camon (ed.) (1941), *Compendio de Arquitectura y Simetría de los templos por Simon Garcia* (Salamanca: Hijos de Francisco Nuñez).
Babelon, Jean-Pierre (1991), *Demeures parisiennes sous Henri IV et Louis XIII* (Paris: Hazan).
Bachmann, Erich (1970), *Schloss Aschaffenburg und Pompeijanum* (Munich: Bayerische Verwaltung der Staatlichen Schlösser, Gärten und Seen).
Backemeyer, Sylvia, and Gronberg, Theresa (eds.) (1984), *W. R. Lethaby, 1857–1931: Architecture, Design, and Education* (London: Lund Humphries).
Bacon, Edmund Norwood (1974), *Design of Cities* (New York: Viking).
Badovici, Jean (1923), *Maisons de Rapport de Charles Plumet* (Paris: Morancé).
—(1925), *Intérieurs Français* (Paris: Morancé).
—(1926–30), *L'Architecture Russe en URSS* (Paris: Morancé).
—(1931), *Grandes Constructions* (Paris: Morancé).
—(1937), *Architecture de Fêtes: Arts et Techniques* (Paris: Morancé).
—(ed.) (1975), *L'Architecture Vivante* (New York: Da Capo).
—and Gray, Eileen (1929), *E-1027: Maison en Bord de Mer* (Paris: Morancé).
Baedeker, Karl, *Handbook for Travellers* (Leipzig: Baedeker, various dates before 1939). These excellent guides often contain valuable architectural information, and the volumes published from 1900 to 1939 are mines of factual data.
Bahns, Jörn (1971), *Johannes Otzen* (Munich: Prestel).
Bailey, Brian (1988), *Almshouses* (London: R. Hale).
Baillairgé, Charles Philippe Ferdinand (1899), *Bilan de M. Baillairgé*, etc. (Quebec: n.p.).
—(1900), *Rapport de l'ex'Ingénieur de la Cité* (Quebec: Darveau).
—(1979), *C. Baillairgé: Arct. Ing. dessins architecturaux* (Quebec: Ministry of Cultural Affairs).
Baker, Herbert (1934), *Cecil Rhodes by His Architect* (London: Oxford UP).
—(1944), *Architecture and Personalities* (London: Country Life).
Baker, James McFarlan (1915), *American Churches* (New York: American Architect).
Baker, Paul R. (1980), *Richard Morris Hunt* (Cambridge, Mass.: MIT Press).
Bakonyi, Tibor, and Kubinszky, Mihály (1981), *Lechner Ödön* (Budapest: Corvina).
Baldini, Umberto, *et al.* (1979), *La Cappella des Principi e le pietre dure a Firenze* (Milan: Electa).
Baldon, Cleo, and Melchior, Ib (1989), *Steps and Stairways* (New York: Rizzoli).
Baldwin, Charles C. (1976), *Stanford White* (New York: Da Capo; reprint of 1931 edn.).

Ball, R, and Cox, P. (1982), *Low Tech* (London: Century).

Ballantyne, Andrew (1997), *Architecture, Landscape, and Liberty: Richard Payne Knight and the Picturesque* (Cambridge: Cambridge UP).

Ballu, Théodore (1868), *Monographie de l'Église de la Sainte-Trinité* (Paris: Dupuis).

Baltard, Louis-Pierre (1818), *Grands-Prix d'Architecture* (Paris: Vaudoyer & Baltard).

—(1875), *Arc de Triomphe* (Paris: Claye).

Baltard, Victor, and Callet, Félix (1863), *Monographie des halles centrales de Paris* (Paris: Morel).

Banham, Mary, and Hillier, Bevis (eds.) (1976), *A Tonic to the Nation: The Festival of Britain 1951* (London: Thames & Hudson).

Banham, Reyner (1960), *Theory and Design in the First Machine Age* (London: Architectural Press).

—(1966), *The New Brutalism: Ethic or Æsthetic?* (London: Architectural Press).

—(1971), *Los Angeles* (New York: Harper).

—(1975), *Age of the Masters: A Personal View of Modern Architecture* (London: Architectural Press).

—(1976), *Megastructure: Urban Features of the Recent Past* (London: Thames & Hudson).

Barbieri, Franco (1952), *Vincenzo Scamozzi* (Verona: Cassa di Risparmio).

Barbon, Nicholas (1976), *An Apology for the Builder* (New York: Scholarly).

Bardazzi, Silvestro, and Castellani, Eugenio (1981), *La villa medicea di Poggio a Caiano* (Prato: Edizioni del Palazzo).

Bardet, Gaston (1978), *L'Urbanisme* (Paris: Presses Universitaires).

Bardi, P. M. (1964), *The Tropical Gardens of Burle Marx* (New York: Reinhold).

Barnard, Toby, and Clark, Jane (1995), *Lord Burlington: Architecture, Art, and Life* (London and Rio Grande, Ohio: Hambledon Press).

Barnes, Carl, F. jun. (1982), *Villard de Honnecourt—the Artist and his Drawings* (Boston: G. K. Hall).

Barr, Alfred H. (1936), *Cubism and Abstract Art* (New York: Museum of Modern Art).

Barratucci, Brunilde, and Russo, Bianca di (1983), *Arata Isozaki: architetture 1959–82* (Rome: Officina).

Barrett, Anthony A., and Liscombe, Rhodri Windsor (1983), *Francis Rattenbury and British Columbia* (Vancouver: University of British Columbia Press).

Barrett, H., and Phillips, T. (1987), *Suburban Style: The British Home 1840–1960* (London: MacDonald).

Barry, Alfred (1867), *Memoir of the Life and Works of the late Sir Charles Barry* (London: J. Murray).

Bartning, Otto (1959), *Kirchen* (Munich: Callwey).

Bassegoda Nonell, Juan (1977), *Antonio Gaudí* (Tarragona: Caja de Ahorros Provincial).

—(1979), *Obras Completas de Gaudí* (Tokyo: Rikoyosha).

Bassi, Elena (1936), *Giannantonio Selva architetto veneziano* (Padua: Milani).

Bassi, Martino (1572), *Dispareri in materia d'architettura . . .* (Brescia: Bassi).

Battisti, Eugenio (1981), *Filippo Brunelleschi: The Complete Work* (New York: Rizzoli).

Bauch, Kurt (1966), *Das Brandenburger Tor* (Cologne: Wallraf-Richartz Museum).

Bauchal, Charles (1887), *Nouveau Dictionnaire Biographique et Critique des Architectes Français* (Paris: Daly).

Baudot, Anatole de (1905), *L'Architecture et le Béton Armé* (Paris: n.p.).

—(1916), *L'Architecture, le Passé, le Présent* (Paris: Laurens).

Bauer, Hermann (1962), *Rocaille, zur Herkunft und zum Wesen eines Ornament-Motivs* (Berlin: de Gruyter).

—and Bauer, Anna (1985), *Johann Baptist und Dominikus Zimmermann: Entstehung und Vollendung des bayerischen Rokoko* (Regensburg: Pustet).

Baum, Julius (1956), *German Cathedrals* (London: Thames & Hudson).

Baur, Christian (1981), *Neugotik* (Munich: Heyne).

Bayer, Herbert (1938), *Bauhaus: 1919–1929* (New York: Museum of Modern Art).

Bazin, Germain (1963), *Aleijadhino et la sculpture baroque au Brésil* (Paris: Le Temps).

—(1964), *Baroque & Rococo* (London, Thames & Hudson).

—(1990), *Paradeisos: The Art of the Garden* (London: Cassell).

Beach, John (1976), *Julia Morgan* (Oakland, Calif.: The Museum).

Beard, Geoffrey (1983), *Stucco and Decorative Plasterwork in Europe* (New York: Harper & Row).

—(1986), *The Work of John Vanbrugh* (London: Batsford).

Becatti, Giovanni (1960), *La colonna coclide istoriata* (Rome: L'Erma di Bretschneider).

Becherer, Richard (1984), *Science plus Sentiment: César Daly's formula for Modern Architecture* (Ann Arbor: UMI Research).

Becker, Annette, Olley, John, and Wang, Wilfried (eds.) (1997), *20th-Century Architecture in Ireland* (Frankfurt: Prestel).

Becker, F. (1977), *User Participation, Personalization, and Environmental Meaning* (Ithaca, NY: Cornell University).

Becker, Paul (1966), *Clemens Holzmeister und Salzburg* (Salzburg: Residenz Verlag).

Bedford, Steven McLeod (1998), *John Russell Pope, Architect of Empire* (New York: Rizzoli).

Beetz, Wilhelm (1929), *Die Hermes-Villa in Lainz* (Vienna: Gerlach & Wiedling).

Beevers, Robert (1988), *The Garden City Utopia: A*

Critical Biography of Ebenezer Howard (London: Macmillan).
Behne, Adolf (1919), *Die Wiederkehr der Kunst* (Leipzig: Wolff).
—(1920), *Ruf zum Bauen* (Berlin: Wasmuth).
—(1926), *Der Moderne Zweckbau* (Munich: Drei Masken Verlag).
—(1988), *Das neue Berlin* (with Martin Wagner) (Basle and Berlin: Birkhäuser).
Behrendt, Walter Curt (1920), *Architektur und Handwerk im letzten Jahrhundert ihrer traditionellen Entwicklung* (Munich: Bruckmann).
—(1937), *Modern Building* (New York: Harcourt Brace).
Behrens, Peter (1901), *Ein Dokument deutscher Kunst: Die Ausstellung der Künstler-Kolonie in Darmstadt 1901* (Munich: Bruckmann).
Belgiojoso, Ludovico (1979), *Intervista sul mestiere di architetto* (Rome: Laterza).
Bell, Quentin (1978), *Ruskin* (New York: Braziller).
Bellamy, Edward (1967), *Looking Backward 2000–1887* (Cambridge, Mass.: Harvard UP; new corrected version of 1888 edn.).
Bellini, Amedeo (1978), *Benedetto Alfieri* (Milan: Electa).
Bellot, Dom Paul (1948), *Propos d'un bâtisseur du bon Dieu* (Montreal: Fides).
Belluzzi, Amedeo, and Conforti, Claudia (eds.) (1986), *Giovanni Michelucci* (Milan: Electa).
Belov, M., *et al.* (1988), *Contemporary Soviet Visionary Architecture* (London: Architectural Association).
Beltrami, Luca (1912), *Vita di Aristotile da Bologna* (Bologna: Libreria Beltrami).
Bence-Jones, Mark (1988), *A Guide to Irish Country Houses* (London: Constable).
Benedetti, Sandro (1973), *Giacomo del Duca e l'architettura del Cinquecento* (Rome: Officina).
Benešová, Marie (1971), *Josef Gočár* (Prague: Academy).
Benevolo, Leonardo (1971), *History of Modern Architecture* (London: Routledge & Kegan Paul).
—(1978), *The Architecture of the Renaissance* (Boulder, Colo.: Westview Press).
Benjamin, Asher (1838, 1854), *The Builder's Guide* (Boston: The Author).
—(1972), *American Builder's Companion* (New York: Da Capo; new version of 1806 edn.).
—(1972*a*), *The Country Builder's Assistant* (New York: Da Capo; new version of 1797 edn.).
—(1976), *The Elements of Architecture* (Boston: Mudsey; new version of 1843 edn.).
—(1976*a*), *The Practical House Carpenter* (New York: Da Capo; new version of 1830 edn.).
—(1976*b*), *The Practice of Architecture* (New York: Da Capo; new version of 1833 edn.).
—(1976*c*), *The Rudiments of Architecture* (New York: Da Capo; new version of 1814 edn.).
Bennett, David (1997), *The Architecture of Bridge Design* (London: Thomas Telford).
Benoît-Lévy, Georges (1911), *La cité-jardin* (Paris: Éditions des Cités-Jardins de France).
—(1932), *Cités-Jardins* (Nice: Benoît-Lévy).
Bentivoglio, Enzo, and Valtieri, S. (1973), *San Martino al Cimino* (Viterbo: Azienda).
Benton, Tim, Benton, Charlotte, and Sharp, Dennis (eds.) (1975), *Architecture and Design: 1890–1939* (New York: Whitney Library).
Bercé, Françoise, and Foucart, Bruno (1988), *Viollet-le-Duc, Architect, Artist, Master of Historic Preservation* (Washington: Trust for Museum Exhibitions).
Berckenhagen, Eckhart (1966), *Barock in Deutschland: Residenzen* (Berlin: Hessling).
—(1975), *St Petersburg um 1800: Architekturzeichnungen Thomas de Thomon* (Berlin: Kunstbibliothek).
—(1976), *Fünf Architekten aus Fünf Jahrhunderten* (Berlin: Mann):
—(ed.) (1977), *Fritz Höger* (Berlin: Kunstbibliothek).
Bergdoll, Barry (1994), *Karl Friedrich Schinkel: An Architecture for Prussia* (New York: Rizzoli).
—(1994*a*), *Léon Vaudoyer: Historicism in the Age of Industry* (New York and Cambridge, Mass.: Architectural History Foundation and MIT Press).
Berger, Robert W. (1969), *Antoine le Pautre: A French Architect of the Era of Louis XIV* (New York: New York UP).
Berlage, Hendrik Petrus (1996), *Thoughts on Style 1886–1909* (Santa Monica, Calif.: Getty Center for the History of Art & the Humanities).
Bernhard, Marianne (1992), *Die Wiener Ringstrasse: Architektur & Gesellschaft* (Vienna: Kremayr & Scheriau).
Berti, Luciano (1967), *Il principe dello studiolo: Francesco I dei Medici e la fine del Rinascimento florentino* (Florence: Edam).
Bertotti-Scamozzi, Ottavio (ed.) (1776–83), *Le fabbriche e i disegni di Andrea Palladio raccolti ed illustrati* (Vicenza: Francesco Modena).
—(1797), *Le Terme dei Romani, disegnate da A. Palladio* (Vicenza: G. Rossi).
Berty, Adolphe (1860), *Les grands architectes français de la Renaissance* (Paris: Aubry).
Berve, Helmut, and Gruben, Gottfried (1963), *Greek Temples, Theatres, and Shrines* (New York: Abrams).
Besset, Maurice (1957), *Gustave Eiffel 1832–1923* (Milan: Electa).
—(1976), *Le Corbusier* (New York: Rizzoli).
Beveridge, Charles E. (1995), *Frederick Law Olmsted: Designing the American Landscape* (New York: Rizzoli).
Beyaert, Henri (1880–92), *Travaux d'architecture*

exécutés en Belgique par Henri Beyaert (Brussels: Lyon-Claesen).

Białostocki, Jan (1972), *Spätmittelalter und beginnende Neuzeit* (Berlin: Propyläen).

Bianchi, Lidia (1955), *Disegni di Ferdinando Fuga . . .* (Rome: Gabinetto Nationale della Stampe).

Biddle, Gordon (1973), *Victorian Stations* (Newton Abbot: David & Charles).

Biederstedt, Rudolf (1961), *Johann Friedrich Eosander. Grundzüge einer Biographie* (Stockholm: Kungl. Vitterhets-Historie- och Antikvitetsakademien).

Biegański, Piotr (1972), *U Źródet Architektury Współczesnej* (Warsaw: PWN).

Biehn, Heinz (1965), *Die Löwenburg im Schlosspark Wilhelmshöhe* (Munich: Verwaltung der Staatlichen Schlösser & Gärten in Hessen).

Biesantz, Hagen, Klingborn, Arne, and Fant, Åke (1980), *The Goetheanum: Rudolf Steiner's Architectural Impulse* (London: Steiner).

Bill, Max (1945), *Wiederaufbau* (Zurich: Verlag für Architektur).

——(1952), *Form: Eine Bilanz über die Formentwicklung um die Mitte des XX. Jahrhunderts* (Basle: Werner).

——(1955), *Mies van der Rohe* (Milan: Il Balcone).

——(1969), *Robert Maillart: Bridges and Constructions* (London: Pall Mall).

Billcliffe, Roger (1977), *Architectural Sketches and Flower Drawings by Charles Rennie Mackintosh* (London: Academy Editions).

Billing, Hermann (1904), *Der Musikraum in der Weltausstellung St-Louis* (Stuttgart: Hoffmann).

Billings, Robert William (1845–52), *The Baronial and Ecclesiastical Antiquities of Scotland* (Edinburgh: Blackwood).

Billington, David P. (1983), *The Tower and the Bridge: The New Art of Structural Engineering* (New York: Basic Books).

——(1990), *Robert Maillart and the Art of Reinforced Concrete* (New York: Architectural History Foundation).

Bindmann, David, and Riemann, Gottfried (1993), *Karl Friedrich Schinkel: 'The English Journey'. Journal of a Visit to France and Britain in 1826* (New Haven and London: Yale UP for Paul Mellon Center for Studies in British Art).

Bingham, Neil (1991), *C. A. Busby, The Regency Architect of Brighton and Hove* (London: RIBA).

Binney, Marcus (1984), *Sir Robert Taylor: From Rococo to Neoclassicism* (London: Allen & Unwin).

——and Pearce, David (eds.) (1979), *Railway Architecture* (London: Orbis).

Birchler, L. (1924), *Einsiedeln und sein Architekt Bruder Caspar Moosbrugger* (Augsburg: n.p.).

Birrell, James (1964), *Walter Burley Griffin* (St Lucia: University of Queensland Press).

Biver, Marie-Louise (1963), *Le Paris de Napoléon* (Paris: Plon).

——(1964), *Pierre Fontaine, premier architecte de l'Empereur* (Paris: Plon).

Bjelajac, David (1997), *Washington Allston, Secret Societies, and the Alchemy of Anglo-American Painting* (Cambridge: Cambridge UP).

Blair, S. S., and Bloom, Jonathan M. (1994), *The Art and Architecture of Islam 1250–1800* (New Haven and London: Yale UP).

Blake, Peter (1949), *Marcel Breuer, Architect and Designer* (New York: Museum of Modern Art).

——(1973), *The Work of Harry Seidler* (Sydney, New York, and Stuttgart: Horowitz, Wittenborn, & Kraemer).

——(1977), *Form Follows Fiasco* (Boston: Little, Brown).

Blaser, Werner (1977), *Mies van der Rohe* (Basle: Birkhäuser).

——(1980), *Filigran Architektur: Metall- und Glaskonstruktion* (Basle and New York: Wepf).

——(1982), *Architecture 70/80 in Switzerland* (Basle and Boston: Birkhäuser).

——(1990), *Santiago Calatrava: Ingenieur–Architektur* (Basle, Boston, Berlin: Birkhäuser).

——(1996), *Mies van der Rohe: West Meets East* (Basle: Birkhäuser).

Blasi, Cesare (1963), *Figini e Pollini* (Milan: Edizioni di Comunità).

Blau, E. (1982), *Ruskinian Gothic: The Architecture of Deane and Woodward (1845–61)* (Princeton: Princeton UP).

Bletter, Rosemarie Haag (1979), *Bruno Taut and Paul Schubart's Vision* (New York: Rizzoli).

——(1986), *The Architecture of Frank Gehry* (New York: Rizzoli).

——(1989), *Remembering the Future: The New York World's Fair from 1939–1964* (New York: Rizzoli).

——and Robinson, Cervin (1975), *Skyscraper Style—Art Deco, New York* (New York: Oxford UP).

Blijstra, Reinder (1962) *Nederlandse bouwkunst na 1900* (Utrecht: Spectrum).

——(1971), *C. van Eesteren* (Amsterdam: Meulenhoff).

——et al. (1970), *Mart Stam: documentation of his works, 1920–1965* (London: RIBA).

Blok, G. A. C. (1937), *Pieter Post: 1608–1669* (Siegen: Vorländer).

Blomfield, Reginald Theodore (1892), *The Formal Garden in England* (London: Macmillan).

——(1897), *A History of Renaissance Architecture in England 1500–1800* (London: Bell).

——(1932), *Memoirs of an Architect* (London: Macmillan).

——(1934), *Modernismus* (London: Macmillan).

——(1938), *Sébastien Le Prestre de Vauban* (London: Methuen).

——(1940), *Richard Norman Shaw* (London: Batsford).

—(1974), *A History of French Architecture* (New York: Hacker; repr. of the 1921 edn.).

Blondel, Jacques-François (1752–6), *L'Architecture Françoise* (Paris: Jombert).

—and Patte, Pierre (1771–7), *Cours d'Architecture* (Paris: Desaint).

Blondel, Nicolas-François (1698), *Cours d'Architecture* (Paris: Mortier).

Bloom, Jonathan, M. (1989), *Minaret, Symbol of Islam* (Oxford: Oxford UP).

Bloomer, Kent, and Moore, Charles (1977), *Body, Memory, and Architecture* (New Haven: Yale UP).

Blore, Edward (1826), *The Monumental Remains of Noble and Eminent Persons, comprising the Sepulchral Antiquities of Great Britain* (London: Harding, Lepard).

Bloxam, Matthew Holbeche (1882), *The Principles of Gothic Ecclesiastical Architecture* (London: George Bell).

Blum, Hans (1550), *Quinque Columnarum exacta descriptio atque deliniatio cum symmetrica earum distributione* . . . (Zurich: Froschouerum); see also *The Booke of Five Columnes of Architecture . . . Gathered . . . by H. Bloome out of Antiquities* (London: Stafford, 1608).

Blundell Jones, Peter (1995), *Hans Scharoun* (London: Phaidon).

Blunt, Anthony (1941), *François Mansart and the Origins of French Classical Architecture* (London: Warburg Institute).

—(1958), *Philibert de L'Orme* (London: Zwemmer).

—(1968), *Sicilian Baroque* (London: Weidenfeld & Nicolson).

—(1975), *Neapolitan Baroque and Rococo Architecture* (London: Zwemmer).

—(1978), *Baroque and Rococo Architecture and Decoration* (London: Elek).

—(1979), *Borromini* (Harmondsworth: Penguin).

—(1982), *Art and Architecture in France: 1500–1700* (Harmondsworth: Penguin).

Boaga, Giorgio (ed.) (1984), *Riccardo Morandi* (Bologna: Zanichelli).

Boardman, Philip (1978), *The World of Patrick Geddes: Biologist, Town Planner, Re-educator, Peace-warrior* (Boston: Routledge & Kegan Paul).

Boase, Thomas Sherrer Ross (1967), *Castles and Churches of the Crusading Kingdom* (London: Oxford UP).

—(1979), *Vasari: The Man and the Book* (Princeton: Princeton UP).

Böck, Hanna (1989), *Einsiedeln: das Kloster und seine Geschichte* (Zurich: Artemis).

Bock, Manfred (ed.) (1997), *Michel de Klerk: Architect and Artist of the Amsterdam School* (Rotterdam: NAI Publishers).

Boehlke, Hans-Kurt (1958), *Simon-Louis du Ry als Stadtbaumeister Landgraf Friedrichs II von Hessen Kassel* (Kassel: Bärenreiter).

—(1980), *Simon-Louis du Ry: ein Wegbereiter klassizistischer Architektur in Deutschland* (Stuttgart: Die Sparkasse).

Boer, Hans-Peter, Lechtape, Andreas, and Buske, Stefan (1995), *J. C. Schlaun: Sein Leben, seine Zeit, sein Werk* (Münster: Aschendorff).

Boesiger, Willy (1966), *Richard Neutra: Buildings and Projects* (New York: Praeger).

—(ed.) (1966–70), *Œuvre complète par Le Corbusier* (Zurich: Les Éditions d'Architecture).

—(1972), *Le Corbusier* (New York: Praeger).

Boëthius, Axel (1960), *The Golden House of Nero: Some Aspects of Roman Architecture* (Ann Arbor: University of Michigan Press).

—and Ward-Perkins, J. B. (1970), *Etruscan and Early Roman Architecture* (Harmondsworth: Penguin).

Boëthius, Gerda Axelina, and Romdahl, Alex Ludvig (1935), *Uppsala Domkyrka 1258 til 1435* (Uppsala: Almqvist & Wiksell).

Bogardus, James (1856), *Cast Iron Buildings: Their Construction and Advantages* (New York: Harrison).

Bognar, Botond (1985), *Contemporary Japanese Architecture: Its Development and Challenge* (New York and Wokingham: Van Nostrand Reinhold).

—(1990–2), *Contemporary Japanese Architecture* (New York: Rizzoli).

Bohigas, Oriol (1968), *Arquitectura Modernista* (Barcelona: Lumen).

—(1970), *Arquitectura española de la segunda república* (Barcelona: Tusquets).

—*et al.* (1991), *Barcelona: City and Architecture* (New York: Rizzoli).

Boito, Camillo (1880), *Architettura del Medio Evo in Italia* (Milan: Hoepli).

—(1882), *I principii del disegno e gli stili dell'ornamento* (Milan: Hoepli).

Boje, A. (1972), *Open-Plan Offices* (London: Business Books).

Bold, John (1989), *John Webb: Architectural Theory and Practice in the Seventeenth Century* (Oxford: Clarendon Press).

Bolton, Arthur T. (1922), *The Architecture of Robert and James Adam (1758–1794)* (London: Country Life).

—(1925), *Architectural Education a Century Ago* (London: Sir John Soane's Museum).

—(ed.) (1927), *The Portrait of Sir John Soane* (London: Sir John Soane's Museum).

—(ed.) (1929), *The Lectures on Architecture by Sir John Soane* (London: Sir John Soane's Museum).

Bonatz, Paul (1950), *Leben und Bauten* (Stuttgart: Spemann).

Bond, Francis (1908), *Fonts and Font Covers* (London: Oxford UP).

—(1908*a*), *Screens and Galleries in English Churches* (London: Oxford UP).

—(1910), *Wood Carvings in English Churches II:*

Stalls and Tabernacle Work, etc. (London: Oxford UP).

Bond, Francis (1912), *Wood Carvings in English Churches I: Misericords* (London: Oxford UP).

—(1913), *An Introduction to English Church Architecture from the Eleventh to the Sixteenth Century* (London: Oxford UP).

—(1916), *The Chancel in English Churches* (London: Oxford UP).

Bond, Frederick Bligh, and Camm, Dom Bede (1909), *Roodscreens and Roodlofts* (London: Pitman).

Bonfanti, Ezio, *et al.* (1973), *Architettura Razionale* (Milan: Angeli).

Bongartz, Norbert, *et al.* (1977), *Paul Bonatz 1877–1956* (Stuttgart: Krämer).

Bonnar, Thomas (1892), *Biographical Sketch of George Meikle Kemp: Architect of the Scott Monument, Edinburgh* (Edinburgh: Blackwood).

Bonwitt, W. (1987), *Michael Searles: A Georgian Architect and Surveyor* (London: Society of Arch. Historians of Great Britain).

Bony, Jean (1979), *The English Decorated Style* (Oxford: Phaidon).

—(1982), *French Gothic Architecture of the Twelfth and Thirteenth Centuries* (Berkeley and London: University of California Press).

Boogaart, E. van den (ed.) (1979), *Johan Maurits van Nassau-Singen 1604–1679* (The Hague: Johan Maurits van Nassau Stichtung).

Booth, M. (1983), *Camp* (London: Quartet).

Booth, Philip, and Taylor, Nicholas (1970), *Cambridge New Architecture* (London: Leonard Hill).

Booz, Paul (1956), *Der Baumeister der Gothik* (Munich: Deutsche Kunstverlag).

Borger, Hugo (ed.) (1980), *Der Kölner Dom im Jahrhundert seiner Vollendung* (Cologne: Museen der Stadt Köln).

Borisova, Elena A., and Kazhdan, Tatiana P. (1971), *Russakaya arkhitektura Konsta XIX–nachala XX veka* (Moscow: Nauka).

Born, Esther (1937), *The New Architecture of Mexico* (New York: *Architectural Record* and William Morrow).

Borràs, Maria Lluïsa (1970), *Lluís Domènech i Montaner* (Barcelona: Polígrafa).

—(1975), *Arquitectura contemporánea japonesa* (Barcelona: Editalia).

—(ed.) (1975*a*), *Sert: Mediterranean Architecture* (Boston: New York Graphic Society).

Borrmann, Richard (1893), *Die Bau- und Kunstdenkmäler von Berlin* (Berlin: Springer).

Börsch-Supan, Eva (1977), *Berliner Baukunst nach Schinkel 1840–1870* (Munich: Prestel).

—(ed.) (1980), *Ludwig Persius: Das Tagebuch des Architekten Friedrich Wilhelms IV, 1840–1845* (Munich: Deutscher Kunstverlag).

Börsch-Supan, Helmut, and Grisebach, Lucius (eds.) (1981), *Karl Friedrich Schinkel: Architektur, Malerei, Kunstgewerbe* (Berlin: Vorwaltung der Staatlichen Schlösser und Gärten).

Borsi, Franco (1966), *L'Architectura dell'Unità d'Italia* (Florence: Le Monnier).

—(1969), *Victor Horta* (Rome: Edizioni del Tritone).

—(1975), *Il Palazzo della Consulta* (Rome: Editalia).

—(1984), *Bernini architetto* (New York: Rizzoli).

—(1989), *Leon Battista Alberti: the Complete Works* (New York: Electa/Rizzoli).

—and Godoli, Ezio (1978), *Paris 1900* (New York: Rizzoli).

——(1986), *Vienna 1900, Architecture and Design* (London: Lund Humphries).

—and Wieser, Hans (1971), *Bruxelles: Capitale de l'Art Nouveau* (Brussels: Volkaer).

Boscarino, Salvatore (1961), *Studi e rilievi di architettura siciliana* (Messina: Raphael).

—(1973), *Juvarra, architetto* (Rome: Officina).

Bosdari, D. De (1954), *Anton Anreith, Africa's First Sculptor* (Cape Town: Balkema).

Bosserman, Joseph Norwood (1968), *Ralph Walker Bibliography* (Charlottesville, Va.: American Association of Architectural Bibliographers).

Both, Wolf von, and Vogel, Hans (1973), *Landgraf Friedrich II von Hessen-Kassel* (Munich: Deutscher Kunstverlag).

Botta, Mario (1991), *Mario Botta, 1980–1990* (Zurich: Verlag für Architektur).

Bottineau, Yves (1962), *L'Art d'Ange-Jacques Gabriel à Fontainebleau 1735–1774* (Paris: Boccard).

Botto, Ida Maria (1968), *Mostra di disegni di Bernardo Buontalenti (1531–1608)* (Florence: Olschki).

Boucher, Cyril Thomas Goodman (1963), *John Rennie 1761–1821: The Life and Work of a Great Engineer* (Manchester: Manchester UP).

Boudon, Françoise, Loyer, François, and Dufournet, Paul (1979), *Hector Horeau 1801–1872* (Paris: Centre d'Études et de Recherches Architecturales).

Bourgeois, Victor (1971), *Victor Bourgeois 1897–1962* (Brussels: Archives de l'Architecture Moderne).

Bourget, Pierre, and Cattaui, Georges (1960), *Jules Hardouin-Mansart* (Paris: Vincent, Fréal).

Bourke, John (1962), *Baroque Churches of Central Europe* (London: Faber & Faber).

Bowie, Theodore (ed.) (1968), *The Sketchbook of Villard de Honnecourt* (Bloomington, Ind., and London: Indiana UP).

Boyd, Julian P. (ed.) (1950–), *The Papers of Thomas Jefferson* (Princeton: Princeton UP).

Boyd, Robin (1962), *Kenzo Tange* (New York: Braziller).

—(1968), *New Directions in Japanese Architecture* (New York: Braziller).

Boyd Whyte, Iain (1982), *Bruno Taut and the Architecture of Activism* (Cambridge & New York: Cambridge UP).

Boyé, Pierre (1910), *Les châteaux du Roi Stanislaus en Lorraine* (Paris: Berger-Levrault).

Bozal, Valeriano (1978), *Historia del arte en España* (Madrid: ISTMO).

Braham, Allan (1980), *The Architecture of the French Enlightenment* (London: Thames & Hudson).

— and Hager, Hellmut (1977), *Carlo Fontana: The Drawings at Windsor Castle* (London: Zwemmer).

— and Smith, Peter (1973), *François Mansart* (London: Zwemmer).

Bramsen, Henrik (1959), *Gottlieb Bindesbøll* (Copenhagen: Selskabet til udgivelse af okrifter om danskte mindesmaerker).

Brandon-Jones, John, *et al.* (1978), *C. F. A. Voysey, Architect and Designer* (London: Lund Humphries).

Brandwood, Geoffrey K. (1997), *Temple Moore: An Architect of the Late Gothic Revival* (Stamford: Paul Watkins).

Branner, Robert (1965), *St Louis and the Court Style in Gothic Architecture* (London: Zwemmer).

Branzi, Andrea (1984), *The Hot House: Italian New Wave Design* (Cambridge, Mass.: MIT Press).

Brauer, Heinrich, and Wittkower, Rudolf (1970), *Die Zeichnungen des Gianlorenzo Bernini* (New York: Reprinted Collectors Editions).

Braunfels, Wolfgang (1938), *François Cuvilliés: ein Beitrag zur Geschichte der künstlerischen Beziehungen zwischen Deutschland und Frankreich im 18. Jahrhundert* (Würzburg: Mayr).

—(1972), *Monasteries of Western Europe: The Architecture of the Orders* (London: Thames & Hudson).

—(1981), *Brunelleschi und die Kirchenbaukunst des frühen Humanismus* (Basle: Helbing & Lichtenhahn).

—(1986), *François Cuvilliés: der Baumeister der Galanten Architektur des Rokoko* (Munich: Süddeutscher Verlag).

Brawne, Michael (1983), *Arup Associates: The Biography of an Architectural Practice* (London: Lund Humphries).

Brayda, Carlo, Coli, Laura, and Sesia, Daria (1966), *Ingegneri e architetti del sei e settecento in Piemonte* (Turin: Società Ingegneri e Architetti).

Brétas, Rodrigo José Ferreira (1951), *António Francisco Lisboa—O Aleijadhino* (Rio de Janeiro: Directoria do Património Histórico).

Brett, Charles E. B. (1967), *Buildings of Belfast 1700–1914* (London: Weidenfeld & Nicolson).

—(1973), *Court Houses and Market Houses of the Province of Ulster* (Belfast: Ulster Architectural Heritage Society).

—(1976), *Roger Mulholland, Architect, of Belfast, 1740–1818* (Belfast: Ulster Architectural Heritage Society).

—(1996), *Buildings of County Antrim* (Belfast: Ulster Architectural Heritage Society and the Ulster Historical Foundation).

Breuer, Marcel (1955), *Sun and Shadow: The Philosophy of an Architect* (New York: Dodd).

Bridenbaugh, Carl (1949), *Peter Harrison, first American Architect* (Chapel Hill, NC: University of North Carolina Press).

Briganti, Giuliano (1962), *Pietro da Cortona* (Florence: Sansoni).

Briggs, Nancy (1991), *John Johnson 1732–1814* (Chelmsford: Essex County Record Office).

Brinckmann, Albert E. (1915–19), *Baukunst des 17. und 18. Jahrhunderts in den Romanischen Ländern* (Berlin: Athenaion).

—(1931), *Theatrum Novum Pedemontii* (Düsseldorf: Schwann).

—(1932), *Von Guarino Guarini bis Balthasar Neumann* (Berlin: DVK).

Brino, Giovanni (1972), *La casa dell'architetto Alessandro Antonelli in Torino* (Turin: n.p.).

— Bernardi, Attilio de, *et al.* (1966), *L'opera di Carlo e Amedeo di Castellamonte* (Turin: Quaderni di Studio).

Brion-Guerry, Liliane (1960), *Philibert de L'Orme* (New York: Universal Books).

Britton, John (1807–26), *The Architectural Antiquities of Great Britain* (London: Longman).

Broadbent, Geoffrey (1991), *Deconstruction: A Student Guide* (London: Academy Editions).

— *et al.* (1980), *Signs, Symbols, and Architecture* (Chichester: Wiley).

Brockman, H. A. N. (1978), *Fry, Drew, Knight, Creamer: Architecture* (London: Lund Humphries).

Brolin, Brent (1976), *The Failure of Modern Architecture* (New York: Van Nostrand Reinhold).

—(1985), *Flight of Fancy: The Banishment and Return of Ornament* (London: Academy Editions).

Brongniart, A.-T. (1986), *Alexandre-Théodore Brongniart 1739–1813* (Paris: Musée Carnavalet).

Brooks, Harold Allen (1972), *The Prairie School* (Toronto: University of Toronto Press).

—(ed.) (1982), *Le Corbusier Archive* (New York: Garland).

—(1984), *Frank Lloyd Wright and The Prairie School* (New York: Braziller).

—(ed.) (1987), *Le Corbusier: the Garland Essays* (New York: Garland).

—(ed.) (1987*a*), *Le Corbusier* (Princeton: Princeton UP).

Brooks, Michael W. (1987), *John Ruskin and Victorian Architecture* (New Brunswick, NJ: Rutgers UP).

Brooks, Neil Conwell (1921), *The Sepulchre of Christ in Art and Liturgy* (Urbana, Ill.: Univ. of Illinois Studies in Language and Literature).

Brown, C. (1976), *Star-spangled Kitsch* (London: Prior).

Brown, Elizabeth Mills (1976), *New Haven: A Guide to Architecture and Urban Design* (New Haven and London: Yale UP).

Brown, Glenn (1970), *History of the United States Capitol* (New York: Da Capo; reprint of 1903 edn.).

Brown, Jane (1982), *Gardens of a Golden Afternoon: The Story of a Partnership—Edwin Lutyens and Gertrude Jekyll* (Harmondsworth: Penguin).

—(1996), *Lutyens and the Edwardians* (London: Viking).

Brown, Nancy A. Houghton (1980), *The Milanese Architecture of Galeazzo Alessi* (New York: Garland).

Brown, R. J. (1986), *Timber-framed Buildings of England* (London: R. Hale).

Brown, Roderick (ed.) (1985), *The Architectural Outsiders* (London: Waterstone).

Brown, Theodore M. (1958), *The Work of Gerrit Rietveld, Architect* (Utrecht: Bruns).

Brownlee, David (ed.) (1986), *Friedrich Weinbrenner, Architect of Karlsruhe* (Philadelphia: University of Pennsylvania Press).

Brownlee, David Bruce (1984), *The Law Courts: The Architecture of George Edmund Street* (Cambridge, Mass.: MIT Press).

Brown-Manrique, G. (1989), *The Ticino Guide* (London: Longman).

Brucker, Günter (1983), *Barockarchitektur in Österreich* (Cologne: Du Mont).

Bruegmann, Robert (1991), *Holabird & Roche, Holabird & Root: An Illustrated Catalogue* (New York: Garland).

Brunhammer, Yvonne (1984), *The Art-Déco Style* (New York: St Martin's Press).

—*et al.* (1975), *Hector Guimard 1867–1942* (Münster: Landesmuseum).

—and Naylor, Gillian (1978), *Hector Guimard* (New York: Rizzoli).

Brunskill, Ronald W. (1987), *Illustrated Handbook of Vernacular Architecture* (London and Boston: Faber & Faber).

—(1990), *Brick Building in Britain* (London: Victor Gollancz).

—(1994), *Timber Buildings in Britain* (London: Gollancz).

Bruschi, Arnaldo (1977), *Bramante* (London: Thames & Hudson).

Bruun, Charles, and Fenger, L. P. (1892), *Thorvaldsens Musaeums Historie* (Copenhagen: Philipsen).

Bruun, Erik, and Popovits, Sara (eds.) (1978), *Kaija and Keikki Sirén, Architects* (Stuttgart: Kramer).

Bryan, John Morrill (1976), *Robert Mills, Architect, 1781–1855* (Columbia, SC: Columbia Museum of Art).

Buchanan, Peter (1996–7), *Renzo Piano Building Workshops* (London: Phaidon).

Bucher, François (1979), *Architector: The Lodge Books and Sketchbooks of Medieval Architects* (New York: Araris Books).

Büchner, Joachim (1964), *Die spätgotische Wandpfeilerkirchen Bayerns und Österreichs* (Nuremburg: Carl).

Buckley, Leonard (1933), *Sir Ninian Comper, 1864–1960 and Howard Martin Otto (Otho) Travers, 1886–1948: A Belated Tribute* (London: Ecclesiological Society).

Buddensieg, Tilmann, and Rogge, Henning (1984), *Industriekultur: Peter Behrens and the A.E.G., 1907–1914* (Cambridge, Mass.: MIT Press).

Buekschmitt, Justus (1963), *Ernst May* (Stuttgart: Koch).

Buffinga, A. (1971), *Gerrit Thomas Rietveld* (Amsterdam: Meulenhoff).

Bulfinch, Ellen Susan (1973), *The Life and Letters of Charles Bulfinch, Architect* (New York: Franklin).

Bullock, Albert Edward (1908), *Some Sculptural Works of Nicholas Stone* (London: Batsford).

Bullrich, Francisco (1969), *New Directions in Latin American Architecture* (New York: Braziller).

Bungaard, Jens Andreas (1957), *Mnesicles: A Greek Architect* (Copenhagen: Gyldendal).

Bunting, Bainbridge, and Nylander, Robert H. (1973), *Survey of Architectural History in Cambridge* (Cambridge, Mass.: Cambridge Historical Commission).

Burckhardt, Lucius (1980), *The Werkbund: History and Ideology 1907–1933* (Woodbury, NY: Barron's).

—and Förderer, Walter Maria (1968), *Bauen ein Prozess* (Teufen: Niggli).

Burdett, Richard (ed.) (1996), *Richard Rogers Partnership: Works and Projects* (New York: Monacelli Press).

Bure, Gilles de (1987), *Ettore Sottsass Jr.* (Paris: Rivages).

Burford, Alison (1969), *The Greek Temple Buildings at Epidauros* (Toronto: University of Toronto Press).

Burger, P. and Gillies, D. (1989), *Interactive Computer Graphics* (Wokingham: Addison-Wesley).

Burke, Doreen Bulger, *et al.* (1986), *In Pursuit of Beauty: Americans and the Æsthetic Movement* (New York: Metropolitan Museum of Art).

Burke, Edmund (1757), *A Philosophical Enquiry into the Origin of our Ideas of the Sublime and Beautiful* (London: Dodsley).

Burke, G. (1976), *Townscapes* (Harmondsworth: Penguin).

Burkhardt, François, Eveno, Claude, and Podrecca, Claude (eds.) (1989), *Jože Plečnik, Architect, 1872–1957* (Cambridge, Mass.: MIT Press).

—— and Lamarová, Milena B. (1982), *Cubismo cecoslovacco* (Milan: Electa).

Burl, Aubrey (1976), *The Stone Circles of the British Isles* (New Haven and London: Yale UP).

Burlington, Lord (1730), *Fabbriche Antiche disegnate da Andrea Palladio Vincentino* (London: The Author).

Burney, Jan (1994), *Ettore Sottsass* (London: HarperCollins).

Burns, Howard (ed.) (1975), *Andrea Palladio 1508–1580: The Portico and the Farmyard* (London: Arts Council of Great Britain).

Burns, J. (1972), *Anthropods: New Design Futures* (New York: Praeger).

Busby, Charles Augustin (1810), *A Collection of Designs for Modern Establishments* (London: Lumley).

—— (1835), *A Series of Designs for Villas and Country Houses* (London: Taylor).

Bush-Brown, Albert (1960), *Louis Sullivan* (New York: Braziller).

—— (1984), *Skidmore, Owings, & Merrill: Architecture and Urbanism, 1973–1983* (London: Thames & Hudson).

Butikov, Georgii Petrovich (1980), *St Isaac's Cathedral, Leningrad* (Leningrad: Aurora Art).

Butler, Arthur Stanley George (1950), *The Architecture of Sir Edwin Lutyens* (London: Country Life).

Cable, Carole (1985), *Italian New Wave Design: Memphis and the Recent Work of Ettore Sottsass* (Monticello, Ill.: Vance).

Cady, John Hutchins (1957), *The Civic and Architectural Development of Providence, 1636–1950* (Providence, RI: Book Shop).

Caemmerer, H. Paul (1970), *The Life of Pierre Charles L'Enfant, Planner of the City Beautiful* (Washington: National Republic).

Caisse Nationale des Monuments Historiques et des Sites (1980), *Soufflot et son temps: 1780–1980* (Paris, CNMHS).

Caldenby, Claes, and Hultin, Olof (eds.) (1986), *Asplund: A Book* (New York: Rizzoli).

Calvesi, Maurizio (ed.) (1967), *Giovanni Battista e Francesco Piranesi* (Rome: CN).

—— and Manieri-Elia, Mario (1970), *Architettura barocca a Lecce e in terra di Puglia* (Rome and Milan: Bestetti).

Cambridge Camden Society (later The Ecclesiological Society) (1842–68), *The Ecclesiologist*.

—— (1847), *A Hand-Book of English Ecclesiology* (London: J. Masters).

Cameron, Charles (1772), *The Baths of the Romans* (London: Scott).

Cameron, Christina (1989), *Charles Baillairgé: Architect & Engineer* (Montreal: McGill-Queen's University Press).

Campbell, Colen (1728–9), *Andrea Palladio's Five Orders of Architecture* (London: Harding).

—— (1967–72), *Vitruvius Britannicus, or the British Architect* (London: 1715–25; repub. New York: Benjamin Blom).

Campbell, Joan (1978), *The German Werkbund: The Politics of Reform in the Applied Arts* (Princeton: Princeton UP).

Camus de Mézières, Nicolas le (1780), *Le Génie de l'architecture ou l'Analogie de cet art avec nos sensations* (Paris: The Author).

Cancro, C. (1992), *Benedetto Alfieri 1699–1767. L'opere astigiani* (Turin: Lindau).

Candilis, Georges (1973), *Recherches sur l'Architecture* (Paris: Eyrolles).

—— (1977), *Bâtir la Vie: Un Architecte Témoin de son Temps* (Paris: Stock).

Canina, Luigi (1828), *Le nuove fabbriche della Villa Borghese denominata* (Rome: Pinciana).

—— (1846). *Richerche sull'architettura più propria dei tempi cristiani* (Rome: Tipi dello Stesso/Canina).

—— (1852), *Particolare genere di architettura domestica . . .* (Rome: Bertonelli).

Cantacuzino, Sherban (1978), *Wells Coates* (London: G. Fraser).

—— (1989), *Re/architecture: Old Buildings/New Uses* (London: Thames & Hudson).

Caplow, Harriet McNeal (1977), *Michelozzo* (New York: Garland).

Caramel, Luciano, and Longatti, Alberto (1988), *Antonio Sant' Elia: The Complete Works* (New York: Rizzoli).

Caramuel de Lobkowitz, Juan (1678–81), *Architectura civil, recta y obliqua* (Vigevana: Corrado).

Carboneri, Nino (ed.) (1961), *Andrea Pozzo architetto (1642–1709)* (Trento: CAT).

—— (1966), *Ascanio Vitozzi: Un architetto tra manierismo e barocco* (Rome: Officina).

—— (1979), *Le Reale Chiesa di Superga di Filippo Juvarra* (Turin: Ages Arti Grafiche).

—— and Viale, Vittorio (1967), *Bernardo Vittone, Architetto* (Turin: Pozzo-Salvati-Gros Monti).

Cardwell, Kenneth H. (1977), *Bernard Maybeck: Artisan, Architect, Artist* (Santa Barbara, Calif.: Peregrine Smith).

Carli, Enzo (1966), *Pienza, la città di Pio II* (Rome: Editalia).

Carlo, Giancarlo de (1965), *Questioni di Architettura e Urbanistica* (Urbino: University).

—— (1970), *Urbino* (Cambridge, Mass.: MIT).

Caronia Roberti, Salvatore (1935), *Ernesto Basile* (Palermo: Ciuni).

Carpenter, Rhys (1970), *The Architects of the Parthenon* (Harmondsworth: Penguin).

Carrogis, Louis (1779), *Jardin de Monceau* (Paris: Delafosse).

Carrott, Richard G. (1978), *The Egyptian Revival: Its*

Sources, Monuments, and Meaning 1808–1858 (Berkeley: University of California Press).

Carstensen, Georg John Bernhard, and Gildemeister, Charles (1854), *The New York Crystal Palace* (New York: Riker, Thorne).

Carter, Edward C. *et al.* (eds.) (1977, 1980), *The Journal of Benjamin Latrobe* (New Haven: Yale UP).

Carter, Peter (1974), *Mies van der Rohe at Work* (New York: Praeger).

Carvalho, Armino Ayres de (1960–2), *Don João V e arte do seu temps* (Lisbon: Mafra).

Casanelles, E. (1968), *Antonio Gaudí: A Reappraisal* (Greenwich, Conn.: Graphic Society).

Casey, Christine, and Rowan, Alistair (1993), *Buildings of Ireland: North Leinster* (Harmondsworth: Penguin).

Casper, Dale E. (1988), *Paolo Soleri: Master Architect* (Monticello, Ill.: Vance).

Cassou, Jean (1984), *The Concise Encyclopaedia of Symbolism* (Ware: Omega).

Castagnoli, Ferdinando (1956), *Ippodamo di Mileto e l'urbanistica a pianta ortogonale* (Rome: De Luca).

—(1971), *Orthogonal Town Planning in Antiquity* (Cambridge, Mass.: MIT Press).

Castan, Auguste (1891), *L' "Architecteur" Hugues Sambin* (Besançon and Dijon: n.p).

Castedo, Leopoldo (1969), *A History of Latin American Art and Architecture* (New York: Praeger).

Cellini, Francesco, Amato, Claudio d', and Valeriani, Enrico (eds.) (1979), *L'architettura di Ridolfi e Frankl* (Rome: De Luca).

Cennamo, Michelle (1973), *La Prima Esposizione Italiana di Architettura Razionale* (Naples: Fausto Fiorentino).

—(1976), *Materiali per l'Analisi dell'Architettura Moderna Il MIAR* (Naples: Società Editrici Napoletane).

Centre d'Études Supérieures de la Renaissance (1985), *L'Escalier dans l'architecture de la Renaissance* (Paris: Picard).

Cerdá, Ildefonso (1968), *Teoría general de la urbanización* (Madrid: Instituto de Estudios Fiscales).

Cesarini, Dante (1983), *Giuseppe Piermarini, architetto neoclassico* (Foligno: Ediclio).

Cetto, Max C. (1961), *Modern Architecture in Mexico* (New York: Praeger).

Chadwick, George F. (1961), *The Works of Sir Joseph Paxton, 1803–65* (London: Architectural Press).

Chambers, Sir William (1759), *A Treatise on Civil Architecture, in which the Principles of that Art are laid down; and illustrated by a Great Number of Plates, accurately designed, and elegantly engraved by the best hands* (London: Haberkorn). See also the edition with an essay by John B. Papworth (London: J. Taylor, 1826, repub. Farnborough: Gregg, 1969).

—(1968), *A Treatise on the Decorative Part of Civil Architecture* (New York: Blom).

—(1969), *Designs of Chinese Buildings, Furniture, Dresses, Machines, and Utensils* (London: The Author, 1757; repub. Farnborough: Gregg).

—(1972), *Dissertation on Oriental Gardening* (Farnborough: Gregg).

Champeaux, Alfred de, and Gauchery, Paul (1894), *Les Traveaux d'arts exécutés pour Jean de France, Duc de Berry* (Paris: Champion).

Champigneulle, Bernard (1959), *Perret* (Paris: Arts & Métiers Graphiques).

Champneys, Basil (1875), *A Quiet Corner of England* (London: Seeley).

—(ed.) (1901), *Memoirs and Correspondence of Coventry Patmore* (London: Bell).

Chapman, J. M., and Chapman, Brian (1957), *The Life and Times of Baron Haussmann: Paris in the Second Empire* (London: Weidenfeld & Nicolson).

Chareau, Pierre (1929), *Meubles* (Paris: Moreau).

Chastel, André (1959), *Art et Humanisme à Florence* (Paris: Presses Universitaires).

—(1988), *La Grottesque* (Paris: Le Promeneur).

Châteauneuf, Alexis de (1839), *Architectura domestica* (London: Ackerman).

—(1860), *Architectura publica* (Berlin: Ernst & Korn).

Chermayeff, Serge, and Alexander, Christopher (1963), *Community and Privacy: Towards a New Architecture of Humanism* (Garden City, NY: Doubleday).

—and Tzonis, Alexander (1971), *Shape of Community, Realization of Human Potential* (Baltimore: Penguin).

Cherry, Gordon Emanuel (1986), *Holford: A Study in Architecture, Planning, and Civic Design* (London: Mansell).

Chevalier, Pierre, and Rabreau, Daniel (1977), *Le Panthéon* (Paris: Caisse Nationale des Monuments Historiques).

Chevalley, Denis André (1973), *Der grosse Tuilerienentwurf in der Überlieferung Ducerceaus* (Berne and Frankfurt: Lang).

Chiat, Marilyn Joyce Segal (1982), *Handbook of Synagogue Architecture* (Chico, Calif.: Scholars Press).

Chiaveri, Gaetano (1743–4), *Ornamenti Diversi di Porte e Finestre* (Dresden: Zucci).

Chilvers, Ian, and Osborne, Harold, with Farr, Dennis (eds.) (1988), *The Oxford Dictionary of Art* (Oxford: Oxford UP).

Chirol, Pierre (1920), *Jean-Antoine Alavoine* (Rouen: Lainé).

Chitham, Robert (1985), *The Classical Orders of Architecture* (London: Architectural Press).

Choay, Françoise (1960), *Le Corbusier* (New York, Braziller).

—(1965), *L'Urbanisme* (Paris: Seuil).

Choisy, Auguste (1873), *L'Art de bâtir chez les Romains* (Paris: Boucher).
—(1883), *L'Art de bâtir chez les Byzantines* (Paris: Librairie de la Société anonyme de publications périodiques).
—(1883*a*), *Études sur l'architecture Grecque* (Paris: Librairie de la Société anonyme de publications périodiques).
—(1899), *Histoire de l'Architecture* (Paris: Gauthier-Villars).
—(1904), *L'Art de bâtir chez les Égyptiens* (Paris: Rouveyre).
—(1910), *Vitruve* (Paris: Lahure).
Christ-Janer, Albert (1979), *Eliel Saarinen: Finnish-American Architect and Educator* (Chicago: University of Chicago Press).
Christophe, Paul (1902), *Le Béton Armé* (Paris: Béranger).
Christovich, Mary Louise, *et al.* (eds.) (1972–7), *New Orleans Architecture 2* (Gretna, La.: Pelican).
Chrościcki, Juliusz A., and Rottermund, Andrzej (1977), *Atlas Architektury Warszawy* (Warsaw: Arkady).
Chueca Goitia, Fernando (1951), *La catedral nueva de Salamanca* (Salamanca: University of Salamanca).
—(1953), *Arquitectura del Siglo XVI* (Madrid: Plus-Ultra).
—(1965), *Historia de la Arquitectura Española* (Madrid: Dosset).
—and Miguel, Carlos de (1949), *La vida y las obras del arquitecto Juan de Villanueva* (Madrid: Carlos-Jaimé).
Clark, Kenneth Mackenzie (1974), *The Gothic Revival: An Essay in the History of Taste* (London: John Murray).
Clark, Robert Judson (1966), *Louis Christian Mullgardt: 1866–1942* (Santa Barbara, Calif.: University of California).
Clarke, Basil Fulford Lowther (1958), *Anglican Cathedrals outside the British Isles* (London: SPCK).
—(1963), *The Building of the Eighteenth-Century Church* (London: SPCK).
—(1966), *Parish Churches of London* (London: Batsford).
—(1969), *Church Builders of the Nineteenth Century: A Study of the Gothic Revival in England* (Newton Abbot: David & Charles).
Clausen, Meredith L. (1987), *Frantz Jourdain and the Samaritaine* (Leiden: Brill).
Clay, Jean (1981), *Romanticism* (Oxford: Phaidon).
Clayssen, Dominique (1983), *Jean Prouvé: l'idée constructive* (Paris: Dunod).
Clayton, Peter A. (1982), *The Rediscovery of Ancient Egypt: Artists and Travellers in the 19th Century* (London: Thames & Hudson).
Clérisseau, Charles-Louis (1778), *Monumens des Nismes*: part 1 of *Antiquités de la France* (Paris: Philippe-Denis-Pierres).
Clifton-Taylor, Alec (1987), *The Pattern of English Building* (London: Faber & Faber).
Clough, Rose Trillo (1961), *Futurism: The Story of a Modern Art Movement* (New York: Philosophical Library).
Cockerell, Charles Robert (1830), *Antiquities of Athens and Other Places of Greece, Sicily, etc.* (London: Priestley).
—(1860), *The Temples of Jupiter Panhellenius at Aegina and of Apollo Epicurius at Bassae* (London: Weale).
Coe, Peter, and Reading, Malcolm (1981), *Lubetkin and Tecton: Architecture and Social Commitment* (London: Arts Council of Great Britain).
Coffin, David Robbins (1960), *The Villa d'Este at Tivoli* (Princeton: Princeton UP).
—(1979), *The Villa in the Life of Renaissance Rome* (Princeton: Princeton UP).
—(1994), *The English Garden: Meditation and Memorial* (Princeton: Princeton UP).
Cole, David (1980), *The Work of Sir George Gilbert Scott* (London: Architectural Press).
Collins, George Roseborough (1960), *Antonio Gaudí* (New York: Braziller).
—(1973), *Antonio Gaudí and the Catalan Movement, 1870–1930* (Charlottesville, Va.: University Press of Virginia).
—(1973*a*), *The Discovery of Maillart as an Artist* (Princeton: Princeton UP).
—(ed.) (1979), *Visionary Drawings of Architecture and Planning* (Cambridge, Mass.: MIT Press).
—*et al.* (1968), *Arturo Soria y la Ciudad Lineal* (Madrid: Revista de Occidente).
—and Bassegoda Nonell, Juan (1983), *The Designs and Drawings of Antonio Gaudí* (Princeton: Princeton UP).
—with Collins, Christiane C. (1986), *Camillo Sitte: The Birth of Modern City Planning* (New York: Rizzoli).
Collins, Peter (1959), *Concrete: The Vision of a New Architecture: A Study of Auguste Perret and his Precursors* (London: Faber & Faber).
—(1965), *Changing Ideals in Modern Architecture (1750–1950)* (London: Faber & Faber).
Collins Baker, C. H., and Collins Baker, M. I. (1949), *The Life and Circumstances of James Bryges, Duke of Chandos* (Oxford: Clarendon Press).
Collymore, Peter (1982), *The Architecture of Ralph Erskine* (London: Granada).
Colombier, Pierre du (1949), *Jean Goujon* (Paris: Michel).
—(1953), *Les Chantiers des cathédrales* (Paris: Picard).
—(1955), *L'architecture française en Allemagne au XVIII*ᵉ *siècle* (Paris: Presses Universitaires de France).

Colombo, Cesare (1964), *Giancarlo de Carlo* (Milan: Bassoli).

Colston, James (1881), *History of the Scott Monument, Edinburgh* (Edinburgh: The Magistrates and Council).

Colvin, Howard Montagu (ed.) (1973, 1976), *The History of the Kings' Works* (London: HMSO).

—(1991), *Architecture and the After-Life* (New Haven and London: Yale UP).

—(1995), *A Biographical Dictionary of British Architects 1600–1840* (New Haven and London: Yale UP).

—and Craig, Maurice (eds.) (1964), *Architectural Drawings in the Library of Elton Hall by Sir John Vanbrugh and Sir Edward Lovett Pearce* (Oxford: Oxford UP).

—and Harris, John (eds.) (1970), *The Country Seat: Studies in the History of the British Country House presented to Sir John Summerson* (London: Allen Lane).

Commission des Sciences et Arts d'Égypte (1820–30), *Description de l'Égypte* . . . (Paris: Panckoucke).

Comper, John Ninian (1893), *Practical Considerations of the Gothic English Altar and Certain Dependent Ornaments* (Aberdeen: Albany Press).

—(1897), *The Reasonableness of the Ornaments Rubric Illustrated by a Comparison of the German and English Altars* (London: Harrison).

—(1933), *Further Thoughts on the English Altar* (Cambridge: Heffer).

—(1940), *The Atmosphere of a Church* (London: Sheldon).

—(1950), *Of the Christian Altar and the Buildings which Contain it* (London: SPCK).

Conant, Kenneth John (1979), *Carolingian and Romanesque Architecture: 800–1200* (Harmondsworth: Penguin).

Condit, Carl W. (1952), *The Rise of the Skyscraper* (Chicago: University of Chicago Press).

—(1960), *American Building Art: the Nineteenth Century* (New York: Oxford UP).

—(1961), *American Building Art: the Twentieth Century* (New York: Oxford UP).

—(1964), *The Chicago School of Architecture: A History of Commercial and Public Building in the Chicago Area* (Chicago: University of Chicago Press).

—(1968), *American Building: Materials and Techniques from the First Colonial Settlements to the Present* (Chicago: University of Chicago Press).

—(1973), *Chicago, 1910–29: Building, Planning, and Urban Technology* (Chicago: University of Chicago Press).

Conforti, Claudia (1980), *Carlo Aymonino. L'architettura non è un mito* (Rome: Officina).

Connely, Willard (1960), *Louis Sullivan as He Lived* (New York: Horizon).

Conner, Patrick (1979), *Oriental Architecture in the West* (London: Thames & Hudson).

Connors, Joseph (1980), *Borromoni and the Roman Oratory: Style and Society* (New York: Architectural History Foundation).

Conrads, Ulrich (ed.) (1970), *Programmes and Manifestos on Twentieth-Century Architecture* (London: Lund Humphries).

—and Sperlich, Hans (1960), *Phantastische Architektur* (Stuttgart: Hatje).

——(1962), *The Architecture of Fantasy: Utopian Buildings and Planning in Modern Times* (New York: Praeger).

Contant d'Ivry, Pierre (1769), *Les Œuvres d'Architecture* (Paris: Dumont, Huquier, Joullain).

Contet, Frédéric (1914–34), *Les vieux hôtels de Paris* (Paris: Contet).

Cook, Clarence C. (1972), *A Description of the New York Central Park* (New York: Blom).

Cook, Jeffrey (1978), *The Architecture of Bruce Goff* (New York: Harper & Row).

Cook, Peter (1970), *Experimental Architecture* (London: Studio Vista).

—(ed.) (1991), *Archigram* (Basle: Birkhäuser, 1991).

Coop Himmelblau (1983), *Architecture is Now: Projects, (Un)buildings, Actions, Statements*, etc. *1968–1993* (New York: Rizzoli).

Coope, Rosalys (1972), *Salomon de Brosse and the Development of the Classical Style in French Architecture 1565–1630* (University Park, Pa.: Pennsylvania State University).

Cooper, Jackie (ed.) (1984), *Mackintosh Architecture: The Complete Buildings and Selected Projects* (London: Academy Editions).

Corbusier, Le: *see* Jeanneret-Gris.

Cordemoy, J.-L. de (1714), *Nouveau Traité de Toute L'Architecture, ou L'Art de bastir; utile aux entrepreneurs et aux ouvriers . . . Avec un Dictionnaire des Termes d'Architecture* (Paris: J.-B. Coignard).

Cornell, Elias (1965), *Ragnar Östberg Svensk arkitekt* (Stockholm: Byggmästerens forlag).

Correa, Charles (1996), *Charles Correa* (with an essay by Kenneth Frampton) (London: Thames & Hudson).

Costa, Lúcio (1962), *Sôbre Arquitetura* (Pôrto Alegre: Centro dos Estudantes Universitarios de Arquitetura).

Cotton, Vere Egerton (1964), *The Book of Liverpool Cathedral* (Liverpool: Liverpool UP).

Coudenhove-Erthal, Eduard (1930), *Carlo Fontana und die Architektur des römischen Spätbarocks* (Vienna: Schroll).

Coulton, J. J. (1976), *The Architectural Development of the Greek Stoa* (Oxford: Clarendon Press).

—(1977), *Ancient Greek Architects at Work* (Ithaca, NY: Cornell UP).

Council of Europe (1995), *Art and Power: Europe*

under the Dictators 1930–45 (London: Hayward Gallery).
—(1972), *The Age of Neo-Classicism* (London: Arts Council of Great Britain).
Courtonne, Jean (1725), *Traité de la perspective pratique, avec les remarques sur l'architecture* (Paris: Jombert).
Craig, James (1786), *Plan for Improving the City of Edinburgh* (Edinburgh: The Author).
Craig, Lois A. (1978), *The Federal Presence: Architecture, Politics, and Symbols in United States Government Building* (Cambridge, Mass.: MIT Press).
Craig, Maurice (1969), *Dublin 1660–1960: A Social and Architectural History* (Dublin: Figgis).
—(1982), *The Architecture of Ireland from the Earliest Times to 1880* (London: Batsford).
Cram, Ralph Adams (1924), *Church Building* (Boston: Marshall Jones).
—(1925), *The Substance of Gothic* (Boston: Marshall Jones).
—(1930), *The Catholic Church and Art* (New York: Macmillan).
—(1966), *Impressions of Japanese Architecture and the Allied Arts* (New York: Dover; reprint of 1905 original).
—(1967), *Ministry of Art* (Freeport, NY: Books for Libraries Press; reprint of 1914 edition).
—(1969), *My Life in Architecture* (Boston: Little, Brown; reprint of 1936 edn.).
Cramail, Alfred (1888), *Le Château de Rueil et ses Jardins* (Fontainebleau: Bourges).
Cramer, Max, Grieken, Hans von, and Pronk, Heleen (1981), *W. M. Dudok 1884–1974* (Amsterdam: van Gennep: Stichting Architectuur Museum).
Crawford, Alan (1985), *C. R. Ashbee, Architect, Designer, and Romantic Socialist* (New Haven and London: Yale UP).
Creese, Walter L. (ed.) (1967), *The Legacy of Raymond Unwin: A Human Pattern for Planning* (Cambridge, Mass.: MIT Press).
—(1992), *The Search for Environment: The Garden City, Before and After* (Baltimore: Johns Hopkins UP).
Creswell, Harry Bulkeley (1929), *The Honeywood File: An Adventure in Building* (London: Architectural Press).
—(1930), *The Honeywood Settlement: A Continuation of the 'Honeywood File'* (London: Architectural Press).
—(1931), *Jago v. Swillerton & Toomer* (London: Architectural Press).
—(1935), *Diary from a Dustbin* (London: Faber).
—(1942), *Grig* (London: Faber).
—(1943), *Grig in Retirement* (London: Faber).
Crippa, Maria Antonietta (1986), *Carlo Scarpa: Theory, Design, Projects* (Cambridge, Mass.: MIT Press).
Cristinelli, Giuseppe (1978), *Baldassare Longhena* (Padua: Marsilio).
Croft-Murray, Edward, and Hulton, Paul (1960), *Catalogue of British Drawings in the British Museum* (London: British Museum).
Croix, Horst de la (1972), *Military Considerations in City Planning* (New York: Braziller).
Crook, Joseph Mordaunt (1964), 'Haileybury and the Greek Revival: The Architecture of William Wilkins', in *The Haileybury and I.S.C. Chronicle* (Hoddesdon: Haileybury).
—(1972), *The British Museum* (London: Allen Lane).
—(1972a), *The Greek Revival: Neo-Classical Attitudes in British Architecture 1760–1870* (London: John Murray).
—(1981), *William Burges and the High Victorian Dream* (London: John Murray).
—(1987), *The Dilemma of Style* (London: John Murray).
—(1995), *John Carter and the Mind of the Gothic Revival* (London: Society of Antiquaries of London).
—and Port, Michael H. (1973), *History of the King's Works* (London: HMSO).
Crosby, Sumner McKnight (1987), *The Royal Abbey of Saint-Denis* (New Haven: Yale UP).
Cross, N. (ed.) (1972), *Design Participation* (London: Academy Editions).
Crossley, Fred H. (1921), *English Church Monuments AD 1150–1550* (London: Batsford).
Cruickshank, Dan (1985), *A Guide to the Georgian Buildings of Britain and Ireland* (London: Weidenfeld & Nicolson).
—(ed.) (1996), *Sir Banister Fletcher's A History of Architecture* (Oxford: Architectural Press).
Crunden, John (1767), *Convenient and Ornamental Architecture* (London: The Author).
Cullen, Gordon (1973), *The Concise Townscape* (London: Architectural Press).
Culot, Maurice, and Meade, Martin (eds.) (1996), *Dom Bellot: Moine-Architecte 1876–1944* (Paris: Institut Français d'Architecture/Éditions Norma).
Curjel, Hans (ed.) (1955), *Henry van de Velde* (Munich: Piper).
Curl, James Stevens (1983), *The Life and Work of Henry Roberts (1803–76), Architect* (Chichester: Phillimore).
—(1986), *The Londonderry Plantation, 1609–1914* (Chichester: Phillimore).
—(1990), *Victorian Architecture* (Newton Abbot: David & Charles).
—(1991), *The Art and Architecture of Freemasonry: An Introductory Study* (London: Batsford).
—(1992), *Classical Architecture: An Introduction to its Vocabulary and Essentials* (London: Batsford).
—(1993), *A Celebration of Death: An Introduction to some of the Buildings, Monuments, and Settings of*

Funerary Architecture in the Western European Tradition (London: Batsford).
Curl, James Stevens (1993*a*), *Encyclopædia of Architectural Terms* (London: Donhead).
—(1993*b*), *Georgian Architecture* (Newton Abbot: David & Charles).
—(1994), *Egyptomania: The Egyptian Revival as a Recurring Theme in the History of Taste* (Manchester: Manchester UP).
—(1995), *Victorian Churches* (London: Batsford & English Heritage).
Current, William (1974), *Greene and Greene: Architects in the Residential Style* (Dobbs Ferry, NY: Morgan).
Curry, David Park, and Pierce, Patricia Dawes (eds.) (1979), *Monument: The Connecticut State Capitol* (Harford, Conn.: Old State House Association).
Curtis, William (1995), *Denys Lasdun: Architecture, City, Landscape* (London: Phaidon).
—(1995*a*), *Le Corbusier: Ideas and Forms* (London: Phaidon).
—(1996), *Modern Architecture since 1900* (London: Phaidon).
Cuypers, P. J. H. (1917), *Het Werk van Dr P. J. H. Cuypers: 1827–1917* (Amsterdam: van Holkema & Warendorf).
Dacos, Nicole (1969), *La découverte de la Domus Aurea et la Formation des Grotesques à la Renaissance* (London: Warburg Institute).
Dahinden, Justus (1972), *Urban Structures for the Future* (New York: Praeger).
Dal Co, Francesco (ed.) (1985), *Kevin Roche* (New York: Rizzoli).
—(1987), *Mario Botta: Architecture 1960–1985* (Milan: Electa).
—(1996), *Tadao Ando: Complete Works* (London: Phaidon).
—and Forster, Kurt W. (1998), *Frank O. Gehry: The Complete Works* (New York: Monacelli).
—and Mazzariol, Giuseppe (eds.) (1985), *Carlo Scarpa: The Complete Works* (New York: Electa/Rizzoli).
Dale, Anthony (1947), *Fashionable Brighton: 1820–1860* (London: Country Life).
—(1956), *James Wyatt* (Oxford: Blackwell).
Daly, Denis-César (1840–90), *Revue générale de l'architecture et des travaux publics* (Paris, n.p.).
—(1848), *Profession de foi du citoyen Daly* (Paris: Martinet).
—(1864), *L'Architecture privée au XIXme siècle sous Napoléon III, Nouvelles Maisons de Paris et des environs* (Paris: Morel).
—(1869), *Motifs historiques d'architecture et de sculpture d'ornement I* (Paris: Morel).
—(1871), *L'architecture funéraire contemporaine* (Paris: Ducher).
—(1871*a*), *L'Architecture privée au XIXme siècle: Deuxième série* (Paris: Ducher).
—(1877), *L'Architecture privée au XIXme siècle: Troisième série* (Paris: Ducher).
—(1880), *Motifs historiques d'architecture et de sculpture d'ornement II* (Paris: Librairie Générale de l'architecture et des travaux publics).
—(n.d.), *Motifs divers de Serrurerie I* (Paris: André, Daly).
—(n.d.) *Motifs divers de Serrurerie II* (Paris: Ducher).
—and Davioud, Gabriel (1874), *L'architecture contemporaine: Les théatres de la place du Châtelet* (Paris: Ducher).
Danesi, Silvia, and Patetta, Luciano (eds.) (1976), *Il Razionalismo e l'architettura in Italia durante il fascismo* (Venice: Biennale).
Daniel, Ann Miner (1980), *The Early Architecture of Ralph Adams Cram: 1889–1902* (Ann Arbor: University Microfilms).
Daniel, Glyn Edmund (1972), *Megaliths in History* (London: Thames & Hudson).
Danz, Ernst (1962), *Architecture of Skidmore, Owings, & Merrill* (New York: Praeger).
Darby, Michael (1983), *John Pollard Seddon* (London: Victoria & Albert Museum).
—and Physick, John (1973): *see* Physick.
Darley, Gillian (1975), *Villages of Vision* (London: Architectural Press).
Davey, Norman (1961), *A History of Building Materials* (London: Phoenix House).
Davey, Peter (1980), *Architecture of the Arts and Crafts Movement: The Search for an Earthly Paradise* (New York: Rizzoli).
—(1995), *Arts and Crafts Architecture* (London: Phaidon).
Davidoff, Paul (1965), 'Advocacy and Pluralism in Planning', *Journal of the American Institute in Planning*, 31/4 (Nov.), 331–8.
Davies, Colin (1988), *High Tech Architecture* (London: Thames & Hudson).
—(1995), *Hopkins: The Work of Michael Hopkins & Partners* (London: Phaidon).
Davis, Alexander J. (1980), *Rural Residences* (New York: Da Capo; repr. of 1838 edn.).
Davis, Terence (1973), *John Nash: the Prince Regent's Architect* (Newton Abbot: David & Charles).
—(1974), *The Gothick Taste* (Newton Abbot: David & Charles).
Davison, T. Raffles (1916), *Port Sunlight* (London: Batsford).
Deane, Philip (1965), *Constantinos Doxiadis: Master Builder for Free Men* (Dobbs Ferry, NY: Oceana).
Debenedetti, Elisa (1979), *Valadier* (Rome: Bulzoni).
—(1988), *Carlo Marchionni* (Rome: Multigrafica).
Decker, Paul (1711–16), *Fürstlicher Baumeister* (Augsburg: Wolff).
Deconchy, M.-F. (1875), *Victor Baltard, sa vie, ses œuvres* (Paris: Ducher).
Defilippis, Felice (1968), *Il palazzo reale di Caserta e i Borboni di Napoli* (Naples: Mauro).
Dehio, Ludwig (1961), *Friedrich Wilhelm IV von*

Preussen, ein Baukünstler der Romantik (Berlin: Deutscher Kunstverlag).

Delaborde, Henri (1879), *Institut de France: Notice sur la vie et les ouvrages de M. Duc* (Paris: Académie des Beaux-Arts).

—(1887), *Institut de France: Notice sur la vie et les ouvrages de M. Théodore Ballu* (Paris: Firmin-Didot).

—(1890), *Institut de France. Académie des Beaux-Arts. Notice sur la vie et les ouvrages de M. Questel* (Paris: Firmin-Didot).

Delaire, Edmond (1907), *Les architectes élèves de l'école des Beaux-Arts 1793–1907* (Paris: Librairie de la Construction Moderne).

Delevoy, Robert L. (1958), *Victor Horta* (Brussels: Elsevier).

—*et al.* (1963), *Henry van de Velde* (Brussels: PVS).

Delorme, Jean (1960), *Gymnasion: étude sur les monuments consacrés à l'éducation en Grèce* (Paris: Boccard).

Deming, Mark K. (1984), *La Halle au blé de Paris* (Brussels: Archives d'architecture moderne).

Dennis, Richard, and Jesse, John (1972), *Christopher Dresser: 1834–1904* (London: Fine Art Society).

Denon, Dominique Vivant (1802), *Voyage dans la Basse et la Haute Égypte* (Paris: Didot, and London: Crosby).

Dent, R. (1971), *Principles of Pneumatic Architecture* (London: Architectural Press).

Dernie, David, and Carew-Cox, Alastair (1995), *Victor Horta* (London: Academy Editions).

——(1996), *The Villa d'Este at Tivoli* (London: Academy Editions).

Descharnes, Robert (1982), *Gaudí the Visionary* (New York: Viking).

Desgodetz, Antoine (1771–95), *The Ancient Buildings of Rome* (London: George Marshall).

Deshairs, Léon (1914), *Dessins Originaux des Maîtres Décorateurs: Nicolas et Dominique Pineau* (Paris: Longuet).

Desideri, Paolo, *et al.* (eds.) (1979), *Pier Luigi Nervi* (Bologna: Zanichelli).

Design Council (1974), *Street Furniture* (London: Design Council).

Dethier, J. (1983), *Down to Earth: Mud Architecture* (London: Thames & Hudson).

Dezzi Bardeschi, Marco (1965), *La Cathédrale di Burgos* (Florence: Sadea Sansoni).

Dhuys, Jean François (1983), *L'architecture selon Émile Aillaud* (Paris: Dunod).

Diamonstein, Barbaralee (ed.) (1980, 1985), *American Architecture Now* (New York: Rizzoli).

Dickson, D. (1974), *Alternative Technology and the Politics of Technical Change* (London: Fontana Collins).

Dickson, E. (1989), *Colefax & Fowler: The Best in English Interior Decoration* (London: Barrie & Jenkins).

Dictionary of American Biography (DAB) (1929–) (New York: Scribner).

Dictionary of National Biography (DNB) (1917–) (London and Oxford: Oxford University Press).

Dietterlin, Wendel (1598), *Architectura von Ausztheilung. Symmetria und Proportion der Fünff Seulen, und aller darausz folgender Kunst Arbeit, von Fenstern, Caminen, Thürgerichten, Portalen, Bronnen und Ephitaphien.* (Nuremberg: B. Caymor). Another edition was published in Nuremberg by Pauluss Fürst (1655), and a French version was published in 1861–2.

Dilettanti, Society of (1814), *Report of the Committee of the Society of Dilettanti, appointed by the Society to superintend the expedition lately sent by them to Greece and Ionia* (London: Society of Dilettanti).

Dini, Massimo (1984), *Renzo Piano, Projects and Buildings, 1964–1983* (New York: Electa/Rizzoli).

Dinsmoor, William Bell (1950), *The Architecture of Ancient Greece* (London: Batsford).

Dirsztay, Patricia (1978), *Church Furnishings: A NADFAS Guide* (London: Routledge & Kegan Paul).

Dischinger, Gabriele (1977), *Johann und Joseph Schmuzer* (Sigmaringen: Thorbecke).

Dixon, Roger, and Muthesius, Stefan (1985), *Victorian Architecture* (London: Thames & Hudson).

Dober, Richard (1992), *Campus Design* (New York: J. Wiley).

Dobson, Margaret Jane (1885), *A Memoir of John Dobson* (London: Hamilton-Adams).

Doebber, Adolph (1911), *Das Schloss in Weimar* (Jena: Fischer).

—(ed.) (1916), *Heinrich Gentz ein Berliner Baumeister von 1800* (Berlin: Carl Heymanns Verlag).

Döhmer, Klaus (1976), *Im welchem Style sollen wir bauen? Architekturtheorie zwischen Klassizismus u. Jungendstil* (Munich: Prestel).

Dolgner, Dieter (1971), *Die Architektur des Klassizismus in Deutschland* (Dresden: Verlag der Kunst).

—(1993), *Historismus: Deutsche Baukunst 1815–1900* (Leipzig: Seemann).

Domenech Girbau, Luis (1968), *Arquitectura española contemporánea* (Barcelona: Blume).

Dorfles, G. (ed.) (1969), *Kitsch: An Anthology of Bad Taste* (London: Studio Vista).

Doumato, Lamia (1980), *Filippo Brunelleschi: 1377–1446* (Monticello, Ill.: Vance).

—(1980*a*), *Heikki and Kaija Sirén* (Monticello, Ill.: Vance).

—(1981), *Jules Hardouin-Mansart* (Monticello, Ill.: Vance).

—(1983), *Jørn Utzon* (Monticello, Ill.: Vance).

—(1987), *Hugh A. Stubbins* (Monticello, Ill.: Vance).

Dow, Alden Ball (1965), *Retrospective Exhibition of Architecture* (Flint, Mich.: The Institute of Arts).
—(1970), *Reflections* (Midland, Mich.: Northwood Institute).
—(*c*.1970), *A Way of Life* (Midland, Mich.: Centre for the Arts).
Dowling, Elizabeth Meredith (1989), *Philip Trammell Shutze* (New York: Rizzoli).
Downes, Kerry (1966), *English Baroque Architecture* (London: Zwemmer).
—(1977), *Vanbrugh* (London: Zwemmer).
—(1980), *Hawksmoor* (Cambridge, Mass.: MIT Press).
—(1982), *Sir Christopher Wren* (London: Whitechapel Art Gallery and Trefoil Books).
—(1987), *Sir John Vanbrugh* (New York: St Martin's Press).
—(1988), *The Architecture of Wren* (Reading: Redhedge).
—(1988*a*), *Sir Christopher Wren: The Design of St Paul's Cathedral* (London: Trefoil and Guildhall Library).
Downing, Andrew J. (1967), *Cottage Residences* (Watkins Glen, NY: Library of Victorian Culture; repr. of 1842 edn.).
—(1967*a*), *A Treatise on the Theory and Practice of Landscape Gardening* (New York: Funk; repr. of 1841 edn.).
—(1968), *The Architecture of Country Houses* (New York: Da Capo; repr. of 1850 edn.).
Downing, Antoinette F. (1937), *Early Homes of Rhode Island* (Richmond, Va.: Garrett).
—and Scully, Vincent J. (1967), *The Architectural Heritage of Newport, Rhode Island, 1640–1915* (New York: Bramhill).
Doxiadis, Constantinos A. (1963), *Architecture in Transition* (New York: Oxford UP).
—(1966), *Between Dystopia and Utopia* (Hartfield, Conn.: Trinity College Press).
Drachmann, Aage (1963), *The Mechanical Technology of Greek and Roman Antiquity* (Copenhagen: Munksgaard, London: Hafner, Madison, Wis.: University of Wisconsin Press).
Dresser, Christopher (1862), *The Art of Decorative Design* (London: Day).
—(1873), *Principles of Decorative Design* (London: Cassell).
—(1882), *Japan: Its Architecture, Art, and Art Manufactures* (London: Longman, Green).
Drew, Philip (1972), *Third Generation: The Changing Meaning of Architecture* (London: Pall Mall Press).
—(1976), *Frei Otto: Form and Structure* (London: Crosby Lockwood).
—(1982), *The Architecture of Arata Isozaki* (London: Granada).
Drexler, Arthur (1960), *Ludwig Mies van der Rohe* (New York: Braziller).
—(1973), *Charles Eames: Furniture from the Design Collection* (New York: Museum of Modern Art).
—(ed.) (1977), *The Architecture of the École des Beaux Arts* (New York: Museum of Modern Art).
—(1980), *Transformations in modern architecture* (London: Secker & Warburg).
—and Hines, Thomas S. (eds.) (1982), *The Architecture of Richard Neutra: From International Style to California Modern* (New York: Museum of Modern Art).
Duboy, Philippe (1987), *Lequeu: An Architectural Enigma* (Cambridge, Mass.: MIT Press).
Duffy, Eamon (1992), *The Stripping of the Altars: Traditional Religion in England c.1400–c.1580* (New Haven and London: Yale UP).
Duffy, F. (1969), *Office Landscaping* (London: Anbar).
Dufournet, Paul (1981), *Horeau précurseur, idées, techniques, architectures* (Paris: Académie d'Architecture).
Duiker, Johannes (1930), *Hoogbouw* (Rotterdam: Brusse).
Dülfer, Martin (1914), *Ausgefürte Bauwerke* (Berlin: Wasmuth).
Dunbar, John F. (1966, 1978), *The Historic Architecture of Scotland* (London: Batsford).
—(1970), *Sir William Bruce, 1630–1710* (Edinburgh: Scottish Arts Council).
Dunster, David (ed.) (1997), *Arups on Engineering* (Berlin: Ernst & Sohn).
Dupérac, Étienne (1973), *I vestigi dell' antichità di Roma* (London: Warren; repr. of 1575 edn.).
Duportal, Jeanne (1931), *Charles Percier* (Paris: Rousseau).
Durand, Jean-Nicolas-Louis (1802–9), *Précis des Leçons d'Architecture données à l'École Polytechnique . . .* (Paris: Durand).
—(1809), *Essai sur l'Histoire Générale de l'Architecture . . . pour servir de texte explicatif au receuil et parallèle des édifices de tout genre, anciens et modernes, remarquables par leur beauté, leur grandeur, ou leur singularité . . .* (Paris: L.-C. Soyer).
Duverger, Josef (1933), *De Brusselsche Steenbickeleren* (Ghent: Vyncke).
Dyssegaard, Soren (1971–2), *Arne Jacobsen: A Danish Architect* (Copenhagen: Ministry of Foreign Affairs).
Eastlake, Charles Locke (1970), *A History of the Gothic Revival*, with an Introduction by J. Mordaunt Crook (Leicester: Leicester UP).
Eaton, Leonard K. (1972), *American Architecture comes of Age: European Reactions to H. H. Richardson and Louis Sullivan* (Cambridge, Mass.: MIT Press).
Ebhardt, Manfred (1975), *Die Salzburger Barockkirchen* (Baden-Baden: Körner).
Eckardt, Wolf von (1960), *Eric Mendelsohn* (New York: Braziller).

Edestrand, Hans, and Lundberg, Erik (1968), *Isak Gustaf Clason* (Stockholm: Norstedt).
Edis, Robert William (1973), *Decoration and Furniture of Town Houses* (New York: British Book Centre; repr. of 1881 edn.).
Edwards, Brian (1995), *Basil Spence 1907–1986* (Rutland: Rutland Press).
Edwards, Iowerth Eiddon Stephen (1985), *The Pyramids of Egypt* (Harmondsworth: Penguin).
Edwards, William Churchill (1954), *Historic Quincy, Massachusetts* (Quincy, Mass.: Franklin).
Egbert, Donald Drew (1980), *The Beaux Arts Tradition in French Architecture* (Princeton: Princeton UP).
Egelius, Mats (1988), *Ralph Erskine, Arkitekt* (Stockholm: Byggförlaget).
Eggert, Klaus (1963), 'Friedrich von Gärtner, der Baumeister König Ludwigs I', *Neue Schriftenreihe des Stadtarchivs München*, 15: 1–208.
—(1976), *Der Wohnbau der Wiener Ringstrasse im Historismus: 1855–1896* (Wiesbaden: Steiner).
Egli, Ernst (1976), *Sinan: der Baumeister osmanischer Glanzzeit* (Erlenbach-Zurich and Stuttgart: Rentsch).
Egli, Hans G. (1997), *Sinan: An Interpretation* (Philadelphia and Istanbul: EGE Yayinlarii).
Egorov, I. A. (1969), *The Architectural Planning of Saint Petersburg* (Athens, Ohio: Ohio UP).
Ehrenkrantz, E. (1989), *Architectural Systems* (New York: McGraw Hill).
Ehrensvaerd, Carl August (1786), *De fria konster philosophi* (Stockholm: Tryckt I Kongl Tryckeriet).
—(1922–5), *Skrifter* (Stockholm: Bonniers).
—(1948), *Resa til Italien, 1780, 1781, 1782* (Stockholm: Sällskapet Bokvännerna; repr. of 1786 edn.).
Ehrle, Francesco (1908), *Roma prima di Sisto V: La pianta di Roma Du Pérac-Lafréry del 1577* (Rome: Danesi).
—(ed.) (1932), *Roma al tempo di Benedetto XIV: La pianta di Roma di Giambattista Nolli del 1748* (Vatican City: Vatican Press).
Ehrmann, J. (ed.) (1970), *Structuralism* (New York: Doubleday).
Eidlitz, Leopold (1977), *The Nature and Function of Art, more especially of Architecture* (New York: Da Capo; repr. of 1881 edn.).
Eimer, Gerhard (1970–1), *La fabbrica di Sant'Agnese in Navona* (Stockholm: Almqvist & Wiksell).
Eitel, H. (1952), *Friedrich von Thiersch* (Munich: Baumeister).
Eitelberger, Rudolf von, and Ferstel, Heinrich (1860), *Das bürgerliche Wohnhaus und das Wiener Zinshaus* (Vienna: Gerold).
Elbert, Claudia (1988), *Die Theater Friedrich Weinbrenner: Bauten und Entwürfe* (Karlsruhe: C. F. Müller).
Elia, Mario Manierir (1996), *Louis Henry Sullivan* (New York: Princeton Architectural Press).
Ellenius, Allan (1971), *Den offentliga konsten och ideologierna* (Stockholm: Almqvist & Wiksell).
Ellis, Malcolm Henry (1966), *Francis Greenway: His Life and Times* (San Francisco: Tri-Ocean).
Emanuel, Muriel (ed.) (1980), *Contemporary Architects* (London: Macmillan).
—(1994), *Contemporary Architects* (Detroit: St James Press).
Embury, Aymar (ed.) (1917), *Asher Benjamin* (New York: Architectural Book Publishing).
Emery, Marc (1971), *Un Siècle d'Architecture Moderne en France* (Paris: Horizons).
Ende, Horst (1971), *Schloss Schwerin* (Leipzig: VEB Seemann).
Endell, August (1896), *Um die Schönheit: Eine Paraphrase über die Münchener Kunstausstellung in 1896* (Munich: Franke).
Engel, Carl Ludvig (1990), *Carl Ludvig Engel 1778–1840* (Helsinki: Exhibition (7 Aug. 1990–14 Sept. 1990) Catalogue, Näyttely Helsingin Tuomiokirkon Kryptassa).
Ennis, Robert B. (1982), *Thomas U. Walter, Architect, 1804–1887* (Philadelphia: The Athenaeum).
Éri, Gyöngyi, and Jobbágyi, Zsuzsa (1990), *A Golden Age: Art and Society in Hungary 1896–1914* (London: Barbican Art Gallery, and Miami: Center for the fine Arts).
Erickson, Arthur (1988), *The Architecture of Arthur Erickson* (New York: Harper & Row).
Eriksen, Svend (1974), *Early Neo-Classicism in France* (London: Faber).
Eschapasse, Maurice (1963), *L'architecture bénédictine en Europe* (Paris: Éditions des Deux-Mondes).
Escher, Frank (1994), *John Lautner, Architect* (Zurich: Artemis).
Escritt, Stephen (1997), *Art Déco Style* (London: Phaidon).
'Espinasse, Margaret (1962), *Robert Hooke* (London: Heinemann).
Estape, Fabian (1971), *Vida y obra de Ildefonso Cerdá* (Madrid: Instituto de Estudios Fiscales).
Etchells, Frederick (1947), *The City of Tomorrow and Its Planning*, translation of Le Corbusier's *Urbanisme* with a new preface by Etchells (London: Architectural Press; facsimile of 1929 edn.).
—(1989), *Towards a New Architecture*, translation of Le Corbusier's *Vers une architecture* with an introduction by Etchells (London: Butterworth Architecture; new edn. of 1927 edn. with new introduction).
—and Addleshaw, G. W. O. (1948), *The Architectural Setting of Anglican Worship: An Inquiry into the Arrangements for Public Worship in*

the Church of England from the Reformation to the Present Day (London: Faber).

Etlin, Richard (1984), *The Architecture of Death: The Transformation of the Cemetery in Eighteenth-Century Paris* (Cambridge, Mass., and London: MIT Press).

—(1991), *Modernism in Italian Architecture, 1890–1940* (Cambridge, Mass.: MIT Press).

—(1994), *Frank Lloyd Wright and Le Corbusier: The Romantic Legacy* (Manchester: Manchester UP).

Ettinghausen, Richard, and Grabar, Oleg (1988), *The Art and Architecture of Islam 650–1250* (Harmondsworth: Penguin).

Ettlinger, Leopold D. (1937), *Gottfried Semper und die Antike* (Bleicherode: Nieft).

Evans, Joan (1972), *The Romanesque Architecture of the Order of Cluny* (Farnborough: Gregg).

Faber, Colin (1963), *Candela The Shell Builder* (London: Architectural Press).

Faber, John, and Alsop, David (1976), *Reinforced Concrete Simply Explained* (London: Oxford UP).

Faber, Tobias (1963), *A History of Danish Architecture* (Copenhagen: Dansk Selskab).

—(1964), *Arne Jacobsen* (London: Tiranti).

—(1966), *Arkitekten Kay Fisker 1893–1965* (Copenhagen: Arkitektens Forlag).

Fagiolo dell' Arco, Marcello (1863), *Funzioni simboli valori della regia di Caserta* (Rome: dell' Arco).

Fagiolo dell' Arco, Maurizio, and Carandini, Silvia (1977–8), *L'Effimero barocco* (Rome: Bulzoni).

Fairbairn, William (1849), *An Account of the Construction of the Britannia and Conway Tubular Bridges* (London: Weale).

—(1869), *Iron—Its History, Properties, and Processes of Manufacture* (Edinburgh: Black).

—(1870), *On the Application of Cast and Wrought Iron to Building Purposes* (London: Longmans).

—and Pole, William (1970), *The Life of Sir William Fairbairn* (Newton Abbot: David & Charles; repr. of 1877 edn.).

Fanelli, Giovani (1968), *Architettura moderna in Olanda 1900–1940* (Florence: Marchi & Bertolli).

Fant, Åke, Klingborn, Arne, and Wilkes, A. John (1969), *Die Holzplastik Rudolf Steiners in Dornach* (Dornach: Philosophisch-Anthroposophischer Verlag am Goetheanum).

Fara, Amelio (1979), *Buontalenti: architettura e teatro* (Florence: La Nuova Italia).

—(1988), *Bernardo Buontalenti: l'architettura, la guerra, e l'elemento geometrico* (Genoa: Sagep).

Fasolo, Furio (1949), *Le chiese di Roma nel '700* (Rome: Danesi).

—(1961), *L'opera di Hieronimo e Carlo Rainaldi* (Rome: Ricerche).

Faulkner, T. and Greg, A. (1987), *John Dobson: Newcastle Architect* (Newcastle: Tyne & Wear Museum Service).

Fawcett, Jane (ed.) (1976), *Seven Victorian Architects* (London: Thames & Hudson).

Fehr, Götz (1961), *Benedikt Ried: ein deutscher Baumeister zwischen Gotik und Renaissance in Böhmen* (Munich: Callwey).

Félibien des Avaux, André (1687), *Recueil historique de la vie et des ouvrages des plus célèbres architectes* (Paris: Mabre-Cramoisy).

—(1699), *Des Principes de L'architecture* . . . etc.; 3rd edn. of the book originally published in 1676 (Paris: Coignard).

Fellows, Richard A. (1985), *Sir Reginald Blomfield* (London: Zwemmer).

Felstead, Alison, Franklin, Jonathan, and Pinfield, Leslie (1993), *Directory of British Architects 1834–1900* (London: Mansell).

Fenwick, Hubert (1970), *Architect Royal: The Life and Works of Sir William Bruce, 1630–1710* (Kineton: Roundwood).

Feo, Vittorio de (1988), *Andrea Pozzo: architettura e illusione* (Rome: Officina).

Ferguson, George (1961), *Signs and Symbols in Christian Art* (New York: Oxford UP).

Ferguson, Hugh (1995), *Glasgow School of Art: The History* (Glasgow: Foulis Press).

Fergusson, James (1847), *An Essay on the Ancient Topography of Jerusalem* (London: Weale).

—(1847*a*), *Picturesque Illustrations of Ancient Architecture in Hindustan* (London: Hogarth).

—(1849), *An Historical Inquiry into the True Principles of Beauty in Art More Especially with Reference to Architecture* (London: Longman).

—(1851), *The Palaces of Nineveh and Persepolis Restored* (London: Murray).

—(1855), *Illustrated Handbook of Architecture: Being a Concise and Popular Account of the Different Styles of Architecture Prevailing in All Ages and Countries* (London: Murray).

—(1862), *A History of the Modern Styles of Architecture* (London: Murray).

—(1862–7), *A History of Architecture in All Countries, from the Earliest Times to the Present Day* (London: Murray).

—(1874), *A History of Ancient and Mediaeval Architecture* (London: Murray).

—(1876), *A History of Indian and Eastern Architecture* (London: Murray).

—(1878), *The Temples of the Jews and the Other Buildings in the Haram Area of Jerusalem* (London: Murray).

—(1883), *The Parthenon: An Essay on the Mode by which White Light was Introduced into Greek and Roman Temples* (London: Murray).

Fergusson, Peter (1984), *Architecture of Solitude: Cistercian Abbeys in Twelfth-Century England* (Princeton: Princeton UP).

Ferlenga, Alberto (ed.) (1987), *Aldo Rossi: architettura 1959–1987* (Milan: Electa).
—— (1992), *Aldo Rossi: architettura 1988–1992* (Milan: Electa).
Fernández Arenas, José (1972), *Mozarabic Architecture* (Greenwich, Conn.: New York Graphic Society).
Fernández Ordóñez, José A. (1978), *Eugène Freyssinet* (Barcelona: Zc. Ediciones).
Ferrara, Miranda, and Quinterio, Francesco (1984), *Michelozzo di Bartolomeo* (Florence: Salimbeni).
Ferraz, Gilberto (1965), *Warchavchik e la introdução da nova arquitectura no Brasil 1925 a 1940* (São Paulo: Museu de Arte).
Ferrero, Mercedes Viale (1970), *Filippo Juvarra scenografo e architetto teatrale* (Turin: Pozzo).
Ferrey, Benjamin (1861), *Recollections of A. N. Welby Pugin, and his Father, Augustus Pugin* (London: E. Stanford).
Ferriday, Peter (ed.) (1963), *Victorian Architecture* (London: Cape).
Ferriss, Hugh (1929), *The Metropolis of Tomorrow* (New York: Ives Washington).
—— (1953), *Power in Buildings: An Artist's View of Contemporary Architecture* (New York: Columbia UP).
Ferry, W. Hawkes (ed.) (1987), *The Legacy of Albert Kahn* (Detroit: Wayne State UP).
Feuchtmüller, Rupert (1951), *Die Spätgotische Architektur und Anton Pilgram* (Vienna: Österreichische Staatsdruckerei).
—— (1960), essay in *Jakob Prandtauer und sein Kunstkreis*, exhibition catalogue for the Prandtauer exhibition, Stift Melk, 1960 (Vienna: Österreichische Staatsdruckerei).
—— (1978), *Der Wiener Stephansdom* (Vienna: Wiener Dom-Verlag).
Feuerstein, G. (1988), *Visionäre Architektur, Wien, 1958–88* (Berlin: Ernst & Sohn).
Fichera, Francesco (1934), *G. B. Vaccarino e l'architettura del Settecento in Sicilia* (Rome: Reale Accademia d'Italia).
Fichet, Françoise (ed.) (1979), *La théorie architecturale à l'âge classique* (Brussels: Mardaga).
Fiddes, Valerie, and Rowan, Alistair (eds.) (1976), *David Bryce 1803–1876* (Edinburgh: Talbot Rice Arts Centre, University of Edinburgh).
Filarete, Antonio Averlino (1965), *Treatise on Architecture* (New Haven: Yale UP).
Fils, Alexander (1988), *Brasilia: Moderne Architektur in Brasilien* (Düsseldorf: Beton-Verlag).
Fink, August, and Appuhn, Horst (1965), *Die Marienkirche ... in Wolfenbüttel* (Wolfenbüttel: Landeskirchenamt).
Finnimore, B. (1989), *Houses from the Factory: System Building and the Welfare State* (London: Rivers Oram Press).
Fiocco, Giuseppe (1931), *Giuseppe Jappelli: Architetto* (Padua: Stedir).
Fiore, Gaspare de (1963), *Baccio Pontelli architetto fiorentino* (Rome: Edizione dell' Ateneo).
Firpo, L. (ed.) (1963), *Leonardo: Architetto e Urbanista* (Turin: Unione Tipografico Editrice Torinese).
Fischer, Manfred (1977), *Fritz Schumacher* (Hamburg: Christians).
Fischer, Theodor (1903), *Stadterweiterungsfragen mit besonderer Rücksicht auf Stuttgart* (Stuttgart: Deutsche Verlags-Anstalt).
—— (1917), *Für die deutsche Baukunst* (Munich: Müller).
Fischer von Erlach, Johann Bernhard (1964), *Entwurff eines historischen Architektur* (1725) (Ridgewood, NJ: Gregg).
Fisher, Geoffrey, *et al.* (eds.) (1981), *The Scott Family*. Catalogue of the RIBA Drawings Collection (London: Gregg).
Fishman, Robert (1977), *Urban Utopias in the Twentieth Century: Ebenezer Howard, Frank Lloyd Wright, and Le Corbusier* (New York: Basic Books).
—— (1987), *Bourgeois Utopias: The Rise and Fall of Suburbia* (New York: Basic Books).
Fisker, Kay, and Yerbury, F. R. (1927), *Modern Danish Architecture* (New York: Scribner).
Fitch, James Marston (1960), *Walter Gropius* (New York: Braziller).
—— (1961), *Architecture and the Esthetics of Plenty* (New York: Columbia UP).
—— (1973), *American Building* (New York: Schocken).
—— and Waite, Diana S. (1974), *Grand Central Terminal and Rockefeller Center: A Historic-Critical Estimate of Their Significance* (Albany, NY: New York State Parks and Recreation).
Fitzgerald, Desmond, *et al.* (1963), *Juste-Aurèle Meissonnier* (New York: Seiferheld).
Fleig, Karl (ed.) (1963–78), *Alvar Aalto 1922–1978* (New York: Praeger).
Fleming, John (1962), *Robert Adam and His Circle* (London: Murray).
Fletcher, Sir Banister, see Cruickshank, Dan (ed.).
Flores Lopez, Carlos (1961), *Arquitectura española contemporánea* (Madrid: Aguilar).
Flouquet, Pierre-Louis (1952), *Victor Bourgeois: Architecture 1922–1952* (Brussels: Éditions Art et Technique).
Focillon, Henri (1967), *Giovanni Battista Piranesi* (Bologna: Alfa).
Fogaccia, Piero (1945), *Cosimo Fanzago* (Bergamo: Istituto italiano d'arti grafiche).
Fogelmarck, Stig (1957), *Carl Fredrik Adelcrantz, arkitekt* (Stockholm: Almqvist & Wiksell).
Fontana, Domenico (1604), *Della Trasportatione dell'Obelisco Vaticano* (Naples: The Author).

Fontana, Vincenzo (1988), *Fra Giovanni Giocondo, architetto, 1435–c.1515* (Vicenza: Neri Pozza).
Förderer, Walter Maria (1964), *Kirchenbauten von Heute für Morgen* (Zurich: NZN).
—(1975), *Walter Maria Förderer, Architektur und Skulptur* (Neuchâtel: Éditions du Griffon).
Forester, T. (1987), *High-Tech Society* (Oxford: Blackwell).
Forsmann, Erik (1981), *Karl Friedrich Schinkel: Bauwerke und Baugedanken* (Munich: Schnell & Steiner).
Forster, Kurt Walter (1961), *Benedetto Antelami: der grosse romanische Bildhauer Italiens* (Munich: Hirmer).
Fossi, Mazzino (1967), *Bartolomeo Ammannati, Architetto* (Naples: Morano).
Foster, H. (ed.) (1983), *The Anti-Aesthetic* (Port Townsend, Wash.: Bay Press).
Foucart, Bruno (ed.) (1980), *Viollet-le-Duc* (Paris: Réunion des Musées Nationaux).
Fox, Helen Morgenthau (1962), *André Le Nôtre, Garden Architect to Kings* (New York: Crown).
Frampton, Kenneth (1980), *Modern Architecture: A Critical History* (New York: Oxford UP).
—(1991), *Tadao Ando* (New York: Museum of Modern Art).
—*et al.* (1975), *Five Architects* (New York: Oxford UP).
—and Drew, Philip (1992), *Harry Seidler: Four Decades of Architecture* (London and New York: Thames & Hudson).
Franca, Jose-Augusto (1965), *Une ville des lumières: La Lisbonne de Pombal* (Paris: SEVPEN).
Francastel, Pierre (ed.) (1959), *Les Architectes célèbres* (Paris: Mazenod).
France-Lanord, Albert (1984), *Emmanuel Héré, architecte du Roi Stanislas* (Nancy: Presses Universitaires).
Francis, Dennis Steadman (1980), *Architects in Practice, New York City, 1840–1900* (New York: Committee for the Preservation of Architectural Records).
Franciscono, Marcel (1971), *Walter Gropius and the Creation of the Bauhaus in Weimar* (Urbana, Ill.: University of Illinois Press).
Franck, Klaus (1960), *The Works of Affonso Eduardo Reidy* (New York: Praeger).
Franclieu, Françoise de (ed.) (1981–2), *Le Corbusier Sketchbooks* (New York: Architectural History Foundation).
Franco, Barbara (ed.) (1976), *Masonic Symbols in American Decorative Arts* (Lexington, Mass.: Museum of Our National Heritage).
Frank, Dietrich von (1985), *Joseph Effners Pagodenburg: Studien zu einer Maison de Plaisance* (Munich: Tuduv).
Frank, Suzanne Shulof (1984), *Michael de Klerk, 1884–1923: An Architect of the Amsterdam School* (Ann Arbor: UMI Research Press).
Franke, H. (1985), *Computer Graphics—Computer Art* (Berlin: Springer).
Frankl, Paul (1960), *The Gothic: Literary Sources and Interpretations through Eight Centuries* (Princeton: Princeton UP).
—(1962), *Gothic Architecture* (Harmondsworth: Penguin).
Fransen, Hans, and Cook, Mary Alexander (1978), *The Old Houses of the Cape* (Cape Town: Balkema).
Franz, Erich (1985), *Pierre-Michel d'Ixnard 1723–1795: Leben und Werk* (Weissenhorn: Konrad).
Franz, Heinrich Gerhard (1942), *Die Kirchenbauten des Christoph Dientzenhofer* (Brno, Munich, and Vienna: Rohrer).
—(1943), *Die Deutsche Barockbaukunst Mährens* (Munich: Bruckmann).
—(1943*a*), *Studien zur Barockarchitektur in Böhmen und Mähren* (Brno, Munich, and Vienna: Rohrer).
—(1953), *Zacharias Longuelune und die Baukunst des 18. Jahrhunderts in Dresden* (Berlin: Deutscher Verein für Kunstwissenschaft).
—(1962), *Bauten und Baumeister der Barockzeit in Böhmen* (Leipzig: Seemann).
Fraser, Douglas, Hibbard, Howard, and Lewine, Milton J. (eds.) (1967), *Essays in the History of Architecture Presented to Rudolf Wittkower* (London: Phaidon).
Fraser Reekie, R. (1946), *Draughtsmanship* (London: Arnold).
Fréart de Chambray, Roland (1650), *Parallèle de l'Architecture Antique et de la Moderne, avec un recueil des dix principaux autheurs qui ont écrit des cinq ordres: sçavoir Palladio et Scamozzi, Serlio et Vignola, D. Barbaro et Cataneo, L. B. Alberti et Viola Bullant et De Lorme*, . . . etc. (Paris: Martin). This appeared in a translation by John Evelyn as *A Parallel of the Ancient Architecture with the Modern* (London: Roycroft & Place, 1664).
Freeden, Max Herman von (1952), *Residenz Würzburg* (Munich: Deutsche Kunstverlag).
—(1963), *Balthasar Neumann als Stadtbaumeister* (Würzburg: Freunde Mainfränkischer Kunst und Geschichte).
—(1981), *Balthasar Neumann: Leben und Werk* (Munich and Berlin: Deutscher Kunstverlag).
Freeland, John M. (1968), *Architecture in Australia: A History* (Melbourne: Cheshire).
Freeman, Jennifer Margaret (1990), *W. D. Caröe: His Architectural Achievement* (Manchester: Manchester UP).
Freixa, Jaume (ed.) (1979), *Josep Ll. Sert* (Barcelona: Gili).
Freixa, Mireia (1991), *El Modernisme a Catalunya* (Barcelona: Barcanova).
Fremantle, Katharine (1959), *The Baroque Town*

Hall of Amsterdam (Utrecht: Haentjens, Dekker & Gumbert).

Freyre, Gilberto (1940), *Vauthier: Engenheiro francês no Brasil*, Coleçao Documentos Brasileiros, 26 (Rio de Janeiro: Olympio).

Frézier, Amédée-François (1716), *Relation du voyage de la mer du sud, aux côtes du Chily et du Pérou fait pendant les années 1712, 1713, et 1714* (Paris: Nyon).

—(1737–9), *La théorie et la pratique de la coupe des pierres et des bois pour la construction des voûtes ..., ou, traité de stéréotomie, à l'usage de l'architecture* (Strasbourg: Doulsseker).

—(1738), *Dissertation sur les Ordres d'Architecture* (Strasbourg: Doulsseker).

—(1747), *Traité des feux d'artifice pour le spectacle* (Paris: Quai des Augustins; original publication 1706).

Friedman, Joseph (1993), *Spencer House: Chronicle of a Great London Mansion* (London: Zwemmer).

Friedman, Mildred (ed.) (1982), *De Stijl, 1917–1931—Visions of Utopia* (Minneapolis: Wallow Art Center).

Friedman, Terry (1984), *James Gibbs* (New Haven and London: Yale UP).

Friedman, Yona (1970), *L'Architecture Mobile* (Paris: Casterman).

—(1975), *Towards a Scientific Architecture* (Cambridge, Mass.: MIT Press).

Frodl-Kraft, Eva (1955), *Tiroler Barockkirchen* (Innsbruck: Inn-Verlag).

Fröhlich, Marie, and Sperlich, Hans-Günter (1959), *Georg Moller: Baumeister der Romantik* (Darmstadt: Roether).

Fröhlich, Martin (1974), *Gottfried Semper* (Basle: Birkhäuser).

Frommel, Christoph Luitpold (1973), *Der römischen Palastbau der Hochrenaissance* (Tübingen: E. Wasmuth).

—(ed.) (1994), *The Architectural Drawings of Antonio da Sangallo the Younger and his Circle* (New York: Architectural History Foundation, and Cambridge, Mass.: MIT Press).

—(ed.) (1995), *Michele Sanmichele Architettura* (Milan: Electa).

—*et al.* (1984), *Raffaello Architetto* (Milan: Electa).

—*et al.* (1989), *Giulio Romano* (Milan: Electa).

Fromonot, Françoise (1995), *Glenn Murcutt: Works and Projects* (London: Thames & Hudson).

Fry, Edwin Maxwell (1944), *Fine Building* (London: Faber).

—(1969), *Art in a Machine Age* (London: Methuen).

—(1975), *Autobiographical Sketches* (London: Elek).

—and Drew, Jane B. (1947), *Village Housing in the Tropics* (London: Lund Humphries).

——(1956), *Tropical Architecture in the Humid Zone* (London: Batsford).

——(1964), *Tropical Architecture in the Dry and Humid Zones* (London: Batsford).

——(1976), *Architecture and the Environment* (London: Allen & Unwin; originally published as *Architecture for Children* in 1944).

Frykenstedt, Holger (1965), *Carl August Ehrensvaerd (1745–1800): An Original Swedish Aesthetician and an Early Functionalist* (Uppsala: Almqvist & Wiksell).

Fuhrmann, Franz (1950), *Salzburg and its Churches* (Vienna: Kunstverlag Wolfrum).

Fuller, Richard Buckminster (1971), *Nine Chains to the Moon* (Garden City, NY: Doubleday; repr. of 1938 edn.).

—(1975), *Synergetics: Explorations on the Geometry of Thinking* (New York: Macmillan).

—(1979), *Synergetics 2* (New York: Macmillan).

—(1981), *Critical Path* (New York: St Martin's).

Funari, Lucia (1990), *Robert A. M. Stern: modernità e tradizione* (Rome: Kappa).

Fusco, Renato de (ed.) (1973), *Luigi Vanvitelli* (Naples: ESI).

Futagawa, Yukio (ed.) (1975), *Global Architecture 33: Bruce Goff–Bavinger House and Price House* (Tokyo: ADA Edita).

—(1975*a*), *Roche and Dinkeloo Associates* (Tokyo: ADA Edita).

—(1981), *Cesar Pelli/Gruen Associates* (Tokyo: ADA Edita).

Fyfe, Theodore (1936), *Hellenistic Architecture: An Introductory Study* (Cambridge: Cambridge UP).

Gaehtgens, Thomas W. (1974), *Napoleon's Arc de Triomphe* (Göttingen: van den Hoeck & Ruprecht).

—(1986), *Johann Joachim Winckelmann 1717–1768* (Hamburg: F. Meiner).

Gaidos, Elizabeth (ed.) (1972), *The Creative Spirit of Cranbrook* (Bloomfield Hills, Mich.: Cranbrook Academy).

Gaillard, Jeanne (1977), *Paris la Ville: L'Urbanisme parisien a l'heure d'Haussmann* (Paris: Champion).

Gallagher, Helen Mar Pierce (1935), *Robert Mills* (New York: Columbia UP).

Gallego y Burín, Antonio (1952), *La Capilla Real de Granada* (Madrid: Consejo Superior de Investigaciones Cientificas).

—(1956), *El Barroco Granadino* (Granada: University of Granada).

Gallet, Michel (1964), *Demeures Parisiennes; l'époque de Louis XVI* (Paris: Le Temps).

—(1972), *Paris Domestic Architecture of the 18th Century* (London: Barrie & Jenkins).

—(1972*a*), *Stately Mansions: Eighteenth-Century Paris Architecture* (New York: Praeger).

—(1980), *Claude-Nicolas Ledoux: 1736–1806* (Paris: Picard).

—*et al.* (1980), *Soufflot et son temps* (Paris: Caisse

National des Monuments Historiques et des Sites).
Gallet, Michel and Bottineau, Yves (1982), *Les Gabriel* (Paris: Picard).
—and Garms, Jörg (1986), *Germain Boffrand 1667–1754* (Paris: Herscher).
Galli da Bibiena, Ferdinando (1703–8), *Varie opera di prospettive* (Bologna: Camillo).
—(1711), *L'Architettura civile preparata su la geometria, e ridotta alle prospettive* (Parma: Monti).
Gallier, James (1973), *Autobiography of James Gallier, Architect* (New York: Da Capo; repr. of 1864 edn.).
Ganay, Ernest, Comte de (1962), *André Le Nostre, 1613–1700* (Paris: Vincent, Fréal).
Gandon, James (1969), *The Life of James Gandon, Esq., MRIA, FRS, etc.* (Dublin: Hodges & Smith, 1846; new edn.).
Garnham, Trevor (1994), *Melsetter House, Orkney* (London: Phaidon).
—(1995), *St Andrew's Church, Roker, Sunderland, 1905* (London: Phaidon).
Garnier, Charles (1871), *Le Théâtre* (Paris: Hachette).
—(1874), *Notice sur Victor Baltard* (Paris: Didot).
—(1878–81), *Le nouvel Opéra de Paris* (Paris: Ducher).
Garnier, Tony (1920), *Les Grands Travaux de la Ville de Lyon* (Paris: Massin).
—(1932), *Une Cité Industrielle: Étude pour la construction des villes* (Paris: Vincent; originally published in 1918).
—(1938), *L'Œuvre de Tony Garnier* (Paris: Morancé).
—(1951), *Tony Garnier, 1869–1948* (Lyons: Durand-Girard).
Garstang, Donald (1984), *Giacomo Serpotta and the stuccatori of Palermo, 1560–1790* (London: Zwemmer).
Gary, M. N. de (1979), *La Maison Pompéienne du Prince Napoléon, 1856: Dessins de l'architecte Alfred Normand* (Paris: Musée des Arts-Décoratifs).
Gau, Franz Christian (1822–7), *Antiquités de la Nubie* (Stuttgart: Cotta).
—(1829–38), *Ruines de Pompeii* (Paris: Didot).
Gaya Nuño, J. A. (1966), *Arte del siglo XIX* (Madrid: Plus-Ultra).
Gayle, Margot, and Gillon, Edmund V. (1974), *Cast-Iron Architecture in New York* (New York: Dover).
Gazaneo, Jorge O., and Scarone, Mabel M. (1959), *Lúcio Costa* (Buenos Aires: Instituto de Arte Americano e Investigaciones Estéticas).
Gazzola, Piero (ed.) (1960), *Michele Sanmicheli* (Venice: Neri Pozza).
Gebhard, David (1953), *Purcell and Elmslie: Architects* (Minneapolis: Walker Art Center).
—(1965), *A Guide to Architecture in Southern California* (Los Angeles: Los Angeles County Museum of Art).
—(1965*a*), *The Work of Elmslie and Purcell* (Park Forest, Ill.: Prairie School).
—(1975), *C. F. A. Voysey, Architect* (Los Angeles: Hennessey & Ingalls).
—(1980), *Schindler* (Santa Barbara, Calif.: Peregrine Smith).
—and Breton, Hariette von (1971), *Lloyd Wright Architect* (Santa Barbara, Calif.: University of California).
——and Winter, Robert (1979), *Samuel and Joseph Cather Newsom* (Santa Barbara, Calif.: University of California, Santa Barbara Art Museum).
Geddes, Norman Bel (1932), *Horizons* (Boston: Little, Brown).
—(1940), *Current Biography* (New York: Wilson).
—(1940*a*), *Magic Motorways* (New York: Random House).
Geddes, Patrick (1918), *Town Planning Towards City Development* (Indore: Holkar State Press).
—(1973), *City Development* (New Brunswick, NJ: Rutgers UP; repr. of 1904 edn.).
Geffrye Museum (1972), *George Dance, the Elder (1695–1768); the Younger (1741–1825)* (London: Geffrye Museum).
Geist, Johann Friedrich (1983), *Arcades: The History of a Building Type* (Cambridge, Mass.: MIT Press).
Gelder, Hendrik E., and Duverger, J. (eds.) (1954), *Kunstgeschiedenis der Nederlanden* (Utrecht: De Haan).
Geldner, Ferdinand (1965), *Matthäus Roritzer: Das Büchlein von der Fialen Gerechtigkeit* (Wiesbaden: Pressler).
Gell, Sir William, and Gandy, John Peter (1852), *Pompeiana: The Topography, Edifices, and Ornaments of Pompeii* (London: Bohn).
Gendrop, Paul, and Heyden, Doris (1986), *Pre-Columbian Architecture of Mesoamerica* (London: Faber & Faber, and Milan: Electa).
Gentil, Philippe (ed.) (1990), *Vienne 1815–1848: Un nouvel art de vivre à l'époque Biedermeier* (Paris: Atelier Philippe Gentil).
Geretsegger, Heinz, and Peintner, Max, *et al.* (1983), *Otto Wagner 1841–1918* (Salzburg and Vienna: Residenz Verlag).
Gerkan, Armin von (1929), *Der Altar des Artemis-Tempels in Magnesia am Mäander* (Berlin: Schötz).
Gerkens, Gerhard (1974), *Das fürstliche Lustschloss Salzdahlum und sein Erbauer Herzog Anton Ulrich von Braunschweig-Wolfenbüttel* (Brunswick: Selbstv. d. Braunschweigischen Geschichtsvereins).
Gerland, Otto (1895), *Paul, Charles, und Simon-Louis du Ry. Eine Künstlerfamilie der Barockzeit* (Stuttgart: Neff).

Germann, Georg (1972), *Gothic Revival in Europe and Britain: Sources, Influences, and Ideas* (London: Lund Humphries).

Germer, Stefan, and Preiss, Achim (eds.) (1991), *Giuseppe Terragni, 1904–43: Moderne und Faschismus in Italien* (Munich: Klinkhardt & Biermann).

Gerson, Horst, and Ter Kuile, E. H. (1960), *Art and Architecture in Belgium 1600 to 1800* (Harmondsworth: Penguin).

Geyer, Albert (1936), *Geschichte des Schlosses zu Berlin* (Berlin: Deutscher Kunstverlag).

Geymüller, H. von (1887), *Les Du Cerceau, leur vie, leur œuvre* (Paris: Rouam).

Ghiberti, Lorenzo (1947), *I Commentarii: A Cura di Ottavio Morisani* (Naples: Riccardi).

Ghyka, Matila Costiescu (1976), *Le Nombre d'Or: rites et rythmes pythagoriciens dans le dévelopement de la civilisation occidentale* (Paris: Gallimard).

Gibberd, Frederick (1952), *Harlow New Town* (Harlow: Development Corporation).

—(1968), *Metropolitan Cathedral of Christ the King* (London: Architectural Press).

—(1970), *Town Design* (London: Architectural Press).

—(1980), *Harlow: The Story of a New Town* (Stevenage: Publications for Companies).

—and Yorke, F. R. S. (1978), *Modern Flats* (London: Architectural Press).

Gibbs, James (1728), *A Book of Architecture, Containing Designs of Buildings and Ornaments* (London: n.p.).

—(1732), *Rules for Drawing the Several Parts of Architecture, in a More Exact and Easy Manner* . . . etc. (London: Bowyer).

—(1747), *Bibliotheca Radcliviana* (London: The Author).

Giedion, Sigfried (1922), *Spätbarocker und romantischer Klassizismus* (Munich: Bruchman).

—(1928), *Bauen in Frankreich: Eisen, Eisenbeton* (Leipzig & Berlin: Klinkhardt & Biermann).

—(1954), *A Decade of Modern Architecture* (Zurich: Birkhäuser).

—(1954*a*), *Walter Gropius: Work and Teamwork* (New York: Reinhold).

—(1958), *Architecture, You and Me* (Cambridge, Mass.: Harvard UP).

—(1962–4), *The Eternal Present: The Beginnings of Architecture* (New York: Pantheon).

—(1967), *Space, Time, and Architecture: The Growth of a New Tradition* (Cambridge, Mass.: Harvard UP).

—(1969), *Mechanization Takes Command* (New York: Norton; repr. of 1948 edn.).

—(1971), *Architecture and the Phenomena of Transition* (Cambridge, Mass.: Harvard UP).

Giersberg, Hans-Joachim, and Schendel, Adelheid (1982), *Potsdamer Veduten: Stadt- und Landschaftsansichten vom 17. bis 20. Jahrhundert* (Potsdam–Sanssouci: Staatlichen Schlösser und Gärten).

Giesz, L. (1971), *Phänomenologie des Kitsches* (Munich: Fink).

Gifford, John (1989), *William Adam 1689–1748: A Life and Times of Scotland's Universal Architect* (Edinburgh: Mainstream).

—McWilliam, Colin, and Walker, David (1984), *Buildings of Scotland: Edinburgh* (Harmondsworth: Penguin).

Gilchrist, Agnes Addison (1969), *William Strickland, Architect and Engineer, 1788–1854* (New York: Da Capo; repr. of 1950 edn.).

Gill, Brendan (1987), *Many Masks: A Life of Frank Lloyd Wright* (New York: Putnam).

Gilly, David (1797), *Über Erfindung: Construction und Vortheile der Bohlen-Dächer* (Berlin: The Author).

—(1797–8), *Handbuch der Landbaukunst* (Berlin: The Author).

—(ed.) (1797–1806), *Sammlung nützlicher Aufsätze und Nachrichten die Baukunst betreffend* (Berlin: The Author).

Gilly, Friedrich (1994), *Essays on Architecture 1796–1799* (Chicago: University of Chicago Press).

—and Frick, Friedrich (1965), *Schloss Marienburg in Preussen* (Düsseldorf: Galtgarben).

Ginsburg, Moisei Yakovlevich (1982), *Style and Epoch* (Cambridge, Mass.: Harvard UP).

Giorgio di Martini, Francesco di (1967), *Trattato di Architettura* (Milan: Polifilo).

Gioseffi, Decio (1963), *Giotto architetto* (Milan: Comunità).

Giovannoni, Gustavo (1959), *Antonio da Sangallo, il Giovane* (Rome: Tipi Regionale).

Girouard, Mark (1966), *Robert Smythson and the Architecture of the Elizabethan Era* (London: Country Life).

—(1977), *Sweetness and Light: The 'Queen Anne' Movement, 1860–1900* (Oxford: Clarendon Press).

—(1979), *The Victorian Country House* (New Haven: Yale UP).

—(1979*a*), *Victorian Pubs* (London: Yale UP).

—(1983), *Robert Smythson and the Elizabethan Country House* (New Haven: Yale UP).

—(1990), *Alfred Waterhouse and the National History Museum* (London: Natural History Museum).

—(1998), *Big Jim: The Life and Work of James Stirling* (London: Chatto & Windus).

Giuliana Alajmo, Alessandro (1950), *L'architetto della Catania settecentesca: G. B. Vaccarini e le sconosciute vicende della sua vita* (Palermo: Industrie Grafiche).

Giurgola, Romaldo, and Mehta, Jaimini (1975), *Louis I. Kahn* (Boulder, Colo.: Westview).

Givelet, François (1897), *L'église et l'abbaye de Saint-Nicaise de Reims* (Rheims: n.p.).

Glaeser, Ludwig (1972), *The Work of Frei Otto* (New York: Museum of Modern Art).

—(1977), *Ludwig Mies van der Rohe: Furniture and Furniture Drawings* (New York: Museum of Modern Art).

Glancey, Jonathan (1989), *New British Architecture* (London: Thames & Hudson).

—(1989*a*), *Pillar Boxes* (London: Chatto & Windus).

Glare, P. G. W. (ed.) (1982), *Oxford Latin Dictionary* (Oxford: Clarendon Press).

Glazier, Richard (1926), *A Manual of Historic Ornament* (London: Batsford).

Glendinning, Miles, *et al.* (1996), *A History of Scottish Architecture* (Edinburgh: Edinburgh UP).

Glin, Desmond Fitzgerald, the Knight of (1964), 'Richard Castle', *Irish Georgian Society Quarterly Bulletin*, 7: 31–8.

Gočár, Josef (1930), *Josef Gočár* (Geneva: Meister der Baukunst).

Godfrey, Walter Hindes (1955), *The English Almshouse With Some Account of its Predecessor, the Medieval Hospital* (London: Faber & Faber).

Goldberger, Paul (1981), *The Skyscraper* (New York: Knopf).

Golding, John (1973), *Ozenfant* (New York: Knoedler).

Goldstein, B. (ed.) (1977), *Architecture: Opportunity, Achievements* (London: RIBA).

Goldstone, Harmon H., and Dalrymple, Martha (1974), *History Preserved: A Guide to New York City Landmarks and Historic Districts* (New York: Simon & Schuster).

Goldthwaite, Richard (1980), *The Building of Renaissance Florence: An Economic and Social History* (Baltimore and London: Johns Hopkins UP).

Gollins, Melvin, & Ward (1974), *Architecture of the Gollins, Melvin, Ward Partnership* (London: Lund Humphries).

Gomme, Andor, and Walker, David (1987), *Architecture of Glasgow* (London: Lund Humphries).

Goode, James M. (1979), *Capital Losses: A Cultural History of Washington's Destroyed Buildings* (Washington: Smithsonian Institute).

Goodhart-Rendel, Harry Stuart (1924), *Hawksmoor* (London: Benn).

—(1949), 'Rogue Goths of the Victorian Era', *Journal of the RIBA*, 3rd ser., 56/6: 251–9.

—(1989), *English Architecture Since the Regency: An Interpretation* (new edition, London: Century; previously published London: Constable, 1953).

Goodwin, Godfrey (1971), *A History of Ottoman Architecture* (London: Thames & Hudson).

Gould, Jeremy H. (1977), *Modern Houses in Great Britain* (London: Soc. of Architectural Historians of Great Britain).

Goulet, Patrice (1994), *Jean Nouvel* (Paris: Regard).

Gourlier, Biet, Tardieu, Grillon, and Tardieu, Feu (1825–50), *Choix d'édifices publics projetés et construits en France depuis le commencement du XIXe siècle* (Paris: Colos).

Gowans, Alan (1955), *Church Architecture in New France* (Toronto: University of Toronto Press).

Gozak, Andrei, and Leonidov, Andrei (1988), *Ivan Leonidov: The Complete Works* (New York: Rizzoli).

Grabar, André (1972), *Martyrium: recherches sur le culte des reliques et l'art Chrétien antique* (London: Variorum Reprints).

Grabar, Igor, Lazarev, V. N., and Kemenov, V. S. (eds.) (1963), *Istoriya Russkogo Iskusstva* (Moscow: Knebel).

Gradidge, Roderick (1981), *Edwin Lutyens: Architect Laureate* (London: Allen & Unwin).

Graf, Otto Antonia (1985), *Otto Wagner, 1841–1918* (Vienna: Böhlau, 1985).

Graham, F. Lanier (1970), *Hector Guimard* (New York: Museum of Modern Art).

Graillot, Henri (1914), *Nicholas Bachelier, Imagier et Maçon de Toulouse au XVIe siècle* (Toulouse: Edouard Privat).

Grassi, Giorgio (1982), *Progetti e disegni 1965–1980* (Mantua: Exhibition Centre).

—(1989), *Architecture, Dead Language* (New York: Rizzoli).

Grassi, Liliana (1966), *Razionalismo architettonico dal Lodoli a G. Pagano* (Milan: Bignami).

Graupner, G. (1931), *Paul Bonatz und seine Schüler* (Stuttgart: n.p.).

Gravagnuolo, Benedetto (1982), *Adolf Loos, Theory and Works* (New York: Rizzoli).

Gray, A. Stuart (1985), *Edwardian Architecture: A Biographical Dictionary* (London: Duckworth).

Greene, Charles Sumner, and Greene, Henry Mather (1977), *The Architecture and Related Designs* (Los Angeles: Municipal Art Gallery).

Greeves, T. Affleck (1975), *Bedford Park* (London: Bingley).

Gregor, Joseph (1953), *Clemens Holzmeister: Das Architektonische Werk* (Vienna: Österreichische Staatsdruckerei).

Gregotti, Vittorio (1968), *New Directions in Italian Architecture* (New York: Braziller).

Greiff, Constance M. (1979), *John Notman, Architect* (Philadelphia: The Athenaeum).

Greig, Doreen E. (1970), *Herbert Baker in South Africa* (Cape Town: Purnell).

Grimm, German G. (1940), *Arkitektor Andreyan Zakharov* (Moscow: Akademii Arkitektury SSSR).

Grimschitz, Bruno (1947), *Hans Buchsbaum* (Vienna: Wolfrum).

—(1947*a*), *Wiener Barockpaläste* (Vienna: Wiener Verlag).
—(1959), *Johann Lucas von Hildebrandt* (Vienna: Herold).
Grioni, John S. (1975), *Le edicole sacre di Roma* (Rome: Editalia).
Gritella, Gianfranco (1992), *Juvarra: l'architettura* (Modena: Panini).
Grodecki, Louis (1986), *Gothic Architecture* (London: Faber & Faber, and Milan: Electa).
Gropius, Walter (1945), *Rebuilding Our Communities* (Chicago: Theobald).
—(1952), *Architecture and Design in the Age of Science* (New York: Spiral).
—(1962), *The Scope of Total Architecture* (New York: Collier; new version of 1955 edn.).
—(1965), *The New Architecture and the Bauhaus* (Cambridge, Mass.: MIT Press).
—(1968), *Apollo in the Democracy* (New York: McGraw-Hill).
—and Harkness, Sarah P. (eds.) (1966), *Architects Collaborative: 1945–1965* (Tenfel: Niggli).
Grossman, Elizabeth Greenwell (1966), *The Civic Architecture of Paul Cret* (Cambridge: Cambridge UP).
Gruen, Victor (1964), *The Heart of Our Cities* (New York: Simon & Schuster).
—(1973), *Centers for the Urban Environment* (New York: van Nostrand).
—and Smith, Larry (1960), *Shopping Towns USA* (New York: Reinhold).
Grundmann, Günther (1957), *Jenisch Haus und Jenisch Park* (Hamburg: Christians).
Guarini, Guarino (1660), *La Pieta Trionfante* (Messina: n.p.).
—(1665), *Placita Philosophica* (Paris: Thierry).
—(1671), *Euclides Adauctus* (Turin: Zapatae).
—(1674), *Modo di Misurare le fabriche* (Turin: Gianelli).
—(1675), *Compendio della sfera celeste* (Turin: n.p.).
—(1676), *Trattato di Fortificazione* (Turin: Gianelli).
—(1678), *Leges Temporum et Planetarum* (Turin: Janelli).
—(1683), *Coelistis Mathematicae* (Milan: Montiae).
—(1966), *Desegni d' 'Architettura Civile e Ecclesiastica' di Guarino Guarini e l'arte del maestro* (Turin: Albra; facsimile of edn. of 1686 with critical notes).
—(1968), *Architettura Civile* (Milan: Polifilo; originally published in 1737).
Gubitosi, Camillo, and Izzo, Alberto (eds.) (1974), *Pietro Belluschi: Edifici e Projetti* (Rome: Officina).
——(1976), *Van den Broek/Bakema* (Rome: Officina).
——(1981), *Frank Lloyd Wright: Three-Quarters of a Century of Drawings* (New York: Horizon).
Gubler, Hans-Martin (1972), *Der Vorarlberger Barockbaumeister Peter Thumb, 1681–1766* (Sigmaringen: Thorbecke).
Gubler, Jacques (1975), *Nationalisme et Internationalisme dans l'architecture moderne de la Suisse* (Lausanne: L'Âge d'Homme).
—(1978), *Alberto Sartoris* (Zurich: ETH).
Guedes, Amancio (1977), *Fragments from an Ironic Autobiography* (Johannesburg: n.p.).
Guedes, P. (1981), *Taller de Arquitectura: Ricardo Bofill* (London: Architectural Association).
Guêpière, Pierre-Louis-Phillipe de la (1759), *Recueil d'esquisses d'architecture* (Stuttgart: Cotta).
Guiffrey, Jules (1915), *Artistes Parisiens des XVIe et XVIIe siècles* (Paris: Imprimerie Nationale).
Guimard, Hector (1907), *Fontes Artistiques pour Constructions . . . , Style Guimard* (Paris: Fonderies de Saint-Dizier).
Gunnis, Rupert (1968), *Dictionary of British Sculptors 1660–1851* (London: Abbey Library).
Günschel, Günter (1966), *Grosse Konstrukteure. Freyssinet, Maillart, Dischinger, Finsterwalder* (Berlin, Frankfurt, and Vienna: Ullstein).
Gunther R. T. (ed.) (1928), *The Architecture of Roger Pratt . . . From His Note-Books* (Oxford: Oxford UP).
Gurlitt, Cornelius (1891), *Andreas Schlüter* (Berlin: Wasmuth).
—(1907–12), *Baukunst Konstantinopels* (Berlin: Wasmuth).
—(1924), *August der Stärke: Ein Fürstenleben aus der Zeit des deutschen Barock* (Dresden: Sibyllen).
Gutiérrez de Ceballos, Alfonso Rodríguez (1971), *Los Churriguera* (Madrid: Instituto Diego Velázquez).
Gwilt, Joseph (1811), *Treatise on the Equilibrium of Arches* (London: Priestley & Weale).
—(1818), *Notitia Architectonicae Italiana* (London: Egerton).
—(1822), *Sciography, or Examples of Shadows, with Rules for their Projection* (London: Bohn).
—(ed.) (1825), new edition of Chambers's *A Treatise on the Decorative Part of Civil Architecture*, including an essay on Greek Architecture (London: Priestley & Weale).
—(1826), *The Architecture of Marcus Vitruvius Pollio in Ten Books* (London: Priestley & Weale).
—(1826*a*), *Rudiments of Architecture* (London: Taylor).
—(1837), *Elements of Architectural Criticism* (London: Williams).
—(1848), new edition of Nicholson's *Principles of Architecture* (London: Bohn).
—(1903), *An Encylopaedia of Architecture, Historical, Theoretical, and Practical* (London: Longmans, 1842, with subsequent editions of 1845, 1854, 1859, 1867, 1876, and 1889 (the last three editions by Wyatt *Papworth,

whose edn. is that referred to in the present work)).
Habachi, Labib (1984), *The Obelisks of Egypt: Skyscrapers of the Past* (Cairo: American University in Cairo Press).
Habbel, Josef (ed.) (1943), *Dominikus Böhm* (Regensburg: Habbel).
Habraken, Nicholas (1972), *Supports: An Alternative to Mass Housing* (London: Architectural Press).
Hackney, Rod (1990), *The Good, the Bad, and the Ugly: Cities in Crisis* (London: Muller).
Hadamowsky, Franz (1962), *Die Familie Galli-Bibiena in Wien* (Vienna: Pracher).
Hadfield, Miles, Harling, Robert, and Highton, Leonie (1980), *British Gardeners: A Biographical Dictionary* (London: Zwemmer).
Haesler, Otto (1930), *Zum Problem des Wohnungsbaues* (Berlin: Reckendorf).
—(1957), *Mein Lebenswerk als Architekt* (Berlin: Henschel).
Hager, Helmut (1970), *Filippo Juvarra* (Rome: De Luca).
Hager, Luisa (1955), *Nymphenburg: Schloss, Park, und Burgen* (Munich: Hirmer).
—and Hojer, Gerhard (1976), *Schleissheim: Neues Schloss und Garten* (Munich: Bayerische Verwaltung der staatlichen Schlösser, Gärten, und Seen).
Hager, Werner (1942), *Die Bauten des deutschen Barocks 1690–1770* (Jena: Diederichs).
Hague, Graham, and Hague, Judy (1986), *The Unitarian Heritage: An Architectural Survey of Chapels and Churches in the Unitarian Tradition in the British Isles* (Sheffield: P. B. Godfrey).
Hahn, Robert, *et al.* (eds.) (1988), *Coop Himmelblau: The Power of the City* (Darmstadt: Büchner).
Hahnloser, Hans Robert (1937), *Villard de Honnecourt* (Vienna: Schroll).
Haigh, Diane (1995), *Baillie Scott: The Artistic House* (London: Academy Editions).
Haiko, Peter (1991), *Friedrich von Schmidt* (Vienna: Museum der Stadt Wien).
—and Krimmel, Bernd (1988), *Joseph Maria Olbrich* (New York: Rizzoli).
Halévy, Daniel (1925), *Vauban* (New York: MacVeagh).
Halfpenny, William (1731), *Perspective Made Easy* (London: Oswald).
—(1747), *The Builders Pocket Companion* (London: Ware; based on 1728 edn.).
—(1748), *Arithmetick and Measurement* (London: Ware).
—(1749), *A New and Compleat System of Architecture* (London: Brindley).
—(1752), *Geometry Theoretical and Practical* (London: Sayer).
—(1752*a*), *Rural Architecture in the Gothic Taste* (London: Sayer).
—(1752*b*), *Useful Architecture in Twenty-One New Designs for Erecting Parsonage-Houses, Farm-Houses, and Inns* (London: Sayer).
—(1757), *The Modern Builder's Assistant* (London: Sayer; with Robert Morris and Timothy Lightoler).
—(1774), *Twelve Beautiful Designs for Farm Houses* (London: Sayer).
—(1965), *Practical Architecture* (New York: Blom; repr. of 1724 edn.).
—(1968), *The Art of Sound Building* (New York: Blom; repr. of 1725 edn.).
—(1968*a*), *Chinese and Gothic Architecture Properly Ornamented* (New York: Blom; repr. of 1752 edn.).
—(1968*b*), *Magnum in Parvo, or, The Marrow of Architecture* (New York: Blom; repr. of 1728 edn.).
—(1968*c*), *Rural Architecture in the Chinese Taste* (New York: Blom; repr. of 1750–2 edn.).
Hall, F. G. (1949), *The Bank of Ireland, 1783–1946* (Oxford: Blackwell).
Hall, Lee (1995), *Olmsted's America* (London: Little, Brown).
Hall, Marcia B. (1979), *Renovation and Counter-Reformation: Vasari and Duke Cosimo in Sta Maria Novella and Sta Croce* (Oxford: Clarendon Press).
Hall, Thomas (ed.) (1981), *Stenstadens Arkitektur* (Stockholm: Akademilitteratur).
Hamilton, George Heard (1983), *The Art and Architecture of Russia* (Harmondsworth: Penguin, 1954, revised edn.).
Hamlin, Talbot F. (1953), *Architecture through the Ages* (New York: Putnam).
—(1955), *Benjamin Henry Latrobe* (New York: Oxford UP).
—(1964), *Greek Revival Architecture in America* (New York: Dover; repr. of 1944 edn.).
Hammacher, Abraham Marie (1967), *Die Welt Henry van de Veldes* (Antwerp: Mercator).
Hammer, Karl (1968), *Jacob Ignaz Hittorff: Ein Pariser Baumeister, 1792–1867* (Stuttgart: Hierjehann).
Hammond, Peter (ed.) (1962), *Towards a Church Architecture* (London: Architectural Press).
Hamon, Françoise, and MacCallum, Charles (eds.) (1991), *Louis Visconti 1791–1853* (Paris: Délégation à l'Action artistique de la Ville de Paris).
Hancocks, David (1971), *Animals and Architecture* (London: Evelyn).
Handler, B. (1970), *Systems Approach to Architecture* (New York: Elsevier).
Handlin, David P. (1985), *American Architecture* (London: Thames & Hudson).
Hannmann, Eckart (1975), *Karl Ludwig Wimmel, 1786–1845: Hamburgs erster Baudirektor* (Munich: Prestel).
Hansen, Hans Jürgen (1971), *Architecture in Wood:*

A History of Wood Building and its Techniques in Europe and North America (London: Faber).

Harbron, Dudley (1936), 'Samuel Beazley', *Architectural Review*, 79: 131–4.

—— (1949), *The Conscious Stone: The Life of Edward William Godwin* (London: Latimer House).

Harksen, Marie Luise (1973), *Erdmannsdorff und Seine Bauten in Wörlitz* (Wörlitz: Staatliche Schlösser und Gärten).

Harmon, Robert Bartlett (1983), *The Shingle Style in American Architecture* (Monticello, Ill.: Vance).

Harris, Cyril M. (1983), *Illustrated History of Historic Architecture* (New York: Dover).

Harris, Eileen (ed.) (1979), *Thomas Wright's Arbours and Grottos* (London: The Scolar Press).

—— (1990), *British Architectural Books and Writers 1556–1785* (Cambridge: Cambridge UP).

Harris, John (1970), *Sir William Chambers, Knight of the Polar Star* (London: Zwemmer).

—— (1981), *The Palladians* (London: Trefoil).

—— (1982), *William Talman, Maverick Architect* (London: Allen & Unwin).

—— and Higgot, Gordon (1989), *Inigo Jones: Complete Architectural Drawings* (London: Zwemmer).

—— Orgel, Stephen, and Strong, Roy (1973), *The King's Arcadia: Inigo Jones and the Stuart Court* (London: Arts Council of Great Britain).

—— and Snodin, Michael (eds.) (1996), *Sir William Chambers: Architect to George III* (New Haven: Yale UP).

—— and Tait, A. A. (1979), *Catalogue of the Drawings by Inigo Jones, John Webb, and Isaac de Caus at Worcester College, Oxford* (Oxford: Clarendon Press).

Harriss, Joseph (1989), *The Tallest Tower: Eiffel and the Belle Epoque* (Washington: Regnery Gateway).

Hart, Franz, Henn, W., and Sontag, H. (1985), *Multi-Storey Buildings in Steel* (London: Collins).

Hartt, Frederick (1958), *Giulio Romano* (Northford, Conn.: Elliot).

Hartung, Giselher (1983), *Eisenkonstruktion des 19. Jahrhunderts* (Munich: Schirmer).

Hartung, Hugo (1896–1902), *Motive der mittelalterlichen Baukunst in Deutschland* (Berlin: Wasmuth).

—— (1902), *Studienentwürfe, Aufnahmen und Ausführungen* (Berlin: Wasmuth).

—— (1912), *Ziele und Ergebnisse der italienischen Gotik* (Berlin: Ernst).

Harvey, John Hooper (1987), *English Medieval Architects: A Biographical Dictionary down to 1550* (Gloucester: Alan Sutton).

Haslam, Richard (1979), *Powys: Buildings of Wales* (Harmondsworth: Penguin).

—— (1995), *Clough Williams-Ellis* (London: Academy Editions).

Hatch, Alden (1974), *Buckminster Fuller: At Home in the Universe* (New York: Crown).

Hatch, C. Richard (ed.) (1984), *The Scope of Social Architecture* (New York: Van Nostrand Reinhold).

Haupt, Georg (1952–4), *Die Bau- und Kunstdenkmäler der Stadt Darmstadt* (Darmstadt: Roether).

Haus-Rucker-Co (1984), *Haus-Rucker-Co 1967 bis 1983* (Brunswick: Vieweg).

Haussmann, Georges-Eugène (1890–3), *Mémoires de Baron Haussmann* (Paris: Victor-Havard).

Hautecœur, Louis (1912), *L'architecture classique à Saint-Pétersbourg à la fin du XVIIIe siècle* (Paris: Champion).

—— (1943–57), *Histoire de l'architecture classique en France* (Paris: Picard).

Hautmann, Hans, and Hautmann, Rudolf (1980), *Die Gemeindebauten des Roten Wien, 1919–1934* (Vienna: Schönbrunn).

Hauttmann, Max (1913), *Der Kurbayerische Hofbaumeister Joseph Effner* (Strasbourg: Heitz).

—— (1921), *Geschichte der kirchlichen Baukunst in Bayern, Schwaben, und Franken 1550–1780* (Munich: Schmidt).

Haviland, John (1830), *The Builder's Assistant* (Baltimore: The Author).

—— (ed.) (1830*a*), *Young Carpenter's Assistant by Owen Biddle* (Philadelphia: n.p.).

Havlíček, Josef (1964), *Návrhy a stavby 1925–1960* (Prague: STWL).

Hawkes, Dean (1986), *Modern Country Homes in England: The Arts and Crafts Architecture of Barry Parker* (Cambridge: Cambridge UP).

Hayter, William (1970), *William of Wykeham: Patron of the Arts* (London: Chatto & Windus).

Hazlehurst, Franklin Hamilton (1980), *Gardens of Illusion: The Genius of André Le Nostre* (Nashville: Vanderbilt UP).

Headley, Gwyn, and Meulenkamp, Wim (1986), *Follies* (London: Jonathan Cape).

Heber, Wiltrud (1986), *Die Arbeiten des Nicolas de Pigage in den Ehemals Kurpfälzischen Residenzen Mannheim und Schwetzingen* (Worms: Wernersche Verlagsgesellschaft).

Heckmann, Herbert (1972), *Matthäus Daniel Pöppelmann (1662–1736), Leben und Werk* (Munich and Berlin: Deutsches Kunstverlag).

—— (1986), *Matthäus Daniel Pöppelmann und die Barockbaukunst in Dresden* (Stuttgart: Deutsche Verlags-Anstalt).

Hederer, Oswald (1960), *Karl von Fischer: Leben und Werk* (Munich: Callwey).

—— (1964), *Leo von Klenze: Persönlichkeit und Werk* (Munich: Callwey).

—— (1976), *Friedrich von Gärtner, 1792–1847: Leben, Werk, Schüler* (Munich: Prestel).

—— (1976*a*), *Klassizismus* (Munich: Heyne).

Hedicke, Robert (1913), *Cornelis Floris und die Florisdekoration* (Berlin: Bard).
Hegemann, Hans W. (1943), *Die deutsche Barockbaukunst Böhmens* (Munich: Bruckmann).
Hegemann, Werner (1911), *Amerikanische Parkanlagen* (Berlin: Wasmuth).
—(1911–13), *Der Städtebau nach den Ergebnissen der allgemeinen Städtebau-Austellung in Berlin* (Berlin: Wasmuth).
—(1923), *Gothenburg 1923: International Cities and Town Planning Exhibition* (Gothenburg: Zachrissons).
—(1929), *German Bestelmayer* (Berlin: Hübsch).
—(1929*a*), *Reihen- und Geschäftshaus-Fassaden* (Berlin: Wasmuth).
—(1936–8), *City Planning: Housing* (New York: Architectural Book Publishing).
—(1976), *Das steinerne Berlin: Geschichte der grössten Mietskasernstadt der Welt* (Brunswick, Vieweg; originally published 1930).
—and Peets, Elbert (1972), *The American Vitruvius: An Architect's Handbook of Civic Art* (New York: Blom; originally published 1922).
Heideloff, Karl Alexander von (1838–55), *Die Ornamentik des Mittelalters* (Nuremberg: Geigers).
—(1844), *Die Bauhütte des Mittelalters in Deutschland* (Nuremberg: Stein).
—(1855), *Die Kunst des Mittelalters in Schwaben* (Stuttgart: Ebner & Seubert).
—(1855*a*), *Nürnbergs Baudenkmale der Vorzeit, oder Musterbuch der Alt-Deutschen Baukunst* (Nuremberg: Lotzbeck; originally published 1838–43).
Heimbürger Ravalli, Minna (1971), *L'architetto militare Marcantonio De Rossi* (Rome: Istituto di Studi Romani).
—(1977), *Architettura, Scultura, e Arti Minori nel Barocco Italiano* (Florence: Olschki).
Heinz, Thomas A. (1982), *Frank Lloyd Wright* (New York: St Martin's).
Hempel, Doris (ed.) (1987), *Friedrich Wilhelm von Erdmannsdorff 1736–1800: Leben, Werk, Wirkung* (Wörlitz: Staatliche Schlösser & Gärten).
Hempel, Eberhard (1924), *Francesco Borromini* (Vienna: Schroll).
—(1955), *Gaetano Chiaveri: Der Architekt der katholischen Hofkirche zu Dresden* (Dresden: W. Jess).
—(1965), *Baroque Art and Architecture in Central Europe . . .*, etc. (Harmondsworth: Penguin).
Hénard, Eugène-Alfred (1903–9), *Études sur les transformations de Paris* (Paris: Librairies Imprimeries Réunies).
Henderson, Philip (1967), *William Morris: His Life, Work, and Friends* (London: Thames & Hudson).
Hennebique, François (1908), *The Hennebique Armored Concrete System* (New York: Hennebique).
Hensoldt, H. C. (1845), *Die neue Stadt-Pfarrkirche in Sonneberg* (Nuremberg: Stein).
Hentrich-Petschnigg & Partners (1969, 1975), *Bauten 1953–1969 and 1972–1975* (Düsseldorf: Hentrich-Petschnigg).
Hentschel, Walter, and May, Walter (1973), *Johann Christoph Knöffel, der Architekt d. sächs. Rokokos* (Berlin: Akademie-Verlag).
Herbert, Gilbert (1984), *The Dream of the Factory-Made House: Walter Gropius and Konrad Wachsmann* (Cambridge, Mass.: MIT Press).
Herdeg, K. (1985), *The Decorated Diagram: Harvard Architecture and the Failure of the Bauhaus Legacy* (Cambridge, Mass.: MIT Press).
Héré de Corny, Emmanuel (1753), *Plans et élévations de la place royale de Nancy* (Paris: François).
—(1753–6), *Recueil des plans, élévations et coupes . . . des châteaux, jardins, et dépendances . . . en Lorraine* (Paris: François).
Herman, Morton (1954), *The Early Australian Architects and Their Work* (Sydney: Angus & Robertson).
—(1963), *The Blackets: An Era of Australian Architecture* (Sydney: Angus & Robertson).
Herrera Casado, Antonio (1975), *El Palacio del Infantado en Guadalajara* (Guadalajara: Institución Provincial de Cultura).
Herrmann, Wolfgang (1962), *Laugier and Eighteenth Century French Theory* (London: Zwemmer).
—(1973), *The Theory of Claude Perrault* (London: Zwemmer).
—(1977), *Deutsche Baukunst des 19. und 20. Jahrhunderts* (Basle: Birkhäuser).
—(1984), *Gottfried Semper: In Search of Architecture* (Cambridge, Mass.: MIT Press).
Hersey, George L. (1972), *High Victorian Gothic: A Study in Associationism* (Baltimore and London: Johns Hopkins UP).
—(1988), *The Lost Meaning of Classical Architecture: Speculations on Ornament from Vitruvius to Venturi* (Cambridge, Mass.: MIT Press).
Hertz, R., and Klein, N. (1990), *Twentieth-Century Art Theory: Urbanism, Politics, and Mass Culture* (Englewood Cliffs, NJ: Prentice Hall).
Hertzen, Heikki von, and Speiregen, Paul D. (1973), *Building a New Town: Finland's New Garden City, Tapiola* (Cambridge, Mass.: MIT Press).
Herzog, Thomas (1977), *Pneumatic Structures: A Handbook for the Architect and Engineer* (London: Crosby Lockwood).
Hess, Jacob (ed.) (1934), *Vite de' pittori, scultori, ed architetti . . . in Roma* (Vienna: Schroll).
Hesse, Fritz (1964), *Erinnerungen an Dessau* (Hanover: Schmorl & von Seefeld).
Hesse, Ludwig F. (1854–5), *Ländliche Wohngebäude in der Umgegend von Sanssouci und Potsdam* (Berlin: Riegel).

—(1854–6), *Sanssouci in seinen Architekturen unter der Regierung Seiner Majestät Friedrich Wilhelm IV von Preussen* (Berlin: Riegel).

Heuss, Theodor (1939), *Hans Poelzig: Bauten und Entwürfe* (Stuttgart: Wasmuth).

Hewison, Robert (1976), *John Ruskin: The Argument of the Eye* (London: Thames & Hudson).

Hewitt, Barnard (ed.) (1958), *The Renaissance Stage: Documents of Serlio, Sabbattini, and Furttenbach* (Coral Gables, Fla.: University of Miami Press).

Heydenreich, Ludwig Heinrich, and Lotz, Wolfgang (1974), *Architecture in Italy 1400–1600* (Harmondsworth: Penguin).

Heyer, Paul (1978), *Architects on Architecture: New Directions in America* (New York: Walker).

Heym, Sabine (1984), *Henrico Zuccalli, um 1642–1724: der kurbayerische Hofbaumeister* (Munich: Schnell & Steiner).

Hibbard, Howard (1962), *The Architecture of the Palazzo Borghese* (Rome: American Academy in Rome).

—(1965), *Bernini* (Harmondsworth: Penguin).

—(ed.) (1967), *Essays in the History of Architecture Presented to Rudolf Wittkower* (London: Phaidon).

—(1971), *Carlo Maderno and Roman Architecture, 1580–1630* (London: Zwemmer).

Hieber, Hermann (1923), *Elias Holl* (Munich: Piper).

Hilbersheimer, Ludwig Karl (1925), *Grossstadtbauten* (Hanover: Apos).

—(1927), *Grossstadt Architektur* (Stuttgart: Hoffmann).

—(1927*a*), *Internationale Neue Baukunst* (Stuttgart: Hoffmann).

—(1929), *Beton als Gestalter* (Stuttgart: Hoffmann).

—(1944), *The New City* (Chicago: Theobald).

—(1949), *The New Regional Pattern* (Chicago: Theobald).

—(1955), *The Nature of Cities* (Chicago: Theobald).

—(1956), *Ludwig Mies van der Rohe* (Chicago: Theobald).

—(1963), *Contemporary Architecture: Its Roots and Trends* (Chicago: Theobald).

—(1963*a*), *Einfaltung einer Planungsidee* (Berlin: Ullstein).

Hildebrand, Grant (1974), *Designing for Industry: The Architecture of Albert Kahn* (Cambridge, Mass.: MIT Press).

Hill, Oliver, and Cornforth, John (1966), *English Country Houses: Caroline, 1625–1685* (London: Country Life).

Hillenbrand, Robert (1994), *Islamic Architecture: Form, Function, and Meaning* (Edinburgh: Edinburgh UP).

Hillier, Bevis (1985), *Art Deco of the 20s and 30s* (New York: Schocken Books).

Hines, Thomas (1974), *Burnham of Chicago: Architect and Planner* (New York: Oxford UP).

—(1994), *Richard Neutra and the Search for Modern Architecture* (Berkeley: University of California Press).

Hinrichs, Walter Th. (1909), *Carl Gotthard Langhans, ein schlesischer Baumeister, 1733–1808* (Strasbourg: Heitz).

Hinz, Berthold (1979), *Art in the Third Reich* (New York: Pantheon).

Hiscock, Walter George (1960), *Henry Aldrich of Christ Church 1648–1710* (Oxford: Holywell Press).

Hitchcock, Henry-Russell (1931), *J. J. P. Oud* (Paris: Éditions Cahiers d'Art).

—(1938), *Marcel Breuer and the American Tradition in Architecture* (Cambridge, Mass.: MIT Press).

—(1939), *Rhode Island Architecture* (Providence, RI: Museum Press).

—(1954), *Early Victorian Architecture in Britain* (New Haven and London: Yale UP).

—(1955), *Latin-American Architecture since 1945* (New York: Museum of Modern Art).

—(1966), *The Architecture of Henry Hobson Richardson and His Times* (Cambridge, Mass.: MIT Press).

—(1966*a*), *Philip Johnson, Architecture, 1949–1965* (New York: Holt).

—(1966*b*), *Richardson as a Victorian Architect* (Baltimore: Barton-Gillet).

—(1968), *German Rococo: the Zimmermann Brothers* (Baltimore: Penguin).

—(1968*a*), *Rococo Architecture in Southern Germany* (London: Phaidon).

—(1973), *In the Nature of Materials* (New York: Da Capo; repr. of 1942 edn. on Frank Lloyd Wright's work).

—(1976), *American Architectural Books* (New York: Da Capo).

—(1977), *Architecture: Nineteenth and Twentieth Centuries* (Harmondsworth: Penguin, 1958, rev. edn.).

—(1981), *German Renaissance Architecture* (Princeton: Princeton UP).

—(1993), *Modern Architecture: Romanticism and Reintegration* (New York: Da Capo; first pub. 1929).

—and Johnson, Philip (1966), *The International Style: Architecture since 1922* (New York: Norton; originally pub. 1932).

—and Seale, William (1976), *Temples of Democracy: The State Capitols of the USA* (New York: Harcourt).

Hitchmough, Wendy (1992), *Hoover Factory: Wallis, Gilbert, & Partners* (London: Phaidon).

—(1995), *C. F. A. Voysey* (London: Phaidon).

Hittorff, Jakob Ignaz (1851), *Architecture polychrome chez les Grecs* (Paris: Firmin-Didot).

—(1987), *Hittorff, Jakob Ignaz: ein Architekt aus*

Köln in Paris des 19. Jahrhunderts: exhibition catalogue (Cologne: Museum).

Hittorff, Jakob Ignaz, and Lecointe, Jean (1827), *Description des cérémonies . . .* (Paris: Renouard).

—and Zanth, Ludwig (1827), *Architecture antique de la Sicile* (Paris: Donnard).

——(1835), *Architecture moderne de la Sicile* (Paris: Renouard).

Hitzig, Friedrich (1850–9), *Ausgeführte Bauwerke* (Berlin: Ernst & Korn).

—(1867), *Die Börse in Berlin* (Berlin: Ernst & Korn).

—(1875), *Das Palais des Herrn von Kronenberg in Warschau* (Berlin: Ernst & Korn).

Hix, John (1996), *The Glass House* (London: Phaidon).

Hoag, John D. (1986), *Islamic Architecture* (London: Faber & Faber, and Milan: Electa).

Hoak, Edward Warren, and Church, Willis Humphrey (1930), *Masterpieces of Architecture in the United States* (New York: Scribner).

Hobhouse, Hermione (1975), *A History of Regent Street* (London: Macdonald & Jane's with Queen Anne Press).

—(1983), *Prince Albert, His Life and Work* (London: Hamilton).

—(ed.) (1986), *Survey of London*, xlii: *Southern Kensington* (London: Athlone Press).

—(1995), *Thomas Cubitt, Master Builder* (Didcot: Management Books).

Hoefer, Johann Christian Ferdinand (ed.) (1857), *Nouvelle biographie générale* (Paris: Firmin-Didot).

Hoeljte, Georg (1964), *Georg Ludwig Friedrich Laves* (Hanover: Steinback).

Hoff, August (1928), *Emil Fahrenkamp: Ein Ausschnitt seines Schaffens aus den Jahren 1924–1927* (Stuttgart: Hoffmann).

—Muck, Herbert, and Thoma, Raimund (1962), *Dominikus Böhm: Leben und Werk* (Munich: Schnell & Steiner).

Hoffmann, Donald (ed.) (1967), *The Meanings of Architecture: Buildings and Writings by John Wellborn Root* (New York: Horizon Press).

—(1973), *The Architecture of John Wellborn Root* (Baltimore: Johns Hopkins UP).

Hoffmann, Hans-Christoff (1966), *Die Theater-Bauten von Fellner und Helmer* (Munich: Prestel).

Hoffmann, Paola (1967), *Il Monte Pincio e la Casina Valadier* (Rome: Mondo).

Hoffmann, Walter (1968), *Schloss Pommersfelden* (Nuremberg: Carl).

Høller, Viggo Sten (1973), *Amalienborg* (Copenhagen: Rhodas).

Holmdahl, Gustav, *et al.* (eds.) (1981), *Gunnar Asplund, Architect, 1885–1940* (Stockholm: Byggförlaget).

Holt, Elizabeth G. (ed.) (1958), *A Documentary History of Art* (Garden City, NY: Doubleday).

Holzmeister, Clemens (1937), *Bauten, Entwürfe, und Handzeichnungen* (Salzburg: Pustet).

—(1976), *Architekt in der Zeitenwende* (Salzburg: Bergland).

Honour, Hugh (1961), *Chinoiserie: The Vision of Cathay* (London: John Murray).

—(1977), *Neo-Classicism* (Harmondsworth: Penguin).

—(1979), *Romanticism* (Harmondsworth: Penguin).

Hood, Raymond M. (1931), *Raymond M. Hood* (New York: McGraw).

Hope, Thomas (1804), *Observations on the Plans and Elevations designed by James Wyatt, Architect, for Downing College, Cambridge* (London: Shuny).

—(1835), *An Historical Essay on Architecture* (London: Murray).

—(1962), *Costumes of the Greeks and Romans* (New York: Dover; repr. of *Costumes of the Ancients* (1809)).

—(1971), *Household Furniture and Interior Decoration* (New York: Dover; repr. of 1807 edn.).

Hôpital, Winifred de l' (1919), *Westminster Cathedral and its Architect* (London: Hutchinson).

Hoppenbrouwers, A., *et al.* (1975), *Victor Horta, architectonografie* (Brussels: Confédération nationale de la construction).

Horeau, Hector (1841–6), *Panorama d'Égypte et de Nubie avec un portrait de Méhémet Ali* (Paris: Horeau).

Horn, Walter William, and Born, Ernest (1979), *The Plan of St Gall: A Study of the Architecture and Economy of and Life in a Paradigmatic Carolingian Monastery* (Berkeley: University of California Press).

Hornblower, Simon, and Spawforth, Antony (eds.) (1996), *The Oxford Classical Dictionary* (Oxford: Oxford UP).

Hornig, Christian (1981), *Oscar Niemeyer: Bauten und Projekten* (Munich: Moos).

Horn-Oncken, Alste (1981), *Friedrich Gilly, 1772–1800* (Berlin: Mann).

Hoster, Joseph, and Mann, Albrecht (eds.) (1973), *Vom Bauen, Bilden, und Bewahren* (Cologne: Greven).

Houfe, Simon (1980), *Sir Albert Richardson* (London: White Crescent Press).

Howard, Deborah (1975), *Jacopo Sansovino: Architecture and Patronage in Renaissance Vienna* (New Haven: Yale UP).

—(1980), *The Architectural History of Venice* (London: Batsford).

—(1995), *Scottish Architecture from the Reformation to the Restoration, 1560–1660* (Edinburgh: Edinburgh UP).

Howard, Ebenezer (1898, 1902, 1946, 1965),

Tomorrow: A Peaceful Path to Real Reform (London: Swan Sonnenschein; later re-issued as *Garden Cities of Tomorrow*).

Howarth, Thomas (1977), *Charles Rennie Mackintosh and the Modern Movement* (London: Routledge & Kegan Paul, 1977).

Howell, Peter (ed.) (1970), *Victorian South Wales* (London: Victorian Society).

—and Sutton (eds.) in conjunction with The Victorian Society (1989), *The Faber Guide to Victorian Churches* (London: Faber & Faber).

Howland, R. H., and Spencer, E. (1953), *The Architecture of Baltimore* (Baltimore: Johns Hopkins UP).

Howley, James (1993), *The Follies and Garden Buildings of Ireland* (New Haven: Yale UP).

Hubala, Erich (1987), *Balthasar Neumann 1687–1753* (Stuttgart: Cantz).

—(1989), *Baroque and Rococo* (New York: Universe Books).

—and Schweikhart (eds.) (1978), *Festschrift Herbert Siebenhüner* (Würzburg: Kommissionsverlag Ferdinand Schöningh).

Hubbard, Edward (1986), *The Buildings of Wales, Clwyd* (Harmondsworth: Penguin).

—(1991), *The Work of John Douglas* (London: Victorian Society).

Huber, Benedikt, and Steinegger, Jean-Claude (eds.) (1971), *Jean Prouvé: Prefabrication: Structures and Elements* (New York: Praeger).

Huelsen, Christian von (ed.) (1910), *Il libro di Giuliano da Sangallo* (Leipzig: Harrassowitz).

Hughes, James Quentin (1964), *Seaport: Architecture and Townscape in Liverpool* (London: Lund Humphries).

Humann, Karl (1904), *Magnesia am Mäander* (Berlin: Reimer).

Humbert, Jean-Marcel (1989), *L'Égyptomanie dans l'Art Occidental* (Paris: ACR).

—(ed.) (1996), *L'Égyptomanie à l'épreuve de l'archéologie* (Paris: Musée du Louvre, and Brussels: Éditions du Gram).

—Pantazzi, Michael, and Ziegler, Christiane (1994), *Égyptomania: L'Égypte dans l'art occidental* (Paris: Réunion des musées nationaux, and Ottawa: Musée des Beaux-Arts du Canada, and Paris: Spadem, Adago).

Hunt, John Dixon (1987), *William Kent, Landscape Garden Designer* (London: Zwemmer).

Hurry, J. B. (1928), *Imhotep, the Vizier and Physician of King Zoser* (London: Oxford UP).

Hussey, Christopher (1931), *The Work of Sir Robert Lorimer* (London: Country Life).

—(1958, 1965), *English Country Houses* (London: Country Life).

—(1967), *English Gardens and Landscapes, 1700–1750* (London: Country Life).

—(1967*a*), *The Picturesque* (London: Cass).

—(1989), *The Life of Sir Edwin Lutyens* (Woodbridge, Suffolk: Antique Collectors' Club).

Hüter, Karl Heinz (1967), *Henry van de Velde* (Berlin: Akademie Verlag).

—(1976), *Das Bauhaus in Weimar* (Berlin: Akademie Verlag).

Hüttinger, Eduard (1977), *Max Bill* (Zurich: ABC).

Hutton, Edward (1950), *The Cosmati: The Roman Marble Workers of the XIIth and XIIIth Centuries* (London: Routledge & Kegan Paul).

Huxley, G. L. (1959), *Anthemius of Tralles: A Study in Later Greek Geometry* (Cambridge, Mass.: Harvard UP).

Huxtable, Ada Louise (1960), on Kiesler in *New York Times* (27 Mar.): 2, 13.

—(1960*a*), *Pier Luigi Nervi* (London: Mayflower).

—(1961), *Museum of Modern Art* (New York: Doubleday).

—(1964), *Classic New York: Georgian Gentility to Greek Elegance* (New York: Doubleday).

—(1970), *Will They Ever Finish Bruckner Boulevard?* (New York: Macmillan).

—(1976), *Kicked a Building Lately?* (New York: Quadrangle).

—(1984), *The Tall Building Artistically Reconsidered: The Search for a Skyscraper Style* (New York: Pantheon).

—(1986), *Architecture, Anyone?* (New York: Random House).

—(1986*a*), *Goodbye History, Hello Hamburger* (Washington: Preservation Press).

—(1997), *The Unreal America: Architecture and Illusion* (New York: The New Press).

Iglauer, Edith (1981), *Seven Stones: A Portrait of Arthur Erickson* (Vancouver: Harbour).

Imbesi, Giuseppe, *et al.* (1991), *Riccardo Morandi* (Rome: Gangemi).

Ind, Rosemary (1983), *Emberton* (London: Solar Press).

Inskip, P. (1979), *Edwin Lutyens* (London: Academy Editions).

Inwood, Henry (1827), *The Erechtheion in Athens* (London: Carpenter).

—(1834), *The Resources of Design in the Architecture of Greece, Egypt, and Other Countries* (London: n.p.).

Ionides, Julia (1999), *Thomas Farnolls Pritchard of Shrewsbury* (Ludlow: Dog Rose Press).

Irizarry, Florita Z. Louie de (1983), *Louis Barragán, the Architect and his Work* (Monticello, Ill.: Vance).

Irving, Robert Grant (1981), *Indian Summer: Lutyens, Baker, and Imperial Delhi* (New Haven and London: Yale UP).

Isaacs, Reginald R. (1983–4), *Walter Gropius: Der Mensch und sein Werk* (Berlin: Mann).

Ison, Walter (1969), *The Georgian Buildings of Bath* (Bath: Kingsmead).

Iversen, Erik (1968), *Obelisks in Exile* (Copenhagen: Gad).

Iwicki, Zygmunt (1980), *Der Hochaltar der Kathedrale in Oliva* (Freiburg: HSV).
Ixnard, Pierre-Michel d' (1791), *Recueil d'Architecture* (Strasbourg: Treutel).
Jackson, Frank (1985), *Sir Raymond Unwin: Architect, Planner, and Visionary* (London: Zwemmer).
Jacobs, Jane (1961), *The Death and Life of Great American Cities* (New York: Random House).
—(1969), *The Economy of Cities* (New York: Random House).
—(1984), *Cities and the Wealth of Nations: Principles of Economic Life* (New York: Random House).
—(1992), *Systems of Survival: A Dialogue on the Moral Foundations of Commerce and Politics* (New York: Random House).
—(1996), *Edge of Empire: Postcolonialism and the City* (London: Routledge).
Jacobus, John (1962), *Philip Johnson* (New York: Braziller).
Jacques, David (1983), *Georgian Gardens: The Reign of Nature* (London: Batsford).
Jaffé, Hans L. C. (1956), *De Stijl 1917–1931* (Amsterdam: Meulenhoff).
James, Warren A. (ed.) (1988), *Ricardo Bofill: Taller de Arquitectura. Buildings and Projects 1960–1985* (New York: Rizzoli).
Jamot, Paul (1927), *A. G. Perret et l'architecture du béton armé* (Paris: Vanoest).
Jankel, A., and Morton, R. (1984), *Creative Computer Graphics* (Cambridge: Cambridge UP).
Janofske, Eckehard (1984), *Architektur-Räume: Idee und Gestalt bei Hans Scharoun* (Brunswick: Vieweg).
Jeanneret-Gris, Charles-Édouard (Le Corbusier) (1964, 1973–7), *The Complete Works* (London: Thames & Hudson, from 1964; see also the Zurich: Girsberger & Artemis edn., 1973–7).
—(1968), *The Modulor* (Cambridge, Mass.: MIT Press).
—(1973), *The Athens Charter* (New York: Grossman).
Jencks, Charles (1968), 'Adhocism on the South Bank', *Architectural Review*, 144/857 (July): 27–30 .
—(1971), *Architecture 2000: Predictions and Methods* (London: Studio Vista).
—(1972), *Adhocism* (London: Secker & Warburg).
—(1973), *Le Corbusier and the Tragic View of Architecture* (London: Allen Lane).
—(1973*a*), *Modern Movements in Architecture* (Harmondsworth: Penguin).
—(1977), *The Language of Post-Modern Architecture* (New York: Rizzoli).
—(1979), *Bizarre Architecture* (London: Academy Editions).
—(1980), *Late-Modern Architecture and Other Essays* (London: Academy Editions).
—(1980*a*), *Post-Modern Classicism* (London: Academy Editions).
—(1982), *Current Architecture* (London: Academy Editions).
—(1982*a*), *Free Style Classicism* (London: Academy Editions).
—(ed.) (1983), 'Abstract Representation', *Architectural Design*, 53, 7/8.
—(1985), *Towards a Symbolic Architecture* (London: Academy Editions).
—(1987), *What is Post-Modernism?* (London: Academy Editions).
—(1988), *Architecture Today* (London: Academy Editions).
—(1988*a*), *Post-Modernism: The New Classicism in Architecture and Urbanism* (London: Academy Editions).
—(1990), *The New Moderns* (London: Academy Editions).
—and Baird, G. (eds.) (1969), *Meaning in Architecture* (London: Barrie & Rockliff).
Jenkins, Charles E. (1895), 'A White Enamelled Building', *Architectural Record*, 4: 299–306.
Jensen, Robert, and Conway, Patricia (1983), *Ornamentalism: The New Decorativeness in Architecture and Design* (London: Allen Lane).
Jericke, Alfred, and Dolgner, Dieter (1975), *Der Klassizismus in der Baugeschichte Weimars* (Weimar: Böhlhaus).
Jervis, Simon (1983), *High Victorian Design* (Woodbridge: Boydell Press).
—(1984), *The Penguin Dictionary of Design and Designers* (London: Allen Lane).
Jessen, Peter (1892), *Das Ornamentwerk des Daniel Marots* (Berlin: Wasmuth).
Jodard, Paul (1994), *Raymond Loewy* (London: HarperCollins).
Jodice, Romano (1988), *L'architettura del ferro: gli Stati Uniti (1776–1876)* (Rome: Bulzoni).
Jodidio, Philip (1993), *Contemporary American Architects* (Cologne: Taschen).
—(1995), *Contemporary California Architects* (Cologne: Taschen).
—(1995*a*), *Contemporary European Architects*, iii (Cologne: Taschen).
—(1996), *Contemporary American Architects*, ii (Cologne: Taschen).
—(1996*a*), *Contemporary European Architects*, iv (Cologne: Taschen).
—(1997), *Contemporary American Architects*, iii (Cologne: Taschen).
—(1997*a*), *Contemporary Japanese Architects*, ii (Cologne: Taschen).
Joedicke, Jürgen (1963), *Shell Architecture* (London: Tiranti).
—(ed.) (1963*a*), *Das Werk van den Broek und Bakema* (Stuttgart: Krämer).
—(1976), *Architectengemeenschap van den Broek en Bakema* (Stuttgart: Krämer).

—and Plath, Christian (1968), *Die Weissenhofsiedlung* (Stuttgart: Krämer).
Johnson, Diane Chalmers (1979), *American Art Nouveau* (New York: Abrams).
Johnson, Donald Leslie (1977), *The Architecture of Walter Burley Griffin* (South Melbourne: Macmillan of Australia).
—(1980), *Australian Architecture 1901–51* (Sydney: Sydney UP).
Johnson, J. Stewart (1980), *Eileen Gray—Designer* (London: Debrett).
Johnson, Philip (1969), *Machine Art* (New York: Museum of Modern Art & Arno Press; repr. of 1934 edn.).
—(1978), *Mies van der Rohe* (New York: Museum of Modern Art).
—and Wigley, Mark (1988), *Deconstructivist Architecture* (New York: Museum of Modern Art).
Jones, Barbara (1974), *Follies and Grottoes* (London: Constable).
Jones, Bernard E. (1956), *Freemason's Guide and Compendium* (London: Harrap).
Jones, Cranston (ed.) (1962), *Marcel Breuer: Buildings and Projects* (New York: Praeger).
Jones, Owen (1843), *Views on the Nile* (London: Graves & Warmsley).
—(1854), *An Apology for the Colouring of the Greek Court at the Crystal Palace* (London: Bradbury & Evans and Crystal Palace Library).
—(1863), *Lectures on Architecture and the Decorative Arts* (London: n.p.).
—(1868), *Grammar of Ornament* (London: Quaritch).
—and Bonomi, Joseph (1854), *Description of the Egyptian Court Erected at the Crystal Palace* (London: Crystal Palace Library).
—and Goury, Jules (1836–45), *Plans, Elevations, Sections, and Details of the Alhambra* (London: Jones).
Jordan, Terry G. (1985), *American Log Buildings* (Chapel Hill, NC: University of North Carolina Press).
Jordy, William H. (1976), *American Buildings and Their Architects* (Garden City, NY: Anchor).
—and Coe, Ralph (eds.) (1961), *American Architecture and Other Writings* (Cambridge, Mass.: Belknap).
Jørgensen, Lisbet Balslev (1979), *Enfamiliehuset* (Copenhagen: Gyldendal).
Josephson, Ragnar (1930), *L'Architecte de Charles XII, Nicodème Tessin* (Paris and Brussels: Van Oest).
—(1930–1), *Tessin* (Stockholm: Norstedt).
—(1963), *Carl August Ehrensvaerd* (Stockholm: Norstedt).
Jourdain, Frantz (1893), *L'Atelier Chantorel* (Paris: Charpentier & Fasquelle).
—(1895), *Les Décorés* (Paris: Empnis).
—(1902), *De Choses et d'Autres* (Paris: Empnis).
—(1914), *Propos d'un Isolé en Faveur de Son Temps* (Paris: Figuière).
Jullian, René (1989), *Tony Garnier, constructeur et utopiste* (Paris: Sers).
Junghanns, Kurt (1970), *Bruno Taut: 1880–1938* (Berlin: Henschelverlag).
Jurecka, Charlotte (1986), *Brücken. Historische Entwicklung—Faszination der Technik* (Vienna: A. Schroll).
Kadatz, Hans-Joachim (1983), *Georg Wenzeslaus von Knobelsdorff: Baumeister Friedrichs II* (Munich: Beck).
—(1986), *Friedrich Wilhelm von Erdmannsdorff: Wegbereiter des deutschen Frühklassizismus in Anhalt-Dessau* (Berlin: Verlag für Bauwesen).
Kahn, Albert (Associated Architects and Engineers Incorporated) (1948), *Architecture* (New York: Albert Kahn Associated).
Kahn, Ely Jacques (1935), *Design in Art and Industry* (New York: Scribner).
—(1969), *A Building Goes Up* (New York: Simon & Schuster).
Kahn, Louis Isadore (1969), *Louis I. Kahn: Talks with Students* (Houston, Tex.: Rice University).
—(1973), *The Notebooks and Drawings of Louis I. Kahn* (Cambridge, Mass.: MIT Press).
—(1975), *Light is the Theme: Louis I. Kahn and the Kimbell Art Museum* (Fort Worth, Tex.: Kimbell Art Foundation).
—(1977), *The Complete Works 1935–1974* (Boulder, Colo.: Westview).
—and Cantacuzino, Sherban (eds.) (1974), *Carlo Scarpa* (London: RIBA).
Kallmann, George (1959), 'The "Action" Architecture of a New Generation', *Architectural Forum*, 111/4 (Oct.): 132–7, 244.
Kallmorgen, Werner (ed.) (1969), *Schumacher und Hamburg* (Hamburg: Christians).
Kalman, Harold (1968), *The Railway Hotels and the Development of the Château Style in Canada* (Victoria: University of Victoria, Maltwood Museum).
—(1994), *A History of Canadian Architecture* (Toronto, New York, and Oxford: Oxford UP).
Kalnein, Wend, Graf (1956), *Das Kurfürstliche Schloss Clemensruhe in Poppelsdorf* (Düsseldorf: Schwann).
—(1995), *Architecture in France in the Eighteenth Century* (London: Yale UP).
—and Levey, Michael (1972), *Art and Architecture of the Eighteenth Century in France* (Harmondsworth: Penguin).
Kamerling, Bruce (1979), *Irving Gill* (San Diego, Calif.: Historical Society).
Kamm, Peter (1973), *Roland Rainer: Bauten, Schriften, und Projekte* (Tübingen: Wasmuth).
Kamm-Kyburz, Christine (1983), *Der Architekt*

Ottavio Bertotti-Scamozzi 1719–1790 (Berne: Benteli).

Kaplan, Wendy (1987), *'The Art that is Life': The Arts and Crafts Movement in America 1875–1920* (Boston: Little, Brown).

Karl, Thomas (ed.) (1991), *Die Baumeisterfamilie Munggenast* (St Pölten: Kulturverwaltung der Landeshauptstadt).

Karlinger, Hans (1932), *Theodor Fischer. Ein deutscher Baumeister* (Munich: Callwey).

Karpowicz, Mariusz (1991), *Baroque in Poland* (Warsaw: Arkady).

Kasper, Alfons, and Strache, Wolf (1957), *Steinhausen* (Stuttgart: Strache).

Kastholm, Jørgen (1968), *Arne Jacobsen* (Copenhagen: Høst).

Kaufmann, Edgar (1956), *Louis Sullivan and the Architecture of Free Enterprise* (Chicago: Art Institute).

—(ed.) (1970), *The Rise of an American Architecture* (New York: Praeger).

Kaufmann, Emil (1952), *Three Revolutionary Architects: Boullée, Ledoux, and Lequeu* (Philadelphia: American Philosophical Society).

—(1955), *Architecture in the Age of Reason: Baroque and Post-Baroque in England, Italy, and France* (Cambridge, Mass.: Harvard UP).

Kaufmann, Thomas DaCosta (1995), *Court, Cloister & City: The Art and Culture of Central Europe 1450–1800* (London: Weidenfeld & Nicolson).

Keller, Harald (1971), *Goethe, Palladio, und England* (Munich: Beck).

Kelley, William (ed.) (1960), *Miracle in the Evening: An Autobiography of Norman Bel Geddes* (Garden City, NY: Doubleday).

Kelly, Alison (1990), *Mrs Coade's Stone* (Upton-upon-Severn, Worcestershire: Self Publishing Association).

Kelly, John Frederick (1948), *Early Connecticut Meetinghouses* (New York: Columbia UP).

Kemp, Jim (1987), *American Vernacular: Regional Influences in Architecture and Interior Design* (New York: Viking).

Kemper, Carl (1966), *Der Bau: Studien der Architektur und Plastik des ersten Goetheanums* (Stuttgart: Verlag Freies Geisteleben).

Kennedy, Roger G. (1989), *Greek Revival America* (New York: Stuart, Taburi & Chang).

Kennes, J., Vanderperren, J., and Victoire, J. (1978), *L'architecture éclectique d'Henri Beyaert* (Brussels: Banque Nationale).

Kerber, Bernhard L. (1971), *Andrea Pozzo* (Berlin and New York: de Gruyter).

Kerber, Ottmar (1947), *Von Bramante zu Lukas von Hildebrandt* (Stuttgart: Kohlhammer).

Keynes, Geoffrey (1960), *A Bibliography of Dr Robert Hooke* (Oxford: Clarendon Press).

Khan, Hasan-Uddin (1987), *Charles Correa: Architect in India* (London: Butterworth).

—(1995), *Contemporary Asian Architects* (Cologne: Taschen).

Khan-Magomedov, Selim Omarovich (1975), *M. J. Ginsburg* (Milan: Angeli).

—(1986), *Alexandr Vesnin and Russian Constructivism* (New York: Rizzoli).

—(1987), *Pioneers of Soviet Architecture: The Search for New Solutions in the 1920s and 1930s* (New York: Rizzoli).

Kidder-Smith, G. E. (1964), *The New Churches of Europe* (New York: Holt).

Kidney, Walter C. (1974), *The Architecture of Choice: Eclecticism in America, 1880–1930* (New York: Braziller).

Kienzle, Hermann (1937), *Karl Moser: 1860–1936* (Zurich: Züricher Kunstgesellschaft).

Kiesler, Frederick J. (1964), *Frederick Kiesler: Environmental Sculpture* (New York: Guggenheim Museum).

—(1966), *Inside the Endless House* (New York: Simon & Schuster).

Kieven, Elisabeth (ed.) (1988), *Ferdinando Fuga e l'architettura romana del settecento* (Rome: Multigrafica).

Kikutake, Kiyonori (1973), *Works and Methods: 1956–1970* (Tokyo: Bijutus).

Kilham, Walter Harrington (1974), *Raymond Hood, Architect: Form through Foundation in the American Skyscraper* (New York: Architectural Book Pub. Co.).

Killy, Herta Elisabeth, Pfankuch, Peter, and Scheper, Dirk (1965), *Poelzig-Endell-Moll und die Breslauer Kunstakademie* (Berlin: Akademie der Künste).

Kimball, Sidney Fiske (1966), *Domestic Architecture of the American Colonies and of the Early Republic* (New York: Dover; repr. of 1922 edn.).

—(1966*a*), *Mr Samuel McIntire, Carver: The Architect of Salem* (Gloucester, Mass.: Smith; repr. of 1940 edn.).

—(1968), *Thomas Jefferson, Architect* (New York: Da Capo; repr. of 1916 edn.).

—(1980), *The Creation of the Rococo Decorative Style* (New York: Dover).

King, Anthony (1992), *The Bungalow: The Production of a Global Culture* (London: Routledge & Kegan Paul).

King, David (1991), *The Complete Works of Robert and James Adam* (Oxford: Butterworth, with the University of Stirling).

King, Georgiana Goddard (1927), *Mudéjar* (London and New York: Longmans, Green).

Kirichenko, Evgenia I. (1975), *Fedor Shekhtel* (Moscow: Stroiizdat).

Kirker, Harold (1969), *The Architecture of Charles Bulfinch* (Cambridge, Mass.: Harvard UP).

Kirkham, Patricia (1995), *Charles and Ray Eames:*

Designers of the Twentieth Century (Cambridge, Mass., and London: MIT Press).

Kismarty-Lechner, Jeno (1961), *Lechner Ödön* (Budapest: KA).

Kite, Elizabeth S. (ed.) (1929), *L'Enfant and Washington, 1791–1792* (Baltimore: Johns Hopkins UP).

Klaiber, Hans Andreas Ernst (1959), *Der Württembergische Oberbaudirektor Philippe de la Guêpière* (Stuttgart: Kohlhammer).

Kleiner, Leopold (1927), *Josef Hoffmann* (Berlin: Hübsch).

Klenze, Leo von (1830), *Sammlung architectonischer Entwürfe* (Munich: Cotta).

—(1833), *Anweisung zur Architektur des christlichen Cultus* (Munich: n.p.).

—(1843), *Die Walhalla in artistischer und technischer Beziehung* (Munich: n.p.).

Kliemann, Helga (1973), *Wassili Luckhardt* (Tübingen: Wasmuth).

Klotz, Heinrich (1970), *Die Frühwerke Brunelleschis und die mittelalterliche Tradition* (Berlin: Mann).

—(1977), *Architektur in der Bundesrepublik: Gespräche mit Günter Behnisch* et al. (Frankfurt-am-Main: Ullstein).

—(1984), *Moderne und Postmoderne: Architektur der Gegenwart 1960–80* (Brunswick: Vieweg).

—(ed.) (1986), *Vision der Moderne: das Prinzip Konstruktion* (Munich: Prestel).

—(1988), *The History of Postmodern Architecture* (Cambridge, Mass.: MIT Press).

Knell, Keiner, and Wessenberg, Burkhardt (1984), *Vitruv-Kolloquium des deutschen Archäologen-Verbandes e.v.* (Darmstadt: Die Hochschule).

Knight, Richard Payne (1794), *The Landscape: A Didactic Poem* (London: n.p.).

—(1972), *An Analytical Inquiry into the Principles of Taste* (Westmead: Gregg; repr. of 1805 edn.).

Knoblauch, Gustav, and Hollen, F. (1878), *Die neue Synagoge in Berlin* (Berlin: Ernst & Korn).

Knoop, Douglas, and Jones, G. P. (1949), *The Genesis of Freemasonry* (Manchester: Manchester UP).

Knox, Bryan (1962), *The Architecture of Prague and Bohemia* (London: Faber).

Koch, Alexander (ed.) (1889–1931), *Academy Architecture and Architectural Review* (London: Koch).

—(1901), *Die Ausstellung der Darmstädter Künstlerkolonie* (Darmstadt: Koch).

—(1902), *Meister der Innenkunst: Haus eines Kunstfreundes des M. H. Baillie Scott* (Darmstadt: Koch).

—(1907), *British Competitions in Architecture* (London: Academy Editions).

—(1908), *London County Council Hall: Final Competition* (London: Academy Editions).

Koch, Robert (1966), *Louis C. Tiffany: Rebel in Glass* (New York: Crown).

Koepf, Hans (1969), *Die gotischen Planreise der Wiener Sammlungen* (Vienna: Böhlaus).

Kohlmaier, Georg, and Sartory, Barna von (1986), *Houses of Glass: A Nineteenth-Century Building Type*, tr. John C. Harvey (Cambridge, Mass.: MIT Press).

Kohn, Wendy (ed.) (1996), *Moshe Safdie* (London: Academy Editions).

Koksa, Giorgio (1971), *S. Girolamo degli Schiavoni* (Rome: Marietti).

Kommer, Björn R. (1974), *Nicodemus Tessin der Jüngere und das Stockholmer Schloss* (Heidelberg: Winter).

Konwiarz, Richard (1926), *Die Baukunst Breslau* (Breslau: Grass, Barth).

Koolhaas, Rem (1978), *Delirious New York* (New York: Oxford UP).

Kopp, Anatole (1970), *Town and Revolution* (New York: Braziller).

—(1978), *L'architecture de la période Stalinienne* (Grenoble: Presses Universitaires).

Koppelkamm, Stefan (1981), *Glasshouses and Wintergardens of the Nineteenth Century*, tr. Kathrine Talbot (New York: Rizzoli).

Korn, Arthur (1953), *History Builds the Town* (London: Lund Humphries).

—(1967), *Glass in Modern Architecture* (London: Barrie & Rockliff).

Kornwolf, James D. (1972), *M. H. Baillie Scott and the Arts and Crafts Movement* (Baltimore: Johns Hopkins UP).

Korth, Thomas, and Poeschke, Joachim (eds.) (1987), *Balthasar Neumann: Kunstgeschichtliche Beiträge zum Jubiläumsjahr 1987* (Munich: Hirmer).

Köster, Baldur (1990), *Palladio in Amerika: die Kontinuität Klassizistischen Bauens in den USA* (Munich: Prestel).

Kostof, Spiro (1995), *A History of Architecture: Settings and Rituals* (New York and Oxford: Oxford UP).

Kotěra, Jan (1902), *Meine und meiner Schüler Arbeiten: 1898–1901* (Vienna: Schroll).

Koulermos, Panos (1995), *Twentieth Century European Rationalism*, ed. James Steele (London: Academy Editions).

Krafft, Johann Karl (1801–3), *Plans . . . etc., des plus belles maisons et des hôtels construits à Paris* (Paris: Krafft & Ransonnette).

Krapf, Michael (1979), *Baumeister Gumpp* (Vienna and Munich: Herold).

Krautheimer, Richard (1986), *Early Christian and Byzantine Architecture* (Harmondsworth: Penguin, 1965, revised edn.).

—and Krautheimer-Hess, Trude (1956), *Lorenzo Ghiberti* (Princeton: Princeton UP).

Krečic, Peter (1993), *Plečnik, the Complete Works* (New York: Whitney Library of Design).

Kreis, Wilhelm (1927), *Über die Zusammenhänge von Kultur, Zivilisation, und Kunst* (Berlin: Hübsch).

Kreisel, Heinrich (1932), *Schloss Aschaffenburg und Pompejanum* (Munich: Nimmer).

—— (1953), *Das Schloss zu Pommersfelden* (Munich: Nimmer).

Krejcar, Jaromír (ed.) (1928), *L'architecture contemporaine en Tchécoslovaquie* (Prague: Orbis).

Kretzschmar, Frank Joachim (1981), *Pierre Contant d'Ivry: Ein Beitrag zur französischen Architektur des 18. Jahrhunderts* (Cologne: University).

Kreytenberg, Gert (1974), *Der Dom zu Florenz* (Berlin: Mann).

Kriéger, Antoine (1937), *La Madeleine* (Paris: de Brouwer).

Krier, Léon (1978), *Rational Architecture* (Brussels: Archives d'architecture moderne).

—— (1981), *Léon Krier: Drawings 1967–1980* (Brussels: Archives d'architecture moderne).

—— (ed.) (1985), *Albert Speer: Architecture 1932–1942* (Brussels: Archives d'architecture moderne).

Krier, Rob (1979), *Urban Space* (New York: Rizzoli).

Krimmel, Bernd (ed.) (1978), *Darmstadt in der Zeit des Klassizismus und der Romantik* (Darmstadt: Stadt Darmstadt).

Krinksy, Carol Herselle (1978), *Rockefeller Center* (New York: Oxford UP).

—— (1988), *Gordon Bunshaft of Skidmore, Owings, & Merrill* (Cambridge, Mass.: MIT Press).

—— (1996), *Synagogues of Europe: Architecture, History, Meaning* (New York: Dover).

Kroha, J., and Hrüza, J. (1973), *Sovetska architektonika avant garda* (Prague: Odeon).

Kron, J., and Slesin, S. (1979), *High-Tech: The Industrial Style and Source Book for the Home* (London: Allen Lane).

Kubach, Hans Erich (1986), *Romanesque Architecture* (London: Faber & Faber, and Milan: Electa).

Kubinszky, Mihály (1977), *Bohuslav Fuchs* (Budapest: Akadémiai Kladó).

Kubler, George (1982), *Building the Escorial* (Princeton: Princeton UP).

—— (1984), *Art and Architecture of Ancient America* (Harmondsworth: Penguin, 1962, rev. edn.).

—— and Soria, Martin (1959), *Art and Architecture in Spain and Portugal and their American Dominions 1500–1800* (Harmondsworth: Penguin).

Kuchamov, A. M. (1976), *Pavlovsk: Dvoretsi i Park* (Leningrad: n.p.).

Kuděkka, Zdeněk (1966), *Bohuslav Fuchs* (Prague: Nčvu).

Kuhner, Robert A. (1975), *Eero Saarinen: His Life and Work* (Monticello, Ill.: Council of Planning Librarians).

Kulka, Heinrich (ed.) (1931), *Adolf Loos: Das Werk des Architekten* (Vienna: Schroll).

Kulturmann, Udo (1958), *Wassili und Hans Luckhardt* (Tübingen: Wasmuth).

—— (ed.) (1970), *Kenzo Tange, 1946–1969: Architecture and Urban Design* (New York: Praeger).

Kuran, Aptullah (1987), *Sinan: The Grand Old Master of Ottoman Architecture* (Istanbul: Ada Press).

Kurokawa, Kisho Noriaki (1977), *Metabolism in Architecture* (Boulder, Colo.: Westview Press).

—— (1988), *Kisho Kurokawa: The Architecture of Symbiosis*, with Introduction by François Chaslin (New York: Rizzoli).

—— (1990), *Intercultural Architecture: The Philosophy of Symbiosis* (London: Academy Editions).

—— (1992), *Kisho Kurokawa: From Metabolism to Symbiosis* (London: Academy Editions).

Kurtz, Donna C., and Boardman, John (1971), *Greek Burial Customs* (London: Thames & Hudson).

Kuspit, D., *et al.* (1986), *Neo-Neo-Classicism* (Annadale on Hudson, Bard College: Edith C. Blum Art Institute).

Kuyper, W. (1980), *Dutch Classicist Architecture: A Survey of Dutch Architecture, Gardens, and Anglo-Dutch Architectural Relations from 1625 to 1700* (Delft: Delft UP).

Labaree, Benjamin Woods (ed.) (1957), *Samuel McIntire: A Bicentennial Symposium 1757–1957* (Salem, Mass.: Essex Institute).

Labò, Mario (1947), *Giuseppe Terragni* (Milan: Il Balcone).

Labrouste, Henri (1877), *Les Temples de Paestum* (Paris: Firmin-Didot).

Labrouste, Léon (1885), *La Bibliothèque Nationale* (Paris: Lutier).

—— (1902), *Esthétique monumentale* (Paris: Schmid).

Ladendorff, Heinz (1935), *Der Bildhauer und Baumeister Andreas Schlüter* (Berlin: Deutscher Verein für Kunstwissenschaft).

Lafever, Minard (1829), *The Young Builder's General Instructor* (Newark, NJ: Tuttle).

—— (1838), *The Modern Practice of Staircase and Handrail Construction* (New York: Appleton).

—— (1856), *The Architectural Instructor* (New York: Putnam).

—— (1968), *The Beauties of Modern Architecture* (New York: Da Capo; repr. of 1835 edn.).

—— (1969), *The Modern Builder's Guide* (New York: Dover, and Magnolia, Mass.: Smith; repr. of 1833 edn.).

Laloux, Victor-A.-F. (1888), *L'Architecture Grecque* (Paris: Quantin).

Lambot, Ian (1989–91), *Norman Foster: Team 4 and Foster Associates: Buildings and Projects* (London and Hong Kong: Watermark).

Lambourne, Lionel (1980), *Utopian Craftsmen:*

The Arts and Crafts Movement from the Cotswolds to Chicago (London: Astragal Books).
—(1996), *The Aesthetic Movement* (London: Phaidon).
Lammert, Marlies (1964), *David Gilly: Ein Baumeister des deutschen Klassizismus* (Berlin: Akademie-Verlag).
Lampl, Sixtus (1979), *Johann Baptist Zimmermanns Schlierseer Anfänge* (Schliersee: Lampl).
Lampugnani, Vittorio Magnano (1982), *Visionary Architecture of the Twentieth Century* (London: Thames & Hudson).
—(ed.) (1988), *Encylopaedia of 20th Century Architecture* (London: Thames & Hudson).
Lancaster, Clay (1985), *The American Bungalow 1880–1930* (New York: Abbeville Press).
Landale-Drummond, Andrew Alastair (1934), *The Church Architecture of Protestantism* (Edinburgh: T. & T. Clark).
Landau, Royston (1968), *New Directions in British Architecture* (London: Studio Vista).
Landau, Sarah Bradford (1979), *Edward T. and William A. Potter: American Victorian Architects* (New York: Garland).
—and Condit, Carl W. (1986), *The Rise of the New York Skyscraper 1865–1913* (New Haven: Yale UP).
Landisch, Bohumil (1968), *Prague* (Prague: Olympia).
Landy, Jacob (1970), *The Architecture of Minard Lafever* (New York: Columbia UP).
Lane, Barbara Miller (1985), *Architecture and Politics in Germany 1918–1945* (Cambridge, Mass.: Harvard UP).
Langberg, Harald (1950), *Omkring C. F. Hansen* (Copenhagen: Prior).
Lange, Gunter (1965), *Alexis de Châteauneuf: Ein Hamburger Baumeister (1799–1853)* (Hamburg: Verlag Weltarchiv).
Langenskiöld, Erik (1938), *Michele Sanmicheli, the Architect of Verona* (Uppsala: Almqvist & Wiksell).
—(1959), *Pierre Bullet: Royal Architect* (Stockholm: Almqvist & Wiksell).
Langhans, Karl Ferdinand (1810), *Über Theater oder Bemerkungen über Katakustik in Beziehung auf Theater* (Berlin: Hayn).
Langley, Batty (1724), *An Accurate Description of Newgate* (London: Warner).
—(1726), *Practical Geometry* (London: Innys).
—(1728), *A Sure Method of Improving Estates* (London: Clay & Browne).
—(1729), *Pomona* (London: Strahan).
—(1729*a*), *Sure Guide to Builders* (London: Wilcox & Heath).
—(1734), *Young Builder's Rudiments* (London: Millan).
—(1736), *Ancient Masonry* (London: The Author).
—(1738), *The Builder's Compleat Assistant* (London: Ware).
—(1739), *The Builder's Chest-Book* (London: Wilcox & Hodges).
—(1742), *The Measurer's Jewel* (London: Wilcox).
—(1745), *The City and Country Builder's and Workman's Treasury of Designs: Or the Art of Drawing and Working the Ornamented Parts of Architecture* (London: S. Harding—new edn. of original of 1740).
—(1747), *Gothic Architecture improved by Rules and Proportions in many Grand Designs* (London: Millan).
—(1756), *The Workman's Golden Rule* (London: Ware).
—(1970), *The Builder's Director or Bench-Mate* (New York: Blom; repr. of 1751 edn.).
—(1970*a*), *The Builder's Jewel* (New York: Blom; repr. of 1757 edn.).
—(1971), *New Principles of Gardening* (Farnborough: Gregg; repr. of 1728 edn.).
Langmead, Donald (1996), *Willem Marinus Dudok, a Dutch Modernist: A Bio-Bibliography* (Westport, Conn.: Greenwood Press).
Lankilde, Hans Erling (1960), *Arkitekten Kay Fisker* (Copenhagen: Arkitektens Forlag).
Lapadula, Attilio (1969), *Roma e la regione nell'epoca napoleonica* (Rome: IEPI).
Laprade, Albert (1960), *François d'Orbay architecte de Louis XIV* (Paris: Vincent, Fréal).
Larmour, Paul (1987), *Belfast: An Illustrated Architectural Guide* (Belfast: Friar's Bush Press).
—(1992), *The Arts and Crafts Movement in Ireland* (Belfast: Friar's Bush Press).
Larsson, Lars Olof (1983), *Albert Speer: Le Plan de Berlin 1937–1943* (Brussels: Archives d'Architecture Moderne).
Lasdun, Denys (1984), *Architecture in an Age of Scepticism* (New York: Oxford UP).
—& Partners (1976), *A Language and a Theme: The Architecture of Denys Lasdun & Partners* (London: RIBA).
Lassalle, Émile (1846), *Les Principaux Monuments Funéraires du Père-Lachaise* . . . etc. (Paris: Bédelet).
Lassus, Jean-Baptiste-Antoine (1842–67), *Monographie de la Cathédrale de Chartres* (Paris: Imprimerie Nationale).
—(1858), *Album de Villard de Honnecourt* (Paris: Imprimerie Nationale).
Latham, Ian (1980), *Joseph Maria Olbrich* (New York: Rizzoli).
—(ed.) (1980*a*), *New Free Style: Arts and Crafts: Art Nouveau: Secession* (London: Architectural Design).
Laugier, Marc-Antoine (1753), *Essai sur l'Architecture* (Paris: Duchesne). Another edition, augmented with a Dictionary of terms and plates to explain the terms was published in Paris in 1755. *See also* the version translated

by W. & A. Hermann (Los Angeles: Hennessey, 1977).

Laugier, Marc-Antoine (1753*a*), *Jugement d'un amateur sur l'exposition des tableaux* (Paris: Duchesne).

—(1765), *Observations sur l'Architecture* (The Hague: Desaint).

Lavagnino, Emilio (1961), *L'arte moderna dai neo-classici ai contemporanei* (Turin: Unione Tipografico-Editrice Torinese).

Lavedan, Pierre (1952–60), *Histoire de l'urbanisme* (Paris: Laurens).

—(1975), *Histoire de l'urbanisme à Paris* (Paris: Hachette).

Lavin, Irving (1980), *Bernini and the Unity of the Visual Arts* (New York: Morgan Library, and Oxford: Oxford UP).

—*et al.* (1981), *Drawings by Gianlorenzo Bernini from the Museum der Bildenden Künste, Leipzig* (Princeton: Art Museum).

Lawrence, Arnold Walter (1983), *Greek Architecture* (Harmondsworth: Penguin, 1957, revised edn.).

Layna Serrano, Francisco (1941), *El Palacio del Infantado en Guadalajara* (Madrid: Hauser & Menet).

Lazard, Pierre E. (1934), *Vauban: 1633–1707* (Paris: Alcan).

Leach, Peter (1988), *James Paine* (London: Zwemmer).

Leeds, William Henry (ed.) (1836), *Moller's Memorials of German Gothic Architecture* (London: Weale).

—(1839), *The Travellers' Club House* (London: Weale).

—(ed.) (1862), *A Treatise on the Decorative Part of Civil Architecture by William Chambers* (London: Lockwood).

—(1904), *Rudimentary Architecture: The Orders and their Aesthetic Principles* (London: Crosby; corrected version of original edn. of 1848).

Leemans, Herthe (1972), *De Sint-Gommaruskerk te Lier* (Antwerp and Utrecht: Nederlandsche Boekhandel).

Lees-Milne, James (1951), *Tudor Renaissance* (London: Batsford).

—(1953), *The Age of Inigo Jones* (London: Batsford).

—(1970), *English Country Houses* (Feltham: Country Life).

Leet, Stephen (ed.) (1990), *Franco Albani: Architecture and Design 1934–1977* (Princeton: Princeton UP).

Leeuwen, Thomas A. P. van (1988), *The Skyward Trend of Thought: The Metaphysics of the American Skyscraper* (Cambridge, Mass.: MIT Press).

Legner, Anton (ed.) (1978–80), *Die Parler und der schöne Stil 1350–1400* (Cologne: Museen der Stadt Köln).

Lehman, Karl (1980), *Thomas Jefferson, American Humanist* (Chicago: University of Chicago Press; repr. of 1947 edn.).

Lehoux, Françoise (1966–8), *Jean de France, duc de Berry* (Paris: Picard).

Leich, Jean Ferriss (1980), *Architectural Visions: The Drawings of Hugh Ferriss* (New York: Whitney Library of Design).

Lelievre, Pierre (1988), *Nantes au XVIIIe siècle: Urbanisme et Architecture* (Paris: Picard).

Lemaresquier, Charles-Henri-Camille (1938), *Institut de France. Académie des Beaux-Arts. Notice sur la vie . . . de Victor Laloux* (Paris: Firmin-Didot).

Lemoine, Bertrand (1984), *Gustave Eiffel* (Paris: Hazan).

—(1986), *L'architecture du fer: France, XIXe siècle* (Seyssel: Champ Vallom).

Lenning, Henry (1951), *Art Nouveau* (The Hague: Nijhoff).

Léon, Paul (1951), *La Vie des Monuments Français* (Paris: Picard).

Leonhardt, Fritz (1984), *Bridges, Æsthetics and Design* (Cambridge, Mass.: MIT Press).

Leoni, Giacomo (1742), *The Architecture of A. Palladio, Revis'd, Design'd, and Publish'd by Giacomo Leoni, a Venetian: Architect to His Most Serene Highness, the Elector Palatine* (London: Ward; later version of the 1715–20 edn.).

—(1755), *The Architecture of Leon Battista Alberti* (London: Owen; later version of the 1726 edn.).

Lesage, Pierre-Charles (1806), *Notice pour servir à l'éloge de M. Perronet* (Paris: Bernard).

Lescaze, William Edmond (1942), *On Being an Architect* (New York: Putnam).

Leśnikowski, Wojciech (ed.) (1996), *East European Modernism: Architecture in Czechoslovakia, Hungary, & Poland between the Wars* (London: Thames & Hudson).

Lethaby, William Richard (1935), *Philip Webb and his Work* (Oxford: H. Milford for Oxford UP).

Leutheusser, Sabine (1993), *Die Barocken Ausstattungs Programme der Ehemaligen Zisterzien Abteikirchen Waldsassen, Fürstenfeld, Raitenhaslach* (Munich: Tuduv).

Lever, Jill, and Harris, John (1993), *Illustrated Dictionary of Architecture 800–1914* (London: Faber & Faber).

Levi, Rino (1974), *Rino Levi* (Milan: Edizione di Comunità).

Levine, Neil (1996), *The Architecture of Frank Lloyd Wright* (Princeton: Princeton UP).

Lévi-Strauss, Claude (1963), *Structural Anthropology* (New York: Basic Books).

Lewcock, Ronald (1963), *Early Nineteenth-Century Architecture in South Africa* (Cape Town: Balkema).

Lewell, J. (1985), *Computer Graphics* (London: Orbis).

Lewis, Douglas (1979), *The Late Baroque Churches of Venice* (New York and London: Garland).

Lewis, Philippa, and Darley, Gillian (1986), *Dictionary of Ornament* (London: Macmillan).

Lewis, W. Sheldon (1960), *Horace Walpole* (New York: Pantheon).

—(1973), *A Guide to the Life of Horace Walpole* (New Haven: Yale UP).

Lhotsky, Alphons (1941), *Die Baugeschichte der Museen und den neun Burg* (Vienna: Kunsthistorisches Museum).

Licht, Hugo (ed.) (1877), *Die Architektur Berlins* (Berlin: Wasmuth).

—(1879–82), *Die Architektur Deutschlands* (Berlin: Wasmuth).

—(1882), *Die Architektur der Gegenwart* (Berlin: Wasmuth).

—(1886–1900), *Die Architektur der Gegenwart* (Berlin: Wasmuth).

—(1900), *Architektonische Details von ausgeführten Bauwerken* (Berlin: Wasmuth).

—(1901–6), *Charakteristische Details zu ausgeführten Bauwerken* (Berlin: Wasmuth).

—(1901–14), *Die Architektur des XX. Jahrhunderts: Zeitschrift für moderne Baukunst* (Berlin: Wasmuth).

Lieb, Norbert (1941), *Münchener Barockbaumeister: Leben und Schaften in Stadt und Land* (Munich: Schnell & Steiner).

—(1976), *Barock-Baumeister* (Munich: Schnell & Steiner).

—(1982), *Johann Michael Fischer: Baumeister und Raumschöpfer im späten Barock Süddeutschlands* (Regensburg: Pustet).

—(1988), *München. Die Geschichte seiner Kunst* (Munich: Callwey).

—(1992), *Barockkirchen zwischen Donau und Alpen* (Munich: Hirmer).

—and Dieth, Franz (1976), *Die Vorarlberger Barockbaumeister* (Munich and Zurich: Schnell & Steiner).

—and Hufnagel, F. (eds.) (1979), *Leo von Klenze: Gemälde und Zeichnungen* (Munich: Residenz).

Lieberman, Ralph (1982), *Renaissance Architecture in Venice 1450–1540* (London: Frederick Muller).

Liedke, Volker, Nussbaum, Norbert, and Puchta, Hans (1986) *Beiträge zum Leben und Werk des Meisters Hanns von Burghausen* (Burghausen: Stadt Burghausen).

Lilius, Henrik, *et al.* (1990), *Carl Ludvig Engel 1778–1840* (Helsinki: Opetusministeriö).

Lind, Sven Ivar, Romans, Bengt, and Sterner, Nils (1950), *L. I. Wahlman* (Stockholm: Byggmästeren).

Lindsay, Ian G., and Cosh, Mary (1973), *Inveraray and the Dukes of Argyll* (Edinburgh: Edinburgh UP).

Linn, Björn (1967), *Osvald Almqvist: En arkitekt och hans arbete* (Stockholm: Byggmästeren).

Linstrum, Derek (1972), *Sir Jeffry Wyatville: Architect to the King* (Oxford: Clarendon Press).

—(1978), *West Yorkshire: Architects and Architecture* (London: Lund Humphries).

Linze, Georges (1959), *Victor Bourgeois* (Brussels: Elsevier).

Lippert, Karl-Ludwig (1969), *Giovanni Antonio Viscardi, 1645–1713* (Munich: Seitz & Höfling).

Lipstadt, Hélène, and Mendelsohn, Harvey (1980), *Architecte et ingénieur dans la presse: Polémique, débat, conflit* (Paris: Corda-Ierau).

Liscombe, Rhodri Windsor (1980), *William Wilkins, 1778–1839* (Cambridge: Cambridge UP).

—(1985), *The Church Architecture of Robert Mills* (Easley, SC: Southern Historical Press).

—(1994), *Altogether American: Robert Mills, Architect & Engineer 1781–1855* (Oxford: Oxford UP).

Lissitzky, El (1970), *Russia: An Architecture for World Revolution* (Cambridge, Mass.: MIT Press).

—(1981), *Lissitzky* (New York: Matthews).

Lissitzky-Küppers, Sophie (1980), *El Lissitzky, Life, Letters, Texts* (London: Thames & Hudson).

Litten, Julian (1991), *The English Way of Death* (London: Hale).

Little, Bryan (1955), *The Life and Work of James Gibbs 1682–1754* (London: Batsford).

Littlejohn, David (1984), *Architect: The Life and Work of Charles W. Moore* (New York: Holt, Rinehart, & Winston).

Lloyd, J. S. (ed.) (1978), *W Curtis Green RA: Architect and Draughtsman, 1875–1960* (London: Green, Lloyd, & Adams).

Lloyd, Nathaniel (1925), *A History of English Brickwork* (London: Montgomery, and New York: Helborn).

Lloyd, Seton, and Müller, Hans Wolfgang (1986), *Ancient Architecture* (London: Faber, and Milan: Electa).

Lodder, Christina (1983), *Russian Constructivism* (New Haven: Yale UP).

Loeber, Rolf (1981), *A Biographical Dictionary of Architects in Ireland 1600–1720* (London: John Murray).

Loewy, Raymond Fernand (1937), *The Locomotive* (London: The Studio).

—(1951), *Never Leave Well Enough Alone* (New York: Simon & Schuster).

—(1975), *The Designs of Raymond Loewy* (Washington: Smithsonian Institution Press).

—(1988), *Industrial Design* (London: Fourth Estate).

Lohmeyer, Karl (1931), *Die Baumeister des rheinisch-fränkischen Barocks* (Vienna and Augsburg: Filser).

Long, David Gilson (1977), *The Architecture of Bruce Goff: Buildings and Projects, 1916–1974* (New York: Garland).

Long, David Gilson (1988), *Bruce Goff: Towards Absolute Architecture* (Cambridge, Mass.: MIT Press).

—(1996), *Frank Lloyd Wright: Designs for an American Landscape* (London: Thames & Hudson).

Longstreth, Richard W. (1977), *Julia Morgan, Architect* (Berkeley: Berkeley Architectural Heritage Ass.).

—(1979), *A Matter of Taste: Willis Polk's Writings on Architecture in the Wave* (San Francisco: Book Club of California).

—(1983), *On the Edge of the World: Four Architects in San Francisco at the Turn of the Century* (Cambridge, Mass.: MIT Press).

Loos, Adolf (1962), *Sämtliche Schriften* (Vienna: Herold).

Lopen, A. (1965), 'Harlem's Streetcorner Architects', *Architectural Forum*, 123/5 (Dec.): 50–1.

Lorck, Carl von (1972), *Landschlösser und Guthäuser in Ost- und Westpreussen* (Frankfurt: Weidlich).

Lorentz, Stanisław, and Rottermund, Andrzej (1984), *Klasycyzm w Polsce* (Warsaw: Wydawnictwo Arkady).

Lorenz, Helmut (1991), *Domenico Martinelli* (Vienna: Österreichischen Akademie der Wissenschaft).

Lotz, Wolfgang (1977), *Studies in Italian Renaissance Architecture* (Cambridge, Mass.: MIT Press).

Loudon, John Claudius (1834), *An Encyclopædia of Cottage, Farm, and Furniture* . . . etc. (London: Longman, Rees, Orme, Brown, Green, & Longman, with many subsequent edns.).

—(1981), *On the Laying Out, Planting, and Managing of Cemeteries* (Redhill, Surrey: Ivelet Books; facsimile of 1843 edn. with a new Introduction).

Loukomski, G. (1943), *Charles Cameron* (London: Nicholson & Watson).

Lovero, Pasquale (ed.) (1975), *Giuseppe Samonà* (Milan: Angeli).

Loyer, François (1983), *Architecture of the Industrial Age 1789–1914* (Geneva: Skira).

—(1986), *Victor Horta: Hôtel Tassel* (Brussels: Archives d'architecture moderne).

—(1987), *Paris XIXe siècle: L'immeuble et la rue* (Paris: Hazan).

—(1991), *Dix Ans d'Art Nouveau: Paul Hankar, architecte* (Brussels: Archives d'architecture moderne).

Lozano, E. (1991), *Community Design and the Culture of Cities* (Cambridge: Cambridge UP).

Luciani, Roberto (1987), *Pietro Lombardi architetto* (Rome: Officina).

Lund, Hakon, and Küster, Christian, L. (1968), *Architekt C. F. Hansen: 1756–1845* (Hamburg: Altonaer Museum).

Lund, Hakon, and Thygesen, Anne Lise (1995), *C. F. Hansen I & II* (Copenhagen: Danish Architectural Press).

Luporini, Eugenio (1964), *Brunelleschi: Forma e ragione* (Milan: Edizioni di Communità).

Lurçat, André (1929), *Architecture* (Paris: Sans Pareil).

—(1953–7), *Formes, Compositions, et Lois d'Harmonie* (Paris: Vincent Fréal).

Lüttichau, Mario-Andreas von (1983), *Die Deutsche Ornamentkritik im 18. Jahrhundert* (Hildesheim: Olms).

Lux, Joseph August (1914), *Otto Wagner* (Munich: Delphin).

—(1919), *Joseph M. Olbrich* (Berlin: Wasmuth).

Lyall, Sutherland (1988), *Dream Cottages: From Cottage Orné to Stockbroker Tudor* (London: Hale).

Lynch, Gerard (1990), *Gauged Brickwork* (London: Donhead).

—(1994–6), *Brickwork: History, Technology, and Practice* (London: Donhead).

Lyotard, J.-F. (1984), *The Post-Modern Condition* (Manchester: Manchester UP).

McAndrew, John (1980), *Venetian Architecture of the Early Renaissance* (Cambridge, Mass.: MIT Press).

McArdle, Alma Dec, and Bartlett, Deirdre (1978), *Carpenter's Gothic* (New York: Whitney Library of Design).

Macartney, Mervyn Edmund (1907–27), *The Practical Exemplar of Architecture* (London: Architectural Press).

—(1908), *English Houses and Gardens in the 17th and 18th Centuries* (London: Batsford).

— and Belcher, John (1901), *Later Renaissance Architecture in England* (London: Batsford).

Macaulay, James (1975), *The Gothic Revival 1745–1845* (Glasgow: Blackie).

—(1987), *The Classical Country House in Scotland 1660–1800* (London: Faber & Faber).

McCarter, Robert (1997), *Frank Lloyd Wright* (London: Phaidon).

McCarthy, Michael (1987), *The Origins of the Gothic Revival* (New York and London: Yale UP).

McCoy, Esther (1960), *Richard Neutra* (New York: Braziller, and London: Mayflower).

—(1962), *Modern California Houses—Case Study Houses 1945–1962* (New York: Reinhold).

—(1968), *Craig Ellwood: Architecture* (New York: Walker).

—(1974), *Gunnar Birkerts & Associates* (Tokyo: ADA Edita).

—(1975), *Five California Architects* (New York: Reinhold, 1960, later edn. published by Praeger).

—(1977), *Case Study Houses 1945–1962* (Los Angeles: Hennessey & Ingalls).

—(1979), *Vienna to Los Angeles: Two Journeys* (Santa Monica, Calif.: Arts & Architecture Press).

—(1983), *The Second Generation* (Salt Lake City: Smith).

—(1989), *Blueprints for Modern Living: History and Legacy of the Case Study Houses* (Cambridge, Mass.: MIT Press).

—(1990), *Arts and Architecture: Essays* (Cambridge, Mass.: MIT Press).

—and Goldstein, Barbara (1982), *Guide to US Architecture, 1940–1980* (Santa Monica, Calif.: Arts & Architecture Press).

McCue, George (1976), *The Octagon* (Washington: AIA Foundation).

MacDonald, C., *et al.* (1986), *Figurative Architecture: The Work of Five Dublin Architects* (London: Architectural Association).

MacDonald, William Lloyd (1965–86), *The Architecture of the Roman Empire* (New Haven and London: Yale UP).

—and Pinto, J. (1995), *Hadrian's Villa and its Legacy* (New Haven and London: Yale UP).

MacDougall, Elizabeth B. (1980), *John Claudius Loudon and the Early 19th Century in Great Britain* (Washington: Dumbarton Oaks, Trustees for Harvard University).

MacFadyen, Dugald (1970), *Sir Ebenezer Howard and the Town Planning Movement* (Cambridge, Mass.: MIT Press).

McFadzean, Ronald (1979), *The Life and Work of Alexander Thomson* (London: Routledge & Kegan Paul).

MacGibbon, David, and Ross, Thomas (1887–92), *The Castellated and Domestic Architecture of Scotland from the Twelfth to the Eighteenth Century* (Edinburgh: David Douglas).

McGrath, Raymond (1934), *Twentieth-Century Houses* (London: Faber).

—and Frost, A. C. (1937), *Glass in Architecture and Decoration* (London: Architectural Press).

McIntire, Samuel: *see* Labaree (1957).

Mack, Charles Randall (1987), *Pienza: The Creation of a Renaissance City* (Ithaca, NY: Cornell UP).

McKay, Ian, and Boyd, Robin (1971), *Living and Partly Living: Housing in Australia* (Melbourne: Nelson).

McKay, W. B. (1957), *Building Construction* (London: Longmans Green).

McKean, Hugh F. (1980), *The 'Lost' Treasures of Louis Comfort Tiffany* (New York: Doubleday).

McKean, John (1988), *Learning from Segal: Walter Sega's Life, Work, and Influence* (Basle: Birkhäuser).

MacKeith, Margaret (1986), *The History and Conservation of Shopping Arcades* (London: Mansell).

Mackowsky, Hans (1912), *Paul Wallot und seiner Schüler* (Berlin: Wasmuth).

McLaughlin, Charles C. (ed.) (1977–), *The Papers of Frederick Law Olmsted* (Baltimore: Johns Hopkins UP).

MacLeod, Robert (1971), *Style and Society: Architectural Ideology in Britain 1835–1914* (London: RIBA).

—(1983), *Charles Rennie Mackintosh* (London: Collins).

McParland, Edward (1985), *James Gandon, Vitruvius Hibernicus* (London: Zwemmer).

—Rowan, Alistair, and Rowan, Ann Martha (1989), *The Architecture of Richard Morrison (1767–1849) and William Vitruvius Morrison (1794–1838)* (Dublin: Irish Architectural Archive).

Macrae, Marion, and Adamson, Anthony (1963), *Domestic Architecture of Upper Canada* (Toronto: Clarke, Irwin).

—(1975), *Church Architecture of Upper Canada* (Toronto: Clarke, Irwin).

McWilliam, Colin (1978), *The Buildings of Scotland, Lothian* (Harmondsworth: Penguin).

Maddex, Diane (1973), *Historic Buildings of Washington DC* (Pittsburg, Pa.: Ober Park).

Mádl, Karel B. (1922), *Jan Kotěra* (Prague: Štenc).

Madsen, Stephan Tschudi: *see* Tschudi-Madsen.

Maeyer, Charles de (1963), *Paul Hankar* (Brussels: Meddens).

Magnée, R. N. H. (1954), *Willem M. Dudok* (Amsterdam: van Saane).

Maguire, Robert, and Murray, Keith (1965), *Modern Churches of the World* (New York: Dutton).

Maher, James T. (1975), *The Twilight of Splendor* (Boston: Little, Brown & Co.).

Mainstone, Rowland J. (1975), *Development in Structural Form* (London: Allen Lane).

—(1988), *Hagia Sophia: Architecture, Structure, and Liturgy of Justinian's Great Church* (London: Thames & Hudson).

Maki, Fumihiko (1972), *Investigations in Collective Form* (St Louis: School of Architecture, Washington University).

Makinson, Randell L. (1974), *A Guide to the Works of Greene and Greene* (Salt Lake City: Peregrine Smith).

—(1977–9), *Greene & Greene* (Salt Lake City: Peregrine Smith).

Makowski, Zygmunt Stanisław (1965), *Steel Space Structures* (London: Michael Joseph).

Malet, Henri (1973), *Le Baron Haussmann et la Rénovation de Paris* (Paris: Éditions Municipales).

Malevich, Kasimir (1959), *The Non-Objective World* (Chicago: Theobald).

Mallet-Stevens, Robert (1922), *A Modern City* (London: Benn).

—(1929), *Grands Constructions* (Paris: Moreau).

—(1937), *Vitraux Modernes* (Paris: Moreau).

Mallgrave, Harry Francis (1996), *Gottfried Semper: Architect of the Nineteenth Century* (New Haven and London: Yale UP).

Mallgrave, Harry Francis and Herrmann, Wolfgang (1988), *Gottfried Semper: The Four Elements of Architecture and Other Writings* (Cambridge and New York: Cambridge UP).

Mallory, Nina A. (1977), *Roman Rococo Architecture from Clement XI to Benedict XIV (1700–1758)* (New York: Garland).

Malone, Dumas (1948–74), *Jefferson and his Time* (Boston: Little, Brown).

Maltby, Sally, MacDonald, Sally, and Cunningham, Colin (1983), *Alfred Waterhouse, 1830–1905* (London: RIBA).

Mandowsky, Erna, and Mitchell, Charles (eds.) (1963), *Pirro Ligorio's Roman Antiquities in MS.XIII B 7 in the National Library of Naples* (London: Warburg Institute of the University of London).

Mang, Karl (1977), *Kommunaler Wohnungsbau in Wien. Aufbruch, 1923–1932* (Vienna: Presse-u.-Informations-Dienst die Stadt).

Mango, Cyril (1972), *The Art of the Byzantine Empire 312–1453: Sources and Documents* (Englewood Cliffs, NJ: Prentice-Hall).

—(1986), *Byzantine Architecture* (London: Faber & Faber, and Milan: Electa).

Manieri-Elia, Mario (1997), *Louis Henry Sullivan* (New York: Princeton Architectural Press).

Mansuelli, Guido Achille (1958), *Le ville de mondo romano* (Milan: Pleion).

—*et al.* (1979), *Studi sull' arco onorario romano* (Rome: L'Erma di Bretschneider).

Mantero, Enrico (ed.) (1969), *Giuseppe Terragni e la città del razionalismo italiano* (Bari: Dedalo).

—(1984), *Il Razionalismo Italiano* (Bologna: Zanichelli).

Maranesi, D. Francesco (1929), *Un grande architetto marchigiano: Giuseppe Sacconi* (Fermo: PSCT).

March, Lionel, and Sheine, Judith (eds.) (1993), *R. M. Schindler: Composition and Construction* (London: Academy Editions).

Marchi, Virgilio (1924), *Architettura Futurista* (Foligno: Campitelli).

—(1931), *Italia Nuova, Architettura Nuova* (Foligno: Campitelli).

Marchini, Giuseppe (1943), *Giuliano da Sangallo* (Florence: Sansoni).

Marcianò, Ada Francesca (1987), *Giuseppe Terragni: opera completa, 1925–1943* (Rome: Officina).

Marco Dorta, Enrique (1951), *Fuentes para la Historia del Arte Hispano-Americano* (Seville: Instituto Diego Velasquez).

Marconi, Paolo (1964), *Giuseppe Valadier* (Rome: Officina).

Maré, Eric de (1955), *Gunnar Asplund: A Great Modern Architect* (London: Art & Technics).

Marfany, Joan-Lluís (1975), *Aspectes del Modernisme* (Barcelona: Curial).

Marie, Alfred, and Marie, Jeanne (1972), *Mansart à Versailles* (Paris: Fréal).

Mariette, Jean (1927–9), *L'architecture français* (Paris and Brussels: van Oest).

Marini, Remigio (1959), *Andrea Pozzo Pittore (1642–1709)* (Trento: CAT).

Marks, Robert W. (1973), *The Dymaxion World of Buckminster Fuller* (Garden City, NY: Anchor; repr. of 1960 edn.).

Marot, Jean (1969), *Recueil des plans . . . de plusiers palais . . . etc. . . . bâtis dans Paris* (Farnborough: Gregg; repr. of 1655 edn.).

—(1970), *Architecture Française* (Paris: Laget; repr. of 1670 edn.).

Marot, Pierre (1954), *Emmanuel Héré (1705–1763)* (Nancy: Berger-Levrault).

—(1966), *La place royale de Nancy* (Paris: Berger-Levrault).

Marschall, Horst K. (1981), *Friedrich von Thiersch (1852–1921): Ein Münchner Architekt des Späthistorismus* (Munich: Prestel).

Martin, K. (1930), *Hermann Billing* (Berlin: Hübsch).

Martin, Roland (1956), *L'Urbanisme dans la Grèce antique* (Paris: Picard).

—(1986), *Greek Architecture* (London: Faber & Faber, and Milan: Electa).

Martinell, César (1975), *Gaudí: His Life, his Theories, his Work* (Cambridge, Mass.: MIT Press).

Martiny, V. G. (1980), *Bruxelles: L'architecture des origines à 1900* (Brussels: Vokaer).

Martley, Robert H., and Urbin, R. Denny (eds.) (1867), *Afternoon Lectures on Literature and Art* (London: Bell & Daldy, and Dublin: Hodges, Smith & McGee).

Marx, Harald (1989), *Matthäus Daniel Pöppelmann: der Architekt des Dresdner Zwinger* (Münster: Westfälisches Landesmuseum, and Leipzig: Seemann).

Masaryková, Anna (1967), *Bedřich Feuerstein* (Prague: Special Exhibition Catalogue).

Masini, Laura Vinca (ed.) (1974), *Riccardo Morandi* (Rome: De Luca).

Massari, Antonio (1971), *Giorgio Massari architetto veneziano del settecento* (Vicenza: Pozzo).

Matteucci, Anna Maria (1969), *Carlo Francesco Dotti e l'architettura bolognese del Settecento* (Bologna: Alfa).

Matthiae, Guglielmo (1952), *Ferdinando Fuga e la sua opera romana* (Rome: Fratelli Palombi).

Maxwell, Robert (1972), *New British Architecture* (London: Thames & Hudson).

May, J. (1985), *Computer Graphics* (London: Secker & Warburg).

Mayer, Hans F. (1958), *Der Baumeister Otto Bartning* (Heidelberg: Lambert & Schneider).

—and Rehder, Gerhard (1953), *William Kreis* (Essen: Vulkan).

Mayer, Marcel (1953), *Le Château d'Anet* (Paris: Firmin-Didot).

Mayo, Bernard (ed.) (1970), *Jefferson Himself: The Personal Narrative of a Many-Sided American* (Charlottesville, Va.: University Press of Virginia; repr. of 1942 edn.).

Mayor, Alpheus Hyatt (1945), *The Bibiena Family* (New York: Bittner).

Mazzi, Giuliana (ed.) (1982), *Giuseppe Japelli e il suo tempo* (Padua: Liviana).

Mead, Christopher Curtis (ed.) (1989), *The Architecture of Robert Venturi* (Albuquerque, NM: University of New Mexico Press).

—— (1991), *Charles Garnier's Paris Opéra* (Cambridge, Mass.: MIT Press).

Mebes, Paul, and Behrendt, Walter Curt (1920), *Um 1800. Architektur und Handwerk im letzten Jahrhundert: ihrer traditionellen Entwicklung* (Munich: Bruckmann).

Meek, Harold Alan (1988), *Guarino Guarini and His Architecture* (New Haven: Yale UP).

Meeks, Carroll Louis Vanderslice (1964), *The Railroad Station: An Architectural History* (New Haven: Yale UP).

—— (1966), *Italian Architecture 1750–1914* (New Haven and London: Yale UP).

Meier, Richard (1984), *Richard Meier, Architect, 1964–1984*, with an introduction by Joseph Rykwert (New York: Rizzoli).

—— *et al.* (1996), *Richard Meier Houses* (London: Thames & Hudson).

Meintjes, Johannes (1951), *Anton Anreith, Sculptor 1754–1822* (Cape Town: Juta).

Meintzschel, Joachim (1963), *Studien zu Maximilian von Welsch* (Würzburg: Schöningh).

Meissner, Carl (1925), *William Kreis* (Essen: Baedeker).

Mellor, D. (ed.) (1987), *A Paradise Lost: The Neo-Romantic Imagination in Britain 1935–55* (London: Barbican Art Gallery, and Lund Humphries).

Melograni, Carlo (1955), *Giuseppe Pagano* (Milan: Il Balcone).

Memmo, Andrea (1973), *Elementi d'architettura Lodoliana* (Milan: Mazzotta).

Menges, Axel (1974), *Architecture of Skidmore, Owings, & Merrill* (London: Architectural Press).

Merényi, Ferenc (1970), *Magyar építészet: 1867–1967* (Budapest: Müszaki Könyvkladó).

Messina, Vittorio, Taut, Max, and Lauterbach, Heinrich (1969), *Hans Scharoun* (Rome: Officina Edizione).

Metcalf, Priscilla (1977), *The Hall of the Fishmongers' Company: An Architectural History of a Riverside Site* (Chichester: Phillimore).

—— (1978), *The Park Town Estate and the Battersea Tangle* (London: Topographical Society).

—— (1980), *James Knowles, Victorian Editor and Architect* (Oxford: Clarendon Press).

Meyer, Adolf (1925), *Ein Versuchshaus des Bauhauses in Weimar* (Munich: Langen).

Meyer, Edina (1972), *Paul Mebes* (Berlin: Seitz).

Meyer, Esther da Costa (1995), *The Work of Antonio Sant'Elia: Retreat into the Future* (New Haven and London: Yale UP).

Meyhöfer, Dirk (1995), *Contemporary European Architects*, ii (Cologne: Taschen).

Mezzanotte, Gianni (1966), *Architettura neoclassica in Lombardia* (Naples: Edizione Scientifiche Italiane).

Michelucci, Giovanni (1978), Exhibition at the RIBA (Calenzano: Modulo Books).

Middleton, Robin D. (ed.) (1982), *The Beaux-Arts and Nineteenth Century French Architecture* (London: Thames & Hudson).

—— and Watkin, David (1987), *Neo-Classical and Nineteenth Century Architecture* (London: Faber/Electa).

Mikellides, Byron (ed.) (1980), *Architecture for People* (New York: Holt).

Milizia, Francesco (1785), *Memorie degli architetti antichi e moderni* (Bassano: Remondini).

Millar, John Fitzhugh (1987), *Classical Architecture in Renaissance Europe 1419–1585* (Williamsburg, Va.: University Press).

Millech, Knud (1951), *Danske Arkitekturstrømninger 1850–1950* (Copenhagen: Udgivet af Østifternes kreditforening).

—— (1960), *Bindesbølls Museum* (Copenhagen: Thorvaldsens Museum).

Miller, Mary (1986), *Helmut Jahn* (New York: Rizzoli).

Miller, Mervyn (1989), *Letchworth: The first Garden City* (Chichester: Phillimore).

—— (1992), *Raymond Unwin: Garden Cities and Town Planning* (Leicester: Leicester UP).

—— and Gray, A. Stuart (1992), *Hampstead Garden Suburb* (Chichester: Phillimore).

Miller, Nory (1979), *Johnson/Burgee Architecture* (New York: Random House).

Miller, Philip (1981), *Decimus Burton* (London: Building Centre).

Millon, Henry A. (1961), *Baroque and Rococo Architecture* (New York: Braziller).

—— (1980), *Studies in Italian Art and Architecture 15th through 18th Centuries* (Cambridge, Mass.: MIT Press).

—— (1984), *Filippo Juvarra: Drawings from the Roman Period, 1704–1714* (Rome: dell' Elefante).

—— (ed.) (1996), *Italian Renaissance Architecture: From Brunelleschi to Michelangelo* (London: Thames & Hudson).

—— and Nochlin, Linda (1978), *Art and Architecture in the Service of Politics* (Cambridge, Mass.: MIT Press).

—— and Smyth, Craig Hugh (1988), *Michelangelo Architect: The Façade of San Lorenzo and the Drum and Dome of St Peter's* (Milan: Olivetti).

Mills, Edward D. (1953), *The New Architecture in Great Britain (1946–1953)* (London: Standard).

Milner, John (1983), *Vladimir Tatlin and the Russian Avant-Garde* (New Haven: Yale).

Mindlin, Henrique (1956), *Modern Architecture in Brazil* (New York: Reinhold).

Mittig, Hans E., and Plagemann, Volker (eds.) (1972), *Denkmäler in neunzehnten Jahrhundert* (Munich: Prestel).

Moholy-Nagy, Dorothea Maria Pauline Alice Sibyl (1964), *Carlos Raúl Villanueva and the Architecture of Venezuela* (London: Tiranti).

—(1970), *Introduction to the Architecture of Paul Rudolph* (New York: Praeger).

Mohri, Takenobu (1970), *Bruce Goff in Architecture* (Tokyo: Kenchiku).

Mojon, Luc (1967), *Der Münsterbaumeister Matthäus Ensingen* (Berne: Bonteli).

Moller, Georg (1815–44), *Denkmäler der deutschen Baukunst* (Darmstadt: Leske).

Monneret de Villard, Ugo (ed.) (1908), *L'architettura di Giuseppe Sommaruga* (Milan: Preiss & Bestetti).

Monroe, Harriet (1966), *John Wellborn Root* (Park Forest, Ill.: Prairie School Press).

Montagu, Jennifer (1985), *Alessandro Algardi* (New Haven and London: Yale UP).

Montferrand, Auguste-Ricard de (1845), *L'Église cathédrale de Saint-Isaac* (St Petersburg: Bélizard).

Montgomery-Massingberd, Hugh, and Watkin, David (1980), *The London Ritz: A Social and Architectural History* (London: Aurum).

Moore, Rowan (ed.) (1995), *Structure, Space, and Skin: The Work of Nicholas Grimshaw & Partners* (London: Phaidon).

Morales de los Rios Filho, Adolfo (1942), *Grandjean de Montigny* (Rio de Janeiro: Empresa a Noite).

Morey, Mathieu Prosper (1868), *Richard Mique* (Nancy: Raybois).

Morgan, Ann Lee, and Naylor, Colin (1987), *Contemporary Architects* (Chicago and London: St James Press).

Morisani, Ottavio (1951), *Michelozzo architetto* (Turin: Einaudi).

Morison, M. Pitt, and White, John (eds.) (1979), *Western Towns and Buildings* (Perth: University of Western Australia Press).

Morosini, Luigi (1929), *Giuseppe Saccone* (Rome: Biblioteca d'Arte).

Morper, Johann Joseph (1940), *Das Czernin-Palais in Prag* (Prague: Volk & Reich).

Morris, William (1966), *Collected Works* (New York: Russell).

Morselli, Piero, and Corti, Gino (1982), *La Chiesa di Santa Maria delle Carceri in Prato* (Florence: Edam).

Moschini, Francesco (ed.) (1979), *Aldo Rossi: Projects and Drawings 1962–1979* (London: Academy Editions).

—(1979*a*), *Franco Albini* (London: Academy Editions).

—(1984), *Giorgio Grassi, progetti 1960–1980* (Florence: Centro Di).

Mossakowski, Stanisław (1973), *Tylman z Gameren: architekt polskiego baroku* (Wrocław: Zakład Narodowy im Ossolinskich).

Mosser, Monique, and Rabreau, Daniel (1979), *Charles de Wailly: peintre architecte dans l'Europe des Lumières* (Paris: Caisse Nationale des Monuments Historiques et des Sites).

—and Teyssot, Georges (eds.) (1991), *The History of Garden Design: The Western Tradition from the Renaissance to the Present Day* (London: Thames & Hudson).

Mowl, Tim (1996), *Horace Walpole: The Great Outsider* (London: John Murray).

—(1998), *William Beckford: Composing for Mozart* (London: John Murray).

—and Earnshaw, Brian (1985), *Trumpet at a Distant Gate: The Lodge as Prelude to the Country House* (London: Waterstone).

—(1988), *John Wood: Architect of Obsession* (Bath: Millstream).

——(1995), *Architecture without Kings—the Rise of Puritan Classicism under Cromwell* (Manchester: Manchester UP).

Mrusek, Joachim (1972), *Die Albrechtsburg zu Meissen* (Leipzig: Seemann).

Muccigrosso, Robert (1980), *American Gothic: The Mind and Art of Ralph Adams Cram* (Washington: University Press of America).

Mujica, Francisco (1929), *History of the Skyscraper* (Paris: Archaeology and Architecture Press).

Mulder, Bertus (1975), *Rietveld Schröder Huis 1925–1975* (Utrecht: Bruna & Zoon).

Mulvany, Thomas J. (1969), *The Life of James Gandon, Esq.*, ed. Maurice Craig (London: Cornmarket Press).

Mumford, Lewis (1922), *The Story of Utopias* (New York: Boni & Liveright).

—(1924), *Sticks and Stones* (New York: Boni & Liveright).

—(1931), *The Brown Decades* (New York: Harcourt Brace).

—(1934), *Technics and Civilization* (New York: Harcourt Brace).

—(1938), *The Culture of Cities* (London: Secker & Warburg).

—(1944), *The Condition of Man* (London: Secker & Warburg).

—(1946), *City Development: Studies in Disintegration and Renewal* (London: Secker & Warburg).

—(1952), *Art and Technics* (Oxford: Oxford UP).

—(1952*a*), *The Conduct of Life* (London: Secker & Warburg).

—(1961), *The City in History* (New York: Harcourt Brace).
—(1963), *The Highway and the City* (New York: Harcourt Brace).
—(1967, 1970), *The Myth of the Machine*, i–ii (New York: Harcourt Brace).
—(1975), *Architecture as a Home for Man* (New York: Architectural Record Books).
Mungenast, Emmerich (1963), *Josef Munggenast der Stiftsbaumeister 1680–1741* (Vienna: Bergland Verlag).
Muñoz, Antonio (1944), *Domenico Fontana Architetto, 1543–1607* (Rome: Cremonese).
Müntz, Eugène (1889), *Histoire d'art pendant la Renaissance* (Paris: Hachette).
Münz, Ludwig, and Künstler, Gustav (1966), *Adolf Loos: Pioneer of Modern Architecture* (New York: Praeger).
Muraro, Maria Teresa, and Povoledo, Elena (eds.) (1970), *Disegni teatrali dei Bibiena* (Venice: Fondazione Giorgi Cini).
Muraro, Michelangelo (1986), *Venetian Villas: The History and Culture* (New York: Rizzoli).
Murphy, William, and Muller, Louis (1970), *Bruce Goff: A Portfolio* (New York: Architectural League).
Murray, Peter (1969), *The Architecture of the Italian Renaissance* (London: Thames & Hudson).
—(1986), *Renaissance Architecture* (London: Faber & Faber, and Milan: Electa).
Murrell, K. (1965), *Ergonomics: Man in his Working Environment* (London: Chapman & Hall).
Musgrave, Clifford (1959), *Royal Pavilion: An Episode in the Romantic* (London: Leonard Hill).
Musgrove, John (ed.) (1987), *Sir Banister Fletcher's A History of Architecture* (London: Butterworth).
Muthesius, Hermann (1902), *Der Kirchenbau der Englischen Secten* (Halle: Waisenhauses).
—(1979), *The English House*, tr. Janet Seligman (Oxford: BSP).
Muthesius, Stefan (1972), *The High Victorian Movement in Architecture, 1850–70* (London: Routledge & Kegan Paul).
—(1974), *Das Englische Vorbild: Eine Studie zu den Reformbewegungen in Architektur, etc. . . .* (Munich: Prestel).
—(1982), *The English Terraced House* (New Haven: Yale UP).
Myles, Janet (1996), *L. N. Cottingham 1787–1847: Architect of the Gothic Revival* (London: Lund Humphries).
Mylne, Robert Scott (1893), *The Master Masons to the Crown of Scotland and their Works* (Edinburgh: Scott & Ferguson).
Nagy, Elemér (1974), *Erik Gunnar Asplund* (Budapest: n.p.).
Nairn, Ian (1955), *Outrage* (London: Architectural Press).
—(1959), *Counter Attack against Subtopia* (London: Architectural Press).
Nasoni, Niccolò (1991), *Niccolò Nasoni, 1691–1773: un artista italiano a Oporto* (Florence: Ponte alle Grazie).
National Institute for Architectural Education (1964), *Winning Designs 1904–1963: Paris Prize in Architecture* (New York: The Institute).
Navone, P., and Orlandini, B. (1974), *Architettura 'radicale'* (Milan: Documenti di Casabella).
Naylor, Gillian (1971), *The Arts and Crafts Movement* (London: Studio Vista).
—(1985), *The Bauhaus Reassessed: Sources and Design Theory* (London: Herbert Press).
Negri, E. de (1977), *Ottocento e rinnovamento urbano: Carlo Barabino* (Genoa: Saged).
Negroponte, N. (1970), *The Architecture Machine: Towards a More Human Environment* (Cambridge, Mass.: MIT Press).
—(1974), *Soft Architecture Machines* (Cambridge, Mass.: MIT Press).
Nénot, Henri-Paul (1895), *La Nouvelle Sorbonne* (Paris: Colin).
—(1903), *Monographie de la Nouvelle Sorbonne* (Paris: Imprimerie Nationale).
Nerdinger, Winfried (1980), *Klassizismus in Bayern, Schwaben, und Franken* (Munich: Stadtmuseum).
—(ed.) (1982), *Richard Riemerschmid: von Jugendstil zum Werkbund* (Munich: Prestel).
—(1987), *Romantik und Restauration: Architektur in Bayern zur Zeit Ludwigs I. 1825–1848* (Munich: Stadtmuseum).
Nervi, Pier Luigi (1956), *Structures* (New York: Dodge).
—(1965), *Aesthetics and Technology in Building* (Cambridge, Mass.: Harvard UP).
Nettleton, E. (1836), *Nettleton's Guide to Plymouth, Stonehouse, Devonport, and the Neighbouring County* (Plymouth: Nettleton).
Neuman, Robert (1994), *Robert de Cotte and the Perfection of Architecture in Eighteenth-Century France* (Chicago: University of Chicago Press).
Neumann, Eckhard (ed.) (1970), *Bauhaus and Bauhaus People* (New York: Van Nostrand).
Neumann, Jaromir (1970), *Das Böhmische Barock* (Prague: Odeon).
Neutra, Richard (1954), *Survival Through Design* (New York: Oxford UP).
—(1962), *Life and Shape* (New York: Appleton).
Neuwirth, Josef (1890), *Die Wochenrechnungen und der Betrieb des Prager Dombaues in den Jahren 1372–1378* (Prague: Calve).
—(1891), *Peter Parler von Gmünd* (Prague: Calve).
Newhouse, Victoria (1989), *Wallace K. Harrison, Architect* (New York: Rizzoli).
Newman, John (1995), *Buildings of Wales, Glamorgan* (Harmondsworth: Penguin).
Newsom, Joseph Cather (1890), *Picturesque and*

Artistic Homes and Buildings of California (San Francisco: n.p.).
Newsom, Joseph Cather (1893), *Modern Homes of California* (San Francisco: n.p.).
—(1895), *Artistic City Buildings, Flats, and Residences* (San Francisco: n.p.).
—(1895*a*), *Artistic Country Homes* (San Francisco: n.p.).
—(ed.) (1897–99), *Up-to-Date Architecture* (San Francisco: n.p.).
—(1981), *Artistic Buildings and Homes of Los Angeles* (Los Angeles: Calliope Press; repr. of 1888 edn.).
— and Newsom, Samuel (1978), *Picturesque California Homes* (Los Angeles: Hennessey & Ingalls; repr. of 1884–5 edn.).
Newton, Roger Hale (1942), *Town & Davis, Architects, Pioneers in American Revivalist Architecture, 1812–1870*, etc. (New York: Columbia UP).
Nichols, Frederick D. (ed.) (1978), *Thomas Jefferson's Architectural Drawings* (Boston: Massachusetts Historical Society).
— and Bear, James A. (1967), *Monticello* (Monticello, Va.: Jefferson Memorial Foundation).
Nichols, Karen Vogel, Burke, Lisa, and Burke, Patrick (eds.) (1995), *Michael Graves: Buildings and Projects, 1990–1994* (New York: Rizzoli).
— Burke, Patrick J., and Hancock, Caroline (eds.) (1990), *Michael Graves: Buildings and Projects, 1982–1989* (New York: Princeton Architectural Press).
Nicholson, Peter (1823), *A New Practical Builder, and Workman's Companion: Containing a Full Display and Elucidation of the most recent and skilful Methods, pursued by Architects and Artificers . . .* (London: Thomas Kelly).
—(1835), *An Architectural and Engineering Dictionary* (London: John Weale). Also *A New Improved Edition of Nicholson's Dictionary*, ed. Edward Lomax and Thomas Gunyon (London: Peter Jackson, 1852).
Nicoletti, Manfredo (1978), *L'architettura liberty in Italia* (Rome: Laterza).
Niemann, Georg, and Feldegg, Ferdinand (1893), *Theophilus Hansen und seine Werke* (Vienna: Schroll).
Niemeyer, Oscar (1975), *Oscar Niemeyer* (Milan: Mondadori).
—(1978), *A forma na architectura* (Rio de Janeiro: Avenir).
Nilsson, Nils Martin Persson (1932), *The Origin of the Triumphal Arch* (Lund: n.p.).
Nolhac, Pierre de (1910), *Hubert Robert, 1733–1808* (Paris: Goupil).
Noppen, Luc, Paulette, Claude, and Tremblay, Michael (1979), *Québec: Trois Siècles d'Architecture* (Quebec: Libre Expression).
Norberg-Schulz, Christian (1968), *Kilian Ignaz Dientzenhofer e il barocco boemo* (Rome: Officina).
—(1986), *Baroque Architecture* (London: Faber & Faber, and Milan: Electa).
—(1986*a*), *Late Baroque and Rococo Architecture* (London: Faber & Faber, and Milan: Electa).
Nordberg, Tord Karl Gustaf Olsson (1970), *De La Vallée: En arkitektfamilj i Frankrike, Holland, och Sverige* (Stockholm: Almqvist & Wiksell).
Normand, Charles (1852), *Nouveau Parallèle des Ordres d'Architecture des Grecs, des Romains . . .* etc. (Paris: Normand Ainé & Carilian).
Normand, Louis-Marie (1832), *Monumens Funéraires choisis dans les Cimetières de Paris* (Paris: Normand Fils).
Norris, C. (1982), *Deconstruction* (London: Methuen).
— and Benjamin, A. (1988), *What is Deconstruction?* (London: Academy Editions).
North, Arthur Tappan (1931), *Ralph Adams Cram* (New York: McGraw-Hill).
Norton, Christopher, and Park, David (1986), *Cistercian Art and Architecture in the British Isles* (Cambridge: Cambridge UP).
Norton, Paul F. (1977), *Latrobe, Jefferson, and the National Capitol* (New York and London: Garland).
Nussbaum, Norbert (1994), *Deutsche Kirchenbaukunst der Gotik* (Darmstadt: Wissenschaftliche Buchgesellschaft).
Nuttgens, Patrick (ed.) (1988), *Mackintosh and his Contemporaries in Europe and America* (London: John Murray).
Nyberg, Dorothea (ed.) (1969), *Œuvre de Juste-Aurèle Meissonier* (New York: Blom).
— and Mitchell, Herbert (eds.) (1975), *Piranesi Drawings and Etchings at the Avery Architectural Library, Columbia University, New York* (New York: Columbia University).
Ochsner, Jeffrey Karl (1982), *H. H. Richardson (1838–1886): Complete Architectural Works* (Cambridge, Mass.: MIT Press).
O'Donovan, Donal (1998), *God's Architect: A Life of Raymond McGrath* (Bray: Kilbride Books).
O'Dwyer, Frederick (1997), *The Architecture of Deane and Woodward* (Cork: Cork UP).
Oechslin, Werner (1970), In *Guarino Guarini e l'internationalità del Barocco: Atti del Convegno Internazionale Promosso dall'Accademia delle Scienze di Torino*, September–October 1968 (Turin: Accademia delle Scienze).
—(ed.) (1972), *Bildungsgut und Antikenrezeption im frühen Settecento in Rom, Studien zum römischen Aufenthalt Bernardo Antonio Vittones* (Zurich: Atlantis-Verlag).
—(1973), *Die Vorarlberger Barockbaumeister* (Einsiedeln and Bregenz: Benziger).
Oettinger, Karl (1951), *Anton Pilgram und die Bildhauer von St Stephan* (Vienna: Verlag Herold).

Offermann, Klaus (1989), *Coop Himmelblau* (Stuttgart: IRB).

—(ed.) (1993), *Architekten, Bruno Taut* (Stuttgart: IRB).

Office for Metropolitan Architecture, Koolhaas, Rem, and Mau, Bruce (1995), *S, M, L, XL* (Rotterdam: OIO Publishers).

O'Gorman, James F. (1987), *The Architecture of Frank Furness* (Philadelphia: Philadelphia Museum of Art).

Ohle, Walter (1960), *Schwerin-Ludwigslust* (Leipzig: VEB Seemann).

Oldham, Ray, and Oldham, John (1978), *Western Heritage* (Perth: University of Western Australia Press).

Olivato, Loredano (1975), *Ottavio Bertotti-Scamozzi studioso di Andrea Palladio* (Vicenza: N. Pozza).

Oliver, Paul, *et al.* (1981), *Dunroamin: The Suburban Semi and its Enemies* (London: Barrie & Jenkins).

—(ed.), (1997), *Encylopaedia of Vernacular Architecture of the World* (Cambridge: Cambridge UP).

Oliver, Richard (1983), *Bertram Grosvenor Goodhue* (New York: Architectural History Foundation, and Cambridge, Mass.: MIT Press).

Olivero, Eugenio (1920), *Le opere di Bernardo Antonio Vittone* (Turin: Tipografia del Collegio degli Artigianelli).

Olmsted, Frederick Law, jun., and Hubbard, Theodore Kimball (eds.) (1973), *Frederick Law Olmsted, Landscape Architect, 1822–1903* (Cambridge, Mass.: MIT Press).

Oncken, Älste (1935), *Friedrich Gilly: 1772–1800* (Berlin: Deutscher Verlag für Kunstwissenschaft).

O'Neal, William Bainter (1960), *Jefferson's Buildings at the University of Virginia* (Charlottesville, Va.: University Press of Virginia).

—(ed.) (1966), *Walter Gropius* (Charlottesville, Va.: American Association of Architectural Bibliographers).

Onians, John (1979), *Art and Thought in the Hellenistic Age* (London: Thames & Hudson).

—(1988), *Bearers of Meaning: The Classical Orders in Antiquity, the Middle Ages, and the Renaissance* (Cambridge: Cambridge UP).

Onofrio, Cesare d' (1957), *Le Fontane di Roma* (Rome: Staderini).

—(1963), *La Villa Aldobrandini di Frascati* (Rome: Staderini).

—(1978), *Castel Sant'Angelo e Borgo tra Roma e Papato* (Rome: Società Romana).

Oorthuys, Gerrit, and Moller, Werner (1995), *Mart Stam* (Milan: Rassegna).

Oosterman, Arjen (ed.) (1995), *William Marinus Dudok: Architekt-Stedebouwkundige 1884–1974* (Naarden: V & K Publishing/Immerc).

Orazi, Anna Maria (1982), *Jacopo Barozzi da Vignola, 1528–1550* (Rome: Bulzoni).

Orme, Philibert de l' (1567), *Architecture* (Paris: F. Morel).

Ortner, Eugen (1978), *Der Barockbaumeister Balthasar Neumann* (Munich: Ehrenwirth).

Ortolani, Sergio (1927), *San Carlo ai Catinari* (Rome: Treves).

Osborne, Harold (ed.) (1970), *The Oxford Companion to Art* (Oxford: Clarendon Press).

—(1975), *The Oxford Companion to the Decorative Arts* (Oxford: Clarendon Press).

Oshchepkov, Grigori D. (1955), *I. V. Zholtovskii* (Moscow: ILPSIA).

Östberg, Ragnar (1908), *Auswahl von schwedischer Architektur der Gegenwart* (Stockholm: Aktiebolaget Ljus).

Ostwald, Hans (1948), *Otto Wagner* (Baden: Verlag Buchdruckerei).

Ottenheym, Koen (1989), *Philips Vingboons (1607–1678), Architect* (Zutphen: Walburg).

Otto, Christian F. (1979), *Space into Light: The Churches of Balthasar Neumann* (New York: The Architectural History Foundation).

Otto, Frei (1961), *Structures: Traditional and Lightweight* (New Haven: Yale UP).

—(1963), *Lightweight Structures* (Berkeley: University of California Press).

Ousiannikov, Iurii (1982), *Franchesko Bartolomeo Rastrelli* (Leningrad: Iskusstvo).

Ouvrard, Nicole, Bouniort, Jeanne, and Huet, Sabine (1986), *Vienne 1880–1938: L'Apocalypse Joyeuse* (Paris: Éditions du Centre Pompidou).

Overy, Paul (1969), *De Stijl* (London: Studio Vista).

—*et al.* (1988), *The Rietveld–Schröder house* (Cambridge, Mass.: MIT Press).

Oxford English Dictionary (OED) (1933) (Oxford: Clarendon Press).

Ozenfant, Amédée (1968), *Mémoires, 1886–1962* (Paris: Seghers).

—and Jeanneret-Gris, Charles-Édouard (1975), *Après le Cubisme* (Turin: Bottega d'Erasmo; repr. of 1918 edn.).

Ozinga, M. D. (1939), *Daniel Marot: De Schepper van den Hollandschen Lodewijk XIV-Stijl* (Amsterdam: Paris).

Paatz, Walter, and Paatz, Elisabeth (1940–54), *Die Kirchen von Florenz* (Frankfurt: Klostermann).

Paavilainen, Simo (ed.) (1982), *Nordic Classicism 1910–1930* (Helsinki: Museum of Finnish Architecture).

Padover, Saul K. (ed.) (1946), *Thomas Jefferson and the National Capitol* (Washington: US Government Printing Office).

Paetow, Karl (1929), *Klassizismus und Romantik auf Wilhelmshöhe* (Kassel: Bärenreiter).

Paine, Judith (1979), *Theodate Pope Riddle: Her Life and Work* (Washington: National Park Service).

Paley, F. A. (1844), *Illustrations of Baptismal Fonts* (London: van Voorst).

Palladio, Andrea (1570), *I Quattro Libri dell' Architettura* (Venice: D. de' Franceschi). See also *The Architecture of A. Palladio in four books . . . to which are added several notes and observations made by Inigo Jones . . .* (London: Leoni, 1715–20).

—(1965), *The Four Books of Andrea Palladio's Architecture* (New York: Dover).

—(1997), *The Four Books of Architecture*, tr. R. Tavernor and R. Schofield (Cambridge, Mass.: MIT Press).

Pallasmaa, Juhani (ed.) (1980), *Aulis Blomstedt: Architect* (Helsinki: Museum of Finnish Architecture).

Pampaloni, Guido (1963), *Palazzo Strozzi* (Rome: Istituto nazionale della assicuriazioni).

Pane, Robert (1956), *Ferdinand Fuga* (Naples: Edizione Scientifiche Italiane).

—(1964), *Antonio Gaudí* (Milan: Comunità).

Panizza, Giorgio, and Mazzottas, Adele Buratti (1990), *Pellegrino Pellegrini 1527–1596* (Milan: Polifilo).

Panofsky, Erwin (ed.) (1979), *Suger, Abbot of Saint-Denis, 1081–1151* (Princeton: Princeton UP).

Papachristou, Tician (1970), *Marcel Breuer: New Buildings and Projects* (New York: Praeger).

Papadaki, Stamo (1960), *Oscar Niemeyer* (New York: Braziller).

Papadakis, A (ed.) (1989), *The Architecture of Pluralism* (London: Academy Editions).

—and Watson, H. (1990), *New Classicism* (London: Academy Editions).

Papanek, V. (1985), *Design for the Real World* (London: Thames & Hudson).

Papini, Roberto (1946), *Francesco di Giorgio architetto* (Florence: Electa).

Papworth, John Buonarotti (1832), *Rural Residences . . .* (London: Sedding & Tuttle).

Papworth, Wyatt Angelicus van Sandau (1852, 1887, 1892), *The Dictionary of Architecture* (London: The Architectural Publication Society, published by Thomas Richards, vols. i–vi (from 1852)), and Whiting & Co. (vols. vii (1887) and viii (1892)).

—(1879), *J. B. Papworth, Architect to the King of Wurtemburg* (n.p.).

Pare, Richard (1997), *Tadao Ando: The Colours of Light* (London: Phaidon).

Parent, Michel, and Verroust, Jacques (1971), *Vauban* (Paris: J. Fréal).

Pariset, François-Georges (1980), *Victor Louis, 1731–1800* (Bordeaux: Bibliothèque municipale).

Parissien, Steven (1997), *Station to Station* (London: Phaidon).

Parker, John Henry (1850), *A Glossary of Terms used in Grecian, Roman, Italian, and Gothic Architecture* (Oxford: The Author, and London: David Bogue).

Parreaux, André, and Plaisant, Michèle (eds.) (1977), *Jardins et Paysages: le style anglais* (Villeneuve d'Ascq: Publications de l'Université de Lille).

Pascoli, Lione (1965), *Vite de' pittori, scultori, ed architetti moderni* (Amsterdam: Israel; repr. of 1736 edn.).

Pastine, D. (1975), *Juan Caramuel* (Florence: Nuova Italia).

Paterson, A. N. (1921), 'Sir Robert Rowand Anderson', *Journal of the Royal Institute of British Architects*, ser. 3/28: 511–13.

Patetta, Luciano (1972), *L'Architettura in Italia, 1919–1943: Le Polemiche* (Milan: Clup).

—(1987), *L'architettura del quattrocento a Milano* (Milan: Clup).

—(ed.) (1990), *L'architettura della Compagnia di Gesù in Italia* (Brescia: Grafo).

Patrick, James A. (1980), *Architecture in Tennessee: 1768–1897* (Knoxville, Tenn.: University of Tennessee Press).

Paul, Sherman (1962), *Louis Sullivan: An Architect in American Thought* (Englewood Cliffs, NJ: Prentice-Hall).

Paulsson, Thomas (1958), *Scandinavian Architecture: Buildings and Society in Denmark, Finland, Norway, and Sweden from the Iron Age until Today* (London: Leonard Hill).

Paulus, Richard (1912), *Der Baumeister Henrico Zuccalli am kurbayerischen Hofe zu München* (Strasbourg: Heitz).

Pawley, Martin (1994), *Future Systems: The Story of Tomorrow* (London: Phaidon).

Pawlowski, Christophe (1967), *Tony Garnier et les débuts de l'urbanisme functionnel en France* (Paris: Centre de recherche d'urbanisme).

Pawson, John (1996), *Minimum* (London: Phaidon).

Pedretti, Carlo (1985), *Leonardo, Architect* (New York: Rizzoli).

Pehnt, Wolfgang (1970), *German Architecture 1960–1970* (New York: Praeger).

—(1973), *Expressionist Architecture* (London: Thames & Hudson).

—(1991), *Rudolf Steiner, Goetheanum, Dornach* (Berlin: Ernst & Sohn).

Peisch, Mark L. (1964), *The Chicago School of Architecture: Early Followers of Sullivan and Wright* (London: Phaidon).

Peña, Ignacio (1996), *The Christian Art of Byzantine Syria* (Reading: Garnet).

Penfold, Alastair (ed.) (1980), *Thomas Telford, Engineer* (London: Thomas Telford).

Penman, A. (1989), *The CAD Systems Handbook* (London: ADT/Longman).

Pereda de la Reguera, Manuel (ed.) (1951),

Rodrigo Gil de Hontañon (Santander: Imp. y Enc. de la Librería Moderna).

Perks, Sydney (1922), *The History of the Mansion House* (Cambridge: Cambridge UP).

Pérouse de Montclos, Jean-Marie (1974), *Étienne-Louis Boullée 1728–1799: Theoretician of Revolutionary Architecture* (New York: Braziller).

Perrault, Claude (1683), *Ordonnance des cinq espèces de colonnes selon la méthode des anciens* (Paris: J.-B. Coignard). See also the translation by John James, *A Treatise of the Five Orders of Architecture* (London: printed by Motte and sold by Sturt, 1708).

Perret, Auguste (1959), *Perret: Catalogue de l'exposition organisée à l'occasion de la remise au Conservatoire du fonds A. G. Perret* (Paris: Conservatoire National des Arts et Métiers).

Perriand, Charlotte (1985), *Charlotte Perriand: un art de vivre* (Paris: Musée des Arts Décoratifs).

Perrin, Louis-Jean-Sainte-Marie (1889), *Pierre Bossan, Architecte* (Lyons: Mougin-Rhiand).

—(1912), *La Basilique de Fourière* (Lyons: Vitte).

Persius, Friedrich Ludwig (1843–9), *Architektonische entwürfe für den Umbau vorhandener Gebäude* (Potsdam: Ferdinand Riegel).

Peschken, Goerd, and Klünner, Hans-Werner (1982), *Das Berliner Schloss* (Frankfurt-am-Main: Propyläen).

Petersen, A. D. (ed.) (1968), *De Stijl* (Amsterdam: Athenaeum).

Peterson, Charles E. (ed.) (1976), *Building Early America* (Radnor, Pa.: Chilton).

Petsch, Joachim (1978), *Baukunst und Stadtplanung im Dritten Reich* (Munich: Hanser).

Pettena, Gianni (ed.) (1981), *Richard Meier* (Venice: Marsilio).

—(1982), *Superstudio, 1966–1982* (Florence: Electa).

—(ed.) (1988), *Hans Hollein, Opere, 1960–88* (Florence and Milan: Electa).

Petzet, Michael (1961), *Soufflots Sainte-Geneviève und der französische Kirchenbau des 18. Jahrhunderts* (Berlin: de Gruyter).

Pevsner, Nikolaus (1960), *An Outline of European Architecture* (Harmondsworth: Penguin).

—(1963), *The Choir of Lincoln Cathedral: An Interpretation* (London: Oxford UP).

—(1968), *Studies in Art, Architecture and Design* (London: Thames & Hudson).

—(1969), *Ruskin and Viollet-le-Duc: Englishness and Frenchness in the Appreciation of Gothic Architecture* (London: Thames & Hudson).

—(1972), *Some Architectural Writers of the Nineteenth Century* (Oxford: Clarendon Press).

—(ed.) (1974), *The Picturesque Garden and its Influence outside the British Isles* (Washington: Dumbarton Oaks, Trustees for Harvard University).

—(1974*a*), *Pioneers of Modern Design* (Harmondsworth: Penguin).

—(1976), *A History of Building Types* (London: Thames & Hudson).

—*et al.* (1951–), *The Buildings of England* series (Harmondsworth: Penguin).

——(1979–), *The Buildings of Ireland* (Harmondsworth: Penguin; see also Casey and Rowan (1993) and Rowan (1979)).

——(1978–), *The Buildings of Scotland* (Harmondsworth: Penguin; see also Gifford, McWilliam, and Walker (1984), and Williamson, Riches, and Higgs (1990)).

——(1979–), *The Buildings of Wales* (Harmondsworth: Penguin; see also Hubbard (1986) and Newman (1995)).

—and Richards, J. M. (eds.) (1973), *The Anti-Rationalists* (London: Architectural Press).

Pfankuch, Peter (1974), *Hans Scharoun: Bauten, Entwürfe, Texte* (Berlin: Akademie der Künste).

Pfister, Rudolf (1968), *Theodor Fischer: Leben und Wirken eines deutschen Baumeisters* (Munich: Callwey).

Phillips, L. (1989), *Frederick Kiesler* (New York: Norton).

Physick, John Frederick, and Darby, Michael (1973), *Marble Halls: Drawings and Models for Victorian Secular Buildings* (London: Victoria & Albert Museum).

Piacentini, Marcello (1930), *Architettura d'oggi* (Rome: Cremonesi).

Piano, Renzo (1989), *Renzo Piano and Building Workshop: Buildings and Projects, 1971–1989* (New York: Rizzoli).

Pica, Agnoldomenico (1936), *Nuova architettura italiana* (Milan: Hoepli).

—(1969), *Pier Luigi Nervi* (Rome: Editalia).

Piccinato, Giorgio (1965), *L'architettura contemporanea in Francia* (Rocca San Casciano: Capelli).

Picon, Antoine (1988), *Claude Perrault, 1613–1688, ou, la Curiosité d'un Classique* (Paris: Picard).

Picton, J. A. (1875), *Memorials of Liverpool* (London: Longmans).

Pierson, William Harvey, and Jordy, William H. (1970–86), *American Buildings and their Architects* (New York: Doubleday).

Pigage, Nicholas de (1805), *La galerie électorale de Düsseldorf: ou, catalogue raisonné et figuré de ses tableaux* (Düsseldorf: Daenzer).

Pile, John (1994), *Dictionary of 20th-Century Design* (New York: Da Capo).

Pilyavski, V. I. (1970), *Zodchii Vasilii Petrovich Stasov* (Leningrad: Soyuz S. A. SSR).

Pinelli, Antonio (1971), *Genga architetto: Aspetti della Cultura Urbinate del primo 500* (Rome: Bulzoni).

Pinkney, David H. (1958), *Napoleon III and the Rebuilding of Paris* (Princeton: Princeton UP).

Pintarič, V. Horvat (1989), *Vienna 1900: The*

Architecture of Otto Wagner (London: Studio Editions).

Pinto, John A. (1986), *The Trevi Fountain* (New Haven: Yale UP).

Piranesi, Giovanni Battista (1769), *Diverse maniere d'adornare i Cammini* (Rome: Salomoni).

Pirr, Margot (1940), *Die Architektur des Wendel Dietterlin* (Gräfenhainischen: Schulze).

Pirrone, Gianni (1971), *Palermo Liberty* (Rome: Sciascia).

Pisano, Niccolò (1958), *Barocco in Sicilia* (Syracuse: Isola d'Ora).

Pitz, Helge, and Brenne, Winfried (1980), *Siedlung Onkel Tom, Zehlendorf, Ein familienhäuser 1929, Architekt: Bruno Taut* (Rome: Punto).

Pizzi, Emilio (1991), *Mario Botta* (Barcelona: Gustavo Gili).

Place, Charles A. (1968), *Charles Bulfinch: Architect and Citizen* (New York: Da Capo).

Placzek, Adolf K. (1968), *The Phantastic Engravings of Wendel Dietterlin* (New York: Dover).

—(ed.) (1982), *Macmillan Encyclopaedia of Architects* (London and New York: The Free Press).

Pla Dalmáu, José María (1951), *La Arquitectura Barroca española y el Churriguerismo* (Gerona: Editorial Dalmáu Carles, Pla).

Plagemann, Volker (1967), *Das deutsche Kunstmuseum 1790–1870* (Munich: Prestel).

Platt, Charles Adams (1913), *Monograph of the Work of Charles A. Platt* (New York: Architectural Books).

Platz, Gustav A. (1927), *Die Baukunst der neuesten Zeit* (Berlin: Propyläen).

Poelzig, Hans (1954), *Der Architekt* (Tübingen: Wasmuth).

Poensgen, Georg (1930), *Die Bauten Friedrich Wilhelms IV. in Potsdam* (Berlin: Deutscher Kunstverlag).

Polano, Sergio (1988), *Hendrik Petrus Berlage: Complete Works 1856–1934* (New York: Rizzoli).

Pollak, Ernst (1926), *Die Baumeister Otto Bartning* (Berlin: The Author).

Polleross, Friedrich (1995), *Fischer von Erlach und die Wiener Barocktradition* (Vienna: Böhlau Verlag).

Pommer, Richard (1967), *Eighteenth-Century Architecture in Piedmont: The Open Structures of Juvarra, Alfieri, & Vittone* (New York: New York UP).

—(1988), *In the Shadow of Mies: Ludwig Hilbersheimer, Architect* (Chicago: Art Institute and Rizzoli).

—and Otto, Christian F. (1991), *Weissenhof 1927 and the Modern Movement in Architecture* (Chicago: University of Chicago Press).

Poncetton, François (1939), *Eiffel: le magicien du fer* (Paris: Tournelle).

Ponti, Lisa Licitra (1990), *Gio Ponti: The Complete Work, 1923–1978* (Cambridge, Mass.: MIT Press).

Pope-Hennessy, John (1958), *Italian Renaissance Sculpture* (London: Phaidon).

Popp, Hermann (1924), *Die Architektur der Barock- und Rokokozeit in Deutschland und der Schweiz* (Stuttgart: Hoffmann).

Popp, Joseph (1916), *Bruno Paul* (Munich: Bruckmann).

Porphyrios, Demetri (1982), *Sources of Modern Eclecticism: Studies on Alvar Aalto* (London: Academy Editions).

Port, Michael Harry (1961), *Six Hundred New Churches: A Study of The Church Building Commission 1818–56* (London: SPCK).

—(ed.) (1976), *The Houses of Parliament* (New Haven and London: Yale UP).

Portman, John, and Barnett, Jonathan (1976), *The Architect as Developer* (New York: McGraw-Hill).

Portoghesi, Paolo (1956), *Guarino Guarini* (Milan: Electa).

—(1960), *Metodo e poesia nell' architettura di Bernardo Antonio Vittone* (Turin: Societá Piemontese de Archeologia e Belle Arti).

—(1964), *Michelangelo architetto* (Turin: Einaudi).

—(1966), *Bernardo Vittone* (Rome: Elefante).

—(1968), *L'eclettismo a Roma 1870–1922* (Rome: De Luca).

—(1970), *Roma Barocca: The History of an Architectonic Culture* (Cambridge, Mass.: MIT Press).

—(1982), *Borromini nella cultura europea* (Rome-Bari: Laterza).

—(1983), *Postmodern: The Architecture of the Postindustrial Society* (New York: Rizzoli).

—(1990), *Francesco Borromini* (Milan: Electa).

Posener, Julius (1970), *Hans Poelzig: gesammelte Schriften und Werke* (Berlin: Mann).

—(1979), *Berlin auf dem Wege zu einer neuen Archittekur* (Munich: Prestel).

—(1992), *Hans Poelzig: Reflections on his Life and Work* (New York: Architectural History Foundation).

Powell, Caryll Nicolas Peter (1959), *From Baroque to Rococo: An Introduction to Austrian and German Architecture from 1580 to 1790* (London: Faber & Faber).

Powell, Kenneth (1995), *Edward Cullinan Architects* (London: Academy Editions).

Powers, Alan (ed.) (1987), *Real Architecture* (London: Building Centre Trust).

Pozzetto, Marco (1966), *Max Fabiani Architetto* (Gorizia: Comune di Gorizia).

—(1979), *La Scuola di Wagner, 1894–1912* (Trieste: Comune di Trieste).

Prager, Frank D., and Scaglia, Giustina (1970), *Brunelleschi: Studies of his Technology and Inventions* (Cambridge, Mass.: MIT Press).

Prelovšek, Damjan (1979), *Josef Plečnik: Wiener Arbeiten 1896–1914* (Vienna: Tusch).

—— (1997), *Jože Plečnik* (New Haven and London: Yale UP).

Prévost, Jean (1929), *Eiffel* (Paris: Reider).

—— (1948), *Philibert Delorme* (Paris: Gallimard).

Preziosi, D. (1979), *Semiotics of the Built Environment* (Bloomington, Ind.: Indiana UP).

Price, Cedric (1971), *Air Structures: A Survey Commissioned by the Ministry of Public Buildings and Works* (London: HMSO).

—— (1984), *Works* (London: Architectural Association).

Price, Uvedale (1810), *Essays on the Picturesque as compared with the Sublime and Beautiful . . .* (London: Mawman).

Pride, Glen L. (1996), *Dictionary of Scottish Building* (Edinburgh: Rutland Press).

Prisbrey, Tessa (1967), *Grandma's Bottle Village* (n.p.: privately printed).

Probst, Hartmut, and Schädlich, Christian (1986–8), *Walter Gropius* (Berlin: Ernst).

Proulx, M. (1977), *Electric Art* (New York: Rizzoli).

Puget, Wanda (ed.) (1994), *Kwartalnik Architektury i Urbanistyki Teoria i Historia*, 38/3–4 (Warsaw: Wydawnictwo Naukowe PWN).

Pugin, Augustus Welby Northmore (1841), *The Present State of Ecclesiastical Architecture in England* (London: Dolman).

—— (1843), *An Apology for the Revival of Christian Architecture in England* (London: John Weale).

—— (1843a), *The True Principles of Pointed or Christian Architecture* (London: Henry G. Bohn; originally published in 1841).

—— (1973), *Contrasts* (Leicester: Leicester UP; originally published in 1836).

Pugsley, Sir Alfred (ed.) (1980), *The Works of Isambard Kingdom Brunel: An Engineering Appreciation* (Cambridge: Cambridge UP).

Puppi, Lionello (1971), *Michele Sanmicheli* (Padua: Marsilio).

—— (1975), *Andrea Palladio* (London and New York: Phaidon).

—— (1980), *Andrea Palladio* (Vicenza: Electa).

—— (1980a), *Il Caffè Pedrocchi di Padova* (Vicenza: Pozza).

—— *et al.* (eds.) (1982), *Longhena* (Milan: Electa).

Puppi, Loredana Olivato, and Puppi, Lionello (1977), *Mauro Codussi* (Milan: Electa).

Puttemans, Pierre (1976), *Modern Architecture in Belgium* (Brussels: Vokaert).

Puyfontaine, H. Roy de (1972), *Louis-Michel Thibault, 1750–1815* (Cape Town: Tafelberg).

Quaglio, Johann Maria von (1823), *Praktische Anleitung zur Perspektive mit Anwendung auf die Baukunst* (Munich: Kunst-Anstalt an der Feyertags-Schule).

Quantrill, Malcolm (1995), *Finnish Architecture and the Modernist Tradition* (London: E. & F. N. Spon).

Quarenghi, Giacomo (1821), *Fabbriche e disegni di Giacomo Quarenghi architetto de S. M. l'Imperatore di Russia cavaliere di Malta e di S Walodimiro illustrate dal Cav. Giulio suo figlio* (Milan: Paolo Antonio Tosi).

Quaroni, Ludovico (1980), *Giovanni Michelucci* (Florence: Vallecchi).

Quatremère de Quincy, Antoine-Chrysostôme (1788–1825), *Dictionnaire d'Architecture* in the *Encylopédie Méthodique* (Paris: Panckoucke).

—— (1803), *De l'architecture égyptienne considerée dans son origine, ses principes, et son goût, et comparée sous les mêmes rapports à l'architecture grecque* (Paris: Barrois).

—— (1814), *Le Jupiter Olympien ou l'art de la sculpture antique considerée sous un nouveau point de vue* (Paris: Debure).

—— (1823), *Essai sur la Nature* (Paris: Treuttel & Würtz).

—— (1828), *De l'invention et de l'innovation dans les Beaux-Arts* (Paris: Firmin-Didot).

—— (1830), *Histoire de la vie et des œuvres des plus célèbres architectes du XIe siècle jusqu'à la fin du XVIIIe* (Paris: Renouard).

—— (1832), *Dictionnaire Historique d'Architecture* (Paris: Leclère).

—— (1834), *Recueil de Notices Historiques lues dans les Séances Publiques de l'Académie Royale des Beaux-Arts* (Paris: Leclère).

Queysanna, Bruno (1986), *J. B. Santini-Aichel: un architecte baroque-gothique en Bohème, 1677–1723* (Grenoble: École d'architecture).

Quilici, Vieri, and Scolari, Massimo (eds.) (1975), *Ivan Leonidov* (Milan: Angeli).

Quiney, Anthony (1979), *John Loughborough Pearson (1817–1897)* (New Haven and London: Yale UP).

Radice, Barbara (1993), *Ettore Sottsass: A Critical Biography* (New York: Rizzoli).

Rados, Jenö (1975), *A magyar építészettörtenete* (Budapest: Müszaki Könyvkladó).

Raeburn, Michael (ed.) (1991), *The Twilight of the Tsars* (London: South Bank Centre).

—— and Wilson, Victoria (eds.) (1987), *Le Corbusier: Architect of the Century* (London: Arts Council of Great Britain).

Raev, Svetlozar (1982), *Gottfried Böhm: Bauten und Projekte 1950–1980* (Cologne: König).

Raggi, O. (1857), *Della vita e delle opere di L. Canina* (Casal Monferrato: Nani).

Randall, Frank A. (1949), *History of the Development of Building Construction in Chicago* (Urbana, Ill.: University of Illinois Press).

Rankin, Peter (1972), *Irish Building Ventures of the Earl Bishop of Derry 1730–1803* (Belfast: Ulster Architectural Heritage Society).

Raschdorff, Julius (1879), *Entwürfe und*

Bauausführungen im Stile deutscher Renaissance (Berlin: Wasmuth).

Raschdorff, Julius (1886–1922), *Palast-Architektur von Ober-Italien und Toscana von XIII. bis XVII. Jahrhundert* (Berlin: Wasmuth).

Rasmussen, Steen Eiler (1940), *Nordiske Baukunst* (Berlin: Wasmuth).

Rau, Julia, Gräfin von der Schulenburg (1973), *Emmanuel Héré: premier architecte von Stanislas Leszcynski in Lotharingen (1705–1763)* (Berlin: Mann).

Ray, K. (ed.) (1980), *Contextual Architecture: Responding to Existing Style* (New York: McGraw-Hill).

Ray, Stefano (1969), *Il contributo svedese all' architettura contemporanea e l'opera di Sven Markelius* (Rome: Officina).

—(1974), *Raffaello architetto: linguaggio artistico e ideologia nel Rinascimento romano* (Rome: Laterza).

—(1978), *Ralph Erskine: architettura di bricolage e partecipazione* (Bari: Dedalo).

Raymond, Antonin (1973), *Antonin Raymond: An Autobiography* (Rutland, Vt.: Tuttle).

Reau, Louis, Lavedan, Pierre, *et al.* (1954), *L'Œuvre du Baron Haussmann* (Paris: Presses Universitaires).

Rébelliau, Alfred (1962), *Vauban* (Paris: Fayard).

Recht, Roland (ed.) (1989), *Les bâtisseurs de cathédrales gothiques* (Strasbourg: Éditions les musées de la ville de Strasbourg).

Redslob, Edwin (ed.) (1922), *Alt-Dänemarck* (Munich: Delphin).

Reed, Henry Hope, and Duckworth, Sophia (1967), *Central Park: A History and a Guide* (New York: C. N. Potter).

Reese, Thomas Ford (1976), *The Architecture of Ventura Rodríguez* (New York: Garland).

Reichensperger, Auguste (1866), *Georg Gottlob Ungewitter* (Leipzig: Wiegel).

Reidelbach, Hans (1888), *König Ludwig I. von Bayern und seine Kunstschöpfungen* (Munich: Roth).

Reiff, Daniel D. (1977), *Washington Architecture 1791–1861* (Washington: US Commission of Fine Arts).

Reilly, Charles (1931), *Representative British Architects of the Present Day* (London: Batsford).

—(1972), *McKim, Mead, & White* (New York: Blom; repr. of 1924 edn.).

Reinink, Adriaan Wessel (1975), *Amsterdam en de Beurs van Berlage* (The Hague: Staatsuitgeverij).

Remnant, G. L. (1969), *A Catalogue of Misericords in Great Britain* (Oxford: Clarendon Press).

Rensselaer, Mrs Schuyler van (1969), *Henry Hobson Richardson and his works* (New York: Dover).

Reps, John W. (1967), *Monumental Washington* (Princeton: Princeton UP).

Retera, W. K. (1928), *P. Kramer* (Amsterdam: van Munster).

Reudenbach, Bruno (1979), *G. B. Piranesi: Architektur als Bild* (Munich: Prestel).

Reutersward, Patrik (1965), *The Two Churches of the Invalides* (Stockholm: National Museum).

Reuther, Hans (1960), *Die Kirchenbauten Balthasar Neumanns* (Berlin: Hessling).

—(1969), *Barock in Berlin* (Berlin: Rembrandt).

Rey, Robert (1923), *Frantz Jourdain* (Paris: La Connaissance).

Reyburn, Wallace (1972), *Bridge across the Atlantic: The Story of John Rennie* (London: Harrap).

Reynolds, R. (1987), *Computing for Architects* (London: Butterworth).

Rheims, Maurice, and Vigne, Georges (1988), *Hector Guimard* (New York: Abrams).

Rhodes James, Robert (1983), *Albert, Prince Consort* (London: Hamilton).

Rice, Tamara Talbot, and Tait, A. A. (1967–8), *Charles Cameron* (London: Arts Council).

Richards, J. (1973), *The Castles on the Ground: The Anatomy of Suburbia* (London: Murray).

Richards, James Maude (1958), *The Functionalist Tradition in Early Industrial Buildings* (London: Architectural Press).

—(1966), *A Guide to Finnish Architecture* (London: Evelyn).

—(1978), *800 Years of Finnish Architecture* (Newton Abbot: David & Charles).

—Serageldin, Ismael, and Rastorfer, Darl (1985), *Hassan Fathy* (Singapore: Concept Media).

Richardson, Albert E. (1914), *Monumental Classic Architecture in Great Britain and Ireland during the Eighteenth and Nineteenth Centuries* (London: Batsford).

Richardson, Margaret (1980), 'George Aitchison: Lord Leighton's Architect', *Journal of the Royal Institute of British Architects*, 39: 37–40.

—(1983), *Architects of the Arts and Crafts Movement* (London: Trefoil Books).

Richardson, Sara (1987), *Gottfried Böhm* (Monticello, Ill.: Vance).

Riche de Prony, Gaspard-Clair-François-Marie (1829), *Notice historique sur Jean-Rudolphe Perronet* (Paris: Firmin-Didot).

Richter, H. (1958), *El Lissitzky: Sieg über die Sonne. Zur Kunst des Konstruktivismus* (Cologne: Czwiklitzer).

Rickman, Thomas (1848), *An Attempt to Discriminate the Styles of Architecture in England from the Conquest to the Reformation* (London and Oxford: John Henry Parker, revised edn.).

Riedl, D. (1977), *Henrico Zuccalli: Planung und Bau des Neuen Schlosses Schleissheim* (Munich: Riedl).

Riemann, Gottfried (ed.) (1981), *Karl Friedrich Schinkel 1781–1841* (Berlin: DEB).

Rijksmuseum (1975), *Nederlandse Architectuur 1880–1930, Americana* (Otterloo: Rijksmuseum).
Riseboro, B. (1983), *Modern Architecture and Design: An Alternative History* (Cambridge, Mass.: MIT Press).
Rispa, Raúl (ed.) (1996), *Barragán: The Complete Works* (London: Thames & Hudson).
Rittich, Werner (1938), *Architektur und Bauplastik* (Berlin: Rembrandt).
Roberts, E. S. (ed.) (1912), *The Works of John Caius* (Cambridge: Cambridge UP).
Roberts, Henry D. (1939), *A History of the Royal Pavilion, Brighton* (London: Country Life).
Robertson, Donald Struan (1945), *A Handbook of Greek and Roman Architecture* (Cambridge: Cambridge UP; revised edn. 1969).
Robertson, Donald W. (1974), *Mind's Eye of Richard Buckminster Fuller* (New York: Vantage).
Robertson, E. Graeme (1970), *Early Buildings of Southern Tasmania* (Melbourne: Georgian House).
Robertson, Howard (1924), *The Principles of Architectural Composition* (London: Architectural Press).
Robertson, Pamela (1995), *Charles Rennie Mackintosh: Art is the Flower* (London: Pavilion Books).
Robins, C. (1985), *The Pluralist Era: American Art 1968–81* (New York: Harper & Row).
Robinson, John Martin (1979), *The Wyatts: An Architectural Dynasty* (Oxford: Oxford UP).
—and Artley, Alexandra (1985), *The New Georgian Handbook* (London: Ebury Press).
Robinson, Sidney K. (1983), *The Architecture of Alden B. Dow* (Detroit: Wayne State UP).
Robson, Edward Robert (1972), *School Architecture* (Leicester: Leicester UP; new edn. of 1874 publication).
Rochas d'Aiglun, Albert de (ed.) (1910), *Vauban, sa famille et ses écrits* (Paris: Berger-Levrault).
Rochester, University of (1972), *A Rediscovery: Harvey Ellis: Artist, Architect* (Rochester, NY: Memorial Art Gallery of the University of Rochester & Margaret Woodbury Strong Museum).
Rochowanski, Leopold (1950), *Joseph Hoffmann* (Vienna: Österreichische Staatsdrückerei).
Rock, Joe (1984), *Thomas Hamilton, Architect, 1784–1858* (Edinburgh: The Author and Talbot Rice Art Centre).
Roeck, Bernd (1985), *Elias Holl: Architekt einer europäischen Stadt* (Regensburg: Pustet).
Rogerson, Robert W. C. K. (1986), *Jack Coia: His Life and Work* (Glasgow: The Author).
Rohe, Wilhelm (1934), *Karl Ferdinand Langhans: Ein theaterbaumeister des Klassizismus* (Bückeburg: Prinz).
Roland, Conrad (1970), *Frei Otto: Tension Structures* (New York: Praeger).
Rolt, L. T. C. (1957), *Isambard Kingdom Brunel: A Biography* (London: Longmans, Green).
—(1958), *Thomas Telford* (London and New York: Longmans, Green).
—(1960), *George and Robert Stephenson* (London: Longmans, Green).
Romanini, Angiola Maria (1980), *Arnolfo di Cambio e lo stil novo del gotico italiano* (Florence: Sansoni).
Rondelet, Antoine-J.-B. (1852), *Notice Historique sur l'église de Sainte-Geneviève* (Paris: Remquet).
Rondelet, Jean-Baptiste (1790), *Memoire sur l'Architecture* (Paris: Gueffier).
—(1802–17), *Traité théorique et pratique de l'art de bâtir* (Paris: The Author).
Ronner, Heinz (1987), *Louis I. Kahn: Complete Works, 1935–1974* (Basle: Birkhäuser).
Roper, Laura Wood (1973), *F. L. O.: A Biography of Frederick Law Olmsted* (Baltimore: Johns Hopkins UP).
Roseberry, Cecil (1964), *Capitol Story* (Albany, NY: State of New York).
Rosenau, Helen (ed.) (1953), *Boullée's Treaty on Architecture* (London: Tiranti).
—(1975), *The Ideal City in its Architectural Evolution* (New York: Harper & Row).
—(1976), *Boullée and his Visionary Architecture* (London: Academy Editions).
Rosenberg, H. P. R. (1972), *De 19de-eeuwse kerkelijke bouwkunst in Nederland* (The Hague: Staatsuitgeverij).
Rosenberg, Jakob, Slive, Seymour, and Ter Kuile, E. H. (1966), *Dutch Art and Architecture 1600–1800* (Harmondsworth: Penguin; revised edn. 1977).
Rosenblum, Robert (1967), *Transformations in Late-Eighteenth-Century Art* (Princeton: Princeton UP).
Rosenfeld, Myra Nana (1978), *Sebastiano Serlio on Domestic Architecture* (New York: Architectural History Foundation).
Rosenthal, Earl E. (1961), *The Cathedral of Granada* (Princeton: Princeton UP).
—(1985), *The Palace of Charles V in Granada* (Princeton: Princeton UP).
Rossi, Aldo (ed.) (1967), *Étienne-Louis Boullée, Architettura* (Padua: Marsilio).
—(1982), *The Architecture of the City* (Cambridge, Mass.: MIT Press).
—*et al.* (1973), *Architettura Razionale, XV di Milano* (Milan: Franco Angelli Editore).
Rosso, Franco (1989), *Alessandro Antonelli 1798–1888* (Milan: Electa).
Rossow, Walter, *et al.* (1980), *Arbeitsrat für Kunst: Berlin* (Berlin: Akademie der Künste).
Roth, Alfred (1946), *La Nouvelle Architecture* (Zurich and Erlenbach: Éditions d'architecture).

Roth, Alfred (1973), *Begegnung mit Pionieren* (Basle: Birkhäuser).
—(1977), *Zwei Wohnhäuser von Le Corbusier und Pierre Jeanneret* (Stuttgart: Krämer; repr. of 1927 original).
Roth, Leland M. (ed.) (1973), *A Monograph of the Works of McKim, Mead, & White 1879–1915* (New York: Blom; new edn. of 1915 publication).
—(1980), *A Concise History of American Architecture* (New York: HarperCollins).
—(1983), *McKim, Mead, & White, Architects* (New York: Harper & Row).
Rotili, Mario (1951), *Filippo Raguzzini e il rococò romano* (Rome: Palombi).
—(1982), *Filippo Raguzzini nel terzo centenario della nascita* (Naples: Società editrice napoletana).
Rotondi, Pasquale (1950–1), *Il Palazzo Ducale di Urbino* (Urbino: Istituto Statale d'Arte per Libro).
—(1970), *Francesco di Giorgio nel Palazzo Ducale di Urbino* (Milan: Provinciale Spotorno).
Roullet, Anne (1972), *The Egyptian and Egyptianizing Monuments of Imperial Rome* (Leiden: Brill).
Rovere, Lorenzo, Viale, Vittorio, and Brinckmann, Albert E. (1973), *Filippo Juvarra* (Turin: Crudo).
Rowan, Alistair (1979), *The Buildings of Ireland, North West Ulster* (Harmondsworth: Penguin).
—(1985), *Designs for Castles and Country Villas by Robert and James Adam* (Oxford: Phaidon).
Rowe, Colin (1976), *The Mathematics of the Ideal Villa and Other Essays* (Cambridge, Mass., and London: MIT Press).
—(1994), *The Architecture of Good Intentions: Towards a Possible Retrospect* (London: Academy Editions).
—(1996), *As I was Saying: Recollections and Miscellaneous Essays* (Cambridge, Mass., and London: MIT Press).
— and Koetter, Fred (1984), *Collage City* (Cambridge, Mass., and London: MIT Press).
Rowland, K. (1973), *The Modern Movement in Art, Architecture, and Design* (New York: van Nostrand Reinhold).
Rubens, Godfrey (1986), *William Richard Lethaby: His Life and Work, 1857–1931* (London: Architectural Press).
Ruffinière du Prey, Pierre de la (1982), *John Soane: The Making of an Architect* (Chicago and London: University of Chicago Press).
—(1994), *The Villas of Pliny from Antiquity to Posterity* (Chicago and London: University of Chicago Press).
Ruiz de Arcaute, Agustin (1936), *Juan de Herrera* (Madrid: Espasa-Calpe).
Runciman, Steven (1975), *Byzantine Style and Civilization* (Harmondsworth: Penguin).
Rupprecht, Bernhard (1959), *Die Bayerische Rokokokirche* (Kallmünz: Lassleben).
— and Mülbe, Wolf-Christian von der (1987), *Die Brüder Asam: Sinn und Sinnlichkeit im bayerischen Barock* (Regensburg: Pustet).
Ruskin, John (1903–12), *Works* (London, Longmans, Green).
Russack, Hans H. (1942), *Deutschen Bauen in Alten* (Berlin: Limpert).
Russell, Frank (ed.) (1979), *Art Nouveau Architecture* (London: Academy Editions).
Ryan, William, and Guinness, Desmond (1980), *The White House: An Architectural History* (New York: McGraw Hill).
Rykwert, Joseph (ed.) (1966), *Alberti's Ten Books on Architecture*, tr. Leoni (New York: Transatlantic Arts).
—(1973), *On Adam's House in Paradise* (New York: Museum of Modern Art).
—(1980), *The First Moderns: The Architects of the Eighteenth Century* (Cambridge, Mass.: MIT Press).
— and Rykwert, Anne (1985), *Robert and James Adam: The Men and the Style* (London: Collins).
Saalman, Howard (1971), *Haussmann: Paris Transformed* (New York: Braziller).
—(1980), *Filippo Brunelleschi: The Cupola of Santa Maria del Fiore* (London: Zwemmer).
Saarinen, Aline B. (ed.) (1968), *Eero Saarinen on His Work* (New Haven: Yale UP).
Saarinen, Eliel (1931), *The Cranbrook Development* (Bloomfield Hills, Mich.: Cranbrook Academy).
Sack, Manfred (1995), *Lluís Domènech i Montaner, Palau de la Música Catalana, Barcelona* (Stuttgart: Axel Menges).
Saddy, Pierre (1977), *Henri Labrouste, architecte, 1801–1875* (Paris: Caisse Nationale des Monuments Historiques et des Sites).
Safran, Yehuda, and Wang, Wilfried (eds.) (1985), *The Architecture of Adolf Loos* (London: Arts Council).
Saint, Andrew (1976), *Richard Norman Shaw* (New Haven and London: Yale UP).
—(1987), *Towards a Social Architecture: The Role of School Building in Post-War England* (New Haven and London: Yale, UP).
Saisselin, R. (1985), *Bricabracomania* (London: Thames & Hudson).
Saliga, Pauline, and Woolever, Mary (1995), *The Architecture of Bruce Goff* (London: Thames & Hudson).
Salokorpi, Asko (1970), *Modern Architecture in Finland* (London: Weidenfeld & Nicolson).
Sambrook, John (1989), *Fanlights* (London: Chatto & Windus).
Sanfaçon, Roland (1971), *L'Architecture Flamboyante en France* (Quebec: Presses de l'Université Laval).

Sanpaolesi, Piero (1975), *Il Duomo di Pisa* (Pisa: Nistri-Lischi).

Sarnitz, August (ed.) (1988), *R. M. Schindler, Architect: 1887–1953* (New York: Rizzoli).

Sartoris, Alberto (1936), *Gli elementi dell'architettura funzionale: sintesi panoramica dell'architettura moderna* (Milan: Hoepli).

—— (1948–54), *Encylopédie de l'architecture nouvelle* (Milan: Hoepli).

Satkowski, Leon George (1979), *Studies on Vasari's Architecture* (New York: Garland).

—— (1993), *Giorgio Vasari: Architect and Courtier* (Princeton: Princeton UP).

Sauliol, René (1931), *Le Maréchal de Vauban: Sa Vie, Son Œuvre* (Paris: Lavauzelle).

Saumarez Smith, Charles (1990), *The Building of Castle Howard* (Chicago: University of Chicago Press).

Saunders, Matthew (1982), *The Churches of S. S. Teulon* (London: The Ecclesiological Society).

Saur, K. G. (1991–   ), *Allgemeines Künstlerlexikon* (Leipzig and Munich: Saur).

Sauvage, Henri, and Sarazin, Charles (1904), *Éléments d'Architecture Moderne* (Paris: Schmid).

Savage, Peter (1980), *Lorimer and the Edinburgh Craft Designers* (Edinburgh: Harris).

Savi, Vittorio (1976), *L'Architettura di Aldo Rossi* (Milan: Angeli).

—— (1980), *Luigi Figini e Gino Pollini architetti* (Milan: Electa).

Saxl, Fritz, and Wittkower, Rudolf (1969), *British Art and the Mediterranean* (London: Oxford UP).

Scamozzi, Vincenzo (1615), *L'Idea dell'Architettura Universale* (Venice: Scamozzi, printed by Giorgio Valentino).

Schaffer, Daniel (1982), *Garden Cities for America: The Radburn Experience* (Philadelphia: Temple UP).

Schavo, Armando (1956), *La Fontana di Trevi e le altre opere di Nicola Salvi* (Rome: Istituto Poligrafico dello Stato).

Scheele, Godfrey (1977), *The Prince Consort: Man of Many Faces* (London: Oresko).

Schildt, Göran (1984–91), *Alvar Aalto* (New York: Garland).

Schinkel, Karl Friedrich (1989), *Collection of Architectural Designs* (Guildford: Butterworth Architecture).

Schirmer, Wulf (ed.) (1984), *Egon Eiermann, 1904–1970: Bauten und Projekte* (Stuttgart: Deutsche Verlags-Anstalt).

Schliepmann, Hans (1892), *Martin Gropius* (Berlin: n.p.).

—— (1913), *Paul Wallot* (Berlin: Wasmuth).

Schmädecke, Jürgen (1970), *Der Deutsche Reichstag* (Berlin: Hande & Spener).

Schmalenbach, Werner (1970), *Kurt Schwitters* (New York: Abrams).

Schmid, Elmar D. (1987), *Joseph Effner, 1687–1745: Bauten für Kurfürst Max Emanuel* (Munich: Bayerische Verwaltung der Staatl. Schlösser, Gärten und Seen).

Schnaidt, Claude (ed.) (1965), *Hannes Meyer: Bauten, Projekte, und Schriften* (Teufen: Niggli).

Schneider, Donald David (1977), *The Works and Doctrine of Jacques-Ignace Hittorff 1792–1867* (New York: Garland).

Schneider, Ernst (1937), *Paul Decker der Ältere (1677–1713): Beiträge zu seinem Werk* (Frankfurt-am-Main: Düren).

Schneider, Louis, and Langhans, Karl Ferdinand (1845), *Die Geschichte der Oper und des königlichen Opernhauses in Berlin* (Berlin: Duncker & Humboldt).

Schneider, René (1910), *L'Esthétique classique chez Quatremère de Quincy* (Paris: Hachette).

—— (1910*a*), *Quatremère de Quincy et son Intervention dans les Arts (1788–1830)* (Paris: Hachette).

Schnell, Hugo (1981), *Die Wies* (Munich: Schnell & Steiner).

—— and Schedler, Uta (1988), *Lexikon der Wessobrunner Künstler und Handwerker* (Munich: Schnell & Steiner).

Scholfield, P. H. (1958), *The Theory of Proportion in Architecture* (Cambridge: Cambridge UP).

Schönberger, Angela (ed.) (1990), *Raymond Loewy: Pioneer of American Industrial Design* (Munich: Prestel).

Schreyl, Karl Heinz (1972), *Joseph Maria Olbrich* (Berlin: Mann).

Schubert, Otto (1924), *Historia del barroco en España* (Madrid: Calleja).

Schull, Diantha Dow (1980), *Landmarks of Otsego County* (Syracuse, NY: Syracuse UP).

Schulze, Franz (1985), *Mies van der Rohe: A Critical Biography* (Chicago: University of Chicago Press).

—— (1994), *Philip Johnson: Life and Work* (New York: Knopf).

Schulze-Battman, Elfriede (1939), *Giuseppe Valadier. Ein klassizistischer Architekt Roms* (Dresden: Zetsche).

Schumacher, Thomas L. (1991), *Surface and Symbol: Giuseppe Terragni and the Architecture of Italian Rationalism* (New York: Princeton Architectural Press).

Schumann-Bacia, Eva (1989), *Die Bank von England und ihr Architekt John Soane* (Zurich: Verlag für Architektur Artemis).

—— (1990), *Sir John Soane und die Bank of England, 1788 bis 1833* (Hildesheim and New York: Olms).

Schürer, Oskar (1938), *Elias Holl: Der Augsburger Stadt Werkmeister* (Berlin: VDI).

Schuyler, David, and Censer, Jane Turner (eds.) (1992), *The Papers of Frederick Law Olmsted, vi: The Years of Olmsted, Vaux, and Company 1865–1874* (Baltimore: Johns Hopkins UP).

Schuyler, Hamilton (1931), *The Roeblings* (Princeton: Princeton UP).
Schuyler, Montgomery (1961), *American Architecture and Other Writings* (Cambridge, Mass.: Harvard UP).
Schuyt, Michael, and Elffers, Joost (1980), *Fantastic Architecture: Personal and Eccentric Visions* (London: Thames & Hudson).
Schwartz, Frederic J. (1997), *The Werkbund: Design Theory and Mass Culture before the First World War* (New Haven and London: Yale UP).
Schwartzmann, John B. (1962), *Raymond Hood: The Unheralded Architect* (Charlottesville, Va.: University of Virginia Press).
Schwarz, Maria, and Conrads, Ulrich (1979), *Rudolf Schwarz, Wegweisung der Technik und andere Schriften zum neuen Bauen 1921–1961* (Wiesbaden: Vieweg).
Schwarz, Rudolf (1958), *The Church Incarnate* (Chicago: Regnery).
—(1960), *Kirchenbau: Welt vor der Schwelle* (Heidelberg: Kerle Verlag).
Scott, George Gilbert (1995), *Personal and Professional Recollections*, with an introduction by Gavin Stamp (Stamford: Paul Watkins).
Scott, Ian Jonathan (1975), *Piranesi* (London: Academy Editions).
Scott, Mackay Hugh Baillie (1906), *Houses and Gardens* (London: Newnes; with a later edn., published by Architecture Illustrated, 1933).
—(1910), *Garden Suburbs, Town Planning, and Modern Architecture* (London: Unwin).
Scott, Quinta, and Miller, Howard S. (1979), *The Eads Bridge* (Columbia, Mo.: University of Missouri Press).
Scotti, A. (1969), *Ascanio Vitozzi* (Florence: Nuova Italia).
Scott-Moncrieff, William Walter (1924), *John Francis Bentley* (London: E. Benn).
Scully, Arthur (1973), *James Dakin, Architect: His Career in New York and the South* (Baton Rouge, La.: Louisiana State University Press).
Scully, Vincent Joseph (1962), *Louis I. Kahn* (New York: Braziller).
—(1971), *The Shingle Style and the Stick Style* (New Haven: Yale UP).
—(1974), *The Shingle Style Today: or, the Historian's Revenge* (New York: Braziller).
—(1988), *American Architecture and Urbanism* (New York: Holt).
—(1989), *The Architecture of the American Summer: The Flowering of the Shingle Style* (New York: Rizzoli).
Searing, H. and Reed, H. (1981), *Speaking a New Classicism: American Architecture Now* (Northampton, Mass.: Smith College Museum of Art).
Sedding, John Dando (1891), *Garden-Craft Old and New* (London: Kegan Paul).
—(1893), *Art and Handicraft* (London: Kegan Paul).
Sédille, Paul (1886), *Théodore Ballu, architecte (1817–1885)* (Paris: Chaix).
Sedlmayr, Hans (1930), *Österreichische Barockarchitektur (1690–1740)* (Vienna: Filser Verlag).
—(1976), *Johann Bernhard Fischer von Erlach* (Vienna: Herold).
Seibt, Ferdinand (ed.) (1985), *Renaissance in Böhmen* (Munich: Prestel).
Seidler, Harry (1954), *Houses, Interiors, and Projects* (Sydney: Associated General Publications).
—(1963), *Harry Seidler* (New York, Stuttgart, and Sydney: Wittenborn, Kraemar & Horowitz).
Sekler, Eduard Franz (1956), *Wren and his Place in European Architecture* (London: Faber & Faber).
—(1985), *Joseph Hoffmann: The Architectural Work* (Princeton: Princeton UP).
Sembach, Klaus-Jürgen (1989), *Henry van de Velde* (New York: Rizzoli).
Semper, Gottfried (1851), *Die Vier Elemente der Baukunst* (Brunswick: Vieweg).
—(1860–3), *Der Stil in den technischen und tektonischen Künsten oder praktische Aesthetik* (Munich: Bruckmann).
—(1884), *Kleine Schriften von Gottfried Semper* (Berlin and Stuttgart: Spemann).
—(1966), *Wissenschaft, Industrie, und Kunst* (Berlin and Mainz: Kupferberg).
Sereny, Gitta (1995), *Albert Speer: His Battle with Truth* (London: Macmillan).
Serlio, Sebastiano (1584), *Libro d'architettura* (Venice: Franceschi).
—(1611), *The Booke of Architecture* (London: E. Stafford).
—(1663), *Architettura di S. Serlio Bolognese, in sei libri divisa . . .* (Venice: Gio. Giacomo Hertz).
—(1964), *Tutte l'opere d'architettura* (Ridgewood, NJ: Gregg).
—(1996), *On Architecture*, tr. Vaughan Hart and Peter Hicks (New Haven and London: Yale UP).
Service, Alastair (1975), *Edwardian Architecture and its Origins* (London: Architectural Press).
—(1977), *Edwardian Architecture: A Handbook to Building Design in Britain, 1890–1914* (London: Thames & Hudson).
Seta, Cesare de' (1972), *La cultura architettonica in Italia tra le due guerre* (Bari: Laterza).
—(1979), *Giuseppe Pagano Fotografico* (Milan: Electa).
—(ed.) (1976), *Architettura e città durante il fascismo: Giuseppe Pagano* (Bari: Laterza).
Sethe, Kurt (1902), *Imhotep, der Asklepios Der Ägypter* (Leipzig: Hinrichs).
Seymour, William Wood (1898), *The Cross in Tradition, History, and Art* (New York and London: Putnam).
Shafer, H. B. (ed.) (1973), *The Writings and Sketches*

of Matthew Nowicki (Charlottesville, Va.: University of Virginia Press).
Shand-Tucci, Douglass (1975), *Ralph Adams Cram, American Medievalist* (Boston: Boston Public Library).
—(1994), *Ralph Adams Cram: Life and Architecture* (Amherst, Mass.: University of Massachusetts Press).
Sharp, Dennis (1967), *Modern Architecture and Expressionism* (New York: Braziller).
—(1967*a*), *Planning and Architecture* (London: Barrie & Rockliff).
—(ed.) (1972), *Glass Architecture by Paul Scheerbart and Alpine Architecture by Bruno Taut* (New York: Praeger).
—(1978), *The Rationalists: Theory and Design in the Modern Movement* (London: Architectural Press).
Shearman, John K. G. (1967), *Mannerism* (Harmondsworth: Penguin).
Sheehy, Jeanne (1977), *J. J. McCarthy and the Gothic Revival in Ireland* (Belfast: Ulster Architectural Heritage Society).
Shelby, Lonnie Royce (1977), *Gothic Design Techniques: The Fifteenth-Century Design Booklets of Matthäus Roriczer and Hans Schuttermayer* (Carbondale, Ill.: Southern Illinois UP).
Sheppard, F. H. W. (ed.) (1973), *Survey of London*, xxxvii: *Northern Kensington* (London: Athlone Press, for the GLC).
—(1975), *Survey of London*, xxxviii: *The Museums Area of South Kensington and Westminster* (London: Athlone Press).
—(1983), *Survey of London*, xli: *Southern Kensington: Brompton* (London: Athlone Press).
Shinohara, Kazuo (1976), *11 Houses and Architectural Theory* (Tokyo: Bijutsu Shuppan-sha).
Shute, John (1563), *The first and Chief Grounds of Architecture* (London: Thomas Marshe).
Shvidkovsky, Dimitri (1996), *The Empress and the Architect* (New Haven and London: Yale UP).
Shvidkovsky, Oleg Aleksandrovich (1970), *Building in the USSR: 1917–1932* (London and New York: Studio Vista & Praeger).
Siemon, Alfred (ed.) (1958), *Otto Bartning* (Bramsche: Rasch).
Simo, Melanie Louise (1988), *Loudon and the Landscape: From Country Seat to Metropolis* (New Haven and London: Yale UP).
Simpson, Duncan (1979), *C. F. A. Voysey and the Architecture of Individuality* (London: Lund Humphries).
Simson, Jutta von (1976), *Das Berliner Denkmal für Friedrich den Grossen* (Frankfurt: Propyläen).
Singelenberg, Pieter (1972), *Hendrik Petrus Berlage: Idea and Style—The Quest for Modern Architecture* (Utrecht: Haentjens Dekker & Gumbert).
—and Bock, Manfred (1975), *H. P. Berlage, Bouwmeester 1856–1934* (The Hague: Gemeentemuseum).
Sissons, M., and French, P. (eds.) (1964), *Age of Austerity* (Harmondsworth: Penguin).
SITE, *et al.* (1980), *SITE: Architecture as Art* (London: Academy Editions).
Sitte, Camillo (1965), *City Planning According to Artistic Principles* (London: Phaidon).
Sitwell, Sacheverell, and Schneiders, Toni (1959), *Austria* (London: Thames & Hudson).
Skempton, A. W. (ed.) (1981), *John Smeaton, FRS* (London: T. Telford).
Skriver, Poul Erik, *et al.* (1971), *Arne Jacobsen, a Danish Architect* (Copenhagen: Presse & Kulturabteilung).
Sky, Alison, and Stone, Michelle (1976), *Unbuilt America* (New York: McGraw-Hill).
Šlapeta, Vladimír (1978), *1900–1978: Guide to Modern Architecture* (Prague: Narodni Technicke Museum).
Slater, Gregory John (1995), *Mackay Hugh Baillie Scott, an Architectural History* (Isle of Man: Amulree).
Slesin, S., and Cliff, S. (1984), *English Style* (London: Thames & Hudson).
Sloan, Samuel (1867), *City and Suburban Architecture* (Philadelphia: Lippincott).
—(1868), *American Houses* (Philadelphia: Baird).
—(1870), *Sloan's Homestead Architecture* (Philadelphia: Lippincott).
—(1873), *The Model Architect* (Philadelphia: Lippincott).
—(1873*a*), *Sloan's Constructive Architecture* (Philadelphia: Lippincott).
—and Lukens, Charles J. (eds.) (1868–70), *The Architectural Review and American Builder's Journal* (Philadelphia: The Editors).
Smart, C. M. (1990), *Muscular Churches: Ecclesiastical Architecture of the High Victorian Period* (Fayetteville, Ark.: University of Arkansas Press).
Smeaton, John (1813), *A Narrative of the Building . . . of the Eddystone Lighthouse* (London: Longmans).
—(1837), *Reports of the Late John Smeaton* (London: Taylor).
Smiles, Samuel (1862), *Lives of the Engineers* (London: Murray).
Smith, C. Ray (1977), *Supermannerism: New Attitudes in Post-Modern Architecture* (New York: Dutton).
Smith, Clive Bamford (1967), *Builders in the Sun: Five Mexican Architects* (New York: Architectural Book Pub. Co.).
Smith, Graham (1977), *The Casino of Pius IV* (Princeton: Princeton UP).
Smith, J. Boulton (1975), *The Golden Age of Finnish*

Architecture (Helsinki: Ministry of Foreign Affairs).
Smith, Robert Chester (1968), *The Art of Portugal 1500–1800* (London: Weidenfeld & Nicolson).
Smith, Roy S. (1962), *John Lee Archer: Tasmanian Architect and Engineer* (Hobart: Tasmania Historical Research Association).
Smith, W. Stevenson, and Simpson, W. Kelley (1992), *The Art and Architecture of Ancient Egypt* (New Haven and London: Yale UP).
Smithson, Alison Margaret (ed.) (1968), *Team 10 Primer* (Cambridge, Mass.: MIT Press).
— and Smithson, Peter (1967), *Urban Structuring* (London: Studio Vista).
— — (1968), *The Euston Arch and the Growth of the London, Midland, & Scottish Railway* (London: Thames & Hudson).
— — (1975), *Bibliography of the Work of Alison and Peter Smithson* (London: The Authors).
— — (1981), *The Heroic Age of Modern Architecture* (New York: Rizzoli).
— — (1991), *Team 10 Meetings: 1953–1984* (New York: Rizzoli).
Snodgrass, Adrian (1985), *The Symbolism of the Stupa* (Ithaca, NY: Southeast Asia Program, Cornell University).
Snodin, Michael (ed.) (1991), *Karl Friedrich Schinkel: A Universal Man* (New Haven and London: Yale UP, in association with the Victoria & Albert Museum, London).
Soane, John (1830), *Description of the House and Museum on the North Side of Lincoln's Inn Fields* (London: James Moyes).
Sodré, Nelson Werneck (1978), *Oscar Niemeyer* (Rio de Janeiro: Graal).
Sokolov, N. B. (1952), *A. V. Shchusev* (Moscow: GILSA).
Soleri, Paolo (1969), *Arcology: The City in the Image of Man* (Cambridge, Mass.: MIT Press).
— (1971), *The Sketchbooks of Paolo Soleri* (Cambridge, Mass.: MIT Press).
Solomon, Barbara (1988), *Green Architecture and the Agrarian Garden* (New York: Rizzoli).
Sommer, R. (1974), *Tight Spaces: Hard Architecture and How to Humanize It* (Englewood Cliffs, NJ: Prentice-Hall).
— (1983), *Social Design: Creating Buildings with People in Mind* (Englewood Cliffs, NJ: Prentice-Hall).
Soria y Puig, Arturo (1979), *Hacia una teoría general de la urbanizacíon* (Madrid: Colegio de Ingenieros de Caminos).
Soriano, Marc (1972), *Le Dossier Perrault* (Paris: Hachette).
Sottsass, Ettore (1976), *Sottsass's Scrap-Book* (Milan: Casabella).
— (1983), *Storia e progetti* (Florence: Alinea).
— (1985), *Ettore Sottsass: Furniture and a Few Interiors* (Milan: Mondadori).
— (1987), *Design Metaphors* (New York: Rizzoli).
— (1988), *Essays* (New York: Rizzoli).
— (1993), *Arrêt sur l'image* (Milan: Archivolto).
— (1993*a*), *Ettore Sottsass: Designer, Artist, Architect* (Tübingen: Wasmuth).
— (1994), *Ouvrage* (Paris: Centre Pompidou).
— (1995), *Ettore Sottsass Ceramics* (London: Thames & Hudson).
Spade, Rupert (1971), *Eero Saarinen* (New York: Simon & Schuster).
— (1971*a*), *Oscar Niemeyer* (London: Thames & Hudson).
— (1971*b*), *Richard Neutra* (London: Thames & Hudson).
— (1971*c*), *Paul Rudolph* (London: Thames & Hudson).
Spagnesi, Gianfranco (1964), *Giovanni Antonio de Rossi: Architetto Romano* (Rome: Officina).
Sparke, Penny (ed.) (1981), *Design by Choice* (London: Academy Editions).
— (1982), *Ettore Sottsass* (London: Design Council).
— (1988), *Italian Design: 1870 to the Present* (London: Thames & Hudson).
Speer, Albert (1970), *Inside the Third Reich* (London: Weidenfeld & Nicolson).
— (1976), *Spandau: The Secret Diaries* (New York: Macmillan).
— (1981), *The Slave State* (London: Weidenfeld & Nicolson).
Spence, Basil (1964), *Phoenix at Coventry* (London: Bles).
— (1973), *New Buildings in Old Cities* (Southampton: The University).
— *et al.* (1964), *The Idea of a New University: An Experiment in Sussex* (London: Deutsch).
— and Snoek, H. (1963), *Out of the Ashes: A Progress through Coventry Cathedral* (London: Bles).
Spencer, Brian A. (ed.) (1979), *The Prairie School Tradition* (New York: Whitney Library & Watson-Gupthill).
Spiers, Phené (1893), *The Orders of Architecture, Greek, Roman and Italian, Selected from Normand's Parallel and other Authorities* (London: Batsford).
Spitzner, Alfred (1913), *Deutschlands Denkmal der Völkerschlacht* (Leipzig: Breitkopf & Härtel).
Spoerry, F. (1989), *Spoerry: L'architecture douce: de Port Grimaud à Port-Liberté* (Paris: Robert Laffont).
Sponsel, Jean-Louis (1893), *Die Frauenkirche zu Dresden* (Dresden: Baensel).
— (1924), *Der Zwinger, die Hoffeste und die Schlossbaupläne zu Dresden* (Dresden: Stengel).
Sprague, Paul (1979), *The Drawings of Louis Henry Sullivan* (Princeton: Princeton UP).
Staber, Margit (1964), *Max Bill* (St Gallen: Erker, and London: Methuen).
Stalley, Roger A. (1987), *The Cistercian Monasteries*

of Ireland . . . 1142–1540 (New Haven and London: Yale UP).

Stalling, Gesine (1974), *Studien zu Dominikus Böhm* (Berne: Herbert Lang).

Stamm, Günther (1984), *J. J. P. Oud: Bauten und Projekte* (Mainz: Kupferberg).

Stamp, Gavin (1977), *Silent Cities* (London: RIBA).

—(1981), *Robert Weir Schultz and His Work for the Marquesses of Bute* (Mount Stuart: privately printed).

—(1989), *Telephone Boxes* (London: Chatto & Windus).

—and Amery, Colin (1980), *Victorian Buildings of London: 1837–1887* (London: Architectural Press).

—and Harte, Glynn Boyd (1979), *Temples of Power* (London: Cygnet).

—and McKinstry, Sam (1994), *'Greek' Thomson* (Edinburgh: Edinburgh UP).

Stansky, Peter (1996), *Redesigning the World: William Morris, the 1880s and the Arts and Crafts* (Palo Alto, Calif.: Soc. Promotion of Science).

Stanton, Phoebe B. (1968), *The Gothic Revival and American Church Architecture: An Episode in Taste, 1840–56* (Baltimore: Johns Hopkins UP).

—(1971), *Pugin* (London: Thames & Hudson).

Starr, J. Frederick (1978), *Melnikov: Solo Architect in a Mass Society* (Princeton: Princeton UP).

Starr, Kevin (1973), *Americans and the California Dream* (New York: Oxford UP).

Stavenow, Åke (1927), *Carl Hårleman* (Uppsala: Almqvist & Wiksell).

Stearns, Elinor, and Yerkes, David N. (1976), *William Thornton: A Renaissance Man in the Federal City* (Washington: American Institute of Architects Foundation).

Steele, James (1994), *Charles Rennie Mackintosh: Synthesis in Form* (London: Academy Editions).

—(1994*a*), *Hassan Fathy* (London: Academy Editions).

Stein, Susan R. (ed.) (1986), *The Architecture of Richard Morris Hunt* (Chicago: University of Chicago Press).

Steinberg, R. (ed.) (1975), *Nazi-Kitsch* (Darmstadt: Melzer).

Steinhauser, Monika (1970), *Die Architektur der Pariser Oper* (Munich: Prestel).

Steinitz, Kate (1968), *Kurt Schwitters* (Berkeley: University of California Press).

Steinmann, Martin (1979), *CIAM: Dokumente 1928–1939* (Basle: Birkhäuser).

—and Boga, Thomas (eds.) (1975), *Tendenzen: Neuere Architektur im Tessin* (Zurich: ETH).

Steinweg, Klara (1929), *Andrea Orcagna* (Strasbourg: Heitz).

Stephan, Hans (1939), *Die Baukunst im Dritten Reich* (Berlin: Junker & Dünnhaupt).

—(1944), *Wilhelm Kreis* (Oldenburg: Stalling).

Stephenson, Flora, and Pool, Phoebe (1944), *A Plan for Town and Country* (London: Pilot Press).

Stern, Robert A. M. (1975), *George Howe: Towards a Modern Architecture* (New Haven: Yale UP).

—(1977), *New Directions in American Architecture* (New York: Braziller).

—(ed.) (1979), *Philip Johnson: Writings* (New York: Oxford UP).

—(1982), *Raymond Hood* (New York: Institute for Architecture & Urban Studies).

—(1988), *Modern Classicism* (New York: Rizzoli).

—(1996), *Buildings* (New York: Monacelli Press).

—*et al.* (1995), *New York 1960: Architecture and Urbanism between the Second World War and the Bicentennial* (New York: Monacelli Press).

Sternberg, J. (1971), *Les chefs d'œuvre du Kitsch* (Paris: Éditions Planète).

Stevenson, David (1988), *The Origins of Freemasonry. Scotland's Century 1590–1710* (Cambridge: Cambridge UP).

Stevenson, John James (1880), *House Architecture* (London: Macmillan).

Stillman, Damie (1966), *Decorative Work of Robert Adam* (London: Tiranti).

—(1988), *English Neo-Classical Architecture* (London: Zwemmer).

Stockhorst, Erich (1967), *Fünftausend Köpfe: Wer war Was im Dritten Reich* (Bruchsal, Baden: Blick & Bild).

Stoll, Robert (1967), *Architecture and Sculpture in Early Britain* (London: Thames & Hudson).

Stone, Edward Durell (1962), *The Evolution of an Architect* (New York: Horizon).

—(1967), *Recent and Future Architecture* (New York: Horizon).

Storrer, William Allin (1974), *The Architecture of Frank Lloyd Wright* (Cambridge, Mass.: MIT Press).

—(1993), *The Frank Lloyd Wright Companion* (Chicago: University of Chicago Press).

Strack, Johann Heinrich (1843), *Das altgriechische Theatergebäude* (Potsdam: Riegel).

—(1858), *Architektonische Details* (Berlin: Ernst & Korn).

—and Gottgetreu, M. (1857), *Schloss Babelsberg* (Berlin: Ernst).

—and Kugler, Franz (1833), *Architektonische Denkmäler der Altmark Brandenburg* (Berlin: Sachse).

Stratton, A. (1972), *Sinan* (New York: Scribner).

Strazzullo, Franco (1972), *Sinan* (London: Macmillan).

—(ed.) (1976–7), *Le lettere di Luigi Vanvitelli* (Galatina: Congedo).

Street, Arthur Edmund (1972), *Memoir of George Edmund Street, R. A., 1824–1881* (New York: Blom; repr. of 1888 edn.).

Street, George Edmund (1855, 1874), *Brick and*

Marble in the Middle Ages (London: John Murray).

Street, George Edmund (1867), *Explanation and Illustrations of His Designs for the Proposed New Courts of Justice* (London: Taylor).

—(1969), *Some Acccount of Gothic Architecture in Spain* (New York: Blom; repr. of 1865 edn.).

Streichhan, Annaliese (1932), *Knobelsdorff und das friderizianische Rokoko* (Burg bei Magdeburg: Hopfer).

Strobl, Alice (1961), *Das k.k. Waffenmuseum im Arsenal* (Graz: Böhles).

Stroud, Dorothy (1950), *Henry Holland, 1745–1806* (London: Art & Technics).

—(1962), *Humphry Repton* (London: Country Life).

—(1966), *Henry Holland: His Life and Architecture* (London: Country Life).

—(1971), *George Dance, Architect, 1741–1825* (London: Faber).

—(1975), *Capability Brown* (London: Faber).

—(1984), *Sir John Soane, Architect* (London: Faber).

Stuart, James, and Revett, Nicholas (1762–1816), *The Antiquities of Athens* (London: Haberkorn, etc.).

Stubblebine, Jo (ed.) (1953), *The Northwest Architecture of Pietro Belluschi* (New York: Dodge).

Stubbs, William (ed.) (1879), *The Historical Works of Gervase of Canterbury* (London: Longmans).

Stubenvoll, Beda (1875), *Die Basilika und das Benedictinerstift St. Bonifax in München* (Munich: Stahl).

Stüler, Friedrich August (1853–66), *Bauwerke* (Berlin: Ernst & Korn).

—(1861), *Vortrag über die Wirksamkeit Friedrich Wilhelm IV. in dem Gebiete der bildende Künste* (Berlin: Ernst & Korn).

—Prosche, E., and Willebrand, H. (1869), *Das Schloss zu Schwerin* (Berlin: Ernst & Korn).

Sturgis, Russell (1971), *A Critique of the Work of Peabody and Stearns* (New York: Da Capo; repr. of the 1896 edn.).

—(1971*a*), *A Review of the Work of George B. Post* (New York: Da Capo; repr. of the 1896 version).

—(1977), *The Works of Bruce Price* (New York: Da Capo; repr. of 1899 original).

—*et al.* (1901–2), *A Dictionary of Architecture and Building* (New York and London: Macmillan).

Sturm, Leonhard Christian (1694), *Sciagraphia Templi Hierosolymitani* (Leipzig: Krügerl).

—(1712), *Architektonisches Bedenken von der protestantischen Klein Kirchen Figur und Einrichtung* (Hamburg: The Author).

Stüssi, Fritz (1974), *Othmar H. Ammann. Sein Beitrag zur Entwicklung des Brückenbaus* (Basle: Birkhäuser Verlag).

Stutchbury, Howard Edward (1967), *The Architecture of Colen Campbell* (Cambridge, Mass.: Harvard UP).

Sudjic, Deyan (1986), *Norman Foster, Richard Rogers, James Stirling: New Directions in British Architecture* (London: Thames & Hudson).

—(1995), *The Architecture of Richard Rogers* (New York: Abrams).

—Meade, J., and Cook, P. (1988), *English Extremists: The Architecture of Campbell, Zogolovitch, Wilkinson, and Gough* (London: Blueprint, Fourth Estate).

Suida, William Emil (1953), *Bramante pittore e il Bramantino* (Milan: Ceschina).

Sullivan, Louis Henry (1956), *The Autobiography of an Idea* (New York: Dover; repr. of 1924 edn.).

—(1967), *A System of Architectural Ornament* (New York, Eakins; repr. of 1924 edn.).

—(1980), *Kindergarten Chats* (New York: Dover; repr. of 1934 edn.).

Summerson, Sir John Newenham (1948), *Architecture in England since Wren* (London: Longmans Green).

—(1952), *Sir John Soane, 1753–1837* (London: Art & Technics).

—(1963), *Heavenly Mansions and other Essays on Architecture* (New York: W. W. Norton).

—(1965), *Sir Christopher Wren* (London: Collins).

—(1966), *Inigo Jones* (Harmondsworth: Penguin).

—(ed.) (1968), *Concerning Architecture* (London: Allen Lane).

—(1970), *Victorian Architecture: Four Studies in Evaluation* (New York: Columbia UP).

—(1976), *The Architecture of Victorian London* (Charlottesville, Va.: University of Virginia Press).

—(1980), *The Classical Language of Architecture* (London: Thames & Hudson).

—(1980*a*), *The Life and Work of John Nash, Architect* (London: Allen & Unwin).

—(1986), *Architecture of the Eighteenth Century* (London: Thames & Hudson).

—(1988), *Georgian London* (London: Barrie & Jenkins).

—(1990), *The Unromantic Castle and other Essays* (London: Thames & Hudson).

—(1993), *Architecture in Britain 1530–1830* (Harmondsworth: Penguin, 1953, revised edn. 1983; with later edition published by Yale UP).

—*et al.* (1983), *John Soane* (Architectural Monographs Series; London: Academy Editions).

Suner, Bruno (1988), *Pei* (Paris: Hazan).

Suolahti, Eino E. (1973), *Helsinki: A City in a Classical Style* (Helsinki: Otava).

Sutcliffe, Sheila (1973), *Martello Towers* (Rutherford, NJ: Farleigh Dickinson UP).

Sutton, S. B. (ed.) (1979), *Civilizing American Cities: A Selection of Frederick Law Olmsted's Writings* (Cambridge, Mass.: MIT Press).

Svácha, Rotislav (1995), *The Architecture of New*

Prague, 1895–1945 (Cambridge, Mass., and London: MIT Press).
Svanberg, Jan (1983), *Master Masons* (Stockholm: Carmina).
Sweeney, James Johnson, and Sert, Josep Lluís (1970), *Antonio Gaudí* (New York: Praeger).
Sweeney, Robert Lawrence (1978), *Frank Lloyd Wright: An Annotated Bibliography* (Los Angeles: Hennessey & Ingalls).
Swenarton, Mark (1981), *Homes for Heroes* (London: Heinemann).
—(1989), *Artisans and Architects: The Ruskinian Tradition in Architectural Thought* (New York and London: St Martin's Press).
Swillens, P. T. A. (1961), *Jacob van Campen: Schilder en Bouwmeester* (Assen: van Gorcum).
Swoboda, Karl Maria (1943), *Peter Parler* (Vienna: Schroll).
—(ed.) (1964), *Barock in Böhmen* (Munich: Prestel).
Symes, Michael (1993), *A Glossary of Garden History* (Princes Risborough: Shire).
Symondson, Anthony (1988), *Sir Ninian Comper, the Last Gothic Revivalist* (London: RIBA).
Szambien, Werner (1984), *Jean-Nicolas-Louis Durand, 1760–1834* (Paris: Picard).
Tadgell, Christopher (1978), *Ange-Jacques Gabriel* (London: Zwemmer).
Tadisi, J. A. (1760), *Memora della vita di Mons. G. Caramuel* (Venice: n.p.).
Tafuri, Manfredo (1964), *Ludovico Quaroni* (Milan: Edizioni di Comunità).
—(1966), *L'architettura del Manierismo nel cinquecento europeo* (Rome: Officina Edizione).
—(1972), *Jacopo Sansovino e l'architettura del '500 a Venezia* (Padua: Marsilio).
—(1976), *Architecture and Utopia: Design and Capitalist Development* (Cambridge, Mass.: MIT Press).
—(1980), *Theories and History of Architecture* (New York: Harper).
—(1989), *History of Italian Architecture, 1944–1985* (Cambridge, Mass.: MIT Press).
— and Dal Co, Francesco (1986), *Modern Architecture* (London: Faber & Faber, and Milan: Electa).
Tallmadge, Thomas E. (1941), *Architecture in Old Chicago* (Chicago: University of Chicago Press).
Tamburini, Luciano (1968), *Le chiese di Torino* (Turin: Le Bouquiniste).
Tange, Kenzo (1960), *Katsura, Tradition, and Creation in Japanese Architecture* (New Haven: Yale UP).
—(1970), *Kenzo Tange 1946–1969* (New York: Praeger).
Tanner, Howard (1976), *Australian Housing in the Seventies* (Sydney: Ure Smith).
Taranovskaia, Marianna Zenonovna (1980), *Karl Rossi, arkitektor* (Leningrad: Stroiizdat).
Tarn, John Nelson (1971), *Working-Class Housing in Nineteenth-Century Britain* (London: Architectural Association).
Tate, A., and Smith, C. Ray (1986), *Interior Design in the Twentieth Century* (New York: Harper & Row).
Taut, Bruno (1920), *Die Auflösung der Städte* (Hagen: Volkwang-Verlag).
—(1924), *Die Neue Wohnung* (Leipzig: Klinkhardt & Biermann).
—(1927), *Bauen: der neue Wohnbau* (Leipzig: Klinkhardt).
—(1929), *Modern Architecture* (London: Studio).
—(1929*a*), *Die Neue Baukunst in Europe und Amerika* (Stuttgart: Hoffmann).
—(1930), *Ein Wohnhaus* (Stuttgart: Keller).
—(1934), *Nippon Seen with European Eyes* (Tokyo: Meiji-Shobo).
—(1939), *Fundamentals of Japanese Architecture* (Tokyo: K.B.S.).
—(1958), *Houses and People of Japan* (Tokyo: Sansaido).
—(ed.) (1963), *Frühlicht* (Berlin: Ullstein; originally published 1920–1).
—(1972), *Alpine Architecture* (New York: Praeger; translation of 1919 edn.).
—(1977), *Architekturlehre* (Hamburg: VSA; new version of 1936 edn.).
—*et al.* (1919), *Die Stadtkrone* (Jena: Diederichs).
Taut, Max (1927), *Bauten und Pläne* (Berlin: Hübsch).
Tavernor, Robert (1991), *Palladio and Palladianism* (London: Thames & Hudson).
Taylor, Brian Brace (1986), *Geoffrey Bawa* (Singapore: Concept Media).
Taylor, R. (1974), *The World in Stone: The Rôle of Architecture in the National Socialist Ideology* (Berkeley: University of California Press).
Teague, Walter Dorwin (1946), *Design this Day: The Techniques of Order in the Machine Age* (London: The Studio).
Teeters, Negley K., and Shearer, John D. (1957), *The Prison at Philadelphia* (New York, Columbia UP).
Teige, Karel (1933), *Práce Jaromíra Krejcara* (Prague: Petr).
Teitelman, Edward, and Longsteth, Richard W. (1974), *Architecture in Philadelphia* (Cambridge, Mass.: MIT Press).
Telford, Thomas (1838), *Life of Thomas Telford, Civil Engineer* (London: Payne & Foss).
Temko, Allan (1962), *Eero Saarinen* (New York and London: Braziller).
Tempel, Egon (1968), *New Finnish Architecture* (London: Architectural Press).
Temple, Nigel (1979), *John Nash and the Village Picturesque* (Gloucester: Alan Sutton).
Templer, John (1992), *The Staircase: History and Theories* (Cambridge, Mass.: MIT Press).
Ternois, Daniel, and Pérez, Marie-Félicie (eds.)

(1982), *L'œuvre de Soufflot à Lyon* (Lyons: L'Institut d'histoire de l'art).
Tessari, Cristiano (1995), *Baldassare Peruzzi: il progetto dell' antico* (Milan: Electa).
Tessenow, Heinrich (1919), *Handwerk und Kleinstadt* (Berlin: Cassirer).
—(1921), *Das Land in der Mitte: Ein Vortrag* (Hellerau: Hegner).
—(1927), *Der Wohnhausbau* (Munich: Callwey).
Teufel, Richard (1953), *Balthasar Neumann: Sein Werk in Oberfranken* (Lichtenfels: Schulze).
—(1957), *Vierzehnheiligen* (Lichtenfels: Schulze).
Teut, Anna (ed.) (1967), *Architektur im Dritten Reich* (Berlin: Ullstein).
Teyssèdre, Bernard (1967), *L'art français au siècle de Louis XIV* (Paris: Poche).
Thau, Carsten, and Vindum, Kjeld (1998), *Arne Jacobsen* (Copenhagen: Arkitektens Forlag).
Thibiage, — de (1846), *Histoire pittoresque et anecdotique des anciens châteaux, demeures féodales, forteresses, citadelles*, etc. (Paris: B. Renault).
—(1846a), *Geschichte der berühmtesten Ritterburgen und Schlösser Frankreichs, Englands, Deutschlands, der Schweiz*, etc. (Merseburg: n.p.).
Thieme, Ulrich, and Becker, Felix (1932), *Thieme und Becker Kunstlerlexikon* (Leipzig: Seemann).
Thiersch, Heinz (1961), *German Bestelmeyer: Sein Leben und Werken für Baukunst* (Munich: Callwey).
Thiersch, Hermann (1925), *Friedrich von Thiersch: Der Architekt* (Munich: Bruckmann).
Thollier, Félix (1891), *L'Œeuvre de Pierre Bossan* (Montbrisson: Brassart).
Thompson, F. (ed.) (1981), *The Rise of Suburbia* (Leicester: Leicester UP).
Thompson, Paul Richard (1971), *William Butterfield* (London: Routledge & Kegan Paul).
—(1993), *The Work of William Morris* (Oxford: Oxford UP).
Thon, Christina (1977), *Johann Baptist Zimmermann als Stukkator* (Munich: Schnell & Steiner).
Thorne, Robert (ed.) (1990), *The Iron Revolution: Architects, Engineers, and Structural Innovation 1780–1880* (London: RIBA Heinz Gallery).
Tiberi, Claudio (1964), *Mnesicle l'architetto dei Propilei* (Rome: Officina).
Tiberia, Vitaliano (1974), *Giacomo della Porta. Un architetto tra manierismo e barocco* (Rome: Bulzoni).
Tigler, Peter (1963), *Die Architekturtheorie des Filarete* (Berlin: de Gruyter).
Tisdall, Caroline, and Bozzolla, Angelo (1977), *Futurism* (London: Thames & Hudson).
Todd, John Emerson (1982), *Frederick Law Olmsted* (Boston: Twayne).
Toplis, Ian (1987), *The Foreign Office: An Architectural History* (London and New York: Mansell).
Torcellan, Gianfranco (1963), *Una figura della Veneziana settecentesca: Andrea Memmo* (Rome and Venice: Fondazione Cini).
Torre, Stefano della (1994), *Pellegrino Tibaldi architetto* (Milan: San Fedele edizione).
Torre, Susana (ed.) (1977), *Women in American Architecture* (New York: Watson-Guptil).
Torroja, Eduardo (1958), *Philosophy of Structure* (Berkeley: University of California Press).
Toudouze, Georges (1954), *Monsieur de Vauban* (Paris: Berger-Levrault).
Towers, Graham (1995), *Building Democracy: Community Architecture in the Inner Cities* (London: UCL Press).
Town, Ithiel (1835), *The Outline of a Plan for Establishing in New York an Academy and Institution of the Fine Arts* (New York: Hopkins).
—(1842), *Important Notice to All Colleges, State, and Other Public Libraries* (New York: Vinten).
Toynbee, J. M. C. (1971), *Death and Burial in the Roman World* (London: Thames & Hudson).
Trabucco, Marcelo A. (1965), *Mario Roberto Álvarez* (Buenos Aires: Instituto de Arte Americano).
Trachtenberg, Alan (1965), *Brooklyn Bridge* (New York: Oxford UP).
Trachtenberg, Marvin (1971), *The Campanile of Florence Cathedral, 'Giotto's Tower'* (New York: New York UP).
Traulos, Ioannes (1967), *Neoklasike architektonike sten Ellada* (Neoclassical architecture in Greece) (Athens: n.p.).
Trevisiol, Robert (1990), *Otto Wagner* (Rome: Laterza).
Troche, N. M. (1857), *L'architecte Lassus* (Paris: Leclerc).
Troost, Gerdy (1941), *Das Bauen im neuen Reich* (Bayreuth: Gauverlag Bayerische Ostmark).
Trost, Brigitte (1973), *Domenico Quaglio, 1787–1837* (Munich: Prestel).
Troy, Nancy J. (1983), *The De Stijl Environment* (Cambridge, Mass.: MIT Press).
Tschudi-Madsen, Stephan (1965), *The Works of Châteauneuf in London and Oslo* (Oslo: Norske Fortidsminnesmerkers Bevaring).
—(1967), *Art Nouveau*, tr. R. I. Christopherson (New York: McGraw-Hill).
Tugnutt, A., and Robertson, M. (1987), *Making Townscape: A Contextual Approach to Building in an Urban Setting* (London: Mitchell).
Tummers, N. H. M. (1968), *J. L. Mathieu Lauweriks* (Hilversum: van Saane).
Tunnard, Christopher, and Pushkarev, Boris (1981), *Man-Made America, Chaos or Control?* (New York: Harmony Books).
Turak, Theodore (1986), *William Le Baron Jenney: A Pioneer of Modern Architecture* (Ann Arbor: UMI Research Press).
Turner, Jane Shoaf (ed.) (1996), *The Dictionary of Art and Architecture* (London: Macmillan).

Turner, Paul Venable (1987), *Campus: An American Planning Tradition* (New York: Architectural History Foundation).

Twombly, Robert C. (1979), *Frank Lloyd Wright: His Life and his Architecture* (New York: Wiley).

—(1986), *Louis Sullivan: His Life and Work* (New York: Viking).

Tyack, Geoffrey (1992), *Sir James Pennethorne and the Making of Victorian London* (Cambridge: Cambridge UP).

Tyng, Alexandra (1984), *Beginnings: Louis I. Kahn's Philosophy of Architecture* (New York: Wiley).

Tyrwhitt, Jaqueline (ed.) (1947), *Patrick Geddes in India* (London: Lund Humphries).

Tyszkiewicz, Maryla (1928), *Bernardo Rossellino* (Florence: Stamperia Polacca).

Underhill, Sarah Mollma (ed.) (1989), *Stanley Tigerman: Buildings and Projects* (New York: Rizzoli).

Ungers, O. M. (ed.) (1963), *Die Gläserne Kette: Visionäre Architekturen aus dem Kreis um Bruno Taut, 1919–1920* (Berlin: Akademie der Künste).

Unwin, Raymond (1908), *Cottage Plans and Common Sense* (London: Fabian Society).

—(1909), *Town Planning and Modern Architecture at the Hampstead Garden Suburb* (London: Unison).

—(1918), *Nothing Gained by Overcrowding: How the Garden City Type of Development May Benefit Both Owner and Occupier* (London: Garden Cities and Town Planning Association).

—(1971), *Town Planning in Practice: An Introduction to the Art of Designing Cities and Suburbs* (New York: Blom; new version of 1909 edn.).

Upjohn, Everard Miller (1935), *Buffington and the Skyscraper* (New York: College Art Association of America).

—(1939), *Richard Upjohn, Architect and Churchman* (New York: Columbia UP).

Upjohn, Richard (1975), *Upjohn's Rural Architecture* (New York: Da Capo; repr. of 1852 edn.).

Urban, Joseph (1929), *Theatres* (New York: Theatre Arts).

Urban, Martin (1960), *Wenzel Hablik* (Kiel: Landesmuseum).

Vachon, Marius (1907), *Une famille parisienne de maistres-maçons aux XV, XVI, XVII siècles: Les Chambiges* (Paris: Librairie la Construction Moderne).

Vagnetti, Luigi (ed.) (1978), *2000 anni di Vitruvio* (Florence: Edizione della Cattedra di Composizione Architettonica la della Facoltà di Architettura di Firenze).

Valdenaire, Arthur (1919, 1926, 1976), *Friedrich Weinbrenner: Sein Leben und Seine Bauten* (Karlsruhe: Müller).

—(1926), *Heinrich Hübsch* (Karlsruhe: Braun).

Vale, B., and Vale, R. (1991), *Towards a Green Architecture* (London: RIBA).

Vallance, Aymer (1920), *Old Crosses and Lychgates* (London: Batsford).

—(1947), *Greater English Church Screens* (London: Batsford).

Vallet, Albert (1982), *La céramique architecturale* (Paris: Dessain & Tolra).

Vanbrugh, John (1927–8), *Complete Works* (London: Nonesuch).

Vance, Mary A. (1983), *Stucco and Stuccowork: A Bibliography* (Monticello, Ill.: Vance).

Vanvitelli, Luigi (1975), *Vita di Luigi Vanvitelli* (Naples: ESI).

Varriano, John L. (1986), *Italian Baroque and Rococo Architecture* (New York and Oxford: Oxford UP).

Vasari, Giorgio (1568), *Le Vite de più eccelenti pittori, scultori, e architettori* (Florence: Sansoni).

—(1912–15), *Lives*, translated by G. du C. de Vere (London: Medici Society).

Vaudremer, Émile (1871), *Monographie de la Maison d'arrêt et de correction pour hommes construite à Paris par Émile Vaudremer* (Paris: The Author).

Vaux, Calvert (1970), *Villas and Cottages* (New York: Dover; repr. of 1864 edn.).

Vegesack, Alexander von (ed.) (1992), *Czech Cubism: Architecture, Furniture, and Decorative Arts, 1910–1925* (Montreal: Canadian Centre for Architecture).

Velde, Henry van de (1903), *Die Renaissance im moderne Kunstgewerbe* (Berlin: Cassirer).

—(1962), *Geschichte meines Lebens* (Munich: Piper).

Vellay, Marc (1985), *Pierre Chareau: Architect and Craftsman 1883–1950* (New York: Rizzoli).

Ven, Cornelis van de (1980), *Space in Architecture: The Evolution of a New Idea in the Theory and History of the Modern Movement* (Assen: van Gorcum).

Venturi, Adolfo (1967–   ), *Storia dell' Arte Italiana* (Nendeln: Kraus (and other volumes)).

Venturi, Robert (1966), *Complexity and Contradiction in Architecture* (New York: Museum of Modern Art).

—(1996), *Iconography and Electronics upon a Generic Architecture: A View from the Drafting Room* (Cambridge, Mass.: MIT Press).

—and Rauch, John (1978), *Venturi and Rauch: The Public Buildings* (London: Academy: Editions).

—Scott Brown, Denise, and Izenour, Steven (1977), *Learning from Las Vegas* (Cambridge, Mass.: MIT Press; originally published 1972).

Verheyen, Egon (1977), *The Palazzo del Tè in Mantua: Images of Love and Politics* (Baltimore: Johns Hopkins UP).

Vermeulen, Frans A. J. (1941), *Handboek tot de*

geschiedenis der Nederlandsche Bouwkunst (The Hague: Nijhoff).
Veronesi, Giulia (1947), *Tony Garnier* (Milan: Il Balcone).
—(1948), *Joseph Maria Olbrich* (Milan: Il Balcone).
—(1953), *Difficoltà politiche dell'architettura in Italia, 1920–40* (Milan: Editrice Politecnica Tamburini).
—(1953*a*), *J. J. Pieter Oud* (Milan: Il Balcone).
—(1956), *Joseph Hoffmann* (Milan: Il Balcone).
—(1957), *Luciano Baldessari Architetto* (Trent: Collana di Artisti Trentini).
—(ed.) (1964), *Edoardo Persico: Tutte le Opere, 1923–1935* (Milan: Edizione di Comunità).
—(ed.) (1965), *L'opera di Mario Chiattone, architetto* (Pisa: Lischi & Figli).
Viale, Vittorio (ed.) (1966), *Catalogo della Mostra di Filippo Juvarra* (Messina: University).
—(1972), *Bernardo Vittone e la disputà* (Turin: Academia delle Scienze).
Victoria & Albert Museum (1971), *Victorian Church Art* (London: HMSO).
—(1978), *Sir Gilbert Scott (1811–78): Architect of the Gothic Revival* (London: Victoria & Albert Museum).
Vidler, Anthony (1987), *The Writing of the Walls: Architectural Theory in the Late Enlightenment* (Princeton: Princeton UP).
—(1990), *Claude-Nicolas Ledoux* (Cambridge, Mass., and London: MIT Press).
Vignola, Giacomo Barozzi da (1596), *Regola delli Cinque Ordini d'Architettura* (Venice: Porro). See also *The Five Orders of Architecture according to Vignola*, arranged by Pierre Esquié and ed. Arthur Stratton (London: Tiranti, 1926).
Vignon, Alexandre-Pierre (1806), *Mémoire . . . de la nouvelle église de la Madeleine* (Paris: Vignon).
—(1816), *Monuments commémoratifs projetés en l'honneur de Louis XVI et de sa famille* (Paris: Perroneau).
Vilímková, Milada, and Brucker, Johannes (1989), *Dientzenhofer: eine bayerische Baumeisterfamilie in der Barockzeit* (Rosenheim: Rosenheimer Verlagshaus).
Villari, Sergio (1990), *J.-N.-L. Durand: Art and Science of Architecture* (New York: Rizzoli).
Viollet-Le-Duc, Eugène-Emmanuel (1874), *Description . . . du Château de Pierrefonds* (Paris: Morel).
—(1875), *Dictionnaire Raisonné de l'Architecture Française du XIe au XVIe siècle* (Paris: Morel).
—(1876), *Habitations of Man in All Ages* (London: Low, Marston, Searle & Rivington; translation of the *Histoire de l'habitation* . . . of 1875).
—(1877), *L'Art Russe* (Paris: Morel).
—(1959), *Discourses on Architecture* (London: Allen & Unwin; translation of the *Entretiens* . . . of 1858–72).
—and Narjoux, Félix (1979), *Habitations Modernes* (Brussels: Mardaga; repr. of 1875–7 edn.).
Vitruvius Pollio, Marcus (1567), *De Architectura*, edn. published in Venice with plates by Palladio.
—(1955–6), *De Architectura*, tr. Frank Granger (Cambridge, Mass. : Harvard UP, and London: Heinemann).
—(1960), *Architettura*, ed. Ferri (Rome: Palombi).
Vits, Gisela (1973), *Joseph Effners Palais Preysing: Ein Beitrag zur Münchener Profanarchitektur des Spätbarock* (Berne and Frankfurt: Lang).
Vlaamse Toeristen-Bond (1977), *De Onze-Lieve-Vrouwkathedraal van Antwerpen* (Antwerp: VTB).
Vogel, Hans Martin Erasmus (1958–9), *Heinrich Christoph Jussow, 1754–1825* (Kassel: Hessisches Landesmuseum).
Vogel, Robert M. (1971), *Roebling's Delaware and Hudson Canal Aqueducts* (Washington: Smithsonian Institution).
Vogt, Adolf Max (1969), *Boullées Newton-Denkmal* (Basle and Stuttgart: Birkhäuser).
—(1974), *Russische und französische Revolutions-Architektur* (Cologne: Du Mont Schauberg).
—Reble, Christina, and Frohlich, Martin (eds.) (1976), *Gottfried Semper und die Mitte des 19. Jahrhunderts* (Basle: Birkhäuser).
Vogt-Göknil, Ulya (1993), *Sinan* (Tübingen: Wasmuth).
Vollmar, Joseph E. (1974), *James B. Eads and the Great St Louis Bridge* (St Louis: Engineers Club).
Vondrová, Alena *et al.* (eds.) (1978), *Architektura Česky Funkcionalismus 1920–1940* (Prague and Brno: Umělecko Prümyslové Museum and Moravská Galerèe).
Voss, Knud (1971), *Arkitekten Nicolai Eigtved, 1701–1754* (Copenhagen: Nyt Nordisk Forlag).
Vostell, W., and Higgins, D. (1969), *Fantastic Architecture* (New York: Something Else Press).
Vriend, J. J. (1949–50), *De bouwkunst van ons Land* (Amsterdam: Scheltama).
Vries, Paulus Vredeman de (1617), *Les cing rangs de l'Architecture, a sçavoir, Tuscane, Dorique, Ionique, Corinthique, et Composée . . . avec l'instruction fondamentale faicte par H. H.* [Henrik Hondius the Younger]. *Avec . . . quelques belles ordonnances d'architecture, mises en perspective, inventées par J. Vredeman Frison et son fils* (Amsterdam: Jean Janson).
—(1651), *L'Architecture . . . avec quelques belles ordonnances d'Architecture, mises en perspective per J. Vredman Frison* [and P. V. de V.] (Amsterdam: Jean Janson). Many versions were published following the first Antwerp edition of 1577 entitled *Architecture* . . .
Vynckt, Randall J. van (ed.) (1993), *International Dictionary of Architects and Architecture* (Detroit, London, and Washington: St James Press).

Wachsmann, Konrad (1961), *The Turning-Point in Building* (New York: Reinhold).
—(1988), *Vom Sinn des Details: zum Gesamtwerk von Konrad Wachsmann* (Cologne: Müller).
Wackernagel, Martin (1915), *Die Baukunst des 17. und 18. Jahrhunderts in den germanischen Ländern* (Berlin: Akademische Verlagsgesellschaft Athenaion).
Wagner, Martin (1918), *Neue Bauwirtschaft* (Berlin: Heymann).
—(1923), *Alte oder Neue Bauwirtschaft* (Berlin: Vorwärts-Buchdruckerei).
—(1925), *Amerikanische Bauwirtschaft* (Berlin: Vorwärts-Buchdruckerei).
—(1929), *Städtebaulichen Probleme in Amerikanischen Städten* (Berlin: Deutsche Bauzeitung).
—(1932), *Das Wachsende Haus* (Berlin: Bong).
Wagner, Otto (1914), *Die Baukunst unserer Zeit* (Vienna: Schroll).
—(1988), *Modern Architecture*, tr. H. F. Mallgrave (Santa Monica, Calif.: Getty Center for the History of Art & the Humanities).
Wagner-Rieger, Renate (1970), *Wiens Architektur im 19. Jahrhundert* (Vienna: Österreichischer Bundesverlag).
—(1980), *Die Wiener Ringstrasse: Bild einer Epoche* (Vienna: Böhlaus).
Walcher Casotti, M. (1960), *Il Vignola* (Trieste: Istituto di storia dell' arte).
Walker, John A. (1992), *Glossary of Art, Architecture, and Design since 1945* (London: Library Association Publishing).
Walker Art Center (1974), *Naives and Visionaries* (New York: Dutton).
Wall, Donald (1971), *Visionary Cities: The Arcology of Paolo Soleri* (New York: Praeger).
Walter, Renate von (1972), *Das Augsburger Rathaus* (Augsburg: Mühlberger).
Walton, Ann Thorson (1994), *Ferdinand Boberg, Architect* (Chicago: MIT Press).
Wangerin, Gerda, and Weiss, Gerhard (1976), *Heinrich Tessenow: Ein Baumeister 1876–1950* (Essen: Bacht).
Wanscher, Vilhelm (1903), *Arkitekten G. Bindesbøll* (Copenhagen: Koster).
Warburg, Karl (1893), *Karl August Ehrensvaerd* (Stockholm: Beijer).
Ward, Alastair (1988), *The Architecture of Ferdinando Sanfelice* (New York: Garland).
Ward, James, and Tomkins, Calvin (1984), *The Artifacts of Richard Buckminster Fuller: A Complete Collection of his Designs and Drawings* (New York: Garland).
Ward, P. (1991), *Kitsch in Sync: A Consumer's Guide to Bad Taste* (London: Plexus).
Ward, William Henry (1976), *The Architecture of the Renaissance in France* (New York: Hacker).
Ward-Jackson, Peter W. (1967), article on strap-work in *Victoria & Albert Museum Bulletin* (April), vol. 3 (London: HMSO, 1965–8).
—(1967*a*), article on arabesques in *Victoria & Albert Museum Bulletin* (July), vol. 3 (London: HMSO, 1965–8).
Ward-Perkins, John Bryan (1974), *Cities of Ancient Greece and Italy: Planning in Classical Antiquity* (New York: Braziller).
—(1981), *Roman Imperial Architecture* (Harmondsworth: Penguin).
—(1986), *Roman Architecture* (London: Faber & Faber, and Milan: Electa).
Ware, Isaac (1756–7), *The Complete Body of Architecture. Adorned with Plans and Elevations, from Original Designs* (London: Osborn & Shipton, Hodges, Davis, Ward, & Baldwin).
Ware, William Robert (1866), *An Outline of a Course of Architectural Instruction* (Boston: Wilson).
—(1878), *Greek Ornament* (Boston: Tilton).
—(1900), *Modern Perspective* (New York: Macmillan).
—(1912–13), *Shades and Shadows* (Scranton, Pa.: International Textbook).
—(1977), *The American Vignola* (New York: Norton; repr. of 1901 edn.).
Ware, William Rotch (ed.) (1923), *The Georgian Period* (New York: UPC).
Warsaw Polytechnic (1967), *Warszawska szkoła architektury 1915–1965* (Warsaw: Polish Scientific Publishers PWN).
Waterfield, Giles (ed.) (1996), *Soane and Death* (London: Dulwich Picture Gallery).
Waterhouse, Alfred (1867), *Courts of Justice Competition* (London: Eyre & Spottiswoode).
Waterman, Thomas Tileston (1945), *The Mansions of Virginia, 1706–1776* (Chapel Hill, NC: University of North Carolina Press).
Wates, N., and Knevitt, C. (1987), *Community Architecture* (Harmondsworth: Penguin).
Watkin, David (1968), *Thomas Hope 1769–1831 and the Neo-Classical Idea* (London: John Murray).
—(1974), *The Life and Work of C. R. Cockerell* (London: Zwemmer).
—(1977), *Morality and Architecture* (Oxford: Clarendon Press).
—(1979), *English Architecture: A Concise History* (London: Thames & Hudson).
—(1982), *Athenian Stuart: Pioneer of the Greek Revival* (London: Allen & Unwin).
—(1982*a*), *The English Vision: The Picturesque in Architecture, Landscape, and Garden Design* (London: John Murray).
—(1986), *A History of Western Architecture* (London: Barrie & Jenkins).
—(1996), *Sir John Soane: Enlightenment Thought and the Royal Academy Lectures* (Cambridge: Cambridge UP).

Watkin, David and Mellinghoff, Tilman (1987), *German Architecture and the Classical Ideal 1740–1840* (London: Thames & Hudson).

Weaver, Lawrence (1915), *Memorials and Monuments* (London: Country Life).

—(1981), *Houses and Gardens by Edwin Lutyens* (London: Antique Collectors' Club).

Webb, Geoffrey Fairbank (1937), *Wren* (London: Duckworth).

—(1965), *Art and Architecture in Britain: The Middle Ages* (Harmondsworth: Penguin).

Webb, Michael (1969), *Architecture in Britain Today* (Feltham: Country Life).

Weber, E. Parkes (1914), *Aspects of Death in Art and Epigram* (London and Leipzig: Unwin, and London: Quaritch).

Weber, Helmut (1961), *Walter Gropius und das Fagus-Werk* (Munich: Callwey).

Weber, Wilhelm (ed.) (1966), *Peter Behrens (1868–1940)* (Kaiserslautern: Pfalzgalerie).

Webster, Richard James (ed.) (1976), *Philadelphia Preserved* (Philadelphia: Temple UP).

Weilbach, Philip (1896–7), *Nyt Dansk Kunstnerleksikon* (Copenhagen: Hoest).

—(1947–), *Weilbachs Dansk Kunstnerleksikon* (Copenhagen: Aschehoug Dansk Forlag, and later edn., published by Munksgaard-Rosinante, from 1994).

Weiser, Armand (1927), *Clemens Holzmeister* (Berlin, Leipzig, and Vienna: Hübsch).

—(1930), *Joseph Hoffmann* (Geneva: Meister der Baukunst).

Weiss, Roberto (1969), *The Renaissance Discovery of Classical Antiquity* (London: Blackwell).

Weller, Allen Stuart (1943), *Francesco di Giorgio* (Chicago: University of Chicago Press).

Werbrouck, M. (1949), *Le temple d'Hatshepsout à Deir el Bahari* (Brussels: Fondation égyptologique reine-Elisabeth).

Wertheim, Paul (ed.) (1927), *Neuere Arbeiten von O. R. Salvisberg* (Berlin: Hübsch).

West, Robert C. (1988), *A Complete Guide to the Ancient Art of Thatching* (Newton Abbot: David & Charles).

Westfehling, Uwe (1977), *Triumphbogen im 19. und 20. Jahrhundert* (Munich: Prestel).

Weston, Richard (1995), *Alvar Aalto* (London: Phaidon).

—(1996), *Modernism* (London: Phaidon).

Westphal, Carl J. (ed.) (1938), *Fritz Höger der niederdeutsche Backsteinbaumeister* (Lübeck: Wolfshagen-Scharbeutz).

Weyres, Willy, and Mann, Albrecht (1968), *Handbuch zur rhenischen Baukunst des 19. Jahrhunderts* (Cologne: Greven).

Wheeler, Karen Vogel, Arnell, Peter, and Bickford, Ted (eds.) (1982), *Michael Graves: Buildings and Projects 1966–1981* (New York: Rizzoli).

Wheeler, Sir Mortimer (1964), *Roman Art and Architecture* (London: Thames and Hudson).

Wheildon, William W. (1865), *Memoirs of Solomon Willard* (Boston: Monument Association).

Whiffen, Marcus (1950), *Architecture of Sir Charles Barry in Manchester and Neighbourhood* (Manchester: Royal Manchester Institution).

—(1950*a*), *Thomas Archer: Architect of the English Baroque* (London: Art & Technics).

—and Koeper, Fredrick (1983), *American Architecture 1607–1976* (Cambridge, Mass.: MIT Press).

Whinney, Margaret (1964), *Sculpture in Britain 1530 to 1830* (Harmondsworth: Penguin).

—(1971), *Christopher Wren* (London: Thames & Hudson).

Whistler, Laurence (1954), *The Imagination of Vanbrugh and his Fellow Artists* (London: Batsford).

Whitaker, C. H. (ed.) (1925), *Bertram Grosvenor Goodhue* (New York: American Institute of Architects Press).

White, Anthony G. (1990), *Kenzo Tange: A Selected Bibliography* (Monticello, Ill.: Vance).

White, James F. (1962), *The Cambridge Movement: The Ecclesiologists and the Gothic Revival* (Cambridge: Cambridge UP).

White, John (1987), *Art and Architecture in Italy 1250–1400* (Harmondsworth: Penguin, revised version of 1966 edn.).

White, Theophilus Ballou (1973), *Paul Philippe Cret: Architect and Teacher* (Philadelphia: Art Alliance).

Whitehill, Walter Muir (1968), *Boston: A Topographical History* (Cambridge, Mass.: Harvard UP).

—(1970), *Museum of Fine Arts, Boston: A Centennial History* (Cambridge, Mass.: Belknap).

—and Nichols, Frederick Doveton (1976), *Palladio in America* (Milan: Electa).

Whittick, Arnold (1956), *Eric Mendelsohn* (London: Leonard Hill).

—(1974), *Encyclopedia of Urban Planning* (New York: McGraw-Hill).

Whitwell, William L. (1975), *The Heritage of Longwood* (Jackson, Miss.: University Press of Mississippi).

Whone, Herbert (1990), *Church Monastery Cathedral: An Illustrated Guide to Christian Symbolism* (Longmead, Shaftesbury: Element Books).

Wibiral, Norbert, and Mikula, Renata (1974), *Heinrich von Ferstel: Die Bauten und ihre Architekten* (Wiesbaden: Steiner).

Wichmann, Siegfried (ed.) (1968), *Hermann Obrist* (Munich: Stuck Villa).

Wickberg, Nils Erik (1962), *Finnish Architecture* (Helsinki: Otava).

Wickersham, George W. (1977), *The Cathedral Church of St John the Divine* (New York: Conroy).
Wiebenson, Dora (1969), *Sources of Greek Revival Architecture* (London: Zwemmer).
—(1978), *The Picturesque Garden in France* (Princeton: Princeton UP).
—(1970), *Tony Garnier, the Cité Industrielle* (New York: Braziller).
Wiener Sezession (1972), *Wiener Sezession* (Vienna: Wiener Secession).
Wietek, Gerhard (1972), *J. A. Arens: Eine Hamburger Architekt des Klassizismus* (Hamburg: Altonaer Museum).
Wigginton, Michael (1996), *Glass in Architecture* (London: Phaidon).
Wildung, Dietrich (1977), *Imhotep und Amenhotep* (Munich: Deutscher Kunstverlag).
Wilenski, R. (1957), *The Modern Movement in Art* (London: Faber).
Wilhelm, Karin (1985), *Architekten Heute: Portrait Frei Otto* (Berlin: Quadriga Verlag J. Severin).
Wilhide, E. (1995), *The Mackintosh Style—Decor and Design* (London: Pavilion Books).
Wilkes, Lyall (1980), *John Dobson: Architect and Landscape Gardener* (Stocksfield: Oriel).
—and Dodds, Gordon (1964), *Tyneside Classical: The Newcastle of Grainger, Dobson, and Clayton* (London: Murray).
Wilkins, William (1807), *The Antiquities of Magna Graecia* (London: Longman).
—(1816), *Atheniensia, or Remarks on the Topography and Buildings of Athens* (London: Murray).
—(1817), *The Civil Architecture of Vitruvius* (London: Longman).
—(1836), *An Apology for the Designs of the Houses of Parliament* (London: Clowes).
—(1837), *Prolusiones Architectonicae: or, Essays on Subjects Connected with Greek and Roman Architecture* (London: Weale).
Willard, Solomon (1843), *Plans and Sections of the Obelisk on Bunker's Hill* (Boston: Dickinson).
Williamson, Elizabeth, Riches, Anne, and Higgs, Malcolm (1990), *Buildings of Scotland, Glasgow* (Harmondsworth: Penguin).
Williamson, Hugh Ross (1949), *Four Stuart Portraits* (Sir Balthazar Gerbier, Lancelot Andrews, Sir John Eliot, and Col. Thomas Rainsborough) (London: Evans).
Willis, Carol (1995), *Form Follows Finance: Skyscrapers and Skylines in New York and Chicago* (Princeton: Princeton Architectural Press).
Willis, Peter (1977), *Charles Bridgeman and the English Landscape Garden* (London: Zwemmer).
—(1997), *Dom Paul Bellot, Architect and Monk, and the Publication of* Propos d'un bâtisseur du Bon Dieu 1949 (Jesmond: Elysium Press).
Wilson, Henry *et al.* (1892), *A Memorial to the late J. D. Sedding* (London: Batsford).
Wilson, Michael I. (1984), *William Kent: Architect, Designer, Painter, Gardener, 1685–1748* (London: Routledge & Kegan Paul).
Wilson, R. *et al.* (1986), *The Machine Age in America (1918–41)* (New York: Brooklyn Museum & Abrams).
Wilson, Richard Guy (1983), *McKim, Mead, & White, Architects* (New York: Rizzoli).
Wilton-Ely, John (1972), *Giovanni Battista Piranesi: The Polemical Works* (Farnborough: Gregg).
—(1978), *The Mind and Art of Giovanni Battista Piranesi* (London: Thames & Hudson).
—(1978*a*), *Piranesi* (London: Arts Council of Great Britain).
Windsor, Alan (1981), *Peter Behrens: Architect and Designer* (London: Architectural Press).
Wines, James (1987), *De-Architecture* (New York: Rizzoli).
—*et al.* (1989), *SITE* (New York: Rizzoli).
Wingler, Hans Maria (1969), *The Bauhaus: Weimar, Dessau, Berlin, and Chicago* (Cambridge, Mass.: MIT Press).
Winslow, Carleton (1980), *The Enchanted Hill* (Milbrae, Calif.: Celestial Arts).
Winter, Robert (ed.) (1997), *Towards a Simpler Way of Life: The Arts and Crafts Architects of California* (Berkeley: University of California Press).
Winther, Annemarie (1973), *Cosimo Fanzago und die Neapler Ornamentik des 17. und 18. Jahrhunderts* (Bremen: Hauschild).
Wiseman, Carter (1990), *I. M. Pei: A Profile in American Architecture* (New York: Abrams).
Wisłocka, Izabella (1968), *Awangardowa Architektura Polska: 1918–1939* (Warsaw: Arkady).
Wittkower, Rudolf (1964), *La Cupola di San Pietro di Michelangelo* (Florence: Sansoni).
—(1974), *Gothic v. Classic: Architectural Projects in Seventeenth-Century Italy* (New York: G. Braziller).
—(1974*a*), *Palladio and English Palladianism* (London: Thames & Hudson).
—(1975), *Studies in the Italian Baroque* (London: Thames & Hudson).
—(1978), *Idea and Image: Studies in the Italian Renaissance* (London: Thames & Hudson).
—(1981), *Gian Lorenzo Bernini* (Oxford: Phaidon).
—(1982), *Art and Architecture in Italy 1600–1750* (Harmondsworth: Penguin, revised version of 1965 edn.).
—(1988), *Architectural Principles in the Age of Humanism* (London: Tiranti, 1962, revised edn., London: Academy Editions).
—and Brauer, Heinrich (1970), *Bernini's Drawings* (New York: Collectors Editions).
—and Jaffé, Irma B. (eds.) (1972), *Baroque Art: The Jesuit Connection* (New York: Fordham).
—and Saxl, Fritz (1969), *British Art and the Mediterranean* (Oxford: Oxford UP; revised version of 1948 edn.).
Wodehouse, Lawrence (1976), *American Architects*

from the Civil War to the First World War (Detroit: Gale).

Wodehouse, Lawrence (1988), *White of McKim, Mead, and White* (New York: Garland).

Wojtowicz, Robert (1996), *Lewis Mumford and American Modernism* (Cambridge: Cambridge UP).

Wolf, Friedrich (1967), *François de Cuvilliés: Der Architekt und Dekorschöpfer* (Munich: Historischer Verein).

Wolf, Peter M. (1969), *Eugène Hénard and the Beginning of Urbanism in Paris 1900–1917* (The Hague: International Federation for Housing and Planning and Centre de Recherche d'Urbanisme).

Wolfe, Tom (1981), *From Bauhaus to Our House* (New York: Farrar, Straus & Giroux).

Woltersdorf, Arthur (1924), 'A Portrait Gallery of Chicago Architects: Charles B. Atwood', *Western Architect*, 33/8: 89–94.

Wood, Margaret E. (1965), *The English Mediaeval House* (London: Phoenix House).

Woodbridge, Sally (ed.) (1976), *Bay Area Houses* (New York: Oxford UP).

Woods, May (1996), *Visions of Arcadia: European Gardens from Renaissance to Rococo* (London: Aurum).

— and Warren, Arete Swartz (1988), *Glass Houses: A History of Greenhouses, Orangeries, and Conservatories* (New York: Rizzoli).

Woods, Shadrach (ed.) (1968), *Candilis, Josic, Woods: Building for People* (New York: Praeger).

Woodward, Christopher (1970), *Skidmore, Owings, & Merrill* (New York: Simon & Schuster).

Wörner, Hans Jakob (1979), *Architektur des Frühklassizismus in Süddeutschland* (Munich: Schnell & Steiner).

Wortmann, Reinhard (1977), *600 Jahre Ulmer Münster* (Ulm: Stadtarchiv).

Wrangel, Fredrik Ulrik (1912), *Tessinska Palastet* (Stockholm: Palmqvist).

Wrede, Stuart (1980), *The Architecture of Erik Gunnar Asplund* (Cambridge, Mass.: MIT Press).

— (1986), *Mario Botta* (New York: Museum of Modern Art).

Wright, Frank Lloyd (1939), *An Organic Architecture: The Architecture of Democracy* (repr. London: Lund Humphries 1970).

— (1943), *An Autobiography* (New York: Duell, Sloan & Pearce).

— (1945), *When Democracy Builds* (Chicago: University of Chicago Press).

Wurm, Heinrich (ed.) (1984–), *Baldassare Peruzzi: Architekturzeichnungen* (Tübingen: Wasmuth).

Wurm-Arnkreuz, Alois von (1919), *Architekt Ferdinand Fellner und seine Bedeutung für den modernen Theaterbau* (Vienna and Leipzig: Verlag für Technik und Industrie).

Wurman, Richard Saul (ed.) (1986), *What Will Be Has Always Been: The Words of Louis I. Kahn* (New York: Access).

Wüsten, Ernst (1951), *Die Architektur des Manierismus in England* (Leipzig: Seemann).

Wycherley, R. E. (1962), *How the Greeks Built Cities* (London: Macmillan).

Yamasaki, Minoru (1979), *A Life in Architecture* (New York: Weatherhill).

Yatsuka, Hajime, and Stewart, David B. (1991), *Arata Isozaki: Architecture 1960–1990* (Los Angeles: Museum of Contemporary Art).

Yeang, Ken (1997), *The Skyscraper: Bioclimatically Considered* (London: Academy Editions).

Yorke, Francis Reginald Stevens (1947), *The Modern House in England* (London: Architectural Press; reissue of 1937 edn.).

— (1951), *The Modern House* (London: Architectural Press; revised version of 1934 edn.).

— and Penn, Colin (1939), *A Key to Modern Architecture* (London: Blackie).

— and Whiting, Penelope (1954), *The New Small House* (London: Architectural Press).

Yorke, Rosenberg, & Mardall (1972), *The Architecture of Yorke, Rosenberg, Mardall, 1944–72* (London: Lund Humphries).

York Georgian Society (1973), *The Works in Architecture of John Carr* (York: York Georgian Society).

Young, Andrew McLaren (1968), *Charles Rennie Mackintosh 1868–1928* (London: Victoria & Albert Museum and Scottish Arts Club).

Young, Edgar B. (1980), *Lincoln Center: The Building of an Institution* (New York: New York UP).

Youngson, A. J. (1966), *The Making of Classical Edinburgh 1750–1840* (Edinburgh: Edinburgh UP).

Zachwatowicz, Jan, *et al.* (1952), *Architektura Polska* (Warsaw: PWT).

Zádor, Anna (1960), *Pollack Mihály 1773–1855* (Budapest: Akademiai Klado).

— (1985), *Revival Architecture in Hungary: Classicism and Romanticism* (Budapest: Corvina).

Zahar, Marcel (1959), *D'une doctrine d'architecture Auguste Perret* (Paris: Vincent, Fréal).

Zaitzevsky, Cynthia (1969), *The Architecture of William Ralph Emerson 1833–1917* (Cambridge, Mass.: Fogg Art Museum).

Zanella, Vanni (1988), *Giacomo Quarenghi: architetto a Pietroburgo* (Venice: Albrizzi).

Zanten, David van (ed.) (1970), *Walter Burley Griffin: Selected Designs* (Palos Park, Ill.: Prairie School Press).

— (1977), *Architectural Polychromy of the 1830s* (New York: Garland).

— (1987), *Designing Paris: The Architecture of Duban, Labrouste, Duc, and Vaudoyer* (Cambridge, Mass.: MIT Press).

Zevi, Bruno (1950), *Towards an Organic Architecture* (London: Faber).
—(1960), *Biagio Rossetti architetto ferrarese* (Turin: Einaudi).
—(1973), *Storia dell'Architettura Moderna* (Turin: Einaudi).
—(1974), *Poetica dell'architettura neo-plastica* (Milan: Einaudi).
—(1978), *The Modern Language of Architecture* (Seattle, Wash.: University of Washington Press).
—(1979), *Frank Lloyd Wright* (Bologna: Zanichelli).
—(1980), *Architecture as Space: How to Look at Architecture* (New York: Horizon; originally published in Italian in 1948).
—(1980*a*), *Giuseppe Terragni* (Bologna: Zanichelli).
—(1985), *Erich Mendelsohn* (New York: Rizzoli).
—(1999), *Erich Mendelsohn: The Complete Works* (Basle: Birkhäuser).
Zhadova, Larissa Alekseevna (1982), *Malevich: Suprematism and Revolution in Russian Art 1910–1930* (New York: Thames & Hudson).
—(ed.) (1988), *Tatlin* (New York: Rizzoli).
Zieler, Otto (1913), *Potsdam: Ein Stadtbild des 18. Jahrhunderts* (Berlin: Weide).
Zimmer, Erich (1971), *Rudolf Steiner als Architekt von Wohn- und Zweckbauten* (Stuttgart: Verlag Freies Geistesleben).
Zocca, Emma (1959), *La basilica dei SS. Apostoli Roma* (Rome: Canella).
Zorzi, Giangiorgio (ed.) (1959–), *Le opere di Andrea Palladio* (Venice: Pozza).
Zucchi, Benedict (1993), *Giancarlo de Carlo* (London: RIBA).
Zucker, Paul (1959), *Town and Square: From the Agora to the Village Green* (New York: Columbia UP).
Zuk, W., and Clark, R. (1971), *Kinetic Architecture* (New York: van Nostrand Reinhold).
Zukowsky, John (ed.) (1986), *Mies Reconsidered: His Career, Legacy, and Disciples* (New York: Rizzoli).
—(ed.) (1987), *Chicago Architecture 1872–1922: The Birth of a Metropolis* (Chicago: Art Institute of Chicago).
—(ed.) (1993), *Chicago Architecture and Design 1923–1993: Reconfiguration of an American Metropolis* (Chicago: Art Institute of Chicago).
—(1994), *The Many Faces of Modern Architecture: Building in Germany between the World Wars* (Munich: Prestel).
—(1994*a*), *Karl Friedrich Schinkel (1781–1841): The Drama of Architecture* (Tübingen: Wasmuth).
Zürchner, Richard (1977), *Rokoko-Schlösser* (Munich: Heyne).
Zurko, Edward Robert de (1957), *Origins of Functionalist Theory* (New York: Columbia UP).
Zuydewijn, H. J. F. de Roy van (1969), *Amsterdamse Bouwkunst: 1815–1940* (Amsterdam: De Bussy).
Zwirner, Ernst Friedrich (1842), *Vergangenheit und Zukunft des Kölner Dombaues* (Cologne: Zwirner).